THE USA
AND CANADA
1990

THE USA AND CANADA 1990

EUROPA PUBLICATIONS LIMITED

First Edition 1989

Australia and New Zealand
James Bennett (Collaroy) Pty Ltd, 4 Collaroy Street,
Collaroy, NSW 2097, Australia

India
UBS Publishers' Distributors Ltd,
POB 7015, 5 Ansari Road, New Delhi 1-10002

Japan
Maruzen Co Ltd, POB 5050, Tokyo International 100-31

British Library Cataloguing in Publication Data
The USA and Canada. — 1990-
1. North America   #003876280
970-053'8
ISBN 0-946653-55-0
ISSN 0956-0904

Printed and bound in England by
Staples Printers Rochester Limited,
Love Lane, Rochester, Kent.

FOREWORD

This first edition of THE USA AND CANADA aims to provide a comprehensive guide to the political, economic and social structures, and international roles of these two neighbouring North American nations. Various types of information (essays, statistics and directory) normally only accessible from diverse and separate sources for each country, have been brought together in a single volume.

Individual sections for each country provide introductory historical, geographical and demographic data; essays on the political and administrative system, the economy, social issues, and international relations and defence; and extensive statistical and directory material organized under the headings of Public Affairs, The Economy, Society, Transport and Utilities, and Tourism. Where appropriate, detailed coverage of these subjects at state, provincial or territorial level is provided.

Bridging the two sections is a group of essays which examines topics affecting the USA and Canada equally—the current relationship between the two nations (brought into focus by the historic US–Canada Free Trade Agreement, effective from January 1989), the position of the native peoples and the economic development of the far north of the continent.

With the depth of expert analysis in the essays, the detail of the statistical coverage and the exhaustiveness of the directory, where telephone, telex and fax numbers are included wherever possible, it is hoped that THE USA AND CANADA will provide its users with an invaluable reference aid.

October 1989

ACKNOWLEDGEMENTS

The editors would like to acknowledge the co-operation, enthusiasm and advice given by the authors and others who have contributed to this volume. Consultants Phil Davies, David McKay and David Robertson provided unfailingly helpful and knowledgeable assistance, and special thanks are also due to contributors Robert Burchell, John Davis, Alan Hallsworth, Cedric May and Alan Williams; to Denis Balsom of the University College of Wales; to Peter Boyle of the University of Nottingham; to Michael Hellyer of the Canadian High Commission in London; to Professor Peter Parish of the Institute of United States Studies at the University of London; and to Robert Estall and Jim Potter, both of the London School of Economics.

We are also indebted to the staff of the Canada House Library and the USIS Reference Center, and to the many other organizations, state, provincial and territorial government departments and national statistical and information offices whose kind assistance in providing up-to-date information is greatly appreciated. In addition, thanks are due to Edward Oliver for drawing the maps which are included in this volume.

Our publication makes extensive use of statistical information published by the US Bureau of the Census and by Statistics Canada, and we also acknowledge with thanks the use of defence statistics from *The Military Balance 1988–1989*, published by the International Institute for Strategic Studies, 23 Tavistock Street, London WC2E 7NQ.

EXPLANATORY NOTE ON STATISTICAL TABLES

In the tables contained in this volume, a dash (—) is to be taken to represent zero, while 0 is used to indicate less than one half-unit: for example, where the unit used is one thousand US dollars (US $'000), 0 represents less than $500.

CONTENTS

CONTENTS

CONTENTS

THE CONSULTANTS

Philip John Davies. Lecturer in the Department of American Studies at the University of Manchester, specializing in US domestic government and politics, especially urban and regional affairs, and US elections.

David McKay. Reader in Government at the University of Essex and Executive Director of the European Consortium for Political Research.

David Robertson. Fellow and Tutor in Politics at St Hugh's College, University of Oxford.

OTHER CONTRIBUTORS

Bruna Angel. Research Assistant in the Center for Agricultural and Rural Development at Iowa State University.

Ken Atkinson. Senior Lecturer in the Department of Geography at the University of Leeds, specializing in natural-resource studies.

Alec T. Barbrook. Director of the School of Continuing Education at the University of Kent.

R. A. Burchell. Senior Lecturer in American History and Institutions in the Department of American Studies at the University of Manchester.

Lyndhurst Collins. Senior Lecturer in the Department of Geography at the University of Edinburgh, and Vice-Dean of the University's Faculty of Social Sciences.

Ian M. Cuthbertson. Research Associate at the Institute for East–West Security Studies, New York.

P. W. Daniels. Professor of Geography, and Director of the Service Industries Research Centre, at Portsmouth Polytechnic.

John F. Davis. Senior Lecturer in the Department of Geography at Birkbeck College, University of London, and Co-Director of the Birkbeck Centre for Canadian Studies.

Martin Edmonds. Reader in Political and Defence Studies at the University of Lancaster.

Richard Goodenough. Head of the Department of Geography at Christ Church College of Higher Education, Canterbury.

Wyn Grant. Reader in Politics at the University of Warwick, specializing in economic and industrial policy.

Alan Hallsworth. Senior Lecturer in the Department of Geography at Portsmouth Polytechnic, specializing in retailing and Canadian studies.

Freda Hawkins. Professor Emeritus in Political Science at the University of Toronto, specializing in the study of immigration and international migration.

Michael D. Helmar. Research Associate in the Center for Agricultural and Rural Development at Iowa State University.

Richard Hodder-Williams. Reader in Politics at the University of Bristol, specializing in the politics of the US Supreme Court.

Joseph Hogan. Professor and Head of Management at Birmingham Polytechnic Business School.

Stanley Johnson. Professor of Economics and Director of the Center for Agricultural and Rural Development at Iowa State University.

John Killick. Lecturer in Economic History in the School of Business and Economic Studies at the University of Leeds.

Peter Lyon. Academic Secretary of the Institute of Commonwealth Studies, and Reader in International Relations, at the University of London.

Cedric May. Former Director of Canadian Studies at the University of Birmingham.

Geoffrey Mercer. Senior Lecturer in the Department of Social Policy and Sociology at the University of Leeds, specializing in the sociology of Canadian society.

Calum Paton. Senior Lecturer in the Centre for Health Planning and Management at the University of Keele, specializing in US, British and international health policy.

Gillian Peele. Fellow and Tutor in Politics at Lady Margaret Hall, University of Oxford, specializing in the government of the USA.

Marissa Quie. Recognized Lecturer in the Department of Social and Political Sciences at the University of Cambridge and Samuel Reichmann Fellow in Canadian Studies at Queens' College, Cambridge.

Michael Rush. Head of the Department of Politics at the University of Exeter, specializing in the study of parliamentary systems.

Alan F. Williams. Director of Canadian Studies at the University of Birmingham.

Phil Williams. Professor in International Security in the Graduate School of Public and International Affairs at the University of Pittsburgh.

Graham Wilson. Professor of Political Science at the University of Wisconsin—Madison, specializing in US politics and the comparative study of interest groups and executives.

ABBREVIATIONS

AB	Alberta	ID	Idaho
Adj.	Adjutant	IL	Illinois
admin	administration	IN	Indiana
admin.	administrative	Inc	Incorporated
AK	Alaska	incl.	including
AL	Alabama	Ind.	Independent
AR	Arkansas	Int.	International
asscn	association	IR	Independent Republican
asst	assistant		
Att.	Attorney	Jan.	January
attn	attention	Jr	Junior
Aug.	August		
ave	avenue	km	kilometre(s)
AZ	Arizona	KS	Kansas
		KY	Kentucky
BC	British Columbia		
Bd	Board	LA	Louisiana
Bldg	Building	lb	pound(s)
Blvd	Boulevard	Lib.	Liberal
Brig.	Brigadier	Lt, Lieut	Lieutenant
CA	California	m	metre(s)
Capt.	Captain	m.	million
CEO	Chief Executive Officer	MA	Massachusetts
Chair.	Chairman; Chairwoman; Chairperson	Maj.	Major
circ.	circulation	Man.	Manager; Managing
cnr	corner	MB	Manitoba
Co	Company	MD	Maryland
CO	Colorado	ME	Maine
c/o	care of	mem.	member
Col	Colonel	mfrs	manufacturers
Comm.	Commission	MI	Michigan
Commdr	Commander	MJ	megajoules
Commr	Commissioner	MN	Minnesota
COO	Chief Operating Officer	MO	Missouri
Corpn	Corporation	Mon.	Monday
CP	Case Postale, Casilla Postale (Post Office Box)	MS	Mississippi
Cres.	Crescent	MT	Montana
Ct	Court		
CT	Connecticut	N.	North(ern)
Cttee	Committee	n.a.	not available
cwt	hundredweight	Nat.	National
		NB	New Brunswick
DC	District of Columbia	NC	North Carolina
DE	Delaware	ND	North Dakota
Dec.	December	NDP	New Democratic Party
Dem.	Democratic; Democrat	NE	Nebraska; North-east(ern)
Dept	Department	NF	Newfoundland
DFL	Democratic-Farmer-Labor	n.i.e.	not included elsewhere
Dir	Director	no(.)	number
Div.	Division(al)	Nov.	November
Dr	Doctor	NH	New Hampshire
Dr.	Drive	NJ	New Jersey
		NM	New Mexico
E.	East(ern)	NS	Nova Scotia
Econ.	Economic(s)	NT, NWT	Northwest Territories
Edif.	Edificio (Building)	NV	Nevada
edn	edition	NW	North-west(ern)
EEC	European Economic Community	NY	New York
excl.	excluding		
Exec.	Executive	Oct.	October
		OH	Ohio
f.	founded	OK	Oklahoma
fax	facsimile	ON	Ontario
Feb.	February	OR	Oregon
Fed.	Federal	org.	organization
FL	Florida		
fmr	former	p.	page
fmrly	formerly	PA	Pennsylvania
Fri.	Friday	PC	Progressive Conservative
		PE	Prince Edward Island
GA	Georgia	Pkwy	Parkway
GDP	gross domestic product	Pl.	Place
Gen.	General	POB	Post Office Box
GNP	gross national product	PQ	Québec
Govt	Government	Pres.	President
grt	gross registered ton(s)	Prof.	Professor
		publ.	publication; published
Hon.	Honorary	publr	publisher
Hwy	Highway		
IA	Iowa		

ABBREVIATIONS

R. & D.	research and development		SW	South-west(ern)
Rd	Road		tel.	telephone
reorg.	reorganized		Thur.	Thursday
Rep.	Republic; Representative		TN	Tennessee
Repub.	Republican		Treas.	Treasurer
Rev.	Reverend		Tue.	Tuesday
RI	Rhode Island		TV	television
Rm	Room		TX	Texas
RR	Rural Route			
Rt	Right		UK	United Kingdom
			UN	United Nations
S.	South(ern); San		US	United States
Sat.	Saturday		USA	United States of America
SC	South Carolina; Social Credit		USSR	Union of Soviet Socialist Republics
SD	South Dakota		UT	Utah
SE	South-east(ern)			
Sec.	Secretary		VA	Virginia
Sept.	September		VT	Vermont
SK	Saskatchewan			
Soc.	Society		W.	West(ern)
sq	square (in measurements)		WA	Washington (state)
Sq.	Square		Wed.	Wednesday
Sr	Senior		WI	Wisconsin
St	Street; Saint		WV	West Virginia
Ste	Sainte		WY	Wyoming
Sun.	Sunday			
Supt	Superintendent		YT	Yukon Territory

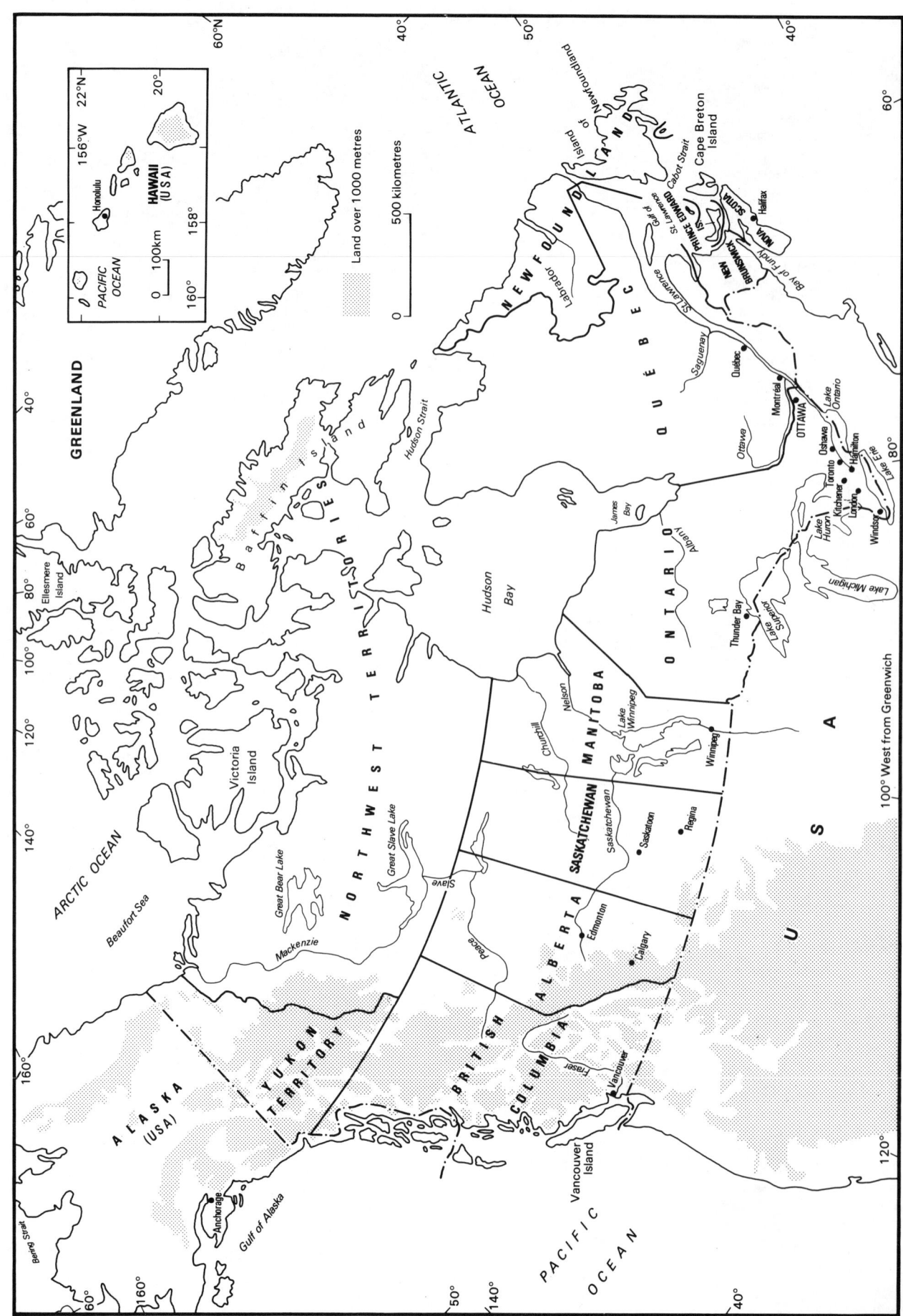

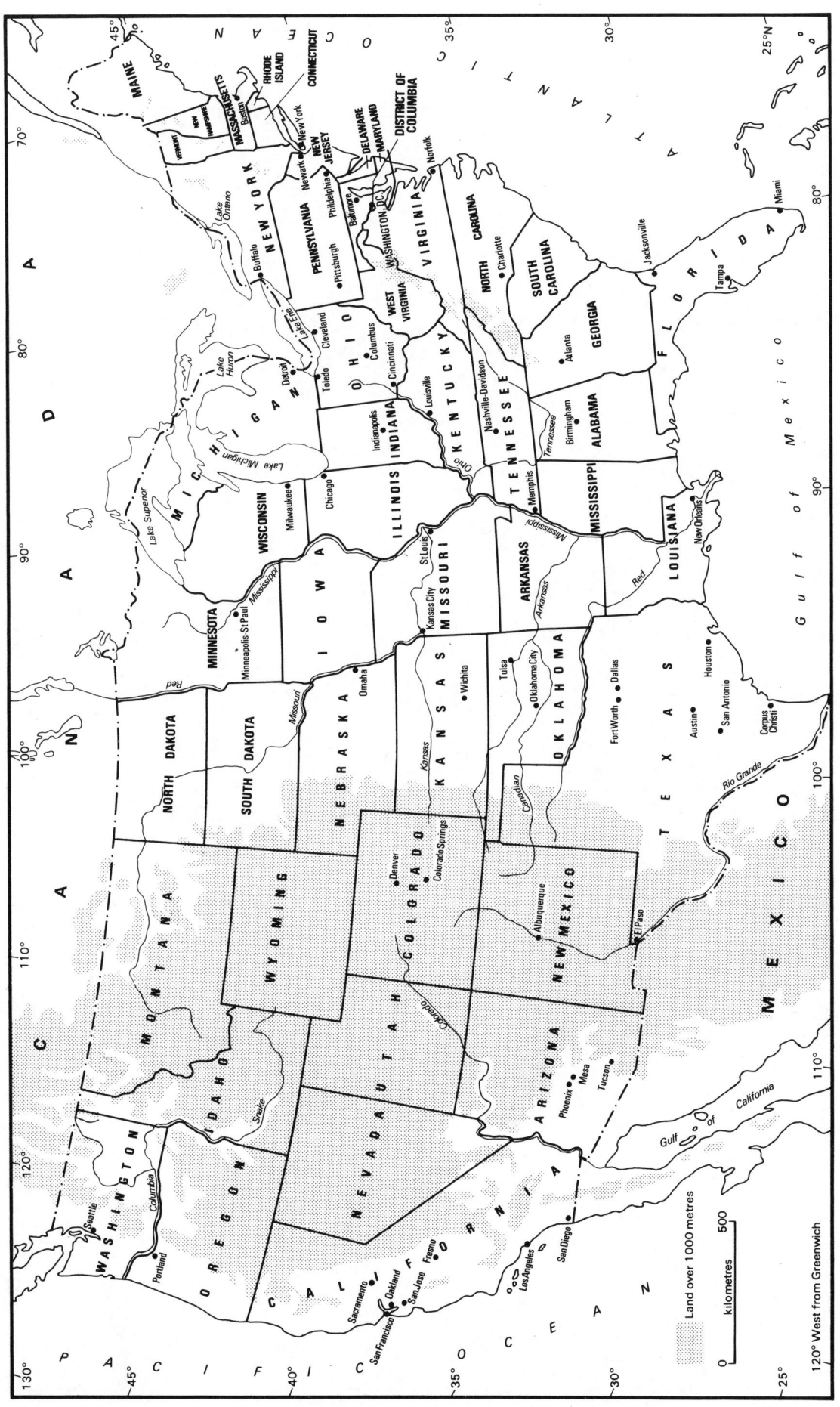

THE USA

INTRODUCTION

THE USA: A CHRONOLOGY SINCE COLONIZATION

1492: Christopher Columbus landed in the present-day Bahamas.

1565: The Spanish explorer Pedro Menendez de Aviles established the first permanent European settlement at St Augustine, now in Florida.

1607: The first permanent English settlement was established at Jamestown, now in Virginia.

1620: The 'Pilgrim Fathers' settled at Plymouth, now in Massachusetts; settlements subsequently established along coast of 'New England'.

1624-26: Dutch settlers established colony of 'New Netherland', with fur-trading posts at Fort Orange (now Albany) and New Amsterdam (New York City).

1630s: Rapid expansion of New England. Maryland founded as an English, predominantly Roman Catholic, colony. 'New Sweden' founded in present-day Delaware and New Jersey by Swedish and Finnish settlers.

1655: New Sweden conquered by Dutch and incorporated into New Netherland.

1663: Colony of Carolina founded.

1665: New Netherland acquired by King Charles II of England during the second Anglo–Dutch naval war. The colony and the city of New Amsterdam were both renamed New York in honour of the Duke of York, with the area east of the Delaware River becoming known as New Jersey.

1675-76: Remaining Indian peoples disappeared from southern New England as a result of King Philip's War.

1682: Lower Mississippi country claimed for France and named Louisiana. William Penn signed treaty with Delaware Indians and colonized Pennsylvania.

1718: New Orleans founded as the administrative centre for Louisiana.

1733: Colony of Georgia founded.

1740-41: Vitus Bering, a Danish captain employed by Russia, sailed to Alaska and the Aleutian islands.

1756-63: French and Indian War (known in Europe as the 'Seven-Years War'). Britain gained control over French Canada and that portion of Louisiana lying east of the Mississippi River, while the western portion was ceded to Spain; Spain surrendered Florida to the British.

1773: Massachusetts citizens occupied three ships in Boston harbour and threw overboard their cargoes of tea in protest against the imposition of tax on tea.

1774: First Continental Congress met in Philadelphia and voted anti-British measures.

1775: Forces of the 13 colonies, under the command of George Washington, entered into battle with the British army.

1776: Declaration of Independence adopted.

1783: Ratification of the Treaty of Paris with Britain; this recognized the independence of the USA.

1781: Entry into effect of the Articles of Confederation (adopted by the Continental Congress in 1777); these constituted the original framework for government of the 13 states.

1783: Florida returned to Spain.

1787: Formation of a constitutional convention in Philadelphia to revise the Articles of Confederation. The Constitution of the United States was subsequently adopted by delegates, and was ratified by Delaware, Pennsylvania and New Jersey during 1787. The constitution was officially adopted in June 1788.

1788: Georgia, Connecticut, Massachusetts, Maryland, South Carolina, New Hampshire, Virginia and New York ratified the US Constitution and were admitted to the Union.

1789: George Washington was elected to be the first president of the USA in February; the constitution came into effect in March and the first Congress met in New York City in April. The US Supreme Court was created in September. North Carolina was admitted to the Union.

1790: Rhode Island became the last of the 13 original states to be admitted to the Union.

1791: The 10 original amendments to the constitution (Bill of Rights) came into effect. Vermont admitted to the Union.

1792: Kentucky admitted to the Union.

1796: Tennessee admitted to the Union.

1800: Napoleon signed an agreement with Spain returning Louisiana to France.

1803: Supreme Court established the power of judicial review in *Marbury v. Madison*. Napoleon sold all of Louisiana, which stretched from the Gulf of Mexico to what is now the Canadian border, and had an open western boundary, to the USA for $15m. under the Louisiana Purchase. Ohio admitted to the Union.

1804-06: The Lewis and Clark expedition (ordered by President Jefferson) explored the north-western USA, starting from St Louis.

1812: Louisiana admitted to the Union.

1812-14: War of 1812 with Britain; unsuccessful attempt by USA to drive British out of North America.

1816: Indiana admitted to the Union.

1817: Mississippi admitted to the Union.

1818: Illinois admitted to the Union.

1819: Spain sold Florida to USA for $5m. Alabama admitted to the Union.

1820: Missouri Compromise bill allowed slavery in Missouri, but outlawed it in areas west of the Mississippi River and north of a line extending from the southern boundary of Missouri. Maine admitted to the Union.

1821: Missouri admitted to the Union.

1828: Democratic-Republican Party became the Democratic Party.

1835-42: War with Seminole Indians in Florida, ending with Indians being sent to Oklahoma.

1836: Texas declared its independence from Mexico; Texan army defeated Mexicans at San Jacinto. Arkansas admitted to the Union.

1837: Michigan admitted to the Union.

1842: US-Canadian border in Maine and Minnesota fixed by Webster–Ashburton Treaty.

1845: Florida admitted to the Union. Texas also admitted after Texans voted for annexation to the USA.

1846: Western US-Canadian boundary fixed at 49th parallel. Iowa admitted to the Union.

1846-48: Mexican War, ending with Mexico ceding claims to Texas, California, Arizona, Nevada, New Mexico, Utah and part of Colorado under the Treaty of Guadalupe-Hidalgo.

1848: Wisconsin admitted to the Union.

1850: California admitted to the Union, with slavery outlawed, but New Mexico and Utah made territories without decision on slavery being made, under the Compromise of 1850.

1854: Republican Party founded.

1858: Minnesota admitted to the Union.

1859: Slavery abolitionists, led by John Brown, captured US Armory at Harper's Ferry; Armory recaptured by US marines, and Brown hanged for treason. Oregon admitted to the Union.

1860: Abraham Lincoln elected president; South Carolina became first state to secede from the Union over abolition-of-slavery issue.

1861: Secessionist Confederate States of America founded, with 11 member states; first major battle of Civil War at Bull Run. Kansas admitted to the Union.

1862: Inconclusive campaigns in the east, but Union forces captured New Orleans and the southern Mississippi River.

1863: Lincoln's Emancipation Proclamation came into effect, 'freeing all slaves in areas still in rebellion'; major Unionist victory at Gettysburg in July, followed by gaining of control of the entire Mississippi River. West Virginia admitted to the Union.

1864: Unionist troops marched through Georgia, led by Gen. William T. Sherman, taking Atlanta and Savannah. Nevada admitted to the Union.

1865: Confederate troops surrendered at Appomattox Court House, Virginia; Lincoln assassinated; slavery abolished by 13th Amendment to the constitution.

1867: Russia sold Alaska to USA for $7.2m. Nebraska admitted to the Union.

1872: Civil rights restored to Southern citizens, barring 500 confederate leaders.

1876: Defeat of Col George A. Custer in Sioux Indian War at Battle of the Little Big Horn. Colorado admitted to the Union.

1877: Congress awarded presidency to Republican, Rutherford B. Hayes, despite receiving minority of votes, after Republicans promised to end Reconstruction of the South.

1881: Pres. James A. Garfield shot in July, died in September.

1889: North Dakota, South Dakota, Montana and Washington admitted to the Union.

1890: Battle of Wounded Knee, South Dakota, last major conflict between Indian and US troops. Idaho and Wyoming admitted to the Union.

1896: Supreme Court approved racial segregation under 'separate but equal' doctrine. Utah admitted to the Union.

1898: USA defeated Spain in war; Spain ceded Guam, Philippines and Puerto Rico to the USA. Hawaii, previously an independent republic, annexed by USA.

1901: Pres. William McKinley shot in September, died eight days later.

1903: Treaty for construction of Panama Canal signed.

1907: Oklahoma admitted to the Union.

1912: New Mexico and Arizona admitted to the Union.

1914: Pres. Woodrow Wilson proclaimed US neutrality in First World War.

1915: Sinking of British ship, *SS Lusitania*, with heavy US losses.

1916: USA bought Danish West Indies (now US Virgin Islands) for $25m. First woman elected to Congress.

1917: USA declared war on Germany on 6 April; conscription introduced.

1918: Over 1m. US troops in Europe by July; war ended with defeat of Germany in November.

1919–33: Prohibition of alcoholic beverages introduced by the 18th Amendment and ended by the 21st Amendment to the constitution.

1920: US membership of League of Nations blocked by Senate. Women receive right to vote under the 19th Amendment.

1921: National quota system set to restrict immigration.

1924: All Indians made citizens by Law of Congress.

1929: Stock Market crash marked beginning of Great Depression which lasted for most of the 1930s.

1933: 'New Deal' domestic legislation passed by Congress. Isolationist policy confirmed by declaration that USA would not become militarily involved in affairs of Western Hemisphere nations.

1939: Pres. Franklin D. Roosevelt declared US neutrality in Second World War.

1941: USA entered Second World War following Japanese attack on Pearl Harbor, Hawaii.

1942: USA inflicted the first major defeat on Japan at Battle of Midway, in June; US and British forces invaded North Africa in November.

1943: US forces invaded Italy in September.

1944: US and Allied forces invaded northern Europe in June; US forces landed in the Philippines in October.

1945: US forces landed on Iwo Jima and Okinawa, Japan, in February and April respectively; war with Germany ended 7 May; explosion of first atomic bomb in July at Alamogordo, New Mexico; atomic bombs dropped on Hiroshima, 6 August, and Nagasaki, 9 August; Japan surrendered 16 August; US forces moved into Korea, replacing Japanese, in September.

1946: Philippines granted independence by USA.

1947: Announcement of Truman Doctrine, linked to granting of aid to Greece and Turkey to combat communist insurgency, which became the cornerstone of US policy of containment. Marshall Aid programme to nine European countries began; $12,000m. granted over next four years.

1948: Creation of Organization of American States.

1949: US troops withdrew from Korea. Creation of North Atlantic Treaty Organization (NATO).

1950: Production of hydrogen bomb authorized by Pres. Harry S Truman. USA answered United Nations request for peace-keeping troops to be sent to Korea after northern Communists invaded the south.

1953: Korean conflict ends.

1954: Senator Joseph McCarthy led hearings into alleged communist influence in the US Army. Supreme Court ruled, in *Brown v. Board of Education of Topeka*, that 'separate educational facilities are inherently unequal' and therefore that the 'separate but equal' doctrine was in violation of the equal-protection clause of the 14th Amendment.

1955: The USA began to provide military-adviser assistance to South Vietnamese army.

1958: *Explorer 1*, first US earth satellite, launched.

1959: Alaska and Hawaii admitted to the Union as the 49th and 50th states. Opening of St Lawrence Seaway admitted ocean-going ships to the Great Lakes. Nikita Khrushchev became the first Soviet premier to visit the USA.

1961: Unsuccessful attempt to overthrow Cuban premier, Fidel Castro, in 'Bay of Pigs' invasion by US-armed and -directed Cuban exiles. US military advisers in Vietnam authorized to fight with the units they were training.

1962: Cuban Missile Crisis defused when US naval blockade and interception of Soviet merchant fleet carrying nuclear missiles forced Soviet premier Khrushchev to back down.

1963: Partial Test Ban Treaty signed by the USA, the USSR and the UK confined nuclear-explosives testing to underground sites. Pres. John F. Kennedy assassinated in Dallas, Texas. Total of 15,000 US troops in Vietnam by the end of the year.

1964: Civil Rights Act banned discrimination in places of public accommodation and in employment. Tonkin Resolution passed by Congress authorizing presidential action in Vietnam following reports of North Vietnamese attack on two US destroyers.

1965: Pres. Lyndon B. Johnson ordered bombing raids on North Vietnam. Voting Rights Act banned use of tests and other devices to deny right to vote to certain minority groups. National-origins quota system for immigration abolished.

1966: Medicare and Medicaid introduced.

1967: Domestic opposition to (undeclared) war in Vietnam increased.

1968: Communist forces launched *Tet* offensive against Saigon and 36 provincial towns in January; North Vietnamese suffered heavy casualties, but public perception of physical and financial cost of war prompted Pres. Johnson to propose cease-fire talks (at this time more than 500,000 US troops were in Vietnam); policy of Vietnamization announced under which South Vietnamese would gradually assume entire fighting role. Martin Luther King, Jr, and Senator Robert Kennedy assassinated, in May and June respectively.

1969: US forces began to withdraw from Vietnam. Neil Armstrong became first man to set foot on the Moon.

1970–71: Invasions launched into Cambodia and Laos to interrupt North Vietnamese supply lines.

1971: Voting age lowered to 18 by 26th Amendment.

1972: Pres. Richard M. Nixon visited both China and the USSR; Strategic Arms Limitation Treaty signed with USSR. North Vietnamese made attacks across demilitarized zone; USA resumed bombing of Hanoi and Haiphong and mined North Vietnamese ports; last US combat troops left in August; peace talks broke down; 'Christmas bombing' of North Vietnamese cities. Five men were arrested following a break-in at the offices of the Democratic National Committee in the Watergate complex, Washington, DC.

1973: Cease-fire in Vietnam in January. Watergate case hearings began. Vice-Pres. Spiro Agnew resigned over charges of tax evasion. Embargo imposed on petroleum exports to the USA by Arab oil-producing nations following the outbreak of the Arab–Israeli war.

1974: House of Representatives Judiciary Committee opened impeachment hearings against Pres. Nixon in May, and in July recommended three articles of impeachment against him; Nixon resigned in August and received an unconditional pardon from his successor, Gerald Ford, in September.

1975: North Vietnamese launched offensive in January; remaining US personnel evacuated and South Vietnamese surrendered in April.

1978: Senate voted to hand jurisdiction over the Panama Canal to Panama in December 1999.

1979: Major accident at Three Mile Island nuclear reactor, Pennsylvania, caused a radical alteration in attitudes to nuclear-power stations in the USA. Militant Islamic fundamentalist students took 63 US citizens hostage in US Embassy in Iran.

1980: Embargoes placed on sale of grain and high-technology products to the USSR following invasion of Afghanistan. Eruption of Mount St Helens volcano in state of Washington.

1981: US hostages in Iran freed following agreement on the return of $8,000m. in frozen assets to Iran. First reusable spacecraft, the Space Shuttle, launched.

1983: US Marines and rangers participated in invasion of Grenada to overthrow hardline Marxist regime.

1984: First woman chosen as vice-presidential candidate: Geraldine Ferraro stood for the Democrats.

1986: USA launched bombing raids on Tripoli and Benghazi, Libya, in retaliation for bombing of US troops in West Germany and other terrorist attacks. Iran-Contra affair gradually revealed following reports that the USA had sent military spare parts and ammunition to Iran, and channelled the profits to the Contra forces seeking to overthrow the Nicaraguan government.

1987: USA and USSR sign Intermediate Nuclear Forces Treaty for the phasing-out of all land-based nuclear missiles in the 300–3,400-mile (500–5,500-km) range.

PRESIDENTS OF THE USA

April 1789–March 1797: GEORGE WASHINGTON (Federalist).

March 1797–March 1801: JOHN ADAMS (Federalist).

March 1801–March 1809: THOMAS JEFFERSON (Democratic–Republican).

March 1809–March 1817: JAMES MADISON (Democratic–Republican).

March 1817–March 1825: JAMES MONROE (Democratic–Republican).

March 1825–March 1829: JOHN QUINCY ADAMS (National Republican).

March 1829–March 1837: ANDREW JACKSON (Democrat).

March 1837–March 1841: MARTIN VAN BUREN (Democrat).

March 1841–April 1841: WILLIAM HENRY HARRISON (Whig).

April 1841–March 1845: JOHN TYLER (Whig).

March 1845–March 1849: JAMES K. POLK (Democrat).

March 1849–July 1850: ZACHARY TAYLOR (Whig).

July 1850–March 1853: MILLARD FILLMORE (Whig).

March 1853–March 1857: FRANKLIN PIERCE (Democrat).

March 1857–March 1861: JAMES BUCHANAN (Democrat).

March 1861–April 1865: ABRAHAM LINCOLN (Republican).

April 1865–March 1869: ANDREW JOHNSON.*

March 1869–March 1877: ULYSSES S. GRANT (Republican).

March 1877–March 1881: RUTHERFORD B. HAYES (Republican).

March 1881–September 1881: JAMES A. GARFIELD (Republican).

September 1881–March 1885: CHESTER A. ARTHUR (Republican).

March 1885–March 1889: GROVER CLEVELAND (Democrat).

March 1889–March 1893: BENJAMIN HARRISON (Republican).

March 1893–March 1897: GROVER CLEVELAND (Democrat).

March 1897–September 1901: WILLIAM MCKINLEY (Republican).

September 1901–March 1909: THEODORE ROOSEVELT (Republican).

March 1909–March 1913: WILLIAM H. TAFT (Republican).

March 1913–March 1921: WOODROW WILSON (Democrat).

March 1921–August 1923: WARREN G. HARDING (Republican).

August 1923–March 1929: CALVIN COOLIDGE (Republican).

March 1929–March 1933: HERBERT C. HOOVER (Republican).

March 1933–April 1945: FRANKLIN D. ROOSEVELT (Democrat).

April 1945–January 1953: HARRY S TRUMAN (Democrat).

January 1953–January 1961: DWIGHT D. EISENHOWER (Republican).

January 1961–November 1963: JOHN F. KENNEDY (Democrat).

November 1963–January 1969: LYNDON B. JOHNSON (Democrat).

January 1969–August 1974: RICHARD M. NIXON (Republican).

August 1974–January 1977: GERALD R. FORD (Republican).

January 1977–January 1981: JIMMY CARTER (Democrat).

January 1981–January 1989: RONALD REAGAN (Republican).

January 1989– : GEORGE BUSH (Republican).

* Andrew Johnson, a Democrat, was nominated vice-president by the Republicans and elected with Lincoln on a 'National Unity' ticket, and succeeded to the presidency on Lincoln's assassination.

AREA AND POPULATION

Source (unless otherwise indicated): US Bureau of the Census, Department of Commerce, Washington, DC 20233.

Area, Population and Density*

Historical Summary (census results, selected years)

	Area ('000 sq km)				Population per sq km of land area
	Land	Water	Gross	Population	
2 August 1790	2,240	62	2,309	3,929,214	1.8
4 August 1800	2,240	62	2,309	5,308,483	2.4
1 June 1850	7,615	137	7,748	23,191,876	3.0
1 June 1900	7,692	136	7,825	75,994,575	9.9
1 April 1950	9,200	163	9,373	151,325,798	16.4
1 April 1960	9,171	192	9,373	179,323,175	19.6
1 April 1970	9,169†	203†	9,373	203,302,031†	22.2
1 April 1980	9,167	206	9,373	226,545,805	24.7

* Area figures represent area on indicated date including, in some cases, considerable areas not then organized or settled, and not covered by the census. Total area figures for 1790–1970 have been recalculated on the basis of the remeasurement of states and counties for the 1980 census. The land- and water-area figures for past censuses have not been adjusted and are not strictly comparable with the total area data for comparable dates because the land areas were derived from different base data, and these values are known to have changed with the construction of reservoirs, draining of lakes, etc. Density figures are based on land-area measurements as reported in earlier censuses.

† Figures corrected after 1970 final reports were issued.

1980: Males 110,053,161; Females 116,492,644.

States (1 July 1987)

State	Area (sq km)			Population ('000)	Population per sq km of land area
	Land	Water	Gross		
Alabama	131,487	2,428	133,915	4,083	31.1
Alaska	1,478,458	52,243	1,530,700	525	0.4
Arizona	293,986	1,274	295,260	3,386	11.5
Arkansas	134,883	2,872	137,754	2,388	17.7
California	404,814	6,235	411,049	27,663	68.3
Colorado	268,311	1,285	269,596	3,296	12.3
Connecticut	12,618	380	12,997	3,211	254.5
Delaware	5,005	290	5,295	644	128.7
District of Columbia	162	16	178	622	3,839.5
Florida	140,256	11,683	151,939	12,023	85.7
Georgia	150,365	2,211	152,576	6,222	41.4
Hawaii	16,641	118	16,759	1,083	65.1
Idaho	213,447	2,985	216,432	998	4.7
Illinois	144,120	1,814	145,934	11,582	80.4
Indiana	93,064	656	93,720	5,531	59.4
Iowa	144,950	803	145,753	2,834	19.6
Kansas	211,805	1,293	213,098	2,476	11.7
Kentucky	102,743	1,917	104,660	3,727	36.3
Louisiana	115,310	8,366	123,677	4,461	38.7
Maine	80,277	5,879	86,156	1,187	14.8
Maryland	25,477	1,615	27,092	4,535	178.0
Massachusetts	20,265	1,191	21,456	5,855	288.9
Michigan	147,511	4,075	151,586	9,200	62.4
Minnesota	206,030	12,571	218,601	4,246	20.6
Mississippi	122,333	1,183	123,516	2,625	21.5
Missouri	178,568	1,948	180,516	5,103	28.6
Montana	376,555	4,293	380,848	809	2.1
Nebraska	198,508	1,842	200,350	1,594	8.0
Nevada	284,624	1,728	286,352	1,007	3.5
New Hampshire	23,292	739	24,032	1,057	45.4
New Jersey	19,342	827	20,169	7,672	396.6
New Mexico	314,258	667	314,925	1,500	4.8
New York	122,707	4,483	127,190	17,825	145.3
North Carolina	126,504	9,909	136,413	6,413	50.7
North Dakota	179,486	3,633	183,119	672	3.7
Ohio	106,201	843	107,044	10,784	101.5
Oklahoma	177,817	3,369	181,186	3,272	18.4
Oregon	249,117	2,302	251,419	2,724	10.9
Pennsylvania	116,260	1,088	117,348	11,936	102.7
Rhode Island	2,732	408	3,140	986	360.9
South Carolina	78,227	2,355	80,582	3,425	43.8
South Dakota	196,715	3,014	199,730	709	3.6
Tennessee	106,591	2,561	109,152	4,855	45.5
Texas	678,623	12,407	691,030	16,789	24.7
Utah	212,569	7,320	219,889	1,680	7.9
Vermont	24,017	883	24,900	548	22.8
Virginia	102,832	2,754	105,586	5,904	57.4
Washington	172,264	4,215	176,479	4,538	26.3
West Virginia	62,468	291	62,760	1,897	30.4
Wisconsin	140,964	4,472	145,436	4,807	34.1
Wyoming	251,202	2,125	253,326	490	2.0
Total	9,166,759	205,858	9,372,614	243,400	26.6

Population by State, Race and Hispanic Origin

(1980 census, '000)

State	White	Black	Asian and Pacific Islander	American Indian, Eskimo and Aleut	Others	Total	Hispanic population as % of total
Alabama	2,873	996	10	8	8	3,894	0.9
Alaska	310	14	8	65	6	402	2.4
Arizona	2,241	75	22	153	227	2,718	16.2
Arkansas	1,890	374	7	9	6	2,286	0.8
California	18,031	1,819	1,254	201	2,363	23,668	19.2
Colorado	2,571	102	30	18	169	2,890	11.8
Connecticut	2,799	217	19	5	69	3,108	4.0
Delaware	488	96	4	1	5	594	1.6
District of Columbia	172	449	7	1	9	638	2.8
Florida	8,185	1,343	57	19	142	9,746	8.8
Georgia	3,947	1,465	25	8	19	5,463	1.1
Hawaii	319	17	583	3	43	965	7.4
Idaho	902	3	6	11	23	944	3.9

(continued)

POPULATION BY STATE, RACE AND HISPANIC ORIGIN—*continued*

State	White	Black	Asian and Pacific Islander	American Indian, Eskimo and Aleut	Others	Total	Hispanic population as % of total
Illinois	9,233	1,675	160	16	343	11,427	5.6
Indiana	5,004	415	21	8	43	5,490	1.6
Iowa	2,839	42	12	6	16	2,914	0.9
Kansas	2,168	126	15	15	40	2,364	2.7
Kentucky	3,379	259	10	4	9	3,661	0.7
Louisiana	2,912	1,238	24	12	20	4,206	2.4
Maine	1,110	3	3	4	5	1,125	0.4
Maryland	3,159	958	64	8	28	4,217	1.5
Massachusetts	5,363	221	50	8	96	5,737	2.5
Michigan	7,872	1,199	57	40	94	9,262	1.8
Minnesota	3,936	53	27	35	26	4,076	0.8
Mississippi	1,615	887	7	6	5	2,521	1.0
Missouri	4,346	514	23	12	22	4,917	1.1
Montana	740	2	3	37	5	787	1.3
Nebraska	1,490	48	7	9	16	1,570	1.8
Nevada	700	51	14	13	22	800	6.7
New Hampshire	910	4	3	1	3	921	0.6
New Jersey	6,127	925	104	8	201	7,365	6.7
New Mexico	978	24	7	106	188	1,303	36.6
New York	13,961	2,402	311	40	845	17,558	9.5
North Carolina	4,458	1,319	21	65	19	5,882	1.0
North Dakota	626	3	2	20	2	653	0.6
Ohio	9,597	1,077	48	12	64	10,798	1.1
Oklahoma	2,598	205	17	170	35	3,025	1.9
Oregon	2,491	37	35	27	43	2,633	2.5
Pennsylvania	10,652	1,047	64	10	91	11,864	1.3
Rhode Island	897	28	5	3	14	947	2.1
South Carolina	2,147	949	12	6	8	3,122	1.1
South Dakota	640	2	2	45	2	691	0.6
Tennessee	3,835	726	14	5	11	4,591	0.7
Texas	11,198	1,710	120	40	1,161	14,229	21.0
Utah	1,383	9	15	19	35	1,461	4.1
Vermont	507	1	1	1	1	511	0.6
Virginia	4,230	1,009	66	10	32	5,347	1.5
Washington	3,779	106	103	61	84	4,132	2.9
West Virginia	1,875	65	5	2	3	1,950	0.7
Wisconsin	4,443	183	18	30	32	4,706	1.3
Wyoming	446	3	2	7	12	470	5.2
Total	188,372	26,495	3,500	1,420	6,761	226,546	6.4

Population by State and Age

(preliminary estimates as at 1 July 1986, '000)

State	Under 18 years	18–24 years	25–34 years	35–64 years	65 years and over	Total
Alabama	1,115	478	690	1,273	497	4,052
Alaska	171	66	109	169	18	534
Arizona	911	378	591	1,031	410	3,319
Arkansas	645	271	369	744	343	2,372
California	7,109	3,028	5,215	8,782	2,848	26,981
Colorado	866	375	679	1,053	294	3,267
Connecticut	758	363	528	1,117	423	3,189
Delaware	160	78	114	209	72	633
District of Columbia	137	71	132	209	77	626
Florida	2,630	1,207	1,831	3,935	2,071	11,675
Georgia	1,713	744	1,082	1,957	608	6,104
Hawaii	286	129	196	348	103	1,062
Idaho	311	110	171	298	112	1,002
Illinois	3,058	1,317	2,050	3,740	1,386	11,552
Indiana	1,477	646	965	1,760	657	5,504
Iowa	747	322	493	874	415	2,851
Kansas	646	276	441	767	330	2,460
Kentucky	1,009	448	647	1,177	448	3,729
Louisiana	1,347	552	821	1,327	454	4,501
Maine	302	138	196	380	156	1,173
Maryland	1,111	539	796	1,544	473	4,463
Massachusetts	1,341	705	1,065	1,928	793	5,832
Michigan	2,470	1,083	1,625	2,927	1,039	9,145
Minnesota	1,110	487	772	1,319	526	4,214
Mississippi	801	324	423	763	314	2,625
Missouri	1,309	570	860	1,633	694	5,066
Montana	231	89	145	255	100	819
Nebraska	427	182	281	490	217	1,598
Nevada	240	104	198	322	100	963
New Hampshire	260	122	187	338	119	1,027

(continued)

POPULATION BY STATE AND AGE (preliminary estimates as at 1 July 1986, '000)—*continued*

State	Under 18 years	18–24 years	25–34 years	35–64 years	65 years and over	Total
New Jersey	1,831	863	1,233	2,713	981	7,619
New Mexico	444	176	258	458	144	1,479
New York	4,375	2,034	2,961	6,119	2,283	17,772
North Carolina	1,624	767	1,126	2,085	731	6,333
North Dakota	190	80	126	196	88	679
Ohio	2,854	1,215	1,850	3,514	1,320	10,752
Oklahoma	899	378	580	1,037	411	3,305
Oregon	686	280	512	858	362	2,698
Pennsylvania	2,850	1,328	1,983	3,990	1,737	11,888
Rhode Island	227	116	171	319	142	975
South Carolina	937	425	605	1,055	355	3,377
South Dakota	198	81	120	210	99	708
Tennessee	1,250	553	833	1,578	589	4,803
Texas	4,930	1,937	3,146	5,089	1,583	16,685
Utah	619	198	308	406	134	1,665
Vermont	140	67	100	170	64	541
Virginia	1,438	717	1,064	1,962	606	5,787
Washington	1,156	489	861	1,437	520	4,462
West Virginia	504	214	321	618	261	1,918
Wisconsin	1,271	563	842	1,486	624	4,785
Wyoming	154	56	111	144	42	507
Total	63,271	27,739	42,784	78,111	29,172	241,078

Principal Metropolitan Statistical Areas*

(estimated population at 1 July 1986)

New York–Northern New Jersey–Long Island, NY–NJ–CT (CMSA)	17,968,000
Los Angeles–Anaheim–Riverside, CA (CMSA)	13,075,000
Chicago–Gary–Lake County, IL–IN–WI (CMSA)	8,116,000
San Francisco–Oakland–San Jose, CA (CMSA)	5,878,000
Philadelphia–Wilmington–Trenton, PA–NJ–DE–MD (CMSA)	5,833,000
Detroit–Ann Arbor, MI (CMSA)	4,601,000
Boston–Lawrence–Salem, MA–NH (CMSA)	4,056,000
Dallas–Fort Worth, TX (CMSA)	3,655,000
Houston–Galveston–Brazoria, TX (CMSA)	3,634,000
Washington, DC–MD–VA (CMSA)	3,563,000
Miami–Fort Lauderdale, FL (CMSA)	2,912,000
Cleveland–Akron–Lorain, OH (CMSA)	2,766,000
Atlanta, GA	2,561,000
St Louis, MO–IL	2,438,000
Pittsburgh–Beaver Valley, PA (CMSA)	2,316,000
Minneapolis–St Paul, MN–WI	2,295,000
Seattle–Tacoma, WA (CMSA)	2,285,000
Baltimore, MD	2,280,000
San Diego, CA	2,201,000
Tampa–St Petersburg–Clearwater, FL	1,914,000
Phoenix, AZ	1,900,000
Denver–Boulder, CO (CMSA)	1,847,000
Cincinnati–Hamilton, OH–KY–IN (CMSA)	1,690,000
Milwaukee–Racine, WI (CMSA)	1,552,000
Kansas City, MO–KS	1,518,000
Portland–Vancouver, OR–WA (CMSA)	1,364,000
New Orleans, LA	1,334,000
Norfolk–Virginia Beach–Newport News, VA	1,310,000
Columbus, OH	1,299,000
Sacramento, CA	1,291,000
San Antonio, TX	1,276,000
Indianapolis, IN	1,213,000
Buffalo–Niagara Falls, NY (CMSA)	1,182,000
Providence–Pawtucket–Fall River, RI–MA (CMSA)	1,108,000
Charlotte–Gastonia–Rock Hall, NC–SC	1,065,000
Hartford–New Britain–Middletown, CT	1,044,000
Salt Lake City–Ogden, UT	1,041,000
Oklahoma City, OK	983,000
Rochester, NY	980,000
Louisville, KY–IN	963,000
Memphis, TN–AR–MS	960,000
Dayton–Springfield, OH	934,000
Nashville, TN	931,000
Birmingham, AL	911,000
Greensboro–Winston-Salem–High Point, NC	900,000
Orlando, FL	898,000
Jacksonville, FL	853,000
Albany–Schenectady–Troy, NY	844,000
Honolulu, HI	817,000
Richmond–Petersburg, VA	810,000

* According to the standards adopted in January 1980, an area qualifies as a Metropolitan Statistical Area (MSA) if it includes either a city with 50,000 or more inhabitants, or a Census Bureau-defined urbanized area of at least 100,000 (75,000 in New England). As well as the county in which the central city is located, an MSA includes other counties having strong economic and social ties to that central county. If an area has one million or more inhabitants, and certain specified criteria are met, it is designated a Consolidated Metropolitan Statistical Area (CMSA).

Principal Cities

(estimated population at 1 July 1986)

New York, NY	7,262,700	San Francisco, CA	749,000
Los Angeles, CA	3,259,340	Indianapolis, IN	719,820
Chicago, IL	3,009,530	San Jose, CA	712,080
Houston, TX	1,728,910	Memphis, TN	652,640
Philadelphia, PA	1,642,900	Washington, DC (capital)	626,000
Detroit, MI	1,086,220	Jacksonville, FL	609,860
San Diego, CA	1,015,190	Milwaukee, WI	605,090
Dallas, TX	1,003,520	Boston, MA	573,600
San Antonio, TX	914,350	Columbus, OH	566,030
Phoenix, AZ	894,070	New Orleans, LA	554,500
Baltimore, MD	752,800		

Cleveland, OH	535,830	Atlanta, GA	421,910
Denver, CO	505,000	Long Beach, CA	396,280
El Paso, TX	491,800	Portland, OR	387,870
Seattle, WA	486,200	Pittsburgh, PA	387,490
Nashville–Davidson, TN	473,670*	Miami, FL	373,940
Austin, TX	466,550	Tulsa, OK	373,750
Oklahoma City, OK	446,120	Honolulu, HI	372,330
Kansas City, MO	441,170	Cincinnati, OH	369,750
Fort Worth, TX	429,550	Albuquerque, NM	366,750
St Louis, MO	426,300	Tucson, AZ	358,850
		Oakland, CA	356,960

(continued)

8

PRINCIPAL CITIES (estimated population at 1 July 1986)—*continued*

Minneapolis, MN . . 356,840	Louisville, KY . . 286,470	Arlington, TX . . 249,770	Shreveport, LA . . 220,380
Charlotte, NC . . 352,070	Fresno, CA . . . 284,660	Baton Rouge, LA . 241,130	Jersey City, NJ . . 219,480
Omaha, NE . . . 349,270	Tampa, FL . . . 277,580	Anaheim, CA . . 240,730	Aurora, CO . . . 217,990
Toledo, OH . . . 340,680	Birmingham, AL . . 277,510	St Petersburg, FL . 239,410	Richmond, VA . . 217,700
Virginia Beach, VA 333,400	Norfolk, VA . . . 274,800	Santa Ana, CA . . 236,780	Lexington-Fayette,
Buffalo, NY . . . 324,820	Colorado Springs, CO 272,660	Rochester, NY . . 235,970	KY† 212,900
Sacramento, CA . . 323,550	Corpus Christi, TX . 263,900	Anchorage, AK . . 235,000	Jackson, MS . . . 208,420
Newark, NJ . . . 316,240	St Paul, MN . . . 263,680	Akron, OH . . . 222,060	Mobile, AL . . . 203,260
Wichita, KS . . . 288,870	Mesa, AZ . . . 251,430		

* Urban population of Nashville and Davidson County.   † Lexington and Fayette County were consolidated in 1974.

Immigration
(year ending 30 September)

Country of last permanent residence	1985	1986	1987
Europe.	69,526	69,224	67,967
Austria	1,930	2,039	1,769
France	3,530	3,876	3,809
Germany, Fed. Repub . . .	10,028	9,853	9,923
Greece	3,487	3,497	4,087
Ireland (excl. N. Ireland) . . .	1,288	1,757	3,032
Italy	6,351	5,711	4,666
Netherlands	1,235	1,263	1,303
Poland	7,409	6,540	5,818
Portugal	3,811	3,804	4,009
Romania	3,764	3,809	2,741
Spain.	2,278	2,232	2,056
Sweden	1,171	1,197	1,168
Switzerland	980	923	964
USSR	1,532	1,001	1,139
United Kingdom	15,591	16,129	15,889
Yugoslavia	1,521	1,915	1,793
Asia	255,164	258,546	248,293
Cambodia	5,754	4,502	3,979
China (incl. Taiwan)	33,095	32,389	32,669
Hong Kong	10,795	9,930	8,785
India	24,536	24,808	26,394
Iran	12,327	12,031	10,323
Korea, Repub.	34,791	35,164	35,397
Laos	4,750	3,654	3,331
Philippines	53,137	61,492	58,315
Thailand	17,577	19,086	16,489
Vietnam	20,367	15,010	13,073
North and South America . . .	225,519	254,078	265,026
Argentina	1,925	2,318	2,192
Brazil	2,580	2,693	2,729
Canada	16,354	16,060	16,741
Colombia	11,802	11,213	11,482
Cuba	17,115	30,787	27,363
Dominican Repub.	23,861	26,216	24,947
Ecuador	4,601	4,518	4,656
El Salvador	10,093	10,881	10,627
Guatemala	4,447	5,253	5,843
Guyana	8,080	9,908	10,894
Haiti	9,872	12,356	14,643
Jamaica	18,277	18,916	22,430
Mexico	61,290	66,753	72,511
Panama	3,188	3,067	2,799
Peru	4,117	4,813	5,795
Trinidad and Tobago . . .	2,788	2,844	3,546
Africa	15,236	15,500	15,730
Australia and New Zealand . .	2,501	2,423	2,312
Not specified	2,063	1,937	2,188
Total (all countries)	570,009	601,708	601,516

Source: Immigration and Naturalization Service, US Department of Justice.

AN INTRODUCTION TO THE STATES

Alabama

Gross Area: 133,915 sq km (51,705 sq miles).
Resident Population* (1 July 1987): 4,083,000.
State Capital: Montgomery.
Principal Cities (estimated population at 1 July 1986): Birmingham 277,510; Mobile 203,260; Montgomery (capital) 194,290; Huntsville 163,420.

LOCATION, TOPOGRAPHY AND CLIMATE

The State of Alabama (nicknamed 'The Heart of Dixie') lies in the south of the USA and is bordered by Tennessee to the north, Georgia to the east, Florida and the Gulf of Mexico to the south and Mississippi to the west. The southern half of the state is a low-lying coastal plain through which the Alabama and Tombigbee Rivers flow before joining to form the Mobile, which runs down into the Gulf of Mexico. Stretching across the south of the state is the 'Black Belt', a band of rich, chalky soil. The land rises towards the north of the state, which is traversed by the Tennessee River. Alabama's highest elevation is Cheaha Mountain in the north-east, at 734 m (2,407 ft). The climate is subtropical in the south, with long, hot summers, mild winters and high rainfall. Towards the north of the state, however, the climate is temperate and there is occasionally snow in winter.

HISTORICAL LANDMARKS

The first permanent European settlement in Alabama, Fort Louis de la Mobile, was established by the French in 1702. The Louisiana Purchase of 1803 brought most of modern Alabama under US control, and Gen. Andrew Jackson's victory at Horseshoe Bend in 1814 weakened the presence of the Cherokee, Chickasaw, Choctaw and Creek Indians. In 1817 the region was granted territorial status and Alabama was admitted to the Union as the 22nd state on 2 August 1819. Due to the power of pro-slavery plantation owners the state played an important role in the Civil War; Montgomery was the site of Jefferson Davis's inauguration as President of the Confederation in 1861. Confederacy troops suffered a major naval defeat in Mobile Bay in 1864. More recently, Alabama featured prominently in the civil-rights demonstrations of the 1950s and 1960s, with Dr Martin Luther King, Jr leading a march from Selma to Montgomery in 1965.

Alaska

Gross Area: 1,530,700 sq km (591,004 sq miles).
Resident Population* (1 July 1987): 525,000.
State Capital: Juneau (population 19,528 at 1980 census).
Principal City: Anchorage (estimated population 235,000 at 1 July 1986).

LOCATION, TOPOGRAPHY AND CLIMATE

The State of Alaska, situated to the extreme north-west of the North American continent, is the largest state in the Union, covering 16% of the total US land area. Its borders are formed by the Beaufort Sea to the north, Canada (the Yukon Territory and British Columbia) to the east, the Pacific Ocean to the south, and the Bering Sea to the west. Alaska's mainland is surrounded by numerous islands, including the volcanic Aleutian Islands, sweeping south-west from the Alaska Peninsula, and the Alexander Archipelago, extending along the narrow strip of coast in the south-east. The interior of the state is mountainous, and contains the USA's 17 highest peaks, five of which mark the border with Canada. The two principal mountain ranges are the Brooks Range, within the Arctic Circle, and the Alaska Range in the south, which includes Mount McKinley, the highest point in North America at 6,194 m (20,320 ft). The main lowland area is in the centre of the state, where the Yukon River runs westwards from Canada towards the Bering Sea. There are many lakes, the largest of which is Iliamna Lake at about 2,600 sq km (1,000 sq miles). Northern Alaska has a 'tundra' climate, with a permanently frozen subsoil, while in the central lowlands the winters are long and harsh but the short summers may be hot. Towards the south-east of the state the climate becomes milder. Heavy rainfall occurs across the south and also in the west.

HISTORICAL LANDMARKS

Aleuts and Inuit, originally from Siberia, were the first peoples to occupy Alaska. As a result of exploration by Russian groups in 1741, Europeans started arriving in Alaska to exploit the hunting skills of the Aleuts for the fur trade; their first permanent settlement was established on Kodiak Island in 1784. The fur trade was monopolized by the Russian–American Company, but its success wavered in the first half of the 19th century and in 1867 US Secretary of State William H. Seward persuaded the Russians to part with their American territory for $7.2m. Gold was discovered at Juneau in 1880, following which Alaska's population expanded rapidly; the Organic Act of 1884 granted it a government and courts. The region was granted territorial status in 1912. By 1915 the gold-rush had subsided and fishing had become the primary industry. In 1957 oil was discovered on the Kenai Peninsula and further discoveries led to the building of the Trans-Alaska Pipeline System, completed in 1977. Alaska became the 49th state of the USA on 3 January 1959. In 1989 an oil tanker grounded outside Valdez, spilling 50,000 cu m of oil into Prince William Sound and causing widespread damage to the environment.

Arizona

Gross Area: 295,260 sq km (114,000 sq miles).
Resident Population* (1 July 1987): 3,386,000.
State Capital: Phoenix.
Principal Cities (estimated population at 1 July 1986): Phoenix (capital) 894,070; Tucson 358,850; Mesa 251,430; Tempe 136,480; Glendale 125,820; Scottsdale 111,140.

LOCATION, TOPOGRAPHY AND CLIMATE

The State of Arizona (nicknamed 'The Grand Canyon State') lies in the west of the USA and is bordered by Utah to the north, New Mexico to the east and California and Nevada to the west. To the south is the border with Mexico. In the north of Arizona is the Colorado Plateau, a high, arid region cut by the canyons of the Colorado and Little Colorado Rivers. The Colorado, which flows through the one-mile-deep Grand Canyon, also forms most of the state's western boundary. Arizona's highest point, Humphreys Peak (3,860 m—12,663 ft) lies within the plateau, which is divided from the Sonoran Desert, to the south, by a rocky escarpment, the Mogollon Rim, and a high central region of forest-covered ranges stretching from north-west to south-east. Some fertile land in the south has been created by the irrigation of the Gila and Salt river valleys. Arizona's climate is hot and very sunny. The central region has the highest rainfall in the state (which otherwise receives an extremely low level of precipitation) and also has heavy snowfall in winter.

HISTORICAL LANDMARKS

Among the Indians inhabiting what is now Arizona when the first Spanish explorers arrived in the 16th century were the Apache, Navaho, Pima–Papago and Hopi tribes. Missionaries and silver-prospectors followed the explorers, and a military outpost was established at Tubac in 1752. In 1821 much of the region was annexed by Mexico. After the Mexican War (1846–48) most of Arizona was ceded to the USA as part of the territory of New Mexico. The Gadsden Purchase of 1853 added the southern strip. Arizona succeeded in establishing itself as a new territorial entity in 1863, during the turmoil of the Civil War. With the discovery of gold, silver and copper in the 1870s–1890s, settlers began to pour into the region. Agricultural potential in Arizona was increased by the Salt River Project set up in 1917, the first of many major irrigation projects in the state. Before Arizona became the 48th state on 14 February 1912, 14 out of 17 federally-appointed governors had been Republicans. Statehood coincided with a period of dominance by the Democratic Party, which lasted until the 1950s, when Barry Goldwater was first elected to the US Senate, heralding a new era in the fortunes of the Republicans in Arizona.

Arkansas

Gross Area: 137,754 sq km (53,187 sq miles).
Resident Population* (1 July 1987): 2,388,000.
State Capital, Principal City: Little Rock (estimated population 181,030 at 1 July 1986).

---

* Provisional. Excludes armed forces overseas.

LOCATION, TOPOGRAPHY AND CLIMATE

The State of Arkansas (nicknamed 'The Land of Opportunity') lies in the south of the USA. Its borders are formed by Missouri to the north, Tennessee and Mississippi to the east, Louisiana to the south, and Texas and Oklahoma to the west. The south-east is low-lying and fertile and forms part of both the Gulf Coastal Plain and the Mississippi Alluvial Plain. The Mississippi River, which forms the eastern boundary of Arkansas, is fed by numerous rivers running across the state from the forested uplands in the north-west, where the Arkansas River divides the Ozark Plateau from the Ouachita Mountains. The highest point in the state is Magazine Mountain, at 839 m (2,753 ft). Arkansas has a temperate climate.

HISTORICAL LANDMARKS

When the Spanish arrived in Arkansas in 1541 Indian tribes occupying the area included Quapaw, Caddo and Osage. The first white settlement was established by the French in 1686 at Arkansas Post. Arkansas, as part of Louisiana, came under Spanish control in 1762, was returned to the French in 1800 and was transferred to the USA under the Louisiana Purchase in 1803. In 1819 Arkansas became a territory, joining the Union as the 25th state on 15 June 1836. During the Civil War Arkansas was on the side of the Confederacy. It was at the forefront of national politics in 1957 when President Eisenhower sent troops to enforce a federal court order to integrate the Central High School at Little Rock, which had maintained segregation on the orders of Democrat Governor Orval E. Faubus. Faubus served six terms as governor until 1966, when Winthrop Rockefeller became the first Republican governor since post-Civil War Reconstruction.

California

Gross Area: 411,049 sq km (158,706 sq miles).
Resident Population* (1 July 1987): 27,663,000.
State Capital: Sacramento.
Principal Cities (estimated population at 1 July 1986):

Los Angeles	.	3,259,340	San Bernardino .	. 138,620
San Diego	.	1,015,190	Torrance . .	. 135,570
San Francisco	.	749,000	Garden Grove	. 134,850
San Jose	. .	712,080	Modesto . .	. 132,940
Long Beach	. .	396,280	Pasadena . .	. 129,900
Oakland	. . .	356,960	Oxnard . .	. 126,980
Sacramento (capital)		323,550	Chula Vista .	. 118,840
Fresno	. . .	284,660	Pomona . .	. 115,540
Anaheim	. . .	240,730	Ontario . .	. 114,320
Santa Ana	. .	236,780	Sunnyvale .	. 112,130
Riverside	. .	196,750	Fullerton . .	. 108,750
Huntington Beach		183,620	Concord . .	. 105,980
Stockton	. . .	183,430	Berkeley . .	. 104,110
Glendale	. .	153,660	Inglewood .	. 102,550
Fremont	. .	153,580	Hayward . .	. 101,520
Bakersfield	. .	150,400	Orange . . .	. 100,740

LOCATION, TOPOGRAPHY AND CLIMATE

The State of California (nicknamed 'The Golden State') lies in the west of the USA, and is bordered by Oregon to the north, Nevada and Arizona to the east, Mexico to the south and the Pacific Ocean to the west. Parallel to the coast in the east of the state is the Sierra Nevada mountain range. In the east of the state are the Mojave and Colorado Deserts. The highest and lowest points of the 48 conterminous states of the USA are found within a relatively short distance of each other: Mount Whitney, which has an elevation of 4,418 m (14,494 ft), in the Sierra Nevada, and Death Valley, which is 86 m (282 ft) below sea level, in the Mojave Desert. The Central Valley, enclosed to the east by the Sierra Nevada and to the west by the Coast Ranges, is drained in the north by the Sacramento River and in the south by the San Joaquin River. Both rivers flow into the Pacific Ocean at San Francisco Bay, the only point at which the Coast Ranges are broken. There are two groups of islands off the coast of California: the Santa Barbara Islands and the Farallon Islands. The Salton Sea, in the extreme south of the state, and Lake Tahoe, on the border with Nevada, are among the USA's largest natural lakes. The climate in California is varied, but generally summers are long, hot and dry, and winters are mild and wet. Temperatures are colder in high regions.

HISTORICAL LANDMARKS

When the first permanent settlements were established in the 1760s, California was inhabited by at least 100 different Indian

tribes. Mexico controlled California from 1821 until 1848, when it was handed over to the USA under the Treaty of Guadalupe-Hidalgo. In the same year gold was discovered along the America River, and California's population expanded rapidly, as the gold-rush lasted into the 1870s, helped by improved communications provided by the transcontinental railway (completed in 1869). On 9 September 1850 California was admitted to the Union as the 31st state and, under the Compromise of 1850, slavery was excluded from the state. A major earthquake in 1906 which virtually demolished the city of San Francisco did nothing to deter the influx of people; by 1963 California had the highest population of any state in the USA.

Colorado

Gross Area: 269,596 sq km (104,091 sq miles).
Resident Population* (1 July 1987): 3,296,000.
State Capital: Denver.
Principal Cities (estimated population at 1 July 1986): Denver (capital) 505,000; Colorado Springs 272,660; Aurora 217,990; Lakewood 122,140; Pueblo 101,240.

LOCATION, TOPOGRAPHY AND CLIMATE

The State of Colorado (nicknamed 'The Centennial State') is in the west of the USA and is bordered by Wyoming to the north, Nebraska to the north and east, Kansas to the east, Oklahoma and New Mexico to the south and Utah to the west. Its eastern third consists of high plateau, part of the western Great Plains, which rises towards the foothills of the Rocky Mountains in the centre of the state. The east and west slopes of the Rockies are separated by the Continental Divide. Colorado has the largest number of peaks over 14,000 ft of any state in the USA, the highest point being Mount Elbert at 4,399 m (14,433 ft). It is also the state with the highest mean elevation, at 6,800 ft. To the west of the mountains is *mesa* country—flat tableland with deep ravines and gorges. Six major rivers flow through Colorado: the Colorado, South Platte, North Platte, Rio Grande, Arkansas and Republican. Colorado has a highland continental climate—dry and sunny in summer, with cold, snowy winters in the high mountains.

HISTORICAL LANDMARKS

When French explorers and Spanish gold prospectors arrived in the 18th century Colorado was inhabited by the Ute, Commanchero, Cheyenne, Arapaho and Kiowa Indians. Although much of Colorado was handed over to the USA under the Louisiana Purchase of 1803 it was not until after 1848, when the rest of the state was acquired from Mexico under the Treaty of Guadalupe-Hidalgo, that the first permanent settlement was established at San Luis. Gold discoveries during the second half of the 19th century led to the founding of many mining towns, including Denver and Boulder. Colorado fought for the Union during the Civil War. The 1860s saw a period of warfare against the Indians, beginning in 1864 with a brutal attack at Sand Creek by a force led by Col John Chivington, and ending with two heavy Indian defeats at Beecher Island (1868) and Summit Spring (1869). In 1861 the region was granted territorial status and Colorado entered the Union as the 38th state on 1 August 1876.

Connecticut

Gross Area: 12,997 sq km (5,018 sq miles).
Resident Population* (1 July 1987): 3,211,000.
State Capital: Hartford.
Principal Cities (estimated population at 1 July 1986): Bridgeport 141,860; Hartford (capital) 137,980; New Haven 3,450; Waterbury 102,300; Stamford 101,080.

LOCATION, TOPOGRAPHY AND CLIMATE

Connecticut (nicknamed 'The Constitution State') is one of the six states constituting New England and is bordered by Massachusetts to the north, Rhode Island to the east, the waters of Long Island Sound to the south and New York to the west. In the centre of Connecticut are lowlands formed by the river valleys of the Quinnipiac and Connecticut Rivers. The latter bisects the state from north to south and is the longest river in New England. The Eastern and Western Highlands lie to either side of the central lowlands, with the land gradually rising from the coastal plain to the north of the state, where the highest elevations are to be found. Connecticut's highest mountain is Mount Frissell, at 725 m (2,380 ft). The coast consists of gravel and sand beaches, and rocky peninsulas. The climate is generally temperate.

---

* Provisional. Excludes armed forces overseas.

HISTORICAL LANDMARKS

The first European settlers to arrive in Connecticut were the Dutch, who built a fort on the site of Hartford in 1633. The Dutch were shortly followed by the English, who established settlements at Windsor (1633), Wethersfield (1634) and Hartford (1636). Most of the region's Algonquian-speaking Indian inhabitants were wiped out by European-spread diseases or during King Philip's War (1675–76). In 1639 the three communities formed the Connecticut Colony, which received royal recognition in 1662, and in 1665 was joined by the colony of New Haven (established in 1638). Connecticut operated as an almost autonomous republic during the colonial period and was an American patriot stronghold during the Revolution. Connecticut joined the Union as the fifth state on 9 January 1788. During the Civil War the state sent 55,000 men to fight for the Union.

Delaware

Gross Area: 5,295 sq km (2,045 sq miles).

Resident Population* (1 July 1987): 644,000.

State Capital: Dover (population 23,507 at 1980 census).

Principal City: Wilmington (population 70,195 at 1980 census).

LOCATION, TOPOGRAPHY AND CLIMATE

The State of Delaware (nicknamed 'The First State') lies on the east coast of the USA and is bordered by Pennsylvania to the north, by the Delaware River, Delaware Bay and the Atlantic Ocean to the east and by Maryland to the south and west. Most of the state lies within the Atlantic Coastal Plain. The rolling hills of the Piedmont Plateau in the north of the state slope down towards low-lying fertile plains and marshes in the east, with sandy beaches and dunes along the coast. Delaware's many rivers include the Christina, Appoquinimink, Leipsic and Nantichoke; there are also numerous freshwater lakes. The state's mean elevation is 18 m (60ft), the lowest in the USA. The climate is temperate and humid.

HISTORICAL LANDMARKS

When Henry Hudson, in the pay of the Dutch West India Company, sailed up Delaware Bay in 1603 the region now known as Delaware was inhabited by Indians including the Leni–Lanape (Delaware), Nautichoke and Assateague tribes. The first white settlement, Swanendael (present-day Lewes), was established in 1631 but was destroyed by Indians in the following year. Delaware was subsequently colonized by the Swedes and the Dutch again before coming under English rule and being granted to William Penn by the Duke of York (later King James II) in 1682. Delaware was granted an elected assembly in 1704 but remained under Pennsylvania until the Revolution in 1776. On 7 December 1787 Delaware became the first state to ratify the federal constitution. The state was on the side of the Union during the Civil War, although it had not abolished slavery and blacks were not enfranchised until 1890.

District of Columbia

Gross Area: 178 sq km (69 sq miles).

Resident Population* (1 July 1987): 622,000.

LOCATION, TOPOGRAPHY AND CLIMATE

The District of Columbia is bordered by Maryland to the north-west, east and south, and by the Virginia bank of the Potomac River to the south-west. The district lies within the Atlantic Coastal Plain and is mainly low-lying, with marshes surrounding the Potomac River and reclaimed land flanking the Anacostia River in the south-east. Rock Creek flows from the north-west plateau into the Potomac river. The highest area of the district is the north, where there are rolling hills. The District of Columbia has a temperate climate, with hot, humid summers and mild winters.

HISTORICAL LANDMARKS

Algonquian-speaking Indians inhabited the region now called the District of Columbia until the early 18th century, by which time they had been driven out and the land, part of the Maryland colony, was covered in plantations. In 1791 Pres. George Washington chose the site for the federal government and Pierre L'Enfant was appointed to design the city. The district became the nation's capital on 1 December 1800, and in 1802 it was granted a federally-appointed mayor and elected council. Residents of the District of Columbia were barred from voting in national elections, and from electing their own officials, until the 23rd Amendment to the constitution was passed in 1961 which permitted them to vote for the president and vice-president. In 1970 legislation was passed allowing the district one congressional delegate to the House of Representatives, who can only vote in committee.

Florida

Gross Area: 151,939 sq km (58,664 sq miles).

Resident Population* (1 July 1987): 12,023,000.

State Capital: Tallahassee.

Principal Cities (estimated population at 1 July 1986): Jacksonville 609,860; Miami 373,940; Tampa 277,540; St Petersburg 239,410; Hialeah 161,760; Fort Lauderdale 148,620; Orlando 145,900; Hollywood 120,910; Tallahassee (capital) 119,450.

LOCATION, TOPOGRAPHY AND CLIMATE

The State of Florida (nicknamed 'The Sunshine State') is situated at the south-eastern extremity of the USA and is bordered by Alabama and Georgia to the north. It has coastlines with the Atlantic Ocean to the east, the Straits of Florida to the south (separating it from the Bahamas and Cuba) and the Gulf of Mexico to the south-west. Large areas of the Florida peninsula are covered in marshes. In the south-east and south is the Everglades, a vast sawgrass swamp with occasional mounds where cypress and mahogany grow, and to the west and north of the Everglades is Big Cypress Swamp. The centre of the peninsula is gently undulating and scattered with lakes. Inlets and bays characterize the west coast, while sandbanks lie along the east coast. Curving south-west into the Gulf of Mexico from the extreme south of Florida are the 'Ten Thousand Islands', the most southerly of which, Key West, is also the southernmost point of the 48 conterminous states of the USA. In south-central Florida is Lake Okeechobee, one of the largest lakes entirely within the USA, at about 1,800 sq km (700 sq miles). The state has numerous caves, springs and rivers. Major rivers are the St Johns, flowing into the Atlantic at Jacksonville; the Suwannee, flowing south from Georgia into the Gulf of Mexico; and the Apalachicola, also running south into the Gulf of Mexico. Florida has a humid, mild and sunny climate, tropical in the extreme south and subtropical in the north.

HISTORICAL LANDMARKS

When Juan Ponce de Léon claimed Florida for Spain in 1513 the land was inhabited by numerous Indian tribes, among them the Apalachee, Timucua and Tocobaga. Most were destroyed by European-spread diseases or in battles against the settlers. Creek Indians moved into northern Florida at the end of the 18th century, but these people were defeated by US troops during the (Second) Seminole War of 1835–42 and most were forcibly removed to Oklahoma. Pedro Menendez de Aviles drove out the French Huguenots, who had attempted to claim the land for France, and built a fort at St Augustine in 1565—the first permanent settlement in the USA, and still standing. Florida came under British rule in 1763, and was returned to the Spanish in 1783; it was eventually transferred to the USA (after much wrangling) in 1821 and was granted territorial status in 1822. On 3 March 1845 Florida joined the Union as the 27th state. The state was on the side of the Confederacy during the Civil War. More recently, the first American in space was launched from Cape Canaveral (now Cape Kennedy) in 1961, which has also been the site of subsequent manned missions.

Georgia

Gross Area: 152,576 sq km (58,910 sq miles).

Resident Population* (1 July 1987): 6,222,000.

State Capital: Atlanta.

Principal Cities (estimated population at 1 July 1986): Atlanta (capital) 421,910; Columbus 180,180; Savannah 146,800; Macon 118,420.

LOCATION, TOPOGRAPHY AND CLIMATE

The State of Georgia (unofficially nicknamed 'The Empire State of the South') is bordered by Tennessee and North Carolina to the north, South Carolina and the Atlantic Ocean to the east, Florida to the south and Alabama to the west. Lying off the Atlantic coast are the Sea Islands, of which the largest are Tybee, Ossabaw, St Catherines, Sapelo, St Simons, Sea Island, Jekyll and Cumberland. The south of the state consists of flat, coastal plain

---

* Provisional. Excludes armed forces overseas.

with marshy areas along the coast, and the Okefenokee Swamp in the south-east. A ridge of sandy hills marks the beginning of the Piedmont Plateau, its rolling hills occupying central Georgia. The Blue Ridge Mountains extend into the north, and the state's highest point is reached at Brasstown Bald, at 1,458 m (4,784 ft). Georgia's main rivers are the Savannah, which forms part of the border with South Carolina; the Chattahoochee, flowing across the state before forming the southern half of the Alabama boundary; the Ocmulgee and Oconee, joining to form the Altamaha which flows east into the Atlantic; and the Flint, which meets with the Chattahoochee to form the Apalachicola. The Suwannee River rises in the Okefenokee Swamp and runs into Florida. Georgia has hot summers and mild winters. Temperatures are cooler in the mountainous north.

HISTORICAL LANDMARKS

Before the Spanish established missions on the Sea Islands of St Simons and Jekyll, around 1566, the region now known as Georgia was inhabited by Creek and Cherokee Indians. In 1742 James Oglethorpe defeated the Spanish at the Battle of Bloody Marsh and from 1754 to 1782 Georgia was a British colony. On 2 January 1788 Georgia became the fourth state to ratify the Constitution of the USA. Ceding its western lands to Alabama and Mississippi, the state took on its present form in 1802. During the Civil War Georgia fought on the side of the Confederacy because of the interests of the cotton-plantation owners who relied on black slaves. The Unionist march through Georgia in 1864 marked a decisive stage in the war.

Hawaii

Gross Area: 16,759 sq km (6,471 sq miles).
Resident Population* (1 July 1987): 1,083,000.
State Capital, Principal City: Honolulu (estimated population 372,330 at 1 July 1986).

LOCATION, TOPOGRAPHY AND CLIMATE

The State of Hawaii (nicknamed 'The Aloha State') consists of an archipelago of 132 islands stretching for 2,451 km (1,523 miles) from Kure Island to Hawaii Island, and lying about 3,900 km (2,400 miles) south-west of San Francisco in the northern Pacific Ocean. The eight major islands, extending roughly north-west to south-east, are Niihau, Kauai, Oahu, Molokai, Lanai, Maui, Kahoolawe and Hawaii. Hawaii is the largest island, at 10,451 sq km (4,035 sq miles). The islands, mountainous and mostly fertile, were formed by volcanic eruptions. Mauna Loa, on Hawaii Island, is still an active volcano. The state's highest peak is Mauna Kea (4,205 m— 13,796 ft), also on the island of Hawaii. Hawaii's climate is tropical, tempered by strong, cool winds. Rainfall varies greatly, the islands' interiors and high mountain slopes being mainly dry, and the north-eastern slope of the islands receiving heavy precipitation.

HISTORICAL LANDMARKS

When Captain James Cook reached the islands of Hawaii in 1778 they were inhabited by Polynesians, who had arrived from South Pacific Islands between AD 500–1000. By 1810 Hawaii was united under King Kamehameha I. During the reign of Kamehameha III (1824–54) Honolulu became the kingdom's capital and sugar plantations began to dominate the economy, many of them run by former American missionaries. The Chinese, who arrived in the 1850s, were the first of many groups of immigrants who came to work on the plantations. An increasing US presence on the islands and a weakening of the Kamehameha dynasty led to a bloodless revolution in 1893 when the last monarch, Queen Liliuokalani, was deposed, and Hawaii declared a republic with Sanford B. Dole as president. Hawaii was annexed by the USA in 1898 and Dole became its first territorial governor in 1900. The Japanese attack on the US Pacific fleet at Pearl Harbor in 1941 brought the USA into the Second World War. Hawaii became the 50th state of the Union on 21 August 1959.

Idaho

Gross Area: 216,432 sq km (83,564 sq miles).
Resident Population* (1 July 1987): 998,000.
State Capital, Principal City: Boise City (estimated population 108,390 at 1 July 1986).

LOCATION, TOPOGRAPHY AND CLIMATE

The State of Idaho (nicknamed 'The Gem State') lies in the west of the USA and is bordered by Montana to the north-east, Wyo-

ming to the east, Utah and Nevada to the south, and Oregon and Washington to the west. To the north there is also a short border with the Canadian province of British Columbia. The northern two-thirds of Idaho are very mountainous, the largest ranges being Bitterroot, Clearwater, Salmon River, Sawtooth, Lost River and Lemhi. Borah Peak in the Lost River Range is the state's highest elevation, at 3,859 m (12,662 ft). Curving across the state from east to west at the southern end of the main mountain region is the Snake River, one of the longest rivers in the USA. The river then bends northward to form part of Idaho's western boundary, passing through Hell's Canyon, one of the deepest gorges in North America. South of the Snake River Plain the land is arid and hilly, except in the state's south-eastern extremity, where there is a greener and more mountainous area. In the far north of the state is the lake of the Pend Oreille, covering 383 sq km (148 sq miles). The climate in Idaho varies according to altitude, with hot, dry summers in the south of the state, and cold, snowy winters in the mountains. Eastern Idaho has a continental climate, with greater extremes of temperature.

HISTORICAL LANDMARKS

In 1805, when Meriwether Lewis and William Clark explored the region, Idaho was inhabited by the Shoshone, Northern Paiute, Salishan and Shapwailutan Indians. Idaho officially became part of the USA in 1846 but the first permanent settlement was not created until 1860, when Mormons established Franklin. In the same year a flood of speculators arrived when gold was discovered in northern Idaho. Idaho Territory was organized in 1863 and Boise became the capital in the following year. The increasing occupation of the land by white settlers led to battles with the Indians in the 1870s, which culminated in the surrender of Chief Joseph of the Nez Percé in 1877. A second influx of speculators occurred in the 1880s, when large deposits of silver and lead were discovered. Idaho became the 43rd state to join the Union on 3 June 1890.

Illinois

Gross Area: 145,934 sq km (56,345 sq miles).
Resident Population* (1 July 1987): 11,582,000.
State Capital: Springfield.
Principal Cities (estimated population at 1 July 1986): Chicago 3,009,530; Rockford 135,760; Peoria 110,290; Springfield (capital) 100,290.

LOCATION, TOPOGRAPHY AND CLIMATE

The State of Illinois (nicknamed 'The Prairie State') lies in the Midwest region of the USA, bordered by Wisconsin to the north, Lake Michigan and Indiana to the east, Kentucky to the south-east, and Missouri and Iowa to the west. The state lies within the Central Plains and is therefore mainly flat; however, the land becomes hilly in the north-west, towards the Driftless Area of Wisconsin, and in the south, where it rises towards the Ozark Plateau. The Mississippi River forms Illinois's western border and the Ohio and Wabash its southern and eastern boundaries respectively. The Illinois River traverses the state from north-east to south-west before flowing into the Mississippi River at Grafton, a little north of the confluence of the Mississippi and Missouri. Illinois's climate is generally temperate, with hot, wet summers and cold, snowy winters.

HISTORICAL LANDMARKS

Algonquian-speaking Indians inhabited Illinois by the time whites were exploring the state in the 17th century. The first permanent European settlement was a mission built by the French near what is now St Louis in 1699. The British took control in 1763 and most of the inhabitants were Loyalists during the Revolution. Granted territorial status in 1809, Illinois was admitted to the Union as the 21st state on 3 December 1818 and Springfield became the capital in 1839. Until the 19th century Illinois was only sparsely populated by white settlers, but the defeat of the Indians in the Black Hawk War of 1832 made fertile land available in the south and many farmers from Kentucky moved into the state. Illinois was at first very divided over the slavery issue, but in 1856 slavery was abolished and the state fought for the Union during the Civil War.

Indiana

Gross Area: 93,720 sq km (36,185 sq miles).
Resident Population* (1 July 1987): 5,531,000.
State Capital: Indianapolis.

---

* Provisional. Excludes armed forces overseas.

Principal Cities (estimated population at 1 July 1986): Indianapolis (capital) 719,820; Fort Wayne 172,900; Gary 136,790; Evansville 129,480; South Bend 107,190.

LOCATION, TOPOGRAPHY AND CLIMATE

The State of Indiana (nicknamed 'The Hoosier State') is in the Midwest region of the USA, with Michigan and Lake Michigan to its north, Ohio to its east, Kentucky to its south and Illinois to its west. Undulating land in the north of the state gives way to rougher hill-country in the south. The most fertile region of Indiana is in the north-central area which has numerous lakes and streams. Indiana's major rivers are the Wabash, flowing across the state from north-east to the west and turning south to form the southern half of the boundary with Illinois, and the Ohio, forming the boundary with Kentucky. The climate is humid and continental.

HISTORICAL LANDMARKS

When French explorers Jacques Marquette and Robert Cavelier, Sieur de la Salle, arrived in Indiana in the 1670s the region was inhabited by the Miami, Potawatomi, Kickapoo and Wea Indians. In the early 18th century white settlements were established at Detroit, Fort Miami, Kekionga (now Fort Wayne) and Vincennes. Indiana was part of the territory ceded by France to England in 1763. The first US settlement was Clarksville, established in 1784. Indiana was granted territorial status in 1800, assumed its present boundaries in 1809 and joined the Union as the 19th state on 11 December 1816. Indianapolis became the capital in 1825. The state fought for the Union during the Civil War, although there was initially some sympathy with the southern cause.

Iowa

Gross Area: 145,753 sq km (56,275 sq miles).

Resident Population* (1 July 1987): 2,834,000.

State Capital: Des Moines.

Principal Cities (estimated population at 1 July 1986): Des Moines (capital) 192,060; Cedar Rapids 108,370.

LOCATION, TOPOGRAPHY AND CLIMATE

The State of Iowa (nicknamed 'The Hawkeye State') lies in the Midwest region of the USA and is bordered by Minnesota to the north, Wisconsin and Illinois to the east, Missouri to the south, and Nebraska and South Dakota to the west. Iowa's intensely-cultivated rolling plain gradually rises in altitude from the south-east to the north-west. The land is drained by two major rivers: the Mississippi, which forms the eastern boundary of the state, and the Missouri, which provides the southern two-thirds of the western boundary. Numerous tributaries running across Iowa flow into these two rivers. The state has a humid, continental climate.

HISTORICAL LANDMARKS

Among the Indians occupying Iowa when Frenchmen Louis Joliet and Jacques Marquette travelled through the region in 1673 were the Illinois, Sioux and Iowa tribes. Before the USA took control of Iowa under the Louisiana Purchase of 1803 the only person to have exploited the land was French Canadian Julien Dubuque, who had opened up a lead mine in 1788. After the Black Hawk War of 1832 Indian land became increasingly available and white settlers poured into the region to take advantage of the fertile prairie. Granted territorial status in 1838, Iowa joined the Union on 28 December 1846 as the 29th state, and Des Moines became the capital in 1857. Iowa was fiercely anti-slavery and fought on the side of the Union during the Civil War.

Kansas

Gross Area: 213,098 sq km (82,277 sq miles).

Resident Population* (1 July 1987): 2,476,000.

State Capital: Topeka.

Principal Cities (estimated population at 1 July 1986): Wichita 288,870; Kansas City 162,070; Topeka (capital) 118,580.

LOCATION, TOPOGRAPHY AND CLIMATE

The State of Kansas (nicknamed 'The Sunflower State') is in the Midwest region of the USA, bordered by Nebraska to the north, Missouri to the east, Oklahoma to the south and Colorado to the west. The western part of Kansas forms the eastern extremity of the Great Plains and is the highest region of the state, reaching

1,231 m (4,039 ft) at Mount Sunflower. The land slopes down from the arid country near the Colorado border towards the east. The Smoky Hills and the Central Plains lie in the centre of the state. South of the Kansas River in the east are the Osage Plains, Flint Hills and Arkansas River Lowlands. The major rivers of Kansas are the Missouri, which forms the state's north-eastern boundary; the Arkansas, curving across the state from Colorado to Oklahoma; and the Kansas and its tributaries, flowing across the state to join the Missouri at Kansas City in the east. Kansas has a continental climate with great annual and seasonal variations. High winds and tornadoes frequently sweep across the state.

HISTORICAL LANDMARKS

The first European explorer to enter Kansas was Francisco Coronado in 1541. At this time the region was inhabited by the Wichita, Pawnee, Kansa and Osage Indians. France and Spain claimed the area in the 18th century, but in 1803 Kansas was sold to the USA by the French as part of the Louisiana Purchase. Having been granted territorial status in 1854, there was much dispute as to whether Kansas would be a free state or pro-slavery. Several violent incidents related to this dispute led to the state becoming known as 'Bleeding Kansas'. Kansas eventually entered the Union as a free state (the 34th state) on 29 January 1861, and as such fought on the side of the Union in the Civil War. Prohibition of alcoholic beverages was in force between 1880 and 1948.

Kentucky

Gross Area: 104,661 sq km (40,410 sq miles).

Resident Population* (1 July 1987): 3,727,000.

State Capital: Frankfort (population 25,973 at 1980 census).

Principal Cities (estimated population at 1 July 1986): Louisville 286,470; Lexington–Fayette 212,900.

LOCATION, TOPOGRAPHY AND CLIMATE

The Commonwealth of Kentucky (nicknamed 'The Bluegrass State') lies in the South region of the USA. Its northern boundary is marked by the Ohio River and is bordered by Illinois, Indiana and Ohio; the north-eastern boundary is formed by the Big Sandy River, dividing Kentucky from West Virginia; the south-east shares a border with Virginia; and the south and west are bordered respectively by Tennessee and by Missouri (across the Mississippi River). The south-east of Kentucky is dominated by the Appalachian Mountains, rising to 1,263 m (4,145 ft) at Black Mountain. The Cumberland Plateau, at the edge of the mountains, slopes down towards the Lexington Plain in the north—'Bluegrass' country—and the hilly terrain of the Pennyroyal in the south-centre of the state. The limestone Pennyroyal region contains some of the world's largest caves, the most famous of which is Mammoth Cave. The extreme south-western part of the state lies in the low coastal plain of the Mississippi River. In addition to those forming its boundaries, Kentucky's rivers include the Kentucky, Green, Tradewater, Licking and Cumberland. Kentucky has a temperate and humid climate, with colder winters in the mountainous south-east.

HISTORICAL LANDMARKS

Kentucky was used as a hunting ground by the Shawnee and Cherokee Indians when Thomas Walker and Christopher Gist first explored the region in 1750 and 1751. The first permanent white settlement was established by James Harrod, a Virginian, at Harrodsville (now Harrodsburg) in 1774. In 1776 Kentucky became a county of Virginia. During the second half of the 18th century the area became the main route for migration into the Mississippi Valley and new settlements sprang up, particularly in the 'Bluegrass' region. Kentucky entered the Union as the 15th state on 1 June 1792. Kentucky was divided over the slavery issue prior to the Civil War and initially declared itself neutral before opting for the Union side in 1861. Both Union and Confederacy leaders, Abraham Lincoln and Jefferson Davis, were native Kentuckians.

Louisiana

Gross Area: 123,677 sq km (47,752 sq miles).

Resident Population* (1 July 1987): 4,461,000.

State Capital: Baton Rouge.

Principal Cities (estimated population at 1 July 1986): New Orleans 554,500; Baton Rouge (capital) 241,130; Shreveport 220,380.

LOCATION, TOPOGRAPHY AND CLIMATE

The State of Louisiana (nicknamed 'The Pelican State') is in the South region of the USA and is bordered by Arkansas to the

---

* Provisional. Excludes armed forces overseas.

north, Mississippi to the east, the Gulf of Mexico to the south and Texas to the west. The state lies entirely within the area known as the Gulf Coastal Plain. In the south-east of Louisiana is the Mississippi Delta, which features Lake Pontchartrain, a coastal lagoon covering 1,619 sq km (625 sq miles). The region of coastal lowlands stretching west from the Delta consists of flood plains, bayous and marshes. Off the coast are numerous islands. Louisiana's main rivers are the Mississippi, forming the northern half of the border with the state of the same name; the Red, flowing across the state from north-west to east to join the Mississippi; the Pearl, which provides the southern part of the boundary with Mississippi; and the Sabine, which flows out of the Toledo Bend Reservoir, on the border with Texas. The Atchafalaya branches off from the Mississippi and channels about 25% of its outflow to the Gulf of Mexico. The land gradually rises towards the north of the state, where there are rolling hills to the east and west of central alluvial plains. Louisiana has a subtropical climate.

HISTORICAL LANDMARKS

Among the Indians inhabiting Louisiana when Spanish explorers arrived in the region in the 16th century were the Caddo, Atakapa, Muskogean, Natchez and Tunican-speaking tribes. Robert Cavelier, Sieur de la Salle, claimed the entire Mississippi valley for Louis XIV in 1682, but the French did not succeed in building Natichitoches, their first permanent settlement in Louisiana, until 1714. New Orleans was established in 1718. In 1762 Louisiana passed from French to Spanish control; it was then returned to France in 1800 before being sold to the USA in 1803—thus doubling the size of US territory—for the sum of $15m. In 1804 the area south of 33°N was separated and named the Territory of Orleans which, along with the west of what was then Florida, entered the Union as Louisiana, the 18th state, on 30 April 1812. At the end of the War of 1812, in 1814–15, the army of Gen. Andrew Jackson inflicted a major defeat on the British, who were attempting to capture New Orleans. Due to the economic and political power of the pro-slavery plantation owners, Louisiana fought for the Confederacy during the Civil War.

Maine

Gross Area: 86,156 sq km (33,265 sq miles).
Resident Population* (1 July 1987): 1,187,000.
State Capital: Augusta (population 21,819 at 1980 census).
Principal City: Portland (population 61,572 at 1980 census).

LOCATION, TOPOGRAPHY AND CLIMATE

The State of Maine (nicknamed 'The Pine Tree State') is in the Northeast region of the USA. It is one of the six states of New England and is the most easterly state in the Union. Maine is bordered to the north-west, north and east by the Canadian provinces of Québec and New Brunswick, to the south and south-east by the Atlantic Ocean and to the south-west by New Hampshire. In the west and centre of Maine is the high land of the Longfellow Mountains, the northernmost range of the Appalachian chain, reaching 1,606 m (5,268 ft) at Mount Katahdin. North of the mountains is a region of high plateau. The land is low-lying around the river basins of the St John River in the north, the Penobscot River in the east and the Androscoggin, Kennebec and Saco rivers in the south. The state has numerous rivers and over 2,000 lakes, of which the largest is Moosehead Lake, at 303 sq km (117 sq miles). The coast has sandy beaches in the south-west, becoming more rocky towards the north-east with deep inlets and jagged promontories. There are hundreds of offshore islands. The climate is dry in the north with cool summers and cold winters. The northern interior of the state has heavy snow in winter. Temperatures are more moderate in the coastal region.

HISTORICAL LANDMARKS

When Giovanni da Verrazano, a Florentine explorer, visited Maine in 1524 (the first recorded visit of a European) the region was inhabited by Abnaki Indians. Maine lands were first granted to Sir Ferdinando Gorges by the Council of New England (which he dominated) in 1622. The first permanent European settlements were established on the Saco River in 1623 and at York in 1624. The region came under the jurisdiction of Massachusetts in 1659, following the death of Gorges. The first naval skirmish of the Revolution took place in 1775 when the Americans captured a British vessel in Machias Bay. Maine, the 23rd state, was admitted to the Union as a free state on 15 March 1820 (under the Missouri Compromise). In 1851 Maine became the first state to introduce a prohibition law, which was later adopted as part of its constitution, and was not repealed until 1934.

* Provisional. Excludes armed forces overseas.

Maryland

Gross Area: 27,092 sq km (10,460 sq miles).
Resident Population* (1 July 1987): 4,535,000.
State Capital: Annapolis (population 31,740 at 1980 census).
Principal City: Baltimore (estimated population 752,800 at 1 July 1986).

LOCATION, TOPOGRAPHY AND CLIMATE

The State of Maryland (nicknamed 'The Old Line State' and 'The Free State') is in the South region of the USA and is bordered by Pennsylvania to the north, Delaware to the east, the Atlantic Ocean to the south-east, Virginia to the south and west, the District of Columbia to the west, and West Virginia to the north-west. The Potomac River forms the western and north-western boundary and flows out into Chesapeake Bay, which divides Maryland from north to south, extending 314 km (195 miles) inland from the Atlantic Ocean. The Susquehanna River flows into the bay in the north. West of the Atlantic Coastal Plain which surrounds Chesapeake Bay is the Piedmont Plateau, an area of undulating hills rising towards the Appalachian mountain chain in the far north-west of the state, with a peak of 1,024 m (3,360 ft) at Backbone Mountain. Maryland has hot summers and mild winters in the coastal region and around Chesapeake Bay, with cooler temperatures occurring in the western uplands.

HISTORICAL LANDMARKS

Maryland was inhabited by Algonquian-speaking Indians when European explorers entered the Chesapeake region in the 16th century. George Calvert, Baron of Baltimore, a Catholic, was granted land north of the Potomac River by King Charles I of England in the 1620s, and his descendants had extensive governmental powers over the region until the American Revolution. Maryland joined the Union as the seventh state on 28th April 1788. The state was officially unionist during the Civil War, but many of its landowners relied on slave labour for their tobacco plantations and there was considerable sympathy with the South. A major military confrontation took place in the state in 1862, the Battle of Antietam. By 1864 the government of Maryland was fully behind the Union and the state's new constitution included the abolition of slavery.

Massachusetts

Gross Area: 21,456 sq km (8,284 sq miles).
Resident Population* (1 July 1987): 5,855,000.
State Capital: Boston.
Principal Cities (estimated population at 1 July 1986): Boston (capital) 573,600; Worcester 157,770; Springfield 149,410.

LOCATION, TOPOGRAPHY AND CLIMATE

The Commonwealth of Massachusetts (nicknamed 'The Bay State'), one of the six states of New England, lies in the Northeast region of the USA, with Vermont and New Hampshire to the north, the Atlantic Ocean to the east and south-east, Rhode Island and Connecticut to the south-west, and New York to the west. Eastern Massachusetts is a region of coastal lowlands. South of hook-shaped Cape Cod are Massachusetts' largest islands, Martha's Vineyard and Nantucket Island. The coast is rocky, and higher in the north than the south, rising towards the interior eastern uplands where there are forest-covered hills. Massachusetts' main rivers are the Merrimack, in the north-east; the Taunton, flowing into Mount Hope Bay in the south; and the Connecticut, running southward through west-central Massachusetts. West of the Connecticut River Valley are the Berkshire Hills and the Taconic Mountains, part of the Appalachian chain, with the state's highest point at Mount Greylock, 1,064 m (3,491 ft). The climate in Massachusetts is temperate, with cold, dry winters and cool summers in the west of the state.

HISTORICAL LANDMARKS

The main Indian tribes inhabiting the Massachusetts area in the early 17th century were the Nauset, Massachuset, Wampanoag, Nipmuc and Pocumtuc. The first permanent European settlement was established at Plymouth in 1620 by a group of British Puritans, known as the Pilgrim Fathers, who arrived in the *Mayflower*. In 1630 a larger group of Puritans settled the Massachusetts Bay Colony in Salem. The two separate colonies were united under a royal charter in 1692. Strict trade regulations imposed by the colonial power in the 1760s were very unpopular and the dumping of tea into Boston harbour in 1773 (the 'Boston Tea Party') to prevent Britain from benefiting from its taxation signalled an all-out resistance to British rule. The Battle of Bunker Hill and the British evacuation of Boston in 1775 were also major developments in the American Revolution. On 6 February 1788 Massachusetts became the sixth state to join the Union. The state was a Unionist stronghold during the Civil War, and Yankee Republicans dominated state politics from the 1850s until 1928, when the Democrats began to emerge as the leading party.

Michigan

Gross Area: 151,586 sq km (58,527 sq miles).
Resident Population* (1 July 1987): 9,200,000.
State Capital: Lansing.
Principal Towns and Cities (estimated population at 1 July 1986): Detroit 1,086,220; Grand Rapids 186,530; Warren 149,800; Flint 145,590; Lansing (capital) 128,980; Sterling Heights 111,960; Ann Arbor 107,800; Livonia 100,540.

LOCATION, TOPOGRAPHY AND CLIMATE

The state of Michigan (nicknamed 'The Wolverine State') is in the Midwest region of the USA and consists of two peninsulas. The Upper Peninsula is bordered to the north and east by the Canadian province of Ontario, the boundary passing through St Mary's River and Lake Superior; to the south by Lake Huron and Lake Michigan (separated by the Straits of Mackinac); and to the west by Wisconsin. The Lower Peninsula is bordered to the north by Lake Michigan and Lake Huron; to the east by Ontario, the boundary passing through Lake Huron, the St Clair River, Lake St Clair and the Detroit River; to the south-east by Lake Erie, bordered by Ontario and Ohio; to the south by Ohio and Indiana; and to the west by Lake Michigan. Michigan is mainly flat, with areas of higher land in the west of both peninsulas. In the east of the Lower Peninsula is low, rolling land, while the east of the Upper Peninsula is marshy with hills along the shore of Lake Michigan and sandstone ridges on that of Lake Superior. In addition to its Great Lakes waters, Michigan has thousands of smaller lakes and ponds. Michigan's climate is temperate with well-defined seasons. Temperatures are colder in the Upper Peninsula.

HISTORICAL LANDMARKS

When European settlement of what is now the state of Michigan began in the early 17th century, the region was inhabited by Algonquian-speaking, Winnebago and Huron Indians. Fur-trading and missionary posts were established by the French at Sault Sainte Marie in 1668 and St Ignace in 1671. In 1701 a permanent settlement was created on the site of present-day Detroit. After the defeat of the French in the French and Indian War (1756–63) Michigan came under British authority. The region did not come under US authority until 1796. After being captured by the British during the war of 1812, Michigan was finally returned to the USA under the Treaty of Ghent in 1814. Given territorial status in 1805, Michigan entered the Union as the 26th state on 26 January 1837. The state was controlled by the Democratic Party until the 1850s, when the slavery issue brought the Republicans to power as the proponents of anti-slavery; Michigan fought for the Union during the Civil War. Republicans continued to dominate the government until the 1930s.

Minnesota

Gross Area: 218,601 sq km (84,402 sq miles).
Resident Population* (1 July 1987): 4,246,000.
State Capital: St Paul.
Principal Towns and Cities (estimated population at 1 July 1986): Minneapolis 356,840; St Paul (capital) 263,680.

LOCATION, TOPOGRAPHY AND CLIMATE

The state of Minnesota (nicknamed 'The North Star State') is in the Midwest region of the USA and is bordered by the Canadian provinces of Manitoba and Ontario to the north, Lake Superior and Wisconsin to the east, Iowa to the south, and South Dakota and North Dakota to the west. The state is characterized by its large number of lakes and rivers, including Lake of the Woods at 3,846 sq km (1,485 sq miles) and Rainy Lake at 894 sq km (345 sq miles) in the north (both shared with Canada); Lower and Upper Red Lake, at 1,168 sq km (451 sq miles); Mille Lacs, at 536 sq km (207 sq miles); and Leech Lake, at 456 sq km (176 sq miles). The Mississippi River runs south from its source at Lake Itasca in the north-west and forms the state's south-eastern boundary. Other

major rivers in Minnesota are the St Croix, forming part of the eastern boundary with Wisconsin; the Red River of the North, flowing north into Canada and forming the north-western boundary with North Dakota; and the Minnesota River, flowing across the south of the state into the Mississippi. Minnesota lies at the edge of the Central Plains region of the USA and the land is mainly flat, particularly in the north-west. In the south-east are undulating hills, and in the north-east are the rugged, forested Mesabi and Vermilion Ranges. Minnesota has a continental climate, with cold winters and warm summers.

HISTORICAL LANDMARKS

When the French began to explore Minnesota in the 1650s the region was mainly inhabited by two Indian groups, the Dakota and the Ojibwa. In 1679 Daniel Greysolon claimed the area for France. Part of the region came under British rule in 1763 following the French and Indian War, and became US land after the Revolution; the rest was bought from the French under the Louisiana Purchase of 1803. Minnesota was granted territorial status in 1849 and on 11 May 1858 became the 32nd state to join the Union. Loss of their lands after a series of treaties in 1837 caused a revolt by the Indians and the Dakota War in 1862. On the side of the Union during the Civil War, Minnesota was politically dominated by the anti-slavery Republican Party until the early 20th century when it was challenged by the Democrats and others, including the Non-Partisan League, founded in 1915 by Minnesotan Arthur C. Townley, and its offshoot, the Farmer–Labor Party which emerged in the 1920s and later merged with the Democratic Party.

Mississippi

Gross Area: 123,516 sq km (47,689 sq miles).
Resident Population* (1 July 1987): 2,625,000.
State Capital, Principal City: Jackson (estimated population 208,420 at 1 July 1986).

LOCATION, TOPOGRAPHY AND CLIMATE

The State of Mississippi (nicknamed 'The Magnolia State') lies in the South region of the USA and is bordered by Tennessee to the north, Alabama to the east, the Gulf of Mexico and Louisiana to the south, and Arkansas to the west. The Mississippi River forms the western boundary of the state. To the east of it is the Mississippi Alluvial Plain, or Delta, a broad band of flat, fertile land which becomes narrower towards the south. The rest of the state lies within the Gulf Coastal Plain, rising towards the highest region in the north-eastern corner, and including the Red Clay Hills of east-central Mississippi and the Piney Woods of the south. Sandy beaches extend along the coast. Numerous oxbow lakes, which were once part of the Mississippi River, lie along the state's western boundary. Other major rivers are the Pearl, flowing south into the Gulf of Mexico; and the Big Black and Yazoo Rivers, flowing south-west into the Mississippi. Mississippi has long, humid summers and short winters. Winters are milder in the south, which has a subtropical climate.

HISTORICAL LANDMARKS

Choctaw, Chickasaw and Natchez Indians were the main tribes which inhabited what is now Mississippi when the French began to settle the area in the late 17th century. The first French settlement was established at Biloxi Bay in 1699 and Mississippi was initially part of the French Louisiana territory. Passing frequently between French, Spanish and English control from the 1760s, the region came under US control in 1795. From 1798 until 10 December 1817, when Mississippi became the 20th state of the Union, the USA administered the whole of Alabama and Mississippi as the Mississippi Territory. Cotton plantations and black slave labour were introduced when fertile northern land became available as a result of three treaties with Indians made between 1820 and 1832, and Mississippi went on to become a leading Confederate state. A key area during the Civil War, Mississippi was the scene of three major Union victories: at Corinth and Iuka in 1862, and at Vicksburg in 1863.

Missouri

Gross Area: 180,516 sq km (69,697 sq miles).
Resident Population* (1 July 1987): 5,103,000.
State Capital: Jefferson City (population 33,619 at 1980 census).
Principal Cities: (estimated population at 1 July 1986): Kansas City 441,170; St Louis 426,300; Springfield 139,360; Independence 112,950.

---

* Provisional. Excludes armed forces overseas.

LOCATION, TOPOGRAPHY AND CLIMATE

The State of Missouri (nicknamed 'The "Show Me" State') is in the Midwest region of the USA and is bordered by Iowa to the north; Illinois, Kentucky and Tennessee to the east (across the Mississippi River); Arkansas to the south; and Oklahoma, Kansas and Nebraska to the west. The Missouri River forms the western boundaries with Nebraska and part of Kansas and then flows east across the state to join the Mississippi, which forms the eastern boundary; these two rivers are the longest in the USA. North of the Missouri is a region of undulating hills and fertile plains known as the Dissected Till Plains. South of the Missouri, stretching into Arkansas, is the Ozark Plateau, the highest area of the state. In the west of the state are the low hills and prairies of the Osage Plains, and in the south-eastern corner of the state are the fertile lowlands of the Mississippi Alluvial Plain. Other principal rivers include the White and the Osage. Missouri has a continental climate. The south-east receives the heaviest precipitation.

HISTORICAL LANDMARKS

In 1673, when Jacques Marquette and Louis Joliet travelled down the Mississippi River, Missouri's main inhabitants were Algonquian-speaking and Siouan Indians. Fur-trading and missionary posts were established by the French, who continued to dominate the settlement of Missouri until it became US territory as part of the Louisiana Purchase of 1803. Missouri Territory was established in 1812. Under Spanish rule (1762–1800) many slave-owning farmers had settled in the region and Missouri was the 24th state to enter the Union on 10 August 1821, as a slave-holding state under the Missouri Compromise. Despite substantial support for the Confederacy cause, Missouri was officially on the side of the Union during the Civil War. The Battle of Westport, which saw the defeat of Confederate forces in 1864, was one of the many confrontations which took place on Missouri soil. In 1865 Missouri became the first slave state to free all black slaves. After Reconstruction, when the Radical Republicans threatened to disfranchise all Confederacy sympathizers, there was a general swing towards the Democratic Party, which remained in power into the 20th century.

Montana

Gross Area: 380,848 sq km (147,046 sq miles).
Resident Population* (1 July 1987): 809,000.
State Capital: Helena (population 23,938 at 1980 census).
Principal City: Billings (population 66,842 at 1980 census).

LOCATION, TOPOGRAPHY AND CLIMATE

The State of Montana (nicknamed 'The Treasure State') is in the West region of the USA and is bordered by the Canadian provinces of British Columbia, Alberta and Saskatchewan to the north; North Dakota and South Dakota to the east; Wyoming to the south; and Idaho to the south-west and west. The Rocky Mountains extend along the west of the state, the crest of the Bitterroot Range forming part of the border with Idaho. The Continental Divide passes through Montana, from the Lewis Range in the north-west to the Bitterroot Range in the south-west. The high, undulating land of the northern Great Plains forms the central and eastern regions of the state. The highest elevation in Montana is Granite Peak, at 3,901 m (12,799 ft), near the Wyoming border. The state's main rivers are the Missouri, which has its source in the south-west and flows north and then east across Montana; and the Yellowstone, flowing from the south-east to join the Missouri in North Dakota. Montana has a continental climate, with heavy snow in the west.

HISTORICAL LANDMARKS

Sioux, Blackfoot, Arapaho and Cheyenne Indians were among those occupying Montana at the beginning of the 19th century. In 1803 most of Montana became part of the USA under the Louisiana Purchase; an expedition led by Meriwether Lewis and William Clark in 1804–06 explored the rest of Montana and it became US land. Fur traders were the main settlers until gold was discovered near present-day Drummond in 1858, following which miners started to pour into the region. Another influx occurred in 1880, with the discovery of copper at Butte. It was not until the Indians had been subdued and removed onto reserves that farmers, particularly cattle and sheep ranchers, began to move into the area. One of the most famous Indian victories took place in Montana: the Battle of the Little Big Horn (1876), where Col George Custer and all 266 men of a unit from the Seventh US Cavalry regiment were killed by Sioux and Cheyenne Indians led

by Chiefs Sitting Bull, Crazy Horse and Gall. Granted territorial status in 1864, Montana became the 41st state of the Union on 8 November 1889.

Nebraska

Gross Area: 200,350 sq km (77,355 sq miles).
Resident Population* (1 July 1987): 1,594,000.
State Capital: Lincoln.
Principal Cities (estimated population at 1 July 1986): Omaha 349,270; Lincoln (capital) 183,050.

LOCATION, TOPOGRAPHY AND CLIMATE

The State of Nebraska (nicknamed 'The Cornhusker State') is in the Midwest region of the USA, bordered by South Dakota to the north, Iowa and Missouri to the east, Kansas to the south, Colorado to the south-west and Wyoming to the west. The land in Nebraska slopes down from tableland in the west (the edge of the Rocky Mountains) to prairie in the central region, part of the Great Plains, and the alluvial lowlands of the Missouri valley in the east. In the north-west is a region of grass-covered sand-dunes and small lakes. The state's main rivers are the Missouri, forming part of the northern border with South Dakota, and forming the entire eastern boundary; and the Platte and the Niobrara, which both flow from west to east to join the Missouri. Nebraska has a continental climate with greatly variable temperatures. Precipitation is heaviest in the east.

HISTORICAL LANDMARKS

By the beginning of the 19th century Nebraska was occupied by the Pawnee, Ponca, Omaha and Oto Indians. French and Spanish fur traders travelled through the region in the 18th century. The land became US territory through the Louisiana Purchase of 1803. Bellevue, established in 1823, was the first permanent white settlement. Although the Indian Intercourse Act of 1834 forbade white settlement west of the Mississippi River, thousands of people crossed Nebraska in the mid-19th century on their way westwards to California, and military forts were set up in the 1840s to protect them from Indian attack. Granted territorial status in 1854, Nebraska became the 37th state to join the Union on 1 March 1867.

Nevada

Gross Area: 286,352 sq km (110,561 sq miles).
Resident Population* (1 July 1987): 1,007,000.
State Capital: Carson City (population 32,022 at 1980 census).
Principal Towns and Cities (estimated population at 1 July 1986): Las Vegas 191,510; Reno 110,430.

LOCATION, TOPOGRAPHY AND CLIMATE

The State of Nevada (nicknamed 'The Silver State') is in the West region of the USA and is bordered by Oregon and Idaho to the north, Utah to the east, Arizona to the south-east, and California to the south and west. Nevada lies largely in the Great Basin, a high region of short, rugged ranges and arid basins stretching in a north–south direction. Ranges include the Ruby, Egan, Snake, Schell Creek, Hot Creek, Monitor, Toiyabe and Carson. The state's highest elevation is Boundary Peak in the White Mountains near the border with California, at 4,006 m (13,143 ft). Nevada's rivers frequently dry up, and many flow into saline marshes or lakes: these include the Humboldt, the state's longest river, which flows south-west into Humboldt Sink. Nevada's extreme south-eastern boundary is formed by the Colorado River. Among the state's lakes are Pyramid Lake, Nevada's largest at 487 sq km (188 sq miles); Lake Tahoe, shared with California; and Lake Mead, created by the Hoover Dam on the Colorado and shared with Arizona. Nevada is the driest state in the USA, although there is heavy snow in the mountains. Temperatures vary greatly from day to day, but generally winters are very cold in the north and summers are extremely hot in the south.

HISTORICAL LANDMARKS

When Francisco Garcés, a Spanish priest, entered Nevada in 1776 the region was inhabited by the Southern Paiute, Northern Paiute, Shoshoni and Washo Indians. The first permanent white settlement was established at Mormon Station (later Genoa) in 1850. Carson City was founded in 1858. In 1859 the discovery of the Comstock Lode, a vast silver and gold deposit, attracted a flood of settlers to the area. Nevada Territory was created in 1861 and on 31 October 1864 Nevada became the 36th state to join the Union.

---

* Provisional. Excludes armed forces overseas.

Further discoveries of gold and silver at Tonopah in 1900, of gold at Goldfield and copper at Ely in 1902 gave another boost to the mining industry after Comstock Lode was exhausted. Gambling was legalized in 1931, rapidly becoming the economic mainstay of the state, and particularly of the cities of Las Vegas and Reno, but bringing with it links with organized crime. Underground nuclear-explosion testing is carried out at the Nevada Test Site.

New Hampshire

Gross Area: 24,032 sq km (9,279 sq miles).

Resident Population* (1 July 1987): 1,057,000.

State Capital: Concord (population 30,400 at 1980 census).

Principal City: Manchester (population 90,936 at 1980 census).

LOCATION, TOPOGRAPHY AND CLIMATE

The State of New Hampshire (nicknamed 'The Granite State') is in the Northeast region of the USA and is one of the six states which constitute New England. It is bordered by the Canadian province of Québec to the north and north-west, Maine to the east, the Atlantic Ocean to the south-east, Massachusetts to the south, and Vermont to the west. New Hampshire is mainly rocky, hilly and tree-covered. In the south and west are the New England Uplands, a region with numerous lakes, of which the largest is Lake Winnipesaukee (181 sq km—70 sq miles). In the north are the White Mountains (part of the Appalachian chain), including Mount Washington at 1,917 m (6,288 ft). Lowlands characterize the coastal region in the south-east. Three of the nine rocky Isles of Shoals, in the Atlantic, belong to New Hampshire. The state's main rivers are the Connecticut, which forms the border with Vermont; the Merrimack, forming part of the border with Massachusetts; the Salmon Falls and Piscataqua Rivers, forming part of the border with Maine; and the Androscoggin in the north-east. The climate is temperate and changeable, with severe, snowy winters in the mountains and cool summers inland. Temperatures are warmer on the coast.

HISTORICAL LANDMARKS

Algonquian-speaking Indians inhabited what is now New Hampshire when the Dutch, English and French explored the coast in the 17th century. First to penetrate the region were Martin Pring in 1603, Samuel de Champlain in 1604 and Captain John Smith in 1614. New Hampshire was a province of Massachusetts from 1643 to 1680, when it became a separate colony, although its boundary with Massachusetts remained under dispute until 1740. In 1776 New Hampshire became the first of the original 13 colonies to set up a government independent of Britain; and on 21 June 1788 it became the ninth state to join the Union. Concord became the state capital in 1808. New Hampshire fought with the Unionist forces during the Civil War, but was too far north to witness any fighting within its boundaries.

New Jersey

Gross Area: 20,169 sq km (7,787 sq miles).

Resident Population* (1 July 1987): 7,672,000.

State Capital: Trenton (population 92,124 at 1980 census).

Principal Cities: (estimated population at 1 July 1986): Newark 316,240; Jersey City 219,480; Paterson 139,130; Elizabeth 106,540.

LOCATION, TOPOGRAPHY AND CLIMATE

The State of New Jersey (nicknamed 'The Garden State') is in the Northeast region of the USA and is bordered by New York to the north, the Hudson River, New York Bay and the Atlantic Ocean to the east, Delaware Bay and Delaware to the south, and Pennsylvania to the west. The southern two-thirds of New Jersey lie in the Atlantic Coastal Plain, with sandy beaches, many barrier islands and narrow peninsulas, swamps and an area of pines and marshes known as the Pine Barrens. To the north and east is a region of gently rolling plains interrupted by the high traprock ridges of the Watchungs, Sourlands and Pallisades. Towards the west is a highland region, including the Ramapo Mountains, part of the Appalachian system, and many lakes. The state's highest elevations are in the Kittatinny Mountains in the north-west. New Jersey's main rivers are the Delaware, forming the western boundary with Pennsylvania, the Raritan, Passaic and Hackensack. New Jersey has a temperate climate, with warm, humid summers and cold winters.

---

* Provisional. Excludes armed forces overseas.

HISTORICAL LANDMARKS

When Giovanni da Verrazano, the Florentine navigator, sailed into Newark Bay in 1524 the region now known as New Jersey was inhabited by the Leni–Lanape (or Delaware) Indians. In 1609 Henry Hudson claimed the area for the Dutch and called it New Netherland. After being taken by the English in 1664 it was divided into two provinces until 1702, when the entire region came under the government of New York. New Jersey did not have its own government until 1738, when Lewis Morris became its first governor. Loyalties were divided during the American Revolution and many major battles were fought on New Jersey soil during the war, including the Battle of Trenton (1776) and the Battle of Monmouth (1778). On 18 December 1787 New Jersey became the third state to ratify the US constitution. Although strong sympathies towards the South existed, mainly due to economic links, New Jersey sent troops to fight on the Unionist side during the Civil War.

New Mexico

Gross Area: 314,925 sq km (121,593 sq miles).

Resident Population* (1 July 1987): 1,500,000.

State Capital: Santa Fe (population 49,160 at 1980 census).

Principal City: Albuquerque (estimated population 366,750 at 1 July 1986).

LOCATION, TOPOGRAPHY AND CLIMATE

The State of New Mexico (nicknamed 'The Land of Enchantment') lies in the West region of the USA, and is bordered by Colorado to the north, Oklahoma to the north-east, Texas to the east and south-east, Mexico to the south-west and Arizona to the west. The east of the state forms the western extremity of the Great Plains. The southern Rocky Mountains comprise the north-central part of New Mexico and include the state's highest elevation, Wheeler Peak at 4,011 m (13,161 ft), in the Sangre de Cristo Mountains. Towards the north-west of the state lie the Colorado Plateau and the Chuska Mountains, and across the south of New Mexico are the ranges of San Mateo, Caballo, San Andres, Sacramento and Guadalupe. The main rivers of New Mexico are the Rio Grande, which bisects the state as it flows south from Colorado; the San Juan, looping across the north-west corner; the Pecos, flowing south into Texas, and the Canadian, curving across the north-east into Texas. The Continental Divide runs from north-central to south-western New Mexico. The state has a semi-arid climate, the hottest temperatures being in the south. There is heavy snowfall in the northern mountains.

HISTORICAL LANDMARKS

Navaho, Apache and Pueblo Indians inhabited New Mexico when the first European explorers arrived in the area in the 16th century. The first major European expedition to the area was led by Francisco Vasquez de Coronado in 1540. In 1599 the first permanent white settlement was set up by Don Juan de Oñate. Santa Fe became the capital in 1610. In 1821 Mexico gained its independence from Spain, and New Mexico came under Mexican rule until 1846 when Gen. Stephen Kearney captured Santa Fe for the USA during the Mexican War. Two years later the region was officially ceded to the USA through the Treaty of Guadalupe–Hidalgo. General uncertainty caused by land disputes between new settlers, Spanish inhabitants and Indians, the Civil War and the Lincoln County War of 1878–81, waged between cattlemen and merchants, delayed New Mexico's entry into the Union until 6 January 1912, when it became the 47th state. In 1945 the state was the scene of the explosion of the first atomic bomb, at White Sands Proving Ground.

New York

Gross Area: 127,190 sq km (49,108 sq miles).

Resident Population* (1 July 1987): 17,825,000.

State Capital: Albany (population 101,727 at 1980 census).

Principal Cities (estimated population at 1 July 1986): New York 7,262,700; Buffalo 324,820; Rochester 235,970; Yonkers 186,080; Syracuse 160,750.

LOCATION, TOPOGRAPHY AND CLIMATE

The State of New York (nicknamed 'The Empire State') is in the Northeast region of the USA and is bordered by Lake Ontario and the Canadian provinces of Ontario and Québec to the north; Vermont, Massachusetts and Connecticut to the east; New Jersey and Pennsylvania to the south (apart from where Long Island extends into the Atlantic Ocean); and Pennsylvania, Lake Erie and Ontario to the west. Extensive highland areas cover much of the state. The Adirondack Mountains in the north-east contain New York's highest elevations, including Mount Marcy, at 1,629 m (5,344 ft). In the south of the state are the Catskill Mountains and the Kittatinny Mountain Ridge, both belonging to the Appalachian Highlands stretching across southern New York. The Great Lakes Plain and the coastal area of Long Island are the state's main lowland regions. New York's major rivers are the Hudson, flowing from the north-east to New York Bay in the south; the Mohawk, flowing west from east-central New York to join the Hudson; and the St Lawrence, forming the boundary with Ontario in the north. Other rivers include the Oswego, the Black and the Geneseo, flowing into Lake Ontario; the Poultney, forming part of the eastern boundary; and the Delaware, forming part of the southern boundary. The state's most outstanding natural feature is Niagara Falls, on the Niagara River (the boundary with Canada between Lakes Erie and Ontario). There are numerous lakes in New York (apart from the Great Lakes), including the 11 long, narrow Finger Lakes in the south. New York has a humid, continental climate. The south-east is the warmest region, and the Great Lakes Plain area experiences some of the heaviest snowfall in the USA.

HISTORICAL LANDMARKS

The main Indian tribes inhabiting New York when Florentine navigator Giovanni da Verrazano sailed into New York harbour in 1524 belonged to the Iroquois language group. In 1609 Henry Hudson sailed up the Hudson River almost as far as Albany and claimed the region for the Netherlands. New Amsterdam was founded in 1626. In 1664 the British forced the Dutch to surrender the colony and both it and New Amsterdam were renamed New York. Many battles were fought on New York soil during the American Revolution, including what was probably the turning point of the war when the British were defeated at Saratoga in 1777. On 26 July 1788 New York became the 11th state to ratify the US constitution, and in New York City, which served as the US capital between 1785 and 1790, on 30 April 1789 George Washington was inaugurated as the first president of the USA. In 1825 the Erie Canal between Albany and Buffalo was opened and New York became a primary trade route as well as being the nation's commercial and financial centre.

North Carolina

Gross Area: 136,413 sq km (52,669 sq miles).
Resident Population* (1 July 1987): 6,413,000.
State Capital: Raleigh.
Principal Cities (estimated population at 1 July 1986): Charlotte 352,070; Raleigh (capital) 180,430; Greensboro 176,650; Winston–Salem 148,080; Durham 113,890.

LOCATION, TOPOGRAPHY AND CLIMATE

The State of North Carolina (nicknamed 'The Tar Heel State') is in the South region of the USA and is bordered by Virginia to the north, the Atlantic Ocean to the east, South Carolina to the south and Tennessee to the west. A chain of narrow offshore islands of shifting sandbanks, called the Outer Banks, runs parallel to the entire coastline. In the west of North Carolina are the highest ranges of the Appalachian system, principally the Great Smoky and Blue Ridge Mountains; separating these two ranges are the Black Mountains, with the state's highest elevation, Mount Mitchell, at 2,037 m (6,684 ft). To the east is the rolling land of the Piedmont Plateau, which stretches for 200 miles (320 km) across the centre of North Carolina, gradually descending until a sudden drop occurs along a line between the Roanoke Rapids and Rockingham. The east of the state lies in the Atlantic Coastal Plain, with higher fertile land towards the interior and swampy regions on the coast. From the mountains the New River, Watauga, French Broad, Little Tennessee and Hiwassee rivers flow westward towards the Mississippi; and east of the Blue Ridge the Chowan, Roanoke, Tar, Neuse and Cape Fear are among those rivers flowing towards the coast. North Carolina's climate is humid and subtropical, with long, hot summers and short, mild winters. Temperatures are cooler in the mountain region.

HISTORICAL LANDMARKS

When Europeans explored the region in the 16th century North Carolina was inhabited by Algonquian-, Siouan-, and Iroquoian-speaking Indians. One of the first white men to arrive in North Carolina was Florentine navigator Giovanni da Verrazano in 1524. In 1585 expeditions to colonize Roanoke Island organized by Sir

Walter Ralegh failed. In 1629 Charles I of England claimed all the land from 30°N to 60°N for England, and in 1663 Charles II divided the land between eight proprietors. The proprietors' heavy-handed attempts to collect royal taxes caused much anger among early settlers, resulting in Culpepper's Rebellion of 1677. In 1776 North Carolina's provincial congress voted for independence from Britain. North Carolina ratified the US constitution on 21 November 1789, when it joined the Union as the 12th state. North Carolina was the last of the southern states to secede from the Union in 1861. In 1865 the last major Confederate army surrendered to Gen. William T. Sherman at Bennet House near Hillsborough.

North Dakota

Gross Area: 183,119 sq km (70,702 sq miles).
Resident Population* (1 July 1987): 672,000.
State Capital: Bismarck (population 44,485 at 1980 census).
Principal City: Fargo (population 61,308 at 1980 census).

LOCATION, TOPOGRAPHY AND CLIMATE

The State of North Dakota (nicknamed 'The Flickertail State', 'Sioux State' and 'The Peace Garden State') lies in the Midwest region of the USA, and is bordered by the Canadian provinces of Saskatchewan and Manitoba to the north, Minnesota to the east, South Dakota to the south, and Montana to the west. The eastern boundary is formed by the Red River of the North as it flows towards Canada. The land rises from the flat Red River Valley towards the Drift Prairie which covers most of the eastern half of the state. The Missouri River flows into the state from the north-west, then loops south-east into South Dakota. Inside the river's curve the Missouri Plateau forms the highest area of the state, rising to White Butte at 1,069 m (3,506 ft), and is divided from the Drift Prairie by the Missouri Escarpment. North Dakota has a continental climate, with short, hot summers and very cold winters. Precipitation is low, particularly in the west.

HISTORICAL LANDMARKS

Indians inhabiting North Dakota at the beginning of the 18th century included the Hidatsa, Arikara and Mandan tribes. French fur trader Pierre Gaultier de Varennes, Sieur de la Vérendrye, was one of the first Europeans to explore the region in 1738. The American Fur Company set up a post at Fort Union in 1828. The first permanent community was established at Pembina in 1851. Once the Northern Pacific Railroad had reached as far as Fargo (1872) and the Indians had been confined to reservations settlers began to pour into the region. On 2 November 1889 North Dakota joined the Union as the 39th state. For 58 of the years between 1889 and 1960 power in the state government was held by the Republican Party. However, between 1916 and 1921 the Non-Partisan League held the governorship, losing it in a recall election.

Ohio

Gross Area: 107,044 sq km (41,330 sq miles).
Resident Population* (1 July 1987): 10,784,000.
State Capital: Columbus.
Principal Cities (estimated population at 1 July 1986): Cleveland 535,830; Columbus (capital) 566,030; Cincinnati 369,750; Toledo 340,680; Akron 222,060; Dayton 178,920; Youngstown 104,690.

LOCATION, TOPOGRAPHY AND CLIMATE

The State of Ohio (nicknamed 'The Buckeye State') is in the Midwest region of the USA and is bordered by Michigan and Lake Erie (through which the border with Ontario, Canada, runs) to the north, Pennsylvania to the east, West Virginia to the south-east, Kentucky to the south and Indiana to the west. In the east of the state are the rugged foothills of the Allegheny Mountains. The Allegheny Plateau gradually declines in altitude as it extends westwards towards the Central Plains. Immediately south of Lake Erie is a flat, marshy area. A low ridge stretches from the middle of the border with Indiana to the north-east: the Maumee, Portage, Sandusky, Vermilion, Cuyahoga, and Grand Rivers drain from it into Lake Erie. The rolling hills of the south decline towards the Ohio River which forms the state's southern boundary. Among the rivers flowing into the Ohio from south of the low ridge are the Miami, Little Miami, Scioto, Raccoon, Hocking and Muskingum. Ohio has a humid, temperate climate, with cold winters.

HISTORICAL LANDMARKS

When European exploration of Ohio began in the 17th century the region was inhabited by Wyandot, Leni–Lanape (Delaware), Miami

---

* Provisional. Excludes armed forces overseas.

and Shawnee Indians. Probably the first European to penetrate the area was Robert Cavelier, Sieur de la Salle, in 1669. Separate claims to the region by the French and British in the middle of the 18th century led to the French and Indian War, ending in French defeat in 1763. The first permanent settlement was established at Marietta in 1788. The increasing presence of white settlers caused Indian unrest which culminated in the Battle of Fallen Timbers in 1794 and the surrender of Indian land in southern Ohio. On 1 March 1803 Ohio became the 17th state to join the Union. The War of 1812 saw the defeat of a British fleet by Commodore Oliver Hazard Perry at Put In Bay on Lake Erie. There was considerable sympathy with the cause of the Confederacy in Ohio before the Civil War, but the state eventually fought for the Union, providing 320,000 volunteers.

Oklahoma

Gross Area: 181,186 sq km (69,956 sq miles).
Resident Population* (1 July 1987): 3,272,000.
State Capital: Oklahoma City.
Principal Cities (estimated population at 1 July 1986): Oklahoma City (capital) 446,120; Tulsa 373,750.

LOCATION, TOPOGRAPHY AND CLIMATE

The State of Oklahoma (nicknamed 'The Sooner State') is in the South region of the USA, with Colorado and Kansas to the north, Missouri and Arkansas to the east, Texas to the south and southwest, and New Mexico to the west. The state's highest elevation is Black Mesa at 1,516 m (4,973 ft) in the north-west corner, near the Colorado and New Mexico borders. Western Oklahoma is in the high Great Plains, which give way to prairie towards the centre of the state. In the south of Oklahoma are the Wichita and Arbuckle ranges, while in the east are the Ouachita and Boston Mountains, the latter forming part of the Ozark Plateau. The south-east tip of Oklahoma lies in the Gulf Coastal Plain. The state's major rivers are the Arkansas, looping across the northeast; the Red, forming the southern boundary; and the Canadian and the Cimarron, which run from the west and north-west respectively to join the Arkansas. Oklahoma has a continental climate, with hot summers and cold winters. The south and east are humid.

HISTORICAL LANDMARKS

Oklahoma was only sparsely populated by Indians when Spanish explorers arrived in the 16th century, among them Hernando de Soto and Francisco Vasquez de Coronado. Most of Oklahoma became part of the USA through the Louisiana Purchase in 1803. The Indian Removal Act of 1830 resettled the Cherokee, Chickasaw, Choctaw, Creek and Seminole Indians in Oklahoma. During the Civil War the so-called Five Civilized Tribes, some of which were slave-owners by this time, fought for the Confederacy and in 1866 much of their western land was confiscated in retaliation. Indian unrest culminated in their defeat by Col George Custer and the Seventh Cavalry regiment at the Battle of Washita in 1868. A flood of white settlers to western Oklahoma began in the late 19th century as Indian land became available for farming and as the state's coal, lead, zinc and oil resources began to be exploited. The west of what is now Oklahoma was granted territorial status in 1890, the east, Indian territory, remaining separate until 1906. Oklahoma became the 46th state to join the Union on 16 November 1907.

Oregon

Gross Area: 251,419 sq km (97,073 sq miles).
Resident Population* (1 July 1987): 2,724,000.
State Capital: Salem (population 89,233 at 1980 census).
Principal Cities (estimated population at 1 July 1986): Portland 387,870; Eugene 105,410.

LOCATION, TOPOGRAPHY AND CLIMATE

The State of Oregon (nicknamed 'The Beaver State') lies in the West region of the USA and is bordered by Washington to the north, Idaho to the east, Nevada and California to the south and the Pacific Ocean to the west. The sandy beaches and promontories of the Pacific coast rise to the Coast Range and Cascade Mountains, the latter containing Oregon's highest point, Mount Hood, at 3,424 m (11,235 ft), a dormant volcano. Between the two ranges are fertile valleys, the largest being that of the Willamette River in the north. East of the Cascades is an arid plateau consisting of

undulating hills in the north, and rising towards the Wallowa and Blue Mountains in the north-west of the state. In the south-east is the Great Basin, a bare, dry region. Oregon's main rivers are the Columbia, the fourth largest river in the USA in terms of outflow, forming the western two-thirds of the northern border; the Willamette, draining into the Columbia; and the Snake, forming the northern half of the eastern border and flowing through Hell's Canyon, one of the deepest gorges in North America. The state's largest lake is Upper Klamath Lake, covering 229 sq km (142 sq miles); Crater Lake, formed after the eruption of Mount Mazama, is the deepest lake in the USA, at 589 m (1,932 ft). Oregon's climate is generally temperate; there is heavy precipitation in the west, while the east is dry with greater extremes of temperature.

HISTORICAL LANDMARKS

Among the Indians inhabiting Oregon before the arrival of Europeans were the Bannock, Klamath, Nez Percé and Shoshone tribes. Various European voyagers made sightings of the Oregon coast in the 16th–18th centuries, but the first to sail up the Columbia River (named after his ship) was Robert Gray, an American, in 1792. The Lewis and Clark Expedition reached the mouth of the Columbia River in 1805, and in 1811 a fur-trading post was established at Astoria. Britain and the USA agreed to joint occupation of the region in 1818. The first large influx of settlers occurred in the early 1840s; these people formed a provisional government in 1843 which remained intact until Oregon became a territory in 1849, three years after the British had accepted the Canadian boundary along the 49th parallel. In 1859 Oregon was reduced to its present size, and became the 33rd state on 14 February of that year. The state remained isolated until the completion of the transcontinental railway in 1883.

Pennsylvania

Gross Area: 117,348 sq km (45,308 sq miles).
Resident Population* (1 July 1987): 11,936,000.
State Capital: Harrisburg (population 53,264 at 1980 census).
Principal Cities (estimated population at 1 July 1986): Philadelphia 1,642,900; Pittsburgh 387,490; Erie 115,270; Allentown 104,360.

LOCATION, TOPOGRAPHY AND CLIMATE

The Commonwealth of Pennsylvania (nicknamed 'The Keystone State') is in the Northeast region of the USA and is bordered by Lake Erie and New York to the north; New Jersey to the east; Delaware, Maryland and West Virginia to the south; and West Virginia and Ohio to the west. From the Delaware river, which forms the eastern border of the state, the land slopes up to the rolling hills of the Piedmont Plateau in the south-east and the high Pocono Plateau in the north-east. West of the Great Valley, curving from north-east to south, are the ridges of the Allegheny Mountains, part of the Appalachian system. To the west and north is the Allegheny High Plateau, with Mount Davis in the southwest, at 979 m (3,213 ft), the state's highest peak. In the northwest tip the land slopes down to form a narrow lowland region around Lake Erie. Much of Pennsylvania is drained by the Susquehanna River, which flows through the Appalachians and down into Chesapeake Bay. The west is drained by the Allegheny and Monongahela rivers which join to form the Ohio. South-eastern Pennsylvania has long, warm summers and mild winters, while the high Appalachian region has short, cool summers and harsh winters. Around Lake Erie summers are long and there is heavy snowfall in winter.

HISTORICAL LANDMARKS

Pennsylvania was inhabited by Leni–Lanape (Delaware), Nantichoke, Shawnee, and Iroquoian-speaking Indians when Cornelis Jacobssen, a Dutchman (probably the first European to arrive in the region), entered Delaware Bay in 1614. Swedes began farming along the Delaware River in 1638 and the region was known as New Sweden until the Dutch took the land in 1655, surrendering it to the British in 1664. In 1781 Charles II granted the region to William Penn in payment for his father's services in the war against the Dutch. British taxation of the American colonies and the Proclamation of 1763, which aimed to prevent settlement west of the Allegheny Mountains, infuriated Pennsylvanians. In 1774 Philadelphia became the meeting place for the Continental Congress and in 1776 the Declaration of Independence was proclaimed from Independence Hall. After the American Revolution Philadelphia served as US capital from 1778 to 1783, and again from 1790 to 1800. On 12 December 1780 Pennsylvania became the second state to join the Union. The state fought for the Union during the Civil War, the Battle of Gettysburg, fought on Pennsylvanian soil in 1863, being a turning point in the fortunes of the Union. A

---

* Provisional. Excludes armed forces overseas.

disaster was narrowly averted at Three Mile Island in 1979 when a nuclear reactor malfunctioned.

Rhode Island

Gross Area: 3,140 sq km (1,212 sq miles).
Resident Population* (1 July 1987): 986,000.
State Capital, Principal City: Providence (estimated population 157,200 at 1 July 1986).

LOCATION, TOPOGRAPHY AND CLIMATE

The State of Rhode Island and Providence Plantations (nicknamed 'Little Rhody'), is the smallest of the 50 states. One of the six states comprising New England, it lies in the Northeast region of the USA and is bordered by Massachusetts to the north and east, the Atlantic Ocean to the south, and Connecticut to the west. Block Island, the largest of the 38 offshore islands, is 14 km (9 miles) south-west of Point Judith; Narragansett Bay, extending inland for 48 km (30 miles), contains three of the largest islands of the state: Rhode Island itself (also known as Aquidneck), Prudence and Conanicut. In the state's southern and eastern coastal region there are sandy beaches, marshes and lagoons. Towards the interior the land rises, and western Rhode Island lies within the New England Uplands—rugged, forest-covered hills which are scattered with lakes. The state's main rivers are the Blackstone, which flows from north-eastern Rhode Island into Providence River; and the Pawtucket, flowing into Block Island Sound. Rhode Island's climate is humid with short summers and cold winters.

HISTORICAL LANDMARKS

The main Indian tribes inhabiting Rhode Island in the 16th century were the Narragansett and Wampanoag. The first permanent European settlement in Rhode Island was established by the British at Providence in 1636, to be followed by Portsmouth (1638), Newport (1639) and Warwick (1642). In 1644 these settlements were united as a single colony, the Providence Plantations. Increasing settlement caused Indian unrest, resulting in King Philip's War (1675–76) in which the Indians were defeated. In 1776 Rhode Island declared itself independent from Britain. On 29 May 1790 the region became the last of the 13 original states to join the Union. Despite the increasing development of industry during the 19th century, political power remained in the hands of the landowners until a new constitution was drawn up in 1843. The state was thereafter dominated by the Republican Party until the 1930s, when the Democrats became the major political force.

South Carolina

Gross Area: 80,582 sq km (31,113 sq miles).
Resident Population* (1 July 1987): 3,425,000.
State Capital, Principal City: Columbia (population 101,229 at 1980 census).

LOCATION, TOPOGRAPHY AND CLIMATE

The State of South Carolina (nicknamed 'The Palmetto State') is in the South region of the USA and is bordered by North Carolina to the north, The Atlantic Ocean to the east, and Georgia to the south-west. Marshes and numerous islands lie along the coast of the state. The low-lying Atlantic Coastal Plain extends inland for about 160 km (100 miles), the land rising very gradually towards the undulating Piedmont Plateau in the north-west. In the north-west corner are the Blue Ridge Mountains, part of the Appalachian system, with Sassafras Mountain, at 1,085 m (3,560 ft), the state's highest point. South Carolina's main rivers are the Pee Dee, flowing from the north-east into Winyah Bay; the Santee, running through the centre of the state; and the Savannah, forming the boundary with Georgia. South Carolina's climate is humid and subtropical.

HISTORICAL LANDMARKS

When the Spanish and French attempted to establish settlements in what is now South Carolina in the 16th century, the region was inhabited by Indian tribes including the Cherokee, Catawba and Yamasee. The first permanent European settlement was established by the British at Albemarle Point, moving to the present site of Charleston in 1680. South Carolina was the scene of many battles during the American Revolution, including two major American victories at King's Mountain (1780) and Cowpens (1781). South Carolina became the eighth state to ratify the US constitu-

tion on 23 May 1788. By 1860, when South Carolina became the first state to secede from the Union, more than half the state's population were black slaves. The Civil War's first battle took place at Fort Sumter, Charleston harbour, in 1861.

South Dakota

Gross Area: 199,730 sq km (77,116 sq miles).
Resident Population* (1 July 1987): 709,000.
State Capital: Pierre (population 11,973 at 1980 census).
Principal City: Sioux Falls (population 81,343 at 1980 census).

LOCATION, TOPOGRAPHY AND CLIMATE

The State of South Dakota (nicknamed 'The Coyote State' and 'The Sunshine State') is in the Midwest region of the USA and is bordered by North Dakota to the north, Minnesota and Iowa to the east, Nebraska to the south, and Wyoming and Montana to the west. The eastern half of South Dakota lies within the Central Lowlands of the USA and consists of fertile prairie. West of the Missouri River, which bisects the state from north to south, is the Missouri Plateau, part of the Great Plains. Included in the Missouri Plateau are the Black Hills in the south-west, and the High Plains in the south. North-west of the High Plains are the Badlands, a bare region with fossil deposits and eroded gullies. South Dakota's highest point is Harney Peak, at 2,207 m (7,242 ft), in the Black Hills. Tributaries of the Missouri flowing through the state include the Grand, Moreau, Cheyenne, Bad and White in the west; and the James, Vermilion and Big Sioux in the east. South Dakota has a continental climate, with hot summers, cold winters, low precipitation and high winds.

HISTORICAL LANDMARKS

When the Lewis and Clark Expedition of 1804–06 arrived in what is now South Dakota, the main Indian tribes inhabiting the region were the Hidatsa, Mandan and Arikara. Fur traders and missionaries were the only white men to exploit the region until 1874, when the discovery of gold in the Black Hills started a flood of prospectors to the area. Dakota Territory (including Wyoming, Montana and North and South Dakota) was formed in 1861 and South Dakota became the 40th state to join the Union on 2 November 1889. The state included nine Indian reservations. Wars against the Indians culminated in 1890 with the massacre of hundreds of Sioux at Wounded Knee; 200 Indians occupied Wounded Knee for 70 days in 1973 as a protest against the removal of their land in the Black Hills.

Tennessee

Gross Area: 109,152 sq km (42,144 sq miles).
Resident Population* (1 July 1987): 4,855,000.
State Capital: Nashville.
Principal Cities (estimated population at 1 July 1986): Memphis 652,640; Nashville–Davidson 473,670; Knoxville 173,210; Chattanooga 162,170.

LOCATION, TOPOGRAPHY AND CLIMATE

The State of Tennessee (nicknamed 'The Volunteer State') lies in the South region of the USA and is bordered by Kentucky and Virginia to the north; North Carolina to the east; Georgia, Alabama and Mississippi to the south; and Arkansas and Missouri to the west. Western Tennessee lies in the Gulf Coastal Plain and has fertile land sloping down towards the low-lying Mississippi Flood Plains. In the centre of the state is the rolling land of the Central Basin, encircled by the Highland Rim. The Cumberland Plateau covers much of east-central Tennessee and includes the Cumberland Mountains in the north. The Unaka Mountains, in the extreme east of the state, are part of the Appalachian system. The state's highest point is Clingman's Dome in the Great Smoky Mountains, at 2,025 m (6,643 ft). Tennessee's main rivers are the Mississippi, which forms the western border; the Tennessee, which flows southwards through the Great Valley, separating the Cumberland Plateau from the Unaka Mountains, into Alabama and then back into Tennessee on its way northwards to Kentucky; and the Cumberland, which enters from Kentucky, and then curves across northern Tennessee before flowing back into Kentucky. Tennessee's climate is generally temperate, with warm summers and mild winters. Summers are humid in the west and winters are severe in the mountainous east.

HISTORICAL LANDMARKS

Creek, Yuchi, Cherokee, Chickasaw and Shawnee Indians inhabited the region now known as Tennessee when Hernando de

---

* Provisional. Excludes armed forces overseas.

Soto explored the area in 1540. In 1790 the region was given territorial status as the Southwest Territory, and on 1 June 1796 it was admitted to the Union as the 16th state. The state opted for the Confederacy in 1861 and was a major theatre of battle during the Civil War. Fort Donelson and Fort Henry were taken by the Union in 1862; in 1863 Confederate troops routed Union forces in the Battle of Chickamauga; and the following year Confederate Gen. John Hood received a crushing defeat at Nashville. An important development of the 20th century was the creation of the Tennessee Valley Authority in 1933 which, through building dams and generating electricity, sought to make the state attractive to industry. In 1968 civil-rights leader Dr Martin Luther King, Jr was assassinated in the city of Memphis.

Texas

Gross Area: 691,030 sq km (266,807 sq miles).
Resident Population* (1 July 1987): 16,789,000.
State Capital: Austin.
Principal Towns and Cities (estimated population at 1 July 1986):

Houston	1,728,910	Amarillo	165,850
Dallas	1,003,520	Irving	128,530
San Antonio	914,350	Beaumont	119,900
El Paso	491,800	Pasadena	118,050
Austin	466,550	Laredo	117,060
Fort Worth	429,550	Abilene	112,430
Corpus Christi	263,900	Plano	111,030
Arlington	249,770	Waco	105,220
Lubbock	186,400	Brownsville	102,110
Garland	176,510	Odessa	101,210

LOCATION, TOPOGRAPHY AND CLIMATE

The State of Texas (nicknamed 'The Lone Star State') lies in the South region of the USA and is the largest of the conterminous states of the USA. It is bordered by Oklahoma to the north; Arkansas to the north-east; Louisiana to the east; the Gulf of Mexico to the south-east; the Mexican states of Tamaulipas, Nuevo León, Coahuila and Chihuahua to the south-west; and New Mexico to the west. Between the Pecos and Rio Grande Rivers in the west of Texas is the mountainous trans-Pecos region, including the highest point in Texas, Guadalupe Peak at 2,667 m (8,751 ft), near the New Mexico border. Extending into the north from Edwards Plateau in west-central Texas are the Great Plains, separated from the North Central Plains by Cap Rock Escarpment. The North Central Plains largely consist of rolling prairie, but also include the Burnet–Llano Basin and Hill Country. Dividing the North Central Plains from the eastern Coastal and southern Rio Grande Plains is the Balcones Escarpment, which stretches across Central Texas. The Gulf Coastal Plain in the east consists of the north-eastern Piney Woods, the flat Post Oak Belt and the undulating prairie of the Blackland Belt towards central Texas. The state's main rivers include the Rio Grande, forming the southwestern boundary with Mexico; the Colorado (which is to be distinguished from the longer river of the same name which flows through the West region), crossing central Texas on its way to the Gulf of Mexico; the Red, forming part of the northern border; the Canadian, passing through northern Texas on its way from New Mexico to Oklahoma; and the Sabine, forming part of the eastern boundary. Texas has an extremely varied climate due to its size. Generally the Gulf Coast region has a maritime climate with heavy precipitation in the north-east; the interior of the state has a continental climate, semi-arid in the trans-Pecos region.

HISTORICAL LANDMARKS

Indians belonging to the Coahuiltecan, Karankawa, Tonkawa, Caddo, and Jumano groups inhabited Texas when Spanish explorer Alonso Alvarez de Pineda entered the region in 1519. The establishment of Fort St Louis by the French in 1685 spurred the Spanish into setting up mission-forts in the area, including San Antonio de Bexar in 1718, near present-day San Antonio. After the Spanish abandoned Mexico in 1821, Texas began to be settled by Americans, and by 1835 the latter outnumbered Mexicans by four to one. Declaring their independence, the Texans defeated the Mexicans at San Jacinto in 1836, and Texas existed as an independent republic for 10 years, with Sam Houston as president. Controversy over Texas's slave-owning status delayed its admission to the Union (the 28th state) until 29 December 1845. Texas fought for the Confederacy during the Civil War and the last battle of the war was fought at Palmito Ranch, near Brownsville, in 1865. Important developments of the early 20th century include the growth of the cattle and petroleum industries. President John F. Kennedy was assassinated in the city of Dallas in 1963.

Utah

Gross Area: 219,889 sq km (84,899 sq miles).
Resident Population* (1 July 1987): 1,680,000.
State Capital, Principal City: Salt Lake City (estimated population 158,440 at 1 July 1986).

LOCATION, TOPOGRAPHY AND CLIMATE

The State of Utah (nicknamed 'The Beehive State') is in the West region of the USA, bordered by Idaho and Wyoming to the north, Colorado to the east, Arizona to the south and Nevada to the west. In the south and east of Utah is the Colorado plateau, cut by numerous canyons, including the Glen Canyon, formed by the Colorado River. To the north are the Rocky Mountain ranges of Uinta and Wasatch: King's Peak, at 4,123 m (13,528 ft), the state's highest point, is near the Wyoming border in the Uintas. Western Utah is dominated by the Great Basin. In the north-west the Great Salt Lake, 5,827 sq km (2,250 sq miles) in 1984, although the area varies greatly with weather cycles, and the Great Salt Lake Desert, are the remains of a prehistoric sea. The largest body of fresh water in the state is Utah Lake (363 sq km–140 sq miles). Utah's main rivers are the Colorado; the Green, flowing from the north into the Colorado; and the Sevier, running through central and southern Utah. Utah's climate is generally arid, the highest temperatures being in the south-west. The eastern, mountainous region is cooler, with greater precipitation.

HISTORICAL LANDMARKS

Indian groups living in Utah before the arrival of Spanish and Mexican traders in the mid-18th century were the Ute, Goshiute, Southern Paiute and Navaho. Most Indians were removed to reservations after the Walker War of 1853–54 and the Black Hawk War of 1865–68. After the death of Joseph Smith, founder of the Church of Jesus Christ and the Latter-day Saints, in Illinois, the new leader, Brigham Young, and his Mormon followers set out for the Great Basin in 1847. The region became part of the USA as a result of the Treaty of Guadalupe–Hidalgo in 1848 and was granted territorial status in 1850. From the 1850s Utah's non-Mormon population began to increase as miners came to the region to take advantage of the discovery of ore deposits in south-west Utah. The Mormons' political domination of the region caused clashes with the federal government, particularly over their practice of polygamy. In 1890 the Mormon Church renounced polygamy, and on 4 January 1896 Utah joined the Union as the 45th state.

Vermont

Gross Area: 24,900 sq km (9,614 sq miles).
Resident Population* (1 July 1987): 548,000.
State Capital: Montpelier (population 8,241 at 1980 census).
Principal City: Burlington (population 37,712 at 1980 census).

LOCATION, TOPOGRAPHY AND CLIMATE

The State of Vermont (nicknamed 'The Green Mountain State') is in the Northeast region of the USA and is one of the six states constituting New England. It is bordered by the Canadian province of Québec to the north, New Hampshire to the east, Massachusetts to the south and New York to the west. Dominating Vermont are the forest-covered Green Mountains which extend from Canada to Massachusetts. The state's highest point is Mount Mansfield, at 1,339 m (4,393 ft) in the Green Mountains. In the south-west and reaching into New York are the lower Taconic Mountains. Lying to the west of the Green Mountains in the north of the state are the narrow Valley of Vermont, through which the Poultney River flows, and the broad Champlain Valley, alongside Lake Champlain. East of the Green Mountains in the north is the Vermont Piedmont. The eastern border of the state is formed by the Connecticut River. Vermont has a temperate climate, with heavy precipitation and severe winters in the mountains.

HISTORICAL LANDMARKS

When Samuel de Champlain explored Vermont in 1609 the region was inhabited by Algonquian-speaking Indians. The first permanent settlement established by Europeans was Fort Dummer, built by the British in 1724 near present-day Brattleboro. Disputes over land ownership between New Hampshire and New York caused problems for settlers who in 1770, led by Ethan Allen, organized themselves into a force called the Green Mountain Boys. In 1775 Allen's men captured Fort Ticonderago from the British, and in 1777 Vermont troops won a victory for the patriots at Bennington. Vermont was admitted to the Union as the 14th state on 4 March 1791, after New York's claims had been settled. In 1864, during

---

* Provisional. Excludes armed forces overseas.

the Civil War, Confederates crossed the Canadian border to raid Vermont banks.

Virginia

Gross Area: 105,586 sq km (40,767 sq miles).
Resident Population* (1 July 1987): 5,904,000.
State Capital: Richmond.
Principal Cities (estimated population at 1 July 1986): Virginia Beach 333,400; Norfolk 274,800; Richmond (capital) 217,700; Newport News 161,700; Chesapeake 134,400; Hampton 126,000; Portsmouth 111,000; Alexandria 107,800; Roanoke 101,900.

LOCATION, TOPOGRAPHY AND CLIMATE

The Commonwealth of Virginia (nicknamed 'Old Dominion') is in the South region of the USA and is bordered by West Virginia to the north-west, Maryland and the District of Columbia to the north-east, the Atlantic Ocean to the east, North Carolina and Tennessee to the south and Kentucky to the west. In south-eastern Virginia the Tidewater, a low-lying plain cut by the James, York, Rappahanock and Potomac rivers, gradually slopes up towards the fertile, rolling hills of the Piedmont Plateau. The piedmont covers much of the centre of Virginia, broadening out towards the south. Parallel with the West Virginia and Kentucky borders are the Blue Ridge and the Allegheny Mountains (parts of the Appalachian system), divided by the Valley of Virginia. Mount Rogers, the state's highest point at 1,746 m (5,729 ft), is in the Blue Ridge Mountains near the border with North Carolina. Virginia has a mild, humid climate. Temperatures are cooler in the mountainous west.

HISTORICAL LANDMARKS

When the first Europeans arrived in Virginia the region was mainly inhabited by Algonquian-speaking Indians. The first permanent British settlement in America was established at Jamestown in 1607 by the Virginia Company. In 1619 the colonists formed their first representative assembly. Virginia became a royal colony in 1624. Resistance to British rule led the colony to declare independence (the first to do so) in 1775. Playing a major part in the American Revolution, Virginia was the scene of British Gen. Charles Cornwallis's surrender to George Washington in 1781. On 25 June 1788 Virginia became the 10th state to join the Union. The state was divided over the slavery issue but in 1861 seceded from the Union, Richmond becoming the capital of the Confederacy; this step led to the western third of Virginia setting itself up as West Virginia, the latter being admitted to the Union in 1863. Virginia was the main scene of battle during the Civil War, including Confederate Gen. Robert E. Lee's victories at Bull Run (1861), Fredericksburg (1862) and Chancellorsville (1864); Lee eventually surrendered at Appomattox in 1865.

Washington

Gross Area: 176,479 sq km (68,139 sq miles).
Resident Population* (1 July 1987): 4,538,000.
State Capital: Olympia (population 27,447 at 1980 census).
Principal Cities (estimated population at 1 July 1986): Seattle 486,200; Spokane 172,890; Tacoma 158,950.

LOCATION, TOPOGRAPHY AND CLIMATE

The State of Washington (nicknamed 'The Evergeen State') is in the West region of the USA and is bordered by the Canadian province of British Columbia to the north, Idaho to the east, Oregon to the south and the Pacific Ocean to the west. In the west of the state are the northernmost mountains of the Coast Ranges, consisting of the Olympic Mountains in the north-west Olympic Peninsula, and the Willapa Hills in the south-west. Cutting 130 km (80 miles) southward into the state between the Coast Ranges and the higher Cascade Range is Puget Sound. The Cascades include the highest mountains in the state—all volcanic: Mount Baker, Glacier Peak, Mount Rainier (the highest point in Washington at 4,392 m—14,410 ft), Mount St Helens (which erupted destructively in 1980) and Mount Adams. The two lowland areas of the state are the Western Corridor, formed by Puget Sound, and the Columbia Plateau, east of the Cascades. In north-eastern Washington are the Okanogan Highlands, and in the south-east are the Palouse Hills and Blue Mountains. The main rivers are the Columbia, flowing south-west from Canada to become part of the state's southern boundary, and the Snake, curving across

south-eastern Washington from Idaho and joining the Columbia. The Cascades divide Washington into two climatic regions: mild weather with heavy precipitation predominates in the west, while in the east there are seasonal extremes of temperature and low rainfall.

HISTORICAL LANDMARKS

When the Spanish explored the region in the 18th century Washington was inhabited by Indians of the Nootkin, Salishan and Shahaptian language groups. The first documented exploration of the coast was by Juan Pérez in 1774. In 1792 US Captain Robert Gray discovered the mouth of the Columbia River. The Lewis and Clark Expedition of 1804–06 excited the interest of fur trappers, and in 1836 the first missionaries established a settlement at Waiilatpu, near present-day Walla Walla. In 1848 Oregon Territory, which included Washington, was organized; Washington (including part of Idaho) became a separate territory in 1853. The discovery of gold in the Walla Walla region and the completion of the Northern Pacific Railroad in 1883 increased the flow of settlers to the area and on 11 November 1889 Washington became the 42nd state to join the Union. In 1919 Washington was the scene of the first general strike in the USA. The eruption of Mount St Helens caused widespread destruction in 1980.

West Virginia

Gross Area: 62,760 sq km (24,232 sq miles).
Resident Population* (1 July 1987): 1,897,000.
State Capital: Charleston.
Principal Cities (population at 1980 census): Charleston (capital) 63,968; Huntington 63,684.

LOCATION, TOPOGRAPHY AND CLIMATE

The State of West Virginia (nicknamed 'The Mountain State') is in the South region of the USA and is bordered by Ohio on the north-west, Pennsylvania and Maryland on the north-east, Virginia on the south-east and Kentucky on the south-west. The east of Virginia lies in the Ridge and Valley region of the Appalachian Highlands. Much of the south-eastern border runs parallel with the Allegheny Mountains which include West Virginia's highest point, Spruce Knob, at 1,482 m (4,863 ft). The land drops abruptly at the Allegheny Front, giving way to the rugged Allegheny Plateau which covers the rest of the state. Flowing through the Allegheny Plateau and into the Ohio River, which forms the boundary with the state of the same name, are the Big Sandy, Guyandotte, Kanawha, Little Kanawha and Monongahela Rivers. The main river in the east of the state is the Potomac, forming the border with Maryland. West Virginia has hot, humid summers and cool winters.

HISTORICAL LANDMARKS

Iroquois, Cherokee, Shawnee, Tuscarora and Leni-Lanape (Delaware) Indians inhabited the region now called West Virginia when the French and English explored the Ohio Valley in the 17th century. West Virginia was part of Virginia when Virginia joined the Union in 1788. By the early 19th century small West-Virginian farmers and industrialists were feeling unrepresented in the state legislature, which was dominated by the slave-holding plantation-owners of the east. When Virginia joined the Confederacy in 1861 West Virginia refused to secede from the Union and set up the Reorganized Government at Wheeling, becoming the 35th state to join the Union on 20 June 1863.

Wisconsin

Gross Area: 145,436 sq km (56,153 sq miles).
Resident Population* (1 July 1987): 4,807,000.
State Capital: Madison.
Principal Towns and Cities (estimated population at 1 July 1986): Milwaukee 605,090; Madison (capital) 175,830.

LOCATION, TOPOGRAPHY AND CLIMATE

The State of Wisconsin (nicknamed 'The Badger State') is in the Midwest region of the USA and is bordered by Lake Superior and the state of Michigan to the north, Lake Michigan to the east, Illinois to the south, and Iowa and Minnesota to the west. The Apostle Islands, in Lake Superior, and Washington Island, in Lake Michigan, belong to Wisconsin. In the north of the state, below Lake Superior, are the forest-covered hills of the Superior Upland—the highest region of the state. Craggy, unglaciated hills known as the Driftless Area cover the south-west of Wisconsin.

---

* Provisional. Excludes armed forces overseas.

The centre of the state consists of a broad, sandy plain, occasionally broken by buttes. Lowland prairie occupies the south-east and east of Wisconsin, around Lake Michigan and Green Bay. The state has large areas of fresh water, with over 8,000 lakes. The largest inland lake in Wisconsin is Lake Winnebago in the east, covering 557 sq km (215 sq miles). The Mississippi River and its tributary, the St Croix, form most of the western boundary; flowing from south to south-west is the Wisconsin River. Other rivers include the Chippewa, Black, Fox, Wolf, and Menominee. Wisconsin has a continental climate, with warm summers and severe winters.

HISTORICAL LANDMARKS

When the first Frenchmen arrived in Wisconsin in the 17th century the region was inhabited by Indian tribes including the Ojibwa, Sauk, Fox, Potawatomi and Kickapoo. French dominance of the region ended following the French and Indian War of 1756–63, when it became part of Québec under British rule. Wisconsin was ceded to the USA in 1783 but was not granted territorial status until 1836. On 29 May 1848 Wisconsin joined the Union as the 30th state. The state supported the abolition of slavery and fought for the Union during the Civil War. Following a tradition of reform Wisconsin became the first state to pass old-age pension and unemployment compensation acts, in 1925 and 1932 respectively.

Wyoming

Gross Area: 253,326 sq km (97,809 sq miles).
Resident Population* (1 July 1987): 490,000.
State Capital: Cheyenne (population 47,283 at 1980 census).
Principal City: Casper (population 51,016 at 1980 census).

---

* Provisional. Excludes armed forces overseas.

LOCATION, TOPOGRAPHY AND CLIMATE

The State of Wyoming (nicknamed 'The Equality State' and 'The Cowboy State') is in the West region of the USA and is bordered by Montana to the north, South Dakota and Nebraska to the east, Colorado and Utah to the south, and Utah, Idaho and Montana to the west. Much of the eastern half of Wyoming belongs to the flat Great Plains. The land rises to the Black Hills in the north-east corner, the Big Horn Mountains in the north, and the Laramie and Medicine Bow Mountains in the south. In the south-west of Wyoming is the flat Wyoming Basin, an extension of the Great Plains, which divide the Southern and Middle Rocky Mountains, the latter occupying the north-west of the state. Gannett Peak in the Rocky Mountains is Wyoming's highest point, at 4,207 m (13,804 ft). The Continental Divide runs in a north-west–south direction through the state. Except for the North Platte, which curves across the south-east from Colorado to Nebraska, all Wyoming's major rivers have their sources within its boundaries: the Yellowstone, Powder, Big Horn, Green, Snake, Belle Fourche, Cheyenne, Bear and Niobrara. The state's largest lake is Yellowstone, at 347 sq km (134 sq miles). Wyoming has a continental, semi-arid climate.

HISTORICAL LANDMARKS

Among the Indian tribes living in Wyoming in the 18th century were the Shoshone, Sioux, Cheyenne, Arapaho and Crow. French-Canadian traders, including François and Louis-Joseph Vérendrye in 1743, were the first Europeans to arrive in Wyoming. In 1806–07 John Colter, a US fur trader, travelled across the north-west of the region. It was not until the discovery of gold in California in 1848 that thousands of people began to cross Wyoming as they travelled the Oregon Trail, and supply towns began to develop along the route. The arrival of the Union Pacific Railroad in 1867 encouraged settlement in the region, and in 1868 it was given territorial status. In 1869 the territorial legislature became the first in the USA to grant suffrage to women. Wyoming became the 44th state of the Union on 10 July 1890.

ESSAYS

US POLITICAL AND ADMINISTRATIVE AFFAIRS

THE CONSTITUTIONAL STRUCTURE OF THE USA*

DAVID McKAY

Introduction

Compared with other constitutional systems, that of the United States of America has a number of unusual and, in one or two respects, unique features. The first of these is its relative longevity: neither the wording of the US constitution nor the basic political relations it lays down has changed a great deal since its ratification in June 1788. It has been amended on just 16 occasions (exclusive of the amendments contained in the Bill of Rights—see below), and present-day US politics remain dominated by the federal system and separation of powers which were initially laid down by the constitution. A second notable characteristic of the system lies in the unusual and extensive powers granted to Congress, the national legislature. Few constitutions give their assemblies or parliaments such sweeping powers; in even fewer are executives so constrained by legislators in terms of the day-to-day exercise of power.

A third feature is the high esteem in which the US constitution is held by the country's population. This has applied virtually throughout the history of the republic. Even during the Civil War of 1861–65, the Confederate states believed that the federal government had violated the constitution's prescription for federalism: the document itself was not the target of their grievances. Certainly today it is impossible to find a significant social or economic group which believes that the constitution should be abolished, replaced or changed in any fundamental sense.

Constitutional Provisions on Government

THE LEGISLATURE

Article I of the constitution is devoted to Congress, and in this respect the legislature was assigned pre-eminence over other institutions. The powers given to Congress were carefully defined: they include the power to tax and spend, to declare war, to regulate commerce between the states, to ratify treaties and to confirm appointments to the executive branch. Originally only the House of Representatives was to be elected directly by the people; the Senate was to assume the status of a more deliberative body, with two senators from each state being chosen indirectly by the individual state legislatures to serve a six-year term. (The election of senators by direct popular vote was introduced by the 17th Amendment, ratified in 1913.) The House of Representatives was considered to be the 'people's' assembly; representatives were elected for just two years and the House was given special powers over those areas of public policy which had been so central to the grievances of colonial America—taxation and spending.

The 55 state delegates, or Founding Fathers, who drew up the US constitution wanted to achieve a balance between popular representation (the apportionment of seats in the House of Representatives was, and is, proportional to population, with a minimum of one representative per state) and territorial representation (two senators were to be elected

from each state, irrespective of its population). Most legislation (see below) may be introduced in either house of Congress, and bills must be passed by both before being presented to the president for approval. However, each house has independent sources of political power in addition to their joint sources: only the House of Representatives may originate bills for raising revenue, while the Senate was given special powers to ratify foreign treaties and to confirm executive appointments (thus having an enhanced responsibility for exercising checks upon the executive branch).

THE EXECUTIVE

Article II of the constitution defines the power of the executive, all of which was vested in the president. The most heated debates among the framers of the constitution concerned the relationship between the legislature and the executive. They were determined to prevent the possibility of the abuse of power by the chief executive—a direct consequence of their perception of King George III of England's conduct. However, the experience of very weak central authority, as provided for under the Articles of Confederation (which were the basis of government in 1781–89), pointed to a need for a stronger national executive. The eventual solution was a system of separation of powers, with built-in checks and balances to prevent one branch from usurping the power of the other. So, although the president was given the executive power—as well as being designated US commander-in-chief and having the authority to recommend to Congress 'such measures as he shall judge necessary and expedient' in a 'state-of-the-union' address made 'from time to time' (by convention given annually)—, senior appointments are subject to the 'advice and consent of the Senate'. The Senate has to approve all foreign treaties by a two-thirds majority, and war can only be declared by Congress.

The president was given the power to veto any bill passed by Congress, while Congress, in turn, was enabled to override the veto by a two-thirds majority of a quorum in both the House of Representatives and the Senate (Figure 1 shows some of these basic relationships). The president's powers are thus constrained by having only a limited authority over the crucial law-making process. Moreover, the presidential constituency is a national one, whereas those of members of the House of Representatives are essentially local and those of senators are state-wide.

The Founding Fathers were cautious about vesting too much power in the mass of the population. This is reflected in the original provisions for the indirect election of senators and also in the creation of an electoral college responsible for electing the president. Each state was to appoint 'a number of electors, equal to the whole number of Senators and Representatives to which the State may be entitled in the Congress', the method by which each state did so being determined by its legislature. Whereas it was intended that the electoral college would comprise wise and senior citizens who would exercise an independent choice, the development of political groups and parties meant that electors became increasingly partisan. Eventually, during the early 19th century, the states voted to allow the electorate to choose electoral-college members, and this system has continued, resulting in a *de facto* direct election of the US president.

---

* For text of the US constitution, please see pp. 119–124.

THE JUDICIARY

The system of checks and balances extends to the judicial branch. While all judicial power is vested in the US Supreme Court (Article III), responsibility for nominating its members lies solely with the president. Congress, in turn, may regulate the appellate jurisdiction of the Court, and the Senate must confirm all presidential appointments. The constitution is highly ambiguous on the question of judicial review, or whether the Supreme Court has the power to determine what is, and what is not, compatible with the constitution. This power was, however, established as early as 1803 in *Marbury v. Madison* (see The Judicial System of the USA, p. 33). Since then, it has been the Court's responsibility to review acts of Congress, presidential decisions and the actions of state and local government in order to determine their constitutionality. Although used sparingly, this power has had a profound impact in dealing with such diverse issues as the separation of powers, civil rights and liberties, abortion and federal–state relations.

Figure 1: The Separation of Powers and the Law-making Process

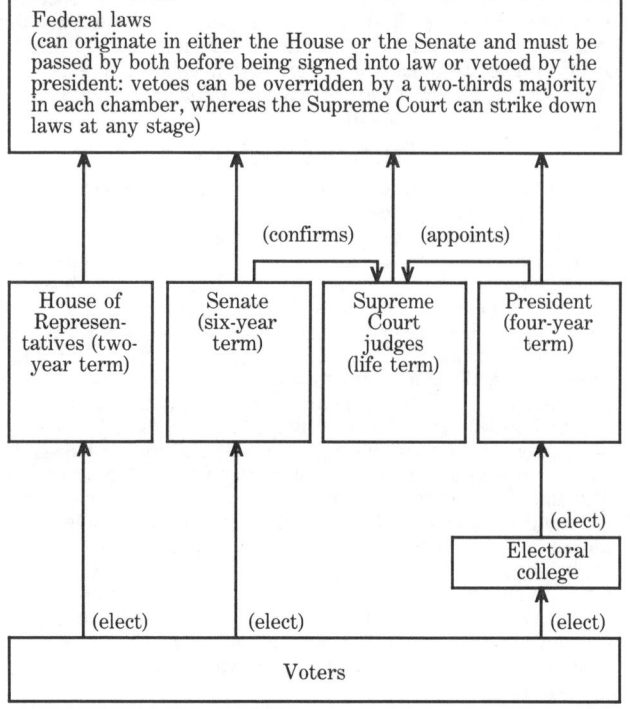

FEDERALISM

A further distinguishing feature of the US constitutional system is its federalism, or the notion that sovereignty is shared between the federal and state levels of government. In fact the constitution says very little about federalism, in that very little is guaranteed to the states (they are assured of equal representation in the Senate, territorial integrity, a republican form of government and protection against invasion and domestic violence). The 10th Amendment, however, does guarantee that 'The powers not delegated to the United States by the Constitution, nor prohibited by it to the States, are reserved to the States respectively, or to the people'. In other words, anything not specifically assigned as a federal responsibility in the constitution is assumed to be a state responsibility. The problem is that the constitution says very little about which level of government is responsible for which functional policy areas. Foreign affairs and certain aspects of economic policy (printing and coining money, for example) are clearly federal tasks, but beyond that much ambiguity remains. As will be discussed later, the USA clearly retains a federal system of government: while each state retains a separate legal system (see pp. 181–190) and a structure of political institutions (governors and state legislatures—see pp. 136–166— and

courts—see pp. 181–190), the federal government has gradually assumed more and more domestic policy responsibilities in relation to the states.

Constitutional Amendments

The Founding Fathers imposed upon the constitution a very cumbersome amendment process which required the agreement of more than a simple majority of elected officials at several levels in the system. As can be seen from Figure 2, the most commonly-used method of amendment has been proposal by a two-thirds vote in both houses of Congress followed by ratification by three-quarters of all state legislatures.

Figure 2: Constitutional Amendments in the US System

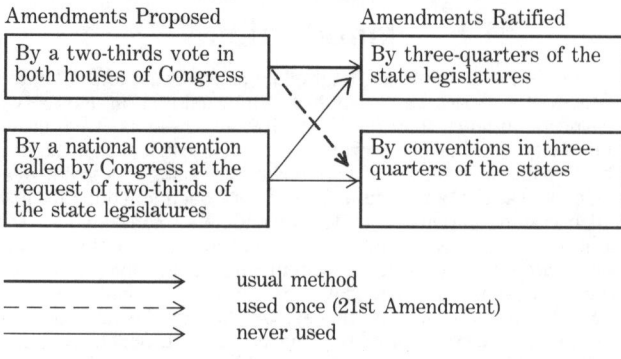

In December 1791, less than four years after ratification of the original seven Articles, 10 amendments came into effect which collectively are known as the Bill of Rights. These 10 provisions guarantee basic liberties (of religion, speech, press, association, assembly and petition) and freedom from arbitrary government action (such as freedom from search and seizure, the right of trial by jury and due process of law) and were added at the insistence of those states which feared that the new federal government might threaten the rights of citizens.

Of the 16 amendments adopted since the ratification of the Bill of Rights, the most important are those affecting elections. In most cases these have either extended the suffrage or have introduced elections to particular institutions. Hence the 15th Amendment (ratified in February 1870) extended the right to vote—at least in theory—to all races; the 17th (April 1913) provided for the popular election of senators; the 19th (August 1920) extended voting to women; and the 23rd (March 1961) awarded three electoral-college votes to the District of Columbia. The 24th Amendment (January 1964) abolished payment of the poll tax as a requirement for voting in federal elections and the 26th (June 1971) lowered the voting age to 18 years. Of the remaining amendments two (the 18th and the 21st) were devoted to the adoption and rejection of prohibition (a legal ban on the manufacture, transportation or sale of liquor). Only four others can be deemed to have had a lasting effect on the substance of policy and on the powers of the federal government. The 13th Amendment (December 1865) abolished slavery, while the 14th (July 1868) extended the due process of law as expressed in the Bill of Rights to apply to the states as well as to the federal government. (In practice this was not implemented fully until the 1950s and 1960s.) The 16th Amendment (February 1913) established a graduated national income tax, and the 22nd (February 1951) limited presidents to a maximum of 10 years in office, or two full terms plus two years of the previous president's elected term.

Constitutional Changes by Interpretation

Overall, many more far-reaching changes in the US constitution have been wrought by interpretation than by amendment. All constitutions are subject to changes by interpretation, but that of the USA has been more flexible than most—partly because the document is both short and, in places, quite vague. Four major interpretative changes can be identified.

THE RISE OF FEDERAL POWER

However measured, the federal government plays a much more dominant role in the system than that envisaged by the Founding Fathers. On the fiscal level, state and local governments are now in receipt of federal aid to help finance a wide range of services. While it was originally envisaged that almost all domestic functions of government would be performed by the states and localities, a combination of factors, such as fiscal stress, the need to achieve some degree of equality in the provision of services and the increasing complexity of society, have increased the role of the federal government. This also applies to civil liberties and civil rights: since the 1940s both have been subject to federalizing or nationalizing trends as the Supreme Court has insisted on the application of national standards. Each state retains considerable *de facto* autonomy in such areas as education, land-use planning, law enforcement and the administration of justice, but there are few legal limits on how far the federal government can extend its influence into these areas.

THE RISE OF EXECUTIVE POWER

The executive branch, with the president at its apex, is now much more powerful than originally intended. While the ascendancy of executives over legislatures is common to all democracies, it is especially noteworthy in the US context because of the very considerable constitutional autonomy of Congress. Presidents have been able to assert their ascendancy, if not their dominance, over Congress for a number of reasons. As the USA has acquired vast overseas responsibilities and a major defence capability, so the president, as commander-in-chief, has assumed responsibility for military and foreign policy. While it can be assumed that such was always intended, the scale of these responsibilities has grown immeasurably since the 1930s.

With the onset of economic depression in the late 1920s following the rapid industrialization of the country, the federal government was expected to take on the job of managing the economy. After the Second World War the crucial function of keeping the economy growing at something approaching full employment was added to Washington's responsibilities. While Congress plays some role here, the major part of the task has fallen to the executive branch and to the presidency, with the result that the US population tends to look first to the presidency to take policy initiatives—and to assume responsibility for the outcome of the latter. A general increase in the size and complexity of government apparatus has also added to the executive branch's responsibilities since, having access to the detailed information available to those responsible for the implementation of policy, the executive branch has developed a clear advantage in relation to Congress. Partly as a result of these developments, the president has become the chief legislator: it is the president's programme, not that of Congress, which determines the national policy agenda.

THE DEMOCRATIZATION OF US POLITICS

The spread of mass democracy is, of course, related to formal changes in the constitution, but the democratization of US politics has gone much further than these changes imply. Increasingly, both the president and Congress are expected to respond quickly and appropriately to the people's will. This 'electoral connection' is much stronger than in most comparable countries, partly because the USA has developed a more populist political culture, but also because the society is highly individualist in its values. Individual voters expect a great deal from individual senators, representatives and presidents, and so the pressures on elected officials to 'perform' are very great.

THE GROWING PROTECTION OF INDIVIDUAL RIGHTS

Until the 20th century the Supreme Court failed to interpret the Bill of Rights and the 14th Amendment (which guarantees all citizens the equal protection of the law) in ways which extended protection to state laws. Hence the civil rights and liberties of groups such as southern blacks were violated with relative impunity. Since the 1940s, however, the Supreme Court has extended these constitutional guarantees to all laws enforceable within the USA. In addition, the Supreme Court has been increasingly active in its insistence that, under federal law, the rights of individuals often take precedence over those of the state (or the federal government). As a result, while protection is in no sense absolute, freedom of speech, assembly and religion is better protected in the USA than in most comparable countries. Citizens' access to the affairs of government is also very considerable.

The US Constitutional System: An Assessment

For almost all of its history, the USA has enjoyed relative domestic political stability. Indeed, since the Civil War no threat to the US regime has emanated from domestic political movements. Few democracies have experienced such a long period of stability. The achievement is all the more remarkable when it is remembered that the USA has been buffeted by truly dramatic changes over the course of its history: it has been transformed by immigration, industrialization, centralization and territorial expansion. Indeed, the building of the 'New Society' has always been founded on the bringing together of diverse peoples, whether defined in national, religious, linguistic, ethnic or racial terms.

This being accepted, critics point to a number of features of the constitutional structure which may put the USA at a disadvantage in relation to some other developed nations. Of these, two in particular dominate—the separation of powers and the federal system.

THE SEPARATION OF POWERS

Because political parties are unusually weak in the USA, and because Congress and the presidency are elected by completely different constituencies, there is very little to oblige the executive and legislative branches to act in harmony. In the modern period (since the election of Franklin D. Roosevelt in 1932) there have, indeed, been few occasions when these two branches have worked easily together. The early 'New Deal' period (1933–35), the Second World War and the 'Great Society' period (1964–66) stand out as exceptions. It may be argued that, before the USA acquired its massive global responsibilities and became the effective economic locomotive of the world economy, this lack of co-operation was an affordable cost for the working of a healthy democracy. Today, however, critics argue that the system so inhibits efficient policy-making that the USA finds itself at a disadvantage in relation to other countries.

Budget-making, for example, must involve both executive and legislature. However, the incentive on the part of individual representatives and senators to put the national or public interest (balancing the budget) before the interests of their constituents is low. This problem is compounded by the fact that as political parties have grown weaker and political behaviour has become more personalized, so the link between members of the Congress and constituents has grown stronger. Thus the pressures on the system are greater: by the late 1980s the USA faced domestic economic problems and foreign-policy problems far more complex than those experienced 30 years previously—but the capacity to respond had grown weaker.

A further problem associated with the constitutional separation of powers is the relative isolation of the executive branch. All executive power is vested in the president, who alone is responsible for running a vast federal bureaucracy. Unlike most parliamentary systems, there is no collective responsibility among prominent members of the executive. Nor is there the sort of party peer-group review which, in the Japanese and British systems, for example, acts as something of a check on the suitability and qualifications of cabinet members and other top officials. Instead, presidents rely more on networks of personal contacts when staffing the executive branch. As a result, the potential for errors and the placing of inappropriate men and women in key positions is probably higher in the USA than elsewhere. (The fact that the president is also head of state compounds this problem, since heads of state are traditionally held to be 'above politics'.)

Finally, the institution of judicial review has attracted many critics. The Supreme Court is today called upon to deliberate on the constitutionality of a wide range of issues: from banking deregulation to abortion, and from civil rights to genetic engineering. Unlike comparable courts in other countries, the US Supreme Court's function extends further than the clarification of the law, or stating whether Congress, the president or the states have acted beyond the law—it is actually to make policy. Critics of judicial review argue that Congress and the president should assume the main responsibility for law-making.

FEDERALISM AND POLITICAL FRAGMENTATION

A second major problem concerns the division of the country into 50 states, among which there is much inequality of size, population and wealth. As already noted, although the federal government has intervened in the affairs of the states increasingly as time has gone by, they retain considerable *de facto* autonomy and variety in the policy-making sphere. As a result there are great disparities to be found in such areas as labour law, the penal system (particularly over the vexed question of capital punishment), levels of taxation and environmental protection. Critics argue that, whether the chief line of defence be justice, economic efficiency or protection from environmental pollution, the need for national standards is pressing. This

is not so much a legal as a political problem—although neither Congress nor the president is inhibited by the courts from insisting on national standards, they have tended to be very sensitive to pressures from the states or to be committed ideologically to some degree of decentralization.

Each of these apparent disadvantages of the US constitutional structure has, however, a corresponding advantage. The separation of powers ultimately prevents the concentration of power in just one branch. While the system of checks and balances may not encourage the development of the most efficient policy-making procedures, it does increase accountability, thus preventing the federal government from making large and serious mistakes. Judicial review may take the courts into unknown policy-making territory, but it also provides the US population with a decision-making reference point which at least appears to be above the highly-politicized world of president and Congress. Finally, while federalism may encourage inconsistencies and anomalies in public policy, it can also provide for more variety and for responsive government at a level more directly involving the electorate.

Ultimately, the success of the US constitutional system must be judged in relation to that of other political systems. When this is done, it is clear that it has been remarkably successful. Almost all of its diverse citizenry supports it, and it has endured more than 200 years already, with the minimum of amendment. No internal threat to the US regime exists, while the country's population has achieved an average level of personal wealth which is among the highest in the world.

US POLITICS AND GOVERNMENT

ALEC T. BARBROOK

The US political system has its basis in both the country's written constitution, as described above, and in those distinct organizations and practices which have grown up as a result of implementing the constitution. This has become a considerable instrument of government, adapting itself to the ever-changing circumstances of two centuries of US history with the minimum of amendment. While institutions such as parties and pressure groups are not mentioned as such in the constitution, they have developed as a result of the defined arrangements for elections and the enshrined rights (especially those listed in the First Amendment) and today constitute vital organs of US democracy.

Elections, Parties and Pressure Groups

Much of the extra-constitutional apparatus of US government has evolved as a result of the perceived need to influence and select those who are elected to office in the country. A great deal of this pressured activity is conducted between elections, but the choice (and support) of candidates by groups, parties and the voters is a dynamic element in the political process. It is not without reason that the USA is referred to as the land of 'continuous election'. The federal system encourages the delegation of political power to subsidiary levels of government, thereby ensuring that electioneering is an ongoing process. Federal senators are probably the most insulated from the process, with a six-year term, one-third of the Senate being subject to the electorate every two years. In contrast, the federal House of Representatives is re-elected in full every two years—however, the electoral advantages of incumbency are such that the vast majority of those of the 435 members who wish to seek re-election are so returned (in 1988, only 6 incumbents out of more than 350 seeking re-election were defeated). The presidency is a special case, for the four-year term has been renewable once only since the 22nd Amendment, ratified in 1951; previously the same held, but only by a convention, which was effectively destroyed by Franklin Roosevelt's four terms in office (1933–45).

The separation of powers at federal level is mirrored at state level by the election of executive officers, legislators and also, in some states, of judges. The governor is the chief (sometimes the sole) elected official of each state: gubernatorial terms are usually two or four years, with less restriction on re-election than was common some years ago. Other constitutional offices (such as lieutenant-governor, attorney-general and secretary of state) are, in most cases, elective. Legislatures (bicameral except in the case of Nebraska) are elected, almost always at two-yearly intervals. Beneath this lie counties (often used for judicial-election purposes) and even smaller units, such as the township (found in New England, where it elects a board of 'selectmen'), providing the lowest tier of government, though even here there are supplementals, such as the school-board elections for the group which controls local education. Cities generally have elected mayors and councils, although alternative systems such as the city-manager or the commission have been tried as reforming devices.

The multiplicity of elections is one reason given for the low turnout in US elections (barely 50% for the 1988 presidential election, although this represented more than 80% of registered voters). An additional burden to the voter at election time is the growing proliferation of referendums or 'questions', which led in 1988 to an (unsuccessful) attempt in California, with probably the largest ballot paper of the year, to limit the amount of time that a voter could spend in the voting booth. Registration is the necessary precursor of voting and usually requires a prior attendance at polling stations early in election year. This can involve three trips in all over a matter of months (registration, primary, general election) if civic duty is to be complete. All voters must be 18 years of age at the date of the general election (while some states allow 17-year-olds to vote in primary elections) and US citizens.

THE ELECTORAL SYSTEM

Proportional representation is literally foreign to the US voter; its nearest equivalent is the 'run-off' of the top two candidates in some civic elections, such as that for the Boston mayoralty and in many state primaries in the south of the country. The more usual 'first-past-the-post' system means that victory requires a plurality rather than a majority. The primary election effectively narrows down the field as far as major parties are concerned, while excluding neither minor-party candidates nor 'independents'. Primaries are essentially intraparty elections designed to place selection of candidates in the hands of the rank-and-file. Party membership is a vaguer concept in the USA than almost anywhere else (entailing little, if anything, in the way of card-carrying or dues-paying) which is why voter registration is all-important. In some states only those registered as supporters of a certain political party can vote in that party's primary (which is consequently termed 'closed'); in other states 'crossover' is permitted, which allows minority-party supporters to participate in a majority party's primary.

While primaries are used for elections at almost all levels, it is the presidential-election primaries which attract most public attention. This system involves some degree of candidate choice and also, usually, the selection of delegates for the national party convention (who may be 'committed' to the primary-voter's choice, at least on the first ballot). The New Hampshire primary, held in the February of each presidential-election year, is justly renowned as a bellwether because of its early indication of candidate popularity and its record of forecasting each major party's electoral choice. Primaries, when first introduced in the early part of the 20th century, were held to be a reforming device; during the 1970s and 1980s their use has increased, so that in 1988 a total of 34 states and the District of Columbia conducted a primary for one or both main parties. The second principal method of presidential-candidate choice is the 'caucus' method, based around private meetings of party members. The Iowa caucus, which is the first to be held in each presidential-election year, has a similar standing to the New Hampshire primary in terms of forecasting eventual candidate choice.

US elections are now largely contested through the mass media which means, for the more important posts, television. This is a high-cost medium and is supplemented by other expensive apparatus such as computer hardware, telephone banks, political consultants and other 'experts', the total cost of which, for a presidential or senatorial race, can amount to many millions of dollars. For the post-convention period, a presidential candidate can now expect to spend in the region of $100m. Public financing will account for about 40% of this, but the rest has to be raised and spent under the restrictions of the Federal Election Campaign Acts (FECA) of 1971–79. In theory, presidential candidates should depend almost solely on public finance for the general (presidential) elections, but the use of national parties' 'soft money', directed at state level, pushes the final expenditure to a level much higher than allowed for by that source alone.

The most expensive senatorial race up to 1988 was the 1984 Helms–Hunt contest in South Carolina, where at least $26m. was spent by the two candidates. Before the 1970s candidates for this level of office would tend to call on wealthy donors if at all possible; these so-called 'fat cats' could contribute tens of thousands of dollars, which meant that a few contributions could make up a substantial 'war-chest' for a candidate. The FECA tried to place strict constraints on this process by placing limits on contribution levels at federal level—these were set at $1,000 per election for individuals (primary and general elections being considered separate) and $5,000 for specified groups. Limits on how much individual candidates could themselves spend on an election campaign were struck down by the Supreme Court's *Buckley v. Valeo* decision of 1976. A by-product of the FECA was the ruling (by the Federal Election Commission) that Political Action Committees (PACs), originally established by organized labour in order to raise and distribute campaign funds, could be set up by other organizations under certain easily-met criteria. As a result the number of PACs increased rapidly at federal level to total over 4,000 by the mid-1980s, most of which were set up by labour organizations, corporations or professional associations. The PACs provide a means by which small sums can be amassed into large donations in that the $10,000 combined limit for primary and general elections can be utilized. Money can also be funnelled outside these rules by the device of 'independent expenditure', which allows payment to be made in support of a cause or candidate providing there is no collusion between the supporting individual, PAC or other group and the candidate's official campaign organization. As a general indication, PACs now contribute about one-third of campaign expenditure, although in certain cases the proportion is much higher (and in others much lower; some candidates refuse to take money from PACs at all).

Each state has a body of legislation which governs the amassing and disbursement of campaign expenditure—in general, this mirrors the FECA, with variations in each state. As at the federal level, disclosure of where money comes from is the fulcrum of this state legislation, although many states have experimented, for example, with patterns of public financing, now used for candidates or parties in about one-third of the 50 states. Measures to restrain the influence of PACs have been introduced in the US Congress, notably in 1987–88, but so far there has been some reluctance to pass more restrictive legislation on campaign finance—perhaps because incumbents benefit from the existing system.

The new technology being brought to bear on elections in the USA is perhaps but an extension of past trends at making elections predictable in every sense of the term: since the turn of the century increasingly sophisticated polling methods have been employed in an attempt to anticipate election results, and in some cases these are thought to exercise a degree of influence over those results.

POLITICAL PARTIES

It is widely claimed that the nature of electoral politics over the last 20 to 30 years has diminished the electoral role of the political party which, despite the above-mentioned strictures, has been a considerable organizing force in the overall US political system since the 19th century. Apart from a few, relatively brief, periods in the early 19th century, and especially since the Civil War of 1861–65, the tendency has been for a two-party system to dominate. The Republican Party won the presidency in 1860 after being in existence since only about 1854, while the Democrats claim links back to the Democratic–Republican party of Jefferson (inaugurated as president in 1801), but effectively date from the 1830s and the organizing force of Martin van Buren.

It is customary to describe the balance between the two major parties as an 'alignment' and to look for changes in this balance from time to time. In broad terms there have been three distinct periods since the 1860s. With the exception of the presidencies of Grover Cleveland (1885–89 and 1893–97) and Woodrow Wilson (1913–21), the northern-based, eventually business-dominated Republicans carried their Civil War victory into decades of relative hegemony at federal level over the Democrats, a Southern-associated, more agrarian party but one which eventually attracted the newer immigrants of the cities. Franklin Roosevelt's victories in the presidential elections of 1932, 1936, 1940 and 1944 subsequently led to the creation of what is usually known as the 'New Deal' coalition, based on blue-collar workers, ethnic voters (such as Irish, Italian and Eastern European immigrants), blacks—some of whom were won over from the 'party of Lincoln'—poor farmers and the intelligentsia. This powerful coalition dominated until the early 1950s, but has since undergone a gradual decline. Debate rages over whether the post-Second World War period has seen a realignment or a 'de-alignment', where there has been no permanent majority party but a series of shifting coalitions dependent on electoral circumstances. A presidency mostly in the hands of the Republicans balanced by a Congress almost permanently controlled by the Democrats suggests that a 'detachment' of the presidential elections has taken place, with the Republicans able to provide candidates in the accepted leadership mould while the Democrats have tended to alienate major voting blocks which they attracted in the past (as with the so-called 'Reagan Democrats').

Much has been made of the supposed decline of party identification as a benchmark in voting behaviour. The increased importance of the primary (see above) is held to be significant here. There has also sometimes been a tendency for candidates to wear the party badge lightly, especially if running in a state or district where the other party has dominated. 'Vote the man . . .' was a slogan which crept into post-1945 US politics and often cut across party ties. Another factor was said to be the confusion, in the 1960s and 1970s, over issues which transcended party allegiance, such as the Vietnam War, the excesses of the young and racial issues, all of which could lead to intraparty disagreement. In the 1980s, however, these have largely disappeared and party organization has improved, especially at national level where previously it was often weak. The increasing incidence of direct-mail fund-raising, first by the Republicans and more recently by the Democrats, has led to some reversal of the old generalization that party organization became weaker as one ascended from local to state to national level. Both parties, and especially the Republicans, are now partially funding state- and local-party organization from national fund-raising. Parties in the USA are often criticized for not being more like Western European parties in that they lack a clear mandate, yet federalism and the separation of powers would make that style of party activity difficult. US political parties perform a necessary role in the country's political process: for example, the organizing power of parties is seen not only in the electoral process, which otherwise would be chaotic and confusing for the voter, but in the legislative process, where Congress and the state legislatures are organized on party lines. Admittedly party discipline never approaches the levels that result from the British 'whipped' system but, even though a legislator must at times vote in line with specific local interests, he or she will tend to vote along party lines most of the time. Distinction between party programmes in the late 1980s is more similar to that prevailing at mid-century than during much of the intervening period, and this can only encourage the revival of party as a guide to the voter.

PRESSURE GROUPS

If the USA has an indigenous political theory of its own, it lies in the concept of group-orientation or pluralism. Electoral analysis is often couched in group terms, with age, social class, income, education, religious and ethnic affiliation and regional origin all being used to determine where candidates are strong or weak. For example, the Reagan and Bush candidacies for the presidency in the 1980s were perceived as appealing to the majority of white voters but to only a small minority of black voters, to men more than to women, and to inhabitants of the southern and western—Rocky Mountain—states even more than to inhabitants of the 'rustbelt'—the industrial states of the Northeast. Much of this differentiation reflects the coalitions of the past and recent past, and encompasses electoral trends such as the shift in the black vote towards the Democrats during the 20th century. Two major population groups have entered the electorate in the post-war period. While the extension of the franchise to southern blacks (provided for in the 17th Amendment, ratified in July 1868) did not become fully effective until after 1965, the 26th Amendment (ratified in June 1971) enfranchised all US citizens aged 18 or over. In general, parties have a specific image in any given period, and population groups tend to identify or not to identify with a party according to their perception of it and of themselves.

The most intrusive effect of the 'group' in US politics is probably in the articulation of common causes by what are termed 'pressure groups' or 'interest groups'. From the time of Madison's *Federalist Paper Number 10* (published in 1787–88), the role of interest articulation within the US political system has grown until it is now regarded as a vital motivating force which can have both beneficial and detrimental consequences. Classic interest-group analysis concentrated especially on economic difference as being perhaps the most important dividing dimension among interest groups, with stress being placed on agriculture, business and industry, and organized labour as the three strands on which the activities of most interest groups were focused. Farming has declined as a major economic force, accounting for less than 3% of total US employment in the late 1980s; as a consequence, its pressures have been mainly defensive in recent years. Organized labour in the USA has never achieved the same power as have the great European labour movements, although the American Federation of Labor and Congress of Industrial Organizations

(AFL–CIO, formed by merger in 1955) does represent many millions of US workers.

In the 1960s and 1970s a new wave passed through the 'interest-group society', with the idea of the 'public interest' becoming dominant. John Gardner's 'Common Cause', the Ralph Nader consumer-rights movement, environmental groups and an increased range of women's groups (such as the National Organization for Women) rode high in the public consciousness for some years, but declined in relative importance during the 1980s. Business, industry and the professions tend to be regarded as the 'big spenders' in terms of interest-group activity. Published figures do not always corroborate this, but these are unreliable because of the largely ineffective legislation on lobbying. Through the use of the FECA (see above), such groups as the Business–Industry Political Action Committee funnel large sums into the electoral process. Some right-wing cause groups such as NCPAC (National Conservative Political Action Committee) were also very active in the early 1980s, targeting liberal legislators; their influence seemed to have declined in the latter part of the decade.

Interests can range over a wide spectrum of human attributes and activity. In the 'pluralist' interpretation, US political society can supply a dynamic which can encompass both unfair practice (such as the occasional bribery scandal) and the expression of genuine grass-roots opinion, which is why there is always so much ambivalence about the interest group's contribution to democracy in the USA. Combined with free (and frequent) elections and a party system that is at least flexible, the formal interest-group universe does provide a range of access to government which is wider than in most other political systems.

Law-making

The formal structures of US government, as set out in the constitution, are based around the three branches indicated by the concept of the separation of powers. For most of US history the mainspring (as indicated in Woodrow Wilson's title for his *Congressional Government: A Study in American Politics*, published in 1885) was regarded as the United States Congress; today it is often argued that power has moved to any president who wishes to take advantage of the potential of that office. Yet Congress is still in theory the main creator of laws, even if it is rarely the instigator or initiator of the main items of the legislative programme.

THE ROLE OF CONGRESS

The US Congress is a representative body, the 'compromise' of the original constitution ensuring that both the states and the people were represented by the final system adopted. The House of Representatives' 435 members come from districts of roughly equal population, which means that California sends 45 representatives to Washington whereas a sparsely-populated state such as South Dakota sends only one 'at-large'. The Senate, with its six-year term for members (as against the two-year term for members of the House) and its smaller size (100 members, two from each state), is regarded as the more prestigious of the two and, after the president, a US senator has probably the highest standing of any US politician. The 'advice and consent' of the Senate has to be sought by the president for treaty-making and major federal appointments, which provides it with considerable leverage. The only comparable unique power possessed by the House of Representatives is that to originate money bills, but this has not provided the dominance that, for example, the House of Commons enjoys in the British system. There are other divided powers in areas such as impeachment or the election of the president and vice-president in the case of deadlock in the electoral college, but these are rarely used. However, it is generally accepted that the most prominent single office in both houses is that of the Speaker of the House of Representatives who, of late, seems to have regained some (though not all) of the power held by the Speakers in the early part of the century. The Senate is chaired by the vice-president in theory (although rarely in practice) while both houses have majority and minority leaders, the former of whom, particularly in the Senate, occupies a crucial leadership position.

Congress occupies a vital educative and communicatory role within the US political system. Constituents exercise influence via district or state on members of both houses and research has long indicated that senators and representatives (also known as congressmen/congresswomen) pay especial heed to strong waves of opinion among the voters who elect them. At the same time, organized interests of the type previously discussed are in a position to exert leverage, often because of the assistance they provide with money or with personnel at election time. Federal legislators, while insisting that they cannot be 'bought' (an old Washington joke suggested that they could be 'rented'), admit that organized groups which provide campaign funds are given what is termed 'access', or the opportunity to put their case on specific issues which may come before Congress. This provides an obvious advantage over the less vocal or less financially-powerful groups.

Congressional procedures are complex and tend to encourage the demise of a bill rather than its passage; defenders of the system suggest that this ensures that any legislation reaching the statute book has been well scrutinized and thus has a chance of being good law. Much of the scrutiny takes place through the committee system where, it is argued, the main work of Congress as a law-making body takes place. Committees are of several types; they usually consist of members from either Senate or House, but there are some important joint committees. Standing committees, usually designated by subject (Foreign Relations, Budget, Judiciary, for example), are the key committees, for it is to these that legislation is referred from the floor of each chamber. Their membership reflects the balance between the parties in the chambers and members are generally ranked according to seniority. Junior senators and representatives slot into the bottom range of the committees to which they are allocated and climb slowly as senior members leave through resignation, electoral defeat or death. Chairmen have traditionally been chosen by virtue of seniority of service on the majority side of a standing committee—however, since the 1970s it has not been unknown for the senior member to be passed over. The power of standing-committee chairmen used to be extensive, especially concerning the scheduling of meetings, control of agendas and the very decision whether to consider or to 'pigeon-hole' a bill. This power has now become diffused, especially with the rise of the subcommittee. By the mid-1980s there were about 230 subcommittees operating within Congress, and these had an important voice in current legislative business referred to standing committees. Whether or not these recent reforms in the committee system can be described as substantive is arguable, but there is no doubt that they have ended the stranglehold that a small clique of elderly committee chairmen wielded over legislation in the 1960s.

Among the more notable committees is the notorious Rules Committee in the House of Representatives, which regulates the flow of bills to the floor: early in his presidency John Kennedy launched an important drive to enlarge the committee's membership and dilute its power. Special select committees, such as that set up to investigate the Watergate scandal in 1972, can play a crucial role in the political process. The final stage of the *cause célèbre* which ensued from the Watergate break-in was played out before the House Judiciary Committee in 1974 which recommended the articles of impeachment prior to Richard Nixon's resignation. The Senate Judiciary Committee is also on occasion in the public eye in connection with the ratification of presidential Supreme Court appointments, as when it overturned President Reagan's nomination of Judge Robert Bork in October 1987.

Apart from the changes noted, much pressure has been exercised over recent years for both chambers of Congress to reform themselves and to make themselves into more efficient representative and legislative bodies. After Watergate, Congress tried to exercise more control over the executive's role in taxing and peacekeeping, but neither attempt has been markedly successful. Ethical considerations have also been forced on Congress from time to time when bribery and other scandals have surfaced. Congress tries to police itself in these matters, but successive ethics codes do not appear to have

prevented the occasional irregularity in behaviour of the members of democracy's most-observed legislature.

PRESIDENTIAL POWER

If the attempt to revive the power of Congress had only a limited success, the question arises whether the initiative, as far as policy-making is concerned, has remained in, or returned to, the hands of the president. Much of the *raison d'être* for the congressional attempt to regain at least some of the initiative came from the argument that the USA had, in the 20th century, produced an 'imperial' presidency, notably in terms of foreign policy, and that there should be more of a balance of power between the legislative and executive branches. It is true that Congress can wield much more independent power in domestic affairs and that this limits the validity of the imperialist thesis, but its influence still lingers.

The presidential emphasis would seem to date principally from the 'New Deal' of the 1930s, even if it had flickered earlier in the century during the administrations of Theodore Roosevelt (1901–09) and Woodrow Wilson (1913–21). The crises of the 20th century have been more suited to the presidential capacity for constant reaction than to the more deliberative approaches of Congress. Presidential power, as defined in the (comparatively short) Article II of the Constitution, has been utilized by 'strong' presidents to lead the nation through the complex foreign and domestic problems it has encountered. For example, as commander-in-chief, the president is empowered to intervene immediately in overseas incidents where the nation's interests seem to be at stake (as with the execution of Maurice Bishop in Grenada in October 1983, following which 1,900 US troops entered the island). Indeed, it is noticeable that, while there has not been a declaration of war since 1941, the USA has seen its forces committed to action time and time again through presidential initiative since the end of the Second World War.

The president has a range of other roles. Executive power is accorded by the opening sentences of Article II. Treaty-making, senior administrative appointments and the implementation of law-making buttress the power to ensure that 'the laws be faithfully executed' (II.3); the initiating of laws is clearly suggested by this latter section, which allows the president to recommend to the consideration of Congress 'such measures as he shall judge necessary and expedient'.

THE FEDERAL BUREAUCRACY

A considerable personal machine has evolved around the president during the 20th century, and this provides access to an unparalleled range of advice and often to the means to carry out policy based on that advice. The White House Office, the National Security Council, the Council of Economic Advisers and the Office of Management and Budget are just some constituent elements of the constellation through which the president carries on day-to-day, week-to-week policy formulation. The presidential cabinet consists mainly of political appointees acting as heads of the 14 departments which oversee the main governmental activity; they hold office at the pleasure of the president. Responsible to them are more than 3m. federal employees: these are not only resident in Washington, but spread all over the USA (every state capital has its federal building) and, indeed, in many parts of the world.

The federal bureaucracy has not increased at the same rate as has state and local bureaucracy over the last 20 years, but it remains a formidable force, and is often claimed to act as a brake on dramatic change when a new inhabitant occupies the White House. In the early 1980s the opposition to the seemingly revolutionary changes advocated in the Department of the Interior by the Secretary, James Watt, and his political assistants led to resistance inside the department, as well as from groups outside, and a more moderate regime ensued on Watt's resignation. In theory, the US civil service is now mainly a merit-motivated organization, with a comparatively thin veneer of political appointees seeking to implement the president's policies by direction from the upper echelons of the departmental administration. There have been attempts to regularize the position of the very senior civil servants who have a status almost equivalent to that of political appointees, and whose jobs are often viewed enviously when there is a new president wanting to make sweeping changes. Over the last few years, with much talk of waste, inefficiency and cost overruns (particularly in the field of defence appropriation), some encouragement has been given to 'whistle-blowing' (the exposing of agency errors by bureaucrats), but the Reagan administration latterly resisted attempts to modify this, on the grounds that it leads to mischief-making. Many of the agencies that nestle in the shadow of the executive branch often develop quasi-independent tendencies. This allegation was made about J. Edgar Hoover's reign at the Federal Bureau of Investigation (FBI) and about some of the covert operations of the Central Intelligence Agency (CIA). Other regulatory agencies do not receive this pitch of criticism, yet their influence extends into almost every corner of US life.

Much has been written both about an inertia in the US bureaucracy and about its tendency to act as a 'state-within-a-state', yet the two do not appear to be effectively reconcilable. The US political culture is not especially conducive to bureaucracy; criticism of the operations of the civil service often finds an echo in popular feeling. If the presidency is to be the final arbiter of the development of the bureaucracy, it will, as in other political systems, find that the latter has a life of its own and that change in its structure or its attitudes can only be brought about in piecemeal fashion.

The relationship between president and Congress, or between each and the bureaucracy, provides a web (especially when interest groups are added to the equation) in which policy-making is conducted in a pragmatic fashion, with a considerable amount of bargaining taking place. The old cliché in Washington was that 'the President proposes, the Congress disposes', yet today the process is more interactive. For example, it is rare that both houses of Congress and the presidency are held by the same party or, when that happens (as during the presidency of Jimmy Carter), there may still be a contrast in ethos between the executive and legislative branches. All the actors in the principal branches of government appeal to different constituencies (national, local and specific interest groups), and, while this interchange can produce effective policy on occasion, it can also from time to time produce a degree of *immobilisme*.

JUDICIAL REVIEW

The final actor in the federal law-making process is the federal court system, with the US Supreme Court at its apex. (See following essay, The Judicial System of the USA.) Judicial review, or the power of the Supreme Court to declare government actions as unconstitutional, dates from the early years of the republic and was enshrined in US democratic practice by the classic *Marbury v. Madison* case of 1803. The Supreme Court has often been at the centre of controversy as, for example, when Franklin Roosevelt tried to extend its membership from nine to 15 when it resolutely opposed the 'New Deal' legislation he and the Congress had enacted. Since the federal bench is appointed by the president, with the advice and consent of the Senate, a two-term president can change its composition for many decades (Supreme Court judges are appointed for life). By the end of his second term, for example, Ronald Reagan had made new appointments to about one-half of the federal bench. He was less successful in radically changing the character of the Supreme Court, but the election of George Bush in November 1988 ensured that the prevailing conservative leaning of the Court would continue into the early 1990s.

The process of judicial review involves the selection of cases from a long potential list which would provide an impossible workload. The Court's choice tends to centre on those cases with important constitutional or social implications, and many of the Court's decisions have had profound effects on US politics and society. One such was *Brown v. Board of Education of Topeka* in 1954, which—if slowly—transformed educational systems in the southern states so that public schools became racially desegregated. Precedent is all-important in the Court but, as in the Brown case, it can be overturned if societal change or new knowledge so requires. The nine judges have to interpret anew the US constitution, the basic law of the country, in each generation and ensure that current law-making does not clash with its intent.

INTRAGOVERNMENT INTERACTION

The emphasis that is laid on the separation of powers in the constitution belies the fact that the three branches of government interact continually. The legislative process culminates in the president signing a bill into law after Congress has painstakingly processed it. The president can 'veto' a bill by refusing to sign, or by failing to sign if Congress adjourns within 10 days (the 'pocket veto'). Congress can override the veto with a two-thirds majority in each chamber, whereupon the bill becomes law. Presidents, unlike many state governors, do not have the power to veto separate items in a bill (the 'item veto'), and thus can only sign or veto the bill in its entirety. The Supreme Court can be brought in at a later stage if a specific case decides that the bill collides with a provision of the constitution, in which case the latter will prevail. A similar example of the tripartite interaction lies in the procedure for a Supreme Court nomination. First of all the president puts forward a name, whereupon the Judiciary Committee of the Senate recommends to the full Senate either acceptance (which means that the Court will be replenished) or rejection, in which case another name must be put forward. This constant measure of interaction provides an essential dynamic to the system.

State and Local Government

In a short description it is inevitable that one concentrates on the federal level, yet it is in the government of the states, and to some extent the localities, that innovation is more frequently to be found (see State Governments, pp. 136–166). This is particularly true in the 1980s, when some retreat by the federal government from the welfare programmes and other citizen-orientated programmes, initiated largely by the 'Great Society' domestic legislation of the 1960s, has provoked the more progressive states to intervene with proposals of their own. As noted, the state bureaucracies have been increasing faster than the federal since the early 1970s, although initially this was due to the need to administer federal grants. With a federal system comprising 50 states there is no such thing as an optimum shape of state politics, although inevitably patterns emerge. States use the separation of powers in a similar tripartite way to the federal government. Governors are the usual initiators of legislation, which is deliberated and passed by state legislators. Since each state has a written constitution (most of them being much longer and more detailed than the federal document), the courts may also enter the political process—however, they still spend most of their time on routine civil and criminal cases. The political cultures of individual states may vary widely as a result of historical, economic, racial and other cultural factors; one classification suggested that pure types of state culture were either individualistic, moralistic or traditional, with each state lying somewhere between the ideal types depicted in the model. Most far-northern states tend to the moralistic whereas further to the south the culture is more individualistic and the 'Deep South' itself tends more to the traditional ethos.

States vary enormously in terms of both size and population. The three most populous states, California, New York and Texas, tend to be particularly dominant in the political system—for example, they account for a total of 112 of the 538 electoral-college votes exercised at the time of a presidential election. Large states often encompass a variety of party, ethnic and cultural divisions. Northern California, for example, tends to be more Democratic than Republican, while in the southern part of the state the position is reversed. New York similarly balances a largely Democratic downstate (New York City especially) with a Republican upstate. Although an individual state may seem relatively small and discrete compared to the union as a whole, political feuding and infighting, even within one party, can be considerable (an internal feud in the Texas Democratic Party, for example, was one of the reasons that President John Kennedy visited Dallas, the scene of his assassination, in November 1963). In addition, even smaller states can provide pointers to development and experimentation in government. For example, there are wide variations as to the number of executive-branch officials which are elected and the number which are appointed by a state's governor, thus giving particular governors a particularly strong presence *vis-à-vis* their counterparts in other states. States continually experiment with fund-raising methods, such as taxes and lotteries. The sales tax, state income taxes and excise taxes (on tobacco and alcohol) are permutated differently in each state (sub-state units use property taxes and, occasionally, a city sales tax). A recent attempt by the Florida state government to impose a tax on certain service-sector activities was repealed following a major protest campaign by the advertising industry.

It is generally agreed that the quality of state government has improved since the 1960s, with a better-trained, more expert bureaucracy, a higher calibre of state politician and a public which expects much from the tax dollars it hands over to state government (hence the attempts to curb state taxing by the voters). The growing complexity of state government is indicated by the profusion of referendum questions which proliferate at election time (most notably in California) which

give the voting public a direct stake in the legislative and administrative processes. Federal aid in 1988 was equivalent to the same percentage (17%) of state and local outlays as it was in 1968, having risen to 26% in 1978. This reflects a shrinkage in the funding of federal-aid programmes during the 1980s, given that the number of such programmes has remained intact at over 400. What has been termed 'fend-for-yourself-federalism' is likely to persist for the foreseeable future.

The resurgence of the individual state's postion in the federal system indicates that the US constitution is highly resilient and can adapt to changing conditions better than can those of most political systems. The intricate nature of US politics is inevitable given the diversity of the subcontinent occupied by the USA. Attempts are made, sometimes successfully, sometimes less so, to introduce a high degree of popular sovereignty to a nation where only the common adherence to certain basic principles and the common feeling of being 'American' holds together a community with such a great potential to become fragmented.

THE JUDICIAL SYSTEM OF THE USA

RICHARD HODDER-WILLIAMS

Introduction

The 13 original states of the Union were colonies of the British crown before they revolted and declared their independence in 1776. This revolution was followed by the introduction of a system of law and government which exemplified both continuity and change. On the side of continuity were a number of British traditions such as the common law, the adversarial principle of litigation and a commitment to jury trials. On the side of change were the ratification of a written constitution to be the supreme law of the land and a populist belief in democratic accountability, even, in some instances, for judges.

The division of powers between one national government and several state governments, which is a central principle of the federal compact enshrined in the constitution, permitted the individual states a high degree of independence in structuring and regulating their domestic affairs. Each state, therefore, controls its own constitution (provided, of course, that no part violates any provision of the national constitution) and, among other things, devises its own system of justice. There is consequently a considerable variety among the states in the formal arrangements of their court systems. However, three practices are essentially common to all systems.

Firstly, the common-law tradition survives throughout the USA—except in Louisiana, a former French colony where a form of the Code Napoléon survives. Judges are regularly faced with claims for which no legislation or constitutional provision provides absolute guidance, and must therefore 'make law' according to their notions of justice and precedents. This exercise of judicial power gains its legitimacy from a belief in a 'higher law' than mere man-made law. However, the massive growth in regulatory laws throughout the country has reduced the range of disputes in which judges can still exercise their common-law powers.

Secondly, the USA employs 'adversarial' proceedings, rather than the 'inquisitorial' system used on the European continent. Civil cases are initiated by a party who can claim to have suffered a personal loss, and claimants prosecute and present their own cases. It is believed that partisan presentation of evidence most favourable to each side is more likely to uncover the truth than the disinterested investigation of a third party, and that in 'adversarial' proceedings it is less likely that any relevant piece of evidence or argument will be omitted from a trial. The same principle applies in criminal trials, in which the judge acts as the neutral arbiter between the state and the accused.

Thirdly, the USA is characterized by a commitment to trial by jury. The Sixth and Seventh Amendments to the constitution guarantee the right to trial by jury in criminal prosecutions and civil suits in the federal courts. The Four-

teenth Amendment extended this right to defendants in state criminal proceedings as well. However, in many cases the litigants waive this right and are tried by a judge alone. In such cases, there may be negotiated outcomes or 'plea bargaining', by which a defendant agrees to enter a guilty plea in return for providing useful information to the police forces.

Above all, however, the US population is highly litigious. In the words of the professor and writer James Q. Wilson, the American Revolution gave 'to American political thought and culture a preoccupation with the assertion and maintenance of rights.' The struggle for equality in the USA took the form of a contest for legal entitlements—a contest in which blacks, women and, lately, Hispanics won many victories. Because there is now an extraordinarily-high level of personal mobility with its consequential tendency for localities to be unintegrated, disputes often can no longer be managed through social means and community pressure: consequently, courts are turned to for the redress of grievances. The paucity of informal institutions of arbitration and reconciliation add another pressure towards litigation. For these cultural and institutional reasons, the courts in the USA are employed by its inhabitants to deal with more disputes per head of population than in any other country in the world. Over 25m. cases are filed each year (or one for every 10 persons) and more than 550,000 lawyers (one for every 450 persons) are qualified to service these litigious demands.

Court Systems

Article III of the constitution establishes the judicial branch of the federal government, but it says little about its organization. 'The judicial Power of the United States', it begins, 'shall be vested in one supreme Court, and in such inferior Courts as the Congress may from time to time ordain and establish.' The structure of the federal judiciary, therefore, has been developed through acts passed by Congress. The first, the Judiciary Act, passed in 1789, laid down a general framework which has been refined, over time, into the present arrangements.

There are three layers of courts. At the base of the pyramid are the 94 district courts, at least one of which must exist in each state. They are presided over by individual judges, normally themselves inhabitants of that district. The intermediate layer is composed of the 12 Circuit Courts of Appeals and the Court of Appeals for the Federal Circuit. These hear appeals from the district courts and normally sit as panels of three judges, although, in special circumstances, the full bench may hear a case of special significance *en banc*.

At the top of the pyramid is the Supreme Court itself. The number of justices is fixed by congressional legislation: as the

USA has grown in size and population, the number of justices has also increased. The only level of the judicial system which has not expanded in size in recent decades has been the Supreme Court. The 1789 Act created six justiceships; later acts increased this number, originally to reflect the westward movement of the frontier, and, on one occasion, reduced the number. However, since the 1869 Act the number has been set at nine. Although it is possible for the Congress to increase (or reduce) this number, nine is now the firm constitutional convention, dramatically affirmed in 1937 when President Roosevelt's plans to increase its numbers were convincingly defeated.

As the amount and complexity of litigation also increased, the pressure for more courts, and in some cases more specialist courts, was heeded. Although the central principle of the federal court system is a system of courts with general jurisdiction, there are also tax courts, bankruptcy courts, a Claims Court and a Court of International Trade. In addition, some administrative agencies (such as the US Immigration and Naturalization Service) operate as quasi-courts, conducting hearings and arbitrating disputes. The findings of these tribunals can be appealed to the Circuit Courts of Appeals and ultimately, if it is a matter of sufficient national significance, to the Supreme Court itself.

Each state has its own particular structure, but most have established four levels of courts. At the bottom of the hierarchy are courts of limited and specialized jurisdiction (making up three-quarters of all state courts), devoted, for example, specifically to traffic offences, juvenile cases or civil claims. Above them are courts of general jurisdiction, which may hear cases deemed too important for the specialized courts as well as appeals from them. Above them, in more than half of the states, are intermediate appellate courts, with the obligation to hear appeals from the lower courts. At the apex of the judicial pyramid are the state supreme courts (although they are not always so named) and they, like the US Supreme Court, usually have discretionary power over which cases to hear. Most disputes are resolved in the courts of first instance (70% involve traffic offences) and less than 1% proceed to the appeal stage.

Judicial Power

State and local courts dispose of more than 99% of all civil and criminal cases filed in the USA. This reflects the reality of the federal system, in which the vast majority of regulations affecting ordinary people and their businesses are made in state political institutions. In the larger states the importance and complexity of the caseload is matched by the quality and competence of the judges, especially at the highest levels. Since both states and federal government often act upon US citizens in a particular area, litigants can sometimes choose whether to use the state courts or the federal courts. As the Supreme Court became a less friendly forum for civil-liberties claims in the 1980s, many people took their cases to some of the state courts, where the judges were more liberal and the state laws more helpful to their claims.

The jurisdiction of the federal courts is, with one set of exceptions, established by congressional legislation. Article III of the constitution sets out a few instances where the Supreme Court shall exercise original jurisdiction. These are in all cases 'affecting Ambassadors, other public Ministers and Consuls, and those in which a State shall be Party'. Otherwise, 'the judicial Power shall extend to all Cases, in Law and Equity, arising under this Constitution, the Laws of the United States, and Treaties made': in these cases 'the supreme Court shall have appellate Jurisdiction, both as to Law and Fact, with such Exceptions, and under such Regulations as the Congress shall make.'

There are, therefore, two different sources of cases litigated in the federal courts. The first source is the laws and treaties of the US government itself. Like courts in most countries, the federal courts have the responsibility of interpreting the laws of the land; like the courts of most countries, their interpretations, if deemed incorrect by the law-making bodies, may be reversed by the passage of amendments to the act in dispute. In this respect, the power of the federal courts differs little from that of other national courts of last resort.

Considering the second source, the federal courts may also hear cases in which the application of the constitution, the supreme law of the land, is in dispute. It is now accepted that the Supreme Court's decision in such matters is final. Only a formal amendment can reverse its interpretation of the constitution. The Supreme Court first claimed this right in *Marbury v. Madison* (1803) when it invalidated part of the 1789 Judiciary Act; it asserted this right over state law in *Fletcher v. Peck* (1810). Although some legal scholars and politicians have questioned whether the Founding Fathers intended this power of judicial review, the fact now is that the Supreme Court can invalidate the laws of both Congress and the individual states as well as the actions of their officials if it decides, in a case properly brought to it, that some provision of the constitution has been violated.

It is this power of judicial review which gives the Supreme Court its unique characteristic. Part of the design of the Founding Fathers was to limit the power of government, and this was to be achieved, in the main, by the dispersal of formal powers between the states and the federal government on the one hand and between the branches of the federal government on the other. To emphasize governmental limitations and to establish 'a government of laws, not men', great respect was given to the constitution as the supreme law of the land.

However, many US citizens were still concerned that their individual rights might be denied through the partisan action of temporary legislative majorities in the national legislature, and the first Congress began its business by proposing amendments to the constitution. These first 10 amendments collectively became known as the Bill of Rights and were originally only applicable against the national government. The 14th Amendment (ratified in 1868) has, in recent years, 'incorporated' virtually all of the Bill of Rights and thereby made it applicable against the state governments; thus individuals now have a constitutional bulwark against all governments and their agents who attempt to deprive them of their constitutional rights. In protecting those rights, the Supreme Court, which is directly accountable to no voters, must on occasions deny to elected majorities the fruits of their electoral victories. That is one of the major paradoxes of the US political system.

The Congress has used its power to regulate the judicial branch on many occasions—almost always, however, on purely organizational matters. The establishment of the Circuit Courts of Appeals in 1891 was one such occasion; the 1925 Act, which granted the Supreme Court limited discretion over which cases to hear, was another. Before 1925, all cases which met jurisdictional requirements were entitled to be appealed right up to the Supreme Court. This overburdened the highest court and so Congress, after lobbying from the chief justice of the day, enacted legislation which required most litigants to seek a 'writ of *certiorari*' from the Supreme Court before their case could be taken. The writ was only to be granted when issues of general significance were raised, it being felt that a trial in the district court and one appeal before a Circuit Court would protect most individuals from grievous injustice.

However, Congress continued to pass some laws which entitled aggrieved citizens to appeal to the Supreme Court for final adjudication. The wisdom of this was called into question in the early 1970s when the court's docket expanded greatly. In the period from October 1982 to July 1988, the average number of cases appealed to the Supreme Court each year was 4,249 and the average number of cases decided with full opinion only 131. The remaining cases were either dismissed, by refusing to grant a writ of *certiorari*, or summarily affirmed or reversed if they fell under a statute establishing the right of appeal to the Supreme Court. In 1988 Congress passed legislation which finally gave the court complete discretion over its docket (apart from the very few cases arising out of its original jurisdiction). Now litigants in any case before the Supreme Court must persuade it that the issues involved warrant a full hearing.

The Supreme Court thus hears four distinguishable types of cases. First are those very few instances where it exercises original jurisdiction; second are those which arise out of the laws and treaties of the USA and have been litigated through the federal courts; third are those which involve interpretation of the constitution and which have been litigated through the federal courts; fourth are those in which a constitutional issue was raised in a state court of first instance and has been appealed through the relevant state court systems.

The Appointment of Judges

FEDERAL APPOINTMENTS

The constitution provides that judges to the federal courts be nominated by the president and confirmed by the Senate. In choosing district-court judges, presidents have traditionally consulted with, and listened to, the senators from the state in which the vacancy occurs, especially where senators and president come from the same party. The individuals suggested often have political links with their state party and may well have been active politicians themselves; there is no requirement to have had court experience and, for many, the first direct contact with a trial court is the first case they judge.

Nominations to the Circuit Courts of Appeals are more exclusively the concern of the executive branch. Within the US Department of Justice a committee is responsible for seeking out and considering candidates. Although the senators covered by the Circuit Court where there is a vacancy will make suggestions, their claims are competing; this allows a greater freedom to the president and his advisers. There is no career structure by which judges progress from a district court to a Circuit Court of Appeals. Some do, but most are appointed direct from academic positions, private law firms or political posts.

Appointments to the Supreme Court are very much the prerogative of the president, although his attorney-general usually plays a major part in the selection of possible candidates. Because filling any vacancy contains the possibility of a long-term and significant impact on the Supreme Court's jurisprudence, there is considerable lobbying from interested parties. Once again, there is no career pattern, although recent Republican presidents have tended to prefer candidates who have had some experience of work as an appellate judge.

Justices leave the Supreme Court, it has been said, only 'by an act of will or an act of God'. They can only be removed involuntarily through the process of impeachment, a process only once attempted and then unsuccessfully. On average, there is a vacancy about every 27 months, but vacancies do not occur evenly over time. President Carter had no vacancy to fill; President Reagan had three vacancies, including the Chief Justice, in his two terms; President Bush may have as many in the duration of a four-year term alone.

STATE APPOINTMENTS

The individual states select their judges through a variety of processes. Twelve states employ partisan elections in which candidates run under the label of their political party. A further 12 states have non-partisan elections, in which candidates compete but without any party identification being explicit. Eight states follow the federal model with the governor nominating the judges. Four states leave the selection to the legislature, while the remaining 14 employ what is called a merit plan. Under this scheme a judicial nominating board of judges, lawyers and lay persons is established to scrutinize applications, after which it sends a short list of the most suitable candidates to the governor for final selection. Most judges hold office for fixed terms, which can normally be renewed. In some states there is provision for recall so that judges can be voted off the state's highest court.

The federal system attempts to isolate the justices from political forces and give them a real independence. One result is that the voting records of some justices disappoint their presidential nominators, but they cannot be removed or replaced. In some states, by contrast, the fear of such lack of accountability outweighs the virtue of independence; accordingly judges are seen as extensions of the popular will and therefore subject to popular accountability.

The Warren and Burger Supreme Courts

The Supreme Courts presided over by Chief Justice Earl Warren (1953–69) and Chief Justice Warren Earl Burger (1969–86) made a number of decisions which radically affected US politics and society. Many of these resulted from incorporating most of the Bill of Rights into the so-called 'due-process' clause of the 14th Amendment. This revolutionized many state practices, forcing changes in the drawing of electoral boundaries, in educational and prison systems, in police procedures, and in the treatment of blacks and women.

The court's first duty, however, is to mark the boundaries between the three branches of the federal government and between the federal and state governments. It outlawed the legislative veto (*Immigration and Naturalization Service v. Chadha*, 1983) and that part of the Gramm–Rudman–Hollings amendment which granted the General Accounting Officer the power to decide upon budgetary cuts in the event of the legislature and executive not agreeing, on the grounds that the legislature was trespassing on executive turf (*Bowsher v. Synar*, 1986), but it upheld the law authorizing special prosecutors (*Morrison v. Olson*, 1988).

On the federal dimension, it continued to accept Congress's right to use the interstate commerce and general-welfare clauses to regulate almost any economic activity within the states (*Katzenbach v. McClung*, 1964), but in 1976 it decided Congress had overreached itself in prescribing minimum wage standards for state employees (*National League of Cities v. Usery*, 1976). This, however, was reversed in 1985 (*Garcia v. San Antonio Metropolitan Transit Authority*) and the responsibility for defending state autonomy shifted to the political branches.

The court's second duty is to adjudicate claims that the legislature or executive have exceeded their constitutional authority. The court has regularly found congressional acts unconstitutional, but mainly because they were held to violate provisions of the Bill of Rights or the 14th Amendment rather than being *ultra vires* Article I. Article II's grant of executive power was held not to encompass Nixon's impounding of funds (*Train v. City of New York*, 1975), unauthorized wire-tapping (*District Court v. United States*, 1972) or his claims for executive privilege (*United States v. Nixon*, 1974), although in the last case the existence of some executive privilege was for the first time acknowledged. Carter was permitted to abrogate a treaty without the senatorial approval needed for its initial ratification (*Goldwater v. Carter*, 1979) and Reagan was permitted unilaterally to suspend private claims against Iran as part of his deal to free US hostages (*Dames & More v. Regan*, 1981).

The court has also seen itself as the guardian of the electoral process which provides the legitimacy for all governments. In 1964 it required electoral districts in the states to be drawn on the principle of 'one man, one vote, one value' (*Reynolds v. Sims*, 1964) and applied this requirement most stringently to congressional districts also (*Wesberry v. Sanders*, 1964; *Karcher v. Daggett*, 1983), thus shifting political power from overrepresented rural areas to the cities and suburbs. In 1986 it agreed to consider whether gerrymandering (the redrawing of electoral districts in such a way as to enhance a party's political power) was unconstitutional (*Davis v. Bandemer*).

The court's third duty, and the one which brought it so much into the public eye, was its responsibility to enforce the Bill of Rights and the equal-protection and due-process clauses of the 14th Amendment. Fulfilling this particular duty has been essentially a post-Second World War phenomenon. The First Amendment has provided the court with especially difficult problems. In the 1960s it sought to establish a wall of separation between church and state, outlawing the compulsory saying of a prayer (*Engel v. Vitale*, 1962) or the reading of a passage from the Bible (*School District of Abington Township v. Schempp*, 1963) at the beginning of the day in state schools. Legislatures continued to attempt to assist Christian religion generally or religious schools in particular and the court tried hard to set down rules which would define an infringement of the so-called 'establishment' clause (*Lemon v. Kurtzman*, 1971), but in vain. In 1985 it outlawed an attempt in Alabama to introduce 'a moment of silence' for meditation or prayer (*Wallace v. Jaffree*, 1985).

'The right to communicate', now protected under the First Amendment, has also provided difficulties. The court has struck down limitations on the electoral expenditures of individuals and groups as well as overall spending limits (*Buckley v. Valeo*, 1976; *Federal Election Commission v. National Conservative Political Action Committee*, 1985), constraints on advertising (*Bigelow v. Virginia*, 1975; *Metromedia Inc v. City of San Diego*, 1981), most attempts to control pornography in its many forms (*Roth v. United States*, 1957; *Miller v. California*, 1973) without actually saying it was 'protected speech', and efforts by the government to 'quarantine' the press (*New York Times v. United States*, 1971).

The Fourth, Fifth and Sixth Amendments essentially cover procedural matters dealing with the rights of suspects. Here the court applied the exclusionary rule (*Mapp v. Ohio*, 1961) which required the exclusion of all evidence unconstitutionally gathered, and later a set of procedures to be followed by police officers before confessions or other self-incriminatory evidence could be used in court (*Miranda v. Arizona*, 1966). It also held that individuals were entitled to be provided with a lawyer in all felony cases (*Gideon v. Wainwright*, 1963). These protections for suspects were cut away at the edges during the Burger Court as exceptions to the inflexible application of the Miranda rules and the Mapp exclusionary rule were made (*Harris v. New York*, 1971; *United States v. Leon*, 1984; *Nix v. Williams*, 1984; *New York v. Quarles*, 1984).

The Eighth Amendment's prohibition of 'cruel and unusual punishments' was raised in death-penalty cases but was never applied by a majority against the death penalty as such. Although *Furman v. Georgia* (1972) found the death penalty, as then practised, unconstitutional, *Gregg v. Georgia* (1976) readmitted it as a constitutionally-proper punishment, given that certain safeguards were provided and a distinction was made between the processes of ascertaining guilt and deciding sentence. The clause was, however, applied, especially by lower-court judges, to outlaw some prison systems (*Finney v. Hutto*, 1978).

The most contentious parts of the court's work derived from its reading of the equal-protection clause of the 14th Amendment. The landmark case was *Brown v. Board of Education of Topeka, Kansas* (1954–55), which outlawed single-race schools. This led to the requirement to desegregate in other walks of life. Southern school boards, however, retained single-race schools so that in *Alexander v. Holmes County* (1969), the court demanded the immediate end to one-race schools and in *Swann v. Charlotte–Mecklenburg Board of Education* (1971) it gave constitutional blessing to busing as one method of doing this. Differentiation in terms of race now required 'strict scrutiny' to ensure that it was not due to unconstitutional discrimination.

The equal-protection clause was also applied to the treatment of women. In *Reed v. Reed* (1970) the court for the first time found discrimination on grounds of gender. Several cases confirmed the protection afforded women by the equal-protection clause (*Frontiero v. Richardson*, 1973; *Stanton v. Stanton*, 1975; *Craig v. Boren*, 1976), but the level of scrutiny called for was less strict than where allegations of racial discrimination were concerned (*Personnel Administrator of Massachusetts v. Feeney*, 1979), but it was certainly stricter than in the majority of cases involving differential treatment when only a rational explanation for differential treatment was needed to ensure that the challenged law or regulation passed constitutional examination.

Problems arose in devising remedies for discrimination. Not all affirmative-action programmes were deemed constitutional, especially those which involved inflexible quotas (*Regents of the University of California v. Allan Bakke*, 1978) or the deprivation of seniority rights (*Fire Fighters Local Union No. 1784 v. Stotts*, 1984). Where the affirmative action involved consideration of race or gender as one appropriate factor, involved the distribution of new advantages like jobs or promotion, involved redressing past discrimination, or resulted from negotiated local agreements, 'postive discrimination' was permitted (*Regents of the University of California v. Allan Bakke*, 1978, *United Steelworkers v. Weber*, 1979; *Johnson v. Santa Clara County*, 1987).

Perhaps the Supreme Court's most controversial development of the law was the creation of a 'right to privacy'. First asserted in *Griswold v. Connecticut* (1965), it provided the main rationale for the 1973 decision in *Roe v. Wade*, which established a constitutional right to an abortion in the first three months of pregnancy. This decision was assailed by many 'pro-life' groups and cherished by many·'pro-choice' groups— and became a major political issue. The court's support for Roe narrowed from 7–2 in 1973 to 6–3 in 1983 (*City of Akron v. Akron Center for Reproductive Health*) and to 5–4 in 1986 in *Thornburgh v. American College of Obstetricians and Gynecologists*.

Much of the most visible work of the court is in the field of constitutional adjudication, but its statutory interpretations are also important. It has strengthened the force of the Voting Rights Act Amendments and, in recent years, weakened the force of the Sherman and Clayton Acts as well as interpreting the National Labor Relations and Occupational Health and Safety Acts more to the benefit of employers than employees. In short, in whatever area it is active, the court is making decisions with profound political consequences.

The Rehnquist Supreme Court

When Ronald Reagan became president in January 1981 it was widely expected that he would be able to shape the Supreme Court in his own image. At the time, Chief Justice Burger was 74 years of age, Justice Brennan 75, Justice Powell 74, Justice Marshall 73, and Justice Blackmun 73. Brennan, Marshall and, for the most part, Blackmun had been the main defenders of the liberal positions associated with the Warren Court, and Powell had often made up the fifth vote in matters of high saliency, especially on church–state cases, abortion and affirmative action. Reagan and his supporters were, however, sadly disappointed.

Justice Stewart was the first to resign. He was replaced by the first woman ever to be nominated to the Supreme Court, Sandra Day O'Connor, a jurist slightly more conservative than the retiring Stewart. In 1986 Chief Justice Burger retired and was replaced by sitting Justice William Rehnquist; the latter's postion was taken by Antonin Scalia, a man of conservative views similar to Rehnquist's. When Powell retired in 1987 Reagan had his first opportunity substantially to shift the ideological balance of the court. However, his nominee, Robert Bork, was deeply opposed both by civil-rights groups and by moderate Democrats and Republicans, who believed his conservative views were not in the nation's interest. Bork's appointment was not confirmed by the Senate. Ultimately, Powell's place was taken by Anthony Kennedy, a cautious but undoctrinaire conservative.

The appointment of Kennedy has begun the transformation of the Rehnquist Court. Within a few years, the stalwarts of a liberal jurisprudence (Brennan, Marshall and Blackmun) will be replaced, most probably by nominees of President Bush. Almost certainly there will be a shift in the ideological centre of the court away from a concern for the individual towards a deference to the elected branches of government, away from the acceptance of regulation towards a concern for free enterprise and property rights.

Because the US political system has so many points of access, civil-rights groups, although they will not cease to litigate in the federal courts, will tend more to prosecute their causes in the state courts where they might hope to receive a friendlier reception; by the same token, economic interests will tend to litigate in the federal courts, where their preferences are likely to be supported. However, there will not be dramatic changes. The conservative principle of state decisions, keeping to precedents, will most probably ensure merely that most of the rights established and extended over the last 30 years will be gently cut back rather than entirely abrogated.

Because the US population is litigious and uses its courts to advance its political interests, new matters of dispute will continue to come before the courts. As de Tocqueville wrote in 1835, 'scarcely any political question arises in the United States that is not resolved sooner or later into a judicial question.' That remains true to this day.

THE BUREAUCRACY OF GOVERNMENT IN THE USA

GRAHAM WILSON

The Character of the Bureaucracy

The desire to constrain and limit government has been strong in the USA since the birth of the nation. The belief that the individual is sovereign and responsible for his or her own destiny, and should be as free as possible from government interference, has been seen as central to a 'liberal tradition' dominating US political culture, together with the thesis that self-help and charity, rather than government, should be the dominant approach to society's problems.

The USA has had a distinctive history as a state because the establishment of judicial authority and mass political parties preceded the establishment of strong central authority and bureaucracy. During the 19th century not only was the machinery of government less developed than in Europe, but the bureaucracy was small and the positions within it were seen to be used primarily as a resource to consolidate support for political parties. Indeed, the bureaucracy did not come to be dominated by a professional civil service until the 'New Deal' era (1932–45), with the proportion of civil-service posts filled on merit having increased from the late 19th century onwards. The slow development of a merit system of recruitment within the bureaucracy has resulted in the civil service in the USA occupying a much less prestigious position than it does in, for example, France or Japan.

A further consequence of the USA's unusual historical development is the survival of a comparatively large number of political appointments to be made within the bureaucracy by the president. An incoming US president can expect to fill about 5,000 government posts, whereas a newly-elected British prime minister, for example, might appoint only 200. As well as its uses for purposes of political patronage, this system can be used to place those with ideological commitments to the policies of the president deep within agencies. However, with the scramble to fill 5,000 posts early in an administration, it is inevitable that the capacity of a president to recruit such ideologically-committed, or even qualified, supporters can be overwhelmed. Appointees generally remain in office for a relatively short time (about two years on average). Particularly as the uncertain latter period of administrations approach, there is a very rapid turnover in these politically-appointed posts, calling for the appointment of little- or unknown people and to the so-called 'government of strangers'. Salaries much lower than those current in the private sector and, since the mid-1970s, tougher ethics laws and closer congressional investigation of nominees' records, have made government service even less attractive. This presence of a large number of political appointees serving only limited terms further works against the prestige and orderliness of the US bureaucracy.

The Structure of the Bureaucracy

In 1985 there were 3,021,000 federal employees, of whom 2,156,000 were classed as white-collar employees; in addition there was a total of 13,669,000 state and local employees, both full- and part-time. The overwhelming majority of officials are now recruited and employed under the merit system. Complex rules and procedures govern the recruitment, promotion, discipline and dismissal of civil servants. Many of these rules, administered by the Civil Service Commission from 1883–1978, and subsequently by the Office of Personnel Management and the Merit Systems Protection Board, have been promulgated in order to reduce the ability of politicians to use civil-service posts as patronage. As in all bureaucracies, most civil servants are in the lower grades handling routine work; in 1985 only 11% of federal white-collar civilian employees were likely to have any direct role in policy-making, while only 0.05% were in the highest grades and so were almost certain to have such a role.

The bureaucracy is organized into a bewildering number and variety of agencies: it has been said that no one is sure how many agencies there are in the federal government. There is certainly no clear organizational logic to the structure of the federal executive. Most federal agencies are located within departments, of which there were 14 in early 1989 (Agriculture, Commerce, Defense, Education, Energy, Health and Human Services, Housing and Urban Development, Interior, Justice, Labor, State, Transportation, Treasury and Veterans' Affairs). The secretaries of these departments constitute the president's cabinet, while cabinet-level status may also be accorded to the US Representative to the United Nations, the National Security Adviser and other selected officials. The US cabinet does not correspond to, for example, its UK counterpart: it has no collective responsibility for administration policy, is not a decision-making body and is only one of many sources of advice to the president. Many departments have been created to please a political force in the USA: Agriculture, Commerce, Labor, Veterans' Affairs and, arguably, Education all fall into this category. There are other very important agencies, such as the Environmental Protection Agency or the Office of the US Trade Representative (which handles trade negotiations) which, while they are not located within any of the 14 departments, possess equivalent, sometimes more far-reaching, responsibilities. Many agencies which do fall under specific departments also enjoy substantial autonomy. The Department of Commerce, for example, has often been regarded as a conglomerate of disparate, highly independent agencies over which the Secretary of Commerce has little influence.

There is also a number of agencies which are independent in the sense that they have been structured so as to minimize the influence which can be exercised over them by presidential control. Independent Regulatory Commissions, for example, are headed by commissioners who are nominated by the president for a fixed term of office, but who cannot be removed by him. Commissioners, like all agency or department chiefs, are subject to confirmation by the Senate. However, Congress and the courts are likely to regard themselves as particularly entitled to intervene in the work of independent commissions. A particularly important independent agency is the Federal Reserve Board, which controls money supply and interest rates in the USA. Members of the Federal Reserve Board are appointed for very long terms (14 years) and its chairman, though appointed for only four years, has a term of office which deliberately does not coincide with that of the US president. Thus presidents have to work with a Federal Reserve Board not of their choosing, and on a number of occasions the Board and the federal administration have pursued different, even conflicting, strategies.

The Cost of the Bureaucracy

It is widely known that total government expenditures in the USA lag behind the average for OECD countries when expressed as a percentage of gross domestic product (GDP). Among industrialized democracies, only Japan commits as small a percentage of its GDP to government. It is less widely appreciated that the share of GDP spent by federal, state and local governments in the USA has increased considerably during the 20th century, and especially in the last 50 years. Measured in terms of constant 1982 dollars, federal expenditures rose from $394,000m. in 1965 to $862,300m. in 1985. Government expenditures in the USA are equivalent to almost one-third of GDP, while taxes are equivalent to a smaller proportion (29.2%), which has led to the creation of a sizeable, and well-publicized, deficit. About two-thirds of total government expenditures are made by the federal government; the remainder, made by state and local governments, are often prompted by federal policies, including promises of grants or 'matching funds'. However, government expenditures are a poor measure of the comparative size of government apparatus in the USA. As Andrew Shonfield noted over 25 years ago,

US governments have used regulations to control society and the economy when other nations have used policy techniques such as nationalization. Regulations typically cost government little to administer but cost those (such as corporations) who obey them thousands of millions of dollars in increased capital or operating costs. In brief, large-scale government—and large-scale national government at that—has come to the USA, and is likely to remain. Although many US citizens profess to believe in individualism and self-reliance in the abstract, the overwhelming majority of government programmes, including all the most expensive ones, enjoy widespread public support. Even President Reagan failed to reduce the public's fondness in practice, though not in theory, for 'big government'.

The Bureaucracy: Constitutionally and in Reality

It is, perhaps, possible to identify five institutions seeking to shape the behaviour of the bureaucracy. These are the presidency, Congress, the courts, the bureaucrats themselves, and interest and pressure groups outside government. Each institution brings with it its own set of advantages. Furthermore, each of the three branches of government, executive, legislative and judicial, exercises some form of mastery over the bureaucracy through their respective constitutional positions.

THE PRESIDENT

The president certainly has the most direct influence over the bureaucracy. Often referred to as the 'chief executive', the president is empowered by the constitution to 'require the Opinion, in writing, of the Principal Officer in each of the executive Departments, upon any Subject relating to the Duties of their respective Offices', to nominate (and by implication to dismiss) top officials or ambassadors and to 'take Care that the Laws be faithfully executed'. The president's control over the permanent bureaucracy has become restricted both by law and by civil-service rules and procedures. However, the Civil Service Reform Act of 1978, which created the Merit Systems Protection Board, also increased the ability of the president to reassign the very highest-level civil servants and to order reductions-in-force (RIFs) for agencies, reducing or abolishing sections as considered necessary or desirable. These last measures, designed to increase efficiency within the bureaucracy, effectively increased the opportunities for a president to pursue personal policy likes and dislikes.

Presidents have their power of political appointment to place ideologically-'sound' staff in key positions within the bureaucracy. This power can also be used to signal presidential sympathy, or at least openness, towards interests such as business, women, trade unions, farmers and racial minorities. However, this system, as discussed above, has its limitations and problems in recruiting and retaining suitable personnel. Even appointees who start out as loyal to a president may, once installed in office, become heavily influenced by their departments' views. Presidents also fear that dismissing appointees will alienate their supporters and may undermine the validity of the original decision.

There is one group of presidential political appointees, the White House staff, which holds a special position. Its members are not subject to Senate confirmation and hold office solely at the pleasure of the president, while their advice to the president is confidential under the doctrine of executive privilege. Although many White House staffers carry out mundane responsibilities, such as answering letters, others are at the very heart of government. The senior staff control the flow of visitors and paper to the president from the bureaucracy, and are better placed to advise the president than are departmental secretaries because of their relative proximity. The White House staff may even implement policies on behalf of the president. In the early 1970s Henry Kissinger, then National Security Adviser, implemented President Nixon's policy of opening diplomatic relations with the People's Republic of China without the State Department even being aware of the policy; similar secrecy covered the action of the White House staff during the so-called 'Iran-Contra' affair in the mid-1980s.

However, the White House staff is also limited in its ability to control the bureaucracy, given its relative small size and frequent lack of experience in Washington circles.

Also at the president's disposal is that body of permanent civil servants working within the presidency—known as the 'institutionalized presidency'. The most important agency within the presidency in the context of controlling the bureaucracy is the Office of Management and Budget (OMB). In theory, federal agencies cannot request money or legislation from Congress without the prior approval of the OMB. Its officials scrutinize budgets and, through 'legislative clearance', proposed legislation in order to ensure that it is 'in accordance with the program of the President'. Many modern presidents have not found the OMB an adequate tool for controlling the bureaucracy: it is better suited to preventing agencies from acting than to motivating them to act, so it is at its most useful under presidents trying to cut programmes. The OMB is also open to circumvention by agencies secretly encouraging 'friendly' legislators to request draft legislation or budgets which those agencies actually already favour, but which have been blocked by the OMB. Finally, the OMB has been distrusted by some recent presidents because it is itself part of the Washington establishment, composed mainly of civil servants—however, the proportion of political appointees within the OMB has been increased in the last 20 years, particularly under President Reagan.

CONGRESS

Congress has its own set of powers with which it can seek to control the bureaucracy, and, indeed, the executive branch itself. (Executive-branch agencies are created not by the constitution, but by Act of Congress. The Senate confirms the president's nominees to top executive-branch posts—even though the president's choices are rarely challenged.) The powers to define or change the structure, missions or budgets of agencies lie with Congress, and are in principle, and sometimes in practice, sufficient to bring about major changes in policy. Congress also decides the fate of agencies' requests for new laws and their annual budget, so agencies incurring the displeasure of Congress may encounter difficulty in obtaining desired legislation or money. 'Appropriations riders' may be attached to budgets giving specific instructions to the bureaucracy on how it is or is not to behave. The use of this power has become much more common in recent years, and has extended to such diverse topics as whether or not the Occupational Safety and Health Administration (OSHA) can inspect small businesses and whether the Central Intelligence Agency (CIA) can attempt to overthrow the government of Nicaragua.

Control over agency budgets and legislation has traditionally been decentralized in Congress, with committees or subcommittees generally enjoying substantial autonomy, and it has become commonplace for legislators to acquire great expertise in their chosen specialized areas. As representatives and senators tend to serve long periods in office, their in-depth knowledge gives them distinct advantages over presidents and political appointees within the bureaucracy, who have relatively short career lives. Furthermore, the quantity and quality of advice available to Congress have increased rapidly in recent decades. Agencies working for Congress as a whole, such as the General Accounting Office (GAO) or the Congressional Budget Office, give Congress its own detailed analysis of policies and the behaviour of the bureaucracy. The GAO in particular provides Congress with a means of monitoring how closely the bureaucracy has followed its instructions.

Congress, however, frequently fails to make full use of its powers. Oversight of agencies is an unglamorous task, bringing little publicity and winning few votes. However, there are many policy areas which are unglamorous, yet which matter considerably to a legislator's constituents. Congress tends to place legislators from districts or states where the work of an agency is particularly important on committees controlling that agency's budgetary and legislative requests. Thus the agriculture committees are almost exclusively composed of legislators representing rural states. Congressional influence on the bureaucracy is often highest where the interest of the general public and the presidency is at its lowest.

THE JUDICIARY

Courts in the USA exercise very close supervision of the work of government agencies in issuing regulations implementing the laws passed by Congress, and have the power to annul them. Challenges may be based on claims that the agency has misconstrued the law under which it is acting, that the agency has followed improper procedure (for example, that those affected by a proposed regulation were not given the opportunity to state their views on it), or that the evidence available to the agency did not warrant the action it took. For example, a regulation issued by the OSHA limiting exposure to benzene was successfully challenged in the courts on the grounds that the agency lacked clear evidence that benzene could seep through human skin and cause leukaemia.

The willingness of the judiciary to impose decisions on the bureaucracy has generally been thought to be highest in areas where civil rights and liberties are at stake. Contrary to popular belief, however, courts have remained a major influence on economic issues. Perhaps the most prominent example of economic-policy-making by the judiciary was the breakup in 1982, under court order, of the American Telegraph and Telephone Co (AT&T) telephone system, and the approval by a federal district judge of the plan for what has become the contemporary US telephone system.

While judges are supposed not to impose their own preferences on agencies, the distinction between declaring that an agency lacks sufficient evidence to act and the judge preferring that the agency not act can sometimes be a thin one. This is particularly so when the law under which the agency acts requires reviewing judges to be satisified that there is 'substantive evidence on the record' to justify the action taken; in other words, that they themselves, when faced with such evidence, would have acted similarly. Courts remain limited by the need to have a suitable case to try in order to make policy, and by widespread acceptance (in theory) of the principle that elected policy-makers should be supreme on economic and social issues.

THE BUREAUCRACY ITSELF

The bureaucracy exists to service the decisions made by the three branches of government, but is able to take advantage of this position by mobilizing alliances with one or other of those branches to 'block' policies which it dislikes. US bureaucrats have their own policy preferences, which may be the result of personal political opinion or, more commonly, of experience, commitment to the prevailing opinion in an agency or loyalty to policies developed by the civil servant in the past (US civil servants tend to be more specialized and change jobs less frequently than, for example, their UK counterparts). The very expertise of the bureaucracy often allows it to frame the alternatives between which politicians choose.

Bureaucrats need to be more politically-minded in the USA than in other Western democracies, as the complexity of the government system creates frequent political dilemmas for them. An agency leader has to calculate the support and opposition which the agency's policies will encounter, and also how to reconcile conflicting powerful influences upon the agency. For example, a conservative White House might wish to be more sympathetic towards business, while a liberal congressional committee, that controls an agency's budget, might favour more stringent protection of the environment, which would put pressure on business. For all these reasons, a president who wishes to control the bureaucracy needs to plot strategy just as carefully as in steering a bill through Congress.

INTEREST GROUPS

Interest groups interact with the bureaucracy partly directly, and partly through their relationship with other actors in the political system. Presidents and members of Congress need to heed the opinions of interest groups for electoral reasons, so policies and legislation will often owe much to initial pressure from this direction. Bureaucrats frequently come into contact with interest-group officials in the line of their duties, and may even come to be influenced by them. The introduction of interest groups to the equation can, it has been said, lead to the formation of 'iron triangles'—impervious coalitions of self-interest formed by an agency, the interest group affected by the agency's work and the legislators on the relevant supervisory committee of Congress. The agency wishes to please legislators to obtain its legislation and budget; the legislators wish to please the interest groups in order to obtain votes and campaign contributions; and the interest groups want a favourable policy from the agency. Closer inspection reveals fewer 'iron triangles' than might be supposed, because disagreements among legislators and affected interest groups cause more conflict than the 'iron triangle' concept can accommodate. In the area of agricultural policy, for example, the increase in the number and variety of interest groups active in Washington has ensured that agricultural associations, themselves often having conflicting goals, are vying for attention with environmental and consumer-protection groups.

WHO RULES THE BUREAUCRACY?

If the bureaucracy is regarded as a battleground in which the president, Congress, the courts, the bureaucrats themselves and interest groups contend for influence, the question may be asked—who wins? There is no straight answer to this question. Certain agencies, such as those within the Departments of State and Defense, have traditionally been regarded as part of an 'inner cabinet' which is particularly susceptible to presidential control. Others, handling issues of vital concern to legislators and the communities they represent, have been regarded as particularly susceptible to congressional control—the Army Corps of Engineers (responsible for many civil-engineering projects) being a favourite example. Some skilled bureaucrats, such as J. Edgar Hoover, for many years director of the Federal Bureau of Investigation (FBI), have been able to establish a considerable degree of independence. In practice, however, the complexity of the bureaucracy defies such simple characterization. In certain respects the Defense Department may be close to the president, but it is undeniable that Congress is a major influence on military-procurement policies. Such traditionally 'congressional' agencies as the Army Corps of Engineers have been faced with closer inspection by OMB officials, using techniques such as cost-benefit analysis, bringing them under closer presidential control.

The Co-ordination of the Bureaucracy

Co-ordinating the different branches of the bureaucracy can be a daunting task in any system, but is unusually difficult in the USA. As in all countries, different agencies have differing attitudes, values and approaches. The USA, however, gives bureaucrats unusual opportunities to build alliances to defy co-ordination. In the 1980s, for example, the Civil Rights and Anti-Trust Divisions of the Justice Department could mobilize the House of Representatives judiciary committee (and, after 1986, that of the Senate) in their defence against the aims of the Reagan White House. Alliances between the permanent bureaucracy in both the Department of the Interior and the Environmental Protection Agency and environmental interest groups ultimately blunted the Reagan administration's campaign to weaken enforcement of the environmental-protection laws. Alliances between political hardliners in the Department of Defense and the CIA with pro-military interest groups and legislators in the late 1970s propelled President Carter into launching the defence build-up, which was later expanded under Reagan. In brief, most agencies can find allies in Congress, among interest groups or even in the courts to help them resist unwelcome attempts to bring their actions into compliance with the general objectives of the prevalent administration.

Congress has little or no part to play in the co-ordination of the bureaucracy. The very decentralized structure which has allowed Congress, through specialization, to avoid the powerlessness of many legislatures *vis-à-vis* the bureaucracy has also made it unable to reconcile the differences and conflicts which exist within the bureaucracy. The decentralized structure of Congress cannot, for example, reconcile the inclination of the Department of the Interior to increase the agriculturally-productive land area of the USA with that of the Department of Agriculture to reduce it by paying farmers not to produce, in order to boost farm prices and incomes. This is because Congress deals with the two departments through entirely separate committee systems.

The US bureaucracy is also unable to co-ordinate itself. It has been said that the French and Japanese bureaucracies, characterized by strong *esprits de corps* inculcated by way of education, training and service, have been able to promote a coherent vision of their nations' futures; all of this is lacking in the USA. Just as there is very little concept of 'the state' in the US political system, so is there very little vision of being a government servant as opposed to being an official in a particular department or agency.

Finally, the courts cannot provide much co-ordination through the disparate cases that reach them, so it follows that only the presidency can provide it. Only that office can be expected to possess the unity and perspective to provide a central guidance overriding the parochialism of agencies. Yet the odds are stacked against the president in this context. The president as an individual has insufficient time or energy even to begin to think about most of the work of government. The White House staff and the OMB do indeed attempt to reconcile agency policies with the overall objectives of the president. However, as described above, such attempts will often produce conflict, not only with the bureaucracy but with powerful allies of the bureaucracy in Congress and among interest groups. The result of this lack of co-ordination contributes to bureaucratic inefficiency and disorderliness, although this, incidentally and ironically, may be in accord with the traditional hostility to strong government in the USA.

SELECT BIBLIOGRAPHY

Aberbach, J. D., Putnam, R. and Rockman, B. *Bureaucrats and Politicians in Western Democracies*. Cambridge, Massachusetts, Harvard University Press, 1983.

Abraham, H. J. *Justices and Presidents* (2nd edn). New York, Oxford University Press, 1985.

Adams, D. K. (Ed.). *Studies in United States Politics*. Manchester, Manchester University Press, 1989.

Bailyn, B. *The Ideological Origins of the American Revolution*. Cambridge, Massachusetts, Harvard University Press, 1967.

Barker, L. J. (Ed.). *New Perspectives in American Politics*. New Brunswick, New Jersey, Transaction Books, 1988.

Berry, J. M. *The Interest Group Society*. Boston, Massachusetts, Little, Brown & Co Inc, 1984.

Blasi, V. (Ed.). *The Burger Court: The Counter-revolution That Wasn't*. New Haven, Connecticut, Yale University Press, 1983.

Campbell, C. *Managing the Presidency: Carter, Reagan and the Search for Executive Harmony*. Pittsburgh, Pennsylvania, University of Pittsburgh Press, 1986.

Chubb, J. E. and Peterson, P. I. (Eds). *Can the Government Govern?* Washington, DC, The Brookings Institution, 1989.

The New Direction in American Politics. Washington, DC, The Brookings Institution, 1985.

Corwin, E. S. *The Constitution and What it Means Today* (14th edn). Princeton, New Jersey, Princeton University Press, 1978.

Cox, A. *The Court and the Constitution*. Boston, Massachusetts, Houghton Mifflin Co, 1987.

Davies, P. J. and Waldstein, F. A. (Eds). *Political Issues in America Today* (Politics Today Series). Manchester, Manchester University Press, 1988.

Farrard, M. *The Framing of the Constitution of the United States*. New Haven, Connecticut, Yale University Press, 1913.

Fisher, L. *Constitutional Dialogues*. Princeton, New Jersey, Princeton University Press, 1988.

Friedman, L. M. *A History of American Law*. New York, Simon & Schuster Inc, 1975.

Halpern, S. C. and Lamb, C. M. (Eds). *Supreme Court Activism and Restraint*. Lexington, Massachusetts, Lexington Books, 1982.

Hartz, L. *The Liberal Tradition in America*. New York, Harcourt Brace, 1955.

Heclo, H. *A Government of Strangers: Executive Branch Politics in Washington*. Washington, DC, The Brookings Institution, 1977.

Kaufman, H. *The Administrative Behavior of Federal Bureau Chiefs*. Washington, DC, The Brookings Institution, 1981.

Keefe, W. J. *Parties, Politics and Public Policy in America*. Eastbourne, Holt–Saunders Ltd, 1984.

Light, P. C. *The President's Agenda: Domestic Policy Choice from Kennedy to Carter*. Baltimore, Maryland, The Johns Hopkins University Press, 1982.

McCloskey, R. G. *The American Supreme Court*. Chicago, Illinois, University of Chicago Press, 1960.

McKay, D. *American Politics and Society* (2nd edn). Oxford and New York, Basil Blackwell Ltd, 1989.

Mackenzie, G. C. *The In and Outers: Presidential Appointees and Transient Government in Washington*. Baltimore, Maryland, The Johns Hopkins University Press, 1987.

Maidment, R. A. *The American Political Process*. London, Sage Publications Ltd, 1986.

Maisel, L. *Parties and Elections in America: The Electoral Process*. New York, Random House Inc, 1987.

Marshall, T. R. *Public Opinion and the Supreme Court*. London, Unwin Hyman Ltd, 1988.

Nathan, R. P. *The Administrative Presidency*. New York, John Wiley & Sons Inc, 1983.

Nelson, M. (Ed.). *The Presidency and the Political System* (2nd edn). Washington, DC, Congressional Quarterly Books, 1988.

O'Brien, D. *Storm Center: the Supreme Court in American Politics*. New York, W. W. Norton & Co Inc, 1986.

Reichley, A. J. (Ed.). *Elections American Style*. Washington, DC, The Brookings Institution, 1987.

Richardson, R. J. and Vines, K. N. (Eds). *The Politics of the Federal Courts: Lower Courts in the United States*. Boston, Massachusetts, Little, Brown & Co Inc, 1970.

Ripley, R. B. *Congress: Process and Policy*. New York, W. W. Norton & Co Inc, 1983.

Robinson, D. L. (Ed.). *Reforming American Government*. Boulder, Colorado, Westview Press Inc, 1985.

Schwartz, B. *Superchief: Earl Warren and his Supreme Court*. New York, New York University Press, 1983.

Seidman, H. and Gilmour, R. *Politics, Position and Power: The Dynamics of Federal Organization*. New York, Oxford University Press, 1980.

Shaw, M. (Ed.). *Roosevelt to Reagan: The Development of the Modern Presidency*. London, C. Hurst & Co Ltd, 1987.

Smith, H. *The Power Game: How Washington Works*. London, William Collins plc, 1988.

Van Horn, C. E. *The State of the States*. Washington, DC, Congressional Quarterly Books, 1989.

Wayne, S. J. 'The United States' in Plowden, W. (Ed.). *Advising the Rulers*. Oxford, Basil Blackwell Ltd, 1987.

THE US ECONOMY

OVERVIEW

DAVID McKAY

Introduction

The US economy remains by far the world's largest. By the end of 1988 the country's gross national product (GNP) totalled $4,900,000m. The next largest capitalist economy was that of Japan, whose GNP was $2,000,000m. in 1988.

Since 1945 the US economy has been through a number of major transitions, of which two stand out: the shift away from agriculture, extractive and manufacturing industries and towards the service sector; and the increasing interdependence with other economies. Interdependence has, by definition, accompanied an erosion of what from 1945 to 1965 was accepted as a US economic hegemony. The USA, and multilateral institutions under its control, effectively dictated the terms of world trade during this period. Since then, however, a number of developed and newly-developing countries have asserted independent economic power. Some, but by no means all, of the USA's economic problems today stem from this fact. This overview will begin with a brief review of US economic performance since 1945, stressing trends in GNP and productivity growth and changes in employment and inflation. Further sections will focus on income and poverty, investment and savings, foreign trade, government finances, research and development, regulation and deregulation, and trade unions and industrial relations.

The US Economy in Perspective

Between 1900 and 1988 the USA experienced an average rate of growth of real GNP of 3.1%. Of the leading industrial nations, only Canada and Japan grew faster. Measured in per-head terms, the growth was slower (1.7%, compared with 3.0% for Japan and 2.7% for the Federal Republic of Germany): however, it must be noted that population growth was more rapid in the USA during this period than in most comparable countries. US economic growth tended to lag behind that of other countries between 1948 and 1973. During this period the economy expanded at 3.7% a year, compared with 9.1% for Japan, 7% for the Federal Republic of Germany and 5.3% for France. Of the leading industrial nations, only the United Kingdom experienced a lower rate of growth (3%). However, since 1981 growth has recovered to surpass that of most competing nations. During the 1980s the US economy grew at an average rate of 3% a year, while West German growth slumped to 1.8%, as did that of France. Only Japan outpaced the USA, recording a 3.8% annual growth rate.

In broader historical perspective, the whole post-war period was one of rapid economic expansion. Indeed, the USA was more adversely affected by the 'Great Depression' of the 1930s than were most other countries. Between 1930 and 1938 the economy grew at just 0.4% a year, compared with Japan's 6.3%, Germany's 4.4% and the UK's 2.2%, so it is misleading to talk of the 1948–73 period in terms of anything but success. During the 1930s serious mistakes in financial management contributed to a very low level of economic activity. The federal authorities reduced the money supply and increased taxation between 1929 and 1933, thereby aggravating deflationary trends. In addition, a series of protectionist measures were enacted, which provoked retaliation by other nations and led to a sharp decline in world trade. Not until the mid-1930s were measures taken to correct these mistakes, but it was the rearmament policies of the late 1930s and early 1940s which eventually allowed the US economy to recover to levels of full capacity.

After the Second World War political leaders were intent on avoiding the mistakes of the past and accordingly adopted an economic strategy designed to keep both the US and other capitalist economies operating at, or near, full capacity. Three broad policies were adopted: firstly, the USA took on the role of leader of the world economy. Britain had effectively abandoned this role in 1931 when it stopped the free convertibility of sterling into gold. At Bretton Woods in 1944 the USA pledged to maintain the convertibility of the dollar into gold at a rate of $35 to one ounce of gold. Britain promised eventually to join the USA in providing a reserve currency by facilitating the free convertibility of sterling into dollars. A system of fixed exchange rates was to be adopted by the capitalist economies, underpinned by the dollar. Only when an economy's currency was grossly under- or over-valued would a formal revaluation of the currency occur. A new multilateral institution, the International Monetary Fund, would provide loans to help prevent national economies from having to impose a devaluation, or to assist in adjusting following a devaluation.

Secondly, the USA also took the lead in pursuing a policy of free international trade. The General Agreement on Tariffs and Trade (GATT) was signed in 1948 by all the leading economies in order to facilitate successive rounds of tariff reductions, the ultimate objective being a completely open international trading system. The 'beggar-my-neighbour' protectionist polices of the 1930s could be avoided because by far the largest economy, that of the USA, would lead the way by permitting goods from protected markets to be sold in the country. Thirdly, in the sphere of domestic economic policy, the USA formally adopted Keynesian demand management through the passage of the 1946 Full Employment Act. In other words, the federal government was committed to pursuing a policy of near-full employment by stimulating the economy should a period of deflation and serious under-utilization of capacity occur.

Few dispute that these policies were successful. From the late 1940s to the late 1960s the US economy grew steadily. Recessions were relatively mild (the deepest occurring in 1958) and were in no way comparable with the earlier economic slowdowns. In addition to a stable domestic and international environment, the USA was able to take advantage of major advances in technology which led directly to a rapid increase in productivity. Uniquely among the major economies, US productivity growth accelerated during the 1940s. In 1938 the six other large economies had productivity levels averaging 57% of the US figure; by 1950 this figure had declined to 43%.

If 1977 is taken as the base year and given the value of 100, in 1947 US output per hour in the business sector (including all commercial farm and non-farm production) was 44.9. Productivity improved steadily to reach 100 in 1977. For the next three years, however, productivity declined, reaching a low of 99.3 in 1980, and even by 1982 output per hour had only recovered to 100.3. Between 1982 and 1987 the picture changes again, with what appeared to be a major recovery. In 1987 output per hour was measured at 111.0.

In an international perspective US post-war performance looks less impressive. Between 1960 and 1973 US total-factor productivity growth per year was 1.5%, compared with 6.3% for Japan, 2.6% for the Federal Republic of Germany, 3.9% for France, 4.8% for Italy and 1.9% for the UK. From 1973 to 1980 the USA continued to lag behind, but after 1980 a considerable narrowing in the gap between the USA and some other countries occurred. (Much of this relative improvement was the result of improved labour productivity rather than enhanced capital productivity.) In spite of these trends, the

US economy remains the most productive in the OECD. In manufacturing, the gap is narrowing, but in the service sector, the USA is maintaining its lead.

As far as inflation and unemployment are concerned, the post-war years can be divided into three periods. Between 1950 and 1970 low levels of inflation and unemployment were recorded. In 1965, for example, inflation (the annual change in the consumer-price index) was 1.9%, while unemployment totalled 4.5% of the labour force. During these years unemployment tended to fluctuate more than inflation, for while the US economic strategy was broadly Keynesian, the trade-off between inflation and unemployment was different in the USA than in other industrial countries. Very generally, US politicians and economists were more willing to accept higher levels of unemployment (up to 5% or 6%) than were the Europeans and the Japanese. US inflation rates were generally lower. In spite of these variations, the period 1950 to 1970 was generally one of price and employment stability.

By the late 1960s, however, signs of strain in both the domestic and international economies were evident. Commodity prices were increasing and, partly because of expenditure on the Vietnam War, the domestic economy was overheating. In addition, a dollar shortage was being replaced by a dollar surplus as the demand for dollars declined.

These problems were acknowledged during the early 1970s by the effective abandonment of the Bretton Woods system of fixed exchange rates in 1973. Since then the value of currencies has fluctuated according to market forces. The major dislocation to the post-war regime came in the form of increased commodity prices, however. The Arab–Israeli War of October 1973 and the rise of OPEC (the Organization of the Petroleum-Exporting Countries) led to an immediate quadrupling in the price of oil. Other commodity prices also rose following a period of rapid economic growth during the early 1970s. The resulting 'stagflation' (stagnation or recession coupled with inflation) had a seriously-disruptive effect on output and productivity growth. A further externally-induced shock occurred in 1979–80 following the Iranian Revolution.

While the US economy did not recover until the early 1980s, that recovery was comprehensive. Output, productivity and employment all rose, while inflation fell—although it began to accelerate once more during the late 1980s. Interestingly, the US recovery was more solidly based than that of most other countries: indeed, the erosion of the country's relative productivity advantage, which had been proceeding since the 1950s, was actually reduced. In employment terms, the US success was even more striking. Between 1981 and 1987 civilian unemployment increased by 3.2% in France, 3.1% in the Federal Republic of Germany, 1.8% in Italy, 1.4% in Canada and 0.7% in Japan, but declined by 2% in the UK and by 1.4% in the USA. This trend can be partly explained by the high levels of unemployment experienced by the USA and the UK during the base year of 1981: however, the recovery since then has been sustained, and there is evidence that uniquely American factors, including a flexible labour market and low wage increases, have helped to account for the continuing ability of the US economy to generate new jobs.

One way of characterizing this recovery is to claim that the USA was more successful in making the transition from a lower-technology, manufacturing-based economy to a higher-technology, manufacturing and service-sector economy than were many other countries. Indeed, by the mid-1980s, some 75% of those in employment in the USA worked in the service sector. This accepted, potentially serious economic problems remain, especially those relating to investment, international trade and government finances.

Income and Poverty

Between 1948 and 1973 the standard of living in the USA improved steadily, with real disposable family income growing by an average of 2.4% a year. Moreover, these benefits applied to all income-groups. The most wealthy 20% of families enjoyed an average 3.1% improvement and the least wealthy 20% an increase of 2.9%. Since 1973 the rate of increase has levelled off and the 'lowest' 20% of families were slightly worse off, in terms of real disposable income, in 1987 than they were in 1973. The 'top' 20% have continued to prosper, however, with increases of around 2% a year since 1973. Finally, single or unrelated individuals have experienced a steady improvement in their standard of living.

The economic downturns of the 1970s and early 1980s account in part for these trends. Lower-income workers and those at the margin of the labour force are more exposed to fluctuations in growth rates than other income groups. Welfare benefits also peaked during the late 1970s and, in response to a more hostile economic environment, employers reduced their relative wage levels across a wide front from the mid-1970s onwards. This is reflected in data for earnings. In constant 1977 dollars, earnings delined from $5.10 per hour in all industries in 1975 to $4.83 per hour in 1982. This decline was most marked in those industries most affected by economic dislocation: in construction, for example, earnings declined from $8.23 per hour in 1975 to $7.16 in 1984. However, the decline applied across the board. In no major sector of the economy was there anything but a marginal increase in earnings per hour in the 1975–85 period.

The USA employs an official measure of poverty (adjustable for family size and local costs of living). The number of families living in poverty declined steadily from over 30% in 1950 to 9.9% in 1975. It increased to 13.6% in 1982 and then declined again, to 12% by 1987. These figures disguise a structural trend in poverty which is only loosely related to the general state of the economy. Full-time, year-round working heads of family are falling as a percentage of the poor, while female-headed families are increasing rapidly as a percentage of poor households. In other words, the incidence of poverty among those in full-time work is declining. Part-time workers and female-headed families account for a large percentage of the poor. Indeed, by 1987 more than 50% of all female-headed families were living in poverty.

As far as the distribution of wealth is concerned, the USA continues to display greater inequalities than most comparable countries. About 40% of the total wealth in the USA is owned by the top 2% of households, compared with 25% in Sweden and less than 20% in Japan. Little change in these figures has been discernible since 1970.

Investment and Savings

As earlier suggested, until the early 1970s US productivity growth was relatively high, reflecting high levels of investment. After 1973, however, investment growth declined, resulting in lower output and productivity levels. Most commentators agree that this decline was a direct result of higher inflation and (partly as a result of inflation) of higher effective tax rates. The incentive to save and to invest fell during these years. In addition, inflation and distortions in the tax code diverted investment away from manufacturing industry and towards residential development. One result was a rapid rise in real-estate prices during the late 1970s. Although economists disagree about the magnitude of the disincentive effects of inflation and higher effective tax rates, they estimate that, in combination, they reduced overall investment by between 20% and 50%. Indeed, the rate of growth of net non-residential capital stock per worker dropped from 2.2% between 1966 and 1973 to 1.4% in the 1973–81 period.

These events led to an increasingly vocal debate on how best to achieve a recovery for the US economy. Left-leaning economists argued that the USA should adopt an industrial policy through provision of government incentives for investment. Loans, grants, infrastructure, and research and training efforts should be directed towards high-growth, high-technology industries. Older, declining industries should be encouraged to modernize or should make the adjustment to lower levels of output at higher productivity levels. Industrial-policy advocates varied in their precise prescriptions for change, but all agreed that governments, and in particular the federal government, should play a leading role in helping industry adjust to economic change.

Economists on the right of the political spectrum argued that such measures would, by distorting the free working of the market, simply make the investment environment worse. In addition, taxes would have to be increased to pay for the industrial-policy measures. In the event, the election of a Republican president, Ronald Reagan, in November 1980 forestalled any chance of the adoption of an industrial policy by the federal government. During 1981 and the early part of 1982 the investment environment deteriorated further, as the new administration pursued a high-interest-rate policy to squeeze inflation out of the economy. From mid-1982 until the end of 1988 investment recovered somewhat. Indeed, gross investment averaged 11.8% of GNP between 1981 and 1987—or 1% above the post-war average.

In spite of this and improvements in productivity, concern about low levels of investment in the USA remain. In fact, net manufacturing investment (gross investment minus depreciation) remains low in the USA relative to other countries—and to Japan in particular. The USA invests much more than comparable countries on consumer durables, housing, services and military capital. Some economists argue that this characteristic, along with historically-low levels of saving, will produce longer-term problems for the economy. Net household savings in the USA remain worryingly low—and they have been falling. In 1987 they totalled 3.3% of disposable income (as against 7.7% in 1981). This compares with 16.8% in Japan, 12.4% in the Federal Republic of Germany, 12.1% in France, 21.9% in Italy and 5.4% in the UK.

One final point on investment concerns the achievement of higher labour-productivity levels during the 1980s. This was mainly the result of more efficient use of existing capital and of falling or constant labour costs, rather than of the utilization of new capital in manufacturing industry.

Foreign Trade

As indicated, until the early 1960s the USA experienced few, if any, problems in foreign economic policy. The major 'problem' for much of the 1945-65 period was a dollar shortage which often worked to the country's advantage rather than to its disadvantage. Since then, three interrelated difficulties have arisen, none of which look resoluble in the near future. Firstly, the USA has acquired a sizeable external trade deficit. Secondly, pressures for protection from domestic industries have risen discernibly. Thirdly, the value of the dollar has fluctuated considerably in ways which have sometimes aggravated the first and second problems.

Between 1960 and 1983 the current account of the USA's balance of payments was approximately in equilibrium. Deficits were recorded in the early and late 1970s, but these were of a low magnitude. During the early 1980s exports increased as the value of the dollar fell, but after 1983 the current-account balance went into serious deficit, reaching –$153,964m. in 1987. Some recovery subsequently occurred, to a projected –$116,000m. in 1989. Unfortunately, measuring precisely why the USA has acquired a trade imbalance is confused by a number of factors, including an exchange rate for the dollar which does not always adjust as it would in a free-market situation. Strictly speaking, the exchange rate should adjust automatically to eliminate surpluses or deficits on the current trading account, but market imperfections often prevent this. For example, during 1985 and 1986 the value of the dollar fell sharply, but so did net exports. Under 'ideal' conditions a depreciating currency should result in fewer imports and increased exports.

There is, of course, a lag between currency changes and the demand for exports and imports—and indeed the relative recovery in the US trade deficit after 1987 may partly be because of this. However, other factors are at work. The US consumer may have acquired a preference for foreign goods (and especially consumer durables) which is resistant to small price changes induced by currency fluctuations. US export performance is also affected by the fact that it is increasingly bipolar in nature. Most exports are in very-high-technology goods (such as computers or aircraft) or in primary products (such as agricultural and other commodities).

The US domestic deficit may also impact on the trade deficit. In order to finance the domestic budget deficit, interest rates have been held high (although this is by no means the only reason they have been held thus). As long as interest rates stay at high levels, the USA remains an attractive destination for mobile international capital. The resulting net inflow of money boosts the dollar and depresses exports. This at least partly accounts for the rapid appreciation of the dollar between 1981 and 1985, during which period the US budget deficit was growing very rapidly.

In response to these problems, the so-called Group of Five (G5) countries (Japan, the USA, the UK, France and the Federal Republic of Germany) have since 1985 attempted to co-ordinate their central banks' activities so as to keep the value of the dollar down to a level which approximates to the real trading position of the USA. Indeed, the dollar's value did decline from 1986 onwards, but during 1989 the dollar began to appreciate sharply again—even in the face of co-ordinated intervention by central banks.

A related problem is the fact that the USA has now become a debtor nation—measured not in terms of international trade or domestic fiscal problems, but in terms of net assets held abroad in comparison with assets held by foreigners in the USA. By the late 1980s this new debt status had been established—but only just. Economists are generally less worried by this trend than by others. Increasing investment by foreigners in the US economy reflects confidence in the US investment environment, which offers especially-high returns, low taxes and increasingly-competitive labour costs. Moreover, this 'debt' status is very small—less than $1,000m. in 1988 and, as with the other indicators, it can change very rapidly in response to sharp fluctuations in exchange rates.

A more volatile international trading environment has raised once more the question of trade barriers and protectionism. Until 1934 the USA was a protectionist state, the original impulse for tariffs being the need to protect US products from cheap British goods. Since the Second World War the USA has, in contrast, been the champion of free trade and has led the way, via the GATT system, through successive rounds of tariff reductions. In 1934 average US tariff rates on all imports were 20%. By 1950 they were down to 6% and by the late 1980s had fallen to between 3% and 4%. The last record of GATT tariff reductions (the Tokyo Round) was completed in 1987. For finished manufactured goods these reduced tariff rates in the USA to 5.7%, in the European Communities to 6.9% and in Japan to 6%. However, these figures disguise wide variations by product and do not take account of 'escape' clauses designed to protect particular industries. Non-tariff barriers, including quotas, also continue to apply.

In the context of increasing dislocation to domestic industries caused by imports, calls for increased protection have grown discernibly during the 1980s. Moreover, US industries claim that they are the victims of unfair trading practices, such as dumping. Anti-dumping measures have been adopted with increasing frequency throughout the industrial world, while the USA has been the most active user of countervailing or retaliatory tariffs. Certain industries—most notably textiles and agriculture—remain highly protected throughout the industrial world and most economists agree that the rise of non-tariff measures is worrying. Within the USA the political pressures for further protection are growing and are likely to remain high as long as import penetration is increasing. Successive federal administrations have been consistent in their formal espousal of free trade, while protectionist sentiment tends to be expressed through Congress.

One final point on international trade is that, in spite of increasing interdependence, the USA remains much more self-sufficient than other industrial economies. Even by 1987, only about 22% of GNP was accounted for by foreign trade. This compares with over 33% for Japan and 51% for the UK.

Government Finances and Economic Management

For most of its history the USA has been a fiscally-conservative country. Taxes have traditionally been held low, budgets balanced and the role of government limited. Even by the mid-1980s government spending as a percentage of GNP was significantly lower in the USA than in most comparable countries. Only 36.7% of GNP was accounted for by government outlays at all levels (federal, state and local) in 1985, compared with 47.2% in the Federal Republic of Germany, 52.4% in France and 47.7% in the UK. Only in Japan was the figure lower (32.7%), but Japanese spending is held low in part because of constitutional limitations on defence spending.

This accepted, government spending did increase rapidly from 1929, when it stood at 10% of GNP, to 1969, when it accounted for 30%. More recently, a serious shortfall between revenues and expenditures has resulted in a sizeable budget deficit. The actual pattern of federal-government spending is broadly similar to that in comparable countries—with the exception that the USA spends significantly more on defence. So in 1989 26% of the federal budget was devoted to defence and 43% to direct benefits to individuals (social security, welfare payments, agricultural subsidies); 11% went in the form of grants to states and localities and 15% as net interest on the national debt. On the income side, individual income taxes accounted for 44% of revenue, social-security (payroll) taxes 37% and corporate income taxes 11%. Borrowing and excise taxes made up the remainder. Again, this is not an untypical distribution of revenue sources.

As far as the functioning of the economy is concerned, debate on government finances dwells on three major areas: the level of spending, including the general level of taxation needed to finance expenditure; the harmful effects of the budget deficit; and the level of military spending. As indicated, federal expenditure levels are not high in comparative terms: however, the two Reagan administrations (1981–89) were concerned that they were high enough to constitute a burden on the economy and, because of high marginal tax rates, created a disincentive to work. Tax and expenditure reductions therefore dominated the Reagan agenda. In 1981 the administration succeeded in passing the largest tax-reduction act in US history, the Economic Recovery Tax Act (ERTA). Some $162,000m. was removed from the revenue side of national income and expenditure. Both corporate and individual income taxes were reduced and the highest marginal rates were cut from 70% to 50% for individuals and from 28% to 20% for corporations. Equally importantly, automatic indexing of deductible allowances was introduced in order to prevent 'fiscal drag' or 'bracket-creeping'. Both measures served to reduce tax revenues in subsequent years.

Expenditures were also reduced in a range of social programmes, although earnings-related social-security benefits (mainly for pensions) survived unscathed. In 1986 a further major tax reform was enacted, designed not so much to reduce total tax revenues as to simplify the tax code and remove 'loophole' tax allowances. Throughout his period in office, President Reagan sought to reduce domestic spending, although military spending was increased.

With relatively few exceptions (mainly enacted in 1981), Congress refused to accept the administration's expenditure cuts, so between 1981 and 1986 the federal deficit first increased and then was maintained at a high level. In 1986 the largest dollar value of the deficit—$220,700m.—was witnessed, although as a percentage of GNP the deficit peaked at 6.1% in 1983. Recession in 1981 and 1982 added to the administration's fiscal problems. In 1985 Congress enacted the Gramm–Rudman–Hollings Deficit Reduction Act, which initially mandated systematic spending cuts to meet deficit targets. The Supreme Court declared the mandatory provision unconstitutional, so Gramm–Rudman–Hollings has become advisory rather than compulsory. By 1989 the deficit-reduction target was $100,000m. (for fiscal 1990), but few commentators believed that it would be met. In fact, if expressed as a percentage of GNP, the federal deficit was about 3% in 1987. This is not high if taken in a comparative perspective. Once surpluses on the Social Security Trust Fund are taken into account (most countries include any social-security tax surpluses or deficits in their national budget accounting) the deficit is reduced further. Furthermore, if these and state and local government balances are included, the US deficit is reduced to 2.3% (in 1987) compared with 2.5% in France, 1.7% in the Federal Republic of Germany, 1.5% in the UK, 0.3% in Japan and 10.5% in Italy.

However, most commentators agree that for the leading economy in the industrial world to experience rapidly-increasing deficits can have distorting effects on interest rates and investment. It also reduces confidence in the US economy. The USA has itself defined it as a serious economic problem. If the country is unable to resolve it through its political system, the suggestion is that other economic problems may not be resoluble.

Defence spending increased rapidly from 1980 to 1985, having experienced a sharp relative decline from 1973 to 1978. Since 1985 defence-spending increases have been modest, although at close on $300,000m. in 1989 defence was set to account for over one-quarter of federal spending. Economists disagree about the precise effects of high levels of military spending on the economy, but all concur that the economy would operate more efficiently with lower levels of spending. Fiscal and world political factors combined in the late 1980s to produce a new consensus that defence spending should be reduced—however, it remained to be seen how this could be achieved.

Monetary policy in the USA is much more insulated from democratic pressures than is fiscal policy. A federally-organized 'central' bank, the Federal Reserve Bank, is responsible for controlling the money supply and setting interest rates. The chairman of the Federal Reserve Board of Governors is a very powerful figure in the general area of monetary policy. Although appointed by the president, the Federal Reserve chairman is widely recognized as relatively independent. Nevertheless, conflict between the two has been infrequent. Paul Volcker, who chaired the board during both the Carter and Reagan administrations, is acknowledged as having been a major force behind the tight monetary policies of the late 1970s and early 1980s. In comparative perspective, therefore, monetary policy in the USA is formulated in a context not unlike that prevailing in other countries—in other words, central bankers and political executives dominate.

Research and Development

The USA spends far more in absolute terms on research and development (R. & D.) than the other leading OECD countries—more in 1986, for example, than the Federal Republic of Germany, France, Japan and the UK combined. Expressed as a percentage of GNP, however, US R. & D. spending is, at about 2.7%, at the same level as that of both Japan and West Germany.

The federal government plays a major role in R. & D. spending, making up some 47% of funding in 1988, compared with 49% provided by industry, 3% by universities and 1% by other non-profit institutions. Of the total, some 14% is basic research, 22% applied and 64% devoted to development. It is generally recognized that the USA is the world leader in scientific discovery and in the development and application of scientific breakthroughs. Nevertheless, problems exist, the most important of which are an over-reliance on defence-related research and the decline of research-related innovation relative to Japan. US R. & D. has been defence-dependent at least since the Second World War. More than two-thirds of all government-sponsored research is conducted by the Department of Defense, with the National Aeronautics and Space Administration (NASA) taking a further 5%. However, these defence- and aerospace-related efforts have been declining as a proportion of the total, and in particular as a proportion of that part of the total which is devoted to basic research.

Judged by the varying proportions of patents issued within the USA, foreign competition in R. & D. is increasing. In 1973 73% of all US-issued patents came from US inventions: by 1987 this proportion had fallen to 52%. Japanese inventors have increased their share by a factor of five. There is also evidence that Japanese research concentrates on processes rather than new products. In other words, the Japanese are more concerned with improving methods of production or with productivity, rather than with creating larger numbers of new products.

Regulation and Deregulation

In all modern industrial societies economic regulation has become a central part of the political agenda. In the USA this applies with particular force. Indeed, regulation has been a major political issue in the USA for most of the 20th century. Two broad areas of economic activity are covered by regulation: those associated with market imperfections and/or market failure, and those associated with monopoly and oligopoly. The former is often labelled social regulation and the latter economic regulation. Recent administrations, both Democratic and Republican, have been active in both spheres, but it is primarily in the area of social regulation that major political differences have occurred.

Social regulation is designed to compensate for what economists call 'externalities', or those adverse consequences of production which producers have no incentive to correct. As a result, government has to intervene to do what the market will not, or cannot, do by providing such benefits as environmental, consumer-protection, occupational-safety and health legislation, and the regulation of financial institutions. Since the mid-1960s social regulation has occurred with increased frequency and, according to many critics, now constitutes a burden on the economy. Certainly, the Reagan administrations believed this and made serious efforts to relax environmental, consumer-protection, and occupational-safety and health regulations. Little evidence exists, however, to suggest that the USA is at a competitive disadvantage because of burdensome social regulation. Many Western European countries and Japan have broadly similar laws. Where the USA is different is in the ways in which such laws are formulated and implemented. Federal, state and local governments are involved, and serious disagreements occur between the executive and legislative branches in this broad area of public policy. Advocates of social regulation are well organized and have good access to law-making institutions—Congress and the state legislatures—even if access to the implementing executive agencies is limited.

Economic regulation is less controversial but no less important. In this area debate has concentrated on the extent to which industries regulated by law should be required to operate in a more competitive environment. Until the 1970s regulations designed to protect the public interest often resulted in advantages for special interests. Hence the telephone companies, airlines, trucking companies and railways all enjoyed elements of price- and/or route-fixing which increased fares and profits. Beginning in the mid-1970s, however, Congress legislated to remove some of the advantages. Since then, passenger and cargo air transport, telephone services, broadcasting, long-distance bus services, oil refining and natural-gas supplies have all been deregulated. Studies vary on the resulting benefits, but airline deregulation has been estimated as producing $15,000m. a year for the economy, while trucking deregulation (not yet fully implemented) may produce benefits up to $60,000m. a year.

Public utilities have also partly been deregulated, but when services have the status of so-called 'natural monopolies' it is impossible to create a truly-competitive trading environment. Such measures as competitive tendering for the construction of power stations have, however, been introduced in many states.

In summary, public policy in the USA is being pulled in two directions in the general area of regulation. On the one hand, the competitive free-market ethos is very strongly established, and this is shown both in support for economic deregulation and in opposition to social regulation. On the other hand, public-interest groups have fought hard for stronger social-regulatory laws. Conflict between such groups and producer interests is likely to continue.

One final area of regulation which has produced serious problems for policy-makers in recent years concerns financial institutions. Since the 1930s a framework of regulation has been created to protect investors and savers from the vagaries of economic dislocation and recession. Most of these laws have provided federal-guaranteed insurance for depositors at banks and savings and loan institutions (the so-called 'thrifts'). At the same time, few changes in the organization of banks and savings and loan institutions have been made. Their day-to-day operations have been regulated under state, not federal

law, resulting in wide interstate variations. This system prevails today and most commentators agree that it has led to considerable inefficiencies in the operations of both sorts of institution. Banks and the thrifts tend to be small compared with those operating in comparable countries and, during periods of recession, may become financially vulnerable. During 1981, for example, over 240 US commercial banks failed. The problem of the thrifts has become more serious as they have ventured into new areas, such as real-estate speculation, in order to reap large profits. Such activities, together with corruption and mismanagement, have resulted in a persistently-high rate of failure among the thrifts—in 1987, for example, more than 150 went bankrupt. Federal insurance will compensate most investors, but the long-term cost is estimated at more than $50,000m. In the late 1980s many commentators were of the opinion that a federally-imposed reform of banks and savings and loans institutions was urgently required.

Trade Unions and Industrial Relations

In the late 1980s less than 19% of the US non-farm labour force was unionized—the lowest figure for any large industrial country. The decline has been considerable since 1945, when 36% of the labour force was unionized. As might be expected, union membership is concentrated in the older manufacturing industries and in extractive industries. Among the most notable unions are the United Automobile, Aerospace and Agricultural Implement Workers of America (United Auto Workers—UAW), the International Brotherhood of Teamsters, Chauffeurs, Warehousemen and Helpers of America ('Teamsters', which represents transport workers) and the American Federation of State, County and Municipal Employees (AFSCME). AFSCME is one of the few unions to have grown in size during the 1980s. Significantly, it is a service-workers' union in the public sector, where union growth generally has been marked in recent years.

Most trade-union activities in the USA are regulated at the state level. The 1935 Wagner Act and subsequent 1947 Taft–Hartley Act do lay down a framework of federal law, including the right to collective bargaining. However, the right to a union ('closed') shop is determined at the state level, as are picketing laws. Generally, the southern and western states have conservative union laws, while those of the northern industrial states tend to be more favourable to organized labour.

Strike activity has been declining for some years as unions have grown weaker and the price of labour—especially in manufacturing industry—has fallen. The USA does, however, have a minimum-wage law which is periodically adjusted at the state level in line with inflation. Most observers agree that union activity and pro-union laws provide relatively little in the way of obstacles to the working of the market economy. In relation to most comparable nations, the USA has a flexible labour market.

Conclusions

Perhaps the most striking thing about the US economy is its continuing resilience. In the mid- and late 1970s many observers claimed that the USA was entering a period of permanent decline. The 1980s demonstrated that this was not so, with the US economy outperforming at least the Western European economies by most measures. Serious problems remain, however, including low levels of net investment and continuing balance-of-payments and budget deficits. The investment and trade problems seem endemic to the US economy and are unlikely to be solved in the short run. The budget-deficit problem is more political than economic in origin. Solutions will have to come through improved co-operation between president and Congress, together with careful financial management.

US AGRICULTURE: HISTORY, POLICIES AND PERSPECTIVES

BRUNA ANGEL, MICHAEL D. HELMAR, STANLEY R. JOHNSON

Introduction

The modern history of US agriculture has been dominated by change, the driving force for which has commonly been seen as technology. As important, however, has been the policy framework that has evolved to support the development and application of technology (and simultaneously to soften the adverse effects of the structural changes resulting from the technology). The results have been a highly-productive agriculture, a low-cost, high-quality food supply and a significant expansion of international trade; meanwhile there have been significant alterations in the structure of the agricultural sector which, in turn, will bring future changes. Farm numbers have been reduced, agriculture has become a relatively small industry within the economy, and adjustments in rural communities responding to the existing structure for agriculture are ongoing.

The contribution of agriculture, forestry and fishing to the USA's gross national product (GNP) fell from 2.9% in 1970 to 2.2% in 1986. The value of agricultural commodity exports was about 17% of total export value in 1970, rising to 21% in the 1970–74 period and falling to 19% in 1980 and to 12.6% in 1986, largely due to prices and domestic policy changes. In 1986 the farm population (all persons living on farms in rural areas) represented 2.2% of the total population and, in overall terms, produced the food and fibre needs for the US population of 241,596,000 in addition to supporting the export of about 29% of crop production. The ratio for the number of persons worldwide who received their requirement of farm commodities from a single US farm worker increased from 48 to one in 1970 to 93 to one in 1986, of which 75 were US citizens and 18 were foreign.

In the 1980s, of the over 2,200m.-acre land area of the USA, about 17% was used for crops. Idled cropland was about 1%, cropland used for pastures about 3%, grassland pastures 26% and forests 29%. Crops and livestock are of equal importance to US agriculture. Corn is the most important crop in terms of value of production and area harvested, followed by wheat, soybeans and hay; other feed grains, cotton, fruits and nuts, and commercial vegetables also contribute significantly to the value of agricultural production and agricultural exports. Beef cattle constitutes the largest livestock industry in terms of value, followed by dairy, poultry and eggs, and hogs. US meat and livestock industries are characterized as producing for domestic consumption, with trade being insignificant relative to production. In 1984 total meat consumption in the USA was 52,600m. lb (retail weight).

While the forested area of the USA has been declining throughout its history, never before has the annual growth increment been greater. In the 1980s forest area has been reduced by 2% but timber volume has increased by 4%. Forest and grasslands are managed with multiple-use objectives that require more than timber production; forage, wildlife, water and recreation are included by law as management objectives.

Real prices for many agricultural products have remained stable or declined in the last two decades. However, the income of farm-operator households has averaged close to that of workers in the rest of the economy, especially in the 1970s and mid- to late 1980s. Farm size has increased and there has been a continuing downward adjustment in farm labour due to the introduction of capital-intensive technology.

Agricultural Policy

The objectives of agricultural programmes have remained basically the same throughout the history of government intervention in agriculture in the USA. These have been to maintain a free and independent farm sector, as the best guarantee of an adequate supply of food at reasonable prices, and to encourage agricultural exports. While government intervention in agricul-

ture dates back more than 200 years, the foundations of current farm programmes were laid in the Agricultural Adjustment Acts of 1933 and 1938 and in the Agricultural Act of 1949. While the Adjustment Acts of the 1930s were initially seen as 'temporary methods of dealing with an emergency', they were still in effect, albeit with some modifications, over 50 years later.

HISTORY

After the First World War agricultural prices collapsed as export demand suddenly declined. This was followed by a decade of declining agricultural prices and rigid non-agricultural prices and wages, resulting in a gap between farm income and costs. The farm depression was one of the causes of the Great Depression, and the Agricultural Acts of the 1930s were aimed at improving the financial situation of the average farmer.

The 1933 Agricultural Adjustment Act attempted to readjust productive acreage to market requirements. It entitled the Secretary of Agriculture to reduce acreage or production by voluntary agreements; farmers could receive rental or benefit payments and the Department of Agriculture could spend money to expand markets or remove surpluses. In subsequent years additional laws were passed and agencies established to address specific farm problems. In 1936 the production-control provisions of the Agricultural Adjustment Act of 1933 were repealed by the Supreme Court as unconstitutional and were replaced by the Soil Conservation and Domestic Allotment Act of 1936. This act, with many modifications, remains the basis of agricultural price-support and production-adjustment law today. It retained a federal role in production management, with the law being administered nationally by the Department of Agriculture. Policy objectives explicitly included maintenance of farm income and welfare as well as improving production efficiency. The Act attempted to reduce production of surplus crops by payments for improved land use and conservation practices. However surpluses continued to accumulate and the Agricultural Adjustment Act of 1938 was passed; this introduced the goal of 'parity' prices and incomes for farmers. The concept of parity prices gave a unit of commodity the same purchasing power as it had in the period 1910–1914, otherwise known as the 'Golden Age' of agriculture. Parity prices were one of the major determinants of support prices until the early 1960s.

During the Second World War major changes took place in land use, agricultural production and farm life. Farm prices rose above 100% of parity and farmers were guaranteed high price-support levels for two years after the cessation of hostilities. The Agricultural Act of 1949 set intervention levels for major commodities at between 75% and 90% of parity. This was a compromise between those who wanted prices supported at a high level of parity and those advocating flexible price supports adjusting to supply and demand conditions.

The Agricultural Trade Development and Assistance Act of 1954, known as Public Law 480 (PL 480), enacted to stimulate foreign demand, and the Soil Bank, established by the Agricultural Act of 1956 to take farmland out of production for up to 10 years, were large-scale efforts to deal with surpluses accumulating during the 1950s. PL 480 has been extended to the present and is a cornerstone of the US foreign food assistance programme, while for many years after the Soil Bank was discontinued there were no long-term programmes to lay land idle. (The current Conservation Reserve Program— see below—retains many of the ideas of the Soil Bank but is targeted more to soil conservation than to supply control.)

Since the early 1970s farm policy has been reviewed systematically, and legislation enacted, every four to five years. This legislation establishes a comprehensive framework within which the Secretary of Agriculture administers agricultural and food programmes. Provisions include acreage limitations, disaster payments and income and price supports for specific commodities such as dairy, wheat, feed grains, cotton, rice, soybeans, sugar, peanuts and wool and mohair. This legislation also establishes general provisions for other commodities, trade, conservation, research and extension, food stamps and marketing.

CROPS

During the early 1970s world crop shortages, increased world demand, export subsidies and the devaluation of the dollar combined to reduce stocks. This was a period of high demand and market prices for farm commodities. The Agriculture and Consumer Protection Act of 1973 was designed to protect farm incomes while encouraging production to respond to increasing world-wide demand for agricultural commodities. Loan rates were set below market prices to encourage commodities to move into the market rather than into government storage. Target prices and deficiency payments (direct payments on crops) were established. Supply-reducing programmes introduced at this time included the Paid Land Diversion Program, a voluntary system of acreage diversion where the government paid farmers to take land out of production, and the Acreage Reduction Program (ARP), introduced in 1978, which required that a certain percentage of farm cropland be taken out of production in return for the right to receive farm programme benefits. Both were annual land-idling programmes.

The Food and Agricultural Act of 1977 was a compromise between farmers' demands for higher support prices as production costs rose and the need to keep potential programme costs at reasonable levels. Loan rates increased during this period and a farmer-owned reserve was established, permitting farmers to hold their grain for three to five years rather than turn stocks over to the government. The Agriculture and Food Act of 1981 extended PL 480, the food-stamp and related programmes and the general pattern of price support through loan rates and target prices, legislated on the basis of expected continuing inflation and expanding markets. However, during the early 1980s export markets and farm prices weakened, leading to the accumulation of surplus farm commodities and inflated farm-programme costs. In 1983 the US Department of Agriculture introduced a payment-in-kind (PIK) programme, offering surplus commodities owned by the government in exchange for agreements to reduce production by cutting crop acreage. A major drought in 1983 combined with the PIK programme to reduce production and eliminate most of the government-held surplus.

Concern over the competitiveness of US agricultural products in world markets, the farm financial crisis and conservation issues helped to shape the Food Security Act of 1985. The Export Enhancement Program (EEP) was introduced and made mandatory from 1 October 1985 until 30 September 1988. Initial EEP funding for use of agricultural commodities equal in value to $1,000m.–$1,500m. was made through the Commodity Credit Corporation Charter Act (with an extension of the EEP beyond $1,500m. being announced in June 1987). The main aims of the EEP were to promote farm exports through market development, to challenge alleged unfair international trade practices and to encourage serious negotiation on agricultural trade issues, particularly with the European Economic Community and Japan. Bonuses were offered to US exporters in the form of Commodity Credit Corporation generic certificates sufficient to allow them to compete successfully with subsidized suppliers from other countries. Reductions in loan rates were also used, beginning in 1985, to encourage the movement of commodities into world markets. However, as a result of the farm financial crisis and to maintain farm income, target prices were not reduced significantly.

Within certain boundaries, the Secretary of Agriculture was given discretion to choose the key provision for the land-set-aside programmes, the Acreage Reduction and Paid Land Diversion Rates. In order to reduce mounting surpluses of major grains, the Secretary selected rates at the higher end of the range. Set-aside rates for 1987 and 1988 were at historically-high levels for the land-idling programmes. The Conservation Reserve Program of the 1985 Act authorized the withdrawal from production of up to 45m. acres of highly-erodible land that had been used to produce crops in two of the five years from 1981 to 1985. Farmers were to withdraw

eligible cropland from production for 10 years and, in return, to receive an annual rental payment and 50% cost-share assistance for converting the withdrawn lands to perennial grasses, wildlife plantings and windbreaks or tree crops. By mid-1989 bids had been accepted to enter about 30.5m. acres into the Conservation Reserve.

Consideration was being given to legislation to replace the Food Security Act of 1985 when it expires at the end of the 1990/91 crop year. Environmental concerns, the impact of the Uruguay Round of the General Agreement on Tariffs and Trade (GATT) negotiations and a continuing adjustment to increased technology in the agricultural sector are major topics for debate.

Government policies have attempted to support and stabilize prices of agricultural commodities. The main policy tools employed have been target prices, loans, storage facilities, direct payments, marketing orders, import quotas and acreage reductions. These programmes have tended to increase expected returns to production and reduce their variability. In general, the benefits from farm programmes have tended to become concentrated on the largest producers and have become capitalized into land values, thereby increasing landowner's wealth. Different sectors have had different rates of protection, with important implications for efficient resource allocation. Feed grains, wheat, rice and cotton have all benefited from price supports, deficiency payments and acreage restrictions; wheat and feed-grains policies have also provided storage incentives to programme participants. Tobacco has been subject to price support and acreage and marketing controls, peanut production has been subject to price support, acreage restriction, import quotas and domestic marketing controls, and sugar beet and sugar-cane have been subject to price support, import quotas, fees and duties.

LIVESTOCK

The government intervenes directly in the livestock sector through import quotas, marketing orders, price supports, federal-level standards for inspection of meat in slaughter establishments, the setting of quality grades and other health and regulatory standards. The sector is also affected indirectly by government policies for feed grains and meal. Dairy is the most heavily-protected of the livestock industries. Rigid import quotas, marketing orders, government price supports and classified pricing have prevailed. Dairy production is the least concentrated of all livestock enterprises, the stability provided by the dairy price-support programmes being the major contributor to the lack of concentration, followed by the relative stability of real prices of dairy products since the early 1950s.

Beef cattle and calves have been subject to import restrictions and to purchases for domestic food-assistance programmes ('Section 32' purchases). Beef producers have spread their risks through 'hedging' on futures markets, spreading ownership of cattle to non-farm investors and, increasingly, by contracting. Hogs, poultry and eggs have been subject only to purchases under Section 32, and in adjusting to risk have become increasingly integrated. Broiler production is almost entirely vertically-integrated, with one individual firm owning the operation from the hatchery flock to the supermarket. Turkey and egg production are not as integrated but still utilize highly-industrialized production and marketing systems. Hog operations, while not exhibiting the degree of industrialization of poultry and eggs, have become more integrated in recent years.

SPECIALITY CROPS

Vegetables, fruits and nuts have been subject to marketing orders and import restrictions. They have also received some assistance through Section 32 purchases. Forward contracting of processing vegetables is commonly used to minimize risk to producers and to ensure adequate supplies of quality produce to processors.

COSTS AND TRANSFERS

Total net Commodity Credit Corporation (CCC) budgetary expenditures for support and related programmes, special activities and PL 480 have varied considerably through time, with most of the variability arising from direct producer-support programmes. PL 480 expenditures remained at between $5,000m. and $1,200m. between 1969 and 1983, rising to $1,700m. in 1985 before falling back to $700m. in 1988. Direct support operations were $3,800m. in 1970 and $600m. in 1975, rising dramatically to $18,700m. in 1982, falling to $7,200m. in 1984, rising again to $25,700m. in 1986 and declining again to $12,400m. in 1988.

The importance of different commodities for net government budgetary expenditures has changed over time. In 1970 expenditures on feed grains and products, wheat and products, and cotton were $1,513m., $1,264m. and $999m. respectively. Expenditures on dairy and tobacco programmes were $176m. and $137m. respectively, while the CCC received revenues of $161m. from the soybean programme. (In the long term, the soybean programme is expected to be a zero-cost programme to the government.) By 1987 net CCC budgetary expenditures for feed grains and products had risen to $14,022m., with wheat and cotton expenditures at $3,443m. and $1,817m. respectively. The dairy-programme expenditures, at $1,179m., were lower than at any time since 1980 as a result of the reduction in dairy-cow numbers through the Dairy Herd Termination programme. Soybeans and tobacco became money-making programmes with receipts of $476m. and $346m. respectively. Expenditure levels were significantly lower in 1988, mainly because of higher market prices. Expenditures on feed grains and products continued to be the largest at $9,104m. Wheat- and cotton-programme expenditures fell by more than one-half, to $1,228m. and $680m. respectively, while revenues from the soybean and tobacco programmes increased to $1,676m. and $453m. respectively. Expenditures on the dairy programme rose by $1,307m. above the 1987 figure because of increased purchases. States receiving the largest transfer payments (under the Stabilization and Conservation Program) in 1976 were Texas, South Dakota and Minnesota; by 1987 the most important recipients were Iowa, Illinois and Texas.

The government has also attempted to increase domestic and foreign demand in order to provide price support. When the government began purchasing agricultural commodities to support farm prices and farm income in the 1930s, certain commodities were distributed free to the urban poor and unemployed. Direct distribution of surplus commodities acquired by the CCC continues, for example, with the distribution of surplus cheese. The government also subsidizes school lunches and donates commodities, including meats, fruits, vegetables, eggs and poultry, to schools.

The largest food-assistance programme is the food-stamp programme, with a federal cost of $2,200m. in 1973, $11,900m. in 1983 and about $11,600m. in 1987. About 10% of the US population participated in the food-stamp programme in the mid-1980s.

FOREST, RANGE AND FISHERIES POLICY

Most forest policy between 1776 and 1891 consisted of acquiring and disposing of public domain lands. This was followed by a brief period, until 1905, during which the government established programmes to reserve or withhold lands from disposition. After this time government programmes were aimed at actively managing the public domain. For almost a century following the Revolutionary War, there was no general legislation dealing with the large tracts of forest land in the public domain. In 1886 the Department of Forestry was formed. The forest reserves were established in 1891 and were administered by the General Land Office of the Interior Department. In 1905 they were transferred to the Department of Agriculture and the US Forest Service was established.

Grazing was allowed on the forest reserves using a permit system in the late 1890s and grazing fees were introduced in 1905. After the First World War forest management made major strides in the areas of fire control, reforestation and forest protection; in 1930 the Knutson-Vandenberg Act provided for funding national forest planting and the operation of nurseries and plantations. Unfortunately, while forest policy was moving forward, range policy was largely ignored.

Important conservation legislation came out of the Great Depression. In 1933 the Civilian Conservation Corps was established, in part to provide for the restoration of the country's depleted natural resources. The work was to be conducted primarily on federal and state lands. The Tennessee Valley Authority was established with one of its many goals being the 'proper method of reforestation of all lands in the drainage basin suitable for reforestation'. During this period, the issue of public-domain grazing lands was addressed in the Taylor Grazing Act of 1934. This act was aimed at stopping injury to the range by preventing over-grazing and at providing for the orderly use, improvement and development of the remaining 142m. acres of public-domain rangelands.

The Second World War put renewed pressure on the natural resources from public lands. Overcutting occurred and, by the end of the war, the Forest Service had become oriented towards production forestry. Although over-grazing was not a grave problem on Forest Service grazing lands, the public-domain lands of the Grazing Service were abused. In the months following the war, the Grazing Service's budget was severely cut, and the agency became ineffective. In 1946 its remnants were consolidated with the General Land Office into the Bureau of Land Management.

As the various use interests conflicted with each other and with the management policies of the Forest Service, the Forest Service wrote and lobbied for the Multiple Use–Sustained Yield Act of 1960. This authorized the Secretary of Agriculture 'to develop and administer the renewable surface resources of the national forests for multiple use and sustained yield of the several products and services'. The Land and Water Conservation Fund Act of 1964 has contributed to the development of park systems and federal land-acquisition programmes in the various land-management agencies. The National Environmental Policy Act of 1969 mandated the assessment of impacts on the environment of activities on range and forest lands.

Two major planning directives were adopted during the 1970s; the Forest and Rangelands Renewable Resources Planning Act of 1974 and the National Forest Management Act of 1976 outlined important additions to the management-planning processes by which the Forest Service and Bureau of Land Management operated. These acts provide for long-range planning to ensure adequate supplies of resources, while at the same time maintaining environmental quality.

As is the case with other natural resources in the USA, management of wildlife did not really begin until after the Civil War. The establishment of licence requirements and creel limits, along with closed seasons for selected species, were introduced in some areas prior to the Civil War, but these were of limited effectiveness until the appropriate agencies developed the capabilities of enforcing them. In 1871 Congress set up the US Fisheries Commission, giving it the responsibility of rehabilitating depleted fisheries. By 1910 most states had fish and game regulations and had established agencies responsible for wildlife protection and replenishing fisheries. Although limited, raising game fish in hatcheries and stocking ponds, lakes, and streams was successful.

Historical Perspective

Up to the end of the 19th century, as settlers colonized the interior of the continental USA, agricultural development was rapid and extensive. While worker productivity increased as some machinery substituted for labour, the ratio of total output to total input increased little. The closure of the frontier in the early 20th century was accompanied by a gradual shift towards more intensive land use; technological development advanced rapidly and included mechanical and chemical as well as biological developments. Agricultural productivity rose dramatically, more than doubling between 1945 and 1985.

1860–1920

Between 1860 and 1920 the US population increased from 31m. to 106m. Demands for food and timber to meet the needs of the growing domestic population and European demand for exports accelerated incentives for development and expansion of agriculture. Farm output doubled during this period, as did the area of cropland, which reached 402m. acres in 1920. Feed for draught animals and livestock was the main use of crops. In 1880 corn was the largest crop, occupying one-third of the harvested area; corn, hay, oats, wheat and cotton together accounted for 85% of cropland used. The US Department of Agriculture and the Land Grant College System were established in 1862 (with the former being elevated to cabinet status in 1889). The objectives of the Department of Agriculture were mainly to collect and distribute agricultural information. Under the Land Grant College System land grants were made to each state so that colleges could be set up to teach agriculture and mechanical arts. In 1887 an act of Congress provided the colleges with funds to establish agricultural experiment stations. This research, education and extension system has played an important role in improving management systems and productivity in agriculture and forestry.

Between 1900 and 1920, in what has become known as the 'Golden Age' of US agriculture, farm income and prices held steady in comparison to the rest of the economy. Both farm population and the number of farm workers reached a peak in 1910, at 32m. and 13.6m. respectively. Crop exports averaged 25% of production, up from 10% in 1860.

1920–45

Foreign agricultural demand fell at the end of the First World War with the recovery of agriculture in Europe. Commodity prices collapsed and the period to 1940 was one of depression for agriculture. Rigid non-agricultural prices and wages led to a cost squeeze on farm incomes. In the 1920s per-head average incomes for the farm population were half those of non-farmers. Agricultural productivity increased overall between 1920 and 1945, with a particularly marked growth occurring after the Depression in response to the introduction of agricultural stabilization programmes and the increased demand which accompanied the onset of the Second World War. Farm-labour productivity and average yields per acre rose as the farm population declined and average farm size increased. One of the main contributions to increases in labour productivity was the adoption of the tractor. In addition, commercial fertilizer and lime use rose significantly. Plant and animal disease control improved and hybrid corn came into use. By 1945 total crop production was 18% above the 1929 figure and livestock production had increased by 38%.

Between 1920 and 1945 the total area of cropland remained stable at about 404m. acres. However, the location of production shifted considerably from the eastern states and the so-called 'cornbelt' of the Midwest to the northern and southern Plains states, the Mountain states and the Pacific coast. This shift was aided by a (heavily-subsidized) 50% expansion in irrigated area, to 21m. acres, and the conversion of rangeland and pasture for the production of wheat and other crops. Meanwhile the number of horses and mules on farms declined by 50%, releasing significant amounts of grassland capacity. Cows kept for dairy increased from 30m. to 41m., especially in the eastern states, while beef cattle increased from 40m. to 45m. head.

1945 TO THE PRESENT

Between 1945 and 1985 the US population increased from 133m. to 239m. Per-head income more than doubled, domestic demand for goods and services increased by a factor of more than 2.5, and agricultural exports quadrupled. However, the total amount of land available for crop, forage and forest production declined by about 5%.

Farm productivity increases during this period have no historical precedent. At a time when domestic population and food demands nearly doubled and export demands were expanding, the acreage of crops harvested fell from 354m. in 1945 to 290m. in 1969. Production per acre grew faster than demand. After 1969 a rapid expansion in world food demand reversed this downward trend and harvested acreage increased to a peak of 366m. in 1981. Export demands in the 1970s and 1980s became the single most important determinant of changes in cropland cultivated. In 1980 exports comprised 31% of total farm production, including livestock, and 39% of crop production; in 1986 they comprised 29% of crop output.

Shifts in production among the regions persisted. While the amount of cropland continued to decline in the eastern states and the southern Plains states (with some 8m. acres being lost

in the latter region between 1945 and 1985), major increases occurred in the cornbelt, with expansions in corn and soybean production. Cattle numbers on farms increased to a peak of 132m. in 1975 from 86m. in 1945. This growth came mainly from increases in the beef-cattle herd, with beef-cow numbers increasing from 16m. to 46m. head. There has been a long-term decline in milk-cow numbers, which fell by 60% between 1945 and 1975, totalling just 10.3m. in 1987. Total milk and milk-fat production during this period increased, however, due to increases in production per cow. Between 1973 and 1987 milk-cow numbers declined by 9.5%, while milk production per cow increased by 36%, from 10,119 lb to 13,786 lb. Therefore total milk production actually increased by 23%. Growth in beef production was largely in response to a growth in consumption in the period 1945 to 1976. Per-head beef consumption grew from 46 lb (retail weight) per year in the 1950–52 period to a peak of 94 lb in 1976. During this period total beef production was increasing faster than both population and per-head disposable income.

After 1976 cattle numbers started a downward trend to 105m. in January 1986, due to the continuing decline in dairy cattle and a reduction in beef-cattle numbers. This decline, which has occurred in all major regions and is particularly marked in the eastern states, reflects the decrease in per-head beef consumption from 94 lb in 1976 to 73 lb in 1987. Over the same period total per-head poultry consumption rose from 52 lb to 78 lb. This shift was associated with a sharp decline in poultry prices relative to beef prices and with growing consumer concerns about the health and nutrition aspects of red-meat consumption. Using 1967 as a base year, real retail beef prices fell by 17% between 1976 and 1985 while real retail broiler prices fell by 34%. Further declines in cattle numbers are expected, given relative prices of red and white meats, changes in the composition of the population and perhaps in preferences for red meat, and further increases in milk production per cow.

PRODUCTIVITY AND TECHNOLOGY

Productivity increases are reflected in terms of the number of people supplied per farm worker, which rose from 15 in 1945 to 77 in 1985. In 1945 less than two of these persons were supplied via exports of US goods while in 1985, 20 were supplied by exports. The number of farm workers, the total farm population and the number of farms have all declined during the post-war period: in 1982 there were 55% fewer farms than in 1945. Meanwhile the average farm size more than doubled, reaching 461 acres in 1987. Farm output doubled and, while the quality and composition of inputs changed, the quantity remained constant.

Mechanization was the main factor which caused both the reduction in farm labour and the increase in farm size. The number of tractors rose from 2.6m. in 1945 to about 4.5m. in the early 1960s, when the numbers stabilized. However, tractor horsepower kept growing as the size and capacity of farm machines increased: total horsepower was 69m. in 1947, 212m. in 1973 and 311m. in 1986. The number of grain combines grew from 465,000 in 1947 to 640,000 in 1986, while corn heads increased from 236,000 to 688,000, pickup balers from 65,000 to 798,000 and field forage harvesters from 30,000 to 281,000 over the same period.

The farm productivity index for the USA (measured in terms of output per unit of input, with the base year of 1977) rose from 55 in 1947 to 128 in 1986. The total-input index fell from 104 to 87 between 1947 and 1986. The labour-input index fell from 297 to 80 during this period, while the real-estate input index remained constant, the mechanical power and machinery input index rose from 54 to 76, the agricultural-chemicals (fertilizers, lime and pesticides) index rose from 15 to 109, and the feed, seed and livestock-purchases index increased from 51 to 102. The index of farm output for the 1947–86 period rose from 58 to 111. The livestock and livestock-product index increased from 65 to 110, with the largest adjustment for the poultry and eggs group, where the index increased from 44 to 133. The crop index rose from 56 to 109, with the largest individual increases occurring in feed grains (39 to 123) and oilseeds (22 to 110). Throughout this period farm prices declined relative to the general price level.

Numerous factors contributed to the rise in agricultural productivity. Firstly, the risk of farming was reduced because of high and stable prices brought about by commodity-support programmes, crop insurance and natural-disaster assistance. Surpluses were controlled by acreage-reduction programmes, low-cost or emergency food assistance to developing countries, and domestic food programmes. Secondly, adequate farm credit was available for equipment, operating purposes and real estate. Thirdly, there was a strong export demand throughout much of the period. The sharp rise in commodity demand in the 1970s absorbed US grain stocks accumulated in previous years and, although the world recession and the rising value of the dollar in the 1980s reduced demand for US crops, exports have subsequently continued at historically-high levels. Fourthly, new farming methods and systems were developed and combined with new technology to increase productivity. Finally, improved education and information systems brought knowledge of new technologies to farm workers. More farm managers had high school and college degrees than was previously the case.

Farming became specialized in order to capture the efficiencies of new technologies; farmers also purchased more of the inputs used in production. More recently, marketing and financial management have become important aspects of the farming system. Increasing farm size and the adoption of new technology have changed the profile of farming during the post-war period. In 1949 79% of all sales came from farms with less than $100,000 of gross sales in 1980 prices. They constituted 99% of all farms. By 1982 these farms accounted for only 31% of all sales and made up 88% of all farms.

Technological factors contributing to the doubling in crop production per acre included the development of new and improved plant varieties and of pesticides, the expanded use of agricultural chemicals, and of irrigation, the drainage of highly productive wetlands, double-cropping and the use of conservation tillage systems. The total area of irrigated croplands increased from 29.5m. acres in 1954 to 49m. in 1982. The largest growth occurred after 1969 as export demand and farm prices rose. One-half of the irrigated land is in the Mountain and Pacific states: the three top-ranking states in 1982 in terms of acreage irrigated were California (8.5m. acres), Nebraska (6m. acres) and Texas (5.7m. acres). In 1982 irrigated lands made up 13% of harvested cropland and accounted for 32% of total crop value. Corn, hay, wheat and cotton used 53% of the irrigated area and contributed 36% of irrigated crop value. In contrast, commercial vegetable and orchard crops used 11% of the irrigated area and contributed 34% of irrigated crop value.

Several factors contributed to the increase in range and beef cattle productivity. Harvested forages and cropland residue grazing increased, mainly in the eastern and Plains states. Irrigation of feed crops, hay lands and improved pastures was expanded. Advances in biochemistry such as plant hormones and herbicides for plant control, antibiotics and animal hormones and tranquillizers to increase the rate of weight gain were extensively adopted. Artificial insemination, better breeding of higher-producing animals and improvements in animal nutrition, feeds and feeding were also important.

The Structure of US Agriculture

The farm population of the USA fell from 2.9% of the total resident population in 1978 to 2.2% in 1986. The contribution of agriculture, forestry and fishing to the country's gross national product (GNP) has also declined, from 2.9% of GNP in 1970 to 2.2% in 1986. Agricultural exports have fluctuated as a share of total exports over the past two decades, reaching a peak in the early 1970s with an annual average of 21%, and accounting for only 12.6% in 1986.

FARM PROFILE

Between 1975 and 1987 the total number of farms fell from 2.5m. to under 2.2m. Over that period land in farms also fell, from 1,059m. acres to 1,002m. acres. Average farm size increased, however, from 420 acres to 461 acres. In 1987 the states with the largest area in farms were Texas (133m. acres), Montana (61m. acres) and Kansas (48m. acres). The states with the largest area used for crops were Kansas (28m. acres), North Dakota (27m. acres), and Texas (26m. acres).

The structure of farm ownership has changed dramatically during the 20th century, but has remained relatively stable since 1969. In 1900 55.8% of farms were under full operator ownership, 7.9% under part-ownership and 35.3% were occupied by tenants. By 1969 the proportion of all farms which were under full ownership had increased to 62.5% and that accounted for by part-owned farms to 24.6%, while the share of tenanted farms had decreased to only 12.9%. In 1982 farms under full ownership accounted for 59.2% of all farms: however, only 34.7% of farmland was under full ownership. Part-owned farms were 29.3% of all farms, but part-owned farmland was 53% of all farmland. The proportion of farms and farmland (taken together) under tenancy agreements was about 11.6%.

In 1980 real estate made up 79% of physical and financial assets on the farm balance sheet, up from 71% in 1972. Decreasing farmland value reduced this figure to 74% in 1986. Real-estate debt was 55% of liabilities in 1972, 54% in 1980 and 50% in 1986. In 1972 livestock and machinery (the latter including motor vehicles) each represented about 10% of total assets. Livestock fell to 6.1% of total assets in 1980 while machinery remained at about 10%. In 1986 livestock was 6.9% and machinery 11.6% of total assets.

In 1970 58.5% of farm cash receipts came from livestock and livestock products and 41.5% from crop products. By 1986 cash receipts from crop products had risen to 47.1% of total cash receipts, while the share of livestock and livestock products cash receipts had declined to 52.9%. The relative decline in livestock and livestock products during this period is attributable to the decline in cash receipts for cattle and calves from 27% of all receipts in 1970 to 21.4% in 1986. The relative importance of cash receipts for feed crops and oil-bearing crops rose over this period to total 13.2% and 7.8% respectively in 1986. The shares of crop receipts derived from food grains and cotton fell slightly to 4.4% and 2.2%, while those for vegetables and for fruit and nuts increased to 6.4% and 5.1% respectively. In 1987 the three states with the largest cash receipts from agriculture were California ($15,500m., with dairy products and cattle as leading commodities, contributing 14% and 10% of cash receipts respectively), Texas ($9,100m., with cattle contributing 50.5% and cotton 10.8%) and Iowa ($8,800m., with hogs contributing 31.2% and cattle 22.2%).

The US Department of Agriculture classifies farm size by value of gross sales. In 1987 73% of farms had gross sales with an annual value of under $40,000. They received 1.8% of net farm income and 19% of government payments, and 95% of their total cash income was made up of off-farm income. In the same year 22.4% of farms were 'middle-size' farms, with sales between $40,000 and $249,999. They received 33.6% of net farm income and 56.9% of government payments, and off-farm income represented 25% of total cash income. Large farms, or those with gross sales of $250,000 and above, constituted 4.6% of all farms and received 64.6% of net farm income and 24.1% of government payments; off-farm income was only 5.5% of total cash income. Of the large farms, those with gross sales above $500,000 annually constituted only 1% of establishments but accounted for 45% of net farm income. Overall in 1987, off-farm income accounted for 45% of total cash income available to farm operators and their households. Off-farm income was especially important in West Virginia and Tennessee and least important in Nebraska and South Dakota.

VEGETABLE CROP PRODUCTION

The most important crops in US agriculture, in terms of area harvested and value of production, are corn, wheat, soybeans and hay. Other major crops are peanuts, sunflower, cotton, edible beans, potatoes, tobacco, sugar beet and sugar-cane. While cropland used for commercial vegetables and fruits and nuts varies around only 1.5%–2% of that used for the principal crops, commercial vegetables and fruits and nuts are very important in terms of their value of production, ranking among the top 10 crops. The value of commercial production of vegetables and of fruit and nuts in 1986 amounted to $4,400m. and $8,000m. respectively, while the values of corn, soybean, hay and wheat production totalled $12,500m., $9,300m., $8,600m. and $5,000m. respectively.

Corn

Area harvested of corn for grain was 62.1m. acres in 1973, 72.9m. acres in 1980, 69.2m. in 1986 and 58.2m. in 1988, with a figure of 65m. being estimated for 1989. Corn yields have risen from 91.3 bushels* per harvested acre in 1973 to 119.4 bushels in 1987. Yields in the drought years of 1983 and 1988 were 81.1 bushels and 84.6 bushels per acre respectively. Overall corn production was 5,700m. bushels in 1973 and 8,200m. bushels in 1986; it decreased to 4,900m. bushels in 1988 as a result of the drought but was projected to recover to an annual average of 8,000m.–8,500m. bushels in the 1990s. Beginning stocks accounted for 18.6% of production in 1985, rising to 69% of production in 1987 and to 86% in 1988, as a result of the drought. Beginning corn stocks were expected to fall back to about 20% of production in the 1990s.

In addition, some corn is harvested for silage: this accounted for 9m. acres in 1973, 11.3m. in 1976, 6.3m. in 1986 and 8.3m. acres in 1988, as some of the drought-affected corn was harvested early.

Wheat

Winter wheat accounts for about 70%–75% of wheat area harvested. The rest consists mainly of other spring wheat and some durum wheat. Wheat area harvested was 54.1m. acres in 1973, 80.6m. in 1981, 60.7m. in 1986 and 53.2m. in 1988. Some winter wheat was affected by drought conditions prevailing in early 1989; the wheat area to be harvested in that year was estimated at 63m. acres. Wheat yields per harvested acre rose from 31.6 bushels in 1973 to 39.4 bushels in 1983; total wheat production rose from 1,700m. bushels in 1973 to 2,785m. bushels in 1981 before commencing an overall decline, falling to 2,100m. bushels in 1987 and to 1,800m. bushels in the 1988 drought year. It was expected to rise to about 2,600m. bushels in the 1990s. Beginning stocks were 59% of production in 1985 and 86% in 1987. After the 1988 drought wheat beginning stocks in 1989 were, at about 500m. bushels, at their lowest level in the preceding decade. They were expected to recover to about 30% of production in the 1990s.

Other Crops

Area harvested for alfalfa and all other hay has fluctuated around 60m. acres since the early 1970s. In 1988 hay area harvested increased to 65.6m. acres as harvesting of hay on some of the acres left idle under government programmes was permitted due to the drought.

Soybean area harvested was 56m. acres in 1973, 70m. acres in 1979, 58m. acres in 1986 and about 57m. acres in both 1987 and 1988. Estimates were for 60m. acres to be harvested in 1989. Soybean yields per harvested acre rose from 27.8 bushels in 1973 to 33.7 in 1987. Yields fell to 26.8 bushels in 1988, a level similar to those of other drought years. Production in 1973 was 1,500m. bushels, rising to 2,300m. bushels in 1979 and to 2,100m. in 1985 before falling to 1,500m. bushels in the 1988 drought. It was expected to recover to an annual average of 2,200m. bushels in the 1990s.

Area harvested for sorghum and barley in 1973 was 16m. acres and 10m. acres respectively. By 1986 sorghum area harvested was 14m. acres, falling to 9m. acres in the 1988 drought year. Barley area harvested was 12m. acres in 1986 and 7.5m. acres in 1988.

Cotton area harvested was about the same in 1973 and 1988, at about 11.9m. acres. During this period cotton area harvested peaked at 13.8m. acres in 1981 and reached a low of 7.3m. acres in 1983. Average cotton yields per harvested acre fluctuated around 500 lb for most of the 1970s. They increased in the mid-1980s, peaking at 702 lb in 1987 and falling to 620 lb in 1988.

Commercial vegetables and fruits and nuts are comparable to individual grains and to hogs and poultry in terms of cash receipts from marketing and value of production. They are produced mainly in the western states of California, Washington and Oregon, in the Midwest states of Wisconsin, Michigan and Minnesota, and on the east coast in Florida and New York.

* A bushel is equal to 56 lb (25.4 kg) for corn and sorghum; 60 lb (27.2 kg) for wheat and soybeans; 32 lb (14.5 kg) for oats; 48 lb (21.8 kg) for barley.

The USA is a leading producer of major crops. In 1985 it was the world's third-largest producer of wheat, after the USSR and the People's Republic of China, producing 13.2% of global output. In the same year it was the largest producer of corn and soybeans, with respectively 46.4% and 58.9% of world production, and was also the second-largest producer of cotton after China, with 16.9% of world production.

LIVESTOCK PRODUCTION

The relative importance of the different sectors of the livestock industry has changed over the past two decades. While beef remains the major meat produced in the USA, it has been losing ground to poultry. Between 1973 and 1986 cattle and calf production fell from 44,200m. lb (live weight) to 40,500m. lb. Hog production totalled 20,100m. lb (live weight) in 1973, increased to 23,400m. lb in 1980 and fell to 19,400m. lb in 1986. Chicken and turkey production almost doubled over this period, increasing from 11,200m. lb to 20,700m. lb and from 2,500m. lb to 4,100m. lb respectively. The total number of eggs produced rose from 66,000m. to 68,300m. between 1973 and 1986, while total output of milk rose continuously, from 115,500m. lb in 1973 to 143,400m. lb in 1986.

While livestock and poultry are produced in all states, most production occurs near major forage or grain sources. In 1984 40% of livestock and poultry production occurred in the Plains states, 25% in the 'cornbelt', 17% in the western states and 13% in the southern states. Extensive beef-cattle production is the principal activity in the western USA, which accounted for about 17% of livestock production in 1984. More than 90% of farms with beef cows have less than 100 cows and only 16% of beef cows are in herds numbering more than 500 in total. Farm feedlots and marketings fell from 11m. in 1970 to 4m. in 1984. This decline has been offset by the increased marketings from large commercial feedlots, which increased by 5m. head during this period. Commercial feedlots have led in the implementation of new technology to improve feed efficiency, cross-breeding and changes in weight and type of cattle placed on feed. Partnerships are an important form of organization in commercial feedlots, while farm feedlots are characterized by individual ownership. Concentration in the slaughter and processing of beef has increased, with 62% of cattle being slaughtered by the top 20 firms in 1982, up from 52% in 1972. Compared with other sectors of the livestock industry (see below) there has been very little vertical integration by processing firms, which accounted for less than 0.1% of production in 1980.

In 1980 about 60% of hogs were produced in 'farrow-to-finish' operations. Hog production is characterized by small enterprises operated in conjunction with feed-grain production and some cow-, calf- and cattle-feeding enterprises. Only 7% of hog enterprises sell more than 1,000 hogs annually, but they account for more than 50% of sales. In 1984 about 85% of hog production took place in the 'cornbelt' and northern Plains states, with the rest occurring in the south-eastern region. Vertical integration of hog production by the processing firms measured about 4% in 1980.

Broiler production is heavily concentrated in the South, which also accounts for about 40% of turkey production. Heavy domination by a small number of vertically-integrated firms has developed in the poultry industry since the mid-1960s. Slaughterers and processors control the quality and quantity of birds arriving at the market. While quality improvements have made poultry more appealing to the consumer, the cost efficiencies associated with vertical integration have made broiler and turkey very low-cost meats. Real prices of poultry products have fallen by more than 75% since 1950, while per-head consumption of poultry more than doubled between 1940 and 1982. Integrated production by slaughter firms was about 99% for broilers and 90% for turkeys in 1980. Integration in the broiler and turkey industries is mainly in the form of contracts between the producer and the slaughter firm, followed by ownership of the birds by the integrator. Between 1972 and 1982 the proportions of broilers and turkeys slaughtered by the top 20 firms rose from 43% to 69% and from 72% to 87% respectively. More than half of broiler and turkey processing takes place in enterprises owned by the top eight firms. The number of broilers and turkeys produced increased by 45% and by 37% respectively between 1975 and 1984. The poultry industry is expected to continue growing, as real prices should remain low relative to other meats and as consumer tastes continue shifting to white meats. Real retail beef and pork prices in 1984 were 20% below 1960 levels, while broiler-meat prices were 51% lower.

Between 1964 and 1984 total consumption of animal products increased by about 45%. However, animal products lost some of their share of consumption to crop products, mainly through declines in the share of milk products and eggs. Per-head beef consumption has been declining since 1976, when it reached its highest level of 93.3 lb (retail weight). In 1987, for the first time, per-head consumption of poultry (77.8 lb retail weight) was greater than that of beef (73.4 lb). In the same year per-head chicken-meat consumption, at 62.7 lb, overtook pork consumption (59.2 lb).

FOREIGN TRADE

During the 1970s and 1980s the USA has been a net exporter of agricultural commodities. Net agricultural exports increased during the 1970s, but decreased between 1982 and 1986 as the value of agricultural exports fell and that of agricultural imports rose. The value of agricultural imports was 47% of the value of agricultural exports in 1983 and 79% in 1986. Net agricultural exports recovered somewhat in 1987 as exports rose and imports fell slightly, to 74% of agricultural exports by value.

Agricultural imports in the 1980s did not grow at the same pace as imports of all commodities. In 1983 agricultural imports were 6.6% of all imports while in 1987 they were 5.3%. During the 1980s imports of animals and animal products and of 'non-competitive', mainly tropical, commodities grew at the expense of vegetable-product imports. In 1987 animal and animal-product imports constituted 24.5% of total imports, while vegetable products accounted for 42.7% and non-competitive imports 32.8%.

The most important agricultural imports are coffee, meat and meat products, dairy products, fruits and preparations, vegetables and preparations, sugar and related products, wine and malt beverages, grains and feeds, and unmanufactured tobacco. The quantity indexes for US agricultural imports indicate that between 1976 and 1987 grains and feeds imports grew the most, followed by wool, unmanufactured tobacco and meat and meat products. Over this period the quantity of sugar-cane or -beet imports declined while that of vegetable-oil and oilseeds imports remained stable.

Trade in livestock products is small compared to domestic production and consumption. However, beef imports have grown since the early 1960s and pork and hog imports have risen sharply in the 1980s. Poultry exports have also risen in the past few years. Net beef imports in 1961 supplied 6% of consumption; they rose to 7.9% of consumption in 1980 before declining to 6.7% in 1985. In addition, imports of live cattle and feeder calves in 1985 were equivalent to 2% of total cattle slaughterings.

Net pork imports supplied about 1% of consumption in both 1961 and 1980. They rose sharply to 5.9% of consumption in 1985. Net imports of live hogs in 1985 were equivalent to 1.3% of consumption. Poultry exports in the past have averaged about 3% of production; they rose to 7% of production in 1980 and fell to 4% in 1985. Dairy products, mainly cheese, are also imported, especially from Western Europe.

Agricultural exports are an important factor in determining the well-being of US agriculture and constitute a major component of demand, especially in the case of crops. The harvested crop area required for exports rose during the 1970s, from 24.6% of total crop area harvested in 1970 to 38.9% in 1980. It fell to 29% in 1986 and rose to 35.5% in 1987. Of the principal crops, 54.8% of wheat production was exported in 1970, 63.6% in 1980 and 49.1% in 1986. Soybean production for export rose to account for 40.3% of production in 1980 from 38.5% in 1970.

Food and feed grains, and oilseeds and associated products are the major agricultural commodities exported by the USA. The share of total agricultural export value made up by food and feed grains rose to 46.4% in 1980, with corn and wheat making up 23.8% and 16.2% respectively. The share of food and feed grains fell to 33.1% in 1986, with corn and wheat

contributing about 12% each. The share of oilseeds has fluctuated from 26.6% in 1970 to 22.8% in 1980 and 24.8% in 1986; that of animal and animal-product exports was 11.9% in 1970, 9.1% in 1980 and 17.3% in 1986. Cotton, fruits, vegetables and nuts exports made up 4.6%, 5%, 4.2% and 2.9% respectively of total agricultural-commodity export value in 1986. Fruits, vegetables and nuts, both fresh and in preparations, are becoming increasingly important exports.

The quantity index for US agricultural exports (with a base year of 1977) gives an indication of export growth in different commodities. The total agricultural export index grew from 97 to 143 between 1976 and 1980; it fell to a low of 103 in 1986 and rose to 118 in 1987. The animal and animal-products index rose consistently between 1976 and 1987 from 91 to 137. Dairy products and poultry and poultry products were the fastest-growing agricultural exports over this period; their export indexes grew from 76 to 515 and from 76 to 188 respectively. The animal-fats export index increased slightly and the meat and meat-products index rose by 45.6%, to 134.

The crop commodity-export indexes fluctuated greatly between 1976 and 1987. Generally, they tended to rise in the early 1980s, then fall to their lowest levels in 1986 and rise again in 1987. The grains and feeds export index rose 43% between 1976 and 1981; it fell below its 1976 level in 1986, then rose to 110 in 1987. The vegetable-oils and oilseeds export index rose from 92 in 1976 to 149 in 1982, and stood at 126 in 1987. The fruit and vegetables export index rose from 104 in 1976 to 159 in 1981, and fell to 111 in 1986 before rising to 127 in 1987. The unmanufactured-tobacco export index fell from 93 to 79 between 1976 and 1987. The cotton export index rose from 74 in 1976 to 193 in 1980, fell to 49 in 1986 and then rose to 126 in 1987.

The USA is an important trader of agricultural commodities. In the 1985/86 crop year the US share of world wheat trade was 29%. This share rose to 40.2% in 1988/89 and was expected to remain at about 40% in the early 1990s. The USA's share of world corn trade was 58% in 1985/86 and 80% in 1988/89, while its share of world soybean trade fell from 77% in the 1985/86 crop year to 61% in 1988/89. The USA also has significant shares of the world markets for cotton, oilseeds and products, fruits and vegetables, and animals and animal products.

Forest Resources

Between the time of settlement and 1920 the forested area of the 48 conterminous states was reduced from about 850m. acres to less than 570m. acres, with the most rapid clearing occurring between 1900 and 1920. With this clearing and other cutting of forests, the standing commercial saw-timber inventory declined from 7,500,000m. board feet to around 2,000,000m. board feet, and continued to decline after 1920. However, because of the regrowth of forests after cutting, net annual growth increased from zero in 1800 to 5,000m. cubic feet by 1920.

The declining timber inventory, reduction of forest area, and concern over water supplies has led to increased management of forestlands. Congress authorized a federal forest agent within the Department of Agriculture in 1876. The Division of Forestry was formed in 1886, becoming the Bureau of Forestry in 1887. Forest reserves were established in 1891 and were transferred to the Department of Agriculture in 1905. At the same time the Bureau of Forestry was renamed the Forest Service. Two years later the forest reserves were renamed the national forests, emphasizing that the forests were to be managed for the use of all US citizens.

In 1885 the states of California, New York, Colorado and Ohio established state forestry programmes. These agencies were small but signalled an awakening realization that government had a responsibility to manage public lands more actively. At the same time a growing conservation movement was emerging: efforts of various interests prompted reservation of public lands, legislation and programmes for resource protection and management, and the regulation of hunting, parklands, natural monuments and historic sites. This movement, coupled with the establishment of the federal and state forestry agencies, slowed the conversion of public lands and the utilization of resources and helped reverse the deterioration in resource conditions and productivity.

The softwood saw-timber inventory of the USA has been fairly steady since the mid-1940s at about 2,000,000m. board feet. Over the same period the hardwood inventory has risen from 400,000m. to 600,000m. board feet. The current timber volume is about one-third the volume in the USA at the time of settlement. About one-half of the decline in volume was a result of forestland conversion to cropland and other uses; the remainder resulted from the harvest of old-growth timber and the subsequent reforestation with more vigorous growing stock.

While the total volume of timber has been growing slowly in the post-war period, the timber area has been declining steadily. In 1962 the USA had 759m. acres of forests, but this area had declined to 737m. acres by 1977 and to 728m. acres by 1987. While more than one-half of the area reduction took place in the northern USA, large areas of forestland were also converted in the south of the country; however, the western USA (taken as a region) has actually experienced an increase in forest area since the 1960s.

Despite the declines in forest area in both the North and the South, commercial saw-timber volume has increased since 1970; in that year commercial timberland totalled 496m. acres, but by 1987 the area had decreased to 483m. acres. All the decrease was in the North, with the South actually gaining 3m. acres of timberland. Timber growth has outpaced timber harvest in both regions due to plantings, improved stand-management practices and more productive second-growth timber. In the West, on the other hand, commercial saw-timber volumes have declined during the same period, even with a slight increase in forest area and stability in the commercial-timberland area. The reason for this seemingly paradoxical situation was that remaining old-growth softwood timber had been harvested, reducing the inventory more rapidly than young growing stock could achieve commercial size.

The replacement of old-growth forests with more vigorous second-growth ones has resulted in an increase in growth rates of the US growing stock of timber. In 1970 new timber growth totalled 18,600m. cubic feet, of which 10,700m. cubic feet was softwood and 7,900m. cubic feet was hardwood. By 1987 growth had increased to 22,400m. cubic feet a year, softwoods comprising 12,700m. cubic feet and hardwoods 9,700m. cubic feet. Of the 1987 increase in growing stock the South accounted for 10,400m. cubic feet (or more than 45%), with 28% growing in the West and the remaining 25% in the North.

Although forestland conversion to other uses is likely to continue, it will probably be slowed somewhat. The spread of urban areas will continue, but conversion of timber to agricultural land will slow, at least temporarily. Excess supply capacity for crops and fairly low agricultural land values provide little incentive to clear more forestland.

The objectives of the Conservation Reserve Program (CRP), authorized by the Food Security Act of 1985, were in part met by paying farmers to establish and maintain a permanent cover of trees or wildlife plantings on highly erodible cropland. One of the goals of this programme was to have 12.5% of the total CRP acreage forested. In the South more than 90% of the enrolled acreage has been planted in trees. This land is eligible to be brought back into production 10 years from the date of enrolment, which process began in 1986. It is hoped that much of this land will be left in trees, adding to the already-expanding timber growing-stock levels.

Removals of timber, from harvesting, cutting during cultural operations and land clearing, have also been on the rise. In 1970 14,000m. cubic feet of timber was cut from the USA's forests; by 1987 this volume had risen to 17,000m. cubic feet, with increased volumes of both hardwood and softwood timber. The increase in timber-cutting was a result of a general expansion of the forest-products industries. Employment in logging and wood-products industries increased from 646,000 nationally in 1970 to 711,000 in 1986. The contribution of forest-products industries to gross national product was $21,600m. in 1986.

Demand for forest products in the USA has been increasing at a faster rate than timber production and harvest. Domestic utilization of construction materials, furniture, and paper products has grown, and exports of softwood logs (primarily to Japan) have increased. This category of demand is constrained, however, by federal regulations which prohibit the export of more than 350m. board feet of logs harvested from federal lands annually. While 13,700m. cubic feet of industrial forest products were produced in 1986, US consumers used 15,800m. cubic feet, necessitating net imports of forest products totalling more than 2,000m. cubic feet, most of which came from Canada.

Since the mid-1970s fuelwood use in the USA has increased from around 600m. to more than 4,000m. cubic feet as a result of the development of alternative energy sources. Adding this to industrial use brings total domestic use of woods in 1986 to 19,900m. cubic feet. Use will increase as the population increases, and the USA will continue to be a net importer of forest products in the future. However, this consumption level of 19,900m. cubic feet is still below the 22,400m. cubic feet of annual timber growth occurring in US forests. With increasing improvements in forest-management practices, a slowing of forest clearing and increased planting of rapidly-growing trees timber production is likely to stay ahead of use, and US forests can remain at sustainable levels, or even expand, into the 21st century.

Grasslands

At the time of settlement in the early 1600s vast grasslands existed in the area of the modern 48 conterminous states of the USA. These grasslands included virtually all of the Great Plains, much of the semi-arid Great Basin area between the Rockies and the Sierra Nevada, the arid south-west and the central and coastal valleys along the Pacific coast. As the USA grew in extent, many of these native grasslands were ploughed and planted with crops. Even in the semi-arid and arid west, irrigation has allowed tilling of some of these grasslands. Nevertheless, these lands have also made important contributions to the livestock industry.

Today the Forest Service and Bureau of Land Management still manage millions of acres of range. On privately-held areas urbanization and increased cropping continue to reduce grasslands. In 1959 there were 633m. acres (just under 1m. square miles) of natural grasslands left in the USA. By 1969 the area had been reduced to 604m. acres, and by 1978 to 587m. acres, as agricultural cropland expanded rapidly in the 1970s. By 1982, however, some land had reverted to grassland. With the CRP, much of the highly erodible land has been planted with permanent grass cover, and it is possible that, after the 10-year retirement period, some of this land will be left in grass. Although some land is being returned to grass, native species of grass will not return in many cases as different species are planted or native ones have difficulty competing against introduced species.

Currently, more than 90% of public grazing lands are in the 11 western states. Although the cattle industry does not rely heavily on public grazing lands on a national level, some 16% of cattle operations in the West are dependent on grazing on these lands. Continued management of these lands, with goals of improvement of range conditions and forage quality, will remain an important public service in the future.

Fisheries

Fish are no longer spawned and raised outside their natural habitat exclusively by government agencies. Because of the increasing importance of fish in the average US diet and a preference for certain species, such as trout and catfish, private individuals have also begun to produce fish. In 1970 5.7m. lb of catfish were raised on farms; by 1987 catfish production on farms had increased to about 50 times the 1970 level, to 280m. lb.

Commercial fishing has also expanded during this period. In 1970 there were just over 87,000 commercial fishing craft operating in the USA and its ocean waters; by 1986 this number had increased to 128,000. Employment in the fishing industry, including processors and wholesalers, increased from 227,000 to 347,000 over the same period.

Per-head consumption of fish and shellfish increased from 11.8 lb annually to 15.4 lb between 1970 and 1987. This implies increased pressure on both freshwater and marine fisheries. While the effects of harvest, pollution and habitat change can be evaluated to a certain extent on the freshwater fisheries, it is more difficult to assess the marine fisheries. There is, however, little doubt that fish are not as abundant in the major fishing grounds of North America as they were in the past.

Conclusion

The above description of US agriculture has documented significant changes in the current century. Specialization, the adoption of more capital-intensive methods and a changing policy institutional structure have shaped US agriculture; it remains highly dependent on international markets; and there are increased concerns about environmental impacts of the technologies which have been responsible for the rapid growth in productivity. As policies evolve for trade and environmental issues, the trends observed for US agriculture may be significantly altered. Multilateral trade negotiations, which may lead to reductions in trade barriers, and policies that have more neutral impacts on agricultural output are the two policy areas that are likely to influence the future course of US agriculture, along with the emergence of environmental legislation.

EXTRACTIVE INDUSTRIES IN THE USA

RICHARD GOODENOUGH

Energy Resources

Few policy-making problems in the economic sphere are so complex and beset by so many uncertainties as those related to energy. Moreover, decisions on energy policy have repercussions for broader social, economic, political and environmental issues. The USA is both incomparably rich in energy resources and a major consumer, and thus has been at the forefront of recent adjustments in response to a less favourable world energy market. In 1960, at a time when comparatively little thought was given to the planning, management or conservation of these finite resources, the USA consumed about 40% of world energy supplies; by 1985 this proportion had declined to just under 25%, while the country's production of primary energy was equivalent to 21% of the global total.

Since 1973, when an embargo on petroleum exports to the USA was imposed by Arab oil-producing nations following the outbreak of the Arab–Israeli war, the US energy industry has been forced to react to several unsettling trends, including price increases, shrinking product markets, energy-price controls, special energy taxes and economic recessions caused by world-wide energy crises. Annual US production of energy increased by 50% between 1960 and 1973, but by only 4% between 1973 and 1986, while annual consumption increased by 70% during the earlier period but by only 0.5% during the latter. In July 1986 US oil prices plummeted to a low of $9.39 per barrel as a result of external forces, including the efforts of the Organization of Petroleum Exporting Countries (OPEC) to defend its market share by increasing sales through price-cutting. Consequently oil and gas production revenues and income fell sharply, and exploration and development activities in the USA fell into a deep recession. Energy companies have also had to react to internal fluctuations in production and consumption. Between July 1987 and July 1988 total US energy production increased by 2.8%, but this figure conceals differences in production for the individual sectors of petroleum (−1.9%), natural gas (+3.8%), coal (+3.6%) and 'other' (+10.7%). The category of 'other' includes hydroelectric, nuclear, geothermal and solar thermal energy. Over the same period petroleum consumption decreased by 3.3%.

COAL

Structural Changes

The corporate composition of the US coal industry has undergone a number of substantial changes in the last decade. The sharp rise in world oil prices since the early 1970s has caused electric utilities to secure long-term coal supplies and has also encouraged the diversification of oil and gas companies into coal production, usually through acquisition of existing coal companies. Western US coal reserves, with their low sulphur content, have been in great demand following the implementation of increasingly stringent environmental regulations. Finally, an escalation of merger activity within the coal industry has raised concerns about the domination of the industry by a few large companies. In 1976 52 'major' producers (i.e. companies producing 3m. short tons or more a year) accounted for 64% of US production. By 1986 the largest 52 companies accounted for 74% of total production.

This trend towards concentration is explained by the need for utilities to secure a large volume of long-term supplies for coal-fired plants. This is particularly significant in relation to thick-seamed western coal reserves, where production has been consolidated by the development of large surface mines. At the same time, falling coal prices have resulted in the closing of many marginal mines and the exit of many small producers. Between 1976 and 1986 the number of mines producing bituminous coal and lignite fell by 32%, from 6,161 to 4,203, while rationalization resulted in a doubling of average production per mine, to 211,000 short tons a year, and productivity increased from 1.8 short tons per miner in 1976 to 3 short tons in 1986.

Regional Production and Concentration

During the last decade changes in coal production have had different effects on each of the three main producing regions of Appalachia, the interior and the West. Appalachia is the most important producing region, accounting for 48% of US production in 1986. It is also the most diverse in terms of variety of coals, and methods and scale of production. Coals are predominantly bituminous, while showing a wide range of sulphur content. Almost two-thirds of the coal is produced from underground mines, although there is extensive strip mining. The region includes some of the nation's largest producers as well as hundreds of small producers. Appalachia remains the principal source of coal used in the metallurgical industry, although this sector of the market declined from 85m. short tons in 1976 to 36m. short tons in 1986—largely because of a slump in the domestic steel industry, increased steel imports and an increase in the importance of some steelmaking processes, such as the electric arc, which require less coke. The region's largest producer is Consolidation Coal, whose production fluctuated in the early 1980s, partly because of marketing problems caused by environmental-protection regulations. However, the acquisition of new mines in 1986 and 1987 has increased production substantially.

The interior region contains those Midwestern states which produce high-sulphur bituminous coal for shipment to electric utilities. Demand has been seriously affected by environmental regulations requiring either the installation of costly stack gas scrubbers or a switch to low-sulphur coal. This impact has been mitigated by recent Clean Air Acts which require all new plants everywhere to use scrubbers, irrespective of sulphur content. In 1986 some 67% of production in the interior region was from surface mines, but depletion of surface deposits and stricter surface-mining regulations, particularly in Kentucky, have attracted more attention towards underground mining. Texas is a major producer of lignite coals, which have a low calorific value and a high moisture content. Production of Texan lignite increased by 66% between 1980 and 1986, while production for the rest of the interior region increased by less than 1% over the same period. Newly-established companies in Texas have been subsidiaries of electric companies seeking lignite to serve power plants close to the mines.

Coal deposits in the western region are mostly situated on federal, Indian or railroad lands. The coal is typically produced from very thick seams, often 40–70 ft (12–21 m) thick, by a few major companies using large-scale mining equipment. Virtually all coal is used by electric utilities at mine-mouth plants. Growth in production in this region has been rapid, increasing from 110m. short tons in 1976 to 265m. short tons in 1986, partly as a result of the entry of several oil and gas companies into the coal industry. Three of the region's top eight producers in 1986 were oil companies (Atlantic Richfield, Exxon and Kerr–McGee). This illustrates the long-term national trend towards increasing participation of oil and gas companies in the coal industry, while independent coal and steel companies have declined in importance.

Outlook

Foreign companies have come to account for an increasing share of US coal production. In 1986 well over 6% of US production was controlled by six companies in which foreign ownership held more than 50% of stock. On the other hand, major US producers have increased their share in foreign coal production in such countries as Australia, Canada (British Columbia), Colombia, the People's Republic of China, Indonesia and Venezuela. The coal industry is therefore becoming increasingly international in scope.

US coal production reached its highest-ever monthly total of 91m. short tons in August 1988. Future production is likely to be influenced by several adverse factors. Legislation aiming to curb the phenomenon of 'acid rain' is causing major coal producers to establish positions in low-sulphur coal markets after experiencing difficulties in marketing high-sulphur coals. Thus large electric utilities are likely to continue to increase their share of coal production, particularly from western fields. This will be accompanied by a decline in production by steel companies because of decreasing coking-coal consumption. Secondly, changes in coal production and consumption will be strongly influenced by prices of alternative fuels for steam-electric utility plants. The significance of this is underlined by the fact that electric utilities account for about 85% of total domestic coal consumption. Finally, increased transportation costs, more vigorous enforcement of surface-mining regulations, increased productivity from underground mines and the depletion of strippable Appalachian reserves are all factors encouraging the shift in the economies and location of coal production back to the developed, underground operations in the east and Midwest.

PETROLEUM AND NATURAL GAS

Production, Productivity and Consumption

The US oil industry is frequently required to respond to sudden and unpredictable fluctuations in price, often as a result of excess of world production and uncertainty in world oil markets. Thus, after several price rises brought crude oil to a peak in 1981, oil prices in the USA began to fall, plummeting from $26.75 per barrel in 1985 to $9.39 per barrel in July 1986, bringing with the collapse the worst financial performance by the US petroleum industry in recent memory. The reduction in oil prices is reflected in the retail prices of petroleum products. For example, the average annual price of unleaded petrol declined from $1.20 per gallon in 1985 to $0.93 in 1986, while that of residential heating oil fell from $1.05 per gallon to $0.84 over the same period. However, the demand for petroleum, petroleum products and natural gas is relatively inelastic in the short term. As a consequence the fall in prices was not compensated by an increase in consumption and the burden of lower prices fell directly on revenue and income.

Of the total US production, 86% comes from onshore wells. The 623,000 producing wells attained an average productivity of 14 barrels per day (b/d) per well in 1986, the same level as the previous year but significantly below the peak productivity of over 18 b/d attained in 1972. Throughout the 1950s and 1960s production capacity in the USA exceeded demand to

such an extent that an import ceiling was introduced to protect domestic production. By the 1970s demand had increased and production neared 100% capacity. Significant increases in Alaskan production at the end of the decade and throughout the 1980s counteracted declines in other oil-producing states. In 1986 Alaska was producing an average of 1,865,000 b/d (compared with 173,000 in 1976), with Texas producing 2,300,000 b/d, Louisiana 1,402,000 b/d and California 1,114,000 b/d. In terms of the consumption of petroleum products, motor gasoline has consistently accounted for the largest share, reaching 40% during the 1970s, but growth in demand has slowed more recently due to greater efficiencies in the use of motor fuel. This is highlighted by the fact that from 1976 to 1986 the average fuel consumed per car in the USA declined from 723 gallons a year to 515.

In response to the severe oil disruptions of the early 1970s the US government established a Strategic Petroleum Reserve (SPR) which was intended to minimize the effects of any future disruptions. The SPR began storing crude oil in 1977 and by the end of 1986 held 512m. barrels, equivalent to about 100 days of net petroleum imports required in the event of a disruption in supplies. US dependence on petroleum imports remains high, reaching a peak of nearly 9m. b/d in 1977. This figure has since fluctuated, but the average figure over the first eight months of 1988 remained at 7m. b/d. Mexico, for some years the major supplier, was overtaken in 1986 by Venezuela, Canada and Saudi Arabia.

The 1986 fall in crude-oil prices referred to earlier in this section triggered declines in the prices of other fossil fuels, notably natural gas. Texas, Louisiana and Oklahoma are the primary producers, together accounting for almost 77% of total US production in 1986. Most withdrawals come from onshore wells, with some also from state and federal offshore sources. In order to meet peak demands for natural gas, seasonal, and even daily, fluctuations are met by withdrawals from storage. When demand is low, natural gas is injected into storage. Throughout the 1950s and 1960s the market was buoyant and expanding, but in 1973 uncertainties about supply coupled with rising energy prices began to erode demand. By the 1980s the situation was serious enough to cause curtailment of production in some areas, with the decline in demand being most severe in the industrial and electricity-generating sectors. Historically, Canada has been the major supplier of US natural-gas imports, together with Mexico and, more recently, Indonesia and Algeria. In 1986, however, Canada supplied virtually all imports.

Exploration for oil and natural gas is closely tied to market conditions, particularly to the price of crude oil. When market prices rise, as in 1974, the number of seismic crews, rotary rigs for drilling and exploratory well completions also increases. Further price rises in 1981 and 1982 sent these indicators to record levels, but subsequently there have been drastic cutbacks in exploration. Although the USA has potential crude-oil reserves of about 300,000m. barrels, much of this lies in small, scattered fields. Tapping this potential will require extensive drilling and expensive recovery techniques, thus making the USA a high-cost producer.

Outlook

The world's principal reserves of low-cost oil remain concentrated in the OPEC nations. Moreover, 80% of the OPEC reserves are concentrated in six of its 13 member states: Iran, Iraq, Kuwait, Libya, Saudi Arabia and the United Arab Emirates. This pivotal position is unlikely to change, and therefore OPEC will continue to dominate the world market for some time. The issue for the USA and other non-OPEC oil-producing nations is whether OPEC can and will use its position to influence oil price and supply.

Apart from such external influences, the prospects for oil and gas depend on the rate of economic growth, the availability of alternatives and the rate of improvement in energy efficiency, all of which are highly interdependent and uncertain. The rate of economic growth in the USA to 1992 is expected to be moderate and to restrain US demand for energy. The prices of all forms of primary energy are also likely to increase progressively. By 1992 the well-head price of US-produced crude oil could be similar to the pre-collapse levels of 1985.

Total US energy consumption is expected to grow two to three times more rapidly than production between 1987 and 1992, and energy import requirements will consequently increase sharply.

How much oil will come from the Outer Continental Shelf (OCS) rather than the continental land area remains a controversial subject in both environmental and political terms. In 1981 the Geological Survey estimated that 32% of the still-undiscovered domestic oil resources and 27% of undiscovered gas resources are located in the OCS. Apart from Alaska, with its severe environmental difficulties, OCS leasing has attracted great interest in the Santa Monica Basin, off California, and the Georges Bank, off Newfoundland. With one-third of the continental land area and all the OCS in the public domain, the federal government is critical in dictating access to remaining reserves.

ALTERNATIVE ENERGY SOURCES

Nuclear

At the beginning of 1987 there were 100 operable nuclear reactors in the USA, producing over 15% of generated electricity. The distribution of units shows a concentration in the east and Midwest, with Illinois alone having 9 operable units and a further 6 in start-up, under construction or on order. The nuclear-energy resource has provoked great technical controversy and political debate, with public opinion swinging against further construction in the 1980s because of concern over disposal of radioactive waste, thermal pollution and the siting of nuclear plants. There is a lack of confidence surrounding the performance of nuclear plants, particularly following the potentially-disastrous nuclear breakdown in the Three Mile Island plant near Harrisburg, Pennsylvania in March 1979.

A sluggish demand for electricity, an adverse economic climate and environmental concern have had a negative effect on the uranium industry. Historically the domestic uranium industry has faced competition from importers of low-cost uranium oxide (U_3O_8). In 1960 net imports actually exceeded domestic production, and although the Atomic Energy Commission responded to this situation in 1966 by effectively suspending imports through curtailing enrichment services for foreign uranium, domestic production remained low until the mid-1970s. Peak production of 43.7m. lb (19.8m. kg) was reached in 1980 but by 1986 output had fallen drastically, to 13.2m. lb (6.0m. kg). Because of the continuing availability of low-cost uranium imports, lower-than-expected demand and the fact that no order has been placed for a nuclear reactor in almost a decade, nuclear-fuel operations continue to be a relatively unprofitable investment for energy companies.

Synthetic fuels

Synthetic fuels are those that have been derived from the conversion of carbon-containing raw materials such as coal, tar sands and oil shale to produce petroleum or gas. The great expectations for synthetic fuel in the late 1970s have faded sharply as one after another 'synfuel' project has been cancelled or deferred. Since 1982 the industry has virtually collapsed because of depressed oil prices and the elimination of subsidies from the Synthetic Fuels Corporation (SFC). This organization was established in 1980 and was to terminate operations in 1997 'but in no event prior to 1992'. Despite this executive order of the president, the corporation ceased to exist in 1986, and with it the potential benefits of a healthy coal-conversion industry. The final project to be sponsored was the Unocal shale-oil mine complex in Parachute, Colorado, which began trucking synthetic crude oil to its pipeline terminal in Lisbon, Utah, in December 1986. Gasification or liquefaction of coal to oil has thus been a short-lived idea and one which will be resurrected with great difficulty, even if the cost of petroleum fuels rise and that of converted coal declines.

Geothermal energy

Geothermal energy is a highly-localized resource which lies deep underground and often in remote locations. Unocal, the world's largest geothermal-energy producer, continues to increase production at geysers in northern California. In addition, the company acquired full ownership of the Salton Sea geothermal reservoir, in the south of the state, in 1987 and a subsidiary began development work on two power plants that were to run on geothermal steam. Chevron similarly expanded investment in 1986 when the company completed a project in Beowawe, Nevada, by purchasing geothermal assets valued at $27m. from Phillips Petroleum. Research and development funding has declined in recent years, suggesting that the optimistic estimates of the future for this resource are not justified by current scientific evaluation.

Hydroelectric power

Hydroelectric power generation reached a peak of 332,000m. kilowatt-hours (kWh) in 1983 but fell back to 250,000m. kWh in 1987. This represents about 10% of US energy generated by electric utilities. Sites are irregularly distributed according to the nature of storage capacity and precipitation levels. Major dams are located in the West: these include those at Glen Canyon, Lake Mead, Shasta, Garrison, Fort Peck and Grand Coulee (which is probably the largest hydro station in the world). Once construction costs are amortized, electricity production becomes economic, but there is environmental concern that ecological costs are too high to justify additional large-scale construction. Concerns focus on the disturbance of silting regimes of rivers, damage to wildlife and groundwater reserves and the destruction of 'wild' rivers, much valued by outdoor recreation enthusiasts. The Pacific census division, which incorporates the states of Alaska, California, Hawaii, Oregon and Washington, has well over one-half of the nation's developed installed capacity of water power and also leads in terms of estimated undeveloped capacity. However, there is considerable feeling that hydro power has already been over-developed.

Other alternative energy sources include solar energy, wind power, tidal power, biomass and ocean thermal-energy conversion. Solar energy probably has the greatest potential for large-scale harnessing. California occupies a fortunate position in relation to solar radiation and the amount of undeveloped land in favourable locations such as the Mojave Desert, the site of the nation's first solar electric plant, opened in 1980. The negative environmental impacts of such schemes are mild in comparison with fossil-fuel and nuclear-power plants, but their success depends on the right economic and political incentives.

CONCLUSION

The energy-resource question is one which is central to the economic growth and urbanization process in the USA. Whatever decisions are made will affect long-established economic, social and political structures. Sudden changes in OPEC production policies and rates of economic growth will force adjustments to an uncertain, fluctuating situation.

On the domestic energy scene, national policy, however vaguely defined, will continue to generate regional conflict. US energy resources of oil, natural gas, coal, uranium, geothermal, hydro and solar power are primarily western energy resources which energy-poor regions regard with envy. The basis of long-standing conflict of interests lies between the producer and consumer states. These contrasts in energy endowment are reflected in the uneven burden of energy costs, with the Northeast and North–Central regions facing considerably higher prices than the South and West. Rates paid in the Northeast for electricity are about 85% higher on average than in the West, where cheap hydroelectric power holds down the average costs. Average energy prices for residential consumption rose by 219% in the USA between 1970 and 1980, with the percentage increase in the Northeast being 263% compared to 193% in the South. Today's winners, however, may well turn out to be tomorrow's losers. Some states, such as Washington and Idaho, have kept energy prices down because of the large hydroelectric power components, but as new non-hydro capacity is brought into production (such as through the establishment of new nuclear-power plants) so costs will rise dramatically, changing the regional differentials and conflicts which they generate.

Apart from variations in energy costs, energy has a significance to states through the collection of severance taxes which are imposed on the removal of natural resources. They are a major source of state revenue and play an important role in the location and profitability of production, since 90% of all severance-tax payments are for the removal of energy resources. The regional importance of these taxes has altered dramatically in recent decades, increasing tenfold between 1972 and 1982 to a peak of $7,800m. (5% of all state tax revenue) in response to a rapid increase in energy prices, particularly those of crude oil and natural gas. In subsequent years this trend has been reversed because of a decrease in production caused by falling oil prices. Severance taxes decreased by 30% between 1986 and 1987, forcing states to respond to falling revenue by either finding alternative sources of funding or cutting public expenditure.

Non-Fuel Mineral Production

Mineral raw materials are consumed directly by a great range of processing establishments such as smelters, refiners, and producers of intermediate goods including steel, aluminium, brick and fertilizers. Although the production of non-fuel mineral products contributed less than 1% to total gross national product (GNP) in the late 1980s, products made directly from minerals accounted for about 9% of GNP. The estimated value of US non-fuel mineral production in 1987 was $25,100m.; in constant dollars this value was only 1.2% above the 1972 level.

The metals component of mineral production has shown a very irregular pattern of growth, reflecting the volatile nature of market prices for metals. This is particularly true for precious metals and, to a lesser extent, for base metals such as copper. In contrast to metals, the value of production for non-metallic minerals such as stone, sand and gravel, clays, phosphate rock and salt showed an almost consistent increase from 1961 to 1987. Rising production trends are not necessarily reflected in employment increases; the growing use of labour-saving equipment has caused a decline in the number of production workers in some sectors. Metal mining, however, showed an increase of 2.9% in employment between 1960 and 1987 as a result of increases in prices for precious metals, particularly gold. Numerous gold mines have opened recently in the USA in response to higher prices, but the financial situation in the mining sector as a whole is far from being entirely favourable. A US Department of Commerce survey of profitability in 40 US industrial sectors has shown that in the second quarter of 1987 the metal-mining sector recorded profits 95% below those for the same period in 1986.

Government regulations, especially those pertaining to environmental quality, have affected the mining and mineral-processing industries significantly. For example, demand for platinum has grown because it is needed for pollution-control devices on motor vehicles. Almost 50% of the domestic consumption of platinum is now used in these devices. The Environmental Protection Agency (EPA) has also been effective in emission control and the regulation of mining waste. Acid-rain control continued to be an issue in 1987, with Congress seeking to reduce sulphur-dioxide emissions by 12m. tons nationwide, and the EPA remains actively involved in monitoring emissions from base-metal smelters and measuring acid levels in lakes.

Lands owned and administered by the federal government contain significant amounts of minerals. About 22% of the total value of domestic coal production and 16% of the value of phosphate production comes from federal and Indian lands. In 1986 total royalties paid to the federal government and Indian tribes amounted to $160m. It is therefore not surprising that the Bureau of Mines and the Geological Survey have tried to stimulate industry interest in developing new domestic sources by evaluating federal lands where minerals exist. This activity raises controversial issues concerning resource development in wilderness areas, because as long as these resources remain 'locked up', ecological disturbance is minimized and outdoor recreation activities can continue. However, the development of these resources will reduce US dependence on foreign sources of many strategic minerals and bring much-needed revenue and employment to local communities.

New techniques for exploration continue to be developed, with significant new finds resulting. Alaska, a little-explored state, has proven deposits of lead, silver, tin, gold, copper, molybdenum, columbium, coal and graphite. By the late 1980s nearly 300 localities throughout Alaska and the adjoining continental shelf had been, or were, under investigation. The Forest Service, an agency of the US Department of Agriculture, has developed new methods of mineral evaluation, and information is being incorporated into land-use management plans, thus providing information on mineral deposits in areas of potential land-use conflict.

Despite its apparent rich endowment of mineral deposits, the USA imports large quantities of chromium, cobalt and manganese, none of which can be mined economically in the USA. The country's share of world production of several metals, including iron, copper and zinc, has declined in recent years. Nevertheless, the USA is self-sufficient in all but a few non-metallic minerals. Canada, Mexico, Western Europe and the market-economy countries of Asia are the main trading partners in raw and processed minerals trade, while imports from South America, including iron ore from Brazil and copper from Chile, increased dramatically in 1987. The performance and market conditions of various non-fuel minerals are assessed below, followed by a survey of future prospects for the industry.

IRON ORE

The iron-ore industry in the USA has been undergoing a major restructuring since 1985, which has involved trading and selling off extensive corporate assets to improve the financial health of the industry. Production of ore declined from 49m. long tons in 1985 to 39m. long tons in 1986, the second worst year for the industry since 1939. Consumption of ore followed a similar pattern. This rapidly-deteriorating situation is partly a result of external factors related to the world supply of iron ore. New mines in Brazil, India and Venezuela have boosted the world supply well above demand, causing a deteriorating situation for many marginal producers in the USA. This loss of market share and associated fall in price has prevented even the most long-established producers from upgrading their facilities. A decline in steel production, a higher level of steel imports and the increasing use of scrap in steel production are additional internal factors which have exacerbated the contraction.

Domestic production of iron ore in 1987 was carried out by 18 companies operating 18 mines, 14 concentration plants and nine pelletizing plants. Almost all the ore mined is 'beneficiated' before shipment. This involves crushing and washing to separate the ore from gangue (valueless or undesirable material) using differences in chemical and physical properties. Agglomeration techniques are also used with fine-grained taconite ores by a process of pelletizing the ore near the mine site. Because of the low-grade nature of these taconite mines, five-six tons of mined rock are required to produce a ton of usable product. Finished pellets contain about 65% ore and make up over 74% of all iron ore consumed in the USA, although high rail rates continue to hamper the sale of pellets to blast furnaces on the Atlantic and Gulf coasts. Transportation of ores from the Great Lakes region has, however, been transformed in recent years. Since 1971 self-loading, supercarrier vessels have been in operation and are now each capable of delivering 2.5m. long tons of ore to the lower lake ports in an eight-month shipping season.

Domestic steel companies have direct control over most of the ore production, and there is an overwhelming concentration of activity around Lake Superior, centred on Illinois, Indiana and Michigan (50% of total output); Ohio and Pennsylvania (31%), and Maryland and West Virginia (13%) are the other major contributors. Consumption of the ore is almost totally by blast furnaces. An important characteristic of mining activity is the reduction in underground methods, with only one active underground pit remaining in 1987. Open pits are favoured because most commercial ore bodies lie close to the surface and have large lateral dimensions, thus making operations high-capacity and cost-effective in comparison with underground pits.

Environmental concerns remain prominent in relation to the iron-ore industry. Careful monitoring of the reclamation and disposal of process water and solid waste is undertaken and efforts are made to reduce dust and noise. Particular emphasis has been laid in the late 1980s on epidemiological studies on the effect of taconite dust on health.

The future for the industry remains uncertain, especially with increasing imports of steel and motor vehicles from Japan, the Republic of Korea and the Federal Republic of Germany. US iron producers have to remain competitive in the face of foreign competition, but the volatility of the financial situation since the fourth quarter of 1987 has made it difficult for companies throughout the heavy-industry sector to make capital expenditures for restructuring and modernization.

COPPER

Copper provides another good illustration of the way in which depressed metal markets have affected not only the US industry but the whole western world. There are few commodities whose real price declined so rapidly as that of copper during the 1980s. In 1980 the average price on the domestic market was 102.4 cents a pound, which stimulated production of copper ore to a figure of 306m. short tons in 1981. By 1985 the price had fallen 66.9 cents and production in 1986 was down to 186m. short tons.

In 1986 copper was mined in 12 states from 87 mines, one-third of which were producing copper ore as a by-product of gold, lead, silver or zinc. Arizona was by far the greatest producer, followed by New Mexico and Michigan. The industry is characterized by integration of operations through to the refining phase, with the 12 largest companies accounting for 97% of domestic mine production, mostly fully-integrated from the mine to the refinery and even to the fabricating facilities such as rod, wire and brass mills. The largest uses of the metal are in electrical and electronic equipment, and telecommunications—where it is facing strong competition from the use of fibre-optics cable.

As with many other metals, the growth rate in consumption for copper has decreased over the long term, although there will always be cyclical surges (such as the 3% increase recorded in 1987). The future will be influenced by the use of substitute materials and the advent of new technologies which do not require the use of copper. There does not appear to be any revolutionary new use for copper on the horizon.

GOLD

Between 1979 and 1986 there was a fourfold increase in US gold production, making the nation the third-largest producing country in the world. Prices have fluctuated wildly from a low of $36 per fine ounce in 1970 to $613 in 1980, settling back to $318 in 1985. This has had a direct effect not only on levels of production but also on methods of mining. High gold prices in recent years have encouraged production from low-grade deposits, often surrounding former areas of production that have been worked intermittently in open-pit mines over the last 100 years. At one large-scale operation, for example, it costs $385 per troy ounce to recover the extremely fine particles of gold distributed throughout the ore. The cost of production was low enough to make a profit in 1987, when prices stayed well over $400 per fine ounce, but in earlier years the mine would not have been an economically-sound proposition. One reason for high prices in 1987 was the threat of a strike by gold miners in South Africa that became a reality during the summer and lasted for several weeks.

In 1986 there were 40 gold mines in operation, mostly in California, Nevada, Colorado and Idaho. Nevada has the greatest production and a recent revival of the industry created over 2,000 new jobs in 1986, thus boosting the state's rural economy. California has experienced a similar revival and for four consecutive years production increased by over 100%. With new technology and better methods of recovery, the prospects for the industry are promising, especially in view of an increase in recent demand for the metal, not only for jewellery and artistic applications, but also from the electronics and aerospace industries.

BAUXITE

Bauxite is the principal ore used in the manufacture of aluminium and is generally located in countries remote from major aluminium-producing centres such as the USA, which has less than 1% of the world's bauxite reserves. In 1988 three companies mined bauxite at four surface mines located in Arkansas, Alabama and Georgia although, with the exception of 1984, production from Arkansas has decreased steadily since 1977. Aluminium has considerable strategic importance because of its high strength-to-weight ratio, making it ideally suited for the construction of military aircraft, missiles and high-speed surface vehicles. It is also becoming increasingly important in the electronics and communications industries as a substitute for copper.

High energy costs for smelting and the limited domestic bauxite reserves are major current problems for the US aluminium industry, but in 1987 a strong world-wide demand for aluminium led to a recovery from the depressed conditions of the preceding years. However, imports continue to supply well over 90% of the country's bauxite requirements, and it is likely that domestic sources are nearing depletion. As the average size of the ore body diminishes and mining depths increase, so the costs escalate.

MOLYBDENUM

Molybdenum is used principally as an alloy in steels and cast irons to enhance strength, hardness, wear and corrosion resistance. The USA produces nearly one-half of the world's production: while domestic mine production decreased from 1985 to 1986, this was not consistent with longer-term trends. The principal producing states are Colorado, Arizona, Idaho and New Mexico. Four corporations, the largest of which is AMAX Inc, account for about 90% of domestic production, mostly from underground mines. Future demand for molybdenum is solely related to the demand for speciality steels and super-alloys.

TIN

Domestic production of tin comes from one mine in Alaska. Production figures are normally withheld to avoid disclosing company data, but total production amounts to only a small fraction of domestic tin requirements. The only tin smelter, at Texas City, Texas, recovers tin from imported and domestic concentrates, much of it from secondary sources such as recycled fabricated parts. Consumption of tin continues to decline because of decreasing industrial activity for tin products. Solder is currently the largest application of primary tin with tinplate a distant second, having lost markets to aluminium in the container business. Imports of tin concentrate continue to increase, with Brazil and Malaysia being the major sources.

ZINC AND NICKEL

In 1987 zinc mine production continued its downward trend for the sixth successive year, resulting in the lowest production since 1966. Poor market conditions contributed to mine closures in Idaho, Mississippi, New Jersey and Tennessee in 1986, leaving Tennessee the principal zinc-producing state.

Nickel has similarly experienced a drop in demand, because of the decline in consumption of stainless steel, the largest single use for nickel. In 1986 the sole US integrated nickel mine–smelter complex, based in Oregon, succumbed to continuing low nickel prices and closed down permanently. This closure has eliminated the USA as a primary nickel producer, since for some time it has been unable to compete with countries which are prepared to subsidize the high-cost mining operations.

CONCLUSION

Non-fuel mineral production has experienced particular problems in recent years. Firstly, there has been a declining intensity of mineral use accompanied by a displacement of mineral applications by organic and composite materials. Other problems are the unfavourable long-term pricing trends and the increased intensity of foreign competition. However, the total value of mineral production is expected to increase gradually in future years and may exceed $30,000m. in 1992 (compared with $24,000m. in 1986). Greater use of advanced technology, such as mining automation and robotics, may make some domestic mines more competitive with those of other countries. However, continuing a long-term trend, US imports are likely to increase and take the form of semi-processed minerals instead of raw minerals as other countries try to obtain a larger share of value added through processing.

Activities related to the mining of sea-bed minerals from the US Exclusive Economic Zone (EEZ) are likely to increase. In 1987 the Congressional Office of Technology Assessment completed a study on the technologies for exploring and developing the zone. The report also reviewed current knowledge of hard mineral resources within the EEZ and the potential of sea-bed resources. Along with other nations, the USA is interested in manganese and metallic sulphide resources, but exploitation of these deposits is not likely until prices rise and more effective recovery methods are developed. Closer to the shore, extensive deposits of heavy-mineral placer deposits, including titanium-rich minerals, have been found off shore from Virginia and Georgia. Construction materials (such as sand, gravel and lime) account for the largest volumes of offshore minerals, but their low value in relation to weight will result in interest being focused on those deposits close to coastal cities. Future decisions on mining beneath the ocean floor are likely to be very strongly influenced by legal and environmental issues, which will require the adoption of strict regulations on leasing and post-leasing activities.

The value of non-fuel minerals is overshadowed by that of energy resources because of the high per-ton value of many energy materials. This is also true in terms of their contribution to foreign trade: it has been remarked, for example, that one day's petroleum imports are of equivalent value to two years' tungsten imports. Clearly, trade in energy and non-fuel minerals is conducted on very different scales. Even so, the Arab oil embargo of 1973–74 caused concern over the dependency of the USA on foreign imports of non-fuel minerals as well as of energy resources. While these imports are vulnerable to interruption through civil disturbances, embargoes and the formation of producer cartels, domestic mineral supplies have also sometimes been unreliable owing to periodic interruptions caused by labour disputes. In spite of these external and internal uncertainties, the USA remains one of the world's largest producers of minerals and, at the same time, one of the world's largest consumers of minerals and mineral products.

MANUFACTURING AND CONSTRUCTION IN THE USA

WYN GRANT

Introduction

In 1986 the industrial sector (manufacturing, construction and mining) accounted for just under 28% of total civilian employment in the USA, compared with 69% in services and 3% in agriculture. The proportion of workers employed in industry was lower than in any of the other major industrialized countries belonging to the 'Group of Seven' apart from Canada, and contrasts particularly sharply with the figures for Japan (34.5%) and the Federal Republic of Germany (40.9%). One interpretation of this situation would be that the USA has a highly efficient manufacturing sector whose well-paid workers spend their income in such a way as to sustain a large service economy. An alternative interpretation is that this low level of employment in industry reflects a 'de-industrialized' economy which has lost ground to foreign competitors. There are elements of truth in both interpretations, but the evidence suggests that the de-industrialization-through-loss-of-competitiveness explanation is the more compelling.

One by-product of the de-industrialization process has been a redistribution of population, production and wealth from the 'rustbelt' of the north to the 'sunbelt' of the south. A slightly different way of looking at this process is in terms of a shift of economic activity from the interior to the coastal states. Expanding sectors of the economy, such as finance and services to business, are concentrated on both coasts, while 'problem' sectors, such as heavy manufacturing, are to be found largely in the country's inland regions. It is clear that there are traditional manufacturing areas in the upper Midwest and in the Northeast which have suffered both from plant closures and from the lack of investment needed to modernize or replace existing units.

In this essay the various manufacturing activities are classified as either heavy industries, consumer industries or high-technology industries. 'Heavy' industries are defined here in terms of intermediate industries making materials which are used as inputs by other industries. The motor-vehicle industry, for example, would be classified as 'heavy' if one was concerned with the actual form of production, but as the emphasis here is on the final destination of the product, it is termed a 'consumer' industry. 'High-technology' industries, in which research and development is of crucial importance and high proportions of scientifically- and technically-qualified staff are employed, deserve to be given their own category; they constitute a sector where the USA has maintained its international competitiveness, and are crucial to the economy's future performance.

OUTPUT AND EMPLOYMENT IN SELECTED US MANUFACTURING INDUSTRIES AND THE CONSTRUCTION SECTOR

(1987, unless otherwise indicated)

	Value of shipments ($ million)	Employment
Chemicals and allied products	210,400	1,023,000
Petrochemicals	85,770	252,000
Synthetic rubber[1]	3,036	9,200
Plastics materials	23,854	55,500
Tyres	11,199	63,600
Miscellaneous plastics products	60,539	580,000
Steel[2]	43,450	230,000
Machine tools[3]	2,748	64,300
Food (excluding drinks)	273,325	1,289,000
Motor vehicles[1]	126,459	265,000
Textiles	57,456	683,000
Consumer electronics[4]	9,493	46,700
Domestic appliances[4]	17,723	125,000
Footwear (including rubber and plastic footwear)	4,756	84,500
Tobacco	18,732	28,900
Alcoholic drinks	19,778	62,000
Construction[5]	397,000	6,400,000
Aerospace[2,6]	110,371	836,000
Computer equipment	63,254	332,000
Biotechnology[7]	550	25,000
Pharmaceuticals	36,331	166,600

[1] Figures for shipments refer to 1988.
[2] Both figures refer to 1988.
[3] Figure for shipments refers to 1986.
[4] Figures for employment refer to 1988.
[5] Shipments defined as the value of new construction put in place; employment figure includes self-employed.
[6] Includes military and civilian aerospace industries.
[7] Estimate: industry in development rather than production stage.

Source: US Department of Commerce publications.

Heavy Industries

CHEMICALS

The chemical industry is the single most important heavy industry in the USA in terms of the value of its products. At US $85,770m. in 1987, the value of products sold by the petrochemical industry alone was twice that of the steel industry, while all chemicals and allied products accounted for shipments of over $210,000m. Even so, the chemical industry did not really recover from the recession of 1982–83 until the late 1980s, with the 1987 *US Industrial Outlook* noting that the industry had suffered from 'a combination of slow growth, depressed prices, and declining profit margins'. In the immediate post-war period the USA dominated the world petrochemical industry, but by the mid-1980s, although the USA still accounted for about one-quarter of world production, total chemical-industry turnover was only just ahead of that of the whole of Western Europe. In an industry which had always been self-sufficient in terms of its basic needs, the decision by the oil companies Exxon and Chevron, in 1988, to form a joint venture to build a terminal for the import of ethylene (the basic 'building block' of the petrochemical industry) on the Houston Ship Canal in Texas has been seen as a significant turning-point. Although the US chemical industry exports a relatively small proportion of its output (10%–20%, compared with 40% for the Federal Republic of Germany and 33% for the UK), it has always maintained a strong trade surplus: however, the 1987 surplus of just over $9,000m. was considerably less than the 1980 peak of $14,000m.

In part, the problems of the US chemical industry are shared by the world chemical industry. The industry is maturing, and growth for its basic products is slow. Like chemical concerns in other countries, US companies are turning away from commodity products (which are increasingly being produced by newly-industrializing countries) in favour of speciality chemicals which offer the prospect of higher profits. Much of the industry's excess capacity was trimmed between 1982 and 1985, with many marginal plants being closed down, and there has been a general trend of business consolidation through mergers and acquisitions. Foreign companies (particularly from Western Europe) have played an important role in such acquisitions, encouraged by a cheap dollar, the attractions of the large US market and the continuing strengths of US research and technology: it was estimated that foreign-owned companies accounted for about 30% of US chemical output by the late 1980s.

The multifactor productivity-growth record of the industry in the post-war period is a good one, but there are signs of a marked slowdown after 1973, which persists even after adjustments are made for the effects of a decline in capacity utilization. Even so, it should be noted that although the chemical industry employed only about 5% of all industrial workers in the late 1980s, it employed more than 10% of the nation's scientists and engineers, reflecting its capital-intensive, research-intensive character.

The US chemical industry faces stringent environmental regulations relative both to other US industries and to chemical industries in other countries, which has forced up both capital expenditure and operating costs. In 1985 the chemical industry incurred pollution-abatement expenditures totalling $740m. and regulation-related operating costs of $2,500m. Both federal and state laws can have a significant impact in this respect. However, the industry does benefit from factors such as readily available supplies of oil and natural gas, a large domestic market, skilled labour and a supporting infrastructure on the Gulf Coast (the main area of production of petrochemicals) including a complex pipeline system for transporting raw materials and liquid products between plants. In basic petrochemical products, much depends on raw-material prices; US producers can expect to be competitive with Middle Eastern producers only if oil prices per barrel are not above the $14–$17 range. In relation to speciality chemicals, much will depend on research and development (R. & D.) successes which will enable them to find profitable market niches in high-performance applications.

Synthetic rubber and plastics materials

Synthetic rubber is one of the most capital-intensive sectors of the chemical industry, with just over 9,000 workers producing goods valued at over $3,000m. in 1988. The USA has maintained a positive trade balance in synthetic rubber for several decades. The industry may be subdivided into general-purpose and speciality rubbers: production of general-purpose synthetic rubbers peaked in 1978 and has since declined, but still accounted for nearly two-thirds of total output in the late 1980s. Speciality rubbers are customized to meet the needs of a specific industry or application, and are produced in small quantities. Demand has increased sharply in the 1980s, particularly for high-performance applications in industries such as aerospace.

The plastics-materials industry, also capital-intensive and highly automated, had a positive trade balance of nearly $2,000m. a year in the late 1980s. In 1987 55,500 workers accounted for production valued at nearly $24,000m. Plastics materials may be subdivided into commodity plastics, produced in large volumes, and more specialized products, such as engineering plastics, produced in smaller quantities. Output of engineering plastics was growing at an estimated 12% a year in the late 1980s. R. & D. costs are high in this area, but financial support has been received from the federal government, particularly from the Department of Defense. This is, however, a highly competitive area in which foreign governments and companies are very active.

Tyres and other rubber and plastics products

Tyres have two markets: in new cars and other vehicles, and for replacement purposes. Sales for new vehicles are affected by the level of domestic production, while mileage driven is the key influence on replacement needs (although frequency of replacement has also been affected by the development of longer-lasting 'radial' tyres). While the US share of total world motor-vehicle production fell from two-thirds in 1960 to about one-third in 1985, the US share of world tyre production fell from 50% in 1960 to less than 30% in 1985, with increased foreign production being an important influence on the industry. Tyre imports have been growing significantly, especially since 1983, while exports have been declining gradually since the late 1970s (Canada is the main export market). More than 20 long-established tyre plants have closed during this period, and employment in the industry was reduced by nearly one-half between the late 1970s and the mid-1980s (from 114,000 in 1977 to 66,500 in 1985). Nevertheless, population growth, causing an increase in the number of vehicles in use, is expected to lead to a growth rate in the US tyre market of 1%–2% a year in the early 1990s: price will be the main influence of the relative growth rates of domestically-produced and imported tyres.

The rubber and plastics hose and belting industry employed just under 25,000 workers in the mid-1980s, with an output of about $2,500m. Major products include conveyor belts, transmission belts, fire hose and garden hose. The industry is dominated by eight large producers, which together account for two-thirds of total output. The success of the industry is closely linked to that of US manufacturing as a whole, although a deteriorating trade balance has undermined its long-term prospects.

Production of miscellaneous rubber products accounted for 91,000 workers in 1987, with output valued at $9,500m. Products range from foam and sponge goods to wall and floor coverings. However, the manufacture of miscellaneous plastics products accounted for 580,000 workers and output valued at $60,539m. in the same year. Plastics products have a variety of uses throughout the economy, such as component parts in motor vehicles, electrical equipment and a wide variety of consumer goods.

STEEL

For much of the post-war period the USA was the world's leading steel producer. For much of the 1980s the industry experienced a severe decline, although towards the end of the decade it recovered somewhat. Even so, the total volume of mill products in 1988 was just 84m. short tons, compared with 100.9m. short tons in 1979. Total industry employment was forecast at 230,000 for 1988, representing a reduction of 52% since 1980, when there were 481,000 workers. While raw steel-making capacity was reduced by 27% between 1982 and 1987, in the latter year the industry was still only operating at about 80% of current capacity. Financial losses of steel companies (from steel operations only) totalled $12,000m. between 1982 and 1986, with more than 10 steel companies filing for bankruptcy in 1986–87. In 1988, however, major producers made operating profits of $2,300m. Further encouragement has come from an expansion in the operation of minimills (see below).

An underlying problem for the industry has been the decline in the 'steel-intensity' of the US economy. Steel-intensive products have lost ground in export markets; automobiles, which are major steel users, have been progressively reduced in size; steel is used more efficiently and hence in smaller quantities; and there continues to be a substitution of steel by other materials, such as engineering plastics. However, other countries have experienced these structural changes and have coped with them more successfully; for example, Canada has a relatively successful steel industry. One problem in the USA is that labour costs in steel production have traditionally accounted for about one-third of total production costs—a higher proportion than in other steel-producing countries—while foreign productivity in steel now meets or exceeds US levels. Production facilities are relatively outdated; only one new integrated steel plant has been built since the 1950s (at Burns Harbour). While plants have been modified to incorporate new innovations, such as basic oxygen furnaces, only 60% of US production is continuously cast, compared with nearly 95% in Japan. (Continuous casting directly converts molten steel into semifinished forms, thus simplifying the production process, raising yields and reducing energy needs.) It is often less costly to keep operating an out-of-date mill rather than meet the costs associated with closure: unprofitable plants have thus kept working, making it difficult to bring supply and demand into balance.

From accounting for only 6% of total domestic steel shipments in 1975, minimills had come to account for 22% by 1987. The minimills melt scrap in electric arc furnaces, generally operating away from traditional steel production centres such as Pittsburgh and the southern side of Lake Michigan. Their output has tended to concentrate on the production of commodity steels, such as reinforcing bars for construction, rod for screws and fasteners, and merchant bar for mesh fencing, but technological advances of the late 1980s were expected to enable them to break into such areas as large structural beams for construction, special-quality bar for automobiles, and—most importantly—flat-rolled steel used in appliances and automobile bodies. (Flat-rolled products account for almost 60% of domestic steel shipments.) The minimills have benefited from flexible labour contracts, which helped them to boost productivity by 36% in the six years to 1988, and production costs can be as much as 15% lower than for 'major' steel plants. The contribution of minimills to the overall US steel market is expected to increase to about 36% by the end of the 20th century.

Steel imports into the USA are controlled through a series of voluntary-restraint agreements with major steel exporters. Even so, import penetration has remained persistently high, amounting to 22.5% of consumption in the first six months of 1987. Exports constitute a negligible proportion of production, accounting for less than 2% of shipments. It is unlikely that there will by any substantial growth in domestic steel consumption: indeed, aluminium, plastics or even ceramics might be used to replace steel in certain aspects of automobile construction. Against this background, excess capacity continues to be the industry's major problem. Given that increased domestic demand is unlikely, at any event in the short to medium term, more will have to be done to remove exit barriers. In 1986 the Reagan administration decided not to back a scheme which would have provided financial assistance to help companies to close plants.

MACHINE TOOLS

Machine tools is another sector in which the USA had a strong position after the Second World War, but in which there has been a marked deterioration in performance in the 1970s and 1980s. The US share of world production of machine tools was about 35% in 1967 but dropped sharply thereafter, to 17% in 1971. By 1978 the US industry had a negative trade balance for the first time in its history, partly because of a deterioration in its technological lead over other countries manufacturing in this sector. Productivity has deteriorated since 1977, although it has undoubtedly been affected by sharp declines in output.

The best indicator of the health of the industry is the value of new orders, and these have fallen sharply. Orders for both high- and low-technology products have increasingly gone to foreign manufacturers producing more inexpensively; imports accounted for 51% of apparent consumption in 1986, compared with 17.2% in 1977, while total new orders in 1986 were valued at $2,125m., or just 38% of the 1979 peak of $5,621m. Similarly, exports, at $582m. in 1987, were just over one-half of their 1981 value. After three years of losses in 1983–85, the industry moved into marginal profitability in 1986. Domestic machine-tool capacity fell by at least 25% between 1981 and 1986, but operating rates have still only been about 50% of capacity. From a 1981 peak of 101,700, employment in the industry had fallen to 64,300 by May 1987. Compared with chemicals and steel, machine tools is a small-company industry, with two-thirds of companies having less than 20 employees.

In May 1986 President Reagan launched a voluntary-restraint agreement programme to give the industry a five-year 'breathing space' to restructure: Japan and Taiwan agreed to limit their exports of machine tools to the USA. In order to help the industry to regain lost competitiveness, the Department of Defense has provided $5m. annually to fund a National Center for the Manufacturing Sciences in Ann Arbor, Michigan, with an equal amount of funding coming from member companies and $2m. a year for three years from the state of Michigan.

In the long term the internationalization of the industry is likely to continue. Many US machine-tool firms have contracted with offshore producers for components, parts and even complete machine tools. Foreign producers are increasing their presence in the USA through distribution, assembly and production facilities, a trend which may be encouraged by import restrictions. There is a growing view in the industry that the advent of new materials and manufacturing technologies is likely to lead to further decline for the classic machine-tools business.

Consumer Industries

FOOD PROCESSING

In 1985 the manufacture of 'food and kindred products' (including beverages) accounted for over 13% of all manufacturing shipments in the USA. The food-processing industry has three principal distinguishing characteristics. Firstly, it is a very heterogeneous industry in that there are substantial differences between its various subsectors. Each subsector uses its own raw materials and its own process technology to produce products with a distinctive consumer profile. Secondly, because of persistent differences in national preference and other factors, imports and exports are less important than in many other industries. The principal market is the domestic market. Many leading US food-processing firms are multinationals, but production generally takes place in or near the foreign markets they serve. For example, H. J. Heinz obtained 42% of its sales from its foreign subsidiaries in 1988, up from 34% in 1985. Thirdly, in many of the subsectors of the food-processing industry there is substantial government involvement, either in terms of import controls or export subsidies, or arrangements for the purchase of surplus products.

The shipments of the food-processing industry (excluding drinks) were valued at an estimated $291,000m. in 1988. Of this, some 84% was provided by six subsectors: meat products ($75,600m.); dairy products ($44,400m.); grain-mill products ($41,600m.); preserved fruits and vegetables ($41,000m.); bakery products ($23,200m.); and sugar and confectionery ($18,600m.). Minor subsectors such as processed fishery products ($6,200m.) and pasta products ($1,400m.) make up the rest of the industry.

Meat products

Meat products constitute the largest subsector in the food-processing industry, and can be subdivided into two major segments: the red-meat industry and the poultry industry. The red-meat industry is by far the larger segment in terms of value of shipments (83% of all meat-products shipments in 1987), but there is less difference in total employment (186,000 in 1988 in red meat; 140,000 in poultry). Moreover, the poultry sector is advancing: poultry meat is increasingly seen as a healthier product than red meat and there has been more innovation in the introduction of new value-added products. Its price advantage means that it is used more often in the preparation of convenience foods. 1987 was the first year in which more poultry than beef was consumed in the USA. The portion of the meat-packing industry which slaughters cattle for steaks and roasts is highly concentrated, with 70% of cattle being slaughtered by only three companies. Hamburgers and canned meats are produced from old breeding stock and dairy cattle, and this side of the industry is less concentrated.

The US government protects the red-meat industry through voluntary-restraint agreements negotiated with the main foreign suppliers, such as Australia. US imports of red meat rose to total $3,600m. in 1988, which was close to the 'trigger level' at which quotas would be imposed. The US government has also purchased beef for export to Brazil and the European Communities.

Dairy products

The federal government purchases a large quantity of dairy products in order to support the farm price of milk. Between 1979 and 1985 government purchases of butter, cheese and non-fat dry milk grew by 11.2% a year to reach $2,400m. (excluding administrative and storage costs). For a variety of reasons, including an increase in demand for milk for manufacturing, the cost of the support programme fell back to $1,200m. in 1987. Butter consumption has shown a long-term decline, while cheese consumption has increased. Yoghurt shipments were growing more slowly in the late 1980s, after rapid growth earlier in the decade. The character of the industry would change significantly if the Food and Drug Administration gave approval for the use of bovine growth hormone, which would substantially increase milk production.

Dairy farming in the USA traditionally has been concentrated in the upper Midwest (particularly in the states of Minnesota and Wisconsin), but the balance of the industry has been upset in recent years by an expansion of production elsewhere in the USA, particularly in California. California is a lower-cost producer, and has substantially expanded its dairy-processing industry. As California has approached self-sufficiency, the market there for producers elsewhere in the USA has disappeared.

Processed fruit and vegetables

This sector can be subdivided into two segments, canned goods and frozen foods, with the former accounting for 64% of total shipments in 1988. Long-term growth prospects for frozen food are good, given the increasing number of two-income and single-parent households and the growing availability of micro-wave ovens.

Grain-mill products

This is very heterogeneous subsector, covering a range of products from flour to pet food. The most important product area is that of cereal-based breakfast foods. Per-head consumption of breakfast cereals has shown an annual growth rate of about 3% for much of the 1980s, although it slowed slightly in 1988.

MOTOR VEHICLES

In the years after the second oil 'shock' of 1979, the US automobile industry went through the most serious crisis of its history. It faced a combination of recession, increased competition from abroad, and a shift in consumer tastes away from its traditional products. Since then, however, the industry has experienced a significant turn-round, manifested by increased sales, improved productivity and higher profits. A total of $84,000m. was invested in plant and equipment between 1978 and 1985.

The industry has made good progress in improving productivity, which increased from an annual output of 14.5 vehicles per hourly employee at the plants of General Motors (GM), Ford and Chrysler in 1980 to 20.4 vehicles in 1985. However, as the Department of Commerce noted in its 1985 survey of the US automobile industry, 'despite major gains in productivity, large fixed-cost reductions and more effective controls over variable costs in recent years, US car manufacturers continue to face a substantial Japanese manufacturing cost advantage in the production of small cars'.

Some 865,000 workers were employed in the motor-vehicle industry in 1986, compared with 788,000 in 1980. Industry output was just over $120,000m. in 1987; output of motor vehicles and car bodies grew at a compound annual rate of 2.5% between 1972 and 1985, in terms of 1982 dollars. Forecast sales of 15.2m. vehicles in 1989, while 4% lower than in 1988, would still give the fourth-highest annual output figure in the industry's history. Sales of trucks and vans, including small passenger vans and sport utility vehicles, have increased steadily in the 1980s and by 1989 one-third of vehicles sold in the USA were classified as trucks. However, these encouraging figures conceal some important changes in industry structure. The total import share of the US car market rose from 12% in 1978 to just under 30% in 1987. US Department of Commerce forecasts suggest that imports will be supplying 37% of the market by 1990.

Moreover, Japanese 'transplant' operations have grown in importance since the early 1980s. It is estimated that by the early 1990s Japanese automobile manufacturers will be able to produce 1.7m. units a year in the USA (and another 350,000 in Canada), giving cars built in the USA by Japanese companies a 12.5% market share. (By that time the North American share of US automobile sales is likely to have fallen to just over 50%, compared with 68.1% in 1986.) New production facilities being built by Japanese manufacturers will increase industry capacity by more than 1.5m. units by the early 1990s. It is estimated that by then the industry will have about 3m. units more capacity than will be required to serve the market, bringing about a 20% loss of market share by traditional US manufacturers and requiring substantial rationalization and job losses.

Traditionally, US car production has been located in the upper Midwest (and across the Canadian border in Ontario), with Michigan and Ohio being the primary automobile-producing states. However, both Nissan and GM have recently chosen Tennessee as the location for new plants—Tennessee is a 'right-to-work' state, which means that workers do not have to belong to a union if they want to work in a union-organized plant. The future competitive record of the US automobile industry will depend to a large extent on cost containment in two areas: labour and supplies. GM, for example, cut employee payrolls by $3,700m. in 1987 and by $4,000m. in 1988, while Ford has announced plans to cut the number of locations from which its North American plants buy parts from 22,000 in 1984 to 1,700 in 1992.

TEXTILES

Historically located in New England, the US textile industry has shifted southwards and westwards to take advantage of lower wages. In 1950 six states in the Northeast accounted for 40.5% of all textile employment; by 1970 they accounted for only 21.7%. The industry has had a stronger productivity-growth record than most other US manufacturing industries—and than the textile industries of most other advanced countries. Annual average multifactor productivity growth was 4.6% from 1948 to 1965, then 2.0% in 1965–73, 5.7% in 1973–79 and 2.6% in 1979–85. Capital expenditure by the textile industry increased steadily throughout the late 1970s and early 1980s, then declined slightly before increasing to an estimated $1,900m. in 1987. Textile manufacturing now involves the widespread use of advanced microprocessor-controlled technology. While restructuring has reduced the number of companies operating in the sector, there is still a large number of relatively small textile companies. A long-term downward trend in employment in the industry was reversed in 1987, when a net gain of 22,000 jobs brought the workforce up to 683,000.

Rising imports are the industry's main problem. Imports grew at a compound annual rate of 8.1% between 1972 and 1985, and at a rate of 12.7% in 1980–85; exports declined by a compound rate of 10.1% a year over the same period. A renewed Multifibre Arrangement, which set the framework for world trade in textiles by limiting the rate of growth of the exports of developing countries, was brought into force in 1987, and more restrictive bilateral arrangements were negotiated with Hong Kong, Taiwan and the Republic of Korea in 1986, and with Japan in 1987. In 1988 the House of Representatives failed by 11 votes to override a presidential veto on a bill that would have restricted growth in textile imports to 1% a year. Under the provisions of the bill 20% of the total value of textile-import quotas would have been auctioned off. Protectionist pressures are likely to persist, particularly from the southern states.

CONSUMER ELECTRONICS

Japan is the world leader in consumer electronics and the US domestic market is now largely served by imports. Domestic manufacturers supplied less than 40% of the home market by 1987. Many products that are in demand abroad are no longer made by US manufacturers: these include radios, portable radio-cassette players and recorders, and televisions that meet foreign standards. The only domestic production of video-cassette recorders involves their assembly by foreign-owned companies. Domestic manufacturing is now limited to large-screen colour televisions. With the sale of General Electric's consumer-electronics division to the French government-owned group Thomson, Zenith is the only major US-owned manufacturer of colour televisions, and most of their production takes place in Mexico. Most domestic production of colour televisions is by foreign-owned firms, with Japanese plants in the USA accounting for 18% of Japanese companies' global production. Companies based in the Netherlands, Taiwan and the Republic of Korea also manufacture in the USA. Against this background it is not surprising that employment levels in the industry are relatively low, with forecast employment of just under 47,000 in 1988.

HOUSEHOLD APPLIANCES

The household-appliance industry is generally characterized by mature products with high market-saturation levels, manufactured by established production processes which are very sensitive to economies of scale. This has encouraged the consolidation of producer companies into five corporations offering a complete range of appliances. New housing starts are a major driving force for sales, accounting for one-quarter of major appliance shipments.

While imports have been increasing steadily in recent years, exports (the main market for which is Canada) decreased at an average annual rate of 8.3% between 1981 and 1986 until the declining dollar caused them to increase by 28% in 1987. However, imports are a major threat only to some small appliances, for example microwave ovens. The manufacturing processes for these products tend to be labour-intensive, and their transport costs are low relative to those of major appliances. Across the industry as a whole imports are estimated to have accounted for less than 15% of total sales in 1987. Labour productivity growth for major household appliances has been steady, if unspectacular: an annual average of 3.2% from 1970–85, with growth of 4.1% a year being achieved in 1980–85. Total employment in the sector was forecast at 125,000 in 1988, showing relatively little decline in recent years.

FOOTWEAR

The US footwear industry has experienced substantial import penetration and a considerable decline in domestic output. The production of footwear is a labour-intensive process, with a very large number of operations being involved in the production of a single pair of shoes. Indeed, one response of US manufacturers has been to export cut footwear parts to developing countries for assembly, with less labour-intensive finishing operations taking place in the USA. In fashion products the US footwear industry has been less competitive than those of countries such as Italy, which has caused it to become largely dependent on the middle-priced segment of the market. There is relatively little scope for economies of scale and relatively few changes have been made in footwear production over the last century: the sector has registered one of the lowest productivity gains of all US industries, with an annual average increase of 0.3% between 1970 and 1985.

In 1987 domestic production of non-rubber footwear declined for the 10th consecutive year, while shipments of rubber and plastic footwear have been declining in volume since 1983. Import penetration of the domestic non-rubber footwear market totals about 80% of consumption, with particularly high proportions in women's footwear (85%) and non-rubber athletic footwear (97%). Production employment has declined since 1968, with total employment at just over 84,000 in the rubber and non-rubber sectors in 1987. Between 1982 and mid-1987, 324 footwear plants closed. Given that many of the weaker firms have closed, and that the larger firms are consolidating and investing in new technology, the decline in the industry is expected to become less severe.

TOBACCO

The tobacco industry has been affected by changing public attitudes towards smoking, reinforced by increasingly restrictive antismoking legislation. Per head consumption of cigarettes by adults has been declining in the USA since 1974: by 1988 the volume of cigarettes produced for the domestic market had declined by 11% from its 1981 peak. As a result of trade concessions in the mid-1980s the industry has obtained much greater access to the Japanese and Taiwanese markets, with the result that the decline in cigarette production in the USA was halted in 1987. Imports are only significant in the cigar market, where they are largely made up of higher-priced cigars.

Total employment in the industry (excluding stemming and redrying activities) declined from 54,900 in 1972 to 38,100 in 1987. Productivity growth has been relatively slow but an average annual percentage increase in labour productivity was recorded between 1970 and 1985. Expressed in terms of 1982 dollars, however, forecast industry shipments of $11,596m. in 1988 were very close to the 1972 level of $11,823m. The industry has not been as much affected by import penetration as have other consumer industries, although the diversification strategies of the tobacco companies are an indicator of its long-term prospects.

ALCOHOLIC DRINKS

Fundamental shifts have occurred in the market for alcoholic drinks in the USA in the 1980s. Real consumer spending on alcoholic drinks increased by just 1% a year between 1976 and 1986, and by only 0.4% a year in 1982–86. It was in this latter period that consumer concern about alcohol abuse, drink-driving, and health and fitness seems to have shown a marked increase, resulting in a greater degree of public support for restrictive legislation; states have been required to enforce a minimum 'drinking age' of 21, or face the loss of federal highway funds.

Distilled-spirit producers have been particularly affected by the shift of some consumers to low-alcohol or alcohol-free drinks. However, the preference for lower-alcohol drinks has not been reflected in patterns of beer consumption, with imported beers, which are perceived as stronger and having more flavour, growing in popularity. Per-head wine production also increased in the 1980s, with particular growth in 'wine coolers' (pre-packaged mixes of wine, fruit flavours, citric acid and carbonated water). The wine-cooler market appeared to stabilize at about 25% of total wine consumption in 1987.

The USA is a major purchaser of imported beers, wines and spirits. Beer is imported from 63 different countries, and the value of beer imports was expected to increase by almost 21%, to $972m., in 1987. Wine and brandy imports remain the largest category by value, at $1,193m. in 1987. In contrast, the USA has a relatively minor role as an exporter of alcoholic drinks. The value of exports did increase by 36%, to $285m., in 1987, but this did not prevent a trade deficit on alcoholic beverages of nearly $3,000m. in that year. The ratification of the US–Canadian Free-Trade Agreement was expected to lead to increased exports of US wines and spirits to Canada.

Foreign firms have made substantial acquisitions in the US alcoholic drinks market. It has been estimated that a relatively small number of Australian, Canadian and European firms may control 60%–65% of the US spirits market, 25%–30% of US wine production, and over 15% of domestic brewing capacity. The industry is likely to experience very slow rates of growth over the next few years, and total employment is likely to remain around the 1987 level of 62,000.

CONSTRUCTION AND HOUSING

The value of new construction, expressed in 1982 dollars, reached a record level of $347,800m. in 1986 (compared with $280,700m. in 1980), falling back slightly, to an estimated $344,000m., in 1988. The value of new construction in 1987 was about 8.9% of gross national product (GNP), well up from a cyclical low of 7.7% of GNP in 1982 but below the post-war peak of 11.9% in 1966. However, construction-industry employment increased by 4% in 1987 to reach a historically high level of 5.1m. employees. In addition, more than 1m. people were self-employed as proprietors and working partners.

Levels of owner–occupation in the USA have not varied very much since 1960, when 61.9% of all housing units were owner–occupied; by 1983, this figure had only increased to 64.7%. Units in public housing projects account for only just over 2% of all units, with just over 1% of private housing units receiving a government rent subsidy. A high level of commercial building in the period to 1985 resulted in record vacancy rates for office buildings, stores, hotels and warehouses in the late 1980s, and supply and demand were not expected to return to equilibrium for some years. A significant number of foreign-owned construction companies has moved into the US market in recent years, obtaining contracts worth about $7,300m. in 1985. Increasing foreign investment in the US real-estate market is likely to lead to further penetration of the US construction sector by foreign companies. The US international construction industry's market position has been eroded over a number of years, with a 50% decline in contract awards to US firms occurring between 1982 and 1986. Part of this decline was due to a general market slowdown, but it was also apparent that US firms were losing out to foreign competitors. However, if macroeconomic conditions remain favourable, the construction industry as a whole should reach new record levels of output in the early 1990s.

High-Technology Industries

CIVILIAN AEROSPACE

The civilian aerospace industry can claim to be one of the most successful US manufacturing industries. Nearly 90% of all civilian aircraft used in the world in the late 1980s were produced in the USA. The military and civilian aerospace industries together continue to be the leading positive contributor to the US balance of trade among all manufacturing industries. Of the total output of the aerospace sector (60% of which consists of military deliveries), more than one-half is sold abroad, largely to the UK, Japan, France and the Federal Republic of Germany. Total employment in the sector was expected to increase by 3% in 1988, to 836,000, and includes a high proportion of scientists and engineers. The industry has, however, experienced its problems: increases in both price competition and the cost of research and development have eroded profit margins (which in any case have tended to be below the average for all manufacturing industries), with the result that in 1986 profits fell to the lowest level recorded since 1972.

The USA's historical dominance of the civilian aircraft sector has been based on the large size of the domestic market and on the country's technological leadership. Direct and indirect research and development (R. & D.) expenditures are estimated to account for around 15% of the cost of product shipments for aircraft and aircraft parts. However, the relative level of US aerospace R. & D. funding has declined steadily at a time when foreign competitors have been increasing their R. & D. spending. The average level of federal government-sponsored R. & D. was 32% lower in the 1970s than in the 1960s and has continued to decline. Although industry-funded R. & D. has increased, it accounts for only one-quarter of total aerospace R. & D. expenditures, and could not compensate for the decline in federal funding.

The US aircraft industry is expected to continue to show a good rate of growth, although air-traffic-control problems could dampen a favourable growth trend in air travel. The US Department of Commerce forecast in 1988 that the aggregate value of aerospace shipments would grow from its then strong base at a compound annual rate of over 4%, although worries about quality-control standards were expressed in early 1989 following a series of aircraft crashes and malfunctions, particularly affecting Boeing.

COMPUTERS

The US computer-equipment industry was the fastest-growing sector of the US economy from 1972 to 1988, with its value increasing almost 90-fold over that period in terms of constant 1982 US dollars. However, the industry has now entered a period of increased foreign competition, reflected in declines in both its trade surplus and its employment level. The trade surplus in computer equipment peaked at $7,000m. in 1981, with a figure of $2,800m. being forecast for 1988. Total employment in the industry in 1988, at 332,000, represented a decline of more than 11% compared with the 1984 level of 374,000. Both the above trends in part reflect moves by some US manufacturers to offshore sites in an effort to remain competitive. Moreover, personal-computer sales, which had previously been expanding by 20%–30% annually, were predicted to grow by only 13% in 1989 and, because by the late 1980s personal computers had come to account for the largest share of the industry's business, overall growth was expected to slow.

In the area of so-called 'supercomputers', which can handle extremely complex tasks, US manufacturers have supplied about 80% of the world market. With mainframe computers (used for large-volume, general-purpose applications), however, Japanese manufacturers have made major gains in the world market, largely at the expense of US suppliers. There has been an increase in imports from the Republic of Korea, Taiwan and Singapore in more basic products such as the cheaper microcomputers, peripheral equipment and components. The value of imports from the Republic of Korea exceeded $500m. in 1987, an increase of 25% over 1986.

Sales of personal computers were expected to account for some 39% of the hardware revenues of US computer firms in 1988. Worries have been expressed that the market could experience a slowing-down, or even a contraction, in growth. Because of the high price of memory chips, prices of personal computers stabilized in the late 1980s, a contrast with the earlier experience of regular decreases in prices. It could be that personal-computer manufacturers are facing a relatively saturated market (although some manufacturers think that will not be a problem until well into the 1990s) and there are also some indications that businesses tend to prefer more sophisticated 'desktop' machines which can be used in networking and can replace minicomputers. Although this development should help the 'big three' manufacturers (IBM, Apple and Compaq), who account for two-thirds of all sales through computer stores, the second-tier producers may be adversely affected.

With its short product cycles, the computer industry has to spend substantial sums of money on research and development. The R. & D. expenditures of leading computer manufacturers grew at a compound rate of 18% in the five years to 1984, with the 33 leading manufacturers spending more than $6,000m. on R. & D. in 1984. The industry continues to hold a leading position in terms of its R. & D. spending, which was equivalent to 8.2% of the value of its sales in 1987. However, it should be noted that the proportion of R. & D. spent on software rather than hardware has been increasing in the late 1980s because so much of the new technology is software-dependent. A continuing shortage of skilled programmers is, however, a significant constraint on software development.

Technological advances in the industry can be expected to continue, but many of the fundamental technologies may be developed by Japanese companies rather than their US counterparts. Firm predictions are difficult to make in such a fast-moving industry, but there is concern that what used to be a broad US lead may continue to be eroded.

FIBRE OPTICS

Fibre-optics technology involves the transmission of voice, data and video by pulses of light passing through strands of hair-thin, ultra-pure glass. It has several advantages for communication purposes over satellites or coaxial cables, including the capability to carry much more data than wire of comparable size (an optical fibre provides at least 250 times the capacity of a copper wire), freedom from interference (including ground static and communications delay in the case of satellites) light weight and small size, and greater security. Fibre optics can be used for high-density telephone transmission, office-automation systems and cable television. A new application would place optical-fibre sensors in the wings of aeroplanes to detect any defects.

The USA is the world's largest producer and consumer of fibre optics, accounting for about 45% of the world market. While telecommunications accounts for about 70% of the market, the military market for fibre optics is also important, with about 15% of domestic sales in the late 1980s. After several years during which annual growth rates reached 20% or higher, the US fibre-optics market began to slow down in the second half of 1986, a trend which continued in 1987. Completion of long-haul telecommunications networks brought the 1987 market to an estimated $820m. Forecasts suggest that the market should expand in 1989 and that this expansion should continue in the 1990s as substantial price reductions, resulting from the standardization of components, permit more extensive applications of this technology. There is a small trade deficit in optical fibre and cables, with $105m. of imports and $65m. of exports in 1985, with imports coming principally from Canada, Japan and the UK. Employment in this capital-intensive industry was estimated at 15,000 in 1985, but is likely to increase as the market expands.

ROBOTICS

Robots are instrumented machines capable of undertaking complex tasks which would otherwise require human operatives, although the line separating robots from merely automated machinery is not always well-defined. The first industrial robot was developed in the USA around 1960: however, the US industry was slow to develop and is regarded as relatively young, with statistics being collected for the first time in 1984. The USA continues to be the world leader in research and design, but in the past decade Japan has overtaken the USA in both the production and use of robots. The installed base of industrial robots in the USA increased from about 6,000 units in 1982 to about 27,000 units in 1987; more than one-half of these units are used in the automobile industry or closely related sectors. Although the industry has expanded significantly, a persistent problem has been low profitability. Since robotics production combines low volume with high unit costs, many small US firms prefer to import the basic robots and add items, such as peripherals and software, to tailor the robot to meet the needs of the domestic user. In 1986 it was calculated that only three of the top companies by sales produced a complete product line in the USA. Imports of robotics in 1987 captured 40% of the US market, with Japan the principal supplier. The number of new orders declined in 1986, and remained low in 1987, but despite this slowdown there was an accumulation of unfilled orders.

The role of the robot in the future will become much more complex as a result of enhanced vision and sensing capabilities. As higher levels of machine intelligence and communication are achieved the most significant gains in industrial productivity will result from the integration of the robot into various forms of automated systems, rather than from its use as an individual production unit. In the late 1980s the USA was investing less in research into new forms of application than were its competitors, while the customer base of the US robotics industry had been diversified very little beyond its traditional ties to the automobile industry.

BIOTECHNOLOGY

Biotechnology, which may be defined as the use of scientifically-engineered biological systems to produce goods and services, is not an industry as such but an enabling technology using a variety of related techniques which can be deployed in a number of industries. It is highly research-intensive, with scientific and technical staff often accounting for between 30%

and 70% of all employees. Very few products are yet available on the market, and biotechnology firms are not profitable. However, capital availability does not seem to have been a constraint, with investment in small biotechnology firms alone totalling an estimated $4,500m. in the first half of 1987.

Because biotechnology is a set of technologies with a number of applications, estimates of the number of companies operating in the field vary considerably. However, they can be divided into two groups: small companies founded to exploit discoveries made in the early to mid-1970s in recombinant DNA and monoclonal antibody technologies (a direct result of federal government support for health research); and over 200 large, established companies from areas such as chemicals and pharmaceuticals which have expanded into biotechnology applications more recently. Their commitment may vary from keeping a foothold in biotechnology to devoting one-quarter of their R. & D. to this area. There are at least 400 small biotechnology companies, with the peak years of establishment being between 1980 and 1984; about one-half of these are located in the states of California, Massachusetts, New York and New Jersey. There are also more than 200 companies which supply materials, instruments, equipment and services. Employment statistics are not available from government sources, but a conservative estimate would put employment at 25,000, largely in relatively well-paid jobs.

Many of the new products of biotechnology are subject to health, safety and environmental regulations. Whether or not speedy regulatory approval can be obtained for the testing, marketing and export of new products greatly influences the attractions and risks of new areas of activity. Small firms are placed at a competitive disadvantage because US Food and Drug Administration (FDA) approvals often take longer than foreign regulatory approvals, and larger companies can afford to produce abroad. However, legislation approved in 1986 permits the export of new drugs not approved by the FDA under certain conditions. Also in 1986 the Office of Science and Technology Policy established an interagency Biotechnology Science Co-ordinating Committee. It is estimated that the annual market value of products derived from biotechnology could reach several thousand million dollars by the early 1990s. The largest applications are expected to be in human health care, reflecting the high value-added nature of medical products, and in genetic manipulation of plants. Applications are also possible in toxic-waste degradation and pollution control, and in energy.

PHARMACEUTICALS

While the USA dominated the world pharmaceutical industry between 1940 and 1960, its share of world pharmaceutical research, innovation, production, sales and exports has since declined. Pharmaceutical products have traditionally provided a surplus for the US trade balance, but a rapid increase in imports in 1987 reduced that trade surplus by 40%, from $765m. to $450m. However, it should be noted that imports accounted for only 7.6% of domestic supply in 1987, whilst exports totalled 9.6% of shipments.

Pharmaceutical innovation is a very risky process because of the long time periods involved. The USA remains the leading world site for pharmaceutical research (26 foreign companies have R. & D. facilities in the country), but the share of such research located in the USA fell from about two-thirds in the early 1960s to about one-third in the late 1980s. Even so, US pharmaceutical manufacturers increased R. & D. expenditure by 18%, to $3,500m., in 1987, equivalent to 9.5% of sales.

Against the background of a compound annual growth rate of 11.3% between 1972 and 1984, long-run increases in labour productivity in pharmaceuticals have not been spectacular, with an average annual increase of 2.7% between 1970 and 1985; the 1986 figure was 2.6%. Total employment in the industry has remained stable over the last few years, at about 165,000. Future growth in the industry depends to a considerable extent on the ability of biotechnology to increase the numbers both of new diagnostics to perform sophisticated tests, and of vaccines for viral diseases.

Conclusions

The USA retains a number of innovative high-technology industries which remain world leaders. Some of its older heavy industries, such as steel, seem to have made a partial recovery from the worst period in their histories. It is in consumer industries, such as consumer electronics and footwear, that the weaknesses of the US industrial economy are most apparent. Increasing concern is being expressed in the USA about growing levels of foreign ownership in a number of sectors, although public attention has focused particularly on purchases of real estate in major cities by foreign nationals. However, foreign investment in the USA is likely to be a significant issue under the Bush presidency. Pressures for protection in the political system, although perhaps past their peak, are still strong, and the USA is likely to continue to safeguard its industries through bilateral trade deals with other countries. The completion of the internal market in the European Communities in 1992 may increase the risk of serious trade disputes between the USA and the EC. The competitiveness of US industry is likely to remain a central issue within domestic politics, although solutions to fundamental problems that can command widely-based political support are hard to reach.

THE DEFENCE INDUSTRIES OF THE USA

MARTIN EDMONDS

A Secure Market

Public interest in and concern about the defence industries of the USA is not confined to the US population. Business, industry and the armed forces of the USA have set both the direction and the pace of post-Second World War defence technology development for the world, leaving allied and non-aligned nations to follow their lead, and adversaries to react. Furthermore, the USA has consistently topped the world 'league table' for the transfer of military weapons and equipment, leading to close international interest in the surplus output of the US defence industry, the support it receives from federal government, the quality of its military hardware and, for potential purchasers, the cost-effectiveness of its products.

Three principal factors can be identified as causes of this international interest in the research, development and production of the US defence industries. Firstly, as US defence industries are almost entirely in private ownership their products are not completely confined to the requirements of the US armed forces, and they are driven by commercial interests. To the extent that the US Department of Defense and Department of State will grant the necessary export licences—and there is no evidence to suggest that they are any more liberal than other arms-exporting countries—the choice of US military equipment is significantly greater, both in type and sophistication, than can be offered by any international competitor. A second factor is the size of the US defence industry as a whole, and the number of constituent industries and individual corporations within it, which makes possible the wide choice of products.

Thirdly, the US policy of containment of the Soviet Union, set down in National Security Council memorandum Number 68 (NSC-68), signed by President Truman in September 1950, has determined that military requirements would of necessity cover a range of capabilities, including nuclear strategy, air superiority, continental defence, victory in a war of attrition (both conventional and nuclear), US military support to European allies (NATO) and the protection of US political and economic interests world-wide. In other words, the US arms market for land, sea and air operations has been both larger than that of any other single nation, and more varied. For the US defence industries this substantial and eclectic demand has proved profitable and, for as long as these perceived national-security requirements do not diminish, it is assured.

There are further aspects of US defence provision and policy which guarantee a regular source of income and employment to the defence industries. Even in peacetime, the sizes of the US armed forces (2,163,200 regular personnel, plus 1,637,900 active reservists, in July 1988) and the procurement budget ($81,000m. in 1988) are enormous. The perceived quantitative and qualitative military-technology 'gaps' with the Soviet Union provide an impulse always to extend, through scientific and technological research and development, the state of the art in weapons and equipment, in order to establish or maintain a lead in military capability over the USSR. This arms race with the Soviet Union has resulted in an exponential increase in equipment costs, caused by a heavy emphasis on the latest-available military technology. Mary Kaldor has described this ever-increasing elaboration of existing weapons systems as a 'baroque arsenal'. It is possible to present an argument that weapons have been introduced to the US inventory sometimes regardless of either their military worth or operational relevance.

In the four decades since NSC-68 the basic assumptions regarding the role of the USA in the world, national-security requirements, and policy towards the Soviet Union and communist expansion have altered little. During the first Reagan administration US policy towards the USSR, likened by the President to an 'evil empire', hardened considerably. Two new major initiatives followed: the first, in April 1981, was to embark on a major 'force modernization programme'; the second, in March 1983, was to initiate a Strategic Defense Initiative (SDI—or 'Star Wars'), in the form of a long-term, and extremely ambitious technologically advanced comprehensive research and development programme leading to a land- and space-based system designed to protect the US continent (CONUS) from Soviet nuclear-missile attack. The two programmes together cost the US Treasury almost one-half of the $3,000,000m., much of it in practice from overseas borrowing, spent on defence over the ensuing eight years. For October 1988–September 1993, planned defence expenditure is put at a further $1,700,000m.: almost 50% of both of these figures would be spent with US industry.

Each programme generated immense interest and concern, for the technologies they heralded would clearly have significant repercussions on the wider international-security environment. No country, large or small, could comfortably ignore the long-term, and potentially destabilizing, implications of this enhanced US military capability. However, a number of subsequent developments are likely to cause reductions in these programmes, and consequently in the level of spending with the US defence industries. These developments include: the progress made in arms control since Mikhail Gorbachev became leader of the Soviet Union; the trend towards international collaboration in weapons-systems development and production; and, perhaps above all, the concern over the US budget deficit, and particularly the strictures of the Gramm-Rudman-Hollings Balanced Budget and Emergency Deficit Control Act of 1985, which required across-the-board government spending cuts to achieve a balanced budget by 1991.

Public Concern

US domestic interest in the industrial production and development of military equipment is not simply a post-Second World War phenomenon. Nor has that interest been manifest just in positive, supportive and competitive ways. Indeed, as often as not, US citizens have generally shared the early concerns of the Founding Fathers of the US constitution that standing peacetime armies, and the industries that support them, are a threat to liberty, a drain on national resources and a serious challenge to democracy. This was a conclusion that President Eisenhower reluctantly drew in his 1961 farewell address, warning the US population of the acquisition of 'unwarranted influence . . . by the military–industrial complex.' It is difficult, however, to strike a balance between, on the one hand, a defence-industrial capacity adequate to meet the requirements of national security and, on the other, overspending on weaponry at the expense of other social and economic priorities; few are wholly convinced that the USA has achieved it.

The Civil War has been credited with being the first conflict in which the new technologies of mass production were harnessed to a need for powerful modern weapons. The superior industrial capacity of the North contributed substantially to its victory, but it also heralded a national awareness of the need for a defence-industrial base for the successful prosecution of war. Mass production was at its most effective during the Second World War, when the ability of the USA rapidly to convert civilian industry to military production to meet the demands of the US forces, and those of several allies, in a lengthy and highly-destructive war became the *sine qua non* for victory. During that war, unlike the First World War, there was a significant emphasis on technological development and basic research. Military advantage was believed to go to the side which could both meet weapons-production targets and deadlines, and introduce new, technologically superior weapons. For most of the period since 1945 the USA has primarily been concerned with the capacity of its defence industries to maintain a technological lead in weaponry; industrial output became of secondary importance as it was assumed that wars would be short in duration and fought with forces-in-being. The more recent shift in strategic planning away from nuclear deterrence and 'nuclear-escalation dominance' towards more conventional deterrence has refocused concern on the need for a defence-industrial 'surge' capability.

However, it tends to be only during war, or periods of crisis, that the need for a defence-industrial capacity is fully appreciated. In time of peace public attitudes to defence-industrial interests have tended to be critical, sometimes wary (except in areas where defence-industrial spending is high). After every major war which has seen US involvement there has been a manifest desire for demobilization, the dismantling of the war economy and the restoration of industrial output to meet civilian requirements. This was largely achieved after 1865 and 1918; similar moves in that direction were made after 1945, but the emergence of the cold war determined that disarmament and industrial reorientation were neither possible, nor, at the time, considered prudent. The maintenance of a strong US military capability at a permanent state of readiness, with highly-trained and well-equipped professional forces, increased the influence of the entire defence community. Public concern grew during the US involvement in Vietnam throughout the 1960s, when increasing numbers of the population came to believe that a highly destructive and costly war was being prosecuted more out of national pride and prestige, and for industrial profit, than in either the public interest or the interests of national security.

Neither the end of US participation in the Vietnam conflict, nor the situation of nuclear parity between the USA and the USSR, brought about a significant reduction in defence-procurement expenditure in the early 1970s. Several explanations have been offered. Some economists have concluded that the US economy has become attuned to high levels of defence spending, without which there would be, in neo-Keynesian terms, over-production, high deflation and economic dislocation; furthermore, the administration would lose one of its major tools for managing the US economy. Political analysts have pointed to the pressure exerted by members of Congress and governors representing areas economically dependent on defence industries for the maintenance of high levels of defence spending in their regions. Finally, the military–industrial complex has a tradition of exaggerating the extent of the Soviet threat to US security, favouring weapons that are expensive,

complex and technologically advanced, and absorbing a disproportionate amount of the country's scientific and engineering talent. The emphasis has, therefore, shifted away from reducing defence-procurement expenditure and towards getting better value for money out of the defence industries. This has led to the search for more 'dual-use' technologies (both civil and military). The long lead times associated with the most advanced and esoteric scientific and technological programmes (such as the SDI) and their commercial exploitation, coupled with the need to find technical conventional substitutes to compensate for manpower shortages as a result of demographic decline, will ensure that the output of US industries with defence interests, and their contribution to the national economy, will continue on a major scale well into the foreseeable future.

Defence-Critical Industries

Paradoxical as it may seem, the US defence industry does not exist as a single entity. Neither are there defence industries, as such; instead, there are numerous industries, some of whose outputs are concerned directly or indirectly with the research, development and production of weapons, and with material specified and ordered by the US armed forces. Nowhere is this more clearly detailed than in an evaluation of the US defence-industrial base prepared for the Department of Defense (DOD) by the Logistics Management Institute (LMI) in 1987. In their Report, LMI identified 185 'defence-critical' industries, and ranked them by performance according to six economic indicators. Defence-critical industries were taken from the Standard Industrial Classification (SIC) of the US Department of Commerce, compiled in accordance with the composition and structure of the economy. The 185 listed were not the only industries with defence interests, but merely those identified as critical to the defence-industrial base.

LMI's definition of a 'defence-critical' industry used a combination of two sources: the Defense Economic Impact Modelling System (DEIMS), an input–output model of the US economy combined with the US defence budget, and the Department of Commerce *Shipments to Federal Agencies*, a publication listing the value of manufacturers' shipments to government departments and employees engaged in work related to government expenditure on manufactured products. While in the judgement of LMI 185 industries were critical to the US defence-industrial base, the DOD's own review identified 215 individual industries which accounted for 95% of its purchases from the US manufacturing sector.

Some industries are clearly more critical than others to the needs of national security. This was implicit both in the rationale of US strategic-bombing targeting during the Second World War, and in the intent behind Section 301 of the 1950 Defense Production Act, which provided for loans (termed 'V' loans) to industries in financial difficulty only where they were deemed essential to national security. How criticality is measured is an imprecise art: one indicator would be gross defence purchases by the government from one particular industry, another the defence share of an industry's total sales. Neither, however, takes into account the utility function, or military worth, of an industry's defence products to national security. Nor do they accommodate value-added factors in the design, assembly and testing of complex military systems.

The DOD's Industrial Resources Office has recently identified five industrial groupings critical to security and in need of support—the semiconductor, gas-turbine, machine-tool, bearings and forgings industries. These particular industries were perceived to be vulnerable to foreign competition, to have had a relatively poor industrial performance in recent years, and to lack the capacity to respond to DOD requirements in the event of a national emergency or security crisis. As a consequence, active policies have been introduced to remedy these apparent shortcomings, as outlined in the Report of the Under-Secretary of Defense (Acquisition) *Bolstering Defense Industries* (July 1988), more commonly known as the 'Costello Report'.

The structure of the US defence industry can also be viewed according to the characteristics of the suppliers. The defence industry is dominated not by the suppliers, but by the principal customer, the DOD. The latter defines the specifications of the products to be purchased, and sets the rules under which they are acquired; the resultant defence 'industry' has come to be hierarchically structured between prime contractors, subcontractors and parts suppliers. There is sound common sense in this arrangement; the extent of government involvement in the procurement process, the wide variety in forms of contract and the plethora of statutory regulations governing defence procurement (16,000 pages of instructions) have made it preferable to keep the number of firms required to be familiar with both the government's procedures and the bureaucracy that goes with them relatively small. When combined with the technological complexity of modern weapons systems, this approach has led to a high degree of specialization among both prime contractors and many subcontractors.

PRIME CONTRACTORS

When commentators refer to the US defence industry it is normally the prime contractors which they have in mind. Some of these large corporations are almost wholly defence-oriented; others are defence-oriented divisions of larger, diversified conglomerates. The percentage of total defence procurement contracted with the prime contractors has changed little since 1960. For example, 70% of defence business by value is still conducted with the top 100 defence companies, 50% with the top 25 and 20% with the top five. Although the trend to concentrate defence purchases on fewer prime contractors tended to rise throughout the 1950s and 1960s, it has since levelled off. When threatened with defence-spending cuts, these large prime contractors, while retaining their defence-market share, have looked for compensation in the civil market. This was a policy pursued by Lockheed in the mid-1960s when it tried to reduce its 93% dependence on the DOD by re-entering the civil-aerospace market with its 'Tristar' L-1011 airliner.

The domination of the defence market by the largest prime contractors is enhanced by the basic research and development (R. & D.) work each does for the DOD in addition to production contracts. This advanced technological work gives them not merely a comprehensive advantage in capital, experience and 'know-how', but often a monopoly in certain categories of weapons system. With the US armed forces' strategic and tactical requirements concentrated on aircraft, missiles, space systems and avionics, the largest defence corporations have tended to become, through vertical integration and specialization, concentrated in the aerospace and related industrial sectors.

The mutually beneficial relationship between the aerospace industry and the armed forces' government agencies has nurtured the progress of many procurement programmes. The names Boeing, General Dynamics, Lockheed, McDonnell Douglas, Northrop, Rockwell, and United Technologies (Pratt and Whitney), figure consistently as the companies receiving the bulk of military contracts awarded in value terms. Together, these companies regularly account for 25% of total DOD production contracts a year, and in excess of 35% of all DOD R. & D. contracts. For NASA (the National Aeronautics and Space Administration), the procurement figure for these companies is even higher, totalling about 36%.

These figures refer to overall defence R. & D. procurement, and to the largest prime contractors. When translated into specific products the market concentration confirms the trend towards vertical integration, product specialization and company monopoly. Figures for 1967 (and evidence suggests that overall percentages have changed little in the subsequent period) reveal that the top four firms received over 90% of DOD contracts for products such as satellites, nuclear submarines, space boosters, fighter aircraft, missile guidance and navigation systems, missile re-entry vehicles, aircraft fire-control systems, transport aircraft, helicopters and jet engines. The dominance of the major contractors has been enlarged by steady horizontal integration in the defence business—principally through company take-overs, absorptions and mergers—to the further detriment of competition and efficiency. Exacerbating this trend is the propensity for the prime defence contractors to subcontract work between them-

selves, especially when the overall DOD procurement budget declines in real terms. Under the Reagan administration this did not happen, although the Bush administration was expected to take measures to reduce defence expenditure as a matter of some urgency.

SUBCONTRACTORS AND PARTS SUPPLIERS

Subcontractors are responsible for subsidiary systems of weapons system programmes. They have to meet the technical specifications of the prime contractors and deliver their products for final assembly. Subcontractors are paid by the prime contractors and generally have no direct involvement with government procurement agencies other than in terms of quality control and their conformity with federal procurement regulations. Supplying both prime contractors and subcontractors are third-tier companies—the parts and components producers. These are companies covering a multitude of industries whose degree of dependence on defence procurement contracts is highly variable. Nevertheless, that they are defence-critical is reflected in the fact that over 50% of all the costs of defence hardware is paid to subcontractors and parts suppliers. Of that 50%, some 35% of all defence contracts by value go to small businesses; legislation exists to encourage their use more extensively. In the fiscal year to September 1987 small businesses received 19.7% of total prime contract awards and 40.6% of total subcontract awards.

DISTRIBUTION OF WORK

So, although a few prominent companies dominate the award of prime contracts, there is a much wider distribution of work by value after subcontracting. For example, on the Minuteman Intercontinental Ballistic Missile system Boeing was the prime contractor, but about 40,000 subcontracted suppliers accounted for 55% of the total value of the project. The federal Small Business Administration estimates that there are about 130,000 small businesses interested in being DOD prime contractors or subcontractors. The DOD has made efforts to open its market to horizontal competition as a means to promote efficiency and stimulate innovation. This makes the field of small, innovative high-technology defence-oriented business a very competitive one, with a concomitant casualty rate among companies.

Furthermore, while defence-industrial businesses tend to concentrate around the locations of the major prime contractors, the latter themselves are widely distributed in geographical terms. In terms of Census divisions, the Pacific and New England states receive the highest total value of defence prime contracts, while the Midwest states receive the least. California, where many large aerospace and electronic corporations are to be found, alone receives about 20% of total DOD procurement and R. & D. contracts; New York, with 9%, and Connecticut and Texas, with about 7% each, follow in prominence.

Annual DOD expenditure on procurement, as declared in the DOD Individual Contracting Action Report (Form DD-350), declined between 1984 and 1987 from $133,500m. to $92,800m.; 4% a year was procured from overseas sources. Since US private industry receives virtually 100% of all DOD production contracts, compared with only 70% of all R. &. D. contracts—the remainder going to government-owned laboratories—it is possible to estimate that an average of about $100,000m. a year was spent with US industries on defence work between 1984 and 1988. (This is excluding spending on 'black-budget' items, such as the Stealth bomber, which has been estimated as high as $15,000m.–$20,000m. a year.) From this total California will have received about $20,000m. a year in prime contract awards, a figure that increases if the concentration of defence-critical subcontractors in that state is taken into consideration. California is an extreme example; but the economies of many other states, regions and, in particular, localities depend heavily on DOD contracts.

The Defence-Industrial Lobby

With the economic importance of the defence industry in many states, regions and localities added to the cost of maintaining military bases and other service facilities, the military–industrial complex carries great weight with members of Congress. The armed forces and defence industries have a common interest in attracting support for their new products and ideas—and both groups are always keen to extend the boundaries of military technology. Professional lobbyists, congressional representatives, corporate representatives, ex-service personnel on their executive staffs and highly sophisticated public-relations strategies are all deployed by defence industries to further their interests in Washington.

Not least important in prosecuting the interests of the defence industries are the industrial and trade associations. These include: the National Security Industrial Association (NSIA), with over 250 members; the Air Force Association with some 200 members added to a personal membership list running into tens of thousands; the Aerospace Industries Association of America (AIA) with over 60 members; the American Defense Preparedness Association with 400 members; and, perhaps the most important of all, the Council of Defense and Space Industry Association which brings together the AIA and NSIA with other industrial associations with defence interests, such as the Shipbuilders Council of America, the Motor Vehicle Manufacturers Association of the United States and the Electronic Industries Association. A relative newcomer to the list is the Armed Forces Communications and Electronics Association which not only seems to have a particularly close relationship with the Pentagon, but has proved itself to be very active and effective in promoting corporate interests in the defence-electronics, information-technology, telecommunications, surveillance, security and communications fields.

Employment

The defence procurement and R. & D. budgets contributed towards the direct employment of five million people in 1987, with a further two million being engaged indirectly in subcontracting and parts supply. These figures accounted for about 5% of total US employment. One estimate is even that one in every 10 jobs in the USA depends directly or indirectly on the defence budget. In states where there is a high concentration of defence contractors, or a low level of general manufacturing, defence procurement accounts for at least 10% of all personal income. This applies to the states of Alaska, Arizona, California, Colorado, Connecticut, Hawaii, Maryland, Massachusetts, Utah, Virginia and Washington. The very high technological content of defence procurement entails the employment of highly-trained and qualified, and mostly 'white-collar', workers. A conservative estimate is that about 20% of all US engineers and 25% of all physicists are engaged in defence work.

The major defence contractors are capital-intensive. They are managed and run by highly-qualified and highly-paid technicians, designers, computer programmers and machinists. The total amount of capital invested in the defence industries is impossible to calculate, partly because the figures do not exist, and partly because of the 'dual-use' technology with which most corporations and industries are involved: the capital investment supports both civil and military R. & D. and production.

Capital Investment

In the past it was generally held that civilian markets benefited from 'spin-off' from defence R. & D. and production. Today there is greater appreciation of the civil foundation upon which most defence industries are based, and of the contribution that civilian work makes to the defence effort. This has proved particularly pertinent in the advanced electronics fields. Nevertheless, the highly specific and often unusual specifications emanating from the DOD procurement agencies in the past have necessitated the use of capital equipment and facilities that are highly product-specific and for which there is also a very restricted market. In these circumstances the Pentagon has found it unreasonable to expect private industry to provide the necessary investment, and has met the requirement itself.

These Government Owned/Company Operated (GOCO) assets, plus government-provided real estate, have been estimated to account for about 40% of the capital used by private corporations working on DOD contracts, and are valued at between $18,000m. and $20,000m.

The size of this figure has invited the criticism that government-provided assets act as a form of subsidy to large corporations that are already wealthy. They not only assist the prime contractors, to whom this support mainly applies, to record a high return on investment on defence work, but also, unfairly, help them to compete in the civil market, since the capital equipment in question is not differentiated by the nature, or subsequent use, of the final product. GOCO equipment further discriminates against open entry into the defence market, since these assets are not easily transferable or available to competitors, and are therefore a constraint on competition. A counter-argument to such criticism is that the investment makes possible a necessary capacity that the US government should pay for, and hold in reserve, in order to meet the requirements of a prolonged conventional war.

The Efficiency of Defence Acquisition

Wherever there are large, complex government contracts involving many thousands of people and corporations, there is ample scope for waste, and potentially for abuse and even fraud. Assessing the costs of projects contracted to the defence industries has proved very difficult. As most projects are by definition working in hitherto inadequately-understood areas, assessing their scale, length and cost has become more of an art than a science. Furthermore, a 1% underestimation on a $30,000m. contract, a valuation which is not unusual in modern times, would lead to a cost overrun of $300m.: the norm allowed for estimating error in industry is plus or minus 5%.

The General Accounting Office, Congress and the Pentagon have long sought to promote efficiency in defence acquisition, to prevent waste, and yet to ensure the delivery of the weapons that the US armed forces say they need. The consensus is that they have not succeeded, and often have made the situation worse. Critics of defence acquisition allege that US weapons are unnecessarily complex, and hence expensive and unreliable; they further accuse the defence industry of dishonesty and inefficient production procedures. The industry's response to such allegations has changed little over the years; constant interference by government agencies and Congressionally-imposed audits, it is claimed, have hindered attempts to manage acquisition projects smoothly and efficiently.

The root of the problem is the acquisition process itself. In the wake of a succession of cost-escalation revelations and scandals concerning the irresponsible use of public money, congressional subcommittees were convened, in 1983, to investigate the problem yet again. Their solution was the Defense Reorganization Act of 1986, which changed the organization and conduct of defence procurement. As in 1969, when President Nixon appointed a Blue Ribbon Commission on Defence Management, because the issue had become a political one, so President Reagan, also for political reasons, was prompted to set up a second such Blue Ribbon Panel in 1985. By coincidence, both panels were chaired by the same man, David Packard, and in 1985 he was forced to conclude that the situation was no better than it had been in 1969 when his panel had found the defence-acquisition process to be in a 'real mess'. Appealing to the Truth in Negotiations Act of 1962, Packard asked in 1969 for greater integrity in government–industry relations, especially in cost estimations. The record shows that either integrity was manifestly absent, or the exercise was beyond the capability of the defence corporations.

The US defence industry is an integral and major part of the defence-acquisition process: it must take its share of the blame. However, the problem really goes deeper, since the defence industries have a divided commitment: the one to the government, often as its sole-source supplier, and the other to shareholders. These commitments are not always compatible, as demonstrated by the need for systems of renegotiation on government and defence contracts. The acquisition process is involved, technically complex, costly, time-sensitive and dynamic. Above all, it is a process that, over time, has accumulated an encyclopedia of rules, regulations and statutory requirements. Many of these, also, are contradictory and counter-productive.

The US public, however, has always been suspicious of big business, and of monopolies in particular. The 1890 Sherman Antitrust Act is as alive today as when it was passed. Suspicions are aroused even further when public money is at risk, where open market principles do not apply, there is little accountability (the DOD does its own audit) and when high-spending public programmes are liable to be determined by politically-flavoured decisions. Defence procurement is all of these things: by their very nature, modern weapons programmes necessitate the involvement of large industrial corporations, great complexity, vast amounts of finance, and sole-source suppliers. Furthermore, defence contracting is also conducted under the cloak of national security and secrecy.

These public concerns have determined that close surveillance of defence contracts is conducted, even though the normal processes of audit inspection and accounting are increasingly impractical and difficult to implement. Instances are reported where defence contractors have had to stop work as often as 30 or 40 times a year to provide government agencies with the detailed figures they require. Not infrequently these exercises, or when there is 'whistle-blowing' from within the DOD or the defence manufacturers, reveal instances of 'fraud, waste or abuse'. Such information is ammunition to headline-seekers and opponents of the 'military–industrial complex'. While there is no way of condoning $100 toilet seats and company 'boondoggles' (wasteful or unproductive activities), these instances have to be put in perspective: in the overall scheme of things the total amount of waste and abuse is trivial indeed compared with overall defence-acquisition costs. Perhaps in an undertaking of such dimensions, and with such technical and military uncertainties, occasional mistakes and failures are allowable. However, no matter how trivial the problem is economically, politically it is highly relevant due to the presence of public suspicions.

Conclusion

The US defence industry has to be seen in the context of US politics, otherwise its performance and controversial nature cannot be properly understood. Defence R. & D. and production is largely a monopolistic activity, operating in an antitrust environment. Firms operate in the country's largest market which, for reasons of security, scarcity, and complexity, has restricted entry; the final assembled products are of such a scale that only large businesses can handle them; and its principal market is the government. However, the US defence industry represents all that the country's population admires in business—technological and financial success—but also all that it fears—monopoly, secrecy, and government control. On balance, the positive side continues to have the upper hand: the US defence industry serves the most powerful nation on earth well; it produces the most advanced products that set the lead that others follow; and it has consistently kept the USA in the forefront in most spheres of modern technology. Certainly it is far from perfect. Its results could be better, and there have been mistakes. But despite all the scandals, it has demonstrated a high level of commitment and integrity, given the political context in which it has to operate, and compares more than favourably with its equivalents elsewhere.

SERVICE INDUSTRIES IN THE USA

P. W. DANIELS

Introduction

The USA is the archetypal service economy; in 1986 service-producing industries provided employment for 77.3m. workers—or 71% of all those in employment. The shift from manufacturing to service industries has been a significant feature of the economy since the mid-1960s. There has been a steady increase in demand for service workers—in part as a result of a slower growth in productivity in services than in manufacturing. Increasing real wages (until the mid-1970s), and more leisure time as working hours have been reduced, have also spurred demand for a wide variety of services which are mainly labour-intensive. The average working time per week for all service-industry workers in 1985 was 35.8 hours, compared with 38.8 hours per week for all wage and salary workers in manufacturing and services. Workers with service occupations (excluding managerial and professional) had even shorter working weeks, averaging 32.3 hours. In 1986 22%, or more than one in five, of all those in employment in the USA were employed in leisure, hotel, and retail and wholesale distribution services compared with just under 7% in finance, insurance and real estate, 7% in transportation, communication and public utilities and 5% in public administration. Professional and related services (health, education, social, legal) also comprise a large group (20% of all employees). It is anticipated that the increasing share of total employment in services will continue well into the 1990s, when more than 75% will be so engaged as manufacturing employment continues to contract. Most of the fast-growing occupations up to 2000 are forecast to be service-related; for example medical assistants (forecast to increase by 90%), computer-systems analysts (76%) and legal assistants (60%).

It will be apparent that the diverse nature of the service sector makes difficult both the identification of its constituent industries and generalizations about the trends they exhibit.

The most common way of characterizing the difference between services and manufacturing is on the basis of output; the former generates largely intangible outputs rather than tangible goods. Yet it soon becomes apparent that the sectors of retail and wholesale distribution, for example, which are essentially low-wage and labour-intensive activities, are very different from the utilities such as gas or electricity supply which are capital-intensive, high-wage activities. These, in turn, differ markedly from many of the financial or professional services which are labour-intensive but exhibit both very high- and low-wage occupations in almost equal measure.

Wage levels in a number of service industries are low, and there tends to be a polarization between a high proportion of low-wage earners and a high proportion of high-wage earners, with a small group of middle-income earners. In 1984 about 29% of full-time workers in manufacturing earned less than $15,000 a year, compared with 41% in services. Less than 20% earned more than $30,000 in services as a whole, compared with 26% in manufacturing. Such statistics do, of course, disguise considerable variations; 45% of males in professional service employment earned more than $30,000 in 1984, but only 28% of female employees did so; for personal services the equivalent figures were 17% and 6% respectively. The high proportion of low-wage service jobs not only reflects the large proportion of female workers in many services but also the ease of entry into service production. The majority of service establishments are small and are not capital-intensive. This in turn tends to reduce productivity and therefore wages. The nature of service production also means greater flexibility in the use of labour, so that part-time employment is more prevalent than in other segments of the US labour market. Self-employment is also more common in service industries and tends to be adopted by high-income workers such as lawyers, dentists or doctors. Part-time working arrangements reduce employer obligations and have the effect of increasing the supply of jobs, expanding the potential work-force and contributing to lower wages.

While factors of this kind have undoubtedly contributed to the expansion of the service industries in the USA, it is also necessary to draw attention to other, equally important, considerations. Services not only contribute to the quality of life (for example amusement, recreation, conservation of historic buildings, sanitation) across the USA but are also increasingly integral to the production process for both tangible goods and intangible services. As products and services have become more specialized and refined, in response both to the need to maintain competitiveness and to consumer preference, the need to invest in a wide range of sophisticated marketing, distribution, production, equipment and human resources, for example, has expanded. It is neither practicable nor cost-effective for many organizations to invest in all their requirements for their exclusive use; they purchase them from specialist firms providing a wide range of consulting, legal, design, market-research and other services. This 'contracting-out' of demand for services also creates a need for lawyers and sales personnel to mediate in both the initial process and subsequent contract renewals. It is also worth noting that most legislation enacted by the US government which affects business or consumers creates an immediate demand for additional or new services.

Transportation and Communications

ROADS

The integration of the USA's domestic economy, as well as the maintenance of overseas trade in services and goods, is dependent on one of the most comprehensive networks of transport services in the world. In 1985 there were 691,000 miles (1.1m. km) of urban roads and 3.2m. miles (5.1m. km) of rural highways, of which 88% were paved. The interstate freeway is the backbone of the nation's highway system, in 1985 carrying more than 20% of total traffic on 44,000 miles (71,000 km) of two- or three-lane, fully-graded, limited-access highway offering low-cost movement of goods and people between all the major metropolitan areas. It is possible, for example, to drive for more than 3,000 miles from the Pacific coast to the Atlantic coast without leaving an interstate freeway. The system has encouraged the redistribution of manufacturing and service firms from the Northeast to the South and West and, where several routes converge on major cities, for example Chicago, St Louis, Atlanta or Dallas–Fort Worth, it has also improved accessibility for workers and businesses within such metropolitan areas. With more than 117m. passenger cars and taxis, 45m. goods vehicles, and 600,000 buses and coaches in use in 1986, an efficient highway system is a paramount need. These figures indicate that the demand for surface travel is largely from private road users, while public transport (bus, rail, tram and metro systems) is relatively insignificant. Cities and towns across the USA have their own publicly- and privately-funded bus systems; exceptions, such as New York, Washington, DC, Chicago and the San Francisco Bay area, also have metro or equivalent systems, while others, such as Portland, San Francisco or Philadelphia, have retained (or introduced) tramways. Individually, the recent investments in these systems (BART in the San Francisco Bay area or the Metro in Washington, DC) have created impressive but often incomplete systems. However, they have hardly changed the significant imbalance between the use of public and private transport services in the USA. Following a decline between 1980 and 1983, the number of passengers carried by the passenger-transit industry (which comprises all privately- and publicly-owned organized local passenger transportation agencies except taxis, suburban railroads, and sightseeing and school buses) increased to almost 9,000m. in 1985, while the number of vehicle-miles it operated in that year totalled 2,453m. (compared with 1,270,000m. vehicle-miles of travel for passenger cars and motorcycles).

RAILWAYS

This pattern has not been aided by the continuing demise of rail transport, which has achieved only modest increases in passenger numbers, to 315m. in 1987. While railroads remain very important for freight, revenues from this source have been declining since 1984. The number of Class I line-hauling companies (i.e. those with gross annual operating revenues of more than $88.5m., measured in 1978 dollars) declined from a peak of 73 in 1975 to 22 in 1986 and the length of line operated by them decreased from 206,000 miles (331,000 km) in 1970 to 154,000 miles (248,000 km) in 1986. Locomotive numbers, station numbers and operating revenues have all been falling since 1981. The rail network is most intensively used along the north-east corridor, between Boston and Washington, DC, and for commuter services into the largest metropolitan areas, notably New York and Chicago. In high-density corridors the publicly-owned AMTRAK, which carried 20.2m. passengers overall in 1986, and some independent railway companies have been able both to invest in new rolling stock and to upgrade track and signalling facilities to provide services that can compete with other forms of transport on time, reliability and cost. For long-distance travel, however, the market remains very small for the slow, unreliable and geographically-limited services provided (mainly by AMTRAK), even though the average trip-distance per passenger has increased from 220 miles (354 km) in 1982 to 249 miles (401 km) in 1986.

AIR

The inability of the railways to compete for anything other than relatively short-distance commuting travel in selected parts of the country is not unrelated to the inexorable growth of the US domestic-airline network. The number of passengers has increased by more than 50% since 1975, to about 400m. in 1988. Passenger-miles increased by 40% between 1984 and 1988, while freight ton-miles increased by 24% and the volume of mail carried by more than 55% over the same period.

Deregulation of the airline industry since 1978 has increased competition between national and regional carriers, brought down fares and made flying more accessible to a greater proportion of the US population. The efforts to remain profitable and competitive have made several carriers vulnerable to take-over or merger, so that the number of operators has declined steadily during the 1980s. New airlines, such as Texas Air, have emerged as major players, while larger established companies such as TWA (Trans World Airlines), United Airlines and American Airlines have had to consolidate by gaining control of local or regional carriers that can then be used to provide 'feeder' services to the hub-and-spoke pattern that is now such a dominant feature of the organization of the US airline network. The aim has been to reduce total transportation costs. Each major airline has chosen a major city— possibly two—as a focus for their operations (Delta Air Lines, for example, has chosen Atlanta, TWA St Louis and Northwest Minneapolis–St Paul) with a view to implementing economies of scale in aircraft servicing, utilization, passenger transfer and the range of destinations served that might not otherwise be possible using direct flights. As passenger numbers have grown and travel demand is concentrated into certain peak periods, the hub-and-spoke system has offered fewer clear advantages to passengers, especially business travellers who use airline services because of their time-saving advantages. By concentrating so many aircraft movements and increasing the number of landings and take-offs on specific airports, the airlines' performance in relation to punctuality declined in the late 1980s and there have been some calls for re-regulation in an effort to improve both the service to passengers and safety in the air and on the ground. In 1985 the 25 largest 'hubs' (some of which—such as Chicago and Los Angeles—include more than one airport) handled 60% of all scheduled departures and 69% of all passengers enplaned.

WATER

Coastal, lake and other internal waterways (mainly river systems such as those of the Mississippi and Columbia) also carry freight traffic; especially bulk products such as coal, timber, grain and petroleum. The volume of domestic intercity freight traffic on inland waterways totalled 425,000m. short-ton-miles in 1979, declining to 351,000m. in 1982 before increasing again, to 382,000m. short-ton-miles in 1985. Of this some 59%

(225,000m. short-ton-miles) is transported on the Mississippi River system (which includes the Mississippi, Illinois, Missouri and Ohio Rivers and their tributaries). The absence of a clear trend suggests that annual fluctuations in freight carried are in part related to the effects of winter conditions or summer droughts on the navigability of some parts of the inland-waterway system.

Measured in terms of shipping weight, 99.7% of general imports into the USA are transported by vessel rather than air. The most significant change during the 1980s has been the increase in the relative importance of the Pacific seaboard in terms of the value of imports, even though the total tonnage has grown at a slower rate than for the Atlantic or Gulf ports. Increasing trade with Pacific Rim countries in high-value-added goods, such as vehicles, accounts for this change.

There is also an unseen, but vital, transportation system comprising petroleum and natural-gas pipelines. Transport operators and domestic consumers benefit from these pipelines, which distribute products that would otherwise require transport using road or rail haulage. Petroleum pipeline length has remained much the same, at about 170,000 miles (275,000 km), during the 1980s and most is trunk line for interstate deliveries of crude oil and derivative products. Domestic consumers depend more on natural-gas pipeline systems, the total length of which has expanded from 178,000 miles (286,000 km) in 1982 to 190,000 miles (305,000 km) in 1985. However, the bulk of operating revenues (60%) are attributable to commercial and industrial areas.

Retailing and Wholesaling

RETAILING

During the early 1980s wholesale and retail trade consistently provided about 16% of the USA's total gross national product (GNP). In 1986 wholesale trade was worth $294,600m. (in current prices) and retailing $407,900m. Retail sales, assets and net income have become more concentrated throughout the 1980s; in 1986 just 10 companies commanded 55% of the sales of the 50 largest retailers—they also held 65% of the assets and 51% of the net income. In terms of constant (1982) dollars, total retail sales rose every year between 1983 and 1986, at annual rates varying between 4.9% and 7.3%, and per-head sales increased from $4,609 in 1982 to $5,639 in 1986. Retailers can be divided into the two categories of durable-goods stores (selling, for example, furniture, motor vehicles and hardware) and non-durable-goods stores (including apparel stores, gasoline service stations, food stores, liquor stores, and so on). Sales from durable-goods stores increased by 89% in nominal terms between 1980 and 1986, compared with an increase of just 35% for non-durable-goods stores. In 1986 automotive dealers accounted for 59% of durable-store sales, while sales by food stores and by general-merchandise stores are most prominent among non-durables, accounting for 33% and 18% respectively of sales in the latter category in 1986.

Shopping Centres

During the mid-1980s the US retail sector has been experiencing structural and organizational changes very similar to those which have taken place in financial and professional services and in hotel and related services (see below). Thus, although retail sales have been growing, the number of retail establishments has begun to decline. There are some differences in the various areas of activity; numbers of food stores and automotive dealers have declined, while those of apparel and accessory stores and of furniture and home-furnishing stores have stabilized. Such differences reflect the ability of some segments of the retail sector to derive economies of scale (in terms of, for example, distribution, prices, labour costs and ability costs) from large-scale operating units. The most notable examples are to be found among food stores and general-merchandise stores, which are anchor retailers in the numerous regional shopping centres and malls which are located on the outskirts of most US cities or along major 'ribbon' shopping streets. In most smaller suburban shopping centres the key tenant is a supermarket, but in larger centres there is also a requirement for a drugstore and a hardware store. Up to 50% of the leasable floor space in neighbourhood shopping centres is occupied by supermarkets. (Neighbourhood centres have a catchment-area population of up to 40,000, whereas community retail centres have catchments up to 150,000 and regional shopping centres catchments well in excess of 150,000.) The major tenants in community centres are small department stores (regional chains), variety stores and discount stores; in regional centres the anchor function is exercised by at least one, possibly two, major department stores, usually part of national chains such as J. C. Penney. The department store provides the primary attraction for consumers, who also then provide a market for a range of shopping-goods, such as general-merchandise, apparel, and furniture and home-furnishing stores. Locations for regional shopping centres are primarily suburban, at the intersection of radial and ring freeways and with large areas for parking at ground level. They are also often supplemented with entertainment services such as bowling alleys, movie theatres and drive-in banks and fast-food restaurants.

In recent years retailing development has focused on even larger, superregional shopping centres: these are mainly situated in the major metropolitan areas and provide high-quality retail services accessible primarily to high- and middle-income consumers. These centres are usually developed by major international companies with a detailed knowledge of retail-market trends and the expertise to assemble the finance necessary for shopping centres which typically comprise four to six department stores, at least 100 other shop units and a wide range of supporting services. There are more than 300 superregional shopping centres, mainly in the South and West of the USA, where population growth and economic growth have been fastest throughout the 1980s. There has been a relative decline in shopping-centre activity in those parts of the country, such as the Northeast and the Midwest, with the longest-established centre tradition. Some of the most modern and innovative shopping centres have been located in states such as Washington or Missouri with a well-established, but slower-growing, shopping-centre industry.

Franchising

Franchising has been an even more significant feature during the 1980s. Few segments of US retailing are not participants in this method of marketing or distribution. The total number of franchised establishments increased from 442,000 in 1983 to 499,000 in 1987, most of which were franchisee-owned. Average annual sales per establishment increased by 57% over the 1980–87 period, from $760,000 in 1980 to $1.2m. in 1987. The USA has dominated in the development of international franchising—in 1986 more than 350 US companies were operating more than 30,000 foreign outlets. (McDonalds, the fast-food chain, has been particularly prominent in this respect, having opened some 1,400 restaurants in 31 overseas countries in addition to its 5,500 outlets in the USA.) In 1987 gasoline service stations comprised 23% of all domestic franchisees and accounted for 16% of franchise sales, compared with 28% in 1980. This provides an indication of the extent to which franchising has been adopted in other areas of retailing, notably restaurants (which accounted for 17% of franchisees in 1987), non-food retailing (10%) and auto and truck dealerships (6%). The latter sector generated almost 52% of all franchise sales in 1987 through 25,100 franchised new-car dealers, over one-half of whom handled both domestic and imported vehicles. Some data on advertising expenditure by new-car dealerships also illustrate the interdependence between different areas of the US service economy. In 1986 more than $3,400m. was expended on vehicle advertising, in nominal terms almost three times the 1980 figure of $1,200m. It is therefore not surprising that advertising is one of the most buoyant business services at the present time.

General Trends

While the number of retail establishments increased by 15% in 1980–85, from 1,222,900 to 1,406,800, total employment in the sector expanded by only 12% over the same period. The real effect of this may be exaggerated since a substantial proportion of recent recruitment has involved part-time workers for whom sales work, for example, is well suited. Employment in eating and drinking places thus expanded by

18% during the early 1980s, that in miscellaneous retailing (for example drug stores, liquor stores and florists) by 11% and that in food stores (mainly grocery stores) by 16%. As ownership concentration in US retailing continues, many small, independent retailers are disappearing. One indication of this is the reduction in the number of self-employed retailers from 1.6m. in 1984 to 1.5m. in 1987, even though the numbers of self-employed nationally increased by 3%. This is also a symptom of the continuing competitive uncertainty in retailing. As consumer tastes evolve, shopping habits and preferred shopping locations change; this now requires more complex decision-making and more sophisticated information to help managers to make the right investment and location decisions. A state of maturity has been reached in US retailing, and this is reflected in numerous mergers and take-overs, falling returns on investment, increased advertising expenditures, extensive price competition and some stagnation in gross margin trends. In 1986 there were 147 mergers within the retail industry, with a nominal value of $13,683; this represents a 71% increase since 1982, when there were 86 mergers with a nominal value of $1,948m. Over the same period the total annual number of mergers in the US economy increased by 42%.

WHOLESALING

Wholesale trade performs a crucial connecting role between manufacturers and retailers and is very amenable to economies of scale through large-scale operations and carefully-chosen locations with good access to interstate highway and, where appropriate, rail or air services. Information technology has also helped in inventory management and control, and the planning of distribution-vehicle routing and networks. Thus the number of wholesale establishments grew by almost 9% between 1977 and 1982. Over the same period sales increased by 59% but the number of employees by only 13%. Capital investment in new technology and fewer, but larger, wholesale outlets continue to maintain these differentials. The proportion of all establishments with sales exceeding $1m. annually had reached 46% in 1982 compared with 40% in 1977. Merchant wholesalers dominate this part of the service sector, with 58% of the sales of all establishments in 1982. The value of inventories held by wholesalers has increased greatly, largely because of the diversity of product ranges resulting from even more-sophisticated customer demand. This is especially true for the durable-goods sector, where the value of inventories increased by 19% between 1980 and 1987, compared with the non-durable-goods sector, which registered a corresponding increase of 16%.

Media Services

RADIO AND TELEVISION

The USA has what is possibly the most diverse and dynamic media industry in the world. Interstate radio and television broadcasting is regulated by the Federal Communications Commission and individual states issue licences to almost 4,000 FM radio stations and almost 5,000 AM stations. In addition there are more than 1,270 licensed educational FM radio stations as well as 50 radio programme networks. It has been estimated that there are almost two radio receivers per person in use and these receive output mainly from individual commercial stations, with a limited range and centred on urban areas, or from commercial networks, ranging from the National Broadcasting Co Inc (NBC), with 554 affiliated stations nation-wide, to the Keystone Broadcasting System, which has about 1,140 affiliated stations providing a transcription network for rural parts of the country, and the National Black Network, which has 140 affiliated stations. There are a few non-commercial stations, such as National Public Radio, which has member stations in 48 states and the District of Columbia, or the Voice of America, which broadcasts in 42 languages to all areas of the world. There are also radio stations operated by associations such as the National Education Association. These are supported by public subscription rather than the sale of air time for advertising. A large number of private radio stations (some 2.5m.) are also licensed for use by aviation, marine

police, fire and forestry services, for example, as well as for personal use.

A dichotomy between public and commercial broadcasting also exists for television services. The major non-profit station is an educational service financed by private subscription and by government funds. The Public Broadcasting Service co-ordinates and provides programming for 314 affiliated non-commercial TV stations across the USA. With one exception the commercial TV networks are run by the same companies operating the commercial radio networks; all are roughly the same size, with five owned and operated stations each and more than 200 affiliated stations. Turner Broadcasting operates the one commercial television-only network, although in 1988 there were a further 46 national cable television networks with some 4.8m. subscribers. The total for all cable television system subscribers was 42.3m. in 1988, compared with 15.5m. in 1980. Projections to 1995 suggest a further increase to 55m. subscribers by that date. As with radio, national networks are paralleled by a large number of independent, local television stations, which numbered more than 1,000 in 1988, together with 325 educational television stations.

With so many radio and television stations (including cable and pay-TV networks) dependent on commercial revenues, there is concern in the USA about the negative relationship between the quantity (broadcast hours) and quality of broadcasting. The 'ratings' of programmes are vital to the attraction of advertising revenues (worth $29,534m. in 1986) so that specialist documentary, drama, educational or in-depth news programmes tend to be displaced by soap operas, films, talk shows, and quiz and game shows, which attract larger audiences. Expenditure on advertising via radio, television and the press doubled in nominal terms between 1980 and 1986, with regional/local advertising accounting for about 45% of the total and national advertising about 55%. Since more than 90m. US households own at least one television set, there is no doubt that the medium can be used to convey information to more people than is the case with newspapers and periodicals.

THE PRESS

Even though there were 1,657 daily newspapers in 1986 with a combined circulation of 62.5m., the majority are oriented towards local or regional markets. At one end of the scale, Wyoming's 10 daily papers had a total combined circulation of just 99,000 in 1986, while the circulation of papers such as the *New York Times* or the *Los Angeles Times* exceeds 1m. each. Papers such as the *New York Times*, the *Wall Street Journal* and the *Washington Post* have a national readership and comprehensive coverage of national and international news. Geography has in some respects been the enemy of the press in the USA; until appropriate technology became available in the 1980s, distribution of other regions' news or newsprint in time to appear on news-stands and to arrive at homes early in the morning was costly, given the distances between the major markets (for example from the Northeastern industrial complex to California or even to industrial centres in the Midwest such as Illinois and Ohio). Telecommunications and satellite technology has allowed this problem to be overcome by allowing news copy assembled at one location to be transmitted simultaneously to printing facilities strategically located around the USA. Only one paper, *USA Today*, has so far taken advantage of this technology and issued its first edition in 1982. It has also pioneered extensive use of colour, especially for charts and maps, in a daily, general-interest paper. By 1988 its daily circulation had increased to about 1.5m.

In most cases the Sunday editions of national and local papers (of which there were 820 in 1987) have larger circulations; 150–200-page issues are not uncommon, and while news is certainly included it is swamped by advertising copy. There are also some 7,400 weekly and semi-weekly newspapers and more than 11,000 periodicals; these two categories had a circulation of more than 200m. in 1986. In common with other media-service activities, the newspaper industry has undergone considerable concentration of ownership through merger and take-over. This has largely resulted from increasing production costs and contracting sales. As a result few daily local newspapers are now produced by independent proprietors, the majority (1,212 in 1987) being owned by one of 143 newspaper groups such as the Gannett Co Inc, which publishes 90 daily newspapers, including *USA Today*.

In 1985 US book publishers (excluding the government) brought out a total of 50,070 new books and new editions. The US market for academic books is the largest in the developed world since a large proportion of the eligible population participates in a higher-education system which makes extensive use of set books for many courses, thus ensuring a very large market for academic books in comparison with most other countries.

A small number of US newspapers and periodicals are part- or wholly-owned by overseas companies. One such example is the *New York Post*, which has been owned since 1985 by Rupert Murdoch's UK-based News International group. Several of the publishing houses, especially those in New York, are US subsidiaries or affiliates of British or other European publishing houses. This is but a small part of the growing exposure in recent years of US service industries to competition through direct investment by overseas firms and through mergers and acquisitions with existing operations in the country. Internationalization is a new and still-evolving feature of the development of US service industries, and is most advanced among the wide-ranging activities of financial services (see below).

Recreation and Tourism

The share of total personal consumption expenditure accounted for by recreation has been increasing steadily during the 1980s to reach 7.1% in 1986 ($198,000m.). Increases in per-head disposable income and shorter working hours have released resources for this consumption, which encompasses a wide range of activities from the purchase of books and maps to admissions to motion-picture theatres, spectator sports and involvement in clubs or similar organizations. These figures do not include expenditures connected with travel and tourism services, either within the USA or to other countries. Almost one-half of all trips of 100 miles or more away from home are made to visit friends and relatives or for other 'pleasure' purposes. The proportion is even higher (76%) if the figures are converted to person-trips. Measured another way, the 354m. vacation trips undertaken in 1986 comprised 60% of all trips or 61% of all person-trips (in both cases in excess of 100 miles). In all instances the trend suggests that these proportions will continue to grow, together with the absolute number of trips. The majority of trips are taken by automobile; the growth of air travel for tourism and recreation purposes has been slower.

The diversity of US landscapes also makes the country a major destination for overseas visitors and the expenditures generated in this way also help to maintain the hotels, restaurants and other services which support the tourist industry. The national parks, for example, are a major tourist attraction. Covering almost 76m. acres (30.7m. hectares) of federal land, the 338 areas in the National Park System attracted 365m. visits (of which 281m. were recreational) in 1986, up by 6% since 1985. The pattern of recreational visits to Yellowstone National Park (which extends into the states of Idaho, Montana and Wyoming) is typical, in that more than one-half of the 2.4m. visitors in 1986 stayed for at least one night. The number of visitors from overseas has been increasing since 1984 in overall terms. As regards short-term trends in the numbers arriving from individual countries, much continues to depend on the strength of the dollar relative to those countries' currencies. For example, the numbers of tourists arriving from the UK increased rather more quickly in the early 1980s because a favourable exchange rate placed the USA within reach by tourists also benefiting from airline deregulation and the attendant intensive price competition on air routes across the North Atlantic. Receipts from tourism have also continued to increase since 1984. 'Packaged' visits are popular as car hirers, hotel chains and airlines put together services which reduce the time and complexity of completing long-distance travel arrangements for many first-time visitors to the USA.

Business receipts in the travel industry have been growing at annual rates of about 7% in the 1980s, with the most rapid increases being recorded by hotels, motels and eating and drinking places. As a result the travel industry has generated more jobs in labour-intensive activities, notably restaurants, bars and hotels, motels and tourist courts. In the mid-1980s, with hotel- and motel-occupancy rations remaining steady at about 65%, but the ratio of net income before income tax to sales becoming negative for full-service and resort hotels, there were reductions in employment in some sections of the industry. As in other parts of the service sector, rising costs and more-demanding customers have made it difficult for small independent hotel and motel operations to survive. The industry is dominated by major intercontinental hotel operators, such as Holiday Inn or Sheraton, and several national and regional hotel and motel chains such as Howard Johnson or Best Western, an increasing number of which are being operated as franchises. These arrangements allow independent operators to use the name and supporting services of a well-known hotel or motel chain in a prescribed manner, over a certain period of time and in a specified place, in return for an initial fee and a share of the profits. This allows the franchiser to benefit from economies of scale (while limiting exposure to failure) and the franchisee to gain access to expertise, support and markets that would otherwise be costly to obtain. Restaurants have also been prominent participants in franchising. Between 1985 and 1987 sales by franchised hotels and motels increased by 13% and those by franchised restaurants by 22%, compared with the 9% increase recorded by the franchised sector overall.

Receipts from foreign visitors for travel and passenger fares do not compensate, however, for expenditures by US citizens on international travel services. In 1984–86, for example, expenditures by US citizens abroad (excluding travel from the USA) exceeded the total amount of receipts from foreign visitors to the USA. In the mid-1980s overseas travel involved more than 12m. US citizens a year, principally travelling to tourist and business destinations in Europe and the Mediterranean area, and the Caribbean and Central America. The average length of stay is falling, but average expenditures per trip and per day (excluding transatlantic passenger fares) are increasing. A combination of more rapid jet-airliner travel and higher disposable incomes account for these apparently contradictory relationships.

As the above analysis indicates, recreation and tourism services cannot be readily separated from other parts of the service sector. The employment effects of tourist expenditures spread across a wide range of industries, including agriculture. It is therefore difficult to be clear about the present or future contribution of leisure services to job-creation and to wealth. The seasonality of many aspects of tourism further complicates the situation. Job trends will not only be dependent on national and international tourism and patterns of expenditure, they will depend on whether the industry shifts from full-time to part-time employment, replaces seasonal with permanent recruitment or moves from manual to non-manual labour. There is relatively little scope for substituting jobs with technology, so job growth in these services, especially part-time work in hotels and restaurants, is likely to continue. The number of waiters and waitresses is expected to increase by 44% between 1986 and 2000, that of dining-room and cafeteria attendants by 46% and that of food-preparation workers by 34%.

Financial Services

Banking, finance, insurance and real-estate services accounted for 16.4% (in current dollars) of US gross national product (GNP) in 1986. US financial markets have experienced numerous changes during the 1980s: capital markets have become increasingly internationalized; there has been extensive restructuring of domestic financial markets; and competition between different parts of the sector has intensified. Until inflation exaggerated the gap between interest charged to borrowers and paid to depositors in the late 1970s and early 1980s, it had been possible for firms to function effectively on the basis of providing a small number of standardized products. As depositors began to find more lucrative places in which to put their money, such as mutual funds, the scene was set for increased competition for borrowers. As the savings banks and commercial banks became more sophisticated, so too did depositors, who were learning how to negotiate more advantageous arrangements. Borrowers were also becoming more discriminating as information technology allowed them, from the mid-1980s onwards, to look beyond traditional US sources to overseas markets in London and elsewhere. In addition, it allowed their funds to be moved around much more quickly than in the past. This encouraged further attempts by the US financial-services industry to find new ways of keeping corporate customers; one of these was the creation of markets in commercial papers for short-term funds at rates more favourable than those charged for borrowing from commercial banks. In the late 1970s such markets did not exist, but by 1985 nearly one-quarter of the total corporate debt of $350,000m. was in the form of outstanding commercial paper. Changes too numerous to detail here have tended to favour investment banks or mutual funds rather than insurance companies, savings centres and commercial banks. Thus in recent years the latter have pressed for greater domestic deregulation and more liberal rules for participation in international financial markets. The banking industry provides an example of the consequences.

BANKING

Until recently the regulatory framework for US banks has protected the interests of locally-based banks (mainly small institutions) over those of large, non-local banks. It has also limited competition within and between regional and state markets; promoted savings rather than investments; and discouraged rapid (and therefore efficient) circulation of capital even though telecommunications technology has made it possible for a decade or more. The US banking system is still one of the most decentralized and fragmented in the world; there were more than 14,000 commercial and stock savings banks in 1985 with over 47,000 operating establishments (compared with 42,000 in 1980). The number of mutual savings banks increased from 2,223 to 2,500 over the same period. Banking employment has increased by 60% since 1970 and in 1985 accounted for almost one in four of the just over 6m. jobs in financial services. That such growth has occurred in spite of the volatility of the financial environment during the last decade (culminating in the stock-market crash that started in New York in October 1987) is an indication of the way in which banking has diversified and changed. Technology has been used to enhance service to customers through the introduction, from the early 1980s onwards, of automatic teller machines, point-of-sale terminals, home banking (using home computers) and a wide range of credit and debit cards. Among other innovations, facilities for transporting funds electronically both between remote locations within the USA and overseas have been introduced to enhance services to corporate clients for, among others, money transfer and payments, cheque processing and clearing and currency transfers. Upward pressures on costs have further encouraged banks to deploy technology in this way. Processing costs have been reduced and electronic networks between banks have brought some greater flexibility and integration into a very fragmented system.

National banks cannot establish branches at will; they are subject to the banking laws of each state concerned. In 1988 22 states permitted state-wide banking of national banks, while 18 allowed limited banking and 10 allowed no branches to be set up. Within states local banks are similarly subject to state controls on the number and geographical extent of their branching activity. Thus in 1988 well over 60% of the USA's commercial banks had assets of less than $100m., and only 3% had assets valued at $500m. or more. The majority also have relatively small deposits (40% of insured commercial banks have less than $25m.) and this has made them vulnerable to merger and acquisition. The preferred method of merger and acquisition is through bank holding companies, which are under the jurisdiction of the Federal Reserve System. There are now almost 6,500 of these companies controlling more than 90% of bank assets. Not only have they allowed banks to extend their markets into other geographical areas, they have allowed them to engage in 'non-bank' activities such as financial planning, insurance, mortgages, finance and leasing. Hence the banks are now better placed to face greater competition if the eventual abolition of the regulations on interstate banking is achieved. Most of the smaller banks in metropolitan areas across the country are vulnerable to absorption by wholly-owned subsidiaries of bank holding companies and, ultimately, there will be increasing horizontal mergers between state-wide banks competing in the same markets.

Banks have also faced growing competition in their traditional area of activity from non-bank institutions. Insurance companies, investment banks, retailers and brokerage firms have been offering savers and investors a wide range of financial services by means of 'one-stop' financial supermarkets. There are few geographical restrictions on their operation and some of the largest firms such as Sears (retailing), Merrill Lynch (brokerage), American Express (travel services) and Prudential (insurance) now supply nation-wide credit and cash cards, a range of personal loans, real estate and investment advice, checking accounts and other facilities.

US banking services must also now function within a more internationalized banking system. Following the International Banking Act (1978) a regulated system of chartering foreign banks (at federal and state level) has, along with related requirements, increasingly allowed foreign-owned banks to operate in the USA. By 1986 263 foreign banks had established a total of 638 offices in the USA, with total assets of $468,000m. and total deposits of $255,000m. Japan, the UK and Canada are the leading overseas representatives, with Japanese banks accounting for 14% of all foreign banking offices in the USA in 1986 and owning 43% of foreign-owned banking assets. The location of most foreign banks is confined to the country's major financial centres, mainly New York (which had 405 foreign banking offices in 1985), Los Angeles (111), Chicago (79) and San Francisco (69). The total number of foreign banks in the USA has been increasing steadily throughout the 1980s.

Indeed, there is a close association between the tendency towards centralization of growth in financial services as a whole and the regeneration of large cities. New York was on the brink of bankruptcy in the mid-1970s, while at the same time Los Angeles, Boston and Philadelphia were losing office employment and population to surrounding suburban or rural areas. During the 1980s they have experienced growth again because of the advantages which they offer for advanced financial, business and professional services requiring international telecommunications, high accessibility within the country, skilled labour, and opportunities for specialization and innovation which are best supported at the local scale. Thus 34 of the top 200 financial firms (bank holding companies, life-insurance companies and diversified financial firms), ranked by accumulated assets, were controlled from New York in 1985. The next four cities in the list were Los Angeles (16), San Francisco (7), Hartford (8) and Chicago (7). The top 10 cities had 106 of the top 200 firms and controlled 76% of their total assets of more than $3,000m. New York gained some 118,000 jobs in financial services between 1979 and 1986, while Los Angeles and Dallas gained 85,600 and 66,400 jobs respectively.

STOCK MARKETS

Another measure of New York's key role as a financial-services centre, both nationally and internationally, is the growth in the volume and value of shares traded on its Stock Exchange. In 1986 a total of 36,009m. shares were traded (three times as many as in 1980) at a value of $1,388,800m. (3.6 times as much as in 1980). The number of companies listed by the National Association of Securities Dealers increased by almost 53% over the same period, to 4,417 in 1986. Another growth area on a number of exchanges in New York, Chicago and San Francisco has been that of futures trading. Prior to 1980 most deals struck concerned grain, livestock or metals, but since 1981 there has been a rapid expansion in trade in financial instruments and currencies, neither of which were traded at all as recently as 1970. Since 1982 the number of contracts traded in the category of financial instruments has exceeded those in all other categories, accounting for 53% of all futures trading on US exchanges in 1986, while currencies became the second most important category in 1985 and accounted for 10% of all futures trading in 1986.

It has already been mentioned that information technology has greatly facilitated the expansion of financial services. It has also placed them at the forefront of using technology to improve the range of services to customers by providing automatic teller machines (ATMs), facilities for point-of-sale (POS) transactions and drive-in banks. In POS transactions the customer uses a debit card issued by financial institutions that are linked through electronic networks to pay for goods or services at a remote location such as a supermarket or gas station. Supermarkets and oil companies are the biggest users of this new payments technology, which meets their needs to reduce the costs of handling cheques, credit cards and cash for business that is high on volume and low on margins. In recent years department stores and some speciality retailers have also adopted POS payment systems. ATM cards were owned by 46% of families in 1986 and almost 70% used them to withdraw cash. Since 71% of US families used credit cards in 1986, there is clearly scope for ATM technology to continue to reduce the demand for labour-intensive direct-deposit or cash-withdrawal facilities at banks and at all other financial institutions offering customer accounts.

International Trade in Services

The USA is both the world's largest exporter of services and its largest importer. In 1984 it provided 12.1% of total world exports of services by value and took 11.5% of imports. On the export side, while travel and passenger services (for tourism and business purposes) have been important, the main positive contributions to the current account have arisen from property services, interest payments and 'other' services such as royalties and licence fees, films, contractors' fees and other private services traded between affiliated companies. This reflects the intercorporate character of US trade in services, which itself may result in an underestimation of trade in 'other' services and of its overall contribution to the US surplus in services. Trade in these 'other' services is growing relative to other external payments. Advances in telecommunications and information technology have facilitated the tradability of financial, information, computing and some professional services, providing US firms with a strong competitive advantage in the world market. The most important imported services are in the fields of shipping, travel and passenger services. There is little doubt that large international capital flows have become commonplace in recent years, enabling the USA to sustain the overall growth of its economy in spite of its massive trade and budget deficits.

However, there are still many barriers to the expansion of international trade in services and the USA has been trying to dismantle these through negotiations started during the Uruguay Round of GATT (the General Agreement on Tariffs and Trade) and by entering into bilateral agreements. The only example of the latter to date is the US–Canadian Free-Trade Agreement (1988) on trade in services and the rights of maintaining foreign establishments in support of services trade. In 1987 trade in goods and services between the USA and Canada totalled some $166,000m., with a 17%–20% increase occurring in 1988 alone. The agreement covers services, temporary cross-border movements of business employees, financial services and investment. US service firms in Canada are assured that their service provision will benefit from the following: national treatment according to Canada's general rules for the conduct of that service; the right to establish branches, agencies or distribution networks; certification or licences for professional workers using the same criteria; less 'red tape' on the entry of managerial and professional personnel required to support the provision of a service in Canada; free entry of services produced in the USA for consumption in Canada; no discrimination in investment for facilities; and no limits on repatriation of profits. Canadian service firms will receive similar treatment in the USA. The direct impact of the agreement on US banking, however, is likely to be limited because it has a strong, if fragmented, banking sector upon

which restrictions on interstate banking still prevail, while Canada has maintained its restrictions on foreign ownership of its large banks. Perhaps the economies of border states will be most affected, so that US service firms in northern New York state or Illinois, for example, will be able to develop cross-border links rather than being confined to regional markets along one side of the border.

Services have contributed to the USA's very large balance-of-payments deficits in the mid- and late 1980s. Because US interest rates have generally been higher than elsewhere, foreign investors have been prepared to lend their dollar earnings in prospect of an acceptable return. The dollar has weakened somewhat since 1985, however, and in order to prevent their currencies from appreciating too far a number of countries have become important holders of dollar assets invested in US government securities. An important part of these investments has been portfolio investment in purely financial assets such as bank deposits, corporate stocks and bonds and government securities. These assets are held purely for commercial gain, often on a very short-term basis. There has been some concern recently about the build-up of these private portfolio investments; they account for over 60% of the USA's $1,500,000m. debt to foreigners which has been growing at an average annual rate of more than 15% between 1980 and 1987. If foreign investors begin to believe these holdings are excessive and begin to sell, US interest rates would rise and the foreign-exchange value of the dollar would fall. The price of borrowed money would rise and inflationary pressures would be rekindled.

Services and Metropolitan Development

The marked shift to service industries during the 1980s represents a profound change in the structure of the US economy. One of the symptoms of the change is the tendency towards a centralization of the associated growth in major US cities. This reverses the strongly-developed tendency towards decentralization of population, manufacturing and, to some extent, service employment, during the 1960s and 1970s. A combination of forces, including rapid technological change and the diversification or specialization of service-industry products, increasing competition, deregulation, increasing efficiency in communication systems and the emergence of small enterprises, has promoted this change. Some of these factors have been mentioned above. They have created a need for service businesses to locate in centres of innovation, in places where they can fulfil an increasing demand for skilled labour, or where they can achieve economies of scale due to their easy access to large markets. All these things have discouraged many service industries, especially those with products destined for other industries rather than for the final consumer, from moving down the urban hierarchy to smaller cities and towns. Large cities offer an array of opportunities that are unavailable in smaller cities. They have a superior infrastructure, more comprehensive public services, larger and more diverse labour markets, a wider mix of financial, commercial and consulting services and a greater variety of cultural and life-style amenities. The effects of airline deregulation have been to encourage 'hub-and-spoke' networks focusing on large cities; in financial services, deregulation has brought down the barriers between formerly-separate services such as banking and insurance. Market uncertainty has been increased and as a result the effects of this and related problems are best minimized by agglomeration in large cities. Thus, several cities in the Northeast and Midwest, such as Boston, Philadelphia and St Louis, have experienced a revival which is service-industry-driven, while cities such as Houston, Atlanta and Phoenix in the South and West also continue to grow, largely as a result of the centralization of service-industries growth and location.

THE EXTERNAL TRADE OF THE USA

JOHN KILLICK

Introduction

Foreign competition has only recently become an important issue in the USA. In 1914 foreign trade amounted to only about 4% of the country's gross national product (GNP) and the USA was self-sufficient in most goods. After the Second World War the need for a global balance of power was written into US foreign policy and it recognized the importance of world prosperity for good international relations. While US politicians played a major role in creating the new international economic system after the war, the US economy was still so self-sufficient, and US industry generally so successful, that in contrast to most Western European countries, especially Britain, there was no concern about the balance of payments. Even when unpleasant reality—for instance the run on the dollar at the time of the international financial crisis in 1971—struck, US policy-makers were unprepared to make foreign economic affairs a major concern.

Since 1960 the contribution of foreign trade to the economy has grown rapidly. In 1985 imports accounted for 11.2% of the USA's GNP, with exports at 9.2%. Many industries now rely on, or are exposed to, foreign trade and the USA has gradually lost its self-sufficiency in many vital raw materials, instead importing large quantities of manufactured goods. An increasing proportion of these come from Japan and other Pacific Rim nations. More dramatically, since 1983 the USA has accumulated a very large trade deficit, partly as a result of attempts to break out of domestic stagnation. This deficit seems likely to persist, despite radical changes in relative currency levels, and to threaten the basis of the USA's postwar free-trade policy.

Figure 1: US Balance of Payments, 1960–88
($'000 million; % of GDP × 50)

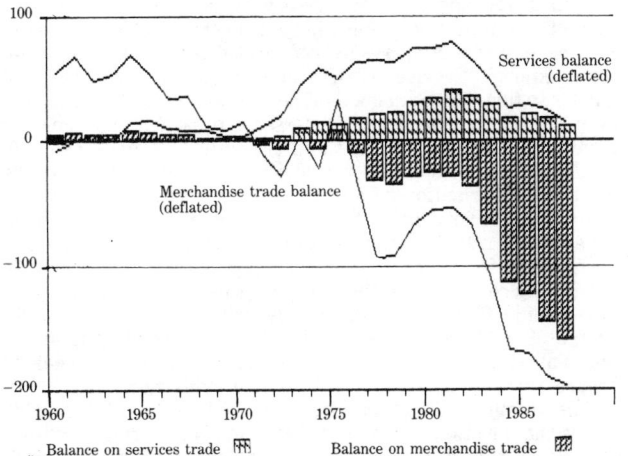

Source: OECD.

The crude figures (represented by bars in Figure 1) show that US trade in merchandise and services, taken together, was approximately in balance between 1960 and 1983. After 1983 the merchandise-trade balance went massively into deficit, while the net returns on foreign investment—the major component of services—, which had formerly been growing at such a rate as to offset the merchandise-trade deficits, declined as the USA borrowed more in order to finance its imports. This suggests that the massive increase in the size of current-account deficits after 1983 has been due mostly to a failure to manage the current (1980s') cycle. However, given that the merchandise-trade balance had already been in deficit for some years, moving from a surplus roughly equivalent to 1% of gross domestic product (GDP) in the mid-1960s to deficits of 2% of GDP in the late 1970s and 3% in the mid-1980s, it is

apparent that longer-run factors are in existence and that there may be no easy macroeconomic solution.

The Changing Composition of US Trade

During the early part of the 20th century the USA's leading exports were food, raw materials such as cotton, wheat and oil, and the high-technology products of the time such as typewriters, cash registers, radios, machine tools and automobiles. These exports were the product, in varying proportions, of cheap land and raw materials, generally (but not always) highly-skilled labour, and advanced marketing techniques. With such great natural advantages, once the USA had industrialized it was difficult for European countries to sell industrial goods there. Instead the latter balanced their transatlantic purchases by large sales to less-developed countries. These, in turn, sold tropical products, such as coffee, sugar, rubber and special raw materials, to the USA. While the USA usually earned large trading surpluses during this period, they were partly balanced by substantial capital exports—which enabled foreigners to buy US goods. In 1945, with so much of European industry destroyed as a result of the ravages of the Second World War, US predominance spread over the whole range of manufacturing. Since then, however, as Western Europe and Japan have recovered and industrialization has spread in the Far East, US exports have been forced back into more specialized highly-skilled areas, and the products of the country's lower-skilled industries have declined in importance.

The broad changes in US specialization since 1960 are shown in Table 1. Traditional exports of food, raw materials and fuel have slowly declined, with some fluctuations: wheat exports, for instance, rose temporarily in the 1970s because of poor harvests in the rest of the world (exports to the USSR, in particular, increased during this period), but by the late 1980s seemed to have resumed a long-term decline. The USA's more advanced specialization in exporting chemicals, machinery and transport equipment has been confirmed, but its performance has been somewhat weaker in the category of 'other manufactured goods'. On the import side, the decline in the shares of foods and raw materials, and the corresponding increase in the contribution of goods in the category of 'machinery and transport equipment', summarize a revolution in US trading patterns.

As mentioned above, immediately following the end of the Second World War the USA dominated world production of many simple mass-produced consumer and producer goods. Gradually, however, first Western Europe and then Japan began to dispense with US imports and to export their own products to the USA. In the 1950s the Volkswagen 'Beetle' became the first European-manufactured car to sell in substantial numbers in the USA. By the 1970s and 1980s large quantities of well-made and fuel-efficient Japanese cars were flooding on to the US market and challenging the Detroit-based domestic industry. By the early 1980s it appeared that most cars on US roads were either small, new and imported, or large, old and domestic. When US manufacturers began producing their own small cars in the late 1970s they found that Japanese capacity was not just based on cheap labour, but also on very efficient production and marketing methods. Similar problems were experienced in the case of textiles: here the USA had never been a great exporter because of British and Japanese competition, but had dominated its own market using cheap southern labour and raw materials. In the 1970s and 1980s, however, that market was invaded by cheap textiles from south-east Asia, and domestic production declined.

In the 1980s the Japanese challenge extended to the manufacture of high-technology optical and electrical goods. Since the 1960s Japan had exported vast numbers of cameras, televisions

TABLE 1: DISTRIBUTION OF US EXPORTS AND IMPORTS, 1960–86

(Selected commodity groups, as % of all merchandise trade)

Exports

	1960	1970	1980	1986
Food, live animals, beverages and tobacco	16	12	14	10
Crude materials, inedible, except fuels	14	11	11	8
Mineral fuels and related materials	4	4	4	4
Chemicals and related products	9	9	10	11
Machinery and transport equipment	34	42	39	46
Other manufactured goods	19	18	18	15

Imports

	1960	1970	1980	1986
Food, live animals, beverages and tobacco	23	16	8	7
Crude materials, inedible, except fuels	18	8	4	3
Mineral fuels and related materials	11	8	34	10
Chemicals and related products	5	4	4	4
Machinery and transport equipment	10	28	25	44
Other manufactured goods	30	33	23	29

Source: Bureau of the Census, US Department of Commerce, *Statistical Abstract of the United States*, 1975 and 1988 edns.

and other goods to the USA and had slowly displaced domestic production in that country. These goods typify Japan's comparative advantage. They use few raw materials, are made by skilled mass-production techniques, are very attractive to high-income-earners and create large profits. This specialization lent itself to the production of semiconductors, and the Japanese have begun to challenge the dominance of the computer products of California's 'Silicon Valley'. While IBM remains the world's largest computer firm and dominates the mainframe market, it is being strongly challenged in the production of personal computers. Both imports and exports of computers and business machines grew very strongly in the 1980s.

The USA has retained strong specializations in many areas—especially those of medium and heavy engineering, chemicals and very advanced production such as genetic engineering, space technology and mainframe computers. Many US companies are world leaders in their chosen field of technology. In aircraft production, for example, Boeing has made far shrewder assessments of the future passenger market than its European competitors and continues to dominate an industry which requires economies of scale, skilled (but not mass-production) labour, relatively heavy engineering and a large market. Similarly, the Japanese have found it far harder to break into the markets for heavy construction or generating equipment than into domestic car production. Many advanced engineering markets are effectively closed to foreign companies because they are tied to local service industries—for instance power generation or communications. Finally, the USA has been able to dominate in the production and sale of military hardware because of a high degree of government support, the reluctance of the Japanese to compete, and diversity among European manufacturers, causing compatibility problems.

The USA's imports and exports of staple foods and raw materials have declined, partly as a result of long-term factors, such as resource exhaustion and technical change, and partly as a result of a temporary lack of demand and low prices affecting all staple producers. Oil, for instance, was a major export from 1870, but by about 1970 the USA had become a major oil importer, seemingly increasingly dependent on the production of member countries of OPEC (the Organization of Petroleum-Exporting Countries). An interesting feature of the 1980s, therefore, was a decline in the value of oil imports as OPEC price increases encouraged conservation, domestic sources were developed, and the international price of oil fell.

The same forces have limited US coal exports, which in the late 1970s seemed very promising.

In agriculture, cotton, produced by cheap southern labour, was still an important export in 1950, but has been displaced since then by foreign peasant production. The wheat and meat of the Midwest and Great Plains, however, which have always been produced by highly-paid skilled labour on large farms, are still potent forces in international trade. The current problem is that most countries prefer domestic production, and the US supply is treated as a reserve, only needed when other harvests fail. The European Communities, in particular, have encouraged wheat production as part of the Common Agricultural Policy: they have limited US imports and exported surplus Western European grain at low prices to developing countries. This has made the wheat market very difficult to predict. In the 1970s there were poor harvests in many countries and US exports rose; in the 1980s harvests were better and US exports fell. In the late 1980s European surpluses were being reduced by quotas, but there was concern that persistent droughts in the Midwest could limit US capacity to take advantage of this.

The decline in the USA's earnings from merchandise trade has been partly offset by earnings from overseas investment. The USA became a creditor country during the First World War and since then has received substantial earnings from overseas investments (see 'The Balance of Payments' below for a discussion of their components). These grew very rapidly in the 1960s and in the 1970s were sufficient to offset the country's growing merchandise-trade deficits (see Figure 1). The swing in the trade balance in the 1980s, however, was so strong, and US borrowing abroad rose so rapidly, that net earnings from foreign investment peaked in 1981 and were down to insignificant levels by 1986. The other substantial source of income has been from services. The USA was originally a very mercantile economy, but in the late 19th century its shipping and service trades were pushed aside by the growth of primary and manufactured exports and by British competition.

In the last 30 years, however, in the USA as in all the developed economies, services have grown at the expense of manufactures and are now a very large proportion of total economic output. Inevitably this is reflected by an increase in service exports, which now constitute about one-quarter of total exports. Service exports are so diverse that they are harder to quantify than goods. The leading items are transportation, banking, insurance, overseas construction, tourism, advertising, motion pictures and accounting. A good example of the new high-technology services being provided are the electronic information databases that are increasingly spanning the world and in which US companies have an obvious advantage. Some of these, such as banking and advertising, are net earners but in others, such as shipping and tourism, the USA spends more overseas than it produces in its domestically-based and offshore operations. Overall, the USA has a net surplus in services, reflecting its well-organized institutions and skilled labour force, and the country continues to seek to secure overseas markets for its service industries.

This account of the changing commodity basis of US trade raises the question of whether that trade is suffering a general decline, or merely evolving into more specialized areas, and if the former, if this is a symptom of a major turning point or 'climacteric' in US economic performance similar to that experienced by the UK in the late 19th century. It is sufficient to say here that it is too early to describe rising import penetration and distress in some prominent industries, such as automobiles, textiles or steel, as symptoms of a general decline. Problems in these areas have been matched by success stories elsewhere and, in general, US industry seems to have held up well during the 1980s. Few industries have suffered both import penetration and falling employment: most have gained from rising domestic demand, but have had to share part of their success with foreign importers. In electrical components, for instance, imports rose rapidly in the 1980s but domestic production rose even more rapidly. Surveys show that US industry seems to have remained remarkably dynamic and flexible and to be adapting rapidly to new opportunities. What seems to have happened to trade is that a remarkably-broad absolute advantage in many industrial sectors in 1950 has slowly been whittled down to an absolute advantage in only a few areas, as other countries recovered from the war and industrialization spread. The USA, therefore, inevitably lost its comparative advantage in many mass-produced goods which it now imports, and its foreign trade has become more specialized. The easy predominance it enjoyed earlier is over and in future it will have to compete hard with efficient overseas producers. However, its relatively high current rate of technical change and employment growth, and its comparative advantage in high-skilled, capital- or land-intensive areas provide some reassurance for the future.

The Geographical Pattern of US Overseas Trade

One of the most interesting aspects of US external affairs in the 1970s and 1980s has been the changing geographical direction of the country's economic and social interests. In 1914 Europe was still the USA's principal market and source of capital, migrants and cultural ideas. Between 1914 and 1950 the USA became the dominant partner, actively concerned in European affairs in many ways. However, the volume of economic contacts across the Atlantic fell relatively as US interests diversified around the globe, and some trading arrangements hitherto exclusively made with Europe came to change dramatically. Between the wars there was little market either in the USA for European manufactures or in Europe for US raw materials. Immediately after the Second World War Western Europe resumed heavy buying of US food and industrial supplies, but most US imports still came from primary producers in the Americas or elsewhere. Since 1970, while cultural and political ties with Western Europe have remained strong, the USA's economic and social ties across the Atlantic have weakened further and have been increasingly replaced by connections across the Pacific.

Figure 2: Sources of Imports into the USA, 1950–85

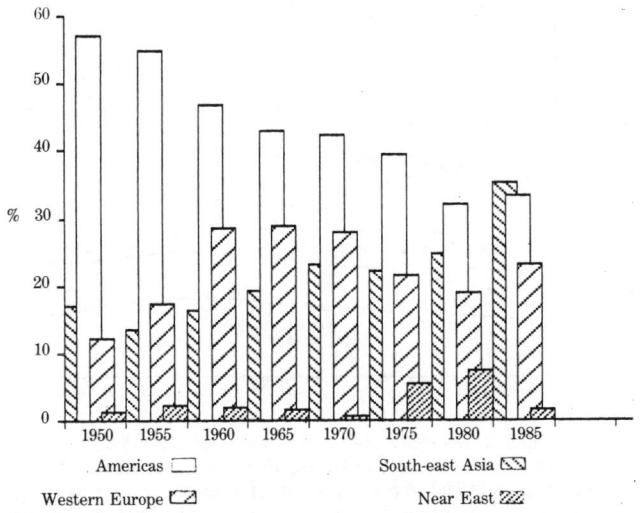

Source: Bureau of the Census, US Department of Commerce, *Statistical Abstract of the United States*, 1960–88.

US TRADE WITH WESTERN EUROPE

US trade with Western Europe grew very rapidly after 1950. Initially the European countries were desperate to rebuild their shattered economies after the war and only the USA could provide the necessary food, raw materials and capital equipment. The post-war dollar shortages often forced them to find other (short-term) sources of supply, and to increase their exports to the USA, but through the 1960s and 1970s the USA continued to run comfortable surpluses with Western Europe. In the 1980s this surplus vanished, partly because of the trade distortion caused by the Reagan boom (see 'The Balance of Payments', below) and partly because of long-term

trends. The latter are due to the gradual decline in US exports of food, raw materials and manufactures other than machinery and transport equipment. Western European countries have gradually replaced these goods with domestic production, although they still need substantial volumes of high-technology products such as advanced computers and passenger aircraft. The ultimate reason for this lies in increasing self-sufficiency in food and raw materials and the adoption of US methods in manufacturing. These trends are being aggravated by the development of the internal European market: the EEC Common Agricultural Policy, for example, has limited US exports to both Community member states and many third countries. This trend was expected to increase with the creation of the unified market by 1992.

US TRADE WITH THE PACIFIC RIM

Since 1950 US trade with the Far East has grown even more rapidly than its trade with Western Europe. While Japan did not benefit from US aid under the Marshall Plan in the post-Second World War era, the country recovered very rapidly when it became a forward base in the Korean and Vietnam Wars. Once recovery had begun, Japanese industry specialized in products suitable for the high-income US market, and by the 1980s Japan was earning a massive surplus on its trade with the USA. Meanwhile, the Japanese market for US products was growing far more slowly—only about one-quarter as fast between 1960 and 1985. Initially, like Western Europe, Japan needed US capital equipment in order to rebuild; as the country's economy recovered, successive imports were excluded and by the mid-1980s it was importing only a few high-technology goods (such as fast computers and passenger aircraft) and a limited volume of luxury high-value consumer goods. Neither has the USA been able to sell Japan many of its traditional agricultural products because, despite very high food prices, Japanese agriculture is even more tightly protected than that of the EEC. Similarly, US sales of services and high-technology public-utility installations have been obstructed by invisible non-tariff barriers.

US trade with Japan is part of a developing US relationship with the whole Pacific Rim, in which Japan itself is under considerable pressure from other countries in its region (South Korea, Hong Kong, Taiwan and Singapore). These countries have set up successful competitors to Japan's older industries, such as textiles, shipbuilding and steel, and have forced Japan to develop its 'high' technologies even further in order to preserve its hold on US trade. Simultaneously, however, they provide Japan with cheap raw materials and simple components for its advanced industries, and with a market for its capital goods and investment. Many Japanese firms have moved their factories to these new areas as wages and costs in Japan have increased. In this way Japanese influence in south-east Asia is being extended peacefully under indirect US protection. In principle the USA should be able to find markets in this densely-populated area for its food and raw materials that are decreasingly required by Western Europe: although exports in these commodities have increased sharply, Asian consumers are still very conservative, saving a substantial proportion of their incomes and preferring traditional goods and services. East Asian trade is also partly balanced by purchases of oil and raw materials from the Gulf, Australia and elsewhere. However, the combination of the imbalance with the USA (and, to a lesser extent but for similar reasons, with Western Europe) and current low commodity prices have left the Pacific Rim countries with large trade surpluses which cannot easily be spent. These, therefore, accumulate in the Japanese money-market, earning minimal returns, or are exported overseas, principally to the USA: in this way they help to finance the US trade debt and compensate for the low US savings rates (see 'The Balance of Payments' and 'Capital Movements' below). Therefore the USA, still with spare land and natural resources, is developing what is in many ways a symbiotic relationship with the Pacific Rim similar to the traditional Atlantic partnership but without, of course, the traditional shared cultural heritage.

The developing tensions in US trade with Western Europe and Asia have been complemented by changes within the industrial structure of the USA itself. Although the traditional westward movement and the more recent recovery of the southern 'sunbelt' states were mostly internally generated by domestic forces, the changing direction of foreign trade has also had a considerable influence. For instance, East Asian competition has had its worst effects on the old Midwestern heavy-industrial 'rustbelt' and the south-eastern cotton textile areas. By contrast, Japanese competiton has not really harmed the newer industries on the west coast, such as computers or aerospace, and the already well-established mining and lumbering industries in that area have found new, potentially vast, markets in East Asia. The port of Los Angeles has grown rich on Pacific trade, while New York's Atlantic trade has stagnated.

Both internal and external pressures are also helping to unify the North American market. Thus the vigorous Central American and Caribbean immigration into southern California, Texas and Florida (some of which is illegal) is generated by population pressure, poverty and disorder, but the low-cost work-force which it provides is a useful ingredient in maintaining US labour flexibility and meeting Asian competition. Together with a smaller (but rapidly-growing) Asian immigration this is also reducing the European element in the population—slowly overall, but very quickly in large cities such as Los Angeles, Miami and New York. In addition, the availability of relatively-cheap Canadian power and raw materials and the Canadian market provide important stimuli for US industry (see essays on US–Canadian relations, pp. 341–346). The conclusion of the Free Trade Agreement with Canada in 1988 and the ongoing plans for free trade with Mexico are, therefore, not surprising in view of the growing competitiveness of south-east Asia and the agreement to unify the European market by 1992.

The Balance of Payments

As Figure 1 shows, since the early 1980s the USA has accumulated a massive deficit on the current account of its balance of payments. The previous discussion has indicated some of the more long-term causes of this, but the difficulties have been aggravated by flawed domestic policies. These originated as deliberate attempts to deal with the slow growth and inflation of the 1970s. After a long recovery from the recession of 1973–74, the economy was already badly overheated in 1979, and an increase in the price of OPEC oil forced President Carter to tighten monetary and fiscal policy. This reaction contributed to his losing the election in late 1980, but President Reagan continued the monetary squeeze when he took office in early 1981. Although the consequent recession, in 1981–82, cooled the economy and temporarily improved the trade balance, the monetary tightening and consequent rise in US interest rates was one cause of the trade deficit.

In addition, President Reagan's mandate was to tackle the underlying causes of slow US growth. The problems were analysed in his 'Program for Economic Recovery' of 1981 and taxes were cut and government controls reduced. The aim was to encourage growth by improving the long-term prospects for entrepreneurship and investment. The extent of the reductions, however, and the maintenance of a tough monetary policy through the recession and into the recovery to discourage inflation were new and had dramatic domestic consequences: the effect was increased by the Reagan administration's foreign policy, which increased defence spending, and Congress's refusal to match tax reductions with cuts in social-services expenditure. The federal budget therefore went severely into deficit and the fiscal boost given to the economy was very large. Consequently, domestic output rose very rapidly, investment recovered and unemployment fell to substantially-lower levels than in many Western European countries. Simultaneously, inflation remained at acceptably-low levels. The stagnation of the 1970s seemed to have been conquered and, despite some unease about the deficits, President Reagan's policies were endorsed at the polls in 1984 and 1988.

Although the budget and trade deficits were closely related, the exact connections are complex. Thus, firstly, the trade deficit was partly caused by the faster rate of growth in the USA than elsewhere, creating more demand in the USA for foreign goods than existed abroad for US goods: a relatively faster rate of growth overseas would have restricted the deficit. Secondly, the combination of relatively greater increases in government, investment and consumer expenditure in the USA as a proportion of national income than elsewhere, indicating a relatively high propensity by government and consumers to spend a large proportion of their income, created greater demand for imports. Again, therefore, a change in spending and savings habits overseas could have reduced the deficit. For example, the high savings ratios found in Japan helped to finance US imports. Finally, the deficit was partly caused by changes in the portfolio investment choices of US citizens and foreigners alike. It could only continue at the level of the mid-1980s because US citizens reduced their customary purchases of foreign assets, freeing these funds for import purchases, and foreigners continued to be attracted by US assets, thus providing additional money for imports.

Some popularly-suggested causes of the deficit can be eliminated quickly. Many US observers blamed restrictive foreign tariff or non-tariff barriers, or low foreign wages, but the deficit worsened so rapidly, and was so geographically widespread, that more general causes must have been responsible. Similarly, it is unlikely that changes in personal consumption or savings habits were important, as these are normally slow to develop. Corporate investment plans, while they can move quickly, also normally follow government action, so macroeconomic policies must have been the principal cause of the deficit. While US policy changes were the most dramatic, they occurred at a time when many Western European governments were introducing tough anti-inflationary policies. In quantitative terms, the US deficit rose by about 3.5% of gross national product (GNP) from 1980–85, while deficits of some other foreign governments fell by 2.5% of GNP, and the combined effect (assuming the appreciation of the dollar, discussed in the following paragraph) may explain about two-thirds of the US trade deficit.

Figure 3: Selected US Dollar Exchange Rates, 1980–88

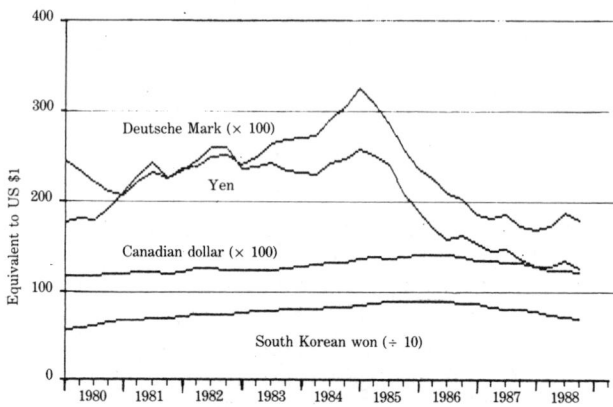

US policies also affected the value of the dollar, which appreciated dramatically between 1980–85 and then fell equally rapidly. The initial reason for the rise of the dollar was the increase in US interest rates begun by the Carter administration in late 1979. President Reagan maintained this pressure and by 1982 the value of the dollar was soaring against every other major currency, each 1% increase in the interest rate causing a 6%–8% appreciation of the dollar. As the budget deficit increased, government borrowing and rising corporate investment encouraged by the recovery maintained the pressure. By 1984 the trade deficit was so large that uncertainty would have depressed the value of almost any other currency, especially when monetary policy eased in 1984, and the difference between US and foreign interest rates narrowed. However, the boom had made US assets attractive, and many foreigners, concerned about investment prospects elsewhere, chose the USA as a 'safe haven' for their funds despite the high currency cost. Only in 1985 did concerted action by central bankers begin to bring the dollar down to more reasonable levels. The explanations for the appreciation of the dollar therefore antedate the Reagan administration, and are only partly explained by the budget deficit. The appreciation, however, acted to reduce US exports to nearly all markets and was responsible for a significant, but minor, proportion of the trade deficit.

The trade deficit has persisted (although it declined slightly in 1988 and was projected to do so again in 1989) despite the depreciation of the dollar to levels similar to those in 1980 when there was no overall deficit. This did not initially cause disquiet because the common experience of trade deficits caused by overvalued currencies is that they generally get worse before improving sharply—the so-called 'J curve'. The immediate effect of devaluation is to change prices without affecting volumes, but after suitable lags increasing volumes more than compensate for the reduction in price. In the case of the USA, however, the recovery was delayed for an exceptionally long time because, although the dollar sank against other major currencies (such as the Deutsche Mark and the yen) and US exports to countries such as the Federal Republic of Germany and Japan rose rapidly from 1987, it did not fall significantly against the currencies of several of the other leading exporter nations—Taiwan, Singapore, South Korea, Brazil and Canada—, and exports from these countries to the USA continued at high levels.

Many leading foreign companies have shown great determination to hold on to their share of the US market. Initially they 'priced their goods to market' (that is, they offered low prices to attract customers, and then, when they had established a connection, increased prices to market levels). During the boom they made very large profits, but when the dollar fell they had sufficient margin to hang on at much lower prices. By contrast, most US companies simply priced their exports at domestic prices plus shipping costs. Foreign markets were marginal for them, and they have only recently begun to develop separate pricing and marketing strategies for each foreign market. Similarly, the operation of US quota systems, which limit imports but raise profits on each item, and the growth of oligopoly, which increases the opportunity for strategic pricing, dull the market response to changes in relative currency levels and prolong the delaying aspect of the 'J curve'. A more fundamental possibility, implied by Figure 1 (p. 77), is that a ratchet-like deindustrialization of the US economy is occurring, causing a step-like increase in imports after each boom. As shown above, however, the US economy is still flexible enough to slow this process considerably, but only at the cost of substantial reductions in relative wages and living standards.

US Foreign Trade Policy

Foreign trade deficits of the size experienced during most of the 1980s could be expected to challenge the USA's post-war free-trade policy. This policy originated as a reaction first to the Depression of the 1930s and then to the Second World War. Until 1934 US policy had traditionally been very protectionist, the famous Fordney McCumber (1922) and Smoot Hawley (1930) tariff acts symbolizing US isolationism. It was recognized by 1934 that the latter, in particular, had encouraged a whole round of international protectionism which had exacerbated the Depression. Accordingly, in 1934 President Roosevelt, encouraged by his secretary of state, Cordell Hull, passed the Reciprocal Trade Agreements Act which modestly began to bargain down international tariff barriers in the late 1930s. During the Second World War tariff reduction became an essential part of US foreign policy in accordance with the theory that 'if trade does not cross frontiers, soldiers will'. After the war the administration took advantage of US economic dominance to create as open as possible a post-war world, attempting to impose multilateral trading and stable exchange rates at Bretton Woods (1944) and other conferences, and within the framework of the GATT, the IMF and the Marshall Plan.

Despite initial difficulties, this foreign-trade policy was very successful in the long term. Combined with the Marshall Plan, Korean War spending in Japan and, of course, strong indigenous forces, Western Europe and the Far East recovered very rapidly after the Second World War. In the 1950s and 1960s the opening of the huge US market, continuing tariff reductions such as those achieved under the Kennedy Round of GATT negotiations (1964–67) and relative world currency stability encouraged massive increases in the volume of international trade and consolidated the USA's position at the centre of the Atlantic and Pacific trading systems. The dollar became the key currency around which all others revolved. This central role gave the USA many trading privileges, much immediate prosperity and a decisive advantage in the cold war. However, as dominant economies have discovered in the past, there were also long-term costs attached to world leadership, such as enormously-expensive defence programmes, the overvaluing of the dollar and the removal of the protective tariff shield against cheaper production overseas. In this sense the USA's current problems are an indirect result of its successful post-war foreign economic policy which seems to have provided some of the conditions for its own decline.

It took a very long time, however, for foreign competition to begin to influence US policy. Despite substantial increases in imports in the 1970s and serious distress in some industries such as steel, textiles, footwear, and many consumer-electronic goods, few overt concessions were made to protectionism during that decade. In international terms a turning point was marked by the oil price increases of 1973–74, and the consequent recession in many industrial countries, including the USA. From that time on the trend to freer trade was reversed and many countries began to impose a wide variety of controls on imports, such as voluntary export restraints (VERs), which threatened strict controls unless there was voluntary restraint, or health and environmental controls which were difficult for importers to meet. Nevertheless, the main traditional limit on imports, tariff levels, still continued downwards as a result of the Tokyo Round of GATT negotiations (1973–79) and the US administration, especially, was reluctant to grant requests from distressed US industries for VERs. The main reason for this was probably the official policy of encouraging international trade. In any case, by the 1970s far more firms had developed international interests than before the Second World War. Many firms now received important components or supplies from overseas or were involved in cross-trades that would have been damaged by increased protectionism. Hence, whereas between the wars there had been unanimous lobbying by threatened industries, in the 1970s the larger multinationals frequently opposed lobbying efforts by smaller domestic firms. In semiconductors, for example, the industry split between the larger firms like IBM and Texas Instruments, which bought many components in the Far East, and smaller firms like Motorola, which wanted to protect their domestic production, and thus the market remained open.

The large increases in imports in the 1980s have weakened this resistance to protection. Now even the largest and most technically-advanced US industries are being pressed by foreign competition, and demands for protection, especially against Japan, have reached new heights. For example, by the mid-1980s the semiconductor industry had been made distraught by the influx of cheap Asian semiconductors and in 1986 persuaded the Reagan administration to conclude price-maintenance agreements with Japan. The theoretical justifications for free trade have also weakened somewhat. Until about 1980 the US balance of payments was approximately in equilibrium, and it was possible to describe Japanese and Western European competition as a natural and beneficient catching-up process. By the end of the 1980s Far Eastern competition had become so vigorous that it was seen as a threat to the system rather than a support. While the Republican administrations of the 1980s frequently vetoed protectionist measures, there was still a discernible move towards protection. For example, the 1988 Trade Act gave the administration the means to break into markets hitherto closed to US exports, while concealing large elements of old-fashioned protectionism. In addition, some US theorists and many industries began to ask for a 'strategic trade policy' that, combined with an industrial policy, could 'pick winners' and give selected industries or firms protection. If the USA chose such a policy it would have very severe consequences for the Atlantic and Pacific trading systems and the formal and informal alliances under-pinned by them, reversing much US policy since 1945. It would also have very large internal consequences, modifying the relative role of the executive and Congress, since only a far more-informed and -powerful administration could effectively wield these powers. Whether the USA travels down this road will depend on the success of its exports in rounding the 'J curve' and the willingness of foreigners to continue financing the US trade deficit.

Capital Movements

The USA's trade deficit in the 1980s has necessarily been balanced by massive offsetting capital flows, a major reversal of the traditional pattern. Between 1920 and 1980 the current account of the balance of payments had generally been in surplus, and the USA had exported large sums of capital overseas. These were invested in overseas property and com-panies, and in 1980 many US firms were among the world's leading multinational companies, remitting substantial invest-ment income. Meanwhile Western European and (later) Japanese investment continued in the USA but at a much lower rate, with the UK accounting for about 50% of all direct investment (about three times as much as Japan). By the mid-1980s, as shown in Table 2, these trends had been reversed. Very large inflows of short-term capital had helped to finance the trade deficit, while US investment overseas had slowed very substantially. Japanese companies were becoming increas-ingly prominent in multinationals rankings, and foreign multi-national investment in the USA had increased enormously.

TABLE 2: MAJOR US CAPITAL FLOWS, 1960–85
($'000 million, at current prices. Minus (−) denotes outflows)

	1970	1975	1980	1985
US military aid, net	−3	−2	−1	0
Other unilateral transfers, net .	−3	−5	−8	−15
US government grants . .	−2	−3	−5	−11
Other	−2	−2	−3	−4
US purchases abroad, net . .	−9	−40	−86	−31
US official reserve assets, net .	2	−1	−8	−4
Other US government assets .	−2	−3	−5	−3
US private assets, net . .	−10	−35	−73	−25
Direct investments abroad .	−8	−14	−19	−17
Foreign securities . . .	−1	−6	−4	−7
Claims reported by US non-banking concerns . . .	−1	−1	−3	1
US bank claims . . .	−1	−14	−47	−1
Foreign purchases in the USA, net	6	16	58	130
Foreign official assets, net . .	7	7	15	−1
Other foreign assets, net . .	−1	9	43	131
Direct investments . .	1	3	17	19
US Treasury securities . .	0	3	3*	20
Other US securities . .	2	3	5	51
US non-banking liabilities .	2	0	7	0
US bank liabilities . .	−6	0	11	41

* Includes foreign-currency notes sold to private residents abroad.
Source: Bureau of the Census, US Department of Commerce, *Statistical Abstract of the United States: 1988.*

The precise reasons for the change in capital flows varied according to the sources and type of capital. All flows of funds are either government or private in origin. After the Second World War US government grants, such as the aid distributed under the Marshall Plan, were very important, but by the 1980s such aid was growing very slowly and was relatively insignificant. Similarly, military aid, once an important element in the flow of funds, declined as US foreign policy changed. By contrast the flow of US private assets overseas grew steadily in the 1960s and 1970s as multinational firms estab-lished themselves overseas. It was this flow that declined rapidly after 1982, as US firms and investors switched their funds to domestic investments and US banks were attracted by higher domestic interest rates and repelled by fear of foreign defaults. Similarly, in the late 1970s, US banks had been loaning very large volumes of recycled Arab oil money

to developing countries, but this flow stopped as the third-world debt crisis grew. Some of this money returned by various routes in the 1980s, increasing foreign assets held in the USA. Even so, a very large volume of US or recycled funds remained overseas under permanent threat of repudiation by countries such as Mexico, Argentina or Brazil, and some US banks wrote off part of these obligations. Simultaneously, many foreign companies (especially British and Dutch firms) which had been investing steadily in the USA in the 1970s increased their direct investment in the USA after 1982, to take advantage of the US boom or to avoid quotas or tariffs. Japanese firms also began heavy investment after about 1980, as they realized that they would have to invest in the USA or face punitive import restraints. Furthermore, the US government deficit forced the sale of large volumes of Treasury securities, some of which went overseas. Finally, US banks borrowed liberally overseas as domestic demand rose and domestic savings proved inadequate.

The result of the above-described changes in capital flows was that the net investment position of the USA had moved dramatically into deficit by the late 1980s. US assets abroad have continued to grow slowly—but foreign assets in the USA have expanded enormously. The growth of the deficit has not been geographically even: while the USA has retained its traditional surpluses with Canada and Latin America, its debts with Western Europe and (more especially) Japan have increased rapidly. US firms continued to extend their Euro-pean interests slowly, but there has been a massive increase in European investment in the USA first from investors attracted by the boom and then from companies taking advan-tage of the low dollar to buy US concerns. In fact British investors and companies, despite the imminence of the implementation of the EEC-single integrated market by 1992, have shown far more interest in the USA than in other Western European countries. US investment in Canada has continued to consolidate its dominant position, but there has recently been a growth of Canadian purchases in the USA. The importance of bank lending in US investment in Latin America (and vice versa) has already been mentioned. The interesting feature of US lending to Japan is the low proportion of direct investment, reflecting the exclusiveness of the Japanese system. The large increase in Japanese lending to the USA is partly explained by the very high Japanese savings ratio, which has inflated Japanese stock and real-estate prices to such an extent that investors have accepted the currency risks of US investment in order to earn a reasonable return. In a sense, therefore, Japanese investment in the USA (and thus the Japanese trade surplus which it helps to finance) is a function of the difference between the savings ratios of the two countries. These reflect, in turn, a too-slow adjustment by consumers in Japan to commercial success, and, in the USA, a frustrated determination to increase consumption even when real wages are stagnant.

Since 1945 no country has sustained such large trade deficits, or increased its foreign debts so rapidly, for more than two or three years without a major correction. In the late 1980s the USA suffered both a sharp stock-exchange crash and a major depreciation of the dollar but, although trade volumes subse-quently improved, trade values were slow to change, suggest-ing that any adjustment will be gradual. In addition, the deficit had reached such large proportions by the late 1980s that extremely large yearly increases in exports would be needed to first close the gap with imports, then cover the increasing interest charges on the debt and finally begin to reduce the accumulated debt. However, it was just possible to visualize eliminating the deficit relatively quickly if all went well. Con-tinuation of the theoretically-tough Gramm-Rudman-Hollings regulation is one necessary condition to reduce gradually the federal budget deficit. In addition, a fairly accommodating monetary policy is needed to prevent the dollar appreciating again. Useful assistance could come from higher foreign demand for US exports. Although in some countries, such as the UK, relatively high demand (and perhaps, by some indirect route, the improvement in US trade) is already producing substantial deficits, there is still plenty of room for expansion in others, such as West Germany. The avoidance of further trade restrictions on all sides is, of course, a vital ingredient for success. Finally, if the USA was able to build on its increasing productivity relative to its trade partners, or to find some way of substituting domestic products for attractive Japanese goods, then the twin deficits could be cured over the medium term. This would mean, however, five years of substantial increases in GNP coupled with a diversion of resources into new investment and exports, rather than into domestic consumption. Such an outcome is mathematically possible, if all went well, but it would be politically difficult—especially given President Bush's famous election-campaign promise: 'Read my lips; no new taxes!' Indeed, it has proved very difficult to cut the US budget according to the Gramm-Rudman-Hollings schedule, although the developing *détente* with the USSR may result in a decrease in military expenditure. Furthermore, any sign of trade or budget progress in the USA, or difficulties elsewhere in the world, seems to have the perverse effect (shown in early 1989) of forcing up the dollar and making the trade adjustment more difficult.

Fortunately, at least until the late 1980s, investors have purchased sufficient US assets to sustain the trade deficit, but it is difficult to define just what the sustainable limits of such a debt might be. Prior to 1914, the debt–income ratio of many primary-producing countries was far higher than that of the USA today, but at that time there was a larger proportion of relatively-safe public utilities to sell, and in modern times investors have been far more cautious. However, the wealth and conservatism of the USA make it an ideal borrower with a very wide range of assets to offer, particularly where Japanese investors are concerned. The USA seemed to benefit from a decisive shift in the 1980s towards international balance in investors' portfolios, but it remained uncertain how permanent this shift would be. The sums required annually to balance the deficit, large though they are, are not so great when measured in relation to wealth, international investment funds, or the product of some quite low additional taxes, for example on gasoline; but many investors may come to a decision that they have enough US exposure. Clearly, as the limits of sustainable lending approach, US borrowers would have to offer higher rates, which could inhibit the adjustment process described above, and thus in turn dramatically change overseas investors' perceptions of their US risk. Obviously the possibility exists for some sort of chaotic solution—for example, a free-fall of the dollar. However, the modern international economy seems marvellously adept at avoiding such dramatic solutions, and the political and economic interests vested in the present system are so large that this is unlikely to be allowed to occur.

Conclusion

Many commentators warned, during the mid- and late 1980s, of the possible dangers if the twin US deficits do not improve.

They have argued that a downward spiral could start at many points. The dollar could become even more erratic; more developing countries could repudiate their debts; substantial parts of the US banking system could fail and overwhelm the Federal Reserve System; or a reciprocal escalation of protectionism could halt world trade. A generation ago, such possibilities would have been denied by orthodox economists, but now many economists have argued that the Keynesian antidote no longer seems potent because the growing interdependence of the world economy has not been matched by equivalent political cohesion. The course of the Reagan boom suggests that even the largest and most self-sufficient economy may not be able to sustain an isolated Keynesian boom for ever. Finally, observers argue that although appropriate capital flows have eased the tensions enormously, there is a disturbing lack of domestic political understanding of the international issues at stake. Members of Congress lobby to protect their local industries while West German officials explain why faster growth is impossible and Japanese importers evade the spirit of free trade.

Yet, despite these warnings, the stock-market crash of October 1987 had little effect on the real economy; during the first half of 1989 the dollar rose against all major currencies. This probably reflected some improvements in the US trade balance, expectations that President Bush would act to reduce the budget deficit, and some slowing down in the US economy—possibly leading to the hoped-for 'soft landing'. This improvement in the face of the continuing deficits also seems to show how much relative confidence overseas investors still have in the US system. It is often argued that the US economy has retained much flexibility despite its problems. Recent scholars have shown that smaller imbalances in the 1920s were ultimately disastrous, but now the main actors know that far more important interests are committed to making the system work. Since the Second World War US and Western foreign policy has been built upon the encouragement of relatively-free trade between the USA and its allies, and this commitment can not be forsaken without fundamental political consequences. Since 1960 many domestic vested interests have become far more dependent on the success of the international economy. Thus US and other consumers prefer many imported goods and oppose tariffs. Similarly, many leading US, Japanese and Western European companies and investors own multinational offshoots or have interests in the USA, and have a vested interest in their success. It is commonplace to claim that modern governments have lost much of their independence because of the massive growth of world trade and finance. Conversely, the benefits, in the US case at any rate, seem to be that investors sense the greater security this gives the system and are more ready to allow the economy scope to adjust.

US GOVERNMENT FINANCES

JOSEPH HOGAN

Trends in National Income and Expenditure

The USA has experienced great economic growth in the post-Second World War period. Between 1940 and 1964 the country's gross national product (GNP—the sum of personal consumption expenditures, gross private domestic investment, net exports and government purchases of goods and services) increased from $100,000m. to $622,000m. With prices more than doubling over this period, the increase in real GNP was somewhat less—from $246,000m. to $622,000m., measured in constant 1964 dollars. A 47% increase in the size of the US population, from 132m. in 1940 to an estimated 194m. in 1964, meant that in per-head terms the level of personal income after taxes increased less rapidly than GNP—from $576 in 1940 to $2,248 in 1964. In constant 1964 terms this represented a

real increase in per-head income of about 67%, from $1,329 to $2,248.

The country's GNP rose from $482,000m. in early 1961 to just under $720,000m. in the last quarter of 1968. Disposable personal income per head—after taxes and adjustment for price increases—increased by 33% over this period. The average annual percentage increase in GNP, as measured in 1958 dollars, amounted to 4.8% between 1960 and 1968, compared with 2.7% between 1952 and 1960. By the time President Nixon took office in 1969 the economy had been expanding for nine years, and inflation had been running at between 4% and 5% for three years, primed by a gradual escalation in expenditure related to the Vietnam War. At the end of 1969 GNP totalled $897,600m. in current prices. The adoption of anti-inflation policies led to depressed economic figures for 1970: while GNP reached $947,100m. for the year, in terms of constant prices this represented a decline of 0.5% compared with 1969.

The Nixon administration made a surprise switch in mid-1971 to wage, price and rent controls to combat inflation. GNP expanded vigorously during the fourth quarter of the year, bringing the annual total to $1,065,000m. The expansion continued through 1972: GNP was measured at $1,152,100m. (representing a real growth rate of 6.5% compared with 1971) and inflation at just over 3%.

The US economy endured severe jolts in 1973-74. Beginning in 1973, a sharp rise in world oil prices caused the worst price inflation since after the Second World War, which in turn was followed by the deepest recession since the 1930s. Consumer prices rose by 11% during 1974, and the unemployment rate reached 8.5% in 1975. In terms of annual performance, real GNP grew in 1973 by 5.5%, to reach just over $1,350,000m., but declined by 1.7% in 1974 and by a further 1.8% in 1975. The boom in output that carried over from 1973 spent itself in the first quarter of 1974, and actual growth slowed drastically during the rest of the year. The first-quarter decline in output moderated slightly between April and September but spread into a general collapse in the final quarter. Real GNP fell at an annualized rate of 7.5% between October and December, while a sharp decline in personal consumption was evidenced by a collapse of automobile sales and a marked slow-down in business investment. Real disposable personal income fell for the first time since 1947, as price increases outpaced wage and salary gains. The downturn continued into 1975, reaching its nadir in a 9.9% first-quarter drop in actual output before the slide was initially checked in April. Economic recovery in 1976 was uncertain. Actual output grew at an annualized rate of 9.2% between January and March, but its growth slowed progressively during the rest of the year. Overall, real GNP increased by 6.1% for the year, despite recording an annualized growth rate of just 2.6% in the final quarter.

Between 1976 and 1980 the US economy experienced both rapid slow-downs in output and sudden bursts of inflation. The producer- and consumer-price indexes both rose by more than 11% in 1979, and by more than 13% in 1980. (It was the first time since the First World War that the nation had endured two consecutive years of double-digit inflation.) By the end of 1980 real GNP had increased by 13% compared with 1976: most of the growth occurred in 1977-78, with real output dropping briefly, but sharply, during mid-year downturns in both 1979 and 1980. In the April–June quarter of 1980 real GNP fell at an annualized rate of 9.9% (which matched the decline recorded in the first quarter of 1975), while a real decline of 0.2% was recorded for the year as a whole. (The decline amounted to 3% in nominal terms—see below.) Unemployment totalled 7.1% of the labour force in 1980.

During his two terms in the White House, President Ronald Reagan challenged the trend towards increasing government intervention in the economy which had been in evidence (and had been almost uninterrupted) since the 1930s. The Reagan administration's first budget, in 1981, proposed sharp reductions in many domestic spending programmes and in individual and business taxation rates. These policies, based on 'supply-side' economic theories, were aimed at stimulating private enterprise (thereby, it was claimed, creating a basis for sustained economic growth) and were largely maintained throughout Reagan's eight-year presidency. The president surprised many political observers in 1981 when he secured congressional approval for much of his economic agenda. This success changed the terms of debate about economic policy in Washington, but marked the last time that the Reagan administration and Congress reached broad agreement on economic policies.

The new president's policies did not, however, bring the quick improvement in economic performance that he had promised. Reagan had inherited a deteriorating economic situation, which was evidenced by a decline of 3% in nominal GNP during 1980. Following a slight recovery in the first half of 1981, the economy deteriorated sharply in the second half, declining by an annualized rate of 4.9% in the final quarter. The recession deepened and lasted throughout 1982: unemployment climbed to 9.7%, which was the highest level reached that he had since the 'Great Depression' of the 1930s, while real GNP declined by 2.1% over the year. The recession lowered inflation sharply (from

10.4% in 1981 to 6.1% in 1982). Recovery began in early 1983: real GNP increased by 3.7% in that year, and by 6.8% in 1984—the greatest annual expansion since 1951. GNP growth consolidated thereafter at an average annual rate of about 3% through to 1988.

The 1983-88 recovery represents the longest sustained period of economic growth in the post-war era. Unemployment was reduced to 5.3% at the end of 1988 and inflation to 1.9% in 1986 (although the latter had increased again, to 4.7%, by December 1988). The need to set high interest rates in order to attract foreign credit to finance the budget deficit led to dollar appreciation and made US exports less competitive, while it made the domestic economy vulnerable to foreign penetration. This led to record trade deficits, reaching a peak of $170,000m. in 1987, and to the USA moving from being the world's leading creditor nation to becoming its leading debtor economy.

Federal Budget Outlays by Category

Expenditure under the US administrative budget rose from $9,000m. in fiscal 1940 to $98,300m. in 1944, declining to a post-war low of $33,000m. in 1948 before climbing almost steadily to $97,700m. in 1964. (Fiscal years for the federal government ran from 1 July to 30 June until 1976, since when they have run from 1 October to 30 September; a fiscal year is designated by the calendar year in which it ends.) Deficits ranging from $1,800m. to $12,400m. were incurred in 12 of the 18 fiscal years between 1947 and 1964. However, the administrative budget figures did not reflect the large amounts of income and expenditure that were channelled through federal trust funds for social security and other purposes. According to the consolidated cash budget, which also covered these trust-fund operations, federal payments to the public increased from $36,500m. in fiscal 1948 to $120,300m. in 1964, in which year cash payments by state and local governments to individuals amounted to another $50,700m.

Expenditure on national defence was by far the largest item in the federal budget between 1946 and 1964. Annual expenditure from the federal administrative budget on national defence averaged just over $12,000m. for fiscal 1948-50, escalating to $22,400m. in 1951, $44,000m. in 1952 and $50,400m. in 1953. It subsequently declined to total $40,600m. by 1956, but then steadily increased again, reaching $54,100m. in 1964. Interest payments on the national debt constituted the second-largest expenditure category, increasing steadily from $5,200m. in fiscal 1948 to $10,700m. in 1964. Federal expenditures on agriculture and agricultural resources, natural resources, commerce and transportation, health, labour and welfare, and education all increased significantly between 1946 and 1964, while expenditures on international affairs and finance fell.

The separate consolidated cash statement of federal expenditure covers the payments from trust funds to finance civil-service retirement benefits, railroad retirement benefits, old-age and survivors' insurance, unemployment compensation benefits and veterans' life insurance. Collectively, these payments amounted to relatively little before the war but grew rapidly thereafter, reaching $9,100m. in fiscal 1954 and $30,300m. in 1964.

Federal budget policy during the presidency of Lyndon Johnson (1963-69) had not only to take into account the escalation in expenditures on the war in Vietnam but also the initiation of the Johnson administration's costly and ambitious social-policy programmes to assist the poor. Between the fiscal years of 1965 and 1968 total federal budget outlays increased by just over one-third in nominal terms, growing from $118,400m. in 1965 to $178,900m. in 1968, and accounting for 21.7% of GNP in the latter year compared with 18.1% three years previously. Throughout this period the federal budget sustained a deficit, which varied from $1,600m. in fiscal 1965 to $25,200m. in 1968.

In 1967, following the acceptance by Congress and the Johnson administration of recommendations made by a special Presidential Commission on the Federal Budget, a unified federal-budget statement, which included the administrative budget and the consolidated cash budget, replaced the existing multiplicity of budgetary tabulations. According to unified budget figures calculated for the fiscal period 1965–68, expenditure on national defence increased from $49,600m. in fiscal 1965 to $80,500m. in 1968, making this again the largest single-outlay category. Expenditure on health and welfare programmes became the second-largest category, increasing from $27,200m. in fiscal 1965 to $43,500m. in 1968. Outlays on net interest thus took third place overall, increasing from $10,300m. in fiscal 1965 to $13,700m. in 1968. Outlays for the unified budget in fiscal 1969 reached $184,500m. (20.6% of total GNP), $196,600m. in 1970 (20.6%), $223,650m. in 1971 (21.0%) and $236,600m. in 1972 (21.7%).

As US involvement in the Vietnam War approached its end, the federal budget showed a marked readjustment of spending priorities from defence to domestic expenditure. Of total outlays under the fiscal 1971 budget, 41% was allocated for human-resource programmes and 37% for defence spending. This pattern continued in 1972, when the figures were 42% and 34% respectively, and in 1973, when they were 45% and 32%. Most of the shift was attributable to large increases in payments for social-security, welfare, and other income-security programmes. (These increases were beyond the control of Congress and the administration, since all applicants who meet the eligibility requirements of these programmes are entitled to a benefit payment—hence the term 'entitlements-spending'.) Spending for these programmes increased from $37,700m. in fiscal 1969 to $64,900m. in 1972 and to an estimated $69,700m. in 1973. Over the same period, debt charges increased from $15,700m. to $20,500m.

Federal budget outlays grew almost without restraint between 1973 and 1976, and there were deep divisions between Congress and the executive branch on the question of how to control expenditures. Indeed, Congress revised its budget procedures to obtain more control over fiscal policy-making and also benefited from a general decline in presidential authority following the Watergate scandal of 1972–74. This enabled Congress regularly to exceed the spending levels sought by the executive branch and, as a result, both expenditures and budget deficits set peacetime records. A sharp recession hit the economy in 1973–74 (see above) and encouraged Congress to vote for new spending programmes to stimulate the economy: these measures led to budget outlays totalling $326,100m. in fiscal 1975. The economy's continued decline prompted the adoption of further stimulative measures in fiscal 1976, resulting in actual budget outlays of $366,500m., which produced a peacetime record deficit of over $66,000m. (In addition, in 1976 there was a transitional quarter between July and September, to account for the relocation of the start of the federal-government fiscal year from 1 July to 1 October, during which budget outlays totalled about $100,000m.) In fiscal 1977 federal budget outlays surpassed $413,000m.

Budget outlays between 1973 and 1976 continued to shift away from defence towards more direct federal distributions to the elderly and the poor. Income-security outlays increased from $64,200m. to about $140,000m. (an increase of 118% in nominal terms), while defence outlays increased from $75,100m. to just over $100,000m. (+33%). This development was sustained in the late 1970s. As a result, a total of 77% of all federal spending was devoted to relatively uncontrollable entitlements-spending on social-security benefits. The fastest-growing spending area was that of health and income-security programmes, which grew 63% during the fiscal period 1977–81.

From 1981, President Ronald Reagan launched a dramatic assault on the growth in budget outlays by proposing massive across-the-board cuts in all areas of domestic spending, except middle-class entitlements. At the same time, however, he proposed a sharp escalation in defence spending (see below). The president surprisingly obtained congressional support to reduce domestic discretionary spending by $130,600m. in the fiscal period 1982–86; this portion of outlays was reduced from $141,000m. in fiscal 1980 to $112,000m. in 1981, but rose again to total $137,000m. by 1983. Outlays reached $173,000m. in fiscal 1985 but then rose only marginally to 1988. While the president failed in his later attempts to cut domestic discretionary spending, he did lower its rate of growth and hence its share of overall budget outlays, which fell from 26% in fiscal 1980 to 19% in 1985. By comparison, entitlements spending

rose from $267,000m. in fiscal 1980 to $345,000m. in 1982 and to $440,000m. by 1985, with an estimated figure of $532,000m. being put forward for fiscal 1989.

In 1981 President Reagan succeeded in securing an increase in defence spending from the $136,000m. of fiscal 1980 to $160,000m. and $187,000m. for 1981 and 1982 respectively. This initial rate of increase was sustained, leading to defence outlays of $210,000m. in 1983 and $253,000m. by 1985. In 1986 Congress moderated the rate of growth in defence spending, which was forecast to reach almost $300,000m. in fiscal 1989. Over his two terms, President Reagan increased defence spending from 23% of total budget outlays in fiscal 1980 to 27% in 1985, with a marginal increase on that level estimated for fiscal 1989.

The president's promise to balance the budget by 1984 gave way instead to a series of record peacetime budget deficits. In turn, this led to a dramatic increase in federal outlays spent on servicing the national debt. These outlays increased from $52,000m. in fiscal 1980 to $129,000m. in 1985 and were forecast to reach $166,000m. in 1989. Thus President Reagan did succeed in reordering federal budget outlays, but at the expense of a rapid growth in the deficit and in debt charges. To put the level of federal budget expenditure in some perspective, total outlays rose, in terms of constant 1982 dollars, from under $400,000m. in 1965 to over $860,000m. in 1987.

Federal Budget Receipts

Federal taxes on individual and corporate income were raised sharply during the Second World War, and remained essentially unchanged (and steeply progressive) until 1964. Thus income taxes accounted for about 80% of administrative-budget receipts in 1963, as they did in 1945. Because of their sensitivity to changes in the rate of economic activity, income taxes were a major counter-cyclical force in the post-war economy, serving to brake declines and booms alike. For example, tax accruals on corporate profits at higher rates soared from $11,700m. in fiscal 1950 to $21,800m. in 1951, but dropped to $2,700m., $3,100m. and $2,000m. respectively during the 1953–54, 1957–58 and 1960–61 recessions. During the fiscal period 1946–64 annual federal receipts grew from $43,500m. to $115,500m., albeit with periodic declines. By 1962, however, the Kennedy administration had concluded that the existing income-tax rate structure was too high for optimum growth purpose, because it tended to halt expansionary forces before they reached full-employment levels. As a result the administration proposed—and Congress in 1964 finally approved—an $11,000m. cut in individual and corporate income-tax rates, for the explicit purpose of stimulating private demand.

Federal budget receipts grew from $116,800m. in fiscal 1965 to $153,700m. in 1968, and as a proportion of GNP from 17.9% to 18.7% over the same period. In 1967 President Johnson came to the realization that the nation could not afford both the Vietnam War and his ambitious social-policy initiatives within the limits of existing tax revenues, and decided to seek an increase in taxes and to hold down expenditures. In August of that year he sent to Congress a proposal for a 10% surcharge on personal and corporate income taxes; in June 1968 a law was passed enacting this surcharge.

Total federal budget receipts increased sharply to $187,800m. in fiscal 1969 as a result of the surcharge tax, then totalled $193,700m. in 1970 and $188,400m. in 1971 before rising steeply, to $208,700m., in 1972. In an effort to stimulate the economy, the 1971 Revenue Act cut individual and business taxes by an average of $8,600m. a year between 1971 and 1973. Also in 1971, President Nixon obtained congressional support to restore the 7% investment tax credit, which amounted to a tax cut of an estimated $2,400m. in fiscal 1972, rising to $4,000m. by 1974. Higher-than-expected revenues, due to a short-lived economic boom, raised actual revenues to almost $264,000m. for fiscal 1974. However, the calamitous downturn in the economy experienced in mid-year (associated with the sharp increases in the price of oil in 1973–74 and an inflation rate of 11% in 1974—see above) meant that the $281,000m. revenue collected in fiscal 1975 represented a substantial real decline. To deal with the economic collapse, Congress in 1975 passed a $22,800m. tax-reduction bill. Final revenues for fiscal

1976 amounted to $300,000m., while outlays reached $366,500m.: the resulting deficit was a peacetime record.

Federal tax policy shifted during the late 1970s as a result of inflation. Bursts of inflation pushed taxpayers into higher tax brackets and thus fuelled sharp increases in revenues, which rose from $358,000m. in fiscal 1977 to $402,000m. in 1978, $466,000m. in 1979, $520,000m. in 1980 and $603,000m. in 1981. The increasing burden of taxation eventually led to a 'taxpayers' rebellion' by middle-income taxpayers and even the wealthy, as well as businesses. This movement, which gained much support from the success of 'Proposition 13' in California (an initiative, approved by 65% of the state's voters, to cut property taxes in the state by 57%), changed the tax debate from the traditional approach of cutting taxes for those on lower incomes in favour of adopting massive across-the-board reductions in individual and business taxes.

Preident Reagan aligned himself with this movement and claimed, after his election in 1980, that he had an electoral mandate to retrench federal spending. In early 1981 he proposed to cut personal income taxes by 30% over three years and also to slash business taxes. To win congressional approval for his radical tax agenda, the president was forced to accept modifications to the proposals, and individual income-tax rates were instead reduced by 25% over three years. President Reagan accepted a proposal to index individual tax rates beginning in 1985. This would effectively prevent the process known as 'bracket-creeping', in which taxpayers were pushed into higher tax-payment bands because of inflation. The president also accepted a much more generous business depreciation tax regime to win support for the most radical reordering of federal tax policies in the post-war period.

According to official estimates, these decisions—along with the recession between mid-1981 and early 1983—led to a loss in tax revenues of about $1,000,000m. in the fiscal period 1981–86. Revenues fell from $617,800m. in fiscal 1982 to $600,600m. in 1983 before rising to $666,500m. in 1984. Economic recovery prompted a rise to $734,100m. in fiscal 1985 and to $769,100m. the following year. In 1986 President Reagan once more persuaded Congress to reform individual taxes by dropping top rates sharply and by taking many people off the tax rolls. The decision was very popular with voters and also effectively prevented Congress from using tax increases to reduce the budget deficit. Sustained economic growth increased revenues to over $900,000m. in fiscal 1988. In that year, individual income taxes amounted to $393,400m., while corporate income taxes amounted to $105,600m. and social-insurance taxes to $331,500m. Excise taxes and user fees contributed $78,600m.

Federal Debt

The US government borrowed more than $200,000m. to help finance the cost of the Second World War, raising the accumulated public debt to almost $280,000m. early in 1946. By use of its large cash reserves and an $8,400m. budget surplus in fiscal 1948, the Treasury cut the outstanding debt to about $250,000m., but deficits in subsequent years raised the accumulated debt to about $275,000m. by 1955. Surpluses totalling $3,200m. were recorded in 1956–57, but deficits in seven of the next eight fiscal years lifted the total debt to about $317,000m. by mid-1965. In fiscal 1945 the administrative budget allocated $3,600m. to interest payments on the public debt, whereas the corresponding figure for 1965 was $11,200m. The increase was largely the result of higher interest rates and mostly occurred after 1954, when monetary policy was adjusted to combat inflation and capital outflows.

From the 1960s the deficit grew considerably. During the Johnson presidency the total federal debt increased from $323,100m. in fiscal 1965 to $369,700m. in 1968. After the Vietnam War surcharge had generated a budget surplus of $3,200m. in fiscal 1969, President Nixon experienced great difficulties in managing the federal budget. The annual federal budget deficit measured between $23,000m. and $25,000m. for the fiscal period 1971–73, and as a result the federal debt increased from $365,000m. in fiscal 1969 to $465,000m. in 1973. Intense conflicts in the mid-1970s between the White House

and Congress over spending and taxing policies frequently resulted in Congress spending more and taxing less than Presidents Nixon and Ford had proposed in their annual budget submissions. Added expenditures to tackle economic contraction, especially during the 1973–75 recession, further increased the accumulated deficit. The combination of political and economic factors led to higher annual deficits, and those occurring in the fiscal years of 1975, 1976 and 1977—respectively $45,100m., $66,500m. and about $60,000m.—were far larger than any previous peacetime deficits. As a result the public debt increased to over $720,000m. in fiscal 1977.

The federal budget deficit remained persistently high during the period in office of the Carter administration, totalling $44,900m. in fiscal 1977, $44,800m. in 1978, $27,700m. in 1979 and $59,600m. in 1980. These persistent shortfalls reflected, in part, the lingering impact of the 1973–75 recession, but were also perpetuated by the administration and Congress in that policy actions were taken that enlarged the gap between revenues and spending.

President Reagan came to office with the intention of tackling the growing deficit burden. However, the bold promise he made in 1981 that his supply-side fiscal policies would balance the budget in 1984 gave way instead to a string of record budget deficits during his first term. The deficit increased from the $59,600m. of fiscal 1980 to $79,100m. in 1981 and to $128,100m. in 1982. The combination of policy mistakes and recession pushed the deficit to record peacetime figures of $208,400m. in fiscal 1983, $212,300m. in 1985 and $220,700m. in 1986. Between 1980 and 1986 the accumulated deficit as a proportion of GNP increased from 34.2% to 51.2%, and federal government debt increased from $914,000m. to $2,133,000m. Towards the end of Reagan's second term, a combination of revenue increases (due to economic growth and moderation in defence spending) and skilful budgetary manoeuvring lowered the federal deficit to the $150,000m.–$160,000m. range. By 1987, however, the national debt had increased to an estimated $2,370,000m., and the massive federal budget deficit had been established as the major economic legacy of the Reagan era.

Trends in Federal Employment

Civilian employment in the federal career system—which includes staff in the US Postal Service and other independent agencies, the executive branch, the legislative branch and the judiciary—surpassed 1m. in 1940. By 1945, as a result of US involvement in the Second World War, some 3.8m. were on the civilian payroll and 11.6m. in uniform. After the Second World War civilian government employment stabilized at about 2m. until the Korean War caused it to increase to 2.5m. in 1951. There was a slight drop, to 2.4m., during President Eisenhower's two administrations (1953–61), but civilian employment then returned to 2.5m.

In fiscal 1965, with total federal civilian employment still standing at about 2.5m., some 1.47m. staff were working in civilian agencies and just over 1m. civilian staff were employed by the Department of Defense. These figures increased to, respectively, 1.71m. and 1.31m. in fiscal 1968, when overall federal civilian employment totalled just over 3m. During this period the US Postal Service employed the single greatest number of federal civilian staff (595,512 in 1965, increasing to 730,977 in 1968), but its growth was outpaced by that of the Department of Health, Education and Welfare (reorganized into two separate departments in 1979), which increased its employment from 87,316 in 1965 to 177,115 in 1968. Overall, the Veterans' Administration constituted the second-largest civilian agency, employing 165,059 in fiscal 1965 and 175,668 in 1968.

Federal civilian-employment costs reached an all-time peak of $22,400m. in fiscal 1968, which was $1,900m. more than in 1967 and some $5,200m. more than in 1965. The fiscal 1968 total comprised $13,000m. for employment costs in civilian agencies and $9,400m. for civilian employment in military agencies. Although the period saw significant growth in federal employment, many more persons were employed by state and local governments to implement, in part, federal spending programmes. In all, some 9.4m. persons were employed by state and local governments in fiscal 1968, compared with 7.7m. in 1965.

These trends and patterns have subsequently remained in place. Federal employment levels have fluctuated between 2.7m. and 3m. since the late 1960s. Executive-branch civilian employment fell from a peak of 3,032,817 in fiscal 1968 to 2,756,744 in 1972. The Nixon administration had resolved to retrench federal employment by several means, most notably by attempting to transfer responsibility for certain federal programmes to state and local governments. These and other measures led to a reduction in civilian employment in the Department of Defense from 1,313,049 in fiscal 1969 to 1,073,471 in 1972. Over the same period, employment in the Department of Health, Education and Welfare fell from 117,115 to 114,065, while employment in the US Postal Service fell from 730,977 to 675,197. Employment in the Department of the Treasury, on the other hand, increased from 89,125 to 105,326, and that in the Veterans' Administration from 175,688 to 187,561. The post-Watergate and post-Vietnam Congress continued to reduce civilian employment levels in the Department of Defense, with the result that total federal civilian employment was pegged at about 2.7m.

During the presidencies of Jimmy Carter and Ronald Reagan, the increase in the amount of money spent on federal programmes continued to outpace that in the number of federal employees. However, the number of persons employed by state and local governments continued to rise, totalling over 15m. in 1981. President Reagan's perennial attempts to retrench the federal bureaucracy, even including proposals to abolish the Departments of Education (founded in 1979) and Energy, were rebuffed by Congress, with the result that the president achieved only marginal reductions, bringing total federal employment down to about 2.6m. It is significant to note that since 1950 the level of federal employment has not increased substantially (only from about 2m. to about 2.6m.); taking into account the simultaneous 60% increase in the size of the US population, there has even been a proportional decline. The increase in government employment over this period has taken place at state and local level.

Federal Aid to State and Local Governments

Federal grants-in-aid to state and local governments have been used as a means of achieving national objectives since the first such programme was introduced in 1862. Their total value increased tenfold during the immediate post-war years, from $847m. in fiscal 1946 to $8,600m. in 1963. Of the 80 grant-in-aid programmes established by the end of 1964, 57 had been enacted after the Second World War. As a result the structure of US federalism was substantially altered because the growth in both the size and the variety of federal assistance was made conditional upon state and local governments accepting an increase in federal regulation.

The 80 programmes enacted to 1964 varied widely in terms of their purpose, scope, administration and allocation of funds. Expenditures on highway programmes, for example, constituted the largest area of funding, increasing from $318m. in 1948 to $2,750m. in 1962. Over the same period, expenditures on social programmes increased from $724m. to $2,450m., while funds spent on education rose from $418m. to $1,170m. By comparison, expenditures on health and hospital programmes increased from $55m. in 1948 to $168m. in 1962, while spending on housing and urban renewal increased from only $11m. in 1952 to $352m. in 1962.

Federal grant-in-aid expenditures grew rapidly during the Johnson presidency, more than doubling in value between 1963 and 1968 to account for over $22,000m. (12% of all federal expenditures) in the latter year. Unusually rapid rates of expansion were experienced in the field of welfare legislation as a result of President Johnson's 'Great Society' initiative. The example of community-action programmes, funded by the Office of Economic Opportunity (established by the Economic Opportunity Act of 1964) is illustrative of how social-policy expenditures grew rapidly during Johnson's presidency. The 1964 legislation authorized spending totalling $236.7m. for fiscal 1965 to establish the community-action programme, and expenditure on it rose to $847m. in 1968. By late 1972 there were 1,054 federal domestic-assistance programmes, conducted by 60 federal agencies, offering grants and loans to state and local government, non-profit groups and individuals, and by fiscal 1972 the total value of federal grants-in-aid had increased to over $29,000m.

President Nixon proposed to rationalize this labyrinth of grants by enacting a system of general revenue-sharing. This consisted of a programme of sharing tax revenues, but without major federal interference on the use of funds. The proposal was aimed at shifting many responsibilities from the federal level to state and local governments. Nixon claimed that the proposal promised more federal dollars, with no narrow-purpose guidelines and less federal regulation, and that as a result there would be significant savings in administrative and other overhead costs (which would thus reduce the overall amount of federal aid to state and local governments). The initiative thus promised to start reversing the post-war trend towards both more federal regulation of, and spending on aid to, state and local governments. The president's proposal was eventually enacted in part in the form of the State and Local Fiscal Assistance Act of 1972. This legislation entailed a five-year programme to share $30,200m. in federal revenues. Nixon's related proposals to combine a series of categorical grants (which finance specially-designated programmes, such as school aid for disadvantaged children) into large block grants (which would give recipient governments wide latitude as to how they used grant funds within a broad area such as education) were, however, rejected by Congress.

The general revenue-sharing programme was extended in 1975 for five years. Despite misgivings among many of its members (which took two years to resolve) Congress retained the basic non-interventionist approach of the revenue-distribution programme that successive Republican administrations had endorsed as a necessary transfer of federal power back to state and local governments. The $25,600m. extension was, however, less than was sought by the administration because Congress had doubts about the 'New Federalism' concept—pioneered by President Nixon—of sharing federal tax revenues without federal control over their use. Federal aid to state and local governments remained largely constant at about 11.5% of budget outlays in the late 1970s. Due to the general consolidation of categorical grant programmes, the overall number of federal-aid programmes was reduced. The general revenue-sharing block-grant programme was extended in 1980 for a further three years at existing levels: however, state governments were excluded from it for fiscal 1981.

In 1981 President Reagan proclaimed his intention to redirect power—and spending—from the federal government to state and local governments. The main vehicle for this change was an updated 'New Federalism' plan, which involved a proposal to convert 88 categorical-grant programmes into seven block grants, again claiming that such a reduction in federal tutelage would also lower administrative overheads and hence costs. Congress, however, approved the amalgamation of just 57 of these categorical grants—mainly affecting health, education and community services—into the seven block grants. The decision reduced their funding levels by about 25%.

In 1982 President Reagan made a more radical proposal to thoroughly restructure federal, state and local responsibilities. The administration proposed to shift to the states about 40 programmes—in the areas of social policy and transportation—and to provide additional revenues to finance them in the early phase. In return, the federal government would assume the full cost of Medicaid (the federal–state health programme for the poor). While this plan was not in fact implemented, the Reagan administration did manage to reduce the overall total of expenditures on aid to state and local governments from $95,000m. in fiscal 1981 to $88,000m. in 1983, and subsequently to restrain their rate of growth to a considerable degree.

SELECT BIBLIOGRAPHY

Aaron, H. et al. *Economic Choices: 1987.* Washington, DC, The Brookings Institution, 1986.

Adams, G. *The Politics of Defense Contracting.* New York, Transaction Books, 1984.

Adelman, M. A. *Energy Resources in an Uncertain Future: Coal, Gas, Oil and Uranium Supply Forecasting.* Cambridge, Massachusetts, Ballinger Publishing Co, 1984.

Baily, M. N. and Chakrabarti, A. K. *Innovation and the Productivity Crisis.* Washington, DC, The Brookings Institution, 1988.

Bertsch, K. and Shaw, L. *The Nuclear Weapons Industry.* Washington, DC, Investor Responsibility Research Center, 1984.

Blackburn, J. O. *The Renewable Energy Alternative.* Durham, North Carolina, Duke University Press, 1987.

Brandin, D. H. and Harrison, M. A. *The Technology War.* New York, John Wiley & Sons Inc, 1987.

Cagan, P. *Essays in Contemporary Economic Problems: The Impact of the Reagan Program.* Washington, DC, American Enterprise Institute for Public Policy Research, 1986.

Cash, D. E. *US Energy Policy: Crisis and Complacency.* Norman, Oklahoma, University of Oklahoma Press, 1984.

Castle, E. N. and Price, R. A. (Eds). *US Interests and Global Natural Resources.* Washington, DC, Resources for the Future, 1982.

Chubb, J. E. and Paterson, P. I. *Can the Government Govern?* Washington, DC, The Brookings Institution, 1989.

Cochrane, W. W. *The Development of American Agriculture: A Historical Analysis.* Minneapolis, Minnesota, University of Minnesota Press, 1979.

Congress and the Nation Vols 1–6, covering 1945–84. Washington, DC, Congressional Quarterly Inc.

Coulan, R. *Illusions of Choice.* Princeton, New Jersey, Princeton University Press, 1977.

Cuff, D. J. *The US Energy Atlas.* New York, Macmillan Publishing Co, 1985.

Cuomo, M. *The Cuomo Commission Report: A New American Formula for a Strong Economy.* New York, Simon & Schuster Inc, 1988.

Dana, S. T. and Fairfax, S. K. *Forest and Range Policy.* New York, McGraw-Hill Inc, 1980.

Denison, E. F. *Trends in American Economic Growth, 1929–82.* Washington, DC, The Brookings Institution, 1985.

Economic Report of the President: 1989. Washington, DC, Government Printing Office, 1989.

Edmonds, M. 'Accountability and the Military-Industrial Complex' in Smith, B. (Ed). *The New Political Economy.* London, Macmillan, 1975.

Ender, R. L. and Kim, J. C. (Eds). *Energy Resources Development.* New York, Quorum Books, 1987.

Ethier, W. J. *Modern International Economics.* New York and London, W. W. Norton & Co Inc, 1988.

Feldstein, M. (Ed). *The United States in the World Economy.* Chicago, Illinois, University of Chicago Press, 1988.

Fitzgerald, E. *The High Priests of Waste.* New York, W. W. Norton & Co Inc, 1972.

Food and Agriculture Policy Research Institute. *FAPRI US and World Agricultural Outlook* (Staff Report No. 2/89). Iowa State University/University of Missouri–Columbia, FAPRI, 1989.

Frieden, J. A. *Banking on the World: The Politics of American International Finance.* New York, Harper & Row, Publishers Inc, 1987.

Fuchs, V. *The Service Economy.* New York, National Bureau of Economic Research/Columbia University Press, 1968.

Gansler, J. *The Defense Industry.* Cambridge, Massachusetts, The MIT Press, 1980.

General Accounting Office. *Industrial Base: Defense-Critical Industries.* Washington, DC, GAO/NSIAD, 1988.

Goldfield, M. *The Decline of Organized Labour in the United States.* Chicago, Illinois, University of Chicago Press, 1987.

Grimwade, N. *International Trade.* London, Routledge, 1989.

Halberstram, D. *The Reckoning.* New York, Avon Books, 1986.

Hansen, A. H. *The Postwar American Economy: Performance and Problems.* New York, W. W. Norton & Co Inc, 1964.

Hibbs, D. A. *The American Political Economy: Macroeconomics and Electoral Politics in the United States.* Cambridge, Massachusetts, Harvard University Press, 1987.

Hooper, P. and Mann, C. L. 'The US external deficit: its causes and persistence' in *International Finance Discussion Papers* (No. 316). Washington, DC, Federal Reserve Board, November 1987.

IMF. *International Financial Statistics.* Washington, DC, monthly.

Kaldor, M. *The Baroque Arsenal.* London, Sphere, 1983.

Kennedy, P. *The Rise and Fall of the Great Powers: Economic Change and Military Conflict from 1500 to 2000.* London, Unwin Hyman Ltd, 1988.

Kirn, T. J. 'Growth and Change in the Service Sector of the US: A Spatial Perspective' in *Annals, Association of American Geographers,* No. 77, 1987.

Landsberg, H. H., Tilton, E. and Haas, R. B. 'Non-Fuel Minerals' in Portney, P. R. (Ed). *Natural Resource Policy.* Washington, DC, Resources for the Future, 1982.

Libicki, M., Nunn, J. and Taylor, W. *US Industrial Base: Dependence/Vulnerability* (Phase II). Washington, DC, National Defense University Mobilization Concepts Development Center, 1987.

Mayer, C. J. *Public Domain, Private Dominion: A History of Public Mineral Policy in America.* San Francisco, California, Sierra Club Books, 1985.

Miller, J. B. and Bluestone, R. *Prospects for Service Sector Employment in Non-Metropolitan America.* Washington, DC, Government Printing Office, 1987.

Milner, H. V. *Resisting Protectionism: Global Industries and the Politics of International Trade.* Princeton, New Jersey, Princeton University Press, 1988.

Noyelle, T. J. (Ed). *New York's Financial Markets: The Challenge of Globalization.* Boulder, Colorado, Westview Press Inc, 1988.

Obey, D. and Sarbanes, P. (Eds). *The Changing American Economy.* Oxford, Basil Blackwell Ltd, 1986.

OECD. *Economic Outlook.* Paris, semiannual.

The United States (Economic Surveys). Paris, annual.

Packard, D. *A Quest for Excellence* (Report of the President's Blue Ribbon Commission on Defense Management). Washington, DC, 1986.

Pechman, J. A. *Federal Tax Policy.* Washington, DC, The Brookings Institution, 1987.

Peck, M. J. and Scherer, F. M. *The Weapons Acquisition Process.* Cambridge, Massachusetts, Harvard University Press, 1964.

Portney, P. R. *Natural Resources and the Environment: The Reagan Approach.* Washington, DC, The Urban Institute Press, 1984.

Price, K. A. *Regional Conflict and National Policy.* Washington, DC, Resources for the Future, 1982.

Rabin, M. R. and Huber, M. T. *The Knowledge Industry in the United States.* Princeton, New Jersey, Princeton University Press, 1986.

Regens, J. L., Rycroft, R. W. and Daneke, G. A. (Eds). *Energy and the Western United States: Politics and Development.* New York, Praeger Publishers, 1982.

Reppy, J. 'The United States' in Ball, N. and Leitenburg, M. (Eds). *The Structure of the Defense Industry.* London, Croom Helm, 1983.

Riddle, D. *Service-Led Growth: The Role of the Service Sector.* New York, Praeger Publishers, 1986.

Sauvant, K. *International Trade in Services: The Politics of Transborder Data Flow.* Boulder, Colorado, Westview Press Inc, 1987.

Shoven, J. *Government Policy towards Industry in the United States and Japan.* Cambridge, Cambridge University Press, 1988.

Sommers, A. T. and Blau, L. R. *The US Economy Demystified.* Lexington, Massachusetts, Lexington Books, 1988.

Spinney, F. *The Defense Facts of Life.* Boulder, Colorado, Westview Press Inc, 1985.

Stanback, T. M. *Understanding the Service Economy: Employment, Productivity, Location.* Baltimore, Maryland, The Johns Hopkins University Press, 1979.

Stanback, T. M., Bearse, P. J., Noyelle, T. J. and Karasek, R. A. *Services: The New Economy.* Totowa, New Jersey, Allanheed, Osman & Co, 1981.

Stein, H. *Presidential Economics: The Making of Economic Policy from Roosevelt to Reagan and Beyond.* New York, Simon & Schuster Inc, 1985.

Stern, R. M. (Ed). *US Trade Policies in a Changing World Economy.* Cambridge, Massachusetts, The MIT Press, 1987.

Sternlieb, G. and Hughes, J. W. (Eds). *Shopping Centers: USA.* New Brunswick, New Jersey, Rutgers University Press, 1981.

The US Budget In Brief: Fiscal Year 1990. Washington, DC, Government Printing Office, 1989.

US Bureau of the Census. *Annual Survey of Manufactures.* Washington, DC, Government Printing Office, annual.

Historical Statistics of the United States, Colonial Times to 1970. Washington, DC, Government Printing Office, 1975.

State and Metropolitan Area Data Book 1986. Washington, DC, Government Printing Office, 1986.

Statistical Abstract of the United States. Washington, DC, Government Printing Office, annual.

US Bureau of Economic Analysis. *Survey of Current Business.* Washington, DC, monthly.

US Congressional Budget Office. *How Federal Policies Affect the Steel Industry.* Washington, DC, Government Printing Office, 1987.

US Department of Agriculture. *Agricultural Statistics.* Washington, DC, Government Printing Office, annual.

Agricultural Policy Review: Commodity Program Perspectives (Agricultural Economic Report No. 530). Washington, DC, Government Printing Office, 1985.

Crop Production Reports. Washington, DC, Government Printing Office, monthly and annual.

Economic Indicators of the Farm Sector. Washington, DC, Government Printing Office, series of five annual issues.

Economics of the US Meat Industry (Economic Research Service, AIB 545). Washington, DC, Government Printing Office, 1988.

World Grain Situation and Outlook. Washington, DC, Government Printing Office, annual.

World Oilseed Situation and Market Highlights. Washington, DC, Government Printing Office, annual.

US Department of Commerce. *An Assessment of US Competitiveness in High-Technology Industries.* Washington, DC, Government Printing Office, 1983.

A Competitive Assessment of the US Ethylene Industry. Washington, DC, Government Printing Office, 1986.

Fisheries of the United States. Washington, DC, Government Printing Office, annual.

The US Automobile Industry, 1985 (Report to the Congress from the Secretary of Commerce). Washington, DC, Government Printing Office, 1985.

US Department of Defense. *Bolstering Defense Industrial Competitiveness* (The Costello Report). Washington, DC, Department of Defense, 1988.

US Department of Energy. *The Changing Structure of the US Coal Industry, 1976-86* (Energy Information Administration—Report DOE/EIA 0513). Washington, DC, Government Printing Office, 1986.

Performance Profiles of Major Energy Producers, 1986 (Energy Information Administration—Report DOE/EIA 0106). Washington, DC, Government Printing Office, 1986.

US Department of the Interior. *Mineral Facts and Problems* (Bureau of Mines Bulletin No. 675). Washington, DC, Government Printing Office, 1985.

(Bureau of Mines) *Minerals Year Book* (Vols I and II). Washington, DC, Government Printing Office, annual.

US Forest Service. *An Analysis of the Timber Situation in the United States, 1952-2030.* Washington, DC, Government Printing Office, 1982.

The Evolving Use and Management of the Nation's Forests, Grasslands, Croplands and Related Resources: A Technical Document Supporting the 1989 RPA Assessment (Draft). Washington, DC, Government Printing Office, 1988.

US International Trade Administration. *US Industrial Outlook.* Washington, DC, annual.

Vawter, R. *US Industrial Base: Dependence/Vulnerability* (Phase I, Survey). Washington, DC, National Defense University Mobilization Concepts Development Center, 1987.

Vietor, R. H. K. *Energy Policy in America since 1945: a Study of Business-Government Relations.* Cambridge, Cambridge University Press, 1984.

Zysman, J. and Tyson, L. (Eds). *American Industry in International Competition.* Ithaca, New York, Cornell University Press, 1983.

CONTEMPORARY SOCIAL ISSUES

DEMOGRAPHIC MOVEMENTS WITHIN THE USA

PHILIP JOHN DAVIES

Mobility in the USA

The United States of America is rightly thought of as a nation with a highly mobile population. The rate of mobility, however, alters over time, and a number of such alterations have occurred in the post-war period. Between 1 April 1960 and 31 March 1961 just over 20% of the population moved residence within the USA, but over the next 20 years the annual mobility rate declined slowly and steadily, reaching a low of just over 16% in 1982/83. The mid-1980s have seen this trend reversed, starting in 1983/84, when the rate increased to almost 17%, and continuing into 1985/86, when 18% of the population, or about 42m. persons, moved residence within the USA.

These consistently high annual mobility rates clearly confirm the image of the USA as a mobile nation, but it has to be stressed that most of this internal migration does not result in the individuals concerned moving very long distances. In 1985/86, as in previous years, two-thirds of the movers stayed within the county of their former residence, and only one-sixth of those moving took up residence in a different state. Nevertheless, the pattern of population movement is significant both at local and at national level, as it reflects the changing demographic structures of communities, states and regions within the USA.

Population movement is often a response to economic or other stimuli. The tendency for members of a population to 'vote with their feet' can provide the analyst with broad insights into the historical success and future potential of areas with the characteristics that appear to attract or repel population groups at any particular time. Population mobility also has political consequences: communities and states devise policies aimed at providing those qualities which attract economic and population growth. Those that are successful gain an additional advantage, since the boundaries of a state's congressional and other electoral constituencies are redrawn every 10 years on the basis of census returns. Thus those places with an increased population are rapidly accorded increased political influence. Furthermore, any gain or loss of population has a life-cycle of its own. The most mobile age-groups are 20–34 (i.e. the most fertile sector of the population) and 0–9 (i.e. the children of the former). Therefore the areas that gain new settlers from the in-migration of these groups are likely to find population growth being maintained through the next generation, and those that are losing population are faced with the prospect of decreased fertility, compounding current migration loss with a future declining birth-rate.

Metropolitan Migration

Most mobility is relatively localized, with people generally moving within the geographical area with which they are already familiar. The major single pattern of local migration since 1950 has been the 'suburbanization' of urban areas. Many urban problems derive in part from the cities' historical success in acting as centres of cultural and service excellence, and in providing both economic opportunity for individuals and economically efficient environments for business. Such success has encouraged the development of large urban populations, as people are attracted from non-metropolitan areas by the opportunities offered in the cities, the size and population density of which eventually exacerbate the difficulties faced by individuals and local governments. Overcrowding accelerates housing deterioration and puts excessive burdens on education,

health and other services; industrial concentration can create a blanket of pollution which will not easily disperse. Communities become economically segregated, and the poor, often living in neighbourhoods of people similarly disadvantaged, find that a problem shared is not halved, but compounded.

Many major cities developed suburbs in the late 19th century, especially as the invention of faster forms of mass transportation, such as suburban railways and electrically-powered railed streetcars (trams), increased the distance that could be covered in an acceptable commuting time. As urban areas grew, the affluent were tempted to move to the more 'countrified' fringes of the cities. The late 20th-century predominance of the private automobile over public transportation—and of the truck over the railroad—means that the inner cities are no longer the obvious locations for industry or housing. While city roads have become more crowded and massive government investment in highways since the 1950s has provided access to outlying areas, the suburbs have become the logical sites for growth and relocation, attracting migrants both from the inner cities and from non-metropolitan areas. Post-war mass-production techniques have reduced the unit cost of new housing, but the move to the suburbs may still not be cheap. The people who have migrated to the suburbs have been predominantly middle-class whites; with only about 6% of the suburban population being black, against about 12% in the total US population.

In the 1970s the non-metropolitan population growth rate outpaced that for metropolitan areas for the first time in a century, indicating a lessening attraction towards urban areas. Between the 1 April 1980 census and 1 July 1986, however, with the national population increasing by 6.1% overall, the metropolitan population grew by 7.2% and the non-metropolitan population by 3.9%, thereby apparently re-establishing the pattern of 'metropolitanization' of the USA. The pattern has regional variations, with most of this differential growth concentrated in the South, where the metropolitan population grew by 12.3% in the six years to 1986, while the rest of the country has shown a more even pace of growth in metropolitan and non-metropolitan areas. Nevertheless the US population has, on average, become increasingly concentrated, with 76.6% living in areas classified as metropolitan in 1986, as opposed to 56.1% in 1950.

Much of this metropolitan growth has been concentrated in suburban areas. Measured nationally, central-city growth stopped almost completely during the 1970s (while individual cities, of course, continued to experience different rates of growth or decline). The 1980s have seen the return of some growth in the populations of inner cities, but there are still considerable individual differences, and in most metropolitan areas the suburban population is still increasing at a greater rate. Of the nation's 20 largest cities, those in the South and West showed most growth betwen 1980 and 1986. For example, the central-city population of San Diego grew by 16%, of Dallas by 10.9%, Phoenix by 13.1%, and Jacksonville by 12.7%. However, in these cities of vibrant growth the suburbs were growing even faster, at rates of 20.3%, 32.8%, 39.9% and 34.3% respectively. Those inner cities with static or declining populations over this period were concentrated in the Northeast and Midwest regions. For example, Chicago's population growth was just 0.1% over the six-year period, while there were declines of 2.7% in Philadelphia, 4.3% in Baltimore and 9.7% in Detroit. Each city nevertheless experienced modest suburban population increases, of 4%, 5.1%, 7% and 8.1% respectively.

Nationally, then, the population is still attracted to the suburbs, and these differential rates of growth can only be explained by migration. People are still moving to the suburbs of their own metropolis, but the figures also suggest that people moving to other cities and other regions are more likely to choose a suburban location for their new home. Nevertheless, these net measures of population movement are made up of complex and overlapping shifts to and from every area. Places are not just losing or gaining people, they are exchanging people. The most recent estimates of this network of movement cover 1983/84. In that year, for example, inner cities made a net gain of 4,000 people from non-metropolitan areas. This apparently marginal change was, however, made up of 1,037,000 people leaving the inner cities for non-metropolitan areas, being replaced by 1,041,000 migrants from non-metropolitan areas into the cities. If these millions of people form significantly different sectors of the population, then the apparently marginal net change may in fact disguise a significant shift in the character of the populations of both living environments. In the same year 2.3m. people left suburban areas for the inner cities, while slightly over 4m. made the opposite journey, and 1.2m. left the suburbs for non-metropolitan areas, with almost 1.6m. going the other way.

It is difficult to assess the social and economic characteristics of these exchanging populations, but analyses of similar patterns in the 1970s suggest that those leaving the inner cities are more affluent than those moving in; in spite of the fact that 'gentrification' has certainly attracted professional households into some city neighbourhoods, it is still likely that cities are losing more household income than they are gaining from current migration. In the 1970s cities were losing individuals and families with an aggregate income approaching $7,000m. annually, with a consequent dramatic effect on purchasing power within the cities. Urban migration has also been racially selective, and in 1980 about 60% of the black population lived in central cities, compared with 27% of all whites.

Regional Migration

Regional population mobility has also followed distinct patterns over time. The US Bureau of the Census has calculated the geographical position of the 'centre of population' for the USA for each census since the first was taken in 1790. This notional 'centre' moved steadily west through the 19th and the first half of the 20th centuries. In 1800 the US population was centred on a point between Baltimore and Washington, DC. By 1850 it had shifted 250 miles west, to a point about 50 miles north of Charleston, West Virginia. In 1900 the 'centre of population' had moved another 250 miles, and was some 50 miles south of Indianapolis, Indiana. The rate of the westward shift of the 'centre of population' slowed by about one-half in the next half-century, but it continued to edge across Indiana and, by 1950, into Illinois. Since 1950 the 'population centre' has resumed its 19th-century westward pace, and the trend has, in addition, developed a distinct tendency towards the south, so that by 1980 the population was centred on a point some 50 miles south-west of St Louis, Missouri. This single, cumulative indicator traces the growing significance of the West and, more recently, the South in attracting settlement.

There has been much discussion of the rise of the 'sunbelt' ever since Republican commentator Kevin Phillips invented the term in 1969 in *The Emerging Republican Majority*. The inclusive term 'sunbelt' is too unspecific to define the areas of real economic and population growth of recent years, but it is true to say that some Southern and Western states have been the locations of significant development. These areas have become increasingly accessible to creative investment in the post-World War II period, with the development of an efficient highway system, a highly-developed trucking industry, and the domestic air service. The environmental attraction of a 'sunbelt' climate is evident, and its excesses have been made much more bearable by the development of air-conditioning. Some Southern and Western locations had extra incentives for the employer, since, compared to the recognized industrial heartlands of the Northeast and Midwest, land was relatively inexpensive, the cost of living relatively low, and the trade unions weak. The incentives for relocation had existed for some

time, and with the international decline of heavy industry, accompanied by the development of light engineering and service industries less tied to the location of raw materials, investment (and therefore employment) could be moved to different areas of the country.

By the early 1970s these changes were beginning to have a dramatic effect upon US employment statistics. Between 1970 and 1975 non-agricultural employment in the West grew by 30.1%, and in the South by 35.8%, while the Midwest had a growth rate of only 14.7%, and the Northeast actually lost 0.6% of its jobs. The second half of the 1970s was a period of more general growth, but the regional inequalities remained, with Western employment growth at 21.3%, Southern at 18.5%, Midwestern at 10.4%, and Northeastern at 9.2%. The early 1980s saw a sustained, if modest, recovery in Northeastern figures, with 8.5% employment growth between 1980 and 1986, but the Midwest has slumped further, only managing 3% growth, while the South and West maintain their rapid growth with 11.6% and 11.9% respectively. In 1970 the Northeast and Midwest regions of the USA accounted for almost 40m. of the nation's 77m. jobs, or 52% of the total. By 1986 growth in the Northeast and Midwest had raised employment to 46.8m. jobs, but the even faster economic growth of the rest of the nation meant that this was now only 47% of the national total. The South and West had become the major employing regions of the nation. It is evident that such sustained differentials in employment growth serve to stimulate migration, as people move to where the new jobs are appearing.

Recent censuses have confirmed a population shift away from the Northeast and Midwest, towards the South and West. The pattern of differential population change follows closely the pattern of employment shifts. Between 1970 and 1980 the national population increased by 11.4%. However, the South (20%) and the West (23.9%) grew at about twice the national rate, while the Midwest (4%) and the Northeast (0.2%) were almost standing still in comparison. From 1980 to 1986 national population growth was 6.4%, a somewhat lower annual rate than in the previous decade, but the regional pattern is repeated. The South (10.1%) and the West (12.9%) grew at almost double the national rate, while the total population figures in the Northeast and Midwest have remined relatively unchanged, with growth rates of just 1.8% and 0.8% respectively.

Regional differentials are also apparent as regards natural population growth rates. Between 1980 and 1986 there were two births for every death in the population of the South and West, while the replacement rate in the Northeast and Midwest was only 1.6 births for each death. To some extent this must reflect the different age structures of the population. The South and West have younger populations than the North and East: in 1986, for example, only 10.6% of the Western population was over 65 years of age, while 13.4% of the Northeastern population was in this age-group. In addition, the proportion of the population in the fertile age-group of 18–44 in 1986 was just over 42% in both the Northeast and the Midwest, but approached 43% in the South, and was almost 45% in the West. One contribution to these regional differences has been the migration of fertile populations between the regions, reflected in subsequent birth and death rates, and adding a generational echo to geographical movement. Projections to the end of the century suggest that while these regional differences will narrow, they will not disappear. By 2000 the population age structures in the Midwest and the South are expected to be converging, while the Northeast will still have a population older than the national average, and Western growth rates in particular will still be benefiting from a younger age structure with an above-average proportion of the population in the fertile 18–44-year age-group.

While natural population growth may reflect the effects of migration, in the combined figures of population change it in fact masks the migration figures. The net migration figures calculated by the Bureau of the Census include foreign as well as domestic migrants, but the pattern is dramatically clear. Between 1980 and 1986 a net 386,000 people left Northeastern states, and 2m. left the Midwest. During the same period over 4m. people moved into the South and 2.6m. into the Western states. Complicated though this is by the inclusion of foreign migrants, it is quite clear that migration between regions in the USA in the 1980s continued the pattern of the immediately preceding decades. The regional rates of migration have shown some change in recent years, however. The South and West have continued to gain by immigration a similar, even slightly higher, annual increase in population than that established throughout the 1970s, but the regional element of this increase has, in the 1980s, come increasingly from the Midwest rather than the Northeast.

In the Northeast, losing out-migrants at the average rate of 288,800 a year in the 1970s, out-migration was at 64,300 a year between 1980 and 1986. In the Midwest, average out-migration of 270,300 annually in the 1970s increased to an average of 336,200 a year between 1980 and 1986. This may indicate the different economic influences operating on the Northeast and Midwest. While the overall picture of these regions is one of steady relative decline since 1960, the trough appears to be moving across the region from the north-eastern seaboard as different parts of the economy, and consequently different areas within these regions, have faced problems and undergone restructuring. In the 1975 recession New England suffered worse, in economic terms, than any other area of the USA, and the unemployment rate in Massachusetts was higher than that of any other Northeastern state. By 1988 Michael Dukakis could challenge for the US Presidency on the basis of the 'Massachusetts miracle', an apparent state economic regeneration with regional potential.

In fact, Massachusetts and its immediate neighbours first began to feel the cold winds of economic change in the 1920s, when the state's traditionally-strong textiles industry began to decline in the face of southern competition. The subsequent loss of heavy engineering that affected the steel, automobile and related industries of the Midwest with devastating impact in the 1970s and 1980s was just a later, and relatively more minor, stage in a longer pattern of change in the states of New England. Furthermore, while the newly-developing industries of recent decades have found the South and West hospitable, some were persuaded to maintain a foothold in the Northeast. New developments such as microtechnology, micro-electronic engineering, and similar high-technology industries need investment and the support of a highly-educated research sector. New England has the largest concentration of prestigious universities in the world, and its business community has appeared enthusiastic in the provision of venture capital to support new ideas. In addition, the politicians of the region have had the influence to attract government support for some ventures. By the early 1980s New Hampshire, Massachusetts, Vermont and Connecticut were ranked as the leading four among all states in terms of the share of total employment taken by high-technology industries. Additional employment advances have been made in service industries and in tourism, and the remaining heavy industry of New England has benefited from a period of high government spending on defence.

Other parts of the Northeast and Midwest have tried to emulate this change. Philadelphia has its own 'high-tech highway' in Route 202; New Jersey's American Telegraph and Telephone Co (AT&T) headquarters remains among the world leaders in modern communications developments, and the automobile-producing states of the Great Lakes area have become world leaders in the development and use of industrial robots. These may be among the potential building blocks of an economic recovery that can move across the Northeast and Midwest, ultimately providing markedly increased job opportunities and reversing the incentives to out-migrate.

However, even if this scenario turns out to be accurate, there is not likely to be any marked change in recent regional differentials in population growth until the 21st century.

The regions identified by the census are large, and while overall patterns of growth or decline are in their way accurate, they may sometimes disguise the existence of states and localities where the figures do not follow the regional trend, or where the stimuli for migration may differ from those common in the region. For example, between 1980 and 1986 out-migration from the Midwest reflected considerable regional homogeneity, since there was net out-migration from every Midwestern state in this period. The same was not true, however, in the Northeast, where several states had modest in-migration, and New Hampshire, a low-tax 'haven' adjacent to the developing high-technology areas of New England, received substantial in-migration.

The benefits of growth were similarly unevenly distributed in the South and West. The relatively poor states of West Virginia and Mississippi, along with Kentucky and Oregon, suffered net out-migration, while others such as Alabama, Arkansas and Louisiana grew only negligibly as a result of in-migration. In-migration had much more impact in North Carolina, Georgia, Florida, Texas, Arizona, Nevada, California and Alaska, where it was so considerable that it exceeded natural population growth. While the differential pull of economic opportunity, even within regions, accounts for much of this diversity, there can be other reasons too. Some states, especially Florida, have become attractive to retired people. Florida's net 1.7m. in-migrants in 1980–86 added almost 17% to the state's population, and helped to confirm its position as the state with the highest proportion of population over the age of 65 years (17.7% in 1986).

Outlook

The South and West continue to dominate in population growth, both as regions and in terms of the location of the fastest-growing metropolitan areas. While the attraction of these areas appears to be levelling off, they are still likely to experience regional growth in excess of the national figures during the rest of the 20th century, both by immigration, and because of the higher birth-rate that often accompanies the continuing arrival of new, relatively young, in-migrants. Politically this will lead to a further shift of influence from the Northeast and Midwest to the South and West as seats in the federal House of Representatives and votes in the presidential Electoral College are reallocated in accordance with the census returns. It is estimated that about 16 House seats (out of 435), and therefore the same number of Electoral College votes (out of 538), will be reallocated from the Northeast and Midwest to states in the South and West following the 1990 census, continuing a trend that saw 17 seats move in that direction after the 1980 census and eight seats after the 1970 census. While in 1970 the Northeast and Midwest had between them held 275 Electoral College votes, and the South and West held 263, current predictions suggest that the South and West may hold 304 votes in the 1990s. While this increased national political power may give these regions the capability, at both presidential and congressional levels, to influence national policies to their advantage, the differences that exist between states within regions are likely to limit the potential for coherent regional hegemony over national policy.

HEALTH AND WELFARE POLICY IN THE USA

CALUM PATON

Introduction—US Ideologies

The mainstream ideologies in the USA which affect health and welfare policy are, as in other policy arenas, liberalism and conservatism. US (as opposed to European or classical) liberalism consists of a belief in government intervention to help the poor and lower classes. Unlike European socialism and social democracy, it does not generally involve notions of public ownership and public provision. Instead it is concerned with the provision of equality of opportunity and the avoidance of domination of the economy by monopolistic and special interests. US conservatism consists in a belief in unfettered markets and a *laissez-faire* approach to social policy. Emphasis on voluntaristic and private solutions to social problems is strong in this ideology. US conservatism generally lacks the paternalistic strand evident in certain European variants. Thus the concept of, for example, a national health service is unpalatable to US conservatives in a way that it is not to many mainstream British conservatives.

Major Influences on Welfare Policy

THE POLITICAL STRUCTURE

The US political structure involves, firstly, federalism (primarily the division of governmental responsiblity between the national government and the various state governments) and, secondly, a separation of powers between the presidency, Congress and the judiciary, especially the federal Supreme Court. These two basic features make a considerable amount of consensus and co-operation necessary for national health and welfare programmes to be passed. Social planning, as understood in Europe, is difficult to organize in the USA, and health and welfare policy tends to lead to a complex mosaic of programmes provided for the benefit of separate social groups, rather than to nationally-provided uniform services.

The two most significant periods of social reform in the 20th century which spawned health and welfare programmes were the 'New Deal' under President Franklin Roosevelt in the 1930s and the 'Great Society' under President Lyndon Johnson in the mid-1960s. In particular, the 89th Congress of 1965–66 is credited with being the most liberal Congress in recent times. In political terms the so-called New Deal Coalition is the left-of-centre coalition of particular groups—workers, rural interests and the public sector in particular—which has supported government intervention to provide health and welfare programmes. A reaction to the depression of the late 1920s and early 1930s, the formation of the New Deal Coalition represented a major realignment in US politics: the voting patterns of various classes and social groups underwent significant change, rather than witnessing a mere temporary swing of the political pendulum. It was not until the late 1980s that the New Deal Coalition was widely acknowledged to be in final decline. For, despite Republican dominance of the presidency, from Richard Nixon in 1969 to George Bush in 1989, with only the four-year interregnum of Jimmy Carter of 1977–81, Democratic ascendancy in Congress has been complete since the late 1950s, with the exception of temporary Republican control of the Senate in the early 1980s.

FISCAL POLITICS

The massive budget deficit in the USA has significant implications for health and welfare policy. The universal phenomenon whereby public expenditure is popular, yet taxation to finance it is not, is considerably increased in the USA by the fragmented way in which welfare policy is produced. This fragmentation has contributed to a widespread perception that liberal policies are unaffordable; a conservative reaction against policies of, for example, the 1960s and early 1970s is evident. A contrast with other countries may be instructive. In Britain,

for example, the National Health Service is a centrally-planned and -budgeted service, which is characterized by strict cost control as well as by attempts at social equity. In the USA, however, liberal reforms have attempted to spread the benefits of expensive private provision of health care to hitherto excluded or disadvantaged groups, such as those who have previously had no, or inadequate, health insurance. As a result, liberal reforms are seen as unaffordable.

Overall, a conservative reaction against the fiscal problems caused by public expenditure on health and welfare is leading to demands that the federal government take a more positive role in co-ordinating welfare programmes. This is a paradoxical development, in that conservatives have traditionally believed in as small a role as possible for the federal government. Common to the Republican presidencies of Nixon, Ford and Reagan was the belief that, instead of spending money on specific health and welfare programmes itself (so-called categorical programmes), the federal government ought to make block grants to the states, which would then have the responsibility for allocating resources for specific purposes. A more recent current of thought argues that, as well as or instead of this approach, the federal government ought to take more direct responsibility for health and welfare programmes as a means to cost control and tighter public management.

Health and welfare policies are, of course, seen as investments in the economic future of the country, as well as attempts at social justice and equity. Given this fact, it is perhaps not surprising that, for example, US health-care benefits are often workplace-based: firms will invest in their workers, with government help or tax incentives to do so, rather than the state investing in both the productive and unproductive. US health and welfare policy is therefore a complex amalgam, not only of different specific programmes for specific groups, but also representing different social needs—to provide legitimacy for the existing social order, to 'invest in the future' and to co-ordinate the pieces into a whole that is both manageable and fiscally controllable. The most interesting current controversies in US health and welfare policy are informed by this last imperative.

Health Policy

US health care relies on the private sector for both provision and finance to a greater extent than the health-care systems of other developed Western countries. Private insurance is the linchpin of the financing system and private hospitals, whether non-profit or for-profit, are that of the system of provision. In considering the government role in financing health care it is important to consider both overt government programmes and tax allowances for individuals and groups. The main government programmes are Medicare (Parts A and B, dealing with hospitals and ambulatory care respectively) for those over 65 and for certain categories of disabled people, and Medicaid for certain low-income categories. Medicare is more broadly financed than Medicaid, but consists basically of federally-purchased private insurance. Medicaid's costs are shared between the federal government and the states, with the federal contribution depending upon a number of factors, primarily each state's willingness to spend and various indicators of need for health care in the various states. Individuals and companies receive tax allowances for the purchase of private health insurance or membership in health programmes such as a Health Maintenance Organization (see below), and in 1985 it was estimated that the cost to the Treasury of this was greater than the total cost of the Medicaid programme.

Health care has traditionally been provided in private, non-profit hospitals, for secondary care, and through private 'office physicians' for primary and less-specialized care. The rise of the for-profit private hospital in the USA has been a recent phenomenon, and many non-profit institutions are now being taken over by the for-profit sector. In general, a 'rationalization' of the health-care system is occurring as the economic imperative of financial solvency becomes more acute.

BALANCING COSTS WITH ACCESS

The two most significant characteristics of US health care are costs, which continue to rise, and the need to increase equity and access of the health-care system. Most recent innovations in US health policy are geared to cost control, especially those made by the federal government for its own programmes.

In the 1970s, following the enactment of Medicare and Medicaid in 1965, it was widely perceived that more significant health planning to rationalize the system, in order to control costs, would be necessary if further access to the health-care system by the disadvantaged was to be affordable. Thus in 1974, with bipartisan support, the National Health Planning and Resources Development Act was passed; this was intended to delegate responsibility to Health Systems Agencies (HSAs), working in co-operation with state governments, both to restrict unnecessary expansion and to direct funds to underserved areas. However, the HSAs were dominated by coalitions of providers and consumers who preferred to allow as much expansion as possible rather than to plan. The failure of planning to achieve its ambitiously-stated goals, let alone to mobilize new resources for the underinsured and underserved communities, was the consequence of expecting too much of the US political system, which is not geared to the demands of such programmes. As a result planning has become discredited, and most health-care policy analysts, in the 1980s, prefer to rely on the open market rather than on planning.

A more significant policy sponsored by the federal government in the 1970s was reflected in a series of Health Maintenance Organization (HMO) acts and amendments. The HMO seeks to provide a cost-effective alternative to fee-for-service medicine, whereby a private doctor is paid a fee for every item of service provided. Private fee-for-service medicine has been thought to be expensive, in that the consumer and provider have an incentive to overcharge a third-party payer, namely the insurer. The HMO seeks to merge the roles of insurer and provider. An individual pays a premium to join an HMO, for a year in most cases, and the HMO will then be financially liable to provide the necessary care (with exclusions perhaps stipulated) as required. Some companies subscribe to an HMO on behalf of their employees. HMOs did not expand as much as the federal government had hoped during the 1970s, because interventionist legislation demanded that HMOs, if they were to receive federal subsidies, must not charge higher premiums to the poorer and sicker, and that they must accept all applications. This formula, however, meant that HMOs could not survive such regulation without corresponding financial support. In the 1980s, gradually freed from the details of federal regulation, HMOs flourished as a major feature of private corporate health care. HMOs generally have become freer to turn away people considered bad risks, or to charge them higher membership premiums. In the early 1980s the annual rate of growth of HMOs reached about 25%, and by the late 1980s about 30m. US citizens belonged to an HMO. By that time the rate of expansion seemed to be slowing a little, as HMOs faced bankruptcy on a greater scale than earlier in the decade.

Some HMOs employ all their staff directly and provide their health care through directly-owned institutions such as hospitals. These generally are considered to be 40% cheaper than the traditional fee-for-service health-care sector. Other HMOs neither own all their own facilities nor employ all their own doctors and other medical workers: instead they contract with group practices of doctors to provide health care by paying them a capitation fee for each patient registered. This is the so-called 'Group' HMO model. Finally, some HMOs merely engage traditional fee-for-service doctors to provide for the patients who are registered with them: it is this type of HMO which has the least impressive record in controlling costs.

The Preferred Provider Organization is another means of attempting to cut costs in the system, whereby both private firms and state or local governments, acting on behalf of their dependent populations, contract with certain providers of health care to provide at lower costs than the norm. This is essentially 'bulk buying', and is controversial as it limits the right of a programme member to receive health care anywhere: instead he or she must go to the stipulated providers.

The federal government has been seeking to control costs directly as well by stimulating new forms of provision both in the public and private sectors. A system of Diagnosis Related Groups (DRGs) has been instituted whereby the fees payable by the federal government for Medicare patients are dependent upon the diagnosis: the scheme operates, effectively, as a national system of price regulation. Seen as a much-needed response to the spiralling costs of the health-care system, DRGs were sponsored by a Republican administration and received bipartisan support.

It seemed in 1985 that cost control in the US health-care system was beginning to take effect. However, figures from the late 1980s show a reborn cost explosion, with almost 12% of US gross domestic product (GDP) going to health care. This compares, for example, with less than 6% in the UK (of a GDP per head which was, moreover, less than two-thirds that of the USA in 1987) and figures ranging from 7% to 11% in the other major Western European countries, Canada and Australasia. As well as the overall cost problems, particular price regulations are beginning to have obvious consequences, particularly where the poor and uninsured are concerned. Hitherto they have relied on charitable care, especially in public and charitable hospitals (such as the major city hospitals), which has been subsidized from the surplus gained from conventional paying patients. However, regulatory-based limitations on reimbursement are restricting the capacity to do this, as surpluses are diminished. As a result charitable care for the poor is being thrust even more firmly at the door of the federal government. The same dynamics are evident with medical education. This is creating a paradoxical position for the government: as the logical consequences of political fragmentation, manifested in an inability to co-ordinate the health-care system and provide a coherent national health-care policy, work through the system, a stronger federal role may at last emerge.

When Medicare and Medicaid were authorized in 1965 through amendments to the Social Security Act, they were in fact a compromise, as liberal reformers had sought a system of national health insurance. It is generally agreed that 1974 was the last year when any enactment of national health insurance, or at least its passage by Congress, was even a remote possibility. However, as inequity worsens within the system, the issue is being reborn. Massachusetts has enacted a state-wide health-insurance programme under Governor Michael Dukakis, and this formed the basis of his campaign promises on health care in 1988 when he was the Democratic presidential candidate. Essentially the Dukakis plan calls for employer-provided insurance with the state insuring those not covered in this way, financed through a combination of payroll taxes and cost-saving measures. Nationally the provision and financing of health care for lower-income groups varies significantly: some states are relatively generous, for example Massachusetts (even before the implementation of the Dukakis plan in 1988) and New Jersey, and some providing almost nothing for their poor populations. An extreme example of the latter is found in Arizona, which declined to participate in the Medicaid programme at all, and only provided health care for some of its indigent population in the 1980s, when the opportunity to buy them into relatively cheap prepaid health-care schemes arose.

The recurrent themes in US health policy are, therefore, the search for equity and greater access by the poor and uninsured, and—politically much more dominant—cost control by a variety of mechanisms, ranging from national regulation through a policy of Diagnosis Related Groups (whereby the expected cost of treating a particular disease is estimated) to competing Health Maintenance Organizations, which it is believed will reduce costs both through competition and through financial incentives within the HMO. Overall, US health-care policy has been characterized by the dominant characteristics of US politics. However, this has created such complexity that a stronger co-ordinating role for federal government may emerge, less as a point of political controversy than as an acknowledged need on both sides of the political spectrum.

Income Maintenance

In contrast to the position in many Western European countries, federal unemployment benefit is only temporarily available after the loss of a job in the USA. Different states and localities have varying kinds and levels of protection for the needy, the disabled and the unemployed. There is no national 'safety net' of the type found in developed welfare states.

The most fundamental disagreement over policy for income maintenance has been whether transfers to the poor ought to be cash or 'in-kind'. In general, Democrats have supported categorical programmes which provide specific benefits, sometimes in-kind; the food stamp is an example of the latter. Republicans have tended to support cash transfers, in line with the ideology of letting the market work after the necessary redistribution of income. However, as with so many issues in social-welfare policy, there is no clear party (or indeed left–right) division on matters such as these. Economists sometimes favour cash transfers on the grounds that they do not distort pricing in the market-place in the same way as can the free provision of specific goods. However, if it is believed that an item constitutes a basic right—as many believe with health care, for example—specific provision of that item may be logical policy.

As is true in many countries, there are three main objectives to be met in designing a coherent policy for income maintenance. The policy must protect the poorest members of society and raise the incomes of those below the poverty line; the cost must be affordable to central government; and it must not institute perverse or bad incentives, such as those associated with the so-called 'poverty trap' and 'unemployment trap'. It is difficult to meet all three objectives. Poverty and unemployment traps can result when individuals lose benefit and/or become susceptible to tax when they raise their income or find a job, but actually have a lower disposable income as a result of having gained employment, or their gross income having been increased otherwise. In the USA some programmes contribute to such a trap. For example, the Aid to Families with Dependent Children programme was restricted after the budget of 1981, as embraced by the 'Omnibus Budget Reconciliation' Act of that year. The Aid to Families with Dependent Children programme was cut, and in practice denied to single mothers who found work. Thus the incentive for them to do so was removed, contrary to the philosophy of the government. A means of evading such traps is to introduce a sliding scale whereby, as income increases, benefit or income support is only removed gradually. However, the more generous the protection (through the income floor guaranteed by the government) and the more gradual the operation of the sliding scale, the more expensive the programme is overall. Accompanying administrative difficulties, expense rather than coherence is the reason why sudden or total loss of benefit on reaching a certain threshold is common.

An idea which has attracted both liberals and conservatives, both Democrats and Republicans, is the idea of the 'negative income tax' as a means of income support. This is a means of unifying the welfare and taxation systems whereby below a certain threshold a subsidy is received according to a formula, but above that threshold tax is paid according to the same formula. Conservatives have been attracted to it because it avoids government-controlled categorical programmes, liberals because, if adequately funded, it can achieve redistribution of money to the lowest income groups. A major initiative of this kind was the Family Assistance Programme, devised in the early 1970s during the Nixon administration. The measure failed at the Senate Finance Committee stage, and was widely agreed to be the victim of opposition from both liberal Democrats antagonistic to Nixon initiatives and conservative Republicans antagonistic to redistributive policies.

A more recent controversy, which finds liberals and conservatives in both support and opposition, concerns so-called 'workfare' programmes, which require work or job training to be taking place before a claimant can qualify for welfare or income support. In Texas, for example, this has generally been viewed as conservative policy and opposed by political liberals; in Massachusetts, however, a variant of workfare involving more creatively-designed education and training programmes has been sponsored by Governor Dukakis and many liberals.

Education
EARLY EDUCATION

At one stage in the 1988 presidential campaign day-care was debated in some depth. A traditional Republican–Democrat divide in fact emerged: George Bush advocated income transfer to allow the more needy to purchase their own day-care, and Michael Dukakis advocated federally-provided day-care. The issue is likely to grow in importance in US politics, as it is increasingly a favoured issue of the women's movement. As a result it has overtones of a moral controversy and, as such, is discussed not only in terms of its utility (its regulatory and distributive implications) but also in terms of civic rights.

Early childhood education holds a special place in what can be termed the American ideology, given the centrality of equality of opportunity and classlessness in that ideology. Headstart, instituted as part of President Johnson's 'Great Society' legislation, is a federal programme providing nursery and early-childhood education for the disadvantaged. It is significant that it survived relatively unharmed by the years of conservative retrenchment under President Reagan (protected largely by the Democratic-controlled Congress).

SCHOOL

Apart from current controversies over the adequacy of the high-school curriculum in preparing students for work and life, two of the most significant educational controversies have concerned affirmative action to remove racial discrimination and segregation, and the financing of public education. The 1954/55 Supreme Court decision in *Brown v. Board of Education of Topeka* led, eventually, to the desegregation of schools, and in turn to the 'busing' of children in order to provide racial balance in schools. These developments have been surrounded, at every step, by controversy.

The provision of effective and well-financed education was the subject of a separate controversy during the early 1970s, although one which overlapped with the debate on racial integration. A series of Supreme Court decisions, both at state and federal level, asserted that the constitution guaranteed the right to public education financed at the same level as the next person's, wherever that person happened to live. The implication of this was that both state and federal governments had to equalize finance for schools, by redistributing revenue from rich to poor local authorities. This dictated that a local authority School Board (responsible for the provision of education in the USA) need not institute a higher property-tax rate than any other in order to provide the same level of financing for education. Naturally, poor areas with a low property-tax base find it more difficult to finance high-quality education without supplementary assistance. However, this is an area where policy was still not clear in the late 1980s. As in so many other areas of public policy, the focus in the late 1980s has been on results, quality and efficiency rather than on equity and access. Current debates about education focus upon both basic literacy and numeracy and the utility of the curriculum.

UNIVERSITY EDUCATION

The cost of university education is becoming a significant worry for both working-class and middle-class parents in the USA. While state universities generally charge low fees for students from within the state, the cost of private education and even some state education is growing at a rate to cause concern, particularly to the middle classes. As such it became an issue during the 1988 presidential election. The Democratic candidate, Michael Dukakis, proposed that students should be allowed to borrow money for their education and then pay it back during their working lives as a percentage of their income, rather than as a fixed amount. The victorious Republican candidate, George Bush, called for tax-free savings bonds as an incentive for families to save for their children's college education.

Other Social and Welfare Policies
CIVIL RIGHTS

The general policy of affirmative action to redress discrimination has caused considerable controversy, with some seeing it as an assertion of minority rights and others seeing it as reverse discrimination. Under Title IV of the Civil Rights Act of 1964, minority groups include not only blacks but also Hispanics, Asian or Pacific Islanders and native Americans or Alaskans. (Other legislation stipulates other groups.) The Civil Rights Act of 1866 followed the civil war and granted citizenship to all people born in the USA, but federal activism to protect blacks was short-lived and it was only in the late 1950s that Congress returned to civil-rights legislation. The Commission on Civil Rights was created in 1957 and was responsible for much of the groundwork for legislation, although the influence of the peaceful but powerful action organized by the Southern Christian Leadership Conference (SCLC) should not be underestimated. Very soon after President Kennedy's assassination, President Johnson strongly sponsored the passage of the 1964 Civil Rights Bill in Congress. The Civil Rights Act of 1964 contained significant clauses on employment. It created the Equal Employment Opportunity Commission (EEOC), which was to investigate individuals' claims of discrimination and to give help to employers and unions seeking to obey the Civil Rights Act. The Equal Employment Opportunity Act of 1972 had its origins in an attempt significantly to strengthen the EEOC, but a legislative compromise was interpreted as a defeat for civil-rights groups.

It is worth mentioning briefly the Voting Rights Act of 1965, intended to establish the unequivocal right of blacks to vote. In recent years controversies over the Voting Rights Act have involved the concept of affirmative action in voting. For example, if blacks or Hispanics are a minority and the elections for a city council are held 'at large' (meaning that all candidates are to be elected city-wide), it may be the case that no minority candidates are elected. Various court decisions have established the rights of blacks to elections based on the district or territorial division, or in some cases even the right, when casting a multiple vote for more than one candidate, to cast all of those votes for a single candidate in an attempt to provide a concentration of votes sufficient to elect some minority candidates. This has predictably been a very controversial policy. As with all cases of affirmative action, a particular controversy arises over who and what constitutes a minority.

President Jimmy Carter gave strong support to civil rights and equal employment opportunity. There were important Supreme Court cases decided during his presidency, and the Justice Department was active in fighting for civil rights. The Democratic platform for the elections of 1980 built on this record, and was consequently opposed vigorously by the Republicans. The ensuing Reagan administration argued that no separate policy for blacks and other minorities was necessary, and that economic growth was the answer to the economic problems of all. When in office, President Reagan replaced most of the personnel on the Commission on Civil Rights, and its opposition to the Reagan administration's eschewal of affirmative action and busing was removed. In the early period of the Bush administration the very future of the Commission itself was in doubt.

ABORTION

Abortion is another controversial area where the Supreme Court has played a prominent role. In *Roe v. Wade* (1973) rights to abortion were affirmed; however, in practical terms, abortion is available to those willing or able to pay for it—there is no right to federally-funded abortion. Congress took action in the late 1970s to limit abortions for people covered under Medicaid; gradually the right to a Medicaid abortion has been reduced to cases of 'medical necessity', where there is a risk to the mother's life. With a conservative majority on the Supreme Court, after President Reagan's appointments, it is possible that the Roe decision may be amended or overturned.

POVERTY

In the 1960s federal agencies such as the Office of Economic Opportunity sponsored specific anti-poverty programmes, which incorporated medical and other social-service provision. More recent administrations have stressed the need for a dynamic entrepreneurial economy to achieve universal prosperity. In the late 1980s, however, poverty was being redis-

covered: one in six children in the USA were living below the official poverty level. Key programmes under consideration in early 1989 which could mitigate poverty in early life and health problems in later life covered prenatal care, immunization and preventive health care, and Headstart (the pre-school programme for children). In October 1988 Congress agreed on a new programme for low-income mothers with dependent children (estimated to number about 4m. and 7m. respectively). Under this law, states are required to set up programmes to help poor women to find jobs (either in the private sector or in unpaid jobs in the public sector). However, after a year in such a job, a woman ceases to be eligible for Medicaid and subsidized day-care.

HOUSING

During the 1980s the number of families buying houses declined. High interest rates led to high mortgage costs and resulted in almost no houses being within the financial reach of the poor. According to the Joint Centre for Housing Studies at Harvard, the price for first homes was generally 92% higher in real terms in 1987 than in 1975. Significant moves away from the provision of low-cost public housing by the federal government and other public agencies has exacerbated the situation whereby access to cheap housing (whether bought or rented) is much diminished, and has increased concerns over housing and homelessness in general.

CRIME

The main political debate about crime again stems from the ideological argument between liberalism and conservatism, with adherents of the former stressing the rights of individuals (including criminals) and the latter stressing law and order. Rising crime has been accompanied by renewed support for capital punishment. Again the Supreme Court has been significant in this area, with its decision in *Gregg v. Georgia* in 1976 that the death penalty for those convicted of murder would not constitute a 'cruel and unusual punishment'—outlawed by the Eighth Amendment to the US constitution. Political controversy over crime has also been concerned with issues such as interrogation of suspects and the presence of a lawyer.

At a broader level, the crime debate is one, familiar in many countries, between those who have social and sociological explanations of crime and those who consider the criminal to be a blameworthy individual. While it should be remembered that the states have responsibility for most public policy concerning crime, it can be said that there has been a broad swing since the early 1960s away from the view that crime is a socioeconomic problem.

ENVIRONMENT: NATIONAL AND URBAN

The environment, both on a national and localized level, is a further policy area which significantly affects the health and welfare of US society. The main environmental issues are clean air and water, acid rain, waste disposal, the protection of public lands and the general control of pollution. The Republican election campaign of 1988 stressed the importance of new technologies in improving the environment, whereas the Democrats generally emphasized regulation.

On inner-city policy there is an unusual degree of consensus between liberals and conservatives. The free market is seen as having a greater role in this area than in many other countries, and public intervention is increasingly partnered by private initiative; this form of partnership at inner-city level may consequently form part of the new policy agenda in the USA.

The Political Context

It was alleged by *The Economist* during the 1988 presidential election campaign that 'if America's middle classes conclude their way of life is sliding down-hill, they will choose Michael Dukakis; if they conclude that they are managing pretty well, they will choose George Bush'. *The Economist* went on to allege that 'a middle-class family with middle-class standards should be doing fine so long as both husband and wife were working, so long as they have already bought their house, and so long as they decide to educate their children at a state university or college and not one of the smarter private institutions. And, of course, so long as no member of the family is struck down by an illness that requires long-term uninsurable medical treatment. Many families succeed in obeying all these rules.' Following a similar line of argument, further health and welfare reform will be off the agenda as long as standards of living are perceived to be rising, and firmly on the agenda should they be perceived to be falling. The prospects at the moment are equivocal. While real incomes per head have risen, it is mostly because of the increase in the number of working women and the birth of fewer children: men's earnings have stayed, in real terms, at their early 1970s' levels. Furthermore, although the proportion of US families earning less than $20,000 a year (in 1987 dollars in real terms) remains static, this masks an important change in demography. The elderly are doing increasingly well as a result of indexation of pensions, whereas single-parent families and children now dominate the ranks of the poor.

When President George Bush came to office in 1989, he pledged to increase the financing of Headstart, the pre-school programme for school children, because at that time only one out of five children could benefit. He had promised to ask Congress for $500m. a year for schools that are recognized as 'national merit schools', and would give (a small amount of) money to states which supported 'magnet schools'—schools offering special curriculums. On social policy as a whole, Bush had generally proposed incremental extensions of access to existing social programmes rather than significant new programmes. Just as in health care he had promised to seek federal money to allow the uninsured to 'buy into' Medicaid at a subsidized price, so he proposed tax credits in child care worth up to $1,000 for each child under four to working parents earning less than $20,000 a year. On housing, candidate Bush stressed the voluntary role and—showing continuity with the Reagan administration's approach to social policy—stressed the overall economic policy of low interest rates as the best contribution to cheap housing. On drugs and crime, Bush favoured capital punishment for drug-related murders, but did not favour tighter gun control. As Vice-President Bush was part of an administration that was identified with strong anti-crime measures, but paid little attention to social programmes to alleviate what some see as the causes of crime.

Conclusion

US social policy, including health and welfare, has recently been dominated by so-called neoliberal and neoconservative ideologies. Neoliberalism is essentially a restrained and modified version of liberalism which is, furthermore, less hostile to the market; neoconservatism generally entails the view that the objectives of social policy should not necessarily be shunned, but should be achieved through an amalgam of market mechanisms and voluntary action rather than by government intervention on the 1960s model. Neoconservatism should not be confused with what is termed the 'New Right', which refers to social and cultural conservatives whose main policy agenda concerns emotive social issues such as prayer in schools and abortion and which is identified with a strong anti-libertarianism. Both ideologies stress cost-effectiveness more than traditional liberalism. This also is in reaction to the perception that welfare expenditure reached high proportions during the 'Great Society' of the 1960s, yet that welfare programmes had a low overall cost-effectiveness.

Furthermore, the new conservative coalition which has produced Republican domination at the presidential level (though not elsewhere in the political system) combines a number of interests: traditional East Coast conservatives (with whom President Bush was formerly identified) and the new economic right wing identified with the 'sunbelt' states, supply-side economics, the virtual extinction of corporate income tax and a belief in a minimal government role in regulating domestic policy. It is in this context that reassessment of health and welfare policy ought to be understood. Much confusion in policy is based on an inability to achieve consensus on policy among liberals or among conservatives, let alone between both camps. Conservatives in general wish to see a return of power to the states. Ironically, in early American history it was progressives and reformers who believed in greater power to the states, as a protection of direct democracy. Today, however, the federal government is seen by liberals as the best source of protection for the disadvantaged.

Political tradition in the USA has a significant bearing on welfare policy. Unlike in Western Europe, where ideologies divide countries, there is 'an American creed'. This creed consists in a set of political ideals (whether or not compatible) including liberty and equality, democracy and the rule of law, government by the majority and respect for minority rights. Conflict arises in promoting the means to achieve these various ideals, particularly during idealistic periods of reform in the country's history. It is fair to cite both the New Deal of the 1930s and the Great Society legislation of the 1960s as examples of idealistic reforming periods. There are signs that the conservative reaction to the 1960s is weakening: the question for the future of US welfare policy is whether it will be replaced by a return to normal interest-group activity, or by a new reforming era which will lead to a significant new policy agenda for health and welfare.

At the broadest level the ideological debate in the USA, as in other countries, is between privatization and a reliance on the market on the one hand and public provision or regulation on the other. The decline of traditional liberalism, involving traditional 1930s- and 1960s-style programmes, has encouraged an increased use of the market even where redistributive welfare policy is accepted. Even if the political pendulum swings, a new welfare agenda is not likely to be characterized by government-dominated centralism. This is not to deny that there is a radical and indeed moralistic component to US politics which has implications for welfare policy. The Jesse Jackson presidential campaigns of 1984 and 1988 represent this sector of politics. However, it remains to be seen what effect this will have upon public policy in future years.

Another current of thought affecting health and welfare policy which has been generated by disillusionment with 1960s programmes is a rather iconoclastic and nihilistic one. If health-care programmes do not significantly improve the health status of the population, then why bother with them? If schools and increased federal financing of schools in poor areas do not increase educational achievement and social success, then why invest in them? This approach is unnecessarily pessimistic; a more constructive course of action is to call for better targeting of social programmes.

Finally, both liberals and conservatives can agree that a major challenge is the co-ordinating of health and welfare programmes. for example, the USA spends over $100,000m. a year on programmes related to disability (including both national and state programmes). However, these programmes are uncoordinated: for example, some imply that the handicapped should work and join the mainstream, whereas others imply that they should retire and be segregated from the rest of the population. As with much of health and welfare policy in the USA, each programme represents a specific, 'single-issue', regulatory solution to a problem of its time, and in aggregate they fail to meet contemporary needs in an effective manner. The challenge acknowledged by most politicians is not to dismantle health and welfare programmes but to make them more effective.

SOCIAL GROUPINGS IN THE USA

GILLIAN PEELE

Introduction

The USA possesses an unusually high degree of social heterogeneity compared with other modern nation-states. To the divisions of gender, age, income and sexual preference which mark every society, there are added in the USA the numerous divisions of ethnic or national origin and religious adherence which make the country unique. Many of these divisions are the product of the waves of immigration which have occurred during the course of US history; others—such as the existences of the black population and the Mormon Church (Church of Jesus Christ of Latter-day Saints)—are the results of other factors in US history.

The pluralism of US society is a fact of major political significance. Not all social divisions are politically relevant, but in the USA—as Alexis de Tocqueville, the French historian, noticed in the early 19th century—there has always been a tendency to organize in order to protect and promote group interests. Indeed, some theorists have seen an understanding of the groups which exist in US society as the key to understanding the US political system. Certainly no one can understand the dynamics of US political life without understanding the character of the most important social groups at any one time, the nature of their particular agendas and their political strategies and strengths.

It would, of course, be a mistake to see the spectrum of the USA's social groups as being neatly demarcated. There is much difficulty of definition and much need for caution in generalizations. For example, are Jewish Americans to be treated as an ethnic or a religious group? Does it make sense to treat Hispanics as a single group when they include Americans from so many different parts of Latin America as well as Mexico? To what extent does it make sense to talk about women as a social group when so many other factors—of ethnicity, of income and of education—divide them?

In addition there is a high degree of overlapping of issue agendas and political strategies. For example, one of the most marked characteristics of US society in the 1980s has been the so-called 'feminization of poverty'—the process whereby the problems associated with low incomes have been found to be specially concentrated in female-headed households. Many of these women are also black, so that the issue agendas of the poor, of blacks and of women to that extent overlap. Such overlapping does, of course, aid the various groups in the political process for it means that they can build coalitions beyond the confines of their immediate constituency.

The US political system is one in which groups find it easy to operate. The carefully-constructed mechanism of the US constitution was designed to prevent the concentration of power in any one branch of government, and it is frequently the case that groups which at any one time find themselves with little influence in one branch of the federal system (as, for example, blacks and liberal civil-rights leaders had little weight in the executive during the Reagan presidency) have been able to press their case on the legislature and the judiciary. In addition to the horizontal fragmentation of power, the vertical fragmentation between the federal government, the states, and city and local governments offers additional opportunities for groups whose interest might be very much a minority one nationally to exert influence at the state or local levels. For example, the Mormon Church, while only one among many churches nationally, is the most powerful religious influence in the state of Utah and is able to exercise a good deal of political 'clout' both there and in the neighbouring states. Gay pressure groups which have demanded legal reforms to prevent discrimination against them and to take account of homosexual relationships have made progress in some cities such as San Francisco, although they have made little progress nationally. Thus San Francisco in 1989 became the first major city to validate a public registration for 'domestic partnership' in the same manner as marriage licences.

It is not simply the constitutional structure of the US political system which encourages the country's various social groups to organize around their special agendas. The loose party structure and the electoral system encourage presidential, congressional, gubernatorial and mayoral candidates to put together their own coalitions of support. Once elected, any public official will find that he or she is unlikely to be able to rely on partisan loyalty alone to secure a political objective. The House of Representatives is composed of districts which are sufficiently small to allow minority groups to exercise substantial electoral influence—the demographic character of a particular district will affect its politicians' behaviour at least as much as its party identity. At reapportionment time, party politicians and representatives will watch carefully for any slight shift in the composition of a district which will make it more or less attractive to their interests and the courts will be faced with difficult balancing acts to protect the representation of voting rights. In the USA, as Tip O'Neill, the former Speaker of the House of Representatives, remarked, 'all politics is local' which means not only that a member of Congress must pay careful attention to the special needs of his or her constituents, but that anyone who wants that member's support must do so too.

The manner in which various social groups can get a hearing in the context of an electoral campaign emerges especially clearly during a presidential election. During the nomination process the candidates will tailor their strategies to the sequence of state contests, emphasizing any links they may have with the individual states and different populations of the states. In the general election itself the candidate will try to maximize his or her own associations and appeals to particular groups, while trying to ensure that those associations do not alienate other parts of the electorate. Thus in the 1988 election campaign Democratic candidate Michael Dukakis celebrated his Greek origins and the fact that he was of recent immigrant extraction—in contrast to George Bush. Both candidates sought to appeal to Hispanics—Bush by virtue of family connections, Dukakis by emphasizing his ability to speak Spanish. Dukakis's wife being Jewish gave him an advantage among that group and was an additional help in the New York primary when his main rival, Jesse Jackson, found it difficult to shake off accusations of anti-Semitism.

How to integrate the various social groups into an election campaign has been the subject of recent debate within the Democratic Party in particular. In 1986—in part as a response to new technological developments and in part as a contribution to the modernization of the Democratic Party organization—the Democrats abolished their ethnic and special-interest co-ordinators. Instead of focusing on divisions of race, religion, colour, sex and ethnicity, the Democrats decided to divide the USA into four regions and to appoint a co-ordinator for each one. This reorganization did not mean that the underlying social divisions of the country ceased to be relevant: rather it suggested that the party was seeking new ways of targeting them without labelling the Democratic Party as one geared primarily to the interests of minorities.

Race, Ethnicity and Nationality

A number of factors account for the USA's remarkable ethnic diversity. In addition to the native Indians who predated the arrival of European settlers (and whose tiny numbers have made it difficult for them to operate as an effective pressure group), an early distinctive group in the USA were the blacks. The need for slaves resulted in the importation to the USA of a black population of African and West Indian origin. The territorial expansion of the USA during the 19th century brought into the USA areas with a Spanish-speaking population. Above all, it was the waves of immigration which brought new groups to the USA—from different parts of Europe and from Asia.

The presence of new immigrant groups has always been a source of tension in US society. The Irish (who emigrated in large numbers to the USA in the 19th century) felt the force of nativist hostility to them in employment and in social life generally: 'No Irish Need Apply' was a commonly-seen sign. The Irish responded by developing their own protective networks and becoming politically active. At the time of the 1980 census there were some 40,166,000 US citizens of Irish or part-Irish ancestry. However, the distinctiveness of the group has in one sense become very much reduced. Whereas in the 1860s only about 10% of Irish-American males married outside their group, by the 1960s (according to Thomas Sowell) over one-half of them did so. Although US citizens of Irish ancestry are still aware of their distinct cultural heritage, social mobility has erased any evidence of disadvantage, and indeed the Irish do remarkably well by comparison with other groups on scores which relate national origin to income. The fact that two recent US presidents (John Kennedy and Ronald Reagan) have been of Irish origin has underlined the integration of the Irish into the mainstream of US society.

The Irish were not the only group to feel the hostility of those who were already in the USA. Although there had been small numbers of Jews in the country from the time of Columbus, the 19th century saw a massive expansion of the Jewish communities. The immigration of Jews—especially from Germany and Eastern Europe—in the 19th century caused the number of active Jewish congregations to multiply eightfold between 1800 and 1880 and transformed aspects of Judaism in the USA. Jewish immigrants encountered widespread prejudice, as did the Greeks, Italians, Serbs and Poles who came to the USA to find a better life. Sometimes the hostilities of the original country were reproduced in the USA, and national sensitivities were thereby injected into US politics. This has certainly been true of the Irish-Americans, so that Congress will sometimes be responsive to anti-British sentiments on the subject of Northern Ireland. However, it has also been true in relation to Greek–Turkish conflicts, as, for example, when some members of Congress with Greek sympathies voted to cut off aid to Turkey in the wake of the Turkish invasion of Cyprus in 1974. In addition, voluntary groups such as the Polish Falcons have been an important factor in maintaining support for the trade-union organization Solidarność (Solidarity).

Much of the hostility between different ethnic groups was in large part the reaction of the newly-established to the next generation of newcomers. But it was also—and continues to be in some cases—the result of different attitudes, values and life styles which generated dislike and hostility, especially when the different ethnic groups were forced to live in close proximity to each other. One result of the suspicion generated by the pressures of immigration, however, has been that controls over entry have been continuously on the political agenda, although their impact has not always been seen as equally severe on all national and ethnic groups and the USA has always tried to retain an 'open-door' policy for those which its government recognizes as genuine refugees. In addition, political history has given some emigrants a special status—for example Cuban exiles, who form an important minority in some states (especially Florida).

The original assumption about immigrants was that—whatever their origin—they would, after one or two generations, be absorbed into the 'melting-pot' of the USA. Yet this assumption was seen by many as the assumption of superiority by a US establishment of white Anglo-Saxon Protestants (WASPs) who denigrated (explicitly or implicitly) the cultural inheritance of the various ethnic groups of the USA. During the 1970s and 1980s there has been a conscious assertion of national origin and identity. Indeed, to be a member of the WASP élite is in a sense to be a member of a disadvantaged minority of its own; the white non-Hispanic population (77.6% of the total in 1987) was projected to decline to only about 69.5% of the total in 2020. Certainly it was clear in the 1988 election campaign that George Bush had to counteract his WASP credentials by such devices as being seen driving trucks and wearing working clothes. Neither is the minority status of WASPs entirely illusionary. Although the 1986 *Statistical Abstract of the United States* reported that 49,598,000 US citizens reported their ancestry as English, this was not much more than the second-highest group, the Germans, and only slightly higher than the Irish.

Whatever the desirability of submerging ethnic origin in a single all-embracing US culture, the processes of educational achievement, social mobility and integration proved altogether more difficult for blacks.

BLACK AMERICANS

While black Americans constitute just over 12% of the US population, they remain disadvantaged in comparison with whites by every criterion. Inevitably the economic status of blacks will be affected by the condition of the broader US economy, but there are also special features of black participation in the economy which affect the black community's economic status. The 1960s saw a determined effort by the federal government to reduce the level of poverty in the USA. The 'war on poverty' had a direct impact on the most disadvantaged groups in US society, notably blacks. The political rejection of strategies of federal intervention to alleviate poverty—combined with the experience of economic recession—have affected the black poverty rate. Thus the *Yearbook of Black America* showed that in 1986 the national poverty rate for blacks (i.e. the proportion of all black people with incomes below the official poverty level) was 31.1%. An estimated 8,983,000 black persons were in households with incomes below the official poverty level and 42.7% of all black children under the age of 18 were officially classified as poor. The poverty rates for blacks had risen during the early 1980s and stood in sharp contrast to those of the late 1960s and early 1970s. A 1988 report from the Bureau of the Census recorded that while the poverty rate for whites declined slightly from 11% in 1986 to 10.5% in 1987, the poverty rate for blacks rose from 31.1% to 33.3%. Poverty rates for blacks are not uniform regionally. However, one of the marked areas of improvement since the 1960s, has been in the South—the region where, until the 1950s, effective segregation of the races existed.

Black participation in the work-force is affected both by the legacy of disadvantage in education and income and by the experience of discrimination. The decline of some traditional manufacturing industries has tended not only to reduce the number of jobs where blacks were disproportionately concentrated but to replace them with less well-paid service-sector jobs. As a result the participation rate of black males in the labour force has been declining in the 1980s.

Black groups have been mobilized politically for a number of causes. The 1950s and 1960s saw black groups organizing to promote the cause of racial equality in the civil-rights movement. The political strengthening of blacks was reflected in the growing number of blacks elected to public office in the 1970s and 1980s. The 101st Congress (elected in 1988) had a record number of black members. There were 24 black members of the House of Representatives, although no black person has won election to the Senate since the defeat of Massachusetts Senator Edward Brooke in 1978. Because many of the black members of the House sit for safe seats, they have been able to build up seniority. The black caucus in the House has thus gained considerable influence in the past decade, and blacks have chaired committees with special relevance to their agenda such as Education and Labor and the District of Columbia as well as the Narcotics Committee. In addition, a senior black Congressman—William Gray—has chaired the crucial Budget Committee of the House.

The Reagan years (1981–88) were in many ways ones in which black issues were difficult to promote; but there were occasional victories. Thus in 1986 on the issue of South African sanctions—a highly symbolic cause for US blacks—the congressional black caucus passed a bill to impose sanctions over President Reagan's veto. The advent of the Bush administration saw a change of mood. President Bush appointed members of minority groups to senior posts in his administration (for example a black—Dr Louis Sullivan—was made Secretary of Health and Human Resources); but more important even than these somewhat symbolic appointments was the renewed contact between the administration and the black community.

The 1988 presidential election in many ways underlined the political dilemma of blacks in the USA. While the candidacy of the Rev. Jesse Jackson injected excitement and ideological commitment into the Democratic nomination process, it labelled the Democratic Party as 'liberal' in a way which allowed the Republicans to paint the Democrats as being outside the mainstream of US opinion and as the 'captive' of minority groups. From the black perspective, the fact that blacks have been an important part of the Democratic coalition since the 'New Deal' era of the 1930s and 1940s means that their support is often taken for granted and their bargaining power is accordingly reduced.

The 1988 campaign was followed by the selection of a Jackson supporter—Ron Brown—as the chairman of the Democratic National Committee, and there was speculation that changes might occur in the rules governing the nomination process which would further aid another Jackson candidacy.

HISPANICS

By comparison with the black groups, US Hispanics have enjoyed less extensive attention. Yet some 17m. US citizens have roots in Mexico, Cuba, other Latin American nations and Puerto Rico, and there are a number of states in which Americans of Hispanic origin outnumber blacks. These states include California, Texas, New Mexico and Arizona, where there are large numbers of Hispanics, but also a number of western states, such as Utah, where the numbers of blacks are small.

The major significance of the USA's Hispanic community is, however, in its potential impact on US society. The scale of Hispanic immigration (both legal and illegal) and such factors as the fertility rate of the Hispanic community make this one of the fastest-growing social groups in the country. Hispanics are projected to overtake blacks as a proportion of US society by the mid-21st century.

The Hispanic community is not monolithic. Clearly numbers of Hispanics think of themselves as white while others either are, or think of themselves as, black. The fact that many Hispanics (especially those of Mexican-American descent) are either illegal immigrants or fail to acquire naturalization makes their integration into the mainstream of US life difficult and acts as an impediment to the total mobilization of Hispanics as a political force.

The USA's one million Cubans (who constitute 6% of the Hispanic population) are a special subgroup within the broader Hispanic community. They emigrated to the USA primarily for political, rather than economic, reasons—to escape the communist regime of Fidel Castro. Many of the initial immigrants to the USA were wealthy. Their anti-communism and the self-confident nature of a section of the Cuban community gives Republicans a degree of support among Cubans which they find hard to attract from other sections of the Hispanic community. Issues which concern Cubans include aid to anti-communist fighters in Latin America such as the Contras in Nicaragua. Indeed, anti-communism is so salient an issue for many Cubans that it often plays an important role even in local elections in areas such as Miami, where Cubans are a major force and where in November 1985 there was a run-off in the mayoralty election between two Cuban immigrants, Raul Masvidal and Xavier Suarez (the latter winning ultimately).

Other special features of the Hispanic community have, thus far, limited its political effectiveness. Apart from the high percentage of illegal immigrants among the Hispanic population, the age structure of the population is heavily weighted to the younger age-groups (the median age of US Hispanics in 1986 was 25—10 years younger than the median age of the rest of the population). Non-voting is a common feature of younger age-groups, but Hispanics also tend to be among the poorest and least-literate members of US society—factors which correlate with non-voting.

Efforts have been made to remedy the low level of Hispanic participation in the electoral process. In a radical (and some would argue spurious) extension of the principles of the Voting Rights Act of 1965, Congress in 1975 extended the protections against discrimination to cover Hispanics in the south-west. Moreover, in some states ballot papers are printed in Spanish (as well as other minority languages, such as Chinese). The abolition of at-large electoral districts and the use of own-language ballots has caused an increase in Hispanic registration

levels. However, the most important factor in extending participation is undoubtedly the growth of a body of Hispanic elected officials as well as the efforts of groups such as the National Puerto-Rican-Hispanic Voter Registration Project (NPR-HVRP) and the National Association of Latino Elected Officials (NALEO). NALEO found in 1985 that the number of Hispanic elected officials across the country was 3,147—double that of 1970.

The 101st Congress (1989-90) saw 12 Hispanics elected to the House of Representatives. President Bush took care also to nominate Hispanics to his cabinet, appointing Manuel Lujan as Secretary of the Interior and Lauro Cavazos as Secretary of Education. However, the national political power of Hispanics is likely to be felt in the next decade rather than at present, and strategists such as Luis Caban have seen the 1980s as years in which the groundwork for future influence can be laid. Undoubtedly, also, Hispanic influence will be felt at the state and local level long before it is perceived at the national level.

THE CHANGING ASIAN POPULATION

The 6m. Asian-Americans are at present a small force in the country's population, but there is no doubt of their potential significance. The various groups who could be considered Asian-American accounted for 2.1% of the population in 1985 but the group is the USA's fastest-growing minority and could account for 4% of the population by 2000. Both the fact that the USA has a Pacific coast with a 'window' on Asia and the economic dynamism of parts of Asia give this segment of the population an important role in the USA.

Chinese communities have existed in the USA from the 19th century. Although the 1980 census recorded a relatively small Chinese population of just over 800,000 (less than 0.5% of the total), it is a fast-growing population, having recorded a very high growth rate since 1970—partly as a result of immigration. Although the Chinese population is the longest-established Asian-origin group in the USA, the Filipinos constitute the largest group—it was predicted that there would be some 1.4m. Filipinos in the USA by 1990.

The small communities of Japanese have increased since the Second World War, but the affluence of Japan has meant that immigration from that country is small. At the time of the 1980 census the Japanese community numbered some 700,000—an increase of only 18.5% since 1970. By 1990 the Japanese, the Vietnamese and the Koreans were each expected to number about 800,000, although birth rates suggest that the Vietnamese and Koreans will overtake the Japanese in the next decade.

During the 1970s and 1980s increases in immigration from Vietnam and Korea brought to the USA groups with high educational goals and already these groups have recorded levels of university enrolment well above their proportion in the population as a whole. There is also an unusual degree of self-employment, reflecting the tendency for new immigrants to open businesses, especially restaurants.

Although the USA's Asian community is as yet quite small, it promises to be a growing force in US life, both because of the potential numbers of would-be immigrants and because of the characteristics of those who have already settled in the country. The exercise of political power has been delayed by the denial of citizenship to many of these groups until after the Second World War, and other factors operating to limit participation have included cultural alienation, illiteracy and a certain amount of division between the components of the Asian community. However, in the 1970s a few Asian-Americans (from the mainland as opposed to Hawaii) gained political office at national level. Thus Norman Mineta, a California Democrat of Japanese ancestry, was elected to the House in 1974 and in 1976 California's S. I. Hayakawa was elected to the US Senate.

The Asian-Americans are concentrated in a few centres at present. Los Angeles and New York have received the largest numbers of new Asian immigrants in the 1980s and it is not surprising to find that seven of the 10 congressional districts with the largest percentage of Asian-Americans of voting age are in California. (The remaining three are in Hawaii and New York.) It seems likely, therefore, that the expression of Asian political power within the USA will be felt in a limited number of areas for the foreseeable future, although the local nature of indigenous Asian power may well be compensated for by the USA's increasing concern with its political, economic and trading relationships with the continent.

RELIGION

Religion has always been an important factor in US social life and in the 1980s it has become more significant in the political arena. The diversity of the US religious scene can, in part, be explained by the early tolerance of religious nonconformity in the country—however, differences of national origin and ethnicity, region and even sexual preference have imposed further divisions within the various religious groupings.

Initially, the population of the USA was overwhelmingly Protestant, although there was a substantial Roman Catholic minority in Maryland. The 19th-century influx of immigration from Europe brought large numbers of both Roman Catholics and Jews to the USA. The number of US Jews was estimated at 5.8m. in 1986, while in the same year the Roman Catholic Church reported that it had some 52.7m. members, making it by far the biggest single denomination in the USA. The rapid growth of the country's Hispanic population may be expected to increase the numbers of US Catholics even further over the next 30 years, although evangelical Christianity is gaining support among Latinos.

It was at one time thought possible to categorize the USA's religious divisions into these three broad groupings of Protestantism, Roman Catholicism and Judaism. However, the experience since the Second World War has underlined the extent of the diversity of US religion. For example, the number of Protestant denominations has increased, despite the decision by some churches to amalgamate. An important split within the Protestant camp is that between those churches which are liberal in theological outlook (broadly those churches which adhere to the National Council of Churches) and those which are more conservative or fundamentalist in orientation. Observers of religious developments in the USA have long pointed out that it is in the latter group of churches that growth has been most rapid.

While Roman Catholics remain formally a united entity, there is a remarkable diversity within US Catholicism. Even in the 19th century there was a tendency for Roman Catholics to accommodate to the exceptionalism of US society, and this tendency has persisted in the 20th century, producing a range of special-purpose groups and differences of doctrinal belief, tradition and activism unparalleled in other societies.

US Jewry is also split into at least three tendencies: the Conservative; the Orthodox; and the Reform. Reform Judaism, however, has become virtually synonymous with American Judaism and is by far the most dominant tendency. One special feature of contemporary American Judaism is its political support for the state of Israel. This support—although somewhat dented by recent events in the Middle East—is sustained through a network of pressure groups, such as the American Israel Political Action Committee and the American Jewish Committee, as well as more specialist groups such as B'Nai Brith.

In addition to these Judaeo–Christian groupings, the USA has generated a range of newer groups which stand slightly apart. By far the largest grouping is the Church of Jesus Christ of Latter-day Saints, or Mormon Church. Based in Salt Lake City, Utah, but now enjoying a huge national membership, this church claimed 3.9m. members in the USA in 1986. The Mormon Church is distinctive because of the American context of its doctrine and beliefs. It is a highly conservative church which places a special emphasis on the family and, until recently, did not accord blacks equal membership.

The new immigration to the USA from Asian countries has increased the representation of Eastern religions and sects— for example Buddhism and Shintoism. But it must be remembered that much of the Asian population is Christian. For example, the Korean and Filipino population is heavily Roman Catholic, while the fundamentalist churches have made many converts among recent immigrants.

At one time the distribution of religious adherents was regionally distinctive. Thus the South was predominantly Prot-estant, and it was in the South and Midwest that fundamentalism had its spiritual home. Roman Catholics and Jews, by contrast, were more likely to be found in the cities of the Northeast. However, social mobility and the media have created a much more homogenous religious picture in the USA, although pockets of regional distinctiveness remain—for example in Utah's Mormon population and in the concentration of Roman Catholics in Boston and New York.

The politicization of religion in the USA during the 1980s can be attributed to a number of factors. Firstly, there was the desire of the churches (including those not previously involved in direct political action) to organize in order to defend their life style against permissiveness and secularism. Secondly, there was the search by political entrepreneurs (especially those on the right) for support for political causes and candidates which seemed in line with the views of some churches. There was the rise to public prominence of issues with moral and theological implications, by far the most important of which was the question of abortion. Finally there was the impact of individual personalities whose messages, often conveyed through television programmes, were a blend of the political and the religious.

Evangelism has a long history in the USA, and its most famous proponents (such as Billy Graham and Jerry Falwell) have frequently been courted by politicians or have themselves sought to exert political influence. Although some of the individual preachers have not been able to sustain their following, others, such as Jerry Falwell, have developed extensive organizations which include schools and colleges as well as churches and television stations. These networks are themselves a feature of the US social scene in two senses. Firstly, there is a marked tendency for religious groups in the USA to operate in a way which is like any other pressure group or indeed any other commercial organization. Secondly, there has been a proliferation of the special-purpose groups which promote highly-specific aspects of religious activity. Although these groups have a religious connection, they also exist to further a range of broader interests and operate in a way which is distinct from that of the formal church bodies. Such groups have a long history in the USA and include the Pocket Testament League, the American Bible Society, the Christian Business Committee and eccentric-sounding groups such as the Christian Magicians. The period since 1960 has seen a growth in the number of these groups, with some 300 being founded between 1960 and 1988.

The variety and number of US churches and denominations and the range of groups with religious associations and purposes testify to the vitality of religion in the USA and to its importance as a basis of social identity.

Women

Women constitute a majority of the US population and it might therefore be wondered whether they need, or can achieve, effective political organization. Women were given the vote in the USA in 1920, under the terms of the 19th Amendment, but not until the 1960s was there any real feminist or women's movement, or much evidence of a distinctive female perception of politics. Since the 1970s evidence of a gender gap has accumulated. Women, it seems, are more likely to support the Democratic Party than men, and during the 1980s were less supportive of Reagan and his policies. The nomination of Geraldine Ferraro as the Democratic vice-presidential candidate in 1984 was seen by many as a breakthrough, although the experience of the campaign itself underlined the barriers to successful female candidacies at the highest levels in the USA. Nevertheless, a number of women were mentioned as possible vice-presidential candidates in 1988. President Bush has appointed women (for example Elizabeth Dole and Carla Hills) to senior positions in his administration, while President Reagan nominated the first female Supreme Court justice— Sandra Day O'Connor.

At the elective level of the political system women have had only a limited success. Although the numbers of women elected to Congress have risen since the 1970s, the gains have not been dramatic. In 1971 there were 15 female members of

Congress; in 1986 there were 25, including two female senators. The 1988 elections saw the return of two women to the Senate: Nancy Kassebaum of Kansas and Barbara Mikulski of Maryland. In the House 25 women were returned. This slight numerical improvement conceals the fact that women have done relatively poorly in acquiring leadership positions, so that in the 100th Congress (1987–88) there was no woman chair of any committee. In addition, some women felt that they had to avoid the promotion of women's issues in order to avoid becoming stereotyped. Thus the assumption that more women in Congress means that the legislature will be more responsive to women's issues is not necessarily correct.

A variety of groups are organized around women's issues in the USA. Some, such as the National Organization of Women (NOW) and the National Women's Political Caucus (NWPC) are firmly in the liberal and Democratic camp. Others, such as the League of Women Voters, are bipartisan. There is also a range of specialist groups, such as the Women's Legal Defense Fund, which was founded in 1971 to promote legal equality through court action.

Until the 1980s the women's movement placed the passage of a constitutional amendment to secure equal rights high on its agenda. However, the development of a backlash against feminism in the 1980s as a result of the mobilization of the 'new right' caused the amendment to stall in the ratification process and polarized the debate on women's issues. The various pressure groups working on women's issues therefore found themselves with a double fight on their hands. Firstly, they had to work to try to prevent any retreat on the gains of the 1960s and 1970s. Secondly, they had to try to convince other groups to join them in the battle to secure improvements in legislation on such issues as child-care.

A particular cause of concern was the right to reproductive freedom, and specifically the right to secure an abortion in the first three months of pregnancy. Although the Supreme Court in 1973 enunciated the existence of such a right in *Roe v. Wade*, the opposition to abortion grew in political strength and there was a frequent testing of the limits of the 1973 decision in the courts. The Reagan administration used opposition to *Roe v. Wade* as a means of screening judicial candidates' credentials, and by 1988 the Supreme Court majority for upholding the 1973 decision had narrowed considerably.

Women were also affected by the Reagan administration's reluctance to use the federal government to combat discrimination in employment and education. The cuts in domestic spending pursued by that administration were of special concern to women, since they affected a number of programmes (such as Headstart, school-lunch programmes and student aid) all of which had been designed to remedy disadvantage among poor families. Women's groups have typically found themselves in the liberal Democratic camp as far as coalition politics are concerned, especially since the sharp turn to the right of the Republican Party and its renunciation of the Equal-Rights Amendment (ERA).

Sexual Preference

The growth of the homosexual or gay liberation movement in the 1960s made this a force to be reckoned with in some areas. In the 1970s the goal of the gay-rights movement was primarily to achieve legal equality for homosexuals in such fields as property rights and employment. The shift from a liberal and permissive environment to one of greater conservatism in the 1980s put the gay movement on the defensive. The spread of the Acquired Immunodeficiency Syndrome (AIDS) virus in the 1980s had the effect of giving the gay movement a new agenda. The liberal orientation of homosexual pressure groups made it inevitable that it would align itself firmly in the Democratic

camp, although gay support was not always greatly desired by political candidates.

Age

Differences of age have not generally led to the formation of distinct groups, although of course political observers have frequently noted that different age cohorts have their own concerns and may display distinctive patterns of partisanship. Consciousness about the specific needs of the elderly has, in part, arisen for demographic reasons. In 1986 12% of the US population was over 65 years of age and 5% was over 75. Projections suggest that by 2000 13% of the US population will be over 65. Equally important from the perspective of funding retirees, the ratio of retired to working persons is expected to shift from 1:5 in 1986 to 1:3 by 2020. Some states are especially conscious of the impact of elderly residents. Florida, California and Arizona have especially large proportions of elderly and retired persons in their populations for climatic reasons and are therefore sensitive to the agenda of the elderly.

In the 1970s pressure groups began to form around the agenda of the elderly and attention to these issues was given by politicians such as the late Congressman Claude Pepper of Florida. In addition to the growth of 'gray' pressure groups, it has been noted that Congress itself has been getting older. The 101st (1989–90) Congress had an average age of 52.8 years at its election, making it the oldest since the 91st Congress of 1969–70. The explanation for this trend is in part the ageing of the population, generally combined with the safeness of House seats.

The issues which have been of particular concern to the elderly in the USA in recent years have concerned the viability of the various forms of social-security benefit available to them. Because these funds are only partially financed from the 'pay-as-you-go' contributions, they are very vulnerable both to general budgetary constraints and to demographic fluctuation, which might reduce the numbers in the work-force who are able to provide benefits to support their seniors. Both factors have been present in the calculations of policy-makers (who have anticipated some of the problems relating to pension funding by raising contributions). But the viability of social security and problems of health-care provision remain major issues in US politics. The relative poverty of older members of US society and their likely dependence on governmental services has made the question of governmental responsibility for service delivery a general issue of concern. At the same time, however, there is a growing awareness of the burden which support for the elderly places on younger families and their children.

Conclusion

US society is unique in a number of ways. The continual transformation of the population makes it in one sense a 'permanently unfinished' society. The sheer scale of its immigration continues to be astonishing. The USA, which has about 5% of the world's population, takes over one-half of all legal international migrants. Divisions of age, sex, religion and sexual preference provide endless permutations of society already marked by a colourful diversity. If the impact of technology and mobility has to some extent been to make the regions of the USA more homogeneous, identities of race, religion and gender are likely to remain an important basis of the country's social and political life for the foreseeable future.

RECENT PATTERNS AND POLICIES IN US IMMIGRATION

R. A. BURCHELL

The USA has always been a nation of immigrants. All its inhabitants, apart from native Americans (who constituted just 0.6% of the population at the 1980 census), are either immigrants or the descendants of men and women who have moved there since Europeans first founded permanent settlements in the 17th century. A combination of natural resources, an entrepreneurial culture, external (mainly European) sources of capital and large internal and overseas markets have given the USA two centuries of economic growth since independence and a need for labour which has been met by immigrants. Labour shortages have generally meant high wages, while immigrants have also been attracted by a politically democratic society and its emphasis on maximizing opportunity for individuals, the lack of an overt class system and a state church, and, in the 19th century, the lack of militarism which meant freedom from conscription.

Principal Trends

1820–1900

Immigration figures were first collected in 1820, in which year there were just under 9,000 immigrants. Thereafter numbers increased sharply, with some 750,000 men, women and children arriving between October 1819 and December 1840. The large majority of these immigrants came from Great Britain, Ireland and Germany and, being largely Protestant Christians and, apart from the Germans, English-speaking, they fitted into the receiving society with relative ease. The so-called 'Hungry 'Forties', however, with the famines of the period 1846–54 in Britain, Germany and, above all, Ireland, caused an acceleration in the rate of immigration, with some 4.3m. immigrants arriving between 1841 and 1860, and a change in its composition. The entry of increasing numbers of Catholics was perceived by much of the native-born US population as a challenge to the Protestant Republicanism on which US society was based. The most extreme among native-born Americans, including supporters of the 'Know-Nothing' political movement that wished to restrict the rights of immigrants, claimed that Catholics could never give up their encompassing allegiance to the Pope, and that this made them incapable of taking part in the democratic US experiment. The language of the anxious of the 1850s has interesting connections with that used more recently by those alarmed at present trends in US immigration.

The Civil War of 1861–65 concentrated minds on other matters. A nation at war was less attractive, especially since after 1863 all immigrant males between 20 and 45 years of age resident in the northern states (the destination of a large majority of immigrants) were liable for conscription once they gave notice of intended naturalization. Nevertheless, the USA was now fixed in the European imagination as a destination for the discontented and the post-war period saw a resurgence, with some 13.3m. immigrants, largely from Europe, arriving between 1866 and 1900. About 5.2m. came in the 1880s alone, when major changes occurred in the distribution of European areas exporting population to the USA. The ravages of the famine years and the resultant high death rate led to a decrease in emigration from Ireland. Germany united and industrialized, and the consequent increase in domestic opportunities meant that its rate of emigration declined, after peaking in 1882. The same was true for Great Britain which, in addition, was beginning to direct emigration towards its Empire. Meanwhile, the populations of southern and eastern Europe became more mobile, as much towards the burgeoning cities of their regions as abroad. Improved communications, increases in population in rural areas with insufficient land, the development of world markets in foodstuffs, and the gradual growth of ethnic tensions all contributed to population rearrangements. One of the most significant developments, as far as the USA was concerned, was the growing official and organized persecution of Russian Jews which encouraged increasing numbers to consider emigration. While some tried other European nations, the majority turned to the USA, helping to ensure that from 1896 emigration from southern and eastern Europe to the USA began to exceed that from northern and western Europe.

1901 ONWARDS

Immigration continued strongly into the 20th century, with some 34m. men, women and children arriving between 1901 and 1986. Seventeen million arrived between 1901 and 1925, during which period immigration was still largely unrestricted. Restriction (see below), the world-wide depression of the 1930s and the impact of the Second World War sharply reduced numbers, and there were only 3m. immigrants between 1926 and 1950. Restriction continued through the next quarter-century, but the return of peace, increasing US affluence and the willingness of the country to accept political refugees sent numbers soaring again. A further 8m. immigrants entered the USA between 1951 and 1975, while another 6m. arrived in 1976–86. The net annual civilian immigration rate fluctuated between 1.7 and 2.1 per 1,000 of the US population from 1950 to 1979, but rose sharply thereafter, reaching an annual average of 2.9 per 1,000 between 1980 and 1984, and 2.6 per 1,000 in 1985–86.

The 1970s saw the greatest volume of immigration in 50 years. Whereas between 1950 and 1960 numbers arriving varied between 170,000 and 327,000 per year (the latter figure, reached in 1957, was the highest annual total in the period 1946–65), in 1961–70 the parameters were 271,000 and 454,000 (recorded in 1961 and 1968 respectively). In 1971–80 the parameters moved upwards again, to 370,000 and 601,000 (1971 and 1978), and in 1981–86 they increased even further, to 544,000 and 602,000 (1984 and 1986). Thus immigration is still continuing at a very substantial level, some 60 years after unrestricted immigration was ended.

An outstanding characteristic of recent immigration has been that it has originated from countries that have not traditionally exported population to the USA. Overall, between 1820 and 1965 (the year of a distinct shift in the emphasis of US immigration policy—see below) 81% of all US immigrants came from Europe. However, this proportion had declined to just 37% by the decade 1961–70. At the same time, the proportion arriving from North and Central America (including the Caribbean) had grown to become the greatest source of immigrants, providing 41% in the 1960s. At this point Asians comprised 13% of immigrants, South Americans 7% and newcomers from the rest of the world 2%.

The percentage arriving from Europe fell further, to 18%, in the decade 1971–80. The marked change in these years was in the proportion arriving from Asia, which rose to 36%. That coming from North and Central America fell slightly, to 37%, and from South America to 6%. These trends continued in 1981–85, when the proportion from Europe fell to 11% and that from Asia rose to 48%. The proportion from North and Central America fell to 31%; that from South America remained constant. 1986 figures show the European and Asian totals declining to 10% and 45% respectively, with the North and Central American total increasing to 35%. Altogether, the predominance of non-European immigrants has shaped a new era in US immigration history. It is interesting that in 1964, when Congress debated changing immigration legislation, no one disagreed with the then Attorney-General, Robert Kennedy, when he said that he expected the number of immigrants to arrive from the so-called 'Asia-Pacific triangle' in the first year after liberalization would be about 5,000 and that thereafter 'immigration from that source would virtually disappear'.

Problems and Policies

The immigration of the later 1890s and early 1900s led to frequent questioning as to whether the USA could assimilate so many peoples from unfamiliar societies. Since the native-born American population had already shown itself to be ambivalent on welcoming all immigrants, it was not surprising that many Americans were unwilling to welcome wholeheartedly the 'New Immigrants', as they came to be called. Many of the latter spoke no English; few were Protestants. The diets and clothing of some were viewed as outlandish. There was undoubtedly a cultural distance to be travelled by these new arrivals, as Mary Antin, a successful and prominent immigrant of the period, later recalled in her *Autobiography*, remarking how she and her family on arrival:

> 'had to visit the stores and be dressed from head to foot in American clothing; . . . learn the mysteries of the iron stove, the washboard, and the speaking-tube; . . . to trade with the fruit peddler through the window, and not be afraid of the policemen . . . and above all . . . to learn English.'

This was practical accommodation to the new society. However, something else was being referred to as she went on:

> 'With our despised immigrant clothing we (had to) shed also our impossible Hebrew names.'

Descendants of Antin's generation would later despise this last move, but to do so was to ignore the pressures on newcomers. Immigrants found it impossible to retain every vestige of ancestral cultures while also adjusting to the demands of the new society. These had to be met, at least in part, if the receiving society was not to disintegrate and immigrants were not to fail to advance.

Debate over accommodation and assimilation uncovered three differing views. As the 'Know-Nothings' had already shown, some native-born Americans insisted on a full submission to 'American' ways, demanding what has been termed 'Angloconformity'. In reply, some immigrant leaders suggested that the USA would best benefit by becoming a 'melting pot', a society in which a new culture would emerge from an amalgam of constituents drawn from all settling ethnic groups. In time, social scientists were to pose a third, now widely accepted model—cultural pluralism—which suggested a retention of some and a surrender of other ethnic cultural patterns; it also suggested that the USA could survive with a high degree of cultural heterogeneity in the private lives of its inhabitants, while maintaining a degree of homogeneity in aspects of its public culture such as politics. Groups that have joined fully in the US political process but have never intermarried to any large degree, such as Jews and Roman Catholics, show the distinction to be both real and workable.

RESTRICTION AND REGULATION

Restrictive immigration policies have reflected both public and private doubts. Early restriction and control of immigration proceeded piecemeal, but was motivated by three often-linked sets of feelings. Racial prejudice was apparent from the first; there was also a fear that unskilled immigrant labourers would take away jobs from the native-born; and there was apprehension lest the USA be flooded with the 'morally undesirable'.

The earliest attempt at restricting immigration was aimed at one group in particular, the Chinese, and among them ostensibly at labourers. In 1882 the USA banned the immigration of Chinese labourers for 10 years, subsequently renewing the ban and maintaining it until 1943, when it became difficult to justify in the face of the Chinese–US alliance against Japan. In 1882, also, the USA prohibited the immigration of criminals, paupers, the insane and other 'undesirables', and in 1885 that of all labourers arriving as the result of prearranged contracts. In 1903 anarchists and prostitutes were added to the list, and in 1907–08 the USA and Japan informally agreed to stop the migration of Japanese labourers. On three occasions, in 1896, 1913 and 1915, Congress attempted to control the quality of immigration by imposing a literacy test, but Presidents Cleveland, Taft and Wilson refused to sign the respective acts. In 1917, however, Congress overrode Wilson's veto and

passed such a bill. This stipulated that in future aliens over 16 years of age had to read a passage containing between 30 and 80 words in ordinary use in the English language or another language or dialect to immigration officials in order to gain entry to the USA.

By that time, however, much of the US population felt that piecemeal policies were not enough and that immigration needed wholesale regulation. A fear of foreign radicalisms after the upheavals in Europe in 1918–20, and a desire not to return to the ever-upwardly spiralling immigrant numbers that had characterized the period 1900-14, led in 1921 to the passage by Congress of a law, the most significant effects of which were to establish a maximum number of immigrants to be admitted per year and to set quotas for individual nations. These provisions were further refined in acts of 1924 and 1929, which were all primarily intended to reduce immigration from southern and eastern Europe. Reflecting continuing antipathy to the Chinese and Japanese, oriental immigration was not allowed, while the acts did not cover immigration from the western hemisphere. The Act of 1929, which governed policy for 40 years, set out a quota system, put the maximum annual immigration at 150,000 and stipulated that this should be shared out in the same proportions as nations had contributed to the total US population as of 1920. Minor adjustments were made in the next 30 years. For example, in 1952 the McCarran–Walter Act kept the maximum immigration and quota provisions, but removed the ban against the immigration of Asian and Pacific peoples. In 1953 the Refugee Relief Act provided for the entry into the USA on an emergency basis, outside regular immigration quotas, of 186,000 persons who had left Communist countries.

The results of the 1929 Act were as required. Between 1930 and 1948 the total average annual immigration was 153,929, with Europe alone providing 150,501 of these. Northern and western Europe's quota was 125,853: that for the UK was 65,721, for Germany 25,721, and for the Irish Free State (now the Republic of Ireland) 17,853; by contrast, that for Italy was 5,802. Partly as a result of these quotas, in the 1950s the countries providing the largest numbers of immigrants were Germany, east and west (448,313), Canada (331,284), Mexico (267,103), Italy (172,122) and the UK (144,631). While the British were not fully using their quota, the Italians, and other groups with tiny quotas, were substantially oversubscribing theirs. By the early 1960s the species of prejudice that had brought about the Act of 1929 was weakening fast and it was decided to adopt new principles to reflect changed global circumstances. In 1965 a new act abolished the national-origins quota system and replaced it by a system of preferential admissions, which was intended to be based on the skills offered by individual immigrants. However, immigration officials would also be permitted to take notice of the existence of close family relationships between intending immigrants and persons who were already citizens or permanent residents of the USA. Within the system of preferences, the issue of visas would be on a 'first-come, first-served' basis.

In the event, the second provision has overtaken the first in importance. In 1986 some 601,708 immigrants were admitted into the USA. Some 10,910, or 1.8%, had gained first-preference status (given to unmarried sons and daughters of US citizens, and their children) but no fewer than 110,926, or 18.4%, gained second-preference status (as spouses, unmarried sons and daughters of resident aliens, and their children). Married sons and daughters of US citizens, who had fourth-preference status, totalled 20,702, or 3.4%. Brothers and sisters of US citizens, with fifth-preference status, numbered 70,401, or 11.7%. Together these groups produced 35.3% of immigrants. By contrast, immigrants in professions, with third-preference status, numbered only 11,763, or 2.0%, while 'other workers', with sixth-preference status, numbered just 11,399, or 1.9%; the spouses and children of those with third- and sixth-preference statuses numbered 30,403, or some 5.1% of the total. Immigrants with skills and their dependants thus made up just 9.0% of total immigration, while by far the largest group admitted in 1986 were those joining immediate relatives—some 334,740, or 55.6% in all. Beyond these groups the USA also admitted 104,383 refugees in 1986, 17.3% of the total.

In the census year of 1980 2,199,200 immigrants living in the USA had been born in Mexico, 849,400 in Germany, 842,900 in

Canada, 831,900 in Italy, 607,800 in Cuba and 501,400 in the Philippines. The overall character of the immigrant population is, however, changing rapidly. Many European immigrants are elderly and are not being replaced. By contrast, in 1986 10.9% of the Hispanic population was under five years of age, compared to 7.7% of the total population. Furthermore, the countries providing most immigrants in the years 1984–86 were Mexico (185,863), the Philippines (161,614), the Republic of Korea (102,492), Taiwan and the People's Republic of China (94,593 altogether, of whom the majority were Taiwanese), the Dominican Republic (73,284), and India (72,691). By contrast, only 29,256 West Germans and 18,390 Italians immigrated during this period.

The Cultural Debate

The USA has benefited from immigration from developing countries in one particular way: it has been able to import a highly-educated population. At one extreme, no less than 66.2% of 1986 immigrants from India were college graduates. So were over one-third of immigrants from Hong Kong (42.7%), Iran (42.9%), Israel (34.9%), Korea (34.2%), the Philippines (41.8%) and Taiwan (59.8%). Despite the quality of modern immigration revealed by these figures, contemporary anxieties about the cultural results of changes in the character of the immigrant population have revolved about the ability of newcomers to speak or learn the English language. The relationship between language and culture is a very important but far from simple one, as some authorities have already discovered. Nevertheless, the movement to have English declared the official language of the USA has grown, and continues to gather momentum.

To begin with, the sense that the character of immigration was changing produced remedial action. In 1968 existing bilingual education programmes in primary and secondary public schools were put under federal or state financing. In 1974 it was agreed that students could first be taught in their native tongues and then weaned onto English and, by 1986, 41 states had bilingual education programmes that were financed by the federal government. However, rising numbers of non-English-speaking immigrants undermined the general agreement that this was the way to proceed. Opponents of these arrangements increasingly argued that bilingual teaching delayed the process by which immigrants learned the English language and that, since learning it was an inescapable prerequisite of becoming 'an American', it should, if anything, be accelerated by government. Colorado Governor Richard D. Lamm spoke of English as the nation's 'social glue' and maintained that while the USA should be 'colour blind', it should not be 'linguistically deaf'. The USA could be a 'rainbow' but not a 'cacophony'. It should 'welcome different people, but not adopt different languages'. Such a stance was opposed by bodies like the Mexican-American Legal Defense Group, which saw nativist prejudice in the attempts to teach immigrants in English. Some pointed to a 1985 RAND Corporation study which showed that 90% of first-generation Mexican-Americans were already proficient in English and that one-half of the second generation spoke nothing else, and maintained that matters could safely be left to run their natural course.

Growing numbers of native-born Americans in many states were not convinced. They felt an important matter of principle was at stake. By the end of 1986 voters in Georgia, Illinois, Indiana, Kentucky, Nebraska and Virginia had accepted propositions to make English the official language in their states. Republican Senator Steven Symms of Idaho spoke for them when he introduced a resolution into the US Senate in 1986 that 'the English language shall be the official language of the United States'. In 1980 Dade County, Florida, which includes Miami, banned bilingualism, so that official publications were no longer sent out in Spanish and welfare and hospital forms were printed only in English. Government jobs could no longer be advertised in Spanish-language newspapers and Dade County stopped financing the annual Spanish Heritage Festival. But officials soon discovered the complexities of the subject, as they found it impossible to abandon bilingualism in the

emergency health and safety services and had to continue to broadcast hurricane warnings bilingually. In practice, authorities continued bilingualism in matters of health, safety and tourism; whatever the intention was for the future, it was presently the case that much of the US population did not speak fluent English. Nevertheless, voters continued to back moves for a single official language. In November 1988 84% of those voting in Florida backed a proposition to make English the state's official language, while 61% of Colorado voters and 51% of Arizona voters approved similar propositions in their respective states.

Some of the insistence that English be made the official language with immediate effect stemmed from a sense that multilingualism might become a greater possibility in the not-too-remote future as a result of further immigration of non-English speakers, though this view assumed that these immigrants would wish to retain their own languages. It also tended to neglect their need to communicate with each other, as well as with the host society, through a common language. In California the debate over making English the official language was much affected by the publication, in late 1985, of a study by the California Population Research Unit which suggested that, between 1985 and 2010, the proportion of whites in the state's population would fall from 64% to 47% while that of Hispanics would rise from 22% to 32% and that of Asians from 7% to 13%.

ILLEGAL IMMIGRATION

A second factor was contributing to the general unease, in that it was widely felt that official statistics underestimated the demographic changes occurring in the USA because they could not take account of illegal immigration. Logically, there were no figures for this, although some commentators put the number of illegal immigrants in the USA at 7m. in the early 1980s. Many of these were believed to be from Mexico, given that it was comparatively easy to cross the long common border and that the Mexican work-force was growing at 3.5% a year, a rate with which the Mexican economy could not cope.

Officials faced two problems: what to do about those illegal immigrants already in the USA; and how to control and deter such movement in the future. Mexican-American groups were opposed to any measures that might lead to 'witch-hunts'; US employers of aliens suspected of entering the country illegally were not happy with the possibility of punishment. In 1986, following a number of attempts at legislation, Congress passed and President Reagan signed an Immigration Reform and Control Act regulating the status of aliens in the USA and granting amnesty to illegal aliens who could prove they had been resident there continuously since before 1 January 1982. Those illegal aliens who could prove that they had worked in the USA for at least 90 days in each of the previous three years would become eligible for lawful temporary resident status, which could be made permanent after a further two years. Such men and women would further become eligible for citizenship after another five years. In future, employers of illegal immigrants would be fined to a degree which, it was hoped, would both deter them from employing such labour in the future and dry up at source the sort of jobs that had attracted the labour itself into the USA.

REFUGEE MOVEMENTS

Despite rising anxieties about excessive heterogeneity in its population, the USA has continued to announce that it is ready to accept refugees. In September 1988 the then Secretary of State George Shultz told Congress that the USA planned to accept 94,000 refugees in 1989, some 20,000 more than in 1988. Of these, some 53,000 (56%) were to come from south-east Asia. The USA had already admitted at least 413,000 refugees from that region since 1981: 97,000 from Laos, 116,000 from Kampuchea, and 200,000 from Vietnam. The USA has always distinguished, however, between 'economic' and 'political' refugees, and policy has reflected this distinction. Hostility to refugees fleeing poor economic conditions in their homelands has grown during the early part of 1989, due to a sharply rising tide of refugees from Central America. Like immigrants generally of late, most refugees that have been allowed to stay have tended to have pre-existing ties with the USA and only a few thousand have been admitted with none.

Refugee programmes are expensive to run and vulnerable in an age of budget deficits. Consequently, officials in the USA have, for instance, already had to consider ending the broad guarantee of refugee status and subsequent resettlement assistance for Soviet Jews. Many may have to be given the status of 'parolees', which will mean that they will no longer be reimbursed for the cost of flights out of the USSR, nor will there be any automatic qualification for US citizenship or even for permanent residence. In the past, political refugees have also been given medical assistance, welfare and other social benefits. Budget constraints may well affect the surveillance of illegal immigration by limiting the number of officials administering and patrolling borders and thus creating further tensions in the south-west. Black groups in the region have been particularly anxious about influxes of aliens, whom they expect to compete with black workers for scarce unskilled jobs.

Conclusion

The USA has always been a nation of immigrants and has been largely built by its immigrants. It has also been, in Walt Whitman's words, 'not merely a nation but a teeming of nations', something which has had its implications for the peace of US society. Yet the USA has never lost its faith that it can turn heterogeneous multitudes into Americans and the products of many nations into one. In this it has not been unique, as the histories of Canada, Australia and Brazil, among others, show. No other country, however, has attracted so many immigrants during its history and none, today, continues to accept them in such numbers.

SELECT BIBLIOGRAPHY

Ahlstrom, S. E. *A Religious History of the American People* (2 vols). New Haven, Connecticut, Yale University Press, 1972.

Allen, J. P. and Tucker, E. *We the People: An Atlas of America's Ethnic Diversity*. New York, Macmillan Publishing Co, 1988.

Berkowitz, E. D. *Disabled Policy: America's Programmes for the Handicapped*. Cambridge, UK, and New York, Cambridge University Press, 1987.

Biracre, T. and Biracre, N. *The Almanac of the American People*. New York, Facts on File Inc, 1988.

Bodnar, J. *The Transplanted: A History of Immigrants in Urban America*. Bloomington, Indiana, Indiana University Press, 1985.

Bradbury, K. L., Downs, A. and Small, K. A. *Urban Decline and the Future of American Cities*. Washington, DC, The Brookings Institution, 1982.

Bradshaw, M. *Regions and Regionalism in the United States*. London, Macmillan Publishers Ltd, 1988.

Clark, D. *Post-Industrial America: A Geographical Perspective*. London and New York, Methuen & Co Ltd, 1985.

Dilger, R. J. *The Sunbelt-Snowbelt Controversy: The War Over Federal Funds*. New York and London, New York University Press, 1982.

The Economist. *American Survey*. London, 17 September 1988.

Fox, K. *Metropolitan America: Urban Life and Urban Policy in the United States, 1940–80*. London, Macmillan Publishers Ltd, 1985.

Gann, L. H. and Duignan, P. J. *The Hispanics in the United States: A History*. Stanford, California, Hoover Institution Press, 1988.

Glazer, N. *Clamor at the Gates: The New American Immigration*. San Francisco, California, ICS Press, 1985.

Goggin, M. L. *Policy Design and the Politics of Implementation: The Case of Child Healthcare in the American States*. Knoxville, Tennessee, University of Tennessee Press, 1987.

Griffith, E. S. *The American System of Government* (6th edn). New York and London, Methuen Inc, 1983.

Gutmann, A. (Ed.). *Democracy and the Welfare State*. Princeton, New Jersey, Princeton University Press, 1988.

Handlin, O. *The Uprooted*. Boston, Massachusetts, Little, Brown and Co Inc, 1951.

Higham, J. *Send These to Me: Immigrants in Urban America*. Baltimore, Maryland, The Johns Hopkins University Press, 1984.

   Strangers in the Land: Patterns of American Nativism, 1860–1925. London, Greenwood Press, 1981.

Hoover, K. and Plant, R. *Conservative Capitalism in Britain and the United States: A Critical Appraisal*. London and New York, Routledge, 1989.

House, J. W. (Ed.). *United States Public Policy: A Geographical View*. Oxford, Oxford University Press, 1983.

Howe, I. *World of Our Fathers*. New York, Simon & Schuster Inc, 1976.

Huntington, S. P. *American Politics: The Promise of Disharmony*. Cambridge, Massachusetts, Harvard University Press, 1982.

Jackson, G. *Regional Diversity: Growth in the United States, 1960–90*. Dover, Massachusetts, Auburn House Publishing Co, 1981.

Jones, M. A. *American Immigration*. Chicago, Illinois, University of Chicago Press, 1960.

Kagan, S. L. (Ed.). *America's Family Support Programs: Perspectives and Prospects*. New Haven, Connecticut, Yale University Press, 1988.

Knox, P. L., Bartels, E. H., Bohland, J. R., Holcomb, B. and Johnston, R. J. *The United States: A Contemporary Human Geography*. London, Longman, 1988.

Kotz, N. *Let Them Eat Promises: The Politics of Hunger in America*. New York, Achor Books, 1971.

Lehman Schlozman, K. (Ed.). *Elections in America*. Boston, Massachusetts and London, Allen & Unwin Inc, 1987.

Lieberson, S. *Piece of the Pie: Black and White Immigrants Since 1880*. Berkeley, California, University of California Press, 1981.

Lohr, K. N. and Marquis, M. S. *Medicare and Medicaid: Past, Present and Future*. Santa Monica, California, The RAND Corporation, 1984.

Mann, A. *One and the Many: Reflections on the American Identity*. Chicago, Illinois, University of Chicago Press, 1979.

Marmor, T. R. *Political Analysis and American Medical Care: Essays*. New York and Cambridge, UK, Cambridge University Press, 1983.

Marshall, T. R. *Public Opinion and the Supreme Court*. Boston, Massachusetts and London, Unwin Hyman Inc, 1989.

Morrison, J. and Zabusky, C. *American Mosaic: The Immigrant Experience in the Words of Those Who Lived It*. New York, E. P. Dutton Inc, 1980.

Moynihan, D. P. *The Politics of a Guaranteed Income: The Nixon Administration and the Family Assistance Plan*. New York, Vintage Books, 1973.

National Urban League. *The State of Black America*. New Brunswick, New Jersey, Transaction Books, 1983.

Novak, M. *The Rise of the Unmeltable Ethnics: Politics and Culture in the 1970s*. New York, Macmillan Publishing Co, 1972.

Oxford Analytica. *America in Perspective*. Boston, Massachusetts, Houghton Mifflin Co, 1986.

Paton, C. R. 'British and American Health Policy: Recent Lessons from One System to Another' in *International Journal of Health Planning and Management*, Vol. 1, No. 5. Chichester, West Sussex, John Wiley & Sons Ltd, 1985.

Phillips, K. *The Emerging Republican Majority*. Garden City, New York, Doubleday, 1969.

Pierce, N. R. and Hagstrom, J. *The Book of America: Inside Fifty States Today*. New York, Warner Books Inc, 1984.

Sawers, L. and Tabb, W. K. *Sunbelt-Snowbelt: Urban Development and Regional Restructuring*. New York and Oxford, Oxford University Press, 1984.

Sowell, T. *Ethnic America: A History*. New York, Basic Books Inc, 1981.

Tatalovich, R. and Daynes, B. W. *Social Regulatory Policy: Moral Controversies in American Politics.* Boulder, Colorado and London, Westview Press Inc, 1988.

Taylor, P. *The Distant Magnet: European Emigration to the USA.* New York, Harper and Row, Publishers Inc, 1971.

Thernstrom, S. (Ed.). *The Harvard Encyclopedia of American Ethnic Groups.* Cambridge, Massachusetts, Harvard University Press, 1980.

US Bureau of the Census. *America's Black Population: 1970–82.* Washington, DC, Government Printing Office, 1983.

Population Profile of the United States, 1984–85. Washington, DC, Government Printing Office, 1987.

Statistical Abstract of the United States: 1988 (108th edn). Washington, DC, Government Printing Office, 1987.

Williams, P. M. 'Battle Hymns of the Republic' in *The Times Higher Education Supplement.* London, 7 May 1982.

Wolfe, T. 'Mau-mauing the Flak Catchers' in *The Purple Decades.* London, Penguin, 1984.

Wuthnow, R. *The Restructuring of American Religion.* Princeton, New Jersey, Princeton University Press, 1988.

THE INTERNATIONAL ROLE OF THE USA

US FOREIGN POLICY

PHIL WILLIAMS

Introduction

One of the paradoxes of US foreign affairs since 1945 is that a relatively coherent policy has emerged out of a process which at best is highly fragmented and at worst is chaotic. De Tocqueville, writing in the 19th century, claimed that the USA lacked most of the qualities necessary for the efficient conduct of foreign policy. More recent commentators have made similar observations, arguing that a political system which constantly pits the president against Congress, encourages bureaucratic rivalry and organizational pluralism and places faith in democratic controls is ill-equipped to provide the qualities of leadership, judiciousness and steadfastness which would appear indispensable to a consistent US world role. The difficulties are exacerbated by an approach to foreign policy that often appears to place idealism over realism, regards rhetoric excess as necessary to mobilize popular support and seems insensitive to the problems confronting other nations.

Such analyses are, in many respects, very persuasive. The separation of powers, as has often been noted, is an invitation for the president and Congress to struggle for the privilege of directing US foreign policy. During the first two post-war decades this was not too great a problem. The bipartisan consensus created by the Truman and Eisenhower administrations, together with the widespread belief in Congress that the president needed freedom to act decisively in order to protect US national security, limited the congressional impact on foreign policy. With the US involvement in the Vietnam War from 1961–75, however, and especially after the Watergate scandal of 1972–74, this mood of deference gave way to a new assertiveness and Congress took steps to ensure that it played a much more active role in the policy-making process. The most important measure was the War Powers Act of 1973 which stated that the president could commit US troops to hostilities for only 60 days without congressional approval. (This legislation had not properly been put to the test by mid-1989.) Nevertheless, during the 1970s Congress intruded into the policy-making process and on several occasions severely complicated US policy, especially towards the Soviet Union. In the 1980s, under President Reagan, the National Security Council's attempt to circumvent congressional restrictions on supplying military assistance to opponents of the Nicaraguan government resulted in the Iran–Contra affair.

In addition to the problems stemming from a system based on what the Democrat politician Richard Neustadt described as 'separate institutions sharing powers', there are difficulties resulting from a large and diversified foreign-policy-making system in which government agencies compete vigorously to promote their preferred policies, sometimes obscuring broader conceptions of the national interest. Even when the participants rise above considerations of organizational advantage, this is no guarantee of consensus. In both the Carter and Reagan administrations conflicts among the presidents' leading foreign-policy advisers were rooted as much in differences of outlook and judgement as in competing institutional roles. Under Carter, the main conflict was between the National Security Adviser, Zbigniew Brzezinski, and the Secretary of State, Cyrus Vance; under Reagan it was between the Secretary of Defense, Caspar Weinberger, and the Secretary of State, George Shultz. In the former case the differences were philosophical; in the latter they were tactical. The experience of the last two decades, however, suggests that such conflict—which can be debilitating in its effects—is endemic.

Containment

It is somewhat surprising, therefore, that this rather turbulent and competitive foreign-policy-making process has produced policies which have been remarkably resilient and have been pursued by successive administrations since the late 1940s. This is explicable partly in terms of enduring geopolitical realities, a widespread acceptance of the US leadership role and a broad consensus on policy objectives, albeit combined somewhat uneasily with perennial and sometimes bitter disputes about how policy can best be implemented. Fundamentally, though, it is the policy framework of containment of the Soviet Union, established in the late 1940s, which has supplied this policy consistency.

The immediate post-war period was one of considerable uncertainty about the principles on which international relations would function, about future patterns of co-operation and conflict, and about the future role and responsibilities of the USA. The Truman administration responded to this challenge in a way which not only ended the uncertainty but defined the objectives of post-war foreign policy, established patterns of commitment that did much to determine the allocation of economic and military resources, and mobilized a bipartisan consensus that endured until the late 1960s.

The Truman administration's foreign policy stems partly from the famous telegram, sent in 1946 from Moscow by George Kennan, which helped to establish the idea of the Soviet Union as an expansionist power; partly from the post-war division of Europe; and partly from the need to mobilize congressional and public opinion to accept a global role. The result was an assessment of the Soviet Union as implacably hostile to the values of the West, and a policy designed to prevent the spread of Soviet power and ideology. The containment policy was outlined in the Truman Doctrine of March 1947 and, apart from the first two years of the Carter administration, has provided the overriding objective of US policy ever since. However, the geographical focus of containment has expanded and contracted at various times, and the means to implement the policy have been changed on several occasions; there were several shifts in implementation even between 1947 and the end of the Truman presidency.

Initially containment was confined to Western Europe and emphasized economic recovery. Western Europe was to be given economic aid sufficient to eliminate the poverty and dissatisfaction which allowed communist parties to flourish, especially in France and Italy, and offered the Soviet Union opportunities to extend its influence. The Marshall Plan was intended to revive Western Europe and thereby re-establish an indigenous counter-weight to the Soviet Union in Europe. This was to prevent the USA from becoming too deeply entangled, politically and economically, in the affairs of the continent and to encourage the emergence of a pluralist world order. It was somewhat ironic, therefore, that Marshall aid, which was initially intended to limit US involvement in Europe, became the rationale for extending this involvement and eventually led to the deployment of US troops in Europe. As relations with the Soviet Union deteriorated—largely because of the Western decision to facilitate West German economic recovery and political rehabilitation—so West European insecurity increased and it became clear that without some kind of security guarantee to boost confidence, the indigenous investment required to bring the Marshall Plan to fruition would not be forthcoming.

The North Atlantic Treaty of April 1949 provided this guarantee, even though at that time there was no significant fear of a Soviet invasion. Several developments within the next 15 months, however, radically altered this assessment. The Soviet explosion of an atomic bomb, combined with Mao Zedong's victory in China, prompted the USA to carry out a reappraisal of its commitments and capabilities. The result was National Security Council memorandum Number 68 (NSC-68), drafted mainly by Paul Nitze, then Head of the Department of State's Policy Planning Staff, arguing that the Soviet threat was essentially a military one and the USA had to make far greater efforts to counter it. This assessment was not accepted by the Truman administration until after the North Korean attack on South Korea in June 1950: it was assumed not only that the Soviet Union was responsible for the North Korean action, but that the war heralded a change in Soviet tactics to include overt aggression and not just political pressure. The US response spread containment to Asia, and effectively transformed it from a political to a military doctrine in Europe. As well as becoming involved in the Korean War, Washington deployed forces to Western Europe, initiated the process of West German rearmament and created an integrated military-command structure. Although Kennan was the initial author of containment, he was appalled at what he saw as a distortion of his conception.

The history of US foreign policy since this time can be seen as one in which Nitze's conception of containment has dominated, but in which Kennan's ideas have occasionally come back to the fore. Nitze's contention that the threat was military was buttressed by his argument that nuclear deterrence would be effective only until the Soviet Union developed a counter-deterrent. At this point Moscow would be free to use its conventional superiority to engage in local and limited aggression. This could only be prevented if the USA was able to match the Soviet Union at the local conventional level. In other words, Nitze advocated what John Gaddis has subsequently termed 'symmetrical containment'.

From Massive Retaliation to Flexible Response

The problem with this approach was its cost in terms of lives, money and domestic political popularity. Not surprisingly, therefore, President Eisenhower, a fiscal conservative greatly concerned about the impact of military spending on economic and social well-being, reverted to asymmetrical containment. Rather than relying on conventional forces to deter conventional aggression, he emphasized the possibility that the USA would retaliate massively at times and places of its own choosing. The debate over this strategy was a vigorous one, with Nitze and other critics, mainly found among the Democrats, demanding greater flexibility.

While the Eisenhower administration retreated only slightly from a rather relaxed notion of how containment should be implemented, its successor reverted to the logic of NSC-68. President John F. Kennedy not only reaffirmed the principle of symmetrical containment, but promised to pursue it with a vigour that was unprecedented. His inaugural address was a cold-war call to arms, a declaration which combined the ideological belligerence of the Truman Doctrine with the crusading zeal and military logic of NSC-68. Massive retaliation was replaced with the strategy of flexible response (although this was not accepted by NATO as a whole until 1967) and the reluctance of Eisenhower to become involved in another ground war in Asia was superseded by a determination to demonstrate to the Soviet Union that it could not benefit from limited aggression either directly or through the use of proxies. Conventional aggression was to be met with a conventional response and Vietnam was the test case to demonstrate to Moscow that its support for wars of national liberation was ineffectual. The deepening US involvement, therefore, was the logical consequence of the idea of symmetrical containment.

Lyndon Johnson, successor to Kennedy on the latter's assassination, feared that conservative reaction to any US withdrawal from Vietnam would undermine domestic support for his presidency and for his 'Great Society' programme, but his escalatory policies had the opposite effect and precipitated a liberal defection from the foreign-policy consensus. Democratic

senators such as William Fulbright and Michael Mansfield, who had not only been among the most stalwart internationalists on Capitol Hill but also among the strongest supporters of presidential power, began demanding withdrawal from Vietnam and a less militarized approach to foreign policy in general. They also took the lead in attempts to re-establish congressional prerogatives to balance the power of the presidency.

The Nixon–Kissinger Era

In 1969, therefore, President Richard Nixon and his National Security Adviser, Henry Kissinger, inherited a foreign policy in disarray: the USA was bogged down in a war that seemed unwinnable, the limits of US power had been revealed by the *Tet* offensive of early 1968 (during which Saigon, Hué and many other towns were attacked), the cold-war consensus had disintegrated and there were demands for the abandonment of containment. The response to this was not to abandon containment but to develop a programme for its implementation that was both imaginative and less burdensome than the symmetrical strategy of the Kennedy–Johnson years.

Many of the basic concepts that underlay US foreign policy during the Nixon and Ford administrations were outlined in a study made by Henry Kissinger shortly before he became National Security Adviser. There were also important echoes of the approach adopted by the Eisenhower administration during the 1950s. The basic premise was that domestic pressures required the USA to restrict its foreign commitments: yet US interests still had to be upheld. The solution was to co-opt allies and adversaries into a US diplomatic and strategic design. Allies were to take a greater share of the burden of Western security: the war in Vietnam was to be fought by the South Vietnamese; Western Europe was to share more of the NATO burden and the Shah of Iran was to act as the US surrogate in the Gulf. Secondly, the People's Republic of China was to be drawn into a system of 'triangular diplomacy' in which the USA could offset the two major communist powers against each other. Thirdly, the Soviet Union was to be persuaded to adopt a policy of self-containment and to refrain from taking advantage of the USA's inability to compete effectively in the Third World. Soviet restraint was to be cultivated through offering Moscow incentives for 'good behaviour' and imposing penalties for transgressions.

There were several problems with the Nixon–Kissinger design, which deprived it of the domestic legitimacy attained by US cold-war policies during the 1950s and early 1960s. It recognized US weakness, yet still assumed that the USA could manipulate other states to conform to US preferences and conceptions. It also required a strong centralized control and the absence of domestic challenge, while *détente* appeared to diminish the need for the presidential dominance which had been evident throughout the years of Soviet–US tensions. Watergate compounded the congressional challenge to presidential dominance over Vietnam, and the result was a power vacuum at the centre of US politics. This was particularly evident when Congress took away first the inducements for Soviet 'good behaviour' by restricting trade and credits with Moscow, and then the penalty for 'bad behaviour' by prohibiting covert aid to the US-supported factions in the Angolan civil war. The final problem was that the Soviet Union did not accept Kissinger's conception of permissible behaviour: for Moscow *détente* was about equality rather than restraint—something that it had earned through the attainment of strategic parity.

Carter's 'World Order'

Thus the Carter administration, like that of Nixon, came to office at a time when US foreign policy appeared to be in a state of considerable confusion. The policy of military containment had been replaced by a political and economic containment which was not proving effective; US power and prestige had declined, and the office of the presidency had been deeply tarnished. Carter sought to reintroduce morality into US foreign policy, to change the agenda so that the USA could still provide leadership and direction, and replace the traditional preoccupation with the Soviet challenge and East–West relations with emphasis on 'world-order' issues and North–South relations. Consequently the first two years of the Carter presidency saw containment relegated to a relatively unimportant place in US foreign policy. It was argued that, while the Soviet Union might make geopolitical gains in the Third World, these would not be enduring given the power of nationalist forces.

This fairly sanguine view of the Soviet challenge was not accepted by domestic critics of the Carter administration. Paul Nitze now became a leading figure in the Committee on the Present Danger (CPD), a bipartisan organization dedicated to alerting the US public to the danger posed by Soviet strategic programmes. The CPD claimed that Moscow was intent on achieving strategic superiority and that the administration was doing nothing to prevent this. SALT (Strategic Arms Limitation Talks) II, which had been initiated by the Nixon administration, was castigated for encouraging a degree of US strategic restraint that was not reciprocated by the Soviet Union.

Although these critics exaggerated the Soviet threat and ignored the US force modernization that took place throughout the 1970s, there were several factors which made their interpretation compelling and eroded support for the 'world-order' foreign policy. Probably the most important of these was Soviet activism in the Third World. In the latter half of the 1970s the Soviet Union exploited instability in several regions, lending credence to the argument that *détente* was fraudulent and that the Carter administration was negligent of US security. Even the National Security Adviser, Zbigniew Brzezinski, contended that Soviet actions had created an 'arc of crisis'. The Soviet Union became a scapegoat for a USA which had suffered a series of foreign-policy reverses and which was increasingly experiencing a sense of malaise. *Détente* became synonymous with decline; accordingly, recovery could take place only if there was a rejection of *détente*.

The End of *Détente*

The Carter administration was unable to remain impervious to congressional and public pressure for more assertive policies and, after two years of the 'world-order' approach, it gradually moved back towards the mainstream. In 1979 Carter attempted to mobilize support for the SALT II Treaty by combining it with a more robust approach to national security. It was the Soviet invasion of Afghanistan in December of that year, however, which crystallized a new cold-war consensus. During 1980 Carter embraced traditional containment policies. His state-of-the-union address warned the Soviet Union that the USA had vital interests in the Gulf, while the emphasis that was placed on the Rapid Deployment Force highlighted the end of the administration's indifference to events in the Third World.

Consequently the transition from Carter to Reagan was less dramatic than is often suggested. The differences were in style and presentation rather than substance, with President Reagan rapidly establishing himself as a much more enthusiastic 'cold warrior' than Carter. The Reagan administration was also more assertive in its foreign policy, emphasizing that the USA was determined to re-establish its status as the leading superpower and that it would only negotiate from positions of strength. The early 1980s was a dismal period in terms of East–West relations during which the Soviet Union was seriously concerned about the possibility of US aggression. Superpower negotiations on arms control were broken off by Moscow when US Intermediate Nuclear Forces (INF) began to arrive in Europe (implementing a decision that had been made by the Carter administration and its European allies), and Reagan described the Soviet Union as the source of evil in the world. The rhetoric was matched by changes in nuclear strategy which appeared to be part of a drive for renewed strategic superiority, with plans for a new generation of land-based missiles and the innovatory Strategic Defense Initiative.

The USA also appeared to be in a strong position in the superpower competition in the Third World. In the first half of the 1980s the Soviet Union was reappraising the benefits of international activism. The gains that had been made in the 1970s were, in the 1980s, a continuing drain on Soviet resources. Furthermore, the administration attempted to go beyond containment. By supporting wars of national liberation against recently-installed Marxist regimes, Reagan hoped to put further pressure on the Soviet Union. Although this policy, embodied in what was termed the 'Reagan Doctrine', had some limited success, it was hampered by congressional reluctance to fund the levels of assistance requested by the executive branch.

The Reagan administration saw regional crises in global terms. Unrest in Central America was attributed to the efforts of the Sandinista government of Nicaragua, supported by Cuba and the Soviet Union, to export revolution. There was nothing new in this. The same kind of attitude had prevailed over Vietnam, and had been evident in Kissinger's policy towards Angola prior to the congressional ban on covert funds for factions fighting the Soviet-backed Movimento Popular de Libertação de Angola (MPLA). Similar reasoning, together with the influence of the Jewish lobby, dictated the often uncritical support for Israel in the USA's Middle East policy. This support, however, acted to compromise US attempts to play the role of even-handed mediator in the Arab–Israeli dispute, while geopolitical considerations, and particularly the desire to exclude the Soviet Union from the peace process, undermined genuine understanding of the subtleties of regional politics. In the last weeks of the Reagan administration, however, the USA did begin a dialogue with the Palestine Liberation Organization (PLO), a development that provoked considerable strains in relations with Israel.

The Gorbachev Era

The more flexible approach displayed towards the PLO was symptomatic of more fundamental changes that, often rather subtly, had taken place in the policy of the Reagan administration. This was especially the case in the relationship with the Soviet Union. During Reagan's second term a dialogue with the Soviet Union was developed that went far beyond anything that had seemed possible during the tense years of the early 1980s. Among the reasons for this was that Reagan believed that he had regenerated US power and could therefore negotiate from strength. This new-found confidence coincided with the appointment, in 1985, of a Soviet leader, Mikhail Gorbachev, far more flexible than his predecessors and anxious to improve East–West relations in order to engage in domestic economic reform and restructuring. Even so, the administration was divided between those who wanted to put pressure on the Soviet Union through an intensified arms race and tight restrictions on technology transfer, and those, such as Secretary of State George Shultz, who wanted a more moderate approach based on negotiation and compromise. Gradually the president came to favour negotiation, and a series of summit meetings with the Soviet leader led to the signing of the INF Treaty in December 1987. This provided for all land-based nuclear missiles with a range between 500 and 5,500 km to be removed from Europe. In June 1988 President Reagan visited Moscow and, although this summit did not yield much of substance, the symbolism of a visit to the heart of what he had once referred to as the 'evil empire' was immense.

At the end of the Reagan administration, the USA remained suspicious about the ultimate goals of Soviet foreign policy, but recognized that the depth of Soviet economic problems made containment far less of a problem than it had appeared during the 1970s. This was fortuitous, as the USA had serious problems of its own. Perhaps the most important concerned what had become known as the issue of US decline. In a sense, the limits of power had been evident since the late 1960s. The administrations of the 1970s had tried to accommodate these limits, albeit in very different ways, while the Reagan administration had attempted to transcend them. Psychologically, President Reagan had been successful, and restored a buoyancy to the US public that had not been evident since the early 1960s. Yet the incoming Bush administration faced several problems, the response to which would do much to determine whether the policy framework that had been dominant since the late 1940s would endure or be modified.

The major item on the presidential policy agenda in January 1989 was the twin deficits—budget and trade. There was a growing consensus that policies which hampered moves towards a balanced budget or an increased US competitiveness in world markets were untenable. Although some commentators argued that the only way of dealing with the budget deficit was to increase taxes, Bush had pledged not to do this. Furthermore, the demands of US security policy, and an actual or potential imbalance between international commitments and the capabilities necessary to maintain them, were identified as major causes of the problem. There was universal acceptance that the Bush administration would have to make painful choices in the defence budget. While many of these choices would be determined as a result of bureaucratic bargaining, others would depend on (and in turn help to determine) the future relationship of the USA with both its allies and its principal adversary.

By embracing a less acrimonious and more co-operative relationship with the Soviet Union the Reagan administration had moved in directions that were not foreseen when it came into office. Although this improvement in superpower relations could be followed by another deterioration, thereby reaffirming the familiar cycle of *détente* and cold war, it seems more likely that the internal changes in the Soviet Union, combined with the increasingly rapid erosion of the bipolar international system, could promote more substantive and enduring changes. Should Gorbachev succeed in restructuring Soviet conventional forces towards a more defensive posture, thus easing many of the traditional concerns of NATO, this would be even more likely.

A further reduction of East–West tensions, accompanied by significant arms reductions at the nuclear and conventional levels, would ease some of the budgetary difficulties facing US security-policy makers. It would also offer more scope for the changes in US alliances called for by those who resent the failure of Western Europe and Japan to shoulder their fair shares of the defence burden. Many mean not so much 'burden-sharing' as 'burden-shedding'—if the allies do more the USA can do less. Even if this sentiment is contained, the Bush administration will almost certainly find it necessary to promote the 'orderly devolution' of roles, risks and responsibilities from the USA to Western Europe and Japan. The Nixon administration's emphasis on a polycentric world was premature, but may yet provide a model for the 1990s and beyond.

A third foreign-policy problem for the Bush administration is how to deal with the Third World. It has become increasingly apparent that the imposition of a superpower template on diverse and individualistic regions of the Third World is both inadequate and ill-advised. Neither can the Third World simply be seen as an arena for US military intervention. Although

the Reagan administration's actions against Libya and Grenada (in April 1986 and November 1983 respectively) and its ongoing involvement in Lebanon appeared to have taken the USA beyond the 'Vietnam Syndrome', Reagan's Secretary of State, George Shultz, believed that the threat of force was essential to effective and credible diplomacy, while his Secretary of Defense, Caspar Weinberger, was always reluctant to use US troops in the Third World, be it the Middle East or Central America. The resolution of this argument will determine whether the (possibly outdated) reliance on superpower military domination can be replaced by a more constructive approach to Third World instability.

Bush's Challenge

In spite of the beginnings of superpower strategic disengagement in the Third World, the problems of insecurity and instability are likely to increase in the 1990s. The spread of ballistic-missile technology, the emergence of new arms suppliers from within the Third World itself and the diffusion of chemical and nuclear capabilities demand a positive US response that has at least some of the vision of the 'world-order' approach briefly adopted by the Carter administration during 1977 and 1978.

The foreign-policy agenda facing the Bush administration, therefore, was both full and formidable. In mid-1989 the ability of the new administration to devise an effective strategy for dealing with the problems had yet to be proved. The fate of Carter's 'world-order' policy suggests that imaginative attempts to deal with new problems have less appeal than traditional means of coping with familiar challenges. While the USA could display continuity and consistency in the pursuit of containment of the Soviet Union, the challenge was a relatively simple one. The challenges of the 1990s and the next century will be both more complex and more differentiated: the international system of bipolarity is in the process of being replaced by one of multipolarity; the traditional instruments of foreign policy, such as the use of force, are regarded as less legitimate and effective than ever before; and the USA's traditional security allies are increasingly becoming its economic adversaries. The US political system, in which bureaucratic parochialism and congressional self-indulgence combine with the volatility of public opinion, makes the devising of a rational response to these challenges fraught with difficulties.

The Bush administration may be tempted to distance itself from the role of global leadership, effectively to return to the isolationism of the 1920s and 1930s, and focus on the resolution of domestic problems. Alternatively it may be able to continue the efforts to maintain international order, even though the USA's position as a determinant of the international system has been seriously eroded.

US DEFENCE POLICY

DAVID ROBERTSON

Introduction

With the possible exception of the Soviet Union, since the Second World War the USA has consistently spent more on defence, both in absolute terms and as a percentage of gross national product (GNP), than any other developed country. At its peacetime height in 1960 (seven years after the end of the Korean War and four years before the first active US involvement in Vietnam) the US defence budget reached a peak as a proportion of all federal spending, at 52%; in the same year it also accounted for more than 9% of GNP. In 1968, during the Vietnam War, the defence budget again exceeded 9% of GNP, but accounted for only 46% of total federal spending. Since then, defence spending has represented significantly lower proportions of both GNP and total federal spend-

ing (partly explained by the increasing importance of other budgetary items, particularly social spending). The lowest figures were reached during the Carter administration (4.8% of GNP in 1978 and 1979, and 22.6% of federal spending in 1980). The relative weight of the defence budget increased again during the 1980s, reaching 6.5% of GNP and 27% of federal spending in the later years of the Reagan administration. The fact that the USA's NATO allies spent an average of only about 3% of their respective GNPs on defence during the 1980s illuminates one of the major debates over the direction of US defence policy.

Despite the consistently-high level of defence spending, at no time since 1945 has the USA been confident that it wielded the forces necessary to carry out the military tasks that the country's security policy has set for the Department of

Defense. This, however, is as much a consequence of the nature of the US defence system as of the level of spending.

As in any country, defence policy in the USA is the result of an interaction between several elements. The most important among these are the perception of military threat, the definition of crucial national interests, the war-fighting doctrines of the military, the technological base and the government's general public-expenditure policies. These are the more definable elements in the equation; in addition, such matters as inter-service rivalry, the structure and expectations of the military profession, the entrenched interests of the defence industries and their political allies in Congress, and public attitudes towards military strength have all affected the development of policy.

A further complication stems from the number of people with legitimate roles in deciding defence policy. Apart from the civilian and military leaders of the Department of Defense, and the President and the White House Office staff, there is the often-autonomous National Security Council and the Armed Services Committees of the two Houses of Congress. At least according to the more critical commentators, the sum effect of all these factors has been to accumulate tasks in excess of capacity, and to ensure that the capacity that does exist is inefficiently designed, over-expensively equipped and unprofessionally wielded to such extent that serious doubts must exist about the USA's ability to defend its interests. Those holding some or all of these views include a large number of influential legislators, probably a majority of defence journalists and civilian defence analysts, and at least large minorities of all groups in the overall 'defence community'.

The Structure of Defence Planning

The post-war era can conveniently be defined as starting in 1947, when the Department of Defense (DOD), the separate services, and other institutions, such as the National Security Council (NSC) and the Central Intelligence Agency (CIA), were set up in their current form. Since then the operational aspects of defence policy have rested on a structure of three armed services—the Air Force (USAF), which had not been an independent service before 1947, the Army and the Navy (USN). (There is a fourth fighting service, the US Marine Corps—USMC—, but it is effectively under the control of the Navy.) Between them these three services operate three different types of military force—strategic nuclear (USAF and USN), tactical nuclear (all three) and conventional (all three).

Individually, the services, with the possible exception of the army, are far from united. The Air Force is effectively split between the strategic nuclear force, known as the Strategic Air Command (SAC), and various commands which carry both the bulk of the conventional tasks and an important tactical nuclear role. The Navy is divided into at least three camps: the submarine service, which includes the navy's strategic nuclear submarines; naval aviation, which, on its huge aircraft carriers, wields the bulk of the Navy's tactical nuclear force and which also constitutes the principal means of long-distance troop transportation; and the main surface-fighting body of frigates, destroyers, cruisers and battleships. In most cases an officer's whole career will be inside one of these subdivisions, with primary loyalty devoted accordingly.

The military and civilian command structure which has to cope with this diversity is itself complex and cumbersome and is often criticized for being unable to exercise any cohesive policy control over it. The task is huge: in 1988 there were about 2.2m. military personnel on active duty, about 1.9m. in the reserves and over 1m. civilian DOD employees.

Control is exercised by parallel civilian and military structures. Each service has an executive department headed by the politically-appointed Secretaries for the Army, Navy and Air Force. To integrate and control these three branches there is, on the civilian side, the Secretary of Defense and the accompanying executive department, known as the Office of the Secretary of Defense (OSD). The principal job of the service secretaries and OSD is to handle procurement, the budget and major overall strategic policy. They do not command the services, and have no direct operational control.

Such overall operational command and planning as there is comes from the Joint Chiefs of Staff (JCS). This consists of the four service chiefs of staff (the head of the Navy is called the Chief of Naval Operations and that of the USMC the Commandant) under the chairmanship of a fifth senior officer, called the Chairman of the Joint Chiefs of Staff, together with a small, non-permanent, staff of military aides drawn from the separate services. Although it represents the pinnacle of the military machine, the JCS has never fulfilled the role of giving central direction to US military policy, neither during states of conflict, nor even in terms of organization, budgeting and procurement in peacetime. Each service chief tends to represent their separate service interests, while serving officers on the JCS staff know that their career hopes lie with pleasing their own service hierarchies, and therefore tender advice strictly from that perspective. Consequently the decisions of the JCS are made by compromising between individual service interests, or by trading and bargaining with support for programmes and policies when this cannot be done. The traditional functions of general staffs include giving sound military advice to the political leaders. Here again the JCS system has failed. Until recently the Chairman was not allowed to present personal advice, but had to report the consensus, often effectively a compromise, of the committee: the Pentagon Reorganization Act of 1986 attempted to reform the JCS system by making the Chairman the official adviser to the President.

Defence Budgeting and Procurement

The biggest single failure of the defence-policy-making establishment is probably its inability to get an adequate return from the huge defence budget. Of course this is typical of most Western defence systems, but there are reasons to suggest that in the US case those factors common to NATO are more extreme, and that there are, in addition, some unique factors. One problem is a consequence of the inter-service rivalry: there are, for example, three separate air forces in the US, one each for the Navy, the Marine Corps and the USAF itself. (If helicopters, widely used by the Army, are taken into account, there are four.) But instead of benefiting from economies of scale, the rivalries lead to separate designs for aircraft with almost identical missions, and to attendant problems of lack of interoperability. Congress has made valiant efforts to enforce joint procurement programmes, but such programmes are regularly given minimum priority, by mutual consent of all the services involved, when it comes to budget proposals.

A similar problem, more familiar amongst other NATO members, is the question of design economies. What is called 'gold-plating', adding every possible technological benefit to a weapon design with concern neither for the costs nor the actual military need, is rife. Stories of $1,000 coffee pots designed to withstand an aircraft crash, though true, trivialize what has become endemic and serious. The fault lies in the close interrelationship between the service officers and the defence industry. To be a project officer on a new fighter, tank or missile is crucial for a middle-ranking officer's career. There are two factors at work here: firstly, appreciation of a fine piece of equipment by service colleagues; secondly, the possibility of a lucrative post-service career within the defence industry (the American terminology for this phenomenon, which is equally applicable to most other parts of the federal bureaucracy, is 'the revolving door'). While corruption, as such, seldom occurs, these factors do nothing to encourage simpler, cheaper, weapons design; the second of these factors is a symptom of the 'military–industrial complex' warned against by President Dwight D. Eisenhower in his farewell address.

The weakness of central control, both from the JCS and from the civilian politicians in the OSD, furthers the problems of economic efficiency because it means that procurement policy does not follow from centrally-set strategic needs. Instead each service seeks to equip itself to meet each and every contingency. The lack of positive direction from the centre of the military allows Congress to assume a major role—one which is another cause of excessive defence expenditure. The defence budget set by the Pentagon has to pass through a series of committees in each House of Congress, most importantly the

House and Senate Armed Services Committees, and the House Appropriations Committee. In theory this should mean that any unnecessary fat in the budget is trimmed away. In practice it often means the opposite. The members of the Armed Services Committees all represent constituencies or states with major defence-industry plants or large military and naval facilities. Whatever their overall views on defence policy, they all fight to keep and expand military expenditure in their areas, often pushing for expenditure *above* that requested by the DOD.

When Congress does succeed in trimming a defence budget, the long-term consequences are often counter-productive. The institutional pressures described combine with the fact that spending authorizations are made on a single-year basis to ensure inefficiency. Told to cut their demands, the military almost never cancel a plan to purchase. Instead they extend the procurement plan for all items, merely buying fewer in the current year. All this does is to increase the unit price of each item bought, as well as bringing the total force on-line later than needed.

Military Doctrine and Reality

These problems of administrative structure and policy-making are not different from other areas of US government, but they are compounded, in a way not relevant to most policy areas, by the genuine difficulty the USA would have in defining a defence policy even under ideal conditions. There is no easy way of defining exactly what US defence policy is, or should be, because the country's vital national interests are so multifarious, and so dependent on subjective judgements. Until the Second World War the USA had been basically isolationist, opposed to alliances, concerned only with its own hemisphere where it had no discernible enemy. The military giant it has become was not anticipated even after that war started. In 1942 the building plans for the Pentagon were opposed on the grounds that there would be nothing for which to use it once the war ended. Though political commitments of a massive scale were made under the Truman administration's 'containment' policy in the late 1940s, and maintained under the 'Eisenhower Doctrine' of massive retaliation after that, there was no immediate attempt to provide the military capacity to back them. The first real surge in defence expenditure was caused by the Korean War, but even that was curtailed by the fiscally-conservative Eisenhower administration. The original definition of US military requirements was known as the 'two-and-a-half war' doctrine. This meant the USA should be able to fight as it had in the Second World War, with a major war effort both in Europe and the Pacific, and also fight a regional war in, for example, the Middle East. Over the years the obvious unattainability of this led to the goal being trimmed to a 'one-and-a-half-war' requirement—a world-war level engagement in Europe, and something of the size of the Vietnam conflict as well. Even this proved to be ambitious, as Vietnam employed over 3m. US troops over the period 1964–74, and the USA was forced to reduce its troop commitment to NATO in order to fight it. The only other serious conflict the USA has faced was in Korea and, in the eyes of many of its own military, it essentially lost that war to the technologically-inferior North Korean and Chinese armies. That war, desperately unpopular, was fought mainly by reservists recalled after their Second World War service. But the USA now no longer has such a pool of experienced ex-soldiers to call on, and, following the abolition of the draft (conscription) in 1973, has far fewer reserves in general.

In reality the USA has never had the military capacity to back its military commitments. In 1989 the Army and USMC between them could only field 21 active-duty divisions. (By contrast the USSR had 20 divisions in East Germany alone.) At no time could the USA have carried out Truman's promise to defend the 'free world' from attack, unless the attackers had co-operated by choosing only one battlefield, and that preferably where US troops were already forward deployed. Part of the problem is deployment itself—getting the troops and equipment where they are needed. Apart from Western Europe and South Korea, there are no sizeable permanent US

garrisons. In the days when Britain tried to play the world policeman role, it kept its troops widely distributed around the world (in India, Africa and the Middle East, for example). US forces would have to be delivered to crisis points after the crisis had started. Because the relevant capacity, troop ships, cargo aircraft and the like, are much less glamorous than aircraft carriers or fighter planes, the services have systematically underinvested in this aspect of preparedness.

An example of why this matters can be taken from US plans for intervention in the Middle East. In 1980 President Carter announced that this region was of vital concern to US national interests and that the USA would defend these interests, if necessary by force. He had already set up the Rapid Deployment Force (RDF), later to be known as Central Command (CENCOM), for this purpose. The RDF, however, has never been seen as capable of fighting a serious conventional war in the event, for example, of a Soviet invasion of Iran (which was seriously feared in the early 1980s). Instead, it was supposed to play a 'tripwire' role. This concept of conventional forces as a trigger mechanism for nuclear war has always been the US method of reconciling its inability to provide sufficient resources to match its commitments. In the Iran invasion scenario, one set of plans drawn up by the JCS called for the use of 200 tactical nuclear weapons on southern parts of the USSR and Iran after the wire had been 'tripped'.

The dependence of the USA on nuclear weapons to give its defence policy credibility dates from the immediate post-Hiroshima period. While changes in emphasis have been made through the publicly-announced, declaratory policy, actual 'nuclear use' plans have changed surprisingly little. This is true despite the huge technical developments that the US nuclear arsenal has undergone, and despite the even more vital changes that have occurred in the relative nuclear strengths of the USA and USSR.

MASSIVE RETALIATION

From the end of the Second World War until 1954 the USA's reliance on nuclear weapons was considerable, but the accompanying strategy was not totally new: the only weapons available—atomic bombs to be delivered by the SAC's bombers—were sufficiently few in number, and of sufficiently low yield, to be treated just as a rather more powerful version of traditional strategic bombing. Initially, the USA also expected to have a massive nuclear advantage over the USSR for a long time. There was very little in the way of organized nuclear planning at this stage, a properly-conceived total nuclear-war plan not being developed until the early 1960s. Largely as a result of the costs and pain of the Korean War, President Eisenhower produced the first declaratory nuclear policy in 1954. Usually described as 'massive retaliation', this policy amounted to a statement that the USA would no longer think in terms of traditional defence of its interests and allies by fighting a defensive war. Instead any incursion by the Soviet Union or its client states on territory the USA was pledged to defend would be met with a huge and paralysing nuclear attack on the Soviet heartland. (One reason for defining the policy in this way was that useful targets for a nuclear attack had been found wanting in Korea, but there could never be a lack of easy targets in the USSR itself.) Massive retaliation was, among other things, a way of making sense of the size of conventional force commitment the USA could afford to make in Europe. The newly-reorganized NATO had defined its conventional requirement against the USSR as 96 divisions, even though it did not then have, and has never had, as much as one-third of that capacity. Why then keep US troops in Europe at all, if they could never meet the assumed threat? Again the answer lies in the 'tripwire' thesis. By placing a US force which would require a major attack by a determined national army to overcome it—such an attack signalling unequivocally the hostile and aggressive intentions of the enemy—, whatever nuclear action was taken would essentially be justified.

Massive retaliation was never a very plausible doctrine, because of the inherent improbability that a limited but successful attack by Soviet conventional forces—one that captured, for example, Hamburg but went no further—really would be met by the destruction of Soviet cities. It rapidly became less plausible as the USSR built up its own strategic nuclear forces.

At the same time nuclear-weapons technology was advancing in such a way as to present a different way of making political use out of this form of warfare. By the early 1960s the USA had in place a nuclear structure, known as the 'triad', which has since become a hallowed and unarguable cornerstone. The nuclear triad consists of three strategic nuclear forces. One is, still, the SAC's air-force bombers, although these are now increasingly armed with Air-Launched Cruise Missiles (ALCMs) rather than traditional gravity bombs. The second, also controlled by the SAC, is the Intercontinental Ballistic Missile (ICBM), principally the various versions of Minuteman, now also the MX and soon, perhaps, the Midgetman. The third, controlled by the Navy, is the Submarine-Launched Ballistic Missile (SLBM), Polaris, later Poseidon and now Trident.

MUTUAL ASSURED DESTRUCTION

These last weapons were a vital element in the strategic doctrine that took over from massive retaliation during the Kennedy administration, called mutual assured destruction (MAD). The submarine-launched missiles were invulnerable. As long as a country had enough of them, it could guarantee, whatever the enemy did to it, to devastate them in return. MAD became the official declaratory policy during McNamara's period as Kennedy's and Lyndon Johnson's Secretary of Defense. It had several purposes as a policy description, apart from being a way of making sense of nuclear weapons in the face of a rapidly-growing Soviet capacity which made a non-sense of massive retaliation. Perhaps the most important purpose was to control the military's procurement ambitions, because by defining what counted as a guaranteed destructive minimum force it set an upper level to the numbers of warheads and delivery vehicles that could be needed. (The definition, destroying one-third of the population and two-thirds of the industrial capacity of the USSR, just happened to be the level that the USA already had planned when McNamara forced the policy through.)

FLEXIBLE RESPONSE

The use of some form of nuclear weaponry has remained central to US war plans ever since their acquisition. The strategic weapons are not seriously thought of as usable, but great reliance has always been put on other weapons, falling into various categories such as 'Theatre Nuclear Forces', 'Intermediate Nuclear Forces' (INF) and 'Tactical Nuclear Forces', which have been at the centre of arms-control negotiations for a decade. At early-1989 levels of conventional-force deployment, neither the US forces in particular, nor NATO in general, is capable of resisting the Warsaw Treaty Organization (WTO) for more than about two weeks, should a real war start in Central Europe. At that stage nuclear weapons would have to be used. To avoid immediate escalation to the massive-retaliation level, the doctrine of flexible response was adopted by NATO in 1967, after several years' advocacy by the USA. Under this doctrine the targets would initially be command and control centres, troop concentrations, and logistical bottle-necks in Eastern Europe, and later, perhaps, similar targets in the western USSR. The hope would be that some degree of escalation control could be achieved by limiting the attacks in this way, and that the mutual assured destruction threatened by strategic nuclear parity would prevent attacks on the mainlands of the two superpowers while intra-war bargaining took place in an attempt to stop the process. But nothing, including both the existing INF Treaty of December 1987 and any proposed Short-Range Nuclear Force Treaty (SNF), can remove the USA's reliance on nuclear weapons.

DECLARATORY POLICY

The official names for US declaratory nuclear policy have changed over time, and a series of important policy documents with cryptic titles like PD59 and NUWEP2 (replaced by NUWEP82) has been issued. In practice nothing has changed for two reasons. The first is that, as soon as the USSR began to get anywhere near nuclear parity, the only intelligent policy had to be pure deterrence, relying heavily on the invulnerable submarine force. The second reason is that the nuclear *use* policy never has changed. Nuclear use policy is laid down in the Single Integrated Operation Plan (SIOP). The first version of this was devised under President Eisenhower as a way to control the rivalry of the different services which had led to hundreds of targets (which could only be destroyed once!) being simultaneously selected by two or more nuclear commanders. Much of the arguments about declaratory policy have focused on the contrast between hitting military (counter-force) targets or civilian (counter-value) targets. The other major argument has been over the choice between a massive all-out attack launched in revenge and limited small-scale attacks on carefully-specified targets, allowing the USA to, in some sense, fight a nuclear war rather than contribute to Armageddon. While these distinctions can be important in reflecting political attitudes, and as means to nuclear-weapons diplomacy, they have never been real. In reality, all versions of the SIOP (SIOP–5 is the current version) have always contained all of these options. In fact the SIOP lists over 40,000 targets, even though the USA has never owned more than about 10,000 strategic warheads.

THE STRATEGIC DEFENSE INITIATIVE AND FUTURE ORIENTATION

The most famous recent aspect of US nuclear policy has been journalistically dubbed 'Star Wars', and more properly known as the Strategic Defense Initiative. The first attempt at Ballistic Missile Defence (BMD) was in the late 1960s, when both the USA and the USSR mounted small-scale anti-ballistic missile (ABM) systems, followed shortly by the controlling of them in the 1972 ABM Treaty. The idea of replacing defence by mutual fear with actual defence was reawakened by President Reagan in 1982, and has become a politically-controversial issue, both within domestic US politics and between the super-powers.

At the moment SDI is just a research programme, and both the hostility of the US Congress to the incredible cost and dubious technical reliability of the programme and the improvement in superpower relations since the accession to power of Mikhail Gorbachev in the Soviet Union make it very unlikely that it will ever be anything more than this. Nevertheless, the very idea of making the USA immune to Soviet nuclear strength strikes a powerful symbolic chord. In a strange way it harmonizes with other pressures inside US politics to untie the USA from what one analyst has called its 'entangling alliances'. Two factors are especially important here. One is the increasing sense in the USA that its eastward orientation towards Europe, and the costly involvement in NATO, may be anachronistic for a nation which also has a Pacific coastline. The notion that the Pacific countries are the real centre of the USA's interest is growing steadily, and carries important defence implications. Consistent with this, though independent, is a modern version of isolationism, often referred to as the 'maritime strategy'. Instead of dangerous, expensive, and static land-force commitments to particular places, mainly Europe, it is suggested that the USA should concentrate on easily-deployable, navy-based forces capable of fighting for specific US interests anywhere in the world. While the Reagan administration was staunch in its defence of the traditional 'Atlanticist' policy, the most visible part of its build-up was the famous '600-Ship Navy', organized around 15 huge aircraft-carrier 'battle groups', a structure essentially more suitable for both the Pacific orientation and the maritime strategy.

THE USA AND NATO

DAVID ROBERTSON

The original North Atlantic Treaty willingly signed by the USA in 1949 was not meant to be the tightly-organized and -integrated structure into which it was soon transformed. At its inception it was seen as a traditional defensive pact whereby each member simply guaranteed to come to the aid of any other member under attack. Neither did it extend to West Germany—the allied forces in the Federal Republic were still there as armies of occupation. It is difficult to believe that the US Senate would have ratified the Treaty had they known that over 300,000 soldiers would still be deployed on the intra-German border 40 years later, and that 60% of the US defence budget would be spent on protecting Western Europe.

It was the outbreak of the Korean War in June 1950 and the French veto of the plans for a European Defence Community (EDC) which led to the creation of a unified military command and to the rearmament of West Germany. Since that time US relations with 'European NATO' have fluctuated from irritation to disappointment and back. Several themes in this relationship can be identified running more or less continuously through NATO's history. To start with, the USA has always wanted NATO to be much stronger in conventional forces than it has ever been. Secondly, the European members have always relied on the US 'nuclear umbrella', although the USA has not always been very happy about providing this. Thirdly, the USA has always thought, not unfairly, that its huge contribution to NATO entitled it to lead what it thinks of as 'the Western Alliance', and has always talked of 'Alliance Management', although European members have seldom been happy with this subservient position. Furthermore, to most Western European governments NATO is just a regional defence pact, *not* a combatant in world-wide ideological conflict.

The story really begins in 1952 when the Lisbon Conference of NATO members worked out what their force goals would have to be to offset the threat from the USSR. The figure arrived at was 96 divisions, at a time when only 28 divisions were actually deployed in Europe. Almost immediately it became clear that these goals could not possibly be achieved with the economic strain of post-war reconstruction, especially as the two major European members, the UK and France, were still heavily engaged militarily in their colonies. (At this time France was spending more money trying to hold on to Indochina than it was receiving under the Marshall aid programme.) The only alternative was to compensate for conventional weakness with nuclear weapons, and only the USA could provide these. France had not properly started its nuclear-weapons development, and even Britain would not have a convincing capacity for some years. The USA, therefore, immediately became absolutely central to NATO's existence—being not just the biggest power, but one that was literally indispensable. When, under Eisenhower's presidency, the doctrine of massive retaliation was enunciated in 1954 (see previous essay, US Defence Policy), the key element in NATO's general strategy, the 'coupling' of US strategic nuclear forces to the defence of Western Europe, was set, and was never to be changed.

The problem was that as soon as the USSR began to build its own strategic nuclear forces, US nuclear coupling took on an ever-increasing aura of improbability. What the doctrine demanded was that a US president was expected to risk the nuclear devastation of, for example, Detroit or New York, by destroying, for example, Leningrad, in order to persuade the USSR not to invade Hamburg or Lille. In the early days of the nuclear guarantee the problem was less evident, because the stress was more on the use of the USA's plentiful supply of battlefield nuclear weapons against Soviet military forces. This was very early official policy: Field Marshal Montgomery, as NATO Deputy Supreme Allied Commander, said as early as 1953 that 'It is not a question of whether nuclear weapons will be used. They will be used. It is a question of when, and the answer is "As late as possible and as soon as necessary."'
This advantage did not survive for long; exercises and simulations by NATO planners conducted since the acquisition of

strategic nuclear strength by the Soviet Union have suggested that a major reliance on tactical nuclear weapons could actually speed up NATO's defeat.

European members of NATO were not blind to the dangers of relying on US nuclear courage, and by the beginning of the 1960s, the fears of the nuclear guarantee breaking down led to a serious challenge to the USA's leadership. The non-nuclear NATO members began to demand a voice in nuclear decision-making, even though it would be the USA which provided the hardware and ran the risks of strategic retaliation. At the same time the USA began to be distinctly worried about the small nuclear forces in the hands of the French and British, which were clearly a threat to US dominance in this area—a particular fear being that one of the small powers would intentionally trigger a war by attacking the USSR as a way of forcing the USA into fulfilling its nuclear guarantee. Things were brought to a head when the Kennedy administration told the world in 1962 that it was abandoning the Eisenhower doctrine of massive retaliation, and then forced NATO to work out an alternative strategy. The French president, de Gaulle, seeing this change in policy as an outright betrayal, and furious at the USA anyway for its opposition to French nuclear forces, in 1966 withdrew from the integrated military structure of NATO, thus weakening its conventional capacity even further.

Finally, in 1967, the USA succeeded in getting the rest of NATO to agree to a new doctrine that had at least a surface plausibility. The coupling of US nuclear weapons to the defence of Europe was retained, but the obviously-improbable massive retaliation was deferred to a later stage of the strategic plan. The new doctrine, known as 'flexible response', has been the cornerstone both of general NATO strategy and of US involvement in Europe ever since. The essence of flexible response is that NATO should have the capacity to respond to Soviet threats at whichever level they are made, and therefore retain the option of either meeting that threat at its own level, or escalating to a higher one. Most vitally, NATO should never be forced, as with massive retaliation, to meet a low-level threat by initiating central strategic warfare. The doctrine raised two particular problems. Firstly, from the US point of view, it *still* required increased conventional forces, and Western Europe was *still* not willing to raise these forces. Secondly, from the European position, flexible response began to sound like a strategy for actually fighting a war in Europe, whereas much European opinion, especially in Germany, held that any war fought, whether purely conventionally or with any degree of nuclear involvement, would be a disaster. European NATO sought to cling as much as possible to a purely-deterrent stance, but the very flexibility of the doctrine seemed like an invitation to the Warsaw Treaty Organization (WTO) to attack because it would limit what they had to fear.

Between the inception of flexible response and about 1975 the USA was in no position to demand anything of its allies, because it was deeply embroiled in Vietnam, and indeed had to reduce its military commitment to Europe in order to fight that war. It was also the period of President Nixon's *détente* with the USSR, and the first stage of the Strategic Arms Limitation Talks, culminating in the signing of the Anti-Ballistic Missile (ABM) Treaty and an Interim Agreement on Strategic Offensive Arms in 1972. Lowered tensions and a degree of superpower conciliation, including West Germany's *Ostpolitik*, its own version of *détente*, allowed NATO to stagnate—but without causing irritation to the USA.

The only exception to this was the first serious political demand by the US Congress for greater European 'burden-sharing' to be backed by a threat. The campaign of Senator Mike Mansfield in the early 1970s tried to persuade the Senate to threaten to cut US troop numbers in Europe by one-half should the Western Europeans refuse to increase the size of their share of total NATO cuts. The Mansfield Amendment, as it was known, was easily defeated, but the threat re-emerged a decade later, and this time proved to be longer-lived. When the issue came back into prominence in the early

1980s the context had changed in two vital ways. Firstly, this was the period of 'new cold war'; but Reagan's cold war was very much more a matter of US perceptions than of Western Europe's. What is technically called the 'threat perception' now differed radically, with Western Europe at least partly affected by Brezhnev's wooing of the anti-nuclear movement. Secondly, the USA became more aware than ever before of Western Europe's relative economic prosperity. No longer was it the case that Europe could not afford to defend itself. Instead, the total GNPs of the European NATO members exceeded that of either the USA or the USSR. The political arguments, at least superficially, behind the second Mansfield Amendment (actually led first by Senator Stevens and then, more powerfully, by Senator Sam Nunn) were very much more persuasive. When a new version of the Mansfield Amendment came to the floor of the Senate in 1984, under Nunn's leadership, it was narrowly defeated. However, it was only meant as a signal, at that time, and even its authors did not intend it to pass. The pressure has not evaporated since, and policy debates on other issues inside NATO have only intensified the danger that the USA will finally reduce its commitment. What that will do to NATO's solidarity cannot be predicted.

Mansfield apart, the next phase of tension in NATO started after 1976, as a direct logical result of the flexible-response doctrine. When, in the mid-1970s, the USSR started to upgrade its theatre nuclear forces with the SS-20 missile system, NATO, partly under prompting from the West German government, called on the USA to produce a matching capacity. The response was to plan to introduce two new missile systems onto European soil—the Pershing–II ballistic missile, and the Ground-Launched Cruise Missile (GLCM). This turned into one of the most confusing and internally-incoherent episodes in the history of NATO. Western European governments wanted the missiles, not so much for technical reasons, but to ensure the symbolic 'coupling' of the US strategic forces. Western European populations in general did *not* want them. The USA, under President Carter, obliged the European governments who, now under intense electoral pressure, began backing down from their original request. The USA was left looking like the villain, presented often by skilful Soviet propaganda as forcing the innocent Western Europeans to accept a terrible burden. The anti-US feelings thus generated contributed to the burden-sharing debate mentioned above, and by the end of the Carter administration Euro–American relations were deeply strained.

The missiles were eventually deployed, or at least deployment began, during President Reagan's second term. However, by then the whole issue had taken a further ironic twist. For the Reagan administration the missiles had become bargaining counters in an arms-control strategy. US determination to sign an arms-control treaty led to a sudden reversal of policy, and the offer to withdraw the Pershing–IIs and GLCMs was made with no consultation at all of the European allies. This was an appalling shock to the governments who had fought so hard to be loyal to NATO, and lost such political credibility in the process. The strain continued with the move towards full denuclearization of Europe, although the issue has twisted yet again. Most European members, but definitely not the British under Margaret Thatcher, wished to negotiate towards removal of all short-range nuclear weapons. The USA shared the British position of seeing short-range nuclear forces as essential to the defence of Western Europe. In May 1989 a compromise was reached, requiring progress in conventional disarmament before any short-range nuclear negotiations should commence, and even these would be for reductions, not for total removal.

A final problem endemic to US–European relations has surfaced seriously in the last decade, giving added reason to believe that, unless some structural changes are made, the USA and Western Europe face a very difficult time ahead. Under Reagan, the USA saw European NATO as failing to shoulder its burden in a second way, over and above financial contribution. The USA still sees itself as engaged in a worldwide fight for democracy and freedom, and is unwilling to accept that NATO activity should be restricted by any rigid regional borders. Not surprisingly, they have started to ask why NATO does not act to protect its vital interests wherever they may be, and why the USA is left having to do it for them. The major example has been the need to protect oil supplies from events in the Persian Gulf, Indian Ocean and similar areas. The demand for such action, usually referred to as 'out-of-theatre' or 'out-of-area' operations, is partly an attempt to release US forces, especially naval forces, to attend to other vital US interests in parts of the world that European NATO genuinely cannot be expected to be concerned about. European NATO's general unwillingness to help, or to expand the definition of its territorial scope (although individual members such as the UK and France have taken some action), compounds the whole US conception of Western Europe as 'selfish', 'weak' and 'ungrateful'. The principal threat to NATO's unity comes from the way these issues play into domestic US politics. The USA has always had a latent isolationist perspective, and NATO can be a very useful issue around which to rally support.

THE USA AND ARMS CONTROL

IAN M. CUTHBERTSON

Domestic Pressure for Arms Control

The USA is almost unique among NATO countries in having no strong domestic party or pressure group which pushes consistently for arms-control and disarmament measures. Public pressure groups tend to be small in membership and focus their financial and organizational resources on lobbying individual members of the Congress and government. Within Congress it is generally the Democratic Party which is more closely identified with supporting arms control, while the Republican Party, under President Reagan, became closely identified with the huge military build-up of the early 1980s. Despite this, however, it has been Republican presidents, Nixon in the case of the Strategic Arms Limitation Talks (SALT) treaties of 1972 and Reagan himself with the Intermediate Nuclear Forces (INF) Treaty of 1987, who have negotiated the two most significant arms-limitation treaties with the Soviet Union.

Furthermore, party-political loyalties in both the House of Representatives and the Senate are weak, and individual members are inclined to take decisions based more on their own personal convictions rather than on any co-ordinated approach based on party lines. It has often been the case that a number of individual members of both houses have chosen to support or oppose a particular arms-control agreement without any serious reference to the wishes of their political party's leadership. A few individual members of the Congress, such as Les Aspin, Chairman of the House Armed Services Committee, and Senator Sam Nunn, Chairman of the Senate Armed Services Committee, have also developed particular expertise on arms-control issues and their views carry great weight with their colleagues in both houses. Both are Democrats, but have shown themselves able to forge alliances across party lines to support or oppose particular measures.

Within the USA, and particularly in Washington, there are also various non-governmental organizations ('think-tanks'), which seek to influence administrations' policies on arms-control and disarmament issues. Some work on contracts from the Departments of State or Defense, analysing particular issues and making policy recommendations (for example the RAND Corporation). Others (for example The Brookings Institution) are wholly independent and carry out their research in parallel to that which is going on within the US government.

Arms Control and the US Government

The following agencies or government bodies are responsible for some aspect of the formulation and implementation of arms-control policy in the USA: the Arms Control and Disarmament Agency (ACDA); the Department of State; the Department of Defense (DOD); the Department of Energy (DOE); the Central Intelligence Agency (CIA); the United States Information Agency (USIA); and the National Security Council (NSC). The appropriate offices within these agencies work continuously to provide relevant information and policy positions on their respective areas of expertise. The information is then used by various representatives of all these agencies in interagency groups which are formed at various levels of the policy-making hierarchy. Proposals are considered and refined at each level of the hierarchy until only the most relevant and pressing issues reach the NSC. The NSC stage of the process determines which issues can be handled within its remit and which items ultimately need to be considered by the Special Co-ordinating Committee (composed of the US Secretaries of State and Defense, the director of the CIA and the chairman of the Joint Chiefs of Staff, and chaired by the NSC adviser), which is charged with addressing short-term policy issues. *Ad hoc* policy groups are also commissioned by the Committee to provide information and policy options as required. The NSC adviser then reports to the president on relevant arms-control issues. Once a US arms-control position is established, clear instructions are given to the US negotiating team, which is made up of representatives of the above-mentioned agencies.

The ACDA plays a unique role in this process. It was established in 1961 to give arms-control policy formulation some freedom from the existing bureaucracy. By statute ACDA is charged with: providing research for arms-control policy formulation; preparing and managing the negotiation process; disseminating information on arms control to the public; and operating any system or regime which will result from the arms-control process. In theory, the US chief negotiator was to be the director of the ACDA. In reality, however, the chief negotiators increasingly have been political appointees who are largely independent of the Agency. Furthermore, the power and direction given to the Agency is extremely vulnerable to the preferences and attitudes of the serving US president. Thus in the first half of the Reagan administration the ACDA was rendered largely ineffectual and almost irrelevant, reflecting the importance which was then placed on arms control by the president.

In the more general arms-control process the importance which each of the large institutional players has depends to a considerable degree on the expertise and political influence of its representative. For example, the NSC under Gen. Brent Scowcroft, appointed National Security Adviser in 1989, was expected to be very influential in arms-control policy over the next few years, because of its leader's knowledge and expertise and his close relationship with President Bush.

THE STRATEGIC DEFENSE INITIATIVE

President Reagan announced the Strategic Defense Initiative (SDI) in March 1983, calling for a space-based defence system which would protect the USA from all ballistic-missile-launched nuclear warheads. Ever since, the cost, technical feasibility and strategic logic of this approach towards protecting the USA have been the subjects of heated debate. The most divisive disagreements over SDI came as a result of the Reagan administration's 'reinterpretation' of the Anti-Ballistic Missile (ABM) Treaty of 1972—one of the fruits of SALT. The traditional (or 'narrow') interpretation of the ABM Treaty was that it specifically banned weapons systems protecting a whole nation and with the capability of intercepting ballistic missiles or interfering with their trajectories. It was also understood by this interpretation that there was to be research only on space-based and land-mobile ABM systems (while there could be research, development and testing of fixed land-based systems).

In October 1985 officials from the Departments of Defense and State, the ACDA and the NSC discussed the 'reinterpretation' of the ABM Treaty. The resulting 'broad' definition, subsequently endorsed by the Reagan administration, was that the Treaty would allow ABM systems based on physical principles or 'new concepts' which had not been in operation in 1972. This reinterpretation was subjected to quick and vociferous congressional opposition, led by Senator Nunn. The advocates of the broad interpretation used two main lines of defending their argument: firstly that the negotiating record leading to the Treaty (rather than the text of the Treaty itself) was vague; secondly that the Soviet Union had never accepted the narrow interpretation of the Treaty and had constructed a phased array radar system at Krasnoyarsk which, it was alleged, was intended for an ABM system (the Soviet Union admitted this in 1989, and offered to dismantle the installation).

The original narrow interpretation of the Treaty was eventually upheld by the so-called Biden Condition, which was attached to the 1987 INF Treaty. In accordance with this, the Senate voted in 1987 to limit fiscal-year 1988 SDI spending to those tests which clearly fell within the ABM Treaty guidelines. The future of SDI remains uncertain. A report prepared for Democratic senators Dale Bumpers, J. Bennet Johnston and William Proxmire suggested that deployment of the early parts of phase I of SDI was not likely in the 20th century. In mid-1989 the position of the Bush administration on SDI was less than clear, but it seemed inevitable that there would be further cuts in the programmes.

STRATEGIC ARMS REDUCTION TALKS

The first significant US proposal in the Strategic Arms Reduction Talks (START) process was formulated in 1982 and eventually evolved into the '50%-reduction' plan proposed at the Reykjavik summit in 1986. However, progress at that summit was blocked by Soviet objection to the SDI and the US reinterpretation of the ABM Treaty. Although the summit collapsed without agreement, the main principles outlined survived; they included the following: a ceiling of 6,000 warheads, on 1,600 'delivery vehicles' (Intercontinental Ballistic Missiles—ICBMs, Submarine-Launched Ballistic Missiles—SLBMs and heavy bombers), to apply to both Soviet and US strategic forces; a sub-limit of 4,900 on the aggregate number of warheads delivered by ICBMs and SLBMs; a sub-limit of 1,540 on heavy multi-warhead missiles (such as the Soviet SS-18 and the US MX); a 50% reduction in total Soviet throw-weight capability (a measure of the lifting ability of ballistic missiles); a ban on mobile ICBMs; and, for counting purposes, the treatment of a bomber fully loaded with gravity bombs as equivalent to the total payload of a single ICBM or SLBM.

There are still many areas to be resolved, including Air-Launched Cruise Missiles (ALCMs), Sea-Launched Cruise Missiles (SLCMs), mobile missiles and the counting of these weapons. Furthermore, SDI, although less prominent as an obstruction to progress, remains a major problem. The Bush administration seemed likely to adhere to the general approach of its predecessor; however, there was a probability that the US insistence on a ban on mobile ICBMs would be relinquished, as that had become the favoured direction for the next generation of US ICBMs.

Comprehensive Test Ban

The USA has been discussing a comprehensive test ban (CTB) at the Conference on Disarmament (also known as the Forty Nations Conference) in Geneva for more than a decade, and has also conducted bilateral discussions with the Soviet Union on the issues concerned. However, the official US position has been that, while a CTB remains a long-term goal, it is not in favour of such a ban at present, as national-security interests require testing to continue for the development of new, more-reliable and -effective warheads in order to maintain nuclear deterrence, and to ensure the viability of existing nuclear-weapon stockpiles. The USA is, however, negotiating with the Soviet Union for a gradual reduction in the yield of nuclear tests, with the object being to limit yields to the lowest reliably-verifiable level. The USA has not stated exactly where it thinks this threshold currently stands.

The USA is also negotiating with the Soviet Union to improve the verification provisions of two existing treaties, the Threshold Test Ban Treaty of 1974 (which restricted underground explosions to a maximum limit of 150 kilotons) and the Peaceful Nuclear Explosives Treaty, both of which it has signed but not ratified. The USA has respected the terms of the treaties, but will only ratify them when it believes they can be reliably verified.

CHEMICAL WARFARE CONVENTION

The USA is involved in two sets of talks on chemical warfare (CW). It has been negotiating a complete ban on the use, possession and manufacture of chemical weapons since 1971. In 1984 the US government tabled a draft treaty in the Conference on Disarmament (CD) calling for a complete ban on the use, manufacture and possession of chemical weapons and for highly-intrusive verification provisions. Those provisions, which include the right to challenge inspection—the ability to inspect any site in any country on demand—remain the USA's basic approach. However, these stringent verification provisions have caused problems not only with the Soviet Union, but also with the USA's European allies and with some in Washington who fear they may give the Soviet Union access to highly-sensitive military or commercial installations.

In 1987 the USA also restarted bilateral CW talks with the Soviet Union, which had been suspended in 1980. These talks parallel the negotiations going on in the CD and cover possession, production and use of chemical weapons. In addition, the talks have recently focused on the issue of chemical-weapons proliferation and use in Third World countries.

CONVENTIONAL FORCES IN EUROPE (CFE)

The Conference on Security and Confidence-Building Measures and Disarmament in Europe (CDE) talks began in January 1984, as a continuation of the Conference on Security and Co-operation in Europe (CSCE). The principal purpose of these talks is to overcome the fear and uncertainty engendered by major military exercises by making provision for mutual inspection and verification. Simultaneously with the CDE talks, in March 1989, the USA and its 15 NATO allies began negotiations with the Soviet Union and its six Warsaw Pact (WP) partners on the reduction and restructuring of conventional forces in Europe. The objective of the negotiations is to reduce the number of troops deployed in Europe, create a more stable balance and eliminate the capacity of either alliance to launch a surprise attack. When the talks began NATO tabled a proposal which called for the reduction of the number of tanks, artillery and armoured personnel carriers possessed by both sides to levels 10% below current NATO levels. For example, NATO would cut its tanks by about 2,000 to a total of 20,000; the WP would be required to cut its tank numbers by 37,000 to reach the same ceiling. In addition, no single member of either alliance would be allowed more than 12,000 tanks, a serious constraint on the Soviet Union, by far the world's largest possessor of tanks.

The USA would reduce not only the number of tanks it has in Europe as the result of any agreement, but also the number of troops it deploys in Europe, because a treaty would require the withdrawal of whole military units from the region. Such an agreement would be welcomed in Congress, where there has been pressure to make unilateral reductions in US troop numbers in Europe in order to cut the US military budget.

ARMS CONTROL AND HUMAN RIGHTS

Human-rights issues have, from time to time, been an important factor in US foreign policy, mainly because of the role of ethnic voting blocks, and especially the Jewish lobby. Certainly during the 1970s, and particularly under the Carter administration, there were attempts to link Soviet progress on human rights with arms-control negotiations. There is little clear-cut evidence that these concerns have ever caused the USA to forfeit a genuine opportunity for progress in arms control. It is true that the principal reason for the US Senate's failure to ratify the SALT II agreement was the Soviet invasion of Afghanistan; but it should be remembered that even this agreement was observed by both countries for several years.

NATO as a whole has used human-rights issues to exert political pressure on the USSR as a means of slowing progress in conventional arms negotiations. Monitoring groups have been allowed some access to the Soviet Union, and arms-control negotiations, have been stalled on occasion due to human-rights concerns, However, with reform in the Soviet Union well under way, the linkage of human rights and arms control has become much less overt, although the USA has made its attendance at a CSCE follow-up meeting on human rights, to be held in Moscow, contingent not only on Soviet domestic behaviour but also on progress in a variety of arms-control negotiations, in particular the CFE talks.

SELECT BIBLIOGRAPHY

Baylis, J., Booth, K., Garnett, J. and Williams, P. *Contemporary Strategy* (Vols I and II). New York, Holmes & Meier Publishers, Inc, 1988.

Betts, R. K. *Soldiers, Statesmen and Cold War Crises.* Cambridge, Massachusetts, Harvard University Press, 1978.

Blacker, C. D. *Reluctant Warriors: The United States, the Soviet Union and Arms Control.* New York, W. H. Freeman & Co Publishers, 1987.

Bowker, M. and Williams, P. *Superpower Détente.* London, Sage Publications Ltd/Royal Institute of International Affairs, 1988.

Calleo, D. P. *Beyond American Hegemony.* Brighton, Wheatsheaf Books Ltd, 1987.

Clark, A. A., Chiarelli, P. W., McKitrick, J. S. and Reed, J. W. (Eds). *The Defense Reform Debate: Issues and Analyses.* Baltimore, Maryland, The Johns Hopkins University Press, 1984.

Coates, J. and Kilian, M. *Heavy Losses: The Dangerous Decline of American Defense.* New York, Viking Penguin Inc, 1985.

Cuthbertson, I. and Robertson, D. *Enhancing European Security: Living in a Less Nuclear Age.* London, Macmillan Publishers Ltd, 1988.

Destler, I. M., Gelb, L. and Lake, A. *Our Own Worst Enemy: The Unmaking of American Foreign Policy.* New York, Simon & Schuster Inc, 1984.

Gaddis, J. L. *Strategies of Containment: Critical Appraisal of Postwar American National Security Policy.* New York, Oxford University Press, 1983.

Garthoff, R. L. *Détente and Confrontation.* Washington, DC, The Brookings Institution, 1985.

Kaplan, L. S. *NATO and the United States: The Enduring Alliance* (Twayne's International History Series). Boston, Massachusetts, Twayne Publishers, 1988.

LaFeber, W. *The American Age: United States Foreign Policy at Home and Abroad since 1750.* New York, W. W. Norton & Co Inc, 1989.

Laird, R. F. *The Soviet Union, the West and the Nuclear Arms Race.* Brighton, Wheatsheaf Books Ltd, 1986.

Luttwak, E. N. *The Pentagon and the Art of War.* New York, Simon & Schuster Inc, 1985.

Miller, S. E. (Ed.). *Strategy and Nuclear Deterrence.* Princeton, New Jersey, Princeton University Press, 1984.

Osgood, R. E. *NATO: The Entangling Alliance.* Chicago, Illinois, University of Chicago Press, 1962.

Palmer, B. *The 25-Year War: America's Military Role in Vietnam.* New York, Simon & Schuster Inc, 1984.

Pringle, P. and Arkin, W. *SIOP: Nuclear War from the Inside.* London, Sphere Books Ltd, 1983.

Schwartz, D. N. *NATO's Nuclear Dilemmas.* Washington, DC, The Brookings Institution, 1983.

Shearman, P. and Williams, P. *The Superpowers, Central America and the Middle East.* Oxford, Brassey's Defence Publishers, 1988.

Talbot, W. *Deadly Gambits: The Reagan Administration and Arms.* New York, Harper & Row, Publishers Inc, 1983.

End Game: The Inside Story of SALT-II. New York, Harper & Row, Publishers Inc, 1979.

PUBLIC AFFAIRS

GOVERNMENT

THE CONSTITUTION OF THE USA

Preamble

We, the people of the United States, in order to form a more perfect Union, establish justice, insure domestic tranquillity, provide for the common defence, promote the general welfare, and secure the blessings of liberty to ourselves and our posterity, do ordain and establish this Constitution for the United States of America.

Article I

Section 1

All legislative powers herein granted shall be vested in a Congress of the United States, which shall consist of a Senate and House of Representatives.

Section 2

1. The House of Representatives shall be composed of members chosen every second year by the people of the several States and the electors in each State shall have the qualifications requisite for electors of the most numerous branch of the State Legislature.

2. No person shall be a Representative who shall not have attained to the age of 25 years and been seven years a citizen of the United States and who shall not, when elected, be an inhabitant of that State in which he shall be chosen.

3. Representatives and direct taxes shall be apportioned among the several States which may be included within this Union according to their respective numbers, which shall be determined by adding to the whole number of free persons, including those bound to service for a term of years, and excluding Indians not taxed, three-fifths of all other persons. The actual enumeration shall be made within three years after the first meeting of the Congress of the United States, and within every subsequent term of 10 years, in such manner as they shall by law direct. The number of Representatives shall not exceed one for every 30,000, but each State shall have at least one Representative; and until such enumeration shall be made, the State of New Hampshire shall be entitled to choose 3; Massachusetts 8; Rhode Island and Providence Plantations 1; Connecticut 5; New York 6; New Jersey 4; Pennsylvania 8; Delaware 1; Maryland 6; Virginia 10; North Carolina 5; South Carolina 5; and Georgia 3.*

4. When vacancies happen in the representation from any State, the Executive Authority thereof shall issue writs of election to fill such vacancies.

5. The House of Representatives shall choose their Speaker and other officers and shall have the sole power of impeachment.

Section 3

1. The Senate of the United States shall be composed of two Senators from each State, chosen by the Legislature thereof, for six years; and each Senator shall have one vote.

2. Immediately after they shall be assembled in consequence of the first election, they shall be divided as equally as may be into three classes. The seats of the Senators of the first class shall be vacated at the expiration of the second year, of the second class at the expiration of the fourth year, and of the third class at the expiration of the sixth year, so that one-third may be chosen every second year, and if vacancies happen by resignation, or otherwise, during the recess of the Legislature of any State, the Executive thereof may make temporary appointments until the next meeting of the Legislature, which shall then fill such vacancies.

3. No person shall be a Senator who shall not have attained to the age of 30 years, and been nine years a citizen of the United

States, and who shall not, when elected, be an inhabitant of that State for which he shall be chosen.

4. The Vice-President of the United States shall be President of the Senate, but shall have no vote, unless they be equally divided.

5. The Senate shall choose their other officers, and also a President *pro tempore*, in the absence of the Vice-President, or when he shall exercise the office of the President of the United States.

6. The Senate shall have the sole power to try all impeachments. When sitting for that purpose, they shall be on oath or affirmation. When the President of the United States is tried, the Chief Justice shall preside; and no person shall be convicted without the concurrence of two-thirds of the members present.

7. Judgment of case of impeachment shall not extend further than to removal from office, and disqualification to hold and enjoy any office of honour, trust, or profit under the United States; but the party convicted shall nevertheless be liable and subject to indictment, trial, judgment, and punishment, according to law.

Section 4

1. The times, places and manner of holding elections for Senators and Representatives shall be prescribed in each State by the Legislature thereof; but the Congress may at any time by law make or alter such regulations, except as to places of choosing Senators.

2. The Congress shall assemble at least once in every year, and such meeting shall be on the first Monday in December, unless they shall by law appoint a different day.

Section 5

1. Each House shall be the judge of the elections, returns, and qualifications of its own members, and a majority of each shall constitute a quorum to do business; but a smaller number may adjourn from day to day, and may be authorized to compel the attendance of absent members in such manner and under such penalties as each House may provide.

2. Each House may determine the rules of its proceedings, punish its members for disorderly behaviour, and, with the concurrence of two-thirds, expel a member.

3. Each House shall keep a journal of its proceedings, and from time to time publish the same, excepting such parts as may in their judgement require secrecy; and the yeas and nays of the members of either House on any question shall, at the desire of one-fifth of those present, be entered on the journal.

4. Neither House, during the session of Congress shall, without the consent of the other, adjourn for more than three days, nor to any other place than that in which the two Houses shall be sitting.

Section 6

1. The Senators and Representatives shall receive a compensation for their services, to be ascertained by law, and paid out of the Treasury of the United States. They shall in all cases, except treason, felony, and breach of the peace, be privileged from arrest during their attendance at the session of their respective Houses, and in going to and returning from the same; and for any speech or debate in either House they shall not be questioned in any other place.

2. No Senator or Representative shall, during the time for which he was elected, be appointed to any civil office under the authority of the United States which shall have been created, or the emoluments whereof shall have been increased during such time; and no person holding any office under the United States shall be a member of either House during his continuance in office.

Section 7

1. All bills for raising revenue shall originate in the House of Representatives, but the Senate may propose or concur with amendments, as on other bills.

* See Amendment XIV.

2. Every bill which shall have passed the House of Representatives and the Senate shall, before it becomes a law, be presented to the President of the United States; if he approve, he shall sign it, but if not he shall return it, with his objections to that House in which it shall have originated, who shall enter the objections at large on their journal and proceed to reconsider it. If after such reconsideration two-thirds of that House shall agree to pass the bill, it shall be sent, together with the objections, to the other House, by which it shall likewise be reconsidered; and if approved by two-thirds of that House it shall become a law. But in such cases the votes of both Houses shall be determined by yeas and nays, and the names of the persons voting for and against the bill be entered on the journal of each House respectively. If any bill shall not be returned by the President within 10 days (Sundays excepted) after it shall have been presented to him, the same shall be a law in like manner as if he had signed it, unless the Congress by their adjournment prevent its return; in which case it shall not be a law.

3. Every order, resolution, or vote to which the concurrence of the Senate and House of Representatives may be necessary (except on a question of adjournment) shall be presented to the President of the United States, and before the same shall take effect shall be approved by him, or being disapproved by him, shall be repassed by two-thirds of the Senate and the House of Representatives, according to the rules and limitations prescribed in the case of a bill.

Section 8

1. The Congress shall have power:

To lay and collect taxes, duties, imposts, and excises, to pay the debts and provide for the common defence and general welfare of the United States; but all duties, imposts, and excises shall be uniform throughout the United States.

2. To borrow money on the credit of the United States.

3. To regulate commerce with foreign nations; and among the several States and with the Indian tribes.

4. To establish a uniform rule of naturalization and uniform laws on the subject of bankruptcies throughout the United States.

5. To coin money, regulate the value thereof, and of foreign coin, and fix the standard of weights and measures.

6. To provide for the punishment of counterfeiting the securities and current coin of the United States.

7. To establish post-offices and post-roads.

8. To promote the progress of science and useful arts by securing for limited times to authors and inventors the exclusive right to their respective writings and discoveries.

9. To constitute tribunals inferior to the Supreme Court.

10. To define and punish piracies and felonies committed on the high seas, and offences against the law of nations.

11. To declare war, grant letters of marque and reprisal, and make rules concerning captures on land and water.

12. To raise and support armies, but no appropriation of money to that use shall be for a longer term than two years.

13. To provide and maintain a navy.

14. To make rules for the government and regulation of the land and naval forces.

15. To provide for calling forth the militia to execute the laws of the Union, suppress insurrections, and repel invasions.

16. To provide for organizing, arming and disciplining the militia, and for governing such part of them as may be employed in the service of the United States, reserving to the States respectively the appointment of the officers, and the authority of training the militia according to the discipline prescribed by Congress.

17. To exercise exclusive legislation in all cases whatsoever over such district (not exceeding 10 miles square) as may, by cession of particular States and the acceptance of Congress, become the seat of Government of the United States and to exercise like authority over all places purchased by the consent of the Legislature of the State in which the same shall be, for the erection of forts, magazines, arsenals, dry-docks, and other needful buildings.

18. To make all laws which shall be necessary and proper for carrying into execution the foregoing powers and all other powers vested by this Constitution in the Government of the United States, or in any department or officer thereof.

Section 9

1. The migration or importation of such persons as any of the States now existing shall think proper to admit shall not be prohibited by the Congress prior to the year 1808, but a tax or duty may be imposed on such importations, not exceeding 10 dollars for each person.

2. The privilege of the writ of habeas corpus shall not be suspended, unless when in cases of rebellion or invasion the public safety may require it.

3. No bill or attainder or *ex post facto* law shall be passed.

4. No capitation or other direct tax shall be laid, unless in proportion to the census or enumeration hereinbefore directed to be taken.

5. No tax or duty shall be laid on articles exported from any State.

6. No preference shall be given by any regulation of commerce or revenue to the ports of one State over those of another, nor shall vessels bound to or from one State be obliged to enter, clear, or pay duties to another.

7. No money shall be drawn from the Treasury but in consequence of appropriations made by law; and a regular statement and account of the receipts and expenditures of all public money shall be published from time to time.

8. No title of nobility shall be granted by the United States. And no person holding any office of profit or trust under them shall, without the consent of the Congress, accept of any present, emolument, office, or title of any kind whatever from any king, prince, or foreign state.

Section 10

1. No State shall enter into any treaty, alliance or confederation, grant letters of marque and reprisal, coin money, emit bills of credit, make anything but gold and silver coin a tender in payment of debts, pass any bill of attainder, *ex post facto* law, or law impairing the obligation of contracts, or grant any title of nobility.

2. No State shall, without the consent of the Congress, lay any imposts or duties on imports or exports, except what may be absolutely necessary for executing its inspection laws, and the net produce of all duties and imposts, laid by any State on imports or exports, shall be for the use of the Treasury of the United States; and all such laws shall be subject to the revision and control of the Congress.

3. No State shall, without the consent of Congress, lay any duty of tonnage, keep troops or ships of war in time of peace, enter into agreement or compact with another State, or with a foreign power, or engage in war, unless actually invaded, or in such imminent danger as will not admit of delay.

Article II

Section 1

1. The Executive power shall be vested in a President of the United States of America. He shall hold his office during the term of four years, and, together with the Vice-President chosen for the same term, be elected as follows:

2. Each State shall appoint, in such manner as the Legislature thereof may direct, a number of electors equal to the whole number of Senators and Representatives to which the State may be entitled in the Congress; but no Senator or Representative or person holding an office of trust or profit under the United States shall be appointed an elector.

3. The electors shall meet in their respective States and vote by ballot for two persons, of whom one at least shall not be an inhabitant of the same State with themselves. And they shall make a list of all the persons voted for, and of the number of votes for each, which list they shall sign and certify and transmit, sealed, to the seat of the Government of the United States, directed to the President of the Senate. The President of the Senate shall, in the presence of the Senate and House of Representatives, open all the certificates, and the votes shall then be counted. The person having the greatest number of votes shall be the President, if such number be a majority of the whole number of electors appointed, and if there be more than one who have such a majority, and have an equal number of votes, then the House of Representatives shall immediately choose by ballot one of them for President; and if no person have a majority, then from the five highest on the list the said House shall in like manner choose the President. But in choosing the President, the vote shall be taken by States, the representation from each State having one vote. A quorum, for this purpose, shall consist of a member or members from two-thirds of the States, and a majority of all the States shall be necessary to a choice. In every case, after the choice of the President, the person having the greatest number of votes of the electors shall be the Vice-President. But if there should remain two or more who have equal votes, the Senate shall choose from them by ballot the Vice-President.*

4. The Congress may determine the time of choosing the electors and the day on which they shall give their votes, which day shall be the same throughout the United States.

---

* This clause is superseded by Amendment XII.

5. No person except a natural born citizen, or a citizen of the United States, at the time of the adoption of this Constitution, shall be eligible to the office of President; neither shall any person be eligible to that office who shall not have attained to the age of 35 years and been 14 years a resident within the United States.

6. In case of the removal of the President from office, or of his death, resignation, or inability to discharge the powers and duties of the said office, the same shall devolve on the Vice-President, and the Congress may by law provide for the case of removal, death, resignation, or inability, both of the President and Vice-President, declaring what officer shall then act as President, and such officer shall act accordingly until the disability be removed or a President shall be elected.*

7. The President shall, at stated times, receive for his services a compensation which shall neither be increased nor diminished during the period for which he shall have been elected, and he shall not receive within that period any other emolument from the United States, or any of them.

8. Before he enter on the execution of his office he shall take the following oath or affirmation:

'I do solemnly swear (or affirm) that I will faithfully execute the office of President of the United States, and will, to the best of my ability, preserve, protect, and defend the Constitution of the United States.'

Section 2

1. The President shall be Commander-in-Chief of the Army and Navy of the United States, and of the militia of the several States when called into the actual service of the United States; he may require the opinion, in writing, of the principal officer in each of the executive departments upon any subject relating to the duties of their respective offices, and he shall have the power to grant reprieves and pardons for offences against the United States except in cases of impeachment.

2. He shall have power, by and with the advice and consent of the Senate, to make treaties, provided two-thirds of the Senators present concur; and he shall nominate, and by and with the advice and consent of the Senate, shall appoint ambassadors, other public ministers and consuls, judges of the Supreme Court, and all other officers of the United States whose appointments are not herein otherwise provided for, and which shall be established by law; but the Congress may by law vest the appointment of such inferior officers as they think proper in the President alone, in the courts of law, or in the heads of departments.

3. The President shall have power to fill up all vacancies that may happen during the recess of the Senate by granting commissions, which shall expire at the end of their next session.

Section 3

He shall from time to time give to the Congress information of the state of the Union, and recommend to their consideration such measures as he shall judge necessary and expedient; he may, on extraordinary occasions, convene both Houses, or either of them, and in case of disagreement between them with respect to the time of adjournment, he may adjourn them to such time as he shall think proper; he shall receive ambassadors and other public ministers; he shall take care that the laws be faithfully executed, and shall commission all the officers of the United States.

Section 4

The President, Vice-President, and all civil officers of the United States shall be removed from office on impeachment for, and conviction of, treason, bribery or other high crimes and misdemeanours.

Article III

Section 1

The judicial power of the United States shall be vested in one Supreme Court, and in such inferior courts as the Congress may from time to time ordain and establish. The judges, both of the Supreme and inferior courts, shall hold their offices during good behaviour, and shall at stated times receive for their services a compensation which shall not be diminished during their continuance in office.

Section 2

1. The judicial power shall extend to all cases in law and equity arising under this Constitution, the laws of the United States, and treaties made, or which shall be made, under their authority; to all cases affecting ambassadors, other public ministers and consuls;

---

* This clause is amended by Amendments XX and XXV.

to all cases of admiralty and maritime jurisdiction; to controversies to which the United States shall be a party; to controversies between two or more States, between a State and citizens of another State, between citizens of different States, between citizens of the same State claiming lands under grants of different States, and between a State, or the citizens thereof, and foreign States, citizens, or subjects.

2. In all cases affecting ambassadors, other public ministers, and consuls, and those in which a State shall be party, the Supreme Court shall have original jurisdiction. In all the other cases before mentioned the Supreme Court shall have appellate jurisdiction both as to law and fact, with such exceptions and under such regulations as the Congress shall make.

3. The trial of all crimes, except in cases of impeachment, shall be by jury, and such trials shall be held in the State where the said crimes shall have been committed; but when not committed within any State the trial shall be at such place or places as the Congress may by law have directed.

Section 3

1. Treason against the United States shall consist only in levying war against them, or in adhering to their enemies, giving them aid and comfort. No person shall be convicted of treason unless on the testimony of two witnesses to the same overt act, or on confession in open court.

2. The Congress shall have power to declare the punishment of treason, but no attainder of treason shall work corruption of blood or forfeiture except during the life of the person attained.

Article IV

Section 1

Full faith and credit shall be given in each State to the public acts, records, and judicial proceedings of every other State. And the Congress may by general laws prescribe the manner in which such acts, records, and proceedings shall be proved, and the effect thereof.

Section 2

1. The citizens of each State shall be entitled to all privileges and immunities of citizens in the several States.

2. A person charged in any State with treason, felony, or other crime, who shall flee from justice, and be found in another State, shall, on demand of the Executive authority of the State from which he fled, be delivered up, to be removed to the State having jurisdiction of the crime.

3. No person held to service or labour in one State, under the laws thereof, escaping into another shall, in consequence of any law or regulation therein, be discharged from such service or labour, but shall be delivered up on claim of the party to whom such service or labour may be due.

Section 3

1. New States may be admitted by the Congress into this Union; but no new State shall be formed or erected within the jurisdiction of any other State, nor any State be formed by the junction of two or more States, or parts of States, without the consent of the Legislatures of the States concerned, as well as of the Congress.

2. The Congress shall have the power to dispose of and make all needful rules and regulations respecting the territory or other property belonging to the United States; and nothing in this Constitution shall be so construed as to prejudice any claims of the United States, or of any particular State.

Section 4

The United States shall guarantee to every State in this Union a republican form of government, and shall protect each of them against invasion, and on application of the Legislature, or of the Executive (when the Legislature cannot be convened) against domestic violence.

Article V

The Congress, whenever two-thirds of both Houses shall deem it necessary, shall propose amendments to this Constitution, or, on the application of the Legislature of two-thirds of the several States, shall call a convention for proposing amendments, which, in either case, shall be valid to all intents and purposes, as part of this Constitution, when ratified by the Legislatures of three-fourths of the several States, or by conventions in three-fourths thereof, as the one or the other mode of ratification may be proposed by the Congress, provided that no amendment which may be made prior to the year 1808 shall in any manner affect the first and fourth clauses in the Ninth Section of the First Article; and that no State, without its consent, shall be deprived of its equal suffrage in the Senate.

Article VI

1. All debts contracted and engagements entered into before the adoption of this Constitution shall be as valid against the United States under this Constitution as under the Confederation.

2. This Constitution and the laws of the United States which shall be made in pursuance thereof and all treaties made, or which shall be made, under the authority of the United States, shall be the supreme law of the land, and the judges in every State shall be bound thereby, anything in the Constitution or laws of any State to the contrary notwithstanding.

3. The Senators and Representatives before mentioned, and the members of the several State Legislatures, and all executives and judicial officers, both of the United States and of the several States, shall be bound by oath or affirmation to support this Constitution; but no religious test shall ever be required as a qualification to any office or public trust under the United States.

Article VII

The ratification of the Conventions of nine States shall be sufficient for the establishment of this Constitution between the States so ratifying the same.

Amendments to the Constitution

Ten Original Amendments, ratified 15 December 1791:

AMENDMENT I

Congress shall make no law respecting an establishment of religion, or prohibiting the free exercise thereof; or abridging the freedom of speech or of the Press; or the right of the people peaceably to assemble and to petition the Government for a redress of grievances.

AMENDMENT II

A well-regulated militia being necessary to the security of a free State, the right of the people to keep and bear arms shall not be infringed.

AMENDMENT III

No soldier shall, in time of peace, be quartered in any house without the consent of the owner, nor in time of war, but in a manner to be prescribed by law.

AMENDMENT IV

The right of the people to be secure in their persons, houses, papers, and effects, against unreasonable searches and seizures, shall not be violated, and no warrants shall issue but upon probable cause, supported by oath or affirmation, and particularly describing the place to be searched, and the persons or things to be seized.

AMENDMENT V

No person shall be held to answer for a capital or otherwise infamous crime unless on a presentment or indictment of a Grand Jury, except in cases arising in the land or naval forces, or in the militia, when in actual service, in time of war or public danger; nor shall any person be subject for the same offence to be twice put in jeopardy of life or limb; nor shall be compelled in any criminal case to be a witness against himself, nor be deprived of life, liberty, or property, without due process of law; nor shall private property be taken for public use without just compensation.

AMENDMENT VI

In all criminal prosecutions, the accused shall enjoy the right to a speedy and public trial, by an impartial jury of the State and district wherein the crime shall have been committed, which districts shall have been previously ascertained by law, and to be informed of the nature and cause of the accusation; to be confronted with the witnesses against him; to have compulsory process for obtaining witnesses in his favour, and to have the assistance of counsel for his defence.

AMENDMENT VII

In suits at common law, where the value in controversy shall exceed 20 dollars, the right of trial by jury shall be preserved, and no fact tried by a jury shall be otherwise re-examined in any court of the United States than according to the rules of the common law.

AMENDMENT VIII

Excessive bail shall not be required, nor excessive fines imposed, nor cruel and unusual punishments inflicted.

AMENDMENT IX

The enumeration in the Constitution of certain rights shall not be construed to deny or disparage others retained by the people.

AMENDMENT X

The powers not delegated to the United States by the Constitution, nor prohibited by it to the States, are reserved to the States respectively, or to the people.

Subsequent Amendments:

AMENDMENT XI
(ratified 7 February 1795)

The judicial power of the United States shall not be construed to extend to any suit in law or equity, commenced or prosecuted against one of the United States, by citizens of another State, or by citizens or subjects of any foreign State.

AMENDMENT XII
(ratified 15 June 1804)

The Electors shall meet in their respective States, and vote by ballot for President and Vice-President, one of whom at least shall not be an inhabitant of the same State with themselves; they shall name in their ballots the person voted for as President, and in distinct ballots the person voted for as Vice-President; and they shall make distinct lists of all persons voted for as President, and of all persons voted for as Vice-President, and of the number of votes for each, which list they shall sign and certify, and transmit, sealed, to the seat of the Government of the United States, directed to the President of the Senate; the President of the Senate shall, in the presence of the Senate and House of Representatives, open all the certificates and the votes shall then be counted; the person having the greatest number of votes for President shall be the President, if such number be a majority of the whole number of Electors appointed; and if no person have such a majority, then from the persons having the highest numbers, not exceeding three, on the list of those voted for as President, the House of Representatives shall choose immediately, by ballot, the President. But in choosing the President, the votes shall be taken by States, the representation from each State having one vote; a quorum for this purpose shall consist of a member or members from two-thirds of the States, and a majority of all the States shall be necessary to a choice. And if the House of Representatives shall not choose a President, whenever the right of choice shall devolve upon them, before the fourth day of March next following, then the Vice-President shall act as President, as in the case of the death or other constitutional disability of the President. The person having the greatest number of votes as Vice-President shall be the Vice-President, if such number be a majority of the whole number of Electors appointed, and if no person have a majority, then, from the two highest numbers on the list, the Senate shall choose the Vice-President; a quorum for the purpose shall consist of two-thirds of the whole number of Senators, and a majority of the whole number shall be necessary to a choice. But no person constitutionally ineligible to the office of President shall be eligible to that of Vice-President of the United States.

AMENDMENT XIII
(ratified 6 December 1865)

1. Neither slavery nor involuntary servitude, except as a punishment for crime whereof the party shall have been duly convicted, shall exist within the United States, or any place subject to their jurisdiction.

2. Congress shall have the power to enforce this article by appropriate legislation.

AMENDMENT XIV
(ratified 9 July 1868)

1. All persons born or naturalized in the United States, and subject to the jurisdiction thereof, are citizens of the United States and of the State wherein they reside. No State shall make or enforce any law which shall abridge the privileges or immunities of citizens of the United States, nor shall any State deprive any person of life, liberty, or property without due process of law, nor deny to any person within its jurisdiction the equal protection of the laws.

2. Representatives shall be apportioned among the several States according to their respective numbers, counting the whole number of persons in each State excluding Indians not taxed. But when the right to vote at any election for the choice of Electors for President and Vice-President of the United States, Representatives in Congress, the executive and judicial officers of a State, or the members of the Legislature thereof, is denied to any of the male inhabitants of such State, being 21 years of age, and citizens of the United States, or in any way abridged, except for participation in rebellion, or other crime, the basis of representation therein shall be reduced in the proportion which the number of such male citizens shall bear to the whole number of male citizens 21 years of age in such State.

3. No person shall be a Senator or Representative in Congress, or Elector of President and Vice-President, or hold any office, civil or military, under the United States, or under any State, who, having previously taken an oath as a member of Congress or as an officer of the United States, or as a member of any State Legislature, or as an executive or judicial officer of any State, to support the Constitution of the United States, shall have engaged in insurrection or rebellion against the same, or given aid and comfort to the enemies thereof. But Congress may, by vote of two-thirds of each House, remove such disability.

4. The validity of the public debt of the United States, authorized by law, including debts incurred for payment of pensions and bounties for services in suppressing insurrection and rebellion, shall not be questioned. But neither the United States nor any State shall assume or pay any debt or obligation incurred in aid of insurrection or rebellion against the United States, or any claim for the loss or emancipation of any slave; but all such debts, obligations, and claims shall be held illegal and void.

5. The Congress shall have power to enforce, by appropriate legislation, the provisions of this article.

AMENDMENT XV
(ratified 3 February 1870)

1. The right of the citizens of the United States to vote shall not be denied or abridged by the United States or by any State on account of race, colour, or previous condition of servitude.

2. The Congress shall have power to enforce this article by appropriate legislation.

AMENDMENT XVI
(ratified 3 February 1913)

The Congress shall have power to lay and collect taxes on incomes, from whatever source derived, without apportionment among the several States, and without regard to any census or enumeration.

AMENDMENT XVII
(ratified 8 April 1913)

1. The Senate of the United States shall be composed of two Senators from each State, elected by the people thereof for six years; and each Senator shall have one vote. The electors in each State shall have the qualifications requisite for electors of the most numerous branch of the State Legislature.

2. When vacancies happen in the representation of any State in the Senate, the executive authority of such State shall issue writs of election to fill such vacancies: Provided that the Legislature of any State may empower the Executive thereof to make temporary appointments until the people fill the vacancies by election as the Legislature may direct.

3. This amendment shall not be so construed as to affect the election or term of any Senator chosen before it becomes valid as part of the Constitution.

AMENDMENT XVIII
(ratified 16 January 1919*)

1. After one year from the ratification of this article the manufacture, sale, or transportation of intoxicating liquors within, the importation thereof into, or the exportation thereof from the United States, and all territory subject to the jurisdiction thereof for beverage purposes is hereby prohibited.

2. The Congress and the several States shall have concurrent power to enforce this article by appropriate legislation.

3. This article shall be inoperative unless it shall have been ratified as an amendment to the Constitution by the Legislatures of the several States, as provided in the Constitution, within seven years from the date of the submission hereof to the States by the Congress.

---

* Repealed by Amendment XXI.

AMENDMENT XIX
(ratified 18 August 1920)

1. The right of citizens of the United States to vote shall not be denied or abridged by the United States or by any State on account of sex.

2. Congress shall have power, by appropriate legislation, to enforce the provisions of this article.

AMENDMENT XX
(ratified 23 January 1933)

Section 1

The terms of the President and Vice-President shall end at noon on the 20th day of January, and the terms of Senators and Representatives at noon on the third day of January, of the years in which such terms would have ended if this article had not been ratified; and the terms of their successors shall then begin.

Section 2

The Congress shall assemble at least once in every year, and such meetings shall begin at noon on the third day of January, unless they shall by law appoint a different day.

Section 3

If, at the time fixed for the beginning of the term of the President, the President elect shall have died, the Vice-President elect shall become President. If a President shall not have been chosen before the time fixed for the beginning of his term, or if the President elect shall have failed to qualify, then the Vice-President elect shall act as President until a President shall have qualified; and the Congress may by law provide for the case wherein neither a President elect nor a Vice-President elect shall have qualified, declaring who shall then act as President, or the manner in which one who is to act shall be selected, and such person shall act accordingly until a President or Vice-President shall have qualified.

Section 4

The Congress may by law provide for the case of the death of any of the persons from whom the House of Representatives may choose a President whenever the right of choice shall have devolved upon them, and for the case of the death of any of the persons from whom the Senate may choose a Vice-President whenever the right of choice shall have devolved upon them.

Section 5

Sections 1 and 2 shall take effect on the 15th day of October following the ratification of this article.

Section 6

This article shall be inoperative unless it shall have been ratified as an amendment to the Constitution by the legislature of three-fourths of the several States within seven years from the date of its submission.

AMENDMENT XXI
(ratified 5 December 1933)

Section 1

The 18th article of amendment to the Constitution of the United States is hereby repealed.

Section 2

The transportation or importation into any State, Territory or Possession of the United States for delivery or use therein of intoxicating liquors, in violation of the laws thereof, is hereby prohibited.

Section 3

This article shall be inoperative unless it shall have been ratified as an amendment to the Constitution by conventions in the several States, as provided in the Constitution, within seven years from the date of the submission hereof to the States by the Congress.

AMENDMENT XXII
(ratified 27 February 1951)

1. No person shall be elected to the office of President more than twice, and no person who has held the office of President, or acted as President, for more than two years of a term to which some other person was elected President shall be elected to the office of President more than once. But this article shall not apply to any person holding the office of President when this Article was proposed by Congress, and shall not prevent any person who may be holding the office of President, or acting as President, during the term within which this Article becomes operative from holding the office of President or acting as President during the remainder of such term.

2. This article shall be inoperative unless it shall have been ratified as an amendment to the Constitution by the Legislatures of three-fourths of the several States within seven years from the date of its submission to the States by the Congress.

AMENDMENT XXIII
(ratified 29 March 1961)

Section 1

The District constituting the seat of Government of the United States shall appoint in such manner as the Congress may direct:

A number of electors of President and Vice-President equal to the whole number of Senators and Representatives in Congress to which the District would be entitled if it were a State, but in no event more than the least populous State; they shall be in addition to those appointed by the States, but they shall be considered, for the purposes of the election of President and Vice-President, to be electors appointed by a State; and they shall meet in the District and perform such duties as provided by the 12th article of amendment.

Section 2

The Congress shall have power to enforce this article by appropriate legislation.

AMENDMENT XXIV
(ratified 23 January 1964)

Section 1

The right of citizens of the United States to vote in any primary or other election for President or Vice-President, for electors for President or Vice-President, or for Senator or Representative in Congress, shall not be denied or abridged by the United States or any State by reason of failure to pay any poll tax or other tax.

Section 2

The Congress shall have power to enforce this article by appropriate legislation.

AMENDMENT XXV
(ratified 10 February 1967)

Section 1

In case of the removal of the President from office or of his death or resignation, the Vice-President shall become President.

Section 2

Whenever there is a vacancy in the office of the Vice-President, the President shall nominate a Vice-President who shall take office upon confirmation by a majority vote of both Houses of Congress.

Section 3

Whenever the President transmits to the President *pro tempore* of the Senate and the Speaker of the House of Representatives his written declaration that he is unable to discharge the powers and duties of his office, and until he transmits to them a written declaration to the contrary, such powers and duties shall be discharged by the Vice-President as Acting President.

Section 4

Whenever the Vice-President and a majority of either the principal officers of the executive departments or of such other body as Congress may by law provide, transmit to the President *pro tempore* of the Senate and the Speaker of the House of Representatives their written declaration that the President is unable to discharge the powers and duties of his office, the Vice-President shall immediately assume the powers and duties of the office as Acting President.

Thereafter, when the President transmits to the President *pro tempore* of the Senate and the Speaker of the House of Representatives his written declaration that no inability exists, he shall resume the powers and duties of his office unless the Vice-President and a majority of either the principal officers of the executive department or of such other body as Congress may by law provide, transmit within four days to the President *pro tempore* of the Senate and the Speaker of the House of Representatives their written declaration that the President is unable to discharge the powers and duties of his office. Thereupon Congress shall decide the issue, assembling within 48 hours for that purpose if not in session. If the Congress, within 21 days after receipt of the latter written declaration, or, if Congress is not in session, within 21 days after Congress is required to assemble, determines by two-thirds vote of both Houses that the President is unable to discharge the powers and duties of his office, the Vice-President shall continue to discharge the same as Acting President; otherwise, the President shall resume the powers and duties of his office.

AMENDMENT XXVI
(ratified 30 June 1971)

Section 1

The right of citizens of the United States, who are 18 years of age or older, to vote shall not be denied or abridged by the United States or by any State on account of age.

Section 2

The Congress shall have power to enforce this article by appropriate legislation.

FEDERAL EXECUTIVE

Head of State

President: GEORGE HERBERT WALKER BUSH (took office 20 January 1989).
Vice-President: JAMES DANFORTH QUAYLE.

The Federal Cabinet
(May 1989)

Secretary of State: JAMES ADDISON BAKER, III.
Secretary of the Treasury: NICHOLAS FREDERICK BRADY.
Secretary of Defense: RICHARD BRUCE CHENEY.
Attorney-General: RICHARD LEWIS THORNBURGH.
Secretary of the Interior: MANUEL LUJAN, Jr.
Secretary of Agriculture: Dr CLAYTON KEITH YEUTTER.
Secretary of Commerce: ROBERT ADAM MOSBACHER.
Secretary of Labor: ELIZABETH HANFORD DOLE.
Secretary of Health and Human Services: Dr LOUIS WADE SULLIVAN.
Secretary of Housing and Urban Development: JACK F. KEMP.
Secretary of Transportation: SAMUEL K. SKINNER.
Secretary of Energy: JAMES DAVID WATKINS.
Secretary of Education: LAURO FRED CAVAZOS.
Secretary of Veteran Affairs: EDWARD JOSEPH DERWINSKI.

OFFICALS WITH CABINET RANK

Chairman of the Council of Economic Advisers: MICHAEL JAY BOSKIN.
Director of the Office of Management and Budget: RICHARD GORDON DARMAN.
United States Trade Representative: CARLA ANDERSON HILLS.

Presidential Election, 8 November 1988

	Popular votes*	% of popular votes	Electoral College votes
GEORGE HERBERT WALKER BUSH (Republican) . .	48,881,011	53.37	426
MICHAEL STANLEY DUKAKIS (Democrat) .	41,828,350	45.67	111
Others	876,511	0.96	1
Total	91,585,872	100.00	538

* Provisional.

Government Departments

Department of Agriculture: 14th St and Independence Ave, SW, Washington, DC 20250; tel. (202) 655-4000; f. 1889.

Department of Commerce: 14th St between Constitution Ave and E St, NW, Washington, DC 20230; tel. (202) 377-2000; f. 1913.

Department of Defense: The Pentagon, Washington, DC 20301; tel. (202) 697-5737; f. 1947.

Department of Education: 400 Maryland Ave, SW, Washington, DC 20202; tel. (202) 245-3192; f. 1979.

Department of Energy: James Forrestal Bldg, 1000 Independence Ave, SW, Washington, DC 20585; tel. (202) 586-5000; fax (202) 586-8134; f. 1977.

Department of Health and Human Services: 200 Independence Ave, SW, Washington, DC 20201; tel. (202) 245-7000; f. 1980.

Department of Housing and Urban Development: 451 7th St, SW, Washington, DC 20410; tel. (202) 755-5111; f. 1965.

Department of the Interior: C St between 18th and 19th Sts, NW, Washington, DC 20240; tel. (202) 343-7351; f. 1849.

Department of Justice: Office of the Attorney-General, 10th St and Constitution Ave, NW, Washington, DC 20530; tel. (202) 633-2007; f. 1870.

Department of Labor: 200 Constitution Ave, NW, Washington, DC 20210; tel. (202) 523-6666; fax (202) 523-6354; f. 1913.

Department of State: 2210 C St, NW, Washington, DC 20520; tel. (202) 647-4000; f. 1789.

Department of Transportation: 400 7th St, SW, Washington, DC 20590; tel. (202) 426-4000; f. 1967.

Department of the Treasury: 15th St and Pennsylvania Ave, NW, Washington, DC 20220; tel. (202) 566-2041; f. 1789.

Department of Veteran Affairs: 810 Vermont Ave, NW, Washington, DC 20420; tel. (202) 389-3775; f. 1989.

Executive Office of the President

Council of Economic Advisors: Old Executive Office Bldg, Washington, DC 20500; tel. (202) 395-5042; Chair. MICHAEL JAY BOSKIN.

Council on Environmental Quality: 722 Jackson Pl., NW, Washington, DC 20503; tel. (202) 395-5080; Chair. A. ALAN HILL.

Intelligence Oversight Board: Old Executive Office Bldg, Washington, DC 20500; tel. (202) 456-2530; Chair. W. GLENN CAMPBELL.

National Security Council: Executive Office Bldg, Washington, DC 20506; tel. (202) 395-3440; Asst to the President for National Security Affairs Gen. BRENT SCOWCROFT.

Office of Administration: Executive Office Bldg, Washington, DC 20500; tel. (202) 395-4980; Dir GORDON RIGGLE.

Office of Federal Procurement Policy: Executive Office Bldg, Washington, DC 20503; tel. (202) 395-5802.

Office of Management and Budget: Old Executive Office Bldg, Washington, DC 20500; tel. (202) 395-4840; Dir RICHARD G. DARMAN.

Office of National Drug Control Policy: Old Executive Office Bldg, Washington, DC 20506; Dir WILLIAM JOHN BENNETT.

Office of Policy Development: Old Executive Office Bldg, Washington, DC 20500; tel. (202) 456-6515; Deputy Asst to the President for Policy Development FRANMARIE KENNEDY-KEEL.

Office of Science and Technology Policy: Old Executive Office Bldg, Washington, DC 20506; tel. (202) 456-7116; Dir Dr WILLIAM R. GRAHAM, Jr.

Office of the United States Trade Representative: 600 17th St, NW, Washington, DC 20506; tel. (202) 395-3204; Rep. for Trade Negotiations CARLA ANDERSON HILLS.

Office of the Vice-President: 1600 Pennsylvania Ave, NW, Washington, DC 20500; tel. (202) 456-2326; telex 440402; Chief of Staff ROBERT M. GUTTMAN.

Regulatory Information Service Center: Executive Office Bldg, Washington, DC 20503; tel. (202) 395-6693; Exec. Dir MARK G. SCHOENBERG.

United States Mission to the United Nations: 799 United Nations Plaza, New York, NY 10017; tel. (212) 415-4000; US Rep. to the United Nations THOMAS R. PICKERING.

The White House Office: 1600 Pennsylvania Ave, NW, Washington, DC 20500; tel. (202) 456-1414; telex 440074; White House Chief of Staff JOHN H. SUNUNU.

Independent Agencies

ACTION: 806 Connecticut Ave, NW, Washington, DC 20525; tel. (202) 634-9282; f. 1971; Dir DONNA M. ALVARADO.

Administrative Conference of the United States: 2120 L St, NW, Washington, DC 20037; tel. (202) 254-7020; f. 1964; Chair. MARSHALL J. BREGER.

African Development Foundation: 1625 Massachusetts Ave, NW, Suite 600, Washington, DC 20036; tel. (202) 673-3916; telex 671-1367; Pres. LEONARD H. ROBINSON, Jr.

American Battle Monuments Commission: 5127 Pulaski Bldg, Washington, DC 20314; tel. (202) 272-0532; f. 1923; Chair. Gen. (retd) ANDREW J. GOODPASTER.

Appalachian Regional Commission: 1666 Connecticut Ave, NW, Washington, DC 20235; tel. (202) 673-7968; f. 1965; Fed. Co-Chair. WINIFRED A. PIZZANO; States' Co-Chair. Gov. CARROLL A. CAMPBELL, Jr (South Carolina).

Board for International Broadcasting: 1201 Connecticut Ave, Suite 400, NW, Washington, DC 20036; tel. (202) 254-8040; f. 1973; Chair. MALCOLM S. FORBES, Jr.

Central Intelligence Agency: Washington, DC 20505; tel. (703) 351-7676; f. 1947; Dir WILLIAM H. WEBSTER.

Commission on Civil Rights: 1121 Vermont Ave, NW, Washington, DC 20425; tel. (202) 523-5571; f. 1957; Chair. WILLIAM ALLEN.

Commission of Fine Arts: 708 Jackson Pl., NW, Washington, DC 20006; tel. (202) 566-1066; f. 1910; Chair. J. CARTER BROWN.

Commodity Futures Trading Commission: 2033 K St, NW, Washington, DC 20581; tel. (202) 254-8630; f. 1974; Chair. WENDY LEE GRAMM.

Consumer Product Safety Commission: 5401 Westbard Ave, Bethesda, MD 20207; f. 1972; Chair. ANNE GRAHAM (acting).

Environmental Protection Agency: 401 M St, SW, Washington, DC 20460; tel. (202) 382-4700; fax (202) 382-7886; telex 892757; f. 1970; Admin. WILLIAM REILLY.

Equal Employment Opportunity Commission: 2401 E St, NW, Washington, DC 20507; tel. (202) 634-6922; fax (202) 634-7332; f. 1965; Chair. CLARENCE THOMAS.

Export–Import Bank of the United States: 811 Vermont Ave, Washington, DC 20571; tel. (202) 566-8144; telex 248460; f. 1934, independent agency since 1945; Chair. WILLIAM RYAN (acting).

Farm Credit Administration: 1501 Farm Credit Dr., McLean, VA 22102-5090; tel. (703) 883-4000; Chair. MARVIN DUNCAN (acting).

Federal Communications Commission: 1919 M St, NW, Washington, DC 20554; tel. (202) 632-7000; f. 1934; Chair. DENNIS R. PATRICK.

Federal Deposit Insurance Corporation: 550 17th St, NW, Washington, DC 20429; tel. (202) 389-4221; f. 1933; Chair. L. WILLIAM SEIDMAN.

Federal Election Commission: 999 E St, NW, Washington, DC 20463; tel. (202) 376-5140; f. 1971; Chair. D. McDONALD.

Federal Emergency Management Agency: 500 C St, SW, Washington, DC 20472; tel. (202) 646-4600; f. 1979; Dir JULIUS W. BECTON, Jr.

Federal Home Loan Bank Board: 1700 G St, NW, Washington, DC 20552; tel. (202) 377-6677; f. 1932; Chair. M. DANNY WALL.

Federal Labor Relations Authority: 500 C St, SW, Washington, DC 20424; tel. (202) 382-0700; f. 1978; Chair. JEAN McKEE (acting).

Federal Maritime Commission: 1100 L St, NW, Washington, DC 20573; tel. (202) 523-5725; f. 1961; Chair. JAMES L. CAREY (acting).

Federal Mediation and Conciliation Service: 2100 K St, NW, Washington, DC 20427; tel. (202) 653-5290; f. 1947; Dir ROBERT P. BAKER (acting).

Federal Reserve System: 20th St and Constitution Ave, NW, Washington, DC 20551; tel. (202) 452-3204; telex 197668; f. 1913; Chair. ALAN GREENSPAN.

Federal Trade Commission: 6th St and Pennsylvania Ave, NW, Washington, DC 20580; tel. (202) 326-2100; f. 1914; Chair. DANIEL OLIVER.

General Accounting Office: 441 G St, NW, Washington, DC 20548; tel. (202) 275-5481; f. 1921; Comptroller-Gen. of the USA CHARLES A. BOWSHER.

General Services Administration: 18th and F Sts, NW, Washington, DC 20405; tel. (202) 535-0800; f. 1949; Admin. RICHARD ASTIN.

Government Printing Office: North Capitol and H Sts, NW, Washington, DC 20401; tel. (202) 275-2034; Public Printer RALPH E. KENNICKELL, Jr.

Inter-American Foundation: 1515 Wilson Blvd, Rosslyn, VA 22209; tel. (703) 841-3800; telex 247008; fax (703) 841-0973; f. 1969; Pres. DEBORAH SZEKELY.

Interstate Commerce Commission: 12th St and Constitution Ave, NW, Washington, DC 20423; tel. (202) 275-7524; f. 1887; Chair. HEATHER J. GRADISON.

Library of Congress: 101 Independence Ave, SE, Washington, DC 20540; tel. (202) 287-5000; telex 8220185; fax (202) 707-9199; f. 1800; Librarian JAMES H. BILLINGTON.

Merit Systems Protection Board: 1120 Vermont Ave, NW, Washington, DC 20419; tel. (202) 653-7124; f. 1978; Chair. HERBERT E. ELLINGWOOD.

National Aeronautics and Space Administration: 400 Maryland Ave, SW, Washington, DC 20546; tel. (202) 453-1000; telex 4979843; fax (202) 755-9234; f. 1958; Admin. RICHARD TRULY.

National Archives and Records Administration: Pennsylvania Ave at 7th St, NW, Washington, DC 20408; tel. (202) 523-3220; f. 1934; Archivist DON W. WILSON.

National Capital Planning Commission: 1325 G St, NW, Washington, DC 20576; tel. (202) 724-0174; f. 1952; Chair. GLEN T. URQUHART.

National Credit Union Administration: 1776 G St, NW, Washington, DC 20456; tel. (202) 357-1100; f. 1970; Chair. ROGER W. JEPSEN.

National Foundation for the Arts and Humanities: 1100 Pennsylvania Ave, NW, Washington, DC 20506; tel. (202) 682-5414; f. 1965; Chair. HUGH SOUTHERN (acting).

National Labor Relations Board: 1717 Pennsylvania Ave, NW, Washington, DC 20570; tel. (202) 254-9430; f. 1935; Chair. JAMES M. STEPHENS.

National Mediation Board: 1425 K St, NW, Washington, DC 20572; tel. (202) 523-5920; f. 1934; Chair. WALTER C. WALLACE.

National Science Foundation: 1800 G St, NW, Washington, DC 20550; tel. (202) 357-7748; f. 1950; Chair. ERICH BLOCH.

National Transportation Safety Board: 800 Independence Ave, SW, Washington, DC 20594; tel. (202) 382-6600; f. 1975; Chair. JAMES L. KOLSTAD (acting).

Nuclear Regulatory Commission: 1717 H St, NW, Washington, DC 20555; tel. (202) 492-7715; f. 1975; Chair. LANDO W. ZECH, Jr.

Occupational Safety and Health Review Commission: 1825 K St, NW, Washington, DC 20006-1246; tel. (202) 634-7943; f. 1970; Chair. E. ROSS BUCKLEY.

Office of Personnel Management: 1900 E St, NW, Washington, DC 20415; tel. (202) 632-6106; telex 4931447; f. 1978; Dir CONSTANCE NEWMAN.

Overseas Private Investment Corporation: 1615 M St, NW, Washington, DC 20527; tel. (202) 457-7010; f. 1970; Pres. and CEO FRED M. ZEDER, III.

Panama Canal Commission: APO Miami, FL 34011-5000; f. 1979; Chair. of Bd of Dirs WILLIAM R. GIANELLI.

Peace Corps: 1890 K St, NW, Washington, DC 20526; tel. (202) 254-7970; f. 1961; Dir PAUL D. COVERDELL.

Pennsylvania Avenue Development Corporation: 1331 Pennsylvania Ave, NW, Suite 1220 North, Washington, DC 20004-1703; tel. (202) 724-9091; f. 1972; Chair. HENRY A. BERLINER.

Pension Benefit Guaranty Corporation: 2020 K St, NW, Washington, DC 20006; tel. (202) 254-4817; f. 1974; Exec. Dir KATHLEEN P. UTGOFF.

Postal Rate Commission: 1333 H St, NW, Washington, DC 20268-0001; tel. (202) 789-6800; f. 1970; Chair. JANET D. STEIGER.

Railroad Retirement Board: 844 Rush St, Room 905, Chicago, IL 60611; tel. (312) 751-4500; fax (312) 751-4923; f. 1935; Chair. THOMAS J. SIMON.

Securities and Exchange Commission: 450 Fifth St, NW, Washington, DC 20549; tel. (202) 272-2650; f. 1934; Chair. RICHARD BREEDEN.

Selective Service Systems: 1023 31st St, NW, Washington, DC 20435; tel. (202) 724-0790; f. 1940; Dir SAMUEL K. LESSEY, Jr.

Small Business Administration: 1441 L St, NW, Washington, DC 20416; tel. (202) 653-6565; f. 1953; Admin. SUSAN ENGELEITER.

Smithsonian Institution: Smithsonian Institution Bldg, 1000 Jefferson Dr., SW, Washington, DC 20560; tel. (202) 357-2700; telex 264729; fax (202) 786-2515; f. 1846; Sec. ROBERT McCORMICK ADAMS.

Tennessee Valley Authority: 400 West Summit Hill Dr., Knoxville, TN 37902; tel. (615) 632-8000; f. 1933; Chair. of Bd of Dirs MARVIN T. RUNYON.

United States Arms Control and Disarmament Agency: 320 21st St, NW, Washington, DC 20451; tel. (202) 632-0392; f. 1961; Dir RONALD F. LEHMAN, II.

United States Information Agency: 301 Fourth St, SW, Washington, DC 20547; tel. (202) 485-7860; f. 1978; Dir BRUCE GELB.

United States International Development Co-operation Agency: 320 21st St, NW, Washington, DC 20523; tel. (202) 647-9620; f. 1979; Dir JAY F. MORRIS (acting).

United States International Trade Commission: 701 E St, NW, Washington, DC 20436; tel. (202) 523-0161; f. 1916; Chair. ANNE E. BRUNSDALE.

United States Postal Service: 475 L'Enfant Plaza West, SW, Washington, DC 20260-0001; tel. (202) 268-2000; f. 1970; Postmaster-Gen. ANTHONY M. FRANK.

United States Railway Association: 955 L'Enfant Plaza North, SW, Washington, DC 20595; tel. (202) 488-8877; f. 1973.

PRESIDENTIAL ELECTIONS

Popular Votes Cast for President, by State

('000, by major political party. Sources: Elections Research Center, Washington, DC; News Election Service.)

	1980 Dem.	1980 Rep.	1984 Dem.	1984 Rep.	1988* Dem.	1988* Rep.
Alabama	637	654	552	873	547	810
Alaska	42	86	62	138	62	102
Arizona	247	530	334	681	447	694
Arkansas	398	403	339	535	345	464
California	3,084	4,525	3,923	5,467	4,448	4,756
Colorado	368	652	455	822	621	728
Connecticut	542	677	570	891	675	747
Delaware	106	111	102	152	99	131
District of Columbia	131	24	180	29	153	26
Florida	1,419	2,047	1,449	2,730	1,632	2,539
Georgia	891	654	707	1,069	716	1,070
Hawaii	136	130	147	185	192	159
Idaho	110	291	109	298	147	253
Illinois	1,981	2,358	2,086	2,707	2,181	2,299
Indiana	844	1,256	841	1,377	851	1,280
Iowa	509	676	606	703	667	542
Kansas	326	567	333	677	422	553
Kentucky	616	635	540	822	579	731
Louisiana	708	793	652	1,037	716	881
Maine	221	239	215	337	241	304

PRESIDENTIAL ELECTIONS—Popular Votes Cast for President, by State ('000, by major political party)—*continued*

	1980 Dem.	1980 Rep.	1984 Dem.	1984 Rep.	1988* Dem.	1988* Rep.
Maryland	726	681	788	880	794	834
Massachusetts	1,054	1,058	1,240	1,311	1,387	1,184
Michigan	1,662	1,915	1,530	2,252	1,673	1,969
Minnesota	954	873	1,036	1,033	1,107	958
Mississippi	429	441	352	582	361	552
Missouri	931	1,074	849	1,274	1,004	1,081
Montana	118	207	147	232	168	190
Nebraska	167	420	188	460	254	389
Nevada	67	155	92	189	133	206
New Hampshire	109	222	120	267	162	280
New Jersey	1,147	1,547	1,261	1,934	1,275	1,700
New Mexico	168	251	202	307	237	261
New York	2,728	2,894	3,120	3,665	3,228	2,975
North Carolina	876	915	824	1,346	890	1,232
North Dakota	79	194	104	200	127	166
Ohio	1,752	2,207	1,825	2,679	1,935	2,412
Oklahoma	402	696	385	862	483	678
Oregon	457	571	536	686	575	518
Pennsylvania	1,938	2,262	2,228	2,584	2,184	2,291
Rhode Island	198	155	197	212	217	170
South Carolina	430	442	344	616	368	600
South Dakota	104	198	116	200	146	166
Tennessee	783	788	712	990	678	939
Texas	1,881	2,511	1,949	3,433	2,331	3,014
Utah	124	440	155	469	207	427
Vermont	82	95	96	136	116	123
Virginia	752	990	796	1,337	861	1,305
Washington	650	865	807	1,052	845	800
West Virginia	367	334	328	405	339	308
Wisconsin	982	1,089	996	1,199	1,122	1,044
Wyoming	49	111	53	133	67	107
Total	**35,484**	**43,904**	**37,577**	**54,455**	**41,016**	**47,946**

* Based on nearly-complete, unofficial returns.

FEDERAL LEGISLATURE (CONGRESS)

The Senate
(May 1989)

Senators' terms are for six years, one-third of the Senate being re-elected every two years.

President of the Senate: Vice-Pres. JAMES DANFORTH QUAYLE.

President Pro Tempore: ROBERT C. BYRD (Dem.).

  Democrats: 55 seats.

  Republicans: 45 seats.

Majority Leader: GEORGE J. MITCHELL (Dem.).

Minority Leader: ROBERT J. DOLE (Rep.).

MEMBERS

(With political party and year in which term expires—on 3 January in all cases)

Alabama
HOWELL T. HEFLIN	Dem.	1991
RICHARD C. SHELBY	Dem.	1993

Alaska
TED STEVENS	Rep.	1991
FRANK H. MURKOWSKI	Rep.	1993

Arizona
JOHN McCAIN, III	Rep.	1993
DENNIS DeCONCINI	Dem.	1995

Arkansas
DAVID H. PRYOR	Dem.	1991
DALE BUMPERS	Dem.	1993

California
ALAN CRANSTON	Dem.	1993
PETE WILSON	Rep.	1995

Colorado
WILLIAM L. ARMSTRONG	Rep.	1991
TIMOTHY E. WIRTH	Dem.	1993

Connecticut
CHRISTOPHER J. DODD	Dem.	1993
JOSEPH I. LIEBERMAN	Dem.	1995

Delaware
JOSEPH R. BIDEN, Jr	Dem.	1991
WILLIAM V. ROTH, Jr	Rep.	1995

Florida
D. ROBERT GRAHAM	Dem.	1993
CONNIE MACK, III	Rep.	1995

Georgia
SAM NUNN	Dem.	1991
WYCHE FOWLER, Jr	Dem.	1993

Hawaii
DANIEL K. INOUYE	Dem.	1993
SPARK M. MATSUNAGA	Dem.	1995

Idaho
JAMES A. McCLURE	Rep.	1991
STEVEN D. SYMMS	Rep.	1993

Illinois
PAUL SIMON	Dem.	1991
ALAN J. DIXON	Dem.	1993

Indiana
DAN COATS	Rep.	1991
RICHARD G. LUGAR	Rep.	1995

Iowa
TOM HARKIN	Dem.	1991
CHARLES E. GRASSLEY	Rep.	1993

Kansas
NANCY LANDON KASSEBAUM	Rep.	1991
ROBERT J. DOLE	Rep.	1993

Kentucky		
A. MITCHELL MCCONNELL	Rep.	1991
WENDELL H. FORD	Dem.	1993
Louisiana		
J. BENNETT JOHNSTON	Dem.	1991
JOHN B. BREAUX	Dem.	1993
Maine		
WILLIAM S. COHEN	Rep.	1991
GEORGE J. MITCHELL	Dem.	1995
Maryland		
BARBARA A. MIKULSKI	Dem.	1993
PAUL S. SARBANES	Dem.	1995
Massachusetts		
JOHN F. KERRY	Dem.	1991
EDWARD M. KENNEDY	Dem.	1995
Michigan		
CARL LEVIN	Dem.	1991
DONALD W. RIEGLE, Jr	Dem.	1995
Minnesota		
RUDOLPH. E. BOSCHWITZ	Rep.	1991
DAVID F. DURENBERGER	Rep.	1995
Mississippi		
THAD COCHRAN	Rep.	1991
TRENT LOTT	Rep.	1995
Missouri		
CHRISTOPHER S. BOND	Rep.	1993
JOHN C. DANFORTH	Rep.	1995
Montana		
MAX BAUCUS	Dem.	1991
CONRAD BURNS	Rep.	1995
Nebraska		
J. JAMES EXON	Dem.	1991
BOB KERREY	Dem.	1995
Nevada		
HARRY M. REID	Dem.	1993
RICHARD BRYAN	Dem.	1995
New Hampshire		
GORDON J. HUMPHREY	Rep.	1991
WARREN B. RUDMAN	Rep.	1993
New Jersey		
BILL BRADLEY	Dem.	1991
FRANK R. LAUTENBERG	Dem.	1995
New Mexico		
PETE V. DOMENICI	Rep.	1991
JEFF BINGAMAN	Dem.	1995
New York		
ALFONSE M. D'AMATO	Rep.	1993
DANIEL P. MOYNIHAN	Dem.	1995
North Carolina		
JESSE A. HELMS	Rep.	1991
TERRY SANFORD	Dem.	1993
North Dakota		
KENT CONRAD	Dem.	1993
QUENTIN N. BURDICK	Dem.	1995
Ohio		
JOHN H. GLENN, Jr	Dem.	1993
HOWARD M. METZENBAUM	Dem.	1995
Oklahoma		
DAVID L. BOREN	Dem.	1991
DON NICKLES	Rep.	1993
Oregon		
MARK O. HATFIELD	Rep.	1991
ROBERT W. PACKWOOD	Rep.	1993
Pennsylvania		
ARLEN SPECTER	Rep.	1993
H. JOHN HEINZ, III	Rep.	1995
Rhode Island		
CLAIBORNE PELL	Dem.	1991
JOHN H. CHAFEE	Rep.	1995
South Carolina		
STROM THURMOND	Rep.	1991
ERNEST F. HOLLINGS	Dem.	1993
South Dakota		
LARRY PRESSLER	Rep.	1991
THOMAS A. DASCHLE	Dem.	1993
Tennessee		
ALBERT GORE, Jr	Dem.	1991
JAMES R. SASSER	Dem.	1995

Texas		
PHIL GRAMM	Rep.	1991
LLOYD M. BENTSEN	Dem.	1995
Utah		
E. JAKE GARN	Rep.	1993
ORRIN G. HATCH	Rep.	1995
Vermont		
PATRICK J. LEAHY	Dem.	1993
JAMES JEFFORDS	Rep.	1995
Virginia		
JOHN W. WARNER	Rep.	1991
CHARLES S. ROBB	Dem.	1995
Washington		
BROCK ADAMS	Dem.	1993
SLADE GORTON	Rep.	1995
West Virginia		
JOHN D. ROCKEFELLER, IV	Dem.	1991
ROBERT C. BYRD	Dem.	1995
Wisconsin		
ROBERT W. KASTEN, Jr	Rep.	1993
HERBERT H. KOHL	Dem.	1995
Wyoming		
ALAN K. SIMPSON	Rep.	1991
MALCOLM WALLOP	Rep.	1995

The House of Representatives

(June 1989)

A new House of Representatives is elected every two years.

Speaker: THOMAS S. FOLEY (Dem.).

Democrats: 259 seats.

Republicans: 172 seats.
(5 vacancies)

Majority Leader: RICHARD GEPHARDT (Dem.).

Minority Leader: ROBERT H. MICHEL (Rep.).

MEMBERS
(with political party, listed in District order)

District	Alabama	Party
1	SONNY CALLAHAN	Rep.
2	WILLIAM L. DICKINSON	Rep.
3	(vacant)	
4	TOM BEVILL	Dem.
5	RONNIE G. FLIPPO	Dem.
6	BEN ERDREICH	Dem.
7	CLAUDE HARRIS, Jr	Dem.
	Alaska	
At Large	DON YOUNG	Rep.
	Arizona	
1	JOHN J. RHODES, III	Rep.
2	MORRIS K. UDALL	Dem.
3	BOB STUMP	Rep.
4	JOHN KYL	Rep.
5	JIM KOLBE	Rep.
	Arkansas	
1	BILL ALEXANDER	Dem.
2	TOMMY F. ROBINSON	Dem.
3	JOHN PAUL HAMMERSCHMIDT	Rep.
4	BERYL ANTHONY, Jr	Dem.
	California	
1	DOUGLAS H. BOSCO	Dem.
2	WALLY HERGER	Rep.
3	ROBERT T. MATSUI	Dem.
4	VIC FAZIO	Dem.
5	NANCY PELOSI	Dem.
6	BARBARA BOXER	Dem.
7	GEORGE MILLER	Dem.
8	RONALD V. DELLUMS	Dem.
9	FORTNEY H. ('PETE') STARK	Dem.
10	DON EDWARDS	Dem.
11	TOM LANTOS	Dem.
12	TOM J. CAMPBELL	Rep.
13	NORMAN Y. MINETA	Dem.
14	NORMAN D. SHUMWAY	Rep.
15	(vacant)	
16	LEON E. PANETTA	Dem.

District		Party
17	CHARLES PASHAYAN, Jr	Rep.
18	RICHARD H. LEHMAN	Dem.
19	ROBERT J. LAGOMARSINO	Rep.
20	WILLIAM M. THOMAS	Rep.
21	ELTON GALLEGLY	Rep.
22	CARLOS J. MOORHEAD	Rep.
23	ANTHONY C. BEILENSON	Dem.
24	HENRY A. WAXMAN	Dem.
25	EDWARD R. ROYBAL	Dem.
26	HOWARD L. BERMAN	Dem.
27	MEL LEVINE	Dem.
28	JULIAN C. DIXON	Dem.
29	AUGUSTUS F. HAWKINS	Dem.
30	MATTHEW G. MARTINEZ	Dem.
31	MERVYN M. DYMALLY	Dem.
32	GLENN M. ANDERSON	Dem.
33	DAVID DREIER	Rep.
34	ESTEBAN EDWARD TORRES	Dem.
35	JERRY LEWIS	Rep.
36	GEORGE E. BROWN, Jr	Dem.
37	AL McCANDLESS	Rep.
38	ROBERT K. DORNAN	Rep.
39	WILLIAM E. DANNEMEYER	Rep.
40	CHRISTOPHER COX	Rep.
41	BILL LOWERY	Rep.
42	DANA ROHRABACHER	Dem.
43	RON C. PACKARD	Rep.
44	JIM BATES	Dem.
45	DUNCAN L. HUNTER	Rep.

Colorado

1	PATRICIA SCHROEDER	Dem.
2	DAVID SKAGGS	Dem.
3	BEN NIGHTHORSE CAMPBELL	Dem.
4	HANK BROWN, Jr	Rep.
5	JOEL HEFLEY	Rep.
6	DANIEL R. SCHAEFER	Rep.

Connecticut

1	BARBARA B. KENNELLY	Dem.
2	SAM GEJDENSON	Dem.
3	BRUCE A. MORRISON	Dem.
4	CHRISTOPHER SHAYS	Rep.
5	JOHN G. ROWLAND	Rep.
6	NANCY L. JOHNSON	Rep.

Delaware

At Large	THOMAS R. CARPER	Dem.

Florida

1	EARL HUTTO	Dem.
2	BILL GRANT	Rep.
3	CHARLES E. BENNETT	Dem.
4	CRAIG JAMES	Rep.
5	BILL McCOLLUM	Rep.
6	CLIFFORD B. STEARNS	Rep.
7	SAM GIBBONS	Dem.
8	C. W. BILL YOUNG	Rep.
9	MICHAEL BILIRAKIS	Rep.
10	ANDY IRELAND	Rep.
11	BILL NELSON	Dem.
12	TOM LEWIS	Rep.
13	PORTER J. GOSS	Rep.
14	HARRY A. JOHNSTON	Dem.
15	E. CLAY SHAW, Jr	Rep.
16	LARRY SMITH	Dem.
17	WILLIAM LEHMAN	Dem.
18	(vacant)	
19	DANTE B. FASCELL	Dem.

Georgia

1	LINDSAY THOMAS	Dem.
2	CHARLES HATCHER	Dem.
3	RICHARD RAY	Dem.
4	BEN JONES	Dem.
5	JOHN LEWIS	Dem.
6	NEWT GINGRICH	Rep.
7	GEORGE ('BUDDY') DARDEN	Dem.
8	J. ROY ROWLAND	Dem.
9	ED JENKINS	Dem.
10	DOUG BARNARD, Jr	Dem.

Hawaii

1	PATRICIA SAIKI	Rep.
2	DANIEL K. AKAKA	Dem.

Idaho

1	LARRY CRAIG	Rep.
2	RICHARD STALLINGS	Dem.

District		Party
	Illinois	
1	CHARLES A. HAYES	Dem.
2	GUS SAVAGE	Dem.
3	MARTY RUSSO	Dem.
4	GEORGE SANGMEISTER	Dem.
5	WILLIAM O. LIPINSKI	Dem.
6	HENRY J. HYDE	Rep.
7	CARDISS COLLINS	Dem.
8	DAN ROSTENKOWSKI	Dem.
9	SIDNEY R. YATES	Dem.
10	JOHN EDWARD PORTER	Rep.
11	FRANK ANNUNZIO	Dem.
12	PHILIP M. CRANE	Rep.
13	HARRIS W. FAWELL	Rep.
14	J. DENNIS HASTERT	Rep.
15	EDWARD R. MADIGAN	Rep.
16	LYNN MARTIN	Rep.
17	LANE EVANS	Dem.
18	ROBERT H. MICHEL	Rep.
19	TERRY L. BRUCE	Dem.
20	RICHARD J. DURBIN	Dem.
21	JERRY COSTELLO	Dem.
22	GLENN POSHARD	Dem.

Indiana

1	PETER J. VISCLOSKY	Dem.
2	PHILIP R. SHARP	Dem.
3	JOHN HILER	Rep.
4	(vacant)	
5	JAMES JONTZ	Dem.
6	DAN L. BURTON	Rep.
7	JOHN T. MYERS	Rep.
8	FRANK McCLOSKEY	Dem.
9	LEE H. HAMILTON	Dem.
10	ANDREW JACOBS, Jr	Dem.

Iowa

1	JIM LEACH	Rep.
2	TOM TAUKE	Rep.
3	DAVID R. NAGLE	Dem.
4	NEAL SMITH	Dem.
5	JIM ROSS LIGHTFOOT	Rep.
6	FRED GRANDY	Rep.

Kansas

1	PAT ROBERTS	Rep.
2	JIM SLATTERY	Dem.
3	JAN MEYERS	Rep.
4	DAN GLICKMAN	Dem.
5	BOB WHITTAKER	Rep.

Kentucky

1	CARROLL HUBBARD, Jr	Dem.
2	WILLIAM H. NATCHER	Dem.
3	ROMANO L. MAZZOLI	Dem.
4	JIM BUNNING	Rep.
5	HAROLD ROGERS	Rep.
6	LARRY J. HOPKINS	Rep.
7	CARL C. PERKINS	Dem.

Louisiana

1	BOB LIVINGSTON	Rep.
2	LINDY BOGGS	Dem.
3	W. J. ('BILLY') TAUZIN, II	Dem.
4	JIM McCRERY	Rep.
5	JERRY HUCKABY	Dem.
6	RICHARD HUGH BAKER	Rep.
7	JIMMY HAYES	Dem.
8	CLYDE C. HOLLOWAY	Rep.

Maine

1	JOSEPH E. BRENNAN	Dem.
2	OLYMPIA J. SNOWE	Rep.

Maryland

1	ROY DYSON	Dem.
2	HELEN BENTLEY	Rep.
3	BENJAMIN L. CARDIN	Dem.
4	THOMAS McMILLEN	Dem.
5	STENY H. HOYER	Dem.
6	BEVERLY B. BYRON	Dem.
7	KWEISI MFUME	Dem.
8	CONSTANCE A. MORELLA	Rep.

Massachusetts

1	SILVIO O. CONTE	Rep.
2	RICHARD E. NEAL	Dem.
3	JOSEPH D. EARLY	Dem.
4	BARNEY FRANK	Dem.
5	CHESTER G. ATKINS	Dem.

District		Party
6	NICHOLAS MAVROULES	Dem.
7	EDWARD J. MARKEY	Dem.
8	JOSEPH P. KENNEDY, II	Dem.
9	JOE MOAKLEY	Dem.
10	GERRY E. STUDDS	Dem.
11	BRIAN J. DONNELLY	Dem.
	Michigan	
1	JOHN CONYERS, Jr	Dem.
2	CARL D. PURSELL	Rep.
3	HOWARD WOLPE	Dem.
4	FRED UPTON	Rep.
5	PAUL B. HENRY	Rep.
6	BOB CARR	Dem.
7	DALE E. KILDEE	Dem.
8	BOB TRAXLER	Dem.
9	GUY VANDER JAGT	Rep.
10	BILL SCHUETTE	Rep.
11	ROBERT W. DAVIS	Rep.
12	DAVID E. BONIOR	Dem.
13	GEORGE W. CROCKETT, Jr	Dem.
14	DENNIS M. HERTEL	Dem.
15	WILLIAM D. FORD	Dem.
16	JOHN D. DINGELL	Dem.
17	SANDER M. LEVIN	Dem.
18	WILLIAM S. BROOMFIELD	Rep.
	Minnesota	
1	TIMOTHY J. PENNY	Dem.
2	VIN WEBER	Rep.
3	BILL FRENZEL	Rep.
4	BRUCE F. VENTO	Dem.
5	MARTIN OLAV SABO	Dem.
6	GERRY SIKORSKI	Dem.
7	ARLAN STANGELAND	Rep.
8	JAMES L. OBERSTAR	Dem.
	Mississippi	
1	JAMIE L. WHITTEN	Dem.
2	MIKE ESPY	Dem.
3	G. V. ('SONNY') MONTGOMERY	Dem.
4	MIKE PARKER	Dem.
5	LARKIN SMITH	Rep.
	Missouri	
1	WILLIAM CLAY	Dem.
2	JACK BUECHNER	Rep.
3	RICHARD A. GEPHARDT	Dem.
4	IKE SKELTON	Dem.
5	ALAN WHEAT	Dem.
6	E. THOMAS COLEMAN	Rep.
7	MEL HANCOCK	Rep.
8	BILL EMERSON	Rep.
9	HAROLD L. VOLKMER	Dem.
	Montana	
1	PAT WILLIAMS	Dem.
2	RON MARLENEE	Rep.
	Nebraska	
1	DOUGLAS K. BEREUTER	Rep.
2	PETER HOAGLAND	Dem.
3	VIRGINIA SMITH	Rep.
	Nevada	
1	JAMES BILBRAY	Dem.
2	BARBARA F. VUCANOVICH	Rep.
	New Hampshire	
1	ROBERT C. SMITH	Rep.
2	CHARLES G. DOUGLAS, III	Rep.
	New Jersey	
1	JAMES J. FLORIO	Dem.
2	WILLIAM J. HUGHES	Dem.
3	FRANK PALLONE, Jr	Dem.
4	CHRISTOPHER H. SMITH	Rep.
5	MARGE ROUKEMA	Rep.
6	BERNARD J. DWYER	Dem.
7	MATTHEW J. RINALDO	Rep.
8	ROBERT A. ROE	Dem.
9	ROBERT G. TORRICELLI	Dem.
10	DONALD PAYNE	Dem.
11	DEAN A. GALLO	Rep.
12	JIM COURTER	Rep.
13	H. JAMES SAXTON	Rep.
14	FRANK J. GUARINI	Dem.
	New Mexico	
1	STEVEN H. SCHIFF	Rep.
2	JOE SKEEN	Rep.
3	BILL RICHARDSON	Dem.

District		Party
	New York	
1	GEORGE J. HOCHBRUECKNER	Dem.
2	THOMAS J. DOWNEY	Dem.
3	ROBERT J. MRAZEK	Dem.
4	NORMAN F. LENT	Rep.
5	RAYMOND J. McGRATH	Rep.
6	FLOYD FLAKE	Dem.
7	GARY L. ACKERMAN	Dem.
8	JAMES H. SCHEUER	Dem.
9	THOMAS MANTON	Dem.
10	CHARLES E. SCHUMER	Dem.
11	EDOLPHUS TOWNS	Dem.
12	MAJOR R. OWENS	Dem.
13	STEPHEN J. SOLARZ	Dem.
14	GUY V. MOLINARI	Rep.
15	BILL GREEN	Rep.
16	CHARLES B. RANGEL	Dem.
17	TED WEISS	Dem.
18	ROBERT GARCIA	Dem.
19	ELIOT L. ENGEL	Dem.
20	NITA M. LOWEY	Dem.
21	HAMILTON FISH, Jr	Rep.
22	BENJAMIN A. GILMAN	Rep.
23	MICHAEL R. McNULTY	Dem.
24	GERALD B. H. SOLOMON	Rep.
25	SHERWOOD L. BOEHLERT	Rep.
26	DAVID O'B. MARTIN	Rep.
27	JAMES T. WALSH	Rep.
28	MATTHEW F. McHUGH	Dem.
29	FRANK HORTON	Rep.
30	LOUISE M. SLAUGHTER	Dem.
31	WILLIAM PAXON	Rep.
32	JOHN J. LaFALCE	Dem.
33	HENRY J. NOWAK	Dem.
34	AMORY HOUGHTON, Jr	Rep.
	North Carolina	
1	WALTER B. JONES	Dem.
2	TIM VALENTINE, Jr	Dem.
3	MARTIN LANCASTER	Dem.
4	DAVID E. PRICE	Dem.
5	STEPHEN L. NEAL	Dem.
6	HOWARD COBLE	Rep.
7	CHARLES G. ROSE, III	Dem.
8	BILL HEFNER	Dem.
9	ALEX McMILLAN, III	Rep.
10	CASS BALLENGER	Rep.
11	JAMES McCLURE CLARKE	Dem.
	North Dakota	
At Large	BYRON L. DORGAN	Dem.
	Ohio	
1	THOMAS A. LUKEN	Dem.
2	BILL GRADISON, Jr	Rep.
3	TONY P. HALL	Dem.
4	MICHAEL OXLEY	Rep.
5	PAUL E. GILLMOR	Rep.
6	BOB McEWEN	Rep.
7	MICHAEL DeWINE	Rep.
8	DONALD E. ('BUZ') LUKENS	Rep.
9	MARCY KAPTUR	Dem.
10	CLARENCE E. MILLER	Rep.
11	DENIS E. ECKART	Dem.
12	JOHN R. KASICH	Rep.
13	DON J. PEASE	Dem.
14	THOMAS C. SAWYER	Dem.
15	CHALMERS P. WYLIE	Rep.
16	RALPH REGULA	Rep.
17	JAMES TRAFICANT, Jr	Dem.
18	DOUGLAS APPLEGATE	Dem.
19	EDWARD F. FEIGHAN	Dem.
20	MARY ROSE OAKAR	Dem.
21	LOUIS STOKES	Dem.
	Oklahoma	
1	JAMES INHOFE	Rep.
2	MIKE SYNAR	Dem.
3	WES WATKINS	Dem.
4	DAVE McCURDY	Dem.
5	MICKEY EDWARDS	Rep.
6	GLENN ENGLISH	Dem.
	Oregon	
1	LES AuCOIN	Dem.
2	ROBERT F. SMITH	Rep.
3	RON WYDEN	Dem.

District		Party		District		Party
4	PETER A. DEFAZIO	Dem.		12	JIM WRIGHT	Dem.
5	MICHAEL J. KOPETSKI	Dem.		13	BILL SARPALIUS	Dem.
	Pennsylvania			14	GREG LAUGHLIN	Dem.
1	THOMAS M. FOGLIETTA	Dem.		15	E. ('KIKA') DE LA GARZA	Dem.
2	WILLIAM H. GRAY, III	Dem.		16	RONALD D. COLEMAN	Dem.
3	ROBERT A. BORSKI	Dem.		17	CHARLES W. STENHOLM	Dem.
4	JOE KOLTER	Dem.		18	MICKEY LELAND	Dem.
5	RICHARD T. SCHULZE	Rep.		19	LARRY COMBEST	Rep.
6	GUS YATRON	Dem.		20	HENRY B. GONZALEZ	Dem.
7	CURT WELDON	Rep.		21	LAMAR SMITH	Rep.
8	PETER H. KOSTMAYER	Dem.		22	TOM DELAY	Rep.
9	BUD SHUSTER	Rep.		23	ALBERT G. BUSTAMENTE	Dem.
10	JOSEPH M. MCDADE	Rep.		24	MARTIN FROST	Dem.
11	PAUL KANJORSKI	Dem.		25	MICHAEL A. ANDREWS	Dem.
12	JOHN P. MURTHA	Dem.		26	RICHARD ARMEY	Rep.
13	LAWRENCE COUGHLIN	Rep.		27	SOLOMON P. ORTIZ	Dem.
14	WILLIAM J. COYNE	Dem.			**Utah**	
15	DON RITTER	Rep.		1	JAMES V. HANSEN	Rep.
16	ROBERT S. WALKER	Rep.		2	WAYNE OWENS	Dem.
17	GEORGE GEKAS	Rep.		3	HOWARD C. NIELSON	Rep.
18	DOUG WALGREN	Dem.			**Vermont**	
19	BILL GOODLING	Rep.		At Large	PETER P. SMITH	Rep.
20	JOSEPH M. GAYDOS	Dem.			**Virginia**	
21	THOMAS J. RIDGE	Rep.		1	HERBERT H. BATEMAN	Rep.
22	AUSTIN J. MURPHY	Dem.		2	OWEN B. PICKETT	Dem.
23	WILLIAM F. CLINGER, Jr	Rep.		3	THOMAS J. BLILEY, Jr	Rep.
	Rhode Island			4	NORMAN SISISKY	Dem.
1	RONALD K. MACHTLEY	Rep.		5	LEWIS F. PAYNE, Jr	Dem.
2	CLAUDINE SCHNEIDER	Rep.		6	JAMES R. OLIN	Dem.
	South Carolina			7	D. FRENCH SLAUGHTER, Jr	Rep.
1	ARTHUR RAVENAL, Jr	Rep.		8	STAN PARRIS	Rep.
2	FLOYD SPENCE	Rep.		9	RICK C. BOUCHER	Dem.
3	BUTLER DERRICK, Jr	Dem.		10	FRANK R. WOLF	Rep.
4	LIZ J. PATTERSON	Dem.			**Washington**	
5	JOHN M. SPRATT, Jr	Dem.		1	JOHN MILLER	Rep.
6	ROBERT TALLON	Dem.		2	AL SWIFT	Dem.
	South Dakota			3	JOLENE UNSOELD	Dem.
At Large	TIM JOHNSON	Dem.		4	SID MORRISON	Rep.
	Tennessee			5	THOMAS S. FOLEY	Dem.
1	JAMES H. QUILLEN	Rep.		6	NORMAN D. DICKS	Dem.
2	JOHN J. DUNCAN, Jr	Rep.		7	JIM MCDERMOTT	Dem.
3	MARILYN LLOYD	Dem.		8	ROD CHANDLER	Rep.
4	JIM COOPER	Dem.			**West Virginia**	
5	BOB CLEMENT	Dem.		1	ALAN B. MOLLOHAN	Dem.
6	BART GORDON	Dem.		2	HARLEY O. STAGGERS, Jr	Dem.
7	DON SUNDQUIST	Rep.		3	ROBERT E. WISE, Jr	Dem.
8	JOHN S. TANNER	Dem.		4	NICK J. RAHALL, II	Dem.
9	HAROLD E. FORD	Dem.			**Wisconsin**	
	Texas			1	LES ASPIN	Dem.
1	JIM CHAPMAN	Dem.		2	ROBERT W. KASTENMEIER	Dem.
2	CHARLES WILSON	Dem.		3	STEVE GUNDERSON	Rep.
3	STEVE BARTLETT	Rep.		4	GERALD D. KLECZKA	Dem.
4	RALPH M. HALL	Dem.		5	JIM MOODY	Dem.
5	JOHN BRYANT	Dem.		6	THOMAS E. PETRI	Rep.
6	JOE BARTON	Rep.		7	DAVID R. OBEY	Dem.
7	BILL ARCHER	Rep.		8	TOBY ROTH	Rep.
8	JACK FIELDS	Rep.		9	F. JAMES SENSENBRENNER, Jr	Rep.
9	JACK BROOKS	Dem.			**Wyoming**	
10	J. J. ('JAKE') PICKLE	Dem.		At Large	(vacant)	
11	MARVIN LEATH	Dem.				

FEDERAL BUDGET

($ million, year ending 30 September. Sources: Office of Management and Budget, Executive Office of the President; Financial Management Service, US Department of the Treasury.)

FEDERAL RECEIPTS (includes off-budget receipts)

	1987	1988	1989*
Individual income taxes . .	392,557	401,181	424,307
Corporation income taxes . .	83,926	94,195	110,992
Social-insurance taxes and contributions	303,318	334,335	357,913
Excise taxes	32,457	35,540	34,494
Estate and gift taxes . .	7,493	7,594	7,795
Customs duties . .	15,085	16,198	17,559
Miscellaneous receipts . .	19,307	19,909	20,450
Total	854,143	908,953	973,510

* Estimates at October 1988.

FEDERAL OUTLAYS
(includes outlays of off-budget federal entities and programmes)

	1987	1988	1989*
National defence . . .	281,999	290,349	293,429
International affairs . .	11,649	10,469	15,696
General science, space and technology . .	9,216	10,876	12,329
Energy	4,115	2,342	4,927
Natural resources and environment . . .	13,363	14,538	16,591
Agriculture	27,356	17,210	20,890
Commerce and housing credit .	6,182	19,064	11,568
Transportation . . .	26,228	27,196	28,066
Community and regional development . .	5,051	5,577	6,626
Education, training, employment and social services	29,724	30,856	35,911
Health	39,968	44,482	49,474
Medicare	75,120	78,798	86,285
Income security . . .	123,250	130,174	135,878
Social security . . .	207,353	219,030	232,597
Veterans' benefits and services	26,782	29,248	28,977
Administration of justice . .	7,548	9,205	8,831
General government . .	7,569	9,506	9,388
Net interest . . .	138,570	151,711	157,561
Allowances	—	—	1,069
Undistributed offsetting receipts	−36,455	−36,576	−37,130
Total	1,004,586	1,064,055	1,118,964

* Estimates at October 1988.

STATE GOVERNMENTS

Votes Cast for US Senators, by State

('000, by major political party. Sources: Elections Research Center, Washington, DC; News Election Service.)

	1984 Dem.	1984 Rep.	1986 Dem.	1986 Rep.	1988* Dem.	1988* Rep.
Alabama .	861	499	609	603	—	—
Alaska .	59	147	80	98	—	—
Arizona .	—	—	341	522	650	471
Arkansas .	502	374	433	262	—	—
California .	—	—	3,647	3,542	4,054	4,828
Colorado .	449	834	529	513	—	—
Connecticut .	—	—	633	340	680	670
Delaware .	148	98	—	—	85	141
Florida .	—	—	1,878	1,552	1,966†	1,966†
Georgia .	1,344	337	624	601	—	—
Hawaii .	—	—	242	87	248	67
Idaho .	106	293	185	197	—	—
Illinois .	2,397	2,308	2,034	1,054	—	—
Indiana .	—	—	595	936	671	1,410
Iowa .	717	564	299	589	—	—
Kansas .	212	757	247	577	—	—
Kentucky .	640	645	504	173	—	—
Louisiana‡ .	—	—	724	646	—	—
Maine .	143	404	—	—	443	103
Maryland .	—	—	675	437	953	589
Massachusetts .	1,393	1,137	—	—	1,620	853
Michigan .	1,916	1,745	—	—	1,987	1,245
Minnesota .	853	1,200	—	—	852	1,171
Mississippi .	372	580	—	—	431	487
Missouri .	—	—	700	778	659	1,407
Montana .	216	154	—	—	175	189
Nebraska .	332	307	—	—	371	272
Nevada .	—	—	131	117	175	161
New Hampshire .	157	226	79	154	—	—

(continued)

VOTES CAST FOR US SENATORS, BY STATE ('000, by major political party)—*continued*

	1984 Dem.	1984 Rep.	1986 Dem.	1986 Rep.	1988* Dem.	1988* Rep.
New Jersey	1,987	1,080	—	—	1,551	1,302
New Mexico	141	361	—	—	311	181
New York	—	—	1,723	2,378	3,890	1,827
North Carolina	1,070	1,157	824	768	—	—
North Dakota	—	—	144	142	171	112
Ohio	—	—	1,949	1,172	2,474	1,870
Oklahoma	906	281	400	493	—	—
Oregon	406	808	376	656	—	—
Pennsylvania	—	—	1,448	1,907	1,409	2,892
Rhode Island	287	108	—	—	174	207
South Carolina	307	645	466	263	—	—
South Dakota	81	235	153	143	—	—
Tennessee	1,001	557	—	—	1,020	535
Texas	2,203	3,116	—	—	3,078	2,068
Utah	—	—	116	315	203	427
Vermont	—	—	124	68	72	162
Virginia	601	1,406	—	—	1,456	591
Washington	541§	672§	677	651	815	840
West Virginia	374	345	—	—	411	223
Wisconsin	—	—	703	755	1,123	1,028
Wyoming	41	146	—	—	89	90

* Preliminary figures.
† Republican candidate won election.
‡ Louisiana holds an open primary election with candidates from all parties running on the same ballot. Any candidate who receives a majority is elected; if no candidate receives 50%, there is a run-off election in November between the top two finishers.
§ 1983 election to fill vacancy caused by death of incumbent senator.

Votes Cast for US Representatives, by State

('000, by major political party. Source: Elections Research Center, Washington, DC.)

	1982 Dem.	1982 Rep.	1984 Dem.	1984 Rep.	1986 Dem.	1986 Rep.
Alabama	677	273	822	308	679	436
Alaska	52	128	86	114	74	102
Arizona	300	395	320	603	260	540
Arkansas*	397	362	341†	91†	387	268
California	3,815	3,537	4,327	4,424	3,744	3,328
Colorado	448	485	436	780	450	566
Connecticut	577	485	668	762	545	434
Delaware	99	87	142	101	106	54
District of Columbia	93	17	155	—‡	102	18
Florida*	1,311	900	1,245	1,191	1,154	987
Georgia	670	225	1,091	430	773	289
Hawaii	267	—‡	227	41	187	135
Idaho	151	170	165	240	163	208
Illinois	2,093	1,508	2,367	2,204	1,623	1,393
Indiana	882	910	1,022	1,147	788	756
Iowa	529	475	595	673	428	461
Kansas	346	401	435	542	313	475
Kentucky	413	280	657	529	375	253
Louisiana§	336	142	402	239	288	102
Maine	187	261	162	375	165	249
Maryland	743	349	955	536	669	394
Massachusetts	1,300	561	1,618	704	1,198	250
Michigan	1,670	1,093	1,861	1,567	1,342	977
Minnesota	956	778	1,061	902	832	558
Mississippi	368	260	523	327	316	208
Missouri	872	653	1,130	903	828	600
Montana	166	142	187	179	172	146
Nebraska	116	402	168	482	197	358
Nevada	114	116	109	155	121	134
New Hampshire	114	154	119	251	84	156
New Jersey	1,206	915	1,508	1,471	803	739
New Mexico	203	192	201	294	179	207
New York¶	2,617	1,940	3,255	2,898	2,132	1,665
North Carolina	708	580	1,131	1,026	890	682
North Dakota	187	72	243	66	216	67
Ohio	1,807	1,457	2,134	2,159	1,512	1,536
Oklahoma*	539	310	646	458	430	291
Oregon	578	437	655	548	585	446
Pennsylvania	1,911	1,652	2,531	2,112	1,763	1,526
Rhode Island	174	158	195	195	130	176
South Carolina	353	295	471	441	453	261
South Dakota	142	134	181	135	171	118

(continued)

VOTES CAST FOR US REPRESENTATIVES, BY STATE ('000, by major political party)—*continued*

	1982		1984		1986	
	Dem.	Rep.	Dem.	Rep.	Dem.	Rep.
Tennessee.	698	470	726	589	636	449
Texas	1,847	935	2,695	1,982	1,717	1,263
Utah	145	312	208	387	197	230
Vermont	38	114	60	148	—‡	168
Virginia	630	690	795	1,003	545	467
Washington	690	604	997	800	768	527
West Virginia.	343	202	429	275	299	97
Wisconsin.	769	667	1,033	1,033	704	669
Wyoming	46	113	46	138	49	111

* State law does not require tabulation of votes for unopposed candidates.
† Excluding data for one of the state's four congressional districts.
‡ No candidate.
§ Data for 1982 and 1984 refer to September open primary; data for 1986 refer to general-election run-offs in two districts.
¶ Includes votes cast by other endorsing parties for Democratic and Republican candidates.

Votes Cast for State Governors, by State

('000, by major political party. Sources: Elections Research Center, Washington, DC; state election administration offices.)

	1982		1984		1986	
	Dem.	Rep.	Dem.	Rep.	Dem.	Rep.
Alabama	651	441	—	—	537	696
Alaska	90	72	—	—	85	77
Arizona	454	236	—	—	299	344
Arkansas	432	357	555	332	440	248
California	3,788	3,881	—	—	2,782	4,507
Colorado	628	303	—	—	616	434
Connecticut	578	498	—	—	576	408
Delaware	—	—	108	135	—	—
Florida	1,740	949	—	—	1,539	1,848
Georgia	734	434	—	—	828	347
Hawaii	141	82	—	—	174	160
Idaho	165	161	—	—	193	190
Illinois	1,811	1,816	—	—	209	1,656
Indiana	—	—	1,037	1,146	—	—
Iowa	483	548	—	—	437	473
Kansas	406	39	—	—	404	436
Kentucky	—	—	562*	455*	—	—
Louisiana†	—	—	n.a.*	n.a.*	—	—
Maine	281	173	—	—	129	170
Maryland	706	433	—	—	907	194
Massachusetts	1,219	750	—	—	1,158	525
Michigan	1,561	1,370	—	—	1,632	754
Minnesota.	1,049	716	—	—	790	607
Mississippi	—	—	409*	289*	—	—
Missouri	—	—	914	1,195	—	—
Montana	—	—	267	100	—	—
Nebraska	277	270	—	—	265	298
Nevada	128	100	—	—	187	65
New Hampshire	132	145	127	257	116	135
New Jersey	—	—	—	—	578‡	1,373‡
New Mexico	216	192	—	—	185	209
New York	2,675	2,495	—	—	2,775	1,364
North Carolina	—	—	1,011	1,208	—	—
North Dakota.	—	—	174	140	—	—
Ohio	1,982	1,304	—	—	1,858	1,207
Oklahoma.	548	332	—	—	405	432
Oregon	374	640	—	—	549	507
Pennsylvania	1,772	1,873	—	—	1,717	1,638
Rhode Island	247	80	163	245	105	209
South Carolina	469	203	—	—	361	385
South Dakota	81	197	—	—	142	153
Tennessee.	501	738	—	—	657	553
Texas	1,698	1,466	—	—	1,585	1,814
Utah	—	—	276	352	—	—
Vermont	74	93	117	113	92	75
Virginia	—	—	—	—	700‡	602‡
Washington	—	—	1,007	882	—	—
West Virginia.	—	—	347	395	—	—
Wisconsin.	897	663	—	—	706	805
Wyoming	106	62	—	—	89	76

* Figures refer to 1983 election.
† Louisiana holds an open primary election with candidates from all parties running on the same ballot. Any candidate who receives a majority is elected; if no candidate receives 50%, there is a run-off election between the top two finishers. In 1983 the primary election was won by the Democratic candidate, with 62.3% of the 1,615,905 votes cast.
‡ Figures refer to 1985 election.

State and Local Government Finances

(Figures are in $ million and refer to years ending 30 June. Source: Bureau of the Census, US Department of Commerce, *Governmental Finances*, Series GF, No. 5.)

SUMMARY

Revenue	1984/85	1985/86	1986/87
From federal government . .	106,158	113,099	114,996
From state and local governments. . . .	613,904	670,251	727,593
General revenue from own sources	491,963	528,359	571,168
Taxes	350,367	373,051	405,149
Property. . . .	103,757	111,710	121,227
Sales and gross receipts	126,376	135,001	144,293
Individual income .	70,361	74,354	83,681
Corporation income .	19,152	19,982	22,672
Other	30,721	32,004	33,277
Charges and miscellaneous	141,596	155,308	166,019
Utility and liquor stores . .	44,772	47,163	49,810
Insurance trust revenue . .	77,170	94,729	106,615
Employee retirement . .	53,212	69,365	79,255
Unemployment compensation . . .	17,640	18,267	18,925
Other	6,319	7,097	8,434
Total	720,062	783,349	842,589

Expenditure	1984/85	1985/86	1986/87
General expenditure . . .	553,997	605,594	656,064
Education	192,686	210,819	226,658
Local schools . . .	131,987	145,111	156,782
Institutions of higher education	52,316	56,535	60,240
Other	8,383	9,173	9,636
Libraries.	2,700	2,948	3,274
Public welfare . . .	71,479	75,868	82,520
Hospitals.	35,967	37,958	40,108
Health	13,711	15,550	16,864
Social-insurance administration . . .	2,592	2,707	2,752
Veterans' services . .	113	122	129
Highways	44,989	49,368	52,199
Other transportation. . .	6,060	6,940	7,621
General public buildings . .	4,105	4,106	4,853
Housing and urban renewal	10,378	11,285	11,766
Police	20,956	22,685	24,684
Fire	8,917	9,587	10,910
Correction	12,839	14,957	16,637
Protection inspection. . .	3,530	4,079	4,420
Parks and recreation. . .	9,160	10,164	10,978
Sewerage and sanitation . .	17,398	19,142	21,324
Natural resources . .	8,357	9,074	9,738
General control . . .	14,314	15,800	17,202
Financial administration .	10,471	11,897	12,841
Interest on general debt .	32,427	37,064	41,816
Other and unallocable .	30,847	33,475	36,770
Utility and liquor stores .	59,798	65,297	68,440
Insurance trust expenditure	44,191	46,538	50,815
Employee retirement . .	14,995	26,521	29,614
Unemployment compensation	24,414	14,887	15,248
Other	4,782	5,130	5,953
Total	657,986	717,430	775,318

REVENUE, EXPENDITURE AND DEBT, BY STATE, (1984/85, estimates)

	General revenue						
	From federal government	From taxes	From current charges	Total (incl. miscellaneous)	Debt outstanding	Direct general expenditure	Capital outlay*
Alabama	1,768	3,981	1,476	8,068	7,740	7,879	1,278
Alaska	525	2,389	421	6,726	9,881	4,954	1,462
Arizona	939	4,386	851	7,324	11,819	7,345	1,835
Arkansas	944	2,282	558	4,219	3,283	3,998	599
California	13,526	43,365	9,170	73,542	50,361	68,429	7,831
Colorado	1,198	4,680	1,189	8,200	8,959	7,784	1,490
Connecticut	1,252	5,765	659	8,599	8,735	7,516	831
Delaware	293	969	296	1,907	2,582	1,672	216
District of Columbia	1,348	1,574	147	3,238	3,437	2,718	519
Florida	3,805	13,428	4,080	23,940	26,071	22,228	4,669
Georgia	2,716	7,061	2,530	13,455	11,251	11,771	2,496
Hawaii	500	1,741	338	2,818	3,055	2,601	369
Idaho	419	1,027	288	1,915	1,147	1,878	315
Illinois	4,970	17,007	2,542	27,399	21,709	25,067	3,430
Indiana	1,941	6,493	1,869	11,256	7,146	10,179	1,241
Iowa	1,144	3,839	1,078	6,603	3,958	6,664	1,062
Kansas	869	3,324	795	5,872	5,994	5,439	815
Kentucky	1,643	3,850	608	7,295	10,365	6,698	909
Louisiana	1,877	5,818	1,501	10,882	15,313	10,344	1,439
Maine	651	1,545	242	2,648	1,963	2,449	237
Maryland	1,848	7,153	1,110	11,308	12,307	10,332	1,555
Massachusetts	2,957	9,987	1,492	15,502	15,439	14,134	1,822
Michigan	4,270	14,619	3,393	24,491	15,214	22,705	1,889
Minnesota.	2,088	7,407	1,797	13,023	13,959	11,918	1,731
Mississippi	1,183	2,398	982	4,929	3,248	4,662	585
Missouri	1,857	5,485	1,331	9,593	7,249	8,927	1,271
Montana	524	1,142	218	2,282	1,884	2,160	401
Nebraska	638	2,010	646	3,721	5,958	3,621	707
Nevada	339	1,351	424	2,436	2,802	2,355	447
New Hampshire	385	1,124	186	1,921	2,485	1,812	226

(continued)

REVENUE, EXPENDITURE AND DEBT, BY STATE (1984/85, estimates)—*continued*

| | General revenue | | | | | | |
	From federal government	From taxes	From current charges	Total (incl. miscellaneous)	Debt outstanding	Direct general expenditure	Capital outlay*
New Jersey	3,112	13,223	2,050	20,700	22,629	18,771	1,837
New Mexico	687	1,810	395	4,168	3,954	3,678	691
New York	11,457	41,500	5,850	64,568	62,454	59,455	7,236
North Carolina	2,332	7,158	1,588	12,205	10,012	11,168	1,697
North Dakota	409	930	348	1,949	1,299	1,847	296
Ohio	4,203	14,296	3,254	24,229	16,642	22,781	2,560
Oklahoma	1,151	4,255	1,135	7,409	7,411	6,713	1,219
Oregon	1,407	3,816	930	7,165	9,863	6,640	882
Pennsylvania	5,096	16,414	2,491	27,163	25,197	24,040	2,492
Rhode Island	530	1,431	242	2,569	3,443	2,459	238
South Carolina	1,257	3,601	1,065	6,425	6,748	5,966	838
South Dakota	375	738	181	1,535	1,584	1,567	405
Tennessee	1,932	4,742	1,470	8,799	8,267	8,300	1,329
Texas	4,889	20,741	4,636	35,579	42,388	32,803	6,358
Utah	865	2,070	486	4,240	7,924	3,827	1,740
Vermont	333	745	146	1,351	1,226	1,282	157
Virginia	1,909	7,460	1,788	12,101	8,760	11,369	1,439
Washington	2,246	6,328	1,550	11,219	17,873	11,093	2,352
West Virginia	851	2,328	463	4,006	4,402	3,840	505
Wisconsin	2,229	7,692	1,677	12,463	8,822	12,160	1,403
Wyoming	470	1,313	252	2,684	2,291	2,121	551
Total	106,158	349,793	74,415	597,640	568,501	552,119	79,901

* Includes general functions, liquor stores and utilities.

Alabama

CONSTITUTION AND GOVERNMENT

The current constitution of Alabama is the state's sixth and became effective on 28 November 1901. Constitutional amendments proposed by the Legislature have to be approved by a three-fifths majority vote in each house, and must then be ratified by a simple majority of state voters. The governor is elected separately from the lieutenant-governor to serve a four-year term of office, and may serve no more than two terms consecutively. The cabinet consists of 24 members who are appointed by the governor and meet at least twice a month. The Legislature consists of 35 senators and 105 representatives, and both chambers are elected every four years. Regular legislative sessions are held annually and are limited to 30 legislative days. A bill becomes law once it has been passed by a majority of a quorum of both houses and has been signed by the governor. The governor has 10 days to consider a bill, after which it becomes law unless vetoed. A gubernatorial veto may be overridden by a majority vote of the elected members in each house. Most enacted bills become effective immediately. In the 1986 gubernatorial election 1,236,000 people voted, representing 52% of the number registered to vote and 42% of the voting-age population. Alabama has 67 administrative counties.

ELECTED EXECUTIVE-BRANCH OFFICIALS

Governor (1987–91): GUY HUNT (Rep.).

Lieutenant-Governor: JIM FOLSOM, Jr (Dem.).

Secretary of State: GLEN BROWDER (Dem.).

Attorney-General: DON SIEGELMAN (Dem.).

Treasurer: GEORGE WALLACE, Jr (Dem.).

Auditor: JAN COOK (Dem.).

Commissioner of Agriculture and Industries: ALBERT McDONALD.

SELECTED GOVERNMENT ADDRESSES

Office of the Governor: State Capitol, Rm 100, 11 South Union St, Montgomery, AL 36130; tel. (205) 261-2500.

Office of the Lieutenant-Governor: State Capitol, Rm 201, 11 South Union St, Montgomery, AL 36130; tel. (205) 261-2500.

Office of the Secretary of State: State Capitol, Rm 105, 11 South Union St, Montgomery, AL 36130; tel. (205) 261-2500.

Office of the Attorney-General: 64 North Union St, Montgomery, AL 36130; tel. (205) 261-2500.

Office of the Treasurer: State Capitol, Rm 111, 11 South Union St, Montgomery, AL 36130; tel. (205) 261-4169.

Office of the Auditor: State Capitol, Rm 107, 11 South Union St, Montgomery, AL 36130; tel. (205) 261-7010.

Bureau of Tourism and Travel: 532 South Perry St, Montgomery, AL 36130; tel. (205) 261-4169; Dir LISA WALSH SHIVERS.

Department of Agriculture and Industries: 1445 Federal Dr., POB 3336, Montgomery, AL 36193; tel. (205) 261-2650; Commr ALBERT McDONALD.

Department of Corrections: 101 South Union St, Montgomery, AL 36130-1301; tel. (205) 834-1227; Commr MORRIS THIGPEN.

Department of Education: 501 Dexter Ave, Montgomery, AL 36130-3901; tel. (205) 261-5156; Supt Dr WAYNE TEAGUE.

Department of Environmental Management: 1751 Federal Dr., Montgomery, AL 36130; tel. (205) 271-7700; Dir LEE PEGUES.

Department of Finance: State Capitol, 11 South Union St, Montgomery, AL 36130; tel. (205) 261-7160; Dir GEORGE R. SWIFT, Jr.

Department of Labor: 651 Administrative Bldg, 64 North Union St, Montgomery, AL 36130; tel. (205) 261-3460; Commr ROBIN REA.

Department of Public Health: State Office Bldg, Rm 381, Montgomery, AL 36130-1701; tel. (205) 261-5052; State Health Officer CLAUDE EARL FOX.

Department of Revenue: 200 Administrative Bldg, 64 North Union St, Montgomery, AL 36130; tel. (205) 261-3362; Commr JAMES M. SIZEMORE, Jr.

Division of Energy Resources: Dept of Economics and Community Affairs, POB 2939, Montgomery, AL 36105; tel. (205) 284-8953; Dir FRED BRASWELL.

Military Department: 1720 Federal Dr., POB 3711, Montgomery, AL 36193-4701; tel. (205) 271-7200; Adj.-Gen. IVAN F. SMITH.

Public Service Commission: State Office Bldg, Montgomery, AL 36130; tel. (205) 261-5209; incorporates Div. of Transportation; Pres. JAMES SULLIVAN.

LEGISLATURE

(May 1989)

Senate: Dem. 28; Rep. 4; Ind. 3; Total 35.

President: Lt-Gov. JIM FOLSOM, Jr (Dem.).
President Pro Tempore: RYAN deGRAFFENRIED, Jr (Dem.).
Secretary: McDOWELL LEE.

House of Representatives: Dem. 87; Rep. 11; Ind. 6; 1 vacancy; Total 105.

Speaker: JAMES S. CLARK (Dem.).
Speaker Pro Tempore: JAMES N. CAMPBELL (Dem.).
Clerk: JOHN W. PEMBERTON.

Alaska

CONSTITUTION AND GOVERNMENT

Alaska's only constitution was adopted in 1956 and became effective on 3 January 1959. A constitutional amendment proposed by the Legislature requires a vote by three-fifths of the elected members of each house, and ratification by a majority of state voters. The governor and lieutenant-governor are elected jointly to serve four-year terms, neither being allowed to serve more than two consecutive terms. The governor may not stand for re-election for four years after completion of a second consecutive term. The 17 members of the cabinet (including the governor) are appointed to specified office and meet at regular intervals. There are 20 senators and 40 representatives in the Legislature, serving terms of four and two years respectively. Alternate halves of the Senate are re-elected every two years. Regular legislative sessions commence in January each year and last for no longer than 120 calendar days. A bill becomes law when it has been approved by both houses of the Legislature and has been signed by the governor. During session the governor has 15 days in which to consider a bill, after which it becomes law unless vetoed. After session a bill becomes law unless vetoed within 20 days of being presented to the governor. The governor's veto may usually be overridden by a two-thirds vote of the elected representatives in each house. Legislation becomes effective 90 days after enactment. In the 1986 election to the US Senate 181,000 people voted, representing 62% of those registered to vote and 49% of the voting-age population. Instead of having administrative counties Alaska has 11 boroughs covering 40% of the state, and the rest of the state comes under one 'unorganized' borough.

ELECTED EXECUTIVE-BRANCH OFFICIALS

Governor (1987–91): STEVE COWPER (Dem.).

Lieutenant-Governor and Secretary of State: STEPHEN A. McAL-PINE (Dem.).

SELECTED GOVERNMENT ADDRESSES

Office of the Governor: Capitol Bldg, 3rd Floor, POB A, Juneau, AK 99811; tel. (907) 465-3500.

Office of the Lieutenant-Governor: Capitol Bldg, 3rd Floor, POB AA, Juneau, AK 99811; tel. (907) 465-3520.

Department of Administration: State Office Bldg, 10th Floor, POB C, Juneau, AK 99811; tel. (907) 465-2200; Commr JOHN M. ANDREWS.

Department of Commerce and Economic Development: POB D, Juneau, AK 99811; tel. (907) 465-2500; incorporates Div. of Tourism and Public Utilities Comm.; Commr LARRY MERCULIEFF.

Department of Corrections: Fuller Bldg, 3rd Floor, Corner of 4th and Harris Sts, POB T, Juneau, AK 99811; tel. (907) 465-3376; Commr SUSAN HUMPHREY-BARNETT.

Department of Education: Goldbelt Bldg, 2nd Floor, 801 West 10th St, POB F, Juneau, AK 99811; tel. (907) 465-2800; Commr WILLIAM G. DEMMERT.

Department of Environmental Conservation: 3220 Hospital Dr., POB O, Juneau, AK 99811; tel. (907) 465-2600; Commr DENNIS KELSO.

Department of Fish and Game: 1255 West 8th St, Capital Office Park, POB 3-2000, Juneau, AK 99802; tel. (907) 465-4100; Commr DON W. COLLINSWORTH.

Department of Health and Social Services: Alaska Office Bldg, Rm 204, POB H, Juneau, AK 99811; tel. (907) 465-3030; Commr MYRA MUNSON.

Department of Labor: 1111 West 8th St, POB 21149, Juneau, AK 99802; tel. (907) 465-2700; Commr JIM SAMPSON.

Department of Law: Capitol Bldg, Rm 412, POB K, Juneau, AK 99811, tel. (907) 465-3600; Att.-Gen. DOUGLAS B. BAILY.

Department of Military and Veterans Affairs: 3601 C St, Suite 660, Anchorage, AK 99503-5989; tel. (907) 249-1565; Adj.-Gen. Maj.-Gen. JOHN W. SCHAEFFER.

Department of Natural Resources: 400 Willoughby Ave, 5th Floor, Juneau, AK 99801; tel. (907) 465-2400; incorporates Div. of Agriculture; Commr LENNIE BOSTON-GORSUCH.

Department of Public Safety: 450 Whittier St, POB N, Juneau, AK 99811; tel. (907) 465-4322; Commr ARTHUR ENGLISH.

Department of Revenue: State Office Bldg, 11th Floor, POB S, Juneau, AK 99811; tel. (907) 465-2300; incorporates State Finance Div.; Commr HUGH MALONE.

Department of Transportation and Public Facilities: 3132 Channel Dr., POB Z, Juneau, AK 99811-2500; tel. (907) 465-3900; Commr MARK S. HICKEY.

Energy Programs Division: Dept of Community and Regional Affairs, 3601 C St, Suite 7221, Anchorage, AK 99503; tel. (907) 563-1955; Dir ROBERT BREAN.

LEGISLATURE
(May 1989)

Senate: Rep. 11; Dem. 9; Total 20.

President: TIM KELLY (Rep.).
Secretary: NANCY QUINTO.

House of Representatives: Dem. 23; Rep. 17; Total 40.

Speaker: SAM COTTEN (Dem.).
Chief Clerk: IRENE CASHEN.

Arizona

CONSTITUTION AND GOVERNMENT

Arizona's only constitution was adopted in 1911 and became effective on 14 February 1912. An amendment to the constitution proposed by the Legislature must be passed by a two-thirds majority in each house; approval by a majority of state voters is then required to ratify the amendment. The governor is elected to serve a four-year term, the secretary of state succeeding to the office of governor in the event of a vacancy or incapacity. Arizona is the only state which elects a mine inspector. The cabinet consists of 15 members (including the governor) who are appointed to specified office and meet weekly. There are 30 senators and 60 representatives in the state Legislature, both houses being re-elected together every two years. Regular legislative sessions commence annually in January and there is no statutory limit to their length. Bills must be passed by both houses and signed by the governor to become law. During session the governor has five days in which to consider a bill, after which it becomes law unless vetoed. After adjournment of the session a bill becomes law unless vetoed by the governor within 10 days. The governor's veto may be overridden by a two-thirds vote from the elected members of each house. Legislation becomes effective 90 days after adjournment of the session. In the 1986 gubernatorial election 867,000 people voted, a figure which represented 54% of those registered to vote and 36% of the state's voting-age population. Arizona has 15 administrative counties.

ELECTED EXECUTIVE-BRANCH OFFICIALS

Governor (1988–91): ROSE MOFFORD (Dem.; succeeded to office in April 1988 after the impeachment, conviction and removal from office of Evan Mecham, and elected in May to serve the remainder of Mecham's 1987–91 term).

Secretary of State: JIM SHUMWAY.

Attorney-General: ROBERT K. CORBIN (Rep.).

Treasurer: RAY ROTTAS (Rep.).

Superintendent of Public Instruction: C. DIANE BISHOP.

Mine Inspector: DOUGLAS K. MARTIN.

SELECTED GOVERNMENT ADDRESSES

Office of the Governor: State Capitol, 1700 West Washington St, Phoenix, AZ 85007; tel. (602) 255-4331.

Office of the Secretary of State: State Capitol, West Wing, Phoenix, AZ 85007; tel. (602) 255-4285.

Office of the Attorney-General: 1275 West Washington St, Phoenix, AZ 85007; tel. (602) 255-4266.

Office of the Treasurer: State Capitol, Rm 150, Phoenix, AZ 85007; tel. (602) 255-5815.

Agriculture and Horticulture Commission: 1688 West Adams St, Rm 421, Phoenix, AZ 85007; tel. (602) 255-4373; Dir IVAN J. SHIELDS.

Department of Administration: State Capitol, Rm 809, Phoenix, AZ 85007; tel. (602) 255-1751; incorporates Div. of Finance; Dir DOUGLAS S. PATINO.

Department of Commerce: State Capitol, West Wing, Phoenix, AZ 85007; tel. (602) 255-5374; Exec. Dir Dr THOMAS CALDWELL.

Department of Corrections: 321 West Indian School Rd, Phoenix, AZ 85013; tel. (602) 255-5497; Dir SAMUEL LEWIS.

Department of Education: 1535 West Jefferson St, Phoenix, AZ 85007; tel. (602) 255-4361; Supt of Public Instruction C. DIANE BISHOP.

Department of Emergency and Military Affairs: 5636 East McDowell Rd, Phoenix, AZ 85008; tel. (602) 273-9710; Adj.-Gen. DONALD L. OWENS.

Department of Health Services: 1740 West Adams St, Phoenix, AZ 85007; tel. (602) 255-1024; incorporates Div. of Environmental Health Services; Dir TED WILLIAMS.

Department of Public Safety: 2310 North 20th Ave, Phoenix, AZ 85005; tel. (602) 262-8359; Dir RALPH T. MILSTEAD.

Department of Revenue: State Capitol, West Wing, Phoenix, AZ 85007; tel. (602) 255-3572; Dir BETSY BAYLESS (acting).

Department of Transportation: POB 2100, Phoenix, AZ 85007; tel. (602) 255-7011; Dir CHARLES MILLER.

Division of Employment and Rehabilitation Services: Dept of Economic Security, 1717 West Jefferson St, Phoenix, AZ 85005; tel. (602) 255-5678; Dir EDDIE BROWN.

Division of Natural Resources: Dept of Land, 1624 West Adams St, 4th Floor, Phoenix, AZ 85007; tel. (602) 255-4621; Commr M. J. HASSESS.

Energy Programs Office: Office of Econ. Planning and Development, State Capitol, West Wing, Phoenix, AZ 85007; tel. (602) 255-5371; Dir MARK GINSBERG.

Governor's Office of Tourism: 1480 East Bethany Home Rd, Suite 180, Phoenix, AZ 85014; tel. (602) 255-3618; Dir VIC HELLER (acting).

Utilities Division: Corporation Comm., 1200 West Washington St, Phoenix, AZ 85007; tel. (602) 255-4251; Dir WAYNE E. RUHTER.

LEGISLATURE
(May 1989)

Senate: Rep. 19; Dem. 11; Total 30.

  President: CARL KUNASEK (Rep.).
  President Pro Tempore: JACK TAYLOR (Rep.).
  Secretary: SHIRLEY WHEATON.

House of Representatives: Rep. 36; Dem. 24; Total 60.

  Speaker: JOE LANE (Rep.).
  Speaker Pro Tempore: BOB DENNY (Rep.).
  Chief Clerk: JANE RICHARDS.

Arkansas
CONSTITUTION AND GOVERNMENT

The current constitution of Arkansas is the state's fifth and became effective on 30 October 1874. Amendments to the constitution, which are proposed by the General Assembly (the state legislature), must be approved by the majority of elected members in each house and then ratified by a majority of voters. The governor and lieutenant-governor are elected separately to serve four-year terms, and the governor may serve no more than two terms. The cabinet, which has 17 members (including the governor), is appointed to specified office and meets regularly. There are 35 senators and 100 representatives in the General Assembly, serving terms of four and two years respectively. Alternate halves of the Senate are elected every two years. Regular legislative sessions take place biennially in odd-numbered years beginning in January, and there is no statutory limit to their length. After a bill has been approved by both houses of the General Assembly it has to be considered by the governor. During session the governor has five days to consider a bill, after which it becomes law unless vetoed. After session a bill becomes law if not vetoed within 20 days. A gubernatorial veto may be overriden by majority votes by the elected members in each house. Enacted legislation becomes effective 90 days after adjournment of the session. In 1986 695,000 people voted in the election to the US Senate, representing 58% of the number registered and 40% of the voting-age population. Arkansas has 75 administrative counties.

ELECTED EXECUTIVE-BRANCH OFFICIALS

Governor (1987–91): BILL CLINTON (Dem.).
Lieutenant-Governor: WINSTON BRYANT (Dem.).
Secretary of State: BILL McCUEN (Dem.).
Attorney-General: STEVE CLARK (Dem.).
Treasurer: JIMMIE LOU FISHER (Dem.).
Auditor: JULIA HUGHES JONES (Dem.).
Land Commissioner: CHARLIE DANIELS.

SELECTED GOVERNMENT ADDRESSES

Office of the Governor: State Capitol, Little Rock, AR 72201; tel. (501) 371-2345.

Office of the Lieutenant-Governor: State Capitol, Rm 301, Little Rock, AR 72201; tel. (501) 371-2144.

Office of the Secretary of State: State Capitol, Little Rock, AR 72201; tel. (501) 371-1010.

Office of the Attorney-General: Justice Bldg, Little Rock, AR 72201; tel. (501) 371-6030.

Office of the Treasurer: State Capitol, Little Rock, AR 72201; tel. (501) 371-5888.

Office of the Auditor: State Capitol, Little Rock, AR 72201; tel. (501) 371-6030.

Department of Commerce: 1501 North University Ave, Suite 364, Little Rock, AR 72207; tel. (501) 371-2231; incorporates Energy Office and Public Service Comm.

Department of Corrections: POB 8707, Pine Bluff, AR 71611; tel. (501) 247-1800; Dir A. L. LOCKHART.

Department of Education: A. W. Ford Bldg, Capitol Mall, Little Rock, AR 72201; tel. (501) 371-1464; Dir TOMMY R. VENTERS.

Department of Finance and Administration: POB 3278, Little Rock, AR 72203; tel. (501) 371-2242; incorporates Div. of Revenue Services; Dir and Comptroller MAHLON A. MARTIN.

Department of Health: 4815 West Markham St, Little Rock, AR 72205-3867; tel. (501) 661-2111; Dir BEN N. SALTZMAN.

Department of Highways and Transportation: POB 2261, Little Rock, AR 72203; tel. (501) 569-2211; Dir HENRY GRAY.

Department of Labor: 1022 High St, Little Rock, AR 72202; tel. (501) 375-8442; Dir DEWEY STILES.

Department of Pollution Control and Ecology: POB 9583, Little Rock, AR 72219; tel. (501) 562-7444; Dir Dr PHYLLIS GARNETT.

Department of Parks and Tourism: 1 Capitol Mall, Little Rock, AR 72201; tel. (501) 371-7777; Dir Jo LUCK WILSON.

Department of State Police: POB 5901, Little Rock, AR 72215; tel. (501) 224-4111; Dir T. L. GOODWIN.

Military Department: Camp Robinson, Box 628, North Little Rock, AR 72118; tel. (501) 758-4053; Adj.-Gen. Maj.-Gen. JAMES A RYAN.

GENERAL ASSEMBLY
(May 1989)

Senate: Dem. 31; Rep. 4; Total 35.

  President: Lt-Gov. WINSTON BRYANT (Dem.).
  President Pro Tempore: EUGENE CANADA (Dem.).
  Secretary: HAL MOODY.

House of Representatives: Dem. 91; Rep. 9; Total 100.

  Speaker: B. G. HENDRIX (Dem.).
  Speaker Pro Tempore: ODE MADDOX (Dem.).
  Chief Clerk: Jo KENSHAW.

California
CONSTITUTION AND GOVERNMENT

California's current constitution is its second and became effective on 4 July 1879. A constitutional amendment proposed by the Legislature has to be approved by two-thirds of the members of both houses and then ratified by a majority of voters. The governor and lieutenant-governor are elected separately for terms of four years, and there is no limit to the number of terms that can be served. Cabinet members, 11 including the governor, are appointed to specified offices and meet every two weeks. There are 40 senators and 80 representatives in the Legislature, serving terms of four and two years respectively. Alternate halves of the Senate are re-elected every two years. Regular sessions of the Legislature begin in the January following an election and last until November of the following year. Bills may be introduced by either house; they are then referred to committees and read three times before each house. Before being presented to the governor, bills must be approved by an absolute majority in each house; a bill becomes law unless vetoed by the governor within 12 days. A gubernatorial veto may be overridden by a two-thirds vote of the elected members of each house. Legislation usually becomes effective in the January following enactment, providing a 90-day period has elapsed. In 1986 7,444,000 people voted in the gubernatorial election, representing 58% of those registered to vote and 37% of the voting-age population. California is divided into 58 administrative counties.

ELECTED EXECUTIVE-BRANCH OFFICIALS

Governor (1987–91): GEORGE DEUKMEJIAN (Rep.).
Lieutenant-Governor: LEO T. McCARTHY (Dem.).
Secretary of State: MARCH FONG EU (Dem.).
Attorney-General: JOHN K. VAN DE KAMP (Dem.).
Treasurer: JESSE M. UNRUH (Dem.).
Controller: GRAY DAVIS (Dem.).
Superintendent of Public Instruction: BILL HONIG.

SELECTED GOVERNMENT ADDRESSES

Office of the Governor: State Capitol, Rm 100, Sacramento, CA 95814; tel. (916) 445-2841.

Office of the Lieutenant-Governor: State Capitol, Rm 1028, Sacramento, CA 95814; tel. (916) 445-8994; incorporates Comm. for Economic Development.

Office of the Secretary of State: 1230 J St, Sacramento, CA 95814; tel. (916) 445-6371.

Office of the Attorney-General: 1515 K St, Rm 511, Sacramento, CA 95814; tel. (916) 324-5437.

Office of the Treasurer: POB 1919, Sacramento, CA 95809; tel. (916) 445-5316.

Office of the Controller: POB 1019, Sacramento, CA 95805; tel. (916) 445-2636.

Commission on Energy: 1516 9th St, Sacramento, CA 95814; tel. (916) 324-3000; Chair. CHARLES R. IMBRECT.

Department of Commerce: 1121 L St, Suite 600, Sacramento, CA 95814; tel. (916) 445-3962; incorporates Office of Tourism; Dir CHRISTY CAMPBELL.

Department of Corrections: 630 K St, Sacramento, CA 94283-0001; tel. (916) 445-7688; Dir DANIEL J. MCCARTHY.

Department of Education: POB 944272, Sacramento, CA 94244-2720; tel. (916) 445-4338; Supt of Public Instruction BILL HONIG.

Department of Employment Development: 800 Capitol Mall, Sacramento, CA 95814; tel. (916) 445-9212; Dir KAYE R. KIDDOO.

Department of Finance: State Capitol, Rm 1145, Sacramento, CA 95814; tel. (916) 445-4141; Dir JESSE R. HUFF.

Department of Food and Agriculture: 1220 N St, Sacramento, CA 95814; tel. (916) 445-7126; Dir CLARE BERRYHILL.

Department of Health Services: 714 P St, Sacramento, CA 95814; tel. (916) 445-1351; Dir KENNETH KIZER.

Department of Revenue: Aerojet Center, Sacramento, CA 95857; tel. (916) 355-0370; Exec. Officer of Franchise Tax Bd GERALD GOLDBERG.

Department of Transportation: 1120 N St, Sacramento, CA 95814; tel. (916) 445-2201; Dir LEO J. TROMBATORE.

Environmental Affairs Agency: POB 2815, Sacramento, CA 95814; tel. (916) 322-5840; Sec. JANANNE SHARPLESS.

Military Department: POB 214405, Sacramento, CA 95821-4405; tel. (916) 920-6513; Commanding Gen. Maj.-Gen. WILLIARD SHANK.

Public Utilities Commission: 505 Van Ness Ave, San Francisco, CA 94102; tel. (415) 557-0647; Pres. STANLEY HULETT.

State Police: State and Consumer Services Agency, 815 S St, Sacramento, CA 95814; tel. (916) 445-7473; Deputy Dir JOE G. SANDOVAL.

LEGISLATURE
(May 1989)

Senate: Dem. 23; Rep. 16; Ind. 1; Total 40.
  President: Lt-Gov. LEO T. MCCARTHY (Dem.).
  President Pro Tempore: DAVID A. ROBERTI (Dem.).
  Secretary: DARRYL WHITE.
Assembly: Dem. 44; Rep. 36; Total 80.
  Speaker: WILLIE BROWN, Jr (Dem.).
  Speaker Pro Tempore: MIKE ROOS (Dem.).
  Chief Clerk: R. BRIAN KIDNEY.

Colorado

CONSTITUTION AND GOVERNMENT

Colorado's only constitution became effective on 1 August 1876. The constitution may be amended if a proposal by the General Assembly is passed by a two-thirds vote in both houses, followed by approval by a majority of voters. The governor and lieutenant-governor are elected together to serve a four-year term. The cabinet members, 21 including the governor, are appointed to specified offices and meet twice monthly. There are 35 senators and 65 representatives in the state General Assembly, serving terms of four and two years respectively. Alternate halves of the Senate are re-elected every second year. Regular legislative sessions are held annually, beginning in January, and are limited to 120 days in even-numbered years. A bill may become law when it has been passed by a majority vote in each house and signed by the governor. During session the governor has 10 calendar days in which to consider a bill, after which it becomes law unless vetoed. Following the adjournment of the General Assembly a bill becomes law unless vetoed by the governor within 30 calendar days. The governor's veto may be overridden by a two-thirds vote

by elected legislators. Legislation becomes effective immediately, unless a date is specified. In the 1986 election to the US Senate 1,061,000 people voted, representing 58% of the registered voters and 44% of the voting-age population. Colorado has 63 administrative counties.

ELECTED EXECUTIVE-BRANCH OFFICIALS

Governor (1987–91): ROY ROMER (Dem.).
Lieutenant-Governor: C. MICHAEL CALLIHAN (Dem.).
Secretary of State: NATALIE MEYER (Rep.).
Attorney-General: DUANE WOODARD (Rep.).
Treasurer: GAIL SCHOETTLER (Dem.).

SELECTED GOVERNMENT ADDRESSES

Office of the Governor: State Capitol, Rm 136, Denver, CO 80203; tel. (303) 866-2471; incorporates Energy Policy Council.

Office of the Lieutenant-Governor: State Capitol, Rm 144, Denver, CO 80203; tel. (303) 866-2087.

Office of the Secretary of State: 1575 Sherman St, Rm 200, Denver, CO 80203; tel. (303) 866-2762.

Office of the Attorney-General: 1525 Sherman St, Rm 300, Denver, CO 80203; tel. (303) 866-3611.

Office of the Treasurer: State Capitol, Rm 140, Denver, CO 80203; tel. (303) 866-2441.

Department of Administration: 1525 Sherman St, 7th Floor, Denver, CO 80203; tel. (303) 866-3221; incorporates Div. of Finance; Exec. Dir FARREST CASON.

Department of Agriculture: 1525 Sherman St, 4th Floor, Denver, CO 80203; tel. (303) 866-2811; Commr TIMOTHY SCHULTZ.

Department of Corrections: 2860 South Circle Dr., Suite 2200, Colorado Springs, CO 80906; tel. (303) 579-9580; Exec. Dir CHASE RIVELAND.

Department of Education: 303 West Colfax Ave, 6th Floor, Denver, CO 80203; tel. (303) 866-6806; Commr CALVIN M. FRAZIER.

Department of Health: 4210 East 11th Ave, Denver, CO 80220; tel. (303) 331-4600; incorporates Div. of Environmental Protection; Exec. Dir THOMAS M. VERNON.

Department of Labor and Employment: 251 East 12th Ave, Rm 306, Denver, CO 80203; tel. (303) 866-2782; Dir CHARLES MCGRATH.

Department of Military Affairs: 300 Logan St, Denver, CO 80203; tel. (303) 777-8669; Adj.-Gen. Maj.-Gen. JOHN L. FRANCE.

Department of Natural Resources: 1313 Sherman St, Rm 718, Denver, CO 80203; tel. (303) 866-3311; Exec. Dir CLYDE O. MARTY.

Department of Public Safety: Bldg B, 1325 South Colorado Blvd, 7th Floor, Denver, CO 80222; tel. (303) 239-4403; Dir of State Patrol JOHN DEMPSEY.

Department of Revenue: 1375 Sherman St, Denver, CO 80203; tel. (303) 866-3091; Exec. Dir ALAN N. CHARNES.

Division of Commerce and Development: Dept of Local Affairs, 1313 Sherman St, Rm 18, Denver, CO 80203; tel. (303) 866-2205; Dir STEVE SCHMITZ.

Public Utilities Commission: Dept of Regulatory Agencies, 1580 Logan St, Denver, CO 80203; tel. (303) 866-3155; Chair. HARRY A. GALLIGAN.

GENERAL ASSEMBLY
(May 1989)

Senate: Rep. 25; Dem. 10; Total 35.
  President: TED STRICKLAND (Rep.).
  President Pro Tempore: HAROLD MCCORMICK (Rep.).
  Secretary: JOAN M. ALBI.
House of Representatives: Rep. 41; Dem. 24; Total 65.
  Speaker: CARL ('BEV') BLEDSOE (Rep.).
  Chief Clerk: LEE BAHRYCH.

Connecticut

CONSTITUTION AND GOVERNMENT

Connecticut's current constitution is its fourth and became effective on 30 December 1965. An amendment to the constitution which is proposed by the General Assembly requires either a vote by three-quarters of the members of each house at one session, or a majority vote in each house in two sessions. After being passed by the General Assembly, the amendment must be ratified by a majority of the voters. The governor is elected jointly with the lieutenant-governor for a period of four years. The cabinet members, 24 including the governor, are appointed to specified offices and meet at the governor's discretion. The General Assembly has 36 senators and 151 representatives, both houses serving two-year terms. Regular sessions are held annually, beginning in January or February. Once a bill has been approved by both houses, it is passed to the governor for signing. After presentation to the governor a bill will automatically become law unless vetoed within five days during legislative sessions, or within 15 days outside session. A gubernatorial veto may be overridden by a vote of two-thirds of the elected legislators in each house. Bills become effective on 1 October following enactment. In 1986 994,000 people voted in the gubernatorial election, representing 59% of the registered voters and 41% of the voting-age population. Connecticut has eight administrative counties.

ELECTED EXECUTIVE-BRANCH OFFICIALS

Governor (1987–91): WILLIAM A. O'NEILL (Dem.).

Lieutenant-Governor: JOSEPH J. FAULISO (Dem.).

Secretary of State: JULIA H. TASHJIAN (Dem.).

Attorney-General: CLARINE NARDI RIDDLE.

Treasurer: FRANCISCO BORGES (Dem.).

Comptroller: J. EDWARD CALDWELL (Dem.).

SELECTED GOVERNMENT ADDRESSES

Office of the Governor: State Capitol, Hartford, CT 06106; tel. (203) 566-4840.

Office of the Lieutenant-Governor: State Capitol, Rm 302, Hartford, CT 06106; tel. (203) 566-2614.

Office of the Secretary of State: State Capitol, Hartford, CT 06106; tel. (203) 566-2739.

Office of the Attorney-General: Trinity St, Hartford, CT 06115; tel. (203) 566-2026.

Office of the Treasurer: 20 Trinity St, Hartford, CT 06115; tel. (203) 566-5050.

Office of the Comptroller: 30 Trinity St, Hartford, CT 06115; tel. (203) 566-5565.

Department of Administrative Services: State Office Bldg, 165 Capitol Ave, Hartford, CT 06106; tel. (203) 566-7528; Commr ELISHA C. FREEDMAN.

Department of Agriculture: State Office Bldg, 165 Capitol Ave, Hartford, CT 06106; tel. (203) 566-4667; Commr KENNETH B. ANDERSEN.

Department of Corrections: 340 Capitol Ave, Hartford, CT 06106; tel. (203) 566-4457; Commr RAYMOND M. LOPES.

Department of Economic Development: 210 Washington St, Hartford, CT 06106; tel. (203) 566-3787; incorporates Divs of Commerce and of Tourism; Commr JOHN J. CARSON.

Department of Education: State Office Bldg, 165 Capitol Ave, Hartford, CT 06106; tel. (203) 566-5061; Commr GERALD N. TIROZZI.

Department of Environmental Protection: State Office Bldg, 165 Capitol Ave, Hartford, CT 06106; tel. (203) 566-2110; Commr STANLEY J. PAC.

Department of Health Services: 150 Washington St, Hartford, CT 06106; tel. (203) 566-2279; Commr DOUGLAS S. LLOYD.

Department of Labor: 200 Folly Brook Blvd, Wethersfield, CT 06109; tel. (203) 566-5160; Commr P. JOSEPH PERARO.

Department of Policy and Management: 80 Washington St, Hartford, CT 06106; tel. (203) 566-4298; incorporates Divs of Finance and of Energy; Sec. ANTHONY V. MILANO.

Department of Public Utility Control: 1 Central Park Plaza, New Britain, CT 06051; tel. (203) 827-1553; Chair. JOHN T. DOWNEY.

Department of Revenue Services: 92 Farmington Ave, Hartford, CT 06105; tel. (203) 566-7120; Commr JOHN G. GROPPO.

Department of Transportation: 24 Wolcott Hill Rd, Wethersfield, CT 06109; tel. (203) 566-3477; Commr J. WILLIAM BURNS.

Division of State Police: 100 Washington St, Hartford, CT 06106; tel. (203) 566-3200; Commr LESTER T. FORST.

Military Department: National Guard Armory, 360 Broad St, Hartford, CT 06105; tel. (203) 524-4953; Adj.-Gen. JOHN T. GERESKI.

GENERAL ASSEMBLY
(May 1989)

Senate: Dem. 25; Rep. 11; Total 36.

 President: Lt-Gov. JOSEPH J. FAULISO (Dem.).

 President Pro Tempore: JOHN B. LARSON (Dem.).

 Clerk: THOMAS SHERIDAN.

House of Representatives: Dem. 91; Rep. 59; 1 vacancy; Total 151.

Speaker: IRVING J. STOLBERG (Dem.).
Deputy Speaker: WILLIAM J. CIBES, Jr (Dem.).
Clerk: PENN J. RITTER.

Delaware
CONSTITUTION AND GOVERNMENT

Delaware's current constitution is its fourth and became effective on 10 June 1897. Constitutional amendments proposed by the General Assembly have to be approved by two-thirds of the elected members of each house in two successive sessions with an election in between. Delaware is the only state where a constitutional amendment need not be ratified by the electorate. The governor is elected separately from the lieutenant-governor to serve a four-year term, and may hold office no more than twice. The cabinet, which has 19 members in total, is appointed by the governor with the consent of the Senate and meets at the governor's discretion. There are 21 senators and 41 representatives in the state General Assembly, serving four- and two-year terms respectively. Elections for alternate halves of the Senate are held every two years. Regular legislative sessions are held annually, lasting from January to June. A bill becomes law when it has been passed by both houses of the General Assembly and has been signed by the governor. During session a bill also becomes law unless vetoed within 10 days of presentation to the governor. Outside session a bill dies if it remains unsigned for 30 days after adjournment of the legislature. A gubernatorial veto may be overridden by three-fifths of the elected members of each house. Enacted legislation becomes effective immediately. In 1986 161,000 people voted in elections to the US House of Representatives, representing 54% of the registered US voters and 34% of the voting-age population. Delaware has three administrative counties.

ELECTED EXECUTIVE-BRANCH OFFICIALS

Governor (1989–93): MICHAEL N. CASTLE (Rep.).

Lieutenant-Governor: DALE E. WOLF (Rep.).

Attorney-General: CHARLES M. OBERLY, III (Dem.).

Treasurer: JANET C. RZEWNICKI (Rep.).

Auditor: R. THOMAS WAGNER, Jr.

Insurance Commissioner: DAVID N. LEVINSON.

SELECTED GOVERNMENT ADDRESSES

Office of the Governor: Legislative Hall, Dover, DE 19901; tel. (302) 736-4101; incorporates Office of Energy Affairs.

Office of the Lieutenant-Governor: Legislative Hall, Dover, DE 19901; tel. (302) 736-4151.

Office of the Attorney-General: 820 North French St, Dover, DE 19901; tel. (302) 571-3838.

Office of the Treasurer: Thomas Collins Bldg, Dover, DE 19903; tel. (302) 736-3382.

Office of the Auditor: Townsend Bldg, POB 1401, Dover, DE 19903; tel. (302) 736-4241.

Department of Administrative Services: Townsend Bldg, POB 1401, Dover, DE 19903; tel. (302) 736-3611; incorporates Div. of Public Utilities Control; Sec. GEORGE HALE.

Department of Agriculture: 2320 South duPont Highway, Dover, DE 19901; tel. (302) 736-4811; Sec. WILLIAM CHANDLER, Jr.

Department of Corrections: 80 Monrovia Ave, Smyrna, DE 19977; tel. (302) 736-5601; Commr JOHN L. SULLIVAN.

Department of Finance: Thomas Collins Bldg, POB 1401, Dover, DE 19903; tel. (302) 736-4201; incorporates Div. of Revenue; Sec. STEPHEN T. GOLDING.

Department of Health and Social Services: Delaware State Hospital, New Castle, DE 19720; tel. (302) 421-6705; Sec. THOMAS P. EICHER.

Department of Insurance: 21 The Green, Dover, DE 19901; tel. (302) 736-4251; Commr DAVID N. LEVINSON.

Department of Labor: 820 North French St, Wilmington, DE 19801; tel. (302) 571-2710; Sec. MATHIAS J. FALLIS.

Department of Natural Resources and Environmental Control: 89 Kings' Highway, POB 1401, Dover, DE 19903; tel. (302) 736-4403; Sec. JOHN E. WILSON, III.

Department of Public Instruction: Townsend Bldg, POB 1402, Dover, DE 19903; tel. (302) 736-4601; Supt Dr WILLIAM B. KEENE.

Department of Public Safety: POB 430, Dover, DE 19903; tel. (302) 736-5911; Supt of State Police Col DANIEL L. SIMPSON.

Department of Transportation: Transportation Admin. Bldg, POB 778, Dover, DE 19903; tel. (302) 736-4303; Sec. KERMIT H. JUSTIS.

Division of Commerce: Dept of Community Affairs, 156 South State St, Dover, DE 19801; tel. (302) 736-4456; Sec. FRANCES WEST.

Division of the National Guard: First Regiment Rd, Wilmington, DE 19808; tel. (302) 995-8555; Adj.-Gen. JOSEPH M. LANK.

Office of the Secretary of State: Townsend Bldg, Dover, DE 19901; tel. (302) 736-4111; Sec. of State MICHAEL E. HARKINS.

GENERAL ASSEMBLY
(May 1989)

Senate: Dem. 13; Rep. 8; Total 21.

  President: Lt-Gov. DALE E. WOLF (Rep.).
  President Pro Tempore: RICHARD S. CORDREY (Dem.).
  Secretary: BETTY JEAN CANIFORD.

House of Representatives: Rep. 22; Dem. 19; Total 41.

  Speaker: TERRY SPENSE (Rep.).
  Chief Clerk: JOANN HEDRICK.

District of Columbia
CONSTITUTION AND GOVERNMENT

The government of the District of Columbia operates according to the Charter of 1974, which allows residents to elect a mayor and City Council. The Council has 13 members, of whom the chairman or -woman and four other members are elected at-large, the remaining members being elected from the district's eight wards. Of those members elected at-large, there may not be more than three affiliated to the same political party. Members are elected to serve a four-year term of office. The mayor, chief executive officer of the district, is also elected to hold office for four years. A bill becomes law when it has been passed by a majority of the Council present at two readings and has been signed by the mayor. The mayor has 10 days to consider a bill, after which it becomes law unless vetoed. The mayor's veto may be overridden by two-thirds of those members of the Council who are present, in which case it is then presented to the President of the USA and becomes law, with presidential approval, after 30 days. Under the federal constitution, all legislation enacted by the District of Columbia may be vetoed by Congress, and Congress may pass laws on any matter affecting the district. In 1982 a constitution was drafted and it was proposed that the district should become the state of New Columbia. The draft constitution was approved by the district electorate.

An amendment to the federal constitution giving the District of Columbia full voting representation in Congress was approved by Congress in 1978 but failed to become law after having been ratified by only 16 states of the requisite 38 before the statutory deadline was reached in August 1985.

ELECTED EXECUTIVE-BRANCH OFFICIALS

Mayor (1987–91): MARION S. BARRY, Jr (Dem.).

Chairman of City Council: DAVID A. CLARKE (Dem.).

SELECTED ADMINISTRATION ADDRESSES

Executive Office of the Mayor: District Bldg, 1350 Pennsylvania Ave, NW, Washington, DC 20004; tel. (202) 727-6319.

Board of Education: 415 12th St, NW, Washington, DC 20004; tel. (202) 724-4222; Supt of Schools FLORETTA McKINSEY.

Department of Corrections: 1923 Vermont Ave, NW, Rm N-207, Washington, DC 20001; tel. (202) 673-7316; Dir HALLEM WILLIAMS (acting).

Department of Employment Services: 500 C St, NW, Rm 600, Washington, DC 20001; tel. (202) 639-1000; Dir F. ALEXIS ROBERSON (acting).

Department of Finance and Revenue: Municipal Center, Rm 4136, 300 Indiana Ave, NW, Washington, DC 20001; tel. (202) 727-6020; Dir MELVIN JONES.

Department of Human Services: 801 North Capitol St, NE, Rm 700, Washington, DC 20002; tel. (202) 727-0310; incorporates Div. of Public Health; Dir BYRON MARSHALL (acting).

Division of Public Health: Dept of Human Services, 801 North Capitol St, NE, Washington, DC 20002; tel. (202) 724-5466; Dir REED V. TUCKSON.

Division of Transportation: Dept of Public Works, The Frank D. Reeves Center for Municipal Affairs, 6th Floor, 2000 14th St, NW, Washington, DC 20009; tel. (202) 939-8000; Dir JOHN TOUCHSTONE.

Metropolitan Police Department: Municipal Center, Rm 5080, 300 Indiana Ave, NW, Washington, DC 20001; tel. (202) 727-4218; Chief MAURICE T. TURNER.

Office of Business and Economic Development: Perpetual Bldg, Suite 700, 1111 E St, NW, Washington, DC 20004; tel. (202) 727-6600; Dir KWASI HOLMAN.

Office of the City Administrator: District Bldg, Rm 507, 1350 Pennsylvania Ave, NW, Washington, DC 20004; tel. (202) 727-6053; City Administrator THOMAS M. DOWNS.

Office of the Corporation Counsel: District Bldg, 1350 Pennsylvania Ave, NW, Washington, DC 20004; tel. (202) 727-6248; Corpn Counsel FREDERICK D. COOKE.

Office of Energy: 613 G St, NW, Washington, DC 20001; tel. (202) 727-1800; Dir CHARLES CLINTON.

Public Service Commission: 451 Indiana Ave, NW, Washington, DC 20001; tel. (202) 727-3070; Chair. PATRICIA MORRIS WORTHY.

CITY COUNCIL
(mid-1989)

Members: Dem. 11; Ind. 2; Total 13.

  Chair.: DAVID A. CLARKE (Dem.).
  Chair. Pro Tempore: NADINE P. WINTER (Dem.).
  Secretary: RUSSELL SMITH.

Florida
CONSTITUTION AND GOVERNMENT

The current constitution of Florida is the state's sixth and became effective on 7 January 1969. An amendment to the constitution introduced by the Legislature requires approval by three-fifths of the elected members of each house followed by a majority of voters. The governor and lieutenant-governor are elected jointly to serve terms of four years, the governor serving no more than two consecutive terms. Cabinet members, six in total, are elected to specified offices and meet every two weeks. There are 40 senators and 120 representatives in the Legislature, elected for four- and two-year terms respectively. Alternate halves of the Senate are re-elected every two years. Regular sessions of the Legislature take place annually in April and last for no longer than 60 calendar days. A bill becomes law when it has been passed by a majority of elected members present in both houses of the Legislature and has been signed by the governor. During session the governor has seven calendar days in which to consider a bill, after which it becomes law unless vetoed. After session a bill becomes law unless vetoed within 15 calendar days. A gubernatorial veto may be overridden by a vote of two-thirds of the elected members in each house. Enacted legislation becomes effective 60 days after adjournment of the session. In 1986 3,430,000 people voted in the election to the US Senate, representing 61% of the registered voters and 38% of the voting-age population. Florida has 67 administrative counties.

ELECTED EXECUTIVE-BRANCH OFFICIALS

Governor (1987–91): BOB MARTINEZ (Rep.).

Lieutenant-Governor: BOBBY BRANTLEY (Rep.).

Secretary of State: JIM SMITH (Rep.).

Attorney-General: BOB BUTTERWORTH (Dem.).

Treasurer, Insurance Commissioner and Fire Marshal: TOM GALLAGHER (Rep.).

Comptroller: GERALD A. LEWIS (Dem.).

Commissioner of Education: BETTY CASTOR (Dem.).

Commissioner of Agriculture: DOYLE E. CONNER (Dem.).

SELECTED GOVERNMENT ADDRESSES

Office of the Governor: The Capitol, Tallahassee, FL 32399-0001; tel. (904) 488-4441.

Office of the Lieutenant-Governor: The Capitol, Tallahassee, FL 32301; tel. (904) 488-4711.

Office of the Secretary of State: The Capitol, Tallahassee, FL 32301; tel. (904) 488-3680.

Office of the Attorney-General: The Capitol, Tallahassee, FL 32301; tel. (904) 487-1963.

Office of the Treasurer: The Capitol, Tallahassee, FL 32301; tel. (904) 488-3440.

Office of the Comptroller: The Capitol, Tallahassee, FL 32301; tel. (904) 488-0370.

Department of Administration: Carlton Bldg, Rm 435, Tallahassee, FL 32399-1550; tel. (904) 488-4116; Sec. ADIS MARIE VILA.

Department of Agriculture and Consumer Services: The Capitol, Tallahassee, FL 32399-0810; tel. (904) 488-3022; Commr DOYLE E. CONNER.

Department of Commerce: Collins Bldg, Suite 510c, Tallahassee, FL 32301; tel. (904) 488-3104; incorporates Div. of Tourism; Sec. Lt-Gov. BOBBY BRANTLEY.

Department of Corrections: 1311 Winewood Blvd, Tallahassee, FL 32399-2500; tel. (904) 488-7480; Sec. RICHARD L. DUGGER.

Department of Education: The Capitol, Tallahassee, FL 32399-0400; tel. (904) 487-1785; Commr BETTY CASTOR.

Department of Environmental Regulation: Twin Towers, 2600 Blair Stone Rd, Tallahassee, FL 32399-2400; tel. (904) 488-4805; Sec. DALE TWATCHMANN.

Department of Health and Rehabilitative Services: 1323 Winewood Blvd, Tallahassee, FL 32399-0700; tel. (904) 488-7721; Sec. GREGORY L. COLER.

Department of Labor and Employment Security: 2590 Executive Center, Circle East, Suite 200, Tallahassee, FL 32399-2152; tel. (904) 488-4398; Sec. HUGO MENENDEZ.

Department of Law Enforcement: POB 1489, Tallahassee, FL 32302; tel. (904) 488-8771; Commr JAMES T. MOORE.

Department of Military Affairs: State Arsenal, POB 1008, St Augustine, FL 32085-1008; tel. (904) 824-8461; Adj.-Gen. Maj.-Gen. ROBERT F. ENSSLIN, Jr.

Department of Natural Resources: 3900 Commonwealth Blvd, Tallahassee, FL 32399-3000; tel. (904) 488-1554; Exec. Dir THOMAS E. GARDNER.

Department of Revenue: 102 Carlton Bldg, Tallahassee, FL 32399-0100; tel. (904) 488-5050; Exec. Dir KATIE D. TUCKER.

Department of Transportation: Haydon–Burns Bldg, 605 Suwannee St, Tallahassee, FL 32399-0450; tel. (904) 488-6721; Sec. KAYE N. HENDERSON.

Division of Finance: Office of the Comptroller, The Capitol, Tallahassee, FL 32301; tel. (904) 487-2583; Dir RANDY HOLLAND.

Energy Office: Office of the Governor, The Capitol, Tallahassee, FL 32399-0001; tel. (904) 488-6764.

Public Service Commission: 101 East Gaines St, Tallahassee, FL 32399-0850; tel. (904) 488-7181; Exec. Dir DAVID SWAFFORD.

LEGISLATURE
(May 1989)

Senate: Dem. 23; Rep. 17; Total 40.

President: BOB CRAWFORD (Dem.).
President Pro Tempore: ARNETT E. GIRARDEAU (Dem.).
Secretary: JOE BROWN.

House of Representatives: Dem. 73; Rep. 47; Total 120.

Speaker: TOM GUSTAFSON (Dem.).
Speaker Pro Tempore: SAM MITCHELL (Dem.).
Clerk: JOHN B. PHELPS, III.

Georgia
CONSTITUTION AND GOVERNMENT

The current constitution of Georgia, the state's 10th, was adopted in 1982 and became effective on 1 July 1983. Constitutional amendments proposed by the General Assembly must be approved by two-thirds of each house and must then be ratified by a majority of state voters. The governor and lieutenant-governor are elected separately, the governor being elected to serve a four-year term and serving no more than two terms consecutively. Georgia has no formal cabinet system. There are 56 senators and 180 representatives in the state General Assembly and both houses are re-elected every two years. Regular sessions of the General Assembly are held annually, beginning in January and lasting for 40 legislative days. A bill becomes law when it has been passed by both houses and has been signed by the governor. During session the governor has to sign or veto a bill within six calendar days of receiving it, otherwise it will automatically become law. After session a bill becomes law unless vetoed within 40 days from adjournment of the session. A gubernatorial veto may be overridden by a vote by two-thirds of the legislators in each house. Enacted legislation generally becomes effective in the following July. In 1986 1,225,000 people voted in the election to the US Senate, representing 48% of registered voters and 28% of the voting-age population. Georgia has 159 administrative counties.

ELECTED EXECUTIVE-BRANCH OFFICIALS

Governor (1987–91): JOE FRANK HARRIS (Dem.).
Lieutenant-Governor: ZELL B. MILLER (Dem.).
Secretary of State: MAX CLELAND (Dem.).
Attorney-General: MICHAEL J. BOWERS (Dem.).
Comptroller-General: WARREN EVANS (Dem.).

Superintendent of Schools: Dr WERNER ROGERS (Dem.).
Commissioner of Agriculture: THOMAS T. IRVIN (Dem.).
Commissioner of Labor: JOE D. TANNER (Dem.).

SELECTED GOVERNMENT ADDRESSES

Office of the Governor: State Capitol, Rm 203, Atlanta, GA 30334; tel. (404) 656-1776.

Office of the Lieutenant-Governor: State Capitol, Rm 240, Atlanta, GA 30334; tel. (404) 656-5030.

Office of the Secretary of State: State Capitol, Rm 214, Atlanta, GA 30334; tel. (404) 656-2881.

Office of the Attorney-General: State Judicial Bldg, Rm 132, Atlanta, GA 30334; tel. (404) 656-4585.

Office of the Comptroller-General: West Tower, 7th Floor, 200 Piedmont Ave, Atlanta, GA 30334; tel. (404) 656-2056.

Department of Administrative Services: West Tower, Suite 1520, 200 Piedmont Ave, Atlanta, GA 30334; tel. (404) 656-5514; Commr LARRY L. CLARK.

Department of Agriculture: Agriculture Bldg, Rm 204, Atlanta, GA 30334; tel. (404) 656-3600; Commr THOMAS T. IRVIN.

Department of Banking and Finance: 2990 Brandywine Rd, Suite 200, Atlanta, GA 30341; tel. (404) 393-7330; Commr EDWARD D. DUNN.

Department of Corrections: 756 East Tower, Floyd Veterans' Memorial Bldg, Atlanta, GA 30334; tel. (404) 656-6002; Commr DAVID C. EVANS.

Department of Defense: POB 17965, Atlanta, GA 30316; tel. (404) 656-6000; Adj.-Gen. Maj.-Gen. JOSEPH W. GRIFFIN.

Department of Education: Twin Towers East, 205 Butler St, SE, Atlanta, GA 30334; tel. (404) 656-2804; Supt of Schools Dr WERNER ROGERS.

Department of Industry and Trade: 230 Peachtree St, NW, POB 1776, Atlanta, GA 30301; tel. (404) 656-3556; incorporates Div. of Tourism; Commr GEORGE BERRY.

Department of Labor: 148 International Blvd, Atlanta, GA 30334; tel. (404) 656-3011; Commr JOE D. TANNER.

Department of Natural Resources: East Tower, 205 Butler St, Suite 1252, Atlanta, GA 30334; tel. (404) 656-3500; incorporates Environmental Protection Div.; Commr J. LEONARD LEDBETTER.

Department of Public Safety: POB 1456, Atlanta, GA 30371; tel. (404) 624-7710; Commr of State Police Col CURTIS D. EARP.

Department of Revenue: 410 Trinity–Washington Bldg, Atlanta, GA 30334; tel. (404) 656-4015; Commr MARCUS E. COLLINS, Sr.

Department of Transportation: 2 Capitol Sq., Atlanta, GA 30334; tel. (404) 656-5206; Commr HAL RIVES.

Health Planning Agency: 4 Executive Park, Suite 2100, Atlanta, GA 30329; tel. (404) 894-4899; Dir C. ANNETTE MAXEY.

Office of Energy Resources: 270 Washington St, SW, Rm 615, Atlanta, GA 30334; tel. (404) 656-5176; Dir PAUL BURKS.

Public Service Commission: 244 Washington St, SW, Rm 174, Atlanta, GA 30334; tel. (404) 656-4556; Commr BOBBY PAFFORD.

GENERAL ASSEMBLY
(May 1989)

Senate: Dem. 44; Rep. 11; 1 vacancy; Total 56.

President: Lt-Gov. ZELL B. MILLER (Dem.).
President Pro Tempore: JOSEPH E. KENNEDY (Dem.).
Secretary: HAMILTON McWHORTER, Jr.

House of Representatives: Dem. 144; Rep. 36; Total 180.

Speaker: THOMAS B. MURPHY (Dem.).
Speaker Pro Tempore: JACK CONNELL (Dem.).
Clerk: GLENN W. ELLARD.

Hawaii
CONSTITUTION AND GOVERNMENT

As a US state, Hawaii has had one constitution which was adopted in 1950 and became effective on 21 August 1959. Constitutional amendments proposed by the Legislature have to be passed by either two-thirds of the elected members in each house at one session, or a majority of each house in two sessions. Amendments must then be ratified by a majority of voters. The governor and lieutenant-governor are jointly elected to serve four-year terms and may serve no more than two terms consecutively. The cabinet, which has 24 members in total, meets at the governor's discretion. The Legislature consists of 25 senators and 51 representatives, serving terms of four and two years respectively. Alternate halves of the Senate are re-elected every two years. Regular sessions of the Legislature take place annually, beginning in January and lasting no longer than 60 days. A bill becomes law when it has been approved by both houses of the Legislature and has been signed by the governor. The governor has 10 days in which to consider a bill, during session, after which it automatically becomes law unless vetoed. Outside session a bill becomes law unless vetoed within 45 days of adjournment. The governor's veto may be overridden by a two-thirds vote of the elected members of the Legislature. Enacted legislation becomes effective immediately. In the gubernatorial election of 1986 334,000 people voted, representing 80% of those registered to vote and 43% of the voting-age population. There are five counties in Hawaii, one of which, Kalawao, is wholly under the authority of the state Department of Health.

ELECTED EXECUTIVE-BRANCH OFFICIALS

Governor (1987–91): JOHN D. WAIHEE, III (Dem.).

Lieutenant-Governor and Secretary of State: BENJAMIN CAYETANO (Dem.).

SELECTED GOVERNMENT ADDRESSES

Office of the Governor: State Capitol, 415 South Beretania St, Rm 500, Honolulu, HI 96813; tel. (808) 548-5420.

Office of the Lieutenant-Governor: State Capitol, 415 South Beretania St, Honolulu, HI 96813; tel. (808) 548-2350.

Department of Agriculture: 1428 South King St, POB 22159, Honolulu, HI 96814; tel. (808) 548-7101; Chair. of Bd of Agriculture SUZANNE D. PETERSON.

Department of Budget and Finance: State Capitol, 415 South Beretania St, Honolulu, HI 96813; tel. (808) 548-2325; Dir YUKIO TAKEMOTO.

Department of Commerce and Consumer Affairs: 1010 Richards St, Honolulu, HI 96813; tel. (808) 548-7505; Dir ROBERT ALM.

Department of Defense: 3949 Diamond Head Rd, Honolulu, HI 96816; tel. (808) 734-2195; Adj.-Gen. Maj.-Gen. ALEXIS T. LUM.

Department of Education: 1390 Miller St, Honolulu, HI 96813; tel. (808) 548-6502; Supt CHARLES T. TOGUCHI.

Department of Health: 1250 Punchbowl St, POB 3378, Honolulu, HI 96813; tel. (808) 548-6505; incorporates Div. of Environmental Protection and Health Services; Dir JOHN C. LEWIN.

Department of Labor and Industrial Relations: 830 Punchbowl St, Honolulu, HI 96813; tel. (808) 548-7575; Dir MARIO R. RAMIL.

Department of Land and Natural Resources: POB 621, Honolulu, HI 96809; tel. (808) 548-6550; Chair. WILLIAM W. PATY.

Department of Planning and Economic Development: POB 2359, Honolulu, HI 96804; tel. (808) 548-6914; incorporates Offices of Energy and of Tourism.

Department of Taxation: 425 South Queen St, Honolulu, HI 96813; tel. (808) 548-7650; Dir RICHARD F. KAHLE.

Department of Transportation: 869 Punchbowl St, Honolulu, HI 96813; tel. (808) 548-3205; Dir EDWARD Y. HIRATA.

Division of Corrections: Dept of Social Services and Housing, 1340 Miller St, Honolulu, HI 96813; tel. (808) 548-6440; Dir THEODORE I. SAKAI.

Office of the Attorney-General: State Capitol, 415 South Beretania St, Room 405, Honolulu, HI 96813; tel. (808) 548-4740; Att.-Gen. WARREN PRICE.

Public Utilities Commission: 465 South King St, Honolulu, HI 96813; tel. (808) 548-3990; Chair. HIDETO KONO.

LEGISLATURE
(May 1989)

Senate: Dem. 21; Rep. 4; Total 25.
  President: RICHARD S. H. WONG (Dem.).
  Vice-President: PATSY K. YOUNG (Dem.).
  Clerk: T. DAVID WOO, Jr.

House of Representatives: Dem. 40; Rep. 11; Total 51.
  Speaker: DANIEL J. KIHANO. (Dem.).
  Vice-Speaker: EMILIO S. ALCON (Dem.).
  Clerk: GERALD I. MIYOSHI.

Idaho

CONSTITUTION AND GOVERNMENT

Idaho's only constitution was adopted in 1889 and became effective on 3 July 1890. An amendment to the constitution proposed by the Legislature has to be passed by two-thirds of the elected members of each house, followed by a majority of voters. The governor and lieutenant-governor are elected separately to serve four-year terms and there is no limit to the number of terms they may serve. There is no formal cabinet system but sub-cabinets have been formed by executive order, the chairmen and -women reporting to the governor. The Legislature has 42 senators and 84 representatives, all serving two-year terms. Regular sessions of the Legislature take place annually, starting in January. A bill becomes law when it has been passed by both houses and has been signed by the governor. During session the governor has five days in which to consider a bill, after which it becomes law unless vetoed. After session a bill becomes law unless vetoed within 10 days after adjournment. A vote by two-thirds of the elected legislators in each house is required to override the governor's veto. Legislation generally becomes effective in the July following enactment. In 1986 387,000 people voted in the gubernatorial election, representing 70% of those registered to vote and 55% of the voting-age population. Idaho has 44 administrative counties.

ELECTED EXECUTIVE-BRANCH OFFICIALS

Governor (1987–91): CECIL D. ANDRUS (Dem.).
Lieutenant-Governor: C. L. ('BUTCH') OTTER (Rep.).
Secretary of State: PETE T. CENARRUSA (Rep.).
Attorney-General: JIM JONES (Rep.).
Treasurer: LYDIA JUSTICE EDWARDS (Rep.).
Auditor and Comptroller: JOE R. WILLIAMS (Dem.).
Superintendent of Public Instruction: JERRY L. EVANS.

SELECTED GOVERNMENT ADDRESSES

Office of the Governor: State House, Rm 200, Boise, ID 83720; tel. (208) 334-2100.

Office of the Lieutenant-Governor: State House, Rm 225, Boise, ID 83720; tel. (208) 334-2200.

Office of the Secretary of State: State House, Rm 203, Boise, ID 83720; tel. (208) 334-2300.

Office of the Attorney-General: State House, Rm 210, Boise, ID 83720; tel. (208) 334-2400.

Office of the Treasurer: State House, Rm 102, Boise, ID 83720; tel. (208) 334-3200.

Office of the Auditor: 700 West State St, Boise, ID 83720; tel. (208) 334-3100.

Department of Administration: 650 West State St, Rm 100, Boise, ID 83720; tel. (208) 334-3380; Dir LOREN NELSON.

Department of Agriculture: 2270 Old Penitentiary Rd, POB 790, Boise, ID 83701; tel. (208) 334-3240; Dir RICHARD RUSH.

Department of Commerce: 700 West State St, Boise, ID 83720; tel. (208) 334-2470; incorporates Div. of Tourism; Dir JAMES HAWKINS.

Department of Corrections: 1075 Park Blvd, Boise, ID 83712; tel. (208) 334-2318; Dir RICHARD VERNON.

Department of Education: Len B. Jordan Bldg, 650 West State St, Rm 200, Boise, ID 83720; tel. (208) 334-3300; Supt of Public Instruction JERRY L. EVANS.

Department of Finance: 700 West State St, Boise, ID 83720; tel. (208) 334-3313; Dir BELTON PATTY.

Department of Health and Welfare: The Towers, 450 West State St, Boise, ID 83720; tel. (208) 334-5500; incorporates Div. of the Environment; Dir RICHARD DONOVAN.

Department of Labor and Industrial Services: 277 North 6th St, Boise, ID 83720; tel. (208) 334-3950; Dir GARY GOULD.

Department of Lands: State Capitol Bldg, Rm 121, Boise, ID 83720; tel. (208) 334-3280; Dir STANLEY F. HAMILTON.

Department of Law Enforcement: 3311 West State St, Rm 129, POB 55, Boise, ID 83707; tel. (208) 334-2521; Dir MACK RICHARDSON.

Department of Revenue and Taxation: 700 West State St, Boise, ID 83720; tel. (208) 334-7660; Chair. LARRY LOONEY.

Department of Transportation: 3311 West State St, POB 7129, Boise, ID 83707; tel. (208) 334-8000; Dir KERMIT KIEBERT.

Energy Resources Division: Dept of Water Resources, State House, Boise, ID 83720; tel. (208) 334-7900; Dir BOB HOPPIE.

Military Department: Gowen Field, POB 45, Boise, ID 83707; tel. (208) 385-5225; Adj.-Gen. DARRELL MANNING.

Public Utilities Commission: State House Mall, 472 West Washington St, Boise, ID 83720; tel. (208) 334-3427; Pres. DEAN MILLER.

LEGISLATURE
(May 1989)

Senate: Dem. 23; Rep. 19; Total 42.
  President: Lt-Gov. C. L. ('BUTCH') OTTER (Rep.).

President Pro Tempore: MICHAEL CRAPO (Rep.).
Secretary: DOROTHEA BAXTER.

House of Representatives: Rep. 64; Dem. 20; Total 84.

Speaker: TOM BOYD (Rep.).
Chief Clerk: PHYLLIS WATSON.

Illinois
CONSTITUTION AND GOVERNMENT

Illinois's current constitution, its fourth, was adopted in 1970 and became effective on 1 July 1971. A constitutional amendment proposed by the General Assembly needs to be approved by three-fifths of the elected members of each house and then ratified by either the majority of those voting in an election or three-fifths of the electorate voting specifically on the amendment. The governor and lieutenant-governor are elected jointly, both serving four-year terms of office. There is no limit to the number of terms which may be served. Cabinet members, 32 in total, are appointed to specified office with the consent of the Senate and meet at the governor's discretion. The General Assembly has 59 senators and 118 representatives, the latter serving two-year terms. The entire Senate is re-elected every 10 years, senators being elected for two four-year terms and one two-year term within each 10-year period. Regular sessions of the General Assembly begin in January of odd-numbered years, and there are no statutory limitations on their length. A bill becomes law when it has been passed by the General Assembly and signed by the governor. The governor is allowed 60 days to consider a bill, after which it becomes law if not acted upon. A gubernatorial veto may be overridden by a vote of three-fifths of the elected legislators in each house unless it concerns an appropriation bill, in which case a majority vote only is required. In 1986 3,144,000 people voted in the gubernatorial election, representing 52% of the number registered and 37% of the voting-age population. Illinois has 102 administrative counties.

ELECTED EXECUTIVE-BRANCH OFFICIALS

Governor (1987–91): JAMES R. THOMPSON (Rep.).
Lieutenant-Governor: GEORGE H. RYAN (Rep.).
Secretary of State: JIM EDGAR (Rep.).
Attorney-General: NEIL F. HARTIGAN (Dem.).
Treasurer: JERRY CONSENTINO (Dem.).
Comptroller: ROLAND W. BURRIS (Dem.).

SELECTED GOVERNMENT ADDRESSES

Office of the Governor: State House, Rm 207, Springfield, IL 62706; tel. (217) 782-6830.
Office of the Lieutenant-Governor: State House, Rm 214, Springfield, IL 62706; tel. (217) 782-7884.
Office of the Secretary of State: State House, Rm 213, Springfield, IL 62706; tel. (217) 782-2201.
Office of the Attorney-General: 500 South 2nd St, Springfield, IL 62706; tel. (217) 782-1090.
Office of the Treasurer: State House, Rm 219, Springfield, IL 62706; tel. (217) 782-2211.
Office of the Comptroller: State House, Rm 201, Springfield, IL 62706; tel. (217) 782-6000.

Department of Agriculture: State Fairgrounds, Springfield, IL 62706; tel. (217) 782-2172; Dir LARRY A. WERRIES.
Department of Commerce and Community Affairs: 620 East Adams St, Springfield, IL 62701; tel. (217) 782-3233; incorporates Divs of Tourism and of Public Utility Regulation; Dir JAY HEDGES.
Department of Corrections: 1301 Concordia Ct, Springfield, IL 62706; tel. (217) 522-2666; Dir MICHAEL P. LANE.
Department of Energy and Natural Resources: 325 West Adams St, 3rd Floor, Springfield, IL 62706; tel. (217) 785-2002; Dir KAREN WITTER.
Department of Labor: Old State Capitol Plaza West, Suite 1, Rm 300, Springfield, IL 62701; tel. (217) 782-6206; Dir GWEN MARTIN.
Department of Military Affairs: 1301 South MacArthur Blvd, Springfield, IL 62706; tel. (217) 785-3500; Adj.-Gen. HAROLD G. HOLESINGER.
Department of Public Health: 535 West Jefferson St, Springfield, IL 62761; tel. (217) 782-4977; Dir BERNARD J. TURNOCK.
Department of Registration and Education: 320 West Washington St, Springfield, IL 62786; tel. (217) 785-0822; Dir STEVE SELCKE.
Department of Revenue: 101 West Jefferson St, Springfield, IL 62708; tel. (217) 785-2602; incorporates Finance and Planning Bureau; Dir ROGER SWEET.

Department of State Police: Armory Bldg, Rm 103, Springfield, IL 62706; tel. (217) 782-7263; Dir JEREMY MARGOLIS.
Department of Transportation: DOT Administration Bldg, 2300 South Dirksen Parkway, Springfield, IL 62764; tel. (217) 782-5597; Sec. GREG BAISE.
Division of Administration: Dept of Central Management Services, William G. Stratton Bldg, Rm 715, Springfield, IL 62706; tel. (217) 782-2141; Dir MICHAEL TRISTANO.
Illinois Environmental Protection Agency: 220 Churchill Rd, Springfield, IL 62706; tel. (217) 782-3397; Dir BERNARD P. KILLIAN.

GENERAL ASSEMBLY
(May 1989)

Senate: Dem. 31; Rep. 28; Total 59.
President: PHILIP ROCK (Dem.).
Secretary: LINDA HAWKER.

House of Representatives: Dem. 67; Rep. 51; Total 118.
Speaker: MIKE MADIGAN (Dem.).
Chief Clerk: JOHN O'BRIEN.

Indiana
CONSTITUTION AND GOVERNMENT

The current constitution of Indiana is the state's second and became effective on 1 November 1851. Constitutional amendments proposed by the General Assembly have to be approved by a majority of the elected members in each house in two successive sessions, and then ratified by a majority of state voters. The governor and lieutenant-governor of Indiana are elected jointly to serve a term of four years, the governor serving no more than two terms consecutively. Indiana has no formal cabinet system. The state General Assembly has 50 senators and 100 representatives, elected to serve four- and two-year terms respectively. Alternate halves of the Senate are re-elected every two years. Regular legislative sessions take place annually, beginning in January. Sessions may last no longer than 61 legislative days in odd-numbered years and 30 days in even-numbered years. A bill becomes law after it has been approved by both houses of the General Assembly and has been signed by the governor. The governor is allowed seven days to consider a bill, after which it becomes law unless vetoed. A gubernatorial veto may be overridden by a majority of the elected legislators in each house. Enacted legislation does not become effective until it has been published and circulated in the counties. In 1986 1,556,000 people voted in the election to the US House of Representatives, representing 54% of the number of voters registered and 39% of the voting-age population. Indiana has 92 administrative counties.

ELECTED EXECUTIVE-BRANCH OFFICIALS

Governor (1989–93): EVAN BAYH (Dem.).
Lieutenant-Governor and Agriculture Commissioner: FRANK O'BANNON (Dem.).
Secretary of State: JOE HOGSETT (Dem.).
Attorney-General: LINLEY E. PEARSON (Rep.).
Treasurer: MARJORIE H. O'LAUGHLIN (Rep.).
Auditor and Comptroller: ANN DEVORE (Dem.).

SELECTED GOVERNMENT ADDRESSES

Office of the Governor: State House, 100 North Senate Ave, Rm 206, Indianapolis, IN 46204; tel. (317) 232-4567.
Office of the Lieutenant-Governor: State House, 100 North Senate Ave, Rm 333, Indianapolis, IN 46204; tel. (317) 232-4545.
Office of the Secretary of State: State House, 100 North Senate Ave, Rm 201, Indianapolis, IN 46204; tel. (317) 232-6531.
Office of the Attorney-General: State House, 100 North Senate Ave, Rm 219, Indianapolis, IN 46204; tel. (317) 232-6201.
Office of the Treasurer: State House, 100 North Senate Ave, Rm 242, Indianapolis, IN 46204; tel. (317) 232-6386.
Office of the Auditor: State House, 100 North Senate Ave, Rm 240, Indianapolis, IN 46204; tel. (317) 232-3301.

Board of Health: 1330 West Michigan St, POB 1964, Indianapolis, IN 46206; tel. (317) 633-8400; incorporates Div. of Environmental Health; Commr WOODROW MYERS, Jr.
Budget Agency: State House, 100 North Senate Ave, Rm 212, Indianapolis, IN 46204; tel. (317) 232-5610; Dir FRANK SULLIVAN, Jr.
Department of the Adjutant-General: POB 41326, Stout Field, Indianapolis, IN 46241; tel. (317) 247-3274; Adj.-Gen. Brig.-Gen. JACK K. ELROD.

Department of Administration: State Office Bldg, 100 North Senate Ave, Rm 507, Indianapolis, IN 46204; tel. (317) 232-3114; Commr JOHN R. WELIEVER.

Department of Commerce: 1 North Capitol St, Suite 700, Indianapolis, IN 46204-2248; tel. (317) 232-8800; incorporates Divs of Agriculture, of Energy and of Tourism Development; Exec. Dir Lt-Gov. FRANK O'BANNON.

Department of Corrections: State Office Bldg, 100 North Senate Ave, Rm 804, Indianapolis, IN 46204; tel. (317) 232-5766; Commr JAMES E. AIKEN.

Department of Labor: 100 North Senate Ave, Rm 103, Indianapolis, IN 46204; tel. (317) 232-2663; Commr KENNETH J. ZELLER.

Department of Natural Resources: State Office Bldg, 100 North Senate Ave, Rm 608, Indianapolis, IN 46204; tel. (317) 232-4020; Dir PATRICK R. RALSTON.

Department of Public Instruction: State House, 100 North Senate Ave, Rm 229, Indianapolis, IN 46204; tel. (317) 232-6667; Supt H. DEAN EVANS.

Department of Revenue: State Office Bldg, 100 North Senate Ave, Rm 202, Indianapolis, IN 46204; tel. (317) 232-2101; Commr JOHN R. GILDEA.

Department of Transportation: Harrison Bldg, 143 West Market St, Suite 300, Indianapolis, IN 46204; tel. (317) 232-1470; Dir ROLAND J. MROSS.

Public Service Commission: State Office Bldg, 100 North Senate Ave, Rm 901, Indianapolis, IN 46204; tel. (317) 232-2704; Chair. WILLIAM N. MONTGOMERY.

State Police Department: State Office Bldg, 100 North Senate Ave, Rm 301, Indianapolis, IN 46204; tel. (317) 232-8241; Supt LLOYD R. JENNINGS.

GENERAL ASSEMBLY
(May 1989)

Senate: Rep. 26; Dem. 24; Total 50.
President: Lt-Gov. FRANK O'BANNON (Dem.).
President Pro Tempore: ROBERT D. GARTON (Rep.).
Principal Secretary: CAROLYN TINKLE.

House of Representatives: Rep. 50; Dem. 50; Total 100.
Democratic Offices:
Speaker: MICHAEL K. PHILLIPS.
Speaker Pro Tempore: CHESTER F. DOBIS.
Principal Clerk: BETTY MASARIU.
Republican Offices:
Speaker: PAUL S. MANNWEILER.
Speaker Pro Tempore: JEFFREY K. ESPICK.
Principal Clerk: SHARON CUMMINS THUMA.

Iowa

CONSTITUTION AND GOVERNMENT

Iowa's constitution, its second, became effective on 3 September 1857. An amendment to the constitution proposed by the General Assembly has to be approved by a majority of the elected members of each house in two successive sessions and then ratified by a majority of state voters. The governor is elected separately from the lieutenant-governor to serve a four-year term of office and there is no limit to the number of terms he or she may serve. Cabinet members, five in total, are elected to specified offices and meet weekly. The General Assembly consists of 50 senators and 100 representatives, serving four- and two-year terms respectively. Alternate halves of the Senate are re-elected every two years. The General Assembly convenes annually in January and there is no limit to the number of days a session may last. A bill must be approved by a simple majority of the elected members in each house before being presented to the governor. During session the governor is allowed three days to consider a bill, after which it becomes law unless vetoed. Outside session a bill becomes law unless vetoed within 30 days from the adjournment of the session. A gubernatorial veto may be overridden by a two-thirds vote in each house of the General Assembly. Legislation generally becomes effective on 1 July following enactment. In 1986 911,000 people voted in the gubernatorial election, representing 56% of those registered to vote and 43% of the voting-age population. There are 99 administrative counties in Iowa.

ELECTED EXECUTIVE-BRANCH OFFICIALS

Governor (1987–91): TERRY E. BRANSTAD (Rep.).
Lieutenant-Governor: JO ANN ZIMMERMAN (Dem.).
Secretary of State: ELAINE BAXTER (Dem.).

Attorney-General: THOMAS J. MILLER (Dem.).
Treasurer: MICHAEL L. FITZGERALD (Dem.).
Auditor: RICHARD D. JOHNSON (Rep.).
Secretary of Agriculture: DALE M. COCHRAN (Dem.).

SELECTED GOVERNMENT ADDRESSES

Office of the Governor: State Capitol, Des Moines, IA 50319; tel. (515) 281-5211.

Office of the Lieutenant-Governor: State Capitol, Des Moines, IA 50319; tel. (515) 281-3421.

Office of the Secretary of State: State Capitol, Des Moines, IA 50319; tel. (515) 281-5864.

Office of the Attorney-General: Hoover State Office Bldg, Suite 200, Des Moines, IA 50319; tel. (515) 281-8373; incorporates Div. of Consumer Protection.

Office of the Treasurer: State Capitol, Des Moines, IA 50319; tel. (515) 281-5366.

Office of the Auditor: State Capitol, Des Moines, IA 50319; tel. (515) 281-5834.

Department of Agriculture: Wallace State Office Bldg, Des Moines, IA 50319; tel. (515) 281-5321; Sec. DALE M. COCHRAN.

Department of Commerce: 1918 Hulsizer Ave, SE, Ankney, IA 50021; tel. (515) 281-7401; incorporates Div. of Public Utilities; Dir. DAVID ROEDERER.

Department of Corrections: Capitol Annex, Des Moines, IA 50309; tel. (515) 281-6783; Dir PAUL GROSSHEIM (acting).

Department of Education: Grimes Bldg, Des Moines, IA 50319-0146; tel. (515) 281-5294; Supt of Public Instruction BILL LEPLEY.

Department of Health: Lucas State Office Building, Des Moines, IA 50319; tel. (515) 281-5605; Commr of Public Health MARY ELLIS.

Department of Natural Resources: Wallace State Office Bldg, Des Moines, IA 50319; tel. (515) 281-5385; incorporates Environment Div.; Dir LARRY J. WILSON.

Department of Public Defense: 7700 Beaver Dr., NW, Camp Dodge, Johnston, IA 50131-1902; tel. (515) 242-5211; Adj.-Gen. Maj.-Gen. WARREN G. LAWSON.

Department of Public Safety: Wallace State Office Bldg, Des Moines, IA 50319; tel. (515) 281-5261; Dir GENE SHEPARD.

Department of Revenue and Finance: Hoover State Office Bldg, Des Moines, IA 50319; tel. (515) 281-3204; Exec. Dir JERRY BAIR.

Department of Transportation: 800 Lincoln Way, Ames, IA 50010; tel. (515) 239-1111; Dir DARRELL RENSINK.

Energy Bureau: Natural Resources Dept, Wallace State Office Bldg, Des Moines, IA 50319; tel. (515) 281-6682; Sec. PHIL SVANOE.

Labor Services Commission: Employment Services Dept, 1000 East Grand Ave, Des Moines, IA 50319; tel. (515) 281-8067; Commr ALLEN J. MEIER.

Office of the Comptroller: State Capitol, Des Moines, IA 50319; tel. (515) 281-3322; incorporates Div. of the Budget; Comptroller WILLIAM KRAHL.

Tourism and Visitors' Bureau: Economic Development Dept, 200 East Grand Ave, Des Moines, IA 50319; tel. (515) 281-3100; Sec. DAVID REYNOLDS.

GENERAL ASSEMBLY
(May 1989)

Senate: Dem. 30; Rep. 20; Total 50.
President: Lt-Gov. JO ANN ZIMMERMAN (Dem.).
President Pro Tempore: GEORGE R. KINLEY (Dem.).
Secretary: JOHN F. DWYER.

House of Representatives: Dem. 62; Rep. 38; Total 100.
Speaker: DONALD D. AVENSON (Dem.).
Speaker Pro Tempore: JOHN H. CONNORS (Dem.).
Chief Clerk: JOSEPH O'HERN.

Kansas

CONSTITUTION AND GOVERNMENT

Kansas's only constitution was adopted in 1859 and became effective on 29 January 1861. Constitutional amendments proposed by the Legislature have to be approved by two-thirds of the elected members in each house and then ratified by a majority of state voters. The governor and lieutenant-governor are elected jointly to serve a four-year term; neither office may be held for more than two terms consecutively. The cabinet, consisting of 15 members in total, is appointed by the governor and meets at least once a month. There are 40 senators and 125 representatives in the state

Legislature, serving terms of four and two years respectively. Regular sessions of the Legislature are held annually in January. In even-numbered years sessions are limited in length to 90 calendar days; in odd-numbered years no limit applies. After approval by a majority of the elected members in each house, a bill is presented to the governor for consideration; it may then become law either by being signed or by remaining unsigned after the 10-day consideration period. A two-thirds vote is required from each house to override a gubernatorial veto. Enacted legislation becomes effective upon publication. In 1986 841,000 people voted in the gubernatorial election, representing 72% of those registered to vote and 46% of the voting-age population. There are 105 administrative counties in Kansas.

ELECTED EXECUTIVE-BRANCH OFFICIALS

Governor (1987–91): MIKE HAYDEN (Rep.).

Lieutenant-Governor: JACK D. WALKER (Rep.).

Secretary of State: BILL GRAVES (Rep.).

Attorney-General: ROBERT T. STEPHAN (Rep.).

Treasurer: JOAN FINNEY (Dem.).

Commissioner of Insurance: FLETCHER BELL (Rep.).

SELECTED GOVERNMENT ADDRESSES

Office of the Governor: State Capitol, Rm 200, Topeka, KS 66612; tel. (913) 296-3232.

Office of the Lieutenant-Governor: State Capitol, Rm 222, Topeka, KS 66612; tel. (913) 296-2213.

Office of the Secretary of State: State Capitol, Rm 200, Topeka, KS 66612; tel. (913) 296-2236.

Office of the Attorney-General: Judicial Center, Rm 200, Topeka, KS 66612; tel. (913) 296-2215.

Office of the Treasurer: 700 Harrison St, Topeka, KS 66601; tel. (913) 296-3171.

Board of Agriculture: 109 Ninth St, SW, Topeka, KS 66612; tel. (913) 296-3556; Sec. SAM BROWNBACK.

Commerce Department: 400 8th St West, Topeka, KS 66612; tel. (913) 296-3481; Sec. HARLAND PRIDDLE.

Corporate Commission: State Office Bldg, 4th Floor, Topeka, KS 66612; tel. (913) 296-3355; incorporates Divs of Energy and of Public Utility Regulation; Chair. C. MICHAEL LENNEN.

Department of Administration: State Capitol, Rm 263-E, Topeka, KS 66612; tel. (913) 296-3011; incorporates Div. of Finance; Sec. H. EDWARD FLENTJE.

Department of Corrections: Landon State Office Bldg, 900 Jackson St, SW, Topeka, KS 66612; tel. (913) 296-3317; Sec. ROGER V. ENDELL.

Department of Education: 120 East 10th St, Topeka, KS 66612; tel. (913) 296-3201; Commr Dr LEE DROEGEMUELLER.

Department of Health and Environment: Forbes Field Bldg, Topeka, KS 66620; tel. (913) 296-1500; incorporates Div. of Natural Resources; Sec. Dr STANLEY C. GRANT.

Department of Human Resources: 401 Topeka Blvd, Topeka, KS 66603; tel. (913) 296-5000; Sec. DENNIS R. TAYLOR.

Department of Insurance: 420 9th St, SW, Topeka, KS 66612; tel. (913) 296-3071; Commr FLETCHER BELL.

Department of Revenue: Docking State Office Bldg, 2nd Floor, Topeka, KS 66612; tel. (913) 296-3909; Sec. HARLEY T. DUNCAN.

Department of Transportation: Docking State Office Bldg, 7th Floor, Topeka, KS 66612; tel. (913) 296-3461; Sec. HORACE B. EDWARDS.

Division of the Highway Patrol: 122 7th St, SW, Topeka, KS 66603; tel. (913) 232-9200; Supt DON PICKERT.

Office of the Adjutant-General: 2800 Topeka Blvd, Topeka, KS 66611; tel. (913) 233-7560; Adj.-Gen. Brig.-Gen. PHILIP B. FINLEY.

Tourism Division: Commerce Dept, 400 8th St, SW, Topeka, KS 66603; tel. (913) 296-2009; Sec. Dir LEWJENE SCHNEIDER.

LEGISLATURE

(May 1989)

Senate: Rep. 22; Dem. 18; Total 40.

  President: PAUL BURKE (Rep.).
  Vice-President: ERIC YOST (Rep.).
  Secretary: LU KENNEY.

House of Representatives: Rep. 67; Dem. 58; Total 125.

  Speaker: JAMES D. BRADEN (Rep.).
  Speaker Pro Tempore: DALE SPRAGUE (Rep.).
  Chief Clerk: JANET E. JONES.

Kentucky

CONSTITUTION AND GOVERNMENT

Kentucky's constitution is the state's fourth and became effective on 28 September 1891. Amendments to the constitution proposed by the General Assembly must be approved by three-fifths of the elected members of each house, and must then be ratified by a majority of state voters. The governor and lieutenant-governor are elected separately to serve terms of four years; no elected state official may serve consecutive terms of office. Cabinet members, 13 in total, are appointed to specified office and meet once a week. There are 38 senators and 100 representatives in the state General Assembly, elected for four- and two-year terms respectively. Alternate halves of the Senate are re-elected every two years. Regular legislative sessions are held biennially in even years in January and may last no longer than 60 legislative days. A bill becomes law when it has been approved by a majority of the General Assembly equal to at least two-fifths of the membership of each house, and has been signed by the governor. The governor has 10 days in which to consider a bill, after which it becomes law unless vetoed. A gubernatorial veto may be overridden by a majority vote by the elected members of each house. Enacted legislation becomes effective 90 days after adjournment of the legislative session. In 1986 677,000 people voted in the election to the US Senate, representing 34% of those registered to vote and 25% of the voting-age population. Kentucky has 120 administrative counties.

ELECTED EXECUTIVE-BRANCH OFFICIALS

Governor (1988–92): WALLACE WILKINSON (Dem.).

Lieutenant-Governor: BRERETON C. JONES (Dem.).

Secretary of State: BREMER EHRLER (Dem.).

Attorney-General: FREDRIC J. COWAN (Dem.).

Treasurer: ROBERT MEAD (Dem.).

Auditor: BOB BABBAGE (Dem.).

Superintendent of Public Instruction: Dr JOHN BROCK.

Commissioner of Agriculture: WARD BURNETTE (Dem.).

SELECTED GOVERNMENT ADDRESSES

Office of the Governor: State Capitol, Frankfort, KY 40601; tel. (502) 564-2611; fax (502) 564-2735.

Office of the Lieutenant-Governor: State Capitol, Rm 142, Frankfort, KY 40601; tel. (502) 564-7562; fax (502) 564-4075.

Office of the Secretary of State: State Capitol, Rm 150, Frankfort, KY 40601; tel. (502) 564-3490.

Office of the Attorney-General: State Capitol, Rm 116, Frankfort, KY 40601; tel. (502) 564-4002.

Office of the Treasurer: Capitol Annex, 1st Floor, West Wing, Frankfort, KY 40601; tel. (502) 564-4722.

Office of the Auditor: Capitol Annex, Rm 125, Frankfort, KY 40601; tel. (502) 564-5841.

Bureau of Health Services: Human Resources Cabinet, 275 East Main St, Frankfort, KY 40601; tel. (502) 564-3970; Dir CARLOS HERNANDEZ.

Commerce Cabinet: Capitol Plaza Tower, 24th Floor, Frankfort, KY 40601; tel. (502) 564-7670; Sec. CARROLL KNICELY.

Corrections Cabinet: State Office Bldg, 5th Floor, Frankfort, KY 40601; tel. (502) 564-4726; Sec. JOHN T. WIGGINTON.

Department of Agriculture: Capitol Plaza Tower, 7th Floor, Frankfort, KY 40601; tel. (502) 564-4696; Commr WARD BURNETTE.

Department of Military Affairs: Boone National Guard Center, Frankfort, KY 40601; tel. (502) 564-8558; Adj.-Gen. Brig.-Gen. MICHAEL W. DAVIDSON.

Education and Humanities Cabinet: Capitol Plaza Tower, 1st Floor, Frankfort, KY 40601; tel. (502) 564-4770; Supt of Public Instruction Dr JOHN BROCK.

Energy Cabinet: Iron Works Pike, POB 11888, Lexington, KY 40578; tel. (606) 252-5535; Sec. GEORGE E. EVANS, Jr.

Finance and Administration Cabinet: Capitol Annex, Rm 301, Frankfort, KY 40601; tel. (502) 564-4240; Sec. L. ROGERS WELLS, Jr.

Labor Cabinet: US 127 South, Frankfort, KY 40601; tel. (502) 564-3070; Sec. CAROL PALMORE.

Natural Resources and Environmental Protection Cabinet: Capitol Plaza Tower, 5th Floor, Frankfort, KY 40601; tel. (502) 564-3350; Sec. CARL H. BRADLEY.

Public Service Commission: 730 Schenkel Lane, Frankfort, KY 40601; tel. (502) 564-3940; Chair. RICHARD D. HEMAN, Jr.

Revenue Cabinet: Capitol Annex, Rm 401, Frankfort, KY 40601; tel. (502) 564-3226; Sec. C. EMMETT CALVERT.

State Police Department: 919 Versailles Rd, Frankfort, KY 40601; tel. (502) 695-6300; Commr W. MICHAEL TROOP.

Tourism Cabinet: Capitol Plaza Tower, 24th Floor, Frankfort, KY 40601; tel. (502) 564-4270; Sec. MARY RAY OAKEN.

Transportation Cabinet: State Office Bldg, 10th Floor, Frankfort, KY 40601; tel. (502) 564-4890; Sec. MILO D. BRYANT.

GENERAL ASSEMBLY
(May 1989)

Senate: Dem. 28; Rep. 8; Vacancies 2; Total 38.

President: Lt-Gov. BRERETON C. JONES (Dem.).
President Pro Tempore: JOHN A. ROSE (Dem.).
Chief Clerk: JULIE HAVILAND.

House of Representatives: Dem. 74; Rep. 26; Total 100.

Speaker: DONALD J. BLANDFORD (Dem.).
Speaker Pro Tempore: PETE WORTHINGTON (Dem.).
Chief Clerk: EVELYN MARSTON.

Louisiana
CONSTITUTION AND GOVERNMENT

The current constitution of Louisiana is the state's 11th and became effective on 1 January 1975. Constitutional amendments proposed by the Legislature must be approved by two-thirds of the elected members of each house, and then ratified by a majority of state voters. The governor is elected separately from the lieutenant-governor to serve a term of four years, and may serve no more than two terms consecutively. Louisiana is the only state which elects an elections commissioner. Cabinet members, 21 including the governor, are elected to specified offices and meet twice a year. The Legislature consists of 39 senators and 105 representatives, all members being re-elected every four years. Regular sessions of the Legislature take place annually, beginning in April and lasting for no longer than 60 days. A bill becomes law after having been approved by both houses of the Legislature and signed by the governor. During session the governor is allowed 10 days in which to consider a bill, after which it becomes law unless vetoed. Outside session, the consideration period is 20 days from adjournment. A two-thirds vote by the elected members in each house is required to override a gubernatorial veto. Enacted legislation becomes effective 60 days after adjournment of the Legislature. In the 1986 election to the US Senate 1,370,000 people voted, representing 63% of those registered to vote and 43% of the voting-age population. Louisiana is divided into 64 'parishes', similar to counties in their political and administrative function.

ELECTED EXECUTIVE-BRANCH OFFICIALS

Governor (1988–92): CHARLES ('BUDDY') ROEMER (Dem.).
Lieutenant-Governor: PAUL HARDY (Dem.).
Secretary of State: WALTER ('FOX') MCKEITHEN (Dem.).
Attorney-General: WILLIAM J. GUSTE, Jr (Dem.).
Treasurer: MARY LANDRIEU (Dem.).
Superintendent of Education: THOMAS G. CLAUSEN.
Commissioner of Agriculture: BOB ODOM.
Commissioner of Insurance: DOUGLAS GREEN.
Commissioner of Elections: JERRY M. FOWLER.

SELECTED GOVERNMENT ADDRESSES

Office of the Governor: POB 94004, Baton Rouge, LA 70804; tel. (504) 342-7015.

Office of the Lieutenant-Governor: State Capitol, POB 44243, Baton Rouge, LA 70804; tel. (504) 342-7009.

Office of the Secretary of State: POB 94125, Baton Rouge, LA 70804; tel. (504) 922-1000.

Office of the Attorney-General: POB 94005, Baton Rouge, LA 70804; tel. (504) 342-7013.

Office of the Treasurer: POB 44154, Baton Rouge, LA 70804; tel. (504) 342-0010.

Department of Agriculture: POB 94302, Capitol Station, Baton Rouge, LA 70804-9302; tel. (504) 342-7011; Commr BOB ODOM.

Department of Commerce: POB 94185, Baton Rouge, LA 70804-9185; tel. (504) 342-5388; Sec. KAY JACKSON.

Department of Corrections: POB 44304, Baton Rouge, LA 70804; tel. (504) 342-6740; Deputy Sec. C. PAUL PHELPS.

Department of Culture, Recreation and Tourism: POB 44291, Baton Rouge, LA 70804; tel. (504) 925-3853; Sec. H. TRUXILLO.

Department of Education: POB 94064, Baton Rouge, LA 70804-9125; tel. (504) 342-3602; Supt THOMAS G. CLAUSEN.

Department of Health and Human Resources: POB 3776, Baton Rouge, LA 70821; tel. (504) 342-6711; Sec. SANDRA L. ROBINSON.

Department of Insurance: POB 94214, Baton Rouge, LA 70804; tel. (504) 342-5900; Commr DOUGLAS GREEN.

Department of Labor: POB 44094, Baton Rouge, LA 70804; tel. (504) 342-3011; Sec. DUDLEY J. PATIN, Jr.

Department of Natural Resources: POB 44396, Baton Rouge, LA 70804; tel. (504) 342-4500; incorporates Offices of Energy and of the Environment; Sec. WILLIAM C. HULS.

Department of Revenue and Taxation: POB 201, Baton Rouge, LA 70821; tel. (504) 925-7680; Sec. SHIRLEY MCNAMARA.

Department of Transportation and Development: POB 94245, Baton Rouge, LA 70804-9245; tel. (504) 342-7501; Sec. ROBERT G. GRAVES.

Division of Administration: POB 44095, Baton Rouge, LA 70804; tel. (504) 342-7000; incorporates Office of Finance; Commr STEPHANIE L. ALEXANDER.

Law Enforcement Commission: 1885 Wooddale Blvd, Rm 610, Baton Rouge, LA 70806; tel. (504) 925-4418; Exec. Dir MIKE RANATZA.

Military Department: Jackson Barracks, New Orleans, LA 70146; tel. (504) 271-6262; Adj.-Gen. B. JIM PORTER.

Office of Elections: POB 94125, Baton Rouge, LA 70804-9125; tel. (504) 342-7305; Commr JERRY M. FOWLER.

Public Service Commission: 1 American Pl., Suite 1630, Baton Rouge, LA 70825; tel. (504) 342-1407; Exec. Sec. LOUIS S. QUINN.

LEGISLATURE
(May 1989)

Senate: Dem. 34; Rep. 5; Total 39.

President: ALLEN BARES (Dem.).
President Pro Tempore: SAMUEL NENEZ (Dem.).
Secretary: MICHAEL S. BAER, III.

House of Representatives: Dem. 87; Rep. 18; Total 105.

Speaker: JIMMY N. DIMOS (Dem.).
Speaker Pro Tempore: HUNTINGTON DOWNER (Dem.).
Clerk: ALFRED SPEER.

Maine
CONSTITUTION AND GOVERNMENT

Maine's only constitution was adopted in 1879 and became effective on 15 March 1920. An amendment to the constitution proposed by the Legislature has to be approved by two-thirds of the elected members of both houses and then ratified by a majority of voters. The governor is the state's only elected executive-branch official. He or she is elected to serve a term of four years and may serve no more than two terms consecutively. There is no lieutenant-governor, and the president of the Senate succeeds in the absence of the governor. Cabinet members, 21 in total, are appointed by the governor with the consent of the Senate and meet at the governor's discretion. The Legislature consists of 35 senators and 151 representatives, both houses being re-elected every two years. The first of two regular sessions of the legislative term begins in December following the election and lasts for a maximum of 100 days. The second session (restricted to budgetary legislation) is limited to 50 days. A bill becomes law when it has been approved by the Legislature and signed by the governor. During session the governor is allowed 10 days in which to consider a bill, after which it becomes law unless vetoed. Bills vetoed after adjournment must be returned to the Legislature for reconsideration within the first three days of the next session. A gubernatorial veto may be overridden by a vote of two-thirds of the elected members in each house. Enacted legislation becomes effective 90 days after adjournment of the session. In 1986 427,000 people voted in the gubernatorial election, representing 54% of those registered to vote and 49% of the voting-age population. The principal units of local government in Maine are its 22 cities and 475 towns.

ELECTED EXECUTIVE-BRANCH OFFICIAL

Governor (1987–91): JOHN R. MCKERNAN, Jr (Rep.).

SELECTED GOVERNMENT ADDRESSES

Office of the Governor: State House, Station 1, Augusta, ME 04333; tel. (207) 289-3531; incorporates State Development Office (includes Divs of Commerce and of Tourism).

Bureau of Health: Dept of Human Services, State House, Station 11, Augusta, ME 04333; tel. (207) 289-3201; Commr Dr WILLIAM S. NERSESIAN.

Corrections Department: State House, Station 111, Augusta, ME 04333; tel. (207) 289-2711; Commr DONALD L. ALLEN.

Department of Agriculture, Food and Rural Resources: Deering Bldg, Augusta, ME 04333; tel. (207) 289-3871; Commr BARBARA GOTTSCHALK.

Department of Defense and Veterans' Services: Camp Keyes, Augusta, ME 04333; tel. (207) 622-9331; Commr and Adj.-Gen. ERNEST C. PARK.

Department of Educational and Cultural Services: State House, Station 23, Augusta, ME 04333; tel. (207) 289-5800; Commr EVE BITHER.

Department of Environmental Protection: State House, Station 17, Augusta, ME 04333; tel. (207) 289-2811; incorporates Div. of Natural Resources; Commr DEAN C. MARRIOTT.

Department of Finance and Administration: State House, Station 78, Augusta, ME 04333; tel. (207) 289-3446; incorporates Div. of Taxation; Commr JEAN MATTIMORE.

Department of Labor: 20 Union St, Augusta, ME 04330; tel. (207) 289-3788; Commr JOHN FITZSIMMONS.

Department of Public Safety: 36 Hospital St, Augusta, ME 04330; tel. (207) 289-2801; Commr of State Police JOHN ATWOOD.

Department of Transportation: Transportation Bldg, State House, Station 16, Augusta, ME 04333; tel. (207) 289-2551; Commr DANA F. CONNERS.

Office of the Attorney-General: State House, Station 6, Augusta, ME 04333; tel. (207) 289-3661; Att.-Gen. JAMES E. TIERNEY.

Office of Energy Resources: State House, Station 53, Augusta, ME 04333; tel. (207) 289-3811; Dir JOHN M. KERRY.

Office of the Secretary of State: State House, Station 29, Rm 223, Augusta, ME 04333; tel. (207) 289-1090; Sec. of State RODNEY S. QUINN.

Public Utilities Commission: 242 State St, Station 18, Augusta, ME 04333; tel. (207) 289-3831; Chair. PETER BRADFORD.

LEGISLATURE
(May 1989)

Senate: Dem. 20; Rep. 15; Total 35.
　President: CHARLES P. PRAY (Dem.).
　Secretary: JOY J. O'BRIEN.

House of Representatives: Dem. 97; Rep. 54; Total 151.
　Speaker: JOHN L. MARTIN (Dem.).
　Clerk: EDWIN H. PERT.

Maryland

CONSTITUTION AND GOVERNMENT

Maryland has had four constitutions. The current constitution became effective on 5 October 1867. Amendments to the constitution proposed by the General Assembly must be approved by three-fifths of the members of each house, and must then be ratified by a majority of state voters. The governor is elected with the lieutenant-governor to serve a four-year term and, after two consecutive terms, is not eligible to stand for office again until a period of four years has elapsed. Cabinet members, 23 in total, are appointed to specified offices with the consent of the Senate and meet at the governor's discretion. There are 47 senators and 141 delegates in the General Assembly, both houses serving terms of four years. Regular sessions are held annually, starting in January and lasting for no longer than 90 calendar days. A bill becomes law by being approved by a majority in both houses and signed by the governor. The governor is allowed six days to consider a bill during session, after which it becomes law unless vetoed. After session a bill becomes law unless vetoed within 30 days of being presented to the governor. A three-fifths vote is required to override a gubernatorial veto. Enacted legislation becomes effective on the following 1 July unless another date is specified. In the 1986 election to the US Senate, 1,113,000 people voted representing 52% of those registered to vote and 33% of the voting-age population. Maryland has 23 administrative counties.

ELECTED EXECUTIVE-BRANCH OFFICIALS

Governor (1987–91): WILLIAM D. SCHAEFER (Rep.).
Lieutenant-Governor: MELVIN A. STEINBERG (Dem.).
Attorney-General: J. JOSEPH CURRAN, Jr (Dem.).
State Treasurer: LUCILLE MAURER.

SELECTED GOVERNMENT ADDRESSES

Office of the Governor: State House, Annapolis, MD 21404; tel. (301) 974-3901; fax (301) 974-3275.

Office of the Lieutenant-Governor: State House, Annapolis, MD 21404; tel. (301) 974-2804.

Office of the Attorney-General: Corner of Calvert and Fayette Sts, Baltimore, MD 21202; tel. (301) 576-6300; fax (301) 576-6404.

Office of the State Treasurer: State Treasury Bldg, Rm 109, Annapolis, MD 21401; tel. (301) 974-3533; fax (301) 974-3530.

Department of Agriculture: 50 Harry S Truman Parkway, Annapolis, MD 21401; tel. (301) 841-5880; fax (301) 841-5914; Sec. WAYNE A. CAWLEY, Jr.

Department of Assessment and Taxation: 301 West Preston St, Rm 808, Baltimore, MD 21201; tel. (301) 225-1184; Dir GENE L. BURNER.

Department of Economic and Community Development: Redwood Tower, 23rd Floor, 217 East Redwood St, Baltimore, MD 21402; tel. (301) 333-6901; Sec. J. RANDALL EVANS.

Department of Education: 200 West Baltimore St, Baltimore, MD 21201; tel. (301) 333-2200; fax (301) 333-2226; Supt of Schools Dr JOSEPH SHILLING.

Department of Fiscal Services: 90 State Circle, Rm 200, Annapolis, MD 21401; tel. (301) 841-3761; Dir WILLIAM S. RATCHFORD, II.

Department of Health and Mental Hygiene: 201 West Preston St, 5th Floor, Baltimore, MD 21201; tel. (301) 225-6505; Sec. ADELE WILZACK.

Department of Natural Resources: Tawes State Office Bldg, 580 Taylor Ave, Annapolis, MD 21401; tel. (301) 974-3041; incorporates Div. of Environmental Services; Sec. Dr TORREY C. BROWN.

Department of Planning: 301 West Preston St, Baltimore, MD 21201; tel. (301) 225-4500; incorporates Office of Energy and Public Service Comm.; Sec. RON KREITNER.

Department of Public Safety and Correctional Services: 6776 Reisterstown Rd, Suite 310, Baltimore, MD 21215; tel. (301) 764-4004; Supt of State Police GEORGE BROSAN; Sec. BISHOP ROBINSON.

Department of Transportation: Baltimore–Washington International Airport, POB 8755, Baltimore, MD 21240; tel. (301) 859-7397; fax (301) 859-7138; Sec. RICHARD TRAINOR.

Division of Labor and Industry: 501 St Paul Pl., Baltimore, MD 21202; tel. (301) 333-4179; Commr DOMONIC FORNARO.

Military Department: 5th Regiment Armory, 29th Division St, Baltimore, MD 21201; tel. (301) 728-3388; fax (301) 576-6191; Adj.-Gen. Maj.-Gen. JAMES F. FRETTERD.

Office of the Secretary of State: Jeffrey Bldg, 16 Francis St, Annapolis, MD 21404; tel. (301) 974-5521; Sec. of State WINFIELD M. KELLY.

Office of Tourist Development: Dept of Econ. and Community Development, 45 Calvert St, Annapolis, MD 21401; tel. (301) 974-2686; Dir KURT ALBERSON.

GENERAL ASSEMBLY
(May 1989)

Senate: Dem. 40; Rep. 7; Total 47.
　President: THOMAS V. MIKE MILLER, Jr (Dem.).
　President Pro Tempore: FREDERICK C. MALKUS, Jr (Dem.).
　Secretary: ODEN BOWIE.

House of Delegates: Dem. 124; Rep. 17; Total 141.
　Speaker: L. CLAYTON MITCHELL (Dem.).
　Speaker Pro Tempore: DONALD B. ROBERTSON (Dem.).
　Chief Clerk: JACQUELINE M. SPELL.

Massachusetts

CONSTITUTION AND GOVERNMENT

Massachusetts' only constitution became effective on 25 October 1780. Constitutional amendments proposed by the General Court (the state legislature) must be approved by a majority of the elected members of each house at two successive sessions and must then be ratified by a majority of state voters. The governor and lieutenant-governor are elected jointly to serve a four-year term and there is no limit to the number of times a governor may hold office. Cabinet members, 12 including the governor, are appointed to specified offices and meet twice monthly. Elections for the 40 senators and 160 representatives in the General Court are held every two years. Regular sessions are called annually in January and there is no statutory limit to the number of days a session may last. A bill must be approved by a majority of members in both houses before being presented to the governor. During session the governor is allowed 10 days to consider a bill, after which it becomes law unless vetoed. After session a bill dies unless it is signed or vetoed within 10 days of being presented to the governor. A gubernatorial veto may be overridden by a two-thirds vote of the members present in each house. Legislation becomes effective 90 days after enactment. In the 1986 gubernatorial election 1,684,000 people voted, representing 56% of the registered voters and 37% of the voting-age population. There are 14 administrative counties in Massachusetts.

ELECTED EXECUTIVE-BRANCH OFFICIALS

Governor (1987–91): MICHAEL S. DUKAKIS (Dem.).

Lieutenant-Governor: EVELYN F. MURPHY (Dem.).

Secretary of State: MICHAEL JOSEPH CONNOLLY (Dem.).

Attorney-General: JAMES M. SHANNON (Dem.).

Treasurer and Receiver-General: ROBERT Q. CRANE (Dem.).

Auditor: A. JOSEPH DE NUCCI (Dem.).

SELECTED GOVERNMENT ADDRESSES

Office of the Governor: State House, Rm 360, Boston, MA 02133; tel. (617) 727-3600.

Office of the Lieutenant-Governor: State House, Rm 259, Boston, MA 02133; tel. (617) 727-2000.

Office of the Secretary of State: State House, Rm 340, Boston, MA 02133; tel. (617) 727-2800.

Office of the Attorney-General: 1 Ashburton Pl., 20th Floor, Rms 2000–2001, Boston, MA 02108; tel. (617) 727-2200.

Office of the Treasurer: State House, Rm 227, Boston, MA 02133; tel. (617) 727-2000.

Office of the Auditor: State House, Rm 230, Boston, MA 02133; tel. (617) 727-2075.

Department of Corrections: Exec. Office of Human Services, 100 Cambridge St, Boston, MA 02202; tel. (617) 727-3301; Commr MICHAEL V. FAIR.

Department of Education: 1385 Hancock St, Quincy, MA 02169; tel. (617) 770-7300; Commr HAROLD REYNOLDS, Jr.

Department of Public Health: Exec. Office of Human Services, 150 Tremont St, Boston, MA 02111; tel. (617) 727-2700; Commr DEBORAH PROTHROW-SMITH.

Executive Office of Administration and Finance: 1 Ashburton Pl., Boston, MA 02108; tel. (617) 727-2922; incorporates Div. of Revenue; Sec. EDWARD LASHMAN.

Executive Office of Economic Affairs: 1 Ashburton Pl., Rm 2101, Boston, MA 02108; tel. (617) 727-8380; incorporates Travel and Tourism Office: Sec. GRADY HEDGESPETH.

Executive Office of Energy Resources: 100 Cambridge St, Rm 1500, Boston, MA 02202; tel. (617) 727-4732; Sec. SHARON M. POLLARD.

Executive Office of Environmental Affairs: 100 Cambridge St, Rm 2000, Boston, MA 02202; tel. (617) 727-9800; incorporates Depts of Food and Agriculture, and of Natural Resources; Sec. JOHN DEVILLARS.

Executive Office of Labor: 1 Ashburton Pl., Rm 2112, Boston, MA 02108; tel. (617) 727-6573; Exec. Sec. PAUL EUSTACE.

Executive Office of Public Safety: 1 Ashburton Pl., Rm 2133, Boston, MA 02108; tel. (617) 782-7775; incorporates State Police Dept; Sec. CHARLES V. BARRY.

Executive Office of Transportation and Construction: 10 Park Plaza, Rm 3510, Boston, MA 02116; tel. (617) 973-7031; Sec. FREDERICK P. SALVUCCI.

Public Utilities Division: Exec. Office of Consumer Affairs and Business Regulation, 100 Cambridge St, Boston, MA 02202; tel. (617) 727-3503; Chair. PAULA W. GOLD.

GENERAL COURT
(May 1989)

Senate: Dem. 32; Rep. 8; Total 40.

President: WILLIAM M. BULGER (Dem.).
Clerk: EDWARD O'NEILL.

House of Representatives: Dem. 128; Rep. 32; Total 160.

Speaker: GEORGE KEVERIAN (Dem.).
Clerk: ROBERT MACQUEEN.

Michigan
CONSTITUTION AND GOVERNMENT

Michigan's constitution, the state's fourth, was adopted in 1963 and became effective on 1 January 1964. An amendment to the constitution proposed by the Legislature has to be passed by a two-thirds vote in each house and must then be ratified by a majority of state voters. The governor and lieutenant-governor are jointly elected to serve a four-year term, and there is no limit to the number of times they may hold office. Cabinet members, 25 in total, are appointed to specified offices and meet at the governor's discretion. There are 38 senators and 110 representatives in the Legislature, serving terms of four and two years respectively. Regular sessions are held annually, starting in January; there is no statutory limit to their length. A bill must be passed by both houses of the Legislature and signed by the governor to become law. The governor is allowed 14 days to consider a bill during session, after which it becomes law unless vetoed. After session a bill dies unless signed within 14 days of the session's adjournment. A two-thirds vote by each house is required to pass bills over the governor's veto. Enacted legislation becomes effective 90 days after adjournment of the session. In 1986 2,397,000 people voted in the gubernatorial election, representing 41% of those registered to vote and 36% of the voting-age population. Michigan has 83 administrative counties.

ELECTED EXECUTIVE-BRANCH OFFICIALS

Governor (1987–91): JAMES J. BLANCHARD (Dem.).

Lieutenant-Governor: MARTHA W. GRIFFITHS (Dem.).

Secretary of State: RICHARD A. AUSTIN (Dem.).

Attorney-General: FRANK J. KELLEY (Dem.).

SELECTED GOVERNMENT ADDRESSES

Office of the Governor: Exec. Office, Capitol Bldg, POB 30013, Lansing, MI 48909; tel. (517) 373-3400.

Office of the Lieutenant-Governor; Capitol Bldg, Lansing, MI 48909; tel. (517) 373-6800.

Office of the Secretary of State: 430 Treasury Bldg, 1st Floor, 430 West Allegan St, Lansing, MI 48918; tel. (517) 373-2510.

Office of the Attorney-General: Law Bldg, 7th Floor, 525 West Ottawa St, Lansing, MI 48913; tel. (517) 373-1110; incorporates Divs of Environmental Protection and of Municipal Affairs and Finance.

Department of Agriculture: Exec. Office, Capitol Bldg, POB 30017, Lansing, MI 48909; tel. (517) 373-1050; Dir Dr PAUL KINDINGER.

Department of Commerce: Law Bldg, 4th Floor, POB 30004, Lansing, MI 48909; tel. (517) 373-7230; incorporates Energy Administration, Travel Bureau and Public Service Comm.; Dir DOUGLAS ROSS.

Department of Corrections: Mason Bldg, 3rd Floor, POB 30003, Lansing, MI 48909; tel. (517) 373-0720; Dir ROBERT BROWN.

Department of Education: Ottawa Office Bldg, South Tower, 608 West Allegan St, POB 30008, Lansing, MI 48909; tel. (517) 373-3354; Supt of Public Instruction DONALD L. BEMIS.

Department of Labor: 309 North Washington Ave, POB 30015, Lansing, MI 48909; tel. (517) 373-9600; Dir ELIZABETH HOWE.

Department of Management and Budget: Lewis Cass Bldg, 1st Floor, POB 30026, Lansing, MI 48909; tel. (517) 373-1004; incorporates Office of Revenue and Tax Analysis and Div. of Administration; Dir ROBERT H. NAFTALY.

Department of Military Affairs: 2500 South Washington Ave, Lansing, MI 48913; tel. (517) 483-5507; Adj.-Gen. Maj.-Gen. VERNON J. ANDREWS.

Department of Natural Resources: POB 30028, Lansing, MI 48909; tel. (517) 373-2329; Dir DAVID HALES.

Department of Public Health: 3500 North Logan St, POB 30035, Lansing, MI 48909; tel. (517) 335-8024; Dir RAJ M. WEINER.

Department of Transportation: POB 30050, Lansing, MI 48909; tel. (517) 373-2114; Dir JAMES P. PITZ.

Department of the Treasury: POB 11097, Lansing, MI 48901; tel. (517) 373-3223; Treasurer and Comptroller ROBERT A. BOWMAN.

State Police Department: 714 South Harrison Rd, East Lansing, MI 48823; tel. (517) 337-6157; Dir Col RITCHIE T. DAVIS.

LEGISLATURE
(May 1989)

Senate: Rep. 20; Dem. 18; Total 38.

President: Lt-Gov. MARTHA W. GRIFFITHS (Dem.).

President Pro Tempore: NICK SMITH (Rep.).
Secretary: WILLIS H. SNOW.

House of Representatives: Dem. 64; Rep. 46; Total 110.

Speaker: LEWIS DODAK (Dem.).
Speaker Pro Tempore: TEOLA P. HUNTER (Dem.).
Clerk: DAVID EVANS.

Minnesota

CONSTITUTION AND GOVERNMENT

Minnesota's only constitution was adopted in 1857 and became effective on 11 May 1858. Amendments to the constitution proposed by the Legislature have to be approved by a majority of elected members in each house and then ratified by a majority of voters in the next election. The governor and lieutenant-governor are elected jointly to serve a four-year term of office. Members of the cabinet, 25 in total, are appointed to specified offices and form five sub-cabinets, meeting at regular intervals throughout the year. There are 67 senators and 134 representatives in the Legislature, serving terms of four and two years respectively. In Minnesota there is legal provision for regular sessions of the Legislature to be held in January in odd-numbered years only, but in practice sessions are also held in even-numbered years. Regular sessions may last no longer than 120 days. Before being presented to the governor a bill must be passed by both houses of the Legislature. During session a bill becomes law unless vetoed within three days of presentation to the governor. Outside session the governor is allowed 14 days to consider a bill, after which it dies unless signed. A gubernatorial veto may be overridden by a two-thirds vote by the elected members of each house. Enacted legislation becomes effective on 1 August following, except for fiscal legislation which becomes effective immediately. In 1986 1,416,000 people voted in the gubernatorial election, representing 54% of the registered voters and 46% of the voting-age population. Minnesota has 87 administrative counties.

ELECTED EXECUTIVE-BRANCH OFFICIALS

Governor (1987–91): RUDY PERPICH (DFL)*.
Lieutenant-Governor: MARLENE JOHNSON (DFL)*.
Secretary of State: JOAN ANDERSON GROWE (DFL)*.
Attorney-General: HUBERT H. HUMPHREY, III (DFL)*.
Treasurer: MICHAEL A. McGRATH (DFL)*.
Auditor: ARNE H. CARLSON (IR)†.
Administration Commissioner: SANDRA J. HALE.

SELECTED GOVERNMENT ADDRESSES

Office of the Governor: South Capitol Bldg, Rm 130, St Paul, MN 55155; tel. (612) 296-3391.

Office of the Lieutenant-Governor: South Capitol Bldg, Rm 121, St Paul, MN 55155; tel. (612) 296-2374.

Office of the Secretary of State: State Office Bldg, 435 Park St, Rm 180, St Paul, MN 55155; tel. (612) 296-3266.

Office of the Attorney-General: South Capitol Bldg, Aurora Ave, Rm 102, St Paul, MN 55155; tel. (612) 296-6196.

Office of the Treasurer: Administration Bldg, 50 Sherburne Ave, Rm 303, St Paul, MN 55155; tel. (612) 296-7091.

Office of the Auditor: 525 Park St, Suite 400, St Paul, MN 55103; tel. (612) 296-2551.

Department of Administration: Administration Bldg, 50 Sherburne Ave, St Paul, MN 55155; tel. (612) 296-3862; Commr SANDRA J. HALE.

Department of Agriculture: 90 West Plato Blvd, St Paul, MN 55107; tel. (612) 297-3219; Commr JAMES NICHOLS.

Department of Corrections: Bigelow Bldg, Rm 300, 450 North Syndicate St, St Paul, MN 55104; tel. (612) 642-0282; Commr ORVILLE B. PUNG.

Department of Education: Capitol Square Bldg, 550 Cedar St, St Paul, MN 55101; tel. (612) 296-2358; Commr RUTH E. RANDALL.

Department of Energy and Economic Development: 150 East Kellog Blvd, 9th Floor, St Paul, MN 55101; tel. (612) 296-6424; incorporates Div. of Tourism; Commr MARK DAYTON.

Department of Finance: Centennial Bldg, Rm 400, 658 Cedar St, St Paul, MN 55155; tel. (612) 296-9721; Commr TOM TRIPLETT.

---

* Democratic–Farmer–Labor Party: official name for Minnesota's Democratic Party.
† Independent–Republican Party: official name for Minnesota's Republican Party.

Department of Health: 717 Delaware St, SE, Minneapolis, MN 55440; tel. (612) 623-5460; incorporates Div. of Environmental Health; Commr Sister MARY MADONNA ASHTON.

Department of Labor and Industry: 443 Lafayette Rd, St Paul, MN 55155; tel. (612) 296-2342; Commr KEN PETERSON.

Department of Military Affairs: Veterans' Service Bldg, 20 West 12th St, St Paul, MN 55155; tel. (612) 296-4662; Adj.-Gen. Brig.-Gen. EUGENE R. ANDREOTTI.

Department of Natural Resources: 500 North Lafayette Rd, St Paul, MN 55155-4001; tel. (612) 296-2549; Commr JOSEPH N. ALEXANDER.

Department of Public Safety: Transportation Bldg, John Ireland Blvd, Rm 211, St Paul, MN 55155; tel. (612) 296-6642; Commr PAUL J. TSCHIDA.

Department of Revenue: 10 River Park Plaza, St Paul, MN 55107; tel. (612) 296-3781; Commr JOHN JAMES.

Department of Transportation: Transportation Bldg, John Ireland Blvd, St Paul, MN 55155; tel. (612) 296-3000; Commr LEONARD W. LEVINE.

Public Utilities Commission: American Center Bldg, 150 East Kellog Blvd, Rm 780, St Paul, MN 55101; tel. (612) 296-2354; Chair. BARBARA BEERHALTER.

LEGISLATURE
(May 1989)

Senate: DFL 44; IR 23; Total 67.

President: JEROME M. HUGHES (DFL).
Secretary: PATRICK E. FLAHAVEN.

House of Representatives: DFL 80; IR 54; Total 134.

Speaker: ROBERT VANASEK (DFL).
Chief Clerk: ED BURDICK.

Mississippi

CONSTITUTION AND GOVERNMENT

Mississippi's current constitution, its fourth, became effective on 1 November 1890. Amendments to the constitution introduced by the Legislature must be approved by two-thirds of the elected members of each house and then ratified by a majority of state voters. The governor, elected separately from the lieutenant-governor, serves a four-year term and may serve no more than two successive terms. Mississippi has no formal cabinet system. The Legislature comprises 52 senators and 122 representatives, both houses serving four-year terms. Regular sessions are held annually in January and the first session of a legislative term is limited to 125 days. Thereafter, sessions have a 90-day limit. A bill has to be approved by both houses of the Legislature before being presented to the governor, who then has five days to consider it, after which it becomes law unless vetoed. After session a bill becomes law unless vetoed within 15 days of being presented to the governor. The governor's veto may be overridden by a two-thirds vote by the elected members of each house. Legislation becomes effective 60 days after enactment. In 1986 524,000 people voted in the election to the US House of Representatives, representing 32% of the number of people registered to vote and 29% of the voting-age population. Mississippi is divided into 82 administrative counties.

ELECTED EXECUTIVE-BRANCH OFFICIALS

Governor (1988–92): RAY MABUS, Jr (Dem.).
Lieutenant-Governor: BRAD DYE (Dem.).
Secretary of State: DICK MOLPUS (Dem.).
Attorney-General: MIKE MOORE (Dem.).
Treasurer: MARSHALL BENNETT (Dem.).
Auditor of Public Accounts and Comptroller: PETE JOHNSON.
Commissioner of Agriculture and Commerce: JIM BUCK ROSS.
Commissioner of Insurance: GEORGE DALE.

SELECTED GOVERNMENT ADDRESSES

Office of the Governor: POB 139, Jackson, MS 39205; tel. (601) 359-3100.

Office of the Lieutenant-Governor: POB 1018, Jackson, MS 39205; tel. (601) 359-3200.

Office of the Secretary of State: POB 136, Jackson, MS 39205; tel. (601) 359-1350.

Office of the Attorney-General: POB 220, Jackson, MS 39205; tel. (601) 359-3680.

Office of the Treasurer: POB 138, Jackson, MS 39205; tel. (601) 359-3600.

Office of the Auditor of Public Accounts: POB 956, Jackson, MS 39205; tel. (601) 359-3561.

Army and Air National Guard: POB 5027, Jackson, MS 39296-5027; tel. (601) 949-6232; Adj.-Gen. Maj.-Gen. ARTHUR J. FARMER.

Department of Agriculture and Commerce: POB 1609, Jackson, MS 39215-1609; tel. (601) 359-3639; Commr JIM BUCK ROSS.

Department of Corrections: 723 North President St, Jackson, MS 39202-3097; tel. (601) 354-6454; Interim Commr CHARLES J. JACKSON.

Department of Economic Development: POB 849, Jackson, MS 39205; tel. (601) 359-3449; incorporates Div. of Tourism; Exec. Dir J. MAC HOLLADAY.

Department of Education: POB 771, Jackson, MS 39205-0771; tel. (601) 359-3513; Supt RICHARD BOYD.

Department of Energy and Transportation: Dickson Bldg, 510 George St, Suite 301, Jackson, MS 39202; tel. (601) 961-4733; Exec. Dir ANDREW JENKINS.

Department of Health: POB 1700, Jackson, MS 39215-1700; tel. (601) 960-7634; incorporates Bureau of Environmental Health; State Health Officer ALTON B. COBB.

Department of Insurance: POB 79, Jackson, MS 39205; tel. (601) 359-3569; Commr GEORGE DALE.

Department of Natural Resources: POB 20305, Jackson, MS 39209; tel. (601) 961-5000; Exec. Dir JAMES PALMER, Jr.

Department of Public Safety: POB 958, Jackson, MS 39205; tel. (601) 987-1212; Exec. Dir LOUISA O. DIXON.

Employment Security Commission: 1520 West Capitol St, POB 1699, Jackson, MS 39215-1699; tel. (601) 354-8711; Exec. Dir LINDA ROSS ALDY.

Fiscal Management Board: POB 267, Jackson, MS 39205; tel. (601) 359-3402; Fiscal Officer CECIL C. BROWN.

Public Service Commission: POB 1174, Jackson, MS 39215-1174; tel. (601) 961-5400; incorporates Utilities Div.; Chief Exec. BRIAN U. RAY.

Tax Commission: POB 1033, Jackson, MS 39205; tel. (601) 359-1105; Exec. Dir LESTER C. HERRINGTON.

LEGISLATURE

(May 1989)

Senate: Dem. 45; Rep. 7; Total 52.

President: Lt-Gov. BRAD DYE (Dem.).
President Pro Tempore: GLEN DeWEESE (Dem.).
Secretary: CHARLES H. GRIFFIN.

House of Representatives: Dem. 111; Rep. 11; Total 122.

Speaker: TIM FORD (Dem.).
Speaker Pro Tempore: CECIL L. SIMMONS.
Clerk: CHARLES JACKSON, Jr.

Missouri

CONSTITUTION AND GOVERNMENT

The current constitution of Missouri is the state's fourth and became effective on 30 March 1945. Constitutional amendments proposed by the General Assembly have to be passed by a majority of elected members in each house and then ratified by a majority of state voters. Neither the governor (elected separately from the lieutenant-governor) nor the treasurer may serve more than two terms of office, a term lasting for four years. Members of the cabinet, 15 in total, are appointed to specified offices and meet at the governor's discretion. There are 34 senators and 163 representatives in the General Assembly, serving terms of four and two years respectively. Alternate halves of the Senate are re-elected every two years. Regular legislative sessions are held annually, beginning in January and ending no later than 30 May. To become law, a bill requires the approval of both houses of the General Assembly and must be signed by the governor. If, after a 15-day consideration period, the governor has neither signed nor vetoed the bill the legislators may present it to the secretary of state for enactment. A bill presented to the governor after session becomes law unless vetoed within 45 days. A gubernatorial veto may be overridden by a vote by two-thirds of the elected members of each house. Enacted legislation becomes effective 90 days after adjournment of the session, except for legislation authorizing the expenditure of state funds which becomes effective at the beginning of the state fiscal year on 1 July. In 1986 1,477,000 people voted in the election to the US Senate, representing 53% of those registered to vote and 39% of the voting-age population. There are 114 administrative counties in Missouri.

ELECTED EXECUTIVE-BRANCH OFFICIALS

Governor (1989–93): JOHN ASHCROFT (Rep.).
Lieutenant-Governor: MEL CARNAHAN (Dem.).
Secretary of State: ROY D. BLUNT (Rep.).
Attorney-General: WILLIAM WEBSTER (Rep.).
Treasurer: WENDELL BAILEY (Rep.).
Auditor: MARGARET B. KELLY (Rep.).

SELECTED GOVERNMENT ADDRESSES

Office of the Governor: State Capitol, Rm 216, POB 720, Jefferson City, MO 65101; tel. (314) 751-3222.

Office of the Lieutenant-Governor: State Capitol, Rm 326, POB 563, Jefferson City, MO 65101; tel. (314) 751-3000.

Office of the Secretary of State: State Capitol, Rm 209, POB 778, Jefferson City, MO 65102; tel. (314) 751-2379.

Office of the Attorney-General: Supreme Court Bldg, POB 889, Jefferson City, MO 65102; tel. (314) 751-3321.

Office of the Treasurer: State Capitol, Rm 229, POB 210, Jefferson City, MO 65102; tel. (314) 751-2411.

Office of the Auditor: State Capitol, Rm 224, POB 869, Jefferson City, MO 65101; tel. (314) 751-4824.

Department of Agriculture: 1616 Missouri Blvd, POB 630, Jefferson City, MO 65102; tel. (314) 751-4211; Dir CHARLES E. KRUSE.

Department of Corrections and Human Resources: 2729 Plaza Dr., POB 236, Jefferson City, MO 65102; tel. (314) 751-2389; Dir DICK D. MOORE.

Department of Economic Development; Truman Bldg, 6th Floor, POB 1157, Jefferson City, MO 65102; tel. (314) 751-2133; Dir CARL M. KOUPAL, Jr.

Department of Elementary and Secondary Education: Jefferson Bldg, Rm 205, POB 480, Jefferson City, MO 65102; tel. (314) 751-4212; Commr ROBERT E. BARTMAN.

Department of Health: 1738 East Elm St, Jefferson City, MO 65101; tel. (314) 751-4815; Dir ROBERT G. HARMON.

Department of Labor and Industrial Relations: 421 East Dunklin St, Jefferson City, MO 65104; tel. (314) 751-4091; Dir JERRY HUNTER.

Department of Natural Resources: 205 Jefferson St, POB 176, Jefferson City, MO 65102; tel. (314) 751-4422; incorporates Divs of Environmental Quality and of Energy; Dir FREDERICK A. BRUNNER.

Department of Public Safety: Truman Bldg, 8th Floor, POB 749, Jefferson City, MO 65102; tel. (314) 751-4905; incorporates Offices of Adj.-Gen. and State Police; Dir RICHARD RICE.

Department of Revenue: Truman Bldg, 6th Floor, POB 311, Jefferson City, MO 65105; tel. (314) 751-4450; Dir DUANE BENTON.

Division of Tourism: Dept of Econ. Development, Truman Bldg, Rm 290, POB 1055, Jefferson City, MO 65102; tel. (314) 751-4133; Dir MARJORIE BEENDERS.

Highway and Transportation Department: Highway and Transportation Office Bldg, POB 270, Jefferson City, MO 65102; tel. (314) 751-2551; Chair. JOHN C. COZAD.

Office of Administration: State Capitol, Rm 125, POB 809, Jefferson City, MO 65102; tel. (314) 751-3311; incorporates Div. of Budget and Planning; Commr JAMES R. MOODY.

Public Service Commission: Dept of Econ. Development, Truman Bldg, POB 360, Jefferson City, MO 65102; tel. (314) 751-3234; Chair. WILLIAM D. STEINMEIER.

GENERAL ASSEMBLY

(May 1989)

Senate: Dem. 22; Rep. 12; Total 34.

President: Lt-Gov. MEL CARNAHAN (Dem.).
President Pro Tempore: JAMES L. MATHEWSON (Dem.).
Secretary: TERRY SPIELER.

House of Representatives: Dem. 104; Rep. 59; Total 163.

Speaker: ROBERT F. GRIFFIN (Dem.).
Speaker Pro Tempore: PATRICK J. HICKEY (Dem.).
Chief Clerk: DOUGLAS W. BURNETT.

Montana

CONSTITUTION AND GOVERNMENT

Montana's constitution, the state's second, was adopted in 1972 and became effective on 1 July 1973. Amendments to the constitution proposed by the Legislature have to be passed by a two-thirds vote in both houses and ratified by a majority of state voters. The governor and lieutenant-governor, elected jointly, serve a four-year term; there are no limits on the number of times they may hold office. Cabinet members, 16 including the governor, are appointed to specified offices and meet six times a year. The Legislature consists of 50 senators and 100 representatives. Following a reapportionment of seats after the 1980 census, lots were drawn for one-half of the senators to serve an initial two-year term, after which they were to serve a four-year term; representatives serve two year terms. Regular sessions of the Legislature are held biennially in odd-numbered years. They begin in January and may last no longer than 90 days. A bill becomes law when it has been passed by a simple majority in both houses and signed by the governor. During session the governor has five days to consider a bill, after which it becomes law unless vetoed. After session a bill becomes law unless vetoed within 25 days. A gubernatorial veto may be overridden by two-thirds of the members present in each house. Legislation becomes effective on the 1 October following enactment, except for fiscal legislation which becomes effective on 1 July. In 1986 318,000 people voted in the election to the US House of Representatives, representing 72% of those registered to vote and 54% of the voting-age population. Montana has 56 administrative counties.

ELECTED EXECUTIVE-BRANCH OFFICIALS

Governor (1989–93): STAN STEPHENS (Rep.).
Lieutenant-Governor: ALLEN C. KOLSTAD (Rep.).
Secretary of State: MIKE COONEY (Dem.).
Attorney-General: MARC RACICOT (Rep.).
Auditor and Insurance Commissioner: ANDREA BENNETT (Rep.).
Superintendent of Public Instruction: NANCY KEENAN (Dem.).

SELECTED GOVERNMENT ADDRESSES

Office of the Governor: Capitol Station, Rm 204, Helena, MT 59620; tel. (406) 444-3111.
Office of the Lieutenant-Governor: Capitol Station, Rm 207, Helena, MT 59620; tel. (406) 444-3111.
Office of the Secretary of State: State Capitol, Rm 202, Helena, MT 59620; tel. (406) 444-2034.
Office of the Attorney-General: Justice Bldg, 215 North Sanders, Helena, MT 59620; tel. (406) 444-2026.
Office of the Auditor: POB 4009, Helena, MT 59604; tel. (406) 444-2040.

Department of Administration: Sam W. Mitchell Bldg, Rm 155, Helena, MT 59620; tel. (406) 444-2032; Dir DAVE ASHLEY.
Department of Agriculture: Capitol Station, Helena, MT 59620; tel. (406) 444-3144; Dir EVERETT SNORTLAND.
Department of Commerce: 1424 9th Ave, Helena, MT 59620; tel. (406) 444-3494; incorporates Divs of Tourism Promotion and of Transportation; Dir MIKE LETSON.
Department of Health and Environmental Sciences: Capitol Station, Helena, MT 59620; tel. (406) 444-2037; Administrator DON PIZZINI.
Department of Labor and Industry: Capitol Station, Helena, MT 59620; tel. (406) 444-3661; Commr MIKE MICONE.
Department of Military Affairs: POB 4798, Helena, MT 59604-4798; tel. (406) 444-6910; Adj.-Gen. GARY BLAIR.
Department of Natural Resources and Conservation: 25 South Ewing, Helena, MT 59601; tel. (406) 444-6697; incorporates Div. of Energy; Dir KAREN BARCLAY.
Department of Revenue: Sam W. Mitchell Bldg, Rm 445, Helena, MT 59620; tel. (406) 444-2460; Dir KEN NORDTVEDT.
Division of Corrections: Dept of Institutions, 1539 11th Ave, Helena, MT 59620; tel. (406) 444-3930; Dir CARROLL SOUTH.
Highway Patrol Division: Dept of Justice, 303 North Roberts, Helena, MT 59620; tel. (406) 444-3000; Administrator ROBERT W. LAMDON.
Office of the Superintendent of Public Instruction: State Capitol Office, Rm 106, Helena, MT 59620; tel. (406) 444-3654; Supt NANCY KEENAN.
Public Service Commission: 2701 Prospect Ave, Helena, MT 59620; tel. (406) 444-6199; Chair. CLYDE JARVIS.

LEGISLATURE
(May 1989)

Senate: Dem. 25; Rep. 25; Total 50.
  President: JACK GALT (Rep.).
  President Pro Tempore: MATT HIMSL (Rep.).
  Secretary: JOHN W. LARSON.

House of Representatives: Rep. 51; Dem. 49; Total 100.
  Speaker: JOHN VINCENT (Dem.).
  Speaker Pro Tempore: KELLY ADDY (Dem.).
  Chief Clerk: LARRY FASBENDER.

Nebraska
CONSTITUTION AND GOVERNMENT

Nebraska's current constitution is the state's second and became effective on 12 October 1875. Constitutional amendments proposed by the unicameral Legislature may be approved by a three-fifths vote from the elected members and ratified by a majority of state voters. The majority vote must amount to at least 50% of the votes cast at the election. The governor is elected jointly with the lieutenant-governor to serve a four-year term and, after two consecutive terms, is not eligible to hold office again until a four-year period has elapsed. Cabinet members, 27 including the governor, are appointed to specified offices and meet weekly. The Legislature consists of 49 senators who are elected to serve four-year terms of office, alternate halves being elected every two years. Regular sessions of the Legislature are held annually in January and are limited in length to 60 days in even-numbered years and 90 days in odd-numbered years. A bill becomes law when it has been passed by a majority in the Legislature and has been signed by the governor; it also becomes law if it remains neither signed nor vetoed five days after having been presented to the governor. A gubernatorial veto may be overridden by a three-fifths vote by the elected members of the Legislature. Legislation becomes effective three months after adjournment. In the 1986 gubernatorial election 564,000 people voted, representing 66% of those registered to vote and 48% of the voting-age population. There are 93 administrative counties in Nebraska.

ELECTED EXECUTIVE-BRANCH OFFICIALS

Governor (1987–91): KAY ORR (Rep.).
Lieutenant-Governor: WILLIAM NICHOL (Rep.).
Secretary of State: ALLEN J. BEERMANN (Rep.).
Attorney-General: ROBERT SPIRE (Rep.).
Treasurer: FRANK MARSH (Rep.).
Auditor of Public Accounts: RAY A. C. JOHNSON (Rep.).

SELECTED GOVERNMENT ADDRESSES

Office of the Governor: State Capitol Bldg, 2nd Floor, Lincoln, NE 68509; tel. (402) 471-2244.
Office of the Lieutenant-Governor: State Capitol Bldg, Rm 2315, Lincoln, NE 68509; tel. (402) 471-2256.
Office of the Secretary of State: State Capitol Bldg, Rm 2300, Lincoln, NE 68509; tel. (402) 471-2554.
Office of the Attorney-General: State Capitol Bldg, Rm 2115, Lincoln, NE 68509; tel. (402) 471-2682.
Office of the Treasurer: State Capitol Bldg, POB 94788, Lincoln, NE 68509; tel. (402) 471-2455.
Office of the Auditor of Public Accounts: State Capitol Bldg, Rm 2303, Lincoln, NE 68509; tel. (402) 471-2111.

Department of Administrative Services: State Capitol Bldg, Rm 1315, Lincoln, NE 68509; tel. (402) 471-2331; Dir LARRY BARE.
Department of Agriculture: 301 Centennial Mall South, POB 94947, Lincoln, NE 68509; tel. (402) 471-2341; Commr ROY FREDERICK.
Department of Banking and Finance: POB 5006, Lincoln, NE 68509; tel. (402) 471-2171; Dir CYNTHIA MILLIGAN.
Department of Correctional Services: West Van Dorn and Folsom Sts, POB 94661, Lincoln, NE 68509; tel. (402) 471-2654; Dir FRANK O. GUNTER.
Department of Education: 301 Centennial Mall South, POB 94987, Lincoln, NE 68509; tel. (402) 471-2465; Commr JOE E. LUTEJEHARMS.
Department of Environmental Control: State Office Bldg, POB 94887, Lincoln, NE 68509; tel. (402) 471-2186; Dir DENNIS GRAMS.
Department of Health: 301 Centennial Mall South, 3rd Floor, POB 95007, Lincoln, NE 68509; tel. (402) 471-2133; Dir GREGG F. WRIGHT.
Department of Labor: POB 94600, Lincoln, NE 68509; tel. (402) 471-9000; Commr VIRGINIA YUELL.
Department of Revenue: 301 Centennial Mall South, POB 94818, Lincoln, NE 68509; tel. (402) 471-2971; Dir JOHN BOEHM.
Department of Roads: POB 94759, Lincoln, NE 68509; tel. (402) 471-2871; Dir STANLEY COOPER.

Department of State Energy: POB 95085, Lincoln, NE 68509-5085; tel. (402) 471-2867; Dir GARY L. REX.

Division of Travel and Tourism: Dept. of Econ. Development, POB 94666, Lincoln, NE 68509; tel. (402) 471-3794; Dir PEGGY BRIGGS.

Natural Resources Commission: 301 Centennial Mall South, POB 94876, Lincoln, NE 68509; tel. (402) 471-2081; Dir DAYLE E. WILLIAMSON.

Office of the Adjutant-General: 1300 Military Rd, Lincoln, NE 68508; tel. (402) 471-1114; Adj.-Gen. STANLEY HENG.

Public Service Commission: POB 94927, Lincoln, NE 68509; tel. (402) 471-3101; Chair DONALD J. ADAMS.

State Patrol: POB 94907, Lincoln, NE 68509; tel. (402) 471-4545; Supt Col HAROLD W. LaGRANDE.

LEGISLATURE
(May 1989)

Nebraska's legislature is unicameral and comprises 49 members elected on a non-partisan basis, all of whom go by the title of senator.

President of the Legislature: Lt-Gov. WILLIAM NICHOL (Rep.).

Speaker of the Legislature: WILLIAM BARRETT (Rep.).

Chair. of Executive Board, Legislative Council: RICHARD PETERSON (Rep.).

Vice-Chair. of Executive Board, Legislative Council: BERNICE LABEDZ (Dem.).

Clerk of the Legislature: PATRICK O'DONNELL.

Nevada
CONSTITUTION AND GOVERNMENT

Nevada's only constitution became effective on 31 October 1864. Amendments to the constitution proposed by the Legislature have to be approved by a majority of elected members in each house in two successive sessions and ratified by a majority of state voters. The governor, elected separately from the lieutenant-governor, serves a four-year term and may serve no more than two terms consecutively. Nevada has no formal cabinet system. There are 21 senators and 42 representatives in the Legislature, serving terms of four and two years respectively; alternate halves of the Senate are re-elected every two years. Regular sessions of the Legislature take place biennially in January in odd-numbered years, and may last no longer than 60 calendar days. A bill becomes law when it has been passed by the Legislature and signed by the governor. During session the governor has 10 days to consider a bill, after which it becomes law unless vetoed. Outside session the consideration period is 10 days from adjournment of the Legislature. A gubernatorial veto may be overridden by a two-thirds vote in each house. Enacted legislation becomes effective on 1 July following, or whenever specified. In 1986 262,000 people voted in the election to the US Senate, representing 71% of those registered to vote and 36% of the voting-age population. Nevada is divided into 16 administrative counties.

SELECTED EXECUTIVE-BRANCH OFFICIALS

Governor (1987–91): RICHARD H. BRYAN (Dem.).

Lieutenant-Governor: BOB J. MILLER (Dem.).

Secretary of State: FRANKIE SUE DEL PAPA (Dem.).

Attorney-General: BRIAN McKAY (Rep.).

Treasurer: KEN SANTOR (Rep.).

Controller: DARRELL DAINES (Rep.).

SELECTED GOVERNMENT ADDRESSES

Office of the Governor: Capitol Bldg, Executive Chambers, Carson City, NV 89710; tel. (702) 885-5670.

Office of the Lieutenant-Governor: Capitol Complex, Carson City, NV 89710; tel. (702) 885-3037.

Office of the Secretary of State: Capitol Complex, Carson City, NV 89710; tel. (702) 885-5203.

Office of the Attorney-General: Capitol Complex, Heroes Memorial Bldg, Carson City, NV 89710; tel. (702) 885-4170.

Office of the Treasurer: Capitol Complex, Carson City, NV 89710; tel. (702) 885-5200.

Office of the Controller: Capitol Annex, Carson City, NV 89710; tel. (702) 885-4330.

Commission on Tourism: 110 East Williams St, Suite 117, Carson City, NV 89710; tel. (702) 885-4332; Exec. Dir STEPHEN B. RICHER.

Department of Administration: Blasdel Bldg, Rm 204, Carson City, NV 89710; tel. (702) 885-4065; Dir WILLIAM A. BIBLE.

Department of Adult Parole and Probation: 1100 East William St, Suite 206, Carson City, NV 89701; tel. (702) 885-5040; Chief ROBERT N. CALDERONE.

Department of Agriculture: 350 Capitol Hill, POB 11100, Reno, NV 89510; tel. (702) 789-0180; Exec. Dir THOMAS BALLOW.

Department of Commerce: Capitol Complex, Carson City, NV 89710; tel. (702) 885-4250; Dir LARRY D. STRUVE.

Department of Conservation and Natural Resources: 201 South Fall St, Capitol Complex, Carson City, NV 89710; tel. (702) 885-4360; incorporates Div. of Environmental Protection; Dir ROLAND D. WESTERGARD.

Department of Education: 400 West King St, Capitol Complex, Carson City, NV 89710; tel. (702) 885-3100; Supt of Public Instruction EUGENE PASLOV.

Department of Taxation: Capitol Complex, Carson City, NV 89710; tel. (702) 885-4892; Exec. Dir JOHN PERRY COMEAX.

Department of Transportation: 1263 South Stewart St, Carson City, NV 89712; tel. (702) 885-5440; Dir GARTH DULL.

Division of Health: Dept of Human Services, 505 East King St, Rm 600, Carson City, NV 89710; tel. (702) 885-4740; Health Officer CATHERINE LOWE.

Highway Patrol Division: Dept of Motor Vehicles, 555 Wright Way, Carson City, NV 89711; tel. (702) 885-5300; Dir WINSTON RICHARDS.

Labor Commission: 505 East King St, Rm 601, Carson City, NV 89710; tel. (702) 885-4850; Commr FRANK T. MacDONALD.

Office of the Adjutant-General: 2525 South Carson St, Carson City, NV 89701; tel. (702) 887-7302; Adj.-Gen. ROBERT J. DWYER.

Public Service Commission: 505 East King St, Carson City, NV 89710; tel. (702) 885-4117; Chair. SCOTT M. CRAIGIE.

LEGISLATURE
(May 1989)

Senate: Dem. 13; Rep. 8; Total 21.

President: Lt-Gov. BOB J. MILLER (Dem.).
President Pro Tempore: LAWRENCE E. JACOBSEN (Rep.).
Secretary: JANICE L. THOMAS.

Assembly: Rep. 30; Dem. 12; Total 42.

Speaker: JOSEPH E. DINI, Jr (Dem.).
Speaker Pro Tempore: JIM SCHOFIELD (Dem.).
Chief Clerk: MOURYNE B. LANDING.

New Hampshire
CONSTITUTION AND GOVERNMENT

New Hampshire's constitution, its second, became effective on 2 June 1784. An amendment to the constitution proposed by the General Court has to be approved by three-fifths of the elected members of each house and ratified by a majority of state voters. The governor, New Hampshire's only elected executive-branch official, is elected to hold office for two years and is succeeded in his absence by the president of the Senate. There is no formal cabinet system in New Hampshire. The General Court has 24 senators and 400 representatives who are re-elected every two years. Regular legislative sessions are held annually in January and may last no longer than 45 legislative days. To become law a bill must be passed by a majority of the General Court and signed by the governor. During session a bill also becomes law unless vetoed within five days of presentation to the governor; after session a bill dies unless signed within five days of presentation. A gubernatorial veto may be overridden by two-thirds of the elected members of each house. Legislation becomes effective 60 days after enactment. In 1986 251,000 people voted in the gubernatorial election, representing 46% of those registered to vote and 32% of the voting-age population. There are 10 administrative counties in New Hampshire.

ELECTED EXECUTIVE-BRANCH OFFICIAL

Governor (1989–91): JUDD GREGG (Rep.).

SELECTED GOVERNMENT ADDRESSES

Office of the Governor: State House, Rms 208–214, Concord, NH 03301; tel. (603) 271-2121; fax (603) 271-2130.

Accountancy Board: 2½ Beacon St, Concord, NH 03301; tel. (603) 271-3286; Chair. MICHAEL SPECTOR.

Department of Administration Services: State House Annex, Rm 120, Concord, NH 03301; tel. (603) 271-3201; Commr MICHAEL BARLOW (acting).

Department of Agriculture: 10 Ferry St, 4th Floor, Concord, NH 03301; tel. (603) 271-3551; Commr STEPHEN H. TAYLOR.

Department of Corrections: POB 769, Concord, NH 03301; tel. (603) 224-5300; Commr Dr RONALD L. POWELL.

Department of Education: 101 Pleasant St, Concord, NH 03301; tel. (603) 271-3144; Commr JOHN MCDONALD.

Department of Environmental Services: Hazen Dr., Concord, NH 03301; tel. (603) 271-3503; Commr ALDEN H. HOWARD.

Department of Health and Human Services: H. & W. Bldg, Hazen Dr., Concord, NH 03301; tel. (603) 271-4501; Commr. MARY MONGAN.

Department of Justice: State House Annex, Rm 208, Concord, NH 03301; tel. (603) 271-3655; Att.-Gen. STEPHEN E. MERRILL.

Department of Labor: 19 Pillsbury St, Concord, NH 03301; tel. (603) 271-3171; Commr RICHARD M. FLYNN.

Department of Resources and Economic Development: 105 Loudon Rd, Prescott Park, Concord, NH 03301; tel. (603) 271-2341; incorporates Vacation Travel Promotion Office; Commr GEORGE JONES.

Department of Safety: Hayes Bldg, Hazen Dr., Concord, NH 03301; tel. (603) 271-4331; Commr RICHARD M. FLYNN.

Department of Transportation: John O. Morton Bldg, Hazen Dr., Concord, NH 03301; tel. (603) 271-3734; Commr WALLACE STICKNEY.

Governor's Energy Office: 2½ Beacon St, 2nd Floor, Concord, NH 03301; tel. (603) 271-2711; Deputy Dir JON OSGOOD.

Office of the Adjutant-General: 1 Airport Rd, Concord, NH 03301; tel. (603) 271-2331; Adj.-Gen. Maj.-Gen. LLOYD M. PRICE.

Office of the Secretary of State: State House, Rm 204, Concord, NH 03301; tel. (603) 271-3242; Sec. of State WILLIAM M. GARDNER.

Office of the Treasurer: State House Annex, Rm 121, Concord, NH 03301; tel. (603) 271-2621; Treasurer GEORGIA E. A. THOMAS.

Public Utilities Commission: 8 Old Suncook Rd, Concord, NH 03301; tel. (603) 271-2431; Chair. VINCENT IACOPINO.

Revenue Administration: 61 South Spring St, Concord, NH 03301; tel. (603) 271-2191; Commr STANLEY R. ARNOLD.

GENERAL COURT
(May 1989)

Senate: Rep. 16; Dem. 8; Total 24.

President: WILLIAM S. BARTLETT, Jr.
President Pro Tempore: ELEANOR P. PODLES (Rep.).
Clerk: WILMONT WHITE.

House of Representatives: Rep. 281; Dem. 119; Total 400.

Speaker: W. DOUGLAS SCAMMON, Jr. (Rep.).
Deputy Speaker: HAROLD W. BURNS (Rep.).
Clerk: JAMES A. CHANDLER.

New Jersey

CONSTITUTION AND GOVERNMENT

The current constitution of New Jersey is the state's third and became effective on 1 January 1948. Constitutional amendments proposed by the Legislature have to be approved by either three-fifths of the elected members of each house at one session, or a majority of elected members at two successive sessions; they must then be ratified by a majority of state voters. The governor is the state's sole executive-branch official: he or she is elected to serve a regular term of four years and may serve no more than two terms consecutively; as there is no lieutenant-governor the governor is succeeded by the president of the Senate. Cabinet members, 21 in total, are appointed to specified offices and meet once or twice monthly. The Legislature consists of 40 senators and 80 representatives, re-elected every four and two years respectively. Regular legislative sessions take place annually, starting in January, and there is no statutory limit to their length. A bill becomes law once it has been passed by the Legislature and signed by the governor. During session a bill also becomes law unless vetoed within 10 days of presentation to the governor. A gubernatorial veto may be overridden by a two-thirds vote of the elected members in each house. Legislation becomes effective on 4 July following enactment, unless another date is specified. In the 1986 election to the US House of Representatives, 1,554,000 people voted, representing 41% of those registered to vote and 27% of the voting-age population. There are 21 administrative counties in New Jersey.

ELECTED EXECUTIVE-BRANCH OFFICIAL

Governor (1986–1990): THOMAS H. KEAN (Rep.).

SELECTED GOVERNMENT ADDRESSES

Office of the Governor: State House, Trenton, NJ 08625; tel. (609) 292-6000.

Department of Agriculture: John Fitch Plaza, CN 330, Trenton, NJ 08625; tel. (609) 292-3976; Sec. ARTHUR R. BROWN, Jr.

Department of Commerce and Economic Development: 1 West State St, CN 820, Trenton, NJ 08625; tel. (602) 292-1581; incorporates Divs of Travel and Tourism and of Energy; Asst Commr HENRY BLEKICKI.

Department of Corrections: Whittlesey Rd, POB 7387, Trenton, NJ 08628, tel. (609) 292-9860; Commr WILLIAM H. FAUVER.

Department of Education: 225 West State St, CN 500, Trenton, NJ 08625; tel. (609) 292-4450; Commr SAUL COOPERMAN.

Department of Environmental Protection: 401 West State St, Trenton, NJ 08625; tel. (609) 292-2885; Commr RICHARD T. DEWLEVY.

Department of Health: CN 360, Trenton, NJ 08625; tel. (609) 292-7837; Commr Dr MALLORY COYE.

Department of Labor: John Fitch Plaza, CN 110, Trenton, NJ 08625; tel. (609) 292-2323; Commr CHARLES SERRAINO.

Department of Transportation: 1035 Parkway Ave, CN 600, Trenton, NJ 08625; tel. (609) 530-3535; Commr HAZEL GLUCK.

Division of State Police: POB 7068, West Trenton, NJ 08625; tel. (609) 882-2000; Supt Col CLINTON PAGANO.

Office of the Attorney-General: Justice Complex, CN 080, Trenton, NJ 08625; tel. (609) 292-4925; Att.-Gen. W. GARY EDWARDS.

Office of the Secretary of State: State Capitol Bldg, CN 300, Trenton, NJ 08625; tel. (609) 984-1900; Sec. of State JANE BURGIO.

Public Utilities Board: 101 Commerce St, Newark, NJ 07102; tel. (201) 648-2027; Pres. BARBARA A. CURRAN.

Treasury Department: State House, CN 002, Trenton, NJ 08625; tel. (609) 292-6748; incorporates Div. of Taxation; Treas. FEATHER O'CONNOR.

LEGISLATURE
(May 1989)

Senate: Dem. 24; Rep. 16; Total 40.

President: JOHN F. RUSSO (Dem.).
President Pro Tempore: CARMEN ORECHIO (Dem.).
Secretary: JOHN J. MCCARTHY.

General Assembly: Rep. 41; Dem. 39; Total 80.

Speaker: CHUCK HARDWICK (Rep.).
Speaker Pro Tempore: JOHN A. ROCCO (Rep.).
Clerk: VIRGINIA E. HAINES.

New Mexico

CONSTITUTION AND GOVERNMENT

New Mexico's only constitution was adopted in 1911 and became effective on 6 January 1912. Most constitutional amendments proposed by the Legislature have to be approved by a majority of elected members in each house before being ratified by a majority of state voters. The governor, elected with the lieutenant-governor, serves a four-year term of office and, until 1991, may not serve consecutive terms. After 1991 he or she will be limited to two consecutive terms. Cabinet members, 15 including the governor, are appointed to specified offices and meet once a week. There are 42 senators and 70 representatives in the Legislature, serving terms of four and two years respectively. Regular legislative sessions take place annually in January and may last no longer than 60 calendar days in odd-numbered years and 30 days in even-numbered years. A bill becomes law when it has been passed by the Legislature and signed by the governor. During session a bill may also become law unless vetoed within three days of presentation to the governor. Outside session a bill dies unless signed by the Governor within 20 days after adjournment of the session. A gubernatorial veto may be overridden by a two-thirds vote from the elected members present in each house. Enacted legislation becomes effective 90 days after the adjournment of the Legislature, except for fiscal legislation, which becomes effective immediately. In 1986 395,000 people voted in the gubernatorial election, representing 62% of those registered to vote and 38% of the voting-age population. New Mexico has 33 administrative counties.

ELECTED EXECUTIVE-BRANCH OFFICIALS

Governor (1987–91): GARREY E. CARRUTHERS (Rep.).
Lieutenant-Governor: JACK L. STAHL (Rep.).
Secretary of State: REBECCA VIGIL-GIRON (Dem.).

Attorney-General: HAL STRATTON (Rep.).
Treasurer: JAMES LEWIS (Dem.).
Auditor: HARROLL H. ADAMS (Dem.).
Commissioner of Public Lands: WILLIAM R. HUMPHRIES (Rep.).

SELECTED GOVERNMENT ADDRESSES

Office of the Governor: State Capitol, Santa Fe, NM 87503; tel. (505) 827-3000.

Office of the Lieutenant-Governor: State Capitol, Rm 421, Santa Fe, NM 87503; tel. (505) 827-3050.

Office of the Secretary of State: State Capitol, Rm 400, Santa Fe, NM 87503; tel. (505) 827-3600.

Office of the Attorney-General: POB 1508, Santa Fe, NM 87504-1508; tel. (505) 827-6000.

Office of the Treasurer: POB 608, Santa Fe, NM 87504-0608; tel. (505) 827-6400.

Office of the Auditor: PERA Bldg, Rm 202, Santa Fe, NM 87503; tel. (505) 827-4740.

Department of Agriculture: POB 30005, Dept 3189, Las Cruces, NM 88003-0005; tel. (505) 646-3008; Dir FRANK DUBOIS.

Department of Corrections: 1422 Paseo de Peralta, Santa Fe, NM 87503; tel. (505) 827-8709; Dir LANE McCOTTER.

Department of Economic Development and Tourism: Joseph Montoya Bldg, 1100 St Francis Dr., Santa Fe, NM 87503; tel. (505) 827-0381; Dir JOHN DENDAHL.

Department of Education: Education Bldg, Santa Fe, NM 87501-2786; tel. (505) 827-6635; Supt ALAN MORGAN.

Department of Energy, Minerals and Natural Resources: Villagra Bldg, Rm 121, Santa Fe, NM 87503; tel. (505) 827-7836; Dir TOM G. BAHR.

Department of Finance and Administration: State Capitol, Rm 425, Santa Fe, NM 87503; tel. (505) 827-3060; Dir WILLARD LEWIS.

Department of Health and Environment: Harold Runnels Bldg, 1190 St Francis Dr., Santa Fe, NM 87503; tel. (505) 827-2613; Dir CARLA MUTH.

Department of Labor: 401 Broadway, NE, Albuquerque, NM 87102; tel. (505) 841-8409; Dir PAUL GARCIA.

Department of Public Safety: New Mexico State Police Complex, Santa Fe, NM 87504-1628; tel. (505) 827-3370; Dir ROBERT KEMBLE.

Department of State Highways and Transportation: 1120 Cerrillos Rd, Santa Fe, NM 87503; tel. (505) 827-5110; Dir DEWEY LONSBERRY.

Department of Taxation and Revenue: Joseph Montoya Bldg, 1100 St Francis Dr., Santa Fe, NM 87503; tel. (505) 827-0341; Dir GAIL REESE.

Office of Military Affairs: POB 4277, Santa Fe, NM 87503; tel. (505) 473-2402; Adj.-Gen. Gen. EDWARD D. BACA.

Public Service Commission: Bataan Memorial Bldg, Rm 236, Santa Fe, NM 87503; tel. (505) 827-6940; Chair. MARILYN O'LEARY.

State Land Office: State Land Office Bldg, Santa Fe, NM 87503; tel. (505) 827-5760; Commr WILLIAM R. HUMPHRIES.

LEGISLATURE

(May 1989)

Senate: Dem. 26; Rep. 16; Total 42.

President: Lt-Gov. JACK L. STAHL (Rep.).
President Pro Tempore: MANNY M. ARAGON (Dem.).
Chief Clerk: JUANITA M. PINO.

House of Representatives: Dem. 45; Rep. 25; Total 70.

Speaker: RAYMOND G. SANCHEZ (Dem.).
Chief Clerk: STEVE ARIAS.

New York

CONSTITUTION AND GOVERNMENT

New York's constitution, its fourth, was adopted in 1894 and became effective on 1 January 1895. An amendment to the constitution proposed by the Legislature needs to be passed by a majority of the elected members in each house in two successive sessions before being ratified by a majority of state voters. The governor and lieutenant-governor are elected jointly to serve a four-year term. State cabinet members, 16 in total, are appointed to specified offices and meet at the governor's discretion. There are 61 senators and 150 representatives in the New York Legislature, both houses being re-elected every two years. Regular sessions take place annually, starting in January; there is no statutory limit to their length. A bill becomes enacted when it has been approved by both houses of the Legislature and signed by the governor. During session the governor has 10 days to consider a bill, after which it becomes law unless vetoed. Outside session a bill dies if it remains unsigned for 30 days after adjournment of the Legislature. A two-thirds vote by the elected members of each house is required to override a gubernatorial veto. Legislation becomes effective 20 days after enactment. In 1986 4,294,000 people voted in the gubernatorial election, representing 53% of the number registered to vote and 32% of the voting-age population. New York state has 62 administrative counties.

ELECTED EXECUTIVE-BRANCH OFFICIALS

Governor (1987–91): MARIO M. CUOMO (Dem.).
Lieutenant-Governor: STAN LUNDINE (Dem.).
Attorney-General: ROBERT ABRAMS (Dem.).
Comptroller and Auditor: EDWARD V. REGAN (Rep.).

SELECTED GOVERNMENT ADDRESSES

Office of the Governor: State Capitol, Executive Chambers, Albany, NY 12224; tel. (518) 474-8390.

Office of the Lieutenant-Governor: State Capitol, Rm 326, Albany, NY 12224; tel. (518) 474-4623.

Office of the Attorney-General: State Capitol, Albany, NY 12224; tel. (518) 474-7330.

Office of the Comptroller: Alfred E. Smith Bldg, Albany, NY 12236; tel. (518) 474-4040.

Department of Agriculture and Markets: Capital Plaza Bldg, Suite 8, Albany, NY 12235; tel. (518) 457-4188; Commr DONALD BUTCHER.

Department of Commerce: Twin Towers, New York, NY 12245; tel. (212) 474-4100; incorporates Divs of Econ. and Corporate Development and of Tourism; Dir of Econ. Development RONALD S. MOSS.

Department of Correctional Services: State Campus, Correctional Services Bldg, Albany, NY 12226; tel. (518) 457-8134; Commr THOMAS A. COUGHLIN, III.

Department of Education: Education Bldg, Washington Ave, Albany, NY 12234; tel. (518) 474-5884; Commr GORDON M. AMBACH.

Department of Environmental Conservation: 50 Wolf Rd, Albany, NY 12223; tel. (518) 457-3446; incorporates Div. of Natural Resources: Commr THOMAS JORLING.

Department of Health: Tower Bldg, Empire State Plaza, Albany, NY 12237; tel. (518) 474-2011; Commr DAVID AXELROD.

Department of Labor: Executive Campus, Dept of Labor Bldg, Albany, NY 12240; tel. (518) 457-2741; Commr LILLIAN ROBERTS.

Department of Public Service: Agency Bldg, Rm 3, Empire State Plaza, Albany, NY 12223; tel. (518) 474-2530; Chair. ANN MEAD.

Department of Taxation and Finance: State Campus, Tax and Finance Bldg, Albany, NY 12227; tel. (518) 457-2244; Commr RODERICK CHU.

Department of Transportation: Campus Bldg, Suite 5, Albany, NY 12232; tel. (518) 457-4422; Commr FRANKLIN C. WHITE.

Division of Military and Naval Affairs: 330 Old Niskayuna Road, Albany, NY 12110; tel. (518) 786-4502; Chief of Staff Maj.-Gen. LAWRENCE P. FLYNN.

Office of the Secretary of State: 162 Washington Ave, Albany, NY 12231; tel. (518) 474-4750; Sec. of State GAIL S. SCHAFFER.

State Police: Executive Campus, Bldg 22, Albany, NY 12226; tel. (518) 457-6721; Supt THOMAS A. CONSTANTINE.

LEGISLATURE

(May 1989)

Senate: Rep. 34; Dem. 27; Total 61.

President: Lt-Gov. STAN LUNDINE (Dem.).
President Pro Tempore: WARREN M. ANDERSON (Rep.).
Secretary: STEPHEN SLOAN.

Assembly: Dem. 92; Rep. 58; Total 150.

Speaker: MELVIN H. MILLER (Dem.).
Speaker Pro Tempore: WILLIAM F. PASSANNANTE (Dem.).
Clerk: FRANCINE MISASI.

North Carolina

CONSTITUTION AND GOVERNMENT

The current constitution of North Carolina, the state's third, was adopted in 1970 and became effective on 1 July 1971. Constitutional amendments proposed by the General Assembly require a vote by three-fifths of the elected members of each house and ratification by a majority of state voters. The governor is elected with the lieutenant-governor to serve a four-year term and may serve no more than two terms. Cabinet members, 10 in total, are appointed by the governor and meet monthly. The General Assembly consists of 50 senators and 120 representatives, both houses being re-elected every two years. There is statutory provision for regular legislative sessions to be held in odd-numbered years, starting in January, but in practice sessions are also held in even-numbered years; there is no statutory limit to their length. North Carolina is the only state in which the governor has no power to approve or veto bills. A bill becomes law when it has been passed by each house of the General Assembly at three readings, and becomes effective 30 days after adjournment. In 1986 1,591,000 people voted in the election to the US Senate, representing 52% of those registered to vote and 34% of the voting-age population. There are 100 administrative counties in North Carolina.

ELECTED EXECUTIVE-BRANCH OFFICIALS

Governor (1989–93): JAMES G. MARTIN (Rep.).

Lieutenant-Governor: JAMES C. GARDNER (Rep.).

Secretary of State: RUFUS L. EDMISTEN.

Attorney-General: LACY H. THORNBURG (Dem.).

Treasurer: HARLAN E. BOYLES (Dem.).

Auditor: EDWARD RENFROW.

Superintendent of Public Instruction: BOB ETHERIDGE.

Commissioner of Agriculture: JAMES A. GRAHAM.

Commissioner of Labor: JOHN C. BROOKS.

Commissioner of Insurance: JAMES E. LONG.

SELECTED GOVERNMENT ADDRESSES

Office of the Governor: State Capitol Bldg, 116 West Jones St, Raleigh, NC 27603-8001; tel. (919) 733-4240.

Office of the Lieutenant-Governor: Legislative Office Bldg, 116 West Jones St, Raleigh, NC 27603-8006; tel. (919) 733-7350.

Office of the Secretary of State: Legislative Office Bldg, 300 North Salisbury St, Raleigh, NC 27603-5909; tel. (919) 733-3433.

Office of the Attorney-General: Justice Bldg, POB 629, Raleigh, NC 27602; tel. (919) 733-3377.

Office of the Treasurer: Albemarle Bldg, 325 North Salisbury St, Raleigh, NC 27611; tel. (919) 733-3951.

Office of the Auditor: Legislative Office Bldg, 300 North Salisbury St, Raleigh, NC 27611; tel. (919) 733-3217.

Department of Administration: 116 West Jones St, Raleigh, NC 27611; tel. (919) 733-7232; Sec. GRACE JEMISON ROHRER.

Department of Agriculture: Agriculture Bldg, 1 West Edenton St, POB 27647, Raleigh, NC 27611; tel. (919) 733-7125; Commr JAMES A. GRAHAM.

Department of Commerce: 430 North Salisbury St, Raleigh, NC 27611; tel. (919) 733-4962; incorporates Divs of Energy, of Finance and of Travel and Tourism Development, and Utilities Comm; Sec. JAMES T. BROYHILL.

Department of Corrections: 840 West Morgan St, Raleigh, NC 27603; tel. (919) 733-4926; Sec. AARON J. JOHNSON.

Department of Education: 116 West Edenton St, Raleigh, NC 27603-1712; tel. (919) 733-3813; Supt of Public Instruction BOB ETHERIDGE.

Department of Insurance: Dobbs Bldg, 430 North Salisbury St, POB 26387, Raleigh, NC 27611; tel. (919) 733-7343; Commr JAMES E. LONG.

Department of Labor: Labor Bldg, 4 West Edenton St, Raleigh, NC 27601; tel. (919) 733-7166; Commr JOHN C. BROOKS.

Department of Natural Resources and Community Development: 512 North Salisbury St, Raleigh, NC 27611; tel. (919) 733-4984; incorporates Div. of Environmental Management; Sec. S. THOMAS RHODES.

Department of Revenue: 2 South Salisbury St, POB 25000, Raleigh, NC 27640; tel. (919) 733-7211; Sec. HELEN A. POWERS.

Department of Transportation: 1 South Wilmington St, Raleigh, NC 27611; tel. (919) 733-2520; Sec. JAMES E. HARRINGTON.

Division of Health Services: Dept of Human Resources, 225 North McDowell St, Raleigh, NC 27602; tel. (919) 733-3446; Dir Dr RONALD H. LEVINE.

Division of the Highway Patrol: Dept of Crime Control and Public Safety, 512 North Salisbury St, Raleigh, NC 27611; tel. (919) 733-7952; Commander JACK F. CARDWELL.

Military Division: Dept of Crime Control and Public Safety, 4105 Reedy Creek Rd, Raleigh, NC 27611; tel. (919) 733-3770; Adj.-Gen. Maj.-Gen. CHARLES E. SCOTT.

Office of the State Budget: 116 West Jones St, Raleigh, NC 27611; tel. (919) 733-7061; Chief State Budget Officer and Comptroller C. C. CAMERON.

GENERAL ASSEMBLY
(May 1989)

Senate: Dem. 37; Rep. 13; Total 50.

President: Lt-Gov. JAMES C. GARDNER (Rep.).

President Pro Tempore: J. J. HARRINGTON (Dem.).

Principal Clerk: SYLVIA FINK.

House of Representatives: Dem. 74; Rep. 46; Total 120.

Speaker: LISTON B. RAMSEY (Dem.).

Speaker Pro Tempore: JOHN J. HUNT (Dem.).

Principal Clerk: GRACE COLLINS.

North Dakota
CONSTITUTION AND GOVERNMENT

North Dakota's only constitution became effective on 2 November 1889. Amendments to the constitution proposed by the Legislative Assembly have to be approved by a majority of the elected members of each house followed by a majority of state voters. The governor and lieutenant-governor are elected jointly to serve a four-year term and there is no limit to the number of times they may hold office. The Legislative Assembly has 53 senators and 106 representatives who hold office for four and two years respectively, alternate halves of the Senate being re-elected every two years. There is no formal cabinet system in North Dakota. Regular sessions of the Legislative Assembly are held biennially, starting in January and lasting no longer than 80 days. A bill becomes law when it has been passed by the Legislative Assembly and signed by the governor. During session the governor has three days to consider a bill, after which it becomes law unless vetoed. Outside session a bill becomes law unless vetoed within 15 days from adjournment. A gubernatorial veto may be overridden by a two-thirds vote from the elected members in each house. Enacted bills become effective on 1 July. In 1986 289,000 people voted in the election to the US Senate, representing 59% of the voting-age population (the state law does not require voter registration). North Dakota has 53 counties.

ELECTED EXECUTIVE-BRANCH OFFICIALS

Governor (1989–93): GEORGE A. SINNER (Dem.).

Lieutenant-Governor: LLOYD OMDAHL (Dem.).

Secretary of State: JIM KUSLER (Dem.).

Attorney-General: NICHOLAS SPAETH (Dem.).

Treasurer: ROBERT HANSON (Dem.).

Auditor: ROBERT PETERSON (Rep.).

Superintendent of Public Instruction: WAYNE SANSTEAD.

Commissioner of Agriculture: SARAH VOGEL (Dem.).

Commissioner of Labor: BYRON KNUTSON.

Commissioner of Insurance: EARL POMEROY (Dem.).

Tax Commissioner: HEIDI HEITKAMP (Dem.).

SELECTED GOVERNMENT ADDRESSES

Office of the Governor: State Capitol, Bismarck, ND 58505; tel. (701) 224-2200.

Office of the Lieutenant-Governor: State Capitol, Bismarck, ND 58505; tel. (701) 224-2200.

Office of the Secretary of State: State Capitol, Bismarck, ND 58505; tel. (701) 224-2900.

Office of the Attorney-General: State Capitol, Bismarck, ND 58505; tel. (701) 224-2210.

Office of the Treasurer: State Capitol, Bismarck, ND 58505; tel. (701) 224-2643.

Office of the Auditor: State Capitol, Bismarck, ND 58505; tel. (701) 224-2241.

Department of Agriculture: State Capitol, Bismarck, ND 58505; tel. (701) 224-2231; Commr SARAH VOGEL.

Department of Highways: Highway Bldg, Bismarck, ND 58505-0178; tel. (701) 224-2581; Dir RICHARD J. BACKES.

Department of Health: State Capitol, Bismarck, ND 58505; tel. (701) 224-2372; Health Officer ROBERT M. WENTZ.

Department of Insurance: State Capitol, Bismarck, ND 58505; tel. (701) 224-2440; Commr EARL POMEROY.

Department of Labor: State Capitol, Bismarck, ND 58505; tel. (701) 224-2661; Commr BYRON KNUTSON.

Department of Parole and Probation: POB 5521, Bismarck, ND 58502; tel. (701) 221-6190; Dir JIM MARION.

Department of Public Instruction: State Capitol, Bismarck, ND 58505; tel. (701) 224-2261; Supt of Public Instruction WAYNE SANSTEAD.

Department of Taxation: State Capitol, Bismarck, ND 58505; tel. (701) 224-2770; Tax Commr HEIDI HEITKAMP.

Division of Environmental Health: Dept of Health, 1200 Missouri Ave, Bismarck, ND 58501; tel. (701) 224-2374; Dir of Environmental Health GENE A. CHRISTIANSON.

Economic Development Commission: Liberty Memorial Bldg, Bismarck, ND 58505; tel. (701) 224-2810; incorporates Travel Div.; Dir WILLIAM PATRIE.

Office of Management and Budget: State Capitol, Bismarck, ND 58505; tel. (701) 224-2680; Dir RICHARD RAYLE.

Office of the Military: POB 1817, Bismarck, ND 58502; tel. (701) 224-5100; Adj.-Gen. Maj.-Gen. ALEXANDER P. MACDONALD.

Public Service Commission: State Capitol, Bismarck, ND 58505; tel. (701) 224-2400; Pres. DALE V. SANDSTROM.

LEGISLATIVE ASSEMBLY
(May 1989)

Senate: Dem. 32; Rep. 21; Total 53.

President: Lt-Gov. LLOYD OMDAHL (Dem.).
President Pro Tempore: HERSCHEL LASHKOWITZ (Dem.).
Secretary: PERRY GROTBERG.

House of Representatives: Rep. 61; Dem. 45; Total 106.

Speaker: WILLIAM E. KRETSCHMAR (Rep.).
Chief Clerk: ROY GILBREATH.

Ohio

CONSTITUTION AND GOVERNMENT

Ohio's constitution, the state's second, became effective on 1 September 1851. An amendment to the constitution proposed by the General Assembly has to be approved by three-fifths of the elected members of each house and ratified by a majority of state voters. The governor, elected with the lieutenant-governor, serves a four-year term of office and may serve no more than two terms consecutively. Cabinet members, 27 in total, are appointed to specified offices and meet at the governor's discretion. The 33 senators and 99 representatives in the General Assembly are re-elected every four and two years respectively, alternate halves of the Senate being re-elected every two years. Regular sessions are held annually, starting in January, and there is no statutory limit to the number of days they may last. Bills require the approval of both houses of the General Assembly before being presented to the governor for signing. During session the governor has 10 days to consider a bill, after which it becomes law unless vetoed. Outside session a bill becomes law unless vetoed within 10 days from adjournment. A gubernatorial veto may be overridden by three-fifths of the elected members in each house. Enacted legislation becomes effective 90 days after being filed with the secretary of state. In 1986 3,121,000 people voted in the election to the US Senate, representing 52% of those registered to vote and 39% of the voting-age population. Ohio has 88 administrative counties.

ELECTED EXECUTIVE-BRANCH OFFICIALS

Governor (1987-91): RICHARD F. CELESTE (Dem.).
Lieutenant-Governor: PAUL R. LEONARD (Dem.).
Secretary of State: SHERROD BROWN (Dem.).
Attorney-General: ANTHONY J. CELEBREZZE, Jr (Dem.).
Treasurer and Comptroller: MARY ELLEN WITHROW (Dem.).
Auditor: THOMAS E. FERGUSON (Dem.).

SELECTED GOVERNMENT ADDRESSES

Office of the Governor: State House, Columbus, OH 43215; tel. (614) 466-3526.

Office of the Lieutenant-Governor: State House, Columbus, OH 43215; tel. (614) 466-3396.

Office of the Secretary of State: 30 East Broad St, 14th Floor, Columbus, OH 43215; tel. (614) 466-4980.

Office of the Attorney-General: 30 East Broad St, Columbus, OH 43215; tel. (614) 466-4320.

Office of the Treasurer: 30 East Broad St, Columbus, OH 43215; tel. (614) 466-3285.

Office of the Auditor: 88 East Broad St, Columbus, OH 43215; tel. (614) 466-4514.

Department of Administrative Services: 30 East Broad St, 40th Floor, Columbus, OH 43215; tel. (614) 466-6511; Dir WILLIAM J. FLAHERTY.

Department of Agriculture: 65 South Front St, 6th Floor, Columbus, OH 43215; tel. (614) 466-2737; Dir STEVE MAURER.

Department of Commerce: 77 South High St, 23rd Floor, Columbus, OH 43266-0544; tel. (614) 466-3638; Dir LINDA K. PAGE.

Department of Development: 77 South High St, POB 1011, Columbus, OH 43266; tel. (614) 466-3379; incorporates Offices of Energy and of Travel and Tourism; Dir DAVID J. BAKER.

Department of Education: 65 South Front St, Columbus, OH 43266-0308; tel. (614) 466-3304; Supt of Public Instruction FRANKLIN B. WALTER.

Department of Health: 246 North High St, Columbus, OH 43266; tel. (614) 466-2253; Dir RONALD L. FLETCHER.

Department of Natural Resources: Building D, Fountain Sq., Columbus, OH 43224; tel. (614) 265-6877; Dir JOSEPH J. SOMMER.

Department of Rehabilitation and Correction: 1050 Freeway Dr. North, Columbus, OH 43229; tel. (614) 431-2763; Dir RICHARD SEITER.

Department of Taxation: 30 East Broad St, 22nd Floor, Columbus, OH 43216; tel. (614) 466-2166; Commr JOANNE LIMBACH.

Department of Transportation: 25 South Front St, Columbus, OH 43215; tel. (614) 466-2335; Dir WARREN J. SMITH.

Environmental Protection Agency: 1800 Watermark Dr., Columbus, OH 43266; tel. (614) 644-2782; Dir RICHARD L. SHANK.

Highway Patrol Division: 660 East Main St, Columbus, OH 43205; tel. (614) 466-2990; Supt Col JACK WALSH.

Office of the Adjutant-General: 2825 West Granville Rd, Worthington, OH 43085-2712; tel. (614) 889-7070; Adj.-Gen. Maj.-Gen. RAYMOND R. GALLOWAY.

Office of Budget and Management: 30 East Broad St, 39th Floor, Columbus, OH 43215; tel. (614) 466-4034; Dir WILLIAM J. SHKURTI.

Public Utilities Commission: 180 East Broad St, Columbus, OH 43266-0573; tel. (614) 466-3204; Chair. JOLYNN BOSTER.

GENERAL ASSEMBLY
(May 1989)

Senate: Rep. 19; Dem. 14; Total 33.
President: STANLEY J. ARONOFF (Rep.).
President Pro Tempore: DAVID HOBSON (Rep.).
Clerk: MARTHA BUTLER.

House of Representatives: Dem. 59; Rep. 40; Total 99.
Speaker: VERNAL RIFFE, Jr (Dem.).
Speaker Pro Tempore: BARNEY QUILTER (Dem.).
Legislative Clerk: WILLIAM W. PFEIFFER.
Executive Secretary: ARISTOTLE HUTRAS.

Oklahoma

CONSTITUTION AND GOVERNMENT

Oklahoma's only constitution became effective on 16 November 1907. Constitutional amendments proposed by the Legislature have to be approved by a majority of the elected members of each house and then ratified by a majority of state voters. The governor, elected separately from the lieutenant-governor, holds office for four years before re-election and may serve no more than two terms consecutively. Cabinet members, 11 in total including the governor, are appointed by the latter and meet at his or her discretion. There are 48 senators and 101 representatives in the Legislature, serving terms of four and two years respectively; alternate halves of the Senate are re-elected every two years. Regular legislative sessions take place annually, starting in February and lasting until no later than the end of May. A bill becomes law when it has been passed by the Legislature and signed by the governor. During session a bill also becomes law if it has not been vetoed and remains unsigned five days after being presented to the governor. After session a bill dies unless signed within 15 days from adjournment of the Legislature. A gubernatorial veto may be overridden by a two-thirds vote from the elected members of each house. Enacted legislation becomes effective 90 days after adjournment. In the 1986 gubernatorial election 910,000 people voted, representing 45% of those registered and 38% of the voting-age population. Oklahoma has 77 administrative counties.

ELECTED EXECUTIVE-BRANCH OFFICIALS

Governor (1987-91): HENRY BELLMON (Rep.).
Lieutenant-Governor: ROBERT S. KERR, III (Dem.).

Attorney-General: ROBERT HENRY (Dem.).
Treasurer: ELLIS EDWARDS (Dem.).
Auditor and Inspector: CLIFTON H. SCOTT (Dem.).
Superintendent of Public Instruction: GERALD HOELTZEL (Rep.).
Insurance Commissioner: GERALD GRIMES (Dem.).

SELECTED GOVERNMENT ADDRESSES

Office of the Governor: State Capitol, Rm 212, Oklahoma City, OK 73105; tel. (405) 521-2342.
Office of the Lieutenant-Governor: State Capitol, Rm 211, Oklahoma City, OK 73105; tel. (405) 521-2161.
Office of the Attorney-General: State Capitol, Rm 112, Oklahoma City, OK 73105; tel. (405) 521-3921.
Office of the Treasurer: State Capitol, Rm 217, Oklahoma City, OK 73105; tel. (405) 521-3191.
Office of the Auditor and Inspector: State Capitol, Rm 100, Oklahoma City, OK 73105; tel. (405) 521-3495.

Department of Agriculture: 2800 North Lincoln Blvd, Oklahoma City, OK 73105; tel. (405) 521-3868; Commr JACK D. CRAIG.
Department of Commerce: 6601 Broadway Extension, Oklahoma City, OK 73116; tel. (405) 521-2401; Exec. Dir DONALD PAULSEN.
Department of Corrections: POB 11400, Oklahoma City, OK 73136; tel. (405) 427-6511; Dir LARRY R. MEACHUM.
Department of Education: 2500 North Lincoln Blvd, Rm 121, Oklahoma City, OK 73105; tel. (405) 521-3301; Supt of Public Instruction GERALD HOELTZEL.
Department of Health: 1000 10th St, NE, POB 53551, Oklahoma City, OK 73152; tel. (405) 271-4200; incorporates Div. of Environmental Health Services; Commr JOAN K. LEAVITT.
Department of Insurance: 1901 North Walnut St, Oklahoma City, OK 73105; tel. (405) 521-2828; Commr GERALD GRIMES.
Department of Labor: 1315 Broadway Pl., Oklahoma City, OK 73103; tel. (405) 521-0530; Commr DEAN CALHOON.
Department of Mines: 4040 North Lincoln Blvd, Suite 107, Oklahoma City, OK 73105; tel. (405) 521-3859; Dir BENNIE COX.
Department of Tourism and Recreation: Will Rogers Bldg, Rm 500, Oklahoma City, OK 73105; tel. (405) 521-2413; Executive Dir ABE L. HESSER.
Department of Transportation: 200 North 21st St, Oklahoma City, OK 73105; tel. (405) 521-2631; Dir V. O. BRADLEY.
Energy Conservation Services: Corporation Comm., Jim Thorpe Bldg, Oklahoma City, OK 73105; tel. (405) 521-3941; Head of Div. LAURIE HAYNES.
Military Department: 3501 Military Circle, NE, Oklahoma City, OK 73111-4398; tel. (405) 427-8371; Adj.-Gen. Maj.-Gen. ROBERT M. MORGAN.
Office of the Secretary of State: State Capitol Bldg, Rm 101, Oklahoma City, OK 73105-4897; tel. (405) 521-3911; Sec. of State HANNAH DIGGS ATKINS.
Office of State Finance: Capitol Bldg, Rm 122, Oklahoma City, OK 73105; tel. (405) 521-2141; Dir ALEXANDER HOLMES.
Public Utilities Division: Corporation Comm., Jim Thorpe Bldg, Oklahoma City, OK 73105; tel. (405) 521-3908; Dir HOWARD MOTLEY.
State Police Department: Bureau of Investigation, POB 11497, Oklahoma City, OK 73136; tel. (405) 682-6724; Dir TED R. LIMKE.
Tax Commission: 2501 Lincoln Blvd, Oklahoma City, OK 73194; tel. (405) 521-3115.

LEGISLATURE
(May 1989)

Senate: Dem. 33; Rep. 15; Total 48.
  President: Lt-Gov. ROBERT S. KERR, III (Dem.).
  President Pro Tempore: RODGER A. RANDLE (Dem.).
  Secretary: LEE SLATER.
House of Representatives: Dem. 69; Rep. 32; Total 101.
  Speaker: JIM BARKER (Dem.).
  Speaker Pro Tempore: LONNIE L. ABBOTT.
  Chief Clerk: LARRY WARDEN.

Oregon

CONSTITUTION AND GOVERNMENT

Oregon's only constitution became effective on 14 February 1859. Amendments to the constitution proposed by the Legislative Assembly require the approval of a majority of elected members of both houses and ratification by a majority of state voters. The governor, elected to serve a four-year term of office, may serve no more than two terms consecutively and is succeeded in his or her absence by the secretary of state. The cabinet, consisting of 21 members in total, is appointed by the governor and meets as often as necessary. The 30 senators and 60 representatives in the Legislative Assembly are re-elected every four and two years respectively, alternate halves of the Senate being re-elected every two years. Regular legislative sessions are held biennially, starting in January, and have no statutory limit to their length. A bill becomes law when it has been passed by a majority in the Legislative Assembly and has been signed by the governor. During session the governor has five days in which to consider a bill, after which it becomes law unless vetoed. After session a bill becomes law unless vetoed within 20 days from the adjournment of the Legislative Assembly. A gubernatorial veto may be overridden by a two-thirds vote of those present in each house. Enacted bills become effective 90 days after the session's adjournment. In the 1986 gubernatorial election 1,060,000 people voted, representing 71% of those registered to vote and 53% of the voting-age population. Oregon has 36 administrative counties.

ELECTED EXECUTIVE-BRANCH OFFICIALS

Governor (1987–91): NEIL GOLDSCHMIDT (Dem.).
Secretary of State: BARBARA ROBERTS (Dem.).
Attorney-General: DAVID B. FROHNMAYER (Rep.).
Treasurer: ANTHONY MEEKER (Rep.).
Superintendent of Public Instruction: VERNE A. DUNCAN.
Commissioner of Labor and Industries: MARY WENDY ROBERTS (Dem.).

SELECTED GOVERNMENT ADDRESSES

Office of the Governor: State Capitol, Rm 254, Salem, OR 97310; tel. (503) 378-3111; fax (503) 378-6075; incorporates Div. of Natural Resources.
Office of the Secretary of State: State Capitol, Rm 136, Salem, OR 97310; tel. (503) 378-4139; fax (503) 373-7414; incorporates Audit Div.
Office of the Attorney-General: Justice Bldg, Rm 100, Salem, OR 97310; tel. (503) 378-6002; fax (503) 378-4017.
Office of the Treasurer: State Capitol, Rm 158, Salem, OR 97310; tel. (503) 378-4329; fax (503) 378-6772.

Bureau of Labor and Industries: 1400 Fifth Ave, SW, Portland, OR 97201; tel. (503) 229-5737; fax (503) 229-6372; Commr MARY WENDY ROBERTS.
Department of Agriculture: Agriculture Bldg, 635 Capitol St, NE, Salem, OR 97310; tel. (503) 378-4152; fax (503) 378-5529; Dir ROBERT BUCHANAN.
Department of Economic Development: 595 Cottage St, NE, Salem, OR 97310; tel. (503) 373-1240; fax (503) 581-5115; incorporates Div. of Tourism; Dir RICHARD G. REITEN.
Department of Education: 700 Pringle Parkway, SE, Salem, OR 97310; tel. (503) 378-3573; fax (503) 378-8434; Supt of Public Instruction VERNE A. DUNCAN.
Department of Energy: Labor and Industries Bldg, Rm 102, Salem, OR 97310; tel. (503) 378-4128; fax (503) 373-7806; Dir DAVID V. YADEN.
Department of Environmental Affairs: 811 Sixth St, SW, POB 1760, Portland, OR 97207; tel. (503) 229-5696; Dir FRED J. HANSEN.
Department of Human Resources: Public Service Bldg, Rm 318, Capitol Hall, Salem, OR 97310; tel. (503) 378-3034; incorporates Divs of Health and of Corrections; Dir KEVIN W. CONCANNON.
Department of Insurance and Finance: Commerce Bldg, 158 12th St, NE, Salem, OR 97310; tel. (503) 378-4271; Dir THEODORE R. KULONGOSKI.
Department of Revenue: Revenue Bldg, Rm 457, 955 Center St, NE, Salem, OR 97310; tel. (503) 378-3363; Dir RICHARD A. MUNN.
Department of State Police: Public Service Bldg, Rm 107, Capitol Mall, Salem, OR 97310; tel. (503) 378-3720; Supt R. B. MADSDEN.
Department of Transportation: Transportation Bldg, Rm 135, Capitol Mall, Salem, OR 97310; tel. (503) 378-6388; fax (503) 373-7376; Dir ROBERT N. BOTHMAN.
Executive Department: 155 Cottage St, NE, Salem, OR 97310; tel. (503) 378-3104; fax (503) 373-7643; incorporates Div. of Budget and Management; Administrator JON YUNKER.
Public Utility Commission: Labor and Industries Bldg, Rm 300, Salem, OR 97310; tel. (503) 378-6611; fax (503) 378-6880; Commr RON EACHUS.

LEGISLATIVE ASSEMBLY
(May 1989)

Senate: Dem. 17; Rep. 13; Total 30.

President: JOHN KITZHABER (Dem.).
President Pro Tempore: FRANK ROBERTS (Dem.).
Secretary: DONNA MERRILL.

House of Representatives: Dem. 31; Rep. 29; Total 60.

Speaker: VERA KATZ (Dem.).
Speaker Pro Tempore: MIKE BURTON (Dem.).
Chief Clerk: RAMONA KENADY.

Pennsylvania
CONSTITUTION AND GOVERNMENT

Pennsylvania's constitution, the state's fifth, became effective in 1968. An amendment to the constitution proposed by the General Assembly has to be approved by a majority of the elected members in each house in two successive sessions and ratified by a majority of state voters. The governor and lieutenant-governor are jointly elected to serve a four-year term of office; neither office may be held for more than two consecutive terms. Cabinet members, 18 in total excluding the governor, are appointed to specified offices and meet at the governor's discretion. The 50 senators and 203 representatives in the state General Assembly are re-elected every four and two years respectively, alternate halves of the Senate being re-elected every two years. Regular legislative sessions are held biennially and there is no statutory limit to their duration. To become law a bill must be passed by the General Assembly and signed by the governor. During session the governor is allowed 10 days to consider the bill, after which it becomes law unless vetoed. Outside session a bill becomes law unless vetoed within 30 days from adjournment. The governor's veto can be overridden by a two-thirds vote from the elected members of each house. Legislation generally becomes effective immediately upon enactment. In 1986 3,388,000 people voted in the gubernatorial election, representing 58% of the people registered to vote and 37% of the voting-age population. There are 67 administrative counties in Pennsylvania.

ELECTED EXECUTIVE-BRANCH OFFICIALS

Governor (1987–91): ROBERT P. CASEY (Dem.).
Lieutenant-Governor: MARK S. SINGEL (Dem.).
Attorney-General: ERNEST D. PREATE (Rep.).
Treasurer: G. DAVIS GREENE, Jr (Dem.).
Auditor-General: BARBARA HAFER (Dem.).

SELECTED GOVERNMENT ADDRESSES

Office of the Governor: Main Capitol Bldg, Rm 225, Harrisburg, PA 17120; tel. (717) 787-2500.

Office of the Lieutenant-Governor: Main Capitol Bldg, Rm 200, Harrisburg, PA 17120; tel. (717) 787-3300.

Office of the Attorney-General: Strawberry Sq., 14th-16th Floors, Harrisburg, PA 17120; tel. (717) 787-3391.

Office of the Treasurer: Finance Bldg, Rm 129, Harrisburg, PA 17120; tel. (717) 787-2991.

Office of the Auditor-General: Finance Bldg, Rm 229, Harrisburg, PA 17120; tel. (717) 787-1381.

Department of Agriculture: 2301 North Cameron St, Rm 211, Harrisburg, PA 17110; tel. (717) 787-5085; Dir BOYD E. WOLFF.

Department of Commerce: Forum Bldg, Rm 433, Harrisburg, PA 17120; tel. (717) 787-3405; incorporates Travel Development Bureau; Dir RAYMOND R. CHRISTMAN.

Department of Corrections: Lisburn Rd, POB 598, Camp Hill, PA 17011; tel. (717) 975-4859; Commr DAVID S. OWENS, Jr.

Department of Education: 333 Market St, Harristown 2, Harrisburg, PA 17126; tel. (717) 787-6788; Dir THOMAS K. GILHOOL.

Department of Environmental Resources: Fulton Bldg, POB 2063, Harrisburg, PA 17120; tel. (717) 783-2300; Dir ARTHUR A. DAVIS.

Department of Health: Health and Welfare Bldg, Rm 802, Harrisburg, PA 17120; tel. (717) 787-2959; Dir Dr N. MARK RICHARDS.

Department of Labor and Industry: Labor and Industry Bldg, Rm 1700, Harrisburg, PA 17120; tel. (717) 787-5279; Dir HARRIS L. WOFFORD, Jr.

Department of Revenue: Strawberry Sq., 11th Floor, Harrisburg, PA 17120; tel. (717) 787-2709; Dir DAVID L. DONAHOE.

Department of State Police: 1800 Elmerton Ave, Harrisburg, PA 17110; tel. (717) 783-5599; Commr RONALD M. SHARPE.

Department of Transportation: Transportation and Safety Bldg, Rm 1200, Harrisburg, PA 17120; tel. (717) 787-2838; Dir HOWARD YERUSALIM.

Energy Council: POB 8010, Harrisburg, PA 17105; tel. (717) 783-9981; Exec. Dir ROBERT A. SHINN.

Military Affairs Department: Indiantown Gap Military Reservation, Annville, PA 17003; tel. (717) 436-8572; Adj.-Gen. Maj.-Gen. GERALD T. SAJER.

Office of Administration: Main Capitol Bldg, Rm 238, Harrisburg, PA 17120; tel. (717) 787-4450; incorporates Div. of Finance; Sec. MURRAY DICKMAN.

Public Utility Commission: POB 3265, Harrisburg, PA 17120; tel. (717) 783-1740; Chair. LINDA TALIA FERRO.

GENERAL ASSEMBLY
(May 1989)

Senate: Rep. 27; Dem. 23; Total 50.

President: Lt-Gov. MARK S. SINGEL (Dem.).
President Pro Tempore: ROBERT C. JUBELIRER (Rep.).
Secretary: MARK CORRIGAN.

House of Representatives: Dem. 103; Rep. 99; 1 vacancy; Total 203.

Speaker: ROBERT W. O'DONNELL (Dem.).
Chief Clerk: JOHN J. ZUBECK.

Rhode Island
CONSTITUTION AND GOVERNMENT

Rhode Island's current constitution is its second and was adopted in November 1986. Constitutional amendments proposed by the General Assembly must be passed by a majority of elected members in both houses and ratified by a majority of voters. The governor, elected separately from the lieutenant-governor, serves a two-year term and there is no statutory limit on the number of terms of office he or she may serve. There is no formal cabinet system in Rhode Island. The state General Assembly has 50 senators and 100 representatives who are re-elected every two years. Regular legislative sessions take place annually, starting in January and generally lasting until May or June. A bill becomes law when it has been passed by the General Assembly and has been signed by the governor. During session a bill may also become law if it remains unsigned six days after being presented to the governor for consideration. Outside session a bill becomes law unless vetoed within 10 days after adjournment of the General Assembly. A three-fifths vote by all members present in each house is required to override a gubernatorial veto. Enacted legislation becomes effective 10 days after adjournment of the session. In the 1986 gubernatorial election 323,000 people voted, representing 62% of the number registered to vote, and 43% of the voting-age population. The main units of local government in Rhode Island are eight cities and 31 towns.

ELECTED EXECUTIVE-BRANCH OFFICIALS

Governor (1989–91): EDWARD D. DIPRETE (Rep.).
Lieutenant-Governor: ROGER N. BEGIN (Dem.).
Secretary of State: KATHLEEN S. CONNELL (Dem.).
Attorney-General: JAMES E. O'NEIL (Dem.).
General Treasurer: ANTHONY J. SOLOMON (Dem.).

SELECTED GOVERNMENT ADDRESSES

Office of the Governor: State House, Rm 222, Providence, RI 02903; tel. (401) 277-2080.

Office of the Lieutenant-Governor: State House, Rm 317, Providence, RI 02903; tel. (401) 277-2371.

Office of the Secretary of State: State House, Rm 218, Providence, RI 02903; tel. (401) 277-2357.

Office of the Attorney-General: 72 Pine St, Providence, RI 02903; tel. (401) 277-4400.

Office of the General Treasurer: State House, Rm 102, Providence, RI 02903; tel. (401) 277-2397.

Department of Administration: State House, Rm 118, Providence, RI 02903; tel. (401) 277-2280; incorporates Div. of Finance; Dir FREDERICK LIPPITT.

Department of Corrections: 75 Howard Ave, Cranston, RI 02920; tel. (401) 464-2611; Dir JOHN J. MORAN.

Department of Economic Development: 7 Jackson Walkway, Providence, RI 02903; tel. (401) 277-2601; incorporates Div. of Tourism; Dir LOUIS A. FAZZANO.

Department of Education: 22 Hayes St, Providence, RI 02908; tel. (401) 277-2031; Commr Dr J. TROY EARHART.

Department of Environmental Management: 9 Hayes St, Providence, RI 02903; tel. (401) 277-2771; incorporates Div. of Agriculture; Dir ROBERT L. BENDICK, Jr.

Department of Health: 75 Davis St, Providence, RI 02908; tel. (401) 277-2231; Dir Dr H. DENMAN SCOTT.

Department of Labor: 220 Elmwood Ave, Providence, RI 02907; tel. (401) 277-2741; Dir JAMES RIGNEY.

Department of Taxation: 289 Promenade St, Providence, RI 02908; tel. (401) 277-3050; Administrator R. GARY CLARK.

Department of Transportation: State Office Bldg, Rm 210, Providence, RI 02903; tel. (401) 277-2481; Dir MATTHEW J. GILL, Jr.

Governor's Office of Energy Assistance: 275 Westminster Mall, Providence, RI 02903; tel. (401) 277-3370; Dir CLEMENT A. GRISCOM.

National Guard: 1050 North Main St, Providence, RI 02904; tel. (401) 457-4100; Adj.-Gen. Maj.-Gen. JOHN W. KIELY.

Public Utilities Commission: 100 Orange St, Providence, RI 02903; tel. (401) 277-3500; Chair. EDWARD F. BURKE.

State Police Headquarters: POB 185, North Scituate, RI 02857; tel. (401) 647-3311; Supt Col WALTER E. STONE.

GENERAL ASSEMBLY
(May 1989)

Senate: Dem. 38; Rep. 12; Total 50.

  President: Lt-Gov. ROGER N. BEGIN (Dem.).
  President Pro Tempore: WILLIAM O'NEILL (Dem.).
  Secretary: KATHLEEN O'CONNELL.

House of Representatives: Dem. 80; Rep. 20; Total 100.

  Speaker: MATTHEW J. SMITH (Dem.).
  First Deputy Speaker: MARION G. DONNELLY (Dem.).
  Reading Clerk: EUGENE McMAHON.

South Carolina
CONSTITUTION AND GOVERNMENT

South Carolina's constitution, the state's seventh, became effective on 1 January 1896. Amendments to the constitution proposed by the Legislative Assembly have to be approved by two-thirds of the elected members of each house, and then by a majority of voters before being returned for consideration at a second session where the approval of a majority of members in each house is required. The governor is elected separately from the lieutenant-governor to serve a four-year term and may serve no more than two terms consecutively. South Carolina is the only state which elects its adjutant-general. The Legislative Assembly has 46 senators and 124 representatives, re-elected every four and two years respectively. There is no formal cabinet system. Regular legislative sessions are held annually, starting in January and not extending beyond the first Thursday in June. A bill becomes law after it has been approved by the Legislative Assembly and signed by the governor. During session the governor has five days to consider a bill, after which it becomes law unless vetoed. A gubernatorial veto may be overridden by a two-thirds vote from the members present in both houses. Legislation becomes effective on a date specified in the act itself. In 1986 754,000 people voted in the gubernatorial election, representing 58% of those registered to vote and 31% of the voting-age population. South Carolina has 46 administrative counties.

ELECTED EXECUTIVE-BRANCH OFFICIALS

Governor (1987–91): CARROLL A. CAMPBELL, Jr (Rep.).
Lieutenant-Governor: NICK A. THEODORE (Dem.).
Secretary of State: JOHN T. CAMPBELL (Dem.).
Attorney-General: TRAVIS T. MEDLOCK (Dem.).
Treasurer: GRADY L. PATTERSON (Dem.).
Comptroller-General: EARLE E. MORRIS, Jr (Dem.).
Superintendent of Education: Dr CHARLIE G. WILLIAMS.
Commissioner of Agriculture: D. LESLIE TINDAL.
Adjutant-General: Maj.-Gen. ESTON MARCHANT.

SELECTED GOVERNMENT ADDRESSES

Office of the Governor: POB 11450, Columbia, SC 29211; tel. (803) 734-9818.

Office of the Lieutenant-Governor: State House, 1st Floor, East Wing, POB 142, Columbia, SC 29202; tel. (803) 734-2080.

Office of the Secretary of State: POB 11350, Columbia, SC 29211; tel. (803) 734-2155.

Office of the Attorney-General: POB 11549, Columbia, SC 29211; tel. (803) 758-3970.

Office of the Treasurer: POB 11778, Columbia, SC 29211; tel. (803) 734-2101.

Office of the Comptroller-General: POB 11228, Columbia, SC 29211; tel. (803) 734-2121.

Budget and Control Board: Wade Hampton Office Bldg, Rm 681, POB 12444, Columbia, SC 29211; tel. (803) 734-2320; Exec. Dir JESSE A. COLES.

Department of Agriculture: Wade Hampton Office Bldg, Rm 527, POB 11280, Columbia, SC 29211-1280; tel. (803) 734-2210; Commr D. LESLIE TINDAL.

Department of Corrections: 4444 Broad River Rd, POB 21787, Columbia, SC 29221-1787; tel. (803) 737-8555; Commr WILLIAM D. LEAKE.

Department of Education: Rutledge Bldg, 1429 Senate St, Columbia, SC 29201; tel. (803) 734-8492; Supt Dr CHARLIE G. WILLIAMS.

Department of Health and Environmental Control: J. Marion Sims Bldg and R. J. Aycock Bldg, 2600 Bull St, Columbia, SC 29201; tel. (803) 734-4880; Commr MICHAEL JARRETT.

Department of Highways and Public Transportation: 955 Park St, POB 191, Columbia, SC 29202; tel. (803) 737-1302; Exec. Dir J. G. RIDEOUTTE.

Department of Labor: 3600 Forest Dr., POB 11329, Columbia, SC 29211-1329; tel. (803) 734-9594; Commr EDGAR L. McGOWAN.

Department of Parks, Recreation and Tourism: 1205 Pendleton St, Suite 248, Columbia, SC 29201; tel. (803) 734-0135; Dir of Div. of Tourism ROBERT G. LIMING.

Division of General Services: POB 12444, Columbia, SC 29211; tel. (803) 758-5650; incorporates Admin. Div.; Dir WILLIAM T. PUTNAM.

Land Resources Conservation Commission: 2221 Devine St, Columbia, SC 29205; tel. (803) 734-9100; incorporates Div. of Energy; Exec. Dir JOHN W. PARRIS.

Law Enforcement Department: POB 21398, Columbia, SC 29221-9990; tel. (803) 737-9000; Chief J. P. STROM.

Office of the Adjutant-General: 100x Assembly St, Columbia, SC 29201; tel. (803) 748-4200; Adj.-Gen. Maj.-Gen. T. ESTON MARCHANT.

Public Service Commission: POB 11649, Columbia, SC 29211; tel. (803) 758-3517; Exec. Dir J. H. STILL.

Revenue Division: POB 125, Columbia, SC 29214; tel. (803) 734-1830; Chair. HUNTER HOWARD.

State Development Board: 1301 Gervais St, POB 927, Columbia, SC 29202; tel. (803) 734-1400; incorporates Div. of Commerce; Dir J. MAC HOLLADAY.

GENERAL ASSEMBLY
(May 1989)

Senate: Dem. 34; Rep. 12; Total 46.

  President: Lt-Gov. NICK A. THEODORE (Dem.).
  President Pro Tempore: REMBERT DENNIS (Dem.).
  Clerk: FRANK CAGGIANO.

House of Representatives: Dem. 89; Rep. 34; 1 vacancy; Total 124.

  Speaker: ROBERT J. SHEEHAN (Dem.).
  Speaker Pro Tempore: JOHN I. ROGERS, III (Dem.).
  Clerk: LOIS T. SHEALY.

South Dakota
CONSTITUTION AND GOVERNMENT

South Dakota's only constitution became effective on 2 November 1889. An amendment to the constitution has to be approved by a majority of elected members in each house of the Legislature and ratified by a majority of state voters. The governor and lieutenant-governor are elected jointly to serve a four-year term of office, neither serving more than two terms consecutively. Cabinet members, 22 in total, are appointed to specified offices by the governor and meet at the governor's discretion. There are 35 senators and 70 representatives in the Legislature, all of whom are re-elected every two years. Regular legislative sessions are held annually, starting in January, and are limited in length to 40 days in odd-numbered years and 35 days in even-numbered years. A bill becomes law when it has been passed by the Legislature and signed by the governor. During session it also becomes law if it remains unsigned five days after being presented to the governor for consideration. Outside session a bill becomes law unless vetoed within 15 days from adjournment of the Legislature. A gubernatorial veto may be overridden by a two-thirds vote of the elected members in each house. Enacted legislation becomes effective on 1 July or, if enacted on or after this date, 91 days after adjournment of the session. In the 1986 election to the US Senate 296,000 people voted, representing 69% of those registered to vote and 58% of the voting-age population. There are 64 administrative counties in South Dakota.

ELECTED EXECUTIVE-BRANCH OFFICIALS

Governor (1987–91): GEORGE S. MICKELSON (Rep.).

Lieutenant-Governor: WALTER D. MILLER (Rep.).

Secretary of State: JOYCE HAZELTINE (Rep.).

Attorney-General: ROGER TELLINGHUISEN (Rep.).

Treasurer: DAVID VOLK (Rep.).

Auditor and Comptroller: VERNON L. LARSON (Rep.).

Commissioner of School and Public Lands: TIMOTHY H. AMDAHL.

SELECTED GOVERNMENT ADDRESSES

Office of the Governor: 500 East Capitol Ave, Pierre, SD 57501; tel. (605) 773-3212.

Office of the Lieutenant-Governor: State Capitol, Pierre, SD 57501; tel. (605) 773-3824.

Office of the Secretary of State: 500 East Capitol Ave, Pierre, SD 57501; tel. (605) 773-3661.

Office of the Attorney-General: State Capitol, Pierre, SD 57501-5090; tel. (605) 773-3215.

Office of the Treasurer: 500 East Capitol Ave, Rm 200, Pierre, SD 57501; tel. (605) 773-3378.

Office of the Auditor: 500 East Capitol Ave, Pierre, SD 57501; tel. (605) 773-3341.

Bureau of Administration: State Capitol, 1st Floor, Pierre, SD 57501; tel. (605) 773-3688; Commr JEFFREY STROUP.

Bureau of Finance and Management: State Capitol, Pierre, SD 57501; tel. (605) 773-3411; Commr JIM HILL.

Department of Agriculture: Anderson Bldg, 445 East Capitol Ave, Pierre, SD 57501; tel. (605) 773-3375; Sec. JAY SWISHER.

Department of Charities and Corrections: Foss Bldg, 523 East Capitol Ave, Pierre, SD 57501; tel. (605) 773-3813; Exec. Dir JIM SMITH.

Department of Commerce and Regulation: 910 Sioux Ave, Pierre, SD 57501; tel. (605) 773-3177; Sec. JEFF STINGLEY.

Department of Education and Cultural Affairs: Kneip Bldg, 700 Governors' Dr., Pierre, SD 57501-2293; tel. (605) 773-3134; Sec. JAMES O. HANSEN.

Department of Health: Foss Bldg, 523 East Capitol Ave, Pierre, SD 57501; tel. (605) 773-3361; Sec. KATHERINE A. KINSMAN.

Department of Labor: Kneip Bldg, 700 Governors' Dr., Pierre, SD 57501; tel. (605) 773-3101; Sec. PETER DE HUECK.

Department of Military and Veterans' Affairs: Anderson Bldg, 445 East Capitol Ave, Pierre, SD 57501; tel. (605) 394-6702; Adj.-Gen. Brig.-Gen. HAROLD SYKORA.

Department of Revenue: Kneip Bldg, 700 Governors' Dr., Pierre, SD 57501-2276; tel. (605) 773-3311; Sec. RON SCHREINER.

Department of Tourism: Capitol Lake Plaza, Pierre, SD 57501; tel. (605) 773-3301; Sec. SUSAN EDWARDS.

Department of Transportation: 700 East Broadway Ave, Pierre, SD 57501; tel. (605) 773-3265; Sec. RICHARD HOWARD.

Department of Water and Natural Resources: Foss Bldg, 523 East Capitol Ave, Pierre, SD 57501; tel. (605) 773-3151; Sec. JOHN J. SMITH.

Governor's Office of Energy Policy: 217½ West Missouri St, Pierre, SD 57501; tel. (605) 773-3603; Commr RON REED.

Public Utilities Commission: Dept of Commerce and Regulations, 500 East Capitol Ave, Pierre, SD 57501; tel. (605) 733-3201; Commr DENNIS EISNACH.

LEGISLATURE
(May 1989)

Senate: Rep. 20; Dem. 15; Total 35.

President: Lt-Gov. WALTER D. MILLER (Rep.).
President Pro Tempore: MARY A. MCCLURE (Rep.).
Secretary: FEE JACOBSEN.

House of Representatives: Rep. 46; Dem. 24; Total 70.

Speaker: DEBRA R. ANDERSON (Rep.).
Speaker Pro Tempore: ROYAL J. WOOD (Rep.).
Chief Clerk: PAUL INMAN.

Tennessee
CONSTITUTION AND GOVERNMENT

The current constitution of Tennessee is the state's third and became effective on 23 February 1870. Constitutional amendments proposed by the General Assembly have to be approved first by the majority and then by two-thirds of members elected to both houses, followed by ratification by a majority of all people voting for the governor at election. The Governor of Tennessee (the only elected executive-branch official) is elected to serve a four-year term of office and may serve no more than two terms consecutively. The speaker of the Senate, who has the statutory title of Lieutenant-Governor, succeeds in the absence of the governor. Members of the cabinet, 27 in total, are appointed to specified offices and meet at the governor's discretion. The 33 senators and 99 representatives in the state General Assembly are elected to serve four- and two-year terms respectively, alternate halves of the Senate being re-elected every two years. Statutory provision is made for regular sessions to be held in odd-numbered years only, beginning in January, but in practice sessions are also held in even-numbered years. Regular sessions are limited in length to 90 days. A bill becomes law when it has been read and passed three times in each house and has been signed by the governor; during session it also becomes law unless vetoed within 10 days of presentation to the governor. After session a bill becomes law unless vetoed within 10 days from adjournment of the General Assembly. A majority vote by the elected members in each house is required to override a gubernatorial veto. Legislation becomes effective 40 days after enactment. In 1986, 1,210,000 people voted in the gubernatorial election, representing 49% of the number registered to vote and 34% of the voting-age population. There are 95 administrative counties in Tennessee.

ELECTED EXECUTIVE-BRANCH OFFICIALS

Governor (1987–91): NED RAY MCWHERTER (Dem.).

SELECTED GOVERNMENT ADDRESSES

Office of the Governor: State Capitol Bldg, Nashville, TN 37219-5081; tel. (615) 741-2001.

Commerce and Insurance Department: 5th Floor, Volunteer Plaza, Nashville, TN 37219; tel. (615) 741-2241; Commr ELAINE A. MCREYNOLDS.

Department of Agriculture: Ellington Agriculture Center, POB 40627, Nashville, TN 37204; tel. (615) 360-0103; Commr L. H. IVY.

Department of Conservation: 701 Broadway, Nashville, TN 37219; tel. (615) 742-6758; Commr ELBERT T. GILL.

Department of Correction: Rachel Jackson Bldg, 4th Floor, Nashville, TN 37219; tel. (615) 741-2071; Commr W. JEFF REYNOLDS.

Department of Education: Cordell Hull Bldg, Rm 100, Nashville, TN 37219; tel. (615) 741-2731; Commr Dr CHARLES E. SMITH.

Department of Finance and Administration: State Capitol Bldg, 1st Floor, Nashville, TN 37219; tel. (615) 741-2401; Commr DAVID L. MANNING.

Department of Health and Environment: Cordell Hull Bldg, Rm 344, Nashville, TN 37219; tel. (615) 741-3111; Commr J. W. LUNA.

Department of Labor: Union Bldg, 2nd Floor, Rm 501, Nashville, TN 37219; tel. (615) 741-2582; Commr JAMES R. WHITE.

Department of Revenue: Andrew Jackson Bldg, Rm 2000, Nashville, TN 37219; tel. (615) 741-2461; Commr CHARLES E. CARDWELL.

Department of Safety: 1150 Foster Ave, Nashville, TN 37210; tel. (615) 251-5166; Commr ROBERT D. LAWSON.

Department of Tourist Development: Rachel Jackson Bldg, 5th Floor, Nashville, TN 37219; tel. (615) 741-1904; Commr SANDRA FULTON.

Department of Transportation: James K. Polk Bldg, 7th Floor, Nashville, TN 37219; tel. (615) 741-2848; Commr JIMMY EVANS.

Economic and Community Development Department: Rachel Jackson Bldg, 8th Floor, Nashville, TN 37219; tel. (615) 741-1888; incorporates Div. of Energy and High Technology; Commr CARL JOHNSON.

Military Department: Houston Barracks, 3041 Sidco Dr., Nashville, TN 37204-1501; tel. (615) 252-3001; Adj.-Gen. CARL D. WALLACE.

Office of the Attorney-General: 450 James Robertson Parkway, Nashville, TN 37219; tel. (615) 741-3491; Att.-Gen. CHARLES BURSON.

Office of the Comptroller of the Treasury: State Capitol, 1st Floor, Nashville, TN 37219; tel. (615) 741-2501; Comptroller WILLIAM R. SNODGRASS.

Public Service Commission: 460 James Robertson Parkway, Nashville, TN 37219; tel. (615) 741-3668; Chair. KEITH BISSELL.

GENERAL ASSEMBLY
(May 1989)

Senate: Dem. 22; Rep. 11; Total 33.

  Speaker: Lt-Gov. JOHN S. WILDER (Dem.).
  President Pro Tempore: ROBERT T. ROCHELLE (Dem.).
  Chief Clerk: CLYDE McCULLOUGH, Jr.

House of Representatives: Dem. 59; Rep. 40; Total 99.

  Speaker: ED MURRAY (Dem.).
  Speaker Pro Tempore: LOIS M. DE BERRY (Dem.).
  Chief Clerk: BRYANT MILLSAPS.

Texas

CONSTITUTION AND GOVERNMENT

The current constitution of Texas, the state's fifth, became effective on 15 February 1876. A constitutional amendment proposed by the Legislature requires the approval of two-thirds of the elected members of each house, followed by ratification from a majority of state voters. The governor is elected separately from the lieutenant-governor and serves a four-year term of office. The Legislature has 31 senators and 150 representatives, elected to serve terms of four and two years respectively; alternate halves of the Senate are re-elected every two years. There is no formal cabinet system. Regular sessions of the Legislature are held every two years, beginning in January in odd-numbered years, and are limited in length to 140 days. A bill becomes law once it has been approved by a majority of the elected members present in each house (which must be equal to at least two-thirds of the entire membership of each house) and has either been signed by the governor or, during session, left unsigned 10 days after being presented to the governor. Outside session a bill becomes law if it remains unsigned for 20 days from adjournment of the session. A gubernatorial veto can be overridden by two-thirds of the elected members present in each house. Enacted legislation becomes effective 90 days after the Legislature's adjournment. In 1986 3,441,000 people voted in the gubernatorial election, representing 47% of those registered to vote and 29% of the voting-age population. Texas has 254 administrative counties.

ELECTED EXECUTIVE-BRANCH OFFICIALS

Governor (1987–91): BILL CLEMENTS (Rep.).

Lieutenant-Governor: WILLIAM P. HOBBY (Dem.).

Attorney-General: JIM MATTOX (Dem.).

Treasurer: ANN W. RICHARDS (Dem.).

Comptroller of Public Accounts: BOB BULLOCK (Dem.).

Commissioner of Agriculture: JAMES HIGHTOWER.

Commissioner of General Land Office: GARRY MAURO.

SELECTED GOVERNMENT ADDRESSES

Office of the Governor: Capitol Station, POB 12428, Austin, TX 78711; tel. (512) 463-2000.

Office of the Lieutenant-Governor: Capitol Station, POB 12068, Austin, TX 78711; tel. (512) 463-0001.

Office of the Attorney-General: Supreme Ct Bldg, POB 12548, Austin, TX 78711; tel. (512) 463-2100; incorporates Div. of Public Finance.

Office of the Treasurer: Capitol Station, POB 12608, Austin, TX 78711; tel. (512) 463-6000.

Office of the Comptroller of Public Accounts: Lyndon Baines Johnson Bldg, POB 13528, Austin, TX 78774; tel. (512) 475-1900.

Bureau of Environmental Health: 1100 West 49th St, Austin, TX 78756; tel. (512) 458-7542; Head of Div. L. DON THURMOND.

Department of the Adjutant-General: Camp Mabry, Bldg 1, POB 5218, Austin TX 78763-5218; tel. (512) 465-5006; Adj.-Gen. Maj.-Gen. WILLIAM C. WILSON.

Department of Agriculture: Stephen F. Austin Bldg, Rm 933, Austin, TX 78701; tel. (512) 475-2760; Commr JAMES HIGHTOWER.

Department of Corrections: POB 99, Huntsville, TX 77340; tel. (409) 295-6371; Dir JAMES E. LYNAUGH (acting).

Department of Economic Development: Capitol Station, POB 12728, Austin TX 78711; tel. (512) 472-5059; Exec. Dir HARDEN H. WIEDEMANN.

Department of Health: 1100 West 49th St, Austin, TX 78756; tel. (512) 458-7111; Commr Dr ROBERT BERNSTEIN.

Department of Highways and Public Transportation: 11th and Brazos Sts, Austin, TX 78701; tel. (512) 475-3525; Engineer-Dir RAYMOND E. STOTZER.

Department of Labor and Standards: POB 12157, Austin, TX 78711; Commr RICHARD L. MORGAN.

Department of Public Safety: 5805 North Lamar St, Austin, TX 78773; Dir Col JOE MILNER.

Education Agency: 1701 North Congress Ave, Austin, TX 78701; tel. (512) 463-8985; Commr WILLIAM KIRBY.

General Land Office: Stephen F. Austin Bldg, 1700 North Congress Ave, Rm 835, Austin, TX 78701; Commr GARRY MAURO.

Public Utilities Commission: 7800 Shoal Creek Blvd, Suite 400 North, Austin, TX 78757; tel. (512) 458-0293; incorporates Div. of Energy Efficiency; Exec. Dir COYLE KELLY.

Tourist Development Agency: Capitol Station, POB 12008, Austin, TX 78711; tel. (512) 463-7400; Exec. Dir LARRY TODD.

LEGISLATURE
(May 1989)

Senate: Dem. 23; Rep. 8; Total 31.

  President: Lt-Gov. WILLIAM P. HOBBY (Dem.).
  President Pro Tempore: CARL PARKER (Dem.).
  Secretary: BETTY KING.

House of Representatives: Dem. 94; Rep. 56; Total 150.

  Speaker: GIBSON LEWIS (Dem.).
  Speaker Pro Tempore: HUGO BERLANGA (Dem.).
  Chief Clerk: BETTY MURRAY.

Utah

CONSTITUTION AND GOVERNMENT

Utah's only state constitution became effective on 4 January 1896. Amendments to the constitution proposed by the Legislature must be passed by two-thirds of the elected members of each house and ratified by a majority of state voters. The governor and lieutenant-governor are jointly elected to serve a four-year term and there is no limit to the number of times they may hold office. Cabinet members, 26 including the governor, are appointed to specified offices and meet monthly. The 29 senators and 75 representatives in the Legislature are re-elected every four and two years respectively, alternate halves of the Senate being re-elected every two years. Regular legislative sessions are held annually in January and are limited in length to 45 days. A bill becomes law when it has been passed by the Legislature and signed by the governor. During session the governor has 10 days in which to consider a bill, after which it becomes law unless vetoed. Outside session a bill becomes law unless vetoed within 20 days from adjournment of the Legislature. A gubernatorial veto may be overridden by a two-thirds vote of the elected members of each house. Enacted legislation becomes effective 60 days after adjournment. In 1986 435,000 people voted in the election to the US Senate, representing 57% of those registered to vote and 41% of the voting-age population. There are 29 administrative counties in Utah.

ELECTED EXECUTIVE-BRANCH OFFICIALS

Governor (1989–93): NORMAN H. BANGERTER (Rep.).

Lieutenant-Governor and Secretary of State: W. VAL OVESON (Rep.).

Attorney-General: R. PAUL VAN DAM.

Treasurer: EDWARD T. ALTER (Rep.).

Auditor: TOM L. ALLEN.

SELECTED GOVERNMENT ADDRESSES

Office of the Governor: Capitol Bldg, Rm 210, Salt Lake City, UT 84114; tel. (801) 538-1000.

Office of the Lieutenant-Governor: Capitol Bldg, Rm 203, Salt Lake City, UT 84114; tel. (801) 538-1040.

Office of the Attorney-General: Capitol Bldg, Rm 236, Salt Lake City, UT 84114; tel. (801) 538-1015.

Office of the Treasurer: Capitol Bldg, Rm 215, Salt Lake City, UT 84114; tel. (801) 538-1042.

Office of the Auditor: Capitol Bldg, Rm 211, Salt Lake City, UT 84114; tel. (801) 538-1025.

Board of Education: 250 East 500 South St, Salt Lake City, UT 84114; tel. (801) 533-5431; Supt of Public Instruction JAMES R. MOSS.

Department of Administrative Services: State Office Bldg, Rm 2100, Salt Lake City, UT 84114; tel. (801) 533-4200; incorporates Div. of Finance; Exec. Dir CAROLYN LLOYD.

Department of Agriculture: 350 North Redwood Rd, Salt Lake City, UT 84116; tel. (801) 533-5421; Commr MILES FERRY.

Department of Community and Economic Development: State Office Bldg, Rm 6290, Salt Lake City, UT 84111; tel. (801) 533-5325; incorporates Div. of Travel Development; Exec. Dir DAVID W. ADAMS.

Department of Corrections: 6065 South 300 East St, Murray, UT 84107; tel. (801) 261-2817; Exec. Dir GARY W. DELAND.

Department of Health: 288 North 1460 West St, Salt Lake City, UT 84116; tel. (801) 533-6111; incorporates Div. of Environmental Health; Exec. Dir SUZANNE DANDOY.

Department of Natural Resources and Energy: 1636 West North Temple St, Salt Lake City, UT 84116; tel. (801) 533-5356; Exec. Dir DEE HANSEN.

Department of Public Safety: 4501 South 2700 West St, Salt Lake City, UT 84119; tel. (801) 965-4518; Commr DOUGLAS BODRERO.

Department of Transportation: 4501 South 2700 West St, Salt Lake City, UT 84119; tel. (801) 965-4113; Dir EUGENE FINDLAY.

Division of Labor: Industrial Comm., 160 East 300 South St, Salt Lake City, UT 84001-5800; tel. (801) 530-6811; Commr JOHN MEDINA.

Division of Public Utilities: Dept of Business Regulation, 160 East 3rd South St, Salt Lake City, UT 84110; tel. (801) 530-6676; Dir RALPH N. CREER.

National Guard: POB 1776, Salt Lake City, UT 84020; tel. (801) 524-3600; Adj.-Gen. Maj.-Gen. JOHN L. MATTHEWS.

Tax Commission: 160 East 300 South St, POB 4000, Salt Lake City, UT 84134; tel. (801) 530-6088; Chair. and Commr HAL HANSEN.

LEGISLATURE
(May 1989)

Senate: Rep. 22; Dem. 7; Total 29.

   President: ARNOLD CHRISTENSEN (Rep.).
   Secretary: SOPHIA BUCKMILLER.

House of Representatives: Rep. 48; Dem. 27; Total 75.

   Speaker: NOLAN E. KARRAS (Rep.).
   Chief Clerk: CAROLE PETERSON.

Vermont
CONSTITUTION AND GOVERNMENT

Vermont's constitution, the state's fifth, became effective on 9 July 1793. Constitutional amendments proposed by the General Assembly must be considered at two sessions, requiring a two-thirds vote by the elected members of the Senate and a majority vote by the House of Representatives at the first session, and a majority vote by both houses at the second. Amendments must then be ratified by a majority of state voters. The governor is elected separately from the lieutenant-governor to serve a term of two years. Members of the cabinet, six in total, are appointed to specified office and meet at the governor's discretion. The General Assembly comprises 30 senators and 150 representatives and both houses are re-elected every two years. Legal provision is made for regular sessions of the General Assembly to be held in odd-numbered years only, but in practice sessions are also held in even-numbered years. Regular sessions convene in January. A bill becomes law when it has been passed by a majority in each house and signed by the governor. During session the governor has five days to consider a bill, after which it becomes law unless vetoed. Outside session a bill dies if it remains unsigned for three days from the adjournment of the General Assembly. A vote by two-thirds of the members present in each house is required to override a gubernatorial veto. Legislation becomes effective on 1 July following enactment. In the gubernatorial election of 1986 197,000 people voted, representing 60% of those registered to vote and 49% of the voting-age population. Vermont has 14 administrative counties.

ELECTED EXECUTIVE-BRANCH OFFICIALS

Governor (1989–91): MADELEINE M. KUNIN (Dem.).
Lieutenant-Governor: HOWARD DEAN (Rep.).
Secretary of State: JAMES H. DOUGLAS (Rep.).
Attorney-General: JEFFREY L. AMESTOY (Rep.).
Treasurer: PAUL W. RUSE, Jr.
Auditor of Accounts: ALEXANDER ACEBO.

SELECTED GOVERNMENT ADDRESSES

Office of the Governor: 109 State St, Montpelier, VT 05602; tel. (802) 828-3333.

Office of the Lieutenant-Governor: State House, Montpelier, VT 05602; tel. (802) 828-2226.

Office of the Secretary of State: 26 Terrace St, Montpelier, VT 05602; tel. (802) 828-2363.

Office of the Attorney-General: 109 State St, Montpelier, VT 05602; tel. (802) 828-3171.

Office of the Treasurer: 133 State St, 2nd Floor, Montpelier, VT 05602; tel. (802) 828-2301.

Office of the Auditor of Accounts: 132 State St, Montpelier, VT 05602; tel. (802) 828-2281.

Agency of Administration: Pavilion Office Bldg, Montpelier, VT 05602; tel. (802) 828-3322; Sec. THOMAS P. MENSON.

Agency of Development and Community Affairs: Pavilion Office Bldg, Montpelier, VT 05602; tel. (802) 828-3211; incorporates Travel Div.; Sec. ELBERT G. MOULTON.

Agency of Transportation: State Administration Bldg, Montpelier, VT 05602; tel. (802) 828-2657; Sec. SUSAN C. CRAMPTON.

Department of Agriculture: State Office Bldg, Montpelier, VT 05602; tel. (802) 828-2413; Commr RONALD ALLBEE.

Department of Corrections: State Office Complex, Waterbury, VT 05676; tel. (802) 241-2263; Commr JOSEPH J. PATRISSI.

Department of Education: State Office Bldg, Montpelier, VT 05602; tel. (802) 828-3135; Commr RICHARD P. MILLS.

Department of Environmental Conservation: State Office Complex, Waterbury, VT 05676; tel. (802) 828-3130; Commr PATRICK PARENTEAU.

Department of Finance and Management: Pavilion Office Bldg, Montpelier, VT 05602; tel. (802) 828-2311; Commr PATRICIA WALTON.

Department of Health: State Office Bldg, Montpelier, VT 05602; tel. (802) 863-7280; Commr Dr ROBERTA R. COFFIN.

Department of Labor and Industry: State Office Bldg, Montpelier, VT 05602; tel. (802) 828-2700; Commr JEANNE VANVLANDREN.

Department of Public Safety: State Office Complex, Waterbury, VT 05676; tel. (802) 244-5194; Commr A. JAMES WALTON.

Department of Public Service: State Office Bldg, Montpelier, VT 05602; tel. (802) 828-2358; incorporates Div. of Energy; Commr GEORGE STERZINGER.

Department of Taxes: Pavilion Office Bldg, Montpelier, VT 05602; tel. (802) 828-2523; Commr NORRIS HOYT.

Military Department: Bldg 1, Camp Johnson, Winooski, VT 05404; tel. (802) 864-1000; Adj.-Gen. Maj.-Gen. DONALD E. EDWARDS.

GENERAL ASSEMBLY
(May 1989)

Senate: Dem. 16; Rep. 14; Total 30.

   President: Lt-Gov. HOWARD DEAN (Rep.).
   President Pro Tempore: DOUGLAS RACINE (Dem.).
   Secretary: ROBERT GIBSON.

House of Representatives: Dem. 76; Rep. 74; Total 150.

   Speaker: RALPH WRIGHT (Dem.).
   Clerk: ROBERT PICHER.

Virginia
CONSTITUTION AND GOVERNMENT

Virginia's current constitution, its sixth, became effective on 1 July 1971. An amendment to the constitution proposed by the General Assembly has to be passed by a majority of the elected members of each house at two consecutive sessions, and then ratified by a majority of state voters. The governor, elected separately from the lieutenant-governor, serves a four-year term and may not serve consecutive terms. Cabinet members, seven in total, are appointed to specified offices and meet at the governor's discretion. There are 40 senators and 100 representatives in the General Assembly, serving terms of four and two years respectively. Regular legislative sessions take place annually, starting in January, and are limited in length to 60 days in odd-numbered years and 90 days in even-numbered years. To become law, a bill must be approved by the General Assembly and signed by the governor. During session a bill becomes law if it remains neither signed nor vetoed seven days after being presented to the governor for consideration. Outside session, if the governor fails to sign a bill within 30 days after adjournment of the General Assembly the bill is treated as if it were vetoed. A gubernatorial veto may be overridden by a two-thirds vote of members present in each house (which must be at least a majority of the elected members). Legislation usually becomes effective on 1 July following enactment. In 1986 1,043,000 people voted in the election to the US House of Representatives, representing 40% of those people registered to vote and 24% of the voting-age population. There are 95 administrative counties in Virginia.

ELECTED EXECUTIVE-BRANCH OFFICIALS

Governor (1986–90): GERALD LEE BALILES (Dem.).

Lieutenant-Governor: L. DOUGLAS WILDER (Dem.).

Attorney-General: MARY SUE TERRY (Dem.).

SELECTED GOVERNMENT ADDRESSES

Office of the Governor: Capitol Bldg, 3rd Floor, POB 1475, Richmond, VA 23212; tel. (804) 786-2211.

Office of the Lieutenant-Governor: Supreme Ct Bldg, 101 North 8th St, Richmond, VA 23219; tel. (804) 786-2078.

Office of the Attorney-General: Supreme Ct Bldg, 101 North 8th St, Richmond, VA 23219; tel. (804) 786-2071.

Corporation Commission: 1220 Bank St, POB 1197, Richmond, VA 23209; tel. (804) 786-3608; incorporates Div. of Energy Regulation; Chair. THOMAS P. HARWOOD, Jr.

Council on the Environment: 9th St Office Bldg, Rm 903, Richmond, VA 23219; tel. (804) 786-4500; Administrator KEITH J. BUTTLEMAN.

Department of Agriculture and Consumer Services: Washington Bldg, 1100 Bank St, Rm 210, POB 1163, Richmond, VA 23209; tel. (804) 786-3501; Commr S. MASON CARBAUGH.

Department of Commerce: 3600 West Broad St, Richmond, VA 23230; tel. (804) 367-8519; Dir DAVID R. HATHCOCK.

Department of Corrections: 4615 West Broad St, POB 26963, Richmond, VA 23261; tel. (804) 674-3119; Dir EDWARD W. MURRAY.

Department of Economic Development: Washington Bldg, Rm 1000, Richmond, VA 23219; tel. (804) 786-3791; Dir HUGH D. KEOGH.

Department of Education: 9th St Office Bldg, Rm 603, POB 1475, Richmond, VA 23212; tel. (804) 786-1151; Sec. DONALD J. FINLEY.

Department of Health: Madison Bldg, 109 Governor St, Rm 400, Richmond, VA 23219; tel. (804) 786-3561; Commr Dr C. M. G. BUTTERY.

Department of Highways and Transportation: 1401 East Broad St, Richmond, VA 23219; tel. (804) 786-2701; Commr RAY D. PETHTEL.

Department of Labor and Industry: 205 North 4th St, POB 12064, Richmond, VA 23241; tel. (804) 786-2377; Commr CAROL A. AMATO.

Department of Planning and Budget: 9th St Office Bldg, Rm 412, POB 1422, Richmond, VA 23211; tel. (804) 786-5375; Dir PAUL W. TIMMEREK.

Department of State Police: 7700 Midlothian Turnpike, POB 27472, Richmond, VA 23261; tel. (804) 674-2087; Supt Col ROBERT SUTHARD.

Department of Taxation: 2220 West Broad St, POB 6-L, Richmond, VA 23282; tel. (804) 257-8005; Tax Commr WILLIAM H. FORST.

Military Affairs Division: 501 East Franklin St, Richmond, VA 23219; tel. (804) 344-4102; Adj.-Gen. Maj.-Gen. JOHN G. CASTLES.

GENERAL ASSEMBLY

(May 1989)

Senate: Dem. 30; Rep. 10; Total 40.

President: Lt-Gov. L. DOUGLAS WILDER (Dem.).
President Pro Tempore: WILLIAM F. PARKERSON, Jr (Dem.).
Clerk: J. T. SHROPSHIRE.

House of Delegates: Dem. 64; Rep. 35; Ind. 1; Total 100.

Speaker: A. L. PHILPOTT (Dem.).
Clerk: JOSEPH H. HOLLEMAN, Jr.

Washington

CONSTITUTION AND GOVERNMENT

Washington's only constitution became effective on 11 November 1889. Amendments to the constitution proposed by the Legislature have to be approved by two-thirds of the elected members of each house and ratified by a majority of state voters. The governor, elected separately from the lieutenant-governor, serves a four-year term and there is no limit on the number of times he or she may hold office. The cabinet members, 26 in total, are appointed to specified office and meet twice monthly. There are 49 senators and 98 representatives in the Legislature, elected to serve terms

of four and two years respectively; alternate halves of the Senate are re-elected every two years. Regular sessions are held annually, starting in January, and last no longer than 105 days in odd-numbered years and 60 days in even-numbered years. A bill becomes law once it has been passed by a majority of the elected members in each house and signed by the governor. During session the governor is allowed five days to consider a bill, after which it becomes law unless vetoed. After session a bill becomes law unless vetoed within 20 days of being presented to the governor. A two-thirds vote of members present in each house is required to override a gubernatorial veto. Enacted legislation becomes effective 90 days after adjournment of the session. In the 1986 election to the US Senate 1,337,000 people voted, representing 60% of those registered to vote and 40% of the voting-age population. Washington has 39 administrative counties.

ELECTED EXECUTIVE-BRANCH OFFICIALS

Governor (1989–93): W. BOOTH GARDNER (Dem.).

Lieutenant-Governor: JOEL PRITCHARD (Rep.).

Secretary of State: RALPH MUNRO (Rep.).

Attorney-General: KENNETH EIKENBERRY (Rep.).

Treasurer and Comptroller: DANIEL K. GRIMM.

Auditor: ROBERT V. GRAHAM.

Superintendent of Public Instruction: JUDITH BILLINGS.

Insurance Commissioner and Fire Marshal: DICK MARQUARDT.

Commissioner of Public Lands: BRIAN BOYLE.

SELECTED GOVERNMENT ADDRESSES

Office of the Governor: Legislative Bldg, Olympia, WA 98504; tel. (206) 753-6780.

Office of the Lieutenant-Governor: Legislative Bldg, Rm 304, Olympia, WA 98504; tel. (206) 786-7700.

Office of the Secretary of State: Legislative Bldg, Rm 306, Olympia, WA 98504; tel. (206) 786-7550.

Office of the Attorney-General: Temple of Justice, Olympia, WA 98504; tel. (206) 753-2550.

Office of the Treasurer: Legislative Bldg, AS-523, Olympia, WA 98504; tel. (206) 753-7130.

Office of the Auditor: Legislative Bldg, AS-21, Olympia, WA 98504; tel. (206) 753-5280.

Corrections Department: POB 9699, Olympia, WA 98504; tel. (206) 753-2500; Sec. CHASE RIVELAND.

Department of Agriculture: Gen. Admin. Bldg, Rm 406, Olympia, WA 98504; tel. (206) 753-5050; Dir J. ALAN PETTIBONE.

Department of Commerce and Economic Development: Gen. Admin. Bldg, Rm 101, AX-13, Olympia, WA 98504; tel. (206) 753-7426; Dir JOHN ANDERSON.

Department of Ecology: Mailstop PV-11, Olympia, WA 98504; tel. (206) 459-6168; Dir CHRIS GREGOIRE.

Department of Energy: 400 East Union Ave, Olympia, WA 98504; tel. (206) 754-0701; Dir DICK WATSON.

Department of Financial Management: Insurance Bldg, Rm 300, Olympia, WA 98504; tel. (206) 753-5450; Dir LEN McCOMB (acting).

Department of General Administration: Gen. Admin. Bldg, Rm 218, Olympia, WA 98504; tel. (206) 753-5434; Dir MARY FAULK.

Department of Labor and Industries: Gen. Admin. Bldg, Olympia, WA 98504; tel. (206) 753-6307; Dir JOE DEAR.

Department of Natural Resources: Public Lands Bldg, Olympia, WA 98504; tel. (206) 753-5317; Commr of Public Lands BRIAN BOYLE.

Department of Public Instruction: Old Capitol Bldg, 600 South Washington St, Olympia, WA 98504; tel. (206) 753-6717; Dir JUDITH BILLINGS.

Department of Revenue: Gen. Admin. Bldg, Suite 415, MS-AX-02, Olympia, WA 98504; tel. (206) 753-5512; Dir BILL WILKERSON.

Department of Social and Health Services: OB-44, Olympia, WA 98504; tel. (206) 753-3395; Sec. JULIE SUGARMAN.

Department of Transportation: Transportation Bldg, MS-KF-01, Olympia, WA 98504; tel. (206) 753-6054; Sec. DUANE BERENTSON.

Military Department: Camp Murray, Tacoma, WA 98430; tel. (206) 964-6201; Adj.-Gen. Maj.-Gen. KEITH EGGEN.

Office of the Insurance Commissioner and State Fire Marshal: Insurance Bldg, AQ-21, Olympia, WA 98504; tel. (206) 753-7301; Commr and Fire Marshal DICK MARQUARDT.

State Patrol: General Admin. Bldg, AX-12, Olympia, WA 98504; tel. (206) 753-6540; Chief GEORGE B. TELLEVIK.

Tourist Promotion Division: Dept of Commerce and Econ. Development, Gen. Admin. Bldg, Rm 101, AX-13, Olympia, WA 98504; tel. (206) 753-5600; Dir BILL TAYLOR.

Utilities and Transportation Commission: Highways–Licenses Bldg, Olympia, WA 98504; tel. (206) 753-6430; Chair. SHARON NELSON.

LEGISLATURE
(May 1989)

Senate: Dem. 25; Rep. 24; Total 49.

President: Lt-Gov. JOEL PRITCHARD (Rep.).
Vice-President: ELLEN CRASWELL.
Secretary: GORDON A. GOLOB.

House of Representatives: Dem. 63; Rep. 35; Total 98.

Speaker: JOSEPH E. KING (Dem.).
Speaker Pro Tempore: JOHN L. O'BRIEN (Dem.).
Chief Clerk: ALAN THOMPSON.

West Virginia
CONSTITUTION AND GOVERNMENT

West Virginia's current constitution, the state's second, became effective on 9 April 1872. Constitutional amendments proposed by the Legislature must be approved by a two-thirds vote by the elected members of each house and ratified by a majority of state voters. The governor, succeeded in his or her absence by the President of the Senate, is elected to serve a four-year term of office and may serve no more than two terms successively. There is no formal cabinet system in West Virginia. The Legislature has 34 senators and 100 delegates, serving terms of four and two years respectively; alternate halves of the Senate are re-elected every two years. Regular sessions of the Legislature are held annually in January or February and may last no longer than 60 days. A bill becomes law when it has been passed by the Legislature and signed by the governor. During session the governor is allowed five days to consider a bill, after which it becomes law unless vetoed. Outside session a bill becomes law unless vetoed within 15 days from adjournment of the legislature, or within five days for appropriation bills. A gubernatorial veto may be overridden by a majority of the elected members of both houses, except where the veto is applied to an appropriation bill, in which case a two-thirds vote is required. Legislation becomes effective 90 days after enactment. In 1986 396,000 people voted in the election to the US House of Representatives, representing 42% of those registered to vote and 28% of the voting-age population. There are 55 administrative counties in West Virginia.

ELECTED EXECUTIVE-BRANCH OFFICIALS

Governor (1989–93): W. GASTON CAPERTON (Dem.).

Secretary of State: KEN HECHLER (Dem.).

Attorney-General: CHARLES BROWN (Dem.).

Treasurer: A. JAMES MANCHIN (Dem.).

Auditor and Comptroller: GLEN B. GAINER, Jr (Dem.).

Commissioner of Agriculture: CLEVE BENEDICT.

SELECTED GOVERNMENT ADDRESSES

Office of the Governor: Capitol Bldg, Charleston, WV 25305; tel. (304) 348-2000.

Office of the Secretary of State: Capitol Bldg, Charleston, WV 25305; tel. (304) 345-4000.

Office of the Treasurer: Capitol Bldg, Rm E26, Charleston, WV 25305; tel. (304) 348-2021.

Office of the Auditor: Capitol Bldg, Rm 100, Charleston, WV 25305; tel. (304) 348-2251.

Department of Agriculture: Capitol Bldg, Charleston, WV 25305; tel. (304) 348-2201; Commr CLEVE BENEDICT.

Department of Corrections: 112 California Ave, Charleston, WV 25305; tel. (304) 348-2036; Commr RON GREGORY.

Department of Economic and Community Development: 1900 Washington St East, Charleston, WV 25305; tel. (304) 348-0400; Dir of Econ. Development JOHN G. REDLINE.

Department of Education: Capitol Complex, Bldg 6, Rm B358, Charleston, WV 25305; tel. (304) 348-2681; State Supt of Schools JOHN PISAPIA.

Department of Energy: 1615 Washington St, Bldg E, Charleston, WV 25311; tel. (304) 348-3500; Commr GEORGE DIALS.

Department of Finance and Administration: Capitol Bldg, Rm E117, Charleston, WV 25305; tel. (304) 348-2300; Commr JOHN F. MCCUSKEY.

Department of Health: 1800 Washington St East, Charleston, WV 25305; tel. (304) 348-2971; Dir DAVID K. HEYDINGER.

Department of Highways: 1900 Washington St East, Charleston, WV 25305; tel. (304) 348-3063; incorporates Div. of Transportation; Commr FRED VANKIRK (acting).

Department of Labor: 1800 Washington St East, Charleston, WV 25305; tel. (304) 348-7890; Commr JESS T. SHUMATE.

Department of Natural Resources: 1800 Washington St East, Charleston, WV 25305; tel. (304) 348-2754; incorporates Environment Div.; Dir ED HAMRICK.

Department of Tax: Capitol Bldg, Rm W300, Charleston, WV 25305; tel. (304) 348-2501; Commr CHARLES LORENSEN.

Office of the Adjutant-General: 1703 Coonskin Dr., Charleston, WV 25311; tel. (304) 348-2754; Adj.-Gen. Maj.-Gen. JOSEPH J. SKAFF.

Public Service Commission: 201 Brook St, Charleston, WV 25301; tel. (304) 340-0300; Chair. MICHAEL D. GREER.

Travel Development Division: Dept of Econ. and Community Development, 1900 Washington St East, Charleston, WV 25305; tel. (304) 348-2286; Man. JOSEPH R. FOWLER.

LEGISLATURE
(May 1989)

Senate: Dem. 30; Rep. 4; Total 34.

President: LARRY TUCKER (Dem.).
President Pro Tempore: TONY WHITLOW (Dem.).
Clerk: TODD C. WILLIS.

House of Delegates: Dem. 80; Rep. 20; Total 100.

Speaker: ROBERT CHAMBERS (Dem.).
Clerk: DONALD L. KOPP.

Wisconsin
CONSTITUTION AND GOVERNMENT

Wisconsin's only constitution became effective on 29 May 1848. An amendment to the constitution proposed by the Legislature must be approved by a majority of the elected members of each house in two consecutive sessions and ratified by a majority of voters. The governor, elected with the lieutenant-governor, serves a four-year term and there is no limit on the number of times he or she may hold office. Cabinet members, nine in total, are appointed to specified offices and meet monthly. The 33 senators and 99 representatives in the Legislature serve four and two-year terms respectively, alternate halves of the Senate being re-elected every two years. Regular legislative sessions are held annually, beginning in January, and there is no statutory limit to their duration. A bill becomes law after being passed by both houses and signed by the governor. During session the governor has six days to consider a bill, after which it becomes law unless vetoed. Outside session a bill dies if it remains unsigned for six days after being presented to the governor. A two-thirds vote by the members present in each house is required to override a gubernatorial veto. Enacted legislation becomes effective the day after publication. In the 1986 gubernatorial election 1,527,000 people voted, representing 43% of the voting-age population (there is no statewide voter registration). Wisconsin has 72 administrative counties.

ELECTED EXECUTIVE-BRANCH OFFICIALS

Governor (1987–91): TOMMY G. THOMPSON (Rep.).

Lieutenant-Governor: SCOTT MCCOLLUM (Rep.).

Secretary of State: DOUGLAS LA FOLLETTE (Dem.).

Attorney-General: DONALD HARAWAY (Rep.).

Treasurer: CHARLES P. SMITH (Dem.).

Superintendent of Public Instruction: HERBERT J. GROBER.

SELECTED GOVERNMENT ADDRESSES

Office of the Governor: POB 7863, Madison, WI 53707-7863; tel. (608) 266-1212.

Office of the Lieutenant-Governor: POB 7970, Madison, WI 53707; tel. (608) 266-1018.

Office of the Secretary of State: POB 7848, Madison, WI 53707; tel. (608) 266-5801.

Office of the Attorney-General: POB 7857, Madison, WI 53707; tel. (608) 266-1221.

Office of the Treasurer: 125 South Webster St, POB 7871, Madison, WI 53707; tel. (608) 266-3711.

Department of Administration: 101 South Webster St, POB 7864, Madison, WI 53707-7864; tel. (608) 266-1741; incorporates Divs of

Finance and Program Management, and of Energy; Sec. JAMES R. KAUSER.

Department of Agriculture, Trade and Consumer Protection: 801 West Badger Rd, POB 8911, Madison, WI 53708; tel. (608) 266-7100; Sec. HOWARD RICHARDS.

Department of Development: POB 7970, Madison, WI 53707; tel. (608) 266-3203; incorporates Div. of Tourism; Dir, Econ. and Community Development RAL WEGENKE.

Department of Health and Social Services: POB 7850, Madison, WI 53707; tel. (608) 266-3681; incorporates Div. of Corrections; Sec. TIMOTHY CULLEN.

Department of Industry, Labor and Human Relations: 149 East Wilson St, POB 7946, Madison, WI 53707; tel. (608) 266-7552; Sec. HOWARD FULLER.

Department of Natural Resources: 101 South Webster St, POB 7921, Madison, WI 53707; tel. (608) 266-2121; incorporates Div. of Environmental Standards; Sec. CARROLL D. BESADNY.

Department of Public Instruction: POB 7841, Madison, WI 53707; tel. (608) 266-1771; Supt HERBERT J. GROBER.

Department of Revenue: POB 8933, Madison, WI 53708; tel. (608) 266-1611; Sec. KAREN CASE.

Department of Transportation: POB 7910, Madison, WI 53707-7910; tel. (608) 266-1113; Sec. RONALD FIEDLER.

Division of Military Affairs: POB 8111, Madison, WI 53708; tel. (608) 241-6312; Adj.-Gen. Maj.-Gen. RAYMOND MATERA.

Public Service Commission: 4802 Sheboygan Ave, POB 7854, Madison, WI 53707; tel. (608) 266-1241; Chair. MARY LOU MUNRA.

LEGISLATURE
(May 1989)

Senate: Dem. 20; Rep. 13; Total 33.

  President: FRED A. RISSER (Dem.).
  Chief Clerk: DONALD SCHNEIDER.

Assembly: Dem. 56; Rep. 43; Total 99.

  Speaker: THOMAS A. LOFTUS (Dem.).
  Speaker Pro Tempore: DAVID E. CLARENBACH (Dem.).
  Chief Clerk: THOMAS MELVIN.

Wyoming

CONSTITUTION AND GOVERNMENT

The Wyoming Constitution, the only constitution the state has had, became effective on 10 July 1890. Amendments to the constitution proposed by the Legislature have to be approved by a two-thirds vote of the elected members of each house and ratified by a majority of voters in election. The governor is elected to serve a four-year term of office and is succeeded in his or her absence by the secretary of state, there being no lieutenant-governor. There is no formal cabinet system in Wyoming. The Legislature has 30 senators and 64 representatives, who are elected to serve terms of four and two years respectively; alternate halves of the Senate are elected every two years. Regular legislative sessions are held annually, starting in January and lasting for no longer than 40 days in odd-numbered years, and starting in February and lasting for a maximum of 20 days in even-numbered years. A bill becomes law when it has been passed by the Legislature and signed by the governor. During session it may also become law if left unsigned for three days after presentation to the governor. Outside session the governor has 15 days from the adjournment of the session to consider a bill, after which it becomes law unless vetoed. A gubernatorial veto may be overridden by a vote by two-thirds of the elected members of each house. Enacted legislation becomes effective immediately. In 1986 165,000 people voted in the gubernatorial election, representing 70% of those registered to vote and 47% of the voting-age population. There are 23 administrative counties in Wyoming.

ELECTED EXECUTIVE-BRANCH OFFICIALS

Governor (1987–91): MIKE SULLIVAN (Dem.).
Secretary of State: KATHY KARPAN (Dem.).
Treasurer: STAN SMITH (Rep.).
Auditor: JACK SIDI (Rep.).
Superintendent of Public Instruction: LYNN SIMONS (Dem.).

SELECTED GOVERNMENT ADDRESSES

Office of the Governor: Capitol Bldg, 200 West 24th St, Cheyenne, WY 82002; tel. (307) 777-7434.

Office of the Secretary of State: Capitol Bldg, 200 West 24th St, Cheyenne, WY 82002; tel. (307) 777-7378.

Office of the Treasurer: Capitol Bldg, 200 West 24th St, Cheyenne, WY 82002; tel. (307) 777-7408.

Office of the Auditor: Capitol Bldg, 200 West 24th St, Rm 114, Cheyenne, WY 82002; tel. (307) 777-7831.

Department of Administration and Fiscal Control: Emerson Bldg, 2001 Capitol Ave, Cheyenne, WY 82002; tel. (307) 777-7201; incorporates Div. of Budget; Dir KEN ERICKSON.

Department of Agriculture: 2219 Carey Ave, Cheyenne, WY 82002; tel. (307) 777-7321; Commr DON ROLSTON.

Department of Education: Hathaway Bldg, 2300 Capitol Ave, Cheyenne, WY 82002; tel. (307) 777-7675; Supt of Public Instruction LYNN SIMONS.

Department of Environmental Quality: Herschler Bldg, 122 West 25th St, Cheyenne, WY 82002; tel. (307) 777-7937; Dir RANDOLPH WOOD.

Department of Health and Social Services: Hathaway Bldg, 2300 Capitol Ave, Rm 117, Cheyenne, WY 82002; tel. (307) 777-7656; Dir Dr LAWRENCE J. COHEN.

Department of Labor Statistics: Herschler Bldg, 122 West 25th St, 2nd Floor East, Cheyenne, WY 82002; tel. (307) 777-7261; Commr MICHAEL J. SULLIVAN.

Department of Probation and Parole: 5801 Osage Ave, Cheyenne, WY 82002; tel. (307) 777-7208; Exec. Dir ROBERT E. ORTEGA.

Department of Revenue and Taxation: Herschler Bldg, 122 West 25th St, Cheyenne, WY 82002; tel. (307) 777-7961; Chair. of State Tax Comm. RUDOLPH ANSELMI.

Economic Development and Stabilization Board: Herschler Bldg, 122 West 25th St, Cheyenne, WY 82002; tel. (307) 777-7284; State Administrator RICHARD LINDSEY.

Energy Conservation Office: Herschler Bldg, 122 West 25th St, Cheyenne, WY 82002; tel. (307) 777-7131; Co-ordinator NICHOLAS GILL.

Office of the Adjutant-General: 5500 Bishop Blvd, Cheyenne, WY 82002; tel. (307) 777-6201; Adj.-Gen. CHARLES J. WING.

Office of the Attorney-General: Capitol Bldg, 200 West 24th St, Rm 123, Cheyenne, WY 82002; tel. (307) 777-7841; Att.-Gen. JOSEPH MEYER.

Public Service Commission: Herschler Bldg, 122 West 25th St, Cheyenne, WY 82002; tel. (307) 777-7427; Chair. JOHN R. SMYTH.

Travel Commission: Norris Travel Center, Cheyenne, WY 82002; tel. (307) 777-7777; Dir GENE BRYAN.

LEGISLATURE
(May 1989)

Senate: Rep. 19; Dem. 11; Total 30.

  President: RUSSELL W. ZIMMER (Rep.).
  Vice-President: TOM STROOCK (Rep.).
  Chief Clerk: ED WREN, Jr.

House of Representatives: Rep. 41; Dem. 23; Total 64.

  Speaker: BILL McILVAIN (Rep.).
  Speaker Pro Tempore: RORY CROSS (Rep.).
  Chief Clerk: HERB POWNALL.

POLITICAL ORGANIZATIONS

Democratic National Committee: 430 South Capitol St, SE, Washington, DC 20003; tel. (202) 863-8000; f. 1848; Chair. RONALD H. BROWN; Sec. DOROTHY BUSH; Treas. SHARON PRATT DIXON.

Republican National Committee: 310 First St, SE, Washington, DC 20003; tel. (202) 863-8500; f. 1854; Chair. LEE ATWATER; Sec. KIT MEHRTENS; Treas. WILLIAM J. MCMANUS.

American Independent Party: 8158 Palm St, Lemon Grove, CA 92045; tel. (619) 460-4484; f. 1968; aims to promote individual citizens' rights; c. 180,000 mems, of which 150,000 in California; Nat. Chair. EILEEN M. SHEARER.

American Party of the United States: POB 22382, Lexington, KY 40522; tel. (606) 272-2659; f. 1969; conservative; Nat. Chair. Dr W. S. KROGDAHL; Sec. DORIS FEIMER.

Citizens Party: 1623 Connecticut Ave, NW, Washington, DC 20009; tel. (202) 232-3996; f. 1969; progressive democratic party; environmentalist; 25,000 mems (1984); Co-Chair. BARRY COMMONER.

Communist Labor Party: POB 3774, Chicago, IL 60654; f. 1974; Marxist.

Communist Party of the USA (Marxist–Leninist): POB 6205, Chicago, IL 60680; f. 1978; Sec. D. WEISS.

Communist Party USA: 235 West 23rd St, New York, NY 10011; tel. (212) 989-4994; f. 1919; Gen. Sec. GUS HALL.

Communist Workers' Party: 72 5th Ave, Brooklyn, New York, NY 11215; tel. (212) 789-0737; f. 1979; Gen. Sec. JERRY TUNG.

Conservative Party: 45 East 29th St, New York, NY 10016; tel. (212) 689-8400; f. 1962; operates within New York State; Exec. Dir SERPHIN R. MALTESE.

Constitution Parties of the United States: Medina, ND 58467; tel. (701) 486-3385; f. 1952; individual autonomous state parties; endorse the original US constitution as the supreme law of the land; Nat. Chair. CLARENCE S. MARTIN.

Expansionist Party of the United States: 446 West 46th St, New York, NY 10036; tel. (212) 265-1081; f. 1977; seeks annexation to the USA of as many areas as are willing to abide by the US constitution, culminating in world union; 150 mems (1984); Chair. L. CRAIG SCHOONMAKER.

Industrial Union Party: POB 80, New York, NY 10159; f. 1980; seeks to bring the US economy under the ownership and control of all the people by establishing industrial unions as the form of government; Gen. Sec. SAM BRANDON.

La Raza Unida Party: 554 Kalisher St, San Fernando, CA 91340; tel. (213) 365-6534; f. 1972; aims to achieve self-determination and greater government representation for Latinos through electoral processes; 4 state groups, 100 local groups; Nat. Chair XENARO G. AYALA.

Libertarian Party: 301 West 21st St, Houston, TX 77008; tel. (713) 880-1776; f. 1971; 19 regional groups, 50 state groups, 300 local groups; Chair. JIM TURNEY; Nat. Dir HENRY MITCHELL; Sec. I. DEAN AHMAD.

Marxist–Leninist Party of the USA: Ontario St Station, POB 11942, Chicago, IL 60611; f. 1980 to succeed Central Org. of US Marxist–Leninists (f. 1973).

National Determination Party: POB 3646, Manchester, NH 03105; f. 1975; patriotic, right-wing party; Chair. ARNOLD MOLTIS.

National Hamiltonian Party: 2734 Parkside Dr., Suite 307, Flint, MI 48502; tel. (313) 234-5552; f. 1962; advocates government by an elite of aristocrats and educated citizens; 1,426 mems (1984); Nat. Chair. ALEC SEBASTIAN.

National Socialist Party of America: 2519 West 71st St, Chicago, IL 60629; f. 1970; advocates an 'all-White America'; 11 state groups.

Nationalist Socialist White People's Party: 2507 North Franklin Rd, Arlington, VA 22201; tel. (703) 524-2175; f. 1959; 25 local groups; Commander MATT KOEHL.

National States Rights Party: POB 1211, Marietta, GA 30061; tel. (404) 427-0283; f. 1958; 'patriotic white racist political order'; 15,000 mems (1984); Chair. J. B. STONER.

New Federalist Party: POB 19908, Baltimore, MD 21211; f. 1976; aims to promote the principles of George Washington and the federalist founders of the USA; 38 state groups, 76 local groups; Nat. Dir ALEXANDER BORA.

Populist Party: 6065 Mission Gorge Rd, POB 211, San Diego, CA 92120; tel. (619) 282-5614; f. 1891 by discontented farmers, reformed 1984; Chair. JOHN COUTURE; Treas. FAYE MILLER.

Progressive Labor Party: 220 East 23rd St, 7th Floor, New York, NY 10010; tel. (212) 685-3650; f. 1962; communist; Chair. MILTON ROSEN.

Prohibition National Committee: POB 2365, Denver, CO 80201; tel. (303) 572-0646; f. 1869; opposes the manufacture and sale of alcoholic drinks, opposes 'anti-social' drugs, abortion and euthanasia, and 'champions individual freedom'; Nat. Chair. EARL F. DODGE; Nat. Sec. RAYFORD G. FEATHER.

Social Democrats, USA: 815 15th St, NW, Washington, DC 20005; tel. (202) 638-1515; f. 1972 to succeed Socialist Party est. in 1901; Pres. DONALD SLAIMAN; Exec. Dir RITA FREEDMAN.

Socialist Labor Party of America: POB 50218, Palo Alto, CA 94303; tel. (415) 494-1532; f. 1877; Marxist; 550 mems (1987); Nat. Sec. ROBERT BILLS; Financial Sec. GENEVIEVE GUNDERSON.

Socialist Party of the USA: 1011 North 3rd St, Suite 232, Milwaukee, WI 53203; tel. (414) 276-0773; f. 1973; democratic socialist party; 10 state groups, 24 local groups; Nat. Sec. RICK KISSELL.

Socialist Workers Party: 14 Charles Lane, New York, NY 10014; tel. (212) 242-5530; f. 1938; Nat. Sec. JACK BARNES.

Workers' World Party: f. 1958; Trotskyist; Chair. SAM MARCY.

World Socialist Party of the USA: POB 405, Boston, MA 02272; f. 1916; Marxist; Sec. RONALD ELBERT.

DIPLOMATIC REPRESENTATION

OVERSEAS DIPLOMATIC AND CONSULAR REPRESENTATION IN THE USA

Afghanistan

Embassy: 2341 Wyoming Ave, NW, Washington, DC 20008; tel. (202) 234-3770; Chargé d'affaires Mr MIAGOL.

Algeria

Embassy: 2118 Kalorama Rd, NW, Washington, DC 20008; tel. (202) 328-5300; Ambassador MOHAMED SAHNOUN.

Antigua and Barbuda

Embassy: 3400 International Dr., NW, Suite 2H, Washington, DC 20008; tel. (202) 362-5211; telex 8221130; Ambassador EDMUND HAWKINS LAKE.

Argentina

Embassy: 1600 New Hampshire Ave, NW, Washington, DC 20009; tel. (202) 939-6400; Ambassador ENRIQUE J. A. CANDIOTI.

Consulate-General: 870 Market St, San Francisco, CA 94102; tel. (415) 982-3050; Consul-Gen. GUSTAVO J. CACERES.

Consulate-General: 25 Second Ave, SE, Suite 722, Miami, FL 33131; tel. (305) 373-1889; Consul-Gen. MARCELO E. HUERGO.

Consulate-General: International Trade Mart, Rm 915, New Orleans, LA 70130; tel. (504) 523-2823; Consul-Gen. ENRIQUE MORESCO.

Consulate-General: 12 56th St West, New York, NY 10019; tel. (212) 397-1400; Consul-Gen. JUAN CARLOS FERNÁNDEZ.

Consulate-General: 2000 Post Oak Blvd South, Suite 1810, Houston, TX 77056; tel. (713) 871-8935; Consul-Gen. JORGE DESCALZI.

Consulate: 3550 Wilshire Blvd, Los Angeles, CA 90010; tel. (213) 739-5959; Deputy Consul JORGE L. VINUELA.

Consulate: 20 Clark St North, Suite 602, Chicago, IL 60602; tel. (312) 263-7435; Consul HERNAN R. PLORUTTI.

Australia

Embassy: 1601 Massachusetts Ave, NW, Washington, DC 20036; tel. (202) 797-3000; Ambassador F. RAWDON DALRYMPLE.

Consulate-General: 3550 Wilshire Blvd, Suite 912, Los Angeles, CA 90010; tel. (213) 380-0980; Consul-Gen. BASIL J. TEASEY.

Consulate-General: 360 Post St, San Francisco, CA 94108; tel. (415) 362-6160; Consul-Gen. DAVID C. RUTTER.

Consulate-General: 1000 Bishop St, Honolulu, HI 96813; tel. (808) 524-5050; Consul-Gen. WILLIAM N. FISHER.

Consulate-General: 111 Wacker Dr. East, Chicago, IL 60601; tel. (312) 329-1740; Consul-Gen. TERENCE B. MCCARTHY.

Consulate-General: 636 Fifth Ave, New York, NY 10020; tel. (212) 254-4000; Consul-Gen. JOHN C. TAYLOR.

Consulate-General: 3 Post Oak Central Bldg, 1990 Post Oak Blvd South, 8th Floor, Houston, TX 77056; tel. (713) 877-8100; Consul-Gen. ROBERT CHRISTOPHER WHITTY.

Austria

Embassy: 2343 Massachusetts Ave, NW, Washington, DC 20008; tel. (202) 483-4474; telex 440010; Ambassador FRIEDRICH HÖSS.

Consulate-General: 3440 Wilshire Blvd, Suite 910, Los Angeles, CA 90010; tel. (213) 380-7550; Consul-Gen. Dr NIKOLAUS SCHERK.

Consulate-General: 31 East 69th St, New York, NY 10021; tel. (212) 737-6400; Consul-Gen. HELGA VINKLER-CAMPAGNA.

Bahamas

Embassy: 600 New Hampshire Ave, NW, Suite 865, Washington, DC 20037; tel. (202) 944-3390; Ambassador MARGARET E. MCDONALD.

Consulate-General: Ingraham Bldg, 25 Second Ave, SE, Miami, FL 33131; tel. (305) 373-6295; Consul-Gen. (vacant).

Consulate-General: 767 Third Ave, New York, NY 10017; tel. (212) 421-6420; Consul-Gen. ANGELA MISSOURI SHERMAN-PETER.

Bahrain

Embassy: 3502 International Dr., NW, Washington, DC 20008; tel. (202) 342-0741; Ambassador GHAZI MOHAMED ALGOSAIBI.

Consulate-General: 2 United Nations Plaza, East 44th St, 25th Floor, New York, NY 10017; tel. (212) 223-6200; Consul-Gen. ABDULLA JASSIM AL-SHAKAR.

Bangladesh

Embassy: 2201 Wisconsin Ave, NW, Washington, DC 20007; tel. (202) 342-8372; Ambassador H. S. ATAUL KARIM.

Consulate-General: 821 United Nations Plaza, 8th Floor, New York, NY 10017; tel. (212) 867-3434; Consul-Gen. SAMUEL STUART BRETZFIELD.

Barbados

Embassy: 2144 Wyoming Ave, NW, Washington, DC 20008; tel. (202) 939-9200; telex 64343; Ambassador Sir WILLIAM R. DOUGLAS.

Consulate-General: 800 Second Ave, 18th Floor, New York, NY 10017; tel. (212) 867-8435; Consul-Gen. EARL W. GLASGOW.

Consulate: 3440 Wilshire Blvd, Suite 1215, Los Angeles, CA 90010; tel. (213) 380-2198; Hon. Consul IVOR HUTSON.

Belgium

Embassy: 3330 Garfield St, NW, Washington, DC 20008; tel. (202) 333-6900; telex 440139; Ambassador HERMAN DEHENNIN.

Consulate-General: 3921 Wilshire Blvd, Suite 600, Los Angeles, CA 90010; tel. (213) 385-8116; Consul-Gen. VINCENT VAN DER MERSCH.

Consulate-General: Peachtree Cain Tower, 229 Peachtree St, NE, Suite 2306, Atlanta, GA 30303; tel. (404) 659-2150; Consul-Gen. JACQUES DE BAENST.

Consulate-General: 333 Michigan Ave North, Rm 2000, Chicago, IL 60601; tel. (321) 263-6624; Consul-Gen. CHARLES VAN OVERSTRAETEN.

Consulate-General: 50 Rockefeller Plaza, Rm 1104, New York, NY 10020; tel. (212) 586-5110; Consul-Gen. FERDINAND DE WILDE.

Consulate-General: 1 Westheimer Plaza, 5718 Westheimer Rd, Suite 760, Houston, TX 77057; tel. (713) 784-8077; Consul-Gen. DENIS A. N. BANNEEL.

Belize

Embassy: 3400 International Dr., NW, Suite 2J, Washington, DC 20008; tel. (202) 363-4505; telex 140997; fax (202) 362-7468; Ambassador EDWARD A. LAING.

Benin

Embassy: 2737 Cathedral Ave, NW, Washington, DC 20008; tel. (202) 232-6656; telex 64155; Ambassador THÉOPHILE NATA.

Bolivia

Embassy: 3014 Massachusetts Ave, NW, Washington, DC 20008; tel. (202) 483-4410; telex 440049; fax (202) 328-3712; Ambassador CARLOS E. DELIUS.

Consulate-General: 483 Spring St South, Suite 1212, Los Angeles, CA 90013; tel. (213) 680-0190; Consul-Gen. (vacant).

Consulate-General: 870 Market St, Suite 355, San Francisco, CA 94102; tel. (415) 495-5173; Consul-Gen. (vacant).

Consulate-General: Ingraham Bldg, 25 2nd Ave, SE, Rm 700, Miami, FL 33131; tel. (305) 358-3450; Consul-Gen. MARÍA DEL CARMEN VALASCO DE COZZI.

Consulate-General: International Trade Mart, Rm 1035, New Orleans, LA 70130; tel. (504) 523-7488; Consul-Gen. ANÍBEL REVOLLO.

Consulate-General: 211 43rd St East, Suite 802, New York, NY 10017; tel. (212) 687-0532; Consul-Gen. ARMANDO FORTUN SALMON.

Consulate-General: 6430 Richmond Ave, Suite 120, Houston, TX 77057; tel. (713) 780-1648; Consul-Gen. GUALBERTO VILLARROEL.

Botswana

Embassy: 4301 Connecticut Ave, NW, Suite 404, Washington, DC 20008; tel. (202) 244-4990; Chargé d'affaires CECIL I. MANYUELA.

Brazil

Embassy: 3006 Massachusetts Ave, NW, Washington, DC 20037; tel. (202) 745-2712; Ambassador MARCÍLIO MÁRQUES MOREIRA.

Consulate-General: 3810 Wilshire Blvd, Suite 1500, Los Angeles, CA 90010; telex 677309; tel. (213) 282-3133; Consul-Gen. LYLE AMAURY TARRISSEE DA FONTOURA.

Consulate-General: 770 Brickell Ave, Miami, FL 33131; tel. (305) 377-1734; Consul-Gen. LUIS F. DE OLIVEIRA E CRUZ BENEDINI.

Consulate-General: Peachtree Cain Tower, 229 Peachtree St, NE, Suite 2420, Atlanta, GA 30303; tel. (404) 659-0660; Consul-Gen. ANNUNCIATA SALGADO DOS SANTOS.

Consulate-General: 20 Wacker Dr. North, Suite 1010, Chicago, IL 60606; tel. (312) 372-2177; Consul-Gen. AGENOR DOS SANTOS.

Consulate-General: International Trade Mart, Rm 1306, New Orleans, LA 70130; tel. (504) 588-9187; Consul-Gen. FERNANDO ANTONIO DE OLIVEIRA SANTOS FONTOURA.

Consulate-General: 630 Fifth Ave, Suite 2720, New York, NY 10111; tel. (212) 757-3080; Consul-Gen. JOÃO PAULO DA SILVA PARANHOS DO RIO BRANCO.

Consulate: 300 Montgomery St, Suite 1160, San Francisco, CA 94104; tel. (415) 981-8170; Consul GERALDO A. MUZZI.

Consulate: World Trade Center, 2050 Stemmons Freeway North, Suite 174, Dallas, TX 75258; tel. (214) 651-1854; Consul MARÍA NATIVIDADE DUARTE RIBIERO PETIT.

Consulate: 1333 West Loop South, Suite 1100, Houston, TX 71027; tel. (713) 961-3063; Consul ROBERTO DE SALVO COIMBRA.

Brunei

Embassy: 2600 Virginia Ave, NW, Suite 300, Washington, DC 20037; tel. (202) 342-0159; telex 904081; Ambassador Dato H. MOHD SUNI.

Bulgaria

Embassy: 1621 22nd St, NW, Washington, DC 20008; tel. (202) 387-7969; Ambassador STOYAN ILIEV ZHULEV.

Burkina Faso

Embassy: 2340 Massachusetts Ave, NW, Washington, DC 20008; tel. (202) 332-5577; telex 440399; Ambassador PAUL-DÉSIRÉ KABORÉ.

Burundi

Embassy: 2233 Wisconsin Ave, NW, Suite 212, Washington, DC 20007; tel. (202) 342-2574; Ambassador EDOUARD KADIGIRI.

Cameroon

Embassy: 2349 Massachusetts Ave, NW, Washington, DC 20008; tel. (202) 265-8790; Ambassador PAUL PONDI.

Canada

Embassy: 501 Pennsylvania Ave, NW, Washington, DC 20001; tel. (202) 785-1400; telex 89664; Ambassador DEREK H. BURNEY.

Consulate-General: 300 Grand Ave South, 10th Floor, Los Angeles, CA 90014; tel. (213) 627-9511; Consul-Gen. JOAN P. WINSER.

Consulate-General: Golden Gateway Center, 1 Maritime Plaza, San Francisco, CA 94111; tel. (415) 981-2670; Consul-Gen. PATRICK REID.

Consulate-General: Omni International Bldg South, Rm 400, Atlanta, GA 30303; tel. (404) 577-6810; Consul-Gen. GEOFFREY ELLIOT.

Consulate-General: 310 Michigan Ave South, Suite 200, Chicago, IL 60604; tel. (312) 427-1031; Consul-Gen. ANTHONY HALLIDAY.

Consulate-General: 3 Copely Pl., Suite 400, Boston, MA 02116; tel. (617) 265-3760; Consul-Gen. (vacant).

Consulate-General: First Federal Bldg, Rm 1900, 1001 Woodward Ave, Detroit, MI 48226; tel. (313) 965-2811; Consul-Gen. MARC C. LEMIEUX.

Consulate-General: 701 Fourth Ave South, 9th Floor, Minneapolis, MN 55402; tel. (612) 236-4641; Consul-Gen. BERNARD A. GAGOSZ.

Consulate-General: 1 Marine Midland Center, Suite 3550, Buffalo, NY 14203; tel. (716) 852-1247; Consul-Gen. CHARLES F. ROGERS.

Consulate-General: 1251 Ave of the Americas, New York, NY 10020; tel. (212) 586-2400; Consul-Gen. ROBERT JOHNSTONE.

Consulate-General: Illuminating Bldg, 55 Public Sq., Cleveland, OH 44113; tel. (216) 861-1660; Consul-Gen. (vacant).

Consulate-General: 3 Parkway Bldg, Suite 1310, Philadelphia, PA 19102; tel. (215) 561-1750; Consul-Gen. PIERRETTE A. LUCAS.

Consulate-General: 750 St Paul's St North, Suite 1700, Dallas, TX 75201; tel. (214) 922-9806; Consul-Gen. DOUGLAS H. M. BRANION.

Consulate-General: Plaza 600, Sixth and Stewart Sts, Rm 412, Seattle, WA 98101; tel. (206) 447-3800; Consul-Gen. IAN WOOD.

Cape Verde

Embassy: 3415 Massachusetts Ave, NW, Washington, DC 20007; tel. (202) 965-6820; Ambassador JOSÉ LUÍS FERNANDES LOPES.

Consulate-General: 535 Boylston St, Boston, MA 02116; tel. (617) 353-0014; Consul-Gen. ALIRIO VICENTE SILVA.

Central African Republic

Embassy: 1618 22nd St, NW, Washington, DC 20008; tel. (202) 483-7800; Ambassador CHRISTIAN LINGAMA-TOLÈQUE.

Chad

Embassy: 2002 R St, NW, Washington, DC 20009; tel. (202) 462-4009; Ambassador MAHAMAT ALI ADOUM.

Chile

Embassy: 1732 Massachusetts Ave, NW, Washington, DC 20036; tel. (202) 785-1746; Chargé d'affaires PATRICIO MATURANA.

Consulate-General: 25 Second Ave, SE, Suite 801, Miami, FL 33131; tel. (305) 373-8623; Consul-Gen. PATRICIO TORRES.

Consulate-General: 333 Michigan Ave North, 7th Floor, Chicago, IL 60601; tel. (312) 726-7097; Consul-Gen. SERGIO ANGELLOTTI.

Consulate-General: 866 United Nations Plaza, New York, NY 10017; tel. (212) 370-1455; Consul-Gen. RIGOBERTO RUBIO.

Consulate-General: 600 Travis St, Suite 3825, Houston, TX 77002; Consul-Gen. VICTORINO GALLEGOS.

China, People's Republic

Embassy: 2300 Connecticut Ave, NW, Washington, DC 20008; tel. (202) 328-2500; fax (202) 234-4055; Ambassador HAN XU.

Consulate-General: 1450 Laguna St, San Francisco, CA 94115; Consul-Gen. ZHAO XIXIN.

Consulate-General: 104 Michigan Ave South, Suite 1200, Chicago, IL 60603; tel. (312) 346-0287; Consul-Gen. DENG CHAOCONG.

Consulate-General: 520 12th Ave, New York, NY 10036; tel. (212) 279-4275; Deputy Consul-Gen. RUAN KESHAN.

Consulate-General: 3417 Montrose Blvd, Houston, TX 77006; tel. (713) 524-0708; Consul-Gen. NI YAOLI.

Colombia

Embassy: 2118 Leroy Pl., NW, Washington, DC 20008; tel. (202) 387-8338; Ambassador VICTOR MOSQUEREA.

Consulate-General: 870 Market St, Suite 509, San Francisco, CA 94102; tel. (415) 362-0080; Consul-Gen. JOAQUÍN MEJIA.

Consulate-General: 280 Aragon Ave, Coral Gables, Miami, FL 33134; tel. (305) 448-5558; Consul-Gen. ROBERTO GARCÍA ARCHILA.

Consulate-General: 220 State St South, Suite 2026, Chicago, IL 60604; tel. (312) 341-0658; Consul-Gen. RAFAEL VANEGAS.

Consulate-General: World Trade Center, 2 Canal St, Suite 1844, New Orleans, LA 70130; tel. (504) 525-5580; Consul-Gen. GABRIEL VELÁSQUEZ.

Consulate-General: 10 46th St East, New York, NY 10017; tel. (212) 949-9898; Consul-Gen. LUIS TORO.

Consulate-General: 2990 Richmond Ave, Suite 544, Houston, TX 77098; tel. (713) 527-8919; Consul-Gen. HUGO AFANADOR.

Consulate: 3600 Wilshire Blvd, Suite 1712, Los Angeles, CA 90010; tel. (213) 382-1136; Consul DOUGLAS MONTGOMERY.

Consulate: 1399 Ninth Ave, Suite 1307, San Diego, CA 92101; tel. (714) 235-4480; Consul (vacant).

Consulate: 2904 Commercial Blvd East, Fort Lauderdale, FL 33308; tel. (305) 772-0612; Consul MARÍA CLARA OSPINA DE LORA.

Consulate: 1211 Westshore Blvd North, ADP Bldg, Suite 411, Tampa, FL 33607; tel. (813) 875-1499; Consul DANIEL LEMAITRE.

Consulate: 1961 North Druid Hills Rd, NE, Suite 102B, Atlanta, GA 30329; tel. (404) 320-9665; Hon. Consul ALVARO CARDOSO.

Consulate: 535 Boylston St, 11th Floor, Boston, MA 02116; tel. (617) 536-6222; Consul RICARDO URIBE-VALENZUELA.

Consulate: Horizon Heritage Plaza Bldg, 24901 Northwestern Highway, Suite 316B, Detroit, MI 48075; Consul MARGARITA DE LA VEGA DE HURTADO.

Consulate: 1015 Chestnut St, Philadelphia, PA 19107; tel. (215) 922-1927; Consul AFFAN BUITRAGO.

Comoros

Embassy: 336 45th St East, 2nd Floor, New York, NY 10017; tel. (212) 972-8010; Ambassador AMINI ALI MOUMIN.

Congo

Embassy: 4891 Colorado Ave, NW, Washington, DC 20011; tel. (202) 726-5500; Ambassador BENJAMIN BOUNKOULOU.

Costa Rica

Embassy: 1825 Connecticut Ave, NW, Suite 211, Washington, DC 20009; tel. (202) 234-2945; Ambassador DANILO JIMÉNEZ.

Consulate-General: 1543 Olympia Blvd West, Los Angeles, CA 90015; tel. (213) 380-7925; Consul CARLOS VALVERDE.

Consulate-General: 4201 Caledonia Dr., San Diego, CA 92111; tel. (619) 277-9447; Consul-Gen. (vacant).

Consulate-General: 870 Market St, Suite 600, San Francisco, CA 94102; tel. (415) 392-8488; Consul-Gen. MARIO A. MADRIGAL-CAVALLINI.

Consulate-General: 28 West Flagler St, Suite 806, Miami, FL 33130; tel. (305) 377-4242; Consul-Gen. SYLVIA LORIA DE PETERS.

Consulate-General: 5285 86th Ave, North Penellas Park, Tampa, FL 33619; tel. (813) 544-1147; Consul-Gen. (vacant).

Consulate-General: International Trade Mart, Suite 934, New Orleans, LA 70130; tel. (504) 525-5445; Consul-Gen. MARIO BONILLA-ANTILLON.

Consulate-General: 7033 Luella Anne Dr., NE, Alburquerque, NM 87109; tel. (505) 822-1420; Consul-Gen. (vacant).

Consulate-General: 80 Wall St, Suite 1117, New York, NY 10005; tel. (212) 425-2620; Consul LUIS ENRIQUE MONGE.

Consulate: 819 Koko Isle Circle, Honolulu, HI 96825; tel. (808) 385-7772; Hon. Consul HILDA AGUILAR DE RICHARDSON.

Consulate: 1002 Balfour Rd, Grosse Pointe Park, Detroit, MI 48230; tel. (313) 924-8721; Consul JULIETA HIDALGO DE WOOD.

Consulate: 5370 Siegle Rd, Lockport, Buffalo, NY 14094; tel. (716) 625-9692; Vice-Consul MARITZA ALVÁREZ.

Consulate: 335 Main St East, Moorestown, Philadelphia, PA 08057; tel. (609) 235-6772; Hon. Consul-Gen. YOLANDA MARIN HARTNETT.

Côte d'Ivoire

Embassy: 2424 Massachusetts Ave, NW, Washington, DC 20008; tel. (202) 797-0300; Ambassador CHARLES P. GOMIS.

Cuba

'Interests' section in the Embassy of Czechoslovakia, 2630 16th St, NW, Washington, DC 20009; tel. (202) 797-8518; Counsellor RAMÓN SÁNCHEZ-PARODÍ.

Cyprus

Embassy: 2211 R St, NW, Washington, DC 20008; tel. (202) 462-7772; telex 440596; Ambassador ANDREAS J. JACOVIDES.

Consulate-General: 820 Second Ave, New York, NY 10017; tel. (212) 686-6016; Consul-Gen. PLATON M. KYRIAKIDES.

Czechoslovakia

Embassy: 3900 Linnean Ave, NW, Washington, DC 20008; tel. (202) 363-6315; Ambassador MIROSLAV HOUSTECKY.

Denmark

Embassy: 3200 Whitehaven St, NW, Washington, DC 20008-3683; tel. (202) 234-4300; telex 440081; Ambassador EIGIL JØRGENSEN.

Consulate-General: 3440 Wilshire Blvd, Suite 904, Los Angeles, CA 90010; tel. (213) 387-4277; Consul-Gen. HENNING KRISTIANSEN.

Consulate-General: 369 Michigan Ave North, Chicago, IL 60601; tel. (312) 329-9644; Consul-Gen. KNUD WERNER RASMUSSEN.

Consulate-General: 825 Third Ave, 32nd and 33rd Floors, New York, NY 10022; Consul-Gen. VILLADS VILLADSEN.

Consulate-General: 2 Post Oak Central Bldg, 1980 Post Oak Blvd, Suite 1710, Houston, TX 77056; tel. (713) 850-9520; Consul-Gen. KAJ HANSEN.

Djibouti

Embassy: 1430 K St, NW, Suite 600, Washington, DC 20006; tel. (202) 347-0254; Ambassador ROBLE OLHAYE.

Dominica

Embassy: 205 Yoakum Parkway, Suite 823, Alexandria, VA 22304; tel. (202) 751-6939; Ambassador MCDONALD P. BENJAMIN.

Dominican Republic

Embassy: 1715 22nd St, NW, Washington, DC 20008; tel. (202) 332-6280; Ambassador EDUARDO LEÓN.

Consulate-General: 548 Spring St South, Suite 309, Los Angeles, CA 90013; tel. (213) 858-7365; Consul-Gen. (vacant).

Consulate-General: 1038 Brickell Ave, Miami, FL 33131; tel. (305) 358-3221; Consul-Gen. FEDERICO ANTUN ABUD.

Consulate-General: 3336 Ashland Ave North, Chicago, IL 60657; Hon. Vice-Consul OSVALDO C. MENA y ARISTY.

Consulate-General: ITM Bldg, 611 Gravier St, Rm 1647, New Orleans, LA 70130; tel. (504) 522-1843; Consul-Gen. TABARE GONZÁLEZ BORRELL.

Consulate-General: 755 Boylston St, Boston, MA 02116; tel. (617) 267-4630; Vice-Consul GEORGIAN ALTAGRACIA MICHELEN STEFAN.

Consulate-General: 17 60th St West, New York, NY 10023; tel. (212) 265-0630; Consul-Gen. JOAQUÍN A. RICARDO GARCÍA.

Consulate-General: Lafayette Bldg Associates, Fifth and Chestnut Sts, Room 422, Philadelphia, PA 19106; tel. (215) 923-3006; Vice-Consul DIAZ DE ALMONTE.

Consulate: 4009 Old Shell Rd, Apartment E-16, Mobile, AL 36608; tel. (205) 342-5648; Consul MARIA R. DALMASI DE DIAZ.

Consulate: 870 Market St, Suite 982, San Francisco, CA 94103; tel. (415) 982-5144; Vice-Consul HILI A. CORDERO.

Consulate: 1919 Beach Way Rd, Suite 6-0, Jacksonville, FL 32207; tel. (904) 398-1118; Vice-Consul MILDRED ALTOGRACIA DE JIMÉNEZ.

Consulate: 2171 Babcock Dr., Troy, MI 48084; tel. (313) 643-7022; Consul AMERICA LÓPEZ DE CASTILLO.

Consulate: Norwest Midland Bldg, 401 Second Ave South, Rm 838, Minneapolis, MN 55401; tel. (612) 341-2636; Hon. Consul-Gen. RALPH S. PARKER III.

Consulate: 3300 Gessner Rd, Suite 113, Houston, TX 77024; tel. (713) 467-4372; Consul MODESTO LUCAS DÍAZ MONTANO.

Ecuador

Embassy: 2535 15th St, NW, Washington, DC 20009; tel. (202) 234-7200; telex 440129; Ambassador JAIME MONCAYO.

Consulate-General: 548 Spring St South, Los Angeles, CA 90013; tel. (213) 628-3014; Consul-Gen. FRANCISCO IBAÑEZ.

Consulate-General: The Flood Bldg, 870 Market St, Suite 858, San Francisco, CA 94102; tel. (415) 391-4148; Consul-Gen. CRISTÓBAL CARRILLO.

Consulate-General: Ingraham Bldg, 25 Second Ave, SE, Suite 1130, Miami, FL 33131; tel. (305) 371-8366; Consul-Gen. JUAN A. ORUZ.

Consulate-General: 612 Michigan Ave North, Rm 618, Chicago, IL 60611; tel. (312) 642-8579; Consul-Gen. GABRIEL RICARDO GERCES JARAMILLO.

Consulate-General: International Trade Mart, 2 Canal St, Rm 1312, New Orleans, LA 70130; tel. (504) 523-3229; Consul-Gen. ROCIO PÉREZ DE TAYLOR.

Consulate-General: 18 41st St East, 18th Floor, New York, NY 10017; tel. (212) 683-7555; Consul-Gen. PATRICIO ÁLVAREZ.

Consulate-General: 10850 Richmond Ave, Suite 140, Houston, TX 77057; tel. (713) 977-8750; Consul-Gen. Gen. EDUARDO LITTUMA ARIZAZA.

Consulate: 530 B St, Suite 1375, San Diego, CA 92101; tel. (714) 233-8640; Consul JORGE GORTAIRE.

Egypt

Embassy: 2310 Decatur Pl., NW, Washington, DC 20008; tel. (202) 232-5400; Ambassador EL-SAYED ABDEL RAOUF EL-REEDY.

Consulate-General: 3001 Pacific Ave, San Francisco, CA 94115; tel. (415) 346-9700; Consul-Gen. ISMAIL M. ABDEL-MOETI.

Consulate-General: 505 Lakeside Dr. North, Suite 6503, Chicago, IL 60611; tel. (312) 670-2633; Consul-Gen. MOHAMED KHALIL EL-AZZAZI.

Consulate-General: 1110 Second Ave, New York, NY 10022; tel. (212) 759-7120; Consul-Gen. ABDEL FATTAH ZAKI.

Consulate-General: Control Data Bldg, 2000 West Loop South, Suite 1750, Houston, TX 88027; Consul-Gen. FOUAD MAHMOUD YOUSSEF.

El Salvador

Embassy: 2308 California St, NW, Washington, DC 20008; tel. (202) 265-3480; Ambassador ERNESTO RIVAS-GALLONT.

Consulate-General: 408 Spring St South, Suite 608, Los Angeles, CA 90013; tel. (213) 623-9275; Consul-Gen. ANA MARGOTH MENDEZ.

Consulate-General: 150 Third Ave, SE, Suite 303, Miami, FL 33131; tel. (305) 371-8850; Consul-Gen. ROBERTO HIRLEMANN-POHL.

Consulate-General: International Trade Mart, Rm 1136, New Orleans, LA 70130; tel. (504) 522-4266; Consul-Gen. STELLA Z. DE GUDIEL.

Consul-General: 46 Park Ave, New York, NY 10016; tel. (212) 889-3608; Consul-Gen. RUTH ANABELLA HENRIQUEZ CHAVEZ.

Consul-General: 6655 Hillcroft St, Suite 112, Houston, TX 77081; tel. (713) 270-6239; Vice-Consul JOSÉ JOAQUÍN CHACÓN CORADO.

Equatorial Guinea

Embassy: 801 Second Ave, Suite 1403, New York, NY 10017; tel. (212) 599-1523; Chargé d'affaires PEDRO MBA MEDJA.

Ethiopia

Embassy: 2134 Kalorama Rd, NW, Washington, DC 20008; tel. (202) 234-2281; Chargé d'affaires GIRMA AMARE.

Fiji

Embassy: 2233 Wisconsin Ave, NW, Suite 240, Washington, DC 20007; tel. (202) 337-8321; telex 4971930; Chargé d'affaires ABDUL H. YUSUF.

Consulate: 1 United Nations Plaza, 26th Floor, New York, NY 10017; tel. (212) 344-7316; Consul (vacant).

Finland

Embassy: 3216 New Mexico Ave, NW, Washington, DC 20016; tel. (202) 363-2430; telex 248268; Ambassador JUKKA VALTASAARI.

Consulate-General: 1900 Ave of the Stars, Suite 1060, Los Angeles, CA 90067; tel. (213) 203-9903; Consul-Gen. JUSSI MONTONEN.

Consulate-General: Finland House, 540 Madison Ave, New York, NY 10022; tel. (212) 832-6550; Consul-Gen. ANTTI LASSILA.

Consulate: 35 Wacker Dr. East, Suite 1900, Chicago, IL 60601; tel. (312) 346-1150; Consul TIMO A. HAIKONEN.

Consulate: 3000 Post Oak Blvd, Suite 1350, Houston, TX 77056; tel. (713) 627-9700; Consul KIMMO J. SAHRAMAA.

France

Embassy: 4101 Reservoir Rd, NW, Washington, DC 20007; tel. (202) 944-6000; Ambassador EMMANUEL JACQUIN DE MARGERIE.

Consulate-General: 8350 Wilshire Blvd, Los Angeles, CA 90211; tel. (213) 653-3120; Consul-Gen. BERNARD MIYET.

Consulate-General: 540 Bush St, San Francisco, CA 94108; tel. (415) 397-4330; Consul-Gen. PIERRE VIAUX.

Consulate-General: 1 Biscayne Tower, 2 Biscayne Blvd South, Miami, FL 33131; Consul-Gen. THIERRY REYNARD.

Consulate-General: 444 Michigan Ave North, Room 3140, Chicago, IL 60611; tel. (312) 787-5359; Consul-Gen. MAX DE CALBIAC.

Consulate-General: 3305 St Charles Ave, New Orleans, LA 70115; tel. (504) 897-6381; Consul-Gen. PIERRE Y. G. BOILLOT.

Consulate-General: 3 Commonwealth Ave, Boston, MA 02116; Consul-Gen. ALAIN M. BRIOTTET.

Consulate-General: 100 Renaissance Center, Rm 2975, Detroit, MI 48243; tel. (313) 568-0990; Consul-Gen. JEAN BERNIER.

Consulate-General: 934 Fifth Ave, New York, NY 10021; tel. (212) 535-0100; Consul-Gen. ANDRÉ G. GADAUD.

Consulate-General: 2727 Allen Parkway, Houston, TX 77019; tel. (713) 528-2183; Consul-Gen. GÉRARD G. E. DUMONT.

Gabon

Embassy: 2034 20th St, NW, Washington, DC 20009; tel. (202) 797-1000; Ambassador JEAN-ROBERT ODAZGA.

The Gambia

Embassy: 1030 15th St, NW, Suite 720, Washington, DC 20005; tel. (202) 842-1356; Ambassador OUSMAN AHMADOU SALLAH.

German Democratic Republic

Embassy: 1717 Massachusetts Ave, NW, Washington, DC 20036; tel. (202) 232-3134; telex 6491073; Ambassador Dr GERHARD HERDER.

Federal Republic of Germany

Embassy: 4645 Reservoir Rd, NW, Washington, DC 20007-1998; tel. (202) 298-4000; telex 248321; Ambassador Dr JÜRGEN RUHFUS.

Consulate-General: 6222 Wilshire Blvd, Los Angeles, CA 90048; tel. (213) 930-2703; Consul-Gen. KLAUS RUPPRECHT.

Consulate-General: 601 California St, San Francisco, CA 94106; tel. (415) 981-4250; Consul-Gen. WALTER KÖNIG.

Consulate-General: Peachtree Cain Tower, 229 Peachtree St, NE, Suite 1000, Atlanta, GA 30043; tel. (404) 659-4760; Consul-Gen. ALEXANDER VON SCHMELING DIRINGSHOFEN.

Consulate-General: 104 Michigan Ave South, Chicago, IL 60603; tel. (312) 263-0850; Consul-Gen. JOSEF ENZWEILER.

Consulate-General: 535 Boylston St, Boston, MA 02116; tel. (617) 536-4414; Consul-Gen. JÜRGEN G. KALKBRENNER.

Consulate-General: Edison Plaza, 660 Plaza Dr., Suite 2100, Detroit, MI 48226; tel. (313) 962-6526; Consul-Gen. Dr GOETZ VON BOEHMER.

Consulate-General: 460 Park Ave, New York, NY 10022; tel. (212) 308-8700; Consul-Gen. Dr PETER SYMPHER.

Consulate-General: 1330 Post Oak Blvd, Suite 1850, Houston, TX 77056; tel. (713) 627-7770; Consul-Gen. PETER MAIER-OSWALD.

Consulate-General: IBM Bldg, 1200 Fifth Ave, Suite 1617, Seattle, WA 98101; tel. (206) 682-4312; Consul-Gen. Dr EVA LINDMANN.

Consulate: 100 Biscayne Blvd North, Suite 1717, Miami, FL 33132; tel. (305) 358-0290; Consul KARL MOESLEIN.

Consulate: International Trade Mart, 2 Canal St, Rm 2834, New Orleans, LA 70130; tel. (504) 524-0356; Vice-Consul HEINZ L. CAPELLMANN.

Ghana

Embassy: 3512 International Dr., NW, Washington, DC 20008; tel. (202) 686-4520; Ambassador ERIC K. OTOO.

Consulate-General: 19 47th St East, New York, NY 10017; tel. (212) 832-1300; Consul-Gen. JOSEPH J. NWANEAMPEH (acting).

Greece

Embassy: 2221 Massachusetts Ave, NW, Washington, DC 20008; tel. (202) 667-3168; Ambassador GEORGE PAPOULIAS.

Consulate-General: Los Angeles, CA; Consul-Gen. (vacant).

Consulate-General: 2441 Gough St, San Francisco, CA 94123; tel. (415) 775-2102; Consul-Gen. ADAMANTROS VASSILAKIS.

Consulate-General: Tower Pl., 3340 Peachtree Rd, NE, Atlanta, GA 30026; tel. (404) 261-3313; Consul-Gen. (vacant).

Consulate-General: 168 Michigan Ave North, Chicago, IL 60601; tel. (312) 372-5356; Consul-Gen. EMMANUEL WLANDIS.

Consulate-General: 69 79th St East, New York, NY 10021; tel. (212) 988-5500; Consul-Gen. GEORGE ASSIMAKOPOULOS.

Consulate: International Trade Mart Bldg, Rm 2318, New Orleans, LA 70130; tel. (504) 523-1167; Consul GEORGE PAIZIS.

Consulate: Park Sq. Bldg, 31 St James Ave, Boston, MA 02116; tel. (617) 542-3240; Consul CHRISTOS P. PANAGOPOULOS.

Grenada

Embassy: 1701 New Hampshire Ave, NW, Washington, DC 20009; tel. (202) 265-2561; Ambassador ALBERT O. XAVIER.

Consulate-General: 141 44th St East, New York, NY 10017; Consul-Gen. (vacant).

Guatemala

Embassy: 2220 R St, NW, Washington, DC 20008; tel. (202) 745-4952; telex 361499; Ambassador RODOLFO ROHRMOSER.

Consulate-General: 548 Spring St South, Suite 1030, Los Angeles, CA 90014; tel. (213) 489-1891; Consul-Gen. LESLIE MISHAAN-ROSSELL.

Consulate-General: 870 Market St, 10th Floor, San Francisco, CA 94102; tel. (415) 781-0118; Consul-Gen. NORMAN ERIC AVILA WHITEHEAD.

Consulate-General: Coral Gables, 300 Sevilla Ave, Suite 210, Miami, FL 33134; tel. (305) 443-4828; Consul-Gen. MAURICIO EDUARDO CORONADO LARA.

Consulate-General: 333 Michigan Ave North, Suite 701, Chicago, IL 60601; tel. (312) 332-1587; Consul-Gen. ALBERTA ESTELA MENDEZ CONTRERAS.

Consulate-General: International Trade Mart Bldg, 2 Canal St, Suite 1601, New Orleans, LA 70130; tel. (504) 525-0013; Consul-Gen. GUSTAVO A. LÓPEZ.

Consulate-General: 57 Park Ave, New York, NY 10016; tel. (212) 686-3837; Consul-Gen. ANTONIO ARIS DE CASTILLA.

Consulate-General: Westchase Central, 9700 Richmond Ave, Suite 218, Houston, TX 77042; tel. (713) 953-9531; Consul-Gen. MARÍA CRISTINA ALVAREZ.

Guinea

Embassy: 2112 Leroy Pl., NW, Washington, DC 20008; tel. (202) 483-9420; Ambassador KEKOURA CAMARA.

Guinea-Bissau

Embassy: 211 43rd St East, Suite 604, New York, NY 10017; tel. (212) 661-3977; Ambassador ALFREDO LOPES CABRAL.

Guyana

Embassy: 2490 Tracy Pl., NW, Washington, DC 20008; tel. (202) 265-6900; telex 64170; Ambassador Dr CEDRIC HILBURN GRANT.

Consulate-General: 622 3rd Ave, 35th Floor, New York, NY 10017; Consul-Gen. SYDNEY SAUL.

Haiti

Embassy: 2311 Massachusetts Ave, Washington, DC 20008; tel. (202) 332-4090; telex 440202; fax (202) 745-7515; Chargé d'affaires PIERRE-FRANÇOIS BENOÎT.

Consulate-General: 919 Michigan Ave North, Suite 3311, Chicago, IL 60611; tel. (312) 337-1603; Consul-Gen. PIERRE JEAN-FÉLIX.

Consulate-General: 15 Court St, Suite 860, Boston, MA 02108.

Consulate-General: 60 42nd St East, Rm 1365, New York, NY 10017; tel. (212) 697-9767; Hon. Consul-Gen. EDZERD RACINE.

Holy See

Apostolic Nunciature: 3339 Massachusetts Ave, NW, Washington, DC 20008; tel. (202) 333-7121; telex 440117; Apostolic Nuncio Archbishop PIO LAGHI.

Honduras

Embassy: 4301 Connecticut Ave, NW, Suite 100, Washington, DC 20008; tel. (202) 966-7700; telex 197689; Ambassador JORGE HERNÁNDEZ.

Consulate-General: 548 Spring St South, Suite 929, Los Angeles, CA 90013; tel. (213) 623-2301; Hon. Vice-Consul SUSANA MARTÍNEZ DE STEVENSON.

Consulate-General: Flood Bldg, 870 Market St, Rms 451-453, San Francisco, CA 94102; tel. (415) 392-0076; Consul-Gen. EDILBERTO DURON.

Consulate-General: Israel Discount Bank Bldg, 14 First Ave, NE, Suite 406, Miami, FL 33132; tel. (305) 358-3477; Hon. Consul OWEN S. FREED.

Consulate-General: 6011 Kenmore Ave North, Apartment 212, Chicago, IL 60660; tel. (312) 772-7090; Hon. Vice-Consul MAURA ROSA ALCERRO PRUDOT.

Consulate-General: 203 Carondelet St, Suite 707, New Orleans, LA 70130; tel. (504) 522-3118; Consul ROSAMALIA M. PASTOR.

Consulate-General: 18 41st St East, Suite 602, New York, NY 10017; tel. (212) 889-3858; Consul-Gen. NORMA MEIJA-RODEZNO.

Consulate: 1914 Beachway Rd, Suite 3-0, Jacksonville, FL 32207; Consul ANTONIO J. VALLADARES.

Consulate: 8233 Keel Ave, POB 1903, Baton Rouge, LA 70821; Consul (vacant).

Consulate: 33 Copley St, Newton, Boston, MA 02158; Consul GRACIELA MENDIZABAL SUÁREZ.

Consulate: 3620 Shady Lane, Detroit, MI 48216; Consul ALMA ROSA C. V. DE ALONZO.

Consulate: 4151 Southwest Freeway, Suite 700, Houston, TX 77027; tel. (713) 622-4572; Hon. Consul NORMA RIVAS DE ORTEZ.

Hungary

Embassy: 2910 Shoemaker St, NW, Washington, DC 20008; tel. (202) 362-6730; Ambassador Dr VENCEL HAZI.

Consulate-General: 8 75th St East, New York, NY 10021; tel. (212) 879-4127; Consul-Gen. GYORGY BANLAKI.

Iceland

Embassy: 2022 Connecticut Ave, NW, Washington, DC 20008; tel. (202) 265-6653; Ambassador INGVI S. INGVARSSON.

Consulate-General: 370 Lexington Ave, New York, NY 10017; tel. (212) 686-4100; Consul-Gen. HELGI GISLASON.

India

Embassy: 2107 Massachusetts Ave, NW, Washington, DC 20008; tel. (202) 939-7000; Ambassador PRATAP KISHEN KAUL.

Consulate-General: 450 Arguello Blvd, San Francisco, CA 94118; tel. (415) 668-0662; Consul-Gen. KISHAN K. S. RANA.

Consulate-General: 230 Michigan Ave North, Chicago, IL 60601; tel. (312) 781-6280; Consul-Gen. DILIP LAHIRI.

Consulate-General: 3 64th St East, New York, NY 10021; tel. (212) 879-7800; Consul-Gen. PASCAL NAZARETH.

Indonesia

Embassy: 2020 Massachusetts Ave, NW, Washington, DC 20036; tel. (202) 775-5200; Ambassador ABDUL RACHMAN RAMLY.

Consulate-General: 3457 Wilshire Blvd, Los Angeles, CA 90010; Consul-Gen. POERWANTO.

Consulate-General: 5 68th St East, New York, NY 10021; tel. (212) 879-0600; Consul MAKSOEM EFFENDI.

Consulate-General: 1990 Post Oak Blvd, Suite 1900, Houston, TX 77056; Consul-Gen. SOEKADARI HONGGOWONGSO.

Consulate: 1111 Columbus Ave, San Francisco, CA 94133; tel. (415) 474-9571; Consul ALEXANDER KAREL LOLONG.

Consulate: 2 Illinois Center, 233 Michigan Ave North, Suite 1422, Chicago, IL 60601; tel. (312) 938-0101; Consul SANDJOTO PAMUNGKAS.

Iran

'Interests section' in the Embassy of Algeria, 2209 Wisconsin Ave, NW, Washington, DC 20007; tel. (202) 965-4990.

Iraq

Embassy: 1801 P St, NW, Washington, DC 20036; tel. (202) 483-7500; Ambassador ABDUL-AMIR ALI AL-ANBARI.

Ireland

Embassy: 2234 Massachusetts Ave, NW, Washington, DC 20008; tel. (202) 462-3939; telex 64160; Ambassador PADRAIC MACKERNAN.

Consulate-General: 655 Montgomery St, 9th Floor, San Francisco, CA 94111; tel. (415) 392-4214; Consul-Gen. ERIC B. NASON.

Consulate-General: 400 Michigan Ave North, Chicago, IL 60611; tel. (312) 337-1868; Consul-Gen. PETER J. CUNNING.

Consulate-General: 535 Boylston St, Boston, MA 02116; tel. (617) 267-9330; Consul-Gen. PATRICK HENRY CURRAN.

Consulate-General: 515 Madison Ave, New York, NY 10022; tel. (212) 319-2555; Consul-Gen. JIM FLAVIN.

Israel

Embassy: 3514 International Dr., NW, Washington, DC 20008; tel. (202) 364-5500; Ambassador MOSHE ARAD.

Consulate-General: 6380 Wilshire Blvd, Suite 1700, Los Angeles, CA 90048; tel. (213) 651-5700; Consul-Gen. EYTAN BENTSUR.

Consulate-General: 220 Bush St, Suite 550, San Francisco, CA 94104; tel. (415) 398-8885; Consul-Gen. YAACOV SELLA.

Consulate-General: 330 Biscayne Blvd, Suite 510, Miami, FL 33132; tel. (305) 358-8111; Consul DAVID COHEN.

Consulate-General: 111 Wacker Dr. East, Chicago, IL 60601; tel. (312) 565-3300; Consul-Gen. ZVI BROSH.

Consulate-General: 1020 Statler Office Bldg, Boston, MA 02116; tel. (617) 542-0041; Consul-Gen. ARTHUR AVNON.

Consulate-General: 800 Second Ave, New York, NY 10017; tel. (212) 697-5500; Consul-Gen. MOSHE YEGAR.

Consulate-General: 225 15th St South, Philadelphia, PA 19102; tel. (215) 546-5556; Consul-Gen. DAVID BEN-DOV.

Consulate-General: 1 Greenway Plaza East, Suite 722, Houston, TX 77046; tel. (713) 627-3780; Consul-Gen. YORAM EYTNA-ETTINGER.

Italy

Embassy: 1601 Fuller St, NW, Washington, DC 20009; tel. (202) 328-6500; telex 64461; fax (202) 462-3605; Ambassador: RINALDO PETRIGNANI.

Consulate-General: 12400 Wilshire Blvd, Suite 300, Los Angeles, CA 90025; tel. (213) 826-5998; Consul-Gen. ALBERTO BONIVER.

Consulate-General: 2590 Webster St, San Francisco, CA 94115; tel. (415) 931-4924; Consul-Gen. ROBERTO ROSSI.

Consulate-General: 500 Michigan Ave North, Chicago, IL 60601; tel. (312) 467-1550; Consul-Gen. LEONARDO BARONCELLI.

Consulate-General: Cotton Exchange Bldg, 231 Carondelet St, Rm 708, New Orleans, LA 70130; Consul-Gen. PAOLO MALFATTI.

Consulate-General: 100 Boylston St, Suite 900, Boston, MA 02116; tel. (617) 542-0483; Consul-Gen. RANIERI FORNARI.

Consulate-General: 690 Park Ave, New York, NY 10021; tel. (212) 737-9100; Consul-Gen. FRANCESCO CORRIAS.

Consulate-General: 421 Chestnut St, Philadelphia, PA 19106; tel. (215) 592-7369; Consul-Gen. LUCA DEL BALZO DE PRESENZANO.

Consulate-General: Allied Bank Towers, 1300 Post Oak Blvd, Houston, TX 77056; Consul-Gen. LUCA BROFFERIO.

Jamaica

Embassy: 1850 K St, NW, Washington, DC 20006; tel. (202) 452-0660; Ambassador KEITH JOHNSON.

Consulate-General: Ingraham Bldg, 25 Second Ave, SE, Rm 842, Miami, FL 33131; tel. (305) 374-8431; Consul-Gen. MARIE ROSE CROOKS WRAY.

Consulate-General: 866 Second Ave, Suite 355, New York, NY 10017; tel. (212) 935-9000; Consul-Gen. LORRELL SYLVESTER BRUCE.

Japan

Embassy: 2520 Massachusetts Ave, NW, Washington, DC 20008; tel. (202) 939-6700; Ambassador: NOBUO MATSUNAGA.

Consulate-General: 909 Ninth Ave West, Suite 301, Anchorage, AK 99501; tel. (907) 279-8428; Consul-Gen. SIJI ARIMATSU.

Consulate-General: 250 First St East, Suite 1507, Los Angeles, CA 90012; tel. (213) 624-8305; Consul-Gen. TAIZO WATANABE.

Consulate-General: 400 Colony Sq. Bldg, 1201 Peachtree St, NE, Suite 1501, Atlanta, GA 30361; tel. (404) 892-2700; Consul-Gen. TADAYUKI NONOYAMA.

Consulate-General: 737 Michigan Ave North, Chicago, IL 60611; tel. (312) 280-0400; Consul-Gen. YOSHIO KARITA.

Consulate-General: International Trade Mart Bldg, 2 Canal St, Rm 1830, New Orleans, LA 70130; tel. (504) 529-2101; Consul-Gen. TAKASHI MIYAZAKI.

Consulate-General: Federal Reserve Plaza, 600 Atlantic Ave, 14th Floor, Boston, MA 02210; tel. (617) 973-9772; Consul-Gen. MINORU TAMBA.

Consulate-General: Commerce Tower, 911 Main St, Rm 2519, Kansas City, MO 64195; tel. (816) 471-0111; Consul-Gen. HIDEO NUMOTO.

Consulate-General: 2400 First Interstate Tower, 1300 Fifth Ave, SW, Portland, OR 97201; tel. (503) 221-1811; Consul-Gen. SHOSAKU TANAKA.

Consulate-General: 1000 Louisiana St, Allied Bank Plaza, Suite 5420, Houston, TX 77002; tel. (713) 652-2977; Consul-Gen. SHIGEMI ANDO.

Consulate-General: Rainier Bank Tower, 1301 Fifth Ave, Rm 3110, Seattle, WA 98101; tel. (206) 682-9107; Consul HIROSHI UGAI.

Jordan

Embassy: 3504 International Dr., NW, Washington, DC 20008; tel. (202) 966-2664; telex 64113; Ambassador HUSSEIN HAMMAMI.

Kenya

Embassy: 2249 R St, NW, Washington, DC 20008; tel. (202) 387-6101; Ambassador DENIS D. AFANDE.

Consulate-General: 9100 Wilshire Blvd, Los Angeles, CA 90212; tel. (213) 274-6635; Consul-Gen. JOSEPH O. ADUO.

Consulate-General: 424 Madison Ave, New York, NY 10017; tel. (212) 468-1300; Consul-Gen. SAMUEL C. OKUNGU.

Republic of Korea

Embassy: 2320 Massachusetts Ave, NW, Washington, DC 20008; tel. (202) 939-5600; Ambassador TONG-JIN PARK.

Consulate-General: 101 Benson Blvd, Suite 304, Anchorage, AK 99503; tel. (907) 561-5488; Consul-Gen. SUK-HONG KANG.

Consulate-General: 5455 Wilshire Blvd, Suite 1101, Los Angeles, CA 90036; tel. (213) 931-1331; Consul-Gen. KI SOO KIM.

Consulate-General: 3500 Clay St, San Francisco, CA 94118; tel. (415) 921-2251; Consul-Gen. HIKANG HYUN.

Consulate-General: Peachtree Cain Tower, 229 Peachtree St, NE, Suite 500, Atlanta, GA 30303; tel. (404) 522-1611; Consul-Gen. YUN PARK.

Consulate-General: 500 Michigan Ave North, Suite 610, Chicago, IL 60611; tel. (312) 822-9485; Consul-Gen. SEUNG KON LEE.

Consulate-General: 460 Park Ave, New York, NY 10022; tel. (212) 752-1700; Consul-Gen. RO MYUNG GONG.

Consulate-General: 3 Post Oak Central Bldg, 1990 Post Oak Blvd, Suite 745, Houston, TX 77056; tel. (713) 961-0186; Consul-Gen. NOH-SOO PARK.

Consulate-General: United Airlines Bldg, 2033 Sixth Ave, Suite 1125, Seattle, WA 98121; Consul-Gen. SAE HOON AHN.

Kuwait

Embassy: 2940 Tilden St, NW, Washington, DC 20008; tel. (202) 966-0702; Ambassador Shaikh SAUD NASIR AL-SABAH.

Laos

Embassy: 2222 S St, NW, Washington, DC 20008; tel. (202) 332-6416; telex 904061; Chargé d'affaires DONE SOMVORACHIT.

Lebanon

Embassy: 2560 28th St, NW, Washington, DC 20008; tel. (202) 939-6300; Ambassador Dr ABDALLAH BOUHABIB.

Consulate-General: 7060 Hollywood Blvd, Suite 510, Los Angeles, CA 90028; tel. (213) 462-5284; Consul-Gen. MICHELINE ABI-SAMRA.

Consulate-General: 2211 East Jefferson St, Suite 645, Detroit, MI 48207; tel. (313) 567-0233; Consul-Gen. FAWZI FAWAZ.

Consulate-General: 9 76th St East, New York, NY 10021; tel. (212) 744-7905; Consul-Gen. VICTOR BITAR.

Lesotho

Embassy: 2511 Massachusetts Ave, NW, Washington, DC 20008; tel. (202) 797-5534; Ambassador WILLIAM T. VAN TONDER.

Liberia

Embassy: 5201 16th St, NW, Washington, DC 20011; tel. (202) 723-0437; Ambassador EUGENIA WORDSWORTH-STEVENSON.

Consulate-General: 820 Second Ave, New York, NY 10017; tel. (212) 687-1025; Consul-Gen. S. KANNAH BOONS.

Libya

'Interests section' in the Embassy of the United Arab Emirates, 600 New Hampshire Ave, NW, Suite 740, Washington, DC 20037; tel. (202) 338-6500.

Luxembourg

Embassy: 2200 Massachusetts Ave, NW, Washington, DC 20008; tel. (202) 265-4171; telex 64130; Ambassador ANDRÉ PHILIPPE.

Consulate-General: Citicorp Center, 1 Sansome St, Suite 830, San Francisco, CA 94104; tel. (415) 788-0816; telex 172500; Consul-Gen. JEAN J. FALTZ.

Consulate-General: 801 Second Ave, New York, NY 10017; tel. (212) 370-9850; Consul NICHOLAS V. DIDIER.

Madagascar

Embassy: 2374 Massachusetts Ave, NW, Washington, DC 20008; tel. (202) 265-5525; Ambassador LEON MAXIME RAJAOBELINA.

Consul-General: 801 Second Ave, Rm 404, New York, NY 10017; tel. (212) 986-9491; Consul-Gen. BLAISE JOSEPH ALBERT RABETFIKA.

Malawi

Embassy: 2408 Massachusetts Ave, NW, Washington, DC 20008; tel. (202) 797-1007; Ambassador ROBERT B. MBAYA.

Malaysia

Embassy: 2401 Massachusetts Ave, NW, Washington, DC 20008; tel. (202) 328-2700; telex 440119; Ambassador ALBERT S. TALALLA.

Consulate-General: World Trade Center, 350 Figueroa St South, Suite 400, Los Angeles, CA 90071; tel. (213) 621-2991; Consul-Gen. AZINAL AZMAN.

Consulate-General: 140 45th St East, 43rd Floor, New York, NY 10017; tel. (212) 490-2722; Consul-Gen. SALLEHUDDIN ABDULLAH.

Mali

Embassy: 2130 R St, NW, Washington, DC 20008; tel. (202) 332-2249; Ambassador NOUHOUN SAMASSEKOU.

Malta

Embassy: 2017 Connecticut Ave, NW, Washington, DC 20008; tel. (202) 462-3611; Ambassador SALV J. STELLINI.

Consulate-General: 249 35th St East, New York, NY 10016; tel. (212) 725-2345; Consul-Gen. MARIO J. DUGO.

Mauritania

Embassy: 2129 Leroy Pl., NW, Washington, DC 20008; tel. (202) 232-5700; Ambassador ABDELLAH OULD DADDAH.

Mauritius

Embassy: 4301 Connecticut Ave, NW, Suite 134, Washington, DC 20008; tel. (202) 244-1491; telex 64362; Ambassador CHITMANSING JESSERAMSING.

Mexico

Embassy: 2829 16th St, NW, Washington, DC 20009; tel. (202) 234-6000; telex 248459; Ambassador GUSTAVO PETRICIOLI.

Consulate-General: 125 Paseo de la Plaza, Los Angeles, CA 90012; tel. (213) 624-3261; Consul-Gen. AGUSTÍN SANTAOLALLA GARCÍA-LÓPEZ.

Consulate-General: 110 A St West, 1333 Front St, San Diego, CA 92101; tel. (619) 231-8414; Consul-Gen. JAVIER ESCOBAR Y CORDOVA.

Consulate-General: 870 Market St, Suite 528, San Francisco, CA 94102; tel. (415) 392-5554; Consul SANDRA CALDRON BARRAZA.

Consulate-General: 707 Washington St, Suite A, Denver, CO 80203; tel. (303) 830-0523; Consul-Gen. ALBERTO SÁNCHEZ-LUNA.

Consulate-General: 300 Michigan Ave North, Suite 200, Chicago, IL 60601; tel. (312) 670-0240; Consul-Gen. MARTÍN BRITO HERNANDEZ.

Consulate-General: World Trade Center Bldg, 2 Canal St, Rm 1140, New Orleans, LA 70130; tel. (504) 522-3596; Consul-Gen. OSCAR RAÚL ARAIZA LÓPEZ.

Consulate-General: 8 41st St East, New York, NY 10017; tel. (212) 689-0456; Consul-Gen. JOAQUÍN BERNAL.

Consulate-General: 1349 Empire Central, Suite 100, Dallas, TX 75247; tel. (214) 522-9740; Consul-Gen. OLIVER ALBERT FARRES MARTINS.

Consulate-General: 810 San Antonio St East, El Paso, TX 79901; tel. (915) 533-3644; Consul-Gen. ENRIQUE BUJ FLORES.

Consulate-General: 127 Navarro St, San Antonio, TX 78205; Consul HECTOR MENDOZA Y CAAMANO.

Consulate: 855 Cochise Ave, Douglas, AZ 85607; tel. (602) 364-2275; Consul JUAN VÍCTOR MANUEL TORRES PÉREZ.

Consulate: 137 Terrace Ave, Suite 150, Nogales, AZ 85621; tel. (602) 287-2521; Consul JOSÉ ANTONIO RIVERA CORTES.

Consulate: 700 Jefferson St East, 1st Floor, Phoenix, AZ 85035; tel. (602) 242-7398; Consul RAÚL LOPEZLIRA-CASTRO.

Consulate: 331–333 Second St West, Calexico, CA 92231; tel. (819) 357-3863; Consul FERNANDO GONZÁLEZ SANTOYO.

Consulate: 2839 Mariposa St, Fresno, CA 93721; tel. (309) 233-9770; Consul CARLOS TIRADO-OLVERA.

Consulate: 1508 South St, Sacramento, CA 95816; tel. (916) 446-4696; Consul FERNANDEZ-ZAPATA.

Consulate: 588 Sixth St West, San Bernardino, CA 92401; tel. (714) 889-9836; Consul EMERENIANO RODRÍGUEZ JOBRAIL.

Consulate: 360 First St North, Suite 102, San Jose, CA 95113; tel. (408) 294-3414; Consul ALBERTO BECERRA-SIERRA.

Consulate: 2153 Coral Way, Suite 604, Miami, FL 33129; tel. (305) 858-2931; Consul FERNANDO SÁNCHEZ MAYANS.

Consulate: Omni International Bldg South, 190 Marietta St, NW, Rm 410, Atlanta, GA 30303; tel. (404) 688-3258; Consul LUISA VIRGINIA JUNCO TASSINARI.

Consulate: Statler Bldg, 20 Park Plaza, Boston, MA 02116; tel. (617) 426-4942; Consul ALBERTO LUCIO CAMPILLO-SAENZ.

Consulate: Book Bldg, Washington Blvd, Rm 1515, Detroit, MI 48226; tel. (313) 965-1868; Consul ROBERTO JOSÉ GONZÁLEZ GUTIERREZ.

Consulate: 386 Wabasha St North, Suite 390, St Paul, MN 55102; tel. (612) 228-1114; Consul DIANA A. MUÑOZ RIOS.

Consulate: 306 12th St East, Suite 822, Kansas City, MO 64106; tel. (816) 421-5956; Consul GABRIEL E. GÓMEZ RADILLA.

Consulate: 1015 Locust St, Suite 922, St Louis, MO 63101; tel. (314) 436-3233; Consul JOSÉ AGUIRRE NORIEGA.

Consulate: Western Bank Bldg, 505 Marquette Ave, NW, Rm 1710, Albuquerque, NM 87102; tel. (505) 247-2139; Consul ASTRID GALINDO SARDOZ.

Consulate: Philadelphia Bourse Bldg, 21 5th St South, Rm 575, Philadelphia, PA 19106; tel. (215) 922-4262; Consul JOSÉ-LUIS ENCISO-RODRÍGUEZ.

Consulate: 510 Congress St South, Suite 201, Austin, TX 78704; tel. (512) 478-2866; Consul VÍCTOR MANUEL ROMERO LOPETEQUI.

Consulate: Elizabeth and Seventh St East, POB 711, Brownsville, TX 78520; tel. (512) 542-4431; Consul FERNANDO LEMUS GAS.

Consulate: Guaranty Bank Plaza Bldg, Suite 160, Corpus Christi, TX 78475; tel. (512) 882-3375; Consul HECTOR RANGEL-OBREGÓN.

Consulate: 1010 Main St South, Del Rio, TX 78840; tel. (512) 775-2352; Consul RUBEN GARCÍA DE LEÓN.

Consulate: 140 Adams St, Eagle Pass, TX 78852; tel. (512) 773-9255; Consul ENRIQUE VÁZQUEZ VÁZQUEZ.

Consulate: 1612 Farragut St, Laredo, TX 78040; tel. (512) 723-6360; Consul JESÚS PRECIADO GARCÍA.

Consulate: 1220 Broadway Ave, Lubbock, TX 79401; tel. (806) 765-8816; Consul (vacant).

Consulate: 1418 Beach St, Suite 104, McAllen, TX 78501; tel. (512) 686-0243; Consul ERNESTINA FERNÁNDEZ PICAZO.

Consulate: 730 O'Reilly St, POB 938, Presidio, TX 79845; tel. (915) 229-3745; Consul JOSÉ ANTONIO ARIAS SIERRA.

Consulate: 182 South 600 St East, Suite 202, Salt Lake City, UT 84102; tel. (801) 521-8502; Consul FRANCISCO JAVIER OLAVARRIA PATINO.

Consulate: Joshua Green Bldg, 1425 Fourth Ave, Suite 612, Seattle, WA 98101; Consul HECTOR BLANCO-MELO.

Morocco

Embassy: 1601 21st St, NW, Washington, DC 20009; tel. (202) 462-7979; telex 248378; Ambassador MOHAMMED BRITEL.

Consulate-General: 437 Fifth Ave, New York, NY 10016; tel. (212) 758-2625; Consul-Gen. ABDESLAM JAIDI.

Mozambique

Embassy: 1990 M St, NW, Suite 570, Washington, DC 20036; tel. (202) 293-7147; telex 248530; Ambassador VALERIANO FERRÃO.

Myanmar

Embassy: 2300 South St, NW, Washington, DC 20008; tel. (202) 332-9044; Ambassador U MYO AUNG.

Consulate-General: 10 77th St East, New York, NY 10021; tel. (212) 535-1310; Consul-Gen. U TIN PE.

Nepal

Embassy: 2131 Leroy Pl., NW, Washington, DC 20008; tel. (202) 667-4550; telex 440085; Ambassador MOHAN MAN SAINJU.

Consulate-General: 820 Second Ave, Suite 1200, New York, NY 10017; tel. (212) 370-4188; Consul-Gen. KESHAV RAJ JHA.

Netherlands

Embassy: 4200 Linnean Ave, NW, Washington, DC 20008; tel. (202) 244-5300; Ambassador RICHARD H. FEIN.

Consulate-General: 3460 Wilshire Blvd, Central Plaza, Suite 509, Los Angeles, CA 90010; tel. (213) 380-3440; Consul-Gen. PAUL LAGENDIJK.

Consulate-General: International Bldg, 601 California St, Rm 1106, San Francisco, CA 94108; tel. (415) 981-6454; Consul-Gen. DIGNUS H. VISSCHER.

Consulate-General: 303 Wacker Dr. East, Suite 410, Chicago, IL 60601; tel. (312) 856-0110; Consul-Gen. JOHAN WILLEM SEMEIJNS DE VRIES VAN DOESBURGH.

Consulate-General: 1 Rockefeller Plaza, 11th Floor, New York, NY 10020; tel. (212) 246-1429; Consul-Gen. ADRIEN FLORIS TIELEMAN.

Consulate-General: Post Oak Bldg, 2200 Post Oak Blvd, Suite 610, Houston, TX 77056; tel. (713) 622-8000; Consul-Gen. FRANCISCUS W. J. M. BROUWERS.

New Zealand

Embassy: 37 Observatory Circle, NW, Washington, DC 20008; tel. (202) 328-4800; Ambassador TIMOTHY FRANCIS.

Consulate-General: Tishman Bldg, 10960 Wilshire Blvd, Suite 1530, Los Angeles, CA 90024; tel. (213) 477-8241; Consul-Gen. PETER G. HEENAN.

Consulate-General: 630 Fifth Ave, Suite 530, New York, NY 10111; tel. (212) 586-0060; Consul-Gen. WINSTON A. COCHRANE.

Nicaragua

Embassy: 1627 New Hampshire Ave, NW, Washington, DC 20009; tel. (202) 387-4371; Chargé d'affaires LEONOR DE HUPER.

Niger

Embassy: 2204 R St, NW, Washington, DC 20008; tel. (202) 483-4224; Ambassador MOUMOUNI ADAMOU DJERMAKOYE.

Nigeria

Embassy: 2201 M St, NW, Washington, DC 20037; tel. (202) 822-1500; Ambassador HAMZAT AHMADU.

Consulate-General: 369–371 Hayes St, San Francisco, CA 94102; tel. (415) 552-0334; Consul-Gen. PIUS IKPEFUAN AYEWOH.

Consulate-General: 225 Peachtree St, NE, Suite 1000, Atlanta, GA 30303; tel. (404) 577-4800; Consul-Gen. ALHAJI MOHAMMAD LAMINO ABUBAKAR.

Consulate-General: 575 Lexington Ave, New York, NY 10022; tel. (212) 715-7200; Consul-Gen. BAMIDELE OLAYEMI AWOKOYA.

Norway

Embassy: 2720 34th St, NW, Washington, DC 20008; tel. (202) 333-6000; telex 892374; Ambassador KJELL ELIASSEN.

Consulate-General: 350 Figueroa St South, Los Angeles, CA 90071; tel. (213) 626-0338; Consul-Gen. PER A. TOLLEFSEN.

Consulate-General: 2 Embarcadero Center, Suites 2930–2935, San Francisco, CA 94111; tel. (415) 986-0766; Consul-Gen. PER H. BORGEN.

Consulate-General: 360 Michigan Ave North, Chicago, IL 60601; tel. (312) 782-7750; Consul-Gen. BJARNE ERLING SOLHEIM.

Consulate-General: 229 Foshay Tower, Minneapolis, MN 55402; tel. (612) 332-3338; Consul-Gen. HARALD LONE.

Consulate-General: 825 Third Ave, 17th Floor, New York, NY 10022; tel. (212) 421-7333; Consul-Gen. BJARNE GRINDEM.

Consulate-General: 2777 Allen Parkway, Houston, TX 77019; tel. (713) 521-2900; Consul-Gen. ARNE B. HONNINGSTAD.

Consulate: 1001 North America Way, Miami, FL 33132; tel. (305) 358-4386; Consul KJELL HALFDAN SANDBERG.

Consulate: 2 Canal St, New Orleans, LA 70130; tel. (504) 522-3526; Hon. Consul ERIK F. JOHNSEN.

Oman

Embassy: 2342 Massachusetts Ave, NW, Washington, DC 20008; tel. (202) 387-1980; telex 440267; Ambassador AWADH BIN BADER BIN MARIE AL-SHANFARI.

Pakistan

Embassy: 2315 Massachusetts Ave, NW, Washington, DC 20008; tel. (202) 939-6200; Ambassador ZULFIQAR ALI KHAN.

Consulate-General: 12 65th St East, New York, NY 10021; tel. (212) 879-5800; Consul-Gen. S. HADI RAZA ALI.

Panama

Embassy: 2862 McGill Terrace, NW, Washington, DC 20008; tel. (202) 483-1407; telex 64371; Ambassador JUAN B. SOSA.

Consulate-General: 548 Spring St South, Suite 1040, Los Angeles, CA 90013; tel. (213) 627-9139; Consul-Gen. SANTIAGO TORRIJOS LÓPEZ.

Consulate-General: 870 Market St, Rm 546, San Francisco, CA 94102; tel. (415) 989-0934; Consul-Gen. AIDA TORRIJOS HERRERA.

Consulate-General: Pan American Bank Bldg, 150 3rd Ave, SE, Suite 501, Miami, FL 33131; tel. (305) 379-7280; Consul-Gen. JOAQUÍN MEZA ICAZA.

Consulate-General: 201 Kennedy Blvd East, Tampa, FL 33602; Vice-Consul RUTH C. PERE.

Consulate-General: 1150 State St North, Suite 320, Chicago, IL 60610; tel. (312) 944-5759; Consul-Gen. JUDITH FLOREZ CAMPODONICO.

Consulate-General: International Trade Mart, Rm 1324, New Orleans, LA 70130; tel. (504) 525-3458; Consul-Gen. RAQUEL JUDITH TAPIERO LADRÓN DE GUEVARA.

Consulate-General: The Lafayette Town House, 638 Congress St, Portland, ME 04101; tel. (207) 773-6641; Consul-Gen. (vacant).

Consulate-General: St Paul St, Apartment 9M, Baltimore, MD 21202; tel. (301) 528-0813; Consul-Gen. (vacant).

Consulate-General: 451 Beacon St, Boston, MA 02401; Consul-Gen. JORGE A. CARRIZO ESQUIVEL.

Consul-General: 1270 Ave of the Americas, Suite 408, New York, NY 10020; tel. (212) 246-3771; Consul-Gen. VALDES CHARRIS.

Consulate-General: 2019 Rittenhouse Sq., Philadelphia, PA 19103; tel. (215) 568-0767; Consul LUZ MARIA QUIJANO DE MURRAY.

Consulate-General: 6406 Brooklake, Dallas, TX 75248; tel. (214) 960-0004; Consul-Gen. LYDA ICAZA DE AROSEMENA.

Consulate-General: 9315 Meadowcroft Dr., Houston, TX 77067; tel. (713) 521-9701; Consul-Gen. JULIA A. MAHER.

Consulate: 231 17th St, Apartment 1620, Fort Lauderdale, FL 33160; tel. (305) 931-7587; Consul (vacant).

Consulate: 5573 Semoran Blvd North, Suite 2101, Winter Park, Orlando, FL 32792; Consul (vacant).

Consulate: 126 Blue Gate Circle, Dayton, OH 45429; tel. (513) 294-6247; Consul (vacant).

Consulate: 144 Summer Ave, Pittsburgh, PA 15221; tel. (412) 271-4002; Consul (vacant).

Papua New Guinea

Embassy: 1330 Connecticut Ave, NW, Suite 350, Washington, DC 20036; tel. (202) 659-0856; Ambassador RENAGI LOHIA.

Paraguay

Embassy: 2400 Massachusetts Ave, NW, Washington, DC 20008; tel. (202) 483-6960; Ambassador MARCOS MARTÍNEZ MENDIETA.

Consulate-General: 611 Gravier St, Suite 903, New Orleans, LA 70130; Consul-Gen. LUIS A. GRENNO.

Consulate-General: 1 World Trade Center, Suite 1609, New York, NY 10048; Consul-Gen. FELIX AGUERO.

Peru

Embassy: 1700 Massachusetts Ave, NW, Washington, DC 20036; tel. (202) 833-9860; telex 197675; Ambassador CÉSAR ATALA NAZZAL.

Consulate-General: 1212 Wilshire Blvd, Rm 202, Los Angeles, CA 90017; tel. (213) 975-1152; Consul-Gen. CARLOS GAMARRA.

Consulate-General: 870 Market St, Suite 482, San Francisco, CA 94102; tel. (415) 362-7136; Consul-Gen. HUMBERTO URTEAGA.

Consulate-General: 2490 Coral Way, Suites 201–202, Miami, FL 33145; tel. (305) 856-1355; Consul-Gen. DOMINGO J. NIETO.

Consulate-General: 8 Michigan Ave South, Suites 2003–2005, Chicago, IL 60603; tel. (312) 782-1599; Consul-Gen. MARIANO GARCIA-GODOS.

Consulate-General: Broadway Bank Bldg, 100 Hamilton Pl., 12th Floor, Paterson, NJ 07505; Consul-Gen. (vacant).

Consulate-General: 805 Third Ave, 14th Floor, New York, NY 10022; tel. (212) 644-2850; Consul-Gen. RAÚL PINTO ALVAREZ.

Consulate-General: 5847 San Felipe Ave, Suite 1481, Houston, TX 77057; tel. (713) 781-5000; Consul-Gen. ADOLFO PAREDES.

Philippines

Embassy: 1617 Massachusetts Ave, NW, Washington, DC 20036-2274; tel. (202) 483-1414; telex 440059; Ambassador EMMANUEL PELAEZ.

Consulate-General: 3460 Wilshire Blvd, Suite 1200, Los Angeles, CA 90010; tel. (213) 387-5321; Consul-Gen. LEOVIGILDO A. ANOLIN.

Consulate-General: Philippine Center Bldg, 447 Sutter St, 6th Floor, San Francisco, CA 94108; tel. (415) 433-6666; Consul-Gen. SHULAN O. PRIMAVERA.

Consulate-General: 2433 Pali Highway, Honolulu, HI 96817; tel. (808) 595-6316; Consulate-Gen. TOMÁS GÓMEZ, III.

Consulate-General: 30 Michigan Ave North, Suite 210, Chicago, IL 60602; tel. (312) 332-6458; Consul-Gen. ELEUTERIO E. ESPINAS.

Consulate-General: Philippine Center, 556 Fifth Ave, New York, NY 10036; tel. (212) 764-1330; Consul-Gen. FRANCISCO RODRIGO, Jr.

Consulate-General: American Gen. Tower Bldg, 8th Floor, 2727 Allen Parkway, Houston, TX 77019; tel. (713) 524-0234; Consul-Gen. MARIANO C. LANDICHO.

Consulate-General: Central Bldg, 810 Third Ave, Suites 422–430, Seattle, WA 98104; tel. (206) 624-7703; Consul-Gen. JAIME S. BAUTISTA.

Poland

Embassy: 2640 16th St, NW, Washington, DC 20009; tel. (202) 234-3800; Ambassador JAN KINAST.

Consulate-General: 1530 Lakeshore Dr. North, Chicago, IL 60610; tel. (312) 337-8166; Consul-Gen. JAN RABS.

Consulate-General: 233 Madison Ave, New York, NY 10016; tel. (212) 889-8360; Consul-Gen. ANDRZEJ OLSZOWKA.

Portugal

Embassy: 2125 Kalorama Rd, NW, Washington, DC 20008; tel. (202) 328-8610; Ambassador JOÃO PEREIRA BASTOS.

Consulate-General: 3298 Washington St, San Francisco, CA 94115; tel. (415) 346-3400; Consul-Gen. GABRIEL MESQUITA DE BRITO.

Consulate-General: 899 Boylston St, Boston, MA 02115; tel. (617) 536-8740; Consul-Gen. FERNANDO DE CASTEO BRANDNÃO.

Consulate-General: 630 Fifth Ave, Suite 655, New York, NY 10020; tel. (212) 246-4580; Vice-Consul LUIS HENRIQUE SILVA DE CARVALHO.

Consulate: 1801 Ave of the Stars, Suite 400, Los Angeles, CA 90067; tel. (213) 277-1491; Vice-Consul EDMUNDO AURELIO REBELO DE MACEDO.

Consulate: 628 Pleasant St, Rm 201, New Bedford, MA 02740; tel. (617) 997-6151; Consul MANUEL PRACANA MARTINS.

Consulate: 1180 Raymond Blvd, Suite 222, Newark, NJ 07102; tel. (201) 622-7300; Vice-Consul JORGE DE SA ARAUJO DE CARDIELLOS.

Consulate: 56 Pine St, Sixth Floor, Providence, RI 02903; tel. (401) 272-2003; Consul MANUEL ROCHA FONTES.

Qatar

Embassy: 600 New Hampshire Ave, NW, Suite 1180, Washington, DC 20037; tel. (202) 338-0111; Ambassador AHMED ABDULLA ZAID AL-MAHMOUD.

Romania

Embassy: 1607 23rd St, NW, Washington, DC 20008; tel. (202) 232-4747; Ambassador ION STOICHICI.

Rwanda

Embassy: 1714 New Hampshire Ave, NW, Washington, DC 20009; tel. (202) 232-2882; Ambassador ALOYS UWIMANA.

Saint Christopher and Nevis

Embassy: 2501 M St, NW, Suite 540, Washington, DC 20037; tel. (202) 833-3550; telex 6387679; Chargé d'affaires ERSTEIN M. EDWARDS.

Saint Lucia

Embassy: 2100 M St, NW, Suite 540, Washington, DC 20037; tel. (202) 342-3800; Ambassador Dr JOSEPH EDSEL EDMUNDS.

Consulate-General: 41 42nd St East, Suite 315, New York, NY 10017; tel. (212) 697-9360; Vice-Consul GERMAINE PATRICIA LOUIS.

São Tomé and Príncipe

Embassy: 801 Second Ave, Suite 1504, New York, NY 10017; tel. (212) 697-4211; Ambassador JOAQUIM RAFAEL BRANCO.

Saudi Arabia

Embassy: 601 New Hampshire Ave, NW, Washington, DC 20037; tel. (202) 342-3800; telex 440132; Ambassador Prince BANDAR BIN SULTAN.

Consulate-General: 10900 Wilshire Blvd, Suite 830, Los Angeles, CA 90024; tel. (213) 208-6566; Consul-Gen. ABDUL HAMEED AL-GAREE.

Consulate-General: 866 United Nations Plaza, Suite 480, New York, NY 10017; tel. (212) 752-2740; Consul-Gen. SAAD O. NAZER.

Consulate-General: 5718 Westheimer Rd, Suite 1500, Houston, TX 77057; tel. (713) 785-5577; Consul-Gen. FAWAZ ABDULLAH KAYAL.

Senegal

Embassy: 2112 Wyoming Ave, NW, Washington, DC 20008; tel. (202) 234-0504; Ambassador IBRA DEGUENE KA.

Seychelles

Embassy: 820 Second Ave, Suite 203, New York, NY 10017; tel. (212) 687-9766; telex 220032; Chargé d'affaires MARC R. MARENGO.

Sierra Leone

Embassy: 1701 19th St, NW, Washington, DC 20009; tel. (202) 939-9265; Ambassador GEORGE CAREW.

Singapore

Embassy: 1824 R St, NW, Washington, DC 20009; tel. (202) 667-7555; Ambassador TOMMY T. B. KOH.

Somalia

Embassy: 600 New Hampshire Ave, NW, Suite 710, Washington, DC 20037; tel. (202) 342-1575; Ambassador ABDULLAHI AHMED ADDOU.

Consulate-General: 747 Third Ave, 22nd Floor, New York, NY 10017; tel. (212) 687-9877; Consul-Gen. (vacant).

South Africa

Embassy: 3051 Massachusetts Ave, NW, Washington, DC 20008; tel. (202) 232-4400; telex 248364; Ambassador Dr PIETER G. J. KOORNHOF.

Consulate-General: 9107 Wilshire Blvd, Suite 400, Los Angeles, CA 90120; tel. (213) 858-0380; Consul-Gen. LESLIE B. LABU-SCHAGNE.

Consulate-General: 5215 Old Orchard Road, Skokie, IL 60077; tel. (312) 828-9200; Consul-Gen. WILHELM P. N. LOTZ.

Consulate-General: 326 48th St East, New York, NY 10017; tel. (212) 838-1700; Consul-Gen. THOMAS F. WHEELER.

Consulate-General: 1980 Post Oak Blvd, Suite 1520, Houston, TX 77056; tel. (713) 850-0150; Consul-Gen. PAUL KRUGER COETZEE.

Spain

Embassy: 2700 15th St, NW, Washington, DC 20009; tel. (202) 265-0190; telex 64125; Ambassador JULIÁN SANTAMARÍA.

Consulate-General: 6300 Wilshire Blvd, Suite 1431, Los Angeles, CA 90048; tel. (213) 658-6050; Consul-Gen. PEDRO TEMBOURY.

Consulate-General: 2080 Jefferson St, San Francisco, CA 94123; tel. (415) 922-2995; Consul-Gen. DOMINGO SÁNCHEZ.

Consulate-General: 151 Sevilla Ave, 2nd Floor, Coral Gables, Miami, FL 33134; tel. (305) 446-5511; Consul-Gen. CARLOS MANUEL FERNÁNDEZ-SHAW.

Consulate-General: 180 Michigan Ave North, Suite 1905, Chicago, IL 60601; tel. (312) 782-4588; Consul-Gen. FERNANDO J. BELLOSO.

Consulate-General: World Trade Center, 2 Canal St, Rm 2102, New Orleans, LA 70130; tel. (504) 525-4951; Consul-Gen. JOAQUÍN CERVINO.

Consulate-General: 545 Boylston St, Suite 803, Boston, MA 02116; tel. (617) 536-2506; Consul-Gen. JUAN LUIS MAESTRO DE LEON BOLETTI.

Consulate-General: 150 58th St East, 16th Floor, New York, NY 10155; tel. (213) 355-4080; Consul-Gen. MANUEL SASSOT.

Consulate-General: 2411 Fountain View Dr., Suite 130, Houston, TX 77057; tel. (713) 783-6200; Consul-Gen. JOSÉ LUIS FERNÁNDEZ DE CASTILLEJO.

Sri Lanka

Embassy: 2148 Wyoming Ave, NW, Washington, DC 20008; tel. (202) 483-4025; Ambassador SUSANTHA DE ALWIS.

Consulate: 640 Third Ave, 20th Floor, New York, NY 10017; tel. (212) 986-7040; Consul MOHAMED M. A. FAROUQUE.

Sudan

Embassy: 2210 Massachusetts Ave, NW, Washington, DC 20008; tel. (202) 338-8565; Ambassador HASSAN EL-AMIN ELBASHER.

Consulate-General: 210 49th St East, New York, NY 10017; tel. (212) 421-2680.

Suriname

Embassy: 2210 Massachusetts Ave, NW, Washington, DC 20008; tel. (202) 338-8565; Ambassador SALAH AHMED..

Consulate-General: Virginia Plaza Bldg, 6555 36th St, NW, Suite 201, Miami, FL 33166; tel. (305) 871-2790; Vice-Consul STEPHANUS MARINUS DENDOE.

Swaziland

Embassy: 4301 Connecticut Ave, NW, Washington, DC 20008; tel. (202) 362-6683; Ambassador ABSALOM VUSANI MAMBA.

Sweden

Embassy: 600 New Hampshire Ave, NW, Suite 1200, Washington, DC 20008; tel. (202) 944-5600; Ambassador ANDERS THUNBORG.

Consulate-General: 1088 Wilshire Blvd, Suite 505, Los Angeles, CA 90024; tel. (213) 470-2555; Consul-Gen. MARGARETA B. HEGARDT.

Consulate-General: 150 Michigan Ave North, Suites 1200/1225/1250, Chicago, IL 60601; Consul-Gen. NILS R. LARSSON.

Consulate-General: 615 Peavey Bldg South, 730 Second Ave, POB 2186, Minneapolis, MN 55402; tel. (612) 332-6897; Consul-Gen. KARL-ERIK H. ANDERSSON.

Consulate-General: 825 Third Ave, 38th Floor, New York, NY 10022; tel. (212) 751-5900; Consul-Gen. MAGNUS J. FAXEN.

Switzerland

Embassy: 2900 Cathedral Ave, NW, Washington, DC 20008; tel. (202) 745-7900; telex 440055; Ambassador EDOUARD BRUNNER.

Consulate-General: 3440 Wilshire Blvd, Suite 817, Los Angeles, CA 90010; tel. (213) 388-4127; Consul-Gen. LEO RENGGLI.

Consulate-General: 235 Montgomery St, Suite 1035, San Francisco, CA 94104; tel. (415) 788-2272; Consul-Gen. ÉMILE HENRI BOVAY.

Consulate-General: 1275 Peachtree St, NE, Suite 425, Atlanta, GA 30309; Consul-Gen. PAUL STUDER.

Consulate-General: 307 Michigan Ave North, Chicago, IL 60601; tel. (312) 782-4346; Consul-Gen. ARTHUR BURKHARDT.

Consulate-General: Allied Bank Plaza, Suite 5670, 1000 Louisiana St, Houston, TX 77002; tel. (713) 650-0000; Consul-Gen. GILBERT MARCEL SCHLAEFLI.

Syria

Embassy: 2215 Wyoming Ave, NW, Washington, DC 20008; tel. (202) 232-6313; Chargé d'affaires BUSHRA KANAFANI.

Tanzania

Embassy: 2139 R St, NW, Washington, DC 20008; tel. (202) 939-6125; telex 64213; Ambassador ASTERIUS M. HYERA.

Thailand

Embassy: 2300 Kalorama Rd, NW, Washington, DC 20008; tel. (202) 483-7200; telex 64232; fax (202) 234-4498; Ambassador VITTHYA VEJJAJIVA.

Consulate: 801 La Brae Ave North, Los Angeles, CA 90038; tel. (213) 937-1894; Consul-Gen. SUMET WASANTAPRUEK.

Consulate-General: 35 Wacker Dr. East, Suite 1834, Chicago, IL 60601; tel. (212) 236-2447; Consul-Gen. CHALERM ACHARRY.

Togo

Embassy: 2208 Massachusetts Ave, NW, Washington, DC 20008; tel. (202) 234-4212; Ambassador ELLOM-KODJO SCHUPPIUS.

Trinidad and Tobago

Embassy: 1708 Massachusetts Ave, NW, Washington, DC 20036; tel. (202) 467-6490; Ambassador ANGUS ALBERT KHAN.

Consulate-General: Graybar Bldg, 420 Lexington Ave, Rms 331–333, New York, NY 10017; tel. (212) 682-7272; Consul-Gen. BABOORAM RAMBISSOON.

Tunisia

Embassy: 1515 Massachusetts Ave, NW, Washington, DC 20005; tel. (202) 862-1850; Ambassador ABDELAZIZ HAMZAOUI.

Turkey

Embassy: 1606 23rd St, NW, Washington, DC 20008; tel. (202) 387-3200; Ambassador SUKRU ELEKDAG.

Consulate-General: 4801 Wilshire Blvd, Los Angeles, CA 90010; tel. (213) 937-0118; Consul-Gen. NIHAT BOZKURT ERMAN.

Consulate-General: 360 Michigan Ave North, Suites 1404–1408, Chicago, IL 60601; tel. (312) 263-0644; Consul-Gen. UGUR ZIYAL.

Consulate-General: 821 United Nations Plaza, New York, NY 10017; tel. (212) 949-0160; Consul-Gen. MURAT SUNGAR.

Consulate-General: Post Oak Central Bldg, 1990 Post Oak Blvd South, Houston, TX 77056; tel. (713) 622-5849; Consul-Gen. SELCUK TARLAN.

Uganda

Embassy: 5905 16th St, NW, Washington, DC 20011; tel. (202) 726-7100; Ambassador STEPHEN KATENTA-APULI.

USSR

Embassy: 1125 16th St, NW, Washington, DC 20036; tel. (202) 628-7551; Ambassador YURI V. DUBININ.

Consulate-General: 2790 Green St, San Francisco, CA 94123; tel. (415) 922-6642; Consul-Gen. VALENTIN MIKHAILOVICH KAMENEV.

United Arab Emirates

Embassy: 600 New Hampshire Ave, NW, Suite 740, Washington, DC 20037; tel. (202) 338-6500; Ambassador AHMAD S. AL-MOKARRAB.

United Kingdom

Embassy: 3100 Massachusetts Ave, NW, Washington, DC 20008; tel. (202) 462-1340; Ambassador Sir ANTHONY ACLAND.

Consulate-General: 3701 Wilshire Blvd, Suite 312, Los Angeles, CA 90010; tel. (213) 385-7381; Consul-Gen. DONALD FRANCIS BALLENTYNE.

Consulate-General: 1 Samsome St, Suite 850, San Francisco, CA 94104; tel. (415) 981-3030; Consul-Gen. GRAHAM S. BURTON.

Consulate-General: 225 Peachtree St, NE, Suite 912, Atlanta, GA 30303; tel. (404) 524-5856; Consul-Gen. BARRY T. HOLMES.

Consulate-General: 33 Dearborn St North, Chicago, IL 60602; tel. (312) 346-1810; Consul-Gen. ROGER J. CARRICK.

Consulate-General: Prudential Tower, Prudential Center, Suite 4740, Boston, MA 02199; tel. (617) 437-7160; Consul-Gen. DAVID A. BURNS.

Consulate-General: 845 Third Ave, New York, NY 10022; tel. (212) 752-8400; Consul-Gen. G. M. JEWKES.

Consulate-General: 1650 Illuminating Bldg, 55 Public Sq., Cleveland, OH 44113; tel. (216) 621-7574; Consul-Gen. ANTHONY VICTOR HAYDAY.

Consulate-General: 601 Jefferson St, Suite 2250, Houston, TX 77002; tel. (713) 659-6270; Consul-Gen. MARTIN HIME.

Consulate: Brickell Bay Office Tower, 100 South Bayshore Dr., Suite 1700, Miami, FL 33131; tel. (305) 374-1522; Consul PETER SPICELEY.

Consulate: 813 Stemmons Tower West, 2730 Stemmons Freeway, Dallas, TX 75207; tel. (214) 637-3600; Consul DAVID A. C. HALLETT.

Consulate: 820 First Interstate Center, 999 Third Ave, Seattle, WA 98104; tel. (206) 622-9255; Consul WILLIAM L. CORDINER.

Uruguay

Embassy: 1918 F St, NW, Washington, DC 20006; tel. (202) 331-1313; Ambassador HÉCTOR LUISI.

Consulate-General: 564 Market St, Suite 200, San Francisco, CA 94101; Hon. Consul JOHN BENNETT RICHIE.

Consulate-General: 747 Third Ave, 37th Floor, New York, NY 10017; tel. (212) 753-8193; Consul-Gen. GUILLERMO ENRIQUE STEWART.

Consulate: 111 Second Ave, NE, Suite 1717, Miami, FL 33132; tel. (305) 358-9350; Consul JULIO C. CESANO.

Consulate: 611 Gravier St, Suite 609, New Orleans, LA 70130; tel. (504) 525-8354; Consul ENRIQUE J. VIDAL GUTIERREZ.

Venezuela

Embassy: 2445 Massachusetts Ave, NW, Washington, DC 20008; tel. (202) 797-3800; Ambassador VALENTÍN HERNÁNDEZ.

Consulate-General: 1052 West Sixth St, Rm 608, Los Angeles, CA 90017; tel. (213) 977-1049; Consul REINALDO R. RASQUIN.

Consulate-General: 2655 Le Jeune Rd, Suite 614, Coral Gables, Miami, FL 33146; Consul-Gen. BENJAMIN ORTEGA-ROMERO.

Consulate-General: 20 Wacker Dr. North, Suite 2052, Chicago, IL 60606; tel. (312) 236-9658; Consul-Gen. IVAN ARTURO TOVAR-SILVA.

Consulate-General: World Trade Center, Suites 1006–1009, New Orleans, LA 70130; tel. (504) 522-3284; Consul-Gen. MAGDA RUIZ-PIÑEDA.

Consulate-General: 1233 Mount Royal Ave West, Baltimore, MD 21217; tel. (301) 962-1362; Consul-Gen. JOSEFINA CARRERO.

Consulate-General: 545 Boylston St, 6th Floor, Boston, MA 02116; tel. (617) 266-9355; Consul-Gen. ASTRID JOSEFINA CONSALVI DE LEPAGE.

Consulate-General: 7 51st St East, New York, NY 10022; tel. (212) 826-1660; Consul TATIANA SUCRE.

Consulate-General: 3 Penn Center Plaza, Suite 806, Philadelphia, PA 19102; tel. (215) 568-0585; Consul-Gen. RAÚL ITRIAGO TORO.

Consul-General: 2700 Post Oak Blvd, Suite 1500, Houston, TX 77027; tel. (713) 961-5141; Consul-Gen. MANUEL J. SOSA D.

Western Samoa

Embassy: 820 Second Ave, New York, NY 10017; tel. (212) 599-6196; telex 960945; fax (212) 972-3970; Ambassador MAIAVA IULAI TOMA.

Yemen Arab Republic

Embassy: 600 New Hampshire Ave, NW, Washington, DC 20037; tel. (202) 965-4760; telex 897027; Ambassador MOHSIN AHMED ALAINI.

Consulate-General: 1 Parklane Blvd, Suite 1028 West, Dearborn, Detroit, MI 48126; tel. (313) 271-0840; Consul ALI AL-HADAD.

Consulate: 120 Montgomery St, Suite 2150, San Francisco, CA 94104; Consul ABDULLAH H. QATH.

Yugoslavia

Embassy: 2410 California Ave, NW, Washington, DC 20008; tel. (202) 462-6566; Ambassador ZIVORAD KOVACEVIĆ.

Consulate-General: 1375 Sutter St, Suite 406, San Francisco, CA 94109; tel. (415) 776-4941; Consul-Gen. LJUBOMIR DJUKIC.

Consulate-General: 307 Michigan Ave North, Suite 1600, Chicago, IL 60601; tel. (312) 332-0169; Consul-Gen. BAHRUDIN BIJEDIC.

Consulate-General: 767 Third Ave, 17th Floor, New York, NY 10017; tel. (212) 838-2300; Consul-Gen. PETAR VIDOVIC.

Consulate-General: Park Center, 1700 East St, Suite 4R, Cleveland, OH 44114; tel. (216) 621-2093; Consul-Gen. IVO VAJGL.

Consulate-General: 625 Stanwix St, Suite 1605, Pittsburgh, PA 15222; tel. (412) 471-6191; Consul-Gen. NIKO NAPICA.

Zaire

Embassy: 1800 New Hampshire Ave, NW, Washington, DC 20009; tel. (202) 234-7690; Ambassador MUSHOBEKWA KALIMBA WATANA.

Zambia

Embassy: 2419 Massachusetts Ave, NW, Washington, DC 20008; tel. (202) 265-9717; Chargé d'affaires LAZAROUS KAPAMBWE.

Zimbabwe

Embassy: 2852 McGill Terrace, NW, Washington, DC 20008; tel. (202) 332-7100; telex 248402; Chargé d'affaires JONATHAN WUTAWUNASHE.

US DIPLOMATIC REPRESENTATION ABROAD

(All diplomatic offices listed below are embassies, unless otherwise indicated.)

Afghanistan: Wazir Akbar Khan Mina, Kabul; tel. (93) 62230; embassy closed Jan. 1989.

Algeria: 4 chemin Cheikh Bachir Ibrahimi, BP 549, Alger Gare, 16000 Algiers; tel. (2) 60-11-86; telex 66047; Ambassador CHRISTOPHER ROSS.

Andorra: c/o Consulate-General, Via Layetana 33, Barcelona, Spain; tel. (91) 3199550; telex 52672; Consul-Gen. RUTH A. DAVIS.

Antigua and Barbuda: Queen Elizabeth Highway, St John's; tel. 23505; telex 2140; Chargé d'affaires ROBERT W. DUBOSE, Jr.

Argentina: Avda Colombia 4300, Palermo, 1425 Buenos Aires; tel. (1) 774-7611; telex 18156; Ambassador TERRENCE TODMAN.

Australia: Chancery, Yarralumla, ACT 2600; tel. (062) 705000; telex 62104; Ambassador MELVIN F. SEMBLER. (Also covers Nauru.)

Austria: 1090 Vienna, Boltzmanngasse 16; tel. (1) 31-55-11; telex 114634; Ambassador HENRY A. GRUNWALD.

Bahamas: Mosmar Bldg, Queen St, POB N-8197, Nassau; tel. 322-4733; telex 20138; Ambassador CHIC HECHT.

Bahrain: Off Sheikh Isa Rd, POB 26431, Manama; tel. 714151; telex 9398; Ambassador Dr SAM H. ZAKHEM.

Bangladesh: Park Rd, Baridhara Model Town, Dhaka 1212; tel. (2) 235093; telex 642319; Ambassador WILLARD A. DE PREE.

Barbados: Canadian Imperial Bank of Commerce Bldg, Broad St, POB 302, Bridgetown; tel. 436-4950; telex 2259; Chargé d'affaires JOHN E. CLARK.

Belgium: 27 blvd du Régent, 1000 Brussels; tel. (02) 513-38-30; telex 21336; Ambassador MAYNARD W. GLITMAN.

Belize: 29 Gabourel Lane, POB 286, Belize City; tel. 77161; telex 213; Ambassador ROBERT G. RICH, Jr.

Benin: rue Caporal Anani Bernard, BP 2012, Cotonou; tel. 30-17-92; Ambassador WALTER E. STADTLER.

Bermuda (Consulate-General): Vallis Bldg, Front St, POB 325, Hamilton HM BX; tel. 51342; Consul-Gen. JAMES M. MEDAS.

Bhutan: (see India).

Bolivia: Edif. Banco Popular del Perú, Calle Colón 290, Casilla 425, La Paz; tel. (02) 350120; telex 3268; Ambassador ROBERT S. GELBARD.

Botswana: POB 90, Gaborone; tel. 353982; telex 2554; Ambassador JOHN KORDEK (designate).

Brazil: SES, Avenida des Nações, Lote 3, 70.403 Brasília, DF; tel. (061) 321-7272; telex (61) 41167; Ambassador RICHARD MELTON (designate).

Brunei: Teck Guan Plaza, 3rd Floor, Corner Jalan Sultan and Jalan McArthur, Banda Seri Begawan; tel. (02) 29670; telex 2609; Ambassador THOMAS C. FERGUSON.

Bulgaria: Sofia, Blvd A. Stamboliisky 1; tel. 88-48-01; telex 22690; Ambassador SOL POLANSKY.

Burkina Faso: BP 35, Ouagadougou; tel. 30-67-23; telex 5290; Ambassador DAVID H. SHINN.

Burundi: chaussée Prince Rwagasore, BP 1720, Bujumbura; tel. 23454; Ambassador JAMES D. PHILLIPS.

Cameroon: rue Nachtigal, BP 817, Yaoundé; tel. 23-40-14; telex 8223; Ambassador MARK L. EDELMAN.

Canada: 100 Wellington St, Ottawa, ON K1P 5T1; tel. (613) 238-5335; telex 053-3582; Ambassador EDWARD N. NEY.

Cape Verde: Rua Hoji Ya Yenna 81, CP 201, Praia, São Tiago; tel. 61-43-63; telex 6068; Ambassador VERNON D. PENNER, Jr.

Central African Republic: blvd David Dacko, BP 924, Bangui; tel. 61-02-00; telex 5287; Ambassador DAVID C. FIELDS.

Chad: ave Félix Eboué, BP 413, N'Djamena; tel. 51-28-62; telex 5203; Ambassador ROBERT L. PUGH.

Chile: Agustinas 1343, 5°, Santiago; tel. 710133; telex 240062; Ambassador CHARLES GILLESPIE.

China, People's Republic: 3 Xiu Shui Bei Jie, Beijing; tel. 523831; telex 22701; Ambassador WINSTON LORD.

Colombia: Calle 38, No 8-61, Bogotá; tel. 2851300; telex 44843; Ambassador THOMAS E. McNAMARA.

Comoros: BP 1318, Moroni; tel. 73-12-03; telex 257; Chargé d'affaires KARL I. DANGA.

Congo: ave Amílcar Cabral, BP 1015, Brazzaville; tel. 83-20-70; telex 5367; Ambassador LEONARD G. SHURTLEFF.

Costa Rica: Calle 1, Avenida 3, Apartado 10.054, San José; tel. 331155; Ambassador DEAN R. HINTON.

Côte d'Ivoire: 5 rue Jesse Owens, 01 BP 1712, Abidjan 01; tel. 32-09-79; telex 23660; Ambassador DENNIS KUX.

Cuba (US Interests Section): c/o Swiss Embassy, Calzada entre L y M, Vedado, Havana; tel. 32-0551; telex 512206; Counsellor JOHN J. TAYLOR.

Cyprus: Dositheos St and Therissos St, Lykavitos, Nicosia; tel. (02) 465151; telex 4160; Ambassador BILL K. PERRIN.

Czechoslovakia: Tržiště 15, 125 48 Prague; tel. (2) 536641; telex 121196; Ambassador SHIRLEY TEMPLE BLACK.

Denmark: Dag Hammarskjölds Allé 24, 2100 Copenhagen Ø; tel. (01) 42-31-44; telex 22216; Ambassador KEITH BROWN.

Djibouti: Villa Plateau du Serpent, Blvd Maréchal Joffré, BP 185, Djibouti; tel. 353995; Ambassador ROBERT S. BARRETT, IV.

Dominican Republic: César Nicolás Pensón, esquina Leopoldo Navarro, Santo Domingo, DN; tel. 541-2171; telex 346-0013; Ambassador PAUL D. TAYLOR.

Ecuador: Avenida 12 de Octubre y Patria 120, Casilla 538, Quito; tel. 562-890; telex 2329; Ambassador RICHARD N. HOLWILL.

Egypt: 5 Sharia Latin America, Cairo (Garden City); tel. (02) 3557371; telex 93773; Ambassador FRANK G. WISNER.

El Salvador: 25 Avda Norte 1230, San Salvador; tel. 26-7100; telex 20648; Ambassador WILLIAM G. WALKER.

Equatorial Guinea: Calle de los Ministros, Apdo 597, Malabo; tel. 25-07; Ambassador CHESTER E. NORRIS, Jr.

Ethiopia: Entoto St, POB 1014, Addis Ababa; tel. 110666; telex 21282; Chargé d'affaires ROBERT G. HOUDEK.

Fiji: 31 Loftus St, POB 218, Suva; tel. 314466; telex 2255; Ambassador LEONARD ROCHWARGER. (Also covers Tonga.)

Finland: Itäinen puistotie 14A, 00140 Helsinki; tel. (90) 171931; telex 121644; Ambassador GIFFEN WEINMANN.

France: 2 ave Gabriel, 75008 Paris; tel. (1) 42-96-12-02; telex 650221; Ambassador WALTER J. P. CURLEY, Jr.

French Guiana: (see Martinique).

Gabon: BP 4000, blvd de la Mer, Libreville; tel. 76-20-03; telex 5250; Ambassador WARREN CLARK, Jr. (Also covers São Tomé and Príncipe.)

The Gambia: Kairaba Ave, Fajara, POB 19, Banjul; tel. 92858; telex 2229; Ambassador HERBERT E. HOROWITZ.

German Democratic Republic: 1080 Berlin, Neustädtische Kirchstr. 4-5; tel. 2202741; telex 112479; Ambassador RICHARD C. BARKLEY.

Germany, Federal Republic: 5300 Bonn 2, Deichmanns Aue 29; tel. (0228) 3391; telex 885452; Ambassador Gen. VERNON A. WALTERS.

Ghana: Ring Road East, POB 194, Accra; tel. 775346; Ambassador STEPHEN R. LYNE.

Greece: Leoforos Vassilissis Sofias 91, 10160 Athens; tel. (01) 7212951; telex 215548; Ambassador JAMES E. GOODBY.

Grenada: Ross Point Inn, POB 54, St George's; tel. (440) 1731; Ambassador JAMES F. COOPER.

Guadeloupe: (see Martinique).

Guatemala: Avda La Reforma 7-01, Zona 10, Guatemala City; tel. 311541; Ambassador JAMES H. MICHEL.

Guinea: BP 603, Conakry; tel. 44-15-20; telex 2103; Ambassador SAMUEL E. LUPO.

Guinea-Bissau: Avda Domingos Ramos, CP 297, Bissau; tel. 212816; Ambassador JOHN DALE BLACKEN.

Guyana: 31 Main St, Georgetown; tel. 54900; telex 2213; Ambassador THERESA A. TULL.

Haiti: blvd Harry-Truman, Cité de l'Exposition, BP 1761, Port-au-Prince; tel. 2-0200; telex 0157; Ambassador BRUNSON McKINLEY.

Holy See: Via Aurelia 294A, 00165 Rome; tel. (06) 6390558; telex 622322; Ambassador FRANK SHAKESPEARE.

Honduras: Avda La Paz, Apdo 26-C, Tegucigalpa; tel. 32-3120; Ambassador EVERETT E. BRIGGS.

Hong Kong (Consulate-General): 26 Garden Rd; tel. 5-239011; telex 63141; Consul-Gen. DONALD M. ANDERSON. (Also covers Macau.)

Hungary: 1054 Budapest, Szabadság tér 12; tel. 126-450; telex 22-4222; Ambassador MARK PALMER.

Iceland: Laufásvegur 21, Reykjavík; tel. (91) 29100; telex 3044; Ambassador L. NICHOLAS RUWE.

India: Shanti Path, Chanakyapuri, New Delhi 110021; tel. (11) 600651; telex 3165269; Ambassador JOHN R. HUBBARD. (Also covers Bhutan.)

Indonesia: Jalan Merdeka Selatan 5, Jakarta; tel. (021) 360360; telex 44218; Ambassador JOHN C. MONJO.

Iran: c/o Swiss Embassy, 13 Boustan Ave, POB 11365-176, Tehran; tel. (021) 268227; telex 212851.

Iraq: 929/7/57 Hay Babel, Masba, POB 2447, Alwiyah, Baghdad; tel. 719-6138; telex 212287; Ambassador APRIL C. GLASPIE.

Ireland: 42 Elgin Rd, Ballsbridge, Dublin 4; tel. (01) 688777; telex 93684; Ambassador RICHARD MOORE.

Israel: 71 Rehov Hayarkon, Tel-Aviv 63903; tel. 03-654338; telex 33376; Ambassador WILLIAM A. BROWN.

Italy: Via Vittorio Veneto 119A, 00187 Rome; tel. (06) 46741; telex 622322; Ambassador PETER SECCHIA.

Jamaica: Mutual Life Centre, 2 Oxford Rd, Kingston 5; tel. 929-4850; Ambassador MICHAEL SOTIRHOS.

Japan: 10-1, Akasaka 1-chome, Minato-ku, Tokyo 107; tel. (03) 583-7141; telex 22118; Ambassador MICHAEL H. ARMACOST.

Jordan: POB 354, Jabal Amman; tel. 644371; telex 21510; Ambassador ROSCOE S. SUDDARTH.

Kenya: Corner of Moi Ave and Haile Selassie Ave, POB 30137, Nairobi; tel. 334141; telex 22964; Ambassador ELINOR G. CONSTABLE.

Korea, Republic: 82 Sejong-no, Chongno-ku, Seoul; tel. 732-2601; telex 23108; Ambassador DONALD GREGG.

Kuwait: POB 77, 13001 Safat, Kuwait City; tel. 2424151; telex 2039; Ambassador NATHANIEL HOWELL.

Laos: rue Bartholonie, BP 114, Vientiane; tel. 2220; Chargé d'affaires HARRIET W. ISOM.

Lebanon: POB 70-840, Antelias, Beirut; tel. (01) 417774; telex 20280; Ambassador JOHN T. McCARTHY.

Lesotho: POB 333, Maseru 100; tel. 312666; telex 4506; Ambassador ROBERT S. SMALLEY.

Liberia: 111 United Nations Dr., Mamba Point, POB 98, Monrovia; tel. 222991; Ambassador JAMES K. BISHOP.

Liechtenstein: c/o Consulate-General, Zolliikerstrasse 141, 8008 Zürich, Switzerland; tel. (01) 552566; telex 53893; Consul-Gen. LOUIS S. SEGESVARY.

Luxembourg: 22 blvd Emmanuel-Servais, 2535 Luxembourg-Ville; tel. 46-01-23; Ambassador FREDERICK BUSH.

Macau: (see Hong Kong).

Madagascar: 14-16 rue Rainitovo, Antsahavola, BP 620, 101 Antananarivo; tel. 21257; telex 22202; Ambassador PATRICIA GATES LYNCH.

Malawi: Area 40, Flat 18, POB 30016, Lilongwe 3; tel. 730166; telex 4627; Ambassador GEORGE A. TRAIL, III.

Malaysia: 376 Jalan Tun Razak, POB 10035, 50700 Kuala Lumpur; tel. (03) 2489011; telex 32956; Ambassador PAUL M. CLEVELAND.

Maldives: (see Sri Lanka).

Mali: angle rue Testard et rue Mohamed V, BP 34, Bamako; tel. 22-58-34; telex 2448; Ambassador ROBERT M. PRINGLE.

Malta: Development House, St Anne St, Floriana; tel. 623653; Ambassador PETER R. SOMMER.

Marshall Islands (US Office): POB 680, Majuro, Marshall Islands 96960; tel. 3348; US Representative SAMUEL B. THOMSEN.

Martinique (Consulate-General): 14 rue Blénac, BP 561, 97206 Fort-de-France; tel. 631303; telex 912670; Consul-Gen. MARY DELL PALAZZOLO. (Also covers French Guiana and Guadeloupe.)

Mauritania: BP 222, Nouakchott; tel. 526-60; telex 558; Ambassador WILLIAM H. TWADDELL.

Mauritius: Rogers House, 4th Floor, President John F. Kennedy St, Port Louis; tel. 082347; Ambassador RONALD F. W. PALMER.

Mexico: Paseo de la Reforma 305, Colonia Cuauhtémoc, 06500 México, DF; tel. 2110042; telex 1773091; Ambassador JOHN D. NEGROPONTE.

Monaco: c/o Consulate-General, 12 blvd Paul Peytral, 13286 Marseille Cédex, France; tel. 91-54-92-00; Consul-Gen. EDMUND VAN GILDER.

Mongolia: Ulan Bator (mailing address as for People's Republic of China); tel. 29095; telex 253; Ambassador RICHARD L. WILLIAMS.

Morocco: 2 charia Marrakech, BP 120, Rabat; tel. 62265; telex 31005; Ambassador MICHAEL USSERY.

Mozambique: CP 783, Maputo; tel. 74729; telex 6143; Ambassador MELISSA F. WELLS.

Myanmar: 581 Merchant St, POB 521, Yangon; tel. (01) 82055; telex 21230; Ambassador BURTON LEVIN.

Nauru: (see Australia).

Nepal: Panipokhari, Kathmandu; tel. 411179; telex 2381; Ambassador MILTON FRANK.

Netherlands: Lange Voorhout 102, 2514 EJ The Hague; tel. (070) 62-49-11; telex 31016; Ambassador (vacant).

Netherlands Antilles (Consulate-General): St Anna Blvd 19, POB 158, Willemstad, Curaçao; tel. 613066; telex 1062; Consul-Gen. MARTIN MCLEAN.

New Zealand: 29 Fitzherbert Terrace, POB 1190, Wellington; tel. (04) 722068; telex 3305; Ambassador DELLA NEWMAN.

Nicaragua: Km 4½, Carretera Sur, Apdo 327, Managua, JR; tel. 66010; Ambassador (vacant).

Niger: Yantala, BP 11201, Niamey; tel. 72-26-61; telex 5444; Ambassador CARL C. CUNDIFF.

Nigeria: 2 Eleke Crescent, Victoria Island, PMB 554, Lagos; tel 610097; telex 23616; Ambassador PRINCETON N. LYMAN.

Norway: Drammensvn 18, Oslo 2; tel. (2) 44-85-50; telex 78470; Ambassador ROBERT D. STUART, Jr.

Oman: POB 966, Muscat; tel. 738231; telex 3785; Ambassador RICHARD W. BOEHM.

Pakistan: Diplomatic Enclave, Ramna 5, POB 1048, Islamabad; tel. (51) 826161; telex 5864; Ambassador ROBERT B. OAKLEY.

Palau (US Liaison Office): POB 6028, Koror, Palau, Western Caroline Islands 96940, USA; tel. 920; Liaison Officer STEVEN R. PRUETT.

Panama: Avda Balboa, entre Calle 37 y 38, Apdo 6959, Panamá 5; tel. 27-1777; telex 3583; Ambassador ARTHUR H. DAVIS.

Papua New Guinea: Armit St, POB 1492, Port Moresby; tel. 211455; telex 22189; Ambassador EVERETT E. BIERMAN.

Paraguay: Avda Mariscal López 1776, CP 402, Asunción; tel. 201041; telex 203; Ambassador TIMOTHY L. TOWELL.

Peru: Avda Garcilaso de la Vega 1400, Apdo 1995, Lima; tel. 338000; telex 25028; Ambassador ALEXANDER F. WATSON.

Philippines: 1201 Roxas Blvd, Metro Manila; tel. (02) 5217116; telex 27366; Ambassador NICHOLAS PLATT.

Poland: 00-540 Warsaw, Aleje Ujazdowskie 29–31; tel. 283041; telex 813304; Ambassador JOHN R. DAVIS, Jr.

Portugal: Avda das Forças Armadas (Sete Rios), 1600 Lisbon Codex; tel. 7266600; telex 12528; Ambassador EDWARD M. ROWELL.

Qatar: POB 2399, Doha; tel. 864701; telex 4847; Ambassador JOSEPH GHOUGASSIAN.

Romania: Bucharest, Strada Tudor Arghezi 7–9; tel. 104040; telex 11416; Ambassador ROGER KIRK.

Rwanda: blvd de la Révolution, BP 28, Kigali; tel. 75601; Ambassador LEONARD H. O. SPEARMAN, Sr.

San Marino: c/o Consulate-General, Lungarno Amerigo Vespucci 38, Florence; tel. (055) 298276; telex 570577; Consul-Gen. DIANE DILLARD.

São Tomé and Príncipe: (see Gabon).

Saudi Arabia: POB 9041, Riyadh 11143; tel. (1) 488-3800; telex 406866; Ambassador WALTER L. CUTLER.

Senegal: ave Jean XXIII, BP 49, Dakar; tel. 21-42-96; telex 517; Ambassador GEORGE E. MOOSE.

Seychelles: POB 148, Victoria; tel. 23921; Ambassador JAMES MORAN.

Sierra Leone: Corner of Walpole and Siaka Stevens Sts, Freetown; tel. 26481; telex 3509; Ambassador Dr CYNTHIA S. PERRY.

Singapore: 30 Hill St, Singapore 0617; tel. 3380251; Ambassador ROBERT D. ORR.

Solomon Islands: Honiara (mailing address and telex as for Papua New Guinea); Chargé d'affaires BILL WARREN.

Somalia: Corso Primo Luglio, POB 574, Mogadishu; tel. 20811; telex 789; Ambassador T. FRANK CRIGLER.

South Africa: Thibault House, 225 Pretorius St, 7th Floor, Pretoria; tel. 284266; telex 322143; Ambassador EDWARD J. PERKINS.

Spain: Serrano 75, Madrid; tel. 2763400; telex 27763; Ambassador JOSEPH ZAPPALA.

Sri Lanka: 210 Galle Rd, POB 106, Colombo 3; tel. (1) 548007; telex 21305; Ambassador JAMES W. SPAIN. (Also covers Maldives.)

Sudan: Sharia Ali Abd al-Latif, POB 699, Khartoum; tel. 74700; telex 22619; Ambassador G. NORMAN ANDERSON.

Suriname: Dr Sophie Redmondstraat 129, POB 1821, Paramaribo; tel. 72900; telex 373; Ambassador RICHARD HOWLAND.

Swaziland: Central Bank Bldg, Warner St, POB 199, Mbabane; tel. 22281; telex 2016; Ambassador MARY A. RYAN.

Sweden: Strandvägen 101, 115 27 Stockholm; tel. (8) 783-53-00; telex 12060; Ambassador CHARLES E. REDMAN.

Switzerland: Jubiläumsstrasse 93, 3005 Berne; tel. (031) 437011; telex 912603; Ambassador JOSEPH B. GILDENHORN.

Syria: rue al-Mansour 2, Damascus; tel. 333052; telex 411919; Ambassador EDWARD P. DJEREJIAN.

Tanzania: POB 9123, 36 Laibon Rd, Dar es Salaam; tel. 37501; telex 41250; Ambassador DONALD K. PETTERSON.

Thailand: 95 Wireless Rd, Bangkok; tel. (02) 252-5040; telex 87008; Ambassador DANIEL A. O'DONOHUE.

Togo: angle rue Pelletier Caventou et rue Vauban, BP 852, Lomé; tel. 21-29-91; Ambassador RUSH W. TAYLOR, Jr.

Tonga: (see Fiji).

Trinidad and Tobago: 15 Queen's Park West, POB 752, Port of Spain; tel. 622-6372; Ambassador CHARLES A. GARGANO.

Tunisia: 144 ave de la Liberté, 1002 Tunis–Belvedere; tel. (1) 782-566; telex 13379; Ambassador ROBERT H. PELLETREAU, Jr.

Turkey: Atatürk Bulvar 110, Ankara; tel. (4) 1265470; telex 43144; Ambassador MORTON I. ABRAMOWITZ.

Uganda: POB 7007, Kampala; tel. 259791; Ambassador JOHN A. BURROUGHS, Jr.

USSR: Moscow, ulitsa Chaikovskovo 19–23; tel. (095) 252-24-51; telex 413160; Ambassador JACK F. MATLOCK, Jr.

United Arab Emirates: POB 4009, Abu Dhabi; tel. (2) 336691; telex 22229; Ambassador DAVID L. MACK.

United Kingdom: 24–32 Grosvenor Sq, London, W1A 1AE; tel. (01) 499-9000; telex 266777; Ambassador HENRY E. CATTO, Jr.

Uruguay: Lauro Muller 1776, Montevideo; tel. 409051; Ambassador MALCOLM R. WILKEY.

Venezuela: Avda Principal de la Floresta, esquina Avenida Francisco de Miranda, Apdo 62291, Caracas 1060-A; tel. 2847111; telex 25501; Ambassador OTTO J. REICH.

Yemen Arab Republic: POB 1088, Beit al-Halali, San'a; tel. (2) 271950; telex 2797; Ambassador CHARLES F. DUNBAR.

Yemen, People's Democratic Republic: c/o British Embassy, 28 Shara Ho Chi Minh, Khormaksar, Aden; tel. 32711.

Yugoslavia: Belgrade, Kneza Miloša 50; tel. 645655; telex 11529; Ambassador WARREN ZIMMERMAN.

Zaire: 310 ave des Aviateurs, BP 697, Kinshasa; tel. 25881; telex 21405; Ambassador WILLIAM C. HARROP.

Zambia: Corner of Independence Ave and United Nations Ave, POB 31617, Lusaka; tel. 214911; telex 41970; Ambassador JEFFREY DAVIDOW.

Zimbabwe: 172 Rhodes Ave, POB 3340, Harare; tel. 794521; telex 24591; Ambassador JAMES W. RAWLINGS.

JUDICIAL SYSTEMS OF THE USA

THE FEDERAL JUDICIAL SYSTEM

Supreme Court of the United States

(Supreme Court Bldg, 1 First St, NE, Washington, DC 20543; tel. (202) 479-3000)

The Supreme Court is the only federal court established by the constitution. It is the highest court in the nation, comprising a chief justice and eight associate justices. Appointments, which are for life or until retirement, are made by the president, subject to confirmation by the US Senate.

Chief Justice: WILLIAM HUBBS REHNQUIST (appointed 1986).
Associate Justices: WILLIAM J. BRENNAN, Jr (1956), BYRON R. WHITE (1962), THURGOOD MARSHALL (1967), HARRY A. BLACKMUN (1970), JOHN PAUL STEVENS (1975), SANDRA DAY O'CONNOR (1981), ANTONIN SCALIA (1986), ANTHONY M. KENNEDY (1988).

US Courts of Appeals

(c/o Administrative Office of the US Courts, Washington, DC 20544; tel. (202) 633-6097)

The country is divided into 12 judicial circuits, including one in the District of Columbia, in each of which there is one Court of Appeals. There is also a Court of Appeals for the federal circuit, having nation-wide specialized jurisdiction.

Federal courts hear cases involving federal law, cases involving participants from more than one state, crimes committed in more than one state and civil or corporate cases that cross state lines.

Federal Circuit: HOWARD T. MARKEY (Chief Judge), DANIEL M. FRIEDMAN, GILES S. RICH, EDWARD S. SMITH, HELEN W. NIES, PAULINE NEWMAN, JEAN GALLOWAY BISSELL, GLENN L. ARCHER, Jr, H. ROBERT MAYER, PAUL R. MICHEL.

District of Columbia Circuit: PATRICIA M. WALD (Chief Judge), SPOTTSWOOD W. ROBINSON, III, ABNER J. MIKVA, HARRY T. EDWARDS, RUTH BADER GINSBURG, KENNETH W. STARR, LAURENCE H. SILBERMAN, JAMES L. BUCKLEY, STEPHEN F. WILLIAMS, DOUGLAS GINSBURG, DAVID B. SENTELLE.

First Circuit (Maine, Massachusetts, New Hampshire, Rhode Island, Puerto Rico): LEVIN H. CAMPBELL (Chief Judge), FRANK M. COFFIN, HUGH H. BOWNES, STEPHEN BREYER, JUAN R. TORRUELLA, BRUCE M. SELYA.

Second Circuit (Connecticut, New York, Vermont): JAMES L. OAKES (Chief Judge), WILFRED FEINBERG, THOMAS J. MESKILL, JON O. NEWMAN, AMALYA LYLE KEARSE, RICHARD J. CARDAMONE, LAWRENCE W. PIERCE, RALPH K. WINTER, Jr, GEORGE C. PRATT, ROGER J. MINER, FRANK X. ALTIMARI, J. DANIEL MAHONEY.

Third Circuit (Delaware, New Jersey, Pennsylvania, US Virgin Islands): JOHN J. GIBBONS (Chief Judge), COLLINS J. SEITZ, A. LEON HIGGINBOTHAM, Jr, DOLORES KORMAN SLOVITER, EDWARD R. BECKER, WALTER K. STAPLETON, CAROL LOS MANSMANN, MORTON I. GREENBERG, ANTHONY J. SCIRICA, WILLIAM D. HUTCHINSON, ROBERT E. COWEN, RICHARD L. NYGAARD.

Fourth Circuit (Maryland, North Carolina, South Carolina, Virginia, West Virginia): HARRISON L. WINTER (Chief Judge), KENNETH K. HALL, DONALD STUART RUSSELL, H. EMORY WIDENER, Jr, JAMES DICKSON PHILLIPS, Jr, FRANCIS D. MURAGHAN, Jr, JAMES M. SPROUSE, SAM J. ERVIN, III, ROBERT F. CHAPMAN, J. HARVIE WILKINSON, III, WILLIAM W. WILKINS, Jr.

Fifth Circuit (Louisiana, Mississippi, Texas): CHARLES CLARK (Chief Judge), THOMAS G. GEE, ALVIN B. RUBIN, THOMAS M. REAVLEY, HENRY A. POLITZ, CAROLYN DINEEN KING, SAMUEL D. JOHNSON, JERRE S. WILLIAMS, WILLIAM D. GARWOOD, E. GRADY JOLLY, PATRICK E. HIGGINBOTHAM, W. EUGENE DAVIS, ROBERT M. HILL, EDITH HOLLAN JONES, JERRY E. SMITH, JOHN M. DUHE, Jr.

Sixth Circuit (Kentucky, Michigan, Ohio, Tennessee): ALBERT J. ENGEL (Chief Judge), GILBERT S. MERRITT, DAMON J. KEITH, BOYCE F. MARTIN, Jr, NATHANIEL R. JONES, ROBERT B. KRUPANSKY, HARRY W. WELLFORD, CORNELIA G. KENNEDY, H. TED MILBURN, RALPH B. GUY, Jr, DAVID A. NELSON, JAMES L. RYAN, DANNY J. BOGGS, ALAN E. NORRIS.

Seventh Circuit (Illinois, Indiana, Wisconsin): WILLIAM J. BAUER (Chief Judge), WALTER J. CUMMINGS, HARLINGTON WOOD, Jr, RICHARD D. CUDAHY, RICHARD A. POSNER, JOHN L. COFFEY, JOEL M. FLAUM, FRANK H. EASTERBROOK, KENNETH F. RIPPLE, DANIEL A. MANION, MICHAEL S. KANNE.

Eighth Circuit (Arkansas, Iowa, Minnesota, Missouri, Nebraska, North Dakota, South Dakota): DONALD P. LAY (Chief Judge), THEODORE McMILLAN, RICHARD S. ARNOLD, JOHN R. GIBSON, GEORGE G. FAGG, PASCO M. BOWMAN, II, ROGER L. WOOLMAN, FRANK J. MAGILL, C. ARLEN BEAM.

Ninth Circuit (Alaska, Arizona, California, Hawaii, Idaho, Montana, Nevada, Oregon, Washington, Guam, Northern Mariana Islands): ALFRED T. GOODWIN (Chief Judge), JAMES R. BROWNING, J. CLIFFORD WALLACE, PROCTER HUG, Jr, THOMAS TANG, JEROME FARRIS, BETTY B. FLETCHER, MARY M. SCHROEDER, HARRY PREGERSON, ARTHUR L. ALARCON, CECIL F. POOLE, DOROTHY W. NELSON, WILLIAM C. CANBY, Jr, WILLIAM A. NORRIS, STEPHEN REINHARDT, ROBERT R. BEEZER, CYNTHIA H. HALL, CHARLES E. WIGGINS, MELVIN BRUNETTI, ALEX KOZINSKI, JOHN T. NOONAN, Jr, DAVID R. THOMPSON, DAIRMUID F. O'SCANNLAIN, EDWARD LEAVY, STEPHEN S. TROTT.

Tenth Circuit (Colorado, Kansas, New Mexico, Oklahoma, Utah, Wyoming): WILLIAM J. HOLLOWAY, Jr, (Chief Judge), MONROE G. McKAY, JAMES K. LOGAN, STEPHANIE K. SEYMOUR, JOHN P. MOORE, STEPHEN H. ANDERSON, DEANELL R. TACHA, BOBBY R. BALDOCK, WADE BRORBY, DAVID M. EBEL.

Eleventh Circuit (Alabama, Florida, Georgia): PAUL R. RONEY (Chief Judge), GERALD B. TJOFLAT, JAMES C. HILL, PETER T. FAY, ROBERT S. VANCE, PHYLLIS A. KRAVITCH, FRANK M. JOHNSON, Jr, JOSEPH W. HATCHETT, R. LANIER ANDERSON, III, THOMAS A. CLARK, J. L. EDMONSON, EMMETT R. COX.

United States Federal District Courts

There are 94 Federal District Courts, with at least one in each state, and one each in the District of Columbia and the US External Territories of Guam, the Northern Mariana Islands, Puerto Rico and the US Virgin Islands. They are the courts of first instance for most federal suits. Although federal in their jurisdiction, these courts are listed by state (see pp. 181-190).

United States Claims Court

(717 Madison Pl., NW, Washington, DC 20005; tel. (202) 633-7257)

Judges: LOREN A. SMITH (Chief Judge), JAMES F. MEROW, JOHN P. WIESE, ROBERT J. YOCK, REGINALD W. GIBSON, LAWRENCE S. MARGOLIS, CHRISTINE COOK NETTESHEIM, MOODY R. TIDWELL, III, MARIAN BLANK HORN, ERIC G. BRUGGINK, JOHN L. NAPIER, BOHDAN A. FUTEY, WILKES C. ROBINSON, ROGER B. ANDEWELT, JAMES T. TURNER, RANDALL R. RADER.

US Court of International Trade

(1 Federal Plaza, New York, NY 10007; tel. (212) 264-2814)

Judges: EDWARD D. RE (Chief Judge), JAMES L. WATSON, GREGORY W. CARMAN, JANE A. RESTANI, DOMINICK L. DiCARLO, THOMAS J. AQUILINO, Jr, NICHOLAS TSOUCALAS, R. K. MUSGRAVE.

United States Tax Court

(400 2nd St, NW, Washington, DC 20217; tel. (202) 376-2754)

Judges: SAMUEL B. STERRETT (Chief Judge), CHARLES R. SIMPSON, WILLIAM A. GOFFE, HERBERT L. CHABOT, ARTHUR L. NIMS, III, EDNA G. PARKER, JULES J. KORNER, III, MEADE WHITAKER, MARY ANN COHEN, PERRY SHIELDS, CHARLES E. CLAPP, II, LAPSLEY W. HAMBLEN, Jr, STEPHEN J. SWIFT, JOEL GERBER, JULIEN I. JACOBS, LAWRENCE A. WRIGHT, CAROLYN MILLER PARR, B. JOHN WILLIAMS, Jr.

STATE JUDICIAL SYSTEMS

Alabama

FEDERAL COURTS

Alabama is in the Eleventh Circuit of the US Courts of Appeals. There are US District Courts at Birmingham, Montgomery and Mobile.

US District Courts

Northern: Federal Courthouse, Rm 138, Birmingham, Al 35203; tel. (205) 731-1709; Judges: SAM C. POINTER, Jr (Chief Judge), JAMES HUGHES HANCOCK, J. FOY GUIN, Jr, ROBERT B. PROPST, E. B. HALTOM, Jr, U. W. CLEMON, WILLIAM M. ACKER, Jr.

Middle: POB 711, Montgomery, AL 36101; tel. (205) 832-7308; Judges: TRUMAN M. HOBBS (Chief Judge), MYRON H. THOMPSON, JOEL F. DUBINA.

Southern: POB 1964, Mobile, AL 36652; tel. (205) 690-2371; Judges: WILLIAM BREVARD HAND (Chief Judge), EMMETT R. COX, ALEX T. HOWARD, Jr.

STATE COURTS

The state Supreme Court has nine judges, including the chief justice. All judges are elected at-large to serve staggered six-year terms. The state courts of appeals are the Court of Criminal Appeals, which has five judges serving six-year terms of office, and the Court of Civil Appeals, which has three judges serving six-year terms.

Supreme Court

POB 218, Montgomery, AL 36101; tel. (205) 261-4599; Judges: SONNY HORNSBY, Jr, (Chief Justice), OSCAR W. ADAMS, Jr, RENEAU P. ALMON, GORMAN HOUSTON, RICHARD L. JONES, HUGH MADDOX, JANIE L. SHORES, HENRY B. STEAGALL, II, MARK KENNEDY.

Alaska

FEDERAL COURTS

Alaska is in the Ninth Circuit of the US Courts of Appeals. There is a US District Court at Anchorage.

US District Court

701 C St, POB 50, Anchorage, AK 99513; tel. (907) 271-5533; Judges: JAMES M. FITZGERALD (Chief Judge), H. RUSSEL HOLLAND, ANDREW J. KLEINFELD.

STATE COURTS

The state Supreme Court has five judges including the chief justice. The judges are selected at-large and, once their appointments have been ratified by the electorate, serve a 10-year term of office. The chief justice is selected by the court to serve a three-year term. The state Court of Appeals has three judges, who serve for terms of eight years.

Supreme Court

303 K St, Anchorage, AK 99501; tel. (907) 264-0618; Judges: WARREN MATTHEWS (Chief Justice), EDMOND W. BURKE, ALLEN COMPTON, JAY A. RABINOWITZ, DANIEL MOORE.

Arizona

FEDERAL COURTS

Arizona is in the Ninth Circuit of the US Courts of Appeals. There is a US District Court in Phoenix.

US District Court

US Courthouse and Federal Bldg, Rm 1400, 230 First Ave North, Phoenix, AZ 82025; tel. (602) 261-3341; Judges: RICHARD M. BILBY (Chief Judge), CHARLES L. HARDY, ALFREDO C. MARQUEZ, EARL H. CARROLL, WILLIAM D. BROWNING, PAUL G. ROSENBLAT, ROBERT C. BLOOMFIELD, ROGER G. STRAND.

STATE COURTS

The state Supreme Court has five judges including the chief justice. Judges are appointed by the governor and serve six-year terms of office. The judges select one of their number ·as chief justice and he or she serves a five-year term of office. The state Court of Appeals has 18 judges, all of whom serve six-year terms of office.

Supreme Court

State Capitol Bldg, West Wing South, Rm 201, Phoenix, AZ 85007; tel. (602) 255-4535; Judges: FRANK X. GORDON, Jr (Chief Justice), JAMES DUKE CAMERON, STANLEY G. FELDMAN, ROBERT J. CORCORAN, JAMES MOELLER.

Arkansas

FEDERAL COURTS

Arkansas is in the Eighth Circuit of the US Courts of Appeals. There are US District Courts at Little Rock and Fort Smith.

US District Courts

Eastern: POB 3684, Little Rock, AR 72203; tel. (501) 378--5960; Judges: GARNETT THOMAS EISELE (Chief Judge), ELSIJANE TRIMBLE ROY, HENRY WOODS, GEORGE HOWARD, Jr.

Western: POB 1523, Fort Smith, AR 72902; tel. (501) 783-6833; Judges: H. FRANKLIN WATERS (Chief Judge), ELSIJANE TRIMBLE ROY, GEORGE HOWARD, Jr, MORRIS S. ARNOLD.

STATE COURTS

The state Supreme Court has seven judges including the chief justice, who is chosen by popular election and serves a term of eight years. The remaining judges, who also serve eight-year terms, are selected at-large. The state Court of Appeals has six judges serving terms of eight years.

Supreme Court

Justice Bldg, Little Rock, AR 72201; tel. (501) 371-5614; Judges: JACK HOLT, Jr, (Chief Justice), ROBERT H. DUDLEY, TOM GLAZE, STEELE HAYS, DARRELL HICKMAN, DAVID NEWBERN, JOHN I. PURTLE.

California

FEDERAL COURTS

California is in the Ninth Circuit of the US Courts of Appeals. There are US District Courts in San Francisco, Sacramento, Los Angeles and San Diego.

US District Courts

Northern: 450 Golden Gate Ave, POB 36060, San Francisco, CA 94102; tel. (415) 556-5646; Judges: ROBERT F. PECKHAM (Chief Judge), WILLIAM W. SCHWARZER, WILLIAM A. INGRAM, ROBERT P. AGUILAR, THELTON E. HENDERSON, MARILYN H. PATEL, EUGENE F. LYNCH, JOHN P. VUKASIN, Jr, CHARLES A. LEGGE, D. LOWELL JENSEN.

Eastern: US Courthouse, Rm 2012, 650 Capitol Mall, Sacramento, CA 95814; tel. (916) 551-2825; Judges: LAWRENCE K. KARLTON (Chief Judge), MILTON L. SCHWARTZ, EDWARD DEAN PRICE, RAUL A. RAMIREZ, ROBERT E. COYLE, EDWARD J. GARCIA.

Central: 312 Spring St North, Los Angeles, CA 90012; tel. (213) 894-3535; Judges: MANUEL L. REAL (Chief Judge), W. MATTHEW BYRNE, Jr, ROBERT M. TAKASUGI, MARIANA R. PFAELZER, TERRY J. HATTER, Jr, A. WALLACE TASHIMA, CONSUELO BLAND MARSHALL, DAVID V. KENYON, RICHARD A. GADBOIS, EDWARD RAFEEDIE, PAMELA A. RYMER, HARRY L. HUPP, ALICEMARIE H. STOTLER, JAMES M. IDEMAN, WILLIAM J. REA, WILLIAM D. KELLER, FERDINAND F. FERNANDEZ, STEPHEN V. WILSON, J. SPENCER LETTS, DICKRAN M. TEVRIZIAN, Jr, JOHN G. DAVIES, RONALD S. W. LEW.

Southern: 940 Front St, San Diego, CA 92819; tel. (619) 293-6480; Judges: GORDON THOMPSON, Jr (Chief Judge), WILLIAM B. ENRIGHT, JUDITH N. KEEP, EARL B. GILLIAM, J. LAWRENCE IRVING, RUDI M. BREWSTER, JOHN S. RHOADES, Sr.

STATE COURTS

The state Supreme Court has seven judges including the chief justice. All appointments are made by the governor, confirmed by the Commission on Judicial Appointments and ratified by the electorate at the next election. Judges serve 12-year terms of office. The state Court of Appeals has 77 judges who also serve 12-year terms of office.

Supreme Court

State Bldg, 350 McAllister St, San Francisco, CA 94102; tel. (415) 557-0587; Judges: MALCOLM M. LUCAS (Chief Justice), ALLEN E. BROUSSARD, STANLEY MOSK, EDWARD PANELLI, DAVID EAGLESON, MARCUS KAUFMAN, JOYCE KENNARD.

Colorado

FEDERAL COURTS

Colorado is in the Tenth Circuit of the US Courts of Appeals. The US District Court is at Denver.

US District Court

US Courthouse, Rm C-224, 1929 Stout St, Denver, CO 80294; tel. (303) 844-4151; Judges: SHERMAN G. FINESILVER (Chief Judge), RICHARD P. MATSCH, JOHN L. KANE, Jr, JIM R. CARRIGAN, ZITA L. WEINSHIENK.

STATE COURTS

The state Supreme Court has seven judges including the chief justice. The judges, who are selected at-large to serve 10-year terms of office, choose one of their number as chief justice to serve a term according to the pleasure of the court. The state Court of Appeals has 10 judges, who serve terms of eight years.

Supreme Court

State Judicial Bldg, Rm 435, 2 East 14th Ave, Denver, CO 80203; tel. (303) 861-1111; Judges: JOSEPH R. QUINN (Chief Justice), WILLIAM H. ERICKSON, HOWARD M. KIRSHBAUM, GEORGE E. LOHR, MARY J. MULLARKEY, LUIS D. ROVIRA, ANTHONY VOLLACK.

Connecticut

FEDERAL COURTS

Connecticut is in the Second Circuit of the US Courts of Appeals. The US District Court is at New Haven.

US District Court

141 Church St, New Haven, CT 06510; tel. (203) 773-2140; Judges: T. F. GILROY DALY (Chief Judge), ELLEN B. BURNS, WARREN W. EGINTON, JOSE A. CABRANES, PETER C. DORSEY, ALAN H. NEVAS.

STATE COURTS

The state Supreme Court has seven judges, including the chief justice, serving eight-year terms of office; they are nominated by the governor and appointed by the General Assembly. The state Appellate Court has nine judges, who serve eight-year terms of office.

Supreme Court

231 Capitol Ave, Hartford, CT 06108; tel. (203) 566-3054; Judges: ELLEN ASH PETERS (Chief Justice), ROBERT J. CALLAHAN, ARTHUR H. HEALEY, ANGELO G. SANTANIELLO, DAVID M. SHEA, ALFRED V. COVELLO, ROBERT D. GLASS.

Delaware

FEDERAL COURTS

Delaware is in the Third Circuit of the US Courts of Appeals. The US District Court is at Wilmington.

US District Court

Lockbox 44, 844 King St, Wilmington, DE 19801; tel. (302) 573-6355; Judges: MURRAY M. SCHWARTZ (Chief Judge), JOSEPH J. LONGOBARDI, JOSEPH J. FARNAN, Jr, JANE R. ROTH.

STATE COURTS

The state Supreme Court has five judges, including the chief justice. All the judges, selected at-large, are appointed by the governor with the consent of the Senate and serve terms of 12 years.

Supreme Court

Carvel State Office Bldg, 820 North French St, Wilmington, DE 19801; tel. (302) 571-2427; Judges: ANDREW D. CHRISTIE (Chief Justice), RANDY HOLLAND, HENRY R. HORSEY, ANDREW G. T. MOORE, II, JOSEPH WALSH.

District of Columbia

FEDERAL COURTS

The District of Columbia constitutes a separate circuit of the US Courts of Appeals. There is also a US District Court in Washington.

US District Court

Washington, DC 20001; Judges: AUBREY E. ROBINSON, Jr (Chief Judge), GERHARD A. GESELL, JOHN H. PRATT, CHARLES R. RICHEY, LOUIS F. OBERDORFER, HAROLD H. GREENE, JOHN GARRETT PENN, JOYCE HENS GREEN, NORMA H. JOHNSON, THOMAS P. JACKSON, THOMAS F. HOGAN, STANLEY S. HARRIS, GEORGE H. REVERCOMB, STANLEY SPORKIN, ROYCE C. LAMBERTH.

DISTRICT OF COLUMBIA COURTS

The District of Columbia's Court of Appeals has nine judges, including the chief justice, and functions as the court of last resort. Judges are selected at-large and serve for a term of 15 years; all District of Columbia judges are nominated by the president of the USA, from a list submitted by the District of Columbia Judicial Nominating Commission, and appointed with the consent of the US Senate. The chief justice is similarly appointed to serve a four-year term of office. In the general trial court, the Superior Court, criminal cases are prosecuted by the US Attorney's Office, a division of the federal Department of Justice.

Court of Appeals

500 Indiana Ave, NW, Washington, DC 20001; Judges: WILLIAM C. PRYOR (Chief Judge), JAMES A. BELSON, JOHN M. FERREN, JULIA COOPER MACK, FRANK Q. NEBEKER, THEODORE R. NEWMAN, Jr, JUDITH W. ROGERS, JOHN A. TERRY.

Florida

FEDERAL COURTS

Florida is in the 11th Circuit of the US Courts of Appeals. US District Courts are situated in Tallahassee, Tampa and Miami.

US District Courts

Northern: 110 East Park Ave, Tallahassee, FL 32301; tel. (904) 681-7550; Judges: WILLIAM H. STAFFORD, Jr (Chief Judge), MAURICE M. PAUL, C. ROGER VINSON.
Middle: POB 2908, Tampa, FL 33601-2908; tel. (813) 228-2112; Judges: WILLIAM TERRELL HODGES (Chief Judge), HOWELL W. MELTON, GEORGE C. CARR, SUSAN H. BLACK, WILLIAM J. CASTAGNA, JOHN H. MOORE, II, ELIZABETH A. KOVACHEVICH, GEORGE K. SHARP, PATRICIA C. FAWSETT.
Southern: 301 North Miami Ave, Miami, FL 33128-7788; tel. (305) 356-5000; Judges: JAMES LAWRENCE KING (Chief Judge), NORMAN C. ROETTGER, Jr, SIDNEY M. ARONOWITZ, WILLIAM M. HOEVELER, JOSE A. GONZALEZ, Jr, JAMES C. PAINE, JAMES W. KEHOE, EUGENE P. SPELLMAN, EDWARD B. DAVIS, ALCEE L. HASTINGS, LENORE C. NESBITT, STANLEY MARCUS, THOMAS E. SCOTT, WILLIAM J. ZLOCH, KENNETH L. RYSKAMP.

STATE COURTS

The state Supreme Court has seven judges, including the chief justice. The judges, who are selected at large by the governor on the advice of the Judicial Nominating Commission, serve terms of six years. The chief justice is chosen by the court and serves a two-year term of office. There is a District Court of Appeals, which has 46 judges serving six-year terms of office. Judges of both these courts may run for election to subsequent terms of office at the general election preceding the expiration of their existing term of office.

Supreme Court

Supreme Court Bldg, Tallahassee, FL 32301; tel. (305) 646-8904; Judges: RAYMOND EHRLICH (Chief Justice), PARKER LEE McDONALD, ROSEMARY BARKETT, STEPHEN GRIMES, GERALD KOGAN, BEN F. OVERTON, LEANDER J. SHAW, Jr.

Georgia

FEDERAL COURTS

Georgia is in the 11th Circuit of the US Courts of Appeals. There are US District Courts at Atlanta, Macon and Savannah.

US District Courts

Northern: US Courthouse, Rm 2211, 75 Spring St, SW, Atlanta, GA 30303; tel. (404) 331-6496; Judges: WILLIAM C. O'KELLEY (Chief Judge), RICHARD C. FREEMAN, HAROLD L. MURPHY, MARVIN H. SHOOB, G. ERNEST TIDWELL, ORINDA DALE EVANS, ROBERT L. VINING, Jr, ROBERT H. HALL, HAROLD T. WARD, J. OWEN FORRESTER.

Middle: POB 65, Macon, GA 31202; tel. (912) 752-3491; Judges: WILBUR D. OWENS, Jr (Chief Judge), J. ROBERT ELLIOTT, DUROSS FITZPATRICK.

Southern: POB 8286, Savannah, GA 31412; tel. (912) 944-4281; Judges: ANTHONY A. ALAIMO (Chief Judge), B. AVANT EDENFIELD, DUDLEY H. BOWEN, Jr.

STATE COURTS

The state Supreme Court has seven judges including the chief justice. The judges are elected at-large and serve for terms of six years. The chief justice is appointed by the Court and serves a four-year term of office. The state Court of Appeals has nine judges who hold office for six years.

Supreme Court

State Judicial Bldg, Rm 514, Atlanta, GA 30334; tel. (404) 656-3473; Judges: THOMAS O. MARSHALL (Chief Justice), RICHARD BELL, HAROLD G. CLARKE, HARDY GREGORY, Jr, WILLIS B. HUNT, GEORGE T. SMITH, CHARLES L. WELTNER.

Hawaii

FEDERAL COURTS

Hawaii is in the Ninth Circuit of the US Courts of Appeals. There is a US District Court in Honolulu.

US District Court

POB 50128, Honolulu, HI 96850; tel. (808) 546-8672; Judges: HAROLD M. FONG (Chief Judge), ALAN C. KAY.

STATE COURTS

The state Supreme Court has five judges, including the chief justice. All the judges, chosen at-large, are appointed by the governor on the advice of the Senate and serve for terms of 10 years. The state has an Intermediate Court of Appeals, with three judges serving 10-year terms of office.

Supreme Court

POB 2560, Honolulu, HI 96804; tel. (808) 548-5930; Judges: HERMAN T. F. LUM (Chief Justice), YOSHIMI HAYASHI, EDWARD NAKAMURA, FRANK PADGETT, JAMES H. WAKATSUKI.

Idaho

FEDERAL COURTS

Idaho is in the Ninth Circuit of the US Courts of Appeals. There is a US District Court at Boise.

US District Court

Box 040, 550 West Fort St, Boise, ID 83724; tel. (208) 334-1693; Judges: MARION J. CALLISTER (Chief Judge), HAROLD L. RYAN.

STATE COURTS

The state Supreme Court has five judges, including the chief justice. Judges are elected at-large and serve terms of office of six years; the chief justice is appointed by the court and serves a four-year term of office. The state Court of Appeals has three judges elected to serve six-year terms of office.

Supreme Court

451 West State St, Boise, ID 83720; tel. (208) 334-3186; Judges: ROBERT E. BAKES (Chief Justice), STEPHEN BISTLINE, BYRON JOHNSON, (2 vacancies).

Illinois

FEDERAL COURTS

Illinois is in the Seventh Circuit of the US Courts of Appeals. There are US District Courts situated in Chicago, Benton and Springfield.

US District Courts

Northern: 219 South Dearborn St, Chicago, IL 60604; tel. (312) 435-5713; Judges: JOHN F. GRADY (Chief Judge), PRENTICE H. MARSHALL, NICHOLAS J. BUA, STANLEY J. ROSZKOWSKI, JAMES B. MORAN, MARTIN E. ASPEN, MILTON I. SHADUR, CHARLES P. KOCORAS, JOHN A. NORDBERG, WILLIAM T. HART, PAUL E. PLUNKETT, ILANA DIAMOND ROVNER, CHARLES R. NORGLE, Sr, JAMES F. HOLDERMAN, Jr, ANN C. WILLIAMS, BRIAN BARNETT DUFF, HARRY D. LIENENWEBER, JAMES B. ZAGEL, JAMES H. ALESIA, SUZANNE B. CONLON.

Central: POB 315, Springfield, IL 62705; tel. (217) 492-4020; Judges: HAROLD ALBERT BAKER (Chief Judge), MICHAEL M. MIHM, RICHARD MILLS.

Southern: POB 677, 301 West Main St, Benton, IL 62812; tel. (618) 438-0671; Judges: JAMES L. FOREMAN (Chief Judge), WILLIAM L. BEATTY, WILLIAM D. STIEHL.

STATE COURTS

The state Supreme Court has seven judges, including the chief justice. The judges are elected by judicial district and serve 10-year terms of office. The Court in turn elects one of its number as chief justice for a term of three years. The state Appellate Court has 34 judges, who serve 10-year terms of office.

Supreme Court

Richard Daley Center, Rm 3080, Chicago, IL 60602; Judges: DANIEL P. WARD (Chief Justice), WILLIAM CLARK, BEN MILLER, THOMAS J. MORAN, HOWARD C. RYAN, JOHN J. STAMOS, HORACE L. CALVO.

Indiana

FEDERAL COURTS

Indiana is in the Seventh Circuit of the US Courts of Appeals. There are US District Courts at South Bend and Indianapolis.

US District Courts

Northern: Federal Bldg, Rm 202, 204 South Main St, South Bend, IN 46601; tel. (219) 236-8250; Judges: ALLEN SHARP (Chief Judge), WILLIAM C. LEE, JAMES T. MOODY, ROBERT L. MILLER, Jr.

Southern: US Courthouse, Rm 123, 46 East Ohio St, Indianapolis, IN 46204; tel. (317) 269-6384; Judges: GENE E. BROOKS (Chief Judge), S. HUGH DILLIN, SARAH E. BARKER, LARRY J. McKINNEY, JOHN D. TINDER.

STATE COURTS

The state Supreme Court has five judges, including the chief justice, who are appointed by the governor on the advice of the Judicial Nominating Commission. The chief justice is chosen by the Judicial Nominating Commission from the serving Supreme Court judges, and serves a five-year term. The state Court of Appeals has 12 judges. Judges in both courts serve for two years, and then for a further 10 years if they are approved by referendum.

Supreme Court

State Capitol Bldg, Rm 324, Indianapolis, IN 46204; tel. (317) 232-2544; Judges: RANDALL SHEPARD (Chief Justice), ROGER O. DeBRULER, BRENT E. DICKERSON, RICHARD M. GIVAN, ALFRED J. PIVARNIK.

Iowa

FEDERAL COURTS

Iowa is located in the Eighth Circuit of the US Courts of Appeals. There are US District Courts at Cedar Rapids and Des Moines.

US District Courts

Northern: POB 4411, Cedar Rapids, IA 52407; tel. (319) 339-2468; Judges: DONALD E. O'BRIEN (Chief Judge), DAVID R. HANSEN.

Southern: US Courthouse, Rm 221, East 1st and Walnut Sts, Des Moines, IA 50309; tel. (515) 284-6237; Judges: HAROLD D. VICTOR (Chief Judge), CHARLES R. WOLLE.

STATE COURTS

The state Supreme Court consists of nine judges, including a chief justice. The judges, who are chosen at-large, are appointed by the governor from lists submitted by nominating commissions, and serve terms of eight years. Once they have served for at least one year, judges' appointments must be ratified by voters at the next general election. The judges select one of their number as chief justice, who then serves for the remainder of the term. The state Court of Appeals has six judges serving six-year terms of office.

Supreme Court

State House Annex, Des Moines, IA 50319; tel. (515) 281-5174; Judges: A. A. McGiverin (Chief Justice), James H. Carter, K. David Harris, Jerry L. Larson, Louis A. Lavorato, Linda Neuman, Louis W. Schultz, Bruce Snell, Jr, James Andreasen.

Kansas

FEDERAL COURTS

Kansas is in the 10th Circuit of the US Courts of Appeals. Wichita is the seat of the US District Court.

US District Court

US Courthouse, Rm 204, 401 North Market St, Wichita, KS 67202; tel. (316) 269-6491; Judges: Earl E. O'Connor (Chief Judge), Richard Dean Rogers, Dale E. Saffels, Patrick F. Kelly, Sam A. Crow.

STATE COURTS

The state Supreme Court has seven judges, including the chief justice. All judges are appointed by the governor from names submitted by the Judicial Nominating Commission. When judges have served at least one year in office voters may approve their retention at the next general election. Thereafter they serve for six years. The most senior judge is appointed as chief justice. The state Court of Appeals has 10 judges; appointments are as for Supreme Court judges, with election to serve a four-year term after an initial one-year term of service.

Supreme Court

Kansas Judicial Center, 301 10th St West, Topeka, KS 66612-1507; tel. (913) 296-5348; Judges: Robert H. Miller (Chief Justice), Donald L. Allegrucci, Kay McFarland, Richard Winn Holmes, Harold Herd, Tyler C. Lockett, Frederick N. Six.

Kentucky

FEDERAL COURTS

Kentucky belongs to the Sixth Circuit of the US Courts of Appeals. US District Courts are located in Lexington and Louisville.

US District Courts

Eastern: POB 741, Lexington, KY 40586; tel. (606) 233-2503; Judges: Eugene E. Siler, Jr (Chief Judge), Scott Reed, William Bertelsman, G. Wix Unthank, Henry R. Wilhoit, Jr.
Western: US Courthouse Bldg, Rm 230, 601 West Broadway, Louisville, KY 40202; tel. (502) 582-5156; Judges: Edward H. Johnstone (Chief Judge), Eugene E. Siler, Jr, Thomas A. Ballantine, Ronald E. Meredith, Charles R. Simpson, III.

STATE COURTS

The state Supreme Court has seven judges, including a chief justice. The judges are elected from court districts for terms of eight years; they then choose one of their number to serve a four-year term as chief justice. The Court of Appeals has 14 judges, who are also elected to serve eight-year terms of office.

Supreme Court

State Capitol Bldg, Rm 231, Frankfort, KY 40601; tel. (502) 564-6755; Judges: Robert F. Stephens (Chief Justice), William Gant, Joseph E. Lambert, Charles M. Leibson, Dan Jack Combs, Roy N. Vance, Donald Wintersheimer.

Louisiana

FEDERAL COURTS

Louisiana is in the Fifth Circuit of the US Courts of Appeals. There are US District Courts in New Orleans, Baton Rouge and Shreveport.

US District Courts

Eastern: US Courthouse, 500 Camp St-C525, New Orleans, LA 70130; tel. (504) 589-6504; Judges: Frederick J. R. Heebe (Chief Judge), Charles Schwartz, Jr, Morley L. Sear, Adrian A. Duplantier, Robert F. Collins, George Arceneaux, Jr,

Veronica D. Wicker, Patrick E. Carr, Peter Beer, A. J. McNamara, Henry A. Mentz, Jr, Martin L. C. Feldman, Marcel Livaudais, Jr.
Middle: Federal Court Bldg, Rm 228, 707 Florida Ave, Baton Rouge, LA 70801; tel. (504) 389-0535.
Western: 500 Fannin St, Shreveport, LA 71101; tel. (318) 226-5260; Judges: Tom Stagg (Chief Judge), Earl Earnest Veron, John M. Shaw, John M. Duhe, Jr, F. A. Little, Jr, Donald E. Walter.

STATE COURTS

The state Supreme Court has seven judges, including the chief justice. The judges are elected from six supreme-court districts, the first district having two judges, for staggered 10-year terms. The chief justice is chosen by seniority of service. The state Court of Appeals has 48 judges, also elected to serve 10-year terms. Louisiana is the only US state to have a judicial system based on Roman Law (based on the Code Napoléon), with judgments made by interpretation of existing statutes and code law, as opposed to Common Law which is founded on legal precedent. However, in practice the conduct of court proceedings in Louisiana differs little from that in other states.

Supreme Court

Supreme Court Bldg, 301 Loyola Ave, New Orleans, LA 70112; tel. (504) 568-5747; Judges: John A. Dixon, Jr (Chief Justice), Pascal F. Calogero, Jr, Luther F. Cole, James L. Dennis, Harry T. Lemmon, Walter F. Marcus, Jr, Jack Crozier Watson.

Maine

FEDERAL COURTS

Maine is in the First Circuit of the US Courts of Appeals. There is a US District Court in Portland.

US District Court

POB 7505 DTS, Portland, ME 04112; tel. (207) 780-3357; Judges: Conrad K. Cyr (Chief Judge), Gene Carter.

STATE COURTS

Maine has a Supreme Judicial Court with seven judges, including a chief justice. All the judges, selected at-large, are appointed by the governor with the consent of the Senate and serve terms of seven years.

Supreme Judicial Court

POB 4910, Portland, ME 04112; tel. (207) 879-4791; Judges: Vincent L. McKusick (Chief Justice), Robert W. Clifford, Caroline D. Glassman, David G. Roberts, Daniel E. Wathen, D. Brock Hornby, Samuel W. Collins, Jr.

Maryland

FEDERAL COURTS

Maryland is in the Fourth Circuit of the US Courts of Appeals. There is a US District Court at Baltimore.

US District Court

101 West Lombard St, Baltimore, MD 21201; tel. (301) 962-4655; Judges: Alexander Harvey, II (Chief Judge), Herbert F. Murray, Joseph C. Howard, Norman P. Ramsey, William E. Black, Jr, John R. Hargrove, J. Frederick Motz, Frederick N. Smalkin.

STATE COURTS

The Maryland state court of last resort is the Court of Appeals. There are seven judges, including the chief judge. Judges are nominated by the Judicial Nominating Commission and appointed by the governor with the consent of the Senate. The appointment of judges has to be ratified by the electorate after a minimum of one year of service. Maryland's intermediate appellate court is the Court of Special Appeals, which has 13 judges nominated and ratified in a way similar to that for Court of Appeals judges. All judges in the state serve 10-year terms of office.

Court of Appeals

401 Bosley Ave, County Courts Bldg, Towson, MD 21204; tel. (301) 583-6500; Judges: Robert C. Murphy (Chief Justice), William

H. Adkins, II, Harry A. Cole, Albert T. Blackwell, Jr, John C. Eldridge, John F. McAuliffe, Lawrence F. Rodowsky.

Massachusetts

FEDERAL COURTS

Massachusetts is in the First Circuit of the US Courts of Appeals. There is a US District Court in Boston.

US District Court

John W. McCormack Post Office and Courthouse Bldg, Rm 1629, Boston, MA 02109; tel. (617) 223-9283; Judges: Frank H. Freedman (Chief Judge), Joseph L. Tauro, Walter J. Skinner, A. David Mazzone, Robert E. Keeton, John J. McNaught, Rya W. Zobel, David S. Nelson, William G. Young, Douglas P. Woodlock, Edward F. Harrington.

STATE COURTS

Massachusetts has a Supreme Judicial Court with seven judges, including a chief justice. The chief judge and other judges are appointed by the governor with the advice and consent of the Governor's Council. They are selected at-large and may hold office until reaching the age of 70. The state Appeals Court has 10 judges, who may also remain in office until attaining the age of 70.

Supreme Judicial Court

New Court House, 13th Floor, Boston, MA 02108; tel. (617) 725-8010; Judges: Paul J. Liacos (Chief Justice), Ruth I. Abrams, Neil L. Lynch, Joseph R. Nolan, Francis P. O'Connor, Herbert P. Wilkins, (1 vacancy).

Michigan

FEDERAL COURTS

Michigan is in the Sixth Circuit of the US Courts of Appeals. US District Courts are located in Detroit and Grand Rapids.

US District Courts

Eastern: US Courthouse, Rm 740, 231 West Lafayette Blvd, Detroit, MI 48226; tel. (313) 226-7457; Judges: Philip Pratt (Chief Judge), James P. Churchill, Julian A. Cook, Jr, Stewart A. Newblatt, Avern Cohn, Anna Diggs Taylor, Horace W. Gilmore, George E. Woods, Richard F. Suhrheinrich, George La Plata, Barbara K. Hackett, Lawrence P. Zatkoff, Patrick J. Duggan.
Western: Federal Bldg, Rm 682, 110 Michigan St, NW, Grand Rapids, MI 49503; tel. (616) 456-2523; Judges: Douglas W. Hillman (Chief Judge), Benjamin F. Gibson, Richard A. Enslen, Robert H. Bell.

STATE COURTS

The state Supreme Court has seven judges, including the chief justice. Judges are elected at-large and serve eight-year terms of office; the chief justice is elected by members of the court and the position is held for two years. The state Court of Appeals has 18 judges who are elected to serve six-year terms of office.

Supreme Court

144 Lafayette Blvd, Detroit, MI 48226; tel. (313) 373-0120; Judges: Dorothy Comstock Riley (Chief Justice), Dennis Wayne Archer, Patricia J. Boyle, James H. Brickley, Michael F. Cavanagh, Robert Griffin, Charles L. Levin.

Minnesota

FEDERAL COURTS

Minnesota is in the Eighth Circuit of the US Courts of Appeals. There is a US District Court in St Paul.

US District Court

Federal Bldg, Rm 760, 316 North Robert St, St Paul, MN 55101; tel. (612) 725-7169; Judges: Donald D. Alsop (Chief Judge), Harry H. MacLaughlin, Robert G. Renner, Diana E. Murphy, Paul A. Magnuson, James M. Rosenbaum, David S. Doty.

STATE COURTS

The state Supreme Court has seven judges, including a chief justice. The judges are elected at-large for six-year terms. The chief justice is elected popularly to hold office for the remainder of the term. The state Court of Appeals has 12 judges, who are also elected to serve terms of six years.

Supreme Court

State Capitol Bldg, Rm 230, St Paul, MN 55155; tel. (612) 296-5037; Judges: Peter S. Popovich (Chief Justice), M. Jeanne Coyne, Glenn E. Kelley, A. M. Keith, John E. Simonett, Rosalie E. Wahl, Lawrence R. Yetka.

Mississippi

FEDERAL COURTS

Mississippi is in the Fifth Circuit of the US Courts of Appeals. There are US District Courts in Oxford and Jackson.

US District Courts

Northern: POB 727, Oxford, MS 38655; tel. (601) 234-1971; Judges: L. T. Senter, Jr (Chief Judge), Neal Biggers, Glen H. Davidson.
Southern: POB 2247, Jackson, MS 39225; tel. (601) 960-4545; Judges: William H. Barbour, Jr (Chief Judge), Walter L. Nixon, Jr, Harry T. Wingate, Tom S. Lee, Walter J. Gex, III.

STATE COURTS

The state Supreme Court has nine judges who are elected by district and serve for eight years. The most senior judge is appointed as chief justice.

Supreme Court

Gartin Justice Bldg, Jackson, MS 39205; tel. (601) 359-3697; Judges: Roy Noble Lee (Chief Justice), Reuben V. Anderson, Armis E. Hawkins, Dan M. Lee, Lenore L. Prather, James L. Robertson, Michael D. Sullivan, Edwin L. Pittman, N. Joel Blass.

Missouri

FEDERAL COURTS

Missouri is in the Eighth Circuit of the US Courts of Appeals. There are US District Courts in St Louis and Kansas City.

District Courts

Eastern: 1114 Market St, St Louis, MO 63101; tel. (314) 425-5603; Judges: John F. Nangle (Chief Judge), Edward D. Filippine, William L. Hungate, Clyde S. Cahill, Jr, Stephen N. Limbaugh, George F. Gunn, Jr.
Western: US Courthouse, Rm 613, 811 Grand Ave, Kansas City, MO 64106; tel. (816) 221-6271; Judges: Scott O. Wright (Chief Judge), Russell G. Clark, Howard F. Sachs, Joseph E. Stephens, Jr, D. Brook Bartlett, Dean Whipple.

STATE COURTS

The state Supreme Court has seven judges, including a chief justice. The judges, who serve 12-year terms of office, are chosen at-large by the governor on the advice of a judicial commission. After an initial term of one year their appointment must be ratified by the electorate. The judges select one of their number to act as chief justice for a term of two years. The Court of Appeals has 32 judges, who also serve terms of 12 years.

Supreme Court

POB 150, Jefferson City, MO 65102; tel. (314) 751-4144; Judges: Charles B. Blackmar (Chief Justice), William H. Billings, Ann K. Covington, Andrew J. Higgins, Albert L. Rendlen, Edward D. Robertson, Jr, Warren D. Welliver.

Montana

FEDERAL COURTS

Montana is in the Ninth Circuit of the US Courts of Appeals. There is a US District Court at Billings.

US District Court

Federal Bldg, Rm 5405, 316 North 26th St, Billings, MT 59101; tel. (406) 657-6366; Judges: James F. Battin (Chief Judge), Paul G. Hatfield, Charles C. Lovell.

STATE COURTS

The state Supreme Court has seven judges, including the chief justice, who are elected at-large to serve eight-year terms of office.

Supreme Court

215 North Sanders, Rm 414, Helena, MT 59620; tel. (406) 444-2621; Judges: JEAN A. TURNAGE (Chief Justice), L. C. GULBRANDSON, JOHN C. HARRISON, WILLIAM E. HUNT, Sr, R. C. McDONOUGH, JOHN C. SHEEHY, FRED J. WEBER.

Nebraska

FEDERAL COURTS

Nebraska is in the Eighth Circuit of the US Courts of Appeals. There is a US District Court in Omaha.

US District Court

POB 1297, Omaha, NE 68101; tel. (402) 221-3615; Judges: LYLE E. STROM (Chief Judge), WARREN K. URBOM.

STATE COURTS

The state Supreme Court has seven judges, including a chief justice. Judges, selected by district, are initially appointed by the governor to serve for a three-year term, after which they must run for retention in the next general election. Following approval by the voters judges serve a six-year term of office. The chief justice, however, is chosen state-wide and is appointed by the governor, remaining in office until retirement.

Supreme Court

State Capitol Bldg, Rm 2214, Lincoln, NE 68509; tel. (402) 471-3732; Judges: WILLIAM C. HASTINGS (Chief Justice), LESLIE BOSLAUGH, D. NICK CAPORALE, DALE FAHRENBRUCH, JOHN T. GRANT, THOMAS M. SHANAHAN, C. THOMAS WHITE.

Nevada

FEDERAL COURTS

Nevada is in the Ninth Circuit of the US Courts of Appeals. There is a District Court in Las Vegas.

US District Court

300 Las Vegas Blvd, South Las Vegas, NV 89101; tel. (702) 388-6351; Judges: EDWARD C. REED, Jr (Chief Judge), LLOYD D. GEORGE, HOWARD D. McKIBBEN, PHILIP M. PRO.

STATE COURTS

The state Supreme Court has five judges, including the chief justice, who are elected at-large and serve terms of six years. The chief justice is selected according to seniority of service and retains the position for one to two years.

Supreme Court

Capitol Complex, Carson City, NV 89710; tel. (702) 885-5190; Judges: C. CLIFTON YOUNG (Chief Justice), JOHN C. MOWBRAY, CHARLES E. SPRINGER, THOMAS L. STEFFEN, ROBERT E. ROSE.

New Hampshire

FEDERAL COURTS

New Hampshire is in the First Circuit of the US Courts of Appeals. There is a US District Court in Concord.

US District Court

POB 892, Concord, NH 03301; tel. (603) 225-6051; Judges: SHANE DEVINE (Chief Judge), MARTIN F. LOUGHLIN.

STATE COURTS

The state Supreme Court has five judges, including a chief justice. The chief justice and all other judges, selected at-large, are appointed by the governor with the consent of the Executive Council and may hold office until reaching the age of 70.

Supreme Court

Supreme Court Bldg, Concord, NH 03301; tel. (603) 271-3415; Judges: DAVID A. BROCK (Chief Justice), WILLIAM F. BATCHELDER, WILLIAM R. JOHNSON, DAVID H. SOUTER, W. STEPHEN THAYER, II.

New Jersey

FEDERAL COURTS

New Jersey is in the Third Circuit of the US Courts of Appeals. There is a US District Court at Newark.

US District Court

US Post Office and Courthouse, POB 419, Newark, NJ 07102; tel. (201) 645-3730; Judges: JOHN F. GERRY (Chief Judge), STANLEY S. BROTMAN, ANNE E. THOMPSON, D. R. DEBEVOISE, H. LEE SAROKIN, HAROLD A. ACKERMAN, JOHN W. BISSELL, MARYANNE TRUMP BARRY, JOSEPH H. RODRIGUEZ, GARRETT E. BROWN, Jr, ALFRED J. LECHNER, Jr, NICHOLAS H. POLITAN, ALFRED M. WOLIN.

STATE COURTS

The state Supreme Court has seven judges, including the chief justice. All judges, including the chief justice, are appointed by the governor with the consent of the Senate and serve terms of seven years. The Appellate Division of the Superior Court has 28 judges who also serve seven-year terms of office.

Supreme Court

313 State St, Perth Amboy, NJ 08861; tel. (201) 324-1600; Judges: ROBERT N. WILENTZ (Chief Justice), ROBERT L. CLIFFORD, MARIE L. GARIBALDI, ALAN B. HANDLER, DANIEL J. O'HERN, STEWART G. POLLOCK, GARY S. STEIN.

New Mexico

FEDERAL COURTS

New Mexico is in the Tenth Circuit of the US Courts of Appeals. There is a US District Court in Albuquerque.

US District Court

POB 38, Albuquerque, NM 87103; tel. (505) 766-1129; Judges: SANTIAGO E. CAMPOS (Chief Judge), JUAN G. BURCIAGA, JOHN E. CONWAY, JAMES A. PARKER.

STATE COURTS

The state Supreme Court has five judges, including a chief justice. The judges, who are elected at-large, serve terms of eight years. They elect one of their number to serve a two-year term as chief justice. The Court of Appeals has seven judges, also elected to serve eight-year terms of office.

Supreme Court

POB 848, Santa Fe, NM 87503; tel. (505) 827-4889; Judges: DAN SOSA, Jr (Chief Justice), TONY SCARBOROUGH, RICHARD E. RANSOM, HARRY E. STOWERS, Jr, JOSEPH F. BACA.

New York

FEDERAL COURTS

New York is in the Second Circuit of the US Courts of Appeals. There are US District Courts in Albany, Brooklyn, New York City (Manhattan) and Buffalo.

US District Courts

Northern: POB 1037, Albany, NY 12201; tel. (518) 472-5651; Judges: HOWARD G. MUNSON (Chief Judge), NEAL P. McCURN, THOMAS J. McAVOY, CON G. CHOLAKIS.

Eastern: 225 Cadman Plaza East, Brooklyn, NY 11201; tel. (718) 330-7569; Judges: JACK B. WEINSTEIN (Chief Judge), MARK A. COSTANTINO, THOMAS C. PLATT, Jr, CHARLES P. SIFTON, EUGENE H. NICKERSON, JOSEPH M. McLAUGHLIN, ISRAEL LEO GLASSER, RAYMOND J. DEARIE, LEONARD D. WEXLER, EDWARD R. KORMAN, REENA RAGGI.

Southern: US Courthouse, Foley Sq., New York, NY 10007; tel. (212) 791-0145; Judges: CHARLES L. BRIEANT (Chief Judge), DAVID N. EDELSTEIN, THOMAS P. GRIESA, ROBERT J. WARD, KEVIN THOMAS DUFFY, RICHARD OWEN, LEONARD B. SAND, MARY JOHNSON LOWE, GERARD L. GOETTEL, CHARLES S. HAIGHT, Jr, VINCENT L. BRODERICK, PIERRE N. LEVAL, ROBERT W. SWEET, JOHN E. SPRIZZO, SHIRLEY WOHL KRAM, JOHN F. KEENAN, PETER K. LEISURE, JOHN M. WALKER, LOUIS L. STANTON, MIRIAM G. CEDARBAUM, RICHARD J. DARONCO, MICHAEL B. MUKASEY, KENNETH CONBOY.

Western: Courthouse, Rm 312, 68 Court St, Buffalo, NY 14202; tel. (716) 846-4134; Judges: JOHN T. CURTIN (Chief Judge), MICHAEL A. TELESCA, DAVID G. LARIMER.

STATE COURTS

The highest state court is the Court of Appeals which has seven judges, including the chief justice, who serve terms of 14 years. Judges are appointed by the governor on the advice of, and with the consent of, the Senate. The Appellate Division of the Supreme Court has 47 judges, who serve five-year terms of office. There is an upper age-limit of 70 years for judges in New York.

Court of Appeals

Hall of Justice, Rm 430, Rochester, NY 14614; Judges: SOL WACHTLER (Chief Justice), FRITZ W. ALEXANDER, II, JOSEPH W. BELLACOSA, STEWART F. HANCOCK, Jr, JUDITH S. KAYE, RICHARD D. SIMONS, VIDO J. TITONE.

North Carolina

FEDERAL COURTS

North Carolina is in the Fourth Circuit of the US Courts of Appeals. There are US District Courts in Raleigh, Greensboro and Asheville.

US District Courts

Eastern: POB 27504, Raleigh, NC 27611; tel. (919) 856-4050; Judges: W. EARL BRITT (Chief Judge), JAMES C. FOX, TERENCE W. BOYLE, MALCOLM J. HOWARD.

Middle: POB V-1, Greensboro, NC 27402; tel. (919) 333-5347; Judges: HIRAM H. WARD (Chief Judge), FRANK W. BULLOCK, Jr, RICHARD C. ERWIN.

Western: POB 92, Asheville, NC 28802; tel. (704) 259-0648; Judges: ROBERT C. POTTER (Chief Judge), JAMES B. MCMILLAN.

STATE COURTS

The state Supreme Court has seven judges, including the chief justice. All judges, including the chief justice, are elected at-large and serve terms of eight years. The state Court of Appeals has 12 judges, who are also elected to serve terms of eight years.

Supreme Court

POB 1841, Justice Bldg, Raleigh, NC 27602; tel. (919) 733-3713; Judges: JAMES G. EXUM (Chief Justice), HENRY E. FRYE, HARRY C. MARTIN, LOUIS B. MEYER, BURLEY B. MITCHELL, Jr, JOHN WEBB, WILLIS P. WHICHARD.

North Dakota

FEDERAL COURTS

North Dakota is in the Eighth Circuit of the US Courts of Appeals. The US District Court is in Bismarck.

US District Court

POB 1578, Bismarck, ND 58502; tel. (701) 225-4011; Judges: PATRICK A. CONMY (Chief Judge), RODNEY S. WEBBE.

STATE COURTS

The state Supreme Court has five judges, including the chief justice, who are elected at-large and serve 10-year terms. The chief justice is selected by the Supreme and District Court judges and serves a five-year term.

Supreme Court

State Capitol Bldg, 1st Floor, Bismarck, ND 58505; tel. (701) 224-2221; Judges: RALPH J. ERICKSTAD (Chief Justice), H. F. GIERKE, BERYL J. LEVINE, HERBERT L. MESCHKE, GERALD W. VANDEWALLE.

Ohio

FEDERAL COURTS

Ohio is in the Sixth Circuit of the US Courts of Appeals. There are US District Courts in Cleveland and Columbus.

US District Courts

Northern: US Courthouse, Rm 302, 201 Superior Ave, NE, Cleveland, OH 44114; tel. (216) 522-4250; Judges: FRANK J. BATTISTI (Chief Judge), THOMAS D. LAMBROS, JOHN M. MANOS, GEORGE W. WHITE, ANN ALDRICH, ALVIN I. KRENZLER, JOHN W. POTTER, DAVID D. DOWD, Jr, SAM H. BELL, ALICE M. BATCHELDER, RICHARD B. MCQUADE, Jr.

Southern: US Courthouse, Rm 328, 85 Marconi Blvd, Columbus, OH 43215; tel. (614) 469-5442; Judges: CARL B. RUBIN (Chief Judge), JOHN D. HOLSCHUH, WALTER H. RICE, S. ARTHUR SPIEGEL, HERMAN JACOB WEBER, JAMES L. GRAHAM, GEORGE C. SMITH.

STATE COURTS

The state Supreme Court has seven judges, including a chief justice. All judges, including the chief justice, are elected at-large for terms of six years. The state Court of Appeals has 53 judges, all of whom also serve six-year terms of office.

Supreme Court

30 East Broad St, Columbus, OH 43215; tel. (614) 466-3627; Judges: THOMAS J. MOYER (Chief Justice), HERBERT R. BROWN, ANDREW DOUGLAS, ROBERT E. HOLMES, ALICE ROBIE RESNICK, ASHER WILLIAM SWEENEY, J. CRAIG WRIGHT.

Oklahoma

FEDERAL COURTS

Oklahoma is in the Tenth Circuit of the US Courts of Appeals. There are US District Courts in Tulsa, Muskogee and Oklahoma City.

US District Courts

Northern: US Courthouse, Rm 4-472, 333 West 4th St, Tulsa, OK 74103; tel. (918) 581-7616; Judges: H. DALE COOK (Chief Judge), JAMES O. ELLISON, THOMAS R. BRETT, DAVID L. RUSSELL.

Eastern: POB 828, Muskogee, OK 74401; tel. (918) 687-2437; Judges: FRANK H. SHEY (Chief Judge), DAVID L. RUSSELL.

Western: POB 1996, Oklahoma City, OK 73102; tel. (405) 231-5153; Judges: RALPH G. THOMPSON (Chief Judge), WAYNE ALLEY, LEE R. WEST, DAVID L. RUSSELL, LAYN R. PHILLIPS.

STATE COURTS

Oklahoma shares the distinction with Texas of having twin state courts of last resort: ultimate appellate jurisdiction resides with the Supreme Court in civil cases, and with the Court of Criminal Appeals in criminal cases. Furthermore, Oklahoma's judicial system is unique in that final rulings by its Courts of Appeals may not be referred to any higher state court. Judges are appointed by district to the Supreme Court and Court of Criminal Appeals by the governor, from lists of three submitted by the Judicial Nominating Commission, for six-year terms. At the general election following completion of at least one year's service, and every six years after appointment, judges must be confirmed in office by the electorate. The chief justice of the Supreme Court and the presiding judge of the Court of Criminal Appeals are elected by the members of each court to serve two-year terms of office. The Court of Appeals has 12 judges, who are elected to serve six-year terms.

Supreme Court

State Capitol Bldg, Oklahoma City, OK 73105; tel. (405) 521-3845; Judges: RUDOLPH HARGRAVE (Chief Justice), JOHN B. DOOLIN, RALPH B. HODGES, YVONNE KAUGER, ROBERT E. LAVENDER, MARIAN P. OPALA, ROBERT D. SIMMS, HARDY SUMMERS, ALMA WILSON.

Court of Criminal Appeals

Judges: EDGAR PARKS, Jr (Presiding Judge), TOM BRETT, HEZ J. BUSSEY.

Oregon

FEDERAL COURTS

Oregon is in the Ninth Circuit of the US Courts of Appeals. There is a US District Court in Portland.

US District Court

US Courthouse, Rm 602, 620 SW Main St, Portland, OR 97205; tel. (503) 221-4190; Judges: OWEN M. PANNER (Chief Judge), JAMES M. BURNS, JAMES A. REDDEN, HELEN J. FRYE, MALCOLM F. MARSH.

STATE COURTS

The state Supreme Court has seven judges, including a chief justice. Judges are elected at-large to serve terms of six years. They elect one of their number as chief justice. Oregon has a Court of Appeals, with 10 judges elected to serve six-year terms of office, and a Tax Court, which has a single judge also serving a term of six years.

Supreme Court

Supreme Court Bldg, Salem, OR 97310; tel. (503) 378-6024; Judges: EDWIN J. PETERSON (Chief Justice), WALLACE P. CARSON, Jr, W. MICHAEL GILLETTE, ROBERT E. JONES, ED FADELY, GEORGE VAN HOOMISSEN, HANS A. LINDE.

Pennsylvania

FEDERAL COURTS

Pennsylvania is in the Third Circuit of the US Courts of Appeals. There are US District Courts in Philadelphia, Scranton and Pittsburgh.

US District Courts

Eastern: US Courthouse, Rm 15614, Independence Mall West, 601 Market St, Philadelphia, PA 19106; tel. (215) 597-0436; Judges: JOHN P. FULLAM (Chief Judge), CHARLES R. WEINER, DANIEL H. HUYETT, III, CLIFFORD SCOTT GREEN, LOUIS CHARLES BECHTLE, JOSEPH L. MCGLYNN, Jr, EDWARD N. CAHN, LOUIS H. POLLAK, NORMA L. SHAPIRO, JAMES T. GILES, JAMES MCGIRR KELLY, THOMAS N. O'NEILL, Jr, MARVIN KATZ, EDMUND V. LUDWIG, ROBERT F. KELLY, FRANKLIN S. VAN ANTWERPEN, ROBERT S. GAWTHROP.

Middle: POB 1146, Scranton, PA 18501; tel. (717) 344-5731; Judges: WILLIAM J. NEALON, Jr (Chief Judge), RICHARD P. CONABOY, SYLVIA H. RAMBO, WILLIAM W. CALDWELL, EDWARD M. KOSIK.

Western: US Post Office and Courthouse, 7th & Grant Sts, Courtroom 3, 8th Floor, Pittsburgh, PA 15219; tel. (412) 644-6482; Judges: MAURICE B. COHILL, Jr (Chief Judge), GERALD J. WEBER, PAUL A. SIMMONS, GUSTAVE DIAMOND, DONALD E. ZIEGLER, ALAN N. BLOCH, GLENN E. MENCER, WILLIAM L. STANDISH.

STATE COURTS

The state Supreme Court has seven judges, who are elected at-large to serve 10-year terms of office. The longest-serving judge is appointed as chief justice. The Superior Court, the state intermediate appellate court, has 15 judges also elected to serve 10-year terms of office. The other court of appeal, the Commonwealth Court, which has jurisdiction over civil cases involving the state, has nine judges serving 10-year terms of office.

Supreme Court

Courthouse, Erie, PA 16501; tel. (814) 456-2006; Judges: ROBERT N. C. NIX, Jr (Chief Justice), JOHN P. FLAHERTY, Jr, WILLIAM D. HUTCHINSON, ROLF LARSEN, JAMES T. MCDERMOTT, NICHOLAS P. PAPADAKOS, STEPHEN A. ZAPPALA.

Rhode Island

FEDERAL COURTS

Rhode Island is in the First Circuit of the US Courts of Appeals. There is a US District Court at Providence.

US District Courts

Federal Bldg and US Courthouse, Rm 314, Providence, RI 02903; tel. (401) 528-5155; Judges: FRANCIS J. BOYLE (Chief Judge), RONALD R. LAGUEUX, ERNEST C. TORRES.

STATE COURTS

The state Supreme Court is composed of five judges, including the chief justice. All Supreme Court judges are elected by the state legislature and hold office for life.

Supreme Court

250 Benefit St, Providence, RI 02903; tel. (401) 277-3775; Judges: THOMAS F. FAY (Chief Justice), THOMAS F. KELLEHER, FLORENCE K. MURRAY, DONALD F. SHEA, JOSEPH R. WEISBERGER.

South Carolina

FEDERAL COURTS

South Carolina is in the Fourth Circuit of the US Courts of Appeals. There is a US District Court in Columbia.

US District Court

POB 867, Columbia, SC 29202; tel. (803) 765-5810; Judges: SOLOMON BLATT, Jr (Chief Judge), C. WESTON HOUCK, FALCON B. HAWKINS, MATTHEW J. PERRY, Jr, GEORGE R. ANDERSON, Jr, CLYDE H. HAMILTON, KAREN L. HENDERSON, JOSEPH F. ANDERSON, Jr.

STATE COURTS

The state Supreme Court has five judges, including the chief justice, who serve terms of 10 years. Judges are elected by the General Assembly (the state legislature) from names submitted by the Judiciary Committee of the legislature. The state Court of Appeals has six judges, elected by the General Assembly to serve six-year terms of office.

Supreme Court

POB 53, Darlington, SC 29532; tel. (803) 393-3531; Judges: GEORGE TILLMAN GREGORY, Jr (Chief Justice), JEAN H. TOAL, A. LEE CHANDLER, ERNEST A. FINNEY, Jr, DAVID W. HARWELL.

South Dakota

FEDERAL COURTS

South Dakota is in the Eighth Circuit of the US Courts of Appeals. There is a US District Court in Sioux Falls.

US District Court

US Courthouse, Rm 413, Pierre, SD 57501; tel. (605) 224-0476; Judges: DONALD J. PORTER (Chief Judge), RICHARD H. BATTEY, JOHN BAILEY JONES.

STATE COURTS

The state Supreme Court has five judges, including a chief justice. Judges, selected by district, are initially appointed by the governor on the advice of the Judicial Qualifications Commission to serve for a three-year term. Thereafter they must run for retention in the next general election. Following approval by the voters, judges serve an eight-year term of office. The judges elect one of their number to a four-year term as chief justice.

Supreme Court

POB 1087, Aberdeen, SD 57402; tel. (605) 622-2266; Judges: GEORGE W. WUEST (Chief Justice), FRANK E. HENDERSON, ROBERT A. MILLER, ROBERT E. MORGAN, RICHARD SABERS.

Tennessee

FEDERAL COURTS

Tennessee is in the Sixth Circuit of the US Courts of Appeals. There are US District Courts in Knoxville, Nashville and Memphis.

US District Courts

Eastern: POB 2348, Knoxville, TN 37901; tel. (615) 673-4227; Judges: THOMAS G. HULL (Chief Judge), JAMES H. JARVIS, R. ALLAN EDGAR.

Middle: US Courthouse, Rm 824, 801 Broadway, Nashville, TN 37203; tel. (615) 251-7013; Judges: THOMAS A. WISEMAN, Jr (Chief Judge), THOMAS A. HIGGINS, JOHN T. NIXON.

Western: Federal Bldg, Rm 1107, 167 North Main St, Memphis, TN 38103; tel. (901) 521-3200; Judges: ODELL HORTON (Chief Judge), JULIA S. GIBBONS, JAMES D. TODD, JEROME TURNER.

STATE COURTS

The state Supreme Court has five judges, including the chief justice, who are elected at-large and serve eight-year terms of office. The chief justice is elected by members of the Court and holds office for 18 months. The state Court of Appeals has 12 judges and the Court of Criminal Appeals has nine judges, all of whom serve eight-year terms; initially appointed by the governor from lists of three submitted by the Appellate Court Nominating Commission, these judges must run for election at subsequent general elections.

Supreme Court

Supreme Court Bldg, Rm 309, Nashville, TN 37219; tel. (615) 741-2528; Judges: FRANK F. DROWOTA, III (Chief Justice), CHARLES H. O'BRIEN, ROBERT E. COOPER, WILLIAM H. D. FONES, WILLIAM J. HARBISON.

Texas

FEDERAL COURTS

Texas is in the Fifth Circuit of the US Courts of Appeals. There are US District Courts in Dallas, Houston, Tyler and San Antonio.

US District Courts

Northern: US Courthouse, Rm 15C22, 1100 Commerce St, Dallas, TX 75242; tel. (214) 767-9511; Judges: ROBERT W. PORTER (Chief Judge), ELDON B. MAHON, MARY LOU ROBINSON, BAREFOOT SANDERS, DAVID O. BELEW, Jr, JERRY BUCHMEYER, A. JOE FISH, ROBERT B. MALONEY, SIDNEY A. FITZWATER, SAMUEL R. CUMMINGS.

Southern: POB 61010, Houston, TX 77208; tel. (713) 221-9505; Judges: JAMES DE ANDA (Chief Judge), NORMAN W. BLACK, GABRIELLE K. McDONALD, GEORGE P. KAZEN, HUGH GIBSON, FILEMAN B. VELA, HAYDEN W. HEAD, Jr, RICARDO H. HINOJOSA, LYNN N. HUGHES, DAVID HITNER.

Eastern: Federal Bldg and US Courthouse, Rm 309, 211 West Ferguson St, Tyler, TX 75702; tel. (214) 592-8195; Judges: WILLIAM WAYNE JUSTICE (Chief Judge), ROBERT M. PARKER, HOWELL COBB, SAM B. HALL, Jr, PAUL N. BROWN.

Western: Hemisfair Plaza, 655 East Durango Blvd, San Antonio, TX 78206; tel. (512) 229-6550; Judges: LUCIUS D. BUNTON, III (Chief Judge), HARRY LEE HUDSPETH, HIPOLITO F. GARCIA, JAMES R. NOWLIN, EDWARD C. PRADO, WALTER S. SMITH, Jr.

STATE COURTS

Texas, like Oklahoma, has a state Supreme Court and a Court of Criminal Appeals, each having nine judges. All judges, including the chief justice of the Supreme Court and the presiding judge of the Court of Criminal Appeals, are popularly elected at-large to staggered six-year terms. The Courts of Appeals have 80 judges, all of whom serve six-year terms.

Supreme Court

POB 12248, Austin, TX 78711; tel. (512) 475-4691; Judges: THOMAS R. PHILLIPS (Chief Justice), RAUL A. GONZALEZ, OSCAR H. MAUZY, C. L. RAY, FRANKLIN S. SPEARS, EUGENE A. COOK, JACK HIGHTOWER, NATHAN L. HECHT, LLOYD DOGGETT.

Court of Criminal Appeals

POB 12308, Austin, TX 78711; Judges: MICHAEL J. McCORMICK Presiding Judge), CHARLES F. CAMPBELL, Jr, SAM HOUSTON CLINTON, WILBUR C. DAVIS, CHARLES MILLER, MARVIN O. TEAGUE, BILL WHITE, M. P. DUNCAN, III, DAVID BERCHELMANN, Jr.

Utah

FEDERAL COURTS

Utah is in the Tenth Circuit of the US Courts of Appeals. There is a US District Court in Salt Lake City.

US District Court

US Courthouse, Rm 251, 350 South Main St, Salt Lake City, UT 84101; tel. (801) 524-5167; Judges: BRUCE S. JENKINS (Chief Judge), J. THOMAS GREENE, DAVID SAM, DAVID K. WINDER.

STATE COURTS

The state Supreme Court has five judges including the chief justice. Judges are appointed by the governor with the consent of the Senate. After an initial three-year term their appointment must be ratified by voters at the next general election; thereafter terms last for 10 years. The chief justice is elected by the members of the court to serve a four-year term of office. The state Court of Appeals has seven judges who also serve for terms of three and then 10 years.

Supreme Court

State Capitol Bldg, Rm 332, Salt Lake City, UT 84114; tel. (801) 533-5282; Judges: GORDON R. HALL (Chief Justice), CHRISTINE M. DURHAM, RICHARD C. HOWE, I. DANIEL STEWART, MICHAEL D. ZIMMERMAN.

Vermont

FEDERAL COURTS

Vermont is in the Second Circuit of the US Courts of Appeals. There is a US District Court in Burlington.

US District Court

POB 522, Burlington, VT 05402; tel. (802) 951-6391; Judges: ALBERT W. COFFRIN (Chief Judge), FRANKLIN S. BILLINGS, Jr.

STATE COURTS

Vermont's Supreme Court has five judges, including the chief justice. All judges are nominated by the Judicial Nominating Board and are appointed by the governor to six-year terms, subject to state Senate confirmation.

Supreme Court

State Office Bldg, 111 State St, Montpelier, VT 05602; tel. (802) 828-3281; Judges: FREDERIC W. ALLEN (Chief Justice), ERNEST W. GIBSON, III, JOHN DOOLEY, JAMES MORSE, LOUIS P. PECK.

Virginia

FEDERAL COURTS

Virginia belongs to the Fourth Circuit of the US Courts of Appeals. There are US District Courts in Alexandria and Roanoke.

US District Courts

Eastern: POB 709, Alexandria, VA 22313; tel. (703) 549-5050; Judges: ALBERT V. BRYAN, Jr (Chief Judge), J. CALVITT CLARKE, RICHARD L. WILLIAMS, JAMES C. CACHERIS, ROBERT G. DOUMAR, CLAUDE M. HILTON, JAMES R. SPENCER, THOMAS S. ELLIS, III.

Western: POB 1234, Roanoke, VA 24006; tel. (703) 982-6224; Judges: JAMES C. TURK (Chief Judge), GLEN M. WILLIAMS, JAMES H. MICHAEL, Jr, JACKSON L. KISER.

STATE COURTS

The state Supreme Court has seven judges, including the chief justice, who are elected at-large by the legislature and serve 12-year terms of office. The longest-serving judge is appointed as chief justice. The state Court of Appeals has 10 judges, who are similarly elected to serve for eight years.

Supreme Court

POB 1315, Richmond, VA 23219; tel. (804) 786-2023; Judges: HARRY LEE CARRICO (Chief Justice), A. CHRISTIAN COMPTON, CHARLES S. RUSSELL, ROSCOE B. STEPHENSON, Jr, JOHN CHARLES THOMAS, ELIZABETH B. LACY, HENRY M. WHITING.

Washington

FEDERAL COURTS

Washington is in the Ninth Circuit of the US Court of Appeals. There are US District Courts in Spokane and Seattle.

US District Courts

Eastern: POB 2136, Spokane, WA 99210; tel. (509) 456-6830; Judges: ROBERT J. McNICHOLS (Chief Judge), JUSTIN L. QUACKENBUSH, ALAN A. McDONALD.

Western: US Courthouse, Rm 705, 1010 5th Ave, Seattle, WA 98104; tel. (206) 442-5410; Judges: BARBARA J. ROTHSTEIN (Chief Judge), JACK E. TANNER, JOHN C. COUGHENOUR, CAROLYN R. DIMMICK, ROBERT J. BRYAN, WILLIAM L. DWYER.

STATE COURTS

The state Supreme Court consists of nine judges, including a chief justice. Justices are popularly elected at-large for staggered terms of six years. The chief justice, serving a two-year term of office, is the most senior judge who has not previously held that position. The state Court of Appeals has 16 judges, who are also elected to serve terms of six years.

Supreme Court

Temple of Justice, Olympia, WA 98504; tel. (206) 753-5091; Judges: KEITH CALLOW (Chief Justice), JAMES M. DOLLIVER, JAMES A. ANDERSEN, ROBERT F. BRACHTENBACH, FRED H. DORE, BARBARA DURHAM, CHARLES Z. SMITH, VERNON R. PEARSON, ROBERT F. UTTER.

West Virginia

FEDERAL COURTS

West Virginia is in the Fourth Circuit of the US Courts of Appeals. There are US District Courts in Elkins and Charleston.

US District Courts

Northern: POB 1275, Elkins, WV 26241; tel. (304) 636-5198; Judges: ROBERT EARL MAXWELL (Chief Judge), WILLIAM M. KIDD.

Southern: POB 2546, Charleston, WV 25329; tel. (304) 342-5154; Judges: CHARLES H. HADEN, II (Chief Judge), ROBERT J. STAKER, JOHN T. COPENHAVER, Jr, ELIZABETH V. HALLANAN.

STATE COURTS

The state Supreme Court of Appeals has five judges, including the chief justice, who are elected to serve 12-year terms of office. The chief justice is appointed according to seniority of service and holds office for one year.

Supreme Court of Appeals

State Capitol Bldg, Charleston, WV 25305; tel. (304) 348-2606; Judges: W. T. BROTHERTON, Jr (Chief Justice), DARRELL V. MCGRAW, Jr, W. T. BROTHERTON, Jr, THOMAS E. MCHUGH, THOMAS B. MILLER, RICHARD NEELY.

Wisconsin

FEDERAL COURTS

Wisconsin is in the Seventh Circuit of the US Courts of Appeals. There are US District Courts at Milwaukee and Madison.

US District Courts

Eastern: US Courthouse, Rm 364, 517 East Wisconsin Ave, Milwaukee, WI 53202; tel. (414) 291-1475; Judges: ROBERT W. WARREN (Chief Judge), TERENCE T. EVANS, THOMAS J. CURRAN, J. P. STADTMUELLER.

Western: POB 591, Madison, WI 53701; tel. (608) 264-5447; Judges: BARBARA B. CRABB (Chief Judge), JOHN C. SHABAZ.

STATE COURTS

The state Supreme Court has seven judges, including a chief justice. Judges are elected at-large for terms of 10 years. The most senior judge serves as chief justice for the remainder of the term. The state Court of Appeals has 13 judges serving six-year terms of office.

Supreme Court

POB 1688, Madison, WI 53701-1688; tel. (608) 266-1886; Judges: NATHAN S. HEFFERNAN (Chief Justice), SHIRLEY S. ABRAHAMSON, WILLIAM A. BABLITCH, WILLIAM G. CALLOW, LOUIS J. CECI, ROLAND B. DAY, DONALD W. STEINMETZ.

Wyoming

FEDERAL COURTS

Wyoming is in the Tenth Circuit of the US Courts of Appeals. There is a US District Court in Cheyenne.

US District Court

POB 985, Cheyenne, WY 82001; tel. (307) 634-6072; Judges: CLARENCE A. BRIMMER (Chief Judge), ALAN B. JOHNSON.

STATE COURTS

The state Supreme Court has five judges, including the chief justice. Judges, selected at-large, are appointed by the governor, from a list submitted by the Judicial Nominating Commission; appointments must be ratified by the voters at the next general election. Upon election judges serve eight-year terms. The chief justice is elected by the members of the court and holds office for two years.

Supreme Court

Wyoming Supreme Court Bldg, Cheyenne, WY 82002; tel. (307) 777-7421; Judges: G. JOSEPH CARDINE (Chief Justice), RICHARD J. MACY, RICHARD V. THOMAS, WALTER C. URBIGKIT, Jr, MICHAEL GOLDEN.

THE ECONOMY

NATIONAL ECONOMIC INDICATORS

Currency and Exchange Rates

MONETARY UNITS

100 cents = 1 United States dollar (US $).

DENOMINATIONS

Coins: 1, 5, 10, 25 and 50 cents; 1 dollar.
Notes: 1, 2, 5, 10, 20, 50 and 100 dollars.

INTERNATIONAL VALUE OF THE DOLLAR
Average Exchange Rates
(units of foreign currency equivalent to US $1)

	1986	1987	1988
Canada (dollar) . . .	1.3895	1.3260	1.2307
France (franc) . . .	6.9261	6.0107	5.9569
Federal Republic of Germany (Deutsche Mark)	2.1715	1.7974	1.7562
Italy (lira) . . .	1,490.8	1,296.1	1,301.6
Japan (yen) . . .	168.52	144.64	128.15
United Kingdom (pound sterling) . . .	0.6817	0.6102	0.5614

Foreign-Currency Equivalents
(30 June 1989)

Canada: US $1 = C $1.198; C $100 = US $83.47.
France: US $1 = ₣6.635; ₣1,000 = US $150.72.
Federal Republic of Germany: US $1 = DM 1.9545; DM 100 = US $51.16.
Italy: US $1 = 1,413 lire; 10,000 lire = US $7.077.
Japan: US $1 = ¥144.0; ¥1,000 = US $6.944.
United Kingdom: US $100 = £64.56; £1 sterling = US $1.549.

CURRENCY AND COIN IN CIRCULATION*
($ million at 30 September)

	1986	1987	1988
Total	200,624	216,765	235,495

* Currency outside Treasury and Federal Reserve banks, including currency held by commercial banks.
Source: Financial Management Service, US Department of the Treasury.

INTERNATIONAL RESERVES
($ million at 31 December)

	1986	1987	1988
US gold stock*. . . .	11,064	11,078	11,060
IMF Special Drawing Rights .	8,395	10,283	9,640
Reserve position in the IMF .	11,730	11,349	9,750
Foreign exchange . . .	17,322	13,088	17,360
Total	48,511	45,798	47,800

* Valued at $42.2222 per troy ounce.
Sources: Financial Management Service, US Department of the Treasury; IMF, *International Financial Statistics*.

Cost of Living
(Consumer Price Index for all urban consumers, average of monthly figures.
Base: 1982–84 = 100)

	1986	1987	1988
Food and beverages	109.1	113.5	118.2
Housing	110.9	114.2	118.5
Rent	118.3	123.1	127.8
House ownership	119.4	124.8	131.1
Fuel and other utilities . . .	104.1	103.0	104.4
Furnishings and maintenance	105.2	107.1	109.4
Clothes and upkeep	105.9	110.6	115.4
Transport	102.3	105.4	108.7
Medical care	122.0	130.1	138.6
Entertainment	111.6	115.3	120.3
Other goods and services	121.4	128.5	137.0
Total	109.6	113.6	118.3

Source: Bureau of Labor Statistics, US Department of Labor.

National Accounts
($'000 million in current prices)

National Income and Product

	1985	1986	1987
Compensation of employees .	2,379.6	2,519.6	2,697.1
Operating surplus	778.5	839.7	898.0
Domestic factor incomes . .	3,158.1	3,359.3	3,595.1
Consumption of fixed capital .	503.3	524.7	551.5
Statistical discrepancy . . .	−4.8	−13.6	−8.1
Gross domestic product (GDP) at factor cost .	3,656.6	3,870.4	4,138.5
Indirect taxes	333.6	348.4	366.3
Less Subsidies	22.8	27.3	31.8
GDP in purchasers' values .	3,967.5	4,191.5	4,472.9
Factor income received from abroad	89.7	87.5	96.1
Less Factor income paid abroad	48.9	52.6	66.6
Gross national product . .	4,008.2	4,226.4	4,502.4
Less Consumption of fixed capital	503.3	524.7	551.5
National income in market prices	3,504.9	3,701.7	3,950.9
Other current transfers received from abroad . .	1.6	2.0	2.7
Less Other current transfers paid abroad	16.7	17.4	15.7
National disposable income .	3,486.6	3,686.3	3,937.9

Expenditure on the Gross Domestic Product

	1985	1986	1987
Government final consumption expenditure	727.9	780.4	832.0
Private final consumption expenditure	2,615.8	2,788.2	2,983.7
Increase in stocks	24.3	20.8	37.1
Gross fixed capital formation .	718.1	741.3	772.6
Total domestic expenditure .	4,086.1	4,330.7	4,625.4
Exports of goods and services .	281.3	291.0	332.0
Less Imports of goods and services	400.0	430.2	484.5
GDP in purchasers' values .	3,967.5	4,191.5	4,472.9
GDP at constant 1980 prices .	3,095.6	3,188.0	3,301.3

Gross Domestic Product by Economic Activity

	1985	1986	1987
Agriculture, hunting, forestry and fishing . .	85.2	86.5	89.2
Mining and quarrying . . .	115.2	83.1	86.4
Manufacturing	797.4	828.4	862.3
Electricity, gas and water* .	127.8	134.2	137.3
Construction	188.6	206.2	220.7
Wholesale and retail trade, restaurants and hotels . .	682.8	724.1	767.7
Transport, storage and communications . . .	249.2	262.4	274.2
Finance, insurance, real estate and business services . .	915.4	1,022.5	1,123.9
Community, social and personal services . .	363.9	392.1	431.8
Government enterprises . .	57.7	60.0	62.6
Producers of government services	477.7	504.4	536.4
Sub-total	4,060.8	4,303.7	4,592.7
Import duties	12.2	13.7	15.4
Statistical discrepancy . . .	−4.8	−13.6	−8.1
Less Imputed bank service charges	100.8	112.3	127.1
GDP in purchasers' values .	3,967.5	4,191.5	4,472.9

* Including sanitary and similar services.
Source: Bureau of Economic Analysis, US Department of Commerce.

Balance of Payments
($ million)

	1986			1987		
	Credit	Debit	Net	Credit	Debit	Net
Merchandise trade (free alongside ship)	223,969	368,516	−144,547	249,570	409,850	−160,280
Military transactions	8,583	12,955	−4,372	11,529	13,897	−2,368
Travel and transport	32,095	41,439	−9,344	37,161	47,442	−10,281
Investment income	90,110	66,968	23,142	103,756	83,381	20,375
Other private services	19,701	7,007	12,694	22,281	8,877	13,404
Other government services	595	1,689	−1,094	526	1,895	−1,369
Total goods and services	375,053	498,573	−123,520	424,823	565,342	−140,519
Government grants (net)	—	11,738	−11,738	—	10,011	−10,011
Other government transfers (net)	—	2,197	−2,197	—	2,212	−2,212
Private transfers (net)	—	1,374	−1,374	—	1,222	−1,222
Current balance (net)	—	138,828	−138,828	—	153,964	−153,964
US government capital (net)	—	2,000	−2,000	1,162	—	1,162
Direct private investments	34,091	27,811	6,280	41,977	44,455	−2,478
Securities	70,969	4,297	66,672	42,213	4,456	37,757
US Treasury securities	3,809	—	3,809	—	7,596	−7,596
Other capital	12,682	—	12,682	52,542	—	52,542
Statistical discrepancy	15,566	—	15,566	18,461	—	18,461
Capital balance (net)	103,009	—	103,009	99,848	—	99,848
Total balance (net monetary movements)	—	35,819	−35,819	—	54,117	−54,117

Note: Details may not add to totals because of rounding.
Source: Bureau of Economic Analysis, US Department of Commerce.

Economically Active Population

('000 persons aged 16 and over)

Agriculture and Mining (1984)

	Agriculture	Mining			Agriculture	Mining
Alabama	n.a.	14	Nebraska		102	2
Alaska	n.a.	9	Nevada		n.a.	7
Arizona	30	13	New Hampshire		n.a.	0
Arkansas	71	6	New Jersey		n.a.	2
California	273	50	New Mexico		n.a.	21
Colorado	50	36	New York		105	7
Connecticut	n.a.	1	North Carolina		163	5
Delaware	n.a.	0	North Dakota		n.a.	7
District of Columbia	n.a.	0	Ohio		120	28
Florida	72	10	Oklahoma		n.a.	75
Georgia	80	8	Oregon		81	2
Hawaii	26	n.a.	Pennsylvania		107	39
Idaho	51	4	Rhode Island		n.a.	0
Illinois	140	25	South Carolina		n.a.	2
Indiana	91	10	South Dakota		n.a.	3
Iowa	186	2	Tennessee		n.a.	8
Kansas	98	18	Texas		220	270
Kentucky	96	45	Utah		n.a.	13
Louisiana	37	81	Vermont		n.a.	1
Maine	n.a.	0	Virginia		68	18
Maryland	n.a.	2	Washington		78	3
Massachusetts	n.a.	1	West Virginia		n.a.	48
Michigan	122	9	Wisconsin		170	2
Minnesota	208	9	Wyoming		n.a.	27
Mississippi	57	9	**Total***		**3,750**	**974**
Missouri	147	6				
Montana	n.a.	8				

* Includes data for states where individual figures not available.

Sources: US Department of Agriculture, *Agricultural Statistics: 1985;* Bureau of the Census, US Department of Commerce, *State and Metropolitan Area Data Book: 1986.*

Manufacturing, Construction and Other Non-Agricultural Industries (1986)

	Manu- facturing	Construction	Transport- ation and public utilities	Wholesale and retail trade	Finance, insurance and real estate	Services	Government
Alabama	358	75	72	320	69	258	297
Alaska	12	13	18	44	13	44	68
Arizona	184	114	66	325	89	326	226
Arkansas	212	36	48	184	37	146	145
California	2,064	522	576	2,713	766	2,756	1,833
Colorado	185	76	88	349	98	325	254
Connecticut	396	71	69	358	139	371	196
Delaware	68	19	13	68	23	67	46
District of Columbia	16	14	24	63	36	221	267
Florida	517	340	245	1,239	340	1,203	697
Georgia	565	156	167	670	145	506	459
Hawaii	22	19	34	117	33	119	94
Idaho	52	15	19	84	24	68	71
Illinois	925	178	278	1,185	347	1,126	714
Indiana	603	96	113	526	111	428	343
Iowa	201	36	52	277	63	239	208
Kansas	175	44	62	247	54	193	195
Kentucky	253	57	67	303	60	259	237
Louisiana	167	91	108	370	86	318	321
Maine	104	27	19	115	23	102	87
Maryland	210	139	91	497	117	504	392
Massachusetts	619	121	39	183	203	134	388
Michigan	998	115	148	814	171	787	597
Minnesota	369	75	98	471	116	448	309
Mississippi	223	36	39	183	37	134	190
Missouri	422	98	141	508	129	489	339
Montana	21	10	20	73	13	62	70
Nebraska	86	25	43	169	47	147	136
Nevada	22	27	27	95	23	207	62
New Hampshire	118	35	17	121	28	108	62
New Jersey	693	154	230	833	209	831	536
New Mexico	38	35	29	127	27	118	138
New York	1,251	309	402	1,676	755	2,126	1,382
North Carolina	832	157	133	607	118	453	427
North Dakota	15	11	16	67	12	59	64
Ohio	1,109	161	206	1,067	232	999	680
Oklahoma	163	40	64	279	63	225	251
Oregon	197	34	57	268	70	230	199
Pennsylvania	1,049	202	240	1,095	277	1,218	680
Rhode Island	119	17	15	99	25	109	58

(continued)

Manufacturing, Construction and Other Non-Agricultural Industries (1986)—*continued*

	Manufacturing	Construction	Transportation and public utilities	Wholesale and retail trade	Finance, insurance and real estate	Services	Government
South Carolina . . .	364	88	56	292	61	223	253
South Dakota	28	10	13	66	14	60	59
Tennessee	492	90	97	450	94	385	314
Texas	960	414	375	1,685	448	1,372	1,119
Utah	92	33	38	153	33	138	141
Vermont	50	15	10	53	11	57	38
Virginia	424	168	137	580	131	579	521
Washington . . .	304	85	96	435	105	393	349
West Virginia . . .	87	23	37	137	24	121	129
Wisconsin	513	64	93	478	108	433	325
Wyoming	8	17	14	46	8	33	53
Total*	18,994	4,904	5,244	23,580	6,297	23,099	16,711

* National totals differ from sum of state figures because of differing benchmarks among states and differing industrial and geographic stratification.

Source: US Bureau of Labor Statistics, *Employment and Earnings*.

STATE ECONOMIES

Alabama

Alabama's principal economic activities are manufacturing, wholesale and retail trade, and finance, insurance and real estate. In 1986 the state's per-head disposable income was $9,591, the third lowest in the USA. The civilian labour force totalled 1,883,000 in 1986, while the unemployment rate was 9.8% (185,000 persons), the fifth highest in the country. In 1982 18.2% of workers in non-agricultural establishments were unionized.

At the time of the 1982 Census of Agriculture farmland accounted for 32% of Alabama's land area, with the average farm covering an area of 211 acres. In 1986 33% of farm income was generated by crop sales and 67% by livestock and livestock products. Alabama's principal agricultural commodities in that year were broilers, cattle, eggs and peanuts. It was ranked second among all states in 1986 for production of peanuts (behind Georgia), third for broilers and ninth for eggs. In 1982 65% of the state was covered by forest, and in 1987 Alabama was the nation's seventh most important timber-producing state. Softwoods accounted for 86% of production in that year.

Coal, petroleum and natural gas were Alabama's most important mineral products, in terms of value, in 1985. Iron ore, the basis of the state's once-powerful steel industry, ceased to be extracted in the early 1980s as cheaper foreign ore became available; the most important non-fuel minerals are now stone, sand and gravel, and cement. The availability of coal and iron ore made the city of Birmingham into an important steel-producing centre from the late 19th century. While the primary-metals sector has remained relatively important as a manufacturing employer, the shipments of the paper, chemical and textile industries were most important in 1982 in terms of value added. In 1985 the total value of Alabama's manufacturing shipments was $36,635m., of which 42% was added during manufacture.

Tourists spent $3,600m. in Alabama in 1987. Direct general expenditure by state and local governments in 1984/85 totalled $7,879m.; revenue totalled $8,068m., of which $1,768m. was provided by the federal government.

Alaska

Government spending, services, trade and contract construction are the leading contributors to Alaska's economy. Since the late 1970s the petroleum industry has contributed a high proportion of state revenues (84% in 1984). In 1986 the state had a per-head disposable income of $15,453, the third highest in the country. The civilian labour force totalled 256,000 in 1986, when the state had the country's fourth-highest unemployment rate (10.8%, or 28,000 persons). Alaska has the country's sixth-highest rate of union membership, which was held by 30.4% of non-agricultural workers in 1982.

Alaska has a negligible amount of commercial agriculture: farmland accounted for only 0.4% of the state's land area in 1982, with the average farm size at 2,323 acres (the sixth largest in the country). Its farm income was the lowest among the 50 states in 1986, with 66% being derived from crops and 34% from livestock and livestock products. Greenhouse and dairy products, hay and potatoes dominate what cultivation there is. Alaska's forestland

totalled 87m. acres in 1982, covering 24% of the state's land area and comprising 13% of the USA's total forest resources. However, only about 11m. acres were under development as commercial timberland, and the state is of only middling importance as a timber producer. Alaska's fish catch, the highest of any state, was valued at $753m. in 1986: salmon is the principal species caught.

In 1986 Alaska was the USA's second-largest producer of crude oil (behind Texas) and was also the eighth-largest producer of natural gas. Over 90% of Alaska's oil production originates from fields in the extreme north of the state (by far the largest of which is Prudhoe Bay) and is transported southwards, via the Trans-Alaska Pipeline System, to the ice-free port of Valdez. Non-fuel mining is scarce, with the principal products being sand and gravel, gold and stone.

In 1982 Alaska's most important industries, in terms of value added, were food (especially seafood) processing, petroleum refining and the manufacture of lumber and wood products. Anchorage is the leading manufacturing centre. The total value of Alaska's manufacturing shipments in 1985 was $2,512m., of which 34% was added during manufacture—the seventh-lowest proportion among the 50 states and the District of Columbia.

Alaska's still relatively unspoilt scenery gives it great tourist potential. In 1984 690,000 people visited the state.

Direct general expenditure by state and local governments was $4,954m. in 1984/85, while revenue amounted to $6,726m. in that year. Federal government transfers totalled $525m.

Arizona

Arizona's principal economic activities are manufacturing, tourism and travel, mining and agriculture. In 1986 the state's per-head disposable income was $11,767, and its civilian labour force totalled 1,586,000, of which 110,000 (6.9%) were unemployed. In 1982 12.8% of non-agricultural workers were union members.

Farmland constituted 52% of Arizona's land area in 1982, and the average size of farms was 5,148 acres—the largest in the USA. In 1986 53% of farm income was derived from crops and 47% from livestock and livestock products. Irrigation schemes are in operation throughout the state. Arizona's principal commercial crops are cotton (the state was the USA's fourth-largest producer in 1986), vegetables (especially lettuce) and hay. Cattle are the dominant livestock product, and dairy products are also an important source of income. Forestland covers 25% of Arizona's land area: national forests comprise about two-thirds of all forest, with commercial timberland accounting for only about one-fifth.

In 1985 the value of Arizona's non-fuel mineral production was the fourth highest in the USA. The state provided 69% of the country's copper in 1986, and 31% of its molybdenum; sand and gravel, cement, silver, gold and stone are also valuable minerals. There is some coal-mining, but in general fossil-fuel extraction was still under development in the mid-1980s.

Manufacturing is the state's foremost economic activity, with abundant supplies of land, electricity and labour and a favourable tax structure having assisted its development in centres such as Phoenix and Tucson during the post-war period. Electrical and electronic equipment, non-electrical machinery and transportation equipment were the principal industries in 1982 in terms of value added. In 1985 the total value of Arizona's manufacturing shipments was $16,721m., of which 48% was added during manufacture.

Tourism and travel is Arizona's second-largest industry in terms of receipts; in 1985 tourists spent $5,600m. in the state. While most visitors are US citizens, Arizona also attracts tourists from Mexico.

Direct general expenditure by state and local governments in 1984/85 totalled $7,345m., with revenue at $7,324m. The federal-government contribution to revenue was $939m.

Arkansas

Manufacturing, wholesale and retail trade, agriculture and mining are the principal economic activities in Arkansas. The state had a per-head disposable income of $9,857 in 1986, the eighth lowest in the country. In the same year its civilian labour force numbered 1,073,000, while its unemployment rate was 8.7% (94,000 workers). In 1982 13.2% of non-farm workers were unionized.

The 1982 Census of Agriculture calculated Arkansas's farmland at 44% of the state's total land area and the average farm size at 291 acres. In 1986 crops supplied 33% of farm income, while livestock and livestock products contributed 67%. Arkansas is the USA's leading producer of broilers and in 1986 was ranked fourth for turkeys and sixth for eggs; cattle also provide an important contribution to livestock shipments. The state is the USA's largest producer of rice, providing 41% of the national total in 1986, and its sixth-largest cotton producer. Soybeans, wheat and sorghum are also important cash crops. Forestland comprised 52% of the state's land area in 1982 and almost all of it was commercial timberland. Arkansas was the USA's 10th most important timber producer in 1987; softwoods accounted for 86% of output. Fish (especially catfish and minnow) farming is an important agricultural activity, and provided output valued at $45m. in 1983.

Arkansas's principal mineral products in 1985 were natural gas, crude oil and bromine. The state possesses the USA's only diamond field.

Manufacturing activity was dominated in 1982 (in terms of value added) by the food, electronic equipment and paper and allied products industries, with processing of rice and timber reflecting the resource-based nature of the economy. The total value of manufacturing shipments in 1985 was $21,840m., of which 38% was added during manufacture.

Tourists spent $2,000m. in Arkansas in 1987. Direct general expenditure by state and local governments in 1984/85 totalled $3,998m. Revenue was $4,219m., of which $944m. was provided federally.

California

California leads the USA in many areas of economic activity and has a larger economy, in terms of its gross state product, than most countries of the world. Manufacturing, services, government and wholesale and retail trade are the foremost contributors to California's income. In 1986 the state had a per-head disposable income of $14,553, the fifth highest in the USA. The civilian labour force numbered 13,365,000 in 1986, when unemployment affected 892,000 workers (6.7%). Union membership was held by 25.4% of non-agricultural workers in 1982.

Farmland covered 32% of the state's total land area in 1982, and the average size of farms was 390 acres. California has only 3% of the nation's farmland, but in 1986 accounted for over 10% (the largest proportion of any state) of the USA's farm income, with 68% of the state total coming from crops and 32% from livestock and livestock products. Agriculture is very well diversified, and California led the 50 states in the production of more than 40 commodities in 1983. Dairy products contribute the greatest value, followed by cattle, greenhouse products and grapes (used primarily for the manufacture of wine). Virtually all California's cropland is under irrigation, with agriculture consuming 85% of the state's water supplies. California's forests covered 37% of the state and accounted for almost 6% of the nation's total forestland in 1982—a proportion surpassed only by Alaska. In 1987 the state ranked second in the production of lumber. Commercial fishing is well established; in 1986 California's catch was sixth by value among the 50 states. The principal species fished are tuna and mackerel.

In 1985 California was the leading producer of non-fuel minerals among the 50 states, and came high on the list for total mineral production. Its leading mineral products, in terms of value, are petroleum, natural gas and cement: it is the USA's largest producer of cement, sand and gravel, its second-largest producer of gold (behind Nevada), its fourth-largest producer of crude oil and its sixth-largest producer of natural gas. In total some 40 minerals are mined commercially in the state.

As in so many other sectors of the economy, California dominates in manufacturing, which is centred on the metropolitan areas surrounding San Francisco and Los Angeles. The total value of its shipments in 1985 was $227,086m., almost 10% of the US total. Of this value, 49% was added during manufacture. In 1982 the leading industries in terms of value added were electrical and electronic equipment, transportation equipment and non-electrical machinery. (California ranks second to Michigan in transportation equipment, but leads the country in the other two industry groups.) Paper manufacturing, petroleum refining and food processing are also important.

California has a well-rooted and thriving banking industry, and in 1986 was second only to New York state in terms of total assets held. The Pacific Stock Exchange is situated in San Francisco.

Tourism, both domestic and international, is a major industry in California, which is second only to Florida in terms of the number of international visitors it attracts. Tourism generated 5% of California's employment in 1983, and in 1987 $34,000m. was spent by tourists in the state.

Direct general expenditure by state and local governments in 1984/85 totalled $68,429m.; revenue totalled $73,542m., of which $13,526m. was provided federally.

Colorado

Colorado's principal economic activities are manufacturing, wholesale and retail trade, services and government. It also has an important mining industry. In 1986 Colorado's per-head disposable income was $12,765; its civilian labour force numbered 1,694,000 in that year, with an unemployment rate of 7.4% (126,000 persons). In 1982 18% of the non-farm work-force was unionized.

Agricultural land accounted for 51% of Colorado's total land area in 1982, with average farm size at 1,237 acres. Livestock and livestock products provided 71% of farm income in 1986, with crops providing the remaining 29%. Colorado's leading agricultural products in 1986 were cattle, wheat, corn and dairy products. The state is the USA's fifth-largest cattle producer and its largest sheep producer, accounting for 1.3m. slaughterings of sheep and lambs (22% of the national total) in 1986. Forests covered 30% of the state in 1982, contributing 3% to total US timberland. However, there is relatively little commercial forestry activity.

Colorado's principal mineral products in 1985 were petroleum, natural gas and coal. Although non-fuel minerals accounted for only 19% of the total in that year, these are widely mined, and include silver (of which Colorado is a leading producer), gold, zinc, lead, copper, molybdenum, vanadium, cement, and sand and gravel.

Much of the manufacturing activity of the Rocky Mountain states is concentrated in Colorado. In 1982 the main industries in terms of value added were non-electrical machinery, scientific and medical instruments and related products, and food products. The total value of manufacturing shipments in 1985 was $20,619m., of which 49% was added during manufacture.

Tourism is very important to the state: in 1984 travel and tourism generated expenditure of about $4,000m., of which about $1,200m. was related to skiing.

Direct general expenditure by state and local governments in 1984/85 totalled $7,784m., with revenue at $8,200m., of which $1,198m. was provided by the federal government.

Connecticut

Manufacturing, particularly defence-related, is the mainstay of Connecticut's strong economy. Other important sectors include wholesale and retail trade, and services. The state was the richest in the USA in 1986 in terms of per-head disposable income, which amounted to $16,672. Its civilian labour force totalled 1,740,000 in 1986, when the state's unemployment rate was the second lowest in the country (above that of New Hampshire and equal to Massachusetts), at 3.8% (66,000 workers). Union membership was held by 18% of the non-agricultural work-force in 1982.

Farmland covered just 13% of the state in 1982, and the average size of farms was also relatively low, at 118 acres. Crops made up 44% of farm income in 1986 and livestock and livestock products 56%, with the principal commodities being eggs, greenhouse and dairy products, and tobacco. In 1982 56% of the state was covered by forest, and some lumber is produced.

As in other states of New England, mining is very limited. Connecticut has no significant fuel resources, and non-fuel mining production was dominated in 1985 by stone, sand and gravel, and feldspar.

Connecticut's total manufacturing shipments were valued at $34,980m. in 1985, of which 59%—the second-highest proportion in the country, behind the District of Columbia—was added during manufacture. In 1982 the state's principal industries, in terms of value added, were transportation equipment, non-electrical machinery and electrical and electronic equipment. It is a leading manufacturer of aircraft engines, submarine parts, and military and civilian helicopters. Metal products, chemicals, scientific and medical instruments and related products, primary metals, printing and publishing, and food products are also important.

Financial services are an important industry, with many insurance companies being headquartered in Hartford. Tourism is growing in importance, out-of-state visitors spending $2,500m. in 1985.

Direct general expenditure by state and local governments in Connecticut totalled $7,516m. in 1984/85; revenue in that year was $8,599m., of which $1,252m. was provided federally.

Delaware

Delaware's principal economic activity and source of income is manufacturing. In 1986 the state had a per-head disposable income of $12,745, and its civilian labour force numbered 325,000. Unemployment in that year was 4.3% (14,000 persons) the fifth-lowest rate in the USA. In 1982 20.3% of non-agricultural workers were members of trade unions.

In 1982 57% of the state was in agricultural land, while the average size of farms was 196 acres. Some 77% of the value of farm sales was comprised of livestock and livestock products in 1986, with crops accounting for the remaining 23%. The principal agricultural products in that year were broilers (of which Delaware was the USA's eighth-largest producer), soybeans, corn and greenhouse products. Forestland covered 32% of the state in 1982, of which nearly all was commercial timberland. Fishing was traditionally important to the state but has declined in recent decades.

Delaware has the smallest output of minerals of any state: principal contributors to the value of production in 1985 were magnesium compounds, sand and gravel, and greensand. The state has no known fossil-fuel resources.

Chemicals, food products and instruments and related products constituted the most important manufactures of the state in 1982 in terms of value added. The chemical company E. I. du Pont de Nemours & Co (Du Pont), based in Wilmington, is the USA's seventh-largest industrial corporation. Other important industries include transportation equipment and paper and allied products. In 1985 the total value of Delaware's manufacturing shipments was $10,789m., of which 31%—the fifth-lowest proportion nationwide—was added during manufacture.

Travel and tourism is the state's second most important industry after manufacturing, generating 6.5% of state employment in 1982.

Direct general expenditure by state and local governments in 1984/85 was $1,672m. Revenue totalled $1,907m., of which $293m. came from the federal government.

District of Columbia

Economic activity in the District of Columbia is centred on government, which employs over 40% of the local work-force. The District of Columbia has no agricultural, forestry, fishing or mineral industry; printing and publishing is the major manufacturing activity.

The district's per-head disposable income was $15,955 in 1986, higher than any state except Connecticut. Its civilian labour force numbered 328,000 in 1986, when unemployment affected 7.7% of the work-force (25,000 persons). The federal government is the district's biggest single employer. Union membership was held by 33.4% of workers in 1982, a proportion only exceeded by the states of New York and Michigan.

In 1985 the total value of the district's manufacturing shipments was $1,787m., but of this 68% was added during manufacture—by far the highest proportion in the country, reflecting the fact that printing and publishing accounts for over 85% of all manufacturing shipments. The next most significant industry is food products.

Almost 45,000 jobs are generated by tourism, which provides an income of about $1,000m. annually.

Direct general expenditure by local government totalled $2,718m. in 1984/85; revenue totalled $3,238m., of which $1,348m. was provided by the federal government.

Florida

Manufacturing, wholesale and retail trade and services are the principal economic activities in Florida, while tourism and agriculture are also important sources of income. In 1986 the state had a per-head disposable income of $12,576; its civilian work-force numbered 5,588,000 and its unemployment rate was 5.7% (320,000 workers). In 1982 the state had the fourth-lowest rate of trade-union membership in the USA, at 9.6% of non-farm workers.

At the time of the 1982 Census of Agriculture farmland accounted for 37% of Florida's land area, and the average size of its farms

was 353 acres. It had the ninth-highest farm income in 1986, of which 79% was contributed by crops and 21% by livestock and livestock products. Florida's principal agricultural commodities are greenhouse products, citrus fruits (especially oranges), tomatoes and sugar; it is the nation's leading producer of both citrus fruit and sugar-cane (accounting for 66% and 44% respectively of national production in 1986) and comes second for tomatoes (behind California) and third for lettuces (behind California and Arizona). Soybeans are the next most important field crop, behind sugar-cane. Cattle are the most important livestock product. In 1982 47% of Florida was under forest, constituting 2.5% of the USA's total timber resources; however, the state's lumbering industry is relatively modest. Fishing is an important commercial activity: Florida's 1986 catch was the fifth most valuable in the country. Shrimp and black mullet are among the principal species caught.

The value of Florida's non-fuel mineral production was the third highest in the USA in 1985. In order of value, the principal minerals produced in that year were phosphate, petroleum and stone. Florida is the country's largest producer of phosphate rock (used in the manufacture of fertilizers) and also of titanium materials, while it ranks second in the production of stone. Other important minerals are dolomite, clays and sand and gravel.

Much of Florida's manufacturing activity is centred on the processing of agricultural and other raw materials found in the state; the cities of Miami, Tampa, St Petersburg, Fort Lauderdale and Orlando all have important industrial bases. The major sectors in 1982, in terms of value added, were food products, electrical and electronic equipment and transportation equipment; chemicals (especially agricultural) and non-electrical machinery were also important. In 1985 the total value of Florida's manufacturing shipments was $49,691m., with 44% of this being added during manufacture.

The combined assets of Florida's banks ranked the state in sixth place for commercial banking activity in 1986. Florida is a major tourist centre with many attractions, and income from out-of-state visitors was estimated at $22,000m. in 1987.

Direct general expenditure by state and local governments in 1984/85 was $22,228m.; revenue totalled $23,940m., of which $3,805m. was supplied by the federal government.

Georgia

Georgia's chief economic activity is manufacturing, followed by retail and wholesale trade and services. Agriculture, which dominated the economy before the Second World War, has lost much importance in the post-war period. In 1986 the state had a per-head disposable income of $11,122; its civilian labour force numbered 3,014,000, and the unemployment rate was 5.9% (178,000 persons). In 1982 12.7% of the non-agricultural labour force was unionized.

Agricultural land accounted for 33% of Georgia's land area in 1982, and average farm size in that year was 248 acres. In 1986 some 41% of the value of farm marketings was derived from crops and 59% from livestock and livestock products. The most important agricultural products, in terms of value, were broilers, peanuts, eggs and cattle. Georgia is the USA's leading producer of peanuts (with 44% of national output in 1986) and of pecans, and is also important for peaches. It is second (to Arkansas) in the value of its chickens and broilers and fourth for eggs. Georgia has the largest area of commercial timberland of any state in the USA; 64% of the state was wooded in 1982. The timber industry is important and productive; in 1987 Georgia produced the USA's fourth-largest amount of lumber, of which over 90% was softwood, predominantly pine. Commercial fishing is well established in the state, but its contribution to the economy is small.

Georgia was seventh among the states in the production of non-fuel minerals in 1985. Its only recoverable fossil-fuel resources are provided by small amounts of coal. The state's principal mineral products in 1985 were clays, stone and cement. It is the USA's leading producer of clays (particularly white clay or kaolin), marble and crushed granite. Bauxite and iron ore are both mined in small quantities.

Reflecting the state's cotton-growing history, textiles constitute the most important manufacturing industry in terms of value. It is the USA's second most important textile producer, behind North Carolina. Georgia's most famous manufacture is without doubt Coca-Cola; the soft-drinks manufacturer, Coca-Cola Co, is based in Atlanta. Food and kindred products, and chemicals followed textiles in order of value added in 1982, while other important industries include transportation equipment, paper and allied products, apparel (in which Georgia ranks third nationally) and electrical and electronic equipment. The total value of Georgia's manufacturing shipments in 1985 was $63,057m., of which 43% was added during manufacture.

Travel and tourism is Georgia's second-largest industry in terms of employment, and it was estimated that visitors spent $7,600m. in 1983.

Direct general expenditure by state and local governments in 1984/85 amounted to $11,771m., while revenue totalled $13,455m., of which $2,716m. was provided federally.

Hawaii

The economy of Hawaii is heavily dependent on tourism, national defence programmes and agriculture. Manufacturing is a relatively unimportant contributor to the state's income. Hawaiians' per-head disposable income was measured at $12,893 in 1986, when the civilian labour force numbered 488,000, of which 24,000 (4.8%, the ninth-lowest rate in the USA) were unemployed. Union members made up 31.5% of the non-agricultural work-force in 1982, the fifth-highest rate in the country.

Farmland constituted 49% of Hawaii's total land area in 1982, and the average size of farms was 426 acres. In 1986 85% of farm income was derived from crops and 15% from livestock and livestock products. The dominant agricultural products were sugar-cane, pineapples, greenhouse products and macadamia nuts; Hawaii is the USA's second-largest producer of sugar-cane (behind Florida) and ranks third for sugar beets and barley. Cattle are the most important livestock commodity. Forestland covered 26% of the state in 1982, mostly on the island of Hawaii. Commercial forestry is limited. Fishing is an expanding economic force.

Hawaii has no known fossil-fuel resources. In 1985 its principal mineral products were stone, cement, sand and gravel.

Hawaii's principal manufactures in 1982, ranked by value added, were food products, textiles, and stone, clay and glass products. The canning and preserving of locally-produced fruit and vegetables provides a major source of employment, as does the manufacture of sugar and confectionery products. The value of Hawaii's manufacturing shipments totalled $3,477m. in 1985, of which value added during manufacture contributed 34%—the eighth-lowest rate nation-wide.

The state's revenue from tourism totalled $4,000m. in 1983, and travel and tourism were held to have directly or indirectly generated over one-half of the state's jobs in that year. About two-thirds of visitors in 1983 were US citizens, while 17% came from Japan and 6% from Canada.

Direct general expenditure by state and local governments in 1984/85 was $2,601m.; revenue totalled $2,818m., of which $500m. came from the federal government.

Idaho

Government, wholesale and retail trade, manufacturing and services were the main contributors to Idaho's economy in 1980, with agriculture not far behind. Per-head disposable income in the state in 1986 was $9,873, the ninth lowest in the country. The civilian labour force totalled 468,000 in 1986, and unemployment in that year was 8.7% (41,000 workers). In 1982 16.1% of workers in non-agricultural establishments were members of trade unions.

In 1982 farmland made up 26% of Idaho's land area, and the average farm size was 563 acres. Crops provided 54% of the value of farm marketings in 1986, with livestock and livestock products contributing the remaining 46%. Cattle, dairy products, potatoes and wheat were the principal agricultural products in terms of value in 1986, while hay, barley, sugar beets and wool were also important. Idaho is the USA's largest potato producer, with 25% of national output in 1986. In 1982 34% of the state was covered by forest, and Idaho was the fifth-largest timber producer among the states in 1987. Production was composed entirely of softwood.

Idaho's mining industry is restricted to non-fuel minerals. The state is the USA's major source of silver (producing 33% of national output in 1986) and its second-largest producer of lead, behind Missouri. It also ranks highly for gold, zinc and phosphate rock.

Manufacturing activity in the state is concentrated in the areas of food products, non-electrical machinery and chemicals, which were the leading industry groups in 1982 in terms of value added. Lumber and wood products are also important. Idaho's manufacturing shipments were valued at $5,821m. in 1985, of which 44% was added during manufacture.

Travel and tourism generated an estimated $1,100m. in business revenues in 1982, and employed 27,200 people.

Direct general expenditure by state and local governments in 1984/85 totalled $1,878m.; revenue totalled $1,915m., of which $419m. was provided by the federal government.

Illinois

The principal economic activities in Illinois are manufacturing, wholesale and retail trade, finance, insurance and real estate and services. Agriculture is also very important. In 1986 it was the ninth most wealthy state in the USA in terms of per-head disposable income, which totalled $13,518. The civilian labour force numbered 5,686,000 in 1986; unemployment affected 461,000 workers, or 8.1% of the work-force, in that year. In 1982 27.5% of non-farm workers (the eighth-highest proportion in the USA) were members of trade unions.

Agricultural land accounted for 81% of Illinois's total land area in 1982, and the average size of farms was 292 acres. In 1986 crops accounted for 69% of farm income and livestock products for the remaining 31%. Illinois ranked fifth among the states in farm income in 1986. Its most valuable agricultural commodities in that year were corn, soybeans, hogs and cattle. In national terms in 1986 the state ranked first in production of soybeans, second in corn (behind Iowa), third in hogs (behind Iowa and Minnesota) and eighth in cattle and calves. Forestland covered just 10% of the state's land area in 1982, and is concentrated in the south.

Coal is widely mined in Illinois; the state is the USA's fifth-largest producer and coal formed its most valuable mineral product in 1985, followed by petroleum and stone. Sand and gravel, cement, clay, copper and lead are also important minerals.

Manufacturing activity is centred on Chicago, but occurs throughout the state and is well diversified. The major industry groups in 1982 (in terms of value added) were non-electrical machinery, food products and electrical and electronic equipment. However, petroleum and coal products, chemicals, fabricated metal products, printing and publishing, primary metal industries and rubber and plastics are also important. (Illinois was ranked in the top four for each of these industry groups in 1985.) Illinois's manufacturing shipments were valued at $124,402m. in 1985 (the fifth-highest total of any state), with 45% of this value being added during manufacture.

Chicago became established as the financial centre of the Midwest states at the time of the Civil War. In 1986 Illinois banks ranked fourth in the country in terms of total assets held. The state is also the nation's second most important insurance centre, behind Hartford (Connecticut), and the Midwest Stock Exchange is second only to that of New York in size.

As the country's most important convention centre, Chicago is a major tourist attraction. Out-of-state visitors spent $8,900m. in Illinois in 1986.

Direct general expenditure by state and local governments in 1984/85 was $25,067m. Revenue in that year was $27,399m., of which $4,970m. was provided by the federal government.

Indiana

Manufacturing, trade, government and services are the main contributors to the economy of Indiana. Per-head disposable income in the state totalled $11,291 in 1986; the civilian labour force numbered 2,750,000 in the same year, with unemployment affecting 185,000 workers (6.7%). In 1982 25.1% of non-farm workers were unionized.

Farmland took up 71% of Indiana's land area at the time of the 1982 Census of Agriculture. The average farm size was 211 acres. In 1986 about 55% of the value of farm sales was derived from crops and about 45% from livestock and livestock products. Indiana's total farm income ranked 10th in the USA in 1986. Its principal agricultural products (in terms of value) in that year were corn, hogs, soybeans and cattle. The state ranked fifth overall in the production of soybeans and corn and ninth for hog slaughterings. Other important crops include hay, tobacco and oats, while poultry makes an important contribution to livestock products. Indiana was the USA's second-largest producer of eggs (behind California) and its seventh-largest producer of turkeys in 1986. In 1982 17% of Indiana's land was covered by forest; there is some commercial lumbering activity.

Indiana's principal mineral products in terms of value in 1985 were coal, petroleum, and cement, stone, sand and gravel, and clays. The state is the USA's 10th most important producer of coal.

While much manufacturing activity is centred around Indianapolis, the city of Gary is an important steel-making centre. Indiana's manufacturing shipments were valued at $76,654m. in 1985 (the ninth-highest value of any state), and of this 43% was added during manufacture. The principal industries in 1982 (measured by value added) were electrical equipment, primary metal products and transportation equipment. Indiana ranked second in the USA for primary metal products in 1985.

Tourism is not of major importance to Indiana's economy: in 1985 tourists spent an estimated $3,000m.

Direct general expenditure by state and local governments totalled $10,179m. in 1984/85; revenue in that year came to $11,256m., of which $1,941m. was provided federally.

Iowa

Iowa is the USA's most important agricultural state, behind California. Its manufacturing activity is focused on the processing of farm products and the manufacture of agricultural equipment. In 1986 the state had a per-head disposable income of $11,540; the civilian labour force numbered 1,432,000 in that year, with unemployment at 7% of the work-force (100,000 persons). In 1982 20.5% of the non-farm labour force held union membership.

Farmland covered 91% of Iowa's land area in 1982, with the average farm occupying 283 acres. The state had the second-highest farm income of any state other than California in 1986, at $9,106m. Of this, 55% came from livestock and livestock products, and 45% from crops. Iowa's most important products in 1986, in terms of value, were hogs, corn, cattle and soybeans. The state ranked first in the USA in 1986 in the production of corn for grain, with output of 1,627m. bushels (20% of the national total) and in the slaughter of hogs (18.7m. head—24% of US production). It was second in production of soybeans, behind Illinois, and fourth for cattle and sheep. Wheat is grown towards the south of the state, and poultry-farming is also important. Forestland covered only 3% of Iowa's land area in 1982, and the lumbering industry is relatively insignificant.

The state's most valuable mineral products in 1985 were stone, cement and sand and gravel. Gypsum and coal are mined in small quantities.

Iowa's first manufacturing activity was in the areas of food-processing and the manufacture of agricultural equipment. These industries have remained prominent into the 1980s, with non-electrical machinery and food and kindred products being the leading industries by value added in 1982. Also important are electrical equipment and chemicals. In 1985 the total value of Iowa's manufacturing shipments was $32,237m.; of this, 41% was added during manufacture.

Tourism is not a major contributor to state income: tourists in Iowa spent an estimated $2,000m. in 1986.

Direct general expenditure by state and local governments totalled $6,664m. in 1984/85; revenue totalled $6,603m. The federal government provided revenue of $1,144m.

Kansas

The principal economic activities in Kansas are manufacturing, government, wholesale and retail trade, and services. Agriculture is very important, and is dominated by wheat production. In 1986 Kansans had an average per-head disposable income of $12,500; the civilian labour force totalled 1,224,000 in that year, with unemployment affecting 67,000 workers, or 5.4% of the labour force. In 1982 12% of non-farm workers were unionized, the eighth-lowest rate in the country.

Farmland covered 90% of Kansas's land area at the time of the 1982 Census of Agriculture, and the average farm size was 642 acres. In 1986 the state's farm income was the seventh-largest in the country, 64% being derived from sales of livestock and livestock products and 36% from crops. The principal farm products in 1986, in order of value, were cattle, wheat, sorghum (for grain) and corn (also for grain). Kansas was the USA's leading producer of cattle and calves in 1986, its 6.5m. slaughterings accounting for 16% of the US total; it also led in wheat production, supplying 337m. bushels or 18% of national output, and in production of sorghum for grain, with 311m. bushels, or 33% of national supply. Other important agricultural products include soybeans, hogs, sheep and chickens. Only 3% of Kansas's land area was covered by forest in 1982.

Petroleum, natural gas and cement were Kansas's most important mineral products by value in 1985. The state is the USA's eighth-largest producer of petroleum and its seventh-largest natural-gas supplier. Other widely-found minerals are stone, sand and gravel, salt and clay.

Manufacturing industry is concentrated in and around Kansas City, Topeka and Wichita. Reflecting the economy's agricultural base, food products are one of the leading industries, outranked in 1982 (in terms of value added) only by the transportation-equipment sector. Kansas has a very important aircraft industry, based in Wichita. The state's total manufacturing shipments were valued at $31,630m. in 1985, of which 37% was added during manufacture.

Tourism does not play a great part in the economy of the state; in 1985 out-of-state visitors spent $1,900m. in Kansas.

Direct general expenditure by state and local governments in 1984/85 totalled $5,439m. in 1984/85, while revenue totalled $5,872m. The federal-government contribution was $869m.

Kentucky

In Kentucky the most important sectors of the economy are manufacturing, coal mining and agriculture. In 1986 the state's per-head disposable income totalled $9,933. The civilian labour force totalled 1,690,000 in that year, while the unemployment rate reached 9.3% (156,000 persons), the sixth highest in the country. In 1982 20.4% of workers in non-agricultural employment belonged to a trade union.

At the time of the 1982 Census of Agriculture farmland comprised 56% of Kentucky's land area, while the average farm size was low, at just 140 acres. In 1986 livestock and livestock products accounted for 55% of farm income, while crop sales provided 45%. Tobacco was Kentucky's most important agricultural product in that year in terms of value, followed by horses, cattle and dairy products. In 1986 Kentucky ranked second to North Carolina in tobacco production. Forest covered 47% of the state in 1982.

In 1986 Kentucky ranked first among states in the production of coal, with an output of almost 154m. short tons (all bituminous). Petroleum and natural gas followed coal in order of value in 1985. The most important non-fuel minerals produced are stone, sand and gravel, and clay.

In 1983 Kentucky was the leading producer of American whisky and also a major supplier of the nation's motor vehicles. Food products, non-electrical machinery and chemicals accounted for the highest percentage of value added by manufacture in 1982. In 1985 the total value of Kentucky's manufacturing shipments was $38,404m., with 40% being added during manufacture.

Income from the tourist trade amounted to $3,200m. in 1985. Direct general expenditure by state and local governments in 1984/85 totalled $6,698m., while general revenue totalled $7,295m., including $1,643m. provided by the federal government.

Louisiana

Louisiana's principal economic activities are manufacturing, wholesale and retail trade, services and mining (particularly oil and gas extraction). In 1986 the state's per-head disposable income totalled $9,827, the sixth lowest in the country. The civilian labour force totalled 1,988,000 in 1986, with an unemployment rate of 13.1% (261,000 persons), which was the highest in the USA. In 1982 13.8% of workers in non-agricultural employment belonged to a trade union.

At the time of the 1982 Census of Agriculture 31% of Louisiana's land area consisted of farmland; the average farm covered an area of 282 acres. In 1986 55% of agricultural income derived from sales of livestock and livestock products, with 45% coming from crops. Soybeans, rice, sugar and cotton are among Louisiana's most important crops—the state was the USA's third-largest producer of sugar-cane in 1986. Louisiana is also a major producer of broilers, ranking sixth in 1986. Forest covered 49% of Louisiana's area in 1982; in 1981 the state was the USA's leading supplier of plywood and pulpwood, while in 1987 it ranked 14th overall for timber production. In 1986 the value of Louisiana's commercial fish catch was $313m., the second highest in the country behind Alaska. The most important species caught are shrimp, oysters, menhaden and blue crab.

In 1985 Louisiana's most important mineral products by value were petroleum, natural gas and sulphur. While production of natural gas and petroleum has declined since the 1970s, the state still ranked second nationally (behind Texas) for natural gas and third (behind Texas and Alaska) for petroleum in 1986. It also ranked second, again to Texas, for sulphur, and led all states in salt production, with an output exceeding 11.6m. short tons. Other non-fuel minerals produced in the state include cement, sand and gravel, and stone.

Since the early 20th century the expanding petrochemical industry has played a leading role in the state's economy. By value added, the most important industrial groups in 1982 were chemicals, petroleum and food products. Nationally, the state ranked second for petroleum and coal products and third for chemicals in 1986. The total value of Louisiana's manufacturing shipments in 1985 was $52,828m., of which 23% was added during manufacture, the second-lowest proportion in the USA.

In 1985 out-of-state tourists in Louisiana spent $3,800m. In 1984/85 direct general expenditure by state and local governments amounted to $10,344m.; revenue totalled $10,882m., of which $1,877m. was contributed by the federal government.

Maine

The most important elements of Maine's economy are manufacturing (particularly papermaking), wholesale and retail trade, services, and finance, insurance and real estate. Forestry and fishing are also important sources of income. In 1986 the state's per-head disposable income amounted to $11,106. The civilian labour force was 562,000 in that year and the unemployment rate 5.3% (30,000 persons). In 1982 18.5% of workers in non-agricultural employment belonged to a trade union.

At the time of the 1982 Census of Agriculture just 8% of Maine's land area consisted of farmland (the lowest proportion of any state other than Alaska), with the average farm covering an area of 210 acres. In 1986 69% of farm income derived from livestock and livestock products, and 31% from crops. Maine's most important agricultural commodities, in order of value, were dairy products, potatoes, eggs and cattle. Forestland accounted for 89% of Maine's area in 1982, the highest percentage of any state; the state ranked 15th in the USA for lumber production in 1987. Fishing is also important to Maine's economy; the state ranked eighth in the nation in 1986 in terms of the value of its commercial catch. The most valuable fishery product is lobster.

Maine had the USA's fifth-lowest total value of non-fuel mineral production in 1986. The principal mineral products are sand and gravel, cement and stone. Maine is the USA's leading producer of garnets.

Until the end of the 19th century shipbuilding and lumber dominated Maine's manufacturing economy; today papermaking and wood products are the most important industries. Wood-related industries accounted for a large share of value added in manufacturing in 1982, while the leather and food-products industries are also important. Maine ranked third in the manufacture of leather and leather products in 1985, behind New York and Missouri. In 1985 the total value of Maine's manufacturing shipments amounted to $9,778m., with 48% being added during manufacture.

Travel and tourism was the state's largest employer in 1982. In 1986 tourists in Maine spent $1,600m.

In 1984/85 direct general expenditure by state and local governments totalled $2,449m.; revenue totalled $2,648m., of which $651m. was provided by the federal government.

Maryland

In Maryland the principal sectors of the economy are manufacturing, government, construction, wholesale and retail trade, and services. In 1986 the state's per-head disposable income totalled $14,091, the sixth highest in the country. The civilian labour force numbered 2,358,000 in 1986, and the unemployment rate was 4.5% (105,000 persons), the sixth lowest in the country. In 1982 18.6% of workers in non-agricultural employment belonged to a trade union.

At the time of the 1982 Census of Agriculture farmland comprised 41% of Maryland's land area, with the average farm covering an area of 158 acres. In 1986 sales of livestock and livestock products accounted for 69% of farm income, with crops providing 31%. Maryland's principal agricultural commodities, in terms of value, were broilers, dairy products, greenhouse products and cattle. Tobacco is a long-established crop, but is gradually declining in significance. In 1982 38% of the state consisted of forestland, principally composed of hardwood timber.

Maryland's most important mineral products in 1985 were stone, cement and coal (all bituminous), in order of value. Sand and gravel, clays and lime are also produced. Coal, Maryland's only exploited fossil-fuel resource, is mined along the border with Pennsylvania.

About one-third of Maryland's manufacturing activity takes place in the city of Baltimore, which from the early 18th century has been an important centre for the production of machinery and steel, and later for motor vehicles. In 1982 the shipments of the electrical and electronic equipment, food-products and chemicals industries led in importance in terms of value added. The total value of the state's manufacturing shipments was $25,328m. in 1985, of which 47% was added during manufacture.

In 1985 visitors to the state spent an estimated $4,400m. Direct general expenditure by state and local governments totalled $10,332m. in 1984/85; revenue totalled $11,308m., with $1,848m. being provided by the federal government.

Massachusetts

In Massachusetts the principal economic activity is manufacturing, followed by services, trade and finance. In 1986 the state's per-head disposable income was $14,836, fourth highest in the nation. The civilian labour force totalled 3,051,000 in 1986, with an unemployment rate of 3.8% (117,000 persons), second lowest in the USA. In 1982 19.7% of workers in non-agricultural employment belonged to a trade union.

Farmland accounted for just 12% of Massachusetts' land area at the time of the 1982 Census of Agriculture; the average farm covered an area of only 113 acres. In 1986 crop sales provided 69% and livestock and livestock products 31% of farm income. Greenhouse products, cranberries, dairy products and eggs were the principal commodities by value. Massachusetts is the leading producer of cranberries in the USA. Although 56% of the state was composed of forestland in 1982, forestry is a relatively minor industry. In 1986 the value of Massachusetts' fish catch was fourth highest in the USA, although the fishing industry has become progressively less important to the state economy. The major species caught are cod, haddock, mackerel and lobster.

Massachusetts produces no fossil fuels. Its non-fuel mineral output is relatively small but outranks that of any other state of New England; in 1985 the principal minerals in order of value were stone, sand and gravel, and lime.

Massachusetts was the first major industrial state in the USA and has remained a regional manufacturing centre. In 1982 the most important industrial groups (by value added) were non-electrical machinery, electrical and electronic equipment and instruments and related products. The total value of Massachusetts' manufacturing shipments was $60,610m. in 1985, with 54% added during manufacture, the fourth-highest proportion in the nation.

By the mid-19th century Boston had become an important banking centre, and banking continues to be a principal sector of the state's economy. The Boston Stock Exchange was founded in 1846.

In 1985 tourists spent an estimated $4,400m. in the state. Massachusetts' beaches (especially Cape Cod) represent a major tourist attraction.

In 1984/85 direct general expenditure by state and local governments amounted to $14,134m., while revenue totalled $15,502m., of which $2,957m. was provided by the federal government.

Michigan

The principal elements in Michigan's economy are manufacturing (particularly motor vehicles), agriculture and tourism. In 1986 the state's per-head disposable income totalled $12,598. The civilian labour force numbered 4,393,000 in 1986, and the unemployment rate was 8.5% (385,000 persons), the 10th highest in the USA. In 1982 33.7% of workers in non-agricultural employment belonged to a trade union, the second-highest percentage in the country (behind New York).

At the time of the 1982 Census of Agriculture 30% of Michigan's land area consisted of farmland, with the average farm covering an area of 187 acres. In 1986 54% of farm income was generated by crop sales and 46% by livestock and livestock products. The state's leading agricultural commodities in that year (in order of value) were dairy products, corn, cattle and hogs; Michigan was the USA's fifth-ranked hog producer in 1986, and was third in production of apples, behind Washington and New York. Some 50% of the state was covered by forestland in 1982, nearly all of which was commercial timberland. Michigan was the USA's leading lumber-producing state in the latter part of the 19th century: while production has undergone a relative decline during the 20th century, the lumber industry remains the principal economic activity in the western part of the Upper Peninsula.

Petroleum, iron ore and natural gas were the state's most valuable mineral products in 1985. Michigan was the USA's sixth most important source of non-fuel minerals in that year, with sand and gravel, salt, gypsum, lime and crushed stone following iron ore in importance. Copper and silver are mined in the Upper Peninsula.

The development of the motor-vehicle industry in the early 20th century helped the state to become one of the world's principal manufacturing areas. In 1985 the total value of the state's manufacturing shipments was $134,043m. (the fifth highest of any state), with 40% being added during manufacture. The industrial groups of transportation equipment, non-electrical machinery and fabricated metal products accounted for the largest share of value added in 1982; in 1985 Michigan led the nation in the manufacture of transportation equipment, ranking second behind Ohio for fabricated metal products and third for furniture and fixings. Detroit is the principal manufacturing centre.

Michigan has been an important banking centre since the 1840s, and tourism has also played an important role in the state's economy since the 19th century; in 1987 out-of-state visitors spent an estimated $8,300m.

In 1984/85 direct general expenditure by state and local governments totalled $22,705m.; revenue totalled $24,491m., of which $4,270m. was provided by the federal government.

Minnesota

Trade, manufacturing and construction are principal sectors of Minnesota's economy. It is also an important agricultural state. Per-head disposable income was $13,117 in 1986, in which year the civilian labour force totalled 2,213,000, with an unemployment rate of 5.3% (118,000 persons). In 1982 24.5% of workers in non-agricultural employment belonged to a trade union.

At the time of the 1982 Census of Agriculture farmland accounted for 54% of Minnesota's land area, with the average farm covering an area of 294 acres. In 1986 56% of the state's farm income (which was the sixth highest in the USA) derived from sales of livestock and livestock products, and 44% from crop marketings. Minnesota's principal agricultural commodities by value in that year were dairy products, corn, cattle and hogs: it ranked second in hog production, behind Iowa; second for turkeys, behind North Carolina; second for hay, behind Wisconsin; fourth for milk; and led in the production of sugar beets. In 1982 31% of the state consisted of forestland; there is some lumbering activity.

In 1985 Minnesota ranked fifth in the USA in terms of the value of its non-fuel mineral output. It ranks first among the states in the production of iron ore, with an output of almost 29m. long tons in 1986. The next most valuable mineral products in 1985 were sand and gravel. Peat is Minnesota's only known fossil-fuel resource, and production accounts for almost one-half of the US total (excluding Alaska).

Canning and meatpacking became important industries in the early 20th century, and food processing remains a leading industrial activity. The total value of Minnesota's manufacturing shipments in 1985 was $42,532m., with 46% being added during manufacture. Non-electrical machinery, food products and fabricated metal products contributed the largest shares of value added in 1982. Much of the state's manufacturing activity is concentrated on the Minneapolis–St Paul area.

Out-of-state visitors to Minnesota spent an estimated $3,100m. in 1986, and in 1983 tourism provided about 110,000 jobs.

In 1984/85 direct general expenditure by state and local governments amounted to $11,918m.; revenue totalled $13,023m. of which $2,088m. was provided by the federal government.

Mississippi

Mississippi's economy is dominated by manufacturing, trade and services; until the Second World War it was principally dependent on the cotton industry. In terms of per-head disposable income, in 1986 Mississippi was the poorest state in the union, with an average of just $8,395. The civilian labour force totalled 1,163,000 in that year; the unemployment rate of 11.7% (136,000 persons) was the third highest among the states in the USA. In 1982 9.3% of workers in non-agricultural employment belonged to a trade union, the third-lowest proportion in the country.

At the time of the 1982 Census of Agriculture 41% of Mississippi's land area consisted of farmland, while the average farm covered an area of 293 acres. In 1986 58% of farm income derived from sales of livestock and livestock products and 42% from crops. Mississippi's leading agricultural products in that year were broilers (for which it ranked fifth nationally), cotton (for which it ranked third, behind Texas and California), soybeans and cattle. Forestland comprised some 55% of Mississippi's land area in 1982; in 1987 the state ranked sixth in the USA in timber (principally softwood) production. Commercial fish landings are generally high in volume but low in value; however, Mississippi ranked first among the states for catfish farming in 1985.

Mississippi's principal mineral products by value in 1985 were petroleum, natural gas and sand and gravel. It ranked 11th among petroleum-producing states in 1986. Crushed stone and clays are also extracted.

The total value of Mississippi's manufacturing shipments amounted to $22,723m. in 1985, of which 40% was added in manufacture. Transportation equipment, food products and electrical and electronic equipment contributed the largest shares of value added in 1982; lumber and wood production was also important in terms of shipments.

Out-of-state visitors to Mississippi spent an estimated $1,300m. in 1986, and in 1982 tourism was the third-largest employer in the state.

Direct general expenditure by state and local governments in 1984/85 totalled $4,662m.; revenue was $4,929m., of which $1,183m. was provided by the federal government.

Missouri

Manufacturing, farming, trade, tourism, services and mining are all important elements of Missouri's economy. In 1986 the state's per-head disposable income amounted to $11,933. The civilian labour force totalled 2,529,000 in that year, with an unemployment rate of 6.1% (154,000 persons). In 1982 26.6% of workers in non-agricultural employment belonged to a trade union.

At the time of the 1982 Census of Agriculture farmland comprised 66% of Missouri's land area, while the average farm covered an area of 260 acres. In 1986 55% of farm income derived from sales of livestock and livestock products and 45% from crops. The

principal agricultural commodities by value in that year were soybeans, cattle, hogs and corn. Missouri was the USA's third most important producer of soybeans, behind Illinois and Iowa, its fifth-largest producer of turkeys and its eighth-largest of hogs. Winter wheat, grain sorghum, rice, cotton and cattle are also important. Some 28% of Missouri's land area was covered by forestland in 1982; some lumber is produced commercially, with hardwood predominating.

In terms of value, the most important mineral products in 1985 were cement, stone and lead. The state's output of almost 320,000 metric tons of lead in 1986 represented more than 94% of total US production of the metal. Zinc is also mined in large quantities, and there is some iron ore. Fossil-fuel resources are scarce, but small quantities of bituminous coal and petroleum are extracted.

The leading manufacturing centres of Missouri are the St Louis and Kansas City areas. By value added during manufacture the leading industrial groups in 1982 were transportation equipment (mainly motor vehicles and aeroplanes), food products and chemicals. In 1985 the state ranked fourth overall in transportation equipment and second (behind New York) for leather and leather products. The total value of Missouri's manufacturing shipments in that year was $54,872m., with 40% being added during manufacture.

In 1982 tourists spent an estimated $4,100m. in Missouri, and the tourist industry provided about 97,800 jobs.

Direct general expenditure by state and local governments totalled $8,927m. in 1984/85; revenue was $9,593m., of which $1,857m. was contributed by the federal government.

Montana

The principal elements of Montana's economy are manufacturing, mining, agriculture and tourism. In 1986 the state's per-head disposable income totalled $10,446. The civilian labour force was 407,000 in 1986, and the unemployment rate 8.1% (33,000 persons). In 1982 21.7% of workers in non-agricultural employment belonged to a trade union.

Some 65% of Montana's land area consisted of farmland at the time of the 1982 Census of Agriculture, while the average farm covered an area of 2,568 acres. In 1986 59% of farm income derived from sales of livestock and livestock products and 41% from crops. Cattle, wheat, barley and hay were Montana's most valuable agricultural products in that year; it ranked second to North Dakota in barley production, and its wool clip was the fifth largest in the USA. Dairy products also provide a significant source of income. In 1982 20% of the state was covered by forestland, and in 1987 Montana ranked eighth among all states for timber production.

The state ranks first in the USA for size of its known coal reserves; it ranked ninth overall for coal production in 1985. Petroleum, coal and natural gas were the most valuable minerals produced in that year. Non-fuel mineral products include gold, silver, copper and lead.

Montana's manufacturing activity is based on its mineral, forestry and agricultural resources. By value added, the most important industry groups in 1982 were lumber and wood products, food products, petroleum and coal. In 1985 the total value of Montana's manufacturing shipments was $3,510m., of which 25%, the third-lowest share in the USA, was added during manufacture.

Out-of-state visitors to Montana spent about $423m. in 1983, and about 20,200 jobs in the state were related to travel and tourism.

In 1984/85 direct general expenditure by state and local governments amounted to $2,160m.; revenue totalled $2,282m., with $524m. being provided by the federal government.

Nebraska

Nebraska's economy, including its manufacturing and service sectors, is dependent on agriculture. In 1986 the state's per-head disposable income totalled $12,051. The civilian labour force was 803,000 in 1986, and the unemployment rate 5% (40,000 persons). In 1982 16.3% of workers in non-agricultural employment belonged to a trade union.

According to the 1982 Census of Agriculture some 92% of Nebraska's land area—the highest proportion of any state—was composed of farmland, with the average farm covering an area of 746 acres. Some 6m. acres of farmland was under irrigation in that year. In 1986 Nebraska's farm income was the fourth highest of any state, with 61% being contributed by sales of livestock and livestock products and 39% by crops. The principal agricultural products in 1986, by order of value, were cattle, corn, hogs and soybeans; in that year Nebraska was the third most important state for slaughterings of cattle and calves and for the production of both corn and sorghum for grain, and ranked fourth for hog slaughterings. Wheat, hay, sugar beets, potatoes and barley are subsidiary crops. Forestland comprised just 2% of Nebraska's land area in 1982.

In 1985 Nebraska's most important minerals, in terms of value, were petroleum, cement and sand and gravel. Crushed stone and natural gas are also extracted in the state.

Manufacturing is a small but developing sector of Nebraska's economy. By value added the most important industry groups in 1982 were food products, non-electrical machinery, and chemicals. About one-third of the state's manufacturing activity takes place in Omaha. In 1985 the total value of Nebraska's manufacturing shipments was $15,215m., with 35% being added during manufacture.

Tourists spent an estimated $1,400m. in Nebraska in 1987, and in 1982 tourism was the state's second-largest employer, providing 32,000 jobs.

In 1984/85 direct general expenditure by state and local governments totalled $3,621m.; revenue was $3,721m., of which $638m. was contributed by the federal government.

Nevada

Tourism and gambling revenues are the principal contributors to Nevada's economy, though mining continues to be of significant economic importance. In 1986 the state's per-head disposable income was $13,071. The civilian labour force totalled 541,000 in 1986, with an unemployment rate of 6% (32,000 persons). In 1982 22.1% of workers in non-agricultural employment belonged to a trade union.

Farmland constituted 14% of Nevada's land area at the time of the 1982 Census of Agriculture, while the average farm size was relatively high, at 3,671 acres. Irrigation is used throughout the state. In 1986 69% of farm income was derived from sales of livestock and livestock products and 31% from crops. The main agricultural products by value in 1986 were cattle, hay, dairy products and potatoes. Only 10% of the state was composed of forestland in 1982.

In 1985 the state's principal mineral products by value were gold, petroleum and diatomite. Nevada ranks first among the states in the production of gold (with an estimated output of almost 2.1m. troy ounces in 1986), barite and mercury. Other non-fuel mineral resources include silver, copper, fluorspar, iron ore, lithium and molybdenum.

Nevada's industrial activity is small but diversified. In 1982 the major industry groups, measured by value added during manufacture, were food products, printing and publishing, and fabricated metals. The total value of Nevada's manufacturing shipments in 1985 was $1,946m., the second lowest among the states, of which 53%, the fifth-highest proportion in the USA, was added during manufacture.

Tourism remains of primary importance to Nevada's economy. In 1987 out-of-state visitors spent an estimated $6,500m., and in 1982 some 30% of all jobs in the state were related to the tourist industry. Casino revenues alone represent a large share of the total income from tourism.

Direct general expenditure by state and local governments in 1984/85 totalled $2,355m.; revenue totalled $2,436m., with $339m. being provided by the federal government.

New Hampshire

The economy of New Hampshire is dominated by manufacturing, although the tourist industry is expanding rapidly. The state's per-head disposable income was $13,891 in 1986, ranking eighth highest in the nation. The civilian labour force totalled 562,000 in that year, while New Hampshire's unemployment rate, at 2.8% (16,000 persons), was the lowest of any state in the union. In 1982 12.3% of employees in non-agricultural establishments (the ninth-lowest proportion nation-wide) belonged to a trade union.

Only 9% of New Hampshire's land area consisted of farmland at the time of the 1982 Census of Agriculture, with the average farm covering an area of 170 acres. New Hampshire's farm income is one of the lowest in the USA (only exceeding those of Rhode Island and Alaska); in 1986 65% was contributed by livestock and livestock products and 35% by crops. The state's principal commodities in that year were dairy products, greenhouse products, apples and cattle. In 1982 84% of the state was covered by forestland, the second-highest proportion (behind Maine) of any state. There is a little commercial fishing activity.

Mining plays a minor role in the state's economy; non-fuel mineral production ranked fourth lowest in the nation in 1985. The principal mineral products in that year were sand and gravel, stone and clays. The state is nicknamed after its granite quarries.

Shipbuilding, formerly New Hampshire's principal industry, was superseded as such during the 19th century by textiles. In 1982

the major industry groups, measured in terms of value added during manufacture, were non-electrical machinery, electrical and electronic equipment, and paper and allied products. In 1985 the total value of manufacturing shipments was $9,050m., of which 56%, the third-highest proportion among the states, was added during manufacture.

After manufacturing, tourism is the most important industry to the state economy. In 1985 out-of-state visitors to New Hampshire spent about $1,000m.

Direct general expenditure by state and local governments in 1984/85 totalled $1,812m.; revenue was $1,921m., with $385m. being provided by the federal government.

New Jersey

Manufacturing is New Jersey's principal economic activity, while construction and wholesale and retail trade are expanding rapidly. The state's per-head disposable income in 1986 amounted to $15,927, ranking second highest in the USA. The civilian labour force totalled 3,892,000 in 1986, with an unemployment rate of 5% (196,000 persons). In 1982 19.9% of workers in non-agricultural employment belonged to a trade union.

According to the 1982 Census of Agriculture 19% of New Jersey's land area consisted of farmland, while the average farm covered an area of just 111 acres. In 1986 74% of farm income derived from crop sales and 26% from livestock and livestock products. The most valuable agricultural commodities in that year were greenhouse products, dairy products, eggs and peaches. New Jersey is a major producer of fresh market fruit and vegetables; it is the nation's second-ranked producer of blueberries. In 1982 41% of New Jersey's land area was covered by forest; the modest lumber industry is now of little economic importance. New Jersey has a significant commercial fish catch.

Stone, sand and gravel and zinc were the state's principal mineral products, in order of value, in 1985. New Jersey was the USA's leading producer of zinc in the late 19th century, but its importance has since declined, so that it ranked fifth among zinc-producing states in 1984.

Since the early 19th century New Jersey has been an important manufacturing centre of the USA. In 1985 the principal manufactures, ranked by value added, were chemicals and allied products, food products, and electrical and electronic equipment. New Jersey ranked second overall for chemicals and allied products, behind Texas, but first in pharmaceuticals; it ranked highly in most areas of manufacturing activity. The total value of manufacturing shipments in 1985 was $75,554m. (10th among the states), with 48% being added during manufacture.

The city of Newark is the financial centre of New Jersey; the state is among the leaders nationally in banking activity, but is overshadowed considerably in this respect by the financial activities of nearby New York City and Philadelphia. The tourist industry is of significant economic importance, with tourists spending an estimated $11,400m. in 1987. The gambling industry of Atlantic City accounts for a large share of the total income from tourism.

Direct general expenditure by state and local governments amounted to $18,771m. in 1984/85. Revenue totalled $20,700m., of which $3,112m. was provided by the federal government.

New Mexico

Agriculture dominated the economy of New Mexico until the 1940s; mining, manufacturing and tourism are also currently of importance to the state economy. The state's per-head disposable income totalled $9,890 in 1986, the 10th lowest in the USA. The civilian labour force was 672,000 in 1986, and the unemployment rate 9.2% (62,000 persons), the seventh highest among all states. In 1982 12.8% of employees in non-agricultural establishments belonged to a trade union.

At the time of the 1982 Census of Agriculture farmland constituted some 61% of New Mexico's land area, with the average farm size being relatively high, at 3,493 acres. Water resources are very scarce in the state. In 1986 sales of livestock and livestock products accounted for 70% of farm income, with the remaining 30% being derived from crops. New Mexico's principal agricultural commodities in that year (by value) were cattle, dairy products, hay and chilli peppers. In 1982 22% of the state was covered by forest.

In order of value, the state's most important mineral products in 1985 were natural gas, petroleum and coal. New Mexico is a leading producer of both fuel and non-fuel minerals. It ranked fourth among states in the production of natural gas in 1986 and seventh in petroleum. It was also the USA's largest producer of potash, with an output of 987,000 metric tons, or 96% of the national total. Copper, uranium and coal (bituminous) are also mined in significant quantities.

The total value of New Mexico's manufacturing shipments in 1985 amounted to $4,074m., the 10th-lowest total of any state; 40% of value was added during manufacture. By value added, the most important industries in 1982 were petroleum and coal products, electrical and electronic equipment, and food products. Most of New Mexico's industry is located in the Albuquerque area.

Actively encouraged by the state government, tourism has become a major economic activity. In 1987 out-of-state visitors spent $2,000m. in New Mexico, and in 1982 8% of all jobs in the state were tourist-related.

Direct general expenditure by state and local governments in 1984/85 amounted to $3,678m.; revenue was $4,168m., of which $687m. was provided by the federal government.

New York

Services, manufacturing, trade, finance and communications (all based in New York City) are among New York's principal economic activities, and the state remains a leading power in these sectors. Mining and agriculture are of local importance but are less essential to the overall economy. The state's per-head disposable income in 1986 was $14,070, seventh highest in the USA. The civilian labour force totalled 8,408,000, with an unemployment rate of 6.3% (526,000 persons). New York state has the most highly-unionized work-force in the USA; in 1982 35.8% of workers in non-agricultural employment belonged to a trade union.

At the time of the 1982 Census of Agriculture 30% of New York's land area consisted of farmland, the average farm covering an area of 218 acres. In 1986 livestock and livestock products accounted for 71% of farm income and crops for the remaining 29%. By value, the leading agricultural commodities in 1986 were dairy products, greenhouse products, cattle and eggs. New York ranked third in milk production among the states in 1986 (behind Wisconsin and California) and second in apple production (behind Washington). Field crops produced include hay, corn (for grain and for silage), potatoes, oats and wheat. Some 53% of the state was covered by forest in 1982; lumbering activity is of modest proportions.

New York's most valuable mineral products in 1985 were stone, cement and salt. The state ranked third nationally in 1986 for salt production; it also ranks second for zinc (behind Tennessee) and fourth for lead. Talc, silver and garnets are also important non-fuel products. Estimated reserves of petroleum and natural gas in New York are relatively small; there is some production of both.

Until the 1970s New York led the nation in industrial production of many kinds; however, by 1985 the total of its manufacturing shipments ($138,217m.) was only the fourth highest in the country. Of this value, 53% was added during manufacture, the fifth-highest proportion nationally. In terms of value added, the most important industries in 1985 were printing and publishing, instruments and related products, and electrical and electronic equipment. The state led all others in 1986 in the categories of printing and publishing, instruments, apparel and leather goods; it ranked second behind California in electrical and electronic equipment, third behind California and Illinois for non-electrical machinery and eighth in food products.

Banking is of major economic importance to New York. In 1986 the state's commercial banks held assets of $423,300m. and deposits of $255,500m., ranking it first in the nation in both categories. New York City is the USA's primary banking centre; it is also an important base for life insurance and the centre of US securities trading. It houses the nation's two foremost securities markets, the New York Stock Exchange and the American Stock Exchange.

New York state, with its two main attractions of New York City and Long Island, was visited by 4.8m. foreign tourists in 1983 and regularly attracts more than 60m. US travellers annually. In 1986 it was estimated that tourists spent $17,200m. in the state.

In 1984/85 direct general expenditure by state and local governments totalled $59,455m., while revenue totalled $64,568m., with $11,457m. being provided by the federal government.

North Carolina

North Carolina's economy was dominated by agriculture (particularly tobacco-growing) until industrialization accelerated in the late 19th century. Manufacturing then expanded to replace agriculture as the backbone of the economy. In 1986 the state's per-head disposable income totalled $10,543. The civilian labour force numbered 3,914,000, and the unemployment rate 5.3% (170,000 persons). In 1982 North Carolina had the second-lowest level of unionization in the USA (behind South Carolina); just 8.9% of workers in non-agricultural employment belonged to a trade union.

Farmland accounted for some 33% of North Carolina's land area at the time of the 1982 Census of Agriculture, while the average farm covered a relatively small area—142 acres. In 1986 57% of farm income derived from livestock and livestock products and 43% from crop sales. The leading agricultural products (by value) were tobacco, broilers, hogs and turkeys; North Carolina was the USA's largest producer of tobacco and turkeys in 1986, its third-largest supplier of peanuts, its fourth-largest of broilers and its seventh-largest of eggs. Sweet potatoes, corn, grapes and soybeans are also important crops. Some 60% of the state was covered by forestland in 1982, concentrated along the coast and beyond the Blue Ridge; in 1987 North Carolina was the USA's ninth-largest timber producer. There is a small but well-established commercial fishing industry.

North Carolina's most valuable mineral products in 1985 were stone, phosphate and lithium. The state leads the nation in production of feldspar and lithium, and is a major producer of phosphate rock.

North Carolina has been a leading industrial state for most of the 20th century, ranking second among southern states (behind Texas) and eighth overall in 1985 in the value of its manufacturing shipments. This totalled $81,985m., of which 48% was added during manufacture. The state was the USA's largest manufacturer of textile-mill products, tobacco products and furniture and fixings in 1985. By value added the major industrial groups in 1982 were textile-mill products, tobacco products and electrical and electronic equipment.

In 1984 tourism and travel provided about 165,000 jobs in North Carolina. An estimated $5,700m. was spent in the state by non-resident tourists in 1986.

Direct general expenditure by state and local governments in 1984/85 totalled $11,168m.; revenue totalled $12,205m., with $2,332m. being provided by the federal government.

North Dakota

North Dakota's economy is dominated by agriculture, agriculture-related wholesale trade and manufacturing, and the mining of petroleum and coal. In 1986 the state's per-head disposable income was $11,100. The total civilian labour force in 1986 numbered 331,000, the unemployment rate being 6.3% (21,000 persons). In 1982 14.2% of those employed in non-agricultural work belonged to a trade union.

At the time of the 1982 Census of Agriculture 91% of North Dakota's land area was farmland, an average farm occupying an area of 1,104 acres. In 1986 71% of farm income came from crop sales and 29% from livestock and livestock products; the state's major products, ranked by value, were wheat, cattle, barley and sunflowers. North Dakota ranked first in the USA in barley production in 1986 and second (behind Kansas) for wheat. Flaxseed, oats, soybeans, hay and potatoes are also important sources of income. In 1982 just 1% of the state was covered by forest—the lowest proportion in the USA—and forestry products contribute little to the economy.

Petroleum, coal and natural gas were North Dakota's most important mineral products by value in 1986. The state ranked ninth nationally in that year for petroleum production and 12th for coal. (The state has the largest known recoverable reserves of coal in the USA.) Sand and gravel are the only significant non-fuel mineral products.

In terms of value added, North Dakota's most important manufacturing industries in 1982 were those relating to food, non-electrical machinery, and printing and publishing. The total value of the state's manufacturing shipments in 1986 was $2,492m. (fourth lowest in the USA), of which 30% was added in manufacture (also the fourth-lowest proportion nation-wide).

Tourism is of importance to North Dakota's economy; in 1983 an estimated $651m. was spent by tourists in the state. Direct general expenditure by state and local governments in 1984/85 totalled $1,847m.; revenue totalled $1,949m., of which $409m. was provided by the federal government.

Ohio

Ohio's main economic activities are manufacturing, service industries, wholesale and retail trade, transportation and utilities, construction, finance, insurance and real estate. In 1986 the state's per-head disposable income was $12,015. The civilian labour force totalled 5,234,000 in that year, and the unemployment rate was 8.1% (426,000 persons). In 1982 27.4% of workers in non-agricultural employment belonged to a trade union, the 10th-highest proportion in the country.

Agriculture provides a significant contribution to the state's economy. Farmland accounted for 59% of Ohio's land area in 1982, the average farm covering 177 acres. In 1986 57% of farm income was generated by crop sales and 43% by livestock and livestock products. In 1986 the main agricultural commodities produced by the state (measured by value) were corn, soybeans, dairy products and hogs; Ohio ranked fifth in egg production and seventh in hog slaughterings in that year. Other important crops were tomatoes, wheat and oats. Forestland accounted for 26% of the state's land area in 1982.

Coal, natural gas and petroleum were the principal minerals produced in Ohio in 1985 in terms of their value. In 1986 Ohio ranked eighth in the USA in coal production. Important non-fuel minerals are stone, sand and gravel, salt (in which it ranked fourth in 1986), lime, clays (in which it ranked second, behind Georgia) and cement.

In the late 19th century Ohio led the nation in the production of machine tools and was the second-ranking steel-producing state; the state was among the leaders in the establishment of an automobile industry. In 1982 the state's major industry groups, in terms of value added, were transportation equipment, non-electrical machinery and fabricated metal products. In 1985 Ohio ranked first in the USA in the value of its output of primary metal products, rubber and plastics products and fabricated metal products, and ranked third in transportation equipment. Motor-vehicle tyre manufacturing companies are particularly well represented in the state. Food products and chemicals are also important to the economy. The total value of shipments for Ohio in 1985 was $145,482m. (third highest in the nation), of which 44% was added during manufacture.

In 1982 tourists spent $5,400m. in Ohio. Direct general expenditure by state and local governments in 1984/85 totalled $22,781m.; revenue totalled $24,229m., of which $4,203m. was provided by the federal government.

Oklahoma

Oklahoma's main economic activities are manufacturing, wholesale and retail trade, services, finance, insurance and real estate. Agriculture and the extraction of oil and gas are also of importance to the state's economy. In 1986 Oklahoma's per-head disposable income was $9,837, the seventh lowest in the USA. The civilian labour force totalled 1,593,000 in that year, while the unemployment rate was 8.2% (131,000 persons). In 1982 12.9% of workers in non-agricultural establishments belonged to a trade union.

Farmland accounted for 74% of Oklahoma's land area at the time of the 1982 Census of Agriculture, an average farm covering 446 acres. In 1986 72% of farm income was generated by sales of livestock and livestock products and 28% by crops. The state's main agricultural products by value were cattle, wheat, dairy products and broilers, and it ranked third behind Kansas and North Dakota for wheat output. Other important sources of income are peanuts, hay, sorghum for grain, soybeans, hogs and pigs, and poultry. Forestland covered 15% of the state in 1982.

Oklahoma's most valuable minerals in 1985 were natural gas, petroleum and coal. In 1986 the state ranked third in the USA for natural gas (behind Texas and Louisiana) and fifth for petroleum. Non-fuel minerals contributing to the state's economy are iodine, limestone, gypsum, cement, stone, sand and gravel, and clays.

Until recently Oklahoma's manufacturing industry was based on the processing of agricultural products and petroleum, but it has become more diversified. In 1982 the state's leading manufacturing product groups, in terms of value added, were non-electrical machinery, fabricated metal products, and rubber and plastics products. The total value of Oklahoma's manufacturing shipments in 1985 was $25,025m., of which 37% was added during manufacture.

In 1982 tourism was the second-largest employer in the state. Tourists spent $2,700m. in 1986.

Direct general expenditure by state and local governments in 1984/85 totalled $6,713m.; revenue totalled $7,409m., of which $1,151m. was provided by the federal government.

Oregon

Manufacturing (particularly lumber-related), service industries, tourism and research-related businesses are Oregon's main economic activities. The state's per-head disposable income was $10,726 in 1986. The total civilian labour force numbered 1,347,000 in 1986, while the unemployment rate was 8.5% (114,000 workers). The proportion of non-agricultural workers belonging to a trade union in 1982 was 27.5%, the eighth-highest rate in the country.

At the time of the 1982 Census of Agriculture farmland accounted for 29% of Oregon's land area, an average farm occupying 520 acres. In 1986 64% of farm income came from crops and 36% from livestock and livestock products. In terms of their value the leading agricultural commodities in 1986 were cattle, greenhouse products, dairy products and wheat. Other products of importance include hay and potatoes. Oregon was the nation's third most important

potato producer in 1986, behind Idaho and Washington. In 1982 48% of the state was forestland; Oregon's forests accounted for 4.5% of the US total. Although the industry is declining, Oregon was still the nation's leading timber producer in 1987, with an output of 8,455m. board feet, and, in terms of its value, the lumber and forest products industry contributes more than any other to the state's economy. There is some commercial fishing activity, the most valuable species fished being salmon.

In 1985 Oregon's principal minerals, in terms of their value, were stone, sand and gravel, and cement. Gold, upon which the state's fortunes rested at the end of the 19th century, is no longer of significance to its economy.

The lumber and wood products industry dominates Oregon's manufacturing activity, accounting for one-third of the value of all manufacturing shipments in 1985. After lumber and wood, those sectors with the most value added by manufacture in 1982 were food and kindred products, and scientific and medical instruments. Other major industries in 1985 were paper and allied products, primary metal industries, non-electrical machinery, and electrical and electronic equipment—a fast-growing sector. In 1985 the total value of manufacturing shipments in Oregon was $21,004m., of which 45% was added during manufacture.

Oregon's rugged coast and extensive system of national and state parks make it a major US tourist attraction, and in 1982 the tourist industry was the state's third largest employer.

Direct general expenditure by state and local governments in 1984/85 totalled $6,640m.; revenue totalled $7,165m., of which $1,407m. was provided by the federal government.

Pennsylvania

Despite growth in industries such as the manufacture of non-electrical machinery, tourism, service industries and wholesale and retail trade, Pennsylvania's economy has not yet recovered from the dramatic decline in its production of coal and oil in the first half of the 20th century, and from the loss of industries to foreign competitors and to the 'sunbelt' states. In 1986 the state's per-head disposable income was $12,403. The civilian labour force totalled 5,634,000 in 1986, with an unemployment rate of 6.8% (386,000). In 1982 27% of non-agriculture workers were unionized.

Farmland accounted for 29% of Pennsylvania's land area at the time of the 1982 Census of Agriculture, and the average size for farms in the state was 149 acres. In 1986 71% of farm income was generated by sales of livestock and livestock products and 29% by crops. Dairy products, cattle, greenhouse products and eggs were the most valuable agricultural commodities in 1986. Other important sources of farm income were hay, corn, oats, soybeans, wheat, barley, hogs and pigs, and poultry. The state was ranked third in the nation for egg production (behind California and Indiana), fifth for milk and ninth for cattle and calves. In 1982 57% of the state's land area was forestland, but lumber production is no longer a major industry in the state.

Pennsylvania's most valuable mineral commodities in 1985 were coal, natural gas and stone. The state ranked fourth in US coal production in 1986; it is the only major US producer of anthracite coal. Other important minerals are stone and cement (for both of which Pennsylvania ranked third in 1986), sand and gravel, and clays.

Despite its diminishing role as a contributor to the total US economy, Pennsylvania is still a major manufacturing centre. In 1982 the state's leading industries, in terms of value added during manufacture, were non-electrical machinery, food and kindred products and primary metal products. Other important manufacturing groups were chemicals and allied products, electrical and electronic equipment, and fabricated metal products. In 1985 Pennsylvania ranked second in the USA (behind Wisconsin) in the value of its output of paper and allied products, and third (behind Ohio and Indiana) in the value of its primary metal products. In 1985 the total value of Pennsylvania's manufacturing shipments was $110,319m., of which 47% was added during manufacture.

Pennsylvania is a prominent centre for both banking and insurance; in 1986 its banks held assets valued at $136,200m., the fifth-highest total of any state. The Philadelphia Stock Exchange is the country's oldest and was for many years its most important. Tourism also plays an important role in the state's economy and was Pennsylvania's second-largest employer in 1982; in 1985 non-residential visitors spent $8,900m. in the state.

Direct general expenditure by state and local governments in 1984/85 was $24,040m. in total; revenue totalled $27,163m., of which $5,096m. was provided by the federal government.

Rhode Island

The principal economic activity in Rhode Island is manufacturing, with lesser contributions being made by agriculture, mining, forestry, fishing, real estate, wholesale and retail trade, and services. In 1986 the state's disposable income averaged $12,834 per head. The civilian labour force totalled 510,000 in 1986, while the unemployment rate was 4% (21,000 persons), the fourth lowest in the USA. In 1982 19.4% of workers in non-agricultural establishments belonged to a trade union.

Farmland occupied 15% of Rhode Island's total land area at the time of the 1982 Census of Agriculture, an average farm covering an area of 86 acres, the smallest average size found in any state. In 1986 84% of farm income came from crop sales and 16% was generated by livestock and livestock products. In terms of their value, the leading agricultural products in 1986 were greenhouse products, dairy products, eggs and potatoes. In 1982 some 58% of the state was forestland, most of it usable as commercial timberland. Commercial fishing also contributes to the state's economy; the value of Rhode Island's catch in 1986 ranked it 10th among the states.

In 1985 the value of Rhode Island's non-fuel mineral output was the lowest of any state other than Delaware. The principal minerals, in terms of value, were stone, sand and gravel, and gemstones.

Manufacturing is the state's main source of income, the leading product groups, in terms of value added in manufacture, being miscellaneous manufacturing (especially jewellery), fabricated metal products and electrical and electronic equipment. Primary metal products and non-electrical machinery also provide a significant contribution to the economy. The total value of Rhode Island's manufacturing shipments in 1985 was $8,238m., of which 52% was added in manufacture, the seventh-highest proportion in the USA.

Tourists in Rhode Island spent an estimated $1,100m. in 1987. Direct general expenditure by state and local governments in 1984/85 totalled $2,459m.; revenue totalled $2,569m., of which $530m. was provided by the federal government.

South Carolina

Until the end of World War II South Carolina's economy was largely dependent upon agriculture and the textile industry. Today there is greater diversification, with other industries, transportation, wholesale and retail trade, and services playing important roles in the state's economy. In 1986 South Carolina's per-head disposable income was $9,685, the fifth-lowest in the USA. The civilian labour force totalled 1,602,000 in 1986, while the unemployment rate was 6.2% (100,000 workers). In 1982 only 5.8% of non-agricultural workers belonged to a trade union, by far the lowest proportion in the country.

At the time of the 1982 Census of Agriculture farmland made up 29% of the state's land area, an average farm covering 224 acres. In 1986 sales of livestock and livestock products accounted for 51% of farm income and crop marketings for 49%. South Carolina's principal farm products, in terms of value, were tobacco, cattle, soybeans and dairy products. The state also produces cotton (the major crop in the 19th century and the basis of the important textile-mill industry), wheat, peaches, hogs and pigs, milk and poultry. There is some commercial fishing. In 1982 63% of the state was forestland, nearly all of it classed as commercial timberland.

Mining is not a major source of income in South Carolina. In 1985 the principal minerals in terms of value were cement, stone and clays.

Textile-mill products (in which South Carolina ranked third in the USA according to value of shipments in 1985, behind North Carolina and Georgia), chemicals and allied products, and non-electrical machinery were the state's leading industry groups in terms of value added during manufacture in 1982. Food and kindred products, paper and allied products, apparel and other textile products, and electrical and electronic equipment are also of importance to the economy. The total value of manufacturing shipments was $33,869m. in 1985, of which 43% was added during manufacture.

In 1983 tourism provided about 69,300 jobs in South Carolina, with visitors spending an estimated $2,600m. Direct general expenditure by state and local governments in 1984/85 totalled $5,966m.; revenue totalled $6,425m., of which $1,257m. was provided by the federal government.

South Dakota

South Dakota's main economic activites are agriculture, manufacturing, mining and tourism. In 1986 the state's per-head disposable income was $10,730. The civilian labour force totalled 345,000, while the unemployment rate was 4.6% (16,000 persons), the eighth lowest in the country. In 1982 10.3% of workers in non-agricultural employment were unionized—the fifth-lowest proportion in the USA.

Farmland accounted for 90% of South Dakota's land area at the time of the 1982 Census of Agriculture. An average farm occupied an area of 1,179 acres. In 1986 livestock and livestock products accounted for 62% of farm income while crop sales generated 38%. Cattle, hogs, corn and wheat were the chief agricultural commodities (in terms of value) in that year. Other important contributors to farm income are hay, soybeans, oats, barley, sheep and lambs, dairy produce and poultry. South Dakota ranked third in the USA for hay production in 1986 (behind Wisconsin and Minnesota) and fifth for sheep and lambs. In 1982 only 3% of the total land area of the state was forested.

South Dakota ranked second in the USA (after Nevada) in its production of gold in 1984. In 1985 the state's most important minerals, in terms of value, were gold, petroleum and cement. In general, however, fossil-fuel resources in South Dakota are negligible.

In 1982 the state's most important manufacturing industry groups, in terms of value added during manufacture, were food and kindred products, non-electrical machinery and electrical and electronic equipment. Lumber and wood products, and printing and publishing, although insignificant on a national scale, make a significant contribution to state income. In 1985 the total value of the state's manufacturing shipments was $3,585m., of which 39% was added during manufacture.

In 1982 tourists spent an estimated $460m. in South Dakota. Direct general expenditure by state and local governments in 1984/85 totalled $1,567m.; revenue amounted to $1,535m., of which $375m. was provided by the federal government.

Tennessee

Manufacturing industry, agriculture and tourism are Tennessee's most valuable economic activities. In 1986 the state's per-head disposable income was measured at $10,395. The civilian labour force numbered 2,301,000, and the unemployment rate was 8% (185,000 persons). In 1982 17.3% of non-agricultural workers were members of a trade union.

At the time of the 1982 Census of Agriculture farmland made up 47% of the land area of Tennessee, the average farm covering an area of just 138 acres. In 1986 54% of farm income was generated by sales of livestock and livestock products, with crops accounting for 46%. The principal agricultural commodities, in terms of value, were cattle, dairy products, greenhouse products and soybeans. Cotton, corn and tobacco were the leading crops until the 1950s and still make a significant contribution to farm income. Tennessee is the USA's third most important tobacco-producing state, behind North Carolina and Kentucky. Hogs and pigs, poultry, eggs and horses are also raised. Forestland covered 49% of Tennessee's land area in 1982, 97% of it commercial timberland. Hardwood timber accounts for 80% of production.

In 1985 Tennessee's most valuable minerals were bituminous coal, stone and zinc. The state is the USA's leading zinc producer. Petroleum, copper, iron, lead, manganese, gold, clays, cement, sand and gravel are also mined.

In 1982 Tennessee's principal manufactures, in terms of value added, were chemicals and allied products, food and kindred products and non-electrical machinery. Other important manufacturing groups are transportation equipment, paper and allied products, apparel and other textile products, and electrical and electronic equipment. In 1985 the total value of Tennessee's manufacturing shipments was $50,611m., of which 44% was added during manufacture.

Tourism is probably the third-largest employer in Tennessee; in 1987 out-of-state visitors spent an estimated $3,000m. Direct general expenditure by state and local governments in 1984/85 totalled $8,300m.; revenue totalled $8,799m., of which $1,932m. was provided by the federal government.

Texas

Since the 1970s the economy of Texas has relied largely upon its oil and natural-gas resources. Agriculture still makes a significant contribution, as does the manufacturing industry. Other important economic activities are wholesale and retail trade, finance, insurance, and real estate, and service industries.

In 1986 the state's per-head disposable income was $11,569. The civilian labour force totalled 8,159,000 in 1986, while the unemployment rate was 8.9% (726,000 persons), the ninth-highest unemployment rate among the 50 states. In 1982 12.5% of non-agricultural workers were trade union members, the 10th-lowest rate nationally.

At the time of the 1982 Census of Agriculture 78% of the land area of Texas was farmland, an average-sized farm being 710 acres. Irrigation is essential in much of the state. In 1986 65% of farm income came from livestock and livestock products and 35% from crops. Texas ranked third after California and Iowa in that year in terms of total farm income, the leading commodities by value being cattle, cotton, dairy products and greenhouse products. However, many other products are cultivated. Texas led the nation in the production of both cotton and wool in 1986; it ranked second for grain sorghum and cattle (behind Kansas in both cases), third for sheep and lambs, seventh for broilers and eighth for eggs.

Forestland accounted for just 8% of Texas's land area in 1982. Repeated infestations by pine bark beetle and the incidence of forest fires caused massive destruction of the state's forests between 1976 and 1984. Production of timber, however, continues to play a stable part in the economy. Texas's commercial fish catch ranked third in the USA by value in 1986, at $246m.; shrimp accounts for virtually all the catch value.

In 1985 Texas accounted for 24% of the total value of US mineral production. It led the nation in the production of fuels and ranked second to California in the value of its non-fuel minerals. Petroleum, natural gas and coal were the state's most valuable mineral products in 1985; in 1986 it led in the production of petroleum (with 27% of national output), natural gas (36%), sulphur (60%) and stone (8%) and ranked second for cement and salt and sixth for coal. Other valuable minerals include sand and gravel, lime, fluorspar, helium, magnesium and iron ore.

In terms of value added, the leading manufacturing sectors in Texas in 1982 were non-electrical machinery, chemicals and allied products (particularly petrochemicals), and food and kindred products. Texas ranked first in the USA in 1985 in the value of its output both of chemicals and allied products and of petroleum and coal products, supplying 30% of national output in the latter category. In the same year it ranked third for food and kindred products. Other major manufacturing industry groups are fabricated metal products, transportation equipment, electrical and electronic equipment, and primary metals. The total value of Texas's manufacturing shipments in 1985 was $171,543m. (second highest in the country, behind California), of which 32% was added during manufacture, the sixth-lowest proportion in the USA.

Texas is a major US financial centre. Assets valued at $201,300m.—the third-highest total of any state—were held by its banks in 1986, and it has the second-highest number of insurance companies of any state.

The state is also an important domestic and international tourist centre, the travel and tourism industry being the third-largest employer in Texas in 1982. In 1986 out-of-state visitors spent $17,300m.

Direct general expenditure by state and local governments in 1984/85 totalled $32,803m.; revenue totalled $35,579m., of which $4,889m. was provided by the federal government.

Utah

Trade, government, services and manufacturing are the main employers in Utah. In 1982 more than 28% of personal income came from government salaries. The federal government, military, and defence industries are major employers. In 1986 the state's per-head disposable income was $9,665, the fourth lowest in the USA. The civilian labour force totalled 755,000 and the unemployment rate was 6% (45,000 persons). In 1982 16.8% of workers in non-agricultural establishments belonged to a trade union.

At the time of the 1982 Census of Agriculture farmland occupied 19% of the state's land area, the average farm covering an area of 699 acres. In 1986 76% of farm income was generated by sales of livestock and livestock products and 24% by crops. Principal agricultural commodities in that year were cattle, dairy products, turkeys and hay. The state also produces wheat, apples, sheep and lambs, and hogs and pigs. In 1982 29% of Utah's land area was forestland. There is some lumbering activity.

Petroleum, coal and natural gas were Utah's principal minerals, in terms of value, in 1985; the state was the USA's 10th-largest petroleum producer in 1986. Non-fuel minerals of importance to the economy include copper, gold, silver, iron ore, phosphate rock, potash, and sand and gravel.

Leading manufactures (in terms of value added) in 1982 were non-electrical machinery, transportation equipment, and food and kindred products. Petroleum and coal products, primary metal products and printing and publishing are also important industry groups. In 1985 the total value of Utah's manufacturing shipments was $10,941m., of which 44% was added during manufacture.

In 1986 tourists in Utah spent an estimated $2,000m. Direct general expenditure by state and local governments in 1984/85 totalled $3,827m.; revenue totalled $4,240m., of which $865m. was provided by the federal government.

Vermont

Vermont's principal economic activities are manufacturing, tourism, agriculture, construction, wholesale and retail trade, and

service industries. In 1986 the state's disposable income averaged $11,354 per head. The civilian labour force totalled 292,000, and the unemployment rate was 4.7% (14,000 persons), the seventh lowest in the country. In 1982 11.9% of those employed in non-agricultural establishments belonged to a trade union—the seventh-lowest percentage of any state.

Farmland accounted for 27% of the state's land area at the time of the 1982 Census of Agriculture, the average farm covering 249 acres. Farm marketings have one of the lowest values of any state. In 1986 91% of farm income was generated by sales of livestock and livestock products and 9% by crop marketings. The main sources of income were dairy products, cattle, hay and apples. Forestland covered 75% of Vermont's land area (the third-highest proportion of any state) in 1982, much of it used as commercial timberland. The state is the largest producer of maple syrup in the USA.

In 1985 Vermont's most important minerals, in terms of value, were stone, sand and gravel, and talc.

Leading manufacturing sectors in the state in 1982, in terms of value added, were electrical and electronic equipment, non-electrical machinery and fabricated metal products. Food and kindred products, paper and allied products, and printing and publishing were also of economic importance. In 1985 the total value of Vermont's manufacturing shipments was $3,574m. (eighth lowest in the country), of which 49% was added in manufacture.

Tourism is a major industry in Vermont, due, in part, to its facilities for skiing. In 1982 tourism accounted for 20% of the gross state product, and in 1986 visitors to the state spent an estimated $1,200m.

Direct general expenditure by state and local governments in 1984/85 totalled $1,282m.; revenue totalled $1,351m., of which $333m. was provided by the federal government.

Virginia

Manufacturing, services and trade are important economic activities in Virginia, but government is the largest employer, partly due to the number of military bases in the state, and partly because many state residents work for federal-government offices in Washington, DC. In 1986 the state's per-head disposable income was $12,993. The civilian labour force totalled 2,885,000, while the unemployment rate was 5% (145,000 workers). In 1982 10.9% of those in non-agricultural work were trade union members, the sixth-lowest rate nationally.

At the time of the 1982 Census of Agriculture farmland accounted for 37% of the state's land area, the average farm occupying 182 acres. In 1986 70% of farm income came from sales of livestock and livestock products and 30% from crops. The main agricultural commodities were cattle, dairy products, broilers and turkeys. Other important crops are tobacco, peanuts, sweet potatoes, apples and peaches. Hogs and sheep are also a significant source of income; Virginia ranked sixth in the USA in the production of both hogs and turkeys in 1986. In 1982 62% of the land area of Virginia was covered by forest (the eighth-highest proportion nation-wide), and there is some commercial forestland in every county. In 1986 the state ranked eighth in the value of its commercial fishing catch; shellfish are particularly important.

In 1985 Virginia's principal minerals, in terms of their value, were bituminous coal, stone and cement. In 1986 the state ranked seventh in the value of both its coal production and its stone production. Virginia ranks first in US production of cyanite, and also produces sand, gravel, lime and clay.

In 1982 the state's principal manufacturing industries, in terms of value added, were tobacco products, chemicals and allied products, and food and kindred products. Virginia ranked second to North Carolina in tobacco products in 1986. Other major industry groups are electrical and electronic equipment, transportation equipment, textile-mill products and printing and publishing. The total value of Virginia's manufacturing shipments in 1985 was $45,554m., of which 48% was added during manufacture.

Tourism contributes significantly to Virginia's economy, with out-of-state visitors spending an estimated $3,900m. in 1986. Direct general expenditure by state and local governments in 1984/85 totalled $11,369m.; revenue totalled $12,101m., of which $1,909m. was provided by the federal government.

Washington

Washington's principal economic activities are wholesale and retail trade, manufacturing (particularly lumber products and aerospace—Boeing is the state's leading company), agriculture, lumbering and tourism. Per-head disposable income in the state in 1986 was $13,194, 10th highest in the USA. The civilian labour force totalled 2,178,000 and the unemployment rate was 8.2%

(179,000 persons). Of those workers employed in non-agricultural establishments 32.9% belonged to a trade union, the fourth-highest proportion in the USA.

Farmland made up 39% of Washington's total land area at the time of the 1982 Census of Agriculture, the average farm covering 456 acres. In 1986 crop sales accounted for 65% of farm income, and livestock and livestock products accounted for 35%. Washington's principal agricultural commodities by value in 1986 were dairy products, cattle, apples and wheat. The state is the USA's leading apple producer, with 39% of national output in 1986, and ranks second (to Idaho) for potatoes and 10th for cattle and calves. Hops, cherries, grapes, apricots, prunes, plums, pears, barley, corn, hogs and pigs, and sheep and lambs also contribute to farm income.

Some 43% of Washington's land area was forested in 1982, most of it commercial timberland; in 1987 it produced the most timber of any state other than Oregon and California. In 1986 the state ranked seventh in the value of its commercial fishing catch; salmon are the most valuable fish caught.

Cement, sand and gravel, and gold were the principal minerals produced, in order of value, in 1985. Other minerals of importance to the state economy include coal, stone, clay, silver, copper, uranium, peat, gypsum, lime, talc and tungsten.

In 1982 the state's leading manufacturing industries, in terms of value added, were transportation equipment, food and kindred products, and lumber and wood products. In 1986 Washington ranked third in the USA in the manufacture of lumber and wood products (behind Oregon and California) and in 1984 it led the nation in aluminium production (using imported bauxite). Printing and publishing, paper and allied products, petroleum and coal products, and primary metal industries are also of importance. In 1985 the total value of Washington's manufacturing shipments was $40,458m., of which 37% was added during manufacture.

Tourism was the fourth-largest employer in the state in 1982, and in 1986 $3,400m. was spent by non-residential visitors.

In 1984/85 direct general expenditure by state and local governments amounted to $11,093m.; revenue totalled $11,219m., of which $2,246m. came from the federal government.

West Virginia

Extractive industries, manufacturing industry, agriculture and tourism are West Virginia's most important economic activities. In 1986 the state's per-head disposable income was $9,479, the second lowest in the USA. The civilian labour force totalled 743,000, while the unemployment rate was 11.8% (88,000 persons), the second highest in the country. In 1982 28.9% of non-agricultural workers were trade union members, the seventh-highest rate nationally.

At the time of the 1982 Census of Agriculture farmland accounted for 23% of West Virginia's land area, an average farm occupying 190 acres. It had the fourth-lowest farm income of any state in 1986, of which 69% was generated by sales of livestock and livestock products and 31% was derived from crops. The state's principal farm commodities in that year, in terms of value, were dairy products, broilers, apples and cattle. Hay, corn for grain and silage, tobacco, hogs and pigs, and turkeys also contribute to farm income. Forestland covered 75% of West Virginia's land area in 1982 (the third-highest proportion in the country), most of the timber being hardwood; reafforestation was a major priority in the mid-1980s.

Bituminous coal, natural gas and petroleum were the state's most valuable minerals in 1985. In 1986 West Virginia ranked third in the USA (behind Kentucky and Wyoming) in its production of coal. Non-fuel minerals of some importance to the state's economy include stone, cement, clays, salt, lime, sand and gravel.

West Virginia's leading industrial sectors in 1982, in terms of value added by manufacture, were chemicals and allied products, primary metal industries, and stone, clay and glass products. Other industries of importance to the economy are fabricated metal products, food and kindred products, and non-electrical machinery. In 1985 the total value of West Virginia's manufacturing shipments was $10,603m., of which 45% was added during manufacture.

In 1982 West Virginia's tourist industry earned an estimated $1,400m. and provided 40,165 jobs. Direct general expenditure by state and local governments in 1984/85 totalled $3,840m.; revenue totalled $4,006m., of which $851m. was provided by the federal government.

Wisconsin

Wisconsin's most important economic activities are manufacturing and agriculture—in particular dairy farming. Areas of growth in

the early 1980s were retail trade, construction and service industries. The state's per-head disposable income in 1986 was $12,055. The civilian labour force numbered 2,399,000, while the unemployment rate was 7% (169,000 persons). In 1982 24.5% of non-agricultural workers belonged to a trade union.

Farmland made up 49% of the state's total land area at the time of the 1982 Census of Agriculture, the average farm covering an area of 210 acres. Wisconsin's farm income was the eighth largest in the USA in 1986: livestock and livestock products accounted for 82% and crops 18%. The state is the seventh most important cattle supplier and the leading supplier of dairy products in the USA; cattle, corn and hogs followed dairy products in order of value in 1986. Wisconsin also produces hay, of which it was the biggest supplier in 1986, cabbages, beets, snap beans, peas, cranberries, oats, carrots, cherries, potatoes and apples, as well as chickens and turkeys. In 1984 Wisconsin's mink ranches produced more pelts than any other state. Forestland covered 43% of the state in 1982, hardwoods making up two-thirds of the lumber produced.

Mining does not contribute greatly to Wisconsin's economy. In 1985 the principal minerals produced, in terms of value, were sand, gravel, stone and lime. Peat is also produced. There are no known major fuel resources in the state.

In 1982 Wisconsin's main manufacturing industries, in terms of value added by manufacture, were non-electrical machinery, food and kindred products, and paper and allied products (in which it led the nation in 1985). Transportation equipment, electrical and electronic equipment, and fabricated metal products also make a significant contribution to the economy of the state. The total value of Wisconsin's manufacturing shipments in 1985 was $62,837m., of which 44% was added during manufacture.

Wisconsin has a thriving tourist industry, with out-of-state visitors spending an estimated $5,000m. in 1987. Direct general expenditure by state and local governments in 1984/85 amounted to $12,160m., while revenue totalled $12,463m., of which $2,229m. was provided by the federal government.

Wyoming

Agriculture and mining are the chief bases of economic activity in Wyoming. In 1986 the state's disposable income was $10,675 per head. The civilian labour force totalled 249,000 persons, the smallest in the USA, and the unemployment rate stood at 9% (22,000 persons) the eighth-highest rate in the country. In 1982 15.6% of those employed by non-agricultural establishments belonged to a trade union.

At the time of the 1982 Census of Agriculture farmland accounted for 54% of Wyoming's total land area. The state has the second-largest average farm size in the USA (behind Alaska), at 3,781 acres. Sales of livestock and livestock products made up 80% of farm income in 1986, with crops accounting for 20%. Cattle, sheep, sugar beets and hay were the most important agricultural commodities, in terms of value; Wyoming was the second most important wool producer among the states in 1986, behind Texas. Barley, wheat, oats, potatoes, dry beans, hogs and pigs, and chickens also contribute to farm income. Forestland covered just 9% of Wyoming's land area in 1982, of which about one-half was under commercial development.

The state has the three largest producing coal mines in the country and in 1986 had the second-largest output of coal, behind Kentucky. In terms of value, the principal minerals in 1985 were petroleum, coal and natural gas; Wyoming ranked sixth in the nation for petroleum output and fifth for natural gas. In 1983 the state ranked second in uranium output, and about 35% of known uranium deposits in the USA are in Wyoming. Non-fuel minerals produced include soda ash, bentonite, sand and gravel, and clay.

Manufacturing does not make a major contribution to the state economy. In 1982 the leading manufacturing sectors, in terms of value added by manufacture, were chemicals and allied products, non-electrical machinery and food and kindred products. Other industrial sectors include petroleum and coal products, and fabricated metal products. The state's manufacturing shipments were valued at $2,311m. in 1985, of which 20% was added during manufacture, the lowest proportion in the country.

In 1982 tourists spent an estimated $657m. in Wyoming. Direct general expenditure by state and local governments in 1984/85 amounted to $2,121m.; revenue totalled $2,684m., of which $470m. was provided by the federal government.

AGRICULTURE, FORESTRY AND FISHING
Land Use
(Source: Economic Research Service, US Department of Agriculture.)

Historical Summary (million acres)

	1959	1969	1974	1978	1982
Cropland used for crops[1]	359	333	361	369	383
Idle cropland	33	51	21	26	21
Cropland used only for pasture	66	88	83	76	65
Grassland pasture[2]	633	604	598	587	597
Forestland[3]	728	723	718	703	655
Total land area (including special-use areas and other land)[4]	2,271	2,264	2,264	2,264	2,265

[1] Cropland harvested, crop failure and cultivated summer fallow.
[2] Grassland and other non-forest pasture and range.
[3] Excludes reserved and other forestland duplicated in parks and other special uses of land.
[4] Changes in total land area are due to variable methods and materials used in periodic remeasurements and to the construction of artificial reservoirs.

States (1982; '000 acres, estimates, unless otherwise stated)

	Cropland Used for crops[1]	Cropland Idle	Cropland Used only for pasture	Grassland pasture[2]	Forestland[3]	Total land area (including special-use areas and other land)	Land in farms (census results)
Alabama	3,806	362	1,474	1,865	21,179	32,491	10,200
Alaska	26	21	6	1,281	87,045	365,333	1,300
Arizona	1,174	230	129	41,565	17,846	72,645	37,800
Arkansas	7,975	476	2,055	2,948	17,324	33,330	14,700
California	9,579	642	1,345	22,580	37,043	100,031	32,200
Colorado	9,377	493	1,000	28,198	19,809	66,301	33,500
Connecticut	181	11	43	48	1,745	3,118	400
Delaware	538	9	12	12	394	1,237	700
District of Columbia	—	—	—	—	—	40	—
Florida	2,752	345	1,072	6,229	16,325	34,658	12,800
Georgia	5,372	462	1,290	1,850	23,768	37,156	12,300
Hawaii	156	155	34	1,131	1,067	4,112	2,000
Idaho	5,624	216	763	20,408	17,880	52,744	13,900
Illinois	23,615	560	1,070	1,773	3,551	35,613	28,700
Indiana	12,779	381	798	1,352	3,878	22,996	16,300
Iowa	25,208	826	2,500	2,065	1,227	35,818	32,600
Kansas	28,352	1,318	3,232	13,907	1,359	52,338	47,100
Kentucky	5,354	711	3,453	1,669	11,948	25,388	14,200
Louisiana	5,115	420	916	2,073	13,998	28,494	8,900
Maine	475	67	87	94	17,565	19,837	1,500
Maryland	1,579	71	197	222	2,420	6,296	2,600
Massachusetts	214	16	52	48	2,811	5,008	600
Michigan	7,642	606	566	1,881	18,078	36,451	10,900
Minnesota	21,772	1,205	1,206	1,689	15,643	50,911	27,700
Mississippi	6,143	437	1,441	2,369	16,505	30,229	12,400
Missouri	14,024	827	5,587	6,540	12,348	44,125	29,300
Montana	15,247	469	1,123	48,395	18,936	93,048	60,500
Nebraska	20,816	966	2,397	21,232	796	49,052	45,000
Nevada	614	58	190	45,909	7,272	70,332	10,000
New Hampshire	127	8	31	46	4,839	5,756	500
New Jersey	628	33	64	26	1,940	4,779	900
New Mexico	1,690	229	450	51,217	16,805	77,654	47,100
New York	4,649	360	891	904	15,939	30,321	9,200
North Carolina	5,154	476	806	1,010	18,604	31,260	10,300
North Dakota	26,900	1,021	1,575	11,028	515	44,352	40,200
Ohio	10,845	419	982	1,430	6,837	26,243	15,400
Oklahoma	10,935	650	3,860	18,396	6,810	43,939	32,400
Oregon	4,324	175	858	22,011	29,477	61,558	17,700
Pennsylvania	4,619	309	862	949	16,294	28,728	8,300
Rhode Island	29	3	5	3	391	675	100
South Carolina	2,713	201	484	443	12,084	19,330	5,600
South Dakota	17,657	426	2,309	23,529	1,610	48,609	43,800
Tennessee	5,052	453	2,608	1,370	12,965	26,339	12,500
Texas	25,963	3,129	10,029	103,890	14,080	167,691	131,300
Utah	1,409	116	470	23,238	15,443	52,527	9,800
Vermont	561	18	205	260	4,432	5,935	1,600
Virginia	2,978	252	1,523	1,717	15,872	25,410	9,400
Washington	7,559	309	612	7,705	18,557	42,567	16,500
West Virginia	786	87	676	557	11,509	15,436	3,600
Wisconsin	10,404	411	1,229	2,009	14,877	34,833	17,200
Wyoming	2,264	53	461	45,594	5,640	62,073	33,500
Total	382,755*	21,498†	65,028‡	596,664§	655,280¶	2,265,147‖	986,800**

* 154,901,000 hectares.   † 8,700,000 hectares.   ‡ 26,317,000 hectares.   § 241,470,000 hectares.
¶ 265,192,000 hectares.   ‖ 916,705,000 hectares.   ** 399,358,000 hectares.

[1] Cropland harvested, crop failure and cultivated summer farrow.   [2] Grassland and other non-forest pasture and range.
[3] Excludes reserved and other forestland duplicated in parks and other special uses of land. Includes forested grazing land.

Production of Principal Crops

(Source: National Agricultural Statistics Service, US Department of Agriculture.)

Summary

		1985		1986*		1987*
		Quantity	Value ($ million)	Quantity	Value ($ million)	Quantity
Wheat	(million bushels[1])	2,425	7,648	2,087	4,861	2,105
Corn for grain	(million bushels[1])	8,877	21,029	8,253	12,387	7,064
Barley	(million bushels[1])	591	1,169	610	946	527
Sorghum for grain	(million bushels[1])	1,120	2,538	942	1,316	741
Soybeans for beans	(million bushels[1])	2,099	10,571	2,007	9,326	1,905
Rice	(million cwt[2])	135	893	134	528	128
Hay	(million short tons)	149	9,437	155	8,644	149
Cotton	(million bales[3])	13.4	3,645	9.7	2,441	14.7
Tobacco	(million lb)	1,512	2,487	1,166	1,778	1,226
Sugar beets	(million short tons)	22.5	761	25.2	n.a.	28.0
Sugar-cane	(million short tons)	28.2	752	30.3	n.a.	n.a.
Peanuts	(million lb)	4,123	1,003	3,701	1,065	3,586
Potatoes	(million cwt[2])	407.1	1,571	354.5	1,740	385.8
Lettuce	(million cwt[2])	61.8	675	58.6	701	n.a.
Tomatoes	(million cwt[2])	173.4	1,198	179.4	1,265	n.a.
Apples	(million lb)	7,834	916	7,865	1,068	9,944
Grapes	(million short tons)	5.6	959	5.2	1,170	5.2
Strawberries	(million short tons)	0.5	451	0.5	504	n.a.
Citrus fruits[4]	(million boxes[5])	252.3	n.a.	263.5	n.a.	n.a.

* Preliminary figures.

[1] A bushel is equivalent to 60 lb (27.2 kg) for wheat and soybeans; 56 lb (25.4 kg) for corn and sorghum; 48 lb (21.8 kg) for barley.
[2] Short hundredweight: equivalent to 100 lb.
[3] A bale of cotton is 480 lb net weight.
[4] Includes grapefruit, lemons, limes, tangelos, tangerines and temples. Figures refer to production during season ending in year stated.
[5] Net content of box varies from 95 lb to 67 lb according to state and type of fruit.

States (1986, preliminary figures)

	Wheat ('000 bushels[1])	Corn for grain ('000 bushels[1])	Barley ('000 bushels[1])	Sorghum for grain ('000 bushels[1])	Soybeans for beans ('000 bushels[1])	Rice ('000 cwt[2])
Alabama	5,720	15,390	—	4,000	14,490	—
Arizona	8,688	2,640	2,900	1,044	—	—
Arkansas	31,980	8,480	—	40,920	69,300	55,120
California	51,525	38,000	23,600	2,210	—	27,727
Colorado	96,430	99,400	21,000	11,700	—	—
Delaware	1,530	14,027	3,050	—	6,000	—
Florida	3,100	9,920	—	—	3,220	—
Georgia	15,400	42,340	—	2,706	15,300	—
Hawaii	—	—	72,150	—	—	—
Idaho	81,750	7,800	—	—	—	—
Illinois	36,080	1,404,000	—	19,000	366,000	—
Indiana	30,100	695,400	—	—	161,500	—
Iowa	1,680	1,626,750	—	—	363,125	—
Kansas	336,600	181,560	10,440	311,250	59,840	—
Kentucky	8,910	139,840	527	4,275	37,440	—
Louisiana	7,350	44,660	—	23,800	38,220	19,380
Maryland	6,815	42,340	4,920	—	10,920	—
Michigan	30,600	257,250	3,245	—	30,400	—
Minnesota	103,666	707,600	55,000	—	170,400	—
Mississippi	6,200	13,500	—	14,400	44,100	10,692
Missouri	18,810	280,720	—	92,340	177,550	3,434
Montana	138,520	1,495	85,020	—	—	—
Nebraska	76,000	896,000	5,535	139,730	95,550	—
Nevada	1,720	—	2,970	—	—	—
New Jersey	1,290	11,128	1,240	—	3,393	—
New Mexico	10,120	8,250	1,040	10,350	—	—
New York	7,595	64,350	—	—	—	—
North Carolina	14,260	93,840	1,620	1,350	38,400	—
North Dakota	289,820	49,290	175,950	—	16,685	—
Ohio	48,300	476,160	—	—	150,470	—
Oklahoma	150,800	5,220	1,260	23,030	4,800	—
Oregon	58,405	4,800	20,805	—	—	—
Pennsylvania	9,680	127,720	3,900	—	5,600	—
South Carolina	7,500	21,160	588	1,024	14,960	—
South Dakota	108,660	233,700	35,910	14,030	41,230	—
Tennessee	10,725	56,980	—	10,725	37,500	—
Texas	120,000	148,960	1,750	213,750	4,370	18,063
Utah	9,750	2,250	11,552	—	—	—
Virginia	6,970	21,600	3,960	—	14,750	—
Washington	116,850	20,400	45,000	—	—	—
West Virginia	396	6,300	—	—	11,520	—
Wisconsin	8,040	365,800	4,845	—	—	—
Wyoming	8,445	5,814	10,720	—	—	—
Total	2,086,780	8,252,834	610,497	941,634	2,007,033	134,416

[1] A bushel is equivalent to 60 lb (27.2 kg) for wheat and soybeans; 56 lb (25.4 kg) for corn and sorghum; 48 lb (21.8 kg) for barley.
[2] Short hundredweight: equivalent to 100 lb.

(*continued*)

PRODUCTION OF PRINCIPAL CROPS—States (1986, preliminary figures)—*continued*

	Hay ('000 short tons)	Cotton ('000 bales[1])	Tobacco ('000 lbs)	Sugar beets ('000 short tons[2])	Sugar-cane ('000 short tons)	Peanuts ('000 lbs)
Alabama	1,120	330	—	—	—	494,940
Arizona	1,262	823	—	—	—	—
Arkansas . . .	1,945	602	—	—	—	—
California . . .	8,628	2,245	—	4,669	—	—
Colorado . . .	3,642	—	3,062	46	—	—
Connecticut . .	209	—	—	—	—	—
Delaware . . .	50	—	—	—	—	—
Florida	676	28	13,303	—	13,446	233,160
Georgia	901	185	67,890	—	—	1,632,575
Hawaii	—	—	—	3,496	8,587	—
Idaho	4,720	—	—	—	—	—
Illinois. . . .	3,664	—	—	—	—	—
Indiana	2,236	—	12,095	—	—	—
Iowa	8,000	—	—	—	—	—
Kansas . . .	6,390	1	—	—	—	—
Kentucky . . .	3,588	—	314,940	—	—	—
Louisiana . . .	781	673	—	—	7,371	—
Maine	448	—	—	—	—	—
Maryland . . .	509	—	24,300	—	—	—
Massachusetts. .	325	—	622	—	—	—
Michigan . . .	5,743	—	—	2,325	—	—
Minnesota . . .	9,675	—	—	5,088	—	—
Mississippi . .	1,160	1,190	—	—	—	—
Missouri . . .	6,028	196	4,389	—	—	—
Montana . . .	4,320	—	—	811	—	—
Nebraska . . .	7,258	—	—	1,229	—	—
Nevada	1,376	—	—	—	—	—
New Hampshire . .	198	—	—	—	—	—
New Jersey . .	297	—	—	—	—	—
New Mexico . .	1,319	79	—	—	—	28,700
New York. . .	5,280	—	—	—	—	—
North Carolina .	573	109	444,790	—	—	440,440
North Dakota . .	5,425	—	—	2,423	—	—
Ohio	4,307	—	13,574	258	—	—
Oklahoma . . .	4,295	210	—	—	—	184,500
Oregon	3,134	—	—	319	—	—
Pennsylvania . .	5,124	—	21,830	—	—	—
Rhode Island . .	23	—	—	—	—	—
South Carolina .	328	87	75,480	—	—	25,530
South Dakota . .	9,330	—	—	—	—	—
Tennessee. . .	2,092	396	82,707	—	—	—
Texas	7,460	2,576	—	833	907	385,000
Utah	2,135	—	—	—	—	—
Vermont . . .	938	—	—	—	—	—
Virginia . . .	1,464	2	73,524	—	—	275,900
Washington . .	2,874	—	—	—	—	—
West Virginia .	801	—	2,640	—	—	—
Wisconsin . . .	10,775	—	10,781	—	—	—
Wyoming . . .	2,445	—	—	1,032	—	—
Total	155,271	9,731	1,165,927	22,529	30,311	3,700,745

[1] A bale of cotton is 480 lb net weight.
[2] Crop of 1985.

	Potatoes ('000 cwt[1])	Lettuce ('000 cwt[1])	Tomatoes ('000 cwt[1])	Apples (million lb)	Grapes ('000 short tons)	Citrus fruits[2] ('000 boxes[3])
Alabama	1,668	—	280	—	—	—
Arizona	1,298	10,646	—	—	23	8,650
Arkansas . . .	—	—	400	10	6	—
California . . .	18,457	42,182	137,544	535	4,770	80,100
Colorado . . .	20,296	613	217	18	—	—
Connecticut . .	225	—	—	47	—	—
Delaware . . .	1,311	—	n.a.*	27	—	—
Florida	8,543	2,343	15,830*	—	2	174,250
Georgia	—	—	270	30	—	—
Hawaii	—	88	68	—	—	—
Idaho	87,320	—	—	94	—	—
Illinois. . . .	783	—	n.a.*	90	—	—
Indiana	990	—	2,927	37	—	—
Iowa	332	—	n.a.*	6	—	—
Kansas . . .	—	—	—	3	—	—
Kentucky . . .	—	—	—	4	—	—
Louisiana . . .	35	—	38	—	—	—
Maine	21,000	—	—	88	—	—
Maryland . . .	272	—	976	87	—	—
Massachusetts. .	667	—	127	95	—	—
Michigan . . .	11,190	240	2,953	700	32	—
Minnesota . . .	15,293	—	—	19	—	—

(continued)

PRODUCTION OF PRINCIPAL CROPS—States (1986, preliminary figures)—*continued*

	Potatoes ('000 cwt[1])	Lettuce ('000 cwt[1])	Tomatoes ('000 cwt[1])	Apples (million lb)	Grapes ('000 short tons)	Citrus fruits[2] ('000 boxes[3])
Missouri	—	—	—	37	3	—
Montana	2,233	—	—	—	—	—
Nebraska	2,399	—	—	—	—	—
Nevada	2,800	—	—	—	—	—
New Hampshire . .	—	—	—	50	—	—
New Jersey . . .	1,944	429	1,727	100	—	—
New Mexico . . .	2,745	725	n.a.*	6	—	—
New York . . .	7,780	620	286*	900	164	—
North Carolina . .	2,264	—	232*	120	2	—
North Dakota . .	21,600	—	—	—	—	—
Ohio	2,377	99	8,371	90	8	—
Oregon	23,172	—	—	105	—	—
Pennsylvania . .	5,160	—	1,624	620	60	—
Rhode Island . .	416	—	—	6	—	—
South Carolina . .	—	—	1,200*	30	1	—
South Dakota . .	2,340	—	—	—	—	—
Tennessee . . .	234	—	1,050	—	—	—
Texas	3,591	437	240*	9	—	530
Utah	1,760	—	n.a.*	34	—	—
Vermont . . .	20	—	—	49	—	—
Virginia . . .	1,112	—	554*	460	—	—
Washington . . .	60,180	216	—	—	156	—
West Virginia . .	—	—	—	3,100	—	—
Wisconsin . . .	20,125	157	—	230	—	—
Wyoming . . .	536	—	—	56	—	—
Total	**354,468**	**58,795**	**179,268***	**7,891**	**5,226**	**263,530**

* Figures for production of tomatoes for processing are not given individually for these states but are included in total.

[1] Short hundredweight: equivalent to 100 lb.
[2] Figures refer to production during season ending in 1986.
[3] Net content of box varies from 95 lb to 67 lb according to state and type of fruit.

Livestock and Poultry on Farms

(Source: National Agricultural Statistics Service, US Department of Agriculture.)

Summary ('000 head at 1 January, unless otherwise stated)

	1986		1987*		1988*
	Quantity	Value ($ million)	Quantity	Value ($ million)	Quantity
All cattle	105,468	41,300	102,031	41,500	98,994
Hogs and pigs[1]	52,313	3,600	50,960	4,700	53,795
Sheep and lambs	9,983	673	10,328	782	10,774
Chickens[1,2]	368,548	700	368,681	690	377,516

* Preliminary figures.

[1] At 1 December of preceding year.
[2] Excludes commercial broilers.

States (preliminary figures; '000 head at 1 January 1987, unless otherwise stated)

	Cattle				Hogs and pigs[1]	Sheep and lambs	Chickens[1,2]
	Cows and heifers	Steers and bulls	Calves	All cattle			
Alabama	1,186	174	490	1,850	380	n.a.	16,515
Alaska	6	1	2	10	1	2	58
Arizona	447	315	238	1,000	155	283	528
Arkansas	1,216	161	463	1,840	460	n.a.	24,382
California	2,750	900	1,100	4,750	150	980	40,900
Colorado	1,495	710	395	2,600	190	690	2,935
Connecticut . . .	63	4	16	83	7	9	6,634
Delaware . . .	18	6	7	31	60	n.a.	938
Florida	1,610	115	415	2,140	140	n.a.	13,610
Georgia	1,083	143	424	1,650	1,100	n.a.	25,696
Hawaii	122	28	45	195	50	n.a.	1,185
Idaho	960	275	315	1,550	80	314	1,270
Illinois	1,310	430	510	2,250	5,000	119	3,270
Indiana	845	235	390	1,470	4,150	91	27,915
Iowa	2,305	1,135	1,210	4,650	12,600	375	7,700

(continued)

LIVESTOCK AND POULTRY ON FARMS—States
(preliminary figures; '000 head at 1 January 1987 unless otherwise stated)—*continued*

	Cattle				Hogs and pigs[1]	Sheep and lambs	Chickens[1,2]
	Cows and heifers	Steers and bulls	Calves	All cattle			
Kansas	2,700	1,885	1,335	5,920	1,450	236	2,370
Kentucky	1,537	314	599	2,450	880	32	2,300
Louisiana	852	67	241	1,160	53	8	2,250
Maine	85	8	27	120	8	18	6,508
Maryland	240	26	64	330	190	25	5,129
Massachusetts	65	4	16	85	32	15	1,310
Michigan	798	227	300	1,325	1,250	106	8,100
Minnesota	1,950	523	677	3,150	4,260	237	12,800
Mississippi	930	105	338	1,373	210	n.a.	8,275
Missouri	2,770	570	1,260	4,600	2,900	110	8,000
Montana	1,724	292	384	2,400	190	523	1,010
Nebraska	2,940	1,430	1,130	5,500	3,900	173	4,000
Nevada	345	53	152	550	14	86	17
New Hampshire	46	4	12	62	9	12	430
New Jersey	66	8	16	90	40	14	2,070
New Mexico	786	251	323	1,360	36	480	1,615
New York	1,491	59	335	1,885	128	64	6,700
North Carolina	597	85	268	950	2,360	13	21,560
North Dakota	1,302	241	357	1,900	275	185	290
Ohio	1,080	310	410	1,800	1,950	300	20,400
Oklahoma	2,840	1,035	1,325	5,200	220	105	4,500
Oregon	884	189	327	1,400	115	415	3,365
Pennsylvania	1,333	236	381	1,950	890	104	22,050
Rhode Island	5	1	1	7	5	n.a.	253
South Carolina	412	59	149	620	430	n.a.	8,450
South Dakota	2,165	517	918	3,600	1,520	605	1,850
Tennessee	1,540	215	645	2,400	770	13	3,500
Texas	7,620	2,880	2,900	13,400	510	1,930	17,500
Utah	516	109	145	770	25	464	2,409
Vermont	257	8	60	325	6	16	315
Virginia	1,108	342	410	1,860	360	120	4,971
Washington	858	232	210	1,300	50	59	5,700
West Virginia	386	57	117	560	37	90	670
Wisconsin	2,985	304	971	4,260	1,330	83	4,453
Wyoming	864	175	261	1,300	35	775	25
Total	61,494	17,453	23,084	102,031	50,960	10,328*	368,681

* Includes other states not shown separately.
[1] At 1 December 1986.
[2] Excludes commercial broilers.

Livestock Products

Summary

		1986	1987	1988
Beef:				
Commercial slaughterings	('000 head)	37,288	35,647	n.a.
Production	(million lb)	24,213	23,405	23,436
Pork:				
Commercial slaughterings	('000 head)	79,598	81,081	n.a.
Production	(million lb)	13,998	14,312	15,611
Lamb and mutton:				
Commercial slaughterings	('000 head)	5,635	n.a.	n.a.
Production	(million lb)	331	309	328
Veal:				
Commercial slaughterings	('000 head)	3,408	2,815	n.a.
Production	(million lb)	509	416	388
Broilers	(million lb)	14,266	15,502	16,149
Turkeys	(million lb)	3,133	3,717	3,933
Eggs	(million)	68,460	69,564	68,808
Milk	(million lb)	143,381	142,557	145,527
Manufactured dairy products:				
Butter	(million lb)	1,202	1,104	1,208
Cheese, American	(million lb)	2,798	2,717	2,757
Cheese, other	(million lb)	2,411	2,628	2,815
Non-fat dry milk	(million lb)	1,284	1,057	979
Frozen dessert (ice cream, ice milk and hard sherbet)	(million gallons)	1,249	1,261	1,247
Wool (mill consumption, scoured)	(million lb)	137	131	144

Source: Economic Research Service, US Department of Agriculture.

Livestock Slaughterings by State
(1986, '000 head slaughtered in federally-inspected and other establishments. Excludes animals slaughtered on farms.)

	Cattle	Hogs	Sheep and lambs	Calves
Alabama	306.5	208.8	0.2	1.3
Arizona	411.7	69.3	1.8	n.a.*
Arkansas	71.0	275.7	1.0	1.4
California	1,520.7	1,733.8	876.7	325.2
Colorado	1,919.5	162.0	1,261.2	0.4
Connecticut[1]	n.a.	n.a.	n.a.	n.a.
Delaware[2]	n.a.	n.a.	n.a.	n.a.
Florida	224.7	88.2	0.6	147.7
Georgia	272.9	1,850.3	1.1	4.5
Hawaii	62.0	44.7	0.2	n.a.*
Idaho	794.6	102.8	5.4	2.5
Illinois	1,394.0	5,772.8	296.7	199.0
Indiana	190.1	3,427.3	11.5	242.7
Iowa	1,969.0	18,711.2	520.5	0.2
Kansas	6,493.8	1,417.3	337.5	0.3
Kentucky	148.0	2,262.9	9.0	1.1
Louisiana	41.4	58.1	4.1	162.3
Maine[1]	n.a.	n.a.	n.a.	n.a.
Maryland[2]	n.a.	n.a.	n.a.	n.a.
Massachusetts[1]	n.a.	n.a.	n.a.	n.a.
Michigan	423.3	4,624.7	207.4	100.2
Minnesota	1,013.2	5,862.1	347.1	3.7
Mississippi	268.3	1,683.7	—	28.7
Missouri	470.9	3,632.8	17.0	8.6
Montana	28.1	28.5	2.9	0.3
Nebraska	5,700.2	4,999.8	3.1	0.2
Nevada	4.7	2.7	2.4	n.a.*
New Hampshire[1]	n.a.	n.a.	n.a.	n.a.
New Jersey	97.4	160.4	40.6	136.5
New Mexico	156.7	5.7	133.0	0.5
New York	218.9	89.9	54.4	523.9
North Carolina	163.4	2,549.0	1.1	3.6
North Dakota	146.7	81.0	0.8	0.4
Ohio	524.1	3,659.0	24.9	112.2
Oklahoma	618.0	129.9	2.9	3.4
Oregon	94.6	205.9	8.5	12.6
Pennsylvania	1,125.5	1,526.7	130.7	287.2
Rhode Island[1]	n.a.	n.a.	n.a.	n.a.
South Carolina	122.4	508.1	0.2	27.3
South Dakota	756.9	3,424.2	358.2	0.2
Tennessee	276.4	2,270.2	1.6	n.a.†
Texas	6,207.1	992.9	561.9	247.3
Utah	392.4	221.6	40.1	1.0
Vermont[1]	n.a.	n.a.	n.a.	n.a.
Virginia	112.5	4,499.7	152.7	3.8
Washington	928.2	29.5	155.4	118.0
West Virginia	29.2	24.4	0.8	0.5
Wisconsin	1,428.3	2,062.3	7.5	392.2
Wyoming	5.6	4.6	1.3	0.1
Total	37,288.3	79,598.2	5,635.0	3,408.0

* Figures are not given for states, to avoid disclosing individual operations, but are included in total.

[1] Combined figures for New England: Cattle 99,900; Hogs 67,100; Sheep and lambs 32,700; Calves 181,000 (all included in relevant totals).
[2] Combined figures for Delaware and Maryland: Cattle 55,800; Hogs 66,200; Sheep and lambs 18,400; Calves 31,800 (all included in relevant totals).

Source: National Agricultural Statistics Service, US Department of Agriculture.

Other Livestock and Poultry Production by State (1986)

	Chickens sold (million)	Broilers produced (million)	Turkeys raised (million)*	Eggs (million)†	Milk (million lb)	Shorn wool ('000 lb)‡
Alabama	10.0	587.6	n.a.	2,723	529	—
Alaska	0	n.a.	n.a.	13	32	19
Arizona	0.2	n.a.	n.a.	121	1,368	1,977
Arkansas	16.0	786.8	16.5	3,731	755	—
California	19.7	184.8	21.9	7,850	17,240	8,229
Colorado	1.0	n.a.	n.a.	575	1,188	5,331
Connecticut	3.1	n.a.	0	1,281	600	55
Delaware	0.8	196.8	n.a.§	135	146	—
Florida	5.2	111.9	n.a.	2,683	2,157	—
Georgia	16.5	697.4	2.4	4,318	1,260	—
Hawaii	0.4	2.3	n.a.	227	156	—
Idaho	0.6	n.a.	n.a.	230	2,389	2,683
Illinois	2.0	n.a.	0.3	663	2,741	922
Indiana	16.6	n.a.	9.4	5,561	2,455	617
Iowa	4.5	2.7	7.0	1,441	3,879	3,054
Kansas	1.7	n.a.	0.1	463	1,301	1,502

(continued)

Other Livestock and Poultry Production by State (1986)—*continued*

	Chickens sold (million)	Broilers produced (million)	Turkeys raised (million)*	Eggs (million)†	Milk (million lb)	Shorn wool ('000 lb)‡
Kentucky	1.3	3.0	n.a.	420	2,327	203
Louisiana	1.2	n.a.	n.a.	336	887	58
Maine	4.6	n.a.	n.a.	1,239	694	108
Maryland	2.6	263.9	n.a.§	890	1,620	124
Massachusetts	1.2	n.a.	0.1	315	559	85
Michigan	5.3	0.6	2.7	1,644	5,404	764
Minnesota	7.7	29.7	34.2	2,312	10,614	1,629
Mississippi	7.8	335.7	n.a.	1,274	841	—
Missouri	4.0	n.a.	13.5	1,397	2,930	715
Montana	0.6	n.a.	n.a.	201	338	5,225
Nebraska	1.6	0.8	1.4	829	1,350	1,192
Nevada.	0	n.a.	n.a.	2	274	760
New Hampshire	0.4	n.a.	0	95	373	71
New Jersey	1.4	n.a.	0.1	501	479	62
New Mexico	0.6	n.a.	n.a.	280	1,092	4,313
New York	5.6	2.0	0.3	1,523	11,723	376
North Carolina.	11.8	450.5	39.1	3,400	1,695	66
North Dakota	0.4	n.a.	1.0	61	1,074	1,509
Ohio	11.9	9.9	3.1	3,868	4,936	1,956
Oklahoma	3.1	79.5	n.a.	809	1,190	640
Oregon.	1.5	15.8	1.5	659	1,471	2,825
Pennsylvania	16.5	101.9	7.8	4,692	10,152	683
Rhode Island	0.3	n.a.	n.a.	58	41	—
South Carolina	4.5	63.8	3.9	1,615	565	—
South Dakota	1.0	n.a.	2.0	395	1,722	4,372
Tennessee	1.9	n.a.	n.a.	663	2,221	62
Texas	10.3	238.6	n.a.	3,355	4,089	16,400
Utah	0.9	n.a.	3.4	457	1,157	4,668
Vermont	0.2	n.a.	n.a.	57	2,448	94
Virginia	2.6	154.2	14.3	914	2,151	1,104
Washington	3.4	25.1	n.a.	1,295	3,762	533
West Virginia	0.4	29.0	2.2	109	375	458
Wisconsin	2.2	11.6	6.1	830	24,500	672
Wyoming	0	n.a.	n.a.	5	131	8,240
Total	**216.9**	**4,646.3¶**	**207.0¶**	**68,515**	**143,381**	**84,356**

* Number raised; based on turkeys hatched between 1 September 1984 and 31 August 1985. Excludes young turkeys lost.
† Year ending 30 November 1986.
‡ Preliminary figures.
§ Combined figure for Delaware and Maryland is 125,000 and is included in total.
¶ Includes other states for which individual figures not available.
Sources: Economic Research Service and National Agricultural Statistics Service, US Department of Agriculture.

Forestry

(Sources: Forest Service, US Department of Agriculture and Bureau of the Census, US Department of Commerce.)

Roundwood Removals (million cu feet)

	1985	1986	1987*
Industrial	12,450	13,885	14,585
Softwoods	9,680	10,605	11,315
Hardwoods	2,770	3,250	3,270
Fuelwood	4,080	4,105	4,000
Total	**16,530**	**17,960**	**18,585**

* Preliminary figures.

Lumber Production—Summary
(sawnwood and railway sleepers, million board feet)

	1985	1986	1987*
Softwoods	30,479	34,815	37,422
Hardwoods	5,966	7,184	7,471
Total	**36,445**	**41,999**	**44,893**

* Preliminary figures.

Lumber Production—States
(1987; million board feet, preliminary figures for sawnwood and railway sleepers)

	Softwoods	Hardwoods	Total		Softwoods	Hardwoods	Total
Alabama	1,791	293	2,084	Nebraska	0	n.a.[3]	n.a.[3]
Alaska	n.a.*	0	n.a.*	Nevada	n.a.*	n.a.*	n.a.*
Arizona	407	—	407	New Hampshire	148	27	175
Arkansas	1,226	223	1,449	New Jersey	n.a.*	n.a.*	8
California	n.a.*	n.a.*	5,099	New Mexico	n.a.*	n.a.*	193
Colorado	n.a.*	n.a.*	135	New York	53	268	321
Connecticut	n.a.[1]	n.a.[1]	n.a.[1]	North Carolina	1,150	524	1,674
Delaware	n.a.[2]	n.a.[2]	n.a.[2]	North Dakota	—	—	—
Florida	572	25	597	Ohio	0	303	303
Georgia	2,287	241	2,528	Oklahoma	n.a.*	n.a.*	309
Hawaii	n.a.*	0	n.a.*	Oregon	8,395	60	8,455
Idaho	2,146	—	2,146	Pennsylvania	13	592	605
Illinois	0	107	107	Rhode Island	n.a.[1]	n.a.[1]	n.a.[1]
Indiana	n.a.*	n.a.*	397	South Carolina	1,110	209	1,319
Iowa	0	45	45	South Dakota	186	0	186
Kansas	0	n.a.[3]	n.a.[3]	Tennessee	139	557	696
Kentucky	21	398	419	Texas	1,038	117	1,155
Louisiana	618	158	776	Utah	n.a.*	n.a.*	n.a.*
Maine	694	75	769	Vermont	75	68	143
Maryland	n.a.[2]	n.a.[2]	n.a.[2]	Virginia	460	549	1,009
Massachusetts	72	27	99	Washington	4,669	191	4,860
Michigan	119	226	345	West Virginia	9	363	372
Minnesota	63	89	152	Wisconsin	53	362	415
Mississippi	1,715	421	2,136	Wyoming	318	—	318
Missouri	43	340	383	**Total**	37,422	7,471	44,893
Montana	1,802	—	1,802				

* Data withheld to avoid disclosing figures for individual companies.

[1] Combined production figures for Connecticut and Rhode Island (million board feet): Softwoods 11; Hardwoods 54; Total 65.
[2] Combined production figures for Delaware and Maryland (million board feet): Softwoods 74; Hardwoods 91; Total 165.
[3] Combined production figures for Kansas and Nebraska (million board feet): Hardwoods 22; Total 22.

Fishing

(US domestic landings. Source: National Oceanic and Atmospheric Administration, National Marine Fisheries Service, US Department of Commerce.)

Summary (principal species)

	1986		1987		1988*	
	Quantity (million lb)	Value ($ million)	Quantity (million lb)	Value ($ million)	Quantity (million lb)	Value ($ million)
Cod, Atlantic	61.1	36.1	59.1	44.2	76.1	42.9
Cod, Pacific	104.4	11.3	170.6	31.4	267.2	38.4
Flounders	169.1	124.6	199.7	145.1	228.6	140.1
Grouper	n.a.	n.a.	9.5	16.1	12.2	21.7
Haddock	11.0	10.9	6.7	8.5	6.4	7.0
Halibut	77.7	82.9	76.1	88.3	81.6	72.7
Herring, Pacific	130.8	44.6	122.6	47.9	131.4	57.4
Mackerel, Pacific	85.4	6.4	93.8	6.4	100.3	7.5
Menhaden	2,391.4	93.8	2,712.3	104.4	2,086.1	105.7
Mullets	21.6	6.0	30.1	8.2	32.6	11.2
Pollock, Alaska	n.a.	n.a.	552.0	45.8	1,257.3	95.3
Pollock, Atlantic	54.5	14.0	45.6	17.9	33.1	11.1
Rockfishes	92.0	28.3	117.9	38.2	124.0	38.7
Sablefish	84.9	45.9	102.7	58.1	107.5	91.8
Salmon	658.5	493.9	562.0	596.4	606.1	910.7
Scup or porgy	16.2	9.5	14.3	9.8	14.4	9.6
Sea trout, grey	20.6	7.1	17.9	7.5	20.5	7.9
Sharks (other than dogfish)	n.a.	n.a.	7.7	5.3	14.6	8.5
Snapper	n.a.	n.a.	8.9	18.7	11.0	20.8
Swordfish	9.7	30.5	9.8	35.0	12.8	42.7
Tilefish	n.a.	n.a.	8.0	8.9	4.6	7.2
Tuna	87.8	54.6	100.1	95.8	111.3	121.0
Whiting	39.9	8.3	34.7	11.6	35.6	8.6
Total fish (incl. others)	4,870.8	1,319.1	5,708.2	1,629.0	5,905.6	2,023.2
Clams	145.4	134.9	134.4	132.9	131.7	134.8
Crabs	355.7	270.1	386.4	321.9	455.6	383.6
Lobsters, American	46.1	120.6	45.6	133.6	48.6	145.2
Oysters	40.5	78.1	39.8	92.4	31.9	78.5
Scallops, calico	n.a.	n.a.	8.2	8.9	11.9	12.5
Scallops, sea	20.0	97.4	32.0	132.3	30.6	128.2
Shrimp	400.2	662.7	363.1	578.1	330.9	506.0
Total shellfish (incl. others)	1,159.9	1,443.7	1,187.5	1,485.7	1,287.0	1,497.0
Total	6,030.6	2,762.8	6,895.7	3,114.7	7,192.6	3,520.3

* Preliminary figures.

Regions and States (1988, preliminary figures)

	Quantity (million lb)	Value ($ million)
New England	569.9	493.6
Connecticut	9.1	17.4
Maine	157.3	123.9
Massachusetts	286.5	274.0
New Hampshire	10.8	8.8
Rhode Island	106.2	69.4
Middle Atlantic	156.4	129.0
Delaware	5.5	3.1
New Jersey	112.6	71.9
New York	38.5	54.2
Chesapeake Bay	730.5	148.4
Maryland	79.7	44.1
Virginia	650.8	104.3
South Atlantic	280.1	173.6
Florida (east coast) . . .	56.0	55.2
Georgia	16.6	21.5

(continued)	Quantity (million lb)	Value ($ million)
North Carolina	191.3	75.8
South Carolina	16.2	21.1
Gulf States	1,937.4	708.3
Alabama	22.3	39.7
Florida (west coast) . . .	126.2	114.4
Louisiana	1,356.5	317.3
Mississippi	336.4	61.2
Texas	96.0	175.7
Great Lakes[1]	40.1	18.8
Pacific Coast	3,457.0	1,808.8
Alaska	2,639.3	1,339.4
California	495.6	199.3
Oregon	148.6	97.7
Washington	173.6	172.3
Hawaii	21.1	39.7
Total	**7,192.6**	**3,520.3**

[1] Collected largely by state fishery agencies and compiled by National Marine Fisheries Service. Includes, in addition to the Great Lakes, small amounts for Lake St Clair, Lake of the Woods, Namakan Lake and Rainy Lake.

Selected Agricultural, Forestry and Fisheries Organizations

Agricultural Council of America: 1250 Eye St, NW, Suite 601, Washington, DC 20005; tel. (202) 682-9200; f. 1973; 2,000 mems; Pres. ORVILLE L. FREEMAN.

American Angus Association: 3201 Frederick Blvd, St Joseph, MO 64501; tel. (816) 233-3101; f. 1883; 22,000 mems; Exec. Vice-Pres. RICHARD L. SPADER.

American Brahman Breeders' Association: 1313 La Concha Lane, Houston, TX 77054; tel. (713) 795-4444; f. 1924; 3,700 mems; Exec. Vice-Pres. WENDELL E. SCHRONK.

American Dairy Association: 6300 North River Rd, Rosemont, IL 60018; tel. (312) 696-1880; f.1940; c. 205,000 mems; Pres. JOSEPH B. KELSCH.

American Dairy Goat Association: POB 865, Spindale, NC 28160; tel. (704) 286-3801; f. 1904; 12,500 mems; Sec.-Treas. ELIZABETH STONER.

American Egg Board: 1460 Renaissance Dr., Suite 301, Park Ridge, IL 60068; tel. (312) 296-7044; f. 1939; mems: 18 orgs; Pres. LOUIS B. RAFFEL.

American Farm Bureau Federation: 225 Touhy Ave, Park Ridge, IL 60068-5874; tel. (312) 399-5700; f. 1919; mems: 49 states and Puerto Rico; Pres. DEAN R. KLECKNER.

American Fisheries Society: 5410 Grosvenor Lane, Suite 110, Bethesda, MD 20814-2199; tel. (301) 897-8616; f. 1870; 8,300 mems; Exec. Dir CARL R. SULLIVAN.

American Forest Council: 1250 Connecticut Ave, NW, Suite 320, Washington, DC 20036; tel. (202) 463-2455; f. 1932; c. 75 mems; Pres. LAURENCE D. WISEMAN.

American Forestry Association: 1516 P St, NW, Washington, DC 20005; tel. (202) 667-3300; f. 1875; 40,000 mems; Exec. Vice-Pres. R. NEIL SAMPSON.

American Guernsey Association: POB 666, Reynoldsburg, OH 43068-0666; tel. (614) 864-2409; f. 1877; 2,000 mems; Exec. Sec.-Treas. ERICK A. METZGER.

American Hereford Association: POB 4059, Kansas City, MO 64101; tel. (816) 842-3757; f. 1881; 9,000 mems; Exec. Vice-Pres. M. M. DICKENSON.

American International Charolais Association: 11700 North West Plaza Circle, POB 20247, Kansas City, MO 64195; tel. (816) 464-5977; f. 1957; 3,200 mems; Exec. Vice-Pres. Dr JOE GARRETT.

American Jersey Cattle Club: 6486 East Main St, Reynoldsburg, OH 43068-2349; tel. (614) 861-3636; f. 1868; 2,800 mems; Exec. Sec. MAURICE E. CORE.

American Sheep Producers' Council: 200 Clayton St, Denver, CO 80206; tel. (303) 399-8130; f. 1955; 77 mems; Exec. Dir ROGER L. WASSON.

American Society of Farm Managers and Rural Appraisers: 950 South Cherry St, Suite 106, Denver, CO 80222; tel. (303) 758-3513; f. 1929; 4,200 mems; Exec. Vice-Pres. JOHN OLSON.

American Soybean Association: POB 27300, 777 Craig Rd, St Louis, MO 63141-1700; tel. (314) 432-1600; f. 1920; 29,000 mems; CEO KENNETH L. BADER.

American Wood Council: 1250 Connecticut Ave, NW, Suite 230, Washington, DC 20036; tel. (202) 833-1595; f. 1968; mems: seven orgs; Pres. CARL E. DARROW.

American Yorkshire Club: 1769 US 59 West, West Lafayette, IN 47906; tel. (317) 463-3593; f. 1935; c. 4,500 mems; Pres. BRUCE LEMAN.

Beefmaster Breeders Universal: 6800 Park Ten Blvd, Suite 290 West, San Antonio, TX 78213; tel. (512) 732-3132; f. 1961; 4,200 mems; Exec. Vice-Pres. GENE KUYKENDALL.

Brown Swiss Cattle Breeders' Association of the USA: 800 Pleasant St, POB 1038, Beloit, WI 53511-1038; tel. (608) 365-4474; f. 1880; 1,100 mems; Sec.-Treas. GEORGE G. HARRIS.

California Redwood Association: 403 Enfrente Dr., Suite 200, Novato, CA 94949; tel. (415) 382-0662; f. 1916; mems: eight orgs; Exec. Vice-Pres. L. KEITH LANNING.

Farmers' Educational and Co-operative Union of America: 10065 East Harvard Ave, Denver, CO 80251; tel. (303) 337-5500; f. 1902; mems: 250,000 families; Pres. LELAND H. SWENSON.

Fertilizer Institute: 501 Second St, NE, Washington, DC 20002; tel. (202) 861-4900; f. '1970; mems: c. 315 orgs; Pres. GARY D. MYERS.

Future Farmers of America: National FFA Centre, POB 15160, Alexandria, VA 22309-0160; tel. (703) 360-3600; f. 1928; 404,900 mems; Nat. Advisor Dr LARRY D. CASE.

Holstein Association of America: One Holstein Pl., POB 808, Brattleboro, VT 05301; tel. (802) 254-4551; f. 1885; 45,000 mems; CEO ZANE ATKINS.

Interstate Producers' Livestock Association: 1705 West Luthy Dr., Peoria, IL 61615; tel. (309) 691-5360; f. 1962; 26,600 mems; Sec. EUGENE KUNKLE.

Livestock Marketing Association: 7509 Tiffany Springs Parkway, Kansas City, MO 64190; tel. (816) 891-0502; f. 1976; 1,400 mems; Gen. Man. JAMES ED FROST.

National Agri-Marketing Association: 12345 West 95th St, Shawnee Mission, KS 66207; tel. (913) 492-0220; f. 1956; 2,500 mems; Exec. Dir REX PARSONS.

National Association of Animal Breeders: POB 1033, Columbia, MO 65205; tel. (314) 445-4406; f. 1947; mems: 35 orgs; Pres. GORDON A. DOAK.

National Association of Wheat Growers: 415 Second Street, NE, Suite 300, Washington, DC 20002; tel. (202) 547-7800; f. 1950; 60,000 mems; Exec. Vice-Pres. CARL SCHWENSEN.

National Broiler Council: 1155 15th St, NW, Suite 614, Washington, DC 20005; tel. (202) 296-2622; f. 1954; mems: c. 138 orgs; Pres. GEORGE B. WATTS.

National Cattlemen's Association: 5420 South Québec St, POB 3469, Englewood, CO 80155; tel. (303) 694-0305; f. 1977; 35,000 mems; Exec. Vice-Pres. JOHN MEETZ.

National Cooperative Business Association: 1401 New York Ave, NW, Suite 1100, Washington, DC 20005; tel. (202) 638-6222; f. 1916; mems: 300 orgs and 400 individuals; Pres. and CEO ROBERT D. SCHERER.

National Corn Growers' Association: 1000 Executive Parkway, Suite 105, St Louis, MO 63141; tel. (314) 275-9915; f. 1957; 22,000 mems; CEO JEFF GAIN.

National Cotton Council of America: 1918 North Parkway, POB 12285, Memphis, TN 38182; tel. (901) 274-9030; f. 1938; c. 285 mem. delegates; Exec. Vice-Pres. EARL W. SEARS.

National Farmers' Organization: 720 Davis Ave, Corning, IA 50841; tel. (515) 322-3131; fax (515) 322-3743; f. 1955; c. 35,000 mems; Pres. DEVON R. WOODLAND.

National Fisheries Institute: 2000 M St, NW, Suite 580, Washington, DC 20036; tel. (202) 296-5090; f. 1945; 1,100 mems; Exec. Vice-Pres. LEE J. WEDDIG.

National Hardwood Lumber Association: POB 34518, Memphis, TN 38184-0518; tel. (901) 377-1818; f. 1898; mems: 1,225 orgs; Exec. Man. ERNEST J. STEBBINS.

National Live Stock and Meat Board: 444 North Michigan Ave, Chicago, IL 60611; tel. (312) 467-5520; f. 1922; mems: 28 orgs; Pres. JOHN L. HUSTON.

National Milk Producers' Federation: 1840 Wilson Blvd, 4th Floor, Arlington, VA 22201; tel. (703) 243-6111; f. 1916; mems: 48 orgs; CEO JAMES C. BARR.

National Peanut Council: 1500 King St, Suite 301, Alexandria, VA 22314; tel. (703) 838-9500; f. 1940; c. 275 mems; Pres. and CEO C. EDWARD ASHDOWN.

National Pecan Marketing Council: 219 North Main, Suite 513, Bryan, TX 77803; tel. (409) 775-4009; f. 1979; 300 mems; Exec. Dir NORMAN WINTER.

National Pork Producers' Council: POB 10383, Des Moines, IA 50306; tel. (515) 223-2600; f. 1954; 100,000 mems; Exec. Vice-Pres. ORVILLE K. SWEET.

National Potato Promotion Board: 1385 South Colorado Blvd, Denver, CO 80112; tel. (303) 790-1141; f. 1948; 12,000 mems; Exec. Dir RON WALKER.

National Red Cherry Institute: POB 30285, Lansing, MI 48909-7785; tel. (517) 321-1231; f. 1947; mems: three orgs; Sec. PHILIP J. KORSON, II.

National Turkey Federation: 11319 Sunset Hills Road, Reston, VA 22090; tel. (703) 435-7206; f. 1939; c. 2,250 mems; Exec. Vice-Pres. G. L. 'LEW' WALTS.

North American Limousin Foundation: 100 Livestock Exchange Bldg, Denver, CO 80216; tel. (303) 296-8835; f. 1968; 10,000 mems; Exec. Vice-Pres. JERRY FITZGERALD.

Rice Council of America: POB 740123, Houston, TX 77274; tel. (713) 270-6699; f. 1957; 35,000 mems; Exec. Vice-Pres. BILL GOLDSMITH.

Rice Millers' Association: 1235 Jefferson Davis Highway, Arlington, VA 22202; tel. (703) 920-1281; f. 1899; mems: c. 35 orgs; Pres. J. STEPHEN GABBERT.

Southern Forest Products Association: POB 52468, New Orleans, LA 70152; tel. (504) 443-4464; telex 756854; fax (504) 443-6612; f. 1914; mems: c. 188 orgs; Pres. KARL LINDBERG.

Supima Association of America: 4141 East Broadway Rd, Phoenix, AZ 85040-8803; tel. (602) 437-1364; f. 1955; 1,500 mems; Pres. JESSE W. CURLEE.

United Dairy Industry Association: 6300 North River Rd, Rosemont, IL 60018-4289; tel. (312) 696-1860; f. 1971; mems: 47 orgs; CEO MARION F. BRINK.

United Egg Producers: 3951 Snapfinger Parkway, Suite 580, Decatur, GA 30035; tel. (404) 288-6700; f. 1968; mems: five orgs; Vice-Pres. KEN KIPPEN.

United Fresh Fruit and Vegetable Association: 727 North Washington St, Alexandria, VA 22314; tel. (703) 836-3410; telex 101240; f. 1904; c. 2,750 mems; Pres. ROGER J. STROH.

Western Forest Industries Association: 1500 South West Taylor St, Portland, OR 97205; tel. (503) 224-5455; f. 1947; 125 mems; Pres. JOSEPH W. McCRACKEN.

Western Wood Products Association: Yeon Building, 522 South West Fifth Ave, Portland, OR 97204-2122; tel. (503) 224-3930; f. 1964; mems: 300 orgs; Pres. H. A. ROBERTS.

MINING
Mineral Fuels

Summary

		1985		1986		1987*	
		Quantity	Value ($ million)†	Quantity	Value ($ million)	Quantity	Value ($ million)
Coal:							
Bituminous . . .	(million short tons)	614 }	22,060 {	620 }	21,000 {	636 }	20,990
Sub-bituminous . .	(million short tons)	193 }		190 }		199 }	
Lignite . . .	(million short tons)	72 }		76 }		78 }	
Anthracite . . .	(million short tons)	5	220	4	190	4	180
Crude oil‡ . . .	(million barrels)	3,274	78,880	3,168	39,630	3,033	46,740
Natural gas (dry) .	('000 million cu ft)	16,380	43,170	15,990	32,570	16,350	29,350
Total		n.a.	144,330	n.a.	93,390	n.a.	97,260

* Preliminary.   † Marketed production.   ‡ Includes lease condensates.

Uranium (million lb): 11.31 in 1985; 13.51 in 1986; 13.01 in 1987 (preliminary).

Source: Energy Information Administration, US Department of Energy, *Annual Energy Review*.

States (1986)

	Coal ('000 short tons)	Crude oil (million barrels)	Natural gas* ('000 million cu ft)	(continued)	Coal ('000 short tons)	Crude oil (million barrels)	Natural gas* ('000 million cu ft)
Alabama	25,826	21	107	Montana	33,978	27	49
Alaska	1,570	681	306	Nebraska	—	7	n.a.
Arizona	11,556	—	—	New Mexico . . .	21,496	76	710
Arkansas	167	16	132	New York	—	1	n.a.
California	—	407	469	North Dakota . . .	25,640	46	60
Colorado	15,237	29	158	Ohio	36,441	13	n.a.
Florida	—	9	9	Oklahoma	3,048	149	1,917
Illinois	61,866	27	n.a.	Pennsylvania . . .	71,648	4	n.a.
Indiana	32,852	5	n.a.	Tennessee	6,870	—	—
Iowa	484	—	—	Texas	48,590	840	6,092
Kansas	1,486	67	448	Utah	14,269	39	88
Kentucky	153,933	6	n.a.	Virginia	41,178	—	—
Louisiana	2,254	512	4,889	Washington	4,601	—	—
Maryland	3,906	—	—	West Virginia . . .	129,907	3	130
Michigan	—	26	127	Wyoming	136,826	121	495
Mississippi	—	30	143	**Total**	890,315	3,168	16,809†
Missouri	4,687	—	—				

* Preliminary figures.   † Includes other states for which individual figures not available.

Source: Energy Information Administration, US Department of Energy, various publications.

Metals

(Source (unless otherwise stated): Bureau of Mines, US Department of the Interior, *Minerals Yearbook*.)

Summary

		1985		1986		1987	
		Quantity	Value ($ million)	Quantity	Value ($ million)	Quantity	Value ($ million)
Bauxite	('000 metric tons)	674	13	510	10	576	11
Copper	('000 metric tons)	1,106	1,632	1,147	1,671	1,256	2,284
Gold	('000 troy oz)	2,427	771	3,739	1,377	4,966	2,225
Iron oxide pigments (crude)	('000 short tons)	47	3	41	3	43	4
Iron ore*	('000 long tons)	n.a.	n.a.†	38,825	n.a.†	46,894	n.a.†
Lead	('000 metric tons)	414	174	340	165	311	247
Magnesium	('000 short tons)	n.a.	n.a.	138	424	137	382
Manganiferous ore (gross)	('000 short tons)	20	n.a.†	14	n.a.†	19	n.a.†
Mercury	(76-lb flasks)	16,530	n.a.†	n.a.	n.a.†	n.a.†	n.a.†
Molybdenum . . .	(million lb)	112	348	95	240	70	179
Nickel	('000 short tons)	6	n.a.†	2	n.a.†	—	—
Silver	('000 troy oz)	39,433	242	34,524	189	39,790	279
Tungsten	(metric tons)	983	9	817	6	n.a.†	n.a.†
Zinc	('000 metric tons)	227	202	203	170	217	201
Other		n.a.	2,235	n.a.	1,563	n.a.	1,637
Total		n.a.	5,629	n.a.	5,817	n.a.	7,447

* Source: Bureau of Economic Analysis, US Department of Commerce, *Survey of Current Business*.
† Withheld to avoid disclosing company proprietary data, but included in 'Other'.

States (1986, selected products)

	Copper (metric tons)[1]	Gold (troy oz)[1]	Iron ore ('000 long tons)[2]	Lead (metric tons)[1]	Molybdenum ('000 lb)	Silver ('000 troy oz)[1]	Zinc (metric tons)
Alaska . . .	—	48,271	—	—	—	n.a.*	—
Arizona . . .	789,175	n.a.*	—	n.a.*	29,382	4,202	—
California . . .	n.a.	425,617	n.a.	—	n.a.	155	—
Colorado . . .	n.a.	120,347	—	n.a.	n.a.	645	n.a.
Idaho . . .	n.a.*	70,440	—	9,951	n.a.	11,207	351
Illinois . . .	n.a.	—	—	n.a.	—	n.a.	n.a.
Michigan . . .	n.a.	n.a.	10,957	—	—	n.a.	—
Minnesota . . .	—	—	28,779	—	—	—	—
Missouri . . .	n.a.*	—	803	319,900	—	1,459	37,919
Montana . . .	n.a.*	n.a.*	n.a.	n.a.*	n.a.	4,773	—
Nevada . . .	n.a.	2,098,929	n.a.	—	—	6,409	—
New Jersey . . .	—	—	—	—	—	—	n.a.
New Mexico . . .	n.a.	39,856	n.a.	10	n.a.	n.a.	—
New York . . .	—	—	—	n.a.	—	n.a.	n.a.
North Carolina . . .	—	12	—	—	—	—	—
Oregon . . .	—	n.a.	—	—	—	—	—
South Carolina . . .	—	n.a.	—	—	—	n.a.	—
South Dakota . . .	—	n.a.*	—	—	—	n.a.*	—
Tennessee . . .	n.a.	—	—	—	—	n.a.	102,118
Texas	—	—	n.a.	—	—	—	—
Utah	n.a.	n.a.*	n.a.	—	—	n.a.	—
Washington . . .	—	n.a.	—	—	—	n.a.	—
Total†	1,147,277	3,733,190	n.a.	339,793	95,066	34,220	202,983

[1] Recoverable content of ores, etc.   [2] Usable; gross weight.
* Withheld to avoid disclosing company proprietary data.   † Includes data for states where individual figures are not available.

Non-Metallic Minerals

(Excluding fuels. Source: Bureau of Mines, US Department of the Interior, *Minerals Yearbook*.)

Summary

		1985		1986		1987	
		Quantity	Value ($ million)	Quantity	Value ($ million)	Quantity	Value ($ million)
Asbestos . . .	('000 metric tons)	57	20	51	17	51	17
Barite	('000 short tons)	739	22	297	12	448	16
Boron minerals . .	('000 short tons)	1,269	405	1,251	426	1,385	475
Bromine* . . .	(million lb)	320	80	310	93	335	107
Cement:							
Masonry . . .	('000 short tons)	3,187	213	3,525	232	3,680	260
Portland . . .	('000 short tons)	74,250	3,817	75,181	3,760	74,868	3,647
Clays	('000 short tons)	44,974	4,011	44,620	1,095	47,657	1,202
Diatomite . . .	('000 short tons)	635	127	628	128	658	134
Feldspar . . .	('000 short tons)	700	23	735	26	720	26
Fluorspar . . .	('000 short tons)	66	n.a.†	78*	n.a.†	69	12

(continued)

NON-METALLIC MINERALS—Summary—(*continued*)

		1985 Quantity	1985 Value ($ million)	1986 Quantity	1986 Value ($ million)	1987 Quantity	1987 Value ($ million)
Garnet (abrasive) . .	('000 short tons)	37	3	33	3	43	4
Gem stones		n.a.	7*	n.a.	9	n.a.	21
Gypsum	('000 short tons)	14,414	112	15,403	100	15,612	107
Helium:							
Crude	(million cu ft)	n.a.†	n.a.†	432	10	730	16
Grade A . . .	(million cu ft)	1,865	70	1,941	73	2,230	83
Lime	('000 short tons)	15,690	809	14,474	758	15,733	786
Mica (scrap) . . .	('000 short tons)	138	6	148	7	161	8
Peat	('000 short tons)	882	22	1,038	24	958	26
Perlite	('000 short tons)	507	17	507	16	533	16
Phosphate rock . .	('000 metric tons)	50,835	1,235	40,320	897	40,954	793
Potash (K₂O equivalent).	('000 metric tons)	1,266	178	1,147	152	1,485	196
Pumice	('000 short tons)	508	5	554	6	392	4
Salt	('000 short tons)	40,067	740	36,663	665	36,493	684
Sand and gravel:							
Construction . .	('000 short tons)	800,100*	2,438*	883,000	2,747	896,200	3,003
Industrial . . .	('000 short tons)	29,430	374	27,420	359	28,010	364
Sodium carbonate (natural) . . .	('000 short tons)	n.a.†	n.a.†	n.a.†	n.a.†	8,891	594
Sodium sulphate (natural) . . .	('000 short tons)	389	36	396	34	382	33
Stone:							
Crushed* . . .	('000 short tons)	1,000,800	4,053	1,023,200*	4,255*	1,200,100	5,249
Dimension* . . .	('000 short tons)	1,104	172	1,163*	173*	1,184	190
Sulphur (Frasch) . .	('000 metric tons)	4,678	574	4,180	509	3,610	389
Talc and pyrophyllite .	('000 short tons)	1,269	29	1,302	31	1,349	29
Vermiculite . . .	('000 short tons)	314	32	317	34	303	33
Other		n.a.	1,047	n.a.	994	n.a.	375
Total		n.a.	**17,678**	n.a.	**17,647**	n.a.	**18,899**

* Estimated figures.   † Withheld to avoid disclosing company proprietary data, but included in 'Other'.

States (1986, selected products)

	Cement ('000 short tons)	Clays ('000 short tons)[1]	Lime ('000 short tons)	Phosphate rock ('000 metric tons)	Salt ('000 short tons)	Sand and gravel ('000 short tons)	Stone ('000 short tons)[2]
Alabama	3,744	2,077	1,180	—	n.a.	11,214	24,008
Alaska	n.a.	—	—	—	—	27,762	2,000
Arizona	n.a.	201	505	—	n.a.	40,468	5,600
Arkansas	n.a.	974	n.a.	—	—	8,971	15,505
California	9,490	2,499	371	—	n.a.	130,771	38,523
Colorado	n.a.	242	n.a.	—	—	23,233*	8,004
Connecticut . . .	—	157	—	—	—	7,254	7,724
Delaware	—	—	—	—	—	1,547	—
Florida	3,541	726	n.a.*	n.a.	—	29,700	69,000
Georgia	n.a.	9,827	—	—	—	8,126*	56,899
Hawaii	294	—	3	—	—	605	7,100
Idaho	n.a.	2	89	2,625	—	5,708	3,700
Illinois	2,118	283	n.a.	—	—	31,906	44,202
Indiana	2,531	744	n.a.	—	—	19,835	22,791
Iowa	1,867	486	n.a.	—	—	14,511	23,400
Kansas	1,814	903	—	—	1,656†	15,741	16,600
Kentucky	n.a.	721	n.a.	—	—	7,194	38,400‡
Louisiana	n.a.	332	n.a.	—	11,608	14,548	5,400‡
Maine	n.a.	46	—	—	—	8,572	1,600
Maryland	1,785	362	10	—	—	18,173	26,421
Massachusetts . . .	—	140	n.a.*	—	—	19,245	10,079
Michigan	4,970	1,402	556	—	n.a.†	45,857	27,806
Minnesota	—	n.a.	n.a.	—	—	24,055*	8,328
Mississippi . . .	n.a.	928	—	—	—	15,080	1,600
Missouri	4,809	1,321	n.a.	—	—	10,263	51,200
Montana	n.a.	222	n.a.*	n.a.	—	8,066	2,200
Nebraska	n.a.	221	n.a.	—	—	9,675	4,000
Nevada	n.a.	10	n.a.	—	n.a.	12,715	1,500
New Hampshire . . .	—	n.a.	—	—	—	8,418	1,882
New Jersey . . .	—	133	—	—	—	16,340	15,300
New Mexico . . .	n.a.	60	—	—	n.a.	8,471	3,922
New York	n.a.	619	n.a.	—	5,071	31,231	40,616
North Carolina . . .	—	2,658	—	n.a.	—	9,007	43,541
North Dakota . . .	—	n.a.	74	—	n.a.	5,135	n.a.
Ohio	1,844	2,833	1,648	—	4,115	38,027	39,336
Oklahoma	1,629	933	n.a.	—	n.a.	11,569	30,919
Oregon	n.a.	204	n.a.	—	—	13,441	15,100
Pennsylvania . . .	6,681	1,234	1,417	—	—	16,061	63,772
Rhode Island . . .	—	—	—	—	—	2,291	1,000
South Carolina . .	2,306	1,986	—	—	—	8,000	18,208

(*continued*)

States (1986, selected products)—*(continued)*

	Cement ('000 short tons)	Clays ('000 short tons)[1]	Lime ('000 short tons)	Phosphate rock ('000 metric tons)	Salt ('000 short tons)	Sand and gravel ('000 short tons)	Stone ('000 short tons)[2]
South Dakota . . .	639	119	n.a.	—	—	9,713	3,655
Tennessee . . .	n.a.	1,164	n.a.	1,232	—	7,848	40,706
Texas	9,092	2,515	1,173	—	8,520	60,864	84,249
Utah	1,014	305	232	n.a.	1,112	16,458	4,500
Vermont . . .	—	—	—	—	—	4,834	1,705
Virginia . . .	n.a.	890	624	—	—	11,670	52,010
Washington . .	1,218	252	n.a.	—	—	26,342*	9,001
West Virginia . .	n.a.	215	—	—	n.a.*	1,501	9,800
Wisconsin . . .	n.a.	—	350	—	—	26,107	18,723
Wyoming . . .	n.a.	1,762	25	—	—	3,377	1,700
Total	78,706	44,620	14,474	38,710	36,663	910,420	1,024,363

[1] Excludes certain clays.
[2] Estimated figures.
* Wholly or partially withheld to avoid disclosing company proprietary data.
† Excludes salt in brines.
‡ Excludes certain stones.

Selected Mining Organizations

American Institute of Mining, Metallurgical and Petroleum Engineers: 345 East 47th St, New York, NY 10017; tel. (212) 705-7695; f. 1871; mems: four orgs; Exec. Dir ROBERT H. MARCRUM.

American Mining Congress: 1920 N St, NW, Suite 300, Washington, DC 20036; tel. (202) 861-2800; telex 8220126; f. 1897; 450 mems; Pres. JOHN A. KNEBEL.

Asbestos Information Association/North America: 1745 Jefferson Davis Highway, Suite 509, Arlington, VA 22202; tel. (703) 979-1150; f. 1970; mems: 30 orgs; Pres. ROBERT J. PIGG.

Association of Bituminous Contractors: 2020 K Street, NW, Suite 800, Washington, DC 20006; tel. (202) 785-4440; f. 1968; 250 mems; Sec. and Gen. Counsel WILLIAM H. HOWE.

China Clay Producers' Association, Inc: 1275 Pennsylvania Ave, NW, Suite 1000, Washington, DC 20004-2404; f. 1978; mems: six orgs; Gen. Counsel GORDON O. PEHRSON, Jr.

Coalition For Responsible Mining Law: POB 1826, Coeur d'Alene, ID 33814; tel. (509) 467-5700; f. 1979; mems: 300 mining co executives, geologists and others interested in mining law; Pres. WALLACE McGREGOR.

Colorado Mining Association: 1500 Grant St, Suite 330, Denver, CO 80203; tel. (303) 894-0536; f. 1876; 1,500 mems; Admin. Asst SHIRLEY A. HUNTER.

Gold Institute: 1026 16th St, NW, Suite 101, Washington, DC 20036; tel. (202) 783-0500; f. 1976; mems: 65 orgs; Man. Dir JOHN H. LUTLEY.

Mine Inspectors' Institute of America: 1900 Grant Bldg, Pittsburgh, PA 15219; tel. (412) 281-2620; f. 1912; 500 mems; Sec. JOHN D. WOODS.

Mining Club of the Southwest: POB 27225, Tucson, AZ 85726; tel. (602) 622-6257; f. 1971; 450 mems; Pres. MICHAEL N. GREELEY.

Mining and Metallurgical Society of America: 210 Post St, Suite 1102, San Francisco, CA 94108; tel. (415) 398-6925; f. 1908; 350 mems; Exec. Officer HANS W. SCHREIBER.

Mining and Reclamation Council of America: 1130 17th St, NW, Suite 700, Washington, DC 20036; tel. (202) 789-0220; f. 1977; mems: 185 coal-producing cos, industry suppliers and assocns involved in coal mining; Pres. DANIEL R. GERKIN.

National Aggregates Association: 900 Spring St, Silver Spring, MD 20910; tel. (301) 587-1400; f. 1916; c. 375 mems; Pres. VINCENT P. AHEARN, Jr.

National Association of State Land Reclamationists: 542 8th St, Lasalle, IL 61310; tel. (815) 223-3322; f. 1973; 140 mems; Pres. ANTHONY J. DUPLECHIN, Jr.

National Stone Association: 1415 Elliot Pl., NW, Washington, DC 20007; tel. (202) 342-1100; f. 1985; mems: c. 385 orgs; Pres. ROBERT G. BARTLETT.

Northwest Mining Association: 414 Peyton Bldg, Spokane, WA 99201; tel. (509) 624-1158; f. 1895; 2,000 mems: Exec. Dir KARL W. MOTE.

Open Pit Mining Association: Consol Coal-Consol Plaza, Pittsburgh, PA 15241; tel. (412) 831-4440; f. 1945; 500 mems; Sec.-Treas. HENRY E. GILHAM.

Pennsylvania Coal Mining Association: 212 North Third St, Suite 201, Harrisburg, PA 17101; tel. (717) 233-7909; 360 mems; Exec. Vice-Pres. JAMES V. SCAHILL.

Perlite Institute: 600 South Federal St, Suite 400, Chicago, IL 60605; tel. (312) 922-2062; f. 1949; mems: 80 orgs; Man. Dir PAUL J. JULIUS.

Phosphate Rock Export Association: 1775 Pennsylvania Ave, NW, Washington, DC 20006-4680; tel. (202) 862-5378; f. 1970; mems: eight orgs; Sec. HOWARD W. FOGT, Jr.

Pittsburgh Coal Mining Institute of America: 4800 Forbes Ave, Pittsburgh, PA 15213; tel. (412) 621-4500; f. 1976; 800 mems; Sec.-Treas. DONALD W. HUNTLEY.

Rocky Mountain Coal Mining Institute: 2700 Youngfield, Suite 100, Lakewood, CO 80215; tel. (303) 238-9099; f. 1912; mems: 1,000 mine officials, inspectors, personnel, manufacturers of mining equipment; Exec. Sec. DORIS G. FINNIE.

Sellenium—Tellarium Development Association: POB 3096, Darien, CT 06820; tel. (203) 655-0470; f. 1938; mems: 11 orgs; Sec. PRESCOTT C. FULLER.

Silver Institute: 1026 16th St, NW, Suite 101, Washington, DC 20036; tel. (202) 783-0500; f. 1971; mems: 83 orgs; Exec. Dir JOHN H. LUTLEY.

Society of Economic Geologists: POB 571, Golden, CO 80402; tel. (303) 236-5538; f. 1920; 2,500 mems; Sec. JACK MURPHY.

Society of Exploration Geophysicists: POB 702740, Tulsa, OK 74170-2740; tel. (918) 493-3516; f. 1930; 16,000 mems; Exec. Dir JOHN H. NYDEN.

Society of Mineral Analysts: POB 838, Tooele, UT 84074; tel. (801) 268-4447; f. 1986; 287 mems; Chair. CHARLES R. STURGELL.

Society of Mining Engineers: POB 635002, Littleton, CO 80162-5002; tel. (303) 973-9550; f. 1957; 25,000 mems; Exec. Dir CLAUDE L. CROWLEY.

Solution Mining Research Institute: 812 Muriel St, Woodstock, IL 60098; tel. (815) 338-8579; f. 1958; mems: 39 salt and chemical cos, cos providing services to the industry, consultants; Exec. Dir HOWARD W. FIEDELMAN.

Sorptive Minerals Institute: 1440 New York Ave, NW, Suite 300, Washington, DC 20005; tel. (202) 638-1200; f. 1970; mems; eight orgs; Exec. Dir STEVEN B. HELLEM.

United Mining Councils of America: POB 460, Hinkley, CA 92347; tel. (619) 253-7561; f. 1971; 300 mems; Pres. HOWARD DARE.

Vermiculite Association: 600 South Federal St, Suite 400, Chicago, IL 60605; tel. (312) 922-6222; f. 1950; mems: 38 orgs; Dir TAMIE CEBULA.

Women In Mining National: 909 17th St, Suite 418, Denver, CO 80202; tel. (303) 298-1535; f. 1972; mems: 500 individuals employed in the mineral-resource industry; Exec. Sec. MINETTA MILLER.

Manufacturing Production

($ million. Sources: Bureau of the Census, US Department of Commerce, *Annual Survey of Manufactures* and *Current Industrial Reports*.)

Summary

	1984		1985		1986	
	Value added by manufacture[1]	Value of shipments	Value added by manufacture[1]	Value of shipments	Value added by manufacture[1]	Value of shipments
Food and kindred products . . .	98,037	300,000	104,146	301,562	112,191	314,500
Beverages	18,288	41,200	19,293	43,244	20,952	43,900
Tobacco products	10,787	17,400	11,894	18,507	12,725	18,000
Textile-mill products	22,110	55,500	20,693	53,277	22,232	54,600
Apparel and other textile products . .	28,859	n.a.	27,728	56,993	28,451	n.a.
Lumber and wood products . .	21,035	n.a.	21,066	54,185	23,239	n.a.
Furniture and fixtures	15,906	n.a.	16,479	31,294	17,659	n.a.
Paper and allied products . . .	40,885	94,800	40,387	93,414	43,925	103,800
Printing and publishing . . .	67,022	n.a.	73,054	111,885	78,150	n.a.
Newspapers	18,872	n.a.	20,426	27,015	22,169	n.a.
Chemicals and allied products . .	94,728	198,200	95,258	197,311	100,013	198,300
Petroleum and coal products . .	16,163	189,000	17,112	179,315	17,496	129,300
Petroleum refining	12,743	n.a.	13,660	167,502	13,762	n.a.
Rubber and miscellaneous plastics products	34,183	69,500	35,708	71,324	37,236	72,200
Leather and leather products . .	4,511	n.a.	4,108	8,567	3,611	n.a.
Stone, clay and glass products . .	27,707	53,400	28,842	55,064	30,677	56,800
Primary metal industries . . .	42,291	119,100	38,082	110,301	38,092	101,700
Iron and steel foundries . . .	6,497	n.a.	5,973	10,610	5,650	n.a.
Non-ferrous rolling and drawing .	8,838	n.a.	8,715	28,708	9,095	n.a.
Fabricated metal products . . .	67,645	135,900	69,162	139,580	68,621	136,000
Structural metal products . .	15,469	n.a.	16,322	36,684	16,052	n.a.
Machinery, excluding electrical . .	112,346	210,400	110,224	215,080	108,365	205,800
Construction and related machinery .	13,389	27,100	13,067	27,663	11,940	26,600
Metalworking machinery . . .	11,995	n.a.	12,827	19,692	12,825	n.a.
General industrial machinery . .	14,353	n.a.	14,336	25,347	13,926	n.a.
Electrical and electronic equipment .	110,322	187,600	109,862	192,732	112,422	205,600
Household appliances. . . .	7,539	16,300	7,338	16,230	7,555	17,100
Communication equipment . .	35,730	56,700	40,467	65,393	42,077	69,700
Transportation equipment . . .	114,499	281,200	120,953	301,386	125,706	314,100
Motor vehicles and equipment . .	54,705	179,300	57,127	188,536	59,213	194,700
Aircraft and parts	33,580	n.a.	35,798	66,058	37,756	n.a.
Instruments and related products . .	39,870	59,400	40,278	61,008	40,005	60,900
Miscellaneous manufacturing . . .	14,740	n.a.	14,032	26,527	14,622	n.a.

[1] Adjusted value added; takes into account (a) value added by merchandising operations (i.e. difference between the sales value and cost of merchandise sold without further manufacture, processing or assembly) and (b) net change in finished goods and work-in-process inventories between beginning and end of year.

States (value of shipments in 1985)

	Food and kindred products	Tobacco products	Textile-mill products	Apparel and other textile products	Lumber and wood products	Furniture and fixtures
Alabama	3,840	32	2,560	2,283	1,972	n.a.*
Alaska	614	—	—	—	145	—
Arizona	1,279	—	n.a.*	163	391	168
Arkansas	5,193	—	341	329	1,365	481
California	32,059	—	—*	5,776	5,208	3,599
Colorado	4,782	—	—	104	209	134
Connecticut	1,592	—	353	468	110	273
Delaware	1,423	—	85	74	61	52
District of Columbia . . .	101	—	—	—	—	—
Florida	9,767	106	121	1,206	1,650	710
Georgia	8,368	n.a.*	10,997	3,779	2,382	689
Hawaii	1,277	—	—	148	27	8
Idaho	2,237	—	n.a.*	1,136	n.a.†
Illinois	21,161	n.a.*	n.a.*	1,006	668	1,707
Indiana	7,172	—	n.a.*	539	1,439	1,426
Iowa	12,582	—	59	235	336	38
Kansas	8,350	—	—	900	232	106
Kentucky	3,884	1,977	432	875	443	222
Louisiana	3,694	—	n.a.*	323	1,048	n.a.*
Maine	835	—	524	234	1,116	57
Maryland	4,434	—	188	684	448	236
Massachusetts	4,054	—	1,488	1,874	n.a.*	503
Michigan	8,631	—	n.a.*	2,486	842	2,808
Minnesota	9,549	—	132	n.a.*	1,380	301

(continued)

MANUFACTURING PRODUCTION—States (value of shipments in 1985) (*continued*)

	Food and kindred products	Tobacco products	Textile-mill products	Apparel and other textile products	Lumber and wood products	Furniture and fixtures
Mississippi	2,804	—	372	1,259	1,702	1,072
Missouri	8,779	—	52	780	516	632
Montana	404	—	n.a.*	—	756	n.a.†
Nebraska	8,422	—	n.a.*	94	215	210
Nevada	318	—	—	n.a.*	54	15
New Hampshire	625	—	234	106	380	116
New Jersey	9,063	—	1,043	2,468	n.a.*	707
New Mexico	397	—	n.a.*	n.a.*	150	14
New York	12,531	—	1,743	10,562	n.a.*	1,313
North Carolina	7,285	9,510	14,113	3,531	2,616	4,426
North Dakota	878	—	—	n.a.*	25	—
Ohio	13,191	n.a.*	511	1,244	989	1,259
Oklahoma	2,307	—	n.a.*	432	288	96
Oregon	3,014	—	n.a.*	124	7,231	109
Pennsylvania	14,776	153	2,373	3,518	1,760	1,489
Rhode Island	374	—	327	100	56	n.a.*
South Carolina	2,345	n.a.*	7,774	1,456	1,368	281
South Dakota	1,822	—	—	34	129	—
Tennessee	7,778	479	1,476	2,239	926	1,393
Texas	18,920	—	n.a.*	2,945	2,867	945
Utah	1,694	—	15	193	163	139
Vermont	493	—	39	80	208	70
Virginia	6,185	4,489	2,954	1,192	1,680	1,294
Washington	5,736	—	67	285	3,681	139
West Virginia	494	n.a.*	43	102	238	41
Wisconsin	13,956	—	n.a.*	379	1,475	912
Wyoming	105	—	—	—	n.a.*	14
Total‡	301,562	18,507	53,277	56,993	54,185	31,294

	Paper and allied products	Printing and publishing	Chemicals and allied products	Petroleum and coal products	Rubber and miscellaneous plastics products	Leather and leather products	Stone, clay and glass products
Alabama	3,988	875	3,276	1,377	2,146	—	791
Alaska	n.a.*	80	n.a.*	1,248	—	—	49
Arizona	233	875	686	62	284	n.a.*	688
Arkansas	1,823	770	1,131	486	1,072	208	462
California	5,889	10,763	9,806	23,589	6,167	n.a.*	5,696
Colorado	302	1,525	328	943	430	n.a.*	734
Connecticut	1,160	1,983	2,322	69	967	27	468
Delaware	533	132	1,807	n.a.*	360	—	87
District of Columbia	—	1,567	n.a.*	—	—	—	—
Florida	2,278	3,509	5,008	385	1,095	131	2,125
Georgia	5,115	2,073	4,719	n.a.*	1,516	75	2,089
Hawaii	41	n.a.*	52	n.a.*	n.a.†	—	87
Idaho	373	178	585	—	n.a.*	—	87
Illinois	4,084	9,284	11,190	9,530	4,639	173	2,564
Indiana	1,533	2,053	6,403	4,938	3,469	142	1,707
Iowa	673	1,422	2,370	—	1,026	27	698
Kansas	628	1,675	1,847	3,907	1,144	15	662
Kentucky	977	1,540	3,717	n.a.*	1,095	n.a.*	570
Louisiana	2,288	643	12,677	23,841	322	n.a.*	594
Maine	3,144	285	117	54	388	715	76
Maryland	1,085	1,857	2,544	385	817	n.a.*	701
Massachusetts	2,569	4,193	2,450	293	2,815	668	1,016
Michigan	3,153	3,137	5,837	1,647	3,605	n.a.*	1,803
Minnesota	2,276	2,757	1,154	n.a.*	1,336	153	1,775
Mississippi	1,302	405	1,407	n.a.*	570	n.a.*	523
Missouri	1,751	2,911	4,561	354	1,213	723	1,024
Montana	n.a.*	120	120	1,361	—	—	104
Nebraska	130	562	720	—	375	—	244
Nevada	—	218	101	—	84	—	175
New Hampshire	901	505	97	—	654	188	216
New Jersey	3,020	4,541	16,458	5,705	2,942	294	2,276
New Mexico	—	184	117	1,252	23	n.a.*	259
New York	4,228	19,988	9,606	609	2,902	967	2,589
North Carolina	2,781	1,430	7,967	180	3,280	198	1,593
North Dakota	—	100	n.a.*	n.a.*	51	—	38
Ohio	3,836	4,802	10,006	6,880	7,431	n.a.*	4,139
Oklahoma	730	654	1,142	4,514	1,573	n.a.*	1,002
Oregon	1,989	913	474	212	283	n.a.*	249
Pennsylvania	5,971	5,664	8,800	7,930	3,068	603	4,178
Rhode Island	164	433	360	n.a.*	418	n.a.*	235
South Carolina	2,300	582	5,961	139	2,026	n.a.*	1,068
South Dakota	n.a.*	119	25	—	36	—	73

(*continued*)

MANUFACTURING PRODUCTION—States (value of shipments in 1985) (*continued*)

	Paper and allied products	Printing and publishing	Chemicals and allied products	Petroleum and coal products	Rubber and miscellaneous plastics products	Leather and leather products	Stone, clay and glass products
Tennessee	2,678	2,190	7,194	924	2,565	588	1,404
Texas	2,950	4,903	28,198	53,607	2,891	436	4,355
Utah	157	524	228	1,670	58	—	373
Vermont	384	294	37	—	103	n.a.*	113
Virginia	2,205	2,293	5,307	n.a.*	1,706	n.a.*	1,032
Washington	3,216	1,081	1,463	4,681	381	22	542
West Virginia	120	287	3,899	370	79	89	743
Wisconsin	8,038	2,689	1,969	432	1,732	666	903
Wyoming	—	56	217	n.a.*	n.a.*	—	111
Total‡	93,414	111,885	197,311	179,135	71,324	8,567	55,064

	Primary metal industries	Fabricated metal products	Machinery excluding electrical	Electrical and electronic equipment	Transportation equipment	Instruments and related products	Miscellaneous manufacturing
Alabama	3,964	2,021	n.a.*	1,736	2,295	214	373
Alaska	—	41	11	—	—	—	—
Arizona	1,736	664	3,555	3,033	2,142	540	195
Arkansas	1,143	1,519	1,500	2,608	946	316	147
California	4,394	12,653	22,971	31,304	35,332	8,025	2,561
Colorado	351	1,317	2,246	2,312	1,916	2,611	201
Connecticut	1,706	3,560	4,964	3,762	8,120	2,165	901
Delaware	202	49	103	59	n.a.*	425	n.a.†
District of Columbia	—	—	15	—	—	9	n.a.†
Florida	796	2,942	5,966	6,055	4,405	998	439
Georgia	2,003	2,279	2,492	3,180	8,340	497	447
Hawaii	—	91	12	—	14	—	28
Idaho	—	116	697	147	43	—	n.a.*
Illinois	7,221	11,395	16,032	11,713	7,601	2,417	1,568
Indiana	13,063	5,264	6,695	9,237	9,838	1,064	582
Iowa	1,241	1,290	6,182	2,353	891	147	348
Kansas	333	631	2,242	738	7,785	236	184
Kentucky	2,798	1,981	4,624	3,082	7,134	318	n.a.*
Louisiana	638	926	796	1,376	3,335	100	50
Maine	n.a.*	243	466	591	n.a.*	73	57
Maryland	1,962	1,621	1,919	3,734	2,237	233	—
Massachusetts	1,423	4,033	12,012	9,220	5,017	4,811	1,652
Michigan	6,977	13,177	12,244	3,287	62,059	1,325	678
Minnesota	493	3,068	8,418	2,623	2,089	1,678	213
Mississippi	545	989	1,328	1,814	2,431	120	n.a.*
Missouri	1,527	3,242	2,334	3,991	19,745	425	312
Montana	n.a.*	44	n.a.†	n.a.†	—	n.a.†	39
Nebraska	510	650	1,169	697	555	514	48
Nevada	140	160	233	182	28	107	87
New Hampshire	237	443	1,913	1,609	157	542	100
New Jersey	2,613	4,655	4,499	6,231	4,336	2,736	1,491
New Mexico	n.a.*	79	181	547	238	52	n.a.†
New York	4,855	6,312	15,208	15,849	9,121	13,995	4,754
North Carolina	1,339	2,793	6,306	8,539	2,471	1,143	486
North Dakota	—	60	321	n.a.*	n.a.*	—	12
Ohio	13,686	16,313	13,547	9,834	34,216	1,663	1,174
Oklahoma	518	1,455	3,148	2,447	3,952	553	138
Oregon	1,057	889	1,035	953	898	1,086	152
Pennsylvania	12,442	8,156	8,613	8,606	7,370	3,246	1,603
Rhode Island	690	1,134	439	772	186	400	1,523
South Carolina	1,238	1,446	2,482	1,792	911	434	220
South Dakota	50	82	339	292	71	n.a.*	129
Tennessee	2,140	2,691	4,085	4,563	4,013	571	716
Texas	5,062	7,591	13,442	9,266	9,649	2,293	920
Utah	956	533	1,697	630	1,526	251	147
Vermont	35	428	304	711	143	97	n.a.†
Virginia	879	2,104	1,909	4,569	4,357	430	208
Washington	2,425	1,133	1,365	997	12,125	853	281
West Virginia	2,390	619	433	282	138	n.a.*	27
Wisconsin	1,768	4,622	9,906	5,148	6,580	770	533
Wyoming	—	73	63	—	—	—	—
Total‡	110,301	139,580	215,080	192,732	301,386	61,008	26,527

* Data included in total.
† Data withheld.
‡ Figures may not tally because state and total figures were calculated independently.

Construction

(Source: Bureau of the Census, US Department of Commerce, *Construction Reports.*)

Value of new construction put in place (millions of current dollars)

	1984	1985	1986
Private:	270,977	291,665	316,589
Residential buildings[1]	153,849	158,474	187,148
New housing units	113,826	114,662	133,192
Improvements	40,023	43,812	53,956
Non-residential buildings[2]	81,147	95,317	91,171
Farm non-residential	3,161	2,197	2,049
Public utilities	30,915	32,952	33,946
Other	1,905	2,726	2,275
Public:	57,664	64,328	72,228
Buildings	17,883	20,172	23,494
Highways and streets	18,771	21,756	23,359
Military facilities	2,839	3,283	3,919
Conservation and redevelopment	4,654	4,744	4,668
Sewer systems	6,241	7,196	8,105
Water-supply facilities	2,621	2,664	3,370
Miscellaneous	4,654	4,512	5,313
Total	328,641	355,994	388,817

[1] Includes farm residential buildings.
[2] Excludes building by privately-owned public utilities.

Chambers of Commerce

NATIONAL ORGANIZATIONS

American Chamber of Commerce Executives (ACCE): 1454 Duke St, Alexandria, VA 22314; tel. (703) 836-7904; Pres. PAUL J. GREELEY.

ACCE Communications Council: 1454 Duke St, Alexandria, VA 22314; tel. (703) 836-7904; Exec. Vice-Pres. ROSEMARY M. HARPER.

American Chamber of Commerce Researchers Association: c/o ACCE, 1454 Duke St, Alexandria, VA 22314; tel. (703) 836-7904; Staff Liaison ROSEMARY M. HARPER.

Chamber of Commerce of the United States: 1615 H St, NW, Washington, DC 20062; tel. (202) 659-6000; fax (202) 463-5836; Pres. RICHARD L. LESHER.

Chamber of Commerce of the United States—Central Region: 1200 Harger Rd, Suite 606, Oak Brook, IL 60521; tel. (312) 325-7818.

Chamber of Commerce of the United States—Eastern Region: 711 Third Ave, New York, NY 10017; tel. (212) 370-1440.

Chamber of Commerce of the United States—Southern Region: 4835 Lyndon B. Johnson Freeway, Suite 750, Dallas, TX 75234; tel. (214) 387-0404.

Chamber of Commerce of the United States—Western Region: 500 Airport Blvd, Suite 240, Burlingame, CA 94010; tel. (415) 348-0411.

Council of State Chambers of Commerce: 122 C St, NW, Suite 200, Washington, DC 20001; tel. (202) 484-8103; Pres. WILLIAM R. BROWN.

Permanent Secretariat of the Hemispheric Conference: 1716 West Flagler St, Miami, FL 33135; tel. (305) 642-3870; Exec. Dir WALDO CASTRO MOLLEBA.

United States Council for International Business: 1212 Ave of the Americas, New York, NY 10036; tel. (212) 354-4480; Exec. Dir PAXTON T. DUNN.

STATE ORGANIZATIONS

Alabama

Alabama Business Council: 468 South Perry St, POB 76, Montgomery, AL 35202; tel. (205) 834-6000; Pres. E. CLARK RICHARDSON.

Alaska

Alaska State Chamber of Commerce: 310 Second St, Juneau, AK 99801; tel. (907) 586-2323; Pres. GEORGE KRUSZ.

Arizona

Arizona Chamber of Commerce: 1366 East Thomas Rd, Suite 202, Phoenix, AZ 85014; tel. (602) 248-9172; Pres. LOWELL REESE.

Arkansas

Arkansas State Chamber of Commerce: POB 3645, Little Rock, AR 72203; tel. (501) 374-9225; Exec. Vice-Pres. BOB LAMB.

California

California State Chamber of Commerce: 1027 10th St, 4th Floor, POB 1736, Sacramento, CA 95808; tel. (916) 444-6670; Pres. KIRK WEST.

Colorado

Colorado Association of Commerce and Industry: 1860 Lincoln St, Suite 550, Denver, CO 80295-0501; tel. (303) 831-7411; Pres. GEORGE S. DIBBLE.

Connecticut

Connecticut Business and Industry Association Inc: 370 Asylum St, Hartford, CT 06103; tel. (203) 547-1661; Pres. KENNETH O. DECKO.

Delaware

Delaware State Chamber of Commerce Inc: 1 Commerce Center, Suite 200, Wilmington, DE 19801; tel. (302) 655-7221; Pres. WILLIAM C. WYER.

Florida

Florida State Chamber of Commerce: 136 South Bronough St, POB 11309, Tallahassee, FL 32302; tel. (904) 222-2831; Exec. Vice-Pres. FRANK M. RYLL, Jr.

Georgia

Business Council of Georgia: 233 Peachtree St, Suite 200, Atlanta, GA 30303; tel. (404) 223-2264; Pres. GENE DYSON.

Hawaii

Chamber of Commerce of Hawaii: 735 Bishop St, Honolulu, HI 96813; tel. (808) 531-4111; Pres. ROBERT B. ROBINSON.

Idaho

Idaho Association of Commerce and Industry: 805 Idaho St, Suite 200, POB 389, Boise, ID 83701; tel. (208) 343-1849; Pres. GREG S. CASEY.

Illinois

Illinois State Chamber of Commerce: 20 North Wacker Dr., Suite 1960, Chicago, IL 60606; tel. (312) 372-7373; Pres. LESTER W. BRANN, Jr.

Indiana

Indiana State Chamber of Commerce Inc: 1 North Capitol Ave, Suite 200, Indianapolis, IN 46204-2248; tel. (317) 634-6407; Pres. JOHN W. WALLS.

Iowa

Iowa Association of Business and Industry: Employers' Mutual Bldg, Suite 706, 717 Mulberry St, Des Moines, IA 50309; tel. (515) 244-6149; Pres. FARNSLEY L. PETERS.

Kansas

Kansas Chamber of Commerce and Industry: Bank IV Tower, Suite 500, 1 Townsite Plaza, Topeka, KS 66603; tel. (913) 357-6321; Pres. EDWARD G. BRUSKE.

Kentucky

Kentucky Chamber of Commerce: 452 Versaille Rd, POB 817, Frankfort, KY 40602; tel. (502) 695-4700; Exec. Vice-Pres. JAMES M. WISEMAN.

Louisiana

Louisiana Association of Business and Industry: POB 80258, Baton Rouge, LA 70898-0258; tel. (504) 928-5388; Pres. EDWARD J. STEIMEL.

Maine

Maine Chamber of Commerce and Industry: 126 Sewall St, Augusta, ME 04330; tel. (207) 623-4568; Pres. JOHN S. DEXTER, Jr.

Maryland

Maryland Chamber of Commerce: 60 West St, Suite 405, Annapolis, MD 21401; tel. (301) 269-0642; Pres. PETER J. LOMBARDI.

Massachusetts

Massachusetts Association of Chamber of Commerce Executives: c/o Wellesley Chamber of Commerce, 287 Linden St, POB 715, Wellesley, MA 02181; tel. (617) 235-2446; Exec. Vice-Pres. JEANNE LUKAS.

Michigan

Michigan State Chamber of Commerce: 600 South Walnut St, Lansing, MI 48933; tel. (517) 371-2100; Pres. JAMES BARRETT.

Minnesota

Minnesota Chamber of Commerce and Industry: 300 Hanover Bldg, 480 Cedar St, St Paul, MN 55101; tel. (602) 292-4650; Pres. WINSTON BORDEN.

Mississippi

Mississippi Economic Council: POB 1849, Jackson, MS 39215; tel. (601) 969-0022; Pres. BOB PITTMAN.

Missouri

Missouri Chamber of Commerce: 428 East Capitol Ave, POB 149, Jefferson City, MO 65102; tel. (314) 634-3511; Pres. RONALD D. ROBERSON.

Montana

Montana Chamber of Commerce: 2030 11th Ave, POB 1730, Helena, MT 59624; tel. (406) 442-2405; Pres. FORREST H. BOLES.

Nebraska

Nebraska Association of Commerce and Industry: 1320 Lincoln Mall, POB 95128, Lincoln, NE 68509; tel. (402) 474-4422; Pres. JACK SWARTZ.

Nevada

Nevada State Chamber of Commerce: POB 3499, Reno, NV 89505; tel. (702) 786-3030; Exec. Dir FRED DAVIS.

New Hampshire

Business and Industry Association of New Hampshire: 23 School St, Concord, NH 03301; tel. (603) 224-5388; Pres. J. BONNIE NEWMAN.

New Jersey

New Jersey State Chamber of Commerce: 5 Commerce St, Newark, NJ 07102; tel. (201) 623-7070; Pres. FREDERICK A. WESTPHAL.

New Mexico

Greater Albuquerque Chamber of Commerce: 401 2nd St, NW, POB 25100, Albuquerque, NM 87125; tel. (505) 842-0220; Pres. TERRI MAISEL.

New York

Business Council of New York State Inc: 152 Washington Ave, Albany, NY 12210; tel. (518) 465-7511; Pres. RAYMOND T. SCHULER.

North Carolina

North Carolina Citizens for Business and Industry: 336 Fayetteville St Mall, POB 2508, Raleigh, NC 27602; tel. (919) 828-0758.

North Dakota

Greater North Dakota Association—State Chamber of Commerce: 808 Third Ave South, POB 2467, Fargo, ND 58108; tel. (701) 237-9461; Pres. DALE O. ANDERSON.

Ohio

Ohio Chamber of Commerce: 35 East Gay ST, 2nd Floor, Columbus, OH 43215-3181; tel. (614) 228-4201; Pres. I. JOHN REIMERS.

Oklahoma

Oklahoma State Chamber of Commerce and Industry: 4020 North Lincoln Blvd, Oklahoma City, OK 73105; tel. (405) 424-4003; Pres. RICHARD P. RUSH.

Oregon

Eugene Area Chamber of Commerce: 1401 Willamette St, POB 1107, Eugene, OR 97440; tel. (503) 484-1314; Exec. Vice-Pres. LARRY DOUGLAS.

Pennsylvania

Pennsylvania Chamber of Business and Industry: 222 North Third St, Harrisburg, PA 17101; tel. (717) 255-3252; Pres. CLIFFORD L. JONES.

Rhode Island

Newport County Chamber of Commerce: 10 Americas Cup Ave, Newport, RI 02840; tel. (401) 847-1600.

South Carolina

South Carolina Chamber of Commerce: NCNB Tower, Suite 520, 1301 Gervais St, Columbia, SC 29201; tel. (803) 799-4601; Exec. Vice-Pres. KENNETH OILSCHLAGER.

South Dakota

Industry and Commerce Association of South Dakota: POB 190, Pierre, SD 57501; tel. (605) 224-6161; Exec. Dir R. VAN JOHNSON.

Tennessee

Chattanooga Area Chamber of Commerce: Civic Forum, 1001 Market St, Chattanooga, TN 37402; tel. (615) 756-2121; Exec. Vice-Pres. DAVID MAJOR.

Texas

Texas State Chamber of Commerce: 300 West 15th, Suite 875, Austin, TX 78701; tel. (512) 472-1594; Pres. TOM CHAMPION.

Utah

Utah State Chamber of Commerce Association: 8680 South 440 East, Sandy, UT 84070; tel. (801) 566-1561; Pres. JAN CHRISTENSEN.

Vermont

Vermont State Chamber of Commerce: Granger Rd, Berlin, POB 37, Montpelier, VT 05602; tel. (802) 223-3443; Exec. Vice-Pres. CHRISTOPHER G. BARBIERI.

Virginia

Virginia Chamber of Commerce: 9 South 5th St, Richmond, VA 23219; tel. (804) 644-1607; Exec. Vice-Pres. EDWIN C. LUTHER, III.

Washington

Association of Washington Business: POB 658, Olympia, WA 98507; tel. (206) 943-1600; Pres. DONALD I. BARBER.

West Virginia

West Virginia Chamber of Commerce: 1010 Kanawha Valley Bldg, POB 2789, Charleston, WV 25330; tel. (304) 342-1115; Pres. JOHN D. HURD.

Wisconsin

Wisconsin Association of Manufacturers and Commerce: 501 East Washington Ave, POB 352, Milwaukee, WI 53701; tel. (608) 258-3400; Pres. JAMES S. HANLEY.

Wyoming

Casper Area Chamber of Commerce: POB 399, Casper, WY 82602; tel. (307) 324-5311.

Industrial and Employers' Organizations

Chemicals

American Institute of Chemists: 7315 Wisconsin Ave, Bethesda, MD 20814; tel. (301) 652-2447; f. 1923; 7,500 mems; Exec. Dir D. A. H. ROETHEL.

American Pharmaceutical Association: 2215 Constitution Ave, NW, Washington, DC 20037; tel. (202) 628-4410; f. 1852; 50,000 mems; Pres. and CEO JOHN F. SCHLEGEL.

Chemical Manufacturers Association: 2501 M St, NW, Washington, DC 20037; tel. (202) 887-1100; telex 89617; f. 1872; 175 mems; Pres. ROBERT A. ROLAND; Sec. CHARLES W. VAN VLACK.

Chemical Specialities Manufacturers Association: 1001 Connecticut Ave, NW, Washington, DC 20036; tel. (202) 872-8110; f. 1914; 390 mems; Pres. RALPH ENGEL.

Drug, Chemical and Allied Trades Association, Inc: 2 Roosevelt Ave, 3rd Floor, Syosset, NY 11791; tel. and fax (516) 496-3317; 536 mems; Exec. Dir RICHARD J. LERMAN.

The Fertilizer Institute: 1015 18th St, NW, Washington, DC 20036; tel. (202) 861-4900; f. 1955; 301 mems; Pres. GARY D. MYERS.

National Association of Retail Druggists: 205 Daingerfield Rd, Alexandria, VA 22314; tel. (703) 683-8200; f. 1898; 30,000 mems; Exec. Vice-Pres. CHARLES M. WEST.

Pharmaceutical Manufacturers Association: 1100 15th St, NW, Washington, DC 20005; tel. (202) 835-3400; telex 8229494; f. 1958; 110 mems; Pres. GERALD J. MOSSINGHOFF.

Soap and Detergent Association: 475 Park Ave South, New York, NY 10016; tel. (212) 725-1262; f. 1926; 145 mems; Pres. THEODORE E. BRENNER.

Construction
(see also Electricity, and Engineering and Machinery)

American Institute of Constructors: 20 South Front St, Columbus, OH 43215; tel. (614) 464-0598; f. 1971; 1,600 mems; Exec. Dir ED FREEDMAN.

Associated Builders and Contractors: 729 15th St, NW, Washington, DC 20005; tel. (202) 637-8800; f. 1950; 18,500 mems; Exec. Vice-Pres. DANIEL J. BENNET.

Associated General Contractors of America: 1957 E St, NW, Washington, DC 20006; tel. (202) 393-2040; f. 1918; 8,500 mems; Exec. Vice-Pres. HUBERT BEATTY.

Associated Specialty Contractors: 7315 Wisconsin Ave, Washington, DC 20814-3299; tel. (301) 657-3110; f. 1950; 17,600 mems; Pres. DANIEL G. WALTER.

Building Stone Institute: 420 Lexington Ave, New York, NY 10170; tel. (212) 490-2530; f. 1919; 400 mems; Exec. Vice-Pres. DOROTHY KENDER.

Construction Specifications Institute: 601 Madison St, Alexandria, VA 22314; tel. (703) 684-0300; fax (703) 684-0465; f. 1948; 19,000 mems; Exec. Dir J. A. GASCOIGNE.

Mechanical Contractors Association of America, Inc: 5530 Wisconsin Ave, NW, Chevy Chase, MD 20815; tel. (301) 654-7960; f. 1889; 1,700 mems; Exec. Vice-Pres. WALTER M. KARDY.

National Association of Home Builders of the US: 15th and M Streets, NW, Washington, DC 20005; tel. (202) 822-0200; f. 1942; 149,000 mems; Exec. Vice-Pres. KENT W. COLTON.

National Association of Plumbing-Heating-Cooling Contractors: 180 South Washington St, POB 6808, Falls Church, VA 22046; tel. (703) 237-8100; fax (703) 237-7442; f. 1883; 6,300 mems; Exec. Vice-Pres. JOE A. CHILDRESS.

National Ready-Mixed Concrete Association: 900 Spring St, Silver Spring, MD 20910; tel. (301) 587-1400; f. 1930; 950 mems; Pres. VINCENT P. AHEARN, Jr.

Tile Contractors' Association of America, Inc: 112 North Alfred St, Alexandria, VA 22314; tel. (703) 836-5995; f. 1929; 300 mems; Sec. WILHELMINA T. LOOMIS.

Electricity
(see also Construction, and Engineering and Machinery)

American Electronics Association: 5201 Great America Parkway, Suite 520, Santa Clara, CA 95054; tel. (408) 987-4200; f. 1943; 3,300 mems; CEO and Pres. J. RICHARD IVERSON.

Edison Electric Institute: 1111 19th St, NW, Washington, DC 20036-3691; tel. (202) 828-7444; telex 8220132; f. 1933; mems: 175 investor-owned electric utility cos; Pres. WILLIAM MCCOLLAM, Jr; Exec. Vice-Pres. THOMAS R. KUHN.

Electronic Industries Association: 2001 Eye St, NW, Washington, DC 20006; tel. (202) 457-4900; f. 1924; over 1,000 mems; Pres. P. F. MCCLOSKEY.

Institute of Electrical and Electronics Engineers: 345 East 47th St, New York, NY 10017; tel. (212) 705-7900; f. 1963; 210,000 mems; Exec. Dir ERIC HERZ.

National Association of Electrical Distributors: 28 Cross St, Norwalk, CT 06851; tel. (203) 846-6800; f. 1908; 3,000 mems; Exec. Dir MARVIN V. SCHYLLING.

National Electrical Contractors Association: 7315 Wisconsin Ave, Bethesda, MD 20814; tel. (301) 657-3110; f. 1901; 5,600 mems; Exec. Vice-Pres. ROBERT L. HIGGINS.

National Electrical Manufacturers Association: 2101 L St, NW, Washington, DC 20037; tel. (202) 457-8400; telex 904077; f. 1926; 560 mems; Pres. BERNARD H. FALK.

Engineering and Machinery
(see also Electricity and Construction)

Abrasive Engineering Society: 118 Main St, POB 441, Connoquenessi, PA 16027; tel. (412) 221-0909; f. 1956; 750 mems; Exec. Dir JACK MCMILLEN.

Air-Conditioning and Refrigeration Institute: 1501 Wilson Blvd, Arlington, VA 22209; tel. (703) 524-8800; telex 892351; f. 1953; 185 mems; Pres. A. W. BRASWELL.

American Consulting Engineers Council: 1015 15th St, NW, Washington, DC 20005; tel. (202) 347-7474; f. 1973; 5,000 mems; Exec. Vice-Pres. HOWARD MESSNER.

American Institute of Chemical Engineers: 345 East 47th St, New York, NY 10017; tel. (212) 705-7660; f. 1908; 50,000 mems; Pres. EDWARD MCDOWELL; Exec. Dir RICHARD EMMERT (acting).

American Institute of Mining, Metallurgical and Petroleum Engineers, Inc: 345 East 47th St, New York, NY 10017; tel. (212) 705-7695; f. 1871; four constituent socs representing 79,000 mems; Exec. Dir ROBERT H. MARCRUM.

American Railway Engineering Association: 50 F St, NW, Suite 7702, Washington, DC 20001; tel. (202) 639-2190; telex 892352; f. 1899; 4,200 mems; Exec. Dir L. T. CERNY.

American Society of Civil Engineers: 345 East 47th St, New York, NY 10017; tel. (212) 705-7496; telex 422847; fax (212) 980-4681; f. 1852; 108,000 mems; Exec. Dir EDWARD O. PFRANG.

American Society of Heating, Refrigerating and Air Conditioning Engineers: 1791 Tullie Circle, NE, Atlanta, GA 30329; tel. (404) 636-8400; telex 705343; f. 1895; 50,000 mems; Exec. Dir FRANK M. CODA.

American Society of Mechanical Engineers: 345 East 47th St, New York, NY 10017; tel. (212) 705-7722; telex 5815267; f. 1880; 120,000 mems; Exec. Dir PAUL F. ALLMENDINGER.

American Society of Naval Engineers Inc: 1452 Duke St, Alexandria, VA 22314; tel. (703) 836-6727; f. 1888; 8,000 mems; Exec. Dir Capt. (retd) JAMES L. MCVOY.

Engineering Foundation: 345 East 47th St, New York, NY 10017; tel. (212) 705-7835; telex 126022; f. 1914; 19 mems; Dir HAROLD A. COMERER.

Machinery and Allied Products Institute: 1200 18th St, NW, Washington, DC 20036; tel. (202) 331-8430; f. 1933; 500 companies, 21 asscns; Pres. KENNETH MCLENNAN.

National Machine Tool Builders' Association (NMTBA): 7901 Westpark Dr., McLean, VA 22102-4269; tel. (703) 893-2900; telex 353819; fax (703) 893-1151; f. 1902; 350 mems; Pres. JAMES A. GRAY.

Petroleum Equipment Institute: 3739 East 31st St, Tulsa, OK 74114; f. 1951; 1,050 mems.

Society of Automotive Engineers, Inc: 400 Commonwealth Dr., Warrendale, PA 15096-0001; tel. (412) 776-4841; telex 866355; f. 1905; 50,000 mems; Pres. EDWARD MABLEY; Exec. Vice-Pres. MAX E. RUMBAUGH, Jr.

Society of Naval Architects and Marine Engineers: 601 Pavonia Ave, Jersey City, NJ 07306; tel. (201) 798-4800; f. 1893; 12,000 mems; Exec. Dir ROBERT G. MENDE.

Food and Beverages

American Meat Institute: POB 3556, Washington, DC 20007; tel. (703) 841-2400; telex 5270938; f. 1906; 975 mems; Pres. C. MANLY MOLPUS.

DFA of California: 303 Brokaw Rd, POB 270A, Santa Clara, CA 95052; tel. (408) 727-9302; f. 1908; 40 mems; Pres. FRANK A. MOSEBAR.

Distilled Spirits Council of the US, Inc (DISCUS): 1250 Eye St, NW, Suite 900, Washington, DC 20005; tel. (202) 628-3544; f. 1973; 25 active mems and 65 affiliates; Pres. and CEO F. A. MEISTER.

Food Marketing Institute: 1750 K St, NW, Washington, DC 20006; tel. (202) 452-8444; telex 892722; fax (202) 429-4519; f. 1977; over 1,700 mems; Pres. ROBERT O. ADERS.

Grocery Manufacturers of America, Inc: 1010 Wisconsin Ave, NW, Suite 800, Washington, DC 20007; tel. (202) 337-9400; telex 8229364; f. 1908; 130 mems; Pres. and CEO GEORGE W. KOCH.

Millers' National Federation: 600 Maryland Ave, SW, Suite 305-W, Washington, DC 20024; tel. (202) 484-2000; f. 1902; c. 50 mems, accounting for 90% of flour produced in the USA; Pres. ROY M. HENWOOD.

National-American Wholesale Grocers' Association: 201 Park Washington Court, Falls Church, VA 22046; tel. (703) 532-9400; fax (703) 538-4673; f. 1906; 350 mems; Pres. JOHN R. BLOCK.

National Confectioners Association: 7900 Westpark Dr., McLean, VA 22102; tel. (703) 790-5750; f. 1884; 356 mems; Pres. RICHARD T. O'CONNELL.

National Dairy Council: 6300 North River Rd, Rosemont, IL 60018; tel. (312) 696-1020; f. 1915; 600 mems; Pres. Dr ELWOOD W. SPECKMANN.

National Food Brokers Association: 1010 Massachusetts Ave, NW, Washington, DC 20001; tel. (202) 789-2844; f. 1904; 2,400 mems; Pres. (vacant).

National Frozen Food Association: POB 398, Hershey, PA 17033; tel. (717) 534-1601; f. 1945; 1,050 mems; Pres. NEVIN B. MONTGOMERY.

National Grain Trade Council: 1030 15th St, NW, Washington, DC 20005; tel. (202) 842-0400; 54 mems; Pres. ROBERT R. PETERSEN.

National Grocers' Association: 1825 Samuel Morse Dr., Reston, VA 22090; tel. (703) 437-5300; f. 1982; 2,060 mems; Pres. THOMAS K. ZAUCHA.

National Live Stock and Meat Board: 444 North Michigan Ave, Chicago, IL 60611; tel. (312) 467-5520; f. 1923; mems: 28 orgs; Pres. JOHN L. HUSTON.

National Soft Drink Association: 1101 16th St, NW, Washington, DC 20036; tel. (202) 463-6732; telex 510-1004811; fax (202) 463-6731; f. 1919; 1,100 mems, 450 assoc. mems; Pres. DWIGHT C. REED.

National Sugar Brokers Association: 1 World Trade Center, Suite 5011, New York, NY 10048; tel. (212) 938-0990; f. 1903; 217 mems; Exec. Sec. F. E. WALLACE.

United Fresh Fruit and Vegetable Association: 727 North Washington St, Alexandria, VA 22314; tel. (703) 836-3410; telex 101240; f. 1904; c. 2,750 mems; Pres. ROGER J. STROH.

Iron and Steel

American Cast Metals Association: 455 State St, Des Plaines, IL 60016; tel. (312) 299-9160; f. 1987; 360 mems; Pres. PETER DUDCHENKO.

American Hardware Manufacturers Association: 931 North Plum Grove Rd, Schaumburg, IL 60173-4796; tel. (312) 605-1025; f. 1901; 1,000 mems; Pres. and CEO WILLIAM P. FARRELL.

American Iron and Steel Institute: 1000 16th St, NW, Washington, DC 20036; tel. (202) 452-7100; f. 1908; 1,313 mems; Pres. R. MILTON DEANER.

Steel Founders' Society of America: 455 State St, Des Plaines, IL 60016; tel. (312) 299-9160; f. 1902; 100 mems; Exec. Vice-Pres. JACK D. MCNAUGHTON.

Steel Service Center Institute: 1600 Terminal Tower, Cleveland, OH 44113; tel. (216) 694-3630; f. 1909; 550 mems; Pres. ANDREW G. SHARKEY, III.

Leather

Footwear Industries of America: 1420 K St, NW, Suite 600, Washington, DC 20006; tel. (202) 789-1420; telex 704676; f. 1982; 200 mems; Pres. FAWN EVENSON.

Leather Industries of America: 2501 M St, NW, Suite 350, Washington, DC 20037; tel. (202) 785-9400; telex 8220130; fax (202) 872-1356; f. 1917; 350 mems; Pres. CHARLES S. MYERS.

Luggage and Leather Goods Manufacturers of America: 350 Fifth Ave, New York, NY 10118; tel. (212) 695-2340; telex 6700973; f. 1901; 190 mems; Exec. Vice-Pres. ROBERT K. ERMATINGER.

US Hide, Skin and Leather Association: 1707 N St, NW, Washington, DC 20036; tel. (202) 833-2405; f. 1980; 130 mems; Pres. JEROME J. BREITER.

Lumber
(see also Paper)

American Forest Council: 1250 Connecticut Ave, NW, Suite 320, Washington, DC 20036; tel. (202) 463-2455; f. 1932; c. 75 mems; Pres. LAURENCE D. WISEMAN.

American Plywood Association: POB 11700, Tacoma, WA 98411; tel. (206) 565-6600; telex 327430; 124 mems; Pres. W. T. ROBISON.

American Pulpwood Association: 1025 Vermont Ave, NW, Suite 1020, Washington, DC 20005; tel. (202) 347-2900; f. 1934; 360 mems; Pres. K. S. ROLSTON.

National Forest Products Association: 1250 Connecticut Ave, NW, Suite 200, Washington, DC 20036; tel. (202) 463-2700; telex 140950; f. 1902; 169 mems; Pres. BARRY M. CULLEN.

National Lumber and Building Material Dealers Association: 40 Ivy St, SE, Washington, DC 20003; tel. (202) 547-2230; f. 1915; 24 mems; Exec. Vice-Pres. HARLAN W. HUMMEL.

National Wooden Pallet and Container Association: 1625 Massachusetts Ave, NW, Washington, DC 20036; tel. (202) 667-3670; f. 1967; 234 mems; Exec. Vice-Pres. JOHN J. HEALY.

Southern Forest Products Association: POB 52468, New Orleans, LA 70152; tel. (504) 443-4464; telex 756854; fax (504) 443-6612; f. 1914; c. 188 mems; Pres. KARL W. LINDBERG.

Western Forest Industries Association: 1500 SW Taylor, Portland, OR 97205; tel. (503) 224-5455; f. 1947; 125 mems; Exec. Vice-Pres. J. W. MCCRACKEN.

Metals
(see also Iron and Steel)

Aluminum Association, Inc: 900 19th St, NW, Washington, DC 20006; tel. (202) 862-5100; f. 1933; 92 mems; Pres. JOHN C. BARD.

American Mining Congress: 1920 N St, NW, Suite 300, Washington, DC 20036; tel. (202) 861-2800; telex 8220126; f. 1897; 450 mems; Pres. JOHN A. KNEBEL.

ASM International (American Society for Metals): Metals Park, OH 44073; tel. (216) 338-5151; telex 980619; fax (216) 338-4634; f. 1913; 54,000 mems; Man. Dir EDWARD L. LANGER.

Copper and Brass Fabricators Council Inc: 1050 17th St, NW, Washington, DC 20036; tel. (202) 833-8575; f. 1964; Pres. JOSEPH L. MAYER.

Copper Development Association Inc: Greenwich Office Park 2, POB 1840, Greenwich, CT 06836-1840; f. 1963; 100 mems; Pres. GEORGE M. HARTLEY.

Gold Institute: 1026 16th St, NW, Suite 101, Washington, DC 20036; tel. (202) 783-0500; f. 1976; mems: 65 orgs; Man. Dir JOHN H. LUTLEY.

Lead Industries Association: 292 Madison Ave, New York, NY 10017; tel. (212) 578-4750; f. 1928; 80 mem. cos; Exec. Dir J. F. SMITH.

Manufacturing Jewelers and Silversmiths of America, Inc: Omni Biltmore, Kennedy Plaza, Providence, RI 02903; tel. (401) 274-3840; f. 1903; 2,500 mems; Exec. Dir MATTHEW A. RUNCI.

Metal Powder Industries Federation: 105 College Rd East, Princeton, NJ 08540; tel. (609) 452-7700; telex 6852516; f. 1944; 260 corporate mems.

Mining and Metallurgical Society of America: 210 Post St, Suite 1102, San Francisco, CA 94108; tel. (415) 398-6925; f. 1908; 350 mems; Exec. Officer HANS W. SCHREIBER.

Silver Institute: 1026 16th St, NW, Suite 101, Washington, DC 20036; tel. (202) 783-0500; f. 1971; mems: 83 orgs; Exec. Dir JOHN H. LUTLEY.

Zinc Institute, Inc: 292 Madison Ave, New York, NY 10017; tel. (212) 578-4750; f. 1918; 40 mems; Pres. W. T. MEYER.

Paper
(see also Lumber)

American Paper Institute, Inc: 260 Madison Ave, New York, NY 10016; tel. (212) 340-0600; telex 5815104; f. 1964; 166 mems; Pres. RED CAVANEY.

National Paper Trade Association, Inc: 111 Great Neck Rd, Great Neck, NY 11021; tel. (516) 829-3070; f. 1903; 2,200 mems; Pres. JOHN J. BUCKLEY, Jr.

Paper Converters Association: 1133 15th St, NW, Washington, DC 20005; tel. (202) 429-9440; f. 1934; 36 mems; Exec. Dir KENNETH M. SUFKA.

Paper Industry Management Association: 2400 East Oakton St, Arlington Heights, IL 60005; tel. (312) 956-0250; f. 1919; 3,500 mems; Exec. Dir GEORGE J. CALIMAFOE.

Paperboard Packaging Council: 1101 Vermont Ave, NW, Suite 411, Washington, DC 20005; tel. (202) 289-4100; f. 1933; Pres. S. E. ICIEK.

Technical Association of the Pulp and Paper Industry: POB 10513, Technology Park, Atlanta, GA 30348; tel. (404) 446-1400; telex 7570145; 25,000 mems; Pres. WILLIAM H. GRIGGS; Exec. Dir W. L. CULLISON.

Wallcovering Manufacturers Association: 66 Morris Ave, Springfield, NJ 07081; tel. (201) 379-1100; f. 1973; 72 mems; Exec. Dir MAURO A. CHECCHIO.

Petroleum and Fuel

American Association of Petroleum Landmen: 777 Main St, Suite 1470, Fort Worth, TX 76102; tel. (817) 335-2275; f. 1955; 10,000 mems; Exec. Vice-Pres. HARRY L. SPRINKLE.

American Gas Association: 1515 Wilson Blvd, Arlington, VA 22209; tel. (703) 841-8400; f. 1918; 4,758 mems; Pres. GEORGE H. LAWRENCE.

American Petroleum Institute: 1220 L St, NW, Washington, DC 20005; tel. (202) 682-8000; telex 8229586; f. 1919; 5,200 mems; Chair. RICHARD M. MORROW; Pres. CHARLES J. DIBONA.

Coal Exporters' Association of the US, Inc: 1130 17th St, NW, Washington, DC 20036; tel. (202) 463-2654; telex 8221167; f. 1945; 35 mems; Exec. Dir CONNIE D. HOLMES.

Independent Petroleum Association of America: 1101 16th St, NW, Washington, DC 20036; tel. (202) 857-4722; f. 1929; 6,500 mems; Pres. H. B. SCOGGINS, Jr.

Mid-Continent Oil and Gas Association: 711 Adams Office Bldg, Tulsa, OK 74103; tel. (918) 582-5166; f. 1917; 7,500 mems; Sec.-Treas. CLARK SEIBOLD.

National Coal Association: 1130 17th St, NW, Washington, DC 20036; tel. 463-2625; f. 1917; 220 mems; Pres. C. E. BAGGE.

National Petroleum Refiners' Association: 1899 L St, NW, Suite 1000, Washington, DC 20036; tel. (202) 457-0480; f. 1902; 125 regular mems, 115 assoc. mems, 39 foreign mems; Pres. URVAN R. STERNFELS.

Printing and Publishing
(see also Publishers)

Binding Industries of America: 70 East Lake St, Chicago, IL 60601; tel. (312) 372-7606; 300 mems; Exec. Dir JAMES R. NIESEN.

Book Manufacturers' Institute: 111 Prospect St, Stamford, CT 06901; tel. (203) 324-9670; f. 1920; 90 mems; Exec. Vice-Pres. DOUGLAS E. HORNER.

Metropolitan Lithographers Association, Inc: 950 Third Ave, New York, NY 10022; tel. (212) 838-8480; 112 mems; Pres. EDWARD DENBURG; Exec. Dir AILEEN GORSCHMAN.

National Printing Equipment & Supply Association, Inc: 1899 Preston White Dr., Reston, VA 22091; tel. (703) 264-7200; telex 901753; 270 mems; Pres. REGIS J. DELMONTAGNE.

Printing Industries of America, Inc: 1730 North Lynn St, Arlington, VA 22209; tel. (703) 841-8100; f. 1887; 13,000 mems; Chair. HOWARD C. WEBBER, Jr; Pres. RAY ROPER.

Public Utilities

American Public Gas Association: 301 Maple Ave West, Section 4, Suite G, Vienna, VA 22180; tel. (703) 281-2910; f. 1961; 250 mems; Exec. Dir ARIE M. VERRIPS.

American Public Power Association: 2301 M St, NW, 3rd Floor, Washington, DC 20037; tel. (202) 775-8300; f. 1940; 1,400 mems; Exec. Dir LARRY HOBART.

American Public Works Association: 1313 East 60th St, Chicago, IL 60637; tel. (312) 667-2200; f. 1894; 22,000 mems; Exec. Dir ROBERT D. BUGHER.

American Water Works Association: 6666 West Quincy Ave, Denver, CO 80235; tel. (303) 794-7711; telex 450895; f. 1881; 42,000 mems; Exec. Dir PAUL A. SCHULTE.

Rubber

Rubber Manufacturers Association: 1400 K St, NW, Washington, DC 20005; tel. (202) 682-4800; telex 892666; f. 1915; 200 mems; Pres. DONALD G. BROTZMAN; Sec. GEORGE A. WHITE.

Rubber Trade Association of New York Inc: 80 Broad St, 27th Floor, New York, NY 10004; tel. (212) 344-7776; fax (212) 248-1072; f. 1914; 47 mems; Pres. F. J. RANIOLO.

Stone, Clay and Glass Products

Flat Glass Marketing Association: White Lakes Professional Bldg, 3310 Harrison, Topeka, KS 66611; tel. (913) 266-7013; f. 1949; 125 mems; Exec. Vice-Pres. WILLIAM J. BIRCH.

National Aggregates Association: 900 Spring St, Silver Spring, MD 20910; tel. (301) 587-1400; f. 1911; 380 mems; Pres. VINCENT P. AHERN, Jr.

National Glass Association: 8200 Greensboro Dr., McLean, VA 22102; tel. (703) 442-4890; fax (703) 442-0630; f. 1948; 3,000 mems.; Exec. Vice-Pres. and CEO PHILIP J. JAMES.

National Stone Association: 1415 Elliot Pl., NW, Washington, DC 20007; tel. (202) 342-1100; f. 1945, reorg. 1985; 400 mems; Co-Pres. JAMES H. WILLIAMS, WILLIAM L. CARTER.

Textiles

American Apparel Manufacturers Association: 1611 North Kent St, Suite 800, Arlington, VA 22209; tel. (703) 524-1864; f. 1962; 450 mems; Pres. ELLIS E. MEREDITH.

American Textile Manufacturers Institute, Inc: 1101 Connecticut Ave, NW, Suite 300, Washington, DC 20036; tel. (202) 862-0500; telex 8229489; 250 mems; Exec. Vice-Pres. CARLOS MOORE.

The Custom Tailors and Designers Association of America, Inc: 17 East 45th St, New York, NY 10017; tel. (212) 661-1960; f. 1881; 350 mems; Exec. Dir IRMA B. LIPKIN.

Knitted Textile Association: 386 Park Ave South, Suite 901, New York, NY 10016; tel. (212) 689-3807; f. 1965; 160 mems; Exec. Dir DAVID HERRICK.

Linen Trade Association: 11 West 42nd St, New York, NY 10036; tel. (212) 944-2230; f. 1891; 30 mems; Sec. LAURA E. JONES.

Man-Made Fiber Producers Association Inc: 1150 17th St, NW, Washington, DC 20036; tel. (202) 296-6508; 15 mems; Pres. PAUL T. O'DAY.

Menswear Retailers of America: 2011 Eye St, NW, Washington, DC 20006; tel. (202) 347-1932; f. 1916; 9,000 mems; Exec. Dir TOM L. MOORE.

National Knitwear Manufacturers Association: 365 South St, Morristown, NJ 07960; tel. (201) 326-1650; f. 1866; Pres. ROBERT E. BLANCHARD.

National Knitwear and Sportswear Association: 386 Park Ave South, New York, NY 10016; tel. (212) 683-7520; f. 1918; 600 mems; Exec. Dir SETH M. BODNER.

National Outerwear and Sportswear Association: One Penn Plaza, New York, NY 10119; tel. (212) 594-6647; f. 1942; 120 mems; Exec. Dir WILLIAM H. FITZMAURICE.

Northern Textile Association: 230 Congress St, Boston, MA 02110; tel. (617) 542-8220; f. 1854; 300 mems; Pres. KARL SPILHAUS.

Southern Textile Association: 509 Francisca, POB 190, Cary, NC 27511; tel. (919) 467-7189; f. 1908; 1,300 mems; Sec.-Treas. JACK KISSIAH.

United Infants' and Children's Wear Association Inc: 520 Eighth Ave, New York, NY 10018; tel. (212) 244-2953; f. 1933; 50 mems; Exec. Dir ABRAHAM ELIASBERG.

Wool Manufacturers Council: 230 Congress St, Boston, MA 02110; tel. (617) 542-8220; f. 1956; 30 mems; Chair. JOHN L. GLIDDEN.

Tobacco

Retail Tobacco Dealers of America, Inc: Statler Hilton Hotel, Seventh Ave at 33rd St, New York, NY 10001; tel. (212) 244-8650; f. 1932; 5,000 mems; Man. Dir MALCOLM L. FLEISCHER.

Tobacco Associates: 1101 17th St, NW, Suite 912, Washington, DC 20036; tel. (202) 659-1160; telex 64361; f. 1947; 400,000 mems; Pres. C. N. WAYNE, Jr.

Tobacco Merchants Association of the US: 1220 Broadway, New York, NY 10001; tel. (212) 239-4435; f. 1915; 130 mems; Pres. HOWARD B. CONE; Exec. Dir FARRELL DELMAN.

Transport

Aerospace Industries Association of America: 1250 I St, NW, Washington, DC 20005; tel. (202) 371-8400; f. 1919; 48 mems; Pres. DON FUQUA.

Air Transport Association of America: 1709 New York Ave, NW, Washington, DC 20006-5206; tel. (202) 626-4000; f. 1936; mems: 27 airlines representing more than 98% of US scheduled airline passenger traffic; Pres. WILLIAM F. BOLGER.

American Bureau of Shipping: 45 Eisenhower Dr., POB 910, Paramus, NJ 07653; tel. (201) 368-9100; f. 1862; 565 mems; Chair. and Pres. RICHARD T. SOPER.

American Bus Association: 1025 Connecticut Ave, NW, Washington, DC 20036; tel. (202) 293-5890; f. 1926; 3,500 mems; Pres. NORMAN R. SHERLOCK.

American Institute of Merchant Shipping: 1000 16th St, NW, Suite 511, Washington, DC 20036; tel. (202) 775-4399; telex 89424; fax (202) 659-3795; f. 1969; 21 mems; represents owners and operators of US-flag tankers, bulk carriers and container vessels; Pres. ERNEST J. CORRADO.

American Public Transit Association: 1201 New York Ave, NW, Suite 400, Washington, DC 20005; tel. (202) 898-4000; f. 1974; 900 mems; Exec. Vice-Pres. JACK R. GILSTRAP.

American Short Line Railroad Association: 2000 Massachusetts Ave, NW, Washington, DC 20036; tel. (202) 785-2250; f. 1913; 555 mems; Pres. P. HOWARD CROFT.

American Trucking Associations: 2200 Mill Rd, Alexandria, VA 22314; tel. (703) 838-1700; f. 1933; 3,400 mems; Pres. and CEO THOMAS J. DONOHUE.

Association of American Railroads: 50 F St, NW, Washington, DC 20001; tel. (202) 639-2100; f. 1934; mems; 65 system lines comprising 113 railroads in the USA, Canada and Mexico; Pres. and CEO WILLIAM DEMPSEY.

Independent Truck Owner/Operator Association: POB 621, Stoughton, MA 02072; tel. (617) 341-2030; f. 1981; 7,200 mems; Pres. MARSHALL SIEGEL.

Motor Vehicle Manufacturers Association of the US: 300 New Center Bldg, Detroit, MI 48202; tel. (313) 872-4311; telex 1009770; f. 1912; 11 mems; Pres. THOMAS H. HANNA.

National Automobile Dealers Association: 8400 Westpark Dr., McLean, VA 22102; tel. (703) 821-7000; 19,600 mems; Exec. Vice-Pres. F. E. MCCARTHY.

Shipbuilders Council of America: 1100 Vermont Ave, NW, Washington, DC 20005; tel. (202) 775-9060; f. 1920; 74 mems; Pres. JOHN J. STOCKER.

Miscellaneous

American Advertising Federation: 1400 K St, NW, Suite 1000, Washington, DC 20005; tel. (202) 898-0089; f. 1905; 25,000 individual and 300 corporate mems; Pres. HOWARD H. BELL.

American Association of Cost Engineers: 308 Monongahela Bldg, Morgantown, WV 26505; tel. (304) 296-8444; f. 1956; 6,000 mems; Exec. Dir KENNETH K. HUMPHREYS.

American Association of Exporters and Importers: 11 West 42nd St, 30th Floor, New York, NY 10036; tel. (212) 944-2230; f. 1921; 1,200 mems; Pres. EUGENE MILOSH.

American Farm Bureau Federation: 225 Touhy Ave, Park Ridge, IL 60068-5874; tel. (312) 399-5700; f. 1919; 3.3m. mems; Pres. DEAN R. KLECKNER.

American Management Association: 135 West 50th St, New York, NY 10020; tel. (212) 586-8100; f. 1923; 75,000 corporate and individual mems; Pres. and CEO Dr THOMAS R. HORTON.

American Marketing Association: 250 South Wacker Dr., Chicago, IL 60606; 40,000 mems.

American Society of Association Executives: 1575 Eye St, NW, Washington, DC 20005; tel. (202) 626-2723; f. 1920; 12,500 mems; Pres. R. WILLIAM TAYLOR.

American Society of Professional Estimators: 6911 Richmond Highway, Suite 230, Alexandra, VA 22306; tel. (703) 765-2700; f. 1956; 2,200 mems; Exec. Dir BEVERLY S. PERRELL.

American Subcontractors Association: 1004 Duke St, Alexandria, VA 22314; tel. (703) 684-3450; f. 1966; 7,000 mems; Exec. Vice-Pres. CHRIS S. STINEBERT.

Association of Operative Millers: 4901 Main St, Suite 414, POB 30299, Kansas City, MO 64112; tel. (816) 561-4171; f. 1895; 1,500 mems; Exec. Vice-Pres. G. ROBERT COUGHENOUR.

Farmers' Educational and Cooperative Union of America (National Farmers Union): POB 39251, Denver, CO 80251; tel. (303) 337-5500; f. 1902; 250,000 mems; Pres. LELAND SWENSON.

Motion Picture Association of America, Inc: 1133 Ave of the Americas, New York, NY 10036; tel. (212) 840-6161; telex 236317; f. 1922; 8 mems; Pres. JACK J. VALENTI.

National Association of Manufacturers: 1331 Pennsylvania Ave, NW, Suite 1500 North, Washington, DC 20004-1703; tel. (202) 637-3000; f. 1895; 13,500 mems and subsidiary mems; Pres. ALEXANDER B. TROWBRIDGE.

National Association of Purchasing Management: 2055 East Centennial Circle, POB 22160, Tempe, AZ 85285-2160; tel. (602) 752-6276; f. 1915; 29,000 mems; Exec. Vice-Pres. R. J. BAKER.

National Association of Realtors: 430 North Michigan Ave, Chicago, IL 60611; tel. (312) 329-8200; f. 1908; 670,000 mems; Exec. Vice-Pres. W. D. NORTH.

National Cooperative Business Association: 1401 New York Ave, NW, Suite 1100, Washington, DC 20005; f. 1916; Pres. ROBERT D. SCHERER.

National Farmers' Organization: 720 Davis Ave, Corning, IA 50841; tel. (712) 322-3131; fax (515) 322-3743; f. 1955; Pres. DEVON R. WOODLAND.

National Retail Merchants Association Inc: 100 West 31st St, New York, NY 10001; tel. (212) 244-8780; telex 220883; f. 1911; Chair. EDWARD FINKELSTEIN; Pres. J. R. WILLIAMS.

Packaging Institute International: 20 Summer St, Stamford, CT 06901; tel. (203) 325-9010; f. 1939; 3,000 mems; Exec. Dir CAROL M. NEWMAN.

Trade Unions

In 1985 there were 175 trade unions, of which 93 were affiliated to the American Federation of Labor and Congress of Industrial Organizations (AFL-CIO). Many trade unions based in the USA have members throughout North America. About one-third of Canada's trade-union members belong to unions having headquarters in the USA.

American Federation of Labor and Congress of Industrial Organizations (AFL-CIO): 815 16th St, NW, Washington, DC 20006; tel. (202) 637-5000; f. 1955; 90 affiliated unions with total membership of 14.1m. (1987); Pres. LANE KIRKLAND; Sec.-Treas. THOMAS R. DONAHUE.

AFL-CIO Affiliates
(with 50,000 members and over)

Aluminum, Brick and Glass Workers International Union: 3362 Hollenberg Dr., Bridgeton, MO 63044; tel. (314) 739-6142; f. 1982; 55,000 mems; Pres. ERNIE J. LABAFF.

Amalgamated Clothing and Textile Workers' Union: 15 Union Sq., New York, NY 10003; tel. (212) 242-0700; fax (212) 255-7230; f. 1976; 266,000 mems; Pres. JACK SHEINKMAN; Sec.-Treas. CHARLES SALLEE.

Amalgamated Transit Union: 5025 Wisconsin Ave, NW, 3rd Floor, Washington, DC 20016; tel. (202) 537-1645; f. 1892; 165,000 mems; Pres. JAMES LA SALA.

American Federation of Government Employees: 80 F St, NW, Washington, DC 20001; tel. (202) 737-8700; f. 1932; 210,000 mems; Nat. Pres. KENNETH T. BLAYLOCK; Exec. Vice-Pres. JOHN N. STURDIVANT; Sec.-Treas. ALLEN H. KAPLAN.

American Federation of Musicians of the United States and Canada: 1501 Broadway, Suite 600, New York, NY 10036; tel. (212) 869-1330; f. 1896; 200,000 mems; Pres. J. MARTIN EMERSON; Sec.-Treas. KELLY L. CASTLEBERRY, II.

American Federation of State, County and Municipal Employees: 1625 L St, NW, Washington, DC 20036; tel. (202) 452-4800; f. 1936; 1m. mems; Pres. GERALD W. MCENTEE; Sec.-Treas. WILLIAM LUCY.

American Federation of Teachers: 555 New Jersey Ave, NW, Washington, DC 20001; tel. (202) 879-4400; telex 8220009; f. 1916; 680,000 mems; Pres. ALBERT SHANKER; Sec.-Treas. ROBERT PORTER.

American Federation of Television and Radio Artists: 260 Madison Ave, 7th Floor, New York, NY 10016-2401; f. 1937; 67,000 mems; Pres. FRANK MAXWELL.

American Postal Workers' Union: 1300 L St, NW, Washington, DC 20005; f. 1971; 330,000 mems; Pres. MORRIS BILLER; Sec.-Treas. DOUGLAS C. HOLBROOK.

Associated Actors and Artistes of America: 165 West 46th St, New York, NY 10036; tel. (212) 869-0358; 100,000 mems; Pres. FREDERICK O'NEAL; Exec. Sec. JOHN HALL.

Bakery, Confectionery and Tobacco Workers' International Union: 10401 Connecticut Ave, Kensington, MD 20895; tel. (301) 933-8600; f. 1886; 145,000 mems; Pres. JOHN DECONCINI; Sec.-Treas. RENE RONDOU.

Brewery and Soft Drink Workers' Conference—USA and Canada: 1400 Renaissance Dr., Suite 406, Park Ridge, IL 60068; tel. (312) 299-3406; f. 1886; 75,000 mems; Sec.-Treas. CHARLES KLARE.

Brotherhood of Maintenance of Way Employees: 12050 Woodward Ave, Detroit, MI 48203-3596; tel. (313) 868-0490; telex 8685122; f. 1887; 75,000 mems; Pres. GEOFFREY N. ZEH; Sec.-Treas. MAC A. FLEMING.

Brotherhood of Railway Carmen of the United States and Canada: 4929 Main St, Kansas City, MO 64112; tel. (816) 561-1112; f. 1888; 50,000 mems; Gen. Pres. C. E. WHEELER; Sec.-Treas. ORVILLE P. CHANNELL, Jr.

Civil Service Employees' Association, Inc: 143 Washington Ave, Albany, NY 12210; tel. (518) 434-0191; f. 1910; 220,000 mems; Pres. JOSEPH E. MCDERMOTT.

Communications Workers of America: 1925 K St, NW, Washington, DC 20006; tel. (202) 728-2300; f. 1939; 700,000 mems; Pres. MORTON BAHR; Sec.-Treas. JAMES B. BOOE.

Glass Molders, Pottery, Plastics & Allied Workers' International Union: 608 East Baltimore Pike, POB 607, Media, PA 19063; tel. (215) 565-5051; f. 1842; 85,000 mems; Pres. JAMES E. HATFIELD; Sec.-Treas. FRANK W. CARTER.

Graphic Communications International Union: 1900 L St, NW, Washington, DC 20036; tel. (202) 462-1400; f. 1983; 187,000 mems; Pres. JAMES J. NORTON; Sec.-Treas. GUY DEVITO.

Hotel Employees & Restaurant Employees International Union: 1219 28th St, NW, Washington, DC 20007; f. 1981; 330,000 mems; Pres. EDWARD T. HANLEY; Sec.-Tres. HERMAN LEAVITT.

International Alliance of Theatrical Stage Employees and Moving Picture Machine Operators of the US and Canada: 1515 Broadway, Suite 601, New York, NY 10036; tel. (212) 730-1770; f. 1893; 61,000 mems; Pres. ALFRED W. DiTOLLA; Sec.-Treas. JAMES J. RILEY.

International Association of Bridge, Structural and Ornamental Iron Workers: 1750 New York Ave, NW, Suite 400, Washington, DC 20006; tel. (202) 383-4810; f. 1896; 153,000 mems; Pres. JUEL D. DRAKE; Sec. JAKE WEST.

International Association of Fire Fighters: 1750 New York Ave, NW, Washington, DC 20006; tel. (202) 737-8484; f. 1918; 172,000 mems; Pres. ALFRED K. WHITEHEAD; Sec.-Treas. VINCENT J. BOLLON.

International Association of Machinists and Aerospace Workers: 1300 Connecticut Ave, NW, Washington, DC 20036; tel. (202) 857-5200; f. 1888; 800,000 mems; Int. Pres. WILLIAM W. WINPISINGER; Gen. Sec.-Treas. TOM DUCY.

International Brotherhood of Boilermakers, Iron Shipbuilders, Blacksmiths, Forgers and Helpers: 570 New Brotherhood Bldg, 8th and State Ave, Kansas City, KS 66101; tel. (913) 371-2640; f. 1880; 102,000 mems; Pres. CHARLES W. JONES; Sec.-Treas. CHARLES F. MORAN.

International Brotherhood of Electrical Workers: 1125 15th St, NW, Washington, DC 20005; tel. (202) 833-7000; f. 1891; 1m. mems; Pres. J. J. BARRY; Sec. JACK F. MOORE.

International Brotherhood of Painters and Allied Trades: 1750 New York Ave, NW, Washington, DC 20006; tel. (202) 637-0720; f. 1887; 162,000 mems; Gen. Pres. WILLIAM A. DUVAL; Sec.-Treas. ROBERT PETERSDORF.

International Brotherhood of Teamsters, Chauffeurs, Warehousemen and Helpers of America: 25 Louisiana Ave, NW, Washington, DC 20001; tel. (202) 624-6800; f. 1903; 1.7m. mems; Pres. WILLIAM J. McCARTHY; Gen. Sec.-Treas. WELDON L. MATHIS.

International Chemical Workers' Union: 1655 West Market St, Akron, OH 44313; tel. (216) 867-2444; f. 1944; 70,000 mems; Pres. FRANK D. MARTINO; Sec.-Treas. W. J. SPARKS.

International Ladies' Garment Workers' Union: 1710 Broadway, New York, NY 10019; tel. (212) 265-7000; f. 1900; 200,000 mems; Pres. JAY MAZUR.

International Longshoremen's Association: 17 Battery Pl., Rm 1530, New York, NY 10004; tel. (212) 425-1200; f. 1892; 77,000 mems; Pres. THOMAS W. GLEASON; Sec.-Treas. HARRY R. HASSELGREN.

International Printing and Graphic Communications Union: 1730 Rhode Island Ave, NW, Washington, DC 20036; tel. (202) 293-2185; f. 1889; 120,000 mems; Pres. SOL FISHKO; Sec.-Treas. MICHAEL P. McNALLY.

International Typographical Union: POB 157, Colorado Springs, CO 80901; tel. (303) 636-2341; f. 1852; 70,000 mems; Pres. ROBERT S. McMICHEN; Sec.-Treas. THOMAS W. KOPECK.

International Union of Allied Industrial Workers of America: 3520 West Oklahoma Ave, Milwaukee, WI 53215; tel. (414) 645-9500; f. 1935; 70,000 mems; Int. Pres. DOMINICK D'AMBROSIO; Sec.-Treas. WILLIAM J. SALAMONE.

International Union of Bricklayers and Allied Craftsmen: 815 15th St, NW, Washington, DC 20005; tel. (202) 783-3788; f. 1865; 110,000 mems; Pres. JOHN T. JOYCE; Sec.-Treas. EDWARD M. BELLUCCI.

International Union of Electronic, Electrical, Technical, Salaried, Machine and Furniture Workers: 1126 16th St, NW, Washington, DC 20036; tel. (202) 296-1200; f. 1949; 200,000 mems.; Pres. WILLIAM H. BYWATER; Sec.-Treas. EDWARD FIRE.

International Union of Operating Engineers: 1125 17th St, NW, Washington, DC 20036; tel. (202) 429-9100; f. 1896; 375,000 mems; Gen. Pres. LARRY DUGAN, Jr; Gen. Sec.-Treas. FRANK HANLEY.

International Union of Police Associations: 815 16th St, NW, Rm 507, Washington, DC 20006; tel. (202) 628-2740; f. 1978; 20,000 mems; Pres. ROBERT B. KLIESMET.

International Union of United Automobile, Aerospace and Agricultural Implement Workers of America: 8000 East Jefferson Ave, Detroit, MI 48214; tel. (313) 926-5000; f. 1935; 1.2m. mems; Pres. OWEN F. BIEBER; Sec.-Treas. (vacant).

International Woodworkers of America: 1622 North Lombard St, Portland, OR 97217; tel. (503) 285-5281; f. 1936; 100,000 mems; Int. Pres. KEITH JOHNSON; Sec.-Treas. ROBERT GERWIG.

Laborers' International Union of North America: 905 16th St, NW, Washington, DC 20006; tel. (202) 737-8320; f. 1903; 430,000 mems; Pres. ANGELO FOSCO; Gen. Sec.-Treas. ARTHUR E. COIA.

Marine Engineer Beneficial Association/National Maritime Union: 346 West 17th St, New York, NY 10001; 50,000 mems; Pres. C. E. DeFRIES.

National Association of Letter Carriers: 100 Indiana Ave, NW, Washington, DC 20001; tel. (202) 393-4695; f. 1889; 310,000 mems; Pres. VINCENT R. SOMBROTTO; Sec.-Treas. RICHARD P. O'CONNELL.

National Union of Hospital and Health Care Employees: 330 West 42nd St, 19th Floor, New York, NY 10036; tel. (212) 947-1944; f. 1973; 150,000 mems; Pres. HENRY NICHOLAS.

Office and Professional Employees' International Union: 265 West 14th St, Suite 610, New York, NY 10011; tel. (212) 675-3210; telex 3202918; f. 1945; 135,000 mems; Int. Pres. JOHN KELLY; Sec.-Treas. WILLIAM A. LOWE.

Oil, Chemical and Atomic Workers' International Union: POB 2812, Denver, CO 80201; tel. (303) 987-2229; f. 1918; 110,000 mems; Pres. JOSEPH M. MISBRENER; Sec.-Treas. MICHAEL RICIGLIANO.

Operative Plasterers' and Cement Masons' International Association of the United States and Canada: 1125 17th St and K St, NW, Washington, DC 20036; tel. (202) 393-6569; f. 1864; 65,000 mems; Pres. ROBERT J. HOLTON; Sec.-Treas. VINCENT J. PANEPINTO.

Retail, Wholesale and Department Store Union: 30 East 29th St, New York, NY 10016; tel. (212) 684-5300; f. 1937; 200,000 mems; Pres. LENORE MILLER; Sec.-Treas. GUY DICKINSON.

Screen Actors' Guild: 7065 Hollywood Blvd, Hollywood, CA 90028-6007; tel. (213) 465-4600; f. 1933; 71,000 mems; Pres. BARRY GORDON; Nat. Exec. Dir KEN ORSATTI.

Seafarers' International Union of North America: 5201 Auth Way, Camp Springs, MD 20746; tel. (301) 899-0675; f. 1938; 90,000 mems; Pres. FRANK DROZAK; Sec.-Treas. JOSEPH DiGIORGIO.

Service Employees' International Union: 1313 L St, NW, Washington, DC 20005; tel. (202) 898-3200; fax (202) 898-3284; f. 1921; 850,000 mems; Pres. JOHN J. SWEENEY; Sec.-Treas. RICHARD W. CORDTZ.

Sheet Metal Workers' International Association: 1750 New York Ave, NW, Washington, DC 20006; tel. (202) 783-5880; f. 1888; 150,000 mems; Gen. Pres. EDWARD J. CARLOUGH; Sec.-Treas. LONNIE A. BASSETT.

Transport Workers' Union of America: 80 West End Ave, New York, NY 10023; tel (212) 873-6000; f. 1934; 91,000 mems; Int. Pres. JOHN E. LAWE; Sec.-Treas. GEORGE LEITZ.

Transportation and Communications International Union: 3 Research Pl., Rockville, MD 20850; tel. (301) 948-4910; f. 1899; 160,000 mems; Pres. RICHARD I. KILROY; Sec.-Treas. D. A. BOBO.

United Association of Journeymen and Apprentices of the Plumbing and Pipe Fitting Industry of the United States and Canada: 901 Massachusetts Ave, NW, Washington, DC 20001; tel. (202) 628-5823; f. 1889; 325,000 mems; Pres. MARVIN J. BOEDE; Sec.-Treas. JOSEPH A. WALSH.

United Brotherhood of Carpenters and Joiners of America: 101 Constitution Ave, NW, Washington, DC 20001; tel. (202) 546-6206; f. 1881; 650,000 mems; Pres. SIGURD LUCASSEN; Sec. JOHN S. ROGERS.

United Farm Workers of America: La Paz, Keene, CA 93531; tel. (805) 822-5571; f. 1962; 100,000 mems; Pres. CESAR ESTRADA CHAVEZ.

United Food and Commercial Workers International Union: 1775 K St, NW, Washington, DC 20006; tel. (202) 223-3111; f. 1979; 1.3m. mems; Int. Pres. WILLIAM H. WYNN; Int. Sec.-Treas. JERRY MENAPACE.

United Paperworkers International Union: 3340 Perimeter Hill Dr., Nashville, TN 37202; f. 1884; 245,000 mems; Pres. WAYNE E. GLENN; Sec.-Treas. NICHOLAS C. VRATARIC.

United Rubber, Cork, Linoleum and Plastic Workers of America: URWA Bldg, 87 South High St, Akron, OH 44308; tel. (216) 376-6181; f. 1935; 116,000 mems; Pres. MILAN STONE; Sec.-Treas. KENNETH L. COSS.

United Steelworkers of America: 5 Gateway Center, Pittsburgh, PA 15222; tel. (412) 562-2400; f. 1936; 833,000 mems; Int. Pres. LYNN WILLIAMS; Sec. EDGAR BALL.

Utility Workers' Union of America: 815 16th St, NW, Suite 605, Washington, DC 20006; tel. (202) 347-8105; f. 1945; 60,000 mems; Pres. JAMES JOY, Jr; Sec.-Treas. MARSHALL M. HICKS.

Independent Unions
(with 50,000 members and over)

American Association of Classified School Employees: 2000 Pennsylvania Ave, NW, Washington, DC 20006; tel. (202) 429-9725; f. 1958; 200,000 mems; Exec. Dir CRAIG J. RANCOURT.

American Nurses' Association: 1101 14th St, NW, Suite 200, Washington, DC 20005; tel. (202) 789-1800; f. 1896; 53 constituent state asscns comprising 188,000 mems; Pres. LUCILLE A. JOEL; Exec. Dir JUDITH RYAN.

Brotherhood of Locomotive Engineers: 1365 Ontario Ave, Cleveland, OH 44114; tel. (216) 241-2630; f. 1863; 55,000 mems; Pres. R. E. DELANEY; Gen. Sec.-Treas. JOHN D. RINEHART.

Fraternal Order of Police: 2100 Gardiner Lane, Louisville, KY 40205-2962; fax (502) 459-2000; 195,000 mems; Nat. Pres. DEWEY STOKES; Nat. Sec. CHARLES R. ORMS.

International Allied Printing Trades Association: 6025 Chippewa, Rm 302, St Louis, MO 63109; tel. (314) 353-2248; f. 1911; 300,000 mems; Sec.-Treas. LEO L. VOHSEN.

International Longshoremen's and Warehousemen's Union: 1188 Franklin St, San Francisco, CA 94109; tel. (415) 775-0533; f. 1937; 55,000 mems; Pres. JAMES R. HERMAN; Sec.-Treas. CURTIS MCCLAIN.

International Union, United Mineworkers of America: 900 15th St, NW, Washington, DC 20005; tel. (202) 842-7200; f. 1890; 240,000 mems; Int. Pres. RICHARD L. TRUMKA; Sec.-Treas. JOHN J. BANOVIC.

Machinists Non-Partisan Political League: 1300 Connecticut Ave, NW, Washington, DC 20036; tel. (202) 857-5295; f. 1947; 930,000 mems; Dir WILLIAM J. HOLAYTER.

National Alliance of Postal and Federal Employees: 1628 11th St, NW, Washington, DC 20001; tel. (202) 939-6325; f. 1913; 90,000 mems; Nat. Pres. ROBERT L. WHITE.

National Association of American School Employees and Retirees: 13902 Robson, Detroit, MI 48227; tel. (313) 837-0627; f. 1962; 195,000 mems; Pres. WILLIAM B. JOHNSON.

National Education Association of the United States: 1201 16th St, NW, Washington, DC 20036; tel. (202) 833-4000; 1.7m. mems; Pres. MARY H. FUTRELL; Exec. Dir DON CAMERON.

National Federation of Federal Employees: 1016 16th St, NW, Washington, DC 20036; tel. (202) 862-4400; f. 1917; 60,000 mems; Pres. JAMES M. PEIRCE, Jr; Sec.-Treas. ABRAHAM ORLOFSKY.

National Rural Letter Carriers' Association: 1448 Duke St, Suite 100, Alexandria, VA 22314; tel. (703) 684-5545; f. 1903; 72,000 mems; Pres. DALLAS N. FIELDS.

National Treasury Employees Union: 1730 K St, NW, Suite 1101, Washington, DC 20006; f. 1938; 120,000 mems; Nat. Pres. ROBERT M. TOBIAS.

United Transportation Union: 14600 Detroit Ave, Cleveland, OH 44107; tel. (216) 228-9400; f. 1969; 120,000 mems; Pres. FRED A. HARDIN; Sec.-Treas. THOMAS J. MCGUIRE.

University Professors, American Association of: 1012 14th St, NW, Washington, DC 20005; tel. (202) 737-5900; f. 1915; 44,000 mems; Pres. CAROL SIMPSON STERN.

EXTERNAL TRADE

Principal Commodities

($ million, adjusted to balance-of-payments basis, excluding military.
Source: Bureau of Economic Analysis, US Department of Commerce, *Survey of Current Business*.)

Imports

	1986	1987	1988
Food, feeds and beverages . .	24,346	24,809	24,909
Agricultural	17,702	17,266	17,451
Coffee, cocoa and sugar .	5,387	3,664	3,137
Green coffee . . .	4,263	2,710	2,283
Meat products and poultry .	2,820	3,305	3,475
Vegetables, fruits, nuts and preparations . . .	4,092	4,426	4,633
Wine and related products .	1,760	1,916	1,905
Other	3,701	3,955	4,301
Non-agricultural	6,644	7,543	7,458
Fish and shellfish . . .	4,746	5,591	5,422
Whisky and other alcoholic beverages	1,247	1,356	1,501
Industrial supplies and materials	104,263	113,746	122,350
Agricultural	2,730	3,106	3,400
Non-agricultural	101,533	110,640	118,950
Energy products . . .	38,574	46,781	43,394
Fuels and lubricants* . .	37,702	45,796	42,550
Paper and base stocks . .	7,382	8,670	10,211
Textile supplies and related materials.	4,558	5,417	5,497
Chemicals (excl. medicinals)	8,972	9,812	12,369
Building materials (excl. metals)	7,438	7,390	7,400
Other non-metals . . .	4,430	4,546	5,032
Metals and non-metallic products	30,179	28,024	35,047
Steelmaking materials .	1,193	1,277	1,920
Iron and steel products .	9,974	10,822	12,579
Non-ferrous metals . .	15,264	11,894	15,472
Non-monetary gold . .	7,859	3,784	4,860
Other precious metals .	2,159	1,889	2,026
Bauxite and aluminium .	2,654	2,982	3,669
Other	2,592	3,239	4,917
Other metallic and non-metallic products. . .	3,748	4,031	5,076
Capital goods (excl. automotive)	72,139	85,129	101,757
Machinery (excl. consumer-type)	65,025	77,408	93,441
Electric generating machinery, electric apparatus and parts . .	8,047	9,518	11,529

(*continued*)	1986	1987	1988
Non-electric (incl. parts and attachments). . . .	56,978	67,890	81,912
Oil drilling, mining and construction machinery	3,125	3,502	4,229
Industrial engines, pumps and compressors . .	2,682	3,215	3,962
Machine tools and metal-working machinery. .	3,440	3,320	3,672
Measuring, testing and control instruments .	2,032	2,472	2,939
Other industrial, agricultural and service industry machinery .	15,831	18,074	20,889
Computers, peripherals and parts . . .	11,020	14,839	18,331
Semiconductors . . .	5,947	7,784	10,961
Telecommunications equipment	6,924	8,128	9,396
Other office and business machines	3,315	3,605	4,130
Scientific, hospital, and medical equipment and parts	2,662	2,951	3,403
Transportation equipment (excl. automotive) . . .	7,114	7,721	8,316
Civilian aircraft, engines and parts . . .	6,038	6,577	7,544
Civilian aircraft (complete)	1,902	2,081	2,691
Automotive vehicles, parts and engines	78,110	85,174	87,941
From Canada . . .	24,668	24,531	29,200
Passenger cars (new and used)	11,681	10,185	13,256
Trucks, buses and special-purpose vehicles . .	4,231	5,261	6,082
Engines and engine parts .	1,600	1,720	1,977
Other parts and accessories	7,156	7,365	7,885
From other areas . . .	53,442	60,643	58,741
Passenger cars (new and used)	33,469	37,737	33,794
Trucks, buses and special-purpose vehicles . .	6,198	5,483	4,266
Engines and engine parts .	3,035	3,696	4,557
Other parts and accessories	10,740	13,727	16,124

(*continued*)

Imports—(*continued*)

	1986	1987	1988
Consumer goods (non-food; excl. automotive) . .	79,179	88,824	96,379
Consumer non-durables (manufactured). . .	33,393	39,431	43,092
Textile apparel and household goods (excl. rugs).	17,449	20,292	20,764
Footwear	4,878	5,558	5,902
Consumer durables (manufactured). . .	41,236	44,894	47,744
Household and kitchen appliances, and other household goods . .	13,372	16,066	17,215

* Includes nuclear fuel materials and fuels.

(*continued*)	1986	1987	1988
Toys, shooting, and sporting goods (incl. bicycles) .	5,778	7,196	7,982
Television and video receivers. . . .	8,095	6,410	5,822
Radio and stereo equipment (incl. records, tapes and discs) . . .	4,229	4,851	5,630
Unmanufactured consumer goods . . .	4,550	4,499	5,543
Imports not elsewhere classified .	10,388	12,084	13,130
US goods returned . . .	6,450	7,192	7,876
Total	368,425	409,766	446,466

Exports

	1986	1987	1988
Foods, feeds and beverages .	23,273	24,757	32,944
Agricultural	21,351	22,658	30,139
Grains and preparations .	9,758	10,515	15,430
Wheat	3,288	3,272	5,108
Corn	2,659	3,260	5,136
Soybeans	4,315	4,332	4,850
Meat products and poultry .	1,497	1,891	2,639
Vegetables, fruits, nuts and preparations . . .	2,869	3,323	3,921
Other	2,912	2,597	3,299
Non-agricultural . . .	1,922	2,099	2,805
Fish and shellfish . .	1,424	1,797	2,400
Industrial supplies and materials	64,068	68,952	88,824
Agricultural	5,387	6,307	7,319
Raw cotton. . . .	823	1,658	1,987
Tobacco (unmanufactured) .	1,204	1,090	1,254
Hides and skins (incl. furs) .	1,590	1,752	1,838
Other agricultural industrial supplies . .	1,671	1,807	2,240
Non-agricultural . . .	58,681	62,645	81,505
Energy products . .	9,956	9,102	9,519
Fuels and lubricants* . .	9,945	9,092	9,468
Coal and related fuels .	4,060	3,501	4,200
Petroleum and products	4,532	4,533	4,377
Paper and base stocks . .	4,684	6,072	7,664
Textile supplies and related materials . . .	3,145	3,604	4,574
Chemicals (excl. medicinals)	17,163	20,875	25,981
Building materials (excl. metals)	3,332	4,474	6,096
Other non-metals . . .	6,244	5,313	6,641
Metals and non-metallic products	14,157	13,205	21,030
Steelmaking materials .	1,334	1,276	1,733
Iron and steel products .	1,178	1,463	2,265
Non-ferrous metals . .	8,622	6,606	12,297
Non-monetary gold . .	5,648	2,666	5,872
Other precious metals .	350	465	557
Other non-ferrous metals .	2,624	3,475	5,868
Other metallic and non-metallic products. .	3,023	3,860	4,735
Capital goods (excl. automotive) . . .	79,342	87,736	112,352
Machinery (excl. consumer-type) . . .	62,760	70,209	89,895
Electric generating machinery, electric apparatus and parts .	7,544	8,214	10,857
Non-electric (incl. parts and attachments). . . .	55,216	61,995	79,038
Oil drilling, mining and construction machinery	5,355	4,836	6,393
Industrial engines, pumps and compressors . .	2,926	3,007	3,967
Machine tools and metal-working machinery. .	1,848	2,100	2,573

* Includes nuclear fuel materials and fuels.

(*continued*)	1986	1987	1988
Measuring, testing and control instruments .	3,829	4,321	5,397
Other industrial, agricultural and service industry machinery	12,019	14,301	18,565
Computers, peripherals and parts . . .	14,310	17,735	22,374
Semiconductors . . .	4,056	5,434	7,078
Telecommunications equipment . . .	4,074	4,756	5,976
Other office and business machines . . .	1,125	1,448	1,591
Scientific, hospital and medical equipment and parts . . .	3,476	4,057	5,124
Civilian aircraft, engines and parts	14,793	15,936	20,642
Civilian aircraft (complete) .	7,333	7,528	10,282
Other transportation equipment . . .	1,789	1,591	1,815
Automotive vehicles, parts and engines . . .	24,916	27,546	32,514
To Canada . . .	19,407	20,553	22,572
Passenger cars (new and used) . . .	7,002	6,770	7,437
Trucks, buses and special-purpose vehicles . . .	2,431	3,229	3,187
Engines and engine parts .	1,729	2,166	2,069
Other parts and accessories	8,245	8,388	9,879
To other areas . . .	5,509	6,993	9,942
Passenger cars (new and used) . . .	521	1,168	2,429
Trucks, buses and special-purpose vehicles . .	611	734	1,066
Engines and engine parts .	901	932	1,221
Other parts and accessories	3,476	4,159	5,226
Consumer goods (non-food; excl. automotive) . .	14,613	18,290	24,180
Consumer non-durables (manufactured). . .	8,532	10,514	13,106
Medical, dental and pharmaceutical preparations (incl. vitamins). . . .	3,203	3,438	4,179
Consumer durables (manufactured). . .	5,034	6,965	9,962
Household and kitchen appliances, and other household goods . .	2,069	2,906	4,014
Unmanufactured consumer goods	627	811	1,112
Exports not elsewhere classified. . .	17,155	22,985	28,437
Re-exports . . .	7,197	8,926	11,937
Total	223,367	250,266	319,251

Principal Trading Partners

($ million, adjusted to balance-of-payments basis, excluding military.
Source: Bureau of Economic Analysis, US Department of Commerce, *Survey of Current Business*.)

Imports

	1986	1987	1988
Western Europe	88,959	96,127	102,000
European Communities . .	74,162	81,451	85,646
Belgium and Luxembourg .	3,938	4,223	4,502
France.	9,542	10,506	12,118
Germany, Fed. Repub. .	24,526	26,941	26,295
Italy	10,347	10,916	11,502
Netherlands . . .	4,097	4,809	5,951
United Kingdom . .	15,055	17,210	17,680
Other	6,657	6,846	7,598
Western Europe (excl. EC) .	14,797	14,676	16,554
Eastern Europe	1,979	1,920	2,165
Asia*	153,013	176,017	191,825
China, People's Repub. . .	4,690	6,300	8,535
Hong Kong	8,782	9,829	10,238
Japan	80,752	84,578	89,760
Korea, Repub. . . .	12,805	16,964	20,154
Singapore	4,589	6,148	7,943
Taiwan	19,757	24,604	24,856
South America and Caribbean .	42,014	47,291	51,421
Brazil	6,990	8,178	9,448
Mexico	17,664	20,289	23,325
Venezuela	4,811	5,652	5,163
Other	12,549	13,172	13,485
Africa	10,064	11,946	10,861
Canada	69,693	73,599	84,400
Australia	2,595	2,965	3,516

Exports

	1986	1987	1988
Western Europe	60,375	68,605	86,414
European Communities . . .	51,848	59,530	74,510
Belgium and Luxembourg .	5,456	6,147	7,353
France.	7,119	7,949	9,996
Germany, Fed. Repub. .	10,461	11,533	14,036
Italy	4,750	5,466	6,668
Netherlands . . .	7,190	8,026	9,961
United Kingdom . .	11,152	13,752	18,042
Other	5,720	6,657	8,454
Western Europe (excl. EC) .	8,527	9,075	11,904
Eastern Europe	2,074	2,262	3,796
Asia*	62,686	71,313	97,542
China, People's Repub. . .	3,065	3,512	5,028
Hong Kong	2,981	3,974	5,663
Japan	26,354	27,619	37,148
Korea, Repub. . . .	5,862	7,646	10,666
Singapore	3,344	4,044	5,756
Taiwan	5,115	7,096	11,859
South America and Caribbean .	30,757	34,971	43,624
Brazil	3,879	4,082	4,240
Mexico	12,310	14,558	20,573
Venezuela	3,094	3,534	4,525
Other	11,474	12,797	14,286
Africa	5,636	5,581	7,195
Canada	56,503	62,005	73,540
Australia	5,072	5,291	6,804

* Including New Zealand.

External Trade Organizations

American Association of Exporters and Importers: 11 West 42nd St, 30th Floor, New York, NY 10036; tel. (212) 944-2230; f. 1921; 1,200 mems; Pres. EUGENE J. MILOSH.

American Cotton Exporters' Association: POB 3366, Memphis, TN 38173; tel. (901) 525-2272; f. 1975; 53 mems; Sec. EARLE N. BILLINGS.

American League for Exports and Security Assistance: 122 C St, NW, Suite 740, Washington, DC 20001; tel. (202) 783-0051; f. 1977; promotes the sale of US goods and services abroad; 29 mems; Exec. Vice-Pres. JOEL L. JOHNSON.

American–Mideast Business Association: The Graybar Bldg, 420 Lexington Ave, Suite 2431, New York, NY 10017; tel. (212) 986-7229; f. 1951; Pres. I. F. YUSIF.

American Motion Picture Export Company: 1133 Ave of the Americas, New York, NY 10036; tel. (212) 840-6161; f. 1965; eight mems; Vice-Pres. NORMAN ALTERMAN.

American Society of International Executives: 1777 Walton, Suite 419, Dublin Hall, Blue Bell, PA 19422; tel. (215) 643-3040; f. 1964; professional society which sets standards for personnel engaged in international trade; 400 mems; Pres. ANTHONY SWARTZ.

American Toy Export Association: c/o Kraemer Mercantile Corpn. US, Inc: 200 Fifth Ave, Rm 1303, New York, NY 10010; tel. (212) 255-1772; f. 1964; 13 mems; Exec. Officer KURT FEIBELMAN.

American West Overseas Association: 19451 195th Ave, Hudson, CO 80642; tel. (303) 536-4206; f. 1976; manufacturers and wholesalers engaged in the export of American western ware; 163 mems; Exec. Dir WILLIAM R. DIEKROEGER.

Association of Dark Leaf Tobacco Dealers and Exporters: Hail and Cotton, POB 179, Springfield, TN 37172; tel. (615) 384-9576; f. 1947; 22 mems; Pres. RICK COYTE.

Association of Foreign Trade Representatives: POB 300, Planetarium Station, New York, NY 10024-0300; tel. (212) 877-8900; f. 1984; mems; 75 orgs and 200 individuals; Exec. Dir JOHN J. McCABE.

Auto International Association: 11540 East Slauson Ave, Whittier, CA 90606; tel. (213) 692-9402; f. 1983; importers, exporters and distributors of parts for vehicles; 350 mems; Nat. Dir DICK WELLS.

Automotive Products Export Council: 5100 Forbes Blvd, Lanham, MD 20706; tel. (301) 459-5927; f. 1979; mems: six orgs; Exec. Man. JAMES HILBERT.

Bankers' Association for Foreign Trade: 1600 17 St, NW, 7th Floor, Washington, DC 20036; tel. (202) 452-0952; f. 1921; mems: 215 orgs; Exec. Dir MARY CONDEELIS.

California Dried Fruit Export Association: 303 Brokaw Rd, POB 270A, Santa Clara, CA 95052; tel. (408) 727-9302; f. 1925; 31 mems; Sec.-Treas. FRANK A. MOSEBAR.

Cleveland World Trade Association: 690 Huntington Bldg, Cleveland, OH 44115; tel. (216) 621-3300; telex 980356; promotes the export of Cleveland area products; Dir RICHARD N. KIRBY.

Coal Exporters' Association of the US, Inc: 1130 17th St, NW, Washington, DC 20036; tel. (202) 463-2654; telex 8221167; f. 1945; 35 mems; Exec. Dir CONNIE D. HOLMES.

Committee on Canada–United States Relations: c/o Chamber of Commerce of the USA, 1615 H St, NW, Washington, DC 20062; tel. (202) 463-5488; f. 1933; considers trade and investment matters between the USA and Canada.

Council of the Americas: 680 Park Ave, New York, NY 10021; tel. (212) 628-3200; f. 1958; c. 195 corporate mems doing business with Latin America; Pres. GEORGE W. LANDAU.

Council for Export Trading Companies: 1225 Connecticut Ave, NW, Suite 415, Washington, DC 20036; tel. (202) 861-4705; f. 1982; mems: 92 orgs; Exec. Dir RONALD C. WAKEFORD.

FCIB-NACM Corporation: 520 Eighth Ave, 22nd Floor, New York, NY 10018-6571; tel. (212) 947-5070; f. 1919; formerly the Foreign Credit Interchange Bureau, sponsored by the National Association of Credit Management; mems: 1,100 orgs; Exec. Vice-Pres. GERD-PETER LOTA.

Federation of International Trade Associations: 1854 Alexander Bell Dr., Reston, VA 22091; tel. (703) 391-6106; f. 1985; mems: 135 orgs; Chair. NELSON T. JOYNER.

Foreign Commerce Club of New York: One World Trade Center, Suite 3147, New York, NY 10048; tel. (212) 432-2500; f. 1914; industrial and transportation executives engaged in foreign trade; 650 mems; Sec. FRANK FILLS.

Holland Cheese Exporters' Association: 47 Orient Way, Rutherford, NJ 07070; tel. (201) 935-0086; f. 1951; Man. JEROEN DE SCHAAF.

International Business Council Mid America: 203 North Wabash Ave, Suite 1102, Chicago, IL 60602; tel. (312) 368-9197; f. 1919; 800 mems; promotes export trade of the Midwest states; Exec. Dir ROBERT F. McCULLOUGH.

International House—World Trade Center: POB 52020, New Orleans, LA 70152; tel. (504) 522-3591; f. 1943; 2,500 mems; Man. Dir PAUL A. FABRY.

International Trade Council: 750 13th St, SE, Washington, DC 20003; tel. (202) 547-1727; f. 1976; 850 mems; Pres. Dr PETER T. NELSEN.

International Traders Association: 6100 Variel Ave, Woodland Hills, CA 91367; tel. (818) 884-4400; f. 1947; 50,000 mems; Vice-Pres. PETER T. MELLINGER.

Leaf Tobacco Exporters' Association: 3716 National Dr., Suite 114, Raleigh, NC 27612; tel. (919) 782-5151; f. 1939; 45 mems; Vice-Pres. J. T. BUNN.

Meat Importers' Council of America: 1901 North Fort Myer Dr., Arlington, VA 22209; tel. (703) 522-1910; f. 1962; 200 mems; Exec. Dir WILLIAM C. MORRISON.

National Association of Export Companies: 17 Battery Pl., Suite 1425, New York, NY 10004; tel. (212) 809-8023; f. 1965; 150 mems; Man. Dir HELGA JALKIO.

National Association of Foreign-Trade Zones: 1825 I St, NW, Suite 400, Washington, DC 20006; tel. (202) 429-2020; f. 1973; mems: 300 orgs; Pres. CHRISTINE WHORTON.

National Council of Music Importers and Exporters: 135 West 29th St, New York, NY 10001; tel. (212) 564-0251; f. 1966; 55 mems; Exec. Vice-Pres. JEROME HERSHMAN.

National Export Traffic League: 234 Fifth Ave, New York, NY 10001; tel. (212) 697-5895; f. 1946; serves US industry in international transportation; 150 mems; Pres. LAWRENCE P. MANCHESE.

National Foreign Trade Council: 100 East 42nd St, Suite 910, New York, NY 10017; tel. (212) 867-5630; f. 1914; 500 mems; Pres. RICHARD W. ROBERTS.

National Lumber Exporters' Association: 1250 Connecticut Ave, NW, Washington, DC 20036; tel. (202) 463-2723; f. 1900; 38 mems; Exec. Dir STEPHEN M. LORETT.

North American Export Grain Association: 1030 15th St, NW, Suite 1020, Washington, DC 20005; tel. (202) 682-4030; f. 1920; 34 mems; Exec. Dir STEVE McCOY.

North Coast Export Company: POB 1203, Eureka, CA 95501; tel. (707) 443-9348; f. 1971; nine mems; Man. BILL CROSS.

Northwest Fruit Exporters: 1005 Tieton Dr., Yakima, WA 98902; tel. (509) 453-4837; f. 1976; 20 mems; Pres. TED ZACHER.

Pacific Lumber Exporters' Association: POB 4726, Portland, OR 97208; tel. (503) 775-6848; f. 1924; 21 mems; Pres. GARY ROSE.

Pulp, Paper and Paperboard Export Association of the United States: 528 North New St, Bethlehem, PA 18018; tel. (215) 694-0832; f. 1952; 12 mems; Exec. Dir ROBERT L. KERRIDGE.

Sell Overseas America, The Association of American Export: 2512 Artesia Blvd, Redondo Beach, CA 90278; tel. (213) 376-8788; f. 1980; Exec. Officer DAVID THAYER.

Texas Produce Export Association: 6912 West Expressway 83, Harlingen, TX 78552; f. 1980; 24 mems; Sec. W. E. WEEKS.

Trade Relations Council of the US: 808 17th St, NW, Suite 501, Washington, DC 20006; tel. (202) 785-4185; f. 1885; mems: c. 38 orgs; Exec. Sec. EUGENE L. STEWART.

United States Feed Grains Council: 1400 K St, NW, Suite 1200, Washington, DC 20005; tel. (202) 789-0789; f. 1960; mems: 100 orgs; Pres. E. STOLTE.

United States Meat Export Federation: 600 South Cherry St, Suite 1000, Denver, CO 80222-1716; tel. (303) 399-7151; f. 1976; mems: 115 orgs; Pres. ALAN R. MIDDAUGH.

United States Paper Exporters' Council: c/o Aquatex Paper Corpn, 404 Park Ave South, New York, NY 10016; tel. (212) 696-2640; f. 1938; four mems; Pres. ROBERT M. ROBERT.

Western International Trade Group: POB 29744, Phoenix, AZ 85038; tel. (602) 271-6361; f. 1946; 208 mems; Treas. RONALD A. INGERSOLL.

World Trade Center of New Orleans: Two Canal St, Suite 2900, New Orleans, LA 70130; tel. (504) 522-3591; f. 1985; 3,300 mems; Man. Dir EUGENE SCHREIBER.

World Trade Centers Association: One World Trade Center, Suite 7701, New York, NY 10048; tel. (212) 775-1370; f. 1968; Pres. GUY F. TOZZOLI.

Foreign Chambers of Commerce in the USA

American Arab Association for Commerce and Industry, Inc: 420 Lexington Ave, Suite 2431, New York, NY 10017; tel. (212) 986-7229; telex 238790; f. 1951; promotes trade and commerce between the USA and Arab League countries; mems: 175 orgs; Chair. PAUL C. SHEELINE; Pres. I. F. YUSIF.

American-ASEAN Trade Council: 40 East 49th St, Suite 501, New York, NY 10017; tel. (212) 688-2755; f. 1978; 250 mems; Vice-Pres. and Exec. Sec. GEORGE PEABODY.

American Hellenic Institute: 1730 K St, NW, Washington, DC 20006; tel. (202) 785-8430; Exec. Dir GEORGIA DELYANNIS.

American-Israel Chamber of Commerce and Industry, Inc (Chicago): 180 North Michigan Ave, Suite 911, Chicago, IL 60601; tel. (312) 641-2937.

American-Israel Chamber of Commerce and Industry, Inc (Chicago): Cleveland Center, 10800 Brookpark Rd, Cleveland, OH 44130; tel. (216) 267-1200.

American-Israel Chamber of Commerce and Industry, Inc (New York): 500 Fifth Ave, Rm 5416, New York, NY 10110; tel. (212) 354-6510; f. 1953; 500 mems; Chair. MAX RATNER.

American-Indonesian Chamber of Commerce: 711 Third Ave, 17th Floor, New York, NY 10017; tel. (212) 687-4505; f. 1949; 110 mems; Exec. Dir WAYNE FORREST.

American-Southern Africa Chamber of Trade and Industry: 1080 Park Ave, New York, NY 10128; tel. (212) 410-6560; f. 1966; Dir-Gen. ROBERT JOHN.

Argentine-American Chamber of Commerce: 50 West 34th St, 6th Floor, Rm C2, New York, NY 10001; tel. (212) 564-3855.

Association of Asian-American Chambers of Commerce: POB 1933, Washington, DC 20013; tel. (202) 638-5595; f. 1965; 15,000 mems; Exec. Officer EDWARD VON ROTHKIRK.

Australian Trade Commission: 636 Fifth Ave, New York, NY 10111; tel. (212) 245-4000; Exec. Officer GEOFFREY M. HILL.

Belgian-American Chamber of Commerce in the United States: Empire State Bldg, 350 Fifth Ave, Suite 703, New York, NY 10118; f. 1925; 500 mems; Exec. Dir CLAIRE F. RAICK.

Brazil-California Trade Association: 350 South Figueroa St, Suite 226, Los Angeles, CA 90071; tel. (213) 627-0634.

Brazilian-American Chamber of Commerce, Inc (Miami): 1111 South Bay Shore Dr., Miami, FL 33131; tel. (305) 377-6700.

Brazilian-American Chamber of Commerce, Inc (New York): 22 West 48th St, Suite 404, New York, NY 10036; tel. (212) 575-9030; f. 1968; 340 mems; Exec. Dir FRANK J. DEVINE.

British-American Chamber of Commerce (New York): 275 Madison Ave, New York, NY 10016; tel. (212) 889-0680; f. 1920; 600 mems; Exec. Dir FABIENNE EDMEADES.

British-American Chamber of Commerce (San Francisco): 3150 California St, San Francisco, CA 94115; tel. (415) 567-6128.

British-American Chamber of Commerce and Trade Centre of the Pacific Southwest: 1640 Fifth St, Suite 224, Santa Monica, CA 90401; tel. (213) 394-4977.

British Trade Development Office: 845 Third Ave, 11th Floor, New York, NY 10022; tel. (212) 593-2258; Export Dir J. BROWN.

Chamber of Commerce of Latin America: One World Trade Center, Suite 2343, New York, NY 10048; tel. (212) 432-9313; f. 1940; 150 mems; Vice-Pres. RONALD W. RAMIREZ.

China External Trade Development Council, Inc (CETDC): 41 Madison Ave, New York, NY 10010; tel. (212) 532-7055; telex 426299; promotes trade and commerce between the USA and the Republic of China (Taiwan).

Chinese-American Association of Commerce: 737B Grant Ave, San Francisco, CA 94108; tel. (415) 362-4306; f. 1980; 350 mems; Pres. STEVE MA.

Chinese Chamber of Commerce of New York: Confucius Plaza, 33 Bowery, Rm C203, New York, NY 10002; tel. (212) 226-2795.

Chinese Chamber of Commerce of San Francisco: 730 Sacramento St, San Francisco, CA 94108; tel. (415) 982-3000.

Colombian-American Association: 111 Broadway, Rm 1408, New York, NY 10006; tel. (212) 233-7776; f. 1927; 105 mems; Sec.-Treas. PAUL E. CALVERT.

Continental Africa Chamber of Commerce (CACC): 1025 Vermont Ave, Suite 920, Washington, DC 20033; tel. (202) 371-2277; f. 1973; Pres. OTHENE DARKO.

Cyprus Trade Centre: 12 East 40th St, New York, NY 10016; tel. (212) 686-6016; telex 666969.

Danish–American Chamber of Commerce: 825 Third Ave, 32nd Floor, New York, NY 10022; tel. (212) 980-6240; 200 mems; Chair. FLEMING SODERLUND.

Danish Trade Office: Westgate Tower Bldg, 20525 Center Ridge Rd, Cleveland, OH 44116; tel. (216) 331-0550; telex 980319.

Dominican Republic Export Promotion Centre: One World Trade Center, Rm 86065, New York, NY 10048; tel. (212) 432-9498.

Ecuadorean–American Association, Inc: 115 Broadway, Rm 1408, New York, NY 10006; tel. (212) 233-7776.

Egyptian–American Chamber of Commerce: One World Trade Center, Suite 4543, New York, NY 10048; tel. (212) 466-1866; f. 1980; 200 mems; Exec. Dir FAROUK ZAKI.

Finnish–American Chamber of Commerce: 540 Madison Ave, New York, NY 10022; tel. (212) 832-2588; f. 1958; 300 mems; Exec. Sec. JUHANI VEHKAOJA.

Finnish–American Chamber of Commerce of the Midwest: 35 East Wacker Dr., Suite 1900, Chicago, IL 60601; tel. (312) 346-1150.

French–American Chamber of Commerce: 509 Madison Ave, Suite 1900, New York, NY 10022; tel. (212) 371-4466; f. 1896; 3,000 mems; Pres. SERGE BELLANGER.

German–American Chamber of Commerce (New York): 666 Fifth Ave, New York, NY 10103; tel. (212) 974-8830; f. 1947; Exec. Dir WERNER WALBROL.

German–American Chamber of Commerce (Washington, DC): 1 Farragut Sq. South, Washington, DC 20006; tel. (202) 347-0247.

German–American Chamber of Commerce of Chicago: 104 South Michigan Ave, Chicago, IL 60603-5978; tel. (312) 782-8557.

German–American Chamber of Commerce of Los Angeles: One Park Plaza Bldg, 3250 Wilshire Blvd, Suite 1112, Los Angeles, CA 90010; tel. (213) 381-2236.

German–American Chamber of Commerce of the Pacific Coast: 465 California St, Suite 910, San Francisco, CA 94104; tel. (415) 392-2262.

Hellenic–American Chamber of Commerce: 960 Ave of the Americas, New York, NY 10001; tel. (212) 943-8594; f. 1947; Administrator GEORGETTE MITRAKOS.

Hong Kong Trade Development Council: 548 Fifth Ave, 6th Floor, New York, NY 10036; tel. (212) 730-0777; telex 5816302; fax (212) 398-0530; f. 1966; Regional Rep. ANDREW MA.

Honolulu–Japanese Chamber of Commerce: 2454 South Beretania St, Honolulu, HI 96826; tel. (808) 949-5531.

India Chamber of Commerce of America: 445 Park Ave, 18th Floor, New York, NY 10022; tel. (212) 755-7181; f. 1934; Dir M. PATRICIA ERDMAN.

Indo–American Chamber of Commerce: c/o Bank of India, 19 South La Salle St, Chicago, IL 60603; tel. (312) 621-1200.

Ireland–United States Council for Commerce and Industry: 460 Park Ave, New York, NY 10022; tel. (212) 751-2660.

Italian–American Chamber of Commerce (Chicago): 126 West Grand Ave, Chicago, IL 60610; tel. (312) 661-1336; f. 1907; 300 mems; Exec. Sec. LEONORA LI PLUMA GRECO.

Italian–American Chamber of Commerce (New York): 350 Fifth Ave, New York, NY 10118; tel. (212) 279-5520; f. 1887; 1,150 mems; Exec. Sec. ROY A. ROSETTI.

Italian Trade Commission: 499 Park Ave, New York, NY 10022; tel. (212) 980-1500; telex 423792; Commr MARIO CASTAGNA.

Japan Business Association of Southern California: 345 South Figueroa St, Suite 206, Los Angeles, CA 90071; tel. (213) 485-0160.

Japan Economic Institute of America: 1000 Connecticut Ave, NW, Suite 211, Washington, DC 20036; tel. (202) 296-5633; f. 1957; Pres. WILLIAM BARNDS.

Japan External Trade Organization: 1221 Ave of the Americas, New York, NY 10020; tel. (212) 997-0400; f. 1958; Pres. YUKIMASA KITAGAWA.

Japanese Chamber of Commerce and Industry of Chicago: 401 North Michigan Ave, Rm 602, Chicago, IL 60611; tel. (312) 332-6199.

Japanese Chamber of Commerce and Industry of Hawaii: 476A Hinano St, Hilo, HI 96720; tel. (808) 961-6123; f. 1950; 406 mems; Exec. Sec. NANCY CAPELLAS.

Japanese Chamber of Commerce of New York, Inc: 145 West 57th St, New York, NY 10019; tel. (212) 246-9774.

Japanese Chamber of Commerce of Northern California: World Affairs Center, 312 Sutter St, Rm 408, San Francisco, CA 94108; tel. (415) 986-6140.

Japanese Chamber of Commerce of Southern California: 224 South San Pedro St, Rm 504, Los Angeles, CA 90012; tel. (312) 626-3067.

Korea Chamber of Commerce: 981 South Western Ave, Rm 201, Los Angeles, CA 90006; tel. (213) 733-4410.

Korea Trade Promotion Center (KOTRA): 460 Park Ave, 4th Floor, New York, NY 10022; tel. (212) 826-0900; f. 1962; promotes trade and commerce between the USA and the Republic of Korea; Exec. Dir SUNG HO CHO.

Mexican Chamber of Commerce of Arizona: POB 626, Phoenix, AZ 85001; tel. (602) 252-6448.

Mexican Chamber of Commerce of the City of Los Angeles: 125 Paseo de la Plaza, Rm 404, Los Angeles, CA 90012; tel. (213) 688-7330.

Mexican Chamber of Commerce of the United States, Inc: Woolworth Bldg, 655 Madison Ave, 16th Floor, New York, NY 10021; tel. (212) 759-9505.

Netherlands Chamber of Commerce in the United States: One Rockefeller Plaza, 11th Floor, New York, NY 10020; tel. (212) 265-6460; f. 1903; 623 mems; Man. Dir KERSEN J. DE JONG.

Nigerian–American Chamber of Commerce, Inc: 575 Lexington Ave, New York, NY 10022; tel. (212) 715-7200.

North American—Chilean Chamber of Commerce, Inc: 200 East 81st St, New York, NY 10028; tel. (212) 288-5691.

Norwegian–American Chamber of Commerce, Inc (Chicago): Midwest Chicago Chapter, 360 North Michigan Ave, Suite 1908, Chicago, IL 60601; tel. (312) 782-7750.

Norwegian–American Chamber of Commerce, Inc (Los Angeles): World Trade Center, 350 South Figueroa St, Suite 360, Los Angeles, CA 90017; tel. (213) 626-0388.

Norwegian–American Chamber of Commerce, Inc (Minneapolis): Upper Midwest Chapter, 229 Foshay Tower, Minneapolis, MN 55402; tel. (612) 332-3339.

Norwegian–American Chamber of Commerce, Inc (San Francisco): 2 Embarcadero Center, Suite 2930, San Francisco, CA 94111; tel. (415) 986-0766.

Norwegian–American Chamber of Commerce, Inc (Seattle): 1301 Fifth Ave, Suite 2727, Seattle, WA 98101; tel. (206) 682-5250.

Office of the Philippines Trade Representative: Philippine Center, 556 Fifth Ave, New York, NY 10036; tel. (212) 575-7925; telex 620311.

Peruvian–American Association: 50 West 34th St, 6th Floor, Suite C2, New York, NY 10001; tel. (212) 564-3855.

Philippine–American Chamber of Commerce: c/o Philippine Consulate-General, 447 Sutter St, San Francisco, CA 94108; tel. (415) 433-6666.

Philippine–American Chamber of Commerce, Inc: 711 Third Ave, 17th Floor, New York, NY 10017; tel. (212) 972-9326.

Portuguese Trade Commission: 548 Fifth Ave, New York, NY 10036; tel. (212) 354-4610; Dir CAMILO MARTINS DE OLIVEIRA.

Portugal–US Chamber of Commerce: 5 West 45th St, 4th Floor, New York, NY 10036; tel. (212) 354-4627; telex 640175; f. 1979; 200 mems; Pres. ALFONSO G. FINOCCHIARO; Exec. Dir PAULO ALMEIDA D'ECA.

Puerto Rico Chamber of Commerce in the United States: 200 Madison Ave, New York, NY 10036; tel. (212) 561-2028.

Saudi Arabian Council of Chambers of Commerce and Industry: c/o Embassy of Saudi Arabia, 601 New Hampshire Ave, NW, Washington, DC 20037; tel. (202) 342-3800.

Singapore Trade Development Board: Los Angeles World Trade Center, 350 South Figueroa St, Suite 170, Los Angeles, CA 90071; tel. (213) 617-7358; telex 4720209; Regional Dir GEOFFREY LIM.

Spain–United States Chamber of Commerce: 350 Fifth Ave, Suite 3514, New York, NY 10118; tel. (212) 967-2170; f. 1958; Exec. Dir MIGUEL SEBASTIA.

Swedish–American Chamber of Commerce: 825 Third Ave, New York, NY 10022; tel. (212) 838-5530; f. 1906; Pres. and Gen. Man. OLLE WIJKSTROM.

Swedish–American Chamber of Commerce of the Western United States: World Trade Center, San Francisco, CA 94111; tel. (415) 781-4188; f. 1948; 250 mems; Exec. Dir ERIK A. STENSTEDT.

Swedish Trade Office: 825 Third Ave, 40th Floor, New York, NY 10022; tel. (212) 593-0045; telex 147238; Trade Commr OLLE WIJKSTROM.

Swiss–American Chamber of Commerce: New York Chapter, 645 Fifth Ave, New York, NY 10001; tel. (212) 213-0482.

Trade Commission of Norway: 825 Third Ave, New York, NY 10022; tel. (212) 421-9210; f. 1945; Trade Commr THEIS H. PEDERSEN.

Trinidad and Tobago Chamber of Commerce of the USA: c/o Trintoc Services Ltd, 400 Madison Ave, Rm 803, New York, NY 10017; tel. (212) 759-3388.

United States–Korea Society: 725 Park Ave, New York, NY 10021; tel. (212) 517-7730.

United States–Lebanese Chamber of Commerce: One World Trade Center, Suite 1345, New York, NY 10048; tel. (212) 432-1133.

United States–Mexican Quadripartite Commission: Center for Inter-American Relations, 680 Park Ave, New York, NY 10021; tel. (212) 249-8950.

United States–Mexico Chamber of Commerce: 1900 L St, NW, Suite 612, Washington, DC 20036; tel. (202) 296-5198; f. 1973; 170,000 mems; Exec. Vice-Pres. GERARD J. VAN HEUVEN.

United States–Pakistan Economic Council: c/o Morton Zuckerman, 17 Battery Pl., New York, NY 10004; tel. (212) 943-5828.

United States–Yugoslav Economic Council: 18th St, NW, Suite 818, Washington, DC 20005; tel. (202) 857-0170; f. 1974; 195 mems; Pres. RICHARD E. JOHNSON.

US–Arab Chamber of Commerce: One World Trade Center, Suite 4657, New York, NY 10048; tel. (212) 432-0655; f. 1967; 600 mems; Exec. Dir MOHAMED THABET AL-MAHAYNI.

US–Austrian Chamber of Commerce: 165 West 46th St, New York, NY 10036; tel. (212) 819-0117; f. 1949; 200 mems; Admin. Sec. ERIKA BOROZAN.

US–Pakistan Economic Council: 500 Fifth Ave, Suite 935, New York, NY 10110; tel. (212) 221-7070; f. 1980; Administrator MARIAN BALDWIN.

US–USSR Trade and Economic Council: 805 Third Ave, New York, NY 10022; tel. (212) 644-4550; f. 1973; 350 mems; Pres. JAMES H. GIFFEN.

USA–Republic of China Economic Council: 200 Main St, POB 517, Crystal Lake, IL 60014; tel. (815) 459-5875; 375 mems; Pres. WILLIAM N. MORELL, Jr.

Venezuelan–American Association of the US: 115 Broadway, Rm 1110, New York, NY 10006; tel. (212) 233-7776; f. 1936.

Western States Chamber of Commerce with Israel: 6505 Wilshire Blvd, Suite 201, Los Angeles, CA 90048; tel. (213) 658-7910.

World Africa Chamber of Commerce: POB 33144, Washington, DC 20033; tel. (202) 223-3244; f. 1973; Pres. OTHENE DARKO.

FINANCE

BANKING

Introduction

COMMERCIAL BANKING IN THE USA

The US commercial banking system is the largest and, in many respects, the most comprehensive and sophisticated in the world. Banking has, however, been largely subject to state rather than federal jurisdiction, and this has created a structure very different from that in other advanced industrial countries. In general, no bank may open branches or acquire subsidiaries in states other than that in which it is based, although in June 1985 the US Supreme Court ruled that federal legislation prohibiting interstate banks does not preclude state governments from permitting regional interstate banking. A number of such mergers have followed, although some states continue to restrict banks to a single branch, or to operating only in certain counties of the state. Federal antitrust laws also limit mergers of banks within a state. The effect of these measures has been to preserve the independence of a very large number of banks: 14,375 at 30 June 1986. Nevertheless, the dominant banks are the main banks in the big industrial states; at 31 December 1987, of the 10 largest (in terms of deposits), six were based in New York, three in California and one in Illinois.

The possession of bank accounts and the use of banking facilities are perhaps more widespread among all classes and regions in the USA than in any other country. This has had important effects on monetary theory and policy, as bank credit has become much more important than currency supply in the regulation of the economy. The use of current accounts and credit cards is so common that many authorities claim the US can be regarded as effectively a cashless society.

Bank Holding Companies

Since 1956 bank holding companies—corporations that control one or more banks in the USA—have become significant elements in the banking system. At the end of 1986 there were 6,489 bank holding companies in the USA. These organizations control commercial banks which hold over 91% of the total assets of insured commercial banks in the USA.

Expansion Overseas

Since the mid-1960s the leading banks have rapidly expanded their overseas interests. At the end of 1960 there were only eight US banks operating foreign branches, mostly in Latin America and the Far East. By the end of 1988 there were 147 US Federal Reserve System member banks operating 854 foreign branches. At the end of 1987 (the most recent date for which such information is available) foreign branches of US Federal Reserve System member banks had assets of about $350,000m. At the end of 1988 there were 532 International Banking Facilities, with assets held in such accounts (end-1987) exceeding $275,000m.

The main factors behind the expansion overseas are the geographical limitations imposed by law at home; the rapid expansion of US business interests abroad; the faster economic growth of certain foreign markets; and finally the profitability of the 'Eurodollar' capital markets.

In December 1981 the Federal Reserve Board of Governors (see below) sanctioned the establishment of domestic International Banking Facilities (IBF), permitting commercial banks within the US (including US branches and agencies of foreign banks) to transact certain types of foreign deposit and loan business free of reserve requirements and, in most cases, state income-tax liability. By the end of 1985 assets held in such accounts exceeded $260,000m.

SAVINGS INSTITUTIONS

The total number of savings institutions in the 50 states of the USA, the District of Columbia, Guam and Puerto Rico at 31 December 1985 was 3,940, of which savings banks accounted for 743 institutions and savings and loan associations (the principal source of private finance for home construction and purchase in the USA) for 3,197.

Insuring Bodies

The Federal Deposit Insurance Corporation (FDIC—see Independent Agencies, p. 125) was created in 1933 to provide insurance coverage for bank deposits. Under the Banking Act of 1935 the deposits of all banks which are members of the Federal Reserve System (see below) must be insured by the FDIC. At 30 June 1986 there were 14,333 FDIC-insured commercial banks in the 50 states and the District of Columbia: of these, 4,922 were federally-chartered or 'national' banks and 9,411 were state-chartered banks. (All the national banks and 1,090 of the state banks were members of the Federal Reserve System.) Savings banks insured by the FDIC numbered 468 at mid-1986.

The Federal Home Loan Bank Board (see p. 125) was established in 1932 under the Federal Home Loan Bank Act to supervise and regulate the operations of savings and loan associations, and it insured them through its subsidiary, the Federal Savings and Loan Insurance Corporation (FSLIC). At 31 December 1986 a total of 3,208 savings institutions in the 50 states and the District of Columbia were insured with the FSLIC.

Financial Summary

(As at 31 December 1986. Data for commercial banks excludes foreign branches of US banks; data for savings institutions refers only to those insured by the FSLIC.)

	Commercial banks[1]			Savings institutions[3]		
	Assets	Deposits		Number of institutions	Assets	Deposits
	Total ($'000m.)	Total ($'000m.)	Per head ($)[2]		Total ($'000m.)	Total ($'000m.)
Alabama	28.9	23.2	5,726	37	8.6	6.8
Alaska	5.0	4.1	7,610	4	0.6	0.4
Arizona	27.6	23.8	7,168	14	21.5	14.6
Arkansas	17.2	15.8	6,681	39	8.2	7.2
California	251.5	206.5	7,652	216	309.3	218.1
Colorado	25.7	21.3	6,531	38	15.9	11.4
Connecticut	32.8	26.3	8,240	31	11.3	7.8
Delaware	34.2	15.3	24,117	4	0.4	0.3
District of Columbia	14.5	11.7	18,626	6	4.3	2.8
Florida	102.4	86.4	7,401	149	83.0	64.1
Georgia	50.2	37.9	6,206	67	16.2	13.2
Hawaii	10.6	9.3	8,768	6	3.7	2.7
Idaho	7.1	5.9	5,922	9	1.5	1.2
Illinois	148.7	108.8	9,421	267	65.3	55.0
Indiana	48.7	40.4	7,346	115	12.7	11.2
Iowa	30.1	26.0	9,119	52	9.1	7.8
Kansas	24.6	21.5	8,746	58	16.9	12.0
Kentucky	33.1	26.2	7,025	67	7.2	6.3
Louisiana	37.0	31.5	7,003	102	15.5	12.9
Maine	6.1	5.2	4,451	15	1.2	0.9
Maryland	37.8	29.1	6,513	95	19.0	15.7
Massachusetts	77.4	58.6	10,056	33	7.0	5.4
Michigan	76.0	62.0	6,782	51	34.8	21.0
Minnesota	54.3	38.9	9,225	37	16.1	10.6
Mississippi	17.9	15.1	5,756	45	4.8	4.2
Missouri	52.7	43.5	8,592	85	21.9	17.7
Montana	7.3	6.1	7,479	11	1.2	1.0
Nebraska	16.6	14.5	9,053	23	9.1	6.0
Nevada	9.0	5.9	6,142	7	4.2	2.8
New Hampshire	7.9	6.9	6,693	12	1.8	1.5
New Jersey	68.5	58.0	7,618	139	50.2	39.9
New Mexico	9.9	8.5	5,763	25	5.9	4.5
New York	423.3	255.5	14,376	86	48.3	38.7
North Carolina	55.4	38.9	6,144	139	19.3	16.4
North Dakota	6.9	6.1	8,957	6	3.9	2.5
Ohio	87.5	69.1	6,427	232	51.7	43.0
Oklahoma	29.2	25.3	7,652	53	10.1	8.6
Oregon	18.9	14.5	5,361	20	9.7	6.9
Pennsylvania	136.2	102.4	8,617	169	38.1	31.4
Rhode Island	11.3	7.9	8,131	3	3.6	2.6
South Carolina	17.0	13.2	3,901	49	10.4	8.4
South Dakota	18.2	8.1	11,391	12	1.4	1.3
Tennessee	38.8	32.1	6,687	64	10.6	8.9
Texas	201.3	158.2	9,482	281	97.3	80.3
Utah	11.1	9.0	5,403	14	5.9	4.4
Vermont	4.7	4.1	7,665	4	0.4	0.3
Virginia	51.0	40.9	7,070	66	22.9	18.3
Washington	31.4	25.6	5,746	43	17.1	11.5
West Virginia	14.9	12.8	6,670	18	2.1	1.9
Wisconsin	40.5	33.8	7,065	79	15.8	13.7
Wyoming	4.4	3.9	7,716	11	1.3	1.1
Total	2,573.1	1,955.8	8,113	3,208	1,158.3	811.2

[1] Figures reflect revisions submitted by banks after original filing date.
[2] Based on US Bureau of the Census resident population estimates as at 1 July.
[3] Savings and loan associations and savings banks.

Sources: Board of Governors of the Federal Reserve System, *Annual Statistical Digest* and US Federal Home Loan Bank Board, *Savings and Home Financing Source Book*.

The Federal Reserve System

(Board of Governors: 20th St and Constitution Ave, NW, Washington, DC 20551; tel. (202) 452-3204)

The Federal Reserve System was established on 23 December 1913, under the Federal Reserve Act of 1913, to provide the USA with a centralized banking system. The System comprises the Board of Governors, the 12 Federal Reserve Banks and their 25 branches, and the Federal Open Market Committee. The Federal Advisory Council, Consumer Advisory Council and Thrift Institutions Advisory Council are bodies which assist the Board of Governors in specific policy-making areas. At the end of 1987

5,753 of the nation's 14,473 federally- and state-chartered banks, accounting for more than three-quarters of consolidated total assets (assets in the USA as well as foreign offices of US banks), were members of the Federal Reserve System.

THE BOARD OF GOVERNORS

Policy affecting the nation's credit and monetary affairs is made by the Federal Reserve Board of Governors, whose seven members are appointed by the President of the USA, with the advice and consent of the Senate, to serve a 14-year term. The board's chairman and vice-chairman, both of whom are appointed from among its members by the US president, serve renewable four-year terms. In addition to its policy-making responsibilities, the Board of Governors supervises the budgets and operations of the Federal Reserve Banks (see below).

Members
(August 1989)

ALAN GREENSPAN (Chairman)
MANUEL H. JOHNSON (Vice-Chairman)
MARTHA R. SEGER
WAYNE D. ANGELL
EDWARD W. KELLEY, Jr
JOHN P. LAWARE
(1 vacancy)

FEDERAL RESERVE BANKS

The Reserve Banks are empowered to issue Federal Reserve notes fully secured by the following assets, alone or in any combination: gold certificates; US government and agency securities; other eligible assets as described by statute; and Special Drawing Rights certificates. The Reserve Banks may discount paper for depository institutions and make properly secured advances to them. They were established by Congress as the operating arms of the nation's central banking system. Many of the services performed by this network for depository institutions and for the government are similar to services performed by banks and thrift institutions for business customers and individuals. Reserve Banks hold the cash reserves of depository institutions and make loans to them. They move currency and coin into and out of circulation, and collect and process millions of cheques each day. They provide banking services for the Treasury, issue and redeem government securities, and act in other ways as fiscal agent for the US government. They also take part in the primary responsibility of the Federal Reserve System, the setting of monetary policy, through participation on the Federal Market Open Committee (see below).

Each of the 12 Federal Reserve Banks has a board of directors consisting of nine members, three of whom (including the chairman and vice-chairman) are appointed by the Federal Reserve Board of Governors. The latter must also ratify the appointment of the president of each of the Reserve Banks.

Banks and Branches

Boston: Boston, MA 02106; Chair. GEORGE N. HATSOPOULOS; Pres. RICHARD SYRON.

New York: New York, NY 10045; Chair. CYRUS R. VANCE; Pres. E. GERALD CORRIGAN; br. at Buffalo, NY 14240.

Philadelphia: Philadelphia, PA 19105; Chair. NEVIUS M. CURTIS; Pres. EDWARD G. BOEHNE.

Cleveland: Cleveland, OH 44101; Chair. CHARLES W. PARRY; Pres. W. LEE HOSKINS; brs at Cincinnati, OH 45201 and Pittsburgh, PA 15230.

Richmond: Richmond, VA 23219; Chair. ROBERT A. GEORGINE; Pres. ROBERT P. BLACK; brs at Baltimore, MD 21203 and Charlotte, NC 28230.

Atlanta: Atlanta, GA 30303; Chair. BRADLEY CURREY, Jr; Pres. ROBERT P. FORRESTAL; brs at Birmingham, AL 35283, Jacksonville, FL 32231, Miami, FL 33152, Nashville, TN 37203 and New Orleans, LA 70161.

Chicago: Chicago, IL 60690; Chair. ROBERT J. DAY; Pres. SILAS KEEHN; br. at Detroit, MI 48231.

St Louis: St Louis, MO 63166; Chair. ROBERT L. VIRGIL, Jr; Pres. THOMAS C. MELZER; brs at Little Rock, AR 72203, Louisville, KY 40232 and Memphis, TN 38101.

Minneapolis: Minneapolis, MN 55480; Chair. MICHAEL W. WRIGHT; Pres. GRAY H. STERN; br. at Helena, MT 59601.

Kansas City: Kansas City, MO 64198; Chair. IRVINE O. HOCKADAY, Jr; PRES. ROGER GUFFEY; brs at Denver, CO 80217, Oklahoma City, OK 73125 and Omaha, NE 68102.

Dallas: Dallas, TX 75222; Chair. BOBBY R. INMAN; Pres. ROBERT H. BOYKIN; brs at El Paso, TX 79999, Houston, TX 77252 and San Antonio, TX 78295.

San Francisco: San Francisco, CA 94120; Chair. ROBERT F. ERBURU; Pres. ROBERT T. PARRY; brs at Los Angeles, CA 90051, Portland, OR 97208, Salt Lake City, UT 84125 and Seattle, WA 98124.

ADVISORY COUNCILS

Federal Advisory Council: comprises one member from each Federal Reserve district, who is elected annually by the board of directors of the relevant Federal Reserve Bank. The council meets with the Federal Reserve Board of Governors four times a year.

Consumer Advisory Council: statutory body which comprises representatives of both consumers and creditors and which advises the Federal Reserve Board of Governors on the implementation of consumer regulations and other consumer-related matters.

Thrift Institutions Advisory Council: created as a result of the Monetary Control Act of 1980 to provide advice on the special needs and problems of thrift institutions. The council comprises representatives of mutual savings banks, savings and loan associations and credit unions.

PRINCIPAL MEANS OF MONETARY CONTROL

The Federal Reserve System has three main tools at its disposal for the implementation of monetary policy. Firstly, reserve requirements applying to all depository institutions are set by the Board of Governors and determine the proportion of its total reserves which a bank may make available for loan. Secondly, the Board of Governors and the Federal Reserve Banks have joint responsibility for making adjustments to the discount rate—the interest rate at which depository institutions borrow funds from the Federal Reserve Banks. Thirdly, the cost and availability of money and credit can be regulated by what are known as 'open-market operations', which, through the purchase and sale of government bonds, can influence the availability of dollars to depository institutions. Open-market operations are regulated by the Federal Open Market Committee, which comprises the seven members of the Federal Reserve Board of Governors together with the president of the Federal Reserve Bank of New York and four other Reserve Bank presidents (the latter serving one-year terms on a rotation basis). The committee sets annual objectives for growth in the supply of money and credit.

Comptroller of the Currency

(490 L'Enfant Plaza East, SW, Washington, DC 20219; tel. (202) 447-1810)

The comptroller of the currency has supervisory control over all federally-chartered banks (the national banks), which, while they comprise less than one-third of all banks numerically, account for almost 60% of the assets in the US banking system.

Comptroller: ROBERT L. CLARKE.

Trade Bank

Export–Import Bank of the United States (Eximbank): 811 Vermont Ave, Washington, DC 20571; tel. (202) 566-8144; telex 248460; f. 1934; independent agency since 1945; finances and facilitates US export–import trade with other countries, guarantees payment to US foreign traders and banks, extends credit to foreign governmental and private concerns; capital $1,400m. (Dec. 1987); Chair. WILLIAM RYAN (acting).

Foreign Banks in the USA
(Banks are branches, unless otherwise indicated.)

Akbank TAS (Turkey): 800 Third Ave, 29th Floor, New York, NY 10022; tel. (212) 832-1212; telex 667711; rep. office.

Algemene Bank Nederland NV: 335 Madison Ave, 16th and 17th Floors, New York, NY 10017; tel. (212) 503-2400; telex 232445; fax (212) 972-8024; Man. R. A. ARNOLD; 9 other brs.

Allied Irish Banks plc: 405 Park Ave, New York, NY 10022; tel. (212) 223-1230; telex 238461; Exec. Vice-Pres. N. J. BANNON.

Amsterdam–Rotterdam Bank NV (Netherlands): 500 Park Ave, New York, NY 10022; tel. (212) 838-7300; telex 225924; fax (212) 980-1464.

Andelsbanken Danebank (Denmark): 245 Park Ave, New York, NY 10167; tel. (212) 916-7944; telex 424337; Rep. G. I. BERESFORD; rep. office.

Arab Bank Ltd (Jordan): 520 Madison Ave, POB 5377, New York, NY 10150; tel. (212) 715-9700; telex 177365; fax (212) 593-4632.

Ashikaga Bank Ltd (Japan): One World Trade Center, Suite 8467, New York, NY 10048; tel. (212) 432-9465; telex 425407; rep. office.

ASLK–CGER Bank (Belgium): 350 Park Ave, 24th Floor, New York, NY 10022; tel. (212) 421-4900; fax (212) 421-0133; Gen. Man. J. PUTZEYS.

Australia and New Zealand Banking Group Ltd: 120 Wall St, New York, NY 10005; tel. (212) 820-9800; telex 667559; fax (212) 820-9859; Exec. Vice-Pres. (Americas) I. J. BUCKLEY; Gen. Man. B. MAISEY; br. in Chicago; rep. office in Houston.

Awa Bank Ltd (Japan): One Liberty Plaza, 45th Floor, 165 Broadway, New York, NY 10006; tel. (212) 349-2121; telex 214916; Chief Rep. SUSUMU MATSUOKA; rep. office.

Banca Commerciale Italiana SpA: One William St, New York, NY 10004; tel. (212) 607-3500; telex 429048; 2 other brs, rep. office in Washington, DC.

Banca Nazionale dell'Agricoltura SpA (Italy): 19th Floor, 100 Wall St, New York, NY 10005; tel. (212) 480-1150; telex 235560; fax (212) 480-0983; Gen. Man. PAOLO DORSA; rep. office in Los Angeles.

Banca Popolare di Milano Srl (Italy): 350 Park Ave, New York, NY 10022; tel. (212) 758-5040; telex 5814045; fax (212) 838-1077; Man. ANTHONY FRANCO.

Banca San Paolo-Brescia SpA (Italy): Park Avenue Tower, 21st Floor, 65 East 55th St, New York, NY 10022; tel. (212) 688-8301; telex 62434; fax (212) 308-0910; rep. office.

Banca della Svizzera Italiana (Switzerland): Park Ave Tower, 65 East 55th St, New York, NY 10022; tel. (212) 326-3100; telex 884821; fax (212) 326-3222; Man. G. SCHULER.

Banco Bilbao Vizcaya (Spain): 116–118 East 55th St, New York, NY 10022; tel. (212) 826-1320; telex 424706; fax (212) 766-9070; br. in Miami.

Banco Bradesco, SA (Brazil): 450 Park Ave, 32nd and 33rd Floors, New York, NY 10022; tel. (212) 688-9855; telex 661955; fax (212) 754-4032.

Banco do Brasil, SA: 550 Fifth Ave, POB 4450, New York, NY 10036; tel. (212) 730-6700; telex 423149; 3 other brs; 2 rep. offices.

Banco Central (Spain): 245 Park Ave, New York, NY 10167; tel. (212) 557-8100; telex 426147; fax (212) 972-9856; Sub-Dir ALFONSO J. GONZALEZ; br. in San Francisco.

Banco Consolidado, CA (Venezuela): 220 East 51st St, New York, NY 10022; tel. (212) 980-1770; telex 422931.

Banco de Crédito del Perú: 410 Park Ave, 9th Floor, New York, NY 10022; tel. (212) 644-6644; telex 420574.

Banco Econômico, SA (Brazil): 499 Park Ave, 20th Floor, New York, NY 10022; tel. (212) 758-3700; telex 237973; fax (212) 758-3881.

Banco Español de Crédito (Spain): 630 Fifth Ave, Rm 55, New York, NY 10111; tel. (212) 974-0527; telex 422035.

Banco Español del Río de la Plata Ltdo (Argentina): 41 East 75th St, Suite 1705, New York, NY 10022; tel. (212) 838-9180; telex 220740; rep. office.

Banco Espírito Santo e Comercial de Lisboa (Portugal): 555 Madison Ave, New York, NY 10022; tel. (212) 418-0320; telex 420776; Gen. Man. FRANCISCO NORTON DE MATOS.

Banco do Estado de São Paulo, SA (Brazil): 1 Citycorp Center, 153 53rd St, 59th Floor, New York, NY 10022-4660; tel. (212) 888-9544; telex 422450; fax (212) 371-1034.

Banco Exterior de España (Spain): 515 South Figueroa St, Suite 750, Los Angeles, CA 90071; tel. (213) 622-7106; telex 4720681; br. in Miami; rep. office in New York.

Banco Hispano Americano, SA (Spain): Olympic Tower, 9th Floor, 645 Fifth Ave, New York, NY 10022; tel. (212) 486-8170; fax (212) 838-1834.

Banco Industrial de Venezuela, CA: 400 Park Ave, New York, NY 10022; tel. (212) 688-2200.

Banco Itaú, SA (Brazil): 540 Madison Ave, 29th Floor, New York, NY 10022; tel. (212) 371-4706; telex 429544; fax (212) 371-4706.

Banco Mercantil, CA (Venezuela): 410 Park Ave, 15th Floor, New York, NY 10022; tel. (212) 838-4455; telex 426902; fax (212) 371-1711; Gen. Man. JOHN M. TRUM.

Banco Mercantil de São Paulo, SA (Brazil): 450 Park Ave, 31st Floor, New York, NY 10022; tel. (212) 888-0030; telex 424231; fax (212) 888-4631.

Banco Nacional de Panamá: 499 Park Ave, New York, NY 10022; tel. (212) 486-1515; telex 424244.

Banco de Napoli (Italy): 277 Park Ave, New York, NY 10017; tel. (212) 644-8400; telex 233344; fax (212) 644-2426.

Banco Português do Atlântico: 2 Wall St, New York, NY 10005; tel. (212) 306-7800; telex 8956296.

Banco Real, SA (Brazil): 680 Fifth Ave, New York, NY 10019; tel. (212) 489-0100; telex 620469; fax (212) 307-5627.

Banco de la República Oriental del Uruguay: Rockefeller Center, 30th Floor, 1270 Ave of the Americas, New York, NY 10020; tel. (212) 307-9600.

Banco di Roma SpA (Italy): 100 Wall St, New York, NY 10005; tel. (212) 952-9300; telex 127951; Man. GIOVANNI BENEDUCI.

Banco de Sabadell (Spain): Chrysler Bldg, 37th Floor, 405 Lexington Ave, New York, NY 10174; tel. (212) 949-6800; telex 210745; fax (212) 949-6809; rep. office.

Banco Santander (Spain): 375 Park Ave, 29th Floor, New York, NY 10152; tel. (212) 826-4350; telex 423097; Man. FRANCISCO MARTÍN.

Banco di Santo Spirito SpA (Italy): Park Avenue Plaza, 55 East 52nd St, New York, NY 10055; tel. (212) 446-0560; telex 6790506; fax (212) 223-2177.

Banco di Sicilia (Italy): 250 Park Ave, New York, NY 10177; tel. (212) 692-4300.

Bangkok Bank Ltd (Thailand): 29 Broadway, 20th Floor, New York, NY 10006; tel. (212) 422-8200; telex 666297; fax (212) 422-0728; Man. LAURENCE A. AVILASAKUL.

Bank of Baroda (India): 1 Park Ave, New York, NY 10016; tel. (212) 578-4550; telex 428901; fax (212) 578-4565.

Bank Brussels Lambert (Belgium): 630 Fifth Ave, Suite 2020, New York, NY 10111; tel. (212) 632-5300; telex 422934; fax (212) 632-5308.

Bank Bumiputra Malaysia Berhad: 900 Third Ave, 11th Floor, New York, NY 10022; tel. (212) 644-1280; telex 0971684; fax (212) 644-1874; Gen. Man. EMADUDDIN LOKMAN.

Bank Central Asia (Indonesia): 1250 Broadway, New York, NY 10001; tel. (212) 629-8888; telex 276688; fax (212) 629-8922; Man. GUY BENTLEY MEEKER.

Bank of China (People's Republic of China): 410 Madison Ave, New York, NY 10017; tel. (212) 935-3101; telex 423635.

Bank of East Asia Ltd (Hong Kong): 450 Park Ave, 20th Floor, New York, NY 10022; tel. (212) 980-0510; telex 276640; fax (212) 485-3195.

Bank of Fukuoka Ltd (Japan): 30 Broad St, 45th Floor, New York, NY 10004; tel. (212) 363-1900; telex 4973137; Chief Rep. TOSHIHIDE MARUTANI; rep. office.

Bank Handlowy W. Warszawie, SA (Poland): 405 Park Ave, Suite 1101, New York, NY 10022; tel. (212) 371-8390; telex 649270; Rep. EUGENIUSZ SZEWEZYK; rep. office.

Bank Hapoalim BM (Israel): Rockefeller Center, 10 Rockefeller Plaza, New York, NY 10020; tel. (212) 830-2600; telex 425764; fax (212) 765-9773; 6 other brs.

Bank of India: 277 Park Ave, New York, NY 10172; tel. (212) 753-6100; telex 234444; Senior Vice-Pres. G. C. KATHRANI.

Bank Indonesia: One World Financial Center, 6th Floor, 200 Liberty St, New York, NY 10281; tel. (212) 945-1310; telex 232557; fax (212) 945-1316; rep. office.

Bank of Ireland: 640 Fifth Ave, New York, NY 10019; tel. (212) 397-1700; telex 620328; fax (212) 307-5559; Chief Exec. P. J. HOOPER.

Bank of Kinki Ltd (Japan): One World Trade Center, Suite 4531, New York, NY 10048; tel. (212) 466-3031; telex 429140; rep. office.

Bank of Kyoto Ltd (Japan): 2 Wall St, New York, NY 10005; tel. (212) 586-1100; fax (212) 372-3888.

Bank Leu AG (Switzerland): Park Avenue Tower, 22nd Floor, 65 East 55th St, New York, NY 10022; tel. (212) 848-9400; telex 666924; fax (212) 848-9527.

Bank Leumi le-Israel BM: 100 North La Salle St, Chicago, IL 60602; tel. (312) 781-1800; telex 0253753; fax (312) 781-9469.

Bank of Montréal (Canada): 430 Park Ave, New York, NY 10022; tel. (212) 702-1800; telex 12380; 3 other brs.

Bank of Nagoya Ltd (Japan): 360 Madison Ave, New York, NY 10017; tel. (212) 867-7580; telex 7607758; fax (212) 867-9188; rep. office.

Bank of New Zealand: 575 Fifth Ave, 38th Floor, New York, NY 10017; tel. (212) 984-1400; telex 427376; Exec. Vice-Pres. R. F. HIRTEN.

Bank of Nova Scotia (Canada): 67 Wall St, New York, NY 10005; tel. (212) 208-6500; telex 421791.

Bank of the Philippine Islands: 805 Third Ave, 28th Floor, New York, NY 10022; tel. (212) 644-6700; telex 421095.

Bank Polska Kasa Opieki, SA (Poland): 470 Park Ave, South (Corner 32nd St), New York, NY 10016-6880; tel. (212) 684-5320; telex 222759; rep. office.

Bank Saderat Iran: 375 Park Ave, New York, NY 10152; tel. (212) 753-6500; telex 421203; br. in Los Angeles.

Bank of Seoul (Republic of Korea): Texas Commerce Tower, Suite 1160, 600 Travis St, Houston, TX 77002; tel. (713) 227-6155; Chief Rep. JONG BAE LEE; rep. office.

Bank Sepan (Iran): 650 Fifth Ave, New York, NY 10019; tel. (212) 974-1777; telex 427425.

Bank of Tokyo Ltd (Japan): 100 Broadway, New York, NY 10005; tel. (212) 766-3400; telex 222967; 6 other brs, and 4 rep. offices.

Bank of Yokohama Ltd (Japan): 44 Wall St, 20th Floor, New York, NY 10005; tel. (212) 943-5800; telex 422184; fax (212) 363-2870; Man. TOSHIHARU OHKUBO.

Banque Indosuez (France): Radio City Station, POB 1002, New York, NY 10101; tel. (212) 408-5600; telex 220898; fax (212) 408-5757; 2 other brs.

Banque Internationale pour l'Afrique Occidentale, SA (France): 350 Park Ave, 28th Floor, New York, NY 10010; tel. (212) 380-4141; telex 645316; Gen. Man. JEAN-CLAUDE PORCHER.

Banque Nationale de Paris, SA: 499 Park Ave, New York, NY 10022; tel. (212) 750-1400; telex 67270; 4 other brs; rep. office.

Banque Paribas (France): Equitable Tower, 787 Seventh Ave, New York, NY 10019; tel. (212) 841-2000; 2 other brs; 2 rep. offices.

Banque Régionale de l'Ouest, SA (France): 520 Madison Ave, New York, NY 10022; tel. (212) 715-4666; telex 62160.

Banque Sudameris, SA (France): 1200 Brickell Ave, Miami, FL 33131; tel. (305) 372-2200; telex 153713; fax (305) 374-1137; rep. office in New York.

Barclays Bank plc (UK): 75 Wall St, New York, NY 10265; tel. (212) 412-4000; telex 62367; fax (212) 797-3018.

Bayerische Hypotheken- und Wechselbank AG (Federal Republic of Germany): Wall St Plaza, Wall St Station, POB 610, New York, NY 10005; tel. (212) 248-0650; telex 175850; fax (212) 440-0798.

Bayerische Landesbank Girozentrale (Federal Republic of Germany): 560 Lexington Ave, New York, NY 10022; tel. (212) 310-9800; telex 661722; fax (212) 310-9841; Gen. Man. and Exec. Vice-Pres. WILFRIED FREUDENBURGER.

Bayerische Vereinsbank AG (Federal Republic of Germany): 335 Madison Ave, 19th Floor, New York, NY 10017; tel. (212) 210-0300; telex 126745; fax (212) 210-0330; br. in Chicago.

Bergen Bank (Norway): 20 West 55th St, 13th Floor, New York, NY 10019; tel. (212) 581-0600; telex 200642; fax (212) 246-6067; Gen. Man. INGE SKJELFJØRD; rep. office in Los Angeles.

Berliner Handels- und Frankfurter Bank (Federal Republic of Germany): Delmonico Plaza, 55 East 59th St, New York, NY 10022; tel. (212) 546-5500; telex 968510; fax (212) 546-5536.

BfG Bank (Federal Republic of Germany): 400 Park Ave, New York, NY 10022; tel. (212) 546-9000; telex 62345; fax (212) 546-9039.

Caisse Nationale de Crédit Agricole (France): 520 Madison Ave, New York, NY 10022; tel. (212) 418-2273; br. in Chicago; rep. offices in San Francisco and Los Angeles.

Canadian Imperial Bank of Commerce: 425 Lexington Ave, New York, NY 10017; tel. (212) 856-4000; rep. office in New York.

Cassa Centrale di Risparmio VE per le Province Siciliane (Italy): 375 Park Ave, New York, NY 10152; tel. (212) 421-6010; telex 666491; fax (212) 759-6785; rep. office.

Cassa di Risparmio di Firenze (Italy): 375 Park Ave, New York, NY 10152; tel. (212) 421-6010; telex 886529; fax (212) 759-6785; Rep. PAOLO G. PALLI; rep. office.

Cassa di Risparmio delle Provincie Lombarde (Italy): 650 Fifth Ave, New York, NY 10019; tel. (212) 541-6262; telex 175944; fax (212) 603-7840; Gen. Man. M. LANZA.

Chiba Bank (Japan): 45 Broadway, New York, NY 10006; tel. (212) 363-7777; telex 251829; fax (212) 809-5256.

Cho Hung Bank (Republic of Korea): 535 Madison Ave, New York, NY 10022; tel. (212) 935-3500; telex 662314.

Christiana Bank og Kreditkasse (Norway): Rockefeller Center, International Bldg, 630 Fifth Ave, 26th Floor, New York, NY 10111; tel. (212) 698-0600; telex 6716020; fax (212) 245-6852.

Chukyo Bank Ltd (Japan): One Liberty Plaza, Suite 4507, 165 Broadway, New York, NY 10006; tel. (212) 962-5111; telex 244092; fax (212) 962-8085; rep. office.

CIC-Union Européenne, International et Cie (France): 520 Madison Ave, New York, NY 10022; tel. (212) 715-4400; telex 62160; Exec. Vice-Pres. and Gen. Man. SERGE BELLANGER.

Commercial Bank of Korea Ltd (Republic of Korea): 230 West Monroe St, Suite 1400, Chicago, IL 60606; tel. (312) 580-0020; telex 206072; Gen. Man. SEMIN LEE.

Commercial Bank of Kuwait SAK: 350 Park Ave, New York, NY 10022-6022; tel. (212) 207-2420; telex 421744; fax (212) 935-6463; Senior Vice-Pres. and Chief Man. WARREN A. SCHAD.

Commerzbank (Federal Republic of Germany): 55 Broad St, New York, NY 10004; tel. (212) 248-1400; telex 423561; 2 other brs.

Commonwealth Bank of Australia: 599 Lexington Ave, 18th Floor, New York, NY 10022; tel. (212) 848-9200; telex 1777666; fax (212) 755-7585; br. in Chicago; rep. office in Los Angeles.

Compagnie de Banque et d'Investissements (Switzerland): 630 Fifth Ave, Suite 1505, New York, NY 10111; tel. (212) 265-3320; telex 666986; fax (212) 265-4310.

Cooperatieve Centrale Raiffeisen-Borerenleenbank BA (Netherlands): 245 Park Ave, New York, NY 10167; tel. (212) 916-7800; telex 424337; Gen. Man. H. STEENSMA.

Copenhagen Handelsbank A/S (Denmark): 280 Park Ave, New York, NY 10017; tel. (212) 984-8400; telex 425760; fax (212) 370-9239; Gen. Man. JAMES M. STEWART; br. in Los Angeles.

Crédit Commercial de France: 450 Park Ave, 7th Floor, New York, NY 10022; tel. (212) 468-3080; telex 62824; Gen. Man. K. CURRY.

Crédit Industriel de Normandie SA (France): 520 Madison Ave, 36th and 37th Floors, New York, NY 10022; tel. (212) 715-4400; telex 62160.

Crédit Lyonnais, SA (France): 95 Wall St, POB 1022, New York, NY 10005; 6 brs; 3 rep. offices.

Crédit du Nord, SA (France): 520 Madison Ave, 35th Floor, New York, NY 10022; tel. (212) 308-5300; telex 220398; Gen. Man. BERNARD BEAUFILS; 2 rep. offices.

Crédit Suisse (Switzerland): 100 Wall St, New York, NY 10005; tel. (212) 612-8000; telex 232491; br. in Los Angeles; 5 rep. offices.

Creditanstalt-Bankverein (Austria): 717 Fifth Ave, 11th Floor, New York, NY 10022; tel. (212) 308-6400; telex 239895; fax (212) 935-7806; Gen. Man. FREDERICK C. HERTEL; rep. office in San Francisco.

Credito Italiano SpA: 375 Park Ave, New York, NY 10152; tel. (212) 546-9600; telex 424690; rep. office in Chicago.

Credito Romagnolo SpA (Italy): Park Ave Tower, 21st Floor, 65 East 55th St, New York, NY 10022; tel. (212) 688-8301; telex 62434; fax (212) 308-0910; rep. office.

DG Bank (Federal Republic of Germany): 630 Fifth Ave, New York, NY 10111; tel. (212) 246-6000; telex 666755; fax (212) 246-8294; br. in Los Angeles; rep. office in New York.

Dah Sing Bank, Ltd (Hong Kong): 465 California St, Suite 700, San Francisco, CA 94104; tel. (415) 398-3781; telex 67685; Dir JOHN K. L. CHAN.

Dai-Ichi Kangyo Bank Ltd (Japan): One World Trade Center, Suite 4911, New York, NY 10048; tel. (212) 466-5200; telex 420720; Man. Dir and Gen. Man. YUKO OANA; 2 rep. offices.

Daishi Bank Ltd (Japan): 437 Madison Ave, New York, NY 10022; tel. (212) 223-4400; telex 4972585; fax (212) 223-4275; rep. office.

Daiwa Bank Ltd (Japan): 140 Broadway, New York, NY 10005; tel. (212) 480-0300; telex 422391; br. in Chicago; rep. office in Houston.

Den Danske Bank af 1871 A/F (Denmark): Tower 49, 12 East 49th St, New York, NY 10017; tel. (212) 759-5500; telex 6801420; fax (212) 759-0415; Gen. Man. KURT SNEBANG LARSEN.

Den Norske Creditbank (Norway): 600 Fifth Ave, New York, NY 10020; tel. (212) 315-6500; telex 236656; rep. office in Houston.

Deutsch–Sudamerikanische Bank AG (Federal Republic of Germany): 999 Brickell Ave, Miami, FL 33131; tel. (305) 374-6912; telex 441873; fax (305) 374-6912.

Deutsche Bank AG (Federal Republic of Germany): 31 West 52nd St, New York, NY 10019; tel. (212) 940-8000; telex 429166; fax (212) 355-5655; br. in Chicago; rep. office in Los Angeles.

Doha Bank Ltd (Qatar): 127 John St, New York, NY 10038; tel. (212) 509-4030; telex 226605.

Dresdner Bank (Federal Republic of Germany): 60 Broad St, New York, NY 10004; tel. (212) 425-4640; rep. office in Houston.

Fuji Bank Ltd (Japan): One World Trade Center, Suite 6011, New York, NY 10048; tel. (212) 839-5600; telex 232440; Dir and Gen. Man. TORU NONOYAMA; br. in Chicago; rep. office in Miami.

Fukui Bank (Japan): 45 Broadway, 31st Floor, New York, NY 10006; tel. (212) 363-5757; fax (212) 363-5628.

Fukuoka City Bank Ltd (Japan): One World Trade Center, Suite 8419, New York, NY 10048; tel. (212) 321-2929; telex 4977061.

Generale Bank NV (Belgium): Tower 49, 12 East 49th St, 22nd Floor, New York, NY 10017; tel. (212) 838-3301; telex 661444.

Genossenschaftliche Zentralbank AG (Austria): Rockefeller Center, 630 Fifth Ave, New York, NY 10111; tel. (212) 586-8274; telex 666755; Rep. OTTO STECKELHUBER; rep. office.

Girozentrale und Bank der österreichischen Sparkassen AG (Austria): Park Avenue Tower, 65 East 55th St, New York, NY 10022; tel. (212) 644-0660; telex 420914; fax (212) 421-2719; Man. RAIMUND SOLONAR.

Gotabanken (Sweden): 575 Fifth Ave, 36th Floor, New York, NY 10017; tel. (212) 984-0566; telex 424843; fax (212) 972-4557; Rep. LARS LARSSON.

Habib Bank Ltd (Pakistan): 44 Wall St, New York, NY 10005; tel. (212) 422-8353; telex 62315.

Hachijuni Bank Ltd (Japan): One World Trade Center, Suite 8697, New York, NY 10048; tel. (212) 466-0882; telex 6711479.

Hang Seng Bank Ltd (Hong Kong): 27 East Broadway, New York, NY 10002; tel. (212) 608-0070; telex 226046; fax (212) 608-0089.

Hessische Landesbank–Girozentrale (Federal Republic of Germany): 499 Park Ave, New York, NY 10022; tel. (212) 371-2500; telex 238614; fax (212) 838-9218; Mans R. P. HUBE, M. M. MILLER-BRINTNELL.

Hiroshima Bank Ltd (Japan): One Wall St, 31st Floor, New York, NY 10005; tel. (212) 509-5151; telex 226586.

Hokkaido Bank Ltd (Japan): 527 Madison Ave, 11th Floor, New York, NY 10022; tel. (212) 888-9100; telex 6711634; fax (212) 688-7063; Gen. Man. ISAO TOMIZU.

Hokkaido Takushoku Bank Ltd (Japan): Two World Trade Center, 83rd Floor, New York, NY 10048; tel. (212) 466-6060; telex 232230; fax (212) 466-6079; Gen. Man. SHIN-ICHI AIKAWA.

Hokuriku Bank Ltd (Japan): One World Trade Center, Suite 8463, New York, NY 10048; tel. (212) 524-9771; telex 233763; Gen. Man. NOBUO HASHIGAKI.

Hong Kong and Shanghai Banking Corporation (Hong Kong): Church St Station, POB 3140, New York, NY 10008; tel. (212) 415-0600; telex 640200; fax (212) 355-1000; Gen. Man. and CEO (Americas) J. R. H. BOND.

Hyakugo Bank Ltd (Japan): One Wall St, 30th Floor, New York, NY 10005; rep. office.

Hyakujushi Bank Ltd (Japan): Two Wall St, New York, NY 10005; tel. (212) 513-0114; telex 141388.

Hyogo Bank Ltd (Japan): One Wall St, 40th Floor, New York, NY 10005; tel. (212) 422-6600; telex 428834; fax (212) 422-6672; rep. office.

Istituto Bancario San Paolo di Torino (Italy): 499 Park Ave, New York, NY 10022; tel. (212) 750-7600; telex 220045; Man. LUIGI MARANZANA; br. in Los Angeles.

IYO Bank Ltd (Japan): 45 Broadway, 31st Floor, New York, NY 10006; tel. (212) 797-1414; telex 425443; Chief Rep. SHIGERU ONO; rep. office.

Joyo Bank (Japan): 45 Broadway, 10th Floor, New York, NY 10006; tel. (212) 425-2710; telex 4976129; fax (212) 425-2887.

Jugobanka (Yugoslavia): 500 Fifth Ave, New York, NY 10110; tel. (212) 704-2900; telex 661042; 2 rep. offices.

Juroku Bank Ltd (Japan): One World Trade Center, Suite 8353, New York, NY 10048; tel. (212) 466-1600; telex 423914; Chief Rep. HAJIME SUGIYAMA.

Kansallis-Osake-Pankki (Finland): 575 Fifth Ave, 36th Floor, New York, NY 10017; tel. (212) 972-4545; telex 424843; fax (212) 972-4557; Exec. Vice-Pres. PETER MODEEN.

Kiyo Bank Ltd (Japan): 45 Broadway, 19th Floor, New York, NY 10006; tel. (212) 635-5490; telex 4977133; rep. office.

Korea First Bank (Republic of Korea): Boulevard Towers, South Suite 915, 205 North Michigan Ave, Chicago, IL 60601; tel. (312) 819-2525; telex 247371; fax (312) 819-2535; Gen. Man. MUN SHIK SHIN.

Kredietbank NV (Belgium): 555 Madison Ave, 5th Floor, New York, NY 10022; tel. (212) 832-7200; telex 126666; fax (212) 832-8865; Vice-Pres. and Gen. Man. LUC PHILIPS; 2 rep. offices.

Kredietbank SA Luxembourgeoise: 555 Madison Ave, New York, NY 10022; tel. (212) 421-3753; telex 126666; fax (212) 832-8865; Rep. OLIVER WINTRINGER; rep. office.

Krung Thai Bank Ltd (Thailand): Republic Bank Tower, 12th Floor, 452 Fifth Ave, New York, NY 10018; tel. (212) 704-0001; telex 237903.

Kyowa Bank Ltd (Japan): One World Trade Center, Suite 4673, New York, NY 10048; tel. (212) 432-6400; telex 422943; 2 rep. offices.

Landesgirokasse (Federal Republic of Germany): 767 Fifth Ave, 5th Floor, New York, NY 10153; tel. (212) 888-1222; telex 426924; fax (212) 888-1268; Reps PETER KANT, HARALD KORB; rep. office.

Ljubljanska Banka (Yugoslavia): Tower 56, 17th Floor, 126 East 56th St, New York NY 10022; tel. (212) 935-1474; fax (212) 935-0509; Senior Vice-Pres. and Rep. VINKO MIR; rep. office.

Lloyds Bank plc (United Kingdom): One Seaport Plaza, 199 Walter St, New York, NY 10038; tel. (212) 607-4300; telex 62853; tel. (212) 607-5410; Senior Vice-Pres. and Regional Man. R. C. SHIELDS.

Magyar Nemzeti Bank (Hungary): 10 Rockefeller Plaza, Suite 1100, New York, NY 10020; tel. (212) 969-9270; telex 238180; fax (212) 969-9273; Rep. Dr IMRE HOLLAI; rep. office.

Malayan Banking Berhad (Malaysia): 400 Park Ave, 9th Floor, New York, NY 10022; tel. (212) 303-1305; Gen. Man. ONG SEE INN.

Metallbank GmbH (Federal Republic of Germany): 520 Madison Ave, New York, NY 10022; tel. (212) 826-5480; telex 425772; rep. office.

Middle East Bank Ltd (United Arab Emirates): 330 Madison Ave, 25th Floor, New York, NY 10017; tel. (212) 557-2500; telex 238145; fax (212) 986-9166; Gen. Man. K. SAMPATH KUMAR.

Mitsubishi Bank Ltd (Japan): One World Trade Center, Suite 8527, New York, NY 10048; tel. (212) 524-7000; telex 232328; fax (212) 432-1157; br. in Chicago; 2 rep. offices.

Mitsui Bank Ltd (Japan): 277 Park Ave, New York, NY 10172; tel. (212) 644-3131; telex 125435; Dir and Gen. Man. ATSUJI SEKI; br. in Chicago; 5 rep. offices.

Monte dei Paschi di Siena (Italy): 245 Park Ave, 26th Floor, New York, NY 10167; tel. (212) 557-8111.

Multi Commercial Bank (Switzerland): 353 West 56th St, Apartment 9B, New York, NY 10019; tel. (212) 765-3881; rep. office.

Nanyang Commercial Bank Ltd (Hong Kong): 500 Washington St, San Francisco, CA 94111; tel. (415) 398-8866; Man. GILBERT Y. PENG.

National Australia Bank Ltd: Pan Am Bldg, 34th Floor, 200 Park Ave, New York, NY 10166; tel. (212) 916-9500; telex 424725; fax (212) 983-1969; Senior Vice-Pres. D. A. DODGE; br. in Chicago; 4 rep. offices.

National Bank of Canada: 535 Madison Ave, New York, NY 10022; tel. (212) 605-8800; telex 177782; 2 rep. offices.

National Bank of Greece: 33 State St, Boston, MA 02109; tel. (617) 367-2200; telex 940493; rep. office in New York.

National Bank of Kuwait SAK: 299 Park Ave, New York, NY 10171; tel. (212) 303-9800; telex 421486.

The National Bank of New Zealand: One Seaport Plaza, 199 Water St, New York, NY 10038; Rep. S. BETTERIDGE; rep. office.

National Bank of Pakistan: 100 Wall St, POB 500, New York, NY 10005; tel. (212) 344-8831; telex 232455; Sr Exec. Vice-Pres. S. AKHTAR RAZA.

National Commercial Bank (Saudi Arabia): 245 Park Ave, 37th Floor, New York, NY 10167; tel. (212) 916-9000; fax (212) 916-9026.

National Westminster Bank plc (UK): 175 Water St, New York, NY 10038-4924; tel. (212) 602-4000; telex 233563; fax (212) 602-1004; Exec. Vice-Pres. G. H. M. HALL.

Nippon Credit Bank Ltd (Japan): 245 Park Ave, 30th Floor, New York, NY 10167; tel. (212) 984-1200; telex 232496; tel. (212) 490-2867; Gen. Man. NOBORU SAKATA; rep. office in Los Angeles.

Nippon Trust Bank Ltd (Japan): 45 Broadway, 18th Floor, New York, NY 10006; tel. (212) 269-2010; fax (212) 750-0139; rep. office.

Nishi-Nippon Bank Ltd (Japan): 45 Broadway, 6th Floor, New York, NY 10006; tel. (212) 968-1066; telex 4977229; fax (212) 968-1195.

NMB Bank (Netherlands): 450 Park Ave, New York, NY 10022; tel. (212) 715-7300; telex 177792; fax (212) 6440428; Gen. Man. L. C. GRIJNS.

Norinchukin Bank (Japan): One World Trade Center, Suite 8025, New York, NY 10048; tel. (212) 432-6886; telex 6720068; Gen. Man. HIROSUKE SATO.

Nuovo Banco Ambrosiano SpA (Italy): Park Avenue Tower, 65 East 55th St, New York, NY 10022; tel. (212) 688-8301; telex 62434; fax (212) 308-0910; Rep. PETER GIANNOTTI; rep. office.

Österreichische Länderbank AG (Austria): General Motors Bldg, 5th Floor, 767 Fifth Ave, New York, NY 10153; tel. (212) 326-3000; telex 425605; fax (212) 593-0392; Exec. Vice-Pres. and Gen. Man. FRIEDRICH HEIGL.

Overland Trust Bank (Switzerland): 200 East 66th St, New York, NY 10021; tel. (212) 223-0332; telex 640538.

Oversea-Chinese Banking Corpn Ltd (Singapore): Wells Fargo Bldg, Suite 1830, 444 South Flower St, Los Angeles, CA 90071; tel. (213) 624-1189; fax (213) 624-1386; Vice-Pres. and Rep. GEORGE A. BAKER, Jr; rep. office.

Philippine Commercial International: One World Center, Suite 4621, New York, NY 11048; tel. (212) 466-0960; telex 232744.

Philippine National Bank: Philippine Center Bldg, 556 Fifth Ave, New York, NY 10036; tel. (212) 382-3300; telex 62703; Asst Vice-Pres. PEDRO E. REYES, III; br. in Los Angeles.

Postipankki Ltd (Finland): 20 West 55th St, New York, NY 10019; Chief Rep. T. OTAMAA.

Privatbanken A/S (Denmark): 13–15 West 54th St, New York, NY 10019; tel. (212) 603-6900; telex 668788; rep. office in Los Angeles.

Romanian Bank for Foreign Trade: 573–577 Third Ave, New York, NY 10016; tel. (212) 697-8278; telex 429722; rep. office.

Royal Bank of Scotland plc: The Pyramid, 600 Montgomery St, San Francisco, CA 94111; tel. (415) 788-4500; telex 470494; agency and rep. office; 3 other rep. offices.

Saitama Bank Ltd (Japan): 44 Wall St, New York, NY 10005; tel. (212) 248-2690; telex 223410; Gen. Man. Masaaki Saito; rep. office in Dallas.

Sanwa Bank Ltd (Japan): 200 Park Ave, New York, NY 10166; tel. (212) 949-0222; telex 232423; 2 rep. offices.

Schweizerischer Bankverein (Swiss Bank Corporation): 4 World Trade Center, New York, NY 10048; tel. (212) 574-3000; telex 232432; 4 other brs; 2 rep. offices.

Senshu Bank Ltd (Japan): 165 Broadway, 45th Floor, New York, NY 10006; tel. (212) 587-1180; telex 420175.

Shizuoka Bank Ltd (Japan): 707 Wilshire Blvd, Suite 3700, Los Angeles, CA 90017; tel. (213) 622-3233; telex 182355; fax (213) 623-8674; rep. office in New York.

Shoko Chukin Bank (Japan): Two Wall St, New York, NY 10005; tel. (212) 732-9300; telex 6801392; fax (212) 608-3604.

Siam Commercial Bank Ltd (Thailand): Wells Fargo Bank Bldg, 22nd Floor, 444 South Flower St, Los Angeles, CA 90071; tel. (213) 641-1805; telex 181367; fax (213) 622-0049; Vice-Pres. and Man. Phaithoon Kijsamrej.

Skandinaviska Enskilda Banken (Sweden): 245 Park Ave, New York, NY 10167; tel. (212) 286-0600; telex 421618; fax (212) 370-1642; Pres. Bo Rassmuson.

Skopbank (Finland): Rockefeller Center, Bldg 6, Rm 2452, 630 Fifth Ave, New York, NY 10111; tel. (212) 245-3340; telex 175619; fax (212) 245-3369; Rep. Jan Wennstrom; rep. office.

Société Générale (France): 50 Rockefeller Plaza, 14th Floor, New York, NY 10020; tel. (212) 830-6600; telex 428802; fax (212) 830-6799; Gen. Man. J. Bouhet; 3 other brs; 2 rep. offices.

Sparbankernas Bank (SwedBank) (Sweden): Rockefeller Center, 24th Floor, 630 Fifth Ave, New York, NY 10111; tel. (212) 245-3342; telex 175619; Rep. Tomas Hammar; rep. office.

Sparekassen SDS (Denmark): 135 East 57th St, 16th Floor, New York, NY 10022; tel. (212) 935-0300; telex 824142; fax (212) 935-3145; Gen. Man. Steffen Johansen.

State Bank of New South Wales (Australia): 529 Fifth Ave at 44th St, 18th Floor, New York, NY 10017; tel. (212) 682-1300; telex 429964; fax (212) 309-0126; Asst Gen. Man. and Sr Vice-Pres. J. Bartholomew; rep. office in Los Angeles.

State Bank of South Australia: 461 Fifth Ave, 4th Floor, New York, NY 10017; tel. (212) 545-5800; fax (212) 779-3477; Exec. Vice-Pres. R. Sewell.

State Bank of Victoria (Australia): 250 Park Ave, 8th Floor, New York, NY 10177; tel. (212) 984-5100; telex 6720577; fax (212) 818-9440; Gen. Man. J. M. Winders.

Sumitomo Bank Ltd (Japan): One World Trade Center, Suite 9651, New York, NY 10048; tel. (212) 553-0100; telex 420515; fax (212) 524-0612; 3 other brs.

Sumitomo Trust and Banking Co Ltd (Japan): 527 Madison Ave, 3rd Floor, New York, NY 10022; tel. (212) 326-0600; telex 222049.

Svenska Handelsbanken (Sweden): 599 Lexington Ave, 38th Floor, New York, NY 10022; tel. (212) 326-5100; telex 1561322; fax (212) 326-5196; Gen. Man. Magnus Uggla.

Taiyo Kobe Bank Ltd (Japan): 350 Park Ave, New York, NY 10022; tel. (212) 750-1050; telex 222892; br. in Chicago; rep. office in Houston.

Thai Farmers Bank Ltd (Thailand): One World Trade Center, Suite 8373, New York, NY 10048; tel. (212) 432-0890; telex 645303; fax (212) 524-0494; Man. Methee Pattarakornkul.

Tokai Bank Ltd (Japan): One World Trade Center, Suite 8763, New York, NY 10048; tel. (212) 432-2600; telex 422857; fax (212) 524-0224; Gen. Man. Eiichi Kimata; 4 rep. offices.

Tokyo Sogo Bank Ltd (Japan): 61 Broadway, Suite 3010, New York, NY 10006; tel. (212) 797-4747; telex 147293; fax (212) 797-4749; Chief Rep. Tadashi Kumamoto.

Toronto-Dominion Bank (Canada): 42 Wall St, New York, NY 10005; tel. (212) 820-2000; telex 127846; Asst Gen. Man. G. B. MacPherson; 2 rep. offices.

Toyo Trust and Banking Co Ltd (Japan): 437 Madison Ave, New York, NY 10022; tel. (212) 371-3535; telex 222675; fax (212) 371-4963; Dir and Gen. Man. Shunroku Yokosuka; 2 rep. offices.

Türkiye Cumhuriyeti Ziraat Bankası (Turkey): 330 Madison Ave, 32nd Floor, New York, NY 10017; tel. (212) 557-5612; telex 426674; fax (212) 490-8076.

Udružena Banka Hrvatske (UBH Zagreb) (Yugoslavia): 225 West 34th St, Rm 1808, New York, NY 10122; tel. (212) 563-6529; telex 234045; fax (212) 967-4530; rep. office.

Unibanco—União de Bancos Brasileiros, SA (Brazil): 555 Madison Ave, 19th Floor, New York, NY 10022; tel. (212) 832-1700; telex 220011; Rep. Ricardo Figueiredo Lima; rep. office.

Union Bank of Finland: 437 Madison Ave, New York, NY 10022; tel. (212) 371-1090; telex 422511; fax (212) 421-4420; Gen. Man. Jorma Laakkonen; rep. office in Los Angeles.

Union Bank of Switzerland: 299 Park Ave, New York, NY 10171; tel. (212) 715-3000; telex 620317; Man. P. De Weck; 3 other brs; rep. office in San Francisco.

United Bank for Africa Ltd (Nigeria): 551 Madison Ave, 7th Floor, New York, NY 10022; tel. (212) 308-7222; telex 6801178; Gen. Man. A. A. Coker.

United Bank Ltd (Pakistan): 30 Wall St, New York, NY 10005; tel. (212) 943-1275; telex 232576.

United Mizrahi Bank Ltd (Israel): 630 Fifth Ave, New York, NY 10111; tel. (212) 307-1364.

Vereins- und Westbank AG (Federal Republic of Germany): Seagram Bldg, 375 Park Ave, New York, NY 10152; tel. (212) 838-9292; telex 126941; fax (212) 371-6982; rep. office; 1 other rep. office in Atlanta.

Vojvodjanska Banka—Udružena Banka (Yugoslavia): 405 Lexington Ave, New York, NY 10165; tel. (212) 490-8990; telex 0968403; Dir Milka Popović.

M. M. Warburg-Brinckmann, Wirtz & Co (Federal Republic of Germany): 375 Park Ave, Suite 3801, New York, NY 10152; tel. (212) 758-0440; telex 427921; fax (212) 223-2425; rep. office.

Westdeutsche Landesbank Girozentrale (Federal Republic of Germany): 450 Park Ave, New York, NY 10022; tel. (212) 745-1000; telex 420736.

Westpac Banking Corporation (Australia): 335 Madison Ave, New York, NY 10017; tel. (212) 551-2700; telex 425620; fax (212) 818-1499; Sr Vice-Pres. and Chief Man. Owen van der Wall; 3 other brs; rep. office in Houston.

Yapı ve Kredi Bankası AS (Turkey): 40 East 52nd St, 20th Floor, New York, NY 10022; tel. (212) 751-1135; telex 125857; fax (212) 308-3491.

Yasuda Trust and Banking Co Ltd (Japan): One World Trade Center, Suite 8871, New York, NY 10048-0554; tel. (212) 432-2300; telex 421061.

Principal Commercial Banks

(br.(s) = branch(es); cap. = total capital and reserves; dep. = deposits; m. = million; amounts in US dollars)

ALABAMA

AmSouth Bank NA: 1900 Fifth Ave North, POB 11007, Birmingham, AL 35288; tel. (205) 326-5120; telex 6827189; f. 1873; cap. 521m., dep. 6,406m. (Sept. 1988); Chair. and CEO John W. Woods; Pres. and COO Dan L. Hendley; 111 US brs, 1 foreign br.

Central Bank of the South: 701 South 20th St, POB 10566, Birmingham, AL 35296; tel. (205) 933-3010; telex 593004; fax (205) 933-3996; f. 1964; cap. 277.3m., dep. 2,787.4m. (Sept. 1987); Chair. Harry B. Brock, Jr; Pres. W. Dan Puckett.

First Alabama Bank: 106 St Francis St, Mobile, AL 36622; tel. (205) 690-1239; telex 505528; f. 1901; cap. 439.7m., dep. 4,239.0m. (Dec. 1988); Chair., Pres. and CEO Carl E. Jones, Jr; 180 brs.

Southtrust Bank of Alabama NA: 420 North 20th St, POB 2554, Birmingham, AL 35290; tel. (205) 254-5220; telex 59837; fax (205) 254-5656; f. 1887; cap. 186.2m., dep. 2,158.1m. (Dec. 1987); Chair. Roy Gilbert; Pres. and CEO Julian W. Banton.

ALASKA

First National Bank of Anchorage: Fourth Ave at G St, Anchorage, AK 99501; tel. (907) 276-6300; telex 25190; f. 1922; cap. 158.2m., dep. 617.9m. (March 1989); Pres. J. P. Pfeifer; Chair. D. H. Cuddy; 19 brs.

National Bank of Alaska: 301 West Northern Lights Blvd, POB 600, Anchorage, AK 99503; tel. (907) 276-1132; telex 25226; f.

1916; cap. 102.5m., dep. 765.4m. (Dec. 1983); Chair. EDWARD B. RASMUSON; Pres. ROBERT P. GRAY; 25 brs.

ARIZONA

Citibank (Arizona): 3300 North Central Ave, Phoenix, AZ 85012; tel. (602) 248-2200; telex 187250; f. 1968; cap. 317m., dep. 2,211m. (June 1988); Chair. M. WELBORN.

First Interstate Bank of Arizona NA: POB 29744, Phoenix, AZ 85003; tel. (602) 271-6000; telex 165052; f. 1877; cap. 455.9m., dep. 5,332.9m. (June 1986); Chair. and CEO ROBERT H. DUCKWORTH; 191 US brs, 1 foreign br.

Security Pacific Bank Arizona: 101 North First Ave, Phoenix, AZ 85003; tel. (602) 262-2000; telex 6835064; fax (602) 253-2855; f. 1902, known as Arizona Bank until 1989; Pres. and CEO WILLIAM S. THOMAS, Jr.

United Bank of Arizona: 3300 North Central Ave, Phoenix, AZ 85012; tel. (602) 248-2200; telex 165062; fax (602) 263-5837; f. 1959; cap. 142.8m., dep. 1,947.9m. (June 1987); Chair. and Pres. GEORGE H. ISBELL; 45 brs.

Valley National Bank of Arizona: POB 71, Phoenix, AZ 85001; tel. (602) 261-2900; telex 187102; f. 1899; cap. 607m., dep. 9,294m. (Sept. 1988); Chair. and CEO JAMES P. SIMMONS; Pres. RICHARD J. LEHMANN; 236 brs.

ARKANSAS

First National Bank: POB 751, El Dorado, AR 71731; tel. (501) 863-3181; f. 1903; Chair. JIM KELLEY; Pres. R. G. DUDLEY.

First National Bank of Hot Springs: 528 Central Ave, Hot Springs, AR 71901; tel. (501) 321-8000; telex 0536465; f. 1882; Pres. and CEO JAMES P. JETT; 8 brs.

National Bank of Commerce of Pine Bluff: POB 6208, Pine Bluff, AR 71611; tel. (501) 541-8000; f. 1934; cap. 16.5m., dep. 213.0m. (Dec. 1987); Chair. WILLIAM H. KENNEDY, Jr; Pres. JAMES F. STOBAUGH.

Simmons First National Bank of Pine Bluff: Main and Fifth Sts, Pine Bluff, AR 71601; tel. (501) 535-2100; telex 7292910; f. 1903; Pres. HOWELL N. DAVIS; CEO LOUIS L. RAMSAY, Jr; 7 brs.

Union National Bank of Little Rock: 1 Union National Plaza, Little Rock, AR 72201; tel. (501) 378-4000; telex 284794; fax (501) 376-4236; f. 1934; cap. 41.3m., dep. 430.2m. (Dec. 1986); Chair. HERBERT H. MCADAMS.

CALIFORNIA

Bank of America National Trust and Savings Asscn: Bank of America Center, 555 California St, San Francisco, CA 94104; tel. (415) 622-3456; telex 27248; f. 1904; cap. 4,224m., dep. 70,150m. (Dec. 1987); Chair., Pres. and CEO ALDEN W. (TOM) CLAUSEN; 1,110 US brs, 79 foreign brs.

Bank of California, NA: 400 California St, San Francisco, CA 94104; tel. (415) 765-0400; telex 278766; fax (415) 981-3761; f. 1864; cap. 287.7m., dep. 3,211.1m. (Dec. 1987); Chair., Pres. and CEO OSAMU YAMADA; Exec. Vice-Pres. and COO JUNJI HATANO; 27 US brs, 5 foreign brs.

Bank of Canton of California: Bank of Canton of California Bldg, 555 Montgomery St, San Francisco, CA 94111; tel. (415) 362-4100; telex 278774; f. 1937; cap. 83.5m., dep. 662.7m. (Dec. 1987); Chair. H. P. CHIA; 8 brs.

Bank of the West: 180 Montgomery St, San Francisco, CA 94104; tel. (415) 765-4800; telex 278607; f. 1874; cap. 144.6m., dep. 1,193.7m. (Dec. 1987); Chair. EDOUARD FINOT; Pres. MCKENZIE MOSS; 42 brs.

City National Bank: 400 North Roxbury Dr., Beverly Hills, CA 90210; tel. (213) 550-5400; telex 677653; fax (213) 623-1163; f. 1953; cap. 129.6m., dep. 1,721.3m. (March 1985); Chair. BRAM GOLDSMITH; Pres. ALEXANDER L. KYMAN; 24 brs.

Exchange Bank: 545 Fourth St, Santa Rosa, CA 95401; tel. (707) 545-6220; f. 1890; cap. 49.5m., dep. 447.7m. (Dec. 1988); Chair. and Pres. ANDREW J. SHEPARD; 14 brs.

First Interstate Bank of California: 707 Wilshire Blvd, Los Angeles, CA 90017; tel. (213) 614-4111; telex 674421; f. 1905; cap. 1,094.0m., dep. 16,718.7m. (June 1988); Chair., Pres. and CEO WILLIAM E. B. SIART; 318 brs.

First Los Angeles Bank: 2049 Century Park East, 36th Floor, Los Angeles, CA 90067; tel. (213) 557-1211; telex 6831476; fax (213) 556-1294; f. 1973; cap. 57.5m., dep. 668.1m. (Dec. 1987); Chair. CHARLES T. MANATT; Pres. and CEO LUIGI MARANZANA; 9 brs.

Mitsui Manufacturers Bank: 515 South Figueroa St, POB 15099, Los Angeles, CA 90071; tel. (213) 485-0331; telex 674184; f. 1962;

cap. 115.6m., dep. 1,431.8m. (Dec. 1987); Chair. KENICHI KAMIYA; Pres. and CEO YUTARO HAYASHI; 12 brs.

Pacific Western Bank: 333 West Santa Clara St, San Jose, CA 95113; tel. (408) 244-1700; telex 346438; fax (408) 298-7633; f. 1870; Chair. PHILLIP R. BOYCE; Pres. JAMES R. KENNY; 23 brs.

San Diego Trust and Savings Bank: 540 Broadway, POB 1871, San Diego, CA 92112; tel. (619) 238-4715; telex 295845; fax (619) 238-0254; f. 1889; cap. 925m., dep. 1,258.4m. (Dec. 1988); Pres. T. W. SEFTON; 46 brs.

Security Pacific National Bank: Security Pacific Plaza, 333 South Hope St, Los Angeles, CA 90071; tel. (213) 613-6211; telex 674343; f. 1871; cap. 2,316.8m., dep. 36,524.1m. (March 1989); Pres. and CEO ROBERT H. SMITH, III; 586 US brs, 7 foreign brs.

Sumitomo Bank of California: 320 California St, San Francisco, CA 94104; tel. (415) 445-8000; telex 470075; fax (415) 397-1475; f. 1952; cap. 164.6m., dep. 2,471.1m. (Dec. 1984); Pres. KEIZO YOSHIDA; 46 US brs, 1 foreign br.

Union Bank: 350 California St, San Francisco, CA 94119; tel. (415) 445-0200; f. 1975, fmrly California First Bank until the acquisition of Union Bank in 1989; cap. 1,047.2m., dep. 11,911.0m. (Dec. 1988); Chair. TOSHIO NAGAMURA; CEO SEISHICHI ITOH; 113 US brs, 4 international brs.

Wells Fargo Bank NA: 464 California St, San Francisco, CA 94163; tel. (415) 396-0123; telex 184904; f. 1852; cap. 1,115.3m., dep. 20,554.4m. (Dec. 1983); Chair. and CEO CARL E. REICHARDT; Pres. and COO PAUL HAZEN; 385 US brs, 3 foreign brs.

COLORADO

First Interstate Bank of Denver: 633 17th St, Denver, CO 80270; tel. (303) 293-2211; telex 4322036; f. 1860; cap. 150.0m., dep. 1,275.3m. (Dec. 1988); Chair. and Pres. ROBERT J. MALONE.

First Interstate Bank of Englewood: 3333 South Bannock St, POB 240, Englewood, CO 80110; tel. (303) 761-1000; f. 1951; cap. 11.7m., dep. 123.3m. (Dec. 1988); Pres. and CEO GARY J. DEFRANGE.

First Interstate Bank of Fort Collins: 205 West Oak St, POB 578, Fort Collins, CO 80521; tel. (303) 4824861; f. 1881; cap. 20.5m., dep. 231.7m. (Dec. 1988); Chair. and Pres. TOM J. GLEASON.

United Bank of Denver NA: United Bank Center, 1700 Broadway, Denver, CO 80274; tel. (303) 861-8811; telex 045533; fax (303) 863-4898 f. 1884; cap. 166.6m., dep. 2,052.4m. (June 1987); Chair. RICHARD A. KIRK; Pres. CARROL D. SPECKMAN; 1 foreign br.

CONNECTICUT

Bank of Boston Connecticut: 81 West Main St, Waterbury, CT 06702; tel. (203) 574-7000; telex 4750336; f. 1899; cap. 148.1m., dep. 2,152.4m. (June 1988); Chair., Pres. and CEO PAUL N. VONCKX, Jr; 49 US brs, 1 foreign br.

Citytrust: 961 Main St, Bridgeport, CT 06601; tel. (203) 336-7325; telex 964225; fax (203) 336-7504; f. 1929; cap. 170.0m., dep. 2,226.5m. (March 1989); Chair. and CEO GEORGE F. TAYLOR; Pres. and COO IRWIN ENGELMAN; 43 brs.

Connecticut Bank and Trust Co: One Constitution Plaza, Hartford, CT 06115; tel. (203) 244-5000; telex 994411; f. 1814; cap. 659.7m., dep. 7,509.7m. (Dec. 1988); Chair. DAVID B. PAYNE; Pres. JAMES F. MCNALLY; 166 US brs, 1 foreign br.

Connecticut National Bank: 777 Main St, Hartford, CT 06115; tel. (203) 728-2000; telex 99339; fax (203) 722-9378; f. 1792, merged with Shawmut Bank NA (Boston, MA) in 1988; cap. 708.4m., dep. 7,440.8m. (June 1988); Chair. JOEL B. ALVORD; Pres. and CEO GUNNAR S. OVERSTROM; 185 US brs, 1 foreign br.

Home Bank and Trust Company: 400 East Main St, Meriden, CT 06450; tel. (203) 237-8411; f. 1854; Pres. RAYMOND N. KELLOGG; 10 brs.

New Britain National Bank: West Main St, POB 2230, New Britain, CT 06050; tel. (203) 229-3731; f. 1860; Chair. HENRY A. NEWBURY; Pres. and CEO WILLIAM H. CHADWICK; 8 brs.

Union Trust Company: 300 Main St, Stamford, CT 06904-0700; tel. (202) 348-6211; telex 996410; f. 1969; Chair., CEO and Pres. THOMAS F. RICHARDSON.

DELAWARE

Bank of Delaware: 300 Delaware Ave, Wilmington, DE 19801; tel. (302) 429-1011; telex 6662280; f. 1885; cap. 115.2m., dep. 1,584.6m. (Dec. 1988); Chair. and CEO JEREMIAH P. SHEA; Pres. and COO DAVID MCMILLAN; 32 brs.

Bankers Trust (Delaware): 1001 Jefferson St, Wilmington, DE 19801; tel. (302) 594-4400; telex 4761151; fax (212) 250-5914; f. 1985;

cap. 249.8m., dep. 812.6m. (Dec. 1988); Pres. and CEO JAMES H. STALLKAMP; Chair. GEORGE J. VOJTA.

Delaware Trust Company: 900 Market St Mall, POB 1109, Wilmington, DE 19899; tel. (302) 421-7000; f. 1899; cap. 60.8m., dep. 836.7m. (Dec. 1985); Chair. and CEO J. H. TYLER MCCONNELL; Pres. JOHN F. PORTER, III; 29 brs.

Wilmington Trust Company: Rodney Sq. North, Wilmington, DE 19890; tel. (302) 651-1000; telex 835437; f. 1903; cap. 228.0m., dep. 1,910.7m. (Dec. 1988); Chair., Pres. and CEO BERNARD J. TAYLOR, II; 32 brs.

DISTRICT OF COLUMBIA

American Security Bank NA: 1501 Pennsylvania Ave, NW, Washington, DC 20013; tel. (202) 624-4000; telex 197548; f. 1889; cap. 249m., dep. 3,078m. (Dec. 1985); Chair. DANIEL J. CALLAHAN, III; Pres. WILLIAM G. TULL; 33 US brs, 1 foreign br.

National Bank of Washington: 619 14th St, NW, Washington, DC 20005; tel. (202) 537-2000; telex 8229325; f. 1809; cap. 104m., dep. 1,491m. (Dec. 1986); Chair. LUTHER H. HODGES, Jr; 18 US brs, 1 foreign br.

Petra International Banking Corporation: 1801 K St, NW, Suite 201, Washington, DC 20006; tel. (202) 293-2250; telex 6491150; fax (202) 293-0448; f. 1983; cap. 4.4m., dep. 52.1m. (Dec. 1986); Chair. JAWAD A. H. CHALABI.

Riggs National Bank of Washington, DC: 1503 Pennsylvania Ave, NW, Washington, DC 20013; tel. (202) 835-6000; telex 248363; f. 1896; cap. 372.0m., dep. 5,253.8m. (Dec. 1988); Chair. and CEO JOEL L. ALLBRITTON; Pres. TIMOTHY C. COUGHLIN.

FLORIDA

Bank of Miami: 100 East Flagler St, Miami, FL 33131; tel. (305) 379-3000; telex 519416; f. 1956; cap. 21.3m., dep. 321m. (Dec. 1985); Chair. JOSE LUIS CARRION; Pres. JUSTO LEGIDO.

Barnett Bank of Central Florida NA: 201 South Orange Ave, Orlando, FL 32801; tel. (305) 420-2780; telex 4450012; f. 1877; Chair. CHARLES K. CROSS.

Barnett Bank of Jacksonville NA: 100 Laura St, Jacksonville, FL 32231; tel. (904) 791-7500; telex 4450012; f. 1877; Chair. and CEO HUGH H. JONES, Jr; Pres. ROLAND S. KENNEDY.

Barnett Bank of South Florida, NA: 701 Brickell Ave, POB 010429, Miami, FL 33101-0429; tel. (305) 350-7122; telex 519542; f. 1877; cap. 206m., dep. 3,566.3m. (Dec. 1985); Chair. and CEO HUGH GENTRY; Pres. LEE CHAPLIN.

Barnett Bank of Tampa, NA: 101 East Kennedy Blvd, Tampa, FL 33602; tel. (813) 225-8155; telex 4450012; f. 1926; cap. 56.4m., dep. 1,026.7m. (Dec. 1986); Pres. ALLAN L. MCLEOD, Jr.

Citizens' and Peoples' National Bank of Pensacola: 213 South Palafox St, Pensacola, FL 32501; tel. (904) 433-2299; f. 1893; cap. 28.8m., dep. 204.2m. (June 1987); Chair. G. W. REESE; Pres. L. A. DOMAN; 3 brs.

Citizens and Southern Florida Corporation: 1 Financial Plaza, POB 5367, Fort Lauderdale, FL 33310; tel. (305) 765-2000; telex 6815174; fax (305) 462-7130; f. 1971; Chair. J. JOSEPH TUOHY; Pres. and CEO A. GORDON OLIVER; 125 brs.

Consolidated Bank NA: 900 West 49th St, Hialeah, FL 33012; tel. (305) 558-1000; telex 3727477; f. 1963; cap. 46,368m., dep. 735.0m. (June 1988); Chair., Pres. and CEO MARIO E. DIEZ; 21 brs.

First Florida Bank NA: POB 1810, Tampa, FL 33601; tel. (813) 224-1111; telex 052812; f. 1883; Pres. D. L. MURPHY.

First Union National Bank of Florida: 200 West Forsyth St, POB 2080, Jacksonville, FL 32231-0010; tel. (904) 361-6767; telex 6815184; fax (904) 361-7943; f. 1908; cap. 194.7m., dep. 2,934.3m. (Dec. 1984); Chair. and CEO B. J. WALKER; Pres. BYRON HODNETT; 230 brs.

Florida National Bank: 201 South Biscayne Blvd, Miami, FL 33131; tel. (305) 789-4670; telex 441395; f. 1931; Pres. M. ROBERT DUSSLER, Jr; 14 brs.

Intercontinental Bank: 200 Southeast First St, Miami, FL 33131; tel. (305) 376-6900; telex 518936; f. 1954; Chair. WILLIAM H. ALLEN, Jr; Pres. WILLIAM L. MORRISON; 10 brs.

Miami National Bank: 300 Aragon Ave, Coral Gables, FL 33134; tel. (305) 448-0800; f. 1956; cap. 9.3m., dep. 83.8m. (Dec. 1983); Chair. FRANCISCO DE BORBÓN; Pres. JOHN W. PENNYPACKER; 4 brs.

NCNB National Bank of Florida: 400 North Ashley St, POB 31590, Tampa, FL 33602; tel. (813) 224-5614; telex 6815308; fax (813) 224-5581; f. 1983; Chair. and CEO HUGH L. MCCOLL, Jr; 200 brs.

Southeast Bank NA: One Southeast Financial Center, Miami, FL 33131; tel. (305) 375-7500; telex 6811264; fax (305) 375-7449; f. 1902; cap. 666.3m., dep. 9,555.8m. (Dec. 1986); Chair. CHARLES J. ZWICK; Pres. JOHN E. PORTA.

Sun Bank NA: 200 South Orange Ave, POB 3833, Orlando, FL 32897; tel. (305) 237-4952; telex 803837; f. 1934; cap. 134.9m., dep. 2,183.9m. (Dec. 1984); Chair. and Pres. BUELL G. DUNCAN, Jr; 59 US brs, 1 foreign br.

Sun Bank/North Florida NA: 550 Water St, POB 2494, Jacksonville, FL 32203; tel. (904) 356-2869; telex 568410; f. 1955; Chair. and CEO ROBERT J. TANNER; Vice-Pres. and Gen. Man. GREGORY J. BODALSKI; 12 brs.

Sun Bank of Tampa Bay: 315 Madison St, Tampa, FL 33602; tel. (813) 224-2326; telex 52626; fax (813) 224-2424; f. 1914; cap. 86.5m., dep. 1,115.3m. (Dec. 1987); Chair. and CEO GEORGE W. KOEHN; 14 brs.

GEORGIA

Bank of the South NA: Marietta and Forsyth Sts, Atlanta, GA 30303; tel. (404) 529-4111; telex 542753; f. 1910; Chair. RAWSON HAVERTY; Pres. and CEO ROBERT GUYTON; 30 brs.

Citizens and Southern National Bank: 35 Broad St, NW, Atlanta, GA 30303; tel. (404) 581-2121; telex 542346; fax (404) 581-5061; f. 1887; cap. 423.8m., dep. 5,303.1m. (Dec. 1984); Chair. and CEO JOHN W. MCINTYRE; 475 brs.

First National Bank of Atlanta: 2 Peachtree St, POB 4148, Five Points, Atlanta, GA 30383; tel. (404) 588-5000; telex 542309; f. 1865; cap. 609.2m., dep. 5,530.5m. (March 1988); Chair. JOHN G. MEDLIN, Jr; Pres. D. RAYMOND RIDDLE; 99 US brs, 1 foreign br.

National Bank of Georgia: 2000 River Edge Parkway, Atlanta, GA 30328; tel. (404) 951-4000; telex 4611074; f. 1911; cap. 102m., dep. 1,247.5m. (Dec. 1986); Chair. and CEO R. P. M. CARLSON; Pres. G. W. FREEMAN.

Trust Company Bank: 25 Park Pl., Atlanta, GA 30303; tel. (404) 588-7711; telex 542210; cap. 401.1m., dep. 3,708.0m. (Dec. 1987); Chair. L. PHILLIP HURNANN; Pres. ROBERT R. LONG; 52 US brs, 1 foreign br.

HAWAII

Bank of Hawaii: 111 South King St, Honolulu, HI 96813; tel. (808) 537-8111; telex 7238434, f. 1897; cap. 356.2m., dep. 4,998.4m. (March 1988); Chair. and CEO FRANK MANAUT; Pres. H. HOWARD STEPHENSON; 62 US brs, 12 foreign brs.

City Bank: 810 Richards St, POB 3709, Honolulu, HI 96813; tel. (808) 546-2411; telex 7430169; fax (808) 523-7458; f. 1959; Chair. and CEO JAMES M. MORITA; Pres. EARL HIROTSU; 12 brs.

First Hawaiian Bank: 165 South King St, Honolulu, HI 96813; tel. (808) 525-7000; telex 7238329; f. 1929; cap. 238.5m., dep. 3,621.8m. (Dec. 1988); Chair. and CEO JOHN D. BELLINGER; Pres. HUGH R. PINGREE; 44 US brs, 4 foreign brs.

Hawaii National Bank: 841 Bishop St, POB 3740, Honolulu, HI 96812; tel. (808) 538-5111; telex 723302; fax (808) 538-5109; f. 1960; cap. 15.2m., dep. 209.0m. (Dec. 1988); Chair. K. J. LUKE; Pres. and CEO TAKAO SATO; 10 brs.

IDAHO

First Interstate Bank of Idaho, NA: 700 West Idaho St, POB 51, Boise, ID 83702; tel. (208) 383-5225; telex 4993948; f. 1891; cap. 53.6m., dep. 753.1m. (Dec. 1988); Chair. and CEO JAMES J. CURRAN; 31 brs.

Idaho First National Bank: 101 South Capitol Blvd, POB 8247, Boise, ID 83707; tel. (208) 383-7000; telex 368431; f. 1867; cap. 197.7m., dep. 2,040.4m. (June 1988); Chair. DANIEL R. NELSON; Pres. and CEO ROBERT LANE.

ILLINOIS

American National Bank and Trust Co of Chicago: 33 North LaSalle St, Chicago, IL 60690; tel. (312) 661-5000; telex 25229; fax (312) 853-0290; f. 1928; cap. 232.6m., dep. 3,042.3m. (June 1988); Chair. MICHAEL E. TOBIN; Pres. RONALD J. GRAYHECK; 1 foreign br.

Commercial National Bank of Peoria: 301 Southwest Adams St, Peoria, IL 61631; tel. (309) 655-5000; telex 404311; f. 1885; cap. 42.6m., dep. 370.9m. (June 1988); Pres. and CEO ROBERT T. STEVENSON, Jr.

Continental Bank NA: 231 South LaSalle St, Chicago, IL 60697; tel. (312) 828-2345; telex 25233; fax (312) 828-3820; f. 1857, known as Continental Illinois National Bank and Trust Co of Chicago until 1988; cap. 1,424m., dep. 19,687m. (Dec. 1987); Chair. and CEO THOMAS C. THEOBALD; 5 US regional offices, 9 foreign brs.

Drovers Bank of Chicago: Ashland Ave at 47th St, Chicago, IL 60609; tel. (312) 927-7000; telex 2212624; f. 1883; Chair. FRANK E. BAUDER; Pres. JAMES J. CARMODY.

Exchange National Bank of Chicago: LaSalle and Monroe Sts, Chicago, IL 60603; tel. (312) 781-8000; telex 6871010; f. 1926; cap. 114.9m., dep. 1,412.4m. (Dec. 1986); Chair. and CEO IRA J. KAUFMAN; Pres. JOHN RAU; 1 foreign br.

First National Bank of Chicago: 1 First National Plaza, Chicago, IL 60670; tel. (312) 732-5965; telex 4330253; f. 1863; cap. 1,727.2m., dep. 27,372.4m. (Dec. 1988); Chair. BARRY F. SULLIVAN; Pres. RICHARD L. THOMAS; 12 foreign brs.

First National Bank, Mattoon: 1515 Charleston, Mattoon, IL 61938; tel. (217) 234-7454; f. 1911; Pres. DONALD S. CASON.

First National Bank of Peoria: 416 Main St, Peoria, IL 61602; f. 1863; cap. 24.8m., dep. 196.0m. (Dec. 1987); Pres. RONALD J. MORGAN.

Harris Trust and Savings Bank: 111 West Monroe St, Chicago, IL 60603; tel. (312) 461-2121; telex 253417; f. 1882; cap. 412m., dep. 5,465.6m. (Dec. 1984); Chair. and CEO B. KENNETH WEST; 2 foreign brs.

Heritage Pullman Bank and Trust Company: 1000 East 111th St, Chicago, IL 60628; tel. (312) 785-1000; cap. 14.4m., dep. 205.2m. (Dec. 1986); Pres. JAMES A. GRELL.

LaSalle National Bank: 135 South LaSalle St, Chicago, IL 60603; tel. (312) 443-2000; telex 253879; f. 1927; cap. 101.8m., dep. 1,105.4m. (Dec. 1988); Chair. ROBERT K. WILMOUTH; Pres. HARRISON F. TEMPEST; 1 foreign br.

NBD Elk Grove Bank: 100E Higgins Rd, Elk Grove Village, IL 60007; tel. (312) 439-1666; f. 1963; cap. 15.5m., dep. 250.8m. (June 1988); Pres. JAMES R. LANCASTER.

Northern Trust Co: 50 South LaSalle St, Chicago, IL 60675; tel. (312) 630-6000; telex 824183; f. 1889; cap. 365.5m., dep. 5,165.8m. (Dec. 1988); Chair. WESTON R. CHRISTOPHERSON; 2 US brs, 3 foreign brs.

Unibanctrust Company: 233 South Wacker Dr., Chicago, IL 60606; tel. (312) 876-4200; telex 190275; f. 1931; Chair. and CEO DONALD T. THORNBURG; Pres. B. T. REIDY.

INDIANA

Bank One, Indianapolis, NA: 101 Monument Circle, Indianapolis, IN 46277; tel. (317) 639-3000; telex 027324; fax (317) 639-7965; f. 1839; cap. 265.2m., dep. 2,912.0m. (Dec. 1988); Chair. FRANK E. MCKINNEY, Jr; Pres. JOSEPH D. BARNETTE, Jr; 65 brs.

First Source Bank: 100 South Michigan St, South Bend, IN 46601; tel. (219) 287-1881; f. 1863; Chair. BENTON M. WAKEFIELD, Jr; Pres. CHRISTOPHER J. MURPHY, III; 18 brs.

Fort Wayne National Bank: 110 West Berry St, Fort Wayne, IN 46802; tel. (219) 426-0555; telex 276482; fax (219) 461-6180; f. 1933; Chair. PAUL E. SHAFFER; Pres. JACKSON R. LEHMAN; 17 brs.

Gary National Bank: POB 209, Gary, IN 46402; tel. (219) 738-4000; f. 1908; Chair. W. W. GASSER, Jr; Pres. J. W. MORFEE; 25 brs.

INB National Bank: 1 Indiana Sq., Indianapolis, IN 46266; tel. (317) 266-6000; telex 6876025; f. 1834, known as Indiana National Bank until 1989; cap. 280.8m., dep. 3,462.7m. (Dec. 1988); Chair. THOMAS M. MILLER; Pres. ANDREW J. PAINE, Jr; 50 US brs, 1 foreign br.

Lincoln National Bank and Trust Company of Fort Wayne: 116 East Berry St, Fort Wayne, IN 46802; tel. (219) 461-6000; f. 1905; Pres. and CEO ROBERT J. DELANEY, Jr; 13 brs.

Merchants National Bank and Trust Co of Indianapolis: 1 Merchants Bank Plaza, Indianapolis, IN 46255; tel. (317) 267-7000; telex 27411; fax (317) 267-7152; f. 1865; cap. 189.8m., dep. 2,081.3m. (March 1989); Chair. J. D. MASSEY; Pres. J. W. MAGEE; 45 US brs, 1 foreign br.

Trustcorp Bank, South Bend: 202 South Michigan St, POB 6, South Bend, IN 46624; tel. (219) 237-5258; telex 4949629; fax (219) 237-5520; f. 1869; Chair. and CEO ARTHUR H. MCELWEE, Jr; 11 brs.

IOWA

Bankers Trust Company (Iowa): 665 Locust St, POB 897, Des Moines, IA 50304; tel. (515) 245-5284; telex 283078; fax (515) 282-3917; f. 1917; cap. 36.8m., dep. 400.0m. (Dec. 1988); Chair. and CEO JOHN CHRYSTAL; Pres. and COO DENNIS WOOD; 5 brs.

First Interstate Bank of Des Moines NA: Locust St at Sixth Ave, Des Moines, IA 50304; f. 1895; cap. 25.9m., dep. 329.4m. (Dec. 1988); Pres. and CEO ROBERT G. MILLEN; 3 brs.

Merchants National Bank: 222 Second Ave, SE, Cedar Rapids, IA 52401; tel. (319) 368-4708; telex 464410; fax (319) 368-4866; f. 1881; cap. 53.1m., dep. 622.7m. (Dec. 1988); Pres. HENRY ROYER; 6 brs.

Norwest Bank Des Moines NA: POB 837, Des Moines, IA 50304; tel. (515) 245-3146; telex 478326; fax (515) 245-3139; f. 1929; cap. 76.3m., dep. 1,040.8m. (Dec. 1988); Chair. and CEO JOHN C. NELSON; Pres. H. LYNN HORAK; 6 brs.

Peoples' Bank and Trust Company: Third Ave at First St, SW, Cedar Rapids, IA 52404; tel. (319) 364-0191; f. 1900; cap. 88.5m., dep. 177.7m. (June 1985); Chair. TED J. WELCH; Pres. JOHN M. SAGERS; 3 brs.

KANSAS

Bank IV Wichita, NA: 100 North Broadway, POB 4, Wichita, KS 67201; tel. (316) 261-4444; telex 417481; fax (316) 261-4515; f. 1887; cap. 103.3m., dep. 1,196.9m. (Dec. 1988); Chair. JORDAN L. HAINES; Pres. K. GORDON GREER.

First National Bank in Wichita: Box One, Wichita, KS 67201; tel. (316) 268-1111; telex 1007591; f. 1876; Chair. and Pres. C. Q. CHANDLER.

KENTUCKY

Citizens Fidelity Bank and Trust Co: Citizens Plaza, Fifth and Jefferson Sts, Louisville, KY 40296; tel. (502) 581-3250; telex 204136; fax (502) 581-2824; f. 1944; cap. 303.3m., dep. 3,258.7m. (Dec. 1988); CEO THOMAS H. O'BRIEN; 82 US brs, 1 foreign br.

First National Bank of Louisville: 3700 First National Tower, 101 South Fifth St, Louisville, KY 40202; tel. (502) 581-4200; telex 6842090; f. 1863; cap. 258.3m., dep. 3,147.7m. (Dec. 1988); Chair. A. STEVENS MILES; Pres. and CEO LEONARD V. HARDIN; 50 US brs, 1 foreign br.

First Security National Bank & Trust Company: 1 First Security Plaza, Lexington, KY 40507; tel. (606) 231-1000; f. 1865; Chair. W. L. ROUSE, Jr; 20 brs.

Liberty National Bank and Trust Co: POB 32580, Louisville, KY 40232; tel. (502) 566-2297; telex 204359; fax (502) 566-2200; f. 1854; cap. 134.9m., dep. 1,498.2m. (June 1987); Chair. and CEO FRANK B. HOWER, Jr; 42 brs.

LOUISIANA

American Bank & Trust Co: 200 Carondelet St, POB 61375, New Orleans, LA 70130; tel. (504) 525-7761; telex 6715269; fax (504) 569-0140; cap. 33.1m., dep. 276.4m. (Dec. 1987); Chair. and CEO WILMORE W. WHITMORE; Pres. SHARON T. ROPPOLO.

Commercial National Bank in Shreveport: 333 Texas St, Shreveport, LA 71101; tel. (318) 429-1000; telex 507411; f. 1932; Pres. J. E. BURT, III; 10 brs.

First National Bank of Commerce: 210 Baronne St, POB 60279, New Orleans, LA 70112; tel. (504) 561-1371; telex 58321; fax (504) 561-7082; f. 1933; dep. 2,083.5m. (Dec. 1988); Chair., Pres. and CEO HOWARD C. GAINES.

First National Bank of Lake Charles: 3401 Ryan St, Lake Charles, LA 70605; tel. (318) 477-7630; telex 9727507; f. 1889; Pres. and Chair. ARTHUR HOLLINS, III; 11 brs.

Hibernia National Bank: 313 Carondelet St, New Orleans, LA 70130; tel. (504) 586-5471; telex 587492; fax (504) 586-5739; f. 1933; cap. 284.4m., dep. 3,882.9m. (Sept. 1987); Chair. THOMAS A. MASILLA, Jr.; Pres. C. JERE SHAW, Jr; 68 US brs, 1 foreign br.

Louisiana National Bank of Baton Rouge: 451 Florida St, Baton Rouge, LA 70801; tel. (504) 389-4011; telex 784590; f. 1882; Chair. and Pres. G. LEE GRIFFIN; 25 brs.

Ouachita National Bank in Monroe: 130 DeSiard St, Monroe, LA 71201; tel. (318) 362-7000; telex 588421; f. 1933; cap. 50.7m., dep. 415.0m. (Dec. 1987); Pres. R. L. VANDERPOOL, III.

Whitney National Bank: 228 St Charles St, New Orleans, LA 70161; tel. (504) 586-7272; telex 58393; fax (504) 586-7383; f. 1883; cap. 275.1m., dep. 2,667.7m. (Dec. 1988); Chair. and CEO PATRICK A. DELANEY; 36 US brs, 1 foreign br.

MAINE

Casco Northern Bank NA: 1 Monument Sq., Portland, ME 04101; f. 1933; cap. 52.8m., dep. 811.2m. (June 1985); Pres. JOHN M. DAIGLE.

MARYLAND

First National Bank of Maryland: 25 South Charles St, Baltimore, MD 21201; tel. (301) 244-4500; telex 87600; fax (301) 539-4594; f. 1806; cap. 344m., dep. 4,059m. (Sept. 1987); Chair. JEREMIAH E. CASEY; Pres. and CEO CHARLES W. COLE, Jr; 142 US brs, 2 foreign brs.

Maryland National Bank: 10 Light St, Baltimore, MD 21202; tel. (301) 244-5000; telex 87705; f. 1933; cap. 432.8m., dep. 4,908m. (Dec. 1985); Chair. ALAN P. HOBLITZELL, Jr; Pres. WILLIAM H. DAIGER, Jr; 196 US brs, 1 foreign br.

Mercantile–Safe Deposit and Trust Company: 2 Hopkins Plaza, Baltimore, MD 21201; tel. (301) 257-5304; telex 2341083; f. 1864; Chair. H. FURLONG BALDWIN; Pres. BRUCE P. WILSON; 17 brs.

Signet Bank/Maryland: 7 St Paul St, POB 1077, Baltimore, MD 21203; tel. (301) 332-5000; telex 87638; fax (301) 752-7357; f. 1795; cap. 196.4m., dep. 2,445.4m. (Dec. 1988); Pres. and CEO WILLIAM H. COWIE, Jr.

MASSACHUSETTS

Bank of New England NA: 28 State St, Boston, MA 02109; tel. (617) 742-4000; telex 940191; f. 1831; cap. 794.4m., dep. 9,623.9m. (Dec. 1988); Chair. RICHARD D. DRISCOLL; Pres. M. THOMAS WILSON; 2 foreign brs.

BayBank Boston, NA: 175 Federal St, Boston, MA 02110; tel. (617) 482-1040; telex 921840; fax (617) 426-7178; f. 1978; cap. 32.3m., dep. 554.3m. (Dec. 1988); Chair. and CEO RICHARD F. POLLARD; Pres. THOMAS M. WHITNEY; 16 US brs, 1 foreign br.

First National Bank of Boston NA: 100 Federal St, Boston, MA 02110; tel. (617) 434-2200; telex 940581; f. 1784; cap. 619.3m., dep. 9,981.6m. (June 1981); Chair. and CEO IRA STEPANIAN; 283 US brs, 97 foreign brs.

Shawmut Bank NA: 1 Federal St, Boston, MA 02211; tel. (617) 292-2000; telex 6817133; fax (617) 556-4694; f. 1836, merged with Connecticut National Bank (Hartford) in 1988; cap. 510.3m., dep. 4,989.9m. (Dec. 1987); Chair. and CEO JOEL B. ALVORD; Pres. JOHN P. HAMILL; 27 US brs, 1 foreign br.

South Shore Bank: 1400 Hancock St, Quincy, MA 02169; tel. (617) 472-1000; telex 940803; f. 1836; Chair. and CEO DAVID B. LYNCH; 33 brs.

State Street Bank and Trust Co: 225 Franklin St, Boston, MA 02101; tel. (617) 786-3758; telex 940238; fax (617) 654-3759; f. 1792; cap. 230.7m., dep. 3,211.5m. (Dec. 1984); Chair. WILLIAM S. EDGERLY; 1 foreign br.

MICHIGAN

Comerica Bank—Detroit: 211 West Fort St, POB 64858, Detroit, MI 48264; tel. (313) 222-3300; telex 235393; f. 1849; cap. 553.3m., dep. 7,521.9m. (March 1989); Chair. DONALD R. MANDICH; Pres. EUGENE A. MILLER; 201 brs.

First of America Bank—Ann Arbor: 101 South Main St, Ann Arbor, MI 48107; tel. (313) 995-7700; fax (313) 995-5225; f. 1936; cap. 25.5m., dep. 331.8m. (Dec. 1984); Chair. BRUCE BENNER; Pres. DOUGLAS FREETH; 18 brs.

First of America Bank—Central: 101 South Washington Sq., Lansing, MI 48909; tel. (517) 374-1600; f. 1892; cap. 36.2m., dep. 464.4m. (Dec. 1987); Pres. ROBERT K. KINNING; 21 brs.

First of America Bank—Southeast Michigan NA: Penebscot Bldg, 645 Griswold St, Detroit, MI 48226; tel. (313) 965-1900; telex 4320065; f. 1949, known as First of America Bank—Detroit until 1988; cap. 169.8m., dep. 2,269.4m.; Chair. and CEO DAVID T. HARRISON; Pres. and COO J. MICHAEL HOFMANN; 72 brs.

Genesee Merchants Bank & Trust Co: 1 East First St, Flint, MI 48502; tel. (313) 766-8000; f. 1872; cap. 71.1m., dep. 840.3m.; Pres. WILLIAM H. PIPER; 33 brs.

Michigan National Bank: 124 West Allegan St, Lansing, MI 48901; tel. (517) 377-3111; telex 235503; f. 1940; cap. 88.2m., dep. 1,476.5m. (Dec. 1982); Chair. and CEO ROBERT J. MYLOD; Pres. PETER K. THOMSEN; 200 brs.

National Bank of Detroit: Woodward at Fort, Detroit, MI 48232; tel. (313) 225-1000; telex 4320060; fax (313) 225-2371; f. 1933; cap. 838.1m., dep. 12,029.1m. (June 1988); Chair. and Pres. CHARLES T. FISHER, III; 159 US brs, 3 foreign brs.

NBD Grand Rapids NA: 200 Ottawa Ave, NW, Grand Rapids, MI 49503; tel. (616) 771-7000; telex 2736996; f. 1918; Pres. CRAIG W. SCHOPF; 38 brs.

Old Kent Bank and Trust Company: 1 Vandenburg Center, Grand Rapids, MI 49503, USA; tel. (616) 771-5000; telex 226373; fax (616) 774-1119; f. 1853; Chair., Pres. and CEO JOHN C. CANEPA; 45 US brs, 1 foreign br.

People's State Bank: 9252 Jos Campau St, Hamtramck, MI 48212; tel. (313) 875-2000; f. 1909; cap. 25.7m., dep. 104.0m. (Dec. 1988); Pres. OSCAR L. OLSON.

MINNESOTA

American National Bank and Trust Company: 5th and Minnesota Sts, St Paul, MN 55101; tel. (612) 298-6000; telex 297099; fax (612) 298-6031; f. 1903; cap. 42.0m., dep. 530.6m. (Dec. 1988); Chair., Pres. and CEO JAMES W. REAGAN.

First Bank NA: First Bank Pl., Minneapolis, MN 55480; tel. (612) 370-4144; telex 290169; fax (612) 370-5301; f. 1857; cap. 892.7m., dep. 10,779.8m. (June 1988); Chair. RICHARD W. SCHOENKE; Pres. JAY B. WALTERS; 6 US brs, 1 foreign br.

First Bank Duluth: 130 West Superior St, Duluth, MN 55802; tel. (218) 722-3301; telex 5612530; f. 1902; Pres. and CEO J. JOSEPH LINDSLEY.

First Bank Rochester: POB 4661, Rochester, MN 55903; tel. (507) 285-7800; f. 1864; cap. 10.3m., dep. 248.6m. (Dec. 1987); Pres. and CEO NORBERT J. CONZEMIUS.

First National Bank of Austin: 301 Main St North, Austin, MN 55912; tel. (507) 433-2332; f. 1868; Pres. W. W. STRAUSBURG.

National City Bank of Minneapolis: 75 South Fifth St, POB E 1919, Minneapolis, MN 55480; tel. (612) 340-3000; telex 201683; fax (612) 340-3181; f. 1964; cap. 38.9m., dep. 365.2m. (Dec. 1988); Chair. and CEO JAMES H. HEARON, III; Pres. WALTER E. MEADLEY, Jr.

Norwest Bank Minnesota NA: Sixth St and Marquette Ave, Minneapolis, MN 55479; tel. (612) 667-8123; telex 290734; fax (612) 372-5185; f. 1872; cap. 442.0m., dep. 5,540.7m. (Dec. 1988); Pres. and CEO JAMES R. CAMPBELL; 7 US brs, 1 foreign br.

MISSISSIPPI

Deposit Guaranty National Bank: 1 Deposit Guaranty Plaza, Jackson, MS 39201; tel. (601) 354-8583; telex 585431; fax (601) 968-4767; f. 1925; cap. 221.3m., dep. 2,562.2m. (Sept. 1987); Chair. E. B. ROBINSON, Jr; Pres. HOWARD MCMILLAN, Jr; 72 brs.

Merchants National Bank: 820 South St, Vicksburg, MS 39180; tel. (601) 636-3752; telex 585453; f. 1886; Pres. and CEO THOMAS G. BARKSDALE; 4 brs.

National Bank of Commerce of Mississippi: NBC Plaza, POB 1187, Starkville, MS 39759; tel. (601) 323-1341; f. 1889; Chair. J. R. SCRIBNER; Pres. LEWIS F. MALLORY, Jr; 7 brs.

Trustmark National Bank: POB 291, Jackson, MS 39205; tel. (601) 354-5861; telex 9662613; fax (601) 949-2387; f. 1889; cap. 102.7m., dep. 1,376.4m. (Dec. 1983); Chair. FRANK R. DAY; 43 brs.

MISSOURI

Boatmen's First National Bank of Kansas City: POB 419038, Kansas City, MO 64183; tel. (616) 221-2800; telex 42246; f. 1886; cap. 142.8m., dep. 1,118.9m. (June 1988); Chair. and CEO C. TED MCCARTER; Pres. WILLIAM C. NELSON.

Boatmen's National Bank of St Louis: 100 North Broadway, St Louis, MO 63102; tel. (314) 425-7500; telex 7610560; f. 1847; Chair. and CEO DONALD N. BRANDIN; Pres. WILLIAM H. T. BUSH; 3 brs.

Centerre Bank NA: One Centerre Plaza, St Louis, MO 63101; tel. (314) 554-6000; telex 447389; f. 1919; cap. 210.4m., dep. 2,582.0m. (Dec. 1987); Chair. CLARENCE C. BARKSDALE; Pres. and CEO JOHN PETERS MACCARTHY; 1 foreign br.

Commerce Bank of Kansas City NA: POB 248, Kansas City, MO 64141; tel. (816) 234-2581; telex 424217; f. 1865; cap. 99.3m., dep. 1,197.5m. (Dec. 1988); Chair. DAVID A. RISMILLER; Pres. JONATHAN KEMPER; 2 US brs, 1 foreign br.

Mercantile Bank NA: Mercantile Tower, Eighth and Locust Sts, POB 524, St Louis, MO 63166; tel. (314) 425-2850; telex 4312023; f. 1855; cap. 298.0m., dep. 3,159.4m. (June 1988); Chair. THOMAS H. JACOBSEN; 1 foreign br.

United Missouri Bank of Kansas City NA: 10th and Grand Sts, POB 226, Kansas City, MO 64141; tel. (816) 556-7000; telex 42572; fax (816) 556-4858; f. 1913; Chair. R. CROSBY KEMPER, Jr; Pres. MALCOLM M. ASLIN.

MONTANA

First Interstate Bank of Glacier County: 24 East Main St, POB 2000, Cut Bank, MT 59427; tel. (406) 873-2265; f. 1935; cap. 4.0m., dep. 52.2m. (Dec. 1988); Pres. GEORGE E. WAGGONER.

First Interstate Bank of Great Falls: 425 First Ave North, POB 5010, Great Falls, MT 59401; tel. (406) 761-1750; f. 1881; cap. 8.8m., dep. 94.1m.; Pres. and CEO WILLIAM C. PARKER.

First Interstate Bank of Kalispell NA: 2 Main St, POB 209, Kalispell, MT 59901; tel. (406) 752-5001; f. 1891; cap. 10.5m., dep. 109.5m. (Dec. 1988); Chair., Pres. and CEO ROBERT T. GERHARDT.

First National Bank of Lewiston: POB 540, Lewiston, MT 59457; tel. (406) 538-7471; f. 1924; cap. 6.2m., dep. 72.3m. (June 1985); Pres. D. R. BROWNE.

Norwest Bank Anaconda-Butte NA: 101 North Main St, Butte, MT 59701; tel. (406) 782-8391; f. 1877; cap. 7.7m., dep. 102.4m. (June 1983); Pres. WILLIAM R. TAIT.

NEBRASKA

First National Bank of Omaha: 1 First National Center, Omaha, NE 68103; tel. (402) 341-0500; telex 484410; f. 1857; Chair. J. LAURITZEN; Pres. B. R. LAURITZEN.

FirsTier Bank NA, Lincoln: 13th and M Sts, POB 81008, Lincoln, NE 68501; tel. (402) 471-1231; telex 484356; fax (402) 434-1109; f. 1960; cap. 81.2m., dep. 796.0m. (Dec. 1988); Pres. ORRIN A. WILSON.

National Bank of Commerce Trust and Savings Association: 13th and O Sts, Lincoln, NE 68501; tel. (402) 472-4321; telex 484300; f. 1902; Pres. JAMES F. NISSEN.

Norwest Bank Omaha NA: 20th and Farnam Sts, Omaha, NE 68102; tel. (402) tel. (402) 536-2424; telex 484473; f. 1856; cap. 42.3m., dep. 520.5m. (Dec. 1984); Chair. JOHN R. COCHRAN.

NEVADA

First Interstate Bank of Nevada NA: 3800 Howard Hughes Pkwy, POB 98588, Las Vegas, NV 89193-8588; tel. (702) 385-8011; telex 3957099; f. 1902; cap. 224.5m., dep. 2,822.5m. (June 1988); Chair. and CEO DONALD D. SNYDER; Pres. RONALD M. ZUREK; 67 brs.

NEW HAMPSHIRE

Bank of New Hampshire NA: 300 Franklin St, Manchester, NH 03101; tel. (603) 624-6600; f. 1969; cap. 48.1m., dep. 549.6m. (Dec. 1986); Chair. DAVIS P. THURBER; Pres. and CEO ROBERT L. BAILEY; 16 brs.

Indian Head National Bank: One Indian Head Plaza, POB 647, Nashua, NH 03061; tel. (603) 880-5000; telex 953080; f. 1852; cap. 40.3m., dep. 617.5m. (Dec. 1986); Chair. H. E. HARRINGTON, Jr; Pres. BRUCE N. JOHNSTONE.

Merchants National Bank: 1 Hampshire Plaza, Manchester, NH 03105; tel. (603) 668-5000; f. 1853; cap. 26.6m., dep. 355.8m. (Dec. 1987); Pres. JAMES W. COLEMAN; 5 brs.

NEW JERSEY

Central Jersey Bank and Trust Company: Route 9, Freehold Township, NJ 07728; tel. (201) 462-0011; f. 1932; Pres., Chair. and CEO ELSIE SOKOL; 30 brs.

Chemical Bank New Jersey NA: 334 Madison Ave, Morristown, NJ 07960; tel. (201) 285-2000; telex 275144; fax (201) 285-2737; f. 1890, known as Horizon Bank until 1989; cap. 273.5m., dep. 3,727.1m. (Dec. 1988); Chair. and CEO WILLIAM J. SHEPHERD; Pres. and COO ARISTIDES W. GEORGANTAS; 130 brs.

Citizens First National Bank of New Jersey: 54 East Ridgewood Ave, Ridgewood, NJ 07450; tel. (201) 445-3400; telex 178460; fax (201) 445-9828; f. 1899; cap. 162.4m., dep. 2,401.8m. (March 1989); Chair. and CEO RICHARD G. KELLEY; 48 brs.

Commercial Trust Company of New Jersey; 15 Exchange Pl., Jersey City, NJ 07302; f. 1899; Pres. JOHN G. COLLINS; 27 brs.

First Fidelity Bank NA: 550 Broad St, Newark, NJ 07192; tel. (201) 565-3200; telex 138620; f. 1812; cap. 593.5m., dep. 7,209.8m. (Dec. 1986); Chair. ROBERT R. FERGUSON, Jr; Pres. and CEO EDWARD D. KNAPP; 183 US brs, 1 foreign br.

First Jersey National Bank: 1 Exchange Pl., Jersey City, NJ 07302; tel: (201) 547-7000; telex 620004; f. 1864; cap. 96.2m., dep. 1,441.3m. (June 1985); Chair. THOMAS J. STANTON, Jr; Pres. HERMAN H. SUENHOLZ; 35 brs.

First National Bank of New Jersey: 515 Union Blvd, POB 4000, Totowa, NJ 07512; tel. (201) 790-2000; telex 130426; f. 1864; Chair. C. GORDON JELLIFFE; Pres. DONALD E. PIERCE; 34 brs.

Midlantic National Bank: Metro Park Plaza, POB 600, Edison, NJ 08818; tel. (201) 321-8000; telex 138490; f. 1804; cap. 366.6m., dep. 4,658.3m. (Dec. 1988); Chair. R. VAN BUREN; Pres. D. P. MCDONALD; 436 US brs, 1 foreign br.

Midlantic National Bank/North: 1 Garret Mountain Plaza, West Paterson, NJ 07424; tel. (201) 881-5000; telex 130432; f. 1983; cap. 167.5m., dep. 2,281.1m. (Sept. 1986); Chair. RALPH A. CORBIN; Pres. and CEO ROBERT D. KRESTEL; 68 US brs, 1 foreign br.

National Community Bank of New Jersey: 24 Park Ave, Rutherford, NJ 07070; tel. (201) 845-1000; telex 219418; f. 1895; cap. 163.5m., dep. 2,691.4m. (Dec. 1987); Chair. FARLEIGH S. DICKINSON, Jr; Pres. and CEO ROBERT M. KOSSICK; 82 brs.

National State Bank: 68 Broad St, Elizabeth, NJ 07207; tel. (201) 354-3400; telex 6716459; f. 1812; cap. 115.6m., dep. 1,831.4m. (Dec. 1988); Chair. W. EMLEN ROOSEVELT; Pres. and CEO JOHN J. CONNOLLY; 49 brs.

New Jersey National Bank: CN 1, Pennington, NJ 08534; tel. (609) 771-5700; telex 4990118; f. 1804; Chair. JOHN H. WALTHER; Pres. and CEO JOHN D. WALLACE; 76 brs.

Trust Co of New Jersey: 35 Journal Sq., Jersey City, NJ 07306; tel. (201) 420-2500; f. 1896; cap. 59m., dep. 1,045.5m. (Dec. 1985); Chair. and Pres. SIGGI B.WILZIG; 19 brs.

United Jersey Bank: 210 Main St, Hackensack, NJ 07602; tel. (201) 646-5240; telex 134352; f. 1903; cap. 272.2m., dep. 3,455.9m. (Dec. 1988); Chair. T. JOSEPH SEMROD; Pres. CLIFFORD H. COYMAN; 43 brs.

NEW MEXICO

First Interstate Bank of Albuquerque: 320 Gold Ave, SW, POB 1830, Albuquerque, NM 87103; tel. (505) 766-6000; cap. 28.0m., dep. 405.1m. (Dec. 1988); Pres. and CEO J. A. CLARK.

First Interstate Bank of Lea County: 216–220 West Broadway, POB 400, Hobbs, NM 88240; tel. (505) 397-4511; f. 1928; cap. 8.1m., dep. 148.6m. (June 1988); Pres. and CEO SAMUEL S. SPENCER.

First Interstate Bank of Roswell: 128 West Second St, POB 2057, Roswell, NM 88201; tel. (505) 622-4240; f. 1946; cap. 3.8m., dep. 61.3m. (Dec. 1988); Pres. and CEO DANNY T. SKARDA.

First Interstate Bank of Santa Fe: 150 Washington Ave, POB 969, Santa Fe, NM 87501; tel. (505) 982-3671; f. 1946; cap. 6.0m., dep. 116.4m. (Dec. 1988); Pres. and CEO DAVID R. VLAMING.

First National Bank in Albuquerque: 40 First Plaza, POB 1305, Albuquerque, NM 87103; tel. (505) 765-4000; telex 660439; fax (505) 247-2611; f. 1881; cap. 89.8m., dep. 970.3m. (Dec. 1988); Pres. and CEO NORMAN R. CORZINE; 21 brs.

First National Bank of Santa Fe: The Plaza, Santa Fe, NM 87501; tel. (505) 988-7111; telex 9850671; f. 1870; cap. 12.9m., dep. 189.8m. (Dec. 1984); Chair. EDWARD B. BENNETT, Jr; Pres. MILO L. MCGONAGLE; 9 brs.

Sunwest Bank of Albuquerque NA: POB 25500, Albuquerque, NM 87125-5500; tel. (505) 765-2211; telex 660430; f. 1924; cap. 135.4m., dep. 1,387.0m. (March 1989); Chair. GEORGE S. JENKS; 23 brs.

NEW YORK

Amalgamated Bank of New York: 11–15 Union Sq., New York, NY 10003; tel. (212) 255-6200; f. 1923; cap. 95.6m., dep. 1,105.4m. (Dec. 1986); Pres. and CEO EDWARD M. KATZ; 3 brs.

American Express Bank Ltd: American Express Tower, World Financial Center, New York, NY 10285; tel. (212) 298-5000; telex 421044; cap. 529.0m., dep. 13,035.0m. (Dec. 1988); Chair. and CEO EDMOND J. SAFRA; 46 foreign brs.

Atlantic Bank of New York: 960 Ave of the Americas, New York, NY 10001; tel. (212) 695-5400; telex 422195; f. 1926; cap. 71.7m., dep. 770.9m. (Dec. 1987); Pres. H. S. KOSTAKOPOULOS; 7 brs.

Bank Audi (USA): 600 Fifth Ave, New York, NY 10020; tel. (212) 307-5577; telex 421898; f. 1983; cap. 27.3m., dep. 213.5m. (Dec. 1986); Chair. RAYMOND W. AUDI; Pres. JOSEPH G. AUDI.

Bank Leumi Trust Co of New York: 579 Fifth Ave, New York, NY 10017; tel. (212) 382-4000; telex 420968; f. 1968; cap. 130.4m., dep. 2,696.4m. (Dec. 1983); Chair. E. I. JAPHET; Pres. DAVID NOVICK; 25 US brs, 2 foreign brs.

Bank of New York: 48 Wall St, New York, NY 10286; tel. (212) 495-1784; telex 62763; f. 1784, merged with Irving Bank Corpn in 1988; cap. 4,065.9m., dep. 32,706.4m. (Dec. 1988); Chair. and CEO J. CARTER BACOT; Pres. PETER HERRICK; 190 US brs, 3 foreign brs.

Bank of Tokyo Trust Co: 100 Broadway, New York, NY 10005; tel. (212) 766-3400; telex 420742; fax (212) 732-9560; f. 1955; cap. 376m., dep. 5,361.4m. (Dec. 1987); Chair. TAMOTSU YAMAGUCHI; Pres. HIROSHI HAYASHI; 4 US brs, 1 foreign br.

BankAmerica International: 335 Madison Ave, POB 5938, New York, NY 10017; tel. (212) 503-7000; telex 232037; f. 1950; cap.

707.0m., dep. 1,530.6m. (Dec. 1988); Pres. MERRILL BURNS: 1 foreign br.

Bankers' Trust Co: 16 Wall St, New York, NY 10005; tel. (212) 775-2500; telex 233015; f. 1903; cap. 2,873.4m., dep. 31,985.4m. (Dec. 1987); Chair. and CEO CHARLES S. SANFORD, Jr; 8 US brs, 15 foreign brs.

Barclays Bank of New York, NA: 75 Wall St, New York, NY 10265; tel. (212) 412-4000; telex 62367; fax (212) 797-3019; f. 1971; cap. 198.7m., dep. 2,676.8m. (Dec. 1988); Chair. ROBERT C. VINCENT, Jr; Pres. and CEO JOHN S. SPENCER; 71 brs.

Brown Brothers Harriman & Co: 59 Wall St, New York, NY 10005; tel. (212) 483-1818; telex 42096; fax (212) 493-8526; f. 1818; cap. 90.7m., dep. 964.1m. (June 1988); Operations Man. TERENCE F. COOKE; US Banking Man. JOSEPH P. DONLAN; 7 US brs, 1 foreign br.

Central Trust Company: POB 22900, Rochester, NY 14692; tel. (716) 546-4500; telex 6716204; f. 1988; cap. 55.7m., dep. 723.1m. (Dec. 1987); Pres. and CEO R. CARLOS CARBALLADA; 29 brs.

Chase Manhattan Bank, NA: 1 Chase Manhattan Plaza, New York, NY 10081; tel. (212) 552-2222; telex 232163; f. 1955; cap. 5,182.0m., dep. 58,143.6m. (Dec. 1988); Chair. and CEO WILLARD C. BUTCHER; Pres. THOMAS C. LABRECQUE; 237 US brs, 109 foreign brs.

Chemical Bank: 277 Park Ave, New York, NY 10172; tel. (212) 310-6161; telex 222271; f. 1959; cap. 3,393m., dep. 33,672m. (Dec. 1988); Chair. and CEO WALTER V. SHIPLEY; Pres. THOMAS S. JOHNSON; 280 US brs, 20 foreign brs.

Citibank NA: 399 Park Ave, New York, NY 10022; tel. (212) 559-1000; telex 347; f. 1812; cap. 8,168m., dep. 102,445m. (Dec. 1988); Chair. and CEO JOHN S. REED; Pres. WILLIAM I. SPENCER; 135 foreign brs.

Daiwa Bank Trust Company: 75 Rockefeller Plaza, New York, NY 10019; tel. (212) 399-8500; telex 276626; fax (212) 399-8531; f. 1977; cap. 194.5m., dep. 1,401m. (Dec. 1988); Chair. and Pres. KENJI YASUI.

DNC America Banking Corporation: 600 Fifth Ave, New York, NY 10020; tel. (212) 315-6500; telex 426357; fax (212) 307-1589; f. 1975; Chair. KRISTIAN RAMBJØR; Pres. and CEO JOHN R. NELSON; 1 foreign br.

European American Bank: EAB Plaza, Long Island, New York, NY 11555; tel. (718) 296-5000; telex 177603; f. 1950; cap. 535.2m., dep. 4,385.4m. (Dec. 1988); Chair. and Pres. RAYMOND J. DEMPSEY; 90 brs.

Extebank: 645 Fifth Ave, New York, NY 10022; tel. (212) 688-7500; telex 427549; fax (212) 308-0422; f. 1977; cap. 44.5m., dep. 500.4m. (Dec. 1988); Chair. SIDNEY SHENKMAN; Pres. RAMIRO MATO.

First American Bank of New York: 350 Park Ave, New York, NY 10022; tel. (212) 759-9898; telex 427646; f. 1982; cap. 104.4m., dep. 1,083.3m. (Dec. 1988); Pres. WILLIAM DUNCAN.

French American Banking Corporation: 499 Park Ave, New York, NY 10022; tel. (212) 415-9600; telex 82614; fax (212) 415-9696; f. 1919; cap. 103.8m., dep. 2,462.8m. (Dec. 1987); Chair. JACQUES H. WAHL; Pres. and CEO GERARD DECOURCELLE; 1 foreign br.

Fuji Bank and Trust Company: One World Trade Center, 92nd Floor, New York, NY 10048; tel. (212) 839-6846; telex 425777; f. 1974; cap. 291.7m., dep. 3,232.8m. (Dec. 1988); Pres. KUNITAKE NOMURA; 11 foreign brs.

Fulton County National Bank and Trust Company: 2 North Main St, Gloversville, NY 12078; tel. (518) 725-3181; f. 1852; Pres. and CEO CHARLES E. PRATT; 3 brs.

Israel Discount Bank of New York: 511 Fifth Ave, New York, NY 10017; tel. (212) 551-8500; telex 62411; fax (212) 370-9623; f. 1922; cap. 278.2m., dep. 3,965.9m. (Dec. 1988); Chair. and Pres. ARON KAHANA; 1 foreign br.

Key Bank NA: 60 State St, Albany, NY 12207; tel. (518) 447-3500; telex 145355; f. 1825; cap. 145.9m., dep. 1,815.1m. (Dec. 1988); Pres. and CEO JAMES K. PATRICK; 69 brs.

LBS Bank—New York: Manhattan Tower, 101 East 52nd St, New York, NY 10022; tel. (212) 980-8600; telex 229976; fax (212) 593-1967; f. 1986; cap. 10.1m., dep. 15.4m. (Dec. 1988); Chair. VINKO MIR; Pres. and CEO VLADO L. SODIN.

Manufacturers' Hanover Trust Co: 270 Park Ave, New York, NY 10017; tel. (212) 286-6000; telex 232337; f. 1961; cap. 4,235m., dep. 42,447m. (Dec. 1988); Chair. and CEO JOHN F. MCGILLI-CUDDY; 30 foreign brs.

Manufacturers' and Traders' Trust Co—M & T Bank: One M & T Plaza, Buffalo, NY 14203; tel. (716) 842-4200; telex 91347; f. 1856; cap. 138.3m., dep. 2,049.7m. (Dec. 1985); Chair. and CEO ROBERT G. WILMERS; 61 US brs, 1 foreign br.

Marine Midland Bank: 140 Broadway, New York, NY 10015; tel. (212) 797-4000; telex 421800; f. 1976; cap. 823.4m., dep. 16,659.1m. (Dec. 1988); Chair. and Exec. Dir RICHARD C. KELLER; Pres. and CEO GEOFFREY A. THOMPSON; 316 brs.

Merchants' Bank of New York: 434 Broadway, New York, NY 10013; tel. (212) 669-6600; telex 232112; fax (212) 226-3667; f. 1926; cap. 57.1m., dep. 594.3m. (Dec. 1988); Chair. SPENCER B. WITTY; Pres. and CEO JAMES G. LAWRENCE; 6 brs.

Merchants' National Bank and Trust Company of Syracuse: 216–220 South Warren St, POB 4950, New York, NY 13221; tel. (315) 472-5561; f.1850; cap. 39.6m., dep. 544.9m. (Dec. 1987); Pres. JOHN W. FINLAY; 23 brs.

Morgan Guaranty Trust Co of New York: 23 Wall St, New York, NY 10015; tel. (212) 483-2323; telex 5814040; f. 1859; cap. 7,257m., dep. 45,122m. (Dec. 1988); Chair. LEWIS T. PRESTON; Pres. DENNIS WEATHERSTONE; 14 foreign brs.

National Bank of Geneva: 2 Seneca St, Geneva, NY 14456; tel. (315) 789-2300; f. 1817; cap. 9.1m., dep. 92.6m. (Dec. 1987); Pres. M. E. HAYES.

National Westminster Bank USA: 175 Water St, New York, NY 10038; tel. (212) 602-1000; telex 232369; f. 1967; cap. 435m., dep. 9,146m. (June 1987); Chair. and CEO WILLIAM T. KNOWLES; Pres. ROBERT F. WALLACE.

PKbanken International (US) Banking Corporation: 555 Theodore Fremd Ave, Suite B-300, New York, NY 10580; tel. (914) 925-2300; telex 6801479; fax (914) 967-0519; f. 1986; cap. 16.0m., dep. 11.3m. (Dec. 1987); Pres. ÅKE SVENSON.

Republic National Bank of New York: 452 Fifth Ave, New York, NY 10018; tel. (212) 930-6000; telex 421434; f. 1966; cap. 1,631.1m., dep. 13,897.3m. (Dec. 1988); Chair. WALTER H. WEINER; Pres. DOV C. SCHLEIN; 30 US brs, 7 foreign brs.

Sterling National Bank and Trust Company of New York: Madison Ave and 55th St, New York, NY 10022; tel. (212) 826-2200; telex 3766895; fax (212) 826-2424; f. 1929; cap. 76.2m., dep. 445.0m. (Dec. 1988); Chair. THEODORE H. SILBERT; Pres. and CEO JOHN C. MILLMAN; 5 brs.

UBAF Arab American Bank: 40 East 52nd St, New York, NY 10022; tel. (212) 644-2000; telex 666880; fax (212) 755-6944; f. 1976; cap. 10.1m., dep. 783.5m. (Dec. 1988); Chair. ALY MOHAMED MEGM; Pres. and CEO FAKHRUDDIN KHALIL.

UMB Bank and Trust Company: 10 Rockefeller Plaza, New York, NY 10020; tel. (212) 541-8070; telex 666557; fax (212) 307-1364; f. 1978; cap. 57.7m., dep. 380.5m. (Dec. 1988); Chair. MICHAEL ZVINERI; Pres. EMANUEL GENAUER.

United States Trust Co of New York: 45 Wall St, New York, NY 10005; tel. (212) 806-4500; telex 420003; f. 1853; cap. 176.7m., dep. 2,391.6m. (Dec. 1986); Chair. and CEO H. MARSHALL SCHWARZ; Pres. JEFFREY S. MAURER; 1 foreign br.

NORTH CAROLINA

First Union National Bank: First Union Plaza, Charlotte, NC 28288; tel. (704) 374-6565; telex 572422; f. 1908; cap. 782.1m., dep. 8,061.1m. (Dec. 1987); Chair. EDWARD E. CRUTCHFIELD, Jr; Pres. JOHN R. GEORGIUS; 211 US brs, 1 foreign br.

NCNB National Bank of North Carolina: One NCNB Plaza, Charlotte, NC 28255; tel. (704) 374-5000; telex 575297; f. 1960; cap. 995.7m., dep. 10,585.0m. (Dec. 1987); Chair. and CEO HUGH L. MCCOLL, Jr.

OHIO

AmeriTrust Co NA: 900 Euclid Ave, Cleveland, OH 44101-0937; tel. (216) 687-5680; telex 980198; fax (216) 621-4834; f. 1894; cap. 539.2m., dep. 6,895.4m. (June 1987); Chair. and CEO JERRY V. JARRETT; Pres. JAMES D. RODE; 140 US brs, 1 foreign br.

Bancohio National Bank: 155 East Broad St, Columbus, OH 43251; tel. (614) 463-6957; telex 246610; f. 1888; cap. 336.6m., dep. 3,983.9m. (Dec. 1988); Chair. ARTHUR D. HERRMANN; Pres. GARY A. GLASER; 136 US brs, 1 foreign br.

Bank One, Cleveland, NA: 1255 Euclid Ave, OH 44115; tel. (216) 781-3333; telex 4332131; fax (216) 781-4427; f. 1972; Chair. and CEO KAREN N. HORN; Pres. DAVID L. STITH; 50 brs.

Bank One, Columbus, NA: 100 East Broad St, Columbus, OH 43271-0135; tel. (614) 463-5855; telex 4949515; fax (614) 248-5649; f. 1868; cap. 229.0m., dep. 3,013.6m. (Dec. 1988); Chair. ROBERT H. POTTS; Pres. WILLIAM M. BENNETT; 62 US brs, 1 foreign br.

Bank One, Dayton, NA: Kettering Tower, Dayton, OH 45401; tel. (513) 449-8778; telex 288068; fax (513) 461-3302; f. 1857; cap. 144.1m., dep. 1,695.7m. (Dec. 1988); Chair. and CEO THOMAS E. HOAGLIN; 44 US brs, 1 foreign br.

Central Trust Co NA: Fifth and Main Sts, Cincinnati, OH 45202; tel. (513) 651-8562; telex 214187; f. 1862; cap. 149.7m., dep. 1,790.6m. (Dec. 1985); Chair. O. W. BIRCKHEAD; Pres. and CEO GARY N. KOCHER; 51 brs.

Fifth Third Bank: 38 Fountain Sq. Plaza, Cincinnati, OH 45263; tel. (513) 579-5300; telex 214567; f. 1927; cap. 204.2m., dep. 2,341.5m. (Dec. 1987); Pres. CLEMENT BUENGER; 74 US brs, 1 foreign br.

First National Bank: 1 First National Plaza, Dayton, OH 45402; tel. (513) 226-2000; telex 28825; fax (513) 226-2020; f. 1871; cap. 59.8m., dep. 771.7m. (Dec. 1987); Pres. FREDERICK W. SCHANTZ; 27 brs.

First National Bank of Ohio: 106 South Main St, Akron, OH 44308; tel. (216) 384-8000; fax (216) 253-1849; f. 1934; cap. 180.6m., dep. 1,662.6m. (March 1989); Pres. and CEO HOWARD L. FLOOD; 65 brs.

First National Bank of Toledo: 606 Madison Ave, Toledo, OH 43604; tel. (419) 259-6895; telex 240090; fax (419) 259-6939; f. 1931; cap. 69.0m., dep. 785.4m. (Dec. 1988); Pres. and CEO C. L. MCKELVY, Jr; 28 brs.

Huntington National Bank: 41 South High St, POB 1558, Columbus, OH 43260; tel. (614) 463-4323; telex 245475; f. 1866; cap. 201.7m., dep. 3,075.1m. (Dec. 1983); Chair. WILLIAM A. ARGO; 162 US brs, 1 foreign br.

National City Bank: 1900 East Ninth St, Cleveland, OH 44114; tel. (216) 575-2943; telex 212537; fax (216) 696-3849; f. 1845; cap. 428.1m., dep. 5,511.7m. (Dec. 1988); Pres. DAVID A. DABERKO; 87 US brs, 1 foreign br.

Ohio Citizens' Bank: 405 Madison Ave, Toledo, OH 43604; tel. (419) 259-7700; telex 286044; f. 1932; cap. 72.3m., dep. 921.4m. (Dec. 1988); Chair. WILLARD I. WEBB, III; Pres. and CEO ROBERT G. SIEFERS.

Society National Bank: 800 Superior Ave, Cleveland, OH 44114; tel. (216) 622-9000; telex 985517; f. 1849; cap. 375.7m., dep. 4,607.4m. (Dec. 1988); Chair. GORDON E. HEFFERN; Pres. and CEO ROBERT W. GILLESPIE; 90 US brs, 1 foreign br.

Star Bank NA, Cincinnati: POB 1038, Cincinnati, OH 45201; tel. (513) 632-4130; telex 214515; fax (513) 632-4888; f. 1863, known as First National Bank of Cincinnati until 1988; cap. 203.7m., dep. 1,961.6m. (June 1988); Chair. OLIVER W. WADDELL; 42 brs.

Trustcorp Bank, Ohio: Three SeaGate, Toledo, OH 43603; tel. (419) 259-8598; telex 4421606; f. 1868; cap. 175.4m., dep. 2,255.7m. (Dec. 1987); Chair. GEORGE W. HAIGH; Pres. and CEO JOEL P. EPSTEIN; 96 brs.

OKLAHOMA

Bank of Oklahoma NA: Bank of Oklahoma Tower, Tulsa, OK 74192; tel. (918) 588-6000; telex 492388; fax (918) 588-6026; f. 1933; cap. 118.7m., dep. 1,509.5m. (June 1988); Chair. and CEO LEONARD J. EATON, Jr; Pres. GREGORY J. FLANAGAN.

Fidelity Bank NA: Fidelity Plaza, Robinson at Robert S. Kerr, Oklahoma City, OK 73124; tel. (405) 272-2000; telex 747240; f. 1908; Chair. and CEO DALE MITCHELL; Pres. ROYCE HAMMONS.

First National Bank and Trust Co of Oklahoma City: First National Center, Oklahoma City, OK 73102; tel. (405) 272-4283; telex 796112; f. 1889; cap. 132m., dep. 1,681.9m. (Dec. 1984); Pres. JAMES G. CAIRNS, Jr.

First National Bank and Trust Co of Tulsa: POB 1, Tulsa, OK 74193; tel. (918) 586-1000; telex 158197; f. 1985; cap. 56.8m., dep. 624.2m. (June 1988); Chair. and CEO K. GORDON GREER; Pres. JAMES A. WHITE; 1 foreign br.

Liberty National Bank and Trust Co: Liberty Tower, 100 Broadway, POB 25848, Oklahoma City, OK 73125; tel. (405) 231-6000; telex 747278; f. 1918; cap. 129.9m., dep. 1,853m. (Dec. 1984); Chair. J. W. MCLEAN; Pres. FRED M. MOSES.

OREGON

First Interstate Bank of Oregon NA: 1300 SW Fifth Ave, POB 3131, Portland, OR 97208; tel. (503) 225-2111; telex 360188; f. 1865; cap. 338.0m., dep. 4,853.4m. (Dec. 1988); Chair. and CEO BRUCE G. WILLISON; Pres. ROBERT AMES; 172 US brs, 1 foreign br.

United States National Bank of Oregon: 321 SW Sixth Ave, Portland, OR 97204; tel. (503) 275-6111; telex 360540; f. 1891; cap. 653.4m., dep. 6,351.3m. (March 1989); Chair. ROGER BREEZLEY; Pres. KEVIN KELLY; 193 US brs, 1 foreign br.

PENNSYLVANIA

Bank of Pennsylvania: 50 North Fifth St, Reading, PA 19601; tel. (215) 378-3920; f. 1913; Chair. FREDERICK E. RUCCIUS, Jr; Pres. WALTER A. MORRISSEY; 24 brs.

Commonwealth National Bank: 10 South Market Sq., POB 1010, Harrisburg, PA 17108; tel. (717) 564-9500; telex 842340; f. 1969; cap. 86.7m., dep. 1,196.4m. (June 1986); Chair., Pres. and CEO CHARLES F. MERRILL; 42 brs.

Continental Bank: Main and Swede Sts, Norristown, PA 19041; tel. (215) 564-7000; telex 4761112; fax (215) 564-7491; f. 1965; cap. 238.4m., dep. 3,174.6m. (Dec. 1988); Chair. and CEO ROY T. PERAINO; Pres. RICHARD C. RISHEL.

Equibank: 2 Oliver Plaza, Pittsburgh, PA 15222; tel. (412) 288-5000; telex 4423037; fax (412) 288-5111; f. 1871; cap. 165.7m., dep. 2,233.7m. (Dec. 1987); Chairs and CEOs ALAN S. FELLHEIMER, CLAIRE W. CARGALLI; Pres. JAMES H. MCLAUGHLIN; 55 brs.

Fidelity Bank NA: Broad and Walnut Sts, Philadelphia, PA 19109; tel. (215) 985-6000; telex 0834480; f. 1866; cap. 482.6m., dep. 6,857.9m. (Dec. 1987); Chair. and CEO LES GOODMAN; Pres. and COO ROSEMARY B. GRECO; 130 US brs, 2 foreign brs.

First Pennsylvania Bank NA: Centre Sq., 15th and Market Sts, Philadelphia, PA 19101; tel. (215) 786-7793; telex 834278; fax (215) 786-8899; f. 1782; cap. 343.0m., dep. 4,328.3m. (June 1988); Chair. GEORGE A. BUTLER; Pres. FRANK E. REED; 78 US brs, 7 foreign brs.

Fulton Bank: 1 Penn Sq., Lancaster, PA 17604; tel. (717) 291-2492; telex 6720525; f. 1882; Chair. and Pres. ROBERT GARNER; 22 brs.

Hamilton Bank: 110 North Queen St, Lancaster, PA 17604; tel. (717) 569-8731; telex 848416; f. 1970; cap. 185.5m., dep. 2,263.2m. (June 1987); Chair. WILSON D. MCELHINNY; Pres. and CEO WILLIAM M. FENIMORE, Jr; 62 US brs, 1 foreign br.

McDowell National Bank: East State at Chestnut, Sharon, PA 16146; tel. (412) 981-1411; f. 1868; cap. 22.4m., dep. 324.9m. (Dec. 1987); Pres. ROY F. BUCHMAN, Jr; 10 brs.

Mellon Bank NA: One Mellon Bank Center, Pittsburgh, PA 15258; tel. (412) 234-5000; telex 199103; f. 1869; cap. 1,469.5m., dep. 15,049.6m. (Dec. 1986); Chair. NATHAN W. PEARSON (acting); GEORGE T. FARRELL; 124 brs.

Mellon Bank (East) NA: Mellon Bank Center, Philadelphia, PA 19102; tel. (215) 585-2000; telex 834398; f. 1982; cap. 305m., dep. 3,486.8m. (Dec. 1986); Chair. and CEO FRANK V. CAHOUET; Pres. ANTHONY TERRACCIANO; 75 US brs, 1 foreign br.

Meridian Bank: 35 North Sixth St, POB 1102, Reading, PA 19603; tel. (215) 320-2500; f. 1901; cap. 500.7m., dep. 5,535.6m. (Dec. 1987); Chair. and CEO SAMUEL A. MCCULLOUGH; Pres. EZEKIEL S. KETCHUM; 1 foreign br.

Philadelphia National Bank: Broad and Chestnut Sts, POB 7618, Philadelphia, PA 19101; tel. (215) 629-3100; telex 845297; f. 1803; cap. 650.3m., dep. 6,492.7m. (June 1988); Chair. FREDERICK HELDRING; Pres. ROBERT B. PALMER; 64 US brs, 2 foreign brs.

Pittsburgh National Bank: Pittsburgh National Bldg, Pittsburgh, PA 15265; tel. (412) 355-2000; telex 866533; f. 1864; cap. 690.6m., dep. 10,045.6m. (Dec. 1988); Chair. ROBERT C. MILSOM; Pres. JAMES E. ROHR; 114 US brs, 2 foreign brs.

PNC International Bank: 1000 Pittsburgh National Bldg, Pittsburgh, PA 15265; tel. (412) 762-7413; telex 866603; f. 1964; 63.5m.; dep. 176.9m. (Dec. 1987); Chair. LEE D. CUTRONE, Jr; Pres. WILLIAM V. ARMITAGE; 3 brs.

Provident National Bank: Broad and Chestnut Sts, Philadelphia, PA 19101; tel. (215) 585-5000; telex 845270; f. 1847; cap. 304m., dep. 3,049m. (Dec. 1983); Chair. ROGER S. HILLAS; 54 US brs, 1 foreign br.

RHODE ISLAND

Fleet National Bank: 111 Westminster St, Providence, RI 02903; tel. (401) 278-6000; telex 927513; f. 1791; cap. 320.9m., dep. 3,945.2m. (Dec. 1985); Chair. and Pres. J. TERRENCE MURRAY; 46 US brs, 2 foreign brs.

Rhode Island Hospital Trust National Bank: 1 Hospital Trust Plaza, Providence, RI 02903; tel. (401) 278-8680; telex 4430090; f. 1867; cap. 183.0m., dep. 2,339.0m. (Dec. 1988); Chair., Pres. and CEO ALDEN M. ANDERSON; 37 brs.

SOUTH CAROLINA

Citizens and Southern National Bank of South Carolina: 46 Broad St, Charleston, SC 29401; tel. (803) 554-0860; telex 573429; f. 1874; cap. 123.8m., dep. 1,879m. (Dec. 1984); Chair. HUGH M. CHAPMAN; Pres. ROBERT V. ROYALL, Jr; 122 brs.

South Carolina National Bank: 1241 Main St, Columbia, SC 29226-0001; tel. (803) 765-3000; telex 4613057; fax (803) 765-3887; f. 1834; cap. 360.1m., dep. 4,028.1m. (Dec. 1988); Chair. and CEO JAMES G. LINDLEY; 161 US brs, 1 foreign br.

SOUTH DAKOTA

First National Bank in Sioux Falls: 100 South Phillips Ave, Sioux Falls, SD 57102; tel. (605) 335-5100; f. 1885; Pres. W. S. BAKER.

Northwestern National Bank of Sioux Falls: Ninth and Phillips Sts, Sioux Falls, SD 57101; tel. (605) 339-7300; f. 1935; cap. 29.6m., dep. 558.3m. (Dec. 1982); Pres. and CEO C. P. MOORE; 13 brs.

TENNESSEE

First American National Bank: First American Center, Nashville, TN 37237; tel. (615) 748-2821; telex 4621020; fax (615) 798-6088; f. 1883; cap. 100.1m., dep. 1,200.4m. (Dec. 1987); Chair. KENNETH ROBERTS; Pres. and COO ANDREW HIGGINS; 24 US brs, 1 foreign br.

First Tennessee Bank NA, Memphis: POB 84, 165 Madison Ave, Memphis, TN 38101; tel. (901) 523-4436; telex 53834; fax (901) 523-4438; f. 1864; cap. 331.1m., dep. 4,231.4m. (June 1988); Chair. RONALD TERRY; Pres. JOHN P. DULIN; 143 US brs, 1 foreign br.

National Bank of Commerce, Memphis: 1 Commerce Sq., Memphis, TN 38150; tel. (901) 523-3122; telex 4621042; fax (901) 523-3293; f. 1873; cap. 103.2m., dep. 1,158.3m. (Dec. 1988); Chair. BRUCE E. CAMPBELL, Jr; 19 brs.

Sovran Bank/Central South: 1 Commerce Pl., Nashville, TN 37219; tel. (615) 749-3333; telex 6823004; f. 1916; fmrly Commerce Union Bank; cap. 103.8m., dep. 1,025.3m. (Dec. 1982); Pres. and CEO OWEN G. SHELL, Jr.

Third National Bank in Nashville: POB 76, Nashville, TN 37202; tel. (615) 748-4832; telex 4621024; f. 1927; cap. 175.8m., dep. 2,070.7m. (Dec. 1986); Pres. and CEO JOHN W. CLAY, Jr.

Union Planters National Bank: 67 Madison Ave, POB 387, Memphis, TN 38147; tel. (901) 523-6821; telex 6828045; fax (901) 523-6784; f. 1869; cap. 169.9m., dep. 1,549.6m. (Dec. 1987); Chair. RICHARD A. TRIPPEER, Jr; Pres. ARMISTEAD SMITH; 32 brs.

TEXAS

First City, Texas–Houston: 1001 Main St, POB 2557, Houston, TX 77002; tel. (713) 658-6670; telex 762429; fax (713) 658-6800; f. 1956, known as First City National Bank of Houston until 1989; cap. 152.8m., dep. 3,321.3m. (Dec. 1986); Chair. of Bd (vacant); Pres. FRED L. BOLLERER; 3 foreign brs.

First Interstate Bank of Texas NA: 1000 Louisiana St, POB 3326, Houston, TX 77253; tel. (713) 224-6611; telex 166488; f. 1973, known as Allied Bank of Texas until 1988; cap. 190.9m., dep. 6,073.6m. (Dec. 1988); Chair. D. KENT ANDERSON; Pres. LINNET F. DIELY.

First RepublicBank Dallas NA: Pacific and Ervay Sts, POB 225961, Dallas, TX 75265; tel. (214) 922-5000; telex 730492; f. 1875; cap. 775.4m., dep. 8,431.2m. (Dec. 1987); Chair. and CEO ALBERT V. CASEY; Pres. JOHN T. STUART, III; 3 foreign brs.

First RepublicBank Fort Worth NA: One Burnett Plaza, Fort Worth, TX 76113; tel. (817) 390-6079; telex 163171; f. 1877; cap. 64.4m., dep. 755.3m. (Dec. 1987); Chair. THOMAS G. BARKSDALE; Pres. and CEO JAMES R. PERRY; 1 foreign br.

First RepublicBank Houston NA: 700 Louisiana St, POB 299001, Houston, TX 77002; tel. (713) 247-6000; telex 762742; f. 1875; cap. 132.6m., dep. 1,787.3m. (June 1987); Chair. RONALD BROWN.

Frost National Bank of San Antonio: 100 West Houston St, POB 1600, San Antonio, TX 78296; tel. (512) 220-4011; telex 767412; f. 1899; cap. 110.5m., dep. 1,475.4m. (Dec. 1987); Chair. and CEO C. LINDEN SLEDGE.

MBank Alamo: POB 900, San Antonio, TX 78293; tel. (512) 271-8200; f. 1890; cap. 46.4m., dep. 755.9m. (Dec. 1986); Chair. and CEO ROBERT G. DAVIS.

MBank Austin: POB 2266, Austin, TX 78780; tel. (512) 479-5400; f. 1890; cap. 28.6m., dep. 517.3m. (Dec. 1986); Chair. and CEO WILLIAM J. RENFRO; Pres. and COO DEAN O. COCHRAN, Jr.

MBank Brownsville: POB 2219, Brownsville, TX 78520; tel. (512) 546-2421; f. 1914; cap. 22.3m., dep. 420.7m. (Dec. 1988); Chair. and CEO E. A. GIBBS, Jr; Pres. JAMES S. SCOTT.

MBank Dallas NA: 1704 Main St, POB 655415, Dallas, TX 75265-5415; tel. (214) 698-6000; telex 732625; fax (214) 290-5598; f. 1916; cap. 253.3m., dep. 4,928.6m. (March 1987); Chair. and CEO JAMES B. GARDNER; 1 foreign br.

MBank El Paso: 1 MBank Plaza, POB 1072, El Paso, TX 79901; tel. (915) 546-4267; fax (915) 532-7071; f. 1881; cap. 55.8m., dep. 927.6m. (Dec. 1986); Chair. and CEO H. M. DAUGHERTY, Jr; Pres. HENRY B. ELLIS.

MBank Fort Worth NA: POB 50608, Fort Worth, TX 76105; tel. (817) 334-9333; telex 758424; fax (817) 334-9336; f. 1903; Chair. and

CEO MICHAEL L. DIETRICH; Pres. and COO ROBERT W. SEMPLE; 1 foreign br.

MBank Houston NA: POB 2629, Houston, TX 77252; tel. (713) 751-6100; telex 762613; f. 1907; cap. 235m., dep. 3,668.9m. (Dec. 1987); Chair. and CEO JOHN T. CATER; Pres. BEN B. McANDREW, III.

MBank Port Arthur: 8200 Highway 69, POB 1000, Port Arthur, TX 77640; tel. (409) 727-0123; f. 1900; Chair. TOM R. SNODGRASS; Pres. WILLIAM G. McNINCH.

Paribas Bank International (Texas) Inc: 2 Allen Center, Suite 3100, Houston, TX 77002; tel. (713) 659-4811; telex 792604; f. 1979; Pres. PHILIPPE BLAVIER.

Texas American Bank/Fort Worth NA: POB 2050, Fort Worth, TX 76113; tel. (817) 884-4195; telex 758275; fax (817) 870-2454; f. 1873; cap. 114m., dep. 1,886m. (June 1987); Chair. and CEO JOSEPH M. GRANT; 1 foreign br.

Texas Commerce Bank: POB 2558, Houston, TX 77252-2558; tel. (713) 236-4865; telex 775418; f. 1964; cap. 625m., dep. 6,704m. (March 1988); Chair. MARC J. SHAPIRO; Pres. W. MERRIMAN MORTON; 1 foreign br.

Victoria Bank and Trust Company: 120 Main Pl., 1 O'Connor Plaza, Victoria, TX 77902; tel. (512) 573-5151; f. 1875; cap. 41.2m., dep. 523.7m. (Dec. 1986); Chair. and CEO CHARLES R. HRDLICKA.

UTAH

First Interstate Bank of Utah: 180 South Main St, Salt Lake City, UT 84101; tel. (801) 350-7000; telex 3789455; fax (801) 350-7340; f. 1859; cap. 57.6m., dep. 837.7m. (Dec. 1988); Chair. and CEO RICHARD W. KIEFFER; 38 brs.

First Security Bank of Utah NA: 2404 Washington Blvd, POB 9936, Ogden, UT 84409; tel. (801) 626-9500; telex 3789450; fax (801) 350-5992; f. 1881; cap. 200.7m., dep. 2,332.7m. (Dec. 1988); Chair. ROBERT T. HEINER; Pres. SCOTT NELSON; 92 US brs, 1 foreign br.

VERMONT

Howard Bank: 111 Main St, Burlington, VT 05402; tel. (802) 658-1010; f. 1870; cap. 31.4m., dep. 445.7m. (Sept. 1986); Chair. LUTHER F. HACKETT; Pres. WILLIAM H. CHADWICK; 26 brs.

VIRGINIA

Central Fidelity Bank NA: Third and Broad Sts, POB 27602, Richmond, VA 23261; tel. (804) 782-4481; telex 240518; fax (804) 697-6869; f. 1865; cap. 223.4m., dep. 3,236.5m. (Dec. 1986); Chair. and CEO CARROLL L. SAINE; Pres. WILLIAM F. SHUMADINE, Jr; 134 brs.

Crestar Bank: 919 East Main St, POB 26665, Richmond, VA 23219; tel. (804) 782-5000; telex 827420; f. 1865; cap. 497.6m., dep. 7,291.1m. (Dec. 1988); Chair. and CEO RICHARD G. TILGHMAN; Pres. JAMES M. WELLS, III; 238 US brs, 1 foreign br.

Signet Bank/Virginia: 7 North Eighth St, Richmond, VA 23219; tel. (804) 747-2000; telex 827475; f. 1922; cap. 417.7m., dep. 5,353.7m. (Dec. 1985); Chair. and CEO FREDERICK DEANE, Jr.

Sovran Bank NA: 12th and Main Sts, POB 27025, Richmond, VA 23251; tel. (804) 441-4000; telex 823468; fax (804) 788-2525; f. 1963; cap. 600.8m., dep. 7,763.9m. (June 1986); Chair. C. COLEMAN McGEHEE; Pres. RANDOLPH W. McELROY; 268 US brs, 1 foreign br.

WASHINGTON

First Interstate Bank of Washington NA: First Interstate Center, 999 Third Ave, POB 160, Seattle, WA 98104; tel. (206) 292-3111; telex 160550; f. 1970; cap. 218.3m., dep. 2,938.1m. (Dec. 1988); Chair. and Pres. WILLIAM RANDALL; 106 brs.

Key Bank of Puget Sound: POB 90, Seattle, WA 98111; tel. (206) 684-6000; telex 4740070; fax (206) 684-6247; f. 1905; cap. 59.3m., dep. 759.1m. (Dec. 1988); Chair. WILLIAM H. STEVENS; 30 brs.

Seattle-First National Bank: 701 Fifth Ave, POB 3586, Seattle, WA 98124; tel. (206) 583-3131; telex 320249; f. 1870; cap. 661.8m., dep. 7,537.6m. (March 1987); Chair. and CEO RICHARD P. COOLEY; 156 US brs, 1 foreign br.

Security Pacific Bank Washington, NA: Security Pacific Bank Tower, POB 3966, Seattle, WA 98124; tel. (206) 621-4111; telex 185242; known as Rainier National Bank until 1989; f. 1889; cap. 457.7m., dep. 5,683.6m. (Dec. 1988); Chair. JOHN D. MANGELS; Pres. JOHN C. GETZELMAN; 128 US brs, 1 foreign br.

US Bank of Washington: 1414 Fourth Ave, POB 720, Seattle, WA 98111; tel. (206) 344-2300; telex 4740153; f. 1889, name changed on merger of Old National Bank of Washington and People's National Bank of Washington in 1988; cap. 263.7m., dep. 3,417.2m.; Chair. and CEO JOSHUA GREEN, III; Pres. and COO GERRY CAMERON; 140 brs.

WEST VIRGINIA

First Huntingdon National Bank: 1000 Fifth Ave, Huntingdon, WV 25701; tel. (304) 526-4200; f. 1872; cap. 21.1m., dep. 264.2m. (March 1985); Pres. DONALD P. RAY.

Kanawha Valley Bank NA: POB 1793, Charleston, WV 25326; tel. (304) 348-7000; telex 9301816; f. 1867; cap. 30.7m., dep. 366.6m. (Sept. 1983); Pres. ROBERT F. BARONNER.

WISCONSIN

Bank One, Milwaukee NA: 111 East Wisconsin Ave, Milwaukee, WI 53202; tel. (414) 765-3000; telex 191115; f. 1930, name changed on merger of Banc One Corporation (Columbus, Ohio) and Marine Bank, NA in 1988; cap. 105.8m., dep. 1,208.0m. (June 1988); Chair. and CEO FREDERICK L. CULLEN; Pres. and COO RONALD C. BALDWIN; 13 US brs, 2 foreign brs.

First Interstate Bank of Wisconsin: 16001 West Cleveland Ave, New Berlin, WI 53151; tel. (414) 224-4270; telex 260180; fax (414) 224-4234; f. 1984; cap. 38.7m., dep. 427.9m. (Dec. 1988); Vice-Pres. ANDREW RUMAN.

First Wisconsin National Bank of Fond du Lac: Main St at Forest Ave, Fond du Lac, WI 54935; tel. (414) 922-3200; f. 1855; cap. 12.2m., dep. 178.7m. (Dec. 1988); Pres. LEON A. LAUTERS; 2 brs.

First Wisconsin National Bank of Milwaukee: 777 East Wisconsin Ave, Milwaukee, WI 53202; tel. (414) 765-5705; telex 26635; fax (414) 765-6207; f. 1863; cap. 202.6m., dep. 2,808.6m. (Dec. 1987); Chair. JOHN H. HENDEE, Jr; Pres. JOHN A. BECKER; 14 brs.

M & I Marshall & Ilsley Bank: 770 North Water St, Milwaukee, WI 53201; tel. (414) 765-7700; telex 269572; f. 1847; cap. 180.1m., dep. 1,791.7m. (Dec. 1987); Chair. J. A. PUELICHER; Pres. and CEO JAMES B. WIGDALE; 1 foreign br.

WYOMING

American National Bank: 1912 Capitol Ave, Cheyenne, WY 82001; tel. (307) 634-2121; f. 1919; Pres. and CEO JACK CREWS.

First Interstate Bank of Casper NA: 104 South Wolcott St, POB 40, Casper, WY 82602; tel. (307) 235-4201; telex 318407; f. 1889; cap. 11.9m., dep. 192.0m. (Dec. 1988); Pres. and CEO CHARLES E. PEDERSEN.

First Interstate Bank of Commerce: 4 South Main St, POB 2007, Sheridan, WY 82801; tel. (307) 674-7411; f. 1893, known as First Interstate Bank of Sheridan until 1989; cap. 17.1m., dep. 240.0m. (Dec. 1988); Chair., Pres. and CEO HOMER SCOTT, Jr.

First Interstate Bank of Laramie: 221 Ivinson Ave, POB 1307, Laramie, WY 82070; tel. (307) 745-4874; f. 1873; cap. 7.2m., dep. 100.0m. (Dec. 1988); Chair. and CEO ELWOOD J. HAINES, Jr.

First Interstate Bank of Riverton: 323 East Main St, POB 233, Riverton, WY 82501; tel. (307) 856-2211; f. 1934; cap. 4.8m., dep. 58.3m. (Dec. 1988); Pres. JOHN L. WARDEN.

Selected Savings Institutions

(dep. = deposits; m. = million; amounts in US dollars)

SAVINGS BANKS

Binghamton Savings Bank: 58–68 Exchange St, Binghamton, NY 13902; tel. (607) 773-2525; f. 1867; dep. 660m.; Pres. and CEO W. H. RINCKER.

Cambridge Savings Bank: 1374 Massachusetts Ave, Cambridge, MA 02238; tel. (617) 864-8700; f. 1834; dep. 392m.; Chair. and CEO D. P. NOYES.

Citizens Commercial and Savings Bank: One Citizens Banking Center, Flint, MI 48502; tel. (313) 766-7500; f. 1890; dep. 963m.; Chair. D. E. JOHNSON.

Citizens Savings Bank, FSB: 870 Westminster St, Providence, RI 02903; tel. (401) 456-7000; f. 1871; dep. 1,101m.; Chair and CEO GEORGE GRABOYS.

The Cumberland Federal Savings Bank: 200 West Broadway, Louisville, KY 40202; tel. (502) 562-5200; f. 1987; dep. 692m.; Chair. and Pres. H. D. HALE.

Dime Savings Bank of New York: 1225 Franklin Ave, Garden City, NY 11530; tel. (516) 351-1550; f. 1859; dep. 6,691m.; Chair., Pres. and CEO H. W. ALBRIGHT, Jr.

First American Savings Bank, FSB: 400 West Tuscarawas St, Canton, OH 44702; tel. (216) 452-0633; f. 1887; dep. 675m.; Chair. and CEO C. F. BAYLOR.

Great Southern Federal Savings Bank: 132 East Broughton St, POB 8206, Savannah, GA 31412-8206; tel. (912) 944-6200; f. 1935; dep. 796m.; Chair. N. C. BRANAN.

Green Point Savings Bank: 807 Manhattan Ave, Brooklyn, NY 11222; tel. (212) 670-7500; f. 1868; dep. 1,067m.; Chair., Pres. and CEO I. J. LASURDO.

Home Savings Bank: 315 Wyckoff Ave, Brooklyn, NY 11237; tel. (718) 417-2440; f. 1905; dep. 1,191m.; Chair., Pres. and CEO R. A. KRAEMER.

Hudson City Savings Bank: 80 West Century Rd, Paramus, NJ 07652; tel. (201) 967-1900; f. 1868; dep. 2,487m.; Chair. and CEO K. L. BIRCHBY.

Mechanics and Farmers Savings Bank: 930 Main St, POB 1460, Bridgeport, CT 06601; tel. (203) 382-6363; f. 1871; dep. 764m.; Pres. and CEO D. J. SULLIVAN, Jr.

Northeast Savings, FA: Northeast Plaza, 50 State St, Hartford, CT 06103; tel. (203) 280-1000; f. 1834; dep. 3,187m.; Chair., Pres. and CEO KENT DIXON.

SAVINGS AND LOAN ASSOCIATIONS

Alabama Federal Savings and Loan Association: 201 Office Park Dr., Birmingham, AL 35223; tel. (205) 877-0200; f. 1925; dep. 665m.; Chair. and CEO J. H. SHANNON; 4 subsidiaries.

Bay View Federal Savings and Loan Association: 2121 South El Camino Real, San Mateo, CA 94403; tel. (415) 573-7300; f. 1911; Pres. and CEO R. E. BARNES; 1 subsidiary.

Columbia Savings and Loan Association: 8840 Wilshire Blvd, Beverly Hills, CA 90211; tel. (213) 657-6134; f. 1958; dep. 5,142m.; Chair. ABRAHAM SPIEGEL; 2 subsidiaries.

Commonwealth Savings and Loan Association of Florida: 2000 West Commercial Blvd, Fort Lauderdale, FL 33309; tel. (305) 493-5100; f. 1980; dep. 1,007m.; Chair. and CEO B. E. CHAPNICK; 2 subsidiaries.

Downey Savings and Loan Association: 3200 Bristol St, POB 6000, Costa Mesa, CA 92626; tel. (714) 549-8811; f. 1957; dep. 1,929m.; Pres. M. L. MCALISTER; 2 subsidiaries.

First Federal Savings and Loan Association of South Carolina: 301 College St, Greenville, SC 29601; tel. (803) 271-7222; f. 1933; dep. 1,427m.; Chair. and CEO H. R. DAVIS; 14 subsidiaries.

Florida Federal Savings and Loan Association: 360 Central Ave, POB 1509, St Petersburg, FL 33731; tel. (813) 893-1131; dep. 3,433m.; Chair., Pres. and CEO ERIC STATTIN; 5 subsidiaries.

Metropolitan Federal Savings and Loan Association: 230 North Fourth Avenue, POB 995, Nashville, TN 37202-0995; tel. (615) 259-2800; f. 1948; dep. 754m.; Chair. and CEO G. L. LAWRENCE; 1 subsidiary.

San Antonio Savings Association: 601 North West Loop 410, POB 1810, San Antonio, TX 78296; tel. (512) 340-7272; f. 1921; dep. 1,662m.; Chair. and CEO W. W. MCALLISTER, III; 11 subsidiaries.

Sooner Federal Savings and Loans Associations: Sooner Federal Tower, 5100 East Skelly Dr., Tulsa, OK 74101; tel. (918) 665-6600; f. 1934; dep. 1,300m.; Chair. W. R. HAGSTREM; 1 subsidiary.

Valley Federal Saving and Loan Association: 6842 Van Nuys Blvd, Van Nuys, CA 91405; tel. (818) 904-3000; f. 1925; dep. 2,067m.; Chair. J. R. BIAFORA; 3 subsidiaries.

Washington Federal Savings and Loan Association: 425 Pike St, Seattle, WA 98101; tel. (206) 624-7930; f. 1917; dep. 838m.; Chair., Pres. and CEO E. K. KNUTSON; 2 subsidiaries.

Banking Associations

There is a State Bankers' Association in each state.

American Bankers Association: 1120 Connecticut Ave, NW, Washington, DC 20036; tel. (202) 663-5000; telex 892787; fax (202) 296-9274; f. 1875; 11,000 mem. orgs; Exec. Vice-Pres. DONALD G. OGILVIE.

American Society of Bank Directors: POB 12329, Arlington, VA 22305; tel. (703) 683-3030; f. 1974; 3,000 mems; Exec. Vice-Pres. ANDREW MCDONAGH.

Association of Bank Holding Companies: 730 15th St, NW, Washington, DC 20005; tel. (202) 393-1158; f. 1958; 125 mem. orgs; Pres. DONALD L. ROGERS.

Association of Reserve City Bankers: 1710 Rhode Island Ave, NW, Suite 500, Washington, DC 20036; tel. (202) 296-5709; f. 1912; Exec. Dir Dr ANTHONY T. CLUFF.

Bank Administration Institute: 60 Gould Center, 2550 Golf Rd, Rolling Meadows, IL 60008; tel. (312) 228-6200; telex 701344; f. 1924; 8,000 mems; Pres. RONALD G. BURKE.

Bank Association for Foreign Trade: 1600 M St, NW, 7th Floor, Washington, DC 20036; tel. (202) 452-0952; f. 1921; 300 mem. orgs; Exec. Dir M. CONDEELIS.

Bank Capital Markets Association: c/o National Press Bldg, Suite 200, Washington, DC 20045; tel. (202) 662-8766; f. 1972; 176 mem. orgs; Exec. Dir RICHARD L. DeCAIR.

Bank Marketing Association: 309 West Washington St, Chicago, IL 60606; tel. (312) 782-1442; f. 1915; 4,500 mems; Exec. Vice-Pres. RAYMOND M. CHESELDINE.

Bankers' Committee: 1615 M St, Suite 220, Washington, DC 20036; tel. (202) 446-8308; f. 1950; 1,000 mem. orgs; Chair. ARTHUR T. ROTH.

Banking Law Institute: 22 West 21st St, New York, NY 10010; tel. (201) 645-7880; f. 1983; 460 mems; Sr Vice-Pres. JAMES F. SLABE.

Consumer Bankers Association: 1300 North 17th St, Arlington, VA 22209; tel. (703) 276-1750; f. 1919; 625 mems.

The Electronic Banking Economics Society: 314 West 53rd St, New York, NY 10019; tel. (203) 295-9788; f. 1981; 74 mems; Pres. LINDA FENNER ZIMMER.

Independent Bankers Association of America: One Thomas Circle, NW, Suite 950, Washington, DC 20005; tel. (202) 659-8111; f. 1930; 6,800 mem. orgs; Exec. Vice-Pres. KENNETH A. GUENTHER.

Institute of Foreign Bankers: 200 Park Ave, Suite 303E, New York, NY 10166; tel. (212) 682-2533; f. 1966; Exec. Officer NICOLA G. STOCK.

National Association for Bank Cost and Management Accounting: POB 27448, San Francisco, CA 94127; tel. (415) 953-4512; f. 1980; 600 mems; Pres. PAUL F. MCATEE, Jr.

National Association of Bank Women: 500 North Michigan Ave, Suite 1400, Chicago, IL 60611; tel. (312) 661-1700; f. 1921; 29,500 mems; Exec. Vice-Pres. PHYLLIS HAEGER.

National Association of Urban Bankers: 111 East Wacker Dr., Suite 600, Chicago, IL 60601; tel. (312) 644-6610; f. 1975; 1,200 mems; Pres. LAFAYETTE JONES.

National Association of Mutual Savings Institutions: 1101 15th St, NW, Washington, DC 20005; tel. (202) 857-3100; f. 1983; 600 mem. orgs; Exec. Vice-Pres. GEORGE HANC.

National Bankers Association: 122 C St, NW, Suite 580, Washington, DC 20001; tel. (202) 783-3200; f. 1927; 47 mems; Pres. JOHN P. KELLY, Jr.

National Independent Bank Equipment and Systems Association: 1411 Peterson Ave, Park Ridge, IL 60068; tel. (312) 825-8419; f. 1973; 250 mems; Exec. Dir ANNE WALK.

National Marine Bankers Association: 401 North Michigan Ave, Suite 2950, Chicago, IL 60611; tel. (312) 836-4747; f. 1980; 150 mems.

New York Clearing House Association: 100 Broad St, New York, NY 10004; tel. (212) 612-9200; f. 1853; 12 mem. orgs; Pres. WILLARD C. BUTCHER; Chair. Clearing House Cttee DANIEL P. DAVISON; Exec. Vice-Pres. and Sec. JOHN F. LEE.

Robert Morris Associates—National Association of Bank Loan and Credit Officers: Philadelphia National Bank Bldg, Philadelphia, PA 19107; tel. (215) 665-2850; f. 1914; 3,100 mems; Exec. Vice-Pres. CLARENCE R. REED.

United States League of Savings Institutions: 1709 New York Ave, NW, Suite 801, Washington, DC 20006; tel. (202) 637-8900; f. 1892; 3,400 mems; Pres. FREDERICK L. WEBBER.

FINANCIAL MARKETS

Principal Stock Exchanges

American Stock Exchange: 86 Trinity Pl., New York, NY 10006; tel. (212) 306-1000; telex 3496761; f. 1849; 864 mems; Chair. JAMES R. JONES; Pres. KENNETH R. LEIBLER.

Boston Stock Exchange, Inc: One Boston Pl., Boston, MA 02108; tel. (617) 723-9500; f. 1834; 196 mems; Chair. and CEO WILLIAM G. MORTON, Jr.

Chicago Board Options Exchange: 400 South LaSalle St, Chicago, IL 60605; tel. (312) 786-5600; f. 1973; 2,017 mems; Chair. and CEO ALGER B. CHAPMAN.

Cincinnati Stock Exchange: 205 Dixie Terminal Bldg, Cincinnati, OH 45202; tel. (513) 621-1410.

Midwest Stock Exchange: 440 South LaSalle St, Chicago, IL 60605; f. 1882; 441 mems; Chair. and CEO JOHN G. WEITHERS; Pres. and COO C. V. DOHERTY.

New York Futures Exchange: 20 Broad St, New York, NY 10005; tel. (212) 656-4949.

New York Stock Exchange, Inc: 11 Wall St, New York, NY 10005; f. 1792; 1,366 mems; Chair. and CEO JOHN J. PHELAN, Jr; Pres. RICHARD A. GRASSO.

Pacific Stock Exchange, Inc: 301 Pine St, San Francisco, CA 94104; tel. (415) 393-4000; telex 203025; f. 1882; 539 mems; Chair. and CEO MAURICE MANN; Pres. HERBERT G. KAWAHARA.

Philadelphia Stock Exchange, Inc: Stock Exchange Bldg, 1900 Market St, Philadelphia, PA 19103; tel. (215) 496-5000; telex 902636; f. 1790; 505 mems; Chair. MARTIN L. LONGSTRETH, Jr; Pres. NICHOLAS A. GIORDANO.

SUPERVISORY BODY

Securities and Exchange Commission: 450 Fifth St, NW, Washington, DC 20549; tel. (202) 272-2650; f. 1934 under the Securities Act of 1934 as a federal body which administers the federal securities laws and oversees the nation's securities and financial markets; Chair. RICHARD BREEDEN.

SALES OF STOCKS AND OPTIONS ON REGISTERED EXCHANGES, 1986
(excludes over-the-counter trading)

	Volume of trade (million)		Market value of trade ($'000 million)		
	Shares sold[1]	Options contracts traded[2]	Shares sold[1]	Options contracts traded[2]	Total, all sales[3]
American	2,999	65	43	19	63
Chicago	—	180	—	56	56
Midwest	2,784	—	102	—	102
New York	39,150	—	1,446	—	1,451
Pacific	1,750	—	51	—	55
Philadelphia	—	—	—	—	35
Total[4]	48,229	289	1,702	88	1,794

[1] Includes voting trust certificates, American Depository Receipts, and certificates of deposit for stocks.
[2] Includes non-equity options.
[3] Includes market value of rights and warrants. Excludes the value of options exercised.
[4] Includes other registered exchanges, not shown separately.

Source: Bureau of the Census, US Department of Commerce, *Statistical Abstract of the United States.*

Commodity Exchanges

Amarillo Grain Exchange: 1300 South Johnson St, Amarillo, TX 79101; tel. (806) 372-8511.

Board of Trade of the City of Chicago: 141 West Jackson Blvd, Chicago, IL 60604; tel. (312) 435-3500; f. 1848; 3,400 mems; Pres. THOMAS R. DONOVAN.

Board of Trade of Kansas City, Missouri: 4800 Main St, Suite 303, Kansas City, MO 64112; tel. (816) 753-7500; f. 1856; 269 mems; Pres. and CEO MICHAEL BRAUDE.

Board of Trade of the Wholesale Seafood Merchants: Seven Dey St, Suite 805, New York, NY 10007; tel. (212) 732-4340; f. 1933; 400 mems; Exec. Sec. DENNIS F. RYAN.

Chicago Mercantile Exchange: 30 South Wacker Dr., Chicago, IL 60606; tel. (312) 930-1000; f. 1898; 2,724 mems; Pres. WILLIAM J. BRODSKY.

Cincinnati Board of Trade: 5675 Kilby Rd, Harrison, OH 45030; tel. (513) 367-4518; f. 1918; 18 mems; Pres. JAMES CORNELIUS.

Coffee, Sugar and Cocoa Exchange: Four World Trade Center, 8th Floor, New York, NY 10048; tel. (212) 938-2800; f. 1882; 527 mems; Pres. BENNETT J. CORN.

Commodity Exchange: Four World Trade Center, New York, NY 10048; tel. (212) 938-2900; f. 1933; 772 mems; Pres. ARNOLD F. STALOFF.

Dallas Cotton Exchange: 608 North St Paul St, Suite 100, Dallas, TX 75201; tel. (214) 880-0282; f. 1907; 100 mems; Pres. BOBBY WALTON.

Forth Worth Grain Exchange: POB 4422, Fort Worth, TX 76106; tel. (817) 626-8213; f. 1907; 36 mems; Exec. Vice-Pres. C. G. MATHEWS.

Galveston Cotton Exchange and Board of Trade: 2102 Mechanic St, Galveston, TX 77550; tel. (713) 765-5761; f. 1875; Sec. and Gen. Man. L. C. OLIVER.

Greenwood Cotton Exchange: POB 884, Greenwood, MS 38930; tel. (601) 453-5252; f. 1927; 35 mems; Sec.-Treas. CHARLES J. SWAYZE.

Hutchinson Board of Trade Association (Grain): 819 Wiley Bldg, Hutchinson, KS 67501; tel. (316) 663-1171; f. 1917; 33 mems; Pres. JIM MCVEY.

Los Angeles Grain Exchange: 515 West Commonwealth Ave, Suite 213, Fullerton, CA 92632; tel. (714) 870-0770; f. 1913; 48 mems; Pres. THOMAS PROKOP.

Memphis Cotton Exchange: POB 3150, Memphis, TN 38173; tel. (901) 525-3361; f. 1873; 100 mems; Exec. Vice-Pres. RETA J. MARTIN.

Merchants' Exchange of St Louis: 5100 Oakland Ave, St Louis, MO 63110; tel. (314) 535-2400; f. 1836; 150 mems; Exec. Vice-Pres. MORRIS L. LARSON.

Midamerica Commodity Exchange: 444 West Jackson Blvd, Chicago, IL 60606; tel. (312) 341-3000; f. 1868; 1,205 mems; Pres. THOMAS R. DONOVAN.

Minneapolis Grain Exchange: 150 Grain Exchange Bldg, 400 South Fourth St, Minneapolis, MN 55415; tel. (612) 338-6212; f. 1881; 402 mems; Pres. PAUL A. TATTERSALL.

Montgomery Cotton Exchange: POB 100, Montogomery, AL 36192; tel. (202) 269-1551; f. 1912; 6 mems; Pres. STUART FRASER.

New England Fish Exchange: Administration Bldg, Boston Fish Pier, Boston, MA 02210; tel. (617) 574-4600; f. 1908; 26 mems; Pres. GERRY FRATTOLLILO.

New Orleans Commodity Exchange: 308 Board of Trade Pl., New Orleans, LA 70130; tel. (504) 524-2184; f. 1976; 500 mems; Pres. RUSSELL F. MCDONALD.

New York Cotton Exchange: Four World Trade Center, New York, NY 10048; tel. (212) 938-2650; f. 1870; 396 mems; Pres. JOSEPH J. O'NEILL.

New York Mercantile Exchange: Four World Trade Center, New York, NY 10048; tel. (212) 938-2222; f. 1872; 180 mems; Pres. R. PATRICK THOMPSON.

Peoria Board of Trade (Grain): 330 Washington St, NW, Peoria, IL 61602; tel. (309) 674-7169; f. 1869; 31 mems; Agent HAROLD D. CADY.

Pine Bluff Cotton Exchange: 408 West Second St, Pine Bluff, AR 71601; tel. (501) 535-1330; f. 1910; 10 mems; Pres. ROGER STONE.

Portland Grain Exchange: 200 Market St, SW, Suite 220, Portland, OR 97201; tel. (503) 228-4361; f. 1929; 55 mems; Sec. RICHARD A. COPELAND.

St Joseph Grain Exchange: 105 Kirkpatrick Bldg, St Joseph, MO 64501; tel. (816) 233-2531; f. 1915; 25 mems; Exec. Sec. W. T. DRANNAN.

Salina Board of Trade (Grain): 1700 East Iron Ave, Salina, KS 67401; tel. (913) 823-6301; f. 1915; 37 mems; Pres. DON SOUKUP.

Sioux City Grain Exchange: 518 Eighth St, Suite B, Sioux City, IA 51101; tel. (712) 255-1418; f. 1907; 22 mems; Sec.-Treas. DOUGLAS PALMER.

Wine Futures Exchange: 31826 Village Center Rd, Suite C, Westlake Village, CA 91361; tel. (818) 991-5589.

INSURANCE

Life Insurance in Force and Benefit Payments

(Source: American Council of Life Insurance, *Life Insurance Fact Book*, annual.)

Summary: Life Insurance in Force in the USA

		1982	1983	1984	1985	1986
Number of policies .	(million)	390	387	385	386	391
Value (total) .	($'000 million)	4,477	4,966	5,500	6,053	6,720
Ordinary .	($'000 million)	2,217	2,544	2,888	3,247	3,658
Group .	($'000 million)	2,066	2,220	2,392	2,562	2,801
Industrial .	($'000 million)	33	31	30	28	27
Credit[1] .	($'000 million)	161	171	190	216	234
Average size of policy:						
Ordinary .	($)	15,140	17,380	19,970	22,780	25,540
Group .	($)	16,630	17,530	18,780	19,720	20,720
Industrial .	($)	630	630	630	640	650
Credit[1] .	($)	2,410	2,650	2,880	3,100	3,310
Average amount per family[2] .	($)	49,300	54,200	58,700	63,400	69,100
Disposable income per family[2] .	($)	23,900	25,500	27,500	29,800	31,100

[1] Insures borrower to cover consumer loan in case of death.　　[2] Definition includes families, subfamilies and unrelated individuals.

States (1986)

	Insurance in force			Benefit payments ($ million)[1]
	Policies ('000)	Value ($'000 million)	Average per family ($)	
Alabama .	11,877	107	69,500	844
Alaska .	866	15	66,200	115
Arizona .	4,940	86	64,000	852
Arkansas .	2,804	44	47,300	392
California .	29,740	723	62,100	6,402
Colorado .	5,164	104	73,600	905
Connecticut .	5,773	120	94,800	1,279
Delaware .	1,415	26	103,300	281
District of Columbia .	2,179	44	138,000	424
Florida .	16,994	279	54,700	3,116
Georgia .	12,434	182	77,500	1,300
Hawaii .	1,805	34	83,500	308
Idaho .	1,304	22	56,900	230
Illinois .	19,620	347	75,500	4,001
Indiana .	9,286	146	66,200	1,591
Iowa .	4,595	80	68,800	951
Kansas .	4,100	73	71,400	723
Kentucky .	6,145	79	55,300	793
Louisiana .	9,219	119	69,900	1,017
Maine .	1,893	27	56,400	284
Maryland .	8,055	138	78,700	1,432
Massachusetts .	8,744	179	73,600	1,895
Michigan .	14,069	262	73,300	2,934
Minnesota .	6,318	127	74,900	1,170
Mississippi .	4,173	54	56,300	380
Missouri .	8,447	141	67,800	1,414
Montana .	1,132	19	54,700	209
Nebraska .	2,564	49	75,000	532
Nevada .	1,452	23	54,000	202
New Hampshire .	1,677	29	68,700	282
New Jersey .	11,516	250	84,600	3,171
New Mexico .	1,831	34	59,700	304
New York .	27,592	534	74,200	6,155
North Carolina .	12,813	167	66,100	1,540
North Dakota .	925	19	67,400	158
Ohio .	18,480	299	71,100	3,450
Oklahoma .	4,446	81	59,900	965
Oregon .	3,094	62	51,800	705
Pennsylvania .	22,207	326	69,000	3,938
Rhode Island .	1,901	29	72,800	343
South Carolina .	8,107	89	68,800	656
South Dakota .	952	19	65,000	173
Tennessee .	9,830	131	70,300	1,230
Texas .	25,549	480	73,200	4,034
Utah .	2,409	42	71,000	346
Vermont .	856	14	58,500	147
Virginia .	12,853	179	79,900	1,532
Washington .	5,239	113	58,600	1,081
West Virginia .	3,022	38	51,200	476
Wisconsin .	7,655	123	65,200	1,520
Wyoming .	658	13	63,200	123
Total .	390,719	6,720	69,100	68,305

[1] Comprises death payments, matured endowments, disability and annuity payments, surrender values and policy dividends.
[2] Definition includes families, subfamilies and unrelated individuals.

Principal Companies

Acacia Mutual Life Insurance Co: 51 Louisiana Ave, NW, Washington, DC 20001; tel. (202) 628-4506; f. 1869; operating in 35 states and the District of Columbia; Chair. DANIEL L. HURSON; Pres. and CEO CHARLES T. NASON.

Aetna Life and Casualty Co: 151 Farmington Ave, Hartford, CT 06156; tel. (203) 273-0123; telex 099241; f. 1853; operating in two states and the District of Columbia; Chair. JAMES T. LYNN; Pres. RONALD E. COMPTON.

Allendale Mutual Insurance Co: 1301 Atwood Ave, Johnston, RI 02919; tel. (401) 275-3000; f. 1835; operating in all states, the District of Columbia, Puerto Rico, the Virgin Islands and Canada; Chair. G. R. WEST; Pres. and CEO J. J. CAREY.

Allstate Insurance Co: Allstate Plaza, Northbrook, IL 60062; tel. (312) 291-5000; f. 1931; operating in all states, the District of Columbia, the Virgin Islands and Puerto Rico; Chair. and CEO D. F. CRAIB, Jr; Pres. R. J. HAAYEN.

American General Corpn: 2929 Allen Parkway, Houston, TX 77019; tel. (713) 522-1111; f. 1926; operating in all states, Canada and Guam; Chair. and CEO HAROLD S. HOOK; Pres. MICHAEL J. POULOS.

American Mutual Liability Insurance Co: Quannapowitt Pkwy, Wakefield, MA 01880; tel. (617) 245-6000; f. 1887; operating in all states, the District of Columbia, Puerto Rico and Canada; Chair. R. E. ROBERSON; Pres. and CEO J. JOHN WORTMAN.

American Mutual Life Insurance Co: Liberty Bldg, Des Moines, IA 50309; tel. (515) 280-1331; f. 1897; operating in 30 states; Pres. W. R. ENGEL.

American National Insurance Co: One Moody Plaza, Galveston, TX 77550; tel. (409) 763-4661; f. 1905; operating in 49 states, the District of Columbia, Canada, Puerto Rico and Guam; Chair. R. L. MOODY; Pres. and CEO O. C. CLAY.

American Security Insurance Co: 3290 Northside Parkway, NW, Atlanta, GA 30327; tel. (404) 261-9000; f. 1983; operating in all states, Puerto Rico and the Virgin Islands; Chair. A. R. FREEDMAN; Pres. M. G. GADDY.

American United Life Insurance Co: 1 West 26th St, Indianapolis, IA 46206; tel. (317) 927-1877; f. 1877; Chair. and CEO JACK E. REICH; Pres. JERRY D. SEMLER.

Ameritas Life Insurance Corpn: 5900 O St, Lincoln, NE 68501; tel. (402) 467-1122; f. 1887; Chair. and CEO NEAL E. TYNER; Pres. LAWRENCE J. ARTH.

Baltimore Life Insurance Co: 901 North Howard St, Baltimore, MD 21201; tel. (301) 539-7900; f. 1882; operating in 13 states and the District of Columbia; Chair. and CEO G. G. RADCLIFFE.

Bankers' Life & Casualty Co: 4444 West Lawrence Ave, Chicago, IL 60630; tel. (312) 777-7000; f. 1880; Chair. and CEO R. T. SHAW; Pres. J. W. GARDINER.

Berkshire Life Insurance Co: 700 South St, Pittsfield, MA 01201; tel. (413) 499-4321; f. 1851; operating in 49 states; Pres. and CEO ALBERT C. CORNELIO.

Business Men's Assurance Co of America: BMA Tower, 1 Penn Valley Park, Kansas City, MO 64108; tel. (816) 753-8000; f. 1909; operating in 48 states and the District of Columbia; Chair. W. D. GRANT; Pres. and CEO W. T. GRANT, II.

California–Western States Life Insurance Co: 2020 L St, Sacramento, CA 95814; tel. (916) 444-7100; f. 1910; operating in 28 states and Canada; Pres. and CEO R. W. REVER.

Capitol Life Insurance Co: 1600 Sherman St, Denver, CO 80203; tel. (303) 861-4065; telex 454464; f. 1905; operating in 49 states; Pres. SANFORD MERKIN.

Central Life Assurance Co: 611 Fifth Ave, Des Moines, IA 50306; tel. (515) 283-2371; f. 1896; Pres. and CEO R. K. BROOKS.

CIGNA Corpn: 1 Logan Sq., Philadelphia, PA 19103; tel. (215) 241-4000; f. 1982 by merger; operating in all states and the District of Columbia, Canada and Puerto Rico; Chair. and CEO ROBERT D. KILPATRICK; Pres. and CEO WILSON H. TAYLOR.

Colonial Life Insurance Co of America: 1 Granite Pl., Concord, NH 03301; tel. (603) 224-7741; f. 1897; operating in all states, the District of Columbia, Puerto Rico and the Virgin Islands; Chair. and CEO DEAN R. O'HARE.

Combined Insurance Co of America: 123 North Wacker Dr., Chicago, IL 60616; tel. (312) 701-3000; f. 1949; operating in all states, the District of Columbia, the Virgin Islands, Puerto Rico, Canada and overseas; Chair. W. CLEMENT STONE; Pres. and CEO P. G. RYAN.

Commercial Union Insurance Companies: One Beacon St, Boston, MA 02108; tel. (617) 725-6000; f. 1861; Pres. and CEO ANTHONY L. BREND.

Commonwealth Life Insurance Co: 680 Fourth Ave, Louisville, KY 40232; tel. (502) 587-7371; f. 1904; operating in 7 states; Chair., Pres. and CEO DAVID E. SAMS, Jr.

Connecticut Mutual Life Insurance Co: 140 Garden St, Hartford, CT 06154; tel. (203) 727-6500; f. 1846; operating in all states and the District of Columbia; Chair. and CEO DENIS F. MULLANE.

Continental American Life Insurance Co: 300 Continental Dr., Newark, DE 19713; tel. (302) 454-5150; f. 1907; operating in 41 states and the District of Columbia; Chair., Pres. and CEO WILLIAM G. COPELAND.

Continental Assurance Co/Continental Casualty Co: CNA Plaza, 333 South Wabash Ave, Chicago, IL 60685; tel. (312) 822-5000; operating in all states, Canada, Guam and Puerto Rico; Chair. and Pres. E. J. NOHA.

The Continental Insurance Co: 180 Maiden Lane, New York, NY 10038; tel. (212) 440-3000; f. 1853; operating in all states and Puerto Rico; Chair. and CEO J. P. MASCOTTE.

Country Mutual Insurance Co: 1701 Towanda Ave, Bloomington, IL 61701; tel. (309) 557-2111; f. 1925; Pres. JOHN WHITE, Jr.

Credit Life Insurance Co: One South Limestone St, Springfield, OH 45501; tel. (513) 328-2200; f. 1925; operating in all states, the District of Columbia and Canada; Chair. D. W. HOLLENBECK.

Equitable of Iowa Companies: 699 Walnut St, 20th Floor, Des Moines, IA 50306; tel. (515) 282-1335; f. 1867; operating in all states and the District of Columbia; Chair. and CEO J. W. HUBBELL, Jr.

Equitable Life Assurance Society of the US: 787 Seventh Ave, New York, NY 10019; tel. (212) 554-1234; f. 1859; operating in all states, the District of Columbia, Puerto Rico and Canada; Pres. and CEO JOHN B. CARTER.

Equitable Life Insurance Co: 8300 Greensboro Dr., McLean, VA 22101; tel. (703) 827-0039; f. 1885; operating in 23 states and the District of Columbia; Pres. and CEO ROBERT S. MARCOTTE.

Excelsior Insurance Co: 1065 James St, Syracuse, NY 13221; tel. (315) 422-3183; f. 1919; operating in 15 states and the District of Columbia; Pres. ALAN JAGLINSKI.

Farmers Group Inc: 4680 Wilshire Blvd, Los Angeles, CA 90010; tel. (213) 932-3200; operating in 25 states; Chair., Pres. and CEO LEO E. DENLEA, Jr.

Federal Home Life Insurance Co: 78 West Michigan Ave, Battle Creek, MI 49017; tel. (616) 968-5500; f. 1906; Chair. J. WILLIAM BRANDER.

Federal Insurance Co: 15 Mountain View Rd, Warren, NJ 07060; tel. (201) 580-2000; f. 1901; operating in all states, the District of Columbia and Puerto Rico; Chair., Pres. and CEO HENRY U. HARDER.

Fidelity & Casualty Co of New York: 180 Maiden Lane, New York, NY 10038; tel. (212) 440-3000; f. 1875; operating in all states, the District of Columbia and Puerto Rico; Chair. and CEO J. P. MASCOTTE; Pres. J. H. BRETHERICK, Jr.

Fidelity Mutual Life Insurance Co: 250 King of Prussia Rd, Radnor, PA 19087; tel. (215) 964-7000; f. 1878; operating in 39 states; Chair. and CEO J. C. LADD; Pres. W. W. DEAKINS.

Fireman's Fund Insurance Co: 777 San Marin Dr., Novato, CA 94947; tel. (415) 899-2000; f. 1863; operating in all states, the District of Columbia, Puerto Rico and Canada; Chair., Pres. and CEO W. M. McCORMICK.

Firemen's Insurance Co of Newark, NJ: 180 Maiden Lane, New York, NY 10038; tel. (212) 440-3000; f. 1855; operating in all states and Puerto Rico; Chair. J. P. MASCOTTE.

Franklin Life Insurance Co: Franklin Sq., Springfield, IL 62713; tel. (217) 528-2011; f. 1884; Chair. W. J. ALLEY; Pres. and CEO HOWARD C. HUMPHREY.

General American Life Insurance Co: 700 Market St, St Louis, MO 63101; tel. (314) 231-1700; f. 1933; operating in 49 states; Chair., Pres. and CEO H. EDWIN TRUSHEIM.

Great American Insurance Co: 580 Walnut St, Cincinnati, OH 45202; tel. (513) 369-5000; f. 1976; operating in all states, the District of Columbia and Puerto Rico; Chair. CARL H. LINDER.

Great Southern Life Insurance Co: 3121 Buffalo Speedway, Houston, TX 77098; tel. (713) 552-4300; f. 1909; operating in 41 states; Chair. ROBERT T. SHAW; Pres. JOHN W. GARDINER.

Guarantee Mutual Life Co: Guarantee Center, 8801 Indian Hills Dr., Omaha, NE 68114; tel. (402) 390-7300; f. 1901; operating in 30 states; Pres. E. A. CONLEY.

The Guardian Life Insurance Co of America: 201 Park Ave South, New York, NY 10003; tel. (212) 598-8000; f. 1860; operating in all states and the District of Columbia; Chair. and CEO JOHN C. ANGLE; Pres. ARTHUR FERRARA.

Gulf Insurance Co: 3015 Cedar Springs Rd, Dallas, TX 75219; tel. (214) 559-1500; f. 1925; operating in all states and the District of Columbia; Pres. and CEO D. W. BANNISTER.

Gulf Life Insurance Co: 1301 Gulf Life Dr., Jacksonville, FL 32207-9048; tel. (904) 390-7000; f. 1911; operating in 34 states; Pres. and CEO R. O. PURCIFULL.

Hanover Insurance Co: 100 North Parkway, Worcester, MA 01605; tel. (617) 853-7200; f. 1973; operating in all states, the District of Columbia and Canada; Chair. F. FEDELI; CEO JOHN F. O'BRIEN.

Hawkeye National Life Insurance Co: 2700 Westown Parkway, Suite 400, West Des Moines, IA 50265; tel. (515) 223-2700; f. 1966; operating in 24 states; Pres. D. L. BLAESS.

Home Beneficial Life Insurance Co: 3901 West Broad St, Richmond, VA 23230; tel. (804) 358-8431; f. 1899; operating in 6 states and the District of Columbia; Chair., Pres. and CEO R. W. WILTSHIRE.

The Home Insurance Co: 59 Maiden Lane, New York, NY 10038; tel. (212) 530-7000; f. 1853; operating in all states, the District of Columbia, Puerto Rico and Canada; Pres. JAMES J. MEENAGHAN.

Home Life Insurance Co: 253 Broadway, New York, NY 10007; tel. (212) 306-2000; f. 1860; operating in all states and the District of Columbia; Pres. and CEO K. C. NICHOLS.

Illinois Mutual Life and Casualty Co: 300 South West Adams St, Peoria, IL 61634; tel. (309) 674-8255; f. 1912; operating in 23 states; Chair. R. A. McCORD; Pres. M. A. McCORD.

Indianapolis Life Insurance Co: 2960 North Meridian St, Indianapolis, IN 46208; tel. (317) 927-6500; f. 1905; operating in 42 states and the District of Columbia; Pres. and CEO EUGENE M. BUSCHE.

Integon Corpn: 500 West Fifth St, POB 3199, Winston-Salem, NC 27152; tel. (919) 725-7261; f. 1920; operating in 43 states and the District of Columbia; Pres. JAMES R. RIDLEY.

Kansas City Life Insurance Co: 3520 Broadway, Kansas City, MO 64141-6139; tel. (816) 753-7000; f. 1895; operating in 43 states and the District of Columbia; Chair. and Pres. JOSEPH R. BIXBY.

Lamar Life Insurance Co: 317 East Capitol St, POB 880, Jackson, MS 39201; tel. (601) 354-5481; f. 1906; operating in 11 states; Pres. JACK P. DEAN.

Liberty Life Insurance Co: Liberty Life Bldg, West Hampton Blvd, Greenville, SC 29615; tel. (803) 268-8111; f. 1905; operating in 37 states and the District of Columbia; Chair. W. HAYNE HIPP; Pres. R. GLENN HILLIARD.

Liberty Mutual Insurance Co: 175 Berkeley St, Boston, MA 02117; tel. (617) 357-9500; Pres. and CEO GARY L. COUNTRYMAN.

Liberty National Life Insurance Co: 2001 Third Ave South, Birmingham, AL 35233; tel. (205) 325-2722; f. 1900; operating in 37 states and the District of Columbia; Chair. R. K. RICHEY; Pres. J. S. P. SAMFORD.

Life Insurance Co of Georgia: 5780 Powers Ferry Rd, NW, Atlanta, GA 30327-4390; tel. (404) 980-5100; f. 1891; operating in 12 states; Chair. and CEO LYNN H. JOHNSTON.

Life Insurance Co of Virginia: 6610 West Broad St, Richmond, VA 23261; tel. (804) 281-6000; f. 1871; operating in 47 states and the District of Columbia; Pres. and CEO S. H. TURNER.

Lincoln National Life Insurance Co: 1300 South Clinton St, Fort Wayne, IN 46801; tel. (219) 427-2000; telex 232673; f. 1905; operating in 49 states and Canada, Guam, Puerto Rico and the District of Columbia; Pres. and CEO IAN M. ROLLAND.

Maccabees Mutual Life Insurance Co: 25800 Northwestern Highway, Southfield, MI 48037; tel. (313) 357-4800; f. 1885; operating in 49 states, the District of Columbia, Puerto Rico and Canada; Chair. and Pres. J. L. PALLONE.

Manhattan Life Insurance Co: 111 West 57th St, New York, NY 10019; tel. (212) 484-9300; f. 1850; operating in all states, the District of Columbia and Puerto Rico; Chair. and CEO D. M. FORDYCE.

Massachusetts Mutual Life Insurance Co: 1295 State St, Springfield, MA 01111; tel. (413) 788-8411; f. 1851; operating in all states, the District of Columbia, Puerto Rico and Canada; Chair. WILLIAM J. CLARK; Pres. and CEO THOMAS B. WHEELER.

Metropolitan Life Insurance Co: 1 Madison Ave, New York, NY 10010; tel. (212) 578-2211; f. 1868; operating in all states, the District of Columbia, Puerto Rico and Canada; Pres. and CEO JOHN J. CREEDON; Chair. ROBERT G. SCHWARTZ.

Millers National Insurance Co: 29 North Wacker Dr., Chicago, IL 60606; tel. (312) 236-8355; f. 1865; operating in 39 states and the District of Columbia; Pres. J. E. CROWLEY.

Minnesota Mutual Life Insurance Co: 400 North Robert St, St Paul, MN 55101; tel. (612) 298-3500; f. 1880; operating in 49 states and the District of Columbia; Chair., Pres. and CEO COLEMAN BLOOMFIELD.

Monarch Life Insurance Co: 1250 State St, Springfield, MA 01109; tel. (413) 785-5811; f. 1901; operating in all states and the District of Columbia; Pres. BRUCE BROWN.

Mutual Benefit Life Insurance Co: 520 Broad St, Newark, NJ 07102; tel. (201) 481-8000; f. 1845; operating in 49 states and the District of Columbia; Chair. and CEO ROBERT V. VAN FOSSAN.

Mutual Life Insurance Co of New York (MONY): 1740 Broadway, New York, NY 10019; tel. (212) 708-2000; f. 1842; operating in all states, the District of Columbia and Puerto Rico; Chair. and CEO JAMES A. ATTWOOD.

Mutual of Omaha Insurance Co: Mutual of Omaha Plaza, Omaha, NE 68175; tel. (402) 342-7600; f. 1909; operating in all states, the District of Columbia, the Virgin Islands, Puerto Rico and Canada; Chair. and CEO THOMAS J. SKUTT; Pres. JOHN W. WEEKLY.

National Life Insurance Co: National Life Dr., Montpelier, VA 05602; tel. (802) 229-3333; f. 1848; operating in all states and the District of Columbia; Chair. and CEO F. H. BERTRAND.

Nationwide Mutual Insurance Co: One Nationwide Plaza, Columbus, OH 43216; tel. (614) 249-7111; f. 1925; operating in all states, the District of Columbia and Puerto Rico; Chair. FRANK B. SOLLARS; CEO JOHN E. FISHER; Pres. and Gen. Man. P. A. DONALD.

New York Life Insurance Co: 51 Madison Ave, New York, NY 10010; tel. (212) 576-7000; f. 1845; operating in all states, the District of Columbia and Canada; Chair. D. K. ROSS; Pres. J. B. UNDERHILL.

Niagara Fire Insurance Co: 180 Maiden Lane, New York, NY 10038; tel. (212) 440-3000; f. 1850; operating in 49 states, the District of Columbia, Puerto Rico and Canada; Chair. J. P. MASCOTTE.

North American Reassurance Co: 237 Park Ave, New York, NY 10017; tel. (212) 907-8000; f. 1923; operating in 28 states, the District of Columbia, Puerto Rico and Canada; Pres. MICHEL SALES.

Northwestern Mutual Life Insurance Co: 720 East Wisconsin Ave, Milwaukee, WI 53202; tel. (414) 271-1444; f. 1857; operating in all states and the District of Columbia; Pres. and CEO D. J. SCHUENKE.

Northwestern National Life Insurance Co: 20 Washington Ave South, Minneapolis, MN 55440; tel. (612) 372-5432; telex 4310138; f. 1885; operating in 49 states and the District of Columbia; Chair. and CEO J. E. PEARSON; Pres. J. G. TURNER.

The Ohio National Life Companies: W. H. Taft at Highland Ave, Cincinnati, OH 45219; tel. (513) 861-3600; f. 1909; operating in 43 states and the District of Columbia; Pres. and CEO BRADLEY L. WARNEMUNDE.

Old Line Life Insurance Co of America: 707 North 11th St, POB 401, Milwaukee, WI 53201; tel. (414) 271-2820; f. 1910; operating in 49 states and the District of Columbia; Pres. and CEO JAMES A. GRIFFIN.

Pacific Mutual Life Insurance Co: 700 Newport Center Dr., Newport Beach, CA 92660; tel. (714) 640-3011; telex 910-5961376; f. 1868; operating in 49 states, the District of Columbia, Puerto Rico and Canada; Pres. and CEO HARRY G. BUBB.

Peerless Insurance Co: 62 Maple Ave, Keene, NH 03431; tel. (603) 352-3221; f. 1901; operating in 48 states and the District of Columbia; Chair. and CEO J. H. YOUNGS; Pres. B. D. REED, Jr.

Penn Mutual Life Insurance Co: Independence Sq., Philadelphia, PA 19172; tel. (215) 629-0600; f. 1847; operating in all states and the District of Columbia; Chair. J. E. TAIT.

Peoples Life Insurance Co: 601 New Hampshire Ave, NW, Washington, DC 20048; tel. (202) 337-3000; f. 1903; operating in 18 states and the District of Columbia; Chair. and CEO A. W. CLARK.

Philadelphia Life Insurance Co: One Independence Mall, Philadelphia, PA 19106; tel. (215) 629-9800; f. 1906; Pres. and CEO R. M. HOWE.

Phoenix Mutual Life Insurance Co: One American Row, Hartford, CT 06115; tel. (203) 275-5000; f. 1851; operating in 49 states, the District of Columbia, Puerto Rico and Canada; Chair. and CEO JOHN GUMMERE.

Protective Life Insurance Co: 2801 Highway 280 South, Birmingham, AL 35223; tel. (205) 879-9230; telex 810-7333592; f. 1907; operating in 38 states, the District of Columbia and Guam; Chair. WILLIAM J. RUSHTON, III.

Provident Life and Accident Insurance Co: Fountain Sq., Chattanooga, TN 37402; tel. (615) 755-1011; f. 1887; operating in 49 states and Canada; Pres. and CEO WINSTON W. WALKER.

Provident Mutual Life Insurance Co of Philadelphia: 1600 Market St, Philadelphia, PA 19103; tel. (215) 636-5000; f. 1865; Chair. and CEO JOHN A. MILLER; Pres. L. J. ROWELL, Jr.

The Prudential Insurance Co of America: Prudential Plaza, Newark, NJ 07101; tel. (201) 877-6000; f. 1875; operating in all states and Canada; Chair. and CEO ROBERT C. WINTERS; Pres. DAVID J. SHERWOOD.

Reliance Insurance Co: 4 Penn Center Plaza, Philadelphia, PA 19103; tel. (215) 864-4000; f. 1817; operating in all states, the District of Columbia, Puerto Rico and Canada; Chair. and CEO ROBERT M. STEINBERG.

Republic National Life Insurance Co: 3988 North Central Expressway, Dallas, TX 75204; tel. (214) 824-0131; f. 1928; operating in 49 states, the District of Columbia, the Virgin Islands and Puerto Rico; Pres. and CEO H. L. KORN.

The Paul Revere Life Insurance Co: 18 Chestnut St, Worcester, MA 01608-1528; tel. (617) 799-4441; f. 1930; operating in all states, the District of Columbia and Canada; Pres. A. K. REID, Jr.

SAFECO Corpn: Safeco Plaza, Seattle, WA 98185; tel. (206) 545-5000; f. 1929; operating in all states and the District of Columbia; Chair. and CEO R. M. TRAFTON; Pres. BRUCE MAINES.

St Paul Companies: 385 Washington St, St Paul, MN 55102; tel. (612) 221-7911; telex 297082; f. 1853; Chair. and CEO ROBERT J. HAUGH.

Security Insurance Co of Hartford: 9 Farm Springs Dr., Farmington, CT 06032; tel. (203) 674-6600; f. 1841; operating in 49 states, the District of Columbia and Canada; Pres. R. B. SANBORN.

Security Mutual Life Insurance Co of New York: 100 Court St, POB 1625, Binghamton, NY 13902; tel. (607) 723-3551; f. 1886; operating in 48 states and the District of Columbia; Pres. and CEO P. H. PEARSON.

Southland Life Insurance Co: 6400 Legacy Dr., Plano, TX 75024; tel. (214) 403-2500; f. 1908; operating in 45 states, the District of Columbia and Puerto Rico; Pres. and CEO M. T. MURRAY.

Southwestern Life Insurance Co: 500 North Akard, Suite 100, Dallas, TX 75201; tel. (214) 954-7111; f. 1903; operating in 36 states and the District of Columbia; Pres. and CEO R. M. HOWE.

Standard Insurance Co: 1100 SW Sixth Ave, Portland, OR 97204; tel. (503) 248-2700; f. 1906; operating in 29 states and the District of Columbia; Pres. and CEO BENJAMIN R. WHITELEY.

State Farm Life Insurance Co: One State Farm Plaza, Bloomington, IL 61701; tel. (309) 766-2311; f. 1929; Chair. MARVIN D. BOWER; Pres. EDWARD B. RUST, Jr.

State Farm Mutual Automobile Insurance Co: One State Farm Plaza, Bloomington, IL 61701; tel. (309) 766-2311; f. 1922; operating in all states, the District of Columbia and Canada; Pres. EDWARD B. RUST, Jr.

State Life Insurance Co: 141 East Washington St, Indianapolis, IN 46204; tel. (317) 632-3551; f. 1894; operating in 41 states and the District of Columbia; Chair. and Pres. ARTHUR L. BRYANT.

State Mutual Life Assurance Co of America: 440 Lincoln St, Worcester, MA 01605; tel. (617) 852-1000; f. 1844; operating in all states, the District of Columbia, Canada and Puerto Rico; Pres. and CEO FREDERICK FEDELI.

Sun Life Insurance Co of America: Sun Life Bldg, Charles Center, Baltimore, MD 21201; tel. (301) 727-0400; f. 1890; operating in 49 states and the District of Columbia; Pres. and CEO ROBERT P. SALTZMAN; Chair. ELI BROAD.

Transamerica Insurance Co: 1150 South Olive St, Los Angeles, CA 90015; tel. (213) 742-4242; f. 1984; operating in all states, the District of Columbia and Canada; CEO GERALD A. ISOM.

Transamerica Occidental Life Insurance Co: Hill and Olive at 12th St, Los Angeles, CA 90015; tel. (213) 742-2111; telex 3422111; f. 1906; Chair. and CEO DAVID R. CARPENTER.

Travelers Insurance Co: 1 Tower Sq., Hartford, CT 06115; tel. (203) 277-0111; f. 1893; operating in all states, the District of Columbia, Puerto Rico, Guam and Canada; Chair. THOMAS H. MCABOY; Pres. RICHARD W. MCLAUGHLIN.

Unigard Security Insurance Co: 1215 Fourth Ave, Seattle, WA 98161; tel. (206) 641-4321; f. 1901; operating in 48 states and the District of Columbia; Chair. and CEO LAURENCE P. O'CONNOR; Pres. DONALD K. SHANKS.

Union Central Life Insurance Co: 1876 Waycross Rd, Cincinnati, OH 45201; tel. (513) 595-2200; f. 1867; operating in all states and the District of Columbia; Pres. and CEO C. C. HINCKLEY.

United Insurance Co of America: One East Wacker Dr., Chicago, IL 60601; tel. (312) 661-4500; f. 1955; operating in 48 states and the District of Columbia; Chair. J. V. JEROME; Pres. RICHARD C. VIE.

United Life and Accident Insurance Co: 1 Granite Pl., Concord, NH 03301; tel. (603) 224-7741; f. 1913; operating in 49 states and the District of Columbia; Chair. DEAN R. O'HARE.

United of Omaha Life Insurance Co: Mutual of Omaha Plaza, Omaha, NE 68175; tel. (402) 342-7600; f. 1926; operating in 49 states, the District of Columbia, Panama, Puerto Rico, Europe, Japan and Pacific Islands; Chair. and CEO T. J. SKUTT; Pres. WILLIAM J. HETZLER.

United States Fidelity & Guaranty Co: 100 Light St, Baltimore, MD 21202; tel. (301) 547-3000; telex 87538; f. 1896; operating in all states, the District of Columbia and Canada; Chair. and CEO JACK MOSELEY; Pres. PAUL SCHEEL.

United States Life Insurance Co: 125 Maiden Lane, New York, NY 10038; tel. (212) 709-6000; f. 1850; operating in all states, the District of Columbia and Guam; Chair., Pres. and CEO GORDON E. CROSBY, Jr.

UNUM Life Insurance Co: 2211 Congress St, Portland, ME 04112; tel. (207) 770-2211; f. 1848; operating in all states, the District of Columbia, Puerto Rico and Canada; Pres., Chair and CEO JAMES F. ORR, III.

Volunteer State Life Insurance Co: Volunteer Bldg, 9th and Georgia Ave, Chattanooga, TN 37402; tel. (615) 756-3480; f. 1903; operating in 42 states and the District of Columbia; Pres. and CEO H. E. RUCK.

Washington National Insurance Co: 1630 Chicago Ave, Evanston, IL 60201; tel. (312) 570-5500; f. 1911; operating in 49 states, the District of Columbia and Canada; Chair. and CEO R. W. PATIN; Pres. GEORGE P. KENDALL, Jr.

Western Life Insurance Co: 500 Bielenberg Dr., St Paul, MN 55125; tel. (612) 738-4000; f. 1910; operating in 49 states and the District of Columbia; Pres. J. K. CLAYTON.

Western & Southern Life Insurance Co: 400 Broadway, Cincinnati, OH 45202; tel. (513) 629-1800; f. 1888; operating in 41 states and the District of Columbia; Chair. and CEO Dr C. M. BARRETT.

Wisconsin National Life Insurance Co: 220–222 Washington Ave, Oshkosh, WI 54901; tel. (414) 235-0800; f. 1908; operating in 33 states and the District of Columbia; Pres. A. DEAN ARGANBRIGHT.

Insurance Organizations

American Association of Insurance Services: 1035 South York Rd, Bensenville, IL 60106; f. 1936; tel. (312) 595-3225; advisory org. for property and casualty cos; 330 mems; Pres. PAUL A. BAIOCCHI.

American Council of Life Insurance: 1001 Pennsylvania Ave, NW, Washington, DC 20004-2599; tel. (202) 624-2000; f. 1976; 640 mem. cos; Pres. RICHARD S. SCHWEIKER.

American Institute of Marine Underwriters: 14 Wall St, New York, NY 10005; tel. (212) 233-0550; f. 1898; mems: 120 marine insurance cos representing 90% of the US marine insurance market; Chair. GEORGE S. ZACHARKOW; Pres. WARD L. MAUCK.

American Insurance Association: 85 John St, New York, NY 10038; tel. (212) 669-0400; f. 1964; 198 mems; Chair. EDWARD H. BUDD; Pres. ROBERT E. VAGLEY.

American Risk and Insurance Association: College of Business, University of Central Florida, Orlando, FL 32816; tel. (305) 275-2525; f. 1932; society of insurance educators; 2,000 mems; Exec. Dir DAVID KLOCK.

American Society of Chartered Life Underwriters: 270 Bryn Mawr Ave, Bryn Mawr, PA 19010; tel. (215) 526-2500; f. 1927; 32,000 mems.

Captive Insurance Companies Association: 205 East 42nd St, New York, NY 10017; tel. (212) 687-4501; f. 1973; 177 mem. orgs; Exec. Officer LISA MUELLER.

Casualty Actuarial Society: One Penn Plaza, 250 West 34th St, New York, NY 10119; tel. (212) 560-1018; f. 1914; Pres. KEVIN M. RYAN.

Consumer Credit Insurance Association: 542 South Dearborn St, Suite 400, Chicago, IL 60605; tel. (312) 726-9895; f. 1951; mems: 205 insurance cos underwriting consumer credit insurance; Exec. Vice-Pres. WILLIAM F. BURFEIND.

Direct Marketing Insurance Council: Six East 43rd St, New York, NY 10017; tel. (212) 689-4977; mems: 175 direct-response divisions of insurance cos; Vice-Pres. JOHN M. CAVANAUGH.

Health Insurance Association of America: 1750 K St, NW, Suite 600, Washington, DC 20006; tel. (202) 331-1336; f. 1956; 306 corporate mems.

Insurance Accounting and Systems Association: POB 8857, Durham, NC 27707; tel. (919) 683-2356; f. 1928; 1,600 mems; Sec.-Treas. ELAINE S. POWELL.

Insurance Crime Prevention Institute: 15 Franklin St, Westport, CT 06880; tel. (203) 226-6347; f. 1971; mems: 385 cos investigating fraud in connection with insurance claims; Dir WENDELL C. HARNESS.

Insurance Economics Society of America: 303 Atlantic Ave, Suite 206, Virginia Beach, VA 23451; tel. (202) 393-2541; f. 1917; 8,000 mems; Pres.-Man. Dir JOHN B. O'DAY.

Insurance Industry Meetings Association: 2330 South Brentwood Blvd, St Louis, MO 63144; tel. (314) 961-2300; f. 1980; 468 mems; Vice-Pres. VICTOR V. VIATOR.

Insurance Information Institute: 110 William St, New York, NY 10038; tel. (212) 669-9200; f. 1959; mems: 300 property and liability insurance cos; Pres. MECHLIN D. MOORE.

Insurance Loss Control Association: 3707 Woodview Trace, POB 68700, Indianapolis, IN 46268; tel. (317) 875-5250; f. 1931; loss prevention specialists for fire and casualty insurance cos; 700 mems; Dir ROGER S. RONK.

Insurance Marketing Communications Association: 62 Northgate Rd, Wellesley, MA 02181; tel. (617) 266-8400; f. 1923; mems: 300 advertising, marketing and sales executives of insurance cos; Exec. Dir WILLIAM T. HADLEY.

Insurance Society of New York: One Insurance Plaza, 101 Murray St, New York, NY 10007; tel. (212) 962-4111; f. 1901; parent organization of the College of Insurance, an educational institution located in New York; 462 mems; Pres. LINDA LAMEL.

Life Insurance Marketing and Research Association, Inc: POB 208, Hartford, CT 06141; tel. (203) 677-0033; telex 643952; f. 1916; a sales research and service org. of life insurance cos; c. 615 mems; Chair. ROBERT D. BATES; Pres. ERNEST E. CRAGG.

Life Office Management Association: 100 Colony Sq., Atlanta, GA 30361; tel. (404) 892-7272; f. 1924; 636 mem. cos; Chair. E. JAMES MORTON; Pres. LYNN G. MERRITT.

National Association of Life Underwriters: 1922 F St, NW, Washington, DC 20006; tel. (202) 331-6001; f. 1890; 120,000 mems.

National Association of Mutual Insurance Companies: POB 68700, Indianapolis, IN 46268; tel. (317) 875-5250; f. 1895; 1,284 mems; Chair. BRUCE N. HEATON; Pres. LARRY L. FORRESTER.

New York Insurance Exchange, Inc: 111 Fulton St, New York, NY 10038; tel. (212) 618-9200; telex 961087; f. 1980; mems: 44 syndicates and 108 brokers; Pres. JOSEPH FAHYS; Gen. Counsel and Sec. A. WILLIAM URQUHART.

Reinsurance Association of America: 1819 L St, NW, 7th Floor, Washington, DC 20036; tel. (202) 293-3335; f. 1969; 32 mems; Pres. ANDRÉ MAISONPIERRE.

Society of Certified Insurance Counsellors: POB 27027, Austin, TX 78755-1027; tel. (512) 345-7932; f. 1969; 10,300 mems; Pres. WILLIAM T. HOLD.

Society of Insurance Research: POB 933, Appleton, WI 54912; tel. (414) 730-8858; f. 1970; mems: 600 individuals involved in insurance research; Admin. Dir DEBRA KRUEGER.

Society of Insurance Accountants: POB 61, Bates Rd, Hollowville, NY 12530; tel. (518) 851-9780; f. 1960; c. 850 mems; Admin. Services ROBERT BAUER.

SOCIETY

TELECOMMUNICATIONS AND BROADCASTING

INTRODUCTION

The USA constitutes the world's biggest market for communications and broadcasting systems. In March 1987 telephones were in use in 92.5% of occupied housing units while in December and January of that year respectively 99% of households were recorded as using radio sets and 98% had television sets. In February 1987 48.7% of households were receiving cable television, while an equal percentage used video-cassette recorders.

Telecommunications

There were 151m. company, private and service telephones in the USA in 1982. The provision of telecommunications services was dominated by the Bell System, operated by the American Telegraph & Telephone Company (AT&T), until the early 1980s when AT&T's role was modified following the settlement of an antitrust suit first brought by the US Department of Justice in 1974. In exchange for permission to retain its long-distance and manufacturing operations and research divisions and to enter into the competitive manufacture of computers and the provision of computerized information-transmission services, AT&T made independent the 22 local Bell operating companies in which it held more than a 50% stake. In January 1984 ownership of the local companies was transferred to seven new regional telephone companies (which have become popularly known as 'Baby Bells'): Nynex, Bell Atlantic Corporation, American Information Technologies Corporation (Ameritech), BellSouth Corporation, Southwestern Bell Corporation, Pacific Telesis Group and US West, Inc. It was estimated in 1986 that the former Bell operating companies still accounted for about 80% of the telephone service market.

AT&T received about 89% of revenue from long-distance telephone operations in 1984, when four other long-distance carriers (MCI Communications, US Sprint, Allnet and Satellite Business Systems—part of the IBM group) together accounted for the remaining 11%. Domestic telegraph services in the USA are provided by the Western Union Corporation, based in Saddle River, New Jersey, through its subsidiary, the Western Union Telegraph Company.

Radio and Television

In 1986 there were 3,969 licensed FM radio stations, 1,272 licensed educational FM stations, 4,887 licensed AM stations and almost 50 radio programme networks. In 1987 the average US household had 5.4 radio sets in use.

In 1988 commercial television stations numbered 1,017 and educational TV stations 325; there were 46 national cable networks in operation. Cable systems in use totalled some 7,900 in January 1987, serving 39.7m. subscribers. The average US household had 1.86 television sets in use in 1987, with average viewing per household amounting to 7.2 hours per day. The USA has the highest ratio of radio and TV receivers per head of population of any country in the world.

Regulatory Bodies

Telecommunications services are regulated within individual states by the state public utility commissions (see Government, pp. 136–166). The seven-member Federal Communications Commission was established under the Communications Act of 1934 to regulate all interstate and international communications by radio, television, wire and cable, 'in the public interest'. Its responsibilities were extended under the Communications Satellite Act of 1962.

Federal Communications Commission (FCC): 1919 M St, NW, Washington, DC 20554; tel. (202) 632-7000; fax (202) 653-5402; f. 1934; Chair. ALFRED C. SIKES.

Use of Selected Media, 1985–87

		1985	1986	1987
Households with:				
Telephone service[1] . . . (%)		91.8	92.2	92.5
Radio sets[2] . . . . (%)		99	99	99
Average number of sets (no.)		5.5	5.4	5.4
Television sets[3] . . . (million)		84.9	85.9	87.4
Television sets[3] . . . (%)		98	98	98
Colour set households[3] . (million)		77.7	80.1	82.7
Average viewing per day[4] . . . . . (hours)		7.1	n.a.	7.2
Average number of sets[3,5] . . . . (no.)		1.83	1.83	1.86
Cable television[6] . . . (%)		44.6	46.8	48.7
Video-cassette recorders[5,6] (%)		20.8	36.0	48.7
Commercial radio stations[7]:				
AM . . . . . (no.)		4,718	4,863	n.a.
FM . . . . . (no.)		3,875	3,944	n.a.
Television stations: Total . (no.)		1,182	1,235	1,290
Commercial . . . (no.)		883	919	968
Cable television[3]:				
Systems . . . . (no.)		6,844	7,600	7,900
Subscribers served . (million)		31.3	37.5	39.7

[1] As of March.   [2] As at 1 December.
[3] As of January.   [4] Calendar year data.
[5] Excludes Alaska and Hawaii.   [6] As of February.
[7] As at 31 December except for 1985, which is as of February 1986.

Sources: Bureau of the Census, US Department of Commerce, *Statistical Abstract of the United States, 1988*; Radio Advertising Bureau, New York, NY, *Radio Facts*, annual (copyright); A. C. Nielsen Company, Northbrook, IL, *Nielsen Report on Television* (copyright), *VCR Trends* (copyright); Television Bureau of Advertising, Inc, *Trends in Television 1950 to Date*, March 1986 (copyright), *Television and Cable Factbook*, annual (copyright).

MAJOR TELECOMMUNICATIONS NETWORKS

Allnet Communications Services, Inc: 30300 Telegraph Rd, Suite 350, Birmingham, MI 48010; tel. (313) 647-6920; f. 1985; long-distance carrier.

American Information Technologies Corporation (Ameritech): 30 South Wacker Dr., Chicago, IL 60606; tel. (312) 750-5000; serves c. 11m. customers in five states through five subsidiaries; Chair. and CEO WILLIAM L. WEISS.

  Illinois Bell Telephone Co: 225 West Randolph St, Chicago, IL 60606; tel. (312) 727-9411; former Bell operating co; Pres. FRANK R. ZIMMERMAN.

  Indiana Bell Telephone Co: 240 North Meridian St, Indianapolis, IN 46204; tel. (317) 265-2266; former Bell operating co; Pres. RAMON L. HUMKE.

  Michigan Bell Telephone Co: 444 Michigan Ave, Detroit, MI 48226; tel. (313) 223-9900; former Bell operating co.

  Ohio Bell Telephone Co: 45 Erieview Plaza, Cleveland, OH 44114; tel. (216) 822-9700; former Bell operating co; Pres. EDWARD F. BELL.

  Wisconsin Bell Telephone Co: 722 North Broadway, Milwaukee, WI 53202; tel. (414) 456-3000; former Bell operating co; Pres. LOUIS J. RUTIGLIANO.

American Satellite Company (ASC): 1801 Research Blvd, Rockville, MD 20850; tel. (301) 251-8333; telex 828-0489; provides satellite telecommunications; Pres. and CEO GEORGE ROBERTS.

American Telegraph and Telephone Co (AT&T): 550 Madison Ave, New York, NY 10022; tel. (212) 605-5500; f. 1885; in 1984

AT&T split, giving up its Bell operating companies and retaining its long-distance operations; Chair. and CEO ROBERT E. ALLEN.

Bell Atlantic Corporation: 1600 Market St, Philadelphia, PA 19103; tel. (215) 963-6000; f. 1983; serves six states and the District of Columbia through eight subsidiaries; Chair and CEO RAYMOND SMITH; Pres. ANTON J. CAMPANELLA.

Bell Telephone Co of Pennsylvania: 1 Parkway, Philadelphia, PA 19102; tel. (215) 466-9900; former Bell operating co; Pres. and CEO GILBERT A. WETZEL.

Chesapeake and Potomac Telephone Cos/HQ: 1710 H St, NW, Washington, DC 20006; tel. (202) 392-9900; former Bell operating co; Pres. and CEO THOMAS M. GIBBONS.

Chesapeake and Potomac Telephone Co of Maryland: 1 East Pratt St, Baltimore, MD 21202; tel. (301) 539-9900; former Bell operating co; Vice-Pres. J. HENRY BUTTA.

Chesapeake and Potomac Telephone Co of Virginia: 703 East Grace St, Richmond, VA 23219; tel. (804) 772-2000; former Bell operating co; Vice-Pres. HUBERT R. STALLARD.

Chesapeake and Potomac Telephone Co of Washington: 2055 L St, NW, Washington, DC 20036; tel. (202) 392-9900; former Bell operating co; Vice-Pres. DELANO E. LEWIS.

Chesapeake and Potomac Telephone Co of West Virginia: 1500 MacCorkle Avenue, SE, Charleston, WV 25314; tel. (304) 343-9911; former Bell operating co; Vice-Pres. THOMAS C. BURNS.

Diamond State Telephone Co: Wilmington, DE; tel. (302) 571-1571.

New Jersey Bell Telephone Co: 540 Broad St, Newark, NJ 07101; tel. (201) 649-9900; former Bell operating co; Pres. and CEO JAMES CULLEN.

BellSouth Corporation: 675 West Peachtree St, NE, Atlanta, GA 30375; tel. (404) 420-8600; f. 1983; serves c. 15m. customers through two subsidiaries; Chair., Pres. and CEO JOHN L. CLENDENIN.

South Central Bell Telephone Co: 600 North 19th St, Birmingham, AL 35203; tel. (205) 321-1000; former Bell operating co; Pres. CARL F. BAILEY.

Southern Bell Telephone and Telegraph Co: 675 West Peachtree St, NE, Atlanta, GA 30375; tel. (404) 529-8611; former Bell operating co; Pres. B. FRANKLIN SKINNER.

Centel Corporation: 245 Perimeter Center Parkway, Atlanta, GA 30345; tel. (404) 391-8000; serves c. 2.3m. customers in 30 states; Pres and CEO DONALD W. WEBER.

Central Telephone and Utilities Corporation: O'Hare Plaza, 5725 East River Rd, Chicago, IL 60631; tel. (312) 399-2500.

Cincinnati Bell Inc (CBI): POB 2301, Cincinnati, OH 45201; tel. (513) 397-9900.

C-Tec Corporation: 46 Public Sq., Wilkes-Barre, PA 18703-3000; tel. (717) 825-1112; c. 155,000 telephone customers and c. 43,000 cable television customers; Chair. ANDREW J. SORDONI, III.

MCI Communications Corporation: 1133 19th St, NW, Washington, DC 20036; tel. (202) 872-1600; f. 1968; long-distance carrier; c. 5m. customers; Chair. WILLIAM McGOWAN.

Mid Continent Telephone Corporation: 100 Executive Parkway, Hudson, OH 44236; tel. (216) 650-7000.

Nynex Corporation: 335 Madison Ave, New York, NY 10017; tel. (212) 370-7400; serves c. 10.5m. customers in the north-eastern USA through two subsidiaries; Chair. and CEO DELBERT C. STANLEY.

New England Telephone and Telegraph Co: 185 Franklin St, Boston, MA 02107; tel. (617) 743-9800; former Bell operating co; Pres. and CEO GERHARD M. FRECHE.

New York Telephone Co: 1095 Ave of the Americas, New York, NY 10036; tel. (212) 395-2121; former Bell operating co; Pres. and CEO FREDERICK V. SALERNO.

Pacific Telesis Group: 116 New Montgomery St, Suite 800, San Francisco, CA 94105; tel. (415) 882-8482; f. 1983; provides services to California and Nevada through two principal subsidiaries; Chair., Pres. and CEO DONALD E. GUINN.

Nevada Bell Telephone Co: 645 East Plumb Lane, Reno, NV 89520; tel. (702) 789-6000; former Bell operating co; Pres. and CEO R. K. VAN ALLEN.

Pacific Bell Telephone Co: 140 New Montgomery St, San Francisco, CA 94105; tel. (415) 542-9000; former Bell operating co; Chair. and CEO SAM L. GINN; Pres. T. J. SAENGER.

RCA American Communications, Inc: Four Research Way, Princeton, NJ 08540; tel. (609) 987-4000; telex 244010.

Rochester Telephone Corporation: 100 Executive Parkway, Hudson, OH 44236; tel. (216) 650-7000.

Southern New England Telecommunications Corporation (SNET): 227 Church St, New Haven, CT 06506; tel. (203) 771-5200; f. 1882; serves c. 1.5m. customers in Connecticut.

Southern Pacific Co: Southern Pacific Bldg, One Market Plaza, San Francisco, CA 94105; tel. (415) 541-1000.

Southwestern Bell Corporation: One Bell Center, St Louis, MO 63101-3099; tel. (314) 235-9800; f. 1983; Chair. and CEO ZANE E. BARNES.

United Telecommunications, Inc (United Telecom): POB 11315, Kansas City, MO 64112; tel. (913) 676-3000; f. 1898; serves 19 states through 20 local telephone cos of its United Telephone System; Pres. and CEO WILLIAM T. ESREY.

US Sprint Communications Co: 2330 Shawnee Mission Parkway, Shawnee Mission, KS 66205; tel. (913) 676-3000; f. 1986; long-distance carrier.; Pres. CHARLES M. SKIBO

US West, Inc: 7800 East Orchard Rd, Englewood, CO 80111; tel. (303) 793-6500; f. 1983; Chair. and CEO JACK A. MACALLISTER.

Mountain Bell Telephone Co: 931 14th St, Denver, CO 80202; tel. (303) 624-2424; former Bell operating co; Pres. ROBERT C. BLANZ.

Northwestern Bell Telephone Co: 1314 Douglas-on-the-Mall, Omaha, NE 68102; tel. (402) 422-2000; former Bell operating co; Pres. THOMAS F. MADISON.

Pacific Northwest Telephone Co: 1600 Bell Plaza, Seattle, WA 98191; tel. (206) 345-2211; former Bell operating co; Pres. ANDREW V. SMITH.

RADIO AND TELEVISION

Radio

DOMESTIC NETWORKS

American Public Radio: 700 Meritor Tower, 444 Cedar St, St Paul, MN 55101; tel. (612) 290-1466; serves 320 public radio stations via satellite; Pres. and CEO STEPHEN SALYER.

Cadena Radio Centro/CRC Radio Network: 1425 Greenway Dr., Suite 210, Irving, TX 75038; tel. (214) 580-1223; Pres. CARLOS J. AGUIRRE.

Capital Cities/ABC, Inc: 1330 Ave of the Americas, New York, NY 10019; tel. (212) 887-7777; f. 1986; by merger; radio network and 13 owned radio stations; Chair. and CEO THOMAS S. MURPHY; Pres. Radio Network AARON DANIELS.

CNN Radio Network: 1050 Techwood Dr., NW, POB 105264, Atlanta, GA 30348-5264; tel. (404) 827-1500; Pres. BURT RHEINHARDT.

Columbia Broadcasting System, Inc (CBS): 51 West 52nd St, New York, NY 10019; tel. (212) 975-4321; 18 owned radio stations and 244 affiliated stations; Pres. and CEO LAURENCE A. TISCH; Chair. WILLIAM S. PALEY; Pres. CBS Broadcasting Group

HOWARD STRINGER; Chair. CBS Broadcasting Group GENE F. JANKOWSKI; Pres. CBS Radio Division NANCY C. WILDMAN.

Dow Jones Radio Network: 200 Liberty St, 14th Floor, New York, NY 10281; tel. (212) 416-2381; Dir ROBERT RUSH.

Educational Broadcasting Corporation: 356 West 58th St, New York, NY 10019; tel. (212) 560-2000.

Family Stations, Inc: 290 Hegenberger Rd, Oakland, CA 94621; tel. (415) 568-6200; non-profit, Christian programming; 17 radio affiliates; Pres. HAROLD CAMPING.

Gear Broadcasting, Inc (GBI): Weybosset St, POB 23172, Providence, RI 02903; tel. (401) 331-6072; Chair. and Pres. JACK G. THAYER.

Moody Broadcasting Network: 820 North LaSalle Dr., Chicago, IL 60610; tel. (800) 621-7031; has 200 radio affiliates and is on 60 cable systems serving c. 997,700 subscribers.

Mutual Broadcasting System Inc (MBS): 1755 South Jefferson Davis Highway, 12th Floor, Arlington, VA 22202; tel. (703) 685-2090; telex 4979296; fax (703) 685-2197; f. 1934; 713 affiliated stations; Pres. JACK CLEMENTS.

National Black Network: 10 Columbus Circle, 10th Floor, New York, NY 10019; 140 affiliated stations; Chair. SYDNEY L. SMALL.

National Broadcasting Co, Inc (NBC): 30 Rockefeller Plaza, New York, NY 10112; tel. (212) 664-4444; f. 1926; 2 owned stations and 554 affiliated stations; Pres. and CEO ROBERT C. WRIGHT; Pres. NBC Radio Stations RANDALL D. BONGARTEN.

National Public Radio: 2025 M St, NW, Washington, DC 20036; tel. (202) 822-2000; telex 440391; network of mem. stations in 48 states, District of Columbia and Puerto Rico; Chair. JACK W. MITCHELL; Pres. DOUGLAS J. BENNET, Jr.

RKO Radio Networks: 1440 Broadway, New York, NY 10018; 12 owned stations; Pres. THOMAS F. BURCHILL.

Sheridan Broadcasting Network: 1811 Blvd of the Allies, Pittsburgh, PA 15129; tel. (212) 575-0099; 105 affiliated stations; Pres. E. J. WILLIAMS, Jr; Network Dir GERALD A. LOPES.

Sun Radio Network: POB 7000, Tampa, FL 33673; tel. (813) 238-3145; Pres. and CEO CHARLES E. HARDER.

TNNR: 2644 McGavock Pike, Nashville, TN 37217; tel. (615) 871-6710; Gen. Man. BOB MEYER.

Transtar Radio Network: 660 South Pointe Court, Suite 300, Colorado Springs, CO 80906; tel. (719) 576-2620.

United Stations Radio Networks: 1440 Broadway, 5th Floor, New York, NY 10018; tel. (212) 575-6100; fax (212) 575-4548; 1,053 radio affiliates; Pres. NICHOLAS J. VERBITSKY.

UPI Radio Network: 1400 Eye St, NW, 9th Floor, Washington, DC 20005; tel. (202) 898-8000; Chair. and CEO MARIO VAZQUEZ-RANA.

USA Radio Network: 2290 Springlake Rd, Suite 107, Dallas, TX 75234; tel. (212) 484-3900; Pres. and CEO MARK MADDOUX.

Wall Street Journal Radio Network: c/o Dow Jones Radio Network, 200 Liberty St, 14th Floor, New York, NY 10281; tel. (212) 416-2381.

Westinghouse Broadcasting and Cable, Inc: 888 Seventh Ave, New York, NY 10106; tel. (212) 247-8700; 15 owned stations; Chair. and CEO BURTON B. STANIAR.

EXTERNAL RADIO SERVICES

ABC International Development: 1330 Ave of the Americas, New York, NY 10019; tel. (212) 887-7461; telex 422003; division of Capital Cities/ABC, Inc: 50 stations in Latin America, Japan, Australia, Canada and elsewhere; Vice-Pres. in Charge JAMES T. SHAW.

Department of Defense, American Forces Radio and Television Service (AFRTS): 10888 La Tuna Canyon Rd, Los Angeles, CA 91352-2098; tel. (818) 504-1200; telex 6831327; govt-operated; provides US radio and TV programming in English by satellite and mail for use by AFRTS networks and stations where US military personnel are stationed; c. 800 radio and TV outlets in more than 20 countries; Commdr Capt. JOHN A. MARTIN.

Radio Free Europe/Radio Liberty: 1201 Connecticut Ave, NW, Washington, DC 20036; tel. (202) 457-6900; f. 1950; financed by the federal govt; broadcasts from Munich, Federal Republic of Germany to Eastern Europe and the USSR; c. 1,000 hours weekly in 23 languages; Pres. E. EUGENE PELL; Dirs A. ROSS JOHNSON (RFE Div.), S. ENDERS WIMBUSH (Radio Liberty Div.).

Radio Station KGEI Inc/The Voice of Friendship: POB 15, San Francisco, CA 94101; tel. (415) 591-7374; f. 1939; owned and operated by Far East Broadcasting Co Inc; short-wave broadcasts in English, Spanish, German (to Latin America); Russian, Byelorussian, Polish, Ukrainian (to the Western USSR); Pres. R. H. BOWMAN; Station Man. JACK BROOKS.

Voice of America: US Information Agency, 400 C St, SW, Washington, DC 20547; tel. (202) 485-7860; f. 1942; govt-controlled; broadcasts in 42 languages to all areas of the world; Dir CHARLES Z. WICK.

Television

NETWORKS
(See Radio section for full addresses)

Capital Cities/ABC, Inc: 5 owned and 211 affiliated stations; Pres. and CEO ABC-TV Network JOHN B. SIAS.

Central Educational Network: 1400 East Tuohy Ave, Suite 260, Des Plaines, IL 60018; tel. (312) 390-8700; Ohio Educational Broadcasting Network Chair. DAVE FORNSHELL; Wisconsin Network Vice-Chair. JEFF CLARKE; Central Education Network, Chicago, Pres. JAMES A. FELLOWS.

Columbia Broadcasting System, Inc (CBS): 5 owned and operated and 215 affiliated stations; Pres. CBS-TV Network THOMAS F. LEAHY.

Eastern Educational Television Network: 120 Boylston St, Boston, MA 02116-4611; tel. (617) 338-5369; Chair. JERRY FRANKLIN; Pres. JOHN S. PORTER; Vice-Chair. WARD CHAMBERLIN.

Fox Television: 205 East 67th St, New York, NY 10021; tel. (212) 452-5555; Chair. and CEO BARRY DILLER.

Hughes Television Network: 260 Madison Ave, 19th Floor, New York, NY 10016; tel. (212) 684-7900; CEO JOSEPH M. COHEN.

International Television Network (ITN): 1000 Kennecott Bldg, Salt Lake City, UT 84133; tel. (801) 321-7779; 26 television affiliates, 18 affiliated cable systems; Pres. and CEO CARL J. SABATINO.

Metromedia, Inc: 205 East 67th St, New York, NY 10021; tel. (212) 734-1000; Chair., Pres. and CEO JOHN W. KLUGE.

National Broadcasting Co, Inc (NBC): 5 owned and operated and 215 affiliated stations; Pres. NBC-TV Stations ALBERT D. JEROME; Pres. NBC-TV Network PIERSON G. MAPES.

Pacific Mountain Network: 12596 West Bayaud Ave, Suite 215, Lakewood, CO 80228; tel. (303) 980-1411; Pres. JOSEPH P. ZESBAUGH.

Public Broadcasting Service (PBS): 1320 Braddock Pl., Alexandria, VA 22314; tel. (703) 739-5000; fax (703) 739-0775; f. 1969; non-profit making; financed by private subscriptions and federal govt funds; provides programming to 314 affiliated, non-commercial TV stations; Pres. and CEO BRUCE L. CHRISTENSEN.

Southern Educational Communications Association: 2628 Millwood Ave, Columbia, SC 29205; tel. (803) 799-5527; Chair. HENRY J. CAUTHEN.

Turner Broadcasting: One CNN Center, POB 105366, Atlanta, GA 30348-5366; tel. (404) 827-1500; operates cable television network.

Univision: 9200 Sunset Blvd, Suite 1100, Los Angeles, CA 90069; tel. (213) 859-7200; 512 satellite interconnected television affiliates; Pres. LUIS NOGALES.

Westinghouse Broadcasting and Cable, Inc: 5 owned stations.

Wold Communications: 3415 South Sepulveda Blvd, Los Angeles, CA 90034; tel. (213) 390-5455; Chair. and Pres. ROBERT N. WOLD.

Broadcasting Associations

Associated Press Broadcasters: c/o 1825 K St, NW, Suite 615, Washington, DC 20006; tel. (202) 955-7212; f. 1941; 5,900 mems; 50 state groups; Exec. Dir JOHN H. BENNITT.

Association of Independent Television Stations (INTV): 1200 18th St, NW, Suite 502, Washington, DC 20036; tel. (202) 887-1970; f. 1972; 300 mems; Pres. PRESTON R. PADDEN.

Corporation for Public Broadcasting: 1111 16th St, NW, Washington, DC 20036; tel. (202) 955-5100; f. 1968; a non-profit, non-governmental agency; aims to promote and finance non-commercial radio and television.

National Association of Broadcasters (NAB): 1771 N St, NW, Washington, DC 20036; tel. (202) 429-5300; telex 350085; f. 1922; a private asscn of radio and TV stations and networks; over 6,000 mems; Pres. EDWARD O. FRITTS.

National Association of Public Television Stations (NAPTS): 1818 N St, NW, Suite 410, Washington, DC 20036; tel. (202) 887-1700; f. 1980; 165 mems.

National Cable Television Association (NCTA): 1724 Massachusetts Ave, NW, Washington, DC 20036; tel. (202) 775-3550; f. 1952; 3,073 mems; Pres. JAMES P. MOONEY.

National Education Association: 1201 16th St, NW, Washington, DC 20036; tel. (202) 833-4000; telex 8229367; f. 1925; 50 state affiliates; 1.7m. mems; Pres. MARY H. FUTRELL.

National Radio Broadcasters Association: 1771 N St, NW, Washington, DC 20036; tel. (202) 429-5300; f. 1922; CEO and Pres. EDWARD O. FRITTS.

THE PRESS

INTRODUCTION

The USA publishes more newspapers and periodicals than any other country. Most dailies give a greater emphasis to local news because of the strong interest in local and regional affairs and the decentralized structure of many government services. These factors, together with the distribution problem inherent in the size of the country, are responsible for the lack of national newspapers. Almost every small town has its own paper.

Most influential and highly respected among the few newspapers with a national readership are the *New York Times* (which introduced a national edition in 1980), the *Washington Post, Los Angeles Times, Christian Science Monitor* and *Wall Street Journal*, the financial and news daily with editions in New York City, California, Illinois and Texas, and a European and an Asian edition. In 1982 the first national general-interest newspaper, *USA Today*, with editorial headquarters near Washington, DC, was introduced by Gannett. An international edition was launched in 1984.

In 1987, 39 daily newspapers had circulations of over 250,000 copies. Among the largest of these, in order of daily circulation, were *The Wall Street Journal, USA Today, New York Daily News, Los Angeles Times, New York Times, Chicago Tribune, Washington Post, New York Post* and *Detroit News*.

At the end of 1987 there were 1,645 English-language daily newspapers (512 morning, 1,165 evening) with a total circulation of 62,826,273 copies per day. The Sunday edition is an important and distinctive feature of US newspaper publishing; many Sunday newspapers run to over 200 pages. At the end of 1987 there were 820 Sunday newspapers with a total circulation of 62,829,875. In addition, there were 7,498 weekly papers with a total circulation of 51,691,451.

A total of 11,229 periodicals were published in the USA in 1987. During the second half of that year 11 magazines achieved total average paid circulation of more than 5m. copies: in order, these were *TV Guide, Modern Maturity, Reader's Digest, NRTA/AARP News Bulletin, National Geographic, Better Homes and Gardens, Woman's Day, Family Circle, McCall's, Good Housekeeping* and *Ladies' Home Journal.*

The total number of new books and new editions published in the USA in 1986 was 42,793.

The famous tradition of press freedom in the USA is grounded in the First Amendment to the Constitution which declares that 'Congress shall make no law . . . abridging the freedom of speech or of the Press . . .' and confirmed in the legislations of many states which prohibit any kind of legal restriction on the dissemination of news.

Legislation affecting the press is both state and federal. A source of controversy between the press and the courts has been the threat of the encroachment by judicial decrees on the area of courtroom and criminal trial coverage. In 1972 the Supreme Court ruled that journalists were not entitled to refuse to give evidence before grand juries on information they have received confidentially. Since then the frequent issuing of subpoenas to journalists and the jailing of several reporters for refusing to disclose sources has led to many 'shield' bills being put before Congress and state legislatures calling for immunity for journalists from both federal and state jurisdiction.

Newspapers, Periodicals and Books— Number and Circulation

Summary

	1985	1986	1987
Number of newspapers[1]			
Daily: Total[2]	1,676	1,657	n.a.
Morning	482	499	n.a.
Evening	1,220	1,188	n.a.
Sunday	798	802	n.a.
Circulation (million)[3]			
Daily: Total	62.8	62.5	n.a.
Morning	36.4	37.4	n.a.
Evening	26.4	25.1	n.a.
Sunday	58.8	58.9	n.a.
Number of periodicals . . .	11,090	11,326	11,593
Weekly	1,367	1,383	1,400
Semimonthly[4]	801	789	858
Monthly	4,088	4,066	4,031
Bimonthly	1,361	1,387	1,402
Quarterly	1,759	1,895	1,984
New books and new editions published: Total[5] . . .	50,070	42,793*	n.a.

* Preliminary figure.

[1] As at 1 February of the following year.
[2] All-day newspapers are included under both 'Morning' and 'Evening' but are only counted once under 'Total'.
[3] As at 30 September.
[4] Includes fortnightly.
[5] Excludes government publications; books sold only by subscription; dissertations; periodicals and quarterlies; and pamphlets with less than 49 pages.

Sources: Gale Research Co, *Gale Directory of Publications, 1987* (copyright); Editor & Publisher Co, Inc, *Editor & Publisher International Year Book* (copyright).

Daily and Sunday newspapers by state (1986)

	Daily		Sunday	
	Number	Net paid circulation ('000)*	Number	Net paid circulation ('000)*
Alabama	28	758	20	763
Alaska	8	131	4	141
Arizona	19	675	11	714
Arkansas	32	504	16	535
California	117	6,221	61	6,150
Colorado	27	941	10	1,117
Connecticut	24	896	11	816
Delaware	3	144	2	162
District of Columbia	3	2,311	1	1,079
Florida	49	2,888	33	3,329
Georgia	36	1,099	16	1,184
Hawaii	6	237	6	250
Idaho	12	205	8	217
Illinois	70	2,652	24	2,699
Indiana	74	1,546	20	1,286
Iowa	37	753	11	751
Kansas	46	545	18	498
Kentucky	25	711	13	655
Louisiana	27	792	21	898
Maine	9	291	2	178
Maryland	15	688	4	570
Massachusetts	46	2,134	11	1,727
Michigan	52	2,549	15	2,468
Minnesota	25	917	12	1,046
Mississippi	23	402	12	334
Missouri	48	1,253	19	1,249
Montana	11	192	7	190
Nebraska	19	472	7	435
Nevada	7	253	4	304
New Hampshire	9	215	4	139
New Jersey	26	1,714	17	1,846
New Mexico	20	302	13	272
New York	73	7,707	33	5,747
North Carolina	54	1,427	29	1,328
North Dakota	10	188	6	173
Ohio	87	2,828	31	2,774
Oklahoma	51	796	43	902
Oregon	20	654	10	647
Pennsylvania	91	3,321	23	2,907
Rhode Island	7	303	3	302
South Carolina	18	639	11	631

Daily and Sunday newspapers by state (1986)—*continued*

	Daily		Sunday	
	Number	Net paid circulation ('000)*	Number	Net paid circulation ('000)*
South Dakota . . .	12	165	4	129
Tennessee	28	979	15	1,050
Texas	109	3,627	96	4,333
Utah	6	287	6	326
Vermont . . .	8	123	3	90
Virginia	36	1,187	15	939
Washington . . .	26	1,145	14	1,128
West Virginia . .	23	446	10	398
Wisconsin . . .	35	1,190	13	1,044
Wyoming	10	99	4	75
Total	**1,657**	**62,502**	**802**	**58,925**

* Circulation figures are based upon the principal community served by a newspaper, which is not necessarily the same location as the publisher's office.

Source: Editor & Publisher Co, Inc, *Editor & Publisher International Year Book* (copyright).

National Newspaper Groups

In recent years, increased production costs have subjected the industry to considerable economic strain, resulting in mergers and take-overs, a great decline in competition between dailies in the same city, and the appearance of inter-city dailies catering for two or more adjoining centres. A consequence of these trends has been the steady growth of newspaper groups or chains. At the end of 1987 there were 143 newspaper groups publishing 1,212 daily newspapers in the USA.

The following are among the principal daily newspaper groups:

Dow Jones & Co Inc: 200 Liberty St, New York, NY 10281; tel. (212) 416-2000; telex 422221; 23 daily newspapers, including *The Wall Street Journal*; also operates domestic and international news wires and provides radio and television news reports; Chair. WARREN H. PHILLIPS; Pres. RAY SHAW; Gen. Man. KENNETH L. BURENGA.

Gannett Co Inc: 1100 Wilson Blvd, Arlington, VA 22209; tel. (703) 284-6000; f. 1906; largest US newspaper group in terms of total circulation; 90 daily newspapers, including *USA Today* and *Detroit News*; Chair. and CEO JOHN J. CURLEY.

Hearst Corpn: Hearst Magazine Bldg, 959 Eighth Ave, New York, NY 10019; tel. (212) 262-5700; 15 daily newspapers, including *Los Angeles Herald Examiner* and *San Francisco Examiner*; Pres. FRANK A. BENNACK, Jr.

Knight-Ridder Inc: One Herald Plaza, Miami, FL 33132-1693; 33 daily newspapers; Chair. and CEO ALVAH H. CHAPMAN, Jr; Pres. JAMES K. BATTEN.

Newhouse Newspapers: Court and Plains Sts, Newark, NJ 07101; 27 daily newspapers; Pres. DONALD E. NEWHOUSE.

Scripps Howard Newspapers: POB 5380, Cincinnati, OH 45201; tel. (513) 977-3000; 20 daily newspapers; Chair. CHARLES E. SCRIPPS; Pres. and CEO LAWRENCE A. LESER.

Thomson Newspapers: 3150 Des Plaines Ave, Des Plaines, IL 60018; 116 daily and 4 weekly newspapers; Chair. of Board K. R. THOMSON; Pres. ST CLAIR MCCABE.

Times–Mirror Co: Times–Mirror Sq., Los Angeles, CA 90053; tel. (213) 972-3923; f. 1884; 9 daily newspapers, including *Los Angeles Times* and *Newsday*; Chair. and CEO ROBERT F. ERBURU; Pres. DAVID LAVENTHOL.

Tribune Company Group: Tribune Tower, 435 North Michigan Ave, Chicago, IL 60611; tel. (312) 222-3232; 9 daily newspapers, including *Chicago Tribune* and *New York Daily News*; Pres. STANTON R. COOK.

PRINCIPAL DAILY AND SUNDAY NEWSPAPERS

(Ind. = politically independent; Dem. = Democrat; Rep. = Republican; Mon. = Monday; Fri. = Friday; Sat. = Saturday; Sun. = Sunday; Publr = Publisher; papers are published seven days a week (Monday to Sunday) unless otherwise indicated.)

Alabama

Anniston Star: POB 189, Anniston, AL 36202-0189; tel. (205) 236-1551; f. 1883; Mon. to Fri. evening, Sat. and Sun. morning; Publr and Editor H. BRANDT AYERS; circ. Mon. to Fri. 31,798, Sat. 33,377, Sun. 32,964.

Birmingham News: 2200 North Fourth Ave, POB 2553, Birmingham, AL 35202; tel. (205) 325-2222; f. 1888; Mon. to Sat. evening, Sun. morning; Publr V. H. HANSON, II; Editor JAMES E. JACOBSON; Ind.; circ. Mon. to Fri. 169,059, Sat. 146,775, Sun. 210,805.

Decatur Daily: 201 First Ave, SE, POB 1527, Decatur, AL 35602; tel. (205) 353-4612; f. 1912; morning; Publr and Editor BARRETT C. SHELTON, Jr; circ. Mon. to Fri. 25,649, Sat. 25,817, Sun. 28,829.

Eagle: POB 1968, Dothan, AL 36302; tel. (205) 792-3141; f. 1902; morning; Publr R. M. JOSEY; circ. Mon. to Sat. 22,603, Sun. 25,651.

Huntsville Times: 2317 Memorial Pkwy, POB 1487, West Station, Huntsville, AL 35807; tel. (205) 532-4000; f. 1910; Mon. to Sat. evening, Sun. morning; Publr WILLIAM C. GREEN, Jr; Editor PATRICK MCCAULEY; Ind.; circ. Mon. to Sat. 58,313, Sun. 76,123.

Mobile Register/Mobile Press-Register: 304 Government St, POB 2488, Mobile, AL 36630; tel. (205) 433-1551; f. 1830; morning (Register) and Mon. to Sat. evening (Press-Register); Publr WILLIAM J. HEARIN; Editor TOM TAYLOR; Ind.-Dem.; circ. Mon. to Fri. morning 54,421, Mon. to Fri. evening 47,031, Sat. 88,183, Sun. 107,620.

Montgomery Advertiser: 200 Washington St, Montgomery, AL 36102; tel. (205) 262-1611; f. 1828; morning; Publr RICHARD H. AMBERG, Jr; Editor WILLIAM BROWN; Ind.-Dem.; circ. Mon. to Fri. 50,682, Sat. 63,078, Sun. 84,316.

Post Herald: 2200 North Fourth Ave, POB 2553, Birmingham, AL 35202; tel. (205) 325-2214; f. 1887; Mon. to Sat.; morning; Editor JAMES H. DENLEY; Ind.; circ. Mon. to Fri. 61,329, Sat. 53,760.

Times Daily: POB 797, Florence, AL 35630; tel. (205) 766-3434; f. 1869; morning; Publr STEVEN AINSLEY; Editor DONALD A. BROWN; circ. Mon. to Sat. 31,173, Sun. 34,206.

Tuscaloosa News: Sixth St and 20th Ave, POB Drawer One, Tuscaloosa, AL 35401; tel. (205) 345-0505; f. 1818; Mon. to Fri.

evening, Sat. and Sun. morning; Publr CHARLES H. LAND; Editor DONALD A. BROWN; circ. Mon. to Fri. 38,300, Sun. 39,200.

Alaska

Anchorage News: POB 149001, Anchorage, AK 99514-9001; tel. (907) 786-4200; f. 1946; morning; Publr JERRY GRILLY; Man. Editor HOWARD WEAVER; Ind.; circ. Mon. to Sat. 56,084, Sun. 70,768.

Anchorage Times: POB 40, Anchorage, AK 99510; tel. (907) 263-9000; f. 1915; Mon. to Fri. evening, Sat. and Sun. morning; Publr ROBERT B. ATWOOD; Editor WILLIAM J. TOBIN; circ. Mon. to Fri. 36,208, Sun. 46,913.

Arizona

Arizona Daily Star: POB 26887, Tucson, AZ 85726-6807; tel. (602) 573-4400; f. 1877; morning; Publr and Editor MICHAEL E. PULITZER; circ. 80,766.

Arizona Republic: POB 1950, Phoenix, AZ 85001; tel. (602) 271-8000; f. 1890; morning; Publr PAT MURPHY; Editor ALAN MOYER; circ. Mon. to Sat. 343,723, Sun. 539,323.

Mesa Tribune: Cox Arizona Publications, Inc/Tribune Newspapers, POB 1547, Mesa, AZ 85201; tel. (602) 898-6500; f. 1890; morning; Publr DAVID SCOTT; Editor MAX JENNINGS; circ. Mon. to Sat. 40,829, Sun. 58,312.

Phoenix Gazette: POB 1950, Phoenix, AZ 85001; tel. (602) 271-8000; f. 1880; Mon. to Sat.; evening; Editor LYNNE HOLT; circ. 105,333.

Tucson Citizen: Tucson Newspapers, Inc, 4850 South Park Ave, POB 26767, Tucson, AZ 85726; tel. (602) 721-2929; f. 1870; Mon. to Sat.; evening; Publr and Editor C. DONALD HATFIELD; circ. 60,496.

Arkansas

Arkansas Democrat: Capitol Ave and Scott St, POB 2221, Little Rock, AR 72203; tel. (501) 378-3400; f. 1871; morning; Publr

WALTER E. HUSSMAN, Jr; Man. Editor JOHN R. STARR; Ind.; circ. Mon. to Sat. 82,156, Sun. 158,011.

Arkansas Gazette: 112 West Third Ave, POB 1821, Little Rock, AR 72203; tel. (501) 371-3700; f. 1819; morning; Publr WILLIAM T. MALONE; Editor WALKER LUNDY; Ind.-Dem.; circ. Mon. to Sat. 139,448, Sun. 201,733.

Jonesboro Sun: 518 Carson, Jonesboro, AR 72401; tel. (501) 935-5525; f. 1903; Mon. to Sat.; morning; Publr and Editor JOHN TROYTT, Jr; circ. 24,100.

Pine Bluff Commercial: POB 6469, Pine Bluff, AR 71611-6469; tel. (501) 534-3400; f. 1881; Mon. to Fri. evening, Sat. and Sun. morning; Editor MIKE HENGEL; Gen. Man. DAN SMITH; circ. Mon. to Sat. 21,436, Sun. 22,750.

Southwest Times Record: 920 Rogers Ave, POB 1359, Fort Smith, AR 72902; tel (501) 785-7700; f. 1882; Mon. to Fri. all day, Sat. and Sun. morning; Publr DONALD W. REYNOLDS; Editor JACK MOSELEY; circ. Mon. to Fri. 42,676, Sun. 46,489; Sat. 42,830.

California

Argus: Alameda Newspapers, 37427 Centralmont Pl., Fremont, CA 94536; tel. (415) 794-0111; f. 1960; morning; Publr ALLAN MEATH; Editor BOB WYNNE; circ. Mon. to Sat. 23,801, Sun. 24,263.

Bakersfield Californian: 1707 Eye St, Bakersfield, CA 93301; tel. (805) 395-7500; f. 1866; morning; Publr DONALD FRITTS; Editor ALFRED T. FRITTS; Ind.; circ. Mon. to Sat. 81,721, Sun. 87,185.

Californian: Salinas Newspapers, Inc, POB 81091, Salinas, CA 93912; tel. (408) 424-2221; f. 1871; Mon. to Fri. evening, Sat. morning; Publr KAREN A. WITTMER; Editor DAVE DOUCETTE; circ. 22,684.

Copley Los Angeles Newspapers: 5215 Torrance Blvd, Torrance, CA 90509; tel. (213) 540-5511; f. 1894; Mon. to Sat. evening, Sun. morning; Publr BERTRAM WINROW; Editor JAMES BOX; circ. Mon. to Sat. 131,194, Sun. 124,750.

County Telegram Tribune: 1321 Johnson Ave, POB 112, San Luis Obispo, CA 93406; tel. (805) 595-1111; f. 1869; Mon. to Fri. evening, Sat. morning; Editor GEORGE L. DEBORD; circ. Mon. to Fri. 28,275, Sat. 33,320.

Daily Californian: 1000 Pioneer Way, POB 1565, El Cajon, CA 92022; tel. (619) 442-4404; f. 1892; Tues. to Fri. evening, Sat. and Sun. morning; Vice-Pres. DAVE REESE; circ. 22,499.

Daily News: 21221 Oxnard St, Woodland Hills, CA 91367-4200; tel. (818) 713-3000; f. 1911; morning; Editor TIMOTHY KELLY; circ. Mon. to Fri. 143,133, Sat. 134,461, Sun. 161,142.

The Desert Sun: 611 South Palm Canyon Dr., POB 190, Palm Springs, CA 92263; tel. (619) 325-8666; f. 1927; Mon. to Sat. evening; Publr KAREN OPPENHEIM; Editor JOHN BEHRMAN; circ. 32,737.

Enterprise-Record: POB 9, Chico, CA 95927-0009; tel. (916) 891-1234; f. 1853; Mon. to Fri. evening; Sat. and Sun. morning; Editor JACK WINNING; circ. Mon. to Sat. 26,919, Sun. 26,328.

Fresno Bee: 1626 E St, Fresno, CA 93786; tel. (209) 441-6111; f. 1922; morning; Exec. Editor BEVERLY KEES; Ind.; circ. Mon. to Fri. 141,396, Sun. 166,279.

Hemet News: POB 1107, Hemet, CA 92343; tel. (714) 925-0555; f. 1894; Mon. to Fri. evening, Sat. morning; Publr JAMES GILL, III; Editor BOB LAUFLER; circ. paid 21,500, non-paid 29,000.

Herald (Dublin): 6207 Sierra, POB 3000, Dublin, CA 94568; tel. (415) 829-9111; all day; Publr J. ALLEN MEATH; Editor DAVID E. HALVORSEN; circ. Mon.-Sat. 26,596, Sun. 26,750.

Herald (Monterey): Monterey Peninsula Herald Co, Monterey, CA 93940; tel. (408) 372-3311; f. 1922; morning; Editor THOMAS W. WALTON; circ. Mon. to Sat. 33,378, Sun. 34,449.

Hollywood News: 6715 Sunset Blvd, Hollywood, CA 90028; tel. (213) 464-7411; f. 1930; Mon. to Fri. morning; Publr TICHI WILKERSON KASSEL; Editor TERI RITZER; circ. 21,500.

Los Angeles Times: Times–Mirror Co, Times–Mirror Sq., Los Angeles, CA 90053; tel. (213) 972-5000; f. 1881; morning; Publr and CEO TOM JOHNSON; Pres. and COO DONALD F. WRIGHT; Editor and Exec. Vice-Pres. WILLIAM F. THOMAS; Ind.; circ. Mon. to Fri. 1,136,813, Sat. 1,044,406, Sun. 1,421,711.

Marin Independent Journal: California Newspapers, Inc, POB 330, San Rafael, CA 94915; tel. (415) 883-8600; f. 1861; Mon. to Sat. evening, Sun. morning; Publr JAMES BARNES, Jr; Editor JAY SILVERBERG; circ. Mon. to Sat. 40,214, Sun. 43,083.

Merced Sun-Star: 3033 North G St, POB 739, Merced, CA 95341-0739; tel. (209) 722-1511; f. 1869; Mon. to Sat.; morning; Publr DEAN S. LESHER; Editor BURTON FOGELBERG; circ. 23,305.

Modesto Bee: 1325 H St, POB 3928, Modesto, CA 95352; tel. (209) 578-2000; f. 1884; morning; Editor ALAN TRUAX; Ind.; circ. Mon. to Fri. 76,445, Sun. 82,227.

Napa Register: 1615 Second St, POB 150, Napa, CA 94559; tel. (707) 226-3711; f. 1863; Mon. to Sat.; evening; Publr BILL G. DANIEL; Editor LYNN PENNY; circ. 20,987.

LA Opinion: Lozano Enterprises, 1436 South Main St, Los Angeles, CA 90015; tel. (213) 748-1191; f. 1926; morning; Publr JOSÉ LOZANO; Man. Editor MONICA LOZANO; circ. Mon. to Sat. 75,292, Sun. 60,782.

Orange Coast Daily Pilot: 330 West Bay St, POB 1560, Costa Mesa, CA 92626; tel. (714) 642-4321; f. 1923; Mon. to Fri. evening, Sat. and Sun. morning; Publr HOWARD MULLENARY; Editor TOM TAIT; circ. paid 22,000, non-paid 28,000.

Orange County Register: 625 North Grand Ave, POB 11626, Santa Ana, CA 92711; tel. (714) 835-1234; f. 1905; all day; Editor N. CHRISTIAN ANDERSON; circ. Mon. to Fri. 307,776, Sat. 347,723, Sun. 300,557.

Press-Democrat: 427 Mendocino Ave, Santa Rosa, CA 95402; tel. (707) 546-2020; f. 1857; morning; Editor ART VOLKERTS; circ. Mon. to Sat. 77,234, Sun. 85,848.

Press Enterprise: 3512 14th St, POB 792, Riverside, CA 92501; tel. (714) 684-1200; f. 1878; morning; Publr and Editor HOWARD H. HAYS, Jr; circ. Mon. to Fri. 140,941, Sun. 147,148.

Press-Telegram: Twin Coast Newspapers, Inc, 604 Pine Ave, Long Beach, CA 90844; tel. (213) 435-1161; f. 1888; morning; Pres. and Publr DANIEL H. RIDDER; Editor LARRY ALLISON; Man. Editor RICH ARCHBOLD; circ. Mon. to Fri. 124,506, Sat. 123,879, Sun. 141,646.

Progress Bulletin: POB 2708, Pomona, CA 91769; tel. (714) 622-1201; f. 1885; Mon. to Fri. evening, Sat. and Sun. morning; Publr DONALD RUSSEL; Editor JIM FULTON; circ. Mon. to Sat. 40,939, Sun. 43,290.

Report: 212 East B St, Ontario, CA 91761; f. 1910; Mon. to Sat. evening; Sun. morning; Publr JAMES L. DIMMIT; circ. Mon. to Sat. 42,235, Sun. 43,340.

Review: 116 West Winton Ave, Hayward, CA 94544; tel. (415) 783-6111; f. 1891; Mon. to Fri. evening, Sat. and Sun. morning; Publr F. L. SPARKS; circ. Mon. to Sat. 47,697, Sun. 47,766.

Sacramento Bee: 21st and Q Sts, Sacramento, CA 95852; tel. (916) 321-1001; f. 1857; morning; Exec. Editor GREGORY FAVRE; Ind.; circ. Mon. to Sat. 245,377, Sun. 289,083.

Sacramento Union: 301 Capitol Mall, Sacramento, CA 95812; tel. (916) 442-7811; f. 1851; morning; Publr RICHARD M. SCAIFE; Editor BRUCE WINTERS; Ind.; circ. Mon. to Sat. 90,888, Sun. 89,561.

San Bernardino Sun: 399 D St, San Bernardino, CA 92401; tel. (714) 889-9666; f. 1873; daily (except Sat.) morning; Publr BROOKS JOHNSON; Editor ARNOLD GARSON; Ind.; circ. Mon. to Fri. 82,413, Sun. 88,028.

San Diego Tribune: POB 191, San Diego, CA 92112; tel. (619) 299-3131; f. 1895; Mon. to Sat.; evening; Publr HELEN COPLEY; Editor NEIL MORGAN; circ. 123,000.

San Diego Union: POB 191, San Diego, CA 92112; tel. (619) 299-3131; f. 1868; morning; Editor GERALD L. WARREN; circ. Mon. to Sat. 252,686, Sun. 415,588.

San Francisco Chronicle: 901 Mission St, San Francisco, CA 94103; tel. (415) 777-1111; f. 1865; morning; Publr and Editor RICHARD T. THIERIOT; Ind.; circ. Mon. to Fri. 568,088, Sat. 517,069.

San Francisco Examiner: 925 Mission St, San Francisco, CA 94103; tel. (415) 777-5700; f. 1865; evening; Publr and Editor WILLIAM R. HEARST, III; Ind.; circ. Mon. to Fri. 142,335, Sun. 112,034.

San Gabriel Valley Daily Tribune: POB 1259, Covina, CA 91722; tel. (818) 962-8811; morning; Editor JOE BLACKSTOCK; circ. Mon. to Sat. 66,000, Sun. 86,000.

San Jose Mercury News: 750 Ridder Park Dr., San Jose, CA 95190; tel. (408) 920-5000; f. 1883; Mon. to Fri. all day, Sat. and Sun. morning; Publr WILLIAM A. OTT; Exec. Editor ROBERT INGLE; Ind.; circ. Mon. to Fri. 264,492, Sat. 248,100, Sun. 308,247.

Santa Barbara News-Press: PO Drawer NN, Santa Barbara, CA 93102; tel. (805) 966-3911; f. 1880; Mon. to Sat. evening; Sun. morning; Publr and Editor B. DALE DAVIS; circ. Mon. to Sat. 48,799, Sun. 57,189.

Santa Cruz Sentinel: POB 638, Santa Cruz, CA 95061; tel. (408) 423-4242; f. 1856; daily (except Sat.) morning; Publr FRED MCPHERSON, III; Editor BRUCE MCPHERSON; circ. Mon. to Fri. 28,239, Sun. 30,830.

Star-News: 525 East Colorado Blvd, Pasadena, CA 91109; tel. (818) 578-6300; f. 1886; morning; Publr WILLIAM R. APPLEBEE; Editor PATRICIA BURNETT; circ. Mon. to Sat. 40,550, Sun. 45,528.

Stockton Record: 530 East Market St, POB 900, Stockton, CA 95202; tel. (209) 943-6397; f. 1895; morning; Publr CHRISTOPHER SCOVELL DIX; Exec. Editor PHILIP BOOKMAN; Ind.; circ. Mon. to Fri. 51,415, Sat. 55,120, Sun. 55,489.

Times and News Leader: 1080 South Amphlett Blvd, San Mateo, CA 94402; tel. (415) 348-4321; f. 1889; Mon. to Sat. evening; Publr JOHN H. CLINTON; Editor J. HART CLINTON; circ. 44,529.

Times-Standard: POB 3580, Eureka, CA 95502; tel. (707) 442-1711; f. 1854; morning, also Mon. to Fri. evening; Publr GERALD COLBY; circ. Mon. to Sat. 20,486, Sun. 22,163.

Times-Tribune: 245 Lytton Ave, Palo Alto, CA 94301; tel. (415) 853-5243; f. 1893; Mon. to Fri. evening, Sat. and Sun. morning; Editor MICHAEL KIDDER; circ. Mon. to Sat. 52,971, Sun. 56,995.

Tribune: 409 13th St, POB 24304, Oakland, CA 94612; tel. (415) 645-2000; f. 1874; morning; Publr and Editor ROBERT C. MAYNARD; Ind.-Rep.; circ. Mon. to Fri. 151,669, Sat. 147,394, Sun. 156,343.

Ventura County Star-Free Press: John P. Scripps Newspaper Group, 5250 Ralston St, POB 6711, Ventura, CA 93003; tel. (805) 656-4111; f. 1875; Mon. to Fri. evening, Sat. and Sun. morning; Editor JOHN L. BOWMAN; circ. Mon. to Sat. 49,402, Sun. 56,047.

Colorado

Coloradoan: POB 1577, Fort Collins, CO 80522; tel. (303) 493-6397; f. 1873; morning; Publr ORAGE QUARLES, III; Editor DAVID FREILING; circ. Mon. to Fri. 20,134, Sun. 25,308.

Daily Camera: POB 591, 1048 Pearl St, Boulder, CO 80302; tel. (303) 442-1202; f. 1891; morning; Publr JOHN L. DOTSON, Jr; Editor BARRIE HARTMAN; circ. Mon. to Sat. 30,429, Sun. 39,306.

Daily Sentinel: POB 668, Grand Junction, CO 81502; tel. (303) 242-5050; f. 1893; Mon. to Fri. evening, Sat. and Sun. morning; Publr GEORGE ORBANEK; Editor DENNIS HERZOG; circ. Mon. to Fri. 28,894, Sun. 32,235.

Denver Post: 650 15th St, POB 1709, Denver, CO 80201; tel. (303) 820-1010; f. 1895; morning; Publr RICHARD SCHLOSBERG; Editor DAVID HALL; Ind.; circ. Mon. to Sat. 227,105, Sun. 425,454.

Gazette Telegraph: 30 South Prospect St, POB 1779, Colorado Springs, CO 80903; tel. (303) 632-5511; f. 1872; morning; Editor TOM MULLEN; Ind.; circ. Mon. to Fri. 105,666, Sat. 105,159, Sun. 116,707.

Pueblo Chieftain: POB 4040, Pueblo, CO 81003; tel. (303) 544-3520; f. 1872; morning; Publr ROBERT H. RAWLINGS; circ. Mon. to Sat. 51,581, Sun. 55,392.

Rocky Mountain News: 400 West Colfax Ave, Denver, CO 80204; tel. (303) 892-5000; f. 1859; morning; Editor RALPH E. LOONEY; Ind.; circ. Mon. to Sat. 347,778, Sun. 379,984.

Tribune: 714 Eighth St, POB 1138, Greeley, CO 80631; tel. (303) 352-0211; f. 1870; Mon. to Fri evening, Sat. and Sun. morning; Publr RICHARD LARSEN; Editor RONALD J. STEWART; circ. Mon. to Sat. 23,182, Sun. 24,045.

Connecticut

Advocate: Southern Connecticut Newspapers Inc, 75 Tresser Blvd, Stamford, CT 06904; tel. (203) 964-2200; f. 1829; Mon. to Fri. evening; Sat. and Sun. morning; Publr WILLIAM J. ROWE; Editor KENNETH M. BRIEF; circ. Mon. to Sat. 30,660, Sun. 37,440.

American: American-Republican Inc, 389 Meadow St, POB 2090, Waterbury, CT 06722; tel. (203) 574-3636; f. 1866; Mon. to Fri.; evening; Publr WILLIAM J. PAPE, II; Editor EUGENE L. MARTIN; circ. 28,419.

Bridgeport Post: 410 State St, Bridgeport, CT 06604; tel. (203) 333-0161; f. 1883; evening; Publr ELIZABETH M. PFRIEM; Editor STEPHEN J. WINTERS; Ind.; circ. Mon. to Sat. 63,218, Sun. 91,488.

Daily Republican: 389 Meadow St, POB 2090, Waterbury, CT 06722; tel. (203) 574-3636; f. 1844; morning; Publr WILLIAM J. PAPE, II; Editor EUGENE L. MARTIN; circ. Mon. to Sat. 39,856, Sun. 73,105.

The Day: POB 1231, New London, CT 06320-1231; tel. (203) 442-2200; f. 1881; morning; Publr and Editor REID MacCLUGGAGE; circ. Mon. to Sat. 37,363, Sun. 40,028.

Hartford Courant: 285 Broad St, Hartford, CT 06115; tel. (203) 241-6206; f. 1764; morning; Publr and CEO MICHAEL J. DAVIES; Exec. Editor MICHAEL WALLER; Ind.; circ. Mon. to Sat. 221,962, Sun. 309,329.

Herald: 1 Herald Sq., New Britain, CT 06050; tel. (203) 225-4601; f. 1880; Mon. to Sat.; evening; Publr and Editor JUDITH W. BROWN; circ. 40,340.

The Hour: 346 Main Ave, Norwalk, CT 06851; tel. (203) 846-3281; f. 1871; Mon. to Sat.; evening; Publr WALTER WHITTON; Editor JOHN P. REILLY; circ. 21,230.

Manchester Enfield Journal Inquirer: 306 Progress Dr., Manchester, CT 06040; tel. (203) 646-0500; f. 1968; Mon. to Fri. evening, Sat. morning; Publr ELIZABETH ELLIS; circ. 43,466.

New Haven Register: Long Wharf, 40 Sargent Dr., New Haven, CT 06511; tel. (203) 562-1121; f. 1755; morning; Publr LIONEL S. JACKSON, Jr; Editor THOMAS G. INGERSOLL; Ind.; circ. 103,004.

News-Times: 333 Main St, Danbury, CT 06810; tel. (203) 744-5100; f. 1883; morning; Publr FORREST C. PALMER; circ. Mon. to Sat. 39,479, Sun. 45,789.

Norwich Bulletin: 66 Franklin, Norwich, CT 06360; tel. (203) 887-9211; f. 1791; morning; Publr RICHARD S. FEENEY; Editor WILLIAM F. MUNGO; circ. Mon. to Sat. 34,638, Sun. 37,094.

Record Journal: 11 Crown Street, Meriden, CT 06450; tel. (203) 235-1661; f. 1867; morning; Publr CARTER H. WHITE; Editor BARBARA C. WHITE; circ. Mon. to Sat. 31,073, Sun. 30,006.

Delaware

Journal: 831 Orange St, POB 1111, Wilmington, DE 19899; tel. (302) 573-2000; f. 1871; Mon. to Fri.; evening; Publr BRIAN DONNELLY; Editor J. DONALD BRANDT; circ. 50,869.

News: 831 Orange St, POB 1111, Wilmington, DE 19899; tel. (302) 573-2000; f. 1880; Mon. to Fri.; morning; Editor J. DONALD BRANDT; circ. 67,384.

News-Journal: 831 Orange St, POB 1111, Wilmington, DE 19899; tel. (302) 573-2000; f. 1975; Sat. and Sun.; Editor J. DONALD BRANDT; circ. Sat. 113,621, Sun. 132,374.

District of Columbia

USA Today: POB 500, Washington, DC 20044; tel. (703) 276-3400; telex 64606; f. 1982; morning; national general interest newspaper, also publishes international edition; Publr CATHIE BLACK; Editor JOHN C. QUINN; Ind.; circ. 1,324,223.

Washington Post: 1150 15th St, NW, Washington, DC 20071; tel. (202) 334-6000; f. 1877; morning; Publr DONALD E. GRAHAM; Exec. Editor BENJAMIN C. BRADLEE; Man. Editor LEONARD DOWNIE, Jr; Ind.; circ. Mon. to Fri. 796,659, Sat. 753,762, Sun. 1,112,802.

Washington Times: 3600 New York Ave, NW, Washington, DC 20002; tel. (202) 636-3000; f. 1982; Mon. to Fri.; morning; Editor ARNAUD DE BORCHGRAVE; Man. Editor WESLEY PRUDEN; circ. 104,890.

Florida

Bradenton Herald: 102 Manatee Ave West, POB 921, Bradenton, FL 33506; tel. (813) 748-0411; f. 1926; morning; Publr and Pres. FRANK McCOMAS; Editor WAYNE H. POSTON; circ. Mon. to Sat. 43,544, Sun. 42,718.

Daytona Beach News-Journal: 901 Sixth St, Daytona Beach, FL 32017; tel. (904) 252-1511; f. 1904; morning; Publr and Editor HERBERT M. DAVIDSON; circ. 82,935.

Diario Las Americas: 2900 NW 39th St, Miami, FL 33142; tel. (305) 633-3341; f. 1953; Tues. to Sun.; morning; Publr and Editor HORACIO AGUIRRE; Ind.; circ. Tues. to Sat. 63,989, Sun. 67,982.

Florida Times-Union: 1 Riverside Ave, Jacksonville, FL 32202; tel. (904) 359-4111; f. 1864; morning; Publr WILLIAM S. MORRIS, III; Exec. Editor FREDERICK W. HARTMANN; Ind.; circ. Mon. to Fri. 160,405, Sat. 184,941, Sun. 228,584.

Florida Today: Gannett Company, Inc, Gannett Plaza, POB 363000, Melbourne, FL 32936; tel. (407) 242-3500; f. 1966; morning; Publr FRANK VEGA; Editor EDWARD E. MANASSAH; circ. Mon. to Sat. 66,686, Sun. 89,180.

Gainesville Sun: PO Drawer A, Gainesville, FL 32602; tel. (904) 374-5000; f. 1876; morning; Publr JOHN FITZWATER; Editor DIANE McFARLIN; circ. Mon. to Sat. 56,298, Sun. 54,220.

Jacksonville Journal: Morris Communications Corpn, 1 Riverside Ave, Jacksonville, FL 32202; tel. (904) 359-4111; f. 1887; Mon. to Fri. evening; Publr W. S. MORRIS, III; Editor FRED HARTMANN; circ. 41,935.

Leesburg/Commercial: 212 East Main St, Leesburg, FL 32748; tel. (904) 787-4515; f. 1876; Mon. to Sat. evening, Sun. morning; Publr E. A. NICHOLS, Jr; Editor J. M. ARCHER; circ. Mon. to Sat. 24,796, Sun. 28,093.

Ledger: POB 408, Lakeland, FL 33802; tel. (813) 687-7000; f. 1924; morning; Publr LYNN MATTHEWS; Editor LOUIS MICHAEL PEREZ; circ. Mon. to Sat. 79,023, Sun. 96,990.

Miami Herald: One Herald Plaza, Miami, FL 33101; tel. (305) 350-2111; f. 1910; morning; Publr RICHARD G. CAPEN; Editor HEATH MERIWETHER; Ind.; circ. Mon. to Sat. 437,223, Sun. 546,980.

Miami News: POB 615, Miami, FL 33152; tel. (305) 350-2200; f. 1896; Mon. to Sat.; evening; Publr DAVID KRASLOW; Editor HOWARD KLEINBERG; Ind.; circ. 56,928.

News (Fort Lauderdale): 101 North New River Dr. East, Fort Lauderdale, FL 33302; tel. (305) 761-4000; f. 1910; Mon. to Fri.; evening; Publr BRYON C. CAMPBELL; Editor GENE CRYER; circ 66,622.

News (Naples): 1075 Central Ave, Naples, FL 33940; tel. (813) 262-3161; f. 1923; Mon. to Fri. evening, Sun. morning; Publr CORBIN A. WYANT; circ. Mon. to Fri. 34,380, Sun. 44,716.

News Herald: POB 1940, Panama City, FL 32402; tel. (904) 763-7621; f. 1931; morning; Publr SCOTT FISCHER; Editor BILL SALTER; circ. Mon. to Sat. 36,564, Sun. 41,060.

News-Press: 2422 Anderson Ave, Fort Myers, FL 33901; tel. (813) 335-0200; f. 1884; morning; Publr TERRY G. HOPKINS; Editor KEITH MOYER; circ. Mon. to Sat. 73,304, Sun. 93,405.

News and Sun-Sentinel: 101 North New River Dr. East, Fort Lauderdale, FL 33302; tel. (305) 761-4000; f. 1910; Sat. and Sun.; morning; circ. Sat. 232,659, Sun. 308,052.

News Tribune: POB 69, Fort Pierce, FL 34954; tel. (305) 461-2050; f. 1903; morning; Publr JAMES MCMILLEN; Editor BOB ENNS; circ. Mon. to Sat. 21,653, Sun. 24,098.

Ocala Star-Banner: 2121 19th Ave, SW, POB 490, Ocala, FL 32678; tel. (904) 867-4010; f. 1866; Mon. to Fri. evening; Sat. and Sun. morning; Editor BERNARD WATTS; circ. Mon. to Sat. 44,586, Sun. 51,461.

Orlando Sentinel: 633 North Orange Ave, Orlando, FL 32801; tel. (305) 420-5000; f. 1876; all day; Publr HAROLD R. LIFVENDAHL; Editor L. JOHN HAILE; Ind.; circ. Mon. to Sat. 258,915, Sun. 340,588.

Palm Beach Post: 2751 South Dixie Highway, West Palm Beach, FL 33405; tel. (305) 837-4100; f. 1910; morning; Publr DAN MAHONEY; Editor THOMAS A. KELLY; Ind.; circ. Mon. to Fri. 109,138, Sat. 128,009, Sun. 174,065.

Pensacola News Journal: One News Journal Plaza, Pensacola, FL 32501; tel. (904) 435-8500; f. 1889; morning; Publr CLIFFORD W. BARNHART; Editor KENT W. COOKSON; Ind.; circ. Mon. to Sat. 60,592, Sun. 75,944.

Playground Daily News: POB 2949, 200 Race Track Rd, NE, Fort Walton Beach, FL 32549; tel. (904) 863-1111; f. 1946; daily except Sat.; morning; Publr MARVIN DeBOLT; Editor TOM CONNORS; circ. 36,600.

Press-Journal: POB 1268, Vero Beach, FL 32961-1268; tel. (407) 562-2315; f. 1919; morning; Publr and Editor J. J. SCHUMANN; circ. Mon. to Sat. 25,000, Sun. 27,000.

Sarasota Herald Tribune: 801 South Tamiami Trail, POB 1719, Sarasota, FL 33578; tel. (813) 953-7755; f. 1925; morning; Publr J. E. GRUBBS; Editor BILL McILWAIN; circ. Mon. to Sat. 106,446, Sun. 130,722.

St Petersburg Times: 490 First Ave South, POB 1121, St Petersburg, FL 33731; tel. (813) 893-8111; telex 522217; f. 1906; morning; Pres., Editor and CEO ANDREW BARNES; Ind.; circ. Mon. to Sat. 307,944, Sun. 394,962.

Stuart News: POB 9009, Stuart, FL 34995-9009; tel. (407) 287-1550; f. 1913; morning; Editor THOMAS E. WEBER, Jr; circ. Mon. to Sat. 26,230, Sun. 29,847.

Sun: POB 2078, Clearwater, FL 33517; tel. (813) 462-2000; f. 1914; morning; Publr and Editor RICHARD W. COSGRAVE; circ. Mon. to Sat. 27,507, Sun. 28,212.

Sun-Sentinel: 101 North New River Dr. East, Fort Lauderdale, FL 33302; tel. (305) 761-4000; f. 1960; Mon. to Fri.; morning; Publr BRYON C. CAMPBELL; circ. 176,093.

Sun-Tattler: 2600 North 29th Ave, Hollywood, FL 33020; tel. (305) 929-8100; f. 1935; Mon. to Sat.; mornings; Editor MIKE PHILLIPS; circ. 32,696.

Tallahassee Democrat: 277 North Magnolia Dr., POB 990, Tallahassee, FL 32302-0990; tel. (904) 599-2100; f. 1905; morning; Publr J. CARROL DADISMAN; Editor BOB STIFF; circ. Mon. to Sat. 56,056, Sun. 67,701.

Tampa Tribune: 202 Parker St, Tampa, FL 33606; tel. (813) 272-7711; f. 1893; all day; Publr R. F. PITTMAN; Man. Editor A. P. HOGAN; Ind.; circ. Mon. to Sat. 271,288, Sun. 362,459.

Georgia

Albany Herald: POB 48, Albany, GA 31703; tel. (912) 888-9300; f. 1891; Mon. to Sat. evening, Sun. morning; Publr and Editor JAMES H. GRAY, Jr; circ. Mon. to Sat. 38,070, Sun. 44,730.

Atlanta Constitution: 72 Marietta St, Atlanta, GA 30303; tel. (404) 572-5151; f. 1868; Mon. to Fri.; morning; Publr JAY R. SMITH; Editor BILL KOVACH; circ. 264,812.

Atlanta Journal: 72 Marietta St, GA 30303; tel. (404) 572-5151; f. 1883; Mon. to Fri.; evening; Editor BILL KOVACH; circ. 188,617.

Atlanta Journal-Constitution: 72 Marietta St, GA 30303; tel. (404) 572-5151; f. 1950; Sat. and Sun; Editor BILL KOVACH; circ. Sat. 501,479, Sun. 645,916.

Augusta Chronicle: POB 1928, Augusta, GA 30913-1928; tel. (404) 724-0851; f. 1785; Mon. to Fri.; morning; Publr W. S. MORRIS; Editor DENNIS SODOMKA; circ. 62,630.

Augusta Chronicle-Herald: POB 1928, Augusta, GA 30913-1928; tel. (404) 724-0851; Sat. and Sun.; Publr W. S. MORRIS; circ. Sat. 87,145, Sun. 85,262.

Columbus Enquirer: 17 West 12th St, Columbus, GA 31901; tel. (404) 324-5526; f. 1828; Mon. to Sat.; morning; circ. Mon. to Fri. 34,654; Sat. 56,594.

Columbus Ledger: 17 West 12th St, Columbus, GA 31901; tel. (404) 324-5526; f. 1886; Mon. to Fri.; evening; Editor BILL BROWN; circ. 25,433.

Gwinnett Daily News: 394 Clayton St, POB 1000, Lawrenceville, GA 30246; tel. (404) 963-0311; f. 1858; Mon. to Fri. evening, Sat. and Sun. morning; Publr ROBERT D. FOWLER; Editor JIM OSTEEN; circ. Mon. to Sat. 27,436, Sun. 30,851.

Journal: 580 Fairground St, Marietta, GA 30060; tel. (404) 428-9411; f. 1866; Mon. to Sat. evening, Sun. morning; Publr OTIS A. BRUMBY, Jr; Editor BOBBY NESBIT; circ. Mon. to Sat. 24,649, Sun. 25,974.

Macon Telegraph and News: 120 Broadway, POB 4167, Macon, GA 31213; tel. (912) 744-4200; f. 1826; morning; Publr ED OLSON; Editor RICK THOMAS; Ind.; circ. Mon. to Sat. 72,601, Sun. 96,957.

News: 111 West Bay St, POB 1088, Savannah, GA 31402; tel. (912) 236-9511; f. 1850; Mon. to Sat.; morning; Publr DON HARWOOD; Editor W. M. DAVIS, Jr; circ. 55,665.

News-Press: 111 West Bay St, POB 1088, Savannah, GA 31402; tel. (912) 236-9511; f. 1966; Sun.; Editor W. M. DAVIS, Jr; circ. 76,064.

Times: POB 838, Gainesville, GA 30503; tel. (404) 532-1234; f. 1947; Mon. to Sat. evening, Sun. morning; Publr DENISE BANNISTER; Editor MIKE CONNELL; circ. 24,500.

Hawaii

Honolulu Advertiser: 605 Kapiolani Blvd, Honolulu, HI 96813; tel. (808) 525-8000; f. 1856; morning; Publr PHILIP T. GIALANELLA; Editor BUCK BUCHWACH; circ. 95,437.

Honolulu Star-Bulletin: POB 3080, Honolulu, HI 96802; tel. (808) 525-8000; f. 1882; Mon. to Sat.; evening; Publr CATHERINE SHEN; Editor JOHN FLANAGAN; circ. 98,485.

Sunday Star-Bulletin and Advertiser: 605 Kapiolani Blvd, Honolulu, HI 96813; tel. (808) 525-8000; f. 1956; Sun.; Editor BUCK BUCKWACH; circ. 203,277.

Idaho

Idaho Statesman: 1200 North Curtis Rd, POB 40, Boise, ID 83707; tel. (208) 377-6200; f. 1864; morning; Publr GORDON R. BLACK; Man. Editor BILL STEINAUER; Ind.; circ. Mon. to Sat. 54,772, Sun. 71,611.

Post-Register: POB 1800, Idaho Falls, ID 83401; tel. (208) 522-1800; f. 1880; Mon. to Fri. evening, Sun. morning; Publr and Editor J. ROBB BRADY; circ. Mon. to Fri. 24,662, Sun. 25,406.

Tribune: 505 C St, Lewiston, ID 83501; tel. (208) 743-9411; f. 1892; morning; Publr and Editor A. L. ALFORD, Jr; circ. Mon. to Sat. 23,778, Sun. 24,768.

Illinois

Arlington Heights Daily Herald: POB 280, Arlington Heights, IL 60006; tel. (312) 870-3600; f. 1872; morning; Editor DANIEL E. BAUMANN; circ. Mon. to Sat. 73,323, Sun. 71,701.

Beacon-News: 101 South River St, Aurora, IL 60506; tel. (312) 844-5844; f. 1846; Mon. to Fri. evening, Sat. and Sun. morning; Publr and Editor JOHN W. CURLEY; circ. Mon. to Sat. 40,421, Sun. 43,520.

Belleville News-Democrat: POB 427, 120 South Illinois St, Belleville, IL 62222; tel. (618) 234-1000; f. 1855; daily (except Sat.) morning; Publr GARY BERKLEY; Editor GREG EDWARDS; Mon. to Fri. 45,399, Sun. 53,322.

Bloomington Pantagraph: 301 West Washington, POB 2907, Bloomington, IL 61701; tel. (309) 829-9411; f. 1846; morning; Publr JOHN R. GOLDRICK; Man. Editor BILL WILLS; Ind.; circ. Mon. to Sat. 52,982, Sun. 56,452.

Chicago Defender: 2400 Michigan Ave, Chicago, IL 60616; tel. (312) 225-2400; f. 1956; Mon. to Fri.; evening; Publr FREDERICK SENGSTACKE; Editor JOHN H. SENGSTACKE; circ. 27,611.

Chicago Sun-Times: 401 North Wabash Ave, Chicago, IL 60611; tel. (312) 321-3000; f. 1948; morning; Publr ROBERT E. PAGE; Editor KENNETH TOWERS; Ind.; circ. Mon. to Fri. 612,686, Sat. 420,501, Sun. 625,935.

Chicago Tribune: 435 North Michigan Ave, Chicago, IL 60611; tel. (312) 222-3232; f. 1847; Mon. to Fri. all day, Sat. and Sun. morning; Publr STANTON R. COOK; Editor JAMES D. SQUIRES; Ind.-Rep.; circ. Mon. to Fri. 758,464, Sat. 601,946, Sun. 1,126,293.

Daily Courier News: 300 Lake St, Elgin, IL 60120; tel. (312) 888-7800; f. 1874; Mon. to Fri. evening, Sat. and Sun. morning; Publr and Editor D. RAY WILSON; circ. Mon. to Sat. 33,240, Sun. 33,541.

Daily Despatch: 1720 Fifth Avenue, Moline, IL 61265; tel. (309) 764-4344; f. 1868; Mon. to Fri. evening, Sat. and Sun. morning; Publr GERALD TAYLOR; circ. Mon. to Sat. 33,300, Sun. 38,052.

Herald-News: The Copley Press Inc, 300 Caterpillar Dr., Joliet, IL 60436; tel. (815) 729-6161; f. 1839; Mon. to Fri. evening, Sat. and Sun. morning; Editor GEORGE H. FISK; circ. Mon. to Sat. 47,520, Sun. 49,474.

Journal Star: 1 News Plaza, Peoria, IL 61643; tel. (309) 686-3000; f. 1855; Mon. to Sat. all day, Sun. morning; Publr JOHN T. McCONNELL; Editor MARGE FANNING; Ind.; circ. Mon. to Sat. 99,197, Sun. 114,536.

Journal: Eight Dearborn Sq., Kankakee, IL 60901; tel. (815) 937-3300; f. 1884; Mon. to Sat. evening, Sun. morning; Publr and Editor JEAN ALICE SMALL; circ. Mon. to Sat. 30,429, Sun. 33,133.

News-Gazette: POB 677, Champaign, IL 61820; tel. (217) 351-5252; f. 1852; Mon. to Fri. evening, Sat. and Sun. morning; Publr MARAJEN S. CHINIGO; Editor JOHN R. FOREMAN; circ. Mon. to Fri. 45,988, Sat. 46,131, Sun. 51,424.

Northwest Herald: 109 South Jefferson, Woodstock, IL 60098; tel. (815) 338-1300; f. 1856; Mon. to Sat.; morning; Publr ROBERT H. SHAW; circ. 30,504.

Quincy Herald Whig: 130 South Fifth St, POB 909, Quincy, IL 62301-0909; tel. (217) 223-5100; f. 1835; Mon. to Fri. evening, Sat. and Sun. morning; Publr T. A. OAKLEY; Editor JOE CONOVER; circ. Mon. to Fri. 27,900, Sat. 25,553, Sun. 31,746.

Rockford Register Star: 99 East State St, Rockford, IL 61104; tel. (815) 987-1200; f. 1888; morning; Publr MICHAEL COLEMAN; Exec. Editor MARK SILVERMAN; circ. Mon. to Sat. 88,100, Sun. 86,485.

Southern Illinoisan: 710 North Illinois, Carbondale, IL 62901; tel. (618) 529-5454; f. 1877; morning; Publr STEVE BURGESS; Editor PETE SELKOWE; circ. Mon. to Sat. 28,353, Sun. 34,097.

State Journal-Register: One Copley Plaza, POB 219, Springfield, IL 62705; tel. (217) 788-8600; f. 1831; morning; Publr JOHN P. CLARKE; Man. Editor PATRICK COBURN; circ. Mon. to Sat. 68,339, Sun. 76,160.

Telegraph: 111 East Broadway, Alton, IL 62002; tel. (618) 463-2500; f. 1836; Mon. to Fri. evening, Sun. morning; Publr BRUCE SPOTLESON; Editor STEVE JACOB; circ. 36,673.

Indiana

Anderson Herald-Bulletin: Anderson Newspapers Inc, 1133 Jackson St, Anderson, IN 46015; tel. (317) 643-5371; f. 1868; morning; Publr JEANNE C. TOWAR; Editor JAMES L. BANNON; circ. Mon. to Fri. 33,479, Sun. 34,064.

Evansville Courier: 201 Second St, NW, POB 268, Evansville, IN 47702; tel. (812) 424-7711; f. 1845; daily (except Sat.) morning; Editor THOMAS W. TULEY; Ind.; circ. Mon. to Fri. 63,122, Sun. 115,634.

Herald-Telephone: POB 909, Bloomington, IN 47402-0909; tel. (812) 332-4401; f. 1877; Mon. to Fri. evening, Sat. and Sun. morning; Publr SCOTT C. SCHURZ; Editor ROBERT ZALTSBERG; circ. Mon. to Fri. 43,610, Sun. 44,190.

Indianapolis News: 307 North Pennsylvania St, Indianapolis, IN 46204; tel. (317) 633-1240; f. 1869; Mon. to Fri.; evening; Publr EUGENE S. PULLIAM; Editor HARVEY JACOBS; circ. 124,292.

Indianapolis Star: 307 North Pennsylvania St, Indianapolis, IN 46204; tel. (317) 633-1240; f. 1903; Mon. to Sun.; morning; Editor JOHN H. LYST; circ. Mon. to Sat. 221,001, Sun. 401,008.

Journal and Courier: Gannett Co Inc, 217 North Sixth St, Lafayette, IN 47901; tel. (317) 423-5511; f. 1829; morning; Publr RICHARD L. HOLTZ; Editor JUDI AUSTIN; circ. Mon. to Sat. 36,164, Sun. 36,506.

Journal-Gazette: 600 West Main St, POB 88, Fort Wayne, IN 46801; tel. (219) 461-8333; f. 1863; morning; Publr RICHARD G.

INSKEEP; Editor CRAIG KLUGMAN; circ. Mon. to Fri. 60,113, Sun. 132,654.

Kokomo Tribune: 300 North Union St, Kokomo, IN 46901; tel. (317) 459-3121; f. 1850; evening, also Sat. and Sun. morning; Publr ARDEN A. DRAEGER; Editor JOHN C. WILES; circ. Mon. to Sat. 27,168, Sun. 28,265.

Muncie Star: Central Newspaper Inc, High and Jackson Sts, POB 2408, Muncie, IN 47302; tel. (317) 747-5700; f. 1889; morning; Publr EUGENE S. PULLIAM; Editor W. W. SPURGEON; circ. Mon. to Sat. 29,574, Sun. 35,133.

News-Sentinel: 600 West Main St, Fort Wayne, IN 46802; tel. (219) 461-8222; f. 1833; Mon. to Sat.; evening; Publr PHIL DE MONTMOLLIN; Editor STEWART SPENCER; circ. 57,414.

Post-Tribune: 1065 Broadway, Gary, IN 46402; tel. (219) 881-3000; f. 1909; morning; Publr JANE SCHOLZ; Editor TERRY O'ROURKE; Ind.; circ. Mon. to Sat. 74,498, Sun. 88,270.

South Bend Tribune: 225 West Colfax Ave at Lafayette Blvd, South Bend, IN 46626; tel. (219) 233-6161; f. 1872; Mon. to Fri. evening, Sat. and Sun. morning; Publr and Editor JOHN J. McGANN; Ind.; circ. Mon. to Sat. 92,132, Sun. 123,560.

The Times: 417 Fayette St, Hammond, IN 46325; tel. (219) 932-3100; f. 1906; Mon. to Sat. evening, Sun. morning; Publr W. J. McCARTHY; Exec. Editor WILLIAM NANGLE; circ. Mon. to Fri. 66,009, Sat. 63,896, Sun. 74,211.

Tribune-Star: 721-25 Wabash Ave, Terre Haute, IN 47808; tel. (812) 231-4200; f. 1903; morning; Publr JOSEPH ZLOMEK; circ. Mon. to Sat. 36,081, Sun. 40,245.

Iowa

Cedar Rapids Gazette: 500 Third Ave, SE, Cedar Rapids, IA 52401; tel. (319) 398-8211; f. 1883; morning; Publr and Editor J. F. HLADKY, III; Ind.; circ. Mon. to Sat. 70,486, Sun. 80,710.

Des Moines Register: 715 Locust St, POB 957, Des Moines, IA 50304; tel. (515) 284-8000; f. 1849; morning; Publr CHARLES C. EDWARDS, Jr; Editor JAMES P. GANNON; Ind.; circ. Mon. to Sat. 221,869, Sun. 364,727.

Quad City Times: 124 East Second St, POB 3828, Davenport, IA 52808; tel. (319) 383-2200; f. 1855; Mon. to Sat. all day, Sun. morning; Publr JOHN GARDNER; Editor FORREST KILMER; circ. Mon. to Sat. 58,427, Sun. 82,271.

Sioux City Journal: 515 Pavonia St, Sioux City, IA 51105; tel. (712) 279-5075; f. 1870; morning; Publr D. A. KRENZ; Editor CAL OLSON; Ind.; circ. Mon. to Fri. 51,640, Sat. 51,135, Sun. 49,045.

Telegraph Herald: West Eighth and Bluff Sts, POB 688, Dubuque, IA 52001; tel. (319) 588-5611; f. 1836; Mon. to Fri. evening, Sat. and Sun. morning; Publr P. SCOTT McKIBBEN; Editor BRIAN COOPER; circ. Mon. to Fri. 35,001, Sun. 38,800.

Waterloo Courier: Courier Bldg, POB 540, Waterloo, IA 50704; tel. (319) 291-1400; f. 1854; Mon. to Fri. evening; Sun. morning; Publr JAMES W. LEWIS; Editor SAUL SHAPIRO; circ. Mon. to Fri. 48,111, Sun. 52,631.

Kansas

Hutchinson News: 300 West Second St, POB 190, Hutchinson, KS 67504-0190; tel. (316) 662-3311; f. 1872; daily; Publr and Editor RICHARD E. BUZBEE; circ. Mon. to Fri. 42,755, Sun. 46,226.

Topeka Capital-Journal: 616 Jefferson St, Topeka, KS 66607; tel. (913) 295-1111; f. 1879; morning; Publr and Editor LEE PORTER; Ind.; circ. Mon. to Fri. 67,250, Sun. 76,441.

Wichita Eagle-Beacon: 825 East Douglas St, Wichita, KS 67202; tel. (316) 268-6000; f. 1872; morning; Publr REID ASHE; Editor W. DAVIS MERRITT, Jr; Ind.; circ. Mon. to Sat. 128,865, Sun. 193,502.

Kentucky

Courier-Journal: 525 West Broadway, Louisville, KY 40202; tel. (502) 582-4011; f. 1868; Mon. to Sat. all day, Sun. morning; Publr GEORGE N. GILL; Editor DAVID V. HAWPE; circ. Mon. to Sat. 237,660, Sun. 329,869.

Lexington Herald-Leader: Main St and Midland Ave , Lexington, KY 40507; tel. (606) 231-3100; f. 1860; morning; Publr CREED C. BLACK; Editor JOHN S. CARROLL; circ. Mon. to Sat. 116,582, Sun. 144,120.

Messenger-Inquirer: Owensboro Publishing Co, POB 1480, Owensboro, KY 42302; tel. (502) 926-0123; f. 1875; morning; Publr LAWRENCE W. HAGER; Publr and Editor JOHN S. HAGER; circ. Mon. to Sat. 32,276, Sun. 34,258.

Sun: POB 2300, Paducak, KY 42002-2300; tel. (502) 443-1771; f. 1871; Mon. to Fri. evening, Sun. morning; Publr FRED PAXTON; Editor JAMES PAXTON; circ. Mon. to Fri. 31,867, Sun. 35,291.

Louisiana

Advertiser: POB 3268, Lafayette, LA 70502; tel. (318) 235-8511; f. 1865; Mon. to Sat. evening, Sun. morning; Publr RICHARD E. D'AQUIN; circ. Mon. to Sat. 30,034, Sun. 37,926.

Alexandria Daily Town Talk: McCormick and Co Inc, 1201 Third St, Alexandria, LA 71301; tel. (318) 487-6397; f. 1883; morning; Publr TOM J. HARDIN; Editor JIM BUTLER; circ. Mon. to Sat. 39,773, Sun. 41,270.

American Press: POB 2893, Lake Charles, LA 70602-2893; tel. (318) 439-2781; f. 1895; morning; Publr WILLIAM H. SHEARMAN; circ. Mon. to Sat. 39,582, Sun. 44,397.

Baton Rouge Advocate: 525 Lafayette St, Baton Rouge, LA 70802; tel. (504) 383-1111; f. 1925; morning; Publr DOUGLAS L. MANSHIP; Editor JAMES H. HUGHES; Ind.; circ. Mon. to Sat. 79,361, Sun. 134,557.

Morning Advocate: 525 Lafayette St, Baton Rouge, LA 70802; tel. (504) 383-1111; f. 1904; morning; Publr and Editor DOUGLAS L. MANSHIP; circ. Mon. to Sat. 79,361, Sun. 134,557.

New Orleans Times-Picayune/States-Item: 3800 Howard Ave, New Orleans, LA 70140; tel. (504) 826-3448; f. 1880; Mon. to Fri. all day, Sat. and Sun. morning; Publr ASHTON PHELPS, Jr; Editor CHARLES A. FERGUSON; Ind.-Dem.; circ. 278,248.

News-Star World: POB 1502, Monroe, LA 71210; tel. (318) 322-5161; f. 1909; morning; Publr and Editor BODIE MCCRORY; circ. Mon. to Sat. 37,190, Sun. 48,068.

Shreveport Journal: 222 Lake St, POB 31110, Shreveport, LA 71130; tel. (318) 459-3200; f. 1896; Mon. to Sat.; evening; Publr CHARLES BEAIRD; Editor STANLEY R. TINER; circ. 23,616.

State Times: 525 Lafayette St, Baton Rouge, LA 70802; tel. (504) 383-1111; f. 1842; Mon. to Sat.; evening; Publr and Editor DOUGLAS L. MANSHIP; circ. 29,911.

The Times: 222 Lake St, POB 30222, Shreveport, LA 71130-0222; tel. (318) 459-3200; f. 1872; morning; Pres. and Publr W. HOWARD BRONSON, Jr; Editor FRANK SUTHERLAND; circ. Mon. to Fri. 77,082, Sun. 110,043.

Maine

Bangor News: 491 Main St, Bangor, ME 04401; tel. (207) 942-4881; f. 1834; Mon. to Sat.; morning; Publr and Editor RICHARD J. WARREN; Ind.; circ. Mon. to Fri. 77,795, Sat. 93,674.

Maine Sunday Telegram: 390 Congress St, POB 1460, Portland, ME 04104; tel. (207) 775-5811; f. 1887; Sun.; Publr JEAN GANNETT HAWLEY; Editor JOHN K. MURPHY; circ. 137,273.

Portland Press Herald: 390 Congress St, POB 1460, Portland, ME 04104; tel. (207) 775-5811; f. 1862; Mon. to Sat.; morning; Publr JEAN GANNETT HAWLEY; Editor JOHN K. MURPHY; circ. 62,183.

Sun: Lewiston Sun-Journal/Sunday, 104 Park St, Lewiston, ME 04240; tel. (207) 784-5411; f. 1893; morning; circ. 35,826.

Maryland

Baltimore Sun: 501 North Calvert St, Baltimore, MD 21278; tel. (301) 332-6000; f. 1837; Mon. to Fri. all day, Sat. and Sun. morning; Publr REG MURPHY; Man. Editors JAMES I. HOUCK, JOHN M. LEMMON; circ. Mon. to Fri. morning 223,334, Mon. to Fri. evening 187,304, Sat. 373,390, Sun. 489,771.

The Capital: 2000 Capital Dr., POB 911, Annapolis, MD 21404; tel. (301) 268-5000; f. 1884; Mon. to Sat. evening, Sun. morning; Publr PHILIP MERRILL; Editor EDWARD D. CASEY; circ. Mon. to Sat. 41,926, Sun. 42,180.

Montgomery Journal: Two Research Ct, Rockville, MD 20850-3285; tel. (703) 750-8100; f. 1973; Mon. to Fri.; morning; Publr GEOFFREY H. EDWARDS; Editor ED MILLER; circ. 40,086.

Prince George's Journal: The Journal Newspapers, 9410 Annapolis Rd, Lanham, MD 20706; tel. (703) 750-8100; f. 1975; Mon. to Fri.; morning; Publr GEOFFREY H. EDWARDS; Editor LINDA SEARLING; circ. 39,000.

Massachusetts

Berkshire Eagle: 33 Eagle St, Pittsfield, MA 01201; tel. (413) 447-7311; f. 1889; morning; Publr and Editor LAWRENCE K. MILLER; circ. 33,591.

Boston Globe: 135 Morrissey Blvd, Boston, MA 02107; tel. (617) 929-2000; f. 1872; Mon. to Fri. all day, Sat. and Sun. morning; Publr WILLIAM O. TAYLOR; Editor JOHN S. DRISCOLL; circ. Mon. to Fri. 500,106, Sat. 453,599, Sun. 798,118.

Boston Herald: One Herald Sq., Boston, MA 02106; tel. (617) 426-3000; telex 940005; f. 1825; morning; Publr PATRICK PURCELL; Editor KENNETH A. CHANDLER; Ind.; circ. Mon. to Fri. 355,494, Sat. 277,507, Sun. 265,548.

Cape Cod Times: Dow Jones/Ottaway, 319 Main St, Hyannis, MA 02601; tel. (617) 775-1200; f. 1936; morning; Publr SCOTT HIMSTEAD; Editor WILLIAM BREISKY; circ. Mon. to Sat. 414,188, Sun. 52,499.

Christian Science Monitor: 1 Norway St, Boston, MA 02115; tel. (617) 262-2300; telex 174188; f. 1908; Mon. to Fri. morning; Editor RICHARD J. CATTANI; Ind.; circ. 186,195.

The Enterprise: 60 Main St, Brockton, MA 02403; tel. (617) 586-6200; f. 1880; Mon. to Fri. evening, Sat. and Sun. morning; Publr M. F. FULLER; Exec. Editor BRUCE P. SMITH; Ind.; circ. Mon. to Fri. 58,248, Sat. 57,569, Sun. 64,038.

The Gazette: 20 Franklin St, Worcester, MA 01613-0666; tel. (617) 793-9100; f. 1866; Mon. to Sat.; evening; Editor KENNETH J. BOTTY; circ. 81,029.

Herald News: 207 Pocasset St, Fall River, MA 02722; tel. (617) 676-8211; f. 1872; Mon. to Fri. evening, Sat. and Sun. morning; Publr EDWARD F. ST JOHN; Editor PAUL BERNIER; circ. Mon. to Sat. 37,708, Sun. 37,162.

Lawrence Eagle-Tribune: 100 Turnpike St, North Andover, MA 01845; tel. (508) 685-1000; f. 1868; Mon. to Fri. evening, Sat. and Sun morning; Publr IRVING E. ROGERS, Jr; Editor DANIEL WARNER; circ. Mon. to Sat. 56,596, Sun. 59,377.

Lowell Sun: 15 Kearney Sq., Lowell, MA 01852; tel. (617) 458-7100; f. 1878; Mon. to Sat. evening, Sun. morning; Pres. JOHN H. COSTELLO; Editor JOHN H. COSTELLO, Jr; Ind.; circ. Mon. to Sat. 56,564, Sun. 55,463.

Middlesex News: 33 New York Ave, POB 800, Framingham, MA 01701-8880; tel. (508) 626-3800; f. 1897; Mon. to Fri. evening, Sat. and Sun. morning; Publr JAMES HOPSON; Editor KENNETH O'HARTNET; circ. Mon. to Sat. 46,663, Sun. 51,907.

Patriot Ledger: 13–19 Temple St, Quincy, MA 02169; tel. (617) 786-7000; f. 1837; Mon. to Fri. evening, Sat. morning; Publr K. PRESCOTT LOW; Editor WILLIAM B. KETTER; Ind.; circ. Mon. to Fri. 89,840, Sat. 96,977.

Salem Evening News: Salem News Publishing Co, 155 Washington St, Salem, MA 01970; tel. (508) 744-0600; f. 1880; Mon. to Sat.; evening; Publr and Editor CYRUS J. NEWBEGIN; circ. 30,916.

Sentinel Enterprise: 808 Main St, Fitchburg, MA 01420; tel. (617) 343-6911; f. 1838; Mon. to Sat.; evening; Publr JOSEPH DRYDEN; Editor GORDON NEWELL; circ. 22,026.

Springfield Republican: 1860 Main St, Springfield, MA 01102; tel. (413) 788-1212; f. 1878; Sun.; Publr DAVID STARR; Editor ARNOLD FRIEDMAN; circ. 155,677.

Springfield Union–News: 1860 Main St, Springfield, MA 01102; tel. (413) 788-1212; f. 1864; Mon. to Sat.; all day; Publr DAVID STARR; Editor ARNOLD FRIEDMAN; circ. 111,931.

Standard-Times: Standard-Times Publishing Co, 555 Pleasant St, New Bedford, MA 02742; tel. (508) 997-7411; f. 1850; Mon. to Fri. evening, Sat. and Sun. morning; Publr ORREN B. ROBBINS; Editor JAMES M. RAGSDALE; circ. Mon. to Sat. 46,881, Sun. 51,091.

Transcript-Telegram: 120 Whiting Farms Rd, Holyoke, MA 01040; tel. (413) 536-2300; f. 1882; Mon. to Fri. evening, Sat. morning; Publr and Editor TOM SCHUMAKER; circ. 24,367.

Worcester Telegram: 20 Franklin St, Worcester, MA 01613-0666; tel. (617) 793-9100; f. 1884; morning; Publr ROBERT C. ACHORN; Editor KENNETH J. BOTTY; circ. Mon. to Sat. 58,199, Sun. 127,951..

Michigan

Ann Arbor News: 340 East Huron Street, Ann Arbor, MI 48104; tel. (313) 994-6989; f. 1835; Mon. to Fri. evening, Sat. and Sun. morning; Publr TIMOTHY O. WHITE; Editor BRIAN S. MALONE; circ. Mon. to Sat. 49,910, Sun. 59,114.

Citizen Patriot: 214 South Jackson St, Jackson, MI 49204; tel. (517) 787-2300; f. 1837; Mon. to Fri. evening, Sat. and Sun. morning; Publr F. T. WEAVER; Editor ROBERT D. LUDWIG; circ. Mon. to Sat. 38,187, Sun. 42,330.

Daily Tribune: 210 East Third St, Royal Oak, MI 48068; tel. (313) 541-3000; f. 1902; Mon. to Fri. evening, Sat. morning; Publr JEANNE TOWAR; Editor JAMES SNEDDON; circ. 39,501.

Detroit Free Press: 321 West Lafayette Blvd, Detroit, MI 48226; tel. (313) 222-6400; f. 1831; morning; Publr DAVID LAWRENCE, Jr; Editor JOE H. STROUD; Ind.; circ. Mon. to Fri. 639,720, Sat. 575,093, Sun. 724,342.

Detroit News: 615 Lafayette Blvd, Detroit, MI 48231; tel. (313) 222-2095; f. 1873; Mon. to Sat. all day, Sun. morning; Pres. and Publr LOUIS A. WEIL, III; Exec. Editor ROBERT H. GILES; Ind.; circ. Mon. to Fri. 686,787, Sat. 633,779, Sun. 837,511.

Enquirer: 155 West Van Buren St, Battle Creek, MI 49016; tel. (616) 964-7161; f. 1900; Mon. to Fri. evening, Sat. and Sun. morning; Publr R. B. MILLER, Jr; Editor AAVIL SMITH; circ. Mon. to Fri. 29,419, Sat. 28,928, Sun. 38,077.

Flint Journal: 200 East First St, Flint, MI 48502; tel. (313) 766-6100; f. 1876; Mon. to Fri. evening, Sat. and Sun. morning; Publr DANNY R. GAYDOU; Editor ALFRED L. PELOQUIN; Ind.; circ. Mon. to Fri. 112,161, Sat. 109,137, Sun. 123,792.

Grand Rapids Press: 155 Michigan St, NW, Grand Rapids, MI 49503; tel. (616) 459-1400; f. 1892; Mon. to Fri. evening, Sat. and Sun. morning; Editor MICHAEL S. LLOYD; Ind.; circ. Mon. to Sat. 136,511, Sun. 182,388.

Herald Palladium: 3450 Hollywood Rd, POB 128, St Joseph, MI 49085; tel. (616) 429-2400; f. 1919; Mon. to Sat.; evening; Publr W. J. BANYON; circ. 36,733.

Kalamazoo Gazette: 401 South Burdick St, Kalamazoo, MI 49003; tel. (616) 345-3511; f. 1883; Mon. to Sat. evening, Sun. morning; Publr DANIEL M. RYAN; Editor JAMES R. MOSBY, Jr; Ind.; circ. Mon. to Sat. 63,416, Sun. 75,945.

Lansing State Journal: 120 East Lenawee St, Lansing, MI 48919; tel. (616) 487-4611; f. 1855; morning; Publr MALCOLM W. APPLEGATE; Editor EDWARD MANASSAH; Ind.-Rep.; circ. Mon. to Sat. 64,883, Sun. 83,982.

Macomb Daily: Macomb Daily Bldg, 67 Cass Ave, POB 707, Mount Clemens, MI 48046; tel. (313) 469-4510; f. 1860; Mon. to Sat. evening, Sat. morning; Publr J. GENE CHAMBERS; Editors MITCH KEHEMAN, MAURICE VINCENT; circ. 50,021.

Monroe Evening News: Monroe Publishing Co, 20 West First, POB 1176, Monroe, MI 48161; tel. (313) 242-1100; f. 1825; Mon. to Fri. evening, Sat. morning; Publr GRATTAN GRAY; Editor STEVE GRAY; circ. 27,374.

Muskegon Chronicle/The Sunday Chronicle: 981 Third St, POB 59, Muskegon, MI 49443; tel. (616) 722-3161; f. 1857; Mon. to Fri. evening, Sat. and Sun. morning; Publr GARY OSTROM; Editor D. GUNNAR CARLSON; circ. Mon. to Sat. 47,611, Sun. 51,742.

Oakland Press: 48 West Huron St, POB 9, Pontiac, MI 48056; tel. (313) 332-8181; f. 1843; Mon. to Fri. evening, Sat. and Sun. morning; Publr BRUCE H. MCINTYRE; Editor NEIL J. MUNRO; Ind.; circ. Mon. to Fri. 71,227, Sat. 70,361, Sun. 79,034.

Saginaw News: 203 South Washington Ave, Saginaw, MI 48605; tel. (517) 752-7171; f. 1859; Mon. to Fri. evening, Sat. and Sun. morning; Publr DAVID D. WIERMAN; Editor PAUL CHAFFEE; Ind.; circ. Mon. to Sat. 57,133, Sun. 63,558.

Times: 311 Fifth St, Bay City, MI 48708-5853; tel. (517) 895-8551; f. 1872; Mon. to Fri. evening, Sat. and Sun. morning; Publr REX H. THATCHER; Editor ROBERT H. LONGSTAFF; circ. Mon. to Sat. 38,803, Sun. 47,374.

Times Herald: 911 Military, Port Huron, MI 48060; tel. (313) 985-7171; f. 1872; evening, Sat. and Sun. morning; Publr DAW A. MARTIN; Editor GORDON T. WELLER; circ. Mon. to Sat. 27,442, Sun. 32,239.

Minnesota

Duluth News-Tribune: 424 West First St, POB 169000, Duluth, MN 55816-9000; tel. (218) 723-5281; f. 1892; daily (except Sat.); morning; Publr JAMES V. GELS; Editor ROBERT W. JODON; Ind.; circ. Mon. to Fri. 65,000, Sun. 82,000.

Post-Bulletin: 18 First Ave, SE, Rochester, MN 55903-6118; tel. (507) 284-2511; f. 1892; Mon. to Sat.; evening; Publr and Editor WILLIAM BOYNE; circ. Mon. to Fri. 38,680, Sat. 41,110.

Star Tribune: 425 Portland Ave, Minneapolis, MN 55488; tel. (612) 372-4141; telex 506387; f. 1867; morning; Publr ROGER P. PARKINSON; Exec. Editor JOEL R. KRAMER; Man. Editor TIM J. MCGUIRE; Ind.; circ. Mon. to Sat. 382,832, Sun. 625,504.

St Paul Pioneer Press and Dispatch: 345 Cedar St, St Paul, MN 55101; tel. (612) 222-5011; f. 1849; Mon. to Fri. evening, Sat. and Sun. morning; Publr JOHN T. HENRY; Exec. Editor JOHN R. FINNEGAN; Ind.; circ. Mon. to Fri. 188,488, Sat. 175,135, Sun. 247,492.

Mississippi

Clarion-Ledger: 311 East Pearl St, Jackson, MS 39205; tel. (601) 961-7000; f. 1837; Mon. to Fri.; morning; Publr KENNETH W. ANDREWS; Editor JOHN JOHNSON; circ. 68,296.

Clarion Ledger-News: 311 East Pearl St, Jackson, MS 39205; tel. (601) 961-7000; f. 1954; Sat. and Sun.; Editor JOHN JOHNSON; circ. Sat. 96,286, Sun. 114,820.

Hattiesburg American: 825 North Main St, POB 1111, Hattiesburg, MS 39401; tel. (601) 582-4321; f. 1907; Mon. to Fri. evening, Sat. and Sun. morning; Publr SANDRA BAKER; Editor G. EDWARD BAKER; circ. Mon. to Sat. 24,742, Sun. 27,951.

Jackson Daily News: 311 East Pearl St, Jackson, MS 39205; tel. (601) 961-7000; f. 1892; evening; Publr KENNETH W. ANDREWS; Editor JOHN JOHNSON; circ. 31,843.

Northeast Mississippi Daily Journal: Journal Publishing Co, POB 909, Tupelo, MS 38801; tel. (601) 842-2611; f. 1870; morning; Publr GENE ROBERTS; Editor TOM PITTMAN; circ. 36,542.

Star: 814 22nd Ave, POB 1591, Meridian, MS 39301; tel. (601) 693-1551; f. 1879; Mon. to Sat. evening, Sun. morning; Publr JAMES B. SKEWES; Editor JIM WYNN; circ. Mon. to Sat. 25,951, Sun. 26,528.

Sun Herald: Gulf Publishing Co Inc, POB 4567, Biloxi, MS 39535-4567; tel. (601) 896-2100; f. 1884; morning; Publr ROLAND WEEKS, Jr; Exec. Editor PIC FIRMIN; circ. Mon. to Sat. 48,984, Sun. 51,149.

Missouri

Globe: 117 East Fourth St, Joplin, MO 64801; tel. (417) 623-3480; f. 1896; morning; Publr RICHARD P. BARKER; Editor JAMES R. ELLIS; circ. Mon. to Sat. 37,024, Sun. 45,340.

Kansas City Times: 1729 Grand Ave, Kansas City, MO 64108; tel. (816) 234-4141; f. 1868; Mon. to Sat.; morning; Publr JAMES H. HALE; Editor JOE MCGUFF; circ. Mon. to Fri. 285,962, Sat. 314,095.

Kansas City Star: 1729 Grand Ave, Kansas City, MO 64108; tel. (816) 234-4141; f. 1880; Mon. to Fri. evening, Sun. morning; Editor JOE MCGUFF; circ. Mon. to Fri. 195,644, Sun. 436,241.

News-Leader: 651 Boonville Ave, Springfield, MO 65801; tel. (417) 836-1100; f. 1890; morning; Publr BRUCE Q. MACKEY; Editor BILL SOUTHERLAND; circ. Mon. to Sat. 61,500, Sun. 100,200.

St Joseph Gazette: Ninth and Edmond Stations, St Joseph, MO 65402; tel. (816) 279-5671; f. 1845; Mon. to Sat.; morning; Publr HENRY H. BRADLEY; Editor DAVID R. BRADLEY, Jr; circ. 44,098.

St Louis Post-Dispatch: 900 North Tucker Blvd, St Louis, MO 63101; tel. (314) 622-7000; f. 1878; morning; Chair. JOSEPH PULITZER, Jr; Ind.; circ. Mon. to Fri. 357,314, Sat. 316,161, Sun. 548,955.

Montana

Billings Gazette: 401 North Broadway, POB 2507, Billings, MT 59103; tel. (406) 657-1200; f. 1885; morning; Publr WAYNE SCHILE; Editor RICHARD J. WESNICK; circ. Mon. to Sat. 57,620, Sun. 60,144.

Great Falls Tribune: Cowles Media, 205 River Dr. South, POB 5468, Great Falls, MT 59403; tel. (406) 761-6666; f. 1885; morning; Publr STEVEN A. STUDT; Editor TERRY DWYER; circ. Mon. to Sat. 34,943, Sun. 41,537.

Missoulian: Lee Enterprises, POB 8029, Missoula, MT 59807; tel. (406) 721-5200; f. 1873; morning; Publr PHIL BLAKE; Editor BRAD HURD; circ. Mon. to Sat. 28,240, Sun. 29,625.

Nebraska

Journal: Journal Star Printing Co, 926 P St, Lincoln, NE 68508; tel. (402) 475-4200; f. 1867; Mon. to Sat.; evening; Editor GARY SEACREST; circ. 43,781.

Omaha World-Herald: World-Herald Sq., Omaha, NE 68102; tel. (402) 444-1000; f. 1885; Mon. to Sat. all day, Sun. morning; Editor G. WOODSON HOWE; Ind.; circ. Mon. to Fri. morning 120,062, Mon. to Fri. evening 101,991, Sat. 212,243, Sun. 290,197.

Star: Journal Star Printing Co, 926 P St, Lincoln, NE 68508; tel. (402) 475-4200; Mon. to Sat.; morning; Editor TOM WHITE; circ. 36,818.

Nevada

Gazette Journal: POB 22000, Reno, NV 89520-2000; tel. (702) 788-6200; f. 1870; morning; Publr SUE CLARK-JACKSON; Editor EV LANDERS; circ. Mon. to Fri. 61,962, Sun. 75,897.

Las Vegas Review-Journal: 1111 West Bonanza, POB 70, Las Vegas, NV 89101; tel. (702) 383-0211; f. 1908; Mon. to Fri. all day, Sat. and Sun. morning; Publr DONALD W. REYNOLDS; Editor THOMAS KEEVIL; circ. Mon. to Fri. 114,269, Sat. 107,638, Sun. 135,407.

Las Vegas Sun: POB 4275, Las Vegas, NV 89127; tel. (702) 385-3111; f. 1950; morning; Publr and Editor H. M. GREENSPUN; Ind.; circ. 71,467.

New Hampshire

New Hampshire Sunday News: 35 Amherst St, POB 780, Manchester, NH 03105; tel. (603) 668-4321; f. 1946; Sun.; Publr NACKEY S. LOEB; Editor J. W. McQUAID; circ. 86,283.

Union Leader: 35 Amherst St, POB 780, Manchester, NH 03105; tel. (603) 668-4321; f. 1862; Mon. to Sat.; morning; Publr NACKEY S. LOEB; Editor J. W. McQUAID; circ. 68,718.

New Jersey

Asbury Park Press: 3601 Highway 66, POB 1550, Neptune, NJ 07754; tel. (201) 922-6000; f. 1879; Mon. to Sat. evening, Sun. morning; Publr JULES L. PLANGERE, Jr; Editor E. DONALD LASS; Ind.; circ. Mon. to Sat. 139,954, Sun. 205,007.

Burlington Country Times: Route 130, Willingboro, NJ 08046; tel. (609) 871-8000; f. 1958; Mon. to Fri. evening, Sun. morning; Publr JOSEPH A. BROWNE; Editor BILL NEWILL; circ. Mon. to Fri. 41,662, Sun. 47,406.

Courier-News: 1201 Highway 22 West, POB 6600, Bridgewater, NJ 08807; tel. (201) 722-8800; f. 1884; Mon. to Fri. evening, Sat. and Sun. morning; Publr FRED FOSTER; Exec. Editor CHARLES W. NUTT, Jr; Ind.; circ. 52,000.

Courier-Post: 301 Cuthbert Blvd, POB 5300, Cherry Hill, NJ 08034; tel. (609) 663-6000; f. 1875; Mon. to Fri. evening, Sat. and Sun. morning; Publr ROBERT T. COLLINS; Ind.; circ. Mon. to Fri. 104,565, Sat. 100,583, Sun. 99,386.

Daily Record: 629 Parsippany Rd, Parsippany, NJ 07054; tel. (201) 428-6200; f. 1900; morning; Publr and Editor NORMAN B. TOMLINSON, Jr; circ. Mon. to Fri. 60,243, Sat. 57,795, Sun. 72,150.

Dispatch: 409 39th St, Union City, NJ 07087; tel. (201) 863-2000; f. 1873; Mon. to Sat.; morning; Publr RICHARD J. VEZZA; Editor BERT WALTER; circ. 32,496.

Home News: 123 How Lane, POB 551, New Brunswick, NJ 08903; tel. (201) 246-5500; f. 1879; Mon. to Sat. evening, Sun. morning; Publr WILLIAM M. BOYD; Editor WATSON SIMS; Ind.; circ. Mon. to Sat. 59,052, Sun. 74,657.

Jersey Journal: 30 Journal Sq., Jersey City, NJ 07306; tel. (201) 653-1000; f. 1867; Mon. to Sat.; evening; Editor AUGUST LOCKWOOD; Ind.; circ. Mon. to Fri. 59,193, Sat. 56,936.

Journal: 295 North Broad St, Elizabeth, NJ 07207; tel. (201) 354-5000; f. 1779; evening; Sat. morning; Publr CHARLES PETTIT; Editor PHIL READ.

News: 988 Main Ave, POB 988, Passaic, NJ 07055; tel. (201) 365-3000; f. 1890; Mon. to Sat.; morning; Publr CHARLES JACOBS; Editor RAY BODE; circ. Mon. to Fri. 45,021, Sat. 44,569.

The Press: 1900 Atlantic Ave, Atlantic City, NJ 08404; tel. (609) 345-1234; f. 1895; morning; Publr and Editor CHARLES C. REYNOLDS; Ind.; circ. Mon. to Sat. 78,000, Sun. 87,000.

The Record: 150 River St, Hackensack, NJ 07602; tel. (201) 646-4000; telex 9905275; f. 1895; Mon. to Fri. evening, Sun. morning; Publr MALCOLM A. BORG; Exec. Editor ROBERT COMSTOCK; Ind.; circ. Mon. to Fri. 159,151, Sun. 231,030.

Star-Ledger: Star-Ledger Plaza, Newark, NJ 07101; tel. (201) 877-4141; f. 1917; morning; Publr MARTIN BARTNER; Editor MORT PYE; Ind.; circ. Mon. to Fri. 461,080, Sat. 416,492, Sun. 681,802.

The Times: 500 Perry St, POB 847, Trenton, NJ 08605; tel. (609) 396-3232; f. 1882; morning; Publr RICHARD BILOTTI; Exec. Editor LINDA CUNNINGHAM; Ind.; circ. Mon. to Sat. 65,474, Sun. 84,117.

Trentonian: Southard and Perry Sts, Trenton, NJ 08602; tel. (609) 989-7800; f. 1946; morning; Publr EDWARD L. HOFFMAN; Editor EMIL G. SLABODA; Ind.; circ. Mon. to Sat. 68,532, Sat. 66,272, Sun. 65,582.

New Mexico

Albuquerque Journal: 7777 Jefferson, NE, Albuquerque, NM 87109-4343; tel. (505) 823-7777; f. 1880; morning; Publr T. H. LANG; Editor GERALD J. CRAWFORD; circ. Mon. to Sat. 105,182, Sun. 143,166.

Albuquerque Tribune: 7777 Jefferson St, NE, Albuquerque, NM 87109; tel. (505) 823-3600; f. 1922; Mon. to Fri.; evening; Publr T. H. LANG; Editor TIM GALLAGHER; circ. 44,853.

New York

Albany Times Union: News Plaza, POB 15000, Albany, NY 12212; tel. (518) 454-5694; f. 1856; morning; Publr JOSEPH T. LYONS; Editor HARRY M. ROSENFELD; Ind.; circ. Mon. to Sat. 89,049, Sun. 176,080.

Binghamton Press/Sun Bulletin: Vestal Parkway East, Binghamton, NY 13902; tel. (607) 798-1234; f. 1904; Publr DAVID J. MACK; Editor LOU ZIEGLER; Ind.; circ. Mon. to Sat. 66,187, Sun. 88,486.

The Buffalo News: 1 News Plaza, POB 100, Buffalo, NY 14240; tel. (716) 849-3434; f. 1880; Mon. to Fri. all day; Sat. and Sun. morning; Publr STANFORD LIPSEY; Editor MURRAY B. LIGHT; Ind.; circ. Mon. to Fri. 315,252, Sat. 286,158, Sun. 378,485.

Democrat and Chronicle: 55 Exchange Blvd, Rochester, NY 14614; tel. (716) 232-7100; f. 1883; morning; Editor BARBARA HENRY; circ. Mon. to Fri. 128,869, Sat. 188,062, Sun. 256,933.

Herald Journal: Clinton Sq., POB 4915, Syracuse, NY 13221; tel. (315) 470-0011; f. 1877; Mon. to Sat.; evening; Editor TIMOTHY BUNN; circ. 101,980.

Post-Standard: Clinton Sq., POB 4915, Syracuse, NY 13221; tel. (315) 470-0011; f. 1829; Mon. to Sat.; morning; Publr STEPHEN A. ROGERS; Editor ROBERT C. ATKINSON; circ. 84,877.

Post-Star: Lawrence and Cooper Sts, Glens Falls, NY 12801; tel. (518) 792-3131; f. 1904; morning; Publr JIM MARSHALL; Editor MARK BEHAN; circ. 35,980.

Poughkeepsie Journal: Poughkeepsie Newspapers Inc, 85 Civic Center Plaza, Poughkeepsie, NY 12602; tel. (914) 454-2000; f. 1785; morning; Editor JOHN C. QUINN, Jr; circ. Mon. to Sat. 44,600, Sun. 61,400.

Press: 221 Oriskany Plaza, Utica, NY 13503; tel. (315) 797-9150; f. 1882; Mon. to Sat.; morning; Publr SAL DE VIVO; Editor DONNA HAGEMANN; circ. Mon. to Fri. 36,299, Sat. 53,190.

Rochester Times-Union: 55 Exchange Blvd, Rochester, NY 14614; tel. (716) 232-6920; tel. (716) 232-7100; f. 1826; Mon. to Fri.; evening; Publr VINCENT E. SPEZZANO; Editor BARBARA HENRY; circ. 99,500.

Schenectady Gazette: 332 State St, Schenectady, NY 12301; tel. (518) 374-4141; f. 1894; Mon. to Sat.; morning; Man. Editor JOHN E. N. HUME, III; Ind.; circ. 71,674.

Star-Gazette: 201 Baldwin St, POB 285, Elmira, NY 14902-9976; tel. (607) 734-5151; f. 1853; morning; Publr JANET R. KRAUSE; Editor RICHARD O. PRICE; circ. Mon. to Sat. 36,557, Sun. 50,620.

Times Herald-Record: 40 Mulberry St, Middletown, NY 10940; tel. (914) 343-2181; f. 1956; morning; Publr JOHN VAN KLEECK; Editor E. CURTISS PIERSON; circ. Mon. to Sat. 86,265, Sun. 99,956.

Times Record: 501 Broadway, Troy, NY 12181; tel. (518) 272-2000; f. 1974; evening; Publr HARRY R. HORVITZ; Editor ROLAND BLAIS; circ. Mon. to Sat. 44,108, Sun. 46,106.

Watertown Daily Times: 260 Washington St, Watertown, NY 13601; tel. (315) 782-1000; f. 1861; Mon. to Fri. evening, Sat. and Sun. morning; Publr and Editor JOHN B. JOHNSON; circ. Mon. to Sat. 42,247, Sun. 37,573.

Yonkers Herald Statesman: Westchester Rockland Newspapers Inc, One Gannett Dr., White Plains, NY 10604; tel. (914) 694-9300; f. 1863; Mon. to Fri. evening, Sat. and Sun. morning; circ. Mon. to Sat. 213,767, Sun. 254,192.

NEW YORK CITY

El Diario/La Prensa: 143–155 Varick St, New York, NY 10013; tel. (212) 807-4600; f. 1913; daily (except Sat.) morning; Publr CARLOS D. RAMÍREZ; Editor MANUEL DEDIOS; circ. 70,000.

New York Daily News: 220 East 42nd St, New York, NY 10017; tel. (212) 210-2100; f. 1919; morning; Publr JAMES HOGE; Editor F. GILMAN SPENCER; Ind.; circ. Mon. to Fri. 1,278,118, Sat. 1,005,714, Sun. 1,631,688.

New York Post: 210 South St, New York, NY 10002; tel. (212) 815-8000; telex 125484; f. 1801; Mon. to Fri. all day, Sat. and Sun. morning; Publr PATRICK PURCELL; Exec. Editor ROGER WOOD; Ind.-Dem.; circ. Mon. to Fri. 740,123, Sat. 550,390, Sun. c. 400,000.

New York Times: 229 West 43rd St, New York, NY 10036; tel. (212) 556-1234; f. 1851; morning; Publr ARTHUR OCHS SULZBERGER; Exec. Editor MAX FRANKEL; Ind.; circ. Mon. to Fri. 1,056,924, Sat. 818,235, Sun. 1,645,060.

Newsday: 235 Pinelawn, Melville, NY 11747; tel. (516) 454-2020; f. 1940; morning; Editor ANTHONY MARRO; circ. Mon. to Fri. 689,389, Sat. 572,385, Sun. 703,555.

People's Daily World: 239 West 23rd St, New York, NY 10011; tel. (212) 924-2523; f. 1968; Mon. to Sat.; morning; Publr HERBERT APTHEKER; Editor MICHAEL ZAGARELL; circ. 60,000.

Staten Island Advance: 950 Fingerboard Rd, Staten Island, New York, NY 10305; tel. (212) 981-1234; f. 1886; Mon. to Sat. evening,

Sun. morning; Publr RICHARD E. DIAMOND; Editor LES TRAUT-MANN; Ind.-Dem.; circ. Mon. to Fri. 77,654, Sat. 75,394, Sun. 88,328.

Wall Street Journal: 200 Liberty St, New York, NY 10281; tel. (212) 416-2000; f. 1889; Mon. to Fri.; morning; Publr PETER R. KANN; Editor ROBERT BARTLEY; Ind.; circ. 2,026,276.

North Carolina

Charlotte Observer: 600 South Tryon St, POB 32188, Charlotte, NC 28232; tel. (704) 379-6300; f. 1886; morning; Publr ROLFE NEILL; Editor RICH OPPEL; Ind.; circ. Mon. to Sat. 218,501, Sun. 275,180.

Citizen: Asheville, NC 28802; tel. (704) 252-5611; f. 1870; Mon. to Fri.; morning; Publr RICHARD B. WYNNE; Editor LARRY POPE; circ. 47,698.

Daily Times-News: Freedom Family, 707 South Main St, POB 481, Burlington, NC 27215; tel. (919) 227-0131; f. 1887; Mon. to Fri. evening, Sat. and Sun. morning; Publr DAVID RUTLEDGE; Editor DAN BOLDEN; circ. Mon. to Fri. 29,335, Sat. 29,042, Sun. 30,810.

Enterprise: POB 1009, High Point, NC 27261; tel. (919) 881-5700; f. 1886; Mon. to Fri. evening, Sat. and Sun. morning; Publrs R. B. TERRY, Jr, J. P. RAWLEY; Editor JOE BROWN; circ. Mon. to Fri. 32,235, Sun. 32,823.

Fayetteville Observer: Fayetteville Publishing Co, 458 Whitfield St, POB 849, Fayetteville, NC 28302; tel. (919) 323-4848; Mon. to Fri.; evening; Publr RAMON L. YARBOROUGH; circ. 46,242.

Fayetteville Times: 458 Whitfield St, POB 849, Fayetteville, NC 23802; tel. (919) 323-4848; f. 1973; Mon. to Fri.; morning; Publr RAMON L. YARBOROUGH; Editor ROY PARKER, Jr; circ. 28,255.

Gazette: 2500 East Franklin Blvd, POB 1538, Gastonia, NC 28053; tel. (704) 864-3291; f. 1880; Mon. to Fri. evening, Sat. and Sun. morning; Publr JOHNATHON SEGAL; Editor BILL WILLIAMS; circ. Mon. to Sat. 40,408, Sun. 44,151.

Greensboro News and Record: 200 East Market St, POB 20848, Greensboro, NC 27420-0848; tel. (919) 373-7000; f. 1905; morning; Publr R. D. BENSON; Exec. Editor BEN J. BOWERS; Ind.; circ. Mon. to Sat. 112,424, Sun. 126,037.

Herald: Durham Herald Co Inc, 115 Market St, Durham, NC 27702; tel. (919) 682-8181; f. 1894; morning; Editor ROBERT C. ROULE; circ. Mon. to Sat. 46,324, Sun. 64,642.

News and Observer: 215 South McDowell St, Raleigh, NC 27602; tel. (919) 829-4500; f. 1865; morning; Publr FRANK DANIELS, Jr; Editorial Dir CLAUDE SITTON; Ind.-Dem.; circ. Mon. to Sat. 139,432, Sun. 182,891.

Raleigh Times: 215 South McDowell St, POB 191, Raleigh, NC 27602; tel. (919) 829-4500; f. 1879; Mon. to Sat.; evening; Publr FRANK DANIELS, Jr; Editor A. C. SNOW; circ. 34,234.

Star: POB 840, Wilmington, NC 28402; tel. (919) 343-2000; f. 1867; Mon. to Sat.; morning; Publr DON R. WHITWORTH; Editor CHARLES M. ANDERSON; circ. 46,848.

Winston-Salem Journal: 418 North Marshall St, POB 3159, Winston-Salem, NC 27102; tel. (919) 727-7394; f. 1897; morning; Publr JOE DOSTER; Man. Editor JOE GOODMAN; Ind.; circ. Mon. to Sat. 91,831, Sun. 103,219.

North Dakota

Bismarck Tribune: 707 East Front Ave, POB 1498, Bismarck, ND 58501; tel. (701) 223-2500; f. 1873; morning; Publr WILLIAM N. ROESGEN; Editor KEVIN GILES; circ. Mon. to Sat. 29,070, Sun. 28,599.

The Forum: 101 5th St, POB 2020, Fargo, ND 58107; tel. (701) 235-7311; f. 1878; morning; Publr WILLIAM C. MARCIL; Editor WILLIAM JOSEPH DILL; Ind.-Rep.; circ. Mon. to Sat. 54,957, Sun. 66,016.

Grand Forks Herald: POB 6008, Grand Forks, ND 58206-6008; tel. (701) 780-1100; f. 1879; morning; Publr MICHAEL MAIDENBERG; Editor MIKE JACOBS; circ. Mon. to Sat. 38,360, Sun. 39,291.

Minot Daily News: 301 Fourth St, SE, POB 1150, Minot, ND 58702; tel. (701) 852-3341; f. 1884; Mon. to Sat. evening, Sun. morning; Publr DONALD W. REYNOLDS; Editor STEPHEN TROSLEY; circ. Mon. to Sat. 26,833, Sun. 25,207.

Ohio

Akron Beacon Journal: 44 East Exchange St, Akron, OH 44328; tel. (216) 375-8111; f. 1839; morning; Publr JOHN M. MCMILLION; Editor DALE ALLEN; Ind.; circ. Mon. to Sat. 155,023, Sun. 225,741.

The Blade: 541 Superior St, Toledo, OH 43660; tel. (419) 245-6000; f. 1835; Mon. to Fri. evening, Sat. and Sun. morning; Publr WILLIAM BLOCK; Editor TOM WALTON; Ind.; circ. Mon. to Sat. 160,835, Sun. 219,293.

Canton Repository: 500 Market Ave South, Canton, OH 44702; tel. (216) 454-5611; f. 1815; Mon. to Fri. evening, Sat. and Sun. morning; Publr S. JOHN SIAM; Editor MICHAEL E. HANKE; Rep.; circ. Mon. to Sat. 58,451, Sun. 77,044.

Chronicle-Telegram: 225 East Ave, Elyria, OH 44036; tel. (216) 323-3321; f. 1829; Mon. to Sat. evening, Sun. morning; Publr ARTHUR D. HUDNUTT; circ. Mon. to Sat. 35,518, Sun. 35,611.

Cincinnati Enquirer: 617 Vine St, Cincinnati, OH 45201; tel. (513) 721-2700; f. 1841; morning; Publr JOHN P. ZANOTTI; Editor GEORGE R. BLAKE; Ind.; circ. Mon. to Sat. 191,645, Sun. 323,390.

Cincinnati Post: 125 East Court St, Cincinnati, OH 45202; tel. (513) 352-2000; f. 1881; Mon. to Fri. evening, Sat. morning; Editor PAUL F. KNUE; Ind.; circ. 115,718.

Cleveland Plain Dealer: 1801 Superior Ave, Cleveland, OH 44114; tel. (216) 344-4500; f. 1842; morning; Publr and Editor THOMAS VAIL; Ind.; circ. Mon. to Fri. 452,343, Sat. 552,401, Sun. 429,783.

Columbus Dispatch: 34 South Third St, Columbus, OH 43216; tel. (614) 461-5000; f. 1871; daily except Sat.; morning; Publr JOHN F. WOLFE; Editor LUKE FECK; Ind.; circ. Mon. to Fri. 257,638, Sun. 384,835.

Dayton Daily News: Fourth and Ludlow Sts, Dayton, OH 45401; tel. (513) 225-2085; f. 1808; morning; Publr BILL TILLSON; Editor MAX JENNINGS; circ. Mon. to Sat. 196,417, Sun. 228,680.

The Journal: 1657 Broadway, Lorain, OH 44052; tel. (216) 245-6901; f. 1879; Mon. to Fri. evening, Sat. and Sun. morning; Publr HARRY R. HORVITZ; Editor JOHN COLE; circ. Mon. to Sat. 44,200, Sun. 47,615.

Lake County News-Herald: 38879 Mentor Ave, POB 351, Willoughby, OH 44094; tel. (216) 951-0000; f. 1880; Mon. to Fri. evening, Sat. and Sun. morning; Publr JOSEPH A. COCOZZO; Editor JAMES K. COLLINS; circ. Mon. to Fri. 54,062, Sun. 61,739.

The Lima News: 121 East High Street, Lima, OH 45802; tel. (419) 223-1010; f. 1884; Mon. to Fri. evening, Sat. and Sun. morning; Publr F. WILLIAM POWER; Editor RON VARLAND; circ. Mon. to Sat. 40,890, Sun. 50,507.

News-Journal: 70 West Fourth St, Mansfield, OH 44903; tel. (419) 522-3311; f. 1885; Mon. to Fri. evening, Sat. and Sun. morning; Publr HARRY R. HORVITZ; Editor K. ROBERT MAY; circ. Mon. to Sat. 40,732, Sun. 54,775.

Springfield News-Sun: Springfield Newspapers Inc, 202 North Limestone St, Springfield, OH 45501; tel. (513) 328-0300; f. 1928; morning; Publr EDWARD W. O'NEIL, Jr; Editor NORM PEARSON; circ. Mon. to Sat. 37,045, Sun. 44,068.

Tribune Chronicle: 240 Franklin St, SE, Warren, OH 44482; tel. (216) 841-1600; f. 1812; Mon. to Fri. evening, Sat. and Sun. morning; Publr WILLIAM J. RUSH; Editor GERALD GUY; circ. Mon. to Sat. 41,398, Sun. 48,159.

The Vindicator: Vindicator Sq., POB 780, Youngstown, OH 44501-0780; tel. (216) 747-1471; f. 1868; Mon. to Sat. evening, Sun. morning; Publr and Editor BETTY H. BROWN JAGNOW; Ind.; circ. Mon. to Sat. 95,974, Sun. 146,849.

Oklahoma

Oklahoman: POB 25125, Oklahoma City, OK 73125; tel. (405) 232-3311; f. 1894; morning; Pres., Publr and Editor EDWARD L. GAYLORD; Ind.; circ. Mon. to Fri. 242,214, Sat. 228,551, Sun. 336,518.

Tulsa Tribune: 315 South Boulder Ave, POB 1770, Tulsa, OK 74102; tel. (918) 581-8400; fax (918) 584-1037; f. 1904; Mon. to Sat. evening; Publr JENKIN L. JONES; Editor JENK JONES, Jr.; Ind.; circ. 75,710.

Tulsa World: 315 South Boulder Ave, POB 1770, Tulsa, OK 74102; tel. (918) 581-8300; f. 1906; morning; Publr BYRON V. BOONE; Exec. Editor BOB HARING; Ind.; circ. Mon. to Sat. 131,816, Sun. 231,473.

Oregon

The Oregonian: 1320 SW Broadway, Portland, OR 97201; tel. (503) 221-8327; f. 1850; morning; Publr FRED A. STICKEL; Editor WILLIAM HILLIARD; circ. Mon. to Fri. 321,677, Sat. 312,448, Sun. 404,186.

The Register-Guard: 975 High St, POB 10188, Eugene, OR 97440; tel. (503) 485-1234; f. 1867; morning; Chair. EDWIN M. BAKER; Editor ALTON F. BAKER, III; Ind.; circ. Mon. to Sat. 69,551, Sun. 73,094.

Statesman Journal: 280 Church St, NE, POB 13009, Salem, OR 97309; tel. (503) 399-6611; f. 1851; morning; Publr WILLIAM STONE;

Editor WILLIAM FLORENCE; Ind.; circ. Mon. to Sat. 54,008, Sun. 57,580.

Pennsylvania

Altoona Mirror: 1000 Green Ave, Altoona, PA 16603; tel. (814) 946-7411; f. 1874; Mon. to Fri. evening, Sat. and Sun. morning; Publr ALBERT J. HOLTZINGER, II; Editor DAVID M. CUZZOLINA; circ. 34,038.

Beaver County Times: 400 Fair Ave, POB 400, Beaver, PA 15009; tel. (412) 775-3200; f. 1946; Mon. to Fri. evening, Sun. morning; Publr F. WALLACE GORDON; Editor LEONARD BROWN; circ. Mon. to Fri. 45,785, Sun. 50,594.

Bucks County Courier Times: Route 13, Levittown, PA 19057; tel. (215) 752-6701; f. 1954; daily (except Sat.); morning; Pres. GROVER J. FRIEND; Editor LEONARD R. BROWN; circ. Mon. to Fri. 64,061, Sun. 70,368.

Citizens' Voice: 75 North Washington St, Wilkes-Barre, PA 18711; tel. (717) 821-2091; f. 1978; Mon. to Sat.; morning; Publr ROBERT MANGANIELLO; Editor PAUL GOLIAS; circ. 48,199.

Daily Intelligencer: 333 North Broad Street, POB 858, Doylestown, PA 18901; tel. (215) 345-3000; f. 1804; daily (except Sat.); morning; Publr CHARLES P. SMITH; Editor JAMES P. MCFADDEN; circ. 41,750.

Daily Local News: Daily Local News Co, 250 North Bradford Ave, West Chester, PA 19382; tel. (215) 696-1776; f. 1872; Mon. to Sat. evening, Sun. morning; Publr MURRAY D. SCHWARTZ; Editor HANNAH GARDNER; circ. Mon. to Sat. 39,403, Sun. 39,837.

Daily Times: 500 Mildred Ave, Primos, PA 19018; tel. (215) 622-8800; f. 1876; daily (except Sat.); morning; Publr FRANK GOTHIE; Editor STUART ROSE; circ. Mon. to Fri. 61,884, Sun. 46,584.

Eagle: Eagle Printing Co Inc, 114 West Diamond St, Butler, PA 16001; tel. (412) 282-8000; f. 1869; Mon. to Sat.; evening; Editor JOHN LAING WISE, Jr; circ. 30,955.

Express: 30 North Fourth St, Easton, PA 18042; tel. (215) 258-7171; f. 1855; Mon. to Fri. evening, Sat. and Sun. morning; Publr HAL NEITZEL; Man. Editor BRUCE FRASSINELLI; circ. Mon. to Sat. 45,324, Sun, 47,349.

Harrisburg Patriot: 812 Market St, Harrisburg, PA 17105; tel. (717) 255-8100; f. 1854; Mon. to Sat.; morning; Publr RAYMOND L. GOVER; Editor RONALD MINARD; circ. Mon. to Fri. 50,425, Sat. 94,740.

Intelligencer Journal: Lancaster Newspapers Inc, 8 West King St, POB 1328, Lancaster, PA 17603; tel. (717) 291-8600; f. 1794; Mon. to Sat.; morning; Editor WILLIAM R. SCHULTZ; circ. 43,745.

Johnstown Tribune Democrat: 425 Locust St, Johnstown, PA 15907; tel. (412) 536-0711; f. 1853; morning; Publr RICHARD H. MAYER; Editor GEORGE FATTMAN; Ind.-Rep.; circ. Mon. to Sat. 50,836, Sun. 53,799.

Lancaster New Era: 8 West King St, POB 1328, Lancaster, PA 17603; tel. (717) 291-8600; f. 1877; Mon. to Sat.; evening; Editor ROBERT J. KOZAK; circ. 57,224.

Morning Call: POB 1260, Sixth and Linden Sts, Allentown, PA 18105; tel. (215) 820-6500; f. 1888; morning; Publr GARY K. SHORTS; Editor LAWRENCE HYMANS; circ. Mon. to Sat. 135,571, Sun. 179,334.

Observer-Reporter: Observer Publishing Co, 122 South Main St, Washington, PA 15301; tel. (412) 222-2200; f. 1808; morning; Publrs W. B. NORTHROP and JOHN L. S. NORTHROP; Editor JOHN E. CROUSE; circ. Mon. to Sat. 37,529, Sun. 33,202.

Philadelphia Daily News: 400 North Broad St, Philadelphia, PA 19101; tel. (215) 854-5905; f. 1925; Mon. to Sat.; evening; Editor ZACHARY STALBERG; circ. Mon. to Fri. 259,381, Sat. 177,900.

Philadelphia Inquirer: 400 North Broad St, Philadelphia, PA 19101; tel. (215) 854-2000; f. 1829; morning; Editor EUGENE ROBERTS, Jr; circ. Mon. to Sat. 508,496, Sun. 984,109.

Pittsburgh Post-Gazette/Sun Telegraph: 34 Blvd of the Allies, POB 957, Pittsburgh, PA 15230; tel. (412) 263-1100; f. 1786; Mon. to Sat.; morning; Publr WILLIAM BLOCK; Editor JOHN G. CRAIG, Jr; Ind.; circ. Mon. to Fri. 168,444, Sat. 155,546.

Pittsburgh Press: 34 Blvd of the Allies, Pittsburgh, PA 15230; tel. (412) 263-1100; f. 1884; Mon. to Sat. evening, Sun. morning; Editor ANGUS MCEACHRAN; Ind.; circ. Mon. to Fri. 232,887, Sat. 203,649, Sun. 564,569.

Reading Eagle: POB 582, Reading, PA 19603-0582; tel. (215) 373-4221; f. 1868; Mon. to Sat. evening, Sun. morning; Publr WILLIAM S. FLIPPIN; Editor EDWARD A. TAGGERT; circ. Mon. to Sat. 35,188, Sun. 111,638.

Reading Times: POB 582, Reading, PA 19603-0582; tel. (215) 373-4221; f. 1858; Mon. to Sat.; morning; Publr WILLIAM S. FLIPPIN; Editor EDWARD A. TAGGERT; circ. 44,950.

Scranton Times: 149 Penn Ave, POB 3311, Scranton, PA 18505; tel. (717) 348-9100; f. 1879; Mon. to Sat. evening, Sun. morning; Publr and Editor EDWARD J. LYNETT, Jr; Ind.; circ. Mon. to Sat. 58,397, Sun. 62,037.

Scranton Tribune: 338 North Washington Ave, Scranton, PA 18501; tel. (717) 344-7221; f. 1856; Mon. to Sat.; morning; Publr NELSON GOODMAN; Editor HAL LEWIS; circ. 37,935.

Sunday News: 8 West King St, POB 1328, Lancaster, PA 17603; f. 1923; Sun.; Editor DAVID M. HENNIGAN; circ. 98,121.

Sunday Patriot News: 812 Market St, Harrisburg, PA 17105; tel. (717) 255-8100; f. 1949; Sun.; Editor RONALD MINARD; circ. 166,444.

Times: 12th and Sassafrass St, POB 400, Erie, PA 16534; tel. (814) 456-8531; f. 1888; Mon. to Sat.; evening; Publrs EDWARD MEAD, MICHAEL MEAD; Editor LEN KHOLOS; circ. 43,024.

Times Herald: POB 591, Norristown, PA 19404; tel. (215) 272-2500; f. 1799; Mon. to Sat.; evening; Publr DAVID S. JOHN; Editor CARROLL SHELTON; circ. 31,821.

Tribune-Review: Tribune Review Bldg, Cabin Hill Dr., Greensburg, PA 15602; tel. (412) 834-1151; f. 1886; morning; Publr R. M. SCAIFE; Editor GEORGE BEIDLER; circ. Mon. to Sat. 51,857, Sun. 80,591.

York Daily Record: 1750 Industrial Highway, York, PA 17402; tel. (717) 757-4842; f. 1795; morning; Publr J. K. SPENCER; Editor SAM FOSDICK; circ. 40,446.

York Dispatch: 15–21 East Philadelphia St, York, PA 17401; tel. (717) 854-1575; f. 1876; Mon. to Fri. evening, Sat. morning; Publr JOHN L. REYNOLDS; Man. Editor PHILIP M. KLINEDINST; circ. 49,152.

Rhode Island

Call: 75 Main St, POB A, Woonsocket, RI 02895-0992; tel. (401) 762-3000; f. 1892; Mon. to Fri. evening, Sat. and Sun. morning; Publr and Editor PAUL A. LEBRECHE; circ. Mon. to Sat. 30,152, Sun. 29,631.

Evening Times: 23 Exchange St, POB 307, Pawtucket, RI 02860; tel. (401) 722-4000; f. 1885; Mon. to Sat.; evening; Publr RAYMOND H. LACAILLADE; Editor RANDALL SZYBA; circ. 26,676.

Providence Bulletin: 75 Fountain St, Providence, RI 02902-9985; tel. (401) 277-7000; f. 1863; Mon. to Fri.; evening; Editor CHARLES McC. HAUSER; circ. 110,180.

Providence Journal: 75 Fountain St, Providence, RI 02902-9985; tel. (401) 277-7000; f. 1829; daily (except Sat.); morning; Publr MICHAEL P. METCALF; Editor CHARLES McC. HAUSER; circ. Mon. to Fri. 93,578, Sun. 260,404.

South Carolina

Anderson Independent-Mail: 1000 Williamston Rd, POB 2507, Anderson, SC 29622; tel. (803) 224-4321; f. 1899; morning; Publr JOHN C. GINN; Editor BOB COCHNAR; circ. 42,453.

Evening Post: 134 Columbus St, Charleston, SC 29403-4800; tel. (803) 577-7111; f. 1894; Mon. to Fri. evening, Sat. and Sun. morning; Publr IVAN V. ANDERSON; Editor BARBARA S. WILLIAMS; circ. 39,000.

Greenville News: POB 1688, South Main St, Greenville, SC 29602; tel. (803) 298-4100; f. 1874; Mon. to Fri.; morning; Publr W. DE B. MEBANE; Editor JOHN S. PITTMAN; circ. 86,613.

Herald: POB 29731, Rock Hill, SC 29730; tel. (803) 329-4000; f. 1877; morning; Publr WAYNE T. PATRICK; Editor TERRY PLUMB; circ. Mon. to Sat. 27,129, Sun. 26,792.

Herald Journal: POB 1657, Herald Sq., Spartanburg, SC 29304; tel. (803) 582-4511; f. 1872; morning; Publr HUBERT HENDRIX; Editor RUDY RIVERS; circ. Mon. to Sat. 55,404, Sun. 59,294.

News: 141 South Irby St, POB 711, Florence, SC 29501; tel. (803) 669-1771; f. 1923; morning; Publr RICHARD G. MOISIO; Editor JOE B. RICKENBAKER; circ. Mon. to Sat. 30,937, Sun. 31,503.

The News and Courier: 134 Columbus St, POB 758, Charleston, SC 29403; tel. (803) 577-7111; f. 1803; morning; Publr HALL T. McGEE, Jr; Exec. Editor R. L. SCHREADLEY; Ind.; circ. Mon. to Fri. 73,427, Sat. 112,232, Sun. 120,131.

News-Piedmont: South Main St, POB 1688, Greenville, SC 29602; tel. (803) 298-4100; f. 1974; Sat. and Sun.; morning; Editor JOHN S. PITTMAN; circ. Sat. 112,519, Sun. 126,553.

The State: 1401 Shop Rd, Columbia, SC 29202; tel. (803) 771-6161; f. 1891; morning; Publr FRANK M. MCCOMAS; Exec. Editor THOMAS N. MCLEAN; Ind.; circ. Mon. to Sat. 140,000, Sun. 153,217.

Sun-News: Knight-Ridder, POB 406, Myrtle Beach, SC 29578-0406; tel. (803) 626-8555; f. 1936; morning; Publr J. MICHAEL PATE; Editor GIL THELEN; circ. Mon. to Sat. 31,379, Sun. 35,776.

South Dakota

Argus Leader: 200 South Minnesota Ave, POB 5034, Sioux Falls, SD 57117-5034; tel. (605) 331-2200; f. 1881; morning; Publr LARRY FULLER; Exec. Editor RICHARD N. THIEN; Ind.; circ. Mon. to Sat. 45,095, Sun. 64,842.

Rapid City Journal: POB 450, Rapid City, SD 57709; tel. (605) 342-0280; f. 1878; morning; Publr DAVID SHARP; Editor JOE KARIUS; circ. Mon. to Sat. 33,847, Sun. 36,715.

Tennessee

The Commercial Appeal: 495 Union Ave, Memphis, TN 38103; tel. (901) 529-2211; f. 1840; morning; Publr JOSEPH R. WILLIAMS; Editor DAVID W. BROWN; Ind.; circ. Mon. to Sat. 224,248, Sun. 295,623.

Journal: 210 West Church Ave, POB 911, Knoxville, TN 37901; tel. (615) 522-4141; f. 1839; Mon. to Sat. evening, Sun. morning; Editor RONALD D. McMAHAN; circ. 44,093.

Kingsport Times-News: 701 Lynn Gardens Dr., POB 479, Kingsport, TN 37662; tel. (615) 246-8121; f. 1920; Mon. to Fri. all day, Sat. and Sun. morning; Publr DAVID A. RAU; Editor TED COMO; circ. Mon. to Fri. 47,293, Sat. 45,587, Sun. 47,349.

Knoxville News-Sentinel: 204 West Church Ave, POB 59038, Knoxville, TN 37902-9038; tel. (615) 523-3131; f. 1886; morning; Editor HARRY MOSKOS; Ind.; circ. Mon. to Sat. 102,340, Sun. 163,108.

Nashville Banner: 1100 Broadway, Nashville, TN 37202; tel. (615) 259-8000; f. 1876; Mon. to Sat.; evening; Publr IRBY C. SIMPKINS; Man. Editor JOE WORLEY; Ind.; circ. 67,408.

News–Free Press: 400 East 11th St, POB 1447, Chattanooga, TN 37401; tel. (615) 756-6900; f. 1888; Mon. to Sat. evening, Sun. morning; Publr ROY McDONALD; Editor LEE S. ANDERSON; circ. Mon. to Fri. 58,351, Sat. 54,741, Sun. 115,695.

The Tennessean: 1100 Broadway, Nashville, TN 37202; tel. (615) 259-8000; f. 1812; morning; Publr JOHN SEIGENTHALER; Dem.; circ. Mon. to Sat. 119,120, Sun. 255,318.

Times: Times Printing Co, 117 East 10th St, POB 951, Chattanooga, TN 37401-0951; tel. (615) 756-1234; f. 1869; Mon. to Sat.; morning; Publr RUTH S. HOLMBERG; Editor PAUL NEELY; circ. 48,000.

Texas

Austin American-Statesman: 166 East Riverside Dr., Austin, TX 78704; tel. (512) 445-3500; f. 1871; morning; Publr ROGER KINTZEL; Editor ARNOLD ROSENFELD; Ind.; circ. Mon. to Fri. 166,919, Sat. 168,350, Sun. 203,790.

Beaumont Enterprise: 380 Walnut St, POB 3071, Beaumont, TX 77704; tel. (409) 833-3311; f. 1889; morning; Publr GEORGE B. IRISH; Editor BEN HANSEN; Ind.; circ. Mon. to Sat. 69,569, Sun. 79,640.

Corpus Christi Caller-Times: POB 9136, Corpus Christi, TX 78469; tel. (512) 884-2011; fax (512) 886-3777; f. 1883; morning; Publr EDWARD HARTE; Editor ROBERT E. RHODES; circ. Mon. to Sat. 70,085, Sun. 90,867.

Dallas Morning News: Communications Center, Dallas, TX 75265; tel. (214) 977-8222; f. 1885; morning; Pres. and Editor BURL OSBORNE; Ind.-Dem.; circ. Mon. to Sat. 390,987, Sun. 531,417.

Dallas Times Herald: 1101 Pacific Ave, Dallas, TX 75202; tel. (214) 720-6556; telex 732229; f. 1876; Mon. to Sat. all day, Sun. morning; Publr TOM JOHNSON; Editor WILL JARRETT; Ind.-Dem.; circ. Mon. to Sat. 246,370, Sun. 338,963.

El Paso Times: 401 Mills Ave, POB 20, El Paso, TX 79999; tel. (915) 546-6100; f. 1881; morning; Pres. HAROLD E. BURDICK; Editor BARBARA FUNKHOUSER; Ind.; circ. Mon. to Sat. 59,273, Sun. 94,266.

Fort Worth Star-Telegram: 400 West Seventh St, POB 1870, Fort Worth, TX 76101; tel. (817) 390-7400; f. 1895; Mon. to Fri. all day, Sat. and Sun. morning; Publr RICHARD L. CONNOR; Exec. Editor MIKE BLACKMAN; Ind.; circ. Mon. to Fri. morning 136,305, Mon. to Fri. evening 130,606, Sat. 265,013, Sun. 318,936.

Houston Chronicle: 801 Texas St, Houston, TX 77002; tel. (713) 220-7171; f. 1901; Mon. to Fri. all day, Sat. and Sun. morning; Editor-in-Chief PHIL WARNER; Ind.-Dem.; circ. Mon. to Sat. 408,084, Sun. 531,528.

Houston Post: POB 4747, Houston, TX 77210-4747; tel. (713) 840-5600; f. 1885; morning; Editor PETER O'SULLIVAN; Ind.; circ. Mon. to Sat. 314,581, Sun. 365,946.

Lubbock Avalanche-Journal: Eighth St and Ave J, POB 491, Lubbock, TX 79408; tel. (806) 762-8844; f. 1922; Mon. to Fri. all

day, Sat. and Sun. morning; Gen. Man. FRANK T. ANDERSON; Editor T. JAY HARRIS; Ind.-Dem.; circ. 70,883.

News: Ninth and Harrison Sts, POB 2091, Amarillo, TX 79166; tel. (806) 376-4488; f. 1909; Mon. to Sat.; morning; Publr JERRY HUFF; Editor GARET VON NETZER; circ. 44,147.

Reporter-News: POB 30, Abilene, TX 79604; tel. (915) 673-4271; f. 1881; morning; Publr A. B. SHELTON; Editor GLENN DROMGOOLE; circ. Mon. to Sat. 43,634, Sun. 55,564.

San Antonio Express-News: Ave E and Third St, San Antonio, TX 78205; tel. (512) 225-7411; f. 1864; all day; Publr and Editor CHARLES O. KILPATRICK; Ind.; circ. Mon. to Fri. 178,812, Sat. 188,620, Sun. 249,397.

San Antonio Light: McCullough and Broadway, POB 161, San Antonio, TX 78291; tel. (512) 271-2700; fax (512) 271-2800; f. 1881; Mon. to Fri. all day, Sat. and Sun. morning; Publr GEORGE B. IRISH; Exec. Editor TED WARMBOLD; Ind.; circ. Mon. to Sat. 142,050, Sun. 206,026.

Standard Times: Harte-Hanks Communications Inc, 34 West Harris Ave, San Angelo, TX 76903; tel. (915) 653-1221; f. 1884; morning; Publr KEVIN J. BARRY; Editor SOREN NIELSEN; circ. Mon. to Fri. 34,257, Sun. 40,506.

Texarkana Gazette: Texarkana Newspapers Inc, 315 Pine St, POB 621, Texarkana, TX 75504; tel. (214) 794-3311; f. 1875; morning; Editor LES MINOR; circ. Mon. to Sat. 33,275, Sun. 36,115.

Times Record News: Time Publishing Co Inc, POB 120, Wichita Falls, TX 76307; tel. (817) 767-8341; f. 1907; morning; Publr JAMES D. LONERGAN; Editor DON JAMES; circ. Mon. to Fri. 43,710, Sun. 50,145.

Tyler Morning Telegraph: POB 2030, Tyler, TX 75710; tel. (214) 597-8111; f. 1877; Mon. to Sat.; morning; Publr CALVIN CLYDE, Jr; Editor NELSON CLYDE; circ. 37,450.

Victoria Advocate: 311 East Constitution St, Victoria, TX 77901; tel. (512) 575-1451; f. 1846; morning; Publr JOHN M. ROBERTS; Editor JAMES RECH; circ. Mon. to Fri. 36,322, Sun. 37,652.

Waco Tribune-Herald: 900 Franklin Ave, Waco, TX 76702; tel. (817) 757-5757; f. 1911; morning; Publr RAYMOND R. PREDDY; Editor BOB LOTT; Ind.; circ. Mon. to Sat. 54,102, Sun. 69,211.

Wall Street Journal (SW Edition): Dow Jones and Co Inc, 1233 Regal Row, Dallas, TX 75247; tel. (214) 631-7250; f. 1948; Mon. to Fri.; morning; Editor ROBERT BARTLEY; circ. 218,819.

Utah

Desert News: 30 East First St South, POB 1257, Salt Lake City, UT 84110; tel. (801) 237-2100; f. 1850; Mon. to Fri. evening, Sat. and Sun. morning; Pres. and Publr WILLIAM JAMES MORTIMER; Man. Editor LaVARR WEBB; Ind.; circ. Mon. to Fri. 63,067, Sun. 71,412.

Ogden Standard-Examiner: 455 23rd St, Ogden, UT 84401; tel. (801) 394-7711; f. 1888; Mon. to Fri. evening, Sat. and Sun. morning; Man. Editor RANDALL C. HATCH; circ. Mon. to Sat. 52,531, Sun. 54,643.

Salt Lake Tribune: 143 South Main St, POB 867, Salt Lake City, UT 84110; tel. (801) 237-2800; f. 1871; morning; Publr PAUL J. O'BRIEN; Editor WILL FEHR; Ind.; circ. Mon. to Fri. 112,625, Sun. 142,644.

Vermont

The Free Press: 191 College St, Burlington, VT 05401; tel. (802) 863-3441; f. 1827; morning; Publr DONNA M. DONOVAN; Editor JAMES E. WELCH; circ. Mon. to Sat. 49,169, Sun. 53,890.

Virginia

Charlottesville Progress: POB 9030, Charlottesville, VA 22906; tel. (804) 978-7200; f. 1892; Mon. to Fri. evening, Sat. and Sun. morning; Publr WILLIAM A. KIRKLAND, Jr; Editor LAWSON H. MARSHALL; circ. Mon. to Sat. 31,783, Sun. 33,072.

Fairfax Journal: 6885 Commercial Dr., Fairfax, VA 22159; tel. (703) 750-2000; f. 1972; Mon. to Fri.; evening; Publr GEOFFREY K. EDWARDS; Editor RICHARD STARNES; circ. 59,718.

The Free Lance-Star: 616 Amelia St, Fredericksburg, VA 22401-3886; tel. (703) 373-5000; f. 1885; Mon. to Sat.; evening; Publr JOSIAH P. ROWE, III; Editor CHARLES S. ROWE; circ. 36,335.

Herald-Courier: 320 Morrison Blvd, Bristol, VA 24201; tel. (703) 669-2181; f. 1870; daily; Publr ARTHUR S. POWERS; circ. Mon. to Fri. 41,885, Sat. 41,743, Sun. 43,228.

Ledger-Star: 150 West Brambleton Ave, Norfolk, VA 23510; tel. (804) 446-2000; f. 1876; Mon. to Fri.; evening; Publr RICHARD F. BARRY, III; Editor SANDRA ROWE; circ. 79,043.

Newport News Press: 7505 Warwick Blvd, Newport News, VA 23607; tel. (804) 247-4600; f. 1896; morning; Editor JACK DAVIS; Ind.; circ. Mon. to Sat. 69,899, Sun. 114,920.

News and Daily Advance: 101 Wyndale Dr., POB 10129, Lynchburg, VA 24506-0129; tel. (804) 237-2941; f. 1866; Mon. to Fri. all day, Sat. and Sun. morning; Publr T. GEORGE WASHINGTON; Exec. Editor WILLIAM CLINE; circ. Mon. to Sat. 42,399, Sun. 44,834.

Richmond News Leader: POB C-32333, Richmond, VA 23293; tel. (804) 649-6000; f. 1896; Mon. to Sat.; evening; Publr J. STEWART BRYAN, III; circ. 109,103.

Richmond Times-Dispatch: 333 East Grace St, Richmond, VA 23293; tel. (804) 649-6000; f. 1850; morning; Publr J. STEWART BRYAN, III; circ. Mon. to Sat. 139,667, Sun. 242,142.

Roanoke Times & World-News: POB 2491, Roanoke, VA 24010-2491; tel. (703) 981-3100; Mon. to Fri. all day, Sat. and Sun. morning; Publr WALTER RUGABER; Exec. Editor FORREST M. LANDON; Ind.; circ. Mon. to Fri. 121,851, Sat. 124,760, Sun. 121,968.

Times Herald: Tribune Co, 7505 Warwick Blvd, Newport News, VA 23607; tel. (804) 247-4600; f. 1900; Mon. to Fri.; evening; Publr JOSEPH D. CANTRELL; Editor JACK W. DAVIS, Jr; circ. 35,674.

Virginian-Pilot: 150 West Brambleton Ave, Norfolk, VA 23510; tel. (804) 446-2000; f. 1865; morning; Publr RICHARD F. BARRY, III; Editor SANDRA ROWE; Ind.; circ. Mon. to Fri. 144,224, Sat. 229,959, Sun. 227,487.

Washington

Bremerton Sun: 545 Fifth St, Bremerton, WA 98310; tel. (206) 377-3711; f. 1935; Mon. to Sat.; evening; Editor GENE GISLEY; circ. 39,049.

Columbian: POB 180, Vancouver, WA 98666; tel. (206) 694-3391; Mon. to Fri. evening, Sun. morning; Publr DON CAMPBELL; circ. Mon. to Fri. 46,963, Sun. 52,227.

The Herald: Grand and California, POB 930, Everett, WA 98206; tel. (206) 339-3000; f. 1891; Mon. to Fri. evening, Sat. and Sun. morning; Publr LARRY HANSON; Exec. Editor JOANN BYRD; Ind.; circ. Mon. to Sat. 55,314, Sun. 58,256.

Seattle Post-Intelligencer: 101 Elliot Ave West, POB 1909, Seattle, WA 98119; tel. (206) 448-8000; f. 1863; morning; Publr VIRGIL FASSIO; Exec. Editor J. D. ALEXANDER; Ind.; circ. Mon. to Fri. 203,726, Sat. 170,813, Sun. 500,781.

Seattle Times: Fairview Ave North and John St, POB 70, Seattle, WA 98111; tel. (206) 464-2111; f. 1896; Mon. to Fri. evening, Sat. morning; Publr FRANK A. BLETHEN; Editor MICHAEL R. FANCHER; Ind.; circ. Mon. to Fri. 231,207, Sat. 226,707.

Spokane Chronicle: West 999 Riverside, POB 2160, Spokane, WA 99210; tel. (509) 459-5045; f. 1886; Mon. to Fri.; evening; Publr W. H. COWLES, III; Editor CHRISTOPHER PECK; circ. 34,671.

Spokane Spokesman-Review: West 999 Riverside, POB 2160, Spokane, WA 99210; tel. (509) 459-9000; f. 1883; morning; Publr W. H. COWLES, III; Man. Editor CHRISTOPHER PECK; Ind.; circ. Mon. to Fri. 86,321, Sat. 126,223, Sun. 134,189.

Tacoma News Tribune: 1950 South State St, POB 11000, Tacoma, WA 98411; tel. (206) 597-8511; f. 1883; morning; Publr WILLIAM L. HONEYSETT, II; Editor JOHN D. KOMEN; Ind.; circ. Mon. to Fri. 116,646, Sun. 126,456.

Tri-City Herald: POB 2608, Pasco, WA 99302; tel. (509) 582-1500; f. 1947; morning; Publr KELSO GILLENWATER; Editor RICHARD K. PETERSEN; circ. Mon. to Sat. 33,211, Sun. 36,183.

West Virginia

Charleston Gazette: 1001 Virginia St East, Charleston, WV 25301; tel. (304) 348-5140; f. 1973; Mon. to Sat.; morning; Publr ROBERT L. SMITH, Jr; Editor DON S. MARSH; circ. 54,000.

Gazette-Mail: 1001 Virginia St East, Charleston, WV 25301; tel. (304) 348-5150; f. 1958; Sun.; Publrs ROBERT L. SMITH, Jr, and JOHN F. McGEE; circ. 109,000.

Wisconsin

Green Bay Press-Gazette: 435 East Walnut St, POB 19430, Green Bay, WI 54307-9430; tel. (414) 435-4411; f. 1915; Mon. to Fri. evening, Sat. and Sun. morning; Publr MICHAEL B. GAGE; Editor ROBERT GALLAGHER; Ind.; circ. Mon. to Sat. 55,533, Sun. 76,966.

Milwaukee Journal: 333 West State St, POB 661, Milwaukee, WI 53201; tel. (414) 224-2000; telex 269460; f. 1882; Mon. to Sat. evening, Sun. morning; Editor SIG GISSLER; circ. Mon. to Sat. 289,254, Sun. 516,890.

Milwaukee Sentinel: 918 North Fourth St, POB 371, Milwaukee, WI 53201; tel. (414) 224-2140; telex 269471; f. 1837; Mon. to Sat.; morning; Editor ROBERT H. WILLS; circ. Mon. to Fri. 188,988, Sat. 187,495.

Post-Crescent: 306 West Washington St, POB 59, Appleton, WI 54912; tel. (414) 733-4411; f. 1920; Mon. to Fri. evening, Sat. and Sun. morning; Editor MICHAEL WALTER; circ. Mon. to Sat. 52,614, Sun. 63,943.

Wisconsin State Journal: 1901 Fish Hatchery Rd, POB 8058, Madison, WI 53708; tel. (608) 252-6100; f. 1839; morning; Publr JAMES E. BURGESS; Editor FRANK DENTON; circ. Mon. to Fri. 79,269, Sat. 83,463, Sun. 145,297.

Wyoming

Star-Tribune: POB 80, Casper, WY 82601; tel. (307) 266-0500; f. 1914; morning; Publr ROBIN HURLESS; Editor RICHARD HIGH; Ind.; circ. Mon. to Sat. 34,993, Sun. 39,522.

SELECTED PERIODICALS

AAA Going Places: 1515 North Westshore Blvd, Tampa, FL 33607; tel. (813) 872-5923; f. 1982; 8 a year; Publr MARVIN L. HOLLOWAY; Editor PHYLLIS W. ZENO; circ. 585,000.

AAA Today Magazine: Automobile Club Publications, 1380 Dublin Rd, Suite 109, Columbus, OH 43215-1025; tel. (614) 481-8088; f. 1921; 6 a year; Editor LISA ANN DUAC; circ. 1,648,000.

ABA Journal, The Lawyer's Magazine: 750 North Lake Shore Dr., Chicago, IL 60611; tel. (312) 988-6003; f. 1915; 12 a year; Publr and Editor LAURENCE BODINE; circ. paid 350,000, non-paid 33,000.

Adventure Road: Amoco Enterprises Inc, 200 East Randolph Dr., Chicago, IL 60601; tel. (312) 856-2583; f. 1961; 6 a year; Publr R. E. MARCINKO; Editor M. HOLSTEIN; circ. 1,524,000.

American Bible Society Record: American Bible Society, 1865 Broadway, New York, NY 10023; tel. (212) 581-1400; f. 1818; 10 a year; Editor CLIFFORD MacDONALD; circ. 400,000.

American Health: 80 Fifth Ave, New York, NY 10011; tel. (212) 242-2460; f. 1982; 10 a year; Editor T. GEORGE HARRIS; circ. 900,000.

American Heritage: 60 Fifth Ave, New York, NY 10011; tel. (212) 206-5500; f. 1954; 8 a year; Editor BYRON DOBELL; circ. 225,000.

American Historical Review: 914 Atwater, Indiana University, Bloomington, IN 47405; tel. (812) 855-7609; f. 1895; 5 a year; Editor DAVID L. RANSEL; circ. 17,000.

The American Hunter: c/o National Rifle Asscn, 470 Spring Park Plaza, Suite 1000, Herndon, VA 22070; tel. (703) 481-3383; f. 1973; monthly; Editor THOMAS FULGHAM; circ. 1,413,000.

American Journal of Psychiatry: American Psychiatric Asscn, 1400 K St, NW, Washington, DC 20005; tel. (202) 682-6020; monthly; Editor Dr JOHN C. NEMIAH; circ. 44,000.

American Legion Magazine: 700 North Pennsylvania St, POB 1055, Indianapolis, IN 46206-1055; tel. (317) 635-8411; f. 1919; monthly; organ of the American Legion; Publr DANIEL S. WHEELER; circ. 2,649,000.

American Motorcyclist: POB 6114, Westerville, OH 43081-6114; tel. (614) 891-2425; f. 1947; monthly; Exec. Editor GREG HARRISON; circ. 131,000.

American Photographer: 1515 Broadway, New York, NY 10036; tel. (212) 719-6265; f. 1978; monthly; Publr JOHN J. MILLER; Editor SEAN CALLAHAN; circ. 255,000.

American Political Science Review: 1527 New Hampshire Ave, NW, Washington, DC 20036; tel. (202) 483-2512; f. 1903; quarterly; Editor SAMUEL C. PATTERSON; circ. 13,000.

The American Rifleman: c/o National Rifle Asscn, 470 Spring Park Plaza, Suite 1000, Herndon, VA 22070; tel. (703) 481-3383; f. 1871; monthly; Editor BILL PARKERSON; circ. 1,362,000.

American Scientist: Sigma xi, The Scientific Research Society, 345 Whitney Ave, New Haven, CT 06511; tel. (203) 624-2566; f. 1913; 6 a year; Publr EDWARD J. POZIOMEK; Editor MICHELLE PRESS; circ. 124,000.

American Teacher: 555 New Jersey Ave, NW, Washington, DC 20001; tel. (202) 879-4430; f. 1916; 8 a year; Editor TRISH GORMAN; circ. 617,000.

American West: 7000 East Tangue Verde Rd, No. 30, Tucson, AZ 85715; tel. (602) 886-9959; f. 1964; 6 a year; Pres. and Editor THOMAS W. PEW, Jr; circ. 208,000.

Americana Magazine: 29 West 38th St, New York, NY 10018; tel (212) 398-1550; f. 1973; 6 a year; Publr JACK ARMSTRONG; Editor SANDRA J. WILMOT; circ. 335,000.

Amnesty Action: Amnesty International USA, 322 Eighth Ave, New York, NY 10001; tel. (212) 807-8400; f. 1971; 6 a year; Editor RON JAJOIE; circ. 300,000.

Ampersand: 303 North Glenoaks, Suite 600, Burbank, CA 91502; tel. (818) 848-4666; f. 1977; quarterly; Publr ALEXANDER AUERBACH; Editor CHARLOTTE WOLTER; circ. 1,505,000.

Architectural Digest: 5900 Wilshire Blvd, Los Angeles, CA 90036; tel. (213) 937-4740; f. 1920; monthly; Publr GEORGE OESTREICH, Jr; circ. 615,000.

Architectural Record: 1221 Ave of the Americas, New York, NY 10020; tel. (212) 512-2139; f. 1891; monthly; Editor MILDRED SCHMERTZ; circ. 76,000.

Arizona Highways: 2039 West Lewis Ave, Phoenix, AZ 85009; tel. (602) 258-6641; f. 1925; monthly; Publr HUGH HARELSON; Editor MERILL WINDSOR; circ. 408,000.

Army Reserve Magazine: Headquarters, Dept of the Army, DAAR-PA, Washington, DC 20310-2400; tel. (202) 696-3962; f. 1954; quarterly; Publr Maj.-Gen. WILLIAM F. WARD, Jr; Editor Maj. J. M. KROESEN; circ. 580,000.

The Atlantic Monthly: 420 Lexington Ave, Suite 2304, New York, NY 10170; tel. (212) 687-2424; f. 1857; monthly; Editor WILLIAM WHITWORTH; circ. 454,000.

Aviation Week and Space Technology: 1221 Ave of the Americas, New York, NY 10020; tel. (212) 463-1770; f. 1916; weekly; Editor-in-Chief DONALD E. FINK, Jr; circ. 146,000.

Awake: Watchtower Bible and Tract Society of New York Inc, 25 Columbia Heights, Brooklyn, NY 112201; tel. (718) 625-3600; f. 1919; 2 a month; circ. 11,350,000.

Baby Talk: 185 Madison Ave, New York, NY 10016; tel. (212) 679-4400; f. 1935; monthly; Publr RICHARD HUTTNER; Editor PATRICIA IRONS; circ. 960,000.

Barbie: The Magazine For Girls: Welsh Publishing Group, 300 Madison Ave, New York, NY 10017; tel. (212) 687-0680; f. 1983; quarterly; Publr DONALD E. WELSH; Editor KAREN TINA HARRISON; circ. 650,000.

Barron's National Business & Financial Weekly: 200 Liberty St, New York, NY 10281; tel. (212) 416-2758; f. 1921; weekly; Editor ALAN ABELSON; circ. 280,000.

Better Homes and Gardens: Locust St at 17th St, Des Moines, IA 50336; tel. (515) 284-3000; f. 1922; monthly; Editor DAVID JORDAN; circ. 8,012,000.

Better Living: 1775 Broadway, New York, NY 10019-1995; tel. (212) 581-2000; f. 1980; quarterly; Editor JOSEPH QUEENAN; circ. 200,000.

Better Nutrition: 390 Fifth Ave, New York, NY 10018; tel. (212) 613-9700; f. 1938; monthly; Publr MICHAEL KELMAN; Editor PATTI SEIKUS; circ. 575,000.

Black Enterprise: 130 Fifth Ave, New York, NY 10011; tel. (212) 242-8000; f. 1970; monthly; Publr and Editor EARL G. GRAVES; circ. 235,000.

Boating: One Park Ave, New York, NY 10016; tel. (212) 725-3517; f. 1956; monthly; Editor J. SAMUEL HUEY; circ. 190,000.

Bon Appetit: 5900 Wilshire Blvd, Los Angeles, CA 90036; tel. (213) 937-1025; telex 910-3212437; f. 1955; monthly; Editor-in-Chief WILLIAM J. GARRY; circ. 1,341,000.

Boy's Life: 1325 Walnut Hill Lane, Irving, TX 75038-3096; tel. (214) 580-2000; f. 1912; monthly; Editor WILLIAM B. McMORRIS; circ. 1,362,000.

Bride's: 350 Madison Ave, New York, NY 10017; tel. (212) 880-8800; f. 1934; 6 a year; Editor BARBARA D. TOBER; circ. 413,000.

Broadcasting: 1705 De Sales St, NW, Washington, DC 20036; tel. (202) 659-2340; fax (202) 429-0651; f. 1931; weekly; Publr LAWRENCE B. TAISHOFF; circ. 34,000.

Business Month: 488 Madison Ave, New York, NY 10022; tel. (212) 605-9400; f. 1983; monthly; Editor ARLENE HERSHMAN; circ. 301,000.

Business Week/World Wide: 1221 Ave of the Americas, New York, NY 10020; tel. (212) 512-1221; f. 1929; weekly; Editor-in-Chief LEWIS H. YOUNG; circ. 879,000.

Cape Cod Guide: Prescott Visitor Magazines, 495 Station Ave, South Yarmouth, MA 02664; tel. (617) 760-2027; f. 1946; 30 a year; Editor LAURA ROZAK; circ. 977,000; free publication.

Capper's: 616 Jefferson St, Topeka, KS 66607; tel. (913) 295-1108; f. 1879; fortnightly; Editor NANCY PEAVLER; circ. 400,000.

Car Craft: 8490 Sunset Blvd, Los Angeles, CA 90069; tel. (213) 854-2320; f. 1953; monthly; Publr JIM ADOLPH; Editor CAM BENTY; circ. 408,000.

Car and Driver: 2300 West Big Beaver, Troy, MI 48084; tel. (313) 649-1950; f. 1955; monthly; Editor DON SHERMAN; circ. 919,000.

Cat Fancy Magazine: POB 57900, Los Angeles, CA 90057-0900; tel. (213) 385-2222; f. 1966; monthly; Publr NORMAN RIDKER; circ. 218,000.

Catholic Digest: St Paul's Sq., POB 64090, St Paul, MN 55164; tel. (612) 647-5298; f. 1936; monthly; Editor HENRY LEXAU; circ. 584,000.

Changing Times: 220 East 42nd St, Suite 3010, New York, NY 10017; tel. (212) 599-0454; f. 1947; monthly; personal finance and consumer matters; Editor TED MILLER; circ. 1,380,000.

Chemical and Engineering News: American Chemical Society, 1155 16th St, NW, Washington, DC 20036; tel. (202) 872-4501; f. 1923; weekly; Editor MIKE HEYLIN; circ. 127,000.

Chemical Week: 810 Seventh Ave, New York, NY 10019; tel. (212) 586-3430; f. 1914; weekly; Editor PETER R. SAVAGE; circ. 50,000.

Child Life: 1100 Waterway Blvd, POB 567, Indianapolis, IN 46206; tel. (317) 636-8881; f. 1921; 8 a year; Editor STEVE CHARLES; circ. 75,000.

Children's Digest: 1100 Waterway Blvd, POB 567, Indianapolis, IN 46206; tel. (317) 636-8881; f. 1929; 8 a year; Publr G. A. NEELY; Editor KATHY MOSHER; circ. 300,000.

Children's Playmate Magazine: 1100 Waterway Blvd, POB 567, Indianapolis, IN 46206; tel. (317) 636-8881; f. 1929; 8 a year; Publr GARTLEY A. NEELY; Editor KATHLEEN B. MOSHER; circ. 290,000.

Christian Herald: 40 Overlook Dr, Chappaqua, NY 10514; tel. (914) 769-9000; f. 1878; monthly; Editor DEAN MERRILL; circ. 150,000.

Christianity Today: 465 Gundersen Dr., Carol Stream, IL 60188; tel. (312) 260-6200; f. 1956; fortnightly; Editors TERRY MUCK, HAROLD SMITH; circ. 180,000.

Circus Magazine: Three West 18th St, New York, NY 10011; tel. (212) 685-5050; f. 1969; monthly; Publr and Editor GERALD ROTHBERG; circ. paid 251,000, non-paid 6,000.

Civil Engineering: 345 East 47th St, New York, NY 10017-2398; tel. (212) 705-7514; telex 422847; f. 1930; monthly; Editor VIRGINIA FAIRWEATHER; circ. 99,000.

College Women: Alan Weston Communications, 303 North Glenoaks Blvd, Suite 600, Burbank, CA 91502; tel. (818) 848-4666; f. 1985; quarterly; Publr JEFF DICKEY; Editor NANCY GOTTESMAN; circ. 500,000.

Colonial Homes: 1790 Broadway, New York, NY 10019; tel. (212) 830-2900; f. 1975; 6 a year; Publr DAVID J. MOORE; Editor RICHARD BEATTY; circ. paid 622,000, non-paid 14,000.

Columbia: Knights of Columbus, PO Drawer 1670, New Haven, CT 06507; tel. (203) 772-2130; f. 1920; monthly; Editor RICHARD McMUNN; circ. 1,450,000.

Conde Nast's Traveler: Conde Nast Publications Inc, 360 Madison Ave, New York, NY 10017; tel. (212) 880-8800; f. 1987; monthly; Publr RON GALOTTI; Editor-in-Chief HAROLD EVANS; circ. 853,000.

Congressional Digest: 3231 P St, NW, Washington, DC 20007; tel. (202) 333-7332; f. 1921; 10 a year; Publr N. T. N. ROBINSON, III; Editor MARTIN L. SKUBINNA.

Consumer Reports: 256 Washington St, Mount Vernon, NY 10553; tel. (914) 667-9400; fax (914) 667-2701; f. 1936; monthly; Editor IRWIN LANDAU; circ. 3,800,000.

Consumers Digest: 5705 North Lincoln Ave, Chicago, IL 60659; tel. (312) 275-3590; f. 1959; 6 a year; Editor JOHN MANOS; circ. 902,000.

Cooking Light: Southern Living Inc, 820 Shades Greek Parkway, Birmingham, AL 35209; tel. (205) 877-6000; f. 1987; 6 a year; Publr JEFFREY C. WARD; Editor KATHERINE M. EAKIN; circ. paid 556,000, non-paid 30,000.

Cosmopolitan: 224 West 57th St, New York, NY 10019; tel. (212) 262-5700; monthly; women's; Editor HELEN GURLEY BROWN; circ. 2,873,000.

Country Home: 1716 Locust St, Des Moines, IA 50336; tel. (515) 284-2015; f. 1979; 6 a year; Publr JERRY KAPLAN; Editor JEAN LEMMON; circ. 880,000.

Country Living: 224 West 57th St, New York, NY 10019; tel. (212) 649-3511; f. 1978; monthly; Editor RACHEL NEWMAN; circ. 1,600,000.

CQ Weekly Report: 1414 22nd St, NW, Washington, DC 20037; tel. (202) 887-8500; f. 1945; publ. by Congressional Quarterly Inc; politics and government; Exec. Editor NEIL SKENE.

Crafts Magazine: PJS Publications Inc, News Plaza, POB 1790, Peoria, IL 61656; tel. (309) 682-6626; f. 1978; monthly; Publr JERRY CONSTANTINO; Editor JUDITH BROSSART; circ. 431,000.

Crafts 'N' Things: Clapper Publishing Co Inc, 14 Main St, Park Ridge, IL 60068; tel. (312) 825-2161; f. 1975; 8 a year; Publr MARIE PETERSEN; Editor NANCY TOSH; circ. 320,000.

Creative Ideas for Living: 810 Seventh Ave, New York, NY 10019; tel. (212) 246-4640; f. 1970; monthly; Editor KATHLEEN STUART; circ. 710,000.

Cumulative Book Index: The H. W. Wilson Co, 950 University Ave, Bronx, NY 10452; tel. (212) 588-8400; f. 1898; monthly; Editor NANCY WONG; circ. 6,000.

Dav Magazine: 807 Maine Ave, SW, Washington, DC 20024; tel. (202) 554-3501; f. 1920; monthly; Editor JERRY ATCHISON; circ. 1,100,000.

Decision: The Billy Graham Evangelistic Asscn, 1300 Harmon Pl., Minneapolis, MN 55403; tel. (612) 338-0500; f. 1960; 11 a year; Editor ROGER PALMS; circ. 2,000,000.

Decorating Remodeling: 110 Fifth Ave, New York, NY 10011; tel. (212) 463-1000; f. 1986; 6 a year; Publr JOHN HILLOCK; Editor CAROL SHEEHAN; circ. 550,000.

Discover: 3 Park Ave, New York, NY 10016; tel. (212) 340-9200; f. 1980; monthly; popular science; Editor PAUL HOFFMAN; circ. 925,000.

Discovery: 3801 West Lake Ave, Glenview, IL 60025; tel. (312) 291-6223; f. 1961; quarterly; Publr ROBERT GORMAN; Editor CLAIRE McCREA; circ. 1,500,000.

Eagle Magazine: Fraternal Order of Eagles, 2401 West Wisconsin Ave, POB 25916, Milwaukee, WI 53225-0916; tel. (414) 933-5646; f. 1913; quarterly; Editor ROBERT W. HANSON; circ. 699,000.

Early American Life: Historical Times, Inc, 2245 Kohn Rd, POB 8200, Harrisburg, PA 17105; tel. (717) 657-9555; f. 1974; monthly; Publr JAMES KEOUGH; Editor FRANCIS W. FINN; circ. 325,000.

Ebony: 820 South Michigan Ave, Chicago, IL 60605; tel. (312) 322-9200; f. 1945; monthly; news and illustrated; Exec. Editor HERBERT NIPSON; circ. 1,703,000.

Editor & Publisher—The Fourth Estate: 11 West 19th St, New York, NY 10011; tel. (212) 675-4380; f. 1884; weekly; Editor ROBERT U. BROWN; circ. 25,000.

Electronics: 1221 Ave of the Americas, New York, NY 10020; tel. (212) 512-2000; telex 4998204; f. 1930; fortnightly; Editor-in-Chief ROBERT W. HENKEL; circ. 131,000.

Elks Magazine: 425 West Diversey Parkway, Chicago, IL 60614; tel. (312) 528-4500; f. 1922; monthly; Exec. Editor FRED D. OAKES; circ. 1,524,000.

Elle: 551 Fifth Ave, New York, NY 10176; tel. (212) 808-5800; monthly; Publr ANNE SUTHERLAND FOUCHS.

Ellery Queen's Mystery Magazine: 380 Lexington Ave, New York, NY 10017; tel. (212) 557-9100; f. 1941; monthly; Editor ELEANOR SULLIVAN; circ. 251,000.

Endless Vacation: POB 80260, Indianapolis, IN 46280-0260; tel. (317) 871-9500; f. 1975; 6 a year; Publr ROBERT M. ANCELL; Editor HELEN A. WERNLE; circ. 572,000.

Esquire: 2 Park Ave, New York, NY 10016; tel. (212) 561-8100; f. 1933; monthly; Editor LEE EISENBERG; circ. 692,000.

Essence: 1500 Broadway, New York, NY 10036; tel. (212) 730-4260; f. 1970; monthly; Editor-in-Chief SUSAN L. TAYLOR; circ. 800,000.

Everybody's Money: Credit Union National Asscn Inc, POB 431, Madison, WI 53701; tel. (608) 231-4092; f. 1961; quarterly; Editor JAMES HANSON; circ. 1,400,000.

Family Circle: 110 Fifth Ave, New York, NY 10011; tel. (212) 463-1000; f. 1932; every 3 weeks; Editor ARTHUR HETTICH; circ. 6,247,000.

Family Computing: 730 Broadway, New York, NY 10003; tel. (212) 505-3580; f. 1983; monthly; Publr SHIRREL RHOADES; Editor CLAUDIA COHL; circ. 435,000.

Family Handyman: 1999 Shepard Rd, St Paul, MN 55116; tel. (612) 690-7328; f. 1951; 10 a year; Editor GARY HAVENS; circ. 1,202,000.

Family/The Magazine for Military Wives: 169 Lexington Ave, New York, NY 10016; tel. (212) 532-0660; f. 1958; monthly; Publr JOSEPH A. MUGNAI; Editor MARY JANE RYAN; circ. non-paid 551,000.

Family Safety and Health: National Safety Council, 444 North Michigan Ave, Chicago, IL 60611; tel. (312) 527-4800; f. 1961; quarterly; Publr GORDON F. BEIBERLE; Editor BEVERLEE A. BURKE; circ. 2,300,000.

Farm Journal: 230 Washington Sq., Philadelphia, PA 19105; tel. (215) 829-4700; f. 1877; monthly; Editor EARL AINSWORTH; circ. 840,000.

Field and Stream: 1515 Broadway, New York, NY 10036; tel. (212) 719-6000; f. 1895; monthly; Editor DUNCAN BARNES; circ. 2,002,000.

Flex: 21100 Erwin St, Woodland Hills, CA 91367; tel. (818) 715-0632; f. 1983; monthly; Publr JOE WEIDER; Editor RUTH SILVERMAN; circ. 175,000.

Flower and Garden Magazine: 4251 Pennsylvania Ave, Kansas City, MO 64111; tel. (816) 531-5730; f. 1957; 6 a year; Editor RACHEL SNYDER; circ. 631,000.

Forbes: 60 Fifth Ave, New York, NY 10011; tel. (212) 620-2200; f. 1917; fortnightly; Publr CASPAR W. WEINBERGER; Editor JAMES W. MICHAELS; circ. 727,000.

Ford Times: One Illinois Center, 111 East Wacker Dr., Suite 1700, Chicago, IL 60601; tel. (312) 565-1200; f. 1908; monthly; free publication; Publr ROLAND WILLIAMS; Editor THOMAS KINDRE; circ. 1,135,000.

Foreign Affairs: 58 East 68th St, New York, NY 10021; tel. (212) 734-0400; f. 1922; 5 a year; Editor WILLIAM G. HYLAND; circ. 91,000.

Fortune: 1271 Ave of the Americas, New York, NY 10020; tel. (212) 586-1212; f. 1930; fortnightly; Man. Editor MARSHALL R. LOEB; circ. 744,000.

Friendly Exchange: Farmers Insurance Group of Cos/Meredith Corpn, Locust St at 17th St, Des Moines, IA 50336; tel. (515) 284-2257; f. 1981; quarterly; free publication; circ. 4,200,000.

Games: PSC Publications, 810 Seventh Ave, New York, NY 10019; tel. (212) 246-4640; f. 1977; 6 a year; Publr GERARD CALABRESE; Editor R. WAYNE SCHMITTBURGER; circ. paid 632,000, non-paid 32,000.

Gentlemen's Quarterly: 350 Madison Ave, New York, NY 10017; tel. (212) 880-7915; f. 1957; monthly; Publr JACK KLIGER; Editor ARTHUR COOPER; circ. 663,000.

Glamour: 350 Madison Ave, New York, NY 10017; tel. (212) 880-8800; f. 1939; monthly; Editor RUTH WHITNEY; circ. 2,386,000.

'Go': AAA Carolina Motor Club, POB 30008, Charlotte, NC 28230; tel. (704) 377-3600; f. 1922; 6 a year; Editor QUENTIN ANDERSON, Jr; circ. 258,000.

Golden State, The Magazine of California: 555 19th St, San Francisco, CA 94107; tel. (415) 621-0220; f. 1984; quarterly; free publication; Publr TOM ELLIOT; Editor ANNE EVERS; circ. 3,025,000.

Golf Digest: 5520 Park Ave, POB 0395, Trumbull, CT 06611; tel. (203) 373-7000; f. 1950; Editor JERRY TARDE; circ. 1,300,000.

Golf Magazine: 2 Park Ave, New York, NY 10016; f. 1959; tel. (212) 687-3000; Editor GEORGE PEPER; circ. 1,000,000.

Good Food Magazine: Triangle Communications Inc, 850 Third Ave, New York, NY 10022; tel. (212) 759-8100; f. 1986; 6 a year; Publr ROBERT F. YOUNG; Editor ANN PLESHETTE MURPHY; circ. 785,000.

Good Housekeeping: 959 Eighth Ave, New York, NY 10019; tel. (212) 262-5700; f. 1885; monthly; Editor JOHN MACK CARTER; circ. 5,222,000.

Gourmet—The Magazine of Good Living: 560 Lexington Ave, New York, NY 10022; tel. (212) 371-1330; f. 1941; monthly; Editor JANE MONTANT; circ. 818,000.

Grit: 208 West Third St, Williamsport, PA 17701; tel. (717) 326-1771; f. 1882; weekly; Editor MICHAEL RAFFERTY; circ. 575,000.

Guideposts: Seminary Hill Rd, Carmel, NY 10512; tel. (914) 225-3681; f. 1945; monthly; Publr NORMAN VINCENT PEALE; Editor VAN VARNER; circ. 4,339,000.

Harper's Bazaar: 1700 Broadway, New York, NY 10019; tel. (212) 935-5900; monthly; Editor-in-Chief ANTHONY T. MAZZOLA; circ. 728,000.

Harper's Magazine: 666 Broadway, New York, NY 10012; tel. (212) 614-6500; f. 1850; monthly; Editor LEWIS H. LAPHAM; circ. 181,000.

Harvard Business Review: Soldiers' Field, Boston, MA 02163; tel. (617) 495-6800; f. 1922; 6 a year; Editor THEODORE LEVITT; circ. 207,000.

Health: 3 Park Ave, New York, NY 10016; tel. (212) 340-9260; f. 1969; monthly; Editor DIANNE PARTIE LANGE; circ. 1,016,000.

HG (House & Garden): 350 Madison Ave, New York, NY 10017; tel. (212) 880-8800; f. 1901; monthly; Publr KEVIN MADDEN; Editor-in-Chief NANCY NOVOGROD; circ. 573,000.

Highlights for Children: 2300 West Fifth Ave, POB 269, Columbus, OH 43216; tel. (614) 253-1080; f. 1946; 11 a year; Editor KENT L. BROWN, Jr; circ. 3,000,000.

Home and Away Magazine: AAA Chicago Motor Club, 999 East Touhy Ave, Des Plaines, IL 60018; tel. (312) 390-9000; f. 1980; 6 a year; Publr NELS L. PIERSON; Editor B. WADE; circ. 1,757,000.

Home Magazine: Knapp Communications, 140 East 45th St, New York, NY 10017; tel. (212) 682-4040; f. 1955; monthly; Publr MICHAEL C. STANKE; Editor CHANNING DAWSON; circ. 900,000.

Home Mechanix: 1515 Broadway, New York, NY 10036; tel. (212) 719-6576; f. 1928; monthly; Editor JOSEPH R. PROVEY; circ. 1,208,000.

The Homeowner: Three Park Ave, New York, NY 10016; tel. (212) 340-9200; f. 1974; 10 a year; Publr MARTIN J. TUBRIDY; Editor JOE CARTER.

Hot Rod Magazine: 8490 Sunset Blvd, Los Angeles, CA 90069; tel. (213) 854-2280; f. 1948; monthly; Editor JEFF SMITH; circ. 821,000.

House Beautiful: 1700 Broadway, New York, NY 10019; tel. (212) 903-5000; f. 1896; monthly; Editor JO ANN BARWICK; circ. 838,000.

Hustler Magazine: 2029 Century Park East, Suite 3800, Los Angeles, CA 90067; tel. (213) 556-9200; f. 1974; monthly; men's; Publr LARRY FLYNT; circ. 1,067,000.

Industry Week: 1100 Superior Ave, Cleveland, OH 44114; tel. (216) 696-7000; f. 1882; fortnightly; Editor PERRY J. PASCARELLA; circ. 329,000.

Jet: 820 South Michigan Ave, Chicago, IL 60605; tel. (312) 322-9200; f. 1951; weekly; Exec. Editor ROBERT JOHNSON; circ. 790,000.

Journal of Accountancy: 1211 Ave of the Americas, New York, NY 10036; tel. (212) 575-6272; f. 1905; monthly; Editor SUSAN Z. FRAYMAN; circ. 298,000.

Journal of the American Medical Association (JAMA): 535 North Dearborn St, Chicago, IL 60610; tel. (312) 280-7233; f. 1883; weekly; Editor Dr GEORGE D. LUNDBERG; circ. 359,000.

Journal of Home Economics: American Home Economics Asscn, 2010 Massachusetts Ave, NW, Washington, DC 20036-1028; tel. (202) 862-8300; f. 1909; quarterly; Editor LISA GARBUS; circ. 28,000.

Junior Scholastic: 730 Broadway, New York, NY 10003; tel. (212) 505-3071; f. 1937; fortnightly; Editor LEE BAIER; circ. 748,000.

Ladies' Home Journal: Meredith Corpn, 100 Park Ave, New York, NY 10017; tel. (212) 953-7070; f. 1883; monthly; Editor-in-Chief MYRNA BLYTH; circ. 5,014,000.

Lear's: Lear Publishing Co, 505 Park Ave, New York, NY 10022; tel. (212) 888-0007; f. 1988; 6 a year; Publr MICHELE S. MAGAZINE; Editor FRANCES LEAR; circ. 200,000.

Life Magazine: 1271 Ave of the Americas, New York, NY 10020; tel. (212) 522-1212; f. 1978; monthly; Man. Editor PATRICIA RYAN; circ. 1,719,000.

Listen: Pacific Press Publishing Asscn, POB 7000, Boise, ID 83707-1000; tel. (208) 465-2500; f. 1947; monthly; Editor GARY B. SWANSON; circ. 100,000.

Lion Magazine: 300 22nd St, Oak Brook, IL 60570; tel. (312) 571-5466; f. 1918; monthly; business and professional; Editor ROBERT KLEINFELDER; circ. 641,000.

MacGuide Magazine: 550 South Wadsworth, Suite 500, Lakewood, CO 80226; tel. (303) 825-8166; f. 1987; quarterly; Publr DAVID G. DUTY; Editor PATRICIA BENSKY; circ. 100,000.

Mademoiselle: 350 Madison Ave, New York, NY 10017; tel. (212) 880-8800; f. 1935; monthly; Editor AMY LEVIN COOPER; circ. 1,298,000.

Management Review: American Management Asscn, 135 West 50th St, New York, NY 10020; tel. (212) 903-8393; fax (212) 903-8168; f. 1923; monthly; Editor ROD WILLIS; circ. 140,000.

Maryknoll Magazine: Maryknoll, NY 10545; f. 1906; monthly; Publr RONALD SAUCCI; Editor MOISES SANDOVAL; circ. 1,115,000.

Materials Engineering: 1100 Superior Ave, Cleveland, OH 44114; tel. (216) 696-7000; telex 4218245; f. 1929; monthly; Editor FRANCIS J. LAVOIE; circ. 61,000.

Mature Outlook Magazine: 3701 West Lake Ave, Glenview, IL 60025; tel. (312) 291-4739; f. 1984; 6 a year; Publr ROBERT GORMAN, Jr; Man. Editor ELIZABETH BREWSTER; circ. 800,000.

McCall's Magazine: 230 Park Ave, New York, NY 10169; tel. (212) 551-9500; f. 1876; monthly; women's; Editor A. ELIZABETH SLOAN; circ. 5,275,000.

Metropolitan Home: Locust St at 17th St, Des Moines, IA 50336; tel. (515) 284-3000; f. 1969; monthly; Publr STEPHEN R. BURZON; Editor DOROTHY KALINS; circ. 729,000.

Michigan Living: Automobile Club of Michigan, 17000 Executive Plaza, Dearborn, MI 48126; tel. (313) 336-1516; f. 1918; monthly;

Publr RON STEFFENS; Editor LEONARD R. BARNES; circ. paid 991,000, non-paid 15,000.

Midwest Living: Meredith Corpn, Locust St at 17th St, Des Moines, IA 50336; tel. (515) 284-3000; f. 1987; 6 a year; Publr TOME BENSON; Editor DAN KAERCHER; circ. 450,000.

Modern Maturity: American Association of Retired Persons, 3200 East Carson St, Lakewood, CA 90712; f. 1957; 6 a year; Editor IAN LEDGERWOOD; circ. 17,400,000.

Modern Photography: 825 Seventh Ave, New York, NY 10019; tel. (212) 265-8360; fax (212) 887-8579; f. 1937; monthly; Editor BARRY TANENBAUM; circ. 727,000.

Modern Screen: 355 Lexington Ave, New York, NY 10017; tel. (212) 391-1400; f. 1930; monthly; Editor MARK BEGO; circ. 84,000.

Money: 1271 Ave of the Americas, New York, NY 10020; tel. (212) 522-1212; f. 1972; monthly; Man. Editor LANDON Y. JONES; circ. 1,862,000.

Moneysworth: 555 West 57th St, Suite 1515, New York, NY 10019-1802; tel. (212) 581-2000; f. 1970; quarterly; Publr RALPH GINZBURG; Editor JOE QUEENAN; circ. 350,000.

Moose Magazine: Loyal Order of Moose, Mooseheart, IL 60539; tel. (312) 859-2000; f. 1917; 10 a year; free publication; Editor RAYMOND DICKOW; circ. 1,300,000.

Mother Earth News: POB 70, Hendersonville, NC 28791; tel. (704) 693-0211; f. 1970; 6 a year; Editor BRUCE WOODS; circ. 700,000.

Motor: 555 West 57th St, New York, NY 10019; tel. (212) 399-5658; f. 1903; monthly; Editor WADE A. HOYT; circ. 135,000.

Motor Trend: 8490 Sunset Blvd, Los Angeles, CA 90069; tel. (213) 854-2222; f. 1949; monthly; Editor MIKE ANSON; circ. 777,000.

Motorland: 150 Van Ness Ave, San Francisco, CA 94102; tel. (415) 565-2620; f. 1917; 6 a year; Editor JOHN G. HOLMGREN; circ. 1,693,000.

Ms Magazine: One Times Sq., New York, NY 10036; tel. (212) 719-9800; f. 1972; monthly; Editor ANNE SUMMERS; circ. 500,000.

Nation: 72 Fifth Ave, New York, NY 10011; tel. (212) 242-8400; telex 667155; f. 1865; weekly; Editor VICTOR NAVASKY; politics and the arts; circ. 85,000.

Nation's Business: 1615 H St, NW, Washington, DC 20062; tel. (202) 659-6000; f. 1912; monthly; Editor ROBERT T. GRAY; circ. 862,000.

National Enquirer: 600 South East Coast Ave, Lantana, FL 33464; tel. (305) 586-1111; f. 1952; weekly; Editor IAIN CALDER; circ. 4,381,000.

National Geographic Magazine: National Geographic Society, 17th and M Sts, NW, Washington, DC 20036; tel. (202) 857-7000; f. 1888; monthly; Editor WILBUR E. GARRETT; circ. 10,765,000.

National Geographic World: National Geographic Society, 17th and M Streets, NW, Washington, DC 20036; tel. (202) 857-7000; f. 1975; monthly; Editor PAT ROBBINS; circ. 1,200,000.

National Review: 150 East 35th St, New York, NY 10016; tel. (212) 679-7330; f. 1955; fortnightly; Editor WILLIAM F. BUCKLEY, Jr; circ. 117,000.

National Wildlife: National Wildlife Federation, 8925 Leesburg Pike, Vienna, VA 22180; tel. (703) 790-4510; f. 1962; 6 a year; Editor BOB STROHM; circ. 850,000.

Nea Today: Nat. Education Asscn, 1201 16th St, NW, Washington, DC 20036; tel. (202) 822-7200; f. 1982; 8 a year; Publr ROBERT E. HARMAN; Editor ANN KURZIUS; circ. paid 1,735,000, non-paid 4,000.

New Republic: 1220 19th St, NW, Suite 600, Washington, DC 20036; tel. (202) 331-7494; f. 1914; weekly; Editor MICHAEL KINSLEY; circ. 90,000.

New Woman: New Woman Inc, 215 Lexington Ave, New York, NY 10016; tel. (212) 685-4790; f. 1970; monthly; Publr and Editor PAT MILLER; circ. 1,200,000.

New York Magazine: 755 Second Ave, New York, NY 10017-5998; tel. (212) 880-0700; f. 1968; weekly; Editor EDWARD KOSNER; circ. 433,000.

New York Review of Books: 250 West 57th St, New York, NY 10107; tel. (212) 757-8070; f. 1963; fortnightly; Editors ROBERT SILVERS, BARBARA EPSTEIN; circ. 120,000.

The New Yorker: 25 West 43rd St, New York, NY 10036; tel. (212) 840-3800; f. 1925; weekly; Editor ROBERT A. GOTTLIEB; circ. 633,000.

Newsweek: Newsweek Bldg, 444 Madison Ave, New York, NY 10022; tel. (212) 350-4000; f. 1933; weekly; Publr HOWARD W. SMITH; Editor-in-Chief RICHARD M. SMITH; circ. 3,181,000.

NRTA/AARP News Bulletins: 420 Lexington Ave, New York, NY 10170; tel. (212) 599-1880; f. 1959; monthly; Publr ROB WOOD; Editor JOE DOOLEY; circ. 13,170,000.

Off Duty America: 3303 Harbor Blvd, Suite C2, Costa Mesa, CA 92626; tel. (714) 549-7172; f. 1980; 6 a year; Publr WALTER B. RIOS; Editor BRUCE THORSTAD; circ. non-paid 500,000.

Omni: 1965 Broadway, New York, NY 10023-5965; tel. (212) 496-6100; f. 1978; monthly; Editor PATRICE ADCROFT; circ. 858,000.

Organic Gardening: 33 East Minor St, Emmaus, PA 18049; tel. (215) 967-5171; f. 1942; monthly; Editor ROBERT RODALE; circ. 1,000,000.

The Original Pennysaver: 2830 Orbiter St, Brea, CA 92621; tel. (714) 996-8900; f. 1962; weekly; Publr and Editor HARRY BUCKEL; circ. non-paid 3,100,000.

Outdoor Life: 380 Madison Ave, New York, NY 10017; tel. (212) 687-3000; f. 1898; monthly; Editor CLARE CONLEY; circ. 1,521,000.

Parents' Magazine: 685 Third Ave, New York, NY 10017; tel. (212) 878-8700; f. 1926; monthly; Editor-in-Chief ANN PLESHETTE MURPHY; circ. 1,722,000.

Partisan Review: 236 Bay State Rd, Boston, MA 02215; tel. (617) 353-4260; f. 1934; quarterly; Editor WILLIAM PHILLIPS; circ. 8,000.

Pennysaver: Capital Cities/ABC Inc; 27742 Forbes Rd, Laguna Niguel, CA 92677; tel. (714) 582-2800; f. 1964; weekly; Pres. WESLEY R. TURNER; circ. non-paid 1,600,000.

Penthouse: 1965 Broadway, New York, NY 10023-5965; tel. (212) 496-6100; f. 1969; monthly; Publr and Editor BOB GUCCIONE; circ. 2,379,000.

People Weekly: 1271 Ave of the Americas, New York, NY 10020; tel. (212) 522-1212; f. 1974; weekly; Man. Editor JAMES R. GAINES; circ. 3,038,000.

Philip Morris Magazine: Philip Morris USA, 120 Park Ave, New York, NY 10017; tel. (212) 878-2742; f. 1985; quarterly; Publr GUY SMITH; Editor FRANK GANNON; circ. non-paid 12,000,000.

Playbill: 71 Vanderbilt Ave, Suite 320, New York, NY 10169; tel. (212) 557-5757; f. 1884; monthly; Publr ARTHUR T. BIRSH; Editor JOAN ALLEMAN; circ. non-paid 1,040,000.

Playboy: 919 North Michigan Ave, Chicago, IL 60611; tel. (312) 751-8000; telex 190166; f. 1953; monthly; men's; Publr and Editor HUGH M. HEFNER; circ. 3,672,000.

Political Science Quarterly: 2852 Broadway, New York, NY 10025-7885; tel. (212) 866-6754; f. 1886; quarterly; Editor DEMETRIOS CARALEY; circ. 11,000.

Popular Mechanics: 224 West 57th St, New York, NY 10019; tel. (212) 262-4284; f. 1902; monthly; Editor JOE OLDHAM; circ. 1,635,000.

Popular Photography: One Park Ave, New York, NY 10016; tel. (212) 503-3700; f. 1937; monthly; Editor SEAN CALLAHAN; circ. 750,000.

Popular Science: 380 Madison Ave, New York, NY 10017; tel. (212) 687-3000; f. 1872; monthly; Editor-in-Chief C. P. GILMORE; circ. 1,800,000.

Portals of Prayer: Concordia Publishing House, 3558 South Jefferson Ave, St Louis, MO 63118-9988; tel. (314) 664-7000; f. 1937; quarterly; circ. 950,000.

Preservation News: National Trust for Historic Preservation, 1785 Massachusetts Ave, NW, Washington, DC 20036; tel. (202) 673-4075; f. 1961; monthly; Publr MARGARET BYRNE HEIMBOLD; Editor ARNOLD BERKE; circ. paid 175,000, non-paid 2,000.

Prevention: 33 East Minor St, Emmaus, PA 18098; tel. (215) 967-5171; f. 1950; monthly; Editor ROBERT RODALE; circ. 2,821,000.

Preview Magazine: 180 East End Ave, New York, NY 10128; tel. (212) 535-5051; f. 1963; monthly; Publr and Editor JACK WINTER; circ. 200,000.

Progressive Architecture: 600 Summer St, POB 1361, Stamford, CT 06904; tel. (203) 348-7531; fax (203) 348-4023; f. 1920; monthly; Editor JOHN MORRIS DIXON; circ. 73,000.

Progressive Farmer: 820 Shades Creek Parkway, POB 2581, Birmingham, AL 35202; tel. (205) 877-6000; f. 1886; monthly; Editor TOM CURL; circ. 536,000.

Psychology Today: 80 Fifth Ave, New York, NY 10011; tel. (212) 242-2460; monthly; Editor JULIA KAGAN; circ. 967,000.

The Public Employee: American Federation of State, County and Municipal Employees, 1625, L St, NW, Washington, DC 20036; tel. (202) 429-1144; f. 1936; 8 a year; Editor MARSHALL O. DONLEY, Jr; circ. 1,157,000.

Publishers Weekly: Bowker Magazine Group, 249 West 17th St, New York NY 10011; tel. (212) 645-0067; telex 127703; f. 1872; weekly; Publr NEIL A. PERLMAN; Editor-in-Chief JOHN F. BAKER; circ. 36,000.

QST: American Radio Relay League, 225 Main St, Newington, CT 06111; tel. (203) 666-1541; telex 650215-5052; fax (203) 665-7531; f. 1915; monthly; Publr DAVID SUMNER; circ. 155,000.

Railfan & Railroad: POB 700, Newton, NJ 07860; tel. (201) 383-3355; f. 1909; monthly; Editor JAMES BOYD; circ. 50,000.

Ranger Rick Magazine: National Wildlife Federation, 8925 Leesburg Pike, Vienna, VA 22184-0001; tel. (703) 790-4283; f. 1967; monthly; Editor E. GERALD BISHOP; circ. 800,000.

Reader's Digest: Pleasantville, NY 10570; tel. (914) 769-7000; f. 1922; monthly; Editor-in-Chief KENNETH O. GILMORE; circ. 16,250,000.

Redbook Magazine: 224 West 57th St, New York, NY 10019; tel. (212) 649-3450; f. 1903; monthly; Editor ANNETTE CAPONE; circ. 4,009,000.

The Renovator's Supply: Renovator's Old Mill, Millers Falls, MA 01349; tel. (413) 659-2211; f. 1978; 6 a year; Publr and Editor CLAUDE JEANLOZ; circ. 1,000,000.

Road and Track: 1499 Monrovia Ave, Newport Beach, CA 92663; tel. (714) 720-5300; f. 1947; monthly; Editor THOMAS L. BRYANT; circ. 740,000.

Rolling Stone: 745 Fifth Ave, New York, NY 10151; tel. (212) 758-3800; f. 1967; fortnightly; Man. Editor ROBERT WALLACE; circ. 1,110,000.

The Rotarian: Rotary International, 1 Rotary Center, 1560 Sherman Ave, Evanston, IL 60201; tel. (312) 866-3000; telex 724465; f. 1911; monthly; Editor W. L. WHITE; circ. 528,000.

Runners' World: 33 East Minor St, Emmaus, PA 18409; tel. (215) 967-5171; f. 1966; monthly; Publr MICHAEL S. PERLIS; Editor JAMES C. MCCULLAGH; circ. 300,000.

Sassy: One Times Sq., New York, NY 10036; tel. (212) 719-9800; monthly; Editor JANE PRATT; circ. 280,000.

Saturday Evening Post: 1100 Waterway Blvd, Indianapolis, IN 46202; tel. (317) 636-8881; f. 1821; 9 a year; Exec. Editor TED KREITER; circ. 600,000.

School and Community: Missouri State Teachers Asscn, POB 458, Columbia, MO 65205-0458; tel. (314) 442-3127; f. 1915; quarterly; Editor SANDY BARKS; circ. 30,000.

Science: 1333 H St, NW, Washington, DC 20005; tel. (202) 326-6500; f. 1880; weekly; publ. by the American Asscn for the Advancement of Science; Editor DANIEL E. KOSHLAND, Jr; circ. 155,000.

Science News: 1719 N St, NW, Washington, DC 20036; tel. (202) 785-2255; f. 1921; weekly; Editor PATRICK YOUNG; circ. 257,000.

Scientific American: 415 Madison Ave, New York, NY 10017; tel. (212) 754-0550; telex 236115; f. 1845; monthly; Pres. and Editor JONATHAN B. PIEL; circ. 592,000.

Scouting Magazine: 1325 Walnut Hill Lane, Irving, TX 75062; tel. (214) 659-2000; f. 1913; 6 a year; Editor WALTER BABSON; circ. 964,000.

Self: 350 Madison Ave, New York, NY 10017; tel. (212) 880-8800; f. 1979; monthly; Editor VALORIE GRIFFITH WEAVER; circ. 1,090,000.

Sesame Street Magazine: Children's Television Workshop, One Lincoln Plaza, New York, NY 10023; tel. (212) 595-3456; f. 1970; 10 a year; Publr NINA B. LINK; Editor-in-Chief MARGE KENNEDY; circ. paid 1,272,000, non-paid 12,000.

Seventeen: 850 Third Ave, New York, NY 10022; tel. (212) 759-8100; f. 1944; monthly; Editor MIDGE RICHARDSON; circ. 1,853,000.

Signs of the Times: POB 7000, Boise, ID 83707-1000; tel. (208) 465-2500; f. 1874; monthly; Publr EUGENE STYLES; Editor K. J. HOLLAND; circ. 400,000.

Ski America: Riverview Rd, POB 737, Lenox, MA 01240; tel. (413) 637-9810; f. 1972; quarterly; Publr and Editor BARRY HOLLISTER; circ. 400,000.

Skiing: Times-Mirror Magazines, 1515 Broadway, New York, NY 10036; tel. (212) 719-6244; f. 1948; 7 a year; Publr HENRY KAISER; Editor WILLIAM GROUT; circ. 449,000.

Smithsonian Magazine: 900 Jefferson Dr., Washington, DC 20560; tel. (202) 357-2600; f. 1970; monthly; Editor DON MOSER; circ. 2,302,000.

Soap Opera Digest: 45 West 25th St, New York, NY 10010; tel. (212) 645-2100; f. 1975; fortnightly; Editor MEREDITH BERLIN; circ. 1,000,000.

Southern Living: POB 523, Birmingham, AL 35201; tel. (205) 877-6000; f. 1966; monthly; Editor GARY E. MCCALLA; circ. 2,272,000.

Southern Travel: The New York Times Co Magazine Group, 110 Fifth Ave, New York, NY 10011; tel. (212) 463-1469; f. 1987; quarterly; Publr REBECCA MCPHETERS; circ. 210,000.

Special Libraries: Special Libraries Asscn, 1700 18th St, NW, Washington, DC 20009; tel. (202) 234-4700; f. 1909; quarterly; Publr DAVID R. BENDER; Editor MARIA C. BARRY; circ. 15,000.

Sport Magazine: 119 West 40th St, New York, NY 10018; tel. (212) 869-4700; f. 1946; monthly; Editor NEIL COHEN; circ. 932,000.

Sporting News: 1212 North Lindbergh Blvd, St Louis, MO 63132; tel. (314) 997-7111; f. 1886; weekly; Editor TOM BARNRIDGE; circ. 725,000.

Sports Afield: 250 West 55th St, New York, NY 10019; tel. (212) 649-4000; f. 1888; monthly; Publr WILLIAM S. DAVID; Editor TOM PAUGH; circ. paid 521,000, non-paid 12,000.

Sports Illustrated: 1271 Ave of the Americas, New York, NY 10020; tel. (212) 522-1212; f. 1954; weekly; Man. Editor MARK R. MULVOY; circ. 2,975,000.

Star: 660 White Plains Rd, Tarrytown, NY 10591; tel. (914) 332-5000; f. 1974; weekly; Editor RICHARD KAPLAN; circ. 3,744,000.

Stereo Review: Diamandis Communications Inc, 1515 Broadway, New York, NY 10036; tel. (212) 719-6000; f. 1958; monthly; Publr TONY JOHNSON; Editor LOUISE BOUNDAS; circ. 555,000.

Success Magazine: 342 Madison Ave, New York, NY 10173; tel. (212) 503-0700; f. 1954; 10 a year; Publr GERALD MOSS; Editor SCOTT DEGARMO; circ. 425,000.

Sunset Magazine: 80 Willow Rd, Menlo Park, CA 94025; tel. (415) 321-3600; telex 348343; f. 1898; monthly; Editor WILLIAM MARKEN; circ. 1,442,000.

Take One: Falcon Publications, Inc, 1601 Broadway, POB 1028, Little Rock, AR 72203; tel. (501) 375-6923; f. 1981; monthly; Publr GLORIA REDMAN; Editor JAMES H. FAULKNER; circ. 1,040,000.

'TEEN: 8490 Sunset Blvd, Los Angeles, CA 90069; tel. (213) 657-5100; f. 1957; monthly; Editor ROXIE CAMRON; circ. 1,124,000.

1,001 Home Ideas: 3 Park Ave, New York, NY 10016; tel. (212) 340-9250; f. 1941; monthly; Editor ELLEN FRANKEL; circ. 1,527,000.

Time: 1271 Ave of the Americas, New York, NY 10020; tel. (212) 586-1212; f. 1923; weekly; Editor-in-Chief JASON MCMANUS; Man. Editor HENRY MULLER; circ. 4,720,000.

Time in Canada: Time and Life Bldg, New York, NY 10020; tel. (212) 522-1212; f. 1943; weekly; Publr ROBERT L. MILLER; Editor HENRY MULLER; circ. 361,000.

Travel/Holiday: 28 West 23rd St, New York, NY 10010; tel. (212) 633-4633; f. 1901; monthly; Man. Editor DIANE MARSHALL; circ. 807,000.

Travel & Leisure: 444 Madison Ave, New York, NY 10022; tel. (212) 350-4173; f. 1971; monthly; Editor-in-Chief PAMELA FIORI; circ. 1,118,000.

True Story: 215 Lexington Ave, New York, NY 10016; tel. (212) 340-7500; f. 1919; monthly; Editor HELEN VINCENT; circ. 1,405,000.

TV Guide: Triangle Publications, POB 500, Radnor, PA 19088; tel. (215) 293-8500; f. 1953; weekly; Editors DAVID SENDLER, ROGER YOUMAN; circ. 16,800,000.

The Upper Room: The Upper Room Inc, 1908 Grand Ave, POB 189, Nashville, TN 37202-0189; tel. (615) 340-7250; f. 1935; 6 a year; Editor MARY LOU REDDING; circ. 2,175,000.

US: One Dag Hammarskjold Plaza, New York, NY 10017; tel. (212) 836-9200; f. 1977; fortnightly; Editor JANN S. WENNER; circ. 1,040,000.

US News & World Report: 2400 N St, NW, Washington, DC 20037; tel. (202) 955-2000; f. 1933; weekly; Editor ROGER ROSENBLATT; circ. 2,366,000.

USA Weekend: Gannett Co Inc, 535 Madison Ave, New York, NY 10022; tel. (212) 715-2000; f. 1953; weekly; Publr PATRICIA HAEGELE; circ. 1,420,000.

Vanity Fair: 350 Madison Ave, New York, NY 10017; tel. (212) 880-8800; f. 1983; monthly; Publr DOUG JOHNSTON; Editor TINA BROWN; circ. 418,000.

Variety: 475 Park Ave South, New York, NY 10016; tel. (212) 779-1100; telex 126335; f. 1905; weekly; Editor ROGER WATKINS; circ. 35,000.

VFW Magazine: 34th and Broadway, Kansas City, MO 64111; tel. (816) 756-3390; f. 1912; 11 a year; Editor WARREN MAUS; circ. 1,951,000.

Vista USA: Exxon Travel Club, POB 161, Convent Station, NJ 07961-0161; tel. (201) 538-7600; f. 1965; 4 a year; Editor KATHLEEN M. CACCAVALE; circ. 925,000.

Vogue: 350 Madison Ave, New York, NY 10017; tel. (212) 880-8800; f. 1892; monthly; Editor ANNA WINTOUR; circ. 1,282,000.

Weight Watchers Magazine: 360 Lexington Ave, New York, NY 10017; tel. (212) 370-0644; fax (212) 687-4398; f. 1968; monthly; Editor LEE HAIKEN; circ. 1,000,000.

Western Pennsylvania Motorist: West Penn Motor Club, 202 Penn Circle West, Pittsburgh, PA 15206; tel. (412) 362-3300; f. 1931; monthly; Editor ANN REED ROSE; circ. 270,000.

Westways: POB 2890, Terminal Annex, Los Angeles, CA 90051; tel. (213) 741-4760; f. 1909; monthly; Publr GEORGE T. MILLER; Editor MARY ANN FISHER; circ. 464,000.

Woman's Day: 1515 Broadway, New York, NY 10036; tel. (212) 719-6000; 15 a year; Editor ELLEN LEVINE; circ. 5,513,000.

Woman's World: Heinrich Bauer North America, Inc, POB 6700, Englewood, NJ 07631; tel. (201) 569-0006; f. 1981; weekly; Pres. KONRAD WIEDERHOLZ; Editor DENNIS NEELD; circ. 1,397,000.

Wood: Meredith Corpn, Locust St at 17th St, Des Moines, IA 50336; tel. (515) 284-3439; f. 1984; 6 a year; Publr JERRY KAPLAN; Editor LARRY CLAYTON; circ. 500,000.

The Workbasket: 4251 Pennsylvania, Kansas City, MO 64111; tel. (816) 531-5730; f. 1935; 10 a year; Editor ROMA JEAN RICE; circ. 1,779,000.

Working Mother: 230 Park Ave, New York, NY 10169; tel. (212) 551-9500; f. 1978; monthly; Publr CAROL EVANS; Editor OLIVIA BUEHL; circ. 565,000.

Working Woman Magazine: 342 Madison Ave, New York, NY 10173; tel. (212) 309-9800; f. 1976; monthly; Editor ANNE MOLLEGEN SMITH; circ. 950,000.

Yale Review: 1902A Yale Station, New Haven, CT 06520; tel. (203) 432-0499; f. 1911; quarterly; Editor KAI ERIKSON; circ. 6,000.

Yankee Magazine: Main St, Dublin, NH 03444; tel. (603) 563-8111; f. 1935; monthly; Editor JUDSON D. HALE; circ. 1,018,000.

YM: Gruner and Jahr USA, 685 Third Ave, New York, NY 10017; tel. (212) 878-8700; f. 1946; 10 a year; Publr ALEX MIRONOVICH; Editor NANCY COMER; circ. 825,000.

You and Your Health: POB AP, Los Altos, CA 94023; tel. (415) 941-3955; f. 1985; 6 a year; free publication; Publr and Editor JEROLD K. KARABENSH; circ. 400,000.

NEWS AGENCIES

US News and Features Syndicates

Advance News Service Inc: 2000 Pennsylvania Ave, NW, Washington, DC 20006; tel. (202) 785-0101.

Alburn Bureau: POB 5745, Tucson, AZ 85703; tel. (602) 624-0721.

Allied Feature Syndicate: Citizen Bldg, Suite 520, 850 Euclid Ave, Cleveland, OH 44114; tel. (216) 781-6700.

American Features Syndicate: 150 East 58th St, New York, NY 10155; tel. (212) 371-6488.

American Syndicate Inc: POB 41359, Cincinnati, OH 45241; tel. (513) 771-1220.

American Way Features: 128 Lighthouse Dr., Jupiter, FL 33458; tel. (305) 746-7815.

Amusement Features Syndicate: 218 West 47th St, New York, NY 10036; tel. (212) 221-2627.

Arcadia Feature Syndicate: POB 5263, Chicago, IL 60608; tel. (312) 276-0715.

Artists and Writers Syndicate: 1034 National Press Bldg, Washington, DC 20045; tel. (202) 882-8882.

Associated Press (AP): 50 Rockefeller Plaza, New York, NY 10020-1666; tel. (212) 621-1500; f. 1848; Pres. and Gen. Man. LOUIS D. BOCCARDI; Vice-Pres. and Asst to the Pres. JAMES F. TOMLINSON; 1,697 newspaper mems in the US, 6,000 broadcast mems and over 8,500 subscribers abroad.

Authenticated News International: 29 Katonah Ave, Katonah, NY 10536; tel. (914) 232-7726.

Black Press Service Inc: 166 Madison Ave, New York, NY 10016; tel. (212) 686-6850.

Buddy Basch Feature Syndicate: 771 West End Ave, New York, NY 10025; tel. (212) 666-2300.

Business Newsfeatures: 20490 Harper Ave, Detroit, MI 48225; tel. (313) 884-1140.

Business Wire: 44 Montgomery St, Suite 2150, San Francisco, CA 94104; tel. (415) 986-4422.

Capitol News Service: POB 38607, Los Angles, CA 90038; tel. (213) 462-6371.

Caruba Organization: POB 40, Maplewood, NJ 07040; tel. (201) 763-6392.

Chronicle Features: 870 Market St, San Francisco, CA 94102; tel. (415) 777-7212.

City Desk Features: 110 71st Rd, Forest Hills, NY 11375; tel. (718) 261-4061.

City News Bureau of Chicago: 35 East Wacker Dr., Suite 792, Chicago, IL 60601; tel. (312) 782-8100.

College Press Service: 2629 18th St, Denver, CO 80211; tel. (303) 458-7216.

Columbia Features Inc: 36 West 44th St, New York, NY 10036; tel. (212) 840-1812.

Commodity News Services Inc: POB 6053, Leawood, KS 66206; tel. (913) 642-7373.

Commodity Quotations Inc: 670 White Plains Rd, Scarsdale, NY 10583; tel. (914) 725-3477.

Community and Suburban Press Service: POB 639, Frankfort, KY 40602; tel. (502) 223-1736.

Computer Features: Five Currier Rd, East Brunswick, NJ 08816; tel. (201) 238-2123.

Congressional Quarterly Service: 1414 22nd St, NW, Washington, DC 20037; tel. (202) 887-8500.

Copley News Service: POB 190, San Diego, CA 92112; tel. (619) 293-1818.

Cowles Syndicate: 715 Locust St, Des Moines, IA 50304; tel. (515) 284-8244.

Dickinson Multi-Media Services Inc: 271 Madison Ave, New York, NY 10016; tel. (212) 532-0170.

Dow Jones News Service: 200 Liberty St, New York, NY 10281; tel. (212) 416-2310.

Dunkel Sports Research Service: POB 2167, Ormond Beach, FL 32074; tel. (904) 677-6100.

Editorial Research Reports: 1414 22nd St, NW, Washington, DC 20037; tel. (202) 887-8500.

Editors' Copy Syndicate: 419 Green St, Orangeburg, SC 29115; tel. (803) 534-1110.

Editors' Press Service Inc: 330 West 42nd St, New York, NY 10036; tel. (212) 563-2252.

Exclusive Press Syndicate: 108 East 66th St, New York, NY 10021; tel. (212) 988-5190.

Fairchild Syndicate: Seven East 12th St, New York, NY 10003; tel. (212) 741-4315.

Feature News Service: 2330 South Brentwood Blvd, St Louis, MO 63144-2096; tel. (314) 961-2300; f. 1924; serves 87 weekly newspapers; Assoc. Editors GEORGE G. WHITE, Sr, LEROY BLITZ.

Financial Advisory Services: 517 Leesville Rd, Lynchburg, VA 24502; tel. (804) 239-7526.

Gannett News Service: POB 7858, Washington, DC 20044; tel. (703) 276-5800.

General Press Review: 1307 Fourth St, NE, Washington, DC 20044; tel. (703) 276-5800.

General Press Features: 116 Parklane St, Kew Gardens, NY 11418; tel. (718) 441-2574.

Global Press Review: 1307 Fourth St, NE, Washington, DC 20002; tel. (202) 543-9428.

Hearst Newspapers: 959 Eighth Ave, New York, NY 10019; tel. (212) 262-7796.

Heritage Features Syndicate: 214 Massachusetts Ave, NE, Washington, DC 20002; tel. (202) 543-0440.

Hispanic Link News Service: 1420 N St, NW, Washington, DC 20005; tel. (202) 234-0280.

Hollywood Inside Syndicate: POB 49957, Los Angeles, CA 90049; tel. (714) 678-6237.

Hopkins Syndicate Inc: Hopkins Bldg, Mellot, IN 47958; tel. (317) 295-2253.

Intermedia News and Feature Service: 799 Broadway, Rm 325, New York, NY 10003; tel. (212) 777-8383.

International Business Information Service: POB 4082, Irvine, CA 92716; tel. (714) 552-8494.

International Medical Tribune Syndicate: 257 Park Ave South, 19th Floor, New York, NY 10010; tel. (212) 674-8500.

Interpress of London and New York: 400 Madison Ave, New York, NY 10017; tel. (212) 832-2839.

Keister-Williams Newspaper Services Inc: POB 8005, Charlottesville, VA 22906; tel. (804) 293-4709.

King Features Syndicate Inc: 235 East 45th St, New York, NY 10017; tel. (212) 682-5600.

Knight News Wire: 790 National Press Bldg, Washington, DC 20045; tel. (202) 383-6080.

Knight-Ridder Financial News: POB 6053, Leawood, KS 66206; tel. (913) 642-7373.

Los Angeles Times/Washington Post News Service: 1150 15th St, NW, Washington, DC 20071; tel. (202) 334-6173.

McGraw-Hill News Service: 5151 Belt Line Rd, Dallas, TX 75240; tel. (214) 458-2400.

McNaught Syndicate Inc: 537 Steamboat Rd, Greenwich, CT 06830; tel. (203) 661-4990.

Midcontinent Feature Syndicate: POB 1662, Pittsburgh, PA 15230; tel. (412) 562-4067.

National News Bureau: 2019 Chancellor St, Philadelphia, PA 19103; tel. (215) 569-0700.

National Press Syndicate: 300 East 40th St, New York, NY 10016; tel. (212) 682-3891.

New York Times News Service: 229 West 43rd St, New York, NY 10036; tel. (212) 556-7087.

New York Times Syndication Sales Corporation: 130 Fifth Ave, New York, NY 10011; tel. (212) 645-3000.

Newhouse News Service: 2000 Pennsylvania Ave, NW, Washington, DC 20006; tel. (202) 383-7800.

Newspaper Enterprise Association Inc: 200 Park Ave, New York, NY 10166; tel. (212) 692-3700.

Newsvertising-Congressional Monitoring Retrieval Services: 1868 Columbia Rd, NW, Washington, DC 20009; tel. (202) 332-2001.

Numismatic Informational Service: Rossway Rd, Pleasant Valley, NY 12569; tel. (914) 635-2361.

Oceanic Press Service: POB 6538, Buena Park, CA 90622; tel. (714) 527-5651.

Ohio Washington News Service: 1822 Corcoran St, NW, Washington, DC 20009; tel. (202) 462-1777.

Ottaway News Service: 815 15th St, NW, Suite 628, Washington, DC 20005; tel. (202) 628-7200.

Pacific News Service: 604 Mission St, San Francisco, CA 94105; tel. (415) 986-5690.

PR Newswire: 150 East 58th St, New York, NY 10155; tel. (212) 832-9400.

Press Associates Inc: 806 15th St, NW, Suite 632, Washington, DC 20005; tel. (202) 638-0444.

Press Features International: 150 East 35th St, New York, NY 10016; tel. (212) 532-2508.

Religious News Service: POB 1015, Radio City Station, New York, NY 10101; tel. (212) 315-0870; world-wide coverage of domestic and foreign religious news; Exec. Editor JUDY WELDMAN.

Retail News Bureau: 101 Fifth Ave, New York, NY 10003; tel. (212) 255-9595.

Science Service: 1719 N St, NW, Washington, DC 20036; tel. (202) 785-2255.

Scripps-Howard News Service: 1110 Vermont Ave, NW, Washington, DC 20005; tel. (202) 833-9520.

Senior News Service: 500 Fesler St, El Cajon, CA 92020; tel. (619) 442-4404.

Seven Arts-Worldwide News Service: 165 West 46th St, New York, NY 10036; tel. (212) 575-9370.

SIPA News Service: 59 East 54th St, New York, NY 10022; tel. (212) 759-5571.

Singer Media Corpn: 3164 Tyler Ave, Anaheim, CA 92801; tel. (714) 527-5650; includes OPS-Oceanic Press Service; news and features services to 300 publs in 35 countries; Chair. KURT SINGER; Editor JOHN KEARNS.

Speciality Features Syndicate: 17255 Redford Ave, Detroit, MI 48219; tel. (313) 533-1846.

Star Service Syndicate: POB 15610, Fort Lauderdale, FL 33318; tel. (305) 472-8794.

States News Service: 1333 F St, NW, Washington, DC 20004; tel. (202) 628-3100.

Transworld Feature Syndicate Inc: Two Lexington Ave, Suite 1021, New York, NY 10036; tel. (212) 254-0586.

Tribune Media Services Inc: 64 East Concord St, Orlando, FL 32801; tel. (305) 422-8181.

United Feature Syndicate Inc: 200 Park Ave, New York, NY 10166; tel. (212) 692-3700.

United Media Enterprises (UME): 200 Park Ave, New York, NY 10166; tel. (212) 692-3700; telex 238506; f. 1978; includes United Feature Syndicate (UFS) and Newspaper Enterprise Asscn (NEA); news features; Pres. and CEO ROBERT ROY METZ; Sr Vice-Pres. and Editorial Dir DAVID HENDIN.

United Press International (UPI): 1400 I St, NW, Washington, DC 20005; tel. (202) 898-8000; f. 1907; Pres. PAUL STEINLE; Exec. Editor AL ROSSITER, Jr; serves 8,000 news outlets world-wide.

Universal Press Syndicate: 4900 Main St, 9th Floor, Kansas City, MO 64112; tel. (816) 932-6600.

Washington Post Writers' Group: 1150 15th St, NW, Washington, DC 20071; tel. (202) 334-6375.

Wideworld News Service: POB 20056, St Louis, MO 63144; tel. (314) 361-1552.

World Wide Information Services: 360 First Ave, New York, NY 10010; tel. (212) 677-7839.

Principal Foreign Bureaux

Canada

Canadian Press (New York): 50 Rockefeller Plaza, Suite 1006, New York, NY 10020; tel. (212) 421-1357; Bureau Chief CAL WOODWARD.

Canadian Press (Washington, DC): 2021 K St, NW, Rm 606, Washington, DC 20036; tel. (202) 223-8813; Bureau Chief JOHN VALORZI.

China (People's Republic)

Xinhua (New China) News Agency (New York): 155 West 66th St, New York, NY 10023; tel. (212) 787-3554; telex 424465; Bureau Chief CHEN JI.

Xinhua (New China) News Agency (Washington, DC): 1740 North 14th St, Arlington, VA 22209; tel. (703) 875-0082.

China (Taiwan)

Central News Agency Inc: 220 East 42nd St, New York, NY 10017; tel. (212) 682-8583; also offices in Washington, DC, San Francisco, Chicago, Boston, Los Angeles and Houston.

Czechoslovakia

Československá tisková kancelář–ČTK (New York): 330 East 46th St, Suite 11C, New York, NY 10017; tel. (212) 682-3409; telex 224192.

France

Agence France-Presse—AFP (New York): 50 Rockefeller Plaza, Suite 1007, New York, NY 10020; Correspondent ANNICK BENOIST-GIANESSINI.

Agence France-Presse—AFP (Washington, DC): 400 City Bldg, 1612 K St, NW, Washington, DC 20006; tel. (202) 293-9380; telex 248465; Bureau Chief PHILIPPE GUSTIN.

German Democratic Republic

Allgemeiner Deutscher Nachrichtendienst—ADN (New York): UN Secretariat Bldg, Rm 482, United Nations Plaza, New York, NY 10017; tel. (212) 963-0203; Man. FRED BÖTTCHER.

Allgemeiner Deutscher Nachrichtendienst—ADN (Washington, DC): 1600 South Joyce St, Suite A1709, Arlington, VA 22202; Man. Dr ANDREAS KABUS.

Germany, Federal Republic

Deutsche Presse-Agentur–dpa (New York): UN Bldg, Rm S352, 405 East 42nd St, New York, NY 10017; tel. (212) 355-0318; Bureau Chief Mr ZEHM.

Deutsche Presse-Agentur—dpa (Washington, DC): National Press Bldg, Suite 969, 592 14th St, Washington, DC 20045; tel. (202) 783-5097; telex 197984; Bureau Chief HERBERT WINKLER.

Hungary

Magyar Távirati Iroda—MTI (Washington, DC): 8515 Farrell Dr., Chevy Chase, MD 20815; tel. (301) 565-2221; telex 440137; Correspondent ANDREAS HELTAI.

Italy

Agenzia Nazionale Stampa Associata—ANSA (New York): 866 United Nations Plaza, Suite 476, New York, NY 10017; tel. (212) 319-6802; telex 177614; Correspondent FABIO CANNILLO.

Agenzia Nazionale Stampa Associata—ANSA (San Francisco): 1890 Clay St, Suite 1004, San Francisco, CA 94109; tel. (415) 775-8094; Correspondent JORGE BRIGNOLE.

Agenzia Nazionale Stampa Associata—ANSA (Washington, DC): National Press Bldg, Suite 416, 592 14th St, Washington, DC 20045; tel. (202) 628-3317; telex 275369; Correspondent RICCARDO BENOZZO.

Inter Press Service—IPS (New York): POB 462, Grand Central Station, New York, NY 10017; tel. (212) 963-6156; telex 175600; fax (212) 371-9020; Dir MARCO NAPOLI.

Inter Press Service—IPS (Washington, DC): National Press Bldg, Suite 1293A, 592 14th St, Washington, DC 20045; tel. (202) 662-7160; Correspondent SEEMA SIROHI.

Japan

Jiji Tshushin-Sha (Chicago): Insurance Exchange Bldg, Suite A655, 175 West Jackson Blvd, Chicago, IL 60604; tel. (312) 427-5865; fax (312) 427-5870; Correspondent HITOSHI OZAWA.

Jiji Tshushin-Sha (Los Angeles): 530 West 6th St, Suite 505, Los Angeles, CA 90014; tel. (213) 488-0958; fax (213) 488-1319; Correspondent MASAHIRO NAKATA.

Jiji Tshushin-Sha (New York): 30 East 42nd St, Rm 1012, New York, NY 10017; tel. (212) 986-8250; telex 2342056; Bureau Chief YASUHIKO SAEKI.

Jiji Tshushin-Sha (San Francisco): 564 Market St, Suite 418, San Francisco, CA 94104; tel. (415) 986-3933; fax (415) 986-6192; Correspondent KENJI MIYAZAWA.

Jiji Tshushin-Sha (Washington, DC): National Press Bldg, Suite 1193, 592 14th St, Washington, DC 20045; tel. (202) 783-4330; fax (202) 783-6093; Correspondent HIROSHI KANASHIGE.

Kyodo Tshushin (Los Angeles): 250 East First St, Suite 1107, Los Angeles, CA 90012; tel. (213) 680-9448; Correspondent Mr J. KIHARA.

Kyodo Tshushin (New York): 50 Rockefeller Plaza, Suite 816, New York, NY 10020; tel. (212) 586-0152; Correspondent Mr I. SAITA.

Kyodo Tshushin (Washington, DC): National Press Bldg, Suite 400, 592 14th St, Washington, DC 20045; tel. (202) 347-5767; telex 2342056; Bureau Chief HIROSHI FUJITA.

Spain

Agencia EFE (Miami): 2125 Biscayne Blvd, Suite 50, Miami, FL 33137; Correspondent JEANINE CAMPS.

Agencia EFE (New York): United Nations Bldg, Rm 484, New York, NY 10017; Bureau Chief DIEGO CARCEDO.

Agencia EFE (Washington, DC): 1400 Eye St, NW, Suite 952, Washington, DC 20005; tel. (202) 745-7692; telex 216486; Bureau Chief JOAQUÍN RABAGO.

United Kingdom

Reuters Information Services Inc (Boston): 53 State St, 26th Floor, Boston, MA 02109; tel. (617) 227-6020.

Reuters Information Services Inc (Chicago): Board of Trade Bldg, Suite 1860, 141 West Jackson Blvd, Chicago, IL 60604; tel. (312) 922-6038; telex 256123.

Reuters Information Services Inc (Dallas): 1999 Bryan St, Dallas, TX 75201; tel. (214) 953-0744.

Reuters Information Services Inc (Detroit): Free Press Bldg, Rm 749, 321 West Lafayette Blvd, Detroit, MI 48226; tel. (313) 961-8370.

Reuters Information Services Inc (Houston): 2 Allen Center, 1200 Smith St, Suite 680, Houston, TX 77002; tel. (713) 659-2450.

Reuters Information Services Inc (Kansas City): 4800 Main St, Kansas City, MO 64112; tel. (314) 561-8671.

Reuters Information Services Inc (Los Angeles): 445 South Figueroa St, Suite 2000, Los Angeles, CA 90071; tel. (213) 680-4800.

Reuters Information Services Inc (Miami): Brickell Bay Tower, Suite 1601, 1001 South Bayshore Dr., Miami, FL 33131; tel. (305) 374-5013.

Reuters Information Services Inc (Minneapolis): Piper Jaffray Tower, Suite 2920, 222 South 9th St, Minneapolis, MN 55402; tel. (612) 339-5940.

Reuters Information Services Inc (New York): 1700 Broadway, 31st Floor, New York, NY 10019; tel. (212) 582-4030; telex 276522; Editor EVELYN LEOPOLD.

Reuters Information Services Inc (San Francisco): 153 Kearny St, Suite 301, San Francisco, CA 94108; tel. (415) 989-3555.

Reuters Information Services Inc (Washington, DC): 1333 H St, NW, Suite 410, Washington, DC 20005; tel. (212) 628-9212; telex 892387.

USSR

Agentstvo Pechati Novosti—APN (Washington, DC): 1706 18th St, NW, Washington, DC 20009.

Telegrafnoye Agentstvo Sovetskovo Soyuza—TASS (New York): 50 Rockefeller Plaza, New York, NY 10020; tel. (212) 245-4250; telex 223346; fax (212) 245-4258; Bureau Chief IGOR Y. MAKURIN; also offices in Washington, DC (tel. (202) 662-7080) and San Francisco.

PAP (Poland), Ghana News Agency, Prensa Latina (Cuba) and JTA (Israel) are also represented.

NATIONAL PRESS ASSOCIATIONS

Alternative Press Syndicate: 211 East 43rd St, 20th Floor, New York, NY 10017; tel. (212) 972-8484; f. 1967; 300 mems; Dir R. J. SMITH.

American Jewish Press Association: St Louis Jewish Light, 12 Millstone Campus Dr., St Louis, MO 63146; tel. (314) 432-3353; f. 1943; 176 mems; Pres. ROBERT A. COHN.

American Newspaper Publishers Association (ANPA): POB 17407, Dulles Airport, Washington, DC 20041; tel. (703) 648-1000; f. 1887; 1,388 mems representing 90% of US daily newspaper circulation; Chair. ARTHUR OCHS SULZBERGER; Pres. JERRY W. FRIEDHEIM.

American Press Institute Inc: 11690 Sunrise Valley Dr., Reston, VA 22091; tel. (703) 620-3611; Dir FRANK QUINE.

American Society of Business Press Editors: 4445 Gilmer Lane, Cleveland, OH 44143; tel. (216) 531-8306; f. 1949; 340 mems; Exec. Vice-Pres. JEANNE RIBINSKAS.

American Society of Magazine Editors: 575 Lexington Ave, New York, NY 10022; tel. (212) 752-0055; 600 mems; Exec. Dir ROBERT E. KENYON, Jr.

American Society of Magazine Photographers: 205 Lexington Ave, New York, NY 10016; tel. (212) 889-9144; f. 1944; 5,000 mems; Exec. Dir PATRICE GARRISON.

American Society of Newspaper Editors: POB 17004, Dulles Airport, Washington, DC 20041; tel. (703) 648-1144; fax (703) 620-4557; f. 1922; 1,000 mems; Pres. LOREN F. GHIGLIONE.

Associated Press Broadcasters: 1825 K St, NW, Suite 615, Washington, DC 20006; tel. (202) 955-7212; f. 1941; 5,900 mems; Exec. Dir JOHN H. BENNIT.

Associated Press Managing Editors: 50 Rockefeller Plaza, New York, NY 10020; tel. (212) 621-1552; f. 1933; 1,000 mems; Pres. ROBERT E. RHODES.

Association of Business Publishers Inc: 205 East 42nd St, New York, NY 10017; tel. (212) 661-6360; f. 1906; mems: 123 publrs, 692 periodicals, 3 associates (suppliers); Pres. WILLIAM G. O'DONNELL.

Audit Bureau of Circulations: 900 North Meacham Rd, Schaumburg, IL 60173; tel. (312) 605-0909; fax (312) 605-0483; 5,200 mems; Chair. ROBERT J. GALLOWAY; Pres. and Man. Dir M. DAVID KEIL; Sec. JOSEPH W. OSTROW.

Catholic Press Association: 119 North Park Ave, Rockville Centre, NY 11570; tel. (516) 766-3400; f. 1911; 600 mems; Exec. Dir JAMES A. DOYLE.

City and Regional Magazine Association: 801 Second Ave, Suite 1400, New York, NY 10017; tel. (212) 697-3580; f. 1978; 40 mems; Exec. Dir C. W. MCDOWELL.

Computer Press Association: 1832 Woodhaven Way, Oakland, CA 94611; tel. (415) 339-8562; f. 1984; 200 mems; Treas. TAY VAUGHAN.

Coordinating Council of Literary Magazines (CCLM): 666 Broadway, New York, NY 10012-2301; tel. (212) 614-6551; f. 1967; aids non-commercial literary magazines; 400 mems; Chair. RICHARD BRAY.

Foreign Press Association: 18 East 50th St, New York, NY 10022; tel. (212) 826-4452; f. 1918; 450 mems; Exec. Dir ISABELLE SILK.

Gay and Lesbian Press Association: POB 8185, Universal City, CA 91608; tel. (213) 877-1045; f. 1980; 325 mems; Admin. Dir R. J. CURRY.

International Motor Press Association: 211 West 56th St, Suite 26J, New York, NY 10019; f. 1962; 500 mems; Pres. WADE HOYT.

International Newspaper Marketing Association: 11690 Sunrise Valley Dr., Reston, VA 22091; tel. (703) 648-1094; telex 292810; f. 1930; 1,450 mems.

International Press Institute, American Committee: 819 North Kiowa St, Allentown, PA 18103; tel. (215) 432-6700; f. 1951; 1,800 mems; Sec. GENE GIANCARLO.

International Society of Weekly Newspaper Editors: Dept of Journalism, Northern Illinois University, DeKalb, IL 60115; tel. (815) 753-1925; f. 1954; 305 mems; Exec. Sec. DONALD F. BROD.

Investigative Reporters and Editors: POB 838, Columbia, MO 65205; tel. (314) 882-2042; f. 1975; 3,000 mems; Exec. Dir STEVE WEINBERG.

Magazine Publishers of America: 575 Lexington Ave, New York, NY 10022; tel. (212) 752-0055; fax (212) 888-4217; f. 1919; 250 mems; Chair. PETER DIAMANDIS; Pres. DONALD D. KUMMERFELD.

Media Credit Association: 575 Lexington Ave, New York, NY 10022; tel. (212) 752-0055; 269 mems; Vice-Pres. JAMES E. VAN METER, Jr.

National American Legion Press Association: 2975 Catalina Dr., Decatur, GA 30032; tel. (404) 284-2480; f. 1923; 1,800 mems; Exec. Dir GEORGE W. HOOTEN.

National Federation of Press Women: 621 Mehring Way, Suite 1106, Cincinnati, OH 45202; tel. (816) 229-1666; f. 1937; 5,000 mems; Pres. NAOMI WHITSEL.

National Newspaper Association: 1627 K St, NW, Suite 400, Washington, DC 20006; tel. (202) 466-7200; f. 1885; 5,000 mems; Exec. Vice-Pres. DAVID SIMONSON.

National Press Club: National Press Bldg, Rm 1386, 529 14th St, NW, Washington, DC 20045; tel. (202) 662-7500; f. 1908; 4,600 mems; Gen. Man. HARRY BODAAN.

National Press Photographers' Association: 3200 Croasdaile Dr., Suite 306, Durham, NC 27705; tel. (919) 383-7246; f. 1946; 9,000 mems; Exec. Dir CHARLES H. COOPER.

Newspaper Advertising Bureau: 1180 Ave of the Americas, New York, NY 10036; tel. (212) 921-5080; f. 1913; 1,000 mems; Pres. CRAIG C. STANDEN.

Newspaper Food Editors and Writers Association: Dallas Morning News, Dallas, TX 75265; tel. (214) 977-8417; f. 1974; 200 mems; Pres. DOTTY GRIFFITH.

The Newspaper Guild: 8611 Second Ave, Silver Spring, MD 20910; tel. (301) 585-2990; f. 1933; affil. to AFL-CIO, Canadian Labour Congress, Int. Fed. of Journalists; 34,000 mems; Chair. PETER MCLAUGHLIN; Pres. CHARLES DALE; Sec.-Treas. JOHN C. EDGINGTON.

Newspaper Systems Group: Knight-Ridder Inc, One Herald Plaza, Miami, FL 33101; tel. (516) 454-2020; f. 1967; 40 mems; Pres. DENNIS O'LEARY.

Overseas Press Club of America: 310 Madison Ave, Suite 2116, New York, NY 10017; tel. (212) 983-4655; f. 1939; 1,500 mems; Pres. HERBERT KUPFERBERG.

Periodical & Book Association of America Inc: 120 East 34th St, Suite 7K, New York, NY 10016; tel. (212) 689-4952; 40 mems; Exec. Dir MICHAEL MORSE.

Periodicals Institute: POB 899, West Caldwell, NJ 07007; tel. (201) 882-1130; f. 1979; 550 mems; Pres. JOHN E. FITZMAURICE, Jr.

Small Magazine Publishers Group: One Main St, Freedom, ME 04941; tel. (207) 382-6200; f. 1979; 1,000 mems; Dir GEORGE FRANGOULIS.

Suburban Newspapers of America: 111 East Wacker Dr., Chicago, IL 60601; tel. (312) 644-6610; f. 1971; 200 mems; Exec. Dir JAMES E. ELSENER.

PUBLISHING

Publishers

Abaris Books Inc: 24 West 40th St, New York, NY 10018; tel. (212) 354-4588; f. 1973; visual arts, philosophy, history, music; Editor-in-Chief WALTER L. STRAUSS.

Abbeville Press Inc: 488 Madison Ave, 23rd–24th Floors, New York, NY 10022; tel. (212) 888-1969; telex 428141; fax (212) 644-5085; f. 1977; fine arts and illustrated books; Pres. and Publr ROBERT E. ABRAMS.

ABC–CLIO: 2040 Alameda Padre Serra, POB 4397, Santa Barbara, CA 93140; tel. (805) 963-4221; f. 1955; political science, humanities and reference; Pres. RONALD J. BOEHM.

Abingdon Press: 201 Eighth Ave South, Nashville, TN 37202; tel. (615) 749-6000; fax (615) 749-6512; f. 1789; religious, general; Gen. Man. NEIL M. ALEXANDER.

Harry N. Abrams, Inc: 100 Fifth Ave, New York, NY 10011; tel. (212) 206-7715; telex 175975; fax (212) 645-8437; division of Times Mirror Co; art, architecture, natural history, popular culture; Pres., CEO and Editor-in-Chief PAUL GOTTLIEB.

Academic Press, Inc: 1250 Sixth Ave, San Diego, CA 92101; tel. (619) 231-0926; telex 568364; fax (619) 669-6320; f. 1942; division of Harcourt Brace Jovanovich, Inc; medical, scientific and technical books and journals; Pres. STEVEN A. DOWLING.

Addison-Wesley-Longman Group: 95 Church St, White Plains, NY 10601; tel. (914) 993-5000; telex 6801023; f. 1988; educational, trade, scientific, engineering, and language teaching materials; Pres. BRUCE S. BUTTERFIELD.

Africana Publishing Co: IUB Bldg, 30 Irving Pl., New York, NY 10003; tel. (212) 254-4100; telex 236845; f. 1969; division of Holmes & Meier Publishers, Inc; general humanities, social sciences; Pres. and Publr MAX J. HOLMES.

Andrews, McMeel & Parker, Inc: 4900 Main St, Kansas City, MO 64112; tel. (816) 932-6700; telex 437007; fax (816) 932-6648; f. 1933; humour, journalism, do-it-yourself; Pres. GEORGE L. PARKER.

Appleton & Lange: 25 Van Zant St, East Norwalk, CT 06855; tel. (203) 838-4400; f. 1825; division of Simon & Schuster, Inc; medical, nursing, health care; Pres. and CEO LIN PATERSON.

Jason Aronson, Inc: 230 Livingston St, Northvale, NJ 07647; tel. (201) 767-4093; f. 1965; psychiatry, psychoanalysis and behavioural sciences; Judaica; Pres. JASON ARONSON.

Aspen Publishers Inc: 1600 Research Blvd, Rockville, MD 20850; tel. (301) 251-5000; telex 6014543; f. 1959; health, business and professional textbooks, reference; Pres. JOHN R. MAROZSAN.

Associated Faculty Press/Kennikat Press: 19 West 36th St, New York, NY 10018; tel. (212) 307-1300; f. 1981; scholarly and reprints; Pres. LINDA B. CAHILL.

Atheneum Publishers: 866 Third Ave, New York, NY 10022; tel. (212) 702-2000; telex 225925; f. 1959; division of Macmillan, Inc; fiction and non-fiction, poetry, drama; Pres. and Publr THOMAS A. STEWART, Jr.

Atlantic Monthly Press: 19 Union Sq. West, New York, NY 10003; tel. (212) 645-4462; telex 147105; f. 1917; fiction, biography, history, social science, poetry; Publr CARL NAVARRE; Editorial Dir GARY FISKETJON.

Augsburg Fortress, Publishers: 426 South Fifth St, POB 1209, Minneapolis, MN 55440; tel. (612) 330-3300; fax (612) 330-3455; f. 1890; religious; Pres. ALBERT E. ANDERSON.

August House Inc, Publishers: POB 3223, Little Rock, AR 72203; tel. (501) 663-7300; f. 1979; Southern regional, history, humour and folklore; Pres. TED PARKHURST.

Avery Publishing Group, Inc: 89 Baldwin Terrace, Wayne, NJ 07470; tel. (201) 696-3359; f. 1976; college textbooks, trade books specializing in childbirth, child care, health and military science; Pres. RUDY SHUR.

Avon Books: 105 Madison Ave, New York, NY 10016; tel. (212) 481-5600; telex 880261; f. 1941; division of Hearst Corpn; reprints and originals; Pres. and Publr CAROLYN REIDY.

Baker Book House: POB 6287, Grand Rapids, MI 49506; tel. (616) 676-9185; fax (616) 676-9573; f. 1939; religious (Protestant); Pres. RICHARD BAKER.

Ballantine/Del Rey/Fawcett Books: 201 East 50th St, New York, NY 10022; tel. (212) 751-2600; f. 1952; division of Random House Inc; fiction, non-fiction, paperbacks and reprints; Pres. SUSAN J. PETERSEN.

Ballinger Publishing Co: 54 Church St, Harvard Sq., Cambridge, MA 02138-3730; tel. (617) 492-0670; fax (617) 661-3281; division of Harper & Row, Publishers Inc; professional, reference, textbooks; Pres. CAROL FRANCO.

Bantam Doubleday Dell Publishing Group: 666 Fifth Ave, New York, NY 10103; tel. (212) 765-6500; telex 237992; f. 1945; general fiction and non-fiction; Pres. and Publr LINDA GREY; Editor-in-Chief STEPHEN RUBIN.

Barnes and Noble Books: 10 East 53rd St, New York, NY 10022; tel. (212) 207-7000; telex 62501; fax (212) 207-7145; f. 1873; division of Harper & Row, Publishers Inc; educational and general; Editor CAROL COHEN.

Barron's Educational Series, Inc: 250 Wireless Blvd, Hauppauge, NY 11788; tel. (516) 434-3311; telex 143160; fax (516) 434-3723; f. 1945; general non-fiction, educational, juvenile; Pres. MANUEL H. BARRON.

Basic Books Inc, Publishers: 10 East 53rd St, New York, NY 10022; tel. (212) 207-7057; telex 981585; fax (212) 207-7145; f. 1953; division of Harper & Row, Publishers Inc; social, physical, political, behavioural and natural sciences, natural history; Pres., Publr and Editorial Dir MARTIN KESSLER.

Beacon Press: 25 Beacon St, Boston, MA 02108; tel. (617) 742-2110; f. 1854; world affairs, religion, general non-fiction; Dir WENDY J. STROTHMAN.

Beekman Publishers Inc: POB 888, Woodstock, NY 12498; tel. (914) 679-2300; f. 1972; new titles, imported titles from England and Russia; Chair. STUART A. OBER.

Matthew Bender and Co Inc: 11 Penn Plaza, New York, NY 10001; tel. (212) 967-7707; f. 1887; division of Times Mirror Co; legal, accountancy, insurance and banking texts and treatises; Pres. L. W. PETERSON.

The Benjamin-Cummings Publishing Co, Inc: 2725 Sand Hill Rd, Menlo Park, CA 94025; tel. (415) 854-0300; telex 348398; f. 1977; division of Addison-Wesley Publishing Co; life, physical and health sciences, mathematics, computer science, general science; Pres. DONALD R. HAMMONDS.

Berkley Publishing Group: 200 Madison Ave, New York, NY 10016; tel. (212) 951-8800; telex 422386; fax (212) 213-6706; f. 1954; division of the Putnam Berkley Group; paperback; Pres. DAVID SHANKS.

Bethany House Publishers: 6820 Auto Club Rd, Minneapolis, MN 55438; tel. (612) 829-2500; f. 1956; religious (Evangelical); Publr GARY L. JOHNSON.

Birkhäuser Boston Inc: 675 Massachusetts Ave, Cambridge, MA 02139; tel. (617) 876-2333; telex 951041; f. 1979; scientific and technical, German language, architecture and design; Pres. and Publr JOLANDA VON HAGAN.

Black Rose Books Ltd: 340 Nagel Dr., Cheektowaga, NY 14225; tel. (716) 683-4547.

Basil Blackwell Inc: 432 Park Ave South, Suite 1503, New York, NY 10016; tel. (212) 684-2890; telex 3331796; fax (212) 213-6183; f. 1984; trade, academic and college texts; Exec. Vice-Pres. CHRISTOPHER R. KERR.

The Borgo Press: POB 2845, San Bernardino, CA 92406; tel. (714) 884-5813; f. 1975; academic and scholarly texts in history, social sciences and literature; Publr ROBERT REGINALD.

Thomas Bouregy and Co Inc: 401 Lafayette St, 2nd Floor, New York, NY 10003; tel. (212) 598-0222; f. 1950; romantic fiction, adventure, westerns; Pres. J. COLLINS COFFEE; Editor BARBARA J. BRETT.

R. R. Bowker Co: 245 West 17th St, New York, NY 10011; tel. (212) 645-9700; telex 127703; fax (212) 242-6987; f. 1872; division of Reed Publishing USA; trade journals, reference and bibliographies; Pres. IRA T. SIEGEL.

Braille Inc: C-3 Heritage Pl., 205 Worcester Ct, Falmouth, MA 02540-3917; tel. (508) 540-0800; f. 1971; fiction, non-fiction, mathematics, science, educational and computer materials in Braille transcription; Exec. Dir JOAN B. ROSE.

Branden Press, Inc: 17 Station St, POB 843, Brookline Village, Boston, MA 02147; tel. (617) 734-2045; f. 1903; art, music, classics, fiction, general non-fiction; Pres. and Treas. ADOLPH CASO.

George Braziller, Inc: 60 Madison Ave, New York, NY 10010; tel. (212) 889-0909; telex 422144; f. 1955; fiction and non-fiction, art; Pres. GEORGE BRAZILLER.

Broadman Press: 127 Ninth Ave North, Nashville, TN 37234; tel. (615) 251-2533; fax (615) 251-2440; f. 1891; religious (Protestant), fiction, non-fiction, music, juvenile; Pres. DESSEL ALDERHOLT.

The Brookings Institution: 1775 Massachusetts Ave, NW, Washington, DC 20036; tel. (202) 797-6000; fax (202) 797-6004; f. 1927; economics, government, foreign policy; Dir of Publs ROBERT L. FAHERTY.

Brooks/Cole Publishing Co: 511 Forest Lodge Rd, Pacific Grove, CA 93950-5098; tel. (408) 373-0728; fax (408) 375-6414; f. 1966; college textbooks; Pres. MICHAEL V. NEEDHAM.

Wm C. Brown Publishers: 2460 Kerper Blvd, Dubuque, IA 52001; tel. (319) 588-1451; telex 468541; fax (319) 589-2955; college textbooks, religious, trade; Chair. WILLIAM C. BROWN; Pres. and CEO MARK C. FALB.

Burgess International Group Inc: 7110 Ohms Lane, Edina, MN 55435; tel. (612) 831-1344; telex 299458; fax (612) 831-3167; f. 1925; college textbooks and manuals; Pres. BERNARD BREY.

Butterworth Publishers: 80 Montvale Ave, Stoneham, MA 02180; tel. (617) 438-8464; telex 880052; fax (617) 438-1479; f. 1975; division of Reed Publishing USA; medical, scientific, security, photography; Pres. ERIC J. NEWMAN.

Cambridge University Press: 32 East 57th St, New York, NY 10022; tel. (212) 688-8885; Dir ALAN WINTER.

Carolrhoda Books Inc: 241 First Ave North, Minneapolis, MN 55401; tel. (612) 332-3345; telex 5106011731; fax (612) 332-7615; f. 1969; juvenile, fiction and non-fiction; Editorial Dir EMILY KELLEY.

Carroll & Graf Publishers Inc: 260 Fifth Ave, New York, NY 10001; tel. (212) 889-8772; f. 1983; original hardcovers, trade and mass-market paperbacks; Publr and Exec. Editor KENT CARROLL.

Castle Books, Inc: 110 Enterprise Ave, Secaucus, NJ 07094; tel. (201) 864-6341; telex 126117; fax (201) 864-8722; f. 1971; art, history, sports, hobbies; Chair. ARNOLD HAUSNER.

The Catholic University of America Press: 620 Michigan Ave, NE, Washington, DC 20064; tel. (202) 635-5052; telex 292016; fax (202) 861-0621; f. 1939; scholarly; Dir DAVID J. McGONAGLE.

The Caxton Printers Ltd: 312 Main St, Caldwell, ID 83605; tel. (208) 459-7421; f. 1903; Western Americana; Pres. GORDON GIPSON.

Chartwell Books Inc: 110 Enterprise Ave, Secaucus, NJ 07094; tel. (201) 864-6341; telex 126117; fax (201) 864-8722; f. 1975; regional, art, history, sports, hobbies; Chair. ARNOLD HAUSNER.

Chelsea House Publishers: 95 Madison Ave, New York, NY 10016; tel. (212) 683-4400; telex 4974068; f. 1966; history, trade, young adult, reference; Pres. PHILIP D. COHEN.

Chicago Review Press Inc: 814 North Franklin St, Chicago, IL 60610; tel. (312) 337-0747; f. 1973; general non-fiction; Pres. E. CURTIS MATTHEWS.

Children's Press: 5440 North Cumberland Ave, Chicago, IL 60656; tel. (312) 693-0800; telex 2215226; fax (312) 693-0574; f. 1944; division of Grolier Inc; juvenile educational; Pres. JOHN WINTER.

The Child's World Inc: 980 North McLean Blvd, Elgin, IL 60123; tel. (312) 741-7591; f. 1968; childhood education; Pres. JANE BUERGER.

Chilton Co: Chilton Way, Radnor, PA 19089-9931; tel. (215) 964-4000; telex 173223; fax (215) 964-4745; f. 1955; crafts and hobbies, automotive, business and technical; Pres. and CEO LAWRENCE A. FORNASIERI.

Churchill Livingstone Inc: 1560 Broadway, New York, NY 10036; tel. (212) 819-5400; telex 662266; fax (212) 302-6598; f. 1979; division of Addison-Wesley-Longman Group; medical; Pres. and CEO TONI M. TRACY.

Citadel Press: 120 Enterprise Ave, Secaucus, NJ 07094; tel. (201) 866-4199; fax (201) 866-8159; f. 1939; general fiction and non-fiction; Pres. ROBERT SALOMON.

Cliffs Notes Inc: POB 80728, Lincoln, NE 68501; tel. (402) 423-5050; fax (402) 423-9254; f. 1957; study and teaching aids, language study, photo humour; Pres. J. R. SPELLMAN.

Collector Books: 5801 Kentucky Dam Rd, Paducah, KY 42001; tel. (502) 898-6211; f. 1971; antiques and collectibles; CEO BILL SCHROEDER.

Columbia University Press: 562 West 113th St, New York, NY 10025; tel. (212) 316-7100; telex 752794; fax (212) 316-7169; f. 1893; trade, educational, scientific, reference; Pres. JOHN D. MOORE.

Commerce Clearing House, Inc: 4025 West Peterson Ave, Chicago, IL 60646; tel. (312) 583-8500; telex 2212587; taxation and business law; Pres. RICHARD T. MERRILL; Man. Editor ALLEN E. SCHECHTER.

Compton's Learning Co: 310 South Michigan Ave, Chicago, IL 60604; tel. (312) 347-7337; telex 190203; fax (312) 347-7399; f. 1922; division of Encyclopaedia Britannica, Inc; reference; Editor DALE GOOD.

Concordia Publishing House: 3558 South Jefferson Ave, St Louis, MO 63118; tel. (314) 664-7000; telex 44896; fax (314) 664-1492; f. 1869; religious (Protestant), fiction, music; Pres. JOHN W. GERBER.

The Conference Board Inc: 845 Third Ave, New York, NY 10022; tel. (212) 759-0900; telex 237282; f. 1916; studies in management practices, economics and public affairs; Pres. JAMES T. MILLS.

Congressional Quarterly Books: 1414 22nd St, NW, Washington, DC 20037; tel. (202) 887-8500; f. 1945; business, education and government; directories; Publr WAYNE P. KELLEY; Pres. ANDREW BARNES.

Contemporary Books Inc: 180 North Michigan Ave, Chicago, IL 60601; tel. (312) 782-9181; fax (312) 782-3987; f. 1947; general non-fiction, juvenile, adult education; Pres. HARVEY PLOTRICK.

David C. Cook Publishing Co: 850 North Grove Ave, Elgin, IL 60120; tel. (312) 741-0800; fax (312) 741-2444; f. 1875; poetry, reference, religion, juvenile, general titles; Chair. DAVID C. COOK, III.

Cornell University Press: 124 Roberts Pl., POB 250, Ithaca, NY 14851; tel. (607) 257-7000; telex 6713054; fax (607) 255-7116; f. 1869; scholarly, non-fiction; Publr DAVID H. GILBERT.

Council of State Governments: Iron Works Pike, POB 11910, Lexington, KY 40578; tel. (606) 252-2291; f. 1935; reference publications on state government subjects.

CPI (Contemporary Perspectives Inc): 145 East 49th St, New York, NY 10017; tel. (212) 753-3800; f. 1976; school and library textbooks, trade, microcomputer software, multimedia; Pres. STEPHEN P. BERNER.

CRC Press Inc: 2000 Corporate Blvd, NW, Boca Raton, FL 33431; tel. (407) 994-0555; telex 568689; f. 1913; medical, scientific and technical reference books; Pres. JOHN DILL.

Creative Education, Inc: 123 South Broad St, POB 227, Mankato, MN 56001; tel. (507) 388-6273; f. 1932; juvenile; Pres. GEORGE R. PETERSON, Jr.

Crown Publishers, Inc: 225 Park Ave South, New York, NY 10003; tel. (212) 254-1600; telex 427195; f. 1936; division of Random House Inc; general fiction and non-fiction, illustrated books, educational materials, reprints; Sr Vice-Pres. (Publishing) MICHELLE SIDRANE.

John Curley & Associates Inc: POB 37, South Yarmouth, MA 02664; tel. (617) 394-1282; f. 1976; popular authors, large-print books; Pres. JOHN F. CURLEY.

Da Capo Press Inc: 233 Spring St, New York, NY 10013; tel. (212) 656-5033; telex 421139; f. 1964; division of Plenum Publishing Corpn; scholarly; Pres. MARTIN E. TASH.

F. A. Davis Co: 1915 Arch St, Philadelphia, PA 19103; tel. (215) 568-2270; telex 834837; f. 1879; medical, nursing and allied health textbooks; Chair. and Pres. ROBERT H. CRAVEN.

DAW Books, Inc: 1633 Broadway, New York, NY 10019; tel. (212) 397-8017; telex 236109; f. 1971; science fiction, fantasy; Publr DONALD A. WOLLHEIM; Pres. and Editor-in-Chief BETSY WOLLHEIM.

Walter de Gruyter Inc: 200 Saw Mill River Rd, Hawthorne, NY 10532; tel. (914) 747-0110; telex 646677; fax (914) 747-1326; f. 1971; scholarly, scientific, journals, reprints; Vice-Pres. and Gen. Man. ECKART A. SCHEFFLER.

Marcel Dekker, Inc: 270 Madison Ave, New York, NY 10016; tel. (212) 696-9000; telex 421419; fax (212) 685-4540; f. 1963; textbooks and reference; Pres. MARCEL DEKKER.

Delmar Publishers Inc: 2 Computer Dr., POB 15015, West Albany, NY 12212; tel. (518) 459-1150; f. 1945; textbooks, technology, health care, mathematics and vocational studies, travel; Pres. GREGORY C. SPATZ.

Devin-Adair Co: 6 North Water St, Greenwich, CT 06830; tel. (203) 531-7755; f. 1911; general non-fiction, nature, health, conservative politics, revisionist history, gardening, cookery, Irish interest; Publr CLAUDINE DE LA BELLE ISSUE; Man. Dir ROGER LOURIE.

Dial Books For Young Readers: 2 Park Ave, New York, NY 10016; tel. (212) 725-1818; telex 125836; fax (212) 532-6568; f. 1961; division of New American Library (Penguin USA); children's picture books, trade, fiction and non-fiction; Pres., Publr and Editor-in-Chief PHYLLIS J. FOGELMAN.

Dodd, Mead & Co Inc: 71 Fifth Ave, New York, NY 10003; tel. (212) 627-8444; f. 1839; general fiction and non-fiction; Chair. JEROME GROSSMAN; Pres. JONATHAN DODD; Publr LYNNE A. LUMSDEN.

The Dorsey Press: 224 South Michigan Ave, Suite 440, Chicago, IL 60604; tel. (312) 322-8400; telex 277972; f. 1959; division of Richard D. Irwin, Inc; educational, political science; Publr DAVID C. FOLLMER.

Doubleday: 666 Fifth Ave, New York, NY 10103; tel. (212) 492-9799; telex 237019; fax (212) 492-9700; f. 1897; division of Bantam Doubleday Dell Publishing Group; general fiction and non-fiction; Pres. and Publr NANCY EVANS.

Dover Publications, Inc: 31 East Second St, Mineola, NY 11501; tel. (516) 294-7000; telex 127731; fax (516) 742-5049; f. 1941; trade, reprints, scientific, classics, language, arts and crafts; Pres. HAYWARD CIRKER.

Dow Jones–Irwin: 1818 Ridge Rd, Homewood, IL 60430; tel. (312) 798-6000; telex 254382; f. 1965; division of Richard D. Irwin, Inc; business; Pres. and CEO ROBERT A. SCHMITZ.

Drama Book Publishers: 260 Fifth Ave, New York, NY 10001; tel. (212) 725-5377; f. 1967; performing arts texts and plays; Pres. and Editor-in-Chief RALPH PINE.

The Dramatic Publishing Co: 311 Washington St, POB 109, Woodstock, IL 60098; tel. (815) 338-7170; f. 1884; plays; Pres. CHRISTOPHER SERGEL.

Dufour Editions, Inc: POB 449, Chester Springs, PA 19425; tel. (215) 458-5005; f. 1946; literary, political science, humanities, music, history; Pres. KRISTIN DUFOUR.

Duke University Press: POB 6697, College Station, Durham, NC 27708; tel. (919) 684-2173; telex 802829; f. 1922; scholarly; Dir RICHARD C. ROWSON.

Duquesne University Press: 600 Forbes Ave, Pittsburgh, PA 15282; tel. (412) 434-6610; f. 1927; scholarly; Dir JOHN DOWDS.

E. P. Dutton, Inc: 2 Park Ave, New York, NY 10016; tel. (212) 725-1818; telex 125836; fax (212) 532-6568; f. 1852; division of New American Library (Penguin USA); general; Pres. and Publr RICHARD MAREK.

Ediciones Universal: 3090 Eighth St, Miami, FL 33135; tel. (305) 642-3234; telex 6811258; f. 1965; Spanish language fiction and non-fiction; Man. JUAN MANUEL SALVAT.

Wm B. Eerdmans Publishing Co: 255 Jefferson Ave, SE, Grand Rapids, MI 49503; tel. (616) 459-4591; telex 234111; fax (616) 459-6540; f. 1911; social concerns, religious, scholarly, juvenile, regional history; Chair. HERO BRATT.

Elsevier Science Publishing Co, Inc: 52 Vanderbilt Ave, New York, NY 10017; tel. (212) 370-5520; telex 420643; fax (212) 916-1288; f. 1962; scientific, medical, technical, multilingual technical journals; Pres. MICHAEL G. BOSWOOD.

Encyclopaedia Britannica, Inc: 310 South Michigan Ave, Chicago, IL 60604; tel. (312) 347-7000; telex 2213243; f. 1768; encyclopedias, atlases, dictionaries; Chair. of Board ROBERT P. GWINN; Pres. PETER B. NORTON.

Lawrence Erlbaum Associates Inc: 365 Broadway, Hillsdale, NJ 07642; tel. (201) 666-4110; telex 132318; f. 1974; scholarly, behavioural sciences, communications, computer science; Pres. LAWRENCE ERLBAUM.

M. Evans & Co, Inc: 216 East 49th St, New York, NY 10017; tel. (212) 688-2810; f. 1960; adult and juvenile fiction and non-fiction; Pres. GEORGE C. DE KAY.

Faber & Faber Inc: 50 Cross St, Winchester, MA 01890; tel. (617) 721-1427; telex 888878; fax (617) 729-2783; f. 1976; fiction and non-fiction; Pres. and Publr THOMAS KELLEHER.

Facts on File Inc: 460 Park Ave South, New York, NY 10016; tel. (212) 683-2244; telex 238552; f. 1940; division of Commerce Clearing House Inc; non-fiction, reference, general trade; Pres. HOWARD M. EPSTEIN.

Fairleigh Dickinson University Press: 285 Madison Ave, Madison, NJ 07940; tel. (201) 377-4700; f. 1966; scholarly; Editor HARRY KEYISHIAN.

Farrar, Straus & Giroux, Inc: 19 Union Sq. West, New York, NY 10003; tel. (212) 741-6900; telex 667428; fax (212) 633-9385; f. 1946; general, new writing; Pres. ROGER W. STRAUS; Chair. ROBERT GIROUX.

J. G. Ferguson Publishing Co: 111 East Wacker Dr., Chicago, IL 60601; tel. (312) 861-0666; telex 2212707; f. 1940; reference; Pres. STEWART W. LAPHAM.

Fodor's Travel Publications: 201 East 50th St, New York, NY 10022; tel. (212) 751-2600; telex 425592; fax (212) 572-2248; division of Random House Inc; travel guides; Editorial Dir MICHAEL SPRING.

Folcroft Library Editions/Norwood Editions: 842 Main St, Darby, PA 19203; tel. (215) 583-4550; f. 1968; reprints, textbooks, trade; Pres. and Editor-in-Chief MARK B. WEIMAN.

Fordham University Press: University Box L, Bronx, NY 10458-5172; tel. (212) 579-2319; fax (212) 579-2708; f. 1907; scholarly; Dir H. GEORGE FLETCHER.

Fortress Press: 426 South Fifth St, POB 1209, Minneapolis, MN 55440; tel. (612) 330-3300; fax (612) 330-3455; f. 1855; religious education (Lutheran); Pres. ALBERT E. ANDERSON.

Foundation Press Inc: 615 Merrick Rd, Westbury, NY 11590; tel. (516) 832-6950; telex 960216; f. 1931; law; Pres. HAROLD R. ERIV.

Franciscan Herald Press: 1434 West 51st St, Chicago, IL 60609; tel. (312) 254-4462; f. 1917; Roman Catholic; Man. Rev. GABRIEL BRINKMAN.

W. H. Freeman & Co, Publishers: 41 Madison Ave, New York, NY 10010; tel. (212) 576-9400; telex 12326; fax (212) 689-2383; f. 1946; textbooks; Pres. and Editor LINDA CHAPUT.

Samuel French, Inc: 45 West 25th St, New York, NY 10010; tel. (212) 206-8990; fax (212) 206-1429; f. 1830; plays; Man. Dir ABBOTT VAN NOSTRAND.

Funk & Wagnalls: 70 Hilltop Rd, Ramsey, NJ 07446; tel. (201) 934-7500; telex 62477; f. 1876; encyclopedias, general reference, juvenile; Pres. and CEO EDWARD A. VOLKWEIN.

Futura Publishing Co Inc: 295 Main St, POB 330, Mount Kisco, NY 10549; tel. (914) 666-3505; telex 420170; f. 1970; medical and scientific; Chair. and Publr STEVEN E. KORN.

Gale Research Inc: Book Tower, Detroit, MI 48226; tel. (313) 961-2242; telex 2217086; fax (313) 961-6241; f. 1954; reference; Pres. T. A. PAUL; Exec. Vice-Pres. and Editorial Dir DEDRIA BRYFONSKI.

Garland Publishing Inc: 136 Madison Ave, New York, NY 10016; tel. (212) 686-7492; telex 424588; fax (212) 889-9399; f. 1969; reprints, reference, college textbooks, law; Chair. GAVIN G. BORDEN.

Bernard Geis Associates: 128 East 56th St, New York, NY 10022; tel. (212) 752-1975; f. 1958; general fiction and non-fiction; Pres. BERNARD GEIS.

Genealogical Publishing Co: 1001 North Calvert St, Baltimore, MD 21202; tel. (301) 837-8271; f. 1959; genealogy, immigration studies, heraldry, local history; Pres. MICHAEL TEPPER.

Gessler Publishing Co Inc: 55 West 13th St, New York, NY 10011; tel. (212) 627-0099; telex 503770; f. 1932; books and visual material for langauge teaching; Pres. SETH C. LEVIN.

The K. S. Giniger Co, Inc: 1133 Broadway, Suite 1301, New York, NY 10010; tel. (212) 645-5150; telex 955439; f. 1965; general non-fiction; Pres. KENNETH S. GINIGER.

Michael Glazier Inc: 1935 West Fourth St, Wilmington, DE 19805; tel. (302) 654-1635; f. 1977; law, history and religion; Pres. MICHAEL GLAZIER.

Glencoe Publishing Co: 15319 Chatsworth St, Mission Hills, CA 91345; tel. (818) 898-1391; f. 1972; textbooks; Pres. JACK E. WITMER.

Gordon & Breach, Science Publishers Inc: 50 West 23rd St, New York, NY 10010; tel. (212) 206-8900; telex 236735; fax (212) 645-2459; f. 1961; scientific and technical books and journals; Chair. MARTIN B. GORDON; Editorial Dir PHILIP C. MANOR.

Gower Publishing Co: Old Post Rd, Brookfield, VT 05036; tel. (802) 276-3162; telex 759615; f. 1979; professional, scholarly and reference; Pres. JAMES W. GERARD.

Warren H. Green, Inc: 8356 Olive Blvd, St Louis, MO 63132; tel. (314) 991-1335; fax (314) 997-1788; f. 1966; medical, science, technology, philosophy; Pres. WARREN H. GREEN.

Stephen Greene Press: 15 Muzzey St, Lexington, MA 02173; tel. (617) 861-0170; telex 2404974; fax (617) 861-3807; f. 1957; division of Viking Penguin Inc; general non-fiction; Pres. and Publr THOMAS L. BEGNER.

Greenwillow Books: 105 Madison Ave, New York, NY 10016; tel. (212) 889-3050; telex 224063; fax (212) 779-0965; f. 1974; juvenile; Vice-Pres. and Editor-in-Chief SUSAN HIRSCHMAN.

Greenwood Press: 88 Post Rd West, POB 5007, Westport, CT 06881; tel. (203) 226-3571; telex 4573586; fax (203) 222-1502; f. 1967; business reference and non-fiction; Pres. ROBERT HAGELSTEIN.

Grolier Inc: Sherman Turnpike, Danbury, CT 06816; tel. (203) 797-3500; telex 969641; fax (203) 797-3197; f. 1895; encyclopedias, reference, educational; Chair. and CEO R. B. CLARKE; Pres. and COO ERIC LAFFONT.

Grove Press: 841 Broadway, New York, NY 10003-4793; tel. (212) 614-7850; telex 6720753; fax (212) 614-7886; fiction and non-fiction, college textbooks; Pres. ANN GETTY.

Gulf Publishing Co, Book/Software/Video Division: POB 2608, Houston, TX 77252; tel. (713) 529-4301; telex 275418; fax (713) 529-4438; f. 1916; texts and computer software on chemical and mechanical, engineering, petroleum, business, construction, videotape training; Vice-Pres. and Dir CLAYTON A. UMBACH, Jr.

Hacker Art Books Inc: 54 West 57th St, New York, NY 10019; tel. (212) 757-1450; f. 1946; art history originals and reprints; Pres. LINDA B. HACKER.

G. K. Hall & Co: 70 Lincoln St, Boston, MA 02111; tel. (617) 423-3990; telex 940037; fax (617) 423-3999; f. 1942; division of Macmillan Publishing Co; reference, art, literary criticism, biography, history, social sciences, large-print; Publr THOMAS T. BEELER; Editor-in-Chief ELIZABETH B. KUBIK.

Hammond Inc: 515 Valley St, Maplewood, NJ 07040; tel. (201) 763-6000; telex 136585; fax (201) 763-7658; f. 1900; maps, atlases, travel, home reference; Chair. CALEB D. HAMMOND; Pres. and CEO C. DEAN HAMMOND, III.

Harcourt Brace Jovanovich Inc: 1250 Sixth Ave, San Diego, CA 92101; tel. (619) 231-6616; telex 181726; fax (619) 699-6320; f. 1919;

fiction, textbooks, general; Chair. WILLIAM JOVANOVICH; Pres. and CEO RALPH CAULO.

Harlequin Enterprises: 300 East 42nd St, New York, NY 10017; tel. (212) 682-6080; telex 127806; f. 1979; romantic fiction; Pres. DAVID GALLOWAY.

Harper & Row, Publishers Inc: 10 East 53rd St, New York, NY 10022; tel. (212) 207-7000; telex 62501; fax (212) 207-7145; f. 1817; fiction, non-fiction, religious, children's, medical, general; Pres. and CEO GEORGE CRAIG.

Harvard University Press: 79 Garden St, Cambridge, MA 02138; tel. (617) 495-2600; telex 921484; fax (617) 495-5898; f. 1913; educational, scientific, classics, fine arts, philosophy, religion, history and government; Dir ARTHUR J. ROSENTHAL; Editor-in-Chief MAUD WILCOX.

Hastings House Publishers, New York Ltd: 9 East 40th St, New York, NY 10016; tel. (212) 685-2928; fax (212) 685-3087; f. 1936; communication, arts, media, travel, children's; Pres. ERIC M. KAMPMANN.

The Haworth Press Inc: 12 West 32nd St, New York, NY 10001; tel. (212) 279-1200; telex 4932599; fax (212) 629-0482; f. 1973; technical, social and behavioural sciences; Pres. PATRICK MCLOUGHLIN.

D. C. Heath & Co: 125 Spring St, Lexington, MA 02173; tel. (617) 860-1340; telex 923455; fax (617) 860-1508; f. 1885; textbooks; Pres. LOREN KORTE.

Hemisphere Publishing Corpn: 79 Madison Ave, Suite 1110, New York, NY 10016; tel. (212) 725-1999; telex 2509620; fax (212) 213-8368; f. 1974; division of Taylor and Francis Ltd; scientific, professional, reference, textbooks; Pres. and Publr WILLIAM BEGELL.

Hero Books: 10392 Democracy Lane, Fairfax, VA 22030; tel. (703) 591-3674; telex 904059; fax (703) 591-6109; f. 1983; military history, political science, Russian studies; Publr GUY P. CLIFTON.

Lawrence Hill Books: 642 West 227th St, 3rd Floor, Riverdale, NY 10463; tel. (212) 601-5806; f. 1972; history, international politics, African studies; Dir SHIRLEY A. CLOYES.

Hill and Wang: 19 Union Sq. West, New York, NY 10003; tel. (212) 741-6900; telex 667428; fax (212) 633-9385; f. 1956; division of Farrar, Straus & Giroux, Inc; general, drama, history; Publr STEVE WASSERMAN.

Hippocrene Books Inc: 171 Madison Ave, New York, NY 10016; tel. (212) 685-4371; telex 4933449; f. 1971; trade, history, music, travel, foreign-language dictionaries; Pres. and Editorial Dir GEORGE BLAGOWIDOW.

Holden Day, Inc: 4432 Telegraph Ave, Oakland, CA 94609; tel. (415) 428-9400; telex 337109; f. 1959; textbooks, scientific, reference, mathematics, statistics, management, computer science; Chair. and Pres. FREDERICK H. MURPHY.

Holiday House Inc: 18 East 53rd St, New York, NY 10022; tel. (212) 688-0085; fax (212) 421-6134; f. 1935; juvenile; Pres. JOHN H. BRIGGS, Jr.

Holmes & Meier Publishers, Inc: 30 Irving Pl., New York, NY 10003; tel. (212) 254-4100; telex 236845; f. 1969; history, political science, area studies, general non-fiction, foreign literature in translation, college texts and scholarly; Publr MAX J. HOLMES.

Henry Holt & Co: 115 West 18th St, New York, NY 10011; tel. (212) 886-9200; telex 424632; fax (212) 633-0748; f. 1866; Pres. and Publr BRUNO QUINSON.

Holt, Rinehart & Winston, Inc: Orlando, FL 32887; tel. (407) 345-2000; f. 1866; division of Harcourt Brace Jovanovich Inc; school textbooks; Sr Vice-Pres. MARGARET MARY McQUILLAN.

Hoover Institution Press: Stanford University, Stanford, CA 94305-6010; tel. (415) 723-3373; telex 348402; fax (415) 723-1687; f. 1962; scholarly; Exec. Editor SUE E. FACTOR.

Houghton Mifflin Co: One Beacon St, Boston, MA 02108; tel. (617) 725-5000; telex 4430255; fax (617) 227-5409; f. 1832; general and educational; Chair., Pres. and CEO HAROLD T. MILLER; COO ROBERT F. BAKER.

Human Sciences Press Inc: 72 Fifth Ave, New York, NY 10011; tel. (212) 243-6000; f. 1965; medicine, health, behavioural and social sciences; Chair. and Pres. SHELDON R. ROEN.

Humanities Press International Inc: 171 First Ave, Atlantic Highlands, NJ 07716-1289; tel. (201) 872-1441; telex 752233; fax (201) 872-0717; f. 1950; scholarly, humanities and social sciences; Pres. KEITH M. ASHFIELD.

Indiana University Press: 10th and Morton Sts, Bloomington, IN 47405; tel. (812) 855-4203; telex 272279; fax (812) 335-5678; f. 1950; trade and scholarly non-fiction; Dir JOHN GALLMAN.

International Universities Press, Inc: 59 Boston Post Rd, Madison, CT 06443; tel. (203) 245-4000; telex 282986; fax (203) 245-0775; f. 1943; psychology, psychiatry, medicine, social sciences and journals; Pres. MARTIN V. AZARIAN; Editor-in-Chief Dr MARGARET EMERY.

The Interstate Printers & Publishers Inc: 19 North Jackson St, POB 50, Danville, IL 61834-0050; tel. (217) 446-0500; f. 1914; vocational and special education, teacher education; Chair. and Pres. VERNIE L. THOMAS.

Iowa State University Press: 2121 South State Ave, Ames, IA 50010; tel. (515) 292-0140; f. 1924; scholarly non-fiction; Dir RICHARD R. KINNEY.

Richard D. Irwin, Inc: 1818 Ridge Rd, Homewood, IL 60430; tel. (312) 798-6000; telex 277972; fax (312) 798-6296; f. 1933; economics, business; Chair., Pres. and CEO ROBERT A. SCHMITZ.

JAI Press Inc: 55 Old Post Rd, Number 2, POB 1678, Greenwich, CT 06836; tel. (203) 661-7602; f. 1975; economics, business, science, social and behavioural sciences; Pres. and Publr HERBERT M. JOHNSON.

Jewish Publication Society: 1930 Chestnut St, Philadelphia, PA 19103-4599; tel. (215) 564-5925; f. 1888; Pres. EDWARD E. ELSON.

Johns Hopkins University Press: 701 West 40th St, Baltimore, MD 21211; tel. (301) 338-6975; telex 1012202; fax (301) 338-6998; f. 1878; social and physical sciences, humanities, health sciences, economics, literary criticism, history; Dir JACK G. GOELLNER; Exec. Editor HENRY Y. K. TOM.

Jossey-Bass, Inc, Publishers: 350 Sansome St, San Francisco, CA 94104; tel. (415) 433-1740; fax (415) 433-0499; f. 1966; textbooks, social and behavioural sciences, higher and adult education, management, health; Pres. and Editor-in-Chief ALLEN JOSSEY-BASS.

Augustus M. Kelley, Publishers: 300 Fairfield Rd, Fairfield, NJ 07006-0008; tel. (212) 685-7202; f. 1947; reprints of economic classics; Editor FREDERICK S. CHEESMAN.

Kendall/Hunt Publishing Co: 2460 Kerper Blvd, Dubuque, IA 52001; tel. (319) 588-1451; telex 468541; fax (319) 589-2955; f. 1944; division of Wm C. Brown Publishers; college and professional texts; Pres. RONALD R. MALONE.

Kluwer Academic Publishers: 101 Philip Dr., Norwell, MA 02061; tel. (617) 871-6600; telex 200190; fax (617) 871-6528; f. 1978; scientific, technical, medical, scholarly and professional books and journals; Pres. F. W. B. VAN EYSINGA.

Alfred A. Knopf, Inc: 201 East 50th St, New York, NY 10022; tel. (212) 751-2600; fax (212) 572-2593; f. 1915; division of Random House Inc; fiction, textbooks, general literature; Pres. and Editor-in-Chief S. MEHTA.

Kraus Reprint & Periodicals: Route 100, Millwood, NY 10546; tel. (914) 762-2200; telex 6818112; fax (914) 762-1195; f. 1946; Pres. HERBERT J. COHEN.

R. E. Krieger Publishing Co Inc: POB 9542, Melbourne, FL 32902; tel. (407) 724-9542; fax (407) 727-7289; f. 1970; technical, medical and scientific reprints; Pres. R. E. KRIEGER.

KTAV Publishing House Inc: 900 Jefferson St, POB 6249, Hoboken, NJ 07030; tel. (201) 963-9524; f. 1924; Jewish literature, juvenile, textbooks; Pres. SOL SCHARFSTEIN.

David S. Lake Publishers: 500 Harbor Blvd, Belmont, CA 94002; tel. (415) 592-7810; telex 171853; fax (415) 595-8143; educational, trade, special education and professional; Pres. DAVID S. LAKE.

Peter Lang Publishing Inc: 62 West 45th St, 4th Floor, New York, NY 10036-4202; tel. (212) 302-6740; telex 6973364; fax (212) 302-7574; f. 1982; monographs in humanities and social sciences; Exec. Dir BRIGITTE D. McDONALD.

Lea & Febiger: 600 Washington Sq., Philadelphia, PA 19106; tel. (215) 922-1330; telex 6701972; fax (215) 629-0060; f. 1785; medical, dental, veterinary and other life sciences; Partners C. C. F. SPAHR, C. C. F. SPAHR, Jr, J. F. SPAHR, J. F. SPAHR, Jr, R. N. SPAHR.

Leisure Books: 6 East 39th St, Suite 900, New York, NY 10016; tel. (212) 725-8811; telex 238198; f. 1982; mass-market, fiction and non-fiction, reprints; Pres. and Publr GERARD BRISMAN.

Lexington Books: 125 Spring St, Lexington, MA 02173; tel. (617) 862-6650; telex 923455; fax (617) 860-1508; f. 1969; division of D. C. Heath & Co; scholarly, professional and trade; Gen. Man. ROBERT BOVENSCHULTE.

J. B. Lippincott Co: East Washington Sq., Philadelphia, PA 19105; tel. (215) 238-4200; telex 834566; fax (215) 238-4227; f. 1792; division of Harper & Row Publishers, Inc; medical; Pres. and CEO PETER D. NALLE.

Little, Brown and Co, Inc: 34 Beacon St, Boston, MA 02108; tel. (617) 227-0730; telex 940928; fax (617) 227-4633; f. 1837; fiction, biography, history, current affairs, general trade, juveniles, medical, law, college textbooks, photography, art; Pres. and CEO KEVIN L. DOLAN.

Littlefield, Adams & Co: 81 Adams Dr., Totowa, NJ 07512; tel. (201) 256-8600; telex 130483; f. 1949; scholarly, professional, dictionaries, non-fiction; Chair. GILBERT RAFF.

Longman Inc: Longman Bldg, 95 Church St, White Plains, NY 10601; tel. (914) 993-5000; telex 6801023; f. 1973; college and professional, languages, social sciences, business; Pres. BRUCE S. BUTTERFIELD.

Longwood Publishing Group Inc: North Line Rd, Wolfeboro, NH 03894-2069; tel. (603) 569-4576; telex 953008; fax (603) 569-5451; f. 1966; academic, reference, music, history, reprints; Pres. JOHN PIZEY.

Lothrop, Lee and Shepard Books: 105 Madison Ave, New York, NY 10016; tel. (212) 889-3050; telex 224063; fax (212) 779-0965; f. 1859; division of William Morrow & Co Inc; juveniles; Editor-in-Chief DOROTHY BRILEY.

Loyola University Press: 3441 North Ashland Ave, Chicago, IL 60657; tel. (312) 281-1818; f. 1912; Dir DANIEL L. FLAHERTY.

McCutchan Publishing Corpn: 2940 San Pablo Ave, Berkeley, CA 94702; tel. (415) 841-8616; professional and college textbooks; Chair. STEPHEN A. ZELLERBACH; Publr JOHN MCCUTCHAN.

McGraw-Hill, Inc: 1221 Ave of the Americas, New York, NY 10020; tel. (212) 512-2000; telex 127960; f. 1888; information texts and services for business, industry, government and the general public; Chair. and Pres. JOSEPH L. DIONNE.

David McKay Co Inc: 201 East 50th St, New York, NY 10022; tel. (212) 751-2600; telex 425592; division of Random House Inc; non-fiction, languages, dictionaries; Vice-Pres. JONATHAN B. SEGAL.

Macmillan Publishing Co: 866 Third Ave, New York, NY 10022; tel. (212) 702-2000; telex 960868; scientific, technical and medical; Chair. ROBERT MAXWELL; Pres. WILLIAM F. REILLY.

Meckler Corpn: 11 Ferry Lane West, Westport, CT 06880; tel. (203) 226-6967; telex 955239; fax (203) 454-5840; f. 1971; library and information sciences, directories, general; Pres. and Publr ALAN M. MECKLER.

Meredith Corpn: 1716 Locust St, Des Moines, IA 50336; tel. (515) 284-3000; telex 478421; f. 1902; trade; Chair. and CEO ROBERT A. BURNETT; Pres. JACK D. REHM.

Merriam-Webster Inc: 47 Federal St, Springfield, MA 01102; tel. (413) 734-3134; telex 981608; fax (413) 731-5979; f. 1831; affiliate of Encyclopaedia Britannica Inc; dictionaries, reference; Pres. WILLIAM A. LLEWELLYN; Vice-Pres. JAMES W. WITHGOTT.

Merrill Publishing Co: 936 Eastwind Dr., Westerville, OH 43081; tel. (614) 890-1111; telex 4821155; f. 1842; textbooks, supplementary materials, software and videos; Pres. GARY D. EISENBERGER.

Michigan State University Press: 25 Manly Miles Bldg, 1405 South Harrison Rd, East Lansing, MI 48823; tel. (517) 355-9543; Dir RICHARD E. CHAPIN.

The MIT Press: 55 Hayward St, Cambridge, MA 02142; tel. (617) 253-5646; telex 921473; f. 1932; computer sciences, architecture, design, linguistics, economics, philosophy, general science, neuroscience, cognitive science and engineering; Dir FRANK URBANOWSKI.

Moody Press: 820 North LaSalle Dr., Chicago, IL 60610; tel. (312) 329-2101; fax (312) 329-2144; f. 1894; religious; Man. GREG THORNTON.

Joshua Morris Publishing Inc: 167 Old Post Rd, Southport, CT 06490; tel. (203) 259-4700; telex 221957; fax (203) 259-5534; f. 1981; children's books; Co-Chairs JOSH GASPERO and MIKE MORRIS.

William Morrow & Co Inc: 105 Madison Ave, New York, NY 10016; tel. (212) 889-3050; telex 224063; fax (212) 779-0965; f. 1926; division of Hearst Corpn; fiction, non-fiction, juveniles; Chair. and CEO ALLEN MARCHIONI.

The C. V. Mosby Co: 11830 Westline Industrial Dr., St Louis, MO 63146; tel. (314) 872-8370; telex 442402; division of Times-Mirror Co; medical, dental and nursing education, bio-sciences, physical education, social sciences, business and economics; CEO PATRICK A. CLIFFORD.

Mouton de Gruyter: 200 Saw Mill River Rd, Hawthorne, NY 10532; tel. (914) 747-0110; telex 646677; fax (914) 747-1326; f. 1956; scholarly; Vice-Pres. and Gen. Man. ECKART A. SCHEFFLER.

National Academy Press: 2101 Constitution Ave, NW, Washington, DC 20418; tel. (202) 334-3318; telex 248664; f. 1863; division of National Academy of Sciences; scientific and technical reports, abstracts, bibliographies, catalogues; Dir VIRGINIA B. MARTIN.

National Education Association Publications: 1201 16th St, NW, Washington, DC 20036; tel. (202) 822-7250; f. 1857; professional; Gen. Man. GORDON H. FELTON; Editor CHARLOTTE MCGOWAN.

National Learning Corpn: 212 Michael Dr., Syosset, NY 11791; tel. (516) 921-8888; f. 1967; professional and vocational study guides; Pres. MICHAEL P. RUDMAN.

National Textbook Co: 4255 West Touhy Ave, Lincolnwood, IL 60646; tel. (312) 679-5500; telex 2230736; f. 1962; elementary, secondary and university textbooks; Pres. S. WILLIAM PATTIS.

Thomas Nelson Inc: Nelson Pl. at Elm Hill Pike, Nashville, TN 37214; tel. (615) 889-9000; telex 4990852; fax (615) 391-5225; f. 1961;

bibles, religious (Roman Catholic), juveniles, trade; Pres. SAM MOORE.

Nelson-Hall Publishers: 111 North Canal St, Chicago, IL 60606; tel. (312) 930-9446; f. 1909; general interest non-fiction and educational; Pres. and Publr STEPHEN A. FERRARA.

The New American Library, Inc: 1633 Broadway, New York, NY 10019; tel. (312) 397-8000; telex 236109; f. 1948; division of Penguin USA; all categories except textbooks; Chair. and CEO ROBERT G. DIFORIO.

New Directions Publishing Corpn: 80 Eighth Ave, New York, NY 10011; tel. (212) 255-0230; f. 1936; modern literature, poetry, criticism, belles-lettres; Pres. and Publr JAMES LAUGHLIN.

New Hampshire Publishing Co: 9 Constitutional Way, POB 70, Somersworth, NH 03878; tel. (603) 692-3727; f. 1969; non-fiction, regional New England history and genealogy; Pres. JOHN BALLENTINE.

New York University Press: 70 Washington Sq. South, New York, NY 10012; tel. (212) 998-2575; telex 235128; fax (212) 995-3533; f. 1916; scholarly, non-fiction, general; Dir COLIN H. JONES; Man. Editor DESPINA GIMBEL.

Northwestern University Press: 625 Colfax St, POB 1093, Evanston, IL 60201; tel. (312) 491-5313; f. 1958; scholarly; Dir JONATHAN BRENT.

W. W. Norton & Co Inc: 500 Fifth Ave, New York, NY 10110; tel. (212) 354-5500; telex 220014; fax (212) 869-0856; f. 1924; general fiction and non-fiction, college textbooks, paperbacks; Chair. and Pres. DONALD S. LAMM.

Oceana Publications Inc: 75 Main St, Dobbs Ferry, NY 10522; tel. (914) 693-1394; telex 5640834; fax (914) 693-0402; f. 1957; international law and trade; Pres. and Publr PHILIP F. COHEN.

Octagon Books: 171 Madison Ave, New York, NY 10016; tel. (212) 685-4371; telex 4933449; fax (718) 454-1391; scholarly reprints; Pres. and Editor-in-Chief GEORGE BLAGOWIDOW.

Ohio State University Press: 1050 Carmack Rd, Columbus, OH 43210; tel. (614) 292-6930; f. 1957; general scholarly non-fiction; Dir PETER JOHN GIVLER.

Ohio University Press: Scott Quad., Ohio University, Athens, OH 45701; tel. (614) 593-1155; f. 1964; Dir DUANE SCHNEIDER.

Open Court Publishing Co: 315 Fifth St, Peru, IL 61354; tel. (815) 223-2520; telex 798927; fax (815) 223-4486; f. 1887; general non-fiction; Pres. and Publr M. BLOUKE CARUS.

Orbis Books: Walsh Bldg, Maryknoll, NY 10545; tel. (914) 941-7590; telex 4901122; f. 1970; religious studies of the developing countries; Exec. Dir ROBERT GORMLEY; Editor-in-Chief ROBERT ELLSBERG.

Ottenheimer Publishers Inc: 300 Reisterstown Rd, Baltimore, MD 21208; tel. (301) 484-2100; telex 198110; fax (301) 486-8301; f. 1890; encyclopedias, dictionaries, self-help books, children's colouring books; Chair. ALLAN T. HIRSH, Jr.

Outlet Book Co: 225 Park Ave South, New York, NY 10003; tel. (212) 254-1600; telex 427195; f. 1933; non-fiction and adult fiction; Pres. ALAN MIRKEN.

Oxford University Press Inc: 200 Madison Ave, New York, NY 10016; tel. (212) 679-7300; telex 130479; f. 1896; non-fiction, trade, religious, reference, bibles, college textbooks, medical, music; Pres. EDWARD W. BARRY.

Paladin Press: POB 1307, Boulder, CO 80306; tel. (303) 443-7250; telex 364412; fax (303) 442-8741; f. 1970; military science and history; Chair. and Pres. PEDER C. LUND.

Pantheon Books Inc: 201 East 50th St, New York, NY 10022; tel. (212) 751-2600; telex 126575; fax (212) 872-8026; division of Random House Inc; fiction, non-fiction, history, philosophy, art, juvenile, illustrated editions; Man. Dir ANDRÉ SCHIFFRIN.

Paragon House: 90 Fifth Ave, New York, NY 10011; tel. (212) 620-0518; fax (212) 633-0518; f. 1982; general trade non-fiction, university texts, reference; Dir JOHN MANIATIS; Editor-in-Chief BEVERLY JANE LOO.

Paulist Press: 997 Macarthur Blvd, Mahwah, NJ 07430; tel. (201) 825-7300; f. 1866; religious, philosophical, social; Publr KEVIN A. LYNCH.

Pennsylvania State University Press: 215 Wagner Bldg, University Park, PA 16802; tel. (814) 865-1327; f. 1956; scholarly non-fiction; Dir CHRIS W. KENTERA.

Pergamon Press Inc: Maxwell House, Fairview Park, Elmsford, NY 10523; tel. (914) 592-7700; telex 137328; fax (914) 592-3625; f. 1952; science, technology, education, medicine, liberal arts; Chair. and CEO L. STRAKA.

Philosophical Library, Inc: 200 West 57th St, Suite 510, New York, NY 10019; tel. (212) 265-6050; f. 1941; educational, reference, scholarly non-fiction; Pres. and Publr ROSE MORSE RUNES.

Phoenix Books, Publishers: POB 32008, Phoenix, AZ 85064; tel. (602) 952-0163; telex 4996467; fax (602) 840-8948; f. 1970; general trade, directories, reference, maps; Dir BOYE LAFAYETTE DE MENTE.

Playmore Inc, Publishers: 200 Fifth Ave, New York, NY 10159; tel. (212) 924-7447; telex 238198; f. 1942; juvenile; Pres. and Editor JON HORWICH.

Plenum Publishing Corpn: 233 Spring St, New York, NY 10013; tel. (212) 620-8000; telex 421139; scientific and technical books and journals, dictionaries, translations and medical; Chair. and Pres. MARTIN E. TASH.

Pocket Books Inc: 1230 Ave of the Americas, New York, NY 10020; tel. (212) 698-7000; telex 6720471; f. 1939; division of Simon & Schuster, Inc; reprints and originals; Pres. and Publr IRWYN APPLEBAUM; Editorial Dir WILLIAM R. GROSE.

Clarkson N. Potter Inc: 225 Park Ave South, New York, NY 10003; tel. (212) 254-1600; telex 427195; f. 1959; division of Crown Publishers, Inc; general; Chair. NAT WARTELS; Editorial Dir CAROL SOUTHERN.

Praeger Publishers, Inc: One Madison Ave, New York, NY 10010; tel. (212) 685-5300; telex 4573586; f. 1950; general non-fiction, reference, scholarly, academic; Gen. Man. RONALD D. CHAMBERS.

Price Stern Sloan Inc: 360 North La Cienega Blvd, Los Angeles, CA 90048; tel. (213) 657-6100; telex 4720816; fax (213) 855-8993; f. 1964; non-fiction, juvenile, humour, adult self-help; Chair. and Publr LAWRENCE SLOAN.

Princeton University Press: 41 William St, Princeton, NJ 08540; tel. (609) 452-4900; telex 6852306; fax (609) 895-1081; f. 1905; scholarly; Dir WALTER H. LIPPINCOTT, Jr; Editor-in-Chief SANFORD G. THATCHER.

The Psychological Corpn: 555 Academic Court, San Antonio, TX 78204; tel. (512) 299-1061; fax (512) 270-0327; division of Harcourt Brace Jovanovich Inc; educational, psychological and clinical texts; Pres. THOMAS A. WILLIAMSON.

The Putnam Berkley Group Inc: 200 Madison Ave, New York, NY 10016; tel. (212) 576-8900; telex 422386; fax (212) 213-6706; f. 1838; general; Pres. and CEO PHYLLIS GRANN.

Raintree Publishers: 310 Wisconsin Ave, Milwaukee, WI 53203; tel. (414) 273-0873; telex 2444858; fax (414) 273-0877; f. 1972; juvenile non-fiction, general reference, teaching aids; CEO JAMES F. MIRRIELEES.

Rand McNally & Co: 8255 Central Park Ave, Skokie, IL 60076; tel. (312) 673-9100; telex 2233631; f. 1856; maps, atlases, travel guides; Chair. ANDREW MCNALLY, III; Pres. ANDREW MCNALLY, IV.

Random House Inc: 201 East 50th St, New York, NY 10022; tel. (212) 751-2600; telex 126575; f. 1925; originals, reprints, paperbacks, juvenile, series, textbooks; Chair., Pres. and CEO ROBERT L. BERNSTEIN.

Raven Press: 1185 Ave of the Americas, New York, NY 10036; tel. (212) 930-9500; telex 640073; fax (212) 869-3495; f. 1964; professional, scientific textbooks and journals; Pres. ALAN M. EDELSON.

Reader's Digest Association: Reader's Digest Rd, Pleasantville, NY 10570; tel. (914) 769-7000; telex 646672; reference and non-fiction; Chair. and CEO GEORGE V. GRUNE; Vice-Pres. and Dir of Books JOHN BOHANE.

Reed Publishing USA: 275 Washington St, Newton, MA 02158; tel. (617) 964-3030; telex 940573; Chair. SAUL GOLDWEITZ; Pres. and CEO RONALD G. SEGEL.

Regal Books: 2300 Knoll Dr., Ventura, CA 93003; tel. (805) 644-9721; fax (805) 644-4729; f. 1933; religious, educational, juvenile; Chair. CYRUS N. NELSON.

Fleming H. Revell Co: 184 Central Ave, Old Tappan, NJ 07675; tel. (201) 768-8060; fax (201) 768-2749; f. 1870; religious (Protestant); Pres. and CEO DAVID J. DANZAK.

Review & Herald Publishing Association: 55 West Oak Ridge Dr., Hagerstown, MD 21740; tel. (301) 791-7000; telex 705600; f. 1861; religion, health care; Chair. K. J. MITTLEIDER.

Lynne Rienner Publishers Inc: 948 North St, Suite 8, Boulder, CO 80302; tel. (303) 444-6684; f. 1984; scholarly; Pres. LYNNE RIENNER.

The Riverside Publishing Co: 8420 West Bryn Mawr Ave, Suite 1000, Chicago, IL 60631; tel. (312) 693-0040; fax (312) 693-0325; f. 1979; educational; Pres. ROBERT JANAS.

Rizzoli International Publications Inc: 597 Fifth Ave, New York, NY 10017; tel. (212) 223-0100; telex 424514; fax (212) 888-3736; f. 1975; fine arts, performing arts, architecture; Pres., CEO and Publr GIANFRANCO MONACELLI.

Roth Publishing Inc: 185 Great Neck Rd, Great Neck, NY 11021; tel. (516) 466-3676; f. 1976; indexes, reference, bibliographies; Pres. HARVEY PAUL ROTH.

Fred B. Rothman & Co: 10368 West Centennial Rd, Littleton, CO 80127; tel. (303) 979-5657; fax (303) 973-8420; f. 1945; legal; Pres. PAUL A. ROTHMAN.

Routledge, Chapman & Hall: 29 West 35th St, New York, NY 10001; tel. (212) 244-3336; telex 6801368; fax (212) 563-2269; f. 1977; division of International Thomson Organization; scholarly, professional, trade, humanities, sciences; Pres. JOHN VON KNORRING.

Rowman & Littlefield, Publishers: 81 Adams Dr., Totowa, NJ 07512; tel. (201) 256-8600; telex 130483; f. 1969; business and economics, sciences, government, philosophy, health services; Pres. GILBERT RAFF.

Rutgers University Press: 109 Church St, New Brunswick, NJ 08903; tel. (201) 932-7762; fax (201) 932-7039; scholarly and regional; Dir KENNETH ARNOLD.

William H. Sadlier Inc: 11 Park Pl., New York, NY 10007; tel. (212) 227-2120; f. 1832; textbooks; Publr ELINOR R. FORD.

SAE (Society of Automotive Engineers, Inc): 400 Commonwealth Dr., Warrendale, PA 15096; tel. (412) 776-4841; telex 866355; fax (412) 776-5760; f. 1905; scientific and technical; Pres. GEORGE D. ARAVOSIS.

Sage Publications Inc: 2111 West Hillcrest Dr., Newbury Park, CA 91320; tel. (805) 499-0721; telex 5101000799; fax (805) 499-0871; f. 1964; professional and reference, social and behavioural sciences; Chair. SARA MILLER-MCCUNE.

St Martin's Press Inc: 175 Fifth Ave, New York, NY 10010; tel. (212) 674-5151; telex 5816459; fax (212) 420-9314; f. 1952; general, scholarly, college textbooks, reference; Chair. and CEO THOMAS J. MCCORMACK.

Salem House Publishers Ltd: 462 Boston St, Topsfield, MA 01983; tel. (617) 887-2440; fax (710) 437-0535; f. 1981; general non-fiction; Pres. PETER ACKROYD.

Howard W. Sams & Co Inc, Publishers: POB 7092, Indianapolis, IN 46268; tel. (317) 298-5400; telex 027343; division of Macmillan, Inc; textbooks, scientific and technical; Gen. Man. T. V. SURBER.

Santillana Publishing Co, Inc: 257 Union St, Northvale, NJ 07647; tel. (201) 767-6961; telex 642822; fax (201) 767-8833; f. 1972; juvenile non-fiction, educational, trade, art and hobbies; Chair. JESÚS DE POLANCO.

W. B. Saunders Co: The Curtis Center, Independence Sq. West, Philadelphia, PA 19106; tel. (215) 238-8406; telex 834795; fax (215) 238-7883; f. 1888; medical, dental and allied health sciences textbooks; Pres. LEWIS REINES; Editor-in-Chief THOMAS MACKEY.

KG Saur: 245 West 17th St, New York, NY 10011; tel. (212) 337-7023; fax (212) 242-6781; f. 1983; division of R. R. Bowker Co; library catalogues, biographical archives, bibliographies and reference; Chair. KLAUS G. SAUR.

Scarecrow Press, Inc: 52 Liberty St, POB 4167, Metuchen, NJ 08840; tel. (201) 548-8600; f. 1950; division of Franklin Watts, Inc; reference, textbooks, library science; Chair. ROBERT B. CLARKE; Pres. ALBERT W. DAUB.

Scholastic, Inc: 730 Broadway, New York, NY 10003; tel. (212) 505-3000; telex 5812057; f. 1920; children's periodicals and school textbooks; Chair., Pres. and CEO M. RICHARD ROBINSON.

Scott, Foresman and Co: 1900 East Lake Ave, Glenview, IL 60025; tel. (312) 729-3000; telex 729371; fax (312) 729-3065; f. 1896; educational; Chair. GEORGE ARTANDI; Pres. RICHARD E. PETERSON.

Shoe String Press Inc: 925 Sherman Ave, POB 4327, Hamden, CT 06514; tel. (203) 248-6307; f. 1952; scholarly and general non-fiction; Pres. and Editorial Dir JAMES THORPE, III.

Silver Burdett & Ginn: 250 James St, Morristown, NJ 07960; tel. (201) 285-7700; telex 134523; f. 1867; division of Simon & Schuster, Inc; school textbooks and related material; Pres. CHARLOTTE GEMMEL.

Simon & Schuster, Inc: 1230 Ave of the Americas, New York, NY 10020; tel. (212) 698-7000; telex 6720471; fax (212) 586-3468; f. 1924; trade, juvenile, reference, educational, elementary and secondary school textbooks, business and professional; Chair. and CEO RICHARD E. SNYDER; Pres. and Chief Publishing Officer JEREMIAH KAPLAN.

Slavica Publishers Inc: POB 14388, Columbus, OH 43214-0388; tel. (614) 268-4002; f. 1966; textbooks and scholarly works in Slavic and Eastern European languages; Pres. and Editor CHARLES GRIBBLE.

Peter Smith Publisher, Inc: 6 Lexington Ave, Magnolia, MA 01930; tel. (617) 525-3562; f. 1929; reprints; Pres. MARY ANN LASH.

W. H. Smith Publishers Inc: 112 Madison Ave, New York, NY 10016; tel. (212) 532-6600; telex 238449; fax (212) 683-5768; f. 1978; fiction and non-fiction; Pres. BRADFORD M. PURCELL.

Smithsonian Institution Press: 955 L'Enfant Plaza, Rm 2100, Washington, DC 20560; tel. (202) 287-3738; telex 264729; f. 1848;

history, science, art, anthropology, aviation, reference; Dir FELIX C. LOWE.

Southern Illinois University Press: POB 3697, Carbondale, IL 62902-3697; tel. (618) 453-2281; f. 1953; scholarly non-fiction; Dir KENNEY WITHERS.

Springer-Verlag New York, Inc: 175 Fifth Ave, 19th Floor, New York, NY 10010; tel. (212) 460-1500; telex 232235; fax (212) 473-6272; scientific, technical and medical; Pres. and CEO JOLANDA L. VON HAGEN.

SRA (Science Research Associates Inc): 155 North Wacker Dr., Chicago, IL 60606; tel. (312) 984-7000; f. 1938; educational and instructional material; Pres. J. E. GUTH, Jr.

Stackpole Books: Cameron and Kelker Sts, POB 1831, Harrisburg, PA 17105; tel. (717) 234-5041; f. 1930; general non-fiction, outdoor activities; Pres. M. DAVID DETWEILER.

Standard Educational Corpn: 200 West Monroe St, Chicago, IL 60606; tel. (312) 346-7440; telex 724451; f. 1909; encyclopedias, children's; Pres. PETER EWING.

Stanford University Press: Stanford, CA 94305; tel. (415) 723-9434; fax (415) 725-3457; f. 1925; Dir GRANT BARNES.

State University of New York Press: State University Plaza, Albany, NY 12246; tel. (518) 472-5000; f. 1966; scholarly; Editorial Dir WILLIAM D. EASTMAN.

Steck-Vaughn Co: POB 26015, Austin, TX 78755; tel. (512) 343-8227; fax (512) 343-8293; f. 1936; educational; Pres. ROY MAYERS.

Sterling Publishing Co, Inc: 387 Park Ave South, New York, NY 10016; tel. (212) 532-7160; telex 666156; fax (212) 213-2495; f. 1949; non-fiction, reference, textbooks; Pres. and Editor BURTON H. HOBSON.

Lyle Stuart Inc: 120 Enterprise Ave, Secaucus, NJ 07094; tel. (201) 866-0490; telex 127117; fax (201) 866-8159; f. 1956; general fiction and non-fiction; Pres. LYLE STUART.

Syracuse University Press: 1600 Jamesville Ave, Syracuse, NY 13244-5160; tel. (315) 443-5534; f. 1943; scholarly, general, Middle East, Irish studies; Dir CHARLES BACKUS.

TAB Books Inc: Blue Ridge Summit, PA 17214; tel. (717) 794-2191; telex 820562; f. 1964; technical, scientific, arts and crafts; Pres. LAWRENCE JACKEL.

Taplinger Publishing Co Inc: 132 West 22nd St, New York, NY 10011; tel. (212) 741-0801; f. 1955; general fiction and non-fiction; Pres. LOUIS STRICK.

Taylor and Francis: 1900 Frost Road, Suite 101, Bristol, PA 19007-1598; tel. (215) 785-5800; telex 244489; fax (215) 785-5515; f. 1972; scientific, technical and reference; Pres. BOB ROONEY.

TFH Publications Inc: One TFH Plaza, Union and Third Aves, Neptune, NJ 07753; tel. (201) 988-8400; telex 132468; fax (201) 988-5466; f. 1952; pets; Pres. HERBERT R. AXELROD.

Charles C. Thomas, Publisher: 2600 South First St, Springfield, IL 62794-9265; tel. (217) 789-8980; f. 1927; textbooks and reference on education, medicine, psychology and criminology; Pres. PAYNE E. L. THOMAS.

Thorndike Press: POB 159, Thorndike, ME 04986; tel. (207) 948-2962; fax (207) 948-2863; f. 1977; large-print books; Chair. and Treas. PHILLIPS TRELEAVEN.

Time-Life Books Inc: 777 Duke St, Alexandria, VA 22314; tel. (703) 838-7000; telex 899162; fax (703) 684-5224; f. 1961; general non-fiction; Pres. and CEO CHRISTOPHER T. LINEN.

Times Books: 201 East 50th St, New York, NY 10022; tel. (212) 872-8104; telex 126575; f. 1959; division of Random House Inc; general trade non-fiction; Editorial Dir JONATHAN B. SEGAL.

Transaction Books: Rutgers University, New Brunswick, NJ 08903; tel. (201) 932-2280; f. 1962; social sciences, textbooks, reference; Chair. DANIEL YANKELOVICH.

Charles E. Tuttle Co Inc: 28 South Main St, POB 410, Rutland, VT 05701-0410; tel. (802) 773-8930; fax (802) 773-6993; f. 1832; the Far East, particularly Japan, languages, art, Americana, culture, juveniles; Pres. DONALD E. BERG.

The Ungar Publishing Co: 370 Lexington Ave, New York, NY 10017; tel. (212) 532-3650; telex 4974569; fax (212) 532-4922; f. 1940; non-fiction, film and literary criticism, reference; Chair. WERNER MARK LINZ.

United Nations Publishing Service: Sales Section, Room DC2-0853, New York, NY 10017; tel. (212) 963-8302; f. 1946; world and national economies, international trade, social questions, human rights, international law; Chief of Section THOMAS HINDS.

Universe Books: 381 Park Ave South, New York, NY 10016; tel. (212) 685-7400; f. 1956; art, architecture, history, natural history, current affairs, music, dance, horticulture; Pres. GILMAN PARK.

University of Alabama Press: POB 2877, Tuscaloosa, AL 35487; tel. (205) 348-5180; f. 1945; scholarly non-fiction; Dir MALCOLM M. MACDONALD.

University of Arizona Press: 1230 North Park Ave, Suite 102, Tucson, AZ 85719; tel. (602) 621-1441; telex 187167; fax (602) 621-4624; f. 1959; scholarly, popular, regional, non-fiction; Dir STEPHEN COX.

University of Arkansas Press: Fayetteville, AR 72701; tel. (501) 575-3246; f. 1980; general humanities, literature, regional studies, natural history; Dir MILLER WILLIAMS.

University of California Press: 2120 Berkeley Way, Berkeley, CA 94720; tel. (415) 642-4247; telex 2959492; fax (415) 643-7127; f. 1893; academic, scholarly; Dir JAMES H. CLARK.

University of Chicago Press: 5801 Ellis Ave, Chicago, IL 60637; tel. (312) 702-7700; telex 2500484; fax (312) 702-9756; f. 1891; scholarly books and journals, general; Dir MORRIS PHILIPSON.

University of Georgia Press: Athens, GA 30602; tel. (404) 542-2830; f. 1939; academic, scholarly, poetry, short fiction, literary trade; Dir MALCOLM L. CALL.

University of Hawaii Press: 2840 Kolowalu St, Honolulu, HI 96822; tel. (808) 948-8257; telex 7238409; fax (808) 988-6052; f. 1947; Dir WILLIAM H. HAMILTON.

University of Idaho Press: POB 3368, University Station, Moscow, ID 83843; tel. (208) 885-6245; f. 1972; scholarly, regional studies; Dir JAMES J. HEANEY.

University of Illinois Press: 54 East Gregory Dr., Champaign, IL 61820; tel. (217) 333-0950; fax (217) 244-8082; f. 1918; scholarly, poetry and short fiction; Dir RICHARD L. WENTWORTH.

University of Massachusetts Press: POB 429, Amherst, MA 01004; tel. (413) 545-2217; f. 1964; scholarly non-fiction; Dir BRUCE G. WILCOX.

University of Michigan Press: 839 Greene St, POB 1104, Ann Arbor, MI 48106; tel. (313) 764-4394; f. 1930; academic, textbooks, paperbacks; Dir COLIN DAY.

University Microfilms International: 300 North Zeeb Rd, Ann Arbor, MI 48106; tel. (313) 761-4700; telex 0235569; fax (313) 665-5022; f. 1938; on-demand publishing of periodicals, dissertations, out-of-print books; Pres. JOSEPH J. FITZSIMMONS.

University of Minnesota Press: 2037 University Ave SE, Minneapolis, MN 55414; tel. (612) 624-2516; f. 1927; scholarly, textbooks, general; Mans TERRY COCHRAN, BEVERLY KAEMMER, MARGARET ROSER.

University of Missouri Press: 200 Lewis Hall, Columbia, MO 65211; tel. (314) 882-7641; Dir BEVERLY JARRETT.

University of Nebraska Press: 901 North 17th St, Lincoln, NE 68588-0520; tel. (402) 472-3581; telex 484340; f. 1941; general scholarly non-fiction, regional history; Dir WILLIS G. REGIER.

University of New Mexico Press: Journalism Bldg, Albuquerque, NM 87131; tel. (505) 277-2346; telex 660461; f. 1929; scholarly, regional studies; Dir ELIZABETH C. HADAS.

University of North Carolina Press: POB 2288, Chapel Hill, NC 27515-2288; tel. (919) 966-3561; fax (919) 966-3829; f. 1922; biographical, regional, scholarly non-fiction; Dir MATTHEW HODGSON.

University of Notre Dame Press: Notre Dame, IN 46556; tel. (219) 239-6346; telex 953008; f. 1949; humanities and social sciences; Dir JAMES R. LANGFORD.

University of Oklahoma Press: 1005 Asp Ave, Norman, OK 73019; tel. (405) 325-5111; fax (405) 325-5068; f. 1928; scholarly; Dir GEORGE W. BAUER; Editor JOHN DRAYTON.

University of Pennsylvania Press: Blockley Hall, 418 Service Dr., Philadelphia, PA 19104; tel. (215) 898-6261; telex 6700328; fax (215) 898-5756; scholarly; Dir T. M. ROTELL.

University of Pittsburgh Press: 127 North Bellefield Ave, Pittsburgh, PA 15260; tel. (412) 624-4110; f. 1936; scholarly; Dir FREDERICK A. HETZEL.

University of South Carolina Press: 508 Assembly St, Columbia, SC 29208; tel. (803) 777-5243; scholarly, regional studies; Dir KENNETH J. SCOTT.

University of Tennessee Press: 293 Communications Bldg, Knoxville, TN 37996-0325; tel. (615) 974-3321; f. 1940; scholarly and regional non-fiction; Dir CAROL ORR.

University of Texas Press: POB 7819, Austin, TX 78713-7819; tel. (512) 471-7233; telex 776453; fax (512) 320-0668; f. 1950; general scholarly non-fiction; Dir JOHN H. KYLE.

University of Utah Press: 101 USB, Salt Lake City, UT 84112; tel. (801) 581-6771; telex 3789459; f. 1949; scholarly, regional and Middle East studies; Dir DAVID CATRON.

University of Washington Press: POB 50096, Seattle, WA 98145-5096; tel. (206) 543-4050; telex 4740096; fax (206) 543-3932; f. 1920; general, scholarly, non-fiction, reprints; Dir DONALD R. ELLEGOOD; Editor-in-Chief NAOMI B. PASCAL.

University of Wisconsin Press: 114 North Murray St, Madison, WI 53715; tel. (608) 262-4928; telex 265452; fax (608) 262-0123; scholarly non-fiction; Dir ALLEN N. FITCHEN.

University Press of America Inc: 4720 Boston Way, Lanham, MD 20706; tel. (301) 459-3366; f. 1974; scholarly; Pres. RAYMOND FELLERS; Publr JAMES E. LYONS.

University Press of Kansas: 329 Carruth, Lawrence, KS 66045; tel. (913) 864-4154; f. 1946; scholarly; Dir FRED M. WOODWARD.

University Press of Kentucky: 663 South Limestone St, Lexington, KY 40506-0336; tel. (606) 257-2951; fax (606) 257-4000; f. 1943; scholarly, regional; Dir KENNETH CHERRY; Editor JEROME CROUCH.

University Press of Mississippi: 3825 Ridgewood Rd, Jackson, MS 39211; tel. (601) 982-6205; fax (601) 982-6610; f. 1970; scholarly, non-fiction, regional; Dir RICHARD ABEL.

University Press of New England: 17½ Lebanon St, Hanover, NH 03755; tel. (603) 646-3349; f. 1970; general scholarly; Dir THOMAS L. MCFARLAND.

University Press of Virginia: POB 3608, University Station, Charlottesville, VA 22903; tel. (804) 924-3468; f. 1963; bibliography, literary criticism, history, religious studies.

University Presses of Florida: 15 NW 15th St, Gainesville, FL 32603; tel. (904) 392-1351; f. 1945; general, scholarly, regional; Dir GEORGE C. BEDELL; Man. Editor JUDITH K. GOFFMAN.

Unwin Hyman Inc: Eight Winchester Pl., Winchester, MA 01890; tel. (617) 729-0830; fax (617) 729-4866; f. 1976; college textbooks, monographs, trade, social sciences, humanities, sciences; Exec. Vice-Pres. ROBERT E. PAUL.

Van Nostrand Reinhold: 115 Fifth Ave, Fourth Floor, New York, NY 10003-1085; tel. (212) 254-3232; telex 272562; f. 1980; textbooks, reference, trade; Pres. CHESTER C. LUCIDO.

Vanderbilt University Press: 1211 18th Ave South, Nashville, TN 37212; tel. (615) 322-3585; f. 1940; scholarly; Dir JOHN W. POINDEXTER.

Ventana Press: POB 2468, Chapel Hill, NC 27515; tel. (919) 942-0220; fax (919) 942-1140; f. 1986; computers; Pres. JOSEF WOODMAN.

Viking Penguin Inc: 40 West 23rd St, New York, NY 10010; tel. (212) 337-5200; telex 233776; fax (212) 243-7676; f. 1925; fiction, non-fiction and juvenile; Pres. and Publr MARVIN S. BROWN.

Wadsworth, Inc: 10 Davis Dr., Belmont, CA 94002; tel. (415) 595-2350; telex 348383; fax (415) 595-2350; f. 1956; division of International Thomson Organization; professional, reference, college textbooks; Pres. JACK N. THORNTON.

J. Weston Walch Publisher: 321 Valley St, POB 658, Portland, ME 04104-0658; tel. (207) 772-2846; f. 1927; educational; Chair. J. WESTON WALCH.

Walker & Co: 720 Fifth Ave, New York, NY 10019; tel. (212) 265-3632; f. 1959; specialized educational and general; Pres. and Publr SAMUEL S. WALKER, Jr.

Warner Books Inc: 666 Fifth Ave, New York, NY 10103; tel. (212) 484-2900; telex 237283; f. 1961; reprints, fiction and non-fiction, trade; Chair. WILLIAM SARNOFF.

Warren, Gorham & Lamont Inc: One Penn Plaza, New York, NY 10019; tel. (212) 971-5000; f. 1846; division of International Thomson Organization; law, business, engineering, taxation, finance; Pres. and CEO WALTER LAESSIG.

Franklin Watts, Inc: 387 Park Ave South, New York, NY 10016; tel. (212) 686-7070; telex 236537; fax (212) 213-6435; f. 1942; division of Grolier Inc; fiction and non-fiction; Pres. JONATHAN N. GILLETT.

Wayne State University Press: 5959 Woodward Ave, Detroit, MI 48202; tel. (313) 577-4601; fax (313) 577-6131; f. 1941; Dir ROBERT MANDEL.

West Publishing Co: 50 West Kellogg Blvd, POB 64526, St Paul, MN 55164; tel. (612) 228-2500; telex 297098; f. 1876; legal, school and college textbooks; Pres. D. D. OPPERMAN.

Western Publishing Co, Inc: 1220 Mound Ave, Racine, WI 53404; tel. (414) 633-2431; telex 2712398; f. 1907; juvenile, general; Pres. and CEO JOSEPH A. MARINO.

Westminster/John Knox Press: 100 Witherspoon St, Louisville, KY 40202; tel. (502) 569-5096; f. 1938; religious (Presbyterian), scholarly, reference, general; Publr ROBERT D. MCINTYRE.

Westview Press Inc: 5500 Central Ave, Boulder, CO 80301; tel. (303) 444-3541; telex 239479; fax (303) 449-3356; scholarly, scientific; Chair. and Publr FREDERICK A. PRAEGER.

John Wiley and Sons, Inc: 605 Third Ave, New York, NY 10158; tel. (212) 850-6000; telex 127063; f. 1807; scientific, technical, medical and social science; Chair. W. BRADFORD WILEY; Pres. ANDREW H. NEILLY, Jr.

Williams & Wilkins: 428 East Preston St, Baltimore, MD 21202; tel. (301) 528-4000; telex 87669; f. 1890; medical, dental, veterinary, scientific; Pres. G. JAMES GALLAGHER.

H. W. Wilson Co: 950 University Ave, Bronx, NY 10452; tel. (212) 588-8400; fax (212) 538-2716; f. 1898; book and periodical indices, reference; Pres. LEO M. WEINS.

World Book International: 510 Merchandise Mart Plaza, Chicago, IL 60654; tel. (312) 245-3456; telex 254915; f. 1917; reference; Chair. and CEO STEPHEN H. FULLER.

Worthy Publishing Co: 3950 Fossil Creek Blvd, Suite 240, Fort Worth, TX 76106; tel. (817) 232-3166; f. 1947; bibles, trade, children's; Pres. and Publr BYRON WILLIAMSON.

Yale University Press: 302 Temple St, New Haven, CT 06511; tel. (203) 432-0960; telex 963531; fax (203) 432-0948; f. 1908; scholarly; Dir JOHN G. RYDEN.

Year Book Medical Publishers, Inc: 200 North LaSalle St, Chicago, IL 60601-1080; tel. (312) 726-9733; telex 206155; fax (312) 726-6075; f. 1901; division of Times Mirror Co; Pres. and CEO JOHN F. DILL.

Zebra Books: 475 Park Ave South, New York, NY 10016; tel. (212) 889-2299; f. 1975; mass-market, fiction and non-fiction; Chair. WALTER ZACHARIUS.

Zondervan Publishing House: 1415 Lake Dr., SE, Grand Rapids, MI 49506; tel. (616) 698-6900; f. 1931; division of Harper & Row, Publishers Inc; religious (Protestant); Pres. BRUCE RYSKAMP.

GOVERNMENT PUBLISHING HOUSE

Government Printing Office: North Capitol and H Sts, NW, Washington, DC 20401; tel. (202) 275-2034; Public Printer RALPH E. KENNICKELL, Jr.

Publishers' Organizations and Associations

Agricultural Publishers' Association: 111 East Wacker Dr., Chicago, IL 60601; tel. (312) 644-6610; f. 1909; 30 mems; Exec. Dir WALTER G. PURCELL.

American Book Producers' Association: New York, NY 10022; tel. (212) 982-8934; f. 1980; 56 mems; Pres. PAUL FARGIS.

American Booksellers' Association (ABA): 137 West 25th St, New York, NY 10001; tel. (212) 463-8450; fax (212) 463-9353; f. 1900; 7,000 mems; Exec. Dir BERNARD E. RATH.

American Medical Publishers' Association: c/o William F. Keller, POB 944, Crystal Lake, IL 60014; tel. (815) 459-3712; f. 1960; Pres. BRAXTON D. MITCHELL.

American Society of Composers, Authors and Publishers: One Lincoln Plaza, New York, NY 10023; tel. (212) 595-3050; f. 1914; 35,000 mems; Pres. MORTON GOULD.

Association of American Publishers, Inc (AAP): 220 East 23rd St, New York, NY 10010; tel. (212) 689-8920; f. 1970; 300 mems; Pres. NICHOLAS A. VELIOTES; Exec. Vice-Pres. THOMAS D. MCKEE.

Association of American University Presses, Inc: 584 Broadway, New York, NY 10012; tel. (212) 889-6040; f. 1937; 99 mems; Pres. THOMAS MCFARLAND; Exec. Dir E. H. PHILLIPS.

Association of Business Publishers: 205 East 42nd St, New York, NY 10017; tel. (212) 661-6360; f. 1965; 665 mems; Pres. WILLIAM G. O'DONNELL.

Association of Jewish Book Publishers: 838 Fifth Ave, New York, NY 10021; tel. (212) 249-0100; f. 1962; 35 mems; Pres. BERNARD I. LEVINSON.

Association of North American Directory Publishers: 351 Longley Rd, Groton, MA 01450; tel. (617) 331-4230; f. 1898; 80 mems; Exec. Dir CAROL HILL.

Baltimore Publishers' Association: POB 5584, Baltimore, MD 21285; tel. (301) 363-6400; f. 1981; 152 mems; Chair. MARJORY SPRAYCAR.

Black Women in Publishing: POB 6275, FDR Station, New York, NY 10150; tel. (212) 772-5951; f. 1979; Pres. ELAINE RAY.

Book Industry Study Group: 160 Fifth Ave, New York, NY 10010; tel. (212) 929-1393; f. 1976; 190 mems; Man. Agent SANDRA K. PAUL.

Book Manufacturers' Institute: 111 Prospect St, Stamford, CT 06901; tel. (203) 324-9670; f. 1920; 90 mems; Exec. Vice-Pres. DOUGLAS E. HORNER.

The Children's Book Council Inc: 67 Irving Pl., New York, NY 10003; tel. (212) 254-2666; 60 mems; Chair. DORIS BASS; Pres. JOHN DONOVAN.

Christian Science Publishing Society: One Norway St, Boston, MA 02115; tel. (617) 262-2300; f. 1898; Man. JOHN H. HOAGLAND, Jr.

Church Music Publishers' Association: POB 158992, Nashville, TN 37215; tel. (615) 790-1730; f. 1925; 33 mems; Pres. FRED BOCK.

Copyright Society of the USA: c/o New York University Law Center, 40 Washington Sq. South, New York, NY 10012; tel. (212) 998-6194; f. 1953; 800 mems; Pres. BERNARD KORMAN.

Cosmep, The International Association of Independent Publishers: POB 703, San Francisco, CA 94101; tel. (415) 922-9490; f. 1969; 1,300 mems; Exec. Dir RICHARD MORRIS.

Evangelical Christian Publishers' Association: POB 2439, Vista, CA 92083; tel. (619) 941-1636; f. 1974; 65 mems; Exec. Dir C. E. ANDREW.

Freelance Network: POB 36838, Miracle Mile Station, Los Angeles, CA 90036; tel. (213) 655-4476; f. 1979; 98 mems; Pres. MICHAEL UTVICH.

International Association of Book Publishing Consultants: 19 West 44th St, Rm 1200, New York, NY 10036; tel. (212) 302-6473; Sec. JOSEPH MARKS.

Magazine Publishers' Association: 575 Lexington Ave, New York, NY 10022; tel. (212) 752-0055; f. 1919; 215 mems; Exec. Officer DONALD D. KUMMERFELD.

Manhattan Publishing Group: 175 West 12th St, New York, NY 10011; tel. (212) 880-8207; f. 1979; 100 mems; Chair. JANET ROSEN.

National Association of Advertising Publishers: 111 East Wacker Dr., Suite 600, Chicago, IL 60601; tel. (312) 644-6610; f. 1950; 300 mems; Exec. Dir HENRY S. GIVRAY.

National Association of Independent Publishers: 2299 Riverside Dr., POB 850, Moore Haven, FL 33471; tel. (813) 946-0293; 300 mems; Exec. Dir BETTY WRIGHT.

National Association of Publishers' Representatives: 114 East 32nd St, Suite 1400, New York, NY 10016; tel. (212) 683-1836; f. 1950; 300 mems; Exec. Dir THOMAS F. KENNY.

National Music Publishers' Association: 205 East 42nd St, 18th Floor, New York, NY 10017; tel. (212) 370-5330; f. 1917; 350 mems; Pres. EDWARD P. MURPHY.

Professional Publishers Marketing Group: POB 86, New York, NY 10101; tel. (212) 316-7125; f. 1980; 100 mems.

Protestant Church-Owned Publishers' Association: 201 Eighth Ave South, POB 801, Nashville, TN 37202; tel. (615) 749-6405; f. 1951; 34 mems; Exec. Sec. HAROLD L. FAIR.

Publishers' Ad Club: Denhard & Stewart, 240 Madison Ave, New York, NY 10016; tel. (212) 481-3200; f. 1920; 140 mems; Pres. CAROLINE A. BARNETT.

Publishers' Alliance: 26662 South Newton Dr., Sun Lakes, AZ 85248; f. 1978; 90 mems; Pres. THOMAS N. HORTON.

Publishers' Information Bureau: 575 Lexington Ave, New York, NY 10022; tel. (212) 752-0055; f. 1945; 150 mems; Pres. P. ROBERT FARLEY.

Publishers' Library Marketing Group: E. P. Dutton Co, Two Park Ave, New York, NY 10016; tel. (212) 725-1818; f. 1965; 50 mems; Pres. DONNE FORREST.

Publishers' Publicity Association: John Wiley & Sons Inc, 605 Third Ave, New York, NY 10158; tel. (212) 850-6259; f. 1963; 250 mems; Pres. ARLYNN GREENBAUM.

Religion Publishing Group: c/o Mary Ruth Howes, Guideposts Books, 757 Third Ave, New York, NY 10017; tel. (212) 371-6060; f. 1973; 275 mems; Pres. STEPHEN WILBURN.

Society for Scholarly Publishing: 2000 Florida Ave, NW, Suite 305, Washington, DC 20009; tel. (202) 328-3555; f. 1978; 1,200 mems; Admin. Officer ALICE O'LEARY.

Women in Scholarly Publishing: 50 East 42nd St, Rm 513, New York, NY 10017; tel. (212) 687-8340; f. 1979; 400 mems; Pres. AMANDA MECKE.

Women's National Book Association: 160 Fifth Ave, Rm 604, New York, NY 10010; tel. (212) 675-7805; f. 1917; 1,200 mems; Pres. CATHY RENTSCHLER.

HEALTH AND WELFARE

INTRODUCTION

US health and welfare programmes are dependent upon a mixture of federal and state government funds, private-sector finance and philanthropy. The Social Security Administration administers three principal programmes: Old Age, Survivors' and Disability Insurance, which includes the Medicare programme; Supplemental Security Income; and Aid to Families with Dependent Children.

Federal government involvement in health care takes the form of Medicare. Medicare is a national health-insurance programme for social-security beneficiaries over the age of 65 and disabled people under 65 who have been entitled to social-security disability benefits for at least two years. The programme also covers insured workers and their dependents in need of dialysis treatment or kidney transplants. Medicare has two components: hospital insurance and a voluntary supplementary medical insurance, financed in part by monthly premiums paid by the beneficiary. The programme is financed largely by federally-purchased private insurance. Those unable to qualify for Medicare may be eligible for Medicaid, which is a state-administered programme supported partly by the federal government. Basically, Medicaid covers the old, blind, disabled and members of families with dependent children where one parent is unemployed, absent or incapacitated. Although there are broad national guidelines as to the form of the programme, eligibility, payment to medical staff, and organization varies from state to state. Individuals and companies (on behalf of employees) are encouraged, through tax incentives, to purchase private health insurance or to join a Health Maintenance Organization (HMO). Upon acceptance by an HMO the individual pays a premium and is then entitled to receive both necessary medical attention and preventive care, thus avoiding the fee-for-service method of private medical insurance. Those who are turned away by the above systems—the destitute and uninsured—either receive charitable care or are paid for by the surplus from fee-paying patients.

Old Age, Survivors' and Disability Insurance, or 'Social Security', is an insurance programme administered by the federal government under the provisions of the Social Security Act of 1935. It aims to provide retirement income for elderly persons, benefit for insured workers under 65 with a prolonged disability and for the workers' dependents, survivor benefit for the dependents of deceased insured workers, and medical care for the elderly (see above). Disability benefit is also paid at age 50 to disabled widows or widowers of deceased insured workers, and a lump sum is usually paid to the spouse or minor children of a deceased insured worker. To qualify, a certain percentage of a person's wage must have been contributed to social security for a specified amount of time, the cost being shared equally between the employee and employer. Self-employed persons also contribute. A worker becomes eligible for full benefit at the age of 65, reduced benefit being payable from the age of 62.

In 1972 the Supplemental Security Income programme was established, whereby a minimum income is paid monthly to those with limited resources who are over 65, blind or disabled. The programme is administered by the federal government and is financed by general funds from the Treasury rather than by social security payments. Entitlement is based on income and assets. The federal payment may be further supplemented by the states.

Aid to Families with Dependent Children was set up under the Social Security Act of 1935 with the aim of providing basic support for children living with one parent or relative. It is administered by the states with federal assistance and works according to national government regulations.

Unemployment-compensation programmes are state-administered and vary from state to state, in terms of both the length of time for which a person is eligible to receive benefit and the amount paid. Common to the various state unemployment-insurance programmes, however, is the entitlement of workers to receive benefit related to past earnings provided that they (a) have worked for a specified period in employment covered by the scheme (about 97% of workers are covered); (b) are registered for work at a public employment office and are able and willing to work; and (c) have not wantonly brought about their own state of unemployment. Benefits, in most states, are payable for 26 weeks. In times of high unemployment the benefit may be payable over an extended period under a federal–state programme. Unemployment insurance is funded from a federal unemployment tax which is levied on the taxable payrolls of employers.

Workers' compensation, for employment-related injuries and deaths, is provided by all states and is usually related to the worker's salary. Federal employees, longshoremen and harbour workers, and private employees in the District of Columbia are covered by federal law. The federal government also provides compensation for coal miners disabled by pneumoconiosis, their survivors and dependents.

National government assistance and private philanthropy co-incide through a federal agency, ACTION, which was established in 1971 to co-ordinate various social-service agencies, among them being VISTA, or Volunteers in Service to America.

SELECTED STATISTICS

Health

National health expenditures, by type
($ million, except percentages)

	1984	1985	1986
Health services and supplies .	224,689	240,658	262,485
Direct patient premiums .	98,414	105,306	116,128
Insurance premiums[1] . .	121,464	130,139	140,726
Other	4,811	5,214	5,631
Medical research . . .	363	377	387
Medical facilities construction .	6,296	5,577	5,645
Total private expenditures .	**231,348**	**246,612**	**268,517**
Health services and supplies .	150,752	166,501	179,473
Medicare[2]	64,427	72,294	77,721
Public assistance medical payments[3] . . .	38,286	42,191	45,782
Medical research . . .	6,410	6,996	7,825
Medical facilities construction .	2,559	2,484	2,399
Total public expenditures (incl. others)	**159,722**	**175,980**	**189,697**
Percentage federal of public expenditures	69.9	70.7	70.6
Total expenditures . . .	**391,070**	**422,592**	**458,214**

[1] Covers insurance benefits and amount retained by insurance companies for expenses, additions to reserves, and profits (net cost of insurance).
[2] Represents expenditures for benefits and administrative cost from federal hospital and medical insurance trust funds under old-age, survivors', disability and health insurance programmes.
[3] Payments made directly to suppliers of medical care (primarily Medicaid).
Source: US Health Care Financing Administration, *Health Care Financing Review*, Summer 1987.

National health expenditures, by object ($'000 million)

	1984	1985	1986
Spent by:			
Consumers	219.9	235.4	256.9
Government	159.7	176.0	189.7
Philanthropy and industry .	11.5	11.2	11.7
Spent on:			
Health services and supplies	375.4	407.2	442.0
Personal health-care expenses	341.9	371.3	404.0
Hospital care . . .	156.3	167.2	179.6
Physicians' services . .	75.4	82.8	92.0
Dentists' services . .	24.6	27.1	29.6
Other professional services[1] . . .	10.9	12.4	14.1
Drugs and sundries . .	26.5	28.7	30.6
Eyeglasses and appliances[2] .	7.0	7.5	8.2
Nursing-home care . .	31.7	35.0	38.1
Other health services . .	9.4	10.8	11.9
Net cost of insurance and administration[3] . .	22.6	23.6	24.5
Government public-health activities . . .	11.0	12.3	13.4
Medical research . . .	6.8	7.4	8.2
Medical facilities construction .	8.9	8.1	8.0
Total	**391.1**	**422.6**	**458.2**

[1] Includes services of registered and practical nurses in private duty, visiting nurses, podiatrists, physical therapists, clinical psychologists, chiropractors, naturopaths and Christian Science practitioners.
[2] Includes fees of optometrists and expenditures for hearing aids, orthopaedic appliances, artificial limbs, crutches, wheelchairs, etc.
[3] Includes administrative expenses of federally-financed health programmes.
Source: US Health Care Financing Administration, *Health Care Financing Review*, Summer 1987.

Hospitals—Summary

	1981	1982	1983	1984	1985
Number of hospitals	6,933	6,915	6,888	6,872	6,872
Non-federal	6,585	6,569	6,546	6,531	6,529
Short-term general and special	5,879	5,863	5,843	5,814	5,784
Long-term general and special	146	138	131	131	128
Psychiatric	549	558	564	579	610
Tuberculosis	11	10	8	7	7
Federal	348	346	342	341	343
Beds ('000)	1,362	1,360	1,350	1,339	1,309
Non-federal	1,246	1,246	1,237	1,226	1,197
Federal	116	114	113	112	112
Occupancy rate[1]	77.9	77.4	76.1	72.5	69.5
Non-federal	77.8	77.2	75.7	71.9	68.9
Federal	79.0	79.4	80.5	79.0	76.3
Expenses ($ million)[2]	107.1	123.2	136.3	144.1	153.3
Non-federal	98.5	113.7	125.6	133.0	141.0
Federal	8.6	9.5	10.7	11.2	12.3
Personnel ('000)[3]	3,661	3,959	3,707	3,630	3,625
Non-federal	3,378	3,656	3,422	3,339	3,326
Federal	283	302	286	290	299
Personnel per 100 patients[3]	345	376	361	374	398
Non-federal	348	380	365	379	403
Federal	283	302	286	290	299

[1] Ratio of average daily census to every 100 beds.   [2] Excludes new construction.
[3] Includes full-time equivalents of part-time personnel.
Source: American Hospital Association, *Hospital Statistics*, annual (copyright).

Hospitals—States (1985)

	Number of hospitals	Beds ('000)	Patients admitted (million)	Average daily census ('000)[1]	Occupancy rate[2]	Personnel ('000)[3]	Total out-patient visits (million)
Alabama	144	24.9	0.7	16.3	65.7	59	3.8
Alaska	27	1.9	0.1	1.2	62.7	6	0.9
Arizona	85	13.1	0.4	8.4	64.4	40	4.3
Arkansas	101	13.3	0.4	7.9	59.0	32	1.9
California	573	110.0	3.3	73.8	67.0	337	31.1
Colorado	98	14.5	0.4	9.3	64.3	42	4.6
Connecticut	63	16.0	0.4	12.8	80.1	51	4.2
Delaware	13	3.8	0.1	2.8	75.6	10	0.8
District of Columbia	17	8.3	0.2	6.6	80.0	32	2.0
Florida	267	61.5	1.8	40.1	65.2	164	10.5
Georgia	197	33.7	1.0	23.3	68.9	92	7.6
Hawaii	26	4.1	0.1	3.1	76.7	13	1.7
Idaho	52	4.2	0.1	2.4	58.4	10	1.0
Illinois	274	66.6	1.9	45.1	67.7	192	14.0
Indiana	134	29.7	0.8	19.8	66.6	78	6.5
Iowa	139	18.6	0.4	11.5	62.1	43	3.2
Kansas	161	17.1	0.4	10.6	62.1	41	3.4
Kentucky	120	19.4	0.6	12.9	66.5	49	3.9
Louisiana	168	27.0	0.8	17.3	64.0	68	4.6
Maine	47	6.4	0.2	4.6	71.4	19	1.7
Maryland	85	22.6	0.6	17.6	77.9	69	6.1
Massachusetts	176	40.5	0.9	32.0	79.0	130	10.7
Michigan	222	45.2	1.3	32.0	70.8	140	11.2
Minnesota	178	27.1	0.6	18.4	67.8	61	3.3
Mississippi	118	16.9	0.5	10.8	63.8	37	2.1
Missouri	168	32.1	0.9	21.7	67.5	90	5.2
Montana	67	4.9	0.1	2.9	58.9	11	0.9
Nebraska	110	11.6	0.3	7.2	62.1	26	1.8
Nevada	29	3.9	0.1	2.2	56.7	11	1.0
New Hampshire	35	4.5	0.1	3.1	70.0	13	1.5
New Jersey	128	41.7	1.2	33.2	79.6	113	7.7
New Mexico	57	6.6	0.2	4.3	65.6	20	2.4
New York	328	114.9	2.7	98.8	86.0	340	26.7
North Carolina	159	31.4	0.9	21.9	69.7	85	5.8
North Dakota	59	6.1	0.1	3.9	63.5	12	0.8
Ohio	233	59.9	1.7	40.1	67.0	179	13.2
Oklahoma	142	17.2	0.5	10.5	60.6	45	3.4
Oregon	82	11.1	0.4	6.6	59.4	30	2.5
Pennsylvania	305	75.2	2.0	54.9	73.1	217	17.1
Rhode Island	21	5.4	0.1	4.3	79.9	18	1.5
South Carolina	90	15.4	0.5	11.2	72.7	41	4.0
South Dakota	68	5.8	0.1	3.5	60.6	11	0.8
Tennessee	165	31.2	0.9	21.2	68.1	79	4.6
Texas	561	85.9	2.5	52.7	61.4	215	14.2
Utah	42	5.1	0.2	3.2	62.0	17	1.6
Vermont	19	2.9	0.1	2.1	72.2	8	0.5
Virginia	138	30.1	0.8	21.5	71.3	79	6.2
Washington	119	17.0	0.6	10.6	62.6	51	5.0
West Virginia	71	11.6	0.4	7.5	64.4	30	2.4
Wisconsin	159	27.4	0.7	18.0	65.8	64	5.6
Wyoming	32	3.1	0.1	1.8	59.0	6	0.5
Total	6,872	1,308.5	36.3	909.8	69.5	3,625	282.1

[1] Inpatients receiving treatment each day; excludes newborn.
[2] Ratio of average daily census to every 100 beds.
[3] Includes full-time equivalents of part-time personnel.
Source: American Hospital Association, *Hospital Statistics*, annual (copyright).

Physicians, Dentists and Nurses—Summary (As of end of year stated)

	1982	1983	1984	1985	1986
Physicians ('000)[1]	505	523	542	n.a.	577
Per 100,000 population[2]	217	222	228	n.a.	237
Medical and osteopathic schools[3]	142	142	142	142	142
Students ('000)[3]	71.6	72.6	73.5	73.6	n.a.
Graduates ('000)[3]	16.8	17.0	17.1	17.6	17.8
Dentists ('000)	144	147	150	153	156
Per 100,000 population[4]	54	55	56	57	57

(continued)

Physicians, Dentists and Nurses—Summary (As of end of year stated)—*continued*

	1982	1983	1984	1985	1986
Dental schools[5]	60	60	60	60	60
Students ('000)[5]	22.6	22.2	21.4	20.6	19.6
Graduates ('000)[5]	5.6	5.4	5.8	5.3	5.4
Nurses, active registered ('000)	1,327	1,380	1,439	1,486	1,531
Per 100,000 population[2]	578	595	615	629	641
Nursing programmes[6]	1,401	1,432	1,466	1,477	1,473
Students ('000)[6]	235	242	251	237	218
Graduates ('000)[6]	74	74	77	80	82

[1] Includes not classified, inactive, and federal physicians.
[2] Based on US Bureau of the Census resident population estimates as of 1 July.
[3] Based on data from annual surveys conducted by the Association of American Medical Colleges and the American Association of Colleges of Osteopathic Medicine.
[4] Based on Bureau of the Census civilian population estimates as of 1 July.
[5] Based on data from the American Dental Association, Council on Dental Education, *Annual Report on Dental Education*.
[6] Numbers of programmes and students are as of 15 October and numbers of graduates are for academic year ending in year shown; from National League for Nursing, *NLN Data Book* (annual).
Source: Unless indicated otherwise, figures are unpublished data from the US Department of Health and Human Services, Health Resources and Services Administration.

Physicians and Dentists—States
(As at 31 December of year stated. Excludes doctors of osteopathy, and federal physicians and dentists.)

	Active physicians (1985)		Active dentists (1984)	
	Total	Per 100,000 civilian population	Total	Per 100,000 civilian population
Alabama	5,769	144	1,560	39
Alaska	658	132	276	57
Arizona	5,912	187	1,381	45
Arkansas	3,274	140	893	38
California	63,009	242	15,829	62
Colorado	6,373	200	2,025	64
Connecticut	8,900	282	2,400	76
Delaware	1,169	189	284	47
District of Columbia	3,547	573	568	92
Florida	22,295	198	4,927	45
Georgia	9,614	163	2,492	43
Hawaii	2,150	215	636	65
Idaho	1,202	120	538	54
Illinois	23,582	205	6,683	58
Indiana	8,002	146	2,557	47
Iowa	3,999	139	1,643	57
Kansas	4,001	165	1,219	50
Kentucky	5,640	153	1,863	51
Louisiana	7,936	178	1,846	42
Maine	1,966	170	565	49
Maryland	13,680	315	2,836	66
Massachusetts	18,079	311	4,319	75
Michigan	16,179	178	5,583	62
Minnesota	8,658	207	2,858	69
Mississippi	3,081	119	866	34
Missouri	9,244	184	2,677	54
Montana	1,148	140	517	63
Nebraska	2,539	159	1,075	68
Nevada	1,471	159	408	45
New Hampshire	1,813	183	541	56
New Jersey	17,112	227	5,061	68
New Mexico	2,379	166	665	47
New York	52,971	298	12,963	73
North Carolina	10,489	171	2,549	42
North Dakota	1,071	159	351	52
Ohio	20,005	186	5,843	54
Oklahoma	4,563	140	1,403	43
Oregon	5,201	194	1,959	73
Pennsylvania	25,903	219	6,984	59
Rhode Island	2,206	229	512	54
South Carolina	4,912	149	1,335	41
South Dakota	927	132	365	52
Tennessee	8,492	179	2,516	53
Texas	26,683	164	6,768	42
Utah	2,844	174	1,054	65
Vermont	1,276	239	330	62
Virginia	11,075	200	2,905	53
Washington	8,773	202	2,993	70
West Virginia	3,122	161	859	44
Wisconsin	8,356	175	3,207	67
Wyoming	655	130	263	52
Total	483,905	204	132,750	57

Sources: American Medical Association, *Physician Characteristics and Distribution in the US* (copyright); US Department of Health and Human Services, Health Resources and Services Administration.

Welfare

Social Welfare Expenditures under Public Programmes ($ million)

	1983		1984*		1985*	
	Federal	State and local	Federal	State and local	Federal	State and local
Social insurance	274,212	56,846	289,884	52,381	313,107	59,477
Public aid	55,895	29,935	57,666	32,206	61,173	34,792
Health and medical programmes	15,594	20,382	16,496	21,368	18,500	23,180
Veterans' programmes	25,561	265	25,822	305	26,883	338
Education	12,397	129,416	12,979	139,046	13,740	152,153
Housing	8,087	1,003	9,068	1,306	10,339	1,540
Other social welfare	7,046	5,438	7,349	6,096	7,549	6,398
Total	398,792	243,285	419,264	252,707	451,241	277,878

* Preliminary estimates.

Source: US Social Security Administration, *Social Security Bulletin*, June 1987.

Public Income-Maintenance Programmes: Cash Benefit Payments

($'000 million; includes payments outside the USA and benefits to dependents, where applicable)

	1982	1983	1984	1985	1986
OASDI[1]	155.7	166.9	175.5	186.1	193.6
Public employee retirement[2]	51.4	55.0	58.6	63.4	n.a.
Railroad retirement	5.8	6.0	6.1	6.3	6.4
Veterans' pensions, compensation	13.3	13.7	13.8	14.1	14.2
Unemployment benefits[3]	21.1	19.2	13.6	14.4	16.0
Temporary disability benefits	1.6	1.6	1.8	1.8	1.9
Workers' compensation[4]	11.4	12.2	13.3	15.2	16.0
Public assistance	31.0	13.9	14.6	15.3	16.1
Supplemental Security Income	9.0	9.5	10.4	11.1	12.1
Total[5]	283.0	298.9	308.7	327.9	n.a.

[1] Old Age, Survivors' and Disability Insurance under the Federal Social Security Act.
[2] Excludes refunds of contributions to employees who leave service.
[3] Covers state unemployment insurance, Ex-Servicemen's Compensation Act and railroad unemployment insurance only.
[4] Includes pneumoconiosis benefits.
[5] Includes lump-sum death benefits, not shown separately.

Source: US Social Security Administration, *Social Security Bulletin*.

Principal Cash and Non-cash Benefits

(years ending 30 September, unless otherwise indicated)

	Average monthly recipients ('000)		Expenditures ($ million)			
			Total[1]		Federal	
	1985	1986	1985	1986	1985	1986
Medical care[2]	n.a.	n.a.	48,297	51,870	27,548	28,898
Medicaid[3]	21,808[4]	22,592[4]	41,150	44,725	22,655	24,995
Veterans[5]	245[6]	245[6]	3,053*	3,183*	3,053*	3,183*
Cash aid[2]	n.a.	n.a.	38,074	40,799	24,924	26,799
AFDC[3,7]	10,794	10,995	16,736	17,757	8,909	9,536
Supplemental Security Income[3]	4,305	4,449	11,857	12,820	9,603[8]	10,307[8]
Pensions for needy veterans[9]	1,489[10]	1,397[10]	3,842	3,874	3,842	3,874
General assistance	1,323*	1,332*	2,499*	2,605*	—	—
Earned income-tax credit	16,500*	18,930*	1,600	2,043	1,600	2,043
Food benefits[2]	n.a.	n.a.	20,085	20,098	19,056	18,996
Food stamps[3,11]	21,400	20,900	13,470	13,466	12,599	12,528
School lunch programme[12]	11,500[13]	11,600[13]	2,656[14]	2,669[14]	2,656[14]	2,669[14]
Housing benefits[2]	n.a.	n.a.	14,115	13,250	14,115	13,250
Lower-income housing assistance (Section 8)	2,010[15]	2,143[15]	6,818	7,430	6,818	7,430
Low-rent public housing	1,355[15]	1,380[15]	3,408	2,882	3,408	2,882

(*continued*)

Principal Cash and Non-cash Benefits—*continued*
(years ending 30 September, unless otherwise indicated)

	Average monthly recipients ('000)		Expenditures ($ million)			
			Total[1]		Federal	
	1985	1986	1985	1986	1985	1986
Education aid[2]	n.a.	n.a.	10,056	10,583	9,559	10,101
Pell grants	2,797[16]	2,881[16]	2,800[17]	3,862[17]	2,800[17]	3,862[17]
Guaranteed student loans	3,477[16]	3,242[16]	3,889[18]	3,295[18]	3,889[18]	3,295[18]
Jobs and training[2]	n.a.	n.a.	3,976	3,700	3,895	3,626
Services[2]	n.a.	n.a.	3,551	3,389	3,551	3,389
Social services (Title 20)[19]	n.a.	n.a.	2,725	2,584	2,725	2,584
Energy assistance[2]	n.a.	n.a.	2,270	2,131	2,245	2,087

* Estimated.
[1] Includes state and local government expenditures not shown separately.
[2] Includes other programmes not shown separately.
[3] Expenditure data include administrative expenses.
[4] Unduplicated annual number.
[5] Medical care for veterans with a non-service-connected disability.
[6] Estimated number of patients discharged from hospital during year.
[7] Aid to Families with Dependent Children programme. Excludes data for foster-care programme.
[8] Excludes federal sums spent for SSI (state supplements) to Indochinese refugees.

[9] Includes dependents and survivors.
[10] Estimates as of September.
[11] Includes Puerto Rico's nutritional-assistance programme.
[12] Free and reduced-price segments.
[13] Estimated daily average.
[14] Includes estimate of commodity assistance.
[15] Units eligible for payment at end of year.
[16] Total numbers for an award ending July of year shown.
[17] Appropriation available for school year ending in the fiscal year named.
[18] Net obligations for school year beginning in the fiscal year named.
[19] Data are unavailable for non-federal funds spent.

Source: Library of Congress, Congressional Research Service, *Cash and Noncash Benefits for Persons with Limited Income: Eligibility Rules, Recipient and Expenditure Data, FY 1984–86*, Report No. 87-759 EPW, September 1987 and previous reports.

Medicare and Medicaid—States
(1986, preliminary estimates)

	Medicare		Medicaid	
	Enrolment ('000)[1]	Payments ($ million)[2]	Recipients ('000)[3]	Payments ($ million)[4]
Alabama	545	1,139	316	410
Alaska	18	42	29	85
Arizona	416	912	—[5]	—[5]
Arkansas	376	720	203	434
California	2,992	9,138	3,466	4,405
Colorado	310	663	132	304
Connecticut	445	1,066	217	675
Delaware	78	167	39	79
District of Columbia	80	283	99	201
Florida	2,044	5,532	588	1,003
Georgia	667	1,360	484	818
Hawaii	105	210	89	137
Idaho	120	216	40	85
Illinois	1,473	3,951	1,064	1,675
Indiana	711	1,985	298	828
Iowa	445	826	222	374
Kansas	350	851	131	239
Kentucky	504	930	415	537
Louisiana	484	1,051	446	780
Maine	173	335	125	283
Maryland	491	1,321	323	680
Massachusetts	843	2,328	529	1,665
Michigan	1,155	3,040	1,120	1,768
Minnesota	561	1,179	344	1,044
Mississippi	351	720	259	270
Missouri	753	2,002	360	556
Montana	108	198	52	112
Nebraska	232	432	102	188
Nevada	102	269	33	79
New Hampshire	127	228	35	133
New Jersey	1,047	2,707	581	1,281
New Mexico	154	299	92	164
New York	2,478	6,506	2,323	8,251
North Carolina	791	1,393	378	751
North Dakota	95	225	40	121
Ohio	1,439	3,213	1,086	2,050
Oklahoma	430	890	242	422
Oregon	382	800	163	260
Pennsylvania	1,862	4,980	1,099	1,993
Rhode Island	153	363	97	263
South Carolina	388	689	262	394
South Dakota	106	197	37	103

(continued)

Medicare and Medicaid—States (1986, preliminary estimates)—*continued*

	Medicare		Medicaid	
	Enrolment ('000)[1]	Payments ($ million)[2]	Recipients ('000)[3]	Payments ($ million)[4]
Tennessee	642	1,312	395	719
Texas	1,636	3,902	767	1,414
Utah	139	248	76	140
Vermont	71	122	50	95
Virginia	648	1,384	314	595
Washington	546	1,172	358	628
West Virginia	296	647	211	201
Wisconsin	678	1,487	409	920
Wyoming	46	88	21	33
Total[6]	31,107	75,734	20,561	40,645

[1] Hospital and/or medical insurance enrolment as of July 1.
[2] Total disbursements from federal hospital and supplementary medical insurance trust funds for the calendar year.
[3] Persons receiving Medicaid at any time during the fiscal year ending 30 September.
[4] For the fiscal year ending 30 September.
[5] Not applicable.
[6] Includes figures for enrollees with residence unknown.
Source: US Health Care Financing Administration, *Medicare Program Statistics, Selected State Data, 1978–1982*.

Social Security (OASDI)—States
(1986. OASDI = Old Age, Survivors' and Disability Insurance. Average monthly benefits as of December 1986)

	Number of beneficiaries ('000)	Benefit payments ($ million)	Average monthly benefits ($)		
			Retired workers[1]	Disabled workers	Widows and widowers[2]
Alabama	668	3,128	445	460	378
Alaska	27	139	502	507	397
Arizona	516	2,679	494	520	449
Arkansas	449	2,056	429	457	371
California	3,456	18,411	497	497	452
Colorado	374	1,900	477	482	436
Connecticut	504	2,967	536	497	483
Delaware	97	530	509	489	455
District of Columbia	81	381	422	429	375
Florida	2,381	12,425	487	498	449
Georgia	818	3,873	445	456	381
Hawaii	134	667	486	472	414
Idaho	147	744	476	495	437
Illinois	1,701	9,625	520	509	467
Indiana	868	4,806	510	506	459
Iowa	511	2,726	492	481	447
Kansas	394	2,107	498	472	451
Kentucky	617	2,895	443	479	388
Louisiana	610	2,853	453	482	396
Maine	204	1,013	448	451	421
Maryland	575	3,078	488	501	447
Massachusetts	941	5,171	492	482	460
Michigan	1,426	8,039	521	534	468
Minnesota	639	3,311	473	482	439
Mississippi	434	1,876	413	439	346
Missouri	877	4,535	475	480	432
Montana	129	660	478	494	443
Nebraska	261	1,362	483	474	444
Nevada	130	676	491	514	453
New Hampshire	152	814	490	481	456
New Jersey	1,189	6,998	533	513	478
New Mexico	192	914	461	481	399
New York	2,802	16,185	524	509	467
North Carolina	979	4,662	448	450	375
North Dakota	108	529	458	452	415
Ohio	1,724	9,365	502	510	460
Oklahoma	506	2,500	464	470	412
Oregon	458	2,457	497	510	454
Pennsylvania	2,163	12,024	507	508	463
Rhode Island	176	959	489	461	448
South Carolina	497	2,341	450	456	371
South Dakota	124	596	450	449	412
Tennessee	777	3,680	449	457	386
Texas	2,004	9,787	470	472	415
Utah	169	884	501	485	455
Vermont	85	433	478	478	432
Virginia	778	3,802	456	469	402
Washington	654	3,569	507	503	460
West Virginia	360	1,827	483	514	413
Wisconsin	805	4,378	502	491	459
Wyoming	56	291	487	489	443
Total	36,726	193,631	491	490	447

[1] Excludes persons with special benefits.   [2] Non-disabled only.
Source: US Social Security Administration, *Social Security Bulletin*.

State Unemployment Insurance
(1986)

	Average weekly insured unemployment		Average weekly unemployment benefits ($)	Beneficiaries, first payments ('000)	Benefits paid ($ million)
	Number ('000)	(%)[1]			
Alabama	43	3.2	99	175	180
Alaska	17	8.0	158	56	138
Arizona	25	2.0	111	74	106
Arkansas	28	3.6	117	96	124
California	392	3.6	118	1,114	2,074
Colorado	33	2.4	155	102	220
Connecticut	25	1.6	153	111	174
Delaware	6	2.0	143	21	44
District of Columbia	8	2.1	159	22	60
Florida	59	1.4	123	182	291
Georgia	43	1.8	109	220	219
Hawaii	9	2.1	145	27	49
Idaho	15	4.8	133	47	74
Illinois	144	3.2	141	364	857
Indiana	45	2.2	99	151	188
Iowa	29	2.9	139	85	161
Kansas	25	2.6	149	83	159
Kentucky	37	3.2	107	120	177
Louisiana	81	5.4	150	217	538
Maine	12	2.8	122	36	56
Maryland	36	2.1	136	110	206
Massachusetts	64	2.3	153	203	447
Michigan	109	3.2	153	406	733
Minnesota	45	2.5	166	135	340
Mississippi	31	4.0	93	93	107
Missouri	51	2.6	107	172	221
Montana	10	4.0	125	31	52
Nebraska	13	2.1	111	43	60
Nevada	12	2.8	133	41	75
New Hampshire	4	0.8	115	23	18
New Jersey	86	2.6	156	268	630
New Mexico	17	3.5	121	42	81
New York	191	2.5	135	541	1,128
North Carolina	49	1.9	117	224	222
North Dakota	8	3.4	149	22	50
Ohio	118	2.8	148	340	712
Oklahoma	36	3.3	146	112	221
Oregon	42	4.3	138	130	305
Pennsylvania	165	3.7	153	487	1,057
Rhode Island	13	3.1	129	45	72
South Carolina	28	2.3	100	102	110
South Dakota	3	1.5	108	11	14
Tennessee	44	2.5	92	166	172
Texas	164	2.6	160	528	1,205
Utah	14	2.5	154	49	95
Vermont	5	2.5	121	18	27
Virginia	23	1.0	127	124	138
Washington	65	4.1	137	177	362
West Virginia	24	4.3	142	72	143
Wisconsin	59	3.1	141	201	347
Wyoming	8	3.9	164	24	62

[1] Insured unemployment as a percentage of average covered employment in preceding year.
Source: US Employment and Training Administration, *Unemployment Insurance Statistics* and *Annual Report of the Secretary of Labor.*

Aid to Families with Dependent Children (AFDC) and Supplemental Security Income (SSI)—Recipients and Payments, States

	AFDC				SSI		
	Recipients ('000)[1]		Payments for year ($ million)	Average monthly payment per family	Recipients ('000)	Payments for year ($ million)	Public aid recipients as % of population[2]
	1985	1986	1985	1985	1986	1986	1986
Alabama	148	139	70	113	131.1[3]	286[3]	6.8
Alaska	16	18	42	550	3.6[3]	10[3]	4.0
Arizona	72	83	65	213	35.1[3]	92[3]	3.3
Arkansas	65	66	43	164	73.8	150	5.9
California	1,631	1,701	3,427	514	710.6	2,782	8.7
Colorado	83	89	100	300	31.3[3]	75[3]	3.5
Connecticut	119	113	223	450	28.2[3]	74[3]	4.5
Delaware	22	21	26	246	7.7	18	4.6
District of Columbia	56	54	76	286	16.4	47	11.3

(continued)

AFDC and SSI—Recipients and Payments, States—*continued*

	AFDC				SSI		
	Recipients ('000)[1]		Payments for year ($ million)	Average monthly payment per family	Recipients ('000)	Payments for year ($ million)	Public aid recipients as % of population[2]
	1985	1986	1985	1985	1986	1986	1986
Florida	276	286	249	215	189.2	482	3.9
Georgia	234	246	200	199	154.5	342	6.4
Hawaii	49	44	77	404	11.8	34	5.4
Idaho	16	17	19	254	8.7[3]	20[3]	2.6
Illinois	733	731	881	307	145.3[3]	397[3]	7.6
Indiana	163	153	153	224	50.9[3]	123[3]	3.8
Iowa	124	122	160	332	28.8	61	5.4
Kansas	67	73	86	315	21.9	47	3.7
Kentucky	161	161	138	194	100.6[3]	245[3]	7.0
Louisiana	237	256	156	168	128.2	304	8.2
Maine	58	56	81	336	22.5	46	6.9
Maryland	198	186	244	283	53.2	138	5.5
Massachusetts	236	235	426	408	113.0	311	5.9
Michigan	673	653	1,194	446	127.0	367	8.7
Minnesota	157	160	309	495	34.2[3]	73[3]	4.6
Mississippi	157	170	64	104	112.1	250	10.4
Missouri	199	202	198	250	80.3[3]	189[3]	5.5
Montana	25	27	33	341	8.0	19	4.2
Nebraska	46	47	59	319	14.1[3]	31[3]	3.9
Nevada	15	17	13	217	8.6	21	2.5
New Hampshire	13	11	20	318	6.5[3]	15[3]	1.9
New Jersey	360	343	499	336	95.2	274	5.8
New Mexico	51	54	51	237	27.5[3]	66[3]	5.3
New York	1,101	1,079	2,029	453	366.8	1,188	8.2
North Carolina	175	173	167	217	140.3[3]	314[3]	5.0
North Dakota	13	14	19	341	6.9[3]	14[3]	3.0
Ohio	672	667	773	287	133.9	347	7.5
Oklahoma	87	94	91	264	59.2[3]	129[3]	4.5
Oregon	78	81	111	325	26.8[3]	66[3]	4.2
Pennsylvania	582	567	751	335	170.2	475	6.3
Rhode Island	44	43	75	393	16.1	42	6.2
South Carolina	128	130	95	181	87.5[3]	192[3]	6.5
South Dakota	17	18	18	256	8.7	18	3.7
Tennessee	159	177	92	134	129.3	295	6.1
Texas	399	458	241	162	264.8[4]	563[4]	4.1
Utah	38	42	52	334	9.2[3]	23[3]	3.0
Vermont	22	22	38	408	9.5	25	5.6
Virginia	155	151	173	246	87.3[3]	197[3]	4.1
Washington	189	210	340	430	50.6	140	5.6
West Virginia	114	115	94	230	43.5[4]	113[4]	8.2
Wisconsin	297	290	568	490	75.6	208	7.8
Wyoming	10	11	14	307	2.5[3]	6[3]	2.7
Total	10,738	10,875	15,126	n.a.	4,269[5]	11,740[6]	6.2

[1] Includes the children and one or both parents, or one caretaker relative other than a parent, in families where the needs of such adults were considered in determining the amount of assistance.
[2] Data compiled by US Bureau of the Census. Total recipients as of June of AFDC and of federal SSI as percentage of resident population.
[3] Data for persons with federal SSI payments only; state has state-administered supplementation.
[4] Data for persons with federal SSI payments only; state supplementary payments not made.
[5] SSI totals include small number of recipients whose residence was 'unknown'.
[6] Totals reduced to reflect returned cheques and overpayment refunds.

Source: US Social Security Administration, *Social Security Bulletin*, monthly, *Annual Statistical Supplement* to the *Social Security Bulletin*, and *Public Assistance Statistics*, monthly.

HEALTH AND WELFARE AGENCIES AND ORGANIZATIONS

Advisory Council on Employee Welfare and Pension Benefit Plans: Office of Pension and Welfare Benefit Programs, US Dept of Labor, Washington, DC 20210; tel. (202) 523-8753.

Federal Advisory Council on Unemployment Insurance: Unemployment Insurance Service, Employment and Training Administration, US Dept of Labor, 601 D St, NW, Washington, DC 20213; tel. (202) 376-6636; reviews federal–state unemployment insurance programmes and makes recommendations to the Secretary of Labor for their improvement; Designated Federal Employee SUSAN C. SCHLICKEISEN.

Health Care Financing Administration: US Dept of Health and Human Services, Humphrey Bldg, Rm 314G, 200 Independence Ave, SW, Washington, DC 20201; tel. (202) 245-6726; oversees the Medicare and Medicaid programmes.

Health Insurance Association of America: 1025 Connecticut Ave, NW, Washington, DC 20036-3998; tel. (202) 223-7780.

Health Resources and Services Administration: US Dept of Health and Human Services, 5600 Fishers Lane, Rockville, MD 20857; tel. (301) 443-2086.

Medicare: 1946 Green Spring Dr., Timonium, MD 21093; tel. (301) 561-4160.

Office of Community Services: 200 Independence Ave, SW, Washington, DC 20201; tel. (202) 475-0373; administers Community Services grant programmes.

Office of Human Development Services: 200 Independence Ave, SW, Washington, DC 20201; tel. (202) 472-7257; provides human services for disadvantaged.

Pension Benefit Guaranty Corporation: 2020 K St, NW, Washington, DC 20006; tel. (202) 254-4817; govt corporation; guarantees basic pension benefits in covered private plans if they terminate with insufficient assets.

Public Health Service: US Dept of Health and Human Services, 200 Independence Ave, SW, Rm 716G, Washington, DC 20201; tel. (202) 245-6296; Asst Sec. JAMES MASON.

Public Health Service Alcohol, Drug Abuse and Mental Health Administration: US Dept of Health and Human Services, 5600 Fishers Lane, Rockville, MD 20857; tel. (301) 443-3783.

Public Health Service Agency for Toxic Substances and Disease Registry: 1600 Clifton Rd, NE, Atlanta, GA 30333; tel. (404) 452-4113.

Public Health Service Centers for Disease Control: 1600 Clifton Rd, NE, Atlanta, GA 30333; tel. (404) 329-3286; Dir WALTER DOWDLE (acting).

Public Health Service National Center for Health Statistics: 3700 East–West Highway, Hyattsville, MD 20782; tel. (301) 436-8500; conducts surveys on matters including health costs, insurance coverage, use of health services, nutrition, and disability; Dir MANNING FEINLEIB.

Social Security Administration: US Dept of Health and Human Services, 6401 Security Blvd, Baltimore, MD 21235; tel. (301) 594-1234.

US ACTION: 806 Connecticut Ave, NW, Washington, DC 20525; tel. (202) 634-9380; aims to interest private sector in meeting social needs through voluntary activity and financial support for volunteer organizations; Dir DONNA M. ALVARADO.

US Department of Health and Human Services: 200 Independence Ave, SW, Washington, DC 20201; tel. (202) 475-0257; Sec. LOUIS W. SULLIVAN.

US Department of Labor, Employment and Training Administration, Unemployment Insurance Service: 200 Constitution Ave, NW, Washington, DC 20210; tel. (202) 535-0600.

Volunteers in Service to America (VISTA): 806 Connecticut Ave, NW, Rm 10100, Washington, DC 20525; tel. (202) 634-9445; f. 1964; 9 regional groups; assistance programme administered by ACTION; Assistant Dir JANE KENNY.

EDUCATION

INTRODUCTION

Public schools are funded and controlled by local, state or federal government, and public education is free in every state from elementary school to high school. The individual states have their own systems of public education and differ in the ways in which they regulate their private schools. Each school is administered by a local school district. Although the districts levy taxes to fund schools, state governments provide additional support in order to overcome inequality of financial resources. In 1984/85 the federal government provided 8.5% of funding for schools (including institutions of higher education), while state governments provided 38.7%, local government provided 25.6% and 27.1% came from other sources; in that year 81% of total funding went to public schools and 19% to private schools. Federal government expenditure on educational programmes administered by the US Department of Education totalled about $21,700m. in 1987/88. The period for which education is compulsory varies between the states, but most states require attendance between the ages of six and 16 years. At the beginning of the 1987/88 academic year there were 27.9m. pupils enrolled in public elementary schools (grades 1–8) and 12m. in public schools (grades 9–12). Private schools, many of which

have traditionally been affiliated with the Roman Catholic Church, enrolled 4.3m. at elementary level and 1.3m. at high-school level.

In the 1987/88 academic year there were about 3,600 degree-granting universities and colleges, with a total enrolment of about 12.5m. students. Almost all states provide guaranteed loans to state residents who wish to attend institutions of higher education in the USA. The larger states also offer assistance programmes for students in low-income groups. The US Department of Education and various federal agencies offer grants and loans, as do many private organizations. In 1984/85 the federal government provided 12.4% of funding for higher education, while the states provided 29.9%, local government 2.5% and other sources 55%. Of all higher-education funding in 1985, 64.8% went to public institutions and 35.2% to private institutions.

Since 1957 the federal government has had a policy of encouraging desegregation in schools, a problem caused by residential patterns. With the aim of preventing racial segregation, some state authorities have imposed interdistrict busing of pupils.

STATISTICS

(Source (unless otherwise stated): Center for Education Statistics, US Department of Education, *Digest of Education Statistics*, annual.)

Schools: Summary

(Excludes schools not reported by level, such as special education. Schools with both elementary and secondary programmes are included under elementary and secondary)

	1970/71	1976/77	1978/79	1980/81	1984/85
Elementary (including kindergarten):					
Public	65,800	62,600	62,000	61,100	58,800
Private	14,400	16,400	16,100	16,800	n.a.
Secondary:					
Public	25,400	25,400	24,500	24,400	23,900
Private	3,800	5,900	5,800	5,700	n.a.
Colleges:					
Public	1,100	1,500*	1,500*	1,500*	1,500*
Private	1,500	1,600*	1,700*	1,700*	1,800*

* Branch campuses counted separately.

Teachers: Summary

('000, as of fall)

	1970	1975	1980	1985	1986*
Elementary (including kindergarten):					
Public	1,128	1,180	1,177	1,230	1,246
Private*	153	172	212	246	250
Secondary (including junior high):					
Public	927	1,016	985	981	957
Private*	80	83	89	97	98
Higher education†	573	781	846	n.a.	n.a.

* Estimated figures.
† Covers universities, colleges, professional schools, junior and teachers' colleges, both publicly- and privately-controlled, regular session.

Enrolment: Summary

('000, as of fall of year indicated)

	1982	1983	1984	1985	1986
Kindergarten to grade 8:					
Public	27,156	26,997	26,918	27,047	27,355*
Private	4,200	4,315	4,300	4,300	4,300*
Grades 9 to 12:					
Public	12,496	12,355	12,375	12,467	12,357*
Private	1,400	1,400	1,400	1,300	1,300*
Colleges:					
Public	9,696	9,683	9,477	9,479	9,600†
Private	2,730	2,782	2,765	2,768	2,797†

* Estimates.
† Preliminary.

Public Elementary Education by State

	Schools (number 1984/85)[1]	Teachers ('000, (1986/87)[2]	Pupils ('000, fall of 1985)[3]
Alabama	799	19.3	517
Alaska	165	3.0	77
Arizona	622	22.8	386
Arkansas	710	11.8	304
California	4,932	123.2	2,927
Colorado	853	16.6	379
Connecticut	689	20.1	321
Delaware	96	2.8	63
District of Columbia	121	3.5	62
Florida	1,480	52.1	1,086
Georgia	1,295	35.5	757
Hawaii	162	4.5	112
Idaho	368	5.4	149
Illinois	3,037	66.6	1,246
Indiana	1,339	26.5	654
Iowa	1,060	14.4	324
Kansas	1,014	15.2	286
Kentucky	983	23.0	449
Louisiana	952	28.5	571
Maine	569	8.5	140
Maryland	856	18.0	446
Massachusetts	1,335	22.5	559
Michigan	2,742	52.0	1,104
Minnesota	942	20.3	468
Mississippi	448	15.3	330
Missouri	1,359	24.9	544

(continued)	Schools (number 1984/85)[1]	Teachers ('000, (1986/87)[2]	Pupils ('000, fall of 1985)[3]
Montana	560	6.6	108
Nebraska	1,257	9.4	184
Nevada	208	4.2	107
New Hampshire	329	6.2	107
New Jersey	1,703	44.0	740
New Mexico	454	8.1	187
New York	2,676	82.5	1,703
North Carolina	1,388	33.9	749
North Dakota	400	5.0	84
Ohio	2,646	53.1	1,206
Oklahoma	1,186	18.8	414
Oregon	916	15.8	305
Pennsylvania	2,375	48.0	1,093
Rhode Island	218	4.4	90
South Carolina	781	22.2	424
South Dakota	481	5.6	88
Tennessee	1,175	25.8	575
Texas	3,969	98.1	2,261
Utah	464	10.8	299
Vermont	309	2.9	63
Virginia	1,263	34.2	665
Washington	1,092	20.3	507
West Virginia	763	12.7	249
Wisconsin	1,407	26.8	501
Wyoming	283	5.5	74
Total	57,231	1,261.0	27,047

[1] Includes schools beginning with grade 6 or below and no grade higher than 8.
[2] Full-time equivalent. Includes kindergarten teachers. Source: National Education Association, Washington, DC, *Estimates of School Statistics, 1986–87* (copyright).
[3] Preliminary figures for enrolment at levels from pre-kindergarten to grade 8. Includes unclassified students.

Public Secondary Education by State

	Schools (number, 1984/85)[1]	Teachers ('000, 1986/87)[2]	Pupils ('000, fall of 1985)[3]
Alabama	325	17.7	213
Alaska	78	2.3	30
Arizona	216	7.2	162
Arkansas	452	12.3	130
California	1,887	66.5	1,329
Colorado	415	14.1	172
Connecticut	245	13.7	141
Delaware	52	3.0	30
District of Columbia	50	2.2	25
Florida	457	41.5	477
Georgia	439	22.0	323
Hawaii	54	3.9	53
Idaho	188	4.9	59
Illinois	1,024	33.7	580
Indiana	485	25.2	312
Iowa	605	16.0	161
Kansas	469	11.8	125
Kentucky	354	11.5	195
Louisiana	371	15.0	221
Maine	176	4.4	66
Maryland	297	20.2	225
Massachusetts	433	34.4	285
Michigan	896	28.2	586
Minnesota	558	20.7	237
Mississippi	210	11.6	141
Missouri	629	24.0	251

(continued)	Schools (number, 1984/85)[1]	Teachers ('000, 1986/87)[2]	Pupils ('000, fall of 1985)[3]
Montana	214	3.1	46
Nebraska	391	8.1	82
Nevada	83	3.7	48
New Hampshire	87	4.1	54
New Jersey	454	30.5	376
New Mexico	176	6.8	90
New York	1,060	94.3	918
North Carolina	515	24.0	337
North Dakota	250	2.9	35
Ohio	1,100	42.9	588
Oklahoma	663	17.8	178
Oregon	327	10.0	142
Pennsylvania	825	53.2	591
Rhode Island	61	4.3	43
South Carolina	319	12.2	183
South Dakota	239	2.4	37
Tennessee	467	15.6	239
Texas	1,532	85.2	871
Utah	187	6.5	105
Vermont	55	3.5	27
Virginia	458	25.3	303
Washington	518	16.4	243
West Virginia	281	10.2	109
Wisconsin	599	19.4	267
Wyoming	94	2.0	29
Total	22,320	972.0	12,467

[1] Includes schools with no grade lower than 8.
[2] Full-time equivalent. Source: National Education Association, Washington, DC, *Estimates of School Statistics, 1986–87* (copyright).
[3] Grades 9–12, preliminary figures. Includes unclassified students.

Higher Education by State

(1985/86 figures; covers universities, colleges, professional schools, junior and teachers' colleges, both publicly- and privately-controlled, regular session)

	Institutions (number)[1]	Students enrolled ('000)[2]		
		Male	Female	Total
Alabama	78	87	92	179
Alaska	15	12	16	27
Arizona	31	105	112	217
Arkansas	36	35	43	78
California	290	784	866	1,650
Colorado	48	79	82	161
Connecticut	48	72	87	159
Delaware	8	14	18	32
District of Columbia	19	39	40	79
Florida	87	213	239	451
Georgia	80	94	103	197
Hawaii	12	24	26	50
Idaho	10	21	22	43
Illinois	162	315	364	679
Indiana	75	124	127	251
Iowa	59	77	76	153
Kansas	52	66	75	141
Kentucky	45	63	78	142
Louisiana	31	84	93	177
Maine	30	21	31	52
Maryland	56	103	128	232
Massachusetts	121	196	225	421
Michigan	92	238	269	507
Minnesota	69	104	117	221
Mississippi	42	46	55	101
Missouri	92	117	124	241
Montana	16	18	18	36
Nebraska	28	47	51	98
Nevada	8	20	24	44
New Hampshire	28	25	28	52
New Jersey	60	137	161	298
New Mexico	20	32	37	68
New York	301	456	544	1,000
North Carolina	128	148	179	327
North Dakota	19	20	18	38
Ohio	142	259	256	515
Oklahoma	47	82	87	169
Oregon	46	69	69	138
Pennsylvania	206	261	272	533
Rhode Island	13	33	37	70
South Carolina	63	61	71	132
South Dakota	18	15	18	33
Tennessee	80	91	103	195
Texas	158	377	393	770
Utah	14	57	47	104
Vermont	22	14	17	31
Virginia	72	132	161	292
Washington	53	108	124	232
West Virginia	29	34	42	77
Wisconsin	63	133	142	275
Wyoming	8	11	13	24
Total	3,340	5,818	6,429	12,247

[1] Branch campuses counted as separate institutions.

[2] Opening fall enrolment of resident and extension students attending full-time or part-time. Excludes students taking courses for credit by mail, radio or TV, and students in branches of US institutions operated in foreign countries.

Sources: Center for Education Statistics, US Department of Education, *Fall Enrollment in Higher Education*, annual; *Education Directory, Colleges and Universities*, annual.

RELIGION

Christian Church Adherents and Jewish Population, by State

	Christian Church adherents (1980)		Jewish population (1988, '000)
	Number ('000)	As % of population	
Alabama	2,230	57.3	9
Alaska	123	30.6	2
Arizona	1,065	39.2	69
Arkansas	1,282	56.1	2
California	8,082	34.1	906
Colorado	1,052	36.4	49
Connecticut	1,890	60.8	110
Delaware	238	40.1	10
District of Columbia	304	47.6	25
Florida	3,707	38.0	596
Georgia	2,560	46.9	63
Hawaii	319	33.1	8
Idaho	472	50.0	0
Illinois	6,251	54.7	258
Indiana	2,451	44.6	20
Iowa	1,781	61.1	7
Kansas	1,262	53.4	14
Kentucky	1,979	54.1	12
Louisiana	2,404	57.2	16
Maine	461	41.0	9
Maryland	1,673	39.7	210
Massachusetts	3,669	64.0	276
Michigan	3,932	42.5	84
Minnesota	2,644	64.9	31
Mississippi	1,385	54.9	2
Missouri	2,613	53.1	63
Montana	348	44.2	0
Nebraska	990	63.1	7
Nevada	233	29.1	20
New Hampshire	407	44.2	7
New Jersey	3,923	53.3	414
New Mexico	767	58.9	6
New York	8,548	48.7	1,844
North Carolina	3,169	53.9	15
North Dakota	482	73.8	1
Ohio	5,306	49.1	132
Oklahoma	1,751	57.9	5
Oregon	946	35.9	12
Pennsylvania	7,177	60.5	346
Rhode Island	710	75.0	16
South Carolina	1,603	51.3	9
South Dakota	462	66.9	0
Tennessee	2,485	54.1	20
Texas	7,752	54.5	98
Utah	1,097	75.1	3
Vermont	244	47.7	5
Virginia	2,221	41.5	65
Washington	1,275	30.9	23
West Virginia	772	39.6	3
Wisconsin	3,029	64.4	36
Wyoming	207	44.0	0
Total	**111,736**	**49.3**	**5,935**

Sources: (Christian Church adherents) Quinn, B., Anderson, H., Bradley, M., Goetting, P. and Shriver, P., *Churches and Church Membership in the United States 1980*, Glenmary Research Center, Atlanta, GA, 1982 (copyright); (Jewish population) American Jewish Committee and the American Jewish Publication Society, New York, NY, *American Jewish Year Book, 1989* (copyright).

Religious Bodies*

(figures refer to 1985, unless otherwise indicated)

	Membership ('000)	Churches
Roman Catholic Church	52,655	24,251
Southern Baptist Convention . .	14,477	36,898
United Methodist Church[1] . . .	9,267	37,990
Jews	5,835	3,416
National Baptist Convention, USA, Inc .	5,500†	n.a.
Church of Jesus Christ of Latter-day Saints (Mormon)	3,860	8,396
Church of God in Christ[2]	3,710	9,982

RELIGIOUS BODIES—*continued*

	Membership ('000)	Churches
Presbyterian Church (USA)	3,048	11,554
Lutheran Church in America . .	2,898	5,817
Episcopal Church	2,739	7,274
National Baptist Convention of America .	2,669†	n.a.
Lutheran Church—Missouri Synod . .	2,638	5,876
American Lutheran Church . . .	2,332	4,940
African Methodist Episcopal Church[3] .	2,210	6,200
Assemblies of God	2,083	10,761
Greek Orthodox Archdiocese of North and South America	1,950†	n.a.
United Church of Christ	1,684	6,408
American Baptist Churches in the USA .	1,660	5,814
Churches of Christ	1,604	13,150
African Methodist Episcopal Zion Church[1]	1,202	6,057
Baptist Bible Fellowships, International[4]	1,406	3,449
Christian Church (Disciples of Christ) .	1,116	4,214
Christian Churches and Churches of Christ	1,051	5,487
Jehovah's Witnesses	730	8,220
Christian Methodist Episcopal Church[5] .	719	2,340

* Table excludes some groups giving no data. Numbers of Roman Catholics include all baptized persons; numbers of Jews comprise all those in Jewish households, including those not born into the Jewish faith, about 7.4%. Most Protestant churches count only full (confirmed) members, but many Lutheran churches and the Episcopal Church count all baptized persons.

† Figures date from 1978 or earlier.
[1] 1984.
[2] 1982.
[3] 1981.
[4] 1986.
[5] 1983.

Source: partly *Yearbook of American and Canadian Churches*, annual. (Copyright by the National Council of Churches of Christ in the USA, used by permission of Abingdon Press.)

Directory

BAHÁ'Í FAITH

National Spiritual Assembly: 536 Sheridan Rd, Wilmette, IL 60091; tel. (312) 869-9039; f. 1844 in Persia; c. 110,000 mems residing in over 7,000 localities; Chair. Judge DOROTHY W. NELSON; Sec.-Gen. Dr ROBERT C. HENDERSON.

BUDDHISM

American Buddhist Movement: 301 West 45th St, New York, NY 10036; tel. (212) 489-1075; f. 1980; Pres. Dr KEVIN R. O'NEIL.

Buddhist Churches of America: 1710 Octavia St, San Francisco, CA 94109; tel. (415) 776-5600; f. 1899; Hongwanji-ha Jodo Shinshu denomination; 250,000 mems; Leader Bishop SEIGEN H. YAMAOKA.

Nichiren Shoshu Soka Gakkai of America: 525 Wilshire Blvd, Santa Monica, CA 90401; tel. (213) 451-8811; f. 1963; 500,000 mems; Gen. Dir GEORGE M. WILLIAMS.

CHRISTIANITY
Adventist Churches

Advent Christian Church: 1002 Grove Ave, SW, Lenoir, NC 28645; f. 1864; Pres. Rev. DONALD E. WRIGLEY; Sec. Rev. MARSHALL TIDWELL.

Primitive Advent Christian Church: 395 Frame Rd, Elkview, WV 25071; 352 churches; 19,946 mems; Pres. DONALD YOUNG; Sec.-Treas. HUGH W. GOOD.

Seventh-day Adventists: 12501 Old Columbia Pike, Silver Spring, MD 20904; f. 1863; 28,452 churches; 5.6m. mems (world-wide); Pres. NEAL C. WILSON; Sec. G. RALPH THOMPSON.

Anglican Communion

The Episcopal Church in the USA: 815 Second Ave, New York, NY 10017; tel. (212) 867-8400; telex 4909957001; f. 1789; 7,054 churches; 2.5m. mems (1987 estimate); Presiding Bishop and Pres.

Exec. Council Rt Rev. EDMOND LEE BROWNING; Exec. Officer Gen. Convention and Sec. Exec. Council Rev. DONALD A. NICKERSON, Jr.

Baptist Churches

Members (1987 estimate): 26.1m., in 14 bodies.

American Baptist Association: POB 1050, Texarkana, TX 75504; f. 1905; 1,705 churches; 250,000 mems; Pres. KEN ASHLOCK; Recording Clerk W. E. NORRIS.

American Baptist Black Caucus: St John Missionary Baptist Church, 34 West Pleasant St, Springfield, OH 45506; tel. (513) 323-4401; f. 1968; 13,000 mems; Chair. Dr JACOB L. CHATMAN.

American Baptist Churches in the USA: Valley Forge, PA 19482-0851; tel. (215) 768-2000, f. 1907; 5,800 churches; 1.6m. mems; Pres. Dr HAROLD DAVIS; Gen. Sec. Rev. Dr DANIEL E. WEISS.

Baptist General Conference: 2002 South Arlington Heights Rd, Arlington Heights, IL 60005; f. 1879; 762 churches; 131,480 mems; Pres. Dr ROBERT S. RICKER.

Baptist Missionary Association of America: POB 1203, Van, TX 75790; f. 1950, formerly North American Baptist Asscn; 1,359 churches; 228,125 mems; Pres. Rev. RONALD MORGAN; Recording Sec. RALPH COTTRELL.

Conservative Baptist Association of America: POB 66, Wheaton, IL 60189; f. 1947; 1,158 churches; 253,000 mems; Gen. Dir TIM BLANCHARD.

Free Will Baptists: POB 1088, Nashville, TN 37202; f. 1727; 2,483 churches; 205,546 mems; Moderator Rev. RALPH HAMPTON; Exec. Sec. Dr MELVIN WORTHINGTON.

General Association of General Baptists: 801 Kendall, Poplar Bluff, MO 63901; f. 1823; Moderator Rev. DEAN TRIVITT.

General Association of Regular Baptist Churches: 1300 North Meacham Rd, Schaumburg, IL 60195; 1,571 churches; 301,000 mems; Chair. Dr JOHN WHITE; Nat. Rep. Dr PAUL N. TASSELL.

National Baptist Convention, USA, Inc: 52 South Sixth Ave, Mt Vernon, NY 10550; f. 1880; 26,000 churches; 6.3m. mems; Pres. Rev. T. J. JEMISON; Gen. Sec. W. FRANKLYN RICHARDSON.

National Baptist Convention of America: 954 Kings Rd, Jacksonville, FL 32204; 11,398 parishes; 3.5m. mems.

North American Baptist Conference: 210 Summit Ave, Oakbrook Terrace, IL 60681; 253 churches; 42,084 mems; Moderator Rev. ERNIE RADKE; Exec. Dir Dr JOHN BINDER.

Progressive National Baptist Convention Inc: 42nd and Wallace St, Philadelphia, PA 19104; 655 parishes; 521,700 mems; Pres. Rev. LORENZO SHEPARD; Gen. Sec. Rev. C. J. MALLOY, Jr.

Southern Baptist Convention: 901 Commerce St, Nashville, TN 37203; tel. (615) 244-2355; f. 1845; 37,286 churches; 14,727,770 mems; Pres. Dr C. JERRY VINES; Pres. Exec. Cttee Dr HAROLD C. BENNETT.

Brethren Churches

Brethren in Christ Church: POB 245, Upland, CA 91785; f. 1798; 183 churches; 16,693 mems; Moderator Bishop GLENN A. GINDER.

Brethren Church (Ashland, Ohio): RR 1, POB 421, McGaheysville, VA 22840; f. 1882; 122 churches; 14,229 mems; Moderator Dr WARREN K. GARNER; Sec. NORMA WATERS.

Christian Congregation: 804 West Hemlock St, La Follette, TN 37766; f. 1887; 1,450 churches; 105,478 mems; Gen. Supt Rev. ORA WILBERT EADS.

Christian Methodist Episcopal Church: 2805 Shoreland Dr., Atlanta, GA 30331; f. 1870; 2,340 churches; 718,922 mems; Exec. Sec. Dr W. CLYDE WILLIAMS.

Christian and Missionary Alliance: 350 North Highland Ave, Nyack, NY 10960; f. 1887; 1,691 churches; 238,734 mems; Pres. DAVID L. RAMBO; Sec. ELWOOD N. NIELSEN.

Church of the Brethren: 1451 Dundee Ave, Elgin, IL 60120; tel. (312) 742-5100; 1,044 parishes; 164,680 mems; Gen. Sec. Dr ROBERT W. NEFF.

Churches of Christ in Christian Union: POB 188, Alma, GA 31510; 260 churches; 11,400 mems; Gen. Supt Rev. ROBERT KLINE; Gen. Sec. Rev. ROBERT BARTH.

Fellowship of Grace Brethren Church: 855 Turnbull St, Delona, FL 32725; f. 1882; 312 churches; 41,767 mems; Moderator Dr JOHN DAVIES; Sec. Rev. KENNETH KOONTZ.

Lutheran Churches

Members (1987 estimate): 8.6m., in eight bodies.

Association of Free Lutheran Congregations: 402 West 11th St, Canton, SD 57013; f. 1962; 160 churches; 19,508 mems; Pres. Rev. RICHARD SNIPSTEAD; Sec. Rev. RONALD KNUTSON.

Church of the Lutheran Brethren of America: 707 Crestview Dr., West Union, IA 52175; f. 1900; 118 churches; 11,778 mems;

Church of the Lutheran Confession: 620 East 50th St, Loveland, CO 80537; f. 1961; 68 churches; 8,852 mems; Pres. Rev. DANIEL FLEISCHER; Sec. Rev. PAUL F. NOLTING.

Evangelical Lutheran Church in America: 8765 West Higgins Rd, Chicago, IL 60631; tel. (312) 380-2700; telex 4900009321; f. 1988 by merger of the American Lutheran Church, the Association of Evangelical Lutheran Churches and the Lutheran Church in America; 11,133 churches; 5,288,230 mems; Bishop Rev. Dr HERBERT W. CHILSTROM; Sec. Rev. Dr LOWELL G. ALMEN.

Evangelical Lutheran Synod: 106 13th St, Northwood, IA 50459; f. 1853; 120 churches; 19,938 mems; Pres. Rev. GEORGE ORVICK; Sec. Rev. ALF MERSETH.

Lutheran Church—Missouri Synod: 1333 South Kirkwood Rd, St Louis, MO 63122; tel. (314) 965-9000; telex 434452; f. 1847; 5,897 churches; 2,630,588 mems; Pres. Dr RALPH BOHLMANN; Sec. Dr WALTER L. ROSIN.

Wisconsin Evangelical Lutheran Synod: 1201 West Tulsa St, Chandler, AZ 85224; f. 1850; 1,180 churches; 416,493 mems; Pres. Rev. CARL H. MISCHKE; Sec. Prof. DAVID WORGULL.

Methodist Churches

Members (1987 estimate): 12.8m., in nine bodies.

African Methodist Episcopal Church: 2843 Princess Ann Rd, Norfolk, VA 23540; f. 1816; 6,200 churches, 2.2m. mems; Pres. Bishops' Council Bishop JOSEPH D. CAUTHEN; Gen. Sec. Dr RUSSEL S. BROWN.

African Methodist Episcopal Zion Church: POB 183, St Louis, MO 63166; tel. (314) 534-6020; f. 1787; 6,200 churches; 3.5m. mems; Sr Bishop HENRY W. MURPH; Gen. Sec. Dr RICHARD ALLEN CHAPPELLE, Sr.

Free Methodist Church of North America: 901 College Ave, Winona Lake, IN 46590; 1,048 churches; 71,682 mems; Bishops: R. F. ANDREWS, D. BASTIAN, G. E. BATES, D. M. FOSTER, N. NZEYIMANA, C. E. VAN VALIN.

The United Methodist Church: 204 North Newlin St, Veedersburg, IN 47987; tel. (317) 294-2665; f. 1968; 42,785 pastoral charges, 9.7m. mems (world-wide); Sec. Gen. Conference Dr CAROLYN M. MARSHALL.

Orthodox Churches

Members (1987 estimate): 4.2m., in 14 bodies.

Antiochian Orthodox Christian Archdiocese of North America (Greek Orthodox Patriarchate of Antioch and all the East): 358 Mountain Rd, Englewood, NJ 07631; tel. (201) 871-1355; f. 1894; 150 churches; 300,000 mems; Primate Metropolitan PHILIP (SALIBA); Auxiliaries: Archbishop MICHAEL (SHAHEEN), Bishop ANTOUN (KHOURI).

Coptic Orthodox Church: 427 West Side Ave, Jersey City, NJ 07304; 28 churches; 115,000 mems; Archpriest Fr GABRIEL ABDELSAYED.

Diocese of the Armenian Church of America: 630 Second Ave, New York, NY 10016; tel. (212) 686-0710; f. 1889; 52 churches; 500,000 mems; Primate Archbishop TORKOM MANOOGIAN; Vicar-Gen. Very Rev. KHAJAG BARSAMIAN; Exec. Dir SYRAUN PALVETZIAN.

Greek Orthodox Archdiocese of North and South America: 8-10 East 79th St, New York, NY 10021; tel. (212) 570-3500; fax (212) 570-4005; inc. 1922; 600 churches; 2.5m. mems; Primate Archbishop IAKOVOS; Chancellor Bishop ISAIAH of ASPENDOS.

Orthodox Church in America: POB 675, Syosset, NY 11791; tel. (516) 922-0550; f. 1792; 440 churches; 1m. mems; Primate Metropolitan THEODOSIUS; Chancellor Very Rev. DANIEL HUBIAK.

Romanian Orthodox Episcopate of America: 3355 Ridgewood Rd, Akron, OH 44313; f. 1929; 34 churches; 60,000 mems; Ruling Bishop NATHANIEL POPP; Sec. Rev. Father LAURENCE LAZAR.

Serbian Orthodox Church for the USA and Canada: St Sava Monastery, POB 519, Libertyville, IL 60048; Bishops Rt Rev. Bishop FIRMILIAN, Rt Rev. Bishop SAVA, Bishop CHRISTOPHER.

Syrian Orthodox Church of Antioch, Archdiocese of the USA and Canada: 45 Fairmount Ave, Hackensack, NJ 07601; f. 1957; 22 churches; 30,000 mems; Primate Archbishop MAR-ATHENASIUS Y. SAMUEL; Gen. Sec. Very Rev. CHOREPISCOPUS JOHN MENO.

Ukrainian Orthodox Church of the USA: POB 495, South Bound Brook, NJ 08880; f. 1919; Metropolitan Most Rev. MSTYSLAV S. SKRYPNYK.

Ukrainian Orthodox Church in America (Ecumenical Patriarchate): 90-34 139th St, Jamaica, NY 11435; f. 1928; 27 churches; 30,000 mems; Admin. Rt Rev. MICHAEL PAWLYSKYN; Sec. Rt Rev. IVAN TKACZUK.

Pres. Rev. ROBERT M. OVERGARD, Sr; Sec. Rev. RICHARD VETTRUS.

The Albanian, Bulgarian, Carpatho-Russian and Russian Orthodox Churches are also represented.

Pentecostal Churches

Assemblies of God: 1445 Boonville Ave, Springfield, MO 65802; f. 1914; tel. (417) 862-2781; telex 436442; 11,004 churches; 1.3m. mems; Gen. Supt G. RAYMOND CARLSON; Gen. Sec. JOSEPH R. FLOWER.

Bible Way Church of Our Lord Jesus Christ World Wide: 5118 Clarendon Rd, Brooklyn, NY 11226; f. 1927; Presiding Bishop SMALLWOOD E. WILLIAMS; Gen. Sec. Bishop EDWARD WILLIAM.

Church of God: POB 13036, 1207 Willow Brook, Huntsville, AL 35802; f. 1903; Gen. Overseer Bishop VOY M. BULLEN; Gen. Sec.-Treas. MARIE POWELL.

Church of God (Cleveland, Tennessee): Keith St at 25th, NW, Cleveland, TN 37311; f. 1886; 5,346 churches; 505,775 mems; Gen. Overseer RAYMOND CROWLEY; Gen. Sec.-Treas. JOHN NICHOLS.

General Council, Christian Church of North America: POB 141-A, RD Suite 1, Route 18 and Routledge Rd, Transfer, PA 16154; f. 1948; 104 churches; 13,500 mems; Gen. Overseer Rev. GUY BONGIOVANNI; Gen. Sec.-Treas. Rev. RICHARD A. TEDESCO.

International Church of the Foursquare Gospel: 1100 Glendale Blvd, Los Angeles, CA 90026; f. 1927; 1,250 churches; 186,213 mems; Pres. Dr ROLF K. MCPHERSON; Sec. Rev. JOHN W. BOWERS.

National Gay Pentecostal Alliance: POB 1391, Schenectady, NY 12301; f. 1980; Pres. Rev. WILLIAM H. CAREY.

Open Bible Standard Churches: 2020 Bell Ave, Des Moines, IA 50315; f. 1919; 281 churches; 46,000 mems; Gen. Supt RAY E. SMITH; Sec.-Treas. PATRICK L. BOWLIN.

Pentecostal Church of God: 4901 Pennsylvania, POB 850, Joplin, MO 84802; f. 1919; 1,144 churches; 90,900 mems; Gen. Supt Dr JAMES D. GEE; Gen. Sec.-Treas. Dr RONALD R. MINOR.

Pentecostal Fellowship of North America: General Council of the Assemblies of God, 1445 Booneville Ave, Springfield, MO 65802; tel. (417) 862-2781; f. 1948; Chair. Rev. G. RAYMOND CARLSON.

Pentecostal Free Will Baptist Church: POB 1566, Dunn, NC 28334; f. 1959; 130 churches; 10,700 mems; Gen. Supt Rev. DON SAULS; Gen. Sec. Rev. J. T. HAMMOND.

United Pentecostal Church International: 8855 Dunn Rd, Hazelwood, MO 63042; f. 1945; 3,543 churches (USA and Canada); 1m. mems (world-wide); Gen. Supt Rev. NATHANIEL A. URSHAN.

Presbyterian Churches
Members (1987 estimate): 3.4m., in seven bodies.

Cumberland Presbyterian Church: 1978 Union Ave, Memphis, TN 38104; f. 1810; 811 churches; 98,103 mems; Moderator WILBUR S. WOOD; Stated Clerk ROBERT PROSSER.

Evangelical Presbyterian Church: 26049 Five Mile Rd, Detroit, MI 48239; f. 1981; 106 churches; 30,000 mems; Moderator PERRY MOBLEY; Stated Clerk Rev. L. EDWARD DAVIS.

Orthodox Presbyterian Church: 7401 Old York Rd, Philadelphia, PA 19126; f. 1936; 171 churches; 18,502 mems; Moderator JOHN O. KINNAIRD; Stated Clerk JOHN P. GALBRAITH.

Presbyterian Church in America: 1852 Century Pl., Atlanta, GA 30345; tel. (404) 320-3366; f. 1973; 1,100 churches; 168,500 mems; Moderator D. JAMES KENNEDY; Stated Clerk Dr PAUL R. GILCHRIST.

Presbyterian Church (USA): 100 Witherspoon St, Louisville, KY 40202-1396; tel. (502) 569-5000; telex 405139; fax (502) 569-5016; f. 1984; 11,593 churches; 2.9m. mems; Moderator Rev. JOAN SALMON CAMPBELL; Stated Clerk Rev. JAMES E. ANDREWS.

Reformed Presbyterian Church of North America: 1117 East Devonshire St, Phoenix, AZ 85014; f. 1871; 71 churches; 5,111 mems; Moderator Prof. WILLARD MCMILLAN; Clerk Rev. PAUL M. MARTIN.

The Roman Catholic Church

In 1986 there were 24,251 parishes in 150 dioceses and 33 archdioceses; 52.7m. mems in total.

National Conference of Catholic Bishops: 1312 Massachusetts Ave, NW, Washington, DC 20005; tel. (202) 659-6600; Pres. Most Rev. JOHN L. MAY (Archbishop of Saint Louis); Gen. Sec. Mgr DANIEL F. HOYE.

Archbishops

Anchorage: FRANCIS THOMAS HURLEY.

Atlanta: EUGENE A. MARINO.

Baltimore: WILLIAM H. KEELER.

Boston: Cardinal BERNARD F. LAW.

Chicago: Cardinal JOSEPH L. BERNARDIN.

Cincinnati: DANIEL E. PILARCZYK.

Denver: J. FRANCIS STAFFORD.

Detroit: Cardinal EDMUND C. SZOKA.

Dubuque: DANIEL W. KUCERA.

Hartford: JOHN F. WHEALON.

Indianapolis: EDWARD T. O'MEARA.

Kansas City in Kansas: IGNATIUS J. STRECKER.

Los Angeles: ROGER M. MAHONY.

Louisville: THOMAS C. KELLY.

Miami: EDWARD A. MCCARTHY.

Milwaukee: REMBERT G. WEAKLAND.

Mobile: OSCAR H. LIPSCOMBE.

Newark: THEODORE E. MCCARRICK.

New Orleans: FRANCIS BIBLE SCHULTE.

New York: Cardinal JOHN J. O'CONNOR.

Oklahoma City: CHARLES A. SALATKA.

Omaha: DANIEL E. SHEEHAN.

Philadelphia: ANTHONY J. BEVILACQUA, STEPHEN SULYK (Ukrainian, Byzantine Rite).

Pittsburgh: STEPHEN J. KOCISKO (Ruthenian, Byzantine Rite).

Portland in Oregon: WILLIAM J. LEVADA.

Saint Louis: JOHN L. MAY.

Saint Paul and Minneapolis: JOHN ROBERT ROACH.

San Antonio: PATRICK F. FLORES.

San Francisco: JOHN R. QUINN.

Santa Fe: ROBERT F. SANCHEZ.

Seattle: RAYMOND G. HUNTHAUSEN, THOMAS J. MURPHY.

Washington: Cardinal JAMES A. HICKEY.

Other Christian Churches

Association of Church Missions Committees: POB ACMC, Wheaton, IL 60189; tel. (312) 260-1660; f. 1974; 1,100 mems; Exec. Dir COLIN MCDOUGALL.

Christian Church (Disciples of Christ): 222 South Downey Ave, POB 1986, Indianapolis, IN 46206; tel. (317) 353-1491; telex 3413193; f. 1809; 4,214 congregations; 1.1m. mems; Gen. Minister and Pres. Dr JOHN O. HUMBERT.

Christian Reformed Church in North America: 2850 Kalamazoo Ave, SE, Grand Rapids, MI 49560; tel. (616) 246-0744; f. 1857; 697 churches; 223,018 mems; Stated Clerk Rev. LEONARD J. HOFMAN.

Church of Christ, Scientist: 175 Huntington Ave, Boston, MA 02115; tel. (617) 450-2000; f. 1879; 2,895 congregations; Pres. PERLINE B. THOMPSON; Clerk VIRGINIA S. HARRIS.

Church of God: POB 2420, Anderson, IN 46018; f. 1880; 2,296 churches; 188,662 mems; Chair. SAMUEL G. HINES; Exec. Sec. PAUL A. TANNER.

Church of Jesus Christ of Latter-day Saints (Mormon): 47 East South Temple St, Salt Lake City, UT 84150; tel. (801) 240-1000; telex 170416; f. 1830; 7m. mems (world-wide); 16,000 wards and branches (congregations); 225 overseas missions; Pres. EZRA TAFT BENSON; Pres. Council of Twelve Apostles HOWARD W. HUNTER.

Churches of God, General Conference: 153 Second St, West Newton, PA 15089; f. 1825; 353 churches; 34,870 mems; Pres. Pastor LARRY G. WHITE; Journalizing Sec. Rev. HARRY G. CADAMORE.

Evangelical Alliance Mission: POB 969, Wheaton, IL 60187; tel. (312) 653-5300; f. 1890; 1,080 mems; missions from evangelical Protestant denominations; Gen. Dir RICHARD WINCHELL.

Evangelical Covenant Church of America: 5101 North Francisco Ave, Chicago, IL 60625; f. 1885; 566 churches; 85,150 mems; Pres. Dr PAUL E. LARESEN; Sec. Rev. TIMOTHY C. EK.

Evangelical Friends Alliance: 2018 Maple St, Wichita, KS 67213; f. 1965; 217 churches; 24,095 mems; Mid-America YM ED KEY.

Friends General Conference: 1520-B Race St, Philadelphia, PA 19102; tel. (215) 567-1965; f. 1900; 505 churches; 31,600 mems; Gen. Sec. MEREDITH WALTON.

Friends United Meeting: 101 Quaker Hill Dr., Richmond, IN 47374; tel. (317) 962-7573; f. 1902; 175,000 mems (world-wide); Presiding Clerk PAUL ENYART; Gen. Sec. STEPHEN F. MAIN.

General Conference of Mennonite Brethren Churches: c/o 33020 Maclure Rd, Abbotsford, BC V2S 4N3, Canada; 215 churches; 35,170 mems; Chair. HERB BRANDT; Sec. BILL A. WIEBE.

Hungarian Reformed Church in America: 9901 Allen Rd, Allen Park, MI 48101; 40 parishes; 11,110 mems; Rt Rev. DEZSO ABRAHAM.

Hutterian Brethren: Woodcrest Service Comm., Route 213, Rifton, NY 12471; tel. (914) 658-3141; 1,500 mems; JOE KEIDERLING.

Independent Fundamental Churches of America: 2684 Meadow Ridge Dr., Bryon Center, MI 49315; f. 1930; National Exec. Dir Dr RICHARD GREGORY.

Jehovah's Witnesses: 25 Columbia Heights, Brooklyn, NY 11201; f. 1879; 8,336 churches; 752,404 mems; Pres. FREDERICK W. FRANZ.

Mariavite Old Catholic Church—Province of North America: 2803 Tenth St, Wyandotte, MI 48192-4994; tel. (313) 281-3082; f. 1930; 158 churches; 356,128 mems; Prime Bishop Most Rev. Archbishop Dr ROBERT R. J. M. ZABOROWSKI.

Mennonite Church: 528 East Madison St, Lombard, IL 60148; f. 1690; 989 churches; 91,167 mems; Moderator RALPH LEBOLD.

Messianic Jewish Alliance of America: POB 1055, Havertown, PA 19083; tel. (215) 896-5812; f. 1915; fellowship of Jews who believe Jesus is the Messiah; Pres. MICHAEL WOLF.

Missionary Church: 3901 South Wayne Ave, Fort Wayne, IN 46807; tel. (219) 456-4502; 26,869 mems; Pres. Rev. JOHN MORAN.

Moravian Church (Unitas Fratrum): (Northern Province) 1021 Center St, POB 1245, Bethlehem, PA 18016; f. 1740; 101 churches; 32,180 mems; Pres. Dr GORDON L. SOMMERS; (Southern Province) 459 South Church St, Winston-Salem, NC 27108; f. 1740; 56 churches; 21,722 mems; Pres. Rev. GRAHAM H. RIGHTS.

National Association of Congregational Christian Churches: POB 1620, Oak Creek, WI 53154; f. 1955; Moderator Rev. BARBARA JANIKOWSKY; Exec. Sec. J. FRED RENNEBOHM.

Nazarene, Church of the: 6401 The Paseo, Kansas City, MO 64131; f. 1908; 8,931 churches; 873,978 mems; Gen. Sec. B. EDGAR JOHNSON.

North American Old Roman Catholic Church: 4200 North Kedvale Ave, Chicago, IL 60641; f. 1915; 133 churches; 62,611 mems; Archbishop Most Rev. THEODORE J. REMATT.

Polish National Catholic Church of America: 115 Lake Scranton Rd, Scranton, PA 18505; tel. (717) 346-9131; 153 congregations; 100,000 mems; Prime Bishop Most Rev. FRANCIS C. ROWINSKI.

Reformed Church in America, General Synod of: 475 Riverside Dr., New York, NY 10115; tel. (212) 870-3071; f. 1628; 955 churches; 344,836 mems; Pres. Rev. WILBUR WASHINGTON; Gen. Sec. Rev. EDWIN G. MULDER.

Reformed Episcopal Church: 6300 Greenwood Parkway, Sagamore Hills, OH 44067; f. 1873; Pres. and Presiding Bishop Rev. WILLIAM H. S. JARDEN, Jr; Sec. ROGER F. SPENCE.

Reorganized Church of Jesus Christ of Latter-day Saints: The Auditorium, POB 1059, Independence, MO 64051; f. 1830; 1,094 churches; 192,077 mems; Pres. WALLACE B. SMITH; Sec. W. GRANT McMURRAY.

Rosicrucian Fellowship: 2222 Mission Ave, POB 713, Oceanside, CA 92054; tel. (714) 757-6600; f. 1909; Pres. VAN B. DEMICK.

Salvation Army: 799 Bloomfield Ave, Verona, NJ 07044; f. 1880; 1,092 churches; 432,893 mems; National Chief Sec. Col. HAROLD E. SHOULTS.

Society of Rosicrucians: Ten East Chestnut St, Kingston, NY 12401; tel. (914) 339-6335; f. 1912; Pres. LUCIA GROSCH.

Unitarian Universalist Association: 25 Beacon St, Boston, MA 02108; f. 1961; 956 churches; 173,167 mems; Pres. Rev. WILLIAM SCHULZ; Sec. BARRY JOHNSON-FAY.

Unitarian Universalist Christian Fellowship: 110 Arlington St, Boston, MA 02116; tel. (617) 482-2957; f. 1944; 900 mems; Exec. Dir Dr THOMAS D. WINTLE.

United Brethren in Christ: 302 Lake St, Huntington, IN 46750; f. 1789; 256 churches; 26,869 mems; Chair. Bishop C. RAY MILLER.

United Church of Christ: 105 Madison Ave, New York, NY 10016; f. 1957; 6,406 churches; 1.7m. mems; Moderator Rev. ROBERT D. SHERARD; Pres. Rev. AVERY D. POST; Sec. Rev. CAROL JOYCE BRUN.

Universal Fellowship of Metropolitan Community Churches: 5300 Santa Monica Blvd, Los Angeles, CA 90029; 230 churches; 34,000 mems; Moderator Rev. Elder NANCY L. WILSON.

Volunteers of America: 3813 North Causeway Blvd, Metairie, LA 70002; f. 1896; Pres. RAYMOND C. TREMONT.

Wesleyan Church: POB 2000, Marion, IN 46953; f. 1968; 1,704 churches; 109,195 mems; Gen. Supts Dr J. D. ABBOTT, Dr O. D. EMERY, Dr R. W. McINTYRE, Dr EARLE L. WILSON; Gen. Sec. Rev. RONALD R. BRANNON.

Interdenominational Organizations

American Bible Society: 1865 Broadway, New York, NY 10023; tel. (212) 581-7400; f. 1816; 500,000 mems; Pres. JAMES WOOD.

National Association of Evangelicals: POB 28, Wheaton, IL 60189; tel. (312) 665-0500; f. 1942; 4,000,000 mems; represents 50,000 churches from more than 70 denominations; Exec. Dir BILLY A. MELVIN.

National Council of the Churches of Christ in the USA: 475 Riverside Dr., New York, NY 10115; tel. (212) 870-2511; telex 234579; f. 1950; a co-operative agency of 32 Protestant and Eastern Orthodox denominations representing 40m. mems; conducts more than 60 interdenominational programmes; Pres. Very Rev. LEONID KISHKOVSKY; Gen. Sec. Rev. Dr ARIE R. BROUWER.

US Conference for the World Council of Churches: 475 Riverside Dr., Rm 1062, New York, NY 10115; tel. (212) 870-2533; f. 1948; mems are major Protestant and Orthodox Churches; Exec. Dir JOAN B. CAMPBELL.

HINDUISM

Ramakrishna–Vivekananda Center: 17 East 94th St, New York, NY 10128; tel. (212) 534-9445; f. 1933; teachings based on the system of Vedanta, combining the religion and philosophy of the Hindus; Minister SWAMI ADISWARANANDA.

ISLAM

American Druze Society: POB 2352, Livonia, MI 48151; tel. (313) 522-2747; f. 1906; 27,000 mems; Sec. EMMA SALEY.

Federation of Islamic Associations in the US and Canada: 25351 Five Mile Rd, Redford Township, MI 48259; tel. (313) 535-0014; f. 1951; co-ordinating agency for 45 affiliated orgs; Gen. Sec. NIHAD HAMED.

Islamic Center of New York: One Riverside Dr., New York, NY 10023; tel. (212) 362-6800; f. 1966.

Islamic Mission of America: 143 State St, Brooklyn, NY 11201; tel. (718) 875-6607; f. 1938; maintains an educational and training institute; 15,000 mems; Chair. Dr JABER.

JUDAISM

There are an estimated 5.9m. Jews in the USA.

Agudath Israel of America: 84 William St, 12th Floor, New York, NY 10038; tel. (212) 797-9000; f. 1921; 100,000 mems; Exec. Dir B. BERCHAVOLK.

American Council for Judaism: 298 Fifth Ave, Rm 301, New York, NY 10001; tel. (212) 947-8878; f. 1943; Exec. Dir. MARCIA FRIEDMAN.

American Jewish Committee: c/o Institute of Human Relations, 165 East 56th St, New York, NY 10022; tel. (212) 751-4000; f. 1906; 45,000 mems; Exec. Vice-Pres. BERTRAM H. GOLD.

American Jewish Congress: 15 East 84th St, New York, NY 10028; tel. (212) 879-4500; f. 1918; 50,000 mems.

American Zionist Federation: 515 Park Ave, New York, NY 10022; tel. (212) 371-7750; f. 1939; 21 mem. orgs; Exec. Dir KAREN RUBINSTEIN.

Central Conference of American Rabbis: 192 Lexington Ave, New York, NY 10016; tel. (212) 684-4990; f. 1889; Reform; Pres. Rabbi EUGENE J. LIPMAN; Exec. Vice-Pres. Rabbi JOSEPH B. GLASER; 1,475 mems.

The Rabbinical Assembly: 3080 Broadway, New York, NY 10027; tel. (212) 678-8060; f. 1901; Pres. Rabbi ALBERT L. LEWIS; Exec. Vice-Pres. Rabbi WOLFE KELMAN; 1,225 mems.

Synagogue Council of America: 10 East 40th St, New York, NY 10016; f. 1926; a co-ordinating agency for Orthodox, Conservative and Reform bodies; Pres. Rabbi WALTER S. WURZBURGER; Exec. Vice-Pres. Rabbi J. MANDELBAUM.

Union of American Hebrew Congregations: 838 Fifth Ave, New York, NY 10021; tel. (212) 249-0100; fax (212) 570-0895; f. 1873; Reform; 820 affiliated congregations representing 1.3m. mems; Pres. Rabbi ALEXANDER M. SCHINDLER; Sr Vice-Pres. ALBERT VORSPAN.

Union of Orthodox Jewish Congregations of America: 45 West 36th St, New York, NY 10018; tel. (212) 563-4000; f. 1898; 1,700 affiliated congregations representing 1m. mems; Pres. SIDNEY KWESTEL; Exec. Vice-Pres. Rabbi PINCHAS STOLPER.

United Synagogue of America: 155 Fifth Ave, New York, NY 10010; tel. (212) 533-7800; f. 1913; Conservative; 850 affiliated congregations representing 1.5m. mems; Pres. FRANKLIN D. KREUTZER; Exec. Vice-Pres. Rabbi BENJAMIN Z. KREITMAN; Sr Vice-Pres. and CEO Rabbi JEROME M. EPSTEIN.

SIKHISM

There are an estimated 9,500 Sikhs in North America.

Sikh Center: 1649 South Robertson Blvd, Los Angeles, CA 90035; Chief Admin. Siri Sikh Sahib HARBHAJAN SINGH KHALSA YOGIJI; Sec.-Gen. SARDAMI PREMKA KAUR KHALSA.

Sikh Study Circle: 5575 Trowbridge Dr., Dunwoody, GA 30338; f. 1971; conducts services, disseminates information about Sikh religion and culture; Pres. AJIT SINGH SOOD.

OTHER RELIGIONS AND CULTS

3HO Foundation: POB 351149, Los Angeles, CA 90035; tel. (213) 552-3416; f. 1969; 265,000 mems world-wide; Exec. Sec. SHAKTI PARWHA KAUR KHALSA.

Agni Yoga Society: 319 West 107th St, New York, NY 10025; tel. (212) 864-7752; f. 1946; 450 mems; Pres. EDGAR LANSBURY.

Ananda Marga: 38 42nd Ave, Suite 97, Corona, NY 11368; tel. (718) 898-1603; f. 1955; 50 state groups, 100 local groups; Pres. JAMES F. KAESER.

Church of Scientology of California: 5930 Franklin Ave, Los Angeles, CA 90028; tel. (213) 662-9431; f. 1954; 5m. mems; applied religious philosophy, mems are of many religions; Pres. Rev. SUE MCCLAY.

Mazdaznan Association (Zoroastrians): 1701 Aryana Dr., Encinitas, CA 92024; tel. (619) 942-9855; f. 1902; 2,000 mems; Elector HENRY L. SORGE.

Self-Realization Fellowship: 3880 San Rafael Ave, Los Angeles, CA 90065; tel. (213) 225-2471; f. 1920; Pres. DAYA MATA.

Spiritual Frontiers Fellowship: 3310 Baring St, Philadelphia, PA 19104; tel. (215) 222-0619; f. 1956; 5,000 mems; Pres. Emeritus ELIZABETH W. FENSKE.

INTER-FAITH ORGANIZATIONS

American Forum for Jewish–Christian Cooperation: 1407 Montfort Dr., Windsor Farms, Harrisburg, PA 17110; tel. (717) 236-0437; f. 1980; Chair. Rabbi DAVID Z. BEN-AMI.

Interfaith Movement: Maurice Blond Agency, 45 East 33rd St, New York, NY 10016; f. 1937; 120,000 mems; Pres. MAURICE BLOND.

National Conference of Christians and Jews: 71 Fifth Ave, Suite 1100, New York, NY 10003; tel. (212) 206-0006; f. 1928; 75 group mems; Pres. JACQUELINE G. WEXLER.

TRANSPORT AND UTILITIES

TRANSPORT

CO-ORDINATING BODIES AND TRANSPORT ASSOCIATIONS

Advanced Transit Association: 9019 Hamilton Dr., Fairfax, VA 22031; tel. (703) 591-8328; f. 1976; 225 mems; Sec.-Treas. JAROLD A. KIEFFER.

Amalgamated Transit Union: 5025 Wisconsin Ave, NW, 3rd Floor, Washington, DC 20016; tel. (202) 537-1645; f. 1892; 165,000 mems; Pres. JAMES LA SALA.

American Movers Conference: 2200 Mill Rd, Alexandria, VA 22314; tel. (703) 838-1930; f. 1963; companies transporting household goods, office equipment and high-value products; 1,400 mems; Pres. Maj.-Gen. CHARLES C. IRIONS.

American Public Transit Association: 1201 New York Ave, NW, Suite 400, Washington, DC 20005; tel. (202) 898-4000; f. 1974; rapid rail and motor bus transit systems; 900 mems; Exec. Vice-Pres. JACK R. GILSTRAP.

American Society of Transportation and Logistics: POB 33095, Louisville, KY 40232; tel. (502) 451-8150; f. 1946; 2,800 mems; Exec. Dir CARTER M. HARRISON.

American Traffic Safety Services Association: 5440 Jefferson Davis Highway, Fredericksburg, VA 22401; tel. (703) 898-5400; f. 1966; 450 mems; Exec. Dir ROBERT M. GARRETT.

Associated Motor Carriers Tariff Bureau: 302 Chester St, St Paul, MN 55107; tel. (612) 222-0303; f. 1935; motor carriers, water carriers, railroads and air freight lines; Pres. W. A. HALLMAN.

Association for Commuter Transportation: 1776 Massachusetts Ave, NW, Suite 521, Washington, DC 20036; tel. (202) 659-0600; f. 1976; 700 mems; Exec. Dir SANDRA SPENCE.

Association of Transportation Practitioners: 1211 Connecticut Ave, NW, Suite 310, Washington, DC 20036-2701; tel. (202) 466-2080; f. 1929; 2,200 mems; Exec. Dir E. DALE JONES.

Council on the Safe Transportation of Hazardous Articles: c/o Bishop, Cook, Purcell and Reynolds, 1400 L St, NW, Suite 800, Washington, DC 20005; tel. (202) 371-5750; f. 1971; federation of shipper trade associations, traffic conferences and associated companies; 194 mems; Pres. LAWRENCE BIERLEIN.

Hazardous Materials Systems (Bureau of Explosives): 50 F St, NW, Washington, DC 20001; tel. (202) 639-2222; f. 1907; railroads, steamship companies, motor carriers, shippers of hazardous materials; 600 mems; Dir CHARLES L. KELLER.

Household Goods Carriers' Bureau: 1611 Duke St, Alexandria, VA 22314; tel. (703) 683-7410; f. 1936; 1,700 mems; Pres. JOSEPH M. HARRISON.

Intermodal Transportation Association: 6410 Kenilworth Ave, Suite 108, Riverdale, MD 20737; tel. (301) 864-2661; f. 1981; transportation companies from air, motor, rail and water industries; 300 mems; Exec. Dir ALBERT J. MASCARO.

International Institute for Safety in Transportation: POB 20180, London Terrace Station, New York, NY 10011; tel. (212) 627-0979; f. 1977; 110 mems; Pres. Dr EDMUND J. CANTILLI.

International Mass Transit Association: National Press Bldg, Suite 1190, Washington, DC 20045; tel. (202) 662-7171; f. 1984; manufacturers and contractors of public transport vehicles and systems; 41 mems; Exec. Dir C. CARROLL CARTER.

Interstate Carriers Conference: 2200 Mill Rd, Alexandria, VA 22314; tel. (703) 838-1950; f. 1983; 900 mems; Exec. Dir J. TERRY TURNER.

Interstate Commerce Commission: 12th St and Constitution Ave, NW, Washington, DC 20423; tel. (202) 275-7524; f. 1887; federal body with regulatory authority over domestic surface common carriers; jurisdiction extends over rail, inland waterways and motorized traffic; Chair. HEATHER J. GRADISON.

NASSTRAC: 1750 Pennsylvania Ave, Suite 1105, Washington, DC 20006; tel. (202) 393-5505; f. 1952; protects the interests of firms making small shipments by rail, motor or air; 300 mems; Exec. Dir JOSEPH F. H. CUTRONA.

National Association of Freight Transportation Consultants: POB 21418, Albuquerque, NM 87154; f. 1959; 100 mems; Exec. Dir D. F. BEHME.

National Defense Transportation Association: 50 South Pickett St, Alexandria, VA 22304-3008; tel. (703) 751-5011; f. 1944; sea, air and land transportation companies, and their suppliers; 8,090 mems; Pres. NORMAN C. VENZKE.

National Export Traffic League: 234 Fifth Ave, New York, NY 10001; tel. (212) 697-5895; f. 1946; export and import traffic executives; 150 mems; Pres. LAWRENCE P. MANCHESE.

National Freight Transportation Association: POB 16219, Rocky River, OH 44116; tel. (216) 331-6064; f. 1905; 500 mems; Exec. Sec.-Treas. W. C. MAYO.

National Industrial Transportation League: 1090 Vermont Ave, NW, Suite 410, Washington, DC 20005; tel. (202) 842-3870; f. 1907; 1,400 mems; Exec. Vice-Pres. JAMES E. BARTLEY.

National Passenger Traffic Association: 516 Fifth Ave, Suite 406, New York, NY 10036; tel. (212) 221-6782; f. 1969; 900 mems; Exec. Dir PETER LUCIANO.

National Transportation Safety Board: 800 Independence Ave, SW, Washington, DC 20594; tel. (202) 382-6600; f. 1975; seeks to ensure that all types of transportation in the USA are conducted safely; carries out studies and accident investigations; Chair. JAMES L. KOLSTAD (acting).

Nu-Trans Co-operative: 3333 South Iron St, Chicago, IL 60608; tel. (312) 376-2700; f. 1987; associations and companies that ship or receive freight; individuals concerned with product distribution and traffic; 3,000 mems; Man. Dir IRWIN R. BENDER.

Survival and Flight Equipment (SAFE) Association: 25044 Peachland Ave, Suite 205, Newhall, CA 91321; tel. (805) 253-2744; f. 1957; promotes safety in all forms of transportation; 950 mems; Admin. JEANI BENTON.

Southwestern Industrial Traffic League: POB 383, Lubbock, TX 79408; tel. (806) 766-8451; f. 1918; traffic managers and transportation directors; 60 mems; Sec. BILL L. RUSK.

TDCC—The Electronic Data Interchange System: 1101 17th St, NW, Suite 712, Washington, DC 20036; tel. (202) 293-5514; f. 1968; manufacturers, shippers, railroads, motor carriers, airlines, steamships; Pres. EDWARD A. GUILBERT.

Transportation Brokers Conference of America; 14508 John Humphrey Dr., Orlan Park, IL 60462; tel. (312) 460-0010; f. 1979; 1,400 mems; Exec. Dir CHARLES M. NAYLOR.

Transportation Clubs International: 1040 Woodcock Rd, Orlando, FL 32803; tel. (305) 894-8312; f. 1921; personnel in the traffic and transportation fields; 25,000 mems; Exec. Dir CHARLES T. HARPER, Jr.

Transportation Communications International Union: Three Research Pl., Rockville, MD 20850; tel. (301) 948-4910; f. 1899; 200,000 mems; Pres. RICHARD I. KILROY.

Transportation Research Forum: 1133 15th St, NW, Suite 1000, Washington, DC 20005; tel. (202) 293-5910; f. 1961; 700 mems; Exec. Dir DAVID W. BARRACK.

Transport Workers' Union of America: 80 West End Ave, New York, NY 10023; tel. (212) 873-6000; f. 1934; 91,000 mems; Pres. JOHN E. LAWE.

RAILWAYS

Class I Railroads: Summary

	1982	1983	1984	1985	1986
Class I line-hauling companies[1]	33	32	29	23	22
Mileage:					
Railroad line owned ('000)[2]	165	161	157	155	154
Railroad track owned ('000)[3]	275	270	264	257	256
Equipment:					
Locomotives in service	27,073	25,838	24,506	22,932	21,045
AMTRAK passenger traffic:					
Passenger revenue ($ million)	465.1	515.3	556.7	604.9	633.6
Revenue passengers carried ('000)	18,725	19,469	20,065	20,945	20,165
Revenue passenger-miles (million)	4,122	4,343	4,566	4,977	5,015
Average trip per passenger (miles)	220.1	223.1	227.6	237.6	248.7
Freight service:					
Freight revenue ($ million)	25,627	25,835	28,472	26,688	25,344
Revenue-tons carried (million)	1,979	1,932	2,119	1,985	1,938

[1] In 1986 class I railroads were those with annual revenues of at least $88.5m.
[2] Represents the aggregate length of roadway of all line-haul railroads, excluding yard tracks, sidings and parallel lines. Includes estimate for class II and III railroads.
[3] Includes multiple main tracks, yard tracks and sidings. Includes estimate for class II and III railroads.

Sources: Association of American Railroads, Washington, DC, *Yearbook of Railroad Facts, Statistics of Railroads of Class I*, annual, and *Analysis of Class I Railroads*, annual.

Directory

REGULATORY BODIES

Federal Railroad Administration: US Dept of Transportation, 400 Seventh St, SW, Washington, DC 20590; tel. (202) 426-0881; formulates federal railway policies and administers and enforces safety regulations; Admin. JOHN RILEY.

United States Railway Association: 955 L'Enfant Plaza North, SW, Washington, DC 20595; tel. (202) 488-8777; f. 1973; independent federal corpn conducting studies dealing with various issues of rail service.

PRINCIPAL RAILWAYS

Alaska Railroad Corpn: POB 7-2111, Anchorage, AK 99510-7069; tel. (907) 265-2403; telex 26658; f. 1912; operated by the Federal Railroad Administration; 526 track-miles; Pres. and CEO F. G. TURPIN.

AMTRAK (National Railroad Passenger Corpn): 400 North Capitol St, NW, Washington, DC 20001; tel. (202) 383-3000; f. 1970; public corpn operating the passenger services in 43 states of 20 fmrly investor-owned railroads; 23,600 track-miles; Chair. W. GRAHAM CLAYTOR, Jr.

The Atchison, Topeka and Santa Fe Railway Co: 80 East Jackson Blvd, Chicago, IL 60604; tel. (312) 347-3000; telex 253266; 11,700 track-miles; Pres. W. JOHN SWARTZ.

Boston and Maine Corpn: Iron Horse Park, North Billerica, MA 01862; tel. (617) 663-9300; f. 1835; 1,393 track-miles; Pres. and CEO D. A. FINK.

Burlington Northern Railroad Co: 777 Main St, Fort Worth, TX 76102; tel. (817) 878-2000; 28,830 track-miles; Pres. and CEO D. W. GASKINS, Jr.

Chessie System Railroads: POB 6419, Terminal Tower, Cleveland, OH 44113; tel. (216) 623-2200; f. 1980; division of CSX Transportation; 11,140 track-miles; Pres. and CEO J. T. COLLINSON.

Chicago and North Western Transportation Co: 1 North Western Center, Chicago, IL 60606; tel. (312) 599-7000; 8,241 track-miles; Pres. and CEO J. R. WOLFE.

Conrail (Consolidated Rail Corpn): Transportation Center, 6 Penn Center Plaza, Philadelphia, PA 19103; tel. (215) 977-4000; telex 9775567; f. 1975 by federal govt merger of six bankrupt freight carriers in the Midwest and Northeast regions; returned to private-sector ownership in 1987; 25,057 track-miles; Chair., Pres. and CEO STANLEY HILLMAN (acting).

CSX Transportation: 500 Water St, Jacksonville, FL 32202; tel. (904) 359-3100; f. 1980 by merger; 22,001 track-miles; Pres. and CEO JOHN W. SNOW.

Delaware and Hudson Railway Co: D & H Bldg, 40 Beaver St, Albany, NY 12207; tel. (518) 462-7600; 1,698 track-miles; Pres. and CEO C. R. McKENNA.

Denver and Rio Grande Western Railroad Co: One Park Central, 1515 Arapahoe St, Denver, CO 80217; tel. (303) 629-5533; 1,764 track-miles; Chair., Pres. and CEO W. J. HOLTMAN.

Florida East Coast Railway Co: PO Drawer 1048, 1 Malaga St, St Augustine, FL 32085; tel. (904) 829-3421; telex 56334; 541 track-miles; Chair. WINFRED L. THORNTON; Pres. RAYMOND W. WYCKOFF.

Grand Trunk Western Railroad Co: 131 West Lafayette Blvd, Detroit, MI 48226; tel. (313) 237-4000; f. 1838; 1,490 track-miles; Chair. (vacant); Pres. G. L. MAAS.

Guilford Transportation Industries, Inc—Rail Division: 43 Railroad St, Bangor, ME 04401; tel. (207) 945-6562; Chair., Pres. and CEO DAVID A. FINK.

Illinois Central Gulf Railroad Co: 233 North Michigan Ave, Chicago, IL 60601; tel. (312) 565-1600; f. 1851; 6,669 track-miles; Chair. and CEO H. J. BRUCE; Pres. J. E. MARTIN.

Kansas City Southern Railway Co/Louisiana and Arkansas Railway: 114 West 11th St, Kansas City, MO 64105; tel. (816) 556-0303; telex 42327; 1,628 track-miles; Chair. and CEO T. S. CARTER; Pres. W. N. DERAMUS, IV.

Long Island Rail Road Co: 93-02 Sutphin Blvd, Jamaica Station, Jamaica, NY 11435; tel. (212) 990-7400; f. 1834; 323 track-miles; Pres. BRUCE McIVER.

Missouri-Kansas-Texas Railroad Co: Katy Bldg, Dallas, TX 75202; tel. (214) 651-6700; telex 730568; f. 1960; 2,175 track-miles; Chair. and CEO R. N. WHITMAN.

Missouri Pacific Railroad Co: 210 North 13th St, St Louis, MO 63103; tel. (314) 621-5544; f. 1849; division of Union Pacific Corpn; 11,089 track-miles; Chair. and CEO J. C. KENEFICK.

Norfolk Southern Corpn: Sovran Center, One Commercial Pl., Norfolk, VA 23514; f. 1896; 18,259 track-miles; Chair., Pres. and CEO ARNOLD B. McKINNON.

Santa Fe Southern Pacific Corpn: 80 East Jackson Blvd, Chicago, IL 60604; tel. (312) 427-4900; f. 1983; 11,500 track-miles; Chair. JOHN S. REID; Pres. and CEO ROBERT D. KREBS.

Seaboard System Railroad Inc: 500 Water St, Jacksonville, FL 32202; tel. (904) 359-3100; f. 1982; division of CSX Transportation; 15,746 track-miles; Pres. and CEO R. D. SANBORN.

SOO Line Railroad Co: POB 530, Minneapolis, MN 55440; tel. (612) 347-8000; f. 1961; 7,975 track-miles; Chair. and CEO D. M. CAVANAUGH; Pres. R. C. GILMORE.

Southern Pacific Transportation Co: Southern Pacific Bldg, One Market Pl., San Francisco, CA 94105; tel. (415) 541-1000; 9,535 track-miles; Chair., Pres. and CEO DENMAN K. McNEAR.

St Louis Southwestern Railway Co: 12400 Olive Blvd, Suite 310, St Louis, MO 63141; tel. (314) 991-9160; division of Southern Pacific

Transportation Co; 2,070 track-miles; Chair. and Pres. DENMAN K. MCNEAR.

Union Pacific System: 345 Park Ave, New York, NY 10154; tel. (212) 418-7000; telex 5815440; f. 1897; division of Union Pacific Corpn; 9,287 track-miles; Chair. and CEO MICHAEL H. WALSH; Pres. and COO R. G. FLANNERY.

ASSOCIATIONS

Alliance of Rail Citizens for Progress: Think Trains, POB 9395, Silver Spring, MD 20906; f. 1971; citizens and organizations interested in developing rail as a means of public transport; 1,550 mems; Founder LORENA F. LEMONS.

American Association of Railroad Superintendents: 18154 Harwood Ave, Homewood, IL 60430; tel. (312) 799-4650; f. 1896; 1,000 mems; Sec. PATRICIA WEISSMANN.

American Association of Railway Surgeons: POB 503, Daleville, VA 24083; tel. (703) 992-2513; f. 1888; 700 mems; Sec.-Treas. LYNNE B. HARRIS.

American Council of Railroad Women: 201 Mission St, 30th Floor, San Francisco, CA 94105; tel. (415) 974-4677; f. 1944; 100 mems; Pres. SUSAN P. SALTZER.

American Railway Bridge and Building Association: 18154 Harwood Ave, Homewood, IL 60430; tel. (312) 799-4650; f. 1891; employees involved in the construction and maintenance of railways; 700 mems; Sec. PATRICIA WEISSMAN.

American Railway Car Institute: Governors Office Park, Bldg V, 19900 Governors Dr., Suite 10, Olympia Fields, IL 60461; tel. (312) 747-0511; 30 mems; Pres. E. T. AHNQUIST.

American Railway Development Association: Florida Central Railroad, POB 967, Plymouth, FL 32768; tel. (407) 880-8500; f. 1906; marketing, real-estate and industrial development officers of railroads; 112 mems; Pres. GLEN C. HIGHFIELD.

American Railway Engineering Association: 50 F St, NW, Suite 7702, Washington, DC 20001; tel. (202) 639-2190; telex 892352; f. 1899; 4,200 mems; Exec. Dir LOUIS T. CERNY.

American Short Line Railroad Association: 2000 Massachusetts Ave, NW, Washington, DC 20036; tel. (202) 785-2250; f. 1913; 555 mems; Pres. P. HOWARD CROFT.

American Train Dispatchers' Associations: 1401 South Harlem Ave, Berwyn, IL 60402; tel. (312) 242-1691; f. 1917; 2,600 mems; Pres. ROBERT J. IRVIN.

Association of American Railroads: 50 F St, NW, Washington, DC 20001; tel. (202) 639-2100; f. 1934; mems: 65 system lines comprising 113 railroads in the USA, Canada and Mexico; Pres. and CEO WILLIAM DEMPSEY.

Brotherhood of Locomotive Engineers: 1370 Ontario St, Cleveland, OH 44114; tel. (216) 241-2630; f. 1863; 32,000 mems; Pres. L. D. MCFATHER.

Brotherhood of Maintenance of Way Employees: 12050 Woodward Ave, Detroit, MI 48203-3596; tel. (313) 868-0490; f. 1887; 70,000 mems; Pres. GEOFFREY N. ZEH.

Brotherhood of Railroad Signalmen: 601 West Golf Road, POB U, Mount Prospect, IL 60056; tel. (312) 439-3732; f. 1901; 12,500 mems; Pres. V. M. SPEAKMAN.

Brotherhood Railway Carmen/TCU: 4929 Main St, Kansas City, MO 64112; tel. (816) 561-1112; f. 1888; 73,000 mems; Pres. C. E. WHEELER.

Car Department Officers' Association: 1039 South Finley Road, Lombard, IL 60148; tel. (312) 627-4714; f. 1901; individuals and cos involved in the construction and maintenance of railway cars; 600 mems; Sec.-Treas. EDWARD TELLALIAN.

High-Speed Rail Association: 206 Valley Ct, Suite 800, Pittsburgh, PA 15237; tel. (412) 364-9306; f. 1983; promotes high-speed passenger transportation systems; 350 mems; Exec. Dir ROBERT J. CASEY.

Locomotive Maintenance Officers' Association: 5653 South Massasoit, Chicago, IL 60638; tel. (312) 585-0424; f. 1905; railway officials concerned with diesel-engine maintenance; 900 mems; Sec.-Treas. RON PONDEL.

National Association of Railroad Passengers: 236 Massachusetts Ave, NE, Suite 603, Washington, DC 20002; tel. (202) 546-1550; f. 1967; promotes public awareness of rail passenger service; Exec. Dir ROSS CAPON.

National Association of Railroad Property Tax Representatives: Norfolk Southern Corpn, Eight North Jefferson St, Roanoke, VA 24042; tel. (703) 981-5793; f. 1963; 100 mems; Sec.-Treas. NOVA PAINTER.

National Association of Railroad Trial Counsel: 881 Alma Real Dr., Suite 103A, Pacific Palisades, CA 90272; tel. (213) 459-7659; f. 1954; 1,200 mems; Exec. Dir HENRY M. MOFFAT.

National Association of Railway Business Women: 210 Bonny Knoll Rd, Roseville, CA 95678; tel. (916) 783-4650; f. 1941; 3,750 mems; Pres. ROZAN PRIZMICH.

National Railroad Construction and Maintenance Association: 150 South Fifth St, Suite 2300, Minneapolis, MN 55402; tel. (612) 335-1617; f. 1967; manufacturing, supply and service firms; c. 175–200 mems; Exec. Dir DANIEL FOTH.

National Railroad Intermodal Association: POB 337, Palos Park, IL 60464; tel. (312) 974-4363; f. 1957; companies and individuals involved in water, rail or highway transportation; 300 mems; Pres. R. KREHMEYER.

National Railway Labor Conference: 1901 L St, NW, Suite 500, Washington, DC 20036; tel. (202) 862-7200; f. 1963; management collective bargaining agency for the railroad industry; 150 mems; Chair. CHARLES I. HOPKINS, Jr.

Railroad Advancement Through Information and Law Foundation: 70 East State Park Boundary Rd, Chesterton, IN 46304; tel. (219) 926-2224; f. 1969; conducts and sponsors research into improving railroad transportation; Pres. HERB READ.

Railroad Public Relations Association: 50 F St, NW, Washington, DC 20001; tel. (202) 639-2552; f. 1952; 163 mems; Sec.-Treas. CAROL B. PERKINS.

Railway Automotive Management Association: c/o Atchison, Topeka and Santa Fe Railway, 80 East Jackson Blvd, 9th Floor, Chicago, IL 60604; tel. (312) 347-3000; f. 1966; railroad fleet representatives; 50 mems; Pres. C. MICHAEL GUNTER.

Railway Engineering–Maintenance Suppliers' Association: 6120 West North Ave, Suite 202A, Chicago, IL 60639; tel. (312) 622-6653; f. 1965; distributors and manufacturers of track supplies; 290 mems; Exec.-Sec. J. J. STALLMAN.

Railway Fuel and Operating Officers Association: POB 8496, Springfield, IL 62791; tel. (217) 544-7834; f. 1892; 1,250 mems; Sec.-Treas. W. N. HULL.

Railway Labor Executives Association: 400 First St, NW, Suite 804, Washington, DC 20001; tel. (202) 737-1541; f. 1926; chief executive officers of railway labour organizations; 18 mems; Exec. Sec.-Treas. J. J. KENNEDY, Jr.

Railway Progress Institute: 700 North Fairfax St, Alexandria, VA 22314-2098; tel. (703) 836-2332; f. 1908; trade association of the railway equipment and supply industry; 150 mem. cos; Pres. ROBERT A. MATTHEWS.

Railway Supply Association: 1150 Wilmette Ave, Office Suite Three, Wilmette, IL 60091; tel. (312) 251-5476; f. 1962; co-ordinators of railway supply exhibitions; 360 mems; Exec. Dir WILLIAM J. BURRONS.

Railway Systems Suppliers: 561 Middlesex Ave, Suite 5, Metuchen, NJ 08840; tel. (201) 494-2910; f. 1906; 162 mem. cos; Exec. Dir W. EDWARD ROWLAND.

Roadmasters and Maintenance of Way Association of America: 18154 Harwood Ave, Homewood, IL 60430; tel. (312) 799-4650; f. 1883; founded to improve the methods of railway track maintenance; 2,000 mems; Sec. PATRICIA WEISSMAN.

Western Railroad Association: 222 South Riverside Plaza, Suite 1100, Chicago, IL 60606-5945; tel. (312) 648-7800; f. 1970; 37 mems; Pres. JAMES N. BAKER.

ROADS

Highway Mileage by State, 1985

(Urban, rural and federal-aid highway system, as at 31 December.)

| | Urban ('000 miles) | Rural ('000 miles) | Federal-aid highway system [1] | | | |
| | | | Total primary | | Urban (miles) | Secondary (miles) |
			Primary (miles)	Interstate (miles) [2]		
Alabama	14.5	73.3	6,679	875	2,737	11,390
Alaska	1.6	10.0	1,043	1,091	233	1,839
Arizona	10.0	66.9	3,696	1,166	2,857	3,221
Arkansas	7.6	69.5	5,130	542	1,114	7,170
California	66.4	107.7	11,076	2,388	16,740	11,119
Colorado	10.7	65.2	4,292	924	2,259	3,405
Connecticut	10.7	8.9	1,269	339	2,948	902
Delaware	1.5	3.8	432	41	305	602
District of Columbia	1.1	—	173	12	233	—
Florida	31.7	67.3	8,395	1,324	5,566	4,682
Georgia	19.7	86.5	10,050	1,225	3,936	13,962
Hawaii	1.4	2.6	509	37	317	448
Idaho	2.5	66.7	2,665	605	724	4,178
Illinois	31.0	103.7	9,710	1,788	6,668	12,934
Indiana	17.5	73.9	4,968	1,119	4,530	9,331
Iowa	8.6	103.9	8,851	782	2,402	13,437
Kansas	8.6	123.8	8,071	816	1,559	22,589
Kentucky	7.5	62.0	3,779	739	1,847	7,245
Louisiana	12.4	45.9	3,156	686	2,143	7,358
Maine	2.4	19.6	2,007	312	694	2,727
Maryland	11.6	16.0	2,195	386	2,106	1,897
Massachusetts	20.6	13.2	2,215	562	5,903	2,007
Michigan	26.6	91.0	5,963	1,131	4,832	19,019
Minnesota	13.5	118.5	9,321	884	2,090	16,490
Mississippi	7.0	64.7	5,693	686	1,684	11,739
Missouri	15.0	104.1	6,903	1,142	2,362	18,139
Montana	2.3	69.2	5,478	1,169	325	4,722
Nebraska	4.9	87.2	7,227	481	1,064	11,441
Nevada	3.0	40.8	1,850	543	512	2,331
New Hampshire	2.4	12.1	1,136	207	714	1,233
New Jersey	22.4	11.5	1,463	385	5,349	1,720
New Mexico	5.4	48.2	3,556	1,000	596	3,917
New York	37.0	73.1	8,433	1,497	8,670	6,345
North Carolina	17.9	75.4	4,483	795	2,624	10,312
North Dakota	1.6	84.4	5,537	571	433	10,487
Ohio	30.5	82.5	6,645	1,549	7,613	11,592
Oklahoma	12.3	98.4	5,309	927	2,966	10,280
Oregon	8.4	85.6	5,004	716	1,987	7,766
Pennsylvania	29.1	86.6	9,913	1,524	6,983	8,039
Rhode Island	4.4	1.6	436	70	899	197
South Carolina	9.0	54.2	5,607	784	1,157	8,509
South Dakota	1.7	71.5	5,799	677	373	11,202
Tennessee	13.7	70.1	6,072	1,057	3,048	5,335
Texas	69.4	212.8	16,680	3,148	7,510	32,594
Utah	5.1	43.4	2,630	848	847	2,569
Vermont	1.0	13.1	1,110	320	280	1,947
Virginia	13.8	51.7	5,463	1,027	3,266	10,187
Washington	15.4	65.6	5,028	727	3,897	7,205
West Virginia	3.0	32.2	2,450	479	785	6,630
Wisconsin	14.0	94.5	8,880	578	2,869	11,841
Wyoming	1.6	36.6	2,983	912	499	2,287
Total	690.9	3,171.0	257,413	43,593	144,055	398,248

[1] Highway mileage open to traffic.
[2] Although the interstate system is part of the federal-aid primary system, its mileage is shown separately.
Source: Federal Highway Administration, US Department of Transportation, *Highway Statistics*, annual.

Motor-Vehicle Registrations by State

(Figures represent registrations covering publicly-, privately- and commercially-owned vehicles; excludes vehicles owned by military service.)

	Automobiles, trucks and buses ('000)				Automobiles ('000)[1] 1986	Motorcycles ('000)[2] 1986
	1983	1984	1985	1986		
Alabama	3,145	3,202	3,338	3,461	2,417	58
Alaska	350	368	353	348	217	9
Arizona	2,289	2,111	2,235	2,353	1,662	84
Arkansas	1,442	1,317	1,384	1,435	939	30
California	17,767	17,965	18,899	19,703	15,384	677
Colorado	2,649	2,754	2,759	2,769	2,027	107
Connecticut	2,305	2,366	2,465	2,537	2,377	58
Delaware	427	459	465	485	383	11
District of Columbia	295	305	326	345	328	4
Florida	8,808	9,394	9,865	10,349	8,142	226
Georgia	4,208	4,460	4,580	4,686	3,375	115
Hawaii	610	638	651	672	589	18
Idaho	877	849	854	862	528	48
Illinois	7,513	7,598	7,727	7,785	6,137	221
Indiana	3,852	3,950	4,024	4,090	3,035	130
Iowa	2,479	2,443	2,696	2,764	1,988	274
Kansas	2,048	2,122	2,148	2,171	1,490	94
Kentucky	2,621	2,590	2,615	2,641	1,777	38
Louisiana	2,877	2,958	3,012	3,054	2,079	55
Maine	766	800	840	861	641	44
Maryland	3,011	3,193	3,276	3,359	2,771	63
Massachusetts	3,840	3,788	3,738	3,737	3,264	124
Michigan	6,295	6,369	6,727	7,187	5,762	214
Minnesota	3,239	2,968	3,385	3,548	2,744	175
Mississippi	1,560	1,669	1,746	1,810	1,375	25
Missouri	3,433	3,521	3,558	3,593	2,648	78
Montana	829	685	652	628	382	24
Nebraska	1,235	1,257	1,257	1,262	842	40
Nevada	730	745	709	696	502	18
New Hampshire	803	870	974	1,019	854	66
New Jersey	4,941	4,896	4,909	4,926	4,428	128
New Mexico	1,237	1,220	1,176	1,155	732	41
New York	8,417	8,644	9,042	9,373	8,185	253
North Carolina	4,603	4,369	4,450	4,536	3,314	67
North Dakota	666	691	655	649	376	29
Ohio	7,768	7,894	8,102	8,331	6,972	279
Oklahoma	2,769	2,781	2,864	2,915	1,915	105
Oregon	2,121	2,183	2,204	2,223	1,561	84
Pennsylvania	6,844	7,081	7,209	7,340	5,980	215
Rhode Island	598	622	610	615	517	27
South Carolina	2,058	2,128	2,222	2,276	1,715	39
South Dakota	629	643	650	677	429	35
Tennessee	3,537	3,569	3,754	3,914	3,070	105
Texas	11,693	12,172	12,444	12,612	8,606	273
Utah	1,074	1,090	1,099	1,105	733	52
Vermont	367	377	398	418	315	21
Virginia	3,894	4,047	4,253	4,463	3,838	84
Washington	3,338	3,430	3,526	3,767	2,652	136
West Virginia	1,175	1,107	1,143	1,239	860	32
Wisconsin	3,214	3,094	3,187	3,281	2,528	206
Wyoming	502	494	500	507	286	19
Total	163,749	166,249	171,654	176,532	135,671	5,358

[1] Includes taxis. [2] Includes motorcycles used for official purposes.

Source: Federal Highway Administration, US Department of Transportation, *Highway Statistics*, annual, and *Selected Highway Statistics and Charts*, annual.

Directory

REGULATORY BODY

Federal Highway Administration: US Dept of Transportation, 400 Seventh St, SW, Washington, DC 20590; tel. (202) 426-0677; implements federal highway policy and promotes road safety; Administrator THOMAS D. LARSON.

PRINCIPAL COMPANIES

Allen H. W. Co: 321 South Cincinnati Ave, Tulsa, OK 74103; tel. (918) 582-2261; intercity bus lines; Pres. and CEO ROBERT W. ALLEN.

American Transit Corpn: 120 South Central Ave, St Louis, MO 63105; tel. (314) 726-9200; local intercity transportation; Chair. D. J. GIACOMA.

Arrow Stage Lines Inc: 720 East Norfolk Ave, Norfolk, NE 68701; tel. (402) 371-3850; intercity and rural highway passenger transportation; Pres. CHARLES D. BUSSKOHL.

Badger Coaches Inc: 200 West Beltline Highway, Madison, WI 53701; tel. (608) 255-6773; intercity highway and passenger charter transportation; Pres. GERTRUDE J. WATSON.

Blue Bird Coachlines Inc: 502–504 North Barry St, Olean, NY 14760; tel. (716) 372-5500; passenger and charter express transportation; Pres. LOUIS A. MAGNANO.

Bonanza Bus Lines Inc: 27 Sabin St, Providence, RI 02901; tel. (401) 331-7500; intercity bus transportation; Pres. GEORGE M. SAGE.

Citizen Auto Stage Co: 424 Grand Ave, Nogales, AZ 85621; tel. (602) 287-3618; highway bus transportation, long-distance trucking, storage trailer rental; Pres. TOM BRUCE MORGAN.

Continental Panhandle Lines: 400 Monroe, Amarillo, TX 79101; tel. (806) 372-2272; bus lines transportation; Pres. JOHN M. HEKET.

Decatur Transit, Inc: 161 First Ave, NE, Decatur, AL 35601; tel. (205) 353-9601; truck transportation, truck and car rental and leasing; Chair. E. WILLIAMS.

Greyhound Corpn: Greyhound Tower, Phoenix, AZ 85013; tel. (602) 248-5000; intercity bus transportation and package delivery; Chair. JAMES E. CUNNINGHAM.

Gulf Transport Co: 505 South Conception St, Mobile, AL 36603; tel. (205) 433-3647; bus terminal and transportation; Pres. E. A. COLLIER.

Holland Industries Inc: 1 Keeshin Dr., Toledo, OH 43612; tel. (419) 476-4711; bus charter service, intercity and rural highway transportation and taxicabs; Chair. MICHAEL MARGOLIES.

Hudson Transit Corpn: 17 Franklin Turnpike, Mahwah, NJ 07430; tel. (201) 529-3666; intercity and rural highway passenger transportation; Chair. DAVID RUKIN.

Jack Rabbit Lines: 301 North Dakota Ave, Sioux Falls, SD 57102; tel. (605) 336-0885; interstate passenger common carrier; Pres. LOWELL C. HANSEN, II.

Kerrville Bus Co Inc: 429 Sidney Baker St, Kerrville, TX 78028; tel. (512) 257-7451; interstate bus transportation; Pres. and CEO FRED E. KAISER.

Lakeland Bus Lines Inc: 425 East Blackwell St, Dover, NJ 07801; tel. (201) 366-0600; interstate busline; Pres. MARTA M. MAZZARISI.

Martz Frank Coach Co: 239 Old River Rd, Wilkes Barre, PA 18773; tel. (717) 829-6911; bus charter service; Pres. FRANK M. HENRY.

Peerless Stages, Inc: 2040 Castro St, Oakland, CA 94612; tel. (415) 444-2900; intercity and rural highway passenger transportation; Chair. HARRY D. GAETA.

Peter Pan Bus Lines Inc: 1776 Main St, Springfield, MA 01102; tel. (413) 781-2900; intercity bus line, charter buses; Chair. PETER PICKNELLY, Jr.

Red and Tan Enterprises Inc: 126 North Washington Ave, Bergenfield, NJ 07621; tel. (201) 384-2400; regular bus route and charter; Pres. ERNEST CAPITANI, Jr.

Starr Transit Co Inc: 2531 East State St, Trenton, NJ 08619; tel. (609) 587-0626; bus charter and tour service; Pres. MITCHELL SUSSMAN.

Southeastern Stages Inc: 226 Alexander St, NW, Atlanta, GA 30313; tel. (404) 874-2741; bus service; Chair. JAKE W. HUGHES.

Trailways Corpn: 1500 Jackson St, Dallas, TX 75201; tel. (214) 655-7711; bus transportation and manufacture of motor vehicles; Chair. JAMES KERRIGAN.

Transit Management of Washoe: 2050 Villanova Dr., Reno, NV 89502; tel. (702) 826-3273; intercity bus lines; Pres. DAVID DAVIS.

Transport Insurance Co: 4100 Harry Hines Blvd, Dallas, TX 75219; tel. (214) 526-3876; long-distance trucking and bus transportation; Chair. and CEO MIKE McCRARY.

ASSOCIATIONS

American Association of State Highway and Transportation Officials: 444 North Capitol St, NW, Suite 225, Washington, DC 20001; tel. (202) 624-5800; f. 1914; public officials in state agencies responsible for highways and transportation; 63 mems; Exec. Dir FRANCIS B. FRANÇOIS.

American Bus Association: 1025 Connecticut Ave, NW, Washington, DC 20036; tel. (202) 293-5890; f. 1926; 3,500 mems; Pres. NORMAN R. SHERLOCK.

American Road and Transportation Builders' Association: 501 School St, SW, Washington, DC 20024; tel. (202) 488-2722; f. 1902; 4,500 mems; Pres. Dr T. PETER RUANE.

American Trucking Associations: 2200 Mill Rd, Alexandria, VA 22314; tel. (703) 838-1700; f. 1933; 3,400 mems; Pres. and CEO THOMAS J. DONOHUE.

Association of Asphalt Paving Technologists: 1404 Concordia Ave, St Paul, MN 55104; tel. (612) 642-1350; f. 1926; 800 mems; Sec.-Treas. EUGENE L. SKOK, Jr.

Better Roads and Transportation Council: 408 Vaughn Bldg, Austin, TX 78701; tel. (512) 478-9351; f. 1971; seeks to improve US transportation systems by promoting public awareness; 50 mems; Sec.-Treas. EUGENE W. ROBBINS.

Buses International Association: POB 1472, Spokane, WA 99210; tel. (509) 328-9181; f. 1981; 100 mems; Exec. Dir WILLIAM A. LUKE.

Canadian–American Motor Carriers' Association: 119 Jeffrey Ave, Holliston, MA 01746; tel. (617) 429-5920; f. 1978; Pres. WILLIAM M. CLIFFORD.

Equipment Interchange Association: 6410 Kenilworth Ave, Suite 108, Riverdale, MD 20737; tel. (301) 277-8830; f. 1958; truck fleet operators engaged in interstate and foreign commerce; 200 mems; Man. Dir ALBERT J. MASCARO.

Highway Users' Federation for Safety and Mobility: 1776 Massachusetts Ave, NW, Washington, DC 20036; tel. (202) 857-1200; f. 1970; 400 mems; Pres. LESTER P. LAMM.

Independent Truck Owner/Operator Association: POB 621, Stoughton, MA 02072; tel. (617) 341-2030; f. 1981; 7,200 mems; Pres. MARSHALL SIEGEL.

International Bridge, Tunnel and Turnpike Association: 2120 L St, NW, Suite 305, Washington, DC 20037; tel. (202) 659-4620; companies and public agencies operating toll facilities; 212 mems; Exec. Dir NEIL D. SCHUSTER.

International Road Federation: 525 School St, SW, Washington, DC 20024; tel. (202) 554-2106; f. 1948; automotive, oil, rubber and construction firms; 500 mems; Pres. W. GERALD WILSON.

International Taxicab Association: 3849 Farragut Ave, Kensington, MD 20895; tel. (301) 946-5701; f. 1966; 600 mems; Exec. Vice-Pres. ALFRED B. LaGASSE.

The Maintenance Council of the American Trucking Associations: 2200 Mill Rd, Alexandria, VA 22314; tel. (703) 838-1763; f. 1979; 1,200 mems; Exec. Dir PAUL T. DOMER.

Middle Atlantic Conference: POB 397, Riverdale, MD 20737; tel. (301) 779-7710; f. 1935; freight rate and tariff agency motor common carriers; 875 mems; Exec. Vice-Pres. J. ALAN ROYAL.

Mid-West Truckers Association: 2715 North Dirksen Parkway, Springfield, IL 62702; tel. (217) 525-0310; f. 1961; 2,000 mems; Exec. Vice-Pres. ROBERT L. JASMON.

National Agricultural Transportation League: 215 North Second St, Suite A, Leesburg, FL 32748; tel. (904) 326-2188; f. 1954; truckers and others concerned with long-haul agricultural trucking; 6,000 mems; Exec. Sec. JAMES TILLY.

National Asphalt Pavement Association: 6811 Kenilworth Ave, Riverdale, MD 20737; tel. (301) 779-4880; f. 1955; producers of asphalt for paving roads; 950 mems; Pres. JOHN GRAY.

National Association of Women Highway Safety Leaders: 7206 Robin Hood Dr., Upper Marlboro, MD 20772; tel. (301) 868-7583; f. 1967; promotes road safety and police enforcement; 100,000 mems; Exec. Dir AGNES BEATON.

National Bus Traffic Association: 506 South Wabash Ave, Chicago, IL 60605; tel. (312) 922-3700; f. 1933; 333 mems; Chair. L. W. HARLOW.

National Committee for Motor Fleet Supervisor Training: Highway Traffic Safety Program, 70 Kellogg Center, Michigan State University, East Lansing, MI 48824; tel. (517) 353-1790; f. 1945; bus, automobile, insurance and safety organizations; 1,200 mems; Exec. Dir Dr DONALD SMITH.

National Motor Freight Traffic Association: 2200 Mill Rd, Alexandria, VA 22314; tel. (703) 838-1821; f. 1956; 2,000 mems; Exec. Dir MARTIN E. FOLEY.

National Private Trucking Association: 1320 Braddock Pl., Suite 720, Alexandria, VA 22314; tel. (703) 683-1300; f. 1947; 3,500 mems; Exec. Dir THOMAS L. MOORE.

National Trucking Industrial Relations Association: 7111 West Edgerton Ave, Milwaukee, WI 53220; tel. (414) 423-1330; f. 1987; Exec. Dir HERVE AITKEN.

North American Professional Drivers' Association: POB 1170, Temple Hills, MD 20748; tel. (800) 843-2043; f. 1987; 8,000 mems; Exec. Admin. JOHN P. MAY.

Owner Operators of America: 9590 State Rd, Boston, NY 14025; tel. (716) 941-5582; f. 1983; 450 mems; Exec. Sec. CHUCK DeVAUL.

Owner/Operator Independent Drivers' Association of America: POB 88, Oak Grove, MO 64075; tel. (816) 229-5791; f. 1973; 7,000 mems; Pres. JAMES JOHNSTON.

Private Truck Council of America: 2022 P St, NW, Washington, DC 20036; tel. (202) 785-4900; f. 1939; 1,500 mems; Exec. Vice-Pres. RICHARD D. HENDERSON.

Professional Truck Driver Institute of America: 8788 Elk Grove Blvd, Suite M., Elk Grove, CA 95624; tel. (916) 686-5146; f. 1985; Pres. E. KYNASTON.

Professional Trucking Services Association: United Truckers Service, 1385 Iris Dr., Conyers, GA 30208; tel. (404) 922-6200; f. 1984; 18 mems; Pres. ANTHONY L. KEENAN.

Regional and Distribution Carriers' Conference: 2200 Mill Rd, Suite 640, Alexandria, VA 22314; tel. (703) 838-1990; f. 1943; 350 mems; Exec. Dir WARREN WIEDHAHN.

Regular Common Carrier Conference: 2200 Mill Rd, Alexandria, VA 22314; tel. (703) 838-1967; f. 1939; 450 mems; Exec. Dir JAMES C. HARKINS.

Society of Professional Drivers: POB 491, Paoli, PA 19301; tel. (215) 647-0818; f. 1957; Exec. Dir WILLIAM D. SHORE.

Trucking Management, Inc: 2233 Wisconsin Ave, NW, Washington, DC 20007; tel. (202) 965-7660; f. 1963; 41 mems; Pres. ARTHUR H. BUNTE, Jr.

United Bus Owners of America: 1275 K St, NW, Suite 800, Washington, DC 20005; tel. (202) 484-5623; f. 1971; 2,000 mems; Exec. Dir WAYNE J. SMITH.

Western Highway Institute: 1200 Bayhill Dr., San Bruno, CA 94066; tel. (415) 952-4900; f. 1947; 350 mems; Exec. Dir BYRON L. GEUY.

INLAND WATERWAYS

Freight Traffic

(million ton-miles)

	1984	1985	1986
Coastal waterways	593,923	610,976	580,887
Lake waterways	49,784	48,184	43,198
Internal waterways . . .	242,855	232,708	248,117
Local waterways	1,157	1,102	1,197
Total	887,720	892,170	873,401

Source: Transportation Systems Center, US Department of Transportation.

Directory

St Lawrence Seaway Corpn: US Dept of Transportation, POB 44090, Washington, DC 20026-4090; tel. (202) 366-0091; responsible for sections of the St Lawrence Seaway within the territorial limits of the USA.

PRINCIPAL COMPANIES

Allied Marine Industries Inc: 100 Avery Ave, Norfolk, VA 23501; tel. (804) 545-7301; river and canal transportation, towing and tugboat service and marine cargo handling.

Alter Co: 2333 Rockingham Rd, Davenport, IA 52808; tel. (319) 326-2561; Chair. and Pres. BERNARD GOLDSTEIN.

American Barge and Towing Inc: 12400 Olive St, St Louis, MO 63141; tel. (314) 434-5554; river barge transportation; Pres. RONALD MOORE.

American Commercial Barge Line Co: CSX Corpn, One James Center, POB C-32222, Richmond, VA 23261; tel. (804) 782-1400; operates along the Mississippi and Ohio rivers and tributaries to the Gulf Intracoastal Waterway; Pres. H. JOSEPH BOBIZEN, Jr.

American Commercial Lines, Inc: 1701 East Market St, Jefferson, IN 47130; tel. (812) 288-0100; river transportation, shipbuilding; Chair. H. T. WATKINS.

American Steamship Co: 3200 Marine Midland Center, Buffalo, NY 14203; tel. (716) 854-7644; telex 91330; f. 1907; 17 self-unloading cargo vessels on the Great Lakes; Pres. and CEO D. WARD FULLER.

Arthur–Smith Corpn: 8919 Interchange Dr., Houston, TX 77056; tel. (713) 660-9171; coastwise and canal transportation; Pres. O. J. TAUBER, Sr.

Atlas Towing Co: Foot of 12th St, Parkersburg, WV 26102; tel. (304) 428-0341; river transportation; Pres. CHRISTOPHE CRISS.

Bernert Barge Lines Inc: 170 Harding Blvd, Oregon City, OR 97045; tel. (503) 656-8288; river barge transportation; Pres. ROBERT BERNERT.

Bulkfleet Marine Ltd 11: 1800 West Loop South, Suite 1600, Houston, TX 77027; tel. (713) 840-1100; tugboat and barge operation; Pres. J. BARRY SNYDER.

Exchange Building Corpn: 300 West Washington St, 13th Floor, Chicago, IL 60606; tel. (312) 236-6300; Pres. and CEO LESTER CROWN.

Cenac Towing Co Inc: Foot of Palm Ave, Houma, LA 70361; tel. (504) 872-2413; marine towing, contract carrier, river and canal transportation, shipbuilding and repairs; Pres. and CEO CLARK C. CENAC.

Columbia Transportation Division, Oglebay Norton Co: 1100 Superior Ave, Cleveland, OH 44114; services on the Great Lakes; 19 vessels; Pres. JOHN J. DWYER.

Crounse Corpn: 2626 Broadway, Paducah, KY 42001; tel. (502) 444-9611; river freight transportation; Chair. GEORGE P. CROUNSE.

Day Line: Circle Line Plaza, West End of 42nd St, New York, NY 10036; tel. (212) 279-5151; telex 125776; f. 1962; seasonal services on the Hudson River between New York City and Poughkeepsie; Chair. KARL G. ANDREN.

Federal Barge Lines, Inc: 7501 South Broadway, St Louis, MO 63111; f. 1918; all-year direct service on Lower Mississippi, Illinois, Ohio, Arkansas and rivers to the Gulf Intracoastal Waterway; seasonal direct service on Upper Mississippi River; Pres. JACK F. LYNCH, Sr; Vice-Pres. THOMAS F. MALONEY.

Findlay Towing Co Inc: 231 Third St, Northport, AL 35476; tel. (205) 752-5361; Pres. T. H. FINDLAY.

Great Lakes Dredge & Dock Co: 9320 South Ewing Ave, Chicago, IL 60617; tugboats and dredges; 32 vessels; Pres. JOHN A. DOWNS.

Knappton Corpn: 9030 North West St Helens Road, Portland, OR 97203; tel. (503) 286-0631; river and canal transportation, towing and tugboat service, and marine cargo handling; Chair. and Pres. PETER J. BRIX.

Lakeshore Contractors Inc: 740 West Western Ave, Muskegon, MI 49440; 9 vessels on the Great Lakes; Pres. JOHN H. BULTEMA, Jr.

Madison Coal and Supply Co: Port Amherst, Charleston, WV 25306; tel. (304) 925-1171; river and canal transportation; Pres. CHARLES T. JONES.

Merchants Grain and Transporting: 60 East 42nd St, New York, NY 10165; tel. (212) 697-5751; manages towboats and freight barges; Chair. HUGH LEVY.

Midland Enterprises Inc: 580 Walnut St, Cincinnati, OH 45202; tel. (513) 721-4000; river and intercoastal transportation, towing and tugboat service and marine cargo handling; Pres. J. D. GEARY.

Norfolk Baltimore Carolina Line: 937 East Water St, Norfolk, VA 23510; tel. (804) 622-3613; river and canal transportation; Chair. JAMES P. McALLISTER, III.

Patton–Tully Transportation Co: 1242 North Second St, Memphis, TN 38101; tel. (901) 525-3159; river construction and transportation, towing service; Pres. BART C. TULLY, Jr.

Pickands Mather & Co (Interlake Steamship Co): 1100 Superior Ave, NE, Cleveland, OH 44114; freight services on the Great Lakes; 9 vessels; Vice-Pres. DAVID A. GROH.

Puget Sound Freight Lines Inc: 3720 Airport Way South, Seattle, WA 98124; tel. (206) 623-1600; marine transportation, cargo handling and storage; Chair. HOWARD E. LOVEJOY.

Rio Marine Inc: 2102 Broadway, Houston, TX 77012; tel. (713) 649-3232; barge carrier, towing and tugboat service; Pres. RONALD C. DANSBY.

Schno Barge Lines Inc: 12680 Olive Blvd, St Louis, MO 63141; tel. (314) 434-1540; inland water transportation and marine cargo handling; Pres. and CEO FRED S. SHERMAN.

Southern Towing Co Inc: Highway 84 West, Caruthersville, MO 63830; tel. (314) 333-1833; barge transportation; Chair. BAXTER SOUTHERN.

Trinity Industries Leasing Co: Stemmons Freeway, Dallas, TX 75207; tel. (214) 631-4420; freight and cargo transportation, arrangement and transportation on rivers and canals; Pres. and CEO W. RAY WALLACE.

United States Steel Great Lakes Fleet, Inc: 400 Missabe Bldg, Duluth, MN 55802; 31 vessels; Pres. W. B. BUHRMANN.

Walker Towing Corpn: 4540 Clarks River Dr., Paducah, KY 42001; tel. (502) 898-7392; marine towing and transportation; Pres. JOSEPH E. WALKER.

Warrior and Gulf Navigation Co: Viaduct Rd, Chickasaw, AL 36611; tel. (205) 452-6000; river and canal transportation; Pres. N. J. BARCHIE, Jr.

Willis C. G. Inc: 705 Mantua Ave, Paulsboro, NJ 08066; tel. (609) 423-4500; inland waterways transportation and marine cargo handling; Chair. CHAUNCEY G. WILLIS, Jr.

ASSOCIATIONS

American Waterways Operators: 1600 Wilson Blvd, Suite 1000, Arlington, VA 22209; tel. (703) 841-9300; f. 1944; 263 mems; Pres. JOSEPH A. FARRELL, III.

American Waterways Shipyard Conference: 1600 Wilson Blvd, Suite 1000, Arlington, VA 22209; tel. (703) 841-9300; f. 1976; 45 mems; Man. MARCIA Y. KINTER.

Committee for Private Offshore Rescue and Towing: 655 15th St, NW, Suite 310, Washington, DC 20005; tel. (202) 639-4462; f.

1987; trade association for the towing and salvage industry; 90 mems; Exec. Dir JEFFREY C. SMITH.

Estuarine Research Federation: POB 30, Chauvin, LA 70344; tel. (504) 851-2800; f. 1969; promotes research in estuarine and coastal waters; 2,000 mems; Pres. Dr DONALD F. BOESCH.

Inland River Ports and Terminals: 204 East High St, Jefferson City, MO 65101-3207; tel. (314) 634-2028; f. 1974; 150 mems; Exec. Sec. DARLA DAVIDSON.

Lake Carriers' Association: 915 Rockefeller Bldg, Cleveland, OH 44113-1306; tel. (216) 621-1107; f. 1892; 14 mems; Pres. GEORGE J. RYAN.

National Association of Dredging Contractors: 1625 Eye St, NW, Suite 321, Washington, DC 20006; tel. (202) 223-4820; f. 1935; 23 mems; Rep. WORTH HAGER.

National Waterways Conference: 1130 17th St, NW, Suite 200, Washington, DC 20036; tel. (202) 296-4415; fax (202) 835-3861; f. 1960; 500 mems; Press. HARRY N. COOK.

Water Transport Association: c/o Ohio River Co, POB 1460, Cincinnati, OH 45201; tel. (513) 543-7375; f. 1962; bargelines and steamship companies serving on inland waterways; 28 mems; Chair. WILLIAM P. MARELLI.

OCEAN SHIPPING

Statistics

(Source: Transportation Systems Center, US Department of Transportation.)

Sea-going Merchant Vessels

	1985	1986	1987
Number of vessels			
Combination passengers/cargo	37	36	23
Freighters	417	411	406
Bulk carriers	25	26	26
Tankers	258	247	254
Total	737	720	709
Displacement ('000 gross tons)			
Combination passengers/cargo	300	289	181
Freighters	7,353	7,446	7,417
Bulk carriers	1,152	1,270	1,270
Tankers	15,535	15,452	16,877
Total	24,339	24,457	25,745

Vessels Entered and Cleared in Foreign Trade in all Ports

	1985	1986	1987
Entered			
Number	55,531	56,849	59,563
Displacement ('000 net tons)	451,784	488,606	518,000
Cleared			
Number	53,095	55,710	58,307
Displacement ('000 net tons)	461,199	491,453	521,000

Directory

REGULATORY BODIES

Federal Maritime Commission: 1100 L St, NW, Washington, DC 20573; tel. (202) 523-5707; telex 204796; fax (202) 523-3782; f. 1961 to regulate the waterborne foreign and domestic offshore commerce of the USA; comprises 5 mems; Chair. JAMES J. CAREY (acting).

Maritime Administration: US Dept of Transportation, Nasif Bldg, 400 Seventh St, SW, Washington, DC 20590; tel. (202) 366-5807; concerned with promoting the US Merchant Marine; also administers subsidy programme to ship operators; Admin. JOHN GAUGHAN.

PRINCIPAL PORTS

The two largest ports in the USA in terms of traffic handled are New York, handling 157.8m. short tons in 1986, and New Orleans, Louisiana (149.1m. short tons); many other large ports serve each coast, 26 of them handling between 13m. and 100m. tons of traffic annually. The deepening of channels and locks on the St Lawrence–Great Lakes Waterway, allowing the passage of large ocean-going vessels, has increased the importance of the Great Lakes ports, of which the largest, Duluth-Superior, handled over 29.2m. short tons in 1986.

PRINCIPAL COMPANIES

Alcoa Steamship Co, Inc: 1501 Alcoa Bldg, Pittsburgh, PA 15219; tel. (412) 553-2544; telex 232777; fax (412) 553-2624; bulk services world-wide; Pres. R. E. GROSSHEIM.

American President Lines Ltd: 1800 Harrison St, Oakland, CA 94612; f. 1929; serves east and west coasts of North America, Mexico, Caribbean Basin, Middle East and Far East; 23 vessels; Pres. T. J. RHEIN.

Amoco Shipping Co/Coastwise Trading Co, Inc: 200 East Randolph Drive, Chicago, IL 60601; Maritime Transportation Dept; Pres. E. J. ROLAND.

Barber Steamship Lines, Inc: 17 Battery Pl., New York, NY 10004; f. 1883; services to the Mediterranean, Middle East, Far East, western Africa, the Caribbean and South America; Chair. E. J. BARBER; Pres. R. H. POUCH.

Chevron Shipping Co: 555 Market St, San Francisco, CA 94105; tel. (415) 894-7700; telex 470074; world-wide tanker sevices; 44 tankers; Pres. D. C. WOOLCOTT.

Coscol Marine Corpn: 9 Greenway Plaza, Houston, TX 77046; 3 tankers; COO DONALD CAMPBELL.

Crowley Maritime Corpn: 101 California St, San Francisco, CA 94111-5875; tel. (415) 546-2500; telex 340578; f. 1895; 413 vessels; Chair. T. B. CROWLEY.

Delta Steamship Lines Inc (Delta Line): One World Trade Center, Suite 3647, New York, NY 10048; 24 vessels; Sr Vice-Pres. and Gen. Man. RICHARD F. ANDINO.

Energy Transportation Corpn: 1185 Ave of the Americas, New York, NY 10036; tel. (212) 642-9800; telex 427864; 10 vessels.

Exxon Shipping Co: POB 1512, Houston, TX 77251-1512; telex 762149; 17 tankers; Pres. F. J. IAROSSI.

Falcon Carriers, Inc: 277 Park Ave, New York, NY 10017.

Farrell Lines Inc: 1 Whitehall St, New York, NY 10004; f. 1926; regular mail and freight services from US Atlantic to western Africa and the Mediterranean; Chair. and CEO GEORGE F. LOWMAN; Pres. RICHARD V. PARKS.

Gulf Oil Products Co, Marine Dept: POB 4431, Houston, TX 77210; 18 vessels, 2 heavy lift; Vice-Pres. P. E. LUITWIELER.

Hudson Waterways Corpn: 1 Chase Manhattan Plaza, New York, NY 10005; tramp services; Pres. JOHN CORCACAS; Vice-Pres. (Engineering) CHARLES NEALIS.

Keystone Shipping Co: 313 Chestnut St, Philadelphia, PA 19106; 21 vessels; Pres. A. B. KURZ.

Lykes Bros Steamship Co Inc: Lykes Center, 300 Poydras St, New Orleans, LA 70130; f. 1900; routes from US Gulf ports to United Kingdom and northern Europe, Mediterranean, west coast of South America, Africa and the Far East; also US east coast and Great Lakes to Mediterranean; 29 vessels; Chair. W. J. AMOSS; Pres. E. F. McCORMICK.

Matson Navigation Co: 100 Mission St, San Francisco, CA 94105; f. 1901; container and other freight services between US west coast, Hawaii and Guam; Pres. M. H. BLAISDELL.

Moore McCormack Lines Inc: 2 Broadway, New York, NY 10004; services to North and South America, southern and eastern Africa; 10 vessels; Pres. ROBERT E. O'BRIEN.

OSG Bulk Ships: 1114 Ave of the Americas, New York, NY 10036; 17 tankers.

Prudential Lines Inc: One World Trade Center, New York, NY 10048; tel. (212) 775-0550; telex 421064; 4 vessels; Pres. S. S. SKOURAS.

Sea-Land Service, Inc: POB 800, Iselin, NJ 08830; largest US-flag container shipping co; 60 vessels providing containerized services to 78 ports in 64 countries; Pres. J. A. BAKER.

Shell Oil Co: POB 2099, Houston, TX 77001; 8 vessels; Man. Marine Dept (vacant).

Sun Refining and Marketing Co, Marine Operations: POB 2224, Aston, PA 19014; tel. (215) 447-3400; telex 6693769; 10 vessels, 14 tug-barge units; Pres. and Gen. Man. JAMES R. NOLAN; Man. Fleet Operations Capt. J. H. BATES.

United Brands Co: Banana and Meat Co, 1271 Ave of the Americas, New York, NY 10020; tel. (212) 307-2000; telex 177669; f. 1899; New York to Latin America and Europe; 30 vessels; Chair., Pres. and CEO K. LINDER.

United States Lines, Inc (Del): 27 Commerce Drive, Cranford, NJ 07016; containerized freight services to Europe, North and South America, Panama, Hawaii, Guam, Far East, southern and eastern Africa; 12 container vessels; Chair. MALCOM McLEAN; Pres. CHARLES HILTZHEIMER.

Victory Carriers: 645 Fifth Ave, New York, NY 10022; tel. (212) 371-8100; telex 666533; 3 vessels.

Waterman Steamship Co: 120 Wall St, New York, NY 10005; tel. (212) 747-8550; telex 235949; f. 1919; services to the Middle East and South-East Asia; Pres. E. P. WALSH.

ASSOCIATIONS

American Association of Port Authorities: 1010 Duke St, Alexandria, VA 22314; tel. (703) 684-5700; f. 1912; 423 mems; Pres. ERIK STROMBERG.

American Bureau of Shipping: 45 Eisenhower Dr., POB 910, Paramus, NJ 07653; tel. (201) 368-9100; f. 1862; 565 mems; Chair. and Pres. RICHARD T. SOPER.

American Institute for Shippers' Associations: POB 33457, Washington, DC 20036; tel. (202) 628-0933; f. 1961; 143 mems; Exec. Asst CAROL LIPSITZ.

American Institute of Merchant Shipping: 1000 16th St, NW, Suite 511, Washington, DC 20036; tel. (202) 775-4399; telex 89424; fax (202) 659-3795; f. 1969; 21 mems; represents owners and operators of US-flag tankers, bulk carriers and container vessels; Pres. ERNEST J. CORRADO.

American Maritime Association: 485 Madison Ave, New York, NY 10022; tel. (212) 319-9217; f. 1961; employers' asscn which contracts negotiations with the maritime unions; 30 mem. cos; Admin. Asst MARLENA SCHROEDER.

American West African Freight Conference: 50 Broadway, Suite 2100, New York, NY 10004; tel. (212) 269-7430; f. 1945; steamship cos serving US, Canadian and West African ports; 7 mems; Chair. DOMINICK J. MANFREDI.

Boston Shipping Association: 223 Lewis Wharf, Boston, MA 02110; tel. (617) 523-3762; f. 1946; 25 mems; Exec. Dir ROBERT M. CALDER.

Cruise Lines International Association: 17 Battery Pl., New York, NY 10004; tel. (212) 425-7400; f. 1975; passenger cruise lines representing 17,000 travel agents; 33 mems; Pres. JAMES G. GODSMAN.

Federation of American Controlled Shipping: 50 Broadway, New York, NY 10004; tel. (212) 344-1483; telex 701979; f. 1958; 20 mems; Chair. PHILIP J. LOREE; Exec. Sec.-Treas. EUGENE A. YOURCH.

Gulf–European Freight Association: Whitney Bldg, Suite 533, New Orleans, LA 70130; tel. (504) 581-5312; f. 1965; shipping lines providing service from ports on the Gulf of Mexico to northern Europe; 7 mems; Chair C. J. SMITH.

International Marine Transit Association: 34 Otis Hill Rd, Hingham, MA 02043; tel. (617) 749-0078; f. 1977; 350 mems; Sec.-Treas. MARTHA A. REARDON.

Joint Maritime Congress: 444 North Capitol St, NW, Suite 801, Washington, DC 20001; tel. (202) 638-2405; f. 1977; major US-flag ship operating companies; Exec. Dir BRUCE J. CARLTON.

Liberian Shipowners' Council: 420 Lexington Ave, Rm 2656, New York, NY 10170; tel. (212) 867-8145; f. 1974; represents owners and operators of Liberian-flag ships; 82 mems; Exec. Sec. JEREMY M. S. SMITH.

Marine Towing and Transportation Employers' Association: 17 Battery Pl., New York, NY 10004; tel. (212) 344-9097; f. 1948; represents owners and operators of tugs, oil barges and tankers; 9 mems; Sec. VIRGINIA M. THOMAS.

Maritime Association of the Port of New York/New Jersey: 17 Battery Pl., Suite 1006, New York, NY 10004; tel. (212) 425-5704; f. 1873; 12,000 mems; Exec. Dir N. NICK CRETAN.

Maritime Institute for Research and Industrial Development: 1133 15th St, NW, Suite 600, Washington, DC 20005; tel. (202) 463-6505; f. 1980; maritime transportation companies and labour unions; 100 mems; Pres. C. JAMES PATTI.

National Association of Passenger Vessel Owners: 1511 K St, NW, Suite 715, Washington, DC 20005; tel. (202) 638-5310; f. 1971; 400 mems; Exec. Dir ERIC G. SCHARF.

National Maritime Council: 1748 North St, NW, Washington, DC 20036; tel. (202) 785-3754; f. 1971; 10 mems; Pres. WILLIAM B. KELLY.

National Party Boat Owners' Alliance: 181 Thames St, Groton, CT 06340; tel. (203) 535-2066; f. 1952; owners and operators of passenger-carrying vessels; 500 mems; Exec. Dir GEORGE F. GLAS.

New Orleans Steamship Association: 219 Carondelet St, Suite 300, New Orleans, LA 70130; tel. (504) 522-9392; f. 1912; steamship agents, owners and operators; 59 mems; Pres. C. DAVID BURNS.

New York Shipping Industry: Two World Trade Center, 20th Floor, New York, NY 10048; tel. (212) 323-6600; f. 1932; 100 mems; Pres. ANTHONY TOZZOLI.

North Atlantic Ports Association: 36 Evergreen Rd, Reading, MA 01867; tel. (617) 944-1277; f. 1949; cos with an interest in marine terminal facilities in the North Atlantic Range; Exec. Dir CHESTER H. GOURLEY.

Offshore Marine Service Association: 1440 Canal St, Suite 1709, New Orleans, LA 70112; tel. (504) 566-4577; f. 1957; represents owners and operators of vessels serving offshore installations; 140 mems; Vice-Pres. CHARLES HANNEN.

Pacific Maritime Association: 635 Sacramento St, POB 7861, San Francisco, CA 94120; tel. (415) 576-3200; provides industrial relations services for the shipping industry; Pres. WILLIAM E. CODAY.

Professional Mariners Alliance: 55 John St, New York, NY 10038; tel. (212) 608-3081; f. 1983; 5,000 mems; Exec. Dir RANDY O'NEILL.

Propellor Club of the US: 1030 15th St, NW, Suite 430, Washington, DC 20005; tel. (202) 898-0680; f. 1927; promotes the American Merchant Marine, and the development of Great Lakes, waterways and harbours; 17,000 mems; Exec. Vice-Pres. J. DANIEL SMITH.

Seafarers International Union of North America: 5201 Auth Way, Camp Springs, MD 20746-4275; tel. (301) 899-0675; f. 1938; 27 affiliated unions of seamen, fishermen, inland boatmen and associated workers; 90,000 mems; Pres. FRANK DROZAK.

Shippers National Freight Claim Council: POB Z, Huntington, NY 11743; tel. (516) 549-8984; f. 1974; represents claimants' interests in cases of loss, damage and overcharging; 950 mems; Exec. Dir WILLIAM J. AUGELLO.

Society of Marine Port Engineers: 21 West St, Rm 3102, New York, NY 10006; tel. (212) 269-4840; f. 1946; 500 mems; Sec.-Treas. JAMES H. DICKEY.

Southern Transportation League: 3426 North Washington Blvd, Arlington, VA 22201; tel. (703) 525-4050; f. 1918; shippers and shipper organizations, port authorities; 100 mems; Exec. Dir WIL-LIAM P. JACKSON, Jr.

Towboat and Harbor Carriers' Association of New York and New Jersey: 17 Battery Pl., New York, NY 10004; tel. (212) 943-8480; f. 1917; 25 mems; Pres. LINDA O'LEARY.

Transportation Institute: 5201 Auth Way, Camp Springs, MD 20746; tel. (301) 423-3335; f. 1968; US-flag shipping, towing and dredging companies concerned with research and education on transportation problems, particularly waterborne commerce; 140 mems; Pres. JAMES L. HENRY.

United Shipowners of America: 1627 K St, NW, Suite 1200, Washington, DC 20006; tel. (202) 466-5388; f. 1977; concerned with the promotion of the citizen-manned US merchant marine; 8 mem. cos; Pres. WILLIAM P. VERDON.

CIVIL AVIATION

Certificated Route Air Carriers: Summary

	1982	1983	1984	1985	1986
Domestic and international operators[1]	98	96	95	106	98
Fixed-wing aircraft in operation[2]	2,468	2,618	2,692	2,860	3,799
Revenue-miles flown (million)[3]	2,699	2,809	3,133	3,320	3,719
Revenue passengers enplaned (million)[3]	294	319	345	382	418
Revenue passenger-miles flown ('000 million):[3]					
Domestic	210.1	226.9	243.7	270.6	301.8
International	49.5	54.9	61.4	65.8	64.4
Express and freight revenue, ton-miles flown (million)[3]	5,482	6,092	6,566	6,020	7,336
Mail, ton-miles flown (million):[3]					
Domestic	1,004	1,065	1,161	1,214	1,247
International	400	415	457	445	434

[1] Includes all cargo.
[2] Excludes aircraft used for crew training and general utility purposes, or held for disposal; includes aircraft operated by the scheduled all-cargo certificated route air carriers. 1986 figure also includes large aircraft operated by commuters and air taxis.
[3] Scheduled services of all certificated route air carriers; includes all cargo.

Source: US Dept of Transportation, Federal Aviation Administration and Research and Special Programs Administration, *Air Carrier Traffic Statistics*, monthly, and *Air Carrier Financial Statistics*, quarterly.

Airports and Air Carriers by State, 1986

	Airport facilities (civil and joint-use)		Air carriers, all services	
	Total	Private	Passengers ('000)	Freight and mail ('000 tons)
Alabama	169	59	1,353	6.0
Alaska	615	169	2,023	315.9
Arizona	240	159	5,822	25.5
Arkansas	160	60	489	2.8
California	862	575	37,303	608.0
Colorado	321	227	11,811	103.0
Connecticut	105	77	1,421	14.3
Delaware	37	25	n.a.	1.4
District of Columbia	16	14	7,886	66.5
Florida	541	404	22,896	169.3
Georgia	302	181	19,329	245.6
Hawaii	51	37	8,291	111.8
Idaho	196	72	501	3.4
Illinois	909	787	19,344	426.5
Indiana	498	367	1,795	19.3
Iowa	280	123	737	6.3
Kansas	380	219	633	3.7
Kentucky	127	54	1,157	16.2
Louisiana	311	215	3,678	15.6
Maine	146	65	448	6.2
Maryland	147	99	2,297	28.9
Massachusetts	130	76	8,045	135.3
Michigan	422	191	5,996	75.4
Minnesota	492	329	6,062	75.4
Mississippi	181	81	531	2.9
Missouri	419	261	10,462	96.7
Montana	197	70	823	4.4
Nebraska	346	234	1,159	9.9
Nevada	126	55	5,862	11.8
New Hampshire	54	25	n.a.	n.a.
New Jersey	291	227	8,634	69.5
New Mexico	160	81	1,550	6.7
New York	476	282	23,150	407.5
North Carolina	284	156	6,170	44.7
North Dakota	451	344	403	2.0

(continued)

AIRPORTS AND AIR CARRIERS BY STATE, 1986—*continued*

	Airport facilities (civil and joint-use)		Air carriers, all services	
	Total	Private	Passengers ('000)	Freight and mail ('000 tons)
Ohio	678	455	7,395	55.1
Oklahoma	332	156	2,513	13.8
Oregon	341	230	2,365	25.7
Pennsylvania	720	542	10,045	91.1
Rhode Island	18	10	315	1.6
South Carolina	137	65	1,196	4.7
South Dakota	165	86	395	2.7
Tennessee	169	75	4,233	40.9
Texas	1,543	1,121	30,853	214.0
Utah	95	44	3,259	44.7
Vermont	60	40	310	0.3
Virginia	270	185	2,159	6.5
Washington	382	240	5,621	130.8
West Virginia	94	51	279	0.7
Wisconsin	416	260	2,155	13.6
Wyoming	104	56	196	0.9
Total	15,966	10,016	301,348	3,785.7

Source: Bureau of the Census, US Department of Commerce, *State and Metropolitan Area Data Book: 1986.*

Directory

REGULATORY BODY

Federal Aviation Administration: US Dept of Transportation, 800 Independence Ave, SW, Washington, DC 20591; tel. (202) 426-8058; f. 1958; promotes safety in the air, regulates air commerce and assists in development of an effective national airport system; Administrator JAMES B. BUSEY.

PRINCIPAL SCHEDULED COMPANIES

Air Wisconsin, Inc: Outagamie Airport, Appleton, WI 54915; tel. (414) 739-5123; fax (414) 739-5123; fleet of 10 BAE 146-200, 12 Fokker F27, 6 Shorts 3-60; Chair. and CEO F. JOHN BARLOW.

Alaska Airlines, Inc: POB 68900, Seattle, WA 98168; tel. (206) 433-3200; telex 328723; fleet of 1 Boeing 727-100, 19 Boeing 727-200, 6 Boeing 737-200C, 8 MD-82, 9 MD-83; Chair., Pres. and CEO BRUCE R. KENNEDY.

Aloha Airlines, Inc: POB 30028, Honolulu, HI 96816; tel. (808) 836-4101; telex 7430125; fax (808) 836-4210; fleet of 10 Boeing 737-200; Chair. SHERIDAN C. F. ING.

American Airlines Inc: POB 619616, Dallas/Fort Worth Airport, TX 75261-9616; telex 791651; f. 1934; domestic flights, services to Hawaii, Canada, Mexico, Caribbean, South America, Japan, Europe; fleet of 2 Boeing 747-SP, 2 Boeing 737-100, 2 Boeing 737-200C, 6 BAE 146-200, 9 Boeing 737-300, 10 MD-83, 11 DC-10-30, 13 Boeing 767-200, 17 Boeing 767-200ER, 19 Boeing 737-200, 39 Boeing 727-100, 50 DC-10-10, 108 MD-82, 120 Boeing 727-200; Chair., CEO and Pres. ROBERT L. CRANDALL.

Braniff Inc: Dallas, TX 75209; telex 73376; f. 1928, reorganized 1983; services to 18 points in USA and Mexico; fleet of 25 Boeing 727-200; Chair. and CEO J. PATRICK FOLEY; Pres. (vacant).

Continental Airlines Inc: 2929 Allen Parkway, POB 4607, Houston, TX 77210-4607; telex 790275; f. 1934; division of Texas Air Corpn; reorg. 1987; serves 103 US destinations and operates services to 34 points in Europe, Japan, the South Pacific, Mexico and Canada; fleet of 2 Boeing 747-100, 6 Boeing 747-200, 7 DC-10-10, 8 DC-10-30, 12 Airbus A-300-B4, 13 DC-9-10, 13 Boeing 727-100, 33 DC-9-30, 62 MD-80, 92 Boeing 727-200, 97 Boeing 737; Chair. and CEO D. JOSEPH CORR; Pres. (vacant).

Delta Air Lines Inc: Hartsfield Atlanta International Airport, Atlanta, GA 30320-6001; telex 542316; f. 1929; domestic services include 132 cities; international services to 22 destinations in 10 countries including Canada, Bermuda, the Bahamas, the United Kingdom, France and the Federal Republic of Germany; fleet of 1 L-1011-200, 2 L-1011-250, 6 DC-10-10, 6 L-1011-500, 9 Boeing 767-332, 13 DC-8-71, 13 Boeing 737-300, 15 Boeing 767-232, 26 L-1011-1, 34 Boeing 757-232, 36 DC-9-32, 75 Boeing 737-202, 139 Boeing 727-232; Chair. and CEO RON W. ALLEN.

Eastern Air Lines Inc: Miami International Airport, Miami, FL 33148; telex 519242; f. 1926; division of Texas Air Corpn; undergoing reorg. in 1989; serves entire eastern half of US and most of western half, US Virgin Islands and Puerto Rico; international services to Canada, Central and South America; fleet of 2 A300-B2, 20 Boeing 727-100, 22 DC-9-50, 23 Tristar 1, 27 Boeing 757-200, 32 Airbus A-300-B4, 58 DC-9-30, 95 Boeing 727-200; Pres. and CEO PHILIP J. BAKES.

Flying Tiger Line: 7401 World Way West, Los Angeles, CA 90009; telex 674496; f. 1945; world's largest air-cargo carrier; scheduled services and charters serving North America, Asia, Australia, the Middle East and Europe; fleet of 2 Boeing 747-200, 6 DC-8-73F, 8 Boeing 747-100F, 10 Boeing 747-200F, 14 Boeing 727-100C; Chair. and CEO (vacant); Pres. and COO JAMES A. CRONIN.

Hawaiian Airlines Inc: POB 30008, Honolulu International Airport, Honolulu, HI 96820; telex 70483707; f. 1929; fleet of 12 DC-9, 6 DC-8, 8 DH-7, 5 L-1011; Chair. JOHN H. MAGOON, Jr.

Midway Airlines, Inc: Midway Airport, Chicago, IL 60638; tel. (312) 838-0001; telex 270106; fleet of 5 Boeing 737-2L9, 2 Boeing 737-2K9, 1 Boeing 737-2H4, 1 DC-9-14, 8 DC-9-15, 9 DC-9-31, 7 DC-9-32; Chair. and CEO DAVID R. HINSON.

Northwest Airlines, Inc: Minneapolis-St Paul International Airport, St Paul, MN 55111; tel. (612) 726-2111; telex 297024; f. 1926; reorg. 1986; coast-to-coast domestic routes and services to Alaska, Hawaii, Canada, Japan, Hong Kong, the Philippines, China (Taiwan), and Europe; fleet of 5 DC-9-15F, 8 Boeing 747-200F, 8 MD-82, 9 Boeing 727-100, 12 Boeing 747-100, 14 Convair 580, 20 DC-10-40, 20 Boeing 747-200, 28 Boeing 757-200, 28 DC-9-50, 29 DC-9-10, 63 DC-9-30, 71 Boeing 727-200; Pres. and CEO STEVEN G. ROTHMEIER.

Pacific Southwest Airlines: 3225 North Harbour Dr., San Diego, CA 92101; tel. (619) 574-2100; telex 695404; fax (619) 574-4958; division of USAir, Inc; fleet of 31 MD-80, 4 DC-9-30, 24 BAE 146-200.

Pan American World Airways: Pan Am Bldg, 200 Park Ave, New York, NY 10166; tel. (212) 880-1234; telex 126437; f. 1927; coast-to-coast domestic flights; international services (excluding Africa, Australia and the Pacific); fleet of 1 Boeing 737-200C, 6 A-310-300, 7 Boeing 747-200B, 7 A-310-200, 7 Boeing 737-200, 12 Airbus A-300-B4, 51 Boeing 727-200; Chair., Pres. and CEO THOMAS G. PLASKETT.

Piedmont Airlines: One Piedmont Plaza, Winston-Salem, NC 27156-1000; telex 806474; f. 1948; division of USAir, Inc; domestic and international services connecting 124 US cities and 4 points in Canada, the UK and the Bahamas; fleet of 6 Boeing 767-200, 9 Boeing 737-400, 20 F-28-1000, 25 F-28-4000, 34 Boeing 727-200, 42 Boeing 737-300, 62 Boeing 737-200; Pres. THOMAS E. SCHICK.

Texas Air Corporation: 333 Clay St, Suite 4040, Houston, TX 77002; tel. (713) 658-9588; fax (713) 658-8337; Chair. and Pres. FRANK LORENZO.

Trans World Airlines Inc (TWA): 605 Third Ave, New York, NY 10158; tel. (212) 692-3000; telex 960124; f. 1925; domestic and international services connecting 64 US cities and 22 points in Europe, the Middle East, the Bahamas and the Caribbean; fleet of 1 DC-9-30F, 3 DC-9-40, 5 Boeing 747-200B, 7 DC-9-10, 8 Tri-Star 50, 10 Boeing 767-200ER, 11 Tri-Star 100, 12 Boeing 747-100,

14 Tri-Star 1, 22 Boeing 727-100, 23 MD-82, 34 DC-9-30, 56 Boeing 727-200; Chair. CARL C. ICAHN; Pres. RICHARD D. PEARSON.

United Airlines Inc (UAL): POB 66100, Chicago, IL 60666; telex 287419; f. 1931; domestic services from coast to coast, services to Hawaii, Canada, Japan and Australia; fleet of 2 Boeing 747-200, 4 DC-10-30, 4 DC-10-30CF, 6 Tri-Star 500, 11 Boeing 747SP, 13 Boeing 747-100, 19 Boeing 767-200, 21 Boeing 737-300, 29 DC-8-71, 46 DC-10-10, 50 Boeing 727-100, 74 Boeing 737-200, 104 Boeing 727-200; Pres. and CEO STEPHEN M. WOLF.

USAir, Inc: Washington National Airport, Washington, DC 20001; telex 892645; f. 1937; scheduled passenger services to 106 cities in the USA, 3 in Canada; fleet of 10 Boeing 727-200, 11 BAC-111-200, 21 BAE-146, 23 Boeing 737-200, 31 MD-80, 55 Boeing 737-300, 74 DC-9; Chair. and CEO EDWIN I. COLODNY.

ASSOCIATIONS

Aerospace Industries Association of America: 1250 I St, NW, Washington, DC 20005; tel. (202) 371-8400; f. 1919; 48 mems; Pres. DON FUQUA.

Air Courier Conference of America: POB 3583, Reston, VA 22090; tel. (703) 391-0303; f. 1976; 210 mems; Exec. Dir LAWRENCE E. BURTCHAELL.

Air Freight Association of America: 1710 Rhode Island Ave, Second Floor, Washington, DC 20036; tel. (202) 293-1030; f. 1948; 27 mems; Exec. Vice-Pres. STEPHEN A. ALTERMAN.

Air Taxi and Commercial Pilots' Association: 7940-2 Airpark Dr., Gaithersburg, MD 20879; tel. (301) 330-6750; f. 1974; Pres. RICHARD C. BARTELL.

Air Traffic Conference of America: 1709 New York Ave, NW, Washington, DC 20006; tel. (202) 626-4218; f. 1938; US-flag scheduled air carriers with the aim of improving service to the air traveller; 34 mems; Exec. Sec. NESTOR N. PYLYPEC.

Air Traffic Control Association: 21020 North 14th St, Suite 410, Arlington, VA 22201; tel. (703) 522-5717; f. 1956; 2,000 mems; Pres. GABRIEL A. HARTL.

Air Transport Association of America: 1709 New York Ave, NW, Washington, DC 20006-5206; tel. (202) 626-4000; f. 1936; mems: 27 airlines representing more than 98% of US scheduled airline passenger traffic; Pres. WILLIAM F. BOLGER.

Aircraft Owners' and Pilots' Association: 421 Aviation Way, Frederick, MD 21701; tel. (301) 695-2000; f. 1939; 260,000 mems; Pres. JOHN L. BAKER.

Airline Industrial Relations Conference: 1920 North St, NW, Suite 250, Washington, DC 20036; tel. (202) 861-7550; f. 1971; 26 mems.

Airline Operational Control Society: 809 Pinecrest Dr., Miami Springs, FL 33166; tel. (305) 888-1009; f. 1973; 200 mems; Sec.-Treas. STEVE MINOCK.

Airport Ground Transportation Association: 901 Scenic Dr., Knoxville, TN 37919; tel. (615) 525-1108; f. 1945; Exec. Dir RAY A. MUNDY.

Airport Operators' Council International: 1220 19th St, NW, Suite 800, Washington, DC 20036; tel. (202) 293-8500; f. 1948; 235 mems; Exec. Dir J. DONALD REILLY.

Airport Security Council: 570 Elmont Rd, Elmont, NY 11003; tel. (516) 328-2990; f. 1968; air carriers and other groups with an interest in developing security systems; 37 mems; Exec. Dir EDWARD J. McGOWAN.

American Association of Airport Executives: 4224 King St, Alexandria, VA 22302; tel. (703) 824-0500; f. 1928; 2,600 mems; Exec. Vice-Pres. CHARLES M. BARCLAY.

Association of Local Transport Airlines: 1140 19th St, NW, Sixth Floor, Washington, DC 20036; tel. (202) 223-9100; f. 1957; 9 mems; Exec. Dir JOHN L. ZORACK.

Aviation Development Council: POB 699, La Guardia Airport, Flushing, NY 11371; tel. (718) 457-7890; f. 1963; scheduled air carriers with the aim of researching measures against the noise of aircraft; Dir JOHN J. SHELLY.

Aviation Facilities Energy Association: Atlanta Airlines Terminal Corpn, POB 45171, Atlanta, GA 30320; tel. (404) 530-2105; f. 1983; 116 mems; Sec. LINDA WOOD.

Aviation Maintenance Foundation, Inc: POB 2826, Redmond, WA 98073; tel. (206) 823-0633; f. 1972; 4,000 mems; Pres. RICHARD S. KOST, Sr.

Aviation/Space Writers Association: 17 South High St, Suite 1200, Columbus, OH 43215; tel. (614) 221-1900; f. 1938; 1,140 mems; Exec. Dir NIKKI HUGHES.

Council of Defense and Space Industry Associations: 1620 I St, NW, Suite 100, Washington, DC 20006; tel. (202) 659-5013; f. 1964; 8 mems; Exec. Sec. SHERIDAN BRINLEY.

Flight Freedoms Foundation: POB 16161, Portland, OR 97216; tel. (503) 252-9012; f. 1972; committed to educating the public about aviation and its benefits; Pres. R. L. MONTEE.

Flight Safety Foundation: 5510 Columbia Pike, Arlington, VA 22204; tel. (703) 820-2777; f. 1945; 465 mems; Pres. JOHN H. ENDERS.

Future Aviation Professionals of America: 4291 J Memorial Dr., Atlanta, GA 30032; tel. (404) 294-0226; f. 1975; 20,000 mems; Pres. WILLIAM LOUIS SMITH.

Helicopter Association International: 1619 Duke St, Alexandria, VA 22314; tel. (703) 683-4646; f. 1948; 1,047 mems; Pres. FRANK L. JENSEN, Jr.

Helicopter Safety Advisory Conference: POB 60220, Houston, TX 72205; tel. (713) 757-8107; f. 1979; 90 mems; Chair. LYNN CLOUGH.

Independent Federation of Flight Attendants: 630 Third Ave, Fifth Floor, New York, NY 10017; tel. (212) 818-1130; f. 1977; 9,300 mems; Pres. VICTORIA L. FRANKOVICH.

International Business Aviation Council: 1200 18th St, NW, Washington, DC 20036; tel. (202) 783-9005; f. 1981; 7 mems; Exec. Officer WILLIAM H. STINE, II.

International Co-ordinating Council of Aerospace Industries Associations: 1725 De Sales St, NW, Washington, DC 20036; tel. (202) 429-4667; f. 1972; 4 mems; Sec. JOHN P. REESE.

International Council of Aircraft Owner and Pilot Associations: 421 Aviation Way, Frederick, MD 21701; tel. (301) 695-2220; f. 1962; 28 mems; Sec.-Gen. VICTOR J. KAYNE.

International Flight Attendants' Association: 2314 Old New Windsor Pike, New Windsor, MO 21776; f. 1976; 40,000 mems; US Rep. P. R. MILLER.

International Society of Women Airline Pilots: POB 38644, Denver, CO 80238; f. 1978; 220 mems; Exec. Chair. DOROTHY VALLEE.

National Aeronautic Association of the USA: 1763 R St, NW, Washington, DC 20009; tel. (202) 265-8720; f. 1905; 160,000 mems; Exec. Vice-Pres. EVERETT W. LANGWORTHY.

National Air Carrier Association: 1730 M St, NW, Suite 710, Washington, DC 20036; tel. (202) 833-8200; f. 1962; 8 mems; Pres. and CEO EDWARD J. DRISCOLL.

National Air Transportation Association: 4226 King St, Alexandria, VA 22302; tel. (703) 845-9000; f. 1974; 1,200 mems; Pres. LAWRENCE BURIAN.

National Aviation Club: 1745 Jefferson Davis Highway, Suite 308, Arlington, VA 22202; tel. (703) 521-1991; f. 1942; 1,000 mems; Exec. Vice-Pres. G. MOORE LINDSAY.

National Business Aircraft Association: 1200 18th St, NW, 2nd Floor, Washington, DC 20036; tel. (202) 783-9000; f. 1947; 2,900 mems; Sec. DOROTHY W. CHEEK.

Ninety Nines, International Women Pilots: Will Rogers Airport, POB 59965, Oklahoma City, OK 73159; tel. (405) 685-7969; f. 1929; 6,500 mems; Exec. Dir LORETTA JEAN GRAGG.

Organization of Black Airline Pilots: POB 86, La Guardia Airport, New York, NY 11371; tel. (201) 568-8145; f. 1976; 450 mems; Gen. Man. EDDIE R. HADDEN.

Pilots International Association: POB 907, Minneapolis, MN 55440; tel. (612) 588-5175; f. 1965; 5,000 mems; Pres. RICHARD J. WILDBERGER.

Pilots' and Passengers' Association: 7310 Ritchie Highway, Suite 601, Glen Burnie, MD 21601; tel. (301) 787-1140; f. 1984; 1,000 mems; Dir CAROL W. TAYLOR.

Professional Aviation Maintenance Association: 500 Northwest Plaza, Suite 912, St Ann, MO 63074; tel. (314) 739-2580; f. 1972; 2,200 mems; Exec. Admin. PATTI J. CAMPBELL.

Regional Airline Association: 1101 Connecticut Ave, NW, Suite 700, Washington, DC 20036; tel. (202) 857-1170; f. 1975; 390 mems; Pres. DUANE H. EKEDAHL.

Seaplane Pilots' Association: 421 Aviation Way, Frederick, MD 21701; tel. (301) 695-2083; f. 1972; 4,100 mems; Exec. Dir GLENN H. RIZNER.

Society of Professional Pilots: POB 23053, Oklahoma City, OK 74834; tel. (405) 787-5300; f. 1986; 185 mems; Exec. Dir WILLIAM D. HERD.

United States Pilots' Association: 11 South Meramec Ave, Suite 810, St Louis, MO 63105; tel. (314) 862-5000; f. 1981; 6,000 mems; Exec. Dir ARNOLD W. ZIMMERMAN.

Wings Club: 52 Vanderbilt Ave, 18th Floor, New York, NY 10017; tel. (212) 867-1770; f. 1942; 1,505 mems; Man. MARGIE E. GEWIRTZ.

ENERGY

INTRODUCTION

The USA consumes more energy, in both absolute and per-head terms, than any other country in the world. In 1985 consumption amounted to 9,563 kg of coal-equivalent energy per head, compared to a world average of 1,888 kg. In terms of their shares of primary energy production, coal, natural gas and petroleum were virtually equal in 1986, at 30.3%, 29.0% and 28.6% respectively; the remaining 12.1% was accounted for by other sources, principally hydro, nuclear, geothermal and solar. In terms of its share of primary consumption, however, petroleum had a clear lead, at 43.1%, over coal and natural gas at 23.4% and 22.4% respectively. In 1986 the USA consumed 15% more energy than it produced. Of primary energy, the largest share, 36.3% in 1986, is used for electricity generation, 28.0% for transport, 22.6% for industrial and miscellaneous, and 13.1% for residential and commercial.

The electricity-supply and -generating industry is diverse in nature, with ownership divided between federal and state authorities, municipal systems, rural co-operatives and the private sector. There are, in total, over 3,200 electricity-supply concerns, of which about one-quarter own generating capacity, with the remainder being involved in distribution only. Over three-quarters of generating capacity is in privately-owned utility companies. National supply co-ordination is handled by nine regional reliability councils and the North American Electric Reliability Council.

Since 1960 alternative sources of electricity generation, particularly nuclear power and hydropower, have become increasingly important. However, the Three Mile Island (Pennsylvania) accident and escalating costs have delivered a serious set-back to nuclear power-plant expansion plans.

Natural gas accounted for only 16.5% of total energy consumption in 1986, including that used in electricity generation. However, about 60% of domestic heating systems are gas-fired (including 5% fuelled by bottled gas). Electricity and fuel oil supply about 19% and 15% of domestic heating systems respectively; coal and coke have virtually disappeared as domestic heating sources, while wood maintains a share of about 5% of households.

Domestic consumption and expenditure on energy varies considerably between regions of the USA. Average consumption per household in both the South and the West was 85m. British thermal units (Btu) in 1985, in the Northeast 125m. Btu and in the Midwest 129m. Btu. Average household expenditure on energy was by far the lowest in the West in the same year, at $852, while spending in the south, Midwest and Northeast was $1,055, $1,160 and $1,443 respectively. Comparative expenditure is only partially explained by the different levels of consumption: there is also variation in the price of household energy from region to region. The Midwest has the cheapest household energy, at $8.96 per million Btu in 1985, followed by the West, at $10.02. Prices were somewhat higher in the Northeast and South, at $11.52 and $12.39 per million Btu respectively.

The Federal Energy Regulatory Commission, part of the Department of Energy, controls the rates and charges current in many parts of the energy industry, including the transmission and sale of gas, and the transportation of oil. The Nuclear Regulatory Commission is independent of the Department of Energy, and licenses and regulates the nuclear-energy sector.

STATISTICS

Energy Production and Consumption, by Major Source

	1982	1983	1984	1985	1986
Total production (quad. Btu[1])	63.9	61.2	65.8	64.8	64.3
Percentage of total:					
Coal	29.2	28.2	30.0	30.0	30.3
Petroleum[2]	28.7	30.1	28.6	29.3	28.6
Natural gas[3]	32.0	30.6	30.7	29.6	29.0
Other[4]	10.2	11.2	10.7	11.3	12.1
Total consumption (quad. Btu[1])	70.8	70.5	74.1	74.0	73.9
Percentage of total:					
Coal	21.6	22.6	23.0	23.6	23.4
Petroleum[5]	42.7	42.6	41.9	41.8	43.1
Natural gas[6]	26.1	24.6	25.0	24.1	22.4
Other	9.6	10.2	10.0	10.4	11.1

[1] Quadrillion ('000,000,000 million) British thermal units.
[2] Includes crude oil and lease condensate.
[3] Includes natural-gas liquids.
[4] Comprised of hydropower, nuclear power, geothermal energy, and other.
[5] Includes domestically-produced crude oil, natural-gas liquids and lease condensate, plus imported crude oil and products.
[6] Excludes natural-gas liquids.

Source: US Energy Information Administration, *Annual Energy Review*, and unpublished data.

Net Generation of Electricity by Electric Utilities, by Energy Source

('000 million kilowatt-hours)

	1983	1984	1985	1986	1987[1]
Coal	1,259	1,342	1,402	1,386	1,464
Petroleum[2]	144	120	100	137	118
Natural gas	274	297	292	249	273
Nuclear power	294	328	384	414	455
Hydroelectric power	332	321	281	291	250
Total[3]	2,310	2,416	2,470	2,487	2,571

[1] Preliminary.
[2] Includes distillate fuel oil, residual fuel oil, jet fuel and petroleum coke.
[3] Includes geothermal sources, and wood, waste, wind, photovoltaic and solar thermal energy used for electricity distribution.
Source: US Energy Administration, *Annual Energy Review.*

Energy Consumption by End-Use Sector—States, 1985

('000,000 million British thermal units (Btu))

	Residential	Commercial	Industrial	Transportation	Total
Alabama	252	173	633	335	1,394
Alaska	43	51	200	154	448
Arizona	170	157	200	293	821
Arkansas	155	104	299	204	762
California	1,219	1,038	1,692	2,409	6,359
Colorado	219	215	174	276	884
Connecticut	199	160	136	196	691
Delaware	37	27	86	56	205
District of Columbia	35	70	30	30	165
Florida	647	533	425	949	2,553
Georgia	355	253	574	589	1,771
Hawaii	21	19	47	145	232
Idaho	80	70	118	80	347
Illinois	839	673	1,229	728	3,469
Indiana	412	243	1,116	518	2,289
Iowa	226	148	326	220	920
Kansas	181	153	405	269	1,007
Kentucky	254	170	448	321	1,192
Louisiana	289	250	2,051	596	3,185
Maine	73	41	96	94	304
Maryland	274	152	388	316	1,129
Massachusetts	362	274	221	383	1,240
Michigan	679	407	913	612	2,612
Minnesota	302	186	402	333	1,224
Mississippi	155	103	304	254	815
Missouri	399	259	390	430	1,477
Montana	64	55	145	82	347
Nebraska	125	105	127	141	497
Nevada	65	41	89	112	306
New Hampshire	61	28	49	63	200
New Jersey	464	379	501	790	2,134
New Mexico	67	70	159	162	458
New York	913	912	702	845	3,373
North Carolina	382	264	542	492	1,681
North Dakota	55	33	145	69	301
Ohio	789	521	1,524	755	3,588
Oklahoma	267	198	532	342	1,339
Oregon	197	142	220	246	804
Pennsylvania	791	462	1,257	761	3,271
Rhode Island	60	38	48	51	195
South Carolina	191	138	400	265	994
South Dakota	51	28	47	65	192
Tennessee	350	271	585	432	1,639
Texas	1,072	927	4,888	2,037	8,924
Utah	115	62	219	133	529
Vermont	36	18	24	37	115
Virginia	366	310	419	500	1,596
Washington	400	310	552	421	1,682
West Virginia	124	78	379	154	735
Wisconsin	344	226	411	311	1,292
Wyoming	40	36	206	70	351
Total	15,263	11,582	27,058*	20,123	74,023

* Includes −13,500,000m. Btu of net imports of coke not allocated by state.
Source: US Energy Administration, *State Energy Data Report, 1960–85.*

Energy Consumption by Selected Source—States, 1985

('000,000 million British thermal units (Btu))

	Petroleum	Natural gas (dry)	Coal	Hydropower	Nuclear power	Total[1]
Alabama	453	228	663	71	155	1,394
Alaska	221	215	5	8	—	448
Arizona	318	136	345	145	12	821
Arkansas	303	199	220	46	107	762
California	3,098	1,896	43	370	213	6,359
Colorado	333	223	300	24	—	884
Connecticut	437	81	21	3	138	691
Delaware	120	39	72	—	—	205
District of Columbia	40	29	4	—	—	165
Florida	1,298	303	467	3	254	2,553
Georgia	754	290	727	29	110	1,771
Hawaii	228	3	—	1	—	232
Idaho	106	41	9	113	—	347
Illinois	1,138	989	801	1	423	3,469
Indiana	748	436	1,192	4	—	2,289
Iowa	341	227	268	21	21	920
Kansas	396	355	260	0	42	1,007
Kentucky	465	183	713	30	—	1,192
Louisiana	1,352	1,446	159	—	27	3,185
Maine	193	3	2	35	58	304
Maryland	467	156	264	16	107	1,129
Massachusetts	762	224	111	47	66	1,240
Michigan	854	745	785	14	145	2,612
Minnesota	495	259	228	38	125	1,224
Mississippi	337	233	109	—	47	815
Missouri	579	259	521	31	87	1,477
Montana	160	47	99	106	—	347
Nebraska	195	125	115	15	45	497
Nevada	136	42	126	45	—	306
New Hampshire	123	11	39	21	—	200
New Jersey	1,215	392	102	-3[2]	192	2,134
New Mexico	217	159	268	1	—	458
New York	1,604	795	305	460	260	3,373
North Carolina	665	139	555	42	209	1,681
North Dakota	119	29	307	50	—	301
Ohio	1,130	764	1,394	2	21	3,588
Oklahoma	466	612	237	41	—	1,339
Oregon	316	86	10	474	75	804
Pennsylvania	1,197	658	1,364	10	284	3,271
Rhode Island	109	31	0	4	—	195
South Carolina	346	101	258	19	344	994
South Dakota	98	25	34	55	—	192
Tennessee	562	197	588	68	105	1,639
Texas	4,099	3,521	1,171	14	—	8,924
Utah	185	124	204	11	—	529
Vermont	64	5	2	13	32	115
Virginia	671	145	304	9	241	1,596
Washington	586	140	94	806	87	1,682
West Virginia	247	129	882	11	—	735
Wisconsin	455	311	365	26	119	1,292
Wyoming	128	87	408	11	—	351
Total	30,925	17,869	17,520	3,363	4,147	74,023

[1] Includes geothermal, wood and waste, and net interstate sales of electricity, including losses, not shown separately.
[2] Amount of energy expended for pump storage hydropower exceeds amount of energy consumed.
Source: US Energy Information Administration, *State Energy Data Report, 1960–85.*

Nuclear-Power Plants: Number of Units and Net Generation by State, 1986

	Number of units	Net generation (million kWh)	(continued)	Number of units	Net generation (million kWh)
Alabama	5	11,561	Mississippi	1	4,087
Arizona	2	9,976	Missouri	1	7,170
Arkansas	2	8,876	Nebraska	2	7,658
California	6	26,215	New Jersey	4	14,770
Colorado	1	52	New York	5	22,084
Connecticut	4	18,667	North Carolina	4	20,286
Florida	5	22,036	Ohio	2	24
Georgia	2	7,238	Oregon	1	7,081
Illinois	9	42,614	Pennsylvania	7	39,820
Iowa	1	2,993	South Carolina	7	35,625
Kansas	1	6,959	Tennessee	2	−10.5*
Louisiana	2	10,637	Vermont	1	2,058
Maine	1	6,242	Virginia	4	21,215
Maryland	2	12,828	Washington	2	8,439
Massachusetts	2	2,420	Wisconsin	4	11,199
Michigan	5	12,257	**Total**	100	414,038
Minnesota	3	11,052			

* Minus indicates that electric power consumed for plant use exceeded gross generation.
Source: US Energy Information Administration, *Electric Power Annual*, and *Inventory of Power Plants in the United States, 1986*.

NATIONAL ENERGY ORGANIZATIONS AND CO-ORDINATING BODIES

Association of Energy Engineers: 4025 Pleasantdale Rd, Suite 420, Atlanta, GA 30340; tel. (404) 447-5083; f. 1977; 6,200 mems; Exec. Dir ALBERT THUMANN.

Association of Professional Energy Managers: 717 Market St, Suite 404, San Francisco, CA 94103; tel. (415) 777-3566; f. 1983; 1,400 mems; Exec. Dir DANIEL C. FREDERICK.

Bonneville Power Administration: 1002 Holladay St, NE, Portland, OR 97208; tel. (503) 230-3000; covers Oregon and Washington; Administrator PETER T. JOHNSON.

Center for Energy Policy and Research: c/o New York Institute of Technology, Old Westbury, NY 11568; tel. (516) 686-7578; f. 1975; Dean GALE TENEN SPAK.

Consumer Energy Council of America Research Foundation: 200 L St, NW, Suite 802, Washington, DC 20036; tel. (202) 659-0404; f. 1973; 52 mems; Exec. Dir ELLEN BERMAN.

US Department of Energy: 1000 Independence Ave, SW, Washington, DC 20585; tel. (202) 586-5000; provides the framework for a comprehensive and balanced national energy plan through the co-ordination and administration of the energy functions of the federal govt; responsible for long-term, high-risk research and development of energy technology, energy conservation, the nuclear-weapons programme, energy regulatory programmes and a central energy data collection and analysis programme; Sec. JAMES D. WATKINS; Asst Sec. for Nuclear Energy MARY ANN NOVAK (acting); Asst Sec. for Conservation and Renewable Energy, JOHN BERG; Asst Sec. for Fossil Energy J. ALLEN WAMPLER; Asst Sec. for Environment, Safety and Health DIANE KAY MORALES.

National Energy Resources Organization: 11529 Montgomery Rd, Bettsville, MD 20705; tel. (301) 937-2799; f. 1975; 450 mems; Pres. ROBERT K. BOYD.

National Energy Specialist Association: NESA Bldg, 518 Gordon St, NW, Topeka, KS 66608; tel. (913) 232-1702; f. 1984; 1,000 mems; Exec. Dir MICHAEL C. COOPER.

National Hydropower Association: 1133 21st St, NW, Suite 500, Washington, DC 20036; f. 1983; 75 mems; Exec. Dir ELAINE EVANS.

National Old Timers' Association of the Energy Industry: POB 168, Mineola, NY 11501; f. 1926; 1,000 mems; Chair. JOHN M. SIBARIUM.

Solid Fuel Advisory Council of America: Star Route 104, Bristol, NH 03222; tel. (603) 744-5100; f. 1979; Dir C. GEOFFREY HYDE.

Southeastern Power Administration: Samuel Elgert Bldg, Elberton, GA 30635; tel. (404) 283-3261; covers Alabama, Florida, Georgia, Kentucky, Mississippi, North Carolina, South Carolina, Tennessee, Virginia and West Virginia; Administrator HARRY C. GEISINGER.

Southern States Energy Board: 2300 Peachford Rd, POB 1230, Atlanta, GA 30338; tel. (404) 455-8841; covers Alabama, Arkansas, Delaware, Florida, Georgia, Kentucky, Louisiana, Maryland, Mississippi, Missouri, North Carolina, Oklahoma, South Carolina, Tennessee, Texas, Virginia and West Virginia; Exec. Dir KENNETH J. NEMETH.

Southwestern Power Administration: Page Belcher Federal Bldg, Tulsa, OK 74101; tel. (918) 581-7474; covers Arkansas, Kansas, Louisiana, Missouri, Oklahoma and Texas; Administrator RONALD H. WILKERSON.

US Energy Association: 1620 I St, Suite 615, Washington, DC 20006; tel. (202) 331-0415; f. 1924; 113 mems.

Western Area Power Administration: POB 3402, Golden, CO 80401; tel. (303) 231-1511; covers Arizona, California, Colorado, Iowa, Kansas, Minnesota, Montana, Nebraska, Nevada, New Mexico, North Dakota, South Dakota, Texas, Utah and Wyoming.

Western Interstate Energy Board: 333 Quebec St, Denver, CO 80207; tel. (303) 837-5851; covers Alaska, Arizona, California, Colorado, Montana, Nebraska, Nevada, New Mexico, North Dakota, Oregon, South Dakota, Utah, Washington and Wyoming; Exec. Dir DONALD C. LARSON.

Atomic Energy

American Nuclear Energy Council: 410 First St, SE, Washington, DC 20003; tel. (202) 484-2670; f. 1975; supports the peaceful application of nuclear energy; 125 mems; Pres. EDWARD M. DAVIS.

American Nuclear Society: 555 North Kensington Ave, La Grange Park, IL 60525; tel. (312) 352-6611; telex 4972673; f. 1954; 14,000 mems; Exec. Dir OCTAVE J. DU TEMPLE.

Edison Electric Institute: 1111 19th St, NW, Washington, DC 20036; tel. (202) 828-7444; f. 1933; 190 mems; investor-owned electric utility cos; Sec. and Sr Vice-Pres. PRALL CULVINER.

Environmental Protection Agency: 401 M St, Washington, DC 20460; tel. (202) 475-9600; Administrator WILLIAM K. REILLY.

Federal Energy Regulatory Commission: 825 North Capitol St, NE, Washington, DC 20426; tel. (202) 357-8055; Chair. MARTHA O. HESSE.

Fusion Energy Foundation: f. 1974; 20,000 mems; aims 'to provide a forum of independent, high-level scientific discussion of fusion from the standpoint of comprehensive policy-making'.

Fusion Power Associates: Two Professional Dr., Suite 248, Gaithersburg, MD 20879; tel. (301) 258-0545; f. 1979; 50 mems; Pres. STEPHEN O. DEAN.

Institute of Nuclear Power Operations: 1100 Circle 75 Parkway, Suite 1500, Atlanta, GA 30339; tel. (404) 953-3600; f. 1979; electric utilities operating nuclear-power plants; 101 mems; Pres. ZACK T. PATE.

Inter-American Nuclear Energy Commission: c/o Organization of American States, 1889 F St, NW, Rm 410A, Washington, DC 20006.

Los Alamos National Laboratory: Los Alamos, NM 87545; tel. (505) 667-7000; telex 660495; fax (505) 667-1754; Dir S. S. HECKER.

National Council on Radiation Protection and Measurements: 7910 Woodmont Ave, Suite 1016, Bethesda, MD 20814; tel. (301) 657-2652; Exec. Dir W. ROGER NEY.

Nuclear Energy Women: 1776 I St, NW, Suite 400, Washington, DC 20006; tel. (202) 293-0770; f. 1975; individuals in energy industry and citizens' advocacy groups disseminating information about nuclear power; 500 mems; Program Co-ordinator PATRICIA BRYANT.

Nuclear Power Oversight Committee: POB 65084, Washington, DC 20035; tel. (202) 872-1280; fax (202) 872-1282; Chair. JAMES J. O'CONNER; Sec. TERENCE J. SULLIVAN.

Nuclear Regulatory Commission (NRC): Washington, DC 20555; tel. (202) 492-7000; f. 1975; federal licensing and regulatory body; Chair. Adm. (retd) LANDO W. ZECH, Jr; Commrs THOMAS M. ROBERTS, JAMES CURTIS, FREDERICK M. BERNTHAL, Vice-Adm. (retd) KENNETH M. CARR; Exec. Dir for Operations VICTOR STELLO, Jr; Sec. SAMUEL J. CHILK.

Nuclear Safety Analysis Center: 3412 Hillview Ave, POB 10412, Palo Alto, CA 94303; tel. (415) 855-2013; Dir WILLIAM LAYMAN.

Oak Ridge National Laboratory: POB X, Oak Ridge, TN 37831; tel. (615) 574-4160; Dir HERMAN POSTMA.

Professional Reactor Operator Society: POB 181, Mishicot, WI 54228; tel. (414) 863-6996; f. 1981; 700 mems; Pres. JAMES PETERSON (acting).

Saudia National Laboratories Energy Programmes Organization 6000: Albuquerque, NM 87185-5800; tel. (505) 844-2036; telex 169012; Pres. I. WELBER.

Society for the Advancement of Fission Energy: 336 Coleman Dr., Monroeville, PA 15146; tel. (412) 374-2222; f. 1976; 1,200 mems; Pres. JEREMY M. HELLMAN.

US Council for Energy Awareness: 7101 Wisconsin Ave, Bethesda, MD 20814; tel. (301) 654-9260; telex 7108249602; Pres. and COO HAROLD B. FINGER.

US Department of Energy: (see p. 323).

Nuclear Energy Research: US Dept of Energy, Nuclear Energy, Room 5A-115, Washington, DC 20585; tel. (202) 586-6456; provides information on research into nuclear energy, including fuel technology, nuclear-waste management and the administration of nuclear power installations.

Nuclear Safety Information Center (NSIC): Oak Ridge National Laboratory, POB Y, Oak Ridge, TN 37830; tel. (615) 574-0391; collects and disseminates information on the safety aspects of nuclear technology.

Alternative Energy Sources

Alternative Energy Resources Organization: 44 North Last Chance Gulch, Suites 8 and 9, Helena, MT 59601; tel. (406) 443-7272; f. 1974; 600 mems; Exec. Dir AL KURKI.

Alternative Sources of Energy: 107 South Central Ave, Milaca, MN 56353; tel. (612) 983-6892; f. 1971; Dir DONALD MARIER.

American Council for an Energy Efficient Economy: 1001 Connecticut Ave, NW, Suite 535, Washington, DC 20036; tel. (202) 429-8873; f. 1980; Man. Dir Dr CARL BLUMSTEIN.

Biomass Energy Research Association: 1825 K St, NW, Suite 503, Washington, DC 20006; tel. (202) 785-3511; f. 1981; 140 mems; Pres. Dr DONALD L. KLASS.

Council on Alternate Fuels: 1225 I St, NW, Suite 320, Washington, DC 20005; tel. (202) 898-0711; f. 1980; 28 mems; Pres. MICHAEL S. KOLEDA.

Natural Power: 5420 Mayfield Rd, Cleveland, OH 44124; tel. (216) 442-5600; f. 1975; 200 mems; Chair. IRWIN FRIEDMAN.

Renewable Fuels Association: 201 Massachusetts Ave, NE, Suite C4, Washington, DC 20002; tel. (202) 543-3802; f. 1981; 50 mems; Pres. ERIC VAUGHN.

ELECTRICITY

Alabama Power Co: 600 North 18th St, Birmingham, AL 35291; tel. (205) 323-5341; conventional thermal, hydro and nuclear generation; Pres. and CEO J. M. FARLEY.

Alaska Power Administration: POB 50, Juneau, AK 99801; CEO R. J. CROSS.

Allegheny Power System Inc: 320 Power Ave, New York, NY 10022; tel. (212) 752-2121; conventional thermal generation; Chair. and CEO K. BERGMAN.

American Electric Power Co: 1 Riverside Plaza, Columbus, OH 43215; fax (810) 482-1627; conventional thermal, hydro and nuclear generation; Chair. and CEO W. S. WHITE, Jr.

American Public Power Association: 2301 M St, NW, 3rd Floor, Washington, DC 20037; tel. (202) 775-8300; f. 1940; 1,400 mems; Exec. Dir LARRY HOBART.

Appalachian Electric Power Co: 40 Franklin Rd, SW, Roanoke, VA 24009; tel. (703) 344-1411; conventional thermal and hydro generation; Chair. and CEO W. S. WHITE, Jr.

Arizona Public Service Co: 411 North Central Ave, POB 53999, Phoenix, AZ 85072; tel. (602) 250-1000; conventional thermal generation; Chair. K. L. TURLEY.

Arkansas Power and Light Co: POB 551, Little Rock, AR 72203; tel. (501) 377-4000; conventional thermal generation; Pres. and CEO J. L. MAULDEN.

Association of Edison Illuminating Companies: 51 East 42nd St, New York, NY 10017; f. 1885; 95 mems; investor-owned public utilities; Sec.-Treas. ARTHUR N. ANDERSON.

Atlantic City Electric Co: 1199 Black Horse Pike, Pleasantville, NJ 08232; tel. (609) 645-4100; conventional thermal generation; Pres. and CEO B. D. HUGGARD.

Baltimore Gas and Electric Co: Gas and Electric Bldg, POB 1475, Baltimore, MD 21203; tel. (301) 234-5000; nuclear generation; Chair. and CEO B. C. TRUESCHLER.

Boston Edison Co: 800 Boylston St, Boston, MA 02199; tel. (617) 424-2400; conventional thermal and nuclear generation; Chair. and CEO S. T. SWEENEY.

Carolina Power and Light Co: 411 Fayetteville St, POB 1551, Raleigh, NC 27602; tel. (919) 836-6111.

Centerior Energy Corpn: 6200 Oak Tree Blvd, POB 94661, Cleveland, OH 44101; tel. (216) 447-3100; conventional thermal and nuclear generation; Chair. and CEO R. M. GINN.

Central Power and Light Co: POB 2121, Corpus Christi, TX 78403; tel. (512) 881-5300; conventional thermal generation; Pres. and CEO E. R. BROOKS.

Central and South West Corpn: 2121 San Jacinto St, Dallas, TX 75266; tel. (214) 754-1000; conventional thermal generation; distributes gas and heat; Chair. and CEO D. CHALKER.

Cincinnati Gas and Electric Co: 139 East Fourth St, POB 960, Cincinnati, OH 45201; tel. (513) 381-2000; conventional thermal generation; CEO W. H. DICKHONER.

Cleveland Electric Illuminating Co: POB 5000, Cleveland, OH 44101; tel. (216) 622-9800; conventional thermal generation.

Columbus and Southern Ohio Electric Co: 215 North Front St, Columbus, OH 43215; conventional thermal generation; Chair. and CEO W. S. WHITE, Jr.

Commonwealth Edison Co: POB 767, Chicago, IL 60690; tel. (312) 294-4321; conventional thermal, hydro and nuclear generation; Chair. and CEO J. J. O'CONNOR.

Connecticut Light and Power Co: POB 2010, Hartford, CT 06141; tel. (203) 665-5000; nuclear generation; Chair., Pres. and CEO W. B. ELLIS.

Consolidated Edison Co: 4 Irving Pl., New York, NY 10003; tel. (212) 460-4600; conventional thermal and nuclear generation; distributes electricity and gas; Chair. A. HAUSPURG.

Consumers' Power Co: 212 West Michigan Ave, Jackson, MI 49201; tel. (517) 788-0550.

Dallas Power and Light Co: 1506 Commerce St, Dallas, TX 75201; tel. (214) 747-4011.

Dayton Power and Light Co: Courthouse Plaza Southwest, Dayton, OH 45401; tel. (513) 224-6000; conventional thermal generation; distributes electricity and gas; Chair. and CEO R. E. FRAZER.

Detroit Edison Co: 2000 Second Ave, Detroit, MI 48226; tel. (313) 237-8000; conventional thermal and nuclear generation; Chair. and CEO W. J. McCARTHY, Jr.

Dominion Resources: POB 2666, Richmond, VA 23261; tel. (804) 771-3000.

Duke Power Co: 422 South Church St, Charlotte, NC 28242; tel. (704) 373-4011; conventional thermal, hydro and nuclear generation; Chair. and CEO W. S. Lee.

Duquesne Light Co: One Oxford Center, 301 Grant St, Pittsburgh, PA 15279; tel. (412) 456-6000; conventional thermal and nuclear generation; Chair. and CEO J. M. Arthur.

Edison Electric Institute: 1111 19th St, NW, Washington, DC 20036; tel. (202) 828-7444; f. 1933; 190 mems; investor-owned electric utility cos; Sec. and Sr Vice-Pres. Prall Culviner.

Electric Power Board of Chattanooga: Sixth and Market Sts, Chattanooga, TN 37402; tel. (615) 629-3300; Chair. and CEO D. L. Blevins.

Electric Utility Industrial Power Association: Southwestern Public Service, POB 631, Lubbock, TX 79408; tel. (806) 765-2800; f. 1929; 15 mems; investor-owned electric utility cos in the southwestern USA servicing the industry; Pres. Don Turner.

Electrification Council: 1111 19th St, NW, Washington, DC 20036; tel. (202) 778-6901; f. 1951; 20 mems; Man. H. E. Bowles.

Energy Telecommunications and Electrical Association: POB 795038, Dallas, TX 75379; tel. (214) 578-1900; f. 1928; 126 mems; Exec. Man. Martha G. Fike.

Florida Power and Light Co: 9250 West Flagler St, Miami, FL 33174; tel. (305) 552-3552; conventional thermal and nuclear generation; Chair. and CEO J. J. Hudiburg.

Florida Progress Corpn: 3201 34th St South, POB 14042, St Petersburg, FL 33733; tel. (813) 866-5151; conventional thermal generation; Chair. A. H. Hines.

General Public Utilities Corpn: 100 Interpace Parkway, Parsippany, NJ 07054; tel. (201) 263-6500; conventional thermal generation; Chair. W. G. Kuhns.

Georgia Power Co: 333 Piedmont Ave, Atlanta, GA 30308; tel. (404) 526-6526; telex 542259; conventional thermal, hydro and nuclear generation; Chair. R. W. Scherer.

Gulf States Utilities Co: 350 Pine St, POB 2951, Beaumont, TX 77704; tel. (409) 838-6631; conventional thermal generation; Chair. and CEO P. W. Murrill.

Hawaiian Electric Co: POB 2750, Honolulu, HI 96840; tel. (808) 548-7771; conventional thermal generation; Chair. and CEO C. D. Pratt.

Houston Lighting and Power Co: POB 1700, Houston, TX; tel. (713) 228-9211; telex 77001; conventional thermal generation; Chair. D. D. Jordan.

Hydra-Co Enterprises Inc: One Lincoln Center, Suite 1225, Syracuse, NY 13202; tel. (315) 471-2881.

Idaho Power Co: 1220 West Idaho St, POB 70, Boise, ID 83707; tel. (208) 383-2200; hydro generation; Pres. and CEO R. J. O'Connor.

Illinois Power Co: 500 South 27th St, Decatur, IL 62525; tel. (217) 424-6600; conventional thermal generation; Chair. and CEO W. J. Kelley.

Indiana and Michigan Electric Co: One Summit Sq., POB 60, Fort Wayne, IN 46801; conventional thermal and hydro generation; Chair. W. S. White, Jr.

Indianapolis Power and Light Co: 25 Monument Circle, Indianapolis, IN 46206; tel. (317) 216-8261; conventional thermal generation; Chair. Z. D. Todd.

Jersey Central Power and Light Co: Madison Ave at Punch Bowl Rd, Morristown, NJ 07960; tel. (201) 455-8200; nuclear generation; Chair. and CEO W. G. Kuhns.

Kentucky Power Co: 1701 Central Ave, Ashland, KY 41101; conventional thermal generation; CEO W. S. White, Jr.

Kentucky Utilities Co: 1 Quality St, Lexington, KY 40507; tel. (606) 255-1461; conventional thermal generation; Chair. and CEO W. S. White, Jr.

Kingsport Power Co: 422 Broad St, Kingsport, TN 37662; Chair. and CEO W. S. White, Jr.

Long Island Lighting Co: 250 Old Country Rd, Mineola, NY 11501; tel. (516) 228-2890.

Los Angeles Department of Water and Power: 111 North Hope St, POB 111, Los Angeles, CA 90012; tel. (213) 481-4211; conventional thermal and hydro generation; Pres. and CEO J. M. Cain.

Massachusetts Electric Co: 25 Research Dr., Westborough, MA 01582; tel. (617) 366-9011; CEO E. E. Mulligan.

Middle South Utilities, Inc: 225 Baronne St, POB 61005, New Orleans, LA 70161; tel. (504) 529-5262; conventional thermal generation; distributes gas and heat; Chair. E. Lupberger.

Minnkota Power Cooperative, Inc: 1318 Grand Forks, ND 58201; tel. (701) 795-4000.

Mississippi Power and Light Co: POB 1640, Jackson, MS 39215; tel. (601) 969-2311; conventional thermal generation; CEO D. C. Lutken.

Monongahela Power Co: 1310 Fairmont Ave, Fairmont, WV 26554; tel. (304) 366-3000; conventional thermal generation; Chair. K. Bergman.

National Rural Electric Cooperative Association: 1800 Massachusetts Ave, NW, Washington, DC 20036; tel. (202) 857-9500; f. 1942; rural electric co-operative systems, public power districts, and public utility districts in 46 states; 1,000 mems; Exec. Vice-Pres. Bob Bergland.

New England Electric System: 25 Research Dr., Westborough, MA 01581; tel. (617) 366-9011; conventional thermal generation; Chair. and CEO J. T. Bok.

New England Power Service Co: 25 Research Dr., Westborough, MA 01581; tel. (617) 366-9011.

New York State Electric and Gas Corporation: POB 287, Ithaca, New York 14851; tel. (607) 347-4131; conventional thermal generation; Chair. and CEO W. P. Allen.

Niagara Mohawk Power Corpn: 300 Erie Blvd West, Syracuse, NY 13202; tel. (315) 474-1511; conventional thermal, hydro and nuclear generation; distributes electricity and gas; Chair. and CEO J. G. Hoehl, Jr.

North American Electric Reliability Council: 101 College Rd East, Princeton, NJ 08540; tel. (609) 452-8060; f. 1968; regional reliability councils concerned with the reliability of bulk electric power supply in North America; 9 mems; Pres. Michehl R. Gent.

Northeast Utilities: POB 270, Hartford, CT 06101; tel. (203) 666-6911; telex 99370.

Northern Indiana Public Service Co: 5265 Hohman Ave, Hammond, IN 46320; tel. (219) 853-5200; conventional thermal and hydro generation; distributes electricity and gas; Chair. and CEO E. A. Schroer.

Northern States Power Co: 414 Nicollet Mall, Minneapolis, MN 55401; tel. (612) 330-5500; conventional thermal, hydro and nuclear generation; distributes electricity and gas; Chair. and CEO D. W. McCarthy.

Ohio Edison: 76 South Main St, Akron, OH 44308; tel. (216) 384-5100; conventional thermal generation; Pres. and CEO J. T. Rogers.

Ohio Power Co: 301 Cleveland Ave, SW, Canton, OH 44702; tel. (216) 456-8173; conventional thermal and hydro generation; Chair. and CEO W. S. White, Jr.

Oklahoma Gas and Electric Co: 321 North Harvey Ave, Oklahoma City, OK 73101; tel. (405) 272-3000; conventional thermal generation; Chair., Pres. and CEO J. G. Harlow, Jr.

Pacific Gas and Electric Co: 77 Beale St, San Francisco, CA 94106; tel. (415) 972-4211; telex 3103726587; conventional thermal, hydro and nuclear generation; distributes electricity and gas; Chair. and CEO R. A. Clarke.

Pacificorp: 920 6th Ave, SW, Portland, OR 97204; tel. (503) 243-1122; conventional thermal and hydro generation; CEO D. F. Bolender.

Pennsylvania Electric Co: 1001 Broad St, Johnstown, PA 15907; tel. (814) 533-8111; conventional thermal generation; Chair. and CEO W. G. Kuhns.

Pennsylvania Power and Light Co: Two North Ninth St, Allentown, PA 18101; tel. (215) 821-5151; conventional thermal, hydro and nuclear generation; Pres. and CEO R. K. Campbell.

Philadelphia Electric Co: 2301 Market St, Philadelphia, PA 19101, tel. (215) 841-4000; conventional thermal, hydro and nuclear generation; Pres. and CEO J. L. Everett.

Portland General Electric Co: 121 Salmon St, SW, Portland, OR 97204; tel. (503) 226-8333; conventional thermal, hydro and nuclear generation; Chair. and CEO R. H. Short.

Potomac Edison Co: Downsville Pike, Hagerstown, MD 21740; tel. (301) 790-3400; conventional thermal generation; Chair. and CEO K. Bergman.

Potomac Electric Power Co: 1900 Pennsylvania Ave, NW, Washington, DC 20068; tel. (202) 872-2000; conventional thermal generation; Chair. and CEO W. R. Thompson.

Power Authority of the State of New York: 10 Columbus Circle, New York, NY 10019; tel. (212) 297-6225.

Public Service Co of Colorado: 550 15th St, POB 840, Denver, CO 80201; tel. (303) 571-7511; conventional thermal generation; Chair. and CEO R. F. Walker.

Public Service Co of Indiana: 1000 East Main St, Plainfield, IN 46168; tel. (317) 839-9611; conventional thermal generation; Chair. and CEO H. A. Barker.

Public Service Co of Oklahoma: 212 East Sixth St, Tulsa, OK 74102; tel. (918) 599-2000; conventional thermal generation; Pres. and CEO M. E. FATE.

Public Service Electric and Gas Go: 80 Park Pl., Newark, NJ 07101; tel. (201) 430-7000; telex 138182; conventional thermal and nuclear generation; distributes electricity and gas; Chair. and CEO E. J. FERLAND.

Puget Sound Power and Light Co: Puget Power Bldg, Bellevue, WA 98009; tel. (206) 454-6363; conventional thermal and hydro generation; Pres. and CEO J. W. ELLIS.

San Diego Gas and Electric Co: 101 Ash St, San Diego, CA 92101; tel. (714) 232-4252; conventional thermal and nuclear generation; electricity and gas distribution; Chair. and CEO T. A. PAGE.

Scana Corpn: 1426 Main St, Columbia, SC 29218; tel. (803) 748-3000; conventional thermal generation; Chair. and CEO J. A. WARREN.

South California Edison Co: POB 800, Rosemead, CA 91770; tel. (213) 572-1212; conventional thermal, hydro and nuclear generation; Pres. and CEO H. P. ALLEN.

South Carolina Electric and Gas Co: 1426 Main St, Columbia, SC 29218; tel. (803) 748-3000; conventional thermal, hydro and nuclear generation; distributes and gas.

Southern Co: 64 Perimeter Center East, Atlanta, GA 30346; tel. (404) 393-0650; conventional thermal generation; Pres. and CEO E. L. ADDISON.

Southwestern Electric Power Co: 428 Travis St, Shreveport, LA 71156; tel. (318) 222-2141; conventional thermal generation; Pres. and CEO J. W. TURK.

Southwestern Public Service Co: Tyler St at Sixth Ave, POB 1261, Amarillo, TX 79170; tel. (806) 378-2121; conventional thermal generation; Chair. and CEO B. BALLENGEE.

Teco Energy, Inc: 702 North Franklin St, POB 111, Tampa, FL 33601; tel. (813) 228-4111; conventional thermal generation; Chair. and CEO H. L. CULBREATH.

Tennessee Valley Authority: Commercial Bldg, 400 Commerce Ave, Knoxville, TN 37902; tel. (615) 632-2101; conventional thermal, hydro and nuclear generation; Chair. MARVIN RUNYON.

Tennessee Valley Public Power Association: 1201 Chestnut St, Chattanooga, TN 37402; tel. (615) 756-6511; f. 1946; municipal and rural co-operative electric systems that buy power wholesale from the Tennessee Valley Authority; 160 mems; Exec. Dir JERRY CAMPBELL.

Texas Utilities Co: 2001 Bryan Tower, Dallas, TX 75201; tel. (214) 653-4600; conventional thermal generation; Chair. and CEO J. FARRINGTON.

Toledo Edison Co: 300 Madison Ave, Toledo, OH 43652; tel. (419) 259-5000; conventional thermal and nuclear generation.

Union Electric Co: 1901 Gratiot St, St Louis, MO 63103; tel. (314) 621-3222.

Utah Power and Light Co: 1407 West North Temple St, POB 899, Salt Lake City, UT 84110; tel. (801) 535-2000; conventional thermal generation; Pres. and CEO F. N. DAVIS.

Washington Water Power Co: 1411 East Mission Ave, POB 3727, Spokane, WA 99220; tel. (509) 489-0500; conventional thermal and hydro generation; electricity and gas distribution; Chair. and CEO P. A. REDMOND.

West Penn Power Co: Cabin Hill, Greensburg, PA 15601; tel. (412) 837-3000; conventional thermal generation; Chair. and CEO K. BERGMAN.

Wheeling Electric Co: POB 751, Wheeling, VA 26003; Chair and CEO W. S. WHITE, Jr.

Wisconsin Energy Corporation: 231 West Michigan St, POB 2949, Milwaukee, WI 53201; tel. (414) 277-2345; conventional thermal, hydro and nuclear generation; distributes electricity and gas.

Wisconsin Power and Light Co: 222 West Washington Ave, Madison, WI 53701; tel. (608) 252-3311; conventional thermal and hydro generation; electricity and gas distribution.

Wisconsin Public Service Corpn: 700 North Adams St, POB 19001, Green Bay, WI 54307; tel. (414) 433-1598; conventional thermal, hydro and nuclear generation; distributes electricity and gas; Pres. and CEO P. D. ZIEMER.

OIL AND GAS ASSOCIATIONS

American Association of Petroleum Landmen: 777 Main St, Suite 1470, Fort Worth, TX 76102; tel. (817) 335-2275; f. 1955; 10,000 mems; Exec. Vice-Pres. HARRY L. SPRINKLE.

American Gas Association: 1515 Wilson Blvd, Arlington, VA 22209; tel. (703) 841-8400; f. 1918; 4,758 mems; Pres. GEORGE H. LAWRENCE.

American Independent Refiners' Association: 50 F St, NW, Suite 1040, Washington, DC 20001; tel. (202) 743-0643; f. 1983; 27 mems; Exec. Dir RAYMOND F. BRAGG; Jr.

American Petroleum Institute: 1220 L St, NW, Washington, DC 20005; tel. (202) 682-8000; telex 8229586; f. 1919; 5,200 mems; Chair. RICHARD M. MORROW.

American Public Gas Association: POB 1426, Vienna, VA 22180; tel. (703) 281-2910; f. 1961; promotes efficiency among public gas systems; 320 mems; Exec. Dir ROBERT S. CAVE.

American Society of Gas Engineers: POB 936, Tinley Park, IL 60477; tel. (312) 532-5707; f. 1954; 600 mems; Exec. Dir CHARLES R. KENDALL.

Association of Desk and Derrick Clubs: 315 Silvey Bldg, Tulsa, OK 74119; f. 1951; 10,000 mems; women employers and employees in the petroleum and allied industries; Pres. CHERYL RECTORSCHEK.

Association of Oil Pipe Lines: 1725 K St, NW, Suite 1205, Washington, DC 20006; tel. (202) 331-8228; f. 1947; 83 mems; Exec. Dir PATRICK H. CORCORAN.

Distribution Contractors' Association: 531 Harvard Tower, 4815 South Harvard, Tulsa, OK 74135; tel. (918) 743-1513; f. 1961; 130 mems; Man. Dir JAMES R. UPTON.

Gas Processors' Association: 6526 East 60th St, Tulsa, OK 74145; tel. (918) 493-3872; f. 1921; 190 mems; Exec. Dir R. E. CANNON.

Gas Processors Suppliers' Association: 6526 East 60th St, Tulsa, OK 74145; tel. (918) 493-3872; f. 1927; 450 mems; Sec. R. E. CANNON.

Gas Research Institute: 8600 W. Bryn Mawr Ave, Chicago, IL 60631; tel. (312) 399-8100; f. 1976; 255 mems; Pres. HENRY R. LINDEN.

Gulf Oil Wholesale Marketers' Association: Three Dunwoody Park, Suite 103, Atlanta, GA 30338; tel. (403) 394-4297; f. 1974; 250 mems; Exec. Dir H. FROST.

Independent Petroleum Association of America: 1101 16th St, NW, Washington, DC 20036; tel. (202) 857-4722; f. 1929; 6,500 mems; Pres. H. B. SCOGGINS, Jr.

Interstate Natural Gas Association of America: 1660 L St, NW, Suite 601, Washington, DC 20036; tel. (202) 293-5770; f. 1944; 29 mems; transporters of natural gas; Exec. Officer JERALD V. HALVORSEN.

Liaison Committee of Cooperating Oil and Gas Associations: 105 South Broadway, Suite 500, Wichita, KS 67202; tel. (316) 263-7297; f. 1957; 27 mem. orgs; Sec.-Treas. DONALD P. SCHNACKE.

Mid-Continent Oil and Gas Association: 711 Adams Office Bldg, Tulsa, OK 74103; tel. (918) 582-5166; f. 1917; 7,500 mems; Sec.-Treas. CLARK SEIBOLD.

National LP-Gas Association: 1301 West 22nd St, Oak Brook, IL 60521; tel. (312) 573-4800; f. 1962; 4,000 mems; promotes use of propane gas and compiles industry stats; Exec. Vice-Pres. J. D. CAPPS.

National Petroleum Refiners' Association: 1899 L St, NW, Suite 1000, Washington, DC 20036; tel. (202) 457-0480; f. 1902; 300 mems; Pres. URVAN R. STERNFELS.

Natural Gas Supply Association: 1129 20th St, NW, Suite 300, Washington, DC 20036; tel. (202) 331-8900; f. 1967; 65 mems; monitors legislation and economic issues affecting natural-gas producers; Pres. NICHOLAS J. BUSH.

Petroleum Marketers' Association of America: 1120 Vermont Ave, NW, Suite 1130, Washington, DC 20005; tel. (202) 331-1198; f. 1941; 41 mems; Exec. Vice-Pres. PHILIP R. CHISHOLM.

Society of Independent Gasoline Marketers of America: 1730 K St, NW, Suite 907, Washington, DC 20006; tel. (202) 429-9333; f. 1958; 285 mems; Exec. Dir KENNETH A. DOYLE.

Texas Independent Producers and Royalty Owners' Association: 1910 First Republic Bank Tower, Austin, TX 78701; tel. (512) 477-4452; f. 1946; 5,400 mems; independent oil and gas producers; royalty owners; Exec. Vice-Pres. JULIAN G. MARTIN.

Western Oil and Gas Association: 727 West Seventh St, Los Angeles, CA 90017; tel. (213) 627-4866; f. 1907; 100 mem. cos; Exec. Dir DOUGLAS F. HENDERSON.

WATER

Water Withdrawals and Consumption per Day, by State, 1985

(Millions of gallons per day, unless otherwise mentioned. 'Withdrawal' signifies water physically withdrawn from a source.
Includes fresh and saline water.)

		Water withdrawn					
		Per head of population (gallons per day, fresh water)		Use			Consumptive use, fresh water
	Total		Irrigation	Public supply[1]	Industrial[2]	Thermo-electric	
Alabama	8,600	2,140	69	654	851	6,920	541
Alaska	406	727	—	86	133	30	27
Arizona	6,430	1,960	5,520	645	133	58	3,700
Arkansas	5,910	2,500	3,870	317	175	1,090	3,210
California	49,700	1,420	30,600	5,450	1,159	12,180	21,100
Colorado	13,600	4,190	12,400	754	211	110	4,850
Connecticut	3,780	375	3	401	147	3,210	106
Delaware	1,650	222	27	87	410	1,121	39
District of Columbia	348	556	—	218	—	130	24
Florida	17,000	554	2,910	1,939	679	11,351	2,730
Georgia	5,450	899	453	935	656	3,326	838
Hawaii	2,150	1,100	906	215	20	970	132
Idaho	22,300	22,200	20,600	301	334	—	5,290
Illinois	14,500	1,250	71	1,910	639	11,700	686
Indiana	8,030	1,470	47	714	2,751	4,480	454
Iowa	2,770	960	67	415	260	1,810	473
Kansas	5,680	2,320	4,730	366	95	415	4,710
Kentucky	4,200	1,130	8	451	266	3,410	260
Louisiana	10,400	2,210	1,670	675	2,072	5,964	2,010
Maine	1,520	733	2	127	578	745	203
Maryland	6,710	321	34	834	371	5,429	423
Massachusetts	9,660	1,070	16	802	153	8,450	316
Michigan	11,400	1,270	210	1,373	1,385	8,390	611
Minnesota	2,830	676	209	604	457	1,470	768
Mississippi	2,460	868	886	328	188	670	651
Missouri	6,110	1,210	306	699	116	4,930	504
Montana	8,650	10,500	8,300	174	60	67	1,900
Nebraska	10,000	6,250	7,270	272	167	2,210	4,910
Nevada	3,740	3,860	3,350	300	35	23	1,890
New Hampshire	894	688	1	111	239	543	76
New Jersey	6,940	307	132	1,114	1,137	4,546	279
New Mexico	3,280	2,320	2,820	264	83	59	1,530
New York	15,200	508	38	3,051	1,080	10,870	1,400
North Carolina	8,760	1,260	132	764	539	7,266	439
North Dakota	1,160	1,690	154	84	13	892	201
Ohio	12,700	1,180	17	1,559	540	10,500	396
Oklahoma	1,270	386	445	547	113	134	576
Oregon	6,540	2,450	5,710	496	301	12	2,600
Pennsylvania	14,300	1,210	11	1,784	2,208	10,200	589
Rhode Island	412	156	3	126	20	261	23
South Carolina	6,820	2,040	34	421	1,135	5,186	340
South Dakota	675	956	460	96	46	7	361
Tennessee	8,450	1,770	9	697	1,613	6,060	275
Texas	25,300	1,230	8,120	3,095	2,763	11,010	8,650
Utah	4,320	2,540	3,590	453	213	28	2,130
Vermont	126	235	1	65	55	1	26
Virginia	7,250	853	52	691	673	5,760	269
Washington	7,030	1,600	4,940	1,053	559	427	4,700
West Virginia	5,700	2,940	4	172	1,028	4,490	773
Wisconsin	6,740	1,400	84	659	461	5,440	321
Wyoming	6,220	12,200	5,660	111	184	236	2,670

[1] Includes domestic.   [2] Includes mining.

Source: US Geological Survey, *Estimated Use of Water in the United States in 1985*, circular 1005.

Directory

American Water Resources Association: 5410 Grosvenor Lane, Suite 220, Bethesda, MD 20814; tel. (301) 493-8600; f. 1964; 3,500 indiv. and group mems; Exec. Dir KENNETH D. REID.

American Water Works Association: 6666 West Quincy Ave, Denver, CO 80235; tel. (303) 794-7711; Exec. Dir P. SCHULTE.

American Water Works Company, Inc: 3908 Kennett Pike, POB 3539, Wilmington, DE 19807; tel. (302) 656-1681; owns the largest group of investor-owned water utilities in the USA, serving 1.5m. customers (5m. people) in 500 communities in 20 states.

Association of Ground Water Scientists and Engineers: 6375 Riverside Dr., Dublin, OH 43017; tel. (614) 761-1711; f. 1963; 9,000 mems; Exec. Dir Dr JAY H. LEHR.

Association of Metropolitan Water Agencies: 477 H St, NW, Washington, DC 20001.

Conference of State Sanitary Engineers: 150 East Main St, Westminster, MA 21157; tel. (301) 876-8440.

Ground Water Institute: POB 981, Minneapolis, MN 55440; tel. (612) 698-4395; promotes better use and management of national ground water resources.

Groundwater Management Caucus: 1125 Maize Rd, Colby, KS 67701; tel. (913) 462-3915; f. 1974; a unit of the National Water Resources Association; provides forum for exchange of information; 156 mems; Sec. WAYNE A. BOSSERT.

Interstate Conference on Water Policy: 955 L'Enfant Plaza, SW, 6th Floor, Washington, DC 20025; tel. (202) 466-7287; f. 1959; 70 mems; Exec. Dir JOAN M. KOVALIC.

National Association of Water Cos: 1725 K St, NW, Suite 1212, Washington, DC 20006; tel. (202) 833-8383; f. 1895; privately- and commercially-owned water cos, and individuals; 500 mems; Exec. Dir JAMES B. GROFF.

National Rural Water Association: 1503 Bois D'Arc, Duncan, OK 73533.

National Water Resources Association: 955 L'Enfant Plaza, SW, Suite 1202N, Washington, DC 20024; tel. (202) 488-0610; f. 1932; 4,800 mems; Exec. Vice-Pres. THOMAS F. DONNELLY.

National Water Supply Improvement Association: POB 102, St Leonard, MD 20865; tel. (301) 855-1173; f. 1985; 400 mems; Exec. Dir JACK C. JORGENSEN.

National Water Well Association: 500 West Wilson Bridge Rd, Suite 135, Worthington, OH 43085; tel. (614) 846-9355.

New England Interstate Water Pollution Control Compact: 607 Boylston St, Boston, MA 02116; tel. (617) 437-1524; covers Connecticut, Maine, Maryland, New Hampshire, New York, Rhode Island and Vermont; Dir KIRK LAFLIN.

Ohio River Valley Water Sanitation Commission: 414 Walnut St, Cincinnati, OH 45202; tel. (513) 421-1151; covers Illinois, Indiana, Kentucky, New York, Ohio, Pennsylvania and Virginia; Exec. Dir and Chief Engineer LEO WEAVER.

San Jose Water Company: 374 West Santa Clara St, San Jose, CA 95113; tel. (408) 279-7900.

Tennessee-Tombigbee Waterway Development Authority: POB 671, Columbus, MS 39701; tel. (601) 328-3286; covers Alabama, Florida, Kentucky, Mississippi and Tennessee; Administrator DON WALDEN.

United States Committee on Large Dams of the International Commission on Large Dams: POB 15103, Denver, CO 80215; tel. (303) 236-6960; f. 1928; 1,353 mems; Exec. Dir LARRY D. STEPHENS.

Universities Council on Water Resources: 4543 Faner Hall, Southern Illinois University, Carbondale, IL 62901; tel. (618) 536-7571; f. 1962; Exec. Dir DUANE D. BAUMANN.

US Committee on Irrigation and Drainage: POB 15326, Denver, CO 80215; tel. (303) 236-6960; f. 1952; 700 mems; Exec. Vice-Pres. LARRY D. STEPHENS.

US Environmental Protection Agency: 401 M St, SW, Washington, DC 20460; tel. (202) 475-9600; Administrator WILLIAM K. REILLY.

US Senate Committee on Environment and Public Works: Subcommittee on Water Resources, Transportation, and Infrastructure: Dirksen Senate Office Bldg, Suite SD-458, Washington, DC 20510.

Water Quality Association: 4156 Naperville Rd, Lisle, IL 60532; tel. (312) 369-1600; f. 1974; individuals or firms involved in the manufacture or distribution of water treatment equipment and services; 1,550 mems; Exec. Dir DOUGLAS OBERHAMER.

Water Quality Research Council: 4151 Naperville Rd, Lisle, IL 60532; tel. (312) 369-1600; f. 1950; 1,465 mems; Exec. Sec. PETER J. CENSKY.

Water Resources Congress: 3800 North Fairfax Dr., Suite 7, Arlington, VA 22203; tel. (703) 525-4881; f. 1971; 300 mems; Pres. RAY LEONARD.

Western Snow Conference: POB 2646, Portland, OR 97208; tel. (503) 221-2843; f. 1939; researches the use of snow as source of water for irrigation and hydroelectric power; 600 mems; Sec.-Treas. JAMES K. MARRON.

TOURISM

STATISTICS

Domestic Travel Expenditures, by State

($ million)

	1984	1985		1984	1985
Alabama	1,623	1,753	Montana	726	742
Alaska	903	919	Nebraska	1,252	1,280
Arizona	3,845	4,389	Nevada	6,459	6,912
Arkansas	1,822	1,870	New Hampshire	1,504	1,562
California	28,552	32,507	New Jersey	11,441	12,933
Colorado	4,638	5,005	New Mexico	1,726	1,804
Connecticut	2,428	2,635	New York	15,728	16,538
Delaware	556	660	North Carolina	5,251	5,668
District of Columbia	1,144	1,232	North Dakota	629	648
Florida	17,681	18,642	Ohio	6,433	6,849
Georgia	4,862	5,222	Oklahoma	2,788	2,902
Hawaii	2,532	2,781	Oregon	2,303	2,462
Idaho	935	975	Pennsylvania	8,375	9,321
Illinois	7,792	8,662	Rhode Island	431	488
Indiana	2,775	2,965	South Carolina	3,019	3,386
Iowa	1,768	1,918	South Dakota	552	576
Kansas	1,734	1,862	Tennessee	3,333	3,756
Kentucky	2,225	2,290	Texas	15,017	15,685
Louisiana	3,742	3,790	Utah	1,761	1,852
Maine	1,532	1,730	Vermont	1,182	1,228
Maryland	3,806	4,346	Virginia	4,710	5,305
Massachusetts	5,243	5,666	Washington	3,452	3,837
Michigan	6,289	7,172	West Virginia	1,271	1,298
Minnesota	4,955	5,209	Wisconsin	3,858	4,065
Mississippi	1,254	1,369	Wyoming	779	805
Missouri	4,705	4,976	**Total**	223,318	242,443

Source: US Travel Data Center, Washington, DC, *Impact of Travel on State Economies, 1984* and *1985* (copyright).

National Park Service Areas

	Acreage (1986, '000)[1]	Visits (million)			
		1984, total	1985, total	1986 Total[2]	1986 Recreation
Acadia National Park, ME	41	3.9	3.9	4.1	3.9
Big Bend National Park, TX	735	0.2	0.2	0.2	0.2
Blue Ridge Parkway, NC-VA	82	19.2	21.2	21.5	17.1
Cape Cod National Seashore, MA	44	4.6	4.4	4.0	4.0
Chesapeake and Ohio National Historical Park, MD-DC-WV	21	6.4	6.3	4.9*	4.9
Chickamauga and Chattanooga National Military Park, TN	8	17.6	15.5	15.8	1.2
Chicasaw National Recreation Park, OK	9	5.2	6.1	4.3	2.0
Colonial National Historical Park, VA	9	5.7	5.7	5.1	2.0
Death Valley National Monument, CA-NV	2,068	0.6	0.6	0.6	0.6
Delaware Gap National Recreation Area, PA-NJ	66	5.2	4.6	4.6	2.2
Gateway National Recreation Area, NY-NJ	26	8.0	8.7	9.0	8.9
George Washington Memorial Parkway, VA-MD	7	8.2	8.8	9.1	9.1
Glacier National Park, MT	1,014	2.0	1.6	1.6	1.6
Glen Canyon National Recreation Area, AZ-UT	1,237	2.1	2.2	2.5	2.4
Golden Gate National Recreation Area, CA	73	16.8	18.4	21.6	21.6
Grand Canyon National Park, AZ	1,218	2.4	3.0	3.3	3.0
Grand Teton National Park, WY	311	2.2	2.1	2.2	1.3
Great Smoky Mountain National Park, NC-TN	520	13.5	14.4	15.9	9.8
Gulf Island National Seashore, MS-FL	140	5.8	9.9	7.6	7.6
Hot Springs National Park, AR	6	5.4	5.2	5.6	1.2
Independence National Historical Park, PA	0†	4.8	4.9	5.0	5.0
Kings Canyon National Park, CA	462	0.9	0.9	1.0	1.0
Lake Meade National Recreation Area, AZ-NV	1,496	6.5	7.2	8.0	7.8
Lincoln Memorial, DC	0†	4.0	3.8	4.0	4.0
Natchez Trace Parkway, MS-TN-AL	50	20.2	19.4	21.5	14.4
National Capital Parks, DC-MD	6	7.2	8.3	6.6	6.6

(continued)

329

NATIONAL PARK SERVICE AREAS—*continued*

	Acreage (1986, '000)[1]	1984, total	1985, total	1986 Total[2]	1986 Recreation
Olympic National Park, WA	915	3.3	3.0	3.5	2.9
Ozark National Scenic Riverways, MO . . .	81	1.9	2.0	1.9	1.4
Rock Creek Park, DC	2	14.1	14.4	14.7	2.2
Sequoia National Park, CA	403	1.0	0.9	1.1	1.1
Shenandoah National Park, VA . . .	195	1.9	2.0	1.9	1.8
Valley Forge National Historical Park, PA . .	3	13.1	12.9	12.9	4.2
Vietnam Veterans' Memorial, DC . . .	0†	2.3	4.0	5.4	5.4
Yellowstone National Park, ID–MT–WY . . .	2,220	2.3	2.3	2.4	2.4
Yosemite National Park, CA	761	2.8	2.9	3.0	2.9
Zion National Park, UT	147	1.6	1.7	1.9	1.7
Total (incl. others)	79,491	332.7	346.2	364.6	281.1

* Not comparable with earlier years due to temporary closing.   † Less than 500 acres.
[1] Includes non-federal land.
[2] Includes non-recreation visits. In some areas, non-recreation visits can not be counted; therefore, total visits equal recreation visits only.
Source: US National Park Service, *National Park Statistics Abstract*, annual, and unpublished data.

DIRECTORY

NATIONAL ORGANIZATIONS

American Society of Travel Agents Inc: POB 23992, Washington, DC 20026-3992; tel. (703) 739-2782; telex 440203; f. 1931; Pres. and CEO VOIT GILMORE; Vice-Pres. and COO RAY SHOCKLEY; 22,000 mems.

United States Travel and Tourism Administration: US Dept of Commerce, Rm 1865, Washington, DC 20230; tel. (202) 377-0136; f. 1961; promotes US tourist industry and collects and analyses data on tourism; Under-Sec. for Travel and Tourism CHARLES E. COBB, Jr.

STATE TOURIST ATTRACTIONS AND ORGANIZATIONS

Alabama

Alabama's four national park sites, which include Tuskegee Institute National Historical Site and Russell Cave National Monument, were visited by an estimated 1,123,849 tourists in 1984. The 22 state parks, with a total area of 48,027 acres, received an estimated 6,577,000 visits in 1986. Gulf beaches also attract thousands of visitors; Point Clear, in particular, has been a well-known tourist destination since the early 19th century. Fishing proves popular with visitors; 589,053 fishing licences were issued in 1982/83, while the Deep Sea Fishing Rodeo at Dauphin Island presents a major attraction. Places of cultural and historical interest include the First White House of the Confederacy at Montgomery, the Marshall Space and Rocket Center at Huntsville and the Shakespeare Festival and Natural History Museum.

Bureau of Tourism and Travel: 532 South Perry St, Montgomery, AL 36130; tel. (205) 261-4169; Dir LISA WALSH SHIVERS.

Division of Parks: 64 North Union St, Montgomery, AL 36130.

Travel Council: 600 Adams Ave, Suite 254, Montgomery, AL 36104.

Alaska

Alaska offers thousands of miles of scenic landscape, including over 3m. lakes and the 11 highest mountains in the USA. The national parks and wildlife enclosures cover more than 104m. acres. Denali National Park, site of Mount McKinley, Glacier Bay National Park and Katmai National Park are among the principal tourist attractions. Alaska's state parks, which cover an area of 3,132,000 acres, were visited by 6,314,000 tourists in 1986. Outdoor facilities to attract tourists included 22 alpine ski areas, 1,876 miles of hiking trails and 3,314 camp sites in 1982. Cruise travel along the Gulf of Alaska is also becoming increasingly popular with visitors.

Division of Parks: Pouch 7-001, Anchorage, AK 99510; tel. (907) 561-2020.

Division of Tourism: Dept of Commerce, POB D, Juneau, AK 99811; tel. (907) 465-2500.

National Park Service: Parks and Forests Information Center, 2525 Campbell, Anchorage, AK 99503; tel. (907) 261-2643.

Arizona

In 1984 an estimated 7,674,764 tourists visited Arizona's national park areas. The 19 national parks and monuments include Petrified Forest National Park, Saguaro National Monument, and Grand Canyon National Park, which, with 2,173,584 visitors in 1984, proves the most popular. There are also 19 state parks, covering an area of 79,000 acres, which attracted an estimated 2,314,000 visitors in 1986. Arizona offers excellent camping facilities, and the state's Indian reservations are favourite destinations for sightseeing and shopping. Boating and fishing are also popular recreations; licences were issued to 454,045 fishermen in 1982/83, while boat registrations totalled 107,333 in 1983. Lake Havasu, the Colorado River and the Salt River lakes figure among the state's tourist attractions.

Office of Tourism: 3507 North Central Ave, Suite 506, Phoenix, AZ 85012; tel. (602) 255-3618.

State Parks: 1688 West Adams St, Phoenix, AZ 85007.

Arkansas

In early 1983/84 an estimated 2,040,900 tourists visited Arkansas' national parks, while the state parks, totalling 44,000 acres, attracted 6,490,000 visitors in 1986. The resorts of Hot Springs, in the Ouachita Mountains, Eureka Springs, in the Ozark Plateau, and Mammoth Springs, near the Missouri border, are major tourist attractions, offering beneficial mineral water and recreational facilities. Visitors also flock to the Crater of Diamonds, near Mursfreeboro, where they are permitted to keep any diamonds they find. Arkansas is popular for hunting; during 1982/83 883,589 hunting licences were issued. The World's Championship Duck Calling Contest, which is held in Stuttgart, is a primary attraction for hunters.

Department of Parks and Tourism: 1 Capitol Mall, Little Rock, AR 72201; tel. (501) 371-7777; Dir Jo Luck Wilson.

California

California contains some of the largest and finest national parks in the USA, including the Redwood National Park and Lassen Volcanic National Park in the north; Yosemite National Park, which had 2.7m. visitors in 1984; and Sequoia National Park in the Sierra Nevada, which had 980,000 visitors in the same year. State parks cover an area of some 1,247,000 acres and were visited by an estimated 69,254,000 tourists in 1986. However, the San Francisco and Los Angeles metropolitan areas provide the major tourist attractions of the state. The Golden Gate National Recreation Area, consisting of 68 square miles on both sides of the entrance to San Francisco Bay, drew 16.7m. visitors in 1984. Principal attractions are the Disneyland amusement centre at Anaheim, and Hollywood, which offers visits to film and television studios and tours of film stars' homes in Beverly Hills.

Office of Tourism: Dept of Commerce, 1121 L St, Suite 600, Sacramento, CA 95814; tel. (916) 445-3962.

San Diego Convention and Visitors Bureau: 12300 3rd Ave, Suite 824, CA 92101; tel. (916) 232-3101.

Colorado

Colorado contains two national parks, Rocky Mountain, which comprises 263,791 acres in the Front Range, and Mesa Verde, 52,085 acres in the south-west. State parks encompass an area of some 328,000 acres and attracted an estimated 7,737,000 tourists in 1986. Colorado offers excellent facilities for skiing, with 40 ski areas, of which the most popular is the Vail resort centre, followed by Keystone and Steamboat. Apart from skiing the state's leading attraction is the US Air Force Academy, near Colorado Springs. Sites of major historical interest include the fossil beds at Dinosaur National Monument, Indian cliff dwellings at Mesa Verde, Black Canyon of the Gunnison and Colorado National Monument.

Board of Tourism: 1625 Broadway, Suite 1700, Denver, CO 80202; tel. (303) 592-5410.

Denver and Colorado Convention and Visitors Bureau: 225 West Colfax Ave, Denver, CO 80202; tel. (303) 892-1112.

National Park Service: POB 25287, Denver, CO 80255-0287; tel. (303) 236-4648.

State Parks and Recreation: 1313 Sherman St, Suite 618, Denver, CO 80203; tel. (303) 866-3437.

Connecticut

Connecticut's lakes and its seashore recreation areas are an important factor in drawing tourists to the state, including such attractions as the Mystic Seaport restoration, with its aquarium, and Hammonasset beach. The most important aquatic event is the Harvard–Yale regatta, which is held each June on the Thames River in New London. Golf courses, boat-launching sites and ski areas number among the other sporting facilities. The 117 state parks and forests cover an area of 181,000 acres, and were visited by an estimated 6,737,000 tourists in 1986. The Mark Twain Mansion and Harriet Beecher Stowe House in Hartford, and the American Clock and Watch Museum in Bristol, are also principal tourist attractions.

Division of Tourism: Dept of Economic Development, 210 Washington St, Hartford, CT 06106; tel. (203) 566-5061.

Forest and Parks Association: POB 389, East Hartford, CT 06108.

Delaware

Rehoboth Beach on the Atlantic Coast is a famous holiday destination in Delaware, especially popular among federal officials and foreign diplomats. Delaware's annual festivities include Easter services, and Delaware Day ceremonies, which commemorate the state's ratification of the constitution. The main tourist pastimes are fishing, clamming, crabbing, boating and swimming; 17,552 fishing licences were issued in 1982/83. State parks cover some 11,080 acres and attracted an estimated 3,499,000 tourists in 1986. The most notable are the Fenwick Island and Trapp Pond state parks.

Division of Fish and Wildlife: William Penn St, Dover, DE 19901.

State Visitors Service: 630 State College Rd, Dover, DE 19901; tel. (800) 282-8667.

Tourism Office: c/o Delaware Development Office, 99 Kings Highway, POB 1401, Dover, DE 19903; tel. (302) 736-4271; Dir Catherine Wheeler.

District of Columbia

The District of Columbia is one of the world's chief tourist destinations, attracting 17.2m. visitors in 1980. The federal capital offers an abundance of historical and cultural attractions, including the Washington Monument and the White House, Supreme Court, Library of Congress and US Capitol buildings. The leading attraction, however, is the Smithsonian Air and Space Museum, which received 14.4m. visitors in 1983. The Museum of Natural History drew 6.1m. tourists in that year and the Museum of American History 5.4m. National park service areas were visited by 28.8m. tourists in 1984, of which Rock Creek Park received 14.1m., the Vietnam Veterans' Memorial 2.3m. and the Lincoln Memorial 3m.

Travelers Aid: 1015 12th St, NW, Washington, DC 20004; tel. (202) 347-0101.

Visitor Information Center: 1455 Pennsylvania Ave, NW, Washington, DC 20004; tel. (202) 789-7000.

Florida

Florida's beaches are an important asset to its tourist industry, attracting millions of visitors each year. Other major attractions are Walt Disney World, a large amusement park in Orlando, the Kennedy Space Center at Cape Canaveral and the St Augustine historic district. National park service areas were visited by an estimated 6,565,700 tourists in 1983. Most popular were Gulf Islands National Seashore, near Pensacola, which had 4,060,400 visitors, and Canaveral National Seashore, with 1,075,000 visitors. The 28 state parks covered a total area of 272,000 acres and attracted 13,659,000 tourists in 1986. Together with 28 state recreation areas and 18 historical sites, they are part of the wide range of facilities operated by the state's Department of Natural Resources. Outdoor recreational activities for tourists include fishing and boating; in 1983/84 499,364 pleasure craft were registered in the state.

Division of Recreation and Parks: Dept of Natural Resources, 3900 Commonwealth Blvd, Suite 613, Tallahassee, FL 32303; tel. (904) 488-7326.

Division of Tourism: Dept of Commerce, Collins Bldg, Suite 510c, Tallahassee, FL 32301; tel. (904) 488-3104.

US Forest Service: 227 North Bruro St, POB 1050, Tallahassee, FL 32302; tel. (904) 681-7265.

Georgia

The state of Georgia offers two national forests, six national parks and approximately 60 state parks and historic areas. The state parks cover an area of some 61,000 acres and attracted an estimated 12,806,000 tourists in 1986. Other important tourist sites include Stone Mountain near Atlanta, the Okefenokee Swamp in southern Georgia, and the Golden Isles. Georgia is particularly attractive to hunters; in 1982/83 674,641 hunting licences were issued.

Department of Natural Resources: 270 Washington St, SW, Atlanta, GA 30334; tel. (800) 542-7275.

Division of Tourism: Dept of Industry and Trade, 230 Peachtree St, NW, POB 1776, Atlanta, GA 30301; tel. (404) 656-3556.

US Forest Service: 1720 Peachtree St, NW, Atlanta, GA 30309; tel. (404) 347-2385.

Hawaii

Hawaii contains a wide range of recreational facilities, including, in 1983, seven national parks and historic sites, 74 state parks and

626 county parks. In 1986 state parks covered some 25,000 acres and were visited by an estimated 15,256,000 tourists. The national parks of Haleakale (on Kauai) and Hawaii Volcanoes (on Hawaii) are among the major tourist attractions. The island also offers opportunities for activities such as scuba diving, snorkelling, swimming, fishing and sailing. In addition the state provides 57 golf courses and 1,600 recognized surfing sites.

Department of Land and Natural Resources: 1151 Punchbowl St, Honolulu, HI 96813; tel. (808) 548-7455.

Department of Parks and Recreation: 650 South King St, Honolulu, HI 96817; tel. (808) 523-4525.

National Park Services: Prince Kuhio Federal Bldg, Suite 6305, 300 Ala Moana Blvd, Honolulu, HI 96813; tel. (808) 541-2693.

Office of Tourism: Dept of Planning and Economic Development, POB 2359, Honolulu, HI 96804; tel. (808) 548-6914.

Idaho

The state of Idaho is popular for its wide variety of outdoor recreational facilities, offering such pastimes as skiing, hunting, camping, fishing and hiking. During 1982/83, 249,928 hunting licences and 425,717 fishing licences were issued. The greatest of the state's 24 ski resorts is Sun Valley, a year-round resort in the Sawtooth Mountains. The state also contains two national parks: the Craters of the Moon National Monument and the Nez Percé National Historical Park, while other tourist attractions include the Hell's Canyon and Sawtooth national recreational areas. In 1986 state parks covered an area of some 93,000 acres and were visited by an estimated 2,297,000 tourists.

Division of Tourism: Dept of Commerce, 700 West State St, Boise, ID 83720; tel. (208) 334-2470.

Parks and Recreation Department: 2177 Warm Springs Ave, Boise, ID 83720; tel. (208) 334-2154.

Illinois

In 1984 Illinois had a total of 42 state parks, four state forests, 36,659 campsites and 25 state recreation areas, which include the Lincoln Home National Historic Site in Springfield. State parks comprise some 335,000 acres, and attracted an estimated 32,407,000 visitors in 1986. The city of Chicago is a popular tourist destination, with the world's tallest building, the Sears Tower, figuring among its attractions. In addition, the state offers opportunities for swimming, bicycling, hiking, riding, fishing, hunting and wildlife observation; in 1982/83 licences were issued to 764,377 fishermen and 329,240 hunters.

Division of Tourism: Dept of Commerce and Community Affairs, 620 East Adams St, Springfield, IL 62701; tel. (217) 782-3233.

Travel Center: 310 South Michigan Ave, Chicago, IL 60604; tel. (312) 793-4732.

Indiana

There are 18 state parks in Indiana, encompassing 54,000 acres and attracting an estimated 9,119,000 visitors in 1986. The most notable state park is Brown County near Nashville. The state also contains 15 fish and wildlife refuges, which comprise 75,200 acres and include Pigeon River, near Howe, and Willow Slough at Morocco. Other natural attractions are the Indiana Dunes National Lakeshore on Lake Michigan, and Cataract Falls near Cloverdale. The reconstructed village of New Harmony, the Indianapolis Motor Speedway and Museum, and the George Rogers Clark National Historic Park, at Vincennes, are also popular with tourists. Hunting is a favourite outdoor pastime; in 1982/83 655,801 anglers and 338,994 hunters were issued with licences.

Division of State Parks: 616 State Office Bldg, Indianapolis, IN 46204.

Division of Tourism Development: 1 North Capitol St, Suite 700, Indianapolis, IN 46204-2248; tel. (317) 232-8800.

Iowa

Iowa contains some 85,000 acres of lakes and reservoirs, and 19,000 miles of fishing streams. These, together with the state's two main rivers, the Mississippi and the Missouri, provide excellent facilities for water sports, while the Switzerland Range in the north-east is well suited to hiking and camping. Other major tourist attractions include the Effigy Mounds National Monument, near Marquette, and the Buffalo Ranch at Fayette. The State Capitol Building in Des Moines and the Herbert Hoover National Historic Site also draw thousands of visitors each year. There are more than 60 state parks, which in 1986 covered an area of some 83,000 acres and attracted 14,223,000 people. In total the state's recreational areas were paid 14,829,000 visits in 1984.

Tourism and Visitors' Bureau: Economic Development Dept, 200 East Grand Ave, Des Moines, IA 50319; tel. (515) 281-3100; Sec. DAVID REYNOLDS.

Kansas

Among its attractions Kansas boasts 22 state parks, 24 federal reservoirs, 48 state fishing lakes, over 100 campsites, and more than 304,000 acres of public hunting and game management lands. The state parks alone total 37,000 acres and were visited by 4,220,000 tourists in 1986. The state also contains two national historic sites, Fort Larned and Fort Scott, which are 19th-century army bases on the Indian frontier. Topeka is a popular tourist site, offering such attractions as the state historical museum and the Menninger Foundation. The state also features two frontier-town reproductions, Historic Wichita Cowtown, and Old Front Street in Dodge City.

Kansas Park and Resources Authority: 503 Kansas Ave, 6th Floor, Topeka, KS 66603; tel. (913) 296-2281.

Tourism Division: Commerce Dept, 400 8th St, SW, Topeka, KS 66603; tel. (913) 296-2009.

Kentucky

As of 1985 Kentucky operated 15 resort parks, 19 recreational parks and nine shrines. These include Breaks Interstate Park on the Kentucky border, which features the Russell Fork River Canyon. State parks cover an area of 43,000 acres and attracted 23,492,000 tourists in 1986. Kentucky's leading tourist attraction is Mammoth Cave National Park in the Pennyroyal region, containing a vast network of underground passages. The national park system also boasts a re-creation of Abraham Lincoln's birthplace in Hodgenville, and Cumberland Gap National Historical Park.

Department of Parks: Capitol Plaza Tower, Frankfort, KY 40601.

Tourism Cabinet: Capitol Plaza Tower, 24th Floor, Frankfort, KY 40601; tel. (502) 564-4270; Sec. MARY RAY OAKEN.

Louisiana

The lively city of New Orleans is a principal tourist destination in the USA, offering excellent seafood restaurants, jazz clubs, the French Quarter, the Superdome and Preservation Hall. Visitors are attracted by lavish annual festivities, notably Mardi Gras, commencing on the Wednesday before Shrove Tuesday. Other spectacular events include the blessing of the shrimp fleet at the Louisiana Shrimp and Petroleum Festival on Labor Day weekend, and the blessing of the cane fields during the Louisiana Sugar Cane Festival in September. Another popular attraction is the Jean Lafitte National Park, visited by 849,004 tourists in 1984. Louisiana's state parks comprised 38,000 acres and attracted 1,100,000 visitors in 1986.

Department of Culture, Recreation and Tourism: POB 44291, Baton Rouge, LA 70804; tel. (504) 925-3853.

New Orleans/Louisiana Tourist Center: 527 St Ann St, New Orleans, LA 70116; tel. (504) 568-5661.

Office of State Parks: POB 1111, Baton Rouge, LA 70821.

Maine

The state of Maine provides an all-year destination for tourists, who are attracted by the state's sandy beaches, lakes and rivers. Sailing, fishing and boating are the main outdoor activities, while the Allagash Wilderness Waterway in northern Maine is popular for canoeing. In winter the state offers around 60 areas for cross-country skiing. Maine is also a favourite site for hunters; in 1982/83 241,733 hunting licences and 279,648 fishing licences were issued. State parks comprise some 72,000 acres and were visited by an estimated 2,638,000 tourists in 1986. They include Baxter State Park in central Maine, which contains Mount Katahdino. Acadia National Park, totalling 41,000 acres, is also popular; it received an estimated 4.1m. visitors in 1986.

Bureau of Parks and Recreation: State Office Bldg, Augusta, ME 04333; tel. (207) 289-3821.

Division of Tourism: Office of the Governor, State House, Station 1, Augusta, ME 04333; tel. (207) 289-3531.

Forest Service: Bureau of Forestry, Ray Bldg, Augusta, ME 04333; tel. (207) 289-2791.
Publicity Bureau: 97 Winthrop St, Hallowell, ME 04347; tel. (207) 289-2423.

Maryland

Maryland received a total of 4,758,894 visitors in 1984. Among its attractions are 10 recreation areas and 15 state parks; the latter total 270,000 acres and drew 6,777,000 visitors in 1986. Popular destinations include Annapolis, the state capital, which contains the US Naval Academy and the State House, built in 1772. The city of Baltimore features such attractions as Edgar Allan Poe House, Fort McHenry, and the Inner Harbor. Ocean City is the state's leading seaside resort, while many other resort towns are located in Chesapeake Bay.
Forest and Parks Service: Tawes State Office Bldg, Annapolis, MD 21404; tel. (301) 269-3776.
Office of Promotion and Tourism: Brokerage Bldg, 34 Market-place, Suite 310, Baltimore, MD 21202; tel. (301) 837-4636.
Office of Tourist Development: Dept of Econ. and Community Development, 45 Calvert St, Annapolis, MD 21401; tel. (301) 974-2686.

Massachusetts

Massachusetts is a major summer resort destination; its beaches and seashores attracted 11,462,167 visitors in 1984. The most popular site for tourists is Barnstable County (Cape Cod); the Cape Cod National Seashore received 4,560,713 visitors in 1984. Together with Nantucket and Martha's Vineyard, it offers beaches, fishing and attractive villages. The state capital of Boston is next in popularity, with such attractions as Bunker Hill Monument, Faneuil Hall and Old North Church. The Berkshire Hills are the site of summer festivities, including the Berkshire Music Festival at Tanglewood. Salem in Essex County holds Nathaniel Hawthorne's House of Seven Gables, while Middlesex County and Bristol County also have features of interest. Massachusetts contains about 130 state-owned camping areas; state parks comprise 265,000 acres and attracted 11,740,000 visitors in 1986.
Division of Tourism: Dept of Commerce and Development, 100 Cambridge St, Boston, MA 02202; tel. (617) 727-3201.
National Historic Park Tourist Bureau: 15 State St, Boston, MA 02109; tel. (617) 242-5642.

Michigan

The state of Michigan features thousands of inland lakes and streams, which present ample opportunity for swimming and sunbathing. Most famous is the Metropolitan Beach on Lake St Clair, reputedly the largest artificial lake beach in the world. In addition to summer pastimes, ice-fishing, skiing, autumn scenic tours and spring festivals attract visitors during the rest of the year. Camping is also becoming increasingly popular, with the federal government operating extensive camping facilities. 201,179 campers visited state forest campsites in 1983. Other attractions include 89 parks and recreational areas, comprising some 248,000 acres. State parks encompass an area of 251,000 acres and received 22,728,000 visitors in 1986. Among the most popular are Holland and Warren Dunes state parks on Lake Michigan.
Department of Natural Resources: Information Services Center, Steven T. Mason Bldg, POB 30028, Lansing, MI 48909; tel. (517) 373-1220.
Travel Bureau: 333 South Capitol, POB 30226, Lansing, MI 48909; tel. (517) 373-0670; Dir JOHN SAVICH.

Minnesota

Minnesota offers a diversity of outdoor recreational facilities and sites of cultural and historical interest. Principal attractions are Voyagers National Park, totalling 220,000 acres near the Canadian border, and Grand Portage National Monument, a former fur-trading centre in Arrowhead country. Minnesota's attractive waterways are popular for boating, while winter sports, such as snowmobiling and cross-country skiing, also have a substantial following. The state operates about 60 parks (including extensive winter-sports areas), which cover some 3,236,000 acres and attracted an estimated 4,406,000 visitors in 1986. The state also provides 18 canoeing and boating routes, five recreation areas and 288 wildlife refuges.

Division of Tourism: Dept of Energy and Economic Development, 1150 East Kellog Blvd, 9th Floor, St Paul, MN 55101; tel. (612) 296-6424.
Minnesota Tourist Information Center: 240 Bremer Bldg, 419 North Robert St, St Paul, MN 55101; tel. (800) 328-1461.

Mississippi

About 9m. people visited Mississippi in 1984. Popular attractions include the state's mansions and plantations, notably McRaven in Vicksburg, and the Delta and Pine Land Company plantation near Scott, one of the largest in the USA. The annual State Fair is held in Jackson during the second week in October. There are five national parks in the state, including Natchez Trace Parkway, Gulf Islands National Seashore, and Vicksburg National Military Park, which together received 13,056,167 visitors in 1983. The 27 state parks cover an area of some 21,000 acres and attracted 4,691,000 tourists in 1986.
Bureau of Parks and Recreation: POB 10600, Jackson, MS 39209.
Division of Tourism: Dept of Economic Development, POB 849, Jackson, MS 39205; tel. (601) 359-3449.

Missouri

Missouri holds a wide variety of tourist attractions, the most significant being the Gateway Arch in St Louis, the tallest man-made national monument in the USA. Part of the Jefferson National Expansion Memorial, it received 2,406,953 visitors in 1984. In Kansas City, the Crown Center hotels and shopping plaza and the Truman Sport Complex constitute just a few of the attractions. The boyhood home of author Mark Twain is located in Hannibal, and the Harry Truman library and museum in Independence. Missouri's Lake of the Ozarks is one of the USA's principal tourist destinations. In 1983 Missouri contained 24 historic sites and 47 state parks, with the largest, Lake of the Ozarks State Park, totalling 16,872 acres. The state parks were visited by an estimated 11,759,000 tourists in 1986.
Department of Natural Resources: 1915 Southridge, POB 176, Jefferson City, MO 65102; tel. (314) 751-3443.
Division of Tourism: Dept of Economic Development, Truman Bldg, Rm 290, POB 1055, Jefferson City, MO 65102; tel. (314) 751-3311; Dir MARJORIE BEENDERS.

Montana

In 1983, 2,208,352 tourists visited Montana, drawn by the scenic attractions and by the state's former gold-rush camps and ghost towns. Historical sites include the Big Hole National Battlefield, near Wisdom, and the Custer Battlefield Monument. The most celebrated location is Glacier National Park, which comprises 60 glaciers and 200 lakes and streams, and covers an area of some 1,013,595 acres. The state also contains Bighorn Canyon National Recreation Area, and a section of Yellowstone Park. State parks total 51,000 acres and were visited by 3,975,000 tourists in 1986.
Division of Tourism: Dept of Commerce, 1424 9th Ave, Helena, MT 59620; tel. (406) 444-3494.
Natural Forest Information: Northern Region, Federal Bldg, 5115 Highway 93, Missoula, MT 59801; tel. (406) 329-3511.

Nebraska

The state of Nebraska offers six state parks, nine state historical parks, 12 federal areas and 55 recreational areas. Most frequented are Pawnee State Recreation Area, which had 716,500 visitors in 1983, and Fremont State Recreation Area, with 611,250 visitors. State parks cover an area of some 147,000 acres and were visited by an estimated 8,575,000 tourists in 1986. Fort Robinson and Arbor Lodge state parks are among the most popular. Outdoor activities for tourists include fishing, swimming and sightseeing; in 1982/83, 240,330 fishing licences were issued.
Division of Travel and Tourism: Dept of Economic Development, POB 94666, Lincoln, NE 68509; tel. (402) 471-3794; Dir PEGGY BRIGGS.
Game and Parks Commission: 2200 North 33rd St, Lincoln, NE 68503; tel. (402) 464-0641.

Nevada

Nevada's primary attraction for tourists is the gambling industry; visitors are drawn by casinos and resort facilities at Reno and

Las Vegas. Natural resources include Lake Pyramid, Lake Mead National Recreation Area and Lehman Caves National Monument. State parks encompass an area of some 145,000 acres and attracted an estimated 22,578,000 visitors in 1986.

Commission on Tourism: 110 East Williams St, Suite 117, Carson City, NV 89710; tel. (702) 885-4332; Exec. Dir STEPHEN B. RICHER.

Division of State Parks: Nye Bldg, 201 South Fall, Carson City, NV 89701; tel. (702) 885-4384.

New Hampshire

New Hampshire boasts a wide variety of outdoor facilities: as of 1982, these included 85 trailer parks and camps, 10 public golf courses and 33 alpine ski areas. Of particular interest is Mount Washington, the highest peak in New England, which features a cog railway as well as a motor road and many trails. Other attractions include Lake Winnipesaukee, the White Mountain National Forest, and Strawberry Bank, a restored village in Portsmouth. State parks cover an area of some 29,000 acres and were visited by an estimated 3,866,000 tourists in 1986.

US Forest Service: POB 638, 719 Main St, Laconia, NH 03247; tel. (603) 524-6450.

Vacation Travel Promotion Office: Dept of Resources and Economic Development, 105 Loudon Rd, Prescott Park, Concord, NH 03301; tel. (603) 271-2341.

New Jersey

New Jersey is a popular tourist destination; the Jersey shores became a summer vacation spot at the beginning of the 19th century. Atlantic City has been the most important shore resort since the late 19th century but has suffered a loss in popularity from the 1970s, as other resorts have developed on the east coast and transport systems have improved. However, the opening of 10 casino hotels in 1985 has done much to revive tourism in the resort. The state also provides extensive recreational facilities: 10 ski areas, three national wildlife refuges, including Brigantine Wildlife Refuge, 31 public golf courses and 30 amusement parks, including Great Adventure in central Jersey. The Delaware Gap and Gateway National Recreation Areas are popular for canoeing and camping, while the state's inland lakes offer opportunities for fishing. State parks, which include the Monmouth and Washington Crossing battlefield state parks, cover some 298,000 acres in total and attracted 9,559,000 visitors in 1986.

Division of Tourism: Dept of Commerce and Economic Development, 1 West State St, CN 820, Trenton, NJ 08625; tel. (602) 292-1581.

Visitors' Bureau of Atlantic City: 2310 Pacific Ave, Atlantic City, NJ 08401; tel. (609) 348-7044.

New Mexico

New Mexico's recreational facilities have been developed in order to promote tourism in the state. They consist of a national park, Carlsbad Caverns, 27,840 acres of designated wilderness reserves, and 10 national monuments, including Aztec Ruins, Bandelier, El Morro, Gila Cliff Dwellings, Pecos and Salinas, all of which contain ancient Indian relics. State parks comprise some 119,000 acres and attracted an estimated 6,280,000 visitors in 1986. The main outdoor activities are hunting, fishing, camping, boating and skiing; in 1983 licences were issued to 149,466 hunters and 247,368 anglers.

Department of Economic Development and Tourism: Joseph Montoya Bldg, 1100 St Francis Dr., Santa Fe, NM 87503; tel. (505) 827-0381; Dir JOHN DENDAHL.

Park and Recreation Divison: Villagra Bldg, POB 1147, Santa Fe, NM 87504-1147; tel. (505) 827-7465.

US Forest Service: 517 Gold Ave, SW, Albuquerque, NM 87102; tel. (505) 842-3292.

New York

New York City is the principal tourist destination of the state of the same name, attracting an estimated 17.1m. visitors in 1983. The Statue of Liberty, the Empire State and United Nations Buildings, the Rockefeller Center, Bronx Zoo and Chinatown are just a few of the city's diverse attractions. Long Island is second in popularity, offering beaches and racetracks. Other tourist areas include the Hudson Valley, site of the US Military Academy at West Point; Albany, containing the Empire State Plaza and Feni-

more House; Saratoga Springs and the region of the Adirondacks. Among the state's scenic attractions are the resorts of the Catskills, the Fingerlakes region, featuring Taughannock Falls, and Niagara Falls to the west. As of 1984, the Office of Parks, Recreation and Historic Preservation operated a total of 147 state parks, 74 boat-launching sites, and 34 historic sites. State parks encompass an area of some 256,000 acres and received an estimated 36,920,000 visitors in 1986.

Division of Tourism: Dept of Commerce, Twin Towers, New York, NY 12245; tel. (212) 474-4100.

State Office of Parks and Recreation: Agency Bldg 1, Empire State Plaza, Albany, NY 12238; tel. (212) 474-0456.

North Carolina

North Carolina offers both outdoor recreational facilities, such as golf courses, mountain parks and coastal beaches, and sites of particular historical interest. Attractions include the Revolutionary War battlegrounds at Guildford Courthouse and Moore's Creek, Fort Raleigh National Historic Site, and the Wright Brothers National Memorial at Kitty Hawk. There are nine national parks in North Carolina, which drew 15.7m. visitors in 1984, of which Great Smoky Mountains National Park attracted 3.7m. The 27 state parks cover an area of some 124,000 acres, and were visited by 6,262,000 tourists in 1986.

Department of Natural Resources and Community Development: Division of Parks and Recreation, POB 27687, Raleigh, NC 27611.

Division of Travel and Tourism Development: Dept of Commerce, 430 North Salisbury St, Raleigh, NC 27611; tel. (919) 733-7232.

North Dakota

As of 1982 North Dakota's recreational facilities included 11 trailer parks and camps, five public golf courses and 31 sport and recreation clubs. State parks comprise some 15,000 acres, which were visited by an estimated 850,000 tourists in 1986. The Theodore Roosevelt National Park in the Badlands is a favourite destination, attracting 381,920 tourists in 1984. Another top attraction is the International Peace Garden, north of Dunseith, which commemorates friendly US–Canadian relations. North Dakota is also popular for hunting and fishing; 96,232 hunting licences and 183,261 fishing licences were issued during 1982/83.

Parks and Recreation Department: 1424 West Century Ave, Suite 202, Bismarck, ND 58502; tel. (701) 224-4887.

Travel Division: Economic Development Commission, Liberty Memorial Bldg, Bismarck, ND 58505; tel. (701) 224-2810.

Ohio

Ohio's tourist attractions range from beaches and parks around Lake Erie to ski resorts in the eastern Allegheny region and to numerous memorials and sites of historical interest. Among several memorials to US presidents are the William Henry Harrison Memorial at North Bend, Ulysses S. Grant's birthplace at Point Pleasant and the William McKinley memorial at Canton. Other notable tourist areas include Mound City Group National Monument near Chillicothe, which contains prehistoric burial mounds, and Perry's Victory and International Peace Memorial on South Bass Island. Ohio's 71 state parks total some 193,000 acres and received an estimated 64,560,000 visitors in 1986. Alum Creek, East Harbour and Kelleys Island are among the most popular.

Greater Columbus Convention and Visitors' Bureau: 50 West Broad St, Suite 1600, Columbus, OH 43215; tel. (800) 821-5784.

Office of Travel and Tourism: Dept of Development, 77 South High St, POB 1011, Columbus, OH 43266; tel. (614) 466-3379.

Oklahoma

Oklahoma is becoming increasingly popular as a tourist destination, offering 35 state parks, 22 state recreation areas and 140,696 acres of national wildlife reserves, such as Optima, Salt Plains and Wichita Mountains. State parks, comprising 95,000 acres, were visited by 16,042,000 tourists in 1986. Ohio contains one national park, namely Chickasaw National Recreation Area, which centres on the man-made Lake Arbuckle. Cultural attractions include the American Indian Hall of Fame at Anadarko, the T. B. Ferguson Home in Watonga and several museums.

Chamber of Commerce Tourist Information: 4 Santa Fe Plaza, Oklahoma City, OK 73125; tel. (405) 278-8912.
Department of Tourism and Recreation: 500 Will Rogers Bldg, Oklahoma City, OK 73105; tel. (405) 521-2431; Exec. Dir ABE L. HESSER.

Oregon

Oregon's natural resources are a primary attraction to visitors; scenic areas include unspoiled coasts and the Rogue River, offering opportunities for fishing. 1,661,003 fishing licences were issued in 1983. The National Park Service operates the one national park, Crater Lake, as well as three other areas: John Day Fossil Beds National Monument, Oregon Caves National Monument and Fort Clatsop National Memorial. The state park systems are among the most extensive in the USA, comprising around 225 parks and recreation areas, which encompass some 88,493 acres. State parks received an estimated 36,158,000 visitors in 1986.

Department of Fish and Wildlife: 506 Mill St, SW Portland, OR 97208; tel. (503) 229-5551.
Division of Tourism: Dept of Economic Development, 595 Cottage St, NE, Salem, OR 97310; tel. (503) 373-1270.
State Parks: 525 Trade St, SE, Salem, OR 97310; tel. (503) 378-6305.

Pennsylvania

Pennsylvania played a crucial role in the emergence of an independent USA, and the state's historical sites are among its leading attractions. The Independence National Historical Park in Philadelphia, containing the Liberty Bell, Independence Hall, the US Mint and many other buildings of historical and cultural interest, attracted 5m. visitors in 1986. Valley Forge National Historical Park, just outside Philadelphia, attracted a further 4.2m. recreational visitors. Gettysburg National Military Park marks the site of a famous Civil War battle, and the home of President Dwight D. Eisenhower is in Gettysburg town. Camping, fishing and, in the east of the state, skiing are all popular outdoor pursuits. The Delaware Water Gap National Recreation Area, shared with New Jersey, is becoming a popular destination for these activities and received 2.2m. recreational visitors in 1986. State parks, forests and recreational areas covered 282,000 acres and attracted 38.2m. visitors in 1986.

Bureau of State Parks: POB 1467, Harrisburg, PA 17120; tel. (717) 787-8800.
Travel Development Bureau: c/o Dept of Commerce, Forum Bldg, Rm 416, Harrisburg, PA 17120; tel. (717) 787-3003; Dir JAMES O. PICKARD, Sr.

Rhode Island

Rhode Island's principal tourist attractions include the historic mansions of Newport and Providence, and the earliest synagogue (Touro Synagogue National Historic Site) and Baptist church in the USA. There are about 40 other museums and historic sites in the state. Rhode Island's state parks and recreation areas cover only 9,000 acres, but attracted 4.1m. visitors in 1986. Block Island is a noted holiday resort, and water sports, particularly yachting, are popular.

Division of Tourism: 7 Jackson Walkway, Providence, RI 02903; tel. (401) 277-2601.

South Carolina

The tourist industry of South Carolina is concentrated on Charleston and the Myrtle Beach and Hilton Head Island resorts, all on the Atlantic coast. Charleston is famous for its many historic buildings. At the entrance to Charleston harbour is the Fort Sumter National Monument, marking the place where the Civil War began. The Charleston area also has several botanic gardens. In the north of the state the Cowpens National Battlefield Site and the King's Mountain National Military Park also attract many visitors. There are several areas of national forest. In addition, South Carolina has 40 state parks, covering a total of 79,000 acres and attracting 8.4m. visitors in 1986.

Department of Parks, Recreation and Tourism: 1205 Pendleton St, Suite 248, Columbia, SC 29201; tel. (803) 734-0135; Dir of Div. of Tourism ROBERT G. LIMING.
US Forest Service: POB 970, Columbia, SC 29202; tel. (803) 765-5222.

South Dakota

Most of the major tourist attractions of South Dakota lie towards the western border of the state. A large area is covered by the Black Hills National Forest, popular with hikers and skiers, and Wind Cave National Park, Jewel Cave National Monument and Mount Rushmore National Memorial (where the heads of US presidents Washington, Jefferson, Lincoln and Theodore Roosevelt are carved in the mountainside) are all within or adjacent to the forest boundaries. A little to the east is the Badlands National Park, a desolate area rich in fossil deposits. To the south of the Badlands is Wounded Knee Massacre National Historical Site, commemorating the last major conflict between Indian and US troops. State parks covered 92,000 acres and attracted 5.3m. visitors in 1986.

Department of Tourism: Capitol Lake Plaza, Pierre, SD 57501; tel. (605) 773-3301; Sec. SUSAN EDWARDS.
Division of State Parks and Recreation: Capitol Bldg, Pierre, SD 57501; tel. (605) 773-3391.
US Forest Service: Custer, SD 57730; tel. (605) 673-2551.

Tennessee

Areas designated as parts of the national park system in Tennessee are located near the state's borders, and are all shared with other states. The Great Smoky Mountains National Park (520,000 acres, attracting 9.8m. recreational visitors in 1986) is shared with North Carolina, and the Big South Fork National River and Recreation Area and the Land of the Lakes Recreation Area with Kentucky. The Natchez Trace Parkway (14.4m. recreational visitors in 1986) starts at a point in the centre of Tennessee, and stretches south into Alabama and Mississippi. The state has many lakes, broad meandering rivers and mountain streams, and fishing is a popular outdoor pursuit. There are 18 state parks, covering 133,000 acres and attracting 22.3m. visitors in 1986. Nashville is a famous centre for country-and-western music, housing the Grand Ole Opry, while Gracelands mansion, the home of Elvis Presley, is located in Memphis.

Department of Tourist Development: Rachel Jackson Bldg, 5th Floor, Nashville, TN 37219; tel. (615) 741-1904; Commr SANDRA FULTON.
State Parks Information: 701 Broadway, Nashville, TN 37203; tel. (615) 742-6667.

Texas

The tourist industry of Texas is among the largest of any state in the USA. There are numerous scenic and historical attractions throughout the state. In the west are two national parks, Big Bend (covering 735,000 acres) and Guadelupe Mountains. There are four large national forest areas in eastern Texas. Historical attractions include the sites of two famous battles, the Alamo and San Jacinto. The long Gulf coast is scattered with beaches and wildlife refuges. State parks and recreation areas covered 206,000 acres in 1986 and attracted 20.3m. visitors. Fishing (an estimated 3m. Texans participate in fishing each year) and game hunting are popular outdoor pursuits; rodeos are also numerous and popular. The major Texan cities are themselves major tourist attractions, particularly Dallas, San Antonio, Houston and Fort Worth.

State Parks and Recreation Areas: Austin Headquarters Complex, 4200 Smith School Rd, Austin, TX 78744; tel. (512) 463-4630.
Tourist Development Agency: Capitol Station, POB 12008, Austin, TX 78711; tel. (512) 463-7400; Exec. Dir LARRY TODD.
US Forest Service: POB 130, Lufkin, TX 75901; tel. (409) 831-2246.

Utah

All or part of five national parks, Arches, Bryce Canyon, Canyonlands, Capitol Reef and Zion, are within the boundaries of Utah. In addition, there are the Glen Canyon and Flaming Gorge national recreation areas (the former covering 1.2m. acres and receiving 2.4m. visitors in 1986), six national monuments (including the Dinosaur National Monument) and the Golden Spike National Historical Site. Much of the centre of the state is covered by national forest areas. In the north-west of the state are the Great Salt Lake and the Great Salt Lake Desert. Salt Lake City is the world centre of the Church of Jesus Christ of Latter-day Saints (the Mormons), and the Mormon Temple and Tabernacle attract many visitors. Utah's state parks and recreation areas covered 116,000 acres and attracted 5.3m. visitors in 1986.

Division of Travel Development: c/o Dept of Community and Economic Development, State Office Bldg, Rm 6150, Salt Lake City, UT 84111; tel. (801) 533-5325; Exec. Dir DAVID W. ADAMS.

Parks and Recreation: 1636 West North Temple, Salt Lake City, UT 84116; tel. (801) 538-7220.

Travel Council: 300 North State St, Salt Lake City, UT 84114; tel. (801) 530-1030.

Vermont

Although Vermont's tourist industry is perhaps best known for its winter-sports attractions, almost two-thirds of tourism income is received during the summer months. Both summer and winter outdoor pursuits are focused on the Green Mountains, which stretch the entire length of the state, and much of which are covered by the Green Mountain National Forest Area. There are over 50 skiing areas in the state. Vermont's state parks totalled 171,000 acres, and attracted 819,000 visitors in 1986. Just outside Bennington, in south-west Vermont, are the Bennington Battle Monument, commemorating a victory over the British in 1777, and the Bennington Museum.

Travel Division: c/o Agency of Development and Community Affairs, Pavilion Office Bldg, Montpelier, VT 05602; tel. (802) 828-3211; Sec. ELBERT G. MOULTON.

Virginia

Virginia is particularly rich in historical sites from both the settlement and Civil War periods. Jamestown was the first permanent British settlement, and Yorktown the scene of the British surrender to George Washington. Manassas National Battlefield Park is the site of the Battle of Bull Run, and there is another such park at Richmond. Appomattox Court House National Historical Park marks the site of the Confederate states' surrender in 1865. There are many buildings associated with famous Americans of the 18th and 19th centuries. The spectacular Skyline Drive, a continuation of the Blue Ridge Parkway, passes through the Shenandoah National Park in the west of the state, and affords views of the Appalachian Mountain ranges. In 1986 there were 1.9m. visitors to the national park, which covered 195,000 acres. There are 25 state parks, which received 3.4m. visitors in 1986.

Division of State Parks: State Office Bldg, Suite 1201, Richmond, VA 23219; tel. (804) 226-1981.

State Travel Service: Ninth St Office Bldg, 5th Floor, Richmond, VA 23219; tel. (804) 786-2051; Commr MARSHALL E. MURDAUGH.

Washington

The dramatic and varied scenic beauty of Washington is the state's main tourist attraction. The Olympic National Park (915,000 acres, with 3.5m. visitors in 1986) and the Mount Rainier National Park both contain glacier systems, and Mount Rainier's is the largest among the 48 conterminous states. In addition, there is a third national park, North Cascades, and much of the remainder of the state is covered by national forest areas. Mount St Helens National Volcanic Monument was established in 1982, and covers about 110,000 acres of the area devastated by the volcanic eruption two years earlier. Hunting, particularly of deer, elk and game birds, is a popular outdoor pursuit, and there are several skiing areas in the Cascade Range of mountains. To contrast with these features are the waters and islands of Puget Sound and beaches on the Pacific coast. The Klondike Gold Rush and San Juan Island are national historical parks, and Fort Vancouver and the Whitman Mission are national historic sites. The Seattle Center (Opera House, Pacific Science Center and Space Needle Tower) is a more modern attraction. State parks, covering 249,000 acres, received 47.7m. visitors in 1986.

Forest Service/National Park Service Outdoor Recreation Information Office: 1018 1st Ave, Seattle, WA 98104; tel. (206) 442-0170.

State Parks and Recreation Commission: 7150 Clearwater Lane, KY–11, Olympia, WA 98504; tel. (206) 753-2027.

Tourist Promotion Division: c/o Dept of Commerce and Econ. Development, Gen. Admin. Bldg, Rm 101, AX–13, Olympia, WA 98504; tel. (206) 753-5600; Dir BILL TAYLOR.

West Virginia

There are 34 state parks and nine state forests in West Virginia, covering 206,000 acres and drawing a total of 8.9m. visitors in 1986. Harper's Ferry National Historical Park, marking the site of John Brown's raid on the US Armory in 1859, is among the principal tourist attractions; there are also historic buildings in nearby Charles Town. The New River Gorge National River area, in the south of the state, and the more rugged forested areas in the east of the state are some of the prominent scenic assets. West Virginia has several spa, spring and mountain resorts, and skiing is a popular outdoor pursuit.

Division of Parks and Recreation: 1800 Washington St East, Charleston, WV 15305.

Travel Development Division: c/o Dept of Econ. and Community Development, 1900 Washington St East, Charleston, WV 25305; tel. (304) 348-2286; Man. JOSEPH R. FOWLER.

US Forest Service, Supervisor's Office: Sycamore St, Elkins, WV 26241; tel. (304) 636-1800.

Wisconsin

Wisconsin has more than 8,000 lakes within its boundaries, and areas such as the Apostle Islands National Lakeshore (on Lake Superior) and the St Croix and Lower St Croix National Scenic Riverways are major attractions. Various scenic aspects of the state testify to the effects of glaciation, and are protected in the Ice Age National Scientific Reserve. There are 55 state parks and 10 state forests, covering 119,000 acres, which received a total of 11.1m. visitors in 1986. There are over 5,000 campsites, and fishing, deer- and small-game-hunting are popular outdoor pursuits. There are many museums, historical sites and art galleries in Wisconsin, among the most interesting of which is the Circus World Museum at Baraboo, on the site of the original Ringling Brothers Circus.

Division of Tourism: c/o Dept of Development, POB 7970, Madison, WI 53707; tel. (608) 266-3203; Dir, Econ. and Community Development RAL WEGENKE.

Wyoming

Wyoming has two national parks, Yellowstone (the largest national park in the USA, at 2.2m. acres, which is shared with Idaho and Montana) and Grand Teton. Both have large lakes, and Yellowstone is renowned for its 3,000 geysers and hot springs. There were 4.6m. visitors to the two national parks in 1986, many of whom made overnight stays within the park boundaries. The state also has the Devil's Tower and Fossil Butte national monuments, and the Fort Laramie national historic site. There are also 10 state parks, which received 1.9m. visitors in 1986. Wildlife is a major attraction: the state is noted for its population of elk (particularly in the National Elk Refuge) and grizzly bear (particularly in the Yellowstone National Park), and many kinds of game (mammal, birds and fish) are hunted, trapped and fished. There are various reminders of Wyoming's 'wild west' heritage, such as rodeos (Cheyenne Frontier Days is the largest) and the Buffalo Bill Historical Center in Cody.

Game and Fish Department: 5400 Bishop Blvd, Cheyenne, WY 82002; tel. (307) 777-7735.

Recreation Commission: Cheyenne, WY 82002; tel. (307) 777-7695.

Travel Commission: Norris Travel Center, Cheyenne, WY 82002; tel. (307) 777-7777; Dir GENE BRYAN.

PRINCIPAL NATIONAL PARKS

Acadia National Park: POB 177, Bar Harbor, ME 04609; tel. (207) 288-3338.

Arches National Park: 125 West 200 South, Moab, UT 84532; tel. (801) 259-8161.

Badlands National Park: POB 6, Interior, SD 57750.

Big Bend National Park: TX 79834; tel. (915) 477-2251.

Biscayne National Park: POB 1369, Homestead, FL 33030.

Bryce Canyon National Park: Bryce Canyon, UT 84717; tel. (801) 834-5322.

Canyonlands National Park: 446 South Main St, Moab, UT 84532; tel. (801) 259-7165.

Capitol Reef National Park: Torrey, UT 84775; tel. (801) 425-3791.

Carlsbad Caverns National Park: 3225 National Parks Highway, Carlsbad, NM 88220; tel. (505) 785-2232.

Channel Islands National Park: 1901 Spinnaker Dr., Ventura, CA 93001.

Crater Lake National Park: POB 7, Crater Lake, OR 97604; tel. (503) 594-2211.

Denali National Park: POB 9, McKinley Park Station, AK 99755.

Everglades National Park: POB 279, Homestead, FL 33030; tel. (904) 247-6211.

Gates of the Arctic National Park: POB 74680, Fairbanks, AK 99707.

Glacier Bay National Park: Bartlett Cove, Gustavus, AK 99826; tel. (907) 697-2230.

Glacier National Park: West Glacier, MT 59936.

Grand Canyon National Park: POB 129, Grand Canyon, AZ 86023; tel. (602) 638-7888.

Grand Teton National Park: POB 170, Moose, WY 83012; tel. (307) 733-2820.

Great Basin National Park: Baker, NV 89311.

Great Smoky Mountain National Park: Gatlinburg, TN 37738; tel. (615) 436-1200.

Guadalupe Mountains National Park: 3225 National Parks Highway, Carlsbad, NM 88220; tel. (505) 785-2233.

Haleakala National Park: POB 369, Makawao, Maui, HI 96768; tel. (808) 572-9306.

Hawaii Volcanoes National Park: HI 96718; tel. (808) 967-7311.

Hot Springs National Park: POB 1860, Hot Springs, AR 71902; tel. (501) 624-3383.

Isle Royale National Park: 87 North Ripley St, Houghton, MI 49931.

Katmai National Park: POB 7, King Salmon, AK 99613.

Kenai Fjords National Park: POB 1727, Seward, AK 99664.

Kobuk Valley National Park: POB 287, Kotzebue, AK 99752.

Lake Clark National Park: 701 C St, POB 61, Anchorage, AK 99513.

Lassen Volcanic National Park: Mineral, CA 96063.

Mammoth Cave National Park: Mammoth Cave, KY 42259.

Mesa Verde National Park: CO 81330; tel. (303) 529-4465.

Mount Rainier National Park: Tahoma Woods, Star Route, Ashford, WA 98304.

North Cascades National Park: 800 State St, Sedro Woolley, WA 98284; tel. (206) 856-5700.

Olympic National Park: 600 East Park Ave, Port Angeles, WA 98362; tel. (206) 452-4501.

Petrified Forest National Park: AZ 86028.

Redwood National Park: 1111 Second St, Drawer N, Crescent City, CA 95531; tel. (707) 488-3461.

Rocky Mountain National Park: Estes Park, CO 80517; tel. (303) 586-4431.

Sequoia and Kings Canyon National Parks: Three Rivers, CA 93271; tel. (209) 565-3456.

Shenandoah National Park: Luray, VA 22835.

Theodore Roosevelt National Memorial Park: POB 7, Medora, ND 58645; tel. (701) 623-4466.

Voyageurs National Park: US-53, International Falls, MN 56649.

Wind Cave National Park: Hot Springs, SD 57747; tel. (605) 745-4600.

Wrangell–St Elias National Park: POB 29, Glennallen, AK 99588.

Yellowstone National Park: WY 82190; tel. (307) 344-7381.

Yosemite National Park: POB 577, Yosemite National Park, CA 95389; tel. (209) 372-0265.

Zion National Park: Springdale, UT 84767; tel. (801) 722-3256.

THE USA AND CANADA

ESSAYS

US–CANADIAN RELATIONS

GEOGRAPHICAL AND ECONOMIC ISSUES

JOHN F. DAVIS

Introduction

Addressing the Canadian parliament in March 1962, US President John F. Kennedy chose the following words to summarize the two countries' relationship: 'Geography has made us neighbors, history has made us friends, economics has made us partners and necessity has made us allies.' Somewhat earlier, in 1911, President William Taft is credited with originating the phrase 'special relationship' in description of the state of affairs that exists between the two countries. While Kennedy's words provide a rather more precise interpretation of the nature of US–Canadian relations, it is apparent that no single sentence can possibly cover all nuances of this relationship, nor can it give any indication of the problems and stresses that close proximity has brought with it.

The international boundary between Canada and the USA (excluding Alaska), stretching for 3,987 miles (6,416 km) is the longest undefended boundary in the world and is often marked by what appears to be little more than a farm fence. Across this boundary US citizens make more than 34m. trips annually, while Canadian cross-border visits total more than 36m. While it is mainly a land boundary, there is a major section which runs through the Great Lakes and also along the St Clair and St Lawrence Rivers. The fact that the two countries share such waterways undoubtedly aided the formalization of efforts to regularize cross-border relations: for example, it was as a result of the Boundary Waters Treaty of 1909 that the International Joint Commission (IJC) was established. This, which comprises three commissioners from each country, has jurisdiction over transboundary water issues, including questions of navigation, water depth and pollution. Its function is principally to alert both governments of problems in boundary areas and to make recommendations for implementation. Since its foundation the IJC's workload has been concerned to an increasing extent with environmental issues and in particular with pollution, both water- and air-related: indeed, one of its early 'successes' was with regard to the so-called 'Trail Smelter dispute' of 1938, as a result of which the Canadian government paid US $350,000 compensation to the state of Washington in recompense for pollution damage.

In terms of land area, the two countries are virtually identical in size, with the USA comprising 3,539,286 sq miles (9,166,759 sq km) and Canada 3,558,078 sq miles (9,215,430 sq km). However, the USA's population is some nine times as great—243.2m. at 1 July 1987, compared with Canada's 25.6m. at 1 June of the same year. This has obvious implications for both economies of scale and market potential, as the USA, with a much larger domestic market, can invest in larger production runs which frequently result in lower unit costs than do smaller runs. Another important point is that while about 30% of the US population lives within 250 miles (400 km) of the common border, about 90% of Canadians do so. Thus the vast majority of the Canadian market is within easy reach of both the US–Canadian border and the major US producing areas.

In some ways both countries are similar; both are well endowed with mineral, forest and water resources and agricultural land, though the USA, because of its more southerly location, has had the opportunity to develop a wider range of crops and fruits. It also has less land in total which is naturally unsuitable for agriculture. At the same time, the voracious appetite of the US economy for raw-material resources means that it has outgrown its own supplies in many cases and looks elsewhere to make up the deficit. Canada, with its close proximity, easy accessibility, stable economy and extensive range of resources, is an attractive proposition as a source of much of what the US economy needs, whether it is wood pulp and paper, metallic ores, natural gas, electricity, potash or uranium. At the same time, Canada looks to US sources, not only for a range of food products that it cannot produce itself, but also for coking coal (in the east) and, especially in the past, petroleum.

Due to the great latitudinal extent of these two countries, and the fact that the location of regional concentrations of manufacturing activities in each does not always correspond to the location of natural resources, there are a number of examples of reciprocal imports and exports of the same product. Thus, for example, US coal is imported into Ontario and other eastern provinces of Canada, while Canada exports some of its western coal to the USA. Natural gas and oil are also imported and exported between the two countries, as is electricity (although in this case Canada exports about 12 times as much as the USA). Much of the US import of electricity is from Québec into the state of New York and the New England region, while Ontario exports mainly to Michigan. Such transborder movements help to ensure a more efficient provision of electricity, reducing risks of disruption due to breakdown or overload: exports also help to make some power-generation developments more possible. For example, a hydroelectric power development on the south-eastern shore of James Bay, which would have produced far more power than was needed locally, has become economically feasible due to the export potential. During the 1980s, as the amount of electricity generated in Canada from thermal and nuclear sources has increased, the argument has arisen from some quarters that the USA, in providing a ready market for this electricity, is 'exporting' problems of pollution from coal- and nuclear-fired stations to Canada.

Economic Relations

INVESTMENT

A significant number of Canadian resource-development companies and a number of major Canadian manufacturing concerns are partially or totally US-owned. Many have the status of branch plants of US 'parents' (and so are particularly vulnerable to changes in either country's economic climate), while it is argued that some have a 'colonial status'—that is, they produce raw materials which are subsequently shipped to the USA, where they are processed (and most of the value is added) before, perhaps, being shipped back again. US ownership is especially predominant in the Canadian automotive, chemical, electrical-products, oil and gas industries and, in the late 1980s, accounted for about 80% of all foreign ownership of Canadian manufacturing companies, while the UK accounted for the second-largest proportion (about 12%). However, the relative importance of the USA has been declining slowly in recent years as that of other countries, particularly Japan, has increased.

During the late 1970s and early 1980s there was a marked increase in Canadian penetration of the US market, so that in 1986 Canada ranked fourth behind the UK, the Netherlands and Japan in terms of foreign ownership of US assets. In the late 1980s, for example, the Canadian company Northern Telecom had about as many employees in the USA as it did in Canada; several major Canadian forestry companies had established businesses in the USA, and one of the largest US sugar refiners was Canadian-owned. Canadian companies account for the greatest proportion of employment among foreign-owned companies in 16 of the 50 states of the USA—principally in the northern half of the country—and in 1985 the Canadian Federation of Independent Business found that about one in five of its medium-sized businesses had at least one branch in the USA. Again, however, the relative share of Canadian investment in the US economy is set to decrease as competition mounts from other investor nations.

In general, Canadian businesses locating in the USA tend to favour the states lying along and just south of the common border, for obvious reasons of proximity: there is also a significant Canadian presence in those south-eastern states where mining is important, thus reflecting the concentration of Canadian investment resources in mining and in the chemicals and forest-products industries. US companies investing in Canada have also tended to favour locations where resources are being developed—including the Prairie provinces of Alberta, Manitoba and Saskatchewan for oil, natural gas and chemicals, and Labrador and Québec for iron ore—as well as having major holdings in a wide range of manufacturing concerns, particularly in Ontario, the principal manufacturing province. Ontario accounts for more than 90% of Canadian automotive-related production, mainly carried out by Canadian-based factories of the principal US companies. However, as a result of the Automotive Products Agreement of 1965, the proportion of Canadian-made components in 'American'-manufactured cars in the USA has increased at a greater rate than production of these cars, and currently about 80% of Canadian production is exported—in large part to the USA.

A significant proportion of cross-border investment is made in land. While much of this is purchased in bulk by companies for development purposes, some takes the form of much smaller pieces of property. As personal mobility has increased, so has the number of second and 'recreation' homes purchased within accessible distances of major population concentrations. Appreciable numbers of properties in the Canadian Maritime Provinces are being purchased by US residents (particularly in Nova Scotia), as in lakeside Ontario (including Manitoulin Island) and in British Columbia, while significant numbers of Canadians own land and homes in the USA, particularly in states such as Arizona and Florida which are sunny and warm all year round. It is estimated that up to 1m. Canadians visit Florida each winter.

TRADE

In 1987 bilateral trade between the USA and Canada was valued at US $157,940m. (C $184,291m.). The two countries have the greatest amount of reciprocal trade of any two nations in the world, and each is the other's principal customer and source of imports. In 1988 the USA took 73% of Canada's exports and provided 66% of its imports, while Canada took 23% of US exports and supplied 19% of imports. About 55% of Canadian food, drink and tobacco exports, for example, are supplied by the USA, and one-quarter of Canadian exports of the same commodities are purchased by the USA. In 1983 some 68% of all Canadian pulp and paper exports were to the USA, which obtained most of its total import of these products from Canada.

Both countries are major world producers and exporters of primary products, such as coal and wheat, and therefore meet as competitors in the international market-place. While most countries give some government support to their farmers, controversy has arisen from time to time between Canada and the USA as to whether or not one is subsidizing exports of farm products to the detriment of the other. It is exceedingly difficult to reach an unbiased conclusion as to who is right in such cases. (In fact both countries offer their farmers direct and indirect financial support of various types.)

Due to their close trading links, each country is susceptible to and influenced by the economic health of the other. In some ways there is no one view of Canadian–US relations, even at a given moment in time. This is not so much a result of national political views, but rather of sectional or regional ones. Thus an Albertan or Saskatchewan may view US relations very differently from an Ontarian or a Nova Scotian, and in reverse, a New Yorker sees things from a very different perspective from a resident of the West Coast or the Great Plains. Different regions have different resource bases, different needs and different markets, and are placed in different spatial relationships, both with their own national markets and with those of their neighbours. Thus one part of the country may want freer trade, while another seeks more protection for industries, and indeed one group in a region will probably have a different view from another interest group in the same region.

Recently the question of free trade between the two countries has come to the top of the political agenda. Some decades ago, in 1911, the Reciprocity Agreement, partly initiated by the pro-Canada President Taft, passed both Houses of Congress but failed in the Canadian Parliament. In 1987 President Reagan and Prime Minister Mulroney signed a Free-Trade Agreement which, having been ratified by both Congress and the Canadian Parliament, came into effect on 1 January 1989 and will, by 1999, eliminate tariffs and other barriers in what is, in effect, the world's biggest trading partnership. Those in favour see it as a means of creating many additional jobs on both sides of the border by expanding access to each other's markets; the opponents fear that it could herald the decline of many industries as they face competition from larger units across the borders; while still others fear a possible loss of sovereignty over resources, such as petrocarbons or water.

Transport Co-operation

RAILWAYS

The Canadian–US border is said to be the most-used international boundary in the world, with over 70m. crossings each year. Not only are large population concentrations to be found close to the border on either side, but the transport systems of the two countries have a large degree of compatibility, which eases cross-border movement. Both countries use standard gauge for their railways, and their motorists drive on the right-hand side of the road. Railways cross the border at a number of points across the width of the continent and there are several different through passenger routes; indeed, the line linking Montréal to Saint John, New Brunswick runs across the state of Maine, this being a much more practicable option than the very much longer 'all-Canadian' route through north-eastern Québec. In the 19th century the Canadians made a conscious decision not to build branch lines to join the US railways, but to concentrate instead on building Canadian transcontinental lines. It is widely anticipated, however, that the gradual introduction of free trade from 1989 will result in Canadian railway companies having to reduce costs in order to become more competitive—thereby, perhaps, abandoning significant mileage of branch lines and reducing staff. Due to Canada's size and population distribution, Canadian manufacturers have to ship their products some 55% further, on average, than their US counterparts—539 miles (868 km) compared with 348 miles (560 km), according to a Toronto *Globe and Mail* article of November 1988.

A number of cross-border traffic agreements exist between US and Canadian railway companies. For example, Grand Trunk, a subsidiary of Canadian National Railways, originally only had some 60 miles (97 km) of track in the USA, but now has a route mileage in excess of 2,000 (3,220 km), including the Central Vermont Railway, and has an agreement with the Burlington Northern Railroad Company for exchanging car loadings, soliciting traffic jointly and offering joint rates.

SHIPPING

The development of the 'land bridge' concept, whereby traffic in containers enters a port on one side of the continent from overseas and is then transported by rail to the other side before being reloaded onto ships for a further ocean journey, has led to significant increases both in inter-railroad co-operation and in the movement of containers through each country's ports. Selection of port is affected by services offered, reliability, labour issues, port charges and proximity to the final market. (It may be noted that the port of Halifax, Nova Scotia, is about 550 miles (885 km) closer to the western shores of Europe than is any other major North American port.) Transborder container traffic has increased considerably as a result of these developments. In 1976 50,000 US containers entered the continent through Canadian ports and 83,000 Canadian containers via US ports; by 1985 the respective totals were 140,000 and 110,000.

The development of the Great Lakes system and the St Lawrence Seaway, which was opened to commercial traffic in April 1959 and is jointly administered by Canada and the USA, has been a major area of transport co-operation. With so much of both countries' manufacturing industry located around or along the Great Lakes–St Lawrence system, the smooth operation of the waterways for transport has been in both countries' mutual interest. Nevertheless, there have been occasional problems: while it is relatively easy to reach agreement over opening and closing dates for the navigation season and over navigation aids, it is less easy to develop freedom of entry for all carriers to all ports. In order to safeguard its merchant marine, the USA has long insisted that coastal traffic between US ports must be carried in US ships.

Over the years the pattern of Great Lakes trade has changed in terms of both products carried and direction, with one of the most significant trends being the decline of westward coal movements to Lake Superior. This has resulted partly from a reduced demand for coal from manufacturing industry and partly from the increase in exploitation of low-sulphur western coal reserves in response to environmental demands, which has increased the volume of eastward movements from Lake Superior. In addition, the trend towards bulk cargoes and the development of containerization have made the Great Lakes–St Lawrence system less attractive for foreign general cargo. Not only is the seaway system too small to take modern container ships and bulk carriers, but the time taken to get into the Lakes from the sea and back to the sea makes the route unattractive. Nevertheless, the system remains the major Canadian waterway, given that the country lacks a river system comparable to the Mississippi, which serves a vast area of the USA.

PIPELINES

Pipelines are not only used to link markets for oil and gas in one country with sources in another, but also have been laid down through the USA to carry crude oil from the producing regions of western Canada to the refineries of Ontario. Indeed, a major routeway for western Canadian gas and oil to eastern Canadian markets has been through the Midwestern states of the USA, with offshoots being constructed to serve US markets. Discussions have been reopened in the late 1980s concerning the economic feasibility and environmental desirability of constructing pipelines to carry natural gas from Alaska and from the Mackenzie Delta in the Northwest Territories southwards through Alberta and on to the US markets. This scheme would involve some 2,110 miles (3,400 km) of pipeline to carry gas down to the 48 conterminous states.

TRUCKING

During the 1980s a number of major US trucking lines have entered the Canadian market for the first time by offering non-stop delivery to the USA from Canada: there are, however, indications that elements of the various transport-deregulation processes occurring in Canada in the late 1980s will enable Canadian companies to respond to this competition. With the implementation of the Free-Trade Agreement, transborder trucking should become easier, but its effects on some companies on both sides of the border may well not be beneficial and there could be several company failures.

AIR TRANSPORT

The deregulation of the airline industry in the USA from 1978 resulted in a number of US companies adding Canadian points to their feeder lines: the concern has arisen that this could divert further traffic south of the border. Fare structures in the two countries have sometimes meant that it could be cheaper for a Canadian to fly east–west in the USA rather than in Canada. Overall, while freer movement between the two countries could bring benefits to both, there is some fear that Canadian traffic movements could become spokes in the bigger North American, or rather US, transport hub.

Water Resources

Much of the international border is man-made rather than physical, and consequently the border frequently ignores variations in terrain, cutting across mountain barriers and rivers, and through lakes. This inevitably brings about potential complications and conflicts, many of which come under the jurisdiction of the IJC (see above). Complexities upon which the commission has been called to adjudicate in the 1980s extend much further than the questions of freedom of navigation and related matters with which it was initially concerned, and, as mentioned above, it is pollution issues which have become particularly important. Water is seldom static, and thus pollution occurring in one place may be transported downstream. The behaviour of 'upstream' waterside activites are thus of deep concern to 'downstream' communities. In Lake Erie, for example, pollution originating on the south (US) bank may also affect the north (Canadian) shore. In addition, the development of hydroelectric power-plant and irrigation schemes which necessitate the construction of dams and reservoirs in one country can have effects on the other, not only from the point of view of diminishing the flow of water downstream, but also because of the potential for flooding valley floors with dam construction (as in southern British Columbia) or the damage to water quality caused by the influx of chemicals (from fertilizers and fungicides) used in irrigation schemes. Thus it can be seen that both countries have seen the need to question the effects of developments across the border.

In addition, more widespread issues are potentially at stake as regards the exploitation of water resources. Canada, the possessor of the world's largest area of natural freshwater lakes, has a greatly-underused water potential, while many western areas of the USA are water-deficient. Various schemes have therefore been proposed for transferring Canadian water to the USA. Actually, certain areas of British Columbia and southern Alberta and Saskatchewan lie within the drainage systems of the Columbia and Mississippi rivers, while streams from Montana, North Dakota and Minnesota drain ultimately into the Nelson River and Hudson Bay, and streams from Yukon Territory flow into Alaska. The potential issues which may arise from water usage in the future relate as much to questions of overall sovereignty over natural resources as to the environmental difficulties encountered with major international water transfers or the engineering challenges involved in implementing the proposed schemes.

External Relations

The USA and Canada share coastlines on three oceans, and consequently have political interests stretching far beyond their own shores. Historically both have looked primarily eastwards, to Europe, but increasingly, in trade and more general political terms, Pacific rim countries such as Japan and South Korea have come to demand greater attention. Not only has Asian investment in North America markedly increased, and the number of immigrants from Pacific countries risen sharply, but these countries have also come to provide an increasingly important market for both North American raw materials and manufactured products.

Lack of population in the far north is undoubtedly a politically- and strategically-sensitive issue. To the north lie the Arctic Ocean, the North Pole and the USSR. In the age of air transport and intercontinental ballistic missiles, the northern lands of North America have assumed a much greater importance than they once held. Indeed, to some degree the extent of mineral exploration and exploitation in these areas is an indirect outcome of the need to map the region and place within it radio and weather stations, and radar and other defence systems. Changes in technology have occasioned first a decline then an increase in the importance of these northern areas of defence. In a sense they provide a defence in depth for the populated areas to the south; though some Canadians would cynically argue that it really means that Canada provides a defence in depth for the conterminous states of the USA!

Both countries are important members of NATO and other regional and global economic and political systems, while Canada's position is enriched (or complicated), by also being an influential member of the Commonwealth. In many ways both countries have a commonality of purpose in political and strategic matters, though in detail some major problems of sovereignty still exist. Canadians are (perhaps justifiably) sensitive about the dangers of Arctic pollution, and at the same time wish to have some control over traffic through the channels between the Arctic islands and the mainland; the USA, while accepting the environmental issues, argues that the Northwest Passage is an international waterway over which the Canadians have no jurisdiction. In other words, they do not accept that the passage lies within Canadian territorial waters.

While the US-Canadian Free-Trade Agreement promises to retain a significant amount of protection for the Canadian cultural industries, there is inevitably a concern about the 'Americanization' of Canadian culture. With the US market being some nine times the size of the Canadian in population terms, yet only separated from it by a land border, it is difficult to see how US influence can be kept completely at bay—especially as in both countries the same language is dominant. While it is true, for example, that Canadian television and radio programmes can be heard in the USA, it is much more usually the other way round, with some 75% of Canadian TV originating outside the country. Just how separate entities can be maintained alongside close co-operation (both economic and strategic) is really a question of fine judgement and balancing. As the US journalist Andrew Malcolm points out in his book *The Canadians*, when a competition asked people to complete the caption 'As Canadian as . . .', the winning answer was deemed to be ' . . . possible under the circumstances'. A more extreme view was expressed by Dalton Camp, writing in 1980, who said that 'while we would never want to be left alone in the world *without* America, we would also never want to be left alone in the world with America *alone.'*

CANADA'S LINKS TO THE USA:
PROSPECTS FOR THE FREE-TRADE ERA

MARISSA QUIE

Introduction

There is no more important relationship for Canada than its link with the USA. This relationship is now critical to Canada's economic well-being. Although the country has the world's seventh most important market economy, in terms of output, it is inextricably tied to that of the USA. The two countries have the largest amount of bilateral trade of any two nations in the world: in 1988 this was valued at US $157,940m., or C $184,291m. More than 70% of Canada's exports go to the USA and, as a consequence, more than one-fifth of its gross national product (GNP) is generated by sales to that country. While this trade relationship is not as critical from the US point of view, it remains extremely important. The USA engages in far more trade with Canada than it does with any other country.

The US-Canadian Free-Trade Agreement, which came into effect on 1 January 1989, was negotiated faster, and covered more ground, than anything previously achieved by the multilateral negotiations of the General Agreement on Tariffs and Trade (GATT). The Free-Trade Agreement was viewed by many as the most important issue in Canadian politics in the late 1980s. It was the central issue of the general election held on 21 November 1988, as a result of which the Progressive Conservative Party of Brian Mulroney achieved an overall, but reduced, majority, winning 169 out of 295 seats in the House of Commons (compared with 211 in 1984) on a pro-free-trade platform. The issue was also perceived to be of great relevance to the international community, in that it was thought that precedents could be set bilaterally which the USA could then attempt to extend on a multilateral basis.

Conceived as a far-sighted effort to gain secure access for Canadian goods to the USA in the face of growing protectionism, the Free-Trade Agreement has far-reaching implications for Canadian society as a whole. The issue touches on the complex questions of the future direction of a resource-based economy, the preservation of Canadian culture and the sovereignty of Canadian political institutions.

Canadian National Identity

Canada's existence historically has been that of a nation caught between the twin powerful 'empires' of the USA and Britain. Between the two it has attempted to carve out its own identity, culture and economy, and to control its own destiny. At the heart of the free-trade issue is the question of identity, which has always been problematic for Canada. Canadian national identity has been variously described as 'negative', 'plural' or 'decentralized'. All of these descriptions relate to Canada's double colonial inheritance from Britain and France, and to its less-definable economic and cultural relationship with the USA. The problem of identity has also been exacerbated by the Canadian preference for a 'mosaic' structure in which all the linguistic, ethnic and social groups retain their distinctiveness. Canada is not only a mosaic of ethnic and linguistic units, but also one of distinct regions, each with its own sense of identity. The nation therefore exists in a state of heterogeneous tensions (the most central being the division between the English- and French-speaking populations), and it is this heterogeneity which gives Canada its dynamism and uniqueness.

Canada's slow evolution as a nation began with a negative decision: *not* to be part of the American Revolution of 1776, and *not* to become 'Americans'. In eschewing the desire for autonomy and independence, and hence in remaining loyal to the British crown, Canada perpetuated its colonial status and deprived itself of a more positive national identity. From the very beginning, the founders of the USA considered it crucial to define themselves in a way that rendered them distinct from the colonial metropole and from other nations. They saw themselves as part of a new and great civilization. In contrast, Canada's history has been shaped fundamentally by a series of discontinuous power politics: the Dominion of Canada was declared by the British North America Act in 1867; only in 1965 did Canada choose the distinctive maple-leaf flag; and its constitution was not entirely liberated from the UK parliament until 1982. This has made the road from colony to nation more difficult for Canada, and has complicated the questions of political, economic and cultural identity.

Canadian national identity is clearly bound up with neither the ideology of a successful revolution nor a dramatic political movement. Conversely, it is the product of a victorious counter-revolution. The separate paths to development chosen by Canada and the USA have resulted in fundamental differences between the two societies which are still evident today. The choice of counter-revolution has meant that Canada, in a sense, must justify its *raison d'être* by emphasizing the virtues of being separate from the USA. The Canadian sense of nationality has always felt itself threatened by the USA, physically in the earlier days of its existence, and economically and culturally in more recent years. In contrast to the powerful US model, English–Canadian nationalism originally sought to emphasize its connections with and similarities to Britain, and its position within the Commonwealth. In this way it rejected many aspects of US populist democracy and culture in favour of a different mode of political development. As English Canadians sought to isolate Canada from the USA, French Canadians searched for ways to assure the safety of their culture within a continent dominated by English speakers. In that sense both English and French Canadians have had similar objectives: to protect their minority cultures from being absorbed by more powerful neighbours. More recently, many Canadians have sought to defend the integrity of Canada against the USA by defining their own country as being more humane, egalitarian, democratic and anti-imperialist, and less homogeneous, than the USA.

Within the economic sphere, the relationship with the USA has, up until very recently, been ambivalent. Canadian history is full of failed attempts to put trade relations on a more systematic footing. In 1854 the Reciprocity Act removed tariffs on the flow of natural products between the then British colonies and the USA. The USA abrogated this treaty in 1866 but approached Canada again on the topic in 1911; Canada rejected the US offer in a debate in which the British connection and the imperial tie featured significantly. Free trade was again rejected in 1947. Nationalism remained an important issue in the recent debate, and the reduced parliamentary majority Mulroney's party received in 1988 was a clear reminder of the Canadian people's desire not to lose their country's proven values or sense of identity.

The Impact of the FTA

THE ECONOMIC SPHERE

With the conclusion of the Free-Trade Agreement, tariffs between the two countries were gradually to be phased out between 1989 and 1998. Similar goods in each country were to be treated equally with regard to taxes, health standards and other regulations. New businesses in the USA or Canada were to operate under the same rules as domestic investors. Canada was to lift a 25% limit on US ownership of a bank or trust company, but was to retain a 10% limit on individual holdings. However, most of the restrictions on US investment in the Canadian economy were to be removed.

Supporters of free trade believed that secure access to US markets would strengthen the Canadian economy because it would force firms and industries to become more competitive and to improve their cost-effectiveness. Trade liberalization was expected to increase Canadian GNP and to lead to the creation of an estimated 250,000 new jobs across the spectrum of the country's industries. An equally-important internal consequence was expected to be the further removal of barriers to the free flow of goods and services between Canada's own provinces, the existence of which has served to make federal–provincial relations so tense over the years. Those who supported the Agreement also believed that it would reorient the economy along more 'logical' lines. Canada's population is too small to encourage its businesses to operate economies of scale. The country is further handicapped by its geography and patterns of settlement; most of its population is strung thinly along its 3,987-mile (6,416-km) southern border with the USA. In the past, a protected home market forced 'horizontal' (British Columbia to Newfoundland) patterns of commerce on businesses, when a glance at the map confirms that 'vertical' ones (between, for example, the Maritime provinces and New England) make better economic sense.

In spite of all these advantages the Free-Trade Agreement is an illustration of the manifold limitations to what can be agreed, even between two close trading partners. Originally Canada had hoped the deal would give it exemption from action under US unfair-trade legislation. It failed to achieve this, and instead the two countries have agreed to consult on new legislation and to work towards a new common approach to problems of dumping and subsidies: this was to come

into effect within seven years of the agreement's becoming effective.

THE POLITICAL SPHERE

From the Canadian perspective the issue of the link between free trade and national unity is called into question because of that country's peculiar economic and political structure. The national governments of Canada and the USA differ fundamentally in the nature of their respective roles in economic development and regional integration. The US federal government has traditionally assumed a less active role than the Canadian government in economic, social and cultural developments within its regions and states. While it has at times fostered specific regional economic-development projects, the US federal government has not made a consistent effort to use national investment resources to alleviate regional economic disparities. The Canadian government, however, has felt the need to play a very active part in economic development and regional policy to ensure both Canada's independence from the USA and its coherence as a nation. The combination of Canada's enormous size (it is the second-largest country on the globe in terms of land mass) and its sparse population (25.6m. people at 1 June 1987) have necessitated strong public-sector leadership in transportation, communications, population settlement and the utilization of vast natural resources. Moreover, linguistic, ethnic and geographical differences are natural centrifugal forces in Canada, and the federal government historically has been a primary impetus in balancing these forces in an effort to maintain unity without creating social or political homogenization.

In terms of the economic structure of Canada's regions, further trade liberalization will dramatically affect regional disparities. The industries which are predicted to decline or to disappear nationally (such as knitting-mills, footwear and textiles, as well as a range of light industry) are regionally concentrated. In Québec, for instance, the number of trade-sensitive communities is strikingly high. In fact, the distribution of communities dependent on a single industry demonstrates just how vulnerable Canada's regions are to changes in trade.

Efforts to compensate for regional disparities and the disadvantages of provincial geography were included in the original British North America Act of 1867. The Maritime provinces were promised federally-subsidized rail links to central Canada to provide their industries with a convenient replacement for the British and US export markets that were displaced by the Confederation. As the Prairie provinces acceded to the federation, they were guaranteed similar rail access for their agricultural production. An entire network of federal subsidies was pledged to Newfoundland to entice it to join the Dominion of Canada in 1949.

Canada maintains a sophisticated revenue-sharing arrangement between the federal and provincial levels of government. Since the 1930s the federal government has transferred an increasing amount of its revenues to the provinces (although the rate of increase has slowed since the early 1980s) so that provincial governments can carry out the educational, health and social-welfare maintenance roles delegated to them by the constitution.

The Constitution Act of 1982 commits the federal government to 'ensuring that provincial governments have sufficient revenues to provide reasonably comparable levels of taxation'. The formal system of equalization has evolved since the Rowell–Sirois Commission publicized its proposals for reforming Canada's fiscal arrangements in 1941. The Commission asserted that a formal equalization-grant system was required 'to make it possible for every province to provide, for its people, services of average Canadian standards and . . . will thus alleviate distress and shameful conditions which weaken national unity and handicap many Canadians'. The system that developed from these recommendations is set forth in the Federal–Provincial Fiscal Arrangements and Federal Post-Secondary Education and Health Contributions Act of 1987.

Some observers claim that Canada's welfare state and its traditional commitment to the maintenance of balanced growth and income across the country is called into question by the new Free-Trade Agreement. In agreements of this type, there is a persistent pressure for countries to align their policies both on a domestic and on an international level. This is particularly problematic for Canada which is thrust into an unequal relationship with a world superpower. The present agreement, for instance, contains no definition of an 'unfair subsidy' and simply states that this will be worked out over time. Such problems may ultimately prevent Ottawa from assisting disadvantaged regions and so undermine Canada's collectivist value orientations and welfare state. Within this context, the agreement may have detrimental effects on both Canadian national unity and sovereignty.

THE POTENTIAL FOR STRUCTURAL CHANGE

It was also thought that the Free-Trade Agreement might have negative effects in terms of a restructuring of the Canadian economy. The Macdonald Commission revealed that, as a consequence of a comprehensive agreement of this type, over 1.5m. Canadians would be forced to change employment. Equally pessimistic studies carried out on behalf of the Ontario provincial government showed that more than 400,000 jobs were likely to disappear from Ontario's manufacturing sector alone. As US firms rationalize production throughout North America, many existing branch-plant operations would be forced to close down. The most vulnerable areas within this context would include textiles, food processing, furniture, electronics and shoes—it should be noted that these are sectors of the economy where a large number of women work. The loss of inefficient firms may ultimately prove beneficial to the economy. However, the limitations which the Agreement was to impose on the Canadian government's ability to provide job retraining were expected to present a significant disadvantage.

The need for modernization was also expected to constitute a greater threat to Canadian-owned firms. Firstly, with less capital at their disposal, they are more directly sensitive to the market than US subsidiaries operating in Canada, and, secondly, these enterprises have decidedly fewer resources with which to purchase expensive new production technologies. This means that they are less able to upgrade their manufacturing operations than the multinationals still dominant in Canada's relatively weak manufacturing sector. Therefore, many small- and medium-sized Canadian companies were likely to fail within the more competitive environment created by the Free-Trade Agreement.

The new agreement with the USA may also weaken Canada's ability to protect the main foundation of its economy—its large and diverse resource base. Since 1980 the inflation-adjusted prices of metals, minerals, and pulp and paper have dropped substantially. In addition, prices for Canadian oil and gas are predicted to remain substantially depressed into the 1990s. This situation raises many disturbing questions regarding the kinds of adjustments Canada will have to make in the future. The country's resources are high-cost in comparison to those of other suppliers, and the radical changes in the role of resources in the new industrial age could undermine one of the basic historical sources of Canada's comparative advantage in export markets.

INTERNATIONAL RELATIONS

In the area of foreign policy Canada will have to strive hard to be autonomous, and there is a danger that it will be perceived internationally, at least from a symbolic point of view, to have become part of the USA. Strategically, Canada and the USA are locked into a continental relationship through the North American Air Defense Command (NORAD, established in 1958), collaborative anti-submarine warfare (ASW), coastal surveillance and defence production-sharing agreements. Canadian territory is now relatively less essential to the strategic defence of North America due to the advent of new weaponry.

The majority of Canada's post-war governments have chosen to associate Canada closely with US foreign-policy and defence arrangements. This choice stemmed from their recognition of the levels of both economic and strategic reliance on the USA. However, despite the central NATO/NORAD core of Canadian foreign and defence policy, Ottawa has tried to develop a mediating and peace-keeping role which reflects something of the nature and purpose of the Canadian state. Lester Pearson (secretary of state for external affairs from 1948 to 1957, and later prime minister), for example, came to symbolize that role as a skilled negotiator at the United Nations. For his part in promoting peace-by-compromise, in the Middle East (Suez Crisis), he was awarded the Nobel Peace Prize in 1957. Pearson also developed a useful 'middleman' function for Canada in the Commonwealth. Canada has been a vigorous advocate of real equality of status among the white and non-white nations of the multiracial Commonwealth that emerged with full Canadian support at the end of the Second World War, and, for this reason, has gained the special confidence of its Afro-Asian members. Canada has also been less ideological than the USA in its relations with the communist world (for instance, it recognized the People's Republic of China before President Nixon's overtures towards that country). However, the extent to which it can be truly independent in the international arena is questionable, particularly in the light of increased economic integration with the USA.

Conclusion

The area which will suffer most as a result of the Free-Trade Agreement is Canadian culture. Control of a substantial portion of Canadian business activity by US corporations is likely to have a significant impact on the cultural environment. Historically, there has been a continuous 'feedback' relationship between foreign direct investment and Canadian culture, with cultural similarities facilitating foreign direct investment and this, in turn, inducing greater cultural similarities. The issue for Canadian producers is not access to the US market in the face of the flood of US culture. Government policy in Canada has traditionally focused on the protection of national culture through content regulations, restrictions on foreign ownership, public subsidy and public ownership. These are areas which the USA sees in terms of unfair trading practices. At present, the cultural sphere is exempt from the Free-Trade Agreement. However, the USA will no doubt continue to press for the right to set up competing firms in sensitive areas such as publishing and film distribution. Many observers still regard Canadian identity and culture as too incomplete and fragile to withstand the pull of the more powerful and integrated culture of the USA.

ABORIGINAL PEOPLES OF THE USA AND CANADA

GEOFFREY MERCER

The aboriginal peoples of the USA and Canada comprise Native Indians, Inuit (Eskimos), Aleuts and Métis. The Indian population is widely distributed across the whole continent while the Inuit are concentrated in the Arctic coastland areas north of the treeline. In Alaska, the Aleuts are differentiated from American Indians and Eskimos, while, uniquely in Canada, the Métis—descendants of unions between Europeans and Indian women—form a distinctive socio-cultural group. Although they are considered together in this essay, there has always been great diversity between and within the aboriginal groups and communities.

Historical Background

Underpinning 19th-century aboriginal policies in North America was a concerted attempt to displace native peoples from most of their lands. A further aim was to break the hold of traditional cultures and life styles, whether through hostility, conversion or neglect. Government plans alternately offered a custodial regime, protection, and assimilation into white society. The Indian population bore the brunt of white colonialism and paternalism, while the Inuit/Eskimos avoided the full embrace of Europeans until the mid-20th century. In both countries the federal government assumed the major responsibility for native affairs and established a bureaucratic system of administration (in the USA the Bureau of Indian Affairs was officially recognized by Congress in 1832, while in Canada the Indian Department—subsequently renamed—became a federal office in 1868), although local practice did not always conform to central directives.

It was in the USA that population growth and economic development first led to serious encroachments on 'Indian territory'. The inhabitants were relocated, and increasingly moved to reservations. The treaty-making process established a special relationship between many Indian tribes and the US Congress. As a result Congress assumed trusteeship for the special status of Indians in respect of the protection of property, rights to self-government and various other services. Native–white relations in Canada were less constrained by pressures of settlement, but the expansion westward and northward, and extensive treaty activity to 'extinguish' native land rights, occasioned the segregation of Indians on reserves. US policy then proclaimed the merits of expropriating native lands by executive orders rather than by treaties, while the reservation system was criticized as an inefficient way of assimilating the native population. An alternative route, based on forced acculturation and a land-reform package, was taken in the Indian Allotment Act of 1887 (and further elaborated in subsequent legislation). This entailed breaking up tribal lands into individual holdings, and offering any 'surplus' land for sale, and yielded another substantial reduction in the amount of land held by Indians. The Canadian government also promoted assimilation, but by different means. The Indian Act of 1876 consolidated existing legislation on reserves, and instituted band (tribal) governments with limited powers. Federal responsibility was recognized for 'status' Indians, who were eligible to live on reserves and receive other 'treaty benfits', while it was denied to all others—that is, to non-status Indians and Métis. An overall goal was to facilitate 'enfranchisement', by which Indians were granted full citizenship in return for relinquishing their treaty status. There has been no comparable Inuit Act, although in 1939 the Canadian Supreme Court decided that the Inuit were included within the scope of federal jurisdiction.

The basic commitment to native assimilation held firm in the USA despite several policy changes. In the inter-war years the allotment programme was abandoned in favour of a 'New Deal'. This was enshrined in the Indian Reorganization Act of 1934, which offered support for tribal landholdings and institutions, although Congress and state governments displayed less than total enthusiasm. Indian expectations of treaty fulfilment were again raised when an Indian Claims Commission was set up in 1946 to expedite land claims, but its preferred solution was financial compensation rather than the reinstatement of land title. Indeed, in the 1950s more overt assimilationist policies returned to favour as part of a general initiative to 'get the government out of the Indian business'. Legislative action focused on the termination of the federal-Indian trust relationship and assisted removal off reservations. Native identity was threatened but it was not destroyed, although these policies often proved an economic disaster for individuals and tribes. Nor was the role of the Bureau of Indian Affairs greatly diminished. With native discontent increasing, the political agenda in the 1960s was dominated by calls for greater native 'self-determination'. In comparison, Canadian policy towards its aboriginal peoples maintained its chosen neo-colonial course until the 1960s. However, in response to growing concern about the plight of native peoples, the 1876 Indian Act was amended to grant status Indians full citizenship rights. Additional powers were delegated to band councils to make by-laws and raise revenue. The franchise was extended federally in 1960, and was operative in every province by the end of the decade. Yet there was considerable uncertainty about the direction of aboriginal policy: the *Hawthorn Report* of 1966 rejected the assimilation route, whereas in 1969 the government advocated the abolition of the Indian Act, including the status provisions. As in the USA, pressure was mounting to give aboriginal peoples a greater role in administration of their own affairs.

Population Size and Distribution

The count of native peoples has been derived from census questions asking for a self-report of identity. Despite the difficulties introduced by this method, it is generally accepted that the recent rate of population increase has been higher among aboriginal peoples than in all other sections of the US and Canadian populations. For the USA, the count in the 1980 census was 1,420,400—an 'increase' of almost 600,000 compared with 1970. The 1980 total comprised 1,364,033 American Indians, 42,162 Eskimos (Inuit) and 14,205 Aleuts—taken together 0.6% of the whole population. On a regional breakdown, 49% of Indians lived in the West (especially in the states of California, Arizona and New Mexico), 27% in the South (especially in Oklahoma), 18% in the Midwest and 6% in the Northeast. The vast majority of Eskimos and Aleuts were concentrated in Alaska, mostly in rural areas. The percentage of American Indians living in urban areas has increased rapidly during the 20th century, from 0.4% in 1900 to 13.4% in 1950, 27.9% in 1960, 44.5% in 1970 and 49.0% in 1980 (compared with 73.7% of US citizens overall). In 1980 the cities with the highest proportions of Indians were Los Angeles, Tulsa, Phoenix, Oklahoma City and Albuquerque, while about 27% of American Indians were resident in one or other of the 300 federal or 21 state reservations or trust lands. These vary greatly in size: the smallest cover only a few acres, while the largest by far is that held by the Navajo tribe, where 132,000 persons occupy a site which covers 14m. acres (5.7m. hectares) and extends into three states—Arizona, New Mexico and Utah.

In Canada, the 1981 census reported that about 2% of the population defined themselves as aboriginal—status Indian, non-status Indian, Métis or Inuit. However, these figures probably grossly underestimated the numbers of Métis and non-status Indians. Partial census returns for 1986 (with 1981 figures in brackets) were: Indians 286,200 (292,705); Inuit 27,300 (25,390); Métis and non-status Indians 398,200 (173,370). This gave a total of 711,700 (491,465), or about 3% of all Canadians. At the 1981 census native peoples comprised 58% of the total population in the Northwest Territories, 18% in Yukon Territory, slightly less than 5% in the Prairie provinces and British Columbia and less than 1% in the rest of the country. The Prairie provinces and British Columbia contained relatively higher proportions of Indians (both status and non-status), while the Métis were concentrated on the Prairies and 63% of Inuit lived in the Northwest Territories. Native peoples remain the most rural- (but not farm-) based population group in Canada—only 35% live in urban or suburban areas, compared with nearly 80% of all Canadians. While the proportion of status Indians living 'off-reserve' has increased from 18% in the 1960s to 35% in the mid-1980s, non-status Indians still exhibit higher levels of urbanization. There was also considerable mobility on and off the reserves. A change in the location of Inuit was effected during the 1960s and 1970s by the construction of over 40 permanent settlements with an average population of 500. Across the whole of the Territories, almost all the aboriginal groups still inhabit rural or remote areas.

Economic and Social Conditions

The economic and social conditions experienced by the aboriginal peoples of North America have been generally worse than those of any other group. These inequalities have been reduced over recent decades, but they remain significant. Post-war trends demonstrated a gradual move away from traditional subsistence activities towards waged labour, although much of the latter has been seasonal or temporary. Using an unofficial combination of US and Canadian census data from the early 1980s, one-half of the adult population of native peoples was economically active, compared with two-thirds of the non-native population. Most native males were in manual occupations in such sectors as construction, processing, machining, assembling and fabricating. Almost one-quarter of native women had technical and professional jobs, such as teaching, while slightly higher proportions were in clerical and service employment. Unemployment levels for native peoples of both sexes were twice the national rates. These patterns were reflected in the low average income of native peoples, which amounted to only two-thirds of the average for the non-native population. In addition, government transfer payments accounted for a more significant part of native incomes, with almost one-third receiving social assistance. Relatively high proportions in all of the aboriginal groups fell below the poverty line, with status/reservation Indians and Inuit/Eskimos being the most disadvantaged.

This economic deprivation is reflected in a broad range of social indicators. Native peoples have a life expectancy which is about 10 years below the national average, while perinatal and neonatal mortality rates are almost twice as high. They are grossly over-represented among those who have committed suicide, or whose death has been attributed to an accident, violence or poisoning. Poor socio-economic conditions are also suggested in health-status measures, with relatively high levels of tuberculosis and respiratory disease. Native peoples also figure disproportionately among those suffering from alcoholism and drug dependency. Housing conditions were rated as seriously inadequate for a significant minority of native peoples—with the main problems being overcrowding and a lack of basic facilities such as piped water supplies and indoor toilets. In the mid-1980s it was estimated that about one-quarter of on-reserve Indian housing was in need of major repairs. On many other measures of deprivation, from the number of children in care to the proportion serving prison sentences, the pattern of disadvantage is replicated. Governments have increasingly recognized these problems and have invested heavily in social and economic improvement programmes. As a result, significant progress has been made through better public-health and housing standards—especially on reservations. That said, native peoples have suffered comparatively more than other population groups from cut-backs on social security and social services imposed by both Canadian and US governments in the 1980s.

A similar record of inequality and lack of opportunities has been manifested in native education. In the 1950s the aim was still to 'civilize' the aboriginal population into the values and skills of white society. In practice, the segregation of native children in residential, often church, boarding-schools served to inhibit integration, and very few achieved even moderate levels of educational attainment. In the post-war years reservation schools became more common, but a major shift in native education was slow to occur. The new emphasis on 'self-determination' and cultural pluralism were formative influences. On both sides of the border there was a surge of government programmes designed to extend native direction of the educational process. In the USA various legislative reforms from 1967 onwards offered federal funding to promote the recruitment and training of native teachers and the use of Indian and Eskimo languages in the classroom. In Canada a similar scenario for local-community control was outlined by the National Indian Brotherhood in its paper *Indian Control of Indian Education* (1973). A parallel scheme was proposed for Inuit schools. In both countries, government policy was to expand native involvement, although this has fallen short of full control. By the early 1980s some 450 out of 577 Indian bands in Canada were responsible for at least some educational activities within their communities and by 1988 a total of 243 bands had assumed the administration of their own school(s), covering 28% of Indian schoolchildren. However, in most schools native-language instruction was not yet available. Special programmes to train native teachers have been set up in most provinces, as have curriculum projects to highlight native values. The Navajo have implemented similar programmes in the USA. The local Indian School Board was contracted by the Bureau of Indian Affairs to take responsibility for the school, which insisted on instruction in the Navajo language and way of life. A comparison of the educational attainment levels of different generations of native peoples suggests other substantial changes. In the early 1960s few Indians graduated from high school, and even fewer attended university (while the number of those attending US colleges totalled more than 3,400 in 1960, and more than 14,000 in 1970). About 3% of Canadian Indians had post-secondary experience in 1971, but a decade later this figure had risen to 19%—still well below the national figure of 36%. Within the native population, fewer women than men leave high school with only a minimal education, although more men than women have a university degree. In the 1980s the native 'drop-out' rate from high school was estimated to be twice that of the non-native population, with especially high rates among Inuit, and Indians on reserves/reservations.

Native groups have also emphasized the retention of indigenous languages. In 1970 32% of American Indians in the USA claimed a native language as their mother tongue, although this figure rose to 58% for those living on reservations. There was, however, considerable variation between reservations and between different areas of the country, with only 13% being native-language speakers in Washington but 78% in Arizona. In 1981 29% of Canadian aboriginal peoples indicated that one of the native languages was their mother tongue, with the most widespread first languages reported being Cree and Ojibway. Nearly one-half of Indians on Canadian reserves were native-language speakers, compared with only 14% of Métis and non-status Indians. The Inuit claimed the highest proportion, with three-quarters using Inuktitut as their first language. All aboriginal communities displayed a generational gap, with fluency in a native language being about twice as widespread among native people over 65 years of age as among the under-15 age-group.

Aboriginal Rights

The 1960s represented a turning-point for aboriginal policy on both sides of the border, with the reversal of the termination programme in the USA and the emergence of widespread opposition to the proposals of the Canadian government to end the special status of native peoples. At the same time, both federal governments actively encouraged and funded native participation in the policy-making process. This further politicized native organizations and grievances over land claims, aboriginal culture, rights and self-government. Groups began to mobilize—at band, regional and national levels—with women's and youth organizations becoming particularly prominent. International recognition also progressed: for example, an Inuit Circumpolar Conference was established to provide a pan-Inuit forum. In addition, native organizations began to reflect the divisions within and across the aboriginal communities. Since the 1960s aboriginal protest has been advanced by various means—including litigation, negotiation and political campaigns—with particularly significant developments occurring in Canada.

In general, aboriginal land claims have focused on two issues—land title and political rights. In 1974 the Canadian government responded to the growing pressure of criticism and court decisions by establishing a Native Claims Office within the Federal Department of Indian and Northern Affairs. A distinction was drawn between 'specific' (i.e. relating to unfulfilled treaty obligations) and 'comprehensive' claims. The latter are based on traditional land use and occupancy. The significance of these claims stems from the absence of land-cessation treaties in large areas of Canada such as British Columbia and the North. Experience of the claims process led to modifications by the federal government in 1981 and again in 1987 following a critical evaluation in the *Coolican Report* of 1986. Several major settlements have been concluded, including: the James Bay and Northern Québec Agreement (1975); the Northeastern Québec Agreement (1978); and the Inuvialuit Final Agreement (1984). The James Bay Agreement, widely regarded as a landmark decision, followed native opposition to the Québec government's decision to embark on a large hydroelectricity project. As a result of the Agreements in 1975 and 1978, the Cree Indians and Inuit received financial compensation, fishing, hunting and trapping rights, enhanced control of native education, and improved self-government for their communities.

The Inuit of the Northwest Territories have also claimed their own lands—known as Nunavut—which extend across the northern and eastern sections of the territory. The intention has been to create a new structure with powers akin to a province, although extraordinary mechanisms would be needed to guarantee that the Inuit domination of Nunavut will continue if they no longer were to constitute the majority group. The proposed territory has been approved in a territorial plebiscite and has the endorsement of the national government in principle, but various land claims are outstanding and boundaries have to be determined. Other land-claim agreements-in-principle have also been signed, including, in 1987, a pact with 15,000 Dene and Métis of the Northwest Territories which will give them the ownership of 10,000 sq km (3,860 sq miles) of land. The pact includes sub-surface rights, a substantial financial settlement, and participation in land-, wildlife- and water-management decisions. The current emphasis on negotiation rather than legislation has provided a new context for government–native relations, although native leaders have been wary lest the land-claims process affect aboriginal title and self-determination. There has also been considerable activity over specific treaty claims, particularly in British Columbia, with some settlements already finalized and others under consideration.

The new direction in US policy is illustrated by an Alaskan case study. The implementation of ambitious plans for resource development following statehood in 1959 were blocked by extensive native land claims. The federal government imposed a 'land freeze' in 1966, which effectively stopped the new economic developments until the native claims had been resolved. In 1968, while negotiations were proceeding, the largest oilfield in North America was discovered in Prudhoe Bay. This inspired plans for a Trans-Alaska pipeline, which in turn was halted, in large part because of objections from native villages in the interior. The Alaska Federation of Natives campaigned for a settlement which provided both land and financial compensation. In 1971 Congress passed the Alaska Native Claims Settlement Act which awarded the native peoples 44m. acres (18m. hectares) of land—equivalent to 12% of the state's total land area—and included surface and sub-surface rights, customary rights for traditional subsistence activities, and some US $960m. in compensation, in exchange for the extinguishment of all aboriginal claims. The settlement entailed complex financial and land-conveyancing arrangements. The 1971 Act established a tier of regional and village corporations which were to manage the lands and money from the settlement. However, both the distribution of lands and the establishment of individual native beneficiaries proved highly contentious. The adoption of the corporate system signalled a novel, private-enterprise route for native people, which offered an alternative to an existence as 'wards' of the federal government. The long-term fear is that after 1991, when native shares in the corporations may be sold, there is the potential for a non-native 'take-over'. In the short term, however, Alaskan native peoples have become an important political force, and the settlement has paved the way for similar agreements.

Native people have long recognized that their claims for greater self-determination depend on breaking out of their economic and social dependency. The land-claims settlements arranged in Alaska and northern Canada have provided new opportunities for native peoples to manage their own economic development. There has also been increased federal funding in both the USA and Canada to sponsor native economic self-sufficiency. This has led to a considerable expansion of mostly small, family-run or community-owned and -managed enterprises. The Inuit, for example, have established their own system of 46 co-operatives, providing retail stores, crafts, services and hotels in the Northwest Territories and Québec. These have become the major employer, after the government, in Inuit areas. Under the terms of the James Bay agreement, compensation funding was paid into the Cree Regional Authority and the Makivik Corporation (for the Inuit) which have administered economic and social programmes. Recipients of aid have included airlines (Air Creebec and Air Inuit) along with various construction, manufacturing and service companies. These initiatives represent a novel compromise between the demands for commercial economic development, long-term employment and the maintenance of traditional community socio-cultural values and life styles.

The discussion of aboriginal rights in Canada has been further transformed by the passage of the Constitution Act of 1982. This recognized and affirmed existing aboriginal and treaty rights. In addition, the status of the Métis as one of the aboriginal groups was confirmed. A First Ministers' Conference (comprising federal and provincial premiers, and representatives from the main native-peoples' organizations) was mandated for 1983 and it produced two substantive amendments to the constitution. Subsequent conferences, the last in 1987, have failed to agree on further changes. Neither aboriginal rights nor self-government have been defined. One consequence of the entrenchment of aboriginal rights in the constitution has been that the provinces now enjoy a greatly elevated role in determining aboriginal rights. The likely provincial impact on constitutional change also promises to be facilitated by the Meech Lake Accord of 1987. In another important legislative development, the Indian Act was amended in 1985 to stop discrimination against women and children who lost their status rights because of marriage to a non-Indian. The internal composition of Canada's native population will be significantly affected if, as expected, about 100,000 non-status Indians successfully claim reinstatement.

Throughout the 1980s various proposals for native self-government have been advanced. In Canada the *Penner Report* of 1983 recommended that Indian communities should work out new forms of band government to replace the present limited structures under the Indian Act. This envisages a new (fourth) level of government within Canadian federalism. The Department of Indian and Northern Affairs responded by establishing a self-government office to develop community-based self-government schemes. Among those on offer, a municipal model has been agreed and the legislation passed in 1986 for the Sechelt Band of British Columbia, giving it control over lands, resources, education, health and social services and local taxation. Other bands have sought more extensive autonomy and self-sufficiency outside the provisions of the Indian Act. In addition, discussions have started, for example in Manitoba, to negotiate a self-government accord with the Métis population. So far the agreements concluded have been accommodated to the basic municipal–provincial–federal structure rather than providing a replacement.

In the USA native self-government had been given an earlier and more substantial basis under the Indian Reorganization Act of 1934. In practice, the Bureau of Indian Affairs has often exercised its guardianship authority to thwart meaningful self-government. In addition, litigation has played a crucial role, especially since the 1960s, in (re-)defining aboriginal rights, including those relating to the extent and character of tribal self-government. The current powers cover a range of executive, judicial and legislative areas. Tribes have the authority to draw up their own constitution and determine the criteria for tribal membership. Tribal laws and courts have played an important role on most reservations, having jurisdiction over a range of civil, family and minor criminal matters. One restriction on Indian law has been the code of individual rights written into the Indian Civil Rights Act of 1968. This has given rise to litigation between the tribal government and individual members, and some tribal councils have felt their authority has been undermined. Recent US Supreme Court decisions have confirmed that non-Indians on reservations are subject to Indian laws. The tribe also has powers to raise revenue through local taxes, both on individual non-Indians and on companies exploiting reservation resources. Conversely, the Supreme Court decided that individual states were not permitted to impose income tax on reservation Indians. Tribal governments have further powers to license and regulate reservation businesses and land use. The Supreme Court has also been supportive of native attempts to defend traditional rights to land, fishing and hunting, water and natural resources. As well as confirming Indian rights on tribal lands, in 1979 the Supreme Court adjudged that Indians were allowed to fish off-reservation at accustomed places. The extent and cost of litigation over state–tribal disputes has led to the formation of the Commission on State–Tribal Relations to promote co-operative agreements, without prior settlement of jurisdictional disputes. In Arizona alone over 60 agreements have been reached, but the emphasis on negotiated agreements is yet to be widely accepted. The way forward for tribal self-government remains problematic and contentious—not least for native peoples themselves.

Review

The aboriginal peoples of America and Canada have experienced an extraordinary history of dependency, discrimination and cultural corrosion. Yet the conventional view that the native way of life was disappearing and that the 'perpetual inhabitant with diminutive rights' was an anachronism has itself been discarded. From the perspective of the 1980s, a more outstanding impression is of the resilience, adaptability and renewed vitality of aboriginal societies and cultures. There has also been a significant change in government policies and public opinion towards the aspirations of native peoples for aboriginal rights, the settlement of land claims and self-government. Nevertheless, many policy uncertainties and obstacles remain, both in the diagnosis of native grievances and in the presentation of suggested and preferred remedies.

THE ECONOMIC DEVELOPMENT OF ALASKA AND THE CANADIAN NORTH

KEN ATKINSON

Alaska and the Canadian North leave a searing impression on the visitor. Together, Alaska, the Northwest Territories and Yukon Territory account for almost 30% of the total land area of the USA and Canada, covering 1.48m. sq km, 3.29m. sq km and 478,970 sq km respectively. As well as sheer size, the visual landscape is also stunning, with the dense sub-Arctic boreal forest (taiga) being separated by the treeline from the windswept tundra region of the Arctic. The topography shows striking contrasts: Mount McKinley in Alaska (6,194 m) and Mount Logan in Yukon Territory (6,050 m) are the highest peaks in the USA and Canada respectively, yet immense lowland areas are to be found along the Arctic coast and surrounding Hudson Bay. The Rocky Mountains and the Arctic islands support vast and awesome ice-caps and glaciers.

Population and Settlement

The northernmost areas of Canada and the USA are barren, remote and isolated. Yukon Territory and the Northwest Territories together make up 41% of Canada's land area, but supported just 0.3% of its population at the 1986 census, while in the same year Alaska had 16% of the US land area but only 0.2% of its inhabitants. Nevertheless, population numbers in the northern areas had increased rapidly during the 1970s and early 1980s. While the population of Canada grew by 4.2% overall between 1981 and 1986, that of the territories increased by 10.1%, and while the US population grew by 11.4% from 1970–80, that of Alaska increased by 32.8% over the same period—a rate surpassed only in Florida. The population is young (in Alaska 3.4% were over 65 years of age in 1980, compared with 12.1% in the USA as a whole), and is relatively fertile. According to the censuses of 1986 (Canada) and 1980 (USA), native peoples comprised 52% of the population of the Northwest Territories but just 14% of Yukon inhabitants and 16% of Alaskans. Towns are mostly small and widely scattered, with the principal exception being Anchorage, the dominant commercial centre in Alaska, of which the population grew from 126,000 at the 1970 census to 235,000 at mid-1986 (although it is thought to have decreased by 20,000 in 1986–88). Other major Alaskan centres are Fairbanks and the capital Juneau, with 1986 populations of 52,000 and 22,000 respectively. Whitehorse, the capital and economic centre of Yukon Territory, had 15,199 inhabitants at the 1986 census, representing 65% of the territory's total population. By contrast the 11,753 residents of Yellowknife, the capital of the Northwest Territories, represent just 20% of the NWT population. This reflects the wide dispersal in the Northwest Territories of small towns such as Inuvik in the Mackenzie Delta (population 3,500 at the 1986 census), Hay River in the Mackenzie Valley (3,000) and Iqaluit on Baffin Island (2,400).

Land Policy and Native Land Claims

The ownership of much northern land is vested in government—whether federal, state or territorial. Thus government land-use policies play a crucial role in controlling resource use. The 92m. ha of federal land in Alaska consists of national parks, wildlife refuges and national forest, and accounts for 60% of Alaska's land area and one-third of all US federal land.

With statehood in 1959, Alaska's government was given until 1994 to select 42m. ha (28% of its land area) for state lands. Not surprisingly, oil-rich tracts have been chosen, thus channeling the immense royalties and taxes (which in 1985 totalled US $3,600m., or $8,650 for each inhabitant) to the state treasury. In 1980, 40m. ha of federal land was designated as wildlife refuges and national forests under the Alaska National Interest Lands Conservation Act (ANILCA); resource development on this land is only possible with the approval of the US Congress, and the late 1980s saw a dispute over oil development in the Arctic National Wildlife Refuge (ANWR).

Recent resource development has also been influenced by claims made by native peoples to aboriginal land rights where these have not been extinguished by treaty. Alaskan claims were settled quickly by the 1971 Alaska Native Claims Settlement Act to avoid delay to the construction of the Trans-Alaska Pipeline System (TAPS); 198 native villages and 13 native corporations received a total of 18m. ha of land and US $960m. in compensation. Settlement of claims in Canada has proceeded more slowly. The four claims settled by 1988 covered the Inuvialuit (Inuit around the Mackenzie Delta), the Inuit Tapirisat (the eastern Arctic), the Yukon Indians, and the Dene Indian nation of the Mackenzie Valley.

Renewable Resources

Renewable resources have historically served as the basis for economic development in Alaska and the Canadian North. Aboriginal Inuit, Aleuts and Indians subsisted on game, fish and plants for their food and material artefacts. The first overseas exploitation came with the movement of 17th-century fur traders and whalers from Europe into the eastern Arctic, followed in the 18th century by American whalers and then by Russian hunters of sea otters and fur seals, who operated in Alaska until its purchase by the USA in 1867. The early 20th century saw an increase in salmon fishing in south-east Alaska, which resulted in a commercial harvest of timber for fish crates, traps and building materials.

For some policy-makers the fostering of renewable resources offers a more stable and sustainable development than comes from non-renewable resources. This lobby points to the highly cyclical nature of the non-renewable sector and to the social and economic problems caused by mine closures and recessions in oil activity. This view overlaps with that of the 'pro-native peoples' lobby which stresses the cultural, social and psychological values which derive from a life on the land for small communities. The village of Arctic Bay on Baffin Island in the Northwest Territories (population 500) illustrates the value of the traditional wildlife harvest in a small community: about 30% of personal income comes from country food and skins, 28% from employment in territorial and hamlet government, 23% from employment in the non-renewable sector (consisting of the Nanisivik lead and zinc mine and the exploration activities of Panarctic Oil Ltd) and 19% from transfer payments. The economic value of the traditional economy is the subject of controversial debate: those who see the future of the North in minerals, oil and natural gas maintain that such high income estimates for hunting, trapping and fishing are exaggerated gross values, without deductions of costs for weapons, ammunition, traps, petrol and other items. It is argued that the importance of the harvest is greatly reduced if net values are calculated. Such debates are far from being purely theoretical; the 1977 *Berger Report*, published by the federal Department of Supply and Services, was anxious to avoid adverse impacts on the native economy when it proposed a 10-year moratorium on the construction of a Mackenzie Valley gas pipeline.

Despite accounting difficulties, it is estimated that in 1985 3,100 commercial trappers in the Northwest Territories harvested furs to the value of C $3m., with additional income coming from ringed seal (C $100,000) and polar bear skins (C $200,000). In Yukon Territory the total value was C $1.5m. from 800 registered trappers. The fur industry in Alaska has declined since its peak of 500,000 pelts a year in the 1920s to a current annual harvest of about 100,000 pelts from 1,000 families. Fur seals are harvested on the Pribilof Islands, but the commercial hunting of other marine mammals is prohibited. The harvest of sealskins by Inuit in the Northwest Territories has been decimated by the animal-rights movement in general, and by the 1983 ban on sealskin imports into the EEC in particular.

Forest industries in the Canadian North are for local use only. While there are 210,000 sq km of productive forest (5.6% of the territories' total land area), there is only one major sawmill—at Watson (Yukon). Logging is much more important along the southern coasts of Alaska. Log, pulp and chipboard exports total US $300m. a year, and go chiefly to Japan. There is a large sawmill at Wrangell, while pulpmills operate at Sitka and Ketchikan. Agriculture is restricted to barley, fodder and cattle operations, chiefly for local consumption, and there are reindeer and musk-ox herding operations.

Employment in Alaska's renewable-resource industries in 1980 totalled 24,000. Of this, employment in fishing and seafood processing totalled 13,200, that in logging and forest industries 3,200 and that in agriculture 200, with federal and state management employing a further 7,400. Many Alaskan fisheries are seasonal, with some 95% of the catch's annual value coming from salmon, shellfish (crab and shrimps) and halibut, the majority of which is frozen for export—only a small proportion now goes to the once-dominant canneries. The major problems facing the industry in the 1980s concern conservation and harvest regulation as a result of overfishing and stock depletion over the past 80 years. In 1976 the USA extended its jurisdiction over marine resources from 12 to 200 nautical miles (22 to 370 km), with the joint federal–state North Pacific Fisheries Management Council (NPFMC) allocating and policing quotas.

Minerals and Mining

It is widely assumed that Alaska and northern Canada possess great wealth in non-renewable resources. While vast size and relative lack of exploration mean that the probability of large deposits being discovered is higher than elsewhere in North America, ores must be high-grade to compete in national and world markets, as costs of exploration, production and transportation are high.

Non-ferrous mineral production occupies first place in the economies of the Yukon and Northwest Territories. In contrast to the situation in the petroleum sector, activity has increased greatly since the mid-1980s, though output values are very variable in the short term. In 1987 northern mines produced 60% of Canada's lead, 35% of its zinc, 14% of its gold and 12% of its silver. As the deposits are polymetallic, their vulnerability to world price fluctuations is reduced, but the industry remains cyclical, with mines often being short-lived. Crucial factors determining development are world market prices, discoveries of competing resources in southern Canada, and the willingness of federal government to subsidize infrastructure.

In Yukon Territory there are four year-round mines, four small seasonal mines and some 200 seasonal placer-gold operations. (Placer mining involves the extraction of gold metal from river sediments.) Value of shipments totalled C $60m. in 1985, C $184m. in 1986 and C $447m. in 1987. The Faro zinc, lead and silver mine (the largest in the territory, employing 500 of its 800 hard-rock mining workers) was scheduled to decline after 1988, but new deposits were to be developed in the Vangorda Plateau, east of Faro. The Mount Skukum gold and silver lode mine opened in 1986 and the Ketza River gold lode mine in 1987, while the Keno Hill silver, lead and zinc mine continues to expand. There are small seasonal operations in Plata-Inca (silver and lead), Whiskey Lake (coal) and White-horse (coal), and in 1987 the gold-placer industry in the Klondike, Sixty Mile and Carmack areas attained its highest production since 1950. Increased gold activity has helped to compensate for recent mine closures at Whitehorse (copper) and Cassiar (asbestos).

The value of mineral production in the Northwest Territories increased from C $656m. in 1986 to C $824m. in 1987. It comes from four gold mines (Giant, Con and Salmita near Yellowknife, and Lupin at Echo Bay) and two zinc, lead and silver mines on Arctic islands (Polaris on Little Cornwallis Island and Nanisivik on Baffin Island). During 1987 the Northwest Territories, largest mine (at Pine Point) was closed, and the non-Communist world's largest tungsten mine, at Cantung, suspended operations due to price and labour problems. Although large deposits of uranium, iron, copper and gypsum are known, gold projects are attracting most attention, as at Tundra and Ptarmigan, north of Yellowknife.

Placer-gold mining and the Kennecott copper mines at Chitima have attracted investment in Alaska during much of the 20th century. Between 1880 and 1980 gold contributed US $13,600m. to the value of Alaskan mineral production (at 1980 prices), sand and gravel $3,700m. and copper $1,200m. Metal mining is now restricted to many small placer-gold workings and the large Valdez Creek placer-gold mine. In addition, 800,000 metric tons of coal are produced annually at the Usibelli mine for power generation at Healy and Fairbanks.

A number of promising mineral deposits have been identified, and those at Green's Creek (zinc, lead and silver) and Quartz Hill (molybdenum) will probably be developed in the 1990s.

PETROLEUM DEVELOPMENT

The Prudhoe Bay oilfield on the north coast of Alaska was discovered by the Atlantic Richfield Company in 1968 and came into production in 1977 following the completion of the US $9,000m., 1,290-km Trans-Alaska Pipeline System (TAPS), leading from the field to the ice-free port of Valdez. Reserves are estimated at 1,600m. cu m. Alaskan crude-oil production has increased from an average of 8.4m. cu m per year in 1966–70 to 115.7m. cu m in 1988, reflecting the dramatic rise of the Prudhoe Bay field, which now contributes 16% of US petroleum production. Whereas output from many states has declined during the 1980s, that from Alaska has increased. Production from Prudhoe Bay is due to decline in the late 1990s and alternative fields are being explored, both on shore and off shore. The Kuparuk River Field, with estimated reserves of 600m. cu m, is more difficult to exploit than Prudhoe Bay, and the Ugnu deposit is of heavy, costly oil. Plans exist for a future trans-Alaska natural gas pipeline to run alongside the TAPS, serving petrochemical industries, and for an oil refinery at Valdez with a daily capacity of 16,000 cu m. However, all that have been completed are three gas processing plants, one at Prudhoe Bay and two at Kenai. With a throughput of 2,300m. cu m a day, they were all operating at half-capacity in 1987. A small (7,500 cu m a day) oil refinery at Fairbanks supplies internal consumption.

Offshore petroleum production started in 1987 from Endicott field, a reservoir of some 160m. cu m which is jointly owned by Standard Alaska and Exxon and is situated just east of Prudhoe Bay. Production in 1988 totalled 6m. cu m, and was brought on shore to the TAPS by causeway from an artificial gravel production island. Additional offshore leases are being explored, but the 600,000-ha Arctic National Wildlife Refuge (ANWR) between Prudhoe Bay and the Canadian border is thought to be potentially the richest unexplored petroleum area in North America and thus the most promising area to succeed Prudhoe Bay, utilizing the then available capacity of the TAPS. The environmental lobby, supported by the Yukon territorial government, bitterly opposes a development which they feel will be harmful to the Porcupine caribou herd and to native lifestyles. Under the 1980 Alaska National Interest Lands Conservation Act (ANILCA), the US Congress will make the final decision, though in 1986 the US Fish and Wildlife Service recommended development, with safeguards for the main caribou calving area of 100,000 ha.

Oil and gas exploration in the Canadian North has been encouraged by federal government policies since the 1960s, but so far discoveries and production have been modest, compared with the success of Prudhoe Bay. Panarctic Oils Ltd was formed in 1967 to oversee exploration in the Arctic islands and the Canada Oil and Gas Lands Administration (COGLA) was established by the federal government in 1981 to regulate all oil and gas activity on Canada's frontier lands. Especially active in the North have been Esso, Gulf and Petrocanada, a Crown Corporation formed in 1976 to increase the pace of Arctic exploration. The areas of greatest potential are the Mackenzie Delta–Beaufort Sea, which in 1987 was estimated to contain crude-oil reserves totalling 65m. cu m, the Sverdrup Basin, the Banks Basin and Baffin Bay–Davis Strait. Depressed oil prices since 1985 have caused oil companies to suspend activity, though Panarctic (now 54% owned by Petrocanada) still operates in the Arctic Islands. Only two fields are currently producing oil. Production at the onshore Norman Wells field in the Mackenzie Valley, which was opened in 1939 and which supplied oil for the Canol pipeline to Whitehorse during the Second World War, was greatly expanded from 500 cu m a day to 5,600 cu m a day in 1985 following the completion of a three-metre diameter pipeline leading south to Zama (Alberta), and providing a link to Edmonton. The second producing field lies at Bent Horn on Cameron Island, High Arctic, from which crude oil has been transported by ship since 1985 to the Petrocanada refinery in Montréal. Despite an increase in the annual shipment from 16,000 cu m to 35,000 cu m in 1987, Bent Horn oil remains the most expensive oil

produced in the world; its value is symbolic, to demonstrate that oil can be produced in the High Arctic and shipped safely south.

Pollution by oil spills from accidents involving tankers, rigs and pipelines has been a threat which governments and industry have sought to lessen by research, by legislation and by strict codes of practice. Despite all safety measures, however, several sources estimate that 75% of all spills are attributable to human error and negligence. Even with near-perfect technology, northern ecosystems will be polluted, a fact tragically illustrated in March 1989 when the tanker *SS Exxon Valdez* grounded outside Valdez, discharging almost 50,000 cu m of oil into Prince William Sound. This unprecedented ecological disaster is certain to have far-reaching implications for future petroleum development in the Arctic Basin; in the short term, federal and local agencies concerned with environmental protection will receive more recognition and funding, while in the long term the influence of the 'anti-development' lobby seems destined to increase.

Tourism and Conservation

The tourist potential of the northern regions of the USA and Canada is based on their landscape resources of wildlife, rivers, scenic vistas, fish, glaciers, clean air and wilderness. Most planners view tourism as a challenging economic sector which could provide secure jobs for a growing population. This judgement is heightened by the instability and recent relative decline of the non-renewable resource sector. The tourist industry is far more developed in Alaska than in the Canadian North. It is difficult to estimate exactly how many visitors come primarily for recreation rather than for business, but the 850,000 visitors to Anchorage in 1987 spent US $215m. One estimate is that two-thirds of out-of-state visitors come partly for recreation. Sport fishing is a major tourist activity, as is hunting. The number of national parks and reserves in Alaska was increased from five to 17 under the 1980 Alaska National Interest Lands Conservation Act (ANILCA), and about 500,000 visitors, including residents, visit these parks each year.

Tourism in the Canadian North is restricted by its remoteness and inaccessibility. Specialist fishing and wilderness vacations are available in many centres, but tourism on any scale has a better potential in Yukon Territory than in the Northwest Territories because of the former's proximity to Alaska, its more highly-developed road infrastructure and its natural attractions of high mountains and large glaciers.

Environmental groups are wary of tourism, which they regard as a self-destructing resource use. Thus there is a strong lobby to offer as much protection as possible to northern wildlife and its habitats. Governments in both the Canadian territories and Alaska have enacted total protection to threatened species (the bowhead whale and musk ox, for example), while protecting other species, such as the polar bear, by imposing hunting quotas. However, the establishment of national parks and wildlife sanctuaries is seen as the most effective method of preserving particular areas of the fragile Arctic from the inevitable economic demands of the 21st century. Canadian park planners estimate that at least 11 parks will be needed to represent the full range of Arctic landscapes; the six which have already been established are at Wood Buffalo, Nahanni, Kluane, North Yukon, Auyuittuq (Baffin Island) and Ellesmere Island. The North Yukon Park is particularly significant, as it protects the Canadian habitat of the Porcupine caribou herd and has effectively withdrawn this Canadian part of the Yukon northslope from the kind of hydrocarbon developments which are imminent in Alaska.

The Economic Future

With income per head of US $17,796 in 1986, Alaska ranks as the third-richest state in the Union, after Connecticut and New Jersey. This reflects the exploitation of North America's largest oilfield at Prudhoe Bay. The rise in oil prices during the 1970s and early 1980s greatly helped the development of this remote field, although it has to be recognized that the field has very low recovery costs, which to some extent offset the high shipment costs. With the predicted decline of the field in the late 1990s, the economic future of Alaska will depend on the discovery and exploitation of new fields, both on and off shore. Although future projects will meet opposition from the environmentalist lobby, it is doubtful whether the pace of modernization will be halted. The exploitation of Alaskan oil is increasingly seen to be in the national interest of the USA and it is recognized that the oil industry has striven hard to minimize adverse impacts on fragile Arctic ecosystems.

There is an almost mythical belief in the 'southern' heartland of Canada and the USA that the North is a vast storehouse of natural resource wealth, ready for commercial exploitation. However, this view ignores the high costs of northern exploration and development and the fact that many deposits are not competitive in national and international markets; to regard the North as the new 'frontier' is to ignore the realities of location, climate and ecology. The postponement of the development of known Beaufort Sea oil and gas deposits is an immediate response to the drop in world oil prices from US $36

a barrel in December 1985 to $15 a barrel in April 1986. Although these and other known deposits will undoubtedly be developed in the foreseeable future, their vulnerability to world price movements is a salutory reminder that only a few very rich deposits provide real development opportunities, and it is these which will dominate the future economy.

The future of northern economies is frequently portrayed in terms of a conflict between development and conservation. Such a portrayal oversimplifies the debate, however. A more striking contrast has arisen between those who advocate the wise use of renewable resources—fisheries, forests, tourism and wildlife—and those who argue that the future of the North will be dependent on the exploitation of non-renewable resources of minerals, oil and natural gas. Undoubtedly a balanced approach seems necessary, with mineral deposits being exploited where commercially feasible, with strong safeguards for natural ecosystems and native lifestyles, and with royalties from such developments being used to promote employment in renewable systems.

SELECT BIBLIOGRAPHY

Armstrong, T., Rogers, G. and Rowley, G. *The Circumpolar North: Political and Economic Geography of the Arctic and Subarctic.* London, Methuen and Co Ltd, 1978.

Atkinson, K. and McDonald, A. T. *Arctic Canada.* Leeds, University of Leeds Regional Canadian Studies Centre, 1988.

Berger, T. *Northern Frontier, Northern Homeland.* Report of the Mackenzie Valley Pipeline Inquiry, Vols I and II, Ottawa, Supply and Services Canada, 1977.

Boldt, M. and Long, J. A. (Eds). *The Quest for Justice: Aboriginal Peoples and Aboriginal Rights.* Toronto, University of Toronto Press, 1985.

Cameron, D. (Ed.). *The Free Trade Papers.* Toronto, James Lorimer & Co Ltd, 1986.

Department of External Affairs. *Synopsis of the Canada–US Free Trade Agreement.* Ottawa, from the text initialled on 10 December 1987.

Economic Council of Canada. *Western Transition.* Ottawa, 1984.

Grant, G. *Lament for a Nation: The Defeat of Canadian Nationalism.* Toronto, McClelland & Stewart, 1965.

Innis, H. *Essays in Canadian Economic History.* Toronto, University of Toronto Press, 1956.

Levitt, K. *Silent Surrender.* Toronto, University of Toronto Press, 1970.

Long, J. A. and Boldt, M. (Eds). *Governments in Conflict? Provinces and Indian Nations in Canada.* Toronto, University of Toronto Press, 1988.

Lopez, B. *Arctic Dreams: Imagination and Desire in a Northern Landscape.* London, Picador, 1986.

Lumsden, I. (Ed.). *Close to the 49th Parallel: The Americanization of Canada.* Toronto, University of Toronto Press, 1970.

McCann, L. D. *Heartland and Hinterland: A Geography of Canada* (2nd edn). Scarborough, Ontario, Prentice–Hall Canada Inc, 1987.

Morehouse, T. A. (Ed.). *Alaskan Resources Development: Issues of the 1980s.* Boulder, Colorado, Westview Press Inc, 1984.

Owen Saunders, J. (Ed.). *Trading Canada's Natural Resources.* Toronto, Carswell Co Ltd, 1987.

Price, J. A. *Native Studies: American and Canadian Indians.* Toronto, McGraw-Hill Ryerson Ltd, 1978.

Stairs, D. and Winham, G. R. (Eds). *The Politics of Canada's Economic Relationship with the USA.* Toronto, University of Toronto Press, 1985.

Statistics Canada. *Canada Year Book 1988.* Ottawa, Canadian Government Publishing Centre, 1987.

Teeple, G. (Ed.). *Capitalism and the National Question in Canada.* Toronto, University of Toronto Press, 1972.

Thorton, R. *American Indian: Holocaust and Survival.* Norman, Oklahoma, University of Oklahoma Press, 1987.

Tomlin, B. W. and Molot, M. A. *1986 Talking Trade: Canada among Nations.* Toronto, James Lorimer & Co Ltd, 1987.

Tomlin, B. W. and Molot, M. A. (Eds). *Canada Among Nations* (4 vols). Toronto, James Lorimer & Co Ltd for the Norman Paterson School of International Affairs, Carleton University, 1985–88.

US Bureau of the Census. *Statistical Abstract of the United States.* Washington, DC, Government Printing Office, annual.

Waldram, C. *Atlas of the North American Indian.* Oxford, Facts on File Ltd, 1985.

Whalley, J. *Canada–United States Free Trade.* Toronto, University of Toronto Press, 1985.

Whittington, M. S. *The North.* Toronto, University of Toronto Press for the Royal Commission on the Economic Union and Development Prospects for Canada, 1985.

Wilson, E. *O Canada: An American's Notes on Canadian Culture.* New York, Farrar, Straus & Giroux Inc, 1964.

Wornacott, R. J. and Hill, R. *Canada and US Adjustment Policies in a Bilateral Trade Agreement.* Toronto, C. D. Howe Institute, 1987.

CANADA

INTRODUCTION

CANADA: A CHRONOLOGY SINCE COLONIZATION

982–1016: Norse explorers from Greenland thought to have explored and established temporary settlements on eastern coast of present-day Canada.

1497–98: Giovanni Caboto (John Cabot) explored coast between Labrador and Chesapeake Bay.

1522: Temporary settlements established on Newfoundland by European fishermen.

1534: Jacques Cartier sailed up the St Lawrence River to sites of present-day Québec City and Montréal.

1583: Island of Newfoundland claimed for England.

1604–05: First French settlements founded on St Croix River and at Port Royal (later Annapolis Royal).

1608: Québec City founded; it subsequently became the administrative centre of New France.

1610: Henry Hudson discovered Hudson Bay.

1615–16: William Baffin explored northern coastline.

1621: Area known as Acadia was granted to a Scottish nobleman and named Nova Scotia.

1629: English forces occupied Québec City.

1632: Control of New France and Acadia granted to the French by King Charles I of England.

1642: City of Montréal founded.

1663: New France became a French royal colony.

1670: The Hudson's Bay Company received its trading monopoly charter from King Charles II.

1713: The Peace of Utrecht, which followed a series of Franco-British conflicts, awarded control over Newfoundland, mainland Acadia (present-day Nova Scotia and New Brunswick) and the islands of Saint Pierre and Miquelon to Great Britain.

1755: French sympathizers in Acadia began to be forcibly deported.

1756–63: The French and Indian War (known in Europe as the 'Seven-Years War') between France and Britain. The Treaty of Paris of 1763 awarded Britain control over all formerly French-claimed lands in North America except for Saint Pierre and Miquelon.

1758: British North America's first elected legislative assembly met at Halifax.

1763: Boundaries of Québec were set by royal proclamation, and a new government established. Cape Breton Island was annexed to Nova Scotia for the first time, and Labrador was united with Newfoundland.

1774: The Québec Act extended the colony's boundaries and guaranteed subjects religious and linguistic freedom.

1776: North West Company founded by traders in Montréal.

1778: Captain James Cook landed in Nootka Sound off the British Columbia coast.

1784: New Brunswick separated from Nova Scotia.

1786: St John's Island separated from Nova Scotia.

1791: The Constitutional Act established representative government in Canada; the colony was divided into Upper Canada (later Ontario) and Lower Canada (Québec), each with its own system of government.

1799: St John's Island renamed Prince Edward Island.

1802: Saint Pierre and Miquelon, taken by the British in 1793, were returned to France under the Treaty of Amiens.

1812–14: Unsuccessful attempt by the USA to drive the British out of North America.

1815–18: Métis (of French–Indian ancestry) rebelled in Red River area.

1821: The Hudson's Bay and North West Companies merged under the name of the former.

1825: Boundaries of present-day Alaska set by the Anglo–Russian Treaty.

1837: 'Rebellions of 1837' in Montréal and Toronto called for a wider measure of self-government for francophone Canadians.

1840: Passage of the Act of Union, which united Upper and Lower Canada, renaming them Canada West and Canada East respectively.

1842: US-Canadian border in Maine and Minnesota fixed by Webster–Ashburton Treaty.

1846: Western US–Canadian boundary fixed at the 49th parallel, with Great Britain gaining control over Vancouver Island.

1848: Joint 'reform ministry'—the first real cabinet—was formed in Canada.

1855: Newfoundland gained full colonial status and its own government.

1857: Commencement of gold rush in the Fraser and Thompson valleys; led to full colonial status being awarded to British Columbia in 1858; British Columbia united with Vancouver Island in 1866.

1864: Conference held in Charlottetown, Prince Edward Island, to discuss unification of Maritime provinces. Canada obtained permission to attend; the Québec Conference, held less than six weeks later, drafted an agreement for confederation of all colonies.

1867: Dominion of Canada formed from the provinces of Ontario, Québec, New Brunswick and Nova Scotia under the British North America Act of 1867. John Alexander MacDonald took office as the first federal prime minister, and the first parliament convened at Ottawa.

1869–70: Northwest Rebellion by Métis led by Jacques Riel; Rupert's Land and other north-western territories sold to Canada by the Hudson's Bay Company. The Northwest Territories were formally constituted. Manitoba entered the Dominion.

1871: British Columbia entered the Dominion.

1873: Establishment of the North West Mounted Police (later the Royal Canadian Mounted Police); Prince Edward Island entered the Dominion.

1880: An Imperial Order-in-Council formally annexed all British possessions in North America, except Newfoundland but including the Arctic islands, to Canada.

1885: Canadian Pacific railway completed in British Columbia. Métis rebelled in Saskatchewan, again led by Jacques Riel.

1896: Discovery of gold at Bonanza Creek in the Klondike.

1898: Yukon Territory, previously part of the Northwest Territories, became a separate entity.

1903: Alaska–British Columbia border fixed by tribunal; Norwegian expedition completed the first navigation of the Northwest Passage.

1905: The Northwest Territories Act set new boundaries to those territories; Alberta and Saskatchewan joined the Dominion.

1909: The Boundary Waters Treaty estabished the International Joint Commission to settle disputes between the USA and Canada.

1914: The United Kingdom declared war on Germany.

1918: Anticonscription riots took place in Québec City.

1919: Canada joined the League of Nations as an independent member.

1931: The Statute of Westminster guaranteed British recognition of the autonomy of each of the Dominions.

1939: Canada issued a separate declaration of war on Germany and entered the Second World War.

1945: Canada joined the United Nations.

1947: Canadian Citizenship Act passed.

1949: An amendment to the British North America Act of 1867 enabled the Canadian parliament to amend the constitution in matters affecting the federal government. System of appeals to the Judicial Committee of the Privy Council in England abolished in full. Newfoundland joined the Dominion.

1952: Vincent Massey became Canada's first Canadian Governor-General.

1857: Lester B. Pearson, Secretary of State for External Affairs, was awarded the Nobel Peace Prize.

1958: North American Defense Organization (NORAD) founded.

1959: St Lawrence Seaway opened to sea-going vessels.

1960: Canadian Bill of Rights gained royal assent.

1962: Official opening of trans-Canada highway.

1963: The Royal Commission on Bilingualism and Biculturalism was appointed.

1965: The 'maple-leaf' flag became the official flag of Canada.

1982: Proclamation of the Canada Act, which ended Canada's colonial status by empowering it to amend its constitution. The British North America Act of 1867 accordingly became the Constitution Act of 1982.

1987: Meech Lake Accord finalized; this recognized Québec as a 'distinct society' within the Canadian federation and granted each of the provinces new powers in the areas of federal parliamentary reform, judicial appointments and the creation of new provinces, subject to approval by all 10 provinces and the federal parliament.

PRIME MINISTERS OF CANADA

July 1867–November 1873: Sir JOHN A. MACDONALD (Conservative).

November 1873–October 1878: ALEXANDER MACKENZIE (Liberal).

October 1878–June 1891: Sir JOHN A. MACDONALD (Conservative).

June 1891–November 1892: Sir JOHN J. C. ABBOTT (Conservative).

December 1892–December 1894: Sir JOHN S. D. THOMPSON (Conservative).

December 1894–April 1896: Sir MACKENZIE BOWELL (Conservative).

May 1896–July 1896: Sir CHARLES TUPPER (Conservative).

July 1896–October 1911: Sir WILFRID LAURIER (Liberal).

October 1911–October 1917: Sir ROBERT L. BORDEN (Conservative).

October 1917–July 1920: Sir ROBERT L. BORDEN (Unionist).

July 1920–December 1921: ARTHUR MEIGHEN (Unionist).

December 1921–June 1926: W. L. MACKENZIE KING (Liberal).

June 1926–September 1926: ARTHUR MEIGHEN (Unionist).

September 1926–August 1930: W. L. MACKENZIE KING (Liberal).

August 1930–October 1935: R. B. BENNETT (Conservative).

October 1935–November 1948: W. L. MACKENZIE KING (Liberal).

November 1948–June 1957: LOUIS ST-LAURENT (Liberal).

June 1957–April 1963: JOHN G. DIEFENBAKER (Progressive Conservative).

April 1963–April 1968: LESTER B. PEARSON (Liberal).

April 1968–June 1979: PIERRE ELLIOTT TRUDEAU (Liberal).

June 1979–March 1980: JOE CLARK (Progressive Conservative).

March 1980–June 1984: PIERRE ELLIOTT TRUDEAU (Liberal).

June 1984–September 1984: JOHN N. TURNER (Liberal).

September 1984–: M. BRIAN MULRONEY (Progressive Conservative).

AREA AND POPULATION

(Source: Statistics Canada, Ottawa, ON K1A 0T6.)

Area, Population and Density

Summary

Area (sq km)	
Land	9,215,430
Inland water	755,180
Total	9,970,610*
Population (census results)	
1851	2,436,297
1901	5,371,315
1951[1]	14,009,429
1961	18,238,247
1971	21,568,311
3 June 1981	24,343,181
3 June 1986[2]	
Males	12,485,650
Females	12,823,680
Total	25,309,330
Population (official estimates at 1 June)	
1985	25,165,400
1986	25,353,000
1987	25,625,100
Density (per sq km of land area) at 1 June 1987	2.8

* 3,849,674 sq miles.

[1] Newfoundland included for the first time. Excluding Newfoundland, the total would have been 13,648,013.

[2] Excludes census data for one or more incompletely enumerated Indian reserves or Indian settlements.

Provinces and Territories (census of 3 June 1986)

	Area (sq km)			Population[1]	Population per sq km of land area
	Land	Inland water	Total		
Alberta	644,390	16,800	661,190	2,365,825	3.7
British Columbia[2]	929,730	18,070	947,800	2,883,367	3.1
Manitoba[2]	548,360	101,590	649,950	1,063,016	1.9
New Brunswick	72,090	1,350	73,440	709,442	9.8
Newfoundland[2]	371,690	34,030	405,720	568,349	1.5
Northwest Territories[2]	3,293,020	133,300	3,426,320	52,238	0.02
Nova Scotia	52,840	2,650	55,490	873,176	16.5
Ontario	891,190	177,390	1,068,580	9,101,694	10.2
Prince Edward Island	5,660	—	5,660	126,646	22.4
Québec	1,356,790	183,890	1,540,680	6,532,461	4.8
Saskatchewan[2]	570,700	81,630	652,330	1,009,613	1.8
Yukon Territory[2]	478,970	4,480	483,450	23,504	0.05
Total	9,215,430	755,180	9,970,610	25,309,331	2.7

[1] Excludes census data for one or more incompletely enumerated Indian reserves or Indian settlements.
[2] Figures for area were recalculated in 1981.

Population by Province or Territory and Selected Ethnic Origins

(Census of 3 June 1986. Based upon 20% sample data; census figures exclude data for one or more incompletely enumerated Indian reserves or Indian settlements.)

Summary

	Single origins	Multiple origins[1]	Total
Alberta	1,389,930	950,335	2,340,265
British Columbia	1,759,810	1,089,780	2,849,585
Manitoba	681,580	367,740	1,049,320
New Brunswick	504,350	197,505	701,680
Newfoundland	470,280	93,730	564,000
Northwest Territories	39,980	12,040	52,020
Nova Scotia	535,905	328,245	864,150
Ontario	5,952,105	3,049,060	9,001,170
Prince Edward Island	74,105	50,985	125,090
Québec	6,010,010	444,480	6,454,490
Saskatchewan	604,750	391,950	996,695
Yukon Territory	12,855	10,505	23,360
Total	18,035,665	6,986,345	25,022,005

[1] Includes persons who report more than one origin.

Single Origins

	British[1]	French[2]	German	Italian	Ukrainian	Aboriginal peoples[3]	Other	Total
Alberta	592,345	77,585	182,870	23,635	106,760	51,760	355,065	1,389,930
British Columbia	871,070	68,965	148,280	46,755	48,200	61,130	515,410	1,759,810
Manitoba	224,375	55,720	96,160	8,230	79,940	55,410	161,745	681,580
New Brunswick	251,315	232,570	3,760	865	490	3,885	11,465	504,350
Newfoundland	449,760	11,315	1,155	235	105	3,825	3,885	470,280
Northwest Territories	7,015	1,510	1,085	255	400	27,175	2,540	39,980
Nova Scotia	417,690	52,900	21,205	2,260	1,440	5,960	34,450	535,905
Ontario	2,912,830	531,580	285,155	461,375	109,705	55,560	1,595,900	5,952,105
Prince Edward Island	59,275	11,130	535	80	65	410	2,610	74,105
Québec	319,550	5,015,565	26,780	163,880	12,225	49,320	422,690	6,010,010
Saskatchewan	222,115	33,535	128,850	1,950	60,550	55,645	102,105	604,750
Yukon Territory	5,370	775	880	75	340	3,280	2,135	12,855
Total single origins	6,332,725	6,093,160	896,720	709,590	420,210	373,265	3,209,995	18,035,665

[1] Includes the single origins of English, Irish, Scottish, Welsh, British n.i.e. (not included elsewhere) and Other British.
[2] Includes the single origins of French, Acadian, French-Canadian and Québecois.
[3] Includes the single origins of Inuit, Métis and North American Indians.

Population by Age

Summary (census of 3 June 1986)*

	Male	Female	Total	%
Under 4 years	927.8	882.4	1,810.2	7.2
5–9 years	920.1	874.9	1,795.0	7.1
10–14 years	916.8	870.0	1,786.8	7.1
15–19 years	985.3	939.6	1,924.9	7.6
20–24 years	1,131.5	1,121.9	2,253.4	8.9
25–34 years	2,248.8	2,278.4	4,527.2	17.9
35–44 years	1,822.0	1,818.9	3,640.9	14.4
45–54 years	1,276.2	1,269.1	2,545.2	10.1
55–64 years	1,124.1	1,204.2	2,328.3	9.2
65–69 years	414.5	497.2	911.8	3.6
70 years and over	718.8	1,067.0	1,785.8	7.1
Total	12,485.7	12,823.7	25,309.3	100.0

* Excludes census data for one or more incompletely enumerated Indian reserves or Indian settlements.

Provinces and Territories (census of 3 June 1986, '000)*

	Under 20 years	20–24 years	25–34 years	35–64 years	65 years and over	Total
Alberta	743.5	224.9	484.9	721.3	191.4	2,365.8
British Columbia	799.3	229.6	506.6	998.6	349.5	2,883.4
Manitoba	318.2	94.5	181.1	335.5	133.8	1,063.0
New Brunswick	221.9	64.0	122.1	222.6	78.7	709.4
Newfoundland	205.2	51.1	95.6	166.5	50.0	568.3
Northwest Territories	22.3	5.4	10.4	12.7	1.4	52.2
Nova Scotia	259.3	81.6	149.7	278.8	103.8	873.2
Ontario	2,558.5	814.6	1,583.0	3,152.9	992.6	9,101.7
Prince Edward Island	40.2	11.4	20.3	38.7	16.1	126.6
Québec	1,816.6	585.4	1,197.7	2,282.1	650.7	6,532.5
Saskatchewan	324.3	88.9	170.5	297.2	128.6	1,009.6
Yukon Territory	7.7	2.0	5.3	7.6	0.9	23.5
Total	7,316.9	2,253.4	4,527.2	8,514.4	2,697.5	25,309.3

* Excludes census data for one or more incompletely enumerated Indian reserves or Indian settlements.

Census Metropolitan Areas

(census of 3 June 1986)

Toronto	3,427,168	Victoria	255,547*
Montréal	2,921,357*	Windsor	253,988
Vancouver	1,380,729	Oshawa	203,543
Ottawa–Hull	819,263	Saskatoon	200,665
Edmonton	785,465*	Regina	186,521
Calgary	671,326*	St John's (NF)	161,901
Winnipeg	625,304	Chicoutimi–Jonquière	158,468
Québec	603,267	Sudbury	148,877
Hamilton	557,029	Sherbrooke	129,960
St Catharines–Niagara	343,258	Trois–Rivières	128,888
London	342,302	Thunder Bay	122,217
Kitchener	311,195	Saint John (NB)	121,265
Halifax	295,990		

* Excludes population of one or more incompletely enumerated Indian reserves or Indian settlements.

Principal Incorporated Cities and Towns

(census of 3 June 1986)

Montréal	1,015,420	London	269,140	Halifax	113,577	Saint John (NB)	76,381
Calgary	636,104	Windsor	193,111	Thunder Bay	112,272	Brantford	76,146
Toronto	612,289	Brampton	188,498	St John's (NF)	96,216	Saint-Léonard	75,947
Winnipeg*	594,551	Saskatoon	177,641	Nepean	95,490	LaSalle	75,621
Edmonton	573,982	Regina	175,064	Montréal-Nord	90,303	Sherbrooke	74,438
North York	556,297	Québec	164,580	Gloucester	89,810	Niagara Falls	72,107
Scarborough	484,676	Kitchener	150,604	Sudbury	88,717	Sainte-Foy	69,615
Vancouver	431,147	York	135,401	Oakville	87,107	Charlesbourg	68,996
Mississauga	374,005	Longueuil	125,441	Gatineau	81,244	Prince George	67,621
Hamilton	306,728	Oshawa	123,651	Sault Sainte Marie	80,905	Saint-Laurent	67,002
Etobicoke	302,973	St Catharines	123,455	Cambridge	79,920	Victoria	66,303
Ottawa	300,763	Burlington	116,675	Guelph	78,235	Saint-Hubert	66,218
Laval	284,164	Markham	114,597				

* Including St James–Assiniboia.

Immigrant Arrivals

Country of last permanent residence	1983	1984	1985
Europe	24,312	20,901	18,859
Czechoslovakia	1,259	924	903
France	1,651	1,380	1,401
Germany, Fed. Republic	2,518	1,727	1,578
Greece	601	555	551
Hungary	484	374	614
Italy	826	839	650
Netherlands	672	545	466
Poland	5,094	4,499	3,617
Portugal (incl. Azores and Madeira)	1,350	1,342	1,342
Switzerland	423	389	376
United Kingdom	5,737	5,104	4,454
Yugoslavia	527	465	478
Africa	3,659	3,552	3,545
Egypt	498	449	394
Morocco	390	251	338
South Africa	454	321	365
Tanzania	418	420	424
Australasia	478	535	506
Australia	334	377	355
Asia	36,906	41,896	38,597
Cambodia	1,542	1,727	1,803
China, People's Republic	2,217	2,214	1,883
Hong Kong	6,710	7,696	7,380
India	7,041	5,502	4,028
Iran	1,268	1,870	1,728
Iraq	325	495	359
Israel	584	429	676
Korea, Republic	1,017	801	934
Laos	434	870	379
Lebanon	813	1,245	1,657
Malaysia	399	356	332
Pakistan	836	611	479
Philippines	4,454	3,748	3,076
Sri Lanka	166	1,048	815
Taiwan	570	421	536
Vietnam	6,451	10,950	10,404
North and Central America	18,251	16,630	17,817
Haiti	2,827	1,397	1,297
Jamaica	2,423	2,479	2,922
Mexico	512	522	369
Trinidad and Tobago	787	595	670
USA	7,381	6,922	6,669
South America	4,816	4,084	4,356
Chile	757	664	534
Guyana	2,605	1,896	2,301
Oceania	735	616	622
Fiji	552	388	444
Sub-total	89,157	88,214	84,302
Not stated	—	25	—
Total	89,157	88,239	84,302

AN INTRODUCTION TO THE PROVINCES AND TERRITORIES

Alberta

Area: 661,190 sq km (255,285 sq miles).
Population (census of 3 June 1986): 2,365,825.
Capital: Edmonton.
Principal Cities (population at census of 3 June 1986): Calgary 636,104; Edmonton (capital) 573,982; Lethbridge 58,841; Red Deer 54,425.

LOCATION, TOPOGRAPHY AND CLIMATE

The province of Alberta lies in the south-west of Canada and is the westernmost of the three Prairie provinces. It is bordered by Saskatchewan to the east, the Northwest Territories to the north, and the US state of Montana to the south. The range of the Rocky Mountains marks the southern part of Alberta's western boundary with British Columbia, and includes Mount Columbia, Alberta's

highest point at 3,747 m (12,293 ft). The south of the province consists of dry prairie land, while in the north regions of poplar forests and open prairies merge into mixed forests. The greater part of southern Alberta drains through the South and North Saskatchewan Rivers into Hudson Bay; northern Alberta is drained by the Athabasca, Hay and Peace Rivers through the Great Slave Lake (Northwest Territories) and ultimately into the Arctic Ocean. Alberta's two principal lakes are Lake Claire (1,436 sq km) and Lesser Slave Lake (1,168 sq km); Lake Athabasca (7,936 sq km) is shared with Saskatchewan. The province has a cool, temperate climate, with cold winters occasionally moderated by the warm, dry Chinook winds. Low precipitation habitually causes droughts, particularly in the south-west.

HISTORICAL LANDMARKS

In 1754 Anthony Henday of the Hudson's Bay Company (HBC) spent the winter near the site of present-day Edmonton. At that time Indian tribes inhabiting the area now known as Alberta included the Blackfoot, Blood, Peigan, Gros Ventre and Sarcee. The period until 1821 was dominated by rivalry between the HBC and the Montréal-based North West Company; fur-trading posts were established from 1778 along the Athabasca River. Following its absorption of the North West Company in 1821, the HBC controlled the territory until 1869, when it was sold to the government of the newly-formed Dominion of Canada. The area lying between the Rocky Mountains and Manitoba was organized in 1870 as the Northwest Territories of Canada; the Northwest Territories Act of 1875 provided it with a lieutenant-governor and legislature. In 1877 the last major agreement between Indian tribes and the Canadian government was signed with the Blackfoot, Sarcee and Stoney. The province of Alberta was created and admitted to the confederation on 1 September 1905, partly as a result of calls for autonomy of the Northwest Territories.

British Columbia

Area: 947,800 sq km (365,946 sq miles).
Population (census of 3 June 1986): 2,883,367.
Capital: Victoria.
Principal Cities (population at census of 3 June 1986): Vancouver 431,147; Prince George 67,621; Victoria (capital) 66,303; Kamloops 61,773; Kelowna 61,213.

LOCATION, TOPOGRAPHY AND CLIMATE

British Columbia is Canada's westernmost province (only Yukon Territory extends further west). It is bordered by Alberta to the east (the southern half of the boundary being marked by the Rocky Mountains), Yukon Territory and the Northwest Territories to the north, Alaska (USA) to the north-west (a narrow strip of land and archipelagos, separated by straits and sounds, extending south from the main mass of the US state), the Pacific Ocean to the west and the US states of Washington, Idaho and Montana to the south. The Cordilleran Region dominates the province, consisting of parallel mountain ranges running north–south, with an accompanying set of parallel valleys; plateaux occupy much of the centre of the province. These mountain ranges include the Rocky Mountains in the east (rising to Mount Robson at 3,954 m—12,972 ft) and the Coast Mountains in the west. The latter stretch the length of the state, starting from the St Elias mountains in the north, around the border with Yukon Territory and Alaska, which include Mount Fairweather (British Columbia's highest peak at 4,663 m—15,298 ft), which is on the boundary with Alaska. Numerous islands lie off the coast, including the large Vancouver Island and the Queen Charlotte Islands group, separated from the mainland by the Strait of Georgia, Queen Charlotte Strait and Hecate Strait. The western boundary of the Rocky Mountains is formed by the Rocky Mountain Trench, extending 1,500 km from Montana to Yukon Territory. The headwaters of the Kootenay, Columbia, Fraser, Peace and Liard rivers flow from this trench. British Columbia has a variable climate, with mild, wet winters and dry summers in the south-east, and colder weather and moderate precipitation in the north.

HISTORICAL LANDMARKS

Spanish explorer Juan Pérez Hernández sighted and claimed an area of the British Columbia coast for his country in 1774. Four years later James Cook sailed into Nootka Sound on the west coast of present-day Vancouver Island. The Nootka Conventions of 1790–92 gave Spain and Britain equal trading rights in the area, while British claims to ownership strengthened with George Vancouver's charting of the coast. Exploration of the interior began at about this time and fur-trading posts were established under the control of the Hudson's Bay Company (HBC). The 1846 Oregon Treaty fixed the USA's northern boundary along the 49th parallel, but excluding Vancouver Island. The latter was granted to the HBC in 1849, and a legislative assembly was established on the island in 1856. The discovery of gold along the Lower Fraser River the following year precipitated the rapid settlement of the surrounding area, and the mainland colony of British Columbia was established in 1858; in 1866 it was united with Vancouver Island. British Columbia joined the confederation on 20 July 1871, having first made the condition that the federal government construct a transcontinental railway to link it with eastern Canada. The Canadian Pacific Railway reached the south-western coast in 1885, built largely with the assistance of Chinese immigrant workers. The Alaska–British Columbia boundary was fixed by tribunal in 1903.

Manitoba

Area: 649,950 sq km (250,946 sq miles).
Population (census of 3 June 1986): 1,063,016.

Capital and Principal City: Winnipeg (population 594,551 at census of 3 June 1986).

LOCATION, TOPOGRAPHY AND CLIMATE

Manitoba is situated in southern–central Canada and is the easternmost of the three Prairie provinces. Its borders are formed by Saskatchewan to the west, Ontario to the east, the Northwest Territories to the north and the US states of North Dakota and Minnesota to the south. The province is divided into four distinct geographic regions: the Hudson Bay Lowland, the Precambrian Upland, the Lake Agassiz Lowland and the Western Upland. The Lake Agassiz Lowland contains the three largest lakes in the province, Winnipeg, Winnipegosis and Manitoba; the Nelson River carries the waters of Lake Winnipeg into Hudson Bay..The south-western part of the province, the Western Upland, is formed by a series of low plateaux. The Precambrian Upland, consisting of rocky outcrop and numerous lakes, is utilized for hydroelectric generation. The topography of the province varies from arable country in the south-western section to wilderness in the section east of a line drawn from the south-east corner of Manitoba to the border with Saskatchewan at Flin Flon, which constitutes two-thirds of the province and forms part of the Canadian Shield. Other major rivers flowing through Manitoba include the Saskatchewan, the Red, the Assiniboine and the Winnipeg. Manitoba has a continental climate, with very cold winters and moderately warm summers.

HISTORICAL LANDMARKS

The area occupied by present-day Manitoba formed part of the territory known as Rupert's Land which was granted to the Hudson's Bay Company (HBC) by King Charles II of England on its establishment in 1670. HBC employee Henry Kelsey and the La Vérendrye family explored lands to the south-west and west of Hudson Bay respectively during the late 17th and early 18th centuries. Fur-trading posts were supplemented by agricultural settlements from 1812. In 1815–18 a major rebellion arose as a result of the conflict between agricultural expansion and the land rights claimed by the Métis (French–Indian inhabitants) of the Red River Valley area. A second period of unrest and Métis rebellion occurred in 1869–70; in 1870, the year following Canada's purchase of Rupert's Land from the HBC, the area was divided into the Northwest Territories (including present-day Alberta and Saskatchewan) and the new province of Manitoba, which entered the confederation on 15 July of the same year. The province's boundaries were confirmed in 1881. In the period to 1914, when the Panama Canal opened up a cheap east–west sea cargo route, the city of Winnipeg enjoyed increasing supremacy as a transportation centre, being the 'hub' of the growing Canadian rail network. The Winnipeg General Strike of 1919 resulted from a localized economic depression partly arising from the loss of this important east–west trade role.

New Brunswick

Area: 73,440 sq km (28,355 sq miles).
Population (census of 3 June 1986): 709,442.
Capital: Fredericton.
Principal Cities (population at census of 3 June 1986): Saint John 76,381; Moncton 55,468; Fredericton (capital) 44,352.

LOCATION, TOPOGRAPHY AND CLIMATE

The province of New Brunswick, one of the three Maritime provinces, lies in the east of Canada, bordered by Québec to the north, the US state of Maine to the west, the Bay of Fundy to the south and Nova Scotia to the south-east. To the north-east are the Northumberland Strait (which separates New Brunswick from Prince Edward Island) and the Gulf of St Lawrence. The province is composed of uplands in the north and low, rolling hills in the central and eastern regions, while steep hills on the southern coast descend to tidal marshes and a low plain in the south-east. The southern region contains several lakes, including Grand Lake, which is over 30 km in length. New Brunswick has a continental climate, more extreme in the interior than on the coasts, where it is moderated by the proximity of the sea.

HISTORICAL LANDMARKS

Micmac communities had inhabited the area of present-day New Brunswick for many years prior to French attempts at settlement on the Saint Croix River (which today forms part of the border with Maine) and at Port Royal (Nova Scotia) in 1604–05. Following the French move to the Québec region from 1608, the Micmac remained in the St John valley, which the French later used to launch raids against New England in the 1690s. In 1621 New

Brunswick formed part of the area granted to Scottish nobleman Sir William Alexander by James I of England and renamed Nova Scotia. Under the Peace of Utrecht in 1713 most of the area of Nova Scotia (Acadia), including New Brunswick, was transferred to the British; French-sympathizing Acadians were largely deported from 1755, following which the land was occupied by floods of immigrants, many from New England. Loyalist refugees settled on the north shore of the Bay of Fundy following the American Revolution and founded the city of Saint John. New Brunswick received separate colonial status from the rest of Nova Scotia in 1784, and was part of the new confederation at its inception on 1 July 1867. During the 1960s a series of legislative measures was passed in an attempt to rectify severe disparities between standards of living in the urban south of the province and those in the rural north.

Newfoundland

Area: 405,720 sq km (156,648 sq miles).

Population (census of 3 June 1986): 568,349.

Capital and Principal City: St John's (population 96,216 at census of 3 June 1986).

LOCATION, TOPOGRAPHY AND CLIMATE

Newfoundland, Canada's easternmost province, consists of the mainland territory of Labrador and the smaller Island of Newfoundland to its south. Labrador is bounded by the Atlantic Ocean to the east and Québec to the west and south; the Island of Newfoundland lies east of the Gulf of St Lawrence, separated from the mainland by the Strait of Belle Isle. To the south-west of the Island of Newfoundland are the French islands of Saint Pierre and Miquelon. The mainland is generally barren and rugged, dominated by the Torngat Mountains in the north and a vast, forested plateau in the interior. On the Island of Newfoundland the Long Range Mountains extend the length of the west coast, reaching 815 m (2,674 ft) at their highest point at Gros Morne. The mountains are interspersed with valleys and several large bays, including the Bay of Islands and Bonne Bay. The interior of the island is an undulating plateau, drained by the Exploits, Gander, Humber and Terra Nova Rivers. The north-eastern coast is characterized by numerous bays, islands and fiords caused by glaciation. Temperatures are variable, but generally winters are very cold, and summers cool on the coast and warmer inland.

HISTORICAL LANDMARKS

Beothuk Indians inhabited the island of Newfoundland at the time when Leif Ericsson and other Norse voyagers travelling from Greenland are thought to have visited the area. John Cabot, in 1497, charted the coast, and by the 16th century the rich fishing grounds around the island were being plied by fishermen from various European countries. In 1583 the island was claimed for England by Humphrey Gilbert, but permanent settlement did not begin until the end of the 17th century due to the power of so-called 'fishing admirals' who protected their interests fiercely. French claims to the island were negated under the Peace of Utrecht in 1713, but they retained some fishing rights off the north shore. During the French and Indian War years (1756–63) the area was occupied again by French forces; the Treaty of Paris (1763) returned it to Britain but awarded France the islands of Saint Pierre and Miquelon. Also in 1763, Labrador was annexed to Newfoundland. Full colonial status was awarded in 1855 and a government established. Representatives of Newfoundland attended the confederation conferences in the period 1864–67 but declined membership at that time. French fishing rights were curtailed in 1904. In the late 1920s and 1930s Newfoundland was affected severely by the economic depression and eventually resumed colonial status; during World War II it assumed great strategic importance as a military base and economic recovery was completed. Following two referendums and much debate, Newfoundland joined the confederation on 31 March 1949.

Northwest Territories

Area: 3,426,320 sq km (1,322,902 sq miles).

Population (census of 3 June 1986): 52,238.

Capital and Principal City: Yellowknife (population 11,753 at census of 3 June 1986).

LOCATION, TOPOGRAPHY AND CLIMATE

The Northwest Territories, which constitute more than one-third of Canada's total area, comprise all Canadian mainland territory north of the 60th parallel of latitude and west of Hudson's Bay, together with the Arctic Archipelago and all islands in James and Hudson Bays and in the Hudson Strait. The eastern part of the mainland consists of barren Canadian Shield terrain, an undulating, rocky surface of low altitude, intersected by rivers and lakes, and is known as the arctic mainland. Westwards from the Canadian Shield lies the Mackenzie Valley area, rising sharply in the west to the Cordillera mountain region, which contains peaks of over 2,700 m. The territories' main river, the Mackenzie (4,241 km—2,635 miles in length), traverses this area, draining into the Beaufort Sea. The Arctic Archipelago is characterized by high mountain ranges and great fiords on the eastern islands, while the western islands are mainly low-lying. Mount Barbeau, which rises to 2,616 m (8,583 ft) on Ellesmere Island, is the highest point in the archipelago. The variations in climate on the mainland are most extreme in the Mackenzie Valley area, where temperatures can be hot in summer, but very cold in winter. The temperature range is slightly less extreme in the arctic mainland, while that of the archipelago is more moderate, with milder winters and short, cool summers.

HISTORICAL LANDMARKS

The area known as the Northwest Territories encompassed a wide variety of indigenous cultures at the time of white exploration, with the nomadic Inuit inhabiting the area north of the Arctic Circle and the Chipewyan, Yellowknife, Slave, Dogrib, Hare, Nahanni and Kutchin groups in the subarctic region. Norse voyagers from Greenland settlements first visited the area in about 1000; several European expeditions in the late 16th century sought unsuccessfully to locate the Northwest Passage. The area became the property of the Hudson's Bay Company in 1670; employee Samuel Hearne made an overland trip from the bayside settlement of Churchill (now in Manitoba) to the Coppermine River in 1770–71. For the North West Company, Alexander Mackenzie charted the length of the Mackenzie River in 1789; fur-trading posts were later established along his route. (These remained the principal settlements until the 1930s, when mineral exploration led to the further development of the Mackenzie Valley.) The Northwest Territories were formally created on 15 July 1870, with their area being reduced firstly by the reorganization of the borders of Manitoba in 1881, then by the creation of Yukon Territory in 1898 and subsequently by the entry into the confederation in 1905 of Alberta and Saskatchewan. The last discoveries of Arctic islands were made in 1913–18; radar and weather stations were established in the Arctic from the Second World War onwards. In 1953 the federal Department of Northern Affairs and Natural Resources (now the Department of Indian Affairs and Northern Development) was created to aid the development of health, housing, educational and communications facilities in the territories.

Nova Scotia

Area: 55,490 sq km (21,425 sq miles).

Population (census of 3 June 1986): 873,176.

Capital: Halifax.

Principal Cities (population at census of 3 June 1986): Halifax (capital) 113,577; Dartmouth 65,243.

LOCATION, TOPOGRAPHY AND CLIMATE

The province of Nova Scotia, one of the three Maritime provinces, is a peninsula lying in the extreme east of Canada, connected to New Brunswick by the Isthmus of Chignecto. It is bounded by Cabot Strait, the Gulf of St Lawrence and Northumberland Strait to the north, the Atlantic Ocean to the south, and the Bay of Fundy to the west. The Strait of Canso divides Cape Breton Island from mainland Nova Scotia. Cape Breton Island is bisected by the Bras d'Or Lake (1,099 sq km), which stretches from north-east to south-west. The province's highest point is Cape Breton, at 532 m. Nova Scotia has a generally temperate climate, which tends to fog, especially in the spring. The coastal areas are both milder and wetter, with frequent storms in the winter.

HISTORICAL LANDMARKS

Algonquian-speaking Micmac were inhabitants of Nova Scotia at the time of European settlement, which began with the establishment of Port Royal (now Annapolis Royal) in 1605, although John Cabot is claimed to have landed on Cape Breton Island in 1497. In 1621 the area known as Acadia was granted by King James I of England to Scottish nobleman Sir William Alexander and renamed Nova Scotia; it was occupied by both French and English troops several times during the 17th and early 18th centuries. In 1713, under the Peace of Utrecht, Nova Scotia (which then included New Brunswick) was placed under British control: Cape Breton Island (then named Île Royale) and Prince Edward Island (Île

Saint-Jean) remained French until 1763, when they too were put under British control under the Treaty of Paris. The first popularly-elected legislative assembly in British North America met at Halifax in 1758. In 1784 the colonies of New Brunswick and Cape Breton were separated from Nova Scotia; the future Prince Edward Island (by now renamed St John's Island) was separated permanently from 1786. Cape Breton Island was re-annexed to Nova Scotia in 1820. Following the American Revolution there was much Loyalist immigration into Nova Scotia. Despite considerable opposition from sections of the community the province entered the confederation on 1 July 1867. Nova Scotia was at the forefront of the Maritime Rights movement of the 1920s protesting against unfavourable freight rates and the protective tariff.

Ontario

Area: 1,068,580 sq km (412,579 sq miles).

Population (census of 3 June 1986): 9,101,694.

Capital: Toronto.

Principal Cities (population at census of 3 June 1986):

Toronto	612,289	Thunder Bay	112,272
North York	556,297	Nepean	95,490
Scarborough	484,676	Gloucester	89,810
Mississauga	374,005	Sudbury	88,717
Hamilton	306,728	Oakville	87,107
Etobicoke	302,973	Sault Sainte Marie	80,905
Ottawa	300,763	Cambridge	79,920
London	269,140	Guelph	78,235
Windsor	193,111	Brantford	76,146
Brampton	188,498	Niagara Falls	72,107
Kitchener	150,604	Vaughan	65,058
York	135,401	Peterborough	61,049
Oshawa	123,651	Waterloo	58,718
St Catharines	123,455	Kingston	55,050
Burlington	116,675	North Bay	50,623
Markham	114,597		

LOCATION, TOPOGRAPHY AND CLIMATE

Ontario is situated in south–central Canada. It is bordered by Manitoba to the west, Hudson Bay to the north and north-east and Québec to the east; its southern boundary is formed by the St Lawrence River, Lakes Ontario, Erie, Huron and Superior, and the state of Minnesota. Ontario extends further to the south than does any other Canadian province due to its Great Lakes boundary. The province is composed of two geological areas, each with distinctive terrain. The Canadian Shield region contains the eastern Ontario plain, with rolling hills and plains to the west descending into flat country in the extreme south-west. The southern lowlands region is characterized by glacial features, such as morainal hills, drumlins and numerous plains. Lakes (including the Great Lakes) and rivers comprise one-sixth of the province's total land area. Major rivers in addition to the St Lawrence include the Ottawa, Albany and Attawapiskat. The largest lake contained wholly within the province is Lake Nipigon, at 4,848 sq km. The Great Lakes–St Lawrence forest region, an area of mixed forest, stretches eastwards and westwards of Lake Superior. Ontario has wide variations in temperature according to differences in altitude; upland areas are distinctly cooler. Winters throughout the province are generally harsh and stormy.

HISTORICAL LANDMARKS

Algonquian and Iroquoian tribes inhabited the area now known as the province of Ontario at the time when Samuel de Champlain travelled along the Ottawa River in 1613-15. The Ontario region gradually became an important link between French settlements in Québec and the Mississippi region. The British began to settle in the mid-18th century. The 1783 Treaty of Paris, which marked the end of the American Revolution, set the southern border of what is now Ontario. Up to 10,000 Loyalist immigrants are thought to have entered the area as a result of the revolution. The province of Upper Canada was created under the Constitutional Act of 1791, with its first capital at Newark (now Niagara-on-the-Lake); in 1812 it was estimated that up to 80% of the settlers in southern Ontario were of US origin. Following the Rebellions of 1837 in Montréal and Toronto, Upper and Lower Canada were united under the Act of Union (1840) and renamed Canada West and East respectively; the first real cabinet was formed in 1848. Together, Canada West and Canada East attended the Charlottetown conference and proposed the idea of a federation of all the provinces; thus Ontario became a member of the confederation on 1 July 1867 and the federal capital was established at Ottawa. The province's western boundary was not finally set until 1912.

Prince Edward Island

Area: 5,660 sq km (2,185 sq miles).

Population (census of 3 June 1986): 126,646.

Capital and City Charlottetown (population 15,776 at census of 3 June 1986).

LOCATION, TOPOGRAPHY AND CLIMATE

Prince Edward Island, which constitutes Canada's smallest province, is one of the three Maritime provinces and is situated in the Gulf of St Lawrence to the east of the country. Across the Northumberland Strait lie Nova Scotia, to the east and south, and New Brunswick, to the south-west. To the north are the Îles de la Madeleine, part of the province of Québec. The land surface of the island is level in the west, rising to gentle hills in the central and eastern regions. The deep red soil which characterizes the island is interspersed with outcrops of sedimentary rock. Tidal inlets indent the coastline, while sandbanks lie along the north shore. Prince Edward Island has a temperate climate, with long, mild winters and cool summers.

HISTORICAL LANDMARKS

The Micmac had inhabited present-day Prince Edward Island for many generations when Jacques Cartier landed in 1534. French settlement of the island, which was named Île Saint-Jean and was a dependency of Île Royale (Cape Breton Island, now part of Nova Scotia), commenced in the 1720s, and the island was ceded to the British and renamed St John's Island in 1763 under the Treaty of Paris. It remained annexed to Nova Scotia until 1769, when it was given a separate government; was re-annexed between 1784 and 1786, and then was separated again. In 1799 it was renamed Prince Edward Island in honour of the third son of George III. Land-ownership problems dominated the island's political life until confederation. The Charlottetown conference was held in 1864 to discuss a union of the Maritime provinces; Prince Edward Islanders declined to join the larger confederation at its inception, but financial difficulties and other pressures caused it to enter the Dominion of Canada on 1 July 1873.

Québec

Area: 1,540,680 sq km (594,857 sq miles).

Population (census of 3 June 1986): 6,532,461.

Capital: Québec.

Principal Urban Centres (population at census of 3 June 1986):

Montréal	1,015,420	Charlesbourg	68,996
Laval	284,164	Saint-Laurent	67,002
Québec	164,580	Saint-Hubert	66,218
Longueuil	125,441	Beauport	62,869
Montréal-Nord	90,303	Chicoutimi	61,083
Gatineau	81,244	Verdun	60,246
Saint-Léonard	75,947	Hull	58,722
LaSalle	75,621	Jonquière	58,467
Sherbrooke	74,438	Brossard	57,441
Sainte-Foy	69,615	Trois-Rivières	50,122

LOCATION, TOPOGRAPHY AND CLIMATE

In terms of its area, Québec is the largest province in Canada. It is bounded to the north-west by Hudson Bay, to the north by the Hudson Strait, to the north-east by Labrador (part of Newfoundland), to the south-east by the Gulf of St Lawrence, the province of New Brunswick and the US states of Maine, New Hampshire, Vermont and New York; and to the south-west by Ontario, across the Ottawa River. Major islands of the province include the Île d'Anticosti, in the mouth of the St Lawrence River, and the Îles de la Madeleine, north of Prince Edward Island and Nova Scotia. Québec is divided into three distinct geological regions. The Canadian Shield, covering the greater part of the province to the north, consists of a huge plateau, cut by numerous lakes and rivers. The St Lawrence River valley and lowlands to the south is a fertile area, formed by a series of broad terraces which decline towards the river. The third section, the Appalachian foothills south of the St Lawrence River, forms part of the Appalachian mountain range, stretching from Newfoundland Island to Alabama (USA) and intersected by arable plateaux and plains. Québec's most important waterway is the St Lawrence River, which flows for over 3,600 km through the Great Lakes before reaching the Atlantic Ocean and is among the world's greatest rivers. The highest point is Mount Iberville, in the Torngat Mountains, rising to 1,652 m (5,420 ft), in northern Québec—the highest point in mainland Canada east of the Rocky Mountains. The climate is severe, with extreme temperatures and long summers and winters, although the south of the province around Montréal and Québec City receives pleasant summers.

HISTORICAL LANDMARKS

The present-day province of Québec was the site of Canada's first permanent European settlement; Samuel de Champlain established what was to become Québec City on the site of an Iroquois village in 1608. The colony of New France grew slowly as the frequency of wars with the British increased; calm was briefly restored by the Peace of Utrecht in 1713 (whereby France lost much of its claimed territory in Canada) but conflict resumed, and the cities of Québec and Montréal were occupied in 1759 and 1760 respectively by British forces. The Treaty of Paris (1763), which ended the French and Indian War, also ended French claims to the area. The Québec Act of 1774 attempted to recreate the boundaries of New France; the Constitutional Act of 1791 divided the English and Fench majority populations of the area then known as Canada into the colonies of Upper and Lower Canada respectively. Following the Rebellions of 1837 in Montréal and Toronto, the two colonies were reunited under the 1840 Act of Union, with English as the official language. The federal structure of confederation was accepted as a means of increasing control over language, religion and civil law, and Québec became a separate province at confederation on 1 July 1867. The Meech Lake Accord of 1987, which recognized Québec as a 'distinct society' within the Canadian federation, assured constitutional protection for the preservation of its French culture and language.

Saskatchewan

Area: 652,330 sq km (251,865 sq miles).
Population (census of 3 June 1986): 1,009,613.
Capital: Regina.
Principal Cities (population at census of 3 June 1986): Saskatoon 177,641; Regina (capital) 175,064.

LOCATION, TOPOGRAPHY AND CLIMATE

The province of Saskatchewan lies in the south-west of Canada, bordered to the east and west respectively by the other two Prairie provinces of Manitoba and Alberta. To the north are the Northwest Territories and to the south, the US states of Montana and North Dakota. The Canadian Shield, which characterizes the northern third of the province, is a region of rocky outcrops and lakes. To the south lie the prairie lowlands, a fertile, grain-producing area. On the western and south-western boundaries another prairie region is characterized by undulating plains of a higher altitude. The Cypress Hills in the extreme south-west rise to 1,468 m (4,816 ft). About 12% of the province is accounted for by freshwater, including several large lake systems. The Qu'Appelle and Saskatchewan rivers eventually drain into Hudson Bay, by way of Lake Winnipeg (Manitoba). The outflow of the Churchill River is also into Hudson Bay, by way of Churchill Lake and the Southern Indian Lake (Manitoba). Lake Athabasca (7,936 sq km), which is shared with Alberta, feeds into the Mackenzie River by way of the Great Slave Lake (both Northwest Territories), and eventually to the Beaufort Sea. Saskatchewan has a continental climate, dry and warm in summer, with long, cold winters.

HISTORICAL LANDMARKS

Athapaskan-, Algonquian- and Siouan-speaking Indians were present in the area now known as Saskatchewan at the time of the first explorations in the late 17th century. Henry Kelsey of the Hudson's Bay Company (HBC) was the first voyager to penetrate the plains south of the Saskatchewan River. Fur-trading was the overriding preoccupation of the first European settlers. Following the purchase of Rupert's Land from the HBC in 1869 there was much immigration, while the relative presence of the Indian population dropped sharply. Saskatchewan was the site of an important Métis rebellion in 1885. The province entered the confederation on 1 September 1905, following which the southern arable lands were settled quickly. The province became a major agricultural power despite the maintenance of crown lands until 1930.

Yukon Territory

Area: 483,450 sq km (186,660 sq miles).
Population (census of 3 June 1986): 23,504.
Capital and Principal City: Whitehorse (population 15,199 at census of 3 June 1986).

LOCATION, TOPOGRAPHY AND CLIMATE

Yukon Territory lies in the extreme north-west of Canada, bordered by Alaska (USA) to the west, the Northwest Territories to the east, the Beaufort Sea to the north and British Columbia to the south. A large part of the territory consists of plateau, divided by mountain ranges and valleys which stretch westwards into Alaska. The central Yukon Plateau, dissected by numerous valleys, is separated from the Porcupine Plateau by the Ogilvie Mountains on the north. Its eastern boundary is marked by the Selwyn and Mackenzie mountain ranges. In the south-west lie the St Elias and Coast Mountains, including Mount Logan which, at 5,951 m (19,524 ft), is the highest point in Canada and the second-highest peak in North America after Mount McKinley (Alaska). The northernmost part of the territory is occupied by a continuation from Alaska of the Arctic Coastal Plain. The greater part of the territory is drained by the Yukon River (3,185 km), which flows into the Bering Sea at Kwiguk in Alaska. Yukon has a continental climate, with very cold winters and warm summers.

HISTORICAL LANDMARKS

The indigenous inhabitants of the Yukon Territory are all Athapaskan-speaking and, at the time of the first European explorations, included Nahanni in the east and groups such as the Teslin, Tutchone and Tagish in the south and west. Fur-trading was the first motive for exploration, but gold prospectors from British Columbia began to cross into the area from the late 19th century. The most famous gold rush in history began on a tributary of the Klondike River in 1896. The Yukon Territory, formerly part of the Northwest Territories, was created on 13 June 1898 with its capital at Dawson. Whitehorse, the seat of government since 1953, grew in importance during the Second World War as it became a transportation and services hub. The decline of the gold-mining industry commenced as early as 1906, but further mineral developments throughout the territory have served to maintain its fragile economy.

ESSAYS

POLITICS AND ADMINISTRATION IN CANADA

MICHAEL RUSH

Introduction

The British North America Act 1867 (later renamed the Constitution Act 1867) gave Canada a federal system 'with a Constitution similar in Principle to that of the United Kingdom'. Canada therefore has a parliamentary system in which the executive is drawn from and responsible to the legislature, but its federal structure means that there are now 11 such parliamentary systems, one for Canada as a whole and one for each of the 10 provinces. While Canada has a bicameral parliament (consisting of the Senate and the House of Commons), a prime minister and a cabinet, each province has its own legislative assembly, premier (the term usually used for provincial heads of government, rather than prime minister) and an executive council (equivalent to a cabinet). The Queen is represented in each province by a lieutenant-governor, appointed by the Governor-General of Canada on the advice of the federal cabinet.

The administration of Yukon Territory and the Northwest Territories is under the direction of the federal Ministry of Indian and Northern Affairs. Each has a federally-appointed commissioner with functions similar to those of a provincial lieutenant-governor, an elected legislative assembly and an executive council. The legislative assemblies of the territories have jurisdiction over all local affairs excluding issues pertaining to renewable and non-renewable natural resources.

Canada also effectively inherited a British-style judicial system. Each province has exclusive power over the administration of justice within that province, but appeals lie ultimately through federal courts to the Supreme Court of Canada. (Appeals originally lay to the judicial committee of the Queen's Privy Council for Canada, but appeals to it in criminal cases were abolished in 1933 and appeals in all other cases in 1949.) The province of Québec provides a partial, but important, exception to these provisions in that civil law in Québec is based not on English-style common law but on a civil code of Roman law, as practised in many Western European countries. However, appeals in civil cases in Québec still lie ultimately to the Supreme Court of Canada and the province must provide three of the latter's nine members.

While Canada has a written constitution, its system of government relies to a large extent upon a number of constitutional conventions. (These are rules of political practice which have no legal force but which are widely accepted by those engaged in political activity.) Thus, under the Constitution Act, executive authority is vested in the Queen, as represented by the Governor-General (the latter being advised by the Privy Council), but by convention this authority is exercised by the prime minister and the cabinet. Similarly, the Constitution Act contains no provisions relating to the relationship between the executive and the legislature; the establishment of a government with, and dependent upon, the continuing support of a majority of the members of the House of Commons, and the constitutional doctrines of individual and collective ministerial responsibility, are matters of convention.

The Origins of the Federal System

Beyond establishing the framework of the parliamentary system, the Constitution Act lays down the division of legislative powers between the federal and provincial levels of government. The Canadian federal system was much influenced by the political system of its great neighbour to the south, the

USA—not in an imitative sense, but in reaction to that which the Fathers of Confederation perceived as faulty with regard to the American union. The discussions and negotiations between the various British colonies leading to the creation of the Dominion of Canada were conducted during, and in the aftermath of, the American Civil War, and the widespread Canadian view was that too much power had been assigned to the states in the US system, thus rendering that system unstable, vulnerable to secession and lacking central direction. The Canadian politicians therefore sought to establish a federal union which was as centralized as circumstances and opinion would allow, with minimal concessions to provincial and regional sensibilities. For the benefit of French Canadians in general, and the province of Québec in particular, constitutional protection was given to the use of the French language, land tenure and civil law in Québec, and there was provincial control over education, but beyond this provincial jurisdiction was deliberately limited. In practice, the relative extent of provincial *vis-à-vis* federal jurisdiction has increased, partly by constitutional amendment but mostly by judicial review. Even though the centralizing intentions of the Fathers of Confederation were never realized, both levels of government have benefited from the general extension of governmental power that has occurred since the mid-19th century, so that the federal government is a powerful entity and much the most important centre of political power in Canada.

Political Parties and Electoral Behaviour

As the product of a union of, originally, four of the British North American colonies—Ontario, Québec (known respectively as Upper and Lower Canada prior to confederation), New Brunswick and Nova Scotia, Canada was also the inheritor of their political traditions and experience. In particular, the executive and legislative experience of the politicians of Upper and Lower Canada played a major part in bringing about confederation and laying the foundations of the Canadian party system. Thus, in 1854, some 13 years before confederation, Sir John A. Macdonald, Canada's first prime minister, established a powerful electoral coalition to form the Conservative Party, which held power from 1867 to 1873 and again from 1878 to 1896. Macdonald's principal opponents were the Liberals, who first held power under Alexander Mackenzie between 1873 and 1878. The Liberal Party, like the Conservative Party, was formed from a coalition of various interests. While neither party has become at all strongly ideological in its stance or its policies, genuine ideological differences exist. Historically, the Conservatives, known since 1942 as the Progressive Conservative Party (PC), have exhibited a paternalistic and collectivistic strand, a hostility to rapid social change and a strong attachment to the British connection, and the Liberals have placed the emphasis on individualism, a desire to eliminate colonial vestiges, and a relative coolness towards the British connection combined with a strong identity with the French-Canadian population. Even so, both parties are essentially highly-pragmatic, 'brokerage' parties, especially when in office.

Following confederation, therefore, Canada rapidly found itself with a two-party system. While each party enjoyed long, continuous periods of government (the Liberals came to power in 1896 and remained in office until 1911), the balance of electoral support remained remarkably even. In 1917, however, Conservative support in the province of Québec was destroyed when the federal Conservative government (under Sir Robert Borden) introduced conscription, to which the French Canadians were bitterly opposed. In the inter-war period the two-party system was undermined further by the emergence of a number of new political groupings. The Progressives, founded in 1920, won more seats than the Conservatives in the election of 1921—thereafter, their support dwindled rapidly, with more being absorbed by the Liberals than by the Conservatives. In the 1930s two longer-lasting parties were formed: the Co-operative Commonwealth Federation (CCF), founded in Saskatchewan in 1932, was an agrarian protest movement of a leftward, socialist persuasion; Social Credit, founded in Alberta in 1935, was a right-wing agrarian movement with unorthodox economic policies. Both made considerable inroads into the traditional parties' support, eventually winning control of provincial governments in Alberta (where Social Credit held power from 1935–70) and Saskatchewan (CCF in 1944–64). Conservative support was particularly seriously affected by the rise of these parties, so that the Liberals became the dominant party at the federal level, holding power continuously between October 1935 and June 1957.

Leadership has always been an important factor in Canadian elections. In June 1957, under the charismatic leadership of John G. Diefenbaker, the PC secured power as a minority government before winning a large overall majority in March 1958. In fact, Diefenbaker's triumph was relatively short-lived—he lost his overall majority in June 1962, but remained in power at the head of a minority government before losing power to the Liberals, under Lester Pearson, in April 1963. After significant electoral success in the mid-1960s, Social Credit began to fade from the federal arena (despite considerable success in Québec as the Ralliement des Créditistes, while the efforts of the CCF to revive its fortunes by strengthening its ties with the labour movement and by adopting the name New Democratic Party (NDP) in 1961 produced only limited gains.

Following their electoral victory in 1963, the Liberals remained in power continuously (with the sole exception of a nine-month period in 1979–80) until September 1984, with Pierre Trudeau succeeding Pearson as leader and prime minister in April 1968. Trudeau resigned in June 1984 and was replaced by John Turner who, in the following September, led the Liberals to a defeat by the PC under the leadership of Brian Mulroney. The Conservatives won the largest electoral majority in Canadian history at the 1984 election, but had a narrower margin of success in November 1988. It remains to be seen whether the dominance of the PC in the mid-1980s represents a major shift in the party system or a deviation from the earlier pattern of Liberal domination. There are indications of such a shift, but its exact nature remains unclear and commentators are rightly wary of predicting the behaviour of the highly pragmatic Canadian electorate. Canadian politics have been characterized both at the federal and provincial levels by long periods of domination by one party followed by sudden and major shifts in electoral opinion. Electoral behaviour in Canada is not dominated by a single major factor, but is a complex of regional, ethnic, religious and class factors, some of which produce cross-cutting cleavages which militate against strong party identification.

Parliament and the Cabinet

The nature of the party system has important implications for the operation of Canadian political institutions, especially Parliament and the cabinet system. The long period of Liberal dominance created a situation in which there was a quasi-permanent governing party and a quasi-permanent opposition party; consequently the Liberals became inherently government-minded and the Conservatives opposition-minded. This had an important effect on the working of Parliament, in that the 'usual channels' of co-operation between government and opposition were much less highly developed than in the UK, for example, since neither Liberals nor Conservatives expected any imminent reversal of the roles of government and opposition. Similarly, neither party had much incentive to support the development of effective parliamentary scrutiny,

principally through the creation of investigatory committees. It was not until the 1960s, when power was held by a series of minority governments faced with a growing pressure of parliamentary business, that significant reform took place. A more efficient committee system (which both expedited government business and improved the scrutiny of government policy) was introduced and a greater degree of inter-party co-operation developed. More recently, a wider range of legislative committees and parliamentary 'task forces' has been introduced, and government–opposition co-operation in dealing with parliamentary business further improved. However, the upper house of the Canadian parliament—the Senate—remains unreformed.

Ostensibly, the Senate represents the provinces. However, it has never developed a federal role comparable in any way to that of the US Senate, partly because it has no special powers and the provinces are not equally represented, but principally because it is an appointed, rather than an elected, body. Senatorial appointments are made by the Governor-General on the recommendation of the prime minister, and prime ministers have tended almost exclusively to recommend the appointment of members of the governing party. Senatorial appointments were for life until a retirement age of 75 for new senators was introduced in 1965. Not surprisingly, therefore, given the long period of Liberal dominance, the Senate has long had a substantial Liberal majority, which has been reduced only slightly since the election of a Conservative government in 1984. One of the provisions of the 1987 Meech Lake Accord between the federal and provincial governments was that the provinces would be consulted on future senatorial appointments, but this had yet to be implemented in early 1989. Not only has the Senate not developed a distinctive federal role, it has never really developed a distinctive role for itself at all. It does act as a revising chamber for government and other legislation passed by the House of Commons (some legislation is introduced initially in the upper house) and its committees have conducted some valuable investigations, but its profile is much lower than that of the British House of Lords, on which it was originally modelled.

Constitutionally, of course, the parliament is the ultimate focus of power in that the government is dependent upon first securing and then retaining the support of a majority in the House of Commons. As in the UK, however, it is basically the government which controls the parliament rather than the reverse. That control stems from the high level of party discipline or cohesion which characterizes almost all parliamentary systems. Moreover, although Canada has experienced periods of minority government (in 1921–30, 1957–58, 1963–68, 1972–74, and 1979–80), there has only ever been one coalition government, in 1917–21. Governments are normally formed by a single party with a working majority in the House of Commons. Again, this follows the British pattern, but in the formation of the government there are important departures from the British model.

The Canadian government lacks the fairly elaborate hierarchy characteristic of its British counterpart, in which the prime minister and members of the cabinet take precedence over middle- and junior-ranking ministers outside the cabinet. In Canada all ministers are cabinet members, although in recent years a hierarchical element has developed within the cabinet, with the increasing use of the office of minister of state. Some of these appointments have been made to deal with a specific problem, but most are given responsibility for a policy area within a particular department and are therefore subordinate to the minister heading that department. In 1984, when he formed his first cabinet, Brian Mulroney appointed no fewer than 12 ministers of state.

For many years it has been common practice to appoint parliamentary secretaries, who serve outside the cabinet. While the latter are paid an official salary, they have no formal ministerial duties, but act as aides to individual ministers. What work they are given depends entirely on the minister concerned, and some act informally to speak for the government on legislative committees in the Houses of Commons during the committee stage of bills.

The cabinet is constitutionally a committee of the Queen's Privy Council for Canada, but its operation is, in the British tradition, governed almost entirely by constitutional convention. As a result the Canadian cabinet rapidly developed conventions which are not found in the British system, notably those relating to the representation of various interests. In particular, each province is normally represented in the cabinet by at least one minister. Since ministers are drawn almost entirely from the House of Commons, and since the governing party may not have won seats in every province, a province is sometimes left without representation. This most commonly happens in the case of Prince Edward Island, the smallest province, which has only four seats in the House of Commons. One alternative open to the prime minister in such a situation is to appoint a senator from the province concerned, as Joe Clark, the Conservative prime minister, did in 1979 when he appointed three senators from Québec to his cabinet. However, as Clark's senatorial appointments suggest, the conventions go beyond the simple question of provincial representation, in that the two largest provinces, Ontario and Québec, expect more extensive representation, and the principle extends further to ethnic, linguistic, and religious representation. Thus Ontario and Québec would normally expect some 10 ministers each, usually representing different regions and interests within each province, while between one-quarter and one-third of cabinet members are normally French-speaking, and Catholics and Protestants are also represented.

In addition, certain portfolios have customarily been given to ministers from particular provinces—for example, those of fisheries and oceans and of forestry to representatives of the Atlantic provinces or British Columbia, finance to an Ontario minister, and agriculture to a representative of the western provinces. The conventions of cabinet representation have two important effects. Firstly, they are a constraint upon the prime minister's choice of cabinet colleagues to the point that, where a province returns only one member of the governing party to the House of Commons, that individual is almost guaranteed a cabinet place. Secondly, as the number of provinces has increased from the original four to the present 10 (and, of course, as governmental responsibilities have grown), so the cabinet has increased in size. The risk of offending particular interests has militated against the development of a British-style hierarchy, with more ministers outside the cabinet than in it. It has been calculated that, given the conventions on representation, the cabinet must comprise a minimum of 17 members. In practice, however, it has grown much larger, and the Mulroney cabinet named in early 1989 numbered 39 members. Ironically, it is increasingly arguable that the cabinet has been largely superseded as a forum for the expression of provincial interests as a result of a gradual increase in the number of regular federal–provincial conferences. The annual meeting between the prime minister and the provincial premiers has become important in this respect.

Partly because of its size, and partly because of the growth in governmental responsibilities, the cabinet operates through a system of committees, about a dozen of which are permanent and the rest *ad hoc*—being set up to deal with particular matters and disbanded once their task is complete. The most important is the Priorities and Planning Committee, which is chaired by the prime minister. Most of the other permanent committees either perform a co-ordinating role or deal with broad policy areas such as economic and regional development, social policy and external affairs. Priorities and Planning, which consists principally of committee chairmen, tends to act like an inner cabinet and overall co-ordinating body on behalf of the full cabinet. Most of the important policy decisions are made at committee level, subject to ratification by the full cabinet. Commencing in 1979, a system of public expenditure control (known as Policy and Expenditure Management Systems or PEMS) has operated through the cabinet committee system, with Priorities and Planning taking an overview and the four principal policy committees operating expenditure controls within their own policy areas. The cabinet meets about 50 times a year, while there are well over 200 cabinet committee meetings in a twelve-month period.

The cabinet and its committees are serviced by the Privy Council Office (PCO), which is responsible for preparing briefing documents for policy discussions and for maintaining records of meetings and decisions. The PCO has grown considerably since 1945 and had more than 300 staff (excluding support staff) in the late 1980s, all of whom are normally career civil servants. In contrast, political appointees fill the upper echelons of the Prime Minister's Office (PMO), which consists of the prime minister's key advisers and has become a crucial part of the governmental machine; the PMO has also grown considerably, particularly during and since the prime ministership of Pierre Trudeau.

Some observers argue that Canada now has a system of prime-ministerial government, but such a description belies the complexity of modern parliamentary politics. That the prime minister is the key figure in the Canadian political system is beyond question: the power to appoint and dismiss ministers is only the most visible aspect of the extensive powers of patronage which form the basis of the prime minister's ability to set the tone of an administration and largely shape the direction of its policies. Furthermore, barring the eventuality of electoral defeat, the prime minister soon becomes the longest-serving and most experienced member of the cabinet, since in Canada political careers are on average not as long as in many comparable countries. The turnover in the membership of the House of Commons is high, partly because of relative electoral volatility, but mostly because many members choose to leave politics after serving in only one or two parliaments. The route to ministerial office does not generally consist of a fairly long parliamentary apprenticeship and ministerial experience outside the cabinet (as is the norm in the UK), other than occasional and brief service as a parliamentary secretary. Even prime ministers can be politically inexperienced: Pierre Trudeau became prime minister in 1968 after only three years in Parliament and one year in the cabinet; and Brian Mulroney had neither parliamentary nor ministerial experience before becoming prime minister. The extent to which the prime minister dominates depends much on personality, but varies according to issue and circumstances. But no single individual, however forceful, can hope to give equal attention to all matters, and the cabinet, individual ministers, civil servants and pressure groups all play a role in the complex process of policy-making.

The Federal Public Service

The Canadian federal civil service consists of permanent 'career bureaucrats' who are expected to be politically neutral in serving their political masters. Thus, unlike in the USA, an incoming government does not fill the highest echelons of the service with political appointees. Not only did the long Liberal dominance create a situation in which some civil servants were accused of being sympathetic towards Liberal policies, it also led to wilder accusations from some Conservatives that the public service was a crypto-Liberal organization. Certainly, when John G. Diefenbaker led the PC to victory in 1957 and 1958, a number of civil servants chose to resign and a few became active Liberal politicians, but any apparent affinity between the civil service and the Liberal Party probably owed more to the latter's long unbroken period in government than to anything else.

Canadian civil servants were originally recruited exclusively by patronage, with jobs being used, in general, to reward the supporters of the governing party. The principle of recruitment on merit was gradually introduced from 1908, with recruitment being placed in the hands of a Civil Service Commission—now the Public Service Commission—which is responsible for laying down the appropriate qualifications and skills required for various positions, and for organizing recruitment accordingly. The federal public service is divided into six occupational categories: management; scientific and professional; administrative and foreign service; technicians; administrative support; and operational. The service currently employs more than 200,000 individuals. The Canadian public service follows the US practice in that it recruits by grade rather than by broader groupings. At one time the number of grades was nearly 4,000, but in recent years there has been a significant reduction. The Public Service Commission is responsible for training programmes and, more especially, for maintaining and extending the use of Canada's two official languages following the passing of the Official Languages Act in 1969. Considerable concern had been expressed by the Royal Commission on Bilingualism and Biculturalism (appointed in 1963) about the under-representation in the public service of French Canadians and of those able to speak French. Extensive language training was introduced and French-speaking units established, so that by 1983 the proportion of francophone employees in the public service had increased to 27%—comparable to their proportion in the Canadian population.

Pressure Groups and Policy-Making

Politicians and civil servants are two of the key groups of actors in the policy process, with pressure or interest groups constituting a third group of actors of considerable, but varying, importance. Canada, like other industrialized liberal democracies, has the usual range of pressure groups covering business, labour, consumers and an enormous variety of socio-cultural interests. The leading business organizations are the Canadian Manufacturers' Association and the Canadian Chamber of Commerce: there are also a considerable number of trade and industrial associations, while agriculture is represented by the Canadian Federation of Agriculture and the smaller National Farmers' Union. One in three non-agricultural workers are members of trade unions, many of which are affiliated to the Canadian Labour Congress (CLC), which in turn has close links with the NDP. Business interests, while broadly sympathetic to the PC, donate funds to both the Liberals and the Conservatives. Québec also has a number of its own trade unions, mostly affiliated to the Québec-based Confédération des syndicats nationaux. Consumer interests are represented by the Consumers' Association of Canada and the professions by bodies such as the Canadian Medical Association and the Canadian Bar Association. Socio-cultural groups represent interests as diverse as the many ethnic groups in Canada, various churches and other religious groups, environmental interests such as Friends of the Earth and Greenpeace, and many more.

The federal system, with its division of responsibilities, means that in many cases groups need to maintain offices in Ottawa, the national capital, and all or most of the provincial capitals. Otherwise, pressure politics in Canada operates largely in the way it does in other parliamentary systems: this means that the civil service is a prime target for lobbying activity and many groups are regularly consulted, often through membership of advisory committees. Considerable attention is also paid to ministers, and a few organizations, such as the CLC, are invited annually to put their views to the cabinet. Parliament is another important focus of attention, although it is often said that lobbying the legislature is a sign of failure to influence at an earlier stage of the policy process. In reality this is an over-simplistic view: although the most effective way to influence policy is undoubtedly through the bureaucracy and the executive, changes of detail can often be achieved at the parliamentary stage—and it is often with detail that outside interests are concerned. Moreover, parliament is part of a wider and complex policy network which helps to set the parameters of policy formation. Some indication of how important lobbying has become in Canada was given by the passing, in 1988, of the Lobbyists Registration Act which required pressure groups to provide details of their activities to a Registrar of Lobbyists.

Provincial Politics

Much of what has already been said applies to provincial government and politics in Canada, but it should be noted that, to a significant extent, each province has its own distinctive brand of politics and that, in many respects, provincial political systems operate quite separately from the federal level. Québec, of course, is the most distinctive in this respect, being the only province with a French-speaking majority (some 80% of the Québec population). For much of its history since the British conquest in 1759, Québec adopted a basically isolationist, introverted stance towards the rest of Canada. The

post-conquest settlement, essentially confirmed at Confederation in 1867, gave Québec protection over the use of the French language, educational system, land tenure and civil law, all of which contributed to the preservation of French-Canadian culture. In the 1950s, however, the Québécois became increasingly aware that, compared with some other provinces, notably Ontario (then undoubtedly the richest province) they were disadvantaged, and with the election of a reformist Liberal government in the province in 1960 there occurred what became known as the 'Quiet Revolution'. Québec became much more outward-looking and assertive, demanding special treatment and recognition as the home of French-Canadian culture. A separatist movement developed which, although initially divided and enjoying little support (with some elements, such as the Front de libération du Québec—FLQ—, resorting to violence), eventually united to form the Parti Québécois (PQ), led by René Lévesque, a former provincial Liberal cabinet minister. In 1976 Lévesque led his party to victory in provincial elections, but it remained unclear how much the PQ ('Péquiste') victory owed to support for separatism, and how much to economic dissatisfaction.

In 1980 the PQ government held a referendum seeking a mandate to negotiate what it termed 'sovereignty-association'—political independence from and continued economic association with Canada. Sovereignty-association was decisively rejected by a 60% to 40% majority and, although he went on to win a further election, Lévesque allowed the independence issue to subside for the time being. This led to a serious split in the ranks of the PQ, and to a crushing electoral defeat in 1985. For the time being, therefore, outright separatism, which according to opinion polls has never had the support of more than one-quarter of Québécois, has subsided, but could easily return if economic dissatisfaction grew. Quite apart from its unique position and the issue of separatism, Québec is also distinct in being the only province that has frequently had major political parties which operate only at provincial level—notably the Union Nationale (now defunct) and the PQ. Other provinces have, or have had, parties which are particularly strong, but these have always at some point engaged in electoral politics at the federal level.

Although Canadian opinion differs widely on the nature and extent of regionalism in Canada, there is widespread agreement that strong regional or 'sub-national' distinctions exist. These give each of the provinces a perceptible political identity which goes beyond the basic French-speaking/English-speaking divide. Five regions are commonly identified: the Atlantic provinces (Newfoundland, New Brunswick, Nova Scotia and Prince Edward Island); Québec; Ontario; the Prairie Provinces (Manitoba, Saskatchewan and Alberta); and British Columbia. In addition, there are the vast lands to the north (the Northwest Territories and the Yukon Territory), comprising no less than 41% of Canada's land area but containing only 0.3% of its population. The territories are politically important for their economic resources and potential and through the presence of Canada's native population of Indians and Inuit, but the north is only just beginning to emerge as a political force. Historically, it has also been common to see Canada as divided into three huge regions: the east, the centre, and the west, with the centre tending to dominate—a view which remains important, especially in the west.

Each of the five regions are distinctive politically, economically and, in many respects, geographically. The two most industrialized provinces are Ontario and Québec, peopled by more than three-fifths of Canada's population (at the 1986 census, 35.9% lived in Ontario and 25.8% in Québec), whereas the provinces to the east and west have been, and largely remain, economically dependent on natural resources—fishing and forestry in the Atlantic provinces, agriculture (especially grain production) and minerals (especially oil and gas) in the west. The Atlantic provinces have always been the poorest provinces in Canada in terms of income per head of population, while Ontario, traditionally the richest province, has been overtaken by Alberta (as a consequence of post-war developments in oil and gas production, which have brought about considerable economic development in the Prairie provinces) and by British Columbia, which has also benefited from significant economic development, especially resulting from an increased volume of 'Pacific-rim' trade with Japan and South-East Asian countries.

Within each of the regions, there exist significant differences between the provinces. Thus Newfoundland, which did not join the confederation until 1949, has always had a distinctive identity resulting from its relative isolation. In income-per-head terms it is the poorest of the Canadian provinces, followed by Prince Edward Island, which is also the smallest province. While Nova Scotia and New Brunswick have much in common, the latter has the largest French-speaking population outside Québec. The distinctiveness of Québec as a predominantly francophone province has already been noted—but it also has an important anglophone community. Ontario is ethnically mixed, with 17.9% of its population claiming a mother tongue other than French or English at the 1986 census. The three Prairie provinces are distinguished in that significant proportions of their populations are of continental-European descent: German or Ukrainian single origin, for example, was attributed to an estimated 12% of Albertans, 17% of Manitobans and 19% of Saskatchewans in 1986. British Columbia differs yet again, with a high proportion (31%) of its population being calculated to have single British origin in 1986.

These differences form the basis of significant political variations which are reflected in both federal and provincial politics, particularly in terms of electoral support. The Atlantic provinces have tended to be dominated, both federally and provincially, by the traditional parties, with 'third' parties making little or no headway, but third-party intervention has been significant in all other provinces, sometimes at federal level, sometimes at provincial, often both. The overall federal dominance of the Liberals since 1896 has not always been mirrored in the provincial arena, as existence of the Union Nationale and the PQ in Québec have already illustrated. Ontario has seen the development of significant support for the NDP, to the extent that in late 1988 the provincial party held the second greatest number of seats (behind the Liberals) in the Ontario legislature. Further west, however, 'third' parties have not only been significant, but have in several cases effectively replaced one, other or even both of the traditional parties at provincial level. Both the NDP (formerly the CCF) and Social Credit were founded in the west (Saskatchewan and Alberta respectively) and have had their greatest success there, forming provincial governments in Manitoba (NDP), Saskatchewan (CCF/NDP), Alberta (Social Credit), and British Columbia (Social Credit and NDP).

Canadian elections (particularly provincial elections) have always been characterized by higher levels of periodic electoral volatility than is common in either the UK or the USA. While the consequences of such volatility tend to be exaggerated by the combination of the simple plurality or 'first-past-the-post' electoral system and the small size of legislatures, especially at provincial level, it remains a marked feature of Canadian politics. It is all the more marked when linked to another feature, that of the dominance of one party over long periods of time, exemplified not only by federal Liberal dominance, but by similar single-party dominance in most provinces. In Newfoundland, for example, the Liberals held power from confederation in 1949 until 1972, since which year there has been a Conservative administration; in Nova Scotia the Liberals were in power in 1933–56 and the Conservatives in 1956–70; Québec was governed by the Liberals from 1897 to 1936 and by the Union Nationale from 1944 to 1960; the Conservatives ruled Ontario from 1943 to 1985 and the CCF Saskatchewan from 1944 to 1964; Social Credit dominated Alberta between 1935 and 1971, since when the Conservatives have been in power; and Social Credit also governed British Columbia from 1952 to 1972 and have done so again since 1975. In a number of cases, such domination has been partly or wholly associated with particular provincial premiers. It should be noted that federal and provincial party organizations in Canada are separate and, moreover, that it does not necessarily follow that federal and provincial parties of the same name are in sympathy with one another, let alone closely associated. To a marked degree federal and provincial politics operate separately, both in the minds of voters and politicians. Indeed, it has been claimed that the real opposition to the federal government in Ottawa comes not from the official opposition, but from the provincial governments, regardless of their political hue or of that of the federal government.

Federalism

In many respects, provincial government impinges more directly on the lives of Canadians than does the federal government. In fact, in recent years provincial government spending has overtaken federal spending, although the situation is complicated by the varying amounts of grants made by the federal government to the provinces. However, as the responsibilities of provincial governments have grown, so has the need for close co-operation between the two levels of government. Federalism in Canada has passed through a number of phases, marked first by an expansion in provincial responsibilities, largely through judicial review of the British North America Act by the Judicial Committees of the Privy Council, and followed by a period of parallel or dual federalism, marked by both levels of government operating more or less autonomously. Under the economic pressures of the First World War and the Depression, however, most of the provinces became increasingly reliant upon federal financial help and there developed what came to be known as 'co-operative' federalism. The emergence of Québec in the 1960s from its relative isolation ushered in 'executive' or 'diplomatic' federalism, in which the provinces generally have been much more assertive and federalism has operated through direct contact between the federal and provincial governments and their officials.

Federalism in Canada has also been complicated by differing views about the nature of Canadian society, characterized most sharply, perhaps, by an inability until recently to agree on a means of amending the constitution. The traditional French-Canadian concept of federalism, known as the 'compact theory', conceives Canada as the product of *les deux nations*—the two founding peoples, the French and the English—so that for French Canadians all other Canadians are part of English Canada. However accurate this perception may have been originally, it hardly commended itself to the growing number of immigrants and their descendants from other parts of Europe reflected in the diverse nature of provincial politics. The alternative view is therefore that of a multicultural society, of which French Canadians and Québec are merely a part.

That these differing concepts should centre on the constitution is hardly surprising, since it was and is the constitution that sets the parameters of federal and provincial powers and responsibilities. The original amending formula was simply that, at the request of the Governor-General (in effect the Canadian government), the UK parliament would pass a statute amending the British North America Act, while judicial review lay with the Judicial Committee of the Privy Council. In 1949 the UK parliament amended the constitution to allow all but its most fundamental parts to be amended by the Canadian parliament, but the crucial matter of the division of powers remained legally a matter for the UK parliament. In the same year, appeals to the Judicial Committee were abolished and the Supreme Court of Canada became the final court of appeal. Further attempts to agree on an amending formula and to patriate the constitution were unsuccessful until after the rejection of sovereignty-association by the voters of Québec in 1980, when the Trudeau government again took the initiative. There was fierce opposition, however, from eight of the 10 provinces, and it was only after the Supreme Court ruled that, while the federal government could legally and unilaterally request the UK parliament to amend the British North America Act, there was also a constitutional convention, requiring provincial consent, that an agreement was reached on an amending formula by which the constitution could be amended by a joint resolution of the Senate and the House of Commons and by resolutions of at least two-thirds of the provincial assemblies representing at least 50% of the population of Canada. In addition, the provinces had the right to opt out on amendments affecting their status and powers. The UK parliament passed the necessary legislation and the new amendment procedure was enshrined in the Constitution Act 1982, under which the British North America Act was renamed the Constitution Act 1867. These measures were supported by every province except Québec, although the Liberal government of Robert Bourassa, elected in 1985, subsequently gave its assent. The Constitution Act also made another crucial change by adding a Charter of Rights and Freedoms to the constitution, entrenching many existing rights and considerably enhancing the potential for the courts to play a strong role in the Canadian political system in the future, through the power of judicial review. A further agreement, the Meech Lake Accord of 1987, set in train a constitutional amendment which would recognize Québec as a 'distinct society' within Canada and give Québec greater control over immigration into the province. As noted earlier, the Accord also provides for provincial participation in the choice of senators.

Canadian federalism has therefore reached a new stage of development, with relations between the two levels of government having changed considerably since 1867. The complex nature of modern government demands considerable co-operation between the federal and provincial governments, and this has developed most importantly through the device of federal–provincial conferences, which have become a regular annual event in the political calendar. Underpinning the annual meetings of the prime minister and the premiers are other conferences and meetings of ministers and officials, so that an elaborate network of contact, co-operation and collaboration has developed. This does not mean that conflict has been eliminated—it would be surprising if it had, given that individual provinces may have differing interests or different governing parties—but it does mean that the Canadian political system has demonstrated an ability to adapt to changing conditions and situations. While Sir Wilfrid Laurier's proud boast that 'the 20th century shall be the century of Canada' has not been fulfilled, there can be no doubt that Canada belongs to the 20th century.

SELECT BIBLIOGRAPHY

Christian, William and Campbell, Colin. *Political Parties and Ideologies in Canada: Liberals, Conservatives, Socialists, Nationalists.* Scarborough, Ontario, McGraw-Hill Ryerson Ltd, 1983.

Clarke, Harold D., Jenson, Jane, Leduc, Lawrence and Pammett, Jon H. *Political Choice in Canada.* Scarborough, Ontario, McGraw-Hill Ryerson Ltd, 1979.

Doern, G. Bruce and Phidd, Richard W. *Canadian Public Policy: Ideas, Structure, Process.* Toronto, Methuen, 1983.

Dyck, Rand. *Provincial Politics in Canada.* Scarborough, Ontario, Prentice-Hall Canada Inc, 1985.

Franks, C. E. S. *The Parliament of Canada.* Toronto, University of Toronto Press, 1987.

Jackson, Robert J., Jackson, Doreen and Baxter-Moore, Nicolas. *Politics in Canada: Culture, Institutions, Behaviour and Public Policy.* Scarborough, Ontario, Prentice-Hall Canada Inc, 1986.

Kent, Paul. *A Public Purpose: An Experience of Liberal Opposition and Canadian Government.* Kingston, Ontario, McGill-Queen's University Press, 1988.

Mahler, Gregory S. (Ed.). *Contemporary Canadian Politics: An Annotated Bibliography, 1980–87.* London, Greenwood Press, 1989.

McRoberts, Kenneth and Postgate, Dale. *Québec: Social Change and Political Crisis.* Toronto, McClelland & Stewart, 1980.

Olling, R. D. and Westmacott, M. W. (Eds). *Perspectives on Canadian Federalism.* Scarborough, Ontario, Prentice-Hall Canada Inc, 1988.

Penniman, Howard R. (Ed.). *Canada at the Polls, 1984.* Durham, North Carolina, Duke University Press, 1988.

Pross, A. Paul. *Group Politics and Public Policy.* Toronto, Oxford University Press (Canada), 1986.

Punnett, R. M. *The Prime Minister in Canadian Government and Politics.* Toronto, Macmillan Co of Canada Ltd, 1977.

Statistics Canada. *Canada Year Book 1988.* Ottawa, Canadian Government Publishing Centre, 1987.

Stevenson, Garth. *Unfulfilled Union: Canadian Federalism and National Unity.* Toronto, Gage Educational Publishing Co, 1979.

Thorburn, Hugh G. (Ed.). *Party Politics in Canada.* Scarborough, Ontario, Prentice-Hall Canada Inc, 1985.

Ward, Norman. *Dawson's Government of Canada.* Toronto, University of Toronto Press, 1987.

THE CANADIAN ECONOMY

NATURAL RESOURCES AND PRIMARY ECONOMIC ACTIVITIES IN CANADA

JOHN F. DAVIS

Canada is endowed with a richness of animal, vegetable and mineral resources which, for a long time and in various combinations, have made a major contribution to the nation's income. Today, with the increasing importance of the secondary and especially the wide-ranging tertiary sectors of the economy, the primary activities no longer play such a direct and dominant role in the country's economy. However, it must be remembered that these primary activities indirectly create some employment in both the secondary and tertiary sectors. Currently, the natural resources sector of the economy accounts for about one-half of Canada's gross national product (GNP), as well as providing direct employment for about 750,000 people and more than one-third of the country's exports by value.

Agriculture

In spite of Canada's large land area, only about 7% (68m. ha) is devoted to farmland, of which 46m. ha (68%) is in improved land, with 33m. ha (72%) of that being under crops and 13m. ha (28%) under pasture. Farmland occurs in all provinces, but about 81% of the total is located within the three Prairie provinces of Alberta, Manitoba and Saskatchewan. Indeed, farmland is distributed very unevenly between the various parts of Canada. Farm cash receipts in 1986 exceeded C $20,000m., of which about 90% came from southern Ontario and Québec, and the southern parts of the Prairie provinces. Climatic conditions are less conducive for agriculture in the northern part of the country, and there are also large areas of the Canadian Shield (which covers most of east and north-central Canada) where the soils are too thin and the ground too rocky for agriculture. Exports of farm produce amounted to C $9,800m. in 1986, or about one-tenth of the total value of exports. In that year 51% of all agricultural production was exported.

In 1986 Newfoundland had both the smallest total area of farmland (37,000 ha) of any province and also the smallest proportion of farmland in relation to its total land area (0.1%). On the other hand, farmland in Prince Edward Island, at 272,000 ha, accounted for 48% of the province's total area—the highest proportion in Canada. In New Brunswick and Nova Scotia, the other two Maritime provinces, agricultural land accounted for 6% and 8% of total land area respectively. The large areas of Shield partly account for the low proportions of farming land in Québec (3%) and Ontario (6%), although their respective total areas of farmland, at 3.6m. ha and 5.6m. ha, are much greater than those of the Maritime provinces. However, the range of crops grown and the large urban markets mean that Ontario has the largest cash value from farm products of any province (C $5,458m. in 1986). The vast majority of Canada's farmland is concentrated west of the Great Lakes in the Prairies, where Saskatchewan leads with 26.6m. ha (47% of its land area), followed by Alberta with 20.7m. ha (32%) and Manitoba with 7.7m. ha (14%). Finally, in the West, is mountainous British Columbia, where only 2.4m. ha of farmland is found, comprising 2.7% of the province. The Territories, for obvious reasons, have minimal areas of agricultural land.

The overall trend of the past decade has been for the total area of farmland to decline, while that of improved land has increased. Inevitably, however, these are not uniform trends. For example, while land has been converted from unimproved

to improved in southern Ontario, and cropland is being used more intensively, there is much concern at the continued loss of top-grade (Grade I) land to urban expansion—especially along the Lake Ontario lowlands, and in the Niagara escarpment area, location of the Niagara 'fruit belt'. There is a similar concern about the loss of highest-quality land to urban use in the Lower Fraser valley in British Columbia and in the adjacent limited lowland areas. Another general trend in farming has been for fewer people to be employed, which, associated with an increasing average farm size, has resulted in fewer farms. The 624,000 farms of 1951 had been reduced to 293,000 by 1986. In that year family farms accounted for 99.1% of the total and the national average farm size was 231 ha: for individual provinces, this varied from about 56 ha in Newfoundland to over 419 ha in Saskatchewan. These figures mask considerable variations within the provinces; for example, in the Prairie provinces some ranches are well in excess of 2,000 ha, and some grain farms have over 1,000 ha, while speciality crop and dairy farms may be well below 100 ha.

To the outside world, Canada is best known agriculturally for grain. In 1986, Canada was the world's sixth-largest wheat producer, with 31.9m. metric tons, and second only to the USA in terms of exports, with 20% of world trade. Wheat is grown mainly, but not exclusively, in the Prairie provinces, where it accounted for 51% of the cropland harvested in 1986, and Saskatchewan is the main producer, providing 59% of Canadian output in 1986. Traditionally, nearly 90% of Prairie wheat shipments have been exported to the UK and the rest of north-west Europe, but recently an increasing proportion has been going to the Pacific rim countries and to the USSR.

To encourage the production of cereals in the Prairie region, and to help counteract the problem of high transportation costs, the federal government instituted the Crow Rate for rail carriage of a range of crops in 1897. This measure fixed freight rates eastwards to the Great Lakes ports, and to the Hudson Bay port of Churchill, and later westwards to ports on the Pacific coast. From 1984 the rate was abolished and the subsidy began to be phased out. The uneconomic realities of handling grain under the Crow Rate had made it very difficult for the railways to finance the rebuilding and track-doubling programmes which were becoming essential due to the siginificant rise in westward movement of a whole range of natural resources to Pacific rim countries from the Canadian Pacific ports (including coal, potash, pulp, sulphur and wheat). Federal and provincial governments have also been involved with attempts to broaden the agricultural base of the Prairie farm economy, which is very susceptible to world trade fluctuations, especially those connected with variations in the Chinese and Soviet wheat harvests. As a consequence, a variety of other crops have been introduced, including canola (rapeseed) and flaxseed (in the Peace River area of north-west Alberta, for example, where about 800 farms grow wheat and now also canola and grass seed). However, in some areas satisfactory, viable and marketable alternatives to wheat are not easily available.

Apart from grain production the Prairie provinces, particularly Alberta, are also major beef-cattle producers, and it seems likely that, as a result of the abolition of the Crow Rate, it will become increasingly profitable to fatten cattle on the Prairies and ship out the meat, rather than shipping out both cattle and feed to the East for fattening. This trend should also mean an increase in the local demand for some fodder crops. Another factor increasing Prairie agricultural diversification is a recent increase in population, particularly in Alberta, and a consequent increase in demand for a whole range of agricultural products. As one would expect, with the highest populations, Ontario and Québec are also the main centres of dairy production, together accounting for 73% of milk and cream sales off farms. The two provinces also provide 55% of Canadian egg production and 65% of turkey and chicken meat, and account for 63% of pig slaughterings.

Production of other agricultural commodities is more widely scattered. This is particularly true of speciality crops, with potatoes particularly important in Prince Edward Island, New Brunswick, Québec and Nova Scotia; leaf tobacco in Ontario (which provided 88% of total production in 1985), Québec and the Maritime provinces, and fruits and other vegetables in south-west Québec, the extreme south and south-west of Ontario, and the Fraser and Okanagan valleys of British Columbia. However, governments have been encouraging the decline of tobacco production, and the harvest area has decreased by some 40% during the 1980s. Canada produces about 70% of the world's maple syrup—mainly from Québec (94% of total production in 1988), Ontario, Nova Scotia and New Brunswick—and both output and exports have been increasing.

Federal governments have instituted a wide range of services and support programmes to aid farming, as well as a range of farm-assistance programmes. Examples of the latter include the Agricultural Stabilization Act and Prairie Farm Assistance Act. At province level there is also a range of services and support programmes, as well as schemes to conserve the best farmland. Governments are also very much involved in attempts to reduce the impact of wide fluctuations in prices upon farmers' incomes, and various types of price supports and government 'buy-in' programmes exist.

Inevitably, Canada has to import a range of agricultural products, especially those of tropical and subtropical origins, but it is a net agricultural exporter, with a positive balance of about C $3,000m. in 1986. In some respects its major competitor for world markets is the USA; for example, both are major exporters of grain. Indeed, nearly 40% of the total value of 1986 exports was contributed by grains, and Canada is the world's principal exporter of mustard seed as well as a major exporter of canola (rapeseed) products. Other exports include beef, pork, some vegetables, maple syrup and cheese. One problematic area for Canadian agricultural exports is that of the export support or subsidies offered by some individual countries or groups of countries (for example, the heavy subsidies offered by the EEC to its member countries). In Canada there is sometimes a differential between the price charged on the domestic market and that charged to overseas buyers: in 1986, for example, the world price for a bushel of wheat was C $5.00, whereas on the domestic market it was $7.00.

Only 4.2% of the total Canadian labour force were employed in agriculture in 1986. However, primary agriculture contributed some 2.8% of gross domestic product in 1984 (GDP). A further substantial contribution is made by food processing. In only three provinces does agriculture employ 10% or more of the labour force—Alberta (10%), Prince Edward Island (13%) and Saskatchewan (19%).

Forestry

Canada's inventoried forest lands covered some 3.4m. sq km (1.3m. sq miles), or 37% of the country's total land area in 1981, and stretch across the country from ocean to ocean in a virtually unbroken belt which varies in width from 500 to 2,100 km. Of this total, the three provinces of Québec, Ontario and British Columbia account for just under one-half (47%), the Prairie provinces 20%, and the Territories 25%. These extensive forests have been an important renewable resource from the early days of settlement, and currently their products provide about 10% of GNP and 15% of Canada's exports by value: about one job in 10 depends directly or indirectly upon the forestry resource.

Almost two-thirds of the total forest land is in productive forests, and the area considered to be of economic value has been extended in recent years as a result of improvements in forestry technology and transport. In addition, the insatiable demands from the paper industry have made it economically feasible for paper- and pulp-related undertakings to be established in more inaccessible areas than formerly. Softwoods predominate, and about one-third of all timber by volume is spruce (black, white, Sitka and Engelmann); pine (jack, white, lodgepole and Ponderosa), fir (including Douglas fir), poplars and hemlock are other important species of standing timber in terms of volume.

In spite of the vast area under timber, increasing concern has been shown over problems of potential overcutting and a decline in the resource base, and consequently over the need for comprehensively-planned forestry management. This is especially the case in some of the more easily-accessible and heavily-worked parts of the country—in British Columbia, for example, which contains 17% of the total forest land and 21% of the productive forests, but about 45% of the timber land harvested. Fire is also an important hazard, each year destroying, on average, an area equivalent to 10% of the annual cut. As a result federal and provincial governments are increasingly giving attention not only to fire prevention and fire-fighting, but also to the expansion of silviculture and reafforestation programmes. It would be easy for a false sense of security to be built up on account of the large area covered by forest, but some of this is inaccessible, some is badly affected by disease—as on Cape Breton Island, for example—and some is uneconomic to work for other reasons. It should also be remembered that the reafforestation cycle lengthens with proximity to the North Pole, and therefore the need is increased for a larger unit area within which the forest industries must work if they are to maintain production over any significant period of time.

There is much debate concerning both the efficiency and adequacy of conservation and reafforestation methods and provision within Canada. Some of this concern is environmental in nature, although it is also economically necessary, in the long term, to maintain forest quality and quantity, as forestry products fuel a principal export industry as well as constituting a major source of employment in some provinces. In Ontario, for example, forest-related industries provide over 90,000 jobs and supply both the *raison d'être* for some 40 single-industry towns and over C $1,000m. annually in provincial and federal taxes.

The forestry-products industry provides a wide variety of processing plants, ranging from the numerous sawmills to the much larger, and fewer, pulp and paper plants which are often located in places where the export of newsprint can be achieved efficiently. The end use of timber cut in 1986 was: logwood, sawn timber and plywood 69%; pulpwood 26%; fuelwood 3.5%; others 1.5%. The importance of plywood and lumber means that production and exports are much affected by cyclic movements in the domestic and overseas economies, since a high proportion is used by the building trade. Canada is the world's second largest pulp and paper producer, after the USA, and also the largest exporter, with the bulk of exports (68% in 1983) moving southwards to the USA. Among the provinces, Québec is the principal supplier of pulp and paper, followed by British Columbia and Ontario. In recent years there has been an increase in production in the Prairie provinces, particularly in Alberta.

The sawmills are also highly dependent upon exports and upon the buoyancy of the construction industry, both in Canada and, more especially, in the USA. The current discussions about free trade have caused some concern among Canadian producers (for example, shingles producers) as to whether or not their products will get the ease of entry into US markets which they hope for. One of the trends in the forestry-products industry, as in others, is towards increases in both the scale of operations and the size of unit, which will have repercussions upon the economies of the smaller forestry-dependent communities in the future.

As has already been indicated, the export trade in forestry products is dominated by trade with USA, which absorbs 70% by value of such exports. The next most important customers are the UK and Japan. Japan is showing an increasing interest in North American sources for many of its raw-material needs, and is backing this interest, not just by increasing significantly its purchases over the past two decades, but also by investment in companies. The eastern provinces have traditionally supplied

European markets as well as the very large US East Coast market, while at one time western areas really only had the US West Coast market, where they faced competition from suppliers in the north-west Pacific states. Now, with the growth of the Pacific rim market, the western provinces are much better placed to expand exports.

Fisheries

One of the earliest exports from the former colonial lands which are now Canada was fish from Newfoundland. Sea fisheries continue to be important in the economies of the Maritime provinces and British Columbia, and, to a lesser extent, Québec. In 1986 the total weight of Atlantic-coast landings was about six times as great as that landed on the Pacific coast, although differentials in the value of fish varieties landed meant that income from the Atlantic fisheries was only about twice as great as that from the Pacific. The Atlantic-coast fisheries rely on cod, flatfish and herring and, close to the shore, shellfish, especially lobster, oysters and scallops. On the Pacific coast the dependence is on salmon, herring and halibut. Lakes and rivers provide both commercial and sport fishing in virtually all provinces and, having the largest area of freshwater lakes of any country in the world, Canada produces significant amounts of perch, trout, whitefish and other freshwater species.

The fishing industry has experienced a number of problems, including overfishing, shoal movements (especially of herring), water pollution and a number of politically-related difficulties. In January 1977 Canada imposed an economic interest zone extending to 200 nautical miles (370 km) around its shores. This led to a dispute with France, which claimed a similar zone around the islands of Saint-Pierre and Miquelon, a French possession lying about 25 km from the southern coast of Newfoundland and on the western edge of the rich Grand Banks of Newfoundland. Bilateral agreements exist with certain nations which are thereby permitted to fish within the exclusion zone if stocks are deemed to be adequate.

Another source of dispute concerns the salmon fisheries along the coast of British Columbia, where commercial fishermen have periodically come into conflict with both 'sport fishermen' and Canadian native peoples who have traditionally caught salmon. Sensitivity to the risks of pollution and their possible effects on the future of the fish populations is a principal reason for Canada's very great concern over the use and development of the Arctic islands and the sub-Arctic region, especially relating to the movement of oil tankers through the North West Passage.

Canada is the world's largest fish exporter by value. The commercial sea-fishing industry had a total market value of C $2,436m. in 1985, in which year the total export value of fish products was C $1,855m. In 1986 there were 44,000 individuals engaged full-time in commercial sea fishing, of whom 12,500 lived in Newfoundland, 6,800 in British Columbia and 9,400 in Nova Scotia. Commercial freshwater fishing accounted for a further 7,750 individuals, while fish processing plants employed a total of 60,000.

Furs

Furs have been an important primary resource to Canada since the 17th century. Although fashions continue to change, and the range of substitutes to grow, the fur industry is still important, and to some communities represents a major source of income. Of the total value of fur production in 1986/87, just over 50% was obtained by trapping and just under 50% came from fur farms, which mainly produce mink. Fur farming is to be found principally in Ontario, Nova Scotia, British Columbia and Québec, while trapping is carried on in all provinces and territories, with Ontario, Québec and Alberta as the principal producers. Trapping is a seasonal industry and is often carried out in association with other occupations. It is an important source, indeed the primary source, of cash income for some native peoples. Seal hunting contributes some C $10m. annually to the economy of eastern Canada, and about one-third of the

annual income of those actually engaged in sealing. The main locations of seal hunting are off the coasts of Labrador, Newfoundland and Québec.

The main outlets for furs are the auction markets of Edmonton, Montréal, North Bay (Ontario), Vancouver and Winnipeg. While about three-quarters of the raw furs are exported in an unfinished state, the export of fur garments is increasing, thus providing both more indirect employment and a greater value added. Another trend over the past 20 years has been for the market share of fur sales taken by fur farms to decrease from over 60% in the 1960s to just under 50% in 1986/87.

Minerals

Canada possesses an impressive range of minerals of economic importance. The country leads the world in terms of the value of its mineral exports and is the third most important producer of non-fuel minerals, after the USA and the USSR. While events such as the Yukon gold rush of the 1890s meant that for a long time attention was focused on that region, the 20th century has seen an increasingly wide distribution of mineral exploitation. While Canada remains a major producer of gold, it currently produces over 60 different minerals. In 1986 the total value of mineral production, including fuels, was estimated at C $33,854m., while employment in the sector totalled about 188,000. Some 80% of production of minerals other than oil and natural gas was destined for the export market in that year, with 65% of this expected to go to the USA. In terms of the value of production, Alberta is the most productive province, followed by Ontario and British Columbia. Fluctuations in world economic growth inevitably have a significant bearing upon the short-term prosperity of the Canadian mineral industry; in addition, environmental concerns have led to a sharp drop in demand for some minerals (such as asbestos). Canada is the world's largest producer (and exporter) of nickel, uranium and zinc, and the second largest producer of asbestos, potash, sulphur and gypsum.

Mineral resources are widely distributed across the country, with the exception of Prince Edward Island, which produces only sand and gravel in any significant amounts. The Canadian Shield, which covers most of east and north-central Canada, is particularly rich in metallic and non-metallic ores, and as the Canadian North becomes increasingly mapped and surveyed in detail, further new resources will undoubtedly be found. However, the exploitation of resources in some of these remote areas involves a whole series of economic, environmental, political and technological issues. The distances involved, local conditions prevailing and lack of local infrastructure mean that development in such areas is often difficult and time-consuming. International economic conditions thus play an important part in determining the feasibility of development. Issues relating to land claims of indigenous peoples, federal-provincial political sensitivities, and the growing concern about upsetting the ecological balance of the more fragile northern areas are further constraints on rapid mineral development in this region.

FUELS

Among the major categories of minerals, fossil fuels account for the largest share of total mineral production by value, having displaced metallic ores from that position in the early 1970s. This change has been due not so much to a decline in the value of metals, but to a major upsurge in fossil-fuel production.

Coal

For many years coal formed the base of Canadian energy-resource mining. Historically, coal production was located in the western and eastern extremities of the country—Vancouver Island and, more importantly, Nova Scotia and New Brunswick. Difficulties of transport over the long distances involved, the unsuitability of the coal type and the overall inadequacy of Canadian output meant that the major markets of Ontario and southern Québec were supplied not by Canadian, but by US Appalachian coal. However, the period since the mid-1960s has witnessed dramatic changes in Canadian coal output.

Eastern production has declined by some 60%, while that from the western provinces of British Columbia, Alberta and Saskatchewan has risen from 5m. metric tons in 1964—the last year in which the Maritime provinces produced more than the West—to over 50m. tons by the mid-1980s. The coal comes predominantly from western Alberta, extreme south-eastern British Columbia and southern Saskatchewan. At the same time, imports have remained fairly constant, fluctuating between 14m. and 18m. tons annually depending on the prosperity of the steel industry, while exports have increased from 1m. tons in 1964 to average just over 26m. tons in 1984–86. In 1987 coal production was about 60m. tons, with an estimated value of C $1,635m.

A combination of an increased demand for electricity in the Prairie provinces, a need for low-sulphur coal (such as that found in the West) for Ontario power stations, and a massive growth in Japanese purchases of Canadian coal—often on long-term contracts—has brought about this dramatic change in the pattern of coal production. Coal is transported by unit trains to purpose-built terminals on the west coast of British Columbia.

Oil

The oil industry did not really become established in Canada until after the discovery, in 1947, of the Leduc oilfield in southern Alberta. In 1988 Alberta supplied some 82% of domestic crude-oil production of 93.6m. cu m, and Saskatchewan 13%; the rest came mainly from British Columbia (2.0%), the Northwest Territories (1.9%) and Manitoba. Domestic production currently surpasses domestic consumption and some oil is exported, mainly to the USA via pipelines which were built to link the oilfields with the refineries in Ontario; parts of these pipelines actually pass through the Midwest region of the USA. The increasing importance of oil, together with the fact that, in the past, Canadian supplies were inadequate to meet domestic demand, has encouraged the continued search for new reserves, both in the traditional areas and further afield. Three areas in which commercially-viable quantities have been found recently are the Beaufort Sea–MacKenzie Delta area, the Arctic islands region and the waters around the Maritime provinces; indeed, the development of the Hibernia oilfield, at an estimated cost of C $8,500m., will be a stimulant to the Newfoundland economy.

Alberta and Saskatchewan also possess very large deposits of oilsands. Exploitation of the oil sand deposits—which have been known to exist for a long time—has been dependent both on the development of the necessary oil-extraction technology and on the existence of economic conditions which would encourage the necessary capital investment. In the late 1980s the oilsands industry was receiving both provincial- and federal-government support, as world oil prices were not very conducive to the growth of the industry; some recently-developed plant had not been brought into operation. However, as world oil prices improve, and as supplies of traditional crude oil become scarcer, exploitation of the enormous oilsand deposits can be expected to make a significant contribution to Canadian oil production.

Natural Gas

Gas has a similar development history, and often a similar location, to petroleum, with over 85% of production coming from Alberta. Gas is piped to markets as far east as Québec, and pipeline extensions are planned both to the Maritime provinces in the east and to Vancouver Island in the west. Gas production is well in excess of domestic demand and one-third of production is exported—almost exclusively by pipeline to the USA. Some is also exported in liquefied form by tanker—principally from British Columbia to Japan. As with oil, the potentially large deposits in the Canadian North await both the right market conditions and the environmental and political acceptance of the construction of pipelines southwards from the Arctic coast. Production of natural gas totalled 77,578m. cu m in 1987, and that of natural gas liquids 19m. cu m.

The hydrocarbons industry has been the subject of serious political controversy. The provinces own the resources within their boundaries, although the federal government has control over interprovincial and international trade. In the past the federal government was keen to have a low price for oil,

principally because of the major domestic markets in Québec and Ontario, while the western oil-rich provinces wanted a high price for the benefit of their own economies. In the early 1980s the federal government tried to establish higher oil prices, with much of the additional revenue going to the central government, leaving the producer provinces with less revenue than they felt they ought to have. Eventually a compromise was reached, but not until global price changes had overtaken the debate. In addition, the change in federal government in 1984 resulted ultimately in the Western Accord of 28 March 1985 on energy pricing and taxation, and this allowed for a more flexible approach to production and sales. Also in 1985, an Atlantic Accord ended years of acrimony between the federal and the provincial governments over the management of offshore resources, and resulted in a scheme for joint management and revenue-sharing.

METALLIC MINERALS

In 1986 the value of Canada's metallic mineral production totalled C $8,944m., or 26% of the total value of mineral production. Gold accounted for 19% of production by value, followed by copper (18%), lead and zinc (17%), iron ore (14%), nickel (12%), uranium (10%) and silver (3%).

Copper

British Columbia and Ontario are the main copper producers, followed by Manitoba and Québec. Much of British Columbia's production is exported in concentrated-ore form to Japan for refining. The world's largest copper refinery is situated in Montréal, while Copper Cliff and Timmins, both in Ontario, are other important centres. Smelters are located at Flin Flon (Manitoba), Copper Cliff, Falconbridge and Timmins (Ontario) and Rouyn-Noranda and Murdochville (Québec). Production of copper ore totalled an estimated 794,000 metric tons in 1987, making Canada the world's fourth-largest producer.

Gold

Though early attempts to find gold in Canada were unsuccessful, late 19th-century finds led to the Klondike gold rush of the late 1890s. By the 1970s many mines had been closed as being uneconomic to operate, but more recently new discoveries—together with strong world prices—have resulted in a significant expansion of gold production, with a 20% increase in output being recorded between 1985 and 1986. Gold is worked widely, from Newfoundland through Québec, Ontario, Manitoba and Saskatchewan to British Columbia and the Territories, with Ontario as the chief producer. In 1987, with a total output of 116,000 kg, Canada ranked fourth among world gold producers, behind South Africa, the USSR and the USA.

Iron Ore

The largely worked-out iron-ore deposits in Bell Island, Newfoundland, were the key to early steel production in Nova Scotia. By the mid-1950s ore production was focused upon the Shield areas of Ontario, and (more especially) Québec and Labrador, where by 1979 11 companies were operating. In that year Newfoundland was the leading producer province, followed by Québec and Ontario, and production reached a peak of 69.6m. metric tons. A general decrease in world demand for steel during the early 1980s, and the exhaustion of several mines, resulted in significant declines in production, which totalled only 38.7m. tons in 1988. Exports to both the USA and Western Europe have declined and some mines in Labrador and Ontario have been closed. Virtually all ore is either concentrated or made into pellets before export.

Lead and Zinc

Canada is the world's chief source of zinc and its third most important producer of lead, which is chiefly mined in Canada as a co-product of zinc. Lead is obtained mainly from the Northwest Territories, Yukon Territory, New Brunswick and British Columbia, while zinc comes principally from mines in the Northwest Territories, Ontario, New Brunswick, Yukon Territory and British Columbia. Increasingly, production is focused on the lower-cost producers. The zinc is refined mainly at Trail (British Columbia), and also at Valleyfield (Québec),

Timmins (Ontario) and Flin Flon (Manitoba), while lead refineries are located principally at Trail and Belledune, New Brunswick. Much of Canada's production of both lead and zinc is exported. In 1988 334,000 metric tons of lead were produced, and 1.3m. tons of zinc.

Molybdenum

Production of molybdenum, a metal used primarily in alloy form to add strength to steel, has increased significantly since 1985, when one mine was reopened and another expanded. Virtually all of the 1987 output of 11.6m. metric tons came from British Columbia. The fourth largest producer in the world, Canada is also a major exporter, with its principal customers being in Western Europe and Japan.

Nickel

Production of nickel has declined significantly from the early 1970s, with marked effects upon the economies of the main producing areas of Ontario. In 1950 Canada produced three-quarters of the world's nickel, but by the mid-1980s its contribution had declined to just one-quarter. The decrease in production was due to a combination of increased domestic production costs (due to the more accessible ores having been exhausted), an increase in output in other parts of the world, which affected exports and prices, and also a general downturn in demand. In spite of all this, Canada remains one of the world's largest producers and Ontario the world's principal source of nickel, with its main operations centred on Sudbury, while in Manitoba production is focused on the Thompson area. In 1988 production was 189,000 metric tons, of which Ontario accounted for some 66%.

Silver

Canada is the world's fifth-largest producer of silver, with a 1988 output of 1,527 metric tons. Production in that year was concentrated upon British Columbia (28%), Ontario (25%), Yukon Territory (22%), New Brunswick (13%) and Québec (8%). Refining takes place mainly at Montréal (Québec), Trail (British Columbia), and Sudbury and Cobalt (Ontario).

Uranium

Canada has significant uranium resources, though frequent problems of over-supply in the world markets have meant that capacity has not often been fully utilized. Canada and the USA are the two major world producers of uranium, and the two most important Canadian producer provinces are Ontario and Saskatchewan, each of which has four producing areas. Total Canadian uranium production was 13,233 metric tons in 1988. Exports are chiefly to the United Kingdom, the USA, Japan, Sweden and the Federal Republic of Germany. Most domestic consumption is for nuclear-electricity generation (see below).

NON-METALLIC MINERALS

Asbestos

Canada provides about one-fifth of world asbestos production, and is second only to the USSR in output. Production has suffered cut-backs, however, due to declines in demand which are partly due to world economic conditions—especially in developing countries—and partly to concern over the environmental hazards of asbestos dust. As a result mining operations in southern Québec, centred on Thetford Mines and East Broughton, have been curtailed. Production has fallen from 1.5m. metric tons in 1979 to 665,000 tons in 1987. About 95% of production is exported, and of this about one-quarter goes to the USA.

Potash

Potash was discovered during oil exploration in the 1940s and the first commercial mine opened in the early 1960s. Today Canada is the world's second-largest producer and its principal exporter. In 1988 production totalled 8.3m. metric tons (K_2O equivalent). Most production comes from Saskatchewan, although New Brunswick has been a producer since 1984. Exports have been affected by economic conditions overseas, including farming conditions in the USA, where economic pressures on farmers have led to a decline in fertilizer consump-

tion, and therefore to a fall in demand for Canadian potash. At present the industry is working at about two-thirds capacity.

Salt

Production is focused on Ontario (63%), Alberta (11%) and Saskatchewan. Production has been increasing, and in 1988 was 11.0m. metric tons, of which 2.5m. tons were exported. Rock salt comes from mines in Ontario, Québec and Nova Scotia and, as a by-product of potash mining, from Saskatchewan and New Brunswick.

Sulphur

Sulphur comes mainly from Alberta, but also from British Columbia. Production, both elemental and from smelter gases, totalled 7.6m. metric tons in 1986, of which some 85% was exported. In spite of recent export declines, Canada remains the world's chief producer and exporter of elemental sulphur.

Electricity

Canada has one of the highest per-head rates of consumption of electric energy in the world, and derives about two-thirds of its production from water power. With its enormous water resources, and its lack of conventional energy sources in the most-populated provinces, it is not surprising that hydroelectric power (HEP) has played such a major role in electricity generation. Though Canada is rich in potential HEP resources, especially in the Shield areas, there are problems involved with exploiting them. Many of the still-untapped resources are distant from existing markets, and are at or beyond the economic and technological margins for economic transmission. Also, some sites are in areas of environmental sensitivity or in land claimed by the native peoples.

In spite of Canada's rich resources of HEP, the relative importance of water power has declined in recent years as that of thermal sources (such as coal, oil and natural gas) has increased. All provinces obtain at least a part of their power from thermal sources, although in 1985 proportions ranged from 100% for Prince Edward Island, which is entirely dependent on oil-powered generation, to 0.1% for Québec. Alberta and Saskatchewan, in particular, obtain only a small proportion (4% and 16% respectively in 1985) of their electricity from water. Coal-fired power stations are concentrated in Ontario, Alberta and Saskatchewan, and the tonnage used in generation has risen dramatically, from under 5m. metric tons in the early 1960s to 39m. tons in 1985. Alberta is the chief coal user (17m. tons in 1985), followed by Ontario (11m. tons).

At the same time, Ontario is the main source of nuclear-generated power, which in 1985 accounted for about 40% of the province's power production and comes from stations at Pickering and Bruce. New Brunswick and Québec are the other nuclear-power producers. Nuclear-power generation has been steadily increasing in importance and, in 1986, accounted for 15% of total electricity produced. The potential for further nuclear-power production is considerable, and in one sense nuclear generation presents an attractive alternative to coal-fired generation, which causes a certain amount of pollution; however, nuclear power has its long-term waste-disposal problems, as well as shorter-term safety concerns on the part of the public.

Technological developments to enable efficient, economic power transmission over distances of 3,000 km (1,865 miles) or more would open up a number of rich hydro sites for exploitation and would give Canada significant scope for increased exports to the USA. Already power is exported from Québec, Ontario and Manitoba to the USA: in Ontario, with its greater dependence on coal-based power, this has raised the complaint that, indirectly, the USA has exported its pollution to Canada.

Conclusion

It is, therefore, apparent that Canada is very rich in a wide range of primary resources. Given the country's low population density, much of this wealth is exported overseas. While the value of these exports (accounting for over one-third of the total value of Canadian exports) help to give Canada a substantial trade surplus in most years, it is often claimed that Canada is still viewed by many other western nations as a 'mere' provider of raw materials—in fact, virtually as a 'colonial' economy: other countries reap the benefits of greater value

added in economic activity by processing the resources which Canada has produced. The situation is changing in that an increasing proportion of Canadian export income is being contributed by the manufacturing and service sectors, but the primary sector remains important, and will continue to do so for many decades to come.

MANUFACTURING AND CONSTRUCTION IN CANADA

LYNDHURST COLLINS

Introduction

The growth of manufacturing industry in Canada can be attributed to several factors. Canada has immense resources of raw materials (minerals, forests, agriculture and fish) which have acted as a base of supplies for a wide variety of processing industries; it has an abundance of water and petroleum, which provide relatively cheap sources of energy, power and transport; it has easy access to the vast market of the USA, as well as traditional marketing connections with the UK and the Commonwealth; and, as a favoured destination for several generations of European and, more recently, Asian immigrants, it has had a constant and secure supply of highly-trained and compliant labour. Finally, Canada has had easy access to capital, both from its own growing stock markets and from New York and London.

In 1970 the manufacturing sector contributed 23% of Canada's gross domestic product (GDP), but by 1981 this contribution had declined to just 17%. Thus the extent to which Canada could continue to rely on its comparative advantage in terms of these traditional factors of production came into question. Increasing concern about Canada's ability to maintain a competitive position in the increasingly-integrated global economy of the late 1980s prompted the federal government to create, in early 1988, a new Department of Industry, Science and Technology. The accelerated diffusion of information-processing technology across Canadian industry, the advent of microprocessing technology and its rapid diffusion into manufacturing, the widespread changes in telecommunications technology and the continuous development of new materials and new sources of existing materials as substitutes for many Canadian products are all modifying the competitiveness of companies and of entire industries. The future competitiveness of many industries will largely depend on the extent to which interindustrial transfer of technology occurs, and on the way in which technological opportunities in one sector lead to innovations and increased competitiveness of firms in other sectors; it will also depend on the ability of the manufacturing sector as a whole to adapt quickly to both changing degrees of competitiveness caused by fluctuations in exchange rates and the new political–economic framework imposed by the creation of the US–Canadian Free-Trade Area which came into operation on 1 January 1989.

Geographical Distribution

Manufacturing activity is not evenly distributed across Canada, but is heavily concentrated in the provinces of Ontario and Québec. In 1984 these two provinces together accounted for 71% of Canada's manufacturing establishments (Ontario 42% and Québec 29%), whereas at the 1986 census they held 62% of the country's population (Ontario 36% and Québec 26%). At the other extreme, the Atlantic provinces of Newfoundland, New Brunswick, Nova Scotia and Prince Edward Island together had 9% of the population in 1986 but just 5.5% of the manufacturing establishments in 1984. British Columbia is the third most important manufacturing province behind Ontario and Québec, with 11% of establishments in 1984 and 11% of population in 1986. The Prairie provinces of Alberta, Manitoba

and Saskatchewan had 12.5% of manufacturers in 1984 and 18% of population in 1986.

The degree of concentration of manufacturing activity within Ontario and Québec is even more marked when measured in terms of the value of shipments. The total value of manufacturing shipments in 1985 was C \$248,500m., of which Ontario provided 53%, Québec 24%, British Columbia 8%, the Prairie provinces 10% and the Atlantic provinces just 4%. The difference between the relative contributions of the two main manufacturing provinces has widened in the 1970s and early 1980s, with Ontario's share increasing by 1% since 1969 and that of Québec decreasing by more than 3%, largely reflecting the differing industrial bases of the two provinces. For example, while Ontario accounted for 83% of the value of shipments of Canadian-made transportation equipment in 1985, Québec provided only 12%. The transportation-equipment industries, particularly the automotive industries, are very highly concentrated in Ontario, accounting for 27% of the province's total manufacturing shipments by value in 1985—the figure for Québec being only 8.5%. The most important manufacturing sectors in Québec are the food industries (providing 14% of the value of all provincial manufacturing shipments in 1985) and the paper and allied products industries (10%). (While Québec and Ontario each contribute over 33% of the total value of Canadian shipments of paper and allied products, the sector has much less importance in relation to the economy of Ontario, accounting for only 4.5% of its manufacturing shipments.) In general, Québec has the most balanced industrial structure of all the Canadian provinces, in that it is the least dominated by a single sector. Food industries, for example, predominate in Prince Edward Island (where they accounted for 69% of all provincial manufacturing shipments in 1985), Newfoundland (43%), Saskatchewan (30%), Manitoba (31%) and Nova Scotia (21%). New Brunswick derives 23% of the value of its shipments from paper and allied products and 21% from food; Alberta has three dominant industries in refined petroleum and coal products (30% of shipments), food (21%) and chemicals and chemical products (15%); and British Columbia is relatively well diversified, obtaining 26% of the value of its shipments from wood industries, 17% from paper and allied products and 13% each from refined petroleum and coal products, and from food.

Manufacturing activity within the individual provinces tends to be concentrated on the large metropolitan areas. Ontario's automobile industry, however, constitutes an important exception. This industry, by far the largest single contributor to the total value of both provincial and national manufacturing shipments, is located at three main sites—Oakville and Oshawa, both on Lake Ontario and just outside the metropolitan boundaries of Toronto, and Windsor, which is situated just across the border from Detroit and which was the first site to be occupied by a US-owned subsidiary manufacturing automobiles in Canada. Such a location offered immediate economies of production by virtue of its close proximity to the parent company in Detroit; at the same time the cars could be sold in the domestic market as Canadian-made products and were, therefore, free from import tariffs. The US automobile industry has gradually, through the establishment of subsidiaries, sought locations closer to the centre of the Canadian market, namely Toronto. Since the land required for new extensive 'greenfield' sites has proved too expensive within metropolitan

Toronto, Ford has chosen to locate in Oakville, to the west of the metropolitan boundary, and General Motors in Oshawa, to the east. Both towns are within commuting distance of Toronto, and thus have easy access to both the labour and consumer markets.

The pattern of manufacturing activity in and around the major cities has also evolved as a result of redevelopment schemes carried out in the 1970s and 1980s. The industrial core areas of cities such as Toronto, Montréal and Vancouver have been redeveloped and much of the industry has been relocated to 'greenfield' sites in the outer suburban areas. Most of this manufacturing industry has been reaccommodated in clean, purpose-built, single-level buildings, surrounded by ample space for parking and, in some cases, for recreation; much is also within reach of the international airports, which provide rapid links to other parts of Canada, the USA and the rest of the world, or alongside the major freeways, highways, and autoroutes leading into the major cities. Such locations, as well as affording ready access to markets and labour, also provide the opportunity for effective advertising.

This process of 'suburbanization' of manufacturing activity around the major cities, especially in southern Ontario, has reinforced the dominant pattern of industrial development in Canada in what is commonly referred to as the 'Golden Horseshoe'. This is situated around the western extremity of Lake Ontario, beginning on the north shore at Oshawa and extending eastwards through metropolitan Toronto to Guelph, Kitchener–Waterloo and along the southern shore via Hamilton, St Catharines and Niagara-on-the-Lake to the Niagara Peninsula, where large areas of some of the best agricultural land in Canada have been lost to urban- and industrial-development schemes.

Structure and Organization of Manufacturing Activity

As well as changes in the geographical pattern of manufacturing activity over the last few decades, there have also been important changes in its structure and organization. While the number of manufacturing establishments in Canada has increased from 31,145 in 1973 to 36,854 in 1985, the total number of employees recorded in manufacturing increased from 1.9m. in 1973 to 2.0m. in 1987. (These increases probably reflect a longer-term upward trend in recent decades, but such a trend cannot be measured easily and accurately because of changes in the way that manufacturing establishments, and hence manufacturing employment, have been defined for statistical and census purposes.) Although the number of manufacturing employees increased by 88,000 between 1973 and 1986, the average 4.6% increase masked different rates of change within individual sectors. The largest absolute loss occurred in the textiles, knitting-mills and clothing sector, where 24,000 jobs (or 11% of the 1973 total) were lost, while the non-electrical machinery sector experienced the largest proportional loss, of 12.6%, through a reduction of 11,000 employees. Substantial gains were experienced in sectors such as rubber and plastic products (29,000 employees or 51%), printing and publishing (43,000 or 36%) and transportation equipment (38,000 or 19.2%). The overall trend or pattern, therefore, has been one of significant decline in the more traditional resource-based manufacturing activities, but this decline has been more than offset by a corresponding increase in higher-technology industries.

Principal Manufactures

FORESTRY PRODUCTS

This gradual change in emphasis has provided Canada with a mature manufacturing structure that is balanced across the full spectrum of industrial activity; there is no overriding dominant industry. Nevertheless, the manufacture of forestry products, a resource-based activity, can still be viewed as Canada's most important industry. This is so for several reasons.

The forestry-products sector comprises two main manufacturing groups as classified by Statistics Canada; wood industries

and pulp and paper industries. The sector is represented in every province and employed 218,740 persons across Canada in 1984, accounting for 12.7% of all employment in Canadian manufacturing industry. (Even so, employment in the sector was well over 10% down on the 'peak year' of 1979.) In addition to this direct employment it is estimated that another 520,000 jobs are provided in support services; this would mean that almost one job in 10 in Canada is dependent on the forestry-products sector. At a local level this dependency becomes much more critical as it is concentrated into more than 300 communities or 'one-industry towns'.

At the regional level, activities in the forestry-products sector are concentrated in eastern Canada and in British Columbia. The emphasis in eastern Canada, especially in Ontario and Québec, is on the manufacture of pulp and paper; these two provinces accounted for some 71.5% of all Canadian employment in these industries in 1984. British Columbia, on the other hand, contains the major portion of the softwood timber industry when measured by output, accounting for almost 40% of Canada's employment in wood industries in 1984. This cleavage of the industry into two parts reflects the markedly different quality of available timber. Timber stands in eastern Canada are of relatively poor quality in comparison to those found in British Columbia, but are eminently suitable for making wood pulp, the material from which paper, especially newsprint, is subsequently made. Much paper manufactured in Canada is shipped to the huge market in the northeastern USA. Timber harvested in British Columbia, especially the Douglas fir and red cedar, found in coastal locations, is of very high quality and is in great demand for construction purposes, especially in the USA, where Canadian timber can fetch a much higher price than that produced domestically.

During the post-war period two major changes have occurred in the production of pulp in Canada. Firstly, the proportion manufactured in British Columbia has increased from 9% in 1950 (when Québec and Ontario together accounted for over 73% of total production) to 29% in 1986 (when Québec produced 32% and Ontario just 19%). During this period the total volume of wood pulp produced in Canada increased from 7.7m. metric tons to 21.5m. tons, with British Columbia contributing almost 40% of this increase. Almost 65% of all Canadian wood pulp is used in the domestic production of paper and board, and most of this takes place in the integrated mills located in Québec and Ontario. In contrast, over 60% of the wood pulp produced in British Columbia in 1986 was exported. The USA took 76% of this, with other major customers being in Japan and Western Europe.

The second major change that has occurred in the production of wood pulp in Canada has involved the introduction of new technology which has changed the way in which pulp is produced. In 1950 pulps produced by a mechanical process involving the grinding of wood logs between large rollers of stone or steel comprised 61% of Canadian production. By 1986 this figure had fallen to 42%, with pulps made from chemical processes having come to account for 58%. These chemical pulps accounted for 93% of the 7m. metric tons of wood pulp exported from Canada in 1986.

In 1987 the forestry-products sector accounted for almost 15% of Canada's manufacturing gross domestic product (GDP), and in 1986 its net contribution to the balance of trade (in terms of the surplus of exports over imports) was, at C $16,547m., over twice as great as that of the energy-products sector, its nearest rival. Although the output of Canada's forestry-products industry is relatively small compared to that of the USA, for example, the country was the world's leading exporter of forestry products in 1985, with total sales of C $16,200m. accounting for 22% of all world trade. In the late 1980s Canada had 16% of world paper-grade wood-pulp capacity compared with the USA's 34%, but accounted for some 61% of the world's newsprint exports, 29% of market-pulp exports (market pulp being that pulp which is shipped from point of origin for further manufacture into paper or board at another location) and 51% of softwood-lumber exports.

Despite its continuing pre-eminence in terms of exports, the relative importance of the forestry-products sector to the domestic economy has been in decline since 1950, when production of pulp and paper accounted for 5.3% of Canada's gross national product (GNP) and 22.9% of all exports; by 1985 these proportions had decreased to 2.9% and to 8.7% respectively. This relative decline can be attributed to several causes: firstly, the loss of some Canadian export markets (especially those for pulp and paper) as a result of increased competition from other countries such as Brazil, Chile and South Africa; secondly, fluctuations in exchange rates which have enabled Scandinavian producers to be more competitive on the lucrative US market; thirdly, the increasing use of both recycled waste paper (especially in Japan and the Federal Republic of Germany) and substitute materials for packaging (with traditional paper derivatives being supplanted increasingly by plastic materials, for example); and fourthly, and possibly of most importance, the increasing contribution to GNP of higher-technology sectors such as transportation equipment and electrical products.

TRANSPORTATION EQUIPMENT

The transportation-equipment industries, as defined by Statistics Canada, now constitute Canada's single most important branch of manufacturing activity in terms of both value of shipments and contribution to all manufacturers' share of GDP. As well as the automobile industry, which is concentrated in southern Ontario (see above), there is shipbuilding at Sorel and Montréal (both on the St Lawrence River), railway rolling-stock manufacture at Montréal and aerospace at both Montréal and Toronto. The transportation-equipment industries' share of the total value of manufactured shipments has increased from 13% in 1979 (when food and beverage industries led with 17%) to 17.3% in 1985, and they contributed 12.1% to total manufacturing GDP in 1987, making them the largest single contributor among the major industrial sectors. The other major sectors which increased their share of total value of manufactured shipments between 1979 and 1985 were electrical products (from 4.3% to 5.3%), refined petroleum and coal products (from 8.1% to 9.8%) and chemicals and chemical products (from 6.2% to 7.3%).

The recovery of the transportation-equipment sector from the effects of the 1981–82 economic depression played a major part in the strengthening of the Canadian economy in the aftermath of the slump, which caused the longest and most severe decline in real manufacturing production in Canada since the depression of the 1930s. One of the main factors was a strong upturn in automobile production from 1984 in response to a more general improvement in the US economy which, in turn, generated an increased demand in the USA for passenger cars made in Canada.

IRON AND STEEL

The primary-metal industries, especially the iron and steel industry, are probably the most vulnerable to fluctuations in the performance of the transportation-equipment sector. More than 90% of the Canadian iron and steel industry is controlled by private Canadian interests, while the mills of the Sydney Steel Corporation (Sysco) in Nova Scotia and Sidbec Dosco in Québec are both under provincial-government control. In 1986 the industry employed a total of 40,800 and produced shipments valued at C $7,880m., of which 21% were exported. In that year Canada accounted for 2% of world production of raw steel.

The Canadian iron and steel industry consists of two types of producing unit. Firstly, there are the large integrated mills which consume iron ore and supply a wide range of products. These are heavily concentrated in Ontario, which in 1984 accounted for 60% of employment in primary-metal industries and 57% of shipments. The Ontario-based companies of Dofasco Inc and the Algoma Steel Corporation Ltd (which merged in July 1988) and Stelco Inc together provide 75% of Canada's iron and steel capacity. These large integrated producers serve national markets and each tends to specialize in particular product lines. Algoma is heavily oriented towards capital goods and energy markets, and is the only Canadian producer of seamless tube and wide-flanged beams. Dofasco produces only flat-rolled products, such as sheet strip and plate, destined primarily for the consumer-durable market such as the automotive and large home-appliances (white-goods) sectors. These products form the largest single market for steel in Canada

and are responsible for consuming 60% of total Canadian demand. Stelco produces the widest range of steel products, serving both consumer and capital-goods markets, and it is the only integrated mill in Canada that produces large-diameter line pipe and a large range of wire and wire products.

The second type of production unit consists of electric-furnace mills ('minimills') which consume ferrous scrap and supply a limited range of products. These mills have successfully captured markets from the integrated mills since the early 1960s and now compete primarily among themselves for a limited segment of the market which they dominate; this segment involves the production of steel bar, light structural items and, to some extent, rod products. Major exceptions within this classification include Ipsco Inc in Saskatchewan and Sidbec Dosco in Québec, which produce flat-rolled steel and pipe. In early 1987 QIT-Fer et Titane Inc began a 400,000-metric-ton-a-year semi-finished billet-production operation at Tracy in Québec, and in late 1988 an electric furnace, a continuous caster and a new rail mill were being installed at Sysco in Nova Scotia as part of a modernization programme.

The rapid decline in world demand for steel since the early 1970s has reduced both the number of plants and total steel-making capacity in most industrialized countries—however, the performance of the Canadian steel industry has been better than that of most of its competitors. Although employment in the industry declined by just over 8,000 (16%) between 1973 and 1986, the number of establishments increased from 21 to 24 (operated by 14 companies in all) and output increased by 18%, from 9.9m. to 11.7m. metric tons. Thus the number of tons shipped for each employee increased by 42%, from 202 in 1973 to 286 in 1986. This has been achieved through high utilization rates of modern capital-intensive equipment: for example, it has been estimated that the cost of producing hot-rolled steel coils in Canada is 86% of that in the USA, and 87% of that in Japan and the European Communities (EC). The corresponding figures, however, are much lower for Brazil (59% of the US cost) and for the Republic of Korea (56%). The increased competitiveness of the Canadian iron and steel industry is also illustrated by its import and export trade. In 1973 the value of Canada's steel exports was equivalent to about 71% of its imports, but by 1986 the relationship had been reversed, with imports amounting to 69% of exports. A major change occurred in Canada's steel trade with the USA and the EC during the mid-1980s. Whereas in 1982 46% of Canada's steel imports came from the USA and 28% from the EC, the corresponding figures for 1986 were 34% and 38% respectively. Similarly, between 1982 and 1985 the proportion of Canada's steel exports going to the USA increased from 56% to 85%, while that going to the EC declined from 14% to 6%.

FOOD AND BEVERAGES

Food industries and beverage industries together contributed 11.3% to manufacturing GDP in 1987: their combined employment declined between 1973 and 1986, recovering in 1987 to account for 12.4% of all manufacturing employment, second only to the forestry-products sector. This industry is represented in every province, but remains concentrated within the provinces of Ontario (40% of shipments in 1984) and Québec (27%); the degree of concentration, however, is much lower than for the other major sectors. Much of the industry in Ontario and Québec is dependent on processing raw materials (including vegetables, fruit, cereals and meat) which have been produced all over Canada for sale both on the main Canadian market, extending from Windsor in Ontario to Québec City, and also to the nearby market of the north-eastern USA.

ELECTRICAL AND ELECTRONIC PRODUCTS

The electrical and electronic products sector contributed an equivalent amount (11.3%) to manufacturing GDP as did the food and beverages sector (see above) in 1987, but, with 8% of manufacturing employment in that year, was the third largest industry in terms of employees. Post-war developments in the hydroelectricity industry in Canada, especially along the St Lawrence River and the edge of the Canadian Shield (see p. 376), have encouraged the rapid development of the manufacture of electrical machinery, electrical turbines and transformers. Similarly, rapid changes in consumer demand for telephones, telex equipment and 'white goods' such as refrigerators, deepfreezes and washing machines, together with a huge demand for television sets, calculators and computers, have spawned the development of a sophisticated industry throughout the 'Golden Horseshoe', especially in St Catharines, Hamilton, Toronto, Peterborough and Ottawa. In terms of shipments, Ontario had 66% of this industry in 1984 and Québec 26%, with the remaining plants being situated principally in Manitoba, British Columbia and Alberta.

CHEMICALS AND CHEMICAL PRODUCTS

The chemical and chemical-products industries—in particular the petrochemical industry, which acounts for more than 60% of all chemical-manufacturing industry in Canada—has been one of Canada's fastest-growing sectors in recent years. Between 1973 and 1986 the total value of shipments of the petrochemical industry increased eightfold, to C $5,114m., and employment increased overall by 4,819 (52%) to 13,962, a peak of 15,455 being reached in 1982.

Petrochemicals are organic chemicals manufactured from raw materials ('feedstocks') which are derived from crude oil and natural gas. The industry uses about 4% of all crude oil consumed in Canada, both domestic and imported, and 25% of domestic natural-gas sales. Feedstocks are converted into first-stage or primary petrochemicals, such as the olefins, the aromatics and methanol, which are then upgraded to intermediaries, such as styorene, ethylene dichloride and large-volume plastic resins including polyethylene and polyvinyl chloride (PVC). Intermediaries are the raw materials for a wide range of 'downstream' (customer) industries such as synthetic rubber, plastics processing, paints, adhesives and synthetic textiles. The more labour-intensive downstream industries tend to locate near the markets, so most of the downstream employment has again been in Ontario and Québec: industries in these provinces tend to use oil-based raw materials, while a new 'western sector' of gas-based industries has developed in Alberta and British Columbia. Major refineries have been developed in Ontario, first at Sarnia, at the southern extremity of Lake Huron (which was the first terminal of the pipeline from Alberta), then at Burlington, near Hamilton, and at Clarkson, near Toronto. Other refineries in eastern Canada use oil imported by way of the St Lawrence Seaway.

Productivity in Canadian Manufacturing

Although these surveys of the major Canadian industries indicate a generally favourable situation, broader comparative analyses indicate certain weaknesses. One major problem concerns the general productivity levels of Canadian manufacturing, especially in comparison to those of the USA. Productivity is a critical economic variable determined by a combination of factors, including the level of education and skills of the labour force, the level of productive capital and technology, the efficiency of management, and other factors such as degree of specialization and scale of production. The Department of Regional Industrial Expansion (DRIE), in its 1988 report, suggested that a significant productivity gap still existed between the manufacturing sectors of Canada and the USA. In general, because of the relatively small-scale operation of Canadian plants, which in turn reflects a small domestic market, Canadian manufacturing is about 85% as productive as that in the USA, and between 1970 and 1986 the overall Canadian productivity ratio improved by only 1%. In 1986 only three Canadian industrial sectors equalled or exceeded the productivity levels achieved by their US counterparts: pulp and paper industries; transportation equipment; and electrical and electronic products. However, the ratio for pulp and paper industries had actually fallen from its 1970 level, while the transportation-equipment and electrical and electronic-products sectors are both heavily controlled by US ownership. DRIE has also noted that another important factor which influences the level of productivity, especially future productivity, is the amount of research and development (R. & D.) carried out, since this affects the rate of diffusion of technological advance.

Of the 11 major manufacturing western countries Canada ranked 10th in 1985 in terms of the proportion of gross expenditure on R. & D. to total GDP; Canada's ratio was less than one-half that of the USA and significantly less than those of the Federal Republic of Germany, Japan, Sweden, the UK, France and the Netherlands.

The relative importance of manufacturing activity to the Canadian economy, especially in terms of employment, has continued to decline from 1973, when manufacturing accounted for 22% of total employment, to 1987, when it accounted for just 17%. Average weekly earnings in manufacturing in 1988 were, at C $538.35, lower than those in forestry (C $616), construction and transportation (C $587), and public administration (C $577). Within the manufacturing sector the highest-paid industries in 1985 were pulp and paper production (C $668/week) and smelting and refining (C $651); average weekly earnings in the automotive industry were C $590.

Construction and Housing

Construction and housing is not formally part of the manufacturing sector, as defined by Statistics Canada, but it is closely interrelated. One important difference is that, unlike the manufacturing sector, it is highly dependent on the domestic market, and consequently was more severely affected by the economic recession of 1981–82. In terms of constant 1981 dollars, the value of all construction work purchased fell by 12% from C $56,800m. in 1981 to C $50,100m. in 1984; by 1987 its value had recovered to C $63,860m. or just over 12% more than it was in 1981 and 28% more than in 1984.

Building and engineering are the two main divisions of the construction industry. The building division is by far the largest and in 1988 accounted for $58,270m. (current value), or 68% of the total value of construction work purchased in Canada (C $85,270m.). The changing relative proportions of these two divisions between 1977 and 1988 illustrate the effect of the 1981–82 slump. In 1977 the building division accounted for 60% of the value of all construction work purchased, but by 1982 this had declined to 51% before recovering to the high level of 1988. In 1988 most of the C $27,020m. spent on engineering construction was purchased by either utilities (33%), government departments (33%) or mining, quarries and oil wells (27%).

Residential construction is by far the largest component of the building division and in 1988 accounted for C $35,650m., or 42% of the total construction work purchased in Canada. Commercial building was responsible for C $13,090m. (15% of the total), institutional building for C $4,020m. (5%) and industrial building for C $3,340m. (4%). Within the building division, residential construction was affected more by the 1981–82 slump than was manufacturing construction. In both 1977 and 1988 residential construction accounted for 61% of construction in the building division, but a low of 47% was recorded in 1982; on the other hand, manufacturing construction accounted for 8% of building construction in 1977, 10% in 1982 and just 6% in 1988. A similar pattern was experienced by commercial construction, which accounted for 22% of building construction in 1988 compared to 17% in 1977; in 1982 it accounted for 24%.

The changing value of work purchased from the construction industry has been reflected in the number of new houses built ('housing starts'). Residential building peaked in 1976, with 275,000 starts, and since then, except for a slight increase in 1981, the general trend was one of gradual decline to a low of 160,000 in 1982. With the exception of a slight decrease in 1984, the number of starts has subsequently increased steadily, reaching 200,000 in 1986. It is estimated that the average-priced new house in 1986 was 4.4% more expensive in real terms than in 1981. At the metropolitan level, there were noticeable regional changes in price indices for new housing between 1981 and 1985. In Toronto, Windsor and Saskatoon, for example, there was very little change, but in the five eastern metropolitan centres of Halifax, Saint John, Québec, Montréal and Ottawa-Hull, and the three 'Golden-Horseshoe' centres of Hamilton, St Catharines–Niagara and Kitchener, the new-housing price index was at least 20% higher in 1985 than it was in 1981. In contrast, the two Prairie centres of

Calgary and Edmonton had indices that were about 20% lower, while those in the two western centres of Vancouver and Victoria were 25% lower than in 1981.

Foreign Ownership

One important feature of Canadian manufacturing industry is the high degree of foreign ownership. Foreign ownership of manufacturing activity is higher in Canada than in any other major industrialized country, though since 1970 more manufacturing activity has come under Canadian control. Between 1970 and 1981 the extent of foreign control, in terms of manufacturing shipments, declined from 52% to 46% in Canada, but in 1981 foreign ownership accounted for just 23% of manufacturing production in Australia, for 28% in France, for 22% in the Federal Republic of Germany and for 21% in the United Kingdom. While the number of foreign-owned establishments is quite small—3,832 in 1981, or about 11% of all Canadian manufacturing establishments—they account for about 37% of manufacturing employment, having about 180 employees each compared with 36 for the average Canadian-controlled plant. The average figures disguise wide provincial variations within Canada: while in 1981 only 6% of manufacturing activity in Prince Edward Island was foreign-controlled, the figure for the Northwest Territories was more than 60%, that for Nova Scotia 57% and those for the most important manufacturing provinces of Ontario and Québec were 57% and 55% respectively.

The dominance of foreign ownership is particularly apparent when individual sectors are considered. By far the most important is the transportation-equipment sector, in which more than 80% of production was controlled by overseas interests in 1981 (rising to more than 85% in the automotive-products industries); in 1970, however, it was 95% foreign-controlled, with 87% being controlled by US interests. Between 1970 and 1981 US control of this sector declined to 71%, while control by other foreign interests (mainly Japanese) increased to account for more than 15%. Other key sectors dominated by foreign ownership are petroleum and coal products (80% in 1981), chemicals and chemical products (73%), electrical products (58%), non-metallic mineral products (55%) and machinery industries (54%); in other words, principally high-technology and 'sunrise' industries. Canadian control, on the other hand, is concentrated in the so-called 'sunset' industries with lower profit margins, such as printing and publishing (90%), clothing industries (86%), knitting mills (86%), leather industries (84%), primary metals (84%), furniture and fixtures (82%), food and beverages (73%) and the forestry-products industries. Canadian control of the latter has increased from 60% of production in 1970 to 73% in 1981. The high degree of foreign ownership in Ontario and Québec, where many manufacturing companies have US 'parents', has been offered as an explanation for the particularly high concentration of Canadian manufacturing activity in these provinces, in that companies can be located relatively close to their US 'parents' while avoiding tariffs in producing for the Canadian, and in some cases the Commonwealth, market.

Manufacturing Activity and International Trade

Another important feature of manufacturing industry in Canada, and one which is also characteristic of manufacturing activity in most other industrialized countries, especially member states of the European Communities, is the increase in trade orientation for both exports and imports. This phenomenon is referred to as intra-industry trade, and involves the two-way trade of similar or even the same goods. The net result is an increasing integration of international markets. In Canada this is most marked in the automotive industry. This industry's exports were valued at C $29,400m. in 1984, in which year Canada imported C $26,400m.-worth of similar products.

It is generally thought that intra-industry trade encourages international specialization and hence increased productivity. The Canadian evidence supports this notion in that the industries with the largest increases in export orientation and import penetration between 1973 and 1986 were also those which registered the largest increases in employment. The most striking example is the electrical and electronic-products industry, whose export orientation (proportion of exports to total shipments) increased by 25% between 1973 and 1986, while its import penetration (proportion of imports to total market) increased by 29%. Significant increases were also registered in the sectors of transportation equipment, non-electrical machinery and primary metals. The USA is Canada's most important trading partner by far, and the strength of the two countries' trading relationship was expected to be reinforced even further from 1 January 1989 with the introduction of the US–Canadian Free-Trade Area.

Manufacturing Activity and the US–Canadian Free-Trade Agreement

In terms of value, the US–Canadian Free-Trade Area (FTA) represents the largest market in the world. In the two years preceding the creation of the FTA there was much debate in Canada about the wisdom of its creation. Although arguments both for and against the FTA received support right across Canada, two broad divisions emerged: representatives of the resource-based industries in the western and Prairie provinces were for the FTA, while representatives of the intermediate manufacturing industries in central and eastern Canada were opposed. The manufacturing lobby was particularly concerned about the size and importance of competition from the USA where plants, already benefiting from larger economies of scale and higher levels of productivity, could undercut their Canadian competitors. For those Canadian firms that can adjust to the new economic environment the potential advantages are very attractive. They will now have secure access to a market exceeding 270m. consumers as opposed to some 26m. The adjustments required to benefit from this opportunity will include increased specialization, longer production runs, the introduction of new technologies, investment in new and expanded facilities and the retraining of workers. In addition, Canadian firms will be able to take advantage of lower-priced materials and machinery purchased from the USA. The world's largest market will also bring further benefits to Canada in the form of increased investment in manufacturing activity, especially by Japanese and Western European companies.

The FTA is to be phased in over a 10-year period, during which time all tariff and non-tariff barriers are to be eliminated. Since for both countries these barriers are higher in manufacturing than in other sectors, manufacturing should have the greatest potential to realize benefits from trade liberalization through cost reductions and improved efficiency. Immediately prior to the introduction of the FTA the average Canadian import tariff on manufactured goods was 5.2%, while that on US imports was 3.2%. These figures, however, conceal wide variations between industries. The highest Canadian tariff was on knitting mills (22.7%). Other traditional resource-based industries also had high tariffs; these included clothing (19.7%), tobacco (16.5%), leather (15.7%), furniture and fixtures (12.5%) and textiles (11.4%). These industries also tended to have the highest import duties in the USA—20.7% in the case of tobacco, 12.3% for knitting mills and 10.9% for clothing. Most of the other industries had much lower, and similar, tariffs in both countries, though in some industries there were significant differences, such as shipbuilding (Canada 10.1%, USA 0.3%) and furniture and fixtures (Canada 12.5%, USA 2.0%).

Free trade with the USA is going to be only one of the influences to which Canadian industries will need to respond in the 1990s. Other important factors include the globalization of markets and the corresponding growth in interdependence which will be stimulated by the spreading influence of multinational corporations and the increased efficiency of enabling technologies. Canadian manufacturing activity is facing many challenges, but the quality of its labour force, infrastructure and resources provide it with a sound base as long as it can adopt and utilize quickly the emerging new technologies and management systems.

SERVICE INDUSTRIES, EXTERNAL TRADE AND GOVERNMENT FINANCES IN CANADA

ALAN HALLSWORTH

Service Industries

INTRODUCTION

Since the end of the Second World War, growth in the service sector has been the prime generator of overall employment growth in Canada, accounting for over 70% of all industrial employment by the late 1980s. In certain phases, notably around the time of the 1981 oil-price collapse, services have been the only growth sector in the Canadian economy. Examination of the figures shows that employment growth has been at its most prominent in the youth and female markets, especially in the part-time sector: at the time of the 1981 census, three-quarters of the 1.5m. part-time workers were to be found in the wholesale and retail trades, community, business and personal services. Women took almost 1m. of the 1.4m. new jobs created in the service sector between 1975 and 1983, and by 1985 one-quarter of employed women worked part-time, as opposed to less than 8% of men.

Consideration of service-sector employment is usually clouded by the divisions of constitutional power between federal and provincial tiers of government. This factor should not be underestimated since, as in most developed economies, employment in, and the direct provision of services by, levels of government is a key element of the economy. Likewise, federal and provincial governments share regulatory functions that affect the operations of private-sector service providers.

TRANSPORT, COMMUNICATIONS AND UTILITIES

Canada has been described as 'a triumph of transportation over geography'. The federal government department Transport Canada, with an annual budget of about C $3,000m., has responsibility for regulation and administration of federal policy and programmes in an area of vital significance to a huge country with strong trading links. As the Department of Transport, it was created initially in 1936 from the Department of Railways and Canals, the Marine Department and the section of National Defence dealing with civil aviation. Crown corporations reporting to parliament through Transport Canada include Air Canada, Canadian National Railways, VIA Rail Canada Inc and the St Lawrence Seaway Authority.

Shipping

For purposes of regulating water-borne traffic, the Marine Group handles the Canadian Coast Guard, the Harbours and Ports directorate, Canada Ports Corporation (in charge of 15 major ports), the St Lawrence Seaway Authority and four pilotage authorities. In 1988 the sector as a whole comprised 25 deep-water ports and 650 smaller ports. The period 1979–83 saw an overall increase of 33% in revenues for water-transport carriers, despite a decline in 1982. The strongest areas of post-1979 growth were commodities, the major staple of water transport, and passengers. In 1984, however, revenues were well below their 1980 peak for both domestic and international freight.

Ocean transport is dominated in the west by Vancouver, Canada's busiest port, and in the east by ports in Québec, although Thunder Bay (Ontario), which tranships coal and wheat, is technically second in terms of tonnage handled. In 1986 Vancouver's 29 terminals handled nearly 58m. metric tons of shipping, with bulk commodities, especially coal, dominating. In that year, container traffic increased by 25%, while 313,000 cruise passengers passed through the port. The dominant feature of Vancouver's trade is that it is heavily export-oriented; in 1985 the volume of goods exported totalled 51.1m. tons and the volume imported 5.1m. tons. Montréal, the other major city with a vital port function, is an alternative, eastern, outlet for traffic not focused on the Pacific rim and burgeoning links with Japan. Montréal's trade is of a quite different nature from that of commodity-dominated Vancouver, with Montréal handling over 300,000 containers annually. Its position within the Great Lakes and St Lawrence Seaway system means that Montréal has substantially more competition from nearby rival ports than has Vancouver. Recession and some by-passing of the port have lessened the significance of Montréal, but there are still some 20 km of port facilities. The Great Lakes system itself cannot be ignored, since the lakes are used to move substantial quantities of cargo, particularly coal, iron ore and grain. Likewise, river-to-coast transport is significant, especially in the context of logging in British Columbia, where towing revenues rose sharply between 1979 and 1983.

Railways

Railways have traditionally found it difficult to attract financing, because of the distances involved and generally low volumes of traffic, with millions of dollars lost annually on passenger operations. This has represented a continuing tax burden for the country. Management of passenger services (excluding commuter services) was consolidated with the creation of the crown corporation VIA Rail Canada Inc in 1978. At a more local level, some cities have invested in rail-based light rapid-transit systems as well as in commuter underground services. Problems with passenger transport have been paralleled in the rail-freight sector, where enormous losses were associated with the statutory Crows Nest Pass agreement which was only abolished in 1983.

Canadian National (CN) and Canadian Pacific (CP) are the two major rail companies, both having their headquarters in Montréal. The former is a federal crown corporation which, while it recorded a C $120m. profit in 1987, has long-term debts estimated at well over C $2,000m. The third-largest rail company is the Vancouver-based BC Rail, which obtains most of its revenue from the transportation of forest products. Products are frequently moved by trains with 100 wagons or more, running average freight-haul distances in excess of 600 miles (1,000 km): this has led to the implementation of economies of scale and improved competitiveness. This competitiveness has also been increased by better traffic management, which can handle the problems of two-way traffic on single-track lines with limited passing points. Traditionally, too, the railways have been major landowners—CP had extensive holdings in Vancouver, for example—so real-estate-related issues have become more prominent. Many cities are relocating their rail terminus to the periphery. This can leave a developable route into the city centre and free substantial inner-city land. Responsibility for this sector lies with Transport Canada's Surface Group, which also covers ferries and highway transportation. Ferry operations are significant in British Columbia, where they link the mainland city of Vancouver with outlying island areas including Vancouver Island, which houses the provincial capital of Victoria.

Air Transport

Airline communications in Canada have gathered importance in recent years, growth having been facilitated by publicly-financed airport construction and by large increases in business traffic, which still accounts for some 80% of passenger-air travel. Airlines, a crucial communications element in such a large country, have also faced some upheavals in the 1980s. One of the more significant developments was the merger, in 1988, of Pacific Western Airlines and Canadian Pacific Airlines to form a new company, Canadian Airlines International. This created a major national competitor for the crown corporation Air Canada. While all carriers have been affected by inflation, recession and deregulation (the latter firstly in the USA and then in Canada itself), Air Canada has also been the subject of privatization, with 45% of shares being sold to the public in late 1988 and full privatization being scheduled for 1989. Plans for the deregulation of air transport, announced in 1984, had already caused major carriers to consolidate their feeder airlines. Accordingly, by the time deregulation took effect on 1 January 1988, Air Canada was carrying about 50% of the annual total of 25m. passengers and Canadian Airlines about 40%. The latter's position was further consolidated by its acquisition of Wardair in 1988–89.

Specialized air services (frequently providing helicopter services), were thought to number about 600 in 1988. Many are linked to the oil industry and to mineral exploration in general. A further significant development in the context of air transport has been the growth of Short-Take-Off-and-Landing (STOL) aircraft, in part pioneered by De Havilland through their DASH aircraft, which was developed while the company was a crown corporation.

Nineteen of Canada's airports account for more than 80% of all scheduled traffic and all international flights, of which two-thirds are to US destinations. Lester B. Pearson (formerly Toronto International) was the busiest airport in terms of international passenger traffic in 1985, handling 15.8m. passengers, followed by Vancouver (7m.) and Calgary (3.9m.). Montréal–Dorval had the most domestic traffic in that year, with 5.5m. passengers. In 1981 Lester B. Pearson accounted for about 31% of freight traffic, with Montréal's two airports (Dorval and Mirabel) together handling about 25%. The total number of scheduled passengers carried more than doubled between 1970 and 1980, but declined in the recession years of 1981–83. Indeed, 1982 saw the major airline carriers recording operating losses, while minor carriers faced reduced revenues. Recovery to 1980 levels of passenger volume was very slow for some routes. In 1987 passenger traffic increased by just 2.4% compared with 1986.

Pipelines and Roads

With substantial resources being situated in remote and inhospitable regions, it is inevitable that pipeline transport should figure prominently in Canada. Certain pipeline projects across areas that are inhospitable and ecologically fragile, as well as of significance to native peoples, have generated intense public debate. Pipelines carry primarily oil products, but also chemicals and water.

The Trans-Canada Highway system was formally completed on 30 July 1962: additional improvements took a further eight years and brought the total cost to some C $1,000m. This, including ferry links, created a 4,860-mile (7,821-km) national route with its extremities at Victoria, BC and St John's, Newfoundland. The inauguration of the highway system symbolized a major shift away from rail transport of commodities: in the 1930s railways took some 85% of Canada's freight revenue, but by 1985 trucking was taking a 50% revenue share. Fast growth has been experienced during recent years in fast courier or messenger services which offer same-day or next-day delivery.

In 1985 14.8m. vehicles were registered, of which 11.1m. (75%) were passenger vehicles. In terms of volume, passenger bus carriers are dominated by school-bus services, though urban-transit operations take a far greater share of operating revenues. Within urban areas, public transport is still well supported in Canadian cities through bus routes, subway lines and commuter trains. All three are well represented in Toronto, and both Toronto and Montréal have integrated the subway to subterranean shopping galleries. There remains a strong tradition of public funding for mass transit, and Canadians are far more likely than their US counterparts to travel to work by public transport. Heavy winter snowfall imposes extra burdens on municipal authorities, which have the task of keeping highways clear. Ontario alone spent C $1,244m. on highway, road, street and bridge construction (including repairs) in 1984; of this total, C $441m. (35%) was allocated to municipal government spending on roads. Motorized sleds or 'snowmobiles' are in frequent off-road use in winter months.

Telecommunications

The trans-Canada telephone system incorporates both publicly- and privately-owned carriers. Telecom Canada, a consortium comprising nine major telephone companies, together with the satellite owner and operator Telesat Canada, provides the public long-distance telephone service, while CNCP Telecommunications provides the national telex network and Teleglobe Canada, a former crown corporation, is the international carrier. Overall there are about 120 telephone companies, serving some 16.5m. telephones in 1984. The size of the country has encouraged the rapid development of satellite technology, and Canada was the third country, after the USA and the USSR, to put a satellite into orbit. Telesat Canada has several orbiting satellites and a range of TV companies using satellite-relay signals. Canada is also involved in SARSAT, the international collaborative project on satellite search and rescue. Remote northern locations can be integrated via satellite-linked terminals which permit links with urban telecommunications networks. Fibre-optics development has been especially associated with a Saskatchewan Telecommunications project to create the longest fibre-optics system in the world. Several Canadian companies are involved in research on Integrated System Digital Networks (ISDN). This could be a revolutionary factor in a total telecommunications hardware/software market worth possibly C $16,000m. in 1988 and likely to be worth about C $25,000m. by 1992. Videotext is an area of especial concern to Canada, which sees its Telidon system as the North American standard for information systems.

Utilities

Public utilities are generally considered to cover the production and distribution of electricity, gas, water and often telecommunications—especially telephones. In the context of Canada, the electricity industry is dominated by provincial crown corporations, while gas supply is controlled privately. It is argued frequently that the high ratio of assets to revenue determine that electricity is best provided publicly; however, it must also be noted that private electricity utilities do exist; indeed, in Alberta they dominate. However owned, electricity utilities are provincially regulated, except in the case of nuclear-power generation, which is a federal responsibility. The utilities account for perhaps 90% of total energy production, with industries generating the rest for their own use.

RETAILING AND WHOLESALING

Retailing

The retail trade, regulated by the Department of Consumer and Corporate Affairs, is the cornerstone of the Canadian service economy, and employs over 1m. persons. Figures for 1985 suggest retail sales of C $129,446m., with Ontario accounting for the largest share (38%) of the market, followed by Québec (25%), British Columbia (11%) and Alberta (10%). There is substantial market concentration, with 'retail chains' or 'multiple' traders dominating in the department-store, grocery, variety and general merchandising sectors. For example, the Hudson's Bay Co and T. Eaton Co together hold about 75% of the total department-store market. The popularity of the department store has diminished somewhat since the peak years of the 1920s and 1930s, with the sector accounting for just 9.3% of the total value of retail sales in 1985, compared with 10.5% in 1982. The future performance of the sector will in part depend upon its role in the development of 'climate-controlled' shopping centres. Developers of these centres still regard department stores as essential as the focus for any proposed scheme. However, the current trend is to seek to incorporate many more of the smaller specialists in what has become a highly-segmented market. Individual retail companies now commonly use several different store names, with products targeted to specific market sub-sectors. As commercial pressures force frequent redevelopments or refurbishments, there is a tendency for larger stores to be reduced in size to free more space for smaller store units.

There are over 1,000 shopping centres with a total floor space of more than 50,000 sq ft (4,645 sq m), but by far the most significant are the regional shopping centres, which normally have at least two, and sometimes even three, department stores as 'anchor' tenants. The regional centres have commonly dominated suburban shopping facilities as metropolitan growth has accelerated into previously undeveloped areas that had little existing infrastructure. This has led to the development of massive freestanding shopping centres or malls, such as the West Edmonton Mall, which was expanded during the early 1980s to a total area of more than 5m. sq ft (464,500 sq m), making it the world's largest shopping centre by 1985. Mall developments have been seen as especially detrimental to small traders in city and town centres, and schemes aimed at providing assistance to the latter have been initiated at both the federal and the provincial level. In addition, restrictions on new mall developments have resulted in a major return to city-centre redevelopments, the best-known example being the Toronto Eaton Centre, built at a cost of C $265m. and with a gross leasable area of 2.6m. sq ft. Such redevelopments are facilitated by the pattern of land-ownership in major cities, where a few important landowners may dominate. Further benefits are reaped from existence of generally efficient and comprehensive subsidized public-transport systems in major city centres. For example, the Toronto and Montréal developments have underground ped-estrian linkages that are integrated with their respective rail subway systems. Finally, city-centre redevelopments have exploited the leisure/heritage/'festival marketing' trend also found in such US cities as Boston and Baltimore. Unique historical locations such as Montréal's Old Port, Ottawa's Byward Market and Vancouver's Gastown have thereby been exploited for retail opportunities. It has also been suggested that more marginal inner-city retail locations may respond by evolving into 'specialty' retail markets.

It is evident that trends in the Canadian retail market cannot be divorced from their spatial context. Aggregate statistics are not a substitute for analysis of the trading ambience of specific retail developments, and here the malls remain supreme. They are essentially the product of post-war afflu-ence, with many prime retail sites having been developed during the 1960s. Canadian developers may have benefited from funding possibilities offered by the well-developed national banking system and from the existence of planning controls preventing too much debilitating competition. It is also common for cities to offer substantial tax concessions to encourage developers in their locality. Retail developments are also often incidental beneficiaries from redevelopment schemes that may involve municipal, provincial and federal public monies.

The structure of the food-store sector, which accounted for 25% of retail sales in 1985, is being affected in the late 1980s by the development of 'superstores' or 'megamarkets' approaching the size levels found in the UK or France. This move to large freestanding food outlets is a recent one and is generating much competition between the major grocery chains, all of which are now either developing superstores or reacting to their presence. Market concentration is also evident in this sector, with a handful of chains controlling more than one-half of the market, and there has been an increasing trend towards franchising, particularly in those outlets originating in the USA. Franchising is also growing in the convenience-store sector, albeit at a slower rate than for fast food, and has long been established in the sector of automobile dealerships.

Selling that is not store-based is well established in Canada, where T. Eaton Co introduced the first mail-order sales system. The total value of mail-order sales was C $624m. in 1985, comprising 25% of the total value of direct sales and 0.5% of all retail sales.

Wholesaling

Provisional figures put the total volume of wholesale trade at C $213,748m. in 1984, of which 84% (C $180,162m.) was reported by wholesale merchants and 16% (C $33,586m.) by agents and brokers. In general terms, the manufacturers and the retailers have both tended to reduce the trade of the wholesale 'middleman', since manufacturers will undertake direct selling to the public or large retailer, while the retailers may have their own distribution networks. This should not detract from the significance of the wholesale trade, which will serve export trades as well as retailers. The spatial and employment implications of wholesaling, which is generally dominated by the major urban areas, are neither as complex nor as significant for society at large as those of retailing.

MEDIA

The Press

There has been a marked trend towards concentration of newspaper ownership since the peak year of 1913, when 138 newspaper titles were in circulation. The increasing importance first of radio and then of television, and the ensuing competition for advertising space, precipitated mergers and take-overs. (The advertising factor is crucial, since advertising space is a far greater income-generator than revenue from newspaper sales.) Today, while there are still numerous titles (111 in 1988), two media groups, Thomson Newspapers Ltd and Southam Newspaper Group, together account for about 60% of the total circulation of English-language newspapers. This tends to mean that only the largest cities have at least two newspapers from different publishers. The Toronto-based *Globe and Mail*, which publishes regional editions and obtains its second-greatest circulation in Alberta, comes closest of all to the concept of a 'national daily'. Within Toronto, however, it is outsold by the *Toronto Star*, which itself has a close circulation battle with the *Toronto Sun* in respect of Sunday editions. Southam also publishes an extensive range of business periodicals, while Thomson has a number of weekly newspapers and has highly diversified Canadian business interests. Essentially this leaves a very concentrated, monopolistic newspaper market that has parallels in the magazine trade where Maclean–Hunter has a dominant position. Concentration of ownership has attracted government attention, and both a 1980–81 Royal Commission and an earlier Senate special commission dwelt on the topic.

Other recent trends in the newspaper sector include an increase in the number of 'small-city' dailies and the increasing use of new technology, such as in the transmission of copy by satellite for Thomson's regional editions of the *Globe and Mail*. There has also been an increase in the number of free, community-based newspapers: these, too, tend to be published by the major conglomerates. Equally, there are a few minority-language newspapers, serving local Chinese, Italian or other communities. Circulation estimates imply a total weekly circu-lation of over 30m. for daily newspapers, with Toronto, Mont-réal and Vancouver accounting for over 40% of the total. Concentration, in information terms, is compounded by the fact that the newspaper owners also control the leading news agency, the Canadian Press. In noting that newspapers tend to be part of conglomerates, it must be recognized that an established title is a steady and profitable enterprise from which to base expansion. This situation is by no means unique to Canada but explains why most chains have, at the very least, expanded into videotext, screenprint technology and on-line services. As testimony to the enduring power of news-papers, it is estimated that they remain the most important recipients of advertising revenue, still well ahead of television.

Radio and Television

Broadcasting is somewhat less concentrated, in terms of owner-ship, than the newspaper sector. The publicly-owned Canadian Broadcasting Corporation (CBC) provides a national radio and television broadcasting service in English and French, and there are several broadcasting organizations which receive funding from provincial governments. The principal private networks include CTV, Global and TVA (a French-language network).

Since its introduction into Canada in the early 1950s, tele-vision broadcasting has been increasingly influenced by devel-opments in cable-transmission technology. Cable TV, which offers improved reception—particularly in areas where tall buildings create interference—and the ability to pick up distant signals, was received by some 68% of Canadian homes in 1988. There are local monopolies on provision, but the three largest companies together accounted for about one-half of all oper-ations in 1982. Initially, cable broadcasting services were restricted because of fears that they might undermine both national broadcasting aims and objectives and the financial stability of 'over-the-air' broadcasters. Following a number of federal–provincial jurisdictional disputes during the 1970s, the Canadian Radio–Television and Telecommunications Com-mission (CRTC) liberalized its stance in the 1980s and cable services were expanded. As in the USA, services have been targeted at sub-sectors of the community rather than at specific geographical areas. Both satellite technology and fibre-optics have helped to enhance the capacity for wide spatial coverage to selected audiences. With many Canadians living close to the border with the USA (the Great Lakes–St Lawrence Lowlands area, for example, has more than one-half of the total Canadian population), cable TV has also brought good-quality reception of the main US channels to a majority of Canadian homes.

TOURISM AND RECREATION

Tourism is a major contributor to the Canadian economy and involves, directly or indirectly, many different government departments and agencies. However, government activity is primarily co-ordinated and promoted by Tourism Canada, a branch of the federal Department of Regional Industrial Expansion.

Visitors from the USA constitute by far the largest group of foreign tourists. In 1983, for example, the USA provided over 32.5m. tourist visitors, compared with 1.8m. visitors from all other sources. The next major source region was the UK, with 400,926 visitors. In 1986 there were over 38m. visitors from the USA and 2.4m. from other countries. In 1983 direct travel expenditure totalled C $18,500m., or 5% of Canada's gross national product. Of this, almost 80% was spent by Canadians in their own country and the balance came from foreign visitors. Multiplier effects of tourist revenue imply that total income generated from this source in 1983 could be more accurately placed at over C $33,000m. For the smaller provinces tourism is a vital source of income and in the late 1980s it represented the greatest single source of employment for Prince Edward Island. Neither are the larger provinces ignoring tourism for, in 1988, Ontario and Québec signed a joint three-year tourism agreement to attract visitors from Japan and the UK. Through a joint federal, provincial and private-sector initiative, the bulk of the financing is public and worth C $3.1m. This is targeted at specific tourist programmes, however, and the provinces will continue to carry out separate promotional schemes. In 1987 Ontario spent C $350,000 on advertising in Japan and C $358,000 on advertising in the UK.

Tourism is one sector seeking to benefit from a revised UK–Canada air-transport agreement which was to bring effective fare reductions from 1988. While the major cities are key tourist destinations in this highly-urbanized society, it is worthy of note that the National Parks system dates from 1885 and national parks cover an area of 69,500 sq miles (180,000 sq km). The largest, at 17,300 sq miles (44,807 sq km), is Wood Buffalo, which straddles the border between northern Alberta and the Northwest Territories and is a UNESCO World Heritage site. More popular with tourists, however, is Banff, the first National Park to be created, which covers 2,564 sq miles (6,641 sq km), west of Calgary on the eastern slope of the Rocky Mountains and which regularly attracts over 4m. visitors a year. Alberta's Jasper National Park, north of Banff, had 2.2m. visitors in 1987.

There is a source of contradiction in the way that Canada has sought to project itself in the international tourist market. On the one hand, there have been campaigns extolling the virtues of the wild and unspoilt scenery, especially that of the Rocky Mountains. Unfortunately, such attractions are hard to transform into direct tourist revenues, other than from transport. With the notable exception of such famous locations as the Banff Springs Hotel, built in 1888, the hotel-based revenues are major-city dominated. The approach has been to focus 'outdoors' vacations on activity-based ventures such as pony-trekking or white-water rafting. The alternative has been to emphasise the attractiveness, lack of violence and general ambience of Canadian city life. Occasionally, the two are married, as with Calgary-based tours to Banff or Edmonton (and even West Edmonton Mall) linked with Jasper.

Allied to tourism comes an awareness of the growing international conference market, and many cities have upgraded their conference facilities and their international profile. Throughout the 1980s in Canada as a whole there was extensive spending on conference and convention facilities, with eight centres being developed or expanded in an ongoing programme valued at C $1,000m., over one-half of which is federally-funded. Canada now regards itself as a possible destination for the growing incentive travel market, with interest reawakened by the 1988 Winter Olympics, held in Calgary.

In the late 1980s it was estimated that the Canadian hotel industry was worth about C $5,000m. a year. Structurally the industry is more fragmented than its US counterpart, where there is heavy market concentration in a limited number of hotel chains. This fragmented structure had begun to attract the interest of European as well as US groups, interested in establishing a foothold in the market. To a considerable extent, the fate of tourist income generated from abroad depends on the behaviour of US tourists. If they venture further afield, then Canada's tourist industry declines as a result. Terrorist activity across the globe generally tends to benefit the Canadian and US tourist trade.

By the late 1980s, estimates suggested that the economic impact of tourist cruises could be boosting the Vancouver regional economy by as much as C $85m. The 1985 hijacking of the Achille Lauro cruise ship in the Mediterranean, plus the impact of the Expo '86, gave a major boost to cruise-ship vacations centred on Vancouver. The number of passengers handled annually was soon around 300,000; more than double the levels of a decade earlier. Vancouver has the particular advantage of functioning as a foreign port for predominantly US-focused cruises, enabling foreign-registered vessels to comply with the US Passenger Shipping Act, which was in effect in the late 1980s and which restricts foreign vessels from carrying passengers between US ports. Much of the Alaskan cruise industry is based in Vancouver and thus is regarded as 'international'.

Other 'life style' initiatives include a reawakening of interest in the Trans-Canada rail network. The major constraint on expansion of this tourist-related form of transport may be the availability of rolling stock.

Canadians, with a 35–40-hour working week, annual holidays and high disposable incomes, naturally create a substantial leisure market. While the Calgary Stampede and Québec winter '*carnaval*' would contribute to specific tourist trades, leisure and recreation in general is more difficult to define. Outdoor sports are strongly emphasized, with skating and ice hockey strongly associated with Canada, though cross-country skiing more than doubled its participation rate during the 1980s. The federal government specifically promotes fitness and amateur sport and all levels of government contribute to the provision of sporting facilities.

BANKING AND FINANCE

The Canadian financial sector has traditionally been seen as a 'four-pillar' structure, comprising chartered banks, trust companies, insurance companies, and securities dealers. This structure has broadly resulted from the implementation of regulatory procedures separating out the four functions, but has increasingly seemed outdated as the boundaries between the sectors have become less distinct. This trend has been accentuated above all by the growth of powerful conglomerates that combined the operations of trust, insurance and mutual fund (unit trust) companies to give a scope far wider than that of the banks. At the same time, the system has been influenced by the recession of 1981–82 in that companies seeking loans from the financial sector during that period faced vastly increased interest charges on loans, to the further detriment of their already reduced general trading performance. One response was a trend towards funding future growth through the equity market, with particular emphasis on non-voting share issues. In addition, problems arose where banks had been involved in heavy lending to resource groups acquiring rival concerns on the assumption that oil prices would remain high. In 1981 energy stocks accounted for about 25% of the market capitalization of the Toronto Stock Exchange, but by 1987 their share had fallen to under 10%.

Resultant moves away from straightforward loans from banks increased pressure for financial-sector change, while the banks themselves responded by increasing the gap between borrowing and lending rates in order to maintain profits. Pressures had, however, been building since before the recession. High inflation in the 1970s worked in favour of banks, which could offer short-term loans, and against the trust companies, tied into longer-term lending. The trust companies were also facing a reduced demand for mortgages, which forced them to seek closer competition with the banks through personal loans and, to an extent, commercial loans. The trust companies now constitute the banks' greatest trading competitors, as they have moved quickly into deposit and cheque accounts and credit cards. Insurance companies felt similar pressures through a trading decline in their traditional sector of activity and looked to the possibility of purchasing trust companies as a possible solution to their trading position. With outstanding mortgages valued at around C $150,000m. in 1981, this sector has inevitably proved attractive to the lending institutions.

These factors, combined with a traditionally restrictive attitude to foreign competition in general, naturally led to pressures for liberalization by Brian Mulroney's Progressive Conservative government. Examples of restrictions included limitations on individual holdings in chartered banks and restricted scale of operations by foreign banks. These restrictions, from the 1967 Bank Act, were eased in 1980 to allow foreign banks to own subsidiaries (known as Schedule B banks) which numbered 59 in late 1988. It had been noted that one effect of prevailing restrictions was virtually a closed securities-dealing market. This, functioning for a small domestic population, resulted in relatively high commissions. This may also have led to the securities market becoming highly concentrated, a characteristic shared with chartered banks. The bulk of the leading financial concerns are, *de facto*, headquartered in Toronto, which is also the major cheque-clearing centre for the country.

Accordingly, much deregulatory attention focused on securities trading, where again the federal–provincial dichotomy is evident. Securities trading as a provincial concern has, inevitably, concerned Ontario where, as of 1970, trading firms (then numbering about 100) had to be registered with the Ontario Securities Commission. Registration was not open to those who were not residents of Ontario. This restriction on the key securities-trading forum for the country, which was the world's fourth-biggest equity market, was a target for revision of regulatory procedures. The Toronto Stock Exchange was the main focus of attention in a system where, in 1984, the five stock exchanges of Toronto, Montréal, Vancouver, Calgary and Winnipeg had a combined trading value of C $20,200m.

The failure of small banks has become a further pressure for change in the financial system. Between 1985 and 1987 almost one-half of the country's domestically-owned small banks disappeared following a run on deposits. As a result of these pressures for change, the Canadian banking system became subject to a series of disruptive influences, only one of which was the 'Little Bang' regulatory reform of 30 June 1987. The 'Little Bang' was perceived as a measured response to the financial deregulation following London's 'Big Bang' of 1986. Japanese, US and European interests quickly applied for the registration of subsidiaries with the Ontario Securities Commission, though the maximum foreign shareholding in full-service securities dealers was limited to 50% until mid-1988. Initial foreign moves into the Canadian market, which needed approval of the finance minister, appeared to favour companies from countries where Canada had equal trading rights, such as the UK. The effects of deregulation seem, therefore, to have opened the door to foreign interest.

A further influence on the performance of banks has been third-world debts. Foreign assets increased from C $21,700m. in 1973 to C $156,700m. in 1983, by which time many loans were being rescheduled and interest arrears had accumulated. In 1984 four of the top six banks had their credit rating reduced by one half-point by the Canadian Bond Rating service as a result of third-world loans outstanding. This signalled the end of an apparently 'golden' period of consistently-escalating bank profits based on increased assets-to-capital ratios, asset growth and international operations. For the fiscal year ended 31 October 1987, the 'Big Six' banks (Royal Bank of Canada, Canadian Imperial Bank of Commerce, Bank of Montréal, Bank of Nova Scotia, Toronto-Dominion Bank and National Bank of Canada) all made allowances against overseas operations. Accordingly, while domestic operations led to post-tax profits of C $2,460m., some C $3,480m. was set aside against foreign

loans, giving a resultant loss of C $81,020m. Finally, a trend towards the creation of merchant banks has recently become evident in the financial sector.

External Trade

The early development of economic activity in Canada became synonymous with trade through the foundation in 1670 of the Hudson's Bay Company. Trade remains a staple concern of Canada, with foreign trade accounting for about 30% of the country's gross national product (GNP), which is a level far higher than in the USA or Japan. Trade may be examined either in terms of type of product or service or by the country with which trade is undertaken. Overriding all trading concerns is the influence of the USA: in 1988, 69% of Canada's trade was with the USA as compared with 72% in 1987 and 73% in 1986. (Because of the substantial direct and indirect investment by the USA, much of the trade is 'managed trade' in that it takes place between separate parts of the same company; typically, a US 'parent' deals with a Canadian subsidiary). Japan is Canada's second most important trading partner, accounting for 7% of total trade in 1988, and the UK third (3% in 1988), having been overtaken by Japan in the early 1970s. The burgeoning Pacific rim trade and the peculiar status of Hong Kong are having particular effects upon trade through Vancouver, as Canada has become regarded as a safe and stable supplier of commodities. In return for staple exports, Canada imports expensive finished products from Japan. Canada also imports large amounts of labour-intensive finished products from the Far East and has a significant import of oil.

In general terms, exports are dominated by merchandise trade which is some four or five times more significant than service trade. The import picture, however, shows services making a substantial balance-of-payments loss. Automobiles and motor-vehicle parts (except engines) are the dominant categories for both imports and exports in finished goods (with exports showing a slight excess for 1986). Yet Canada's trade in automobiles is inseparable from the development of that industry as a branch of the US automobile industry. Figures on trade in automobiles are dominated by parts imported from the USA: exports are of finished vehicles. Other manufactured products show the marked influence of Japan, and here imports far exceed exports opening up to Japan and Europe as wood-frame housing construction grows. This successful sector once drew a US import surcharge, but this has been replaced by an export levy. In the longer term the threats lie with deficiencies in reforestation and fast-growing eucalyptus varieties as developed in Spain. Agricultural and fish products, energy and crude and semi-processed minerals all show a surplus, with slight deficits in chemicals and fertilizers. Overall a slight trade surplus in merchandise trade or 'visibles' is usually recorded. Also, since the introduction of the 'Investment Canada' programme in 1984, the increased foreign investment has led to an increase in imports as US subsidiaries, for example, have been more inclined than indigenous Canadian firms to use US rather than Canadian suppliers.

Services show a different picture, with nearly 60% of the overall deficit shown in 1983 coming from interest and dividends. Business service and allied transactions made up another 16% or so and travel and tourism more than 12%. This is inexorably bound up with the propensity for foreigners to invest more in Canada than Canadians do abroad. Canada has been ambivalent towards this investment, as shown by the findings of two federal task forces of 1967 (the Watkins report) and 1980 (the Gray report). The former led to the establishment of the Federal Investment Review Agency (FIRA) while the latter concluded that investment was, on balance, favourable but could lead to a truncated economy. In 1978, before the liberalizing Mulroney government took over, foreign direct investment in Canada had reached over C $48,000m., of which about 80% came from the USA. Portfolio investment that year totalled nearly C $58,000m., with the USA rather less dominant. With Investment Canada in place, corporate investment in Canada continues to grow, with UK investors being the second most important group behind those from the USA. In the two years following its creation, Investment Canada reviewed 1,992 foreign-investment applications and approved all of them. Its predecessor, FIRA, allowed 90% of applications, but often not without delay.

Canada's position on tariffs is again bound up with bilateral negotiations with the USA, but the general picture is one of a continual decline in the level of tariffs imposed. Quotas are generally negotiated under the auspices of GATT (the General Agreement on Tariffs and Trade), and these influence textiles, clothing, footwear and some food products.

Government Finances

Expressed as a percentage of GNP, the size of the government sector in Canada has grown substantially in the last 50 years, as has been the case in other OECD countries. Canada is broadly in line with the OECD average in respect of the size of its government sector, which in 1985 was put under pressure from the Mulroney administration intent on trimming the federal budget deficit. Typically, governmental employment, excluding employment in hospitals and education, has averaged about 11% of the total labour force. With the latter two categories added on, the percentage of the (growing) labour force in government employment was about 17.9% in both 1960 and 1980, peaking at 20.5% in 1970.

Canada appears to occupy a 'half-way house' between the traditional European model of substantial government funding of catch-all welfare systems and the more laissez-faire philosophies of the USA and Japan. One area of probable future concern for Canada will be the increasing burden of pension payments as the population ages. In 1988 pension payments were running at a level below those even of the USA and Japan. OECD predictions are, however, for a substantial increase in the dependent population in Canada by 2050. In the late 1980s Canada and Japan had the lowest percentages of population aged 65 or over of the 'Group of Seven'. By 2050, however, projections see Canada overtaking the UK, USA and Italy in terms of the percentage of the total population in this age-sector.

During 1986 both federal government recruitment and discretionary spending were frozen, and federal employment was scheduled for a gradual reduction from 1986 onwards. Changes were also played out against a background of restructuring the national energy policy. Budgetary issues in Canada are impossible to divorce from the changing world economy and evolving federal–provincial relations. At root, the federal government does not have total control of all the key financial sectors simply because the provinces have established powers in so many areas. Fiscal matters form a perpetual source of debate at first-ministers' conferences and policy differences are evident even when the same party is in control in an individual province and in Ottawa. Budgetary matters are, therefore, always seen in the context of intergovernmental finance. A federal government with an ideological commitment to reduction of direct personal taxation would, for example, have restricted scope to prevent provinces from levying increased levels of such taxes. Provinces may even compete between themselves for new employment opportunities, making Canada appear less like an economic union. Liberal governments under Pierre Trudeau had made attempts to reinforce central authority but, by the late 1980s, constitutional debates, culminating in the Meech Lake Accord of 1987, seemed to have transferred power back to the provinces.

BUDGETARY ISSUES

Late-1980s' Canadian budgetary policy has its roots in the recession of the early 1980s and the attendant decline in real production and falls in the value of oil-based resources. This period left the country saddled with a large federal deficit and devalued resources that had been acquired at some expense. The deficit is to a large extent the product of high interest rates, typically in the period 1976–82, when interest payments quadrupled as the bank rate at one point reached 21%. Interest payments alone became responsible for 30% of the increased budget deficit between 1981 and 1985. The 1981 oil-price collapse and recesssion came at a time when Canada had been investing heavily in its own massive, but physically marginal,

oil resources. By 1985, after the first year of the Mulroney government, borrowing was stabilizing at a level well above the OECD average (although below that of Italy). Early efforts of the Mulroney government to cut the deficit went some way towards the targets set, although predicted revenue fell back as the energy sector failed to realize expected profits with oil prices below those predicted. Despite pronouncements implying restraint, 1986 saw growth in the economy with inflation remaining relatively high. Typically, falling resource prices negatively affected provinces such as Alberta, where retail growth also fell, and allowed the manufacturing heartland of Ontario to grow. Services in the latter province also benefited. Thus the Bank of Canada continues to perform an uneasy balancing act in a country where, as in 1987, some provinces may be booming and others remain economically weak. Raising interest rates to slow economic growth in Ontario may be damaging to provincial economies that are still weak.

Detailed budgetary adjustments are played out against a broad strategy outlined in the new Progressive Conservative government's 'Agenda' paper of November 1984. Federal budgets of May 1985, February 1986, February 1987 and February 1988 therefore all sought to achieve reductions in the growth of the public debt, in deficits and in financial requirements, and also aimed to ensure expenditure control and good financial management. These four targets were essentially interactive parts of achieving the campaign issues of reducing budget deficits and in this there had been some visible success by 1988. However, the deficit has not fallen as rapidly as predicted in the 1986 federal budget, which estimated deficits of C $25,900m. in 1987 and C $22,000m. in 1990. Revised figures in 1988 gave a 1987 figure of C $29,300m. and implied a 1990 figure nearer C $26,100m. It was suggested that payments to support grain prices, high interest rates and the legacy of support to small banks were responsible for the results. The figures are lower than the C $38,300m. federal budget deficit at September 1984, when the Progressive Conservatives came to power. An initial budgetary move was towards general rises in taxation that, in 1985, halted the recovery of retail sales in durable goods and automobiles. As part of the continuing programme of tax reform, the federal budget of 1986 saw the previous year's corporate surtax reduced from 5% to 3% and corporate taxes themselves restructured. Certain tax credits and inventory allowances were phased out but with some regional tax credits enhanced. There was also a major cut in federal spending on non-statutory programmes. The 1987 budget noted that falling oil and grain prices had triggered support programmes but still predicted a budget deficit of C $29,300m. This was despite the support to farmers costing C $1,500m. more than was allowed for a year earlier. At the same time, a range of indirect taxes was increased. In both the 1987 and 1988 budgets privatization of crown corporations was set to be continued, while moves towards the full privatization of Air Canada and Petrocanada were temporarily delayed in the wake of the 1987 stock-market crash.

Another target, that of cutting costs in government departments, has been forcefully maintained. The government has suggested that between 1985 and 1988 C $539.2m. was saved by 'good housekeeping'. This included the payments of grants in instalments, acceleration of deposits to the Bank of Canada and cash clawbacks from crown corporations. The 1988 budget also made reference to the possibilities of job growth following the free-trade agreement with the USA. The deficit was said to be on target and government-spending growth was set to be restrained to 4.3%, although an expensive seven-year programme to provide daycare places for children was announced. Emphasis was placed on Atlantic, western and northern development agencies and on higher revenues from a growing economy and employment growth. Reference was also made to cuts in income tax from 1 January 1988, and to revisions of sales tax. For 1989–90 there was to be a C $300m. cut in non-statutory federal spending.

The 1982 Constitution Act required the federal government to ensure that individual provinces have the funds to provide roughly comparable services and a roughly comparable tax burden. This implies a continuing need for substantial 'equalization payments' to be a part of any federal budget calculations. Such payments were around C $4,500m. for the financial year

1982–83, or about 30% of all cash transfers to the provinces. The federal government is also obliged to make transfer payments to cover a wide range of provincial activities. Payments for health and education added a further C $5,900m. for 1982–83, while shared-cost programmes cost C $2,600m. An ageing population profile and continuing unemployment serve to exert further pressure on federal budgets already heavily committed to social expenditures. With a further 20% of federal monies automatically earmarked for provincial transfer, there is restricted scope for manoeuvre. Federal payments comprise about 60% of funds in Prince Edward Island, symbolizing the important nature of equalization payments. Alberta commonly draws closer to 10% of revenue centrally, causing it to spend about C $7,500m. in provincial monies on services.

State Expenditure on Education

Jurisdiction for post-secondary education in Canada is vested in the provinces, whereas occupational training is a joint responsiblity of federal and provincial tiers. This factor, with the inevitable peculiarities of practice by individual provinces, makes analysis of this sector difficult. In total, education spending in Canada amounts to about 8% of GNP and is regulated at provincial level. To a large extent, therefore, education provision is at the mercy of local factors since regulation and some funding is a provincial concern, while the bulk of funding is usually raised at the municipal level. In 1980 some 40% of all municipal expenditure was devoted to education, by some distance the leading spending area, well ahead of transport and communications at about 12%. With such a significant area of spending under municipal control, it is vital to note that a high proportion is raised locally, though this does vary from province to province. Commonly, property 'land' taxes (carefully monitored by the provinces) are used, as poll taxes have fallen from favour due to their regressive nature. This complex funding picture can lead to legislation by one tier of government that must be paid for by another tier. When the Liberals came to power in Ontario in the 1980s, for example, there were pledges on education reform. It has been less than certain whether or not such reform will be provincially-funded. For example, in 1972 the Ottawa board of education drew 42% of its revenue from the province. By 1987 the share had fallen to 13%, which placed a greater burden on local property taxes. Indeed, 73% of the Ottawa school board's revenues came from local taxes, and education spending amounted to about one-half of all revenues raised.

Recent demographic trends have led to falling school rolls, evident in the secondary sector since the mid-1970s. By 1987/88 there were less than 5m. full-time elementary- and secondary-school students, a level 15% below the peak year of 1970/71. Such trends carry with them the implications of class-size adjustments and school-closure decisions. Increased participation rates have seen continued increases in the levels of post-secondary enrolments. For many observers the key issue in relation to schooling is the factor of religious denomination. The Maritime provinces have seen an erosion of the denomination factor in school organization, while the matter has become more complex in Ontario. Immigration from countries such as Italy has increased the proportion of Catholics in Ontario to nearly 40%, with an attendant rise in Catholic denominational schools. The rights of pupils to attend denominational schools has undoubtedly been a major factor in educational change in the last two decades.

A high percentage of Canadians succeed in attending university: for 1987/88, some 486,000 students were enrolled full-time at universities. Federal involvement in post-secondary education and in training was about C $8,000m. in 1985/86, while expenditures on education, at 6.2% of GDP, are close to the OECD average of 6.1%. Until 1967 a vital mode of funding was through flat-rate payment of universities on a per-student basis. This system effectively by-passed the provinces and funds were received directly by the institutions. From 1968 to 1977 the university sector was bolstered by transfer payments to the relevant provincial authorities. From 1977 support was based on block payments related to provincial population levels which tended to exaggerate mismatches between block grants and actual educational expenditures. Perhaps as a result of this, provincial spending on students has declined since 1977, with Ontario showing a gradual decline over the period. British Columbia has been suffering more recently from spending restrictions imposed by Social Credit administrations. In British Columbia (and also Newfoundland, Prince Edward Island, New Brunswick and Manitoba) the amount transferred by the provincial government to the universities has sometimes been less than the amount received from federal funds for that purpose. Neither can universities rely upon fee increases to cover shortfalls, since these may be counter-productive in the long term and in any case rarely cover more than 15% of the total operating costs. One student response to the changes is through part-time enrolment, which has increased substantially.

State Expenditure on Health and Welfare

The roots of a Canadian welfare state can be found in the Great Depression of the 1930s which eventually led to the 1941 Unemployment Insurance Act. Public involvement in health care may be traced back yet further, since in 1919 Saskatchewan permitted municipalities to raise taxes for hospital-building. Further developments took place in the 1950s and 1960s, by which time all provinces had hospital plans in place, giving virtually total coverage for the Canadian population. The catalyst for a truly national health-care system was the Hall Report of 1964, which presaged the introduction of the Medicare system. This federal initiative towards a national health-insurance programme was formalized with the addition of doctors' services to existing hospital schemes. It should, however, be noted that most Canadians had, by this time, acquired hospital cover from private schemes.

The overall package is provincially-run, thus allowing differences in implementation. Some provinces fund Medicare through general taxation, others by health-insurance premiums. The standards must, however, conform to federal criteria in order to ensure cost-sharing. Once funded on a dollar-for-dollar basis, federal finance was amended to relate to a moving average of provincial GDP. Health care, like other aspects of welfare, has come under cost-cutting pressures as a result of inflating costs and the burden of public debt. Though pressure on the welfare state had been growing since the mid-1970s, and the MacDonald Commission later also called for reforms, action was taken by the Progressive Conservative administration elected in 1984. There has been a reduction in the GDP-related formula by two percentage points and there has been relaxation of indexed funding.

Cost-cutting measures have also affected welfare systems such as the Canada Pension and Assistance plans which were also products of the 1960s. Inevitably, welfare-related schemes act as a trigger to almost automatic expenditure growth when the percentage of unemployed or dependent individuals rises. Payments are triggered in much the same way as payments to support grain prices and governments constantly seek to control such escalating costs.

SELECT BIBLIOGRAPHY

Alberta Statistical Review. Edmonton, Government of Alberta, quarterly.

Anton, F. R. *The Canadian Coal Industry.* Calgary, Alberta, Detselig Enterprises Ltd, 1981.

Collins, L. 'Canadian Cities: Recent Developments and the Changing Image' in Robinson, G. H. (Ed.). *A Social Geography of Canada.* Edinburgh, North British Publishing, 1988.

Department of Regional Industrial Expansion. *Industry Profiles* (various). Ottawa, DRIE, 1988.

   The Canada–US Free-Trade Agreement and Industry. Ottawa, DRIE, 1988.

Department of Supply and Services. *Report of a Royal Commission on the Economic Union and Development Prospects for Canada* (3 vols). Chairman: Macdonald, Donald S. Ottawa, 1985.

Doern, G. B. and Toner, G. *The Politics of Energy: The Development and Implementation of the NEP.* Toronto, Methuen, 1985.

Drache, D. 'The Strategy of Canadian Trade Liberalisation' in *British Journal of Canadian Studies,* Vol. 2, No 2. London, 1987.

Economic Council of Canada. *Annual Review.* Ottawa, Canadian Government Publishing Centre, annual.

   Western Transition. Ottawa, Canadian Government Publishing Centre, 1984.

Energy, Mines and Resources Canada. *Energy in Canada: A Background Paper.* Ottawa, Canadian Government Publishing Centre, 1987.

Forbes, J. B., Hughes, R. D. and Warley, T. K. *Economic Intervention and Regulation in Canadian Agriculture.* Ottawa, Canadian Government Publishing Centre/Economic Council of Canada, 1982.

Goldberg, M. and Mercer, J. *The Myth of the North American City.* Vancouver, University of British Columbia Press, 1986.

Gower, D. 'The Labour Market in the '80's: Canada and the United States' in *Canadian Economic Observer,* August 1988. Ottawa, Canadian Government Publishing Centre.

Hallsworth, A. G. *Regional Shopping Centres: some lessons from Canada.* London, TEST, 1988.

Hazeldine, T. and Wigington, I. 'Canadian Auto Policy' in *Canadian Public Policy,* Vol. XIII, No 4. Montréal, Canadian Economics Association, 1987.

House, J. D. *The Challenge of Oil: Newfoundland's Quest for Controlled Development.* St John's, Newfoundland, Memorial University of Newfoundland, 1985.

McCann, L. D. (Ed.). *Heartland and Hinterland: A Geography of Canada* (2nd edn). Scarborough, Ontario, Prentice-Hall Canada Inc, 1987.

Melvin, J. R. 'Regional Inequalities in Canada: Underlying Causes and Policy Implications' in *Canadian Public Policy,* Vol. XIII, No 3, 1987.

Mitchell, B. and Sewell, W. R. *Canadian Resources Policies: Problems and Policies.* Toronto, Methuen, 1981.

Myles, J., Picot, G. and Wannell, T. 'The Changing Wage Distribution of Jobs 1981–1986' in *Canadian Economic Observer,* November 1988. Ottawa, Canadian Government Publishing Centre.

OECD Economic Surveys. Canada. Paris, OECD, annual.

Owen, B. E. and Kops, W. J. *The Impact of Policy Change on Decisions in the Mineral Industry.* Kingston, Ontario, and Montréal, McGill-Queen's University Press, 1979.

Owen Saunders, J. (Ed.). *Trading Canada's Natural Resources.* Toronto, Carswell Co Ltd, 1987.

Page, R. *Northern Development: The Canadian Dilemma.* Toronto, McClelland & Stewart, 1986.

Richards, C. F. J. 'Recent Trends in Canada's Direct Investment Position' in *Canadian Economic Observer,* February 1988. Ottawa, Canadian Government Publishing Centre.

Savoie, D. J. *The Canadian Economy: A Regional Perspective.* Toronto, Methuen, 1986.

Shaffer, E. *Canada's Oil and the American Empire.* Edmonton, Alberta, Hurtig Publishers Ltd, 1983.

Statistics Canada. *Canada Handbook* (51st edn). Ottawa, Canadian Government Publishing Centre, 1986.

   Canada Year Book 1988. Ottawa, Canadian Government Publishing Centre, 1987.

Stelter, G. and Artibise, A. *Power and Place.* Vancouver, University of British Columbia Press, 1986.

US Bureau of the Census. *Statistical Abstract of the United States.* Washington, DC, Government Printing Office, annual.

Veltmeyer, H. *Canadian Corporate Power.* Toronto, Garamond Press, 1987.

Watson, J. W. and Watson, J. *The Canadians: How They Live and Work.* Newton Abbot, Devon, David & Charles (Holdings) Ltd, 1978.

CONTEMPORARY SOCIAL ISSUES

HEALTH AND WELFARE POLICY IN CANADA

GEOFFREY MERCER

Overall Trends

Throughout the early decades of the 20th century economic and political pressure built up in Canada for the introduction of state-backed welfare programmes. The first examples of legislative activity were at the provincial level, but developments were slow and uneven, and encountered considerable opposition from key interests in Canadian society. A major catalyst was the experience of social problems and economic hardship during the economic depression of the 1930s. The onset of the Second World War encouraged and legitimated Ottawa's claim to greatly-augmented revenue sources and other wide-ranging powers. However, the barriers presented by Canadian federalism remained to be overcome. Under the terms of the British North America (BNA) Act of 1867, health and social-welfare responsibilites were allocated to the provinces, although in practice they were usually devolved to the municipalities. When the provinces were pressed to assume a higher profile in the inter-war years, they were deterred because the BNA Act had accorded the Dominion Government control of the primary sources of revenue and taxation.

The alternative was to amend the BNA Act so as to permit federal jurisdiction in the social-policy field. With provincial approval, this tactic was first employed in 1940 (and has been repeated subsequently). The immediate products were the Unemployment Insurance Act of 1941 and the Family Allowances Act of 1944. After the end of the war, this phase of state intervention was sustained by public expectations, a changing balance of political forces within the country and the shift back to a peacetime economy. Even so, the grand designs for comprehensive social reform foundered on federal–provincial disputes over funding, and instead there was a more disjointed advance. Indeed, it was not until after a spate of activity in the 1960s that the core legislation of the contemporary welfare state, covering unemployment insurance, income security and pensions, social assistance and health services was put in place.

In the mid-1970s the continued expansion of post-war welfarism was placed in jeopardy by a downturn in the economy characterized, as in other OECD countries, by rising oil prices, inflation and unemployment. Despite the increased political pressure to control public expenditure, spending on social programmes continued to increase, albeit at a slower rate. There was some consolidation but also an expansion of programmes in certain areas. Nevertheless, the policy initiative veered towards those committed to a period of 'retrenchment' in the inter-governmental welfare state. One early casualty of this 'rise and stall' trend was the 1973–75 social-security review. It signalled a transitional period, with provincial and federal governments being engaged in a reassessment of the aims of social policy and the preferred methods for their implementation.

In this climate of increased fiscal restraint, governments pressed for more favourable cost-sharing arrangements. Transfers of federal funds in support of social programmes were usually in the form of conditional grants, with specific provisions governing their use. In some cases the federal contribution was contingent on provincial expenditure but in others it was linked instead to, for example, per-head expenditures, or the rate of increase in gross national product (GNP). Provincial funds were also affected by equalization payments and tax-collection agreements. Inter-governmental disagreements over the proper apportionment of monies have long been a feature in the development of Canadian social policy. In the early 1970s the federal government decided to end the conditional

grants for selected programmes such as Medicare and post-secondary education because the parity cost-sharing arrangements were deemed too costly. For their part, the provinces—Québec especially—had long complained that the attached conditions were an unacceptable interference in their jurisdiction and inhibited innovation. Following protracted negotiations the Established Programmes Financing (EPF) Act was passed in 1977 and, despite provincial objections, was renewed in 1982 without major revision. The EPF Act instituted a system of block conditional grants of near-equal per-head size, composed of cash transfers and tax points. The growth in EPF funding was set at the rate of increase in GNP. It should be noted that, while state expenditure on social security and health has increased rapidly in the post-war years and represents a significant element in both federal and provincial budgets, in 1981 Canada spent only 21.7% of its gross domestic product (GDP) on social programmes, compared with an OECD average of 25.5%.

Economic considerations also loomed large in 1984 when the federal Progressive Conservative government elaborated its priorities for welfare-state policy: fiscal responsibility, which required improved economic growth and equality of employment prospects, as well as the more efficient delivery of social-security programmes; and social responsibility, which meant that the social-assistance safety net would be retained but made more selective. Other goals included: a reorganization of economic and social policy to encourage self-reliance and efficiency; tax reforms and incentives; an extension of labour-market and job-creation schemes; and a greater role for the family, as well as for the private and voluntary sectors. This 'new direction' for federal social policy was founded far less than hitherto in notions of 'distributive justice', and instead suggested a more residual concept of social welfare. At the provincial level, the newly-elected Social Credit government in British Columbia took the lead in restricting the growth of social expenditures and programmes. In the 1980s it embarked on a wider restructuring of the welfare sector, with the reduction and even termination of some programmes and services, along with the imposition of tight fiscal controls. While most provinces have maintained their general commitment to the welfare state, given Ottawa's determination to reduce its financial contribution, provincial restraint measures have become both more evident and significant in their impact.

Health

The process of establishing a national health-insurance programme first took root in provincial initiatives. By 1950 four provincial schemes were in operation, the first having been introduced by Saskatchewan. The federal government started a national system for in-patient services under the Hospital Insurance and Diagnostic Services Act of 1957 and further extended the services it covered in 1966, under the Medical Care Act. The resulting system of Medicare comprised an interlocking series of provincial insurance plans. Federal funding was dependent on a plan administered on a non-profit basis and satisfying the following conditions: comprehensive coverage of insured services; universal population coverage; interprovincial portability of benefits; and reasonable access to services. This provided prepaid health care, with physicians being reimbursed on a fee-for-service basis. The scale of fees is determined by negotiation with the provincial medical association. Provincial health systems offer distinctive features—for example, some are financed from general revenues, while others charge insurance premiums. Plans may include additional benefits such as dental care, prescription-drug costs for senior citizens and chiropractic services.

The Medicare system has proven better than most in holding down health expenditure, but the latter has nevertheless remained a significant item in government budgets. The introduction of EPF arrangements in 1977 and their revision in 1982 (see above) reduced the federal health-funding commitment, although Ottawa continued to expand its assistance for extended (especially non-hospital) health-care services, and to support health-promotion campaigns. In the early 1980s, with expenditure increasing more rapidly than the federal transfer money, the provinces progressively were being confronted with proportionately larger health bills. At the same time, critics argued that Medicare standards were being eroded by the practice of 'extra-billing' (i.e. billing above agreed rates) and the imposition of user charges. The federal answer was contained in the Canada Health Act of 1984, which reaffirmed the commitment to a universal prepaid health-insurance system run according to nationally-agreed criteria. It also introduced penalties for those provinces which allowed extra-billing and user charges. The initial lack of compliance in some provinces ended in the face of these financial sanctions, while industrial action by physicians (in Ontario, for example) also failed to win public support.

Social Security

The relevant programmes encompass both income security and social-welfare services, with a parallel provincial assistance 'safety net'. These have been designed for specific groups, such as the disabled, families and the elderly. In 1965 the introduction of the Canada Pension Plan and the Québec Pension Plan (CPP/QPP) consolidated and extended existing programmes. They provided a universal pension for those aged over 65 years; survivor's and disability pensions; children's and death benefits. The CPP/QPP was the first national social-security measure to provide for automatic cost-of-living benefit increases. Membership was compulsory and not affected if the individual changed jobs or moved to another province. For those senior citizens with little or no income a Guaranteed Income Supplement was introduced in 1967, followed by a similar allowance for surviving spouses aged 60 to 64 years in 1975. Schemes to supplement the incomes of the working poor have been introduced in several provinces. Other recent changes include a tripling of the value of family allowances in 1973, although these were reduced in 1978 when Child Tax Credit was introduced for each child under 18 years in low-income families. Income-security benefits have been a target for cost-cutting exercises, leading to increased contributions with age, as well as reductions in the scale of payments (for example, pensions and child benefits) and changes in eligibility rules.

Since the 1940s the federal government has been the principal provider of income insurance for the low-paid. The original scheme has been extended considerably, with successive revisions extending coverage to 80% of the workforce by 1970. In the following year further changes raised this figure to 95%, and those at all earning levels were made eligible for benefits. The programme was also broadened to include those unable to work due to sickness, maternity and retirement. All governments have placed an increased emphasis on devising schemes (principally job-creation schemes) to manage the recent high levels of unemployment. Measures have included payments to those engaged in job-training or work-sharing.

The scope for action both on an intergovernmental basis and by individual provinces has been most apparent in areas covered by the Canada Assistance Plan (CAP). This replaced existing grants for specific categories among the 'worthy poor' in 1966. Following the EPF changes in 1977 CAP has been the only major scheme in which costs are shared between federal and provincial governments on an equal basis. Conditional grants are made for programmes which encompass both financial assistance (for basic subsistence requirements) as well as selected social services (such as day care, homemaker and home support, rehabilitation and residential care), and approved work-activity projects. There is no residence requirement and eligibility is based solely on need. Each province identifies its own programmes and benefit structures. Examples include schemes to provide supplementary assistance for senior citizens and for low-income families, and tax credits for housing costs. The Vocational Rehabilitation of Disabled Persons instances a cost-shared service programme under CAP for the physically and mentally disabled.

Review

The post-war expansion of the Canadian welfare state has been noteworthy in terms of both the range of programmes introduced and the level of social expenditures achieved. Their impact has been more variable. Specific programmes, such as Medicare, enjoy considerable public support, while on health and general living standards Canada ranks highly in international league tables. Against this, inequalities in the distribution of income and wealth remain pronounced—some 3m. Canadians are thought to be living below the 'poverty line', and there is still a tendency for recipients of social assistance to feel stigmatized. In addition, the 1980s have witnessed the advent of a neoconservative challenge to post-war welfarism.

Uncertainties over social policies have been intensified by speculation about the impact of proposals contained in the Meech Lake Accord of 1987 and in the 1988 Free-Trade Agreement with the USA. If enacted, the Meech Lake Accord will include an amendment to the Constitution Act of 1982 specifying the federal right to engage in shared-cost programmes in areas which fall within provincial jurisidiction. It would also allow provinces to opt out, with 'reasonable compensation', and establish their own programme 'compatible with the national objectives'. As with the Charter of Rights and Freedoms in the Constitution Act, the social-policy implications of these changes are uncertain, and it is feared that one result might be a wide variation in provincial standards. Similarly, critics have argued that the Free-Trade Agreement with the USA might have deleterious consequences because the continued public funding of social programmes will be challenged on the grounds of 'unfair competition'. For its part, the federal government has denied that schemes such as Medicare and unemployment insurance will suffer. What is less contentious is that there is considerable uncertainty about the future direction of Canadian social policy.

SOCIAL GROUPINGS AND REGIONALISM IN CANADA

ALAN F. WILLIAMS and CEDRIC MAY

Introduction

In a 1981 essay entitled *The Issue of National Unity*, S. D. Clark pondered the question of how Canada could have survived as a political unity during the last 300 years of its history. With a population which has rarely exceeded even one-tenth of that of its neighbour to the south, and which has remained thinly scattered as the nation has grown, with regional differences deeply rooted in history and reinforced by geography, and with two national groups divided by language, religion and culture, it seemed a miracle of nation-building that the country did not 'balkanize' or become absorbed by the USA:

'It would be comforting to believe that Canada remained Canada because the great mass of Canadian people wanted to be Canadian. History, however, will not bear out such an easy explanation of the country's political survival over the years. The truth is that among the great mass of the Canadian population, up almost to the Second World War, there developed no great sense of belonging to a national community. This was a population made up of people largely ethnically bound. The sense of group or collective identity of such people derived from their ethnic heritage.' (S. D. Clark, *The Issue of National Unity*, 1981.)

Who were these people? In the 19th and early 20th centuries Canada attracted many Europeans of various nationalities to join those inhabitants of British and French origins. Group identity was particularly important to the large rural population of French Canada, but it was also evident among the Scots of Nova Scotia and eastern Ontario; the Irish of the Miramichi (New Brunswick) and Ottawa Valleys; the Ukrainians, Poles and Germans in rural western Canada; the Mennonites of southern Manitoba and the Hutterites in their closed colonies in various parts of the west. Many of these people, particularly those from Eastern Europe who found themselves in western Canada on prime farmland, with little contact with either Canadian governmental representatives or established Canadian communities, were forced to develop their own communities and resources. They maintained their traditional cultural patterns and beliefs without interference—and thus the transplanted ethnic communities put down solid roots in the west.

In modern Canada Anglo-Canadians remain the largest ethnic group, with a decisive influence on Canadian culture and institutions. But the old, localizing restraints upon other groups have diminished with time and with the vast broadening of the base of the Canadian middle class. The cultural barriers which separated one element of the population from another have been removed. The new prosperity of the post-Second World War years greatly strengthened the vested interests of nationhood; yet because this was developed upon an ethnic or regional base, this base was also strengthened. Many cultural attributes associated with ethnic heritage may be lost, but ethnic associations, churches and publications still flourish, with the Canadian government made party to them in the name of multiculturalism (see below).

Linguistic Groups

At the time of the 1986 census, of a total population of 25.3m., 21.5m. Canadians had English or French, the two official languages, as their exclusive mother tongue (English 15.3m., French 6.2m.); 2.9m. had a single mother tongue which was neither English nor French. The French and English peoples of Canada are still referred to in some accounts as the 'two founding races', although their differences are cultural, not racial. Traditional descriptions portray the French Canadian as dominated by religion, educated by the Catholic Church, rural, raised within an authoritarian family, submissive in relationships, living in the present, and means- rather than

goal-oriented; they portray the English Canadian as not dominated by religion, educated in a secular school, urban, raised in an egalitarian family structure, individualistic, competitive in personal relationships, living for the future and goal-oriented. Others would see these descriptions as dated, or stereotyped. An alternative characterization is that, in the province of Québec, at least, it is the English who are, today, the more conservative and traditional in their outlook and the French who are more liberal and doctrinaire. It may be unwise to generalize on the attitudes and behaviour of Anglo-Canadians as a whole if we consider regional and historical origins to be important. The original settlers of New France, as it was called, were mainly from north-western France, and their descendants are concentrated in Québec. By contrast, the Anglo-Canadians, or the Anglo-Celtic group as we may call them, are the descendants of those who came from all quarters of the British Isles at different times, and they reveal strong regional distinctions based on where they settled across the nation: Newfoundlanders, Maritimers, westerners and easterners.

Canada's earliest immigrants included United Empire Loyalists (who left the 13 colonies then constituting the USA at the time of the American Revolution) and runaway US slaves. In modern times immigrants have come from all parts of the world; they have included draft-dodgers from the USA, boat people from Vietnam and refugees from Central and Latin America, shuttled through the USA by the sanctuary movements. The proportion of the Canadian population not of British, French or First Nations (native people) origin increased from 8% in 1871 and 10% in 1901 to about 25% in 1971 (comparable figures cannot be calculated for 1981). The province of Ontario—once largely British, French-Canadian and German—has received about half of Canada's post-Second World War immigration, with the result that by the 1980s about one-third of its population was of other ethnic origins. It is estimated that one-half of Toronto's population is foreign-born, with the Italians the biggest single ethnic minority. It is claimed that it was the post-war immigrants who converted the city from a staid Anglo-Celtic town, which was 'seldom exuberant and always closed on Sundays', to a lively place with a rich variety of good restaurants, music and entertainment. Both Toronto and Vancouver have authentic and well-established 'Chinatowns'. That in Vancouver is a large neighbourhood, a mile long and half a mile wide; it is a vigorous inner-directed community with two Chinese-language newspapers. A recent survey of the ethnic press in Canada (that is, of publications emanating from cultures other than French or English) listed over 300 titles in 53 languages.

Native Peoples

The ethnic mosaic of Canada includes, of course, the native peoples, both Indian and Inuit. The Inuit (the alternative, and once more widely-used, term Eskimo means 'eater of raw meat' and was derived from Abenaki and Cree Indian language; Inuit means something like 'human beings') numbered about 30,000 in the late 1980s and are the northernmost people of Canada, anciently of Asiatic origin and now scattered over the Arctic coast and islands. The 'Mackenzie Inuit' live near the mouth of the Mackenzie River; the 'Copper Inuit' live around Coronation Gulf; the 'Central Inuit' live on Baffin and Southampton Islands and on the Melville Peninsula, and the 'Labrador Inuit' live on the coast of Labrador and the Ungava Peninsula of Québec.

Over a million people in Canada (about 5% of the population) can trace their ancestry back to the country's first inhabitants. Of this figure, some 70% are either non-status Indians or are Métis (of mixed blood by intermarriage with whites). Inuit account for about 3%, while the remainder are status Indians registered under the Indian Act. The Canadian Indians are not a single people but can be divided into 10 distinct linguistic groups, each with its own dialects. Indians of Algonquian (eastern woodland) origin are the most numerous, and include the Micmacs of Prince Edward Island, Nova Scotia and New Brunswick, the Montagnais of Québec and the Ojibway, Cree and Blackfoot of Ontario and the Prairie provinces. Iroquoian (agricultural) peoples, including the Hurons, are found in Ontario and Québec, Athapaskan (hunting and gathering) peoples inhabit the Yukon and Northwest Territories, and Siouan (Great Plains) tribes live in parts of Manitoba, Saskatchewan and Alberta.

The Indians and Inuit of Canada are often viewed as the impoverished and demoralized descendants of peoples and cultures which were once thriving and viable. The Inuit in particular have been portrayed as a powerless minority, physically and economically separated from Euro-Canadian society, with an alien government imposed on it. Most Inuit have been gathered together in small, permanent communities somewhat distanced from the resources of land and sea that made their traditional hunting-nomadism viable. Health, education and security are their gains, but so is continuing dependency. The Indian populations, which are encountered from ocean to ocean, are often close to the urban areas, in or out of reserves (of which there are over 2,000). They exhibit various stages of economic and social development, from that of the traditional hunter–fisher to the skilled industrial worker or member of the 'white-collar' professions. Since 1973 an increasing number of Indian bands have assumed control of their schools and other educational programmes. Both Inuit and Indian groups take great pride in their heritage and have organized themselves for effective action in the defence of native rights, and for recognition of their unique contributions to the life of the nation. Both wish to ensure their place, but not their assimilation, in Canadian society.

Canadian Multiculturalism

The cultural mosaic of Canada is often sharply contrasted with the pressures of the 'melting-pot' of cultural assimilation in the USA. The word 'multiculturalism' emerged in Canada in the 1960s to counter the word 'biculturalism', as used in the terms of reference of the Royal Commission on Bilingualism and Biculturalism which examined the anglophone and francophone communities—the 'two solitudes', as they had been called. In October 1971 the federal government proclaimed a policy of multiculturalism within a bilingual English and French framework, and at about the same time several provinces also proclaimed policies of multiculturalism. It is said that the word came to have three meanings: the social policy of encouraging retention of group heritages alongside full participation in Canadian society; the philosophy or ideology of cultural pluralism; and a society characterized by ethnic diversity. Clause 27 in the Constitution Act of 1982 states that the Canadian Charter of Rights and Freedoms 'shall be interpreted in a manner consistent with the preservation and enhancement of the multicultural heritage of Canadians'.

Multiethnic orgins and multicultural development have ensured diverse allegiances and identities in Canada. The evolution of the nation-state by the bonding of colonies and territories has provided still-greater diversity. After the rebellions of 1837–38 (see Canada: A Chronology since Colonization, pp. 357–358), an attempt was made to assimilate the French populations into a unitary nation. The British North America Act, which provided Canada with its federal constitution in 1867, recognized the failure of this experiment. Canada has grown into an untidy confederation of provinces and territories of greatly-varying size, population, economic strength and political power. It is a confederation which seems at times to be united only by a common distrust of the economic and cultural might of its great neighbour to the south. Threats by the province of Québec to secede (Québec is an integral part of the prosperous heartland of Canada, with one-quarter of the nation's population) are merely the best-publicized of the numerous threats to the stability of Canada. British Columbia, beyond the Rockies on the Pacific seaboard, has always steered an independent course, while oil-rich Alberta, chafing at cheap energy policies imposed by the federal government in Ottawa, spawned a vociferous western separatist movement in the late 1970s. In 1987 the recognition of political maturity signified by the creation of a representative assembly, in Yellowknife, for the Northwest Territories has served to articulate the sense of neglect by Ottawa of Canada's northern regions and peoples.

The modern concept of a specific, cultural and political, Québec was elaborated mainly during the period of the so-called 'quiet revolution' in the 1960s. Québec's threat of secession has given way to the articulation of a 'distinct French-speaking society', compatible with a unified Canada. Meanwhile, however, the threat to national stability was perceived as so great in the run-up to Québec's 1980 referendum on its links with the rest of Canada that, at great financial cost, the federal government created a Task Force on National Unity which toured the country, holding forums and workshops on Canada's crisis. The members of this task force returned with the clear conclusion that the confederation served the interests of the prosperous heartland (mainly Ontario) and had not brought adequate economic benefits to the periphery. One informant from the island province of Newfoundland (which, with Labrador, was the last to join the Confederation in March 1949) commented; 'I am a Newfoundlander first, Canadian a very distant second', and this sentiment was echoed across the continent. This provincial loyalty even divides the French-Canadian population. French speakers outside the province of Québec feel threatened by the recognition in the Meech Lake Accord (finalized in June 1987) of 'distinct status' for Québec only. The controversiality of Québec's political attitudes has, on occasions, made the position of French-speaking minorities in the other provinces even more uncomfortable. The Meech Lake Accord raised a number of fundamental constitutional questions. Giving a special 'role' to Québec seemed to many to undermine the principle of equality of the provinces, which is said to be fundamental to the constitution. It was also feared that the 'linguistic duality' and 'distinct society' provisions would encourage 'provincial patriotism' at the expense of national patriotism, and, in the long term, undermine the unity of Canada.

Women

Canada is a nation of sub-cultures and the term minority is not always appropriate. Thus, while barely one-quarter of the population of Canada claims French as its mother tongue, the French-speaking Québécois account for more than 80% of the population of the province of Québec. A recent work on the women's movement in Canada was entitled *The Neglected Majority:* Canada can be viewed as a society of such majorities. As a result, Canadian politics is notably a process of compromise and accommodation. The women's movement has achieved as much by the democratic process as by militant action and extremism. A Royal Commission of Inquiry on the situation of women (the Bird Commission of 1970) led to the establishment, in the early 1970s, of a federal Canadian Consultative Council on the Situation of Women, a Québec government department and a Québec Council on the Status of Women to advise on all matters regarding equality of the sexes and respect for women's rights and status. This reflection on women's role was fired by militant feminism, conferences, publishing of women's writing and the teaching of women's studies in the universities. In a pioneer society, both men and women have always been called upon to be resourceful and self-reliant.

Regional Disparities and Policy Initiatives

One of Canada's best-known women writers, the late Gabrielle Roy, has the heroine of one of her last stories travel to a village 30 miles from Winnipeg on the Prairies. She steps from the train at dead of night and asks the conductor: 'Where is Ely?' He points to a few flickering lights in the distant darkness. This fundamental question in Canadian literature points up poignantly the recurrent theme of isolation in Canadian culture. This is, no doubt, the Canadian counterpart of the universal preoccupation in the post-war world with the existential solitude of man the 'Outsider', but it takes on a new meaning in this land of tiny scattered communities, whether they be towns in the Rockies, isolated farms on the Prairies, mining communities in the great expanses of the rugged Canadian Shield, fishing villages of the Gaspé or Nova Scotia, the outports of Newfoundland or the Indian or Inuit villages of the remote North. At the 1986 census only 45% of Canadians were registered as resident in towns or cities with populations of 45,000 or more.

The impact of modern technology has done much to lessen the sense of irreducible diversity and isolation experienced by many rural communities in Canada. Much of the population is within reach of the powerful magnet of highly-commercialized US television. Canadians make more telephone calls per head of population than the inhabitants of any other nation in the world. Satellite is bringing TV5, a pan-European French-language station, to many corners of North America. Communications by road, rail, water and air are highly efficient and one of Canada's major industries and chief areas of industrial production. However (and perhaps not altogether surprisingly), Canada does not yet have a national newspaper, although Toronto's *Globe and Mail* has a good chance of becoming one, and such is the challenge of Canada's multifarious selfhood that these prodigious efforts in technology and inventiveness barely succeed in creating a unit out of the pieces.

A journey from St John's, Newfoundland along the Trans-Canada Highway, passing through Nova Scotia and New Brunswick before travelling up the St Lawrence Valley to Toronto, brings home forcibly the economic inequalities and the disparities in cultural opportunities from the periphery to the prosperous heart of the nation. Little in the Maritime provinces can match the glittering concert halls and theatres, for example, of Montréal, Ottawa or Toronto. The universities bring pockets of culture to St John's, Halifax, Fredericton, Sherbrooke and to communities away from the cities. Québec created the Université du Québec, with constituent colleges in Montréal, Rimouski, Chicoutimi and Hull. Sherbrooke University, in its early years, imaginatively built a 1,500-seat theatre instead of putting the money into a University Council Chamber.

Canada's vast civil services (federal, provincial and municipal government employment together accounted for 10% of Canada's employment total in 1984) have provided a number of important cultural services, examples of which include Parks Canada, with brilliant reconstructions, imaginatively brought to life in the summer season, at Louisbourg (Cape Breton Island), Lower Fort Garry (Winnipeg) and at numerous other sites, and the Canada Council, which subsidizes theatre, music, ballet and opera, folklore, museums, writers, publishing and writers' associations. The Canadian Broadcasting Corporation has, through radio and television broadcasts in both Canada's official languages, brought employment, patronage, quality broadcasting, a sense of participation in a common endeavour and images of a shared culture to every province.

Canada's economy is a strange mix of interventionism and free-market policies. Research has shown that when a new shopping mall is sited in a settled community, most of the retail space will often be taken by chain stores (fast food, groceries, books, clothing and so on) with head offices in Ontario or Québec where all contracting for trucking, purchasing, advertising, insurance, design and construction will be placed. Local retail outlets are unable to compete, and the devastating effects on a fragile local economy can easily be imagined. Not only does much of the wealth of the periphery find its way to the nation's prosperous core, but there is a similar migration of youth and talent towards the Toronto area and other centres in southern Ontario.

These centripetal forces have always been countered in part by a widespread Canadian tendency to strong attachments to one's local area. The quality of life has improved throughout the country and, against all the odds, equalization is slowly working. The high cost of living in the metropolis is encouraging people to prefer the advantages of small- and medium-town life. There is a high level of second-home-ownership in Canada, with many Canadians seeking to escape from the urban centres to country cottages or winter-sports resorts, to hunting or fishing camps. Canada's Centennial in 1967 brought some fine public buildings to provincial cities: life in these cities and even in small towns is becoming not only possible but positively attractive to urban dwellers. Progressively, through an effort of will and collective determination, Canada is becoming the peaceable kingdom it has long sought to be and a very attractive alternative model for life in North America.

RECENT PATTERNS OF IMMIGRATION AND DEMOGRAPHY IN CANADA

FREDA HAWKINS

Immigration Policy since 1900

Since the beginning of this century immigration and demographic patterns in Canada have been shaped in the main by deliberate political and bureaucratic decisions. Other important factors have included: the degree of demand on the part of would-be migrants to come to North America from Europe and, after the Second World War, from other parts of the world; the extent to which Canada was able to retain its own immigrants before the USA began to control migration across the two countries' joint border; and the state of the Canadian economy. Towards the end of the 19th century Canadian politicians were beginning to believe that immigration brought problems as well as benefits for Canada, and were deciding precisely whom to admit and whom to exclude. Legislation to create a 'White Canada' immigration policy was first introduced in 1911 and extended in 1919. (Australia established a 'White Australia' policy in 1901, while the USA established similar policies after the First World War.)

The 'White Canada' immigration policy, under which only those of European or North American origin (with a very few

exceptions) were considered to be admissible, remained in force until 1962. Canada was the first of the three traditional countries of immigration to abandon its white immigration policy. This was done under the so-called Immi-Regulations introduced by Ellen Fairclough, Minister of Citizenship and Immigration in the Progressive Conservative government led by John G. Diefenbaker. A discriminatory restriction on the sponsorship of Asian relatives was retained at the last moment, but this was removed in 1967. Canada's immigration policy became non-discriminatory and universal from this point on, focusing on three basic categories of immigrants: economic migrants; those entering for reasons of family reunion; and refugees. This emphasis has remained the same to this day.

The change to universality did not come about because of any public protest either in parliament or outside. Instead, it was the work of a very small group of senior politicians and officials who realized that Canada could not function effectively in the United Nations, or in the multiracial Commonwealth of Nations, while retaining a racist immigration policy. The USA followed suit in 1965 and Australia in 1973.

THE MODERN AGE IN CANADIAN IMMIGRATION

Although many were excluded before 1962, a great many migrants and refugees found a new home and new opportunities in Canada, particularly in the years immediately before the First World War and after the Second Warld War. Table 1 shows the growth in Canada's population from the first intercensal decade after Confederation (1861–71) to the most recent one (1971–81).

TABLE 1: IMMIGRATION AND POPULATION IN CANADA, 1861–1981
('000)

Period	Immigration (intercensal years)	Population at end of decade		
		Total	Canadian-born	Foreign-born
1861–71	183	3,689	3,064	625
1871–81	353	4,325	3,722	603
1881–91	903	4,833	4,189	644
1891–1901 . . .	326	5,371	4,672	699
1901–11	1,759	7,207	5,620	1,587
1911–21	1,612	8,788	6,832	1,956
1921–31	1,203	10,377	8,069	2,308
1931–41	150	11,507	9,488	2,019
1941–51	548	14,009[1]	11,949	2,060
1951–61	1,543	18,238	15,394	2,844
1961–71	1,429	21,568	18,273	3,295
1971–81	1,447	24,083	20,216	3,867

Source: Canada Employment and Immigration Commission.

[1] Includes Newfoundland, which had a population of 361,416 in 1951.

It was during the 1960s, however, following the change to universality, that what might be called the modern age in Canadian immigration really began. The period from 1963 to 1968 was a period of very creative government by a Liberal administration under Lester B. Pearson, a politician of broad vision both internationally and nationally. It was also a period when the Canadian economy moved into a phase of very rapid expansion. During these years, a new selection system—the Canadian Points System—was introduced in the Immigration Regulations of 1967. A fully-independent Immigration Appeal Board was created in 1969, together with consultative machinery, within the new Department of Manpower and Immigration, in the shape of a Canada Manpower and Immigration Council, to which four specialist advisory boards were attached. Major improvements were made in Canada's Overseas Immigration Service. More support became available for voluntary agencies concerned with immigrants and refugees, and immigrants entering the labour force benefited from the new manpower-training, mobility and other programmes which were being developed by the new department.

The 1960s were also a period of rapid change world-wide, which saw the ending of the largest colonial empires and the creation of many new states in Africa and elsewhere. A new international emphasis on human rights, and on national and racial equality, emerged, and the major shift from north to south in the global origin of immigrants, which has been such a remarkable feature of the 1970s and 1980s, began to become evident in immigration statistics.

Through a combination of natural increase and immigration, the population of Canada doubled in the three decades following the end of the Second World War, and this was achieved with no particular stress or strain and with no evidence of political discontents or difficulties.

Policy Development in the 1970s

During the 1970s there were further improvements in Canadian immigration policy and management, the most notable of which was the creation of a new Immigration Act in 1976. This was the work of Robert Andras, who became minister of manpower and immigration in 1972, and Alan Gotlieb, his deputy minister, who later became the Canadian ambassador to Washington. When taking over this portfolio Robert Andras determined to get a new and effective Immigration Act to replace the long-outdated act of 1952. He achieved this through a process of extensive consultation and deliberation, involving the preparation of a Green Paper on immigration policy, and the efforts of a Special Joint Committee of Parliament.

The Canadian Immigration Act of 1976 has been viewed widely as a sensible, liberal and innovative piece of immigration legislation. In itself, it created a very positive climate in immigration and refugee policy with a major emphasis on admission instead of exclusion. Its major features include a clear statement of principles, among them Canada's lasting commitment to non-discrimination in immigration policy and to helping refugees. It developed a completely new, and much more public, system of deciding on annual immigration levels, which involved a carefully-planned process of consultation with the provinces, national organizations and interest groups, academics and government departments. This process takes place each year from January onwards and eventually leads to a statement in parliament by the minister of employment and immigration (the 'Annual Report to Parliament on Immigration Levels') early in the parliamentary session, which commences in the autumn, outlining the proposed annual immigration levels, normally for the next three years.

The act and the immigration regulations which complement it, which both came into force in 1978, confirmed that three classes of immigrants would be admitted to Canada. Firstly, there is a family class which refers to the immediate family and dependent children, but also includes parents and grandparents over 60, or under 60 if widowed or incapable of gainful employment. Since April 1978 all parents who are under 60 and their dependents have been included in the family class provided they are sponsored by a Canadian citizen. The second class consists of refugees, including Convention refugees—those coming within the scope of the 1951 United Nations Refugee Convention—or members of a specially-designated class of refugees. The third class consists of other applicants selected on the basis of the Points System—those include independent applicants and what are now called 'assisted relatives', that is, more distant relatives who are sponsored by a family member in Canada. In addition, the act has required all visitors and students wishing to work temporarily or study in Canada to obtain prior authorization abroad; once admitted, neither visitors nor students may change their status in Canada.

The 1976 act has made major changes in the areas of exclusion, control and enforcement and has substantially reduced the excessive degree of ministerial discretion permissible under the the 1952 act. What were known as 'the prohibited classes' under the previous legislation, and the long list of those who were considered undesirable, have been removed. In their place the 1976 act identifies certain broad classes of persons whose entry to Canada might endanger public health, welfare, order, security or the integrity of the immigration programme. Grounds for exclusion now include: a degree of health impairment—judged on an individual's 'total health profile'—which would constitute a threat to public health or safety, or cause excessive demands on health or social services; the lack of means of support or evident capacity to acquire them; serious criminal offences without evidence of rehabilitation; and the involvement in criminal activity, such as organized crime, or in espionage, subversion or acts of violence such as terrorism or hijacking. All offences committed outside Canada are directly related to comparable offences under Canadian law and are judged in relation to the sentence which would have been imposed in Canada. The act also introduced major changes in the way enquiries relating to removal from Canada are conducted, and provided new ways to protect the fundamental rights of persons subject to removal. Instead of deportation in all cases requiring removal, as laid down in the 1952 act, there are now three procedures, depending on the gravity of the case: a deportation order; a 12-month exclusion order; and a departure notice.

There were a number of other interesting provisions in the new act, including a revision of the Points System and several important changes relating to refugees. In relation to refugees, Part I of the act establishes Canada's commitment to fulfil its international legal obligation towards refugees and 'to uphold its humanitarian tradition with respect to the displaced and the persecuted'. It also provides for the establishment by regulation of special selection standards for refugees and special classes of refugees. This was done to meet the needs of groups of displaced persons who are, in fact, refugees, but do not qualify under the definition of a refugee laid down in the Geneva Convention and Protocol of UNHCR (Office of the United Nations High Commissioner for Refugees). The act also established what were thought to be improved procedures for determining refugee status, but these proved to be too cumbersome and slow to handle the unexpectedly-large flow of undocumented migrants claiming refugee status which appeared in the 1980s. After a decade of trial and error which has seen the building up of large backlogs of claimants, a new system has now been devised which involves the creation of an Immigration and Refugee Board designed to adjudicate all refugee claims fairly and quickly.

The immigration regulations of 1978 also set out the details of a new refugee-sponsorship plan which proved to be invaluable for Canada's share of the very large Indo–Chinese refugee movement which took place after the fall of Saigon at the end of the Vietnam War in 1975: this is now a permanent feature of Canada's annual refugee plan. This new sponsorship scheme was a deliberate effort on the part of the government to encourage a more direct involvement of both the voluntary sector and the public in the settlement and adjustment of refugees in Canada. It provides for the sponsorship of a refugee family by any group of not less than five individual Canadian citizens or permanent residents who are over the age of 18 and live in 'the expected community of settlement', or by a corporation which is properly incorporated under the laws of Canada, or of any province, and has representatives in that community. This group or organization must give a written undertaking to the minister 'to make provision for lodging, care, maintenance and resettlement assistance for the Convention refugee and accompanying dependents for a period of one year'. Partly because this commitment, although substantial in the first instance, did not last very long, it proved to be very popular and has remained so through to the late 1980s.

Population Policy

Until very recently Canada showed very little interest in a population policy and politicians of all parties saw no need for one. Partly this was a feature of the country's very strong sense of security—a security guaranteed in the 19th century by the British navy and in the 20th century by the increasing world status of the USA. This relative complacency was shaken, however, by a very important demographic event of the 1970s, which caused population policy to be placed much higher on the national agenda. This development has been described by the American demographer Leon Bouvier in the following way:

'Sometime around 1973, a momentous new demographic phenomenon began to unfold throughout most of the developed world—fertility fell below the level of 2.1 births per woman needed to replace the population in the long run and *remained there* . . . Actual population size did not begin to fall immediately in the early seventies . . . because all of these nations experienced a rise in their fertility rate after World War II; some for just a few years, others like Australia, Canada and the United States for ten to fifteen years . . . Never before in modern history has fertility been so low in so many countries for such a long period as has been the case since 1973.' (Leon Bouvier, *Planet Earth 1984-2034, A Demographic Vision.* Population Bulletin 39, no I (February 1984), a publication of the Population Reference Bureau Inc, Washington, DC.)

By the late 1980s it seemed clear that this had become a very powerful long-term trend, and one that was unlikely to be reversed in the foreseeable future or even changed in more than minor ways. A recent study of Canadian fertility by Anatole Romaniuk of Statistics Canada, entitled *Fertility in Canada; From Baby Boom to Baby Bust,* presents a similar view of Canada's demographic future and stresses the important role which immigration is likely to play in it. He writes that 'The current regime of low fertility and the consequent ageing and slowdown of growth in the Canadian population,

are creating an historically new situation which may affect immigration strategies. Indeed if the fertility rate does not increase substantially and if population growth is a national goal, then large-scale immigration is clearly the alternative.'

The background paper tabled with the Annual Report to Parliament on Immigration Levels in November 1984 raised the issue of future population decline for the first time. In a very clear analysis of the options available to Canada, the paper emphasized that:

'assuming current trends continue, the rest of this century will be the last period of robust demographic growth in Canada. The following twenty-year period (2000 to 2020) will be greatly influenced by the demographic events of 1980–90. Were fertility to stay at or below current levels and annual net immigration to be held at a minimum of 50,000, growth would diminish and decline would begin by about 2020. Lower net immigration would advance the timetable and move the onset of decline closer to the year 2001. (Canada Employment and Immigration Commission, *Background Paper on Future Immigration Levels,* November 1984.)

It was clear in the late 1980s that the Mulroney government was well aware of Canada's population problem and was responding to it in two principal ways. Annual immigration levels were increasing quite rapidly. In May 1986 the then Minister of Health and Welfare, Jake Epp, announced that the cabinet had authorized a 'review of demography and its implications for economic and social policy', to be prepared by his department over the next three years. (The report of this demographic review was not yet available at the time of writing.)

1987: Profile of an Immigration Year

Detailed examination of the figures for a single year, 1987, present a clear picture of the present-day dimensions and composition of the annual movement of immigrants and refugees to Canada. During that year a total of 132,719 immigrants and refugees were admitted to Canada, of which 52,341 (39%) originated from Asia and the Pacific, 24,902 (19%) from European countries other than the UK, 22,054 (17%) from Central and South America, 16,890 (13%) from Africa and the Middle East, 8,381 (6%) from the UK and 7,750 (6%) from the USA.

The family class accounted for just under 40% of total immigration in 1987; Convention refugees and members of the designated classes of refugees made up almost 16% and independent immigrants accounted for the remaining 44% of total landings. Provincial settlement followed the well-established pattern, with Ontario receiving just under 54% of the total movement. Québec 16.3% and British Columbia 13.7%. The other provinces and territories each received under 10% of all the immigrants and refugees admitted to Canada in 1987.

A total of 23,279 refugees were admitted to Canada in 1987: of these, 6,644 (29%) were from Eastern Europe, 5,696 (24%) from Indo-China, 4,711 (20%) from Latin America, 3,803 (16%) from the Middle East and western Asia and 1,377 (6%) from Africa. Just over one-half (53%) of all refugee admissions were government-assisted, while 30% were funded privately, 11% took place under special programmes and 6% were processed through the Refugee Status Advisory Committee (which handles claims to Convention refugee status).

According to population projections prepared by the Canada Employment and Immigration Commission to cover the period 1986/87–2050/51, which assumed, firstly, that fertility would continue to decline before stabilizing in 1996 and, secondly, that the emigration rate would remain constant at 0.28% of the population, it would take something in the order of a total immigration of 125,000 in 1986/87, increasing by between 10,000 and 20,000 per year until 1989/90 and thereafter remaining constant, to maintain Canada's population at its current level. The projections show that if there were to be no net migration between 1986/87 and 2050/51 the country's population would decline by some 20%. Whatever path may be followed by Canadian governments in the formulation of immigration policy, it is evident that immigration will be no less important to Canada in the 21st century than it has been in the past.

SELECT BIBLIOGRAPHY

Adachi, K. *The Enemy That Never Was: A History of the Japanese Candians*. Toronto, McClelland & Stewart, 1976.

Anderson, A. B. and Frideres, J. S. *Ethnicity in Canada: Theoretical Perspectives*. Scarborough, Ontario, Butterworths Canada Ltd, 1981.

Asch, M. *Home and Native Land: Aboriginal Rights and the Canadian Constitution*. Toronto, Methuen, 1984.

Banting, K. G. *The Welfare State and Canadian Federalism* (2nd edn). Kingston, Ontario, and Montréal, McGill-Queen's University Press, 1987.

Breton, R., Reitz, J. G. and Valentine, V. *Cultural Boundaries and the Cohesion of Canada*. Montréal, The Institute for Research on Public Policy, 1980.

Bryon, R. J. (Ed.). *Regionalism in Canada*. Toronto, Irwin Publishing, 1986.

Burnet, J. *Multiculturalism in Canada* (Canadian Studies Resource Guides). Ottawa, Department of the Secretary of State, 1988.

Canada. *Report of a Royal Commission on Bilingualism and Biculturalism*. Ottawa, Queen's Printer, 1967-70.

Canada Employment and Immigration Commission. *Annual Reports and Immigration Statistics*. Ottawa, CEIC, 1978-.

   Annual Reports to Parliament on Immigration Levels. Ottawa, CEIC, 1979-.

   Background Papers on Immigration Levels. Ottawa, CEIC, 1983-.

Canadian Social Trends. Ottawa, Statistics Canada, quarterly.

Clark, S. D. *The Issue of National Unity* (Canada House Lecture Series 10). London, Canadian High Commission, 1981.

Curtis, J. E. and Scott, W. G. (Eds). *Social Stratification: Canada* (2nd edn). Scarborough, Ontario, Prentice-Hall Canada Inc, 1979.

Department of the Secretary of State. *Histories of Canadian Ethnocultural Groups* (The Generation Series). Toronto, McClelland & Stewart/Department of the Secretary of State, 1976-.

Evans, R. G. and Stoddart, G. L. (Eds). *Medicare at Maturity*. Calgary, Alberta, The University of Calgary Press, 1986.

Guest, D. *The Emergence of Social Security in Canada*. Vancouver, University of British Columbia Press, 1980.

Hawkins, F. *Canada and Immigration: Public Policy and Public Concern* (2nd edn). Montréal, McGill-Queen's University Press, 1989.

   Critical Years in Immigration: Canada and Australia Compared. Montréal, McGill-Queen's University Press, 1989.

Ismael, J. A. (Ed.). *Canadian Social Welfare Policy: Federal and Provincial Dimensions*. Kingston, Ontario, and Montréal, McGill-Queen's University Press, 1985.

   The Canadian Welfare State: Evolution and Transition. Edmonton, University of Alberta Press, 1987.

Language and Society. Ottawa, Department of Supply and Services, quarterly.

Mandel, E. and Taras, D. (Eds). *A Passion for Identity: An Introduction to Canadian Studies*. Toronto, Methuen, 1987.

McCann, L. D. (Ed.). *Heartland and Hinterland: A Geography of Canada* (2nd edn). Scarborough, Ontario, Prentice-Hall Canada Inc, 1987.

Metcalfe, W. (Ed.). *Understanding Canada: A Multidisciplinary Introduction to Canadian Studies*. New York and London, New York University Press, 1982.

Palmer, H. (Ed.). 'Geography and Ethnic Groups in Western Canada' in *Canadian Ethnic Studies, Special Issue* Vol. IX, No 2. Canadian Ethnic Studies Association, 1977.

Pepin, J.-L. and Roberts, J. P. *The Task Force on Canadian Unity: A Future Together*. Ottawa, Ministry of Supply and Services, 1979.

Porter, J. *The Vertical Mosaic: An Analysis of Class and Power in Canada*. Toronto, University of Toronto Press, 1965.

Romaniuk, A. *Fertility in Canada: From Baby Boom to Baby Bust*. Ottawa, Statistics Canada, 1984.

Statistics Canada. *Canada Year Book 1988*. Ottawa, Canadian Government Publishing Centre, 1987.

THE FOREIGN AND DEFENCE POLICIES OF CANADA

PETER LYON

Introduction

Canada attained self-government as a Dominion within the British Empire as a result of the British North America Act of 1867. Canada's conduct of an independent foreign policy and the assumption of responsibility for its national defence evolved, however, piecemeal and incrementally over decades, and for a long time was qualified by a certain ambivalence as to how much should be done unilaterally and how much in tandem with a more powerful ally—at first with Britain and then later, and much more comprehensively, with the USA. During the inter-war period and the long spells of Mackenzie King's ascendancy as prime minister and leader of the Liberal Party, Canada's foreign policy seemed preoccupied with the quest for status (in imperial and League of Nations' forums, for example) and with the avoidance of formal commitments in security matters. The extent of Canada's national foreign-policy bureaucracy, missions overseas, defence expertise and armed forces remained small until the Second World War.

This world war brought a rapid increase in Canada's international status and significance and impelled a rapid expansion both of the country's armed forces and of its diplomatic and defence establishments. This was the consequence of Canada's resources, war contributions, and position and importance in relation to the theatres of war. About 1m. Canadian men and women, out of a total population of just over 10m., were directly involved in the Second World War. The wartime period saw the doubling of the country's gross national product (GNP) and its assumption of a role, third only to that of the USA and the UK, as an architect and progenitor of many postwar multilateral organizations—not only the United Nations and its associated family of specialized agencies, but also the Bretton Woods system for international economic matters, the General Agreement on Tariffs and Trade (GATT) and the North Atlantic Treaty Organization (NATO). In the late 1940s Canada also played a part in the refashioning of the Commonwealth, just as it was later instrumental in the launch of the Commonwealth Secretariat in the mid-1960s. During the 1940s and 1950s, especially during the period when Lester Pearson was firstly under-secretary of state for external affairs (1946–48) and then secretary of state for external affairs (1948–57), Canada acquired the commendatory sobriquet of being a constructive 'middle power' in world affairs and an intelligent advocate and practitioner of international functionalism—these characterizations, in general, have been appropriate for much of Canada's foreign and defence policy right through to the late 1980s.

Ironically, it was not the relatively short (and rather stormy) period of Progressive Conservative government under John G. Diefenbaker (who was prime minister between 1957 and 1963) which produced much change in the substance, or even the rhetoric, of Canadian foreign policy, despite Diefenbaker's abrasively polemical and populist style. It was the early years of Pierre Trudeau's premiership (and particularly the 1969–72 period, with much-publicized policy reviews and documents being published on foreign policy and defence) which inspected and challenged the Pearson legacy. However, for some years prior to his second (and final) retirement from the premiership (in February 1984), Trudeau's practice seemed to conform with the broad stream of Canadian Liberal internationalism.

Sometimes the dilemmas and choices before Canadian policy-makers in foreign-policy and defence matters have been represented as a tussle between Canada's history, with ties to its two original mother-countries, Britain and France, and its geography, especially the great gravitational pull Canada experiences from the USA. There is no doubt that, in relative terms, the British connection has diminished significantly for Canada—especially during and as a consequence of two world wars and of the cold war. The US connection, by contrast, has increased greatly, indeed dramatically and multifariously, however much aspects of this may be regretted or challenged by some Canadians. Today, US influence within and over Canada is pervasive and without close rival from any other part of the world, despite the apparently increasing economic power of the European Communities (the EC) and Japan. Yet to be independent and distinct from the USA is a perennial concern to, and a major *raison d'être* of, Canada.

Two recurrent themes in Canada's domestic debates about foreign policy came into prominence again in the late 1980s. The first concerned the question of whether there was significant agreement within the Canadian public at large abut the broad lines of foreign policy, regardless of whether the Liberals or the Progressive Conservative party was in office in Ottawa. The evidence provided by public reactions to the Mulroney government, in power since September 1984 (and re-elected in November 1988), seemed to suggest that there is a considerable amount of persisting Canadian cross-party agreement on the major substantive issues, despite marked verbal differences. The second theme concerned the question of the precise role and significance to be accorded to individual provinces in the formulation and conduct of foreign-policy matters, given that on some issues—such as aspects of foreign trade or maritime jurisdiction for provinces with a coastal boundary, for example—the federal–provincial entanglements are close and complex. While there is no doubt that the formal position is that the federal government has constitutional primacy, prudence and good political sense incline wise federal governments to pay due heed to provincial opinion on such issues as trade, resources, immigration, pollution and other matters touching on federal–provincial relations. In reality provincial influence varies considerably according to the issue, its context and the character and standing of the leaders concerned.

Constructive Multilateralism

By the late 1980s Canada had undoubtedly become a country much entangled by its membership of, and active participation in, a large number of multilateral organizations—notably the United Nations, with its array of specialized associated bodies, but also many other international bodies. Their forums serve as outlets for the expression of much of Canada's foreign and defence policies, even though some bilateral ties, especially those with the USA, are of considerable importance.

The mid-term review conference of the continuing Multilateral Trade Negotiations (MTN) of the GATT, held in Montréal in December 1988, marked the end of a period, stretching over at least 15 months, during which Canada had been the host country for a number of important international conferences on major international events. In terms of their sequence of occurrence, Canada was host to la Francophonie in Québec City in September 1987, to a Commonwealth Heads of Government Meeting in Vancouver in October 1987, to the annual meeting of the Group of Seven industrialized countries in Toronto in June 1988, and then for the Montréal review meeting of the current Uruguay Round of the GATT in December 1988. During this time, also, domestic debate quickened over two matters of considerable immediate and long-term importance to Canada—the proposed Free-Trade Agreement with the USA and the question of Canada's defence planning and weapon and manpower needs for the remaining years of the 20th century.

FRANCE, CANADA AND LA FRANCOPHONIE

Canada and France, to some extent, compete with each other for leadership in la Francophonie, the international association of French-language-user countries, which held a summit meeting in Québec City in September 1987 and in which Canada plays a prominent role. The premiers of Québec and New Brunswick were active participants on terms which had been agreed beforehand and expressed in a formal protocol between the government of Canada and the respective governments of the two provinces.

Bilateral relations between France and Canada were by no means entirely free from friction at this time, especially in regard to maritime and fishing matters. On 14 April 1988 four French politicians and 17 crew-members of a ship from the French overseas *collectivité territoriale* of Saint Pierre and Miquelon, islands off the southern coast of Newfoundland (and tiny remaining fragments of the once-extensive French possessions in North America) were apprehended by Canadian officials in what they considered were Canadian waters. The incident occurred during the French presidential-election campaign and provoked a marked, if relatively brief, inflammation of the long-lasting dispute between the two countries concerning precise maritime jurisdictions and fishing rights in the seas around Saint Pierre and Miquelon. These issues had sharpened in the 1980s as both France and Canada sought to expand, clarify and patrol extensive maritime jurisdictions over territorial waters, exclusive economic zones and fishing zones, given that the world's order of the oceans was subject to so much debate and redefinition. The 21 apprehended men were released on bail on 17 April 1988 following the French government's decision to recall its ambassador from Ottawa to Paris for consultation. On 29 April the two countries agreed to submit this dispute to mediation.

THE COMMONWEALTH

Canada has never had colonies, and most Canadians are proud of their country's non-colonial—even, in some respects, anti-imperialist—past, and regard the Commonwealth as an admirable vehicle for the practice of constructive multilateralism in a forum to which neither the USA nor the USSR belong. An experienced Canadian diplomat, Arnold Smith, was Secretary-General of the Commonwealth (and the first head of the Commonwealth Secretariat) between 1965 and 1975. His tenure of office inducted a new, and continuing, phase of a secretariat-centric Commonwealth, albeit with its headquarters in the UK (in London).

The period 1987-88 was one of considerable Canadian exposure to, and activities within, the Commonwealth, most notably from the time of the Commonwealth Heads of Government Meeting (CHOGM), held in Vancouver in October 1987, and chaired by Canadian prime minister Brian Mulroney. A committee of eight Commonwealth foreign ministers (which Britain refused to join) was set up at the Vancouver CHOGM for the purpose of providing 'high-level impetus and guidance' to further Commonwealth objectives on South Africa. The committee, which was chaired by Canada's Minister of External Affairs, Joseph ('Joe') Clark, also comprised the foreign ministers of Australia, Guyana, India, Nigeria, Tanzania, Zambia and Zimbabwe. It held its first meeting in Lusaka in February 1988, followed by subsequent meetings in Toronto in August 1988, in Harare in February 1989 and in Canberra in August 1989—all intended to lead to further recommendations for the October 1989 CHOGM in Kuala Lumpur.

The committee sought, through its various meetings and other efforts by member countries, to ensure the widening, heightening and intensifying of Commonwealth sanctions against South Africa. Initial findings in some studies undertaken after the Vancouver CHOGM suggested that action by banks, particularly by US banks, was damaging the South African economy more than any other sanction. At their Toronto meeting the foreign ministers considered ways of countering South African censorship and propaganda, and Canada stated a willingness to make C$1m. available for this work. Reports early in 1989 that, in some respects, Canadian dealings with South Africa had increased, not diminished, in 1987-88 were therefore somewhat embarrassing for the Canadian government.

Canada has also expressed concern to promote independence for Namibia, a cause with which Clark had identified himself closely from the time when he was briefly Canada's prime minister, in 1979. Canada provided a small contingent of technician-troops and logistic support to the UN Transition Assistance Group (UNTAG) for Namibia in April 1989.

THE G7: CANADA AND THE INTERNATIONAL ECONOMIC SYSTEM

In June 1988 Prime Minister Mulroney hosted the 14th annual summit meeting of the leaders of the Group of Seven industrialized democracies (known as the G7, of which Canada has been a member since 1976), held in Toronto. While the meetings, as was customary, engaged in *tour d'horizon* surveys of the state of the world economy and related matters, no progress was made on the contentious issue of agricultural subsidies. This question was referred—in effect merely adjourned and deferred—to the mid-term review meeting of the Uruguay Round of the General Agreement on Tariffs and Trade (GATT), which took place in Montréal in early December 1988. Canada had been an advocate and champion of the GATT system and an active participant in its collective proceedings ever since the system's inception in 1948.

The Montréal mid-term review negotiations of the GATT proved to be unproductive principally because of the inability of the USA and the European Communities (EC) to resolve their differences on agriculture, and this despite the efforts of the Cairns Group (which comprises developed and developing agricultural producing states, including Canada and Australia) to put forward a compromise formula. The Cairns Group called for the contracting parties 'to register a firm commitment to negotiate a long-term framework for agricultural trade, involving a programme of progressive reductions in trade distorting agricultural support and protection'. The Group also sought agreement on a package of measures which would enable 'early action' for immediate implementation in price-support schemes in 1989 and 1990. As exporters of agricultural products, the Cairns Group (and Canada not least) had a strong interest in reducing farm subsidies, but it also appreciated the need to avert a damaging rift between the USA and the EC. In the lead-up to the Montréal meeting, the proposals of the Cairns Group seemed to be gaining support, but the compromise ultimately broke down because of US obduracy.

CANADA AND THE EC

In 1976 Canada concluded a framework agreement for commercial and economic co-operation with the European Communities. In the ensuing years, however, the proportion of Canada's overall trade which was conducted with EC member states tended to stay much the same or even to diminish slightly, while trade ties with the USA increased proportionately.

In the first quarter of 1989 about a dozen interdepartmental sectoral committees were set up within the federal bureaucracy in Ottawa to examine the probable consequences for Canada of EC moves to implement the Single European Act by 1992. This spawning of investigatory committees was fuelled by Canadian fears of a possible increase in EC protectionism.

Canada's Connections with the USA

Inescapably and inevitably, much of Canada's foreign and defence policy is inextricably part of the complex Canadian-US relationship, so much so that it is difficult at times to disentangle this from the domestic affairs of the two countries.

In March 1984 President Ronald Reagan and Prime Minister Brian Mulroney inaugurated what in effect become annual Canadian-US bilateral summits—the first of these was termed the 'shamrock summit' by many media observers in reference to the Irish ancestry of the two leaders. Early in January 1988 Joe Clark and George Shultz, then US secretary of state, signed three major bilateral agreements. The first of these was an Arctic co-operation agreement designed to defuse a long-standing dispute arising from Canada's claims to sovereignty over the waters surrounding the Arctic archipelago, including the North West Passage. In this accord the USA agreed that navigation by its ice-breaking vessels within the waters claimed by Canada would be undertaken only with Canada's consent. Nevertheless, the agreement fell short of recognizing Canada's full claims, and Liberal Party critics of the government in Canada denounced it and called for the issue to be taken to the International Court of Justice for settlement. Secondly, they signed a protocol to an extradition treaty between the two countries which broadened the category of extraditable offences to include crimes for which both parties had penalties of more than one year in prison. The amendment applied also to parents who abducted their children and took them over the border; it also narrowed the exemption for 'political offences' to exclude violent acts, such as terrorism. Thirdly, there was a declaration whereby the two countries undertook to exchange intelligence on terrorists, to improve border controls, and to share information on research and development on anti-terrorist measures.

A summit meeting between Reagan and Mulroney, held in Washington, DC in April 1988, ended without agreement on Canadian demands for controls on US emissions of pollution to counter the export of 'acid rain' to Canada. President Reagan did agree, however, not to impede a British tender to provide Canada with nuclear-powered submarines, a prospective deal whose realization depended at least on prior US permission to allow the transfer of nuclear technology.

THE CANADA–US FREE-TRADE AGREEMENT

It was in 1988 that the historic decision was taken to enter into a comprehensive free-trade agreement with the USA. The issue of freer trade with the USA had long been a sensitive and controversial one for Canadians. In its current pertinence the idea that there should be a formal agreement between Canada and the USA had received authoritative endorsement from the Macdonald Commission (the Royal Commission on the Economic Union and Development Prospects for Canada) when it reported in July 1985. Its proposals in this regard were accepted and adopted as a policy aim of the Mulroney government shortly afterwards. (That Donald Macdonald had been a former Liberal minister, while this proposal was adopted by a Progressive Conservative government, showed that attitudes had not polarized along conventional party lines.)

Many Canadians believed that a formal agreement to closer economic relations with the USA would undermine Canada's independence. Advocates of the pact pointed out, however, that already the overwhelming proportion of Canada's trade was with the USA, that about 70% of it was free of duty, and that these factors had not actually impaired Canada's ability to formulate its own policies or to play a distinctive role in world affairs. On three previous occasions, however—in 1891, 1911 and 1948—Canada had rejected proposals for a free-trade treaty with the USA.

Canada's 1988 general-election campaign was dominated by the issue of the free-trade pact, which was widely and keenly debated by the Canadian public. The Mulroney government stressed that the conditions of world trade were changing rapidly and emphasized the need to develop a greater degree of competitiveness in Canada's economy. It claimed that enhanced dealing with US industry and services would stimulate Canadians to prepare for intensifying competition from overseas—especially from the European Communities, as they moved rapidly towards their announced goal of creating a single internal market by 1992, and from the rapid growth economies of the Pacific rim countries. The two main opposition parties, the Liberals and the New Democratic Party (NDP) (then led by John Turner and Ed Broadbent respectively, although both men were to resign following their electoral defeats) laid stress on the dangers which a free-trade pact with the USA would signify for Canada's social and economic policies.

Opposition spokespersons maintained that the USA would assert that Canada's regional economic-support programmes were a form of subsidy and that under the jurisdiction of the free-trade agreement they would have to be phased out. (Subsidies had not been defined in the draft agreement, but had been left for further consideration.) It was alleged that the logic of the free-trade agreement would lead to a dilution of the country's progressive legislation in unemployment and health insurance, and other social and welfare measures. The opposition challenged the government's claims that it had negotiated more assured Canadian access to the US market, maintaining instead that thousands of jobs would be lost in Canada as a consequence of the free-trade agreement; criticism was also levied at the trade-dispute mechanism to be set up under the agreement. The opposition parties asserted that a better course would be for Canada to seek tariff reductions

within the framework of the Uruguay round of the GATT, by which route the country had won significant trading benefits in the past.

Following the Progressive Conservatives' electoral victory in November 1988, Mulroney promised the passage of the free-trade agreement through the Canadian parliament before the beginning of 1989. Accordingly, the newly-elected House of Commons approved the accord by 141 votes to 111 on 24 December, and on 30 December the Senate gave its assent on a voice vote. The agreement was thus enabled to enter into force on 1 January 1989, as originally envisaged.

Canada's Defence Policy in the 1980s . . . and 1990s?

At the heart of Canada's defence arrangements, certainly since the 1950s and in important senses at least since the Second World War, is the connection with the USA. In 1958 NORAD, the North American Air Defense Command, was set up following an exchange of diplomatic notes on the subject between Canada and the USA. It was the first time since Canada had ceased to be a colonial dependency of Britain that Canadian forces based in Canada would no longer be controlled by Canadian commanders alone. In 1968 the Trudeau government had inserted a BMD (Ballistic Missile Defences) restriction clause at the time of its renewal of NORAD. In 1981 aerospace as well as air defence provisions were added to NORAD. In 1986 the NORAD agreement was renewed for another five years, passing through the Canadian Parliament without controversy, though some Canadian commentators said that failure to renew NORAD might lead to adverse consequences for Canada in other fields, notably, for example, with regard to the US–Canadian Free-Trade Agreement. NORAD's continuance was not a controversial issue in Canada's 1988 general election. Indeed, when there is any exception to the prevailing Canadian quietude on NORAD, this tends to be about its terms, not its substance.

In June 1987 the Mulroney government had published a Defence White Paper, entitled *Challenge and Commitment: A Defence Policy for Canada*—this was the first such general review and attempted redefinition of the country's defence policy since 1971. This glossy 90-page review affirmed that Canadian defence policy, as it had evolved since the Second World War and inasmuch as it was based on NATO and close co-operation with the USA, was 'essentially sound' in strategic conception. But it was asserted that 'failure to provide modern equipment has undercut the credibility of the Canadian Forces, weakening Canada's contribution to deterrence and collective defence.' The Mulroney government therefore proposed to take a number of initiatives which, it claimed, would produce a significant and visible increase in the effectiveness of the Canadian Forces. Four matters specifically were singled out: the creation of a modern navy capable of operating in the Atlantic, the Pacific and the Arctic; a bolstered capacity for surveillance and defence of Canadian territory; the enlargement and revitalization of the Reserves; and a consolidation of Canada's land and air commitments in Europe on the central front, rather than the northern flank. Each of these stated priorities occasioned comment and some criticism within Canada.

Despite much active consideration of the question, the Canadian government took no decision in 1988 on whether to choose Britain or France as suppliers of nuclear-powered submarines, in a contract said to be worth about £4,000m. The British company Vickers Shipbuilding and Engineering Ltd was competing with the French government to supply up to 12 nuclear-powered submarines to patrol beneath the Arctic ice-pack. During the year opinion polls seemed to show that most Canadians believed that Canada, facing rapid changes in East–West relations and with a high spending deficit, neither needed nor could afford such a fleet. In late April 1989 the plan was finally dropped by the Mulroney government, quite explicitly on financial grounds. Funding for the submarines had never been fully integrated into the defence budget, being contingent on a cabinet decision each year. Opponents of the project, at home and abroad, had criticized it not only because of the costs involved but also because of general qualms about nuclear proliferation. The matter which the cancellation left unresolved goes to the heart of Canadian defence policy, since the submarines were to be the operational centrepieces of the 1987 White Paper's stress on a broader North American role for Canada's forces. It remained to be seen whether the logic of that paper can be sustained without them.

A report entitled *Defence Update* which was presented to the House of Commons by its Standing Committee on National Defence in March 1988 claimed that the White Paper of the previous year had 'established a blueprint and set the direction of defence policy into the next century'. The report also claimed that significant progress had been made in implementing the new programmes required to give Canada a modern and effective defence posture—though it was admitted that 'implementation has only just begun'. Canada has been pressed frequently by its NATO allies to increase its defence spending, as for many years it has ranked among the lowest contributors in terms of the percentage of gross national product (GNP) devoted to the military. Mulroney's cabinet nevertheless found great difficulty in translating their proclaimed policy into credible operational terms when it became fully aware of the potential costs. For example, estimates of the proposed nuclear-powered submarine fleet ranged from C $5,000m. to C $10,000m., depending on which submarine and which shore facilities were chosen, and how much training and equipment were included. It became increasingly clear that decisions would be governed, at least in part, by how much of the contract work suppliers would place in Canada.

Arguably, Canada has never seriously planned for war, not in peacetime and certainly not to defend the whole of Canada's land, sea and air space by itself. Indeed, the condition and capacity of Canada credibly to defend its whole realm by itself has always been problematical. This is why Canada today is a member of NATO and has symbiotically-close defence links with the USA.

CANADA'S ROLE IN PEACE-KEEPING

Ever since the Pearson era in Canadian foreign policy (notably from 1949 to 1956) Canada has been indelibly associated in many minds as a helpful fixer internationally and as an initiator or contributor to UN peace-keeping efforts, of which the most notable among many such ventures was the Emergency Force (UNEF) in Sinai from late 1956 onwards. (However, the country's roles in Kashmir, the Congo and Cyprus would also have to be taken into account in a full appraisal.) Canada participated in two new peace-keeping operations in 1988, and made clear that it was willing to play an active part in assisting Namibian independence by contributing to an appropriate UN force, if and when requested. This happened early in 1989, and Canada duly sent technicians to help the process of ending fighting in Namibia and to facilitate the emergence of Namibia into independence. In May 1988 five Canadian officers were sent to Afghanistan to observe Soviet troop withdrawals, and in August 1988 Canada provided about 500 military specialists to set up a communications link along the Iraq-Iran border. In

its June 1987 Defence White Paper the Mulroney government had said that, while each request for a Canadian contribution to international peace-keeping would have to be considered on its own merits, a decision would be based on the following criteria:

'Whether there is a clear and enforceable mandate; whether the principal antagonists agree to a ceasefire and to Canada's participation in the operation; whether the arrangements are in fact likely to serve the cause of peace and lead to a political settlement in the long term; whether the size and international composition of the force are appropriate to the mandate and will not damage Canada's relations with other states; whether Canadian participation will jeopardize other commitments; whether there is a single identifiable authority competent to support the operation and influence the disputants, and whether participation is adequately and equitably funded and logistically supported.' (*Challenge and Commitment: A Defence Policy for Canada*. Ottawa, Department of National Defence, June 1987.)

Furthermore, Canada's continuing commitments to international peace-keeping are routinely revised according to these criteria. Up to 2,000 trained Canadian personnel can be called on for peace-keeping duties at any one time. Current deployments overseas, as well as stand-by elements in Canada, are counted within this allocation.

Retrospect and Prospect

Canada will have entered the 1990s as a country with a well-earned reputation for constructive internationalism, practised in the arts of being a middle power and committed to the continuance of its membership of NATO, but notably, and recurrently, reluctant to spend much of its GNP on its own national defences, particularly at times when the federal government is burdened with a considerable national debt. Above all, Canada's North American geography compels an attention to the multifarious nature of its American connections, of which the US–Canadian Free-Trade Agreement, concluded in 1988, has a most important and no doubt a most complex legal expression whose practical implications will be discovered, debated and experienced by Canadians for a long time to come. Thus, Canada's geography proves to be more compelling than its history, remote and recent, even though its connections with Britain and France—not least as filtered through the Commonwealth and la Francophonie—underline the point, often evident in its diplomacy, that Canada is an Arctic-, Atlantic- and Pacific-facing power, actively interested in virtually all and affected by most of the vicissitudes of contemporary world affairs. Federal–provincial relations within Canada also have foreign-policy implications and dimensions. It is appropriate, and perhaps should not be at all surprising, that it was a Canadian, the late Marshall McLuhan, who invented the telling phrase that all humanity nowadays lives in a single 'global village'.

SELECT BIBLIOGRAPHY

Byers, R. B. 'Canadian Security and Defence: The Legacy and the Challenges' in *Adelphi Papers*, No 214. London, International Institute for Strategic Studies, 1986.

Canadian Institute of International Affairs (CIIA). *Behind the Headlines* series. Toronto, CIIA.

  Canada in World Affairs, Vols 1-14. Toronto, CIIA.

  International Journal. Toronto, CIIA.

Clarkson, S. *Canada and the Reagan Challenge: Crisis and Adjustment 1981-85*. Toronto, James Lorimer & Co Ltd, 1985.

Department of External Affairs. *Documents on Canadian External Relations* (Vols I-XI). Ottawa, 1967-89.

  Synopsis of the Canada-US Free Trade Agreement. From the text initialled on 10 December 1987.

Department of National Defence. *Challenge and Commitment: A Defence Policy for Canada*. Ottawa, 1987.

Department of Supply and Services. *Report of a Royal Commission on the Economic Union and Development Prospects for Canada* (3 vols). Chairman: Macdonald, Donald S. Ottawa, 1985.

  Defence Update 1988-89. Presented to the House of Commons by the Standing Committee on National Defence.

Eayrs, J. *The Art of the Possible: Government and Foreign Policy in Canada*. Toronto, University of Toronto Press, 1961.

  In Defence of Canada (Vols I-V). Toronto, University of Toronto Press, 1964-83.

Farrell, R. B. *The Making of Canadian Foreign Policy*. Scarborough, Ontario, Prentice-Hall Canada Inc, 1969.

Glazebrook, G. P. de T. *A History of Canadian External Relations*. Don Mills, Ontario, Oxford University Press/CIIA, 1950.

Granatstein, J. L. *Canadian Foreign Policy: Historical Readings*. Mississauga, Ontario, Copp Clark Pitman Ltd, 1986.

Holmes, J. W. *Canada: A Middle-Aged Power* (Carleton Library, No 98). Toronto, McClelland & Stewart, 1976.

  The Shaping of Peace: Canada and the Search for World Order, 1943-57. Toronto, University of Toronto Press, 1979.

Jockel, J. T. *No Boundaries Upstairs: Canada, the United States and the Origins of North American Air Defence 1945-1958*. Vancouver, University of British Columbia Press, 1987.

Nossal, K. R. *The Politics of Canadian Foreign Policy*. Scarborough, Ontario, Prentice-Hall Canada Inc, 1984.

Regehr, E. *Arms Canada: The Deadly Business of Military Exports*. Toronto, James Lorimer & Co Ltd, 1987.

Reid, E. *Time of Fear and Hope: The Making of the North Atlantic Treaty 1947-1949*. Toronto, McClelland & Stewart, 1977.

Robinson, H. B. *Diefenbaker's World: A Populist in Foreign Affairs*. London, University of Toronto Press, 1989.

Sanger, C. (Ed.). *Canadians and the United Nations*. Ottawa, Canadian Government Publishing Centre, 1988.

Stacey, C. P. *Canada and the Age of Conflict: History of Canadian External Politics* Vol. I, 'The Years to 1921'. Toronto, University of Toronto Press, 1984.

  Vol. II, 'The Mackenzie King Era 1921-48'. Toronto, University of Toronto Press, 1981.

Stairs, D. 'The Foreign Policy of Canada' in *Foreign Policy in a World of Change*. London, Harper & Row Ltd, 1963.

Statistics Canada. *Historical Statistics of Canada* (Eds: Urquhart, M. C. and Buckley, K. A. H.). Ottawa, Canadian Government Publishing Centre, 1965.

Stone, F. *Canada, the GATT and the International Trade System*. Montréal, Institute for Research on Public Policy, 1984.

Thordarson, B. *Trudeau and Foreign Policy*. Toronto, Oxford University Press, 1972.

Tomlin, B. W. and Molot, M. (Eds). *Canada Among Nations* (4 vols). Toronto, James Lorimer & Co Ltd for the Norman Paterson School of International Affairs, Carleton University, 1985-88.

Tucker, M. *Canadian Foreign Policy: Contemporary Issues and Themes*. Toronto, McGraw-Hill Ryerson Ltd, 1979.

Whalley, J. (Research Co-ordinator). *Canada-United States Free Trade*. Toronto, University of Toronto Press/Royal Commission on the Economic Union and Development Prospects for Canada, 1985.

Winham, G. R. *Trading with Canada: The Canada-US Free Trade Agreement—a Twentieth-Century Fund Paper*. New York, Priority Press Publications, 1988.

PUBLIC AFFAIRS

GOVERNMENT

THE CANADA ACT 1982

An Act to give effect to a request by the Senate and House of Commons of Canada. (29th March 1982)

Whereas Canada has requested and consented to the enactment of an Act of the Parliament of the United Kingdom to give effect to the provisions hereinafter set forth and the Senate and the House of Commons of Canada in Parliament assembled have submitted an address to Her Majesty requesting that Her Majesty may graciously be pleased to cause a bill to be laid before the Parliament of the United Kingdom for that purpose:

Be it therefore enacted by the Queen's Most Excellent Majesty, by and with the advice and consent of the Lords Spiritual and Temporal, and Commons, in this present Parliament assembled, and by the authority of the same, as follows:

1. The Constitution Act, 1982 set out in Schedule B to this Act is hereby enacted for and shall have the force of law in Canada and shall come into force as provided in that Act.

2. No Act of Parliament of the United Kingdom passed after the Constitution Act, 1982 comes into force shall extend to Canada as part of its law.

3. So far as it is not contained in Schedule B, the French version of this Act is set out in Schedule A to this Act and has the same authority in Canada as the English version thereof.

4. This Act may be cited as the Canada Act 1982.

Schedule B

The Constitution Act, 1982

PART I. CANADIAN CHARTER OF RIGHTS AND FREEDOMS

Whereas Canada is founded upon principles that recognize the supremacy of God and the rule of law:

Guarantee of Rights and Freedoms

1. The *Canadian Charter of Rights and Freedoms* guarantees the rights and freedoms set out in it subject only to such reasonable limits prescribed by law as can be demonstrably justified in a free and democratic society.

Fundamental Freedoms

2. Everyone has the following fundamental freedoms:
    (a) freedom of conscience and religion;
    (b) freedom of thought, belief, opinion and expression, including freedom of the press and other media of communication;
    (c) freedom of peaceful assembly; and
    (d) freedom of association.

Democratic Rights

3. Every citizen of Canada has the right to vote in an election of members of the House of Commons or of a legislative assembly and to be qualified for membership therein.

4. (1) No House of Commons and no legislative assembly shall continue for longer than five years from the date fixed for the return of the writs of a general election of its members.

    (2) In time of real or apprehended war, invasion or insurrection, a House of Commons may be continued by Parliament and a legislative assembly may be continued by the legislature beyond five years if such continuation is not opposed by the votes of more than one-third of the members of the House of Commons or the legislative assembly, as the case may be.

5. There shall be a sitting of Parliament and of each legislature at least once every twelve months.

Mobility Rights

6. (1) Every citizen of Canada has the right to enter, remain in and leave Canada.

    (2) Every citizen of Canada and every person who has the status of a permanent resident of Canada has the right
    (a) to move to and take up residence in any province; and
    (b) to pursue the gaining of a livelihood in any province.

    (3) The rights specified in subsection (2) are subject to
    (a) any laws or practices of general application in force in a province other than those that discriminate among persons primarily on the basis of province of present or previous residence; and
    (b) any laws providing for reasonable residency requirements as a qualification for the receipt of publicly-provided social services.

    (4) Subsections (2) and (3) do not preclude any law, program or activity that has as its object the amelioration in a province of conditions of individuals in that province who are socially or economically disadvantaged if the rate of employment in that province is below the rate of employment in Canada.

Legal Rights

7. Everyone has the right to life, liberty and security of the person and the right not to be deprived thereof except in accordance with the principles of fundamental justice.

8. Everyone has the right to be secure against unreasonable search or seizure.

9. Everyone has the right not to be arbitrarily detained or imprisoned.

10. Everyone has the right on arrest or detention
    (a) to be informed promptly of the reasons therefor;
    (b) to retain and instruct counsel without delay and to be informed of that right; and
    (c) to have the validity of the detention determined by way of *habeas corpus* and to be released if the detention is not lawful.

11. Any person charged with an offence has the right
    (a) to be informed without unreasonable delay of the specific offence;
    (b) to be tried within a reasonable time;
    (c) not to be compelled to be a witness in proceedings against that person in respect of the offence;
    (d) to be presumed innocent until proven guilty according to law in a fair and public hearing by an independent and impartial tribunal;
    (e) not to be denied reasonable bail without just cause;
    (f) except in the case of an offence under military law tried before a military tribunal, to the benefit of trial by jury where the maximum punishment for the offence is imprisonment for five years or a more severe punishment;
    (g) not to be found guilty on account of any act or omission unless, at the time of the act or omission, it constituted an offence under Canadian or international law or was criminal according to the general principles of law recognized by the community of nations;
    (h) if finally acquitted of the offence, not to be tried for it again and, if finally found guilty and punished for the offence, not to be tried or punished for it again; and
    (i) if found guilty of the offence and if the punishment for the offence has been varied between the time of commission and the time of sentencing, to the benefit of the lesser punishment.

12. Everyone has the right not to be subjected to any cruel and unusual treatment or punishment.

13. A witness who testifies in any proceedings has the right not to have any incriminating evidence so given used to incriminate that witness in any other proceedings, except in a prosecution for perjury or for the giving of contradictory evidence.

14. A party or witness in any proceedings who does not understand or speak the language in which the proceedings are conducted or who is deaf has the right to the assistance of an interpreter.

Equality Rights

15. (1) Every individual is equal before and under the law and has the right to the equal protection and equal benefit of the law without discrimination and, in particular, without discrimination based on race, national or ethnic origin, colour, religion, sex, age or mental or physical disability.

(2) Subsection (1) does not preclude any law, program or activity that has as its object the amelioration of conditions of disadvantaged individuals or groups including those that are disadvantaged because of race, national or ethnic origin, colour, religion, sex, age or mental or physical disability.

Official Languages of Canada

16. (1) English and French are the official languages of Canada and have equality of status and equal rights and privileges as to their use in all institutions of the Parliament and government of Canada.

(2) English and French are the official languages of New Brunswick and have equality of status and equal rights and privileges as to their use in all institutions of the legislature and government of New Brunswick.

(3) Nothing in this Charter limits the authority of Parliament or a legislature to advance the equality of status or use of English and French.

17. (1) Everyone has the right to use English or French in any debates and other proceedings of Parliament.

(2) Everyone has the right to use English or French in any debates and other proceedings of the legislature of New Brunswick.

18. (1) The statutes, records and journals of Parliament shall be printed and published in English and French and both language versions are equally authoritative.

(2) The statutes, records and journals of the legislature of New Brunswick shall be printed and published in English and French and both language versions are equally authoritative.

19. (1) Either English or French may be used by any person in, or in any pleading in or process issuing from, any court established by Parliament.

(2) Either English or French may be used by any person in, or in any pleading in or process issuing from, any court of New Brunswick.

20. (1) Any member of the public in Canada has the right to communicate with, and to receive available services from, any head or central office of an institution of the Parliament or government of Canada in English or French, and has the same right with respect to any other office of any such institution where

(a) there is a significant demand for communications with and services from that office in such language; or

(b) due to the nature of the office, it is reasonable that communications with and services from that office be available in both English and French.

(2) Any member of the public in New Brunswick has the right to communicate with, and to receive available services from, any office of an institution of the legislature or government of New Brunswick in English or French.

21. Nothing in sections 16 to 20 abrogates or derogates from any right, privilege or obligation with respect to the English and French languages, or either of them, that exists or is continued by virtue of any other provision of the Constitution of Canada.

22. Nothing in sections 16 to 20 abrogates or derogates from any legal or customary right or privilege acquired or enjoyed either before or after the coming into force of this Charter with respect to any language that is not English or French.

Minority Language Educational Rights

23. (1) Citizens of Canada

(a) whose first language learned and still understood is that of the English or French linguistic minority population of the province in which they reside, or

(b) who have received their primary school instruction in Canada in English or French and reside in a province where the language in which they received that instruction is the language of the English or French linguistic minority population of the province, have the right to have their children receive primary and secondary school instruction in that language in that province.

(2) Citizens of Canada of whom any child has received or is receiving primary or secondary school instruction in English or French in Canada, have the right to have all their children receive primary and secondary school instruction in the same language.

(3) The right of citizens of Canada under subsections (1) and (2) to have their children receive primary and secondary school instruction in the language of the English or French linguistic minority population of a province

(a) applies wherever in the province the number of children of citizens who have such a right is sufficient to warrant the provision to them out of public funds of minority language instruction; and

(b) includes, where the number of those children so warrants, the right to have them receive that instruction in minority language educational facilities provided out of public funds.

Enforcement

24. (1) Anyone whose rights or freedoms, as guaranteed by this Charter, have been infringed or denied may apply to a court of competent jurisdiction to obtain such remedy as the court considers appropriate and just in the circumstances.

(2) Where, in proceedings under subsection (1), a court concludes that evidence was obtained in a manner that infringed or denied any rights or freedoms guaranteed by this Charter, the evidence shall be excluded if it is established that, having regard to all the circumstances, the admission of it in the proceedings would bring the administration of justice into disrepute.

General

25. The guarantee of this Charter of certain rights and freedoms shall not be construed so as to abrogate or derogate from any aboriginal treaty or other rights or freedoms that pertain to the aboriginal peoples of Canada including

(a) any rights or freedoms that have been recognized by the Royal Proclamation of October 7, 1763; and

(b) any rights or freedoms that may be acquired by the aboriginal peoples of Canada by way of land claims settlement.

26. The guarantee in this Charter of certain rights and freedoms shall not be construed as denying the existence of any other rights or freedoms that exist in Canada.

27. This Charter shall be interpreted in a manner consistent with the preservation and enhancement of the multicultural heritage of Canadians.

28. Notwithstanding anything in this Charter, the rights and freedoms referred to in it are guaranteed equally to male and female persons.

29. Nothing in this Charter abrogates or derogates from any rights or privileges guaranteed by or under the Constitution of Canada in respect of denominational, separate or dissentient schools.

30. A reference in this Charter to a province or to the legislative assembly or legislature of a province shall be deemed to include a reference to the Yukon Territory and the Northwest Territories, or the appropriate legislative authority thereof, as the case may be.

31. Nothing in this Charter extends the legislative powers of any body or authority.

Application of Charter

32. (1) This Charter applies

(a) to the Parliament and government of Canada in respect of all matters within the authority of Parliament including all matters relating to the Yukon Territory and Northwest Territories; and

(b) to the legislature and government of each province in respect of all matters within the authority of the legislature of each province.

(2) Notwithstanding subsection (1), section 15 shall not have effect until three years after this section comes into force.

33. (1) Parliament or the legislature of a province may expressly declare in an Act of Parliament or of the legislature, as the case may be, that the Act or a provision thereof shall operate notwithstanding a provision included in section 2 or sections 7 to 15 of this Charter.

(2) An Act or a provision of an Act in respect of which a declaration made under this section is in effect shall have such operation as it would have but for the provision of this Charter referred to in the declaration.

(3) A declaration made under subsection (1) shall cease to have effect five years after it comes into force or on such earlier date as may be specified in the declaration.

(4) Parliament or the legislature of a province may re-enact a declaration made under subsection (1).

(5) Subsection (3) applies in respect of a re-enactment made under subsection (4).

Citation

34. This Part may be cited as the *Canadian Charter of Rights and Freedoms*.

CANADA

Public Affairs

PART II. RIGHTS OF THE ABORIGINAL PEOPLES OF CANADA

35. (1) The existing aboriginal and treaty rights of the aboriginal peoples of Canada are hereby recognized and affirmed.

(2) In this Act, 'aboriginal peoples of Canada' includes the Indian, Inuit and Métis peoples of Canada.

PART III. EQUALIZATION AND REGIONAL DISPARITIES

36. (1) Without altering the legislative authority of Parliament or of the provincial legislatures, or the rights of any of them with respect to the exercise of their legislative authority, Parliament and the legislatures, together with the government of Canada and the provincial governments, are committed to

(a) promoting equal opportunities for the well-being of Canadians;

(b) furthering economic development to reduce disparity in opportunities; and

(c) providing essential public services of reasonable quality to all Canadians.

(2) Parliament and the government of Canada are committed to the principle of making equalization payments to ensure that provincial governments have sufficient revenues to provide reasonably comparable levels of public services at reasonably comparable levels of taxation.

PART IV. CONSTITUTIONAL CONFERENCE

37. (1) A constitutional conference composed of the Prime Minister of Canada and the first ministers of the provinces shall be convened by the Prime Minister of Canada within one year after this Part comes into force.

(2) The conference convened under subsection (1) shall have included in its agenda an item respecting constitutional matters that directly affect the aboriginal peoples of Canada, including the identification and definition of the rights of those peoples to be included in the Constitution of Canada, and the Prime Minister of Canada shall invite representatives of those peoples to participate in the discussions on that item.

(3) The Prime Minister of Canada shall invite elected representatives of the governments of the Yukon Territory and the Northwest Territories to participate in the discussions on any item on the agenda of the conference convened under subsection (1) that, in the opinion of the Prime Minister, directly affects the Yukon Territory and the Northwest Territories.

PART V. PROCEDURE FOR AMENDING CONSTITUTION OF CANADA

38. (1) An amendment to the Constitution of Canada may be made by proclamation issued by the Governor-General under the Great Seal of Canada where so authorized by

(a) resolutions of the Senate and House of Commons; and

(b) resolutions of the legislative assemblies of at least two-thirds of the provinces that have, in the aggregate, according to the then latest general census, at least fifty per cent of the population of all the provinces.

(2) An amendment made under subsection (1) that derogates from the legislative powers, the proprietary rights or any other rights or privileges of the legislature or government of a province shall require a resolution supported by a majority of the members of each of the Senate, the House of Commons and the legislative assemblies required under subsection (1).

(3) An amendment referred to in subsection (2) shall not have effect in a province the legislative assembly of which has expressed its dissent thereto by resolution supported by a majority of its members prior to the issue of the proclamation to which the amendment relates unless that legislative assembly, subsequently, by resolution supported by a majority of its members, revokes its dissent and authorizes the amendment.

(4) A resolution of dissent made for the purposes of subsection (3) may be revoked at any time before or after the issue of the proclamation to which it relates.

39. (1) A proclamation shall not be issued under subsection 38 (1) before the expiration of one year from the adoption of the resolution initiating the amendment procedure thereunder, unless the legislative assembly of each province has previously adopted a resolution of assent or dissent.

(2) A proclamation shall not be issued under subsection 38 (1) after the expiration of three years from the adoption of the resolution initiating the amendment procedure thereunder.

40. Where an amendment is made under subsection 38 (1) that transfers provincial legislative powers relating to education or other cultural matters from provincial legislatures to Parliament, Canada shall provide reaasonable compensation to any province to which the amendment does not apply.

41. An amendment to the Constitution of Canada in relation to the following matters may be made by proclamation issued by the Governor-General under the Great Seal of Canada only where authorized by resolutions of the Senate and House of Commons and of the legislative assembly of each province:

(a) the office of the Queen, the Governor-General and the Lieutenant-Governor of a province;

(b) the right of a province to a number of members in the House of Commons not less than the number of Senators by which the province is entitled to be represented at the time this Part comes into force;

(c) subject to section 43, the use of the English or the French language;

(d) the composition of the Supreme Court of Canada; and

(e) an amendment to this Part.

42. (1) An amendment to the Constitution of Canada in relation to the following matters may be made only in accordance with subsection 38 (1):

(a) the principle of proportionate representation of the provinces in the House of Commons prescribed by the Constitution of Canada;

(b) the powers of the Senate and the method of selecting Senators;

(c) the number of members by which a province is entitled to be represented in the Senate and the residence qualifications of Senators;

(d) subject to paragraph 41 (d), the Supreme Court of Canada;

(e) the extension of existing provinces into the territories; and

(f) notwithstanding any other law or practice, the establishment of new provinces.

(2) Subsections 38 (2) to (4) do not apply in respect of amendments in relation to matters referred to in subsection (1).

43. An amendment to the Constitution of Canada in relation to any provision that applies to one or more, but not all, provinces, including

(a) any alteration to boundaries between provinces, and

(b) any amendment to any provision that relates to the use of the English or the French language within a province, may be made by proclamation issued by the Governor-General under the Great Seal of Canada only where so authorized by resolution of the Senate and the House of Commons and of the legislative assembly of each province to which the amendment applies.

44. Subject to sections 41 and 42, Parliament may exclusively make laws amending the Constitution of Canada in relation to the executive government of Canada or the Senate and House of Commons.

45. Subject to section 41, the legislature of each province may exclusively make laws amending the constitution of the province.

46. (1) The procedures for amendment under sections 38, 41, 42 and 43 may be initiated either by the Senate or the House of Commons or by the legislative assembly of a province.

(2) A resolution of assent made for the purposes of this Part may be revoked at any time before the issue of a proclamation authorized by it.

47. (1) An amendment to the Constitution of Canada made by proclamation under section 38, 41, 42 or 43 may be made without a resolution of the Senate authorizing the issue of the proclamation if, within one hundred and eighty days after the adoption by the House of Commons of a resolution authorizing its issue, the Senate has not adopted such a resolution and if, at any time after the expiration of that period, the House of Commons again adopts the resolution.

(2) Any period when Parliament is prorogued or dissolved shall not be counted in computing the one hundred and eighty day period referred to in subsection (1).

48. The Queen's Privy Council for Canada shall advise the Governor-General to issue a proclamation under this Part forthwith on the adoption of the resolutions required for an amendment made by proclamation under this Part.

49. A constitutional conference composed of the Prime Minister of Canada and the first ministers of the provinces shall be convened by the Prime Minister of Canada within fifteen years after this Part comes into force to review the provisions of this Part.

PART VI. AMENDMENT TO THE CONSTITUTION ACT, 1867

50. The *Constitution Act, 1867* (formerly named the *British North America Act, 1867*) is amended by adding thereto, immediately after section 92 thereof, the following heading and section:

'Non-Renewable Natural Resources, Forestry Resources and Electrical Energy

92A. (1) In each province, the legislature may exclusively make laws in relation to

405

(a) exploration for non-renewable natural resources in the province;

(b) development, conservation and management of non-renewable natural resources and forestry resources in the province, including laws in relation to the rate of primary production therefrom; and

(c) development, conservation and management of sites and facilities in the province for the generation and production of electrical energy.

(2) In each province, the legislature may make laws in relation to the export from the province to another part of Canada of the primary production from non-renewable natural resources and forestry resources in the province and the production from facilities in the province for the generation of electrical energy, but such laws may not authorize or provide for discrimination in prices or in supplies exported to another part of Canada.

(3) Nothing in subsection (2) derogates from the authority of Parliament to enact laws in relation to the matters referred to in that subsection and, where such a law of a Parliament and a law of a province conflict, the law of Parliament prevails to the extent of the conflict.

(4) In each province, the legislature may make laws in relation to the raising of money by any mode or system of taxation in respect of

(a) non-renewable natural resources and forestry resources in the province and the primary production therefrom, and

(b) sites and facilities in the province for the generation of electrical energy and the production therefrom, whether or not such production is exported in whole or in part from the province, but such laws may not authorize or provide for taxation that differentiates between production exported to another part of Canada and production not exported from the province.

(5) The expression "primary production" has the meaning assigned by the Sixth Schedule.

(6) Nothing in subsections (1) to (5) derogates from any powers or rights that a legislature or government of a province had immediately before the coming into force of this section.'

51. The said Act is further amended by adding thereto the following Schedule:

THE SIXTH SCHEDULE

Primary Production from Non-Renewable Natural Resources and Forestry Resources

1. For the purposes of section 92A of this Act,

(a) production from a non-renewable natural resource is primary production therefrom if

(i) it is in the form in which it exists upon its recovery or severance from its natural state, or

(ii) it is a product resulting from processing or refining the resource, and is not a manufactured product or a product resulting from refining crude oil, refining upgraded heavy crude oil, refining gases or liquids derived from coal or refining a synthetic equivalent of crude oil; and

(b) production from a forestry resource is primary production therefrom if it consists of sawlogs, poles, lumber, wood chips, sawdust or any other primary wood product, or wood pulp, and is not a product manufactured from wood.

PART VII. GENERAL

52. (1) The Constitution of Canada is the supreme law of Canada, and any law that is inconsistent with the provisions of the Constitution is, to the extent of the inconsistency, of no force or effect.

(2) The Constitution of Canada includes

(a) the *Canada Act 1982*, including this Act;

(b) the Acts and orders referred to in this schedule; and

(c) any amendment to any Act or order referred to in paragraph (a) or (b).

(3) Amendments to the Constitution of Canada shall be made only in accordance with the authority contained in the Constitution of Canada.

53. (1) The enactments referred to in Column I of the schedule are hereby repealed or amended to the extent indicated in Column II thereof and, unless repealed, shall continue as law in Canada under the names set out in Column III thereof.

(2) Every enactment, except the *Canada Act 1982*, that refers to an enactment referred to in the schedule by the name in Column I thereof is hereby amended by substituting for that name the corresponding name in Column III thereof, and any British North America Act not referred to in the schedule may be cited as the *Constitution Act* followed by the year and number, if any, of its enactment.

54. Part IV is repealed on the day that is one year after this Part comes into force and this section may be repealed and this Act renumbered, consequentially upon the repeal of Part IV and this section, by proclamation issued by the Governor-General under the Great Seal of Canada.

55. A French version of the portions of the Constitution of Canada referred to in the schedule shall be prepared by the Minister of Justice of Canada as expeditiously as possible and, when any portion thereof sufficient to warrant action being taken has been so prepared, it shall be put forward for enactment by proclamation issued by the Governor-General under the Great Seal of Canada pursuant to the procedure then applicable to an amendment of the same provisions of the Constitution of Canada.

56. Where any portion of the Constitution of Canada has been or is enacted in English and French or where a French version of any portion of the Constitution is enacted pursuant to section 55, the English and French versions of that portion of the Constitution are equally authoritative.

57. The English and French versions of this Act are equally authoritative.

58. Subject to section 59, this Act shall come into force on a day to be fixed by proclamation issued by the Queen or the Governor-General under the Great Seal of Canada.

59. (1) Paragraph 23 (1)(a) shall come into force in respect of Québec on a day to be fixed by proclamation issued by the Queen or the Governor-General under the Great Seal of Canada.

(2) A proclamation under subsection (1) shall be issued only where authorized by the legislative assembly or government of Québec.

(3) This section may be repealed on the day paragraph 23 (1)(a) comes into force in respect of Québec and this Act amended and renumbered, consequentially upon the repeal of this section, by proclamation issued by the Queen or the Governor-General under the Great Seal of Canada.

60. This Act may be cited as the *Constitution Act, 1982*, and the Constitution Acts 1867 to 1975 (No 2) and this Act may be cited together as the *Constitution Acts, 1867 to 1982*.

GOVERNMENT OF CANADA

Head of State and Governor-General

Head of State: HM Queen ELIZABETH II.

Governor-General: (until January 1990): JEANNE SAUVÉ (took office 14 May 1984).

Governor-General (from January 1990): RAY HNATYSHYN.

Federal Ministry
(September 1989)

Prime Minister: M. BRIAN MULRONEY.

Secretary of State for External Affairs: JOE CLARK.

Minister of International Trade: JOHN CROSBIE.

Deputy Prime Minister, President of the Queen's Privy Council for Canada and Minister of Agriculture: DON MAZANKOWSKI.

Minister of Public Works, Minister responsible for the Atlantic Canada Opportunities Agency: ELMER M. MACKAY.

Minister of Energy, Mines and Resources: JAKE EPP.

President of the Treasury Board: ROBERT DE COTRET.

Minister of National Health and Welfare: H. PERRIN BEATTY.

Minister of Finance: MICHAEL WILSON.

Minister of Regional Industrial Expansion and Minister of State for Science and Technology: HARVIE ANDRÉ.

Minister of National Revenue: OTTO JELINEK.

Minister of Fisheries and Oceans: TOM SIDDON.

Minister of Western Economic Diversification and Minister of State for Grains and Oilseeds: CHARLES MAYER.

Minister of National Defence: BILL MCKNIGHT.

Minister of Transport: BENOÎT BOUCHARD.

Minister of Communications: MARCEL MASSE.

Minister of Employment and Immigration: BARBARA MCDOUGALL.

Secretary of State for Canada and Minister of State for Multi-culturalism and Citizenship: GERRY WEINER.

Minister of Justice and Attorney-General, and Government Leader in the House of Commons: DOUG LEWIS.

Minister of the Environment: LUCIEN BOUCHARD.

Minister of Labour: JEAN CORBEIL.

Minister of Veterans' Affairs: GERALD MERRITHEW.

Minister of Supply and Services: PAUL DICK.

Minister of Indian Affairs and Northern Development: PIERRE CADIEUX.

Minister of External Relations: MONIQUE LANDRY.

Minister of Consumer and Corporate Affairs: HARVIE ANDRÉ (acting).

Solicitor-General and Minister of State for Agriculture: PIERRE BLAIS.

Minister of State for Employment and Immigration, and Minister of State for Senior Citizens: MONIQUE VÉZINA.

Minister of State for Forestry: FRANK OBERLE.

Government Leader in the Senate and Minister of State for Federal–Provincial Relations: LOWELL MURRAY.

Minister of State for Youth, Minister of State for Fitness and Amateur Sport and Deputy Government Leader in the House of Commons: JEAN CHAREST.

Minister of State for Small Business and Tourism: TOM HOCKIN.

Minister of State for Privatization and Regulatory Affairs: JOHN MCDERMID.

Minister of State for Transport: SHIRLEY MARTIN.

Associate Minister of National Defence: MARY COLLINS.

Minister of State for Housing: ALAN REDWAY.

Minister of State for Science and Technology: WILLIAM WINEGARD.

Minister of State for Indian Affairs and Northern Development: KIM CAMPBELL.

Minister of State for Finance: GILLES LOISELLE.

Ministries

Office of the Prime Minister: Langevin Block, Parliament Bldgs, Ottawa, ON K1A 0A2; tel. (613) 992-4211; telex 053-3208; fax (613) 995-0101.

Agriculture Canada: Sir John Carling Bldg, 930 Carling Ave, Ottawa, ON K1A 0C5; tel. (613) 995-5222; telex 053-3283; fax (613) 996-9564.

Department of Communications: Journal Tower North, 300 Slater St, Ottawa, ON K1A 0C8; tel. (613) 990-6886; telex 053-3342; fax (613) 952-2429.

Department of Consumer and Corporate Affairs: Pl. du Portage, Ottawa-Hull, ON K1A 0C9; tel. (819) 997-2938; telex 053-3694; fax (819) 997-2721.

Department of Energy, Mines and Resources: 580 Booth St, Ottawa, ON K1A 0E4; tel. (613) 995-3065; telex 053-3117; fax (613) 996-9094.

Department of External Affairs: Lester B. Pearson Bldg, 125 Sussex Dr., Ottawa, ON K1A 0G2; tel. (613) 995-1851; telex 053-3745; fax (613) 996-9288.

Department of Finance: Esplanade Laurier, 140 O'Connor St, Ottawa, ON K1A 0G5; tel. (613) 992-1575; telex 053-3336.

Department of Fisheries and Oceans: 200 Kent St, Ottawa, ON K1A 0E6; tel. (613) 993-0600; telex 053-4228.

Department of Indian Affairs and Northern Development: Les Terrasses de la Chaudière, 10 Wellington St, Ottawa, ON K1A 0H4; tel. (613) 995-5586; telex 053-3711; fax (613) 997-1587.

Department of Industry, Science and Technology: 235 Queen St, Ottawa, ON K1A 0H5; tel. (613) 992-4292; telex 053-4396; fax (613) 952-9073.

Department of Justice: Justice Bldg, Kent and Wellington Sts, Ottawa, ON K1A 0H8; tel. (613) 957-4222; telex 053-3603; fax (613) 954-0811.

Department of National Defence: 101 Colonel By Dr., Ottawa, ON K1A 0K2; tel. (613) 996-4450; telex 053-4218.

Department of National Health and Welfare: Brooke Claxton Bldg, Tunney's Pasture, Ottawa, ON K1A 0K9; tel. (613) 957-2991; telex 053-3270.

Department of Public Works: Sir Charles Tupper Bldg, Confederation Heights, Riverside Dr., Ottawa, ON K1A 0M2; tel. (613) 998-7724; telex 053-4235.

Department of Regional Industrial Expansion: 235 Queen St, Ottawa, ON K1A 0H5; tel. (613) 995-8900.

Department of the Secretary of State for Canada: Ottawa, ON K1A 0M5; tel. (819) 997-0055; fax (819) 953-5382.

Department of Supply and Services: 11 Laurier St, Ottawa-Hull, ON K1A 0S5; tel. (819) 956-2304; telex 053-3703; fax (819) 994-8404.

Department of Transport: Transport Canada Bldg, Pl. de Ville, 330 Sparks St, Ottawa, ON K1A 0N5; tel. (613) 990-2309; telex 053-3130; fax (613) 996-9622.

Department of Western Economic Diversification: Cornerpoint Bldg, Suite 604, 10179 105th St, Edmonton, AB T5J 3N1.

Employment and Immigration Canada: 140 promenade du Portage, Ottawa-Hull, ON K1A 0J9; tel. (819) 994-6013; telex 053-3511; fax (819) 994-0116.

Environment Canada: Les Terrasses de la Chaudière, 10 Wellington St, Ottawa, ON K1A 0H3; tel. (819) 997-2800; telex 053-3608; fax (819) 953-6789.

Labour Canada: Pl. du Portage, 165 Hôtel de Ville St, Ottawa-Hull, ON K1A 0J2; tel; (819) 997-2617; telex 053-3640; fax (819) 953-0176.

Ministry of the Solicitor-General: Sir Wilfrid Laurier Bldg, 340 Laurier Ave West, Ottawa, ON K1A 0P8; tel. (613) 991-2857; telex 053-3768; fax (613) 993-6116.

Department of Science and Technology: Ottawa, ON K1A 1A1; tel. (613) 990-6121; telex 053-4123.

Revenue Canada (Customs & Excise): Connaught Bldg, Mackenzie Ave, Ottawa, ON K1A 0L5; tel. (613) 995-0007; telex 053-3330.

Revenue Canada (Taxation): Headquarters Bldg, 875 Heron Rd, Ottawa, ON K1A 0L8; tel. (613) 995-2960; telex 053-4974.

Treasury Board of Canada: 140 O'Connor St, Ottawa, ON K1A 0R5; tel. (613) 996-2690; telex 053-3336; fax (613) 957-2400.

Department of Veterans' Affairs: POB 7700, Charlottetown, PE C1A 8M9; tel. (902) 566-8888; fax (902) 566-8508.

Selected Federal Government Agencies and Boards

Agricultural Stabilization Board/Agricultural Products Board: Sir John Carling Bldg, 930 Carling Ave, Ottawa, ON K1A 0C5; tel. (613) 995-5880; telex 053-3283; fax (613) 996-9014; provides support prices for selected agricultural commodities; Chair G. LAVOIE.

Atlantic Canada Opportunities Agency: POB 6051, Moncton, NB E1C 9J8; tel. (506) 857-6523; fax (506) 857-7403; Pres. DONALD MCPHAIL.

Atomic Energy Control Board: POB 1046, Ottawa, ON K1P 5S9; tel. (613) 992-9206; telex 053-3771; f. 1946; responsible for all nuclear-regulatory matters; Pres. R. J. A. LÉVESQUE; Sec. P. E. HAMEL.

The Canada Council: 99 Metcalfe St, POB 1047, Ottawa, ON K1P 5V8; tel. (613) 237-3400; telex 053-4573; fax (613) 598-4390; f. 1957; promotes and fosters the arts in Canada; Chair. ALLAN GOTLIEB; Dir PETER ROBERTS.

Canada Labour Relations Board: 240 Sparks St, 4th Floor West, Ottawa, ON K1A 0X8; tel. (613) 996-9466; telex 053-4426; fax (613) 995-9493; Chair. MARC LAPOINTE.

Canada Oil and Gas Lands Administration: Tower B, 15th Floor, 355 River Rd, Ottawa, ON K1A 0E4; tel. (613) 993-3760; regulatory agency responsible for activities associated with the exploration and production of energy and mineral resources in the frontier lands.

Canadian Advisory Council on the Status of Women: 110 O'Connor St, 9th Floor, POB 1541, Station B, Ottawa, ON K1P 5R5; tel. (613) 992-4975; f. 1973; Pres. SYLVIA GOLD.

Canadian Aviation Safety Board: Pl. du Portage, POB 9120, Alta Vista Terminal, Ottawa-Hull, ON K1G 3T8; tel. (819) 994-3741; f. 1984; independent body.

Canadian Dairy Commission: 2197 Riverside Dr., 6th Floor, Ottawa, ON K1A 0Z2; tel. (613) 998-9490; telex 053-3634; fax (613) 998-4492; administers national dairy policy; Chair. ROCH MORIN.

Canadian Forestry Service: Pl. Vincent Massey, 351 blvd St-Joseph, Ottawa-Hull, ON K1A 0C5; tel. (819) 997-1107; aims to promote the wise management, conservation and use of Canada's forest resources.

Canadian Grain Commission: 303 Main St, Suite 600, Winnipeg, MB R3C 3G8; tel. (204) 983-2770; telex 07-57451; fax (204) 983-2751; regulates grain handling in Canada and establishes and maintains quality standards for Canadian grains; Chief Commr G. G. LEITH.

Canadian Human-Rights Commission: 90 Sparks St, Suite 400, Ottawa, ON K1A 1E1; tel. (613) 995-1151.

Canadian International Development Agency: Pl. du Centre, 200 promenade du Portage, Ottawa-Hull, ON K1A 0G4; tel. (819) 997-5456; telex 053-4140; fax (819) 953-5469; Pres. MARGARET CATLEY-CARLSON.

Canadian Wheat Board: 423 Main St, Winnipeg, MB R3C 2P5; tel. (204) 983-0239; telex 07-57801; fax (204) 983-3841; sole marketing agency for western Canadian wheat, oat and barley exports and for domestic sales of those grains for human consumption; Chief Commr W. E. JARVIS.

Correctional Service of Canada: 340 Laurier Ave West, Ottawa, ON K1A 0P9; tel. (613) 993-7501; telex 053-4120; Commr OLE INGSTRUP.

Economic Council of Canada: Tower A, 16th Floor, 333 River Rd, POB 527, Ottawa, ON K1P 5V6; tel. (613) 993-1253; fax (613) 991-4904; f. 1963; independent advisory body; Corporate Sec. W. M. MAIDENS.

Elections Canada: 440 Coventry Rd, Ottawa, ON K1A 0M6; tel. (613) 993-2975; telex 053-4267; fax (613) 954-2874; Chief Electoral Officer JEAN-MARC HAMEL.

Emergency Preparedness Canada: Gillin Bldg, 2nd Floor, 141 Laurier Ave West, Ottawa, ON K1A 0W6; tel. (613) 992-9988; telex 053-4443; fax (613) 996-1901; responsible for co-ordinating planning for the federal response to peacetime emergencies; Exec. Dir W. B. SNARR.

Federal–Provincial Relations Office: 59 Sparks St, Station B, Ottawa, ON K1A 0A3; tel. (613) 957-5300; advisory body.

Fisheries Prices Support Board: Ottawa, ON K1A 0E6; tel. (613) 993-2031; telex 053-4228; fax (613) 996-9055; Chair. HAROLD COLLINS.

Fitness and Amateur Sport Canada: Journal Tower South, 365 Laurier Ave West, Ottawa, ON K1A 0X6; tel. (613) 996-4510.

Foreign Claims Commission: 125 Sussex Dr., POB 432, Ottawa, ON K1N 8V5; tel. (613) 996-9510; Chief Commr PETER HARGADAN.

Immigration and Refugee Board: Ottawa, ON K1A 0K1; tel. (613) 995-6486; fax (613) 952-9083; Chair. GORDON FAIRWEATHER.

Insurance Canada: Jackson Bldg, 122 Bank St, 7th Floor, Ottawa, ON K1A 0H2; tel. (613) 996-8587.

International Boundary Commission (Canadian Section): 615 Booth St, Ottawa, ON K1A 0E9; tel. (613) 995-4951; telex 053-4328; has jurisdiction over regulation and maintenance of the Canada–USA boundary; Commr (Canadian Section) ALEC C. McEWEN.

International Centre for Ocean Development: 5670 Spring Garden Rd, 9th Floor, Halifax, NS B3J 1H6; tel. (902) 426-1512; f. 1985; manages ocean resources.

International Joint Commission (Canadian Section): 100 Metcalfe St, 18th Floor, Ottawa, ON K1P 5M1; tel. (613) 995-2984; fax (613) 993-5583; has jurisdiction over questions arising between Canada and the USA concerning the use and regulation of waters forming or crossing the common boundary; Chair. (Canadian Section) P. A. BISSONETTE; Sec. DAVID G. CHANCE.

Investment Canada: POB 2800, Station D, Ottawa, ON K1P 6A5; tel. (613) 995-0465; fax (613) 996-2515; promotes and facilitates investment in Canada by Canadians and non-Canadians.

Law Reform Commission of Canada: Varette Bldg, 7th Floor, 130 Albert St, Ottawa, ON K1A 0L6; tel. (613) 996-7844; fax (613) 996-8599; Pres. ALLEN M. LINDEN.

Livestock Feed Board of Canada: POB 177, Snowdon Station, Montréal, PQ H3X 3T4; tel. (514) 283-7505; telex 055-67137; fax (514) 283-2754; Chair. DENIS ETHIER.

National Advisory Council on Aging: Jeanne Mance Bldg, Suite 1044, Tunney's Pasture, Ottawa, ON K1A 0K9; tel. (613) 957-1968; telex 053-3270; fax (613) 957-9869.

National Council of Welfare: Brooke Claxton Bldg, Rm 506, Tunney's Pasture, Ottawa, ON K1A 0K9; tel. (613) 957-2961; citizens' advisory body.

National Energy Board: 473 Albert St, Ottawa, ON K1A 0E5; tel. (613) 998-7204; telex 053-3791; fax (613) 990-7900; Chair. J. PRIDDLE; Sec. J. KLENAVIC.

National Farm Products Marketing Council: Martel Bldg, 13th Floor, 270 Albert St, POB 3430, Station D, Ottawa, ON K1P 6L4; tel. (613) 995-2297; advises the minister of agriculture on the establishment and operation of national agricultural marketing agencies.

National Research Council Canada: Montréal Rd, Ottawa, ON K1A 0R6; tel. (613) 993-9101; telex 053-3145; fax (613) 952-7928; carries out research and development in the natural sciences and engineering; Pres. Dr LARKIN KERWIN.

National Transportation Agency of Canada: Ottawa, ON K1A 0N9; tel. (819) 997-0677; telex 053-4254; fax (819) 997-6727; responsible for the economic regulation of transportation in Canada; Sec. SUZANNE CLEMENT.

Natural Sciences and Engineering Research Council: 200 Kent St, Ottawa, ON K1A 1H5; tel. (613) 995-6295; telex 053-4228; fax (613) 992-5337; Pres. ARTHUR W. MAY; Exec. Dir and Treas. GILLES JULIEN.

Northern Pipeline Agency Canada: Centennial Towers, 200 Kent St, Station 210, Ottawa, ON K1A 0E6; tel. (613) 993-7466; oversees the planning and construction of the Canadian portion of the Alaska Highway gas pipeline; Commr G. E. SHANNON.

Office of the Auditor-General of Canada: C. D. Howe Bldg, 240 Sparks St, Ottawa, ON K1A 0G6; tel. (613) 995-3766; fax (613) 952-2245; Auditor-Gen. KENNETH M. DYE.

Office of the Commissioner of Official Languages: 110 O'Connor St, Ottawa, ON K1A 0T8; tel. (613) 996-6368; fax (613) 993-5082; Commr D'IBERVILLE FORTIER.

Office of the Privacy Commissioner: Tower B, Pl. de Ville, 112 Kent St, Ottawa, ON K1A 1H3; tel. (613) 995-2410; investigates complaints from citizens and permanent residents who allege that the federal govt has failed to comply with the Privacy Act (covers rights to personal information); Privacy Commr JOHN W. GRACE.

Prairie Farm Rehabilitation Administration: 1901 Victoria Ave, Regina, SK S4P 0R5; tel. (306) 780-5070; telex 071-2541; fax (306) 780-5018; soil and water conservation and development, and land-use adjustment in the Prairie provinces of Alberta, Manitoba and Saskatchewan.

Public Service Commission: 300 Laurier Ave West, Ottawa, ON K1A 0M7; tel. (613) 996-5010; public-service staffing body; Commrs HUGUETTE LABELLE (Chair.), PETER B. LESAUX, GILBERT H. SCOTT.

Royal Canadian Mounted Police (RCMP): 1200 Alta Vista Dr., Ottawa, ON K1A 0R2; tel. (613) 993-9590; fax (613) 993-0216; f. 1873 as North-West Mounted Police, present name since 1920; Commr N. D. INKSTER.

St Lawrence Seaway Authority: 360 Albert St, Ottawa, ON K1R 7X7; tel. (613) 598-4600; telex 053-3322; fax (613) 598-4620; Pres. W. A. O'NEIL; Sec. V. C. DURANT.

Science Council of Canada: 100 Metcalfe St, Ottawa, ON K1P 5M1; tel. (613) 995-6954; fax (613) 995-0115; f. 1966; national advisory agency on scienc and technology policy; Chair. Dr GERALDINE KENNEY-WALLACE.

Social Sciences and Humanities Research Council: 255 Albert St, POB 1610, Ottawa, ON K1P 6G4; tel. (613) 992-0682; telex 053-3500; fax (613) 992-1787; aims to promote and assist research and scholarship in the social sciences and the humanities; Pres. Dr PAULE LEDUC.

Standards Council of Canada: 350 Sparks St, Suite 1203, Ottawa, ON K1R 7S8; tel. (613) 238-3222; promotes voluntary standardization in specific fields for products and other goods not expressly provided for by law; Pres. GEORGES ARCHER.

Statistics Canada: R. H. Coats Bldg, Tunney's Pasture, Ottawa, ON K1A 0T6; tel. (613) 951-8116; telex 053-3585; fax (613) 951-5116; central statistical agency; Chief Statistician of Canada IVAN P. FELLEGI.

Status of Women Canada: 151 Sparks St, 10th Floor, Ottawa, ON K1A 1C3; tel. (613) 995-7835; fax (613) 957-3359; Co-ordinator KAY STANLEY.

Western Grain Stabilization Administration: 303 Main St, Suite 935, Winnipeg, MB R3C 3H5; tel. (204) 983-3384; telex 07-57451; fax (204) 983-2751; Dir GEORGE HOWARD (acting).

FEDERAL LEGISLATURE

SENATE

(January 1989)

Senators are appointed by the Governor-General on the recommendation of the Prime Minister of Canada. Senators appointed before 2 June 1965 hold their positions for life, while those appointed after that date hold their positions until they attain the age of 75 years.

Speaker of the Senate: GUY CHARBONNEAU.

Leader of the Government: LOWELL MURRAY.

Deputy Leader of the Government: WILLIAM DOODY.

Government Whip: ORVILLE PHILLIPS.

Leader of the Opposition: ALLAN J. MACEACHEN.

Deputy Leader of the Opposition: ROYCE FRITH.

Clerk of the Senate and Clerk of the Parliaments: CHARLES A. LUSSIER.

PARTY STANDINGS

	Liberal	Progressive Conservative	Independent	Vacant	Total
Alberta	4	1	—	1	6
British Columbia	4	—	2	—	6
Manitoba	3	3	—	—	6
New Brunswick	6	3	—	1	10
Newfoundland	2	4	—	—	6
Northwest Territories	1	—	—	—	1
Nova Scotia	5	3	—	2	10
Ontario	14	6	2	2	24
Prince Edward Island	1	3	—	—	4
Québec	11	11	1	1	24
Saskatchewan	4	2	—	—	6
Yukon Territory	1	—	—	—	1
Total	56	36	5	7	104

MEMBERS
(with political party and year of appointment)

Alberta

EARL ADAM HASTINGS	Lib.	1966
HORACE ANDREW ('BUD') OLSON	Lib.	1977
MARTHA P. BIELISH	PC	1979
DANIEL HAYS	Lib.	1984
JOYCE FAIRBAIRN	Lib.	1984
(1 vacancy)		

British Columbia

ANN ELIZABETH BELL	Ind.	1970
EDWARD M. LAWSON	Ind.	1970
GEORGE C. VAN ROGGEN	Lib.	1971
RAYMOND J. PERRAULT	Lib.	1973
JACK AUSTIN	Lib.	1975
LEN MARCHAND	Lib.	1984

Manitoba

DOUGLAS DONALD EVERETT	Lib.	1966
GILDAS L. MOLGAT	Lib.	1970
DUFF ROBLIN	PC	1978
JOSEPH-PHILIPPE GUAY	Lib.	1978
NATHAN NURGITZ	PC	1979
MIRA SPIVAK	PC	1986

New Brunswick

CHARLES ROBERT MCELMAN	Lib.	1966
LOUIS-J. ROBICHAUD	Lib.	1973
MARGARET JEAN ANDERSON	Lib.	1978
L. NORBERT THÉRIAULT	Lib.	1979
CYRIL B. SHERWOOD	PC	1979
ROMÉO LEBLANC	Lib.	1984
EYMARD CORBIN	Lib.	1984
BRENDA MARY ROBERTSON	PC	1984
JEAN-MAURICE SIMARD	PC	1985
(1 vacancy)		

Newfoundland

WILLIAM JOHN PETTEN	Lib.	1968
PHILIP DEREK LEWIS	Lib.	1978
JACK MARSHALL	PC	1978
C. WILLIAM DOODY	PC	1979
ETHEL COCHRANE	PC	1986
GERRY OTTENHEIMER	PC	1987

Northwest Territories

WILLIE ADAMS	Lib.	1977

Nova Scotia

JOHN M. MACDONALD	PC	1960
HENRY D. HICKS	Lib.	1972
BERNARD ALASDAIR GRAHAM	Lib.	1972
ROBERT MUIR	PC	1979
JOHN P. STEWART	Lib.	1984
MICHAEL KIRBY	Lib.	1984
ALLAN J. MACEACHEN	Lib.	1984
FINLAY MACDONALD	PC	1984
(2 vacancies)		

Ontario

DAVID CROLL	Lib.	1955
DAVID J. WALKER	PC	1963
RHÉAL BÉLISLE	PC	1963
DANIEL AIKEN LANG	Ind.	1964
DOUGLAS KEITH DAVEY	Lib.	1966
ANDREW ERNEST THOMPSON	Lib.	1967
RICHARD JAMES STANBURY	Lib.	1968
JOAN NEIMAN	Lib.	1972
ROYCE FRITH	Lib.	1977
PETER BOSA	Lib.	1977
STANLEY HAIDASZ	Lib.	1978
LOWELL MURRAY	PC	1979
PETER STOLLERY	Lib.	1981
PETER M. PITFIELD	Ind.	1982
WILLIAM M. KELLY	PC	1982
JERAHMIEL S. GRAFSTEIN	Lib.	1984
ANNE C. COOLS	Lib.	1984
LORNA MARSDEN	Lib.	1984
COLIN KENNY	Lib.	1984
CHARLES TURNER	Lib.	1984
RICHARD J. DOYLE	PC	1985
NORMAN K. ATKINS	PC	1986
(2 vacancies)		

Prince Edward Island

ORVILLE H. PHILLIPS	PC	1963
MARK LORNE BONNELL	Lib.	1971
HEATH MACQUARRIE	PC	1979
EILEEN ROSSITER	PC	1986

Québec

HARTLAND DE M. MOLSON	Ind.	1955
JACQUES FLYNN	PC	1962
AZELLUS DENIS	Lib.	1964
MARTIAL ASSELIN	PC	1972
MAURICE RIEL	Lib.	1973
PIETRO RIZZUTO	Lib.	1976
DALIA WOOD	Lib.	1979

FERNAND-E. LEBLANC	Lib.	1979
GUY CHARBONNEAU	PC	1979
ARTHUR TREMBLAY	PC	1979
JACQUES HÉBERT	Lib.	1983
E. LEO KOLBER	Lib.	1983
CHARLIE WATT	Lib.	1984
PHILIPPE D. GIGANTES	Lib.	1984
PIERRE DE BANÉ	Lib.	1984
TOM LEFEBVRE	Lib.	1984
PAUL P. DAVID	PC	1985
MICHEL COGGER	PC	1986
JEAN BAZIN	PC	1986
ROCH BOLDUC	PC	1988
SOLANGE CHAPUT-ROLLAND	PC	1988
JEAN-MARIE POITRAS	PC	1988

GÉRALD-A. BEAUDOIN	PC	1988
(1 vacancy)		

Saskatchewan

HAZEN ROBERT ARGUE	Lib.	1966
HERBERT O. SPARROW	Lib.	1968
SIDNEY L. BUCKWOLD	Lib.	1971
DAVID GORDON STEUART	Lib.	1976
R. JAMES BALFOUR	PC	1979
E. W. ('STAFF') BAROOTES	PC	1984

Yukon Territory

PAUL LUCIER	Lib.	1975

HOUSE OF COMMONS
(As of 31 January 1989)

Speaker: JOHN A. FRASER (PC).

PARTY STANDINGS

	Progressive Conservative	Liberal	New Democratic Party	Vacant	Total
Alberta	24	—	1	1	26
British Columbia	12	1	19	—	32
Manitoba	7	5	2	—	14
New Brunswick	5	5	—	—	10
Newfoundland	2	5	—	—	7
Northwest Territories	—	2	—	—	2
Nova Scotia	5	6	—	—	11
Ontario	46	43	10	—	99
Prince Edward Island	—	4	—	—	4
Québec	63	12	—	—	75
Saskatchewan	4	—	10	—	14
Yukon Territory	—	—	1	—	1
Total	168	83	43	1	295

MEMBERS
(with political party)

Alberta

JACK SHIELDS	PC
BRIAN O'KURLEY	PC
LEE RICHARDSON	PC
DOUG FEE	PC
BOBBIE SPARROW	PC
SCOTT THORKELSON	PC
JIM EDWARDS	PC
DON MAZANKOWSKI	PC
ALEX KINDY	PC
DAVID KILGOUR	PC
JOE CLARK	PC
BLAINE THACKER	PC
LOUISE FELTHAM	PC
WALTER VAN DE WALLE	PC
KEN G. HUGHES	PC
JIM HAWKES	PC
MURRAY W. DORIN	PC
STEVE PAPROSKI	PC
ROSS HARVEY	NDP
WILLIE LITTLECHILD	PC
HARVIE ANDRÉ	PC
ALBERT COOPER	PC
AL JOHNSON	PC
ARNOLD MALONE	PC
BOB PORTER	PC
(1 vacancy)	

British Columbia

LYNN HUNTER	NDP
SVEND J. ROBINSON	NDP
JOHN A. FRASER	PC
KIM CAMPBELL	PC
DAWN BLACK	NDP
DAVID BARRETT	NDP
MARY COLLINS	PC
JOHN N. TURNER	Lib.
TOM SIDDON	PC
SID PARKER	NDP
JOHN F. BREWIN	NDP
NELSON RIIS	NDP
DAVID WORTHY	PC
ROBERT L. WENMAN	PC
DAVID D. STUPICH	NDP
STAN WILBEE	PC
ROSS BELSHER	PC
RAYMOND SKELLY	NDP
FRANK OBERLE	PC
AL HORNING	PC
BENNO W. FRIESEN	PC
CHUCK COOK	PC
JIM KARPOFF	NDP
BRIAN L. GARDINER	NDP
MARGARET ANNE MITCHELL	NDP
JOY LANGAN	NDP
IAN WADDELL	NDP
LYLE KRISTIANSEN	NDP
ROBERT E. SKELLY	NDP
JIM FULTON	NDP
LYLE DEAN MCWILLIAM	NDP
JACK WHITTAKER	NDP

Manitoba

DAVID BJORNSON	PC
JOHN HARVARD	Lib.
ROD MURPHY	NDP
CHARLIE MAYER	PC
DOROTHY DOBBIE	PC
RONALD J. DUHAMEL	Lib.
BILL BLAIKIE	NDP
JAKE EPP	PC
BRIAN WHITE	PC
REY PAGTAKHAN	Lib.
LLOYD AXWORTHY	Lib.
DAVID WALKER	Lib.
LEE CLARK	PC
FELIX HOLTMANN	PC

New Brunswick

GEORGE S. RIDEOUT	Lib.
GREG THOMPSON	PC
J. W. BUD BIRD	PC
BOB CORBETT	PC
FERNAND ROBICHAUD	Lib.
DOUGLAS YOUNG	Lib.
G. S. GERRY MERRITHEW	PC
BERNARD VALCOURT	PC
GUY H. ARSENAULT	Lib.
MAURICE A. DIONNE	Lib.

Newfoundland

ROGER SIMMONS	Lib.
GEORGE S. BAKER	Lib.
FRED J. MIFFLIN	Lib.
JOHN C. CROSBIE	PC
ROSS REID	PC
BILL ROMPKEY	Lib.
BRIAN TOBIN	Lib.

Northwest Territories

ETHEL BLONDIN	Lib.
JACK IYERAK ANAWAK	Lib.

Nova Scotia

MARY CLANCY	Lib.
HOWARD E. CROSBY	PC
ELMBER M. MacKAY	PC
PAT NOWLAN	PC
RON MacDONALD	Lib.
COLINE CAMPBELL	Lib.
RUSSELL MacLELLAN	Lib.
FRANCIS G. LeBLANC	Lib.
DAVID C. DINGWALL	Lib.
BILL CASEY	PC
PETER L. McCREATH	PC

Ontario

DOUG LEWIS	PC
PATRICK BOYER	PC
ALBINA GUARNIERI	Lib.
DENNIS MILLS	Lib.
BOB HICKS	PC
BRUCE HALLIDAY	PC
STEVE BUTLAND	NDP
BOB HORNER	PC
LEN HOPKINS	Lib.
SERGIO MARCHI	Lib.
JOSEPH VOLPE	Lib.
NEIL YOUNG	NDP
STAN KEYES	Lib.
JIM JORDAN	Lib.
JOHN MANLEY	Lib.
JEAN-ROBERT GAUTHIER	Lib.
BOB SPELLER	Lib.
JOHN R. RODRIGUEZ	NDP
DEREK BLACKBURN	NDP
KEN MONTEITH	PC
EDNA ANDERSON	PC
KEN JAMES	PC
REX CRAWFORD	Lib.
STEVEN LANGDON	NDP
HOWARD McCURDY	NDP
JOHN REIMER	PC
DON BLENKARN	PC
PAUL DICK	PC
DAVID MacDONALD	PC
BARBARA McDOUGALL	PC
JOE FONTANA	Lib.
JIM KARYGIANNIS	Lib.
JESSE FLIS	Lib.
GILBERT PARENT	Lib.
PAT SOBESKI	PC
OTTO JELINEK	PC
ROSS STEVENSON	PC
MICHAEL WILSON	PC
BILL KEMPLING	PC
PAULINE A. BROWES	PC
DON BOUDRIA	Lib.
BARBARA GREENE	PC
CHARLES CACCIA	Lib.
ED BROADBENT	NDP
RENÉ SOETENS	PC
BERYL GAFFNEY	Lib.
MARLENE CATTERALL	Lib.
MAC HARB	Lib.
GARTH TURNER	PC
PETER MILLIKEN	Lib.
ROY MacLAREN	Lib.
BOB KAPLAN	Lib.
JOHN NUNZIATA	Lib.
BILL WINEGARD	PC
CID SAMSON	NDP
STAN DARLING	PC
BOB WOOD	Lib.
EUGÈNE BELLEMARE	Lib.
TOM HOCKIN	PC
GUS MITGES	PC
MURRAY CARDIFF	PC
IAIN ANGUS	NDP
JOE COMUZZI	Lib.
HERB GRAY	Lib.
LYLE VANCLIEF	Lib.
BOB KILGER	Lib.
BILL SCOTT	PC
HARRY CHADWICK	PC
SHIRLEY MARTIN	PC
JOHN A. MacDOUGALL	PC
JOHN McDERMID	PC
WALTER McLEAN	PC
DIANE MARLEAU	Lib.
HARRY BRIGHTWELL	PC
GEOFF SCOTT	PC
RALPH FERGUSON	Lib.
JERRY PICKARD	Lib.
PERRIN BEATTY	PC
SHEILA COPPS	Lib.
GIRVE FRETZ	PC
KEN ATKINSON	PC
DEREK LEE	Lib.
ROB NICHOLSON	PC
TERRY CLIFFORD	PC
BILL VANKOUGHNET	PC
MAURICE FOSTER	Lib.
JOHN BOSLEY	PC
MAURIZIO BEVILACQUA	Lib.
ALAN REDWAY	PC
ROBER D. NAULT	Lib.
RÉGINALD BÉLAIR	Lib.
BETH PHINNEY	Lib.
WILLIAM ATTEWELL	PC
CHRISTINE STEWART	Lib.
BILL DOMM	PC
JOHN E. COLE	PC
TOM WAPPEL	Lib.
DAN HEAP	NDP
JIM PETERSON	Lib.

Prince Edward Island

JOE McGUIRE	Lib.
LAWRENCE MacAULAY	Lib.
GEORGE PROUD	Lib.
CATHERINE CALLBECK	Lib.

Québec

GILLES ROCHELEAU	Lib.
GABRIEL FONTAINE	PC
LISE BOURGAULT	PC
ANDRÉ OUELLET	Lib.
JACQUES VIEN	PC
RICHARD GRISÉ	PC
MARCEL PRUD'HOMME	Lib.
J.-PIERRE HOGUE	PC
NICOLE ROY-ARSELIN	PC
GABRIELLE BERTRAND	PC
ALFONSO GAGLIANO	Lib.
JEAN-CLAUDE MALÉPART	Lib.
MARK ASSAD	Lib.
JEAN CORBEIL	PC
BOB LAYTON	PC
PIERRE H. VINCENT	PC
CLÉMENT COUTURE	PC
JEAN-GUY HUDON	PC
YVON CÔTÉ	PC
GUY RICARD	PC
JEAN-MARC ROBITAILLE	PC
MONIQUE B. TARDIF	PC
GABY LARRIVÉE	PC
MICHEL CHAMPAGNE	PC
MARC FERLAND	PC
SUZANNE DUPLESSIS	PC
SHIRLEY MAHEU	Lib.
ROBERT de COTRET	PC
JEAN-J. CHAREST	PC
ANDRÉ HARVEY	PC
ANDRÉ PLOURDE	PC
JEAN-GUY GUILBAULT	PC
ALLAN KOURY	PC
BENOÎT BOUCHARD	PC
JACQUES TÉTREAULT	PC
GILLES LOISELLE	PC
GUY ST-JULIEN	PC
NIC LEBLANC	PC

Charles DeBlois	PC
Sheila Finestone	Lib.
Paul Martin	Lib.
Benoît Tremblay	PC
Ricardo Lopez	PC
Vincent Della Noce	PC
David Berger	Lib.
Fernand Jourdenais	PC
Warren Allmand	Lib.
Gilbert Chartrand	PC
Pierre Blais	PC
Louis Plamondon	PC
François Gérin	PC
Marcel R. Tremblay	PC
Andrée Champagne	PC
Gilles Bernier	PC
Marcel Danis	PC
Jean-Luc Joncas	PC
Barry Moore	PC
Denis Pronovost	PC
Maurice Tremblay	PC
Lucien Bouchard	PC
Marcel Masse	PC
Jean-Pierre Blackburn	PC
Pierre H. Cadieux	PC
Gerry Weiner	PC
Darryl Gray	PC
Chales-Eugène Marin	PC
Carole Jacques	PC

Monique Landry	PC
Marie Gibeau	PC
Monique Vézina	PC
Brian Mulroney	PC
Pierrette Venne	PC
Jean Lapierre	Lib.
Charles A. Langlois	PC
Gabriel Desjardins	PC

Saskatchewan

Geoff Wilson	PC
Les Benjamin	NDP
Simon deJong	NDP
Larry Schneider	PC
Len Taylor	NDP
Len Gustafson	PC
Vic Althouse	NDP
Ron Fisher	NDP
Bill McKnight	PC
Lorne Nystrom	NDP
Chris Axworthy	NDP
Rod Laporte	NDP
Ray Funk	NDP
Stan Hovdebo	NDP

Yukon Territory

Audrey McLaughlin	NDP

FEDERAL BUDGET

(C $'000, year ending 31 March. Source: Statistics Canada.)

REVENUE

	1986/87
Taxes	86,645,576
Income taxes	50,743,084
Personal income tax	39,502,544
Corporation income tax	9,884,958
Taxes on payments to non-residents	1,355,582
Consumption taxes	20,980,211
General sales tax	12,022,066
Motive fuel tax	1,491,362
Alcoholic beverages tax	1,016,147
Tobacco tax	1,660,023
Custom duties	4,191,285
Health and social-insurance levies	14,482,345
Unemployment-insurance contributions	9,633,000
Universal pension-plan levies	4,849,345
Miscellaneous taxes	439,936
Natural-resource revenue	522,542
Privileges, licences and permits	168,911
Sales of goods and services	2,703,226
Return on investments	5,846,400
Own enterprises	1,431,589
Interest	1,393,942
Other return on investments	4,414,811
Interest	3,951,732
Other revenue from own sources	848,220
Transfers from provincial governments	23,554
Gross general revenue	96,758,429

1987/88 (preliminary): Personal income tax 45,125,000; corporation income tax 10,878,000; taxes on payments to non-residents 1,162,000; unemployment-insurance contributions 10,426,000; return on investments 4,548,000; gross general revenue 95,459,000.

1988/89 (estimates): Personal income tax 45,410,000; corporation income tax 12,000,000; taxes on payments to non-residents 1,270,000; unemployment-insurance contributions 10,600,000; return on investments 5,060,000; gross general revenue 103,305,000.

1989/90: Estimated gross general revenue 106,310,000.

EXPENDITURE

	1986/87
General services	5,470,791
Administration	2,782,215
Contributions to employee pension plans	1,535,202
Protection of persons and property	11,985,933
National defence	9,321,361
Policing	1,258,581
Transportation and communications	3,536,015
Air transportation	1,302,007

EXPENDITURE—*continued*

	1986/87
Health	7,465,107
Hospital care	5,511,725
Extended health care	1,184,795
Social services	41,711,645
Canada Pension Plan	5,753,667
Old-age security	13,444,662
Unemployment insurance	10,886,038
Family allowances	2,534,420
Veterans' benefits	1,569,269
Social-welfare assistance	4,624,186
Other social welfare	1,479,066
Tax credits and rebates	1,360,482
Education	4,187,210
Post-secondary education	2,670,248
Resource conservation and industrial development	7,072,218
Agriculture	3,238,424
Oil and gas	1,040,509
Trade and industry	1,374,693
Environment	445,727
Recreation and culture	930,788
Labour, employment and immigration	1,364,183
Labour and employment	1,130,650
Housing	1,455,531
General assistance	1,454,574
Foreign affairs and international assistance	2,895,952
Regional planning and development	343,913
Research establishments	1,090,126
General-purpose transfers to other levels of government	7,233,959
Equalization	5,771,828
Transfers to own enterprises	2,702,406
Debt charges	25,150,152
Interest	24,173,669
Other	4,192
Gross general expenditure	125,045,848
Transfers to other levels of government	21,461,719

1987/88 (preliminary): National defence 10,772,000; foreign affairs and international assistance 3,439,000; debt charges 28,976,000; gross general expenditure 125,542,000.

1988/89 (estimates): National defence 11,090,000; foreign affairs and international assistance 3,541,000; debt charges 32,055,000; gross general expenditure 132,250.

1989/90: Estimated gross general expenditure 134,900,000.

PROVINCIAL AND TERRITORIAL GOVERNMENTS

Provincial, Territorial and Local Government Finances

(Source: Statistics Canada.)

FEDERAL TRANSFERS TO PROVINCIAL GOVERNMENTS AND TERRITORIES, BY SELECTED PURPOSES
(C $'000; year ending 31 March 1987)

	Equalization transfers	Other general-purpose transfers	Hospital insurance and diagnostic services	Extended health-care services	Canada assistance plan	Post-secondary education	Other	Total
Alberta	—	223,654	515,509	106,396	427,333	207,367	148,963	1,629,222
British Columbia	360	23,999	779,349	129,389	632,056	311,586	138,824	2,015,563
Manitoba	508,359	19,898	262,586	48,139	154,581	112,455	99,173	1,205,191
New Brunswick	632,762	23,848	181,475	32,173	145,108	75,134	69,916	1,160,416
Newfoundland	736,182	35,200	140,613	25,797	85,460	60,212	67,661	1,151,125
Northwest Territories . . .	—	469,531	9,067	2,261	12,004	3,809	45,131	541,803
Nova Scotia	681,840	28,711	214,925	39,438	124,405	92,188	84,424	1,265,931
Ontario	—	114,355	2,002,812	407,344	1,132,191	809,866	206,468	4,673,036
Prince Edward Island . . .	148,021	9,839	31,107	5,725	19,780	13,340	20,609	248,421
Québec	2,891,426	67,177	1,085,629	294,503	1,107,757	434,803	283,466	6,164,761
Saskatchewan	172,878	2,232	254,591	45,461	160,705	109,255	117,297	862,419
Yukon Territory	—	156,028	5,358	1,039	—	2,281	11,513	176,219
Total	**5,771,828**	**1,174,472**	**5,483,021**	**1,137,665**	**4,001,380**	**2,232,296**	**1,293,445**	**21,094,107**

FEDERAL TRANSFERS TO LOCAL GOVERNMENTS, BY SELECTED PURPOSES
(C $'000; year ending 31 March 1987)

	Grants in lieu of taxes	Transportation and communications	Social welfare	Resource conservation and industrial development	Labour, employment and immigration	Regional planning and development	Other	Total
Alberta	18,255	185	404	—	534	1,610	623	21,611
British Columbia	29,156	3,101	3,152	6,718	76	80	457	42,740
Manitoba	13,514	3,239	3,228	1,096	—	123	1,142	22,342
New Brunswick	19,468	1,361	1,730	—	259	—	191	23,009
Newfoundland	4,547	6,081	3,754	93	—	—	1,681	16,156
Northwest Territories . . .	1,668	385	—	—	—	—	1,338	2,053
Nova Scotia	34,667	779	634	—	—	—	1,338	37,418
Ontario	111,355	10,956	12,676	737	984	—	1,093	137,801
Prince Edward Island . . .	1,521	—	323	—	—	—	—	1,844
Québec	51,974	3,804	3,156	74	860	—	95	59,963
Saskatchewan	290	284	461	158	—	—	—	1,193
Yukon Territory	1,244	—	—	238	—	—	—	1,482
Total	**287,659**	**30,175**	**29,518**	**9,114**	**2,713**	**1,813**	**6,620**	**367,612**

PROVINCIAL AND TERRITORIAL GOVERNMENT FINANCES—SUMMARY
(C $ million; year ending 31 March 1985)

Revenue

	Transfers		Revenue from own sources					
	From federal government and federal-government enterprises	From local governments	Taxes	Natural-resource revenue	Privileges, licences and permits	Sales of goods and services	Return on investment	Gross general revenue*
Alberta	1,596	8	3,211	6,032	136	170	3,097	14,534
British Columbia . . .	1,747	3	5,876	793	213	302	1,147	10,122
Manitoba	1,112	11	1,794	54	45	104	601	3,747
New Brunswick . . .	1,061	2	1,093	27	34	58	216	2,502
Newfoundland . . .	981	0†	790	25	60	55	157	2,075
Northwest Territories .	437	—	76	0†	3	56	33	606
Nova Scotia	1,172	1	1,169	8	43	98	312	2,810
Ontario	4,464	72	17,940	233	702	618	2,387	26,667
Prince Edward Island .	213	—	173	0†	4	17	50	458
Québec	6,295	0†	16,382	130	826	385	2,794	27,576
Saskatchewan. . . .	720	6	1,309	785	64	144	683	3,732
Yukon Territory . . .	149	0†	34	0†	3	6	15	207
Total	**19,947**	**104**	**49,848**	**8,089**	**2,132**	**2,012**	**11,492**	**95,037**

* Includes category of 'Other revenue from own sources'.
† Less than C $500,000.

Expenditure (by major category)

	General services	Transportation and communications	Health	Social services	Education	Resource conservation and industrial development	Debt charges	Gross general expenditure (includes others)
Alberta	698	803	2,870	1,238	2,248	2,502	502	12,449
British Columbia	600	648	2,999	1,812	2,090	648	780	10,959
Manitoba	187	184	1,099	536	801	200	657	4,172
New Brunswick	142	228	614	372	607	127	362	2,738
Newfoundland	107	170	462	252	519	91	396	2,265
Northwest Territories . . .	155	20	63	37	106	28	1	593
Nova Scotia	102	245	804	325	744	199	503	3,238
Ontario	1,156	1,599	8,575	4,392	5,440	792	3,407	28,239
Prince Edward Island . . .	33	46	100	53	106	40	54	462
Québec	1,612	1,378	5,817	6,778	6,170	1,246	2,719	28,632
Saskatchewan	249	203	1,006	541	634	522	689	4,262
Yukon Territory	23	48	22	18	37	9	1	194
Total	5,064	5,572	24,431	16,354	19,504	6,405	10,071	98,204

The Government System in the Provinces

Until 1982 the British North America Act of 1867 was the basis of the federal and provincial systems of government. Under the Constitution Act of 1982 the last traces of British control over Canada were removed, although formal representatives of the crown are still retained. The crown representative in provincial government is the lieutenant-governor, who is appointed by the Governor-General on the advice of the federal cabinet and presides over a unicameral legislature. The legislative assembly of each province is elected by the people for a statutory term of five years. It is customary for the lieutenant-governor to appoint the leader of the majority party as provincial premier. The premier selects his or her cabinet from among the elected members of the legislative assembly, together forming the policy-making executive council. Nearly all cabinet members are portfolio-holding ministers. The size of the cabinet may range from 10 to 30 members.

Bills are generally introduced by the executive council, although private members' bills may be introduced. To become law a bill must receive two readings, a detailed review in committee stage, and a third reading before being passed to the lieutenant-governor for formal assent.

Provincial governments have legislative power over all provincial matters, including public schooling, health, social services, roads and local government. The provinces have authority over natural resources, over which they also have taxing power. Provincial taxation is otherwise limited to direct taxation. The federal government's power to disallow a provincial statute within one year has not been used since 1943.

The system of government operating in each of the territories (as distinct from the provinces) is outlined below.

Alberta

The province of Alberta was admitted to the confederation on 1 September 1905 as a result of the Alberta Act of 20 July 1905. The provincial government consists of the lieutenant-governor; the executive council, comprising the cabinet and premier; and an 83-member legislative assembly. In the 1986 provincial elections 715,376 ballots were cast, representing 47% of those registered on the list of electors. Local government is organized through 16 cities, 108 towns, 172 villages, 20 municipal districts and 30 counties.

PROVINCIAL EXECUTIVE

Lieutenant-Governor: HELEN HUNLEY.

Executive Council

Premier, President of the Executive Council: DONALD GETTY.

Deputy House Leader, Minister of Advanced Education: JOHN GOGO.

Minister of Special Projects: NEIL CRAWFORD.

Minister of Federal and Intergovernmental Affairs: JAMES D. HORSMAN.

Minister of Economic Development and Trade: PETER ELZINGA.

Provincial Treasurer: DICK JOHNSTON.

Minister of Energy: RICK ORMAN.

Minister of Technology, Research and Telecommunications, Government House Leader: FRED STEWART.

Minister of Transportation and Utilities: J. ALLEN ADAIR.

Solicitor-General: DICK FOWLER.

Minister of Forestry, Lands and Wildlife: LEROY FJORDBOTTEN.

Minister of Environment: Dr IAN C. REID.

Minister of Family and Social Services: JOHN OLDRING.

Minister of Tourism: DON SPARROW.

Minister of Career Development and Employment: CONNIE OSTERMAN.

Minister of Public Works, Supply and Services: KEN KOWALSKI.

Minister of Agriculture: ERNIE ISLEY.

Associate Minister of Agriculture: SHIRLEY MCCLELLAN.

Minister of Culture and Multiculturalism: DOUG MAIN.

Minister of Municipal Affairs, Deputy Government House Leader: RAY SPEAKER.

Minister of Recreation and Parks: STEVE WEST.

Minister of Labour: ELAINE MCCOY.

Minister of Health: NANCE BETKOWSKI.

Attorney-General: KEN ROSTAD.

Minister of Consumer and Corporate Affairs: DENNIS ANDERSON.

Minister of Education: JIM DINNING.

Minister of the Environment: RALPH KLEIN.

GOVERNMENT ADDRESSES

Office of the Lieutenant-Governor: Legislature Bldg, Edmonton, AB T5K 2B6.

Office of the Premier: Legislature Bldg, Rm 307, Edmonton, AB T5K 2B6; tel. (403) 427-2251; fax (403) 427-1349.

Alberta Advanced Education: Devonian Bldg, East Tower, 11160 Jasper Ave, Edmonton, AB T5K 0L3; tel. (403) 427-2781; fax (403) 428-9406.

Alberta Agriculture: 7000 113th St, Edmonton, AB T6H 5T6; tel. (403) 427-2151; telex 037-2666; fax (403) 422-6317.

Alberta Career Development and Employment: Park Sq., 10001 Bellamy Hill, Edmonton, AB T5J 3W5; tel. (403) 422-4488.

Alberta Consumer and Corporate Affairs: 10025 Jasper Ave, 22nd Floor, Edmonton, AB T5J 3Z5; tel. (403) 422-3935; fax (403) 422-0775.

Alberta Culture and Multiculturalism: CN Tower, 10004 104th Ave, Edmonton, AB T5J 0K5; tel. (403) 427-6530; telex 037-41652; fax (403) 427-5362.

Alberta Economic Development and Trade: Sterling Pl., 9940 106th St, Edmonton, AB T5K 2P6; tel. (403) 427-0670; telex 037-42815; fax (403) 427-0610.

Alberta Education: Devonian Bldg, 11160 Jasper Ave, Edmonton, AB T5K 0L2; tel. (403) 427-2286; fax (403) 420-0728.

Alberta Energy: 9945 108th St, Edmonton, AB T5K 2G6; tel. (403) 427-3590; fax (403) 422-0800.

Alberta Environment: Oxbridge Pl., 9820 106th St, Edmonton, AB T5K 2J6; tel. (403) 427-6267; fax (403) 422-3571.

Alberta Forestry, Lands and Wildlife: Petroleum Plaza, South Tower, 9915 108th St, Edmonton, AB T5K 2C9; tel. (403) 427-3590; telex 037-3676; fax (403) 422-6068.

Alberta Health: Seventh St Plaza, 10030 107th St, Edmonton, AB T5J 3E4; tel. (403) 427-5541; fax (403) 422-6663.

Alberta Labour: 10808 99th Ave, Edmonton, AB T5K 0G2; tel. (403) 427-5585; telex 037-41625; fax (403) 422-0970.

Alberta Municipal Affairs: 9925 107th St, Edmonton, AB T5K 2H9; tel. (403) 427-8862; fax (403) 422-9105.

Alberta Public Works, Supply and Services: 6950 113th St, 3rd Floor, Edmonton, AB T6H 5V7; tel. (403) 427-6518; telex 053-3703; fax (403) 422-0186.

Alberta Recreation and Parks: Standard Life Centre, 10405 Jasper Ave, Edmonton, AB T5J 3N4; tel. (403) 427-2008.

Alberta Social Services: Seventh St Plaza, 10030 107th St, Edmonton, AB T5J 3E4; tel. (403) 427-4801; fax (403) 422-0031.

Alberta Technology, Research and Telecommunications: Pacific Plaza, 10909 Jasper Ave, 12th Floor, Edmonton, AB T5J 3M8; tel. (403) 422-0567; fax (403) 420-1474.

Alberta Tourism: 10025 Jasper Ave, 18th Floor, Edmonton, AB T5J 3Z3; tel. (403) 427-2280; fax (403) 427-2852.

Alberta Transportation and Utilities: Twin Atria, 4999 98th Ave, Edmonton, AB T6B 2X3; tel. (403) 427-2731; telex 037-3065; fax (403) 468-3143.

Alberta Treasury: Terrace Bldg, Rm 434, 9515 107th St, Edmonton, AB T5K 2C3; tel. (403) 427-9957; fax (403) 428-1341.

Attorney-General's Department: 9833 109th St, Edmonton, AB T5K 2E8; tel. (403) 427-2745; telex 037-3019; fax (403) 427-6821.

Department of Federal and Intergovernmental Affairs: 10025 Jasper Ave, Suite 2200, Edmonton, AB T5J 1S6; tel. (403) 427-2611; telex 037-3300; fax (403) 423-6654.

Department of the Solicitor-General: 10365 97th St, 8th/9th/10th Floors, Edmonton, AB T5J 3W7; tel. (403) 427-7245; fax (403) 427-1903.

LEGISLATIVE ASSEMBLY

Speaker: DAVID J. CARTER (PC).

Clerk: W. J. DAVID MCNEIL.

Election, 20 March 1989

						Seats at election
Progressive Conservative	.	.	.	.	.	59
New Democratic Party	.	.	.	.	.	16
Liberal	.	.	.	.	.	8
Total	.	.	.	.	.	83

British Columbia

British Columbia was admitted to the confederation on 20 July 1871 by the Imperial Order-in-Council of 16 May 1871. The government consists of the lieutenant-governor; the executive council, comprising the premier and cabinet; and the legislative assembly. In 1987 British Columbia was divided into eight 'development regions', each of which is represented by a minister of state in the cabinet. There are 69 members of the legislative assembly. In the 1986 provincial general election 1,366,193 people voted, representing 77% of those registered to vote. Local government is directed through the province's 35 cities, 13 towns, 48 villages and 46 districts. In addition there are regional districts which provide services not only to those municipalities with which they overlap, but also to previously unorganized areas.

PROVINCIAL EXECUTIVE

Lieutenant-Governor: DAVID C. LAM.

Executive Council

Premier, President of the Council: WILLIAM N. VANDER ZALM.

Minister of Tourism and Provincial Secretary: WILLIAM E. REID.

Attorney-General: STUART D. SMITH.

Minister of Forests: DAVE PARKER.

Minister of State for Thompson-Okanagan and Kootenay, responsible for Crown Lands: HOWARD DIRKS.

Minister of Finance and Corporate Relations: MEL COUVELIER.

Minister of Agriculture and Fisheries: JOHN SAVAGE.

Minister of Energy, Mines and Petroleum Resources: JACK DAVIS.

Minister of Education: ANTHONY J. BRUMMET.

Minister of Labour and Consumer Services: LYALL HANSON.

Minister of Regional Development and Minister of State for Mainland/Southwest: ELWOOD N. VEITCH.

Minister of Municipal Affairs, Recreation and Culture: RITA M. JOHNSTON.

Minister of Health and Minister responsible for Seniors: PETER A. DUECK.

Minister of Social Services and Housing: CLAUDE H. RICHMOND.

Minister of Transportation and Highways: NEIL VANT.

Minister of State for Cariboo, responsible for Environment: BRUCE STRACHAN.

Minister of State for Vancouver Island/Coast and North Coast, responsible for Parks: TERRY HUBERTS.

Minister of Advanced Education and Job Training and Minister responsible for Science and Technology: STANLEY B. HAGEN.

Minister of Government Management Services: CLIFF MICHAEL.

Minister of International Business and Immigration: JOHN JANSEN.

Solicitor-General: ANGUS REE.

Minister of State for Nechako and the Northeast, responsible for Native Affairs: JACK WEISGERBER.

GOVERNMENT ADDRESSES

Office of the Lieutenant-Governor: Government House, 1401 Rockland Ave, Victoria, BC V8S 1V9.

Office of the Premier: Legislative Bldgs, Victoria, BC V8V 1X4; tel. (604) 387-6630; telex 049-7135; fax (604) 387-0087.

Ministry of Advanced Education and Job Training: Parliament Bldgs, Victoria, BC V8V 1X4; tel. (604) 387-6276; telex 049-7109; fax (604) 387-2100.

Ministry of Agriculture and Fisheries: Parliament Bldgs, Victoria, BC V8W 2Z7; tel. (604) 387-5121; telex 049-7443; fax (604) 387-5130.

Ministry of the Attorney-General: Parliament Bldgs, Victoria, BC V8V 1X4; tel. (604) 387-1866; fax (604) 387-6411.

Ministry of Education: Parliament Bldgs, Victoria, BC V8V 2M4; tel. (604) 387-4611; fax (604) 356-2504.

Ministry of Energy, Mines and Petroleum Resources: Parliament Bldgs, Victoria, BC V8V 1X4; tel. (604) 387-5178; telex 049-7135; fax (604) 387-3527.

Ministry of Environment: Parliament Bldgs, Victoria, BC V8V 1X5; tel. (604) 387-9422; fax (604) 387-5669.

Ministry of Finance and Corporate Relations: Parliament Bldgs, Victoria, BC V8V 1X4; tel. (604) 387-9278; fax (604) 387-9099.

Ministry of Forests: Parliament Bldgs, Victoria, BC V8V 1X4; tel. (604) 387-5255; fax (604) 387-8485.

Ministry of Government Management Services: Parliament Bldgs, Victoria, BC V8V 1X4; tel. (604) 387-0422; fax (604) 387-1399.

Ministry of Health: Parliament Bldgs, Victoria, BC V8V 1X4; tel. (604) 387-3166; telex 049-7462; fax (604) 387-3537.

Ministry of International Business and Immigration: Parliament Bldgs, Victoria, BC V8W 3C1; tel. (604) 387-6921; fax (604) 387-1899.

Ministry of Labour and Consumer Services: Parliament Bldgs, Victoria, BC V8V 1X4; tel. (604) 387-3194; fax (604) 356-8102.

Ministry of Municipal Affairs, Recreation and Culture: Parliament Bldgs, Victoria, BC V8V 1X4; tel. (604) 387-4050; fax (604) 387-4089.

Ministry of Parks: Parliament Bldgs, Victoria, BC V8V 1X5; tel. (604) 387-5002.

Ministry of Regional Development: Parliament Bldgs, Victoria, BC V8W 3C1; tel. (604) 387-4521.

Ministry of Social Services and Housing: Parliament Bldgs, Victoria, BC V8V 1X4; tel. (604) 387-6485; telex 049-7135; fax (604) 387-5775.

Ministry of the Solicitor-General: Parliament Bldgs, Victoria, BC V8V 1X4; tel. (604) 387-1683; fax (604) 387-4348.

Ministry of Tourism and Office of the Provincial Secretary: Parliament Bldgs, Victoria, BC V8V 1X4; tel. (604) 387-1311; telex 049-7135; fax (604) 387-1420.

Ministry of Transportation and Highways: Parliament Bldgs, Victoria, BC V8V 1X4; tel. (604) 387-3198; telex 049-7379; fax (604) 387-6431.

LEGISLATIVE ASSEMBLY

Speaker: JOHN REYNOLDS (Social Credit).
Clerk: IAN M. HORNE.

Election, 22 October 1986

	Seats at election	Seats at 1 Nov. 1988
Social Credit	47	45
New Democratic Party	22	21
Independent	—	1
Vacant	—	2
Total	69	69

Manitoba

The province of Manitoba was admitted to the confederation on 15 July 1870 by the Manitoba Act of 1870, and the Imperial Order-in-Council of 23 June 1870. The formal head of the provincial government is the lieutenant-governor. Manitoba has a 21-member executive council comprising the premier and the cabinet. The legislative assembly has 57 members. In the 1988 provincial general election 538,738 people voted, representing 74% of those registered to vote. Local government is administered by the province's five cities, 35 towns, 40 villages, 105 rural municipalities and 17 local government districts.

PROVINCIAL EXECUTIVE

Lieutenant-Governor: Dr GEORGE JOHNSON.

Executive Council

Premier, President of the Council, Minister of Federal-Provincial Relations, Chairman of the Treasury Board: GARY ALBERT FILMON.
Minister of Northern Affairs: JAMES ERWIN DOWNEY.
Minister of Health: DONALD WARDER ORCHARD.
Minister of Highways and Transportation and Minister of Government Services: ALBERT DRIEDGER.
Minister of Finance: CLAYTON SIDNEY MANNESS.
Minister of Family Services: CHARLOTTE LOUISE OLESON.
Deputy Premier, Minister of Environment, Chairman of Manitoba Public Insurance Corpn: JAMES GLEN CUMMINGS.
Attorney-General and Government House Leader: JAMES COLLUS MCCRAE.
Minister of Co-operative, Consumer and Corporate Affairs: EDWARD JAMES CONNERY.
Minister of Industry, Trade and Technology, Business Development and Tourism: JAMES ARTHUR ERNST.
Minister of Agriculture: GLEN MARSHALL FINDLAY.
Minister of Education: LEONARD DERKACH.
Minister of Urban Affairs, Minister of Housing: GERALD DUCHARME.
Minister of Culture, Heritage and Recreation: BONNIE ELIZABETH MITCHELSON.
Minister of Natural Resources: HARRY ENNS.
Minister of Energy and Mines: HAROLD JOHAN NEUFELD.

GOVERNMENT ADDRESSES

Office of the Lieutenant-Governor: Legislative Bldg, Winnipeg, MB R3C 0V8.
Office of the Premier: Legislative Bldg, Rm 204, Winnipeg, MB R3C 0V8; tel. (204) 945-3714; telex 07-587589; fax (204) 945-5638.
Attorney-General's Department: Woodsworth Bldg, 9th Floor, 405 Broadway, Winnipeg, MB R3C 3L6; tel. (204) 945-2878; fax (204) 945-4882.
Manitoba Agriculture: Legislative Bldg, Winnipeg, MB R3C 0V8; tel. (204) 945-3433.
Manitoba Community Services: 270 Osborne St North, 1st Floor, Winnipeg, MB R3C 1V7; tel. (204) 945-3267.
Manitoba Co-operative, Consumer and Corporate Affairs: Legislative Bldg, Winnipeg, MB R3C 0V8; tel. (204) 956-2040; telex 07-587589; fax (204) 945-2775.

Manitoba Culture, Heritage and Recreation: 177 Lombard Ave, Winnipeg, MB R3B 0W5; tel. (204) 945-2782; fax (204) 945-1369.
Manitoba Education: 1200 Portage Ave, Suite 116, Winnipeg, MB R3G 0T5; tel. (204) 945-6185.
Manitoba Employment Services and Economic Security: 330 Graham Ave, Suite 611, Winnipeg, MB R3C 4A5; tel. (204) 945-4971.
Manitoba Energy and Mines: 330 Graham Ave, Suite 555, Winnipeg, MB R3C 4E3; tel. (204) 945-4437; telex 07-55839.
Manitoba Environment and Workplace Safety and Health: 330 St Mary Ave, Suite 960, Winnipeg, MB R3C 3Z5; tel. (204) 945-5763; fax (204) 956-2501.
Manitoba Finance: Legislative Bldg, Rm 109, Winnipeg, MB R3C 0V8; tel. (204) 945-3754; telex 07-587589; fax (204) 945-8316.
Manitoba Government Services: Woodsworth Bldg, 405 Broadway, 15th Floor, Winnipeg, MB R3C 3L6; tel. (204) 945-3940; telex 07-57346; fax (204) 945-7610.
Manitoba Health: 175 Hargrave St, Winnipeg, MB R3C 3R8; tel. (204) 945-4072; fax (204) 945-4564.
Manitoba Highways and Transportation: Legislative Bldg, Winnipeg, MB R3C 0V8; tel. (204) 945-3746; fax (204) 945-3988.
Manitoba Housing: 287 Broadway, Winnipeg, MB R3C 0R9; tel. (204) 945-4748.
Manitoba Industry, Trade and Tourism: 155 Carlton St, Winnipeg, MB R3C 3H8; tel. (204) 945-2465; telex 07-587833; fax (204) 957-1793.
Manitoba Labour: 610 Norquay Bldg, Winnipeg, MB R3C 0P8; tel. (204) 945-7625.
Manitoba Municipal Affairs: 800 Portage Ave, 6th Floor, Winnipeg, MB R3G 0N4; tel. (204) 945-2194.
Manitoba Natural Resources: Legislative Bldg, Rm 314, Winnipeg, MB R3C 0V8; tel. (204) 945-3785; telex 07-587589; fax (204) 945-3586.
Manitoba Northern Affairs: 59 Elizabeth Dr., Thompson, MB R8N 1X4; tel. (204) 778-4411.
Manitoba Urban Affairs: Legislative Bldg, Rm 317, Winnipeg, MB R3C 0V8; tel. (204) 945-0073; telex 07-587589.

LEGISLATIVE ASSEMBLY

Speaker: DENIS ROCAN (PC).
Clerk: W. H. REMNANT.

Election, 26 April 1988

	Seats at election	Seats at 1 Oct. 1989
Progressive Conservative* . . .	25	24
Liberal	20	21
New Democratic Party . . .	12	12
Total	57	57

* Formed a minority government following the April 1988 election.

New Brunswick

The province of New Brunswick was admitted to the confederation on 1 July 1867 by the British North America Act of the same year. The government of the province consists of a lieutenant-governor; premier and cabinet, or executive council; and legislative assembly which has 58 members. In the 1984 election to the federal parliament 379,850 votes were polled, representing 77% of voters on the official lists. New Brunswick's local government is directed through its six cities, 26 towns and 85 villages. There are also 282 unincorporated local service districts which perform a similar function to municipal organizations.

PROVINCIAL EXECUTIVE

Lieutenant-Governor: GILBERT FINN.

Executive Council

Premier and Minister responsible for the Advisory Council on the Status of Women, and for Regional Development: FRANK MCKENNA.
President of the Council and Minister responsible for Intergovernmental Affairs: ALDÉA LANDRY.
Attorney-General and Minister of Justice: JAMES LOCKYER.
Minister of Finance and Minister responsible for the New Brunswick Liquor Corporation: ALLAN MAHER.

Chairman of the Board of Management: GÉRALD CLAVETTE.
Minister of Supply and Services: BRUCE SMITH.
Minister of Transportation: SHELDON LEE.
Minister of Natural Resources and Energy: MORRIS GREEN.
Minister of Agriculture: ALAN GRAHAM.
Minister of Health and Community Services: RAY FRENETTE.
Minister of Income Assistance: LAUREEN JARRETT.
Minister of Labour and Minister responsible for Multiculturalism: MICHAEL MCKEE.
Minister of Education: SHIRLEY DYSART.
Minister of Advanced Education and Training: RUSS KING.
Minister of Municipal Affairs and Environment: VAUGHN BLANEY.
Minister of Commerce and Technology: AL LACEY.
Minister of Fisheries and Aquaculture: ALDÉA LANDRY (acting).
Minister of Tourism, Recreation and Heritage: ROLAND BEAULIEU.
Minister of Housing: PETER TRITES.
Chairman of the New Brunswick Electric Power Commission: RAYBURN DOUCETT.
Solicitor-General: CONRAD LANDRY.

GOVERNMENT ADDRESSES

Office of the Lieutenant-Governor: Legislative Bldg, POB 6000, Fredericton, NB E3B 5H1.
Office of the Premier: Centennial Bldg, POB 6000, Fredericton, NB E3B 5H1; tel. (506) 453-2144; telex 014-46230; fax (506) 453-7407.
Department of Advanced Education and Training: POB 6000, Fredericton, NB E3B 5H1; tel. (506) 453-2597.
Department of Agriculture: POB 6000, Fredericton, NB E3B 5H1; tel. (506) 453-2666; fax (506) 453-7170.
Department of Commerce and Technology: POB 6000, Fredericton, NB E3B 5H1; tel. (506) 453-2965; telex 014-46100.
Department of Education: POB 6000, Fredericton, NB E3B 5H1; tel. (506) 453-3678; fax (506) 453-3325.
Department of Finance: Centennial Bldg, POB 6000, Fredericton, NB E3B 5H1; tel. (506) 453-2511; fax (506) 453-7408.
Department of Fisheries and Aquaculture: POB 6000, Fredericton, NB E3B 5H1; tel. (506) 453-2766; telex 014-46196; fax (506) 453-5210.
Department of Health and Community Services: POB 6000, Fredericton, NB E3B 5H1; tel. (506) 453-2536.
Department of Income Assistance: POB 6000, Fredericton, NB E3B 5H1; tel. (506) 453-2001; telex 014-46230; fax (506) 453-7478.
Department of Justice: POB 6000, Fredericton, NB E3B 5H1; tel. (506) 453-2458; fax (506) 453-7408.
Department of Labour: POB 6000, Fredericton, NB E3B 5H1; tel. (506) 453-2303; telex 014-46186; fax (506) 453-3806.
Department of Municipal Affairs and Environment: POB 6000, Fredericton, NB E3B 5H1; tel. (506) 453-3700; telex 014-46230; fax (506) 453-3843.
Department of Natural Resources and Energy: POB 6000, Fredericton, NB E3B 5H1; tel. (506) 453-2614; telex 014-46230; fax (506) 453-4279.
Department of the Solicitor-General: POB 6000, Fredericton, NB E3B 5H1; tel. (506) 453-7414.
Department of Supply and Services: POB 6000, Fredericton, NB E3B 5H1; tel. (506) 453-2998; telex 014-46230; fax (506) 452-7012.
Department of Tourism, Recreation and Heritage: POB 12345, Fredericton, NB E3B 5C3; tel. (506) 453-2377; telex 014-46230; fax (506) 453-2416.
Department of Transportation: POB 6000, Fredericton, NB E3B 5H1; tel. (506) 453-2663; fax (506) 453-2900.
New Brunswick Housing Corporation: POB 611, Fredericton, NB E3B 5B2; tel. (506) 453-7755; telex 014-46230.

LEGISLATIVE ASSEMBLY

Speaker: FRANK BRANCH (Liberal).
Clerk: DAVID L. E. PETERSON.

Election, 13 October 1987

	Seats at election	Seats at 1 Nov. 1988
Liberal	58	57
Vacant	—	1
Total	**58**	**58**

Newfoundland

The province of Newfoundland joined the confederation on 31 March 1949, as a result of the British North America Act (later the Newfoundland Act) of the same year. The provincial government has a lieutenant-governor; an executive council, consisting of the premier and his or her cabinet; and a 52-member house of assembly. 242,491 votes were polled in Newfoundland in the 1984 federal general election, representing 65% of voters on the list. Local government is administered by the province's 312 incorporated municipalities: two cities, one metropolitan area, 169 towns and 140 communities. There are also 113 'local service districts' which are quasi-municipal areas.

PROVINCIAL EXECUTIVE

Lieutenant-Governor: JAMES MCGRATH.

Executive Council
Premier and Minister of Energy: CLYDE WELLS.
Minister of Finance: Dr HUBERT KITCHEN.
President of the Council, President of the Treasury Board and Minister responsible for the Status of Women: WINSTON BAKER.
Minister of Mines and Energy: Dr REX GIBBONS.
Minister of Justice: PAUL DICKS.
Minister of Works, Services and Transportation: DAVID GILBERT.
Minister of Forestry and Agriculture: GRAHAM FLIGHT.
Minister of Municipal and Provincial Affairs: ERIC GULLAGE.
Minister of Fisheries: WALTER CARTER.
Minister of Health: CHRIS DECKER.
Minister of Social Services: JOHN EFFORD.
Minister of Development: CHUCK FUREY.
Minister of Environment and Lands: JIM KELLAND.
Minister of Education: PHIL WARREN.
Minister of Employment and Labour Relations: PATT COWAN.

GOVERNMENT ADDRESSES

Office of the Lieutenant-Governor: Government House, Military Rd, St John's, NF A1C 5W4.
Office of the Premier: Confederation Bldg, 8th Floor, St John's, NF A1C 5T7; tel. (709) 576-3570.
Department of Career Development and Advanced Studies: Confederation Bldg, POB 4750, St John's, NF A1C 5T7; tel. (709) 576-3100; telex 016-4197; fax (709) 576-3669.
Department of Consumer Affairs and Communications: Elizabeth Towers, POB 4750, St John's, NF A1C 5T7; tel. (709) 576-2600; telex 016-4197; fax (709) 576-3627.
Department of Culture, Recreation and Youth: Confederation Bldg, 3rd Floor, POB 4750, St John's, NF A1C 5T7; tel. (709) 576-2922; telex 016-4197; fax (709) 576-5038.
Department of Development and Tourism: Confederation Annex, 4th Floor, POB 4750, St John's, NF A1C 5T7; tel. (709) 576-5600; telex 016-4949; fax (709) 576-5936.
Department of Education: Confederation Bldg, POB 4750, St John's, NF A1C 5T7; tel. (709) 576-2991.
Department of Energy: POB 4750, St John's, NF A1C 5T7; tel. (709) 576-2411; telex 016-4034; fax (709) 576-2508.
Department of Environment and Lands: Confederation Bldg, POB 4750, St John's, NF A1C 5T7; tel. (709) 576-3394; telex 016-4197.
Department of Finance: Confederation Bldg, POB 4750, St John's, NF A1C 5T7; telex 016-4132; fax (709) 576-3627.
Department of Fisheries: Confederation Annex, 5th Floor, POB 4750, St John's, NF A1C 5T7; tel. (709) 576-3707; fax (709) 576-6082.
Department of Forestry: Confederation Complex, 5th Floor, POB 4750, St John's, NF A1C 5T7; tel. (709) 576-3245; fax (709) 576-5798.
Department of Health: Confederation Bldg, POB 4750, St John's, NF A1C 5T7; tel. (709) 576-3141; fax (709) 576-5824.
Department of Justice: Confederation Bldg, POB 4750, St John's, NF A1C 5T7; tel. (709) 576-2890; telex 016-4197; fax (709) 576-3627.
Department of Labour: Confederation Bldg, POB 4750, St John's, NF A1C 5T7; tel. (709) 576-2729.
Department of Mines: Confederation Bldg, POB 4750, St John's, NF A1C 5T7; tel. (709) 576-3660; telex 016-4724; fax (709) 576-6782.
Department of Municipal Affairs: Confederation Bldg, POB 4750, St John's, NF A1C 5T7; tel. (709) 576-3049.

Department of Public Works and Services: Confederation Bldg, POB 4750, St John's, NF A1C 5T7; tel. (709) 576-3374; telex 016-4197; fax (709) 576-3627.

Department of Rural, Agricultural and Northern Development: Confederation Bldg, POB 4750, St John's, NF A1C 5T7; tel. (709) 576-3172; fax (709) 576-5967.

Department of Social Services: Confederation Bldg, POB 4750, St John's, NF A1C 5T7; tel. (709) 576-2478; fax (709) 576-3627.

Department of Transportation: Confederation Bldg, 6th Floor, POB 4750, St John's, NF A1C 5T7; tel. (709) 576-3292; telex 016-3101; fax (709) 576-6934.

Intergovernmental Affairs Secretariat (Executive Council): Confederation Bldg, POB 4750, St John's, NF A1C 5T7; tel. (709) 576-3670; telex 016-4718; fax (709) 576-5038.

Newfoundland and Labrador Housing Corporation: POB 220, St John's, NF A1C 5J2; tel. (709) 745-0100; fax (709) 745-2388.

Treasury Board: Confederation Bldg, POB 4750, St John's, NF A1C 5T7; tel. (709) 576-3559.

HOUSE OF ASSEMBLY

Speaker: (vacant).
Clerk: BETTIE DUFF.

Election, 20 April 1989

	Seats at election
Liberal	20
Progressive Conservative	32
Total	52

Northwest Territories

The Northwest Territories were admitted to the confederation on 15 July 1870 by the Rupert's Land Act of 1868 and the Imperial Order-in-Council of 23 June 1870. The Northwest Territories Act of 1970 provided the present system of government. The government comprises a commissioner, appointed by the federal government and under the direction of the Federal Minister of Indian and Northern Affairs; an executive council of up to eight members including the government leader, all of whom are nominated by the legislative assembly; and a 24-member legislative assembly. Members of the legislative assembly are elected for four years and usually meet twice a year. At present the assembly is not arranged along party lines. A majority of its members are of native descent. As in the provinces, the territorial government has authority over most territorial matters, except for non-renewable resources, forestry, and fire suppression. In the 1987 territorial general election 15,901 votes were cast, representing 72% of the number of electors on the official list. Local government is organized through one city, five towns, two villages, 30 hamlets and 14 settlements.

TERRITORIAL EXECUTIVE

Commissioner: JOHN HAVELOCK PARKER.

Executive Council

Government Leader, Minister of the Executive and Minister responsible for Intergovernmental Affairs: DENNIS PATTERSON.

Minister of Culture and Communications, Minister of Renewable Resources and Associate Minister of Aboriginal Rights and Constitutional Development: TITUS ALLOOLOO.

Minister of Justice, Minister of Finance and Government House Leader: MIKE BALLANTYNE.

Minister of Health, Minister of Energy, Mines and Resources, and Minister of Public Works and Highways: NELLIE COURNOYEA.

Minister of Education and Minister of Aboriginal Rights and Constitutional Development: STEVE KAKFWI.

Minister of Social Services, Minister of Personnel, Minister responsible for the Status of Women and Minister responsible for the Highway Transport Board: JEANNIE MARIE-JEWELL.

Minister of Government Services: THOMAS H. BUTTERS.

Minister of Municipal and Community Affairs, Minister of Economic Development and Tourism, and Minister of Transportation: GORDON WRAY.

GOVERNMENT ADDRESSES

The postal address for all government departments is: POB 1320, Yellowknife, NT X1A 2L9; telex 034-45528.

LEGISLATIVE ASSEMBLY

Speaker: RED PETERSEN.

The Legislative Assembly, elected in October 1987, consists of 24 independent members without formal party affiliation.

Nova Scotia

Nova Scotia was admitted to the confederation on 1 July 1867 by the British North America Act of the same year and the Imperial Order-in-Council of 22 May 1867. The provincial government comprises the lieutenant-governor; the executive council, consisting of the premier and the cabinet, chosen by the premier; and the 52-member House of Assembly. In the 1984 federal general election 462,885 votes were polled, representing 75% of voters on the official provincial list. Local government in Nova Scotia is administered by 24 rural municipalities, within which are 25 incorporated villages. In addition, there are three cities and 39 towns.

PROVINCIAL EXECUTIVE

Lieutenant-Governor: ALAN R. ABRAHAM.

Executive Council

Premier, President of the Executive Council, Chairman of the Policy Board, Minister responsible for the Cabinet Secretariat: JOHN M. BUCHANAN.

Minister of Housing, Deputy Premier, Minister responsible for the Emergency Measures Organization: ROGER S. BACON.

Minister of Mines and Energy, Chairman of the Senior Citizens Secretariat, Minister responsible for the Communications and Information Act: JOHN A. MACISAAC.

Minister of Tourism and Culture, Minister responsible for the Administration of the Nova Scotia Research Foundation Corporation Act, Minister responsible for the Advisory Council on Applied Science and Technology: DONALD M. CAMERON.

Minister of Small Business Development, Minister responsible for the Nova Scotia Business Capital Corporation Act: KENNETH STREATCH.

Minister of Education: RONALD C. GIFFIN.

Chairman of the Management Board, Minister of Government Services, Minister of Intergovernmental Affairs, Chairman of the Economic Development Committee of Cabinet, Minister responsible for the Civil Service Act: TERENCE R. B. DONAHOE.

Attorney-General, Minister responsible for the Administration of the Human Rights Act, Chairman of the Social Development Committee of Cabinet: J. MCINNIS.

Minister of Advanced Education and Job Training: JOEL R. MATHESON.

Minister of Labour, Minister responsible for the Administration of the Liquor Control Act: RONALD S. RUSSELL.

Minister of Finance, Minister responsible for the Administration of the Nova Scotia Sport and Recreation Commission, Minister in Charge of the Lottery Act: J. GREG KERR.

Minister of the Environment: JOHN G. LEEFE.

Minister of Transportation and Communications: GEORGE G. MOODY.

Minister of Health and Fitness, Registrar General, Minister in charge of the Drug Dependency Act, Minister responsible for Reporting on the Handicapped: G. DAVID NANTES.

Minister of Community Services, Minister responsible for Acadian Affairs: GUY J. LEBLANC.

Minister of Municipal Affairs: BRIAN A. YOUNG.

Minister of Fisheries, Minister responsible for the Advisory Council on the Status of Women Act: DONALD MCINNES.

Minister of Consumer Affairs, Minister in charge of the Residential Tenancies Act: R. COLIN D. STEWART.

Minister of Agriculture and Marketing: GEORGE ARCHIBALD.

Minister of Lands and Forests: CHARLES W. MACNEIL.

Solicitor General, Provincial Secretary, Minister in charge of the Regulations Act, Minister responsible for Youth: NEIL J. LEBLANC.

GOVERNMENT ADDRESSES

Office of the Lieutenant-Governor: Government House, Halifax, NS B3J 1Z2.

Office of the Premier: Province House, Halifax, NS B3J 2T3; tel. (902) 424-6600; telex 019-22693; fax (902) 424-7648.

Department of Advanced Education and Job Training: POB 2086, Station M, Halifax, NS B3J 3B7; tel. (902) 424-7747; fax (902) 424-0511.

Department of Agriculture and Marketing: POB 190, Halifax, NS B3J 2M4; tel. (902) 424-3244; telex 019-22734; fax (902) 424-3948.

Department of the Attorney-General: POB 7, Halifax, NS B3J 2L6; tel. (902) 424-4223; telex 019-22693; fax (902) 424-4556.

Department of Community Services: POB 696, Halifax, NS B3J 2T7; tel. (902) 424-4326; fax (902) 424-0502.

Department of Consumer Affairs: POB 998, Halifax, NS B3J 2X3; tel. (902) 424-4690; fax (902) 424-0503.

Department of Education: POB 578, Halifax, NS B3J 2S9; tel. (902) 424-5570.

Department of the Environment: POB 2107, Halifax, NS B3J 3B7; tel. (902) 424-5300; fax (902) 424-0503.

Department of Finance: POB 187, Halifax, NS B3J 2N3; tel. (902) 424-5554; telex 019-22570; fax (902) 429-0257.

Department of Fisheries: POB 2223, Halifax, NS B3J 3C4; tel. (902) 424-4560; telex 019-22799; fax (902) 424-4671.

Department of Government Services: 1505 Barrington St, POB 54, Halifax, NS B3J 2L4; tel. (902) 424-6980; telex 019-22734; fax (902) 424-0500.

Department of Health and Fitness: Joseph Howe Bldg, 12th Floor, 1690 Hollis St, POB 488, Halifax, NS B3J 2R8; tel. (902) 424-4391.

Department of Housing: POB 815, Dartmouth, NS B2Y 3Z3; tel. (902) 424-4483; fax (902) 424-5327.

Department of Industry, Trade and Technology: POB 519, Halifax, NS B3J 2R7; tel. (902) 424-8920; telex 019-22548.

Department of Labour: POB 697, Halifax, NS B3J 2T8; tel. (902) 424-4680.

Department of Lands and Forests: Founders Sq., Hollis St, POB 698, Halifax, NS B3J 2T9; tel. (902) 424-6694; telex 019-22745; fax (902) 424-7735.

Management Board: One Government Pl., 4th Floor, 1700 Granville St, POB 1619, Halifax, NS B3J 2Y3; tel. (902) 424-7750.

Department of Mines and Energy: 1701 Hollis St, POB 1087, Halifax, NS B3J 2X1; tel. (902) 424-6745; telex 019-21690.

Department of Municipal Affairs: POB 216, Halifax, NS B3J 2M4; tel. (902) 424-7563.

Department of Small Business Development: Joseph Howe Bldg, 1690 Hollis St, Suite 700, Halifax, NS B3J 3J9; tel. (902) 424-6660; telex 019-22517; fax (902) 424-6823.

Department of the Solicitor-General: Joseph Howe Bldg, 1690 Hollis St, POB 2599, Station M, Halifax, NS B3J 3N5; tel. (902) 424-7403.

Department of Tourism and Culture: POB 456, Halifax, NS B3J 2R5; tel. (902) 424-5000; telex 019-23525; fax (902) 424-2668.

Department of Transportation and Communications: Provincial Bldg, 6th Floor, POB 186, Halifax, NS B3J 2N2; tel. (902) 424-8687; telex 019-21747; fax (902) 424-6308.

HOUSE OF ASSEMBLY

Speaker: ARTHUR DONAHOE (PC).

Clerk: R. K. MACARTHUR.

Election, 6 September 1988

	Seats at election*
Progressive Conservative	28
Liberal	21
New Democratic Party	2
Independent	1
Total	**52**

* Party standings remained the same at 1 January 1989.

Ontario

Ontario was admitted to the confederation on 1 July 1867 by the British North America Act of the same year. The provincial government comprises the lieutenant-governor; the executive council, consisting of the premier and his or her chosen cabinet; and the legislative assembly, which has 125 members. In the 1984 federal general election 4,461,416 votes were polled, representing 76% of the numbers of voters on the official list. Approximately 95% of the population occupy 10% of the land area of the province, in which local government is organized through one metropolitan municipality, encompassing five cities and one borough; 10 regional municipalities; 27 counties and 10 regional districts. The rest of Ontario comes under direct provincial administration.

PROVINCIAL EXECUTIVE

Lieutenant-Governor: LINCOLN M. ALEXANDER.

Executive Council

Premier, Minister of Intergovernmental Affairs: DAVID PETERSON.

Deputy Premier, Treasurer of Ontario and Minister of Economics: ROBERT NIXON.

Minister of Mines and Government House Leader: SEAN CONWAY.

Minister of the Environment: JAMES BRADLEY.

Attorney-General and Minister responsible for Native Affairs: IAN SCOTT.

Minister of Agriculture and Food: JACK RIDDELL.

Minister of Municipal Affairs: JOHN EAKINS.

Minister of Natural Resources: VINCENT KERRIO.

Minister of Tourism and Recreation: HUGH O'NEIL.

Minister of Community and Social Services: JOHN SWEENEY.

Chairman of Management Board, Chairman of Cabinet and Minister of Financial Institutions: MURRAY ELSTON.

Minister of Consumer and Commercial Relations: WILLIAM WRYE.

Minister of Revenue and Minister responsible for Francophone Affairs: BERNARD GRANDMAÎTRE.

Minister of Skills Development: ALVIN CURLING.

Minister of Transportation: ED FULTON.

Minister of Industry, Trade and Technology: MONTE KWINTER.

Minister of Culture and Communications: LILY ODDIE MUNRO.

Minister of Labour and Minister responsible for Women's Issues: GREGORY SORBARA.

Minister of Health: ELINOR CAPLAN.

Minister of Northern Development: RENÉ FONTAINE.

Minister of Correctional Services: DAVID RAMSAY.

Solicitor-General: JOAN SMITH.

Minister of Education: CHRISTOPHER WARD.

Minister of Housing: CHAVIVA HOSEK.

Minister of Colleges and Universities: LYN MCLEOD.

Minister of Government Services: RICHARD PATTEN.

Minister of Citizenship and Minister responsible for Race Relations and the Ontario Human-Rights Commission: GERRY PHILLIPS.

Minister of Energy: ROBERT WONG.

Minister without Portfolio, responsible for Disabled Persons: REMO MANCINI.

Minister without Portfolio, responsible for Senior Citizens' Affairs: MAVIS WILSON.

GOVERNMENT ADDRESSES

Office of the Lieutenant-Governor: Main Parliament Bldg, Rm 131, Queen's Park, Toronto, ON M7A 1A1.

Office of the Premier: Legislative Bldg, Toronto, ON M7A 1A1; tel. (416) 965-1941; telex 06-219681; fax (416) 963-3065.

Management Board: Frost Bldg South, 7th Floor, Queen's Park, Toronto, ON M7A 1Z6; tel. (416) 586-2101.

Ministry of Agriculture and Food: Parliament Bldgs, Queen's Park, Toronto, ON M7A 1A3; tel. (416) 965-1421; telex 06-22546.

Ministry of the Attorney-General: 18 King St East, 18th Floor, Toronto, ON M5C 1C5; tel. (416) 965-9111; telex 06-218941; fax (416) 363-2814.

Ministry of Citizenship: 77 Bloor St West, Toronto, ON M7A 2R9; tel. (416) 965-0615; fax (416) 965-8622.

Ministry of Colleges and Universities: 101 Bloor St West, Toronto, ON M5S 1P7; tel. (416) 965-6407.

Ministry of Community and Social Services: Hepburn Block, Queen's Park, Toronto, ON M7A 1E9; tel. (416) 965-7852; telex 06-23410; fax (416) 963-0947.

Ministry of Consumer and Commercial Relations: 555 Yonge St, Toronto, ON M7A 2H6; tel. (416) 963-1111; telex 06-219608; fax (416) 963-2046.

Ministry of Correctional Services: 2001 Eglinton Ave East, Scarborough, ON M1L 4P1; tel. (416) 750-3333; fax (416) 750-3486.

Ministry of Culture and Communications: 77 Bloor St West, 6th Floor, Toronto, ON M7A 2R9; tel. (416) 965-0615; fax (416) 965-8622.

Ministry of Education: Mowat Block, Queen's Park, Toronto, ON M7A 1L2; tel. (416) 965-6407.

Ministry of Energy: 56 Wellesley St West, 9th Floor, Toronto, ON M7A 2B7; tel. (416) 963-3728; telex 06-217880; fax (416) 965-1823.

Ministry of the Environment: 135 St Clair Ave West, Toronto, ON M4V 1P5; tel. (416) 323-4324; telex 06-23496; fax (416) 963-0704.

Ministry of Financial Institutions: 555 Yonge St, 8th Floor, Toronto, ON M7A 2H6; tel. (416) 963-0339; fax (416) 324-3447.

Ministry of Government Services: Queen's Park, Toronto, ON M7A 1N3; tel. (416) 965-6683.

Ministry of Health: Hepburn Block, Queen's Park, Toronto, ON M7A 1S2; tel. (416) 965-3101; telex 06-23410; fax (416) 963-3496.

Ministry of Housing: 777 Bay St, 17th Floor, Toronto, ON M5G 2E5; tel. (416) 585-7041; fax (416) 591-8445.

Ministry of Industry, Trade and Technology: Hearst Block, 900 Bay St, Queen's Park, Toronto, ON M7A 2E1; tel. (416) 965-1744; fax (416) 963-0335.

Ministry of Intergovernmental Affairs: Mowat Block, 6th Floor, Queen's Park, Toronto, ON M7A 1C2; tel. (416) 965-4706; telex 06-218562; fax (416) 965-2096.

Ministry of Labour: 400 University Ave, Toronto, ON M7A 1T7; tel. (416) 965-7941.

Ministry of Municipal Affairs: 777 Bay St, 17th Floor, Toronto, ON M5G 2E5; tel. (416) 585-7041.

Ministry of Natural Resources: Whitney Block, 99 Wellesley St West, Toronto, ON M7A 1W3; tel. (416) 965-2000; telex 06-219701; fax (416) 965-6336.

Ministry of Northern Development and Mines: 10 Wellesley St East, 10th Floor, Toronto, ON M4Y 1G2; tel. (416) 965-1683; telex 06-524131; fax (416) 965-5181.

Ministry of Revenue: 33 King St West, Oshawa, ON L1H 8H5; tel. (416) 433-5779; telex 06-981338; fax (416) 579-0641.

Ministry of Skills Development: 101 Bloor St West, 13th Floor, Toronto, ON M5S 1P7; tel. (416) 965-8276; fax (416) 963-1000.

Ministry of the Solicitor-General: George Drew Bldg, 11th Floor, 25 Grosvenor St, Toronto, ON M7A 1Y6; tel. (416) 965-5212.

Ministry of Tourism and Recreation: 77 Bloor St West, Toronto, ON M7A 2R9; tel. (416) 965-7680; fax (416) 965-3766.

Ministry of Transportation: 1201 Wilson Ave, West Tower, Downsview, ON M3M 1J8; tel. (416) 235-3904; telex 06-524145.

Ministry of Treasury and Economics: Queen's Park, Toronto, ON M7A 1Y7; tel. (416) 965-7171; telex 06-217575; fax (416) 965-3067.

Office of Francophone Affairs: Mowat Block, 900 Bay St, 4th Floor, Toronto, ON M7A 1C2; tel. (416) 965-3865.

Office for Senior Citizens: 76 College St, 6th Floor, Toronto, ON M7A 1N3; tel. (416) 965-5106.

LEGISLATIVE ASSEMBLY

Speaker: HUGH EDIGHOFFER (Lib.).
Clerk: CLAUDE DESROSIERS.

Election, 10 September 1987

	Seats at election	Seats at 1 Nov. 1988
Liberal	95	94
New Democratic Party	16	19
Progressive Conservative . . .	19	17
Total	130	130

Prince Edward Island

Prince Edward Island was admitted to the confederation on 1 July 1873 by the Imperial Order-in-Council of 26 June 1873. The provincial government consists of the lieutenant-governor; premier and cabinet, together forming the executive council; and a legislative assembly of 32 members. In the 1984 federal general election 73,801 votes were polled, representing 85% of voters on the official list. Local government is administered by the province's one city, eight towns and 30 villages, all of which are incorporated. There are also 39 community improvement committees which serve the unincorporated areas.

PROVINCIAL EXECUTIVE

Lieutenant-Governor: LLOYD G. MACPHAIL.

Executive Council

Premier and President of the Executive Council: JOSEPH A. GHIZ.

Minister of Finance and Minister of Community and Cultural Affairs: GILBERT R. CLEMENTS.

Minister of Energy and Forestry: ALLISON ELLIS.

Minister of Industry: LEONCE BERNARD.

Minister of Fisheries: JOHNNY ROSS YOUNG.

Minister of Transportation and Public Works: ROBERT MORRISSEY.

Minister of Education: BETTY JEAN BROWN.

Minister of Agriculture: TIM CARROLL.

Minister of Justice and Attorney-General, and Minister of Labour: WAYNE CHEVERIE.

Minister of Tourism and Parks: GORDON E. MACINNIS.

Minister of Health and Social Services: KEITH MILLIGAN.

GOVERNMENT ADDRESSES

Office of the Lieutenant-Governor: 'Fanningbank', Charlottetown, PE C1A 7L9.

Office of the Premier: Province Bldg, POB 2000, Charlottetown, PE C1A 7N8; tel. (902) 368-4400; telex 014-44154; fax (902) 368-4416.

Department of Agriculture: POB 2000, Charlottetown, PE C1A 7N8; tel. (902) 368-4880; telex 014-44154; fax (902) 892-3420.

Department of Community and Cultural Affairs: POB 2000, Charlottetown, PE C1A 7N8; tel. (902) 892-0311; telex 014-44154; fax (902) 892-3420.

Department of Education: POB 2000, Charlottetown, PE C1A 7N8; tel. (902) 368-4600; telex 014-44154; fax (902) 892-3420.

Department of Energy and Forestry: POB 2000, Charlottetown, PE C1A 7N8; tel. (902) 368-5020; telex 014-44154; fax (902) 892-3420.

Department of Finance: POB 2000, Charlottetown, PE C1A 7N8; tel. (902) 368-4050; telex 014-44154; fax (902) 892-3420.

Department of Fisheries: POB 2000, Charlottetown, PE C1A 7N8; tel. (902) 368-5240; telex 014-44154; fax (902) 892-3420.

Department of Health and Social Services: POB 2000, Charlottetown, PE C1A 7N8; tel. (902) 368-4900; telex 014-44154; fax (902) 892-3420.

Department of Industry: POB 2000, Charlottetown, PE C1A 7N8; tel. (902) 368-4240; telex 014-44154; fax (902) 892-3420.

Department of Justice and the Attorney-General: POB 2000, Charlottetown, PE C1A 7N8; tel. (902) 368-4588; telex 014-44154; fax (902) 892-3420.

Department of Labour: POB 2000, Charlottetown, PE C1A 7N8; tel. (902) 368-5550; telex 014-44154; fax (902) 892-3420.

Department of Tourism and Parks: POB 2000, Charlottetown, PE C1A 7N8; tel. (902) 368-5500; telex 014-44154; fax (902) 892-3420.

Department of Transportation and Public Works: POB 2000, Charlottetown, PE C1A 7N8; tel. (902) 368-7431; telex 014-44154; fax (902) 892-3420.

LEGISLATIVE ASSEMBLY

Speaker: EDWARD CLARK (Lib.).
Clerk: AUBIN DOIRON.

Election, May 1989

	Seats at election	Seats at 1 Nov. 1989
Liberal	30	30
Progressive Conservative . . .	2	2
Total	32	32

Québec

Québec was admitted to the confederation on 1 July 1867 by the British North America Act of the same year. The provincial government has a lieutenant-governor; a *conseil exécutif* or *conseil des ministres* (executive council), consisting of the *premier ministre* (premier) and his or her ministers; and the Assemblée Nationale (legislative assembly) which has 125 members. In the 1984 federal election 3,485,815 votes were polled, representing 76% of voters on the official list. One-third of Québec is organized municipally, while the remainder is governed directly by the provincial government. In 1985 the province had 95 regional county municipalities, 257 cities and towns, 1,298 municipalities and 56 native villages.

PROVINCIAL EXECUTIVE

Lieutenant-Governor: GILLES LAMONTAGNE.

Executive Council

Premier: ROBERT BOURASSA.

Deputy Premier and Minister of Energy and Regional Development: LISE BACON.

Minister of Finance: GÉRARD D. LÉVESQUE.

Minister of Education and Minister responsible for the Language Law: CLAUDE RYAN.

Minister of Industry: GÉRALD TREMBLAY.

Minister of Justice and Intergovernmental Affairs: GIL RÉMILLARD.

Minister of International Affairs and Native Affairs: JOHN CIACCIA.

Minister of Health and Social Affairs and Minister for Electoral Reform: MARC-YVAN COTÉ.

Minister of Transport and Public Security: SAM ELKAS.

Minister of Agriculture, Fisheries and Food, and Government House Leader: MICHEL PAGÉ.

Minister of Manpower and Income Security: ANDRÉ BOURBEAU.

Minister of Forestry: ALBERT COTÉ.

Minister of Supply and Services: ROBERT DUTIL.

Minister of Communications: LIZA FRULLA-HEBERT.

Minister for the Status of Women, Minister responsible for Immigration and Cultural Communities: MONIQUE GAGNON-TREMBLAY.

President of the Treasury Boad: DANIEL JOHNSON.

Minister of the Environment: PIERRE PARADIS.

Minister of Municipal Affairs: YVON PICOTTE.

Minister responsible for la Francophonie: GUY RIVARD.

Minister of Cultural Affairs: LUCIENNE ROBILLARD.

Minister of Mines and Junior Minister of Regional Development: RAYMOND SAVOIE.

Minister of Revenue and Minister of Labour: YVES SÉGUIN.

Minister of Tourism: ANDRÉ VALLERAND.

Minister of Recreation, Hunting and Fishing: GASTON BLACKBURN.

Junior Minister for Cultural Communities: NORMAND CHERRY.

Junior Minister of Agriculture, Fisheries and Food: ROBERT MIDDLEMASS.

Junior Minister of Finance: LOUISE ROBIC.

Junior Minister of Health: CHRISTOS SIRROS.

Junior Minister for the Status of Women: VIOLETTE TREPANIER.

Junior Minister of Transport: YVON VALLIÈRES.

GOVERNMENT ADDRESSES

Office of the Lieutenant-Governor: André-Laurendeau Bldg, 1050 rue St-Augustin, Québec, PQ G1A 1A1.

Office of the Prime Minister: 885 Grande-Allée est, Edifice J, 3e étage, Québec, PQ G1A 1A2; tel. (418) 643-5321; telex 051-3523; fax (418) 643-3924.

Ministry of Agriculture, Fisheries and Food: 200A chemin Sainte-Foy, Québec, PQ G1R 4X6; tel. (418) 643-2517.

Ministry of Communications: Edifice G, 1037 rue de la Chevrotière, 3e étage, Québec, PQ G1R 4Y7; tel. (418) 643-1529; fax (418) 643-7721.

Ministry of Cultural Affairs: 225 Grande-Allée est, Québec, PQ G1R 5G5; tel. (418) 643-2183; fax (418) 643-4457.

Ministry of Cultural Communities and Immigration: 355 rue McGill, Montréal, PQ H2Y 2E8; tel. (514) 873-4546; telex 055-60840.

Ministry of Education: Edifice G, 1035 rue de la Chevrotière, 15e étage, Québec, PQ G1R 5A5; tel. (418) 643-7095.

Ministry of Energy and Resources: 200 chemin Sainte-Foy, Québec, PQ G1R 4X7; tel. (418) 643-1809; telex 051-2274; fax (418) 643-0720; incorporates Div. of Mines and Autochtone Affairs and Div. of Forests.

Ministry of the Environment: 3900 rue Marly, Sainte-Foy, PQ G1X 4E4; tel. (418) 643-6071.

Ministry of Finance: 12 rue St-Louis, Québec, PQ G1R 5L3; tel. (418) 691-2233; telex 051-3771; fax (418) 643-4700.

Ministry of Health and Social Services: 1075 chemin Sainte-Foy, Québec, PQ G1S 2M1; tel. (418) 643-3380; telex 051-3967; fax (418) 643-3177.

Ministry of Higher Education and Science: 1033 rue de la Chevrotière, Québec, PQ G1R 5K9; tel. (418) 643-6788; fax (418) 643-8651.

Ministry of Industry and Commerce: 710 pl. de Youville, 6e étage, Québec, PQ G1R 4Y4; tel. (418) 643-5068.

Ministry of International Affairs: 875 Grande-Allée est, Québec, PQ G1R 4Y8; tel. (418) 643-2978; telex 051-3523; fax (418) 643-4135.

Ministry of Justice: 1200 route de l'Eglise, 2e étage, Sainte-Foy, PQ G1V 4M1; tel. (418) 643-5140; incorporates Div. of Canadian Intergovernmental Affairs.

Ministry of Labour: 425 rue St-Amable, 2e étage, Québec, PQ G1R 5M3; tel. (418) 643-5297; telex 051-3847.

Ministry of Manpower and Income Security: 425 rue St-Amable, Québec, PQ G1R 4Z1; tel. (418) 643-9818; fax (418) 643-5188.

Ministry of Municipal Affairs: Edifice Cook-Chauveau, 20 ave Chauveau, Québec, PQ G1R 4J3; tel. (418) 691-2019; telex 051-3334; fax (418) 643-7385.

Ministry of Public Security: 1200 route de l'Eglise, 3e étage, Sainte-Foy, PQ G1V 4T4; tel. (418) 643-2112.

Ministry of Recreation, Fish and Game: 150 blvd St-Cyrille est, Québec, PQ G1R 4Y1; tel. (418) 643-2984; telex 051-3994.

Ministry of Revenue: 3800 rue Marly, Sainte-Foy, PQ G1X 4A5; tel. (418) 652-4935.

Ministry of the Solicitor-General: 1200 route de l'Eglise, 3e étage, Sainte-Foy, PQ G1V 4T4; tel. (418) 644-4851.

Ministry of Supply and Services: 1045 rue de la Chevrotière, 7e étage, Québec, PQ G1R 5L4; fax (418) 643-1612.

Ministry of Tourism: 2 pl. Québec, Bureau 336, Québec, PQ G1R 2B5; tel. (418) 643-5959; fax (418) 643-6149.

Ministry of Transportation: 700 blvd St-Cyrille est, Québec, PQ G1R 5H1; tel. (418) 643-6740; telex 051-3733.

Treasury Board: 1050 rue St-Augustin, Québec, PQ G1R 5A4; tel. (418) 643-5926; fax (418) 643-7824.

Women's Programs Office: 875 Grande-Allée est, Edifice H, 2e étage, Québec, PQ G1R 4Y8; tel. (418) 643-9460; fax (418) 643-4991.

ASSEMBLÉE NATIONALE/ NATIONAL ASSEMBLY

Speaker: PIERRE LORRAIN (Lib.).

Secretary-General: PIERRE DUCHESNE.

Election, 25 September 1989

	Seats at election
Liberal	92
Parti Québécois	29
Equality Party	4
Total	125

Saskatchewan

The province of Saskatchewan was created on 1 September 1905 as a result of the Saskatchewan Act of 20 July 1905. The provincial government consists of a lieutenant-governor; an executive council, consisting of the premier and his or her chosen cabinet; and a legislative assembly of 64 members. In the 1986 provincial general election 549,985 people voted, representing 82% of the number of voters on the official list. Local government in the province is organized through 12 cities, 143 towns, 323 villages, 32 resort villages, 2 northern towns, 10 northern villages, 14 northern hamlets and 299 rural municipalities. The 10 northern villages are administered directly by the province.

PROVINCIAL EXECUTIVE

Lieutenant-Governor: SYLVIA FEDORUK.

Executive Council

Premier, President of the Council and Minister of Agriculture: GRANT DEVINE.

Deputy Premier and Provincial Secretary: ERIC BERNTSON.

Minister of Justice and Attorney-General, and Minister of Trade and Investment: BOB ANDREW.

Minister of Finance and Minister of Telephones: GARY LANE.

Minister of Public Participation: GRAHAM TAYLOR.

Minister of Economic Development and Tourism: JOAN DUNCAN.

Minister of Rural Development: NEAL HARDY.

Minister of Health: GEORGE MCLEOD.

Minister of Energy and Mines: PATRICIA SMITH.

Minister of Education: LORNE HEPWORTH.

Minister of Parks, Recreation and Culture: COLIN MAXWELL.

Minister of Highways and Transportation, and Minister responsible for Indian and Native Affairs Secretariat: GRANT HODGINS.

Minister of Human Resources, Labour and Employment, and Minister of Social Services: GRANT SCHMIDT.

Minister of Urban Affairs: JACK C. KLEIN.

Minister of Science and Technology, and Minister of Consumer and Commercial Affairs: RAY MEIKLEJOHN.

Minister of Environment and Public Safety: HERB SWAN.

GOVERNMENT ADDRESSES

Office of the Lieutenant-Governor: Government House, 4607 Dewdney Ave, Regina, SK S4T 3B7.

Office of the Premier: Legislative Bldg, Regina, SK S4S 0B3; tel. (306) 787-6352; telex 071-2586; fax (306) 787-7270.

Department of Agriculture: Walter Scott Bldg, 3085 Albert St, Regina, SK S4S 0B1; tel. (306) 787-6395.

Department of Consumer and Commercial Affairs: 1871 Smith St, Regina, SK S4P 3V7; tel. (306) 787-3897; fax (306) 787-5638.

Department of Economic Development and Tourism: 1919 Saskatchewan Dr., Regina, SK S4P 3V7; tel. (306) 787-4069; telex 071-2675; fax (306) 787-2198.

Department of Education: 2220 College Ave, Regina, SK S4P 3V7; tel. (306) 787-6030.

Department of Energy and Mines: 1914 Hamilton St, Regina, SK S4P 4V4; tel. (306) 787-2526; telex 071-2786; fax (306) 787-7338.

Department of Environment and Public Safety: 3085 Albert St, Regina, SK S4S 0B1; tel. (306) 787-6113.

Department of Finance: 2350 Albert St, Regina, SK S4P 4A6; tel. (306) 787-6532; fax (306) 787-6605.

Department of Health: 3475 Albert St, Regina, SK S4S 6X6; tel. (306) 787-2743; fax (306) 787-9000.

Department of Highways and Transportation: 1855 Victoria Ave, Regina, SK S4P 3V5; tel. (306) 787-4804; fax (306) 525-2560.

Department of Human Resources, Labour and Employment: 1870 Albert St, Regina, SK S4P 3V7; tel. (306) 787-1545; telex 071-2470; fax (306) 787-3626.

Department of Justice: 1874 Scarth St, Regina, SK S4P 3V7; tel. (306) 787-3765.

Department of Parks, Recreation and Culture: 3211 Albert St, Regina, SK S4S 5W6; tel. (306) 787-2322.

Department of the Provincial Secretary: Legislative Bldg, Rm 322, Regina, SK S4S 0B3; tel. (306) 787-2951; fax (306) 757-2376.

Department of Public Participation: 3085 Albert St, Rm 331, Regina, SK S4S 0B1; tel. (306) 787-1667.

Department of Rural Development: 3085 Albert St, Regina, SK S4S 0B1; tel. (306) 787-2011.

Department of Science and Technology: E. Sedco Centre, 2nd Floor, 15 Innovation Blvd, Saskatoon, SK S7N 2X8; tel. (306) 933-7200; fax (306) 933-8244.

Department of Social Services: 1920 Broad St, Regina, SK S4P 3V6; tel. (306) 787-5089; telex 071-2453; fax (306) 787-0925.

Department of Trade and Investment: 2103 11th Ave, Regina, SK S4P 3V7; tel. (306) 787-9149; telex 071-2675; fax (306) 787-2198.

Department of Urban Affairs: POB 7110, Regina, SK S4P 3V7; tel. (306) 787-2686; fax (306) 787-8748.

LEGISLATIVE ASSEMBLY

Speaker: A. B. TUSA (PC).

Clerk: G. L. BARNHART.

Election, 20 October 1986

	Seats at election	Seats at 1 Nov. 1988
Progressive Conservative	38	37
New Democratic Party	25	26
Liberal	1	—
Vacant	—	1
Total	64	64

Yukon Territory

Yukon Territory was admitted to the confederation on 13 June 1898 by the Yukon Territory Act. The system of government is based on the Yukon Act of 1970 and the Government Organization Act of 1966, which provide for a commissioner and the Yukon Legislative Assembly. The commissioner's role is similar to that of a provincial lieutenant-governor, except that he or she is responsible to the federal government through the federal Minister of Indian and Northern Affairs. Since 1979 the executive council has consisted of a cabinet of five elected members of the legislative assembly, and the majority party leader (not called the premier). The 16 members of the legislative assembly are elected to serve for four years. The assembly has jurisdiction over all local concerns but the government retains control of non-renewable natural resources and forestry. In the Yukon territorial election of 1989 11,726 people voted, representing 78% of those eligible to vote. Local government is administered by Yukon's two cities, one town, four villages, one hamlet and eight unorganized communities. Administration of the unorganized communities is provided by the territorial government.

TERRITORIAL EXECUTIVE

Commissioner: J. KENNETH McKINNON.

Executive Council

Government Leader, Minister of the Executive Council Office and of Health and Human Resources, and Minister responsible for the Yukon Development Corporation: TONY PENIKETT.

House Leader, Minister of Education, of Finance, of Economic Development and of Mines and Small Business: PIERS McDONALD.

Minister of Justice, Minister responsible for the Public Service Commission, Minister responsible for the Workers' Compensation Board and Minister responsible for the Women's Directorate: MARGARET JOE.

Minister of Renewable Resources and of Tourism, Minister responsible for the Yukon Liquor Corporation: ART WEBSTER.

Minister of Community and Transportation Services, Minister of Government Services, Minister responsible for the Yukon Housing Corporation: MAURICE BYBLOW.

GOVERNMENT ADDRESSES

The postal address for all government departments is: POB 2703, Whitehorse, YT Y1A 2C6.

Department of Education: tel. (403) 667-5141.

Department of Finance: tel. (403) 667-5343.

LEGISLATIVE ASSEMBLY

Speaker: SAM JOHNSTON (NDP).

Clerk: PATRICK L. MICHAEL.

Election, 20 February 1989

	Seats at election
New Democratic Party	9
Progressive Conservative	7
Total	16

POLITICAL ORGANIZATIONS

British Columbia Libertarian Party: 922 Cloverly St, North Vancouver, BC V7L 1N3; tel. (604) 980-7370; Pres. BILL TOMLINSON.

British Columbia Social Credit Party: 10711 Cambie Rd, Suite 236, Richmond, BC V6X 3G5; tel. (604) 270-4040, conservative; governing party of British Columbia since 1975; Leader WILLIAM VANDER ZALM.

Christian Heritage Party: POB 22009, Station B, Vancouver, BC V6A 3Y2; tel. (604) 574-0660; Leader E. J. VAN WOUDENBERG.

Citizens for Public Justice: 229 College St, Suite 311, Toronto, ON M5T 1R4; tel. (416) 979-2443.

Communist Party of Canada:

Central Committee: 24 Cecil St, Toronto, ON M5T 1N2; tel. (416) 979-2109; f. 1921; Leader WILLIAM KASHTAN; Gen. Sec. GEORGE HEWISON.

Alberta Provincial Committee: 10565 97th St, Suite 1A, Edmonton, AB T5H 2L4; tel. (403) 426-2097.

Atlantic Region Office: POB 1257, Dartmouth, NS B2Y 4B9.

British Columbia Provincial Committee: 1726 East Hastings St, Vancouver, BC V5L 1S9; tel. (604) 254-9636.

Manitoba Provincial Committee: 387 Selkirk Ave, Winnipeg, MB R2W 2M3; tel. (306) 586-7824.

Ontario Provincial Committee: 24 Cecil St, Toronto, ON M5T 1N2; tel. (416) 593-1080.

Saskatchewan Provincial Committee: 2210 Albert St, Suite 3, Regina, SK S4P 2V2; tel. (204) 522-1260.

Communist Party of Canada (Marxist–Leninist): POB 264, Adelaide Station, Toronto, ON M5C 2J4; tel. (416) 522-1373.

Confederation of Regions Party of Alberta: 6155 99th St, Edmonton, AB T6E 3P1; tel. (403) 435-4185; fax (403) 434-3966.

Equality Party: f. 1989 in province of Québec; claims equal status for the English and French languages within the province.

Family Coalition Party of Ontario: POB 922, Adelaide Station, Toronto, ON M5C 2K3; Leader DON PENNELL.

Freedom Party of Ontario: POB 2214, Station A, London, ON M5S 2R4; tel. (519) 433-8612; Pres. ROBERT METZ.

Green Party of Canada/Parti Vert du Canada: POB 77155, Station 5, Vancouver, BC V5R 5T4; tel. (604) 435-13851; f. 1983; environmentalist; 8,000 mems across Canada; Leader SEYMOUR TRIEGER; Chief Agent E. L. MCDONOUGH.

Provincial associations:

Green Party Political Association in British Columbia (Green Party of Canada in British Columbia): 831 Commercial Dr., Vancouver, BC V5L 3W6; tel. (604) 254-8165; Speakers LAURA PORCHER (Victoria), TRUDY FRISK (Kamloops), MURRAY GUDMUNDSON (Vancouver).

The Ontario Greens (Green Party of Canada—Ontario Wing): POB 1912, Brantford, ON N3T 5W5; tel. (416) 698-8027.

Parti Vert du Canada au Québec/Green Party of Canada in Québec: CP 262, Montréal, PQ H1S 2Z2; tel. (514) 259-3580; fax (514) 843-3757.

Liberal Party of Canada/Parti libéral du Canada: 200 Laurier Ave West, Suite 200, Ottawa, ON K1P 6M8; tel. (613) 237-0740; supports Canadian autonomy, comprehensive social security, freer trade within the North Atlantic Community; Leader JOHN NAPIER TURNER; Pres. MICHEL ROBERT; Sec.-Gen. SHEILA GERVAIS.

Provincial parties and associations:

Liberal Party of Canada in Alberta: Principal Plaza, Suite 520, 10303 Jasper Ave, Edmonton, AB T5J 3N6; tel. (403) 424-1984; Pres. UNA MACLEAN EVANS.

British Columbia Liberal Party: 210 West Broadway, 6th Floor, Vancouver, BC V5Y 3W2; tel. (604) 872-1636; Pres. GRANT BURNYEAT.

Liberal Party in Manitoba: 140 Roslyn Rd, Suite 2, Winnipeg, MB R3L 0G8; tel. (204) 453-7343; Pres. MORRIS KAUFMAN; Exec. Dir TERRY DUGUID.

New Brunswick Liberal Association: 715 Brunswick St, Fredericton, NB E3B 1H8; tel. (506) 453-3950; Leader FRANK MCKENNA; Pres. ALDÉA LANDRY; Exec. Dir GUY THIBODEAU.

Liberal Party of Newfoundland and Labrador: POB 9368, St John's, NF A1A 2Y3; tel. (709) 754-1813; Pres. NORMAN WHALEN.

Northwest Territories Liberal Association: POB 190, Rankin Inlet, NT X0C 0G0; Pres. TERRY FOSTER.

Nova Scotia Liberal Association: 1660 Hollis St, Suite 911, POB 723, Halifax, NS B3J 1V7; tel. (902) 423-6129; Pres. NITA IRVINE; Exec. Dir RON MACDONALD.

Ontario Liberal Party: 10 St Mary St, Suite 310, Toronto, ON M4Y 1P9; tel. (416) 961-3800; Leader DAVID PETERSON; Pres. DON SMITH; Exec. Dir NHANCI DESZCA.

Liberal Party of Prince Edward Island: POB 2559, Charlottetown, PE C1A 8C2; tel. (902) 368-3449; Leader JOE GHIZ; Pres. WALTER MCEWEN; Exec. Dir GLENDA DUNCAN.

Liberal Party of Canada (Québec)/Parti libéral du Canada (Québec): 1000 rue St-Antoine ouest, Suite 307, Montréal, PQ H3C 3R7; tel. (514) 866-6391; Leader ROBERT BOURASSA; Pres. FRANCIS FOX; Dir-Gen. JACQUES W. FORTIER.

Saskatchewan Liberal Association (The Liberal Party of Saskatchewan): 2180 12th Ave, Suite 204, POB 4401, Regina, SK S4P 3W7; tel. (306) 522-8507; Leader RALPH GOODALE; Pres. BOB CROWE; Exec. Dir DOUGLAS ANWEILLER.

Yukon Liberal Association: c/o 273 Alsek Rd, Whitehorse, YT Y1A 4T1; Pres. RON VEALE.

Libertarian Party of Canada: 11 Yorkville Ave, Suite 1004, Toronto, ON M4W 1L3; tel. (416) 323-0020; f. 1973; Leader DENNIS CORRIGAN; Pres. CHRIS BLATCHLY.

Manitoba Libertarian Association: 721 Warsaw Ave, Winnipeg, MB R3M 1B6.

National Citizens' Coalition: 100 Adelaide St West, Suite 907, Toronto, ON M5H 1S3; tel. (416) 869-3838; fax (416) 869-1891.

New Democratic Party/Nouveau Parti Démocratique: 280 Albert St, Suite 600, Ottawa, ON K2P 1P7; tel. (613) 236-3613; f. 1961; social democratic; Leader ED BROADBENT (to 30 Nov. 1989); Pres. JOHANNA DEN HERTOG; Sec. DENNIS YOUNG; 120,000 individual mems, 265,000 affiliated mems (1988).

Provincial parties:

Alberta: 5339 12th Ave, NW, Edmonton, AB T5W 0N6; tel. (403) 474-2415; Sec. LYLE BLEICH.

British Columbia: 3665 Kingsway, Suite 250, Vancouver, BC V5R 5W2; tel. (604) 430-8600; Sec. HANS BROWN.

Manitoba: 656 Broadway, Winnipeg, MB R3C 0X3; tel. (204) 786-4857; Sec. DAVID WOODBURY.

New Brunswick: POB 1041, Fredericton, NB E3B 5C2; tel. (506) 458-5828; Sec. ELIZABETH WEIR.

Newfoundland and Labrador: POB 5275, St John's, NF A1C 5W1; tel. (709) 737-8423; Sec. CLE NEWHOOK.

Northwest Territories: POB 2185, Yellowknife, NT X1A 2P6; Sec. DOUG MARSHALL.

Nova Scotia: 1657 Barrington St, Halifax, NS B3J 2A1; Sec. DENNIS THEMAN.

Ontario: 184 Main St, Toronto, ON M4E 2W1; tel. (416) 699-6637; Sec. BRIAN HARLING.

Prince Edward Island: POB 394, Charlottetown, PE C1A 7K8; Sec. JUDITH WITHAKER.

Québec: 1400 blvd de Maisonneuve est, Montréal, PQ H2L 2A7; tel. (514) 523-3115; Sec. LISE GRATTON.

Saskatchewan: T. C. Douglas House, 1122 Saskatchewan Dr., Regina, SK S4P 0C4; tel. (306) 525-1322; Sec. GARRY SIMONS.

Yukon Territory: 9 Cedar Cres., Whitehorse, YT Y1A 4P2; tel. (403) 633-6216; Sec. YVONNE HARRIS.

Ontario Libertarian Party: 1 St John's Rd, Suite 301, Toronto, ON M6P 4C7; tel. (416) 769-5212; Leader KAY SARGENT; Chair. DANIEL HUNT.

Parti communiste du Québec: 4164 rue Parthenais, Montréal, PQ H2K 3T9; tel. (514) 524-2896.

Parti humaniste du Québec: 531 rue Valois, Suite 4, Montréal, PQ H1W 3L6.

Parti Indépendantiste: 6992 rue St-Hubert, Montréal, PQ H2S 2M9; tel. (514) 272-4654; f. 1984 by breakaway faction of Parti Québécois; seeks full independence for Québec; Pres. PIERRE DE BELLEFEUILLE; Leader GILLES RHÉAUME.

Parti Québécois: 7370 rue St-Hubert, Montréal, PQ H2R 2N3; tel. (514) 270-5400; f. 1968; social democratic; seeks political sovereignty for Québec in an economic association with Canada; c. 7,500 mems (1988); Pres. JACQUES PARIZEAU; Chair. of Nat. Exec. NADIA ASSIMOPOULOS.

Parti des Travailleurs du Québec: 4351 rue de Laroche, Montréal, PQ H2J 3J2; tel. (514) 598-5420; Gen. Sec. GÉRARD LACHANCE.

Parti vert du Québec/Green Party of Québec: 6545 rue Lemay, Montréal, PQ H1T 2L8; tel. (514) 259-3580; Leader Yves Blanchette.

Progressive Conservative Party of Canada/Parti progressiste-conservateur du Canada: 161 Laurier Ave West, Suite 200, Ottawa, ON K1P 5J2; tel. (613) 238-6111; f. 1854; advocates individualism and free enterprise, and continued Canadian participation in NATO; Leader Brian Mulroney; Pres. Bill Jarvis; Nat. Dir Jean-Carol Pelletier.

Provincial offices:

Alberta: 10148 114th St, NW, Edmonton, AB T5K 1R7; tel. (403) 488-7983; fax (403) 488-4995.

British Columbia: 1620 West 8th Ave, Vancouver, BC V6J 1V4; tel. (604) 734-5179.

Manitoba: 120 Fort St, Winnipeg, MB R3C 1C7; tel. (204) 947-0627.

New Brunswick: 391 Brunswick St, Fredericton, NB E3B 1H2; tel. (506) 453-3456.

Newfoundland: Virginia Park Plaza, Suite 252, 60 Newfoundland Dr., St John's, NF A1A 3R5; tel. (709) 579-1717.

Nova Scotia: 1649 Hollis St, Suite 905, Halifax, NS B3J 1V8; tel. (902) 429-9470.

Ontario: 121 Richmond St West, Suite 805, Toronto, ON M5H 2K1; tel. (416) 864-0482.

Prince Edward Island: 53 Queen St, POB 578, Charlottetown, PE C1A 7L1; tel. (902) 892-4204; fax (902) 892-0645.

Saskatchewan: 2150 Scarth St, Suite 200, Regina, SK S4P 2H7; tel. (306) 359-1055.

Québec: 625 ave du Président Kennedy, Suite 803, Montréal, PQ H3A 1K2; tel. (514) 284-0090.

Rassemblement Démocratique pour l'Indépendance: 234 blvd St-Joseph ouest, Montréal, PQ H2T 2P8; tel. (514) 271-0690; f. 1985 by breakaway faction of Parti Québécois, seeks full independence for Québec; Leader Dr Camille Laurin.

Reform Party of Canada: RR8, Edmonton, AB T5L 4H8.

Representative Party of Alberta: 10109 106th St, Edmonton, AB T5J 3L7; tel. (403) 424-3802.

Revolutionary Workers' League: CP 280, succursale de Lorimier, Montréal, PQ H2H 2N7; tel. (514) 521-2791.

Rhinoceros Party of Canada/Parti Rhinocéros: 4534 rue de Bordeaux, Montréal, PQ H2H 2A1.

Socialist Party of Canada: POB 4280, Station A, Victoria, BC V8X 3X8; tel. (604) 382-5927; Gen. Sec. J. G. Jenkins.

United Canadian Party: POB 1158, Station B, Ottawa, ON K1P 5R2; tel. (613) 837-3982.

Western Canada Concept Party of Alberta: 10830 107th Ave, Edmonton, AB T5H 0X3; tel. (403) 425-6378.

Western Democracy Party of Canada: 874 Main St, Winnipeg, MB R2W 3P1; tel. (204) 582-4091.

Western Independence Party: 13025 104th Ave, Edmonton, AB T5N 0V9; tel. (403) 452-5713; Leader Dr F. C. Marshall (acting).

World Federalists of Canada: 145 Spruce St, Suite 207, Ottawa, ON K1R 6P1; tel. (613) 232-0647.

DIPLOMATIC REPRESENTATION

OVERSEAS DIPLOMATIC AND CONSULAR REPRESENTATION IN CANADA

Algeria

Embassy: 435 Daly Ave, Ottawa, ON K1N 6H3; tel. (613) 232-9453; telex 053-3625; Ambassador Mohammed Ghoualmi.

Antigua and Barbuda

High Commission: Pl. de Ville, Tower B, 112 Kent St, Suite 205, Ottawa, ON K1P 5P2; tel. (613) 234-9143; fax (613) 232-0539; High Commissioner Conrad Richards.

Consulate: 60 St Clair Ave East, Suite 205, Toronto, ON M4T 1N5; tel. (416) 961-3143; telex 06-218616; Consul Madeline Blackman.

Argentina

Embassy: 90 Sparks St, Suite 620, Ottawa, ON K1P 5B4; tel. (613) 236-2351; telex 053-4293; fax (613) 235-2659; Ambassador Francisco José Pulit.

Consulate-General: 1010 St Catherine St West, Suite 605, Montréal, PQ H3B 3R3; tel. (514) 866-3819; Consul-Gen. José I. García Ghirelli.

Australia

High Commission: 50 O'Connor St, Ottawa, ON K1P 6L2; tel. (613) 236-0841; telex 053-3391; High Commissioner Robert Stephen Laurie.

Consulate-General: 22nd Floor, Commerce Ct North, POB 69, Toronto, ON M5L 1B9; tel. (416) 367-0783; telex 06-219762; fax (416) 367-0830; Consul-Gen. Graham H. Scott.

Consulate-General: Oceanic Plaza, 1066 Hastings St West, POB 12519, Vancouver, BC V6E 3X1; tel. (604) 684-1177; telex 94-507580; fax (604) 684-1856; Consul-Gen. H. David M. Combe.

Austria

Embassy: 445 Wilbrod St, Ottawa, ON K1N 6M7; tel. (613) 563-1444; telex 053-3290; Ambassador Dr Hedwig Wolfram.

Bahamas

High Commission: 360 Albert St, Suite 1020, Ottawa, ON K1R 7X7; tel. (613) 232-1724; telex 053-3793; fax (613) 232-0097; High Commissioner Idris Reid.

Bahrain

Embassy: c/o 3502 International Dr., NW, Washington, DC 20008, USA; tel. (202) 342-0741; Ambassador Ghazi Mohamed Algosaibi.

Consulate: 1869 blvd René-Lévesque ouest, Montréal, PQ H3H 1R4; tel. (514) 931-7444; telex 055-62235; fax (514) 931-5988; Consul Ahmed M. al-Haddad.

Bangladesh

High Commission: 85 Range Rd, Suite 402, Ottawa, ON K1N 8J6; tel. (613) 236-0138; telex 053-4283; High Commissioner Brigadier A. N. M. Nuruzzaman.

Barbados

High Commission: 151 Slater St, Suite 210, Ottawa, ON K1P 5H3; tel. (613) 236-9517; telex 053-3375; High Commissioner Peter G. Morgan.

Consulate-General: 20 Queen St West, Suite 1508, POB 18, Toronto, ON M5H 3R3; tel. (416) 979-2643; telex 06-218247; fax (416) 979-8726; Consul-Gen. Lolita Applewhaite.

Belgium

Embassy: 85 Range Rd, Suites 601–604, Ottawa, ON K1N 8J6; tel. (613) 236-7267; telex 053-3568; fax (613) 236-7882; Ambassador Jean-François de Liedekerke.

Consulate-General: 1001 blvd de Maisonneuve ouest, Suite 1250, Montréal, PQ H3A 3C8; tel. (514) 849-7394; telex 05-268691; fax (514) 844-3170; Consul-Gen. X. Demoulin.

Consulate-General: 8 King St East, Suite 1901, Toronto, ON M5C 1B5; tel. (416) 364-5283; telex 06-23564; fax (416) 364-4001; Consul-Gen. Ingeborg Kristoffersen.

Consulate-General: 701 Georgia St West, Suite 1250, POB 10119, Vancouver, BC V7Y 1C6; tel. (604) 682-1878; telex 04-53268; fax (604) 682-6794; Consul-Gen. Mr Delfosse.

Belize

High Commission: c/o Embassy, 3400 International Dr., NW, Suite 2J, Washington, DC 20008, USA; tel. (202) 363-4505; telex 140997; fax (202) 362-7468; High Commissioner Edward A. Laing.

Benin

Embassy: 58 Glebe Ave, Ottawa, ON K1S 2C3; tel. (613) 233-4429; telex 053-3630; Ambassador Mme BERNADINE DE RÉGO.

Bolivia

Embassy: 77 Metcalfe St, Suite 608, Ottawa, ON K1P 5L6; tel. (613) 236-8237; Ambassador LUÍS PELAEZ RIOJA.

Consulate-General: 11231 Jasper Ave, Edmonton, AB T5K 0L5; tel. (403) 488-1525; telex 037-2991; fax (403) 488-0350; Consul-Gen. CARLOS PECHTEL.

Consulate: 470 Granville St, Vancouver, BC V6C 1V5; tel. (604) 685-8121; Consul Dr ALAN S. ANDREE.

Botswana

High Commission: c/o Embassy, 4301 Connecticut Ave, NW, Suite 404, Washington, DC 20008, USA; tel. (202) 244-4990; telex 64221; Chargé d'affaires CECIL I. MANYUELA.

Brazil

Embassy: 255 Albert St, Suite 900, Ottawa, ON K1P 6A9; tel. (613) 237-1090; telex 053-4222; Ambassador MARCOS ANTÔNIO DE SALVO COIMBRA.

Consulate-General: 2000 rue Mansfield, Suite 1700, Montréal, PQ H3A 3A5; tel. (514) 499-0968; Consul-Gen. JOSÉ MAURICIO BUSTANI.

Consulate-General: 77 Bloor St West, Suite 1109, Toronto, ON M5S 1M2; tel. (416) 992-2503; telex 06-23730; Consul-Gen. ODILON DE CAMARGO PENTEADO.

Consulate-General: Royal Centre, 1035 Georgia St West, Suite 1700, POB 11152, Vancouver, BC V6E 3P3; tel. (604) 687-4589; telex 04-508631; Consul-Gen. GUILHERME PARREIRAS-HORTA.

Brunei

High Commission: c/o Permanent Mission to the UN, 866 United Nations Plaza, Suite 248, New York, NY 10017, USA; tel. (212) 838-1600; High Commissioner Haji JAYA ABDUL LATIF.

Bulgaria

Embassy: 325 Stewart St, Ottawa, ON K1N 6K5; tel. (613) 232-3215; telex 053-4386; Ambassador BOYKO TARABANOV.

Consulate-General: 100 Adelaide St West, Suite 1410, Toronto, ON M5H 1S3; tel. (416) 363-7307; telex 06-23535; Consul-Gen. YORDAN VELICHKOV.

Burkina Faso

Embassy: 48 Range Rd, Ottawa, ON K1N 8J4; tel. (613) 238-4796; Ambassador LÉANDRE BASSOLE.

Burundi

Embassy: 151 Slater St, Suite 800, Ottawa, ON K1P 5H3; tel. (613) 236-8483; telex 053-3393; Ambassador JULYEN NAHAYO.

Cameroon

Embassy: 170 Clemow Ave, Ottawa, ON K1S 2B4; tel. (613) 236-1522; telex 053-3736; Ambassador PHILEMON YANG YUNJI.

Cape Verde

Embassy: c/o 3415 Massachusetts Ave, NW, Washington, DC 20007, USA; tel. (202) 965-6820; telex 440294; Ambassador JOSÉ LUÍS FERNANDES LOPES.

Central African Republic

Embassy: c/o 1618 22nd St, NW, Washington, DC 20008, USA; tel. (202) 483-7800; Ambassador CHRISTIAN LINGAMA-TOLÈQUE.

Chad

Embassy: c/o 2002 R St, NW, Washington, DC 20009, USA; tel. (202) 462-4009; telex 64225; Ambassador MAHAMAT ALI ADOUM.

Chile

Embassy: 151 Slater St, Suite 605, Ottawa, ON K1P 5H3; tel. (613) 235-4402; telex 053-3774; fax (613) 235-1176; Ambassador JORGE BERGUÑO BARNES.

Consulate-General: 1010 St Catherine St West, Suite 731, Montréal, PQ H3B 3R3; (514) 861-8006; telex 055-62423; Consul-Gen. CÉSAR RAVAZZANO.

Consulate-General: 1240 Bay St, Suite 700, Toronto, ON M5R 3L9; tel. (416) 924-1016; telex 06-218049; Consul-Gen. HUMBERTO ALVAREZ JOHANNSEN.

China, People's Republic

Embassy: 511–515 St Patrick St, Ottawa, ON K1N 5H3; tel. (613) 234-2706; telex 053-3770; Ambassador ZHANG WENPU.

Consulate-General: 240 St George St, Toronto, ON M5R 2P4; tel. (416) 964-7260; telex 06-217601; fax (416) 324-6468; Consul-Gen. XIA ZHONGCHENG.

Consulate-General: 3338 Granville St, Vancouver, BC V6H 3K3; tel. (604) 736-6784; telex 04-54659; fax (604) 737-0154; Consul-Gen. DUAN JIN.

Colombia

Embassy: 150 Kent St, Suite 404, Ottawa, ON K1P 5P4; tel. (613) 230-3760; telex 053-3786; Ambassador JAIME VIDAL PERDOMO.

Consulate-General: 1010 Sherbrooke St West, Suite 420, Montréal, PQ H3A 2R7; tel. (514) 849-4852; Consul-Gen. SARA DE PARDO.

Consulate-General: 1 Dundas St West, Suite 2108, Toronto, ON M5G 1Z3; tel. (416) 977-0098; Consul-Gen. EDUARDO OSORIO MUÑOZ.

Comoros

Embassy: c/o Permanent Mission to the UN, 336 East 45th St, 2nd Floor, New York, NY 10017, USA; tel. (212) 972-8010; Ambassador AMINI ALI MOUMIN.

Congo

Embassy: c/o 4891 Colorado Ave, NW, Washington, DC 20011, USA; tel. (202) 726-5500; telex 897072; Ambassador BENJAMIN BOUNKOULOU.

Costa Rica

Embassy: 150 Argyle Ave, Suite 115, Ottawa, ON K2P 1B7; tel. (613) 234-5762; Ambassador MARCO A. GUILLÉN.

Consulate: 300-G4 rue St-Sacrement, Montréal, PQ H2V 1X4; tel. (514) 499-1355; Consul BERNAL MESEN.

Côte d'Ivoire

Embassy: 9 Marlborough Ave, Ottawa, ON K1N 8E6; tel. (613) 236-9919; Ambassador Gen. ISSOUF KONÉ.

Cuba

Embassy: 388 Main St, Ottawa, ON K1S 1E3; tel. (613) 563-0141; telex 053-3135; Ambassador (vacant).

Consulate-General: 1415 Pine Ave West, Montréal, PQ H3G 2B2; tel. (514) 843-8897; telex 05-25228; Consul-Gen. LOURDES URRUTIA.

Consulate-General: 372 Bay St, Suite 406, Toronto, ON M5H 2W9; tel. (416) 362-3622; telex 06-22226; Consul-Gen. ROLANDO RIVERO.

Cyprus

High Commission: c/o Embassy, 2211 R St, NW, Washington, DC 20008, USA; tel. (202) 462-5772; telex 440596; Ambassador ANDREAS J. JACOVIDES.

Czechoslovakia

Embassy: 50 Rideau Terrace, Ottawa, ON K1M 2A1; tel. (613) 749-4442; telex 053-4224; fax (613) 749-4989; Ambassador JÁN JANOVIČ.

Consulate-General: 1305 Pine Ave West, Montréal, PQ H3G 1B2; tel. (514) 849-4495; fax (514) 849-8983; Consul-Gen. RUDOLF HROMADKA.

Consulate: 1280 St Marc St, Montréal, PQ H3H 2G1; tel. (514) 937-6331; telex 055-60672; Consul VIKTOR HORÁK.

Denmark

Embassy: 85 Range Rd, Suite 702, Ottawa, ON K1N 8J6; tel. (613) 234-0704; telex 053-3114; fax (613) 234-7368; Ambassador BJØRN OLSEN.

Consulate-General: 1245 Sherbrooke St West, Suite 1525, Montréal, PQ H3G 1G2; tel. (514) 849-5391; telex 055-60783; Consul-Gen. JENS H. JENSEN.

Consulate-General: 151 Bloor St West, Suite 310, Toronto, ON M5S 1S4; tel. (416) 962-5661; telex 06-22032; fax (416) 962-3668; Consul-Gen. ERLING H. NIELSEN.

Dominica

High Commission: Pl. de Ville, Tower B, 112 Kent St, Suite 1701, Ottawa, ON K1P 5P2; tel. (613) 236-8952; telex 053-4476; fax (613) 236-3042; High Commissioner Dr J. BERNARD YANKEY.

Dominican Republic

Embassy: c/o 1715 22nd St, NW, Washington, DC 20008, USA; tel. (202) 332-6280; Ambassador EDUARDO LEÓN.

Consulate-General: 1464 rue Crescent, Montréal, PQ H3A 2B6; tel. (514) 843-3418; Consul-Gen. ESMERALDA VILLANUEVA.

Ecuador

Embassy: c/o 2535 15th St, NW, Washington, DC 20009, USA; tel. (202) 234-7200; fax (202) 667-3482; Ambassador Jaime Moncayo.

Consulate-General: 1010 rue St-Catherine ouest, Suite 625, Montréal, PQ H3B 3R3; tel. (514) 874-4071; Consul-Gen. Dr Luís Moreno Guerra.

Consulate: 151 Bloor St West, Suite 670, Toronto, ON M5S 1S4; tel. (416) 968-2077; Consul José E. Nuñez T.

Egypt

Embassy: 454 Laurier Ave East, Ottawa, ON K1N 6R3; tel. (613) 234-4931; telex 053-3340; Ambassador Mahmoud Kassem.

Consulate-General: 3754 chemin Côte des Neiges, Montréal, PQ H3H 1V6; tel. (514) 937-7781; Consul-Gen. Mohamed Mounir Gohar.

Ethiopia

Embassy: c/o Permanent Mission to the UN, 866 United Nations Plaza, Suite 560, New York, NY 10017, USA; tel. (212) 421-1830; Ambassador (vacant).

Fiji

Embassy: c/o Permanent Mission to the UN, One United Nations Plaza, 26th Floor, New York, NY 10017, USA; tel. (212) 355-7316; telex 421409; fax (212) 319-1896; Ambassador Winston Thompson.

Finland

Embassy: 55 Metcalfe St, Suite 850, Ottawa, ON K1P 6L5; tel. (613) 236-2389; telex 053-4462; fax (613) 238-1474; Ambassador Erkki Mäentakanen.

Consulate: 1200 Bay St, Suite 604, Toronto, ON M5R 2A5; tel. (416) 964-0066; telex 062-2513; fax (416) 964-1524; Consul Markku Knappila.

France

Embassy: 42 Sussex Dr., Ottawa, ON K1M 2C9; tel. (613) 232-1795; fax (613) 232-4302; Ambassador François Bujon de L'Estang.

Consulate-General: 300 Highfield Pl., 10010 106th St, Edmonton, AB T5J 3L8; tel. (403) 428-0232; telex 037-42651; fax (403) 426-1450; Consul-Gen. Serge Pinot.

Consulate-General: 250 Lutz Rd, POB 1109, Moncton, NB E1C 8P6; tel. (506) 857-4191; Consul-Gen. Michel Couthures.

Consulate-General: 2 Elysée, pl. Bonaventure, POB 177, Montréal, PQ H5A 1A7; tel. (514) 878-4381; Consul-Gen. Jean-Pierre Beauchataud.

Consulate-General: 1110 ave des Laurentides, Québec, PQ G1S 3C3; tel. (418) 694-0941; Consul-Gen. Daniel Jouanneau.

Consulate-General: 210 Dundas St West, Suite 800, Toronto, ON M5G 2E8; tel. (416) 977-1257; telex 06-217545; fax (416) 977-9671; Consul-Gen. Jacques Royet.

Consulate-General: 736 Granville St, Suite 1201, Vancouver, BC V6Z 1H9; tel. (604) 681-4345; telex 04-53227; Consul-Gen. René Delille.

Consulate: Bow Valley Sq. IV, 250 6th Ave, SW, Suite 2920, Calgary, AB T2P 3H7; tel. (403) 233-2061; telex 03-827597; Consul Jean-Claude Daupeyroux.

Consulate: 1299 rue Joseph-Dandurand, Chicoutimi, PQ G7H 6R6; tel. (418) 545-5048; Consul Jacques Druez.

Gabon

Embassy: 4 Range Rd, Ottawa, ON K1N 8J5; tel. (613) 232-5301; telex 053-4295; Ambassador Simon Ombegue.

The Gambia

High Commission: c/o Embassy, 1030 15th St, NW, Suite 720, Washington, DC 20005, USA; tel. (202) 842-1356; High Commissioner Ousman Ahmadou Sallah.

German Democratic Republic

Embassy: 150 Kent St, Suite 700, Ottawa, ON K1P 5P4; tel. (613) 234-4359; Ambassador Heinz Birch.

Federal Republic of Germany

Embassy: 1 Waverley St, Ottawa, ON K2P 0T8; tel. (613) 232-1101; telex 053-4226; fax (613) 594-9330; Ambassador Wolfgang Behrends.

Consulate-General: CN Tower, 10004 104th Ave, Suite 2500, POB 363, Edmonton, AB T5J 2J6; tel. (403) 422-6175; telex 037-3056; Consul-Gen. Dr Gerhard Braumüller.

Consulate-General: 3455 rue de la Montagne, Montréal, PQ H3G 2A3; tel. (514) 286-1820; telex 05-24483; Consul-Gen. Dr Hermann Hillger.

Consulate-General: 77 Admiral Rd, Toronto, ON M5R 2L4; tel. (416) 925-2813; telex 06-22866; Consul-Gen. Dr Henning Leopold von Hassell.

Consulate-General: 325 Howe St, Suite 501, Vancouver, BC V6C 2A2; tel. (604) 684-8377; telex 04-507769; Consul-Gen. Siegfried Haller.

Ghana

High Commission: 1 Clemow Ave, Ottawa, ON K1S 2A9; tel. (613) 236-0871; telex 053-4276; fax (613) 236-0874; High Commissioner Daniel O. Agyekum.

Greece

Embassy: 80 MacLaren St, Ottawa, ON K2P 0K6; tel. (613) 238-6271; telex 053-3852; fax (613) 238-6273; Ambassador Leonidas Mavromichalis.

Consulate-General: 2015 Peel St, Suite 750, Montréal, PQ H3A 1T8; tel. (514) 845-2105; telex 055-60963; Consul-Gen. Elias P. Dimitrakopoulos.

Consulate-General: 100 University Ave, Suite 902, Toronto, ON M5J 1V6; tel. (416) 593-1636; telex 06-23087; Consul-Gen. John G. Thomoglou.

Consulate: 1200 Burrard St, Suite 501, Vancouver, BC V6Z 2C7; tel. (604) 681-1381; Consul John (Yannis) Lacatzis.

Grenada

High Commission: Pl. de Ville, Tower B, 112 Kent St, Suite 1701, Ottawa, ON K1P 5P2; tel. (613) 236-8952; telex 053-4476; fax (613) 236-3042; High Commissioner Dr J. Bernard Yankey.

Guatemala

Embassy: 294 Albert St, Suite 500, Ottawa, ON K1P 6E6; tel. (613) 237-3941; telex 053-3065; fax (613) 237-0492; Ambassador Frederico Urruela-Prado.

Consulate-General: 1140 blvd Maisonneuve ouest, Suite 1040, Montréal, PQ H3A 1M8; tel. (514) 288-7384; telex 05-25866; Consul-Gen. Gustavo Adolfo Lopez Sandoval.

Guinea

Embassy: Pl. de Ville, Tower B, 112 Kent St, Suite 208, Ottawa, ON K1P 5P2; tel. (613) 232-1133; telex 053-4361; Ambassador Abdoulaye Sylla.

Guinea-Bissau

Embassy: c/o Permanent Mission to the UN, 211 43rd St East, Suite 604, New York, NY 10017, USA; tel. (212) 661-3977; telex 668765; Ambassador Alfredo Lopes Cabral.

Guyana

High Commission: 151 Slater St, Suite 309, Ottawa, ON K1P 5H3; tel. (613) 235-7249; telex 053-3684; High Commissioner (vacant).

Consulate-General: 505 Consumers' Rd, Suite 206, Willowdale, ON M2J 4V8; tel. (416) 494-6040; telex 06-986163; Vice-Consul-Gen. Penelope I. Boyce.

Haiti

Embassy: Pl. de Ville, Tower B, 112 Kent St, Suite 1308, Ottawa, ON K1P 5P2; tel. (613) 238-1628; telex 053-3688; Chargé d'affaires Jean-François Livingston.

Consulate-General: 44 Fundy St, Floor F, pl. Bonaventure, CP 187, Montréal, PQ H5A 1A9; tel. (514) 871-8993; Consul-Gen. Auguste D'Méza.

Holy See

Apostolic Nunciature: 724 Manor Ave, Rockcliffe Park, Ottawa, ON K1M 0E3; tel. (613) 746-4914; telex 053-3380; Apostolic Pro-Nuncio Most Rev. Angelo Palmas.

Honduras

Embassy: 151 Slater St, Suite 300a, Ottawa, ON K1P 5H3; tel. (613) 233-8900; telex 053-4528; Ambassador Juan Ramón Molina Cisneros.

Consulate-General: 1500 Stanley St, Suite 330, Montréal, PQ H3A 1R3; tel. (514) 849-4053; Consul-Gen. Ileana Ulloa de Thuin.

Hungary

Ambassador: 7 Delaware Ave, Ottawa, ON K2P 0Z2; tel. (613) 232-1711; telex 053-3251; Ambassador Rezsoe Banyasz.

Consulate-General: 1 pl. Alexis Nihon, 3400 rue de Maisonneuve ouest, Suite 1250, Montréal, PQ H3Z 3B8; tel. (514) 939-1660; telex 05-25162; fax (514) 939-1662; Consul-Gen. Lajos Szuhay.

Consulate: 102 Bloor St West, Suite 450, Toronto, ON M5S 1M8; tel. (416) 923-3596; telex 06-22551; fax (416) 923-2097; Consul PAL EGERVARI.

Iceland

Embassy: c/o 2022 Connecticut Ave, NW, Washington, DC 20008, USA; tel. (202) 265-6653; telex 248596; Ambassador INGVI S. INGVARSSON.

India

High Commission: 10 Springfield Rd, Ottawa, ON K1M 1C9; tel. (613) 744-3751; telex 053-4172; fax (613) 744-0913; High Commissioner SURBIR JIT SINGH CHHATWAL.

Consulate-General: 2 Bloor St West, Suite 500, Toronto, ON M4W 3E2; tel. (416) 960-0751; telex 06-22242; Consul-Gen. VIRENDRA P. SINGH.

Consulate-General: 325 Howe St, 1st Floor, Vancouver, BC V6C 1Z7; tel. (604) 662-8811; telex 045-08415; Consul-Gen. J. C. SHARMA.

Indonesia

Embassy: 287 MacLaren St, Ottawa, ON K2P 0L9; tel. (613) 236-7403; telex 053-3119; fax (613) 563-2858; Ambassador ADIWOSO ABUBAKAR.

Consulate: 425 University Ave, 9th Floor, Toronto, ON M5G 1T6; tel. (416) 591-6461; telex 06-217804; Consul EDWARD M. RURU.

Consulate: 1455 Georgia St West, 2nd Floor, Vancouver, BC V6G 2T3; tel. (604) 682-8855; fax (604) 662-8366; Consul EDDY SUMANTRI.

Iran

Embassy: 411 Roosevelt Ave, 4th Floor, Ottawa, ON K2A 3X9; tel. (613) 729-0902; telex 053-4229; fax (613) 729-0075; Chargé d'affaires MOHAMMAD ALI MOUSAVI.

Iraq

Embassy: 215 McLeod St, Ottawa, ON K2P 0Z8; tel. (613) 236-9177; telex 053-4310; Ambassador HISHAM I. AL-SHAWI.

Ireland

Embassy: 1780 Metcalfe St, Ottawa, ON K2P 1P3; tel. (613) 233-6281; telex 053-4240; Ambassador: EDWARD J. BRENNAN.

Israel

Embassy: 410 Laurier Ave West, Suite 601, Ottawa, ON K1R 7T3; tel. (613) 237-6450; telex 053-4858; Ambassador ISRAEL GUR-ARIEH.

Consulate-General: Suite 2620, Montréal, PQ H3B 4S5; tel. (514) 393-9372; telex 055-60982; Consul-Gen. (vacant).

Consulate-General: 180 Bloor St West, Suite 700, Toronto, ON M5S 2V6; tel. (416) 961-1126; fax (416) 961-3962; Consul-Gen. BENJAMIN ABILEAH.

Italy

Embassy: 275 Slater St, 11th Floor, Ottawa, ON K1P 5H9; tel. (613) 232-2401; telex 053-3278; fax (613) 233-1484; Ambassador VALERIO BRIGANTE COLONNA ANGELINI.

Consulate-General: 3489 Drummond Ave, Montréal, PQ H3G 1X6; tel. (514) 849-8351; telex 055-61057; Consul-Gen. ALBERTO CANDILIO.

Consulate-General: 136 Beverley St, Toronto, ON M5T 1Y5; tel. (416) 977-1566; telex 06-218725; Consul-Gen. GIANLUIGI LAJOLO.

Consulate-General: 1200 Burrard St, Suite 505, Vancouver, BC V6Z 2C7; tel. (604) 684-7288; telex 04-51138; Consul-Gen. GIANFRANCO A. MANIGRASSI.

Consulate: 10404 Jasper Ave, Suite 1020, Edmonton, AB T5J 3N4; tel. (403) 423-5153; telex 037-2117; Vice-Consul GIOVANNI BINCOLETTO.

Jamaica

High Commission: 275 Slater St, Suite 402, Ottawa, ON K1P 5H9; tel. (613) 233-9311; telex 053-3287; fax (613) 233-0611; High Commissioner H. DALE ANDERSON.

Consulate-General: 214 King St West, Suite 216, Toronto, ON M5H 3S6; tel. (416) 598-3008; Consul-Gen. KAY A. BAXTER.

Japan

Embassy: 255 Sussex Dr., Ottawa, ON K1N 9E6; tel. (613) 236-8541; telex 053-4220; Ambassador HIROSHI KITAMURA.

Consulate-General: 10180 101st St, Suite 2480, Edmonton, AB T5J 3S4; tel. (403) 422-3752; fax (403) 424-1635; Consul-Gen. T. NONOGAKI.

Consulate-General: 600 rue de la Gauchetière ouest, Suite 1785, Montréal, PQ H3B 4L8; tel. (514) 866-3429; telex 05-25376; Consul-Gen. T. SUKASA ABE.

Consulate-General: 1803 Toronto-Dominion Centre, POB 10, Toronto, ON M5K 1A1; tel. (416) 363-7038; telex 065-24187; fax (416) 367-9392; Consul-Gen. YASUO NOGUCHI.

Consulate-General: 1177 Hastings St West, Suite 900, Vancouver, BC V6E 2K9; tel. (604) 684-5868; Consul-Gen. SHUNJI MARUYAMA.

Consulate-General: 215 Garry St, Suite 730, Winnipeg, MB R3C 3P3; tel. (204) 943-5554; fax (204) 957-0374; telex 07-57533; Consul-Gen. YUZUKI KAKU.

Jordan

Ambassador: 100 Bronson Ave, Suite 701, Ottawa, ON K1R 6G8; tel. (613) 238-8090; telex 053-4538; Ambassador HANI KHALIFEH.

Kenya

High Commission: 415 Laurier Ave East, Ottawa, ON K1N 6R4; tel. (613) 563-1773; telex 053-4873; High Commissioner PETER M. NYAMWEYA.

Korea, Republic

Embassy: 85 Albert St, 10th Floor, Ottawa, ON K1P 6A4; tel. (613) 232-1715; Ambassador SOO GIL PARK.

Consulate-General: 1000 Sherbrooke St West, Suite 1710, Montréal, PQ H3A 3G4; tel. (514) 845-3243; telex 055-61212; Consul-Gen. WON CHAN RAH.

Consulate-General: 439 University Ave, Suite 700, Toronto, ON M5G 1Y8; tel. (416) 598-4608; Consul-Gen. SON TACK PARK.

Consulate-General: 1066 Hastings St West, Suite 830, Vancouver, BC V6E 3X1; tel. (604) 681-9581; telex 04-51535; Consul-Gen. KIE OK CHUNG.

Kuwait

Embassy: c/o 2940 Tilden St, NW, Washington DC 20008, USA: tel. (202) 966-0702; telex 64142; Ambassador Shaikh SAUD HASIR AL-SABAH.

Laos

Embassy: c/o 2222 S St, NW, Washington, DC 20008, USA; tel. (202) 332-6416; telex 904061; Chargé d'affaires DONE SOMVORACHIT.

Lebanon

Embassy: 640 Lyon St, Ottawa, ON K1S 3Z5; tel. (613) 236-5825; telex 053-3571; fax (613) 232-1609; Ambassador MARKRAM ABDEL HALIM OUAIDAT.

Consulate-General: 40 chaussee Côte Ste-Catherine, Montréal, PQ H2V 2A2; tel. (514) 276-2638; Consul-Gen. YOUSSEF ARSANIOS.

Lesotho

High Commission: 202 Clemow Ave, Ottawa, ON K1S 2B4; tel. (613) 236-9449; telex 053-4563; Chargé d'affaires THABANG M. TSIETSI.

Liberia

Embassy: 116 Albert St, Suite 805, Ottawa, ON K1P 5G3; tel. (613) 594-5410; Ambassador F. D. F. SHERMAN.

Libya

Embassy: c/o Permanent Mission to the UN, 309–315 East 48th St, New York, NY 10017, USA; tel. (212) 752-5775; telex 666740; fax (212) 593-4787; Ambassador Dr ALI A. TREIKI.

Liechtenstein

(See entry for Switzerland.)

Luxembourg

Embassy: c/o 2200 Massachusetts Ave, NW, Washington, DC 20008, USA; tel. (202) 265-4171; telex 64130; fax (202) 328-8270; Ambassador ANDRÉ PHILIPPE.

Madagascar

Embassy: c/o Permanent Mission to the UN, 801 Second Ave, Suite 404, New York, NY 10017, USA; tel. (212) 986-9491; telex 236545; Ambassador BLAISE RABETAFIKA.

Malawi

High Commission: 7 Clemow Ave, Ottawa, ON K1S 2A9; tel. (613) 236-8931; telex 053-3365; fax (613) 236-1054; High Commissioner M. W. MACHINJILI.

Malaysia

High Commission: 60 Boteler St, Ottawa, ON K1N 8Y7; tel. (613) 237-5182; telex 053-3064; fax (613) 236-1054; High Commissioner Tan Sri Datuk THOMAS JAYASURIYA.

Consulate: 34 King St East, Suite 1201, Toronto, ON M5C 1E5; tel. (416) 869-3886; Consul MOHD. NOR MOHD. SAID.

Mali

Embassy: 50 Goulburn Ave, Ottawa, ON K1N 8C8; tel. (613) 232-1501; telex 053-3361; Ambassador SADIBOU KONÉ.

Malta

High Commission: c/o Embassy, 2017 Connecticut Ave, NW, Washington, DC 20008, USA; tel. (202) 462-3611; telex 64231; fax (202) 387-5470; High Commissioner SALV J. STELLINI.

Mauritania

Embassy: c/o Permanent Mission to the UN, 9 East 77th St, New York, NY 10021, USA; tel. (212) 737-7780; telex 576628; Ambassador MOHAMED MAHJOUB OULD BOYE.

Mauritius

High Commission: c/o Embassy, 4301 Connecticut Ave, NW, Suite 134, Washington, DC 20008, USA; tel. (202) 244-1491; telex 64362; Ambassador CHITMANSING JESSERAMSING.

Mexico

Embassy: 130 Albert St, Suite 1800, Ottawa, ON K1P 5G4; tel. (613) 233-8988; telex 053-4520; Ambassador ALFREDO PHILLIPS O.

Consulate-General: 1000 Sherbrooke St West, Suite 2215, Montréal, PQ H3A 3G4; tel. (514) 288-4916; telex 05-24119; Consul-Gen. JOSÉ LUÍS VALLARTA.

Consulate-General: 60 Bloor St West, Suite 203, Toronto, ON M4W 3B8; tel. (416) 922-3196; telex 065-24628; Consul-Gen. JUAN MIRALLES-OSTOS.

Consulate-General: 625 Howe St, Suite 310, Vancouver, BC V6C 2T6; telex 04-55634; Consul-Gen. ALFONSO HERRERA-SALCEDO.

Mongolia

Embassy: c/o Permanent Mission to the US, 6 East 77th St, New York, NY 10021, USA; tel. (212) 861-9460; telex 62582; Ambassador GENDENGIIN NYMDOO.

Morocco

Embassy: 38 Range Rd, Ottawa, ON K1N 8J4; tel. (613) 236-7391; telex 053-3683; fax (613) 236-6164; Ambassador MAATI JORIO.

Consulate-General: 1010 Sherbrooke St West, Suite 1510, Montréal, PQ H3A 2R7; tel. (514) 228-8750; Consul-Gen. ABDESLAM BENJELLOUN.

Mozambique

Embassy: c/o 1990 M St, NW, Suite 570, Washington, DC 20036, USA; tel. (202) 293-7147; telex 248530; fax (202) 835-0245; Ambassador VALERIANO FERRÃO.

Myanmar

Embassy: 85 Range Rd, Suite 902, Ottawa, ON K1N 8J6; tel. (613) 232-6434; telex 053-3334; fax (613) 232-6435; Ambassador WIN SHEIN.

Nepal

Embassy: c/o 2131 Leroy Pl., NW, Washington, DC 20008, USA; tel. (202) 667-4550; telex 440085; Chargé d'affaires SINGHA B. BASNYAT.

Netherlands

Embassy: 275 Slater St, 3rd Floor, Ottawa, ON K1P 5H9; tel. (613) 237-5030; telex 053-3109; Ambassador J. F. E. BREMAN.

Consulate-General: 1245 Sherbrooke St West, Suite 1500, Montréal, PQ H3G 1G2; tel. (514) 849-4247; telex 055-62362; Consul-Gen. H. O. FRASER.

Consulate-General: 1 Dundas St West, Suite 2106, Toronto, ON M5G 1Z3; tel. (416) 598-2520; Consul-Gen. J. W. JANSEN.

Consulate-General: 475 Howe St, Suite 821, Vancouver, BC V6C 2B3; tel. (604) 684-6448; Consul-Gen. T. J. M. VAN DEN MUIJSENBERG.

Consulate: 10020 101st Ave, Suite 930, Edmonton, AB T5J 3G2; tel. (403) 428-7513; fax (403) 424-2053; Consul J. J. KOSTER.

Consulate: 4114 18th Ave, Regina, SK S4S 0C4; tel. (306) 584-5466; Consul Ir E. H. GROLLE.

Consulate: 35 Airport Rd, POB 219, Winnipeg, MB R3C 2Z4; tel. (204) 633-1771; Consul B. A. VAN RUITEN.

New Zealand

High Commission: Metropolitan House, 99 Bank St, Suite 727, Ottawa, ON K1P 6G3; tel. (613) 238-5991; telex 210534282; fax (613) 238-5707; High Commissioner BRUCE BROWN.

Consulate: 701 Georgia St West, Suite 1260, POB 10071, Pacific Centre, Vancouver, BC V7Y 1B6; tel. (604) 684-7388; telex 04-55186; fax (604) 684-1265; Consul ANTHONY J. PERVAN.

Nicaragua

Embassy: 170 Laurier Ave West, Suite 908, Ottawa, ON K1P 5V5; tel. (613) 234-9361; telex 053-4338; fax (613) 238-7666; Ambassador SERGIO LACAYO.

Consulate-General: 4 Topaz Gate, Willowdale, ON M2M 2Z7; tel. (416) 221-3092; Consul-Gen. PASTOR VALLE-GARAY.

Niger

Embassy: 38 Blackburn Ave, Ottawa, ON K1N 8A2; tel. (613) 232-4291; telex 053-3757; Ambassador OUMAROU MAMANE.

Nigeria

High Commission: 295 Metcalfe St, Ottawa, ON K2P 1R9; tel. (613) 236-0521; telex 053-3285; fax (613) 236-0529; High Commissioner G. O. GEORGE.

Norway

Embassy: Royal Bank Centre, 90 Sparks St, Suite 532, Ottawa, ON K1P 5B4; tel. (613) 238-6571; telex 053-4239; fax (613) 238-2765; Ambassador JAN E. NYHEIM.

Consulate-General: 407 rue McGill, Suite 802, Montréal, PQ H2Y 2G3; tel. (514) 842-6883; telex 055-60794; fax (514) 842-6840; Consul-Gen. IVAR TRAA.

Consulate: 355 Burrard St, Suite 540, Vancouver, BC V6C 2G8; tel. (604) 682-2281; telex 04-508781; fax (604) 682-8376; Consul TOR E. VIRDING.

Consulate: 39 Brookhaven Bay, Winnipeg, MB R2J 2S4; tel. (204) 253-2275; Consul MARTIN E. BENUM.

Oman

Embassy: c/o 2342 Massachusetts Ave, NW, Washington, DC 20008, USA; tel. (202) 387-1980; telex 440267; Ambassador AWADH BIN BADER BIN MARIE AL-SHANFARI.

Pakistan

High Commission: 151 Slater St, Suite 608, Ottawa, ON K1P 5H3; tel. (613) 238-7881; telex 053-4428; High Commissioner NAJMUDDIN A. SHAIKH.

Consulate-General: 3421 Peel St, Montréal, PQ H3A 1W7; tel. (514) 845-2297; telex 055-62154; Consul-Gen. EJAZ AHMAD QURESHI.

Consulate General: 8 King St East, Toronto, ON M5C 1B5; tel. (416) 862-1886; telex 062-18424; Consul-Gen. AFZAL AKBAR KHAN.

Panama

Embassy: c/o 2862 McGill Terrace, NW, Washington, DC 20008, USA; tel. (202) 483-1407; telex 64371; fax (202) 483-6132; Ambassador JUAN B. SOSA.

Consulate: 63 Chadwick Pl., Halifax, NS B3M 3N7; tel. (902) 443-0011; Consul LYNETTE A. KEW.

Consulate: 2315 Bromsgrove Rd, Suite 130, Mississauga, ON L5G 4A6; tel. (416) 822-0488; Consul OLGA DE ALBA.

Papua New Guinea

High Commission: c/o Embassy, 1330 Connecticut Ave, NW, Suite 350, Washington, DC 20036, USA; tel. (202) 659-0856; telex 64440; fax (202) 466-2412; High Commissioner RENAGI LOHIA.

Paraguay

Embassy: c/o 2400 Massachusetts Ave, NW, Washington, DC 20008, USA; tel. (202) 483-6960; telex 248411; Ambassador MARCOS MARTÍNEZ MENDIETA.

Peru

Embassy: 170 Laurier Ave West, Suite 1007, Ottawa, ON K1P 5V5; tel. (613) 238-1777; telex 053-3754; Ambassador Dr OSCAR MAURTUA.

Consulate-General: 550 Sherbrooke St West, Suite 1590, Montréal, PQ H3A 1B9; tel. (514) 932-3692; telex 055-61786; Consul-Gen JORGE PÉREZ-GARREAUD.

Consulate: 1200 Bay St, Suite 503, Toronto, ON M5H 2X6; tel. (416) 963-9696; Consul OSCAR BARRENECHEA.

Consulate-General: 505 Burrard St, Suite 1770, Vancouver, BC V7X 1M6; tel. (604) 662-8880; telex 04-508322;. Consul JAIME POMAREDA.

Philippines
Embassy: 130 Albert St, Suite 606, Ottawa, ON K1P 5G4; tel. (613) 233-1121; Ambassador SERGIO A. BARRERA.
Consulate-General: 111 Avenue Rd, Suite 605, Toronto, ON M5R 3J8; tel. (416) 922-7181; telex 06-218780; Consul-Gen. JUAN A. ONA.
Consulate-General: 470 Granville St, Suites 301–308, Vancouver, BC V6C 1V5; tel. (604) 685-7645; telex 04-51390; Consul-Gen. RUFINO J. MARTINEZ.

Poland
Embassy: 443 Daly Ave, Ottawa, ON K1N 6H3; tel. (613) 236-0468; telex 053-3133; Ambassador ALOJZY BARTOSZEK.
Consulate-General: 1500 Pine Ave West, Montréal, PQ H3G 1B4; tel. (514) 937-9481; telex 055-60366; Consul-Gen. JANUSZ KARSKI.
Consulate-General: 2603 Lake Shore Blvd West, Toronto, ON M8V 1G5; tel. (416) 252-5471; telex 06-23440; Consul-Gen. JERRY PALASZ.

Portugal
Embassy: 645 Island Park Dr., Ottawa, ON K1Y 0B8; tel. (613) 729-0883; telex 053-3756; Ambassador JOÃO UVA DE MATOS PROENÇA.
Consulate-General: 1010 St Catherine St West, Suite 937, Montréal, PQ H3B 3R7; tel. (514) 876-1604; Consul-Gen. CARLOS MARIA DE BARROS DAVID CALDER.
Consulate-General: 121 Richmond St West, 7th Floor, Toronto, ON M5H 2K1; tel. (416) 360-8260; Consul-Gen. ANTONIO TANGER-CORRÀ.
Consulate: Pender Pl., 700 Pender St West, Suite 904, POB 2068, Vancouver, BC V6B 3S3; tel. (604) 688-6511; Vice-Consul JOÃO C. O. VALADAS.

Qatar
Embassy: c/o Permanent Mission to the UN, 747 3rd Ave, 22nd Floor, New York, NY 10017, USA; tel. (212) 486-9335; telex 424346; fax (212) 758-4952; Ambassador HAMAD ABDELAZIZ AL-KAWARI.

Romania
Embassy: 655 Rideau St, Ottawa, ON K1N 6A3; tel. (613) 232-5345; telex 053-3101; Ambassador Dr EMILIAN RODEAN.
Consulate-General: 1111 rue St-Urbain, Montréal, PQ H2Z 1X6; tel. (514) 876-1792; telex 05-268571; Consul-Gen. NICOLAE DRAGOIU.

Rwanda
Embassy: 121 Sherwood Dr., Ottawa, ON K1Y 3V1; tel. (613) 722-5835; telex 053-4522; Ambassador JOSEPH NSENGIYUMVA.

Saint Christopher and Nevis
High Commission: Pl. de Ville, Tower B, 112 Kent St, Suite 1701, Ottawa, ON K1P 5P2; tel. (613) 236-8952; telex 053-4476; fax (613) 236-3042; High Commissioner Dr J. BERNARD YANKEY.

Saint Lucia
High Commission: Pl. de Ville, Tower B, 112 Kent St, Suite 1701, Ottawa, ON K1P 5P2; tel. (613) 236-8952; telex 053-4476; fax (613) 236-3042; High Commissioner Dr J. BERNARD YANKEY.
Consulate: 151 Bloor St West, Toronto, ON M5S 1S4; tel. (416) 961-5606; Consul DUNSTAN FONTENELLE.

Saint Vincent and the Grenadines
High Commission: Pl. de Ville, Tower B, 112 Kent St, Suite 1701, Ottawa, ON K1P 5P2; tel. (613) 236-8952; telex 053-4476; fax (613) 236-3042; High Commissioner Dr J. BERNARD YANKEY.

São Tomé and Principe
Embassy: c/o Permanent Mission to the UN, 801 2nd Ave, Suite 1504, New York, NY 10017, USA; tel. (212) 697-4211; Ambassador JOAQUIM RAFAEL BRANCO.

Saudi Arabia
Embassy: 99 Bank St, Suite 901, Ottawa, ON K1P 6B9; tel. (613) 237-4100; telex 053-4285; fax (613) 237-0567; Ambassador ZIAD SHAWWAF.

Senegal
Embassy: 57 Marlborough Ave, Ottawa, ON K1N 8E8; tel. (613) 238-6392; telex 053-4531; Ambassador PIERRE DIOUF.

Sierra Leone
High Commission: c/o Embassy, 1701 19th St, NW, Washington, DC 20009, USA; tel. (202) 939-9265; telex 248430; High Commissioner SAHR MATTURI.

Singapore
High Commission: c/o Permanent Mission to the UN, 2 United Nations Plaza, 25th Floor, New York, NY 10017, USA; tel. (212) 826-0840; telex 421283; fax (212) 826-2964; High Commissioner KISHORE MAHBUBANI.

Solomon Islands
High Commission: c/o Permanent Mission to the UN, 820 2nd Ave, Suite 800A, New York, NY 10017, USA; tel. (212) 599-6193; High Commissioner FRANCIS JOSEPH SAEMATA.

Somalia
Embassy: 130 Slater St, Suite 1000, Ottawa, ON K1P 6E2; tel. (613) 563-4541; telex 053-4739; Ambassador ABDIKARIM ALI OMAR.

South Africa
Embassy: 15 Sussex Dr., Ottawa, ON K1M 1M8; tel. (613) 744-0330; telex 053-4185; fax (613) 741-1639; Ambassador HENDRIK DE KLERK.
Consulate: 1 pl. Ville-Marie, Suite 2615, Montréal, PQ H3B 4S3; tel. (514) 878-9217; telex 055-61745; fax (514) 878-3973; Consul KLAUS W. PRAEKETT.
Consulate: 2 First Canadian Pl., Suite 2515, POB 424, Toronto, ON M5X 1E3; tel. (416) 364-0314; telex 062-3733; fax (416) 363-8974; Consul W. ZASTRAU.

Spain
Embassy: 350 Sparks St, Suite 802, Ottawa, ON K1R 7S8; tel. (613) 237-2193; telex 053-4510; Ambassador ANTONIO JOSÉ FOURNIER.
Consulate-General: 1 Westmount Sq., Suite 1456, Montréal, PQ H3Z 2P9; tel. (514) 935-5235; Consul-Gen. MARIANO URIARTE Y LLODRA.
Consulate-General: 55 Bloor St West, Suite 1204, Toronto, ON M4W 1A5; tel. (416) 967-0488; telex 06-23525; fax (416) 968-9547; Consul-Gen. GUILLERMO CEBRIAN.

Sri Lanka
High Commission: 85 Range Rd, Suites 102–104, Ottawa, ON K1N 8J6; tel. (613) 233-8449; telex 053-3668; High Commissioner Brig.-Gen. TISSA WEERATUNGA.

Sudan
Embassy: 457 Laurier Ave East, Ottawa, ON K1N 6R4; tel. (613) 235-4000; Ambassador NURI KHALIL SIDDIQ.

Suriname
Embassy: c/o 4301 Connecticut Ave, Suite 108, Washington, DC 20008, USA; tel. (202) 244-7488; fax (202) 244-5878; Ambassador ARNOLD TH. HALFHIDE.

Swaziland
High Commission: c/o 441 Van Ness Centre, 4301 Connecticut Ave, NW, Washington, DC 20008, USA; tel. (202) 362-6683; High Commissioner CARLTON M. DLAMINI (acting).

Sweden
Embassy: 441 MacLaren St, 4th Floor, Ottawa, ON K2P 2H3; tel. (613) 236-8553; telex 053-3331; fax (613) 236-5720; Ambassador OLA ULLSTEN.
Consulate-General: 1155 blvd René-Lévesque ouest, Suite 800, Montréal, PQ H3B 2H7; tel. (514) 866-4019; Consul-Gen. BENGT RÖSIÖ.
Consulate-General: 1177 Hastings St West, Suite 1109, Vancouver, BC V6E 2K3; tel. (604) 683-5838; telex 04-51451; fax (604) 687-8237; Consul-Gen. KARL BERTIL ERIKSSON.

Switzerland
(also responsible for the interests of Liechtenstein)
Embassy: 5 Marlborough Ave, Ottawa, ON K1N 8E6; tel. (613) 235-1827; telex 053-3648; fax (613) 563-1394; Ambassador ERNST ANDRES.
Consulate-General: 1572 ave Dr Penfield, Montréal, PQ H3G 1C4; tel. (514) 932-7181; telex 055-60026; Consul-Gen. THÉODORE PORTIER.
Consulate-General: 100 University Ave, Suite 1000, Toronto, ON M5J 1V6; tel. (416) 593-5371; telex 065-24624; Consul-Gen. ERNST KELLER.

Consulate-General: 999 Canada Pl., Suite 790, Vancouver, BC V6C 3E1; tel. (604) 684-2231; telex 04-51184; Consul-Gen. MAX INHELDER.

Syria

Embassy: c/o 2215 Wyoming Ave, NW, Washington, DC 20008, USA; tel. (202) 232-6313; Chargé d'affaires BUSHRA KANAFANI.

Tanzania

High Commission: 50 Range Rd, Ottawa, ON K1N 8J4; tel. (613) 232-1509; telex 053-3569; High Commissioner FERDINAND RUHINDA.

Thailand

Embassy: 180 Island Park Dr., Ottawa, ON K1Y 0A2; tel. (613) 722-4444; telex 053-3975; fax (613) 722-6624; Ambassador MANASPAS XUTO.

Togo

Embassy: 12 Range Rd, Ottawa, ON K1N 8J3; tel. (613) 238-5916; telex 053-4564; Ambassador KOSSIVI OSSEYI.

Trinidad and Tobago

High Commission: 75 Albert St, Suite 508, Ottawa, ON K1P 5E7; tel. (613) 232-2418; fax (613) 232-4349; High Commissioner GERALD YETMING.

Consulate-General: 365 Bloor St East, Suite 1700, Toronto, ON M4W 3L4; tel. (416) 922-3175; telex 06-218199; Consul-Gen. TREVOR SPENCER.

Tunisia

Embassy: 515 O'Connor St, Ottawa, ON K1S 3P8; tel. (613) 237-0330; telex 053-4161; Ambassador ANOUAR BERRAÏES.

Turkey

Embassy: 197 Wurtemburg St, Ottawa, ON K1N 8L9; tel. (613) 232-4716; telex 053-4716; Ambassador ALI TUYGAN.

Uganda

High Commission: 231 Cobourg St, Ottawa, ON K1N 8J2; tel. (613) 233-7797; telex 053-4469; fax (613) 232-6689; High Commissioner JOSEPH TOMUSANGE.

USSR

Embassy: 285 Charlotte St, Ottawa, ON K1N 8L5; tel. (613) 235-4341; telex 053-3332; Ambassador ALEKSEI RODIONOV.

Consulate-General: 3655 Museum Ave, Montréal, PQ H1W 1S1; tel. (514) 843-5901; Consul-Gen. EVGENI N. KOTCHETKOV.

United Arab Emirates

Embassy: c/o Permanent Mission to the UN, 747 Third Ave, New York, NY 10017, USA; tel. (212) 371-0480; telex 148451; fax (212) 319-5433; Ambassador MOHAMMAD BIN HUSSAIN AL-SHAALI.

United Kingdom

High Commission: 80 Elgin St, Ottawa K1P 5K7; tel. (613) 237-1530; telex 053-3318; fax (613) 237-7980; High Commissioner BRIAN FALL.

Consulate-General: 10025 Jasper Ave, Suite 1404, Edmonton, AB T5J 1S6; tel. (403) 428-0375; fax (403) 426-0624; telex 037-2421; Consul-Gen. J. F. DOBLE.

Consulate-General: 1155 University St, Suite 901, Montréal, PQ H3B 3A7; tel. (514) 866-0202; telex 055-61224; Consul-Gen. P. M. NEWTON.

Consulate-General: College Park, 777 Bay St, Suite 1910, Toronto, ON M5G 2G2; tel. (416) 593-1290; telex 065-24486; fax (416) 593-1229; Consul-Gen. B. SPARROW.

Consulate-General: 1111 Melville St, Suite 800, Vancouver, BC V6E 3V6; tel. (604) 683-4421; telex 04-51287; fax (604) 681-0693; Consul-Gen. B. WATKINS.

USA

Embassy: 100 Wellington St, Ottawa, ON K1P 5T1; tel. (613) 238-5335; telex 053-3582; fax (613) 563-7701; Ambassador EDWARD N. NEY.

Consulate-General: 615 Macleod Trail, SE, Rm 1050, Calgary, AB T2G 4T8; tel. (403) 266-8962; fax (403) 264-6630; Consul-Gen. ROBERT J. KOTT.

Consulate-General: Cogswell Tower, Scotia Sq., Suite 910, Halifax, NS B3J 3K1; tel. (902) 429-2480; Consul-Gen. JAMES DONALD WALSH.

Consulate-General: CP 65, Station Desjardins, Montréal, PQ H5B 1G1; tel. (514) 281-1886; fax (514) 281-1072; telex 02-268751; Consul-Gen. ANDREW F. ANTIPPAS.

Consulate-General: 2 pl. Terrasse Dufferin, CP 939, Québec, PQ G1R 4T9; tel. (418) 692-2095; telex 051-2275; Consul-Gen. ROBERT M. MAXIM.

Consulate-General: 360 University Ave, Toronto, ON M5G 1S4; tel. (416) 595-1700; Consul-Gen. JOHN E. HALL.

Consulate-General: 1075 Georgia St West, Vancouver, BC V6E 4E9; tel. (604) 685-4311; telex 04-55673; fax (604) 685-5285; Consul-Gen. SAMUEL C. FROMOVITZ.

Uruguay

Embassy: 130 Albert St, Suite 1905, Ottawa, ON K1P 5G4; tel. (613) 234-2727; telex 053-3602; Chargé d'affaires ZULMA GUELMÁN.

Consulate: 1889 Workman St, Montréal, PQ H3J 2P1; tel. (514) 931-2138; Consul Dr CHARLES VILLIERS.

Venezuela

Embassy: 294 Albert St, Suite 602, Ottawa, ON K1P 6E6; tel. (613) 235-5151; telex 053-4729; fax (613) 235-3205; Ambassador GILBERTO CARRASQUERO.

Consul-General: 2055 Peel St, Suite 400, Montréal, PQ H3A 1V4; tel. (514) 842-3417; telex 05-267523; Consul-Gen. JOSÉ RAMÓN DOVALE.

Consulate-General: 2 Carlton St, Suite 703, Toronto, ON M5B 1J3; tel. (416) 977-6809; Consul-Gen. C. A. TAYLHARDAT.

Western Samoa

High Commission: c/o Permanent Mission to the UN, 820 Second Ave, New York, NY 10017, USA: tel. (212) 599-6196; telex 960945; fax (212) 972-3970; High Commissioner MAIAVA IULAI TOMA.

Yemen Arab Republic

Embassy: c/o 600 New Hampshire Ave, NW, Suite 840, Washington, DC 20037, USA; tel. (202) 965-4760; telex 897027; fax (202) 337-2017; Ambassador MOHSIN AHMED ALAINI.

Yemen, People's Democratic Republic

Embassy: c/o Permanent Mission to the UN, 413 East 51st St, New York, NY 10022, USA; tel. (212) 752-3066; telex 421166; Ambassador ABDALLA SALEH AL-ASHTAL.

Yugoslavia

Embassy: 17 Blackburn Ave, Ottawa, ON K1N 8A2; tel. (613) 233-6289; telex 053-4203; Ambassador VLADIMIR PAVICEVIĆ.

Consulate-General: 1237 Burrard St, POB 48359, Vancouver, BC V7X 1A1; tel. (604) 685-8391; Consul-Gen. NIKOLA JELENCIC.

Consulate: 377 Spadina Rd, Toronto, ON M5P 2V7; tel. (416) 481-7279; fax (416) 483-1847; Consul MIHAJLO DIKA.

Zaire

Embassy: 18 Range Rd, Ottawa, ON K1N 8J3; tel. (613) 236-7103; telex 053-4314; Ambassador K. BUKASA-MUTEBA.

Zambia

High Commission: 130 Albert St, Suite 1610, Ottawa, ON K1P 5G4; tel. (613) 563-0712; High Commissioner HUMPHREY MULEMBA.

Zimbabwe

High Commission: 332 Somerset St West, Ottawa, ON K1P 0J9; tel. (613) 237-4388; telex 053-4221; High Commissioner M. S. KAJESE.

CANADIAN DIPLOMATIC REPRESENTATION ABROAD

(All diplomatic offices listed below are embassies, unless otherwise indicated.)

Afghanistan: (see Pakistan).

Albania: (see Yugoslavia).

Algeria: BP 225, Alger Gare, 16000 Algiers; tel. 60-66-11; telex 66043; Ambassador GILLES MATHIEL.

Andorra: (see France).

Angola: (see Zimbabwe).

Anguilla: (see Barbados).

Antigua and Barbuda: (see Barbados).

Argentina: Edif. Brunetta 25°, Suipacha 1111, Casilla 1598, 1368 Buenos Aires; tel. (1) 312-9081; telex 21383; Ambassador CLAYTON BULLIS. (Also covers Paraguay and Uruguay.)

Australia (High Commission): Commonwealth Ave, Canberra, ACT 2600; tel. (062) 733844; telex 62017; High Commissioner R. ALLEN KILPATRICK. (Also covers New Caledonia, Papua New Guinea and the Solomon Islands.)

Austria: 1010 Vienna, Luegerring 10/IV; tel. (1) 63-36-91; telex 75320; Ambassador MICHAEL SHENSTONE.

Bahamas (Consulate): POB SS–6371, Nassau; tel. (809) 323-2124; telex 20246; Hon. Consul D. G. JOSS.

Bahrain: (see Kuwait).

Bangladesh (High Commission): POB 569, House CWN 16A, Rd 48, Gulshan Model Town, Dhaka 12; tel. (2) 607071; telex 642328; High Commissioner EMILE GAUVREAU. (Also covers Myanmar.)

Barbados (High Commission): POB 404, Bridgetown, Barbados; tel. (809) 429-3550; telex 2247; High Commissioner ART WRIGHT. (Also covers Anguilla, Antigua and Barbuda, the British Virgin Islands, Dominica, Grenada, Montserrat, Saint Christopher and Nevis, Saint Lucia, and Saint Vincent and the Grenadines.)

Belgium: 2 ave de Tervueren, 1040 Brussels; tel. (2) 513-79-40; telex 21613; Ambassador JACQUES J. A. ASSELIN.

Belize (Consulate): POB 1229, 29 Southern Foreshore, Belize City; tel. (02) 3084; telex 118; Hon. Consul L. GORDON.

Benin (see Ghana).

Bermuda (Commission): c/o Consulate-General, 1251 Ave of the Americas, New York, NY 10020-1175, USA.

Bhutan (see India).

Bolivia (Consulate): Avenida Arce 2342, Casilla 20408, La Paz; tel. (02) 375224; telex 3271; Hon. Consul BARBARA CANEDO PATINO.

Botswana: (see Zimbabwe).

Brazil: SES, Avenida das Nações, Lote 16, CP 07-0961, 70.410 Brasília, DF; tel. (061) 223-7615; telex 611296; Ambassador JOHN P. BELL.

British Virgin Islands: (see Barbados).

Brunei: (see Malaysia).

Bulgaria: (see Yugoslavia).

Burkina Faso: (see Côte d'Ivoire).

Burundi (Consulate): Siruco SARL, BP 5, Bujumbura; tel. 2816; Hon. Consul J. A. M. PERSOONS.

Cambodia: (see Thailand).

Cameroon: Immeuble Stamatiades, BP 572, Yaoundé; tel. 22-10-90; telex 8209; Ambassador ANDRÉ S. SIMARD. (Also covers the Central African Republic and Chad.)

Cape Verde: (see Senegal).

Cayman Islands: (see Jamaica).

Central African Republic: (see Cameroon).

Chad: (see Cameroon).

Chile: Ahumada 11, 10°, Casilla 427, Santiago; tel. (02) 6962256; telex 240341; Ambassador MICHEL DE GOUMOIS.

China, People's Republic: 10 San Li Tun, Chao Yang District, Beijing; tel. 523536; telex 22717; Ambassador EARL G. DRAKE.

Colombia: Calle 76, No 11-52, Apartado Aéreo 53531, Bogotá 2; tel. 217-5555; telex 44568; Ambassador GAETAN LAVERTU.

Comoros: (see Kenya).

Congo: (see Zaire).

Costa Rica: Edif. Cronos 6°, Calle 3 and Avenida Central, Apartado Postal 10.303, San José; tel. 23-04-06; telex 2179; Ambassador STANLEY E. GOOCH. (Also covers El Salvador and Nicaragua.)

Côte d'Ivoire: Immeuble Trade Centre, 23 ave Noguès, 01 BP 4104, Abidjan 01; tel. 32-20-09; telex 23593; Ambassador JEAN-GUY SAINT-MARTIN. (Also covers Burkina Faso and Niger.)

Cuba: Calle 30, No. 518 Esquina a 7a, Miramar, Havana; tel. 2-6421; telex 511586; Ambassador MICHAEL KERGIN.

Cyprus (Consulate): 3 Themistocles Dervis St, POB 2125, Nicosia; tel. (02) 451630; telex 2110; Hon. Consul M. G. IOANNIDES.

Czechoslovakia: Mickiewiczova 6, 125 33 Prague 6; tel. (2) 326941; telex 121061; Ambassador BARRY MAWHINNEY.

Denmark: Kr. Bernikowsgade 1, 1105 Copenhagen K; tel. (01) 12-22-99; telex 27036; Ambassador DOROTHY J. ARMSTRONG.

Djibouti: (see Ethiopia).

Dominica: (see Barbados).

Dominican Republic (Consulate): Mahatma Gandhi 200, Corner Juan Sanchez Ramirez, POB 2054, Santo Domingo 1, DN; tel. (809) 689-0002; telex 346-0611; Hon. Consul J. A. BRACHE.

Ecuador (Consulate): POB 4662, Guayaquil; tel. 303-580; Hon. Consul F. J. C. ECHEVERRIA.

Egypt: 6 Sharia Muhammad Fahmy es-Sayed, Cairo (Garden City); tel. (02) 3543110; telex 92677; Ambassador MARC PERRON. (Also covers Sudan.)

El Salvador: (see Costa Rica).

Equatorial Guinea: (see Gabon).

Ethiopia: African Solidarity Insurance Bldg, Haile Selassie I Sq., POB 1130, Addis Ababa; tel. 151100; telex 21053; Ambassador DAVID MACDONALD. (Also covers Djibouti.)

Fiji: (see New Zealand).

Finland: POB 779, 00101 Helsinki; tel. (90) 17-11-41; telex 121363; Ambassador MARY VANDENHOFF.

France: 35 ave Montaigne, 75008 Paris; tel. (1) 47-23-01-01; telex 280806; Ambassador CLAUDE CHARLAND. (Also covers Andorra.)

French Guiana: (see Trinidad and Tobago).

French Polynesia: (see New Zealand).

Gabon: BP 4037, Libreville; tel. 72-41-54; telex 5227; Ambassador BERNARD DUSSAULT. (Also covers Equatorial Guinea and São Tomé and Príncipe.)

The Gambia: (see Senegal).

German Democratic Republic: (see Poland).

Germany, Federal Republic: 5300 Bonn 1, Friedrich-Wilhelm-Strasse 18; tel. (0228) 231061; telex 886421; Ambassador DONALD S. MCPHAIL.

Ghana (High Commission): 46 Independence Ave, POB 1639, Accra; tel. 228555; telex 2024; High Commissioner SANDELLE SCRIMSHAW. (Also covers Benin and Togo.)

Greece: Odos Ioannou Ghennadiou 4, 115 21 Athens; tel. (01) 7239511; telex 215584; Ambassador ANDRÉ COUVRETTE.

Grenada: (see Barbados).

Guadeloupe: (see Trinidad and Tobago).

Guam: (see Japan).

Guatemala: Edif. Galería España 6°, 7 Avenida 11-59, Zona 9, Apartado 400, Guatemala City; tel. 321411; telex 5206; Ambassador PIERRE TANGUAY.

Guinea: BP 99, Corniche Sud, Coleah, Conakry; tel. 46-36-26; telex 2170; Chargé d'affaires ANDRÉE DUBOIS.

Guinea-Bissau: (see Senegal).

Guyana (High Commission): High and Young Sts, POB 10880, Georgetown; tel. 72081; telex 2215; High Commissioner WILLIAM E. SINCLAIR. (Also covers Suriname.)

Haiti: 18 route de Delmas, BP 826, Port-au-Prince; tel. 2-2358; telex 2030069; Ambassador C. LAVERDURE.

Holy See: Via della Conciliazione 4/D, 00193 Rome, Italy; tel. (06) 6547316; Ambassador THEODORE ARCAND.

Honduras (Consulate): Banco Atlantida, Blvd Centro America, Tente al Centro Comercial Miraflores, Tegucigalpa; tel. 32-7175; telex 1107; Hon. Consul G. BUESO.

Hong Kong (Commission): GPO Box 11142; tel. 5-8104321; telex 73391; Commissioner BERNARD GAGOSZ. (Also covers Macau.)

Hungary: 1121 Budapest, Budakeszi utca 32; tel. 767-312; telex 22-4588; Ambassador (vacant).

Iceland (Consulate-General): Skulagata 20, Reykjavík; tel. (91) 25355; telex 2102; Hon. Consul-Gen. J. H. BERGS.

India (High Commission): 7/8 Shanti Path, Chanakyapuri, POB 5207, New Delhi 110021; tel. (11) 608161; telex 312346; High Commissioner JAMES G. HARRIS. (Also covers Bhutan, Maldives and Nepal.)

Indonesia: 5th Floor, Wisma Metropolitan, Jalan Jendral Sudirman 29, POB 52/JKT, Jakarta; tel. (021) 510709; telex 62131; Ambassador JACK WHITTLETON.

Iran: c/o Royal Danish Embassy, Intersection Africa and Modaress Expressway, Bidar St No. 40, POB 11365-158, Teheran; tel. 297371; telex 212784.

Iraq: 47/1/7 Al-Mansour, POB 323, Baghdad; tel. (01) 542-1459; telex 212486; Ambassador ERIK B. WANG.

Ireland: 65–68 St Stephen's Green, Dublin 2; tel. (01) 781988; telex 93803; Ambassador MICHAEL WADSWORTH.

Israel: 220 Rehov Hayarkon, POB 6410, Tel-Aviv 61063; tel. 03-228122; telex 341293; Ambassador JAMES K. BARTLEMAN.

Italy: Via G. B. de Rossi 27, 00161 Rome; tel. 855341; telex 610056; Ambassador (vacant). (Also covers Libya and San Marino.)

Jamaica (High Commission): 30–36 Knutsford Blvd, POB 1500, Kingston 5; tel. (809) 926-1500; telex 2130; High Commissioner KATHRYN E. McCALLION. (Also covers Cayman Islands.)

Japan: 3–38, Akasaka 7-chome, Minato-ku, Tokyo 107; tel. (03) 408-2101; telex 22218; Ambassador BARRY STEERS. (Also covers Guam.)

Jordan: POB 815403, Pearl of Shmeisani Bldg, Shmeisani, Amman; tel. 666124; telex 23080; Ambassador MICHAEL D. BELL.

Kenya (High Commission): Comcraft House, Haile Selassie Ave, POB 30481, Nairobi; tel. 334033; telex 22198; High Commissioner A. RAYNELL ANDREYCHUK. (Also covers Comoros, Réunion, Somalia and Uganda.)

Kiribati: (see New Zealand).

Korea, Republic: Kolon Bldg, 10th Floor, 45 Mugyo-Dong, Chung-ku, POB 6299, Seoul 100; tel. (02) 753-2605; telex 28425; Ambassador WILLIAM B. SCHUMACHER.

Kuwait: POB 25281, 13113 Safat, Block 1, 28 Quraish St, Nuzha, Kuwait City; tel. 2511451; telex 23549; Ambassador LAWRENCE DICKENSON. (Also covers Bahrain, Oman, Qatar and United Arab Emirates.)

Laos: (see Thailand).

Lebanon: (see Syria).

Lesotho: (see South Africa).

Liberia (Consulate): POB 53, Harbel; tel. 22-39-03; telex 44299; Hon. Consul PETER J. REINIS.

Libya: (see Italy).

Liechtenstein: (see Switzerland).

Luxembourg (Consulate): c/o Price Waterhouse, 20 ave Pasteur, 2310 Luxembourg-Ville; tel. 23-74-2; telex 1231; Hon. Consul W. J. BANNERMAN.

Macau: (see Hong Kong).

Madagascar (Consulate): 20 ave de l'Indépendance, BP 4016, Antananarivo; tel. 29442; telex 22464; Hon. Consul DENISE CLEROUX.

Malawi: (see Zambia).

Malaysia (High Commission): Plaza MBF, 7th Floor, Jalan Ampang, POB 10990, 50450 Kuala Lumpur; tel. (03) 261-2000; telex 30269; High Commissioner GARRETT LAMBERT. (Also covers Brunei.)

Maldives: (see India).

Mali: route de Koulikoro, BP 198, Bamako; tel. 22-22-36; telex 530; Chargé d'affaires GUY GAGNON.

Malta (Consulate): Demajo House, 103 Archbishop St, Valletta; tel. 233-121; Hon. Consul J. M. DEMAJO.

Marshall Islands: (see Philippines).

Martinique: (see Trinidad and Tobago).

Mauritania: (see Senegal).

Mauritius: (see Tanzania).

Mexico: Schiller 529, Colonia Polanco, Apartado 105-05, 11580 México, DF; tel. 2543288; telex 1771191; Ambassador RAYMOND CHRÉTIEN.

Monaco (Consulate): Le Continental, Bloc C, pl. des Moulins, 98100 Monte Carlo; tel. (93) 506534; Hon. Consul N. CARALOPOULOS.

Mongolia: (see USSR).

Montserrat: (see Barbados).

Morocco: 13 bis rue Jañfar as-Sadik, BP 709, Rabat-Agdal; tel. 71375; telex 31964; Ambassador WILFRIED-GUY LICARI.

Mozambique: (see Zimbabwe).

Myanmar: (see Bangladesh).

Nauru: c/o Canadian Consulate-General, AMP Centre, 50 Bridge St, 5th Floor, Sydney, NSW 2000, Australia; tel. (02) 231-6522; telex 20600.

Nepal: (see India).

Netherlands: Sophialaan 7, 2514 JP The Hague; tel. (070) 61-41-11; telex 31270; Ambassador JACQUES GIGNAC.

Netherlands Antilles (Consulate): Maduro and Curiels Bank NV, Plaza JoJo Correa 2–4, Willemstad, Curaçao; tel. 613515; Hon. Consul HAROLD L. FAWCETT.

New Caledonia: (see Australia).

New Zealand (High Commission): ICI Bldg, 67 Molesworth St, POB 12-049, Wellington 1; tel. (04) 739577; telex 3577; High Commissioner A. DOUGLAS SMALL. (Also covers Fiji, French Polynesia, Kiribati, Tonga, Tuvalu and Western Samoa.)

Nicaragua: (see Costa Rica).

Niger: (see Côte d'Ivoire).

Nigeria (High Commission): 4 Idowu Taylor St, Victoria Island, POB 54506, Ikoyi Station, Lagos; tel. 612382; telex 21275; High Commissioner R. L. ELLIOTT. (Also covers Sierra Leone.)

Norway: Oscars Gate 20, 0352 Oslo 3; tel. (2) 46-69-55; telex 56-71880; Ambassador GRAHAM MITCHELL.

Oman: (see Kuwait).

Pakistan (High Commission): Diplomatic Enclave, Sector G-5, POB 1042, Islamabad; tel. (51) 821101; telex 5700; High Commissioner MANFRED VON NOSTIZ. (Also covers Afghanistan.)

Palau: (see Philippines).

Panama (Consulate): Calle Rochet 14, 1°, Suite 1, Apartado 3658, Panama City; tel. 62-1032; Hon. Consul RUTH V. DENTON.

Papua New Guinea: (see Australia).

Paraguay: (see Argentina).

Peru: Federico Gerdes 130, Miraflores, Casilla 18-1126, Lima 18; tel. 444015; telex 25323; Ambassador KEITH A. BEZANSON.

Philippines: Allied Bank Center, 9th Floor, 6754 Ayala Ave, Makati, Metro Manila; tel. (02) 8159536; telex 63676; Ambassador ANDRÉ SIMARD. (Also covers Marshall Islands and Palau.)

Poland: 00-481 Warsaw, Matejki 1/5; tel. 298051; telex 813424; Ambassador ERIC J. BERGBUSCH. (Also covers German Democratic Republic.)

Portugal: Avenida da Liberdade 144–156, 4°, 1200 Lisbon; tel. 563821; telex 12377; Ambassador GEOFFREY BRUCE.

Qatar: (see Kuwait).

Réunion: (see Kenya).

Romania: 71118 Bucharest, Strade Nicolae Iorga 36; tel. 506580; telex 10690; Ambassador SAUL GREY.

Rwanda: (see Zaire).

Saint Christopher and Nevis: (see Barbados).

Saint Helena and Dependencies: (see South Africa).

Saint Lucia: (see Barbados).

Saint Pierre and Miquelon (Consulate): place du Général de Gaulle, BP 297, Saint-Pierre; tel. 414020; Hon. Consul J.-P. ANDRIEUX.

Saint Vincent and the Grenadines: (see Barbados).

San Marino: (see Italy).

São Tomé and Príncipe: (see Gabon).

Saudi Arabia: POB 94321, Riyadh 11693; tel. (1) 488-2288; telex 404893; Ambassador G. DOUGLAS VALENTINE. (Also covers Yemen Arab Republic and Yemen, People's Democratic Republic.)

Senegal: Immeuble Daniel Sorano, 45 blvd de la République, BP 3373, Dakar; tel. 21-02-90; telex 51632; Ambassador JEAN-PAUL HUBERT. (Also covers Cape Verde, The Gambia, Guinea-Bissau and Mauritania.)

Seychelles: (see Tanzania).

Sierra Leone: (see Nigeria).

Singapore (High Commission): 14-00 and 15-01 IBM Towers, 80 Anson Rd, Singapore 0207; tel. 225-6363; telex 21277; High Commissioner SEAN BRADY.

Solomon Islands: (see Australia).

Somalia: (see Kenya).

South Africa: POB 26006, Arcadia, Pretoria 0007; tel. 287062; telex 22112; Ambassador RONALD S. MacLEAN. (Also covers Lesotho, Saint Helena and Dependencies and Swaziland.)

Spain: Apartado 117, 28001 Madrid; tel. 4314300; telex 27347; Ambassador JULIE LORANGER.

Sri Lanka (High Commission): 6 Gregory's Rd, Cinnamon Gardens, POB 1006, Colombo 7; tel. (1) 595841; telex 21106; High Commissioner CAROLYN McASKIE.

Sudan: (see Egypt).

Suriname: (see Guyana).

Swaziland: (see South Africa).

Sweden: Tegelbacken 4, POB 16129, 103 23 Stockholm 16; tel. 23-79-20; telex 10687; Ambassador DENNIS B. BROWNE.

Switzerland: Kirchenfeldstrasse 88, 3005 Berne; tel. 446381; telex 911308; Ambassador JACQUES DUPUIS. (Also covers Liechtenstein.)

Syria: Hotel Sheraton, Pl. des Omayades, POB 3394, Damascus; tel. 229300; telex 412422; Ambassador GARY R. HARMAN. (Also covers Lebanon.)

Tanzania (High Commission): Pan Africa Insurance Bldg, Samora Machel Ave, POB 1022, Dar es Salaam; tel. 20651; telex 41015; High Commissioner B. ROSE. (Also covers Mauritius and Seychelles.)

Thailand: Boonmitr Bldg, 11th Floor, 138 Silom Rd, POB 2090, Bangkok 10500; tel. (02) 234-1561; telex 82671; Ambassador LAWRENCE SMITH. (Also covers Cambodia, Laos and Viet-Nam.)

Togo: (see Ghana).

Tonga: (see New Zealand).

Trinidad and Tobago (High Commission): Huggins Bldg, 72–74 South Quay, POB 1246, Port of Spain; tel. (809) 623-7254; telex 22429; High Commissioner RODNEY IRWIN. (Also covers French Guiana, Guadeloupe and Martinique.)

Tunisia: 3 rue de Senégal, pl. Palestine, BP 31, Belvédère 1002, Tunis; tel. 286-577; telex 15324; Ambassador MARIUS BUJOLD.

Turkey: Nenehatun Caddesi 75, 06700 Gaziosmanpaşa, Ankara; tel. 1361275; telex 42369; Ambassador TERRENCE B. SHEEHAN.

Tuvalu: (see New Zealand).

Uganda: (see Kenya).

USSR: Moscow, Starokonyushenny Pereulok 23; tel. (095) 241-91-55; telex 413401; Ambassador VERNON TURNER. (Also covers Mongolia.)

United Arab Emirates: (see Kuwait).

United Kingdom (High Commission): Macdonald House, 1 Grosvenor Sq., London, W1X 0AB; tel. (01) 629-9492; telex 261592; High Commissioner DONALD S. MACDONALD.

USA: 501 Pennsylvania Ave, NW, Washington, DC 20008; tel. (202) 785-1400; telex 89664; Ambassador DEREK H. BURNEY.

Uruguay: (see Argentina).

Vanuatu: c/o Consulate-General, AMP Centre, 50 Bridge St, 5th Floor, Sydney, NSW 2000, Australia; tel. (02) 231-6522; telex 20600.

Venezuela: Edif. Torre Europa, 7°, Avenida Francisco de Miranda, Chacaito, Apartado 62302, Caracas 1060A; tel. 9516166; telex 23377; Ambassador JOHN GRAHAM.

Vietnam: (see Thailand).

Western Samoa: (see New Zealand).

Yemen Arab Republic: (see Saudi Arabia).

Yemen, People's Democratic Republic: (see Saudi Arabia).

Yugoslavia: 11000 Belgrade, Kneza Miloša 75; tel. 644666; telex 11137; Ambassador TERENCE C. BACON. (Also covers Albania and Bulgaria.)

Zaire: BP 8341, Kinshasa; tel. 27551; telex 21303; Ambassador COLLEN L. CUPPLES. (Also covers Congo and Rwanda.)

Zambia (High Commission): North End Branch, Barclays Bank Bldg, Cairo Rd, POB 31312, Lusaka; tel. 216161; telex 42480; High Commissioner MARION MACPHERSON. (Also covers Malawi.)

Zimbabwe (High Commission): 45 Baines Ave, POB 1430, Harare; tel. 733881; telex 4465; High Commissioner ROGER A. BULL. (Also covers Angola, Botswana and Mozambique.)

JUDICIAL SYSTEMS OF CANADA

INTRODUCTION

Common law is in force in Canada, with the exception of the province of Québec, where *le droit civil* (based on the Code Napoléon) prevails in private law. The right to pass legislation on the various aspects of civil law is shared between the federal parliament and the provincial and territorial legislatures. Provinces and territories have jurisdiction over contract, property and tort laws, while the federal parliament has jurisdiction over banking, bankruptcy and insolvency, and patents and copyrights. Jurisdiction is shared on corporation and tax laws.

The criminal-law system of Canada has its origins in the Constitution Act of 1867 (formerly known as the British North America Act), and subsequent amendments, such as the Criminal Code of Canada (1893). Provincial attorney-generals have responsibility for criminal prosecutions within their province which fall under the terms of the Criminal Code. The Attorney-General of Canada has responsibility for proceedings under federal statutes other than the Criminal Code. All criminal proceedings in the Northwest Territories and Yukon Territory come under the jurisdiction of the Attorney-General of Canada.

According to the Constitution Act, the administration of justice in the provinces, including the constitution, maintenance and organization of provincial courts, in both civil and criminal departments, rests with the provincial government.

THE FEDERAL JUDICIAL SYSTEM

Supreme Court of Canada

(Supreme Court of Canada Bldg, Wellington St, Ottawa, ON K1A 0J1; tel. (613) 995-4330; fax (613) 996-3063)

The Supreme Court of Canada was established in 1875 by the Supreme and Exchequer Court Act. It is the ultimate court of appeal in both civil and criminal cases throughout Canada. The judgment of the Court is final and conclusive. The Supreme Court is also required to advise on questions referred to it by the Governor in Council. Important questions concerning the interpretation of the Constitution Act, the constitutionality or interpretation of any federal or provincial law, the powers of parliament or of the provincial legislatures or of both levels of government, among other matters, may be referred by the government to the Supreme Court for consideration.

In civil cases, appeals may be brought from any final judgment of the highest court of last resort in a province. The Supreme Court will grant permission to appeal if it is of the opinion that a question of public importance is involved, one that transcends the immediate concerns of the parties to the litigation. In criminal cases, the Court will hear appeals as of right concerning indictable offences where an acquittal has been set aside or where there has been a dissenting judgment on a point of law in a provincial court of appeal. Appeals are also heard from the appeal division of the Federal Court of Appeal. The Supreme Court may, in addition, hear appeals on questions of law concerning both summary conviction and all other indictable offences if permission to appeal is first granted by the Court.

There are nine supreme-court judges, including the Chief Justice of Canada, and at least five judges are required to be present for a case to be heard (although it is normal for the full court to sit in most instances). The judges are appointed by the Governor in Council, and hold office until reaching the age of 75 years. Judges may only be removed from office by the Governor-General on address of the federal Senate and House of Commons.

Chief Justice of Canada: R. G. BRIAN DICKSON.

Puisne Judges: JEAN BEETZ, W. R. MCINTYRE, ANTONIO LAMER, BERTHA WILSON, GERALD E. LE DAIN, GÉRARD V. LA FOREST, CLAIRE L'HEUREUX-DUBÉ, JOHN SOPINKA.

Federal Court of Canada

(Supreme Court of Canada Bldg, Kent and Wellington Sts,
Ottawa, ON K1A 0H9; tel. (613) 996-6795; fax (613) 952-7226)

The Federal Court of Canada was established in 1971 under section 101 of the Constitution Act of 1867, and replaced the Exchequer Court of Canada, which had existed since 1875. The court has two divisions—the Federal Court of Appeal and the Trial Division of the Federal Court of Canada.

The Federal Court of Appeal has 10 judges (excluding the Chief Justice) and has jurisdiction over appeals from the Trial Division of the Federal Court of Canada, appeals from federal tribunals, review of decisions of federal boards and commissions, appeals from tribunals and reviews under Section 28 of the Federal Court Act, and references by federal boards and commissions.

The Trial Division of the Federal Court of Canada is headed by the Associate Chief Justice, and has jurisdiction in claims against the Crown, claims by the Crown, miscellaneous cases involving the Crown, claims against or concerning crown officers and servants, relief against federal boards, commissions and other tribunals, interprovincial and federal–provincial disputes, industrial or industrial property matters, admiralty, income-tax and estate-tax appeals, citizenship appeals, aeronautics, interprovincial works and undertakings, residuary jurisdiction for relief if there is no other Canadian court that has such jurisdiction, and jurisdiction in specific matters conferred by federal statutes.

The Federal Court of Canada has one central registry and consists of the principal office in Ottawa and local offices in major centres throughout Canada. Each division of the court can sit in any place in Canada.

FEDERAL COURT OF APPEAL

Chief Justice: FRANK IACOBUCCI.

Judges: LOUIS PRATTE, DARREL V. HEALD, JOHN J. URIE, PATRICK M. MAHONEY, LOUIS MARCEAU, JAMES K. HUGESSEN, ARTHUR J. STONE, MARK R. MACGUIGAN, BERTRAND LACOMBE, ALICE DESJARDINS.

TRIAL DIVISION

Associate Chief Justice: JAMES ALEXANDER JEROME.

Judges: GEORGE A. ADDY, J.-E. DUBÉ, PAUL U. C. ROULEAU, FRANCIS C. MULDOON, BARRY L. STRAYER, JOHN C. MCNAIR, BARBARA J. REED, PIERRE DENAULT, YVON PINARD, L. MARCEL JOYAL, BUD CULLEN, LEONARD A. MARTIN, MAX M. TEITELBAUM, WILLIAM ANDREW MACKAY.

LOCAL OFFICES
Alberta
Calgary: 635 Eighth Ave, SW, 3rd Floor, POB 16, Calgary, AB T2P 3M3; tel. (403) 292-5920.

Edmonton: Tower I, 5th Floor, 10060 Jasper Ave, Edmonton, AB T5J 3R8; tel. (403) 420-4651.

British Columbia
Vancouver: Pacific Centre, 700 West Georgia St, POB 10065, Vancouver, BC V7Y 1B6; tel. (604) 666-3232.

Manitoba
Winnipeg: 363 Broadway St, 4th Floor, Winnipeg, MB R3C 3N9; tel. (204) 949-2509.

New Brunswick
Fredericton: Justice Bldg, Supreme Court of New Brunswick, Rm 202, Queen St, POB 6000, Fredericton, NB E3B 5H1; tel. (506) 452-3016.

Saint John: Provincial Bldg, 4th Floor, Rm 427, 110 Charlotte St, Saint John, NB E2L 2J4; tel. (506) 648-4990.

Newfoundland
St John's: Court House, Duckworth St, POB 937, St John's, NF A1C CM3; tel. (709) 772-6524.

Northwest Territories
Yellowknife: Court House, POB 550, Yellowknife, NT X1A 2N4; tel. (403) 873-2044.

Nova Scotia
Halifax: 154 Anchorage House, Historic Properties, 1869 Upper Walter St, Halifax, NS B3J 1S9; tel. (902) 426-3282.

Ontario
Toronto: Canada Life Bldg, 8th Floor, 330 University Ave, Toronto, ON M5G 1R7; tel. (416) 973-3356.

Prince Edward Island
Charlottetown: Sir Louis Henry Davies Courthouse, 42 Water St, POB 2200, Charlottetown, PE C1A 8B9; tel. (902) 892-9900.

Québec
Montréal: Palais de Justice, 11th Floor, 1 Notre Dame St East, Montréal, PQ H2Y 1B6; tel. (514) 283-4820.

Québec: Palais de Justice, Rm 500, 300 Jean-Lesage Blvd, Québec, PQ G1K 8K6; tel. (418) 648-4920.

Saskatchewan
Regina: Court House, 2425 Victoria Ave, Regina, SK S4P 3V7; tel. (306) 780-5268.

Saskatoon: Court House, 520 Spadina Cres. East, Saskatoon, SK S7K 3G7; tel. (306) 975-4509.

Yukon Territory
Whitehorse: Andrew A. Phillipsen Law Centre, 2134 Second Ave, Whitehorse, YT Y1A 5H6; tel. (403) 668-4314.

Court Martial Appeal Court of Canada

(Supreme Court of Canada Bldg, Kent and Wellington Sts,
Ottawa, ON K1A 0H9)

Chief Justice: PATRICK M. MAHONEY.

Tax Court of Canada

(200 Kent St, Ottawa, ON K1A 0M1; tel. (613) 992-0901; telex
063666; fax (613) 957-9034)

The Tax Court of Canada has jurisdiction over appeals concerning the Income Tax Act, the Canada Pension Plan, the Petroleum and Gas Revenue Tax Act and Part IV of the Unemployment Insurance Act of 1971. Hearings may be held in major centres throughout the country for income-tax appeals, and in even smaller communities for appeals relating to unemployment insurance. Appeals of Tax Court decisions may be heard in the Federal Court of Canada.

Chief Judge: J.-C. COUTURE.

Associate Chief Judge: D. H. CHRISTIE.

Judges: LUCIEN CARDIN, ROLAND ST-ONGE, GUY TREMBLAY, DELMER E. TAYLOR, M. J. BONNER, J. B. GOETZ, A. A. SARCHUK, G. J. RIP, J. A. BRULÉ, W. KEMPO.

LOCAL OFFICES
Ontario
Toronto: Sun Life Centre, Rm 902, 200 King St West, Toronto, ON M5H 3T4; tel. (416) 973-9181; fax (416) 973-5944.

Québec
Montréal: La Maison de Barreau, 3rd Floor, 445 St-Laurent Blvd, Montréal, PQ H2Y 3T8; tel. (514) 283-9912; fax (514) 496-1996.

Québec: Palais de Justice, 5th Floor, 300 Jean-Lesage Blvd, Québec, PQ G1L 8L2; tel. (418) 648-7325.

Office of the Commissioner for Federal Judicial Affairs

(Ottawa, ON K1A 1E3; tel. (613) 992-9175; telex 053-3760)

The Office of the Commissioner for Federal Affairs is responsible for administrative matters relating to the Federal Court of Canada, the Canadian Judicial Council and all federally-appointed judges, with the exception of those of the Supreme Court of Canada.

Commissioner: PIERRE GARCEAU.

Deputy Commissioner: A. LAFRAMBOISE.

PROVINCIAL AND TERRITORIAL JUDICIAL SYSTEMS

The Provincial Court System—General Introduction

Provincial courts are constituted under provincial legislation, and while their actual names may vary from province to province their structures are generally similar. There are three levels of provincial courts.

The highest level of court in a province is the Superior or Supreme Court, which hears serious criminal and civil cases and has the authority to grant divorces. The Superior Court may be a single court with a Trial Division and an Appellate Division, or it may consist of two separate courts—the Court of Queen's Bench and the Court of Appeal. The Appellate Division or the Court of Appeal may also hear appeals in both civil and criminal cases from all the trial courts in the province. Judges are appointed by the federal government, and are compulsorily retired at the age of 75 years.

All provinces except Québec also have an intermediate level of courts, called County or District Courts. These possess immediate jurisdiction, dealing with criminal cases (apart from the most serious) and cases beyond the jurisdiction of the Small Claims Court. Judges are appointed by the federal government; the compulsory age of retirement is 70 years.

Finally, each province has inferior courts which, with some variations, consist of the Juvenile Court, the Family Court, the Provincial Court (Criminal Division) and the Small Claims Court. These cover minor civil and criminal matters and settle the majority of such cases. Judges are appointed by the provincial governments, and are compulsorily retired in accordance with the statutes which established the respective courts—usually at the age of 70 years.

Alberta

Alberta's Provincial Court (the lowest level of courts) includes the Family and Youth Division, the Small Claims Division, and the Criminal Division. There are 15 judicial districts, with headquarters at Calgary, Drumheller, Edmonton, Fort Macleod, Fort McMurray, Grande Prairie, Hinton, Lethbridge, Medicine Hat, Peace River, Red Deer, St Albert, St Paul, Vegreville and Wetaskiwin. The highest level of courts comprises the Court of Appeal and the Court of Queen's Bench.

COURT OF APPEAL

Chief Justice of Alberta: J. H. LAYCRAFT (Calgary).

Calgary: Court of Appeal Bldg, 530 7th Ave, SW, Calgary, AB T2P 0Y3; Justices of Appeal: D. C. PROWSE, A. M. HARRADENCE, R. P. KERANS, M. M. HETHERINGTON, J. D. BRACCO.

Edmonton: Law Courts Bldg, 1A Sir Winston Churchill Sq., Edmonton, AB T5J 0R2; Justices of Appeal: SAMUEL S. LIEBERMAN, W. J. HADDAD, J. W. McCLUNG, R. H. BELZIL, W. A. STEVENSON, R. P. FOISY, J. J. STRATTON, H.L. IRVING, J. E. COTÉ.

COURT OF QUEEN'S BENCH

Chief Justice: W. K. MOORE (Calgary).

Associate Chief Justice: T. H. MILLER (Edmonton).

Calgary: Courthouse, 611 4th St, SW, Calgary, AB T2P 1T5; Justices: M. E. SHANNON, F. H. QUIGLEY, W. R. BRENNAN, V. P. MOSHANSKY, J. H. WAITE, G. R. FORSYTH, H. S. PATTERSON, H. S. ROWBOTHAM, D. H. MEDHURST, H. S. PROWSE, W. G. N. EGBERT, P. C. G. POWER, J. J. KRYCZKA, R. A. DIXON, M. E. LOMAS, P. CHRUMKA, R. A. F. MONTGOMERY, A. M. LUTZ, A. B. SULATYCKY, R. T. G. McBAIN, W. E. O'LEARY, J. L. MacPHERSON, E. A. HUTCHINSON, D. B. MASON, C. G. VIRTUE, C. M. CONRAD, R. V. DEYELL.

Edmonton: Law Courts Bldg, 1A Sir Winston Churchill Sq., Edmonton, AB T5J 0R2; Justices: M. B. O'BYRNE, W. R. SINCLAIR, J. C. CAVANAGH, D. C. McDONALD, J. M. HOPE, S. V. LEGG, J. B. FEEHAN, A. W. CROSSLEY, A. H. WACHOWICH, E. A. McFADYEN, J. B. DEA, R. A. CAWSEY, J. A. AGRIOS, V. W. M. SMITH, W. J. GIRGULIS, J. B. VEIT, E. P. MacCALLUM, N. L. FOSTER, T. W. GALLANT, D. R. MATHESON, A. A. ANDREKSON, R. L. BERGER, E. A. MARSHALL, A. COOKE, E. I. PICARD, M. J. TRUSSLER, A. T. MURRAY, Y. ROSLAK.

Lethbridge: Courthouse, 320 Fourth St South, Lethbridge, AB T1J 1Z8; Justices: L. D. MacLEAN, C. G. YANOSIK.

Red Deer: Courthouse, 4909 48th Ave, Red Deer, AB T4N 3T5; Justices: J. K. HOLMES, J. H. MacKENZIE.

PROVINCIAL COURT

There are 22 provincial-court districts and 103 judges.

Chief Provincial Court Judge: C. A. KOSAWAN.

Assistant Chief Judges: C. L. LIDEN, A. G. LYNCH-STAUNTON, D. L. CROWE, H. G. OLIVER, D. E. PATTERSON, C. H. ROLF, W. G. W. WHITE, J. S. WOODS.

British Columbia

British Columbia has seven County Courts which are located at Cariboo, Kootenay, Prince Rupert, Vancouver, Victoria, Westminster and Yale. The highest provincial court is the Court of Appeal, followed by the Supreme Court. The Governor-General-in-Council appoints all provincial judges.

COURT OF APPEAL

Chief Justice of British Columbia: A. McEACHERN.

Vancouver: Law Courts, 800 Smithe St, Vancouver, BC V6Z 2E1; Justices of Appeal: J. D. TAGGART, P. D. SEATON, A. B. B. CARROTHERS, E. E. HINKSON, W. A. CRAIG, J. S. AIKINS, J. D. LAMBERT, J. A. MacDONALD, R. P. ANDERSON, H. E. HUTCHEON, W. J. WALLACE, C. C. LOCKE, S. M. TOY, MARY F. SOUTHIN, A. B. MACFARLANE.

SUPREME COURT

Chief Justice of Supreme Court: W. A. ESSON.

Vancouver: Law Courts, 800 Smithe St, Vancouver, BC V6Z 2E1; Justices: K. E. MEREDITH, A. A. MACKOFF, J. C. BOUCK, L. G. McKENZIE, G. L. MURRAY, H. P. LEGG, W. J. TRAINOR, P. M. PROUDFOOT, H. A. CALLAGHAN, A. G. MacKINNON, M. R. TAYLOR, P. D. DOHM, R. M. P. PARIS, D. B. HINDS, A. A. W. MACDONELL, J. E. SPENCER, W. H. DAVIES, C. R. LANDER, B. D. MACDONALD, K. M. LYSYK, L. S. G. FINCH, J. WOOD, R. J. GIBBS, G. S. CUMMING, D. B. MacKINNON, W. T. OPPAL, M. A. ROWLES, B. I. COHEN, C. M. HUDDART, J. J. GOW, D. W. SHAW, G. R. B. COULTAS, H. A. HOLLINRAKE, J. C. COWAN, J. E. PROWSE, F. MACZKO, A. M. STEWART.

Victoria: Law Courts, 850 Burdett Ave, Victoria, BC V8W 1B4; Justice: J. G. RUTTAN.

PROVINCIAL COURT

The provincial-court system comprises 44 courts and 116 judges.

Chief Judge of the Provincial Court: I. BRUCE JOSEPHSON.

Vancouver: Suite 501, 700 West Georgia St, POB 10287, Pacific Centre, Vancouver, BC V7Y 1E8; Judges: W. J. DIEBOLT, D. E. FIELD, J. L. McCARTHY, T. D. McGEE (Admin. Judge), A. J. SPENCE.

Manitoba

There are 16 Rural Courts in Manitoba, with administrative and judicial centres in Beausejour, Brandon, Dauphin, Flin Flon, Kilarney, Minnedosa, Morden, Portage la Prairie, Russell, St Boniface, Selkirk, Steinbach, Swan River, The Pas, Thompson and Virden. These handle Court of Queen's Bench and provincial-court matters. The superior courts are the Court of Appeal and the Court of Queen's Bench.

COURT OF APPEAL

Chief Justice of Manitoba: A. M. MONNIN.

Winnipeg: Law Courts Bldg, 408 York Ave, Winnipeg, MB R3C 0P9; Judges of Appeal: G. C. HALL, J. F. O'SULLIVAN, C. R. HUBAND, A. R. PHILP, A. K. TWADDLE, S. R. LYON.

COURT OF QUEEN'S BENCH

Chief Justice of the Court of Queen's Bench: B. HEWAK.

Associate Chief Justice: R. J. SCOTT.

Winnipeg: Law Courts Bldg, 408 York Ave, Winnipeg, MB R3C 0P9; Judges: J. E. WILSORI, W. S. WRIGHT, P. S. MORSE, G. J. KROFT, J. A. SCOLLIN, V. SIMONSEN, K. R. HANSSEN, M. A. MONNIN, G. J. BARKMAN, B. R. COLEMAN, A. DUREAULT, G. O. JEWERS, G. H. LOCKWOOD, D. P. KENNEDY, R. KRINDLE, J. G. SMITH, S. E. SCHWARTZ, T. M. GLOWACKI, A. A. HIRSCHFIELD, W. R. DE GRAVES.

Brandon: Courthouse, 1104 Princess Ave, POB 68, Brandon, MB R7A 5Y6; Judge: J. J. OLIPHANT.

Dauphin: Courthouse, 114 River Ave West, POB 604, Dauphin, MB R7N 2V4; Judge: W. M. DARICHUK.

Portage la Prairie: Courthouse, 3rd St, SE, Portage la Prairie, MB R1N 1M9; Judge: A. C. MILLER.

PROVINCIAL COURT

There are six provincial-court districts and 33 judges.

Chief Judge: I. V. DUBIENSKI (acting).

Associate Chief Judges: E. C. KIMELMAN, C. M. SINCLAIR.

Winnipeg: Law Courts Bldg, 408 York Ave, Winnipeg, MB R3C 0P9.

New Brunswick

New Brunswick comprises eight judicial districts, with headquarters at Bathurst, Campbellton, Edmundston, Fredericton, Moncton, Newcastle, Saint John and Woodstock. The highest courts are the Court of Appeal and the Court of Queen's Bench, which is divided into a Trial Division and a Family Division. In 1979 the former district courts were amalgamated with courts of Queen's Bench.

COURT OF APPEAL

Chief Justice of New Brunswick: S. G. STRATTON.

Fredericton: POB 6000, Fredericton, NB E3B 5H1; Judges: J. C. ANGERS, W. L. HOYT, L. C. AYLES, R. C. RICE, P. A. A. RYAN.

COURT OF QUEEN'S BENCH

Chief Justice, Court of Queen's Bench: G. A. RICHARD (Moncton).

Fredericton: POB 6000, Fredericton, NB E3B 5H1; Judges (Trial Division): D. M. DICKSON (Fredericton), J. PAUL BARRY (Saint John), C. I. L. LEGER (Moncton), R. C. STEVENSON (Fredericton), B. A. JEAN (Bathurst), R. L. MILLER (Moncton), W. L. M. CREAGHAN (Fredericton), R. J. HIGGINS (Saint John), J. T. JONES (Saint John), J. Z. DAIGLE (Edmundston), P. J. M. GODIN (Campbellton), A. J. CORMIER (Moncton), P. S. CREAGHAN (Fredericton), D. H. RUSSELL (Fredericton), J. W. TURNBULL (Saint John), H. H. McLELLAN (Woodstock), A. DESCHENES (Bathurst), THOMAS RIORDON (Newcastle), ROGER SAVOIE (Moncton); Judges (Family Division): H. E. MONTGOMERY (Fredericton), R. E. LOGAN (Saint John), J. A. SIROIS (Edmundston), G. BOISVERT (Bathurst), R. J. GUERETTE (Saint John), M. E. L. LARLEE (Edmundston), J. A. LANDRY (Moncton).

PROVINCIAL COURT

There are 14 courts and 23 judges in the provincial-court system.

Chief Judge: H. HAZEN STRANGE.

Newfoundland

Newfoundland's Provincial Court includes a Juvenile Court and a Traffic Court. There are six judicial centres, which are situated at Gander, Grand Falls, Corner Brook, Brigus, Grand Bank and Happy Valley. The Supreme Court is divided into a Court of Appeal and a Trial Division.

SUPREME COURT

(Court House, 355 Duckworth St, St John's, NF A1C 1H6)

Court of Appeal

Chief Justice: NOEL GOODRIDGE.

Judges: H. B. MORGAN, J. R. GUSHUE, J. W. MAHONEY, JOHN J. O'NEILL, WILLIAM W. MARSHALL, ARTHUR S. MIFFLIN.

Trial Division

Chief Justice: T. A. HICKMAN.

Judges: NATHANIEL S. NOEL, G. LANG, G. STEELE, MARGARET CAMERON, F. AYLWARD, WILLIAM G. ADAMS, DAVID G. RICHE, ROBERT WELLS, RAYMOND J. HALLEY, DAVID L. RUSSELL, DENIS ROBERTS, LLOYD SOPER.

PROVINCIAL COURT

The provincial-court system comprises a total of 18 courts and 33 judges.

St John's: Atlantic Pl., POB 5144, St John's, NF A1C 5V5.

Chief Judge and Clerk of the Peace: C. P. SCOTT.

Associate Chief Judge: E. LANGDON.

Judges: J. P. TRAHEY, J. WOODROW, G. SEABRIGHT, L. W. WICKS, MILTON REID.

Northwest Territories

The Northwest Territories have a Territorial Court, which includes a Criminal Division, Small Claims Division, Juvenile Division, and Family and Citizenship Division. The judiciary consists of one Supreme Court judge, four territorial judges, 15 judicial officers and 102 justices of the peace. Both judges and justices of the peace are appointed by the territories' commissioner. Court sessions are held in Yellowknife and on court circuits throughout the Territories. The superior courts of the Territories are the Court of Appeal and the Supreme Court. The Court of Appeal consists of the judges of the Court of Appeal of Alberta, one judge of the Court of Appeal of Saskatchewan, and the judges and ex-officio judge of the Supreme Court of the Northwest Territories.

COURT OF APPEAL

Chief Justice: J. H. LAYCRAFT.

Judges: N. D. McDERMID, C. F. TALLIS, S. S. LIEBERMAN, A. M. HARRADENCE, D. C. PROWSE, R. P. KERANS, W. A. STEVENSON, W. J. HADDAD, J. W. McCLUNG, H. C. B. MADDISON, R. H. BELZIL, M. M. de WEERDT, T. D. MARSHALL, H. L. IRVING, M. HETHERINGTON, R. FOISY, J. J. STRATTON, J. E. L. COTE.

Yellowknife: Courthouse, POB 550, Yellowknife, NT X1A 2N1.

SUPREME COURT

Judges: M. M. de WEERDT, T. D. MARSHALL, E. RICHARD.

Ex-officio Judge: HARRY C. B. MADDISON (Whitehorse, Yukon Territory).

Yellowknife: Courthouse, POB 550, Yellowknife, NT X1A 2N1.

There are 27 deputy judges from the Superior Courts of Alberta, British Columbia, Québec, Ontario and Saskatchewan.

TERRITORIAL COURT

Chief Judge: J. R. SLAVEN (Yellowknife).

Judges: R. HALIFAX (Hay River), R. M. BOURASSA (Yellowknife), T. DAVIS (Yellowknife), O. J. T. TROY (Iqaluit).

Nova Scotia

Nova Scotia has seven county-court districts. The provincial Supreme Court consists of an Appeal Division and a Trial Division. Its judges are appointed by the provincial cabinet.

SUPREME COURT

Appeal Division

Chief Justice: LORNE O'CLARKE.

Justices: ANGUS L. MacDONALD, MALACHI C. JONES, LEONARD L. PACE, GORDON L. S. HART, KENNETH M. MATTHEWS, DAVID R. CHIPMAN, IAN M. MacKEIGAN.

Trial Division

Chief Justice: CONSTANCE R. GLUBE.

Justices: J. DOANE HALLETT, WILLIAM J. GRANT, K. PETER RICHARD, C. DENNE BURCHELL, R. MacLEOD ROGERS, D. MERLIN NUNN, H. S. NATHANSON, ROBERT MacDONALD, F. B. WILLIAM KELLY, GORDON TIDMAN, JOHN McNAB DAVISON, A. M. MacINTOSH.

PROVINCIAL COURT

There are 13 courts and 28 judges in the provincial-court system.

Chief Judge: HARRY W. HOW.

Ontario

Ontario's Provincial Court includes a Civil Division, Criminal Division and Family Division. The province is divided into eight District Court judicial districts, containing 50 District Courts. The Supreme Court of Ontario consists of the Court of Appeal and the High Court of Justice.

SUPREME COURT

(130 Queen St, West, Toronto, ON M5H 2N5)

Court of Appeal

Chief Justice of Ontario: W. G. C. HOWLAND.

Associate Chief Justice: C. L. DUBIN.

Justices: D. G. Blair, J. W. Brooke, J. J. Carthy, M. A. Catzman, P. DeC. Cory, G. D. Finlayson, A. Goodman, S. G. M. Grange, W. D. Griffiths, L. W. Houlden, H. Krever, M. N. Lacourciere, H. M. McKinlay, J. W. Morden, S. L. Robins, W. S. Tarnopolsky, T. G. Zuber.

High Court of Justice

Chief Justice of the High Court: F. W. Callaghan.
Associate Chief Justice: (vacant).
There are 56 justices.

PROVINCIAL COURT
Civil Division

Administration: Inspector of Legal Offices, North Yurchuk, 18th Floor, 18 King St East, Toronto, ON M5C 1C5.

Criminal Division

Chief Judge: F. C. Hayes.
Administration: 60 Queen St West, Toronto, ON M5H 2M4; tel. (416) 965-7200.

Family Division

Chief Judge: H. T. G. Andrews.
Associate Chief Judge: R. J. K. Walmsley.
Judges: P. W. Dunn, K. Wang.
Administration: Suite 2306, 700 Bay St, Toronto, ON M5G 1Z6; tel. (416) 965-3214.

Prince Edward Island

Prince Edward Island comprises three judicial counties with headquarters at Georgetown, Charlottetown and Summerside. The Supreme Court in the province consists of two branches: an Appeal Division and a Trial Division.

SUPREME COURT

(Sir Louis Henry Davies Law Courts Bldg, 42 Water St, POB 2200, Charlottetown, PE C1A 8B9)

Chief Justice of Prince Edward Island: Norman H. Carruthers.

Appeal Division

Chief Justice: Norman H. Carruthers.
Justices: Gerald E. Mitchell, George R. McMahon.

Trial Division

Chief Justice: Kenneth R. MacDonald.
Justices: Alexander B. Campbell, George J. Mullally, Jacquiline Matheson, Charles R. McQuaid, Frederic A. Large.

PROVINCIAL COURT

Chief Provincial Court Judge: Ralph C. Thompson.
Judges: G. L. Fitzgerald, B. R. Plamondon.
Charlottetown: Law Courts Bldg, POB 2290, Charlottetown, PE C1A 8C1.

Québec

Québec's court system differs from the court hierarchy of other provinces, in that it has no District Courts but a greater number of inferior courts. These have six components: the Provincial Court, the Court of the Sessions of the Peace, which covers both federal and provincial penal matters, and is similar to a District Court in its functions, the Youth Court, which hears cases involving juveniles, the Municipal Court, the Small Claims Court and the Court of Justices of the Peace, which issues warrants and enforces municipal by-laws. The highest courts in the province are the Court of Appeal and the Superior Court.

COUR D'APPEL/COURT OF APPEAL

Montréal: 1 rue Notre-Dame est, Montréal, PQ H2Y 1B6.
Judges: Claude C. Bisson (Chief Judge), Marc Beauregard, Fred Kaufman, Louise Mailhot, Albert Malouf, Gerald McCarthy, Amédée Monet, Marcel Nichols, Rodolphe Paré, William S. Tyndale, Claude Vallerand.
Québec: 300 blvd Jean-Lesage, Québec, PQ G1K 8K6.

Judges: Yves Bernier, Roger Chouinard, André Dubé, Paul-Arthur Gendreau, Maurice Jacques, Louis LeBel, Christine Tourigny.

COUR SUPÉRIEURE/SUPERIOR COURT

The Superior Court system comprises 13 courts and 151 judges.
Chief Justice: Alan B. Gold (Montréal).
Senior Associate Chief Justice: Pierre Côté.
Associate Chief Justice: Lawrence A. Poitras.
Montréal: 1 rue Notre-Dame est, Montréal, PQ H2Y 1B6; tel. (514) 873-3227.
Québec: 300 blvd Jean-Lesage, Québec, PQ G1K 8K6; tel. (418) 649-3501.

COUR PROVINCIALE/PROVINCIAL COURT

The provincial-court system comprises 31 courts and 147 judges.
Chief Justice: Gaston Rondeau (Montréal).
Assistant Chief Justice: Louis Vaillancourt (Montréal).
Associate Chief Justice: Yvon Mercier (Québec).
Montréal: 1 rue Notre-Dame est, Montréal, PQ H2Y 1B6.
Québec: 300 blvd Jean-Lesage, Québec, PQ G1K 8K6.

COUR DES SESSIONS DE LA PAIX/COURT OF SESSIONS OF THE PEACE

This comprises 10 courts and 68 judges.
Chief Justice: Guy Guérin (Montréal).
Associate Chief Justice: Jean-Pierre Bonin (Montréal).
Montréal: 1 rue Notre-Dame est, Montréal, PQ H2Y 1B6.
Québec: 300 blvd Jean-Lesage, Québec, PQ G1K 8K6.

TRIBUNAL DE LA JEUNESSE/YOUTH COURT

The Youth Court system comprises 16 courts with 48 judges.
Chief Justice: Albert Gobeil (Montréal).
Associate Chief Justice: Michel Jasmin (Montréal).
Montréal: 410 rue Bellechasse est, Suite 707, Montréal, PQ H2S 1X3.
Québec: 300 blvd Jean-Lesage, Québec, PQ G1K 8K6.

Saskatchewan

The province of Saskatchewan has 18 judicial centres, which are located at Assiniboia, Battleford, Estevan, Gravelbourg, Humboldt, Kerrobert, Melfort, Melville, Moose Jaw, Moosomin, Prince Albert, Regina, Saskatoon, Shaunavon, Swift Current, Weyburn, Wynyard and Yorkton. The superior courts in the province are the Court of Appeal and the Court of Queen's Bench.

COURT OF APPEAL

Chief Justice of Saskatchewan: E. D. Bayda.
Regina: Courthouse, 2425 Victoria Ave, Regina, SK S4P 3V7; Judges: C. F. Tallis, S. J. Cameron, W. J. Vancise, T. C. Wakeling, M. A. Gerwing, N. M. Sherstobitoff.

COURT OF QUEEN'S BENCH

Chief Justice: D. K. MacPherson (Regina).
Battleford: Courthouse, Battleford, SK S0M 0E0; Judge: C. R. Wimmer.
Estevan: Courthouse, Estevan, SK S4A 2A6; Judge: W. N. Lawton.
Humboldt: Courthouse, Humboldt, SK S0K 2A0; Judge: P. J. Dielschneider.
Melville: Courthouse, Melville, SK S0A 2P0; Judge: T. L. Geatros.
Moose Jaw: Courthouse, Moose Jaw, SK S6H 4P1; Judge: R. A. MacLean.
Prince Albert: Courthouse, Prince Albert, SK S6V 4W7; Judge: J. D. Milliken.
Regina: Courthouse, 2425 Victoria Ave, Regina, SK S4P 3V7; Judges: G. M. Forbes, K. R. Halvorson, K. R. MacLeod, E. C. Malone, W. R. Matheson, G. A. Maurice, J. G. McIntyre, E. A. Scheibel, G. H. M. Armstrong, R. L. Barclay.
Saskatoon: 520 Spadina Cres. East, Saskatoon, SK S7K 2H6; Judges: C. L. B. Estey, W. F. Gerein, I. Grotsky, I. Goldenberg, G. E. Noble, A. L. Sirois, S. J. Walker, D. H. Wright, P. Hrabinsky, J. H. Maher, Marion Wedge.

Swift Current: Courthouse, Swift Current, SK S9H 0J4; Judges: B. H. MOORE, I. D. MCLELLAN.

Yorkton: Courthouse, Yorkton, SK S3N 0C2; Judge: H. A. OSBORN.

PROVINCIAL COURT

Saskatchewan's provincial-court system comprises 15 courts and 43 judges.

Chief Judge: B. P. CAREY (Regina).

Regina: Provincial Court of Saskatchewan, 1815 Smith St, Regina, SK S4P 3V7.

Yukon Territory

The Yukon Territorial Court consists of one superior-court judge, two chief judges and several deputy judges. 45 justices of the peace are appointed by the commissioner. There are permanent courtrooms at Whitehorse, Watson Lake and Dawson, and regular court circuits at other locations. Yukon's superior courts are the Court of Appeal and the Supreme Court. The Court of Appeal is composed of one judge from the Yukon Supreme Court, three from the Supreme Court of the Northwest Territories, and 14 from the British Columbia Court of Appeal.

COURT OF APPEAL

Judges: HARRY C. B. MADDISON (Whitehorse), M. M. DE WEERDT, T. D. MARSHALL, E. RICHARD (all of Yellowknife, NWT), N. T. NEMETZ, J. D. TAGGART, P. D. SEATON, A. B. B. CARROTHERS, E. E. HINKSON, W. A. CRAIG, M. M. MCFARLANE, J. D. LAMBERT, J. A. MACDONALD, R. P. ANDERSON, H. HUTCHEON, W. A. ESSON, W. WALLACE, C. LOCKE (all of Vancouver).

SUPREME COURT

Resident Judge: HARRY C. B. MADDISON (Whitehorse).

Ex-officio Judges: M. M. DE WEERDT, T. D. MARSHALL, E. RICHARD (all of Yellowknife, NWT).

The Supreme Court has 35 deputy judges from the superior courts of British Columbia, Alberta, Québec, Saskatchewan, Ontario and Manitoba.

THE ECONOMY

NATIONAL ECONOMIC INDICATORS

Currency and Exchange Rates

MONETARY UNITS

100 cents = 1 Canadian dollar (C $).

DENOMINATIONS

Coins: 1, 5, 10, 25 and 50 cents; 1 dollar.
Notes: 1, 2, 5, 10, 20, 50, 100 and 1,000 dollars.

INTERNATIONAL VALUE OF THE DOLLAR
Average Exchange Rates
(units of foreign currency equivalent to C $1)

	1986	1987	1988
France (franc)	4.9847	4.5327	4.8400
Federal Republic of Germany (Deutsche Mark). . . .	1.5628	1.3554	1.4269
Italy (lira)	1,072.9	977.4	1,057.6
Japan (yen)	121.28	109.07	104.12
United Kingdom (pound sterling).	0.4906	0.4602	0.4561
USA (dollar)	0.7197	0.7541	0.8125

Foreign-Currency Equivalents
(30 June 1989)

France: C $1 = ₣5.538; ₣1,000 = C $180.58.
Federal Republic of Germany: C $1 = DM 1.6294; DM 100 = C $61.37.
Italy: C $1 = 1,178 lire; 10,000 lire = C $8.482.
Japan: C $1 = ¥120.3; ¥1,000 = C $8.316.
United Kingdom: C $100 = £53.83; £1 sterling = C $1.858.
USA: C $100 = US $83.47; US $1 = C $1.198.

MONEY SUPPLY
(C $ million at 31 December)

	1986	1987	1988
Currency outside deposit money banks . . .	15,590	16,820	18,240
Demand deposits at deposit money banks . . .	64,270	68,020	72,230
Total money (incl. others)	79,860	84,840	90,470

Source: IMF, *International Financial Statistics*.

INTERNATIONAL RESERVES
(US $ million at 31 December)

	1986	1987	1988
Gold	845	920	807
IMF Special Drawing Rights .	247	399	1,349
Reserve position in the IMF .	686	661	505
Foreign exchange	2,318	6,218	13,517
Total	4,096	8,198	16,198

Source: IMF, *International Financial Statistics*.

Cost of Living
(Consumer Price Index. Base: 1981 = 100)

	1986	1987	1988
Food	126.8	132.4	135.9
Housing	132.9	138.3	144.3
Clothing	118.8	123.8	130.2
Transport	135.0	139.9	142.6
Health and personal care . .	132.6	139.2	145.3
Recreation, education and reading	130.3	137.3	145.0
Tobacco and alcohol . . .	172.3	183.9	197.4
All items	132.4	138.2	143.8

Source: Statistics Canada.

National Accounts
(C $ million at current prices. Source: Statistics Canada.)

NATIONAL INCOME AND PRODUCT

	1985	1986	1987
Compensation of employees .	257,344	274,607	295,665
Operating surplus . . .	117,832	118,481	132,684
Domestic factor incomes . .	375,176	393,088	428,349
Consumption of fixed capital .	55,760	59,438	63,302
Gross domestic product at factor cost	430,936	452,526	491,651
Indirect taxes, *less* subsidies .	47,176	53,825	58,011
Statistical discrepancy . .	653	132	30
GDP at market prices . .	478,765	506,483	549,692
Factor income from abroad* .	7,574	7,207	6,987
Less Factor income paid abroad*	21,893	23,761	23,594
Gross national product .	464,446	489,929	533,085
Less Consumption of fixed capital	55,760	59,438	63,302
Statistical discrepancy . .	−653	−132	−30
National income at market prices	408,033	430,359	469,753
Other current transfers from abroad†	1,750	2,449	2,058
Less Other current transfers paid abroad† . . .	2,355	2,554	2,965
National disposable income .	407,428	430,254	468,846

* Remitted profits, dividends and interest only.
† Transfers to and from persons and governments.

EXPENDITURE ON THE GROSS DOMESTIC PRODUCT

	1985	1986	1987
Government final consumption expenditure	95,700	100,468	106,490
Private final consumption expenditure	274,946	297,304	322,970
Increase in stocks	2,981	2,936	1,954
Gross fixed capital formation .	94,216	101,326	114,378
Exports of goods and services .	134,979	137,459	144,213
Less Imports of goods and services	123,404	132,879	140,284
Statistical discrepancy . .	−653	−131	−29
GDP at market prices . .	478,765	506,483	549,692
GDP at constant 1981 prices .	395,217	407,736	424,136

Balance of Payments
(US $ million. Source: IMF, *International Financial Statistics*.)

	1985	1986	1987	1988
Merchandise exports f.o.b.	89,654	88,719	97,871	114,632
Merchandise imports f.o.b.	−77,074	−81,137	−89,111	−106,153
Trade balance	12,580	7,582	8,759	8,479
Exports of services	14,720	15,415	16,201	21,741
Imports of services	−29,317	−31,603	−34,518	−42,859
Balance on goods and services . .	−2,017	−8,606	−9,558	−12,639
Private unrequited transfers (net) .	816	932	2,044	3,844
Government unrequited transfers (net)	−225	131	−461	−319
Current balance	−1,426	−7,543	−7,975	−9,114
Direct capital investment (net)	−5,942	−1,731	−643	−3,320
Other long-term capital (net) . .	5,966	13,568	9,061	11,118
Short-term capital (net) . . .	1,802	−2,473	4,594	9,363
Net errors and omissions . . .	−3,680	−2,395	−2,259	−490
Total (net monetary movements) . .	−3,280	−576	2,778	7,558
Valuation changes (net) . . .	75	112	149	−38
Exceptional financing (net) . . .	3,207	1,055	564	—
Changes in reserves	1	591	3,491	7,521

Economically Active Population

(Source: Statistics Canada.)

Summary* ('000 persons aged 15 years and over)

	1985	1986	1987
Agriculture	488	484	475
Forestry, fishing and trapping	112	106	108
Mines, quarries and oil wells	191	185	182
Manufacturing	1,981	2,015	2,044
Construction	587	627	680
Electricity, gas and water	124	121	120
Transport and communications	760	777	785
Trade	2,001	2,082	2,116
Finance, insurance and real estate	629	654	695
Public administration	802	800	814
Other services	3,648	3,783	3,934
Total employed	11,311	11,634	11,955
Male	6,508	6,657	6,793
Female	4,804	4,977	5,161
Unemployed	1,328	1,236	1,167
Total labour force	12,639	12,870	13,121

* Figures exclude military personnel, inmates of institutions, residents of the Yukon and Northwest Territories, and Indian reserves.

EMPLOYMENT BY PROVINCE OR TERRITORY

('000 employees in selected industries, estimates for May 1989)

Goods-producing Industries

	Forestry	Mines, quarries and oil wells	Manufacturing	Construction	Total
Alberta	1.6	63.6	86.8	51.1	203.1
British Columbia	25.1	14.9	164.0	56.9	261.1
Manitoba	1.0	4.5	57.7	14.1	77.4
New Brunswick	2.2	3.3	38.1	12.2	55.7
Newfoundland	0.7	3.4	21.7	6.3	32.2
Northwest Territories	n.a.	n.a.	n.a.	n.a.	3.5
Nova Scotia	2.0	4.3	42.0	16.7	65.0
Ontario	9.4	29.7	989.0	240.7	1,268.8
Prince Edward Island	—	—	5.2	2.3	7.5
Québec	12.3	18.2	543.7	132.8	706.9
Saskatchewan	0.9	8.7	22.6	12.5	44.6
Yukon Territory	n.a.	n.a.	n.a.	n.a.	1.6
Total	55.5	153.7	1,971.3	547.0	2,727.5

Service-producing Industries

	Transportation, communications and other utilities	Trade	Finance, insurance and real estate	Community, business and personal services	Public administration	Total
Alberta	88.4	181.9	55.1	366.6	70.9	762.9
British Columbia	107.2	199.6	74.7	429.6	63.6	874.7
Manitoba	44.8	69.4	25.9	150.2	28.8	319.1
New Brunswick	21.2	41.8	9.5	78.4	18.0	169.0
Newfoundland	14.2	28.5	5.3	52.1	17.3	117.4
Northwest Territories	2.1	2.2	0.9	6.0	5.4	16.6
Nova Scotia	24.6	58.4	15.8	111.6	28.3	238.8
Ontario	306.6	743.8	290.1	1,465.1	251.3	3,056.8
Prince Edward Island	3.4	6.5	1.5	14.6	4.8	30.7
Québec	210.5	465.8	148.1	901.3	167.1	1,892.7
Saskatchewan	29.1	62.0	18.8	126.4	25.4	261.7
Yukon Territory	1.6	1.6	0.5	3.2	2.7	9.6
Total	853.7	1,861.7	646.1	3,705.2	683.5	7,750.1

PROVINCIAL AND TERRITORIAL ECONOMIES

Alberta

In terms of the numbers of people employed, Alberta's leading industries in May 1989 were service industries, trade, transportation, communications and other utilities, manufacturing, and public administration.

Alberta's per-head disposable income in 1986 was about C $14,000, the second highest (with Yukon Territory) after Ontario. In December 1986 Alberta's labour force was estimated at 1,272,000 persons, and the unemployment rate in the same year stood at 9.8%. Of those employed in 1982, 21.7% were reported to be trade-union members.

Of Alberta's total land area, 32.4% was farmland in 1986, and the average size of a farm was 357.5 hectares, the second-largest area after Saskatchewan. The net income of farmers from farm operations was C $720.1m. Alberta is second to Saskatchewan in wheat production. Other crops of importance include rapeseed, and tame hay, in which Alberta ranked first in Canada in 1988. The province was the leading producer of cattle in the same year, and its pig and sheep farms also made a large contribution to farm income. Additional commodities produced included poultry, eggs, dairy products, sugar beet and vegetables.

In 1986/87 Alberta produced 544,377 animal pelts, the third-highest total in the country. Inventoried forestland covered 51.8% of the province in 1981, and lumber shipments were valued at C $221m. in 1984. The commercial fishing catch in Alberta is relatively small. In 1984 1,420 metric tons of fish were caught, with a landed value of C $1.2m.

Alberta leads the nation in its production of oil and natural gas, which in 1986 were valued at C $6,334m. and C $6,106m. respectively. It is also the second-largest producer of coal, after British Columbia. Non-fuel mineral production had a total value of C $1,186m. in 1986, the fourth highest total of any province. The province is a world leader in its production of elemental sulphur. Other non-fuel minerals produced are sand and gravel, stone, clay, cement, salt, gold and silver.

Alberta's manufacturing shipments had a total value of C $17,192m. in 1985, 31.1% of which was added during manufacture. The province's leading manufacturing industries are related to its raw materials. In 1985 the major sectors were refined petroleum and coal products, food, chemicals and chemical products, and primary metal industries.

Tourism plays a significant part in the provincial economy, as hundreds of thousands of people visit the Rocky Mountains each year. Gross general expenditure by the provincial government totalled C $12,449m. in 1984/85; gross general revenue totalled C $14,534m., of which C $1,596m. was provided from federal sources.

British Columbia

In May 1989 it was estimated that the leading employers in British Columbia were (in order) service industries, trade, manufacturing, and transportation, communications and other utilities.

Per-head disposable income for British Columbia measured about C $13,500 in 1986. The labour force amounted to an estimated 1,465,000 persons in December 1986, and in the same year the unemployment rate was 12.6%. Of those employed in 1982, 38.6% were reported to be trade-union members.

Farmland covered only 2.7% of British Columbia's total land area in 1986, and the average size of a farm was 126.5 hectares. Farmers earned a net income of C $214.6m. from farming operations in that year. The province's main agricultural commodities are cattle and dairy products; however, British Columbia is the country's principal apple producer. Other sources of farm income include wheat, oats, barley, tame hay, poultry, eggs, soft fruit, vegetables and flowering bulbs.

In 1981 inventoried forestland covered 63.3% of British Columbia's total land area. Lumber shipments, worth C $3,057m. in 1984, are by far the most valuable in Canada. The province's fishing catch (169,168 metric tons in 1984, with a landed value of C $242.9m.) is the second most valuable in Canada (behind Nova Scotia) partly due to the large number of Pacific salmon caught.

The province is Canada's leading producer of bituminous coal. In 1986 20,362,000 tons of coal were extracted, with a value of C $940m. Natural gas and crude oil are also mined; the province ranks second to Alberta in natural-gas production. British Columbia leads the country in its production of copper (353,406 metric tons in 1988) and lead (90,086 metric tons). Other minerals of importance to the provincial economy are zinc, iron ore, gold, silver (of which it is Canada's largest producer), gypsum, sand and

gravel, stone and clay. The value of non-fuel mineral production totalled C $1,665m. in 1986, the third-highest value of any province.

In 1985 manufacturing shipments were valued at C $19,863.4m., of which 38.9% was added during manufacture. The main manufacturing industries are related to the province's forestry, agriculture and mining industries. In 1984 the leading manufacturing groups were wood industries, paper and allied products, food and refined petroleum products.

The tourist trade plays a significant part in the economy of British Columbia. In 1987 16.7m. visitors to the province spent about C $3,000m.

Gross general expenditure by the provincial government totalled C $10,959m. in 1984/85; gross general revenue totalled C $10,122m., of which C $1,747m. was provided federally.

Manitoba

Manitoba's foremost employers are service industries (trade, transportation, communications, and other utilities, finance, insurance and real estate, and public administration) and manufacturing.

The province's per-head disposable income in 1986 was about C $13,000. In the same year the labour force totalled an estimated 542,000 persons and the unemployment rate was 7.7%. Of those in employment, 26.4% were members of trade unions in 1982.

Farmland occupied 14.1% of Manitoba's total land area in 1986, and the average size of a farm was 283.2 hectares. The net income of farmers from farming was C $503.1m. in that year. Manitoba is one of Canada's leading agricultural provinces. The main crops produced are wheat and other grains, rapeseed (canola) and flaxseed. Other widely-produced commodities are cattle, pigs, sheep, poultry, dairy produce, vegetables, sugar beet and sunflowers.

The fur trade, Manitoba's oldest industry, still contributes to the provincial economy, though it is not a major source of income. In 1981 inventoried forestland occupied 43.8% of Manitoba's total land area, and in 1984 the value of its lumber shipments was C $14.9m. The fishing catch, most of which comes from Lakes Winnipeg, Manitoba and Winnipegosis, had a landed value of C $18.1m. in 1984.

The province's non-fuel mineral production was valued at C $663.8m. in 1986. Some crude oil is mined, but income is mainly derived from non-fuel minerals, namely nickel, copper, zinc, gold, silver, gypsum, lead, sand and gravel, stone, cement and clay.

In 1985 the value of Manitoba's manufacturing shipments was C $5,549.3m. of which 42.1% was added during manufacture, the second-highest proportion in Canada after Newfoundland. The province's principal industries are food industries, transportation equipment, printing, publishing and allied industries, electrical and electronic products, and fabricated metal products.

Gross general expenditure by the provincial government totalled C $4,172m. in 1984/85; gross general revenue totalled C $3,747m., of which C $1,112m. was provided from federal sources.

New Brunswick

The main areas of employment in New Brunswick are services, trade, manufacturing, and transportation, communications and other utilities.

Per-head disposable income was about C $10,500 in 1986, the third lowest among the provinces and territories. In December 1986 the labour force was estimated at 314,000 persons, with an unemployment rate of 14.4% in that year. In 1982, 30.6% of those in employment were members of trade unions.

Farmland covered 5.7% of New Brunswick's total land area in 1986, and the size of an average farm was 115 hectares. The net income of farm operators from farming was C $61.2m. in 1986, the second lowest among the provinces. Potatoes are the province's chief crop, with New Brunswick ranking second in potato production in 1986. Dairy products are also a major source of farm revenue. Other important agricultural commodities are beef, eggs, poultry, pigs, fruit, vegetables and maple products.

Of New Brunswick's total land area, 90.8% was inventoried forestland in 1981, and in 1984 lumber shipments were valued at C $99.2m. The province's fishing catch totalled 100,012 metric tons in 1984, with a landed value of C $75.6m.

Since the 1950s mining has been of major importance to the New Brunswick economy. In 1986 non-fuel mineral production was valued at C $499.3m. The province's most important mineral resources are coal, zinc, silver, lead, coppper, antimony and bismuth. Sand and gravel, gold and potash are also mined.

Manufacturing activity is based mainly around forestry and agriculture. Paper and allied products, food products, beverages, wood products and non-metallic mineral products were the leading sectors in 1984. Manufacturing shipments were valued at C $4,243.0m. in 1985, of which 29.3% was added in manufacture, the lowest proportion among the provinces.

Gross general expenditure by the provincial government totalled C $2,738m. in 1984/85; gross general revenue totalled C $2,502m., of which C $1,061m. was provided from federal sources.

Newfoundland

Newfoundland's economy is largely based on fishing, mining, minerals processing, and manufacturing linked to fish and forest resources. In addition, government, services, trade, commerce, communications and transportation are important employers. It is hoped that the development of offshore oil and natural gas will bring greater prosperity to the region.

In 1986 the province's per-head disposable income was about C $9,500, the lowest in Canada. The civilian labour force was estimated at 222,000 persons in December 1986, and the unemployment rate in the same year was 20.0%—by far the highest in the country. In 1982, 42.5% of those employed were trade-union members, the highest percentage among the Canadian provinces.

Farmland covered less than 0.1% of Newfoundland's total land area in 1986, an average farm covering 56.2 hectares. The net income of farm operators from farming was C $9.9m., the lowest of the Canadian provinces. Agricultural commodities produced by the province include eggs, poultry, dairy products and tame hay.

Inventoried forestland covered 38.2% of Newfoundland's total land area in 1981. Fishing is of major importance to the province's economy: in 1984 its 450,584 metric-ton catch (the largest in the country in terms of weight) had a landed value of C $162.2m. and was the third most valuable in Canada.

Newfoundland's non-fuel mineral production was valued at $764.2m. in 1986. Minerals of significance to the provincial economy are iron ore, gypsum, stone, clay, zinc, and sand and gravel.

The principal manufacturing industries in Newfoundland are fish-processing and the manufacture of newsprint and non-metallic mineral products. The total value of manufacturing shipments for Newfoundland in 1985 was $1,223.8m., of which 43.8% was added during manufacture—the highest percentage among the provinces and territories.

Gross general expenditure by the provincial government totalled C $2,265m. in 1984/85; gross general revenue totalled C $2,075m., of which C $981m. was provided from federal sources.

Northwest Territories

In 1986 per-head disposable income in the Northwest Territories measured about C $12,400. Economic activity centres around the region's natural resources. Fur-trapping, once the main economic activity, is now of minor significance. Agriculture is of little value, it being cheaper to import products from the south. Inventoried forestland covered 18.7% of the total land area in 1981 and in the same year the Mackenzie Valley produced approximately 59,510 cubic metres of timber. Some commercial fishing takes place, mainly on Great Slave Lake. Hunting and fishing are still important on a local level, especially for those living in small, relatively isolated communities. Art and crafts produced by native people are exported internationally and are an increasing source of income.

The most significant economic activity is mining. In 1986 non-fuel mineral production had a value of C $656.2m. The Northwest Territories ranked fourth in Canada in production of crude oil in 1988, and fifth for natural gas. The region ranked second for its production of both zinc and lead in 1988, and fourth in its gold production. Other minerals produced include silver, copper, sand and gravel, and stone.

Gross general expenditure by the territorial government totalled C $593m. in 1984/85; gross general revenue totalled C $606m., of which C $437m. was provided from federal sources.

Nova Scotia

Service industries are Nova Scotia's largest employer. Other important sectors are tourism, agriculture, forestry, fishing, mining and manufacturing industry. Halifax is a major port but trade has suffered as a result of the introduction of protective tariffs.

In 1986 the province's per-head disposable income was about C $11,000. The labour force comprised an estimated 400,000 people in December 1986, while the unemployment rate for that year was 13.4%. In 1982, 26.5% of those in employment were reported to be members of trade unions.

Farmland accounted for 7.9% of Nova Scotia's total land area in 1986, the average farm measuring 97.2 hectares. In the same year

the net income of farm operators from farming operations totalled C $79.8m. The main agricultural sectors are dairying, egg and poultry production, and beef and hog production. Vegetables, fruit and greenhouse products are also of importance. Nova Scotia's trapping industry produced a total of 345,700 pelts in 1986/87. Inventoried forestland covered 77.6% of the province's land area in 1981 and lumbering makes a significant contribution to the provincial economy. The value of lumber shipments in 1984 was almost C $40m. In 1984 Nova Scotia's fishing catch of 394,504 metric tons had a landed value of C $265.3m., the highest of any provincial catch.

Nova Scotia's non-fuel mineral production was valued at C $180.2m. in 1986. The province's most important mineral resource is bituminous coal, and Nova Scotia ranked fourth overall in Canadian coal production in 1988. Other minerals of importance are copper, gold, silver, zinc, gypsum, salt, and sand and gravel, stone, cement and clay.

Manufacturing industry in Nova Scotia is largely based on the province's agriculture and forestry, though there have been attempts to encourage the establishment of more diversified industries. In 1985 Nova Scotia's manufacturing shipments were valued at C $4,634.8m., of which 32.1% was added during manufacture.

Gross general expenditure by the provincial government totalled C $3,328m. in 1984/85; gross general revenue totalled C $2,810m., of which C $1,172m. was provided from federal sources.

Ontario

Service industries, manufacturing, trade, transportation, communications and other utilities, finance, insurance and real estate, and public administration were estimated as being Ontario's leading employment groups in May 1989.

Ontario's per-head disposable income, at about C $14,800 in 1986, is the highest among the provinces and territories. The labour force numbered 4,943,000 in 1986, and the unemployment rate was 7.0%, the lowest in the country. In 1982 about 27.7% of the province's employed work-force belonged to a trade union.

Of Ontario's total land area, 6.2% was farmland in 1986, and the average size of farms was 77.7 hectares. At C $1,421.6m., Ontario's net income of farmers from farming operations was the highest in Canada. Agriculture is diverse in the province. There are more livestock farms than anywhere else in the country, and in dairying it is second only to Québec. Other commodities of major importance are poultry and eggs, forage crops, grain corn, soybeans, mixed grains, wheat, barley and vegetables. Ontario is a major producer of soft fruit and apples.

In 1986/87 the province produced 1,555,869 fur pelts, making it the leader in this sector. Inventoried forestland accounted for 47.1% of Ontario's total land area in 1981, and in 1984 the value of its lumber shipments was C $432.5m., ranking third behind British Columbia and Québec. Fishing makes a relatively minor contribution to the economy, the landed value of the catch in 1984 being C $35.1m.

Mining is still of major importance to the provincial economy, and in 1986 Ontario's non-fuel mineral production, at C $4,716m., was the most valuable of the provinces and territories. Fuel resources comprise oil and natural gas, but non-fuel minerals are the chief source of income. In 1988 Ontario was Canada's leading producer of gold, nickel, zinc, cement, salt, sand and gravel, stone and clay. Silver, copper, iron ore, lead, uranium and gypsum are among other minerals produced.

Ontario is also Canada's foremost manufacturing province and accounts for over half of all manufacturing by value. In terms of the value of shipments in 1984 the province's leading sectors were transportation equipment, food products, chemicals and chemical products, refined petroleum and coal products, and electrical and electronic products. The total value of Ontario's manufacturing shipments in 1985 was C $131,988.2m., of which 38.9% was added in manufacture.

Toronto is Canada's leading financial centre. All the main chartered banks and Canada's largest stock exchanges are based in the city.

Gross general expenditure by the provincial government totalled C $28,239m. in 1984/85; gross general revenue totalled C $26,667m., of which C $4,464m. was provided from federal sources.

Prince Edward Island

Prince Edward Island's economy has greatly strengthened over recent decades, though it remains heavily reliant upon federal-government assistance. The island's dependence on agriculture, its lack of mineral resources and the cost of transportation makes it one of the poorest provinces.

In 1986 the per-head disposable income of the inhabitants of Prince Edward Island was about C $10,000, the second-lowest (above Newfoundland) among the provinces and territories. The civilian labour force numbered about 59,000 persons in December 1986, and the unemployment rate for that year was 13.4%. In 1982, 21% of workers were members of trade unions—the lowest rate among the provinces.

Farmland occupied 48.1% of Prince Edward Island's total land area in 1986–the highest proportion of any province, and the average size of a farm was 96.2 hectares. The net income of farm operators from farming operations in 1986 was C $50.6m., the second lowest of any province except Newfoundland. Prince Edward Island is Canada's foremost producer of potatoes. Other crops grown include tame hay, wheat, oats and barley. Dairying, cattle and pigs, as well as fruit and vegetables are significant to the island's farming industry.

In 1981 53.0% of Prince Edward Island was covered by inventoried forestland, though much of it was not commercially valuable. Fishing is a major employer. In 1984 the fish catch totalled 38,521 metric tons, with a landed value of C $38.3m.

Non-fuel mineral production was valued at just C $1.7m. in 1986, the lowest total among the provinces and territories. Sand and gravel are the only minerals of significance to the provincial economy.

Prince Edward Island's manufacturing industry relies upon its farm and fishing products. Various government assistance schemes attempt to attract more diverse industries to the island. Manufacturing shipments were valued at C $296.8m. in 1985, of which 31.7% was added during manufacture.

Gross general expenditure by the provincial government totalled C $462m. in 1984/85; gross general revenue totalled C $458m., of which C $213m. was provided from federal sources.

Québec

Québec's economic activities are comparatively diverse. The main sectors, in terms of the numbers of people employed, are services, manufacturing, and wholesale and retail trade.

In 1986 per-head disposable income in Québec totalled about C $12,400. The labour force numbered about 3,235,000 persons, and the unemployment rate was 11%. Of those employed in 1982, 34% were trade-union members.

Farmland accounted for 2.7% of Québec's total land area in 1986 and an average farm was 87.8 hectares. The net income of farmers from farming in that year was C $1,066.4m., second only to Ontario. Québec is Canada's largest producer of dairy products, and in 1988 2,984,000 kilolitres of milk and cream were sold from the province's farms. Other commodities of importance are cattle, poultry, eggs, pigs, fodder corn, tame hay, leaf tobacco, and fruit and vegetables, particularly potatoes. Québec is the country's leading maple-syrup producer.

In 1986/87 the province was the second-largest fur producer in Canada, with a total production of 687,739 pelts. Of the total land area of Québec, 46.0% was forestland in 1981. In terms of the value of its shipments (C $827.8m. in 1984), its lumber industry is second only to that of British Columbia. Fishing makes a moderate contribution to Québec's economy. The province's fish catch totalled 84,240 metric tons in 1984, with a landed value of C $57.7m.

In 1986 the value of Québec's non-fuel mineral production was second only to that of Ontario, at C $2,275.8m. Québec ranked second for production of gold in 1988; other minerals of importance are iron ore, copper, silver, zinc, asbestos (of which it is by far the leading Canadian producer), cement, salt, sand and gravel, and clay.

In 1984 Québec's leading manufacturing industries were food, paper and allied products, primary metal industries, chemicals and chemical products, and clothing. Manufacturing shipments were valued at C $60,459.6m. in 1986 (second only to Ontario), of which 40.8% was added during manufacture, the third-highest rate in Canada.

Gross general expenditure by the provincial government totalled C $28,632m. in 1984/85; gross general revenue totalled C $27,567m., of which C $6,295m. was provided from federal sources.

Saskatchewan

In May 1989 the largest share of non-agricultural employment in Saskatchewan was taken by service industries, followed by trade, transport, communications and other utilities, and public administration.

Per-head income in the province was about C $13,000 in 1986. In December of the same year the work-force totalled some 495,000 persons, and the annual unemployment rate was 7.7%. In 1982, 22.6% of those employed were reported to be members of trade unions.

Almost half of Saskatchewan's land area (46.7%) was farmland in 1986, and the average size of a farm was 419.3 hectares, the largest in Canada. The net income of farm operators from farming in that year was C $738.8m., the third largest among the provinces and territories. The province is Canada's leading producer of wheat and in 1988 produced 1,656 metric tons. Other major crops are rapeseed, mustard seed and flaxseed. Pigs, beef cattle, poultry, eggs, dairy produce, tame hay and vegetables also contribute to farm income.

Forestland covered 21.6% of Saskatchewan's land area in 1981, and in 1984 lumber shipments were valued at C $41.6m., representing a relatively minor contribution to the province's economy. Fish landings were valued at C $4m. in 1984.

Non-fuel mineral production in 1986 amounted to C $1,068.3m., the fifth most valuable in Canada. Saskatchewan is a major oil-producing province, second only to Alberta. Natural gas is also produced. The province's principal non-fuel minerals are potash, and uranium (in which it leads the other provinces). Other minerals include copper, zinc, gold, silver, salt, and sand and gravel.

Saskatchewan is not a major centre for manufacturing industry. Food industries, based on the province's agricultural output, dominate the manufacturing sector. Manufacturing shipments were valued at C $2,982.9m. in 1985, of which 34.1% was added during manufacture.

Gross general expenditure by the provincial government totalled C $4,262m. in 1984/85; gross general revenue totalled C $3,732m., of which C $720m. was provided from federal sources.

Yukon Territory

In May 1989 the main sources of employment in the Yukon Territory were service industries, public administration, trade, and transportation, communications and other utilities. In 1986 the territory's disposable per-head income was about C $14,000, the second highest (on a par with Alberta) after Ontario.

Farming is practised only on a small scale and farm products are mainly sold to local markets. Improved transportation has meant that farmers have had difficulty competing with cheaper imported goods. However, it is thought that there is considerable potential for further agricultural development.

Although inventoried forestland covered 50.0% of the territory's total land area in 1981, it is largely unsuitable for commercial timber production. Furs, though still produced, are no longer of great importance to the economy, and fishing is mainly for consumption within the territory itself.

Mineral production in 1986 was valued at C $183.5m. Gold and silver are probably the most valuable mineral commodities. Other minerals produced include copper, lead, zinc, and sand and gravel. Along with mining, tourism provides the Yukon with its most significant source of income.

Gross general expenditure by the territorial government totalled C $194m. in 1984/85; gross general revenue totalled C $207m., of which C $149m. was provided from federal sources.

AGRICULTURE, FORESTRY, FISHING AND TRAPPING

Farmland Use
(Census results. Source: Statistics Canada.)

Summary (hectares)

	1981	1986
Improved land	46,121,593	46,009,990
Under crops	30,965,813	33,181,234
Improved pasture	4,404,727	3,559,215
Summer fallow	9,701,906	8,499,015
Other	1,049,147	770,526
Unimproved land	21,859,087	21,815,765
Total area of farms	67,980,680	67,825,756
Total land area	922,097,313	922,097,313

Provinces and Territories (1986 census, '000 ha)

	Improved land		Unimproved land	Total farm area	Total land area
	Total	Under crops			
Alberta	12,906	9,163	7,749	20,655	63,823
British Columbia	900	571	1,511	2,411	89,307
Manitoba	5,403	4,519	2,337	7,740	54,770
New Brunswick	169	129	240	409	7,157
Newfoundland	11	5	26	37	37,164
Nova Scotia	158	110	259	417	5,284
Ontario	4,096	3,458	1,551	5,647	91,743
Prince Edward Island	186	156	86	272	566
Québec	2,137	1,744	1,501	3,639	135,781
Saskatchewan	20,044	13,326	6,555	26,599	57,011
Total (includes NWT and Yukon)	46,010	33,181	21,816	67,826	922,097

Production of Principal Crops
(Source: Statistics Canada.)

Summary

		1986	1987	1988
Wheat	('000 metric tons)	31,850	26,342	15,654.9
Oats for grain	('000 metric tons)	3,906	2,995	2,993.4
Barley for grain	('000 metric tons)	15,026	14,382	10,125.1
Rye	('000 metric tons)	670	493	257.0
Mixed grains	('000 metric tons)	1,307	1,087	863.3
Flaxseed	('000 metric tons)	1,067	788	413.9
Rapeseed (canola)	('000 metric tons)	3,887	3,852	4,243.0
Corn for grain	('000 metric tons)	6,694	7,014	5,369.2
Peas, dry	('000 metric tons)	224	442	356.5
Soybeans	('000 metric tons)	988	1,267	1,152.6
Lentils	('000 metric tons)	182	313	63.5
Mustard seed	('000 metric tons)	234	132	122.9
Tame hay	('000 metric tons)	30,663	30,840	29,026.0
Fodder corn	('000 metric tons)	9,525	8,691	6,939.0
Sugar beets	('000 metric tons)	945	959	726.0
Potatoes	('000 metric tons)	2,850	3,033	2,874.3
Apples	('000 metric tons)	n.a.	490	n.a.
Maple syrup	('000 gallons)	2,147	1,854	3,103

Provinces (1988, unless otherwise stated)

	Wheat ('000 metric tons)	Oats for grain ('000 metric tons)	Barley for grain ('000 metric tons)	Rye ('000 metric tons)	Mixed grains ('000 metric tons)	Flaxseed ('000 metric tons)
Alberta	5,285.0	1,650.0	5,813.0	70.8	204.0	27.9
British Columbia	117.0	79.0	128.0	8.9	4.5	—
Manitoba	2,400.9	224.0	1,045.0	48.0	43.0	198.0
New Brunswick	13.9	26.2	35.5	—	—	—
Nova Scotia	11.4	14.5	14.6	—	—	—
Ontario	1,045.4	216.0	501.0	40.6	435.0	—
Prince Edward Island	19.8	21.7	81.0	—	61.0	—
Québec	175.5	284.0	460.0	—	75.0	—
Saskatchewan	6,586.0	478.0	2,047.0	88.7	40.8	188.0
Total	15,654.9	2,993.4	10,125.1	257.0	863.3	413.9

(continued)

PRODUCTION OF PRINCIPAL CROPS—Provinces—*continued*

	Rapeseed ('000 metric tons)	Corn for grain ('000 metric tons)	Peas, dry ('000 metric tons)	Soybeans ('000 metric tons)	Lentils ('000 metric tons)	Mustard seed ('000 metric tons)
Alberta	1,882.0	25.4	119.7	—	1.8	24.0
British Columbia . . .	59.0	—	—	—	—	—
Manitoba	612.0	104.0	78.9	—	7.3	8.2
Nova Scotia	—	5.8	—	—	—	—
Ontario	34.0	3,734.0	—	1,124.0	—	—
Québec	—	1,500.0	—	28.6	—	—
Saskatchewan	1,656.0	—	157.9	—	54.4	90.7
Total	**4,243.0**	**5,369.2**	**356.5**	**1,152.6**	**63.5**	**122.9**

PRODUCTION OF PRINCIPAL CROPS—Provinces—*continued*

	Tame hay ('000 metric tons)	Fodder corn ('000 metric tons)	Sugar beets ('000 metric tons)	Potatoes ('000 metric tons)*	Apples ('000 metric tons)*	Maple syrup ('000 gallons)
Alberta	9,072	218	499	300	n.a.	—
British Columbia . . .	2,540	499	—	110	198	—
Manitoba . . .	1,724	145	227	426	n.a.	—
New Brunswick . . .	381	—	—	662	7	29
Newfoundland	22	—	—	3	n.a.	—
Nova Scotia	463	55	—	—	53	18
Ontario	6,622	4,082	—	323	155	154
Prince Edward Island . .	318	—	—	725	n.a.	—
Québec	6,160	1,940	—	410	76	2,902
Saskatchewan	1,724	—	—	34	n.a.	—
Total	**29,026**	**6,939**	**726**	**3,033**	**490**	**3,103**

* 1987 figures.

Livestock and Poultry on Farms

('000 head at 1 January. Source: Statistics Canada.)

Summary

	1987	1988	1989
Cattle	10,802	10,863	11,004
Pigs	9,996	10,748	10,779
Sheep and lambs	481	475	481

Provinces (1989)

	Cattle Cows and heifers	Cattle Steers and bulls	Cattle Calves	Cattle All cattle	Pigs	Sheep and lambs
Alberta	1,877.0	378.0	1,445.0	3,700.0	1,655.0	134.0
British Columbia	370.5	36.5	206.0	613.0	234.8	35.0
Manitoba	564.5	85.5	275.0	925.0	1,230.0	14.5
New Brunswick	62.7	9.4	23.9	96.0	98.0	6.2
Newfoundland	6.2	0.4	1.5	8.1	16.5	4.9
Nova Scotia	81.0	8.8	30.2	120.0	146.0	24.0
Ontario	1,309.0	319.0	605.0	2,233.0	3,355.0	148.0
Prince Edward Island . . .	49.9	20.1	25.0	95.0	124.0	4.2
Québec	1,039.0	81.0	280.0	1,400.0	3,050.0	76.0
Saskatchewan	1,068.0	136.0	610.0	1,814.0	870.0	34.0
Total	**6,427.8**	**1,074.7**	**.3,501.6**	**11,004.1**	**10,779.3**	**480.8**

Livestock Products

(Source (unless otherwise indicated): Statistics Canada.)

Summary

		1986	1987	1988
Beef:				
Slaughterings	('000 head)	3,118	2,879	2,774
Production[1]	(million lb)	2,184	2,056	2,047
Pork:				
Slaughterings	('000 head)	13,515	13,883	14,480
Production[2]	(million lb)	2,419	2,493	2,620
Lamb and mutton:				
Slaughterings[3]	('000 head)	174	160	168
Production[1]	(million lb)	18	17	17

(*continued*)

LIVESTOCK PRODUCTS—Summary—*continued*

		1986	1987	1988
Veal:				
Slaughterings	('000 head)	448	403	383
Production[1]	(million lb)	100	99	99
Stewing hens	('000 metric tons)	36	37	37
Chickens	('000 metric tons)	488	531	537
Turkeys[4]	('000 metric tons)	105	115	119
Eggs	(million)	5,667	5,706	5,721
Milk[5]	('000 kilolitres)	7,305	7,365	7,601
Creamery butter	('000 metric tons)	99	96	104
Cheddar cheese	('000 metric tons)	112	116	118
Ice-cream mix	('000 kilolitres)	166	164	167

[1] Total cold dressed weight, excludes edible offal.
[2] Total cold trimmed weight, excludes fats and edible offal.
[3] Source: Agriculture Canada, *Livestock Market Review.*
[4] Excludes Newfoundland.
[5] Farm sales of milk and cream.

Livestock Slaughterings by Province
(1988, '000 head slaughtered in federally-inspected establishments)

	Cattle	Pigs	Lambs and sheep[1]	Calves
Alberta	1,210.0	1,509.5	75.5	6.2
British Columbia	80.4	554.2	3.2	11.2
Manitoba	171.3	1,725.0	—	1.3
Ontario	730.3	3,777.9	29.6	94.4
Québec	244.6	5,345.4	58.0	268.3
Saskatchewan	272.2	982.3	—	0.7
Atlantic Provinces[2]	64.9	586.1	2.0	1.1
Total	2,773.6	14,480.5	168.3	383.2

[1] Source: Agriculture Canada, *Livestock Market Review.*
[2] New Brunswick, Newfoundland, Nova Scotia and Prince Edward Island.

Other Livestock and Poultry Production by Province (1988)

	Stewing hens (million)	Chickens (million)	Turkeys (million)	Eggs (million)	Milk ('000 kilolitres)	Shorn wool ('000 lb)
Alberta	2.4	33.9	1.6	488	593	734
British Columbia	3.5	42.1	1.9	708	501	161
Manitoba	2.6	16.8	1.3	661	311	79
New Brunswick	0.5	10.4	0.5	124	138	27
Newfoundland	0.2	5.4	n.a.	101	n.a.	14
Nova Scotia	0.9	14.5	0.7	228	180	109
Ontario	9.1	139.7	7.4	2,167	2,541	693
Prince Edward Island	0	0.9	—	35	101	16
Québec	4.6	113.8	4.7	982	2,984	355
Saskatchewan	0.8	11.0	0.7	227	234	210
Total	24.6	388.4	18.8	5,721	7,601	2,398

Forestry
(Source: Statistics Canada.)

Inventoried Forest Land* by Province or Territory (1981, '000 sq km)

	Productive forest land†				Other inventoried forest land	Total
	Crown provincial	Crown federal	Private and others	Total		
Alberta	199	17	—	216	115	331
British Columbia	437	5	16	458	108	566
Manitoba	132	3	4	140	100	240
New Brunswick	29	2	31	62	3	65
Newfoundland	79	1	4	85	57	142
Northwest Territories	—	143	—	143	472	615
Nova Scotia	6	—	22	29	12	41
Ontario	331	6	39	377	55	432
Prince Edward Island	—	—	3	3	—	3
Québec	469	2	63	533	91	624
Saskatchewan	84	5	—	89	34	123
Yukon Territory	—	67	—	67	175	242
Total	1,767	252	183	2,202	1,223	3,425

* Land primarily intended for, or currently supporting, forest.
† Productive forest land available for growing and harvesting forest crops. Excludes reserved forest land by law not available, as in national parks.

Roundwood Removals—Summary
('000 cu m of merchantable timber)

	1984	1985	1986
Logs and bolts[1]	117,254	119,336	125,384
Pulpwood.	42,051	40,601	42,655
Other roundwood.	1,562	2,048	2,224
Fuelwood	6,635	6,669	6,834
Total	167,502	168,654	177,097

[1] Includes some pulpwood.

Roundwood Removals—Provinces and Territories (1986, '000 cu m of merchantable timber)

	Logs and bolts[1]	Pulpwood	Other roundwood	Fuelwood	Total
Alberta	8,556	1,698	44	89	10,387
British Columbia[2]	77,240	—	263	n.a.	77,503
Manitoba	604	927	59	113	1,703
New Brunswick	2,542	5,745	93	340	8,720
Newfoundland	228	1,732	6	442	2,408
Nova Scotia	1,062	2,471	—	326	3,859
Ontario	13,009	14,841	9	2,327	30,186
Prince Edward Island	114	46	—	316	476
Québec	20,531	14,002	993	2,601	38,127
Saskatchewan	1,433	1,193	713	190	3,529
Northwest Territories and Yukon Territory	65	—	44	90	199
Total	125,384	42,655	2,224	6,834	177,097

[1] Includes some pulpwood.
[2] Figures for fuelwood are included in 'Other roundwood'.

Lumber Production—Summary ('000 cu m)

	1984	1985	1986
Softwoods	47,708	51,099	51,860
Hardwoods	1,281	1,010	1,199
Total	48,989	52,109	53,059

Lumber Production—Provinces (1986, '000 cu m)

	Softwoods	Hardwoods	Total
Alberta	2,943.7	—	2,943.7
British Columbia	30,990.3	6.2	30,996.5
Manitoba	215.3	8.2	223.5
New Brunswick	1,427.5	49.5	1,477.0
Newfoundland	37.2	14.9	52.1
Nova Scotia	436.0	30.1	466.1
Ontario	4,582.5	538.7	5,121.3
Prince Edward Island . .	13.7	—	13.7
Québec	10,757.3	551.5	11,308.8
Saskatchewan	456.7	—	456.7
Total	51,860.2	1,199.1	53,059.4

Fishing

(Source: Statistics Canada.)

Landings—Summary (metric tons, live weight)

	1984	1985	1986*	1987*
Atlantic total	1,071,521	1,188,496	1,245,280	1,265,913
Cod	475,942	480,465	474,720	458,051
Crab	43,572	44,246	42,830	28,798
Small flatfishes	80,116	99,113	89,300	90,629
Haddock	32,654	37,095	44,720	28,071
Halibut	3,142	3,926	3,700	2,417
Pollock	35,216	44,832	49,680	50,223
Redfish	67,302	71,388	79,670	79,016
Herring	132,592	193,401	186,730	248,744
Salmon	858	957	1,320	1,541
Lobsters	28,694	32,639	38,030	39,431
Scallops	36,479	47,208	57,000	73,813
Tuna	254	129	90	222
Pacific total	169,168	209,634	220,260	262,690
Halibut	5,364	4,703	5,389	5,000
Herring	33,703	25,955	16,341	37,360
Salmon	50,431	104,014	100,241	66,060
Canada total†	1,284,119	1,442,130	1,508,740	1,571,603

* Preliminary.   † All sea fish.

Landings—Provinces and Territories
(1984, marine and inland fish and other marine products)

	Quantity (metric tons)[1]	Landed value (C $'000)
Alberta[2]	1,420	1,248
British Columbia[2]	169,168	242,935
Manitoba[2]	13,040	18,106
New Brunswick	100,012	75,567
Newfoundland	450,584	162,244
Nova Scotia	394,504	265,280
Ontario	22,667	35,105
Prince Edward Island	38,521	38,301
Québec	84,240	57,711
Saskatchewan[2]	3,508	3,998
Northwest Territories and Yukon Territory . . .	1,163	1,459
Total	**1,278,827**	**901,954**

[1] Nominal catches refer to the live weight equivalent of landings.
[2] Landed value includes final payments to fishermen.

Trapping
(Source: Statistics Canada.)

Pelt Production—Summary

	1985/86		1986/87	
	Number	Value (C $)	Number	Value (C $)
Wildlife .	2,682,547	50,548,688	3,199,970	75,265,071
Ranch-raised .	1,482,646	49,465,211	1,461,701	74,864,268
Total . .	**4,165,193**	**100,013,899**	**4,661,671**	**150,129,339**

Pelt Production—Provinces and Territories
(1986/87, '000; excludes seals)

	Wildlife	Ranch-raised	Total
Alberta	503.3	41.0	544.4
British Columbia	108.3	222.7	330.9
Manitoba	353.8	56.0	409.8
New Brunswick . . .	51.4	34.4	85.9
Newfoundland[1] . . .	31.9	10.1	42.0
Northwest Territories . .	178.0	—	178.0
Nova Scotia[1]	61.8	283.9	345.7
Ontario	921.1	634.8	1,555.9
Prince Edward Island . .	10.1	32.6	42.7
Québec	544.0	143.8	687.7
Saskatchewan . . .	410.0	2.3	412.3
Yukon Territory . . .	26.3	—	26.3
Total	**3,200.0**	**1,461.7**	**4,661.7**

[1] Lynx are excluded for Nova Scotia but included in Newfoundland total.

Selected Agricultural, Forestry, Fisheries and Fur-Trade Organizations

Agricultural Institute of Canada: 151 Slater St, Suite 907, Ottawa, ON K1P 5H4; tel. (613) 232-9459; fax (613) 594-5190; f. 1920; Pres. JIM WEBSTER.

Alberta Association of Agricultural Societies: 7000 113th St, Edmonton, AB T6H 5T6; tel. (403) 427-2174; 210 mems; Sec. EVELYN M. COCKLE.

Alberta Canada All Breeds' Association (1984): 2504 Toronto Cres., NW, Calgary, AB T2N 3V9; tel. (403) 282-8181; 23 mem. asscns, 4 associate mems; Sec. NORMA B. DUNN.

Alberta Canola Growers' Association: 14315 118th Ave, Suite 170, Edmonton, AB T5L 4S6; tel. (403) 454-0844; 1,500 mems; Pres. HENRY VOS; Sec. NELLIE WASCHUK.

Alberta Wheat Pool: 505 2nd St, SW, POB 2700, Calgary, AB T2P 2P5; tel. (403) 290-4910; telex 038-21643; 60,501 mems; Pres. D. E. LIVINGSTONE; CEO J. W. MADILL.

British Columbia Federation of Agriculture: 846 Broughton St, Victoria, BC V8W 1E4; tel. (604) 383-7171; fax (604) 383-5031; 8,600 individual mems, 72 mem. orgs; Man. JACK WESSEL.

British Columbia Fruit-Growers' Association: 1473 Water St, POB 160, Kelowna, BV V1Y 7N6; tel. (604) 762-5226; Sec. KATHY M. BROWN.

Canada Grains Council: 360 Main St, Suite 760, Winnipeg, MB R3C 3Z3; tel. (204) 942-2254; f. 1969; Pres. Dr DONALD A. DEVER.

Canadian Agricultural Economics and Farm Management Society: 151 Slater St, Suite 907, Ottawa, ON K1P 5H4; tel. (613) 232-9459; fax (613) 594-5190; 488 mems; Sec. BRIAN GOULD.

Canadian Cattle-Breeders' Association: 211 12th Ave, Suite 2, Sherbrooke, PQ J1G 2V5; tel. (819) 567-1258; 115 mems; Sec. JEAN-GUY BERNIER.

Canadian Egg-Producers' Council: 75 Albert St, Ottawa, ON K1P 5E7; tel. (613) 236-3633; fax (613) 236-5749; Sec. PETER MARTEN.

Canadian Federation of Agriculture: 75 Albert St, Suite 1101, Ottawa, ON K1P 5E7; tel. (613) 236-3633; fax (613) 236-5749; Pres. DON KNOERR; Exec. Sec. PETER MARTEN.

Canadian Feed Industry Association: 325 Dalhousie St, Suite 625, Ottawa, ON K1N 7G2; tel. (613) 238-6421; fax (613) 238-6620; 300 mem. orgs; Chair. ROSS ARMSTRONG; Exec. Dir R. E. MARTIN.

Canadian Forestry Association: 185 Somerset St West, Suite 203, Ottawa, ON K2P 0J2; tel. (613) 232-1815; fax (613) 232-4210; 12,000 mems; Pres. W. K. FULLERTON; Exec. Dir A. D. HALL.

Canadian Fruit Wholesalers' Association: 1101 Prince of Wales Dr., Suite 310, Ottawa, ON K2C 3W7; tel. (613) 226-4187; telex 053-36070; fax (613) 226-2984; 560 mems; Exec. Vice-Pres. D. DEMPSTER.

Canadian Honey Council: POB 1566, Nipawin, SK S0E 1E0; tel. (306) 862-3011; Sec. and Treas. LINDA GANE.

Canadian Horticultural Council: 1101 Prince of Wales Dr., Suite 310, Ottawa, ON K2C 3W7; tel. (613) 226-4187; telex 053-36070; fax (613) 226-2984; 116 mem. orgs.

Canadian Institute of Forestry: 151 Slater St, Suite 1005, Ottawa, ON K1P 5H3; tel. (613) 234-2242; 2,600 individual mems, 10 mem. orgs; Exec. Dir J. H. CAYFORD.

Canadian Meat Council: 5233 Dundas St West, Islington, ON M9B 1A6; tel. (416) 239-8411; fax (416) 239-2416; 52 mem. cos, 32 associate cos; Gen. Man. D. M. ADAMS.

Canadian Nursery Trades Association: 1293 Matheson Blvd, Mississauga, ON L4W 1R1; tel. (416) 629-1367; fax (416) 629-4438; Exec. Dir BOB CHEESMAN.

Canadian Organic Growers: Rural Route 3, King City, ON L0G 1K0; tel. (416) 727-8953; 1,500 mems; Pres. ALEX CARON.

Canadian Poultry and Egg-Processors' Council: 1 Eva Rd, Suite 300, Etobicoke, ON M9C 4Z5; tel. (416) 622-8621; 89 mem. orgs, 27 associate mems; Exec. Vice-Pres. D. G. MCKENZIE.

Canadian Seed Growers' Association: POB 8455, Ottawa, ON K1G 3T1; tel. (613) 236-0947; f. 1904; 5,000 mems; Exec. Dir W. K. ROBERTSON.

Canadian Sheep-Breeders' Association: POB 260, Borden, SK S0K 0N0; tel. (306) 997-4881; Sec. REITA A. WIDGILL.

Canadian Society of Agronomy: Crop Development Centre, University of Saskatchewan, Saskatoon, SK S7N 0W0; 300 mems; Sec. Dr B. G. ROSSNAGEL.

Canadian Swine-Breeders' Association: Rural Route 3, Embro, ON N0J 1J0; tel. (519) 475-4806; 530 mems; Sec. Man. KAREN SAMPLE.

Canadian Wood Council: 55 Metcalfe St, Suite 1550, Ottawa, ON K1P 6L5; tel. (613) 235-7221; telex 053-3138; fax (613) 235-9911; 15 mem. orgs; Man. Dir and CEO J. F. SHAW.

Canola Council of Canada: 433 Main St, Suite 301, Winnipeg, MB R3B 1B3; tel. (204) 944-9494; telex 07-57672; Pres. Dr ALLAN EARL.

Conseil de l'Alimentation du Québec: 1600 blvd Henri-Bourassa ouest, Suite 500, Montréal, PQ H3M 3E2; tel. (514) 331-9082; Pres. ANDRÉ MARTEL.

Conseil de l'Industrie Laitière du Québec Inc: 50 blvd Crémazie ouest, Suite 304, Montréal, PQ H2P 2S9; tel. (514) 381-5331; Exec. Pres. CLAUDE LAMBERT.

Dairy Bureau of Canada: 20 Holly St, Suite 400, Toronto, ON M4S 3B1; tel. (416) 485-4453; fax (416) 485-1874; Pres. and CEO C. CHEVALIER.

Dairy Farmers of Canada: 75 Albert St, Suite 1101, Ottawa, ON K1P 5E7; tel. (613) 236-9997; telex 053-4304; fax (613) 236-5749; f. 1934; 19 mem. asscns; Exec. Sec. and Treas. RICHARD DOYLE.

Dairy Producers' Co-operative Ltd: POB 560, Regina, SK S4P 3A5; tel. (306) 924-1300; telex 071-2255; fax (306) 924-1342; 6,000 mems; Man. G. H. PEDERSEN.

Fisheries Association of Newfoundland and Labrador: POB 8900, St John's, NF A1B 3R9; tel. (709) 726-7223; telex 016-4785; fax (709) 739-0195; Pres. B. W. CHAPMAN.

Fisheries Council of Canada: 77 Metcalfe St, Suite 505, Ottawa, ON K1P 5L6; tel. (613) 238-7751; fax (613) 238-3542; 6 mem. asscns, 183 mem. cos, 1 distributor mem., 97 associate mems; Pres. R. W. BULMER.

Flax Council of Canada: 433 Main St, Suite 305, Winnipeg, MB R3B 1B3; Exec. Dir STANLEY C. BAKER.

Fur Council of Canada: 1435 rue St-Alexander, Suite 1270, Montréal, PQ H3A 2G4; tel. (514) 844-1945; fax (514) 844-8593; Exec. Dir DEL HAYLOCK.

Fur Institute of Canada: 10 Lower Spadina Ave, Suite 302, Toronto, ON M5V 2Z1; tel. (416) 597-3877; telex 06-218369; fax (416) 597-3919; Exec. Dir KIRK SMITH.

Fur Trade Association of Canada (Ontario) Inc: 185 Spadina Ave, Toronto, ON M5T 2C6; tel. (416) 593-0324; fax (416) 593-1546; 70 mems; Marketing Dir RACHEL KUIPERS.

National Dairy Council of Canada: 141 Laurier Ave West, Suite 704, Ottawa, ON K1P 5J3; tel. (613) 238-4116; telex 053-3952; fax (613) 238-6247; 140 mem. orgs; Pres. K. L. MATTE.

National Farmers' Foundation: 112 Kent St, POB 2500, Charlottetown, PE C1A 8C2.

National Farmers' Union: 250c 2nd Ave South, Saskatoon, SK S7K 2M1; tel. (306) 652-9465; fax (306) 664-6226; f. 1969; Exec. Sec. STUART THIESSON.

New Brunswick Federation of Agriculture: 1115 Regent St, Fredericton, NB E3B 3Z2; tel. (506) 452-8101; fax (506) 452-1085; Gen. Man. JOSEPH H. RIDEOUT.

New Brunswick Fruit-Growers' Association: 1115 Regent St, Fredericton, NB E3B 3Z2; tel. (506) 452-8101; Sec. and Treas. APRIL SEXSMITH.

Nova Scotia Federation of Agriculture: POB 784, Truro, NS B2N 5E8; tel. (902) 893-2293; fax (902) 893-7063; 4,000 mems in 16 orgs; Sec. LESTER SETTLE.

Nova Scotia Fruit-Growers' Association: Kentville Agricultural Centre, Kentville, NS B4N 1J5; tel. (902) 678-0533; Sec. Man. SUZANNE CORKUM.

Nova Scotia Milk-Producers' Association: POB 784, Truro, NS B2N 5E8; tel. (902) 893-2293; fax (902) 893-7063; 625 mems in 5 orgs.

Ontario Dairy Council: 40 Wynford Dr., Suite 300, Don Mills, ON M3C 1J5; tel. (416) 445-7734; fax (416) 445-7985; 163 mem. orgs; Pres. T. D. KANE.

Ontario Federation of Agriculture: 491 Eglinton Ave West, Suite 500, Toronto, ON M5N 3A2; tel. (416) 485-3333; fax (416) 485-9027; 24,000 individual mems, 26 mem. orgs; Exec. Dir JOANNE SUTHERLAND.

Ontario Fruit- and Vegetable-Growers' Association: Ontario Food Terminal, Rm 301, 165 The Queensway, Toronto, ON M8Y 1H8; tel. (416) 255-4473; Exec. Sec. J. VAN DER ZALM.

Ontario Grain- and Feed-Dealers' Association: 1400 Bishop St, Suite 106, Cambridge, ON N1R 6W8; tel. (519) 622-3800; Exec. Vice-Pres. J. M. CUNNINGHAM.

Prince Edward Island Federation of Agriculture: Farm Centre, 420 University Ave, Charlottetown, PE C1A 7Z5; tel. (902) 892-6913.

Québec Farmers' Association: POB 80, Ste-Anne-de-Bellevue, PQ H9X 3L4; tel. (514) 457-2010; Pres. WARREN GRAPES; Exec. Sec. STEVE GRUBER.

Saskatchewan Wheat Pool: 2625 Victoria Ave, Regina, SK S4T 7T9; tel. (306) 569-4228; fax (306) 569-4708; Sec. A. D. MCLEOD.

Society of Ontario Nut Growers: Rural Route 2, Niagara-on-the-Lake, ON L0S 1J0; tel. (416) 682-4966; 536 individual mems, 11 mem. orgs; Sec. G. ROBERT HAMBLETON.

Unifarm: 14815 119th Ave, Edmonton, AB T5L 4W2; tel. (403) 451-5912; 4,000 individual mems, 12 mem. orgs; Exec. Dir W. J. PLOSZ.

L'Union des Producteurs Agricoles: 555 blvd Roland-Therrien, Longueuil, PQ J4H 3Y9; tel. (514) 679-0530; fax (514) 679-5436; f. 1924; 47,000 mems; Pres.-Gen. JACQUES PROULX; Dir-Gen. JEAN-CLAUDE BLANCHETTE.

United Grain Growers Ltd: 433 Main St, Winnipeg, MB R3B 3A7; tel. (204) 944-5411; telex 07-57809; fax (204) 944-4454; 76,000 mems; Sec. M. SHERMAN.

Western Canadian Wheat-Growers Association: 4401 Albert St, Suite 201, Regina, SK S4S 6B6; tel. (306) 586-5866; fax (306) 586-2707; 11,900 mems.

Women of Unifarm: 14815 119th Ave, Edmonton, AB T5L 4W2; tel. (403) 451-5912; 4,000 mems; Sec. WILLOW WEBB.

MINING

Mineral Fuels

(Source: Statistics Canada.)

Summary

	1986	1987	1988
Coal:			
Bituminous . . ('000 metric tons)	32,199	32,651	38,585
Sub-bituminous . ('000 metric tons)	17,331	18,536	19,910
Lignite . . . ('000 metric tons)	8,281	10,020	12,148
Crude oil . . . ('000 cu m)	85,363	89,032	93,563
Natural gas[1] . . (million cu m)	91,608	99,381	113,709

[1] Net withdrawals.

Provinces and Territories (1988)

	Coal ('000 metric tons)	Crude oil ('000 cu m)	Natural gas (million cu m)
Alberta	29,467.8	76,728.7	98,189.1
British Columbia . . .	24,941.5	1,874.3	10,662.0
Manitoba	—	768.8	—
New Brunswick . . .	541.9	—	2.4*
Northwest Territories . .	—	1,833.1	205.1
Nova Scotia	3,544.1	—	—
Ontario	—	135.5	508.6
Saskatchewan . . .	12,148.4	12,167.7	4,141.5
Total	70,643.7	93,563.2†	113,708.7

* Combined production of New Brunswick and Québec.
† Including other provinces not shown separately.

Metals

(Sources: Statistics Canada; Energy, Mines and Resources Canada, *Canadian Minerals Yearbook*.)

Summary

		1986		1987		1988*	
		Quantity	Value (C $ million)	Quantity	Value (C $ million)	Quantity	Value (C $ million)
Cadmium[1]	(metric tons)	1,484	6	1,481	9	1,742	33
Copper[2]	('000 metric tons)	699	1,426	794	1,923	722	2,317
Gold	(metric tons)	103	1,689	116	2,204	128	2,215
Iron ore[3]	('000 metric tons)	36,167	1,343	37,702	1,396	38,743	1,388
Lead[4]	('000 metric tons)	334	228	373	395	334	n.a.
Nickel[5]	('000 metric tons)	170	1,217	164	979	189	1,273
Silver[6]	(metric tons)	1,088	275	1,375	424	1,527	378
Uranium[7]	(metric tons)	11,502	1,042	13,612	1,182	13,233	1,108
Zinc	('000 metric tons)	988	1,201	1,158	1,475	1,254	2,065

* Provisional figures.

[1] Production of refined cadmium from domestic ores, plus recoverable cadmium content of exported ores and concentrates.
[2] Shipments of anode copper recovered in Canada from domestic concentrates, plus exports of payable copper in concentrates and matte.
[3] Includes shipments of by-product iron ore.
[4] Lead content of base bullion produced from domestic primary materials, plus estimated recoverable lead in domestic ores and concentrates exported.
[5] Refined nickel and nickel in oxides and salts produced, plus recoverable nickel in matte and concentrates exported.
[6] Includes recoverable silver in: ores, concentrates and matte shipped for export; crude gold bullion produced; blister and anode copper produced at Canadian smelters; and base and other bullion produced from domestic ores.
[7] Shipments in metric tons of uranium, contained in concentrate, from ore-processing plants.

Provinces and Territories (1988, provisional figures)

	Copper (metric tons)[1]	Gold (kg)	Iron ore ('000 metric tons)[2]	Lead (metric tons)[3]	Nickel (metric tons)[4]	Silver (kg)[5]	Uranium (metric tons)[6]	Zinc (metric tons)
Alberta . . .	—	20	—	—	—	2	—	—
British Columbia	353,406	13,036	71	90,086	—	420,000	—	119,522
Manitoba	53,304	4,285	—	n.a.*	71,579	28,000	—	57,182
New Brunswick	9,607	74	—	73,289	—	201,500	—	230,125
Newfoundland	—	n.a.*	20,044	—	—	n.a.*	—	29,906
Northwest Territories . . .	n.a.*	11,422	—	67,227	—	27,400	—	290,000
Nova Scotia	n.a.*	n.a.*	—	—	—	n.a.*	—	n.a.*
Ontario	256,629	57,882	2,927	2,268	142,292	386,000	4,543	333,235
Québec	45,191	32,485	15,700	—	—	122,160	—	73,440
Saskatchewan	2,509	2,083	—	—	—	n.a.*	8,690	n.a.*
Yukon Territory	n.a.*	4,304	—	n.a.*	—	340,000	—	118,325
Total	721,588*	127,843*	38,742	333,707*	213,871	1,527,052*	13,233	1,253,580*

* Confidential figures; included in total.

[1] Shipments of anode copper recovered in Canada from domestic concentrates, plus exports of payable copper in concentrates and matte.
[2] Includes shipments of by-product iron ore.
[3] Lead content of base bullion produced from domestic primary materials, plus estimated recoverable lead in domestic ores and concentrates exported.
[4] Refined nickel and nickel in oxides and salts produced, plus recoverable nickel in matte and concentrates exported.
[5] Includes recoverable silver in: ores, concentrates and matte shipped for export; crude gold bullion produced; blister and anode copper produced at Canadian smelters; and base and other bullion produced from domestic ores.
[6] Shipments in metric tons of uranium, contained in concentrate, from ore-processing plants.

Non-Metallic Minerals

(Sources: Statistics Canada; Energy, Mines and Resources Canada, *Minerals Yearbook*.)

Summary ('000 metric tons)

	1986		1987		1988*	
	Quantity	Value (C $ million)	Quantity	Value (C $ million)	Quantity	Value (C $ million)
Asbestos	662	234	665	238	n.a.	n.a.
Cement[1]:						
Masonry[2]	682	46	1,091	71⎫	12,611	1,013
Portland	9,929	778	11,512	926⎭		
Clays and clay products	n.a.	180	n.a.	211	n.a.	185
Gypsum[3]	8,803	83	9,094	87	8,522	88
Potash (K$_2$O equivalent)	6,678	n.a.	7,399	n.a.	8,337	n.a.
Salt	10,332	239	10,129	239	10,975	258
Stone[4]	97,602	489	113,291	583	112,422	601
Sulphur	7,724	930	8,106	750	8,952	692

* Provisional figures.
[1] Producers' shipments, plus quantities used by producers.
[2] Includes amounts of clinker and other cement.
[3] Excludes gypsum produced by or shipped for use by Canadian portland-cement producers.
[4] Excludes stone used in the Canadian cement and lime industries.

Provinces and Territories (1988, provisional figures, unless otherwise indicated)

	Asbestos (metric tons)[1]	Cement (metric tons)[2]	Gypsum (metric tons)	Salt (metric tons)	Stone ('000 tons)[3]
Alberta	—	1,152,500	—	1,218,400	300
British Columbia	78,348	1,511,700	428	—	4,913
Manitoba	—	n.a.*	n.a.*	—	3,500
New Brunswick	—	n.a.*	n.a.*	n.a.*	2,960
Newfoundland	43,300	n.a.*	n.a.*	—	990
Northwest Territories	—	—	—	—	1,300†
Nova Scotia	—	n.a.*	6,331	n.a.*	4,450
Ontario	—	5,540,750	1,459	6,862,900	51,000
Québec	540,733	3,394,000	—	n.a.*	43,007
Saskatchewan	—	—	—	399,500	2
Total	662,381	12,610,550*	8,522*‡	10,974,600*	112,422

* Confidential figures; included in total.
† Combined production of Northwest Territories and Yukon Territory.
‡ Excludes gypsum produced by or shipped for use by Canadian portland-cement producers.

[1] 1986 figures.
[2] Producers' shipments, plus quantities used by producers.
[3] Excludes stone used in the Canadian cement and lime industries.

Selected Mining Organizations

Canadian Gas Association: 55 Scarsdale Rd, Don Mills, ON M3B 2R3; tel. (416) 447-6465; telex 06-966824; fax (416) 447-7067; 535 mems; Pres. IAN C. MACNABB.

Canadian Institute of Mining and Metallurgy: 1130 Sherbrooke St West, Suite 400, Montréal, PQ H3A 2M8; tel. (514) 842-3461; fax (514) 842-4312; 12,500 individual mems, 260 orgs; Exec. Dir PIERRE MICHAUD.

Canadian Petroleum Association: 150 6th Ave, SW, Suite 3800, Calgary, AB T2P 3Y7; tel. (403) 269-6721; fax (403) 261-4622; Pres. IAN R. SMYTH.

Coal Association of Canada: 1000 8th Ave, Suite 301, Calgary, AB T2P 3M7; tel. (403) 262-1544; telex 03-827596; 84 mems; Pres. RICHARD T. MARSHALL.

Gold Information Centre: Canada Trust Tower, 20 Elgin Ave West, Suite 1203, Toronto, ON M4R 1K8; tel. (416) 480-1410.

Independent Petroleum Association of Canada: 707 7th Ave, SW, Suite 700, Calgary, AB T2P 0Z2; tel. (403) 290-1530; fax (403) 290-1680; 350 mems; Exec. Dir BOB REID.

Mining Association of Canada: 350 Sparks St, Suite 809, Ottawa, ON K1R 7S8; tel. (613) 233-9391; fax (613) 233-8897; Man. Dir C. GEORGE MILLER.

  Alberta Chamber of Resources: 10235 101st St, Edmonton, AB T5J 3G1; tel. (403) 420-1020; Man. Dir DON CURRIE.

British Columbia and Yukon Chamber of Mines: 840 West Hastings St, Vancouver, BC V6C 1C8; tel. (604) 681-5328; Man. Dir J. M. PATTERSON.

Chamber of Mineral Resources of Nova Scotia: 5525 Artillery Place, Suite 202, Halifax, NS B3J 1J2; tel. (902) 422-5806; Man. Dir. J. A. VEINOT.

Mining Association of British Columbia: 1066 West Hastings St, POB 12540, Vancouver, BC V6E 3X1; tel. (604) 681-4321; Pres. T. WATERLAND.

Mining Association of Manitoba Inc: 305 Broadway Ave, Suite 700, Winnipeg, MB R3C 3J7; tel. (204) 942-2789; Man. W. K. NEWMAN.

Mining Association of Newfoundland: c/o Iron Ore Co of Canada, POB 1000, Labrador City, NF A2V 2L8; Sec. and Treas. W. A. CAMPBELL.

Mining Society of Nova Scotia: 125 Main St, Glace Bay, NS B1A 4Y5; Sec. and Treas. J. C. MARSH.

New Brunswick Mining Association: 236 St George St, Suite 312, Moncton, NB E1C 1W1; tel. (506) 857-3056; telex 014-2126; Administrator PAULINE ST-LAURENT.

Northwest Territories Chamber of Mines: 4918 50th St, Suite 105, POB 2818, Yellowknife, NT X1A 2R1; tel. (403) 873-5281; f. 1967; Gen. Man. D. NUTTER.

Ontario Mining Association: 111 Richmond St West, Suite 1114, Toronto, ON M5H 2G4; tel. (416) 364-9301; f. 1920; 35 mems; Pres. J. M. GORDON; Exec. Dir PATRICK REID.

Québec Asbestos-Mining Association: c/o Paul Fiteau, 1130 Sherbrooke St West, Suite 410, Montréal, PQ H3A 2M8.

Québec Metal-Mining Association: 2 pl. Québec, Québec, PQ G1R 2B5; Gen. Man. Dr CLAUDE DROUIN.

Saskatchewan Mining Association: 730 Avord Tower, Regina, SK S4P 0R7; tel. (306) 757-9505; Man. Dr R. L. CHEESMAN.

Yukon Chamber of Mines: POB 4427, Whitehorse, YT Y1A 3T5; tel. (403) 667-2090; Sec. DOROTHY HOWETT.

Nickel Development Institute: First Canadian Pl., Toronto, ON M5X 1C4; tel. (416) 361-7511; Pres. J. SHADE.

Petroleum Marketers' Association of Canada: 438 Briar Hill Ave, Toronto, ON M5N 1M7; tel. (416) 485-1826.

Potash and Phosphate Institute of Canada: CN Tower, Suite 704, Midtown Plaza, Saskatoon, SK S7K 1J5; tel. (306) 652-3535; Pres. Dr KENNETH M. PRETTY.

INDUSTRY

Manufacturing Production

(C $ million. Source: Statistics Canada.)

Summary

	1984		1985		1986*	1987†
	Value added by manufacture	Value of shipments	Value added by manufacture	Value of shipments	Value of shipments	Value of shipments
Food industries	10,127	31,624	10,936	32,793	35,039	36,758
Beverage industries	2,838	4,551	2,994	4,864	5,435	5,806
Tobacco products industries	787	1,590	826	1,641	1,594	1,814
Rubber products industries	1,396	2,507	1,463	2,554	2,450	2,387
Plastic products industries	1,596	3,510	1,824	3,861	4,161	4,788
Leather and allied products industries	689	1,271	676	1,308	1,371	1,353
Primary textile industries	1,163	2,729	1,201	2,670	2,755	3,073
Textile products industries	1,161	2,523	1,199	2,650	2,824	3,101
Clothing industries	2,813	5,175	2,914	5,543	5,981	6,336
Wood industries	4,051	9,973	4,688	11,122	12,278	14,882
Furniture and fixture industries	1,581	3,022	1,811	3,399	3,648	3,989
Paper and allied products industries	7,492	17,472	7,524	18,075	20,158	23,305
Printing, publishing and allied industries	5,611	8,659	6,169	9,535	10,309	11,239
Primary metal industries	6,879	16,432	7,042	16,971	16,995	18,884
Fabricated metal products industries	6,001	12,193	6,838	13,971	14,508	16,333
Machinery industries	3,731	6,863	3,889	7,451	7,973	8,972
Transportation equipment industries	13,447	37,916	14,741	43,117	44,561	41,644
Electrical and electronic products industries	6,959	11,632	7,587	13,258	14,381	15,775
Non-metallic mineral products industries	2,788	5,246	3,172	5,879	6,459	7,511
Refined petroleum and coal products industries	2,596	23,337	2,595	24,421	16,931	16,277
Chemical and chemical products industries	7,620	17,175	8,329	18,269	18,822	20,157
Other manufacturing industries	2,717	4,670	2,939	5,065	5,278	5,481
Total, all manufacturing industries	94,045	230,070	101,358	248,493	253,911	269,865

* Preliminary.　† Estimates.

Provinces and Territories (value of shipments in 1985)

	Food industries	Beverage industries	Tobacco products industries	Rubber products industries	Plastic products industries	Leather and allied products industries	Primary textile industries
Alberta	3,538	335	—	n.a.*	208	n.a.*	n.a.*
British Columbia	2,558	454	—	n.a.*	214	n.a.*	15
Manitoba	1,695	163	—	n.a.*	n.a.*	36	n.a.*
New Brunswick	896	155	—	n.a.*	33	n.a.*	n.a.*
Newfoundland	532	87	—	—	n.a.*	n.a.*	—
Northwest Territories	—	—	—	—	—	—	—
Nova Scotia	974	n.a.*	—	n.a.*	44	n.a.*	66
Ontario	12,947	2,229	830	1,590	2,249	773	1,110
Prince Edward Island	205	n.a.*	—	—	—	—	n.a.*
Québec	8,560	1,196	811	n.a.*	975	453	1,419
Saskatchewan	889	n.a.*	—	—	n.a.*	n.a.*	n.a.*
Yukon Territory	—	—	—	—	—	—	—
Total	32,793	4,864	1,641	2,554	3,861	1,308	2,670

(continued)

MANUFACTURING PRODUCTION—Provinces and Territories (value of shipments in 1985)—*(continued)*

	Textile products industries	Clothing industries	Wood industries	Furniture and fixture industries	Paper and allied products industries	Printing, publishing and allied industries	Primary metal industries	Fabricated metal product industries
Alberta	39	96	556	108	462	569	866	781
British Columbia	46	160	5,092	112	3,437	658	807	864
Manitoba	n.a.*	304	162	115	239	334	492	290
New Brunswick	n.a.*	n.a.*	344	17	958	n.a.*	n.a.*	113
Newfoundland	n.a.*	—	26	2	n.a.*	38	n.a.*	19
Northwest Territories	—	—	—	—	—	—	—	—
Nova Scotia	n.a.*	n.a.*	138	13	467	n.a.*	n.a.*	113
Ontario	1,211	1,511	2,103	2,009	6,036	5,023	9,863	7,938
Prince Edward Island	—	n.a.*	10	—	—	14	—	9
Québec	1,245	3,404	2,566	1,014	6.054	2,537	4,585	3,747
Saskatchewan	n.a.*	16	126	9	n.a.*	n.a.*	n.a.*	96
Yukon Territory	—	—	—	—	—	—	—	—
Total	2,650	5,543	11,122	3,399	18,075	9,535	16,971	13,971

MANUFACTURING PRODUCTION—Provinces and Territories (value of shipments in 1985)—*(continued)*

	Machinery industries	Transportation equipment industries	Electrical and electronic products industries	Non-metallic mineral products industries	Refined petroleum and coal products industries	Chemical and chemical products industries	Other manufacturing industries	Total, all manufacturing industries
Alberta	756	140	307	523	5,102	2,543	167	17,192
British Columbia	449	848	316	n.a.*	2,501	659	173	19,863
Manitoba	275	n.a.*	321	160	n.a.*	214	65	5,549
New Brunswick	40	n.a.*	n.a.*	n.a.*	n.a.*	82	n.a.*	4,243
Newfoundland	n.a.*	n.a.*	n.a.*	41	—	n.a.*	5	1,224
Northwest Territories	—	—	—	—	n.a.*	—	n.a.*	54
Nova Scotia	n.a.*	313	74	n.a.*	n.a.*	52	n.a.*	4,635
Ontario	4,665	35,834	8,707	3,008	8,325	10,688	3,339	131,988
Prince Edward Island	n.a.*	7	n.a.*	n.a.*	—	n.a.*	6	297
Québec	1,079	5,137	3,312	1,370	5,582	3,738	n.a.*	60,460
Saskatchewan	155	50	180	n.a.*	n.a.*	168	n.a.*	2,983
Yukon Territory	—	—	—	—	n.a.*	—	n.a.*	5
Total	7,451	43,117	13,258	5,879	24,421	18,269	5,065	248,493

* Figures are confidential, but are included in totals.

Construction

(Source: Statistics Canada.)

Value of construction work purchased (C $ million)

	1986	1987	1988
Building construction	47,427	50,298	54,658
Residential	28,885	32,519	35,224
Industrial	3,201	2,362	2,627
Commercial	10,119	10,486	11,583
Institutional	3,565	3,350	3,401
Other	1,656	1,581	1,803
Engineering construction	24,274	19,622	23,394
Marine	335	231	384
Road, highway and airport runways	5,192	4,075	4,214
Waterworks and sewage systems	2,377	1,947	2,561
Dams and irrigation	243	260	261
Electric power construction	3,370	3,215	4,393
Railway, telephone and telegraph construction	2,753	1,846	1,987
Gas and oil facilities	6,728	5,385	6,795
Other	3,275	2,663	2,799
Total	71,701	69,920	78,052

Chambers of Commerce

NATIONAL AND REGIONAL ORGANIZATIONS

Atlantic Provinces Chamber of Commerce: 236 St George St, Suite 110, Moncton, NB E1C 1W1; tel. (506) 857-3980; fax (506) 859-6131; Pres. JEANNE M. GELDART.

British Columbia and Yukon Chamber of Mines: 840 West Hastings St, Vancouver, BC V6C 1C8; tel. (604) 681-5328; Man. Dir J. M. PATTERSON.

The Canadian Chamber of Commerce: 55 Metcalfe St, Suite 1160, Ottawa, ON K1P 6N4; tel. (613) 238-4000; telex 053-3360; fax (613) 238-7643; f. 1925; mems: 500 community chambers of commerce and boards of trade, 80 national trade asscns and 4,000 business corpns; affiliated with all provincial chambers of commerce and with the International Chamber of Commerce and other bilateral orgs; Chair. JOHN D. HERRICK; Pres. R. B. HAMEL.

Regional offices:

Ontario: 120 Adelaide St West, Suite 2109, Toronto, ON M5H 1T1; tel. (416) 868-4334; fax (416) 868-0189.

Québec: 1080 côte du Beaver Hall, Bureau 1730, Montréal, PQ H2Z 1T2; tel. (514) 866-4334; fax (514) 866-7296.

Canadian Junior Chamber/Jeune Chambre du Canada: 39 Leacock Way, Kanata, ON K2K 1T1; tel. (613) 592-2450; telex 053-3845; Exec. Dir LUC BÉGIN.

Chambre de commerce française au Canada: 360 rue St-François-Xavier, Montréal, PQ H2Y 2S8; tel. (514) 281-1246; fax (514) 289-9594.

International Business Council of Canada: 55 Metcalfe St, Suite 1160, Ottawa, ON K1P 6N4; tel. (613) 238-4000; telex 053-3360; fax (613) 238-7643; Associate Exec. Dirs TIMOTHY I. PAGE, WILLIAM NEIL.

ORGANIZATIONS BY PROVINCE AND TERRITORY

Alberta

Alberta Chamber of Commerce: 10130 103rd St, Edmonton, AB T5J 3N9; tel. (403) 425-4180; Exec. Dir REUBEN HAMM.

Alberta Chamber of Resources: Oxford Tower, Suite 1410, 10235 101st St, Edmonton, AB T5J 3G1; tel. (403) 420-1030; Man. Dir DONALD V. CURRIE.

Calgary Chamber of Commerce: 517 South Centre St, Calgary, AB T2G 2C4; tel. (403) 263-7435; fax (403) 266-3413.

Edmonton Chamber of Commerce: 10123 99th St, Suite 600, Edmonton, AB T5J 3G9; tel. (403) 426-4620; fax (403) 424-7946.

British Columbia

British Columbia Chamber of Commerce: 750 Pacific Blvd West, POB 30, Vancouver, BC V6B 5E6; tel. (604) 681-5541; Man. Dir PATRICK J. RISDON.

Chamber of Mines of Eastern British Columbia: 215 Hall St, Nelson, BC V1L 5X4; tel. (604) 352-5242; Sec.-Treas. T. MAY.

Greater Victoria Chamber of Commerce: 525 Fort St, Victoria, BC V8W 1E8; tel. (604) 383-7191; fax (604) 385-3552; Man. BRIAN SMALL.

Vancouver Board of Trade: 499 Canada Pl., Suite 400, Vancouver, BC V6C 3C1; tel. (604) 681-2111; Man. Dir DARCEY REZAC.

Manitoba

Brandon Chamber of Commerce: 1043 Rosser Ave, POB 548, Brandon, MB R7A 5Z7; tel. (204) 727-5431; Man. JEFF TOEWS.

Manitoba Chamber of Commerce: 167 Lombard Ave East, Suite 750, Winnipeg, MB R3B 0V6; tel. (204) 942-2561; Exec. Dir ANNE DOHERTY.

Winnipeg Chamber of Commerce: 167 Lombard Ave, Suite 500, Winnipeg, MB R3B 3E5; tel. (204) 944-8484; fax (204) 944-8492; Man. WILLIAM DRAPER.

New Brunswick

Saint John Board of Trade: c/o Delta Brunswick Hotel, 39 King St, Saint John, NB E2L 4W3; tel. (506) 634-8111; Gen. Man. LINDA FORESTELL.

Newfoundland

St John's Board of Trade: POB 5127, St John's, NF A1C 5V5; tel. (709) 726-2961; Gen. Man. BRUCE J. TILLEY.

Northwest Territories

Yellowknife Chamber of Commerce: POB 906, Yellowknife, NT X1A 2N7; tel. (403) 920-4944; fax (403) 920-2145; Gen. Man. IRENE K. SIHVONEN.

Nova Scotia

Dartmouth Chamber of Commerce: 12 Portland St, Dartmouth, NS B2Y 1G9; tel. (902) 469-7110; Exec. Dir DAVID W. HARRISON.

Halifax Board of Trade: 5251 Duke St, Suite 400, Halifax, NS B3J 1P3; tel. (902) 420-0223; Exec. Vice-Pres. LEONARD O. GIFFIN.

Mulgrave and Area Chamber of Commerce: POB 3, Mulgrave, NS B0E 2G0; tel. (902) 625-0190; Man. IAN MACKENZIE.

Offshore Trade Association of Nova Scotia: World Trade and Convention Centre, Suite 813, 1800 Argyle St, Halifax, NS B3J 3N8; tel. (902) 425-4774.

Ontario

Board of Trade of Metropolitan Toronto: 3 First Canadian Pl., POB 60, Toronto, ON M5X 1C1; tel. (416) 366-6811; fax (416) 366-4906; Gen. Man. J. A. COLLINS.

Hamilton and District Chamber of Commerce: 100 King St West, Suite 830, Hamilton, ON L8P 1A2; tel. (416) 522-1151; fax (416) 522-1154; Exec. Dir R. J. WHYNOTT.

Kingston District Chamber of Commerce: 209 Wellington St, Kingston, ON K7K 2Y6; tel. (613) 548-4453; Gen. Man. H. REYERS.

London Chamber of Commerce: 379 Dundas St, London, ON N6B 1V5; tel. (519) 432-7551; fax (519) 432-8063; Exec. Vice-Pres. and CEO J. A. MANN.

Ontario Chamber of Commerce: 2323 Yonge St, 5th Floor, Toronto, ON M4P 2C9; tel. (416) 482-5222; fax (416) 482-5879; Gen. Man. J. G. CARNEGIE.

Ottawa-Carleton Board of Trade: 185 Sparks St, 3rd Floor, Ottawa, ON K1P 5B9; tel. (613) 236-3631; Pres. L. HOPKINS.

Sudbury and District Chamber of Commerce: 40 Elm St West, Sudbury, ON P3C 1T5; tel. (705) 673-7133; Gen. Man. D. NICHOLSON.

Prince Edward Island

Greater Charlottetown Chamber of Commerce: POB 67, Charlottetown, PE C1A 7K2; tel. (902) 892-3424; Gen. Man. HARVEY McKINNON.

Québec

Bureau de commerce de Montréal: 1800 côte du Beaver Hall, Bureau 710, Montréal, PQ H2Z 1S9; tel. (514) 878-4651; Man. LUC LACHARITÉ.

Chambre de commerce de Montréal: 772 rue Sherbrooke ouest, Montréal, PQ H3A 1G1; tel. (514) 288-9090; fax (514) 843-7320; Man. ALEX HARPER.

Chambre de commerce du Québec: 500 pl. d'Armes, Bureau 3030, Montréal, PQ H2Y 2W2; tel. (514) 844-9571; Exec. Vice-Pres. J. P. LÉTOURNEAU.

Chambre de commerce et d'industrie du Québec metropolitain: 17 rue St-Louis, Québec, PQ G1R 3Y8; tel. (418) 692-3853; Dir-Gen. PIERRE TALBOT.

Saskatchewan

Regina Chamber of Commerce: 2145 Albert St, Regina, SK S4P 2V1; tel. (306) 757-4658; Exec. Dir R. DALZIEL.

Saskatchewan Chamber of Commerce: 1630 Chateau Towers, 1920 Broad St, Regina, SK S4P 3V2; tel. (306) 352-2671; Exec. Vice-Pres. R. C. FINLAY.

Saskatoon Board of Trade: 306 East 24th St, Saskatoon, SK S7K 4R2; tel. (306) 244-2151; Exec. Dir DWIGHT PERCY.

Yukon Territory

Yukon Chamber of Commerce: 302 Steele St, Suite 101, Whitehorse, YT Y1A 2C5; tel. (403) 667-7545; Man. APRIL NEAVE.

Industrial and Employers' Organizations

The Canadian Manufacturers' Association: One Yonge St, Toronto, ON M5E 1J9; tel. (416) 363-7261; telex 065-24693; f.1871; the nat. organization of manufacturers of Canada; 8,000 mems; Pres. and Exec. Dir J. L. THIBAULT.

Building and Construction

Canadian Construction Association: 85 Albert St, Ottawa, ON K1P 6A4; tel. (613) 236-9455; fax (613) 236-9525; f. 1918; 25,000 mems; Chair. PETER LYSAK; Pres. ROBERT E. NUTH.

Canadian Home-Builders Association: 200 Elgin St, Suite 502, Ottawa, ON K2P 1L5; tel. (613) 230-3060; fax (613) 232-4635; 5,500 mems; COO JOHN K. KENWARD.

Canadian Institute of Steel Construction: 201 Consumers Rd, Suite 300, Willowdale, ON M2J 4G8; tel. (416) 491-4552; telex 069-86547; 50 mems; Pres. H. A. KRENTZ.

Canadian Paint and Coatings Association: 9900 blvd Cavendish, Bureau 103, Ville St-Laurent, PQ H4M 2V2; tel. (514) 745-2611; fax (514) 745-2031; f. 1913; 130 mems; Pres. R. W. MURRAY.

Canadian Steel Construction Council: 201 Consumers Rd, Suite 300, Willowdale, ON M2J 4G8; tel. (416) 491-9898; telex 069-86547; Chair. H. A. KRENTZ.

Canadian Roofing Contractors' Association: 151 Slater St, Suite 606, Ottawa, ON V2J 2B9; tel. (604) 992-8391; Exec. Dir JOHN E. HILL.

Construction Specifications Canada: 1 St Clair Ave West, Suite 1206, Toronto, ON M4V 1K6; tel. (416) 922-3159; f. 1954; 500 mems; Exec. Vice-Pres. RENÉ GAULIN.

National Concrete Producers' Association: 1013 Wilson Ave, Suite 101, Downsview, ON M3K 1G1; tel. (416) 635-7179; 55 mems; Pres. R. GRIMM; Exec. Dir MARK PATAMIA.

Ontario Painting Contractors' Association: 211 Consumers Rd, Suite 305, Willowdale, ON M2J 4G8; tel. (416) 498-1897; fax (416) 498-6757; Exec. Dir MAUREEN MARQUARDT.

Chemicals

Canadian Chemical Producers' Association: 350 Sparks St, Suite 805, Ottawa, ON K1R 7S8; tel. (613) 237-6215; fax (613) 237-4061; Pres. J. M. BELANGER.

Canadian Manufacturers of Chemical Specialities Association: 56 Sparks St, Suite 702, Ottawa, ON K1P 5A9; tel. (613) 232-6616; Exec. Dir M. E. CLOGHESY.

The Chemical Institute of Canada: 1785 Alta Vista Dr., Ottawa, ON K1G 3Y6; tel. (613) 526-4652; 9,000 mems, 2,500 student mems; Exec. Dir ANNE E. ALPER.

Clothing and Textiles

Apparel Manufacturers' Association of Ontario: 1179 King St West, Suite 117, Toronto, ON M6K 3C5; tel. (416) 531-5707; f. 1970; 79 mems; Exec. Dir F. J. BRYAN.

Canadian Allied Textile Trades Association: 49 Front St East, Toronto, ON M5E 1B3; tel. (416) 363-4266; telex 062-3441; Sec. and Treas. ALEX HARDIE.

Canadian Carpet Institute: 275 Slater St, Suite 1610, Ottawa, ON K1P 5H9; tel. (613) 232-7183; fax (613) 232-3072; f. 1961; Pres. D. S. EDWARDS.

Canadian Textiles Institute: 280 Albert St, Suite 502, Ottawa, ON K1P 5G8; tel. (613) 232-7195; fax (613) 232-8722; Pres. ERIC L. BARRY.

Institute of Textile Scientists: 1 rue Pacifique, Sainte-Anne-de-Bellevue, PQ H9X 1C5; tel. (514) 457-2347; 180 mems; Sec. DAVID COONEY.

The Shoe Manufacturers' Association of Canada: 1010 rue Sainte-Catherine ouest, Bureau 710, Montréal, PQ H3B 3R4; tel. (514) 878-9337; fax (514) 878-3321; f. 1918; 154 mems; Pres. NATHAN FINKELSTEIN; Exec. Sec. DIANE CAPPELLA.

Textile Federation of Canada: 1 rue Pacifique, Saint-Anne-de-Bellevue, PQ H9X 1C5; tel. (514) 457-2347; 1,750 mems; Exec. Sec. FRED G. DAFOR.

Electrical and Electronics

Canadian Electrical Association: 1 pl. Westmount, Bureau 500, Montréal, PQ H3Z 2P9; tel. (514) 937-6181; telex 052-67401; f. 1891; 2,300 individual and corporate mems; Pres. WALLACE S. READ.

Canadian Electrical Contractors' Association: 161 Eglinton Ave East, Suite 605, Toronto, ON M4P 1J5; Exec. Vice-Pres. NORMAN W. PURDY.

Canadian Electronic Representatives' Association: POB 294, Kleinburg, ON L0J 1C0; tel. (416) 893-1689; fax (416) 893-2392; 25 mem. orgs; Exec. Dir JIM PREECE.

Electrical Bureau of Canada: 10 Carlson Court, Suite 500, Rexdale, ON M9W 6L2; tel. (416) 674-7410.

Electrical and Electronic Manufacturers' Association of Canada: 10 Carlson Court, Suite 500, Rexdale, ON M9W 6L2; tel. (416) 674-7410; telex 069-89110; fax 674-7412; 220 mem. cos; Pres. N. ASPIN; Chair. D. A. NOBLE.

Institute of Electrical and Electronics Engineers, Inc, Canada: 7061 Yonge St, Thornhill, ON L3T 2A6; tel. (416) 881-1930; fax (416) 881-2057; Man. PAMELA E. WOODROW.

Engineering and Machinery

Association of Consulting Engineers of Canada: 130 Albert St, Suite 616, Ottawa, ON K1P 5G4; tel. (613) 236-0569; telex 053-4943; fax (613) 236-6193; 800 mem. cos.

Canadian Council of Professional Engineers: 116 Albert St, Suite 401, Ottawa, ON K1P 5G3; tel. (613) 232-2474; fax (613) 236-6193; 12 provincial and territorial asscns of 130,000 mems; Exec. Dir DONALD G. LAPLANTE.

Canadian Machine-Tool Distributors Association: 9 Brougham Cres., Etobicoke, ON M9R 1J3; tel. (416) 249-3823; 32 mem. cos; Sec. and Treas. ROBERT W. IDE.

Canadian Society for Professional Engineers: 203 College St, Suite 201, Toronto, ON M5T 1P9; tel. (416) 598-0520; 2,700 mems; Pres. MURRAY McINROY.

Municipal Engineers' Association: 26 Francis St, POB 9000, Lindsay, ON K9V 5R8; 500 mems; Sec. P. J. SEATON.

Food and Beverages

Association of Canadian Distillers: 90 Sparks St, Suite 1100, Ottawa, ON K1P 5T8; tel. (613) 238-8444; telex 053-3783; fax (613) 238-3411; 11 mem. cos; Pres. K. M. CAMPBELL.

Bakery Council of Canada: 1185 Eglinton Ave East, Suite 101, Don Mills, ON M3C 3C6; tel. (416) 423-0262; fax (416) 423-1940; Pres. LINDA J. NAGEL.

Brewers Association of Canada: 155 Queen St, Suite 1200, Ottawa, ON K1P 6L1; tel. (613) 232-9601; telex 053-4370; fax (613) 232-2283; f. 1943; 14 mem. cos; Pres. R. A. MORRISON; Sec. F. T. BAMFORD.

Canadian Council for the Advancement of Food Technologies: 789 Don Mills Rd, Suite 700, Don Mills, ON M3C 3L6; tel. (416) 429-4661; Exec. Dir JEAN ALLEN.

Canadian Council of Grocery Distributors: pl. d'Arc, POB 1082, Montréal, PQ H2W 2P4; tel. (514) 982-0272; fax (514) 744-4408; f. 1919; 60 mems; Pres. JACQUES G. AUGER; Exec. Vice-Pres. CLAUDE PIGEON.

Canadian Food Brokers Association: 50 River St, Toronto, ON M5A 3N9; tel. (416) 368-5921; 241 mems; Pres. IAN C. KENNEDY.

Canadian Institute of Food Science and Technology: 46A Elgin St, Suite 48, Ottawa, ON K1P 5H3; tel. (613) 234-2242; 2,600 individual and corporate mems; Exec. Dir J. H. CAYFORD.

Canadian Meat Council: 5233 Dundas St West, Islington, ON M9B 1A6; tel. (416) 239-9411; fax (416) 239-2416; 82 mem. cos; Gen. Man. D. M. ADAMS.

Canadian National Millers' Association: 155 Queen St, Suite 1100, Ottawa, ON K1P 6L1; tel. (613) 238-2293; telex 053-3964; fax (613) 234-5210; f. 1920; 19 mems; Chair. ALLAN H. JAMES; Sec. STEPHEN P. MARKEY.

Canadian Pork Council: 75 Albert St, Suite 1101, Ottawa, ON K1P 5E7; tel. (613) 236-9239; fax (613) 236-5749; 10 mem. asscns; Pres. W. VAAGS; Exec. Sec. MARTIN RICE.

Chilled and Frozen Food Association of Canada: 1306 Wellington St, Suite 303, Ottawa, ON K1Y 3B2; tel. (613) 728-6306; Exec. Dir CHRISTOPHER J. KYTE.

Confectionery Manufacturers' Association of Canada: 1185 Eglinton Ave East, Suite 101, Don Mills, ON M3C 3C6; tel. (416) 429-1046; fax (416) 429-1940; f. 1919; 252 individual mems, 77 corporate mems; Pres. CAROL HOCHU.

Grocery Products Manufacturers of Canada: 56 Sparks St, Suite 800, Ottawa, ON K1P 5A9; tel. (613) 236-0583; Pres. GEORGE FLEISCHMANN.

Forestry, Lumber and Allied

Canadian Forestry Association: 185 Somerset St West, Suite 203, Ottawa, ON K2P 0J2; tel. (613) 232-1815; f. 1900; 12,000 mems; Pres. W. K. FULLERTON; Exec. Dir A. D. HALL.

Canadian Hardwood Plywood Association: 27 Goulburn Ave, Ottawa, ON K1N 8C7; tel. (613) 233-6205; telex 053-4519; fax (613) 233-1919; 55 mem. cos; Exec. Vice-Pres. J. F. McCABE.

Canadian Lumber Standards: 1475-1055 West Hastings St, Suite 260, Vancouver, BC V6E 2E9; tel. (604) 687-2171; 300 mem. cos; Exec. Dir NILS LARSSON.

Canadian Lumbermen's Association: 27 Goulburn Ave, Ottawa, ON K1N 8C7; tel. (613) 233-6205; telex 053-4519; fax (613) 233-1929; f. 1908; 300 mem. orgs; Exec. Dir J. F. McCRACKEN.

Canadian Pulp and Paper Association: Sun Life Bldg, 19e étage, 1155 rue Metcalfe, Montréal, PQ H3B 4T6; tel. (514) 866-6621; telex 055-60690; fax (514) 866-3035; f. 1913; 62 mem. cos; Pres. HOWARD HART; Exec. Vice-Pres. GORDON MINNES; Sec. ELINOR BLANCHARD.

Ontario Forest Industries Association: 130 Adelaide St West, Suite 1700, Toronto, ON M5H 3P5; f. 1943; 25 mem. cos; Pres. I. D. BIRD; Man. R. M. RAUTER.

Québec Forest Industries Association Ltd: 1200 ave Germain-des-Prés, Bureau 102, Sainte-Foy, PQ G1V 3M7; tel. (418) 651-9352; fax (418) 651-4622; f. 1924; 28 mems; Pres. and Dir-Gen. ANDRÉ DUCHESNE.

Wholesale Lumber Dealers' Association, Inc: 4195 Dundas St West, Unit G2, Toronto, ON M8X 1Y4; tel. (416) 232-2042; 41 corporate and associate mems; Sec. and Treas. THERESA MURPHY.

Hotels and Catering

Canadian Restaurant and Foodservices Association: Nu West Center, 80 Bloor St West, Suite 1201, Toronto, ON M5S 2V1; tel. (416) 923-8416; fax (416) 923-1450; f. 1944; 6,000 mems representing 16,000 outlets; Exec. Vice-Pres. DOUGLAS C. NEEDHAM.

Hotel Association of Canada, Inc: 1505 Carlton St, Winnipeg, MB R3C 3H8; tel. (403) 942-0671.

Hotel and Restuarant Suppliers' Association, Inc: 2435 rue Guenette, St-Laurent, PQ H4R 2E9; tel. (514) 334-5161; 473 mem. orgs; Admin. Man. JEAN CYR.

Leather

Tanners' Association of Canada: 50 River St, Toronto, ON M5A 3N9; tel. (416) 364-2134; Exec. Vice-Pres. IAN C. KENNEDY.

Metals

Canadian Institute of Mining and Metallurgy: 1130 Sherbrooke St West, Suite 400, Montréal, PQ H3A 2M8; tel. (514) 842-3461; fax (514) 842-4312; Exec. Dir PIERRE MICHAUD.

Canadian Mining Equipment Manufacturers' Association: 116 Albert St, Suite 701, Ottawa, ON K1P 5G3; tel. (613) 232-7213; Pres. ARNOLD W. D. GARLICK.

Canadian Steel Industry Research Association: One Yonge St, Suite 1400, Toronto, ON M5E 1J9; tel. (416) 363-7261; telex 065-24693; fax (416) 363-7261; 12 mem. orgs; Man. ALEX C. DICK.

Canadian Steel-Producers' Association: 50 O'Connor St, Suite 1414, Ottawa, ON K1P 6L2; tel. (613) 238-6049; fax (613) 238-1832; 14 mems; Man. Dir DANIEL W. RONANKO.

Mining Association of Canada: 350 Sparks St, Suite 809, Ottawa, ON K1R 7S8; tel. (613) 233-9391; fax (613) 233-8897; Man. Dir C. GEORGE MILLER.

Petroleum and Fuels

Canadian Gas Association: 55 Scarsdale Rd, Don Mills, ON M3B 2R3; tel. (416) 447-6465; telex 069-66824; fax (416) 447-7067; 535 mems; Pres. IAN C. MacNABB.

Canadian Gas-Processors' Association: 640 Fifth Ave, SW, Suite 229, Calgary, AB T2D 0M6; tel. (404) 263-5388; 400 mems.

Canadian Petroleum Association: 150 Sixth Ave, SW, Suite 3800, Calgary, AB T2P 3Y7; tel. (403) 269-6721; fax (403) 261-4622; Pres. IAN R. SMYTH.

Canadian Petroleum Equipment Manufacturers' Association: 116 Albert St, Suite 701, Ottawa, ON K1P 5G3; tel. (613) 232-7213; Pres. ARNOLD W. D. GARLICK.

Canadian Society of Petroleum Geologists: 206 Seventh Ave, SW, Suite 505, Calgary, AB T2P 0W7; tel. (403) 264-5610.

Independent Petroleum Association of Canada: 707 Seventh Ave, SW, Suite 700, Calgary, AB T2P 0Z2; tel. (403) 290-1530; fax (403) 290-1680; 350 mems; Exec. Dir BOB REID.

Petroleum Recovery Institute: 3512 33rd St, NW, Calgary, AB T2L 2A6; tel. (403) 282-1211.

Petroleum Resources Communication Foundation: 801 Sixth Ave, SW, Suite 2030, Calgary, AB T2P 3W2; tel. (403) 264-6064; fax (403) 237-6286; Exec. Dir BOB BUCHANAN.

Pharmaceuticals

Canadian Cosmetic, Toiletry and Fragrance Association: 24 Merton St, Toronto, ON M4S 1A1; tel. (416) 487-8111; fax (416) 487-6379; f. 1928; 285 mem. cos; Pres. KENNETH W. BAKER; Vice-Pres. SHARON WISSLER.

Canadian Drug Manufacturers' Association: 60 St Clair Ave West, Suite 604, Toronto, ON M3J 3H7; tel. (416) 663-2362; fax (416) 663-9829; 21 mem. orgs; Chair. BRENDA DRINKWALTER; Exec. Dir NICHOLAS G. LELUK.

Pharmaceutical Manufacturers' Association of Canada: 1111 Prince of Wales Dr., Ottawa, ON K2C 3T2; tel. (613) 236-9993; telex 053-3122; fax (613) 727-1407; f. 1914; 65 mems; Pres. JUDITH A. EROLA.

Printing and Publishing

(see also Publishers' Organizations—p. 483)

Canadian Music Publishers' Association: 56 Wellesley St West, Suite 320, Toronto, ON M5S 2S4; tel. (416) 926-1966; fax (416) 926-7521; 26 mem. cos; Sec. PAUL M. BERRY.

Canadian Printing Industries Association: 75 Albert St, Suite 906, Ottawa, ON K1P 5E7; tel. (613) 236-7208; Pres. WILLY COOPER.

Composers, Authors and Publishers Association of Canada, Ltd (CAPAC): 1240 Bay St, Toronto, ON M5R 2C2; tel. (416) 924-4427; fax (416) 924-4837.

Council of Printing Industries of Canada: 7 King St East, Suite 1908, Toronto, ON M5C 1A2; tel. (416) 867-1520; fax (416) 867-1168; Gen. Man. FRANKLYN R. SMITH.

Retaili.

Canadian Retail Building Supply Council: 213 Notre Dame Ave, Suite 1004, Winnipeg, MB R3B 1N3; 400 mems; Pres. MIKE KEARNEY.

Canadian Retail Hardware Association: 6800 Campobello Rd, Mississauga, ON L5N 2L8; tel. (416) 821-3470; fax (416) 821-8946; 1,800 mems; Exec. Dir THOMAS M. ROSS.

Retail Council of Canada: 210 Dundas St West, Suite 600, Toronto, ON M5G 2E8; tel. (416) 598-4684; f. 1963; mems represent 70% of total retail-store volume; Chair. M. H. AYRE; Pres. ALASDAIR J. McKICHAN.

Retail Merchants' Association of Canada, Inc: 1780 Birchmount Rd, Scarborough, ON M1P 2H8; tel. (416) 291-7903; f. 1896; nat. asscn of provincial groups; Pres. and CEO JOHN GILLESPIE.

Rubber

The Rubber Association of Canada: 89 The Queensway West, Suite 308, Mississauga, ON L5B 2V2; tel. (416) 270-8322; fax (416) 270-2640; 65 mem. cos; Pres. B. E. JAMES.

Stone, Clay and Glass Products

Clay Brick Association of Canada: 1 Sparks Ave, Suite G1, Willowdale, ON M2H 2W1; tel. (416) 498-0217; Pres. S. GRAY.

Tobacco

Canadian Tobacco Manufacturers' Council: 99 Bank St, Suite 701, Ottawa, ON K1P 6B9; tel. (613) 238-2799; fax (613) 238-4463; Pres. WILLIAM H. NEVILLE.

Transport

(see also Transport—pp. 496–502)

Air Transport Association of Canada: 99 Bank St, Suite 747, Ottawa, ON K1P 6B9; tel. (613) 233-7727; fax (613) 230-8648; f. 1934; Pres. and CEO G. M. SINCLAIR.

Canadian Council of Motor Transport Administrators: 1765 St Laurent Blvd, Ottawa, ON K1G 3V4; tel. (613) 526-0550; mems: federal, provincial and territorial transport depts; Exec. Dir NORMAN BROWN.

Canadian Institute of Traffic and Transportation: 145 Berkeley St, 5th Floor, Toronto, ON M5A 2X1; tel. (416) 363-5696; fax (416) 363-5698; Exec. Vice-Pres. VICTOR S. DEYGLIO.

The Canadian Shippers' Council: 99 Bank St, Suite 250, Ottawa, ON K1P 6B9; tel. (613) 238-8888; telex 053-4888; fax (613) 563-9218; Sec. J. D. MOORE.

Canadian Trucking Association: 130 Albert St, Suite 300, Ottawa, ON K1P 5G4; tel. (613) 236-9426; fax (613) 563-2701; f. 1937; Gen. Man. L. P. TARDIF.

Motor Vehicle Manufacturers' Association: 25 Adelaide St East, Suite 1602, Toronto, ON M5C 1Y7; tel. (416) 364-9333; fax (416) 367-3221; f. 1926; 8 mems; Pres. N. A. CLARK.

Railway Association of Canada: 1117 rue Sainte-Catherine ouest, Bureau 721, Montréal, PQ H3B 1H9; tel. (514) 849-4274; fax (514) 849-2861; 11 member railways and 5 asscns; Pres. J. M. BEAUPRE.

Shipping Federation of Canada: 300 rue Saint-Sacrement, Suite 326, Montréal, PQ H2Y 1X4; tel. (514) 849-2325; telex 055-61042; fax (514) 849-6992; 69 mems; Pres. Capt. F. C. NICOL.

Miscellaneous

Adhesives and Sealants Manufacturers Association of Canada: One Yonge St, Suite 1400, Toronto, ON M5E 1J9; tel. (413) 363-7261; 19 mem. cos; Sec.-Treas. BRIAN D. W. WHEELER.

Canadian Maritime Industries Association: POB 1429, Station B, Ottawa, ON K1P 5R4; tel. (613) 232-7127; telex 053-4848; fax (613) 232-2490; f. 1944; 20 shipyards and ship-repairing cos, 87 allied industries; Pres. J. Y. CLARKE.

Canadian Nuclear Association: 111 Elizabeth St, Toronto, ON M5G 1P7; tel. (416) 977-6152; fax (416) 979-8356; 120 mem. orgs. Pres. MICHAEL A. HARRISON; Vice-Pres. (Member Services) JAMES A. WELLER.

Trade Unions

At the beginning of 1989 there were 3,944,000 trade-union members in Canada, representing 29.7% of the civilian labour force. Of these, 36.3% belonged to unions with headquarters in the USA.

In 1989 unions affiliated to the Canadian Labour Congress represented 57.8% of total union membership.

Canadian Labour Congress: 2841 Riverside Dr., Ottawa, ON K1V 8X7; tel. (613) 521-3400; telex 053-4750; fax (613) 521-4655; f. 1956 by merger of the Canadian Congress of Labour and the Trades and Labour Congress of Canada; 2,280,520 mems (1989); Pres. SHIRLEY G. E. CARR; Sec.-Treas. RICHARD MERCIER.

Principal affiliated unions:

Alliance of Canadian Cinema, Television and Radio Artists: 2239 Yonge St, Toronto, ON M4S 2B5; tel. (416) 489-1311; 9,500 mems; Gen. Sec. GARRY NEIL.

Aluminium, Brick and Glass Workers International Union: 230 Lakeshore Rd East, Mississauga, ON L5G 1G7; tel. (416) 271-2577; 8,000 mems.

Amalgamated Clothing and Textile Workers Union: 15 Gervais Dr., Suite 601, Don Mills, ON M3C 1Y8; tel. (416) 441-1806; 30,000 mems (1989); Canadian Dir JOHN ALLERUZZO.

Amalgamated Transit Union: 15 Gervais Dr., Suite 606, Don Mills, ON M3C 1Y8; tel. (416) 445-6204; 24,000 mems; Exec. Sec. in Canada KEN FOSTER.

American Federation of Musicians of the United States and Canada: 75 Donway West, Suite 1010, Toronto, ON M3C 2E9; tel. (416) 391-5161; fax (416) 391-5165; 27,000 mems (1989); Vice-Pres. in Canada J. ALAN WOOD.

Bakery, Confectionery and Tobacco Workers International Union: 3329 Ontario St East, Montréal, PQ H1W 1P8; tel. (514) 527-9371; 15,500 mems (1989); Int. Vice-Pres. ALPHONSE DE CÉSARÉ.

Canadian Actors' Equity Association: 260 Richmond St East, 2nd Floor, Toronto, ON M5A 1P4; tel. (416) 867-9165; 3,900 mems; Pres. ANGELA FUSCO.

Canadian Brotherhood of Railway, Transport and General Workers: 2300 Carling Ave, Ottawa, ON K2B 7G1; tel. (613) 829-8764; f. 1908; 39,900 mems (1989); Pres. J. D. HUNTER.

Canadian Merchant Service Guild: 1150 Morrison Dr., Ottawa, ON K2H 8S9; tel. (613) 829-9531; 5,032 mems; Pres. Capt. MAURY J. SJOQUIST.

Canadian Paperworkers Union: 255 rue St-Jacques, Montréal, PQ H2Y 1M6; tel. (514) 842-8931; 69,000 mems (1989); Pres. JAMES M. BUCHANAN.

Canadian Postmasters' and Assistants' Association: 281 Queen Mary St, Ottawa, ON K1K 1X1; tel. (613) 745-2095; 9,220 mems; Nat. Pres. H. L. JOHNSON; Nat. Vice-Pres. E. L. BLOIS.

Canadian Union of Postal Workers: 280 Metcalfe St, 3rd Floor, Ottawa, ON K2P 1R7; tel. (613) 236-7238; telex 053-3392; fax (613) 563-7861; 46,000 mems (1989); Pres. JEAN-CLAUDE PARROT.

Canadian Union of Public Employees: 21 Florence St, Ottawa, ON K2P 0W6; tel. (613) 237-1590; telex 053-4878; 356,000 mems (1989); Nat. Pres. JEFF ROSE; Nat. Sec.-Treas. JEAN-CLAUDE LANIEL.

Communications and Electrical Workers of Canada: 350 Sparks St, Suite 307, Ottawa, ON K1R 7S8; tel. (613) 236-6083; fax (613) 236-0287; 40,000 mems (1989); Pres. FRED W. POMEROY.

Energy and Chemical Workers' Union: 9940 106th St, Suite 202, Edmonton, AB T5K 2N2; tel. (403) 422-7932; 35,000 mems (1989); Nat. Dir REGINALD C. BASKEN.

Fraternité nationale des charpentiers-menuisiers, forestiers et travailleurs d'usine: 3750 blvd Crémazie est, Bureau 310, Montréal, PQ H2A 1B6; tel. (514) 374-0952; 16,000 mems (1989); Pres. LOUIS-MARIE CLOUTIER.

Graphic Communications International Union: 1110 Finch Ave West, Suite 600, Downsview, ON M3J 2T2; tel. (416) 661-9761; 22,200 mems (1989); Int. Pres. JAMES J. NORTON; Int. Vice-Pres. LÉONARD R. PAQUETTE.

Hospital Employees' Union: 2006 West 10th Ave, Vancouver, BC V6J 4P5; 28,000 mems (1989); Prov. Pres. BILL MACDONALD.

Hotel Employees' and Restaurant Employees' International Union: 1410 rue Stanley, Bureau 500, Montréal, PQ H3A 1P8; tel. (514) 849-7511; 30,000 mems (1989); Int. Vice-Pres JAMES STAMOS (Montréal), RON BONAR (Vancouver).

International Association of Machinists and Aerospace Workers: 100 Metcalfe St, Suite 300, Ottawa, ON K1P 5M1; tel. (613) 236-9761; 58,483 mems (1989); Gen. Vice-Pres. VALÉRIE E. BOURGEOIS.

International Ladies'-Garment Workers' Union: 9275 Clark St, Suite 200, Montréal, PQ H2N 2K3; tel. (514) 381-4692; 12,787 mems; Vice-Pres. GERALD ROY.

International Longshoremen's Association: 1451 Hollis St., Halifax, NS B3J 1V1; 10,000 mems; Vice-Pres. DAVID QUINN.

International Woodworkers Association of Canada (IWA Canada): 1285 West Pender St, Suite 500, Vancouver, BC V6E 4B2; tel. (604) 683-1117; fax (604) 688-6416; f. 1937; 50,000 mems (1989); Pres. J. J. MUNRO.

Letter Carriers' Union of Canada: 43 Auriga Dr., Ottawa, ON K2E 7V3; tel. (613) 723-8133; 23,000 mems; Nat. Pres. BOB MCGARRY.

Maritime Fishermen's Union: 1200 Main St, POB 1418, Shediac, NS E0A 3G0; tel. (506) 532-2385; 3,000 mems; Pres. HASSE LINDBLAD.

National Automobile, Aerospace and Agricultural Implement Workers Union of Canada (CAW–Canada): 205 Placer Ct, North York, Willowdale, ON M2H 3H9; tel. (416) 497-4110; telex 069-86509; fax (416) 495-6559; 160,410 mems (1989); Pres. ROBERT WHITE; Sec.-Treas. BOB NICKERSON.

National Union of Provincial Government Employees: 2841 Riverside Dr., Suite 204, Ottawa, ON K1V 8N4; tel. (613) 526-1663; fax (613) 526-0477; 297,205 mems (1989); Pres. JOHN L. FRYER; Sec.-Treas. LARRY BROWN.

The Newspaper Guild: 1755 Courtwood Cres., Suite 202B, Ottawa, ON K2C 3J2; tel. (613) 727-0990; 5,150 mems; Canadian Dir WILLIAM H. MCLEMAN.

Office and Professional Employees' International Union: 1290 rue St-Denis, 5th Floor, Montréal, PQ H6X 3J7; tel. (514) 288-6511; 30,000 mems (1989); Canadian Dir and Int. Vice-Pres. ANNE HARVEY.

Printing, Publishing and Media Workers' Sector of CWA: 288 Dalhousie St, Suite B, Ottawa, ON K1N 7E6; 9,462 mems.

Public Service Alliance of Canada: 233 Gilmour St, Ottawa, ON K2P 0P1; tel. (613) 560-4200; telex 053-3724; fax (613) 563-3492; f. 1966; 171,966 mems (1989); Pres. DARYL T. BEAN.

Retail, Wholesale and Department Store Union: 15 Gervais Dr., Suite 310, Don Mills, ON M3C 1Y8; tel. (416) 441-1414; 25,862 mems (1989); Canadian Dir D. G. COLLINS.

Service Employees' International Union: 1 Credit Union Dr., Toronto, ON M4A 2S6; tel. (416) 752-4073; 75,000 mems (1989); Vice-Pres S. E. ROSCOE, LOUIS DUVAL.

Telecommunications Workers' Union: 111 Victoria Dr., Vancouver, BC V5H 4A6; tel. (604) 254-8601; 11,148 mems; Canadian Vice-Pres. JOHN FITZPATRICK.

Transportation–Communications International Union: 130 Albert St, Suite 1700, Ottawa, ON K1P 5G4; tel. (613) 234-5811; 18,000 mems; Canadian Dir FRANK MAZUR.

United Electrical, Radio and Machine Workers of Canada: 10 Codeco Ct., Don Mills, ON M3A 1A2; tel. (416) 447-5196; 12,000 mems; Pres. DICK BARRY.

United Fishermen and Allied Workers' Union: 111 Victoria Dr., Suite 160, Vancouver, BC V5L 4C4; tel. (604) 253-1336; 6,292 mems; Pres. JACK NICHOL.

United Food and Commercial Workers' International Union: 61 International Blvd, Suite 300, Rexdale, ON M9W 6K4; tel. (416) 675-1104; fax (416) 675-6919; f. 1979; 170,000 mems (1989); Canadian Dir CLIFFORD EVANS.

United Paperworkers' International Union: 63 Yawkey Ave, POB 634, Marathon, ON P0T 2E0; Canadian Rep. GARY TALARICO.

United Steelworkers of America: 234 Eglinton Ave East, 7th Floor, Toronto, ON M4P 1K7; tel. (416) 487-1571; 160,000 mems (1989); Dir E. GÉRARD DOCQUIER.

United Transportation Union: 99 Bank St, Suite 709, Ottawa, ON K1P 6B9; tel. (613) 238-3717; 12,830 mems; Canadian Vice-Pres. REAL J. PROULX.

Other Central Congresses

Canadian Federation of Labour: 107 Sparks St, Suite 300, Ottawa, ON K1P 5B5; tel. (613) 234-4141; f. 1982; 13 affiliated unions representing 213,901 mems (1989); Pres. JAMES A. MCCAMBLY.

Affiliated unions include:

Canadian Association of Professional Radio Operators: 309 Cooper St, Suite 502, Ottawa, ON K2P 0G5; tel. (613) 230-6968; 1,200 mems; Nat. Pres. ROGER SWICKIS.

International Association of Heat and Frost Insulators, and Asbestos Workers: 3585 rue Diane, Terrebone, PQ J6W 5C9; tel. (514) 433-2926; 3,400 mems; Vice-Pres. ANDRE CHARTRAND.

International Brotherhood of Boilermakers, Iron-Ship Builders, Blacksmiths, Forgers and Helpers: 1215 Sandcove Rd, Suite 139, POB 3279, Saint John, NB E2M 4X8; tel. (506) 634-8203; 68,500 mems; Int. Vice-Pres. ALEXANDER MACDONALD.

International Brotherhood of Electrical Workers: 45 Sheppard Ave East, Suite 401, Willowdale, ON M2N 5Y1; tel. (416) 226-5155; 64,480 mems (1989); Int. Vice-Pres. KEN J. WOOD.

International Brotherhood of Painters and Allied Trades: 1815 Yonge St, Toronto, ON M4T 2A3; tel. (416) 759-6561; 16,250 mems (1989); Gen. Vice-Pres. ARMANDO COLA FRANCESCHI.

International Union of Bricklayers and Allied Operators: 161 Markwood Dr., Kitchener, ON N2M 2H3; tel. (519) 576-4610; 12,000 mems; Pres. BRIAN STRICKLAND.

International Union of Operating Engineers: 17704 103rd Ave, Suite 105, Edmonton, AB T5S 1J9; tel. (403) 483-0421; fax (403) 486-0816; 36,000 mems (1989); Canadian Dir and Gen. Vice-Pres. N. BUDD COUTTS.

Sheet Metal Workers' International Association: 4445 Calgary Trail South, Edmonton, AB T6H 5R7; tel. (403) 438-5475; fax (403) 436-0674; 16,000 mems; Dir, Canadian Affairs RAYMOND GALL.

United Association of Journeymen and Apprentices of the Plumbing and Pipe Fitting Industry of the United States and Canada: 310 Broadway Ave, Suite 702, Winnipeg, MB R3C 0S6; tel. (204) 942-0836; 40,000 mems (1989); Vice-Pres. and Dir, Canadian Affairs RUSS ST ELOI.

Centrale de l'enseignement du Québec: 1415 rue Jarry est, Montréal, PQ H2E 1A7; tel. (514) 374-6660; f. 1974; 102,314 mems (1989); Pres. LORRAINE PAGÉ; Dir-Gen. MICHEL AGNAIEFF.

Affiliated unions include:

Fédération des enseignantes et des commissions scolaires: 2336 rue Sainte-Foy, CP 5800, Québec, PQ G1V 4E5; tel. (418) 658-5711; 75,000 mems: Pres. LUC SAVARD.

Centrale des syndicats démocratiques: 1259 rue Berri, Bureau 600, Montréal, PQ H2L 4C7; tel. (514) 842-3801; f. 1972; 3 federated and 262 non-federated unions representing 65,713 mems (1989); Pres. CLAUDE GINGRAS.

Affiliated federated unions:

Fédération canadienne des travailleurs du textiles inc.

Federation démocratique de la métallurgie, des mines et des produits chimiques.

Fédération nationale des travailleurs de d'industrie du vêtement inc.

Confederation of Canadian Unions: 1331½A St Clair Ave West, Toronto, ON M6E 1C3; tel. (416) 651-5627; f. 1969; 14 affiliated unions representing 32,420 mems (1989); Pres. JESS SUCCAMORE.

Affiliated unions:

Atlantic Oilworkers.

Bricklayers, Masons Independent Union of Canada.

Canadian Association of Communications and Allied Workers.

Canadian Association of Industrial, Mechanical and Allied Workers.

Canadian Association of Smelter and Allied Workers.

Canadian Overseas Telecommunications Union.

Canadian Textile and Chemical Union.

Canadian Union of Transportation Employees.

Independent Canadian Transit Union.

Pulp, Paper and Woodworkers' Employees.

Sudbury Mine, Mill and Smelter Workers' Union.

Union of Rail Canada Traffic Controllers.

United Oil Workers of Canada.

York University Staff Association.

Confédération des syndicats nationaux: 1601 ave de Lorimier, Montréal, PQ H2K 4M5; tel. (514) 598-2231; f. 1921; 8 federated and 2 non-federated unions representing 211,810 mems (1989).

Affiliated unions with over 15,000 mems:

Fédération des affaires sociales inc: 1601 ave de Lorimier, Montréal, PQ H2K 4M5; tel. (514) 598-2210; 94,675 mems (1989); Pres. CATHERINE LOUMÈDE.

Fédération du commerce-inc: 1601 ave de Lorimier, Bureau 122, Montréal, PQ H2K 4M5; tel. (514) 598-2181; 24,500 mems (1989); Pres. LISE POULIN.

Fédération des employées et employés de services publics inc: 1601 ave de Lorimier, Montréal, PQ H2K 4M5; tel. (514) 598-2231; 27,177 mems (1989); Pres. FRANCINE CHAPUT.

Fédération de la métallurgie: 1601 ave de Lorimier, Montréal, PQ H2K 4M5; tel. (514) 598-2136; 19,000 mems (1989); Pres. BENOÎT CAPISTRAN.

Fédération des travailleurs du papier et de la forêt: 155 blvd Charest est, Québec, PQ G1K 3G6; tel. (418) 647-5775; 15,500 mems (1989); Pres. CLAUDE PLAMONDON.

Other affiliated unions:

Fédération nationale des communications.

Fédération nationale des enseignants et enseignantes du Québec.

Fédération nationale des syndicats du bâtiment et du bois.

Fédération des professionels, professionelles salariés et cadres du Québec.

The American Federation of Labor and Congress of Industrial Organizations (AFL–CIO), with headquarters in Washington, DC, USA, represented 230,360 members, or 5.8% of the total union membership in Canada, at the beginning of 1989. Affiliated unions with over 15,000 members:

International Association of Bridge, Structural and Ornamental Iron Workers: 284 King St West, Suite 501, Toronto, ON M5V 1J1; tel. (416) 593-7155; 19,940 mems (1989); Gen. Vice-Pres. DONALD W. O'REILLY.

International Brotherhood of Teamsters, Chauffeurs, Warehousemen and Helpers of America: 8000 blvd Langelier, Suite 404, St-Léonard, PQ H1P 3K2; tel. (514) 374; 100,000 mems (1989); Int. Dir LOUIS LACROIX.

Labourers' International Union of North America: 1177 Belanger Ave, Suite 101, Ottawa, ON K1H 8N7; tel. (613) 738-3184; 48,420 mems (1989); Dir NELLO SCIPIONI.

United Brotherhood of Carpenters and Joiners of America: 5799 Yonge St, Suite 807, Willowdale, ON M2M 3V3; tel. (416) 225-8885; fax (416) 225-5390; 62,000 mems (1989); Officials in Canada EDWARD RYAN, PATRICK MATTEI.

Other affiliated unions:

International Union of Allied Novelty and Production Workers.

United Telegraph Workers—CWA.

Canadian National Federation of Independent Unions: 331 Major St, Welland, ON L3B 3T7; tel. (416) 735-0531; Pres. VINCE VOCAL.

Principal Unaffiliated Unions

Alberta Teachers' Association: 11010 142nd St, Edmonton, AB T5N 2R1; tel. (403) 453-2411; fax (403) 455-6481; 40,224 mems (1989); Pres. BRENDAN D. DUNPHY.

Association of Postal Officials of Canada: 28 Concourse Gate, Suite 201, Nepean, ON K2E 7T7; tel. (613) 727-1310; 4,100 mems; Nat. Sec.-Treas. M. TADDEO.

British Columbia Nurses' Union: 100-4259 Canada Way, Burnaby, BC V5G 1H1; tel. (604) 433-2268; 20,039 mems (1989); Pres. PAT SAVAGE.

British Columbia Teachers' Federation: 2235 Burrard St, Vancouver, BC V6J 3H9; tel. (604) 731-8121; fax (604) 731-4891; 32,456 mems (1989); Pres. KEN NOVAKOWSKI.

Canadian Air Line Pilots' Association: 1300 Steeles Ave East, Brampton, ON L6T 1A2; tel. (416) 453-8210; telex 069-7725; fax (416) 453-8757; 3,384 mems; Exec. Admin. PHILIP BRADY.

Canadian Air Traffic Control Association: 400 Cumberland St, Ottawa, ON K1N 8X3; tel. (613) 232-9413; 2,000 mems; Man. Dir H. J. BRENNAN.

Canadian Nurses' Association: 50 The Driveway, Ottawa, ON K2P 1E2; tel. (613) 237-2133; fax (613) 237-3520; 135,000 mems; Exec. Dir GINETTE RODGER.

Canadian Teachers' Federation: 110 Argyle Ave, Ottawa, ON K2P 1B4; tel. (613) 232-1505; telex 053-4459; fax (613) 232-1886; Sec.-Gen. Dr STIRLING MCDOWELL.

Canadian Telephone Employees' Association: pl. du Canada, Bureau 360, Montréal, PQ H3B 2N2; tel. (514) 861-9963; 18,000 mems (1989); Pres. ELISABETH H. ROUSSEAU.

Fédération des infirmières et d'infirmiers du Québec: 1425 blvd René Lévesque ouest, 5e étage, Montréal, PQ H3G 1T7; tel. (514) 861-8328; fax (514) 861-9015; 41,529 mems (1989); Pres. DIANE LAVALLÉE.

Fédération des syndicats professionels d'infirmières et d'infirmiers du Québec: 175 rue St-Jean, 4e étage, Québec, PQ G1R 1N4; tel. (418) 647-1102; fax (418) 647-5985; 18,000 mems; Pres. HÉLÈNE PELLETIER.

Federation of Women Teachers' Associations of Ontario: 1260 Bay St, Toronto, ON M5R 2B8; tel. (416) 925-1232; fax (416) 964-9512; 29,000 mems (1989); Pres. HELEN PENFOLD.

Fishermen, Food and Allied Workers' Union: Bond Bldg, 53 Bond St, POB 10, St John's, NF A1C 5H5; 23,000 mems (1988); Pres. RICHARD CASHIN.

International Brotherhood of Locomotive Engineers: 77 Metcalfe St, Suite 704, Ottawa, ON K1P 5L6; tel. (613) 235-1828; fax (613) 235-1069; 4,997 mems in 86 divisions; Canadian Dir S. A. WARNER.

National Federation of Nurses' Unions: 275 Slater St, Suite 405, Ottawa, ON K1P 5H9; tel. (204) 233-1018; 24,000 mems; Pres. KATHLEEN CONNORS.

Ontario English Catholic Teachers' Association:. 65 St Clair Ave East, Suite 400, Toronto, ON M4T 2Y8; tel. (416) 925-2493; fax (416) 925-7764; 29,000 mems (1989); Pres. EILEEN LENNON.

Ontario Nurses' Association: 85 Grenville St, Suite 600, Toronto, ON M5B 2E7; tel. (416) 964-8833; 46,680 mems (1989); Pres. PAT BETHUNE.

Ontario Public-School Teachers' Federation: 1260 Bay St, Toronto, ON M5R 2B7; tel. (416) 928-1128; 22,000 mems (1989); Pres. BILL MARTIN.

Ontario Secondary-School Teachers' Federation: 60 Mobile Dr., Toronto, ON M4A 2P3; tel. (416) 751-8300; 35,722 mems (1989); Pres. JIM HEAD.

Professional Employees' Association: 1001 Wharf St, Suite 201, Victoria, BC V8W 1T6; tel. (604) 385-8791; 1,270 mems; Exec. Dir GEOFF HOLTER.

Professional Employees' Association of Foreign Service Officers: 45 Rideau St, Suite 600, Ottawa, ON K1N 5W8; tel. (613) 234-1391; 1,300 mems.

Professional Institute of the Public Service of Canada: 53 Auriga Dr., Nepean, ON K2E 8C3; tel. (613) 228-6310; fax (613) 237-4754; 21,000 mems (1989); Pres. IRIS CRAIG.

Retail Wholesale Union: 4371 Fraser St, Vancouver, BC V5V 4G4; tel. (604) 879-2996; 2,300 mems; Pres. DARRELL CRAIG.

Syndicat des fonctionnaires provinciaux du Québec: 214 ave St-Sacrement, Bureau 200, Québec, PQ G1N 4N9; tel. (418) 687-3343; 40,000 mems (1989); Pres. JEAN-LOUIS HARGUINDEGUY.

Textile Processors, Service Trades, Health Care, Professional and Technical Employees' International Union: 34 Madison Ave, Toronto, ON M5R 3N6; tel. (416) 960-5523; 5,000 mems; Int. Vice-Pres. T. W. CORRIGAN.

EXTERNAL TRADE

Principal Commodities

(C $ million, customs basis. Source: Statistics Canada.)

Imports

	1986	1987	1988
Live animals	158.7	162.1	118.2
Food, feed, beverages and tobacco	6,542.6	6,629.0	7,109.2
Meat and fish	1,063.9	1,233.8	1,281.5
Meat, fresh, chilled or frozen	412.9	493.4	554.0
Fish and marine animals	612.7	691.0	692.0
Fruits and vegetables	2,373.4	2,501.1	2,635.9
Fresh fruits and berries	954.0	976.4	1,033.8
Other fruits and fruit preparations	472.2	516.3	561.2
Vegetables and vegetable preparations	795.5	860.1	902.1
Other food, feed, beverages and tobacco	3,105.4	2,894.1	3,101.9
Coffee	648.9	461.8	432.2
Crude materials, inedible	7,265.0	7,404.4	7,425.7
Metal ores, concentrates and scrap	1,956.8	1,643.6	1,922.0
Aluminium ores, concentrates and scrap	519.2	550.7	632.8
Other crude materials, inedible	5,308.2	5,760.9	5,503.7
Coal	744.0	724.9	728.9
Crude petroleum	2,884.6	3,179.4	2,828.8
Fabricated materials, inedible	19,981.9	20,856.3	24,687.2
Wood and paper	1,743.0	1,974.9	2,264.6
Paper and paperboard	924.6	1,015.1	1,196.9
Textiles	2,104.6	2,261.3	2,150.2
Chemicals	5,840.7	6,228.1	7,169.6
Inorganic chemicals	523.8	524.1	696.9

Imports—*continued*

	1986	1987	1988
Organic chemicals	1,616.5	1,679.8	1,920.6
Plastics materials, not shaped	973.6	1,098.7	1,350.5
Iron and steel	1,840.0	2,076.1	3,030.8
Plate, sheet and strip, steel	721.5	774.1	1,033.6
Pipes and tubes, iron and steel	288.5	311.1	573.4
Non-ferrous metals	3,073.7	2,485.7	2,911.4
Aluminium, including alloys	765.4	868.8	1,212.5
Precious metals, including alloys	1,869.9	1,138.9	1,071.9
Other fabricated materials, inedible	5,379.9	5,830.1	7,160.6
Fuel oil	733.9	721.9	652.3
Bolts, nuts and screws	330.3	324.2	497.1
Valves	259.2	255.1	587.1
End products, inedible	76,819.9	79,194.8	89,114.1
General-purpose machinery	3,401.5	3,481.2	4,766.6
Electric generators and motors	403.1	375.8	521.5
Special industry machinery	5,782.8	6,146.9	5,568.1
Machine tools, metalworking	702.3	675.5	597.1
Agricultural machinery and tractors	1,727.3	1,657.6	1,677.3
Wheel tractors, new	511.8	449.4	261.6
Tractor engines and tractor parts	307.8	294.8	593.4
Transportation equipment	38,067.7	37,620.1	40,213.0
Passenger automobiles and chassis	12,061.7	12,346.2	12,215.0

(*continued*)

PRINCIPAL COMMODITIES—Imports—*(continued)*

	1986	1987	1988
Trucks, truck tractors and chassis	2,947.2	3,292.9	2,909.7
Motor-vehicle engines	2,486.7	2,114.1	2,610.2
Motor-vehicle engine parts	811.4	890.2	1,135.0
Motor-vehicle parts, except engines	14,652.2	13,952.0	14,257.0
Aircraft, complete with engines	1,117.4	750.6	2,425.0
Aircraft engines and parts	695.8	734.6	839.8
Aircraft parts, except engines	1,197.7	1,274.2	1,177.0
Other equipment and tools	16,781.2	18,497.2	22,996.5
Televisions, radio sets and phonographs	916.3	878.6	988.1
Electronic tubes and semiconductors	1,351.5	1,731.4	2,063.3
Air-conditioning and refrigeration equipment	440.1	540.9	1,119.3
Switchgear and protective equipment	176.0	184.5	553.7
Auxiliary electrical equipment for engines	570.7	660.5	751.6
Medical and related equipment	478.8	500.9	539.9
Furniture and fixtures	543.7	630.2	923.1
Hand tools and cutlery	506.9	530.0	650.9
Electronic computers	4,193.7	5,093.2	5,737.3
Other end products, inedible	11,059.4	11,791.7	12,892.7
Outerwear, except knitted	1,053.8	1,151.5	1,171.3
Outerwear, knitted	697.6	786.8	747.0
Other apparel and apparel accessories	442.5	474.4	522.5
Footwear	665.4	713.7	729.0
Games, toys and children's vehicles	373.1	456.8	513.5
Medicinal and pharmaceutical products, in dosage	447.1	504.8	556.7
Medical, opthalmic and orthopaedic supplies	672.5	742.8	700.4
Newspapers, magazines and periodicals	466.8	488.2	541.2
Books and pamphlets	611.7	586.7	782.1
Containers and closures	485.3	485.9	566.4
Special transactions, trade	1,743.3	1,992.1	2,717.4
Total	112,511.4	116,238.6	131,081.8

Exports (excludes re-exports)

	1986	1987	1988
Live animals	348.6	366.0	618.9
Food, feed, beverages and tobacco	9,531.3	10,243.0	11,110.4
Meat and fish	3,405.1	3,812.0	3,616.3
Meat, fresh, chilled or frozen	939.4	1,003.2	833.0
Fish, whole or dressed, fresh or frozen	513.0	474.5	536.0
Fish, fillets and blocks, fresh or frozen	749.6	906.3	725.6
Cereals and preparations	3,870.1	4,131.2	5,197.5
Barley	568.4	448.2	282.0
Wheat	2,835.8	3,224.0	4,432.4
Other food, feed, beverages and tobacco	2,256.1	2,299.9	2,296.6
Crude materials, inedible	15,390.0	16,800.9	17,062.0
Metal ores, concentrates and scrap	3,492.3	3,920.5	4,135.1
Iron ores and concentrates	1,107.8	986.4	968.0
Copper in ores, concentrates and scrap	594.0	720.5	935.9
Nickel in ores, concentrates and scrap	476.4	510.5	569.7

Exports (excludes re-exports)—*continued*

	1986	1987	1988
Other crude materials, inedible	11,897.7	12,880.4	12,926.8
Rapeseed (canola)	422.3	490.6	607.4
Crude petroleum	3,774.6	4,855.1	4,065.1
Natural gas	2,524.0	2,527.3	2,885.9
Coal and other crude bituminous substances	1,851.0	1,670.0	1,941.0
Sulphur	1,109.0	885.2	866.1
Fabricated materials, inedible	38,442.9	41,820.9	47,712.7
Wood and paper	17,291.5	20,383.0	21,628.0
Lumber, softwood	4,892.7	5,745.0	5,237.7
Wood pulp and similar pulp	4,072.1	5,473.0	6,453.5
Newsprint paper	5,660.9	6,028.6	7,287.4
Other paper for printing	620.6	868.9	283.4
Textiles	356.4	424.7	524.7
Chemicals	5,518.6	6,136.3	7,662.6
Inorganic chemicals	1,466.6	1,421.3	1,642.0
Organic chemicals	1,148.2	1,361.1	1,868.3
Fertilizers and fertilizer material	1,161.6	1,269.7	1,663.3
Synthetic rubber and plastic materials	878.5	1,135.5	1,557.3
Plastics basic shapes and forms	454.9	502.0	468.9
Iron and steel	2,415.5	2,668.0	2,415.5
Plate, sheet and strip, steel	801.5	987.7	865.7
Non-ferrous metals	7,369.6	6,423.1	8,980.3
Aluminium, including alloys	2,339.0	2,751.7	3,487.6
Copper and alloys	733.3	811.9	990.2
Nickel and alloys	558.6	664.5	750.5
Precious metals, including alloys	3,113.0	1,516.4	2,705.3
Zinc, including alloys	442.5	484.4	762.0
Other fabricated materials, inedible	5,491.4	5,785.9	6,501.7
Petroleum and coal products	2,086.4	2,200.3	2,327.4
Metal fabricated basic products	947.7	1,012.1	1,729.4
Electricity	1,086.1	1,199.8	910.2
End products, inedible	52,703.5	51,903.0	57,046.3
Industrial machinery	3,455.0	3,459.1	3,752.9
Materials-handling machinery and equipment	450.9	518.7	317.8
Drilling, excavating and mining machinery	620.6	508.9	724.4
Agricultural machinery and tractors	465.1	551.2	703.8
Transportation equipment	38,025.1	35,996.7	39,156.8
Passenger automobiles and chassis	17,615.5	14,092.2	16,972.3
Trucks, truck tractors and chassis	5,084.6	6,009.7	7,206.1
Other motor vehicles	426.2	437.0	681.9
Motor-vehicle engines and parts	1,795.4	1,923.5	2,324.5
Motor-vehicle parts, except engines	9,291.1	9,611.7	8,180.4
Aircraft complete with engines	382.4	351.7	570.9
Aircraft, engines and parts	720.7	838.6	887.5
Aircraft parts, except engines	1,282.5	1,349.5	1,133.6
Other equipment and tools	4,273.7	5,007.5	6,255.3
Electric lighting and distribution equipment	445.0	434.6	681.5
Office machines and equipment	1,456.7	2,031.3	2,473.2
Other end products, inedible	6,484.5	6,888.4	7,177.4
Printed matter	598.4	598.5	583.2
Photographic goods	344.6	461.6	501.6
Containers and closures	405.4	435.7	572.3
Special transactions, trade	317.2	328.5	646.8
Total	116,733.4	121,462.3	134.197.1

Principal Trading Partners

(C $ million, customs basis. Source: Statistics Canada.)

Imports

	1986	1987	1988
Australia	505.4	564.1	662.6
Austria	212.9	247.5	282.6
Belgium and Luxembourg	608.5	619.0	610.2
Brazil	821.5	850.5	1,180.9
China, People's Repub.	566.1	770.9	955.4
Denmark	233.6	249.0	259.3
Finland	254.0	287.8	342.9
France	1,586.1	1,488.7	2,857.1
Germany, Fed. Repub.	3,453.4	3,534.5	3,836.8
Hong Kong	1,041.5	1,137.6	1,154.8
Ireland	244.8	199.7	213.9
Italy	1,671.4	1,702.8	1,948.6
Japan	7,632.2	7,750.7	9,253.5
Korea, Repub.	1,749.4	1,844.0	2,272.0
Malaysia	150.2	187.3	323.9
Mexico	1,176.5	1,169.6	1,319.8
Netherlands	694.8	750.2	774.6
New Zealand	174.8	199.7	225.0
Nigeria	368.2	251.5	310.5
Norway	168.0	256.8	494.0
Puerto Rico	195.1	226.9	246.7
Singapore	210.0	261.9	466.9
Spain	441.4	485.2	708.2
Sweden	788.3	883.7	932.5
Switzerland	591.5	586.8	701.3
Taiwan	1,744.8	2,023.0	2,258.3
Thailand	150.3	200.8	343.5
United Kingdom	3,735.7	4,339.2	4,632.0
USA	77,123.0	79,069.3	86,449.1
Venezuela	523.9	551.2	463.3
Total (incl. others)	112,511.4	116,238.6	131,554.0

Exports (excludes re-exports)

	1986	1987	1988
Algeria	193.5	200.7	286.6
Australia	624.1	689.1	842.1
Belgium and Luxembourg	823.1	1,137.2	1,151.6
Brazil	656.0	636.8	508.8
China, People's Repub.	1,119.0	1,432.1	2,593.1
Colombia	160.7	224.3	179.8
Cuba	364.5	272.9	225.0
France	965.1	1,037.4	1,173.8
Germany, Fed. Repub.	1,255.1	1,515.2	1,711.4
Hong Kong	319.1	480.1	986.5
India	352.4	271.0	393.1
Indonesia	252.0	305.1	298.7
Italy	694.6	842.8	995.1
Japan	5,942.0	7,036.2	8,679.5
Korea, Repub.	968.0	1,167.4	1,200.2
Mexico	397.4	522.0	486.6
Morocco	154.6	203.6	277.9
Netherlands	978.1	1,021.0	1,391.3
Norway	310.4	310.1	480.4
Puerto Rico	202.4	233.6	244.6
Saudi Arabia	212.0	267.9	202.5
Spain	133.4	212.5	237.5
Sweden	212.3	248.5	301.3
Switzerland	335.1	402.5	682.2
Taiwan	611.4	757.0	967.4
Turkey	201.8	266.1	181.0
USSR	1,215.6	800.6	1,141.9
United Kingdom	2,565.6	2,849.9	3,448.4
USA	90,319.2	91,756.4	97,841.6
Venezuela	323.2	336.7	375.3
Total (incl. others)	116,733.4	121,462.3	134,075.1

External Trade Organizations

Association for the Export of Canadian Books: 1 Nicholas St, Suite 1101, Ottawa, ON K1N 7B7; tel. (613) 233-2553; telex 053-3956; f. 1972; Exec. Dir CLAUDE ST-PIERRE.

Automobile Importers of Canada: World Trade Centre, 60 Harbour St, Toronto, ON M5J 1B7; tel. (416) 862-0002; telex 065-24115; f. 1972; 18 corporate mems; Exec. Dir PETER J. DAWES.

Canadian Association of Fish Exporters: 77 Metcalfe St, Suite 200, Ottawa, ON K1P 5L6; tel. (613) 232-6325; fax (613) 238-3542; f. 1978; 50 mems; Pres. (vacant).

Canadian Association of Regulated Importers: 1673 Cyrville Rd, Suite 202, Gloucester, ON K1B 3L7; tel. (613) 746-7928; fax (613) 745-4097; f. 1986; 40 mems; Exec. Sec. ROBERT G. DE VALK.

Canadian Exporters' Association: 99 Bank St, Suite 250, Ottawa, ON K1P 6B9; tel. (613) 238-8888; telex 053-4888; fax (613) 563-9218; f. 1943; fmrly known as Canadian Export Asscn; 600 mems; 7 chapters nation-wide; Pres. L. JAMES TAYLOR.

Canadian Importers' Association Inc: 210 Dundas St West, Suite 700, Toronto, ON M5G 2E8; tel. (416) 595-5333; telex 065-24115; fax (416) 595-8226; f. 1932; 650 mems; Pres. D. R. MCARTHUR; CEO PETER J. DAWES.

Canadian Toy Importers' Association: 32 Carluke Cres., Suite 510, Willowdale, ON M2L 2J3; tel. (416) 225-4419; f. 1950; 50 mems; Sec. GEORGE H. YOUNG.

Federation of Export Clubs Canada: 67 Yonge St, Suite 1402, Toronto, ON M5E 1J8; tel. (416) 4112; telex 065-28048.

Newfoundland and Labrador Capelin Exporters' Association: 31 Pippy Pl., St John's, NF A1B 3X2; tel. (709) 579-0508; fax (709) 738-1353.

Foreign Chambers of Commerce in Canada

ASEAN–Canada Business Council: 55 Metcalfe St, Suite 1160, Ottawa, ON K1P 6N4; tel. (613) 238-4000; telex 053-3360; fax (613) 238-7643; f. 1986; 800 mems; Deputy Sec.-Gen. HEATHER GIBB.

Asia Pacific Foundation of Canada: 999 Canada Pl., Suite 666, Vancouver, BC V6C 3E1; tel. (604) 684-5986; fax (604) 681-1370.

Brazil–Canada Chamber of Commerce: 100 Adelaide St West, Suite 910, Toronto, ON M5H 1S3; tel. (416) 364-4634; telex 062-18330.

British–Canadian Trade Association: 7050 Woodbine Ave, Suite 206, Markham, ON L3R 4G8; tel. (416) 475-3896; f. 1951; 175 mems; Pres. JOHN SELTZER.

Canada–Arab Business Council: 55 Metcalfe St, Suite 1160, Ottawa, ON K1P 6N4; tel. (613) 238-4000; telex 053-3360; fax (613) 238-7643; f. 1983; 34 mem. cos; Exec. Dir PETER EGYED.

Canada–China Trade Council: 133 Richmond St West, Suite 310, Toronto, ON M5H 2L3; tel. (416) 364-8321; telex 062-17598; fax (416) 364-7894; f. 1978; 120 mems; Exec. Dir DAVE BRUCE.

Canada–India Business Council: 55 Metcalfe St, Suite 1160, Ottawa, ON K1P 6N4; tel. (613) 238-4000; telex 053-3360; fax (613) 238-7643; f. 1982; 60 mems; Exec. Dir PETER EGYED.

Canada–Israel Chamber of Commerce and Industry: 76 St Clair Ave West, Suite 600, Toronto, ON M4V 1N2; tel. (416) 961-7302; f. 1961; 240 mems; Exec. Dir NICHOLAS SIMMONDS.

Canada–Japan Trade Council: 75 Albert St, Suite 903, Ottawa, ON K1P 5E7; tel. (613) 233-4047; Pres. J. E. STRUTHERS.

Canada–Korea Business Council: 55 Metcalfe St, Suite 1160, Ottawa, ON K1P 6N4; tel. (613) 238-4000; telex 053-3360; fax (613) 238-7643; 54 mems; Chair. ROBERT FERCHAT.

Canada–Netherlands Chamber of Commerce: 300 rue St-Sacrament, Suite 304, Montréal, PQ H2Y 1X4; tel. (514) 288-4466; fax (514) 288-9183; f. 1978; 15 individual mems, 80 corporate mems; Sec.-Gen. JANNY LOWENSTEYN.

Canada–Pakistan Business Council: 55 Metcalfe St, Suite 1160, Ottawa, ON K1P 6N4; tel. (613) 238-4000; telex 053-3360; fax (613) 238-7643; f. 1987; Associate Exec. Dir PATRICE DALLAIRE.

Canada-Taiwan Business Association: 55 Metcalfe St, Suite 1160, Ottawa, ON K1P 6N4; tel. (613) 238-4000; telex 053-3360; fax (613) 238-7643; f. 1985; 500 corporate mems; Chair. SYDNEY JACKSON.

Canadian Council for the Americas: 55 Metcalfe St, Suite 1160, Ottawa, ON K1P 6N4; tel. (613) 238-4000; telex 053-3360; fax (613) 238-7643; Exec. Dir PAUL QUINNEY.

Canadian Council for Turkish Trade: 55 Metcalfe St, Suite 1160, Ottawa, ON K1P 6N4; tel. (613) 238-4000; telex 053-3360; fax (613) 238-7643; f. 1988; 48 corporate mems; Exec. Dir PATRICE DALLAIRE.

Canadian-East European Trade Council: 55 Metcalfe St, Suite 1160, Ottawa, ON K1P 6N4; tel. (613) 238-4000; telex 053-3360; fax (613) 238-7643; Exec. Dir PAUL QUINNEY.

Canadian-German Chamber of Industry and Commerce Inc: 480 University Ave, Suite 1410, Toronto, ON M5G 1V2; tel. (416) 598-3355; telex 062-3581; fax (416) 598-1840; 700 individual mems, 50 corporate mems; Exec. Dir UWE HARNACK.

Regional offices:

Edmonton: 1330 Scotia Pl., 10060 Jasper Ave, Edmonton, AB T5J 3R8; tel. (403) 420-6611; fax (403) 420-6612.

Montréal: 1010 rue Sherbrooke ouest, Bureau 1604, Montréal, PQ H3A 2R7; tel. (514) 844-3051; fax (514) 844-1473.

Hong Kong-Canada Business Association: National Bldg, 347 Bay St, Suite 1100, Toronto, ON M5H 2R7; tel. (416) 366-2642; telex 062-18056; fax (416) 366-1569; f. 1984; 2,000 corporate mems; Pres. ROBERT A. BROWN.

Hong Kong Trade Development Council: National Bldg, 347 Bay St, Suite 1100, Toronto, ON M5H 2R7; tel. (416) 366-2642; telex 062-18056; fax (416) 366-1569; f. 1966; Rep. LEE MEISTER.

Italian Chamber of Commerce, Montréal: 550 rue Sherbrooke ouest, Bureau 890, Montréal, PQ H3A 1B9; tel. (514) 844-4249; fax (514) 844-4875.

Italian Chamber of Commerce of Toronto: 901 Lawrence Ave West, Suite 306, Toronto, ON M6A 1C3; tel. (416) 789-7169.

Japan External Trade Organization: 151 Bloor St West, Suite 700, Toronto, ON M5S 1T7; tel. (416) 962-5050; fax (416) 962-1124; Exec. Dir MAMORU IWAMOTO.

Swiss-Canadian Chamber of Commerce (Montréal) Inc: 1572 ave du Docteur Penfield, Montréal, PQ H3G 1C4; tel. (514) 937-5822.

FINANCE

BANKING

(br.(s) = branches; cap. = total capital and reserves; dep. = deposits; m. = million; amounts in Canadian dollars.)

Introduction

The Bank of Canada Act of 1980 reorganized the Canadian banking structure by creating two categories of banking institution: 'Schedule A' banks, comprising the existing chartered banks; and 'Schedule B' banks, which are either subsidiaries of foreign banks (whose total Canadian assets cannot exceed 16% of those of the banking system in total), or Canadian-owned banks under private or semi-private ownership. The Act, which is subject to review at 10-year intervals to allow for changes in government policy and economic conditions, strictly limits the range of permitted operations outside the banking sphere, in order to curtail competition between banks and commercial enterprises. In September 1988 there were seven 'Schedule A' banks (of which no individual shareholder may control more than 10%) and 59 'Schedule B' banks.

In line with deregulatory trends in other leading industrial nations, recent legislation in Canada has aimed to lower the barriers between banks, brokerage houses, insurance companies and trust and loan institutions. On 2 July 1987 two bills came into force which gave authority over financial administration and legislation concerning institutions to the superintendent of financial institutions, a post created from the amalgamation of two former offices, those of the inspector-general of banks and the superintendent of insurance. The superintendent of financial institutions is responsible to the minister of finance. A committee comprising the governor of the Bank of Canada, the deputy minister of finance, the chairman of the Canada Deposit Insurance Corporation and the superintendent of financial institutions was set up in order to facilitate exchange of information on financial matters and to provide an overview of the operations of the financial-services industry. Direct regulatory inspections of the commercial banks are carried out by the superintendent of financial institutions.

CANADA DEPOSIT INSURANCE CORPORATION

The Canada Deposit Insurance Corporation was established in 1967 by the Canada Deposit Insurance Corporation Act. The Corporation insures individual deposits up to a maximum amount, currently C $60,000 per person per institution. Institutions may be banks, trust and loan companies, or provincially-incorporated institutions that accept deposits from the public. The Corporation's board has nine directors, including a chairman appointed by the Governor-in-Council. Other directors include the Governor of the Bank of Canada, the deputy minister of finance, the superintendent and a deputy superintendent of financial institutions.

The Bank of Canada

(234 Wellington St, Ottawa, ON K1A 0G9; tel. (613) 782-8111; telex 053-4241; fax (613) 782-8655)

The Bank of Canada was established as the nation's central bank in 1934 by the Bank of Canada Act, revisions to which were made in 1936, 1938, 1954, 1967, 1980 and 1987. Its principal responsibility is the control of credit through monetary action for the benefit of the smooth running of the economy. The bank is managed by a Board of Directors, comprising the governor (its chief executive officer), the senior deputy governor and 12 part-time directors. The part-time directors are appointed by the minister of finance for three-year terms and they, in turn, appoint the governor for seven-year terms. The deputy minister of finance is a non-voting member of the Board. While the Bank of Canada may operate with a considerable amount of independence, it liaises closely with the government which has ultimate responsibility for monetary policy. Capital and reserves of the Bank of Canada totalled C $30m. at December 1988, with deposits at C $2,758m.

Governor: JOHN W. CROW.

Senior Deputy Governor: GORDON G. THIESSEN.

PRINCIPAL METHODS OF MONETARY CONTROL

The principal methods by which the Bank of Canada controls monetary supply are: a) varying the amount of liquid reserves (deposits at the Bank of Canada, cash, treasury bills, day-to-day loans to investment dealers) that the chartered banks are required to maintain as a percentage of deposit liabilities; b) transferring, as fiscal agent of the federal government, government deposits to the chartered banks, adding to their cash reserves and enabling them to expand their deposit liabilities; c) selling or purchasing government securities, which has the effect of absorbing or adding to cash resources in the banking system, thereby affecting the bank's ability to lend money; and d) changing the rate at which the bank will act as lender of last resort to the money market.

Chartered Banks

The first Canadian commercial bank was founded in 1817. A further 34 banks were established over the next 50 years, and following confederation in 1867 the Bank Act of 1871 gave the federal government regulatory powers over banking operations throughout Canada. Canadian banks operate according to laws set out in the Bank Act and are chartered by the federal parliament. While the number of banks has diminished over the last century, the number of branches has increased greatly. At the end of 1987 there were 7,151 commercial bank branches, holding deposits totalling C $216,889m. The banks' combined assets totalled C $485,997m., of which 39.4% were represented by foreign-currency assets, reflecting the importance of international business in Canadian banking.

Principal Commercial Banks

(All are Schedule 'A' banks apart from Laurentian Bank of
Canada, which is a Schedule 'B' bank.)

Bank of Montréal: 129 rue St-Jacques ouest, Montréal, PQ H2Y
1L6; tel. (514) 877-7110; telex 052-67661; f. 1817; cap. 3,624m., dep.
65,054m. (July 1988); Chair. and CEO William D. Mulholland;
Pres. and COO Matthew Barrett; 1,194 brs.

Bank of Nova Scotia (Scotiabank): 44 King St West, Toronto,
ON M5H 1H1; tel. (416) 866-6161; telex 062-2106; f. 1832; cap.
3,094.1m., dep. 57,597.9m. (July 1988); Chair. and CEO C. E.
Ritchie; Dep. Chair., Pres. and COO J. A. G. Bell; 1,009 brs.

Canadian Imperial Bank of Commerce: Commerce Ct, Toronto,
ON M5L 1A2; tel. (416) 980-2211; telex 065-24116; f. 1961; cap.
4,443m., dep. 72,620m. (July 1988); Chair. and CEO R. Donald
Fullerton; 1,582 Canadian brs; 88 foreign brs.

Canadian Western Bank: 10040 104th St, Edmonton, AB T5J
3X6; tel. (403) 423-8888; telex 037-43148; f. 1987 by merger of the
Bank of Alberta and the Western and Pacific Bank of Canada;
cap. 37.7m., dep. 238.1m. (July 1988); Chair. and CEO David L.
Emerson.

Laurentian Bank of Canada: 1981 ave Collège McGill, Montréal,
PQ H3A 3K3; tel. (514) 284-3931; telex 05-24217; fax (514) 284-7519;
cap. 285.4m. (Feb. 1988); Chair. C. Claude Castonguay; Pres.
and CEO Dominic D'Alessandro.

National Bank of Canada/Banque Nationale du Canada: 600
rue de la Gauchetière ouest, Montréal, PQ H3B 4L2; tel. (514) 394-
4000; telex 052-5181; f. 1979; cap. 1,486m., dep. 24,850m. (July
1988); Pres. and CEO André Bedard; 586 brs.

Royal Bank of Canada: 1 pl. Ville-Marie, CP 6001, Montréal, PQ
H3C 3A9; tel. (514) 874-2110; telex 055-61086; f. 1869; cap. 4,921m.,
dep. 87,882.4m (July 1988); Chair. and CEO Allan Taylor; Pres.
John E. Cleghorn; 1,478 Canadian brs, 50 foreign brs.

Toronto-Dominion Bank: Toronto Dominion Centre, 55 King St
West and Bay St, POB 1, Toronto, ON M5K 1A2; tel. (416) 982-
8222; telex 065-24267; f. 1855; cap. 3,623m., dep. 47,889m. (July
1988); Chair. and CEO Richard M. Thomson; Pres. Robert W.
Korthals; 952 brs in Canada.

Savings Institutions with Provincial Charters

Province of Alberta Treasury Branches: 9925 109th St, POB
1440, Edmonton, AB T5J 2N6; tel. (403) 493-7307; telex 037-43122;
f. 1938; assets 6,153m., dep. 6,198m. (March 1988); Supt A. O.
Bray; 132 brs.

Province of Ontario Savings Office: 33 King St West, 6th Floor,
Oshawa, ON L1H 8H5; tel. (416) 433-5785; f. 1921; Exec. Dir J. S.
Purdon; Dir J. L. Allen; 21 brs.

Development Bank

Federal Business Development Bank: Tour de la Bourse, 800 pl.
Victoria, CP 335, Montréal, PQ H4Z 1L4; tel. (514) 283-5904; f.
1975; authorized cap. 512.6m. (1988); Pres. G. A. Lavigueur.

Foreign Banks in Canada
(Schedule 'B' Banks)

ABN Bank Canada (Netherlands): IBM Tower, Toronto Dominion
Centre, Suite 3402, POB 114, Toronto, ON M5K 1G8; tel. (416)
367-0850; telex 065-24016; Pres. and Gen. Man. R. Toorenvliet.

ANZ Bank Canada (New Zealand): North Tower, Suite 1880,
Royal Bank Plaza, POB 145, Toronto, M5J 2J3; tel. (416) 865-0299;
telex 217530; Gen. Man. Angelo Briganti.

Banca Commerciale Italiana of Canada (Italy): 130 Adelaide St
West, Suite 1800, POB 100, Toronto, ON M5H 3P5; tel. (416) 366-
8101; telex 06-22977; fax (416) 366-2577; f. 1975; cap. 50.9m., dep.
651.8m. (Oct. 1988); Chair. Donald E. Smith; Pres. and CEO
Alfonso F. Lanni.

Banca Nazionale del Lavoro of Canada (Italy): 95 Wellington St
West, Suite 2100, POB 23, Toronto, ON M5J 2N7; tel. (416) 365-
7777; telex 06-218880; cap. 35m., dep. 387.2m. (Oct. 1988); CEO
and Chief Gen. Man. Giovanni A. Bastreri.

Banco do Brasil SA (Brazil): Toronto Dominion Centre, Commercial Union Tower, Suite 2312, POB 244, Toronto, ON M5K 1J5;
tel. (416) 365-2375; telex 622475; rep. office.

Banco Central of Canada (Spain): 330 Bay St, Toronto, ON M5H
2S8; tel. (416) 365-7070; telex 06-218904; fax (416) 365-7850; cap.
12.7m., dep. 91.6m. (Dec. 1988); CEO Miguel Sanchez–Tovar.

Banco Nacional de México (Mexico): One First Canadian Pl.,
Suite 3430, Toronto, ON M5X 1C9; tel. (416) 368-1399; telex 06-217797; fax
(416) 367-2543; rep. office.

Bank of America Canada (USA): 4 King St West, 18th Floor,
Toronto, ON M5H 1B6; tel. (416) 863-5400; telex 6218819; f. 1981;
cap. 55.3m., dep. 86.6m. (Feb. 1988); Chair. J. C. Shelley.

Bank of Boston Canada (USA): 500 blvd René-Lévesque, Suite
1400, Montréal, PQ H2Z 1W7; tel. (514) 397-9600; telex 05-25771;
fax (514) 397-1133; f. 1982; cap. 11m., dep. 240.5m. (Oct. 1988);
Chair. Edward P. Collins; Pres. and CEO James E. Shoniker.

Bank of Credit and Commerce Canada (Luxembourg): 625 blvd
René-Lévesque ouest, Montréal, PQ H3B 1R2; tel. (514) 875-0574;
telex 055-61964; fax (514) 875-0652; f. 1980; cap. 30.4m. (Feb. 1988);
Gen. Man. S. P. Chandavarkar.

Bank Hapoalim (Canada) (Israel): One First Canadian Pl., POB
35, Toronto, ON M5X 1A9; tel. (416) 367-1710; telex 06-218586; fax
(416) 864-9061; f. 1982; cap. 12m. (Feb. 1988); Pres. and CEO
Meshulam H. Druckman.

Bank Leumi le Israel (Canada): Bank Leumi Bldg, 2nd Floor,
3055 Bathurst St, Toronto, ON M6B 3B7; tel. (416) 789-3392; telex
06-218582; f. 1982; cap. 10m., dep. 160.5m. (Oct. 1988); Chair. Dr
M. Heth; Pres. Y. Weiler.

The Bank of Tokyo Canada (Japan): South Tower, Suite 2100,
Royal Bank Plaza, POB 42, Toronto, ON M5J 2J1; tel. (416) 865-

0220; telex 065-24440; cap. 54.3m., dep. 688.1m. (Oct. 1988); Pres.
and CEO M. Hongo.

Banque Nationale de Paris (Canada) (France): BNP Tower, 1981
ave Collège McGill, Montréal, PQ H3A 2W8; tel. (514) 285-6000;
cap. 77m., dep. 1,192.5m. (Oct. 1988); Pres. and CEO F. Jonathan.

Barclays Bank of Canada (UK): Commerce Ct West, Suite 3500,
POB 377, Toronto, ON M5L 1G2; tel. (416) 862-0594; cap. 114.8m.,
dep. 1,376.5m. (Oct. 1988); Pres. and CEO G. D. Farrar.

BT Bank of Canada (USA): North Tower, Suite 1700, Royal Bank
Plaza, POB 100, Toronto, ON M5J 2J2; tel. (416) 865-0770; telex
06-217524; fax (416) 865-0779; f. 1973; cap. 15.9m., dep. 245.2m.
(Oct. 1987); Pres. and CEO Brian E. Walsh.

Chase Manhattan Bank of Canada (USA): 150 King St West,
16th Floor, POB 68, Toronto, ON M5H 1J9; tel. (416) 585-3300;
telex 06-23622; fax (416) 585-3334; f. 1982; cap. 53.6m., dep. 810.8m.
(Oct. 1988); Pres. Thomas C. MacMillan.

Chemical Bank of Canada (USA): 150 York St, 18th Floor,
Toronto, ON M5H 3S5; tel. (416) 869-0042; telex 06-218105; fax
(416) 864-0296; f. 1982; cap. 73.3m. (Feb. 1988); Pres. and CEO
P. R. Pollock.

Citibank Canada (USA): University Pl., 123 Front St West, Suite
1900, Toronto, ON M5J 2M3; tel. (416) 947-5500; cap. 117.7m., dep.
2,506.4m. (Oct. 1988); Pres. and CEO Frederick Copeland, Jr.

Crédit Commercial de France (Canada): 1155 blvd René-
Lévesque ouest, Suite 2305, Montréal, PQ H3B 2K2; tel. (514) 875-
4310; telex 055-62153; fax (514) 875-4309; f. 1981; cap. 20m., dep.
387.2m. (Oct. 1988); Chair. Olivier Lavédrine; Pres. P. J.
Freill.

Crédit Lyonnais Canada (France): 2000 Mansfield St, 18th Floor,
Montréal, PQ H3A 3A6; tel. (514) 288-4848; telex 05-25245; f. 1974;
cap. 42.5m., dep. 643.1m. (Oct. 1988); Chair. J. Giraud; Pres. J.
du Vignaud.

Crédit Suisse Canada (Switzerland): Commerce Ct West, Suite
2400, Toronto, ON M5L 1K2; tel. (416) 860-7900; telex 06-23620;
fax (416) 368-5785; cap. 70.9m., dep. 1,058.3m. (Oct. 1988); Chair.
E. Schneider; Pres. and CEO K. P. Kuebel.

Dai-Ichi Kangyo Bank (Canada) (Japan): Commerce Ct West,
Suite 3740, POB 295, Toronto, ON M5L 1H9; tel. (416) 365-9666;
telex 06-22404; fax (416) 365-7314; cap. 42.6m. (Feb. 1988); Chair.,
Pres. and CEO Hirokazu Ichikawa.

Daiwa Bank Canada (Japan): Sun Life Tower, Suite 2509, Sun
Life Centre, 150 King St West, POB 95, Toronto, ON M5H 1J9;
tel. (416) 979-7177; fax (416) 979-7176; cap. 15.1m. (Feb. 1988); Pres.
T. Makino.

Deutsche Bank Canada (Federal Republic of Germany): Exchange
Tower, Suite 3600, 2 First Canadian Pl., POB 408, Toronto, ON

M5X 1E3; tel.(416) 369-8800; telex 06-218479; fax (416) 367-3287; f. 1981; cap. 63.6m., dep. 821.6m. (Oct. 1988); Chair. HILMAR KOPPER; Pres. and CEO KLAUS LELEWEL.

Dresdner Bank Canada (Federal Republic of Germany): Exchange Tower, Suite 1700, 2 First Canadian Pl., Toronto, ON M5X 1E3; tel. (416) 369-8300; telex 065-24503; fax (416) 369-8362; f. 1981; cap. 25m., dep. 434.5m. (Oct. 1988); Chair. KURT MORGEN; Pres. Dr BERNARD BUFFO.

First Interstate Bank of Canada (USA): Exchange Tower, Suite 800, 2 First Canadian Pl., POB 429, Toronto, ON M5X 1E3; tel. (416) 865-0250; cap. 15.1m. (Feb. 1988); Chair. HAROLD J. MEYERMAN; Pres. MERRI L. JONES.

First National Bank of Chicago (USA): Exchange Tower, Suite 2300, 2 First Canadian Pl., POB 448, Toronto, ON M5X 1E4; tel. (416) 869-1863; telex 06-23118; fax (416) 869-1863; cap. 23m., dep. 116.5m. (Oct. 1988); Pres. and CEO ROBERT S. BUCKLIN.

Fuji Bank Canada (Japan): 130 Adelaide St West, Suite 3200, POB 79, Toronto, ON M5H 3R6; tel. (416) 865-1020; telex 06-22094; fax (416) 865-9618; f. 1982; cap. 26.9m., dep. 407.3m. (Oct. 1988); Chair. TAKOA OISHI; Pres. KIMIYA YAMASHITA.

Hanil Bank Canada (Republic of Korea): 60 Bloor St, Suite 1103, Toronto, ON M4W 3B8; tel. (416) 975-0456; f. 1982; cap. 8.4m., dep. 68.3m. (Oct. 1988); Pres. and CEO KWANG JIB KIM.

Hongkong Bank of Canada: 885 West Georgia St, Suite 300, Vancouver, BC V6C 3E9; tel. (604) 685-1000; telex 04-507750; fax (604) 641-1849; f. 1981; cap. 275m., dep. 4,244.1m. (Oct. 1988); Chair. JOHN R. BOND; Pres. and CEO JAMES H. CLEAVE; 61 brs.

Industrial Bank of Japan (Canada): Commerce Ct North, Suite 1200, POB 429, Toronto, ON M5L 1G3; tel. (416) 365-9550; telex 06-219881; fax (416) 367-3452; f. 1982; cap. 30m., dep. 392.9m.; Chair. KANEO NAKAMURA; Pres. NAOTAKE SUZUKI.

International Commercial Bank of Cathay (Canada) (Taiwan): 150 York St, 9th Floor, Toronto, ON M5H 3S5; tel. (416) 947-2800; telex 06-218002; f. 1982; cap. 10.5m., dep. 60m. (Oct. 1988); Chair. C. D. WANG; Pres. and Chief Gen. Man. PAUL CHIA.

Irving Bank Canada (USA): Sun Life Centre, 150 King St West, Suite 707, POB 54, Toronto, ON M5H 1J9; tel. (416) 974-9575; telex 06-23208; fax (416) 974-9901; f. 1981; cap. 21.1m. (Feb. 1988); Pres. and CEO STEPHEN E. PECK.

Israel Discount Bank of Canada: 150 Bloor St West, Suite M100, Toronto, ON M5S 2Y5; tel. (416) 926-7200; telex 06-218920; f. 1982; cap. 10m., dep. 81.9m. (Oct. 1988); CEO and Chief Gen. Man. A. TUVAL.

Korea Exchange Bank of Canada: Exchange Tower, Suite 1140, 2 First Canadian Pl., POB 402, Toronto, ON M5X 1E3; tel. (416) 364-2890; telex 06-23274; fax (416) 364-3079; cap. 14.8m. (Feb. 1988); Pres. and CEO S. OH.

Lloyds Bank Canada (UK): 130 Adelaide St West, Toronto, ON M5H 3R2; tel. (416) 868-8000; cap. 297.9m., dep. 4,219.8m. (Oct. 1988); CEO D. DRAKE.

Manufacturers' Hanover Bank of Canada (USA): 20 Queen St West, Suite 3400, POB 37, Toronto, ON M5H 3R3; tel. (416) 593-5055; telex 06-218241; cap. 48.5m. (Feb. 1988); Pres. and CEO JOHN R. ALTENAU.

Mellon Bank Canada (USA): South Tower, Suite 2310, Royal Bank Plaza, POB 153, Toronto, ON M5J 2J4; tel. (416) 362-6051; telex 06-218291; fax (416) 367-3400; f. 1983; cap. 20m., dep. 229.7m. (Oct. 1988); Chair. FREDERICK K. BEARD; Pres. WILLIAM B. AMIS, Jr.

Midland Bank Canada (UK): Exchange Tower, 2 First Canadian Pl., POB 411, Toronto, ON M5X 1E3; tel. (416) 869-1840; cap. 55.4m. (Feb. 1988); Pres. and CEO J. H. B. NEDERPELT.

Mitsubishi Bank of Canada (Japan): Commerce Ct West, Suite 2300, POB 20, Toronto, ON M5L 1A1; tel. (416) 365-1940; telex 06-22749; fax (416) 367-3579; f. 1982; cap. 40.5m., dep. 399m. (Oct. 1988); Pres. and CEO T. NAKAYAMA.

Mitsui Bank of Canada (Japan): Exchange Tower, Suite 2531, 2 First Canadian Pl., POB 409, Toronto, ON M5X 1E3; tel. (416) 369-8531; telex 06-23400; fax (416) 369-0268; f. 1982; cap. 25.3m., dep. 370.6m. (Oct. 1988); Pres. and CEO MASAHARU ONO.

Morgan Bank of Canada (USA): Royal Bank Plaza, Bay St and Front St, Suite 2250, POB 80, Toronto, ON M5J 2J2; tel. (416) 865-0650; telex 06-23490; f. 1973; cap. 61.7m. (Feb. 1988); Pres. TOM FLEMING, Jr.

National Bank of Detroit, Canada (USA): North Tower, Suite 1601, Royal Bank Plaza, POB 112, Toronto, ON M5J 2J3; tel. (416) 865-0466; telex 06-218722; fax (416) 363-7574; cap. 24.8m., dep. 335m. (Oct. 1988); Pres. and CEO WILLIAM J. SCHMID.

National Bank of Greece (Canada): 852 Jean Talon St West, Montréal, PQ H3N 1S4; tel. (514) 273-4233; telex 05-825822; f. 1971; cap. 11.5m., dep. 177.4m.; Chair. STYLIANOS PANAGOPOULOS; CEO CONSTANTINE P. ZISSIS.

National Westminster Bank of Canada (UK): Royal Bank Plaza, Suite 2060, POB 10, Toronto, ON M5J 2J1; tel. (416) 865-0170; telex 06-22572; fax (416) 865-0934; cap. 85.1m., dep. 1,094.8m. (Oct. 1988); Chair. A. W. GILLESPIE; Pres. and CEO A. S. YANKOVICH.

Overseas Union Bank of Singapore (Canada): The Standard Life Centre, 121 King St West, 10th Floor, POB 9, Toronto, ON M5H 3T9; tel. (416) 363-8227; telex 06-218004; fax (416) 363-1671; f. 1982; cap. 10m., dep. 8.3m. (Oct. 1988); Chair. LEE HEE SENG; Pres. T. Y. KOH.

Paribas Bank of Canada (France): Exchange Tower, Suite 2520, 2 First Canadian Pl., POB 438, Toronto, ON M5X 1E5; tel. (416) 365-9600; telex 06-218612; fax (416) 947-0086; f. 1981; cap. 20m., dep. 278.2m. (Oct. 1988); Pres. and CEO GILLES ROMAN.

Republic National Bank of New York (Canada) (USA): 1981 McGill College Ave, Montréal, PQ H3A 3A7; tel. (514) 288-5551; telex 055-60059; f. 1983; cap. 24.4m., dep. 412.3m.; Pres. and CEO D. M. SCHWARTZ.

Sanwa Bank Canada (Japan): Commerce Ct West, Suite 3950, POB 427, Toronto, ON M4L 1G3; tel. (416) 366-2583; cap. 37.1m., dep. 353.2m. (Oct. 1988); Chair. TATSUO OKADA; Pres. and Gen. Man. YOSHIZOH YAMANOKUCHI.

Security Pacific Bank Canada (USA): 999 West Hastings St, Suite 600, Vancouver, BC V6C 3J5; tel. (604) 669-7325; cap. 29.2m.; Exec. Vice-Pres. A. JENNER.

Société Générale (Canada) (France): 1155 University St, Suite 1100, Montréal, PQ H3B 3A7; tel. (514) 875-0330; telex 05-27342; fax (514) 876-4215; f. 1974; cap. 73.7m., dep. 844m. (Oct. 1988); Chair. BERNARD LORAIN; Pres. and CEO BERNARD CAUSSIGNAC.

Standard Chartered Bank of Canada (UK): 55 University Ave, POB 14, Toronto, ON M5J 2H7; tel. (416) 363-8521; telex 06-22366; f. 1982; cap. 121.0m., dep. 144.2m. (Oct. 1988); Chair. RODERICK L. HENRY; Pres. PETER DOBSON.

State Bank of India (Canada): North Tower, Suite 800, Royal Bank Plaza, POB 81, Toronto, ON M5J 2J2; tel. (416) 865-0414; fax (416) 865-1735; cap. 6.2m. (Feb. 1988); Pres. S. M. SANT.

Sumitomo Bank of Canada: One First Canadian Pl., Suite 1420, POB 43, Toronto, ON M5X 1A9; tel. (416) 368-4766; cap. 14.9m. (Oct. 1988); Pres. M. UENO.

Swiss Bank Corporation (Canada): 207 Queen's Quay West, Suite 780, POB 103, Toronto, ON M5J 1A7; tel. (416) 865-0190; telex 062-17872; fax (416) 864-7505; f. 1981; cap. 79.4m., dep. 1,657.4m. (Oct. 1988); Chair. A. TOHNI; Pres. and CEO K. FREI.

Taiyo Kobe Bank (Canada) (Japan): One First Canadian Pl., Suite 1060, POB 73, Toronto, ON M5X 1B1; tel. (416) 364-0900; cap. 15.1m. (Feb. 1988); Pres. MASUMI SHIOZAWA.

Tokai Bank Canada (Japan): Sun Life Centre, 150 King St West, Suite 2401, POB 84, Toronto, ON M5H 1J9; tel. (416) 597-2210; fax (416) 591-7415; cap. 15.8m. (Oct. 1988); Pres. K. WATANABE.

Union Bank of Switzerland (Canada): Exchange Tower, Suite 1000, 2 First Canadian Pl., POB 500, Toronto, ON M5X 1E5; tel. (416) 365-2222; telex 06-219882; f. 1981; cap. 41m., dep. 979.8m. (Oct. 1988); Pres. JEAN-PIERRE SCHEIDEGGER; Chair. MATHIS CABIALLAVETTA.

United Overseas Bank (Canada) (Switzerland): 666 Burrard St, Suite 880, Vancouver, BC V6C 2X8; tel. (604) 662-7055; fax (604) 662-3356; cap. 5.9m. (Feb. 1988); Dir and Gen. Man. NG CHEE MENG.

Principal Trust and Loan Companies

(m. = million; amounts in Canadian dollars.)

Canada's first trust company was incorporated in 1872. Today there are about 80 companies in operation, with some 1,050 branches offering full services, and over 650 real-estate offices across the country. Both provincially- and federally-incorporated companies may set up offices in any province upon registration in the province. Trust companies may manage property and investments, offer current account facilities, accept savings deposits and issue Guaranteed Investment Certificates. They may also provide mortgage finance and offer trustee, executor and financial agency services, and services to companies. Total assets administered by trust companies amounted to about C $220,000m. in 1989, of which deposits accounted for about C $80,000m.

Acadia Trust Co: 798 Prince St, Truro, NS B2N 1H1; tel. (902) 895-5484; fax (902) 893-1361; Pres. C. E. STANFIELD.

Atlantic Trust Co of Canada: 1741 Barrington St, POB 2224, Halifax, NS B3J 3C4; tel. (902) 442-1701; fax (902) 423-4316; Pres. and CEO JAMES McCALLION.

Bayshore Trust Co: 825 Eglinton Ave West, 5th Floor, Toronto, ON M5N 1E7; tel. (416) 787-1787; Pres. ROBERT CHRISTOPHER.

Cabot Trust Company: 1055 Wilson Ave, Suite 402, Downsview, ON M3K 1Y9; tel. (416) 633-4400; telex 069-86766; fax (416) 633-0432; Pres. CONSIGLIO DI NINO.

Canada Trustco Mortgage Co and the Canada Trust Co: 320 Bay St, Toronto, ON M5H 2P6; tel. (416) 361-8000; fax (416) 361-8178; f. 1855; assets 67,400m. (1988); Chair. and CEO MERV L. LAHN.

Canwest Trust Co: 1195 West Broadway, Vancouver, BC V6H 3Z1; tel. (604) 734-6515; fax (604) 738-2150; Pres. and CEO C. J. CANN.

Central Guaranty Trustco Ltd (Central Trust Co): 366 Bay St, 9th Floor, Toronto, ON M5H 2W5; f. 1925; Pres. and CEO W. T. HODGSON.

Chancellor Trust Co: 360 Bay St, 5th Floor, Toronto, ON M5H 2V6; tel. (416) 869-7980; Pres. RONALD JANES.

CIBC Mortgage Corporation: Commerce Ct Postal Station, Toronto, ON M5L 1A2; tel. (416) 784-7391; fax (416) 785-8308; Sec. K. F. EBBESEN.

Citizens' Trust Co: 815 West Hastings St, Vancouver, BC V6C 1B4; tel. (604) 682-7171; telex 04-507860; fax (604) 682-3571; Pres. PETER G. ROPCHAN.

Community Trust Co Ltd: 2271 Bloor St West, Toronto, ON M6S 1P1; tel. (416) 763-2291; fax (416) 763-2444; Gen. Man. MICHAEL N. WYTIUK.

Confed Trust Co: 321 Bloor St East, 6th Floor, Toronto, ON M4W 1G9; Exec. Vice-Pres. and COO G. B. WALSH.

Co-operative Trust Co of Canada: 333 Third Ave, North Saskatoon, SK S7K 2M2; tel. (306) 244-1900; fax (306) 244-1704; CEO EDWARD G. GEBERT.

Coronet Trust Co: 160 Bloor St East, Suite 160, Toronto, ON M4W 1B9; tel. (416) 928-3965; fax (416) 928-5180; Pres. and CEO DONALD M. LYONS.

Counsel Trust Co: 36 Toronto St, Suite 300, POB 417, Toronto, ON M5C 2C5; tel. (416) 365-3100; fax (416) 365-1634; Pres. BRENDAN R. CALDER.

Crédit Foncier: 612 rue St-Jacques, Montréal, PQ H3C 1E1; tel. (514) 392-1880; telex 052-68622; f. 1880; total assets 2,700m. (July 1985); Chair. CLAUDE CASTONGUAY; Pres. and CEO MICHEL M. LESSARD.

Dominion Trust Company: 121 King St West, Suite 110, POB 22, Toronto, ON M5H 3T9; tel. (416) 362-8282; Pres. GARY W. GOLDMAN.

Effort Trust Co: 240 Main St East, Hamilton, ON L8N 1H5; tel. (416) 528-8956; fax (416) 528-8182; Pres. T. J. WEISZ; Gen. Man. LARRY J. DUNSDON.

Equitable Trust Co: 150 York St, Suite 1100, Toronto, ON M5H 3S5; Pres. S. VERJEE.

Evangeline Saving and Mortgage Co: 494 King St, Windsor, NS B0N 2T0; tel. (902) 798-8362; Pres. and CEO BARBARA HUGHES.

Evangeline Trust Co: 494 King St, Windsor, NS B0N 2T0; tel. (902) 798-8326; Pres. and CEO BARBARA HUGHES.

Family Trust Corporation: 8 Wellington St West, Markham, ON L3P 1A2; tel. (416) 294-1310; fax (416) 294-0776; Pres. and CEO GERALD T. McGOEY.

Fiducie Canadienne Italienne/Canadian Italian Trust: 6999 blvd St-Laurent, Montréal, PQ H2S 3E1; tel. (514) 270-4124; fax (514) 861-6004; Pres. GUISEPPE DI BATTISTA.

Fiducie du Québec/Québec Trust: Tour Sud, 1 Complexe Desjardins, CP 34, Montréal, PQ H5B 1E4; tel. (514) 286-9441; telex 055-60838; fax (514) 286-1131; Pres. RAYMOND A. REID.

Financial Trust Co: 55 Yonge St, Suite 700, Toronto, ON M5E 1S4; tel. (416) 366-8999; fax (416) 862-5415; Pres. K. W. WINGER.

First City Trust Co: 777 Hornby St, Vancouver, BC V6Z 1S4; tel. (604) 685-2489; telex 04-54515; fax (604) 661-4892; Pres. JAMES WESTAWAY.

Guardian Trust Co: 618 rue St-Jacques, Montréal, PQ H3C 1E3; tel. (514) 842-7161; telex 05-25721; Pres. and CEO H. L. KELLY.

Household Trust Co: 85 Bloor St East, Toronto, ON M4W 1B4; tel. (416) 960-0665; fax (416) 960-5086; Pres. G. H. ARCHAMBAULT.

Huronia Trust Co: 2 Mississauga St East, POB 68, Orillia, ON L3V 6H9; tel. (705) 325-2328; Man. Dir JAMES L. GRAHAM.

Income Trust Co: 181 Main St West, POB 870, Hamilton, ON L8N 3N9; tel. (416) 528-9811; fax (416) 528-9816; Chair. BERNARD S. WALMAN.

Inland Trust and Savings Corporation Ltd: 1054 Portage Ave, Winnipeg, MB R3G 3M2; tel. (204) 786-7801; fax (204) 786-7805; Pres. MANUEL BRICKER.

International Trust Co: North Tower, Royal Bank Plaza, POB 75, Toronto, ON M5J 2J2; tel. (416) 865-0515; telex 065-24601; fax (416) 1642; Pres. J. H. MATTHEWS.

Investors Group Trust Co Ltd: One Canada Centre, 447 Portage Ave, Winnipeg, MB R3C 3B6; tel. (204) 956-8441; Exec. Vice-Pres. R. E. ARCHER.

Lombard Odier Trust Co: 1155 rue Sherbrooke ouest, Bureau 1401, Montréal, PQ H3A 2W1; Chair. and Pres. ERIC SKOVSBO.

London Trust and Savings Corporation: 4950 Yonge St, Suite 908, North York, ON M2N 6K1; Pres. RAY JEWELL.

Merchant Trust Co: 115 King St, Stellarton, NS B0K 1S0; Pres. J. W. GOGAN.

Metropolitan Trust Co: 6 Crescent Rd, Toronto, ON M4W 3K9; tel. (416) 967-1813; Chair. and CEO JURI KOOR.

Monarch Trust Co: 21 St Clair Ave East, Suite 1005, Toronto, ON M4T 1L9; tel. (416) 922-4545; Pres. STANLEY TAUB.

Montréal Trust: 1 pl. Ville-Marie, Montréal, PQ H3B 3L6; tel. (514) 397-7000; telex 055-61286; f. 1889; total assets 1,861.1m. (1983); Chair. and Pres. ROBERT GRATTON.

Morgan Trust Co of Canada: Suite 900, 630 blvd René-Lévesque ouest, Montréal, PQ H3B 1S6; tel. (514) 878-3861; telex 055-61022.

Municipal Trust Co: 70 Collier St, POB 147, Barrie, ON L4M 4S9; tel. (705) 726-7200; telex 06-875524; fax (705) 726-6844; Pres. and CEO MAXWELL L. ROTSTEIN.

Mutual Trust Co: 70 University Ave, Suite 400, POB 17, Toronto, ON M5J 2M4; tel. (416) 598-2665; fax (416) 598-7837; Pres. and CEO RAYMOND DORE.

National Trust Co Ltd: 18 King St East, Toronto, ON M5C 1C4; tel. (416) 364-9141; telex 062-2028; f. 1898; total assets 2,787m. (1982); Chair. and CEO WILLIAM H. SOMERVILLE.

National Victoria and Grey Trust Co: 1 Ontario St, Stratford, ON N5A 6S9; f. 1844; total assets 7,800m. (1984); Pres. J. C. C. WANSBROUGH; Chair. and CEO WILLIAM H. SOMERVILLE.

North West Trust Co: 10201 Jasper Ave, 7th Floor, Edmonton, AB T5J 3R3; Pres. and COO DONALD E. FARNELL.

Pacific and Western Trust Corporation: 242 22nd St East, Saskatoon, SK S7K 0E8; tel. (306) 244-1868; fax (306) 244-4649; Pres. R. G. WALKER.

Peace Hills Trust Co: Kensington Pl., 10th Floor, 10011 109th St, Edmonton, AB T5J 3S8; Pres. THOMAS H. LaPOINTE.

People's Trust Co: 1050 Pender St West, Suite 610, Vancouver, BC V6E 3S7; tel. (604) 683-2881; fax (604) 683-8798; Pres. and CEO RONALD J. FISH.

Premier Trust Co: 1155 Yonge St, Toronto, ON M4T 1W2; tel. (416) 964-1124; Chair. and CEO WILLIAM H. SOMERVILLE.

Regent Trust Co: 877 Portage Ave, Winnipeg, MB R3G 0N8; tel. (204) 783-8995; fax (204) 783-6065; Pres. D. J. SKINNER.

Royal Trustco Ltd: Royal Trust Tower, Toronto, ON M5W 1P9; tel. (416) 864-7000; telex 065-24237; f. 1892; total assets 71,849m. (1986); Chair. HARTLAND M. MacDOUGALL; Pres. and CEO MICHAEL A. CORNELISSEN.

Saskatchewan Trust Co: 171 Second Ave South, Saskatoon, SK S7K 1K6; tel. (306) 244-8744; fax (306) 244-0056; Pres. G. NOREN.

Security Trust: 5300 Yonge St, Suite 205, Willowdale, ON M2N 5R2; Pres. MORRIS FISCHTEIN.

Sherbrooke Trust/La Compagnie Sherbrooke Trust: 455 King St West, Sherbrooke, PQ J1H 6E8; tel. (819) 822-9550; fax (819) 822-0532; subsidiary of Trust Général du Canada; Exec. Vice-Pres. and Man. Dir BRUCE D. ALLANSON.

Société Nationale de Fiducie: 425 blvd de Maisonneuve ouest, Montréal, PQ H3A 3G5; tel. (514) 844-2050; fax (514) 844-5824; Vice-Pres. and CEO G. LOSIER.

Standard Trust Company: 69 Yonge St, Toronto, ON M5E 1K3; tel. (416) 868-6900; fax (416) 868-0468; Pres. and CEO BRIAN R. O'MALLEY.

Sterling Trust Corporation: 220 Bay St, Suite 500, Toronto, ON M5J 2K8; tel. (416) 364-7495; telex 06-22198; fax (416) 364-2670; Pres. and CEO MAURICE JODOIN.

Trust Général du Canada: 1100 rue Université, Montréal, PQ H3B 2G7; tel. (514) 871-7180; telex 055-61407; f. 1928; cap. and res 94m., total assets 3,038m. (1985); Exec. Vice-Pres. and COO MAURICE MYRAND.

Trust La Laurentienne du Canada Inc (Laurentian Trust of Canada Inc): 1981 ave Collège McGill, Montréal, PQ H3A 2Y2; tel. (514) 284-7000; fax (514) 284-3210; Dir, Trust Services PAUL CÔTE.

Trust Prêt et Revenu: 850 pl. d'Youville, Suite 700, Québec, PQ G1K 7P3; tel. (418) 692-1221; telex 051-2273; fax (418) 692-1675; Pres. and Dir-Gen. PAUL TARDIF.

Vanguard Trust of Canada Ltd: 70 University Ave, Suite 1200, POB 7, Toronto, ON M5J 2M4; tel. (416) 591-1133; fax (416) 591-9180; Pres. SERGE ROCHELEAU.

Wellington Trust Co: 95 King St East, Toronto, ON M5C 1G4; Chair. F. ROBERT HEWETT.

Yorkshire Trust Co: 1100 Melville St, Vancouver, BC V6E 4B6; Pres. and CEO NICHOLAS R. DENNYS.

Credit Unions

Canadian credit unions and *caisses populaires* are financial institutions which are consumer-owned and provide various savings and loan services, cheque and travellers' cheque facilities, and financial advice. The Canadian Co-operative Credit Society and the Confédération Desjardins act as co-ordinating bodies for the credit unions and *caisses populaires* respectively. In 1987 there were about 3,000 such institutions in Canada, with assets of about C $56,000m.

Canadian Co-operative Credit Society: 300 East Mall, Islington, ON M9B 6B7; tel. (416) 232-1262; CEO BRIAN DOWNEY; Communications Man. RALPH BESLIN.

Confédération Desjardins: 100 ave des Commandeurs, Levis, PQ G6V 7N5.

Bankers' Organizations

The Canadian Bankers' Association: Exchange Tower, 2 First Canadian Pl., POB 348, Toronto, ON M5X 1E1; tel. (416) 362-6092; telex 062-3402; fax (416) 362-7705; f. 1891; 66 mems; Chair. A. W. MOYSEY; Pres. HELEN SINCLAIR.

Trust Companies Association of Canada Inc: Herbert House, 7th Floor, 335 Bay St, Toronto, ON M5H 2R3; tel. (416) 364-1207; Pres. and CEO JOHN L. EVANS; Dir of Admin. and Sec. J. SAYERS.

FINANCIAL MARKETS

Stock Exchanges

Alberta Stock Exchange: 300 Fifth Ave, SW, 6th Floor, Calgary, AB T2P 3C4; tel. (403) 262-7791; telex 038-21793; fax (403) 237-0450; f. 1914; volume of trade 740m. shares (valued at C $971m.) in 1987; 46 mems; Chair. W. J. WELTON; Pres. T. A. CUMMING.

Montréal Exchange/Bourse de Montréal: Tour de la Bourse, 800 sq. Victoria, CP 61, Montréal, PQ H4Z 1A9; tel. (514) 871-2424; telex 055-60586; fax (514) 871-3530; f. 1874; volume of trade 2,021.9m. shares (valued at C $21,873.9m) in 1987; 76 mems; Chair. TERRENCE REID; Pres. and CEO BRUNO RIVERIN.

Toronto Stock Exchange: The Exchange Tower, 2 First Canadian Pl., Toronto, ON M5X 1J2; tel. (416) 947-4700; telex 062-17759; fax (416) 947-4585; f. 1852; volume of trade 7,393.7m. shares (valued at C $100,224.3m.) in 1987; 73 mems; Pres. and CEO J. P. BUNTING.

Vancouver Stock Exchange: Stock Exchange Tower, 609 Granville St, POB 10333, Vancouver, BC V7Y 1H1; tel. (604) 689-3334; telex 045-5480; fax (604) 688-6051; f. 1907; volume of trade 4,795.1m. shares (valued at C $6,650.3m.) in 1987; 49 mems; Chair. J. L. MATHERS; Pres. DONALD J. HUDSON.

Winnipeg Stock Exchange: One Lombard Pl., Suite 2901, Winnipeg, MB R3B 0Y2; tel. (204) 942-8431; fax (204) 947-9536; volume of trade in 1987: industrials 0.3m. shares (valued at C $0.3m.), mines and oils 0.1m. shares (valued at C $0.1m.); 18 mems; Pres. J. D. BEDNAR.

Commodity Exchange

The Winnipeg Commodity Exchange: 500 Commodity Exchange Tower, 360 Main St, Winnipeg, MB R3C 3Z4; tel. (204) 949-0495; fax (204) 943-5448; f. 1887; Chair. E. WOOD; Pres. R. P. PURVES.

INSURANCE

Principal Companies

Abbey Life Insurance Co of Canada: 3027 Harvester Rd, Burlington, ON L7N 3G9; tel. (416) 639-6200; telex 061-8327; Pres. W. D. MILLAR.

Blue Cross Life Insurance Co: POB 220, Moncton, NB E1C 8L3; tel. (506) 853-1811; telex 014-2233; fax (506) 853-4651; Pres. L. R. FURLONG.

Canada Security Assurance Co: 60 Yonge St, Toronto, ON M5E 1H5; tel. (416) 362-2961; telex 062-19667; f. 1913; Pres. R. H. STEVENS.

Canadian General Insurance Co: POB 4030, Terminal A, Toronto, ON M5W 1K4; tel. (416) 528-6766; f. 1907; Pres. JACK W. ROBERTS.

Canadian Home Assurance Co: 465 blvd René-Lévesque ouest, Montréal, PQ H2Z 1A8; tel. (514) 866-6531; telex 052-5169; f. 1928; Pres. PATRICK J. KING.

Canadian Indemnity Co: 165 University Ave, Toronto, ON M5H 3B9; tel. (416) 362-7231; telex 062-19747; f. 1912; Pres. D. A. WAUGH.

The Canadian Surety Co: Canada Sq., 2180 Yonge St, Toronto, ON M4S 2C2; tel. (416) 487-7195; telex 065-24212; fax (416) 482-6176; Pres. and Gen. Man. J. ROBERTSON.

Confederation Life Insurance Co: 321 Bloor St East, Toronto, ON M4W 1H1; tel. (416) 323-8111; f. 1871; Pres. P. D. BURNS.

Groupe Coopérants, inc, et Les Coopérants, société mutuelle d'assurance-vie: Maison des Coopérants, 600 blvd de Maisonneuve ouest, Montréal, PQ H3A 3J9; tel. (514) 287-6600; fax (514) 287-6515; f. 1876; Pres. of Board PAUL DOLAN; CEO PIERRE SHOONER.

Crown Life Insurance Co: 120 Bloor St East, Toronto, ON M4W 1B8; tel. (416) 928-4500; telex 062-22651; f. 1900; Chair. H. M. BURNS; Pres. and CEO R. F. RICHARDSON.

Dominion Insurance Corpn: POB 4024, Terminal A, Toronto, ON M5W 1K1; f. 1904; Pres. and Gen. Man. W. W. WARD.

Dominion of Canada General Insurance Co: 165 University Ave, Toronto, ON M5H 3B9; tel. (416) 362-7231; telex 062-19747; fax (416) 362-9918; f. 1887; Pres. D. A. WAUGH.

Excelsior Life Insurance Co: 145 King St West, Toronto, ON M5H 3T7; f. 1889; Pres. M. A. STEPHEN.

Federation Insurance Co of Canada: 1080 Beaver Hall Hill, 20th Floor, Montréal, PQ H2Z 1S8; tel. (514) 875-5790; telex 055-61701; fax (514) 875-9769; f. 1947; Pres. W. J. GREEN.

General Accident Assurance Co of Canada: The Exchange Tower, Suite 2600, 2 First Canadian Pl., POB 410, Toronto, ON M5X 1J1; tel. (416) 368-4733; telex 065-24272; f. 1906; Pres. LEONARD G. LATHAM.

Gerling Global General Insurance Co: 480 University Ave, Toronto, ON M5G 1V6; tel. (416) 598-4651; telex 065-24108; fax (416) 598-9507; f. 1955; Pres. Dr R. R. KERN.

Gore Mutual Insurance Co: 252 Dundas St, Cambridge, ON N1R 5T3; tel. (519) 623-1910; telex 069-59304; fax (519) 623-4411; f. 1839; Sec. J. M. GRAY.

The Great-West Life Assurance Co: 100 Osborne St North, Winnipeg, MB R3C 3A5; tel. (204) 946-1190; telex 075-7519; f. 1891; Pres. and CEO K. P. KAVANAGH.

Groupe Commerce, compagnie d'assurances: 2450 blvd Girouard ouest, St-Hyacinthe, PQ J2S 3B3; tel. (514) 773-9701; fax (514) 773-4892; f. 1907; Pres. and CEO GUY ST-GERMAIN.

Guardian Insurance Co of Canada: POB 4096, Station A, Toronto, ON M5N 1N1; tel. (416) 941-5050; fax (416) 941-9791; f. 1911; Chair. GEORGE ALEXANDER; Pres. and CEO ROBERT C. SHATFORD.

Halifax Insurance Co: 75 Eglinton Ave East, Toronto, ON M4P 3A3; tel. (416) 440-1000; fax (416) 440-0799; f. 1809; Pres. and CEO J. N. MCCARTHY.

Imperial Life Assurance Co of Canada: 95 St Clair Ave West, Toronto, ON M4V 1N7; tel. (416) 926-2600; fax (416) 923-1599; f. 1896; Pres. ROBERT ST-JACQUES.

Kings Mutual Insurance Co: POB 10, Berwick, NS B0P 1E0; tel. (902) 538-3187; f. 1904; Pres. M. VISSERS; Man. D. C. COOK.

Laurentian General Insurance Co Inc: 1100 blvd René-Lévesque ouest, Montréal, PQ H3B 4P4; tel. (514) 392-6000; telex 055-62067; fax (514) 392-6328; Pres. JEAN BOUCHARD.

Groupe La Laurentienne: 500 est, Grande-Allée, Québec, PQ G1R 2J7; comprises 18 operating cos; Chair. and CEO CLAUDE CASTONGUAY.

London Life Insurance Co: 255 Dufferin Ave, London, ON N6A 4K1; tel. (519) 432-5281; f. 1874; Chair. A. T. LAMBERT; Pres. and CEO EARL H. ORSER.

Manufacturers Life Insurance Co: 200 Bloor St East, Toronto, ON M4W 1E5; tel. (416) 926-0100; fax (416) 928-4427; f. 1887; Chair. E. S. JACKSON; Pres. and CEO THOMAS A. DIGIACOMO.

Mercantile and General Reinsurance Co of Canada: University Pl., 123 Front St West, Toronto, ON M5J 2M7; tel. (416) 947-3800; telex 065-24320; fax (416) 947-1386; f. 1951; Pres. D. M. BATTEN.

Montréal Life Insurance Co: 630 rue Sherbrooke ouest, Montréal, PQ H3A 1E4; f. 1908; Pres. N. BAUER.

Mutual Life of Canada: 227 King St South, Waterloo, ON N2J 4C5; tel. (519) 888-2290; telex 069-55450; fax (519) 888-2990; f. 1870; Chair. J. H. PANABAKER; Pres. and CEO JACK V. MASTERMAN.

The National Life Assurance Co of Canada: 522 University Ave, Toronto, ON M5G 1Y7; tel. (416) 598-2122; fax (416) 598-2142; f. 1897; Pres. ROBERT BEGIN.

North American Life Assurance Co: 333 Broadway Ave, Winnipeg, MB R3C 0S9; tel. (204) 949-1660; telex 06-22400; f. 1881; Chair. D. G. PAYNE; Pres. W. E. BRADFORD.

Northern Life Assurance Co of Canada: 606 Fourth St, SW, Calgary, AB T2P 1S9; f. 1894; Chair. R. C. BROWN; Pres. and CEO G. L. BOWIE.

Portage La Prairie Mutual Insurance Co: POB 340, Portage la Prairie, MB R1N 3B8; tel. (204) 857-3415; fax (204) 239-6655; f. 1884; Pres. and Gen. Man. H. G. OWENS.

Québec Assurance Co: 10 Wellington St East, Toronto, ON M5E 1L5; tel. (416) 366-7511; telex 065-24124; f. 1818; Pres. R. A. ELMS.

Saskatchewan Government Insurance: 2260 11th Ave, Regina, SK S4P 0J9; tel. (306) 565-1200; telex 071-2417; fax (306) 359-0867; f. 1945; Pres. ALEX G. WILDE.

Sauvegarde Compagnie d'assurance sur la vie: 1 complexe Desjardins, Montréal, PQ H5B 1E2; tel. (514) 285-7700; fax (514) 285-7911; f. 1901; Pres. HENRI LEBLOND; Dir-Gen. SERGE BEAUDOIN.

Seaboard Life Insurance Co: 2165 West Broadway, Vancouver, BC V6K 4N5; tel. (604) 737-9300; fax (604) 734-8221; f. 1953; Pres. J. S. M. CUNNINGHAM.

Société Nationale d'Assurances: 425 blvd de Maisonneuve ouest, Bureau 1500, Montréal, PQ H3A 3G5; tel. (514) 288-8711; telex 055-61190; fax (514) 288-8269; f. 1940; Pres. HENRI JOLI-COEUR; Dir-Gen. PIERRE RENAUD.

Sovereign Life Insurance Co: 606 Fourth St, SW, Suite 1500, Calgary, AB T2P 1S9; tel. (403) 298-5576; telex 038-25817; fax (403) 292-1608; f. 1894; Pres. J. ROYER.

Sun Life Assurance Co of Canada: POB 4150, Station A, Toronto, ON M5W 2C9; tel. (416) 979-9966; telex 065-24389; f. 1865; Chair. and CEO JOHN D. MCNEIL; Pres. JOHN R. GARDNER.

Toronto Mutual Life Insurance Co: 112 St Clair Ave West, Toronto, ON M4V 2Y3; tel. (416) 960-3463; fax (416) 960-0531; Chair. WALTER B. THOMPSON; Pres. JOHN T. ENGLISH.

Travelers Canada: Travelers Tower, 400 University Ave, Toronto, ON M5G 1S7; tel. (416) 586-3000; telex 065-24032; fax (416) 586-2858; Pres. and CEO DANIEL DAMOV.

United Canadian Shares Ltd: 1601 Church Ave, Winnipeg, MB R2X 1G9; tel. (204) 633-7042; telex 075-87636; fax (204) 632-6779; f. 1951; Chair. R. H. JONES; Pres. C. S. RILEY, Jr.

Victoria Insurance Co of Canada: 150 Eglinton Ave East, Toronto, ON M4P 2Z3; tel. (416) 488-4666; telex 062-2237; fax (416) 488-5019; Chair. and CEO R. W. BROUGHTON.

Waterloo Insurance Co: 14 Erb St West, POB 1604, Waterloo, ON N2J 4C8; tel. (519) 886-4940; f. 1863; Gen. Man. K. I. TYERS.

Wawanesa Mutual Insurance Co: 191 Broadway, Winnipeg, MB R3C 3P1; tel. (204) 985-3811; telex 075-7564; f. 1896; Pres. I. M. MONTGOMERY.

Western Assurance Co: 10 Wellington St East, Toronto, ON M5E 1L5; tel. (416) 366-7511; f. 1851; Pres. R. A. ELMS.

York Fire and Casualty Insurance Co: 7501 Keele St, Suite 300, Concord, ON L4K 1Y2; tel. (416) 738-1707; telex 069-64754; Pres. ALEXANDER A. THAIN.

Zurich Life Insurance Co of Canada: 375 University Ave, Toronto, ON M5G 2J7; tel. (416) 593-4444; fax (416) 593-0479; Pres. and CEO P. D. MCGARRY.

Insurance Organizations

Canadian Life and Health Insurance Association: 20 Queen St West, Suite 2500, Toronto, ON M5H 3S2; tel. (416) 977-2221; fax (416) 977-1895; f. 1894; 110 mem. cos; Pres. M. R. DANIELS.

Insurance Brokers Association of Canada: 141 Adelaide St West, Suite 801, Toronto, ON M5H 3L5; tel. (416) 367-1831; f. 1920; Gen. Man. BASIL M. STEGGLES.

Insurance Bureau of Canada: 181 University Ave, 13th Floor, Toronto, ON M5H 3M7; tel. (416) 362-2031; telex 062-23502; 180 corporate mems; Pres. and CEO J. L. LYNDON.

Insurance Institute of Canada: 481 University Ave, 6th Floor, Toronto, ON M5G 2E9; tel. (416) 591-1572; f. 1952; 27,000 mems; Chair. J. PHELAN; Pres. J. C. RHIND.

Insurers' Advisory Organization Inc: 180 Dundas St West, Toronto, ON M5G 1Z9; tel. (416) 597-1200; fax (416) 597-2180; f. 1855; 65 mems; Pres. and CEO G. A. CHELLEW.

Life Insurance Institute of Canada: 20 Queen St, Suite 2500, Toronto, ON M5H 3S2; tel. (416) 977-2221; Sec.-Treas. DEBBIE COLE-GAUER.

Life Underwriters' Association of Canada: 41 Lesmill Rd, Don Mills, ON M3B 2T3; tel. (416) 444-5251; f. 1906; 21,000 mems; Exec. Vice-Pres. and COO GORD WATT.

SOCIETY

TELECOMMUNICATIONS AND BROADCASTING

INTRODUCTION

Regulatory Bodies

Telecommunications services in Canada are provided by both government (federal, provincial and municipal) and private organizations. Telecommunications carriers under federal jurisdiction (Telesat Canada, Bell Canada, British Columbia Telephone Company, Canadian National and Canadian Pacific Telecommunications (CNCP), Northwestel, Terra Nova Telecommunications and Teleglobe) and the broadcasting system (radio, television, cable television and pay television), are regulated by the Canadian Radio-Television and Telecommunications Commission (CRTC). The CRTC was created through the 1968 Broadcasting Act, which also established the Canadian Broadcasting Corporation (CBC). Programming policy is to use predominantly Canadian creative and other resources. Services are operated in both English and French.

Canadian Radio-Television and Telecommunications Commission (CRTC): Ottawa, ON K1A 0N2; tel. (819) 997-0313 (Information); telex 053-4253; f. 1968; regional offices in Montréal, Halifax, Winnipeg and Vancouver; Chair. ANDRÉ BUREAU; Vice-Chair. LOUIS R. SHERMAN (Telecommunications), MONIQUE COUPAL (Broadcasting).

Telecommunications

In 1988 about 120 telephone systems served approximately 9,099,000 households, or 98.4% of all households in Canada. The CRTC's main purpose, with regard to telecommunications services, is to regulate carriers on an interprovincial level and ensure that the rates charged for services are just and reasonable. Telecommunications within the provinces are the responsibility of provincial bodies. The federal Department of Communications is responsible for establishing national policy, most of which is formulated by the CRTC. In 1987 the federal Minister of Communications announced plans to liberalize network services, allowing new users access to facilities previously dominated by large companies.

Telephone companies, of which there are over 100 in Canada, range from small rural co-operatives to large privately-owned or government organizations. The largest company is Bell Canada which is investor-owned and serves about two-thirds of the population. Telecom Canada (previously the Trans-Canada Telephone System), an association of telephone companies, co-ordinates facilities for long-distance services. Since 1979 CNCP Telecommunications has competed with Telecom Canada, interconnecting with the local telephone network of Bell Canada and (since 1981) with the British Columbia Telephone Company. International telecommunications are operated by Teleglobe Canada, previously a crown corporation, which was sold to private interests in 1987. Its monopoly on international traffic is guaranteed until 1992.

Mobile radio and radio-paging services in Canada are provided by about 200 radio common carriers. The federal Department of Communications issues licences to private users. In 1988 Bell Canada introduced the ALEX system in the Montréal area, allowing access to general information through the ordinary telephone linked to a video screen.

The cellular radio system (mobile radio communications) was introduced on a national level in 1985. Cantel Cellular Radio Group and the telephone companies in each province were licensed to provide services. A CRTC decision in 1984 permitted interconnection between radio common carriers and public telephone networks of the federally-regulated carriers.

Canada was the first country to establish a domestic communications satellite system with the launching of Anik A-1 in November 1972, of Anik A-2 in April 1973, of Anik A-3 in May 1975 and, finally, of Anik-B in December 1978. In August 1982 Anik D-1 was put in orbit, followed by Anik C-3 in November 1982, and Anik C-2 in June 1983. These were joined by Anik D-2 in November 1984 and Anik C-1 in April 1985. The Canadian commercial satellite communications system is operated by Telesat Canada, a corporation established in 1969 and owned by the Government of Canada and Canadian telecommunications carriers. Telesat transmits audio and video signals, used mainly by broadcasters, and voice and data signals.

Radio and Television

Radio and television service is available to over 99% of the population: in 1988 69% of households had cable television. Most television programming is in colour and in 1988 95% of homes had colour TV sets.

Many privately-owned television and radio stations have affiliation agreements with the CBC and help to distribute the national services. The major private television networks which also have affiliates are CTV, TVA (which serves the province of Ontario), Quatre Saisons (which also serves the province of Québec) and Global (serving the province of Ontario), as well as the educational networks.

RADIO

The CBC operates two AM and two FM networks, one each in English and French. The CBC's Northern Service provides both national network programming in English and French, and special local and short-wave programmes, some of which are broadcast in the languages of the Indian and Inuit peoples. In March 1987 there were 786 outlets for CBC radio (96 CBC-owned stations, 629 CBC-owned relay transmitters, 61 private affiliates and rebroadcasters). CBC radio service, which is virtually free of commercial advertising, is within reach of 99.5% of the population. Radio Canada International, the CBC's overseas short-wave service, broadcasts daily in 11 languages and distributes recorded programmes free for use world-wide.

TELEVISION

The CBC operates two television networks, one in English and one in French. CBC's Northern Service, created in 1958, now provides both radio and television service to 98% of the 90,000 inhabitants of northern Québec, the Northwest Territories and Yukon Territory. Almost 41% of these inhabitants are native Canadians, and programming is provided in Dene and Inuktitut languages as well as English and French. Broadcast time is also made available to native groups who produce their own programmes. As of March 1988, CBC television was carried on 868 outlets (28 CBC-owned stations, 615 CBC-owned rebroadcasters, 37 private affiliates and 188 private rebroadcasters). CBC television is available to over 98% of the population.

Canadian Satellite Communication Inc (Cancom) of Toronto, Ontario, was licensed in April 1981 by the CRTC to carry on a multi-channel television and radio broadcasting operation via Anik satellite for the distribution of CTV, TVA and independent television and radio programmes (one AM and nine FM radio stations) to serve remote and under-served communities. In 1983 Cancom was authorized to distribute the programme output of four US television networks, via Anik satellite.

There are five educational services: TV-Ontario in Ontario and Radio-Québec in Québec operate their own television stations and networks; the Access network in Alberta purchases time for educational cultural programming on the private TV stations of the province; Knowledge Network is involved in the distribution, development and co-ordination of educational television programming to British Columbia communities via Anik C satellites and cable; and Saskmedia is involved in the production, acquisition and distribution of educationally-orientated media programming.

Canadian pay television has been in operation since 1983. All of the services initially licensed have now been reorganized in one form or another. By August 1985, Canadians had access to three general interest pay television services (one French service in eastern Canada, Premier Choix/TVEC, and two regional English services: First Choice serving eastern Canada, and Allarcom serving western Canada). New speciality discretionary services, such as MuchMusic, The Sports Network, Latinovision and Chinavision became available in 1984, and other speciality services are under consideration. In 1987 the total number of subscribers to such discretionary services represented 17.9% of potential households.

Use of Selected Media

(Source: Statistics Canada.)

	1986	1987	1988
Households with telephone service:			
Number ('000) .	9,156	9,409	9,099
Percentage of all households .	98.1	98.5	98.4
Households with radio (excl. automobile radios):			
Number ('000) .	9,244	9,444	9,124
Percentage of all households .	99.1	98.8	98.7
Households with television sets:			
Number ('000) .	9,204	9,410	9,112
Percentage of all households .	98.6	98.5	98.6
Households with colour television sets:			
Number ('000)	8,699	9,020	8,793
Percentage of all households.	93.2	94.4	95.1
Households with cable television:			
Number ('000) .	6,052	6,424	6,376
Percentage of all households .	64.9	67.2	69.0
Households with video-cassette recorders:			
Number ('000) .	3,273	4,296	4,809
Percentage of all households .	35.1	45.0	52.0
Operating radio stations:			
AM .	n.a.	337	331
FM .	n.a.	142	152
Operating television stations .	n.a.	97	100

MAJOR TELECOMMUNICATIONS NETWORKS

Alberta Government Telephones: 10020 100th St, Edmonton, AB T5J 0N5; tel. (403) 425-2110; supplies services to residents of Alberta.

Bell Canada: 1050 Beaver Hall Hill, Montréal, PQ N2Z 1S4; tel. (514) 870-1511; reorganized 1983; Canada's largest telephone operating company, has local monopoly in most of Québec and Ontario, also supplies services to the Northwest Territories; Chair. LÉONCE MONTAMBAULT; Pres. and CEO J. MONTY.

British Columbia Telephone Company: 3777 Kingsway, Burnaby, BC V5H 3Z7; tel. (604) 432-2151; supplies services to residents of British Columbia.

Canadian National and Canadian Pacific Telecommunications (CNCP): 330 Bloor St West, Toronto, ON M8X 2W9; tel. (613) 232-6050; telex 062-18362; national telex network supplier, also provides private telephone services in British Columbia, Québec and Ontario.

Immedia Telematics Inc: POB 429, Hudson, PQ; tel. (514) 458-2121; telex 062-17780; operating company; Pres. DAVID THOMAS.

Manitoba Telephone System: 489 Empress St, POB 6666, Winnipeg, MB R3C 3V6; tel. (204) 941-4111; fax (204) 956-0836; provincial crown corpn; supplies services to Manitoba residents; Chair. PAUL THOMAS; Pres. REG BIRD.

Maritime Telegraph and Telephone Co Ltd: POB 880, Halifax, NS B3J 2W3; tel. (902) 421-4373; supplies services to residents of Nova Scotia; Pres. and CEO IVAN DUVAR.

New Brunswick Telephone Co Ltd: One Brunswick Sq., POB 1430, Saint John, NB E2L 4K2; tel. (506) 648-2340; supplies services to residents of New Brunswick.

Newfoundland Telephone Co Ltd: POB 2110, St John's, NF A1C 5H6; tel. (709) 739-2000; supplies services to residents of Newfoundland and Labrador; Chair. and Pres. A. A. BRAIT.

Northwestel Inc: formerly Canadian National Telecommunications; subsidiary of Canadian National Railways; together with Terra Nova Telecommunications, provides services to the Northwest Territories, Yukon Territory, parts of Newfoundland and northern British Columbia.

Saskatchewan Telecommunications International: 2121 Saskatchewan Dr., Regina, SK S4P 3Y2; tel. (306) 347-4504; supplies services to residents of Saskatchewan; Asst Vice-Pres. W. A. BRUCE.

Teleglobe Canada Inc: 680 Sherbrooke St West, Montréal, PQ H3A 2S4; tel. (514) 289-7212; telex 055-61104; f. 1949; federal crown corpn; operates international telecommunications services; Pres. and CEO JEAN-CLAUDE DELORME.

Telesat Canada: 333 River Rd, Ottawa, ON K1L 8B9; tel. (613) 746-5920; telex 053-4184; f. 1969 by act of parliament; owns and operates Canada's commercial domestic satellite system; Chair. D. A. GOLDEN; Pres. and CEO ELDON D. THOMPSON.

Terra Nova Telecommunications Inc: subsidiary of Canadian National Railways; together with Northwestel Inc, provides services to the Northwest Territories, the Yukon Territory, parts of Newfoundland and northern British Columbia.

RADIO AND TELEVISION

Broadcasting Networks

Access Network: 16930 114th Ave, Edmonton, AB T5M 3S2; tel. (403) 451-7272; telex 037-3948; educational channel.

Allarcom Ltd: 5325 104th St, Edmonton, AB T6H 5B8; tel. (403) 436-1250; pay television network.

Atlantic Television System (ATV): POB 1653, Halifax, NS B3J 2Z4; tel. (902) 453-4000; telex 019-21826; fax (902) 454-3270.

British Columbia Television (BCTV): POB 4700, Vancouver, BC V6B 4A3; tel. (604) 420-2288; telex 04-354784.

Canadian Broadcasting Corporation (CBC): 1500 Bronson Ave, POB 8478, Ottawa, ON K1G 3J5; tel. (613) 724-1200; telex 053-4260; fax (613) 738-6843; f. 1936; national publicly-owned broadcasting service; 2 nation-wide television networks and 4 radio networks; international short-wave radio service; production facilities and broadcast transmitters in many locations throughout Canada; Pres. W. T. ARMSTRONG; Sr Vice-Pres. A. MANERA.

English Networks: 1255 Bay St, POB 500, Station A, Toronto, ON M5W 1E6; tel. (416) 975-3311.

French Networks: 1400 blvd René-Lévesque est, CP 6000, Montréal, PQ H3C 3A8; tel. (514) 285-3211.

Canadian Satellite Communications Inc: 275 Slater St, Suite 1501, Ottawa, ON K1P 5H9; tel. (613) 232-4814; Chair. J. R. PETERS; Pres. and CEO P. L. MORRISSETTE.

CKO Inc: 30 Carlton St, Toronto, ON M5B 2E9; tel. (416) 591-1222.

Communications Radiomutuel Inc: 1717 blvd René-Lévesque est, Montréal, PQ H2L 4T3; tel. (514) 527-4311; fax (514) 522-3127.

CTV Television Network Ltd: 42 Charles St East, Toronto, ON M4Y 1T5; tel. (416) 928-6000; telex 06-22080; fax (416) 928-0907; 24 privately-owned affiliated TV stations from coast to coast, with 247 rebroadcasters; covers 99% of Canadian TV households; Pres. and CEO M. CHERCOVER.

The Family Channel: 98 Queen St East, Suite 200, Toronto, ON M5C 1S6; tel. (416) 867-8866; national pay television network.

Farm Market Network: 550 Berry St, Winnipeg, MB R3H 0R9; tel. (204) 772-1080.

First Choice Canadian Communications Corporation: 98 Queen St East, Suite 200, Toronto, ON M5C 1S6; tel. (416) 394-9115; pay television network covering area extending from Ontario to Newfoundland.

Global Communications Ltd: 81 Barber Greene Rd, Don Mills, ON M3C 2A2; tel. (416) 446-5311; telex 06-966767; fax (416) 446-5371; one TV station and 9 rebroadcasters serving southern Ontario; Pres. (TV) DAVID MINTZ.

Inuit Broadcasting Corporation: 251 Laurier Ave West, Suite 703, Ottawa, ON K1P 5J6; tel. (613) 235-1892; telex 053-3853; fax (613) 235-1892.

Knowledge Network: 475 West Georgia St, Vancouver, BC V6B 4M9; tel. (604) 668-3300; telex 045-4226; fax (604) 668-3398.

Newfoundland Television (NTV): POB 2020, St John's, NF A1C 5S2; tel. (709) 722-5015; telex 016-3155; fax (709) 726-5107.

Société de Radio-Télévision du Québec: 800 rue Fullum, Montréal, PQ H2K 3L7; tel. (514) 521-2424; telex 05-25808; fax (514) 873-7464; f. 1968; Chair. G. LORD; Pres. and Gen. Man. JACQUES GIRARD.

Superchannel/Alberta: 5324 Calgary Trail, Edmonton, AB T6H 4J8; tel. (403) 437-7744; pay television network covering area extending from Manitoba to British Columbia.

Télémedia Communications Inc: 1010 rue Sherbrooke ouest, Bureau 1610, Montréal, PQ H3A 2R7; tel. (514) 845-6291; fax (514) 842-5591.

Télévision Quatre Saisons: 405 rue Ogilvy, Montréal, PQ H3N 1M4; tel. (514) 271-3535; French-language pay television network operating in province of Québec.

TVA Television Network: 1600 blvd de Maisonneuve est, CP 368, succursale C, Montréal, PQ H2L 4P2; tel. (514) 526-0476; telex 055-60626; f. 1971; French-language network, with 10 stations in Québec and 20 rebroadcasters serving 98% of the province and francophone communities in Ontario and New Brunswick; Pres. and Gen. Man. MICHAEL HÉROUX.

TV-Ontario: 2180 Yonge St, POB 200, Station Q, Toronto, ON M4T 2T1; tel. (416) 484-2600; telex 06-23547; fax (416) 484-2725; Chair. and CEO B. OSTRY; Dir Gen. MIMI FULLERTON.

Vision TV: 315 Queen St East, Toronto, ON M5A 1S7; tel. (416) 366-9221.

Wataway Radio Network: POB 1180, Sioux Lookout, ON P0V 2T0; tel. (807) 737-2760.

YTV Canada Inc: 525 Lakeshore Blvd West, Toronto, ON H5V 2V8; tel. (416) 340-1221; national pay television network.

Broadcasting Associations

Atlantic Association of Broadcasters: c/o ATV Cape Breton, POB 469, Sydney, NS B1P 6H5; Pres. W. A. HOLMES.

British Columbia Association of Broadcasters: 2440 Ash St, Vancouver, BC V5Z 4J6; tel. (604) 873-2599; fax (604) 873-0877; Pres. TOM PEACOCK.

Canadian Association of Broadcasters: 350 Sparks St, Suite 306, POB 627, Station B, Ottawa, ON K1P 5S2; tel. (613) 233-4035; telex 053-3127; fax (613) 233-6961; asscn of over 400 private radio and television stations; Pres. and CEO MICHAEL MCCABE; Sr Vice-Pres. (Television) ELIZABETH MCDONALD; Sr Vice-Pres. (Radio) MICHEL TREMBLAY.

Canadian Association of Ethnic Broadcasters: 637 College St, Toronto, ON M6G 1B6; tel. (416) 531-9991; fax (416) 531-5274; asscn of radio broadcasters; Pres. and Exec. Dir JOHNNY LOMBARDI.

Canadian Cable Television Association: 85 Albert St, Suite 400, Ottawa, ON K1P 6A4; tel. (613) 232-2631.

Central Canada Broadcasters' Association: 350 Sparks St, Suite 306, Ottawa, ON K1R 7S8; tel. (613) 233-4035; telex 053-3127; Exec. Sec. GERRY ACTON.

North American National Broadcasting Association: 1500 Bronson Ave, Ottawa, ON K1G 3JS.

Western Association of Broadcasters: c/o CJOB, 930 Portage Ave, Winnipeg, MB R3G 6P8; tel. (204) 786-2471; Pres. JOHN COCHRANE.

THE PRESS

INTRODUCTION

The daily press in Canada is essentially local in coverage, influence and distribution. Through the use of satellite transmission, a national edition of the Toronto *Globe and Mail*, established in 1981, is available coast to coast, and in 1988 the *Financial Post* began publication of a national edition, also using satellite transmission.

Independently-owned daily newspapers account for 19% of the circulation of Canadian dailies. Chain ownership is predominant: over 47% of daily newspaper circulation is represented by two major groups: Thomson Newspapers Ltd (20.5% of daily newspaper circulation) and Southam Inc (27.0%). In 1987 the Québecor Group accounted for 8.7% of the total circulation, while the Sun Publishing Group also had 8.7%, and the Sterling Group had 0.8%. There are several smaller groups.

In September 1980 the Liberal government appointed a royal commission to investigate the effects of concentration of ownership in the newspaper industry. In August 1981 the commission reported that the existing concentration constituted a threat to press freedom, and recommended that some groups should be compelled to sell some of their newspaper interests in areas where there was extreme ownership concentration. While government action on the report has still to be finalized, it is expected that the Progressive Conservative government will continue to restrict cross-media ownership of newspapers, radio and television, and to prohibit non-media companies from owning daily newspapers.

In March 1988 there were 111 daily newspapers with a combined circulation of over 5.7m., representing 62% of the country's households.

In 1988 about 1,100 weekly and twice-weekly community newspapers reached an estimated 5.2m. people, mainly in the more remote areas of the country. A significant feature of the Canadian press is the number of newspapers catering for ethnic groups: there are over 80 of these daily and weekly publications appearing in over 20 languages.

There are numerous periodicals for business, trade, professional, recreational and special interest readership, although periodical publishing, particularly, suffers from substantial competition from publications originating in the USA. Among periodicals, the only one which can be regarded as national in its readership and coverage is *Maclean's Canada's Weekly Newsmagazine*.

Principal National Newspaper Groups

Southam Newspaper Group: 150 Bloor St West, Suite 910, Toronto, ON M5S 2Y9; tel. (416) 927-1877; Pres. JOHN FISHER.

Sterling Newspapers Ltd: 1827 West Fifth Ave, 2nd Floor, Vancouver, BC V6J 1P5; tel. (604) 732-4443; Pres. F. DAVID RADLER; Vice-Pres. and Gen. Man. STEEN O. JORGENSEN.

Thomson Newspapers Ltd: 65 Queen St West, Toronto, ON M5H 2M8; tel. (416) 864-1710; Chair., Pres. and CEO KENNETH R. THOMSON.

Newspapers, Periodicals and Books—Number and Circulation

(Source: Statistics Canada.)

	1984		1985	
	Number	Average circulation ('000)	Number	Average circulation ('000)
Newspapers				
Daily (total).	117	5,666	115	5,667
English	101	4,551	99	4,653
French	11	987	11	987
Other.	5	28	5	28
Non-daily (total)	1,265	12.3*	1,277	12.3*
Periodicals	1,151	33,500†	n.a.	n.a.
Books published.	4,780	n.a.	n.a.	n.a.

* Per issue.

† Total circulation per issue.

PRINCIPAL DAILY AND SUNDAY NEWSPAPERS

(Mon. = Monday; Wed. = Wednesday; Fri. = Friday; Sat. = Saturday; Sun. = Sunday; Publr = Publisher; papers are published seven days a week (Monday to Sunday) unless otherwise indicated.)

Alberta

Advocate: 2950 Bremner Ave, POB 5200, Red Deer, AB T4N 5G3; tel. (403) 343-2400; fax (403) 342-4051; f. 1901; Mon. to Sat.; evening; Publr HOWARD JANZEN; Man. Editor JOE MCLAUGHLIN; circ. 22,218.

Calgary Herald: Southam Inc, 215 16th St, SE, POB 2400, Station M, Calgary, AB T2P 0W8; tel. (403) 235-7100; telex 038-22793; f. 1883; morning; Publr PATRICK O'CALLAGHAN; Man. Editor GILLIAN STEWARD; circ. Mon. to Sat. 133,064, Sun. 119,382.

Calgary Sun: Toronto Sun Publishing Corpn, 2615 12th St, NE, Calgary, AB T2E 7W9; tel. (403) 250-4200; telex 038-22734; fax (403) 291-4242; f. 1980; daily except Sat.; morning; Publr KEN KING; Editor-in-Chief ROBERT POOLE; circ. Mon. to Fri. 74,760, Sun. 94,890.

Daily Herald-Tribune: 10604 100th St, Grande Prairie, AB T8V 2M5; tel. (403) 532-1110; telex 036-7220; Mon. to Fri.; evening; Publr B. WAYNE JOBB; Editor BILL SCOTT; circ. 8,272.

Edmonton Journal: Southam Inc, POB 2421, Edmonton, AB T5J 2S6; tel. (403) 329-5400; telex 037-3492; fax (403) 429-5479; f. 1903; morning; Publr WILLIAM NEWBIGGING; Editor-in-Chief LINDA HUGHES; circ. weekdays except Fri. 168,561, Fri. 204,346, Sun. 149,037.

Edmonton Sun: Toronto Sun Publishing Corpn, 9405 50th St, NW, Suite 100, Edmonton, AB T6B 2Y2; tel. (403) 368-0100; telex 037-42665; fax (403) 468-0128; f. 1978; morning; Publr PATRICK A. HARDEN; Editor-in-Chief DAVID BAILEY; circ. Mon. to Sat. 86,186, Sun. 125,150.

Fort McMurray Today: 9701 Franklin Ave, POB 4008, Fort McMurray, AB T9H 3G1; tel. (403) 748-8186; telex 037-5240; Mon. to Fri.; evening; Publr NEIL SUTCLIFFE; Editor-in-Chief MIKE BEAUDIN; circ. 5,683.

Lethbridge Herald: 504 Seventh St South, POB 670, Lethbridge, AB T1J 3Z7; tel. (403) 328-4411; telex 038-49220; f. 1907; Mon. to Sat.; evening; Publr and Gen. Man. DON DORAM; Man. Editor JIM HASKETT; circ. 25,034.

News: Southam Inc, 3257 Dunmore Rd, SE, POB 10, Medicine Hat, AB T1A 7E6; tel. (403) 527-1101; telex 038-48191; fax (403) 527-6029; f. 1910; Mon. to Sat.; evening; Publr GEORGE WILLCOCKS; Editor PETER MOSSEY; circ. 14,150.

British Columbia

Alaska Highway News: 9916 98th St, Fort St John, BC V1J 3T8; tel. (604) 785-5631; Mon. to Fri.; evening; Publr LOIS F. ARMAS; Editor DAVE NAGY; circ. 3,182.

Alberni Valley Times: Sterling Newspapers Ltd, 4918 Napier St, POB 400, Port Alberni, BC V9Y 7N1; tel. (604) 723-8171; Mon. to Fri.; evening; Publr NIGEL E. HANNAFORD; Editor-in-Chief ROB DIOTTE; circ. 6,516.

Chinese Times: Chinese Freemason Publrs Ltd, 1 East Pender St, Vancouver, BC V6A 1S9; tel. (604) 685-8575; Mon. to Sat.; evening; Publr WAYNE YEUNG; Editor-in-Chief CHI HONG TSANG; circ. 3,200.

Citizen: Southam Inc, 150 Brunswick St, POB 5700, Prince George, BC V2L 5K9; tel. (604) 562-2441; f. 1957; Mon. to Sat.; evening; Publr AL MCNAIR; Editor-in-Chief ROY K. NAGEL; circ. 21,530.

Daily Bulletin: East Kootenay Newspapers Ltd, 335 Spokane St, Kimberley, BC V1A 1Y9; tel. (604) 427-5333; Mon. to Fri.; evening; Publr CAROL MURRAY; Man. Editor BILL PHILLIPS; circ. 2,140.

Daily Courier: Canadian Newspapers Co Ltd, 550 Doyle Ave, Kelowna, BC V1Y 7V1; tel. (604) 762-4445; f. 1904; Mon. to Sat.; evening; Publr DANIEL F. DOUCETTE; Man. Editor DAVE HENSHAW; circ. 16,735.

Daily Free Press: Thomson Newspapers Co Ltd, 223–225 Commercial St, POB 69, Nanaimo, BC V9R 5K5; tel. (604) 753-3451; f. 1874; Mon. to Sat.; evening; Publr CLYDE T. WICKS; Man. Editor WAYNE CAMPBELL; circ. 9,221.

Daily News (Nelson): News Publishing Co, 266 Baker St, Nelson, BC V1L 4H3; tel. (604) 352-3352; f. 1902; Mon. to Fri.; evening; Publr BOB FIRTH; Man. Editor RYON GUEDES; circ. 6,000.

Daily News (Prince Rupert): Sterling Newspapers Ltd, POB 580, Prince Rupert, BC V8J 3R9; tel. (604) 624-6781; Mon. to Fri.; evening; Publr IRIS CHRISTISON.

Daily News (Vernon): Thomson (BC) Newspapers Ltd, 3309 31st Ave, Vernon, BC V1T 6N8; tel. (604) 545-0671; Mon. to Sat.; evening; Publr GARY OLDFIELD; circ. 8,318.

Daily Times: 1163 Cedar Ave, Trail, BC V1R 4B8; tel. (604) 368-8551; Mon. to Fri.; evening; Publr RAY PICCO; Man. Editor KEITH MCQUIGGAN; circ. 5,757.

Daily Townsman: East Kootenay Newspapers Ltd, 822 Cranbrook St North, Cranbrook, BC V1C 3R9; tel. (604) 426-5201; Mon. to Fri.; evening; Publr CAROL MURRAY; circ. 4,148.

Herald: Canadian Newspapers Co Ltd, 186 Nanaimo Ave West, Penticton, BC V2A 1N4; tel. (604) 492-4002; fax (604) 492-2403; Mon. to Sat.; evening; Publr EDWIN A. CLINE; Editor MIKE INGRAHAM; circ. 8,551.

Kamloops Daily News: Southam Inc, 63 West Victoria St, Suite 106, Kamloops, BC V2C 6J6; tel. (604) 372-2331; fax (604) 374-3884; f. 1982; Mon. to Sat.; evening; Publr BRYSON W. STONE; Editor-in-Chief MEL ROTHENBURGER; circ. 20,785.

Peace River Block News: 901 100th Ave, POB 180, Dawson Creek, BC V1G 4G6; tel. (604) 782-4888; Mon. to Fri.; evening; Publr HEINZ GOLDBACH; Editor-in-Chief MARCHETA LEOPPKY; circ. 3,566.

Province: Pacific Press Ltd, 2250 Granville St, Vancouver, BC V6H 3G2; tel. (604) 732-2513; fax (604) 732-2704; f. 1898; daily except Sat.; morning; Editor-in-Chief IAN HAYSOM; circ. Mon. to Fri. 192,000, Sun. 230,000.

Times Colonist: Canadian Newspapers Co Ltd, 2621 Douglas St, POB 300, Victoria, BC V8W 2N4; tel. (604) 382-7211; telex 049-

7288; f. 1858; morning; Publr COLIN McCULLOUGH; Man. Editor GORDON R. BELL; circ. Mon. to Sat. 78,715, Sun. 76,027.

Vancouver Sun: Pacific Press Ltd, 2250 Granville St, Vancouver, BC V6H 3G2; tel. (604) 732-2513; fax (604) 732-2704; f. 1886; Mon. to Sat.; evening; Publr GERALD HASLAM; Editor BRUCE LARSEN; circ. except Fri. 223,227, Fri. 273,553.

Manitoba

Brandon Sun: The Sun Publishing Co Ltd, 501 Rosser Ave, Brandon, MB R7A 5Z6; tel. (204) 727-2451; fax (204) 725-0976; f. 1882; Mon. to Sat.; evening; Publr and Editor-in-Chief ROB FORBES; Man. Editor JACK GIBSON; circ. 19,000.

Daily Bulletin: 120 First Ave, NE, Dauphin, MB R7N 1A5; tel. (204) 638-4420; Mon. to Fri.; evening; Publr BOB GILROY; Editor-in-Chief RYAN KUSTRA; circ. 1,125.

Daily Graphic: Vopni Press Ltd, 1941 Saskatchewan Ave West, POB 130, Portage la Prairie, MB R1N 3B4; tel. (204) 857-3427; fax (204) 239-1270; Mon. to Sat.; evening; Pres. and Publr HUGH McTAGGART; circ. 4,590.

Reminder: 38 Main St, POB 727, Flin Flon, MB R8A 1N5; tel. (204) 687-3454; f. 1946; Mon. to Fri.; evening; Publr TOM DOBSON; Editor-in-Chief RON DOBSON; circ. 3,775.

Report: POB 1629, Swan River, MB R0L 1Z0; tel. (204) 734-2729; evening.

Winnipeg Free Press: Canadian Newspapers Co Ltd, 300 Carlton St, Winnipeg, MB R3C 3C1; tel. (204) 943-9331; f. 1874; morning and evening; Publr ART WOOD; Man. Editor MURRAY BURT; circ. Mon. to Sat. 171,214, Sun. 148,345.

Winnipeg Sun: 1700 Church Ave, Winnipeg, MB R2X 3A2; tel. (204) 694-2022; fax (204) 632-8709; f. 1980; daily except Sat.; morning; Publr AL DAVIES; Editor-in-Chief BRYAN DUNLOP; circ. Mon. to Fri. 54,000, Sun. 60,616.

New Brunswick

L'Acadie Nouvelle: 217 blvd St-Pierre ouest, CP 1100, Caraquet, NB E0B 1K0; tel. (506) 727-4444; f. 1984; Mon. to Fri.; morning; Gen. Man. CAMILLE McLAUGHLIN; Editor MICHEL DOUCET; circ. 8,666.

Daily Gleaner: University Press of New Brunswick, POB 3370, Fredericton, NB E3B 5A2; tel. (506) 452-6671; fax (506) 452-7405; f. 1880; Mon. to Sat.; evening; Publr TOM CROWTHER; Editor-in-Chief HAL P. WOOD; circ. 29,359.

Evening Times-Globe: NB Publishing Co Ltd, Crown St at Union, POB 2350, Saint John, NB E2L 3V8; tel. (506) 632-8888; Mon. to Sat.; evening; Pres. R. PAUL WILLCOCKS; Editor-in-Chief FRED HAZEL; circ. 32,656.

Le Matin: 95 Foundry St, POB 1249, Moncton, NB E1C 8P9; tel. (506) 853-1920; morning.

Telegraph-Journal: NB Publishing Co Ltd, Crown St at Union, POB 2350, Saint John, NB E2L 3V8; tel. (506) 632-8888; Mon. to Sat.; morning; Pres. R. PAUL WILLCOCKS; Editor-in-Chief FRED HAZEL; circ. Mon. to Fri. 30,752, Sat. 60,476.

Times-Transcript: Moncton Publishing Co Ltd, 939 Main St, POB 1001, Moncton, NB E1C 8P3; tel. (506) 853-9321; fax (506) 853-0481; Mon. to Sat.; evening; Publr JIM D. NICHOL; Man. Editor MIKE BEMBRIDGE; circ. 45,067.

Newfoundland

Telegram: Thomson Newspapers Co Ltd, 400 Topsail Rd, POB 5970, St John's, NF A1C 5X7; tel. (709) 364-6300; f. 1879; Mon. to Sat.; evening; Publr STEPHEN R. HERDER; Editor WILLIAM R. CALLAGHAN; circ. Mon. to Fri. 38,531, Sat. 54,959.

Western Star: Thomson Newspapers Co Ltd, West St, POB 460, Corner Brook, NF A2H 6E7; tel. (709) 634-4348; fax (709) 634-9824; f. 1900; Mon. to Sat.; evening; Publr ROBERT C. MARSHALL; Editor-in-Chief RICHARD G. WILLIAMS; circ. 12,500.

Northwest Territories

There are no daily or Sunday newspapers in the Northwest Territories. The following are the leading weekly newspapers:

News/North: Northern News Services Ltd, POB 2820, Yellowknife, NT X1A 2R1; tel. (403) 873-4033; f. 1945; Mon.; Publr JACK W. SIGVALDASON; Man. Editor CRAIG HARPER; circ. 9,025.

Nunatsiaq News: POB 8, Iqaluit, NT X0A 0H0; tel. (403) 979-5357; fax (403) 979-4763; Fri.; Editor KELLY CURWIN; circ. 6,500.

Yellowknifer: Northern News Services Ltd, POB 2820, Yellowknife, NT X1A 2R1; tel. (403) 873-4031; Wed.; Editor BRIAN JONES; circ. 5,516.

Nova Scotia

Cape Breton Post: Thomson Newspapers Co Ltd, 255 George St, Sydney, NS B1P 6K6; tel. (902) 564-5451; Mon. to Sat.; evening; Publr JAMES P. MILNE; Man. Editor ANGUS MacDONALD; circ. 31,254.

Chronicle-Herald: 1650 Argyle St, POB 610, Halifax, NS B3J 2T2; tel. (902) 426-2898; telex 019-21874; fax (902) 426-3014; Mon. to Sat.; morning; Pres. FRED G. MOUNCE; Man. Editor KEN FORAN; circ. 88,395.

Daily News (Amherst): Cumberland Publishing Ltd, POB 280, Amherst, NS B4H 3Z2; tel. (902) 667-5102; Mon. to Fri.; morning; Publr EARL J. GOUCHIE; Editor JOHN CONRAD; circ. 4,008.

Daily News (Halifax): Robinson–Blackmore Printing and Publishing Ltd, POB 8330, Station A, Halifax, NS B3K 5M1; tel. (902) 465-1222; telex 019-31514; Mon. to Sat.; morning; Gen. Man. MARK RICHARDSON; Editor-in-Chief DOUGLAS MacKAY; circ. 22,825.

Daily News (Truro): Thomson Newspapers Co Ltd, 6 Louise St, POB 220, Truro, NS B2N 5C3; tel. (902) 893-9405; f. 1891; Mon. to Fri. evenings, Sat. morning; Publr TERRENCE W. HONEY; Man. Editor ROBERT PAXTON; circ. 9,132.

Evening News: Canadian Newspapers Co Ltd, 352 East River Rd, POB 159, New Glasgow, NS B2H 5E2; tel. (902) 752-3000; f. 1910; Mon. to Sat.; evening; Publr and Gen. Man. KEN SIMS; Man. Editor DOUG MacNEILL; circ. 11,323.

Mail-Star: 1650 Argyle St, POB 610, Halifax, NS B3J 2T2; tel. (902) 426-2898; telex 019-21874; fax (902) 426-3014; Mon. to Sat.; evening; Pres. FRED G. MOUNCE; Man. Editor KEN FORAN; circ. 59,299.

Ontario

Beacon–Herald: 108 Ontario St, POB 430, Stratford, ON N5A 6T6; tel. (519) 271-2220; fax (519) 271-1026; f. 1854; Mon. to Sat.; evening; Co-Publr and Gen. Man. CHARLES W. DINGMAN; Co-Publr and Editor STANFORD H. DINGMAN; circ. 13,205.

Brampton Times: Canadian Newspapers Co Ltd, 33 Queen St West, Brampton, ON L6Y 1M1; tel. (416) 451 2020; f. 1885; Mon. to Sat.; evening; Publr VICTOR MLODECKI; Man. Editor STEVE RHODES; circ. 9,645.

Burlington Spectator: Southam Inc, 534 Brant St, Burlington, ON L7R 2G8; tel. (416) 681-3900; Mon. to Fri. evenings, Sat. morning; Editor ROB AUSTIN; Deputy Editor JOHN GIBSON; circ. 23,204.

Cambridge Reporter: Canadian Newspapers Co Ltd, 26 Ainslie St South, Cambridge, ON N1R 3K1; tel. (519) 621-3810; f. 1846; Mon. to Sat.; evening; Publr JON BUTLER; Man. Editor ROSS FREAKE; circ. 15,000.

Chatham Daily News: Thomson Newspapers Co Ltd, 45 Fourth St, POB 2007, Chatham, ON N7M 2G4; tel. (519) 354-2000; f. 1862; Mon. to Sat.; evening; Publr F. IAN RUTHERFORD; Man. Editor STEVE ZAK; circ. 16,022.

Chronicle-Journal: 75 South Cumberland St, Thunder Bay, ON P7B 1A3; tel. (807) 344-3535; Mon. to Sat.; evening; Publr F. M. DUNDAS; Man. Editor MICHAEL GRIEVE; circ. 29,576.

Daily Bulletin: 116 1st East, POB 339, Fort Frances, ON P9A 3M7; tel. (807) 274-5373; fax (807) 274-7286; Mon. to Fri.; evening; Publr ROBERT A. CUMMING; Editor HARRY VANDETTI; circ. 2,950.

Daily Miner and News: 33 Main St South, POB 1620, Kenora, ON P9N 3X7; tel. (807) 468-5555; telex 759 2540; Mon. to Fri.; evening; Publr JOHN S. BUCHANAN; Editor ROSS A. PORTER; circ. 4,814.

Daily Press: Thomson Newspapers Co Ltd, 187 Cedar St South, POB 560, Timmins, ON P4N 2G9; tel. (705) 268-5050; f. 1933; Mon. to Sat.; evening; Publr J. C. BUTLER; Editor J. HORNYAK; circ. 13,957.

Daily Racing Form: 245 Carlaw Ave, Toronto, ON M4M 2S7; tel. (416) 465-5487; morning.

Daily Star: Northumberland Publishers Ltd, 415 King St West, POB 400, Cobourg, ON K9A 4L1; tel. (416) 372-0131; Mon. to Fri.; evening; Publr BILL POIRIER; Editorial Dir JIM GROSSMITH; circ. 5,684.

Le Droit: 375 Rideau St, Ottawa, ON K1N 5Y7; tel. (613) 560-747; f. 1913; morning; Publr GILBERT LACASSE; Editor PIERRE ALLARD; circ. except Sat. 39,711, Sat. 45,554.

Examiner (Barrie): Canadian Newspapers Co Ltd, 16 Bayfield St, POB 370, Barrie, ON L4M 4T6; tel. (705) 726-6537; f. 1864; Mon. to Fri. evenings, Sat. morning; Publr PETER KAPYRKA; Editor MARK FURLONG; circ. 15,000.

Examiner (Peterborough): 400 Water St, POB 389, Peterborough, ON K9J 6Z4; tel. (705) 745-4641; f. 1884; Mon. to Sat.; evening; Publr and Gen. Man. BRUCE L. RUDD; Man. Editor ED ARNOLD; circ. 7,295.

Expositor: Southam Inc, POB 965, Brantford, ON N3T 5S8; tel. (519) 756-2020; f. 1852; Mon. to Sat.; evening; Publr J. HOWARD GAUL; Editor K. J. STRACHAN; circ. 33,400.

Financial Post: POB 1156, Station A, Toronto, ON M5W 1G6; tel. (416) 596-5649; telex 062-19547; fax (416) 596-5300; f. 1988; Publr NEVILLE NANKIVELL.

Globe and Mail: 444 Front St West, Toronto, ON M5V 2S9; tel. (416) 585-5000; telex 062-19721; fax (416) 585-5275; f. 1844; Mon. to Sat.; morning; Publr A. ROY MEGARRY; Editor-in-Chief NORMAN WEBSTER; circ. 326,300.

Guide: Northumberland Publishers Ltd, 56 Walton St, POB 296, Port Hope, ON L1A 3W4; tel. (416) 885-2471; Mon. to Fri.; evening; Publr WILLIAM POIRIER; Man. Editor J. T. GROSSMITH; circ. 3,542.

Hamilton Spectator: Southam Inc, 44 Frid St, Hamilton, ON L8N 3G3; tel. (416) 526-3333; fax (416) 522-1696; f. 1846; Mon. to Fri. evenings, Sat. morning; Editor ALEX M. BEER; circ. 144,107.

Intelligencer: Canadian Newspapers Co Ltd, 45 Bridge St East, POB 5600, Belleville, ON K8N 5C7; tel. (613) 962-9171; f. 1870; Mon. to Sat.; evening; Publr and Gen. Man. H. MYLES MORTON; Man. Editor LEE BALLANTYNE; circ. 18,042.

Kitchener-Waterloo Record: 225 Fairway Rd South, Kitchener, ON N2G 4E5; tel. (519) 894-2231; fax (519) 894-3912; f. 1878; Mon. to Sat.; evening; Publr K. A. BAIRD; Man. Editor WAYNE MACDONALD; circ. 7,400.

Lindsay Daily Post: 15 William St North, Lindsay, ON K9V 3Z8; tel. (705) 324-2114; Mon. to Fri.; evening; Pres. JAMIE A. MCQUARRIE; circ 4,856.

London Free Press: 369 York St, POB 2280, London, ON N6A 4G1; tel. (519) 679-1111; telex 064-5837; f. 1849; Mon. to Sat.; morning; Publr MARTHA G. BLACKBURN; Editor-in-Chief PHILIP R. MCLEOD; circ. 129,539.

Mercury: Thomson Newspapers Co Ltd, 8-14 MacDonell St, POB 3604, Guelph, ON N1H 6P7; tel. (519) 822-4310; Mon. to Sat.; evening; Publr J. PETER KOHL; Editor BOB BOXALL; circ. 19,411.

Northern Daily News: Thomson Newspapers Co Ltd, 8 Duncan Ave, Kirkland Lake, ON P2N 3L4; tel. (705) 567-5321; f. 1922; Mon. to Sat.; evening; Publr WILLIAM MACKIE; Editor AL HOGAN; circ. 5,567.

Nugget: Southam Inc, 259 Worthington St, POB 570, North Bay, ON P1B 8J6; tel. (705) 472-3200; f. 1909; Mon. to Sat.; evening; Publr JACK R. OWENS; Editor COLIN P. VEZINA; circ. 24,275.

Observer (Pembroke): Canadian Newspapers Co Ltd, 186 Alexander St, Pembroke, ON K8A 4L9; tel. (613) 732-3691; f. 1855; Mon. to Sat.; evening; Publr and Man. Editor W. H. HIGGINSON; circ. 7,066.

Observer (Sarnia): Thomson Newspapers Co Ltd, 140 South Front St, Sarnia, ON N7T 7M8; tel. (519) 344-3641; f. 1917; Mon. to Sat.; evening; Publr and Gen. Man. T. J. HOGAN; Man. Editor COLIN BRUCE; circ. 23,944.

Ottawa Citizen: Southam Inc, 1101 Baxter Rd, POB 5020, Ottawa, ON K2C 3M4; tel. (613) 829-9100; telex 053-4779; fax (613) 829-5032; f. 1843; Mon. to Sat.; morning and evening; Publr CLARK DAVEY; Editor GORDON FISHER; circ. Mon. to Fri. 192,070, Sat. 248,979.

Packet and Times: Thomson Newspapers Co Ltd, 31 Colborne St East, Orillia, ON L3V 1T4; tel. (705) 325-1355; Mon. to Sat.; evening; Publr JACK C. MARSHALL; Man. Editor MARK FURLONG; circ. 10,252.

Recorder and Times: 23 King St West, POB 10, Brockville, ON K6V 5T8; tel. (613) 342-4441; f. 1821; Mon. to Sat.; evening; Co-Publrs H. S. GRANT, PERRY S. BEVERLEY; circ. 15,844.

Reformer: Thomson Newspapers Co Ltd, 105 Donly Dr., Simcoe, ON N3Y 4L2; tel. (519) 426-5710; fax (519) 426-9255; f. 1858; Mon. to Fri.; evening; Pres. JOHN COWLARD; Man. Editor RON KOWALSKY; circ. 9,545.

Review: Thomson Newspapers Co Ltd, 4801 Valley Way, Niagara Falls, ON L2E 6T6; tel. (416) 358-5711; f. 1879; Mon. to Sat.; evening; Publr GORDON A. MURRAY; Man. Editor DONALD M. MULLAN; circ. 21,798.

Standard: 17 Queen St, St Catharine's, ON L2R 5G5; tel. (416) 684-7251; fax (416) 684-8011; f. 1891; Mon. to Sat.; evening; Pres. and Publr H. B. BURGOYNE; Man. Editor MURRAY G. THOMSON; circ. 43,299.

Standard-Freeholder: Thomson Newspapers Co Ltd, 44 Pitt St, Cornwall, ON K6J 3P3; tel. (613) 933-3160; Mon. to Sat.; evening; Publr DON TOMCHICK; Editor JOAN NETTLE; circ. 17,542.

Star: Southam Inc, 145 Old Garden Rd, POB 460, Sault Sainte Marie, ON P6A 5M5; tel. (705) 759-3030; fax (705) 942-8690; f. 1912; Mon. to Sat.; evening; Publr E. PAUL WILSON; Man. Editor DOUG MILLROY; circ. 26,436.

Sudbury Star: Thomson Newspapers Co Ltd, 33 MacKenzie St, Sudbury, ON P3C 4Y1; tel. (705) 674-5271; f. 1909; Mon. to Sat.; evening; Publr MAURICE H. SWITZER; Man. Editor JOHN A. FARRINGTON; circ. 30,000.

Sun Times: Southam Inc, 290 Ninth St East, POB 200, Owen Sound, ON N4K 5P2; tel. (519) 376-2250; f. 1853; Mon. to Sat.; evening; Publr JOHN G. DOHERTY; Editor ROBERT HULL; circ. 23,735.

Sunday Sun: 333 King St East, Toronto, ON M5A 3X5; tel. (416) 947-2222; telex 062-17688; fax (416) 947-2441; f. 1971; Sun.; morning; Pres. and CEO J. DOUGLAS CREIGHTON; Editor JOHN DOWNING; circ. 450,067.

Times: Thomson Newspapers Co Ltd, 44 Richmond St West, Oshawa, ON L1G 1C8; tel. (416) 723-3474; f. 1871; Mon. to Sat.; evening; Publr A. S. TOPP; Man. Editor D. JAMES PALMATEER; circ. 22,277.

Times-News: 75 South Cumberland St, Thunder Bay, ON P7B 1A3; tel. (807) 344-3535; Mon. to Sat.; evening; Publr F. M. DUNDAS; Man. Editor MICHAEL GRIEVE; circ. 8,708.

Toronto Star: One Yonge St, Toronto, ON M5E 1E6; tel. (416) 367-2000; telex 065-24387; fax (416) 869-4156; f. 1892; all day; Publr DAVID R. JOLLEY; Editor JOHN HONDERICH; circ. Mon. to Fri. 522,971, Sat. 789,401, Sun. 531,223.

Toronto Sun: 333 King St East, Toronto, ON M5A 3X5; tel. (416) 947-2222; telex 062-17688; fax (416) 947-2441; f. 1971; Mon. to Fri.; morning; Pres. and CEO J. DOUGLAS CREIGHTON; Editor JOHN DOWNING; circ. 306,203.

Welland/Port Colborne Tribune: Canadian Newspapers Co Ltd, 228 East Main St, POB 278, Welland, ON L3B 5P5; tel. (416) 732-2411; f. 1863; Mon. to Sat.; evening; Publr JOHN W. VANKOOTEN; Editor JAMES R. MIDDLETON; circ. 17,360.

Whig-Standard: 306 King St East, Kingston, ON K7L 4Z7; tel. (613) 544-5000; fax (613) 544-6994; f. 1834; Mon. to Sat.; morning and evening; Publr MICHAEL L. DAVIES; Editor N. REYNOLDS; circ. 36,084.

Windsor Star: Southam Inc, 167 Ferry St, Windsor, ON N9A 4M5; tel. (519) 255-5787; fax (519) 255-5502; f. 1918; Mon. to Sat.; evening; Publr J. S. THOMSON; Editor CARL MORGAN; circ. Mon. to Fri. 88,000, Sat. 98,000.

Woodstock-Ingersoll Daily Sentinel Review: Canadian Newspapers Co Ltd, 16 Brock St, POB 1000, Woodstock, ON N4S 8A5; tel. (519) 537-2341; f. 1886; Mon. to Sat.; evening; Publr PAUL J. TAYLOR; Man. Editor GARY MANNING; circ. 10,172.

Prince Edward Island

Guardian: Thomson Newspapers Co Ltd, 165 Prince St, POB 760, Charlottetown, PE C1A 4R7; tel. (902) 894-5806; f. 1887; Mon. to Sat.; morning; Man. Editor WALTER MACINTYRE; circ. 18,000.

Journal Pioneer: 4 Queen St, POB 4280, Summerside, PE C1N 4K5; tel. (902) 436-2121; f. 1957; Mon. to Fri.; evening; Publr RALPH HECKBERT; Editor RON ENGLAND; circ. 11,617.

Patriot: Thomson Newspapers Co Ltd, 165 Prince St, POB 760, Charlottetown, PE C1A 4R7; tel. (902) 894-5806; f. 1887; Mon. to Sat.; evening; Man. Editor WALTER MACINTYRE; circ. 5,500.

Québec

Le Devoir: 211 rue St-Sacrement, Montréal, PQ H2Y 1X1; tel. (514) 842-9645; telex 055-61245; fax (514) 286-9255; f. 1910; Mon. to Sat.; morning; Dir BENOÎT LAUZIÈRE; Editor-in-Chief PAUL-ANDRÉ COMEAU; circ. Mon. to Fri. 26,000, Sat. 30,863.

Gazette: 250 rue St-Antoine ouest, Montréal, PQ H2Y 3R7; tel. (514) 282-2750; telex 055-61767; fax (514) 282-2322; f. 1778; morning; Publr DAVID PERKS; Editor NORMAN WEBSTER; circ. Mon. to Fri. 190,747, Sat. 268,971, Sun. 196,453.

Le Journal de Montréal: Groupe Québécor Inc, 4545 rue Frontenac, Montréal, PQ H2H 2R7; tel. (514) 521-4545; telex 058-27591; fax (514) 521-4416; f. 1964; morning; Pres. PIERRE PELADEAU; Editor JOCELYNE PELCHAT; circ. Mon. to Fri. 319,121, Sat. 345,698, Sun. 337,381.

Le Journal de Québec: Groupe Québécor Inc, 450 rue Béchard, CP 2158, Ville de Vanier, PQ G1M 2E9; tel. (418) 683-1573; fax

(418) 688-8181; f. 1967; morning; Gen. Man. JEAN-CLAUDE L'ABBÉE; Chief Editor SERGE CÔTÉ; circ. Mon. to Fri. 104,393, Sat. 105,743, Sun. 92,707.

Montréal Daily News: 980 rue St-Antoine ouest, Montréal, PQ H3C 1A9; tel. (514) 877-6397; fax (514) 845-3365; morning.

Le Nouvelliste: 500 rue St-Georges, CP 668, Trois-Rivières, PQ G9A 5J6; tel. (819) 376-2501; f. 1920; Mon. to Sat.; morning; Publr and Editor CLAUDETTE TOUGAS; Editor-in-Chief BERNARD CHAMPOUX; circ. 57,410.

La Presse: 7 rue St-Jacques, Montréal, PQ H2Y 1K9; tel. (514) 285-7306; telex 052-4110; fax (514) 845-8129; f. 1884; morning; Publr ROGER D. LANDRY; circ. Mon. to Fri. 207,296, Sat. 326,988, Sun. 183,719.

Le Quotidien: 1051 blvd Talbot, Chicoutimi, PQ G7H 5C1; tel. (418) 545-4474; fax (418) 545-9854; f. 1973; Mon. to Sat.; morning; Pres. and Gen. Man. GASTON VACHON; Newsroom Dir BERTRAND GENEST; circ. 31,996.

The Record: 2850 Delorme St, CP 1200, Sherbrooke, PQ J1K 1A1; tel. (819) 569-9525; fax (819) 569-3945; f. 1837; Mon. to Fri.; evening; Publr RANDY KINNEAR; Editor CHARLES BURY; circ. 6,100.

Le Soleil: 390 rue St-Vallier est, Québec, PQ G1K 7J6; tel. (418) 647-3270; telex 051-3755; f. 1896; morning; Pres. and Gen. Man. ROBERT NORMAND; Editor-in-Chief CLAUDE GRAVEL; circ. Mon. to Fri. 119,000, Sat. 137,374, Sun. 96,000.

La Tribune: 1950 rue Roy, Sherbrooke, PQ J1K 2X8; tel. (819) 564-5450; f. 1910; Mon. to Sat.; morning; Pres. and Editor YVON DUBE; Assistant Editor JEAN VIGNEAULT; circ. 40,000.

La Voix de l'Est: 136 rue Principale, Granby, PQ J2G 2V4; tel. (514) 375-4555; f. 1945; Mon. to Sat.; morning; Pres. JEAN-GUY DUBAC; Man. Editor RÉAL MARCHESSEAULT; circ. 16,067.

Saskatchewan

Herald: Canadian Newspapers Co Ltd, 30 10th St East, POB 550, Prince Albert, SK S6V 5R9; tel. (306) 764-4276; fax (306) 763-3331; f. 1917; Mon. to Sat.; evening; Publr and Gen. Man. R. W. GIBB; Man. Editor WAYNE ROZNOWSKY; circ. 10,000.

Leader–Post: 1964 Park St, POB 2020, Regina, SK S4P 3G4; tel. (306) 565-8211; telex 071-3131; fax (306) 565-8350; f. 1883; Mon. to Sat.; evening; Pres. MICHAEL C. SIFTON; Editor-in-Chief IVOR WILLIAMS; circ. 71,806.

Star-Phoenix: Armdale Publrs Ltd, 204 Fifth Ave North, Saskatoon, SK S7K 2P1; tel. (306) 664-8340; telex 034-2475; fax (306) 664-8208; f. 1902; Mon. to Sat.; morning; Pres. MICHAEL C. SIFTON; Editor-in-Chief BILL PETERSON; circ. 62,445.

Times–Herald: Canadian Newspapers Co Ltd, 44 Fairford St West, POB 3000, Moose Jaw, SK S6H 6E4; tel. (306) 692-6441; f. 1889; Mon. to Sat.; evening; Publr PETER E. LEICHNITZ; Editor-in-Chief DAVE MCGEE; circ. 9,713.

Yukon Territory

Whitehorse Star: 2149 Second Ave, Whitehorse, YT Y1A 1C5; tel. (403) 668-2063; Mon. to Fri.; evening; Publr BOB ERLAM; Man. Editor JACKIE PIERCE; circ. 4,000.

SELECTED PERIODICALS

Alberta

Alberta Business: 340 39th Ave, SE, Calgary, AB T2G 1X6; tel. (403) 271-7508; fax (403) 270-7607; f. 1984; 6 a year; Editor JOHN DODD; circ. 8,000.

Alberta Farm and Ranch: 4000 19th St, NE, Calgary, AB T2E 6P8; tel. (403) 250-9311; fax (403) 291-0502; f. 1983; monthly; Editor PETER BROUWER; circ. 87,000.

Alberta Farmagazine: 4000 19th St, NE, Calgary, AB T2E 6P8; tel. (403) 250-6633; f. 1983; monthly; Editor PETER BROUWER; circ. 92,000.

Alberta Report: 17327 106th Ave, Edmonton, AB T5S 1M7; tel. (403) 484-8884; f. 1979; weekly; news magazine; Editor STEPHEN HOPKINS; circ. 54,000.

Calgary Magazine: 139 17th Ave, SW, Suite 200, Calgary, AB T2S 0A1; tel. (403) 265-1054; fax (403) 228-5611; f. 1978; monthly; Editor JACK MCIVER; circ. 60,000.

Energy Equipment News: 1015 Centre St North, Calgary, AB T2E 2P8; tel. (403) 276-7881; fax (403) 276-5026; f. 1982; 6 a year; Editor VIC HUMPHREYS; circ. 24,000.

Oilweek: 1015 Centre St North, Calgary, AB T2E 2P8; tel. (403) 276-7881; fax (403) 276-5026; f. 1948; weekly; Editor VIC HUMPHREYS; circ. 17,000.

Ukrainski Visti (Ukrainian News): 10967 97th St, Edmonton, AB T5H 2M8; tel. (403) 429-2363; f. 1929; weekly; Ukrainian and English; Editor K. SHERMAN; circ. 5,000.

Western Catholic Reporter: 10562 109th St, Edmonton, AB T5H 3B2; tel. (403) 420-1330; weekly; Editor MARJORIE BENTLEY; circ. 37,000.

Wings Canada: 1224 53rd Ave, NE, Suite 158, Calgary, AB T2E 7E2; tel. (403) 275-9457; telex 038-21172; fax (403) 275-3925; f. 1957; 6 a year; aviation and space research; Editor TAMMI GODWIN; circ. 12,000.

British Columbia

1001 Decorating Ideas: 382 West Broadway, Vancouver, BC V5Y 1R2; tel. (604) 879-4144; f. 1948; 8 a year; Editor PAM WITHERS; circ. 160,000.

BC Business: 550 Burrard St, 2nd Floor, Vancouver, BC V6C 2J6; tel. (604) 669-1721; telex 043-57513; fax (604) 684-2376; f. 1973; monthly; Editor BONNIE IRVING; circ. 22,000.

BC Outdoors: 1132 Hamilton St, Suite 202, Vancouver, BC V6B 2S2; tel. (604) 687-1581; fax (604) 687-1925; f. 1945; 7 a year; Editor GEORGE WILL; circ. 48,000.

Canada Poultryman: 9547 152nd St, Suite 105A, Surrey, BC V3R 5Y5; tel. (604) 585-3131; fax (604) 585-1504; f. 1928; monthly; Editor ANTHONY GREAVES; circ. 11,000.

Easy Living: 13281 Comber Way, Surrey, BC V3W 5V8; tel. (604) 591-5101; fax (604) 591-3335; f. 1979; monthly; Editor VIVIAN SINCLAIR; circ. 355,000.

Journal of Commerce: 4285 Canada Way, POB 82230, North Burnaby, BC V5C 6E7; tel. (604) 433-8164; fax (604) 433-9549; 2 a week; construction industry.

Pacific Yachting: 1132 Hamilton St, Suite 202, Vancouver, BC V6B 2S2; tel. (604) 687-1581; f. 1968; monthly; Publr PAUL BURKHART; circ. 17,000.

Vancouver Magazine: 1205 Richards St, Vancouver, BC V6B 3G3; tel. (604) 685-5374; telex 045-1484; fax (604) 669-1900; f. 1957; monthly; Editor BOB MERCER; circ. 82,000.

Western Living: 504 Davie St, Vancouver, BC V6B 2G4; tel. (604) 669-7525; telex 045-1484; fax (604) 669-1900; f. 1971; monthly; Editor MALCOLM PARRY; circ. 239,000.

WestWorld Magazine: 4180 Lougheed Highway, Suite 401, Burnaby, BC V5C 6A7; tel. (604) 299-7311; fax (604) 299-9188; quarterly; Publr PETER LEGGE; Editor CAROL POPE; circ. 731,000.

Manitoba

The Beaver: Exploring Canada's History: 450 Portage Ave, Winnipeg, MB R3C 0E7; tel. (204) 786-7048; f. 1920; 6 a year; Canadian social history; Editor CHRISTOPHER DAFOE; circ. 34,000.

Cattlemen: 1760 Ellice Ave, Winnipeg, MB R3H 0B6; tel. (204) 774-1861; f. 1938; monthly; animal husbandry; Editor GREN WINSLOW; circ. 38,114.

Country Guide: 1760 Ellice Ave, Winnipeg, MB R3H 0B6; tel. (204) 774-1861; f. 1882; monthly; agriculture; Editor DAVID WREFORD; circ. 213,000.

Crops Guide: 1760 Ellice Ave, Winnipeg, MB R3H 0B6; tel. (204) 774-1861; annual; crops and livestock; circ. 138,000.

Dairy Guide: 1760 Ellice Ave, Winnipeg, MB R3H 0B6; tel. (204) 774-1861; circ. 26,000.

Grainews: 433 Main St, POB 6600, Winnipeg, MB R3B 1B3; tel. (204) 944-5561; telex 075-7809; fax (204) 944-5454; f. 1975; 18 a year; grain and cattle farming; Editor and Publr JOHN CLARK; circ. 68,000.

Kanada Kurier: 955 Alexander Ave, Winnipeg, MB R3C 0A5; tel. (204) 774-1883; telex 075-5740; f. 1889; weekly; ethnic German; Editor E. PRIEBE; circ. 20,000.

The Manitoba Co-operator: 220 Portage Ave, 4th Floor, Winnipeg, MB R3C 0A5; tel. (204) 934-0401; telex 075-87562; f. 1925; weekly; agricultural; Editor and Publr W. E. MORRIS; circ. 29,000.

Motor in Canada: 1077 St James St, POB 6900, Winnipeg, MB R3C 3B1; tel. (204) 775-0201; f. 1915; monthly; automotive business; Editor DAN PROUDLEY; circ. 12,000.

Trade and Commerce: 1077 St James St, POB 6900, Winnipeg, MB R3C 3B1; tel. (204) 775-0201; fax (204) 783-7488; f. 1905; monthly; Editor GEORGE MITCHELL; circ. 13,000.

New Brunswick

Atlantic Advocate: POB 3370, Fredericton, NB E3B 5A2; tel. (506) 452-6671; fax (506) 452-7405; f. 1956; monthly; Editor MARILEE LITTLE; circ. 30,000.

Newfoundland

Newfoundland Lifestyle: 197 Water St, POB 2356, St John's, NF A1C 6E7; tel. (709) 726-9300; 6 a year; Man. Editor EDWINA HUTTON; circ. 30,000.

Northwest Territories

L'Aquillon: POB 1325, Yellowknife, NT X1A 2N9; tel. (403) 920-2919; fax (403) 873-2158; weekly; circ. 2,000.

The Drum: POB 2719, Inuvik, NT X0E 0T0; tel. (403) 979-4545; f. 1966; weekly; English; Editor DAN HOLMAN; circ. 2,000.

The Hub: POB 1250, Hay River, NT X0E 0R0; tel. (403) 874-6577; weekly; circ. 2,000.

News/North: POB 2820, Yellowknife, NT X1A 2R1; tel. (403) 873-4033; f. 1945; weekly; Publr JACK W. SIGVALDSON; Man. Editor CRAIG HARPER; circ. 9,025.

Nunatsiaq News: POB 8, Iqaluit, NT X0A 0H0; tel. (403) 979-5357; fax (403) 979-4763; f. 1972; weekly; English and Inuktitut (Eskimo); Editor KELLY CURWIN; circ. 6,500.

Slave River Journal: POB 990, Fort Smith, NT X0E 0P0; tel. (403) 872-2784; fax (403) 872-2126; weekly; circ. 2,000.

Weekender: POB 2820, Yellowknife, NT X1A 2R1; tel. (403) 873-4031.

Yellowknifer: POB 2820, Yellowknife, NT X1A 2R1; tel. (403) 873-4031; Editor BRIAN JONES; circ. 5,516.

Nova Scotia

Atlantic Fisherman: 11 George St, POB 100, Pictou, NS B0K 1H0; tel. (902) 485-8014; fax (902) 752-4816; f. 1984; fortnightly; fishing industry; Editor HEATHER RICHARDS; circ. 9,000.

Atlantic Insight: 1668 Barrington St, Halifax, NS B3J 2A2; tel. (902) 421-1214; monthly; Editor SHARON FRASER; circ. 39,000.

The Dalhousie Review: Dalhousie University Press, Sir James Dunn Science Bldg, Halifax, NS B3H 3J5; tel. (902) 424-2541; f. 1921; quarterly; literary and general; Editor Dr ALAN ANDREWS.

Ontario

Boat Guide: 2570 Haines Rd, Mississauga, ON L4Y 4A3; tel. (416) 270-1440; f. 1984; annual; Editor JACK PURDUE; circ. 60,000.

Bon Vivant: 2115 Finch Ave West, Downsview, ON M3N 2V6; tel. (416) 745-2082; f. 1975; 6 a year; wine and spirit trade; Editor BOB PENNINGTON; circ. 31,000.

Camping Canada: 2077 Dundas St East, Suite 202, Mississauga, ON L4X 1M2; tel. (416) 624-8218; fax (416) 624-6764; f. 1971; 7 a year; Editor PETER TASLER; circ. 52,000.

Canada Gazette: Canadian Government Publishing Centre, Supply and Services Canada, Ottawa, ON K1A 0S9; tel. (819) 997-1988; f. 1867; weekly; official bulletin of the Govt of Canada; Chief BEATE ALAOUI.

Canada Reports: External Information Services Division, Dept of External Affairs, Ottawa, ON K1A 0G2; telex 053-3745; fortnightly; English and French edns; Editor CAROLE STELMACK.

Canada and the World: POB 7004, Oakville, ON L6J 6L5; tel. (416) 338-3394; f. 1937; 9 a year; youth; Editor RUPERT J. TAYLOR; circ. 24,000.

Canadian Aeronautics and Space Journal: 222 Somerset St West, Suite 601, Ottawa, ON K2P 2G3; tel. (613) 234-0191; fax (613) 234-

8039; f. 1954; monthly; Chair. of Editorial Board Dr G. F. MARSTERS; circ. 3,000.

Canadian Architect: 1450 Don Mills Rd, Don Mills, ON M3B 2X7; tel. (416) 445-6641; telex 069-66612; f. 1955; monthly; Publr and Man. Editor ROBERT GRETTON; circ. 10,000.

Canadian Bar Review: Canadian Bar Foundation, 50 O'Connor St, Suite 902, Ottawa, ON K1P 6L2; tel. (613) 237-2925; fax (613) 237-0185; f. 1923; quarterly; Editor A. J. McCLEAN; circ. 34,000.

Canadian Boating: 5200 Dixie Rd, Suite 204, Mississauga, ON L4W 1E4; tel. (416) 625-5277; telex 069-86841; f. 1925; 9 a year; Editor GARY ARTHURS; circ. 17,000.

Canadian Chemical News: 130 Slater St, Suite 550, Ottawa, ON K1P 6E2; tel. (613) 232-6252; fax (613) 232-5862; f. 1949; 10 a year; Editor SANDRA HOLLINGSHEAD; circ. 10,000.

Canadian Construction Record: 1450 Don Mills Rd, Don Mills, ON M3B 2X7; tel. (416) 445-6641; telex 069-66612; fax (416) 442-2077; f. 1888; monthly; Editor TED THALER; circ. 22,000.

Canadian Dental Association Journal: 1815 Alta Vista Dr., Ottawa, ON K1G 3Y6; tel. (613) 523-1770; fax (613) 523-7736; f. 1935; monthly; Editor Dr RALPH CRAWFORD; Scientific Editors Dr ROBERT TURNBULL, Dr PIERRE DESAUTELS.

Canadian Doctor: 625 Cochrane Dr., Suite 701, Markham, ON L3R 9R9; tel. (416) 940-0136; fax (416) 940-1888; f. 1935; monthly; Editor SHEREE L. BOND; circ. 30,000.

Canadian Forest Industries: 1450 Don Mills Rd, Don Mills, ON M3B 2X7; tel. (416) 445-6641; telex 069-66612; fax (416) 442-2077; f. 1880; monthly; Editor TIM TOLTON; circ. 21,000.

Canadian Geographic: 39 McArthur Ave, Vanier, ON K1L 8L7; tel. (613) 745-4629; fax (613) 744-0947; f. 1930; 6 a year; publ. by the Royal Canadian Geographical Soc.; Publr SUSANNE HUDSON; Editor IAN DARRAGH; circ. 225,000.

Canadian Labour: 2841 Riverside Dr., Ottawa, ON K1V 8X7; tel. (613) 521-3400; telex 053-4750; f. 1956; trade union journal; Editors D. HODGSON, M. WALSH.

Canadian Medical Association Journal: 1867 Alta Vista Dr., Ottawa, ON K1G 3Y6; tel. (613) 731-9331; telex 053-3152; fax (613) 523-0937; f. 1911; fortnightly; Editor-in-Chief Dr BRUCE P. SQUIRES; circ. 51,000.

The Canadian Nurse/L'infirmière canadienne: 50 The Driveway, Ottawa, ON K2P 1E2; tel. (613) 237-2133; f. 1908; monthly; journal of the Canadian Nurses' Asscn; Editor JUDITH A. BANNING; circ. 101,000.

Canadian Office: POB 190, Port Credit, ON L5G 4L7; tel. (416) 2271-1601; f. 1970; monthly; office management and automation; Editor BRUCE GLASSFORD; circ. 50,000.

Canadian Pharmaceutical Journal: 1785 Alta Vista Dr., Ottawa, ON K1G 3Y6; tel. (613) 523-7877; fax (613) 523-0445; f. 1869; monthly; Editor JANE DEWAR; circ. 12,500.

Canadian Research: 245 Fairview Mall Dr., Suite 500, Willowdale, ON M2J 4T1; tel. (416) 490-0220; fax (416) 490-0119; f. 1968; 8 a year; scientific; Publr D. DINGELDEN; Editor TOM GALE; circ. 14,400.

The Canadian Sportsman: 25 Townline Rd, POB 603, Tillsonburg, ON N4G 4J1; tel. (519) 842-4824; f. 1870; weekly (May–October), fortnightly (October–May); equestrian; Editor GARY FOERSTER.

Canadian Workshop: 130 Spy Ct, Markham, ON L3R 5H6; tel. (416) 475-8440; f. 1977; monthly; do-it-yourself; Editor CINDY LISTER; circ. 108,000.

Carguide: 2570 Haines Rd, Suite 3, Mississauga, ON L4Y 4A3; tel. (416) 270-1440; f. 1971; annual; Editor JIM KENZIE; circ. 200,000.

CMA: 154 Main St East, POB 176, MPO, Hamilton, ON L8N 3C3; tel. (416) 525-4100; fax (416) 525-4533; f. 1926; 6 a year; journal of the Society of Management Accountants; Editor J. HEWER; circ. 37,000.

Departures: 75 The Donway West, Suite 909, Don Mills, ON M3C 2E9; tel. (416) 441-2080; f. 1981; quarterly; travel and tourism; Editor and Publr DIANNE DUKOWSKI; circ. 130,000.

Design Product News: 135 Spy Ct, Markham, ON L3R 5H6; tel. (416) 477-3222; f. 1973; 6 a year; engineering; Editor J. C. YOUNG; circ. 19,000.

Dogs in Canada: 43 Railside Rd, Don Mills, ON M3A 3L9; tel. (416) 441-3228; f. 1889; monthly; for pedigree-dog-breeders; Publr ELIZABETH M. DUNN; Editor SUSAN E. PEARCE; circ. 22,000.

Electronics and Technology Today: 1300 Don Mills Rd, Don Mills, ON M3B 3M8; tel. (416) 445-5600; fax (416) 445-8149; f. 1977; monthly; computing; Editor BILL MARKWICK; circ. 15,000.

enRoute: 2973 Weston Rd, Weston, ON M9M 2T2; tel. (416) 741-1112; f. 1973; monthly; in-flight business, travel, life style; Editor CAROLYN JACKSON; circ. 100,000.

Hardware Merchandising: 245 Fairview Mall Dr., Suite 500, Willowdale, ON M2J 4T1; tel. (416) 490-0220; fax (416) 490-0119; f.

1988; 9 a year; Publr DANTE PUCCININ; Editor MICHAEL MCLAR-NEY; circ. 18,000.

Hi-Rise: 95 Leeward Glenway, Suite 121, Don Mills, ON M3C 2Z6; tel. (416) 424-1393; f. 1980; monthly; city life style; Editor VALERIE M. DUNN; circ. 55,000.

Hockey News: 85 Scarsdale Rd, Suite 100, Don Mills, ON M3B 2R2; tel. (416) 445-5702; f. 1947; 42 a year; Editor-in-Chief BOB MCKENZIE; circ. 115,000.

Holstein Journal: 335 Lesmill Rd, Don Mills, ON M3B 2V1; tel. (416) 441-3030; fax (416) 441-3038; f. 1938; monthly; farming, livestock; Editor BONNIE E. COOPER; circ. 19,000.

Industrial Product Ideas: 245 Fairview Mall Dr., Suite 500, Willowdale, ON M2J 4T1; tel. (416) 490-0220; fax (416) 490-0119; 8 a year; Publr M. SWAN; circ. 30,000.

Inside Hockey: 85 Scarsdale Rd, Suite 100, Don Mills, ON M3B 2R2; tel. (416) 445-5702; f. 1897; circ. 40,000.

Legion Magazine: 359 Kent St, Suite 504, Ottawa, ON K2P 0R6; tel. (613) 235-8741; f. 1926; 10 a year; Editor MALCOLM JOHNSTON; circ. 522,479.

Metalworking Production and Purchasing: 135 Spy Ct, Markham, ON L3R 5H6; tel. (416) 477-3222; f. 1974; 6 a year; Editor MAURICE HOLTMAN; circ. 24,000.

Modern Medicine of Canada: 1450 Don Mills Rd, Don Mills, ON M3B 2X7; tel. (416) 445-6641; telex 069-66612; fax (416) 442-2077; f. 1946; monthly; English and French; Editor Dr J. A. KELLEN; circ. 35,000.

Modern Purchasing: 245 Fairview Mall Dr., Suite 500, Willowdale, ON M2J 4T1; tel. (416) 490-0220; fax (416) 490-0119; monthly; Publr J. J. RESNICK; circ. 18,000.

Municipal World: 360 Talbot St, POB 399, St Thomas, ON N5P 3V3; tel. (519) 633-0031; f. 1981; monthly; Publr and Editor MICHAEL J. SMITHER; circ. 11,000.

Nature Canada: 453 Sussex Dr., Ottawa, ON K1N 6Z4; tel. (613) 238-6154; f. 1972; quarterly; journal of the Canadian Nature Federation; Editor JUDY LORD; circ. 19,000.

Ontario Milk Producer: 6780 Campobello Rd, Mississauga, ON L5N 2L8; tel. (416) 821-8970; f. 1925; monthly; Publr KEN SMITH; circ. 15,000.

Oral Health: 1450 Don Mills Rd, Don Mills, ON M3B 2X7; tel. (416) 445-6641; telex 069-66612; fax (416) 442-2077; f. 1911; monthly; dentistry; Man. Editor JANET BONELLIE; circ. 15,000.

Photo Life: 135 Spy Ct, Markham, ON L3R 5H6; tel. (416) 475-8440; f. 1976; monthly; Editor NORM ROSEN; circ. 70,000.

Plant Management and Engineering: 245 Fairview Mall Dr., Suite 500, Willowdale, ON M2J 4T1; tel. (416) 490-0220; fax (416) 490-0119; monthly; Publr G. JUSTICE; circ. 23,000.

Presbyterian Record: 50 Wynford Dr., Don Mills, ON M3C 1J7; tel. (416) 441-1111; monthy (except August); Editor JAMES ROSS DICKEY; circ. 73,000.

Purchasing Management Digest: 277 Lakeshore Rd East, Suite 209, Oakville, ON L6J 6J3; tel. (416) 842-2884; fax (416) 842-1470; f. 1978; 6 a year; Editor R. ROBB; circ. 18,000.

Stereo Guide: 6 Byng Ave, Brampton, ON L6Y 1L1; tel. (416) 451-8395; f. 1972; 6 a year; Editor MAURICE HOLTMAN; circ. 25,000.

Style: 85 Scarsdale Rd, Suite 300, Don Mills, ON M3B 2R2; tel. (416) 444-8407; telex 069-86351; fax (416) 444-5308; f. 1888; 16 a year; clothing business; Editor MARILYN BOLTON; circ. 14,000.

Teviskes Ziburiai (Lights of Homeland): 2185 Stayebank Rd, Mississauga, ON L5C 1T3; tel. (416) 275-4672; f. 1949; weekly; Lithuanian; Editor Rev. Dr PR. GAIDA; circ. 6,000.

Trucking Canada: 1450 Don Mills Rd, Don Mills, ON M3B 2X7; tel. (416) 442-2000; fax (416) 442-2077; f. 1885; monthly; circ. 28,000.

TORONTO

Anglican Journal Episcopal: 600 Jarvis St, Toronto, ON M4Y 2J6; tel. (416) 924-9192; telex 065-24128; fax (416) 921-4452; f. 1871; monthly; official publ. of the Anglican Church of Canada; Assoc. Editor CAROLYN PURDEN; circ. 273,000.

Arab News of Toronto (Akhbar El-Arab Toronto): 370 Queen St East, Toronto, ON M5A 1T1; tel. (416) 362-0304; telex 065-2629; f. 1978; fortnightly; Arabic and English; Editor SALAH ALLAM; circ. 6,000.

Aviation and Aerospace: Maclean Hunter Bldg, 777 Bay St, Toronto, ON M5W 1A7; tel. (416) 596-5789; fax (416) 596-5789; f. 1928; monthly; Editor AL DITTER; circ. 20,000.

Best Wishes Magazine: 77 Mowat Ave, Toronto, ON M6K 3E3; tel. (416) 537-3604; f. 1949; quarterly; infant and child care; Editor D. G. SWINBURNE; circ. 71,000.

Books in Canada: 366 Adelaide St East, 4th Floor, Toronto, ON M5A 3X9; tel. (416) 363-5426; f. 1971; 9 a year; Editor DORIS COWAN; circ. 12,000.

Breeder and Feeder: 590 Keele St, Toronto, ON M6N 3E3; tel. (416) 766-9217; f. 1963; 7 a year; Editor JEAN SZKOTNICKI; circ. 22,000.

CA magazine: The Canadian Institute of Chartered Accountants, 150 Bloor St West, Toronto, ON M5S 2Y2; tel. (416) 962-1242; telex 062-22835; fax (416) 962-3375; f. 1911; monthly; Editor NELSON LUSCOMBE; circ 63,000.

The Campus Network: Youthstream Canada Ltd, 1541 Avenue Rd, Suite 203, Toronto, ON M5M 3X4; tel. (416) 787-4911; 30 campus edns; Pres. CAMERON KILLORAN; circ. 257,000.

Campus Plus: 124 Merton St, 3rd Floor, Toronto, ON M4S 2Z2; weekly; circ. 325,000.

Canadian Author and Bookman: 121 Avenue Rd, Suite 104, Toronto, ON M5R 2G3; tel. (416) 926-8084; f. 1919; quarterly; publ. by the Canadian Authors Asscn; Editor DIANE KERNER; circ. 5,000.

Canadian Banker/le Banquier: 2 First Canadian Pl., POB 348, Toronto, ON M5X 1E1; tel. (416) 362-6092; telex 062-3402; fax (416) 362-7705; f. 1893; Editor BRIAN O'BRIEN; circ. 36,000.

Canadian Building: Maclean Hunter Bldg, 777 Bay St, Toronto, ON M5W 1A7; tel. (416) 596-5760; fax (416) 596-5810; f. 1951; monthly; Editor JOHN FENNELL; circ. 20,000.

Canadian Business: 70 The Esplanade, 2nd Floor, Toronto, ON M5E 1R2; tel. (416) 364-4266; fax (416) 364-2783; f. 1927; monthly; Publr MICHAEL REA; Editor WAYNE GOODING; circ. 86,000.

Canadian Datasystems: Maclean Hunter Bldg, 777 Bay St, Toronto, ON M5W 1A7; tel. (416) 596-5919; telex 062-19547; fax (416) 596-5526; monthly; Publr V. G. ZELLERMEYER; circ. 30,000.

Canadian Defence Quarterly: 310 Dupont St, Toronto, ON M5R 1V9; tel. (416) 968-7252; telex 065-28085; fax (416) 968-2377; f. 1971; quarterly; Editor JOHN MARTEINSON; circ. 10,000.

Canadian Electronics Engineering: Maclean Hunter Bldg, 777 Bay St, Toronto, ON M5W 1A7; tel. (416) 596-5731; telex 062-19547; fax (416) 596-5526; f. 1957; monthly; Editor PETER J. THORNE; circ. 20,000.

The Canadian Forum: 70 The Esplanade, 3rd Floor, Toronto, ON M5E 1R2; tel. (416) 364-2431; f. 1920; 10 a year; political, literary and economic; Editor JOHN HUTCHESON; circ. 10,000.

Canadian Grocer: Maclean Hunter Bldg, 777 Bay St, Toronto, ON M5W 1A7; tel. (416) 596-5772; telex 062-19547; fax (416) 596-5526; f. 1886; monthly; Publr and Editor GEORGE H. CONDON; circ. 17,000.

Canadian Hotel & Restaurant: Maclean Hunter Bldg, 777 Bay St, Toronto, ON M5W 1A7; tel. (416) 596-5813; telex 062-19547; f. 1923; monthly; Editor RON STANAITIS; circ. 31,000.

Canadian Journal of Economics: c/o University of Toronto Press, Front Campus, Toronto, ON M5S 1A6; tel. (416) 978-6739; f. 1968; quarterly; Editor ROBIN BOADWAY; circ. 3,000.

Canadian Living: 50 Holly St, Toronto, ON M4S 3B3; tel. (416) 482-8600; fax (416) 485-1093; f. 1975; monthly; Editor-in-Chief BONNIE COWAN; circ. 539,000.

Canadian Machinery and Metalworking: Maclean Hunter Bldg, 777 Bay St, Toronto, ON M5W 1A7; tel. (416) 596-5713; telex 062-19547; fax (416) 596-5526; f. 1905; Publr JIM BARNES; circ. 17,000.

Canadian Musician: 3284 Yonge St, Toronto, ON M4N 3M7; tel. (416) 485-8284; fax (416) 485-8924; f. 1979; 6 a year; Editor DAVID HENMAN; circ. 26,000.

Canadian Travel Press Weekly: 310 Dupont St, Toronto, ON M5R 1V9; tel. (416) 968-7252; telex 065-28085; fax (416) 968-2377; Editor EDITH BAXTER; circ. 19,000.

CAR (Canadian Auto Review): Maclean Hunter Bldg, 777 Bay St, Toronto, ON M5W 1A7; tel. (416) 596-5784; f. 1984; 8 a year; Editor RICHARD JACOBS; circ. 6,000.

Chatelaine: Maclean Hunter Bldg, 777 Bay St, Toronto, ON M5W 1A7; tel. (416) 596-5425; telex 062-19547; fax (416) 593-3197; f. 1928; monthly; women's journal; Editor MILDRED ISTONA; circ. 1,000,000.

City and Country Home: Maclean Hunter Bldg, 777 Bay St, Toronto, ON M5W 1A7; tel. (416) 596-5404; f. 1982; life style and interiors; Editor BARBARA JEAN NEAL; circ. 100,000.

Civic Public Works: Maclean Hunter Bldg, 777 Bay St, Toronto, ON M5W 1A7; tel. (416) 596-5953; telex 062-19547; fax (416) 593-3193; f. 1949; monthly; Editor CLIFF ALLUM; circ. 13,000.

Cycle Guide: 411 Richmond St East, Suite 102, Toronto, ON M5A 3S5; tel. (416) 362-7966; f. 1971; monthly; motorcycling; Publr MARTIN LÉVESQUE; Editor JOHN COOPER; circ. 45,000.

Design Engineering: Maclean Hunter Bldg, 777 Bay St, Toronto, ON M5W 1A7; tel. (416) 596-5833; telex 062-19547; fax (416) 593-3193; f. 1955; monthly; Editor STEVE PURWITSKY; circ. 18,000.

Engineering Digest: 111 Peter St, Suite 411, Toronto, ON M5V 2W2; tel. (416) 596-1624; telex 062-18852; f. 1954; 6 a year; Editor H. W. MEYFARTH; circ. 66,000.

Farm and Country: 950 Yonge St, 7th Floor, Toronto, ON M4W 2J4; tel. (416) 924-6209; fax (416) 924-9951; f. 1936; 18 a year; Publr and Editor-in-Chief JOHN PHILLIPS; circ. 68,000.

The Financial Post: Maclean Hunter Bldg, 777 Bay St, Toronto, ON M5W 1A7; tel. (416) 596-5649; telex 062-19547; fax (416) 596-5672; weekly; Publr J. WARRILOW; circ. 200,423.

Financial Times of Canada: 1231 Yonge St, Suite 300, Toronto, ON M4T 2Z1; tel. (416) 922-1133; f. 1912; weekly; Publr DAVID TAFLER; circ. 110,000.

Flare: Maclean Hunter Bldg, 777 Bay St, Toronto, ON M5W 1A7; tel. (416) 596-5433; telex 062-19547; fax (416) 596-5526; f. 1984; monthly; Editor SHELLEY M. BLACK; circ. 225,000.

Floor Covering News: Maclean Hunter Bldg, 777 Bay St, Toronto, ON M5W 1A7; tel. (416) 596-5940; telex 062-19547; fax (416) 593-3189; f. 1976; 10 a year; Editor MICHAEL J. KNELL; circ. 8,000.

Foodservice and Hospitality: 980 Yonge St, Suite 400, Toronto, ON M4W 2J8; tel. (416) 923-8888; fax (416) 923-6114; f. 1968; monthly; Editor MICHAEL MCVEAN; circ. 30,000.

Heavy Construction News: Maclean Hunter Bldg, 777 Bay St, Toronto, ON M5W 1A7; tel. (416) 596-5844; fax (416) 593-3193; f. 1956; fortnightly; Editor RUSSELL B. NOBLE; circ. 26,000.

Home Goods Retailing: Maclean Hunter Bldg, 777 Bay St, Toronto, ON M5W 1A7; tel. (416) 596-5940; fax (416) 593-3189; f. 1955; 10 a year; Editor MICHAEL J. KNELL; circ. 14,000.

Maclean's Canada's Weekly Newsmagazine: Maclean Hunter Bldg, 777 Bay St, Toronto, ON M5W 1A7; tel. (416) 596-5311; telex 065-24196; f. 1905; weekly; Editor KEVIN DOYLE; circ. 404,000.

Magyar Élet (Hungarian Life): 6 Alcina Ave, Toronto, ON M6G 2E8; tel. (416) 654-2551; f. 1948; weekly; Hungarian; Publr ANDREW LASZLO; circ. 8,000.

Marketing: Maclean Hunter Bldg, 777 Bay St, Toronto, ON M5W 1A7; tel. (416) 596-5835; telex 062-19547; f. 1906; weekly; Editor COLIN MUNCIE; circ. 11,000.

Marquee: 277 Richmond St West, Toronto, ON M5V 1X1; tel. (416) 593-7004; f. 1976; 8 a year; film previews; Editor DAVID HASLAM; circ. 500,000.

Medical Post: Maclean Hunter Bldg, 777 Bay St, Toronto, ON M5W 1A7; tel. (416) 596-5770; telex 062-19547; f. 1965; fortnightly; Editor DEREK CASSELS; circ. 36,000.

Metropolitan Toronto Business Journal: 3 First Canadian Pl., POB 60, Toronto, ON M5X 1C1; tel. (416) 366-6811; fax (416) 366-5620; f. 1910; monthly; circ. 43,000.

Motivational Marketing: 173 Waverly Rd, Toronto, ON M4L 3T4; tel. (416) 699-4890; f. 1985; 6 a year; Editor JOHN DUNLOP; circ. 16,000.

New Equipment News: 111 Peter St, Suite 411, Toronto, ON M5V 2W2; tel. (416) 596-1624; f. 1940; monthly; Editor D.B. LEHMAN; circ. 32,000.

Northern Miner: 7 Labatt Ave, Toronto, ON M5A 3P2; tel. (416) 368-3483; fax (416) 367-4036; f. 1915; weekly; Editor J. S. BORLAND; circ. 28,000.

Now: 150 Danforth Ave, Toronto, ON M4K 1N1; tel. (416) 461-0871; f. 1981; weekly; young adult; Editor MICHAEL HOLLETT; circ. 70,000.

Office Equipment and Methods: Maclean Hunter Bldg, 777 Bay St, Toronto, ON M5W 1A7; tel. (416) 596-5920; telex 062-19547; f. 1954; monthly; Editor TOM KELLY; circ. 60,000.

Ontario Medical Review: 250 Bloor St East, Suite 600, Toronto, ON M4W 3P8; tel. (416) 963-9383; fax (416) 963-8819; f. 1922; monthly; Editor R. DAVID FLETCHER; circ. 18,000.

El Popular: 2413 Dundas St West, POB 1108, Adelaide St Station, Toronto, ON M5C 2K5; tel. (416) 531-2495; f. 1970; daily; Spanish; Editor MIGUEL RAKIEWICZ; circ. 114,000.

Pulp and Paper Journal: Maclean Hunter Bldg, 777 Bay St, Toronto, ON M5W 1A7; tel. (416) 596-5856; telex 062-19547; fax (416) 596-5526; monthly (except June and August); Editor ROMAN HOHOL; circ. 10,000.

Quill and Quire: 70 The Esplanade, 4th Floor, Toronto, ON M5E 1R2; tel. (416) 360-0044; fax (416) 941-9038; f. 1935; monthly; book-publishing industry; Editor TED MUMFORD; circ. 7,000.

Saturday Night: 36 Toronto St, Suite 1160, Toronto, ON M5C 2C5; tel. (416) 368-7237; fax (416) 368-7261; f. 1887; monthly; Editor JOHN FRASER; circ. 110,000.

Snowmobile Sports: 1255 Yonge St, Suite 105, Toronto, ON M4T 1W6; tel. (416) 922-7197; f. 1977; 2 a year; Editor KEVIN BRAZENDALE; circ. 80,000.

Time (Canada edn): 620 University Ave, Suite 1120, Toronto, ON M5G 2C5; tel. (416) 595-1229; telex 062-3245; fax (416) 595-7074; f. 1943; weekly; Man. Dir F. P. LINTOTT; circ. 356,000.

Toronto Life Magazine: 59 Front St East, 3rd Floor, Toronto, ON M5E 1B3; tel. (416) 364-3333; telex 062-19629; fax (416) 585-5275; f. 1966; monthly; Editor MARQ DE VILLIERS; circ. 98,000.

Travel Destination Canada: 310 Dupont St, Toronto, ON M5R 1V9; tel. (416) 968-7252; telex 065-28085; f. 1981; Editor DAN PARLE; circ 25,000.

Truck News: 963A Eastern Ave, Toronto, ON M4L 1A4; tel. (416) 461-0323; f. 1981; monthly; Editor ANDY TURNBULL; circ. 40,000.

TV Guide: 50 Holly St, Toronto, ON M4S 3B3; tel. (416) 482-8600; fax (416) 485-1093; f. 1976; weekly; Editor JOHN KEYES; circ. 816,000.

Prince Edward Island

Prince Edward Island Profiles: POB 36, Charlottetown, PE C1A 7K2; tel. (902) 566-5529; f. 1988; 6 a year; Editor NORMA REVELER; circ. 500.

Québec

A+, Le magazine Affaires+: 465 rue St-Jean, 9e étage, Montréal, PQ H2Y 3S4; tel. (514) 842-6491; telex 055-61971; fax (514) 842-6910; f. 1978; 10 a year; Publr CLAUDE BEAUCHAMP; circ. 103,000.

Action Informatique: 465 rue St-Jean, 9e étage, Montréal, PQ H2Y 3S4; tel. (514) 842-6491; telex 055-61971; fax (514) 842-6910; f. 1988; 22 a year; computing; circ. 17,000.

L'Actualité: 1001 blvd de Maisonneuve ouest, Montréal, PQ H3A 3E1; tel. (514) 845-2543; f. 1976; monthly; general interest; Éditor JEAN PARÉ; circ. 264,000.

Les Affaires: 465 rue St-Jean, 9e étage, Montréal, PQ H2Y 3S4; tel. (514) 842-6491; telex 055-61971; fax (514) 842-6910; f. 1928; weekly; business and financial; Editor JEAN-PAUL GAGNÉ; circ. 86,000.

Autoclub: 2600 blvd Laurier, Québec, PQ G1V 4K8; quarterly; circ. 60,000.

l'Automobile: 310 ave Victoria, Bureau 201, Montréal, PQ H3Z 2M9; tel. (514) 487-2308; fax (514) 442-2077; 6 a year; motor trade; Publr BILL JAMES; Editor J. M. GERMAIN; circ. 12,000.

Le Bulletin des Agriculteurs: 110 blvd Crémazie ouest, Bureau 422, Montréal, PQ H2P 1B9; tel. (514) 382-4350; f. 1918; monthly; circ. 78,000.

Canadian Hardware: 6420 ave Victoria, Bureau 8, Montréal, PQ H3W 2S7; tel. (514) 731-3524; f. 1972; hardware trade; Editor KEITH FREDERICKS; circ. 15,000.

Châtelaine: 1001 blvd de Maisonneuve ouest, Montréal, PQ H3A 3E1; tel. (514) 843-2503; f. 1960; monthly; Editor MARTINE DEMANGE; circ. 272,000.

CIM Bulletin: 3400 blvd de Maisonneuve ouest, Bureau 1210, Montréal, PQ H3Z 3B8; tel. (514) 939-2710; fax (514) 939-2714; monthly; also *CIM Directory* (annual) and *CIM Reporter* (2 a year); publ. by the Canadian Inst. of Mining and Metallurgy; Éditor PERLA GANTZ; circ 11,000.

Cinema Canada: CP 398, Outremont, PQ H2V 9Z9; tel. (514) 272-5354; monthly; Editor CONNIE TADROS; circ. 10,000.

Il Cittadino Canadese: 6274 rue Jean-Talon est, Montréal, PQ H1S 1M8; tel. (514) 253-2332; f. 1941; weekly; Italian; Editor BASILIO GIORDANO; circ. 55,000.

Clin d'Oeil: 7 chemin Bates, Outremont, PQ H2V 1A6; tel. (514) 270-1100; fax (514) 270-7079; monthly; Editor-in-Chief MARIE-JOSÉE DESMARAIS; circ. 100,000.

Commerce: 465 rue St-Jean, 9e étage, Montréal, PQ H2Y 2R6; tel. (514) 842-6491; telex 055-61971; fax (514) 842-6910; f. 1898; monthly; Publr MICHEL LORD; circ. 37,000.

Coup de Pouce: 2001 rue Université, Bureau 900, Montréal, PQ H3A 2A6; tel. (514) 499-0561; f. 1984; monthly; circ. 140,000.

Décormag: 101 Laurier St West, Montréal, PQ H2T 2N6; tel. (514) 273-9773; fax (514) 273-9034; f. 1973; 10 a year; home decorating; circ. 75,000.

Dernière Heure: 5689 Christophe-Colomb, Montréal, PQ H2S 2E9; tel. (514) 273-8336; weekly; Publr JACQUES FRANCOEUR; Editor ROLAND COTE; circ. 17,000.

Echo-Nomie: 16 rue St-Germain est, Rimouski, PQ; tel. (418) 723-4800; f. 1983; weekly; free; Editor ROLAND BELLOVANCE; circ. 20,000.

Echos Vedettes: 801 rue Sherbrooke est, Montréal, PQ H2L 4X9; tel. (514) 525-6400; f. 1963; weekly; Editor MARC CHATELLE; circ. 168,000.

L'Essentiel: 7 chemin Bates, Outremont, PQ H2V 1A6; tel. (514) 270-1100; fax (514) 270-4810; Publr SYLVIE BERGERON; circ. 120,000.

Femme Plus: 7 chemin Bates, Outremont, PQ H2V 1A6; tel. (514) 270-1100; fax (514) 270-4810; Publr SYLVIE BERGERON; circ. 85,000.

Finance: 410 rue St-Nicholas, Suite 505, Montréal, PQ H2Y 2P5; tel. (514) 284-0339; fax (514) 284-0311; f. 1979; weekly; circ. 35,000.

Globe: 1440 rue St-Catherine ouest, Bureau 625, Montréal, PQ H3G 1S2; tel. (514) 866-7744; f. 1956; weekly; Editor CLIFF BARR; circ. 2,057,000.

ICAO Bulletin: 1000 rue Sherbrooke ouest, Montréal, PQ H3A 2R2; tel. (514) 285-8222; telex 052-4513; fax (514) 288-4772; f. 1946; monthly; aviation; Editor CHARLES D. LAFOND; circ. 68,000.

Informatique et Bureaucratique: 465 rue St-Jean, 9e étage, Montréal, PQ H2Y 3S4; tel. (514) 842-6491; telex 055-61971; fax (514) 842-6910; f. 1980; monthly; data systems; Editor GIL TOCCO; circ. 22,000.

Le Journal Industriel du Québec: 9500 Henri-Bourassa ouest, Ville St-Laurent, PQ H4S 1N8; tel. (514) 335-2055; fax (514) 477-0867; f. 1985; 10 a year; Editor YVAN GAUTHIER; circ. 35,000.

Le Lundi: 7 chemin Bates, Outremont, PQ H2V 1A6; tel. (514) 270-1100; fax (514) 270-6900; f. 1976; weekly; Editor MICHEL CHOINIÈRE; circ. 107,000.

Monitor: 6525 ave Somerled, Montréal, PQ H4V 1S7; weekly; circ. 38,000.

Montréal Life: 1310 ave Greene, Bureau 920, Westmount, PQ H3Z 2B5; tel. (514) 933-2555; f. 1971; 11 a year; Publr BOB HARRIS; circ. 54,000.

Moto Journal: 5000 Buchan, Bureau 600A, Montréal, PQ H4P 1T2; tel. (514) 738-9493; f. 1972; monthly; Publr MARTIN LÉVESQUE; Editor JEAN-PIERRE BELMONTE; circ. 20,000.

National Examiner: 1440 rue St-Catherine ouest, Bureau 625, Montréal, PQ H3G 1S2; tel. (514) 866-7744; Editor MICHAEL IRISH; circ. 959,000.

Photo Sélection: 850 blvd Pierre-Bertrand, Suite 440, Ville de Vanier, PQ G1M 3K8; tel (418) 687-3550; fax (418) 687-1679; f. 1980; 8 a year; Chief Editor YOLANDE RACINE; circ. 18,000.

PME: 465 rue St-Jean, 9e étage, Montréal, PQ H2Y 3S4; tel. (514) 842-6491; telex 055-61971; fax (514) 842-6910; f. 1984; 10 a year; circ. 40,000.

Le Producteur de Lait Québécois: 555 blvd Roland-Thérrien, Longueuil, PQ J4H 3Y9; tel. (514) 679-0530; f. 1980; monthly; dairy farming; Dir HUGUES BELZILE; circ. 18,000.

Produits pour l'Industrie Québécoise: CP 357, Pointe Claire, PQ H9R 4P4; tel. (514) 337-2177; f. 1976; 6 a year; Editor D. TERHUNE; circ. 16,000.

Progrès-Dimanche: 1051 blvd Talbot, Chicoutimi, PQ G7H 5C1; tel. (418) 545-4474; weekly; Pres. GASTON VACHON; circ. 51,000.

Le Québec Industriel: 1001 blvd de Maisonneuve ouest, Bureau 1000, Montréal, PQ H3A 3E1; tel. (514) 845-5141; f. 1946; monthly; Editor BERTRAND DIONNE; circ. 16,000.

Québec Science: 2875 blvd Laurier, Ste-Foy, PQ G1V 2M3; tel. (418) 657-3551; telex 051-31623; f. 1969; monthly; Editor JACKI DALLAIRE; circ. 20,000.

Québec Yachting: 465 rue St-Jean, 9e étage, Montréal, PQ H2Y 3S4; tel. (514) 842-6491; telex 055-61971; fax (514) 842-8557; f. 1976; 8 a year; circ. 10,000.

Reader's Digest: 215 ave Redfern, Westmount, PQ H3Z 2V9; tel. (514) 934-0751; fax (514) 920-6571; f. 1943; monthly; French and English edns; Editor ALEXANDER FARRELL; circ. 1,706,000.

Relations: 8100 blvd St-Laurence, Montréal, PQ H2P 2L9; tel. (514) 387-2541; f. 1941; monthly; Roman Catholic review; Editor-in-Chief GISÈLE TURCOT; circ. 5,000.

Rénovation Bricolage: 7 chemin Bates, Outremont, PQ H2V 1A6; tel. (514) 270-1100; f. 1976; monthly; Editor-in-Chief CLAUDE LECLERC; circ. 38,000.

Santé: 101 Laurier St West, Montréal, PQ H2T 2N6; tel. (514) 273-9773; fax (514) 273-9034; f. 1984; 10 a year; health interest; circ. 30,000.

Son Hi-Fi: 101 Laurier St West, Montréal, PQ H2T 2N6; tel. (514) 273-9773; fax (514) 273-9034; f. 1984; 6 a year; hi-fi equipment and records; Editor MICHEL PRIN; circ. 15,000.

La Terre de Chez Nous: 555 blvd Roland-Thérrien, Longueuil, PQ J4H 3Y9; tel. (514) 679-0530; f. 1929; weekly; agriculture and forestry; French; Editor-in-Chief ANDRÉ CHARBONNEAU; circ. 46,000.

This Week in Business: 465 rue St-Jean, 9e étage, Montréal, PQ H2Y 3S4; tel. (514) 842-9988; telex 055-61971; fax (514) 842-8557; f. 1988; weekly; circ. 25,000.

Tourisme+: 465 rue St-Jean, 9e étage, Montréal, PQ H2Y 3S4; tel. (514) 842-6491; telex 055-61971; fax (514) 842-8557; f. 1979; weekly; Editor NICOLE LABONTÉ; circ. 7,000.

TV Hebdo/TV Plus: 2001 rue Université, Bureau 900, Montréal, PQ H3A 2A6; tel. (514) 499-0651; fax (514) 499-1844; f. 1960; weekly; Publr MICHEL TRUDEAU; circ. 336,000.

Wine Tidings: 5165 rue Sherbrooke ouest, Montréal, PQ H4A 1T6; tel. (514) 481-5892; fax (514) 481-9699; Publr J. ROCHESTER; Editor B. LESLIE; circ. 27,000.

Saskatchewan

The Commonwealth: 1122 Saskatchewan Dr., Regina, SK S4P 0C4; tel. (306) 525-8321; f. 1938; 24 a year; Editor MERRIL DEAN; circ. 9,000.

Farm Light and Power: 2352 Smith St, Regina, SK S4P 2P6; tel. (306) 525-3305; f. 1959; 10 a year; Man. Editor DON BLACK; circ. 182,000.

Western Producer: POB 2500, Saskatoon, SK S7K 2C4; tel. (306) 665-3500; fax (306) 653-1255; f. 1923; weekly; world and agricultural news; Editor KEITH DRYDEN; circ. 131,000.

Western Sportsman: POB 737, Regina, SK S4P 3A8; tel. (306) 352-2773; f. 1968; 6 a year; Editor ROGER FRANCIS; circ. 31,000.

Yukon Territory

L'Aurore Boréal: POB 5025, Whitehorse, YT Y1A 4Z1; tel. (403) 873-4031; monthly; circ. 1,000.

Dan Sha News: 22 Nisutlin Dr., Whitehorse, YT Y1A 3S5; tel. (403) 667-6923; f. 1973; monthly; Editor ERIC HUGGARD; circ. 3,000.

Yukon News: 211 Wood St, Whitehorse, YT Y1A 2E4; tel. (403) 667-6285; f. 1960; 2 a week; Editor PATRICIA LIVING; circ. 8,000.

NEWS AGENCIES

The Canadian Press: 36 King St East, Toronto, ON M5C 2L9; tel. (416) 364-0321; telex 062-17715; fax (416) 364-0207; f. 1917; national news co-operative; mems: 474 staff and 109 daily newspapers; Chair. DAVID JOLLEY; Pres. KEITH KINCAID.

Regional bureaux:

Edmonton: 305 Cornerpoint, 10179 105th St, Edmonton, AB T5J 1E2; tel. (403) 428-6107; Bureau Chief HEATHER BOYD.

Halifax: 2021 Brunswick St, Halifax, NS B3J 2L4; tel. (902) 422-8496; Bureau Chief IAN DONALDSON.

Montréal: 245 rue St-Jacques ouest, Montréal, PQ H2Y 1M6; tel. (514) 849-6154; Bureau Chief GUY RONDEAU.

Ottawa: 140 Wellington St, Ottawa, ON K1P 5P7; tel. (613) 238-4142; Bureau Chief GORDON GRANT.

Québec: CP 3367, succursale St-Roch, Québec, PQ G1K 6Z3; tel. (418) 523-0445; Bureau Chief DONALD CHARETTE.

Toronto: 36 King St East, Toronto, ON M5C 2L9; tel. (416) 364-0321; telex 062-17715; fax (416) 364-0207; Man. Editor JIM POLING.

Vancouver: 1455 Seventh Ave West, Vancouver, BC V6H 1C2; tel. (604) 731-3191; Bureau Chief WENDY ECKERSLEY.

Winnipeg: 300 Carlton St, Winnipeg, MB R3C 3A4; tel. (204) 942-8188; Bureau Chief JOE FREEMAN.

Principal Foreign Bureaux

China (People's Republic)

Xinhua (New China) News Agency (Ottawa): 406 Daly Ave, Ottawa, ON K1N 6H2; tel. (613) 234-8424; telex 053-4362; Chief Correspondent YUAN RONGSHENG.

Cuba

Prensa Latina (Montréal): 221 rue du St-Sacrement, Bureau 40, Montréal, PQ H2Y 1X1; tel. (514) 844-2975; Correspondent R. Ramos.

France

Agence France-Presse (Montréal): 1255 rue de l'Université, Bureau 1418, Montréal, PQ H3B 3A8; tel. (514) 875-8877; Bureau Chief Hubert Laverne.

Agence France-Presse (Ottawa): National Press Bldg, 150 Wellington St, Ottawa, ON K1P 5A4; tel. (613) 232-2943.

Germany, Federal Republic

Deutsche Presse–Agentur–dpa (Ottawa): National Press Bldg, 150 Wellington St, Suite 702, Ottawa, K1P 5A4; tel. (613) 234-6024; telex 025-34812; Correspondent Barbara Halsig.

Italy

Agenzia Nazionale Stampa Associata—ANSA (Ottawa): National Press Bldg, 150 Wellington St, Suite 703, Ottawa, ON K1P 5A4; tel. (613) 235-4248; telex 053-4392; Correspondent Piero Lacqua.

Inter Press Service—IPS (Montréal): 1470 rue Peel, Bureau 216, Montréal, PQ H3A 1T1; tel. (514) 843-6459; Correspondent Antoine Char.

Inter Press Service—IPS (Ottawa): 1262 Kingston Ave, Ottawa, ON K1Z 8K6; tel. (613) 992-4517; Stringer John Tackaberry.

Japan

Jiji Tshushin-Sha (Toronto): 366 Adelaide St East, Toronto, ON M5A 3X9; tel. (416) 368-8037; Bureau Chief Mikio Koyama.

Spain

Agencia EFE (Ottawa): 165 Sparks St, Suite 502, Ottawa, ON K1P 5B9; tel. (613) 230-2282.

United Kingdom

Reuters Canada Ltd (Montréal): 231 rue St-Jacques ouest, Suite 880, Montréal, PQ H2Y 1M6; tel. (514) 282-0705.

Reuters Canada Ltd (Ottawa): 165 Sparks St, Suite 500, Ottawa, ON K1P 5P8; tel. (613) 235-6745.

Reuters Canada Ltd (Toronto): POB 403, Commerce Ct Postal Station, Toronto, ON M5L 1J1; tel. (416) 869-3600; telex 062-3637; Man. John Adams.

Reuters Canada Ltd (Vancouver): 409 Granville St, Suite 1023, Vancouver, BC V6C 1T2; tel. (604) 684-9784.

USA

United Press International—UPI (Toronto): 45 Richmond St West, Toronto, ON M5H 1Z2; tel. (416) 340-7276; Man. for Canada Ken Whitehurst; Bureau Man. B. J. del Conte.

United Press International—UPI (Ottawa): c/o Parliamentary Press Gallery, 350 North Centre Block, House of Commons, Ottawa, ON K1A 0A8; tel. (613) 233-3359; Bureau Man. Laurie Watson.

Associated Press (USA) and Central News Agency (Taiwan) are also represented.

NATIONAL PRESS ASSOCIATIONS

Canadian Business Press: 100 University Ave, Suite 508, Toronto, ON M5J 1V6; tel. (416) 593-5497; 126 mems; Chair. Gwen Page; Pres. Cy Summerfield.

Canadian Community Newspapers' Association: 88 University Ave, Suite 705, Toronto, ON M5J 1T6; tel. (416) 598-4277; fax (416) 598-4410; f. 1919; 650 mems; Pres. Ken Sopkow; Exec. Dir Ross E. Mavis.

Canadian Daily Newspaper Publishers' Association: 890 Yonge St, Suite 1100, Toronto, ON M4W 3P4; tel. (416) 923-3567; fax (416) 923-7206; f. 1919; 83 mems; Chair. K. A. Baird; Pres. John E. Foy.

Canadian Magazine Publishers' Association: 2 Stewart St, Toronto, ON M5V 1H6; tel. (416) 362-2546; fax (416) 362-2547; f. 1973; 280 mems; Exec. Dir Catherine Keachie.

Magazines Canada: Maclean Hunter Bldg, 777 Bay St, 7th Floor, Toronto, ON M5W 1A7; tel. (416) 596-2644; Chair. James K. Warrillow; Vice-Chair. Ron Payne.

Newspaper Marketing Bureau Inc: 21 King St East, Suite 1200, Toronto, ON M5C 1A2; tel. (416) 362-8850; fax (416) 864-0161.

PUBLISHING

Publishers

Acta Press: POB 3243, Postal Station B, Calgary, AB T2M 4L8; tel. (403) 270-3616; telex 038-26670; fax (403) 270-8855; f. 1972; business, education, science; Pres. M. H. Hamza.

Addiction Research Foundation: 33 Russell St, Toronto, ON M5S 2S1; tel. (416) 595-4053; f. 1949; education, medicine and psychiatry, scientific and social sciences; Chair. of the Bd William Moher.

Addison-Wesley Publishers Ltd: 26 Prince Andrew Pl., POB 580, Don Mills, ON M3C 2T8; tel. (416) 447-5101; telex 069-86743; fax (416) 443-0948; f. 1916; mathematics, science, language, business and social sciences textbooks, trade, juvenile; CEO Anthony J. Vander Woude.

Thomas Allen and Son Ltd: 390 Steelcase Rd East, Markham, ON L3R 1G2; tel. (416) 475-9126; telex 069-66716; f. 1916; Pres. John D. Allen.

Annick Press Ltd: 15 Patricia Ave, Willowdale, ON M2M 1H9; tel. (416) 221-4802; telex 069-86766; fax (416) 221-8400; f. 1976; children's; Co-Dirs Rick Wilks, Anne W. Millyard.

Arsenal Pulp Press Book Publishing Ltd: 1150 Homer St, Vancouver BC V6B 2X6; tel. (604) 687-4233; f. 1972; literary, native, educational.

Avon Books of Canada: 2061 McCowan Rd, Suite 201, Scarborough, ON M1S 3Y6; tel. (514) 293-9404; Pres. Peter Austin.

Black Rose Books Ltd: CP 1258, succursale Pl. du Parc, Montréal, PQ H2W 2R3; tel. (514) 844-4076; social studies; Pres. Jacques Roux.

Borealis Press Ltd: 9 Ashburn Dr., Ottawa, ON K2E 6N4; tel. (613) 224-6837; f. 1972; Canadian fiction and non-fiction, drama, juveniles.

The Boston Mills Press: 132 Main St, Erin, ON N0B 1T0; tel. (519) 833-2407; f. 1971; Canadian and American history; Pres. Frank Tierney.

Breakwater Books Ltd: 277 Duckworth St, POB 2188, St John's, NF A1C 6E6; tel. (709) 722-6680; f. 1973; fiction, general, children's educational, folklore; Pres. Clyde Rose.

Broadview Press: POB 1243, Peterborough, ON K9J 7H5; tel. (705) 743-8990; f. 1985; Pres. Don le Pan.

Éditions Marcel Brouquet Inc: CP 310, La Prairie, PQ J5R 3Y3; tel. (514) 659-4819; fax (514) 659-4521; f. 1979; fine arts, nature, astronomy; Pres. Marcel Broquet.

Butterworths Canada Ltd: 2265 Midland Ave, Scarborough, ON M1P 4S1; tel. (416) 292-1421; fax (416) 292-6970; f. 1912; legal, professional, academic; Pres. S. G. Corbett.

Camden House Books: 7 Queen Victoria Rd, Camden East, ON K0K 1J0; tel. (613) 378-6661; subsidiary of Camden House Publishing Ltd; Assoc. Publr Frank B. Edwards.

Canada Law Books Inc: 240 Edward St, Aurora, ON L4G 3S9; tel. (416) 773-6300; f. 1855; law reports, law journals, legal textbooks, etc.; Pres. S. G. Corbett.

Canada Publishing Corporation: 164 Commander Blvd, Agincourt, ON M1S 3C7; tel. (416) 293-8141; telex 065-25374; fax (416) 293-9009; f. 1844; education, general trade, professional, reference, music; Chair. and Pres. Ronald D. Besse.

Carswell Co Ltd/Carswell Publications: 2330 Midland Ave, Agincourt, ON M1S 1P7; tel. (416) 291-8421; telex 065-25289; fax (416) 291-3426; f. 1864; law journals, encyclopedias, reports; Pres. A. TURNBULL.

CCH Canadian Ltd: 6 Garamond Ct, Don Mills, ON M3C 1Z5; tel. (416) 441-2992; fax (416) 441-3418; f. 1946.

Centre Educatif et Culturel: 8101 blvd Metropolitain, Anjou, Montréal, PQ H1J 1J9; tel. (514) 351-6010; telex 055-62172; fax (514) 351-3534; f. 1965; textbooks; Pres. and Dir-Gen. ANDRÉ ROSSEAU.

Le Cercle du Livre France, Ltée: 8925 blvd St-Laurent, Montréal, PQ H2N 1M5; tel. (514) 384-4131; telex 058-26756; fax (514) 384-0955; f. 1947; French-language and children's books; Pres. PIERRE TISSEYRE.

Charlton Press: 15 Birch Ave, Toronto, ON M4V 1E1; tel. (416) 964-7580; f. 1963; Pres. WILLIAM K. CROSS.

The Coach House Press: 401 Huron St (rear), Toronto, ON M5S 2G5; tel. (416) 979-2217; telex 055-62172; f. 1956; fiction, poetry; Owner STAN BEVINGTON.

Collier Macmillan Canada Inc: 1200 Eglinton Ave East, Suite 200, Don Mills, ON M3C 3N1; tel. (416) 449-6030; telex 069-59372; f. 1958; trade, textbooks, reference; Chair. ANDRÉ BISSON; Pres. RAY LEE.

The Continuing-Legal Education Society of British Columbia: 1148 Hornby St, Suite 200, Vancouver, BC V6Z 2C3; tel. (604) 669-3544; fax (416) 669-9260; f. 1976; Exec. Dir JACK HUBERMAN.

Copp Clark Pitman Ltd: 2775 Matheson Blvd East, Mississauga, ON L4W 4P7; tel. (416) 238-6074; telex 069-60413; fax (416) 238-6075; f. 1841; educational, business, trade; Pres. and CEO STEPHEN J. MILLS.

Décarie, Editeur Inc: 234 ave Dunbar, Ville Mont-Royal, PQ H3P 2H4; tel. (514) 342-8500; f. 1979; educational, medicine and sciences; Gen. Man. ANDRÉ DÉCARIE.

Deneau Publishers & Co Ltd: 760 Bathurst St, Toronto, ON M5S 2R6; tel. (416) 530-1035; f. 1977; general trade; Pres. and Publr DENIS DENEAU.

Dominie Press Ltd: 1362 Huntingwood Dr., Unit 7, Agincourt, ON M1S 3J1; tel. (416) 291-5857; fax (416) 291-1556; f. 1975; educational, trade, children's books; Pres. RAYMOND YUEN.

Doubleday Canada Ltd: 105 Bond St, Toronto, ON M5B 1Y3; tel. (416) 340-0777; fax (416) 977-8488; f. 1944; general, trade, textbooks, mass market; Chair. ANNA PORTER.

Douglas & McIntyre (Educational) Ltd: 1615 Venables St, Vancouver, BC V5L 2H1; tel. (604) 255-7701; classroom books and materials.

Douglas & McIntyre Ltd: 1615 Venables St, Vancouver, BC V5L 2H1; tel. (604) 254-7191; telex 045-08616; fax (604) 254-9099; f. 1971; general non-fiction, juvenile; Pres. G. SCOTT MCINTYRE.

Dundurn Press Ltd: 1558 Queen St East, Toronto, ON M4L 1E8; tel. (416) 461-1881; f. 1974; Pres. KIRK HOWARD.

ECW Press: 307 Coxwell Ave, Toronto, ON M4L 3B5; tel. (416) 694-3348; f. 1974; reference and educational.

Eden Press Inc: 31A ave Westminster, Montréal, PQ H2P 2L9; tel. (514) 488-2066; f. 1977; scholarly, medical, scientific, general non-fiction; Pres. SHERRI CLARKSON.

Editions Beauchemin Ltée: 6700 Côte de Liesse, Ville St-Laurent, PQ H4T 1E3; tel. (514) 842-1427; f. 1842; educational; Controller FRANCINE MARCOUX.

Editions Bellarmin: 8100 blvd St-Laurent, Montréal, PQ H2P 2L9; tel. (514) 387-2541; fax (514) 387-0206; f. 1891; religious, educational, politics, sociology, ethnography, history, sport, leisure; Pres. and Gen. Man. ANDRÉ BEAUCHAMP.

Les Editions du Boréal: 5450 chemin de la Côte-des-Neiges, Bureau 212, Montréal, PQ H3T 1Y6; tel. (514) 735-6267; fax (514) 735-7684; f. 1963; history, biography, fiction, politics, economics, educational; Dirs PASCAL ASSATHIANY, RAYMOND PLANTE.

Editions L'Etincelle: 4920 blvd de Maisonneuve ouest, Bureau 206, Westmount, PQ H3X 1W1; tel. (514) 488-9531; fax (514) 488-9532; f. 1972; art, social and political sciences, geography, history, juvenile; Pres. ROBERT DAVIES.

Les Editions Fides: 5710 ave Decelles, Montréal, PQ H3S 2C5; tel. (514) 735-6406; fax (514) 735-4985; f. 1937; juvenile, history, theology, textbooks and literature; Dir-Gen. MICHELINE TREMBLAY.

Editions FM: 1113 ave Desnoyers, St Vincent-de-Paul, Ville de Laval, PQ H7C 1Y6; tel. (514) 324-0712; telex 058-26852; fax (514) 384-3345; f. 1969; geography textbooks; Gen. Man. MICHEL PELLETIER.

Les Editions Françaises Inc: 1411 rue Ampère, CP 395, Boucherville, PQ J4B 5W2; tel. (514) 641-0514; telex 052-5107; f. 1951; textbooks; Pres. PIERRE LESPÉRANCE.

Editions France-Québec Inc: 955 rue Amherst, Montréal, PQ H2L 3K4; tel. (514) 323-1182; telex 052-4667; f. 1965; Editor BERNARD PREVOST.

Editions le Griffon d'Argile: 3022 chaussée Sainte-Foy, Sainte-Foy, PQ G1X 3V6; tel. (418) 653-6101; telex 051-3786; f. 1969; academic books; Dir ANDRÉ GOSSELIN.

Edtions Héritage: 300 ave Arran, St-Lambert, PQ J4R 1K5; tel. (514) 672-6710; telex 052-5134; f. 1968; history, biography, sport, juveniles; Pres. JACQUES PAYETTE.

Editions de l'Hexagone: 900 rue Ontario est, Montréal, PQ H2L 1P4; tel. (514) 525-2811; f. 1953; literature; Dir-Gen. ALAIN HORIC.

Editions Hurtubise HMH Ltée: 7360 blvd Newman, Ville Lasalle, PQ H8N 1X2; tel. (514) 364-0323; telex 055-67167; fax (514) 364-7435; f. 1960; general academic; Pres. and Dir-Gen. HERVÉ FOULON.

Les Editions Internationales Alain Stanke Ltd: 2127 rue Guy, Montréal, PQ H3H 2L9; tel. (514) 935-7452; f. 1975; general non-fiction, self-help, biographies; Pres. ALAIN STANKE.

Editions Libre Expression: 244 rue St-Jacques ouest, Montréal, PQ H2Y 1L9; tel. (514) 849-5259; f. 1976; religion, social and political sciences, general fiction and non-fiction, juvenile; Pres. ANDRÉ BASTIEN.

Editions du Noroit: POB 244, St-Lambert, PQ J4P 3N8; tel. (514) 671-7718; f. 1971; Pres. RENÉ BONENFANT.

Editions du Renouveau Pédagogique Inc: 8925 blvd St-Laurent, Montréal, PQ H2N 1M5; tel. (514) 384-2690; telex 058-26756; fax (514) 384-0955; f. 1965; textbooks; Pres. FRANÇOIS TISSEYRE.

Editions du Richelieu: CP 142, Saint-Jean, PQ G3B 5W3; f. 1935; general fiction and non-fiction, Roman Catholic school religious texts; Pres. FÉLICIEN MESSIER.

Editions du Septentrion: 1300 ave Maguire, Sillery, PQ G1T 2R8; tel. (418) 688-3556; fax (418) 527-4978; f. 1956; history, essays, general; Man. DENIS VAUGEOIS.

Encyclopaedia Britannica Publications Ltd: 175 Holiday Dr., POB 2249, Cambridge, ON N3C 3N4; tel. (519) 658-4621; fax (519) 658-8181; f. 1937; Pres. DAVID DURNAN.

Les Enterprises Culturelles Inc: 399 rue des Conseillers, porte 17, La Prairie, PQ J5R 4H6; tel. (514) 659-8958; f. 1890; Gen. Man. SERGE ST-AMOUR.

Fitzhenry & Whiteside Ltd: 195 Allstate Parkway, Markham, ON L3R 4T8; tel. (416) 477-0030; fax (416) 477-9179; f. 1966; textbooks, trade, educational; Pres. ROBERT I. FITZHENRY.

Fraser Institute: 626 Bute St, Vancouver, BC V6E 3M1; tel. (604) 688-0221; fax (604) 688-8539; f. 1974; economics, public-policy issues; Dir M. A. WALKER.

Gage Educational Publishing Co: 164 Commander Blvd, Agincourt, ON M1S 3C7; tel. (416) 293-8141; telex 065-25374; fax (416) 293-9009; f. 1844; Pres. and CEO RONALD J. REID.

General Publishing Co Ltd: 30 Lesmill Rd, Don Mills, ON M3B 2T6; tel. (416) 445-3333; telex 065-25374; fax (416) 445-5967; f. 1934; fiction, history, biography, children's, general, textbooks; Pres. JACK E. STODDART.

Ginn and Co: 3771 Victoria Park Ave, Scarborough, ON M1W 2P9; tel. (416) 497-4600; f. 1929; textbooks; Pres. RICHARD H. LEE.

GLC Publishers Ltd: 115 Nugget Ave, Agincourt, ON M1S 3B1; tel. (416) 291-2926; Pres. NELSON PRISKE.

Grolier Ltd: 16 Overlea Blvd, Toronto, ON M4H 1A6; tel. (416) 425-1924; telex 062-17803; fax (416) 425-4015; f. 1912; reference; Pres. P. M. TRUELAND.

Groundwood Books Ltd: 26 Lennox St, 3rd Floor, Toronto, ON M6G 1J4; tel. (416) 537-2501; telex 043-52848; fax (416) 537-4647; f. 1978; children's books; Publr PATRICIA ALDANA.

Guérin Editeur Ltée: 4501 rue Drolet, Montréal, PQ H2T 2G2; tel. (514) 842-3481; f. 1970; professional and textbooks; Pres. MARC-AIMÉ GUÉRIN.

Hancock House Publishers Ltd: 19313 Zero Ave, Surrey, BC V3S 5J9; tel. (604) 538-1114; f. 1975; Pres. DAVID HANCOCK.

Harcourt Brace Jovanovich, Canada: 55 Horner Ave, Toronto, ON M8Z 4X6; tel. (416) 255-4491; telex 069-67890; fax (416) 255-4046; f. 1922; general, educational, medical, scholarly; Pres. ANTHONY W. CRAVEN.

Harlequin Books: 225 Duncan Mill Rd, Don Mills, ON M3B 3K9; tel. (416) 445-5860; telex 069-66697; f. 1949; fiction, paperbacks; Pres. BRIAN E. HICKEY.

Harper & Collins Books of Canada Ltd: 100 Lesmill Rd, Don Mills, ON M3B 2T5; tel. (416) 445-8221; fax (416) 445-9498; f. 1932; trade, reference, bibles, dictionaries, juvenile, paperbacks, cassettes; Pres. STANLEY COLBERT.

The Frederick Harris Music Co Ltd: 529 Speers Rd, Oakville, ON L6K 2G4; tel. (416) 845-3487; f. 1904; Pres. ANDREW SHAW.

Harvest House Ltd: 1200 ave Atwater, Bureau 1, Montréal, PQ H3Z 1X4; tel. (514) 932-0666; f. 1960; history, biography, environment, natural and social sciences; Dir MAYNARD GERTLER.

Hayes Publishing Ltd: 3312 Mainway, Burlington, ON L7M 1A7; tel. (416) 335-0395; telex 061-8980; f. 1976; juveniles; Pres. CYRIL HAYES.

D. C. Heath Canada Ltd: 100 Adelaide St West, Suite 1600, Toronto, ON M5H 1S9; tel. (416) 362-6483; fax (416) 362-7942; Pres. ROBERT H. ROSS.

Herald Press: 117 King St West, Kitchener, ON N2G 4M5; tel. (519) 743-9731; f. 1974; Man. DALE WAGLER.

Holt, Rinehard & Winston of Canada Ltd: 55 Horner Ave, Toronto, ON M8Z 4X6; tel. (416) 255-4491; telex 069-67890; fax (416) 255-4046; f. 1904; educational, college, reference; Pres. ANTHONY W. CRAVEN.

Les Editions HRW Ltée: 8035 rue Jarry est, Montréal, PQ H1J 1H6; tel. (514) 351-7810; fax (514) 351-4040; f. 1966; textbooks; Pres. and Man. Dir J. G. BLANCHETTE.

Houghton Mifflin Canada Ltd: 150 Steelcase Rd West, Markham, ON L3R 3J9; tel. (416) 475-1755; telex 069-86804; fax (416) 475-5290; f. 1974; educational; Pres. JOHN E. CHAMP.

Hurtig Publishers: 10560 105th St, Edmonton, AB T5H 2W7; tel. (403) 426-2359; fax (403) 429-5996; f. 1961; non-fiction, politics, encyclopedias, Canadiana; Pres. MEL HURTIG.

Hyperion Press Ltd: 300 Wales Ave, Winnipeg, MB R2M 2S9; tel. (204) 256-9204; f. 1978; literature, general non-fiction; Pres. MARVIS TUTIAH.

Institute of Psychological Research Inc: 34 rue Fleury ouest, Montréal, PQ H3L 1S9; tel. (514) 382-3000; fax (514) 382-3007; f. 1964; educational and psychological tests; Pres. JEAN-MARC CHEVRIER.

IPI Publishing Ltd: 44 Charles St West, Suite 2704, Toronto, ON M4Y 1R7; tel. (416) 964-6662; f. 1973; Pres. Dr DANIEL J. BAUM.

Irwin Publishing Inc: 30 Lesmill Rd, Don Mills, ON M3B 2T6; tel. (416) 445-3333; telex 069-88864; fax (416) 445-5967; f. 1945; educational; Pres. BRIAN O'DONNELL.

Jesperson Press: 26A Flavin St, St John's, NF A1C 3R9; tel. (709) 753-5700; fax (709) 753-5507; f. 1974; educational and trade books; Pres. and Publr IVAN F. JESPERSON.

Key Porter Books: 70 The Esplanade, 3rd Floor, Toronto, ON M5E 1R2; tel. (416) 862-7777; telex 062-18092; fax (416) 862-2304; f. 1980; general trade; Pres. ANNA PORTER.

Kids Can Press Ltd: 585½ Bloor St West, Toronto, ON M6G 1K5; tel. (416) 534-6389; fax (416) 534-6152; f. 1973; children, young adult and parenting books; Publr VALERIE HUSSEY.

Lancelot Press Ltd: POB 425, Hantsport, NS B0P 1P0; tel. (902) 684-9129; f. 1966; non-fiction, regional; Pres. WILLIAM POPE.

Leméac Editeur: 3575 blvd St-Laurent, Bureau 902, Montréal, PQ H2X 2T7; tel. (514) 848-1096; f. 1957; literary, academic, general; Pres. JULES BRILLANT; Dir-Gen. LISE P. BERGEVIN.

Lester & Orpen Dennys Ltd: 78 Sullivan St, Toronto, ON M5T 1C1; tel. (416) 593-9602; telex 069-86391; fax (416) 593-7497; f. 1973; fiction, non-fiction, history, young adult, politics, social issues; Pres. MALCOLM LESTER.

Lidec Inc: CP 5000, succursale C, Montréal, PQ H2X 3M1; tel. (514) 843-5991; fax (514) 843-5252; f. 1965; educational, textbooks; Pres. and Dir-Gen. MARC-AIMÉ GUÉRIN.

James Lorimer & Co Ltd: 35 Britain St, Toronto, ON M5A 1R7; tel. (416) 362-4762; fax (416) 363-4029; f. 1971; urban and labour studies, children's, general non-fiction; Pres. JAMES LORIMER.

McClelland & Stewart Inc: 481 University Ave, Suite 900, Toronto, ON M5G 2E9; tel. (416) 598-1114; telex 062-18603; fax (416) 598-7764; f. 1906; trade, illustrated and educational; Chair. and Pres. AVIE BENNETT.

McClelland–Bantam Inc: 60 St Clair Ave East, Suite 601, Toronto, ON M4T 1N5; tel. (416) 340-0777; fax (416) 340-1069; f. 1977; mass market, Canadiana; Pres. and CEO ANNA PORTER.

McGill–Queen's University Press: 3430 McTavish St, Montréal, PQ H3A 1X9; tel. (514) 398-3750; fax (514) 398-4333; f. 1960; scholarly and general interest; Exec. Dir PHILIP J. CERCONE.

McGraw–Hill Ryerson Ltd: 330 Progress Ave, Scarborough, ON M1P 2Z5; tel. (416) 293-1911; telex 065-25169; fax (416) 293-0827; f. 1944; general, educational and medical; Pres. ROBERT M. FREEMAN.

Merrill Publishing: 230 Barmac Dr., Weston, ON M9L 2X5; tel. (416) 747-4626; telex 065-27166; fax (416) 746-7890; Gen. Man. LINDA MILNE.

Methuen Publications: 150 Laird Dr., Toronto, ON M4G 3V7; tel. (416) 425-9200; f. 1965; trade, textbooks, professional; Gen. Man. FRED D. WARDLE.

Micromedia Ltd: 158 Pearly St, Toronto, ON M5H; tel. (416) 593-5211; telex 062-4668; fax (416) 593-1760; f. 1972; reference, business, government; Pres. ROBERT GIBSON.

Modulo Editeur Inc: 233 ave Dunbar, Bureau 300, Mont-Royal, PQ H3P 2H4; tel. (514) 738-9818; telex 052-534; f. 1980; CEO ROGER TURCOTTE.

Mosaic Press: 1252 Speers Rd, Unit 2, POB 1032, Oakville, ON L6J 5E9; tel. and fax (416) 825-2130; f. 1974; literary, scholarly and cultural; Dir of Operations HOWARD ASTER.

The C. V. Mosby Co Ltd: 5240 Finch Ave East, Scarborough, ON M1S 5A2; tel. (416) 298-1588; telex 065-26225; fax (416) 298-8071; f. 1965; Vice-Pres. and Gen. Man. RICK PERRY.

NC Press Ltd: 260 Richmond St West, Suite 401, Toronto, ON M5V 1W5; tel. (416) 593-6284; telex 062-18265; f. 1970; fiction and non-fiction; Pres. CAROLINE M. WALKER.

Nelson Canada: 1120 Birchmont Rd, Scarborough, ON M1K 5G4; tel. (416) 752-9100; telex 069-63813; f. 1914; school and university textbooks; Pres. A. G. COBHAM.

North–South Institute/Institut Nord–Sud: 55 Murray St, Suite 200, Ottawa, ON K1N 5M3; tel. (613) 236-3535; telex 053-3300; f. 1976; foreign policy; Chair. ARNOLD C. SMITH.

Novalis: POB 9700 Terminal, Ottawa, ON K1G 4B4; tel. (613) 560-2552; telex 053-3982; fax (613) 232-4865; f. 1935; juvenile and young adult, trade, religious; Marketing Man. BEDE HUBBARD.

Oberon Press: 350 Sparks St, Suite 401A, Ottawa, ON K1R 7S8; tel. (613) 238-3275; f. 1966; poetry, children's, fiction and general non-fiction; Pres. MICHAEL MACKLEM.

OISE Press: Ontario Institute for Studies in Education, 252 Bloor St West, Toronto, ON M5S 1V6; tel. (416) 923-6641; telex 062-17720; fax (416) 926-4725; f. 1965; educational texts, guidance and test materials and scholarly publications; Editor-in-Chief HUGH OLIVER.

Oxford University Press Canada: 70 Wynford Dr., Don Mills, ON M3C 1J9; tel. (416) 441-2941; fax (416) 444-0427; f. 1904; general, education, religious, juvenile, Canadiana; Man. Dir MICHAEL A. MORROW.

PaperJacks Ltd: 330 Steelcase Rd East, Markham, ON L3R 2M1; tel. (416) 475-1261; fax (416) 475-7139; f. 1971; general paperbacks; Pres. SUSAN STODDART.

Peace Research Institute-Dundas: 25 Dundana Ave, Dundas, ON L9H 4E5; tel. (416) 628-2356; f. 1962; Marketing Man. ARLENE FOX.

Penguin Books Canada Ltd: 2801 John St, Markham, ON L3R 1B4; tel. (416) 475-1571; telex 069-86803; fax (416) 479-1705; f. 1974; general trade, classics; Pres. MORTON MINT.

Polyscience Publications Inc: 555 Legendre East, Suite 24, Montréal, PQ H2M 1G2; tel. (514) 381-0442; f. 1986; Pres. ALBERT H. DU FRESNE.

Pontifical Institute of Mediaeval Studies: 59 Queen's Park Cres. East, Toronto, ON M5S 2C4; tel. (416) 926-7143; f. 1939; scholarly; Dir of Publs Dr RON B. THOMSON.

Prentice-Hall Canada Inc: 1870 Birchmount Rd, Scarborough, ON M1P 2J7; tel. (416) 293-3621; telex 065-25184; fax (416) 299-2529; f. 1960; trade, textbooks; Pres. ROSS M. INKPEN.

Les Presses de l'Université Laval: CP 2447, Québec, PQ G1K 7R4; tel. (418) 656-3001; scholarly books and periodicals; Dir CLAUDE FREMONT.

Les Presses de l'Université de Montréal: CP 6128, succursale A, Montréal, PQ H3C 3J7; tel. (514) 343-6168; f. 1962; scholarly and general; Dir MARIE-CLAIRE BORGO.

Les Presses de l'Université du Québec: CP 250, Sillery, PQ G1T 2R1; tel. (514) 657-3551; telex 051-31623; f. 1969; scholarly and general; Dir-Gen. JACKI DALLAIRE.

Quarry Press: POB 1061, Kingston, ON K7L 4Y5; tel. (613) 376-3584; f. 1965; Pres. BOB HILDERLEY.

Ragweed Press: POB 2023, Charlottetown, PE C1A 7N7; tel. (902) 566-5750; f. 1974; Pres. LIBBY OUGHTON.

Random House of Canada Ltd: 1265 Aerowood Dr., Mississauga, ON L4W 1B9; tel. (416) 624-0672; f. 1944; Pres. GORDON BAIN.

The Readers's Digest Association (Canada) Ltd: 215 ave Redfern, Montréal, PQ H3Z 2V9; tel. (514) 934-0751; telex 052-5800; fax (514) 935-4463; f. 1943; Pres. and CEO RALPH HANCOX.

W. B. Saunders Co Canada Ltd: 55 Horner Ave, Toronto, ON M8Z 4X6; tel. (416) 255-4491; telex 069-67890; fax (416) 255-4046; Vice-Pres. PAUL S. WOLFORD.

Scholastic-TAB Publications: 123 Newkirk Rd, Richmond Hill, ON L4C 3G5; tel. (416) 883-5300; fax (416) 883-4113; f. 1957; Pres. F. C. L. MULLER.

Seal Books: 601-60 St Clair Ave East, Toronto, ON M4T 1N5; tel. (416) 922-4970; fax (416) 920-2776; f. 1977; mass market; Editorial Dir SUSAN RUTLEDGE.

Self-Counsel Press Ltd: 1481 Charlotte Rd, North Vancouver, BC V7J 1H1; tel. (604) 986-3366; fax (604) 986-3947; f. 1970; reference, self-help, business, law; Pres. DIANA R. DOUGLAS.

Sentinel Business Publications: 6420 Victoria Ave, Unit 8, Montréal, PQ H3W 2S7; tel. (514) 731-3523; fax (514) 731-9229; f. 1957; periodicals and directories; Publr RENÉ C. LE JEUNE.

Simon & Pierre Publishing Co Ltd: POB 280, Adelaide St Post Office, Toronto, ON M5C 2J4; tel. (416) 463-0313; fax (416) 463-4155; f. 1972; drama and performing arts, fiction and non-fiction; Pres. and Editor-in-Chief MARIAN M. WILSON.

SOGIDES Ltée: 955 rue Amherst, Montréal, PQ H2L 3K4; tel. (514) 523-1182; fax (514) 597-0370; f. 1958; practical skills including cookery, general-interest, biographies, popular psychology and novels; Pres. PIERRE LESPÉRANCE.

Stoddart Publishing Co Ltd: 34 Lesmill Rd, Don Mills, ON M3B 2T6; tel. (416) 445-3333; telex 069-86664; fax (416) 445-5967; f. 1894; fiction and non-fiction; Pres. and CEO JACK E. STODDART.

Summerhill Press Ltd: 52 Shaftesbury Ave, Toronto, ON M4T 1A2; tel. (416) 924-9682; fax (416) 924-8851; f. 1982; non-fiction trade; Pres. JAMES WILLIAMSON.

Talon Books Ltd: 1019 East Cordova St, Suite 201, Vancouver BC V6A 1M8; tel. (604) 253-5261; f. 1967; fiction and non-fiction, poetry, drama; Pres. and Gen. Man. KARL SIEGLER.

Turnstone Press Ltd: 100 Arthur St, Suite 607, Winnipeg, MB R3B 1H3; tel. (204) 947-1555; f. 1976; literary, regional; Man. Editor MARILYN MORTON.

University of Alberta Press: 141 Athabasca Hall, Edmonton, AB T6G 2E8; tel. (403) 492-3662; telex 037-2979; fax (403) 492-7219; f. 1969; Dir NORMA GUTTERIDGE.

University of British Columbia Press: 6344 Memorial Rd, Vancouver, BC V6T 1W5; tel. (604) 228-3259; telex 045-1233; fax (604) 228-6083; f. 1971; humanities, science, social science and scholarly journals; Exec. Dir JAMES J. ANDERSON.

The University of Calgary Press: 2500 University Dr., NW, Calgary, AB T2N 1N4; tel. (403) 220-7578; telex 038-21545; fax (403) 282-7298; f. 1981; Dir ALAN H. MACDONALD.

University of Manitoba Press: 106 Curry Pl., Suite 244, Winnipeg, MB R3T 2N2; tel. (204) 474-9495; f. 1967; scholarly, general, humanities; Dir PATRICIA DOWDALL.

University of Ottawa Press/Les Presses de l'Université d'Ottawa: 603 Cumberland Ave, Ottawa, ON K1N 6N5; tel. (613) 564-2270; fax (613) 564-9100; f. 1936; university texts, scholarly works in English and French, general; Dir TOIVO ROHT.

University of Toronto Press: 10 St Mary St, Suite 700, Toronto, ON M4Y 2W8; tel. (416) 978-2239; fax (416) 978-4738; f. 1901; academic and general university texts and journals; Dir H. C. VAN IERSSEL (acting).

Waterloo Music Co Ltd: 3 Regina St North, Waterloo, ON N2J 4A5; tel. (519) 886-4990; f. 1922; music publishers; Pres. WILLIAM BRUBACHER.

G. R. Welch Co Ltd: 960 Gateway, Burlington, ON L7L 5K7; tel. (416) 681-2760; f. 1938; religious books; Pres. DONNA HAID.

Western Producer Prairie Books: POB 2500, Saskatoon, SK S7K 2C4; tel. (306) 665-3548; fax (306) 653-1255; f. 1954; history, biography, photography, natural history, young adult, regional interest, Publishing Dir ELIZABETH MUNROE.

Whitecap Books Ltd: 1086 West Third Street, North Vancouver, BC V7P 3J6; tel. (604) 980-9852; fax (604) 980-8197; f. 1977; trade, outdoor guides; Pres. MICHAEL E. BURCH.

Whitman Golden Ltd: 200 Sheldon Dr., Cambridge, ON N1R 5X2; tel. and fax (519) 623-3590; f. 1942; juvenile and young adults; Pres. W. F. WHITE.

John Wiley & Sons Canada: 22 Worcester Rd, Rexdale, ON M9W 1L1; tel. (416) 675-3580; telex 069-89189; f. 1968; textbooks, trade; Chair. of the Bd W. BRADFORD WILEY; Pres. JOHN DILL.

Wilfrid Laurier University Press: Alumni Hall, Wilfrid Laurier University, Waterloo, ON N2L 3C5; tel. (519) 884-1970; fax (519) 886-9351; f. 1974; academic and scholarly; Dir SANDRA WOOLFREY.

Worldwide Library: 225 Duncan Mill Rd, Don Mills, ON M3B 3K9; tel. (416) 445-5860; telex 069-66697; f. 1982; mass-market fiction; Editorial Dir RANDALL TOYE.

Government Publishing House

Canadian Government Publishing Centre: Ottawa, ON K1A 0S9; tel. (819) 997-2560; telex 053-4296; fax (819) 1498; f. 1876; books and periodicals on numerous subjects, including agriculture, economics, environment, geology, history and sociology; Dir PATRICIA HORNER.

Publishers' Organizations and Associations

Association of Canadian Publishers: 260 King St East, Toronto, ON M5A 1K3; tel. (416) 361-1408; fax (416) 361-0643; f. 1976; 136 mem. cos; trade asscn of Canadian-owned English-language book publrs; represents Canadian publishing internationally; Pres. PHILIP J. CERCONE; Exec. Dir GORDON PLATT (acting).

Affiliated groups:

Alberta Publishers' Association: 10523 100th Ave, Suite 123, Edmonton, AB T5J 0A8; tel. (403) 424-5060; 24 mems; Exec. Dir RUTH RICHARDSON.

Association of Book Publishers of British Columbia: 1622 West 7th Ave, Vancouver, BC V6J 1S5; tel. (604) 734-1611; Exec. Dir TONY GREGSON.

Association of Manitoba Book Publishers: 100 Arthur St, Winnipeg, MB R3B 1B3; tel. (204) 942-6135; Exec. Dir MAUREEN DEVANIK.

Atlantic Publishers' Association: 1741 Barrington St, 4th Floor, Halifax, NS B3J 2A4; tel. (902) 420-0711; 40 mems; Exec. Dir DEREK STEPHENS.

Association des éditeurs anglophones du Québec/Québec English-Language Publishers' Association: c/o McGill–Queen's University Press, 3430 McTavish St, Montréal, PQ H3A 1X9; tel. (514) 398-3750.

Canadian Book Information Centre: 260 King St East, Toronto, ON M5A 1K3; tel. (416) 362-6555; Nat. Man. GORDON PLATT.

Regional offices:

West: 1622 West Seventh Ave, Vancouver, BC V6J 1S5; tel. (604) 734-2011; Regional Man. NATALIE CHAPMAN.

Prairies: 100 Arthur St, Suite 205, Winnipeg, MB R3B 1B3; tel. (204) 943-3767; Regional Man. JOHN WEIER.

East: 1741 Barrington St, Halifax, NS B3J 2A4; tel. (902) 420-0688; Regional Man. JOCELYNE MARCHAND.

Literary Press Group: 260 King St East, Toronto, ON M5A 1K3; tel. (416) 361-1408; Dir JANE BISBEC.

Association of Canadian University Presses/Association des Presses Universitaires Canadiennes: c/o Pontifical Institute of Mediaeval Studies, 59 Queen's Park Cres. East, Toronto, ON M5S 2C4; tel. (416) 926-7143; 15 mem. presses; Sec. Dr RON B. THOMSON.

Association Québécoise des Presses Universitaires: CP 6128, succursale A, Montréal, PQ H3C 3J7; tel. (514) 343-6929.

Book and Periodical Development Council: 34 Ross St, Suite 200, Toronto, ON M5T 1Z9; tel. (416) 595-9967; 19 mem. orgs; Exec. Dir NANCY FLEMING.

Book Publishers' Professional Association: 78 Sullivan St, Toronto, ON M5T 1C1; 230 mems.

Canadian Book Publishers' Council: 250 Merton St, Suite 203, Toronto, ON M4S 1B1; tel. (416) 322-7011; fax (416) 322-6999; f. 1910; 42 mem. cos; Pres. JOHN CHAMP; Exec. Dir JACQUELINE HUSHION.

Canadian Music Publishers' Association: 56 Wellesley St West, Suite 320, Toronto, ON M5S 2S4; tel. (416) 926-1666; fax (416) 926-7521; 26 mem. cos; Sec. PAUL M. BERRY.

Composers', Authors' and Publishers' Association of Canada, Ltd (CAPAC): 1240 Bay St, Toronto, ON M5R 2C2; tel. (416) 924-4427; fax (416) 924-4837; Gen. Man. MICHAEL R. ROCK.

Regional offices:

Montréal: 1245 Sherbrooke St West, Suite 1470, Montréal, PQ H3G 1G2; tel. (514) 288-4755.

Vancouver: 1155 Robson St, Suite 703, Vancouver, BC V6E 1B9.

HEALTH AND WELFARE

INTRODUCTION

Health

Federal and provincial governments share the responsibility for health care in Canada. The federal government, through Health and Welfare Canada, administers programmes which cater for the needs of residents of the Northwest Territories and the Yukon Territory, Indians and Inuit, public employees, and specific groups of immigrants and refugees. The Health Protection Branch of Health and Welfare Canada aims to protect the public from hazardous food, drugs and environmental conditions, amongst other dangers. Under the Canada Assistance Plan of 1966 the federal government pays 50% of the cost of health care and social services for those in need. The programme is administered by the provincial governments and benefits therefore vary from province to province. A system of advisory committees and conferences has been established in order to maintain federal–provincial co-operation on health matters.

Health-insurance plans are the responsibility of the individual provinces and territories. The Canada Health Act, which became effective on 1 April 1984, outlined the essential elements required from all provincial health-insurance plans. Hospital insurance programmes include acute, general, chronic and convalescent hospital services. The Medical Care Act of 1966–67 provided for payments to be made by the federal government to provinces operating medical care insurance plans, given that the plans fulfilled certain obligations. As a result, almost all persons are insured for essential medical services. The federal contribution to health care varies according to the average rate of growth in gross national product and the population statistics. The provinces may choose how to finance their share of the cost of health care services. British Columbia, Ontario and the Yukon Territory impose premiums (with assistance for those in need), while the other provinces pay for the cost from general revenue. Apart from the statutory health-care benefits provided through provincial health-insurance plans, additional benefits are available at the discretion of the individual provincial governments; benefits may include the services of osteopaths, psychologists and dentists. Provincial health care provision extends to remote areas which may have to be serviced by special facilities, such as flying ambulance services.

Social Security

The Constitution Act of 1867 (formerly known as the British North America Act) sets out the jurisdictional responsibilities of federal, provincial and municipal governments with regard to social security. In general, the federal government administers some programmes for the aged, families and other selected groups, and is involved in the funding of many provincial initiatives. Provincial and local governments operate direct services and a number of financial assistance programmes.

Income-security programmes funded by the federal government comprise: benefits for senior citizens; family allowances; Child Tax Credit; programmes for native peoples; programmes for veterans of the Canadian Forces; and training allowances. Senior citizens' benefits consist of the Old Age Security Pension (OAS), providing monthly benefits to those over the age of 65 who meet residence requirements; Guaranteed Income Supplement (GIS), for pensioners with little or no other income; and a spouse's allowance. The 1973 Family Allowances Act provides for benefit, linked to the cost of living, to be paid to Canadian families with dependents up to 18 years of age. A Special Allowance is paid to dependent children who are in care. The Act allows provincial governments to specify the amount to be awarded, but by 1987 only Québec and Alberta had set their own rates. An annual refundable Child Tax Credit was introduced by the federal government in 1979.

The federal Department of Indian Affairs and Northern Development aims to maintain levels of assistance for native peoples, especially those who live on reserves, and to encourage the involvement of native peoples in their own assistance programmes. A social assistance programme provides for basic needs. Programmes for veterans of the Canadian Forces are administered by the Department of Veterans' Affairs and four independent agencies: the Canadian Pension Commission, the Pension Review Board, the War Veterans' Allowance Board, and the Bureau of Pensions Advocates. Training allowances are paid through Employment and Immigration Canada to those taking part in the national training programme which aims to encourage workers to upgrade their skills in answer to the demands of the labour market.

In 1966 the Canada Assistance Plan (CAP) was set up to provide direct financial assistance for families and individuals in need. Responsibility is divided between the federal and provincial governments. Eligibility depends upon the needs and means of the applicant. The exact structure of the programme varies from province to province, but there are certain common elements to all programmes, such as the provision of food, shelter and fuel, homes for the elderly and accommodation for battered women and children.

The Unemployment Insurance Act of 1941 introduced Canada's first public income-insurance programme. Since 1971 the programme has applied to almost all paid workers and members of the armed forces. Those exempt include persons over the age of 65 and those who work fewer than 15 hours per week and earn less than 20% of the maximum weekly insurable earnings. The programme is financed largely by employer and employee contributions, with federal government general revenue financing about 20% of the cost of the programme.

Canada's main social-insurance programmes are the Canada Pension Plan (CPP), which applies to all provinces except Québec, and the Québec Pension Plan (QPP). Both plans are financed by equal contributions of 1.8% of contributory earnings from employee and employer. Self-employed persons pay the full 3.6%. The two plans differ in the details of eligibility and levels of benefit, but both provide the same range of benefits. Retirement pensions are available from the age of 60 upwards, although the full rate does not apply to those under 65 years of age. Persons over the age of 65 receive increased benefit. Survivor benefit is available to the dependents of deceased contributors. Disability pensions are paid to those whose condition requires them to stop working. Children's benefits are provided for dependent children of disability pensioners and children of a surviving spouse. Benefit applies until the age of 18, and is extended to the age of 25 if the child is still being educated. Death benefit is paid to the estate of a contributor who dies before retirement and has contributed to the CPP or QPP for at least three years.

The federal government provides funds for various social-support programmes which, unlike Unemployment Insurance, the CPP and QPP, do not involve direct payments. Two such programmes are the New Horizons programme, which aims to help the elderly, and the Vocational Rehabilitation of Disabled Persons programme.

Provincial government boards administer workers' compensation programmes which provide financial benefits and medical and rehabilitative services to those injured at work. The programmes are funded entirely from employers' contributions. Public employees' compensation is funded by the federal government.

Most provincial governments provide supplementary payments to recipients of both OAS and GIS benefits. Disabled people and low-income families may also receive additional benefit from provincial programmes.

SELECTED STATISTICS

(Source: Statistics Canada.)

Health

National health expenditures, by category
(C $ million, provisional; figures refer to public and private expenditures)

	1984	1985
Hospitals.	15,149	15,912
Homes for special care	3,831	4,007
Physicians	5,810	6,249
Dentists	2,014	2,178
Other professional services	490	526
Drugs and appliances	4,455	4,942
All other health costs	5,083	5,354
Total	**36,832**	**39,168**

National health expenditures, by province and territory
(C $ million, provisional; figures refer to public and private expenditures)

	1984	1985
Alberta	3,846	4,062
British Columbia.	4,523	4,672
Manitoba.	1,612	1,730
New Brunswick	936	975
Newfoundland	714	745
Nova Scotia	1,168	1,259
Ontario	13,089	14,099
Prince Edward Island	152	163
Québec	9,130	9,701
Saskatchewan	1,471	1,550
Northwest Territories and Yukon Territory	190	213
Total	**36,832**	**39,168**

Hospitals—Summary

	1984/85	1985/86	1986/87
Number of hospitals	1,231	1,229	1,218
Public	1,048	1,048	1,040
General	846	845	843
Speciality	37	38	35
Rehabilitation	20	21	21
Extended care.	121	120	107
Psychiatric (long-term).	10	10	21
Nursing station, outpost and other	14	14	13
Proprietary	58	59	57
Federal	125	122	121
General	17	16	17
Psychiatric	3	3	3
Nursing station, outpost and other	105	103	101
Approved bed complement	177,294	177,486	178,565
Public	170,523	170,721	171,928
Proprietary	3,678	3,683	3,619
Federal	3,093	3,082	3,018
Patient-days (adults and children, '000)	53,555	53,817	54,261
Public	51,824	52,155	52,501
Proprietary	1,196	1,180	1,234
Federal	535	482	527
Occupancy (%).	83	84	84
Public	84	84	84
Proprietary	91	95	94
Federal	62	62	64
Total operating expenses of public hospitals (C $ million)	14,247	15,198	16,238

Hospitals—Provinces and Territories (1986/87)

	Number of hospitals	Approved bed complement	Patient-days ('000)	Occupancy (%)	Admissions ('000)	Personnel[1]	Operating expenses[2] (C $ million)
Alberta	152	18,369	5,224	78	422	39,316	1,737
British Columbia	133	21,480	6,718	86	441	38,532	1,685
Manitoba	104	6,574	1,785	76	166	16,409	692
New Brunswick	36	5,196	1,527	81	123	11,863	446
Newfoundland	42	3,624	963	74	92	8,111	349
Northwest Territories	47	382	47	45	7	509	22
Nova Scotia	52	5,976	1,596	74	154	15,129	612
Ontario	264	52,013	16,083	85	1,338	126,287	5,776
Prince Edward Island.	9	767	223	81	25	1,672	58
Québec	236	56,460	18,040	88	762	121,039	4,296
Saskatchewan.	138	7,570	2,038	75	211	13,881	565
Yukon Territory	5	154	17	39	4	186	—
Total	**1,218**	**178,565**	**54,261**	**84**	**3,747**	**392,933**	**16,238**

[1] Full-time equivalents.
[2] Public hospitals only—note that in Yukon Territory all 5 hospitals are federal.

Physicians, Dentists and Nurses—Summary (As of 31 December of year stated)

	1981	1982	1983	1984	1985
Physicians[1]	45,542	47,384	48,860	49,916	51,966
Population per physician[1]	538	523	512	506	491
Active licensed dentists	11,484	11,880	12,271	12,624	13,027
Population per dentist	2,134	2,086	2,039	2,001	1,958
Licences issued to professional nurses	239,338	242,564	247,294	248,427	250,428

[1] Includes interns and residents.

Physicians, Dentists and Nurses—Provinces and Territories (1985)

	Physicians[1]		Active licensed dentists[2]		Licences issued to professional nurses[3]
	Number	Population per physician	Number	Population per dentist	
Alberta	4,186	567	1,234	1,923	23,951
British Columbia	6,152	471	1,926	1,505	27,647
Manitoba	2,162	497	497	2,164	9,654
New Brunswick	956	753	214	3,366	7,841
Newfoundland	975	596	137	4,239	5,247
Northwest Territories	40	1,273	33	1,542	341
Nova Scotia	1,805	489	373	2,367	9,336
Ontario	19,481	469	5,327	1,716	101,704
Prince Edward Island	165	775	46	2,780	1,234
Québec	14,393	459	2,855	2,315	54,067
Saskatchewan	1,623	628	366	2,786	9,436
Yukon Territory	28	811	19	1,195	—
Total	51,966	491	13,027	1,958	250,458

[1] As of December 31. Includes interns and residents. [2] As of December 31.
[3] Some nurses are registered (licensed) in more than one province. Also includes those nurses who are registered in one or more provinces but are actually working/living abroad.

Social Welfare

Social-security expenditures by programme (C $ million, fiscal years ending 31 March)

	1981	1982	1983	1984	1985
Federal social security:					
Family Allowances	1,850.9	2,019.5	2,230.6	2,326.6	2,417.8
Child Tax Credits	1,069.0	1,513.5	1,446.8	1,494.3	1,460.4*
Old Age Security	5,322.1	6,140.6	7,005.3	7,649.0	8,215.9
Guaranteed Income Supplement	1,918.1	2,242.0	2,416.3	2,524.5	2,953.0
Spouse's Allowances	177.7	202.8	221.5	232.9	248.8
National training programme	217.2	243.4	219.3	247.0	274.1
Registered Indians, social assistance	142.0	166.6	196.2	216.1	235.4
Registered Indians, social services	37.8	52.4	50.5	59.3	68.1
War veterans' allowances	296.6	347.1	388.3	421.7	464.9
Veteran disability and dependent pensioners	515.1	561.0	621.1	657.8	672.0
Canada Pension Plan/Québec Pension Plan, retirement beneficiaries	1,668.3	2,070.5	2,564.6	3,104.7	3,691.2
Canada Pension Plan/Québec Pension Plan, surviving spouse pensioners	590.1	709.1	866.2	1,036.7	1,218.4
Canada Pension Plan/Québec Pension Plan, disability pensioners	328.6	392.4	498.2	617.4	751.8
Canada Pension Plan/Québec Pension Plan, orphans and dependent children of disabled pensioners	128.7	140.0	159.4	179.3	190.9
Unemployment Insurance, unemployment beneficiaries	3,891.3	4,655.7	8,677.1	8,842.1	8,972.3
Unemployment Insurance, sickness benefits	156.8	167.6	175.2	184.6	209.0
Unemployment Insurance, maternity benefits	243.0	282.8	323.4	353.7	408.7
Unemployment Insurance, retirement benefits	16.3	17.7	18.1	18.6	20.5
Unemployment Insurance, fishing benefits	90.2	102.0	124.3	151.8	170.4
Unemployment Insurance, persons in manpower training	161.6	172.0	211.8	230.6	227.4
Unemployment Insurance, work-sharing benefits	—	1.0	121.1	55.5	32.2
Unemployment Insurance, job creation	—	—	56.7	93.8	130.7
Blind persons' allowances[1]	282.0	—	—	—	—
Disabled persons' allowances[1]	190.0	—	—	—	—
Canada Assistance Plan, general assistance[1]	2,838.2	3,272.4	4,154.8	4,927.5	5,521.7
Canada Assistance Plan, homes for special care[1]	541.7	740.2	760.2	780.8	798.2
Canada Assistance Plan, child welfare[1]	327.0	299.3	357.6	314.4	306.1
Canada Assistance Plan, other welfare services and work activity[1]	756.1	884.9	1,031.5	1,101.0	1,194.8
Vocational rehabilitation of disabled persons[1]	63.3	78.8	110.8	134.8	199.6
Provincial social security[2]:					
Workers' compensation, permanent disability	392.6	471.6	590.6	737.6	871.2*
Workers' compensation, temporary disability	709.1	837.6	1,029.7	1,100.5	1,207.0*
Workers' compensation, medical aid	251.5	318.2	346.3	416.2	445.9*
Tax credits and rebates	1,431.0	1,310.7	1,618.9	1,616.4	1,704.9
Other welfare programmes	1,410.8	1,427.8	1,811.2	2,064.3	1,868.6
Municipal social security[2]	400.7	420.6	471.1	524.2	580.8
Total expenditures[1]	28,415.4	32,261.8	40,874.7	44.415.7	47,732.7

* Preliminary figures.
[1] Total federal–provincial expenditures. [2] Excluding Canada Assistance Plan cost-sharable expenditures.

Society

Family Allowances—Provinces and Territories

	1984			1985		
	Average number of children[1]	Average number of families	Net benefit expenditures (C $ million)	Average number of children[1]	Average number of families	Net benefit expenditures (C $ million)
Alberta	669,534	355,220	236.0	668,544	355,198	246.2
British Columbia	724,023	399,674	253.9	726,468	401,889	267.1
Manitoba	289,853	150,290	101.5	289,446	150,929	106.3
New Brunswick	208,120	111,128	72.6	205,111	111,004	75.0
Newfoundland	197,377	98,138	68.6	192,550	97,794	70.4
Northwest Territories	19,883	8,858	7.1	20,249	9,205	7.5
Nova Scotia	238,329	129,645	83.2	235,544	129,594	86.4
Ontario	2,283,849	1,266,020	800.1	2,271,087	1,264,423	837.0
Prince Edward Island	36,481	18,553	12.7	36,186	18,575	13.2
Québec	1,672,599	950,911	586.4	1,648,493	943,458	598.3
Saskatchewan	291,576	145,176	101.9	293,585	146,666	107.7
Yukon Territory	7,052	3,863	2.5	7,116	3,902	2.6
Total	6,638,676	3,637,476	2,326.6	6,594,381	3,632,637	2,417.8

[1] Number of children on whose behalf family allowances were paid.

Child Tax Credit programme—Summary (taxation years)

	1983	1984	1985*
Families receiving credit	2,578,524	2,542,316	2,437,091
Children claimed for tax	5,129,198	5,084,487	4,911,740
Amount of tax credit (C $ million)	1,446.8	1,494.3	1,460.4

* Preliminary figures.

Child Tax Credit programme—Provinces and Territories
(Taxation year 1985; preliminary figures)

	Families receiving credit	Children claimed for tax	Amount of tax credit (C $ million)
Alberta	216,806	463,576	134.2
British Columbia	258,395	520,888	152.8
Manitoba	112,490	243,821	75.5
New Brunswick	87,370	170,180	55.6
Newfoundland	82,653	168,293	55.7
Northwest Territories	6,019	15,734	5.0
Nova Scotia	95,700	184,799	58.0
Ontario	776,211	1,593,722	441.4
Prince Edward Island	15,576	32,149	10.8
Québec	677,155	1,276,794	397.3
Saskatchewan	103,234	230,603	70.8
Yukon Territory	2,180	4,667	1.4
Outside Canada	3,302	6,514	1.7
Total	2,437,091	4,911,740	1,460.4

Senior Citizens' Benefits—Summary (fiscal years ending 31 March)

	1981	1982	1983	1984	1985
Old Age Security (OAS):					
Average number of beneficiaries	2,276,159	2,342,480	2,403,557	2,464,482	2,529,129
Net benefit expenditures (C $ million)	5,322.1	6,140.6	7,005.3	7,649.0	8,215.9
Guaranteed Income Supplement (GIS):					
Average number of beneficiaries	1,204,594	1,234,823	1,226,770	1,227,810	1,257,439
Net benefit expenditures (C $ million)	1,918.1	2,242.0	2,416.3	2,524.5	2,953.0
Spouse's Allowance (SPA):					
Average number of beneficiaries	81,939	84,527	84,843	86,182	90,415
Net benefit expenditures (C $ million)	177.7	202.8	221.5	232.9	248.8

Senior Citizens' Benefits—Provinces and Territories (fiscal year ending 31 March 1985)

	Old Age Security (OAS)		Guaranteed Income Supplement (GIS)		Spouse's Allowance (SPA)	
	Average number of beneficiaries	Net benefit expenditures (C $ million)	Average number of beneficiaries	Net benefit expenditures (C $ million)	Average number of beneficiaries	Net benefit expenditures (C $ million)
Alberta	174,177	568.3	82,320	192.8	5,760	15.9
British Columbia	317,926	1,032.4	134,663	310.3	9,090	24.0
Manitoba	128,645	416.8	64,751	150.4	4,563	12.7
New Brunswick	76,248	247.7	49,790	121.4	4,212	13.2
Newfoundland	48,086	156.5	38,291	99.0	3,559	13.4
Northwest Territories	1,343	4.4	1,075	3.3	68	0.4
Nova Scotia	99,467	323.0	62,886	150.4	4,845	14.6
Ontario	922,413	3,000.8	373,840	838.8	25,287	61.0
Prince Edward Island	15,618	50.7	10,795	27.0	785	2.5
Québec	616,580	2,006.5	376,382	902.3	27,971	78.6
Saskatchewan	123,448	400.9	60,231	144.0	4,181	12.1
Yukon Territory	762	2.6	382	1.1	23	0.1
International[1]	4,415	5.3	2,033	12.2	72	0.4
Total	2,529,129	8,215.9	1,257,439	2,953.0	90,415	248.8

[1] All persons paid under international agreements, including persons outside Canada.

War veterans' allowances and pensions—Provinces and Territories

	1985			1986		
	Recipients of allowances[1]	Benefit expenditures (C $ million)[2]	Payments, veteran disability and dependent pensioners (C $ million)	Recipients of allowances[1]	Benefit expenditures (C $ million)[3]	Payments, veteran disability and dependent pensioners (C $ million)
Alberta[4] .	4,980	25.7	46.8	4,831	25.9	50.5
British Columbia[5]	12,263	58.8	112.1	11,917	61.0	123.2
Manitoba	3,971	21.3	44.2	3,689	18.7	47.1
New Brunswick .	5,880	34.4	29.8	5,459	31.4	33.3
Newfoundland	5,111	26.1	8.8	4,964	24.5	9.7
Nova Scotia .	8,161	45.1	48.6	7,504	41.5	55.3
Ontario .	30,665	156.0	267.6	29,064	155.7	291.5
Prince Edward Island	1,489	8.6	9.1	1,387	7.9	10.1
Québec .	11,042	61.9	77.2	10,258	58.6	87.4
Saskatchewan	3,276	16.0	26.8	3,100	16.0	28.9
Outside Canada .	1,519	11.0	n.a.	1,653	12.8	n.a.
Total[6] .	88,357	464.9	671.0	83,826	453.9	737.0

[1] As of 31 March.
[2] Figures refer to 1984/85.
[3] Figures refer to 1985/86.
[4] Figures for recipients of allowances and benefit expenditures include Northwest Territories.
[5] Figures for recipients of allowances and benefit expenditures include Yukon Territory.
[6] Figures for payments, veteran disability and dependent pensioners include persons who reside in the territories or outside Canada.

Canada Pension Plan and Québec Pension Plan (fiscal years ending 31 March)

	1981	1982	1983	1984	1985
Annual average number of beneficiaries	1,671,165	1,801,344	1,933,283	2,075,567	2,250,411
Retirement pension	1,042,907	1,124,143	1,202,677	1,284,439	1,401,084
Disability pension.	106,559	116,089	128,535	143,624	159,306
Survivor's pension[1]	335,861	373,738	412,183	452,832	496,753
Children's benefits[2]	185,838	187,374	189,888	194,672	193,268
Net benefit expenditures[3] (C $ million) .	2,715.7	3,312.0	4,088.4	4,938.1	5,852.3
Retirement pension	1,668.3	2,070.5	2,564.6	3,104.7	3,691.2
Disability pension.	328.6	392.4	498.2	617.4	751.8
Survivor's pension[1]	590.1	709.1	866.2	1,036.7	1,218.4
Children's benefits[2]	128.7	140.0	159.4	179.3	190.9

[1] 'Survivor's' includes one-time death benefits.
[2] 'Children's benefits' includes benefits to children of disabled contributors, and orphans.
[3] Includes payments outside Canada.

Direct financial assistance paid under the Canada Assistance Plan—Provinces and Territories (fiscal years ending 31 March)

	1983		1984		1985	
	Beneficiaries[1] (including dependants)	General assistance expenditures[2] (total federal–provincial) (C $ million)	Beneficiaries[1] (including dependants)	General assistance expenditures[2] (total federal–provincial) (C $ million)	Beneficiaries[1] (including dependants)	General assistance expenditures[2] (total federal–provincial) (C $ million)
Alberta .	130,600	367.4	117,100	401.5	124,100	419.6
British Columbia	228,800	635.9	257,100	769.7	267,600	866.5
Manitoba	55,900	95.3	59,200	119.5	62,800	149.9
New Brunswick .	70,100	170.4	68,600	174.6	69,100	192.9
Newfoundland	51,900	79.1	53,300	88.6	49,100	86.1
Northwest Territories	7,300	9.3	7,000	9.5	7,400	9.3
Nova Scotia .	69,000	120.1	67,500	126.3	73,600	139.5
Ontario .	471,200	1,047.1	484,600	1,200.8	485,800	1,406.4
Prince Edward Island	11,300	22.6	9,800	19.2	9,600	21.3
Québec .	675,800	1,472.3	705,900	1,851.8	708,700	2,055.3
Saskatchewan	59,700	132.3	63,700	164.3	64,000	173.0
Yukon Territory.	1,300	2.9	1,100	1.8	1,500	2.0
Total .	1,832,900	4,154.8	1,894,900	4,927.5	1,923,300	5,521.7

[1] As of 31 March of each fiscal year.
[2] Total federal–provincial expenditures are estimates. They have been calculated by doubling the federal amount paid for claims received each year.

Unemployment Insurance claims and average payments

	1981	1982	1983	1984	1985
Persons covered by Unemployment Insurance ('000) . .	10,617	10,648	10,797	11,046	11,340
Claims data ('000):					
Beneficiaries	720	1,138	1,248	1,194	1,145
Initial and renewal claims received	2,947	3,919	3,434	3,492	3,312
Benefit data:					
Number of weeks paid ('000)	37,011	60,441	66,585	61,862	59,788
Average weekly payment ($)	130.45	144.60	154.88	161.62	170.96

Unemployment Insurance benefits by type (C $'000)

	1981	1982	1983	1984	1985
Regular	4,115,789	7,646,025	9,069,503	8,825,126	8,975,315
Sickness	164,261	174,416	179,474	204,559	220,700
Maternity	273,052	315,972	344,168	395,918	432,531
Adoption	—	—	—	3,071	3,845
Retirement	17,582	18,167	18,514	19,158	22,399
Fishing	92,443	111,857	141,836	163,372	179,767
Training	165,147	202,129	225,767	226,846	234,529
Work-sharing	—	83,154	83,140	32,389	25,190
Job creation	—	23,726	106,661	115,186	132,612
Total	4,828,273	8,575,445	10,169,063	9,985,625	10,226,888

HEALTH AND WELFARE AGENCIES AND ORGANIZATIONS

Association des centres hospitaliers et centres d'accueil privés du Québec: 300 Leo-Parizeau, Bureau 1021, POB 1083, Montréal, PQ H2W 2P4; tel. (514) 288-6587; 108 mem. orgs; Pres. CLÉMENCE BOUCHER.

Auxiliaires Bénévolés des Établissements de Santé du Québec: 505 blvd Maisonneuve ouest, Bureau 400, Montréal, PQ H3A 3C2; tel. (514) 842-4861; 114 mem. orgs; Pres. ALINE GOUIN.

Canadian Association of Hospital Auxiliaries: 17 York St, Suite 100, Ottawa, ON K1N 9J6; tel. (613) 238-8005; 10 provincial mem. orgs; Co-ordinator of Services JOAN ROCHE.

Canadian Council on Health Facilities Accreditation: 1815 Alta Vista Dr., Ottawa, ON K1G 3Y6; tel. (613) 523-9154; 14 council mems, 5 mem. bodies; Exec. Dir AMBROSE M. HEARN.

Canadian Hospital Association: 17 York St, Suite 100, Ottawa, ON K1N 9J6; tel. (613) 238-8005; Pres. JEAN-CLAUDE MARTIN.
Provincial bodies:

Alberta Hospital Association: 10009 108th St, Edmonton, AB T5J 3C5; tel. (403) 423-1776; fax (403) 429-1719; Pres. D. A. MACGREGOR.

Association des Hôpitaux du Québec: 505 blvd de Maisonneuve ouest, Bureau 400, Montréal, PQ H3A 3C2; tel. (514) 842-4861; 200 mems.

British Columbia Health Association: 1985 Broadway West, Suite 500, Vancouver, BC V6J 4Y3; tel. (604) 734-2423; telex 04-54300; Pres. H. A. CREWSON.

Hospital Association of Prince Edward Island: 57 Queen St, POB 490, Charlottetown, PE C1A 7L1; tel. (902) 368-3901; Exec. Dir R. S. HAMILTON.

Manitoba Health Organizations, Inc: 360 Broadway, Suite 600, Winnipeg, MB R3C 4G6; tel. (204) 942-6591; Exec. Dir L. L. DESJARDINS.

New Brunswick Hospital Association: 861 Woodstock Rd, RR 3, Fredericton, NB E3B 4X4; tel. (506) 458-9989; fax (506) 453-1465; 56 mems; Exec. Dir MICHEL J. POIRIER.

Newfoundland Hospital and Nursing Home Association: POB 8234, Station A, St John's, NF A1B 3N4; tel. (709) 364-7701; 64 mems; Exec. Dir R. J. BURNELL.

Northwest Territories Hospital Association: POB 1280, Hay River, NT X0E 0R0; tel. (403) 874-2448; telex 034-4340; fax (403) 874-3377; 8 mems; Exec. Dir MAMIE MUNRO.

Nova Scotia Association of Health Organizations: 5614 Fenwick St, Halifax, NS B3H 1P9; tel. (902) 429-4020; fax (902) 429-5882; Exec. Dir J. F. INGRAM.

Ontario Hospital Association: 150 Ferrand Dr., Don Mills, ON M3C 1H6; tel. (416) 429-2661; fax (416) 429-1363; Pres. GORDON R. CUNNINGHAM.

Saskatchewan Health-Care Association: 1445 Park St, Regina, SK S4N 4C5; tel. (306) 525-2741; Exec. Dir C. H. HELMSING.

Catholic Health Association of Canada: 1247 Kilborn Ave, Ottawa, ON K1H 6K9; tel. (613) 731-7148; Pres. EVERETT MACNEIL.

Department of National Health and Welfare: Brooke Claxton Bldg, Ottawa, ON K1A 0K9; tel. (613) 957-2980; telex 053-3270; Dir-Gen. of Communications MONIQUE PLANTE-BOYD.

Health Protection Branch: Dept of National Health and Welfare, Ottawa, ON K1A 0L2; tel. (613) 957-1804; Asst Deputy Minister A. J. LISTON.

Health Services and Promotion Branch: Dept of National Health and Welfare, Brooke Claxton Bldg, Ottawa, ON K1A 0K9; tel. (613) 954-8524; Asst Deputy Minister Dr PETER GLYNN.

Income Security Programs (Canada Pension Plan, Family Allowances, Old Age Security): Ottawa, ON; tel. (613) 957-3111; Asst Deputy Minister D. MAASLAND.

Medical Services Branch: Dept of National Health and Welfare, Ottawa, ON K1A 0L3; tel. (613) 957-7701; Asst Deputy Minister J. D. NICHOLSON.

Policy, Communications and Information Branch: Dept of National Health and Welfare, Brooke Claxton Bldg, Ottawa, ON K1A 0K9; tel. (613) 957-3059; Asst Deputy Minister IAN C. GREEN.

Social Services Programs Branch: Ottawa, ON K1A 1B5; tel. (613) 957-2953; Asst Deputy Minister J. G. SOAR.

Hospice Network of Canada: c/o 3 Clarendon Ave, Toronto, ON M4V 1H8.

Hospital Council of Metropolitan Toronto: 2 Carlton St, Suite 1305, Toronto, ON M5B 1J3; tel. (416) 595-0930; fax (416) 593-6362; mems: 51 hospitals; Exec. Dir DANIEL H. DROWN.

National Advisory Council on Aging: Jeanne Mance Bldg, Tunney's Pasture, Ottawa, ON K1A 0K9; Dir SUZANNE FLETCHER.

National Council of Welfare: Brooke Claxton Bldg, Rm 566, Ottawa, K1A 0K9.

Ontario Association of Directors of Healthcare Volunteer Services: 150 Ferrand Dr., Don Mills, ON M3C 1H6; tel. (416) 429-2661; 150 mems.

EDUCATION

INTRODUCTION

Education in Canada is predominantly the responsibility of provincial governments. However, the federal government has some involvement: through the Department of Indian and Northern Affairs, it pays for the schooling of Indian students in federal, Indian-band-controlled or provincial schools. Governments of the Yukon Territory and the Northwest Territories are responsible for Indian and Inuit education in their own territories. Through the Department of National Defence, the federal government also administers and funds schools for the dependents of the Canadian armed forces serving overseas. The Constitution Act of 1867 (formerly known as the British North America Act) gave legislative power over education to the provincial and territorial governments which are also in charge of the finance and administration of educational establishments, from elementary schools to universities.

Provincial government departments or ministries of education form educational policy which is embodied in School or Education Acts and University and College Acts. Ministries of Education oversee standards of teaching and award teaching certificates; approve programmes of teaching, curricula and textbooks; provide financial assistance; and establish guidelines for members of school boards, principals and teachers. School boards are the local units of administration and are in charge of implementing policy in elementary schools (grades one to six or eight) and secondary schools (grades seven or nine to 12). On the level of higher education, some provinces have grants councils or commissions to which the provincial governments delegate responsibility for the planning and financing of post-secondary education. The individual provincial governments vary as to whether the two levels of education (elementary–secondary and post-secondary) are the responsibility of one department or two. Those having two departments are Alberta, British Columbia, New Brunswick, Newfoundland, Nova Scotia, Ontario and Québec.

All provinces provide elementary and secondary public education which is financed from provincial revenue. Seven of the provinces provide tax support for schools on a denominational basis. Québec's public education system is organized along denominational lines, there being both Roman Catholic and Protestant school boards. Non-sectarian public education is available in British Columbia, Manitoba, New Brunswick, Nova Scotia and Prince Edward Island.

Pre-school, or kindergarten, education for five-year-olds is publicly supported in all provinces except for New Brunswick and Prince Edward Island. Manitoba, Ontario and Québec also provide junior kindergartens for those aged four. Alberta's Early Childhood Services programme provides for the admittance of children aged three-and-a-half upwards. Private kindergartens are licensed by provincial departments of education or of social services. Elementary schools are for children between the ages of six and 11 or 13, while secondary, or 'high', schools for ages 12–14 to 18. Some provinces provide a separate 'junior high' school for ages 12–14, 'senior high' therefore catering for older children. While elementary schools provide a general education in a broad range of subjects, secondary schools have a compulsory 'core' curriculum around which students may select subjects. Most secondary schools offer academic, technical and business (or vocational) courses, to reflect different abilities. Some areas have separate specialist schools for technical and business-oriented courses. Québec's secondary education system is different in that after five years at secondary school students spend two or three years at a collège d'enseignement général et professionnel (CEGEP) from where they may go on to higher education. Private schools may operate providing they meet certain criteria stipulated by the various provincial governments. Financial assistance of some kind is provided in Alberta, British Columbia, Manitoba, Québec and Saskatchewan. In 1987/88 approximately 4,974,000 students were enrolled at about 15,347 elementary–secondary schools across Canada.

The provincial and territorial departments of education are responsible for providing education to those who are unable to reach schools due to their distance from centres of population. This has been made easier recently through the use of advanced telecommunications. 'Distant education' may be funded from the general provincial education budget or from a separate budget. All provinces provide educational facilities for those with special needs, whether due to physical or mental handicap. The overall aim is to integrate such persons into the local educational system.

Vocational and technical education is partly financed by the federal government. Federal-government policy is directed towards providing a work-force armed with skills relevant to a modern industrial nation. Under the 1982 National Training Act a Skills Growth Fund was set up to provide the provinces with finances for training institutions and training facilities. The Canadian Occupational Projection system has the task of identifying areas of need in terms of skill shortages and therefore ensures that resources are targeted at the relevant training courses.

Post-secondary education is available from a variety of institutions, including universities, community colleges, technical institutes, agriculture and art colleges and schools of nursing attached to hospitals. Community colleges vary from province to province, some emphasizing pre-university education, some specializing in courses which lead directly to a career. A unifying factor among community colleges is the availability of education to all people, regardless of their academic prowess. Specialized vocational schools and hospital schools of nursing are increasingly being incorporated into the colleges. There were 67 public degree-granting universities in Canada in 1987/88. Graduation from high school, (in the case of Québec) completion of a two-year programme at a CEGEP, is a prerequisite for university entrance. Each university may decide upon further entrance requirements. Universities charge fees but also receive considerable financial support from the relevant provincial government departments. In 1987/88 about 805,200 students were enrolled at 266 institutions of post-secondary education (community colleges and universities).

STATISTICS

(Source: Statistics Canada.)

Schools: Summary

	1983/84	1984/85	1985/86	1986/87	1987/88*
Elementary–secondary†	15,519	15,595	15,634	15,695	15,347
Post-secondary	260	267	265	265	266
Community colleges	194	200	197	197	199
Universities	66	67	68	68	67
Total	15,779	15,862	15,899	15,960	15,613

* Provisional.
† Includes Department of National Defence Schools overseas.

Teachers: Summary

	1983/84	1984/85	1985/86	1986/87	1987/88*
Elementary–secondary	270,992	267,598	267,620	269,899	276,607
Post-secondary	62,564	63,421	63,401	64,553	59,624†
Community colleges	28,283	28,755	28,230	29,017	23,780†
Universities	34,281	34,666	35,171	35,536	35,844
Total	333,556	331,019	331,021	334,452	336,231

* Provisional.
† Estimated figure.

Enrolment: Summary
('000)

	1983/84	1984/85	1985/86	1986/87	1987/88*
Elementary–secondary†	4,975.0	4,946.1	4,927.8	4,938.0	4,973.9
Post-secondary	766.8	782.6	789.6	796.9	805.2
Community colleges	316.3	321.6	322.3	321.5	319.1
Universities	450.5	461.0	467.3	475.4	486.1
Total	5,741.8	5,728.7	5,717.4	5,734.9	5,779.1

* Provisional.
† Includes data relating to Department of National Defence schools overseas.

Elementary and Secondary Education by Province or Territory
(1987/88, provisional)

	Schools	Teachers ('000)			Enrolment ('000)
		Total	Male	Female	
Alberta	1,699	25.0	10.6	14.4	473.4
British Columbia	1,926	27.1	13.0	14.1	532.2
Manitoba	842	12.8	6.6	6.2	220.2
New Brunswick	477	7.8	3.1	4.7	140.4
Newfoundland	569	8.1	3.8	4.2	136.7
Northwest Territories	73	0.7	0.3	0.4	13.4
Nova Scotia	573	10.4	4.4	6.1	173.0
Ontario	5,205	106.6	45.6	60.9	1,897.3
Prince Edward Island	73	1.3	0.6	0.7	24.9
Québec	2,852	64.9	25.0	39.9	1,138.7
Saskatchewan	1,024	11.4	5.1	6.2	215.3
Yukon Territory	25	0.3	0.1	0.2	4,9
Total	15,347*	276.6	118.5	158.1	4,973.9*

* Includes data relating to Department of National Defence schools overseas.

Post-Secondary Education by Province or Territory
(1987/88, provisional)

	Institutions	Teachers ('000)			Enrolment ('000)
		Total	Male	Female	
Alberta	23	5.4	4.2	1.3	70.5
British Columbia	25	5.0	3.9	1.1	61.9
Manitoba	16	2.1	1.6	0.5	23.4
New Brunswick	12	1.4	1.1	0.3	17.6
Newfoundland	13	1.2	0.9	0.3	13.9
Northwest Territories	1	0*	0*	0*	0.2
Nova Scotia	24	2.3	1.7	0.6	26.8
Ontario	52	20.6	15.2	5.4	287.7
Prince Edward Island	3	0.2	0.2	0*	2.9
Québec	89	19.4	14.4	5.0	276.6
Saskatchewan	7	2.0	1.5	0.4	23.6
Yukon Territory	1	0*	0*	0*	0.1
Total	266	59.6	44.7	14.9	805.2

* Represents less than 50.

RELIGION

Population by Religion and Sex

(Census of 1981, based on 20% sample data. Source: Statistics Canada.)

	Total	Male	Female
Catholic	11,402,605	5,641,850	5,760,755
Roman Catholic	11,210,390	5,544,505	5,665,880
Ukrainian Catholic	190,590	96,505	94,080
Polish National Catholic Church	1,630	840	790
Protestant	9,914,580	4,780,345	5,134,235
Adventist	41,605	18,635	22,975
Anglican	2,436,375	1,166,775	1,269,595
Associated Gospel	7,895	3,705	4,190
Baptist	696,850	332,270	364,580
Brethren in Christ	22,260	10,395	11,865
Christian and Missionary Alliance	33,895	16,110	17,785
Churches of Christ, Disciples	15,350	7,190	8,160
Church of God	10,035	4,820	5,215
Church of the Nazarene	13,360	6,185	7,175
Doukhobors	6,700	3,355	3,345
Orthodox Doukhobors	6,620	3,310	3,310
Evangelical Free Church	5,780	2,990	2,795
Jehovah's Witnesses	143,480	65,160	78,320
Latter-day Saints (Mormons)	89,870	42,795	47,070
Church of Latter-day Saints	82,060	39,325	42,735
Reorganized Church of Latter-day Saints	7,810	3,475	4,335
Lutheran	702,905	349,460	353,440
Mennonite and Hutterite	205,895	102,260	103,635
Mennonite	189,370	94,205	95,170
Hutterite	16,530	8,055	8,470
Methodist bodies	47,840	22,480	25,365
Evangelical	19,030	9,045	9,990
Free Methodist	12,270	5,795	6,470
Missionary Church	7,940	3,720	4,220

(*continued*)	Total	Male	Female
Pentecostal	338,785	158,810	179,980
Plymouth Brethren	8,060	3,785	4,275
Presbyterian	812,105	395,475	416,630
Reformed bodies	104,175	53,190	50,985
Christian Reformed	77,370	39,295	38,075
Canadian Reformed Church	10,560	5,495	5,065
Salvation Army	125,085	61,235	63,850
Unitarian	14,505	6,435	8,070
United Church	3,758,015	1,812,935	1,945,080
Wesleyan	7,770	3,630	4,140
Worldwide Church of God	8,130	3,920	4,215
Eastern Orthodox	361,560	186,285	175,280
Greek Orthodox	314,875	161,970	152,905
Armenian Orthodox	9,430	4,900	4,530
Ukrainian Orthodox	7,200	3,685	3,515
Serbian Orthodox	5,410	2,845	2,560
Eastern non-Christian religions	305,890	160,080	145,810
Islam	98,160	52,625	45,535
Hindu	69,500	35,825	33,675
Sikh	67,710	34,965	32,745
Buddhist	51,955	27,080	24,875
Bahá'í	7,960	3,855	4,105
Jewish	296,425	146,965	149,460
Para-religious groups[1]	13,450	6,855	6,595
No religious preference	1,783,530	1,032,915	750,610
No religion	1,752,380	1,013,410	738,975
Agnostic	10,770	6,745	4,025
Atheist	4,450	3,155	1,295
Other	5,460	3,070	2,395
Total	24,083,495	11,958,360	12,125,135

[1] Includes the categories of native Indian and Inuit, New Thought-Unity-Metaphysical, pagan, Fourth Way, and theosophical groups.

Population by Selected Religion and Province or Territory

(Census of 1981, based on 20% sample data. Source: Statistics Canada.)

	Catholic		Protestant				
	Total	Roman Catholic	Total	Anglican	Lutheran	Presbyterian	United Church
Alberta	613,930	573,495	1,240,000	202,265	144,680	63,890	525,480
British Columbia	538,430	526,355	1,484,925	374,055	122,395	89,810	548,360
Manitoba	318,815	269,070	573,420	108,220	58,830	23,910	240,400
New Brunswick	371,245	371,100	295,785	66,260	1,810	12,070	87,460
Newfoundland	204,470	204,430	352,695	153,530	455	2,700	104,835
Northwest Territories	18,330	18,215	23,670	15,295	660	505	3,725
Nova Scotia	310,725	310,140	487,255	131,130	12,310	38,280	169,605
Ontario	3,036,245	2,986,170	4,418,960	1,164,315	254,180	517,020	1,655,555
Prince Edward Island	56,450	56,415	61,170	6,810	205	12,620	29,645
Québec	5,618,360	5,609,685	407,010	132,115	17,660	34,620	126,275
Saskatchewan	310,005	279,840	557,315	77,725	88,785	16,070	263,375
Yukon Territory	5,595	5,465	12,315	4,665	915	615	3,310
Total	11,402,605	11,210,390	9,914,580	2,436,375	702,905	812,105	3,758,015

(*continued*)

POPULATION BY SELECTED RELIGION AND PROVINCE OR TERRITORY (*continued*)

	Eastern Orthodox	Eastern non-Christian religions	Jewish	Para-religious groups[1]	No religious preference	Other	Total
Alberta	49,275	38,195	10,650	1,585	259,065	955	2,213,650
British Columbia	24,640	78,640	14,680	4,125	566,905	1,260	2,713,615
Manitoba	21,135	7,790	15,670	590	76,045	240	1,013,705
New Brunswick.	575	1,175	845	60	19,650	35	689,370
Newfoundland	65	675	220	20	5,520	85	563,750
Northwest Territories . .	195	255	70	55	2,960	10	45,540
Nova Scotia.	2,345	3,030	2,010	110	34,210	120	839,800
Ontario	167,320	137,115	148,255	5,555	618,600	2,220	8,534,265
Prince Edward Island . . .	55	230	80	—	3,220	15	121,225
Québec	73,275	34,330	102,355	745	132,720	215	6,369,070
Saskatchewan	22,495	4,190	1,580	600	59,995	260	956,440
Yukon Territory	190	275	15	5	4,640	40	23,075
Total	361,560	305,890	296,425	13,450	1,783,530	5,460	24,083,495

[1] Includes the categories of native Indian and Inuit, New Thought-Unity-Metaphysical, pagan, Fourth Way, and theosophical groups.

Directory

BAHÁ'Í FAITH

Bahá'í Community of Canada: 7200 Leslie St, Thornhill, ON L3T 6L8; tel. (416) 889-8168; fax (416) 889-8184; f. 1902; 21,000 mems; Sec. Dr H. B. DANESH.

BUDDHISM

Buddhist Churches of Canada: 918 Bathurst St, Toronto, ON M5R 3G5; tel. (416) 534-4302; f. 1904; Jodo Shinshu of Mahayana Buddhism; Bishop Rev. TOSHIO MURAKAMI.

CHRISTIANITY

About 75% of the population belong to the three main Christian churches: Roman Catholic, United and Anglican. Numerous other religious denominations are represented.

Adventist Church

Seventh-day Adventists: 1148 King St East, Oshawa, ON L1H 1H8; tel. (416) 433-0011; organized 1901; 35,992 mems; Pres. J. W. WILSON; Sec. D. D. DEVNICH.

Anglican Communion

The Anglican Church of Canada (l'Église épiscopale du Canada) comprises four ecclesiastical provinces (each with a Metropolitan archbishop), containing a total of 30 dioceses. The Church had 810,140 members in 1987.

General Synod of the Anglican Church of Canada: Church House, 600 Jarvis St, Toronto, ON M4Y 2J6; tel. (416) 924-9192; fax (416) 924-0211; f. 1893; Gen. Sec. Archdeacon DAVID J. WOELLER.

Primate of the Anglican Church of Canada: MICHAEL GEOFFREY PEERS.

Archbishop of British Columbia: DOUGLAS WALTER HAMBIDGE, Bishop of New Westminister.

Archbishop of Canada: HAROLD LEE NUTTER, Bishop of Fredericton.

Archbishop of Ontario: JOHN CHARLES BOTHWELL, Bishop of Niagara.

Archbishop of Rupert's Land: WALTER HEATH JONES, Bishop of Rupert's Land.

Reformed Episcopal Church: 1544 Broadview Ct, Coquitlam, BC V3J 5X9; Pres. Bishop W. W. LYLE.

Baptist Churches

Association of Regular Baptist Churches—Canada: 337 Jarvis Ave, Toronto, ON M5B 2C7; tel. (416) 925-3261; f. 1957; Pres. Rev. STEPHEN KRING.

Baptist General Conference of Canada: 9833 44th Ave, Suite 3, Edmonton, AB T6E 5E3; tel. (403) 438-9127; Pres. WAYNE WICKS; Exec. Dir Rev. ABE FUNK.

Baptist Union of Western Canada: 838 11th Ave, SW, Suite 202, Calgary, AB T2R 0E5; tel. (403) 234-9044; Exec. Minister Rev. DOUGLAS N. MOFFAT.

Canadian Baptist Federation: 7185 Millcreek Dr., Mississauga, ON L5N 5R4; tel. (416) 826-0191; fax (416) 826-3441; 1,200 churches; 131,472 mems; Pres. ROBERT MACQUADE; Gen. Sec. Dr RICHARD C. COFFIN.

Canadian Convention of Southern Baptists: 5403 Crowchild Trail, NW, Suite 210, Calgary, AB T3B 4Z1; tel. (403) 247-3113; f. 1959; 5,200 mems; Exec. Dir-Treas. ALLEN E. SCHMIDT.

Fellowship of Evangelical Baptist Churches in Canada: 3034 Bayview Ave, Willowdale, ON M2N 6J5; tel. (416) 223-8696; f. 1953; 56,627 mems; Pres. Rev. JOHN S. H. BONHAM.

Free Will Baptists: POB 355, Hartland, NB E0J 1N0; tel. (506) 375-6735; f. 1898; Moderator Rev. FRED D. HANSON.

North American Baptist Conference: 11525 23rd Ave, Edmonton, AB T6J 4T3; Rev. CHARLES LITTMAN.

Brethren Churches

Brethren in Christ Church: 1301 Niagara Parkway, Fort Erie, ON L2A 5N4; tel. (416) 382-3144; f. 1788; 3,440 mems; Moderator Bishop HARVEY R. SIDER.

Christian Brethren (Plymouth Brethren): 156A Danforth Ave, Toronto, ON M4J 1N4; tel. (416) 469-2012; 52,000 mems, exclusive and open; Exec. Dir WILLIAM COFFEY.

Christian and Missionary Alliance in Canada: 105 Gordon Baker Rd, Suite 510, North York, ON M2H 3P8; tel. (416) 492-8775; f. 1890; 63,277 mems; Pres. Dr MELVIN P. SYLVESTR.

United Brethren in Christ, Ontario Conference: 118 Ross Ave, Kitchener, ON N2A 1V4; tel. (519) 576-7647; Supt Rev. MARTIN MAGNUS.

Lutheran Churches

Estonian Evangelical Lutheran Church: 30 Sunrise Ave, Suite 216, Toronto, ON M4A 2R3; f. 1917; 7,222 mems; Rep. Rev. KARL RAUDSEPP.

Evangelical Lutheran Church in Canada: 1512 St James St, Winnipeg, MB R3H 0L2; tel. (204) 786-6707; Pres. Dr DONALD W. SJOBERG.

Lutheran Church—Canada: 2727 Portage Ave, Suite 203, POB 55, Winnipeg, MB R3X 1K9; tel. (204) 885-3273; f. 1959; 94,627 mems; Pres. Rev. ELROY TREIT.

Lutheran Council in Canada: 25 Old York Mills Rd, Willowdale, ON M2P 1B5; tel. (416) 488-9430; f. 1967; co-ordinating agency for Evangelical Lutheran Church in Canada and Lutheran Church—Canada; 1,149 ministers; 1,002 congregations; 296,838 mems (1988); Exec. Dir LAWRENCE R. LIKNESS.

Mennonite Churches

Choritiz (Mennonite) Conference: POB 452, Steinbach, MB R0A 2A0; 2,000 mems; Rep. Bishop WILHELM HILDEBRANDT.

Conference of Mennonites in Canada: 600 Shaftsbury Blvd, Winnipeg, MB R3P 0M4; tel. (204) 888-6781; f. 1902; 28,573 mems; Chair. WALTER FRANZ.

Evangelical Mennonite Brethren Conference: POB 456, Steinbach, MB R0A 2A0; tel. (204) 326-2108; 1,990 mems.

Evangelical Mennonite Conference: 440 Main St, POB 120, Steinbach, MB R0A 2A0; tel. (204) 326-6401; f. 1812; 5,639 mems; Conference Moderator ARDEN THIESSEN.

Evangelical Church in Canada: 2805 13th Ave, SE, Medicine Hat, AB T1A 3R1; 3,664 mems; Gen. Supt Dr GEORGE K. MILLEN.

Evangelical Mennonite Mission Conference: 526 McMillan Ave, Winnipeg, MB R3L 0N5; tel. (204) 477-1213; f. 1936; Moderator Rev. WILF LOEWEN.

Hutterian Brethren: Crystal Spring Colony, St Agatha, MB R0G 1Y0; 9,213 mems.

Mennonite Central Committee Canada: 134 Plaza Dr., Winnipeg, MB R3T 5K9; tel. (204) 261-6381; telex 075-7525; f. 1963; 95,000 mems in 560 congregations; Exec. Dir DANIEL ZEHR.

Mennonite Church—Canada: 131 Erb St West, Waterloo, ON N2L 1T7; f. 1988 in North America; 9,400 mems; Chair. NELSON SCHEIFELE.

Old Colony Mennonite Church in Canada: RR3, Wheatley, ON N0P 2P0; 3,300 mems; Rep. Bishop HENRY REIMER.

Old Order Amish Church: c/o Pathway Publishers, Rte 4, Aylmer, ON N5H 2R3; f. 1824; Rep. DAVID LUTHY.

Old Order Mennonite Church: RR1, Fergus, ON N1M 2W3; 3,280 mems.

Reinlaender Mennonite Church: 223rd St South, Winkler, MB R6W 2V9; f.1958; 700 mems; Rep. Bishop P. A. REMPEL.

Methodist Churches

African Methodist Episcopal Church in Canada: 765 Lawrence Ave West, Toronto, ON M6A 1B7; Rep. Rev. WILLIAM J. DANIEL.

British Methodist Episcopal Church of Canada: 460 Shaw St, Toronto, ON M6G 3L3; tel. (416) 534-3831.

Free Methodist Church in Canada: 4315 Village Centre Ct, Mississauga, ON L4Z 1S2; tel. (416) 848-2600; f. 1880; 6,860 mems; Pres. Bishop DONALD N. BASTIAN.

Wesleyan Church of Canada: 3 Applewood Dr., Belleville, Suite 102, ON K8P 4E3; tel. (613) 966-7527; f. 1889; 8,190 enrolled mems; Gen. Sec. WALTER W. JEWELL.

Orthodox Churches

Antiochian Orthodox Church: 575 rue Jean-Talon est, Bureau 555, Montréal, PQ H2R 1T8; tel. (514) 276-8533; 20,000 mems in North America; Canadian Rep. Very Rev. ANTHONY GABRIEL.

Belarusen Autocephalous Orthodox Church: 524 St. Clarens Ave, Toronto, ON M6H 3W7; tel. (416) 530-1025; f. 1954; Exec. Chair. W. TIELESH.

Canadian Orthodox Church: POB 404, Chilliwack, BC V2P 6J7; tel. (604) 858-7750; Admin. Right Rev. Archimandrite LAZAR PUHALO.

Greek Orthodox Church: 40 Donlands Ave, Toronto, ON M4J 3N6; tel. (416) 462-0833; 316,610 mems (1971 census); Bishop of Toronto His Grace SOTIRIOS.

Orthodox Church in America—Canada: 55 Clarey Ave, Ottawa, ON K1F 2R6.

Patriarchal Parishes of the Russian Orthodox Church in Canada: 9566 101st Ave, Suite 303, Edmonton, AB T5H 0B4; f. 1897; 8,000 mems; Admin. Most Rev. Archbishop NICHOLAS.

Romanian Orthodox Church in America (Canadian Parishes): 103 Furby St, Winnipeg, MB R3C 2A4; tel. (204) 775-3701; f. 1902.

Serbian Orthodox Church—Canada: 5A Stockbridge Ave, Toronto, ON H8Z 4M6; tel. (416) 231-4409; f. 1921 in North America; Rep. Right Rev. GEORGIJE.

Ukrainian Greek Orthodox Church: 9 St John's Ave, Winnipeg, MB R2W 1G8; tel. (204) 586-3093; f. 1918; 280 parishes; 150,000 mems; Metropolitan of Winnipeg and of all Canada Most Rev. WASYLY (FEDAK); Chairman of the Consistory Very Rev. Dr STEPHAN JARMUS.

Other Eastern Churches

Armenian Church of North America, Diocese of Canada: 615 ave Stuart, Outremont, PQ H2V 3H2; tel. (514) 276-9479; f. 1930 in Canada; Canadian Primate Bishop VAZKEN KESHISHIAN.

Armenian Evangelical Church: 42 Glenforest Rd, Toronto, ON M4N 1Z8; tel. (416) 489-3188; f. 1960; Minister Rev. YESSAYI SARMAZIAN.

Coptic Church in Canada: 41 Glendinning Ave, Agincourt, ON M1S 3B2; tel. (416) 494-4449; f. 1964; 40,000 mems; Archpriest Father M. A. MARCOS.

Polish National Church of Canada: 186 Cowan Ave, Toronto, ON M6K 2N6; tel. (416) 532- 8249; Rep. Right Rev. JOSEPH NIEMINSKI.

Pentecostal Churches

Apostolic Church in Canada: 27 Castlefield Ave, Toronto, ON M4R 1G3; tel. (416) 489-0453; f. 1927; Pres. Rev. D. S. MORRIS.

Apostolic Church of Pentecost of Canada, Inc: 807 Manning Rd, NE, Suite 105, Calgary, AB T2E 7M9; tel. (306) 279-5777; f. 1921; Moderator Rev. WESLEY S. SCHINDEL.

Church of God and Prophesy in Canada: 1st Line East, RR2, Brampton, ON L6V 1A1; tel. (416) 843-2379; f. 1903; 2,208 mems; Pres. Bishop JOHN DOROSHUK.

Foursquare Gospel Church of Canada: 7895 Welsley Dr., Burnaby, BC V5E 3X4; tel. (604) 524-1908; f. 1964; 2,391 mems; Pres. VICTOR F. GARDNER.

Independent Assemblies of God—Canada: 1920 Huron St, London, ON N5V 3A7; tel. (519) 542-3480; Gen. Sec. HARRY WUERCH.

Italian Pentecostal Church of Canada: 6724 rue Fabre, Montréal, PQ H2G 2Z6; tel. (514) 721-5614; f. 1912; Gen. Supt Rev. ALBERICO DEVITO.

Open Bible Standard Churches of Canada: 4545 Jane St, Toronto, ON M3N 2K7; tel. (416) 661-6770; f. 1982; 1,000 mems; Supt and Gen. Overseer Rev. C. RUSSELL ARCHER.

Pentecostal Assemblies of Canada: 10 Overlea Blvd, Toronto, ON M4H 1A5; tel. (416) 425-1010; fax (416) 425-8308; f. 1919; 191,607 mems; Gen. Supt Rev. J. M. MacKNIGHT; Gen. Sec. Rev. CHARLES YATES.

Pentecostal Assemblies of Newfoundland: 57 Thorburn Rd, St John's, NF A1B 3N4; tel. (709) 753-6314; f. 1910; Pres. and Gen. Supt ROY D. KING.

Pentecostal Holiness Church of Canada: POB 442, Waterloo, ON N2J 4A9; tel. (519) 746-1310; f. 1971; Gen. Supt. Dr G. H. NUNN.

United Pentecostal Church in Canada: POB 651, Brockville, ON K6V 5V8; 23,000 mems; District Supt Rev. WILLIAM COOLING.

Presbyterian Churches

Presbyterian Church in America (Canadian Section): 10120 Lassam Rd, Richmond, BC V7E 2C2; 1,000 mems; Correspondent Rev. DOUGLAS CODLING.

Presbyterian Church in Canada: 50 Wynford Dr., Don Mills, ON M3C 1J7; tel. (416) 441-1111; fax (416) 441-2825; f. 1875; 1,102 ministers, 1,028 congregations; 156,912 mems (1988); Moderator Rev. HAROLD MORRIS; Principal Clerk Dr EARLE F. ROBERTS.

Reformed Churches

Christian Reformed Church in North America: 3475 Mainway, POB 5070, Burlington, ON L7R 3Y8; tel. (416) 336-2920; fax (416) 336-8341; f. 1857; 83,662 mems; Rep. Rev. ARIE G. VAN EEK.

Reformed Church in Canada: RR4, Cambridge, ON N1R 5S5; tel. (519) 623-4860; f. 1628 in North America; 6,487 mems.

The Roman Catholic Church

For Catholics of the Latin rite, Canada comprises 17 archdioceses (including one directly responsible to the Holy See), 47 dioceses and one territorial abbacy. There are also one archdiocese and four dioceses of the Ukrainian rite. In addition, the Maronite, Melkite and Slovak rites are each represented by one diocese (all directly responsible to the Holy See). In 1989 the Roman Catholic Church had 11,375,914 adherents in Canada.

Canadian Conference of Catholic Bishops/Conférence des évêques catholiques du Canada: 90 Parent Ave, Ottawa, ON K1N 7B1; tel. (613) 236-9461; Pres. Most Rev. JAMES M. HAYES, Archbishop of Halifax; Vice-Pres. Mgr ROBERT LEBEL, Bishop of Valleyfield, PQ.

Latin Rite

Archbishop of Edmonton: JOSEPH N. MacNEIL.

Archbishop of Grouard-McLennan: HENRI LÉGARÉ.

Archbishop of Halifax: JAMES M. HAYES.

Archbishop of Keewatin-Le Pas: PETER ALFRED SUTTON.

Archbishop of Kingston: FRANCIS SPENCE.

Archbishop of Moncton: DONAT CHIASSON.

Archbishop of Montréal: Cardinal PAUL GRÉGOIRE.

Archbishop of Ottawa: JOSEPH-AURÈLE PLOURDE.

Archbishop of Québec: Cardinal LOUIS-ALBERT VACHON.

Archbishop of Regina: CHARLES A. HALPIN.

Archbishop of Rimouski: GILLES OUELLET.

Archbishop of St Boniface: MAURICE ANTOINE HACAULT.

Archbishop of St John's, Nfld: ALPHONSUS L. PENNEY.

Archbishop of Sherbrooke: JEAN-MARIE FORTIER.

Archbishop of Toronto: Cardinal G. EMMETT CARTER.

Archbishop of Vancouver: JAMES FRANCIS CARNEY.
Archbishop of Winnipeg: ADAM EXNER.

United Church of Canada

The United Church of Canada (Église unie du Canada) was founded in 1925 with the union of Methodist, Congregational and Presbyterian churches in Canada. The Evangelical United Bretheren of Canada joined in 1968. In 1988 there were 2,420 pastoral charges, 4,175 congregations, 3,897 ministers and 863,910 members.

Moderator: Rt Rev. SANG CHUL LEE.

General Secretary: Rev. HOWARD M. MILLS, The United Church House, 85 St Clair Ave East, Toronto, ON M4T 1M8; tel. (416) 925-5931; telex 065-28224; fax (416) 925-3394.

Other Christian Churches

Associated Gospel Churches: 280 Plains Rd West, Burlington, ON L7T 1G4; tel. (416) 522-2398; f. 1922; 17,000 worshippers; Pres. Rev. WILLIAM SIFFT.

Bible Holiness Movement: POB 223, Station A, Vancouver, BC V6C 2M3; tel. (604) 498-3895; f. 1949; 27,416 mems worldwide; Leader WESLEY H. WAKEFIELD.

Canadian Unitarian and Universalist Churches and Fellowships: 175 St Clair Ave West, Toronto, ON M4V 1P7; tel. (416) 921-4506; 6,290 mems; Pres. ELINOR R. KNIGHT.

Christadelphians in Canada: POB 221, Weston, ON M9N 3M7.

Christian Church (Disciples of Christ): 55 Cork St East, Suite 303, Guelph, ON N1H 2W7; tel. (519) 823-5190; f. 1830; 4,665 Canadian mems; Moderator Rev. STEVEN DOBBINS.

Christian Community and Brotherhood of Reformed Doukhobors: Site 8, Comp. 50, RR1, Crescent Valley, BC V0G 1H0; f. in 17th century in Russia; 2,108 mems; Rep. STEPHEN S. SOROKIN.

Christian Science: 696 Yonge St, Suite 403, Toronto, ON M4Y 2A7; tel. (416) 922-7473.

Church Army in Canada: 397 Brunswick Ave, Toronto, ON M5R 2Z2; tel. (416) 924-9279; Dir Capt. R. A. TAYLOR.

Church of God: POB 2036, Bramalea, ON L6T 3S3; tel. (416) 793-2213; f. 1919; 4,500 mems; Supt S. A. LANKFORD.

Church of Jesus Christ of Latter-Day Saints (Mormon): 7181 Woodbine Ave, Suite 234, Markham, ON L3R 1A3; tel. (416) 477-8595; 113,000 Canadian mems; Rep. RICHARD R. ROBERTSON.

Church of the Nazarene—Canada: POB 30080, Station B, Calgary, AB T2M 4N7; tel. (403) 276-2204; f. 1902; 10,050 mems; Rev. S. RUDOLF PEDERSEN.

Church of the United Brethren in Christ: 9 Dreger St, Kitchener, ON N2A 2A4; tel. (519) 743-3450; Conference Supt MARTIN MAGNUS.

Evangelical Alliance Mission of Canada, Inc: POB 155, Sub 158, Calgary, AB T1Y 6M0; Gen. Dir Dr RICHARD M. WINCHELL.

Evangelical Covenant Church of Canada: 245 21st St East, Prince Albert, SK S6V 1L9; f. 1904; 1,232 mems; Supt Rev. GERALD V. STENBERG.

Evangelical Fellowship of Canada: POB 8800, Station B, Willowdale, ON M2K 2R6; tel. (416) 479-5885; Exec. Dir Rev. BRIAN C. STILLER.

Evangelical Free Church of Canada: 10008 29th Ave, Suite 4, Edmonton, AB T6N 1A8; tel. (403) 463-9068; f. 1917; 5,600 mems; Pres. Rev. RON SWANSON.

General Church of the New Jerusalem: 279 Burnhamthorpe Rd, Islington, ON M9B 1Z6; tel. (416) 239-3054; f. 1835; Exec. Vice-Pres. Rev. LOUIS D. SYNNESTVELDT.

Grace and Peace Evangelistic Ministry: 1801 Eglinton Ave West, Suite 304, Toronto, ON M6E 2H8; tel. (416) 782-4224.

Independent Holiness Church: RR1, Manotick, ON K0H 2T0; f. 1960; Gen. Sec. DWAYNE REANEY.

Jehovah's Witnesses: POB 4100, Halton Hills, ON L7G 4Y4; tel. (416) 873-4100; f. 1918 in Canada; 88,130 Canadian mems; Exec. Dir K. A. LITTLE.

Missionary Church of Canada: 89 Centre Ave, Willowdale, ON M2M 2L7; tel. (416) 223-3496; Pres. Rev. ALFRED W. REES.

New Apostolic Church—Canada: 65 Northfield Dr., POB 1615, Waterloo, ON N2J 4J2; tel. (519) 884-2862; telex 069-55333; over 2m. mems worldwide; Pres. M. KRAUS.

Overseas Missionary Fellowship: 1058 Avenue Rd, Toronto, ON M5N 2C6; tel. (416) 485-0427; f. 1865; Gen. Dir Dr JAMES H. TAYLOR, III.

Polish National Catholic Church of Canada: 188 Cowan Ave, Toronto, ON M6K 2N6; tel. (416) 532-9576; f. 1904; 6,000 mems; officer Right Rev. JOSEPH NIEMINSKI.

Religious Society of Friends (Quakers): 91A Fourth Ave, Ottawa, ON K1S 2L1; tel. (613) 235-8553; Clerk of Canadian Yearly Meeting EDWARD S. BELL.

Reorganized Church of Jesus Christ of Latter-Day Saints: 390 Speedvale Ave East, Guelph, ON N1E 1N5; f. 1980; 12,465 mems; Bishop of Canada ALBERT K. BENNETT.

Salvation Army in Canada: 20 Albert St, POB 4021, Postal Station A, Toronto, ON M5W 2B1; tel. (416) 598-2071; f. 1882; 102,018 mems; Territorial Commander WILLIAM PRATT.

Swedenborgian Church (Church of the Good Shepherd): 116 Queen St North, Kitchener, ON N2H 2H7; tel. (519) 743-3845; Canadian Pres. Rev. PAUL ZACHARIAS.

Ukrainian Catholic Church in Canada: 235 Scotia St, Winnipeg, MB R2V 1V7; tel. (204) 334-6363; 190,585 mems (1981 census); Archeparch-Metropolitan of Winnipeg Most Rev. MAXIM HERMANIUK.

Union of Spiritual Communities of Christ (Orthodox Doukhobors in Canada): POB 760, Grand Forks, BC V0H 1H0; tel. (604) 442-8252; f. 1889 in Canada; Chair. JOHN J. VERIGIN.

Universal Fellowship of Metropolitan Community Churches: POB 2979, Station D, Ottawa, ON K1P 5W9; tel. (613) 232-0241; f. 1968; District Co-ordinator Rev. RON BERGERON.

Zoroastrian Society of Ontario: 3890 Bayview Ave, Willowdale, ON M2M 3S6; tel. (416) 733-4586; c. 1,200 mems.

Interdenominational Organizations

Atlantic Ecumenical Council: 4 Pinehill Dr., Dartmouth, NS B3A 2E6; tel. (902) 469-4480; Pres. Rev. P. A. MCDONALD.

The Canadian Council of Christians and Jews: 49 Front St East, Toronto, ON M5E 1B3; tel. (416) 364-3101; Exec. Dir ELIZABETH LOWETH.

Canadian Council of Churches/Conseil canadien des Eglises: 40 St Clair Ave East, Toronto, ON M4T 1M9; tel. (416) 921-4152; telex 065-24128; f.1944; 15 mem churches, one assoc. mem.; Gen. Sec. Dr STUART E. BROWN.

New Life League: POB 1017, Three Hills, AB T0M 2A0; tel. (403) 443-7352.

Gospel Missionary Union of Canada: POB 773, Annisfail, AB T0M 1A0; tel. (204) 338-7831; f. 1951; Pres. of Canadian Ministries Rev. CHRIS WILSON.

ISLAM

Ahmadiyya Movement in Islam: 10610 Jane St, Maple, ON L0J 1E0; tel. (416) 832-2669; fax (416) 832-3220; 10m. mems worldwide; Missionary in Charge NASEEM MEHDI.

Canadian Council of Muslim Women: 1 King Way, Edmonton, AB T5H 4G9; tel. (403) 481-6141; Pres. Dr LILA FAHLMAN.

Council of Muslim Communities of Canada: 1521 Trinity Dr., Unit 16, Mississauga, ON L5T 1P6; tel. (416) 672-1566; 140,000 adherents; co-ordinating agency; Pres. Dr MIR IQBAL ALI.

JUDAISM

The Jews of Canada number 305,000. There are 112 synagogues across Canada, of which 53 are Orthodox, 43 Conservative, 14 Reform and 2 Reconstructionist.

Canadian Foundation for Jewish Culture: 4600 Bathurst St, Willowdale, ON M2R 3V2; tel. (416) 635-2883; Pres. MIRA KOSCHITZSKY.

Canadian Jewish Congress: 1590 ave Dr Penfield, Montréal, PQ H3G 1C5; tel. (514) 931-7531; fax (514) 931-0548; f. 1919; Exec. Vice-Pres. ALAN ROSE.

Jewish Community Council: 151 Chapel St, Ottawa, ON K1N 7Y2; tel. (613) 232-7306; fax (613) 563-4393; Pres. Dr ELI RABIN; Exec. Dir GERRY KOFFMAN.

Zionist Organization of Canada: 788 Marlee Ave, Toronto, ON M6B 3K1; tel. (416) 781-3571; Pres. MAX GOODY.

SIKHISM

Federation of Sikh Societies of Canada: POB 91, Station B, Ottawa, ON K1P 6C3; tel. (613) 521-2566; Pres. MOHINDER SINGH GOSAL.

TRANSPORT AND UTILITIES

TRANSPORT

CO-ORDINATING BODIES AND TRANSPORT ASSOCIATIONS

Department of Transport: Transport Canada Bldg, Pl. de Ville, Tower C, 21st Floor, 330 Sparks St, Ottawa, ON K1A 0N5; tel. (613) 996-5861; divisions: Aviation Group, Airports Authority Group, Airports Transition Management, Marine Group, Surface Group, Policy and Co-ordination Group, Canadian Coast Guard, Transportation of Dangerous Goods Office.

National Transportation Agency of Canada: Ottawa, ON K1A 0N9; tel. (819) 997-0677; telex 053-4254; fax (819) 997-6727; federal govt agency; responsible for economic regulation of transport in Canada; Sec. SUZANNE CLEMENT.

Amalgamated Transit Union: 15 Gervais Dr., Suite 606, Don Mills, ON M3C 1Y8; tel. (416) 445-6204; Exec. Sec. KEN FOSTER.

Association québécoise du transport et des routes inc: 6455 ave Christophe-Colomb, Bureau 300, Montréal, PQ H2S 2G5; tel. (514) 274-3573; fax (514) 274-9608; Dir-Gen. GUY PARÉ.

Atlantic Provinces Transportation Commission: 236 St George St, Suite 210, POB 577, Moncton, NB E1C 8L9; tel. (506) 857-2820; telex 014-2842; fax (506) 857-2835; Chair. GEORGE KEY; Gen. Man. RAMSAY ARMITAGE.

Canadian Freight Association: 1162 rue St-Antoine ouest, Montréal, PQ H3C 1B5; tel. (514) 861-8331; Chair. E. F. SMITH.

Canadian Industrial Transportation League: 480 University Ave, Suite 706, Toronto, ON M5G 1V2; tel. (416) 596-7833; fax (416) 596-1272; Pres. J. DAVID LONG.

Canadian Institute of Traffic and Transportation: 573 King St East, Toronto, ON M5A 1M5; tel. (416) 363-5696; fax (416) 363-5698; 2,000 mems; Exec. Vice-Pres. VICTOR S. DEYGLIO.

Canadian Transport Tariff Bureau Association: 155 Rexdale Blvd, Suite 807, Rexdale, ON M9W 5Z8; tel. (416) 741-7805; 170 mem. orgs; Gen. Man. A. A. LANDRY.

Canadian Transportation Research Forum: 170 Metcalfe St, Suite 601, Ottawa, ON K2P 1P3; tel. (613) 235-9556; fax (613) 235-8304; 375 mems; Sec. FRANK J. TROTTER.

Canadian Union of Transportation Employees: 839 Second Ave, Prince George, BC V2L 3A6; tel. (604) 572-4272.

Canadian Urban Transit Association: 55 York St, Suite 1101, Toronto, ON M5J 1R7; tel. (416) 365-9800; mems: 29 individuals and 255 orgs; Exec. Dir AL CORMIER.

Express Transport Association: 2255 Sheppard Ave East, Suite E-325, POB 26, Willowdale, ON M2J 4Y1; tel. (416) 495-9611.

Independent Canadian Transit Union: 5050 Kingsway, Suite 206, Burnaby, BC V5H 4H2.

Transport 2000 Canada: 22 Metcalfe St, Suite 405, POB 858, Station B, Ottawa, ON K1P 5P9; tel. (613) 594-3290; nat. federation of consumers of public transportation engaged in research, education and advocacy; Nat. Pres. TONY TURRITTIN; Exec. Dir ROY JAMIESON.

Transportation Safety Association of Ontario: 80 Bloor St West, Suite 602, Toronto, ON M5S 2V1; tel. (416) 927-4696; Gen. Man. HARRY I. MELNYK.

United Transportation Union: 99 Bank St, Suite 709, Ottawa, ON K1P 6B9; tel. (613) 238-3717; Vice-Pres. REAL J. PROUX.

RAILWAYS

Length of Main-Line Track Operated by Area

(In kilometres. Includes all main-line track operated under ownership, joint-ownership, lease, contract or trackage rights. Source: Statistics Canada.)

	1982	1983	1984	1985	1986
Alberta	3,410	3,486	3,730	4,885	4,521
British Columbia	5,574	5,656	6,300	6,312	6,219
Manitoba	2,712	2,824	2,824	2,654	2,654
New Brunswick	1,109	1,101	1,101	1,101	1,099
Newfoundland	453	449	240	240	421
Northwest Territories	93	—	—	—	—
Nova Scotia	710	711	712	675	747
Ontario	14,880	14,944	15,044	13,294	13,760
Québec	4,506	4,508	4,696	5,554	4,575
Saskatchewan	4,012	4,019	4,019	4,016	4,016
USA	575	575	575	575	577
Total	38,034	38,272	39,242	39,307	38,589

Railway Rolling Stock in Service

(As at 31 December. Source: Statistics Canada.)

	1982	1983	1984	1985	1986
Locomotives	3,900	3,783	3,699	3,509	3,897
Freight cars	155,897	149,432	142,407	130,185	129,509
Passenger cars	1,304	1,337	1,326	1,286	1,295

Summary of Operations

(Seven major rail carriers only. Source: Statistics Canada.)

	1984	1985	1986	1987	1988
Railway revenues (C $ million)	7,354	7,452	7,377	7,716	7,778
Railway expenses (C $ million)	6,857	7,179	7,243	7,325	7,287
Railway net income (C $ million)	498	273	134	391	491
Revenue freight ton-km[1] (million)	244,545	232,035	223,527	261,663	263,689
Revenue passenger-km (million)	2,096	2,228	2,090	1,854	2,141
Freight train-km ('000)	100,848	96,879	96,386	101,521	104,061
Freight car-km ('000)	7,709,099	4,319,842	7,277,092	7,715,464	7,672,521
Passenger car-km ('000)	125,021	132,025	124,978	113,554	121,769

[1] Metric tons.

Directory

The Canadian Pacific (CP) and Canadian National (CN) Railways account for 88% of all rail transportation in Canada. Passenger services are operated over CP and CN tracks by the crown corporation VIA Rail.

PRINCIPAL RAILWAY COMPANIES

Algoma Central Railway: 289 Bay St, POB 7000, Sault Sainte Marie, ON P6A 5P6; tel. (705) 949-2113; telex 067-77146; f. 1899; diversified transportation co moving bulk cargo by rail, water and road; also has interests in commercial property development; Chair. HENRY N. R. JACKMAN; Pres. and CEO L. N. SAVOIE.

British Columbia Hydro Rail: 5935 Glover Rd, Langley, BC V3A 4B5; tel. (604) 533-5611; telex 043-65541; 167 km (104 miles) of track; Man. (Marketing and Sales) R. W. NEWTON.

BC Rail Ltd: 221 West Esplanade, POB 8770, Vancouver, BC V6B 4X6; tel. (604) 986-2012; telex 043-52752; f. 1912; 2,608 km (1,620 miles) of track; Pres. and CEO P. J. McELLIGOTT.

Burlington Northern (Manitoba) Ltd: 963 Lindsay St, Winnipeg, MB R3N 1X6; tel. (204) 453-4415; subsidiary of Burlington Northern Railroad Co, Fort Worth, Texas, USA; Superintendent J. A. LOWRY.

Canada & Gulf Terminal Railway/Chemin de Fer de Matane et du Golfe: 206 ave Hébert, CP 578, Mont-Joli, PQ G5H 1M5; tel. (418) 775-4373; telex 051-86408; 48 km (30 miles) of track; Gen. Man. BERNARD BOURGEOIS.

Canadian National Railways: 935 rue de la Gauchetière ouest, CP 8100, Succursale A, Montréal, PQ H3C 3N4; tel. (514) 399-5430; telex 055-60519; f. 1923; 45,000 km (28,000 miles) of track; Chair. BRIAN O'N. GALLERY (acting); Pres. and CEO R. E. LAWLESS.

Canadian Pacific Ltd (CP Rail): Gare Windsor, Bureau 227, CP 6042, Succursale A, Montréal, PQ H3C 3E4; tel. (514) 395-5151; f. 1881; 24,649 km (15,317 miles) of main-line track; also active in road haulage and marine transport; interests in hotels, property, manufacturing and other activities; Chair. R. W. CAMPBELL; Pres. and CEO W. W. STINSON.

Cartier Railway Co: Route 138, Port-Cartier, PQ G5B 2J6; tel. (418) 768-2432; 444 km (276 miles) of track; Pres. G. MASSOBRIO.

Chesapeake & Ohio Railway: c/o 100N Charles St, Baltimore, MD 21201, USA; tel. (301) 237-2000.

Conrail (Consolidated Rail Corpn): c/o Transportation Center, 6 Penn Center Plaza, Philadelphia, PA 19103, USA; tel. (215) 977-4000; telex 9775567.

Devco Railway: POB 2500, Sydney, NS B1P 6K9; tel. (902) 564-7600; telex 01-935132; 142 km (88 miles) of track; Dir (Surface Operations) R. W. MacKENZIE.

Dominion Atlantic Railway: Kentville, NS B4N 2N3; tel. (902) 678-3223; 445 km (277 miles) of track; Man. M. S. ANDREWS.

Esquimalt & Nanaimo Railway: 200 Granville St, Suite 200, Vancouver, BC V6C 2R3; tel. (604) 665-3108; 313 km (195 miles) of track.

Essex Terminal Railway: 1601 Lincoln Rd, POB 2186, Walkerville Post Office, Windsor, ON N8Y 4R8; tel. (519) 973-8222; telex (064) 77767; freight railway; 38 km (24 miles) of track; Pres. and Gen. Man. M. A. ELDER.

Greater Winnipeg Water District Railway: 598 Plinguet St, St Boniface, MB R2J 2W7; tel. (204) 986-4121; 156 km (97 miles) of track; Railway Supervisor D. E. CARR.

Napierville Junction Railway: 21 rue Sainte-Marie, Lacolle, PQ J0J 1J0; tel. (514) 246-3343; telex 05-831564; 45 km (28 miles) of track; Pres. D. S. FINK.

Norfolk & Western Railway Co: c/o 8 North Jefferson St, Roanoke, VA 24042-0027, USA; tel. (703) 981-5228.

Ontario Northland Railway: 555 Oak Street East, North Bay, ON P1B 8L3; tel. (705) 472-4500; telex 067-76103; an agency of the Govt of Ontario; 919 km (571 miles) of track; Chair. J. W. SPOONER; Gen. Man. P. A. DYMENT.

Roberval & Saguenay Railway: CP 1277, Jonquière (Arvida), PQ G7S 4K8; tel. (418) 548-1121; telex 051-36216; 87 km (54 miles) of track.

VIA Rail Canada Inc: 2 pl. Ville-Marie, CP 8116, succursale A, Montréal, PQ H3B 2C9; tel. (514) 871-6000; telex 052-68530; f. 1977; operates passenger services over existing rail routes throughout Canada; Chair. L. HANIGAN; Pres. and CEO R. E. LAWLESS.

The White Pass and Yukon Corporation Ltd: POB 4070, Whitehorse, YT Y1A 3T1; tel. (403) 668-7621; telex 036-8210; 177 km (110 miles) of track; Exec. Vice-Pres. and COO MARVIN P. TAYLOR.

Wisconsin Central Ltd: c/o One O'Hare Center, 6250 North River Rd, Rosemont, IL 60018, USA; tel. (312) 318-4600.

ASSOCIATIONS

Alberta Pioneer Railway Association: POB 6102, Station C, Edmonton, AB T5B 4K5; tel. (403) 973-6738; 100 mems; Sec. GEOFFREY A. LESTER.

Canadian Brotherhood of Railways Transport and General Workers: 2300 Carling Ave, Ottawa, ON K2B 7G1; tel. (613) 829-8764; fax (613) 829-6815; Nat. Pres. J. D. HUNTER.

Canadian Railroad Historical Association: POB 148, St-Constant, PQ J0L 1X0; tel. (514) 632-2410; Sec. BERNARD MARTIN.

Railway Association of Canada: 1117 rue Sainte-Catherine ouest, Montréal, PQ H3B 1H9; tel. (514) 849-4274; fax (514) 849-2861; 11 mem. railways and 5 associates; Pres. J. M. BEAUPRE.

Scotian Railroad Society: POB 798, Armdale Post Office, Halifax, NS B3L 4K5; 6 mems.

West Coast Railway Association: POB 2790, Vancouver, BC V6B 3X2; tel. (604) 524-1011; 250 mems; Pres. DON EVANS.

ROADS

Length of Roads and Highways by Province or Territory

(In kilometres, as at 31 March 1986. Source: Statistics Canada.)

	Federal	Provincial and territorial	Total
Alberta	3,209	35,123	38,332
British Columbia	2,172	42,061	44,233
Manitoba	1,538	19,181	20,719
New Brunswick	337	17,224	17,561
Newfoundland	253	8,713	8,966
Northwest Territories	407	3,419	3,826
Nova Scotia	247	25,797	26,044
Ontario	1,736	21,267	23,003
Prince Edward Island	51	5,279	5,330
Québec	374	58,045	58,419
Saskatchewan	2,370	25,330	27,700
Yukon Territory	1,112	5,006	6,118
Total	13,806	266,445	280,251

Motor-Vehicle Registrations by Province or Territory

(Figures refer to 1986, although the date on which the registration year ends varies in different provinces or territories. Source: Statistics Canada.)

	Passenger cars[1]	Trucks and buses[2]	Motorcycles and mopeds	Other[3]	Total
Alberta	1,295,635	392,365	42,762	—	1,739,472
British Columbia	1,526,645	618,372	77,700	—	2,222,717
Manitoba	527,485	213,434	17,838	19	758,947
New Brunswick	286,037	121,462	12,566	6,417	426,482
Newfoundland	176,351	77,693	10,766	6,301	273,192
Northwest Territories	17,124	1,218	1,670	79	20,231
Nova Scotia	337,120	145,011	18,546	2,973	505,116
Ontario	4,244,200	946,145	151,271	—	5,367,277
Prince Edward Island	56,224	19,841	2,003	140	78,619
Québec	2,614,312	339,033	122,026	56,318	3,145,116
Saskatchewan	388,671	268,628	7,519	225	669,256
Yukon Territory	7,510	12,454	726	—	20,886
Total	11,477,314	3,155,656	465,393	72,472	15,227,311

[1] Includes taxis and for-hire cars.
[2] Includes other types of motor vehicles, in certain provinces or territories, while certain classes of trucks and/or buses have been included under passenger cars in five provinces.
[3] Includes ambulances, fire trucks and some government vehicles.

Directory

Provincial governments are responsible for roads within their boundaries. The federal government is responsible for major roads in the Yukon Territory and Northwest Territories and in national parks. In 1982 there were 391,792 km of roads (excluding municipal roads) of which 41.9% were paved.

The Trans-Canada Highway extends from St John's, Newfoundland, to Victoria, British Columbia.

NATIONAL REGULATORY AGENCIES

National Transportation Agency: Terrasses de la Chaudière, 15 rue Eddy, Hull, PQ K1A 0N9; tel. (819) 997-6567.

Motor Vehicle Transport Committee: c/o National Transportation Agency, Terrasses de la Chaudière, 15 rue Eddy, Hull, PQ K1A 0N9; tel. (819) 997-0265.

ASSOCIATIONS

Association des Propriétaires d'Autobus du Québec: 225 blvd Charest est, Suite 107, Québec, PQ G1K 3G9; tel. (418) 522-7131; 300 mem. cos; Dir-Gen. and Sec. JACQUES GUAY.

Canadian Advanced Drivers' Association: c/o Allen A. Nield, 46 Ivy Green Cres., Scarborough, ON M1G 2Z3.

Canadian Automobile Association: 1775 Courtwood Cres., Ottawa, ON K2C 3J2; tel. (613) 226-7631; telex 053-4440; fax (613) 225-7383; 2.8m. mems; 7 regional asscns; Exec. Vice-Pres. R. B. ERB.

Canadian Construction Association: 85 Albert St, 2nd Floor, Ottawa, ON K1P 6A4; tel. (613) 236-9455; fax (613) 236-9525; nat. asscn of road builders; 25,000 mems; Pres. and CEO ROBERT E. NUTH.

Canadian Council of Motor Transport Administrators: 1765 St Laurent Blvd, Ottawa, ON K1G 3V4; tel. (613) 526-0550; mems: federal, provincial and territorial transportation depts; Exec. Dir NORMAN BROWN.

Canadian Drivers' Club: 480 University Ave, Suite 1100, Toronto, ON M5G 1V2; tel. (416) 977-6208.

Canadian Bus Association: 170 Metcalfe St, Suite 601, Ottawa, ON K2P 1P3; tel. (613) 238-1800; fax (613) 235-8304; mems: 11 individuals and 40 orgs; Exec. Dir FRANK J. TROTTER; Asscn Man. SHEILAGH McDERMOTT.

Canadian Motorcycle Association: 500 James St North, POB 448, Station B, Hamilton, ON L8L 8C4; tel. (416) 522-5705; fax (416) 522-5716; mems: 6,000 individuals and 200 orgs; Exec. Officer M. BASTEDO.

Canadian Trucking Association: 130 Albert St, Suite 300, Ottawa, ON K1P 5G4; tel. (613) 236-9426; fax (613) 563-2701; f. 1937; Exec. Vice-Pres. A. KENNETH MACLAREN; Gen. Man. L. P. TARDIF.

Provincial associations:

Alberta Trucking Association: 6940 Fisher Rd, SE, Suite 310, POB 5520, Station A, Calgary, AB T2H 1X9; tel. (403) 253-8401; Gen. Man. R. J. DRINNAN.

Association du Camionnage du Québec inc: 4837 Boyer St, Suite 100, Montréal, PQ H2J 3E6; tel. (514) 527-1356; mems: 800 individuals and orgs; Vice-Pres. LOUIS FAHNDRICH.

Atlantic Provinces Trucking Association: 567 Coverdale Rd, Suite 7A, Riverview, NB E1B 3K7; tel. (506) 387-4413; 300 mem. orgs; Exec. Dir DALE ELLIOTT.

British Columbia Trucking Association: 4090 Graveley St North, Burnaby, BC V5C 3T6; tel. (604) 299-7407; fax (604) 299-0586; mems: 400 individuals and orgs; Gen. Man. ROB WESTON.

Manitoba Trucking Association: 25 Bunting St, Winnipeg, MB R2X 2P5; tel. (204) 632-6600; fax (204) 694-7134; Gen. Man. AL HARRIS.

Northwest Territories Motor Transport Association: POB 574, Yellowknife, NT X1A 2N4; tel. (403) 873-2831; 100 mem. orgs; Pres. PAUL LADOBRUK.

Ontario Trucking Association: 555 Dixon Rd, Rexdale, ON M9W 1H8; tel. (416) 249-7401; fax (416) 245-6152; mems: 1,000 individuals and orgs; Exec. Vice-Pres. RAYMOND R. COPE.

Saskatchewan Trucking Association: 1335 Wallace St, Regina, SK S4N 3Z5; tel. (306) 569-9696; Gen. Man. WARREN SMITH.

Dominion Automobile Association: 201 King St, London, ON N6A 4T3; tel. (519) 434-2185; 8 provincial offices.

Industrial Truck Association of Canada: One Yonge St, Suite 1400, Toronto, ON M5E 1J9; tel. (416) 363-7261; telex 065-24693; fax (416) 363-3779; Man. JOHN MARTIN.

Ontario Good Roads Association: 5716 Coopers Ave, Unit 7, Mississauga, ON L4Z 2E8; mems include 732 municipalities, 139 corporations and 13 Indian reserves; Exec. Dir SHEILA RICHARDSON.

Private Motor Truck Council of Canada: 53 Village Centre Pl., Suite 102, Mississauga, ON L4Z 1V9; tel. (416) 273-6275; 300 mems; Exec. Dir R. G. HARDIE.

Roads and Transportation Association of Canada: 1765 St Laurent Blvd, Ottawa, ON K1G 3V4; tel. (613) 521-4052; fax (613) 521-6542; 550 mem. orgs; Exec. Dir NORMAN BROWN.

Western Canada Motor Coach Association: POB 4520, Station C, Calgary, AB T2T 5N3; tel. (403) 244-4487; Exec. Dir MARJORIE ZINGLE.

INLAND WATERWAYS

Traffic

(St Lawrence Seaway, '000 metric tons)

	1985	1986	1987
Montréal—Lake Ontario	37,322	37,582	39,969
Welland Canal	41,952	41,613	42,725

Source: St Lawrence Seaway Authority.

Directory

The St Lawrence River and the Great Lakes provide Canada and the USA with a system of inland waterways extending from the Atlantic Ocean to the western end of Lake Superior, a distance of 3,769 km (2,342 miles). There is a 10.7-m (35-foot) navigation channel from Montréal to the sea and an 8.25-m (27-foot) channel from Montréal to Lake Erie. The St Lawrence Seaway, which was opened in 1959, was initiated partly to provide a deep waterway and partly to satisfy the increasing demand for electric power. Power development has been undertaken by the provinces of Québec and Ontario, and by New York State. In 1987 cargo traffic through the Seaway totalled 50.7m. metric tons. The navigation facilities and conditions are within the jurisdiction of the federal governments of the USA and Canada.

ST LAWRENCE RIVER AND GREAT LAKES SHIPPING

Great Lakes Pilotage Authority Ltd: POB 95, Cornwall, ON K6H 5R9; tel. (613) 933-2995; telex 058-11565; fax (613) 932-3793; provides pilotage services in Canadian waters of the St Lawrence River commencing at the northern entrance of St Lambert Lock, the Great Lakes area and the Port of Churchill, Manitoba; Pres. R. G. ARMSTRONG.

Laurentian Pilotage Authority: 1080 Beaver Hall Hill, Suite 1402, Montréal, PQ H2Z 1S8; tel. (514) 496-1813; telex 05-24664; fax (514) 496-2409; provides pilotage services in the province of Québec north of St Lambert Lock; Chair. JACQUES CHOUINARD; Dir of Operations GUY LAHAYE.

St Lawrence Seaway Authority: 360 Albert St, Ottawa, ON K1R 7X7; tel. (613) 598-4600; fax (613) 598-4620; opened 1959 to allow ocean-going vessels to enter the Great Lakes of North America; operated jointly with the USA; Pres. W. A. O'NEIL.

Canada Steamship Lines Inc: 759 Victoria Sq., Montréal, PQ H2Y 2K3; tel. (514) 288-0231; telex 052-5380; f. 1913; 34 vessels; 750,000 grt; Chair. PAUL E. MARTIN; Pres. RAYMOND LEMAY.

Misener Shipping: 63 Church St, POB 100, St Catharine's, ON L2R 6S1; tel. (416) 688-3500; telex 061-5155; bulk cargo; 11 vessels; 200,000 grt; Pres. DAVID K. GARDNER.

Paterson, N. M., and Sons Ltd: POB 664, Thunder Bay, ON P7C 4W6; tel. (807) 577-8421; telex 073-4566; bulk carriers; 12 vessels; 95,536 grt; Vice-Pres. and Dir ROBERT J. PATERSON.

ULS Corporation: 49 Jackes Ave, Toronto, ON M4T 1E2; tel. (416) 920-7610; telex 065-24157; fax (416) 920-5785; bulk carriers; 20 vessels; 417,604 grt; Chair and Dir J. D. LEITCH; Pres. and CEO D. MAXWELL.

ASSOCIATIONS

Canadian Canal Society: POB 1652, St Catharine's, ON L2R 7K1; tel. (416) 682-0253; mems: 120 individuals and 12 govt agencies.

Canadian Port and Harbour Association: 60 Harbour St, Toronto, ON M5J 1B7; tel. (416) 863-2036; telex 062-19666; fax (416) 863-4830; 27 corporate port mems and 4 associate mems; Sec.-Treas. JOHN JURSA.

International Association of Great Lakes Ports: c/o Kenneth L. Closs, Toronto Harbour Commission, 60 Harbour St, Toronto, ON M5J 1B7; tel. (416) 863-2037; fax (416) 462-9867.

Lake Shippers' Clearance Association: 360 Main St, Winnipeg, MB R3C 3Z3; tel. (204) 942-2424.

OCEAN SHIPPING

Statistics

(Source: Statistics Canada.)

Summary

	1985	1986	1987
Goods ('000 metric tons)			
Loaded	143,421	144,561	158,938
Unloaded	60,669	62,012	68,106
Vessels (number)			
Arrived	26,555	28,086	29,404
Departed	26,438	28,061	29,666

Goods Loaded and Unloaded by Province or Territory

('000 metric tons, international cargoes only)

	1985		1986		1987	
	Loaded	Unloaded	Loaded	Unloaded	Loaded	Unloaded
British Columbia	67,921	5,808	69,143	6,347	80,590	6,503
Manitoba	359	—	591	—	569	—
New Brunswick	3,423	4,879	5,685	6,029	5,564	6,954
Newfoundland	1,296	1,105	1,308	1,117	1,580	2,060
Northwest Territories	—	1	70	3	385	14
Nova Scotia	8,386	5,679	8,760	5,826	10,054	6,641
Ontario	9,828	24,199	9,725	22,617	9,867	24,548
Prince Edward Island	67	10	86	38	65	20
Québec	52,142	18,988	49,193	20,035	50,319	21,286
Total	143,421	60,669	144,561	62,012	158,994	68,026

Directory

British Columbia Ferry Corporation: 1112 Fort St, Victoria, BC V8V 4V2; tel. (604) 381-1401; telex 049-7483; fax (604) 381-5452; operates 38 passenger and car ferries; Chair. of Bd R. W. LONG; Gen. Man. ROD MORRISON.

Esso Petroleum Canada: External Supply and Transportation Division, 55 St Clair Ave West, Toronto, ON M5W 2J8; tel. (416) 968-5309; telex 065-28049; coastal, Great Lakes and St Lawrence River, South American, Caribbean and Gulf ports to Canadian east and US Atlantic ports; 11 vessels; 41,836 grt; Pres. G. H. THOMSON; Man. (Marine Div.) H. M. WESTLAKE.

Fednav Ltd: 600 rue de la Gauchetière ouest, Bureau 2600, Montréal, PQ H3B 4M3; tel. (514) 878-6500; telex 055-60637; fax (514) 878-6642; f. 1944; shipowners, operators, contractors, terminal operators; owned and chartered fleet of c. 50 vessels; Pres. L. G. PATHY.

Marine Atlantic Inc: 100 Cameron St, Moncton, NB E1C 5Y6; tel. (506) 858-3600; telex 014-2833; serves Atlantic coast of Canada; 15 vessels, incl. passenger, roll-on/roll-off and freight ferries; Pres. and CEO R. J. TINGLEY.

Pacific Pilotage Authority: 1199 West Hastings St, Suite 300, Vancouver, BC V6E 4G9; tel. (604) 666-6771; telex 04-53357; fax (604) 666-6093; operates pilotage services in Canadian waters in and around British Columbia; Chair. R. J. SMITH; Sec. E. M. HALL.

Papachristidis (Canada) Inc: 1350 rue Sherbrooke ouest, Penthouse, Montréal, PQ H3G 1J1; tel. (514) 844-8404; telex 052-68780; world-wide services; 4 vessels owned and managed; 52,309 grt; Pres. NIKY PAPACHRISTIDIS.

Ports Canada: 99 Metcalfe St, Ottawa, ON K1A 0N6; tel. (613) 957-6787; telex 053-4127; fax (613) 996-9629; Chair. of the Bd RON HUNTINGTON; Pres. and CEO JEAN-MICHEL TESSIER.

Seaboard Shipping Co Ltd: Oceanic Plaza, 1066 West Hastings St, POB 12501, Vancouver, BC V6E 3W9; UK-Continent, Australia, New Zealand, South Africa, Mediterranean, West Indies, US Atlantic Coast; Pres. C. D. G. ROBERTS.

Soconav Inc: 1801 ave Collège McGill, Bureau 830A, Montréal, PQ H3A 2N4; tel. (514) 284-9535; telex 052-67671; Great Lakes, St Lawrence River and Gulf, Atlantic Coast, Arctic and NWT; 13 tankers, 76,476 grt; Chair. MICHEL GAUCHER; Pres. LOUIS ROCHETTE; Vice-Pres. (Operations) GUY BAZINET.

ASSOCIATIONS

American Bureau of Shipping: POB 446, Station A, Mississauga, ON L5A 2Z7; tel. (416) 279-0911; telex 069-60351; 5 regional offices.

British Columbia Ferry and Marine Workers' Union: 990 Market St, Suite 202, Victoria, BC V8T 2E9; tel. (604) 382-2119; 3,007 mems.

Canadian Ferry Operators' Association: 100 Cameron St, Moncton, NB E1C 5Y6; tel. (506) 858-3643; fax (506) 858-3615; Chair. P. A. HEATHCOTE.

Canadian Marine Officers' Union: 9670 rue Notre-Dame est, Montréal, PQ H1L 3P8; tel. (514) 354-8321; Pres. GILBERT GAUTHIER.

Canadian Maritime Industries Association: 100 Sparks St, Suite 801, POB 1429, Station B, Ottawa, ON K1P 5R4; tel. (613) 232-7127; fax (613) 232-2490.

Canadian Offshore Vessel Operators' Association: POB 5549, Baine Johnston Centre, St John's, NF A1C 5W4; tel. (709) 739-6200; telex 016-4978.

Canadian Shipowners' Association: 350 Sparks St, Suite 705, Ottawa, ON K1R 7S8; tel. (613) 232-3539; telex 053-3522; fax (613) 232-6211; 13 mem. cos; Pres. T. NORMAN HALL.

The Canadian Shippers' Council: 99 Bank St, Suite 250, Ottawa, ON K1P 6B9; tel. (613) 238-8888; telex 053-4888; fax (613) 563-9218; Sec. J. D. MOORE.

Council of Marine Carriers: 1575 West Georgia St, Suite 200, Vancouver, BC V6G 2V3; tel. (604) 687-9677; fax (604) 687-1788; Pres. (vacant).

Dominion Marine Association: 350 Sparks St, Suite 705, Ottawa, ON K1R 7S8; tel. (613) 232-3539; telex 053-3522; fax (613) 232-6211; 15 mem. cos; Pres. T. NORMAN HALL.

Marine Workers' Federation: 3700 Kempt Rd, Halifax, NS B3K 4X8; tel. (902) 455-7279; 2,500 mems; Sec.-Treas. RICK CLARKE.

Shipping Federation of Canada: 300 rue St-Sacrement, Suite 326, Montréal, PQ H2Y 1X4; tel. (514) 849-2325; telex 055-61042; fax (514) 849-6992; f. 1903; 69 mems; Pres. Capt. F. C. NICOL.

Western Canadian Shippers' Association: c/o Terry Garvey, 1176 West Georgia St, Suite 640, Vancouver, BC V6E 4A2.

CIVIL AVIATION

Selected Operational Statistics

(Major Canadian airlines, '000. Source: Statistics Canada.)

	1986	1987	1988
Passengers.	23,157	23,532	24,321
Passenger-km	48,534,364	48,416,913	54,255,154
Available seat-km	69,558,669	68,864,737	76,816,435
Goods ton-km	1,154,658	1,205,185	1,320,714

Principal Airports

(1987. Source: Statistics Canada.)

	Cargo ('000 metric tons)	Mail ('000 metric tons)	Passengers ('000)	Flights ('000)
Toronto (Lester B. Pearson International)	225	45	16,018	171
Vancouver International	90	16	6,687	77
Montréal (Dorval International).	27	13	5,599	75
Calgary International	26	8	3,944	66
Winnipeg International.	12	9	2,138	34
Ottawa International	5	6	1,989	31
Edmonton International	24	7	1,881	31
Halifax International	20	6	1,707	26
Montréal (Mirabel International)	75	4	1,368	18
Edmonton Municipal	1	0*	690	12

* Represents less than 500 metric tons.

Directory

REGULATORY BODIES

In October 1985 the former Canadian Air Transportation Administration, a division of the Federal Department of Transport, was replaced by two new organizational units: the Aviation Group, to be responsible for airline safety, regulation and air navigation, and the Airports Authority Group, to manage and operate federal airports.

Aviation Group: c/o Dept of Transport, Transport Canada Bldg, Pl. de Ville, Tower C, 21st Floor, Ottawa, ON K1A 0N5; tel. (613) 990-3838; telex 053-3130; fax (613) 996-9622; Asst Deputy Minister, Aviation C. LaFrance.

Airports Authority Group: c/o Dept of Transport, Transport Canada Bldg, Pl. de Ville, Tower C, 21st Floor, Ottawa, ON K1A 0N5; tel. (613) 990-3001; telex 053-3130; fax (613) 996-9622; Exec. Dir D. C. McAree.

PRINCIPAL SCHEDULED COMPANIES

Air Atlantic Ltd: POB 9040, St John's, NF A1A 2X3; tel. (709) 570-0791.

Air BC: 4740 Agar Dr., Richmond, BC V7B 1A6; tel. (604) 273-2464; fax (604) 273-1016; Pres. I. Harris.

Air Canada: pl. Air Canada, 500 blvd René-Lévesque ouest, Montréal, PQ H2Z 1X5; tel. (514) 879-7000; telex 062-17537; fax (514) 879-7990; f. 1937; operates services throughout Canada and to the USA, also to the UK, France, the Federal Republic of Germany, Switzerland, Austria, India, Singapore, Antigua, Bermuda, Barbados, Bahamas, Trinidad and Tobago, Guadeloupe, Martinique, Cuba, Jamaica, Saint Lucia, the Dominican Republic and Haiti; fleet of 33 Boeing 727, 6 Boeing 747, 21 Boeing 767, 35 DC-9, 6 DC-73F, 14 L-1011; Chair. Claude I. Taylor; Pres. and CEO Pierre J. Jeanniot.

Air Ontario Ltd: 1 Ontario Dr., London Airport, London, ON N5V 3S4; tel. (519) 453-8440.

Canadian Airlines International Ltd: 700 Second St, SW, Suite 2800, Calgary, AB T2P 2W2; tel. (403) 294-2000; telex 043-55610; fax (403) 294-2066; f.1946; passenger and cargo charters and scheduled services to 68 destinations in Canada and 89 destinations overseas; fleet of 66 Boeing 737-200, 12 DC-10-30; Chair. and CEO Rhys T. Eyton; Pres. and COO Murray Sigler.

Eastern Provincial Airways (EPA): POB 178, Elmsdale, NS B3A 3Y7; tel. (902) 861-4030; telex 019-23646; Chair. D. J. Carty; Pres. and CEO S. T. Stoilen.

Nationair: Montréal International Airport, Administration Bldg, CP 300, Mirabel, PQ J7N 1A3; tel. (514) 476-3318; telex 052-67513; f. 1984; scheduled and charter services to Europe and South America; fleet of 3 DC-8-61, 2 DC-8-62, 2 DC-8-63, 1 DC-8-50F; Pres R. Obadia.

Norcanair: 2103 Airport Dr., Suite 105, Saskatoon, SK S7L 6W2; tel. (306) 652-5530; telex 074-21555; Pres. Richard H. Barton.

Northern Thunderbird Air: POB 1510, Prince George, BC V2L 4V5; tel. (604) 963-9611; telex 047-7549; Pres. and Gen. Man. Jack Stelfox.

Northwest Territorial Airways Ltd: Yellowknife International Airport, POB 9000, Yellowknife, NT X1A 2R3; tel. (403) 920-4567; telex 034-45527; fax (403) 873-3273; scheduled passenger and cargo services within the NWT, international cargo charters and scheduled cargo servcies to Toronto, Edmonton, Winnipeg and Vancouver; fleet of 5 Electra, 1 L-100-30 Hercules, 5 DC-3; Pres. and Chair. of the Board Robert P. Engle.

Québec Aviation: Sixth Ave, Québec Airport, Sainte-Foy, PQ G2E 3L9; tel. (418) 872-2272; Pres. Marc Racicot.

Québecair: Montréal International Airport, CP 490, Dorval, PQ H4Y 1B5; tel. (514) 631-9802; telex 058-24815; f. 1946; regional carrier and charter services; fleet of 8 Convair CV-580, 2 Fokker 28-1000; Chair. Marc Racicot; Pres. and CEO Michel Leblanc.

Trans North Air: Whitehorse Airport, POB 4338, Whitehorse, YT Y1A 3E4; tel. (403) 668-2177; telex 036-8290; fax (403) 668-3420; Pres. R. F. Connelly; Gen. Man. T. A. Kapty.

Trans Provincial Airlines: POB 280, Prince Rupert, BC V8J 3P6; tel. (604) 627-1341; telex 047-89215; Gen. Man. Gene Storey.

Wardair Canada Inc: 3111 Convair Dr., Mississauga, ON L5P 1C2; tel. (416) 671-3100; fax (416) 671-1433; Chair. and CEO Maxwell W. Ward; Pres. and COO G. D. Curley.

ASSOCIATIONS

Aerospace Industries Association of Canada: 116 Albert St, Suite 601, Ottawa, ON K1P 5R1; tel. (613) 232-4297; telex 053-4456; fax (613) 232-1142; 205 mems; Pres. K. A. Lewis.

Air Crew Association Canada: 5925 Airport Rd, Mississauga, ON L4V 1W1; tel. (416) 677-7747; fax (416) 677-4512; 270 mems; Pres. Capt. W. J. Hardy; Exec. Admin. S. Singer.

Air Transport Association of Canada: 99 Bank St, Suite 747, Ottawa, ON K1P 6B9; tel. (613) 233-7727; fax (613) 230-8648; f. 1934; 200 mems; Pres. and CEO G. M. Sinclair.

Aircraft Operations Group Association: 130 Slater St, Suite 330, Ottawa, ON K1P 6E2; tel. (613) 230-5476; 500 mems; Chair. I. S. Banyard; Pres. C. J. Foster.

Canadian Aeronautics and Space Institute: 222 Somerset St West, Suite 601, Ottawa, ON K2P 2G3; tel. (613) 234-0191.

Canadian Air Line Pilots' Association: 1300 Steeles Ave, Brampton, ON L6T 1A2; tel. (416) 453-8210; telex 06-97726; fax (416) 453-8757; 3,384 mems; Exec. Admin. PHILIP BRADY.

Canadian Air Traffic Control Association: 400 Cumberland St, Ottawa, ON K1N 8X3; tel. (613) 232-9413; 2,000 mems; Man. Dir H. J. BRENNEN.

Canadian Business Aircraft Association, Inc: 50 O'Connor St, Suite 1317, Ottawa, ON K1P 6L2; tel. (613) 236-5611; fax (613) 236-2361; mems: 1,000 individuals and 165 orgs; Exec. Dir H. F. PROTHEROE.

Canadian Helicopter Pilots' Association: 4653 Strathcona Rd, North Vancouver, BC V7G 1G7; tel. (604) 929-5551; 75 mems; Sec.-Treas. J. E. SAYRE.

Canadian Owners' and Pilots' Association (COPA): POB 734, Ottawa, ON K1P 5S4; tel. (613) 236-4901; fax (613) 236-8646; more than 20,000 mems; Gen. Man. W. N. PEPPLER.

Canadian Society of Air Safety Investigators: 1900 Markwell Cres., Orleans, ON K1C 3T6; tel. (613) 993-6785; Sec.-Treas. JIM STEWART.

Experimental Aircraft Association of Canada: POB 18, Mount Albert, ON L0G 1M0; tel. (416) 683-3517; fax (416) 428-2415; 1,800 mems.

International Airline Passengers' Association of Canada/Association canadienne des passagers de lignes aériennes internationales: c/o 12 Tanglewood Cres., Kirkland, PQ H9J 2M6.

International Civil Aviation Organization: 1000 rue Sherbrooke ouest, Montréal, PQ H3A 2R2; tel. (514) 285-8219; fax (514) 288-4772.

Ninety Nines, International Women Pilots: c/o Toronto Airways, Buttonville Airport, Buttonville, ON L3P 3J9.

Northern Air Transport Association: POB 2457, Yellowknife, NT X1A 2P8; tel. (403) 920-2985; Pres. LES A. DVORAK; Sec.-Treas. JEAN CARTER.

ENERGY

INTRODUCTION

Consumption of primary energy in Canada in 1987 was about 7,840 petajoules. Of this figure oil accounted for 40.3%, natural gas 24.1%, hydroelectricity 12.4%, coal 14.4%, nuclear energy 3.3% and other forms 5.7%. In terms of the production of electricity, hydraulic generation made up 62.9% in the first half of 1988, while conventional thermal generation accounted for 21.5% and nuclear generation 15.6%. In the first half of 1988 exports took 7% of total electricity generation, a 29% decline from the previous year being largely due to an energy shortage in Québec and a drought affecting the western provinces. The largest exporters of electricity are Québec, Ontario, British Columbia, New Brunswick and Manitoba.

Québec, Canada's largest producer, generated 137,028,000 megawatt-hours (mWh) of electric energy in 1985, of which 98% was hydro, 2% was nuclear and 0.1% was thermal. Ontario produced 121,785,000 mWh, 40% of which was nuclear, 34% hydro, and 26% thermal. Coal was the main primary source for Ontario's thermal energy production. British Columbia's electric energy generation

amounted to 59,124,000 mWh in 1985, 96% of which was hydro, the remainder being thermal. Hydroelectricity accounted for 96% of Newfoundland's total energy production of 41,495,000 mWh, the remainder being thermal. Alberta's electricity production amounted to 33,432,000 mWh, of which 96% was thermally generated, mainly from coal, and 4% was hydro. In 1985 electricity demand was greatest in the provinces of Québec, Ontario, British Columbia, Alberta and New Brunswick.

Of the total electricity supply of 450,275,000 mWh in 1985, hydroelectricity made up 66.9%, nuclear 12.7% and thermal 19.7%; imports accounted for 0.7%. Demand totalled 414,657,000 mWh in 1985 of which domestic demand accounted for 89.5% and exports accounted for 10.5%. The greatest proportion of domestic demand (39.6%) came from the manufacturing sector, while residential use accounted for 27.9%, commercial and transport 0.7%, institutional 20.2%, non-manufacturing industrial use 6.5%, public administration 2.6%, agriculture 2.4% and transport 0.7%.

STATISTICS

(Source: Statistics Canada.)

Electricity Generated and Consumed

(1986, '000 mWh)

	Generation			Domestic demand		
	1984	1985	1986	1984	1985	1986
Alberta	31,160	33,432	34,900	28,968	30,929	32,200
British Columbia	52,379	59,124	50,800	42,154	44,750	45,200
Manitoba	21,489	22,777	24,100	12,806	13,514	13,900
New Brunswick	12,396	11,401	12,200	9,361	9,385	10,600
Newfoundland	45,648	41,494	40,600	8,532	8,633	8,800
Nova Scotia	7,236	7,457	7,400	6,867	6,904	7,200
Ontario	120,606	121,783	125,700	110,357	112,713	117,300
Prince Edward Island	2	2	12	494	522	570
Québec	122,179	137,028	148,600	123,709	132,794	140,100
Saskatchewan	11,543	11,838	11,900	10,919	10,223	10,100
Northwest Territories and Yukon	778	846	950	702	774	880
Total	425,416	447,182	457,162	354,869	371,141	386,850

Electric Energy Generation[1] by Method

(1985, '000 mWh)

	Thermal				Hydro	Nuclear	Total
	Coal	Natural gas	Petroleum	Total (incl. other)			
Alberta	27,786	3,803	32	32,021	1,411	—	33,432
British Columbia	—	581	611	2,072	57,052	—	59,124
Manitoba	242	8	83	367	22,410	—	22,777
New Brunswick	1,054	—	2,447	3,685	2,289	5,427	11,401
Newfoundland	—	—	1,847	1,847	39,648	—	41,495
Nova Scotia	5,540	—	875	6,543	914	—	7,457
Ontario	30,320	1,381	118	31,950	41,376	48,459	121,785
Prince Edward Island.	—	—	2	2	—	—	2
Québec	—	—	140	152	133,696	3,180	137,028
Saskatchewan.	9,369	335	38	9,897	1,941	—	11,838
Northwest Territories and Yukon. . . .	—	—	293	293	553	—	846
Total	74,311	6,108	6,486	88,829	301,290	57,066	447,185

[1] For utilities and industry, total generation shown may be higher than net generation due to some station service included in this table.

Fuels Used to Generate Thermal Electricity[1]

(1985)

	Coal ('000 tons)	Natural gas (million cu m)	Petroleum products ('000 cu m)	Uranium (metric tons)	Other[2] (MJ)
Alberta	17,792	907	7	—	2,000
British Columbia	—	80	124	—	4,400
Manitoba	253	1	25	—	170
New Brunswick	521	—	597	112	920
Newfoundland	—	—	492	—	—
Nova Scotia	2,147	—	197	—	640
Ontario	11,068	342	37	908	655
Prince Edward Island	—	—	7	—	—
Québec	—	—	63	66	60
Saskatchewan	8,290	143	18	—	775
Northwest Territories and Yukon . . .	—	—	78	—	—
Total	39,471	1,473	1,645	1,086	9,620

[1] For utilities, industrial and other producers of thermal electricity.
[2] Includes some petroleum products (tar and coke), manufactured gases, wood, spent pulping liquor and other miscellaneous fuels measured in estimated megajoules.

Nuclear Generating Stations in Canada

(Source: Atomic Energy of Canada Ltd)

Reactor	Province	Energy produced in 1986
NPD (Nuclear Power Demonstration Station)[1]	Ontario	146,225
Pickering A	Ontario }	21,404,209[2]
Pickering B	Ontario }	
Bruce A	Ontario }	36,662,986[3]
Bruce B	Ontario }	
Darlington	Ontario	n.a.
Gentilly 2	Québec	3,792,441
Point Lepreau	New Brunswick	5,227,106

[1] Located near Chalk River, Ontario.
[2] Data applies to all reactors at Pickering A and B.
[3] Data applies to all reactors at Bruce A and B.

NATIONAL AND PROVINCIAL ENERGY ORGANIZATIONS AND CO-ORDINATING BODIES

General

Alberta Energy Communications: North Tower, 9945 108th St, 11th Floor, Edmonton, AB T5K 2G6.

Association of Major Power Consumers in Ontario: 20 Toronto St, Suite 420, Toronto, ON M5C 2B8; tel. (416) 363-9634; fax (416) 363-0888.

Canadian Fluid Power Association: One Yonge St, Suite 1400, Toronto, ON M5E 1J9; tel. (416) 363-7261; fax (416) 363-3779.

Canadian Institute of Energy: 640 Fifth Ave, Suite 229, Calgary, AB T2P 0M6; tel. (403) 262-6969; 600 mems; Nat. Sec. ADAM HEDEYAT.

Energy Branch, New Brunswick Department of Natural Resources and Energy: POB 6000, Fredericton, NB E3B 5H1; tel. (506) 453-3684; fax (506) 453-4279.

Energy Probe: 225 Brunswick Ave, Toronto, ON M5S 2M6; tel. (416) 978-7014.

Energy Resources Conservation Board (Alberta): 640 Fifth Ave, SW, Calgary, AB T2P 3G4; tel. (403) 297-8311; telex 038-21717; fax (403) 297-3366.

Energy Resources Division, Ministry of Energy, Mines and Petroleum Resources: Parliament Bldgs, Victoria, BC V8V 1X4; tel. (604) 387-5993; fax (604) 387-1339.

Manitoba Energy Authority: 191 Lombard Ave, 12th Floor, Winnipeg, MB R3C 0X1; tel. (204) 945-7903; fax (204) 945-8808; Chair. B. RANSOM.

Manitoba Energy Council: 330 Graham Ave, Suite 555, Winnipeg, MB R3C 4E3; tel. (204) 945-4299.

National Energy Board: Trebla Bldg, 473 Albert Sq., Ottawa, ON K1A 0E5; tel. (613) 998-7204; telex 053-3791; fax (613) 990-7000; Chair. R. PRIDDLE.

Northwest Territories Power Corporation: 7909 51st Ave, POB 5700, Station L, Edmonton, AB T6C 4J8; tel. (403) 465-3377; telex 037-2736; fax (403) 469-0485.

Nova Scotia Energy Monument Division: Department of Mines and Energy, POB 1087, Halifax, NS B3J 2X1; tel. (902) 424-5019; telex 019-21690.

Nova Scotia Power Corporation: POB 910, Halifax, NS B3J 2W5; tel. (902) 428-6394; telex 019-21736; fax (902) 428-6100.

Ontario Energy Board: 2300 Yonge St, 26th Floor, POB 2319, Toronto, ON M4P 2B7; tel. (416) 440-7604.

Ontario Energy Corporation: 56 Wellesley St West, 12th Floor, Toronto, ON M7A 2B7; tel. (416) 926-4200; telex 06-217880; fax (416) 965-2368; Pres. DUNCAN ALLAN.

Planetary Association for Clean Energy, Inc: 191 Promenade de Portage, Suite 600, Hull, PQ J8X 2K6; tel. (819) 777-9696; Pres. Dr ANDREW MICHROWSKI.

Prince Edward Island Energy Corporation: 105 Rochford St, POB 2000, Charlottetown, PE C1A 7N8; tel. (902) 368-4220; telex 014-44154; Gen. Man. ROBERT BRANDSON.

Prince Edward Island Public Utilities Commission: 134 Kent St, POB 577, Charlottetown, PE C1A 7L1; tel. (902) 892-3501; fax (902) 566-4076.

Saskpower: 2025 Victoria Ave, Regina, SK S4P 0S1; tel. (306) 566-2120; telex 071-2287; fax (306) 55-66-2777; Pres. G. HILL.

Atomic Energy

Atomic Energy of Canada Ltd: 344 Slater St, Ottawa K1A 0S4; tel. (613) 237-3270; telex 053-3126; fax (613) 996-9638; f. 1952; federal govt agency for nuclear research and development, production of radioactive isotopes and design, development and marketing of power reactors; four operational research reactors at Chalk River, ON, and one under construction at Whiteshell Nuclear Research Establishment, Pinawa, MB; prototype reactor under construction at Chalk River (isotope production); nuclear designer for CANDU (Canadian deuterium uranium) reactors; 17 commercial units now in service at four stations, providing a total capacity of 12,051 MW, representing 15.1% of Canada's total electricity generation; four others under construction in Canada; two units each in service in India, Pakistan, the Republic of Korea and Argentina, and three units under construction in Romania; Pres. and CEO JAMES DONNELLY.

Atomic Energy Control Board: POB 1046, Ottawa, ON K1P 5S9; tel. (613) 995-5894; telex 053-3771; fax (613) 995-5086; Pres. Dr R. J. A. LÉVESQUE; Sec. J. G. MCMANUS.

Canadian Coalition for Nuclear Responsibility: CP 236, succursale Snowdon, Montréal, PQ H3X 3T4; tel. (514) 489-2665.

Canadian Nuclear Association: 111 Elizabeth St, Toronto, ON M5G 1P7; tel. (416) 977-6152; fax (416) 979-8356.

Canadian Nuclear Society: 111 Elizabeth St, Toronto, ON M5G 1P7; tel. (416) 977-7620; fax (416) 979-8356.

Eldorado Nuclear Ltd: 360 Albert St, Suite 700, Ottawa, ON K1R 7X7; tel. (613) 238-5222; telex 053-3382; fax (613) 234-8439; Chair. and CEO G. N. M. CURRIE.

Nuclear Awareness Project: POB 2331, Oshawa, ON L1H 7V4; tel. (416) 725-1565.

Organization of CANDU Industries: One Yonge St, Suite 1400, Toronto, ON M5E 1J9; tel. (416) 363-7261; telex 065-24693; fax (416) 363-3779; Gen. Man. JACK R. HOWETT.

Alternative Energy

Biomass Energy Institute Inc: 1329 Niakwa Rd East, Winnipeg, MB R2J 3TA; tel. (204) 257-3891; 1,000 mems, 250 mem. orgs; Exec. Dir BETH CANDLISH.

Canadian Solar Industries Association Inc: 67A Sparks St, Ottawa, ON K1P 5A5; tel. (613) 237-7000; 88 mem cos; Exec. Dir EARL HANSEN.

Canadian Wind Energy Association Inc: 44A Clarey Ave, Ottawa, ON K1S 2R7; tel. (613) 234-9463; 120 mems; Office Man. DAVID HOFFMAN.

Canadian Wood Energy Institute: 85 Curlew Dr., Don Mills, ON M3A 2P8; tel. (416) 445-6296; fax (416) 420-0231.

Centre québecois de valorisation de la biomasse: Pavillon Comtois, Bureau 1316, Université Laval, Ste-Foy, PQ G1K 7P4; tel. (418) 657-3853; Pres. MARCEL RISI.

Solar Energy Society of Canada Inc: 15 York St, Suite 3, Ottawa, ON K1N 5S7; tel. (613) 236-4594; 800 mems; Exec. Dir BILL EGGERTSON.

ELECTRICITY

Alberta Electric Energy Marketing Agency: Suite 711, Woodward Tower, 400 Fourth Ave South, Lethbridge, AB T1J 4E1; tel. (403) 381-5384.

Association of Municipal Electrical Utilities of Ontario: 620 University Ave, Toronto, ON M5G 1X2; tel. (416) 592-3807.

Canadian Electrical Association Inc: One Westmount Sq., Suite 500, Montréal, PQ H3Z 2P9; tel. (514) 937-6181; fax (514) 937-6498; 2,300 mems, 80 mem orgs; Pres. W. S. READ.

Canadian Electrical Contractors' Association: 161 Eglinton Ave East, Suite 605, Toronto, ON M4P 1J5; tel. (416) 486-1290; Exec. Vice-Pres. NORMAN W. PURDY.

Canadian Electrical Distributors' Association: 1470 Don Mills Rd, Suite 303, Don Mills, ON M3B 2X9; tel. (416) 446-1221; fax (416) 445-3682.

Electric Service League of Manitoba: 395 Berru St, Suite 14, Winnipeg, MB R3J 1N6; tel. (204) 885-3668.

Electrical Bureau of Canada: 10 Carlson Ct, Suite 500, Rexdale, ON M9W 6L2; tel. (416) 674-7410; fax (416) 674-7412.

Electrical Contractors' Association of British Columbia: 4299 Canada Way, Suite 265, Burnaby, BC V5G 1H3; tel. (604) 435-4186; fax (416) 486-1290.

Electrical Contractors' Association of Ontario: 161 Eglinton Ave East, Suite 605, Toronto, ON M4P 1J5; tel. (416) 486-1290.

Electrical Contractors' Association of Saskatchewan: 1939 Elphinstone St, Regina, SK S4T 3N3; tel. (306) 525-0171; fax (306) 347-8595.

Electrical Energy Branch, Federal Department of Energy, Mines and Resources: 460 O'Connor St, Ottawa, ON K1S 5H3; tel. (613) 990-0332; telex 053-3117.

Electrical Energy Marketing Committee: 191 Lombard Ave, 12th Floor, Winnipeg, MB R3C 0X1; tel. (204) 945-7903; fax (204) 945-8808.

Electrical Power Systems Construction Association: 700 University Ave, Suite H2-E1, Toronto, ON M5G 1X6; tel. (416) 592-2515; telex 06-217662; fax (416) 592-2753; 96 mem orgs; Gen. Man. J. G. KNIGHT.

Electrical Utilities Safety Association of Ontario, Inc: 220 Traders Blvd East, Mississauga, ON L4Z 1W7; tel. (416) 890-1011; 1,000 mems; Gen. Man. and Sec.-Treas. C. J. TALLON.

Municipal Electric Assocation: 20 Eglinton Ave West, Suite 1301, POB 2004, Toronto, ON M4R 1K8; tel. (416) 483-7739; fax (416) 483-9039; 315 mems; CEO A. J. BOWKER.

New Brunswick Electric Power Commission: Public Affairs Dept, 515 King St, POB 2000, Fredericton, NB E3B 4X1; tel. (506) 458-4050; telex 014-46194; fax (506) 458-4249.

Ontario Electrical League: 2 Lansing Sq., Suite 302, Willowdale (North York), ON M2J 4P8; tel. (416) 495-0052; Man. R. S. MCCARTEN.

Hydroelectric Power

British Columbia Hydro and Power Authority: 970 Burrard St, Vancouver, BC V6Z 1Y3; tel. (604) 663-2212; telex 04-54512; fax (604) 663-3423.

Hydro-Québec: 75 René-Lévesque Blvd West, Montréal, PQ H27 1A4; tel. (514) 289-2211; Chair. RICHARD DROUIN; Pres. and CEO CLAUDE BOIVIN.

Manitoba Hydro: 820 Taylor Ave, POB 815, Winnipeg, MB R3C 2P4; tel. (204) 474-3535; telex 07-57425; fax (204) 475-9044; Pres. and CEO GARRY H. BEATTY.

Newfoundland and Labrador Hydro: POB 9100, St John's, NF A1A 2X8; tel. (709) 737-1290; telex 016-4503; fax (709) 737-1231.

Ontario Hydro: 700 University Ave, Toronto, ON M5G 1X6; tel. (416) 592-5111; telex 062-17662.

Winnipeg Hydro: Admin. Bldg, 5th Floor, Civic Centre, Winnipeg, MB R3B 1C1; tel. (204) 986-2270; fax (204) 956-4502.

OIL AND GAS ASSOCIATIONS

Alberta Petroleum Marketing Commission: 250 6th Ave, SW, Suite 1900, Calgary, AB T2P 3H7; tel. (403) 297-5500; telex 03-821978; Chair. D. LUCAS.

Association Petrolière du Québec: 1253 ave Collège McGill, Suite 845, Montréal, PQ H3B 2Y5.

British Columbia Petroleum Corporation: 1199 Hastings St West, Suite 1199, Vancouver, BC V6E 3T5; tel. (604) 661-3300; telex 045-4530; fax (604) 661-3324; Chair. JOHN DAVIS.

Canada/Newfoundland Offshore Petroleum Board: TD Pl., 5th Floor, 140 Water St, St John's, NF A1C 6H6; tel. (709) 778-1400.

Canada Oil and Gas Lands Administration: 355 River Rd, Tower B, Vanier, ON K1A 0E4; Admin. M. E. TASCHEREAU.

Canadian Association of Drilling Engineers: 707 Seventh Ave, SW, Calgary, AB T2P 3H6.

Canadian Association of Oil Well Drilling Contractors: 540 5th Ave, SW, Suite 800, Calgary, AB T2P 0M2; tel. (403) 264-4311.

Canadian Gas Association: 55 Scarsdale Rd, Don Mills, ON M3B 2R3; tel. (416) 447-6465; telex 06-966824; fax (416) 447-7067; 535 mems; Pres. I. C. MACNABB.

Canadian Gas Processors' Association: 640 Fifth Ave, SW, Suite 229, Calgary, AB T2P 3G4; tel. (403) 262-7714; 400 mems; Pres. MANLEY FRITH.

Canadian Petroleum Association: 150 Sixth Ave, SW, Calgary, Suite 3800, AB T2P 3Y7; tel. (403) 269-6721; fax (403) 261-4622; Pres. IAN R. SMYTH.

Canadian Petroleum Equipment Manufacturers' Association: 116 Albert St, Suite 701, Ottawa, ON K1P 5G3; tel. (613) 232-7213; Pres. ARNOLD W. D. GARLICK.

Compressed Gas Association Inc: 40 Wychwood Park, Toronto, ON M6G 2V5; tel. (416) 278-2456; 984 mems, 250 mem. orgs; Sec. J. S. JOHNSTON.

Independent Petroleum Association of Canada: 707 Seventh Ave, SW, Suite 700, Calgary, AB T2P 0Z2; tel. (403) 290-1530; telex 038-27681; fax (403) 290-1680; 350 mems; Chair. R. A. GUSELLA; Exec. Dir BOB REID.

Industrial Gas Users' Association: 170 Laurier Ave West, Suite 804, Ottawa, ON K1P 5V5; tel. (613) 236-8021; fax (613) 230-9531; 63 mem. orgs; Exec. Dir TED BJERKELUND.

Manitoba Mineral Resources Ltd: 491 Portage Ave, Suite 603, Winnipeg, MB R3B 2E4; tel. (204) 775-8041; fax (204) 783-7879; Pres. C. WRIGHT.

Manitoba Oil and Natural Gas Conservation Board: 330 Graham Ave, Suite 555, Winnipeg, MB R3C 4E3; tel. (204) 945-2694; Chair. W. M. MCDONALD.

Northern Oil and Gas Management: Dept of Indian Affairs and Northern Development, Ottawa, ON K1A 0H4; tel. (819) 997-0877; telex 053-3711; fax (819) 997-1587.

Petro-Canada: POB 2844, Calgary, AB T2P 3E3; tel. (403) 296-8000; telex 038-25753; fax (403) 296-3030; Chair. and CEO W. H. HOPPER.

Petroleum Monitoring Agency Canada: 580 Booth St, Ottawa, ON K1A 0E4; tel. (613) 992-3300; Dir G. A. REINECKE.

Petroleum Recovery Institute: 3512 33rd St, NW, Calgary, AB T2L 2A6; tel. (403) 282-1211.

Pipe Line Contractors' Association of Canada: 775 St Andrew's Rd, West Vancouver, BC V7S 1V5; tel. (604) 925-2520.

Prairie Petroleum Association—Marketing: 167 Lombard Ave, Suite 500, Winnipeg, MB R3B 3E5; tel. (204) 944-8484.

Propane Gas Association of Canada Inc: 500 Fourth Ave, SW, Suite 1202, Calgary, AB T2P 2V6; tel. (403) 263-0450; fax (403) 266-4035; 245 mem. cos; Man. Dir W. L. KURTZE.

Ontario Natural Gas Association: 77 Bloor St West, Suite 1104, Toronto, ON M5S 1M2; tel. (416) 961-2339; fax (416) 961-1173; Man. Dir PAUL E. PINNINGTON.

Ontario Petroleum Association: 245 Fairview Mall Dr., Suite 407, Willowdale, ON M2J 4T1; tel. (416) 492-5677; fax (416) 492-2514; 9 mem. cos; Exec. Dir G. H. BRERETON.

Ontario Petroleum Institute Inc: 70 Talbot Rd South, POB 340, Lambeth, ON N0L 1S0; tel. (519) 652-9536; 375 mems; Exec. Dir DOUGLAS W. GILBERT.

Petroleum Association for the Conservation of the Canadian Environment (PACE): 275 Slater St, Suite 1202, Ottawa, ON K1P 5H9; tel. (613) 236-9122; Assistant Gen. Man. K. A. MATTILA.

Régie du gaz naturel, Ministère de l'Énergie et des Ressources, Québec: 2100 Drummond, Montréal, PQ H3G 1X1; tel. (514) 873-2452; fax (514) 873-2070; Pres. BERNARD CLOUTIER.

SOQUIP (Oil and Gas Exploration): 1175 rue de Lavigerie, POB 10650, Ste-Foy, PQ G15 4PE; tel. (418) 651-9543; telex 051-31562; fax (418) 651-2292; Pres. and CEO RICHARD POULIOT.

WATER

WATER ORGANIZATIONS AND CO-ORDINATING BODIES

American Water Works Association, Atlantic Canada Section: c/o Halifax Water Commission, POB 8388, Station A, Halifax, NS B3K 5M1; 300 individual mems, 15 mem. orgs.

American Water Works Association, Ontario Section: 45 23rd St, Toronto, ON M8V 3M6; tel. (416) 252-7060; 770 mems; Sec. Treas. DORIS WINDSOR.

American Water Works Association, Western Canada Section: POB 6168, Station A, Calgary, AB T2H 2L4; tel. (403) 291-4882; 394 mems; Man. DOREEN MUNSIE.

Association québécoise des techniques de l'eau: 6290 rue Périnault, Bureau 102, Montréal, PQ H4K 1K5; tel. (514) 337-4446; Dir-Gen. RAYMOND LARIVES.

Canadian Association on Water Pollution Research and Control: Dept of Civil Engineering, McMaster University, Hamilton, ON L8S 4L7; tel. (416) 525-9140; fax (416) 529-9688; 250 mems; Pres. Dr KEITH L. MURPHY.

Canadian Water Quality Association: 472 Lee Ave, Waterloo, ON N2K 1X9; tel. (519) 885-3854; fax (519) 747-9124; Exec. Dir L. J. SMITH.

Canadian Water Resources Association: c/o Lethbridge Northern Irrigation District, 334 13th St North, Lethbridge, AB T1H 2R8; tel. (403) 327-3302; 1,200 individual mems, 300 mem. orgs; Sec. F. A. ROSS.

Canadian Water System Manufacturers' Association: One Yonge St, Suite 1400, Toronto, ON M5E 1J9; tel. (416) 363-7261; telex 065-24693; fax (416) 363-3779; Man. JOHN MARTIN.

Canadian Water and Wastewater Association: 24 Clarence St, Ottawa, ON K1N 5P3; tel. (613) 238-5692; telex 054451; fax (613) 237-2965; Exec. Dir PENINA COOPERSMITH.

Canadian Water Well Association: POB 7662, Saskatoon, SK S7K 4R4; tel. (306) 343-1454; 436 mem. orgs.

  Alberta Water Well Drilling Association: POB 33, Lousana, AB T0M 1K0; tel. (403) 749-2050; Sec.-Treas. CAROL CRAIG.

  L'Association des Puisatiers du Québec: 5800 blvd Louis-H. Lafontaine, Anjou, PQ H1M 1S7; tel. (514) 355-4805; fax (514) 353-4825; 92 mems; Technicienne Juridique MANON CLOUTIER.

  British Columbia Water Well Drilling Association: 14695 Southview Dr., Surrey, BC V3S 1A3; tel. (604) 596-4645; 90 mems; Sec. Man ARN HAMELIN.

  Manitoba Water Well Association: POB 1648, Winnipeg, MB R3C 2Z6; tel. (204) 233-1350; Sec. and Man. MARSHA MATHISON.

  Saskatchewan Water Well Association: POB 9434, Saskatoon, SK S7K 7E9; tel. (306) 244-7551; Exec. Sec. KATHLEEN WATSON.

  Newfoundland Water Well Association: c/o Martin Hammond, POB 249, Clarkes Beach, NF A0A 1W0; tel. (709) 786-3561.

  Nova Scotia Well Drillers' Association: 31 Sandlewood Terrace, Eastern Passage, NS B0J 1L0; tel. (902) 752-8429; Sec. ROBERT MCINTOSH.

  Ontario Water Well Association: RR2, Grand Bend, ON N0M 1T0; tel. (519) 243-3612; Sec. MARY ALDERSON.

  Prince Edward Island Water Well Drillers Association: c/o Watson MacDonald, Cornwall, PE C0A 1H0; tel. (902) 675-2360.

Conservation Authorities and Water Management Branch, Ontario Ministry of Natural Resources: Whitney Block, 99 Wellesley St West, Toronto, ON M7A 1W3; tel. (416) 965-6287; telex 06-23496; Dir MAURICE LEWIS.

Direction générale des Ressources Hydriques, Ministère de l'Environnement, Québec: 3900 rue Marly, Ste-Foy, PQ G1X 4E4; tel. (418) 644-6751.

Environment Canada, Inland Waters Directorate: Ottawa, ON K1A 0E7; tel. (819) 997-1508.

Ontario Municipal Water Association: 8 Bloomfield Dr., London, ON N6G 1P3; tel. (519) 471-0488; mems: 138 utilities; Sec. A. L. FURANNA.

Saskatchewan Water Corporation: Victoria Pl., 111 Fairford St East, Moose Jaw, SK S6H 7X9; tel. (306) 694-3907; fax (306) 694-3944; Pres. V. C. FOWKE.

Société québécoise d'assainissement des eaux (Water Purification Society of Québec): 1055 blvd René-Lévesque est, 10e étage, Montréal, PQ H2L 4S5; tel. (514) 873-7411; Pres. JEAN-YVES BABIN.

Water Management Branch, British Columbia Ministry of Environment: Parliament Bldgs, Victoria, BC V8V 1X5; tel. (604) 387-6989; Dir Dr D. KASIANCHUK.

Water Management Division, Nova Scotia Department of Environment: POB 2107, Halifax, NS B3J 3B7; tel. (902) 424-5300; Chief L. R. LEWIS.

Water Planning and Management Branch, Environment Canada: Ottawa, ON K1A 0H3; tel. (613) 997-2071; Dir R. L. PENTLAND.

Water Quality Branch, Environment Canada: Ottawa, ON K1A 0H3; tel. (613) 997-1920; Dir V. NIEMELA.

Water Quality Branch, Saskatchewan Department of Environment and Public Safety: 3085 Albert St, Regina, SK S4S 0B1; tel. (306) 787-6178; Dir D. A. FAST.

Water Resources Branch, Environment Canada: Ottawa, ON K1A 0H3; tel. (613) 997-1508; Dir DALE KIMMETT.

Water Resources Branch, Environmental Management Division, Prince Edward Island Department of Community and Cultural Affairs: 11 Kent St, POB 2000, Charlottetown, PE C1A 7N8; tel. (902) 892-0311; telex 014-44154; fax (902) 892-3420; Dir RORY FRANCIS.

Water Resources Branch, Manitoba Natural Resources: Legislative Bldg, Rm 314, Winnipeg, MB R3C 0V8; tel. (204) 945-3785; telex 07-587589; fax (204) 945-3586.

Water Resources Branch, Ontario, Ministry of the Environment: 185 St Clair Ave West, Toronto, ON M4V 1P5; tel. (416) 323-4917; Dir J. BISHOP.

Water Resources Division, Newfoundland Department of Environment and Lands: Confederation Bldg, West Block, POB 4750, St John's, NF A1C 5T7; tel. (709) 576-2563; Dir WASI ULLAH.

Water Resources Management Division, Alberta Environment: Oxbridge Pl., 9820 106th St, 3rd Floor, Edmonton, AB T5K 2J6; tel. (403) 427-6168; telex 037-2006; Dir A. R. STROME.

Water Resources Planning Branch, New Brunswick Department of Municipal Affairs and Environment: POB 6000, Fredericton, NB E3B 5H1; tel. (506) 453-2353; fax (506) 453-3843; Dir N. ELHADI.

TOURISM

STATISTICS

(Source: Statistics Canada.)

Domestic Visits and Expenditure, by Province

(trips of one or more nights)

	1982		1984		1982	
	Visits ('000)	Spending (C $ million)	Visits ('000)	Spending (C $ million)	Visits ('000)	Spending (C $ million)[1]
Alberta	10,043	1,370	9,180	1,276	10,486	1,184
British Columbia	6,300	1,537	6,262	1,645	7,227	1,697
Manitoba	4,076	384	3,819	458	4,179	390
New Brunswick	1,895	236	1,599	231	1,940	214
Newfoundland	1,138	223	1,059	212	1,103	165
Nova Scotia	2,339	434	2,179	360	2,573	316
Ontario	26,546	2,837	25,408	3,123	27,824	2,933
Prince Edward Island	218	121	201	100	242	81
Québec	14,963	1,671	14,861	1,804	17,907	1,763
Saskatchewan	4,496	526	4,282	472	4,755	452
Total[2]	70,135	9,499	66,626	9,845	75,275	9,312

[1] Not comparable with earlier years due to changes in collection of expenditure data.
[2] Province visits exceed total visits to Canada as more than one province may be visited in a single trip; spending totals include spending in Yukon Territory, Northwest Territories and 'not stated'.

Tourism in Canada by Residents and Visitors

	1982	1984	1986
Total visits (million)	136.0	131.6	157.2
Canadian residents	101.6	96.7	116.6
US visitors	32.4	33.0	38.2
Other visitors	2.0	1.8	2.4
Total person-nights (million)	325.1	304.9	348.2
Canadian residents	252.6	228.1	256.3
US visitors	47.1	53.1	63.4
Other visitors	25.4	23.8	28.2
Total expenditure (C $ '000 million)	14.0	15.2	16.1*
Canadian residents	11.0	11.4	10.8*
US visitors	2.2	2.9	4.2*
Other visitors	0.8	0.8	1.2*

* Not comparable with earlier years due to changes in collection of expenditure data.

National Parks

	Area (sq km)	(continued)	Area (sq km)
Auyuittuq, Baffin Island, NT	21,471.0	La Mauricie, PQ	543.9
Banff, AB	6,640.8	Mingan Archipelago, PQ	150.7
Bruce Peninsula, ON	n.a.	Mount Revelstoke, BC	262.6
Cape Breton Highlands, NS	950.5	Nahanni, NT	4,765.0
Elk Island, AB	194.3	Northern Yukon, YT	10,168.4
Ellesmere Island, NT	39,500.0	Pacific Rim, BC	388.5
Forillon, PQ	240.4	Point Pelee, ON	15.5
Fundy, NB	205.9	Prince Albert, SK	3,874.6
Georgian Bay Islands, ON	14.2	Prince Edward Island, PE	18.1
Glacier, BC	1,349.4	Pukaskwa, ON	1,877.8
Grasslands, SK	n.a.	Riding Mountain, MB	2,975.9
Gros Morne, NF	1,942.5	St Lawrence Islands, ON	4.1
Jasper, AB	10,878.0	South Moresby Reserve, BC	n.a.
Kejimujik, NS	381.5	Terra Nova, NF	396.5
Kluane, YT	22,015.9	Waterton Lakes, AB	525.8
Kootenay, BC	1,377.9	Wood Buffalo, AB–NT	44,807.0
Kouchibouguac, NB	225.3	Yoho, BC	1,313.1

DIRECTORY

NATIONAL ORGANIZATIONS

Alliance of Canadian Travel Associations: 75 Albert St, Suite 1106, Ottawa, ON K1P 5E7; tel. (613) 238-1361; fax (613) 238-8949; 3,200 mems; Exec. Dir GARETH J. DAVIES; 7 provincial brs.

Canadian Business Travel Association: POB 6021, Station D, Calgary, AB T2P 2C7; tel. (514) 735-2567; fax (514) 735-2569; Pres. DORA SANTSCHI.

Canadian Camping Association: 1806 Avenue Rd, Suite 2, Toronto, ON M5M 3Z1; tel. (416) 781-4717; 9 provincial asscns.

Canadian Country Vacations Association: POB 2580, Winnipeg, MB R3C 4B3; tel. (204) 475-6624; Nat. Co-ordinator FELIX KUEHN; 7 provincial asscns.

Canadian Hostelling Association: 1600 James Naismith Dr., Gloucester, ON K1B 5N4; tel. (613) 748-5638; f. 1933; Exec. Dir LEN BROWN.

CITC (Canadian Institutes of Travel Counsellors): 3300 Bloor St West, Suite 2880, Etobicoke, ON M8X 2X3; tel. (416) 239-4891; fax (416) 233-7064; 4,500 mems; Exec. Dir AVA P. GRITZUK; 6 provincial brs.

Canadian Travellers' Association: 56 Warner Ave, Toronto, ON M4A 1Z4.

Hotel Association of Canada, Inc: 155 Carlton St, Suite 1505, Winnipeg, MB R3C 3H8; tel. (403) 942-0671; 7 provincial asscns.

Tourism Canada: Dept of Industry, Science and Technology, 235 Queen St, 4th Floor East, Ottawa, ON K1A 0H6; tel. (613) 954-3925; telex 053-4123.

Tourism Industry Association of Canada: 130 Albert St, Suite 1016, Ottawa, ON K1P 5G4; tel. (613) 238-3883; fax (613) 238-3878; 225 mem. orgs; Exec. Dir JOHN H. LAWSON; 12 provincial and territorial asscns.

PROVINCIAL AND TERRITORIAL TOURIST ATTRACTIONS AND ORGANIZATIONS

Alberta

Alberta has two very different principal tourist areas. The Rocky Mountains in the west of the province are rich in scenic and natural beauty, protected in the Banff and Jasper National Parks. Activities popular in these parks include winter and summer sports (particularly skiing and golf), walking and camping. To contrast, further east in the province are the towns of Calgary and Edmonton, both with striking modern architecture and reminiscences of their cattle-ranching and gold-rush heritage. Calgary has its annual Stampede rodeo in July, museums and galleries, a zoo and a prehistoric park. Edmonton holds the Klondike Days festival in July each year, and hosts the Canadian finals Rodeo in mid-November; West Edmonton Mall is the world's largest shopping complex, and also holds an assortment of leisure facilities. The province has three other national parks—Waterton Lakes on the border with Montana (USA), which is a continuation of the US Glacier National Park, Elk Island in central Alberta, with large herds of buffalo, deer, elk and moose, and Wood Buffalo, stretching over the northern border into the Northwest Territories, which is noted for wildlife such as bison and whooping crane. There are 141 provincial parks, covering 12,514 sq km.

Alberta Camping Association: c/o YMCA, 332 Sixth Ave, SW, Calgary, AB T2P 0R5; tel. (403) 269-6156.

Alberta Country Vacations Association: POB 217, Trochu, AB T0M 2C0; tel. (403) 442-2207; Sec. WILLIE LYNCH.

Alberta Hotel Association: Centre 104, Suite 401, 5241 Calgary Trail South, Edmonton, AB T6H 5G8; tel. (403) 436-6112; Exec. Vice-Pres. JAMES P. HANSEN.

Alberta Recreation and Parks: Standard Life Centre, 10405 Jasper Ave, Edmonton, AB T5J 3N4; tel. (403) 427-2008.

Alberta Tourism: 10025 Jasper Ave, 18th Floor, Edmonton, AB T5J 3Z3; tel. (403) 427-2280; fax (403) 427-2852.

Alliance of Canadian Travel Associations—ACTA (Alberta): Site 17, RR 2, POB 12, Calgary, AB T2P 2G5; tel. (403) 249-6522.

Calgary Tourist and Convention Bureau: 237 Eighth Ave, SE, Calgary, AB T2G 0K8; tel. (403) 263-8510; fax (403) 262-3809; Pres. BOB FLEMING.

Canadian Institutes of Travel Counsellors—CITC (Alberta): POB 3151, Station B, Calgary, AB T2M 4L7.

Edmonton Convention and Tourism Authority: 9797 Jasper Ave, Suite 104, Edmonton, AB T5J 1N9; tel. (403) 426-4715; Gen. Man. RICK ANTONSON.

Motel Association of Alberta: 54 Airport Rd, NW, Edmonton, AB T5G 0W7; tel. (403) 452-4758; Exec. Dir DALE L. SCHULTZ.

Tourism Industry Association of Alberta: 2635 37th Ave, NE, Suite 250, Calgary, AB T1Y 5V7; tel. (403) 250-2760; Exec. Dir LINDA POETZ.

British Columbia

British Columbia's tourist attractions range from the fiords and islands of the Pacific coast to the glaciers and snowfields of the Rocky Mountains, by way of the province's principal city, Vancouver, and its capital, Victoria. Tourism has become British Columbia's second largest industry, after timber, and is concentrated in the southern half of the province; skiing resorts are spread throughout this part of the province, and there are hot springs resorts in the Rocky Mountains. The tourism potential of the remoter north of the province remains largely undeveloped. The province has six national parks, including South Moresby, one of the most recently created, preserving the ancient rain forest and coastline of the southern Queen Charlotte's Islands; parts of the western coastline of Vancouver Island form the Pacific Rim National Park. The remaining national parks (Mount Revelstoke, Glacier, Yoho and Kootenay) are in the south-eastern part of the province, covering the Rocky Mountains and associated ranges. Vancouver is a modern, cosmopolitan city (with, in particular, a well-established Chinatown) set against a dramatic backdrop of mountains, waterways and islands. There are museums, featuring modern exhibits at Science World and traditional north-west Indian arts at the Museum of Anthropology. Victoria, on Vancouver Island and reached by ferry from Vancouver itself, has many signs of Canada's history as a British colony. It is noted for its traditional architecture, particularly the Parliament Buildings. British Columbia has 367 provincial parks, covering 46,687 sq km.

Alliance of Canadian Travel Associations—ACTA (British Columbia): 744 West Hastings St, Suite 210, Vancouver, BC V6C 1A5; tel. (604) 688-0516.

British Columbia Camping Association: 1367 West Broadway, Vancouver, BC V6H 4A9; tel. (604) 737-7000.

British Columbia Motels, Campgrounds, Resorts Association: Harbour Centre, Suite 980, 555 West Hastings St, POB 12105, Vancouver, BC V6B 4N6; tel. (604) 682-8883; Man. Dir PATRICIA CASHIN.

British Columbia and Yukon Hotels' Association: Hotel Vancouver, 1st Floor, 900 West Georgia St, Vancouver, BC V6C 2W6; tel. (604) 681-7164; Exec. Vice-Pres. F. G. HIGGS.

Canadian Institutes of Travel Counsellors—CITC (British Columbia): 744 West Hastings St, Suite 210, Vancouver, BC V6C 1A5; tel. (604) 688-0516.

Ministry of Parks: Parliament Bldgs, Victoria, BC V8V 1X5; tel. (604) 387-5002.

Ministry of Tourism: Parliament Bldgs, Victoria, BC V8V 1X4; tel. (604) 387-1311; telex 049-7135; fax (604) 387-1420.

Tourism Industry Association of British Columbia: 555 West Hastings St, Suite 980, POB 12108, Vancouver, BC V6B 4N6; tel. (604) 688-4115; Exec. Admin. KELLY MILLIN.

Tourism Vancouver: 562 Burrard St, 2nd Floor, Vancouver, BC V6J 2J6; tel. (604) 6882-2222.

Manitoba

One-sixth of the total area of Manitoba is covered in water, and several of the province's principal tourist attractions are associated with this topographical aspect. Swimming, fishing and boating are all popular activities, and can be pursued in many of Manitoba's 164 provincial parks (which cover 14,316 sq km). The province has only one national park, Riding Mountain, which has lakes, streams and trails for hiking and horse-riding; it is a preserved wilderness area within the dominant prairie farmland.

Alliance of Canadian Travel Associations—ACTA (Manitoba): 1680 Ellice Ave, Suite 9, Winnipeg, MB R3H 0Z2; tel. (204) 783-3883.

Canadian Institutes of Travel Counsellors—CITC (Manitoba): 817 Parkhill St, Winnipeg, MB R2Y 0V4; tel. (204) 832-6522.

Manitoba Camping Association: Admin. Centre for Recreation and Sport, 1700 Ellice Ave, Winnipeg, MB R3H 0B1; tel. (204) 985-4166.

Manitoba Culture, Heritage and Recreation: 177 Lombard Ave, Winnipeg, MB R3B 0W5; tel. (204) 945-2782; fax (204) 945-1369.

Manitoba Farm Vacations: 525 Kylemore Ave, Winnipeg, MB R3L 1B5; tel. (204) 475-6624; Exec. Dir IRVIN KROEKER.

Manitoba Hotel Association: 155 Carlton St, Suite 1505, Winnipeg, MB R3C 3H8; tel. (204) 942-0671; Exec. Vice-Pres. JOHN D. READ.

Manitoba Industry, Trade and Tourism: 155 Carlton St, Winnipeg, MB R3C 3H8; tel. (204) 945-2465; telex 07-587833; fax (204) 957-1793.

Tourism Industry Association of Manitoba: 375 York Ave, Suite 232, Winnipeg, MB R3C 3J3; tel. (204) 943-1551; Exec. Vice-Pres. RITA L. ROELAND.

Travel Manitoba: Dept 9259, Winnipeg, MB R3C 3H8; tel. (204) 945-3777; fax (204) 957-1793.

Winnipeg Convention and Visitors' Bureau: 375 York Ave, Suite 232, Winnipeg, MB R3C 3J3; tel. (204) 943-1970.

New Brunswick

The coastline is the principal tourist attraction of the province of New Brunswick. The highest rise of tidal water in the world has been recorded in the Bay of Fundy; the great volume of water advancing and retreating has sculpted dramatic rock formations, and leaves extensive beaches and mud flats creating a haven for wildlife, particularly birds. At the east end of the Bay of Fundy is Fundy National Park. New Brunswick's other national park, Kouchibouguac, preserves a system of lagoons, barrier beaches, sand dunes and salt marshes at the northern end of the Northumberland Strait. Inland attractions include the Saint John river valley, with several covered bridges and waterfalls, and the forest, hills and streams of the Restigouche Uplands. New Brunswick has 48 provincial parks, covering 233 sq km.

Department of Tourism, Recreation and Heritage: POB 12345, Fredericton, NB E3B 5C3; tel. (506) 453-2377; telex 014-46230; fax (506) 453-2416.

Hospitality New Brunswick: 348 King St, Fredericton, NB E3B 1E3; tel. (506) 454-2615; Exec. Dir KAYE PYNE.

New Brunswick Camping Association: POB 263, Moncton, NB E1C 8K9; tel. (506) 857-0203.

New Brunswick Farm Vacation Association: RR 2, Sussex, NB E0E 1P0; tel. (506) 433-3786; Pres. TOM ANDERSON.

Saint John Visitor and Convention Bureau: POB 1971, Saint John, NB E2L 4L1; tel. (506) 658-2990.

Newfoundland

Tourism in the province of Newfoundland is concentrated on the Island of Newfoundland, the mainland area of Labrador to the north being largely undeveloped. The coastline of the island is rugged, and scattered with fiords and bays; icebergs and ice floes occur frequently in the area. Terra Nova National Park is on the east coast, at Bonavista Bay; Gros Morne National Park, on the west coast at Boone Bay, includes mountains, lakes, forests and fiords. L'Anse-Aux-Meadows National Historic Park, at the northern tip of the island, marks the site of the 10th-century Viking settlement, and is also a UNESCO World Heritage Site. Outdoor pursuits include fishing, hunting (principally for game mammals) and skiing. Newfoundland has 75 provincial parks, covering 3,337 sq km.

Department of Development and Tourism: Confederation Annex, 4th Floor, POB 4750, St John's, NF A1C 5T7; tel. (709) 576-5600; telex 016-4949; fax (709) 576-5936.

Hospitality Newfoundland: POB 13516, St John's, NF A1B 4B8; tel. (709) 722-2000; Man. Dir JOSEPH BENNETT.

Newfoundland and Labrador Camping Association: POB 261, Corner Brook, NF A2H 6C9.

St John's Tourist Bureau: City Hall, POB 908, St John's, NF A1C 5M2; tel. (509) 576-8106.

Tourism Industry Association of Newfoundland and Labrador: POB 13516, St John's, NF A1B 4B6; tel. (709) 722-2000.

Northwest Territories

Tourism is developing steadily in the Northwest Territories, but is hindered both by its remoteness from the major population centres of Canada and by the severe weather and long winters. There is a limited road network in the Mackenzie Valley area, otherwise access is only possible by water and air. There are four national parks in the Northwest Territories, including Wood Buffalo, which is shared with the province of Alberta. Nahanni National Park, in the west, has high waterfalls, canyons, hot springs and opportunities for white-water canoeing; it is also a UNESCO World Heritage Site. Auyuittuq National Park is on Baffin Island, and has fiords, glaciers and mountains. Ellesmere Island National Park, the northernmost part of Canada and separated from northern Greenland by only the narrow Nares Strait, is nevertheless a refuge for mammals such as musk ox and arctic hare.

Tourism Industry Association of the Northwest Territories: 5202 50th Ave, 8th Floor, POB 506, Yellowknife, NT X1A 2N4; tel. and fax (403) 873-2122; Pres. JACK WALKER.

TravelArctic: Government of the Northwest Territories, Yellowknife, NT X1A 2L9; tel. (403) 873-7200; fax (403) 920-2756.

Nova Scotia

With its long coastline along the south-eastern boundary of what is now Canada, Nova Scotia was the location for some of the earliest European settlements, including the earliest agricultural settlement, Port-Royal (now Annapolis Royal). A replica of Port-Royal has been developed as a tourist attraction. There are several other historic sites preserved throughout the province. There are two national parks in Nova Scota: Kejimkujik, south-west of Halifax, a wilderness area with lakes and rivers, and Cape Breton Highlands, which is at the north of Cape Breton Island, with coastline on both sides of a rocky peninsula, and includes the northernmost part of the Cabot Trail. Nova Scotia has 113 provincial parks covering an area of 198 sq km.

Alliance of Canadian Travel Associations—ACTA (Atlantic): World Trade and Convention Centre, 4th Floor, 1800 Argyle St, Halifax, NS B3J 3N8; tel. (902) 422-7311.

Cape Breton Tourist Association: 20 Keltic Dr., Sydney River, NS B1S 1P5; tel. (902) 539-9876; Exec. Dir DON BLACKWOOD.

Department of Tourism and Culture: POB 456, Halifax, NS B3J 2R5; tel. (902) 424-5000; telex 019-23525; fax (902) 424-2668.

Nova Scotia Camping Association: POB 3243, Halifax, NS B3J 3H5; tel. (902) 424-4329.

NS Farm and Country Vacation Association: Newport Station, Hants County, NS B0N 2B0; tel. (902) 798-5864.

Tourism Halifax: POB 1749, Halifax, NS B3J 3A5; tel. (902) 421-6448; telex 019-22641; Dir LEWIS M. ROGERS.

Tourism Industry Association of Nova Scotia: 1800 Argyle St, Halifax, NS B3J 3N8; tel. (902) 423-4480; CEO GORDON HARMER, IV.

Ontario

Ontario accounts for over one-third of all tourist visits in Canada and for almost one-third of tourist spending. The size of the province's area and population are in part responsible for this, but no less so than the attractions of great cities and natural beauty. Ontario is the province of the Great Lakes (parts of Lakes Ontario, Erie, Huron and Superior are within the province's boundaries). Niagara Falls, on the Niagara River linking Lakes Erie and Ontario, is one of the world's most famous tourist attractions. The province's five national parks (Bruce Peninsula, Georgian Bay Islands, Point Pelee, Pukaskwa and St Lawrence Islands) are all located on one or other of the Great Lakes. Ontario's 219 provincial parks (including the massive Algonquin Provincial Park of 7,511 sq km) cover a total area of 56,592 sq km, and offer opportunities for hiking, fishing, camping, skiing and various other outdoor pursuits. To contrast, Toronto is a modern cosmopolitan city, particularly favoured for its architecture, entertainment facilities and general cleanliness. Ottawa, on the border with the province of Québec, is the federal capital, and has a number of national museums and galleries.

Alliance of Canadian Travel Associations—ACTA (Ontario): 3080 Yonge St, Suite 4020, Toronto, ON M4N 3N1; tel. (416) 488-2282.

Canada's Capital Visitors' and Convention Bureau: 222 Queen St, 7th Floor, Ottawa, ON K1P 5V9; tel. (613) 237-5150; fax (613) 560-1373; Exec. Vice-Pres. GLEN T. MOORE.

Canadian Institutes of Travel Counsellors—CITC (Ontario): 3300 Bloor St West, Suite 2880, Etobicoke, ON M8X 2X3; tel. (416) 239-4891.

Metropolitan Toronto Convention and Visitors' Association: Queen's Quay Terminal, 207 Queen's Quay West, POB 126, Toronto, ON M5J 1A7; tel. (416) 368-9990; fax (416) 867-3995.

Ministry of Tourism and Recreation: 77 Bloor St West, Toronto, ON M7A 2R9; tel. (416) 965-7680; fax (416) 965-3766.

Motels Ontario: 1837 Lansdowne St West, Unit 4A, Peterborough, ON K9K 1R4; tel. (705) 745-4982; Pres. BRUCE M. GRAVEL.

Niagara Falls, Canada, Visitor and Convention Bureau: 4673 Ontario Ave, Suite 202, Niagara Falls, ON L2E 3R1; tel. (416) 356-6061; Pres. D. GORDON PAUL.

Ontario Camping Association: 1806 Avenue Rd, Suite 2, Toronto, ON M5M 3Z1; tel. (416) 781-0525.

Ontario Convention and Visitors' Association: 1235 Bay St, Suite 400, Toronto, ON M5R 3K4; tel. (416) 920-1573; Exec. Dir JAMES PREECE.

Ontario Hotel and Motel Association: 34 Ross St, Toronto, ON M5T 1Z9; tel. (416) 596-7676; Exec. Vice-Pres. ROBERT H. WOOLVET.

Ontario Private Campground Association: 55 Nugget Ave, Suite 230, Scarborough, ON M1S 3L1; tel. (416) 293-2090; Man. Dir MARY E. MACCARL.

Ontario Ski Resorts Association: 160 Gibson Dr., Unit 11, Markham, ON L3R 3K1; tel. (416) 479-2113; Exec. Dir DONALD K. MCILVEEN.

Ontario Vacation Farm Association: RR 2, Alma, ON N0B 1A0; tel. (519) 846-9788; fax (519) 846-9378; Exec. Dir SHARON GROSE.

Resorts Ontario: POB 2148, Orillia, ON L3V 6S1; tel. (705) 325-9115; telex 06-875600; Man. Dir CATHIE KEEN.

Prince Edward Island

The tourist industry, though small by comparison with those of Canada's larger provinces, plays an important role in the economic life of Prince Edward Island. The island's coastline is 1,800 km long, and there are many sandy beaches. Prince Edward Island National Park, which occupies the north-central part of the shoreline, is the province's principal tourist attraction, with sand dunes, red sandstone cliffs and fishing villages. There are 31 provincial parks, which cover only 15 sq km. Golf, skiing, deep-sea fishing and horse racing are among the sports available in Prince Edward Island. A number of historic sites, such as Province House in Charlottetown, have been developed as tourist attractions.

Department of Tourism and Parks: POB 2000, Charlottetown, PE C1A 7N8; tel. (902) 368-5500; telex 014-44154; fax (902) 892-3420.

Prince Edward Island Convention Bureau: 11 Queen St, Charlottetown, PE C1A 4A2; tel. (902) 368-3688.

Prince Edward Island Farm Vacations Visitor Services: POB 940, Charlottetown, PE C1A 7M5; tel. (902) 368-4444.

Tourism Industry Association of PEI: 25 Queen St, POB 2050, Charlottetown, PE C1A 7N7; tel. (902) 566-5008; Gen. Man. JIM LARKIN.

Québec

The province of Québec's tourist attractions are extremely varied, from the large city of Montréal to remote wilderness areas. However, perhaps the most distinctive aspect of the province is the predominance of French Canadians, dating from the early French settlement of the area in the 17th century. The province has three national parks: Forillon, at the eastern tip of the Gaspé Peninsula, has rugged cliffs and is noted for its sea birds; the Mingan Archipelago is on the northern side of the St Lawrence River as it opens into the Gulf of St Lawrence, and is also known for its sea birds as well as sea plants; and La Mauricie is a hilly area between Montréal and Québec City, with woods and lakes, and opportunities for fishing and skiing. Fishing and hunting (of deer,

caribou, moose and even black bear) are very popular outdoor pursuits in Québec. Provincial parks, of which there are 91, cover a larger area than in any other province at 92,241 sq km. Montréal is the second-largest French-speaking city in the world, behind only Paris; it has architecture both modern and, in Vieux Montréal, traditional. Québec City's architecture and cultural heritage has been affected remarkably little by the intrusions of modern business life.

Association des Camps du Québec: 4545 ave Pierre-de-Coubertin, Montréal, PQ H1V 3R2; tel. (514) 252-3113.

Association of Canadian Travel Associations—ACTA (Québec): 410 blvd Henri-Bourassa est, Montréal, PQ H3L 1C4; tel. (514) 382-0544.

L'Association des Hôteliers de la Province de Québec/Province of Québec Hotelkeepers' Association: 3744 rue St-Denis, Montréal, PQ H2X 3L7; tel. (514) 282-5135; Gen. Man. GUSTAV BAMATTER.

Association des Terrains de Camping du Québec: 5199 rue Sherbrooke est, Montréal, PQ H1T 3X1; tel. (514) 255-5693; Dir-Gen. MICHEL VALADE.

Canadian Institutes of Travel Counsellors—CITC (Québec/Atlantic): 1010 rue Ste-Catherine ouest, Bureau 322, Montréal, PQ H3B 1E7; tel. (514) 871-9600.

Fédération des Agricotours du Québec (Federation of Country Vacations of Québec): 1413 rue Jarry est, Montréal, PQ H2E 2Z7; tel. (514) 374-4700.

Greater Montréal Convention and Tourism Bureau: 1010 rue Ste-Catherine ouest, Bureau 410, Montréal, PQ H3B 1G2; tel. (514) 871-1129; fax (514) 871-1457; Exec. Vice-Pres. (acting) and Gen. Man. PATRICK DINAN.

Institut de Tourisme et d'Hôtellerie du Québec: 401 rue de Rigaud, Montréal, PQ H2L 4P3; tel. (514) 282-5150; telex 052-5740; fax (514) 873-8684; Dir-Gen. Dr ANTOINE SAMUELLI.

Ministry of Recreation, Fish and Game: 150 blvd St-Cyrille est, Québec, PQ G1R 4Y1; tel. (418) 643-2984; telex 051-3994.

Ministry of Tourism: 2 pl. Québec, Bureau 336, Québec, PQ G1R 2B5; tel. (418) 643-5959; fax (418) 643-6149.

Québec City Tourism and Convention Centre: Communauté urbaine de Québec, 399 rue St-Joseph est, Québec, PQ G1K 8E2; tel. (418) 522-3511; telex 051-2301; fax (418) 529-3121.

Saskatchewan

Saskatchewan has many lakes and rivers, and outdoor pursuits associated with these, particularly fishing, are popular. Skiing is another attraction, and can be pursued in some of the 31 provincial parks (which cover a total area of 9,080 sq km). The province has two national parks: Grasslands, on the southern border with Montana (USA), preserves an area of original short-grass prairie; Prince Albert, in central Saskatchewan, is an area of glacial lakes and other glacial features, forests and prairie grasslands, rich in wildlife including elk, moose, caribou, wolves and beavers. 'Grey Owl' (the noted conservationist Archibald Belaney) had close associations with this park.

Alliance of Canadian Travel Assocations—ACTA (Saskatchewan): 129 Riddell Cres., Regina, SK S4S 5TZ; tel. (306) 525-4200.

Canadian Institutes of Travel Counsellors—CITC (Saskatchewan): POB 3686, Regina, SK S4P 3N8.

Department of Parks, Recreation and Culture: 3211 Albert St, Regina, SK S4S 5W6; tel. (306) 787-2322.

Hotels Association of Saskatchewan: 2020 11th Ave, Suite 404, Regina, SK S4P 0J3; tel. (306) 522-1664; Exec. Dir PETER WILLIAMSON.

Regina Visitor and Convention Bureau: POB 3355, Regina, SK S4P 3H1; tel. (306) 789-5099; Exec. Dir RON COULSON.

Saskatchewan Camping Associations: c/o YMCA, 25 22nd St East, Saskatoon, SK S7K 0C7; tel. (306) 652-7515.

Saskatchewan Country Vacations Association: POB 89, Blaine Lake, SK S0J 0J0; tel. (306) 497-2782; Sec. EDITH VERESHAGIN.

Saskatoon Visitor and Convention Bureau: 347 Second Ave South, Saskatoon, SK S4P 3H1; tel. (306) 242-1206; Exec. Dir MURRAY R. BANTLE.

Yukon Territory

Tourism is crucial to the economy of the Yukon Territory because of the vulnerability of the other economic mainstay, mining, to international commodity market conditions. Mining itself has created one of the territory's principal tourist attractions through the Yukon Gold Rush of the late 19th and early 20th centuries. Dawson City has many reconstructed buildings from the gold-rush period, and the US and Canadian national parks services have combined to develop the Klondike Gold Rush International Historical Park. Much tourist trade is derived from visitors passing through the territory to or from Alaska (USA). The Yukon Territory has two national parks: Kluane, in the south-east corner bordering Alaska and British Columbia, is a largely glaciated area containing the highest point in Canada, Mount Logan (5,950 m); Northern Yukon is a wildlife sanctuary on the north coast, created to protect caribou, grizzly, black and polar bears, and waterfowl.

Klondike Visitors' Association: POB 389, Dawson City, YT Y0B 1G0; tel. (403) 993-5575.

Tourism Industry Association of the Yukon: 302 Steele St, Suite 102, Whitehorse, YT Y1A 2C5; tel. (403) 668-3331; fax (403) 667-7379; Exec. Dir DAVID PHILPOTT.

NATIONAL PARKS

Auyuittuq: Pangnirtung, NT X0A 0R0; f. 1972.

Banff: POB 900, Banff, AB T0L 0C0; f. 1885.

Bruce Peninsula: POB 189, Tobermory, ON N0H 2R0; f. 1987.

Cape Breton Highlands: Ingonish Beach, Cape Breton, NS B0C 1L0; f. 1936.

Elk Island: Site 4, RR 1, Fort Saskatchewan, AB T0B 1P0; f. 1913.

Ellesmere Island: c/o Auyuittuq National Park, Pangnirtung, NT X0A 0R0; f. 1986.

Forillon: POB 1220, Gaspé, PQ G0C 1R0; f. 1970.

Fundy: POB 40, Alma, NB E0A 1B0; f. 1948.

Georgian Bay Islands: POB 28, Honey Harbour, ON P0E 1E0; f. 1929.

Glacier: POB 350, Revelstoke, BC V0E 2S0; f. 1886.

Grasslands: Val Marie, SK S0N 2T0; f. 1981.

Gros Morne: POB 130, Rocky Harbour, NF A0K 4N0; f. 1970.

Jasper: POB 10, Jasper, AB T0E 1E0; f. 1907.

Kejimkujik: POB 36, Maitland Bridge, NS B0T 1N0; f. 1968.

Kluane: Haines Junction, YT Y0B 1L0; f. 1972.

Kootenay: POB 220, Radium Hot Springs, BC V0A 1M0; f. 1920.

Kouchibouguac: Kouchibouguac, Kent County, NB E0A 2A0; f. 1969.

La Mauricie: POB 758, Shawinigan, PQ G9N 6V9; f. 1970.

Mingan Archipelago: POB 1180, Havre-St-Piere, PQ G0G 1P0; f. 1984.

Mount Revelstoke: POB 350, Revelstoke, BC V0E 2S0; f. 1914.

Nahanni: POB 300, Fort Simpson, NT X0E 0N0; f. 1972.

Northern Yukon: c/o Kluane National Park, Haines Junction, YT Y0B 1L0; f. 1984.

Pacific Rim: POB 280, Ucluelet, BC V0R 3A0; f. 1970.

Point Pelee: RR 1, Leamington, ON N8H 3V4; f. 1918.

Prince Albert: POB 100, Waskesiu Lake, SK S0J 2Y0; f. 1927.

Prince Edward Island: POB 487, Charlottetown, PE C1A 7L1; f. 1937.

Pukaskwa: POB 550, Marathon, ON P0T 2E0; f. 1971.

Riding Mountain: Wasagaming, MB R0J 2H0; f. 1929.

St Lawrence Islands: POB 469, Mallorytown Landing, ON K0E 1R0; f. 1914.

South Moresby Reserve: POB 37, Queen Charlotte City, BC V0T 1S0; f. 1987.

Terra Nova: Glovertown, NF A0G 2L0; f. 1957.

Waterton Lakes: Waterton Park, AB T0K 2M0; f. 1985.

Wood Buffalo: POB 750, Fort Smith, NT X0E 0P0; f. 1922.

Yoho: POB 99, Field, BC V0A 1G0; f. 1886.